2001

WOMEN IN WORLD HISTORY

A Biographical Encyclopedia

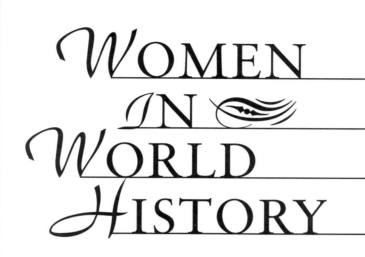

WOMEN IN WORLD HISTORY

A Biographical Encyclopedia

VOLUME

3

Brem-Cold

Anne Commire, Editor

Deborah Klezmer, Associate Editor

YORKIN PUBLICATIONS

GALE GROUP

Detroit
San Francisco
London
Boston
Woodbridge, CT

Yorkin Publications

Anne Commire, *Editor*
Deborah Klezmer, *Associate Editor*
Barbara Morgan, *Assistant Editor*

Eileen O'Pasek, Gail Schermer, Patricia Coombs, James Fox,
Catherine Cappelli, Karen Rikkers, *Editorial Assistants*
Karen Walker, *Assistant for Genealogical Charts*

Special acknowledgment is due to Peg Yorkin who made this project possible.

Thanks also to Karin and John Haag, Bob Schermer, and to
the Gale Group staff, in particular Dedria Bryfonski, Linda Hubbard, John Schmittroth, Cynthia Baldwin,
Tracey Rowens, Randy Bassett, Christine O'Bryan, Rebecca Parks, and especially Sharon Malinowski.

The Gale Group

Sharon Malinowski, *Senior Editor*
Rebecca Parks, *Editor*
Linda S. Hubbard, *Managing Editor, Multicultural Team*

Margaret A. Chamberlain, *Permissions Specialist*
Mary K. Grimes, *Image Cataloger*

Mary Beth Trimper, *Production Director*
Evi Seoud, *Assistant Production Manager*

Cynthia Baldwin, *Product Design Manager*
Tracey Rowens, *Cover and Page Designer*

Barbara Yarrow, *Graphic Services Manager*
Randy Bassett, *Image Database Supervisor*
Robert Duncan and Michael Logusz, *Imaging Specialists*
Christine O'Bryan, *Graphics Desktop Publisher*

Library of Congress Catalog Card Number 99-24692
A CIP record is available from the British Library

ISBN 0-7876-4062-X
Printed in the United States of America.

Library of Congress Cataloging-in-Publication Data

Women in world history : a biographical encyclopedia / Anne Commire, editor, Deborah Klezmer, associate editor.
    p. cm.
    Includes bibliographical references and index.
    ISBN 0-7876-3736-X (set). — ISBN 0-7876-4080-8 (v. 1). —
    ISBN 0-7876-4061-1 (v. 2) — ISBN 0-7876-4062-X (v. 3) — ISBN 0-7876-4063-8 (v. 4)
      1. Women—History Encyclopedias.2. Women—Biography Encyclopedias.
    I. Commire, Anne. II. Klezmer, Deborah.
      HQ1115.W6 1999
      920.72'03—DC21

99-24692

10 9 8 7 6 5 4 3 2 1

Brécourt, Jeanne (b. 1837)

French courtesan and blackmailer. Name variations: Jeanne de la Cour; Brecourt. Born Jeanne Amenaide Brécourt in 1837 in Paris, France; death date unknown; married a grocer named Gras, who deserted her.

One of France's most infamous courtesans, Jeanne Brécourt destroyed a number of her paramours through blackmail and deceit, while feigning an aristocratic background. After plotting to have a wealthy lover blinded to guarantee his dependence, she was brought to trial in 1877 and defended by Charles Lachaud, who had also been the attorney for *Marie Lafarge. The trial, one of the more spectacular of its day, reportedly attracted the elite of Paris, including journalists, playwrights, and even members of the popular Comédie-Française.

Brécourt's early life included a troubled childhood and an abusive marriage. Born in poverty, she was adopted at age five by a wealthy baroness who sought to provide a home for the neglected child. When Brécourt was 11, her parents demanded her back to help support the family. At 18, after seven years on poverty row, she returned to the baroness. Soon after, she married impulsively, living in an abusive relationship for a number of years until her husband abandoned her. Brécourt then tried her hand at writing and acting, before adopting a new persona: she emerged as a beautiful courtesan named Jeanne de la Cour. Professing a devout hatred of all men, she proceeded to use and dismiss a cadre of wealthy lovers, many of whom became suicidal in her wake.

In 1873, Brécourt met Georges de Saint Pierre, a rich and handsome young man 16 years her junior. Faced with his family's disapproval and no marriage plans, Brécourt began to obsess about his fidelity. In a morbid plot, she convinced an old friend, Nathalis Gaudry, to blind Georges by throwing acid in his face, thus causing his dependence on her for the remainder of his life. The plan, which was carried out successfully after she and Georges returned home from a masked ball, eventually fell under the investigation of detective Gustave Macé, who would become one of France's most capable detectives. After months of sleuthing, during which time Brécourt tried to escape to Italy with Georges, Macé wore down Brécourt and located Gaudry. Further implicating Brécourt were letters she had hidden in order to blackmail Georges should he ever try to leave her.

The trial, during which Gaudry confessed to carrying out the crime because of his overwhelming love for Brécourt, culminated in the dramatic testimony of Georges de Saint Pierre, which ultimately clarified Brécourt's guilt. She was convicted and sentenced to 15 years in prison. Little is known of her final years, though by some accounts, she left prison haggard and old, and spent her last days peddling fruit, as she had as a child.

Barbara Morgan,
Melrose, Massachusetts

Bremer, Fredrika (1801–1865)

Swedish writer, considered founder of the Swedish novel, who also wrote well-received travel books dealing with social and political conditions of other countries, and became an emblem for women's emancipation in Sweden. Born Fredrika Bremer near Aabo, Finland, on August 17, 1801; died on December 31, 1865; daughter of Carl Fredric Bremer (a wealthy iron master and merchant) and Brigitta Charlotta (Hollstrom) Bremer; sister of Charlotte Bremer, who edited her letters and works; never married; no children.

Selected works: Teckningar utur hvardagslivet *(translated as* Sketches from Everyday Life, *1828);* Familjen H. *(trans.* The H. Family, *1830–31);* Grannarne *(trans.* The Neighbors, *1837);* Hemmet *(trans.* The Home or Family Cares and Family Joys, *1839);* En Dagbok *(trans.* A Diary, *1843);* Syskonlif *(*Brothers and Sisters, *1849);* England in 1851 *or* Sketches of a Tour in England *(1853);* Hemmen i den nya verlden *(trans.* Homes of the New World,

1853–54); Hertha *(1856);* Fader och dotter *(Father and Daughter, 1858);* Lifvet i gamla verlden *(trans. Life in the old World, 1850–62).*

I will remain unmarried, in order not to attach my heart exclusively . . . but I shall, for the sake of God and of Eternal Love, love all my fellow-men; help and comfort all, as far as lies in my power, which ought to be so much easier when no domestic cares weigh upon my mind. That must be a beautiful and happy life!

—Fredrika Bremer's diary entry (July 9, 1823)

Fredrika Bremer was born in a manor house near Aabo, Finland, where her father Carl, a man of considerable wealth and status, was the ironmaster. At age three, she moved with her parents and her elder sister to Sweden where her father bought a manor house at Aarstad near Stockholm. There, the family spent the clement months of the year, departing for the city with the approach of winter. Fredrika loved the relative freedom of the country where she and her sister were allowed to play outside, though they realized they would never have as much fun as the parson's children who were allowed to roam. Their father, writes Bremer, was "beyond description orderly and punctual"; he ruled the household, backed by their mother and her three principles for children's upbringing. They were to grow up in perfect ignorance of everything evil in the world; they were to learn as much as possible; and they were to eat as little as possible. **Brigitta Bremer** wanted innocent, well-read "ladies," not tall, stout women.

By the time she was five, Fredrika had learned to read both Swedish and French; at seven, she was given music and drawing lessons, and a year later she wrote verses in French. Bremer was an inquisitive child, so eager for information she wore out everyone with her unceasing questions. She further exasperated her teachers and parents by operating on chairs and dolls to examine their contents and by testing the brittleness of porcelain heads against the flagstone hearth. Fredrika was "excessively wild and frolicsome," according to her sister, but she would dissolve in tears when she was chastised, which was often. Bremer would lose her things, tear her dress, or come home late for dinner. Although she had an unusually good memory for her studies, she seemed incapable of heeding daily admonitions, which incurred her parents'

displeasure and resulted in scoldings, sometimes for trifling matters. They appear to have embittered her mind somewhat but to have had no impact on her continued pursuit of knowledge.

Between the ages of nine and twelve, Bremer studied English and German and made considerable headway in history and geography. Always in quest of the nature of things, her selective mind reasserted itself in her precise knowledge of the produce of a country rather than its boundaries, which she found difficult to remember. At 16, in preparation for confirmation, she was encouraged to blindly believe what one could not understand. This stance would lead to subsequent religious scruples that she ultimately transformed into a belief in a religious world order according to which each creature in it had a mission to fulfill.

She was further taught to cook and manage a house, and she became a skilled painter of portraits and a capable pianist. In short, Bremer acquired all the attributes considered desirable for a young woman of the upper-middle class who is destined to make a good match. Fredrika, however, chafed at her constricted, secluded existence. Her diary entries from 1822 to 1823 reveal her impatience at her inactive, unproductive life. "How stagnant, like a muddy pool, is time to youth dragging on a dull and inactive life. . . . I am only twenty-two, and yet I am often tired of the world and wish I were taken from it. But then, we do lead a very dull life." The supposed outcome of this waiting and these accomplishments—marriage—held no attraction for her. "Never marry, Fredrika," she admonished herself. "Be firm; thou wilt bitterly, bitterly repent it if thou allowest the weakness of thy heart to induce thee to such a step. Watch, pray, struggle, and hope." Bremer wanted to commit herself to something worthwhile and considered nursing as a profession. Ultimately, however, she chose writing as a mission worth pursuing and a means to distinguish herself.

Fredrika Bremer's writing began as a way of obtaining funds to help the cottagers on their family estate. She was uncertain of her parents' response to her work; but relying on her worthy purpose, she sent the manuscript of *Teckningar utur hvardagslivet* (*Sketches of Everyday Life*) with her brother as he left for the University of Upsala in the fall of 1828. He found a publisher who was willing to publish the book anonymously, and it received favorable acclaim. Encouraged by that reception, she went on to write *Familjen H.* (*The H. Family*), a continuation of *Sketches*, which became a topic of conversation in all circles of society. Thus empowered, Bremer found the courage to reveal the author's identity to her mother. When shortly afterwards the Swedish Academy awarded her its lesser gold medal, the secret of the authorship was publicly revealed. After her father died in 1830, Bremer began to experience more freedom, living for some years in Norway with a friend.

In the following years, she wrote four full-length novels. Critics have argued that although these novels from the 1830s have "some of the lightness of touch, the playful humor and the realistic impressionism of her early sketches," they have an uneven quality about them due primarily to "excessive moralizing or Romantic posing." Even so, they impress by their probing psychological studies of women and their consistent focus on everyday life. Their style is spontaneous and direct and proved to have in it the vitality necessary to direct Swedish prose from the preciosity of the Romantics to the directness of the Realists.

That her works were translated into other languages and widely read is evidenced by the Swedish Academy granting her its large gold medal, which bore the motto "Genius and Taste." In his presentation speech, the president of the academy reminded his listeners of the earlier award given to "a young genius, whose first essays gave signs of a talent of uncommon order, in a branch of literature for which we hitherto [had] been without models." This award, he continued, was not given as an award but as an acknowledgment of a writer who had "raised the fame of Swedish literature in foreign countries."

Because of the estimable translations of *Mary Howitt, Fredrika Bremer's fame as an author preceded her when she arrived in America in 1849, following the death of her friend. She traveled as far west as St. Paul, in Minnesota Territory, to the deep South and up the Atlantic Coast to the New England states, intent on studying social and political conditions, especially as they reflected the position of women. Her observations were recorded in a series of letters to her younger sister, which were published in three volumes shortly after her return to Sweden. *Hemmen i den nya verlden* (*Homes of the New World*) is true to her childhood's predilection for knowing what a country "produced." Her impressions are recorded from within, depicting her contact with everyday life and people of all kinds and classes. Her reputation had also gained her access to America's most distinguished citizens. She met Henry Wadsworth Longfellow and Nathaniel Hawthorne, as well as Ralph Waldo Emerson whom she especially admired. She was dismayed, however, by his distancing himself from the problems of life, desiring in him "warmer sympathies, larger interest in social questions that touch upon the well-being of mankind, and more feeling for the suffering and sorrowful on earth."

On the whole, Fredrika Bremer was positively inclined towards the new world though not blind to its shortcomings. She thought the American constitution good but considered too many Americans educationally unequipped to sustain the democratic system it advocated. She approved of the American tendency to organize associations for the purpose of accomplishing certain goals or reforms such as abolition of slavery or women's emancipation. And above all, she liked the evidence of religious freedom stimulating an active spiritual life, which, in her opinion, was the cornerstone of democracy.

Influenced by Alexis de Tocqueville's writings about America, she had arrived with high hopes of finding women's position in society considerably more favorable than in the old country. Her expectations were fulfilled to the extent that she found her American sisters to have better educational and professional possibilities than their European counterparts, but even they suffered the isolation and passiveness with which she was well acquainted. She had hoped to find a land in which liberated women were liberating all mankind for pursuit of moral regeneration, but she had to countenance the fact that she was not in Utopia.

Expectedly, Bremer's instinct for independence would lead her to denounce slavery, as indeed she did, emphasizing the disastrous economic and moral consequences of that institution for the slave holders. Her position on this issue was problematic, however, because she thought the black man mentally inferior to his white master and therefore less able to be a free man and a builder of society. In contrast to the abolitionists who wanted immediate emancipation for blacks, Bremer advocated a more protracted process that would allow for a proper

Fredrika Bremer

Christian education to prepare them for the status of free citizens. Characteristically, she supported the move to encourage freed slaves to immigrate to Africa where social structures would be more suitable, it was then assumed, for their "simpler needs and instincts."

In the New England states, she found the highest religious and moral ideals and the richest cultural life. In his analysis of *Homes*, Lars Wendelius points out that Bremer emphasizes two qualities as characteristic of the American people, "on one hand a tendency to further the economic development of the country, on the other hand an equally strong inclination to support its spiritual life." Idealism and common sense, she thought, distinguished the efforts of American society builders, who were individuals as well as social beings working for common purposes. The warm, lively intelligence that informs Bremer's travel books makes them rewarding reading, especially *England in 1815* and *Life in the Old World*. The former concentrates on economic and social concerns whereas the latter focuses on a religious solution to the problems of modern man.

A claim might be made that ultimately Fredrika Bremer contributed more to Swedish culture as a personality than as a writer. As a consequence of her own experience as well as her observations of the world, she made it her aim to labor in the cause of women. On her return from America, she decided to work specifically for the emancipation of Swedish women and their deliverance from the traditional and injurious social restrictions which, in Bremer's opinion, violated their natural rights.

Bremer wanted women to be allowed to study in both elementary schools and universities to become lecturers, professors, judges, physicians, and functionaries in the service of the state. Women, she argued, were owed the same rights to benefit their native country with their talents as men. These views can be found in her most famous novel *Hertha* (1856), as well as in *Fader och dotter* (*Father and Daughter*, 1858).

She took charge of social work as well. When cholera broke out in Stockholm in the summer of 1853, Bremer became the president of a group of women who procured homes for children whose parents had died in the epidemic. Two years later, she placed herself at the head of a small association whose object it was to visit the prisons of the metropolis and the penitentiary for women. In the last years of her life, she devoted her eloquence to calling upon society for money to benefit charitable institutions, such as erection of dwellings for laborers, asylums for aged females, and the so-called Silent School for "deaf-and-dumb" children. Bremer lived to see Sweden pass a law that unmarried women could attain their majority at 25 years of age, and she experienced the introduction in Stockholm of a seminary for the education of female teachers.

In 1856, Bremer set out once again, spending five years on the Continent and in Palestine; her reminiscences were also translated into English. Returning home, she settled at Aarstad, where she lived until her death in December of 1865. In the years following her death, she became the living symbol in Sweden of the struggle for women's rights and for recognition of women's responsibilities. The national women's organization in her country is named the Fredrika Bremer Society.

SOURCES:

Bremer, Charlotte, ed. *Life, Letters, and Posthumous Works of Fredrika Bremer.* Translated by F. Milow. NY: Hurd and Houghton, 1868.

Gustafson, Alrik. *A History of Swedish Literature.* Minneapolis, MN: The Lund Press, 1961.

Wendelius, Lars. *Fredrika Bremers Amerikabild.* Stockholm: Almquist & Wiksell International, 1985.

Inga Wiehl,
Yakima Valley Community College,
Yakima Valley, Washington

Brent, Evelyn (1899–1975)

American leading lady of the silent era. Name variations: appeared in several early films as Betty Riggs. Born Mary Elizabeth Riggs on October 20, 1899, in Tampa, Florida; died in 1975; married Bernie Fineman, 1922 (divorced, 1927); married Harry Edwards (dates unknown); later married Harry Fox (died, 1959).

Films include: The Pit *(1914);* The Shooting of Dan McGrew *(1915);* The Lure of Heart's Desire *(1916);* The Soul Market *(1916);* The Spell of the Yukon *(1916);* The Iron Woman *(1916);* Who's Your Neighbor? *(1917);* Raffles, the Amateur Crackman *(1917);* Daybreak *(1918);* The Other Man's Wife *(1919);* The Glorious Lady *(1919);* Fool's Gold *(1919);* The Shuttle of life *(UK, 1920);* The Law Divine *(UK, 1920);* Sonia *(UK, 1921);* The Spanish Jade *(Spain, 1922);* Held to Answer *(1923);* Loving Lies *(1924);* The Plunderer *(1924);* The Arizona Express *(1924);* The Lone Chance *(1924);* The Desert Outlaw *(1924);* The Dangerous Flirt *(1924);* My Husband's Wives *(1924);* Silk Stocking Sal *(1924);* Midnight Molly *(1925);* Forbidden Cargo *(1925);* Alias Mary Flynn *(1925);* Lady Robinhood *(1925);* Smooth as Satin *(1925);* Three Wise Crooks *(1925);* Queen o' Dia-

Evelyn
Brent

monds *(1926)*; The Impostor *(1926)*; The Jade Cup *(1926)*; Flame of the Argentine *(1926)*; Love 'Em and Leave 'Em *(1926)*; Love's Greatest Mistake *(1927)*; Blind Alleys *(1927)*; Underworld *(1927)*; Women's Wares *(1927)*; Beau Sabreur *(1928)*; The Last Command *(1928)*; The Showdown *(1928)*; A Night of Mystery *(1928)*; The Dragnet *(1928)*; His Tiger Lady *(1928)*; The Mating Call *(1928)*; Interference *(1929)*; Broadway *(1929)*; Fast Company *(1929)*; Woman Trap *(1929)*; Why Bring That Up? *(1929)*; Darkened

Rooms *(1929)*; Slightly Scarlet *(1930)*; Framed *(1930)*; The Silver Horde *(1930)*; Madonna of the Streets *(1930)*; Traveling Husbands *(1931)*; The Mad Parade *(1931)*; Pagan Lady *(1931)*; High Pressure *(1932)*; Attorney for the Defense *(1932)*; The Crusader *(1932)*; The World Gone Mad *(1933)*; Home on the Range *(1935)*; The Nitwits *(1935)*; Hopalong Cassidy Returns *(1936)*; The President's Mystery *(1936)*; (serial) Jungle Jim *(1937)*; Night Club Scandal *(1937)*; The Last Train from Madrid *(1937)*; Daughter of Shanghai *(1937)*; Tip-Off Girls *(1938)*; Mr. Wong—Detective *(1938)*; The Law West of Tombstone *(1938)*; The Mad Empress *(1940)*; (serial) Holt of the Secret Service *(1941)*; Emergency Landing *(1941)*; Westward Ho! *(1942)*; The Seventh Victim *(1943)*; Bowery Champs *(1944)*; The Golden Eye *(1948)*.

Evelyn Brent, under contract to a production company affiliated with Metro known as Popular Plays and Players, began her career as an extra in silents as early as 1915. One of her first leading roles was opposite John Barrymore in *Raffles, the Amateur Crackman* two years later. Following World War I, she sailed to England where she was a chorus girl in the West End production of *The Ruined Lady* (1920).

Brent made a number of films while abroad; though most were British, several were made in Holland. *The Spanish Jade*, filmed in Spain in 1922, was her first success. On the strength of this, she returned to Hollywood to co-star with Douglas Fairbanks, Sr. in *The Thief of Bagdad* (1924), but she was replaced at the last minute. Evelyn Brent went on to make a number of lackluster films for Fox and mediocre photoplays with the Film Booking Office. Several movies for Paramount also flopped. It was Josef von Sternberg's masterpiece 1927 *Underworld* that finally capitalized on Brent's sultry good looks, and she followed this with 1928's *The Last Command*, a small movie that enjoyed enormous success.

Brent's career suffered with the advent of talkies, though her voice was pleasant enough to make the transition. *The Silver Horde* (1930), with Louis Wolheim, received a lukewarm reception, as did *Pagan Lady* (1931) in spite of her popular co-star Conrad Nagel. Brent undertook a vaudeville tour in 1933 and made *Home on the Range* in 1935 with Jackie Coogan. *Golden Eye* (1948) was one of her last cinematic attempts. During the 1950s, Brent worked as an actor's representative for the **Thelma White** Agency. Widowed in 1959, with her fortune gone, she took an apartment in Westwood Village, California, with longtime friend **Dorothy Herzog**. Late

in life, Brent often heard from loyal fans, many who had been born well after her heyday. Bemused by adulation that came too late, she once thanked a fan for his interest while adding, "where were all you people when I needed you?"

SOURCES:
Lamparski, Richard. *Whatever Became of . . . ?* 3rd series. NY: Crown, 1971.

Brent, Linda (1813–1897).
See Jacobs, Harriet A.

Brent, Margaret (c. 1601–1671)
American colonist. Born around 1601; died prior to May 1671; one of 13 children.

Though descended from royalty, Margaret Brent inherited very little on the death of her parents because English inheritance laws were stacked against women. Because of that and because of religious intolerance in then Protestant England, the Catholic Brent, along with her sister Mary and two brothers, immigrated to the newly founded Maryland colony in 1638. Starting with a land grant from Lord Baltimore, Brent began to acquire more and more land in the colony. As far as is known, Mistress Margaret Brent of Maryland, in 1647, was the first woman to demand representation, which was based on property. After several hours of heated debate, her petition was denied.

Brent of Bin-Bin (1879–1954).
See Franklin, Miles.

Brentano, Bettina or Elizabeth (1785–1859).
See Arnim, Bettine von.

Brentano, Sophie (1770–1806).
See Mereau-Brentano, Sophie.

Brereton, Mrs. (1756–1845).
See Kemble, Priscilla.

Breshko-Breshkovskaya, Ekaterina (1844–1934).
See Breshkovsky, Catherine.

Breshkovskaia, Breshkovskaya, or Breshkovskoi, Katerina.
See Breshkovsky, Catherine.

Breshkovsky, Catherine (1844–1934)
Russian revolutionary, educator, political leader, and a vocal opponent of the Bolshevik government who

spent decades in a tsarist prison and exile for her political views. Name variations: Ekaterina Breshko-Breshkovskaya, Katerina Breshkovskaia, Breshkovskaya, or Breshkovskoi; (nickname) "little grandmother of the revolution." Pronunciation: BRESH-kawf-skee. Born Ekaterina Konstantinova Verigo on January 13, 1844, in Ivanovo village, Vitebsk province, Russia; died in Prague, Czechoslovakia, on September 12, 1934; daughter of Konstantine Mikhailovich Verigo (a retired lieutenant in the Russian Imperial Guards who descended from the Polish nobility) and Olga Ivanovna Verigo (née Goremykina, a graduate of the Smolny Institute, a prestigious girl's school in St. Petersburg); though Breshkovsky received no formal education, she was schooled at home; married Nikolai Breshko-Breshkovsky, 1869; children: one child, Nikolai (b. 1874).

Catherine Breshkovsky devoted her life to bringing social and political change to turn-of-the-century Russia. She began her political career as a liberal, although she later discarded the path of reform for a brand of revolutionary activism known as populism. Following years in tsarist exile, she helped found the Socialist Revolutionary Party, a one-time opponent of the Marxist Bolsheviks who eventually came to power. She ended her political career as an avid anti-Bolshevik, then turned to her other great love, teaching, in effective exile in the new Republic of Czechoslovakia. Her years of service to the revolutionary cause earned her the sobriquet "little grandmother of the revolution."

Catherine's parents, Konstantine Mikhailovich Verigo and **Olga Ivanovna Verigo**, were members of Russia's privileged gentry class. She had two sisters and two brothers and most of her childhood years were spent on an estate in Chernigov province, where the family moved shortly after she was born in 1844. Like most girls of the era, she did not go to school; unlike most, however, she received an education at home both from her own voracious reading and from governesses, who taught her, among other subjects, German and French. In addition, she also received extensive religious instruction from her mother.

Catherine
Breshkovsky

Catherine turned 17 in 1861, a year that was to be an important watershed for both her and Russia at large. Following years of rancorous debate, the Russian government dismantled the country's centuries-old practice of serfdom, whereby peasants were tied for life to gentry owners and their land, and the country's 20 million serfs were officially freed. Tsar Alexander II (1855–1881), whose reformist policies allowed the Emancipation to take place, is consequently known as the Tsar Liberator.

A love, an all-absorbing love, boundless love, but not a feeling of abstract duty, was the motive power of all her life. . . . She was able to love not only each from among the simple people, but also all the people collectively.

—P.B. Axelrod

Much anticipated, however, the settlement proved to be a great disappointment to the peasantry and reformers alike, as the nobility was unwilling to give up their serf labor, and the government was unwilling or unable to oppose them. Nonetheless, Catherine was initially greatly excited by the Emancipation, and she decided that she would help the peasants in their new lives by opening a school for them on her family's estate. Although she tried for two years, Catherine was unable to fully motivate the students to learn, and the venture was ultimately a failure. She later wrote that, although the school was unsuccessful, the experience converted her "from a naive young girl to an independent woman."

Following the closure of the school, Catherine traveled to the capital St. Petersburg, where she worked as a governess, one of the few occupations open to women. Since women were forbidden to attend university classes, she sat in on illegal women's courses and went to underground political meetings. While in the capital, she met many of the day's leading liberals and revolutionaries, including the influential anarchist Prince Peter Kropotkin.

In 1866, she returned home at her parents' request. She was at this time fully dedicated to changing Russian society, but only through official channels, and she spent much of her time working with the local *zemstvo*. The *zemstva* were provincial elected bodies that had been recently established by the central government to address educational, medical, and other needs at a community level.

While working on zemstvo initiatives, she met Nikolai Breshko-Breshkovsky, a fellow member of the gentry, whom she married in 1869. Together, they established an agricultural school and cooperative bank on her family estate. She remained a reformer throughout this period, especially as the government of the district was relatively progressive. However, the government changed in 1871, and it became more difficult for Breshkovsky to remain true to her reformist ideals. Eventually, she decided that the only way to bring about true change in Russia was to join the revolutionary cause and bring it about by force.

In 1873, she went to Kiev to do just that, leaving behind both physically and politically her parents and her husband, who refused to join her. At age 30, she was one of the oldest members of Kiev's revolutionary community, as most of the radicals were in their late teens and early 20s. The apartment she shared with her sister **Olga** became the center of the Kiev Commune, which served as a meeting place, training center and occasional living quarters for the city's revolutionary youth. Her sister **Nadezhda** also visited the commune but did not take part in their activities. Olga's participation in the Commune was brief, as she died shortly after it was established.

Cut off from her family, Breshkovsky offered to tutor the students she met to raise money for her living expenses. She also taught French at a private girls' school, and later remembered trying to add some social commentary to the girls' lessons. She was soon forced to abandon the classes, however, as she was unable to maintain them while continuing her political activities.

In the fall of 1873, Breshkovsky returned to St. Petersburg, where she met members of the Chaikovsky circle, one of the most famous of the many revolutionary groups that had sprung up in Russian cities during Tsar Alexander's reign. Her twin interests in education and revolution were evident when she helped convince the group that revolutionary indoctrination of the Russian masses would never be successful without first providing them with a basic education, a stance she would continue to hold throughout her life.

In early 1874, Breshkovsky gave birth to a son Nikolai with whom she had been pregnant when she arrived in Kiev. She soon handed the child over to the care of her brother and sister-in-law, as she knew she would not be able to fully devote herself to both the revolution and to her son. She would not see Nikolai again until he was 22 years old.

Catherine then became involved in one of the most famous and unusual events of the Russian revolutionary era—the "to the people" movement. Because Russian cities, where the revolutionary movement was centered, were isolated from the rural dwellers, many of the young rebels had little or no contact with the peasants who formed the bulk of the Russian population. In the mid-1870s, the revolutionaries decided that they should see the Russian people, the *narod*, face-to-face in an effort to establish links between themselves, an urban, educated minority, and the vast rural, illiterate majority whom they saw as being the heart of Russia.

This movement reached its peak during the summer of 1874, which has become known as the "mad summer" or the "Children's Crusade," when thousands of young people abandoned their families, their studies, and their lives in the cities and fanned out among the peasant population. Sometimes, young people simply met with peasants to observe and attempt to understand them better. Others were more interested in recruiting them to the revolutionary cause.

Because she had far more experience with the peasantry than most of the other participants in the "mad summer," Breshkovsky served as a model for the younger revolutionaries and helped prepare them before they set out to the countryside. She traveled to various workshops to oversee the teaching of skills, such as shoemaking, metal-working, and weaving, that the students would need to be accepted into village life.

Disguised in peasant clothes and having aged her hands and face with acid, Breshkovsky set out that summer with two other activists. Together, they traveled to a number of villages, including Belozerie, Semyela, and Cherkass. Sometimes Catherine simply talked to the women and men she met and gently probed their impressions of their lives. Elsewhere, she was more overt and set up meetings, mostly for the village men, to discuss Russia's political and social situation and try to convince them that it needed to be changed.

The entire effort was short-lived, and in late September Breshkovsky was arrested in the town of Varvaska. As with the hundreds of others who were apprehended that summer, she likely raised the suspicions of the authorities because of her ability to read, which would have been a highly unusual skill for a peasant, particularly a peasant woman. Despite her arrest, she had proven to be one of the most successful of those who went to the people, perhaps because she was older and less impatient, or perhaps because she had worked with the peasantry in the past.

Overall, however, the movement was a disaster from a practical viewpoint. Most of the students did not blend in at all in the villages and were quickly turned over to the police by the peasants. Furthermore, the authorities' harsh reprisals later convinced the students that revolutionary violence was the only recourse left to them.

Following her arrest, Breshkovsky spent the years 1874 to 1877 in Moscow and St. Petersburg prisons. She was a defendant in the Trial of the 193 (October 1877–January 1878), where she was found guilty of spreading revolutionary propaganda and exiled to the Siberian Kara mines. She and several others sentenced with her were the first women in Russian history ever sentenced to hard labor.

In her term of exile, Breshkovsky lived at the Kara mines for ten months, then was sent to the town of Barguzin. She tried to escape in July 1881 but was caught the following month and received another sentence of hard labor as a result. Following that work term, she spent eight years in the town of Seliginsk on the Chinese border. There she was interviewed by George Kennan, an American author who was one of the first to describe the hardships of life in Russian exile in his 1891 work *Siberia and the Exile System*. After four years of free exile, during which she was allowed to travel throughout Siberia on her own, she was permitted to return to European Russia in 1896.

On arrival, Breshkovsky attempted to contact her son, but he did not wish to be associated with her revolutionary politics. Indeed, she immediately resumed her clandestine political work. For two years, she traveled among the peasantry as, unlike many others, she had maintained her faith that the Russian masses must remain at the heart of the revolutionary struggle.

After going underground to avoid the tsarist police in 1898, Breshkovsky spent the next few years helping to establish the Socialist Revolutionary Party (SRs), heir to the 1860s and '70s populist peasant groups in which she had played a part. The SRs placed their hope for Russia's future in a socialist revolution based in the countryside. Like their populist predecessors, they did not shy away from the possibility of using terror to achieve their goals. Breshkovsky helped distribute illegal revolutionary literature and traveled the country raising support for the party. In 1902, she also founded a Peasants' Union in Saratov as an auxiliary to the main SR Party.

In 1903, Breshkovsky fled to Rumania to escape the tsarist police, who were no more amenable to political activism then than they had been in 1874. From Rumania, she went to the United States to raise money for the party as well as general awareness of the revolutionary cause in Russia. Her efforts received a significant boost when Russian police killed hundreds of peaceful demonstrators in front of the Tsar's Winter Palace in January 1905 in what has become known as Bloody Sunday. Through her efforts, she raised approximately 40,000 francs for the SRs. Several months later, she returned to Russia, just in time for the thwarted Revolution of the fall of 1905.

Two years later, Breshkovsky was again arrested by the tsarist police for her illegal political activities. She was jailed in St. Petersburg's Peter and Paul Fortress for two years and tried in 1910 as a revolutionary. Once again found guilty, she was sentenced to a lifetime of Siberian exile in the town of Kerensk on the Lena River; she was 65 years old. While in Kerensk, she met a young lawyer named Alexander Kerensky, who was to play a vital role in Russian politics, as well as Catherine's political life. She again tried to escape in November 1913, although she was once more unsuccessful. Though a campaign was launched among her contacts in the U.S. to pressure the government to release her, she remained in exile for another four years in several towns, including Iakutsk and Minusinsk.

World War I presented the tsarist government with a challenge it could not face after decades of internal and external crises and inadequate leadership. In March 1917, the centuries-old Romanov dynasty was overthrown and a liberal Provisional Government took its place; Alexander Kerensky was appointed minister of justice. One of the new government's first acts was to order the release of all political prisoners held in tsarist jails. Upon her release, Catherine returned to the capital, which had been renamed Petrograd during the war.

That year, Breshkovsky was made an honorary member of the SR Central Committee. She was a fervent supporter of Kerensky and a strong proponent of the Provisional Government policy of remaining in World War I, even though the war was draining the country's resources and causing mounting popular discontent. Many of her fellow party members, known

as the Left SRs, urged the Provisional Government to leave the Alliance with France and England. Those who wished to remain in the war, the Right SRs, were known derisively as "defensists." The issue, among others, eventually led to an irreparable rift in the party. Although Breshkovsky continued to call for a public show of unity, her strong views on the war and unswerving support for Kerensky placed her squarely in the camp of the Right SRs.

Breshkovsky was very active during the period of the Provisional Government. She toured southern Russia to meet with peasants and soldiers and disseminate among them party propaganda, specifically the views of the Right SRs. She also combined her support of the war with her interest in women's issues by supporting the formation of women's battalions. She helped set up a publishing house in Moscow, Zemlia i Volia, and maintained her involvement with the SRs' Society for the Distribution of Literature.

Breshkovsky also retained her contacts with the Americans she had met in 1904–05 and obtained money to establish a printing press. Her ties with American fund raisers were later used against her when claims were made that she accepted their money for the party on the condition that she continue to support the cause of the war and maintain a reformist, rather than a revolutionary, position. Such an arrangement would have made her appear to be working for the Americans' interests. Although not completely incorrect, the allegations were flimsy; her interests coincided with the Americans', they were not dictated by them. Nevertheless, the charges were used by her political enemies to discredit her.

In July 1917, a series of spontaneous riots in the capital, known as the July Days, led to a shift in the Provisional Government, and Alexander Kerensky became the prime minister. As one of his most vocal supporters, Breshkovsky briefly served as his advisor and moved into the Winter Palace, the seat of government. However, the Provisional Government proved as incapable as its tsarist predecessor of handling the war issue or the many other national problems it faced, and, in November 1917, the government was overthrown by the SRs' main socialist rivals, the urban-based Bolshevik Party led by Vladimir Ilyich Lenin. Breshkovsky was a strong opponent of the Bolsheviks, and she often claimed that they were paid German agents, a claim with little or no basis. She left the capital shortly after the revolution and went into hiding in and around Moscow for approximately six months, agitating against the new government. In the spring of 1918, she joined an anti-Bolshevik uprising staged by a Czech Legion stationed on the Volga River. The rebellion was unsuccessful, however, and Breshkovsky fled the country, never to return.

Breshkovsky journeyed to the United States, this time to raise money both for the anti-Bolshevik cause and for the establishment of schools for war orphans. Her second tour was not as successful as her first, partially because of the virulence of her anti-Bolshevik crusade, unwelcome among her supporters, and she soon returned to Europe. In 1919, she settled down to an emigre life in the northern region of the Republic of Czechoslovakia, in an impoverished territory that had been under Russian rule until the Bolshevik government turned it over to the newly established country after the war. For over a decade, she worked as a school administrator and founded Russian-language schools to serve the area's emigre population.

Catherine Breshkovsky retired completely from public life in early 1934, after ten years of poor health. The last few months of her life were spent on a farm outside Prague where she was cared for by Russian emigres. The "little grandmother of the revolution" died there on September 12, 1934, at the age of 90.

SOURCES:

Breshko-Breshkovskaya, Ekaterina. *Hidden Springs of the Russian Revolution.* Stanford, CA: Stanford University Press, 1931.

———, "Rannie gody," in *Novyi Zhurnal.* No. 60, 1960, pp. 179–195.

Good, Jane, and David Jones. *Babushka: The Life of the Russian Revolutionary Ekaterina K. Breshko-Breshkovskaia.* Newtonville: Oriental Research Papers, 1991.

Jones, David R. "Ekaterina Konstantinova Breshko-Breshkovskaya," in *The Modern Encyclopedia of Russian and Soviet History.* Vol. 5. Edited by Joseph L. Wieczynski. Gulf Breeze, FL: Academic International Press, 1977, pp. 164–69.

Kerensky, Alexander. "Catherine Breshkovsky (1844–1934)," in *The Slavonic and East European Review.* Vol. 13, no. 38. January 1935, pp. 428–431.

Radkey, Oliver H. *The Agrarian Foes of Bolshevism: Promise and Default of the Russian Socialist Revolutionaries February to October 1917.* NY: Columbia University Press, 1958.

Stites, Richard. *Women's Liberation Movement in Russia: Feminism, Nihilism and Bolshevism.* Princeton, NJ: Princeton University Press, 1978.

SUGGESTED READING:

Kennan, George, *Siberia and the Exile System.* 2 vols. NY: Century, 1891.

COLLECTIONS:

Blackwell, Alice Stone, ed. *The Little Grandmother of the Russian Revolution: Reminiscences and Letters of Catherine Breshkovskaya.* Boston, MA: Little, Brown, 1918.

Susan Brazier, freelance writer, Ottawa, Ontario, Canada

Breslau, Louise (1857–1927).

See Purser, Sarah for sidebar.

Breslauer, Marianne (1909—)

German photographer. Name variations: (pseudonym) Ipp. Born in Berlin, Germany, in 1909; married Dr. Walter Feilchenfeldt in 1936.

Marianne Breslauer trained in Berlin, then went to Paris where she was a student of Man Ray. There, she photographed extensively, specializing in urban documentation and portraits. Returning to Berlin in 1930, she entered the Ullstein studio under **Elsbeth Heddenhausen**; she was soon back in Paris, however, where she continued her portrait work, photographing artists Pablo Picasso and Ambrois Vollard among others. Breslauer also traveled to Spain and Zurich to photograph for the Mauritius and Academia agencies. Her work was restricted under Hitler's Germany, and she photographed with the Kind agency in 1934 using the pseudonym "Ipp." During the 1930s, she was widely published in German periodicals, including *Frankfurter Illustrierten, Funkstunde, Weltkreir,* and *Weltspiegel.* In 1936, Breslauer married an art dealer and immigrated to Switzerland, where she stopped making photographs to become an art dealer.

Bretagne, Anne de (c. 1477–1514).

See Anne of Brittany.

Bretagne, countess or duchess of.

See Brittany, countess or duchess of.

Brewer, Teresa (1931—)

American popular singer of the 1950s. Born on May 7, 1931, in Toledo, Ohio; married Bob Thiele, 1972.

With her wide eyes and powerful voice, Teresa Brewer began her career on the radio at the age of two. She toured with the Major Bowes talent show for seven years, then dropped out of the business for seven more before resuming her career at 16. In 1950, her recording of "Music! Music! Music!" set her career in motion and, for the next decade, she churned out mega-hits such as "'Til I Waltz Again with You," "Ricochet Romance," and "Let Me Go Lover." Brewer's unusual voice also lent itself to country tunes like "Bo Weevil," "Empty Arms," and "You Send Me." She made one movie, *Those Red Heads from Seattle*, in 1953, and did frequent television and club appearances. Brewer also composed novelty songs, including "I Love Mickey," "Down the Holiday Trail," "There's Nothing as Lonesome as Saturday Night," and "Hush-a-bye Wink-a-bye Do." In 1972, Brewer married Bob Thiele, who had produced some of her early hits. He produced her later albums as well, including several with jazz greats Count Basie, Duke Ellington, and Bobby Hackett.

Brewster, Anne Hampton

(1818–1892)

American fiction writer, poet, essayist, and early female foreign correspondent, who published primarily in Philadelphia, New York, and Boston newspapers, and struggled daily to maintain her independence. Name variations: (pseudonym) Enna Duval. Born Anne Hampton Brewster in Philadelphia, Pennsylvania, on October 29, 1818; died in Siena, Italy, on April 1, 1892; daughter of Francis Enoch Brewster (an attorney) and Maria Hampton Brewster; educated primarily at home by her mother and briefly at Mary Huston's school, Philadelphia; never married; no children.

*G*enevieve [Welling] called me . . . 'a social outlaw' and she is right. I hate the arbitrary rules of privileged society.

—**Anne Hampton Brewster**

Converted to Catholicism (1848); published first poem and first novel (1849); served as an editor at Graham's American Monthly Magazine *for a year (beginning 1850); sued older brother for a portion of their parents' estate (1856); moved to Bridgeton, New Jersey (1858); published second novel (1860); published third novel (1866); moved to Rome, Italy (1868); became foreign correspondent (1869); became member of Arcadia (1873); moved to Siena, Italy (1889).*

Selected publications: Spirit Sculpture *(1849);* Compensation; or, Always a Future *(1860);* Saint Martin's Summer *(1866); at least 52 short stories, 11 pieces of nonfiction, and four poems in* Atlantic Monthly, Blackwood's Edinburgh Magazine, The Cosmopolitan, Cummings Evening Bulletin, Daily Evening Bulletin, Daily Graphic, The Dollar Newspaper, Dwight's Journal of Music, Godey's Lady's Book, Graham's American Monthly Magazine, Harper's Magazine, Knickerbocker, Lippincott's Magazine, Neal's Saturday Gazette, Old and New, Peterson's Magazine, Sartain's Union Magazine *(1845–90); short stories anthologized in* Chaplet of Roses *(1851) and* Short Stories for Spare Moments *(1869); foreign correspondence appeared in* Boston Daily Advertiser *(1870–83),* Boston Sunday Herald *(1887–88),* Chicago Daily News *(1885–88),* Cincinnati Commercial *(1870–71),* Cincinnati Gazette *(1878),* Daily Evening Telegraph *(Philadelphia, 1878–82),* Daily Graphic *(New York, 1876),* European Correspondent *(Paris, 1887),* New York Evening Post *(1886),* New York World *(1876–78),* Newark Courier *(1869–1870),* Parisian *(1879–80),* Philadelphia Evening Bulletin *(1869–78), and* San Francisco Chronicle *(1885).*

At the age of 29, Anne Hampton Brewster wrote in her journal: "I have accomplished nothing in Life yet, all seems but as preparation. I have pictured such fancy scenes—that are never to be realized. . . . Am I to leave this world before the realization of these fancy dreams?" By the time of her death in 1892, Brewster had published numerous poems, essays, reviews, short stories, three novels, and countless newspaper articles. From 1858 on, she had supported herself largely with the earnings from this writing.

Anne Brewster was born in Philadelphia to Francis and **Maria Hampton Brewster**, Anglo-American Protestants of the middle class. Despite several suitors, Anne did not marry, writing in her journal (1845): "I have mind enough & strength to take care of myself. . . . I will never marry for mere convenience." Brewster's attitude toward marriage was relative to her father's abandonment of the family in 1834, when he began living with his mistress and two illegitimate sons. Brewster and her mother became financially dependent on her older brother, Benjamin Harris Brewster.

Anne wrote poetry until 1837, when Benjamin discouraged her. She stopped writing for six years until she found a supportive female role model in the actress *****Charlotte Cushman**, regained her confidence as a writer, and started publishing short stories in 1845 under the pseudonym "Enna Duval." Like most 19th-century American woman's fiction, hers asserted that marriage for financial security is worse than remaining unmarried. Brewster abhorred economic dependency and believed that all women could develop the Victorian qualities of hard work, morality, and social responsibility in order to find happiness.

She converted to Catholicism in 1848, a year before she published her first book, *Spirit Sculpture*, a moderately successful novella concerning religious conversion. In 1849, Brewster also published her first poem, "New Year Meditation," in *Graham's Magazine*, where she secured a position as an editor in March 1850. This appointment lasted until May 1851, resulting in numerous published pieces and a $500 yearly salary.

When Maria and Francis Brewster died in 1853 and 1854, respectively, the estate was split among Francis' three sons. Benjamin planned to support his sister indefinitely, but she sued him for a portion of the estate in 1856. The court case prompted her to spend 15 months in Vevey, Switzerland, and Naples, Italy, beginning in May 1857. Upon her return to America, she settled in Bridgeton, New Jersey, supporting herself by writing and by teaching music and French. Brewster won control of her rental property, but Benjamin retained control of the family estate from which she received periodic payments. She disapproved of this arrangement and became permanently estranged from her older brother.

With the publication of her second novel, *Compensation; Or, Always a Future* (1860), Brewster began publishing under her true name. The story, set in Switzerland, is thematically similar to her short fiction, with discourses on art, music, nature, literature, philosophy, and religion. It was successful enough to warrant a second edition in 1870. Her third and last novel, *Saint Martin's Summer* (1866), is structured as the narrator's travel journal from Switzerland to Naples and explores the superiority of spiritual to physical love.

Brewster's decision to move to Rome in 1868 was fueled not only by a desire to distance herself further from Benjamin, but by a tradition of Italian travel among American writers and artists in the 19th century. With unreliable income from her inheritance, she needed a more profitable vocation than fiction writing and accepted her first newspaper engagements in 1869 as a foreign correspondent with the *Philadelphia Evening Bulletin* and the *Newark Courier*, reporting on the political, religious, scientific, and cultural events in Rome. Her newspaper work, she wrote, was "elevating and beneficial—it confers a double benefit on myself and others." In 1873, Brewster became a member of Arcadia, the poetical academy in Rome, and held a weekly salon where she entertained writers, artists, and musicians.

During the 1880s, income from her inheritance dropped considerably, and Brewster's journalism career declined due to changes in newspaper-writing styles. In 1889, she moved to Siena, Italy, in order to meet expenses without additional income from writing. Anne Hampton

Brewster died in Siena on April 1, 1892, leaving several writing projects unfinished, including a collection of her newspaper correspondence. Through her career, a unique combination of gentility, self-revelation, and scholarship had endeared Brewster to her audience, making her one of the most popular foreign correspondents of her day.

SOURCES:

Baym, Nina. *Woman's Fiction. A Guide to Novels By and about Women in America, 1820–1870*. Ithaca, NY: Cornell University Press, 1978.

Fisher, Estelle. *A Gentle Journalist Abroad: The Papers of Anne Hampton Brewster in The Library Company of Philadelphia*. Philadelphia, PA: The Free Library of Philadelphia, 1947.

Wright, Nathalia. *American Novelists in Italy. The Discoverers: Allston to James*. Philadelphia, PA: University of Pennsylvania Press, 1965.

SUGGESTED READING:

Larrabee, Denise M. *Anne Hampton Brewster: 19th-Century Author and "Social Outlaw."* Philadelphia, PA: Library Company of Philadelphia, 1992.

COLLECTIONS:

Brewster's correspondence, journals, and manuscripts located at The Library Company of Philadelphia.

Denise M. Larrabee,
author and historian,
Philadelphia, Pennsylvania

Brézé, Charlotte de (c. 1444/49–?).

See Diane de Poitiers for sidebar.

Brezhneva, Viktoriya (1908–1995)

First lady of the Soviet Union from 1964 to 1982 who lived in near-total obscurity while her husband was a leading Soviet political figure, though her family would later become a symbol of the favoritism and corruption of an "Era of Stagnation." Name variations: Viktoria Brezhnev. Born Viktoriya Petrovna Denisova in Kursk in 1908; died in Moscow on July 5, 1995; daughter of Pyotr Nikanorovich Denisov (a train engineer) and a housewife mother; married Leonid Brezhnev (1906–1982), in 1928; children: Galina Brezhneva (b. 1929); Yuri (b. 1933).

Until the appearance of *Raisa Gorbachev* as first lady of the Soviet Union in 1985, it was customary for the wives of the Kremlin leadership to remain in the shadows, unreported on in the press, unacknowledged in any official fashion. Viktoriya Brezhneva, wife of Leonid Brezhnev for more than a half-century, was the last of the Soviet leadership's wives to play this self-effacing role.

She was born in Kursk in 1908 into a proletarian family. Her father Pyotr Nikanorovich

Denisov was a train engineer, her mother a housewife who kept busy raising Viktoriya and four other children. Viktoriya was a nursing student in Kursk when she met Leonid Ilyich Brezhnev, an agronomy student, at a school dance. They married in 1928 and their first child, a daughter Galina, was born in 1929; a son Yuri followed in 1933. Uninterested in politics, Viktoriya Brezhneva raised her two children and enjoyed the perquisites that accrued to her and her family as her husband's career in the Communist bureaucracy flourished. After many years in the provinces, the Brezhnevs moved to Moscow in 1952 when Leonid Brezhnev became a member of the Central Committee of the Soviet Communist Party. By 1957, he had become a leading political figure, serving under Nikita Khrushchev. After Khrushchev's fall from power in October 1964, Brezhnev seized the reins and would rule until his death in November 1982. Throughout these years, Viktoriya was a dutiful wife who ignored her husband's many affairs as well as his preoccupations with hunting and expensive foreign automobiles.

While her husband was unchallenged ruler of the Soviet Union, she remained virtually unknown to the Soviet people. Even before he achieved supreme power, she and her family benefited as members of the Communist Party's *Nomenklatura,* the privileged elite who enjoyed material advantages over ordinary Soviet citizens, ranging from superior housing to plentiful food, plush vacations, advanced medical care, and educational advantages for their children. Brezhnev's regime emphasized impressive feats of space exploration, as well as transforming the Soviet army into the largest in the world and making the navy a major geopolitical force. But domestically, the economy stagnated and society became increasingly cynical and graft-ridden.

During the almost two decades of her husband's rule, Viktoriya did not see Leonid for long periods of time. She often went to a one-room apartment of her own that was stacked with boxes of gifts her husband had received over the years. Her acquisitiveness became an obsession. The few family members privileged to visit this room noticed that sealed boxes on the floor were carefully marked with the names of Viktoriya's children, nieces and nephews as well as other members of the next generation of the privileged Brezhnev clan.

Her husband's distinctly non-Socialist love of luxury and her own increasing materialism were coupled with their children's undisciplined natures. **Galina Brezhneva**, an intelligent young woman who studied literature and philosophy,

graduated from Kishinev University, and she soon was attracted to the glittering world of the circus. In 1951, she married Evgenii Milaev, a circus acrobat and strongman. The marriage lasted eight years. Her second marriage to Igor Kio, a man 15 years her junior who was also from the world of the circus, so infuriated her father that Leonid Brezhnev sent the militia to break up the union. She chose as her third husband a lieutenant-colonel of the militia, Iurii Churbanov, whose career prospered due to favoritism. After growing tired of this marriage, Galina took up with a gypsy actor whose career also prospered until, thanks to the Brezhnev family "pull," he found himself engaged by Moscow's famous Bolshoi Theater. Once the full enormity of high-level corruption during the Brezhnev era was exposed, Galina was at the center of several scandals, which included an accusation against her for stealing diamonds. Her husband Churbanov was put on trial and found guilty of various charges of large-scale corruption.

Like his sister, Yuri Brezhnev at first showed promise. He completed his studies in metallurgical sciences and took various engineering jobs. After his father assumed supreme power in 1964, however, nepotism began to determine the nature of his career. By 1976, he had become deputy minister of Foreign Trade and by 1981 was a candidate member of the powerful Central Committee of the Soviet Communist Party. By the time of his father's death in 1982, Yuri's personal life was a shambles and his chronic alcoholism had become well-known in upper echelons. He was dismissed by the new regime of Yuri Andropov in 1983 and sent to work in the provinces.

In her last decades, Viktoriya Brezhneva had little in her life to bring her the consolations some parents derive from their children. Her husband's reputation was in shreds within a few years after his death, his period of rule being universally described in the Soviet Union as an era of stagnation and corruption (*epokha zastoia*). Viktoriya Brezhneva's health declined dramatically; she was physically enfeebled and virtually blind by the end of the 1980s. The lives of her two children had turned into disasters. In one of her last interviews, she stated that her children "gave me much happiness when I was young, but as they grew up they brought me much grief." Virtually forgotten by the peoples of Russia and the former Soviet Union, Viktoriya Brezhneva died in Moscow on July 5, 1995.

SOURCES:

Brezhneva, Luba (Viktoriya Brezhneva's niece). *The World I Left Behind: Pieces of a Past.* Translated by Geoffrey Polk. NY: Random House, 1995.

Opposite page
Mary
Brian

Dornberg, John. *Brezhnev: The Masks of Power.* London: André Deutsch, 1974.

La Penseé Russe, April 1988.

Pozner, Vladimir. *Parting with Illusions: The Extraordinary Life and Controversial Views of the Soviet Union's Leading Commentator.* NY: Avon Books, 1991.

Solovyov, Vladimir, and Elena Klepikova. *Yuri Andropov: A Secret Passage into the Kremlin.* Translated by Guy Daniels in collaboration with the authors. NY: Macmillan, 1983.

Vasilieva, Larissa. *Kremlin Wives.* Translated by Cathy Porter. NY: Arcade, 1994.

"Viktoriya Brezhnev, 87, Widow," in *The New York Times Biographical Service.* July 1995, p. 979.

Vronskaya, Jeanne. "Tormented Prisoner of Russia's Past," in *The European.* June 31–July 2, 1991.

———, and Vladimir Chuguev. *The Biographical Dictionary of the Former Soviet Union.* London: Bowker-Saur, 1992.

John Haag, Associate Professor, University of Georgia, Athens, Georgia

Brian, Mary (1908—)

American film actress. Born Louise Dantzler on February 17, 1908, in Corsicana, Texas; married briefly to artist Jon Whitcomb (marriage dissolved within three months); married film editor George Tomasini, 1937 or 1947 (died, 1967).

Selected films: Peter Pan *(1924);* The Little French Girl *(1925);* Brown of Harvard *(1926);* Beau Geste *(1926);* Running Wild *(1927);* Shanghai Bound *(1927);* Harold Teen *(1928);* Varsity *(1928);* The Man I Love *(1929);* The Virginian *(1929);* The Light of Western Stars *(1930);* The Royal Family of Broadway *(1930);* The Front Page *(1931);* Blessed Event *(1932);* Hard to Handle *(1933);* Girl Missing *(1933);* College Rhythm *(1934);* The Man on the Flying Trapeze *(1935);* Charlie Chan in Paris *(1935);* Killer at Large *(1936);* The Amazing Quest of Ernest Bliss *(UK, 1936);* Navy Bound *(1937);* Calaboose *(1943);* The Dragnet *(1948).*

Remembered as one of the most amiable actresses in pictures, Mary Brian was an unfamiliar face when she was chosen to play Wendy in Paramount's *Peter Pan* (1924) and signed to a seven-year contract. Still a teenager, she attended high school on the studio lot while making as many as seven feature films a year, including the silents *Beau Geste* (1926), *Harold Teen* (1928), and *The Virginian* (1929). The advent of talkies brought roles in such notable films as *Royal Family of Broadway* (1930) and *The Front Page* (1931). She also co-starred with James Cagney in *Hard to Handle* (1933) and W.C. Fields in *The Man on the Flying Trapeze* (1935). In 1936, with her career in decline, Brian accepted

a film offer in England. Returning to America in the late 1930s, she joined a dance act and entertained GIs in Europe and North Africa during World War II. Early in the 1940s, she made a couple of low-budget films that signaled the end of her career. She returned for a brief stint on television in 1955, as the mother of *Janet Waldo in the "Meet Corliss Archer" series.

During the 1930s, Brian's name was linked with Dick Powell, and she was reportedly married briefly to artist Jon Whitcomb. A later marriage to film editor George Tomasini endured until his death in 1967. In later years, she turned her hobby of painting celebrities into a profitable sideline.

SOURCES:
Lamparski, Richard. *Whatever Became of . . . ?* 4th Series. NY: Crown, 1973.

Brianza, Carlotta (1867–1930)

Italian ballerina. Born in Italy in 1867; died in 1930 in Paris, France, possibly a suicide; studied with Carlo Blasis; godmother of Sonia Woizikowska (a dancer and teacher).

Carlotta Brianza made her debut in 1887 at the Arcadia Theater, St. Petersburg, and was subsequently engaged as a guest artist at the Maryinsky Theater (later known as the Kirov), where she made her debut in Lev Ivanov's *Haarlem Tulip*. In 1890, she created the role of Princess Aurora in the Petipa-Tchaikovsky *Sleeping Beauty*. After leaving Russia in 1891, she danced and taught in Italy and Paris. Her final appearance as a dancer was in Diaghilev's London production of *Sleeping Beauty* (then called *The Sleeping Princess*) in 1921.

Brice, Carol (1918–1985)

African-American contralto, the first black American to win the Walter W. Naumberg Award, who performed at the Metropolitan Opera, made many popular recordings, and won a Grammy for Porgy and Bess. Born in Sedalia, North Carolina, on April 16, 1918; died in Norman, Oklahoma, on February 15, 1985; daughter of John Brice (a Presbyterian minister and schoolteacher); niece of Charlotte Hawkins Brown, founder of the Palmer Memorial Institute, a school for black children; attended Talladega College in Alabama and Juilliard School of Music; married Thomas Carey (a vocalist), 1942; children: one son.

Carol Brice was one of a number of remarkable black musicians who established brilliant careers in segregated America. Born in Sedalia, North Carolina, Carol was the youngest of four children. Her father, a minister and school teacher, was frequently absent, so Carol's mother, who found taking care of the large family too great a strain, placed her with her aunt, **Charlotte Hawkins Brown**, when the child was a year old. Brice attended the Palmer Memorial Institute, a school for black children in Sedalia founded by her aunt, then completed her studies at Talladega College in Talladega, Alabama. As early as age three, Brice had shown unusual vocal talent, and she became a member of the Palmer Institute's Glee Club, touring the country as a soloist. In 1939, after completing her Bachelor of Music, she won a fellowship to the Juilliard School of Music. In 1941, she sang at Franklin D. Roosevelt's third presidential inauguration. While still a student in New York, Brice performed in *The Hot Mikado*, Mike Todd's production starring Bill "Bojangles" Robinson, at the 1939 New York World's Fair. Here she met her future husband, Thomas Carey.

In 1944, for her performance as a singer, Brice was the first black to win the Walter W. Naumberg Award. A Town Hall debut followed on March 13, 1945. Shortly afterwards, Columbia Broadcasting System presented her in a televised recital. During the next few years, she performed with the Pittsburgh, Boston, and San Francisco symphonies. Though a wide range of roles was not available to black classical singers in the 1940s and 1950s, Brice still performed frequently. In 1956, she sang the role of the Voodoo Princess in Clarence Cameron White's *Ouanga* at the Metropolitan Opera. She went on to play Addie in Marc Blitzstein's *Regina*, Kakou in Harold Arlen's *Saratoga*, Maude in *Finian's Rainbow*, Queenie in Jerome Kern's *Show Boat*, and Maria in George Gershwin's *Porgy and Bess*. In the 1960s, Brice played *Harriet Tubman in *Gentlemen, Be Seated* and appeared in *Carousel*.

Carol Brice toured extensively in Europe and America. Her brothers, who were musical as well, often traveled with her. Eugene Brice was a Juilliard graduate who sang in numerous Broadway productions while Jonathan was her accompanist, though he had also sung with the Robert Shaw Chorale and the New York City Opera. Carol Brice recorded extensively and won a Grammy for *Porgy and Bess*. With her husband, she joined the music faculty at the University of Oklahoma. Together, they founded the Cimarron Circuit Opera Company and in 1977 were named Oklahoma Musicians of the Year. Known for an outstanding, unforgettable voice, Brice left an indelible mark on the American musical world.

SOURCES:

Smith, Jessie Carney, ed. *Notable Black American Women*. Detroit, MI: Gale Research, 1992.

John Haag,
Athens, Georgia

Brice, Fanny (1891–1951)

American actress, comedienne, and singer, best known as a star of the Ziegfeld Follies *on Broadway and as "Baby Snooks" on radio, whose life served as the basis for the musical and film* Funny Girl. *Born Fania Borach on October 29, 1891, in New York City; died on May 29, 1951, in California; third of four children of Rose and Charles Borach; married Frank White (a businessman), February 14, 1909 (divorced, 1912); married Nick Arnold (real name, Jules Wilford Arnt Stein), June 11, 1919 (divorced, 1927); married Billy Rose (a songwriter and producer), February 2, 1929 (divorced, 1938); children: (second marriage)* **Frances Arnold Stark** *(b. 1919);* William *(b. 1921).*

Began performing in amateur shows in early teens, later appearing in burlesque shows on Broadway as a chorus girl, singer, and dancer; discovered by Florenz Ziegfeld and appeared nearly continuously in his long-running Ziegfeld Follies *(1910–23); through touring, gained a national reputation as a comedienne, bolstered by her later film appearances and her most famous role as "Baby Snooks" on radio.*

Filmography: Night Club *(1928);* My Man *(1928);* Be Yourself! *(1930);* The Man from Blankley's *(1930);* The Great Ziegfeld *(1936);* Everybody Sing *(1938);* Ziegfeld Follies *(1946).*

On a bright early summer day in 1910, pedestrians thronging New York's Great White Way had to make room for a gangly, awkward young woman racing down the crowded Broadway sidewalks. She was waving a piece of paper and shouting something they could barely hear over the clamor of mid-town traffic. As she stopped in front of a burlesque house at Broadway and 47th Street, fellow performers gathered round to look at the piece of paper and hear the amazing news that she, Fanny Brice, had just signed a two-year contract with the legendary Flo Ziegfeld and would be appearing in his *Follies of 1910*. In the entertainment world of the early 1900s, this was considered the pinnacle of success. It was a hard-won victory for a young Jewish woman from New York's Lower East Side, with little formal stage training.

Fanny Brice was the third of four children born to Charlie and **Rose Borach**. Both her parents had come to New York from Europe in the late 19th century. Rose Stern had arrived from a

small village in Hungary and had worked as a children's nurse as well as a "needle worker" in a fur factory before she met Charles Borach, an Alsatian of French-German descent known around the neighborhood as "French Charlie." Charlie was earning $80 a week as a bartender in a Bowery saloon, a considerable sum in those days, and Rose looked forward to improving their condition and maybe even moving uptown someday. But it was the practical Rose that pulled her family up by its collective bootstraps when Charlie quit his job and embarked on a series of ill-conceived get-rich-quick schemes, while playing pinochle and dreaming of fame and fortune.

Fanny, born in October of 1891, spent her first six years amid the jostle and ethnic diversity of the Lower East Side, and would use much of what she absorbed when she first stepped onto a stage. Her most formative years, however, were spent above a candy-and-cigar store the family bought in 1896, in Newark, New Jersey. Blancey's Theater was just down the street, and it was here, when she was supposed to be in school, that Brice spent much of her time, fascinated by the burlesque, vaudeville, and melodramas she glimpsed from her hiding place in the balconies. Though Rose put a stop to it as soon as she found out, Fanny never forgot the laughter and applause.

While Charlie played pinochle and idled away his days with cronies, an increasingly resentful Rose worked hard enough to allow the family to purchase a saloon on Manhattan's Lafayette Street, the first of a group of seven that Rose would manage for a large brewery. Years later, Brice would remember climbing up on the bar on Sunday mornings, when the saloon was closed, to sing and dance for a delighted Charlie and a disapproving Rose. The estrangement between her parents grew deeper, even as the family's finances improved enough for the first of several trips to Europe to visit relatives; after 16 years of marriage, Rose sold the saloon without telling Charlie and moved with her four children to Brooklyn.

At age 14, Fanny made her first stage appearance when she attended Keeney's Theater in downtown Brooklyn for its weekly Amateur Night. Arriving at the theater with only a quarter, she was informed by the box-office clerk that the 50-cent seats were all that were left. Not to be deterred, Brice told the clerk that she was entered in the show, and she was soon ushered into the stage door for free. Though she fully intended to slip away from the lineup of performing hopefuls and join the audience, Frank Keeney was never one for organization and took his acts willy-nilly, regardless of order of entry. Soon, a terrified Fanny found herself thrust out on stage with nothing prepared. All she could think of was a popular ballad of the time, "When You Know You're Not Forgotten by the Girl You Can't Forget." She sang in the same high, clear voice that had so pleased her father on those Sundays in the saloon on Lafayette Street, and by the time she finished the audience was just as delighted. Four dollars in change lay at her feet, and Frank Keeney awarded her the first prize of ten dollars. Rose, for once, was impressed.

> *L*isten, kid. I've done everything in the theater except marry a property man.
>
> —Fanny Brice

Over the next six months, Brice sang at other Amateur Nights at Keeney Theaters throughout Brooklyn, walking away with first prize more often than not. She found that the audiences loved something she'd never thought much about—her knack for dialects, especially the Yiddish and German-Irish patios she had heard growing up on the Lower East Side. Equally as important, she began to "read" an audience and give it what it wanted. "I learned to watch its every move," she later said, "and to beat it to that move. When it wanted sentiment, I gave it tears by the bucketful. When it wanted funny stuff, I clowned to the best of my ability." Watching the money roll in, Rose was soon urging her daughter to try her act in Manhattan, where she could earn $50 a night instead of the $30 that Brooklyn offered. "My mother couldn't read or write," Fanny said, "but she could count like a bugger."

Moving to Manhattan's predominantly German Yorkville section, Brice trooped from audition to audition, like the veteran she would become, and landed a bit part as a chorine in a tawdry melodrama, *The Millionaire's Revenge,* in which she played under the name of "Jenny Waters" and popped out of a giant pie, wearing a flimsy chiffon costume. Next came a bitter disappointment at the hands of George M. Cohan. Fresh from taking Broadway by storm with his *Little Johnny Jones,* Cohan was casting a new show called *The Talk of New York.* Brice sang at the auditions and was hired for the chorus line at $18 a week. But dancing was more prevalent in the show than singing, and this proved Fanny's undoing. Never very graceful, it soon became clear that Fanny's future was not as a dancer. Even though she was in the back row, Cohan no-

ticed the tall, gawky 15-year-old clunking through his choreography and was not pleased. "You!" he bellowed. "You with the St. Vitus' Dance! Back to the kitchen!" Fanny was fired.

Still determined, Brice went on the road as an apprentice in the company of **Rachel Lewis,** a drama-and-dance teacher who made her money by touring shows staffed and acted by pupils who received no pay. Hardly ever on stage, Fanny did seamstress work, cleaned the dingy theaters before show time, and looked after Rachel's dog. But she watched and learned and was clever enough to spot Lewis sneaking out of a hotel in Hazelton, Pennsylvania, about to abandon her troupe and its debts. Brice followed her to the train and forced Lewis to buy her a seat back to New York.

Now 17, Brice finally found a show that would get her noticed: *The Girls From Happyland.* Using the last name of her mother's best friend because "it sounded classy," she appeared for the first time as Fanny Brice and was put in the front row of the chorus line. The show toured the Eastern vaudeville circuit, and, by the time it played Cincinnati, Brice had advanced to a small acting role that attracted enough notice to get her cast in another road show then preparing in New York, *College Girls.* During rehearsals, the show's producer convinced her to do a benefit performance at the Friars' Club. Despite Fanny's protests that she had nothing prepared, she took herself off to Tin Pan Alley to find a song.

Seeking out a music publisher she had dealt with before, Brice was introduced to one of its young songwriters, a man by the name of Irving Berlin, who offered her a song he'd just composed. "Sadie Salome, Go Home" was a spoof on the notorious burlesque number "The Dance of the Seven Veils," then being salaciously performed by the legendary and scantily-clad *Eva Tanguay. Berlin suggested she do the song with a Yiddish accent, and the two created a comedy routine in which Brice appeared in a white sailor's suit and sang: "Don't do that dance, I tell you Sadie./ Dat's not a business for a lady." She brought the house down. "Before the second verse, it happened," Fanny recalled. "The thing that begins to change your life—the clangor, the first thunder on the mountaintop." What Brice didn't confide, until many years later, was that her ill-fitting costume was scrunched and gathered in a most inconvenient spot, forcing her to writhe and wriggle her hips to relieve the discomfort. Whatever the cause, "Sadie Salome, Go Home" caught the attention of show-business luminaries attending the benefit, and Brice in-

corporated it into *College Girls* when the show finally took to the road. She was given several more solo numbers, putting her name in the leading credits of the playbill and prompting the show-business daily, *The New York Clipper,* to call her "a major new find and talent."

As the show trouped through New England, Brice noticed a handsome, impeccably groomed gentleman in the audience at several performances who finally introduced himself one evening as Frank White. The first thing that struck Brice was the smell of his aftershave and talcum powder; and indeed, Frank owned a chain of barber shops in Hartford, Albany, and Springfield, Massachusetts, the city in which he chose to propose marriage. Fanny, never secure about her physical appearance and flabbergasted that such a suave Adonis would be attracted to her, accepted. The two were married on February 14, 1909, when Fanny was 18. Forsaking a honeymoon or even a night alone together, Frank went back to his barber shops, Fanny continued touring with the show, and the two never saw each other again until several months later when Fanny returned to New York. By then, what had been little more than a passing fancy on the part of a stagestruck gigolo had soured, and Frank forced himself on a sexually naive Fanny their first night together in a New York hotel. Leaving him, Brice filed for a legal separation, which was finalized in a divorce three years later.

Another audience member during the *College Girls* tour brought Brice better luck; he was a scout for Florenz Ziegfeld, known as the "Emperor of Broadway." Ziegfeld, who had started his professional life managing a circus strongman, had married a statuesque French actress named *Anna Held, and then built a sophisticated, tuneful revue around her, which he called *The Ziegfeld Follies* ("Glorifying the American Girl!"). As he was now planning his 1910 *Follies,* his scout recommended Brice for a spot on the bill. Ziegfeld was famous for communicating by telegram, even to a close friend a block away, so Fanny was suspicious when she received one asking her to come to his office. Finally convinced it was genuine, she emerged from the meeting waving the precious contract over her head on her dash down Broadway that summer day. Ziegfeld had signed her to a two-year contract, at $75 a week for the first year and $100 a week for the second. When the *Follies* opened on Broadway a month later, Brice was quickly noticed for her natural, apparently spontaneous performance. "This strange, fantastic young woman of the willowy form and the elastic face," said one reviewer, "doesn't sing her songs at all. She just kind of remembers them."

In 1912, the year her divorce from Frank White was finalized, Brice met Nick Arnold (real name, Jules Wilford Arnt Stein). Sophisticated, charming, and good-looking, Nick Arnold arrived with two drawbacks—a mysterious business life he refused to discuss, and a wife from whom he had been separated for several years. While he told Brice about his wife at the start of their relationship, the nature of his "business" never became clear until three years later, when

he was convicted and sentenced on wiretapping charges. "At parties," Fanny remembered nearly 40 years later, "he would be surrounded by people ten minutes after he entered the room. He was a good speaker. Of course, half of the things he would be telling them were lies." During their 15 years together, Fanny would support Nick and raise thousands of dollars in bail by tirelessly trooping show after show on the circuits. She underwent repeated questionings by the district attorney, carried on a clandestine relationship with Nick when he was on the lam from the police, and saw him jailed a second time on a securities fraud conviction. The two were married on June 11, 1919, when Nick finally got a divorce from his first wife. The marriage produced two children—a girl Frances, born in 1919, and a boy William, born two years later. But apart from a few happy years together, with trips to London and an elegant estate on Long Island, the relationship was far from smooth. During the months that led up to the fraud conviction, Nick was in hiding while Fanny was continually dodging police who were on her trail in the midst of a grueling tour schedule. She lost 20 pounds and could only ingest liquids for weeks on end.

But she never stopped working, and by 1915 was earning up to $1,000 a week on the road. Ziegfeld wanted her back for his *Follies of 1915* and sent her the usual telegram proposing a salary of $200 a week. The next day, Fanny sent him one in return:

> FANNY BRICE FOUND DEAD IN HER ROOM IN THE HOTEL STOP THE ONLY CLUE IS A TELEGRAM SIGNED BY F. ZIEGFELD JR WHICH WAS CLUTCHED IN HER HAND STOP

They settled on $500 a week.

Brice would appear in the *Follies* for the next eight years and introduce some of her most famous numbers: "Second Hand Rose," "Rose of Washington Square," and a hilarious ballet spoof set to Mendelssohn's *Spring Song.* Audiences were rapt with attention when she first sang "My Man," clutching her arms to her body and closing her eyes, thinking of the husband that the law kept from her. By now, Brice was a Broadway legend, but, despite the public acclaim, the fancy clothes, expensive hotels and elegant dinners, she never forgot who she really was. The story is told of the night Fanny, waiting in the wings to go on, tried to sell her hat to an admiring chorus girl for $25. When her cue came, Brice told the young woman to stay right there while she went to work. As usual, she brought the house to its feet and had to return for several curtain calls. When she stepped off for the final time, the chorine gushed, "Wonderful, Miss Brice! Just wonderful!" "That's what I was telling you," Fanny said, gesturing at her hat. "For twenty-five bucks, it's a steal!"

By the early 1920s, the strains of her marriage to Nick began to show. In addition to keeping him out of jail while working full-time and raising two children, Brice also discovered Nick's numerous infidelities. The awareness came at a time when she was hoping to break into "legitimate" theater by appearing in a dra-

matic play written especially for her. *Fanny*, produced by David Belasco, ran for only eight weeks and was poorly received. No sooner had the show closed than Nick was sentenced to 18 months in Leavenworth on securities fraud charges, creating what would become a permanent separation. After 15 years with Nick, some of them the happiest of her life, Brice divorced him in 1927. She would later confess to an interviewer, "I can only say he was just a fool."

After the failure of *Fanny*, it was time for a new act to take on the road. Hired to help her de-

Fanny Brice as Baby Snooks.

velop it was one William Samuel Rosenburg, otherwise known as Billy Rose, a songwriter with several pop standards to his credit, among them: "I Found a Million Dollar Baby (In a Five and Ten Cent Store)," and "Paper Moon." In the coming two decades, he would become one of Broadway's most prolific entrepreneurs. Billy Rose was the exact opposite of Nick Arnold. He was short of stature, and pudgy; he dressed badly; and he was often remembered for his scuffed shoes and dirty fingernails. But he was as much a show-business veteran as Fanny, and the two struck up a mutually respectful, later affectionate, relationship. It was Billy who introduced Fanny to Hollywood, although none of her films were successful, and Brice was never comfortable playing in them. "I had such a kisser," she later said, "the camera would stand up and walk away in disgust." And it was in a show that Billy produced for her, *Sweet and Low*, that Fanny's most beloved character was born. Billy and his writers worked up a skit for Brice in which she appeared as a wise-cracking, worldly infant named "Babykins," complete with frilly bonnet, bib, and baby carriage. The audience loved her. By 1934, "Babykins" had become "Baby Snooks," the character Brice would play on stage and radio for nearly 20 years.

While Baby Snooks was gestating, Billy proposed marriage. "I married Frank because he smelled so good," Fanny recalled, "Nick because he looked so good, and Billy because he thought so good." The two became man and wife on February 2, 1929—the diminutive Billy proudly escorting his tall, thin bride to the altar. At cocktail parties, Fanny would poke fun at her husband's physical appearance. "He's just a little shrimp," she would say, "but mentally he's Gary Cooper." During their eight years together, Billy put the finishing touches on Fanny's stature as a national institution at a time when vaudeville and burlesque were beginning their slow retreat before the onslaught of film, radio and, eventually, television. (Brice would make only one TV appearance, in 1950, as Baby Snooks). But Billy always felt himself to be in Fanny's shadow. It wasn't a comfortable position for one of his ambition, and he took solace in the arms of *Eleanor Holm, a swimming sports star of the day for whom he hoped to build a film career. Fanny and Billy Rose were divorced in 1938.

The hectic pace that Brice had maintained for the past 35 years, both personally and professionally, now began to take its toll. Through the 1940s, she would be plagued by numerous health problems and confine much of her work to radio, nearly always as Baby Snooks, in a succession of network radio programs with sponsors such as General Foods, Sanka, and Post Toasties. But she had too many memories of the old days, past glories, bittersweet loves. In 1949, Nick suggested they remarry. She refused. "Love is like a card trick," she told him. "After you see it done once, it loses all of its mystery." It was the last time the two would see each other. Brice spent much of her time in Los Angeles, where she and Billy had bought a house, indulging two of her main interests, interior decorating and landscape painting. She traveled only occasionally to New York. In 1950, she played Baby Snooks for the last time.

Late that year, a young screenwriter was asked to help Brice write her autobiography. But before work on the book advanced very far, Fanny suffered a cerebral hemorrhage at her Westwood home and died five days later, on May 29, 1951, at the age of 60. The writer was left with just a few pages of interview notes. "I lived the way I wanted to live and never did what people said I had to do," she had told him. "And people might open the book and throw it away, and it can be a big flop, my book. But one thing it wouldn't be . . . a lie." Fanny Brice's life story was hardly throwaway material. In 1963, her son-in-law, producer Ray Stark, presented the musical *Funny Girl* on Broadway, with a libretto by *Isobel Lennart and music by Jule Styne. A young **Barbra Streisand** brought Brice back to life. Throughout rehearsals, an elderly man sat silently in the darkened theater. He was Nick Arnold, then 84 years old. He disappeared before rehearsals ended and never attended the opening.

SOURCES:

Brice, Fanny. Unpublished and undated memoirs in the Comden-Green Papers, The New York Public Library, Billy Rose Collection.

Goldman, Herbert G. *Fanny Brice: The Original Funny Girl.* NY: Oxford University Press, 1992.

Grossman, Barbara. *Funny Woman: The Life and Times of Fanny Brice.* Bloomington: Indiana University Press, 1991.

Katkov, Norman. *The Fabulous Fanny: The Story of Fanny Brice.* NY: Alfred E. Knopf, 1953.

RELATED MEDIA:

Funny Girl, starring Barbra Streisand, screenplay by Isobel Lennart, costumes by *Irene Sharaff, directed by William Wyler, Columbia Pictures, 1968.

Funny Lady, starring Barbra Streisand, screenplay by Jay Presson Allen and Arnold Schulman, directed by Herbert Ross, Columbia Pictures, 1975.

Norman Powers, writer/producer, Chelsea Lane Productions, New York, New York

Brico, Antonia (1902–1989)

Dutch-born American conductor, pianist, and musical pioneer who was the first woman to conduct the *Berlin Philharmonic and the New York Philharmonic, as well as many major European and American orchestras, and founded the New York Women's Symphony. Born in Rotterdam, the Netherlands, on June 26, 1902; died in Denver, Colorado, on August 3, 1989; attended University of California, at Berkeley; studied with Karl Muck and Sigismund Stojowski.*

For centuries, prejudice against women musicians, particularly in European society, reflected the notion that music was a male domain. Women were allowed to perform or write "feminine" pieces in the privacy of their homes, but public careers were denied them. Only in the 20th century were women admitted to symphony orchestras, and this occurred after they demanded to be auditioned behind curtains so that judges could not tell the sex of the performer. Given these barriers, it is not surprising that relatively few women have succeeded in this discipline until the late 20th century. It is rather amazing that women made substantial contributions to music despite the gross prejudice against them.

Antonia Brico was a pioneer in music, venturing where few women had gone before. Her career illustrates the frustrations and triumphs women endured for centuries. She decided to become a conductor at a time when this idea was unthinkable for a woman. "Back then there were no women in symphony orchestras," said Brico. "I founded the New York Women's Symphony in 1934, at a time when the New York Philharmonic wouldn't employ a woman harpist, much less a woman conductor. I started the trend. I simply wanted to conduct and I wanted to prove that women could play every single instrument." Struggling to survive in an entirely male-dominated arena, Brico remained optimistic: "I'd never forgive myself if I didn't try. I'd rather die trying."

Antonia Brico was born in the Netherlands and came to the United States at the age of six. She began taking piano at age ten because a doctor felt it would help her to stop biting her nails. Brico often attended concerts in San Francisco parks directed by Paul Steindorff, and her encounters with orchestras made her decide to become a conductor. The obstacles she would face began early, when as a student at a high school in Oakland she had had to petition authorities to be allowed to take a music appreciation course; music, it was assumed, could also only be appreciated by men. Her innate abilities were quickly apparent to the teacher, and Brico began a lifelong struggle to prove that women were as musically gifted as men.

Opposite page
From the movie
Funny Girl,
starring Barbra
Streisand.

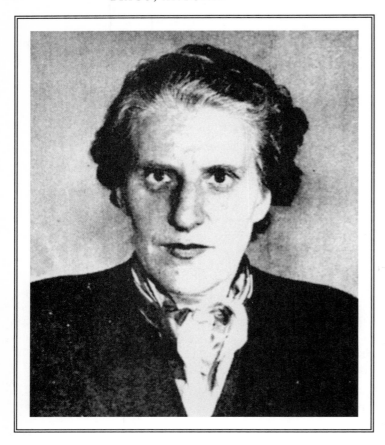

Antonia Brico

Brico started studying at Berkeley and had the opportunity to become the assistant to Paul Steindorff, who conducted the San Francisco Opera as well as a choral group. To support herself as a student she gave recitals. In 1923, Brico graduated with honors, then studied with Sigismund Stojowski for two years. In 1927, she entered the master class of conducting at Germany's Berlin State Academy of Music, which was taught by Julius Prüwer, conductor of the Berlin Philharmonic. During the five years she spent in Europe, Brico also studied with Siegfried Ochs, the choral conductor, and Karl Muck, conductor of the Hamburg Philharmonic. Muck did not accept pupils, and Brico was the sole exception to this general rule. In 1928, she coached at the Bayreuth Wagner Festival. Two years later, in February 1930, she was the first woman to conduct the Berlin Philharmonic, a guest appearance that received rave reviews.

During the 1930s, previously closed doors began to open for women as they began to fly planes, conduct orchestras, and win Nobel prizes. The public was infatuated with these pioneers who often appeared in newspapers, magazines, on radio, and in movie news clips. In 1931, Brico conducted the Hamburg Philhar-

monic. On January 10, 1933, she was the first woman to conduct the Metropolitan Opera orchestra. "With only three rehearsals Miss Brico made that orchestra play as it had never played before," wrote critic Lloyd Morris. Invitations to conduct in Detroit, Buffalo, Washington D.C., and California followed. In 1938, she conducted the New York Philharmonic. Brico's career was clearly on the upswing, as America loved its "symphonic suffragette."

The road ahead, however, would be far from clear. In 1934, Brico founded the New York Women's Symphony Orchestra, which made its first appearance in Town Hall on February 18, 1935. Wrote a *Newsweek* staffer in 1938, "As conductor and as women's orchestra founder Miss Brico has a unity of purpose—to overcome the prejudice against women as orchestral players and conductors. To conduct male orchestras, she feels, is to challenge male conductors on their own grounds. To conduct a female orchestra, as she has been doing, is not only to challenge male orchestral players but to dramatize the competence of women players." Although some grasped Brico's purpose, many did not, and invitations did not continue. "I was a novelty at first," Brico explained. "A woman who wanted to conduct a symphony orchestra. Imagine. But the big New York managers shied away from me like a plague. Nobody wanted to manage a woman." Arthur Judson, who managed most of the leading American conductors, told her that women subscribers would not stand for a woman conductor, and there was some truth to this allegation. *Minnie Guggenheimer, a leading musical figure in New York, was outraged that Brico was conducting and told her, "It's a disgrace for the New York Philharmonic and the only reason you're going to conduct this concert is that we got this petition." Four thousand music devotees had petitioned, asking that Brico be engaged to conduct the Philharmonic in 1938. This appearance, however, proved to be her swan song in the conducting world.

The end of the 1930s and the outbreak of World War II stalled the momentum of the feminist movement as Americans focused their attention elsewhere. In 1942, Brico went to Denver to conduct a semi-professional orchestra and to teach. Enamored with the city and its climate, for the next 27 years she led the Denver Businessman's Orchestra, which was renamed the Brico Symphony in her honor in the late 1960s. Her international conducting career, however, was at an end. "I was buried in an ash heap," she said; though she had never given up her desire to conduct, the male musical world had effectively shut her out. Talent, Brico discovered, was not part of the recipe for success.

The singer **Judy Collins** took piano with Brico from the time she was ten until she reached 16. The two kept in contact even after Collins became a popular singer. In 1974, Collins produced a film about her former teacher that was called *Antonia: Portrait of the Woman*. A complex work, this documentary was a balanced portrayal of Brico's life—of her optimism and despair. The film revived Brico's career. Now in her 70s, Brico was rediscovered and so many offers flooded in that it required two managers to schedule concerts. Brico also recorded for Columbia Records during this period.

When Antonia Brico died in 1989, her career had come full circle. The public was more accepting of a woman on the conductor's podium. The musical world, however, was still dominated by men, and at the time of Brico's death no woman had been made the permanent conductor of a major symphony orchestra. As the 20th century drew to a close, women still had to fight for equality in music.

SOURCES:

"Antonia Brico's Triumph: First of Sex to Wield Baton Over N.Y. Philharmonic," in *Newsweek*. Vol. 12, no. 5. August 1, 1938, p. 21.

Henahan, Donal. "Antonia Brico, at 72, Finds Her Baton in High Demand," in *The New York Times Biographical Service*. May 1975, pp. 568–569.

Kozinn, Allan. "Antonia Brico, 87, a Conductor; Fought Barriers to Women in the 30's," in *The New York Times Biographical Service*. August 1989, p. 742.

Rosen, Majorie. "Antonia Brico: The Orchestra is Her Instrument," in *Ms*. Vol. 3, no. 6. December 1974, pp. 81–84.

John Haag,
Athens, Georgia

Bride.

Variant of Bridget.

Bride (c. 453–c. 524).

See Bridget.

Bridges, Fidelia (1834–1923)

American artist. Born in Salem, Massachusetts, in 1834; died in Canaan, Connecticut, in 1923; daughter of a shipmaster in the China trade; studied painting with William Trost Richards.

Selected paintings: Milkweeds *(1861);* Daisies and Clover *(1871);* Thrush in Wild Flowers *(1974).*

Orphaned as a teenager, nature artist Fidelia Bridges attracted a number of close relationships throughout her life that nurtured her personal and artistic development. One early attachment was with her teacher William Trost Richards, who became her friend and mentor when she set up her own studio in downtown Philadelphia in 1862. He introduced her to his wealthy patrons and welcomed her into his family circle. Richards, a follower of the English Pre-Raphaelite school, strongly influenced Bridges' early artistic style, which utilized small-scale, intimate details to record fragments of nature with botanical accuracy. Many of her early works were exhibited at the Pennsylvania Academy.

Another important early influence was sculptor ***Anne Whitney**, with whom Bridges shared living quarters during a year of study in Rome in 1867. Whitney was a strong role model, urging Bridges to find her own personal style. After her return to the United States, Bridges began to gain recognition for her close-up, fragmented studies of grasses, birds, and flowers, rendered in delicate yet vibrant watercolors. She was elected an associate of the National Academy of Design in 1874 and a member of the Water Color Society in 1875. Her exhibit at the Philadelphia Centennial Exposition brought a number of commissions for chromolithographic prints from Louis Prang and Company. At this time, Bridges became close to the family of artist Oliver I. Lay, spending summers near their home in Stratford, Connecticut. The birds and wildflowers of the region became some of her favorite subjects and inspired such works as *Daisies and Clover* (1871) and *Thrush in Wild Flowers* (1874).

In time, Bridges' work moved away from her all-over detail to a more simplified background, which left orchestrated white space. Her compositions took on an Asian quality and prompted landscape painter John Frederick Kensett to write in *Art Journal*: "Her works are like little lyric poems, and she dwells with loving touches on each of her birds 'like blossoms atilt' among the leaves." A watercolor of this period, *Untitled* (1876), was praised for the shimmering summer air that was said to radiate from the spaces between the flowers.

In 1892, Bridges finally found a home of her own, on a hill in the village of Canaan, Connecticut, and endeared herself to the townspeople. Her later years were spent among the literary and artistic women of the community, and she was often seen riding her bicycle through town as she headed off for a sketching excursion. After her death in 1923, the citizens of Canaan erected a bird sanctuary in her memory.

Barbara Morgan,
Melrose, Massachusetts

Ruby Bridges on her way into school. The Problem We All Live With, *painting by Norman Rockwell. (Printed by permission of the Norman Rockwell Family Trust. Copyright 1964 the Norman Rockwell Family Trust.)*

Bridges, Ruby (c. 1954—)

African-American who was one of four black children chosen to integrate the New Orleans public school system in 1960. Name variations: Ruby Bridges Hall. Born Ruby Bridges in Tylerton, Mississippi, around 1954; oldest of eight children of Abon (a gas station attendant) and Lucile Bridges (a day-care provider and cleaning woman); married Malcolm Hall (a building contractor); children: four sons.

On a November morning in 1960, six-year-old Ruby Bridges, accompanied by U.S. federal marshals, made her way to the New Orleans' William Frantz Elementary School for her first day of first grade. Amid jeers from an angry white mob, Bridges, with a bow in her hair and carrying a lunch box, walked unwittingly into history. "I thought it was Mardi Gras," she would later say of that morning, "I had no idea it was *all* about me."

Bridges had been designated by court order as one of four black children—all girls—to integrate the New Orleans public school system. The other three children were sent to McDonogh 19 school, while Bridges alone went to Frantz. Her months-long ordeal was magnified by loneliness, as all of the white children were kept home by their outraged, fearful parents. Bridges' teacher, **Barbara Henry**, imported from Boston because none of Frantz's faculty would

teach a black student, was amazed at the child's poise under pressure and her sense of purpose. "She enjoyed her time there," she said. "She didn't seem nervous or anxious or irritable or scared. She seemed as normal and relaxed as any child I've ever taught." It was only at the end of the year that Bridges was joined by two white boys in her classroom. By the time she reached the sixth grade and left Frantz, half the students were black. By the close of the 20th century, the school was entirely black.

Bridges, one of eight children, would continue an uphill struggle. Her parents, who had volunteered her as a candidate to integrate the city's schools, split up when she was 12. By 17, she was pregnant and forced to finish her education at a school for expectant mothers. It was only after her marriage four years later, and the start of a career as a travel agent, that her life began to turn around, and only in the 1990s that she found meaning in her history-making childhood experience. "You just can't let that die," she says. "It happened for a reason."

The mother of four boys, Bridges established the Ruby Bridges Educational Foundation in 1994 to encourage parental involvement in schools. Much of the funding for the project came from Robert Coles, a Pulitzer Prize-winning Harvard psychiatry professor and author, who, in 1960, had been caught in a traffic jam and witnessed Bridges' first day at Frantz Elementary School. Coles, then an Air Force psychiatrist stationed in Biloxi, Mississippi, was so moved by the child's ordeal that he spent the next three years as her counselor and devoted his life's work to aiding children in crisis. Not only did he help secure grants for the foundation, but he also pledged royalties from his children's book *The Story of Ruby Bridges* to the project. Bridges' experience also became the subject of Norman Rockwell's famous painting *The Problem We All Live With*, which depicts the little girl on her way into school escorted by four federal marshals. Bridges, who received an honorary degree from Connecticut College in September 1995, became a volunteer parent liaison at the William Frantz Elementary School, where her odyssey had begun over 35 years ago.

SOURCES:

Arellano, Christopher. "Conn Pays Tribute to Woman Who Shaped U.S. History," in *The Day* [New London]. September 1, 1995.
———. "Limelight Shines Again on Civil Rights Pioneer," in *The Day* [New London]. August 31, 1995.
Coles, Robert. *The Story of Ruby Bridges*. NY: Scholastic, 1995.
Jerome, Richard, and Ron Ridenour. "Keeper of the Flame," in *People*. December 4, 1995, pp. 104–106.

RELATED MEDIA:

"Ruby Bridges," starring Chaz Monét, first aired on "The Wonderful World of Disney," ABC-television, January 18, 1998.

Barbara Morgan,
Melrose, Massachusetts

Bridget (c. 453–c. 524)

Patron saint of Ireland who founded the first Irish nunnery at Kildare and ruled there as abbess until her death. Name variations: Brigantia, Brigid, Brigid of Kildare, Brigida, Briget, Brigte; also called Bride. Pronunciation: BRIDGE-it. Born at Faugher or Faughart (then Fochart), near Dundalk, Ireland, around 453; died at Kildare, now in County Louth, on February 1 (her saint's day) in, or around, 524; daughter of Dubhthach (a pagan chieftain) and Broicsech (also spelled Brotsech or Broseach, his bondwoman and concubine); became a nun, reputedly in 467.

Shrouded in the historical obscurity of the early Middle Ages and steeped in centuries of accumulated legend, the life of St. Bridget as it has come down to us must be regarded, beyond its vaguest outlines, more as legend than as biography. Our earliest knowledge of Bridget derives from three saint's lives all written at least a century after her death, making it doubtful that any first-hand recollection of the saint survived to be recorded. In any case, the authors of these narratives were less concerned with elucidating Bridget's life for its own sake than with advancing her cult and thus elevating the prestige of her monastery at Kildare, in the service of their later spiritual and political preoccupations. Our image of the historical Bridget is further clouded by the likelihood that stories about Bridget the Christian saint drew upon the attributes of a Celtic fire goddess of the same name, thereby producing a syncretic figure having both Christian and pagan origins. Whatever her strictly historical standing, however, Bridget ranks with Patrick and Columba as one of the three patron saints of Ireland.

The traditional story of St. Bridget begins with her birth to **Broicsech**, a Christian bondwoman and concubine of Bridget's father Dubhthach, a pagan chieftain. The attention Dubhthach had manifestly bestowed upon Broicsech aroused the envy of his wife, with the result that he was compelled to remove Broicsech from his household while she was still pregnant. He sold her, though reserving his rights to her child, to a druid of Fochart, where Bridget was born around the year 453. Druids were influential priests, soothsayers, or sorcerers of a Celtic religious order who had a passing knowledge of geometry and philosophy, handled affairs of religion and morality, and performed the office of judges. Bridget spent her girlhood in the druid's household, and legends speak of the young Bridget's unexampled goodness and of the miracles that attended her. One such, doubtless conflated with the properties of Bridget the pagan fire goddess, relates how on a certain occasion when Broicsech had left Bridget alone at home, the neighbors noticed the house ablaze, "so that the flame reached from earth to heaven." Yet when they assembled before the house to rescue the child, the fire mysteriously vanished.

As a more mature girl, Bridget expressed a desire to return to her father, and Dubhthach accordingly took her back into his household. There she primarily cared for her stepmother but also displayed to all a characteristic benevolence for which she would be known throughout her life. She nursed the blind and gave to the needy freely of her household's goods, whether sheep from her father's flock or a piece of bacon from his larder or even his costly sword. The scope of her liberality is told in one story of a hungry dog's coming to the door and receiving from Bridget a large share of the family's dinner. Yet Bridget's generosity did not deplete the family's resources, for her energy and industry, which she devoted to good works and the reverence of God, made everything she touched prosper.

This was especially evident when, after some time living with her father, she asked his permission to return to her ailing mother. Though he denied her request, Bridget, displaying a willfulness that seems to have been indelibly etched into her character, departed anyway. She relieved her mother of the task of running the druid's dairy, and under her stewardship it flourished. Apparently impressed by the worldly success that flowed from Bridget's service to God, both the druid and his wife converted to Christianity. The wizard thereupon offered to Bridget not only her freedom from bondage but also the butter and cattle from the dairy. Bridget replied that the druid might keep his cattle if he would only set her mother free as well. Ultimately, the druid gave her Broicsech's freedom; he also tossed in the dairy cattle and butter, which Bridget duly distributed among the poor.

Bridget and her mother then returned to Dubhthach, but his annoyance at Bridget's continued dispersal of his household goods and livestock eventually determined him to sell his daughter, and he offered her to the king of Leinster. When Dubhthach brought Bridget before him, the king asked Dubhthach why he sought to sell his own daughter. He answered, "She stayeth not from selling my wealth and giving it to the poor." The king then inquired of Bridget whether if he bought her she might give his wealth away as she had her father's. To this, Bridget responded that even had she so much wealth and power as the king she would indeed give it all away "to the Lord of the elements." Struck by the assurance and magnanimity of her reply, the king declared that Bridget's merit was too great for mortal bargains, and he freed her from her father instead.

Dubhthach then attempted to secure a marriage for Bridget, but she refused to consider any of his proposed matches and finally prevailed upon her father to consent to her becoming a nun. Bridget, aged about 14, reportedly took the veil from Bishop Macaille in 467, although there seems to be no evidentiary basis for this date. At this early stage of Irish Christianity, monastic foundations did not yet exist, so monks and nuns lived unimmured among their kin, whose frequent retention of pagan customs and beliefs made living the life of a Christian religious all the more difficult. It was Bridget's foremost (and her best attested) achievement to organize, sometime in the late 5th century, the first monastic house for nuns in Ireland, under a large oak

tree; thus, the place was called cill dara or Kildara, "the church of the oak." The city of modern Kildare in the province of Leinster is supposed to have derived its name from St. Bridget's cell. Bridget reputedly traveled the countryside gathering together both bondwomen and freewomen into her protected community, although it has been suggested that the nucleus of the Christian community at Kildare originated from the conversion of a pre-existing college of pagan priestesses. Although no concrete evidence can be cited to support this assertion, hints of continuities between pagan and Christian worship lend the idea plausibility. It happens, for example, that Bridget's saint's day (February 1) coincides with *Imbolc*, one of the four annual pagan festivals. In addition, Geraldus Cambrensis, writing in the 12th century, noted that the religious community at Kildare kept a perpetual flame, surrounded by a fence no man was allowed to enter, for the protection of pilgrims and travelers as well as to honor Bridget, though whether it was the saint or the pagan goddess who was originally honored remains unclear.

Much more certain is that Bridget ruled as an abbess over her monastery at Kildare. Legend has it that at Bridget's consecration Bishop Mel ordained her by invoking a formula used for ordaining bishops, the implication being that Bridget was invested with an authority corresponding to that of a bishop. She continued to rule Kildare even after the addition of a community of men, though eventually she felt that the enormous increase in the size of the community required the presence of a bishop, and consequently her friend Conleth (or Condlaedh) was appointed as bishop and abbot and ruled the monastery jointly with Bridget until his death in 520.

Bridget's youthful vivacity and unstinting benevolence reportedly continued through her adulthood. She habitually made gifts to the poor of the money and goods bequeathed to the monastery, much to the consternation of her fellow sisters and brothers of Kildare. Her energy could also take the form of great emotional warmth: she was known both for her hospitality and love of entertainment as well as for her occasional vehemence when confronted by behavior of which she disapproved. Once during a widespread famine, Bridget, accompanied by a few of her sisters, traveled to a neighboring monastery to beg food for their convent. The nuns were treated to bread and bacon even though it was Lent and those in religious orders customarily refrained from eating meat. Bridget at once began to eat the bacon, but when her sisters demurred she grew angry at their over-tender scruples and put them out of the room. Bridget is also reputed to have traveled widely throughout Ireland. The early lives of St. Bridget speak of at least five journeys around Ireland, chiefly through the provinces of Leinster, Connacht, and Munster. She is even supposed to have met with St. Patrick, though this event is probably a symbolic figuration of a later administrative relationship worked out between Kildare and the rival community at Armagh dedicated to St. Patrick.

Bridget is said to have died in her 70th year on the first of February in the year 523, 524, 526, or 528; the precise date is unknown. Contrary to a later legend that placed her burial in Downpatrick with Saints Patrick and Columba, she was in fact interred at Kildare in a splendid tomb described by an eyewitness in the mid-7th century as decorated with gold, silver, and jewels and situated beside the high altar of the church. On the opposite side of the altar stood the tomb of Bishop (later Saint) Conleth, similarly ornamented. The church itself was divided by a screen separating the men from the women in this dual-sex, or "double" monastery. The women's community at Kildare continued to flourish after Bridget's death, while the community of monks seems to have declined and then become defunct sometime around the 12th century. Perhaps reflecting these contrasting fortunes, the co-equal authority of Conleth and Bridget gave way to the subordination of the bishop's authority to that of the abbess. The nunnery at Kildare survived until 1540–41, when it was closed during the general suppression of the monasteries by Henry VIII of England. The cult of St. Bridget has spread beyond Ireland to neighboring Scotland and England (under the name Saint Bride), and even to northern Italy, Brittany, Wales, Australia, and New Zealand.

SOURCES:

Coulson, John, ed. *The Saints: A Concise Biographical Dictionary.* NY: Guild Press, 1958.

Gwynn, Aubrey, and R. Neville Hadcock. *Medieval Religious Houses: Ireland.* London: Longman, 1970.

Hughes, Kathleen. *The Church in Early Irish Society.* Ithaca, NY: Cornell University Press, 1966.

McCone, Kim. "Brigit in the Seventh Century: A Saint with Three Lives?" and "*Vitae S Brigitae*: The Oldest Texts," in *Peritia.* Vol. 1, 1982, pp. 81–106 and 107–45.

Sharpe, Richard. *Medieval Irish Saints' Lives.* Oxford: Clarendon Press, 1991.

SUGGESTED READING:

O hAodha, D., ed. and trans. *Bethu Brigte.* Dublin, 1978.

Geoffrey Clark, Assistant Professor of History, Emory University, Atlanta, Georgia

Bridget of Sweden (1303–1373)

*Patron saint of Sweden who was the founder of the Catholic order of Brigettines and the mother of Saint Catherine of Sweden. Name variations: Birgitta, Birgitta of Vadstena, Brigit, or Brigitta. Born in 1303; died in 1373; daughter of Sir Birger Persson of Finsta and Lady **Ingeborg**; married Ulf Gudmarsson, prince of Nericia, 1317 (died, 1342); children: first of eight born in 1319 (most of her children either predeceased her or else lived a celibate life, including Catherine, who is known as Saint Catherine of Sweden, c. 1330–1381).*

Became lady-in-waiting and governess to Queen Blanche of Namur (1335); made pilgrimage to Santiago de Compostella (1341); adopted penitential life (1342); departed for Rome just before the Black Death plagued Sweden (1349); made pilgrimage to Holy Land (1372).

Sweden is so far north that it enjoys almost perpetual daylight in the summer months but near total darkness in winter months, which are savagely cold. Its history is likewise extreme and harsh: a saga of dogged men and women living on the rim of the habitable world. It is difficult for English-speaking people to learn much about Sweden's patron saint, Saint Bridget, since almost the only sources on her life are written in Latin, Danish, and Swedish. The exception, Johannes Jorgensen's two-volume biography (written 1940; translated from Danish 1954) is so unsatisfactory that it has to be read with great skepticism. Jorgensen portrayed her as uncannily holy straight from the cradle, rather than as a flesh-and-blood woman; whatever she did he declared to have been supernaturally guided, faultless. Still, it is possible, from information Jorgensen provides, to visit the opposite side of the spectrum and interpret her life as that of a fanatical disciplinarian and political Machiavellian, as extreme as medieval Sweden itself. Like that of many saints, Bridget's history has been clouded behind hundreds of miracle stories, which to contemporary ears depict both the saint and her God more often vengeful and arbitrary than infinite in mercy and tenderness. Her book, the *Revelations,* full of threats of hell and horrible visions side by side with hymns of love for the Virgin Mary, is one of the largest surviving documents from a woman's hand to be written in the 14th century.

The first attempt to convert the Swedes to Christianity had been made in 845 by Saint Ansgar, archbishop of Hamburg, who struggled against the cult of the Nordic gods Thor, Odin, and the rest. But the kingdom as a whole was not converted until 1008, under the influence of Saint Sigfred, an English archbishop of York, who converted King (later Saint) Olaf. For the next five centuries, until the Protestant Reformation carried Sweden into the Lutheran camp, it became the northern extremity of Catholic Europe.

She would create a new army of warriors of God and gather them to fight under a banner as red as blood and bearing on the front a picture of the Cross of Christ, but on the back Mary, the gentle Mother of Mercy, was to stand with open arms.

—Johannes Jorgensen

Bridget was born to a noble Swedish family, one of the country's richest and most powerful, in 1303. Shortly before her birth, her mother Ingeborg had almost drowned in a shipwreck; Ingeborg's providential rescue was taken by later hagiographers as a sign of future greatness. As one of three siblings to survive childhood (four others did not), Bridget became one of the richest people in Sweden upon her father's death. Growing up on the family estates at Finsta Gaard, the girl was well-educated by governesses and priests, becoming literate first in Swedish, later in Latin and Italian. According to legend, she longed for a life of virginity and devotion to God ("Better to die than be a bride!"), but, whatever her wishes, she was married at the age of 14 to a powerful noble, Ulf Gudmarsson, himself 18. They lived "as brother and sister" for the first two years of marriage, but then she gave birth to a child and followed up with seven more, four sons and four daughters, finding time also to teach her hitherto illiterate husband how to read.

Legend has it that in the early days of their marriage, she ordered a fine bed made for herself and her husband; as she gazed upon it, she received a violent blow on the head and a rebuke from Christ, who pointed out that he'd had nowhere soft to lay his head. After that, Bridget took to lying on a sack of straw covered only in bearskin, even in the depths of the Arctic winter, telling surprised observers that the Holy Spirit provided warmth to her soul in compensation for that lost by her body. Both Christ and *Mary the Virgin became regular visitors in a lifetime of frequent visions, and usually in her *Revelations* she spoke not in her own voice but in the voice of Christ or the Virgin. One might speculate that this was a powerful technique for gaining the moral advantage over any challenger.

Bridget also became involved in good works in her district, visiting the poor and sick, rescu-

Opposite page

*B*ridget of *S*weden

ing prostitutes, giving dowries to destitute girls, and introducing her own children to Christian works of mercy. Her daughter Catherine later recalled: "When Mother was reproached with taking us little girls with her, and that we might be infected from the stench of the sick people, she answered that she took us with her just while we were still small, so that we might learn at an early age to serve God in his poor and sick." Bridget undertook fiercely ascetic fasts, dripped burning candle wax onto her arms until they blistered to remind her of Christ's wounds, scratched open the wounds again before they healed, and took to chewing bitter gentian root at all times as a punishment for moments when she had taken pleasure in food and drink.

In addition to these mortifications, Bridget took an interest in the intellectual developments of her age, living as she did shortly after the creative scholastic theologians Albertus Magnus and Thomas Aquinas had reconciled Christian tradition with Aristotelian philosophy. She learned of their work through Master Matthias, a canon of Linkoping Cathedral, near her family home, and became familiar with the intellectual, political, and religious life of greater Europe before ever leaving her homeland. Like Matthias, she was an intense student of the Biblical Book of Revelation and considered herself to be living in the last days of the world, with the Day of Judgment imminent. Many of her "Revelations," like those in the Book of Revelation, are complicated allegories and parables whose meaning is difficult to unravel.

When her husband became an advisor to King Magnus Eriksson (they were cousins), Bridget became a governess and lady-in-waiting to his wife *Blanche of Namur, following the royal wedding of 1335. She was godmother to the royal family's first child but apparently became dissatisfied with the worldly life at court and decided to take up pilgrimages instead. With her husband, in 1341, Bridget set off to Santiago de Compostella, in northwestern Spain, which was then one of the chief pilgrimages of Europe, the place where Saint James was believed to have brought the word of Christ to Iberia and where he was buried. In Spain, she drew attention to herself by harsh condemnations of sinful priests and bishops, and by a slashing indictment of the kings of England and France, whose war with one another (the early days of the Hundred Years' War) had damaged parts of France through which they had passed:

They are like two wild beasts. One of them is greedy to swallow everything it can get, and the more it eats the hungrier it gets, and its hunger is never satisfied. The other animal wants to exalt itself above all men, and to rule over them. Each of the two animals tries to swallow the heart of the other. The terrible voices of these animals is heard far and wide across the world, and their voice and cry is this: "Take gold and the riches of the world, and do not spare the blood of Christian men."

She was dismayed that the pope (then living in Avignon) had been so ineffectual in his efforts to stop the war, and this pilgrimage appears to have hardened her resolve to lead a more active life in reforming a corrupt Christendom. The Avignon popes were notorious for worldliness, nepotism, and self-enrichment; poets like Petrarch and prophets like Joachim of Flora were united in their denunciations of Avignon as a new Babylon. Passing close to the papal court, Bridget pointedly failed to pay a visit.

On the way home from Santiago, her husband Ulf fell dangerously ill. While praying that he might recover, Bridget was rewarded by a vision of Saint Dionysius (St. Paul's disciple) who told her that Ulf would survive but that, from now on, they should live in celibacy. Ulf hung on only for another year and then expired at the monastery of Alvastra. Bridget, now a widow of 40, took up residence there, gaining a dispensation from the usually strict Cistercian rule against the presence of women. The sub-prior of Alvastra, Petrus Olai, became her secretary, and during Bridget's frequent visions and raptures she dictated to him messages she was receiving from God and the saints. Chief among these revelations was that she had been chosen by Christ as His bride with the special task of saving the Swedish people from their sins.

Guided by another vision, she began the work of founding her order, whose first house was raised on land that she had acquired from a greatly beneficent, or possibly terrified, king. (She had warned Magnus that his sins were so wicked that he faced near-certain damnation unless he reformed *and* gave her the royal estate at Vadstena.) In a demonstration to duplicate early Christian fervor, her order was to consist of 60 nuns, under the rule of an abbess. In addition:

> there shall be thirteen priests, after the thirteen apostles, of which the thirteenth, Saint Paul, did not work least. Then there shall be four deacons, who can be priests if they so desire it. They signify the four great doctors of the church: Ambrose, Augustine, Jerome, and Gregory. Next there shall be eight laymen who shall serve the priests. Altogether that makes sixty sisters, thirteen priests, four

deacons and eight servants, which is the same number as the thirteen apostles and the seventy two disciples.

Bridget described living arrangements and the nuns' costume with similar precision and further attempts at allegory. On the white crown of the headdress, she specified, were to be sewn five small pieces of red cloth, like five drops of blood, to signify the crown of thorns. In other respects, the rule was similar to that laid down by Saint Bernard of Clairvaux for the Cistercians, and enjoined on nuns strict vows of poverty and obedience. She sent an envoy to Avignon to obtain the pope's approval for this scheme and to renew her pleas for a peace treaty between England and France. The pope, Clement VI, treated her envoy with scant courtesy, however, and refused to endorse the rule, noting that the Lateran Council of 1215 had judged that no new monastic rules should be introduced; the existing rules (Augustinian, Benedictine, Franciscan, etc.) were sufficient. Bridget received the news with fury, answering the pope (in the voice of Christ):

> [A]s I have let you rise high above all so I shall also let you descend to fearful torment of body and soul, if you do not heed my words. Your boastful tongue shall fall silent, your name, that was famed on the earth, shall be forgotten and dishonored with me and my saints. . . . I shall also question you on how slothful you were to make peace between the kings [of England and France].

Meanwhile, Bridget continued to advise King Magnus and certainly approved of his dynastic schemes against the kings of Norway and Denmark and the Lords of Scania whereby Sweden reached its "natural" boundaries. In one vision justifying Magnus' conquests, Christ told her that Swedes and Danes had originally been together in Noah's Ark. Disembarking after the flood, Christ continued, "the Swedes went towards the east, the Danes towards the west; the Swedes settled on the continent, the Danes on the islands, both were to be content with what they had and live in the land of their fathers, and within the borders of the forefathers." She also agreed with Magnus' plans for a crusade against Finland. She favored an expedition of monks and soldiers—there was a place for peaceful conversions but also, she believed, a place for violence. Her biographer, Johannes Jorgensen, declares: "It may even be an advantage to the heathen to die young—if they were allowed to live longer they would sin more and so get a harder punishment after death."

After early successes, the expedition against Finland turned into a costly disaster—during one retreat, one of Bridget's two surviving brothers died in the city of Riga. Bridget interpreted defeats as a sign of God's wrath against Magnus for his wastefulness and ostentation and urged him to take advantage of the forthcoming holy year (1350) by going to Rome for an indulgence. When Magnus refused, she resolved to do it in his stead, setting out across the Baltic in 1349 as soon as the ice had melted. As it turned out, Bridget was leaving Sweden for the last time. No sooner had she departed than the Black Death swept through Scandinavia, killing two-thirds of the population of Norway and a third of the population of Sweden. King Magnus recalled one of the curses that Bridget had fired at him as a parting shot:

> Thus saith the Son of God: I will visit this kingdom with the sword and lance and with wrath. In vain do they say, "Let us do as it pleaseth us, life is short, God is merciful. He will do us no evil!" Hearken to what I now say to thee. I will rise up in all my power and will not spare either young or old, rich or poor, just or unjust. I will come with my plough and pull up the trees by the roots, so that where there before were a thousand people only a hundred will be left, and their houses shall stand empty.

Like other European rulers he was powerless to prevent the annihilating power of the plague.

On her arrival in Rome, Bridget found the city in a sorry condition; in addition to the ancient Roman ruins and the ruins of earlier Christian ages, there was a new scene of devastation caused by an earthquake in 1348 and signs of the Black Death here too. Worse, two feuding families, the Colonna and the Orsini, kept the city, which the popes had abandoned, in a state of constant civic turmoil; all the Papal States had become the fiefdoms of petty warlords. Vice, crime, simony, nepotism, and a general sense of decay all contributed to Bridget's decision to stay in the hope of inaugurating reforms. Taking up residence in a cardinal's palace but living according to the Brigettine rule she had written, she continued to receive messages from saints and angels. Saint Peter, she said, gave her a summary of the situation in Rome and predicted her future:

> Rome was in times past a city in which dwelt the warriors of Christ, its streets were strewn as if with gold and silver. But now all its precious sapphires are lying in the mire. . . . Toads and vipers build here, and the fishes from my draught are afraid of their poison and dare not lift their heads. Yet shall the fishes still be gathered here, though not so many as in times past, but tasting just as good. . . . Moreover I tell thee that thou shalt live long enough to see with your eyes my

vice regent come back to Rome, and thou shalt hear the people cry "Long Live the Pope."

To prepare Rome for the pope's return (which she interpreted apocalyptically as preparation for Christ's return), she traveled frequently to the churches of Rome, praying in each one. She offered hospitality to visiting Swedish pilgrims, many of whom, by her reckoning, were horrible sinners, drunkards, voluptuaries, liars, and all puffed up with pride. Her visions showed her what would become of these men and women after death, and she passed the word on, depicting lurid torments in purgatory or Hell itself. Several sinners appeared in her visions sitting on a narrow beam suspended over the mouth of Hell, liable to fall into the fiery pit at any moment. Despite her frequent communications with the Virgin Mary whose purity she emphasized, she often described Mary herself carrying out savage eternal punishments on sinners. Bridget's growing dismay with King Magnus, meanwhile, increased when he failed to repay large debts owed to the pope and when he lost a series of conflicts with rival dukes; she approved first of his excommunication in 1358 and then of the baronial conspiracy and rebellion by which he was overthrown in 1365.

Bridget's daughter *Catherine of Sweden, aged 20, either abandoned her husband or was widowed (Lives of Saints says widowed) and came to join Bridget in Rome. Catherine accompanied her mother while Bridget was touring the various kingdoms of Italy, urging corrupt priests and abbots to repent. A blonde Swedish beauty, Catherine became the object of many Italian noble's amorous designs. One, a member of the powerful Orsini family, laid in ambush for her as she was heading for church, but to save Catherine's virtue God struck him blind as she passed by with her mother. Mortified by his sin, the noble followed her to church, helped by his bodyguards, and begged forgiveness for his lecherous schemes. Bridget interceded with God, his sight was restored, and Bridget and Catherine became friends of the admiring Orsinis.

Some Romans, by contrast, took offense at Bridget's unceasing criticism of them, the pope, the Holy Roman emperor, and most of the pilgrims she met—her secretary noted that "when her revelations were made known and read to the inhabitants of Rome they were inflamed with a deadly enmity against the Lady Bridget, and some said that she was a sorceress and wanted her to be burnt as a witch." After she had delivered a new set of divine condemnations

to Rome, a large crowd gathered outside the house, shouted that they would burn it down with her, a sorceress, inside. She consulted her "Bridegroom," Christ, who told her she would come to no harm, and so stayed put, despite her household's terrors, and calmly told her priests to proceed with Vespers.

Shortly afterwards, another of her visions was borne out when, after more than 60 years at Avignon, the papal court under Pope Urban V finally returned to Rome. She contrived to meet him, told him the church in Italy had fallen into a disgraceful state of decay, both material and moral, and that he should set things right forthwith. She renewed her request, first made nearly 20 years earlier, that her convent at Vadstena be recognized, and that her rule guide the lives of its priests and nuns. The pope approved the convent but reasserted his predecessor's judgment that no new rule could be written: she must use the Augustinian rule even though, as she asserted, her own rule had been delivered to her from the lips of Christ himself. Pope Urban did not last more than another year—he thwarted her and then took what she considered the unpardonable step of returning to the Babylon of Avignon, where he at once died.

In 1372, when she was 69 years old, Bridget followed one of her visions and set out on a pilgrimage to Jerusalem. At this time, it was in "moorish" hands and could be reached only by a hazardous journey in the face of great political and environmental odds. En route, she cursed the people of Cyprus for their sinful ways, then her ship was wrecked as it approached the harbor at Jaffa, though all on board were saved. She visited the holy places in Jerusalem, Bethlehem, and the River Jordan, but did not get as far as Nazareth, then returned safely to Rome, via Cyprus and Naples. The journey was not without its scandals. Along the way her son, who had promised to accompany her, began a torrid love affair with *Joanna I, queen of Naples, though both of them were already married. The affair, however, came to an abrupt end with his sudden death.

Bridget also died the following year, receiving (and dictating details of) divine visitations right to the end. Five days before her death, Christ came and stood before the altar in her room and spoke to her with a face of joy:

> I have done with you as the bridegroom does when he hides himself from the bride, so that she may desire him the more greatly. . . . Now it is time for you to make ready. For now shall be fulfilled that which I have

promised you, that you shall be clothed in the habit of a nun before my altar, and from henceforth you shall not only be called my bride, but shall also be called a nun and mother in Vadstena.

Though her remains were first buried in Rome, after five weeks her children came to take back her bones to Vadstena, her convent. Her priest prepared himself for the gruesome task of separating the decaying flesh from the bones, but when he opened the coffin, say the chronicles, all the flesh had miraculously fallen away, there was no odor, and the bones lay clean before him. The bones began to work miracles at once and became prized holy relics. In less than 20 years, Bridget was canonized, after the church heard evidence from her surviving children and secretaries confirming her exemplary life and countless miracles. Her order flourished in Sweden until the Reformation and beyond that elsewhere in Europe, while the story of her life and divine communications became a model for at least two subsequent saints, *Catherine of Siena and *Teresa of Avila.

SOURCES:

Jorgensen, Johannes. *Bridget of Sweden*. 2 vols. Translated from Danish by Ingeborg Lund. NY: Longmans, Green, 1954. (This is the only book on Saint Bridget in English; the only other references to her are short summaries in dictionaries of the saints.)

Patrick Allitt, Assistant Professor of History, Emory University, Atlanta, Georgia

Bridgman, Laura (1829–1889)

First deaf and blind person successfully educated, who paved the way for other disadvantaged people and whose fame spread across America and Europe. Born Laura Dewey Bridgman on December 21, 1829, in Hanover, New Hampshire; died on May 24, 1889, in South Boston, Massachusetts; daughter of Daniel and Harmony Bridgman (both farmers); had two brothers and three sisters, two of whom died from the scarlet fever, which destroyed her senses of sight, hearing, and smell; educated by Dr. Samuel Gridley Howe at the Perkins Institution for the Blind in South Boston, Massachusetts; lived most of her life at the Perkins Institution, in later years helping with the education of blind children; never married; no children.

In 1842, the English novelist Charles Dickens arrived in Boston, the starting point on his long-awaited first visit to the United States. The following morning, his initial stop on this sightseeing tour was a call to the Perkins Institution, the city's school for blind children. Though many distinguished Bostonians waited for a

chance to meet the beloved author, Dickens' decision to head immediately to Perkins was not so unusual. In an age when many people were excited by the possibilities of education, the Perkins Institution, America's first school for the blind, had become one of Boston's most popular tourist attractions. Like so many others, Dickens was impressed by what he saw there, the "good order, cleanliness, and comfort" of the classrooms where blind children learned and played cheerfully. But he was most deeply moved by one particular student, Laura Bridgman, a 12-year-old girl who was both deaf and blind.

Though some of Boston's celebrated poets and politicians were vying for Dickens' attention that morning, he ignored them all, transfixed by the sight of Laura sitting quietly in her room, writing a lesson in her journal. He watched with delight as she finished her assignment, then turned to a teacher sitting nearby and began an "animated conversation," pressing the letters of a finger alphabet into her teacher's outstretched palm and "hearing" replies the same way. "There she was, before me," Dickens recalled, "built up, as it were, in a marble cell, impervious to any ray of light, or particle of sound; with her poor white hand peeping through a chink in the wall, beckoning to some good man for help, that an Immortal soul might be awakened."

A "good man" had come to Laura's aid five years earlier. He was Dr. Samuel Gridley Howe, a liberal reformer from Boston who was the first director of the Perkins Institution. (He was also the husband of *Julia Ward Howe.) In 1837, when Laura was seven, Samuel Howe brought her to the school to see if he could teach her the use of the manual alphabet of the deaf. Until that time, those philosophers and teachers who speculated on the plight of the deaf and blind usually concluded that such people could never be educated. Most felt that a person in Laura's condition was destined to remain beyond the reach of human communication and companionship. Some even speculated that deaf and blind people must be "blank" inside, without a soul or a mind, since they lacked the contact with the outside world, which psychologists of the time said that the brain needs in order to form ideas.

But Howe, aided by Laura's intelligence and curiosity, proved them wrong, demonstrating that such people could learn language and be educated. The story of their accomplishment spread quickly and was hailed by many writers as "a tale of thrilling interest, not surpassed by those of the novelist." Translated into all the major European languages, recounted hundreds

Laura Bridgman

of times in popular magazines, scientific journals, and children's books, Bridgman's story became familiar to thousands of readers in the mid-19th century. A decade after Laura Bridgman had signed her first words, Howe claimed that this humble young girl was one of the most famous women of her day, second only to Queen *Victoria.

Laura was born a normal and healthy child, the third daughter of Daniel and **Harmony Bridgman**, farmers in the New Hampshire village of Hanover. She was two years old, just starting to speak a few words, when she was stricken by scarlet fever. The illness, which killed Laura's two

older sisters, brought her to the brink of death, as she struggled against a high fever and a raging infection, which spread to her eyes and ears. Two weeks later, the doctor informed Harmony Bridgman that her youngest child would live, but that her eyes and ears had been "spoilt" forever.

Laura spent most of the next two years in bed, too weak to leave the cradle that her mother rocked for long hours. At the age of four, her health recovered. With her senses of sight and hearing completely gone and her sense of taste and smell also largely destroyed, the child began the difficult process of orienting herself in her new world of silent darkness. Using her fingers as "feelers," she was soon able to find her way around the Bridgman farmhouse. Eagerly imitating her mother, she even learned to help with some household chores such as setting the table, grinding food, and rocking her younger siblings' cradles.

It is a curious case, this of Laura's. A poor blind and deaf girl, of humble history and humbler hopes,— unconscious of being the object of special regard, and yet every act and word carefully noted down, and more eagerly looked for by thousands in various parts of the world than those of purple-born princesses!

—Samuel Gridley Howe

In spite of these accomplishments, Laura remained cut off from those around her. During her long illness, she had lost any recollection of the spoken language that she was just beginning to learn. The only way she could now communicate with her family was through a primitive set of gestures. "I made signs for my Mother for food and drink," she later recalled, "but it was difficult for her to understand the reality of things whatever I wanted. She was very anxious to satisfy my little hungry mouth." Bridgman's mother tried hard to help her child but found her increasingly difficult to care for. Distracted by household chores and the needs of Laura's younger brothers and sisters, Harmony Bridgman knew that her daughter needed more attention but regretted that she had no time leftover to "study her case." As a result, Laura spent much of her time alone, seated in a rocking chair by the hearth, playing with an old boot that served as a substitute for a doll in the frugal Yankee household.

When Laura was seven, her situation came to the attention of a professor from nearby Dartmouth College medical school. After visiting her, he wrote a short account of her case for the newspapers. In Boston, Howe read this story with much excitement. Not long before, he had visited an asylum for the deaf in Connecticut where he had met ❧▶ **Julia Brace**, the nation's only known case of deaf/blindness at the time. When Brace arrived at the school, her guardians had tried to teach her sign language but had abandoned their efforts as hopeless. Howe began to speculate on ways to reach the intellect of the deaf and blind. "The trial should not be abandoned," he insisted, "though it had failed in her case, as well as in all that had been recorded before." After reading of Laura Bridgman, Howe set out immediately for Hanover to convince her parents to let their child come to Boston.

The Bridgmans agreed to let Howe try his experiment with their child and delivered her to Perkins in the fall of 1837. At first, Laura was confused and frightened by this change, but she quickly adapted, developing an evident affection for both Howe and the school's female teachers. Within a week, Howe began his plan for her education. He started by showing her a set of household objects—a knife, a pin, a pen and so on. To each of these he attached a paper label with the name of the object printed in raised letters. Running her fingers over these objects, Laura learned to associate each label with its matching object, and to match the two when they were separated. As she performed these exercises day after day, Howe was pleased to see "a light of intelligence light her hitherto puzzled countenance." But he felt she had not yet grasped the true use of language. She matched labels with their objects not to communicate, but merely as a rote exercise of "imitation and memory," performed to win the approval of her teachers.

Howe's next step was to break the labels apart into their component letters. Laura soon learned to place each letter in proper order, thus spelling the words herself. At first, Howe found that she also did this mechanically, much like "a very knowing dog" who performed tricks only to win approval. But after months of patient, methodical instruction, she suddenly seemed to understand the true power of those letters. "The truth began to flash upon her," Howe reported. "Her intellect began to work, she perceived that here was a way by which she could herself make up a sign of anything that was in her own mind, and show it to another mind, and at once her countenance lighted up with human expression; it was no longer a dog or parrot,—it was an immortal spirit, eagerly seizing upon a new link of union with other spirits! I could almost fix upon the moment when this truth dawned upon her mind, and spread its light to her countenance. I saw that the great obstacle was overcome."

Bridgman's language skills improved quickly over the next few years. She mastered the finger alphabet within a few months; by age 11, her thoughts flew so rapidly from her fingers that only the most experienced eye could keep up with her. She also learned to write, her pencil guided by specially designed grooved paper, and soon sent regular letters to her mother and a growing host of friends and well wishers. To Howe's delight, Laura proved to be an ideal student, intelligent and incredibly curious about the world. "Can birds study?" she wanted to know. "Why do not flies and horses go to bed?" "Are horses cross all day?" "What did man make red for?" Suffering from the hiccups, she wanted to know "if they were black & where they went when they went away?" She was so full of questions about the world beyond her limited experience that she often left her teachers exhausted by the end of the day.

While Bridgman was a diligent student, her scant exposure to language and her limited experience of the world proved to be formidable obstacles. Her teachers spent long hours trying to help her understand concepts that most children pick up effortlessly. When Laura was ten, for example, Howe reported that "some idea of the difficulty of teaching her common expressions, or the meaning of them, may be found from the fact that a lesson of two hours upon the words *right* and *left* was deemed very profitable, if she in that time really mastered the idea." But Bridgman and her teachers persevered; by the time she was 12, her language skills had improved enough for her to be able to begin lessons in math, geography, and history. After classes, Laura spent the rest of her day doing chores at the school, sweeping and sewing, or taking long walks with her female teacher through the streets of Boston. As they walked, Laura often played a game, stopping suddenly and insisting that her companion describe to her everything she could see and hear from that spot. "She will not be content," her teacher noted, "if she thinks I have not told her objects enough to make up the scene." In this way, Bridgman used her teachers as her own eyes and ears on the world.

After touring North America, Charles Dickens declared that Laura Bridgman was second only to Niagara Falls among the highlights of his trip. His account of their meeting, published in *American Notes,* was widely read, spreading her fame through America and England. Many followed Dickens' lead, coming to Perkins to see the child for themselves. To raise funds for the school, Howe had his students put on weekly exhibitions of their skills. At times, these shows drew more than a thousand visitors a day, most of them straining for a glimpse of Laura Bridgman. One of her instructors complained that the crowd "has become so great at the exhibitions, and presses so closely about Laura, that we are obliged to surround her desk by settees, thus making a little enclosure to protect her." Though she grew tired of the requests, Bridgman provided many hundreds of copies of her autograph to her admirers.

But Bridgman was more than a celebrity and a public curiosity. Her accomplishments confirmed Howe's claim that the deaf-blind could and should be educated. Within a few years, several more deaf-blind children came to Perkins and successfully followed her lead. As her story spread, educators and philanthropists around the world took a new interest in the plight of the deaf and blind. Many of them copied Howe's techniques, bringing the light of language to deaf-blind people in their own communities.

The most notable beneficiary of Bridgman's achievement was *Helen Keller. Keller's parents first learned that their daughter could be educated when they read an account of Laura Bridgman. They wrote to the Perkins school for help and engaged the services of ✥➤ Anne Sullivan (Macy), a teacher at the Perkins Institution. Before she began teaching Keller, Sullivan reviewed all of Howe's writings on Bridgman and sought Laura's own advice. When Keller was an adolescent, preparing to enter college, she came to live at Perkins for a few years and met Bridgman. Years later, she wrote, "The remembrance fills me afresh of the first deaf-blind person in the world to be taught whom I met in the first days of my own glad awakening. Again I feel the dainty lace lengthen as her lovely hands ply the needles. . . . With ever new gratitude I bless Dr. Samuel G. Howe who believed, and therefore was able to raise that child soul from a death-in-life existence to knowledge and joy."

The public's interest in Laura Bridgman slackened after she reached adulthood in the

◆✥
Macy, Anne Sullivan. See Keller, Helen for sidebar.

✥➤ **Brace, Julia** (1806–1884)
American who became famous as the nation's first known case of concurrent deafness and blindness. Born in Newington, Connecticut, on June 13, 1806; died in Bloomington, Connecticut, on August 12, 1884; admitted to the Hartford Asylum when she was 18.

Julia Brace became completely deaf and blind at age five and a half, having learned to read and spell words of two syllables. At age 18, she entered the asylum for the "deaf and dumb" at Hartford. With an acute sense of smell, Brace could differentiate between her own clothes and personal property from those of others. By putting an eye of a cambric needle upon the tip of her tongue, she could feel the thread as it entered the eye and by this had learned to thread a needle. Though her sense of smell was superior to *Laura Bridgman's, Brace was never given the attention and thought-out course of instruction.

early 1850s. While he remained director of Perkins, Howe moved on to new challenges, most notably abolition and the education of the mentally handicapped. Howe continued to look on Laura almost as an adopted daughter, but he believed that institutional life was harmful and that she would be better off returning to her family in New Hampshire. Bridgman moved back to Hanover when she was 22 and developed a close relationship with her mother. But she soon pined for the stimulation and community of the Institution, a place where so many people understood sign language and where she felt she was needed. Less than a year after leaving Perkins, she suffered a nervous breakdown that brought her to the verge of death. Howe brought her back to Perkins, where she soon revived. Recognizing that Laura's true home was really the school, Howe then raised a fund that provided her with a permanent home there.

As Bridgman grew older, she never lost her enthusiasm for learning and for human companionship. She read her raised-letter Bible avidly, maintained a regular correspondence with a wide variety of friends, and even wrote several brief, unpublished autobiographies and some short poems. She also earned money as a seamstress. Her needlework and lacework were eagerly purchased by the school's visitors, valued not just for their novelty but also for their fine artistry. For many years, Bridgman worked at Perkins as an instructor, teaching blind girls how to sew.

Howe died in 1876. At his funeral, Laura passed her hands across his face one last time and wept at the loss of her "best & noble friend." But she took consolation in her faith. Bridgman had been keenly interested in religion since childhood. After the death of one of her sisters in the early 1860s, she experienced a conversion and became an ardent evangelical Baptist. Often she expressed her new faith in the evangelical cliches of the period, but at other times her religious ideas were more her own, giving voice to her unique experience of the world. For example, in a poem that was published and widely admired near the end of her life, Bridgman spoke of heaven as a "holy home" where her senses would be restored:

> I pass this dark home toward light home.
> Earthly home shall perish,
> But holy home shall endure forever.
> Earthly home is wintery.
> Hard it is for us to appreciate the radiance of
>   holy home because of the blindness of our
>   minds.
> How glorious holy home is, and still more than a
>   beam of sun!

On May 24, 1889, Laura Bridgman died, following a brief illness. Her funeral was held in the hall of the Perkins Institution, the place that her achievements had transformed into one of the most talked about schools in America during the 19th century.

SOURCES:

Dickens, Charles. *American Notes*. Gloucester, MA: Peter Smith, 1968 (reprint).

Elliott, Maude Howe, and Florence Howe Hall. *Laura Bridgman: Dr. Howe's Famous Pupil and What He Taught Her*. Boston, MA: Little, Brown, 1904.

Lamson, Mary Swift. *Life and Education of Laura Dewey Bridgman, The Deaf, Dumb, and Blind Girl*. Boston, MA: 1881 (reprinted NY: Arno Press, 1975).

SUGGESTED READING:

Schwartz, Harold. *Samuel Gridley Howe: Social Reformer, 1801–1876*. Cambridge, MA: Harvard University Press, 1956.

COLLECTIONS:

Perkins School for the Blind, 175 North Beacon Street, Watertown, Massachusetts.

> **Ernest Freeberg**, doctoral candidate in American History, Emory University, Atlanta, Georgia

Brigantia (c. 453–c. 524).

See Bridget.

Briggs, Emily Edson (1830–1910)

American journalist. Name variations: (pseudonym) Olivia. Born Emily Pamona Briggs on September 14, 1830, in Burton, Ohio; died in Washington, D.C., on July 3, 1910; married John R. Briggs, in 1854.

Emily Edson Briggs, who distinguished herself as the first woman journalist to cover the White House (1861), was born in Burton, Ohio, and spent her first ten years there until her family moved to the Chicago area in 1840. She taught school briefly before marrying John R. Briggs and settling in Keokuk, Iowa, where John was part owner of the newspaper the *Daily Whig*. In 1861, he was appointed assistant clerk of the U.S. House of Representatives, and the couple took up residence in Washington, D.C.

Briggs soon developed a knack for observing and commenting on the political scene. A letter she sent to the *Washington Chronicle*, defending the efficiency of women in government employment, caught the eye of the paper's owner, John W. Forney, who hired her to write a daily column for the *Chronicle* and its sister paper the *Philadelphia Press*. Using the pseudonym Olivia, Briggs wrote columns that were fashioned as letters to the paper. While her pieces touched upon society and fashion, they also contained political and social insights that set her apart from other women journalists of the day. Under the Lincoln administration, she became the first woman to report from the White House, and later was the first woman admitted to the congressional press gallery. Acquiring a national reputation, Briggs became the first president of the newly formed Women's National Press Association in 1882. In later years, she was a celebrated Washington hostess. Her columns, *The Olivia Letters*, appeared for two decades and were published in book form in 1906 four years before her death on July 3, 1910.

Bright, Dora Estella (1863–1951)

English composer, organist, pianist, and first woman to win the Lucas Medal for composition, whose work was played by the London Philharmonic Orchestra. Name variations: Mrs. Knatchbull. Born in Sheffield, England, on August 16, 1863; died in London on November 16, 1951; daughter of an amateur musician; studied at the Royal Academy of Music under Walter Macfarren and Ebenezer Prout; married a Captain Knatchbull of Bath, in 1892.

Dora Estella Bright was a pioneer in music. She was the first woman to be awarded the prestigious Lucas Medal for composition (1888); the first woman to hear her music performed by the London Philharmonic Orchestra (1892); the first person to give a recital of purely English music, which she called *From Byrd to Cowen* (1892); and the first Englishwoman to play her own concertos in Leipzig, Dresden, and Cologne. In 1880, during a concert tour of Germany, she played her own Piano Concerto in A-Minor with the noted composer Carl Reinecke conducting. Bright wrote eight orchestral pieces as well as compositions for chamber orchestra and piano. Following her marriage in 1892, her public appearances became less frequent. Bright's music for a ballet scena was danced by *Adeline Genée at the Playhouse in 1907.

John Haag,
Athens, Georgia

Bright Eyes (1854–1902).

See La Flesche, Susette.

Brightwell, Ann (b. 1942).

See Packer, Ann.

Brightwen, Eliza (1830–1906)

British naturalist who observed nature from the grounds of her English home. Born Eliza Elder at Banff, Scotland, on October 30, 1830; died at Stanmore, England, on May 5, 1906; daughter of Margaret and George Elder; educated at home; married George Brightwen on June 5, 1855 (died, 1883); no children.

Selected works: My Practical Thoughts on Bible Study *(1871);* Wild Nature Won by Kindness; More about Wild Nature *(1892).*

Eliza Elder was six years old when her mother died, forcing the separation of Eliza and her five siblings from one another and from their Scotland home. Alexander Elder offered to adopt his niece, and Eliza moved to England. Her childhood was isolated and lonely, with playmates limited to cousins who visited occasionally. Each day, she had general lessons, including reading and drawing, and was allowed to play with her pet donkey. A brief venture to boarding school in 1842 made her physically ill from stress. With her aunt and uncle, she traveled around Europe, and she also made solo treks to visit family friends.

On a visit to Stanmore, England, she met George Brightwen, the neighbor of her hosts, and 18 months later she agreed to marry him. "I believe I never knew the keen joy that so many speak of when they are engaged to the man of their choice," Brightwen wrote in her diary. Nevertheless, she was not wealthy, and George was considered a suitable man, which pleased her uncle. They married in 1885 after a three-month engagement and spent two weeks honeymooning in France. The Brightwen estate was named The Grove, and Eliza spent her days drawing, sculpting, and working with indigent children on their Bible studies. She developed friendships with her siblings and kept up regular correspondence with a few sisters. Frequently sick, Brightwen had fainting spells. In 1872, she took to her bed for a decade. "I am now increasingly suffering, and yet must try to keep up and be cheerful for my dear husband's sake; my life is very difficult and far from happy." Her health improved as George fell ill. She nursed him until his February 1883 death.

While she mourned and recuperated, Brightwen began to explore The Grove with renewed interest. Examining the foliage, insects, and animals of her property, she wrote about her findings and experiences. Often invited to lecture, she traveled to host clubs or sponsored day trips to The Grove. She fed, clothed and preached to the poor and lectured on nature to school children. Brightwen took in hurt animals, including a white owl and several mice, which became her pets. Always in poor health, she had two live-in assistants to nurse her. "I have always been so afraid that I was dying," she wrote during her final illness, "and now I am in such dread that I shall not be able to die." Kept company by two squirrels and a robin, Brightwen died on May 5, 1906, at The Grove.

SOURCES:
Chesson, W.H., ed. *Eliza Brightwen: The Life and Thoughts of a Naturalist.* London: T. Fisher Unwin, 1909.

Crista Martin,
Boston, Massachusetts

Brigid.
Variant of Bridget.

Brigid of Kildare (c. 453–c. 524).
See Bridget.

Brigida (c. 453–c. 524).
See Bridget.

Brigit.
See Bridget (c. 453–c. 524) or Bridget of Sweden (1303–1373).

Brigitta (1303–1373).
See Bridget of Sweden.

Brigman, Anne W. (1869–1950)
American photographer and member of the Photo-Secession group. Born Anne Wardrope Knott in Honolulu, Hawaii, in 1869; died in Eagle Rock, California, in 1950; attended Punahou School, 1882–1883; married Martin Brigman, c. 1894 (separated, 1910).

Anne W. Brigman was born in Honolulu, Hawaii, in 1869, a descendant of missionaries who had arrived there in 1828. Around 1886, Brigman moved to California and took up photography. Working on allegorical portraits, nudes, and draped figures in landscapes, she aligned herself with the Photo-Secessionists, a group intent on transforming photography into fine art. Its founders included Alfred Stieglitz, Clarence White, *Gertrude Käsebier, and Edward Steichen. In 1906, Brigman was elected a fellow of the Photo-Secession, forming a close friendship with Stieglitz, who promoted her work.

Brigman's first important exhibitions took place in 1904 at the Corcoran Gallery of Art in Washington, D.C., and the Carnegie Institute in Pittsburgh. She was represented in the opening show of the Photo-Secessionists in New York in 1905. Four years later, in 1909, she won a gold medal at the Alaska-Yukon-Pacific Exhibition in

Seattle, Washington. Her work was first published in *Camera Work* (1909). In 1949, she produced a book with photographs and poetry, *Songs of a Pagan,* and was preparing a second publication, *Child of Hawaii,* at the time of her death in 1950.

Brigue, Jehenna de or Jehenne de (d. 1391).
See French "Witches" (14th–16th centuries).

Brinvilliers, Marie de (1630–1676)
French poisoner. Name variations: Marie-Madeleine Marguerite d'Aubray, marquise de Brinvilliers. Born Marie-Madeleine Marguerite d'Aubray in Paris, France, in 1630; beheaded and body burned on July 16, 1676; daughter of Dreux d'Aubray (a civil lieutenant of Paris); married Antoine Gobelin, marquis de Brinvilliers, in 1651.

Of noble birth, Marie-Madeleine d'Aubray has been described by writers of her day as pretty, petite, and much-courted, with an appealing air of childlike innocence. In 1651, she married French army officer Antoine Gobelin de Brinvilliers, then serving in the regiment of Normandy; in 1659, her husband introduced her to his friend Gaudin de Sainte-Croix, a handsome young cavalry officer of immoderate tastes and shoddy reputation. Marie and Gaudin were soon lovers. Though the affair eventually led to a public scandal, the marquis de Brinvilliers, who had left France to avoid his creditors, made no effort to stop it. Marie's father Dreux d'Aubray, however, was outraged and obtained the arrest of Sainte-Croix on a *lettre de cachet*. For a year, Sainte-Croix was a prisoner in the Bastille, where he supposedly acquired knowledge of poisons from his fellow prisoner, the Italian poisoner Exili. When he left prison, he plotted with his willing mistress revenge upon her father.

Methodically, Marie began to experiment with the potions that Sainte-Croix, possibly with the help of a chemist, Christopher Glaser, prepared, and she found readily available subjects in the poor who sought her charity, and the sick whom she visited in the hospitals. Using a variety of deadly concoctions, it is said that Marie de Brinvilliers poisoned over 50 victims. One of her poisons, *aqua tofana,* was supposedly invented by her Italian counterpart *Tofana.

Meanwhile, Sainte-Croix, completely ruined financially, expanded his original plan. He decided to not only poison Dreux d'Aubray but also Marie de Brinvilliers' sister **Thérèse d'Aubray** and her two brothers. With her relatives dead, Marie would come into possession of the large family fortune. In February 1666, satisfied with the efficiency of Sainte-Croix's preparations and with the ease with which the poisons could be administered without detection, Marie poisoned her father, and in 1670, with the connivance of their valet La Chaussée, her two brothers. A postmortem examination suggested the real cause of death, but no suspicion was directed to the murderers.

Before any attempt could be made on the life of Thérèse d'Aubray, Sainte-Croix suddenly died in 1672, during one of his experiments, possibly by inhaling lethal fumes. As he left no heirs, the police were called in and discovered papers among his belongings that revealed the murders and implicated Marie and La Chaussée. The latter was arrested, tortured into a complete confession, and broken alive on the wheel in 1673, but Marie de Brinvilliers escaped, taking refuge first probably in England, then in Germany, and finally in a convent at Liége, where she was caught by a police agent disguised as a priest. A full account

Marie de Brinvilliers on the way to her execution.

of her life and crimes was found among her papers. Prevented from committing suicide, she was taken to Paris, where she was beheaded and her body burned on July 16, 1676. (See also entry titled *French "Witches."*)

SUGGESTED READING:
Roullier, G. La. *Marquise de Brinvilliers.* Paris, 1883.

Brion, Hélène (1882–1962)

French schoolteacher, union activist, pacifist and feminist who—due to her pacifist stance during World War I—was the first French woman to be tried before a military tribunal, and who, after the war, researched and wrote her own feminist encyclopedia.

Name variations: Helene Brion. Pronunciation: BREE-on. Born Hélène Brion in 1882 (probably January 12) in Clermont-Ferrand, France; died in 1962; orphaned at a young age and raised by her grandmother in the Ardennes; attended the école primaire supérieure Sophie-Germain in Paris; never married; had two children by a Russian immigrant around 1905–1907.

Taught at a nursery school (école maternelle) in Pantin until her revocation in 1917; participated in numerous feminist organizations, including the Feminist University Federation, the League for the Rights of Women, and the French Union for Female Suffrage; belonged to the Socialist Party and to the Confederal Committee of the General Confederation of Work (CGT); during World War I, opened a soup kitchen in Pantin, served as secretary-general of the National Federation of Teachers' Unions (1915–18), helped oversee an orphanage for poor children in Épône, and belonged to the Committee for the Renewal of International Relations; arrested for "defeatism" (1917); found guilty (March 1918) by a military tribunal and given a three-year suspended sentence; returned to teaching after the war (1925) and maintained contact with militant colleagues but retreated from public life; devoted many of her later years to the research and writing of a feminist encyclopedia.

On November 18, 1917, over three years after the beginning of World War I, the front page of the French daily newspaper *Le Matin* announced the shocking news that a traitor had been lurking in their midst. The accused was Hélène Brion, a schoolteacher from the town of Pantin, on the outskirts of Paris. The author of the article claimed Brion to be known throughout the northern suburbs for "the violence of her anti-patriotic feelings." The paper accused her of "malthusianism, defeatism, anti-militarism, and anarchism," as well as of visiting the famous

suffragist, **Emmeline Pankhurst*, in England, and of "exciting women to revolt" in France. According to *Le Matin*, "Toward the end of August 1914, as the German armies were marching on Paris, Hélène Brion rode to the front lines on her bicycle" at a time when "only a spy would have any reason for being there." The paper could only delight in the arrest of this woman whose face they claimed to be "in the least, abnormal," who dressed in masculine clothes, and who, the paper purports, once shouted in the middle of her schoolyard: "Oh how I want to set the Minister of War on fire!"

Some of the accusations in the article were malicious fabrications, which Brion's friends would spend the following months endeavoring to correct. Other charges were based on the truth but filtered through the eye of a nationalistic and chauvinistic press. Brion was indeed a pacifist and a feminist, but, in her mind, neither of these beliefs made her a public enemy. Who was Hélène Brion, and how did she end up the first French woman tried by a military tribunal in France?

We know relatively little about her childhood. She was born in 1882 in Clermont-Ferrand, but by a young age she had lost both her mother and her father, an officer who had fought in the Franco-Prussian war of 1870–71. Raised by her grandmother, Brion spent her childhood in the Ardennes, near the Belgian border, until she left for Paris to attend the école primaire supérieure Sophie-Germain where, according to one classmate, she was voted the award of "good comradeship" by her peers. A teacher of Brion's, Mlle **Jeanne Brochard**, recalled that she was one of the few girls to live alone during her years of study: "denied the tenderness of family, she was obligated to learn quickly to forge her own way in life." At Sophie-Germain, she earned her *brevet*, the minimum requirement to teach elementary school in France at the time (until 1929, one did not necessarily need to train in a normal school), and soon after she took up her post at a nursery school in Pantin.

In early 20th-century France, teaching was one of the few "respectable" careers available to women, and Hélène Brion was determined to be independent. Her close friend **Madeleine Vernet** (who published a pamphlet in Brion's defense during her imprisonment entitled, *Hélène Brion: A Noble Conscience and a Somber Affair*) claimed that Hélène loved children and had a natural aptitude for her job, and the fact that Brion helped Vernet operate an orphanage for destitute children seems to corroborate the claim. Nevertheless, Brion's largest passions in life were the political causes to which she devoted so much of her time: feminism, socialism, and trade unions.

At the time Brion was beginning her career, schoolteachers in France first began to unionize. Although the government denied civil servants the right to unionize, the movement among teachers grew. In 1905, they founded the National Federation of Teachers' Unions, of which Brion was an active member. In addition to her work with the Federation, Brion served on the Confederal Committee of the CGT (Confédération générale du travail), which functioned as an umbrella organization for many unions in France spanning a large variety of professions. Brion was also a member of the leadership of the local section of the Socialist Party. Hence, both at the local and national levels, Brion devoted much of her energy to trying to improve the lot of working people in general, and of schoolteachers in particular.

As devoted as Brion was to working-class politics, however, she never felt entirely comfortable within these circles. As a woman and as a feminist, she devoted the most energy to pressuring left-wing political parties and union organizations to recognize the oppression of women as a problem of as much urgency as the oppression of the working class. Throughout her life, Brion would maintain that neither socialists nor syndicalists (those who adopted a philosophy of radical trade unionism) would ever achieve a true revolution until they accepted equality of the sexes as a necessary prerequisite to a just society.

In an annotated re-publication of Brion's most famous feminist tract, *La Voie féministe* (The Feminist Path), **Huguette Bouchardeau** notes that Brion seldom bothered to critique the positions of the political right, and she justly points out that in criticizing the two groups to which Brion was most devoted—the Socialist Party and the CGT—Brion in no way hoped to undermine their potential success. Nevertheless, Brion used tough language in chastising her male comrades for failing to incorporate women and women's demands into working-class organizations and platforms.

La Voie féministe, which Brion wrote in October 1916, was addressed in general to her unionized male comrades who offered either socialism or syndicalism as the solution to all oppression. But Brion reminded them: "Socialism and syndicalism strive above all else to improve the condition of workers and the poor. But women are even more exploited *as women* by men as a collectivity than they are *as producers* by capital." While Brion criticized working-class movements for not taking seriously the issue of equal salary for equal work, her most bitter complaint was that men failed to recognize the exploitation of women in the home. "It is in the family," Brion wrote, "that the woman is the most oppressed."

Brion knew what she was talking about. In France, at the turn of the century, married women were still legal minors to their husbands. Prior to 1920, a woman could not even join a union without her husband's permission. Brion demanded that her male colleagues recognize that women were not only exploited in the home . . . they were virtual prisoners. Her tract challenged men on the Left to recognize that although they had dedicated their lives to eradicating inequality, they still accepted the domestication of women as natural. Until men overcame their "brutal instinct toward domination," they would never be able to achieve equality or justice.

I am an enemy of war because I am a feminist. War is the triumph of brutal force; feminism can only triumph by moral force and intellectual worth.

—**Hélène Brion**

Brion's impassioned appeal had little immediate impact on the CGT or on the Socialist Party, in part due to timing. Brion penned *La Voie féministe* in the middle of World War I. After fighting erupted at the end of August 1914, the rapid mobilization of hundreds of thousands of men and the exigencies of war meant that neither unions nor political parties had much time or energy left for internal debate. French president Raymond Poincaré dubbed the national war effort the "Sacred Union," and virtually all feminists, union activists, and socialists put their demands on hold in order to support the nation under attack. Union activity among teachers came to a halt as thousands of male teachers were mobilized and others struggled to keep schools running in their absence. Like most of the Left in 1914, Brion felt the French cause to be just due to the presence of the invading German army on French territory, and like so many teachers across France, she sought ways to help her local community, in her case, creating a soup kitchen for those hardest hit by war shortages.

By 1916, however, when Brion wrote *La Voie féministe,* a deep schism had developed within the Left between those who supported the war effort at any cost and those who believed that the government had tricked the working class to serve as cannon fodder for its own nationalist ends. Despite initial reservations, Brion joined the pacifist minority.

Initially, Hélène Brion did not become a pacifist out of deep conviction. She believed France had been unjustly attacked by Germany. Despite government promises in 1914 that the war would be over by Christmas, however, World War I dragged on for four long, murderous years. Life had to go on. With millions of men called to the front, women stepped in to fill their shoes in the fields, in the factories, in schools, and sometimes in positions of even higher authority. Under these conditions, Brion became the first female secretary-general of the National Federation of Teachers' Unions.

From the outset, the Federation maintained a respectful distance from the nationalistic hype surrounding the war, encouraging its members to do their best to provide an education to the nation's youth despite the war. Over the course of 1915, however, some of its members developed a more outright pacifist stance, questioning the government's motives for continuing the war. The French government claimed it would continue to fight *jusqu'au bout* (to the finish), but the teachers of the Federation believed that if their government would show its willingness to negotiate, and state its conditions for peace, then the German enemy would follow suit.

Hélène Brion had many reservations about the evolving pacifist position of the Federation, but as its leader she agreed to follow the wishes of the majority. Furthermore, as a woman and a feminist, Brion felt that war was largely the fault of the male leaders who had dragged the country into the conflict, and she reminded her male comrades in *La Voie féministe* that women "have been able to do nothing to stop the war, because we possess no civil or political rights." Hence, by 1916, Brion joined with other pacifist members of the Federation in calling for an immediate negotiated peace, a decision that would cost Brion her job and eventually land her in jail. It was thus not for her lifelong creed—feminism—which Brion became most known. Hélène Brion became a *cause célèbre* for taking a pacifist stance in the midst of a war of monstrous proportions.

Why exactly was Brion arrested on November 17, 1917? Part of the answer lies in the history of World War I, a war then unprecedented in its scale. By 1917, in the trenches as well as on the homefront, French morale was at its lowest as at any point during the war. Millions of men had already died, war rationing had begun, and the enthusiastic hype in the press seemed more and more distant from the daily reality of protracted war. The more the French people began to grumble, however, the more the government worried about and monitored public opinion. Hence, in midsummer, when a number of legislators and teachers began to receive anonymous notes with the messages: "Peace without annexation, conquest, or indemnity," "Women want their rights and Peace," and "Enough men killed, Peace," the government took the threat to the war effort seriously. A police investigation led to the following conclusion:

> An investigation conducted several months ago after successive mailings of these notes to members of Parliament permitted our suspicion to fall on Hélène Brion, schoolteacher in Pantin, who has since been arrested. A search of her home on July 26, 1917, led to the notable discovery of 14 envelopes addressed to legislators and containing pacifist notes. These envelopes and their contents are identical to those received by the teachers at the Edgar-Quinet and Sophie-Germain schools.

Throughout the following autumn, Brion was called continually before the examining magistrate, while school officials suspended her from teaching. On November 17, 1917, the judge had her arrested, and the following day she was transferred to the Saint-Lazare prison to await trial. Furthermore, the judge determined that Brion's transgression fell under the authority of the military; hence, for the first time in French history, the judicial system sent a woman to be tried before a military tribunal. For the next four months, the Parisian and national press would avidly follow the arrest and trial of the "defeatist schoolteacher."

Although she was to stand trial for alarmist propaganda, Hélène Brion's feminism never ceased to be an issue in the case. A glance through the press coverage of the Brion Affair suggests that reporters were more worried about Brion's appearance than her ideas. *Le Matin* included a picture with its coverage of the Brion Affair with the caption "Hélène Brion in Masculine Clothing." In a March 25, 1918, article, *La Voix nationale* described Brion as she appeared at her trial: "A small man's hat placed devilishly on her blond hair, tied in back without any attempt to please, a loose lavaliere, a jacket that strangely resembles a man's coat, definitely a somewhat masculine and neglected ensemble."

In fact, Brion dressed in a style typical of the feminist teachers of her generation, cutting her hair short, and dressing in more practical, flexible clothing than the corsets and petticoats just beginning to go out of fashion. Indeed, the picture in *Le Matin* captured Brion wearing her cycling outfit, more comfortable for shoveling coal at the Pantin soup kitchen. The press was not alone, however, in making gender an important issue in the trial of the "defeatist schoolteacher." Of all her various causes—pacifism, trade unionism, socialism, and feminism—the last was Brion's true passion, and she saw to it that her trial would serve as a soapbox not only for the pacifism for which she was arrested but also for the feminism that defined all of her political and social action.

During her trial, which lasted from March 25 to March 30, 1918, Brion's lawyer called upon prominent witnesses to speak to the moral integrity of the accused. Several well-known men, including the writer Paul Brulat and the deputy to the National Assembly Jean Longuet, testified to Brion's good character and defended her freedom of opinion. Also on the witness stand were the most distinguished feminists of the period. The socialist-feminist *Séverine (1855–1929) compared Brion to *Louise Michel, the famous 19th-century activist for women and the poor, once maligned by her compatriots, who was later honored with a statue on Montmartre. Séverine reminded the court that history often sees acts of resistance in a very different light. *Marguerite Durand also spoke on Brion's behalf, lecturing the court on the intimate link between feminism and pacifism. She claimed Brion had opinions no different than other women; she was merely more courageous. In all, even the suspicious press seemed impressed by the line-up.

Brion was clearly moved by the support shown her, at times shouting out an emotional "*Merci!*" during the trial, but the most eloquent spokesperson on her behalf was Brion herself. Her lawyer called her personal defense a "profession of faith"; indeed, Brion's speech was much more than a simple plea; it was a statement of creed. "The law should be logical and ignore me when it comes to sanctions just as much as it ignores my existence when it comes to rights," Brion opened. She denied ever calling for peace at any price; she had merely insisted her government make known its willingness to negotiate. Nevertheless, as a feminist, she willingly called herself a natural enemy of war. "I am an enemy of war because I am a feminist," Brion told the court. "War is the triumph of brutal force; feminism can only triumph by moral force and intellectual worth." She claimed that men had been so busy ruling the world that they had lost track of their goals.

> You want to free those who are enslaved . . . [but] you do not realize that in this fight for liberty, we are all losing our rights bit by bit, from the material right to eat and travel as we please all the way to the intellectual right to write, to meet, to think, and most of all, to think justly. All these rights have disappeared little by little because they are incompatible with a state of war.

Hélène Brion's profession of faith put the problems of the world squarely on men's shoulders. That she, a woman, would want to distance herself from the politics of massacre she believed to be only natural, but she also reminded the court that at least one prominent man, President Woodrow Wilson of the United States, had issued calls for peace not far removed from her own. She concluded by quoting 19th-century French socialist Victor Considerant: "The day that women are familiar with social questions, revolutions will no longer be fought with rifles."

Brion's spirited defense and the ardent pleas of witnesses did little to soften the heart of her military judges. She was found guilty and sentenced to three years in prison. Nevertheless, the court gave her a suspended sentence; hence, once the trial was over, Brion was free to return to Pantin.

On November 11, 1918, World War I finally ground to a halt, but not before nearly 1.5 million French men and women had given their lives. It would take a long time for the country to heal its wounds from the war, both physical and emotional. Not until 1925 would Hélène Brion be allowed to return to teaching.

The end of the trial seems to mark the end of Hélène Brion's active public life. According to Bouchardeau, Brion maintained close contact with friends from the Federation as well as from various feminist organizations, but from the 1920s to the end of her life in 1962, she ceased involving herself in political activities. Instead, Brion turned her intellectual and rhetorical talent to another purpose: the research and writing of a massive feminist encyclopedia, a mammoth project that she never completed. To the end of her days, then, Brion remained devoted to the feminist principles and cause that had animated all the turbulent actions of her younger years.

SOURCES:
Brion, Hélène. *La Voie féministe.* Preface, notes, and commentary by Huguette Bouchardeau. Paris: Editions Syros, 1978.

Dossier Brion, in the Bibliothèque Marguerite Durand.

Gerbod, Paul. *Les Enseignants et la politique*. Paris: P.U.F., 1976.

Vernet, Madeleine. *Hélène Brion: Une Belle conscience et une sombre affair*. Épône: l'Avenir Social, 1917.

SUGGESTED READING:

Becker, Jean-Jacques. *The Great War and the French People*. Translated by Arnold Pomerans. U.K.: Berg Publishers, 1985.

Feeley, Francis. "French School Teachers Against Militarism, 1903–1918," in *The Historian*. Vol. 52. Winter 1995, pp. 315–328.

COLLECTIONS:

Correspondence, articles, and manuscripts can be found in the *Dossier Brion* at the Bibliothèque Marguerite Durand in Paris, France.

Mona Siegel, Detling Fellow
and graduate student at the
University of Wisconsin, Madison, Wisconsin

Briouze, Annora de (d. 1241).

See Braose, Annora de.

Briouze, Loretta de (d. 1266).

See Braose, Loretta de.

Brisco-Hooks, Valerie (1960—)

African-American runner and first Olympian to win gold medals in the 200- and 400-meter events. Born in Greenwood, Mississippi, on July 6, 1960; one of ten children of Guitherea and Arguster Brisco; married Alvin Hooks (a wide receiver for the Philadelphia Eagles), 1981 (divorced, 1984); children: Alvin Hooks, Jr.

First Olympian to win the gold medal in both the 200 and 400 meters, in Los Angeles (1984); also won a gold medal in the 4x400-meter relay in Los Angeles; won a silver medal in the 4x400 relay in the Seoul Olympics (1988); first American track-and-field woman to win three Olympic gold medals since Wilma Rudolph in 1960.

Born in Greenwood, Mississippi, Valerie Brisco-Hooks attended Locke High School (near Watts in Los Angeles), where her coach, recognizing great talent, gave the 15-year-old a biography of *Wilma Rudolph. Brisco-Hooks would strive to follow in Rudolph's track shoes and in those of an admired older brother Robert who had been shot to death by a stray bullet while practicing on the high-school track. A short sprinter in high school, in 1977, Brisco-Hooks was timed in the 400 meter in 54.19. In 1979, she ran the 400 meter in 52.08.

Bob Kersee convinced Brisco-Hooks that she could be an Olympic champion if she worked hard. As a member of his World Class Track Club, which included *Jackie Joyner-Kersee and *Florence Griffith-Joyner, Brisco-Hooks trained five days a week, seven hours a day, lifting weights afterward for two or three hours. The workouts ended with 250 push-ups and 1,000 sit-ups. She became an Association for Intercollegiate Athletics for Women (AIAW) champion in the 200 meters while attending California State, Northridge, and was American Athletic Union (AAU) runner-up in the 200 meters. Brisco-Hooks earned a number ten world ranking.

In 1979, she met wide-receiver Alvin Hooks whom she married in 1981. They moved to Philadelphia when he was drafted by the Philadelphia Eagles' football franchise. While Valerie was pregnant with their son, Alvin was released from his football contract in 1982 following a knee injury. After numerous separations and reconciliations, she would divorce him in 1984. Brisco-Hooks had been out of training a couple of seasons when she began working again with coach Bob Kersee. She had gained 40 pounds during her pregnancy but returned to training with a vengeance, even inventing a poor-woman's steamroom in her bathroom by wrapping herself in cellophane while hot water poured from the shower.

In 1984, Brisco-Hooks broke both the American record and the Olympic record of 48.88 set by *Marita Koch from East Germany in 1980, becoming the fourth fastest woman performer of all-time. A week before the 1984 Olympics, Brisco-Hooks ran in The Athletic Congress (TAC) meet, setting a new American record of 49.83 for the 400 meters. In the 1984 Olympics, she won gold medals in both the 200 and 400 meter, becoming the first American—female or male—to do so in the same Olympiad. She ran the 200 meter in 21.81 and the 400 meter in 48.83 (both Olympic records). She also won a gold in the 4x400-meter relay, running the third leg at 49.23, and becoming the first American woman to win three golds in the same Olympiad since Wilma Rudolph's victory nearly 25 years before. In the 1988 Olympics in Seoul, Brisco-Hooks won the silver medal in the 4x400-meter relay.

A winner of three gold medals, she received a number of commercial endorsements after the Olympics. Known for her stylish clothes and braided hair, she became a role model and appeared in antidrug public-service films. After Brisco-Hooks won the 4x400-meter relay at the Pan American Games in Indianapolis, a deaf teenager with impaired eyesight asked if she would pose with him. While the photographer prepared, Brisco-Hooks slipped her Pan-Am gold medal over the boy's neck, then strolled away. She later told a questioning reporter, "It's not that the medal didn't mean anything to me. I am sure it meant more to him."

SOURCES:

Davis, Michael D. *Black American Women in Olympic Track and Field. A Complete Illustrated Reference.* Jefferson, NC: McFarland, 1992.
Page, James A. *Black Olympian Medalists.* Englewood, CO: Libraries Unlimited, 1991.

Karin L. Haag,
Athens, Georgia

Britagne, countess or duchess of.

See Brittany, countess or duchess of.

Britain, Radie (1903—)

American and first woman composer to have work performed at the White House, who created over 30 pieces for orchestra and 30 pieces for mixed chorus. Born near Amarillo, Texas, on March 17, 1903; daughter of Edgar Charles (a rancher) and Katie L. Britain; studied at the Clarendon College Conservatory of Music, the American Conservatory, as well as in Berlin and Munich; married Edgardo Simone, a sculptor (died); married Ted Morton.

Radie Britain was born on a ranch on the high plains in the Texas Panhandle, a windswept and desolate, but often dramatically beautiful, region of the American West, which inspired much of her music. Her parents, who had pioneered as cattle ranchers in the area, recognized their daughter's immense musical talent, and she was provided with the finest musical training. Though her father had said, "No daughter of mine will ever cross the ocean," once he recognized his daughter's determination he helped her to study in Europe. She made her debut as a composer in Munich when the baritone Erich Wildhagen sang several of her songs. A pioneer for American women composers in the 20th century, ironically, she was often mistaken for a man because of her name. In 1930, Britain won the International Award for composition and in 1945 she was the first woman ever to receive the prestigious Juilliard National Prize, for her composition *Heroic Poem*. This piece was dedicated to Charles Lindbergh's flight to Paris in 1929. In 1938, she became a member of the faculty of the American Conservatory of Music in Chicago.

In all, Britain wrote over 150 compositions for orchestra, chamber ensembles, stage works,

choral, piano, violin, harp and voice. In the 1920s and 1930s, many of her works were performed by women's orchestras. These orchestras were created because women of the day were not allowed to perform in major symphony orchestras; this prohibition was later dropped when auditions began to be held behind curtains to force judges to choose on the basis of talent rather than sex.

John Haag,
Athens, Georgia

Brites.

Variant of Beatrice.

Brittain, Vera (1893–1970)

British writer, feminist, and a leading pacifist chronicler of her times. Born Vera Mary Brittain on December 29, 1893, in Newcastle-under-Lyme, Staffordshire, England; died on March 29, 1970, in London; daughter of Thomas Arthur (a paper manufacturer) and Edith Mary (Bervon) Brittain; attended Somerville College, Oxford, 1914–15, 1919–21, M.A., 1925; married George Edward Gordon Catlin, June 27, 1925; children: John and Shirley.

Selected publications: Verses of a V.A.D. *(E. Macdonald, 1918);* The Dark Tide *(Grant Richards, 1923);* Not Without Honor *(Grant Richards, 1923);* Women's Work in Modern England *(N. Douglas, 1928);* Halcyon: The Future of Monogamy *(K. Paul, Trench, Trubner, 1929);* Testament of Youth: An Autobiographical Study of the Years 1900–1925 *(Gollancz, 1933);* Poems of the War and After *(Gollancz, 1934);* Honourable Estate: A Novel of Transition *(Gollancz, 1936, published in America as* Honorable Estate, *Macmillan, 1936);* Thrice a Stranger: New Chapters of Autobiography *(Gollancz, 1938);* Wartime Letters to Peace Lovers *(Peace Book Company, 1940);* Testament of Friendship: The Story of Winifred Holtby *(Macmillan, 1940);* England's Hour *(Macmillan, 1941);* Humiliation with Honour *(A. Dakers, 1942);* Account Rendered *(Macmillan, 1944);* Seeds of Chaos: What Mass Bombing Really Means *(New Vision, 1944, published in America as* Massacre by Bombing, *Fellowship Publications, 1944); (ed. with George Catlin and Sheila Hodges)* Above All Nations *(Gollancz, 1945);* On Becoming a Writer *(Hutchinson, 1947, published in America as* On Being an Author, *Macmillan, 1948);* Born 1925: A Novel of Youth *(Macmillan, 1948);* In the Steps of John Bunyan: An Excursion into Puritan England *(Rich and Cowan, 1950, published in America as* Valiant Pilgrim: The Story of John Bunyan and Puritan England *(Macmil-*

*V*era
*B*rittain

lan, 1950); Search after Sunrise *(Macmillan, 1951)*; Lady into Woman: A History of Women from Victoria to Elizabeth II *(A. Dakers, 1953)*; Testament of Experience: An Autobiographical Story of the Years 1925–1950 *(Gollancz, 1957)*; Selected Letters of Winifred Holtby and Vera Brittain, 1920–1935 *(A.*

Brown, 1960); The Women at Oxford: A Fragment of History *(Harrap, 1960)*; Pethick-Lawrence: A Portrait *(Allen and Unwin, 1963)*; The Rebel Passion: A Short History of Some Pioneer Peace-Makers *(Allen and Unwin, 1964, published in America as* Fellowship of Reconciliation, *1964)*; Envoy Extraordinary: A Study of Vijaya Lakshmi Pandit and Her Contribution to Modern India *(Allen & Unwin, 1965)*; Radclyffe Hall: A Case of Obscurity *(American edition, A.S. Barnes, 1968)*; *(Alan Bishop with Terry Smart, eds.)* Chronicle of Youth: War Diary, 1913–1917 *(Gollancz, 1981)*; *(Paul Terry and Alan Bishop, eds.)* Testament of a Generation: The Journalism of Vera Brittain and Winifred Holtby *(Virago, 1985)*; *(Alan Bishop, ed.)* Chronicle of Friendship: Diary of the Thirties, 1932–1939 *(Gollancz, 1986)*; *(Winifred and Alan Eden-Green, eds.)* Testament of a Peace Lover: Letters from Vera Brittain *(Virago, 1988)*; *(Alan Bishop and Y. Aleksandra Bennett, eds.)* Wartime Chronicle: Vera Brittain's Diary, 1939–1945 *(Gollancz, 1989)*.

On the morning after Christmas, 1915, Vera Brittain, a young British nurse off-duty in Brighton, dressed in her room at the Grand Hotel, awaiting the arrival of her fiancé scheduled to return on furlough from the Western Front. Soon, there was a knock on the door, and she was summoned to the phone; the call was from her fiancé's sister ❧▶ **Clare Leighton.** He would not be arriving, Brittain was told. Then Clare read the cable just received by the family: "Regret to inform you that Lieut. R.A. Leighton 7th Worcesters died of wounds December 23rd. Lord Kitchener sends his sympathy." Roland Leighton had been killed inspecting faulty barbed wire along the trenches at Louvencourt, France. The mission that night had been dangerous: the moon was high and the Germans only a few hundred yards away. Upon hearing the details, Brittain could only ask: "Why did you go so boldly, so heedlessly, in No Man's Land when you knew that your leave was so near?" She later mused, "Hardest of all to bear, perhaps, was the silence which must for ever repudiate that final question." The following Easter, attending services at London's St. Paul's Cathedral, Brittain was struck by an inscription under G.F. Watts' picture of Hagar in the desert: "Watchman, will the night soon pass?" Of herself, she asked, "Will the night pass soon? How much longer can I endure it? What will help me to endure it, if endure it must be?"

But World War I was to last until 1918, and there would be a great deal more to endure. For the next three years, Brittain had a foreboding that her own brother, Edward, also stationed in France on the Western Front, would die in combat. For a brief period, superstition kept her from writing him, as she believed that "if I did he would certainly be dead before the letter arrived." On June 22, 1918, while tending her ill mother in London, she heard the sudden loud

❧▶ **Leighton, Clare** (b. 1899)

British illustrator and wood engraver. Born Clare Veronica Hope Leighton on April 12, 1899, in London, England; daughter of Robert (a literary critic and journalist) and **Marie (Connor) Leighton** *(a novelist); attended Brighton School of Art, Slade School of Fine Art, University of London, 1921–23, and London County Council Central School of Arts and Crafts, Southampton Row; married Henry Noel Brailsford; lived in Woodbury, Connecticut.*

Won *first prize and medal at the International Exhibition of Engraving at the Chicago Art Institute (1930); represented England in wood-engraving at the International Exhibition in Venice (1934); awarded D.F.A., Colby College (1940); works reside in permanent collection of the Victoria and Albert Museum, the British Museum, the National Galleries of Stockholm and Canada, Boston Fine Arts Museum, Baltimore Museum, and the Metropolitan Museum of Art in New York.*

Along with *Wanda Gág, Clare Leighton was one of the foremost practitioners of wood engraving of her day. She grew up in St. John's Wood, a mecca for artists, and was privately educated at home at the dining-room table. "It's useless for you to think you need any serious schooling," her mother would admonish. "I disapprove of education for women. Never forget that a blue stocking is a woman who has failed in her sex, and that the few females who find their way to a university are inevitably far from being the well-bred women of England. A career woman never belongs to the aristocracy." Then her mother would start the morning's dictation of one of her serial installments for the English newspapers that would feed and clothe her three children. Unlike her father's boys' books, her mother's writing brought in large sums of money.

In November of 1935, Leighton arrived in America with plans to travel and sketch. With the advent of World War II, she settled permanently in the U.S. in 1939 and became a naturalized citizen in 1945. Leighton wrote and illustrated *The Farmer's Year* (1933), *Four Hedges*, a month-by-month journal of her garden in the Chiltern Hills (1935), *Country Matters* (1937), *Sometime, Never* (1939), *Southern Harvest* (1942), along with several books for children. She also illustrated **Emily Brontë**'s *Wuthering Heights*, Thornton Wilder's *The Bridge of San Luis Rey*, H.M. Tomlinson's *The Sea and the Jungle*, and Thomas Hardy's *The Return of the Native*. Her autobiography *Tempestuous Petticoat* (Reinhart & Co.) was published in 1947. A close friend of *Vera Brittain and *Winifred Holtby,

knock on the door that always signified the arrival of a telegraph.

For a moment I thought that my legs would not carry me, but they behaved quite normally as I got up and went to the door. . . . I opened and read it in a tearing anguish of suspense. "Regret to inform you Captain E.H. Brittain M.C. killed in action Italy June 22." "No answer," I told the boy mechanically.

Edward had been shot through the head by an Austrian sniper at Asiago Plateau, Italy. The war, Brittain later mused, had condemned her to:

> live to the end of my days in a world without confidence or security, a world in which every dear personal relationship would be fearfully cherished under the shadow of apprehension; in which love would seem threatened perpetually by death; and happiness appear a house without duration, built on the shifting sands of chance. I might, perhaps, have it again, but never again should I hold it.

From the moment of her brother's death, Vera Brittain vowed that she would never again sanction another war.

Vera Mary Brittain had been born at Newcastle-under-Lyme on December 29, 1893. Her mother **Edith Bervon Brittain** was the daughter of a struggling Welsh organist. Her father Thomas Brittain was a prosperous director of Brittain's Ltd., a paper mill near Stoke-on-Trent. Young Vera first grew up in Macclesfield, then after age 11 in Buxton in Derbyshire, a health resort so provincial that she found it a veritable prison. She never lacked for material comfort, though she balked against her parents' "dull life of respectable mediocrity," and her parents never encouraged her intellectual gifts. Fortunately, they were stimulated by Edward, a composer, and his friends at Uppingham School.

From ages 14 through 17, Vera attended St. Monica's, Kingswood, a private girls' school where her intellectual curiosity was aroused by **Louise Heath Jones**, the school's founder. Brittain's incipient feminism was strongly influenced by author *Olive Schreiner's *Women and Labour* (1911), and Vera modeled herself after the heroine of Schreiner's novel, *Story of an African Farm* (1883). In 1912, she became what she called "a provincial debutante," living a life of dances, bridge, tennis, and music lessons. In April 1913, she confided to her diary: "I have not been touched directly yet either by the thrill of joy or the darkness of tragedy; mine has been a very sheltered life."

Prompted by John Marriott, an Oxford don giving a series of extension lectures at Buxton, Brittain applied to Somerville, Oxford's most competitive college for women. In 1914, she won a scholarship, with an entrance essay challenging Thomas Carlyle's pronouncement that history was the biography of great men. It was as a student at Somerville that Brittain had fallen in love with her brother's best friend, the poetic Roland Leighton. The Leightons were a highly talented family. Roland's mother **Marie Connor Leighton** wrote more than 40 novels, his father Robert was a literary critic and journalist who authored some 35 adventure stories for boys, and his sister Clare Leighton later made her mark as a woodcut artist and author.

When WWI first broke out on the European Continent, Brittain supported intervention, believing that a beleaguered France needed rescue. Moreover, she said, "this war is a matter of life & death to us," meaning her own nation. In June 1915, she enrolled as a "VAD," or member of the Voluntary Aid Detachments, a 23-woman unit founded by the British Red Cross and the St. Johns' Ambulance Association to aid the professional nursing services. She served first at Devonshire Hospital, then was assigned in October to First London General, which had been turned into a military institution. In September 1916, she was sent to St. George's Hospital, Malta, and in August 1917 was ordered to No. 24 General Hospital in Étaples, France, where she cared for German war prisoners. Her brother had just been sent to Ypres, not far away, to fight in the opening campaign of the Battle of Passchendaele. She later wrote:

> One day, when I had just finished the gruesome and complicated dress of a desperately wounded soldier, a disturbing thought struck me. Wasn't it odd that I, in Étaples, should be trying to save the life of a man whom my brother up at Ypres had perhaps done his best to kill? And didn't that argue the existence of some fundamental absurdity in the whole tragic situation?

Right after a severe engagement at Cambrai, she wrote her parents:

> I wish those people who write so glibly about this being a Holy War . . . could see a case—to say nothing of ten cases—of mustard gas in its early stages. . . . [T]he only thing one can say is that such severe cases don't last long; either they die soon or they improve—usually the former; they certainly never reach England in the state we have them here, and yet people persist in saying that God made the War, when there are such inventions of the Devil about.

In May 1918, Brittain had to return to England to care for her ill mother. Yet, when she resumed nursing at London's St. Bartholomew's Hospital, she was assigned only the most menial of tasks, "punishment" for technically breaking contract with the VADs. She later referred to herself as "a ghost too dazed to feel the full fury of her own resentment."

Not only did the war see the death of Brittain's fiancé and brother, but also the third of the "Three Musketeers," Victor Richardson, who had been blinded at Arras in June 1917 by a bullet behind the eyes. Brittain had also planned to marry the wounded Richardson. Furthermore, Geoffrey Thurlow, another close friend of Edward and a person to whom Brittain had been closely attached, had been killed that April. In her memoirs, Brittain described the strain of that time:

> The enemy within shelling distance—refugee Sisters [head nurse in a ward] crowding in with nerves all awry—bright moonlight, and aeroplanes carrying machine guns—ambulance trains jolting noisily into the siding, all day, all night—gassed men on stretchers, clawing the air—dying men, reeking with mud and foul green-stained bandages, shrieking and writhing in a grotesque travesty of manhood—dead men with fixed, empty eyes and shiny, yellow faces.

In 1919, after the war's end, Brittain returned to Oxford and shifted her studies from English to history, focusing on modern diplomacy. In 1921, she obtained a disappointing second in her field, but occasionally taught history at St. Monica's. Now her peacekeeping interests led her, along with fellow student *Winifred Holtby, to become a speaker for the League of Nations Union (LNU), a strongly antiwar organization in the 1920s. For three years, she addressed audiences on peace and feminism, sometimes speaking as much as four times a week. Fascism and Nazism, she always maintained, were the inevitable products of the vindictive Versailles Treaty.

All this time Brittain's friendship with Holtby grew. They shared a flat in Maida Vale, London. They often traveled together to Europe, serving as accredited journalists reporting on the League's Assemblies in Geneva and visiting the trenches and cemeteries of the Western Front. Both contributed to *Time and Tide,* a weekly with strong feminist leanings. In 1924, Brittain and Holtby became Socialists, after seeing the misery of London's slums while campaigning for Liberal candidate Sir Percy Harris, a prominent LNU backer. Brittain's socialism grew out of the conviction that:

> no change would come soon enough to save the next generation from the grief and ruin that had engulfed my own so long as the world that I knew endured—the world of haves and have-nots; of Great Powers and little nations, always at the mercy of the wealthy and strong; of influential persons whose interests were served by war, and who had sufficient authority to compel politicians to precipitate on behalf of a few the wholesale destruction of millions.

In 1925, Brittain married George Catlin, who had accumulated a brilliant record at Oxford's New College. Professor of politics at age 28, Catlin taught at Cornell University in Ithaca, New York, from 1924 to 1935. He wrote well-received studies, including *A Study of the Principles of Politics* (1929) and *The Story of the Political Philosophers* (1939). He became a prominent member of the Labour Party, returning frequently to England, where he unsuccessfully ran three times for Parliament.

Brittain and Catlin carried on a lengthy correspondence before they met and became engaged within ten days of their first encounter. Though charmed by the beauty of Ithaca where she spent one winter, Brittain (who kept her maiden name) found herself professionally unfulfilled and returned to London. She called her marriage "semi-detached": her husband journeyed each winter to Cornell, while she remained with Holtby and her two children under one roof at Chelsea. Brittain's love for Catlin was never as intense as it had been for Roland Leighton. Moreover, she could no more adopt his Roman Catholicism than he could share her pacifism. Yet, they remained a devoted couple.

Progressive childrearing now became one of the causes for which Brittain spoke, along with world peace. In 1928, she did a study of British working conditions for women, followed in 1929 by an attack on conventional views of marriage. She remained very much a woman of her class, however, interspersing her activism with hairdresser appointments and luncheons. She supervised four servants, shopped in chic dress shops, attended cocktail parties frequented by prominent literati and political leaders, and enjoyed long spells in the country and at seaside resorts.

Brittain's love of Holtby, while never sexual, grew increasingly intense until 1935, when Holtby died of Bright's disease, shortly after the suicide of Brittain's father. Only Holtby, by then a recognized novelist and critic, had understood Brittain's inner vulnerability as well as her need for both strong support and sharp criticism. The following year, Brittain saw Holtby's most admired novel, *South Riding,* to press and commemorated her in her own book, *Testament of Friendship,* in 1940. She also fell in love with George Brett, her American publisher who was already married. Although Brittain and Brett probably never had an affair, they remained close friends.

Ever since the Great War, Brittain had been writing prodigiously. Two books of poems were published: *Verses of a V.A.D.* (1918) and *Poems of the War and After* (1934). She wrote a novel, *The Dark Tide* (1923), based on her memories of Somerville, which was so critical of the college that it was banned from the senior common room. Another novel, *Not Without Honour* (1924), was drawn from the life of a local curate, Joseph Henry Ward, whom she idolized as an adolescent; it told of an idealistic Anglican priest who lost his faith in Christian orthodoxy.

Brittain's literary efforts met with indifferent success until the appearance of *Testament of Youth* (1933), which offered the first account of the agonies of WWI as seen through the eyes of a woman. Her combination of autobiography, poetry, and diary excerpts ably conveyed the anxieties of her entire generation, and suddenly she became lionized by much of the general public as well as the world of letters. She later wrote, "By enabling me to set down the sorrows of the First War and thus remove their bitterness, *Testament of Youth* became the final instrument of a return to life from the abyss of emotional death." Now famous, she made three lecture tours to the United States, in 1934, 1937 (described in her *Thrice a Stranger*), and 1940.

Brittain's next major book tells her story again, this time in fictionalized form. *An Honorable Estate* (1936) is a *roman à clef* in which a young nurse falls in love with a "very tall, black-haired" soldier who soon dies in battle. Other characters are a 19-year-old feminist, married to a much older Anglican priest, who commits suicide in sheer frustration with her empty life, both of whom were modeled on Catlin's parents.

In the spring of 1936, Brittain traveled with Catlin to France and Germany, and personally heard Adolf Hitler and Hermann Goering address fanatical crowds, instilling her with a strong antipathy toward fascism. Speaking that summer at a large outdoor peace rally in Dorchester, she reached what she called "a turning point in my life" when she became a pacifist. She was strongly influenced by Dick (H.R.L.) Sheppard, canon of St. Paul's Cathedral, and by Bertrand Russell's tract *Which Way to Peace?* (1936). It was Sheppard's influence that caused her to become a practicing Anglican, though in matters of social action she always felt closer to the Quakers.

Early in 1937, Brittain became a sponsor of Sheppard's Peace Pledge Union (PPU), the leading British pacifist organization, and spoke widely at its meetings. She strongly endorsed the Munich agreement, seeing it as necessary to prevent another world conflict. When the Molotov-Ribbentrop pact of August 23, 1939, was signed, she wrote that the Soviets sought to "set Middle and Western Europe by the ears," then "to step in when both sides are exhausted and create revolutions in all the countries involved."

During World War II, Brittain's pacifism was stronger than ever. She wrote on May 23, 1940:

> The present catastrophe has arisen, not from the application of pacifism, but from the total failure of statesmen in all countries to practice its principles when their acceptance was a political possibility. Far from pacifist doctrine being proved wrong, the present calamity demonstrates its correctness.

Brittain's bulletin, "Letters to Peace Lovers," was first published weekly, then fortnightly. It totaled 175 issues and reached 2,000 subscribers. In her graphic account of the bombing of London and the Midlands, *England's Hour* (1941), she wrote, "If we do not learn to forgive, this nation has already lost the peace; and if it loses yet another peace, the war of 1965 will annihilate our children and our London too." Another book, *Humiliation with Honour*, published in 1942, defended her position in the form of letters to her 15-year-old son. In 1945, along with Catlin and **Sheila Hodges**, an editor at Gollancz publishers, Brittain edited *Above All Nations*. The subtitle of the anthology aptly reveals the contents: "Acts of kindness done to enemies, in the war, by men of many nations."

Until May 1940, Brittain advocated a peace with Germany. Once the blitz began, however, she found negotiation infeasible. Now, with the advent of total war, she said she must concentrate on curbing "the flood of hatred" and alleviating the suffering of the innocent. Still, she opposed unconditional surrender, believing it would harden Axis resistance while making the conflict more brutal. On December 9, 1942, she confided to her diary: "How tired I am of this country fighting the Germans (who are so efficient & thorough)—I am sure that the future peace of Europe depends on our ability to be friends with them—& upon little else." Yet, she linked her desire for an immediate truce to the plight of Europe's Jews, saying two days later, "Degree to which Jewish suffering has been extended by war is immeasurable; the worst peace would not have caused one-tenth of it."

Brittain's pamphlets addressed specific wartime issues. "The Higher Retribution" (1942) opposed the policy of revenge she saw propounded by diplomat Lord Vansittart. "We can safely leave the war's criminals . . . to the Almighty," she wrote, "who has claimed vengeance as his." In "Seeds of Chaos" (1944), she severely criticized the saturation bombing of German cities. At one point, she commented, "It is not Hitler upon whom our bombs fall. Our air-raids, like his, wreck humble homes and decimate families living in the East Ends of industrial cities, or close to the dockyards of naval and commercial ports." The pamphlet was endorsed by 28 American Protestant leaders, including Harry Emerson Fosdick of New York's Riverside Church. Her short treatise, "One of These Little Ones" (1943), strongly attacked the Allied blockade. As chair of the PPU's Food Relief Campaign, she hoped that small quantities of special food might reach the innocent civilians of Nazi-occupied Europe, particularly those of Greece and France. Thanks in part to such efforts, the government authorized a thousand tons of food to Greece each month.

Being a pacifist in wartime was not easy. By the spring of 1940, Brittain was subject to police surveillance, saw two vigilante efforts to burn down her office, and along with her husband received a murder threat from an army major. The British government would not allow her to visit the U.S. (where her children had been sent for war refuge), India (whose nationalist cause she strongly endorsed), and Sweden (where she had been asked to lecture). At the same time, Brittain was on the Gestapo round-up list, to be interred as soon as Hitler conquered England.

During the war, Brittain was thwarted in efforts to write biographies of Labour Party leader George Lansbury and aviator *Amy Johnson. She did write a novel, Account Rendered (1944), which told how a sensitive young musician, shell-shocked during World War I, later killed his spouse in a fit of madness. The story was based on the life of Leonard Lockhart, a battle-fatigued physician who in 1939 murdered his beloved wife in a fit of amnesia. As the work graphically showed the brutalizing effects of modern combat, its pacifist message was easy to detect.

As the war came to an end, Brittain hoped for an accommodation with the Soviet Union. Conceding that "several unhappy countries and peoples" under Russian control might face "a period of persecution," she was still optimistic. When such tyrannies lacked an effective opponent, she said, they were "apt to undergo a gradual process of self-modification." Moreover, Russia would be too occupied with reconstruction to make war "on any neighbor who does not actually threaten her." From 1949 to 1951, she was president of PPU. She also was a vice president of the Women's International League for Peace and Freedom and in 1964 wrote a popularized account of the Fellowship of Reconciliation.

After the war, Brittain's work was more diverse. Her pacifism found a new manifestation in her last novel, Born 1925 (1948), which dealt with the generational conflict between a peace-loving father and a son who enlists in World War II. Her life of John Bunyan (1950) analyzed the Puritan author's major works while ably capturing the spirit of religious life in the age of Charles II. Another biography was published in 1963, the life of Frederick (Lord) Pethick-Lawrence, prominent Labourite minister and reformer. In 1967, she updated her memoirs with Testament of Experience, which carried her story down to 1945.

Two of Brittain's books centered on a nation with which she felt a special affinity: India. One, Search after Sunrise (1951), dealt with India in the immediate aftermath of Mahatma Gandhi's assassination. The other, Envoy Extraordinary (1966), focused admiringly on *Vijaya Lakshmi Pandit, prominent diplomat and sister of Indian prime minister Jawaharlal Nehru. Two more Brittain books covered another favorite topic: feminism. Lady into Woman (1953) is a chronological report of women's rights from *Victoria to *Elizabeth II, rich in statistics. Women at Oxford (1960) narrates the struggle for female equality there. Brittain's last book, *Radclyffe Hall: A Case of Obscenity? (1968), involves a defense of Hall's novel The Well of Loneliness (1928), a sympathetic portrayal of lesbianism. After her death, three volumes of Brittain's diary were published, as well as a book of political essays by Brittain and Holtby.

Slight in physique and only five feet tall, Brittain had a reticent personality that conveyed great dignity. In print, all reserve vanished. She was a tireless writer, who often put in ten hours a day on her work. Though her prose could be wordy, her narrative stocked with irrelevant detail, and her thought frustratingly diffuse, at her best she was an extremely sensitive observer and a master of English prose. She will always be remembered as a truly great chronicler of the generation that came of age in World War I and as a courageous defender of pacifism. On March 29, 1970, Vera Brittain died in London.

SOURCES:

Bailey, Hilary. Vera Brittain. Middlesex: Penguin, 1987.

Berry, Paul, and Mark Bostridge. Vera Brittain: A Life. London: Chatto and Windus, 1995.

Brittain, Vera. Testament of Youth: An Autobiographical Study of the Years 1900–1925. London: Gollancz, 1933 (NY: Macmillan).

———. Testament of Experience: An Autobiographical Story of the Years 1925–1950. London: Gollancz, 1957 (NY: Macmillan).

———. Chronicle of Youth: War Diary, 1913–1917. (ed. by Alan Bishop with Terry Smart). London: Gollancz, 1981 (NY: William Morrow, 1982).

———. *Chronicle of Friendship: Diary of the Thirties, 1932– 1939.* Ed. by Alan Bishop. London: Gollancz, 1986.

———. *Wartime Chronicle: Vera Brittain's Diary, 1939–1945.* Ed. by Alan Bishop and Y. Aleksandra Bennett. London: Gollancz, 1989.

SUGGESTED READING:

Brittain, Vera. *Testament of Friendship: The Story of Winifred Holtby.* London: Macmillan, 1940 (NY: Macmillan). Catlin, Sir George. *For God's Sake, Go!: An Autobiography.* Gerards Cross: Colin Smythe, 1972.

RELATED MEDIA:

"Testament of Youth" (five-part television series, each one hour), fictionalized account starring **Cheryl Campbell**, **Jane Wenhan**, Emrys James, Rupert Frazer, and Peter Woodward; script by **Elaine Morgan**; produced by Jonathan Powell; directed by **Moira Armstrong**, BBC, 1979.

COLLECTIONS:

The papers of Vera Brittain are located at McMaster University, Hamilton, Ontario.

Justus D. Doenecke,
Professor of History, New College,
University of South Florida, Sarasota, Florida

Elizabeth Knight Britton

Brittany, countess of.

Brittany, duchess of.

Britton, Elizabeth Knight
(1858–1934)

American botanist. Born Elizabeth Gertrude Knight in New York City, on January 9, 1858; died in New York City on February 25, 1934, daughter and one of five children of James (operator of a furniture factory and sugar plantation) and Sophie (Compton) Knight; attended elementary school in Cuba; graduated from Normal College (later Hunter College), New York, 1875; married Nathaniel Britton, 1885.

Author of close to 350 scientific papers, Elizabeth Britton helped establish and manage the New York Botanical Gardens and was a driving force in conservation efforts. Given the level of Britton's contribution to her field, her ranking as an amateur botanist remains perplexing.

Britton spent most of her childhood in Cuba, where her father ran a furniture factory and sugar plantation. As a teenager, she divided her time between Cuba and New York. In 1875, she graduated from Normal College (later Hunter College) and for ten years served on the staff there, the last two years as assistant in natural science. By 1883, her botanical studies were focused on mosses (bryology), and she had published the first of her numerous scientific papers.

In 1885, Britton married Nathaniel Britton, then an assistant in geology at Columbia College, who shared her interest in botany. The two made numerous botanical expeditions together, and Elizabeth Britton became the unofficial curator of the moss collection at Columbia, which she expanded in 1893 with the acquisition of the collection of August Jaeger of Switzerland. The Brittons were also influential in the establishment of the New York Botanical Garden, which was incorporated in 1891, using the model of the Botanic Gardens of Kew, England. Nathaniel was named director in 1896. When the Columbia College herbarium was transferred there in 1899, Elizabeth became unofficial curator of mosses. She was made honorary curator in 1912.

Throughout her career, Britton was closely associated with a number of botanical associations, including the Torrey Botanical Club. Becoming a member in 1879, she edited the club *Bulletin* from 1886 to 1888. She was a principal founder of the Sullivan Moss Society (later know as the American Bryological Society), serving as its president from 1916 to 1919. Later in her career, Britton turned her attention to wildflower conservation, cofounding in 1902 the Wild Flower Preservation Society of America of which she served as secretary and treasurer. Through lectures and publications, she was instrumental in saving a number of endangered wildflower habitats around the country and also helped push conservation measures through the New York legislature.

Britton died of a stroke in 1934. In spite of her amateur standing, the scientific community recognized her contribution by naming 15 species of plants and a moss genus (*Bryobrittonia*) in her honor.

Barbara Morgan,
Melrose, Massachusetts

Britton, Nan (b. 1896).

See Harding, Florence K. for sidebar.

Broad, Mary (1765–?).

See Bryant, Mary.

Broccadelli, Lucia (1476–1544).

See Lucia of Narni.

Brodbeck, May (1917–1983)

American philosopher and professor. Born in Newark, New Jersey, on July 26, 1917; died on August 2, 1983; granted B.A., New York University (1941); University of Iowa, M.A. 1947, Ph.D. 1947.

Appointed instructor at University of Minnesota (1947–74), professor of philosophy (1959–74), chair, department of philosophy (1967–70), dean of graduate school (1972–74), Carver Professor of Philosophy (1974–83); University of Iowa Professor Emeritus (1983).

Selected works: "Coherence Theory Reconsidered: Professor Werkmeister on Semantics and on the Nature of Empirical Laws," in Philosophy of Science *(Vol. 16, 1949); "Toward a 'Non-Naturalistic' Ethic," in* Philosophical Studies *(Vol. 2, 1951); "An Analytic Principle of Induction?" in* Journal of Philosophy *(Vol. 49, 1952);* Philosophy in America: 1900–1950 *(1952); (ed. with Herbert Fiegel)* Readings in the Philosophy of Science *(1953); "Meaning and Action,"* Philosophy of Science *(Vol. 30, 1963); "Objectivism and Interaction: a Reaction to Margolis," in* Philosophy of Science *(Vol. 33, 1966); (ed.)* Readings in the Philosophy of the Social Sciences *(1968).*

May Brodbeck achieved outstanding success as an academic philosopher at a time when there were few prominent women in philosophy. Widely published, she became chair of her department at the University of Minnesota, prestigious for philosophy of science, and acted as dean of the Graduate School for a few years.

Academically concerned primarily with the philosophy of social science, she examined human behavior, individually and as part of groups. Brodbeck's work also examined the logic, or laws of inference, at work in social science.

Catherine Hundleby, M.A. Philosophy, University of Guelph

Broglie, Duchesse de (1797–1838).

See Staël, Germaine de for sidebar.

Brohan, Augustine (1824–1893).

See Brohan, Augustine Suzanne for sidebar on Josephine Brohan.

Brohan, Augustine Suzanne (1807–1887)

French actress. Name variations: Suzanne or Susanne Brohan. Born in Paris, France, on January 22 (some sources cite 29), 1807; died on August 16 (some sources cite 17), 1887; children: Josephine Félicité Augustine Brohan (1824–1893); Émilie Madeleine Brohan (1833–1900).

Augustine Suzanne Brohan, known on the stage as Suzanne, entered the Paris Conservatoire at the age of 11; she took the second prize for comedy in 1820, and the first in 1821. An extremely graceful, clever, and original actress, she served her apprenticeship in the provinces, making her first Paris appearance at the Odéon in 1832 as Dorine in Molière's *Tartuffe*. Her success earned her a berth at the Comédie Française, where she made her debut on February 15, 1834, as Madelon in *Les Précieuses ridicules*, and as Suzanne in *Le Mariage de Figaro*. Ill health forced her to retire in 1842 at age 35.

Her elder daughter, ❧▸ **Josephine Augustine Brohan** (1824–1893), known on the stage as Augustine Brohan, was admitted to the Conservatoire when very young and twice took the second prize for comedy. The soubrette (or ingenue) part, entrusted for more than 150 years at the Comédie Française to a succession of first-rank

> ❧▸ **Brohan, Josephine Félicité Augustine** (1824–1893)
> *French actress. Name variations: Augustine Brohan. Born in France on December 2, 1824; died on February 16, 1893; daughter of **Augustine Suzanne Brohan** (an actress); married Edmond David de Gheest (secretary to the Belgian legation in Paris), 1866 (died, 1885).*

artists, was vacant when Augustine debuted there on May 19, 1841, as Dorine in *Tartuffe* and Lise in *Rivaux d'eux-mêmes*. She was immediately admitted *pensionnaire* (an actor for hire) and at the end of 18 months unanimously elected *sociétaire* (a member of the company). Known as a remarkably versatile and brilliant actress, Augustine succeeded *Rachel at the Conservatoire and soon became a great favorite in the plays of Molière, Jean de Regnard, and Pierre de Marivaux. Augustine Brohan also wrote plays. On her retirement from the stage in 1866, she wed Edmond David de Gheest (d. 1885), secretary to the Belgian legation in Paris, but the marriage was unhappy.

Suzanne Brohan's second daughter, ◄❧ Émilie Madeleine Brohan (1833–1900), known on the stage as Madeleine, took first prize for comedy at the Conservatoire (1850). She was then engaged by the Comédie Française, but rather than have her debut in a play of the theater's *répertoire*, the management put on a new comedy for her benefit, a play by Augustin Scribe and Gabriel Legouvé, entitled *Les Contes de la reine de Navarre*, in which she created the part of *Margaret of Angoulême on September 1, 1850. A polished soubrette, Madeleine reaped immediate success for her talent and beauty. Less than two years after her debut, she was elected *sociétaire*. In 1853, she married Mario Uchard, from whom she was soon separated (they would divorce in 1884), and in 1858 she returned to the Comédie Française playing leading parts until her retirement in 1886. Her name is associated with a great number of plays, besides those in the classical *répertoire*, notably *Par droit di conquête*, *Les Deux Veuves*, and *Le Lion amoureux*, the last of which brought one of her greatest successes in the role of the marquise de Maupas.

❧► Brohan, Émilie Madeleine (1833–1900)

*French actress. Name variations: Madeleine Brohan. Born in France on October 22, 1833; died in 1900; daughter of **Augustine Suzanne Brohan** (an actress); married Mario Uchard, 1853 (soon separated, divorced 1884).*

Brohan, Madeleine (1833–1900).

See Brohan, Augustine Suzanne for sidebar on Émilie Madeleine Brohan.

Brohan, Suzanne (1807–1887).

See Brohan, Augustine Suzanne.

Bromley, Dorothy Dunbar
(1896–1986)

American editor and writer. *Born Dorothy Ewing Dunbar on a farm near Ottawa, Illinois, on December 25, 1896; died of pneumonia on January 3, 1986, in Pennsylvania; third of four children of Helen Elizabeth (Ewing) and Charles E. Dunbar; attended Hyde Park High School in Chicago; graduated cum laude, Northwestern University, B.A., 1917; married Donald C. Bromley, August 1920 (divorced early 1920s).*

Longtime editor of a substantially transformed "Women's Page" at the New York *Herald Tribune*, Dorothy Dunbar Bromley spent a peripatetic childhood. Her father, unsatisfied with each chosen occupation, moved the family from one small town in Illinois to another, before moving to Toledo, Ohio, then on to Chicago. Following her graduation from Northwestern, Bromley enlisted in the French-speaking women's telephone unit attached to the signal corps; she performed her wartime duties in Atlantic City.

While visiting a sister in Detroit, Bromley was hired as secretary to the editor at the Detroit *Free Press* and was given an opportunity to write reviews. Following her marriage, she and her husband moved to New York where she took a job as reader and editor with Henry Holt and Company (1921–25), until she resigned in order to freelance (1926–34). Bromley's first published article, "Ethics of Alimony," appeared in *Harper's* magazine. Thus began a series of commentaries on women, including "Feminist—New Style," "What Risk Motherhood" (with the input of *Margaret Sanger), and "Diogenes Looks at the Ladies." During a 1932 sojourn in Europe, Bromley interviewed Léon Blum, *Irène Joliot-Curie, and French feminist leaders.

Her first book, *Birth Control: Its Use and Misuse* (1934), contributed to her hiring as columnist on the women's page of the New York *World-Telegram* (1935–38); while there, she collaborated with **Florence Haxton Britten** on *Youth and Sex* (1938). Bromley then signed on as columnist with the New York *Post* (1940–42); in 1942, she was invited to edit the Women's Page of the Sunday edition of the New York *Herald Tribune*. The page was never the same. Replacing club news with national issues, Bromley championed minimum wage for store clerks, asked pointed questions about prisoner of war camps in the U.S., reported on famine in India, and championed equality for racial and religious minorities. Typically, she was the first to interview *Lillian Smith about her controversial new book *Strange Fruit*. Bromley considered Smith a woman of great courage.

Broniewska, Janina (1904–1981)

Polish Communist writer and activist who served as secretary of the Union of Polish Writers. Born in Kalisz, Russian Poland, on August 5, 1904; died in 1981; married Wladyslaw Broniewski (a revolutionary poet).

Born in the last years of Poland's subjugation to foreign rule in the city of Kalisz in Russian Poland on August 5, 1904, Janina Broniewska early exhibited her rebelliousness, spending countless hours in student cafes arguing over the fine points of revolutionary ideology. After graduation, she became a teacher and contributed articles for children to newspapers and journals. Some of her most outstanding work appeared in *Plomyczek* (*Little Flame*), a children's journal published under the auspices of the Polish Association of Teachers and edited by the noted writer **Wanda Wassilewska**. A political militant, Broniewska was a leader in the teacher's union, which she led in a number of dramatic strikes in the 1930s. By the late 1930s, she was moving closer to Communism, in part because her husband, the noted revolutionary poet Wladyslaw Broniewski (1897–1962), was also moving in that direction.

With the Nazi invasion of Poland in September 1939, Janina Broniewska and her husband fled to Soviet-occupied eastern Poland, when that part of the country was annexed to the Ukrainian Soviet Socialist Republic. This was a difficult time for them both, with Wladyslaw serving a term of imprisonment imposed by the NKVD in Lvov; he was released after the Nazi attack on the USSR. With Soviet blessings, Janina joined a Moscow-sponsored political organization, the Union of Polish Patriots. She also became active in Soviet-approved literary activities, serving on the editorial board of the journal *Nowe Widnokregi* (*New Horizons*). Although she knew little about military affairs, in 1944 she became chief editor of the journal *Polska Zbrojna* (*Armed Poland*).

Returning to liberated Poland in 1945, Broniewska became a major literary personality, at least in part because she had gained the trust of Soviet cultural advisors resident in Warsaw. Over the next years, she published books based on her wartime experiences, including *Marching with the First Army* (1946) and *From the Notebooks of a War Correspondent* (1953). A book

written for young readers, *About the Man Who Had No Fear of Bullets* (1948), was a biographical study of Karol Swierczewski, the famous "General Walter" of the International Brigades in the Spanish Civil War. The regime showed its warm regard for Broniewska's literary and political work by awarding her the 1949 City of Warsaw Literary Prize. The most controversial part of her career after 1945 was the role she played as secretary of the Union of Polish Writers, a position that entailed supervising the political loyalty of the organization's members. Watchful of ideological and artistic "deviations," she earned the undying animosity of many of Poland's most talented and independent-minded writers. Broniewska died in 1981 at a time when the rise of the Solidarity movement and a near-universal demand for intellectual freedom made it obvious that Polish cultural life would no longer submit to any form of regimentation.

SOURCES:

"Broniewska, Janina," in *Wielka Encyklopedia Powszechna PWN*. Vol. 2. Warsaw: Panstwowe Wydawnictwo Naukowe, 1963, p. 152.

Toranska, Teresa. *"Them": Stalin's Polish Puppets.* Translated by Agnieszka Kolakowska. NY: Harper & Row, 1987.

John Haag, Associate Professor, University of Georgia, Athens, Georgia

Bronner, Augusta Fox (1881–1966)

American clinical psychologist. Born in Louisville, Kentucky, in 1881; died in Clearwater, Florida, in 1966; attended Columbia University Teachers College, Ph.D., 1914; married William Healy (a neurologist), 1931.

A pioneer in the study of delinquent and mentally challenged girls, Augusta Fox Bronner planned to be a teacher from the age of six. In 1903, supported by her mother who believed she should pursue a career, Bronner enrolled at Columbia University Teachers College, where, in addition to her studies, she was an assistant to educational psychologist Edward L. Thorndike. After graduating, she taught for five years before returning to Columbia for her Ph.D., where her groundbreaking thesis proved that, given equal determinates, girls with mental disabilities were no more likely to behave destructively than girls without disabilities. Published in 1914, the study became a classic, paving the way for increased understanding of the behaviors of both delinquent and mentally challenged youths.

In 1913, Bronner took a summer-school course at Harvard with neurologist William Healy, who would become her mentor, her collaborator, and, much later, her husband. Healy hired Bronner as a research psychologist at the Chicago Juvenile Psychopathic Institute, where she grappled with the difficulties of financing follow-up work with the institute's youngsters. She traveled to Boston, where she secured funding for a clinic to help young offenders. In 1917, with Healy, she opened the Judge Baker Foundation (subsequently renamed the Judge Baker Children's Center). The Foundation became the focus of their professional lives and made them respected experts in their field, although Bronner often let the more established Healy take the public limelight. She lectured at various Boston colleges but published very little, preferring the hands-on clinic setting. The couple married in 1932, after the death of Healy's wife, and retired to Clearwater, Florida, in 1946. Bronner died 20 years later, at the age of 85.

COLLECTIONS:

Bronner's papers are in the Ethel Sturges Dummer Papers in the Schlesinger Library at Radcliffe College, and at the Judge Baker Guidance Center archives in the Francis A. Countway Library of Medicine, Boston, Massachusetts.

Bronsart, Ingeborg von (1840–1913)

German composer and pianist whose greatest success was the 1873 opera Jery und Baetely. *Born Ingeborg Starck in St. Petersburg, Russia, on August 24, 1840, of Swedish parents; died in Munich, Germany, on June 17, 1913; married Hans Bronsart von Schellendorff (known as Hans von Bronsart), in 1862.*

Ingeborg Starck von Bronsart was born in Russia of Swedish parents in 1840, the same year as Peter Ilyitch Tchaikovsky. A child prodigy, her talents as a pianist were carefully cultivated so that she became a mature artist whose talents remained largely intact. Franz Liszt considered her one of his greatest discoveries, and she justified his confidence when, in the early 1860s, she undertook a triumphal concert tour that brought her to numerous German cities, including Leipzig, as well as to Paris and her home city of St. Petersburg. Her marriage to Hans Bronsart in 1862 resulted in the end of her concert career. Because of his position as Intendant of the Court Theater in Hanover, she was forbidden to perform in public. Consequently, her musical energies were put into composition, in which she had been interested since childhood. Confident in all musical forms, she scored her greatest success in 1873 with an opera based on a Goethe text, *Jery und Baetely*. Very popular at its Leipzig premiere, this stage work was also

performed to approving audiences in Berlin, Weimar, Wiesbaden, Königsberg, and Vienna. Her choral works included a patriotic work for mixed choir, *Hurrah Germania*. As late as 1909, she was engaged in the composition of an opera, *Die Sühne*. Several of Ingeborg Starck von Bronsart's compositions have been recorded in recent years, including excerpts from *Jery und Baetely*.

John Haag,
Athens, Georgia

Bronskaya, Eugenia (1882–1953)

Russian soprano and well-known recording artist who taught at the Leningrad Conservatory from 1923 to 1950. Born in St. Petersburg on February 1, 1882; died in Leningrad (St. Petersburg) on December 12, 1953.

Once, while replacing an indisposed colleague, Eugenia Bronskaya assayed the title role in *Lucia di Lammermoor*. When the curtain rose, she knew no more than the Sextet and the Mad Scene but persevered in the best tradition of "the show must go on." Bronskaya studied with her mother and then with **Teresa Arkel** in Milan. She debuted in Tbilisi in 1907 and then went to Kiev for three years. From 1905 to 1907, she performed in Moscow and then returned to Italy. In 1909, Bronskaya was a member of the Boston Opera Company. She became a well-known recording artist in the early 20th century. Returning to Russia in 1911, she was engaged at the Maryinsky and Bolshoi theaters. In 1923, she began to teach at the Leningrad Conservatory where she remained until 1950.

John Haag,
Athens, Georgia

Bronson, Betty (1906–1971)

American film actress. Born Elizabeth Ada Bronson in Trenton, New Jersey, on November 17, 1906; died in 1971; attended Catholic schools in California, where the family moved when she was three; married Ludwig Lauerhaus (a bond specialist), 1932; children: one son.

Selected films: Peter Pan *(1924);* The Golden Princess *(1925);* Are Parents People? *(1925);* A Kiss for Cinderella *(1926);* Everybody's Acting *(1927);* Brass Knuckles *(1927);* Ritzy *(1927);* The Singing Fool *(1928);* Companionate Marriage *(1928);* Sonny Boy *(1929);* The Locked Door *(1929);* Medicine Man *(1930);* The Yodelin' Kid from Pine Ridge *(1937);* Who's Got the Action? *(1962);* Blackbeard's Ghost *(1967);* Evel Knievel *(1971).*

After only a few bit parts, Betty Bronson became an overnight star when Sir James M. Barrie cast her in the title role of the first film version of his play *Peter Pan* (1924). Barrie, who was searching for someone not immediately recognizable for the role, chose Bronson over some of the major stars of her day. With Bronson's overwhelming triumph, Paramount envisioned her as a successor to *Mary Pickford, but she was never able to sustain her initial popularity.

Bronson followed *Peter Pan* with the role of the endearing teenage heroine in *Are Parents People?* (1925). Some of Hollywood's brightest up-and-comers appeared in her subsequent films, which included *Ritzy* (1927), with Gary Cooper, *The Singing Fool* (1928) with Al Jolson (whom she found difficult to work with), and *The Medicine Man* (1930) with Jack Benny in his screen debut. In 1932, Bronson married bond specialist Ludwig Lauerhaus and settled in Asheville, North Carolina, where she wrote a column for the local paper ("Peeping Pixie"), before attempting a comeback in the 1937 *Yodelin' Kid from Pine Ridge* with Gene Autry. Most of her subsequent appearances were on television,

Betty
Bronson

including episodes of *Dr. Kildare, My Three Sons*, and *Marcus Welby, M.D.* In 1969, when Eastman House unearthed a print of *Peter Pan*, they invited Bronson to a showing at the Museum of Modern Art in New York, where she was warmly received by ecstatic film buffs. She died two years later, in 1971.

Brontë, Anne (1820–1849).
See Brontë Sisters.

Brontë, Charlotte (1816-1855).
See Brontë Sisters.

Brontë, Emily (1818–1848).
See Brontë Sisters.

Brontë Sisters

Brontë, Charlotte (1816–1855). *Victorian author of* Jane Eyre *and elder sister to writers Emily and Anne Brontë. Name variations: Charlotte Brontë Nichols; Mrs. Arthur Nichols; (pseudonym) Currer Bell. Born Charlotte Brontë at Thornton in Yorkshire on April 21, 1816; died at Haworth in Yorkshire on March 31, 1855; daughter of* **Maria Branwell Brontë** *and Rev-*

Brontë Sisters

erend Patrick Brontë (a cleric-author); married Arthur B. Nichols on June 29, 1854, at age 38.

By age eight, had lost her mother and two older sisters to childbirth complications and consumption, respectively; briefly attended Cowan Bridge School, which formed the basis for the austere and unhealthy Lowood of Jane Eyre; saw publication of Poems by Currer, Ellis and Acton Bell (male pseudonyms used by Charlotte, Emily and Anne Brontë, 1846); published Jane Eyre, the novel that brought her immediate success (1847); by age 33, saw two younger sisters and only brother die within months of each other; married late in life and died after nine months of her marriage from illness associated with pregnancy and, most likely, consumption.

Writings: Poems of Currer, Ellis and Acton Bell (1846); Jane Eyre (1847); Shirley, A Tale (1849); Villette (1853); The Professor, A Tale (1857); Legends of Angria (1933); The Twelve Adventurers and Other Stories (1925); Five Novelettes (1971).

Brontë, Emily (1818–1848). *Victorian author of* **Wuthering Heights** *and middle sister to writers Charlotte and Anne Brontë. Name variations: (pseudonym) Ellis Bell. Born Emily Jane Brontë at Thornton, near Bradford, Yorkshire, on July 30, 1818; died of consumption at Haworth, on December 19, 1848; daughter of Maria Branwell Brontë and Reverend Patrick Brontë (a cleric-author).*

With younger sister, Anne, developed a rich imaginative world called Gondal, that formed the basis for early poems, which were discovered by elder sister, Charlotte, and published (1846) in Poems by Currer, Ellis and Acton Bell; published Wuthering Heights (1847), sparking great controversy and speculation about author's identity, which she resolutely guarded until her death; contracted consumption (1848), one month after her brother Branwell died of the same disease and less than six months before Anne succumbed as well.

Writings: Poems of Currer, Ellis and Acton Bell (1846); Wuthering Heights (1847).

Brontë, Anne (1820–1849). *Victorian author of* **Agnes Grey** *and* **The Tenant of Wildfell Hall;** *youngest of the Brontë sisters. Name variations: (pseudonym) Acton Bell. Born Anne Brontë at Thornton, near Bradford, Yorkshire, in January 1820; died of consumption in Scarborough on May 28, 1849; youngest child of Maria Branwell Brontë and Reverend Patrick Brontë (a cleric-author).*

Mother died within months of her birth; with elder sister, Emily, developed a world called Gondal; with sisters Charlotte and Emily, published Poems by

Currer, Ellis and Acton Bell (1846); published Agnes Grey based on a brief experience as governess to the Ingham family (1847); worked for four years with the Robinson family, where she witnessed her brother's attempts to seduce Mrs. Robinson; wrote The Tenant of Wildfell Hall as a warning against the type of existence that claimed her brother's life; contracted consumption after the deaths of her brother and elder sister Emily; journeyed to the seaside with Charlotte in hopes of a cure; damp air hastened her demise; was buried in Scarborough within six months of Emily's death.

Writings: Poems of Currer, Ellis and Acton Bell (1846); Agnes Grey (1847); The Tenant of Wildfell Hall (1848).

"You are the three suns," **Ellen Nussey**'s incisive observation to the Brontë sisters upon the unusual appearance of a parhelion in the sky (which looks like three suns), is an apt commentary on their uniqueness. Indeed, how unlikely a phenomenon they were—three females and daughters of a poor cleric whose imaginative genius found expression during a time when, as a rule, women received only a domestic education. Moreover, a professional woman of letters was both laughable and scorned, hence, the need for the Brontës to adopt their respective sexually ambiguous pseudonyms: Currer Bell (Charlotte), Ellis Bell (Emily), and Acton Bell (Anne). Anomalies of the repressive Victorian era and frequent targets of disdain, the Brontës managed to create novels that have survived the major test of time. In fact, the large bulk of critical and biographical studies on the Brontë sisters testifies to their remarkable contribution and place of primacy in the annals of British literature.

Charlotte Brontë's reputation has eclipsed that of her younger sisters, owing to her prodigious literary production. There is ample reason, however, for considering the lives and contributions of the three authors together, for their unusual childhood is largely responsible for their later creative genius. Tragic circumstances led the Brontë children to form a remarkably intimate society, one that was governed by their intellectual precociousness.

Reared by an austere and intellectual cleric-father amid the bleak and secluded Yorkshire moors, the Brontë children created their own rich imaginary world. They developed their budding literary skills in the post-Eve era, which was dominated by the 19th-century view of woman as "Mary." In the Middle Ages, Woman had been cast as the evil and morally reprehensible descendant of her mother, Eve. In the Victorian

Charlotte Brontë

schoolmaster. Possessed of an independent, even eccentric, character, Patrick Brontë freely expressed his evangelical ideas in strongly worded prose and much admired light verse. He claimed to have derived "indescribable pleasure" in writing "from morning till noon, and from noon till night." His literary passions and commitment to education profoundly influenced his children.

At 30, Maria Branwell met and married Patrick Brontë, then 31. Well-read and intelligent, she shared his Methodist faith and political views. Before their marriage she wrote an essay on "The Advantages of Poverty in Religious Concerns." She tempered her husband's stern intellectualism with what **Rebecca Fraser** describes as a "rare passion and freedom from inhibition." Unfortunately, none of her surviving daughters would benefit from her influence.

After bearing six children in quick succession, Maria Brontë suffered complications after the birth of her last, Anne, in January 1820. Within weeks of the difficult birth, the family moved to Haworth, where Patrick Brontë was to become curate. The stress of the move may well have led to Mrs. Brontë's fatal illness, now recognized as an infection of the blood. For seven months, her husband attempted to nurse her back to health. She died in September 1821 when her children were all under eight years old. Charlotte (then five), Emily (three), and Anne (twenty months) would remember nothing of their mother.

Patrick Brontë had asked Maria's eldest sister, the 40-year-old, unmarried **Elizabeth Branwell**, to aid him in caring for the children. She was unequipped, however, to provide emotional or intellectual support. Instead, the Brontë's eldest child, seven-year-old **Maria** (immortalized as Helen Burns in Charlotte's *Jane Eyre*), effectively replaced her mother and namesake.

While Maria served as the family's emotional center, Patrick Brontë firmly guided their intellectual development. His passion for poetry and debate meant that the parsonage was full of books and journals, and his Evangelical faith in the truth was instilled in his children. He expected them to speak their minds. The result was an astounding precocity in all, especially Maria, who was reported to have helped correct the proofs on her father's poems before she had turned 11. She clearly inspired awe in her younger sisters.

In 1824, Maria (age ten) and another sister Elizabeth (nine) were sent to Cowan Bridge school; Charlotte and Emily soon followed. In

era, however, she was placed on a pedestal of virtue. This revised view proved equally confining, for it banned women from the public sphere, that is, from the masculine realm of intellect and commerce. Those of the female sex, and in particular the women of the middle class, were sentenced to the domestic sphere where "the fair sex" was expected to cultivate "feminine" skills and moral virtues only. All of the Brontë sisters resigned themselves to this social precept, but each struggled with its limits, using her imagination in an attempt to transcend its boundaries. While Anne ultimately embraced a staunchly religious view in her life and work, and Emily withdrew into a private imaginative world, Charlotte's creative and passionate nature remained locked in perpetual combat with the moral strictures that governed the famous Victorian "cult of womanhood."

Charlotte, Emily, and Anne were three of six children born to the Reverend Patrick Brontë and **Maria Branwell Brontë** in the short space of six years. Patrick Brontë was a Methodist minister who had transcended his Northern Irish peasant origins. The eldest of ten children, he made his way to Cambridge at the age of 25 after stints as a blacksmith's assistant and as a this repressive and unhealthy institution (the model for Lowood and several major characters in *Jane Eyre*), both Maria and Elizabeth contracted tuberculosis, dying within a two-month period in the summer of 1825. Their loss had lasting effects on the remaining four children, who retreated more deeply into a secret society of their own, headed now by Charlotte.

The family's short tragic history, combined with their isolation from the largely illiterate peasant populace of Hawood, intensified their sense of being "stranger[s] in a strange land," as their father claimed in a letter to a friend. Inspired by their devoted readings of *Blackwood's Magazine* and other political journals, as well as their immersion in Romantic poetry and the apocalyptic paintings of John Martin, the children shaped their own world of the imagination, Glass Town.

In 1826, Patrick Brontë brought his nine-year-old son Branwell twelve wooden soldiers. These were snatched up by his daughters as well and became characters in a separate reality that endured uninterrupted for five years. The group created an entire history, geography, and life for the twelve soldiers and their descendants in the African colony of Glass Town. Charlotte and Branwell wrote daily about their characters' thoughts and actions, producing tiny magazines meant to have been written by the toy soldiers themselves. Their work reflected a keen awareness of contemporary politics and significant historical figures. By the time she was 14, Charlotte had produced 22 volumes. By imitating *Blackwood's Magazine*, Romantic poetry and novels, she developed what Fraser described as an "extraordinary proficiency in the written word." While Emily and Anne participated in this imaginative universe, they appear to have left all writing of its sagas to their elder siblings, preferring to tramp for hours on the moors behind the parsonage. The youngest girls would later hone their own literary skills in creating yet another world: Gondal.

In 1831 at the age of 15, Charlotte began a year of study at Roe Head, which provided governess training for young women who would eventually need to support themselves. The school was managed by the unmarried Wooler sisters, one of whom was the prototype for the kind and pious Miss Temple of *Jane Eyre*. While she found herself placed in a lower grade than her peers—a result of a lack of formal schooling only—Charlotte went on to distinguish herself by her sophisticated grasp of literature and politics. According to Fraser, Charlotte closely re-

Emily Brontë

sembled the character of her creation Jane Eyre—ever-observant, quiet, withdrawn, small and frail. In contemporary language, one might characterize Charlotte as a depressive with anorexic tendencies, although her poor eating habits may have resulted largely from a strict religious upbringing that stressed the mortification of the flesh. Her reclusive nature, moreover, must be viewed in light of the Brontës' secluded environment, coupled with the unusually harsh and bleak circumstances of their life.

You are the three suns.
—Ellen Nussey to the Brontë sisters

Charlotte rose to the occasion at Roe Head, as she often did throughout her life, and performed admirably despite the dis-ease she felt away from her sisters and home. Notably, however, Charlotte formed two close, lifelong friendships with girls as different from each other as they were from their unique friend. **Mary Taylor**, outgoing, independent and an early feminist, sustained a correspondence with Charlotte even after her unconventional move to New Zealand. A more extensive letter-writing rela-

See sidebar on the following page

Taylor, Mary (1817–1893)

English traveler and friend of Charlotte Brontë. Born in York-shire in 1817; died in 1893.

A rebel from childhood, Mary Taylor's "outspoken, independent spirit set her against her Yorkshire kinfolk," writes **Susan Willens**. Taylor journeyed to New Zealand to seek her fortune and temporarily found it as a shopkeeper. Eventually, she would travel, lecture, and write on behalf of women.

Mary Taylor vehemently protested a society that kept middle-class women from earning a living because it was not "nice," imprisoning them as household drudges who played the piano, attended church, and waited for their husbands to make the decisions. Her anger informs her novel *Miss Miles: A Tale of Yorkshire Life Sixty Years Ago*. Willens notes that instead of girl-meets-boy, the novel is more about girl-seeks-profession. It is about four women, each helping the others to achieve their dreams. Notes Willens: "Mary Taylor's one novel makes eye-opening and affecting reading a century after she finished it."

SOURCES:

Willens, Susan P. "The Hope Due to Endeavor," in *Belles Lettres*. Summer 1992, p. 35.

tionship—in addition to periodic visits due to the proximity of their homes—existed between Charlotte and Ellen Nussey, the quintessentially proper Victorian woman. (Shortly after their marriage, Arthur Nichols compelled Charlotte to extract Ellen's promise to destroy all of Charlotte's letters. Fortunately for history, Ellen balked at the coerced promise.) Mary Taylor and Ellen Nussey represent the polar opposites of Charlotte's character: in her fiction and early life, Charlotte was more like Mary Taylor, passionate and strong-willed; with time, she grew to be as pious and conventional as Ellen. Charlotte spent most of her life making sacrifices and caring for her family.

By 1832, she had completed her schooling and returned to her beloved siblings, eager to rejoin their shared imaginative world, but resigned to the necessity of making a living with limited prospects. For three years, Charlotte was content to write romances featuring Byronic heroes with her brother, in addition to producing her own plays and novelettes. Branwell supplied much of the narrative in their shared work, according to Fraser, while Charlotte "elaborated on the characters and relations between them." Perhaps the psychological novelist used her extensive juvenilia as a whetstone to sharpen the mature character studies of later years.

As the only son, Branwell was held in high regard by his sisters and his father. By age 11, he was convinced—in Romantic fashion—that he was destined to be a great poet. But he turned his attention to painting after viewing exhibits of works by the portrait painter William Robinson and the sculptor J.B. Leyland in 1834. His Romanticism led him to choose an artistic career but also to turn to drink and, eventually, opium. His self-indulgence later caused his sisters irreparable harm.

To assist in sending him to the Royal Academy, Charlotte decided to become a governess, one of the few occupations available to women of the time. In 1835, she returned to Roe Head as a teacher with Emily in tow as a student, a partial payment for her teaching services. But within three months, Emily, homesick for her cherished Gondal and the Yorkshire moors, had returned home and exchanged places with Anne. No more content than Emily but older and characteristically stoical, Charlotte suffered the monotony of life at Roe Head. She took no delight in her pupils and longed for the romantic possibilities associated with "Angria," the world that had evolved from "Glass Town." A three-year stint at Roe Head was followed by a period of physical and mental recovery at Haworth before Charlotte assumed the duties of a nursery governess in 1839. Similarly dissatisfied with this experience, Charlotte was back in Haworth within the year.

By the age of 23, Charlotte had already rejected two marriage proposals, one of which came from friend Ellen Nussey's brother. Charlotte apparently preferred the romantic heroes of her imagination to droll flesh and blood Victorian men. She remained occupied with her writing and boldly sought a professional opinion of her poetry, first from the well-known poet Robert Southey, and later, from Hartley Coleridge, son of Samuel Taylor Coleridge and **Sara Fricker Coleridge**. Southey, apparently shocked by the anti-Victorian notion of a professional "woman" writer, almost an "un-woman," took the party line and essentially told her to leave writing to the men. She might write for herself, he advised, but her primary occupation should be domestic pursuits. Coleridge, though more encouraging, was of little help as he referred her to a "ladies" magazine.

Anne was the only Brontë sister to have been content as a governess. After a brief, unhappy stay with the Ingham family, which later provided the material for her novel, *Agnes Grey*, she moved, in 1835, to Thorp Green where she served for four years as governess to the Robinson family. Branwell joined her there as a tutor after a series of failures: unsuccessful as a portrait painter, he had taken work as a clerk in a railway until his debauched existence prevented him from doing his job.

Unlike Anne, Charlotte was convinced of her unsuitability for working and living in the homes of others by another short-term position as governess. With the financial assistance of their Aunt Elizabeth Branwell, the Brontë sisters fixed on the idea of developing their own school, for which purpose Charlotte and Emily enrolled at the Pensionnat de Demoiselles, run by the Heger family in Brussels. This experience had a profound impact on Charlotte's life, since here she met the exacting but charismatic Monsieur Heger, for whom she developed an unrequited passion. Both the characters of Mr. Rochester of *Jane Eyre* and M. Paul Emmanuel of *Villette* are thought to have been based on her hopelessly romantic attachment to M. Heger.

During their stay, both Charlotte and Emily further developed their literary skills. Heger introduced Charlotte to the French Romantics and, thus, to the possibilities of prose, while the reclusive and taciturn Emily secretly composed poems based on the Gondal world in what few moments of solitude she could find. In her studies, Emily surpassed Charlotte, according to Heger. He told *Elizabeth Gaskell (1810–1865):

> Emily had a head for logic, and a capability of argument, unusual in a man, and rare indeed in a woman. . . . She should have been a man—a great navigator. Her powerful reason would have deduced new spheres of discovery from the knowledge of the old; and her strong imperious will would never have been daunted by opposition or difficulty; never to have given way but with life.

Their Aunt Elizabeth Branwell's death called them back after only a year, and gave Emily an excuse not to return, preferring, instead, to tend to house and father. Although torn by duty and her family's needs, Charlotte was fixed on returning to Brussels and the company of Heger. While he obviously admired Charlotte's intellectual prowess and likely flirted with her infatuation, Heger was a Catholic and a family man who withdrew his interest in Charlotte as she grew more obsessed with him. Along with being separated from Emily and the familiar culture of Haworth and England, Charlotte felt increasingly ostracized from the Heger family. But the misery she experienced during the remainder of her time in Brussels did not abate when she returned home. Resigned to being a teacher, having earned

a diploma from the Athenée Royale, Charlotte felt an equal obligation to care for her ailing father and rapidly declining brother Branwell. Moreover, her inclination was to live by her pen, and the probability of being a teacher was almost an anathema to her. But the most profound source of her grief during the post-Brussels period was Heger's stubborn rebuff of her consistent pleas for his attention. While Charlotte was too much a product of Victorian values to identify her feelings for him as sexual and potentially adulterous, her letters offer ample evidence of the true nature of her passion for a married man. Fraser notes that Charlotte's poetry of 1845 onward reflects her concern with illicit love and betrayal. Typically, therefore, the feelings and thoughts that could not be fulfilled in life found expression in her art.

Emily occupied herself by caring for their father, who was gradually losing his sight. She read the papers to him, carried the burden of the housework, and continued, in secret, to write about Gondal. Charlotte and Emily had revived the idea of opening a school, but no students materialized.

In 1845, both Anne and Branwell returned from Thorp Green. Anne's reasons for leaving might have involved her brother, whose unseemly behavior led to his dismissal. He would later claim that Mrs. Robinson had fallen in love with him and had been prepared to leave her husband. He had, at the very least, attempted to seduce her.

Together again at Haworth, the three sisters were writing in earnest. Each began a novel: Charlotte, *The Professor*; Anne, *Agnes Grey*; and Emily, *Wuthering Heights*. Intensely private, Emily hid her work from her sisters. In October 1846, however, she accidently left her poetry notebook on her desk. Charlotte discovered it and saw immediately that the poems should be published. After Emily's death, she wrote in her "Biographical Notice of Ellis and Acton Bell" that "something more than surprise seized me,— a deep conviction that these were not common effusions, nor at all like the poetry women generally write. I thought them condensed and terse, vigorous and genuine. To my ear, they had also a peculiar music—wild, melancholy, and elevating." Charlotte's intrusion into her private world incensed Emily, and it took days for Charlotte and Anne to persuade her that they should publish their poetry together. Adopting the pseudonyms Currer, Ellis, and Acton Bell, the Brontë sisters found a publisher, after they agreed to bear the costs of publication. *Poems by Currer,*

Ellis and Acton Bell appeared in May 1846. Although their volume received favorable reviews, they sold only two copies.

Encouraged by the reviews, the Brontës decided to try to publish their novels with the same firm. All three were rejected. Undaunted, Charlotte continued to search for a publisher and started work on *Jane Eyre.* Anne had begun *The Tenant of Wildfell Hall,* a cautionary tale based on Branwell's intemperate existence.

The three sisters kept their works secret from both their brother and their father. Patrick Brontë had been weakened by cataract surgery, while Branwell continued to be, as Charlotte disclosed to her friend Ellen, "one monstrous species of annoyance." He was threatened with imprisonment for unpaid debts and, one night, set his bed on fire. Emily saved him.

In July 1847, Newby, a small publishing company, accepted *Wuthering Heights* and *Agnes Grey,* but not *The Professor.* As before, however, Emily and Anne had to bear the pub-

lishing costs. Charlotte fared better than her sisters. She sent *The Professor* to the obscure Smith, Elder and Company. William Smith Williams rejected it but wrote so encouragingly that Charlotte sent him *Jane Eyre,* which he published in October 1847, before Emily and Anne's novels had appeared. *Jane Eyre* met with instantaneous success. At age 31, Charlotte was transformed into a *cause celèbre,* even though her identity remained ambiguous and her unconventional novel and heroine had inspired considerable controversy.

Capitalizing on the success of *Jane Eyre,* Newby finally published *Agnes Grey* and *Wuthering Heights* in December 1847. Anne's novel received little attention, but Emily's received strong, condemnatory reviews. While recognizing the power of *Wuthering Heights,* critics objected to its strange wildness. Charlotte and Anne appeared to share their view, believing that Emily had become what **Muriel Spark* and Derek Stanford have termed "death-enamoured."

From the movie Jane Eyre, *starring Orson Welles, Margaret O'Brien, and Joan Fontaine.*

Anne's second novel appeared in July 1848. The unscrupulous Newby presented *The Tenant of Wildfell Hall* as the work of Currer, not Acton, Bell, fueling rumors that the Bells were interchangeable. Determined to disabuse their publishers of this error, Charlotte and Anne set out for London to reveal their true identities. When Emily learned, on their return, that they had revealed hers as well, she again caused an angry scene and forced Charlotte to retract her claim that the Bells were three sisters. As a result, the true author of *Wuthering Heights* was not revealed until after Emily's death.

On September 24, 1848, Branwell died suddenly of consumption. His addiction to alcohol and opium had masked the signs of this highly contagious disease. Emily, who had been closest to Branwell, contracted the disease immediately after his funeral but refused to accept treatment. Instead, she continued to perform her household routines, though visibly weakened and frail. On December 19, hours after she quietly admitted she would see a doctor if her sisters called one, she died on the dining-room sofa. Emily's body had been so wasted by the disease that her coffin was only 16 inches wide.

By the time of Emily's death, Anne was also ill. Unlike her sister, she submitted with religious calm to all medical treatments imposed by her doctors. In May, Charlotte decided to fulfill Anne's wish of seeing the sea. Mistakenly believing that the sea air would alleviate rather than augment Anne's suffering, Charlotte and Ellen took her to Scarborough. Anne died on May 28, 1849, within six weeks of Emily's death.

By 1849, only Charlotte and her aging father survived. Throughout her life, Charlotte remained a steadfast member of the English Church. Added to its prudish strictures was her father's Evangelical influence, which together made an already sensitive nature more impressionable, even morbid. Her novels, however, revealed a different spirit. In *Jane Eyre*, she railed against the fanaticism—the hell, fire and brimstone—of religion, while in *Shirley* and *The Professor*, she critiqued social hypocrisy and the limitations faced by women and the working class. In a letter to her publisher William Smith Williams in September 1848 resisting changes to her manuscript, she expressed the philosophy that guided her artistic vision: "Truth is better than Art. . . . Ignorant as I am, I dare to hold and maintain that doctrine." And so she took an emphatic and independent stand in her work, one she dared not take in her personal life.

From the movie Wuthering Heights, *starring* Laurence Olivier *and* Merle Oberon.

Between 1849 and her marriage to Arthur Nichols in 1854, Charlotte made acquaintances with the likes of novelist William Makepeace Thackeray, publisher G.B. Lewes, and essayist Thomas Carlyle. Her novels won respect, and people were curious to meet the infamous Currer Bell. Charlotte, however, felt extremely uncomfortable in public, almost to the point of physical illness. Hypersensitive and given to migraines and psychosomatic disorders, she confined herself to nurturing comfortable relationships with a few admirers, including Elizabeth Gaskell, her future biographer, and *Harriet Martineau, writer and social reformer. But the most meaningful relationship for Charlotte during this period was the one she developed with George Smith of the publishing house Smith, Williams. Both younger and more attractive than she, Smith became infatuated with Charlotte Brontë, the writer. He arranged visits with Charlotte at his home and on occasional trips elsewhere that were chaperoned by his doting mother. Most likely inadvertently, Smith encouraged romantic expectations in the ever-impressionable and solitary Charlotte Brontë.

Largely at his prodding, she reluctantly entered London artistic society from time to time but persisted in shunning any attention owing to her novels. She found more comfort in the company of her friend, Ellen Nussey, who was also still unmarried, and of kindly Mrs. Gaskell and her family. But Charlotte spent the preponderance of her time in Haworth with her father, where she wrote *Villette,* having published the less well-received *Shirley* in 1949. Ever mindful of her sisters, whose work she greatly admired, she also published new editions of *Wuthering Heights, Agnes Grey,* and *The Poems of Currer, Ellis and Acton Bell* in 1850. Charlotte's own literary acclaim, along with a new introduction she authored, lent credibility to the editions and resulted in renewed interest in the Brontës' work. Suspicion persisted, however, that Charlotte or Currer had also authored the work of the other "Bells," a misconception that Charlotte repeatedly discouraged.

In some ways, Charlotte never fully recovered from her sisters' deaths, as their mutual support and shared literary ambitions had blunted the cold edge of her lonely and introspective nature. While an occasional kind gesture from George Smith lifted her out of her morbid tendencies, she ultimately resigned herself to the fact of the one-sided attachment. Older and more self-possessed, Charlotte avoided the obsequiousness and bitterness associated with her earlier rejection by Heger. While she remained friends with the dashing Smith, she turned to the more realistic offer of marriage from her father's curate, Arthur Nichols. A 37-year-old woman who had earned a considerable sum by her pen, she, nevertheless, demurred when her father irately commanded Nichols to withdraw his proposal and himself from his duties at the parsonage. Patrick Brontë eventually relented, however, and with his blessing Charlotte married Nichols on June 29, 1854.

Within nine months, pregnancy complications and a long-term consumptive condition resulted in Charlotte's death on March 31, 1855, at age 38. She spent her last painful months as she had spent most of her life—at the parsonage in Haworth. Her writing practically ceased altogether in the months following her marriage, and even her longstanding correspondence with Ellen Nussey had diminished to near extinction. The fiercely passionate and independent heroine of Charlotte Brontë's autobiographical novels finally gave way to the conventionally submissive married woman. But the fact remains that Charlotte Brontë had come into the world poor, plain, and obscure, and left it a literary giant.

While Charlotte found early accolades and popularity with *Jane Eyre,* her star has waxed and waned according to the critical mode and views of the day. Emily's work was criticized and overlooked at first, primarily as a result of moral objections. Over time, however, the artistry of her poetry and singular novel *Wuthering Heights* earned her substantial critical respect. In fact, critic **Penny Boumelha** quotes F.R. Leavis as having proclaimed "that 'there is only one Bronte'—and that one is Emily." Anne, often overshadowed by the more readily acknowledged genius of her sisters, made her own distinctive mark in her religious poetry and moralistic novels. French biographer Ernest Dimnet characterized it this way: Anne "had what is called a mystical soul, and wrote poems full of deep religious sentiment."

The women's movement of the 1960s and 1970s, which revived both interest in and the work of women writers, has also served the Brontës well. Feminist criticism has provided new territory in which to explore each of the sister's unique artistry. While Charlotte lived long enough to write four full-length novels, in addition to her poetry and extensive juvenilia, Emily and Anne, unfortunately, died young, denied the encouragement and time necessary to fulfill their ample artistic potential.

SOURCES:
Benvenuto, Richard. *Emily Brontë.* Boston, MA: Twayne, 1982.
Blom, Margaret Howard. *Charlotte Brontë.* Boston, MA: Twayne, 1977.
Boumelha, Penny. *Charlotte Brontë.* Bloomington: Indiana University Press, 1990.
Chitham, Edward. *A Life of Emily Brontë.* Oxford: Basil Blackwell, 1987.
Dimnet, Ernest. *The Brontë Sisters.* Trans. by Louise Morgan Sill. NY: Harcourt, Brace, 1928.
Fraser, Rebecca. *The Brontës: Charlotte Brontë and Her Family.* NY: Fawcett Columbine, 1988.
Gaskell, Elizabeth. *The Life of Charlotte Brontë.* London: Penguin, 1975.
Gérin, Winifred. *Emily Brontë.* NY: Oxford University Press, 1971.
Spark, Muriel, and Derek Stanford. *Emily Brontë: Her Life and Work.* NY: Coward-McCann, 1966.
Tillotson, Kathleen. *Novels of the 1840s.* London: Oxford University Press, 1954.

SUGGESTED READING:
Barker, Janet. *The Brontës.* St. Martin's, 1995.

RELATED MEDIA:
There were three silent movies of *Jane Eyre:* starring Irving Cummings and **Ethel Grand,** 1913; starring Alan Hale and **Louise Vale,** 1915; starring **Mabel Ballin** and Norman Trevor, 1921.

Jane Eyre, starring **Virginia Bruce* and Colin Clive, screenplay by **Adele Comandini**, directed by Christy Cabanne, 1934.

Jane Eyre, starring Orson Welles and **Joan Fontaine*, produced by 20th Century-Fox, directed by Robert Stevenson, screenplay co-authored by Aldous Huxley, 1944.

Jane Eyre, starring Patrick Macnee and **Joan Elan**, 1957 (made for television).

Jane Eyre, starring George C. Scott and **Susannah York**, produced by Omnibus-Saggittarius, directed by Delbert Mann, 1971 (made for British television).

Jane Eyre, starring **Samantha Morton** and Ciaran Hinds, A&E cable television, 1997.

Wuthering Heights, starring **Merle Oberon*, Laurence Olivier and David Niven, produced by Samuel Goldwyn, directed by William Wyler, set design by **Julia Heron**, 1939. (Oscar nominations for Best Picture, Best Screenplay and Best Director.)

Wuthering Heights (*Abismos de Pasion*), starring **Irasema Dilian**, Jorge Mistral, **Lilia Prado**, directed by Louis Buñuel, 1954.

Wuthering Heights, starring **Anna Calder-Marshall**, Timothy Dalton, and Harry Andrews, produced by AIP, directed by Robert Fuest, 1970.

Kate Waites Lamm, Associate Professor, and **Suzanne Ferriss**, Assistant Professor, in the Liberal Arts department of Nova University, Fort Lauderdale, Florida

Brooke, Charlotte (1740–1793)

Irish author and translator of poetry from ancient Irish to English. Born Charlotte Brooke in Rantavan, County Cavan, Ireland, in 1740; died in Kildare, Ireland, in 1793; daughter of Lettice (Digby) Brooke and Henry Brooke (dramatist); educated at home; never married; no children.

Selected works: Reliques of Irish Poetry . . . Translated into English Verse *(1788);* Emma, or the Foundling in the Wood *(1803).*

Charlotte Brooke was raised in Kildare, Ireland, one of **Lettice Brooke** and dramatist Henry Brooke's 21 children. Educated by her father, Charlotte learned Gaelic in addition to traditional lessons. As an adult, she lived at home, sowed a small garden, and drew. Her father introduced her in literary circles, especially during the decade following her mother's death in 1772. Charlotte became her father's primary companion. After Henry died in 1783, his peers, noting Charlotte's talent for writing and translation, encouraged her to publish. She translated a collection of poetry from the ancient Irish, which was published in 1788 to good reviews, and contributed anonymously to other anthologies. Charlotte Brooke died ten years after her father, and her only novel, *Emma, or the Foundling in the Wood*, was released posthumously in 1803.

Crista Martin, Boston, Massachusetts

Brooke, Frances (1724–1789)

English novelist and dramatist. Name variations: Mary Singleton, Spinster. Born Frances Moore in Claypole, Lincolnshire, England, on January 24, 1724; died in Sleaford, Lincolnshire, England, on January 23, 1789; daughter of Mary (Knowles) Moore and William Moore (Anglican minister); grew up in Lincolnshire and Peterborough; educated at home; married Reverend John Brooke, D.D., rector of Colney, Norfolk, in 1756; children: one son, John Moore (b. June 10, 1757).

Selected works: Letters from Juliet, Lady Catesby *(translated from Marie-Jeanne Riccoboni's French novel, 1760);* History of Lady Julia Mandeville *(1763);* The History of Emily Montague *(1769);* The Excursion *(1777).*

An English novelist, poet, and dramatist, Frances Moore was born in Claypole, Lincolnshire, England, on January 24, 1724, the daughter of **Mary Knowles Moore** and Reverend William Moore. When William Moore died three years later, in 1727, Mary Moore moved to her mother's home in Peterborough with her three young daughters. There, Frances Moore and her sister **Sarah** lived and were educated until their mother's death ten years later. (The third sister died in childhood.)

Then a maternal aunt raised the sisters until they turned 21 and inherited £1,000. Frances used her bequest to live independently in London and launch the periodical, *The Old Maid*, writing under the name Mary Singleton, Spinster. She produced 37 issues before ceasing publication in July of 1756, following her marriage to Anglican minister John Brooke who was 15 years her senior. Frances was his second wife.

Enlisting in the army in March of 1757, John Brooke shipped out to Canada where he served as chaplain at the garrison at Quebec; he was part of the British forces fighting the Seven Years' War with France, which included the territorial struggle for Canada. Frances, three months pregnant, went to live with her sister Sarah. Under financial strain because of her husband's absence, Brooke undertook translations, most notably **Marie-Jeanne Ricoboni*'s French epistolary novel, which in English became *Letters from Juliet, Lady Catesby* (1760). She also wrote the successful and sentimental *History of Lady Julia Mandeville* (1763), which had ten subsequent editions.

In 1763, with the war over, Brooke set sail for Canada to join her husband after a six-and-a-half-year separation. She was accompanied by her sister and her son John Moore, born on June 10, 1757, who had yet to meet his father. They arrived on October 4, 1763. John Brooke was the only Protestant minister in Quebec and hoped to lead efforts to convert the largely Roman-Catholic, French-speaking population to the Church of England. Frances advanced John's position within the established colonial government as well as back in England on a 1764 visit. Ultimately John was denied the responsibility of leading the reformation.

In 1767, Frances began *The History of Emily Montague,* a four-volume novel depicting life in Canada, which was well-received and often used as a reference manual by those moving to Canada. The first book to fictionally describe the new North American colony, *Emily Montague* earned Brooke the distinction of having authored the first Canadian novel.

Brooke's greatest love, however, was the theater. She and her friend, actress *Mary Ann Yates, managed the Haymarket Opera House from 1773 to 1778, after Yates' husband and Brooke's brother-in-law bought the property. Brooke's own stage plays—*The Siege of Sinope* (with Yates in the lead) and musicals *Rosina* and *Marian*—were produced in the 1780s and remained popular for many years.

John Brooke, Jr., also became a minister. On a visit to her son's Lincolnshire parish in late 1788, Frances Brooke suddenly became ill and died there on January 23, 1789, two days after the death of her husband in Norfolk and one day shy of her 65th birthday.

SUGGESTED READING:
McMullen, Lorraine. *Frances Brooke and Her Work.* Ontario, Canada: ECW Press, 1983.

Crista Martin,
Boston, Massachusetts

Brooks, Angie (1928—)

Liberian diplomat and lawyer who was president of the 24th session of the United Nations General Assembly. Name variations: Brooks is an anglicized simplification of her father's tribal (Grebo) name. Born Angie Elizabeth Brooks in Virginia, Montserrado County, Liberia, on August 24, 1928; one of nine children of a back-country minister of the African Methodist Episcopal Zion Church; attended Shaw University, Raleigh, North Carolina, B.A. in social science, 1949; University of Wisconsin, Madison, Wisconsin, LL.B and M.Sc. in social science and international relations, 1952; University College law school of London University, 1952–1953; married at 14 (divorced): married Isaac Randolph in Monrovia, Liberia, on April 27, 1970; children: (first marriage) two sons, Wynston and Richard.

In 1969, Angie Brooks, dressed in blue and white robes and a silken turban, took her place at the podium as president of the 24th session of the United Nations General Assembly. The first African woman to serve as assembly president, Brooks, the Liberian delegate for 15 years, was elected overwhelmingly to the post. She did not mince words in her acceptance speech, telling the delegates bluntly that they were a less than dynamic force in the world. Brooks challenged them to "spend less time congratulating each other on so-called diplomatic 'victories' and try more to get their home governments to behave responsibly in the world community."

Angie Brooks was raised in a foster home in Monrovia, the capital of Liberia, because her parents were unable to support all nine of their children. Driven to excel despite limited educational opportunities, she was a self-taught typist at age 11 and earned money copying legal documents. Later, she typed for the Treasury Department and worked as a stenotypist for the Justice Department, while setting her sights on the study of law. After high school, she became a law apprentice under Clarence L. Simpson, who later became foreign minister for Liberia. Only with the help of the pastor of her church and her persistent appeals to the president of her country, William V.S. Tubman, was Brooks finally able to get the money to enroll at Shaw University in Raleigh, North Carolina. She worked a variety of jobs, from scrubbing floors to washing dishes, and endured her first experiences with discrimination. After graduating in 1949, she went to study law at the University of Wisconsin and later did graduate work in international law at London University.

In 1953, Brooks returned to Liberia and was admitted as a counselor-at-law to the Supreme Court. Hoping to inspire women to enter the field of law, she chose to work in the Justice Department and helped establish a department of law at Liberia University, where she taught from 1954 to 1958. Leaving her post of assistant attorney general in 1958, she was appointed assistant secretary of state by President Tubman. Later that year, the president and secretary of state were out of the country at the same time, and Brooks ran the government for ten days.

Brooks soon turned her attention to Liberia's relations with the world. On a visit to the United States in 1954, she began her long association with the United Nations by filling a vacancy on the Liberian delegation at the last minute. The unexpected assignment led to a continuing role as a delegate as well as to a number of important positions within the United Nations. In addition to her leadership in various committees, she was the first woman and the first African to serve as president of the Trusteeship Council, the UN's watchdog over its trust territories. When the UN presidency, which is shifted to a different geographical area each year, fell to an African delegate, Brooks was not shy about campaigning vigorously for the post. Needing the backing of all 40 member states from her continent, she visited some 23 countries in order to win. Only two other Africans had ever served as president, and only one woman had ever held the position, Madame *Vijaya Lakshmi Pandit of India in 1953.

During the 13-week assembly session, Brooks' leadership style combined charm with shrewd diplomacy: "First you must be soft and let it seem they are having their own way. Then you come down hard on them." Using this for-

Angie
Brooks

mula, she attempted to eliminate idle speechifying and long debates; during one committee meeting, she politely cut off the Soviet Ambassador mid-debate and ordered a vote. Although known to be brash at times, Brooks is also noted for her humility. When she heard she was to be honored by Alpha Kappa Alpha, the black sorority she joined at Shaw University, she asked, "But who else are you honoring?"

In addition to raising her own two sons by a marriage entered into when she was only 14, Brooks raised some 47 foster Liberian boys and girls and put them through school. She has championed the advancement of women, particularly Africans, through the United Nations and the International Federation of Women Lawyers. A Baptist, she worked with various projects of the Lott Carey Baptist Foreign Mission, including supervising a high school in Liberia under their sponsorship.

Aware of the UN's imperfections, Brooks stressed that the organization remains the best means of international cooperation we have: "[W]e have to nurse it and cherish it and cultivate it, or else we shall one day perish and not even the moon or the knowledge of space will save us."

SOURCES:
Crane, Louise. *Ms. Africa: Profiles of Modern African Women.* Philadelphia, PA: Lippincott, 1973.
Moritz, Charles, ed. *Current Biography 1970.* NY: H.W. Wilson, 1971.

Barbara Morgan,
Melrose, Massachusetts

Brooks, Charlotte (1918—)

American photographer, specializing in documentation and photojournalism. Born in New York, New York, in 1918; Brooklyn College, New York, B.A., 1940; graduate work in psychology, University of Minnesota, Minneapolis-Saint Paul, Minnesota, 1941.

Charlotte Brooks took a circuitous route to photography. In 1942, she was a social worker in a New York settlement house when she became interested in modern dance. Deciding to photograph instead of perform, Brooks assisted photographer Gjon Mili for a year before obtaining an apprenticeship with dance photographer *Barbara Morgan around 1944. A stint as staff photographer for a chain of newspapers, and a 1,000-picture project for Standard Oil, followed. In 1951, Brooks became the first woman staff photographer for *Look* magazine, a position she held until the magazine folded in 1971. During her later career, she taught and freelanced, traveling to the Soviet Union in

1977. At the International Center of Photography in New York, Brooks participated in the group exhibition *Roy Stryker: U.S.A.* (1943–1950), which later toured. She also had a 1994 solo exhibition at New Britain Museum of American Art, New Britain, Connecticut, entitled *A Poem of Portraits.*

Brooks, Geraldine (1925–1977)

American actress. Born Geraldine Stroock in New York City on October 29, 1925; died of cancer, age 52, in Riverhead, New York, on June 19, 1977; daughter of a costume manufacturer and designer; attended American Academy of Dramatic Arts; married second husband, novelist-screenwriter Budd Schulberg, 1964.

Selected films: Possessed *(1947);* Cry Wolf *(1947);* The Younger Brothers *(1949);* The Reckless Moment *(1949);* Challenge for Lassie *(1950);* Volcano *(1950);* The Green Glove *(1952);* Street of Sinners *(1956);* Johnny Tiger *(1966).*

When Geraldine Brooks arrived at Warner Bros. in 1947, she had already appeared in a stage musical, toured in Shakespeare with the Theater Guild, and studied at the American Academy of Dramatic Arts. After playing ingénue roles in a number of films, she grew disillusioned with the quality of most of her pictures and signed on with Italian director William Dieterle to play *Anna Magnani's younger sister in *Volcano.* Although the movie did not do well, Brooks stayed in Europe to make a few more films before returning to the United States, where she concentrated mostly on stage and television work. In later years, she became an accomplished nature photographer and, in 1975, published a book of bird photographs called *Swan Watch,* with accompanying essays written by her second husband Budd Schulberg.

Brooks, Gwendolyn (1917—)

African-American Pulitzer Prize-winning poet, novelist, and teacher. Born Gwendolyn Brooks on June 7, 1917, in Topeka, Kansas; daughter of David Anderson Brooks (a mechanic and janitor) and Keziah Corine (Wims) Brooks (a teacher and homemaker); graduated from Wilson Junior College, 1936; married Henry Blakely, 1938; children: Henry Jr. (b. October 10, 1940), Nora (b. September 8, 1951).

Awarded numerous honorary degrees; published A Street in Bronzeville *(1945); won Pulitzer Prize for* Annie Allen *(1950); published* In the Mecca *(1968); selected poet laureate of Illinois (1968); appointed po-*

etry consultant to the Library of Congress (1985); received the National Medal of Arts (1995).

Gwendolyn Brooks' literary career has spanned more than 50 years and has included poetry, a novel, criticism, verse and fiction for children, and an autobiography. She has been a teacher of writing and a writer of criticism. Her work has been examined by black and white, male and female commentators. Her writing has been analyzed as "too white" or "too black," as strongly feminist or too conventional in its portrayal of women. She has been the recipient of

more public honors than any other African-American poet, yet not until late in her career was her work widely included in American literature courses. In many ways, her writing, and the public reactions to it, have paralleled developments related to race and gender in the United States during the last half of the 20th century.

Brooks was born in Topeka, Kansas, which was the home of both her parents. David Anderson Brooks, her father, had aspired to study medicine but financial necessity forced him to leave Fisk University after only one year. Her mother

Gwendolyn
Brooks

Keziah Wims Brooks graduated from Topeka High School, attended Emporia State Normal School, and worked in her home town as a fifth-grade teacher. One month after Gwendolyn's birth, her mother took her to join her father who was working in Chicago. Brooks has lived there ever since, with remarkable continuity in her place of residence. She and her brother Raymond, who was born in 1918, grew up in a house on the South Side where she remained until she married in 1940. Then Gwendolyn and her husband Henry Blakely lived for four decades in a house they bought early in their marriage.

She fights with semi-folded arms, . . .

And altogether she does Rather Well.

—Gwendolyn Brooks, from "the weaponed woman"

Like many writers, Brooks was raised in a home that valued books and education. She recounts that she always received books as Christmas gifts, and that she spent long and happy hours reading behind the tree with her book lit by the Christmas lights. Singing and storytelling also probably influenced her poetic development. In her autobiography, Brooks remembers her father as a strong and gentle man. From him, she heard family stories about her ancestors' experiences during and after slavery. Her mother encouraged her interest in writing, promising that young Gwendolyn would grow up to be "the lady Paul Laurence Dunbar." As one who organized children's programs at the church, Keziah Brooks persuaded her daughter to write plays for the other children to perform.

Besides her mother, other female relatives were important role models in Brooks' young life. Her Aunt Eppie married well and lived on a farm in Kalamazoo, Michigan. Aunt Gertrude lived in a "good" neighborhood, was fun loving, and taught her niece to dance the Charleston. Another aunt, Ella, was staunch, despite poverty, while Beulah was the family "queen." A single woman with a career, Beulah had graduated from the University of Chicago, was the chair of her department in a high school, and made stylish clothes for herself and for Gwendolyn.

If her family life was happy and secure, Brooks' social life was unsatisfying. During the 1920s and 1930s, when she was growing up, skin color created a definite hierarchy of beauty among black women, with fair skin and straight hair considered the prettiest. Because of her dark skin and what was considered "bad hair," Brooks felt her peers found her unattractive. In addition, she had some difficulty in finding a satisfactory high school. She first attended Hyde Park, a predominantly white school where she felt ignored. Her experiences there inspired a poem of protest she submitted to the black newspaper, the *Chicago Defender*. At all-black Wendell Phillips High School, Brooks was unpopular for her shyness. She then transferred to integrated Englewood High School. There, things seemed to improve, especially as she received more encouragement for her writing.

During her adolescence, Brooks wrote poems and stories at a prodigious rate. At the age of 13, she published a poem called "Eventide" in *American Childhood* magazine. While in high school, she contributed to a weekly poetry column in the *Chicago Defender*, where she ultimately published nearly 80 poems. At the same time, she had the opportunity to meet two major figures in black literature—James Weldon Johnson and Langston Hughes. Johnson, a poet of the Harlem Renaissance, advised Brooks to become familiar with the writings of modernist poets T.S. Eliot, Ezra Pound, and e.e. cummings. Hughes read and commented on her poetry, as he did with other young poets. He would remain a mentor and promoter of Brooks' work, later dedicating a book of short stories to her.

In 1934, Brooks graduated from Englewood High School and enrolled in Wilson Junior College. There she became active in the National Association for the Advancement of Colored People (NAACP). At one of their meetings, she encountered Henry Blakely, another aspiring writer. Brooks remembered that when she first saw him standing in a doorway, she confided to a friend, "There is the man I am going to marry."

Married in 1938, Brooks and Blakely shared an interest in writing and their life together included frequent visits with friends, discussing social issues, philosophy, and literature. As Brooks recalled, it sometimes seemed that everyone believed society could be changed and improved if they just talked enough. Meanwhile, Gwendolyn enrolled in a poetry workshop for young black writers organized by **Inez Cunningham Stark**. Stark, who had been a reader for *Poetry* magazine, brought books to class from her affluent home and made them available to the students. She introduced them to modern poets and encouraged them to critique each other's work, as well as that of the recognized masters of the genre. How much Brooks' own poetry was influenced by the modernists, such as Eliot and Pound, is debatable. It does seem clear that at that time she began to write more economically and that her work during the 1940s and early 1950s reflects the techniques of the modernists. In addition, Stark was a role model in her devotion to teaching poetry to non-traditional students.

Not long after the workshop, Brooks won the first significant recognition of her work when she received the Midwestern Writers' Conference poetry award in 1943. Several major publishing houses expressed interest in her poetry, and **Elizabeth Lawrence** of Harper and Brothers invited Brooks to submit her work in two years when she would have enough "Negro" poems for a book. Rather than use the time allotted, Brooks wrote feverishly until she had produced the collection, *A Street in Bronzeville,* which was published in 1945. The author recalled when she received the first editions, "I took out the first copy. I turned the pages of the little thing, over and over, My Book."

"Bronzeville" was a sort of generic term for a black urban ghetto, and Brooks used that setting for those poems. As with most of her later writing, the author described average, sometimes anonymous, African-Americans, their struggles, the indignities of racial injustice, and the particular concerns of women. Brooks knew the territory well. She recalled to an interviewer that she wrote about what she saw and heard in the street. "I lived in a small second-floor apartment at the corner; and I could look first on one side and then on the other. That was my material."

During the year that *A Street in Bronzeville* was published, Brooks received recognition from a number of sources. She won four awards at the Midwestern Writers' Conference; she was selected one of the "Ten Young Women of the Year" by *Mademoiselle* magazine, and she received the Society of Midland Authors' "Patron Saint" award. The following year, she won a Guggenheim fellowship and was made a fellow of the prestigious American Academy of Arts and Letters.

In 1949, Brooks published *Annie Allen.* She received the *Eunice Tietjens Memorial Award from *Poetry* magazine, recognition from an internationally influential journal. The next year, *Annie Allen* was named the winner of the Pulitzer Prize for poetry. Gwendolyn Brooks became the first African-American to win the impressive literary honor, and she did so for a collection that was notable for its technical brilliance. *Annie Allen* is arranged in three sections, "Notes from the Childhood and the Girlhood," "The Anniad," and "The Womanhood." The poet was delighted with her achievement, "What a pleasure it was to write that poem!"

she recalled. "I was just very conscious of every word; I wanted every phrase to be beautiful, and yet to contribute to the whole effect."

Three years after her Pulitzer, Brooks published her only novel *Maud Martha.* It may be that Brooks the fiction writer was overshadowed by Brooks the poet or it may be that the novel was ahead of its time. In any event, it did not achieve great sales or success. Later critics, however, writing from the black feminist viewpoint, found it a turning point in African-American fiction. *Maud Martha* was the story of a black woman, not portrayed as a mammy, a sexual object, a mulatto, or a downtrodden heroine, but an ordinary person, growing up to womanhood in all its complexity.

During the decade of the 1950s, Brooks wrote reviews for a number of Chicago newspapers, devoted a great deal of time to raising her two children, and published a book of poetry for children, *Bronzeville Boys and Girls.* Written from the perspective of children, each short poem describes a moment in a child's life. Although developed in a simpler manner, Brooks portrays children facing the same fundamental question that confronts adults. They too consider how to find meaning in a world that seems to ignore or deny their existence as human beings.

Her next major volume of verse, *The Bean Eaters,* appeared in 1960 in the midst of the civil-rights movement in the United States. The collection includes a number of timely poems. One discusses the lynching of black youth Emmett Till in 1955, another focuses on the struggle over the integration of the Arkansas public schools. Some reviewers found the work too strong in its social emphasis. Others thought Brooks' skill with the craft of poetry overshadowed the book's message about racial justice. Unlike her earlier work, *The Bean Eaters* seems to contain a stronger message linking whites with responsibility for the oppression of black Americans. Similarly, Brooks' next publication, *Selected Poems* (1964), continues her concern with racial injustice. A long poem, "Riders to the Blood-Red Wrath," treats black history from its African roots, through the slave trade, to the contemporary protests against segregation by the freedom riders.

If some were troubled by the social concerns expressed in Brooks' poetry, she nonetheless continued to receive recognition at the highest levels. In 1962, President John F. Kennedy invited her to read at the Library of Congress Poetry Festival, and in 1964 she was awarded her first honorary degree, the Doctor of Humane Letters from Columbia College. Brooks would later accept more than 40 honorary degrees from colleges and universities around the country.

She developed other associations with institutions of higher learning during the 1960s. In 1963, she was asked by the president of Columbia College in Chicago to organize a poetry workshop. She also taught creative writing at Elmhurst College, at Northeastern Illinois State, and at the University of Wisconsin. In 1969, she took a position at the City University of New York as Distinguished Professor of the Arts. Although she gave up formal teaching in 1971 after a minor heart attack, she continued to teach informally, especially in settings available to disadvantaged youths.

When Brooks attended the Second Black Writers' Conference at Fisk University in Nashville, Tennessee, in 1967, she experienced an "awakening." There, for the first time, she heard readings by militant young black poets, playwrights, and fiction writers. Their behavior and language were unconventional, and they talked openly about revolution and black power. These artists promoted a "black aesthetic," where art would be at the service of politics. Brooks credited her experience at the Fisk conference with making her more aware of her connection with a black audience. Her subsequent poetry would reflect a stronger racial focus and less concern with intricate form and technique.

The changes in Brooks' perspective would be manifested both in her writings and in her activities. Her next collection, *In the Mecca,* is often labeled a "transitional text." A tribute to the value of the lives of African-Americans, it includes one long poem set in an enormous, labyrinthine tenement building on Chicago's South Side. Although she had always depicted the lives of "common people" in her poetry, the later works, *Riot* (1969), *Family Pictures* (1971), and *Beckonings* (1975), deal more with the black experience while the earlier work seemed to focus more on individuals. This development has been called a passage from egocentric to ethnocentric themes.

In 1968, the same year that *In the Mecca* was published, Brooks was named poet laureate of Illinois. What had been largely a ceremonial position became for Brooks an opportunity to become an advocate for poetry, especially among young people. She gave readings in schools, prisons, colleges, and halfway houses. She sponsored, with her own money, writing contests in penal institutions, drug treatment centers, and homeless shelters as well as in the public schools. After Brooks was appointed poetry consultant for the Library of Congress in 1985, she also used that position to take poetry to the people.

Brooks not only modified the style and content of her poetry to be more reflective of her African-American identity, she also changed publishers. Although Harper and Row had brought out all of her work since *A Street in Bronzeville* in 1945, she decided in 1969 to shift to a new black publisher, Broadside Press of Detroit. No doubt having a bestselling author such as Brooks under contract gave the struggling press the ability to publish the work of many unknown black writers.

In 1972, Brooks published *Report from Part One,* her autobiography. She remained a working poet, even into her 80s. Asked when she would stop writing, she commented, "Every day there's something exciting or disturbing to write about. With all that going on, how could I stop?" Some of her later poems reflect an international focus. For example, in the 1988 collection *Gottschalk and the Grande Tarantelle,* the poem "Winnie" is an imaginary speech by South African **Winnie Mandela**.

In 1995, President Bill Clinton named Gwendolyn Brooks one of 12 Americans to receive the National Medal of Arts. She was among those the president described as "the brightest beacons in American arts and culture . . . people who lift our spirits and illuminate our lives."

SOURCES:

Mootry, Maria K., and Gary Smith, eds. *A Life Distilled: Gwendolyn Brooks, Her Poetry and Fiction.* Urbana: University of Illinois, 1987.

Shaw, Harry B. *Gwendolyn Brooks.* Boston, MA: Twayne, 1980.

Taylor, Henry. "Gwendolyn Brooks: An Essential Sanity," in *The Kenyon Review.* Vol. 13. Fall, 1991, pp. 115–131.

Whitaker, Charles. "Gwendolyn Brooks: A Poet for the Ages," in *Ebony.* June 1987, pp. 154–158.

SUGGESTED READING:

Brooks, Gwendolyn. *Report from Part One.* Detroit, MI: Broadside Press, 1972.

Perry, Margaret. "Gwendolyn Brooks," in *Epic Lives: One Hundred Black Women Who Made a Difference.* Edited by Jessie Carney Smith. Detroit, MI: Visible Ink Press, 1993.

Mary Welek Atwell, Associate Professor of Criminal Justice, Radford University, Radford, Virginia

Brooks, Harriet (1876–1933)

Canadian pioneer nuclear scientist and collaborator with Sir Ernest Rutherford, J.J. Thomson, and Marie

Curie. Born Harriet Brooks on July 2, 1876, in Exeter, Ontario, Canada; died in Montreal on April 17, 1933; one of eight children of George Brooks and Elizabeth Agnes (Worden) Brooks; married Frank Pitcher, 1907; children: three.

Canadian scientist Harriet Brooks made significant contributions to the field of radiation, only to be halted by the pressures of social convention during the early stages of what might easily have developed into a great career. Light was not shed on the magnitude of her advance until two generations after her death and almost a century after her work. Harriet Brooks was born on July 2, 1876, in Exeter, a small town in western Ontario about 30 miles from London, Ontario. By the time of Harriet's birth, her parents George and **Elizabeth Worden Brooks** already had two children; six more would follow. The family was respectable but not wealthy, the latter particularly true after George Brooks' flour mill burned down and was not covered by insurance. From that point on, George supported his large family by working as commercial traveler for a flour firm. Visitors to the Brooks' home were always welcome to a meal, but family members dealt with the economic circumstances through a code that all, young and old, knew by heart: FHB (family hold back) if there was a shortage of food, and MIK (more in kitchen) if there were sufficient groceries on hand in the pantry.

Of the nine Brooks children, only Harriet and her sister **Elizabeth Brooks** would attend a university. Both had an aptitude for mathematics. Elizabeth received a mathematics scholarship for her final two years at McGill University, but being a woman disqualified her for the final two years of her classics scholarship. Harriet entered McGill University in 1894, only six years after McGill graduated its first woman (the first undergraduate degree granted to a Canadian woman was in 1875 by Mount Allison University). An excellent student, Harriet Brooks graduated from McGill with an honors B.A. in mathematics and "natural philosophy" (science) in 1898, the same year that the New Zealand-born Ernest Rutherford (later Sir Ernest Rutherford and Lord Rutherford) moved to McGill from England. Brooks became Rutherford's first graduate student and a key member of what would become his research team.

Even before it was completed in 1901, Brooks' M.A. thesis on the damping of electrical oscillations had already resulted in her first scientific publication, which had appeared in 1899 in the prestigious Transactions of the Canadian

section of the Royal Society. As a promising young researcher, she received an appointment in 1899 as nonresident tutor in mathematics at the newly formed Royal Victorian College, the women's college of McGill University. During these years, her work on the Rutherford team shifted toward the new and exciting field of radium. Papers coauthored by Brooks and Rutherford in 1901 and 1902, and published in the Royal Society Transactions as well as in the venerable *Philosophical Magazine,* announced to the scientific community the appearance of a talent worth watching. Rutherford arranged for her to work with J.J. Thomson in the Cavendish Laboratory at Cambridge University. Although Brooks did some significant laboratory work that was later published, Thomson was preoccupied with his own research and tended to ignore her progress.

In 1903, Brooks returned to the Royal Victorian College to resume her job as a nonresident tutor in mathematics and physics. She also rejoined Rutherford's research group, carrying out work that was published in 1904. In 1905, she began teaching physics at Barnard College in New York. Her life at Barnard was uneventful until the following year when she became engaged to a physics professor at Columbia University, an event that precipitated a crisis in her life. Dean **Laura Gill** of Barnard responded to Harriet's letter about her engagement in the strongest possible terms, noting "that whenever your marriage does take place it ought to end your official relationship with the college." A heated exchange of letters ensued in which Brooks made it clear that she felt she had "a duty" to both her profession and her sex to continue her work even after marriage. Impressed with Brooks' commitment to teaching and research, the head of Barnard's physics department, **Margaret Maltby,* fully backed her Canadian colleague. But Dean Gill ended the dispute by reiterating the view of the college's trustees, which argued that one could not be both a married woman and a successful academic. Soon after, the engagement was broken off, and Brooks initially agreed to stay at Barnard.

In the final months of 1906, Brooks' life took a radical turn. She met John and **Prestonia Martin,** two of the most prominent Fabian Socialists of the day. Through the Martins, she became acquainted with the Russian radical author Maxim Gorky. In October 1906, Brooks accompanied Gorky and his companion **Maria Andreeva* and several other Russians to the Italian island of Capri. During this time, Brooks made contact with ***Marie Curie**, and soon she was in Paris working with Curie as part of her research staff. Although none of her investigations from this period were ever published under her name, Brooks' research was of considerable value and was cited in three contemporary articles published under the aegis of the Curie Institute. At the same time, she attempted to secure a position at the University of Manchester. In his letter of recommendation, Rutherford wrote about Brooks in glowing terms, noting that "next to Mme Curie she is the most prominent woman physicist in the department of radioactivity. Miss Brooks is an original and careful worker with good experimental powers and I am confident that if appointed she would do most excellent research work in Physics."

For reasons that even her excellent biography cannot ascertain, Harriet Brooks then decided to terminate her research in physics and abandon her plans for a university teaching career. In 1907, she married Frank Pitcher, a physics instructor at McGill. In the next years, she became the mother of three children. Brooks remained active in organizations of university women but abandoned all interest in physics. Her married life had more than its share of tragedy, with two of her three children dying while still in their teens. Harriet Brooks died on April 17, 1933, as a result of a lingering illness that was likely related to her years of exposure to radiation. Lord Rutherford wrote a highly laudatory obituary of his former research associate in the journal *Nature*, not surprising in view of the fact that she was repeatedly mentioned in his papers throughout his career.

Not until the 1980s, however, would the importance of the research contributions of Harriet Brooks be recognized as being among the foundations of modern nuclear science. Brooks was the first scientist to show that the radioactive substance emitted from thorium was a gas with a molecular weight of 40 to 100, a discovery crucial to the determination that the elements undergo some transmutation in radioactive decay. During her brief research career, she carried out pioneering studies of radon and actinium. Probably the most crucial contribution made by Brooks to modern physics was her identification of the multiple decays that take place in sequence starting with radium, uranium and thorium. Much more than a promising young researcher, Brooks had the potential to be another Madame Curie.

SOURCES:
Rayner-Canham, Marelene F., and Geoffrey W. Rayner-Canham. "Harriet Brooks—Pioneer nuclear scien-

tist," in *American Journal of Physics*. Vol. 57, no. 10. October 1989, pp. 899–902.
———. *Harriet Brooks: Pioneer Nuclear Physicist*. Montreal: McGill-Queen's University Press, 1992.
———. "Pioneer women in nuclear science," in *American Journal of Physics*. Vol. 58, no. 11. November 1990, pp. 1036–1043.

John Haag, Associate Professor,
University of Georgia, Athens, Georgia

Brooks, Louise (1906–1985)

American actress whose highly memorable performance in the 1929 silent German film Pandora's Box *helped make that film a landmark in the history of the international cinema. Pronunciation: Bruhks. Born November 14, 1906, in Cherryvale, Kansas; died on August 8, 1985, in Rochester, New York; daughter of Leonard Porter Brooks (a lawyer) and Myra Rude Brooks; married Edward Sutherland, 1926 (divorced, 1928); married Deering Davis, 1934 (divorced six months later); children: none.*

Left home at 15 to pursue a career as a dancer in New York City, studying with Ruth St. Denis and Ted Shawn and going on tour with their company (1922); danced in George White's Scandals (1924) and the Ziegfeld Follies (1925); signed a five-year contract with Paramount Motion Picture Studios at age 19 (1925); selected by German filmmaker G.W. Pabst to star in Pandora's Box *(1928); made her final film (1938).*

Selected films: The American Venus *(1926);* It's the Old Army Game *(1926);* The Canary Murder Case *(1928);* A Girl in Every Port *(1928);* Pandora's Box *(later named* Lulu, *1929);* Diary of a Lost Girl *(1929).*

In 1929, a visitor to the Berlin film studio of the celebrated German director G.W. Pabst was startled to discover that the leading lady in the film, a "fascinatingly beautiful" woman, was using the time between filming to read the aphorisms of the philosopher Schopenhauer. Asked if she always read Schopenhauer on the movie set, the actress replied, no; sometimes she read Proust. "I was immediately intrigued by this Louise Brooks," the visitor wrote. "It was her curious blend of passivity and presence that dominated the entire shoot."

Louise Brooks was a unique film actress. Never a "star" in the traditional Hollywood sense, she found that her intelligence and independence gave her an image, in that film capital, of being too "stubborn" and having an "attitude problem." Refusing to renew her contract, she expanded her career into European films, where she became the dominant presence in the landmark 1929 silent German film *Pandora's Box*.

When Hollywood, unlike Europe, still would not recognize her stature as a "film actress," she went into retirement at age 34, spending the rest of her life at hobbies like painting, translating books, and writing penetrating character sketches of Hollywood stars.

The second of four children born to Leonard Porter Brooks, a Kansas lawyer, and **Myra Rude Brooks**, Louise came to admire her parent's honesty and her mother's determination to create her own sense of freedom in the midst of Kansas. Her father, whom she remembered as

hardworking and quiet, dreamed of becoming a federal district judge but, unwilling to play the political games necessary to achieve that, settled for appointment as assistant attorney general for the state of Kansas. "L.P. Brooks," the locals joked, "is so honest that his secretary makes more money than he does."

Louise Brooks described her mother as a "tiny, withdrawn" woman whose health was never very good. Tired of being the disciplinarian for her own brothers and sisters when she was growing up, Myra Brooks told her husband

Louise Brooks

that any "squalling brats" that resulted from their marriage would have to take care of themselves. "When my older brother and I got into a fight, my father would retire to his lawbooks and violin on the third floor, and my mother, who had a sense of the absurd which almost always reduced crime and punishment to laughter, often simply laughed."

Louise wrote that "my mother pursued her [own] freedom by presenting book reviews to her women's club, by delivering lectures on Wagner, and by playing the piano, at which she was extremely talented (and also self-taught)." Brooks "always felt" that the way her mother played Debussy was "incomparable." "It was by watching her face that I first recognized the joy of creative effort."

Louise Brooks is the only woman who had the ability to transfigure no matter what film into a masterpiece.

—Kenneth Tynan

In addition to the delights of creative effort, Brooks also learned perfectionism, and a demanding sense of honesty, from her mother. "My mother did try to make me less openly critical of other people's false faces. . . . I would watch my mother . . . make people feel clever and pleased with themselves, but I could not act that way," she later recalled. "And so I have remained, in cruel pursuit of truth and excellence, an inhumane executioner of the bogus." Her mother, she later concluded, had fostered in her an idea of freedom that was "totally utopian, and a guaranteed source of disillusionment."

Myra Brooks also encouraged her daughter to begin a dancing career. Louise was dancing in public by age ten, at men's clubs and women's clubs. "I was," she later wrote, "what amounted to a professional dancer." When the dancer Ted Shawn presented a dance show in the area—assisted by, among others, *Martha Graham—Myra and Louise attended. Against the opposition of her father, who thought the idea of a dancing career was "just silly," Louise's mother worked to send her to a new dancing school being established by Shawn and *Ruth St. Denis in New York City. At age 15, Louise Brooks was sent off to Manhattan to attend the Denishawn school, accompanied by a middle-aged Kansas woman who also wished to take dance lessons and who was paid to be a chaperon.

Learning to dance was the easiest part. Accustomed to walking barefoot in the Kansas summers, Brooks adapted easily to the school's tradition that dancers practice barefoot, on hard (and splinter-filled) wooden floors. She was even sent on tour with Shawn and St. Denis in 1922 and 1923. But Brooks discovered that her Kansas accent and her style of dress were obstacles in her planned career. Attempting to look sophisticated, she selected clothing that caused her to be evicted from two hotels—from the first hotel because her exercise outfit, while working out, was considered scandalous, and from the second hotel because a short pink dress she had chosen to wear in the lobby made her look 14 years old.

Brooks decided to consult the "people who were experts in such matters—the people at the bottom whose services were supported by the enchantment at the top of New York." To lose her Kansas accent and acquire a more Eastern manner of speaking, she practiced with a soda jerk in a local drugstore, who, she reported, was very good at teaching her to pronounce "water" as if it rhymed with "daughter." For the proper style of dress, she consulted one of the most expensive clothing salons in the city, one that catered to show-business women (and a store that would later use her picture in advertisements). There she was fitted with a dress that accentuated her figure—"it was cut almost to my navel . . . had no upper back," and left me "a nearly naked sight to behold," she reported.

The changes worked. In 1925, she was hired as a chorus girl in George White's *Scandals*; in 1926, she became a dancer in the Ziegfeld *Follies*. In 1925, when she was only 18, both Paramount and Metro-Goldwyn-Mayer studios had also offered her five-year contracts. Her friends suggested that she marry someone of importance in Hollywood, but they failed "to understand that I put no value in my beauty and sexual attractiveness and could not use them as a means to success." Between 1925 and 1929, she appeared in 14 films, including *The American Venus* (1926) and *A Girl in Every Port* (1928). Her signature look was her bangs—dubbed the "puppy look"—an image which, she later revealed, came about because the photographer in one of her early films decided her forehead was too high to photograph properly.

She lived what fan magazines portrayed as the glamorous life, meeting many of the 1930s stars who would become legends and staying regularly at the California castle (designed by *Julia Morgan) of the newspaper magnate William Randolph Hearst. In later life, Brooks would write perceptive and up-close character sketches of many of the stars of the period, including W.C. Fields, whom she saw as a solitary, isolated person who feared being discarded to die on the Hollywood "rubbish heap." Of *Lillian Gish, she wrote, "I can only be eternally grateful that she was able to make so many marvelous pictures before the producers found the trick of curbing a star and standardizing their product according to their own wishes and personal taste."

The Hollywood years were not happy ones for her. She had had a foreboding about this, when, while still in New York City, she had been interviewed by a studio representative. The interviewer was stunned to realize that Brooks was not overwhelmed by the "magic of Hollywood," and that she was leaving the Ziegfeld show only because a screenwriter wanted her to appear in a particular movie. The interviewer saw Brooks as a stupid, lucky girl; Brooks viewed the interviewer as an "artistically retarded" studio employee who did not even realize that a dancing career was the best possible training to appear in silent films.

"Nobody could understand why I hated this terrible destructive place which seemed a marvelous paradise to all others," she wrote. "To me it was like a terrible dream I have—I am lost in the corridor of a big hotel and I cannot find my room." In contrast to Hollywood, "sycophancy had no merit" in the New York theater world where she had been trained. "I was unaware," she later wrote, "that prudent Hollywood actors wooed producers, directors, and writers with a flattering attention." She was viewed as cold or not interested in making motion pictures, an impression she tried to dispel through hard work and a willingness to do some of the stunts herself.

She also discovered that she was fundamentally different from most film actresses and actors. In addition to her habit of reading weighty tomes between "takes," she was not comfortable carrying on constant small talk with the crew—her ironic nickname was "Louise the chatterbox." To a film star, she wrote, to be let alone for an instant was terrifying; whereas Brooks wanted to choose her periods of aloneness and wanted to choose the people with whom she would spend her periods of "non-aloneness."

From the movie It's the Old Army Game, starring Louise Brooks.

Others in Hollywood viewed her as insolent, while she thought she was being totally honest in rejecting the pretentiousness of those around her. She also refused to perpetuate the fiction that actresses and actors were actually anything like the roles they played. When a French interviewer assumed that a particular movie role reflected her real personality, she responded, "You talk as if I were a lesbian in real life." When he replied, "But of course," she lectured him that the public should not believe that an actress' public and private persona were the same.

Her chance to appear in European films came at a time when Hollywood studios were converting to sound. "It was the time of the switchover to talkies, and studios were taking advantage of that fact to cut contract players' salaries." Refusing to accept what would have amounted to a pay cut, she became, in effect, the first Hollywood player to go on strike. She traveled to Europe, accepting an offer from the German film director G.W. Pabst to play the lead in his new film *Pandora's Box.* "In Hollywood, I was a pretty flibbertigibbet whose charm for the executive department decreased with every increase in fan mail. In Berlin, I stepped onto the railroad station platform to meet Pabst and became an actress. I would be treated by him with a kind of decency and respect unknown to me in Hollywood."

The role that Pabst wanted Brooks to play was Lulu, a character in two plays by the 19th-century German playwright Frank Wedekind, *Pandora's Box* and *The Earth Spirit.* Wedekind's Lulu, who becomes a prostitute in the course of the plays, has been described as a "sexual demon—insatiable and destructive." The plays had caused Wedekind constant problems with censors, but censorship was less of a problem in 1920's Berlin. Pabst had considered hiring *Marlene Dietrich for the role, at a time when she had not yet won international fame in *The Blue Angel.* He rejected that idea when he learned that Brooks was available, commenting that the sexual overtones of Dietrich's acting were so obvious that the film would have become a "burlesque" if she played Lulu.

Brooks credited Pabst for motivating much of her characterization of Lulu as amoral, perverse, and child-like. "I revered Pabst," she later wrote, "for his truthful picture of the world of pleasure which let me play Lulu naturally." Pabst selected her wardrobes carefully, arguing that both she and her fellow actors would be aware of what they were wearing. He coaxed another actress into playing a lesbian love scene by convincing her that she was really playing the scene to him, off camera. To play Jack the Ripper in one of the movie's final scenes with Brooks, he cleverly selected one of the few male actors on the set that she found attractive.

But several dimensions of Lulu's character were created by Brooks herself—such as Lulu's disconcerting "sweet innocence" and playfulness, what has been called her "fiery eroticism," and the fact that, as a prostitute, Lulu was portrayed as a victim rather than a villain. She said that the role seemed "perfectly normal to me" and recalled that during her work in the Ziegfeld *Follies,* one of her best friends was a lesbian and that two millionaires in the story were very reminiscent of two studio figures she remembered from Hollywood.

Although the film would become a landmark in the European cinema, Pabst came under criticism for selecting an "American girl" to play "our Lulu." Brooks made only two more films in Europe—*Diary of a Lost Girl,* also directed by Pabst in 1929, and *Prix de Beauté* (1930), based on a script by the French director René Clair.

In 1930's Hollywood, she made seven more pictures after returning from Europe, the last in 1938. After Brooks left Hollywood in 1940, she lived for a time in Wichita, where, she said, citizens could not decide "whether they should dismiss me for having once been a success away from home or for now being a failure in their midst." Finally moving to New York, she was shocked to discover that the "only well-paying career open to me, as an unsuccessful actress of thirty-six," was the career of a call girl.

Cutting herself off from all friends of her movie days, she relied, for a time, on "yellow sleeping pills," until, in 1956, the film curator of Eastman House in Rochester, New York, persuaded her to move to that city. It was while living there, she wrote, that she came to judge her films for their artistic quality rather than the Hollywood standard of the amount of money they drew at the box office. Among the items she wrote was an introduction to a book about W.C. Fields. She also translated into English *Johanna Spyri's *Heidi.*

During the 1950s, Brooks was invited to Paris, where a retrospective of her film career was in progress. When asked why she had left the movies, she replied that she had become bored doing the same thing over and over again. The questioner found that puzzling, since her voice was still "marvelous," and he added that he "couldn't possibly understand why the American directors hadn't brought her back to the screen, like they had Joan Crawford or Bette Davis." Asked by an interviewer if she was unhappy, she replied, "What my friends were searching for—fame, money, and power—were not the things that made me happy. I only began to find a little happiness when I moved to Rochester."

Louise Brooks remained there until her death, spending time at her hobbies or painting, reading, and sometimes watching film from Hollywood's earlier days. She said that she lived like "millions of old people, enslaved by their habits." But, she added, "I was free! Although my mother had left us . . . she was still [present] in me. She brings me comfort every time I read a book."

SOURCES:
Brooks, Louise. *Lulu in Hollywood.* NY: Alfred A. Knopf, 1982.
———. *Louise Brooks: Portrait of an Anti-Star.* Edited by Roland Jaccard. NY: New York Zoetrope, 1980.

SUGGESTED READING:
Paris, Barry. *Louise Brooks.* NY: Anchor Books, 1990.
Tynan, Kenneth. "Profile: Louise Brooks," in *The New Yorker.* June 11, 1979, pp. 45–48.

Niles R. Holt, Professor of History, Illinois State University, Normal-Bloomington, Illinois

Brooks, Matilda M.

American biologist who discovered an antidote for cyanide and carbon monoxide poisoning. Born Matilda Moldenhauer in Pittsburgh, Pennsylvania; daughter of Rudolph and Selma (Neuffer) Moldenhauer; graduated from Girls' High School, Philadelphia; granted B.A. and M.A. degrees from the University of Pittsburgh; granted Ph.D. from Harvard University, 1920; married Sumner Cushing Brooks (a zoologist), 1917.

During a career working with oxidation reductions in living cells, Matilda Brooks discovered that methylene blue acted as a treatment in both cyanide and carbon monoxide poisoning. Methylene blue was first used in 1933 to save a young man who had dosed himself with cyanide of potassium in order to commit suicide.

After emerging from a painfully shy period as a teenager, Brooks received her Ph.D. from Harvard in 1920. She worked as a biologist for the U.S. Public Health Service before her appointment as a research biologist at the University of California, where her husband was also employed as a zoology professor. At the time (1927), husbands and wives were not allowed to both hold salaried positions on the university faculty, so Brooks did not receive pay for her research work, though her expenses were reimbursed and her assistants paid. Under a grant from the National Academy of Sciences, she did research in Bermuda and the South Seas, and in 1930 received a grant from the National Research Council at Naples. When her husband was ill in 1934, and again in 1936, she closed her laboratory and took over his courses at the university.

Brooks and her husband made their permanent home in California but summered in Woods Hole, Massachusetts, where Matilda was a member of the corporation of the Marine Biological Laboratory. The couple also traveled extensively, including one trip around the world. Brooks, though a formidable scientist, had a variety of other interests, including gardening, music, and painting. She thrived on furniture auctions and was a member of the Sierra Club, a California mountain climbing society.

Brooks, Romaine (1874–1970)

American portrait artist whose main theme was "the essential loneliness of the human predicament."
Name variations: Beatrice Romaine Goddard. Born Beatrice Romaine Goddard on May 1, 1874, in Rome, Italy; died on December 7, 1970, in Nice, France; daughter of Major Henry Goddard and Ella Mary Waterman (an heiress); attended St. Mary's Hall, New Jersey, 1882–86; attended Catholic convent school, Italy, 1888; enrolled in Mlle Tavan's Finishing School, Geneva, Switzerland, 1891; studied singing, Paris, 1893; studied art, La Scuola Nazionale, Rome, 1896–97; attended Académie Colarossi, Paris, 1899; married John Ellingham Brooks, June 13, 1903 (separated, 1904); no children.

Went to Capri (1899); had first solo exhibition, Paris (1910); met Natalie Barney (1915); had solo exhibition of drawings, New York (1935); wrote memoirs (1930s); painted last portrait (1961).

Selected paintings: Self-portrait (1900); Portrait of John Rowland Fothergill (1905); Azalées Blanches (1910); The Masked Archer (1910–11); Le Trajet (c. 1911); Gabriele d'Annunzio, Le Poète en Exil (1912); La France Croisée (1914); Jean Cocteau à Epoque de la Grand Roué (1914); Ida Rubenstein (1917); Renata Borgatti au Piano (c. 1920); Miss Natalie Barney, L'Amazone (1920); Una, Lady Troubridge (1924); Marchese Uberto Strozzi (1961).

It might strike one as odd that an artist who excelled in portraiture was a misanthrope to whom the common "herd" was repugnant. Beatrice Romaine Goddard Brooks was a "loner"; she was moody, "mistrustful of others," quick to take offense, completely self-centered, and possessive. A woman of great talent and wealth, her "unfulfilled life" was of her own making; Brooks believed "she was fated not to be happy," and as her biographer notes, this conviction "became tragically self-fulfilling."

In her unpublished memoirs, *No Pleasant Memories,* Romaine Brooks bitterly recollects the fear and rejection that made her childhood a "gothic nightmare." Written in the 1930s, they reveal the life of a "mistreated and emotionally damaged child with the mother as chief tormentor, of a demented brother, and an atmosphere of supernatural evil." Romaine's father, the son of a famous preacher, was an alcoholic, shadowy figure, whose identity and livelihood depended on his wealthy, unstable wife. But it was **Ella Waterman Goddard** who was the ogre in this idiosyncratic family; the daughter of a multimillionaire, Ella imposed a nomadic, dysfunctional lifestyle on her three children after divorcing their father. And from her mother, Romaine Brooks absorbed an "obsessive interest in the supernatural," which pervaded her childhood with ghosts, apparitions, and dire forebodings.

Insult and wound in me the friend, mistress and woman—I can take it—but I beg you, don't insult my art.

—Romaine Brooks

Neglected and unloved, Brooks resented, and yet pitied, her handsome, sickly, demented brother, St. Mar, on whom Ella bestowed all her love. To Romaine, St. Mar was an "Incomplete Being," a "divine fool . . . whose madness had an innocence that protected [him] from life." Little Romaine had no such protection. The first part of Brooks' memoirs, dealing with her childhood and young womanhood, often obscure more than they reveal. Names, places, and dates are falsified, and one is uncertain about the veracity of her recounting of events. For example, in 1881, while residing in New York, Brooks related how her mother sent her to live with an Irish washerwoman, Mrs. Hickey, in a run-down tenement. And in an amazingly matter-of-fact way, Brooks noted that her mother left New York without paying Mrs. Hickey and without leaving a forwarding address. This confirmed Romaine's conviction that she was unlovable, "although she did not know why." Was Mrs. Hickey a figment of Brooks' imagination, a fictitious, loving mother that Romaine so desperately needed? Her biographer admits that she is not certain. Imagined or real, Romaine, at age seven, accepted her fate as an outcast, who was denied a mother's love and was even rejected by the children in Mrs. Hickey's neighborhood.

Brooks' exile ended when her Grandfather Waterman sent his secretary to bring her to his house in Chestnut Hill, Pennsylvania. Shortly thereafter, Brooks was enrolled at St. Mary's Hall, a girls' boarding school. The strict religious atmosphere discouraged self-expression, and Romaine's artistic talents were severely restricted. Her mother had always forbidden her to draw at home, and once again her natural artistic impulses were thwarted. During her four years at St. Mary's, Brooks acquired a belief in God and "a spontaneous flowering of interest in her own sex." She had never liked her father whom she thought to be "a well-intentioned but ineffectual man." Major Henry's rather awkward visits to the school led her to conclude that "belonging to one parent was a disagreeable experience; I had no desire to belong to another," and she dismissed him from her life. Brooks consciously adopted Peer Gynt's maxim, "To thyself be enough," to which she tried to adhere all her life but failed.

After leaving school, Romaine joined her family in London; life was chaotic as they traveled around Europe with a large retinue of servants, a resident doctor, and 22 trunks. At 19, St. Mar was also a problem; frail and prematurely old, he loathed moving about, and his dementia was exacerbated by Ella's odd propensity for eating and sleeping at all hours of the day or night. Living with her mother was like "living on an avalanche," Romaine wrote, and at age 14, she was near nervous collapse. Sent away to a Catholic convent (the family was living in northern Italy), Romaine was forced "to adapt herself to a life of medieval Catholicism." The absence of privacy and personal hygiene and her stubborn refusal to accept the nuances of faith, made her unsuitable as a prospective nun, the vocation her mother and the nuns tried to impose on her. To escape this fate, Brooks decided to become ill, and she did. Finally, the frustrated nuns pronounced her damned and expelled her from school.

Romaine's mother had bought the Château Grimaldi on the Riviera near Mentone, and Romaine joined her family there. The imposing château had 30 rooms on four floors and a large staff of servants and groundskeepers. Brooks had the top floor to herself, but luxurious surroundings could not overcome her feelings of worthlessness: "She turned against herself," she wrote, "finding herself wanting." Outwardly obedient and passive, the 15-year-old had a dread of "descending through a trap door into a private hell" already occupied by St. Mar. But before the trap door sprung open, Romaine was shipped off, in 1891, to Mlle Tavan's Private Finishing School for Young Ladies in Geneva, to be groomed for marriage to some wealthy, acceptable suitor. But Brooks rigorously avoided any attempt to mold her into a decorous mate. She had no interest in academic subjects and filled her notebooks with drawings of "wing spans . . . a wing poised in flight" with which she later signed her work. Unhappy among her classmates, Romaine realized she was different from other women; already she found it difficult to relate to others and took umbrage at the most innocuous remarks, a lifelong trait.

To complete her education, Ella sent Romaine off to Paris to study art and music, and to lose her Swiss accent. Brooks knew that in two years, at age 21, she would be expected to earn a living; as an artist, she would live in poverty, but her musical talent could be turned into a singing career. In September 1893, she became a pupil of M. and **Mme. Givend** and moved into their dark, musty house in a pleasant suburb of Paris. Soon Romaine asserted her independence by moving to a dingy room in the avenue de Clichy and taking a job as an artist's model. Brooks had never asked her mother for money, but she now approached Dr. Alexander Hamilton Phillips to intercede for her with Ella. Phillips had cared for St. Mar for many years, and his ability to handle the young man's violent episodes and to evoke spirits, which delighted Ella, made him indispensable. Romaine hints strongly in her memoirs that Phillips had an affair with Ella whom he wanted to marry. Rejected, he turned to Romaine's older sister **Maya** who had been in love with him for years; they eloped to New York in 1895.

It is often difficult to separate fact from fantasy in Romaine's memoirs, and her own "affair" with Dr. Phillips is especially puzzling. **Meryle Secrest** recounts various possible scenarios without claiming that any are based on known facts. She suggests that Romaine became pregnant and gave birth to a daughter, depositing the baby in a convent where the infant died. To Secrest, this helps to explain why Brooks moved to a remote village for several months, but, she adds, Romaine may have simply been taking her time to plan her future. In any case, Brooks' plea for an allowance to her mother, and to a cousin who managed the Waterman estate, was successful. Romaine received 300 francs a month from her mother until Ella died; she also inherited part of her grandfather's estate.

With an adequate allowance and an unusual degree of freedom for a young "lady" in the 1890s, Brooks sang at a working-class cabaret in Paris for several weeks before leaving for Rome in late 1896, to study art. Able to live frugally, she rented a studio in the Via Sistina. In 1896–97, Romaine studied, free of charge, at La Scuola Nazionale, where she was the only female student, and took a sketch class each evening at the Circolo Artistico. In Rome, Brooks learned how to live in a man's world, how to gain the respect and friendship of men.

While in Rome, Romaine met John Rowland Fothergill, a cultured, handsome graduate of Oxford and protegé of Oscar Wilde. He helped her appreciate the charms of Rome and made her aware of current aesthetic thought. Fothergill left for Greece, and they only met again in 1905, in London. Brooks painted his portrait, one that was "more virile than most." Called Roland in her memoirs, he was one of the few men Romaine liked, but by 1905, she was disappointed to find him changed; he had become "dreary and faded . . . jaded, superficial." And when he evinced an interest in marriage, Romaine "withdrew with finality. But she kept his photograph for seventy years."

Increasingly, Brooks saw herself as an outsider, a martyr (she began using the word *Lapidée*, one who is stoned, i.e., a martyr) incapable of engaging in normal relations with others. Placing a barrier between herself and the "herds" that rejected and misunderstood her, she tried to fashion her life, and her relationships, in light of her adopted maxim, "To thyself be enough," but it led only to an empty existence of her own making.

In the summer of 1899, Romaine went to Capri to try and sell her paintings to earn money for art classes in Paris. She rented a small studio and mingled with the expatriate community of writers and artists who lived on the island. Here she met John Ellingham Brooks, a handsome, charming, English homosexual, about 40 years old. John had studied law at Cambridge but was dedicating his life to translating the Hérédia sonnets and avoiding earning a living; able to live off the generosity of friends, he "dismissed the work ethic as if it never existed." It is not known how they met, but their sexual preferences never precluded their having close friendships with the opposite sex. Secrest points out that John could engage in "tender friendships with women if they did not demand too much from him," an attitude shared by Romaine. But where John was able to tolerate all kinds of people, because he did not expect much of them, Romaine was barely able to tolerate a select few. Aside from his homosexuality, John accepted, and embraced, social convention, "the right ordering of things." On the other hand, Romaine was not concerned about convention, probably because she had never been exposed to the conventional. At this time she received her first commission for a portrait of R. Barra, an American writer living on Capri. In contrast to her later work, she used the brilliant colors of the Capri landscape. The portraits of Barra and of a local Catholic priest reveal Brooks' ability to capture the nuances of character, and only the bright colors seem to place the paintings of this period outside of her corpus of work. Though not satisfied with her efforts, Romaine remembered this as the happiest time of her life.

In Paris during the fall of 1899, Brooks attended the Académie Colarossi while living in real poverty. But when a wealthy Russian fellow student tried to give her a warm fur coat, Romaine refused to accept it. Despite her desperate

Romaine Brooks, Self-Portrait, *1923.*

circumstances, she refused to accept sexual advances from male acquaintances from Capri who contacted her in Paris; R. Barra insisted on having sex with Romaine before he would pay her what he still owed for his portrait. She refused, and he never paid. Another Capri acquaintance, who had shown a sincere interest in her work, suggested that she accompany him on a pleasure trip to England. Romaine's reaction was that men wanted nothing but to exploit women, and she resented being considered a sex object. Fearing for her mental and physical well-being, Brooks sought refuge in a Swiss village until she returned to Capri in the fall of 1901.

Here Romaine learned from a newspaper account that St. Mar had died. She left to join her mother and Maya in Nice. Romaine was shocked at her mother's appearance; shabbily dressed and unkempt, Ella had lost touch with reality. Ten months later, Ella died, uttering her final words of hatred for Romaine. But Brooks was not free; she felt her mother's presence haunting her, and nightly visitations from Ella and St. Mar finally drove Romaine from the château. She was convinced Ella was trying to destroy her, "in death as in life," the evil phantom who stood "between me and life," as she wrote in her memoirs. Whatever her emotional state and the fears that disturbed her might be, the phantasm of poverty no longer haunted her. Brooks was an enormously wealthy heiress. She inherited an apartment in Paris, eight additional apartments around France, and the Château Grimaldi, plus trunks of clothes, furs and linens, and a small fortune in coins. She knew that "the simple, almost monastic life . . . was now over."

During a visit to Capri in the spring of 1903, Romaine unexpectedly married John Brooks. To her annoyance, John insisted on a marriage ceremony, a "bourgeois convention," as she described it. Why she married John is not clear. In her memoirs she noted simply, "Nevertheless, I married him." Romaine assumed they would live separate lives, sharing a "tender friendship," but John thought otherwise. He envisioned Romaine as a "dutiful wife of an English squire" and thoughtlessly talked of how they would spend "our money." An elegant house in London and an active social life were John's idea of "the right ordering of things." Romaine would have none of it; she came to regard him as "the symbol of hateful restriction, a male Ella," and she left for London in 1904, forbidding John to join her there. To avoid a confrontation, Romaine arranged to give John an allowance of £300 a year.

She bought a studio in Chelsea and began to paint again. The influence of her neighbor, James Whistler, is obvious in her work of this period: neutral backgrounds and a more subdued light replaced the bright colors of Capri. Romaine Brooks was discovering her own style, "imposing a point of view upon a work for the first time." Relying on an extremely limited "range of tones"—black, white, and grey—she produced masterful character studies of women, including a stunning self-portrait in three-quarter face, employing the three colors and facial position that became her artistic signature. The warm reception given to her study of a young man's head encouraged her, and Brooks moved to Paris where the Impressionists were beginning to dominate the art world.

Her first exhibit of 13 paintings of women and young girls was in the prestigious Galeries Durand-Ruel and established her reputation as a mature, first-rate artist. The main theme of her work was "the essential loneliness of the human predicament," and her portraits were described as "strong and very cold." Similarly, her elongated nudes were judged "impressively eerie, suggesting a kind of icy eroticism." Depicting a limited range of moods in her work, Brooks painted "with sadness, too much sadness," wrote one critic, seeing "her subjects through a pervasive melancholy." Romaine insisted that she owed nothing to the Impressionists and refused to acknowledge that she was influenced by any of the current art movements.

Living in a fashionable district of Paris, Brooks chose to socialize with "the titled, the famous, the elegantly scandalous, and the intellectual elite" of the Right Bank. But she did not relate well to people, any people; unsympathetic and unduly critical, she rejected people for the most trivial reasons. She dismissed Jean Cocteau, French dramatist and film director, as a "malicious gossip" and "social climber." Brooks' misanthropy and frank expression earned her public censure. She frequented the famous literary salon of **Mme. Muhlfeld** who one day suggested that Romaine might consider marrying Henry Bernstein, the playwright. "I don't want to marry that dirty Jew," Brooks responded to her Jewish hostess. Labelled a bigot by the public, Romaine went on the defensive, portraying herself as "a noble being fated to be misunderstood and victimized."

Thereafter, Brooks shunned Parisian society, but she was unable to avoid human entanglements. She fell in love with the lesbian Princess *Edmond de Polignac (née Winnaretta Singer, American heiress of the Singer Sewing Machine magnate) whose husband was a homosexual, and, even more surprising, with the writer and right-wing Italian patriot Gabriele d'Annunzio. Often described as "short, fat, and ugly," d'Annunzio was irresistible to women. Why Romaine loved him and whether their "affair" was platonic or not is a mystery, but her distaste regarding sexual intercourse was obvious. In one of her notebooks, she stated that "the sexual act was a commotion, rather than an emotion." Eventually, d'Annunzio was forced to distance himself from Brooks whose intense love was too demanding; subsequently, love mellowed into a 30-year friendship, but Romaine got her revenge for being rejected. She took from d'Annunzio his newest love interest, a star of the Ballets Russes in Paris, ⚹▶ Ida Rubenstein. The androgynous Ida adored Romaine who loved d'Annunzio who loved Ida. The ethereal ballerina was the ideal nude for Brooks and is the model for her *Le Trajet* (*The Journey*) of 1911.

⚹▶ Rubenstein, Ida (1875–1961)

Russian ballerina. Born in St. Petersburg, Russia, in 1875; died in 1961; of Russian Jewish parentage; studied with Michel Fokine.

Of Russian-Jewish parentage, Ida Rubenstein was born into wealth. Her parents supported her interest in ballet and paid for private study with Michel Fokine. The androgynous Rubenstein made her debut in 1909, in a private performance of *Salomé*, which was choreographed by Fokine. That same year, she made her Paris debut in the premiere season of Diaghilev's Ballets Russes, dancing the title role in Fokine's *Cléopâtre*. In 1910, she danced Queen Zobeide to *Bronislava Nijinska*'s Golden Slave in Fokine's *Schéhérazade* and "became the rage of smart Paris with her angular, mannish allure set off by a black panther," wrote Nigel Gosling.

Rubenstein stayed with the Ballets Russes, while also financially supporting the world of ballet and other principal artists. She commissioned Maurice Ravel to write "Bolero" for a Fokine ballet; she also commissioned Claude Debussy to write the score for Gabriele d'Annunzio's controversial *Le Martyre de Saint Sébastien* (*The Martyrdom of Saint Sebastian*), a mystery play for soloists, chorus, and orchestra. Again, she played the title role, but it closed after 11 performances. After leaving the Ballets Russes in 1915, Rubenstein formed her own company and hired such greats as Vaslav Nijinsky and Leonide Massine to direct and choreograph. She made her final appearance in the title role of *Orphée* in Paris in 1928 and retired to a life of seclusion in Vence, on the French Riviera. She died there in 1961.

SOURCES:

Gosling, Nigel. *The Adventurous World of Paris 1900–1914.* NY: Morrow, 1978.

Romaine admired Ida, but she found true, all-consuming love with *Natalie Clifford Barney, a wealthy American by birth, but French by choice. A lesbian, a feminist, and an aggressive chaser of women, this "Amazon" was known for her Friday afternoon gatherings in her rue Jacob salon. Unlike Romaine who outwardly conformed to social convention, Natalie "never evaded, explained or apologized. She was what she was." Brooks did some of her best work in the 1920s. Barney, herself a talented writer, admired Romaine's artistic abilities, especially her drawings, which had never been exhibited. Ro-

maine once explained her wraithlike line drawings as rising from the subconscious, "a kind of automatic writing." Brooks craved the approval and admiration of friends, and Barney unselfishly praised and pushed to get Romaine's work more widely appreciated. Romaine had finally found with Natalie Barney the love she desired, the kind of "open marriage" she had wanted with John Brooks. But Natalie was not monogamous, and Romaine suffered acute fits of jealousy. Natalie was humane, witty, intelligent, and gregarious—an undemanding, loyal friend. Romaine, on the other hand, retained her suspi-

Emile d'Erlanger, La Baronne, *painting by Romaine Brooks, 1924.*

cions regarding people's motives, convinced that everyone "was out to get her." Friends for over 50 years, they shared few interests, except that they both cared deeply about Romaine. Everyone was aware that Natalie was the partner who gave, and Romaine was the one who took.

Through Barney, Brooks became acquainted with the literary elite of Paris, *Colette, *Gertrude Stein, Ezra Pound, and others. She also met, and disliked the English couple, *Radclyffe Hall, writer of lesbian novels, and Lady Una Troubridge. Romaine's portrait of Una, dressed in male attire and sporting a monocle, was deemed a caricature; this is in stark contrast to her portrait of Natalie, which displays the warmth and intimacy Romaine felt for her own lover. By the 1930s, interest in Brooks' work was dwindling, and she turned to writing her memoirs, which she revised for the next 30 years. Unfortunately, the memoirs provide little insight into Romaine's views on lesbianism, her marriage, or her long association with Natalie Barney. According to her biographer, the "dominant tone . . . is one of embittered outrage of a woman bent on bringing to justice those who would have destroyed her if they could."

Brooks was bitter, too, that her work did not appeal to or interest Americans. Like *Mary Cassatt, Romaine received recognition from her adopted country, France, but was ignored by her own nation. Brooks' drawings were exhibited in New York in 1935, and she took a studio in Carnegie Hall for the year she spent there; disappointed in the tepid reception her work received, she returned permanently to Europe. She had always thought of herself as American, but she was, as Barney noted, "a stranger everywhere." Bored, dependent on and demanding of Natalie's total affection and attention, and having excluded many people from her life, Romaine slowly and ominously began to take on her mother's aberrant behaviors. Constantly moving about, increasingly hypochondriacal, and convinced she was going blind, Brooks spent weeks secluded in a darkened room, drinking carrot juice and eating herbal concoctions. Barney grew concerned as Brooks became more and more reclusive, but her efforts to get Romaine to see mutual friends created friction between the women. Moreover, since Romaine was often absent from Paris, Natalie had acquired a new lover, and Romaine cruelly severed all contact with her friend, ignoring the fact that Barney was no longer physically able to care for herself. Meanwhile, Brooks was able to spend winters in her apartment in Nice and summers in her villa outside Florence.

Brooks was in fairly good physical health, but she acted irrationally at times—everyone was out to get her, to take advantage of her, even her faithful servants. Alone and consumed with suspicions, she fell madly in love at age 85 with the French portraitist Edouard MacAvoy who had been influenced by her work and encouraged Romaine to resume painting. They agreed to each do a portrait of the other. Romaine never did, but MacAvoy's portrait of the elderly Brooks displeased her, even after he "removed a double chin." She bought the picture, hung it opposite her bed, and concealed it behind a black cloth drape. Jealous and possessive, Brooks finally destroyed their friendship.

By the 1930s, Romaine's work was viewed anachronistic, irrelevant to many in the art world. She had never needed to sell her work to earn a living, and she refused to part with her paintings: the Fothergill portrait was stolen by the subject, Romaine claimed, not given to him. No portrait of John Brooks, who died of cancer in 1929, was ever done, a rather odd omission from her wide-ranging portrait production. Romaine Brooks was, and is, a rather remote figure in black, white, and grey. She never felt completely at ease anywhere or with anyone. Unable to accept that she was subject to normal human frailties, Brooks descended into the dreaded, despised world of Ella; like her mother, she ate and slept at odd hours and inhabited a tomb-like room devoid of all color, except black. Her biographer Secrest wrote that to "have let go of her rage would have removed the barriers between her and life," but the major barrier was the specter of Ella Goddard that was more real to Romaine than life itself.

SOURCES:

Baker, Michael. *Our Three Selves: A Life of Radclyffe Hall.* London: GMP Publishers, 1985.

Secrest, Meryle. *Between Me and Life: A Biography of Romaine Brooks.* Garden City, NY: Doubleday, 1974.

SUGGESTED READING:

Blume, Mary. Article on Romaine Brooks in *Réalités*, December 1967.

Breeskin, Adelyn. Essay on Romaine Brooks in "Thief of Souls." Catalogue of National Collection of Fine Arts exhibition, March 1971.

Kramer, Hilton. "Romaine Brooks: Revelation in Art," in *The New York Times*. April 14, 1971.

"Revival of Romaine Brooks," in *The New York Times*. April 25, 1971.

Young, Mahonri Sharp. Essay on Romaine Brooks in *Apollo*. London, May 1971.

Jeanne A. Ojala, Professor of History, University of Utah, Salt Lake City, Utah

Broom, Mrs. Albert (1863–1939).

See Broom, Christina.

Broom, Christina (1863–1939)

British news and documentary photographer who is often called Britain's first woman press photographer. Name variations: Mrs. Albert Broom. Born Christina Livingston in 1863, probably in London; died in 1939, probably in London; married Albert Broom; children: Winifred; may have been others.

Christina Broom began working as a news photographer at age 40 to help support her ailing husband. Using an old plate-box camera, she took one of her first photographs of the prince and princess of Wales (*Mary of Teck [1867–1953]) opening tramways at Westminster in 1903. Broom's second photo was of the winning horse and jockey on Derby Day at Epson. Shortly after, her pictures were in great demand, and she began selling postcards of her local views through stationery shops.

She was soon documenting national and international events, including the effects of World War I on the home front, 30 years of Oxford and Cambridge boatrace crews, *Edith Cavell's fu-

neral, the arrival of the first women police with *Mary Sophia Allen (1878–1964) standing smartly with her squad, and investitures and deaths of the British monarchs. Broom became especially well known for her important documentation of woman suffrage marches and exhibitions; she also remained the official photographer of the Senior Regiment of the First Life Guards until her death in 1939. "I have photographed all the king's horses and all the king's men," she said, "and I am never happier than when I am with my camera among the crack regiments of Britain."

Notes Val Williams in *The Other Observers*, her survey of Britain's women photographers, Broom's "self-styling as a 'Press Photographer' misleads when considered in contemporary terms, for although she photographed important events and personalities throughout her career, she was essentially a recordist who eschewed the primary task of press photography, which is to dramatise and bring the news to vivid life. This quality, together with the seeming lack of viewpoint or polit-

Photograph of Christabel Pankhurst, at the International Suffragette Fair, Chelsea, 1912, by Christina Broom.

ical centre in her photographs, has made Christina Broom something of an oddity within photographic history and has often deprived her of the serious consideration she deserves."

SOURCES:

Rosenblum, Naomi. *A History of Women Photographers.* NY: Abbeville Press, 1994.

Williams, Val. *The Other Observers.* London: Virago Press, 1991.

Barbara Morgan,
Melrose, Massachusetts

Brophy, Brigid (1929–1995)

British novelist, critic and playwright, who was one of the most entertaining, acute and witty critics of the 1960s and 1970s. Born Brigid Antonia Brophy in London, England, on June 12, 1929; died in Louth, Lincolnshire, on August 7, 1995; daughter of John Brophy and Charis Grundy Brophy; educated at St. Paul's Girls' School; awarded Jubilee Scholarship and studied classics at St. Hugh's College, Oxford; married Sir Michael Levey (author and former director of the National Gallery, London), 1954; children: one daughter, Katharine.

Awards: Cheltenham Literary Festival Prize for first novel (1954); fellow of Royal Society of Literature (1973).

Selected publications: Hackenfeller's Ape *(Hart-Davis, 1953);* The Finishing Touch *(Secker and Warburg, 1963);* Mozart the Dramatist *(Harcourt, 1964);* Don't Never Forget *(Cape, 1966); (with Michael Levey and Charles Osborne)* Fifty Works of Literature We Could Do Without *(Rapp and Carroll, 1967);* Beardsley and His World *(Harmony Books, 1976);* Baroque 'n' Roll *(David and Charles, 1987).*

Brigid Brophy grew up in a literary household. Her mother **Charis Brophy**, a strong feminist, was a teacher, nurse, and prison visitor, and her father John Brophy was a prolific novelist and critic. His best-known novel, *Waterfront* (1934), set on the Mersey River in Liverpool, was turned into a film, as were two other novels. He was chief fiction critic of the *Daily Telegraph* and, during World War II, edited *John O'London's Weekly.* His daughter began writing at a precociously early age, mainly poetry and drama, but gave it up when she found that "there was no great market for blank verse dramas on the Middle Ages." Her father was more percipient, and in 1940 he wrote: "I have a daughter, ten years old, who excels me in everything, even in writing." Brophy and her father were very different: "We never agreed what *is* good art or bad art, yet we were at one in our preoccupation with the problem."

Though of Irish parents, John Brophy was born in Liverpool. Even so, Brigid Brophy described him at the time of his marriage as an Irishman of "poetic temperament, luminous purity and Sinn Fein politics." She was very aware of her Irish background. By nativity, schooling and economics, she acknowledged, she was English but "my exact sociological situation is too complex to allow me to make the simple assertion that I am English." She prided herself on her Irish rationality but confessed that the geography and history of Ireland "hold my imagination in a melancholy magic spell." Dublin and Limerick "are cities beautiful to me not only with some of the most superb and most neglected architecture in Europe but with a compelling litany, a whole folklore, of tragic and heroic associations." She could not sit through Yeats' *Cathleen Ni Houlihan* without crying, but this was not because she was Irish but because the history of Ireland was so sad. She belonged by upbringing to a highly specialized class "those who are reared as *Irish* in England." However, she detested the narrow nationalism and religious intolerance she saw in Ireland and resented the banning of her books by Irish censorship. She was, she concluded, "an awkwardly rational third generation immigrant."

Brophy's classical education contributed precision and clarity to already formidable gifts. Her novels and critical writings reflected a polymathic range of interests: animal rights, atheism, feminism, opera, pacifism, psychoanalysis, and vegetarianism. Her originality was apparent in her first novel, *Hackenfeller's Ape,* which she considered "probably the best I shall ever write," and which dealt with the predicament of a zoologist who sets an ape free from London Zoo because it will be used in a scientific experiment. The theme was an unusual one for the time, but Brophy, a lifelong anti-vivisectionist, had no patience with the cozy anthropomorphism of some animal lovers. "The whole case for behaving decently to animals," she wrote in 1965, "rests on the fact that we are the superior species."

Between 1962 and 1964, Brophy published four novels of which two, *Flesh* and *The Finishing Touch*, are considered among her best. *Flesh* is the story of a young Jewish couple, second generation London Jews, reacting against the social and sexual mores of their parents. *The Finishing Touch*, more controversial, was described by Brophy as a "lesbian fantasy," the story of a young English girl at a French finishing school run by two English lesbians. Lesbianism was also a theme in her 1978 novel *Palace Without*

Chairs, while, in 1969, her experimental novel *In Transit* was an exploration of transsexuality and gender identity. She spoke out strongly against all forms of sexual prejudice, particularly homophobia, at a time when homosexual activity was still illegal in Britain. This prejudice, she argued constantly, led to sexual hypocrisy at the highest levels and to the blackmail of innocent people. Her forthright views on sex led to her being described as the "arch priestess of the permissive society."

In the 1960s and 1970s, Brophy had a high profile on television, radio, and in the press, yet there were contradictions in this. She was a private person and her nervousness was sometimes evident in her media appearances. She also admitted that she hated writing and was impossible to live with when doing so. Some critics thought she should have stuck to "serious writing," which she countered by saying that her journalism *was* serious writing. She was one of the most entertaining, acute and witty critics of the 1960s and 1970s, fearless in tackling controversial subjects and with a mischievous gift for pricking pomposity. Her 1966 collection of essays and reviews, *Don't Never Forget*, discusses subjects as diverse as the rights of animals, the immorality of marriage, the British sense of humor, and *Fanny Hill*. There is a prescient essay on women in which she observed that the invisible barriers restricting women (such as dictates about what constituted "womanly" behavior) were as powerful as the formerly visible ones and that the emancipation of both sexes was necessary, not just women's. The collection also contains an affectionate portrait of her mother whom she compares, tongue-in-cheek, to Lady Macbeth ("I have differed from my mother on every fundamental issue and agreed with her on every practical one"), and a scathing indictment of British sexual hypocrisy in the essay "The Nation in the Iron Mask." This was a talk written for BBC Radio in 1963 at the height of the John Profumo-*Christine Keeler* political and sexual scandal then paralyzing the British establishment. Brophy described the scandal as "the most dazzling free entertainment laid before the British public since the trial of Oscar Wilde" and commented that the British public "comported itself as a dotty old imperial dowager saying 'Hush dear, not in front of the servants.'" The talk was too iconoclastic for BBC tastes and was never broadcast.

Brophy's iconoclasm was demonstrated to further effect in 1967 in a book she published with her husband Michael Levey and a friend, Charles Osborne, *Fifty Works of English (and American) Literature We Could Do Without*. In an "address to the reader" they asked: "Do you *really* like, admire and enjoy the works in question, or do you merely think you ought to?" English Literature "is choked with the implied obligation to like dull books." Some reviewers were outraged by their ruthless puncturing of great reputations, others were hugely entertained. *Jane Eyre* was "like gobbling a jar-full of schoolgirl stickjaw"; Gerard Manley Hopkins wrote "the poetry of a mental cripple"; *To the Lighthouse* was "like some beautifully painted, delicately tinted old parchment which has been made into a lampshade after a labour of several years"; of *Lady Chatterley's Lover,* they commented "all that removes Lady C. from the run of under-the-drier reading is . . . the philistinism with which it ridicules Sir Clifford for reading Racine"; on T.S. Eliot, "It may be that the means whereby T.S. Eliot prevailed upon the world to mistake him for a major poet was the simple but efficient confidence trick of deliberately entitling one or two of his verses 'Minor Poems.'"

On this evidence it is not surprising that Brophy was feared as a critic by authors who were still living. She had a merciless eye and slaughtered with gusto several sacred cows of the English literary establishment. In 1964, she wrote of Evelyn Waugh that only he could write like a baroque cherub but "a baroque cherub on a funerary urn, forever ushering in the *Dies Irae.*" She rubbished comprehensively A.L. Rowse's *William Shakespeare,* which was written "in a prose half-timbered when it is not half-baked, thatched with disintegrating archaisms." She also took aim at *Simone de Beauvoir** whom she considered to be one of the most overrated figures in postwar French writing: "a mind capable of missing entire points, and incapable both of the precision of an artist and of the accuracy of a scholar. Not inspired enough to be slapdash, it was often slipshod. In short, a plodder."

Brophy dismissed those who attacked her as a "controversialist," a term used, as she saw it, by people who disliked making up their minds. "When I think a book a bad work of art I say so to the best of my expository prose. . . . I entertain far too much respect for art to be a 'respecter of persons'—a curious phrase whose meaning has nothing to do with respecting people and everything to do with kowtowing to or fearing powers and influences."

Brophy loved opera and had a particular reverence for Mozart. Her 1964 novel *The Snow Ball* was a modern reworking of *Don Giovanni* and in the same year she published *Mozart the Dramatist*, subtitled "A New View of Mozart, His Operas and His Age," which was strongly influenced by her interest in Freudian psychoanalysis. She later wrote the introduction to Lionel Salter's translations of *The Magic Flute* and *The Seraglio*.

Her fascination with the era of the 1890s was shown in two books on Aubrey Beardsley, *Black and White: A Portrait of Aubrey Beardsley* (1968) and *Beardsley and His World* (1976). One of her most substantial works of nonfiction was *Prancing Novelist* (1973), a biography of Ronald Firbank whose influence on her own fiction was occasionally observed, notably in *The Finishing Touch*. She also wrote the introduction to 1966 Pantheon edition of **Elizabeth Smart's** *By Grand Central Station I Sat Down and Wept* and for the Pan Books edition of *Pride and Prejudice* by ***Jane Austen** who was one of her favorite authors. Her excursions into drama were less successful. She wrote a radio play for the BBC in 1964 *The Waste Disposal Unit*, and in 1968 her only stage play *The Burglar* was produced in London, to a mixed critical reaction.

In the 1970s, Brophy actively took up a cause dear to her father's heart, public lending right (PLR), which would give authors a fee whenever their books were borrowed from public libraries. She and **Maureen Duffy** formed the Writers' Action Group in 1972 to lobby for PLR, which was eventually granted in 1979. (Brophy wrote *A Guide to Public Lending Right* in 1983.) She also served on other writers' organizations; the Writers' Guild of Great Britain from 1975–78 and as vice-chair of the British Copyright Council 1976–80.

A committed atheist, Brophy wrote a number of pamphlets in defense of secularism and against the role of religion in the state. She also attacked the campaign on pornography led by Lord Longford in the early 1970s, which she thought was an invitation to more oppressive censorship.

One of Brophy's last books was *The Prince and the Wild Geese*, a short, charming account of an abortive 19th-century romance between a young Irish girl, **Julia Taaffe**, and a Russian noble, Grégoire Gagarin (whose original drawings provided the illustrations). The following year, 1984, Brophy was diagnosed with multiple sclerosis, an illness that led to increasing physical infirmity. She wrote movingly about the disease in "A Case-Historical Fragment of Autobiography," which was included in her last volume

of essays *Baroque 'n' Roll* (1987). What she most resented about the illness, she wrote, was her dependence on other people, especially those she loved, her family and friends. It was a disgusting illness that "inflicts awareness of loss" and "is accompanied by frustration. . . . I have in part died in advance of the total event." But typically she also used this essay to restate her total opposition to vivisection in the search for a cure for multiple sclerosis.

SOURCES:

Brophy, Brigid. *Baroque 'n' Roll and Other Essays*. London: David and Charles, 1987.

———. *Don't Never Forget: Collected Views and Reviews*. London: Jonathan Cape, 1966.

Contemporary Authors Autobiography Series. Vol. 4. Detroit, MI: Gale Research, 1986.

Contemporary Authors New Revision Series. Vol. 25. Detroit, MI: Gale Research, 1989.

Dictionary of Literary Biography: British Novelists since 1960. Vol. 14. Detroit, MI: Gale Research, 1982.

Deirdre McMahon, Dublin, Ireland, Assistant Editor, *Dance Theatre Journal* (London) and author of *Republicans and Imperialists* (Yale University Press, 1984)

Brough, Louise (1923—)

American tennis player and four-time Wimbledon champion. Name variations: A. Louise Brough, Louise Brough Clapp. Pronunciation: Bruff. Born Althea Louise Brough in Oklahoma City, Oklahoma, on March 11, 1923; daughter of a wholesale grocer; educated at the University of Southern California.

Won the Wimbledon singles title (1948, 1949, 1950, 1955), the Wimbledon doubles title with Margaret Osborne du Pont (1946, 1948, 1949, 1950, 1954), and the Wimbledon mixed doubles (1946, 1947, 1948, 1950); won the British women's singles (1948, 1949, 1950); won the British women's doubles (1946), the French doubles (1946, 1947, 1949), and the U.S. doubles 12 times (1942–50, 1955–57); won the U.S. mixed doubles (1942, 1947, 1948, 1949).

After World War II, Louise Brough was an American powerhouse on national and international tennis courts. Born in Oklahoma City in 1923, she moved at age four with her divorced mother to Beverly Hills, California. Though the athletic ten-year-old found tennis a "bit too prim for her energies," Louise practiced with her brother J.P. on the public courts of Beverly Hills. She quickly lost interest, however, when an aunt forced her to wear a white school dress to the courts. At age 13, Brough again took up the sport under the tutelage of Dick Skeen, who had coached ***Pauline Betz**. Despite an overenthusiastic mother who suffered when she lost, Brough developed a classic forehand and backhand, as well as a winning American twist serve.

A strong singles player, Brough won the Wimbledon singles championship four times and was thrice runner-up. She was also a talented doubles player. Paired with *Margaret Osborne du Pont, Brough won six Wimbledon titles, twelve U.S. doubles titles, and three French titles. *Martina Navratilova and Pam Shriver were the only pair to approach the doubles record set by Brough-Osborne. Singles rivals as well as good friends, Brough and Osborne battled away in two of the longest final matches in major tournament history: the nationals in 1948 (which went to Osborne) and the 1949 Wimbledon (won by Brough). *Billie Jean King noted that the two were as "different as topspin and slice." In mixed doubles, Louise Brough saw four triumphs at Wimbledon and was also a four-time winner in the States. From 1941 to 1950 and again from 1952 to 1960, she was ranked in the top ten.

Around 1950, Brough began having trouble throwing the ball straight up on serve and also developed a case of tennis elbow on a trip to Australia. "I'd throw the ball different places, and they'd call a foot fault on me, and I got tenser and tenser. . . . And then I had a great big suitcase that I carried on and off places with my right arm. I really think the suitcase had more to do with it than anything." She continued to compete long after her prime. Younger players were saddened to watch as she tossed the ball up with a "quivering hand" and caught it again and again. "I played too long," said Brough, "It's hard to give up a trip to Wimbledon." In 1967, Louise Brough was inducted into the International Tennis Hall of Fame.

SOURCES:

King, Billie Jean, with Cynthia Starr. We Have Come a Long Way. NY: McGraw-Hill, 1988.

Markel, Robert, Nancy Brooks, and Susan Markel. For the Record: Women in Sports. NY: World Almanac Publications, 1985.

Robertson, Max, and Jack Kramer. The Encyclopedia of Tennis.

Karin Loewen Haag,
Athens, Georgia

Broughton, Rhoda (1840–1920)

British novelist who published more than 25 works of romantic fiction. Born Rhoda Broughton in Denbighshire, North Wales, on November 29, 1840; died in Headington Hill, Oxford, England, on June 5, 1920; daughter of Jane (Bennett) Broughton (daughter of a Dublin lawyer) and Delves Broughton (a cleric); educated at home; never married; no children.

Selected works: Not Wisely but Too Well (1867); Cometh Up As a Flower (1867); A Fool in Her Folly (1920).

Born in Denbighshire, North Wales, on November 29, 1840, Rhoda Broughton was the youngest of four children of Reverend Delves Broughton and **Jane Bennett Broughton**. She grew up in an Elizabethan manor house, complete with library, and was educated at home by her father, who emphasized reading, particularly poetry. Following the death of her father in 1863 (her mother had died three years previous), Rhoda moved to her sister Eleanor's home, bringing with her an early draft of the novel *Not Wisely but Too Well*. Published in 1867, this work was the beginning of Broughton's routine of a novel every two years. All were published anonymously until *Goodbye Sweetheart* in 1872.

The proceeds from Broughton's extremely popular fiction brought both financial security and celebrity. She became friends with Henry James and enjoyed the social scene. Author Percy Lubbock noted: "There was the cut of her talk, the cheerful slash of her phrase, the snap and crackle of her wit, with all this Rhoda was a personage indeed, not lightly to be engaged, but on no account to be missed or forgotten."

In her provincial hometown, the love affairs Broughton depicted in her fiction were considered risqué, an assessment subsequently made of the author as well. Thus, in 1888, Rhoda and Eleanor moved to London where Broughton was admired instead for her forthright and imposing personality. Eleanor tended their home so that Rhoda might devote her full attention to writing. From then on, Broughton spent a portion of each year in the Chelsea district, becoming a full-time resident in 1890 when she and Eleanor, her constant companion, moved to Richmond. There they remained until 1894, at which time Eleanor's sudden death left Broughton at loose ends.

Returning to the Oxford area, Broughton henceforth lived with a cousin. She was hampered by severe arthritis and, for her final 20 years, frequently dictated her novels. In 1920, she spent a final season in London, receiving friends at a rented flat and working regularly. Rhoda Broughton died in Oxford on June 5 of that year, age 79.

SUGGESTED READING:

Wood, Marilyn. *Rhoda Broughton: Profile of a Novelist.* Stanford, England: Paul Watkins, 1993.

Crista Martin,
Boston, Massachusetts

Brousse, Amy (1910–1963)

American spy, codenamed Cynthia, who managed to acquire Italy's and Vichy France's naval ciphers, a phenomenal boon to the Allies during World War II.

Name variations: Elizabeth Pack; (codename) Cynthia; (pen name) Elizabeth Thomas; (nickname) Betty. Born Amy Elizabeth Thorpe in Minneapolis, Minnesota, on November 22, 1910; died of cancer of the jaw and throat on December 1, 1963; daughter of Major George Cyrus Thorpe, U.S. Marines, and Cora (Wells) Thorpe; married Arthur Pack (a diplomat with the British foreign service, commercial counsellor in the British legation in Santiago, Chile); married Charles Brousse (a French attaché); children: (first marriage) Anthony George Pack (b. October 2, 1930), Denise Avril Beresford Pack (b. January 31, 1934).

She was the "greatest unsung heroine" of World War II, said Sir William Stephenson, the famous Canadian who directed British secret intelligence activities. Known only as Cynthia, Amy Thorpe Pack Brousse did not look like a spy, she looked like an amateur tennis champion. She was wholesome, beautiful, and well-bred, with wide-set green eyes. She was also inordinately restless.

On November 22, 1910, Amy Elizabeth Thorpe was born into a family of achievement. Her father George Cyrus Thorpe was a professional marine who had graduated from Annapolis, obtained a degree in the arts from Brown University, served in the Spanish-American War and in the Philippines after the insurrection, and received the Order of the Star of Ethiopia from Emperor Menelik. Her mother **Cora Wells Thorpe** had graduated *cum laude* from the University of Michigan, then attended Columbia, the Sorbonne, and the University of Munich. With their three children (Jane, George, and Amy), the Thorpes were a family on the move, traveling from post to post. When Amy was five, they moved to Cuba, where they lived throughout World War I.

Amy and her mother were in perpetual conflict, though not to the outside world. Cora was a social butterfly, a believer in manners and ritual, and she was very ambitious for her children. Brousse, in turn, was driven. She told her biographer H. Montgomery Hyde:

> Always in me, even when I was a child, were two great passions: one, to be alone, the other, for excitement. Any kind of excitement—even fear. Anything to assuage my terrible restlessness and the excruciating sense of pressure (that came from where or

what I never knew) that was only released in action, in doing, in exhaustion. I remember when we were very young and running races I always ran past the finish line and ran and ran and ran until I dropped half strangled when my endurance finally gave out. . . . The same drive impelled me to write a novel when I was not yet eleven.

Called *Fioretta*, the story was set in Naples.

The family moved from Cuba to Washington, then on to Hawaii when her father was appointed commander of the Marines at Pearl Harbor in August 1921. When his tour of duty came to an end, he resigned from the service and took his family to Europe. The girls were placed in a school in Territet, Switzerland, overlooking Lake Geneva (Riant Château) for one year. The family returned to the States, and Brousse attended Dana Hall in Wellesley, Massachusetts; she then made her debut in Washington (D.C.) society in the summer of 1929.

Befitting her family status, Amy was soon engaged to a suitable man. Arthur Pack was 19 years her senior and second secretary on the commercial side of the British Embassy in Washington. Married on April 29, 1930, they honeymooned in England where Amy discovered she was pregnant, a jot too early for those who kept monthly accounts. Pack, who was somewhat of a bully, was terrified for his reputation and foreign-service career; he wanted her to abort the child, but she fought to keep it. When her son Anthony George Pack was born in secrecy on October 2, 1930 (five months after the wedding), Pack would not allow her to bring the boy to the United States on their return. Instead, her son was boarded out to a couple in Shrewsbury (who eventually became his foster parents), and Brousse was only allowed a few surreptitious visits when the couple was on leave in England. "He was the most beautiful boy I have ever seen," she told Hyde. "He looked like Rupert Brooke in his younger years." She was to see him rarely.

One year later, as Amy turned 21, Pack was transferred to Santiago, Chile. While there, he received the Order of the British Empire from George V in 1933. Brousse made many friends, went horseback riding, and learned to speak Spanish fluently; she also had an extramarital affair. On January 31, 1934, she gave birth to her daughter Denise Avril Beresford Pack. In spring 1935, her husband was transferred to Madrid, Spain.

They arrived four years after Alphonso XIII had walked away from the throne, and a struggle for control was being waged by the leftists (called the Popular Front, or Republicans, and

Amy
Brousse

Azaña and the Republicans, the British Embassy was less than amused by her efforts.

One year later, following a transfer to Warsaw, Poland, Arthur Pack was diagnosed with a cerebral thrombosis and was invalided home to London to recover. Brousse remained in Warsaw with their daughter until they could ascertain whether or not he would be able to return to his post. She continued to be invited to diplomatic dinners by the Polish Foreign Office and became friends with those in high places. One night in March 1938, a diplomat divulged to her that Hitler was about to invade Czechoslovakia and that Poland planned on gaining from the invasion. She then told a friend at the British Embassy, unaware that he was the principal agent for His Britannic Majesty's Secret Intelligent Service in Poland. He told her to learn all she could, that British Intelligence was extremely interested.

She learned that in the carving up of Czechoslovakia, "Poland was to get the frontier region of Teschen, to the southwest of Cracow, where there was a Polish minority living under Czech rule," wrote biographer Hyde. "She duly reported this piece of news to [her liaison], who relayed it to London. After the Munich agreement, the Czechs were forced to hand over the Teschen district to Poland, who insisted on her share of the spoils, much to the disgust of all her friends in the West." Amy Brousse had become a secret agent.

She was told to cultivate Polish contacts and to entertain discreetly, returning hospitality, for which she was given £20 a month.

> At one of these dinners I found myself sitting beside a fascinating and madly attractive young Pole, whom I shall call Jan. He told me that he was very close to Colonel Beck, the Polish Foreign Minister. In a sense, he was in charge of the minister's private office. This meant that all confidential and even top secret departmental papers passed through his hands. . . . When I heard what his job was, I would have made a dead set at him, even if he had been as ugly as Satan. But happily this wasn't necessary.

She began an affair with her Polish connection.

Brousse was in Warsaw for one year before she returned to her husband, now convalescing in St. Jean-de-Luz. In April 1939, Pack was again posted to Santiago, Chile. When Hitler invaded Poland in September 1939, she was enraged; she was also aware of the pro-Axis feeling in Chile at the time. Under the pen name Elizabeth Thomas, she wrote a pro-Allies column in Spanish in *La Nación,* pouring out a steady stream of inflam-

made up of Socialists and the working class) and rightists (called the Falange, or Nationalists, and composed of landowners, middle class, and the hierarchy of the Roman Catholic Church). When the Packs moved to Spain, the rightists were in power, but the country, with continual strikes, was drifting toward revolution.

Brousse was a perfect handmaiden for a diplomat. She was enthusiastic about each country, learned the language quickly, and jumped into the social swirl, where she was popular with local high society. Her husband encouraged her friendships, especially those he considered useful. Brousse fell in love with a Spaniard, a senior officer in the Spanish Air Force, who worked at the Air Ministry. With the outbreak of Civil War in Spain, the Packs had to evacuate Madrid in July 1936; they set up their embassy at the French border town of St. Jean-de-Luz. From the sidelines, Amy became involved with the International Red Cross in Burgos, raising funds for medical supplies for Francisco Franco's forces. Since Britain was still recognizing only President matory articles. When the German Embassy in Chile, aware of the columnist's identity, eventually put up a squawk, Brousse decided to leave Chile to save face for the British Embassy. She also got in touch with the British Secret Service in London to tell them that she was available.

In August 1940, after writing a letter confessing her dalliances so that her husband might start proceedings for a divorce and save his career, she left for New York to meet with British Intelligence. She was given the codename Cynthia. Told to move to Washington D.C. with her daughter, rent a house, and start entertaining, she was also told to look up an old friend, Albert Lais, now the Italian naval attaché in Washington, and determine why he had been sent there. Amy soon managed to pry the key to Italy's secret cipher from the naval attaché's office. Wrote *Time* magazine in her obituary, "British Intelligence thereafter proved uncannily adept at forestalling Italian fleet movements, notably in the March 1941 sea battle off Greece's Cape Matapan, where the Royal Navy crippled Italy's numerically superior force."

Then asked to penetrate the Vichy French Embassy in Washington, she decided to pose as an American journalist. She contacted the French press attaché and asked for an interview with Ambassador Henry-Haye. The attaché was a married man named Charles Brousse. Initiating an amorous liaison with Brousse, she soon learned that he despised Henry-Haye as well as Pierre Laval, prime minister of Vichy France and an open collaborator with the Germans. Charles was soon sharing valuable information about Vichy underground activities in America. When he learned the Vichy French embassy was about to abolish his post, he had the choice of being transferred back to France or staying in the U.S. where he would work at a lower level with lower pay. Brousse convinced him to stay in America. Since Charles was bitter toward the British, she told him she was an American agent and convinced him that this would be a patriotic way to help her country by divulging secrets of the Vichy Embassy. He agreed. "From then onwards," wrote Hyde, "there was a steady flow of information passing through her hands. This eventually included every happening of importance of which the ambassador had knowledge and deciphered copies of every current official telegram received by and despatched from the Embassy, as well as telegrams of older date which Charles contrived to extract from the chancery files." The information exposed what had long been suspected by British Intelligence. The Vichy ambassador to the States was collect-ing information in America that could hinder the British War effort and passing it on to Vichy and the Nazis in France. One telegram to France's Admiral Jean-François Darlan apprised him of the condition of every British warship docked in American waters for repairs and refitting.

In March 1942, Amy was called to New York and asked to obtain the impossible: the Vichy French naval ciphers. Unbeknownst to her, they were needed for the British-American invasion of North Africa in order to ascertain the composition of the French fleet. By now, the U.S. had entered the war, and the British Service was working closely with American Bill Donovan and his O.S.S. (Office of Strategic Services). At first, she told the British her chance for success was nil; by the time she reached Washington, she was determined to supply the ciphers.

Brousse soon learned that the code room at the Vichy French Embassy was accessed by only two men—the chief cipher officer and his assistant—and that it was guarded night and day. She also learned that the chief cipher officer was retiring. When a meeting with him proved fruitless, she met with his assistant and tried to convince him that his loyalty was to the French people, not to a treasonous government. Again, she had no luck. She told her superiors that, as far as she was concerned, burglary was the only way in. Using a romantic ruse, Charles Brousse then convinced the Embassy doorman that he needed a trysting place. Thus Amy was allowed into the Embassy with Charles while the doorman gallantly looked the other way. The couple met there night after night, as the guard grew used to their presence. On an appointed evening, she secretly let a locksmith, known as the Georgia Cracker, in the front door. Together, they snuck down to the code room, picked the lock of the office door, and, after three attempts, figured out the combination of the safe. At approximately 1 AM, they retrieved the cipher books and handed them to a confederate outside the embassy who took them away to be photographed; the cipher books reappeared promptly at 4 AM, and Amy returned them to the safe. When Hyde asked in later years if she had been afraid something might go wrong, she replied:

> I was not afraid of going to prison, or being shot, or being bitten by the dog. I was afraid of making a mess, especially as we knew there were two FBI cars sitting down the street at the corner of Constitution Avenue and Wyoming Avenue watching every move. If anything had gone wrong, there would have been repercussions on the SIS, on the State Department and all over the place.

Brousse saw intelligence service as the first-line of defense. "Nothing either in cold warfare or hot warfare can be done without good intelligence work," she told Hyde just before her death in 1963. "It is the basis and fundamental principle of everything else, of lives and policies, and of not making mistakes as in the recent Cuban disaster at the Bay of Pigs. A secret intelligence service should attract intelligent people and honest people and patriotic people just as the armed forces do." When American and British troops landed in North Africa they met with little resistance because of the ciphers. Her efforts changed the course of the war.

After World War II, Arthur Pack committed suicide, and Amy married Charles Brousse. Her son, whom she began to know later in life, was killed in action in the Korean War. A heavy smoker, Amy Brousse died of cancer of the jaw and throat on December 1, 1963. By a special dispensation of the French government, she was allowed burial, under the shade of a favorite cedar, on the grounds of the castle of Castellnou, where she and husband Charles Brousse had spent their days following World War II. Of those last days, she said to Hyde, "I hope and believe I was a patriot."

SOURCES:

Hyde, H. Montgomery. *Cynthia*. NY: Farrar, Straus, 1965.

Time magazine (obituary). December 20, 1963.

Brouwenstijn, Gré (1915—)

*Dutch soprano. Name variations: Gre Brouwenstijn. Born Gerada Damphina on August 26, 1915, in Den Helder, the Netherlands; studied with Japp Stroomenbergh, Boris Pelsky, and **Ruth Horna** in Amsterdam.*

Debuted in Amsterdam (1940); joined the Netherlands Opera (1946); made Covent Garden debut (1951), singing roles there until 1964; made Chicago debut (1959) and Glyndebourne (1959); retired (1971).

Gré Brouwenstijn was known as much for her marvelous physical presence as for her voice. She was often called a "great singing actress" in a field that demands both excellent singing and acting. Unfortunately, recordings that documented her career do not do justice to her greatness. Her remarkable interpretation of operatic roles featured an expressive face that was responsive to every nuance of character, and she was known for investing the grandest, most regal heroines with a basic humanity, a feat many singers have never duplicated.

Brown, Ada (1889–1950)

American jazz singer and pianist. Born Ada Scott in Kansas City, Kansas, on May 1, 1889; died in Kansas City on March 31, 1950; daughter of H.W. and Anna (Morris) Scott; cousin of James Scott, noted ragtime composer and pianist.

Billed in her day as "Queen of Blues," Ada Brown is often omitted from the annals of jazz greats. She was born into a musically inclined family and sang in church as a child before launching her career in 1910 at Bob Mott's Pekin Theater in Chicago. She reportedly worked clubs in Paris and Berlin, then became a regular with the Bennie Moten Band during the early 1920s. From the mid-1920s, Brown did widespread theater tours throughout the U.S. and Canada, and appeared in black revues and musical comedies up and down Broadway. Brown was featured at the London Palladium in the late '30s and appeared with Fats Waller in the film *Stormy Weather* (1943). One of her last appearances was in *Memphis Bound* (1945), shortly before her retirement. As a footnote to her career, Brown was one of the original incorporators of The Negro Actors Guild of America in 1936. She moved to Kansas City, Kansas, after leaving music, and died there of kidney disease in 1950.

Brown, Alice (1856–1948)

American novelist and dramatist. Born in Hampton Falls, New Hampshire, on December 5, 1856; died in Boston, Massachusetts, on June 21, 1948; attended local school and Robinson Seminary in Exeter.

Best known for her analysis of New England characters and consciences in her short stories and novels, Alice Brown also authored biographies of *Mercy Otis Warren (1896) and *Louise Guiney (1921), some verse, and a book on English travels. In 1913, Winthrop Ames offered a prize of $10,000 to the best play (to be submitted anonymously) by an American playwright. In June 1914, judges Augustus Thomas, Adolph Klauber, and Ames selected *Children of Earth*, by Alice Brown above nearly 1,700 other manuscripts. In January 1915, Ames produced the play at the Booth Theater in New York.

Brown, Antoinette (1825–1921).

See Brown Blackwell, Antoinette.

Brown, Cleo (c. 1907—)

American jazz pianist and vocalist. Name variations: C. Patra Brown. Born Cleopatra Brown on December 8, 1907, or 1909, in Meridian, Mississippi; sister of pianist Everett Brown.

The daughter of a Baptist minister, Cleo Brown was born on December 8, 1907, or 1909, in Meridian, Mississippi. After the family moved to Chicago in 1919, she studied music, played the piano in church, and learned boogie from her brother, pianist Everett Brown. In the late 1920s, Cleo started touring with shows. Moving on to clubs and radio, she had her first break when she replaced Fats Waller on his New York radio program. This led to recording opportunities and further club bookings in New York, Chicago, Los Angeles, San Francisco, and Las Vegas. During her heyday, Brown had her own series on WABC and led her own group at the Three Deuces in Chicago. Taken seriously ill during the late 1930s, she was in a California sanitarium from 1940 to 1942, then resumed her career until 1953, when she quit the music business to go into nursing. After her retirement in 1973, Brown took up inspirational music, playing and singing under the name C. Patra Brown. The quality of her piano work was said to surpass that of her singing, and her rendition of *Pinetop's Boogie-woogie* influenced many musicians.

Brown, Dorothy (1919–)

First African-American woman surgeon in the American South. Name variations: "D" Brown. Born Dorothy Lavinia Brown on January 7, 1919, in Philadelphia, Pennsylvania; Bennett College, Greensboro, North Carolina, B.A., 1941; Meharry Medical College, Nashville, Tennessee, M.D., 1948; children: one adopted daughter, Lola Cannon Redmon.

Destined to become the first black surgeon in the South, Dorothy Brown would remain ever mindful of her struggle and would devote much of her life to helping others. She was born on January 7, 1919, in Philadelphia, Pennsylvania. Her mother, young and unmarried, left her in a Troy, New York, orphanage as an infant. When mother and daughter were reunited 13 years later, Dorothy was unable to adjust to the relationship and, after running away several times, was placed as a mother's helper in Albany, New York. Encouraged by her employer, she was able to move back to Troy, where she completed high school while living with a foster family. Through the Methodist Church in her community, she won a scholarship to Bennett College in Greensboro, North Carolina, graduating second in her class. In 1944, after working a variety of jobs with the Army Ordinance Department, Brown had saved enough money to enter Meharry Medical College in Nashville, Tennessee. After graduating in the upper third of her class, Brown spent a year as an intern at Harlem Hospital in New York City but was denied a surgical residency at the hospital because of a bias against women surgeons. Undaunted, she returned to Meharry and convinced the chief of surgery to admit her there. After completing her residency in 1954, she continued to practice in Nashville, becoming a fellow of the American College of Surgery. She later became attending surgeon at George W. Hubbard Hospital and professor of surgery at Meharry Medical College.

Brown's life continued to be punctuated by firsts. At the age of 40, she became the first single woman in modern times to adopt a child in the state of Tennessee. She named the little girl Lola Redmon in honor of her foster mother. In 1966, she was the first black woman to be elected to the lower house of the Tennessee State Legislature. She ran for a seat in the Tennessee Senate in 1968, but lost due to her liberal stand on abortion rights.

Brown received honorary doctoral degrees from Bennett College and Cumberland University in Lebanon, Tennessee, and remained an active member of the United Methodist Church. She worked to raise money for the 12 black colleges and universities supported by the denomination.

Brown, Earlene Dennis (1935—)

Three-time Olympian and the first American woman to win an Olympic medal in shot put. Born on July 11, 1935 in Latexo, Texas; attended public elementary and high school; attended Compton Junior College; completed a machinist training program sponsored by the Comprehensive Educational and Training Act (CETA); married; children: Reggie and Lamar.

Won Olympic bronze medal for women's shot put, 53'10⅜;'', took fourth in discus (1960); held American citizen outdoor record in shot put and discus; became Amateur Athletic Union Champion, shot put (1956–62, 1964); won AAU championship, discus (1958–59, 1961); placed sixth in shot put, fourth in discus, in Olympics (1956); won AAU championship, baseball throw (1957); won gold medal in shot put, silver medal in discus, USA-USSR dual meet (1958); took silver medal in shot put, USA-USSR dual meet (1959); was shot put and discus champion, Pan-Amer-

ican Games (1959); placed 12th in shot put, Olympics (1964).

Born in Latexo, Texas, on July 11, 1935, Earlene Brown would make magic when she tried her hand at the shot put. In this difficult event, an athlete does not throw the ball; rather, it is pushed or "put" from the shoulder, using the competitor's body weight to achieve momentum. For a sport in which the weight of the ball (8 pounds 13⅘ ounces, and 4 inches in diameter) must be balanced on the base of the fingers, an athlete needs an accommodating hand. If she holds the ball too high, stiff fingers produce a poor release; if she holds the ball too low in the palm, the release won't be as sharp or quick. Recalled Brown: "My mother told me that the first thing she noticed about me when I was born were my hands."

When I was young I was ashamed of my size. I never thought something of which I was ashamed— my size and strength—could make me feel proud. But I feel proud now.

—**Earlene Brown**

Earlene Brown was an only child whose parents separated when she was three. "One thing I can say about my mother," Brown would later remark, "is that she might not have been rich, but everything I ventured into she tried to help me." From her father, a semipro baseball player with the Negro League in Texas, Brown received her athletic heritage, and she excelled early at a number of sports. Brown was playing outfield in a softball game, about age ten, when a ball slammed toward her: one of those great hands shot up and made a Willie Mays one-handed catch. She wanted to play shortstop, but her coach had other plans; for the next six years, she would travel through Northwest towns as the team's catcher.

With the boys, she played volleyball, softball and football in good weather. "I played house and dolls when it was raining," she recalled. "I would make a little grass doll. I'd take a soda-pop bottle and piece of a clothesline and unravel it. Then I would put a clothespin in the bottle and tie the rope on it. I would take a matchstick and roll the rope around it and make a hairstyle." In later years, Brown, an internationally renowned athlete, would look to hairstyling to make enough money to pay the rent and put food on the table.

As a teenager, she excelled in track and field. A large girl (Brown said she couldn't remember ever weighing less than 180 pounds), she could run the 100-yard dash in 12.8 seconds, fast enough to beat the competition in Los Angeles' city-wide track meets where she competed as a member of the DAP, California's equivalent to New York's Police Athletic League. Before she took on the shot put and discus, Brown anchored the relay team and usually won the basketball throw. In 1958, age 23, she would break the American record for the basketball throw at the Amateur Athletic Union (AAU) indoor meet in Akron, Ohio. On the first day of competition, smaller participants were achieving better distance. That night, Brown crawled into bed annoyed and puzzled: "I dreamed that I took the basketball and ran up with it like you do a javelin; I was holding the basketball just like I would a javelin. I did my cross-over step and buried my left foot and I whipped the ball over." The next morning, she was the first one at the gym: "I took the ball in my hand to see if I could handle it that way and I could. In competition, later, I threw the ball so far that it flapped up against the wall of the gymnasium." During the meet, Brown broke **Amelia Wershoven**'s record. Wrote **Frances Kaszubski** in the *Amateur Athlete*: "Earlene made the old American record of 105 feet 9½ inches seem almost ridiculous by comparison with a throw of 135 feet 2 inches. This was an unbelievable 30 feet over the old record."

Addie Valdez, Brown's high-school gym teacher, first put the discus in those talented hands, and in the schoolyard Brown's history teacher taught her to shot put. Though he showed her a cumbersome method top athletes had by then abandoned, Brown would win a national championship with this, the crossover, technique. With no formal training, Brown's own athletic instinct defined these early victories; later, with little time to train in the push and shove of an impoverished existence, they would define her career.

Brown did not join the AAU until she was 21, by which time she was married and had a son Reggie. When her son was less than six months old, she was informed by Valdez that it was not too late to begin training for the 1956 Olympics in Melbourne, Australia. Brown recalled thinking, "Hey. I didn't know you got to travel overseas. I want to see the world! Wait 'till I tell my husband." But her husband was struggling to find his place in her new life. Despite no coaching or track athletic background, he tried serving as her coach, but the venture was short-lived. Behaving as she thought a "proper wife" should, she deferred to his authority: "To start off with, I asked him if I could go. That was a mistake, because I gave him the authority to tell me whether or not I could go. He ordered me not to go." Unwilling to live with the ultimatum, she and her son moved back home with her mother. To support herself, Brown worked as a domestic, training in her spare time.

All the elements of the shot put came together for Brown in August of 1956 when she competed in the AAU Outdoor Nationals held in Philadelphia. There, she set a new American record with a throw of 45', while also taking second for the discus. It seemed unlikely, however, that Brown would be able to defend her American record at the Olympic trials held a week later in Washington, D.C., because she did not have the money to attend. *The Sentinel*, Los Angeles' black newspaper, took up a collection and sent her; this gesture not only supported Brown as an individual athlete but also opened the door for the sports' history she was to shape. Sportswriters across America began to write about Brown, as she overtook **Lois Testa** in shot put and **Pam Kurrell** in discus to become a double winner and the leading member of the Olympic team. Less than four months after she joined the AAU, Brown held the American records for shot put and discus.

At the 1956 Games, Brown would not medal, though she was to improve her American record. Fans back home heard that she, Pam Kurrell, and *Willye B. White were showing the Nigerians and Russians to rock 'n' roll, and readers enjoyed the image of the easygoing, popular Brown. Athletes of different nationalities sought out the woman whom biographer Michael Davis has described as the "big powerful brown girl in white horn-rimmed glasses who is as light on her feet as a ballerina." Brown was 5'9" and weighed 265 pounds.

Following the Olympics, Brown spent the next two years competing in AAU and national track-and-field competitions. In 1957, at the AAU Outdoor Nationals held in Cleveland, Ohio, she placed second in both the discus and the shot put, a record she was to improve in 1958 at the Outdoor Nationals in Monmouth, New Jersey. The winners of this meet were scheduled to participate in a series of international track-and-field events in Europe, and the prospect of overseas travel was a great motivator for Brown. She competed fiercely and won a gold medal, breaking her old American record in shot put with a throw of 47'5½";. She also won a gold medal in discus with a toss that sailed 152'5½".

The European meets proved a showcase for Brown. "Mrs. Earlene Brown is the toast of Moscow," gushed the Associated Press, "just as she was the most widely known of the United States athletes in the Olympic Village in Melbourne in 1956." She did not disappoint. In the shot put, Brown threw further than any American athlete ever and took the gold medal with a toss of 54'3½". Her performance in the discus was almost as impressive when she took second with a throw of over 162'. At the Warsaw meet, she won the gold medal in both shot put and discus.

The European meets ended in Athens, Greece, where Brown gave a stunning performance. In the discus event, she threw an amazing 153'8¾". Not only did she win the gold medal, but the discus flew out of the stadium and into the crowd, soundly smacking two spectators. When Earlene learned she had hit someone, she went over with an interpreter to apologize. Replied one of the spectators: "That's alright; it doesn't hurt much; but could I have your autograph." Brown hugged the woman to the delight of the crowd.

She returned home with seven gold medals and one silver. Many compared her to *Babe Didrikson Zaharias and said she had the potential to become one of the greatest women athletes ever. In a country that did not provide training, job security, and housing for its amateur athletes, Brown lacked only the finances to fully realize this potential. To fend for herself and her son, she began attending Henrietta's Beauty College to become a beautician. The long hours spent on her feet in a cubicle, inhaling the fumes of hair oils while washing and styling women's hair, made her too tired for the rigorous training undertaken by many of her peers. In addition to the demands of earning a living, Brown rarely had any athletic-club affiliation, no team to support and inspire her. When it came to coaches, she spoke frankly about her personal weaknesses: "Coaches were always asking me to train the way they wanted me to train. They were always telling me to run two laps around the track and do sitting-up exercises. I would run around the track for one lap just to please the coach, but if he wanted two, he would have to run the second one himself."

It is a testament to Brown's outstanding innate abilities that in 1959 she won first place in the AAU Outdoor Nationals and set meet records when she participated in the Pan-American Games later that year. She placed second in the dual USSR-USA meet, making it easy for observers to overlook the toll her lifestyle was taking; nonetheless, her throw was three feet shy of the previous year's.

During the 1960 Olympics in Rome, Brown repeated the role she played in the 1956 Olympics as "mother-hen" to all the team members. She organized card games and dancing and was a close friend to *Wilma Rudolph. After winning the first of her three gold medals, Rudolph abandoned the photographers and well-wishers to run the length of the Olympic stadium to embrace Earlene. After Rudolph's success, Brown and *Barbara Jones awaited her with a towel and comb to help Rudolph "pretty up" before the flash of the cameras. "I was so happy when Wilma started winning her three gold medals," said Brown. "After her first medal I hugged her and went out and threw the shot for the bronze medal." Brown's throw of 53'10⅜" brought the U.S. its first Olympic medal in the shot put competition. Two weeks later, she went on to complete in track-and-field meets in Frankfurt, West Germany, and Greece.

After returning home in 1961, Brown entered the AAU Indoor competition and was again chosen to represent the U.S. in a series of European meets. But financial constraints kept her home. Having just purchased a beauty shop for $10,000 with a $1,000 down payment, she had to find additional beauticians and attract clients. Her status as a world-class athlete was of no consequence to the customers on whom she would have to rely to keep up the mortgage payments. With the 1962 AAU Outdoor Nationals held in Los Angeles, Brown juggled her customers and competition, but she was barely hanging on to fifth place after the first qualifying rounds and used her lunch hour for a training blitz. Brown's last throw with the shot put cleared a distance of 48'10½", giving her the championship once again. She also took second in the discus. The following year, her performance declined. Unable to run the beauty shop and spend adequate time training, she lost her AAU national titles and could not represent the U.S. abroad. Unable to take even second in the shot put or discus, she was deeply hurt by the defeat.

Though many counted her out, Brown did not give up so easily. "A hundred times I've said I'd quit," she said, "but each time I'd get the old urge to travel, and I'd be at it again." Her comeback seemed apparent at the Olympic trials in 1964, where she qualified in shot put though not in discus. With only three days of training with the Olympic team, she was off to Tokyo, Japan. Brown had less than two weeks training at the University of Tokyo before competition, and her Olympic performance showed the lack of preparation. Despite a disappointing 12th-place finish, Brown became the only athlete in the world to ever reach the finals in the shot put in three consecutive Olympics. Davis points out the disparity between Brown's training opportunities and those of other athletes: "It is painful to reflect on what her performance might have been with anything like the three months of intensive training each Russian athlete had before the Tokyo Olympics."

When Brown left amateur sports, she became a Roller Derby superstar and was a member of several professional teams in the 1970s. After retiring from the Roller Derby, Brown worked as a janitor and completed a machinist training program. For Brown, sports and competition had been a road out of the ghetto. "Sports is the greatest thing for any individual to have," she said. "Without sports I would have been nothing. I don't see where life would have had any meaning."

SOURCES:

Davis, Michael D. *Black American Women in Olympic Track and Field.* Jefferson: McFarland, 1992.

Hollander, Phyllis. *100 Greatest Women in Sports.* NY: Grosset and Dunlap, 1976.

Jacobs, Karen F. "Earlene Brown: Down from Olympia," in *Essence.* May 1979, p 12.

Gaynol Langs, independent scholar, Redmond, Washington

Brown, Georgia (1933–1992)

British singer and actress. Born Lillian Claire Laizer Getel Klot in London, England, on October 21, 1933; died in London on June 6, 1992; daughter of Mark (a furrier) and Anne (Kirshenbaum) Klot; attended Central Foundation Grammar School, London; married Gareth Wigan, November 7, 1974; children: one son.

Selected films: A Study in Terror (UK/Ger., 1965); The Fixer (US, 1968); Lock Up Your Daughters (1969); The Raging Moon (Long Ago Tomorrow, 1971); Tales that Witness Madness (1973); Nothing but the Night (1973); Galileo (US/UK, 1975); The Seven Per Cent Solution (US, 1976); The Bawdy Adventures of Tom Jones (1976); Love at Stake (1988).

Born in London in 1933, Georgia Brown gained her early experience as a night-club singer. Her first appearance on the London stage was in 1956 as Lucy Brown in *The Threepenny Opera*, a role she repeated in her New York debut, replacing *Lotte Lenya. Brown's career would include theater, films, television, recordings, and cabaret, as she shuttled back and forth between the United States and England.

In the 1960s, Brown was lauded for her portrayals of Jeannie in *The Lily White Boys* and Nancy in the musical *Oliver!*; for the latter, she received the *Variety* Critics Poll Award (England) in 1961. She also made her Broadway debut in *Oliver!* (1962), receiving a nomination for an **Antoinette Perry* (Tony) Award in 1963. Returning to London, she took over the title role in *Maggie May* and appeared in *Artists Against Apartheid*, both 1965. Her later stage work included Widow Begbick in *Man is Man* (London, 1971) and *Side by Side by Sondheim* (New York, 1977).

Georgia Brown made movies sporadically and was seen on television in the BBC's "Tophat" (1950), "Show Time" (1954), and a production of *Mother Courage* (1960). In the U.S., she appeared on game shows, talk fests, and the "Ed Sullivan Show." She performed cabaret at clubs throughout the world, including the famous Blue Angel in New York. Georgia Brown died in 1992, age 58, after a brief illness.

Brown, Hallie Quinn (c. 1845–1949)

African-American pioneer educator, writer, civil-rights leader, and elocutionist. Born on March 10, around 1845, in Pittsburgh, Pennsylvania; died in Wilberforce, Ohio, on September 16, 1949; daughter of Frances Jane (Scroggins) Brown and Thomas Arthur Brown; granted B.S., Wilberforce University, 1873; never married; no children.

Awards: honorary Master of Arts, Wilberforce University (1890); member of the Royal Geographical Society (1894); honorary Doctorate of Law, Wilberforce University (1936); Hallie Quinn Brown Memorial Library of Central State University named in her honor; Hallie Q. Brown Community House in St. Paul, Minnesota, named in her honor.

Moved to Chatham, Ontario, Canada (1865); returned to U.S. (1870); enrolled Wilberforce University (1870), graduated (1873); taught in South Carolina and Mississippi (1873); appointed dean of Allen University (1875); taught in Dayton, Ohio, public school system (1887); appointed dean of women at Tuskegee Institute, Alabama (1892); appointed professor of elocution, Wilberforce University (1893); addressed the World Congress of Representative Women, Chicago (May 18, 1893); made first trip to Europe (1894); spoke at the World's Women's Christian Temperance Union Conference, London, England (1895); founded the first British Chautauqua, Wales (1895); presented to Queen Victoria (July 7, 1899); elected president of Ohio State Federation of Women's Clubs (1905–12);

represented the Women's Parent Missionary Society of the African Methodist Episcopal Church at the World Missionary Conference in Edinburgh, Scotland (June 14–23, 1910); Julia Emery donated $16,000 to Wilberforce University (1910); Keziah Emery Hall completed (1913); appointed president of the National Association of Colored Women (1920); met Senators Lodge, Shortbridge, McCormick, and President Harding to promote anti-lynching legislation (1922); retired from Wilberforce University (1923); addressed the Republican National Convention (1924); protested segregated seating at the All-American Music Festival of the International Council of Women in Washington, D.C. (1925).

Selected publications: Bits and Odds: A Choice Selection of Recitations for School, Lyceum, and Parlour Entertainment *(Xenia, OH: Chew, 1884);* Trouble in Turkeytrot Church *(printed privately, 1917);* Tales My Father Told Me and Other Stories *(Wilberforce, OH: 1925);* Our Women: Homespun Heroines and Women of Distinction *(Xenia, OH: Aldrine, 1926);* Pen Pictures of Pioneers of Wilberforce *(Xenia, OH: Aldrine, 1937).*

The exact year of Hallie Brown's birth is unknown. We do know, however, that she was born on March 10, around 1845, in Pittsburgh, Pennsylvania, the fifth of six children. Her parents Thomas and **Frances Brown** were freed slaves. Born in Frederick County, Maryland, Thomas Brown, son of Scottish plantation owner Ann Brown and her African-American overseer, purchased his freedom in 1843. Frances Brown was also of mixed parentage. Born in Winchester County, Virginia, she was freed by her white grandfather, a veteran of the American Revolution. The couple wed in 1840. Thomas Brown was employed as a steward and express agent on the river boats that traveled between Pittsburgh and New Orleans; he also owned a substantial amount of real estate prior to the Civil War.

The Brown household became a frequent stop for slaves fleeing to Canada on the Underground Railroad. Thus, Hallie Brown was exposed to the injustices faced by African-Americans at an early age. In 1864, the family moved to Chatham, Ontario, Canada, due to Frances Brown's poor health. It was here that Hallie received her early education. In 1870, the Browns returned to the United States and settled in Wilberforce, Ohio, where they built Homewood Cottage.

In 1868, Hallie Brown enrolled at Wilberforce University, a Methodist Episcopal Church institution for African-Americans. While a student, she heard *Susan B. Anthony speak on women's suffrage. Thus, the rights of women became a lifelong concern. In 1873, Brown graduated sixth in her class with a Bachelor of Science degree. During the summers, she studied at the Chautauqua Lecture School, graduating as the salutatorian of her class in 1886.

Following graduation, Brown was drawn to the South by the pressing need for teachers. In the aftermath of the Civil War, conditions were primitive. At first, she ran a school on the Sonora plantation in Mississippi, teaching both children and adults. Like many plantation schools, the building was in a state of constant disrepair. When her entreaties to local authorities to make repairs to the roof fell on deaf ears, she and one of her students repaired it themselves. Brown's reputation as a devoted and talented teacher spread quickly. She moved to Yazoo City, where she taught public school. Due to the turbulent atmosphere in Mississippi during the 1870s, her mother feared for her safety, however, and Hallie Brown sought employment elsewhere. From 1875 to 1887, she taught at Allen University in Columbia, South Carolina. She also served as dean and administered the university's night-school program.

Returning to Ohio in 1887, Brown taught in the Dayton public-school system for four years and established a night school for adults based on the Allen University model. The plight of African-Americans from the South concerned her greatly. In 1892, Brown briefly accepted the position of dean of women at Booker T. Washington's Tuskegee Institute in Alabama. Afterwards, she returned to Wilberforce University, where she became a professor of elocution in 1893. At Wilberforce, she met two other prominent African-American teachers, *Elizabeth Keckley who taught home economics, and W.E.B. Du Bois, who taught Latin and Greek. In subsequent years, Brown became a member of the Board of Trustees. Until shortly before her death, she would continue to teach Sunday School classes at Wilberforce.

While teaching in Dayton, Brown met Professor Robertson of the Boston School of Oratory and soon enrolled. The event proved to be the beginning of a long career as a public speaker. She frequently performed with the Wilberforce Concert Company, later known as the Stewart Company. A family friend, Bishop Daniel A. Payne, agreed to sponsor a lecture tour in the South in an effort to raise money for Wilberforce. Over the years, Brown lectured in every state in America, with the exception of Maine and Vermont. Her favorite topic was African-American folklore and songs, and she was always well received. Noted the Red Oaks (Iowa) *Express:*

> Miss Hallie Q. Brown has but few equals as an elocutionist. She has a sweet, flexible voice. Her enunciation is distinct, her manner graceful and her gesticulations eminently appropriate to the character of her selections. Some of her humorous selections caused wave after wave of laughter to roll over the audience and were most heartily encored.

On May 18, 1893, Hallie Brown addressed the overwhelmingly white World Congress of Representative Women at the Columbian Exposition in Chicago on the need for African-American women's organizations. Other speakers included *Francis E.W. Harper, *Fannie Jackson Coppin, Sarah J. Early, *Fannie Barrier Williams, and *Anna Julia Cooper.

Brown founded the Neighborhood Club in Wilberforce and welcomed the formation of national organizations for African-American women, such as the Colored Women's League, which was founded in 1894, and the National Federation of Afro-American Women, which was founded in 1895. The mandate of these organizations focused primarily on aiding the poor, the elderly, and the sick, but they were also devoted to the cause of women's suffrage. These groups gave African-American women a national voice for the first time.

From 1894 onwards, Brown undertook several trips to Europe, spending considerable time in Germany, Switzerland, and France, and lecturing throughout Britain. In Edinburgh, Scotland, she became a member of the Royal Geographical Society. Her 1894 tour was sponsored by the noted abolitionist Frederick Douglass, whom she had met in Chicago the year before. Douglass supplied her with letters of introduction to aid her fund-raising efforts for the Wilberforce University library.

Brown was also an organizer and advocate in the Women's Christian Temperance Union. In 1895, she was the American representative to the World's Women's Christian Temperance Union Conference held in London, as well as one of the speakers. In the same year, she founded the first British Chautauqua in Northern Wales. On a subsequent visit to Britain in 1899, Brown was presented to Queen *Victoria and spoke before Her Majesty and *Alexandra of Denmark, princess of Wales. During the celebration of Queen Victoria's jubilee, Brown was the guest of the Lord Mayor of London. While there, she also participated in the International Conference of Women. After the death of Queen Victoria, Brown appeared before King George V and Queen *Mary of Teck in a command performance.

From 1905 to 1912, Hallie Brown served as the president of the Ohio State Federation of Women's Clubs. She also represented the Women's Parent Missionary Society of the African Methodist Episcopal Church in 1910 at World Missionary Conference in Edinburgh, Scotland. She stayed in Britain for seven months, and the *Sheffield Daily Telegraph* dubbed her "one of the finest female elocutionists in the world." While there, Brown persuaded London philanthropist **Julia Emery** to donate half the necessary funds for a dormitory for Wilberforce University. The rest of the building was paid for by Andrew Carnegie. In 1913, the dormitory was named in honor of **Keziah Emery**, Julia Emery's mother.

In 1920, Hallie Brown was appointed president of the National Association of Colored Women and held the position until 1924. As president of the NACW, she supported the efforts of the National Association for the Advancement of Colored People (NAACP) to defeat national and state legislation that would have prohibited interracial marriages. She also established a scholarship for girls unable to afford higher education and sat on the selection committee for many years. Eventually the scholarship was named in her honor. As well, Hallie Brown raised funds for the preservation of Frederick Douglass' home in Washington, D.C.

Hallie Brown was active in national and state politics. At various times, she was vice-president of the Ohio Council of Republican Woman, a member of the Advisory Committee of the National League of Women Voters, a member of the Colored Women's Department of the Republican National Committee, and chair of the executive committee of the Negro Women's National Republican League. In a letter to President Warren Harding in 1921, Brown complained about the opposition of white female federal employees to the appointment of an African-American registrar to the treasury. In her letter, she suggested that if the women were uncomfortable with the appointment, African-American women would be happy to replace them at their jobs at treasury.

Brown often spoke out against discrimination. She met with senators and President Harding in 1922, in an effort to secure anti-lynching legislation. At the Republican National Convention of 1924 in Cleveland, she spoke in support of Harding's nomination. This was probably the first time a woman of color addressed a national political convention. Subsequently, she supported Herbert Hoover's candidacy for the presidency.

In 1925, Hallie Brown delivered an angry speech to the All-American Music Festival of the International Council of Women in Washington, D.C. Initially the Daughters of the American Revolution refused the International Council's request to use Memorial Continental Hall. A compromise was reached, in which African-Americans would sit separately from the rest of the audience. In her speech, Brown protested the segregated seating. Unless the seating arrangements were changed, she threatened to withdraw African-American performers from the conference. Clearly furious, Brown declared that "this is a gathering of women of the world here and color finds no place in it." After her speech, 200 African-American performers refused to take part in the event, which was also boycotted by African-American members of the audience. *The New York Times* tersely reported that "feeling they have been discriminated against, a group of black women walked out of the International Council of Women's Conference."

That same year, Brown published *Tales My Father Told Me and Other Stories.* The collection, based on stories her father had heard while working on the river boats, contained highly romanticized accounts of women escaping from the bonds of slavery. In each tale, the narrator is Brown's father who contrives to rescue the women, though never through force. Brown also included a brief history of African-American spirituals, which she compared to Hebrew songs of the Diaspora. A year later, she published *Our Women: Homespun Heroines and Women of Distinction,* a collection of short biographies of 55 African-American and African-Canadian women. Among those featured were her mother Frances Jane Scroggins Brown, and her aunt, **Eliza Anna Scroggins.** *Our Women* proved to be one of the best early books on the subject.

In 1923, Hallie Brown retired from Wilberforce University due to illness. Never one to remain idle, however, she continued to speak on such diverse topics as education, black culture, the poetry of Paul Laurence Dunbar, African-American women's rights, and the struggle of the black community for equal rights. Brown, who never married, lived in her ancestral Homewood Cottage. On September 16, 1949, she died of coronary thrombosis in Wilberforce, Ohio, and is buried in the Brown family plot in Massie's Creek Cemetery.

As a noted educator, Brown's career as an elocutionist at Wilberforce University spanned 30 years. She did much to promote adult education for African-Americans, and her fund-raising efforts on behalf of Wilberforce led to the construction of much-needed facilities. For her efforts, the Hallie Quinn Brown Memorial Library at Central State University is named in her honor, as is the Hallie Q. Brown Community House in St. Paul, Minnesota.

Hallie Brown's spirituality underpinned a strong belief that social change could be accomplished through religion. Through education, clubs, and political lobbying, she sought to raise the status of African-American women. In public addresses, she linked the political emancipation of African-American women with the well being of the African-American community.

Brown led a rewarding and diverse life, which bridged pre-Civil War America with the modern period. On the political front, she was a tireless campaigner for equal rights, meeting kings and queens, prime ministers, presidents, congressional representatives, and senators.

SOURCES:

Carby, Hazel V. *Reconstructing Womanhood*. Oxford: Oxford University Press, 1987.

Fisher, Vivian Njeri. "Brown, Hallie Quinn," in *Black Women in America*. Edited by Darlene Clark Hine. Brooklyn: Carlson, 1993.

Hendricks, Wanda A. "Brown, Hallie Quinn," in *African American Women*. Edited by Dorothy C. Salem. NY: Garland, 1993.

Lamping, Marilyn. "Hallie Quinn Brown," in *American Women Writers*. Edited by Lina Mainiero. NY: Frederick Ungar, 1979.

Roses, Lorraine Elena, and Ruth Elizabeth Randolf. *Harlem Renaissance and Beyond*. Boston, MA: G.K. Hall, 1990.

SUGGESTED READING:

Locke, Mamie E. "Hallie Brown," in *Notable Black American Women*. Edited by Jessie Carney Smith. Detroit: Gale Research, 1992.

Hugh A. Stewart, M.A., University of Guelph, Guelph, Ontario, Canada

Brown, Helen Gurley (1922—)

American author and editor. Born in Green Forest, Arkansas, on February 18, 1922; daughter of Ira M. and Cleo (Sisca) Gurley; attended Texas State College for Women (now Texas Women's University), 1939–42, and Woodbury Business College, 1942; married David Brown (a motion-picture producer), September 1959.

Selected writings: Sex and the Single Girl *(1962);* Sex and the Office *(1964);* Outrageous Opinions *(1966);* Single Girl's Cookbook *(1969);* Sex and the New Single Girl *(1970);* Having it All *(1982);* The Late Show: A Semiwild But Practical Survival Plan for Women Over 50 *(1993).*

Helen Gurley Brown was a fast-rising star in the advertising business, winning two Frances Holmes Advertising Copywriters awards before her marriage to film producer David Brown and the appearance of her controversial bestseller *Sex and the Single Girl*. She followed this playful celebration of the single lifestyle with *Sex and the Office,* in 1965, the same year of her appointment as editor-in-chief of *Cosmopolitan,* a family magazine in decline. Using ideas developed jointly with her husband, Brown revamped the magazine into a glossy, upbeat publication that appealed to a previously untapped audience of young, newly liberated women. Within a few years, she turned *Cosmopolitan* into one of the five top-selling magazines in the U.S. and had made the "Cosmo Girl" the ideal among her young readers. While many decried the magazine's emphasis on physical attractiveness and what was viewed as male baiting, Brown went on to achieve personal celebrity, espousing her views on television and in further publications, including an autobiographical work, *Having It All* (1982), and a manual for the aging Cosmo girl, *A Semiwild But Practical Survival Plan for Women Over 50* (1993). In 1985, Brown won the New York Women in Communications Award and established a research professorship in her name at Northwestern University. She retired from *Cosmopolitan* in 1997.

Brown, Kay (1903–1995)

American producer and agent. Name variations: Kay Brown Barrett. Born in 1903; died of a stroke in Hightstown, New Jersey, on January 18, 1995; graduated from Wellesley College, 1924; married James Barrett; children: two girls.

A powerful Hollywood agent who once ran Selznick International Pictures in New York, Kay Brown was best known for having prodded David O. Selznick into buying the rights to a book titled *Gone with the Wind,* even though his initial reaction was "A Civil War story won't go." She was also responsible for importing European talent, including *Ingrid Bergman, Alfred Hitchcock, *Vivien Leigh, and Laurence Olivier, as well as handling some of early Hollywood's brightest stars. Known as one of the most tenacious agents in the business, Kay Brown counted among her clients Arthur Miller, *Isak Dinesen, *Lillian Hellman, John Gielgud, and Alec Guinness. Of Dinesen, Brown commented: "I adored her work. But I couldn't get anyone to listen to me about *Out of Africa* in 1952."

Brown, Linda

African-American woman whose Supreme Court case, Brown v. *Board of Education,* *destroyed the legal basis for racial segregation in public schools. Born in Topeka, Kansas; daughter of Reverend Oliver Brown.*

In 1951, as a fourth-grade student at a black elementary school in Topeka, Kansas, Linda Brown unwittingly became the subject of one of the most important Supreme Court decisions to affect racial equality in the United States. Weary of the long walk and bus ride from her home to school each day, Linda applied to attend a nearby public elementary school for white children. When she was turned away, her father, the Reverend Oliver Brown, and 12 other parents, sued the Topeka Board of Education. When a three-judge panel heard the case, it decided that since African-American and white schools in Topeka were equal, or so they maintained, blacks were not discriminated against and therefore could not attend white schools. The Browns and the other parents appealed the decision to the Supreme Court, forcing the judges to confront the explosive issue of segregation in public elementary schools.

The case, which became known as *Brown* v. *Board of Education,* was deliberated for three years. The desegregation decision, handed down in May 1954, simply stated that racially segregated schools were unconstitutional. The passionate reactions to this decision have since been written into the history of school desegregation in the United States, along with the names of Linda Brown, *Ruby Bridges, Charlayne Hunter-Gault, *Daisy Bates, ☘▶ Elizabeth Eckford, and ☘▶ Minnijean Brown.

SOURCES:

Baker, Liva. "With All Deliberate Speed," in *American Heritage.* Vol. XXIV. February 1973.

Brown, Maggie (1867–1932).

See Brown, Molly.

Brown, Marcia (1918–)

American artist and author of children's books. Born in Rochester, New York, on July 13, 1918; one of three daughters of Clarence Edward (a minister) and Adelaide Elizabeth (Zimber) Brown; studied at Woodstock School of Painting, summer, 1938; New York College for Teachers (now State University of New York at Albany), B.A., 1940; studied at New School for Social Research, Art Students League, and Columbia University; studied at Zhejiang Academy of Fine Arts, Hangzhou, China, 1985.

Selected works (all self-illustrated): The Little Carousel *(1946);* Stone Soup: An Old Tale *(1947);* Henry-Fisherman: A Story of the Virgin Islands *(1949);* Dick Whittington and His Cat *(1950);* Skipper John's Cook *(1951);* The Flying Carpet *(1956);* Felice *(1958);* Peter Piper's Alphabet *(1959);* Tamarindo! *(1960);* Once a Mouse . . . *(1961);* Backbone of the King: The Story of Paka'a and His Son Ku *(1966);* The Neighbors *(1967);* How Hippo! *(1969);* The Bun: A Tale from Russia *(1972);* All Butterflies: An ABC *(1974);* The Blue Jackal *(1977);* Listen to a Shape *(1979);* Touch Will Tell *(1979);* Walk with Your Eyes *(1979);* Lotus Seeds: Children, Pictures and Books *(1985).*

Respected as both a storyteller and an illustrator, Marcia Brown grew up with a book in one hand and a pencil in the other. "My interest in making picture books," said Brown, "comes in an almost unbroken line from the constant reading and drawing of my childhood." Encouraged to take pleasure in the visual world, the young Brown also enjoyed music and visiting libraries, particularly the library in Cooperstown that had a small museum on the top floor. After completing college in 1940, she taught English and dramatics for several years before moving to New York City, where she finished her first four books while employed in the children's department of the New York Public Library. Brown would continue her art studies at intervals throughout her career. Between 1956 and 1962, she lived and painted for periods of time in Europe, and as late as 1985, at age 67, she studied at Zhejiang Academy of Fine Arts in Hangzhou, China.

Her first book, *The Little Carousel,* was inspired by Brown's neighborhood in the Italian district of Greenwich Village. "From my apartment window, I saw the little carousel arrive," she recalled, "and the episode that makes the plot of the story happened before my delighted eyes." Her second story, the much loved *Stone Soup,* was the first of her books to be chosen a runner-up for the Randolph Caldecott Medal given by the American Library Association. From 1950 to 1954, Brown produced five more books, four of which were Caldecott honor books and the fifth, *The Steadfast*

☘▶
Eckford, Elizabeth *and* Minnijean Brown. *See* Bates, Daisy (b. 1914) *for sidebar.*

Tin Soldier, was a Caldecott Medal winner. Many of her subsequent books were also award winners, including *Cinderella* (Caldecott Medal), *Once a Mouse . . .* (Caldecott Medal, Lewis Carroll Shelf Award, and *The New York Times* Choice of Best Illustrated Children's Books of the Year), and *Shadow* (Caldecott Medal). In 1977, Brown was also awarded the Regina Medal from the Catholic Library Association for "continued distinguished contribution to children's literature."

As both an illustrator and writer, Marcia Brown was especially concerned with the unity between text and picture, believing that the visual aspect of the book was as important in the revelation of the story as the words: "Rhythm of speech is echoed in rhythm of line and color. Never must there be a mere recounting of the event." Brown's techniques were as varied as her stories and each new work represented a new approach. Ultimately her goal was to present part of her unique self to her young readers. "Those who work with children," Brown offered, "should be encouraged to hand on to them their personal involvement with the world. A child needs the stimulus of books that are fo-

Marcia Brown

cused on individuality in personality and character if he is to find his own."

Barbara Morgan,
Melrose, Massachusetts

Brown, Margaret (1867–1932).

See Brown, Molly.

Brown, Margaret Wise (1910–1952)

American author of the classic children's book Goodnight Moon *and innovator in children's literature. Name variations—pseudonyms: Golden McDonald, Juniper Sage, and Timothy Hay. Born Margaret Wise Brown on May 23, 1910, in New York City; died in Nice, France, on November 13, 1952; daughter of Robert Bruce Brown (an executive with the American Manufacturing Company) and Maude Margaret (Johnson) Brown (a homemaker); educated at Château Brillantmont in Switzerland, Dana Hall School in Wellesley, Massachusetts, and Hollins College, B.A., 1932; never married; no children.*

Published first book, When the Wind Blew *(1937); served on the publications staff of the Bank Street School, New York City; served as editor at W.R. Scott Publishers (1937–41); wrote more than 100 books and lyrics for 21 children's recordings, including* Goodnight Moon.

Margaret Wise Brown once told a publisher that she would write a manuscript for a children's book in 20 minutes—and polish it for a year. She was an amazingly creative writer, one who published over 100 of her own books, as well as adaptations, translations, stories, and poems. Brown's books feature the work of 40 different artists, reflecting her exacting demands that the illustrations be perfectly suited to the text. It was her practice to try out her stories on audiences of young children. Their responses would influence the book's final form. Half of her books are still in print, some have entertained three generations of readers.

Margaret Wise Brown was born in Brooklyn, New York, the middle child of Robert Bruce Brown, a successful businessman, and **Maude Johnson Brown**. When Margaret was quite young, her family moved to Whitestone Landing on Long Island, where she had woods and beaches to explore, as well as the company of dozens of animals. Brown later claimed that she was too busy as a child to remember many books that she read, although she did recall that *The Song of Roland, Black Beauty, Peter Rabbit,* and *Snow White* all seemed true to her, and that

Aladdin was the most exciting of all fairy tales. Even as a child, Brown delighted in making up stories to tell her friends. At the same time, she had a need for privacy that was to be characteristic throughout her life.

Brown attended schools on Long Island until her teen years when she and her sister were sent to the Château Brillantmont School in Switzerland where she developed "a touch of the cosmopolitan," and then to Dana Hall in Wellesley, Massachusetts. There she acquired the nickname "Tim," because her hair was the golden color of timothy grass. Margaret then enrolled in Hollins College in Virginia, her mother's alma mater. One of her former professors later described Brown at Hollins as "an individualist, a nonconformist." She enjoyed people more than the discipline of college work and was known for her eccentric behavior, including carrying a red stool back and forth on the train from New York because she wanted it in both places and it would not fit in her trunk. At Hollins, Brown majored in English and developed the love of literature, which she regarded as necessary for any successful writer. In Brown's words, before becoming a writer, one should have "fallen in love with Chaucer's affectionate naming of all the things in his world about him; Shakespeare's pounding rhythms and certain meanings and some of Wordsworth for his simplicity." When she received her B.A. in 1932 and was asked her plans after graduation, she replied, "Lord knows."

All I want to do is write a story that seems absolutely true to the child who hears it and to myself.

—**Margaret Wise Brown**

Returning to New York, Brown enrolled in a short-story course at Columbia University but dropped out because, in her words, she "couldn't think up any plots." In fact, she tried unsuccessfully throughout her life to write adult fiction. But Brown was more a poet than a storyteller, noted **Louise Seaman Bechtel**.

In 1935, Margaret joined an experimental writing group led by *Lucy **Sprague Mitchell** and associated with the Bureau for Educational Experiment, later known as the Bank Street School. The school broke new ground in the education of young children, integrating developmental research, teacher training, and preschool education. At Bank Street, Brown both listened to children tell their own stories and studied children's responses to stories read to them, a

technique she would use throughout her life to test her own writings. Brown became a sort of protégée of Mitchell, herself a pioneer in children's literature. Mitchell had developed the "here and now" approach to children's books—an attempt to enter the child's world, to see things through the child's eye. Mitchell's books took place in a contemporary urban setting and were characterized by the rhythmic use of children's own speech patterns. Ironically, Brown's first book, *When the Wind Blew* (1937), differed from the "here and now" formula. The book, a fantasy based on a story by Anton Chekov, concerned an old lady who had a toothache, 17 cats, and a kitten who comforted her when the wind blew up from the sea.

Also in 1937, Brown met William Scott and became the first editor at his firm founded to publish books for preschool and nursery-age children. During her initial year with Scott, Margaret published four of her own books and edited such innovative volumes as *Cottontails,* a "feely book" with red glass buttons for apples and a cotton ball for the bunny's tail, designed to be handled by young children. Brown knew that young children would squeeze, bite, throw, and tear books, therefore she had her next work, *Bumble Bugs and Elephants,* printed on heavy cardboard stock. It featured "big and little" creatures, a device that would reappear in many of Brown's stories.

In 1939, Brown wrote *The Noisy Book,* the first of a series in which a little dog with bandaged eyes must guess at the sources of the sounds around him. The child becomes involved in the story as he or she responds by guessing the sound before turning the page. Margaret designed the books for children too young to sit wordlessly still while a story was read to them. "Children wrote these books and I was merely an ear and a pen," she wrote. "And also by some accident, one who shared their pleasure or inattention with them." With her typical sense of the absurd, she noted that dogs would also be interested in listening to the "Noisy Books." *The Noisy Book* proved to be Brown's first big sales success.

While an editor at Scott, Margaret Wise Brown also arranged to have *Gertrude Stein write her only children's book, *The World Is Round or Rose Is a Rose.* During her first few years in the field of children's literature, Brown published seven of her own books and edited numerous others. As Leonard Marcus noted, the late 1930s, "the time of Margaret's professional coming of age," was one of the most dynamic times in the history of children's literature.

Brown left her editorial position at Scott in 1940 over a salary dispute. During the 1940s, she continued to write at least six books a year, working with several different publishers, among them Doubleday, Simon and Schuster, and Harper and Row, and using a number of pseudonyms, including "Golden McDonald," "Juniper Sage," and "Timothy Hay." According to Brown, each name had a different personality. She also believed that it did not matter to a child who had written a book, as long as the story seemed true.

As Golden McDonald, Brown wrote *Red Light, Green Light* (1944) and *Little Lost Lamb* (1944) for Doubleday. She wrote *The Little Island* in 1946, which featured the setting of her summer house at Vinal Haven, Maine, and won a Caldecott medal for the illustrator, Leonard Weisgard. In that book, a kitten learns that his island is part of the larger world, but is also a world of its own. Brown believed that children knew "that the world is as big as the part of it we really know."

During the 1940s, Simon and Schuster brought significant changes to the sphere of children's book publishing with their inexpensively priced Golden Book series. Brown contributed several, such as *The Five Little Firemen* and *Color Kittens,* both of which sold millions of copies in the United States and abroad. Also for Simon and Schuster, Brown published what was, in the eyes of many critics, one of her best books, *Mr. Dog: The Dog Who Belonged to Himself* (1952). It is the story of Crispin's Crispian, named after Brown's own dog, and a small boy who also "belongs to himself." Leonard Marcus has called *Mr. Dog* Brown's "most fully realized tale of self possession."

Margaret Wise Brown's main publisher in the 1940s and '50s was Harper and Row; working there with editor ✎➤ **Ursula Nordstrom,** Brown produced some of her most famous and creative work. In 1942, she completed *The Runaway Bunny,* which is based on an old French love song. In this version, it is told as a dialogue between a bunny and his mother, testing the limits of his freedom and presenting the reassuring message that wherever he goes, his mother will

---

✎➤ **Nordstrom, Ursula** (1910–1988)
American editor and author. Born on February 1, 1910, in New York, New York; died of ovarian cancer on October 11, 1988, in New Milford, Connecticut; daughter of William and Marie (Nordstrom) Litchfield; attended Northfield School for Girls and Scudder Preparatory School.

An editor and innovator for Harper and Row, Ursula Nordstrom was responsible for the publications of E.B. White's *Stuart Little,* and *Charlotte's Web,* Maurice Sendak's *Where the Wild Things Are,* and books by **Ruth Krauss,** Shel Silverstein, Tomi Ungerer, *Laura Ingalls Wilder, M.E. Kerr,* *Louise Fitzhugh* and others. Nordstrom's own book, *The Secret Language,* is believed to have been based on her own experiences at boarding school.

find him and care for him. In 1945, Brown wrote *The House of a Hundred Windows,* which introduced children to contemporary paintings: a cat lives alone in a magical house where, when he looks out the window, he sees one of the pieces of modern art. The year 1946 saw the development of *The Little Fur Family,* originally bound in rabbit skin. Unfortunately, rabbit skin proved to be susceptible to worms and moths, so after the first 100,000 copies were sold, *The Little Fur Family* was produced in a more traditional format.

Brown's greatest success, *Goodnight Moon,* appeared in 1947. The book consists of a child going to bed who says "Good night" to each of the familiar things surrounding him. The illustrations by Clement Hurd are in strong primary colors, yet the effect of the book is soothing. *Goodnight Moon,* noted *Time* magazine, has "put two generations of young insomniacs peacefully to sleep in a 'great green room,'" with its secure universe of a comb and a brush and a bowl full of mush and a quiet old lady whispering "hush." Hurd liked to tell of an 18-month-old boy who, having heard the story read for the fourth or fifth time one evening, gazed intently at the book sitting open in front of him. He then stood up, placed his right foot on the page—the last double-page spread of the darkening room—then the left foot. He waited, then burst into tears, because he could not crawl inside. *Goodnight Moon* sold 6,000 copies during the first year after publication. Then demand declined and leveled off until 1953, when sales growth began again. During the late 1970s, a second generation of readers discovered the book, and its remarkable sales increased, aided by the development of paperback and book club editions. By 1990, *Goodnight Moon* had sold over 4 million copies in the United States alone.

During 1948 and 1949, in addition to her continuous composition of books, Brown also wrote lyrics for children's records and contracted with *Good Housekeeping* to contribute poetry for each monthly issue. She particularly enjoyed the *Good Housekeeping* association, as she was well paid and well treated by the adult publishing world.

In an article Brown wrote for the *Hollins Alumnae Magazine* in 1949, she described her creative process, explaining that she often dreamed her stories or wrote them down very quickly, but that she sometimes spent a year or more trying the story on children to make sure that she did not "include too much of the non-

sense that someone who is no longer a child is apt to put into a children's book."

One of the distinguishing things about Brown's books is the harmony between the text and the illustrations. She collaborated with each artist, among them Clement Hurd, Garth Williams, Leonard Weisgard, and Jean Charlot, making sure that their drawings fulfilled the style and mood of the words. She said that a picture book should be "like a still life or a very short play or a static ballet where the only action is the turning of the pages." Besides her original books for children, Brown translated *The Fables of LaFontaine* and *The Children's Year* from the French. She also adapted the Uncle Remus and the Punch and Judy stories as well as the journals of William Bradford and the log of Christopher Columbus for a modern audience of young people.

As an adult, Brown lived most of the time in New York City, where she had both an apartment and "Cobble Court," an early 19th-century farmhouse in Manhattan, incongruously surrounded by factories and skyscrapers, and heated by wood fires. Here Brown kept her beagling memorabilia—a type of hunting in which one rides with the beagles in search of a jackrabbit—as well as a heterogeneous collection of fur rugs and chairs, and her own efforts as a painter. Brown spent her summers at Vinal Haven, Maine, where she bought "The Only House," a house with no modern conveniences on an isolated island.

Although she had many friends during her life, and a series of older women who served as her mentors, Brown at times was troubled by estrangements within her family and by the failure of several love relationships. In addition, her unwillingness to attend to the financial details of her contracts led to rather pressing money problems during the last years of her life.

In 1952, Brown was planning to be married. That year, she traveled to France for the release of the French translation of *Mr. Dog* and, while there, contracted appendicitis. After a successful operation, she died suddenly of an aneurism. Brown left behind a list of "books under construction," many of which were published posthumously.

Much of Margaret Wise Brown's work still endures. She seemed to enter the child's world, for many of her books center around little things, little animals, even little policemen and firemen. It is a world in proportion to the child, in which someone three feet tall can feel comfortable. It is a warm and secure environment where little fur animals cuddle together. Yet she created a world that stretches children's imagination and encourages the child to think and to explore. "What do you think was inside that egg?" she would ask, or "It began to snow. Could Muffin hear that?"

Brown's books are usually without a plot. In fact, she admitted that she hated writing plots. But to a child whose life is a series of incidents rather than a developing tale, the lack of a plot may more closely mirror reality. She was unsentimental about her work and about children. As Leonard Marcus has said, Margaret Wise Brown's books have "an underlying emotional truthfulness and honesty about them that is both salutary and rare." They show "a clear eyed respect for the young."

SOURCES:
Bechtel, Louise Seaman. "Margaret Wise Brown: Laureate of the Nursery," in *The Horn Book*. Vol. 34. June 1958, pp. 173–186.
Blair, Susie. "As We Remember Her . . . A Tribute to Margaret Wise Brown," in *Hollins Alumnae Magazine*. Vol. XXVI. June 1953, pp. 15–17.
Bliven, Bruce. "Child's Best Seller," in *Life*. December 2, 1946, pp. 59–65.
Brown, Margaret Wise. "Writing for Children," in *Hollins Alumnae Magazine*. Vol. XXII. Winter 1949, pp. 13–14.
Marcus, Leonard S. *Margaret Wise Brown: Awakened by the Moon*. Boston, MA: Beacon Press, 1992.

COLLECTIONS:
Margaret Wise Brown's books, manuscripts, and other biographical materials as well as records and filmstrips are located at the Westerly Public Library, Westerly, Rhode Island.
Hollins College Library, Roanoke, Virginia, also holds some correspondence as well as her books and articles.

Mary Welek Atwell,
Associate Professor of Criminal Justice,
Radford University, Radford, Virginia

Brown, Martha McClellan
(1838–1916)

American temperance leader. Born Martha McClellan in Baltimore, Maryland, on April 16, 1838; died in Dayton, Ohio, on August 31, 1916; graduated from Pittsburgh Female College, 1862; married Rev. W. Kennedy Brown (a Methodist minister), 1858.

Martha Brown, the wife of a Methodist minister, first gained recognition in the temperance movement as a lecturer during the Civil War years. A member of the Order of Good Templars, a fraternal temperance society, she served the state executive committee of the Ohio Templars as grand vice-templar and in 1867 became editor of the *Alliance Monitor*, a post she held until 1876 (the paper was owned by her husband from 1870). Martha Brown helped lay the groundwork for the national Prohibition Party in 1869. Elected world supreme vice-templar in 1874, she was instrumental in founding in Columbus, Ohio, in February of that year, what may have been the first women's state temperance society. In August, she and two others planned a national temperance society, and Brown is believed to have drafted the call for the convention that met in Cleveland in November to organize the Woman's Christian Temperance Union. Unable to win the presidency of that group, possibly because of her identification with the Templars, she withdrew from the organization. She also later withdrew from the Templars when they refused to admit black members. Continuing her efforts through the Prohibition Party, she served on the executive committee from 1876 to 1880. Brown was also a force behind the National Prohibition Alliance, a speakers bureau, of which she served as secretary and principal lecturer until the Alliance's dissolution in 1882. She served variously on the Prohibition Party's executive committee until 1896, when she broke with the party over their failure to adopt the woman suffrage plank. Brown rejoined the Templars in 1881, making several lecture tours of Great Britain. She devoted her later years to local philanthropies in Cincinnati.

Brown, Minnijean (b. 1942).
See Bates, Daisy Lee for sidebar.

Brown, Molly (1867–1932)
American philanthropist who survived the sinking of the Titanic *and became known as known as the Unsinkable Molly Brown. Name variations: Margaret or Maggie Tobin Brown; Mrs. J.J. Brown; "The Unsinkable Molly Brown." Born Margaret Tobin in Hannibal, Missouri, in 1867; died after a stroke on October 26, 1932; briefly attended public school; married miner James J. Brown, 1886 (separated 1909, d. 1922); children: Lawrence and Helen.*

Thirty years after her death in 1932, Molly Brown's legendary rags-to-riches story inspired a stage musical and a film, both entitled *The Unsinkable Molly Brown*. The play, with music and lyrics by Meredith Wilson, lasted over a year on Broadway despite lukewarm reviews. The movie, after a gala premier in Denver where Brown had made her mark, went on to a record-breaking opening at Radio City Music Hall and

Molly Brown

city's most upscale neighborhoods. Outgoing but lacking finesse, Brown was continually snubbed by Denver society who regarded her as uncouth and ignorant. But Brown was undaunted by their dismissals and set out to educate herself with private lessons in English, French, voice, speech, and etiquette. She would eventually master seven languages.

Making frequent trips to Europe, where she hobnobbed with artistic types and the occasional royal, Brown also established a home in fashionable Newport, Rhode Island, where she was finally welcomed among the Astors, Whitneys, and Vanderbilts. She changed her name to Molly in the process of her metamorphosis and distanced herself from her husband, who did not share her fierce desire for acceptance. (Striving for a happy ending, the musical glossed over the chasm that developed between them.)

Returning from Southampton to New York, having visited her daughter at a Paris finishing school, Molly Brown was aboard the ill-fated *Titanic* on its maiden voyage in 1912. Twenty-five minutes after the ship struck an iceberg on the evening of April 15, Molly fought to save as many people as possible, pleading with women to leave their husbands and enter the lifeboats. She was saved on the last lifeboat, No. 6 (capacity 65), and argued fiercely with Quartermaster Robert Hichens to return to the wreck site and pick up more survivors. Hichens refused, fearful that those in the water would swamp the boat. When Hichens dismissed the flare from an approaching ship as a "shooting star," Brown threatened to throw him overboard, took control of the boat, and taught the other women to row, all the while singing an Italian aria in a black velvet, two-piece suit. (The story that Brown took control with a pistol is apocryphal.) Upon the boat's rescue by the liner *Carpathia*, Brown reportedly took up a collection on board and raised $7,000 for the widows of the disaster. "How did you survive?" inquired a reporter who met the returning ship. "I'm unsinkable!" replied Molly. The adjective stuck, and she became a national hero.

Just as she was finally accepted by Denver's Sacred Thirty-Six, Molly abandoned society ratings and devoted her remaining years to charity work. She led an effort to preserve Eugene Field's house in Denver, helped create a Mark Twain Memorial in her hometown of Hannibal, Missouri, and aided children under jurisdiction of Denver's Juvenile Court. During World War I, she volunteered as an army nurse, going overseas at her own expense and entertaining in camps of

won an Academy Award nomination for its spirited star, **Debbie Reynolds**. So great was the film's popularity that in 1965 the spacecraft *Gemini 3* was called "Molly Brown" for luck. Though the capsule missed its return landing site by 60 miles, it bobbed without problems in heavy ocean waves until it was retrieved.

Born in a shanty in Hannibal, Missouri, in 1867, Margaret Tobin was the plucky daughter of a ditch digger. In 1884, then known as Maggie, she was struck with gold fever and followed her brother Daniel to Colorado, where she met and married James Brown, a mine foreman later known as "Leadville Johnny," and set up housekeeping in a tiny log cabin. The couple had two children and moved to larger quarters in Leadville, where James became superintendent and part owner of a silver mine called "Little Jonny." In 1894, Brown's dream of becoming rich came true when the mine yielded a vein of gold, a windfall worth $2.5 million. At Brown's insistence, the family moved to Denver, Colorado, where they built a mansion in one of the

American Expeditionary Forces. In Paris, she led in the rehabilitation of blinded soldiers for which she received a knighthood in Paris' Legion of Honor. Her later projects included a fund-raising campaign for a new wing of St. Joseph's Hospital in Denver and a relief effort for destitute wives and children of miners participating in the Ludlow, Colorado, coal strike.

James Brown died in 1922, leaving no will. After a court battle with her children over the division of money, Molly was awarded $100,000 annually. Her charity work continued up until her death at age 65. A 1930 article in *Fortune* magazine noted: "She is in a fair way to become the Lorenzo de Medici . . . of Denver. . . . She is accused of being a grandstander, but those who know her best insist it is unconscious. She is notably generous, and is guided in her philanthropies only by her emotions." Stories about her persisted long after her death. In March 1955, a news feature written by *Mary Margaret McBride proclaimed: "Molly's life was like one of the old-fashioned movie serials . . . social ostracism . . . then triumphant return to her own country. . . . She remained the unsinkable."

SOURCES:
Roy, Grace Ernestine. *Wily Women of the West.* San Antonio, TX: Naylor, 1972.

RELATED MEDIA:
The Unsinkable Molly Brown (film), based on the Broadway musical, starring Debbie Reynolds and Harve Presnell, MGM, 1964.
Titanic (film), starring **Kate Winslet** and Leonardo DiCaprio, with **Kathy Bates** as Molly Brown, directed by James Cameron, 1997.

Barbara Morgan,
Melrose, Massachusetts

Brown, Olympia (1835–1926)

First woman ordained by a denominational authority (Universalist) in America, whose dual career set a precedent for women in ordained ministry and for obtaining enfranchisement. Name variations: Olympia Brown Willis. Born Olympia Brown on January 5, 1835, in Prairie Ronde, near Schoolcraft, Michigan; died on October 23, 1926, in Baltimore, Maryland; daughter of Asa (a farmer) and Lephia (Brown) Brown (a housewife); attended Mt. Holyoke Seminary (1854–55); graduated from Antioch College, 1860, and St. Lawrence Theological School, 1863; married John Henry Willis, April 1873; children: Henry Parker Willis (b. 1874); Gwendolen Brown Willis (b. 1876).

Graduated from St. Lawrence Theological School, one of the first women to obtain a theology degree, and ordained by Universalist Association (1863); was a founding member of American Equal Rights Association (1866); helped found the New England Woman Suffrage Association (1868); helped found the Federal Suffrage Association (1892); assisted in the final editing of The Woman's Bible *(1898); reorganized the Wisconsin Woman Suffrage Association and served as president for 28 years; was a member and activist for the Congressional Union (1913), which became the Woman's Party (1916); served as publisher of* Racine Times-Call *(1893–1900); helped found and wrote regularly for the suffrage newspaper* The Wisconsin Citizen.

Selected publications: authored the history of Kansas women's suffrage campaign of 1867 for History of Woman Suffrage *(Vol. II, 1881, 1882), "Democratic Ideals—A Sketch of Clara Bewick Colby" (1917),* Acquaintances, Old and New, Among Reformers *(1911), and an unpublished autobiography.*

Olympia Brown

Growing up on the Michigan frontier during the middle of the 19th century, Olympia Brown had the support of a mother who believed in equality for women and a family who valued education. In 1849, at age 14, she discovered an outlet for her early ambitions when she founded a newspaper, along with her sisters and brother and two cousins, named *The Family Museum.* Brown discovered quickly that she liked to express her views, and her forthright editorials show a candor and conviction that foreshadowed the uncompromising principles she later maintained for herself and others. The habits of free activity, inquiry, and expression developed in the environment of her home; they were the source of both courage and conflict as she grew into the roles she pursued throughout her life: as a renowned religious lecturer and staunch worker for women's suffrage.

One early conflict for Olympia was the belief of her father Asa that an elementary education was enough for Olympia. Asa and **Lephia Brown** had left the Green Mountains of Vermont for the open farmland to the west soon after their marriage in 1834, and Olympia was their first child, born in 1835, followed by two more daughters and a son. Olympia was still small when Asa took her with him on rides to other farms, as he gathered support to erect a building and hire a teacher for the community. But in 1849 her father had reservations about sending Olympia and her sister **Oella** into town for further schooling, until his older daughter persuaded him that the education would allow them to be self-supporting rather than dependent on him if they did not marry. Thus, in the fall of 1849, Olympia and Oella became students at Cedar Park Seminary in nearby Schoolcraft, commuting in good weather and staying with relatives in town during the week in winter.

In Schoolcraft, Olympia's appetite for speaking her mind soon provoked a controversy. Despite women like *Angelina and *Sarah Grimké and *Lucy Stone, who were then successes on the lecture circuit, public speaking was generally considered improper behavior for females; while boys at Olympia's new school were required to give speeches and debates, girls were only allowed to read prepared texts. When Brown persuaded a male cousin to present a resolution that girls be allowed to debate, members of the teaching staff were so appalled they threatened to quit, and Olympia declined to push the point.

In 1850, at age 15, Brown taught for one term, then returned to classes in Schoolcraft, knowing she wanted to do something different with her life. Once again she convinced her father to allow continued studies, and she searched for a university or college that accepted female students. Lephia discovered Mt. Holyoke Seminary, and, in the fall of 1854, Olympia and Oella set out for the school in Massachusetts, headed for what would soon prove one of the most unpleasant years of their young lives.

Mt. Holyoke had been established in 1837 by *Mary Lyon, at a time when public sentiment was so antagonistic to higher education for females that the founder had felt it necessary to monitor virtually every activity. In 1854, the school's regulations still included many petty and rigid prohibitions against lingering in doorways and windows, speaking above a whisper in the halls, leaving one's room during study hours, sitting on one's bed. An atmosphere of mistrust was created by the encouragement of students and staff members to report any observed infractions.

The Brown sisters, despite extra studying done at home, found they would not be allowed to sit for examinations to pass their first year's coursework. But they joined a group of young women who were forming a literary society and invited their teachers to attend a meeting. After Olympia and Oella had presented a debate at one of the meetings, they were called in and told that the society must be disbanded or they would have to leave the school. A debate was considered inappropriate behavior because it encouraged opposite viewpoints, and the society risked making the women too independent.

Mt. Holyoke had also retained the evangelical intensity of its founder, which Olympia Brown found confusing. Encouraged by her mother's Universalist teaching of God as full of love and compassion rather than vengeance and punishment, she was so disturbed by visiting preachers speaking of hellfire and brimstone that she wrote for guidance to the Universalist Association in Boston. A letter from her mother gave her the strength to maintain her sense of open-mindedness. Concerned that her daughter would "become the dupe of superstitious bigotry," Lephia wrote, "I suspect the reason why they have you go so slow in your studies is that the mind unoccupied may more easily become their prey." She also suggested a visit to relatives in Vermont, which helped Olympia to relax, but after that year she could not face a return to Mt. Holyoke.

Her father agreed to send her elsewhere, and Olympia chose Antioch College in Ohio, which had a liberal outlook, emphasized character development as well as education, and required no religious instruction. Entering in the fall of 1855, she found the students compatible and professors who encouraged reason and tolerance. The school drew renowned lecturers on controversial topics of the day, including the abolition of slavery and advocacy of women's rights. Brown was instrumental in bringing to campus the Reverend *Antoinette Brown Blackwell, no relation to Olympia but an important role model for her later work in both ordained ministry and women's rights.

After graduating from Antioch in 1860, Brown spent the summer and fall writing essays on religion and women's rights while searching for a theological school to attend. Her applications brought letter after letter of rejection and ridicule. At Christmas, while on a holiday visit with friends in Cleveland, Brown was recruited to help with a petition drive in support of women's property rights that was to be presented to the Ohio state legislature. She surprised organizers with her success at gaining the support of entrepreneurs, was invited to Columbus to assist the state leaders, and then given the honor of carrying the petition into the legislative chamber when it was presented.

In 1861, Brown was admitted to the Universalists' St. Lawrence Theological Seminary. There she proved to have a gift for oratory. Though at first her soft, high-pitched voice was a target for taunts, she silenced her classmates with her sharp wit and accurate critiques. At Christmas, when an area church was in need of a preacher, Brown was hired. Resolutely preparing her services, she soon overcame the initial resistance of members who had not wanted to welcome a "woman preacher."

In spring 1863, Brown requested ordination from the Universalist denomination; the glowing endorsement of one regional board member who had heard her preach overcame all opposition. On June 25, 1863, she became the first woman ordained by any denominational authority in the United States. (Ten years earlier, Antoinette Brown Blackwell had been ordained by the authority of an individual Congregational parish.) Olympia Brown's first ministry was to a small congregation in Marchfield, Vermont, near her beloved Green Mountains, another small church in East Montpelier was soon added.

That fall, she resigned to help nurse her brother in Michigan. After his recovery, she returned east, to Boston, where she had heard of a man who could help correct her speaking deficiencies with vocal and physical exercises. To fund her studies, she sought another church. The head of the Universalist Association, despite his personal opposition, told her of a congregation in need, and Brown was invited to preach. Approved on the first congregational vote, she was formally installed as minister for the Universalist Church in Weymouth Landing, Massachusetts, on July 8, 1864, and served there the next five years. While there was some initial opposition to her ministry, it soon ended. Her sermons and her interest in the congregation and community caused the church to grow, and she instituted lecture programs that made it a meeting place for speakers from Boston and elsewhere. She also grew increasingly involved in the women's rights movement.

*Susan B. Anthony had read some of Olympia Brown's essays, and in 1866 Brown was invited to a convention in New York City, where she gave her first speech on women's rights and helped to organize the American Equal Rights Association. After hearing Anthony, she also taught herself to speak extemporaneously, and that summer she met Lucy Stone in Albany, New York, where their discussion about Stone's refusal to take her husband's name would affect the decision Brown was to later make at the time of her own marriage.

By 1867, a major campaign for women's suffrage was underway in Kansas. When Anthony asked Brown to canvass the state, Brown was given leave by the Weymouth Landing church and crossed the frontier from town to farmstead, not always in the most comfortable or sanitary conditions, gaining recognition as a speaker. Debating publicly with men on the issue of women's right to vote, she converted many to the cause, and although some newspapers took her words out of context and degraded her position, she gained the backing of others.

The Civil War was not long over, and the debate in Kansas centered on whether to approve universal suffrage including women, or only the addition of African-American males to the voting rolls. Brown was accused of championing the rights of women over those of black men. The Republican Party, which had championed the anti-slavery cause and also raised the hopes of many people for women's suffrage, now supported those who were appealing for the black male vote over any vote for women, and Brown saw this as a betrayal, which was to prejudice her view of both Republicans and many working for the suffrage of African-American men for years to come.

Women's suffrage was defeated in Kansas, and Brown returned to her church in Weymouth Landing, where she soon found that parish work no longer brought her satisfaction. When Anthony offered her a salary of $1,000 a year to "take the *World* for your *Pastoral Charge*" by speaking full time for women's rights, Brown agonized over her decision. She admired Anthony and her co-worker, *Elizabeth Cady Stanton, but she believed that three such strong-willed women with such distinct views about women's rights were likely to find themselves constantly at odds, and she finally reached the conclusion that her true calling was the ministry. For the next 20 years, her work for women's rights was to remain on the fringes of the movement.

Regarding the conflict over universal suffrage, major differences between Anthony and Brown had in fact already arisen. Anthony had advised Brown against championing women over African-American men, although she and others were sometimes to use arguments later that were similar to Brown's. After a meeting of the American Equal Rights Association, where

Brown found herself in a public disagreement with Frederick Douglass, she decided the debate was futile and became involved in helping organize the New England Woman Suffrage Association (NEWSA). At its first convention, she cautioned: "This is a woman suffrage convention, and as such, members will work toward the ballot for women to the exclusion of all other issues. Only those willing to work for that cause are invited to join." Her sentiment was not universal among NEWSA members, however, and eventually the movement splintered into the National Woman Suffrage Association and the American Woman Suffrage Association. Brown, fearing each would be run by "a small clique of people with selfish purposes," refused to join either organization, saying that she would work for the cause on her "own hook," as opportunities arose.

While Brown refused to compromise her principles, her confidence in her own position was generally balanced by a fairness that was a hallmark of both her ministry and her suffrage work. She recognized that her inflexibility and aggressiveness were often offensive to others, and through the years she won and lost many colleagues and friends because of outspoken and sometimes unpopular stands. But she also believed firmly in the necessity for many views and voices to be heard in the course of any movement for change.

By 1869, Brown felt her work in Weymouth Landing was done. Despite the vocal opposition of a small group, she was accepted to a new position at Bridgeport, Connecticut, at a salary of $1,500 per year, but she soon noted that the people of the new parish were "apathetic and narrow-minded." Four years later, resistance to her persisted, and the unity of the congregation was threatened. She only decided to stay another year because she was about to marry John Henry Willis.

Willis had met Brown at Weymouth Landing and followed her to Bridgeport, but her family had opposed the union. Lephia worried that marriage would have an adverse effect on the position her daughter had worked so hard to achieve, while workers in women's rights feared the effect on her suffrage work. Once Brown made up her mind, it was unlikely to be changed, however, and Willis proved to be fully supportive of his wife, financially and domestically.

A son and a daughter were born to the couple while they were still in Bridgeport. But as opposition to Brown's ministry became more open,

dissenters put restrictions on the church budget that led the trustees to release her. Brown continued to write essays on religion and equal rights, and occasionally spoke on behalf of women's suffrage from 1876 to 1878, until a visit to the Universalist Church of the Good Shepherd in Racine, Wisconsin, brought about an important change.

Impressed by the city, the people, the business climate, and the view of Lake Michigan, Brown decided to move west, where she remained pastor of the church until 1887, maintaining a favorite lakeview residence until her death. Willis invested in a publishing company, whose publications included *The Racine Times-Call* newspaper, and Lephia Brown, now separated from her husband, joined their family. Her presence in the home enabled her daughter to travel as a preacher and to continue the suffrage campaign. Brown became active in regional Universalist meetings, wrote articles that increased her reputation, and built the Racine church into an educational and social center. In 1880, approached by Anthony, Brown wrote the history of the 1867 Kansas campaign for the second volume of *History of Woman Suffrage*.

In 1883, Brown joined the faltering Wisconsin Woman Suffrage Association. The following year, she was elected its president, a position she held for the next 28 years. In the 1885–86 legislative session, after a limited women's suffrage bill was passed and ratified by voters, it remained unclear whether women were eligible to vote in all elections or only school elections, and Brown approached Anthony for help in getting out the vote in Wisconsin in 1887. When Anthony advised Brown to lead the effort, Brown was faced once again with the choice she had confronted 20 years before, of whether to devote herself to women's suffrage or the ministry. This time she decided, at age 52, to give her time to the enfranchisement for women, and she resigned her Racine pastorate.

In the 1887 general election, Brown was joined by a few women in testing the legal limits of the law. They were refused twice by the inspector at the polls, because separate ballots had not been provided for the women. Despite an internal debate about the effects of a loss, the Wisconsin Woman Suffrage Association filed suit to challenge the action; they won in the initial hearing but lost in the state supreme court, and another 15 years would pass before Wisconsin met its obligation to provide separate ballots for women.

With the support of her husband and mother, Brown now traveled extensively and wrote for *The Wisconsin Citizen,* a suffrage newspaper she had helped to establish. Some of her letters addressed the social restrictions she still found within the suffrage movement, while demonstrating her wry and forthright humor. Addressing rumors about her own behavior, she wrote: "I have never struggled to force my ballot into the box. . . . The women at the Circuit Court in Racine behaved with the utmost dignity and propriety. They kicked up no dust (as reported by the *Herald*), they did nothing but listen in silence." Later, she fended off concerns about her family while she campaigned: "I would like everyone to know that my children are fine. They are being carefully watched over by their father and grandmother and a private tutor is training them in Greek and Latin."

In the mid-1880s, Brown was drawn into another controversy. Proponents of women's suffrage became divided over how to meet the challenge of cultural differences resulting from the influx of immigrants who were becoming naturalized citizens. Many immigrants had customs and beliefs that kept women subservient. In condemning the rights of the new citizens to vote as long as they opposed women's suffrage, Brown alienated many colleagues.

In 1889, when the National and the American Woman's Suffrage Associations voted to merge, Brown saw the prospect of more organizational power struggles at the expense of suffrage and felt further estranged from the mainstream. She refused a request from Anthony for support, and she sent remarks at the time of Anthony's 70th birthday celebration that reflected her lingering resentment. Later, however, when Anthony asked her to join a campaign trip, she willingly agreed.

From 1887 to 1893, Brown's suffrage work continued. Reporters who had once made her a subject of ridicule now wrote that she "warms and mellows and ripens with the years" and "makes more and more eloquent speeches and is more and more lovable in character." In 1893, after Lephia suffered a nervous breakdown, Brown remained at home. Shortly afterward, Willis died of a stroke, and for the next several years, Olympia ran the publishing business, nursed her mother, took on a small pastorate, spoke in other churches, and also assisted in the final editing of *The Woman's Bible,* produced by Stanton.

After her mother's death in 1900, Brown spent winters with her son or her daughter in the East, and summers in Racine. As her own family dwindled with the deaths of two siblings, and her generation of the women's movement numbered fewer and fewer, she fought off loneliness by writing and lecturing, encouraging young college women to become involved in suffrage work. She published two books and a history of women's suffrage in Wisconsin. Encouraged by friends and family, she began an autobiography but had so little interest in the past that she left it for her daughter to complete. She preferred spending her time on gardening and cooking.

Ever controversial, Brown was in her 80s when she marched with *Alice Paul in the Woman's Party protests, which were scorned as unladylike by many suffrage workers. When the women's suffrage amendment was finally passed and ratified by Congress, in August 1920, Brown noted that the ballot did not create equal rights, it only gave women voting rights, and urged women to work for an equal rights amendment. In the presidential election on November 2, 1920, among the millions of women casting their national ballots for the first time, Olympia Brown and Antoinette Brown Blackwell were the only survivors of the first generation of suffragists.

A few weeks earlier, on September 12, Brown had preached her last sermon at the Racine church. Entitled "The Opening Doors," it pointed out reforms that had happened in the 40 years since she moved there. In 1926, at 91, she took a trip to Europe with her daughter, Gwendolen. Perhaps feeling free to break from the somber appearance of a pastor, she bought a hat of dark purple silk, fringed with pansies, and a shawl of black Chantilly lace. After a brief illness, Olympia died that fall and was buried in Racine. Tributes came from across the country and newspapers marked the event with moving editorials, recalling the barriers she had broken as a minister, public speaker and suffrage worker.

In her later life, Brown wondered if she had made the right decision by staying in the ministry rather than devoting her time to the suffrage movement, but she had never really neglected either. Throughout her life, the two vocations had been woven together; in her personal ministry, improving the status of women meant improving the world. As one eulogist remarked at her funeral, perhaps the tribute that would please Olympia Brown most would be for every woman to vote in the next election.

SOURCES:

Coté, Charlotte. *Olympia Brown: The Battle for Equality.* Racine, WI: Mother Courage Press, 1988.

Stanton, Elizabeth Cady, Susan B. Anthony, and Matilda Joslyn Gage, eds. *History of Woman Suffrage.* Vol. II. NY: Fowler and Wells, Publishers, 1881, 1882.

SUGGESTED READING:

The Feminist Papers: From Adams to de Beauvoir. Edited and with an introduction by Alice S. Rossi. NY: Columbia University Press, 1973.

Stanton, Elizabeth Cady, Susan B. Anthony, and Matilda Joslyn Gage, eds. *History of Woman Suffrage.* Vols. I & II. NY: Fowler and Wells, Publishers, 1881, 1882; Vols. III & IV. Rochester, NY: Susan B. Anthony, 1886, 1902; Vols. V & VI. NY: National American Woman's Suffrage Association, 1922.

COLLECTIONS:

Correspondence and papers collected at the Arthur and Elizabeth Schlesinger Library on the History of Women in America, Radcliffe College, Cambridge, Massachusetts; additional information available from Racine County (Wisconsin) Historical Society and Museum, and from the Unitarian Universalist Association, Boston, Massachusetts.

Margaret L. Meggs, Assistant to the Director, Women's Studies Program, Vanderbilt University, and lecturer in Women's Studies, Middle Tennessee State University

Brown, Pamela (1917–1975)

English actress. Born on July 8, 1917, in London, England; died on September 18, 1975; attended St. Mary's Convent, Ascot; dramatic training at the Royal Academy of Dramatic Art; briefly married to actor Peter Copley (divorced, 1953).

Selected films: One of Our Aircraft is Missing (1942); I Know Where I'm Going (1945); Tales of Hoffmann (1951); The Second Mrs. Tanqueray (1952); Personal Affair (1953); Richard III (1956); The Scapegoat (1959); Becket (1964); Secret Ceremony (1968); Wuthering Heights (1970); On a Clear Day You Can See Forever (1970; Lady Caroline Lamb (1972).

Known for her unconventional appearance and husky voice, Pamela Brown made her stage debut in 1936 as Juliet and would continue to distinguish herself in Shakespearean roles throughout her career, performing many with the Oxford Repertory Company and the Old Vic.

In her early days, Brown spent the summers of 1938 and 1939 in Perranporth, where a performing company under the direction of Peter Bull and Robert Morley attempted to introduce American-style summer stock to British audiences. Her first outstanding London success came in 1942 with the title role of *Rose Franken's Claudia*; this was followed by a performance of Ophelia in *Hamlet* (1944) that was criticized as "over-intelligent." In 1947, her New York debut as Gwendolyn in *The Importance of Being Earnest* was greeted with rave reviews, but her career did not peak until 1949 with the role of the suspect-witch Jennet Jourdemayne in *The Lady's Not for Burning*, a play Christopher Fry had written especially for her.

When the show came to New York in 1950, Brooks Atkinson wrote: "Pamela Brown gives a warm, rich and fluent performance that gleams with humorous coquetry."

Brown continued to delight theatergoers between London and New York in plays like *The Way of the World, The Country Wife, Heartbreak House,* and *A Question of Fact.* Her offbeat image in *A Question of Fact* was noted by critic Richard Buckle, who praised the director for casting her. "[I]t was very clever to choose an actress so odd and special as Pamela Brown . . . we might have been irritated by an ordinary, nice, appealing little woman. She plays intelligently, and her bizarre personality removes any suspicion of conventional sweetness from the love scenes." Brown's last stage appearance was in Jack Ronder's *This Year, Next Year,* in 1960.

During her career, Pamela Brown also made occasional films; most memorably, she was seen in the non-speaking role of *Jane Shore in Olivier's *Richard III* (1955). She also made sporadic television appearances, including a 1961 Hallmark Hall of Fame production of *Victoria Regina,* for which she received an Emmy. Brown was married briefly to actor Peter Copley. She died in September 1975, at age 58.

SOURCES:

Hartnoll, Phyllis, and Peter Found, ed. *The Concise Oxford Companion to the Theatre.* NY: Oxford University Press, 1992.

Morley, Robert. *The Great Stage Stars.* London: Angus & Robertson, 1986.

Brown, Rachel Fuller (1898–1980).

See joint entry under Hazen, Elizabeth Lee.

Brown, Rosemary (1930—)

*Feminist activist and first black woman to be elected to any parliament in Canada. Born Rosemary Wedderburn on June 17, 1930 at Kingston, Jamaica; retired in Vancouver, British Columbia, Canada; second child of Ralph Wedderburn (a businessman) and Enid James; attended Westwood Boarding School, Wolmer's High School, McGill University (graduated Bachelor of Arts) and the University of British Columbia (graduated Master of Social Work); married William (Bill) Brown, 1955; children: **Cleta Brown** (b. 1957); Gary (b. 1959); Jonathon (b. 1965).*

Jamaica became independent nation (1960); election of first New Democratic Party (NDP) government in Canada (1972); Brown given the Black Award, National Black Coalition of Canada (1974);

Rosemary Brown

awarded honorary doctorate in Human Letters from St. Vincent University, Halifax, Nova Scotia (1981).

Selected writings: Being Brown *(1989);* Problems of Social Change in Canada: A Feminist Perspective *(1977).*

Rosemary Brown was born on June 17, 1930, in Kingston, Jamaica, which was then part of the British West Indies. Her father Ralph Wedderburn, a prominent businessman on the island, died when she was four years old. Shortly thereafter, her mother **Enid** remarried and moved away, leaving her children to be raised by aunts and uncles and, in particular, by their maternal grandmother. It was the latter, **Imogene Wilson-James**, who had the greatest formative impact on Rosemary's early life and upbringing.

Imogene Wilson-James had arrived in Jamaica in 1848, a small child among the many indentured laborers then being brought to the island by the British. Through a combination of hard work, financial acumen, and good luck, she managed to accumulate sufficient monetary assets to enable her to pursue a series of highly profitable investments in land. Indeed, by the time Rosemary was born, Imogene's large household had become one of the leading and most successful in Jamaica. Wilson-James' interests extended beyond finance to politics where she was one of the founding members of the left-wing People's National Party (PNP). For many

years, she played a leading role in the movement to bring about universal suffrage and fair labor practices. Many other members of the family also rose to positions of prominence within the community. For example, **Leila James-Tomlinson**, one of Imogene's daughters, worked to help develop the Jamaican welfare system and later, following the nation's independence, became an eminent judge.

After attending a local elementary school in Kingston (where she displayed, at an early age, a keen interest in English literature), Rosemary was sent to the highly prestigious and socially exclusive Westwood private boarding school for girls. She remained there until she was 16 before being enrolled at Wolmer's high school for girls, another distinguished and reputable institution that had previously been attended by her mother and aunts. It was there that she began to develop her own interest in politics. She joined the youth wing of the PNP and could often be found handing out leaflets on the streets of Kingston as well as sending letters of protest to newspapers and government officials on various issues of social concern. At this time, Rosemary also developed a strong interest in religion (another influence that she received from her grandmother).

Many of Brown's close relations had traveled abroad, usually to England, in order to complete their higher education. In August 1950, Rosemary decided to follow in the same path but chose to enroll at McGill University in Montreal, Quebec, Canada. During her four years there, Brown was consistently shocked by the extent of institutionalized racism that existed in the community. She found it extremely difficult to find suitable accommodation and, when looking for summer employment, had to be content with low-paying, menial jobs. Immigration officers, to whom Brown had to apply every year for an extension of her visa, were also a source of worry. As a member of the West Indian student community, many of whom professed radical left-wing views, she constantly faced the possibility of deportation. Despite these trials, however, Brown successfully completed her Bachelor of Arts degree in literature and graduated in 1954.

All feminists may not be socialists, but all socialists must be feminists.

—Rosemary Brown

It was during the course of her studies that she met her future husband Bill Brown. Bill had come to McGill University from his home in Georgia to complete a doctoral degree in biochemistry. After the couple decided to marry, he left in 1953 for the medical school at the University of British Columbia in Vancouver where he was to complete his studies in clinical psychiatry. As soon as Rosemary finished her own degree, she traveled to Vancouver to join Bill, and they were married in 1955.

Once again, Rosemary Brown was dispirited by the extent of racist attitudes that prevailed in society. Locating a suitable apartment was a trying and onerous task, and the only job that she could find was as a clerk in the offices of the Registered Nurses Association of British Columbia. Following the birth of her first child, a daughter named Cleta in 1957, Brown became more closely involved in the black community in Vancouver. She joined the newly formed British Columbia Association for the Advancement of Coloured People (BCAACP), an activist organization patterned after the NAACP in the United States. Brown was later elected to the executive committee of this association, which pressed for the introduction of human rights' legislation to combat racist attitudes in housing, employment, and education.

Brown's activities were not, however, confined to the struggle against racism. By 1958, she was working as a volunteer at the Vancouver Crisis Intervention and Suicide Prevention Centre located at Vancouver General Hospital where

her husband was also then working. More significantly, perhaps, she also became involved in the growing feminist and peace movements and spent much of her time lobbying politicians, organizing demonstrations, and writing letters to newspapers. This more active and public role was partially the result of the fact that she and her husband had now become Canadian citizens. She no longer had to face the threat of deportation for her political activities.

During these years, Bill constantly encouraged his wife to seek a career for herself. Rosemary tried writing (but with little success) and briefly considered attending law school. Thanks to her work for the Children's Aid Society of British Columbia, she eventually decided to take a graduate degree in social work, which she received in 1964. In the next few years, Brown achieved an increasingly prominent position in a variety of advocacy groups in British Columbia. She combined these activities with a new job in the counseling service at Simon Fraser University (which is also located in Vancouver).

Brown's principal concern, however, was with the women's rights movement. In the late 1960s, she joined the Vancouver Status of Women Council, a broad feminist coalition that was working to implement the proposals contained in the federal government's Royal Commission on the Status of Women. The council had established special sub-committees to deal with such issues as education, finance, and the media and asked Brown to design and develop an advocacy structure for women. Between 1970 and 1972, she ran an ombudservice where women could bring specific complaints on a wide range of issues, such as unfair labor practices, equal pay, family violence, and inequitable divorce settlements. Brown's job was to not only press for changes in existing legislation, but to help women facing these concerns gain access to adequate legal aid.

It was during this period that she joined the provincial wing of the left-leaning New Democratic Party (NDP). Shortly after, she was approached by members of the party leadership and asked to run for election to the provincial legislature in the forthcoming election. This request was endorsed by Brown's colleagues on the Status of Women Council who were willing to support any woman running for elective office, regardless of party political affiliation, as long as that woman would pledge to work for improvements in women's rights. Brown was initially reluctant to accept this invitation. Few women had ever been elected to office in British

Columbia, and she suffered from the additional disadvantage of being a black immigrant. Nevertheless, she finally did accept the nomination for the riding of Vancouver-Burrard. In August 1972, Brown was elected as part of the first ever NDP government in the history of the province.

Although the new government did introduce several measures that had a progressive effect for women (for example, health collectives, childcare services, and a human rights code outlawing discrimination on the basis of sex or marital status), many feminists were unhappy about the pace and extent of the reforms. In particular, they were angry that Dave Barrett, then NDP leader and premier of the province, refused to establish a Ministry of Women (despite the fact that this was official party policy) or to take Brown into his cabinet. Part of the reason for this was the fact that Barrett and Brown disliked one another intensely, and the latter lost no opportunity in attacking the government when she felt it was ignoring the needs and wishes of the people. Specifically, she focused on the plight of immigrant women, the lack of affordable housing, foreign ownership of natural resources, and corporate control of the environment.

More than anything else, however, Brown was relentlessly dedicated to increasing the amount of female representation in the NDP and attacking the sexism and paternalism that she believed was rampant in the party. This deepening commitment to the feminist movement was practically demonstrated through her membership on the National Action Committee on the Status of Women and the federal-government-sponsored Advisory Council on the Status of Women. In these endeavors, Brown adopted the motto of the Council of Women, a turn-of-the-century feminist organization: "truth, honesty, purity, justice and righteousness should be the foundation for women's involvement in politics."

Early in 1975, David Lewis, then leader of the federal NDP party, unexpectedly resigned. Shortly after, a number of prominent feminists associated with the women's wing of the party approached Brown and asked her to run in the forthcoming leadership convention in Winnipeg, Manitoba. Once again, she demonstrated a great deal of reluctance to be considered for this post. Brown's main concerns centered around the considerable responsibilities that such a prestigious position entailed as well as the effect that this could potentially have on her family. In addition, she recognized certain negative factors militating against her candidacy. She had little or no experience of federal politics and could not speak

French (a crucial factor in national Canadian politics). More specifically, she was widely perceived by the media as well as many members of the NDP as representing the most left-wing faction of the party. On the other hand, Brown recognized that the leadership contest offered her a real and unique chance to make a significant and lasting impact on the policy practices of the NDP.

Throughout the early months of 1975, Brown traveled throughout Canada bringing her message of equal opportunity and rights for all. In the course of this campaign, she received a great deal of grass-root support from women (considerable numbers of whom were not even affiliated to the NDP). At the close of the leadership convention in July, Brown concluded her speech to the assembled delegates with words that described her vision of a new Canada. The task, she declared, was to become "the government that will build a truly socialist, truly humane society—here in Canada." When the final ballot was counted, Brown had managed to attain a very credible second place finish to the victor Ed Broadbent.

In the aftermath of the convention, Broadbent asked Brown to consider standing as a candidate in the next federal election. Although she was greatly tempted by this offer, she refused, largely because of the imminent provincial election in British Columbia that was called in November 1975. Premier Barrett's policies had eventually managed to alienate a substantial proportion of the feminist movement, but Brown felt that an NDP government was the only real alternative to the opposition, right-wing, Social Credit Party. In that election, however, the NDP suffered a crushing defeat, though Brown was able to retain her seat (although by a greatly reduced majority).

Over the next few years, Brown focused her efforts on preventing the new government from rolling back the progressive legislation enacted by the previous administration. Perhaps her greatest moment in the legislature was the filibuster she initiated to avert the government's closure of the Vancouver Resource Board. At serious cost to her own health, Brown talked for over 13 hours in the assembly in what ultimately proved to be a futile attempt to save one of the most prominent and effective advocacy groups in the province.

Following a redrawing of constituency boundaries, Brown was reelected in the new riding of Burnaby-Edmonds in the provincial election of 1979. During this term of office, she found it increasingly difficult to make any substantial contribution to the legislative process. In the climate of the early 1980s, the emerging ideology of neo-conservativism rendered it extremely hard to advance any kind of progressive cause. For this reason, Brown's interests turned increasingly towards extra-parliamentary activities, in particular, the campaign against apartheid in South Africa. She also became passionately involved in the struggle for nuclear disarmament. Brown traveled widely throughout Canada and abroad, speaking in the cause of peace and international co-existence. She became a founding member of Women for a Meaningful Summit, an international organization dedicated to monitoring meetings of NATO and the superpower disarmament talks between the United States and the Soviet Union. At a meeting in Moscow of the International Women's Conference on Peace, Brown stated that "peace remains the number one priority in my life."

In 1982, when Dave Barrett resigned as leader of the NDP in British Columbia, Brown was asked once again to run for the leadership of the party. This time, however, she refused, principally because she was extremely dispirited by the lack of cohesion and direction in the NDP and the disorganized state of its feminist wing. She considered resigning her seat but was persuaded to stand again in the 1983 election. The new NDP leader, Bob Skelley, did little to reverse the decline in the party's fortunes, and this only served to alienate Brown further from the political process. When another election was called in October 1986, she announced that she no longer wished to be considered for office. After her retirement from parliament, Brown continued to speak and lecture throughout Canada on feminist issues and remained active in the international campaign to promote peace.

SOURCES:

Brown, Rosemary. *Being Brown*. Toronto: Random House Publishers of Canada, 1989.

————. "Problems of Social Change in Canada: A Feminist Perspective," in *Queen's Quarterly*. Summer 1977.

SUGGESTED READING:

Hodgins, Bruce. *Canadian History Since Confederation*. Georgetown, Ontario: Irwin-Dorsey, 1976.

Dave Baxter, Department of Philosophy, Wilfrid Laurier University, Waterloo, Ontario, Canada

Brown, Ruth (1928—)

African-American jazz and rhythm-and-blues singer who was inducted into the Rock and Roll Hall of Fame in 1993. Born Ruth Weston in Portsmouth, Virginia, in 1928; grew up in North Carolina; married three times; children: two sons.

Ruth Brown was a small child when she started singing in the church where her father was choir director. She recalled it as the most natural place to begin training: "You had to sing in church. That was required learning. If you could carry a tune, it would start in the church and then, naturally, in the school groups." Brown grew into a somewhat more rebellious teenager, often skipping music class and occasionally sneaking out of the house to sing the so-called devil's music at the USO shows on the local army bases. An early marriage was her ticket out of Portsmouth, Virginia, but Brown knew music was her gift. After singing around Detroit and a stint on the road with the Lucky Millinder band, she met *Blanche Calloway, a bandleader and sister of Cab Calloway, who hired her to sing at her club, the Crystal Caverns; later, Blanche would become her manager. When Duke Ellington and disc jockey Willis Conover (from radio's *Voice of America*) heard her sing one night, they arranged an audition at Atlantic records. On her way to sign a contract and make an appearance at the famed Apollo theater, Brown was involved in an auto accident that sidelined her for an entire year.

Her first release on Atlantic Records was "So Long" (with "It's Raining" on the flip side), which reached number six on the R&B charts in 1949 and led to such a string of hits that Atlantic became known as "The House that Ruth Built." "Teardrops From My Eyes" (1950) put her number one on the charts and was followed by "5-10-15 Hours," "(Mama) He Treats Your Daughter Mean," "Mend Your Ways," "Miss Rhythm," "Oh What a Dream," and "Mambo Baby." In 1957, Brown crossed over to the pop charts with "Lucky Lips," which reached number 25.

When Ruth Brown toured the segregated South during the 1950s, she was banned from the "better" hotels and restaurants. She recalled, however, that there was always a white audience, who was "either upstairs or separated on the main floor because of the rules of the South." But it was a more subtle kind of segregation that gnawed away at Brown's career. Once rock and roll's commercial viability had been established (as Brown put it, "When the white kids started to dance to it"), white artists began recording material, known as cover versions, initially popularized by black performers. With the lyrics sanitized from the more earthy originals, record companies could circumvent the potential controversy of rock and roll while exploiting the genre's commercial potential. Although the sanitized cover versions often lacked the fire of the originals (Pat Boone's renditions of Little Richard's "Tutti Frutti" and Fats Domino's "Ain't That a Shame" are examples), they had the edge in distribution. Brown, who was shut out of the pop charts when her songs were covered by white artists such as *Georgia Gibbs and *Patti Page, left Atlantic Records in 1960 and stumbled around on other labels with little success. She eventually quit the business completely, working as a domestic and driving a bus, until she attempted to get her career on track again in 1976.

With the help of Howell Begle, an avid music fan and attorney, Brown recovered some lost record royalties and started up the Rhythm & Blues Foundation, which established an R&B archive based in the Smithsonian Institution's National Museum of American History. The foundation has awarded money and recognition to R&B artists through its Pioneer Awards Program and, since its inception, has also offered grants to R&B performers who are in need of financial assistance. A number of recording stars have subsequently joined the board of trustees of the foundation, including **Bonnie Raitt** who has been particularly active.

In the 1980s, Brown's career took off again with a role in a workshop production of Allen Toussaint's *Staggerlee;* this led to a part in the hit *Black and Blue,* which ran for eight months in Paris in 1984. Returning to the U.S., Brown rejoined *Staggerlee* off-Broadway and also became the host of the national radio program *Harlem Hit Parade* (later known as *BluesStage*). In 1988, she won a role in John Waters' film *Hairspray,* playing the part of Motormouth Mabel, an R&B record-store owner and DJ. When *Black and Blue* opened on Broadway in 1989, she rejoined the cast, winning a Tony for her performance. She subsequently won a Grammy for her album *Blues on Broadway.* On her 65th birthday, in 1993, Brown was inducted into the Rock and Roll Hall of Fame. To celebrate the event, she and longtime friend Bonnie Raitt sang Brown's 1953 hit "(Mama) He Treats Your Daughter Mean."

While aware of the changes in the music industry over the years, Brown knew that the business still had a way to go; even with her newfound recognition, there were still venues that would not invite her to appear because of her skin color. Nonetheless, Brown noted that singers like herself "went out front and kind of took the blows a little bit," and in so doing

paved the way for the new generation of black performers, like **Whitney Houston, Anita Baker,** and **Janet Jackson.**

SOURCES:

Clarke, Donald, ed. *The Penguin Encyclopedia of Popular Music.* NY: Viking Press, 1989.

Garr, Gillian. *She's a Rebel: The History of Women in Rock and Roll.* Introduction by Yoko Ono. Seattle, WA: Seal Press, 1992.

Jet. Vol. 83. February 1, 1993, pp. 56–57.

SUGGESTED READING:

Brown, Ruth, with Andrew Yule. *Miss Rhythm: The Autobiography of Ruth Brown, Rhythm and Blues Legend.* NY: Donald I. Fine, 1996.

Barbara Morgan,
Melrose, Massachusetts

Brown, Vera Scantlebury

(1889–1946)

Australian doctor who was instrumental in establishing state infant welfare clinics. Born Vera Scantlebury in Australia on August 7, 1889; died on July 14, 1946 (some sources cite 1945); daughter of G.J. (a doctor) and Catherine (Baynes) Scantlebury; attended Toorak College, a small private school; M.D., University of Melbourne, 1913; married Edward Brown (a professor of engineering, University of Melbourne), September 1926; children: two.

Vera Brown was instrumental in establishing a system of infant welfare clinics throughout Victoria, Australia, through her work in preventative health care for children. During Brown's youth, her independent-minded mother oversaw her education, which culminated in graduation from the University of Melbourne in 1913 with an M.D. After her residency at Children's Hospital, Melbourne, Brown worked in a London military hospital during World War I before returning to Melbourne in 1919. But she was unable to get a private practice under way and had to accept several short-term appointments before assuming the position of medical officer of the newly established Victorian Baby Health Centres Association, where she lectured on mother and infant care to nurse trainees.

With increasing commitment to the infant care movement, Brown completed specialized training in children's diseases in 1924 and made a study tour to New Zealand, Canada, and the United States. Upon her return, she was asked by the Victorian government to work with an English doctor, **Henrietta Main**, on a study comparing infant welfare in Victoria with that in New Zealand, where a State supported system of clinics was already in place. The report, completed in 1926, maintained that infant mortality rates would further decline with the establishment of a position of director of Infant Welfare and a network of well-staffed clinics throughout Victoria. Given her own responsibilities as a wife and mother, Brown accepted the recommended position of director on a part-time basis. She worked to bring together rival factions in the infant welfare movement and to standardize training and procedure in the clinics. Her own testing of infant formulas and measuring implements resulted in a manual on artificial feeding. Her interests eventually broadened to include maternal health, and she later added preschools to her department. In 1938, Brown was awarded an OBE for her work, which she continued in spite of her own poor health. She died on July 14, 1946.

Brown, Virginia Mae (1923–1991)

American lawyer and chair of the Interstate Commerce Commission. Born in Pliny, Virginia, in 1923; died in Charleston, West Virginia, on February 24, 1991; graduated from University of West Virginia (Morgantown), 1945; graduated from University of West Virginia School of Law, 1947; married; children: two daughters.

Following the independent spirit of her mother, who was the president of a small bank, Virginia Mae Brown passed the bar in 1947 before many woman were practicing law. Hers would be a career dominated by firsts. She was the first woman executive secretary to the Judicial Council of West Virginia (1944–1952); she was also the first woman to be an assistant attorney general (1952–61) and the first to be appointed state insurance commissioner (1962).

While raising her two daughters, Brown served as council to the governor of West Virginia and as a member of the state public-utilities commission. Though surprised in 1964 when President Lyndon B. Johnson appointed her to serve on the 11-member Interstate Commerce Commission, she was well prepared. She chaired the commission from 1969 to 1970, during which time she fought to maintain public rail transportation in spite of claims of decreased ridership, and she broke with tradition by forbidding ICC employees to accept free trips or other gifts. Her tenure ended with the election of Richard Nixon.

Brown Blackwell, Antoinette
(1825–1921)

First ordained female minister in the U.S. and well-known public speaker on women's rights, temper-ance, and abolition, who successfully combined a career with marriage and motherhood. Name variations: Antoinette Brown; Antoinette Brown-Blackwell. Born Antoinette Louisa Brown on May 20, 1825, in Henrietta, New York; died in New Jersey on November 5, 1921; daughter of Joseph Brown (a farmer) and Abigail Morse Brown; sister-in-law of Elizabeth Blackwell, Emily Blackwell, and Lucy Stone; aunt of *Alice Stone Blackwell (1857–1950); attended Monroe County Academy, 1838–1840; graduated Oberlin College, B.A., 1847, M.A. in theology, 1850 (not recognized by Oberlin until 1908), M.A. (honorary), 1879, D.D. (honorary), 1908; married Samuel Blackwell on January 24, 1856; children: Florence Blackwell (b. 1856); Mabel Blackwell (b. 1858); Edith Blackwell (b. 1860); Grace Blackwell (b. 1863); Agnes Blackwell (b. 1866); Ethel Blackwell (b. 1869).

After graduating from Oberlin College and completing studies at the master's level, began her public speaking career on the lyceum circuit in the northeastern United States, lecturing on women's rights, temperance, and abolition (1847); ordained as the first female minister in U.S. and installed as pastor of a Congregational Church (1853); became the first woman in the U.S. to officiate at a marriage ceremony (1853); after her marriage and the birth of her first daughter (1856), curtailed, but did not eliminate, her public speaking, continuing to tour with Susan B. Anthony and to preach in New York City; turned increasingly to writing, as more compatible with her maternal responsibilities, and wrote several volumes and articles on women's rights and religion, as well as a novel; participated in the founding of the Association for the Advancement of Women (1873); became a Unitarian and was recognized as a Unitarian minister (1878); founded and preached monthly at a Unitarian Church in Elizabeth, New Jersey (1903); was a featured speaker at the International Council of Women (1888) and the World Parliament of Religions (1893); testified before the Senate on behalf of federal suffrage for women (1906).

Selected writings: (novel) The Island Neighbors (1871); The Sexes Throughout Nature (1875); The Philosophy of Individuality (1893); The Making of the Universe (1914); The Social Side of Mind and Action (1915).

Eight-year-old Antoinette Brown astounded her family one Sunday evening by spontaneously contributing a short and simple prayer to the family's regular religious observance. In an age when most children obeyed the injunction to be

Antoinette Brown Blackwell

seen and not heard, Brown's older relatives were curious as to why the child had been emboldened to raise her voice in prayer. The young Antoinette answered honestly, "Because I think I am a Christian, and why should I not pray?" Later that year, the Congregational Church attended by the Brown family voted unanimously to accept Antoinette into full membership, despite her age. The deeply felt religious faith expressed by the young Antoinette Brown would sustain her in the ensuing years as she defied even more strongly held social taboos to become the first ordained woman minister in the United States and a well-known public speaker and writer on the controversial subjects of abolition, temperance, and women's rights.

Antoinette Brown, born on May 20, 1825, in Henrietta, New York, was the seventh child of a farming couple, **Abigail Morse Brown** and Joseph Brown. In 1819, her parents had moved from Connecticut to what was then a frontier region in the vicinity of Rochester. The Brown family was extremely religious and, during Brown's youth, was often caught up in the various religious revival movements that swept across the United States. They belonged to a less strict branch of the Congregational Church, which emphasized God's mercy and forgiveness rather than dwelling on the sinfulness of man.

Brown received her early education in a small local school. In 1838, she went to the co-educational Monroe County Academy where she studied mathematics, composition, rhetoric, and French, graduating in 1840. According to the mores of the time, though Brown was only 16, she was considered equipped to pass on her scant learning to other youngsters. Thus, she began a teaching career in local grammar schools situated near her family's farm. Teaching was virtually the only employment option for young girls like Brown in the 1840s, other than marrying, raising a large family and sharing in the back-breaking labor of running a family farm, as Brown's mother had done. From the beginning, however, Brown was discontented with teaching. She later wrote to a friend, "so far as the school is concerned I have not the least ambition. God never made me for a school teacher."

In what portion of the [Bible] do we find any commandment forbidding woman to act as a [preacher], provided she has a message worth communicating, and will deliver it in a manner worthy of her high vocation? Surely nowhere.

—Antoinette Brown Blackwell

Brown decided instead that God intended her to be a minister. This was a surprising career choice. In virtually all Protestant denominations, except the Quakers, it was unheard of for women to preach, much less to serve as recognized ministers. Realizing that she would need further education to follow her chosen path, she rejected the idea of attending one of the many women's seminaries, "where the great object is to make mere butterflies of females. I wish to go where not only the intellect, but the moral principle will be cultivated, disciplined and trained for active service in the vineyard of the Lord."

Brown concluded that Oberlin College in Ohio could provide her with the requisite moral and intellectual training and left New York in the spring of 1846. The town of Oberlin had been established as a model community and in 1834 a Collegiate Institute, the predecessor of the college, was founded to train ministers, missionaries, and teachers. Brown had some family connections with the college. Her older brother William had graduated from Oberlin Theological Seminary in 1841, and Charles Grandison Finney, the president of Oberlin during Brown's student years, had been a minister in upstate New York and spiritual mentor to her parents.

Oberlin was a very unusual institution. The school required all students to perform some sort of manual labor, for which they were remunerated at very low rates, to build character and instill self-reliance. Politically, the school was known as a hotbed of abolitionism. Officially, the college favored a moderate anti-slavery position known as Christian abolition. Oberlin eschewed the ideology of radical abolitionist William Lloyd Garrison and his followers who argued that opponents of slavery should sever all connections with institutions that included slave holders, including churches. Instead, the college's position was that abolitionists could work through institutions that included slave-owning members in order to mitigate and eventually to eradicate the evil of slavery.

Not the least unusual aspect of Oberlin was its acceptance of students of both genders at a time when women were usually barred from serious higher education. However, while classes were coeducational, female students at Oberlin did not receive the same education as their male colleagues. The college believed its duty lay in training women for their domestic roles, as the wives of ministers and teachers and the mothers of progressive Christian children. Male students, on the other hand, received the rigorous intellectual and practical training necessary for careers in the ministry and education. Thus, women were not schooled in public speaking and rhetoric, two skills essential for any aspiring minister, and, indeed, were not permitted to speak publicly in coeducational classes. Oberlin even offered two courses of study: a demanding classical course, pursued by most of the men, and a less rigorous literary curriculum, in which most female students, including Antoinette Brown, enrolled.

Brown, however, was not to be dissuaded from her plans to prepare herself for a career in the ministry. If Oberlin refused to provide her with the skills and opportunities necessary to develop her preaching talents, then Brown would create those opportunities herself. In this endeavor she was aided by her close friend and fellow student, *Lucy Stone. Stone and Brown met shortly after the latter arrived at Oberlin. Stone, the elder by several years, already had a reputation as a radical Garrisonian abolitionist and an ardent advocate of women's rights. She would go on to achieve renown as a public advocate of abolition and a leader of the women's rights movement in the United States. In 1846, Brown, Stone, and a few other women reactivated the moribund Ladies' Literary Society of Oberlin to provide a forum for training themselves in the public speaking and rhetorical skills denied to them by the college.

In the summer of 1847, the two friends finished their undergraduate work at Oberlin. While Stone left to begin public lecturing on the abolition question, Brown decided to return to Oberlin to undertake the formal study of theology. Oberlin, however, was unwilling to recognize Brown as a regular student in the theology division because of institutional opposition to women's public speaking. Thus, the school refused officially to enroll Brown, but rather considered her a "resident graduate" during her three years of theological study. Oberlin also created financial difficulties for Brown by refusing to allow her to teach in the Preparatory Division of the college. She was reduced to working for three cents an hour until she established herself as a drawing instructor independently of the school. Brown began to speak out in class, and was eventually admitted to the Theological Literary Society, the forum for public speaking maintained by Oberlin's graduate theological students. Although Brown thus succeeded in muting the initial hostility of many professors and fellow students, Oberlin would not formally recognize her successful completion of the graduate program for another 58 years.

Lucy Stone had objected vigorously to Brown's acquiescence in her second-class treatment by Oberlin. She called Oberlin's handling of Brown "dishonorable" and scolded her friend for her meek acceptance of the degrading terms: Oberlin "trampled your womanhood and you did not spurn it. I do believe that even *they* would have thought better of you if you had stayed away." Brown, however, was willing to sacrifice some principles to more pragmatic considerations. She believed that she could benefit greatly from the training and credentials grudgingly provided by Oberlin. Stone also disapproved of Brown's study of theology and her continued adherence to organized religion. Stone perceived religion as not only moribund but also as a major force in the historic oppression of women. In later years, as the burgeoning women's rights movement in the United States came to share many of Stone's negative perceptions of religion, Brown was increasingly at odds with her fellow activists because of her belief in the necessity of institutionalized Christianity and of women's active participation in organized religion.

In 1850, Brown finished her theological studies. The organization empowered to license Oberlin graduates to preach decided that, while they would not prevent Brown from public preaching, they could not officially recognize her preaching by the grant of a license. She returned home to New York dejected and seemingly thwarted in her ministerial ambitions. Brown began to write for the *North Star,* the abolitionist paper of ex-slave Frederick Douglass. She also attended the National Woman's Rights Convention in Worcester, Massachusetts, held in 1850. Her speech, refuting St. Paul's injunction against women's speaking in church, was positively received.

Perhaps because of her success at the convention, Brown decided to embark on a tour as a speaker on the lyceum circuit. Her family vigorously opposed this plan, urging her to pursue, instead, the more acceptably feminine professions of teacher or missionary. Brown persevered, however, lecturing throughout the Northeast on several "hot topics" of the day: abolition, temperance, and women's rights. Although women generally received lower compensation than male speakers, Brown demanded and got equal treatment. Her fame grew—in part because of her unique qualification as a female preacher—and the Brown family became more supportive of their increasingly well-known and successful daughter. Public speaking was commonly believed to be incompatible with feminine modesty, yet Brown suffered no such qualms in her lecturing career. "It was never a real trial," she later wrote, "not even a hard or difficult thing to face the public with a thought which I really wished to impress upon their attention. From first to last there never was any real self-sacrifice in my chosen work—it was merely self-expression."

Despite the success of her lecturing career, Brown had not abandoned her dream of becoming a minister with a church of her own. In 1853, she moved to the small town of South Butler, New York, to become minister of its Congregational Church at the lowly salary of $300 per year. The church was apparently quite open to innovation—indeed, one of Brown's predecessors as pastor had been an African-American male. Because the Congregational Church has no institutional hierarchy, individual congregations have wide latitude to act on their own initiative in hiring, and even ordaining, ministers. On September 15, 1853, when the South Butler Congregational Church recognized Antoinette Brown as its minister, she became the first ordained woman minister in the United States. A few months later, she made history again, becoming the first woman to officiate at a marriage ceremony, an event that received widespread press coverage. Brown's notoriety as a woman minister also boosted her public-speaking career; she could now command almost any price for her lectures.

Despite these significant successes, Brown often found the life of a women's rights pioneer to be both lonely and enervating. As early as her Oberlin days, she had discovered that many people strongly disapproved of women as preachers. She had written to Lucy Stone that when people discovered her ministerial ambitions they "sometimes believe I am joking, sometimes stare at me with amazement and sometimes seem to start back with a kind of horror." Brown was very much alone in her struggle to open up the ministry to women. No other woman was ordained for nearly ten years. She also felt keenly the lack of support from many of her friends and family. Brown later wrote, "It was one of my odd experiences to see some of my old intimates of my own age look at me with a kind of curious incredulity, as utterly unable to comprehend the kind of motive which could lead me to take so peculiar a position in life. No attitude of strangers could have affected me half so much." In 1854, suffering from ill health brought on by the physical and emotional demands of her pastoral work, and also burdened by a spiritual crisis, Brown left her church in South Butler and returned to her parents' home to recuperate.

The issue of women's rights became increasingly important to Brown. Her experiences at the 1853 World Temperance Convention in New York City underscored the disabilities under which women still labored in making their voices heard on public issues. Brown attended the convention as a credentialed delegate of two temperance societies, but the men chairing the meeting refused to allow her to speak. Horace Greeley, the editor of the *New York Tribune* and a friend and supporter of Brown, described the proceedings in his paper: "First Day—Crowding a woman off the platform. Second Day—Gagging her. Third Day—Voting that she shall stay gagged."

However, Brown continued to have a problematic relationship with the established women's movement in the United States. Although she supported the movement for women's suffrage, believing that because men and women were fundamentally different men could not represent women politically, her first priority was to improve women's social and economic position. She refused to wear "bloomers," the outfit of tunic, knee-length skirt and pants adopted by many women's rights activists of the period, believing that ridicule of the costume would detract from more important issues. Brown continued to argue that organized religions could provide a meaningful role for women, although many important leaders of the women's movement such as Stone and *Elizabeth Cady Stanton had severed all ties with their churches. Nonetheless, Brown eventually succeeded in her long campaign to convince her fellow activists to open and close women's rights conventions with a prayer. Finally, although Brown agreed with other women's rights leaders that women needed greater control over their persons and their property within marriage, she strenuously disagreed that making divorce easier was the solution to women's marital disabilities.

Brown had never considered marriage an option for herself. She feared that the responsibilities of a husband and family would interfere with her work as lecturer and minister. Furthermore, she believed that single women could provide to a skeptical public an example of women's vast, untapped abilities. While at Oberlin, she had written to Lucy Stone, who also disavowed marriage, "Let [people] see that woman can take care of herself and act independently without the encouragement and sympathy of her 'lord and master,' that she can think and talk as a moral agent is privileged to. Oh no, don't let us get married. I have no wish to." In 1854, however, while in New York City preaching, doing social work, and writing about her experiences for the *New York Tribune*, Brown met Samuel Blackwell. Blackwell's family were longtime staunch abolitionists and his sisters, *Elizabeth and *Emily Blackwell, were pioneers in women's entry into the medical profession. In addition, his brother Henry Browne Blackwell was assiduously courting a reluctant Lucy Stone. In 1855, shortly after Stone and Henry Blackwell were wed, Antoinette Brown accepted Samuel Blackwell's proposal. They were married on January 24, 1856.

Brown did not intend that her position as wife (and soon, as mother) would hinder her career. She wrote, "It is entirely understood between Mr. Blackwell and myself that my public work would be as nearly uninterrupted as circumstances would allow." Although Brown continued to lecture and preach, the birth of six daughters (five of whom survived infancy) forced her to cut back on her public engagements. After the Civil War, with her family responsibilities increasing and the women's movement riven by factionalism and focused almost exclusively on women's suffrage rather than on the social issues of greater concern to her, Brown abandoned public speaking and turned to writing. Though she authored some fictional works, including a novel, her writings mainly addressed the attempt to reconcile science and religion.

Although distancing herself from the two established women's rights organizations, the National Woman Suffrage Association, led by Brown's former colleagues on the lyceum circuit, *Susan B. Anthony and Elizabeth Cady Stanton, and the American Woman Suffrage Association, headed by her sister-in-law, Lucy Stone, Brown remained committed to progress for women. She was a founder and active member of the Association for the Advancement of Women, which addressed issues such as women's education, science, and dress reform, that the suffrage organizations disdained. In many of her writings, Brown argued that women could and should combine professional and domestic duties. In her own life, she was quite fortunate, for Samuel Blackwell was willing to share household responsibilities with his wife. Perhaps drawing on these experiences, Brown was one of the first writers to propose that, not only should women move into masculine professions, but that men should undertake traditionally feminine domestic duties as well. However, Brown apparently believed that women's first concern should be home and family and that professional responsibilities must be shaped to accommodate domestic requirements. Her writing also did not dwell on women's engaging in paid employment outside the home; rather, she argued that women must remain intellectually alive and engaged while fulfilling their household duties.

As Brown grew older, she reaped the rewards of her earlier pioneering activities. By 1880, there were over 200 female ministers in the United States. Brown's eldest daughter, **Florence Blackwell**, became a lay preacher in the Methodist Church. (Two other daughters, **Edith** and **Ethel**, became doctors.) Brown had herself become a Unitarian in 1878 and was recognized as a minister by the Unitarian Church. In 1903, she helped found a Unitarian church in her hometown of Elizabeth, New Jersey. Accorded the title of "Minister Emeritus," Brown preached once a month.

Oberlin College belatedly acknowledged her achievements. In 1879, her alma mater granted her an honorary masters degree and in 1908 she received an honorary Doctor of Divinity degree. Her intellectual achievements in the debate on science and religion were also recognized in 1881, when she was elected to membership in the American Association for the Advancement of Science, and in 1893, when she presented a paper at the Parliament of Religions held in Chicago. Her work as an early activist in the women's movement was acclaimed in 1888 at the International Council of Women at which she, along with other luminaries such as Lucy Stone, Henry Blackwell, and Elizabeth Cady Stanton, were honored at a "Conference of Pioneers." In 1890, her quiet efforts to reconcile the leaders of the two major women's rights groups were rewarded with the merger of the organizations as the National American Woman Suffrage Association. Brown also testified before the Senate Committee on Woman Suffrage in 1906 in favor of a federal suffrage amendment. She was one of the few original women's rights leaders to live to see that amendment ratified in 1920. Antoinette Brown Blackwell triumphantly voted in the presidential election of 1920, casting her ballot for the Republican candidate Warren Harding.

Although left a widow after Samuel Blackwell's death in 1901 and increasingly plagued by deafness and blindness, Brown maintained an active and involved life throughout her later years. She traveled extensively both abroad and in the United States, visiting the Middle East in 1903 and attending a suffrage convention in Portland, Oregon, in 1905. She continued to write and published her first collection of poems, *Sea Drift,* to generally favorable reviews in 1902. Antoinette Brown Blackwell died in New Jersey on November 5, 1921.

SOURCES:

Cazden, Elizabeth. *Antoinette Brown Blackwell.* Old Westbury, NY: The Feminist Press, 1983.

Lasser, Carol, and Marlene Deahl Merrill. *Friends and Sisters: Letters between Lucy Stone and Antoinette Brown Blackwell.* Urbana: University of Illinois Press, 1987.

SUGGESTED READING:

Flexner, Eleanor. *Century of Struggle.* Cambridge: The Belknap Press, 1959.

Kerr, Laura. *The Lady in the Pulpit.* NY: Woman's Press, 1951.

COLLECTIONS:

Blackwell Family Papers at the Schlesinger Library, Radcliffe College, Cambridge, Massachusetts, and The Library of Congress, Washington, D.C.

Mary A. Procida, University of Pennsylvania, Philadelphia, Pennsylvania

Brown-Miller, Lisa (1966—).

See Team USA: Women's Ice Hockey at Nagano.

Browne, Anne (d. 1511)

*Duchess of Suffolk. Died in 1511; daughter of Sir Anthony Browne and *Lucy Neville; married Charles*

Brandon (1484–1545), 1st duke of Suffolk (r. 1514–1545), around 1508; children: *Anne Brandon (d. 1557); **Mary Brandon** (d. around 1542, who married Thomas Stanley, Lord Monteagle).

Browne, Augusta (1820–1882)

American composer, organist and author who was one of the most prolific woman composers in the U.S. in the period before 1870. Born Augusta Garrett in Dublin, Ireland, in 1820; died in Washington, D.C., on January 11, 1882.

Brought to U.S. sometime in the late 1820s; served as organist at the First Presbyterian Church in Brooklyn (1840s and 1850s); began to publish successful parlor songs and salon piano pieces (1840s); some of her most important pieces are The Chieftain's Halls *(1844) and* The Warlike Dead in Mexico *(1848); was also a prominent musical journalist, arguing for women's right to a complete and equal musical education.*

Augusta Browne was a confident composer who made a significant impact on the American musical scene in the years before and after the Civil War. Born in Ireland, she had no apparent problems in adapting herself to the musical environment of a vibrant, bustling New York City. Though her parlor songs and piano pieces appear to modern observers as hopelessly naive, in their own day they summed up personal romantic yearnings and national aspirations in times of war and peace. A strong-willed and opinionated individual, Browne resisted using American vernacular styles in her compositions, insisting that to rely on them would be "taste-corrupting." She was equally adamant on the subject of a woman's right to a full and complete musical education, a topic she expounded in the strongest possible terms in her article "A Woman on Women," which appeared in the *Knickerbocker Monthly* in 1863.

John Haag,
Athens, Georgia

Browne, Coral (1913–1991)

Australian-born actress. Born Coral Edith Brown in Melbourne, Australia, on July 23, 1913; died of breast cancer on May 29, 1991, in Los Angeles, California; daughter of Leslie Clarence and Victoria Elizabeth (Bennett) Brown; attended Claremont Ladies' College, Melbourne; studied painting at the Working Men's College, Melbourne; married Philip Westrope Pearman, June 26, 1950 (died); married Vincent Price (an actor), 1974.

Selected films: The Amateur Gentleman *(1936);* Black Limelight *(1938);* Let George Do It *(1940);* Piccadilly Incident *(1946);* Auntie Mame *(US, 1958);* The Roman Spring of Mrs. Stone *(US/UK, 1961);* Dr. Crippen *(1964);* The Night of the Generals *(1967);* The Legend of Lylah Clare *(US, 1968);* The Killing of Sister George *(US, 1968);* The Ruling Class *(1972);* Theater of Blood *(1973);* The Drowning Pool *(US, 1975);* American Dreamer *(US, 1984);* Dream Child *(1985).*

An accomplished tragic actress as well as an acclaimed comedienne, Coral Browne was as comfortable in the role of Shakespeare's Lady Macbeth as she was cavorting as Vera Charles, the delightfully cynical actress in *Auntie Mame.* In her 50-year career, Browne was seen on stages in Australia, England, and the United States, as well as in a number of films.

Born in Melbourne, Australia, Browne studied to be a painter before taking up the theater. She made her professional debut in 1931, as Margaret Orme in the Melbourne Comedy Theatre production of *Loyalties,* and had 28 plays to her credit before leaving Australia for England, where she hoped to find character roles suited to her statuesque bearing and deep resonant voice. Her first engagement in London, as an understudy to **Nora Swinburne** in *Lover's Leap* (1934), became an actor's dream come true when Swinburne took ill the night after the play opened. Browne stepped in, and her success led to a series of substantial roles. Between 1935 and 1950, she played in such London hits as *Mated* (1935), *Death Asks a Verdict* (1936), and *The Taming of the Shrew* (1937). She portrayed Maggie Cutler in *The Man Who Came to Dinner* (1941), Ruth Sherwood in *My Sister Eileen* (1943), Mrs. Cheyney in *The Last of Mrs. Cheyney* (1944), and Lady Frederick Berolles in Somerset Maugham's *Lady Frederick* (1946).

Browne's long association with the Old Vic Company began in 1951, when she made her debut as Emilia in *Othello.* She went on to play numerous Shakespearean roles, including Lady Macbeth in 1956, which entailed months of study. She told New York *World-Telegram and Sun* reporter William Peper, "I find Shakespeare very difficult to learn. I mumbled lines everywhere I went and even started to rub the blood off my hands on a bus." After a successful run in London, Browne brought her performance to New York. Critic Brooks Atkinson was ecstatic, calling her work "an extraordinary piece of acting." The following year, in the comic role of Helen of Troy in the Old Vic production of *Troilus and Cressida,* Browne delighted Washington *Post and Times Herald* critic Richard L. Coe, who wrote: "Helen, a busty middle-aged bawd, tinkles on a white piano to her boyish young Paris. . . . Coral Browne's all-too-brief Helen of Troy is a hilarious spoof."

Browne's Broadway debut in Christopher Marlowe's *Tamburlaine the Great*, opposite Anthony Quayle, was a critical success but closed after only three weeks. Throughout the 1960s, Browne continued to delight audiences in new plays such as *Toys in the Attic*, as well as in countless classic roles, many played on tour with the Old Vic. Comparing English audiences to those in America, she noted that the British tended to be noisier, while New Yorkers were inexcusably late getting to the theater.

Browne was married to actors' agent Philip Westrope Pearman in 1950. After his death, she married actor Vincent Price. The actress seems to have left the stage around 1970, although she later made the films *American Dreamer* (1984) and *Dream Child* (1985). Coral Browne died of breast cancer in 1991.

Barbara Morgan, Melrose, Massachusetts

Browne, Ethel (1885–1965).
See Harvey, Ethel Browne.

Browne, Felicia Dorothea (1793–1835).
See Hemans, Felicia D.

Browne, Frances (1816–1879)

Irish author. Name variations: Blind Poetess of Donegal. Born Frances Browne in Stranolar, County Donegal, Ireland, on January 16, 1816; died in London on August 25, 1879; educated at home; never married; no children.

Selected works: The Star of Alteghei (1844); Granny's Wonderful Chair and the Stories It Told (1856); My Share in the World (1861).

Frances Browne was born in Stranolar, County Donegal, Ireland, on January 16, 1816; at 18 months, she lost her sight due to smallpox. The seventh of eleven children, Frances remained at home while her siblings attended school and did their chores in exchange for their reading aloud to her at night from schoolbooks or volumes borrowed from neighbors. By age seven, she composed poetry to amuse her family, and her siblings acted as secretaries, writing down her recitations. In adulthood, Browne's work was published regularly in journals and periodicals. She moved with a sister to Edin-

burgh in 1847, then to London in 1852, to facilitate her career. Literary pensions and wealthy supporters, including the marquess of Landsdowne, kept her comfortable and productive. *Granny's Wonderful Chair and the Stories It Told* (1856) was Browne's most popular work and was kept in print long after her 1879 death.

Crista Martin, Boston, Massachusetts

Browne, Mary K. (1891–1971)

American tennis champion and golfer. Born in Ventura, California, on June 3, 1891; died in Laguna Beach, California, on August 19, 1971.

Distinguishing herself in tennis before taking up golf, Mary K. Browne is the only person to have played in championship rounds of both sports. She held the U.S. National Tennis Singles title (1912 to 1914), the National Doubles (1913 and 1914, and the National Mixed Doubles (1912 to 1914, 1921). She then crossed over to golf, reaching the final round of the USGA

Mary K. Browne (left) with Louise Riddell Williams.

Women's Amateur. In 1924, she beat *Glenna Collett in the championship semifinal, then lost to *Dorothy Campbell Hurd in the final. In 1925, Browne made it to the quarterfinal before losing to **Alexa Stirling Fraser**. In her last attempt in 1934, she lost in the second round to Dorothy Hurd.

Browne, Rosalind Bengelsdorf

(1916–1979)

American artist and founding member of the American Abstract Artists. Name variations: Rosalind Bengelsdorf. Born Rosalind Bengelsdorf in 1916 in New York, New York; died in 1979 in New York; studied art at the Art Students League, the Annot School, and with Hans Hofmann at his newly established school on 57th Street, New York; married Byron Browne (an abstract artist), 1940.

A founding member of the American Abstract Artists, Rosalind Browne devoted a life-

Kady Brownell

time to the advancement of the abstract art movement. She began her own career studying with realist teachers at the Art Students League and was unimpressed by the first painting of Pablo Picasso she viewed at the Museum of Modern Art. Browne was more formally introduced to abstract art at the Annot School and later was influenced by Hans Hofmann, a leader in the Abstract Expressionist movement of the 1940s and 1950s. Advocating the use of colored spaces to provide balance, movement, and tension, Hofmann taught that, through color, forms can be submerged or brought forward from the background of the canvas.

Browne not only integrated Hofmann's ideas into her own abstract compositions but set out to win acceptance for the controversial movement. She contributed her time and talent to the American Abstract Artists, helping the fledgling organization raise money to pay for its first exhibition in 1937; one of her lithographs was included in a printed folio the artists sold to raise money. In the statement of intent that she wrote for the organization in 1938, Browne argued that abstraction was a new way of looking at spatial relationships, not just an escape from reality. That same year, she was one of a handful of abstract artists to win funding from the Federal Art Project, for a mural for the Central Nurses Home. Although the mural was eventually destroyed, the preliminary oil-on-canvas, *Study for Mural for Central Nurses Home* (1937–38), became part of the collection of the University Art Museum at the University of New Mexico. After her marriage to fellow abstract artist Byron Browne in 1940, Rosalind Bengelsdorf Browne cut back on her painting but continued as a critic, teacher, and writer until her death in 1979.

Browne, Sidney Jane (1850–1941)

British nurse, known as "the modern Florence Nightingale." Name variations: Dame Sidney Browne. Born on January 5, 1850; died on August 13, 1941.

In a life dedicated to nursing soldiers, Dame Sidney Jane Browne served in four campaigns, including the Egyptian War, the Sudan campaign, the Boer War, and the First World War. She was recognized with numerous honors and also served as the first president of the Royal College of Nursing.

Brownell, Kady (b. 1842)

American Civil War hero who served with the Rhode Island Volunteers. Name variations: Kate. Born in

Caffraria, on the African coast, in 1842; death date unknown; daughter of a soldier in the British army; married Robert S. Brownell.

During the American Civil War, camp followers—fathers, mothers, brothers, sisters, wives, and sweethearts—were a fact of life. Tents often housed entire families who had found their way into a regiment camp to be with a loved one. While many wives were satisfied to visit their husband on the battlefield or act as volunteer nurses in camp hospitals, others were brave and spirited enough to enlist along with their husbands. In 1861, Kady Brownell joined her husband's Rhode Island infantry company. Becoming an excellent markswoman, she was assigned as color-bearer and fought alongside her husband Robert in several battles. Brownell is credited with saving the day at Newbern when the regiment, traveling through a dense forest, was fired upon by another group of Union soldiers who mistook them for the enemy. Brownell rushed forward, waving the regimental flag until the attackers realized their mistake. Unfortunately, many were wounded in the confusion including her husband, whose leg was shattered by cannon fire. Although Robert recovered, he and his wife were discharged from the regiment. Brownell kept her flag and sword as souvenirs but reportedly gave a rifle she had confiscated to a soldier friend who fought with it until the end of the war.

Brownell, Kate (b. 1842).

See Brownell, Kady.

Browning, Elizabeth Barrett

(1806–1861)

English poet who wrote some of the most exquisite love poems in the English language—the first cycle of Petrarchan love sonnets to be written from the woman's rather than the man's point of view. Name variations: Elizabeth Barrett (1806–1846), Elizabeth Barrett-Browning (1846–1861). Born Elizabeth Barrett Moulton in County Durham, England, on March 6, 1806; died on June 30, 1861, in Florence, Italy; oldest of 12 children of Edward Barrett Moulton (who would change his name to Barrett for reasons of inheritance) and Mary Graham-Clarke; married Robert Browning (the poet), September 12, 1846; children: Robert Wiedemann Browning (b. 1849).

Selected writings: An Essay on Mind and Other Poems *(1826);* Prometheus Bound and Miscellaneous Poems *(1833);* The Seraphim and Other Poems *(1838);* Poems by E. Barrett Browning *(1844);* A Drama of Exile and Other Poems *(1845);* The Runaway Slave at Pilgrim's Point *(1849);* Poems by E.B. Browning *(1850);* Sonnets from the Portuguese *(1850);* Casa Guidi Windows *(1851);* Two Poems *(1854);* Aurora Leigh *(1857);* Poems before Congress *(1860);* Last Poems *(1862); and numerous volumes containing her letters to her sister, as well as* **Mary Russell Mitford**, *R.H. Horne, Robert Browning, and others.*

The marriage of English poets Robert Browning and Elizabeth Barrett is one of the great romantic true stories of the 19th century, in which a dashing 34-year-old poet wooed an ailing poet of 40 and wedded her secretly. They became intimate through a huge correspondence of 573 letters, stole away from their respective homes one day in 1846, married quietly, returned home separately without mentioning it, then immigrated together to Italy the following week. In some respects, however, they were characteristic models of Victorian rectitude rather than romantic rebels. They suffered little disapproval or ostracism, except from Elizabeth's inflexible father, and they never aimed to flout public conventions.

Elizabeth Barrett was born in 1806, oldest of twelve children, nine of whom lived into adulthood. She was born in County Durham but moved as a young child to Hope End, Hertfordshire, north of London, where she lived for the next 21 years. She soon proved exceptionally gifted academically and out-competed her brother Edward in all lessons, though she was denied the opportunity to go away to school. She was passionately devoted to Edward, whom she called "Bro"; as an adult he had no career. At the age of four, she began writing poetry and was a master of poetic genres by the time she was ten. She had also read most of Shakespeare, Pope, and even Milton. As a teenager, she contributed poetry to London journals regularly and published her first book, *An Essay on Mind with Other Poems* (1826), anonymously, at the age of 20. By then, she had learned to read in Italian, French, Greek, Latin, and Hebrew well enough to peruse the Old Testament straight through.

She followed up her initial triumphs with an 1833 translation of Aeschylus' *Prometheus Bound* (a less successful venture that she later revised), and a further book of poetry, *The Seraphim and Other Poems* (1838), which for the first time carried her name on the title page. Until then, her poetic voice had carefully veiled her sex. The main poem, of almost 80 pages, consists of a discussion between two angels in Heaven at the time of Christ's crucifixion. The others are shorter romantic verses, which scored a great hit with

English critics. By the early 1840s, Barrett was probably the best-known and most admired woman poet in Britain. After her marriage, she remained the more famous half of the couple, and, when William Wordsworth died in 1850, her name was mentioned among the candidates for poet laureate.

The family's wealth was based on a West Indies slave plantation, much to her shame, but in her father's generation the business went into decline due to serious mismanagement of the estate. In 1832, four years after the death of Elizabeth's mother **Mary Graham-Clarke**, Edward Barrett was forced to sell Hope End, his country estate, and move to a humbler (though still decidedly affluent) setting. For a while, the family lived in Sidmouth on the Devonshire coast, and then moved to London in 1835 where they lived first in Gloucester Place and then in an elegant townhouse on Wimpole Street. Edward Barrett never discussed his declining fortunes with his children, and they sometimes only learned of problems through the gossip of friends. Like most Victorian patriarchs, he assumed that his sons would later take up work in the world, but unlike most, he did not want his daughters to marry. Instead, he apparently intended that all should remain permanently at home, and as his business and fortune deteriorated he became increasingly autocratic.

Elizabeth developed a serious ailment, a form of tuberculosis, and some biographers have speculated that it was a psychosomatic stratagem, brought on by the tensions of her family life or by resentment at being denied the opportunities granted her brother. She also suffered from a spinal injury incurred in a riding accident. Despite her illness, she worked hard from her sickroom, studied poetry, philosophy, and languages, and enjoyed several close friendships with men. One of them, the Reverend George Hunter, became an ardent suitor, but she turned down cold his frequent marriage proposals in the early 1830s. Her letters show that she was highly critical of gender relations in her world, and disapproved of many marriages that she witnessed because of the men's tendency towards tyranny and the women's lack of education and gravity. She enjoyed a more successful and stable longterm friendship with John Kenyon, a wealthy patron of the arts who first introduced her to Robert Browning's work and helped spark the great literary romance.

At the end of the 1830s, Elizabeth's medical condition was worse than ever and her doctor urged her to spend the winter in the warmer climate of Torquay, a coastal town in southwest England. It took a great battle of wills with her father to be allowed to go, and while she was there in 1840 her brother Edward was drowned in a sailing accident. The loss tormented her with grief, and she convinced herself that she was to blame for his death, since he had come there as her companion. She suffered a complete nervous breakdown as a result, returning to London sobered and subdued a year later. She was so affected by her brother's death that she could never bear to mention it directly for the rest of her life, but only by the most allusive indirection. In the following years, she wrote two more volumes of poetry, which further enhanced her reputation when she published them in 1844. Among the poems in this collection, many of them melancholy, was "The Children's Cry," a protest against the prematurely overworked children in the English coal mines and factories:

> Our knees tremble sorely in the stooping,
> We fall upon our faces, trying to go;
> And underneath our heavy eyelids drooping
> The reddest flower would look as pale as snow.
> For all day we drag our burden tiring
> Through the coal-dark underground;
> Or all day we drive the wheels of iron
> In the factories, round and round.

She also became in those years what would now be described as an opium addict. She was, she wrote a friend, "in the habit of taking forty drops of laudanum a day, and cannot do with less." She spent virtually all her time in her work room, allowing only a small circle of close friends, including Kenyon, to visit her, doing no domestic work, doted on by her siblings, and still studying voraciously.

She and Robert Browning exchanged greetings in January 1845 after he wrote her a letter of admiration for her collected poems (in one of which she had compared him with Wordsworth and Tennyson), and they now began an ardent, 19-month correspondence. He had resolved to have no career except that of poet and had persuaded his baffled but adoring family to go along with his plans and support him financially far into adulthood. He was already well-known and had enjoyed literary acclaim in the 1830s for his long poem *Paracelsus* (1835) and for a play *Strafford* (1837) but his complicated poem *Sordello* (1840) was a flop, and he was still in no position to support himself financially. After that, despite a prolific output, it would be more than a decade before he could enjoy public approval and a decent income from his writing. Robert Browning was excited at discovering a kindred spirit in Elizabeth and told her that until

Elizabeth Barrett Browning

they met he had despaired of finding a woman his intellectual equal, with whom he could be "love's slave" for life. They met frequently in her room and she wrote him a series of sonnets, the most famous of which, still popular today, is: "How do I love thee? Let me count the ways." They were later published as *Sonnets from the Portuguese* to disguise their intensely personal origins, and were the first cycle of Petrarchan love sonnets to be written from the woman's rather than the man's point of view.

The couple slipped away from home and married on September 12, 1846, saying nothing to their families. Still furtive, they set out for Italy on September 19th. Almost at once Elizabeth's health began to improve, and she enjoyed their journey to Italy, apart from getting a furious letter from her father, disowning her for her secret disobedience. For the first six months, they lived in Pisa on money Elizabeth had inherited from her grandmother and uncle, attended by her faithful maid **Elizabeth Wilson**. In March of 1847, not realizing until the last minute that she was pregnant, Elizabeth Browning had a miscarriage, and her loss of blood terrified Robert that his passion had endangered his new wife's life. She recovered and felt buoyant at the evidence of her fertility rather than depressed by the loss.

Later that year, they moved to Florence and into an apartment in an old stone palace, the Casa Guidi. Their son "Pen," Robert Wiedemann Barrett Browning, was born there in 1849, when Elizabeth was 43. She doted on him. Though Florence became a permanent home, they moved frequently back and forth across Europe in the following years, spending time alternately in London, Paris, Rome, and the Alps. Elizabeth continued to have a horror of the sea and ships, ever since her brother's drowning, but braved the crossings of the English Channel to visit London. "It was a little mortifying for both Robert and Elizabeth," writes **Margaret Forster** of their early months together, "to face up to the fact that they were not nearly so well suited to a Bohemian or a gypsy life as they liked to imagine." Elizabeth had always been surrounded by servants and could not cook, sew, or take care of the household. Elizabeth Wilson, who had originally been hired as a lady's maid but was now expected to be housekeeper, dressmaker, and general servant too, served their needs for a modest £16 per year. Elizabeth Barrett Browning never revealed her upper-class origins more clearly than when she indignantly denied Wilson's request for a pay-raise, arguing that she should be grateful for the family's emotional warmth as adequate compensation and claiming, quite unfairly, that she could not afford it. It was all very well for Elizabeth to make impassioned pleas on behalf of oppressed women, American slaves, overworked factory children, and the Italians suffering under the Austrian yoke, political views for which she was renowned, but when it came to her own convenience and comfort the servants were expected to buckle under.

American and British visitors came to see the Brownings in Florence, usually drawn more to Elizabeth than to her husband, whose work at that stage was less widely respected. *Margaret Fuller, a leading light among the American transcendentalists, visited her, while back in America *Emily Dickinson was one of many American authors to admire her from afar. Elizabeth's biggest writing project of the 1850s was *Aurora*

From the movie The Barretts of Wimpole Street, *starring Sir John Gielgud and Jennifer Jones.*

Leigh (1857), a blank verse, book-length poem in the form of an autobiography, full of echoes of her own life, emphasizing the heroine's intellectual precocity and loneliness, her travels in Italy and England, and her ultimate marriage to her true love. It has a strong current of feminist sensibility, criticizing the stifling of women's intellect in contemporary England, and an equally fervent denunciation of the suffering workers in the industrial cities. Sub-plots deal with the discrediting of utopian socialism, the melodramatic kidnapping of a poor girl into a Parisian brothel, a good man blinded in a fire (reminiscent of Mr. Rochester in *Charlotte Brontë*'s *Jane Eyre*), and several of the startling coincidences favored by her contemporaries, including Dickens as well as the Brontës. The poem was a commercial success despite what was, for its time, an unusually frank account of female sexuality.

The Brownings were both excited by the Italian liberal uprisings of 1848 and dismayed by Pope Pius IX's radical change of political views from liberal to reactionary. Throughout the 1850s, Elizabeth followed the development of the Italian unification movement closely and was jubilant to witness its successes in 1859 and 1860. She wrote poems on these events, praising the French Emperor Napoleon III, whom she idealized as a benevolent strong man, and sometimes criticizing English policy that was less sympathetic to the Italian cause. She was dismayed when another hero, Count Camillo di Cavour, prime minister of a newly unified north Italian kingdom, died in 1861, and it prompted a crisis in her own health. She had been frail throughout much of her life, despite her revival after marriage, and now was unable to regain her strength.

Elizabeth Barrett Browning died in June 1861 and was buried in the Protestant Cemetery in Florence where she has an elaborate, elevated stone tomb. Robert Browning abandoned Florence and came back to England where he would live until 1889, publishing her *Last Poems* in 1862 as a tribute. Obituaries praised Elizabeth Barrett Browning in extravagant terms, with one major journal, the *Edinburgh Review*, claiming that such a talented female writer had never before lived. "Such a combination of the finest genius and the choicest results of cultivation and wide-ranging studies has never been seen before in any woman." Her reputation went into eclipse between 1900 and 1930 and by the early 20th century critics and literary historians had come to regard her husband as the greater poet. The contradictory and paradoxical aspects of her character have fascinated a new generation of feminist critics, however, and the discovery and publication of hundreds of her letters in the last three decades have made her as fascinating for them as for her poetry.

SOURCES:

Karlin, Daniel. *The Courtship of Robert Browning and Elizabeth Barrett.* Oxford: Oxford University Press, 1985.

Kenyon, Frederick, ed. "Elizabeth Barrett Browning," in *Poetical Works.* NY: Macmillan, 1899.

Kintner, Elvan, ed. *The Letters of Robert Browning and Elizabeth Barrett-Browning.* Cambridge, MA: Harvard University Press, 1969.

Mander, R. *Mrs. Browning: The Story of Elizabeth Barrett.* London: Widenfeld and Nicolson, 1980.

Raymond, Meredith, and Mary Rose Sullivan, eds. *The Letters of Elizabeth Barrett-Browning to Mary Russell Mitford.* 3 vols. Baylor University: Wedgestone Press, 1983.

Taplin, Gardner. "Elizabeth Barrett Browning" in *Dictionary of Literary Biography.* Vol. 32. Detroit, MI: Gale, 1984, 53–68.

SUGGESTED READING:

Dennis, Barbara. *Elizabeth Barrett Browning: The Hope End Years.* Dufour, 1996.

COLLECTIONS:

Wellesley College Library; New York Public Library; Huntington Library; Baylor University; British Museum; University of Texas.

RELATED MEDIA:

The Barretts of Wimpole Street, play by Rudolph Besier, starring *Katharine Cornell (opened on Broadway in 1931).

The Barretts of Wimpole Street (110 min.), MGM, 1934, film starring *Norma Shearer (who was nominated for an Academy Award for Best Actress), *Maureen O'Sullivan, and Fredric March; screenplay by Claudine West, Donald Ogden Stewart, and Ernest Vajda; directed by Sidney Franklin.

The Barretts of Wimpole Street (105 min.), MGM, 1957, film starring *Jennifer Jones, John Gielgud, Virginia McKenna, and Bill Travers; directed by Sidney Franklin.

Patrick Allitt, Assistant Professor of History, Emory University, Atlanta, Georgia

Browning, Peaches (b. 1911).

See Kuhn, Irene Corbally for sidebar.

Brownrigg, Elizabeth (1720–1767)

English murderer. Born Elizabeth Harkly (or Hartley) in 1720; hanged at Tyburn, England, on September 14, 1767; married James Brownrigg (an apprentice plumber); children: sixteen, three of whom survived childhood.

Married to a prospering plumber, Elizabeth Brownrigg lost 13 of her 16 children in infancy, and, in light her subsequent behavior, it is possible that she was at least a contributory factor in their deaths. She went on to build a successful, respected midwifery practice, which kept her so busy that she was forced to take in apprentices from the local workhouse, where unwanted children were housed and put up for hire. Brownrigg abused three successive teenage apprentices, all named Mary, starving and beating the girls at will and forcing them to work 18 hours a day. The abuse grew increasingly severe with each victim and was often carried out in front of her husband and son, who were said to enjoy their participation as spectators. Brownrigg managed to avoid investigation for a long time, even after one of the girls escaped and made her way to a foundling hospital.

Brownrigg's crimes were not disclosed until the stepmother of the third apprentice demanded to see her child and was turned away; consequently, authorities searched the house and found the victim, who had been severely beaten, crammed into a small cupboard. The child later died of her massive injuries. After an unsuccessful escape attempt, Brownrigg was captured and brought to trial for murder. Silent and offering no defense, she was condemned to execution, while her husband and son were given six-months in prison and fined one shilling each. On September 14, 1767, Elizabeth Brownrigg was hanged in front of one of the largest, and angriest, crowds ever assembled for a public execution in England.

Bruce, Christian (d. 1356)

*Countess of Mar. Name variations: Lady Christian Bruce; Lady Christian Seton; Christian Moray or Murray; Christina Bruce. Died in 1356; daughter of Robert Bruce, earl of Carrick, and *Marjorie of Carrick (c. 1254–1292); sister of Robert I the Bruce (1274–1329), king of Scotland (r. 1306–1329); married Garnait also known as Gratney, 7th earl of Mar, around 1292; married Christopher Seton, in 1305; married Andrew Murray also known as Andrew Moray of Bothwell, after October 12, 1325; children: (first marriage) Donald, 8th earl of Mar; Helen of Mar (who married John Mentieth, lord of Arran, and Sir James Garioch); (third marriage) John Moray, lord of Bothwell; Sir Thomas Moray.*

During Scotland's wars for independence (1296–1328), Lady Christian Bruce defended Kildrummy Castle when it came under siege.

Bruce, Christina (d. 1356).

See Bruce, Christian.

Bruce, Isabel (c. 1278–1358)

*Queen of Norway. Born around 1278; died in 1358; daughter of Robert Bruce, earl of Carrick, and *Marjorie of Carrick (c. 1254–1292); sister of Robert I Bruce (1274–1329), king of Scotland (r. 1306–1329); became second wife of Eirik the Priest-Hater also known as Eric II Magnusson (1268–1299), king of Norway (r. 1280–1299), in 1293; children: Ingeborg Ericsdottir (b. 1297, who married Waldemar, duke of Finland). Eric II's first wife was *Margaret of Norway (1261–1283).*

Bruce, Isabella (d. 1296).

See Isabella of Mar.

Bruce, Margaret (c. 1286–?)

*Scottish royal. Born around 1286; daughter of Robert Bruce, earl of Carrick, and *Marjorie of Carrick (c. 1254–1292); sister of Robert I the Bruce (1274–1329), king of Scotland (r. 1306–1329); married William de Carlyle; children: William de Carlyle; John de Carlyle.*

Bruce, Margaret (1296–1316)

*Scottish princess. Name variations: Marjory or Marjorie Bruce. Born in 1296 (some sources cite 1297); died in an accident at age 20 on March 2, 1316, in Paisley, Strathclyde, Scotland; interred at Paisley Abbey; daughter of Robert I the Bruce (1274–1329), king of Scotland (r. 1306–1329), and *Isabella of Mar (died in 1296, shortly after giving birth to Margaret); married Walter Stewart or Stuart (d. 1326), 6th High Steward of Scotland, in 1315; children: Robert II (1316–1390), king of Scotland (r. 1371–1390).*

In 1306, Margaret Bruce was captured by the English, along with her aunt, *Mary Bruce (fl. 1290–1316), and *Isabella of Buchan (fl. 1290–1310). When the king of England, Edward I Longshanks, ordered Isabella and Mary imprisoned in cages at Roxburgh and Berwick, he also demanded a cage be prepared for ten-year-old Margaret to be located in the Tower of London. Because of her age, however, he relented and placed her in a nunnery in Yorkshire. In 1314, Margaret was exchanged for English prisoners after the battle of Bannockburn and returned to Scotland; in 1315, she married Walter Stewart. The following year, a pregnant Margaret was killed when she fell from her horse; her baby, successfully delivered from her dead body, would succeed to the throne in 1371 as the first Stewart monarch of Scotland, Robert II.

Bruce, Margaret (d. 1346)

*Scottish princess. Died in childbirth in 1346 (some sources cite 1347); daughter of Robert I the Bruce (1274–1329), king of Scotland (r. 1306–1329), and *Elizabeth de Burgh (d. 1327); married William Sutherland, 5th earl of Sutherland, 1343 or 1345; children: John (b. around 1346).*

Bruce, Marjorie (c. 1254–1292).

See Marjorie of Carrick.

Bruce, Marjorie (1296–1316).

See Bruce, Margaret.

Bruce, Mary (fl. 1290–1316).

See Isabella of Buchan for sidebar.

Bruce, Matilda (c. 1285–c. 1326)

*Countess of Ross. Name variations: Matilda Ross; Maud Bruce. Born around 1285; died around 1326; interred at Fearn, Scotland; daughter of Robert Bruce, earl of Carrick, and *Marjorie of Carrick (c. 1254–1292); sister of Robert I the Bruce (1274–1329), king of Scotland (r. 1306–1329); married Hugh Ross (d. 1333), 4th earl of Ross, around 1308; children: Euphemia Ross (d. 1387).*

Bruce, Matilda (d. 1353)

*Scottish princess. Died on July 20, 1353, in Aberdeen Grampian, Scotland; buried in Dunfermline Abbey, Fife, Scotland; daughter of Robert I the Bruce (1274–1329), king of Scotland (r. 1306–1329), and *Elizabeth de Burgh (d. 1327); married Thomas Isaac; children: *Joan Isaac, Lady of Lorn (fl. 1300s); Katherine Isaac.*

Bruddland, Gro Harlem (b. 1939).

See Bruntland, Gro Harlem.

Bruell, Ilse (1925–1942).

See Brüll, Ilse.

Bruha, Antonia (1915—)

Austrian activist against German Nazism who organized a resistance group in the women's concentration camp Ravensbrück. Born in Vienna, Austria, in 1915 into a Czech-speaking working-class family; married.

Active along with her husband in an anti-Nazi resistance cell; arrested (1941) and sent to Ravensbrück concentration camp; survived and was liberated (1945); remained active in anti-Fascist educational work in Vienna.

Born in Austria in 1915 into a working-class family, Antonia Bruha grew up as a member of Vienna's Czech minority. Many Viennese—perhaps one-third of the population—are of Czech origins, but only a small minority retained a distinct Czech linguistic and cultural identity into the 20th century. Politically and culturally militant, Antonia became a Communist early in life and was convinced that only the small but conspiratorially well-organized Austrian Communist Party had a chance of successfully surviving the dual challenges of domestic Fascism and German Nazism.

Soon after the Nazi annexation of Austria in March 1938, Bruha and her husband became members of a tightly knit cell of Viennese Czech Communists. For several years, Bruha's group of resistance workers were able to avoid detection, spending most of their time writing, printing and distributing anti-Nazi literature. In 1941, however, their luck ran out as a Gestapo agent in their midst brought about the destruction of their cell. Bruha had just given birth at the time. Arrested, she was taken to Vienna's infamous Gestapo headquarters at the Morzinplatz (later destroyed in an air raid and now the site of a noted monument to victims of Fascism), while her three-month-old remained with her husband. More than the tortures she endured at the hands of the Gestapo, uncertainty about her child's fate would prove the most difficult part of her next four years.

Without having revealed the names of her fellow resisters, Bruha was transferred from Vienna first to Prague and then to the Ravensbrück women's concentration camp in northern Germany. Here she witnessed scenes of indescribable brutality and suffering. Benefitting from the strong, indeed lifesaving, solidarity of many of her fellow prisoners, Bruha quickly learned to trust and rely on fellow-Austrian *Rosa Jochmann. Although they maintained great ideological differences (Jochmann was a convinced Social Democrat, while Bruha remained a militant Communist), both women respected one another and were united by their common humanity and a shared hatred of the evils of Nazism. Among the countless atrocities Bruha witnessed in Ravensbrück was the beating murder of an elderly Austrian peasant woman who had been sent to the camp for giving a piece of bread to a prisoner from the Mauthausen concentration camp as she passed his column while she herself returned from church. Arrested for this action, she was found innocent by the judge, but his militantly Nazi legal superiors sentenced her to a term in Ravensbrück. Here she lasted only eight days, before being beaten to death by a particularly brutal female camp official.

The witnessing of such bureaucratized evil strengthened Bruha's resolve to resist the Nazi regime. Working as a member of the cutting room of the tailor's shop, and also as a message courier, she emerged as an important organizer of a resistance organization that maintained prisoner morale, supplied them with drugs and additional food when they were ill, and warned them of particularly dangerous situations. The solidarity practiced by Antonia Bruha saved not only her own life but the lives of many of her comrades. By the end of 1943, a well-functioning resistance organization in Ravensbrück included not only Bruha and Jochmann but other Austrian anti-Nazi women as well, including **Mela Ernst** and **Frieda Günzburg** ("Mara"), both of whom had served as nurses on the Republican side in the Spanish Civil War.

Antonia Bruha was among the almost 15,000 women who remained alive at Ravensbrück when it was liberated by the Soviet Army in late April 1945. Along with other Austrian survivors, she returned to find Vienna a city in ruins; many of her prewar friends were dead or permanently missing as victims of the Holocaust and Nazism. When the emaciated Bruha returned home to her husband and child, it took many months for her to be accepted as a mother. Yet in time, her life began to regain certain aspects of normalcy. Determined not to let the world forget what had happened to her and to countless others, she became an active member of the Austrian Resistance Documentation Archive, which researches Austrian insurgency during the era of Nazism and Fascism of the 1930s and 1940s. Despite her advancing years, she often spoke at schools and political rallies, warning a younger generation of Austrians about the dangers of racism and extreme nationalism. In 1984, she published her memoirs, entitled with characteristic modesty, *I Was Not a Heroine*. Others would argue to the contrary.

SOURCES:

Brauneis, Inge. "Widerstand von Frauen gegen den Nationalsozialismus 1938–1945." Unpublished Ph.D. dissertation, University of Vienna, 1974.

Bruha, Antonia. *Ich war keine Heldin*. New ed. Vienna: Europa Verlag, 1995.

Dokumentationsarchiv des österreichischen Widerstandes, Vienna, file folder on resistance activities of Antonia Bruha, file #5796.

Dokumentationsarchiv des österreichischen Widerstandes, Vienna. *Widerstand und Verfolgung in Wien 1934–1945: Eine Dokumentation*. 2nd ed. 3 vols. Vienna: Österreichischer Bundesverlag, 1984.

Luza, Radomir V. *The Resistance in Austria, 1938–1945*. Minneapolis: University of Minnesota Press, 1984.

Sporrer, Maria, and Herbert Steiner, eds. *Rosa Jochmann, Zeitzeugin*. 3rd ed. Vienna: Europa Verlag, 1987.

Weinzierl, Erika. "Österreichische Frauen in nationalsozialistischen Konzentrationslagern," *Dachauer Hefte*. Vol. 3, no. 3. November 1987, pp. 166–204.

John Haag, Associate Professor, University of Georgia, Athens, Georgia

Brüll, Ilse (1925–1942)

Austrian-Jewish girl who became a symbol in Austria of the millions of young girls murdered during the Holocaust. Name variations: Bruell. Born on April 28, 1925, in Innsbruck, Austria; murdered at Auschwitz in early September 1942; daughter of Rudolf Brüll and Julie Brüll; educated at primary and secondary public schools in Innsbruck.

Schooling ended (November 1938) due to Kristallnacht pogrom; went to the Netherlands (April 1939); taken to Hertogenbosch camp (August 1941); deported to occupied Poland and killed at Auschwitz (early September 1942); parents survived imprisonment and returned to Innsbruck (1945).

As was true of Holland's **Anne Frank*, Austria's Ilse Brüll became a symbol to her nation of the millions of young girls murdered during the Holocaust. She was born and grew up in Innsbruck, the capital of the Austrian province of Tyrol. The beauty of the charming city, which is surrounded by the breathtaking Alps, has masked episodes of human cruelty and intolerance at different points in history. Throughout the middle ages, the burghers of Innsbruck sometimes welcomed, and then persecuted and expelled, a small but often influential Jewish community. In 1674, the Jews were once again expelled, and, although a few families achieved the status of "tolerated" Jews, in 1748 the empress **Maria Theresa* (1717–1780) proclaimed Innsbruck a "Jew-free city." By 1867, Austrian Jews finally achieved full legal equality, and in 1869 a census of the Innsbruck Jewish community counted 27 individuals, comprising 0.4% of the city's total population.

By 1914, the small but vibrant Jewish community of Innsbruck had been successfully integrated into Austro-German culture, and its members were regarded as pillars of municipal economic, social and cultural life. Despite this, a lingering spirit of religious animosity remained, particularly among the less educated Innsbruckers who believed that only a Roman Catholic could be a loyal Austrian. Economic insecurity and the trauma of a lost war after 1918 were instrumental in unleashing a new and much more violently racist anti-Semitism among students and some professors at the University of Innsbruck, an institution long known as a hotbed of extremist Pan-German nationalism. The new radicals, some of whom were members of a growing Nazi movement, regarded the Jewish communities in Vienna, Berlin, and elsewhere as biologically subversive groups plotting to frustrate the emergence of a strong, proud and racially pure Germany.

Few of these facts troubled the young Ilse Brüll, the vivacious only child born to **Julie Brüll** and the prosperous furniture manufacturer Rudolf Brüll on April 28, 1925. In the 1920s, the Jews of Innsbruck numbered about 200, a community that increased to 317 in 1934 (0.5% of the total population of Innsbruck). Busy with school and friendships, Ilse Brüll lived a normal life until March 1938, when Nazi Germany annexed Austria.

Within days of the German takeover, Jewish shops and businesses were boycotted by the vast majority of the population. Soon, these enterprises were "Aryanized" as Jewish owners were pressured to sell their property at absurdly low prices, mainly to opportunistic Nazi officials. The Jewish community was systematically stripped of its assets, its archives were confiscated, and the passports of all Jews were seized. By the fall of 1938, it was clear that the life of the Innsbruck Jewish community was to be numbered in days and weeks, not years. The rabbi and others sought to emigrate as quickly as possible. On the terror-filled Kristallnacht (the night of broken glass) of November 9–10, 1938, the houses of Innsbruck's Jews were raided and demolished, the synagogue and cemetery desecrated. Three community leaders were brutally murdered and their bodies thrown into the icy Inn river. Ilse Brüll was with an aunt in Munich during these horrible events, and from there went to Vienna to stay with other relatives while her desperate parents made plans for her emigration.

Ilse was able to leave Austria in late April 1939 with a group of Jewish children accepted for resettlement by the Netherlands. After some time in Rotterdam, she settled with a group of refugee children in the town of Eersel near Eindhoven. Here they were well treated at the St. Jakobus Home, run by a Roman Catholic organization. The German invasion of May 1940 changed everything for Ilse and her friends, some of whom were converts to Catholicism; conversion was inconsequential in the eyes of the Nazi occupying forces that singled out chil-

dren for "special treatment" based on their "race," not their religion. Unlike some of her friends, Ilse had not converted and in fact now felt more Jewish than ever. Proud of her heritage, she faced the future optimistically even when she was shipped to the Hertogenbosch concentration camp. In the last documentation of her brief life, she noted in a letter of August 1942 to her cousin, "Things should also be all right in Poland. Auf Wiedersehen."

After a brief stay in the Dutch camp Westerbork, Ilse Brüll was transported on August 31, 1942, to Niederkirch, one of the outlying camps of Auschwitz. Precise documentation is lacking, but surviving evidence indicates that she was among the individuals who were killed by SS poison gas at Niederkirch on September 3, 1942. Unlike their only child, Rudolf and Julie Brüll survived the hell of Nazism. They lived through several years of privation and fear at the Theresienstadt-Terezin concentration camp near Prague. Despite all that had been done to them, the Brülls still regarded Innsbruck as their home, and so they returned to what could only have been devastatingly painful memories. Rudolf Brüll began a new life by reopening his furniture store at its old location, Anichstrasse 7. For

Ilse Brüll

months, the Brülls hoped to discover that Ilse too had survived the Holocaust, but in time the bitter truth of her death had to be accepted by the grieving parents. Julie and Rudolf Brüll bore their pain in silence and with great dignity. He became president of the reconstituted Jewish community of Tyrol and the neighboring province of Vorarlberg, serving in that post until his death. Ilse Brüll was never forgotten.

SOURCES:

Gehler, Michael. "Spontaner Ausdruck des 'Volkszorns'? Neue Aspekte zum Innsbrucker Judenpogrom vom 9./10. November 1938," in *Zeitgeschichte.* Vol. 18, no. 1–2, 1990–91, pp. 2–21.

Plat, Wolfgang. "Ilse Brüll: vergangen wie ein Rauch," in Wolfgang Plat, ed., *Voll Leben und voll Tod ist diese Erde: Bilder aus der Geschichte der Jüdischen Österreicher (1190–1945).* Vienna: Verlag Herold, 1988, pp. 272–273.

Rimalt, Elimelech S. "The Jews of Tyrol," in Josef Fraenkel, ed., *The Jews of Austria: Essays on their Life, History and Destruction.* 2nd ed. London: Vallentine Mitchell, 1970, pp. 375–384.

Rosenkranz, Herbert. *"Reichskristallnacht" 9.* November 1938 in Österreich. Vienna: Europa-Verlag, 1968.

———. *Verfolgung und Selbstbehauptung: Die Juden in Österreich 1938–1945.* Vienna: Verlag Herold, 1978.

John Haag, Associate Professor, University of Georgia, Athens, Georgia

Brûlon, Angélique (1772–1859)

French woman who defended Corsica disguised as a man. Name variations: Angelique Brulon. Born Marie-Angélique Josephine Duchemin around 1772; died in 1859.

By the time Angélique Brûlon, fighting in male guise, had been identified as a woman, she was so valuable to the French army that she remained in service, known popularly as Liberté the Fusilier. Between 1792 and 1799, Brûlon fought in seven campaigns in defense of the island region of Corsica, displaying particular courage at Calvi and at the attack on Fort Gesco. Those at the garrison at Calvi attested to her acts of heroism, recounting that when her right arm was slashed with a sword she continued to fight with a dagger in her left hand. Brûlon retired in 1822, at the age of 51 and received the rank of lieutenant as well as the red ribbon of the French Legion of Honor from Napoleon III. Even as an old woman, she was said to have worn her lieutenant's uniform.

Brunechildis.

Variant of Brunhilda.

Brunechildis (c. 533–613).

See Fredegund for sidebar on Brunhilda.

Brunehaut or Brunehilde.

Variant of Brunhilda.

Brunhilda (c. 533–613).

See Fredegund for sidebar.

Brunhilde.

Variant of Brunhilda.

Brunner, Josefine (1909–1943)

Austrian Socialist, who was a leading member of Waldemar von Knoeringen's resistance network in the anti-Nazi underground. Born Josefine Ragnes in Innsbruck, Austria, on February 26, 1909; executed with husband Alois at the Stadelheim prison, Munich, on September 9, 1943; married Alois Brunner (1907–1943).

Member of the Austrian Social Democratic Party (1932–34); the Brunners remained committed Socialists and anti-Nazis after 1933; joined von Knoeringen's underground organization (1936) and underwent special training in use of espionage techniques; worked as courier and provided important military, economic and political information to the anti-Nazi underground; arrested (1942) on charges of high treason; sentenced to death (May 28, 1943).

Josefine Brunner was one of many thousands of Austrian men and women who lost their lives fighting Fascism and Nazism during the years 1934–1945. Though Austria was in many ways the birthplace of National Socialism—Adolf Hitler's spiritual home was pre-1914 Linz and Vienna—there were many Austrians who steadfastly opposed his movement. By May 1945, at least 2,700 Austrian anti-Nazis had been executed by the Third Reich, while a further 16,493 died in concentration camps. German jails cost the lives of 9,687 Austrian men and women anti-Fascists, while a further 6,420 Austrians, most of them political refugees, died in the jails of Nazi-occupied Europe. These individuals died to liberate their country from an ideology based on racism and the glorification of war. As active foes of the Hitler regime, they willingly risked, and in many instances sacrificed, their lives in the fight for human decency and freedom.

Josefine Brunner was born into a working-class family in Innsbruck on February 26, 1909. Attracted to the militantly egalitarian and democratic ideals of the Austrian Social Democratic movement, she joined the party in the depression year of 1932. Her husband Alois Brunner, who worked for the railroad, was also a committed Socialist. Despite the bloody suppression of the Social Democratic Party and the establishment of a Fascist dictatorship in Austria in February 1934, the Brunners remained strong in their belief in Socialism and democracy. Within weeks of the creation of the Austro-Fascist regime, the remnants of the Social Democrats reconstituted themselves as an illegal organization, optimistically defining themselves as Revolutionary Socialists. As dedicated members of the Tyrolian branch of the Revolutionary Socialists, Josefine and Alois Brunner became acquainted with an energetic Socialist refugee from Nazi Germany, Waldemar von Knoeringen, who, from his base in the town of Wörgl on the Austrian-German border, headed a resistance network that stretched from Czechoslovakia to Nazi Germany. Despite the great risks involved, the Brunners decided to carry on resistance work to make any contribution possible to destroy the scourge of Nazism.

The German annexation of Austria in March 1938 greatly increased the risks to those like the Brunners who were members of anti-Nazi underground cells. Using the underground name "Erika," Josefine Brunner became a key member of the von Knoeringen network. Well-trained, she was skilled at the use of secret ink and microfilms. With less of a political record than her husband and less chance of being arrested, Josefine worked as a courier. The German takeover of Austria, at first enthusiastically supported by the great majority of the population, did not deceive Josefine and her husband. As Socialists, they deplored the savage persecution of Austria's Jewish minority; as humanists and democrats, they saw the dehumanization and brutalization of society that was at the heart of the new "Greater German Reich" that came into existence as Nazism triumphed in 1938. Determined to fight Nazism in a practical fashion, the Brunners passed valuable data to Waldemar von Knoeringen that included details on the number and movements of German military forces, the construction of industrial plants and Wehrmacht barracks, and the changing morale of the civilian population.

The German military catastrophe at the gates of Leningrad and Moscow in the winter of 1941–1942 brought a new optimism to the von Knoeringen circle. Overestimating the revolutionary spirit of the German working class, they now believed the time had come to expand their cells to prepare for the final crisis of the Third Reich, which they saw as imminent. The German leader of the underground, Bebo Wager, determined that their group would take a bold step by preparing "to take over the leadership in the event of a revolutionary situation."

In place of their previously cautious conspiratorial tactics, they now took ever greater risks. Some of the Austrian members of the group, including the Brunners, were given iron filings to sabotage the railway line through the Brenner Pass, which supplied German forces in Italy and Rommel's Afrika Korps in North Africa. Veteran members were encouraged by new recruits, one of whom was a Gestapo agent. Josefine Brunner and her husband were arrested in 1942 and found guilty of "preparation for high treason" by the Nazi People's Court on May 28, 1943. They were sentenced to death and executed in Munich's Stadelheim prison on September 9, 1943.

SOURCES:

Carsten, F.L. *The German Workers and the Nazis*. Aldershort, Hants., England: Scolar Press, 1995.

Dokumentationsarchiv des österreichischen Widerstandes, Vienna. *Widerstand und Verfolgung in Tirol 1934–1945: Eine Dokumentation*. 2 vols. Vienna: Österreichischer Bundesverlag, 1984.

Dokumentationsarchiv des österreichischen Widerstandes, Vienna. *Widerstand und Verfolgung in Wien 1934–1945: Eine Dokumentation*. 2nd ed. 3 vols. Vienna: Österreichischer Bundesverlag, 1984.

Luza, Radomir V. *The Resistance in Austria, 1938–1945*. Minneapolis: University of Minnesota Press, 1984.

Mehringer, Hartmut. *Waldemar von Knoeringen: Eine politische Biographie. Der Weg vom revolutionären Sozialismus zur sozialen Demokratie*. Munich: K.G. Saur, 1989.

Schärf, Paul. *Otto Haas: Ein revolutionärer Sozialist gegen das Dritte Reich*. Vienna: Europa-Verlag, 1967.

Spiegel, Tilly. *Frauen und Mädchen im österreichischen Widerstand*. Vienna: Europa Verlag, 1967.

Szecsi, Maria, and Karl Stadler. *Die NS-Justiz in Österreich und ihre Opfer*. Vienna: Verlag Herold, 1962.

John Haag, Associate Professor, University of Georgia, Athens, Georgia

Brunnhilde.

Variant of Brunhilda.

Brunschvicg, Cécile (1877–1946)

French feminist who was at the heart of her country's women's suffrage movements. Name variations: Cecile Brunschwicg. Pronunciation: say-SEEL BROON-shvig. Born Cécile Kahn in 1877; died in 1946; daughter of Arthur Kahn; married Léon Brunschvicg (a philosopher at the Lycée Henri IV and the Sorbonne), 1889 (died, 1944); children: four, born 1901–19.

Cécile Brunschvicg was the daughter of Arthur Kahn, an Alsatian industrialist who opposed girls' education. She passed her *brévet supérieur* secretly and then married Léon Brunschvicg (1869–1944), a celebrated philosopher at the Lycée Henri IV and later the Sorbonne. She became politically awakened during the Dreyfus Affair (1894–1906), and her husband acquainted her with doctrines of sexual equality and of equivalence theory that stressed that women and men differ but have complementary qualities and thus are equal. At first, Brunschvicg involved herself in labor and rights issues that impacted women and children. In 1909, she founded the Réchauds de Midi, which provided working women with warm places to eat. In time, however, her husband persuaded her that women would gain little unless they had the vote.

Brunschvicg joined the suffrage section of the National Council of French Women (CNFF), attended the 1908 Amsterdam congress of the International Women's Suffrage Alliance (IWSA), and in 1909 joined *Jeanne Schmahl's newly founded (February 1909) French Union for Women's Suffrage (UFSF). In December 1909, she was made head of a membership and propaganda committee she and **Mme. Pichon-Landry** had proposed. Her talent and energy resulted in a dramatic surge in membership. Schmahl, jealous of her authority and charging that Brunschvicg's outspoken (though moderate) republicanism was violating the non-partisan character of the UFSF and thus endangering prospects of recruiting Catholic women, challenged Brunschvicg at a meeting of the central committee in December 1910. Brunschvicg won out; Schmahl, refusing to be relegated to an honorary role, resigned as president, and Brunschvicg was named secretary-general, from which post she thereafter ran the UFSF, assuming the presidency in the mid-1920s.

Under Brunschvicg's leadership, the UFSF became openly republican but welcomed Catholics and conservatives providing they did not oppose the regime. Under the presidency of **Marguérite Witt-Schlumberger** (1856–1924) after 1912, the UFSF also took on a social coloration by promoting traditional women's causes such as opposition to alcoholism and prostitution. The combination of moderate republicanism and social feminism was especially successful in attracting women of the urban middle class and in reaching out to the provinces, where the UFSF achieved its greatest successes, due in large part to tactics devised by Brunschvicg. By 1914, the UFSF had 12,000

members and was established as the principal women's suffrage organization in France.

During the First World War (1914–18), Brunschvicg was awarded the Legion of Honor for her work in finding lodgings for 25,000 refugee families from the invaded provinces. In 1917, she founded a school to train women factory inspectors to deal with problems arising from the huge wartime employment of women; she was also cofounder of a league, Pour la vie (For Life), which promoted raising the French birthrate.

In 1919, the Chamber of Deputies passed a women's suffrage bill, but in 1922 the Senate defeated it and continued to block the bill until the end of the Third Republic in 1940. The suffrage campaign continued in the meantime. Brunschvicg became president of the UFSF, the director (1926–34) of the monthly *La Française,* and in 1924 joined the Radical-Socialist Party (France's principal centrist party in the 1920s and 1930s), where she had long cultivated friendships with the leadership despite (or because of) the fact that the party included many of the most influential opponents of women's suffrage. The UFSF grew to 100,000 members by 1928. Its continued adherence to moderate tactics, however, caused *Louise Weiss (1893-1983) to found a more militant group, La femme nouvelle (The New Woman); through the 1920s, Weiss became a leading presence in the suffragist movement and was openly critical of Brunschvicg.

Brunschvicg was a founder of the Estates-General of Feminism, which convened in 1929, 1931, and 1937; amidst great publicity, it set women's grievances before the nation. She reached the peak of her prominence when Léon Blum made her one of three women under-secretaries of state—a historic first in France—in his Popular Front government (June 4, 1936–June 21, 1937): she at National Education, *Irène Joliot-Curie at Scientific Research, and **Suzanne Lacore** (1875–1975) at Public Health. Brunschvicg saw to the creation of 1,500 new school canteens, instituted a certificate for teachers of slow-learning children, initiated a reform of disciplinary schools, and involved herself in the education of sailors' children. She pressed the Ministry of the Interior for the revision (enacted in February 1938) of Article 215 of the Code requiring husbands to give consent for wives to enroll in schools, open bank accounts, or obtain passports; and she intervened with the ministries of Colonies, Labor, and Foreign Affairs to admit women to their competitive examinations. Nevertheless, she was criticized by Weiss and others for doing little or nothing to advance the suffrage cause. It had soon appeared, in fact, that Blum, while making the gesture to include women in his cabinet, had no intention of moving on the issue in the foreseeable future. To her critics, Brunschvicg had appeared too ready to accept, or remain in, office under these conditions.

With the German invasion in 1940, Brunschvicg and her husband fled to southern France to escape anti-Semitic persecution. She was employed at a girls' school in Valence under the name of "Madame Valéry." Her husband died in 1944. With the Liberation of 1944–45, Charles de Gaulle granted women the vote at last. At the end of her life, Brunschvicg was internationally known, sitting on United Nations commissions and the executive committee of the International Democratic Federation of Women; she was also honorary president of the National Council of Radical-Socialist Women.

Brunschvicg joined high intelligence with administrative and organizational skills and reforming zeal. She worked for practical reforms, if necessary on a piecemeal basis, and while a fervent, outspoken republican supporting the Third Republic she was moderate in her views and methods. She worked for social and civil equality for women but would have nothing to do with a loosening of sexual morals: "We demand the unity of morals not so that the woman should have the morals of the man, but that the man should have the morals of the woman" (1924). These views spread into her work for the suffrage, where she succeeded in drawing large numbers of women to the cause but where her critics charged that she was not sufficiently militant. Whatever the case may be, it should be noted that women's suffrage was an even more complicated and divisive issue in France than in America and Protestant Europe: class divisions were intrusive, union leaders resented "interference" by bourgeois women reformers, Catholics feared for the future of the family, Socialists feared the Revolution would be postponed, and liberals often feared for the future of the republic itself.

Cécile Brunschvicg, exceptionally well-connected in political and, through her husband, intellectual circles, was by most accounts "the *grande dame* of the feminist movement" in France from the 1920s until her death. She lived to see the victory, being the only pre-1914 leader of the women's suffrage movement to survive to cast a first ballot in 1944.

SOURCES:

Albistur, Maïté, and Daniel Armogathe. *Histoire du féminisme français, du moyen âge à nos jours.* 2 vols. Paris: Éditions des Femmes, 1977.

Biographical Dictionary of French Political Leaders. David S. Bell, Douglas Johnson, and Peter Morris, eds. NY: Simon & Schuster, 1990.

Dictionnaire de biographie française. A. Balteau, M. Barroux, M. Perrot *et al,* directeurs. Paris: Letouzey et Ané, 1933—.

Hause, Steven C., with Anne R. Kenney. *Women's Suffrage and Social Politics in the Third French Republic.* Princeton, NJ: Princeton University Press, 1984.

Klejman, Laurence, and Florence Rochefort. *L'Égalité en marche: Le féminisme sous la Troisième République.* Paris: Presses de la Fondation nationale des sciences politiques, 1989.

McMillan, James F. *Housewife or Harlot: The Place of Women in French Society 1870–1940.* NY: St. Martin's Press, 1981.

Rabaut, Jean. *Histoire des féminismes français.* Paris: Stock, 1978.

Weiss, Louise. *Mémoires d'une européenne.* Vol. 3: *Combats pour les femmes, 1934–1939.* Éd def. Paris: Albin Michel, 1980.

David S. Newhall, Professor of History Emeritus, Centre College; author of *Clemenceau: A Life at War* (Edwin Mellen Press, 1991)

Brunswick, duchess of.

See Catherine of Pomerania (d. 1526).
See Elizabeth of Brandenburg (1510–1558).
See Elizabeth of Denmark (1573–1626).
See Anne-Eleanor of Hesse-Darmstadt (1601–1659).
See Mary-Elizabeth of Padua (1782–1808).

Brunswick, Ruth Mack (1897–1946).

See Gardiner, Muriel for sidebar.

Brunswick-Lüneburg, duchess of.

See Helen of Denmark (d. 1233).
See Matilda of Brandenburg (d. 1261).
See Braunschweig-Luneburg, Sophie Elisabeth (1613–1676).
See Victoria Louise (1892–1980).

Brunswick-Wolfenbuttel, duchess of.

See Philippine Charlotte (1716–1801).
See Augusta Guelph (1737–1813).

Bruntland, Gro Harlem (1939—)

Norwegian politician and first woman prime minister of Norway. Name variations: Bruddland, Brundtland. Born in Oslo, Norway, in 1939; attended university in Oslo and Harvard University; married Arne Olav, 1960; children: four.

A physician with a particular interest in public health, Gro Harlem Bruntland gained her reputation as a sharp and savvy political mind while serving in various local health-care organizations, including the Ministry of Health and Social Affairs, the Oslo City Health Department,

Gro Harlem Bruntland

and the Oslo School Health Services. In 1974, she was appointed Minister of Environmental Affairs and in 1975 became vice chair of the Labor Party. After leaving government service in 1979, Bruntland ran for president of the Labor Party, winning overwhelming support from local constituencies. In 1980, upon the resignation of Odvar Nordli, she took over as head of the minority government.

Bruntland became the first woman prime minister of Norway in 1981 but served for only an eight-month period. Upon her reelection in 1986, she appointed a number of women to Cabinet posts and facilitated the election of more women to governmental positions. Bruntland also worked on a plan to ease Norway's economic decline and, as chair of the United Nations Commission of the Environment, has led discussions on corporate responsibility for environmental health. One of Norway's most influential politicians abroad, Gro Bruntland surprised her nation when she resigned in 1996.

Brunton, Elizabeth (1799–1860).

See Yates, Elizabeth.

Brunton, Louisa (c. 1785–1860)

English actress. Name variations: Countess of Craven. Born Louisa Brunton around 1785; died in 1860; married William, 1st earl of Craven, 1807.

Famed for her remarkable beauty, Louisa Brunton made her debut as an actress as Lady Townley in *Provoked Husband* and Beatrice in *Much Ado About Nothing* in 1803. Brunton became countess of Craven upon her marriage to William, first earl of Craven, in 1807, then retired from the stage.

Brunton, Mary (1778–1818)

Scottish novelist. Born Mary Balfour on November 1, 1778, on the island of Barra, Orkney, on the west coast of Scotland; died in Edinburgh, Scotland, on December 19, 1818; daughter of Captain Thomas Balfour of Elwick; married Alexander Brunton (minister of Bolton in Haddingtonshire and later professor of oriental languages at Edinburgh), in 1798.

Though Mary Brunton did not attend school, she studied French, Italian, and music while running her father's household. Following her marriage in 1798, she lived with her husband, a minister, in East Lothian, in the parish of Bolton, for five years. She died at the age of 40, 12 days after giving birth to a stillborn son in 1818. Brunton was the author of two novels, which were popular in her day: *Self-control,* published anonymously in 1811, was sold out in one month, and *Discipline,* published in 1814, was also successful. As well, she authored a fragment, *Emmeline* (1819), which, together with a memoir, was published by her husband after her death. Wrote a contemporary critic for the *London Monthly Review:* "Among the pleasing expounders of morality Mrs. Brunton stood preeminent, as well for the good taste and style, as for the soundness, of her works."

Brusselsmans, Anne

Englishwoman who operated escape lines in Brussels during World War II. Name variations: Brusselmans.

A quiet English housewife who lived in Brussels, Anne Brusselsmans was one of the unsung heroes of World War II. For four years, from her apartment where she kept house and raised her two small children, she operated an escape line for Allied soldiers, supervising the passage of more than 150 British and American pilots out of Nazi-controlled territory. Brussels-mans, who was possessed of a quick wit and iron nerves, survived at least three searches of her apartment by the Gestapo. Of those involved in the escape network, she was the only one to avoid being killed or captured.

Bruttia Crispina (d. 185)

Roman empress. Died around 185 CE; married Marcus Aurelius Commodus (161–192), Roman emperor (r. 180–192).

Banished by her husband Emperor Commodus in 177 and replaced by *Marcia, Bruttia Crispina died in 185 CE or shortly thereafter.

Bryant, Lane (1879–1951)

American clothing designer and entrepreneur. Born Lena Himmelstein in Lithuania in 1879; died in 1951.

Lane Bryant, the first American designer to address the fashion needs of larger women, immigrated to the United States from Lithuania and set up shop as a seamstress specializing in lingerie and maternity clothing. When a pregnant client asked her to make a presentable dinner dress for her, Bryant was inspired to offer her clothing to the general public. In 1910, she opened her first retail shop, catering to pregnant and larger women. Droves of oversized women, usually passed over by the better department stores, clamored for her merchandise. By 1917, Lane Bryant stores had sold over a million dollars in merchandise. The company continued to expand and was later sold to another clothing retailer, The Limited, Incorporated.

Bryant, Louise (1885–1936)

American journalist who witnessed the Soviet revolution in Russia and became one of its outspoken defenders. Born Anna Louisa Mohan on December 5, 1885, in San Francisco, California; died on January 6, 1936, in Paris, France; daughter of Hugh J. (a journalist) and Anna Louisa (Flick) Mohan (a dressmaker); attended University of Nevada, University of Oregon; married Paul Trullinger, November 13, 1909 (divorced, 1917); married John Reed, November 9, 1916 (died, October 19, 1920); married William C. Bullitt, December 23, 1923 (divorced, March 1930); children: (third marriage) Anne Bullitt (b. 1924).

Parents divorced (1888); mother married Sheridan Daniel Bryant (1892); entered liberal arts college, University of Nevada (1904); entered University of Oregon (1906); spoke for suffrage in Oregon (1912); served as society editor of the Portland Spectator *(1913); moved to New York (1916); traveled to Russia (August 1917); returned to New York (February 1918); testified before Senate subcommittee on Russia (February 1919); joined suffrage picket of White House (1919); went on speaking tour of U.S. (1919); returned to Soviet Union (August 1919); traveled to Middle East (1920–21); diagnosed with incurable disease (1928).*

Selected writings: Six Red Months in Russia *(1918);* Mirrors of Moscow *(1923).*

When Louise Bryant arrived in Petrograd in the summer of 1917, she found the ancient Russian city under the rule of a Provisional Government, which had replaced the tsar's regime after the February revolution. The city was threatened by reactionary forces. Quickly, Bryant and her companion, the poet and journalist John Reed, became persuaded that the future of the Russian Revolution lay not with the narrow base supporting the mildly socialist premier Alexander Keren-

Louise Bryant

sky but with the urban working class and revolutionary socialists, especially the Bolsheviks, currently led by V.I. Lenin and Leon Trotsky.

Few American journalists were on the scene. Of them, Bryant, who had been steeped in the cultural radicalism of the New York avant-garde, was exceptionally observant of details relating to women and sexuality. "Russian women are peculiar in regard to dress," she wrote in one dispatch. "If they are interested in revolution they almost invariably refuse to think of dress at all, and go about looking noticeably shabby—if they are not interested, they care exceedingly for clothes and manage to array themselves in the most fantastic *inspirations.*"

As she spoke with revolutionary leaders, Bryant was particularly impressed by the women. She was fond above all of *Catherine Breshkovsky, who was known by the nickname "Grandmother of the Revolution." She also was struck by *Alexandra Kollontai, the most prominent female Bolshevik: "She often disagrees with Lenin and Trotsky, but she told me herself that she would never desert the ranks of the proletariat, 'if they made every mistake on the calendar!'" Her support for the Russian Revolution did not deter Bryant from the frankest assessment of its partisans. She admired Lenin, while depicting him as "sheer intellect, . . . absorbed, cold, unattractive, impatient at interruption."

Louise Bryant was born Anna Louisa Mohan in 1885. Her father had also been a radical and journalist, but that familial legacy was shrouded from her knowledge. Bryant knew little about her father since he left the family when she was barely a toddler. Hugh Mohan, an Irish Roman Catholic, had grown up in the anthracite region of Pennsylvania, where he worked in coal mines as a boy. In 1876, he was secretary of the Workingman's State Anti-Monopoly Convention in Harrisburg, and later he worked for three Catholic Congressional representatives in Washington. For most of his life, he was a journalist. His marriage to Anna Louisa Flick, a dressmaker in San Francisco, was brief. Their daughter Louise was only three years old when **Anna Mohan** was granted a divorce on the grounds that her husband was habitually drunk, improvident, and absent.

In 1892, when Louise was six, her mother married Sheridan Daniel Bryant, a brakeman and later conductor on the Southern Pacific railroad. Each of the three Mohan children took their new father's last name. Louise was sent for a time to be raised on the ranch of her mother's stepfather in the Nevada desert, where she was educated by an ancient Chinese overseer. At 14, she returned to her mother in Wadsworth, Nevada. She underwent rigorous preparation for higher education, which her mother thought very important, by attending Wadsworth High School and taking classes at the University of Nevada's high school in Reno.

In 1904, Bryant entered the liberal arts college of the University of Nevada, where she joined the staff of the *Student Record* and the literary magazine *Chuckawalla*. In September 1906, she registered as a student at the University of Oregon in Eugene, where she stood out as a free spirit among her 500 contemporaries. With four other young women, she started the Chi Omega sorority chapter on campus, serving as its first president, and she created a small scandal as the first student to wear rouge.

Bryant secretly married Dr. Paul Trullinger, a dentist, in 1909 after she moved to Portland, the largest city in Oregon. One of their acquaintances at the time would later describe Trullinger as "a nice but unintellectual man, not the kind of man to hold a woman like Louise." The couple lived in a houseboat in the Oregon Yacht Club harbor on the Willamette River, but Bryant kept her name and maintained an independent studio, where she sketched. Two of Portland's prominent radicals, ❦▶ **Sara Bard Field** and C(harles) E(rskine) S. Wood, introduced Bryant to the fight for women's suffrage during the campaign of 1912 and to the Industrial Workers of the World (IWW). Bryant began publishing sketches and occasional articles in the *Spectator,* a Portland weekly for which she became society editor in 1913, and she solicited subscriptions from her friends for *The Masses,* a left-wing magazine published in New York.

When John Reed, one of *The Masses'* most vivid writers, visited Oregon on a speaking and fundraising tour for the magazine in December 1915, Bryant sought him out. Reed had grown up in Portland, graduated from Harvard, and won national fame as a brilliant journalist. He was known as one of the finest writers of the American left, a daring correspondent who had ridden with Pancho Villa in the Mexican Revolution. He and Bryant immediately fell in love. "She's wild, brave and straight—and graceful and lovely to look at," Reed wrote to a friend. "I think she's the first person I ever loved without reservation."

Leaving her husband behind and shattered (he would divorce her in 1917), Bryant arrived at Grand Central Station in New York City on

January 4, 1916. Reed was waiting for her on the platform. They lived together in an apartment off Washington Square in Greenwich Village. Soon Bryant was immersed in Reed's world of poets, sexual radicals and revolutionaries. "I used to drop in on them," recalled Albert Boni, a bookstore owner whose shop was a magnet for Village literary life. "I'd go in and find them in bed and I'd just pull up a chair and we'd talk. Jack and Louise had a lovely relationship."

That summer, Reed and Bryant rented a furnished house along the Cape Cod shore at Provincetown, Massachusetts, where other writers and artists, including Max Eastman and *Mary Heaton Vorse, were spending the season. After a week, Reed had to leave for Chicago and St. Louis to cover the Republicans' and Democrats' national political conventions. Bryant began to become a more serious writer. She wrote "The Poet's Revolution," an essay on the Easter Rebellion in Ireland that was published in *The Masses,* and when she sent *Masses* editor Floyd Dell six of her poems, he replied, "These poems hit me hard. I think they are almost terribly beautiful—like Greek fragments."

Theater was a focus of creativity for the Bohemian summer colony in Provincetown. Bryant wrote *The Game: A Morality Play* and portrayed the Dancer in *Thirst,* a drama by Eugene O'Neill, the hottest new talent in the circle of young artists and writers. Soon she and O'Neill could be seen talking for hours on the beach together. Bryant claimed she was trying to wean O'Neill from the bottle, but she was fascinated by him, and O'Neill had fallen head over heels. "When Louise touches me with the tip of her little finger it's like a flame," he wrote to a friend.

Despite rumors of an affair, Reed did not permit O'Neill to stand between himself and Bryant when he returned from his journalistic assignments. When summer ended, much of the group went back to New York. O'Neill took up an apartment close to Reed and Bryant. That fall, the Provincetown Players opened on Macdougal Street in Greenwich Village, showcasing for New York the experimental theatrical productions of the summer. Reed played death in Bryant's *The Game,* but the show was overshadowed by O'Neill's *Bound East for Cardiff.*

In October, Reed bought a house at Croton-on-Hudson, 30 miles from New York, putting it in Bryant's name. On November 9, Reed and Bryant married in Peekskill, the union prompted by Reed's fear that he might die from diseases that troubled him from the time of his coverage of the war in Serbia. Bryant herself was afflicted with a tubular abscess. Though both kept writing—Bryant's poem, "Lost Music," appeared in the January *Masses*—they spent the winter recuperating.

In May 1918, Bryant visited O'Neill in Provincetown for a week but returned to Reed in Croton after receiving a telegram that read, "Peach trees blooming and wrens have taken their house." That was the last of her affair with O'Neill, which he may later have dramatized in his play *Strange Interlude* (1928), in which a man shares a lover with a friend.

Field, Sara Bard (b. 1882)

American poet. Born Sara Bard Field in Cincinnati, Ohio, in 1882; sister of Mary Field Parton (head of a social settlement in Chicago); moved to Detroit at age three; married a minister named Ehrgott (1900); children: one son (b. 1901), another son and a daughter.

In 1900, Sara Bard Field married a minister named Ehrgott, many years her senior, who had just been accepted by a Eurasian Baptist Church in Rangoon, Burma. While there, Field beheld the English-Christian exploitation of a "brave, free, simple, and essentially spiritual people. I saw the famine sufferers from India whose distress, I knew, had drawn pennies from the ragged pockets of bootblacks and washerwomen in America, and watched quantities of rice, wheat, and tea being exported from the land by the wealthy landlords. I saw 'pagans' whose morality shamed many Christians. These things wakened my mind and soul. I grew up." Field's ill health forced the family's return to America, where she audited courses at Yale while living in New Haven, Connecticut; it was there, in a short span of a few months, that she was told by her professor that she was a poet.

The family then moved to a poor parish in Cleveland, where she and her husband continued to mingle with liberals and socialists, meeting Clarence Darrow, and reading books supplied by her sister **Mary Field Parton** who was the head of a settlement house. When the "wealthy and orthodox" trustees of the church asked for their resignation, the family moved once more to Portland, Oregon. There, Field organized the College Equal Suffrage League, helped in the Nevada campaign for suffrage, and traveled throughout the country speaking in the interests of national suffrage. Called "one of the finest spirits of our time," by William Rose Benet, who found her poetry to be "coruscatingly imaginative" and "poignantly human," Field's writings included *The Pale Woman* (1927); *Barabbas* (1932); and *Darkling Plain* (1936).

SOURCES AND SUGGESTED READING:
Saturday Review. December 19, 1936.

After her return, Bryant learned that Reed, too, had had occasional brief affairs. Outraged by the news, she decided to leave for Europe as a war correspondent. Reed helped her get press credentials from the just-organized Bell Syndicate, and she sailed on June 9, 1917, passing through the submarine-ridden Atlantic. She and Reed began to write one another before her boat had left the harbor. "I have always loved you my darling ever since I first met you," wrote Reed, "and I guess I always will. This is more than I've ever felt for anyone, honestly. I know that the one thing I cannot bear any more is consciously to hurt you, honey." Bryant drafted a story that Reed combined with more vivid parts of her letters, rearranging more than rewriting, and sold to the *New York American*. The separation made both aware of their love. Consumed with loneliness and longing, Bryant returned home in August.

Within weeks, both were aboard a steamer bound for Russia by way of Stockholm. Bryant bore credentials from *Metropolitan* magazine and Bell Syndicate. Reed—one of the best-known and best-paid reporters in the country prior to the war—had achieved notoriety by his principled opposition to the war. His credentials were from *The Masses* and the *New York Call*, newspapers of the Socialist Party. From Stockholm, the couple took a train through the forests of northern Sweden into Russia, reaching the Finland Station in Petrograd at the end of August on the Russian calendar.

Revolutions do not run along set formulas.

—Louise Bryant

Reed and Bryant made the Russian Revolution their own and eagerly pursued its every development. The Provisional Government was wobbly, beleaguered. The Bolsheviks had obtained a majority of delegates in the Moscow and Petrograd soviets—those multiparty councils organized by workers, peasants, and soldiers, which constituted a "dual power," as Lenin put it. Their publicity called for withdrawal from the European war, land for the peasantry, and bread for all. In late October (November 6–7 on the modern calendar), Bryant and Reed were present as the Bolsheviks initiated the Soviet Revolution in Petrograd. After six days, they traveled to Moscow on the first train to enter the city since the Soviet Revolution. They filed press reports all the while, and the dramatic scenes they witnessed would serve as the subject of Bryant's first book, *Six Red Months in Russia* (1918), and Reed's famous *Ten Days that Shook the World* (1919).

Russia was an inspiring new backdrop for the combination of romanticism and revolution, personal passion and radical ardor, that Reed and Bryant had cultivated in Greenwich Village. Bryant's poem to Reed in Christmas 1917 emphasized the tie between their comraderie and love:

I want you to know that sometimes when I am
  thinking
About you
I have a lump in my throat
And I am a little bit awed.
You are the finest person I know
On both sides of the world
And it is a nice privilege to be your comrade.

When she returned to New York in February 1918, Bryant devoted herself to telling the American public what she had seen in Russia. Her 32 stories ran in over 100 papers in the U.S. and Canada, with publisher's interest high because eyewitness reports on events in Russia were rare. Bryant simultaneously strove to achieve the release of Reed, who had been detained in Norway on the trumped-up charge that he was a Bolshevik agent. None of Bryant's letters were permitted to reach him, and the State Department only allowed one of his to reach her. Finally, Reed reached the U.S. on April 28, 1918, where he was detained all day, and Naval Intelligence officers seized his papers, posters, clippings and notes on daily events in Russia.

Bryant and Reed, persuaded of the coming of world revolution, threw themselves into defense of the first workers' government in history. In October 1918, Bryant's book was published and favorably received. On February 2, 1919, she and Albert Rhys Williams, who had been a companion of Reed and Bryant in Moscow, spoke in Washington on "The Truth About Russia" to several thousand. Bryant was so engaging that the *Washington Post* called her a female Trotsky.

Bryant joined a picket line outside the White House for women's suffrage, and on February 20, 1919, she testified before a subcommittee of the Senate Judiciary Committee on Bolshevik propaganda, headed by Senator Lee S. Overman (Dem., S.C.). The first witness to criticize the senators' presumptions about the new republic to the East, she was frequently interrupted and bullied by committee members. Asked a series of questions about her religious beliefs, Bryant replied drily, "It seems to me as if I were being tried for witchcraft." She appealed for non-intervention: "I think the Russians ought to settle their internal troubles, and I think it is a shame to have American boys killed determining what form of government there should be in Russia."

Catapulted to renown by her testimony, Bryant embarked on a national speaking tour in 1919. From Detroit, Chicago, and Minneapolis, where Sinclair Lewis came to hear her speak, she proceeded as far west as Spokane, Seattle, and Tacoma. She addressed thousands of people hungry for reliable knowledge about the new-born revolution, often in union halls. In Tacoma, still vibrant from Seattle's recent general strike, Bryant called the Soviet revolution "one great general strike against the governments of the whole world." In her old haunt, Portland, 4,000 filled the Civic Auditorium and watched as Bryant tossed back her cape at the end of her oration to reveal that it was lined in red.

Bryant had told the Overman subcommittee that she was a socialist, but she did not join the Socialist Party. In a personal letter in 1919 to the editor of Soviet Russia, she explained that she had kept beyond "the limits of any organization, . . . even the Socialist Party," because of her belief that it was the only way "to be honest with my own conscience." She was sanguine about the prospects of revolution in the U.S., even though 1919, a year of massive strikes in steel and other basic U.S. industries, also brought the Palmer raids and Red Scare. Bryant, in an article in *Voice of Labor*, declared, "Jails full of political prisoners are the most faithful indicators of how near a country is to revolution."

When the left wing of the Socialist Party split into bickering factions and both factions sought to join the Communist International, Reed, a Socialist Party member, left for Russia as representative of the newly created Communist Labor Party to compete for Comintern affiliation with his erstwhile comrade Louis Fraina, now representative of the Communist Party. The Comintern instructed the two groups to merge. In March 1920, while he tried to return from Russia, Reed was captured in Finland, a nation controlled by counter-revolutionary forces. On April 9, newspapers carried the erroneous report that he had been executed. In June, Reed was finally delivered into Russian hands in exchange for three Finnish professors returned by the Soviets.

Bryant decided to rejoin Reed. Refused a passport, she posed as a Swedish businessman's wife, passing through Scandinavia to Petrograd in August. But when she got there she found Reed gone, removed by train to Baku in the Caucasus for the "first congress of the peoples of the East," where he delivered a speech against U.S. imperialism in Cuba, the Philippines, and Central America.

When they were at last reunited on September 15, Bryant and Reed promised each other that they would never again be separated and talked of having children. At the Second Congress of the Comintern, Reed had pleaded the cause of blacks in the U.S. and had lost a stiff fight on trade union policy, but when Reed took Bryant to meet Lenin she sensed warmth between the two men despite their recent strategic disagreements. Lenin's interview with Bryant was the first he had granted to an American newspaper or press association, and Reed also introduced her to Trotsky and Bela Kun, whom she interviewed for Hearst's International News Service.

In mid-October, Reed fell ill. His disease, at first mistaken for influenza, was typhus contracted during his journey to Baku, and he became delirious and unable to speak. After Bryant spent five days by his bedside, Reed clenching her hand, he died on October 17, 1920, at age 32, a victim of the capitalist blockade that had deprived Moscow hospitals of medications. During the funeral procession from the Labor Temple to Red Square—with Alexandra Kollontai, *Emma Goldman*, Alexander Berkman, Big Bill Haywood, Nikolai Bukharin and Karl Radek in attendance—Bryant fainted and was removed to her hotel room to rest. "Jack's illness and his death brought me closer to him than all our life together did," she wrote. "And when he had gone I found myself alone in a strange world and everything smashed to hell."

Bryant paid a visit to Lenin and told him she wished to travel to the Middle East. He readily assented, giving her a letter insuring passage on any train and a room in any government hotel, as well as a two-soldier escort. Her train, moving across the icy steppes, was stopped by snowfall at night. Going as far as the "edge of Persia and Afghanistan, . . . the only reporter who has been there in six years," Bryant found Soviet policy toward the Muslims remarkably sensitive, particularly in comparison to the tsarist past and British present. In the Ukraine, she met Christian Rakovsky, the region's most powerful Communist, who spoke frankly of ongoing problems: pogroms against Jews, banditry, feudal residues.

In 1921, Bryant returned to the U.S. A new series of 16 of her stories ran in Hearst newspapers in August. Of the Soviet leadership, she wrote, "Lenin I knew best and liked most," for he was "a terrific fighter" with "the tenacity of a bulldog." The mood of her writing, though still evocative and impressionistic, was more sober than the rapture of her earliest reports. Kollontai, Bryant reported, had talked of "the gray days of the revolution" and warned her, "If you look for that high elation you saw here in 1917 you will be disappointed." Bryant spoke at a memorial meeting of 2,000 for John Reed on October 17, 1921, in the Central Opera House of New York, appealing for an end to the starvation of Russia by blockade. Shortly after a stroke paralyzed Lenin in 1922, Bryant wrote a series of stories on him and his lieutenants called "Mirrors of Moscow," and she gave the same title to a book of her portraits of Soviet leaders published the following year.

In 1922, Bryant returned to Russia, still without passport, and then journeyed to Italy, where she interviewed Benito Mussolini. Sometime during this period, while in Paris, Bryant met William Christian Bullitt, offspring of a distinguished Philadelphia family. Few of her radical acquaintances could believe she had become involved with a high society scion, even though Bullitt was a former diplomat under Woodrow Wilson who had resigned in protest of Wilson's policy toward Russia and advocated U.S. recognition of the USSR. After marrying in Paris on December 10, 1923, the two spent their honeymoon in a Constantinople palace. In 1924, a daughter Anne was born to Bryant (who kept her maiden name through all her marriages).

When Bryant returned briefly with Bullitt and the child to the U.S. in September 1926, she granted an interview to the *New York American*. Not only did she reaffirm her opposition to Wilsonian policy—noting the ineffectuality of the League of Nations in the face of Italian imperialism and the issuance of dictatorship instead of democracy after the war in Spain, Italy, Turkey, Hungary, Poland, and Belgium—but she gave a caustic and prescient assessment of the course of Russia under Stalin. "I look to see Russia become one of the conservative nations of the world," she told her interviewer, "and I believe all signs point toward this and most certainly against any possibility of the much-planned realization of the slogan, 'Workers of the World, Unite.'"

Bullitt, it turned out, was an extremely intricate and erratic figure. Fearing that he had a suicide complex, he sought analysis under Sigmund Freud in Vienna. (Eventually he would co-author a book with Freud on Woodrow Wilson.) Bryant's own life was increasingly miserable. Like many expatriates in Paris during the 1920s, she drank heavily. She encouraged young voices, such as Harlem Renaissance writer Claude McKay, but her own work tapered off. Bryant suffered from a baffling illness that doctors in 1928 finally diagnosed as adiposis dolorosa, a rare, incurable, disfiguring disease that is not fatal but induces misery.

At a hearing without Bryant present, William Bullitt sought a divorce in Philadelphia in December 1929; he alleged, without foundation, that she was guilty of lesbianism, excessive drinking, and attempted suicide, never mentioning her chronic disease. Bullitt, who went on to become an ambassador under President Franklin Roosevelt in the 1930s, was granted the divorce in March 1930 and full custody of Anne. Bryant was never permitted to see her daughter again.

Bryant's criticism of the new conservatism and dictatorship in Soviet Russia never led her to renounce the goals of 1917. She gave thought to writing a biography of John Reed and began work on a memoir of her life, but she was emotionally volatile and experienced great fluctuations in weight due to her disease. Friends suspected that she was escaping her pain through heavy drinking and drug use. On January 6, 1936, at the age of 50, Louise Bryant died in a Paris hospital of a cerebral hemorrhage soon after collapsing while climbing the stairs to her modest room in the Hotel Liberia.

SOURCES:

Bryant, Louise. *Six Red Months in Russia* (1918). London: Journeyman, 1982.
———. *Mirrors of Moscow.* NY: Thomas Seltzer, 1923.
Gardner, Virginia. *"Friend and Lover": The Life of Louise Bryant.* NY: Horizon, 1982.
Homberger, Eric, ed. *John Reed and the Russian Revolution.* NY: St. Martin's, 1992 (contains article jointly written by Reed and Bryant).

SUGGESTED READING:

Balabanoff, Angelica. *My Life as a Rebel.* NY: Harper, 1938.
Dearborn, Mary V. *Queen of Bohemia: The Life of Louise Bryant.* NY: Houghton Mifflin, 1995.
Goldman, Emma. *Living My Life* (1931). Garden City, NY: Garden City, 1934.
Hicks, Granville. *John Reed: The Making of a Revolutionary.* NY: Macmillan, 1937.
O'Connor, Richard, and Dale L. Walker. *The Lost Revolutionary: A Biography of John Reed.* NY: Harcourt, Brace and World, 1967.
Robbins, Jack Alan, ed. *The Complete Poetry of John Reed.* Washington: University Press of America, 1983.
Rosenstone, Robert A. *Romantic Revolutionary: A Biography of John Reed* (1975). NY: Vintage, 1981.

COLLECTIONS:

John Reed Papers, Houghton Library, Harvard University, Cambridge, Massachusetts.

RELATED MEDIA:

Reds (3 hrs.), an epic Hollywood film directed and produced by Warren Beatty, with **Diane Keaton** as Louise Bryant, Paramount Pictures, 1981.

Christopher Phelps,
Rush Rhees fellow in U.S. history,
University of Rochester, Rochester, New York

Bryant, Mary (1765–?)

English highway robber and one of only a handful of convicts to escape from the notorious penal colony at Botany Bay. Name variations: Mary Bryant of Fowey; Mary Braund or Broad. Born Mary Broad in Cornwall, England, and baptized on May 1, 1765 (birth date unknown); death date unknown; daughter of William (a mariner) and Grace Broad; married Will Bryant; children: Charlotte Spence (b. September 8, 1787); Emmanuel (b. March 1790).

In 1776, while the British navy was occupied on the other side of the Atlantic in a war against American colonists, the Spanish and French fleets sided with the Americans and preyed on British merchant mariners. As a result, Cornish fishermen were kept from leaving port, and a poor diet killed many in the area of Cornwall. By 1785, Britain had lost the war, mad George III was king, and taxes to pay for the failed conflict rose 20% in five years. There was a land tax, a candle tax, a salt tax (in an area where salt was used to cure fish), even a tax on each window in a household. Thus, citizens were not only starving but living in the dark, having blocked out half the windows in their homes. Employing legal chicanery, landowners grabbed up land, driving out small farmers. Villages were deserted, miners laid off. The disparity between poor and rich grew, with its inevitable creation of a large underclass. Writes **Judith Cook** in *To Brave Every Danger:* "The dispossessed young, with no work, no prospects and no homes, turned not surprisingly to crime."

Mary Bryant, born Mary Broad, grew up in the coastal town of Fowey, near Cornwall, where her mariner father taught her to navigate a small sailing boat with skill. She had an older sister Dolly and a younger brother; two other siblings died in infancy. Except for skeletal facts from the parish register, Bryant's life does not emerge for the historian until age 20 when she and two accomplices were apprehended for highway robbery.

In the tumultuous days of 18th-century England, highway robbery and smuggling were two of Cornwall's major occupations. Smugglers were known as free traders. As the government cracked down, more and more crimes, nearly 200, became capital offenses punishable by hanging; these included highway robbery, sodomy, criminal bankruptcy, forgery, armed smuggling, sacrilege, picking pockets for anything more than a shilling, shoplifting for anything valued over five shillings, cutting down a landowner's tree, and escaping from transportation. Citizens avidly read of each day's hangings. On October 9, 1782, the *London Evening Post* reported:

> Yesterday morning about 9 o'clock the following malefactors were brought out of Newgate and carried to Tyburn in three carts where they were executed according to their sentences, viz: Henry Berthand, for feloniously impersonating one, Michael Groves; . . . Charles Woolett, for robbing Bernard Cheale on the highway of a metal watch; . . . Charlotte Goodall and John Edmonds, for stealing from the house of Mrs Fortescue at Tottenham where Goodall lived as a servant, a quantity of linen. . . . They all behaved very penitent.

At 20, Mary Bryant was 5'4", slim with long dark hair, grey eyes, a good complexion, who had offered "forest dweller" as place of origin, or so it said on her dossier. During the month of January 1786, Mary and two accomplices, **Catherine Fryer** and **Mary Haydon** (alias Mary Shepherd), held up one **Agnes Lakeman** who was walking on the main road to Plymouth. It is thought that Lakeman must have resisted because Bryant attacked the woman before absconding with a silk bonnet and valuables worth nearly £12. All three were caught, jailed, and brought before the Exeter Lent Assizes (a court session). On March 20 or 21, Bryant was sentenced to be hanged.

It was tradition at the end of the Exeter Assizes for judges to review the cases and arbitrarily reprieve some of those condemned. Mary Bryant and her accomplices were spared in this fashion; instead, all were given seven-years transport. "While there was no sentiment over hanging women, unless they were pregnant and could 'plead their bellies,'" writes Cook, "it is certain that in some cases women had their death sentences commuted to transportation for a very basic reason: they could service the male convicts and so keep them quiet. From young teenagers without any sexual experience to middle-aged women, all were classed as whores once they became convicted felons."

With the jails crammed, criminals were transported to penal colonies outside the country, and England was desperately casting about for a new place to offload its malefactors. Previously, felons had been sent to America or Nova Scotia, but most of them had joined the insurrecting colonists. The climate of Africa had proved prohibitory, with convicts dying by the gross as soon as they were put ashore. As options dimmed, it was recommended that felons be kept along England's shore, anchored in obsolete warships, so that convicts could then be used constructively. Shackled waist to ankle, they were brought ashore under an overseer to work on roads and quays (stone wharves), or as pile drivers. Soon, the warships too would be filled to bursting. Mary Bryant was assigned to the first prison ship to take women, the *Dunkirk*, which was anchored off the coast of Devenport. Writes Cook:

> In no time male and female prisoners were separated and then hustled below to their quarters, the hulk "stink" hitting them in the face like a physical blow, the stench made up of closely packed, unwashed bodies, rotting food, stagnant bilge-water and "the necessaries," the buckets in which they had to urinate and defecate which were only emptied once a day. . . . The headroom was hardly enough to allow a moderately sized person to stand upright.

Soon aware that sexual favor would earn her favors in return—a wash, a comfortable bunk, decent food—Bryant became the mistress of one of the officers.

The off-shore prisons became floating breeders for infectious diseases. With Members of Parliament beginning to fear possible epidemics on shore, Sir Joseph Banks, botanist on Captain James Cook's voyage, advocated the foundation of a penal settlement in Australia. It was decided that a colony be established at Botany Bay, on the coast of New South Wales, and Lord Thomas Sydney, the home secretary, chose Arthur Phillip as the colony's first governor. After receiving his appointment on October 12, 1786, Phillip immediately organized the expedition. Mary Bryant was newly pregnant when she was put on board the *Charlotte* of the First Fleet on January 7, 1787. Also aboard was a professional fisherman named Will Bryant, who had been sentenced two years previously to seven-years transport for smuggling, and Watkin Tench, a captain-lieutenant in the British marines and a liberal advocate of the teachings of Rousseau and Voltaire. Tench, assigned as a prison guard, was not only solicitous of the convicts but would keep a journal. He wrote that the pregnant Cornish girl was intelligent, mysterious, and decidedly independent.

On another of the ships, the *Lady Penrhyn*, which carried only female prisoners, a large portion of the women on board were servants who had stolen from their mistresses. One had taken two flat irons, two forks, and two spoons. Another had taken some cheese, bacon, butter, raisins and some flour. **Dorothy Handland**, age 82, was being transported for perjury. On arrival to Botany Bay, she would hang herself, the first recorded suicide in Australian history. **Elizabeth Beckford**, 70, had also snatched cheese from the pantry of her mistress. **Elizabeth Hayward**, 13, had stolen a gown, bonnet and cloak from the wife of her master to whom she had been apprenticed.

For four more months the ships sat in port while the convicts lay in constant motion below decks, nauseated by the swaying and the stench, not allowed up for fresh air and daylight. There were food and clothing shortages, scarcity of tools, no medical supplies, and no funds available for purchases and payrolls for the marine guards. Arthur Phillip, realizing that his superiors were more interested in the removal of the convicts than their health or safety, engaged in many bureaucratic confrontations. On April 25, 1787, the situation improved when the government issued Phillip his formal commission and instructions.

On Sunday, May 13, his fleet of 11 ships sailed from Portsmouth harbor. The convicts and their supplies were carried in the *Charlotte, Lady Penrhyn, Alexander, Scarborough, Friendship, Prince of Wales* and the storeships *Fishburn, Borrowdale,* and *Golden Grove.* The admiralty had also commissioned the H.M. *Sirius*, Phillip's flagship, and its tender-ship *Supply* to convoy the transport fleet. The number of convicts on the First Fleet varies in numerous records, but approximately 729 set sail. This number included about 565 men, 153 women and 11 children. The marine detachment included 19 officers, 192 enlisted men, 30 wives and 12 children. Once en route, Phillip allowed those who behaved to be relieved of their shackles and given some fresh air on deck at regular intervals. The convicts, including Mary and Will, became acquainted. Tench continued to be impressed by Mary, noting in his journal that she was sensible and practical.

Phillip plotted an indirect route that included supply stops in the Canary Islands, Rio de Janeiro, and Cape Town. On September 8, 1787, the fleet's medical records noted: "Mary Broad, a convict, was delivered of a fine girl." When the fleet reached Cape Town in October, the baby was christened Charlotte Spence on the 28th by a minister on board; since Mary would not offer the father's name, the baby was listed as a bastard. The last leg of the trip was plagued by gales. After eight months, 15,000 miles away from home, shore was sighted on January 19, 1788. En route, 56 had died.

Botany Bay proved anything but hospitable. The original Australians—the Aborigines—whose land it was, greeted the ships' arrival with an instinctive "Warra!" (go away). It was summer and incredibly hot. Devoid of protection from the rough seas, vegetation consisted of eucalyptus trees, cabbage palms, and stubby bushes. There was no grassland, no building materials, poor soil for farming, and no edible fruit.

Phillip looked further, arriving in a cove called Port Jackson, which he renamed Sydney Cove. While the women remained on board for another two weeks, the male convicts came ashore on January 26 to clear the land, pitch tents, and offload supplies. Will Bryant was given fish hooks, a net, and the small boats available, and asked to start the colony's fishing industry. About to wed Mary and take on responsibility for her child, he agreed to his assignment on condition that he be given a hut for his family rather than be quartered with other convicts. He also mentioned to others that he did not deem such a marriage binding back in England once his sentence was up, though Mary was unaware of this.

Arthur Phillip was concerned about putting the women ashore, and his fears were tragically well-founded. He had been warned that there were not enough women convicts to service the sexual needs of the marines, sailors, and male convicts. The women disembarked on February 6. Writes Cook:

> [I]t was a night of almost unimaginable horror. Young virgin girls in their mid-teens, old women long past childbearing age, all were fair game. Men queued up to gang rape victims held down for them by their roaring, laughing friends. With every realization of the strength of sexual appetites which had been denied any real relief, it is still chilling to read the justification for what happened (that is, if it was thought worthy of mention at all) in the books of the predominantly male historians. What happened was "only natural," "only to be expected," even some of the more liberal-minded concluded it was probably for the best. Thwarted, the men might well have taken their frustration out on the guards. . . . Morning dawned on a desolate scene. The ground of Sydney Cove was nothing but a morass of red mud. Bruised, battered women, covered in mud and blood, sat shivering in the cold, some moaning, some weeping, some hardly able to walk.

Incensed, Phillip called the prisoners together and warned them that stealing food would bring mandatory death and any man who forced himself on a woman would be shot on sight.

Those women who had previously paired up with men and had posted banns for marriage were more fortunate. Mary, now thin and reserved, though she spoke in the vernacular of the felons, married Will Bryant on Sunday, February 10. Unable to write, she signed her name on the church register with a cross.

As hunger became the constant companion of both convicts and officers, scurvy, cholera, dysentery, and influenza ran rampant, spreading to the Aborigines. Phillip appealed to Britain for additional supplies and for free farmers to settle and teach agricultural methods to the convicts. During the wait for London's response, he established a vigorous system of rationing. He dispatched the *Sirius* to South Africa for food, moved many of the convicts to a second farm at Rose Hill and, pursuant to his orders, sent some convicts to establish a colony on the reputed fertile soil of Norfolk Island.

Though constantly hungry and concerned with feeding her small child, Mary lived a better life than most, thanks to her industry and that of her husband. They subsisted on a diet of fish until February 1789 when, with colony stores further depleted, Will lost the privilege of keeping a small portion of his catch. Where the couple had previously been mindful of authority, now Will secretly held back some fish for eating and barter. As the Bryants had been the subject of envy for other convicts, someone informed the judge-advocate and embellished the criminal details. Will was sentenced to "receive 100 Lashes; to be deprived of the Direction of the Fish and the Boat; and to be turned out of the Hut he is now in alone with his family." Mary and her daughter were moved to the huts of the other women. She would later report that she endured only with the knowledge that she would attempt an escape.

Though the colony had momentary relief when the ship *Sirius* arrived with fresh stores, Phillip was soon desperately in need of fish; he returned the Bryants to their hut, and Will was allowed to take Phillip's boat, a cutter with three sets of oars and a sail, and push further and further out to sea for greater catches. Around March 31, 1790, Mary gave birth to a son, called Emmanuel.

Though Will's sentence was up in March 1791 and Mary's in March 1793, the two began to plan their escape when they received news of an impending Third Fleet with 1,000 more convicts and scant supplies. England had made no provision for bringing transports back home, and the Bryants knew that, unless they acted, they would be in New South Wales for life. They needed a boat to get them to the nearest landfall, the Dutch East Indies, 3,000 miles away in unchartered waters. Mary urged Will to take Phillip's boat. It is supposed they had outside help from the Aborigines, whom they had befriended, most especially the colony's interpreter Bennelong, whose children played with little Charlotte Bryant, and whose wife and sister visited Mary. Soon Will was taking Bennelong and his family on fishing trips, possibly learning more about the currents and reefs along the Eastern coast. Then the Bryants chose seven other men to join them in the escape.

Will also made friends with Detmer Smith, captain of the Dutch vessel *Waaksamheyd* (The Good Lookout), who put into port at Sydney harbor and was shunned because he had negotiated a hard bargain to use his ship as charter to help the ailing colony. Mary offered to do the captain's laundry, invited him to dinner in their hut, and was seen in Smith's company quite often. By February, Smith was listening to their escape plans with sympathy. Mary negotiated for a navigational quadrant and a compass, while Will bartered for rice, saltpork and flour. Smith threw in two old muskets and some ammunition, a 10-gallon barrel of water, and a chart. The Bryants told the others to horde their rations, and Will built a secret cache in their hut under a false floor. They would have to leave by the end of March before the seasonal gales began.

On the eve of March 28, 1791, Mary—with her daughter Charlotte, now three and a half, and Emmanuel, still at her breast—snuck down to the cove with Will and their entourage. It is said that Bennelong swam out and cut the cutter off its mooring in deep water and brought it closer to shore. Provisions were stowed, children were put on board, and, at midnight, they silently glided out of the harbor with the tide. When they rounded the point, they hoisted sail, leaving behind no vessel in the colony large enough to pursue them.

Two journals would recount the Bryant voyage, one left behind by Will and one by James Martin, another escapee. Martin's manuscript was found in the 1940s in a collection of papers belonging to Jeremy Bentham. In his travels, William Bligh came upon Will Bryant's journal in October 1792 and commissioned a scribe to copy it; all that remains of Will's account is the quarter that the scribe managed to copy.

From all reports, once the convicts left the land, Mary's courage sustained them. Though they owed their survival to Will's seamanship, he would often be discouraged, while Mary never lost heart. Will and Mary shared the navigation with two others, sailing for miles along the length of the eastern coast of Australia, navigating between the Great Barrier Reef and shore, through the Torres Strait, then turning west toward the uncharted Arafura Sea. Because it sat so low with passengers, the cutter leaked continually and took in water in a high wind. Every two days, they put ashore for two days—where they located fresh supplies and often recaulked the cutter with rosin and beeswax.

At one landing, they were attacked by Aborigines and had to leave without fresh water or food. When they finally landed again, having run out of rosin, they caulked with soap. Twenty miles later, a monsoon hit. As the rain and high waves deluged the boat, the escapees heaved all possessions overboard to stay buoyant. The men despaired of living, but Mary snatched one of their hats and began bailing, shaming them to fight for their lives. After organizing the bailing effort, she took the tiller and fought the seas; she and her children, said Mary, had no intention of drowning. Between the shore and the Great Barrier Reef, the seas calmed. They put to shore on an islet, dining on turtle and resting for six days. Ahead, however, lay the open Arafura Sea where they would no longer be able to hug the coast. As they passed into the Gulf of Carpenteria, dotted with islands containing unfriendly natives, two enormous war canoes charged out to sea, carrying 30 to 40 warriors. They changed course and headed directly for Timor across the Gulf some 500 miles away.

On June 5, 1791, 69 days out, the convicts sighted land. They had sailed 3,254 miles, 1,200 of which in uncharted ocean waters, in an open boat. Will Bryant's journal said that his wife and two children "bore their suffering with more fortitude than any among them." Their navigation proved superb; that evening, the boat tied up at the wharf in Kupang, island of Timor, in the Dutch East Indies, an exact landfall.

Will told the Dutch that he was a British merchant mariner whose ship had sunk off the Great Barrier Reef. Unfortunately, he added that other members of the crew might be alive and still show up. This would be a fatal embellishment. The Dutch governor allowed the group to replenish their stores under the assumption that he could send the bills to England. Making use of Mary's maiden name, Will signed the bills William Broad. When the Dutch heard of Mary's part in their survival, her fame spread throughout Kupang; indeed, she is still a national heroine in Holland. But her luck would run out in two months' time.

Long before the Bryants' arrival, Captain William Bligh had landed in Kupang after the mutiny on his ship the *Bounty*. When Bligh landed in London in March 1790 and told his story, the British navy sent out the notorious Captain Edward Edwards on the 74-gun warship HMS *Pandora* to find the *Bounty* mutineers. On August 28, 1791, two months after the Bryants pulled into Kupang, Edwards smashed his ship on the Great Barrier Reef; four boats, bearing 89 crew members, came ashore at Kupang harbor on September 15. Edwards was greeted with the news that part of his crew had already arrived.

Within days, the convicts were arrested. Edwards, thrilled at the prizes he was about to bring back to England, hired the Dutch *Rembang* to transport his charges to Batavia (modern-day Djakarta on the island of Java), where they would find a boat back to England. On October 5, Mary and the crew, now fit and healthy after their rest, were turned over to Edwards and confined below on the *Rembang*. The health of her husband and son quickly deteriorated in the deplorable conditions, and they were thoroughly soaked after a cyclone. Arriving at Batavia, the prisoners, ill with fever, were transferred to a hospital, but Batavia was infamous for its fevers brought about by stagnant water. Emmanuel died in his mother's arms on December 1, 1791. Three weeks later, December 22, Will Bryant died.

Mary and the other convicts were put on three different ships and sent to the Cape of Good Hope, a three-month voyage. Edward's instructions were to keep them below in irons, with one hour release a day. Fever killed more of the convicts, and one of them jumped overboard. When Mary and her daughter Charlotte were taken ill, the Dutch captain took off Mary's irons so she could care for her remaining child. At the Cape of Good Hope, the convicts were transferred to the ship *Gorgon*, which set sail for England on April 5, 1792, The new captain insisted that Mary have proper accommodations to nurse her obviously dying child. Another passenger's journal reads for May 6: "Last night the child belonging to Mary Broad . . . died at 4 o'-clock. Committed body to the deep." The only thing Mary Bryant had to look forward to on her arrival in England was a public hanging.

On June 18, the *Gorgon* anchored off the coast of Portsmouth, disembarked passengers, then journeyed on to London with the convicts. At the time, James Boswell had just published *The Life of Samuel Johnson* and was enjoying the beginning of fame and a possible fortune. Boswell, who abhorred injustice and executions, saw the newspaper spread that headlined "Escape of Convicts from Botany Bay." The article quoted Mary as saying: "I would sooner suffer death than return to Botany Bay." James Boswell arrived at Newgate Prison where the prisoners were being retained and offered his services. Mary declined, leaving him amazed by her self-possession and dignity.

The convicts were brought up before magistrate Nicholas Bond, who was also impressed with Mary's responses and demeanor. "She answered her questions intelligently and in a clear voice," wrote biographer Cook, "which only faltered slightly when he asked her about the fate of her family." Bond had already been apprised that it was Mary's force of character that had saved the inhabitants of the small boat. Asked if she was repentant of her crime, Mary Bryant answered that indeed she was.

Court observers who were sympathetic to the plight of the convicts took up a collection, and the press too was supportive. Again Boswell offered to help save her from execution, but Mary responded that she had no desire to spend the rest of her life in prison. Then what about a full pardon?, replied Boswell. A determined magpie, he irritated everyone in the Home Office for so long that on May 2, 1793, Mary Bryant was granted a full pardon by Henry Dundas, home secretary.

With the help of charitable friends, Boswell installed Mary in an apartment on Little Titchfield Street and gave her money for clothes. She soon learned that her father had been left a considerable sum of money and that her sister Dolly was a cook in a household in London; the sisters met with great delight. Boswell then put her on a vessel for Cornwall, taught her how to sign her name, and promised her a biyearly annuity—all she need do was acknowledge receipt. For the next 18 months, the written record of Mary Bryant continues as she acknowledges receipt of three payments. Upon Boswell's death in October 1794, his family put an end to the annuities and to any evidence of the further life and last days of Mary Bryant. She retreats again into obscurity at the age of 29, her story to be eclipsed for more than a century.

In the 1930s, *The Strange Case of Mary Bryant* was penned by a military man named Rawson, but it was mostly fiction of the bodice-ripping class. At the same time, however, two scholarly monographs were also printed, including Professor Frederick Pottle's *Boswell and the Girl from Botany Bay,* contributing to some of the record, enlarging some of the myth. Judith Cook's *To Brave Every Danger,* published in 1993, uses all available documentation to present the most in-depth and accurate biography of one of the few convicts to escape the notorious penal colony at Botany Bay.

SOURCES:

Anonymous. *The Voyage of Governor Phillip to Botany Bay, with an Account of the Establishment of the Colonies of Port Jackson and Norfolk Island.* Reprint of 1789 ed. Angus & Robertson, 1970.

Cook, Judith. *To Brave Every Danger.* London: Macmillan, 1993.

Eldershaw, M. Barnard. *Phillip of Australia: An Account of the Settlement at Sydney Cove, 1788–92.* Angus & Robertson, 1972.

Hughes, Robert. *The Fatal Shore: The Epic of Australia's Founding.* Knopf, 1987.

Mackaness, George. *Admiral Arthur Phillip, Founder of New South Wales, 1738–1814.* Angus & Robertson, 1937.

SUGGESTED READING:

Clark, C.M.H. *A History of Australia: From the Earliest Times to the Age of Macquarie.* Vol. I. Melbourne University Press, 1962.

Taylor, Peter. *Australia: The First Twelve Years.* Allen & Unwin, 1982.

RELATED MEDIA:

Wertenbaker, Timberlake (play), *Our Country's Good,* 1988.

Bryceland, Yvonne (1926–1992)

South African stage actress who originated many roles for the plays of Athol Fugard. Born Yvonne Heilbluth on November 18, 1926, in Cape Town, South Africa; died on January 13, 1992, age 66, in London, England; daughter of Adolphus Walter and Clara Ethel (Sanderson) Heilbluth; attended St. Mary's Convent, Cape Town; married Daniel Bryceland (divorced); married Brian Astbury; children: three daughters.

Yvonne Bryceland first appeared on stage in 1947 in the role of a movie actress in *Stage Door.* In her seven years with the Cape Performing Arts Board (1964–1971), she played a variety of roles including Mme. Desmortes in *Ring Round the Moon,* Miss Madrigal in *The Chalk Garden,* and Mme. Ranevskaya in *The Cherry Orchard.*

From 1969 on, Bryceland's association with playwright Athol Fugard played a prominent part in her career. The leading actor in many of his plays, she created Millie in *People Are Living There* and Lena in *Boesman and Lena* in which

she also made her London debut (July 1971). After leaving Cape Performing Arts to tour with Fugard, Bryceland, with her second husband Brian Astbury, founded The Space, Cape Town (March 1972), where she portrayed such diverse characters as Frieda in Fugard's *Statements after an Arrest under the Immorality Act,* Amanda Wingfield in *The Glass Menagerie,* as well as Mother Courage and Medea. She later toured Europe in *Statements* and repeated that role again in London (1975).

Bryceland appeared in the Edinburgh Festival in 1975 and joined the National Theatre Company in 1978, where she played a Witch in *Macbeth* and Hecuba in *The Woman.* During the 1979–80 season, she appeared as Queen Margaret in *Richard III* and Emilia in *Othello.* In 1980, she appeared in Fugard's *Road to Mecca,* traveling with the play to London and New York and winning both the Theater World Award and an Obie. Bryceland recreated the role of Lena in the film version of *Boesman and Lena* (1972) and appeared on television in *People Are Living There* and Fugard's *Hello and Goodbye.* The actress died of cancer on January 13, 1992, in London.

Bryher (1894–1983).

See Ellerman, Winifred.

Brystygierowa, Julia (1902–1980)

Polish Communist activist and departmental director in the Ministry of Public Security from 1944 to 1956. Name variations: Julia Preiss. Born Julia Preiss in 1902; died in 1980; married.

Member of the Hashomer Zionist Scout organization (1920s); joined Communist Party of Poland (1930); graduated from University of Lvov; joined Communist Party of Ukraine (1939); director of International Workers' Relief, Lvov (1939–41); active in Union of Polish Patriots (1943–45); acted as a major figure in the repression of anti-Communists and other dissidents (1945–56); removed from office (September 1956) and retired to private life.

Born into a Polish-Jewish family in Russian-occupied Poland in 1902, Julia Preiss experienced cataclysmic historical changes in her early years, including the Bolshevik Revolution of 1917 and the restoration of Polish independence in 1918. Like many of her contemporaries, she was torn between an attraction to the ideals of Zionism and those of Marxism. She was at first an active member of the Hashomer Scouts, a

Zionist youth group, but by the late 1920s was drawn to the messianic ideals of Communism. In 1930, she joined the Polish Communist Party, a small and illegal group of conspirators and idealists. Now married and known as Julia ("Luna") Brystygierowa, she lived in the Galician city of Lvov (Lemberg), editing the underground Communist paper published there until the late 1930s. Though Joseph Stalin abolished the Polish Communist Party in 1938 on trumped-up charges of having been infiltrated by Fascists and Trotskyites, militant Marxists like Brystygierowa remained dedicated revolutionaries. Strongly drawn to ideas, she also earned a degree in history at the University of Lvov.

The Hitler-Stalin Pact of August 1939 sealed the fate of Poland, which ceased to exist as a sovereign nation after the German attack of September 1939. Lvov was annexed to the Ukrainian Soviet Socialist Republic as a result of the Nazi-Soviet alliance. Despised and persecuted until now, Polish Communists like Brystygierowa were almost immediately granted positions of power by Soviet occupation officials. She was granted membership in the Ukrainian Communist Party and received the position of director of the Lvov branch of the International Workers' Relief organization, which gave her control over a significant staff and budget. In June 1941, she was able to flee Lvov when Nazi forces attacked the Soviet Union, and after a series of adventures found herself settled far behind the front lines in Samarkand in Soviet Central Asia.

In the next months, Stalin released the Polish prisoners of war still alive in the Soviet Union, allowing them to form an army and a political organization, the Union of Polish Patriots (UPP). One of the few women to occupy a high position in the UPP, Julia Brystygierowa held the important post of director of the UPP's organizational department. She also served as an active member of the UPP executive committee and, between June and September 1944, was a presidium secretary of this pro-Soviet group. Her return to Poland in 1944 brought her to the city of Lublin, where she worked closely with leading Polish Communist militants from the Soviet Union who now declared themselves to be the legitimate government of a liberated Polish Republic.

As strongly committed to Marxist ideals as she had been in her youth, in 1944 Brystygierowa joined the newly reconstituted Polish Communist movement, which now called itself the Polish Workers Party. As a member of the party's control commission, she was a fierce and cunning political infighter who rapidly built up a power base within the new, Soviet-dominated Polish government. By 1947, rigged elections had turned Poland into a Soviet satellite state. In 1948, potential resistance on the Left was nipped in the bud when Social Democrats were merged with Communists in a new, all-dominating political party, the Polish United Workers Party. During these years, Brystygierowa became an important figure in the repressive machinery of "People's Poland," serving as a department director in the Ministry of Public Security. Her responsibility was in the area of cultural affairs, particularly the infiltration of the intelligentsia, non-Communist youth organizations, and the Roman Catholic Church. She was also a member of the supersecret Committee for Public Security, a small core of trusted Communists who were "advised" by high Soviet diplomatic, military, and intelligence officials stationed in Poland.

As the only woman to achieve a high position in the security apparatus of Stalinized Poland, Brystygierowa was occupied for more than a decade in the cat-and-mouse game of attempting to outwit a nation overwhelmingly hostile to its Soviet-imposed Communist regime. Not involved in the harsher aspects of "people's rule"—such as forced confessions, rigged trials, or anti-guerrilla warfare—she was, in the words of fellow-Marxist leader Stefan Staszewski, an exceptional individual within the security apparatus in that she was "[c]ultured, eloquent, not at all shrill." On a number of occasions, she was able to persuade imprisoned enemies of the regime that they could attain their goals after their release from prison; psychologically perceptive, she judged them to be no longer a threat to the regime. Although a fanatical Communist, there were a number of occasions when Brystygierowa made serious efforts to resist the "suggestions" of Soviet officials. Her motives for such behavior are not clear, but perhaps she believed herself to be a Polish patriot as well as a Marxist revolutionary. Regardless, Brystygierowa's career in the Polish Communist hierarchy ended with her abrupt removal in September 1956 when as a result of the growing anti-Stalinist movement in the Soviet Union, a "thaw" caused a national upsurge of reform that ended the terror-based regime in Warsaw. Retiring into private life, she spent her final decades writing novels under her maiden name of Julia Preiss.

SOURCES:
Clark, John, and Aaron Wildavsky. *The Moral Collapse of Communism: Poland as a Cautionary Tale.* San Francisco, CA: ICS Press, Institute for Contemporary Studies, 1990.
Held, Joseph. *Dictionary of East European History since 1945.* Westport, CT: Greenwood Press, 1994.

Polonsky, Antony, and Boleslaw Druiker. *The Beginnings of Communist Rule in Poland.* London, 1980.

Toranska, Teresa. *"Them": Stalin's Polish Puppets.* Translated by Agnieszka Kolakowska. NY: Harper & Row, 1987.

John Haag, Associate Professor,
University of Georgia, Athens, Georgia

Buber, Margarete (1901–1989).

See Buber-Neumann, Margarete.

Buber-Neumann, Margarete

(1901–1989)

German author, Communist activist, and prisoner in the Soviet Gulag before being deported to Nazi Germany and incarcerated in the infamous Ravensbrück concentration camp, who devoted the remainder of her life to exposing Stalinist tyranny. Name variations: Grete Buber, Margarete Buber, Margaret Buber Neumann. Born Margarete Thüring on October 21, 1901, in Potsdam, Germany; died in Frankfurt am Main, Germany, on November 6, 1989; daughter of Heinrich Thüring (a brewery manager) and Else (Merten) Thüring; had two sisters, Babette Gross and Gertrud ("Trude") Thüring, and two brothers; trained as a kindergarten teacher; common-law marriage to Rafael Buber (son of the philosopher Martin Buber), beginning in 1921; common-law marriage to Heinz Neumann (a linguist and Communist revolutionary), around 1928; married Helmuth Faust (divorced); children: (with Rafael Buber) two daughters, Barbara (b. 1921) and Judith (b. 1924).

Joined the Communist Youth League of Germany (1921); joined Communist Party of Germany (KPD, 1926); worked in Berlin as a member of the editorial staff of Inprekorr, *journal of the Communist International; fled Germany (1933) with Heinz Neumann, her second common-law husband, going to Spain, Switzerland, France, and the Saar territory; immigrated to Soviet Union (1935); arrested and convicted of being a "socially dangerous element" and sentenced to five years' loss of freedom (1938); expelled from USSR to Nazi Germany (1940); imprisoned in Ravensbrück concentration camp until 1945; became a noted author after 1945, whose books played a significant role in exposing the Soviet Gulag; after release, spent five years in Sweden; returned to Frankfurt in 1950; in Munich, wrote and published* Milena—Kafkas freundin *(1977, published as* Milena: The Story of a Remarkable Friendship, *Schocken, 1988); continued to write and speak out against Stalinist oppression.*

Margarete Buber-Neumann's life, like the century, began in a time described by the Austrian writer Stefan Zweig as "a golden age of security." Her father Heinrich Thüring (1866–1942) provided a financially comfortable, solidly respectable lifestyle for his large family. Born into an Upper Franconian peasant family, Heinrich was an ambitious and authoritarian man who had risen to a management position by dint of hard work and determination, becoming director of an important brewery. Although he was raised as an easygoing South German, he had adopted Prussian authoritarian values and drove himself without mercy, expecting the same devotion from his workers and his own family. In her memoirs, Margarete described her father as a combination Prussian drill-sergeant, peasant patriarch, self-made man, who customarily worked 12 or more hours a day. A capitalist through and through, he had no use for socialist doctrine of any kind.

In dramatic contrast to Buber-Neumann's rigidly authoritarian father was her remarkably freethinking mother, **Else Merten Thüring** (1871–1960). The last of twelve children, she was one of six who survived as half of her siblings died of diphtheria. Else was born in the small village of Schmergow in the Prussian district of Brandenburg but grew up in Potsdam, where she was raised by a brother who was almost two decades older. Her brother was broadminded and sympathetic to socialist ideas, so Else grew up with his perspective. Like him, she rejected Prussia's monarchical, authoritarian, and militaristic ideals. Even after her marriage to Heinrich, Else never lost her nonconformist spirit, which she passed on to her children.

When Else became a mother, she regarded each new member of the family as a unique and precious entity never to be bullied or crushed. Since her husband had little time to spend with his children, Else left her mark on them, particularly on her daughters. Margarete and **Babette (Gross)** both grew up to be political and social rebels. Buber-Neumann cherished early memories of her mother's disdain for Prussian militarism, especially one incident. To celebrate May Day, soldiers in Potsdam paraded before assembled schoolchildren. During this military review, Margarete's mother made scathing comments under her breath, describing the elaborate ritual as "comic theater" and characterizing the kaiser as a "megalomaniacal saber-rattler."

While Margarete loved her mother, she had few happy memories of her father. At age three, she had visited a neighbor who owned a pet monkey and was thrilled when the monkey took a piece of lettuce she offered it. Full of childish enthusiasm, Margarete ran home to tell her family about this fascinating encounter. Her father did not respond at all to his little daughter's joy and, instead, beat her severely for leaving home without permission. As this was a typical encounter between father and daughter, they were estranged all their lives.

School brought more dealings with Prussian authoritarianism. Margarete and her classmates were exposed to a constant barrage of propaganda, singing patriotic doggerel like *"Der Kaiser ist ein lieber Mann und wohnet in Berlin, und wär es nicht so weit von hier, so ging' ich heute hin"* (The kaiser is a fine man who lives in Berlin, and were it not so far from here I'd go there today). The young girl did not assimilate this philosophy well. In December 1915, Buber-Neumann joined the Alt Wandervogel, part of the German Youth Movement. Love of unspoiled nature bound these young people together. At first, Margarete was intoxicated by hiking in the forest, singing folk music, and celebrating traditional German nature festivals. The Wandervogel rejected conventional morality, embracing freer relations between the sexes and a simpler lifestyle. As World War I drew to a close, however, Buber-Neumann became increasingly disillusioned with youthful Romantics entranced by nature. By 1918, four years of carnage had wiped out an entire generation in Europe. At one meeting, a male leader stressed that members must defend German culture just as the Teutonic knights had done in the Middle Ages. An incensed Margarete asked, "Of what relevance are the ancient Teutons to us today? We would be better advised if we concerned ourselves with the things that are taking place in today's Germany."

In 1919, Margarete enrolled at the Pestalozzi-Fröbel-Haus in Berlin-Schöneberg to become a kindergarten teacher. The collapse of the German monarchy and the loss of the war unleashed a chaotic but creative period of artistic and intellectual ferment. The young woman threw herself into expressionist art as well as lectures on free love, Marxism, and world revolution. In March 1920, she witnessed the Kapp Putsch, a failed coup of extreme rightists who wanted to overthrow the German Republic. Soldiers supporting the coup wore black swastikas on their helmets. After a series of political arguments, Buber-Neumann's father threw her out of the house. For a time, she lived in the home of Karl Wilker, director of the Linderhof, an experimental reform school. One of her friends was **Trude Marcell**, a teacher at the Fröbel-Haus who shared many of Margarete's anti-authoritarian

Margarete Buber-Neumann

views. Through Trude, she met and fell in love with Rafael Buber, son of the famous Jewish philosopher, Martin Buber. Espousing free love, the two contracted a common-law marriage, and in 1921 their first daughter, Barbara, was born. A second daughter, Judith, would arrive in 1924.

In 1921, Margarete Buber, as she now called herself, attended a huge memorial demonstration for the martyred Communist leaders, Karl Liebknecht and *Rosa Luxemburg. Deeply moved, she committed herself to the Communist movement. That same year, she received her diploma as a kindergarten teacher and relocated to Heidelberg where Rafael was pursuing his studies. Shortly after, she joined the German Communist Youth League while Rafael began working in a cement factory to support his family. When the Communist Party had him steal dynamite for its underground work, the police got wind of the Bubers' Communist connections and searched their apartment but found nothing. Soon thereafter, however, Rafael was caught handing out Communist pamphlets and was expelled from the university. Rafael went to Jena to continue his studies, and Margarete moved in with her in-laws who provided a more secure environment for the children.

In 1926, Buber-Neumann returned alone to Potsdam, joined the Communist Party, and took a job at the large Tietz department store where she soon organized a Communist cell consisting of department store employees. Her sister Babette, also a Communist militant, introduced Margarete to many revolutionaries. Buber-Neumann joined the League Against Imperialism and the editorial staff of *Internationale Presse-Korrespondenz* (*Inprekorr*), the Comintern's German language publication. For some time, Buber-Neumann's common-law marriage had been failing, and by 1928 the relationship had ended. Rafael's mother instituted court proceedings to take Margarete's daughters from her. Though Buber-Neumann was deeply disappointed when the courts awarded custody to the Buber family, the event proved fortunate for the little girls. Their emigration from Nazi Germany to Palestine with their Jewish grandparents in 1933 probably saved their lives.

I believe it is my duty to let the world know on the basis of first-hand experience what can happen, what does happen, what must happen when human dignity is treated with cynical contempt.

—Margarete Buber-Neumann

In the late 1920s, Margarete Buber had met Heinz Neumann (1902–1937), a brilliant linguist who had studied at the University of Berlin. Heinz was a committed Communist revolutionary and a rising star in the Communist International (Comintern). He first visited Soviet Russia in 1922 and served on the German Communist Party's Central Committee and its Politburo. In those heady days, international revolution seemed inevitable. Margarete fell in love with the dynamic Heinz and soon contracted a common-law marriage with him, taking the name Buber-Neumann. Heinz had already traveled to China in 1927 at the behest of Joseph Stalin, whom he strongly supported at the time. The couple visited the USSR in 1931 and again in 1932. By the end of 1932, however, Heinz Neumann was no longer a supporter of Stalin and no longer served on the German Communist Party's politburo or the Comintern's executive committee.

When Adolf Hitler came to power in January 1933, Margarete Buber-Neumann had just returned to Berlin from the Soviet Union. Soon the Nazis began to systematically exterminate leftists, and she fled the country using a fake passport. She joined Heinz, who had gone to Spain in 1932 on a Comintern assignment. In November 1933, she and Heinz went to Zurich, Switzerland, where they carried out more conspiratorial work, but this time their luck ran out. Heinz was arrested and imprisoned in December 1934. Margarete feared for his life when Swiss officials threatened to deport him to Nazi Germany, a certain death sentence. Eventually he was released, and the couple moved on to Paris where Margarete worked with Willi Münzenberg (1889–1940), a leader of the German Communist Party propaganda division. In January 1935, she helped organize a plebiscite in the Saar territory, allowing citizens to choose whether they would reunite with Germany, remain independent, or unite with France. Despite massive propaganda efforts by anti-Nazi forces, the left suffered an enormous defeat when the largely working-class population of the Saar voted overwhelmingly to join Nazi Germany. Many of Buber-Neumann's illusions about the revolutionary spirit of the masses were shattered by the Saar experience.

By 1935, Margarete Buber-Neumann and her husband realized that Stalinism was apparently as great an evil as Nazism. Nevertheless, they remained dedicated Communists, hoping that the Soviet Union might still correct its course. Consolidating his power in the USSR, Stalin had begun to eliminate anyone who posed a possible threat. Margarete Buber-Neumann and her husband were internationalists; Stalin was not. The Neumanns detested Nazism both morally and ideologically; Stalin was a cynic who once told Heinz that if Germany became fascist, this would allow the Soviet regime time to industrialize. It was already clear that Stalin was planning to make a deal with Hitler. Faced with deportation to the Third Reich, Margarete and Heinz had few options, however. They chose the lesser of two evils and moved to the Soviet Union in the spring of 1935.

The Neumanns became residents of the Hotel Lux in Moscow, a hotel reserved for Comintern staff and special foreign "guests." They soon discovered that they were virtual prisoners. Because they were known anti-Stalinists, few of their neighbors dared talk to them. When the Soviet purges began in 1936, a Lux resident was taken away by the secret police almost nightly, never to return. Despite the atmosphere of terror, a pseudo-normal life somehow emerged. Margarete and Heinz took well-paid jobs as translators with the Foreign Workers Publishing House. They even vacationed in the Crimea at Sochi, where Stalin had his villa.

On the night of April 27/28, 1937, agents of the secret police came for Heinz. Margarete never saw him again and never knew his fate. Soviet archives, opened at the end of the Cold War, indicate he was sentenced to death on November 26, 1937, and executed the same day. Margarete lost her job and was forced to move in with friends who endangered their own lives to shelter her. She sold personal belongings in order to survive while she tried to learn her husband's fate. On June 19, 1938, she was arrested and taken first to the infamous Lubianka prison and then to Butirka where she was kept for several months. Though Buber-Neumann refused to admit she had committed any crime, she was nonetheless sentenced to five years in the Gulag as a "socially dangerous element."

Although conditions had been far from good in Moscow prisons, much worse was to come. Buber-Neumann became prisoner #174,475 at the Karaganda camp in Siberia. It was brutally cold on the steppe; there was little food; and there were no washing facilities. Political prisoners were housed with common criminals whose status was much higher. These criminals often consorted with the guards to make the lives of the political prisoners as miserable as possible. After a time, Buber-Neumann was transferred to Birma in Kazakhstan where she did agricultural labor. Though the work was hard, she had always been a fighter and refused to give in to the system.

In the fall of 1939, Buber-Neumann's conditions suddenly improved. She and several of her fellow prisoners were transported back to Butirka in Moscow and given clean clothes, blankets, and good food. Since they had been committed Communists who had done nothing wrong, they happily awaited their release. It was not to be. In late August 1939, the Hitler-Stalin pact had been signed, pledging that the two countries would not attack each other. One part of the agreement was that Stalin would send anti-Fascists back to Nazi Germany where thousands had already been exterminated in the Third Reich. In February 1940, Buber-Neumann and some of her fellow prisoners were put on a train, destination unknown. They desperately hoped they would be released in Lithuania and held onto this hope until the train reached Brest Litovsk, at the border of the Soviet Union and German-occupied Poland. Here they were handed over to the Gestapo and SS.

Buber-Neumann was sent to Alexanderplatz prison in Berlin to be interrogated by the Gestapo. Although she had committed no crime except for adhering to her political beliefs, she was charged with high treason. In August 1940, she was transported to the infamous Ravensbrück concentration camp for women where she met and formed a tight bond with the journalist *Milena Jesenská. Buber-Neumann was put in charge of many Jehovah's Witnesses, a sect of religious fundamentalists the Nazis hated and with whom she had little in common. She lost many of her Jewish friends and comrades at Ravensbrück as they were immediately executed or sent to Auschwitz. Some of the Polish women were used in heinous medical experiments. There was no news from the outside world, but Buber-Neumann and her fellow prisoners pieced together scraps of newspaper set aside for toilet paper to read what passed for truth in the German press. Once again Buber-Neumann fought authoritarian oppression in Ravensbrück. Snubbed by most of the Stalinists in the camp, she nearly died in solitary confinement after one encounter with the Nazis. In January 1945, she withstood blood poisoning and lived only because Inka, a Czech Communist friend stole the drugs that saved her.

In April, the Soviet army finally liberated Ravensbrück, but Buber-Neumann's near brushes with death continued. Released with other prisoners when Nazi control of the camp evaporated, she was almost shot by machine-gun fire from an Allied plane. Having survived more than five years at the hands of the Nazis, she was desperate to avoid being picked up by Soviet forces. Luck was with her when an American soldier let her pass through to the Western zones, telling her, "O.K., sister. Go through."

Soon Buber-Neumann made it to Sweden where she began to write her memoirs, *Under Two Dictators*, first published in Germany in 1948 and then translated into many other language editions. Over the next few years, she patched her life back together; after learning her two daughters were living in Israel, she established strong ties with them. She testified in several trials in the postwar period. Her testimony against the Ravensbrück camp commander helped secure his conviction and eventual execution for war crimes. In 1949, Buber-Neumann was involved in the Victor Kravchenko trial in France. Her shattering testimony convinced many that Stalin's Gulag system was comparable to the horrors in Nazi concentration camps and played a significant role in eroding the prestige of the French Communist Party among that country's intellectuals.

Returning to Germany in 1950, Buber-Neumann settled in Frankfurt am Main. In 1951, she became editor of the political journal *Die Aktion,* speaking out forcefully against Soviet Communism. During the chilliest days of the Cold War, she reminded Germans that Stalinist oppression, not Socialist humanism, was at the heart of the Soviet experience. When she died in Frankfurt am Main on November 3, 1989—three days before the fall of the Berlin Wall—many Germans had forgotten who she was or regarded her as just another Cold War relic. Margarete Buber-Neumann experienced terror and degradation inflicted by two of the 20th century's most heartless regimes and yet she survived. She spent the rest of her life warning of the evils that inevitably surface when political dogma becomes a religion.

SOURCES:

Buber, Margarete. *Under Two Dictators.* Translated by Edward Fitzgerald. NY: Dodd, Mead, 1949.

Buber-Neuman, Margarete. *Der kommunistische Untergrund: Ein Beitrag zur Geschichte der kommunistischen Geheimarbeit.* Kreuzlingen: Neptun Verlag, 1970.

———. *Von Potsdam nach Moskau—Stationen eines Irrweges.* Hohenheim: Edition Maschke, 1981.

Des Pres, Terrence. *The Survivor: An Anatomy of Life in the Death Camps.* Oxford: Oxford University Press, 1976.

"Erbswurst und Karnickel," in *Der Spiegel.* Vol. 12, no. 17. April 23, 1958, p. 23.

In den Fängen des NKWD: Deutsche Opfer des stalinistischen Terrors in der UdSSR. Berlin: Dietz Verlag, 1991.

Lazitch, Branko, and Milorad M. Drachkovitch. *Biographical Dictionary of the Comintern.* Rev ed. Stanford, CA: Hoover Institution Press, 1986.

Mayenburg, Ruth von. *Hotel Lux.* Frankfurt am Main: Ullstein Sachbuch, 1981.

McDermott, Kevin. "Stalinist Terror in the Comintern: New Perspectives," in *Journal of Contemporary History.* Vol. 30, no. 1. January 1995, pp. 111–130.

Müller, Reinhard. "Linie und Härasie: Lebensläufe aus den Kaderakten der Komintern (II)," in *Exil.* Heft 1, 1991, pp. 46–69.

Read, Anthony, and David Fischer. *The Deadly Embrace: Hitler, Stalin and the Nazi-Soviet Pact 1939–1941.* NY: W.W. Norton, 1988.

Schafranek, Hans. *Zwischen NKWD und Gestapo: Die Auslieferung deutscher und österreichischer Antifaschisten an Nazideutschland 1937–1941.* Frankfurt am Main: isp-Verlag, 1990.

Schumacher, Martin, ed. *M.d.R. Die Reichstagsabgeordneten der Weimarer Republik in der Zeit des Nationalsozialismus. Politische Verfolgung, Emigration und Ausbürgerung 1933–1945: Eine biographische Dokumentation.* Düsseldorf: Droste Verlag, 1991.

Wall, Irwin M. *French Communism in the Era of Stalin: The Quest for Unity and Integration, 1945–1962.* Westport, CT: Greenwood Press, 1983.

Weber, Hermann. "Weisse Flecken" in der Geschichte: Die KPD-Opfer der Stalinschen Säungen und ihre Rehabilitierung.* 2nd ed. Frankfurt am Main: isp-Verlag, 1990.

John Haag, Associate Professor of History, University of Georgia, Athens, Georgia

Bubley, Esther (1921—)

American industrial photographer, known for her use of "picture story" technique. Born in Phillips, Wisconsin, in 1921; attended Superior State Teachers College, Superior, Wisconsin, 1937–38; studied art and photography at Minneapolis College of Art and Design, 1939.

Esther Bubley was set on becoming a painter when she discovered photography. Encouraged by winning a $1,000 prize in *Life* Magazine's Contest for Young Photographers, she spent some of her early years in Washington, D.C., microfilming rare books at the National Archives. After a stint as staff photographer for the Office of War Information, in 1943 she got her break in New York, freelancing for Roy Stryker, then director of Standard Oil's photographic activities. Her first assignments included photographing America's bus system and Texas oil boomtowns. Between 1948 and 1960, Bubley worked on photojournalism assignments for the *Ladies' Home Journal* series, "How America Lives." She also did a number of assignments for *Life* magazine. Her photographs appeared in periodicals, including *McCall's, Woman's Day, Saturday Evening Post,* and *Good Housekeeping.*

One of the first to use the 35-mm camera and the "picture story" technique in industrial work, Bubley was known to climb oil rigs, ride cranes, and stand at the mouths of blast furnaces to get her shots. She was also known for her sensitive images of children, for which she traveled to almost every imaginable environment the world over. Her studies of children in South and Central America, and in many other countries, culminated in a series commissioned by the United Nations' International Children's Emergency Fund.

Bubley's approach remained fresh, and she kept her photographs—including her work in industry and photojournalism—out of the realm of commercialism. In her book on New York's Central Park, for example, she surprises the viewer with images of owls, rabbits, turtles, and even an empty champagne bottle floating in the lake.

In the 1960s, a poll of the nation's leading photographic editors and writers named Esther Bubley one of the top women photographers. Her work has been included in a number of exhibitions through the years. In 1948, her photographs were featured in an exhibition curated by Edward Steichen called *In and Out of Focus* at the Museum of Modern Art in New York. She was also represented in two other Steichen exhibitions at the Museum of Modern Art: *Diogenes with a*

Camera (1952) and *The Family of Man* (1955). Bubley had solo exhibitions at Limelight Gallery (1956) and Ledel Gallery (1982), both in New York, and at the Kathleen Ewing Gallery (1989) in Washington, D.C. In 1989, she was featured with *Marion Post Wolcott in a two-person exhibition at the Art Institute of Chicago. Once when asked why she chose her profession, Bubley's unassuming answer was simply, "I like it."

Barbara Morgan,
Melrose, Massachusetts

Bucca, Dorotea (fl. 1390–1430).

See Bocchi, Dorotea.

Buchan, countess of.

See Isabella of Buchan (fl. 1290–1310).
See Joan Beaufort (c. 1410–1445) for sidebar on Mary Stewart (d. 1465).

Buchan, Elspeth (1738–1791)

Scottish founder of a religious sect known as the Buchanites. Name variations: Elspeth Simpson. Born Elspeth Simpson near Banff, Scotland, in 1738; died near Dumfries, Scotland, in 1791; daughter of John Simpson (an innkeeper near Banff); married Robert Buchan (a potter of Greenock); children.

Separated from her husband Robert Buchan, a potter in Greenock, Elspeth Buchan settled with her children in Glasgow in 1781. In 1783, deeply impressed by a sermon preached by Hugh White, minister of the Relief Church at Irvine, she moved there and persuaded White and others that she was a saint with a special mission. She convinced White that she was the woman described in *Revelations xii* in whom the light of God was restored to men, and that God was the son she had brought forth. White was condemned by the presbytery, and in 1784 the magistrates expelled White, Buchan, and her Buchanite sect, which ultimately numbered 46 disciples. The group settled on a communal farm, known as New Cample, which consisted of one room and a loft in Closeburn, Dumfriesshire, where they lived on funds provided by the richer members. Claiming prophetic inspiration, Elspeth Buchan maintained that she could bestow the spirit of the Holy Ghost into her followers by breathing on them; she also convinced them that the millennium was near. They would not die, however, only be transposed. In a letter dated August 1784, the poet Robert Burns describes the sect as idle and immoral. Elspeth Buchan published a *Divine Dictionary* (1785) with White, who was unable to keep the sect together after Buchan's death in 1791.

Buchanan, Vera Daerr (1902–1955)

U.S. Representative, Democrat of Pennsylvania, 82nd–84th Congresses, July 24, 1951–November 26, 1955. Born Vera Daerr in Wilson, Pennsylvania, on July 20, 1902; died in McKeesport, Pennsylvania, on November 26, 1955. married Frank Buchanan (Congressman 1946–1951), in 1929.

Vera Buchanan was sworn in as a member of Congress on August 1, 1951, after winning a special election to fill a vacancy left by her husband's death the previous April. She defeated Republican nominee, McKeesport city controller Clifford W. Flegal, whose sharp criticism of President Harry S. Truman and the foreign policy of Secretary of State Dean Acheson cost him the election. Buchanan was reelected twice by her largely Democratic, pro-labor constituency.

Growing up in Duquesne, Pennsylvania, Vera Daerr Buchanan attended public and parochial schools. After her marriage in 1929, she ran a beauty shop in McKeesport and was active in the Democratic Women's Guild. Her husband, after serving a term as mayor of McKeesport, was elected to Congress in 1946 and had employed Vera as his secretary.

Vera Buchanan's terms in Congress were marked by service on the Committee on Merchant Marines and Fisheries, the Committee on Banking and Currency, and the Committee on Public Works. Staunchly behind the Truman administration, she supported unions and the rights of laborers, and backed housing legislation and the Turtle Creek Valley Flood Control Project.

Buchinskaia, Nadezhda Aleksandrovna (1872–1952).

See Teffi, N.A.

Büchner, Luise (1821–1877)

German poet and novelist. Name variations: Luise Buchner. Born in Germany on June 12, 1821; died on November 28, 1877, in Darmstadt, Germany; sister of Georg Büchner (1813–1837, a poet), Friedrich Karl Christian Ludwig Büchner (1824–1899, a German physician and philosopher), and Alexander Büchner (1827–1904, a critic and historian).

Noted as a champion of women's rights, Luise Büchner published *Die Frauen und ihr*

See following page for photograph

Vera Daerr Buchanan

Beruf (Woman and Their Calling) in 1855. This work commanded much attention and reached a fifth edition in 1883. Büchner followed with many other books about women. She also wrote *From Life* (1861), *Poet-Voices of Home and Foreign Lands,* a volume of tales, several original poems for *Woman's Heart,* and some Christmas stories.

Buck, Carrie (?–1983)

First American woman sterilized under the Virginia Compulsory Sterilization Law. Born Carrie Buck in Charlottesville, Virginia; died in 1983 in Waynesboro, Virginia; only daughter of Emma and Frank Buck; *married William Davis Eagle, on May 14, 1932 (died); married Charles Albert Detamore, April 25, 1965; children: one child, Vivian Elaine, born out of wedlock (d. 1932).*

Sometimes an event goes virtually unnoticed only to later surface as an incident of monumental consequence. The operation to sterilize Carrie Buck, carried out on the cloudy morning of October 19, 1927, at the State Colony for Epileptics and the Feebleminded in Lynchburg, Virginia, was performed without Buck's understanding or agreement and was sanctioned by the U.S. Supreme Court. The procedure ultimately altered the lives of thousands in the States, and, arguably, had worldwide implications, influencing the German policy of eugenics or "Aryan cleansing" under the Nazi regime, causing the sterilization of over two million.

From early childhood, Carrie Buck was victimized by local and state court systems, which, lacking provisions for child advocacy, eventually led to her surgery under Virginia's Compulsory Sterilization Law. Her natural mother Emma, widowed at an early age, had to make her living on the street in order to provide for Carrie and Carrie's half siblings Doris and Roy. At age three, Carrie became the ward of J.T. and **Alice Dobbs**, who sought to save her from the squalor of the street but were unable to provide a warm and nurturing environment; much of the time, she was treated like household help, leaving her feeling alienated and lonely.

Buck attended school through the fifth grade before she was withdrawn to help with family chores. She was considered a normal student, and her last teacher pronounced her "very good" in deportment and lessons. Around the age of 16, she was raped by a member of the Dobbs family, a nephew she had known and trusted. When she became pregnant, the family sought to rid themselves of her as quickly as possible by having her certified feebleminded by the local court. J.T. Dobbs understood the workings of the system, having overseen Buck's mother's commitment on the same charge three years earlier. **Emma Buck** remained institutionalized for 24 years, until she died of pneumonia on April 19, 1944. Buck's half-sister Doris would also be admitted to the Colony in December 1927. Her half-brother Roy was evidently legally adopted by another family, thereby escaping institutionalization.

After hearing testimony attesting to her hallucinations, temper tantrums, dishonesty, and morally delinquency, the Court for the City of Charlottesville pronounced Carrie Buck a suitable candidate for institutionalization. She was admitted to the Virginia Colony on June 4, 1924, after giving birth to a baby girl, Vivian Elaine, who remained in the care of the Dobbses. Carrie was allowed to visit Vivian only a few times before the child died of measles in 1932.

When Buck entered the Virginia Colony, the superintendent was Dr. Albert Sidney Priddy, a proponent of eugenics (human improvement through genetic control) who was classifying women at the Colony feebleminded on the basis of their sexual behavior alone and sterilizing them under the guise of treating them for pelvic diseases. After six months of observation, he determined Buck to be "feebleminded of the lowest grade Moron classification." He further judged her "a moral delinquent but physically capable of earning her own living if protected against childbearing by sterilization." At the time Buck was under evaluation, the institution was looking for a test case by which compulsory sterilization could be made law in Virginia. Buck was an ideal litigant, especially given her "feebleminded" mother and illegitimate baby.

Arguing Buck's fate in the courtroom were Aubrey Strode, a prominent Virginia politician and attorney for Albert Priddy, the Colony, and Virginia, and Buck's lawyer, Irving Whitehead, a close friend of Strode's. Presiding over the courtroom was Judge Bennett Gordon, who had known both lawyers since childhood. Strode's testimony was based on characterizations of the Buck family as poverty stricken, sexually promiscuous, and mentally retarded. Neighbors, teachers, and social workers corroborated his argument, which culminated with testimony from an expert and zealous supporter of compulsory sterilization from the Eugenics Record Office on Long Island. By all accounts, Whitehead's defense of Buck paled in light of Strode's prosecution. He called no witnesses and did not argue that there were contradictions in Buck's commitment record, nor that the Virginia sterilization law violated the U.S. Constitution, depriving Buck due process or equal protection under the law.

Judge Gordon took only a few weeks to decide in favor of the State, and he ordered Buck to be sterilized. Dr. Priddy, who died of Hodgkins disease before the judgment, was succeeded by Dr. J.H. Bell, his assistant at the Virginia Colony. The verdict was subsequently sent to the Virginia Court of Appeals as *Buck* v. *Bell,* where it was affirmed. The case was heard by the Supreme Court in April of 1927. Justice Oliver Wendell Holmes delivered the majority opinion (there was but one dissenting judge on the nine-member Court), which found that "Virginia's sterilization act satisfied both due process requirements and equal protection guarantees." Holmes went on to argue that sterilization was "not too great a sacrifice" to ask of Carrie Buck, and that "three generations of imbeciles" were indeed "enough."

Buck's sterilization was followed by 4,000 others at the Virginia Colony, including that of her sister Doris, who was told she was undergoing an appendectomy and did not discover what had been done to her until years later. Within ten years, more than 27,000 compulsory sterilizations had been performed in the United States, and 30 states had passed sterilization laws, many of them based on the Virginia model. In July 1934, the model sterilization act, developed in the United States and used in Virginia, became law in Germany, implemented by Adolf Hitler as the Hereditary Health Law, to insure that the inferior genes of "less worthy" members of the Third Reich were not passed on. It has been estimated that by the end of the first year that the law was in effect, over 56,000 in Germany were found defective and had been sterilized; between 1933 and 1945, two million in Germany met the same fate. Testimony at the Nuremberg war trials cited the Carrie Buck case as the precedent for Nazi race hygiene and sterilization programs.

After Buck's sterilization, the Dobbses refused to take her back, and she was placed in the home of a family named Coleman as a domestic servant. A subsequent placement with the Newbery family in Bland, Virginia, proved to be a nurturing environment for Buck, perhaps her first. Writing to the institution, Mrs. Newbery remarked on Buck's seemingly normal intelligence and inquired why she had ever been institutionalized. During this time, Buck also began a correspondence with her mother, proving that neither of them was illiterate.

In 1932, Buck married a 63-year-old widower and appeared to enjoy a comfortable, loving married life, attending church activities and taking great pleasure in gardening. After her husband died in 1941, she worked at a number of different jobs and suffered a period of ill health, losing a breast to cancer. She was finally hired by **Lucille Lewis**, who nursed her back to health and employed her as a companion for her aging parents, remarking "there was nothing wrong with that woman's mind." Buck married Charles Detamore, an orchard worker, in 1965.

In 1970, with her health beginning to fail, Buck and her husband returned to Charlottesville. They were brought to the District Home in Waynesboro, Virginia, after they were found living in poverty. Buck's final days were spent as an active resident of the Home. She enjoyed reading and music and was completely devoted to her husband. In 1980, Dr. K. Ray Nelson, then director of the Lynchburg Training Center (formerly the Virginia Colony), accompanied Buck and her sister back to the Colony so they could visit their mother's grave for the first time. Three years later, in 1983, Carrie Buck died and was buried with her daughter Vivian in the old section of Charlottesville.

Buck's half-sister Doris became part of a 1980 lawsuit brought by the American Civil Liberties Union on behalf of 8,300 men and women who had been sterilized in Virginia institutions before the practice was halted in 1972. The hearing generated nationwide media coverage and brought to light the shocking revelation that 50,000 Americans, termed mentally ill or retarded, had been sterilized following the Supreme Court decision in the Carrie Buck case. In 1985, two years after Buck's death, a settlement was reached allowing for notification to former residents of state institutions that they could inquire, and be informed, as to whether or not they had been sterilized; the settlement also provided for psychological counseling. One year later, in 1986, a member of the Virginia Board of Social Services sent a letter to the General Assembly suggesting sterilization of welfare mothers as a way to break the welfare cycle among the poor.

SOURCES:
Smith, David J., and K. Ray Nelson. *The Sterilization of Carrie Buck.* Far Hills, NJ: New Horizon Press, 1989.

RELATED MEDIA:
"Against Her Will: The Carrie Buck Story," cable-television movie, starring **Melissa Gilbert** and **Marlee Matlin**, 1994.

Barbara Morgan,
Melrose, Massachusetts

Buck, Pearl S. (1892–1973)

First American woman to win the Nobel Prize in Literature, who was the widely read author of over 100 books and has been translated into 69 foreign languages. Name variations: (occasional pseudonym) John Sedges. Born Pearl Comfort Sydenstricker on June 26, 1892, in Hillsboro, Pocahontas County, West Virginia; died on March 6, 1973, in Danby, Vermont; daughter of Absalom and Caroline Stulting Sydenstricker (Presbyterian missionaries); spent her childhood and youth in China; taught at home by her mother and Chinese tutors; attended boarding school in Shanghai; graduated from Randolph-Macon Woman's College; Cornell University, M.A. in English, 1936; married John Lossing Buck (an agricultural missionary) 1917 (divorced, 1935); married Richard J. Walsh (editor of Asia Magazine and head of John Day Company), in 1935; children: (first marriage) two daughters, Carol and Janice; (adopted) many.

Awards: Pulitzer Prize, William Dean Howells Medal for Distinguished Fiction, Nobel Prize for Literature, Wesley Award for Distinguished Service to Humanity, Gimbel Award (for unique service to humanity), numerous other awards, citations and honorary degrees, memberships in the National Institute

Pearl S. Buck

of Arts and Letters and the American Academy of Arts and Letters.

Had immediate and greatest success with second published novel The Good Earth *(1931); published sequels,* Sons *(1932) and* A House Divided; *published numerous other books of fiction and nonfiction for both children and adults, including* Dragon Seed, The Exile, *and* Fighting Angel, *and biographies of her parents; settled with second husband at Green Hills Farm, Perkasie, Pennsylvania, with large family of adopted children; founded East West Association (1941), Welcome House (1949) and Pearl S. Buck Foundation (1964); made countless appearances urging interracial understanding and world peace. A Bio-*

graphical Sketch of Pearl S. Buck, *published by the Ralston Press, has credited her with publishing 107 books and over 200 short stories, a total that does not include her numerous articles, letters and addresses.*

In 1938, when Pearl S. Buck became the first American woman to receive the Nobel Prize in Literature, the 1930 recipient Sinclair Lewis advised her: "Don't let anyone minimize the receiving of the Nobel Prize. It is a tremendous event, the greatest of an author's life." As moving as the Stockholm ceremony was, the new Laureate looked up into the face of the Swedish king and thought she was seeing the face of her long dead father. The king's family, she learned, had originated in the area of Bavaria from which her 18th-century Sydenstricker forebears had fled to America in search of religious freedom.

Buck's maternal grandparents, prosperous artisans from Utrecht, Holland, had also immigrated to the United States to escape laws limiting religious liberty. Cornelius Stulting and his wife arrived in Virginia in 1847 and, in 1849, settled in Hillsboro in what would become, at the time of the Civil War, Pocahontas County, West Virginia. There they built a large "brick-knobbed" farmhouse that boasted vertical Jenny Lind paneling and a graceful, two-storied portico. In the interior were "horsehair plaster" walls, wide bay windows, black walnut trim, and a fine stairway ornamented with hand-carved scrolling. This serene and lovingly tended house, looking out from its plateau onto a green mountain world, would always haunt the dreams of the Stultings' daughter Caroline. It was there that Caroline's own daughter, Pearl Comfort, was born on June 26, 1892.

For rich and genuine epic portrayals of the Chinese peasant life and for masterpieces of biography.

—Nobel Prize citation for award to Pearl S. Buck

Caroline and her husband, Absalom Sydenstricker, were deeply dedicated Presbyterian missionaries who returned to their post in China within a few months of their daughter's birth. Caroline would give birth to seven children, losing four of them to diseases contacted in the Orient. Pearl was one of the three whom she would raise to adulthood.

The little girl spent her childhood in the ancient city of Chinkiang, situated at the junction of China's Grand Canal and the Yangtze River. She would later say that, as an adult entering 20th-century American life, she had come out of the Middle Ages.

Though the child learned to speak Chinese before she spoke English, her first formal instruction in reading and writing was in English with her mother as teacher. An illiterate and much loved Chinese *amah* introduced Buck to the riches of Chinese folklore. Her tutor, a Confucian scholar, brought her knowledge of the traditional Chinese novel, a sprawling, story-telling genre looked down upon by the learned, but greatly loved by ordinary people. The English language literature available in the Sydenstricker home included the King James Bible, Shakespeare, and the novels of

Scott, Thackeray, George Eliot (*Mary Anne Evans) and Dickens, the latter Buck's favorite for many years. Caroline insisted that her daughter write regularly and submitted her work to the *Shanghai Journal*, an English language newspaper, under the pseudonym "Novice."

At 15, Buck was sent to boarding school in Shanghai. At 17, she went "home" to matriculate at Randolph-Macon Woman's College in Lynchburg, Virginia. In that cloistered environment, where she felt in many ways an alien, she nevertheless became a student leader, was chosen class president, elected to Phi Beta Kappa, won literary prizes, and taught psychology for a term after her graduation in 1914.

Caroline Sydenstricker's illness brought her daughter back to China. There Pearl nursed her frail patient back to tentative health, and there she met John Lossing Buck, an agricultural expert whom she married after a brief courtship. Chinese etiquette did not allow prolonged contact between young men and women. The bride's parents opposed the marriage, thinking the couple too different in temperament and interests, but there is a time, Buck would say later, when one is "ready" for marriage.

The Bucks went to live in Nanhsüchou in Anhwei (Anhui) province in North China. There Pearl became head of the local girls' school and accompanied her husband John on trips about the bleak northern countryside, he instructing the poverty stricken peasants in new farming methods, she talking with the women and children in whom she found a fascinating basic humanity. It was this sympathetic immersion in Chinese peasant life that would in time give her material for her major novels.

After five years, the Bucks left the north to accept appointments at the University of Nanking (Nanjing) in the ancient Yangtze River city some hundred miles from Shanghai. John, known as Lossing, taught rural economics, while Pearl taught English literature. She taught irregularly, also, at Southeastern University and at Chung Yang University, both in Nanking. In 1925, the couple returned to the United States for graduate study at Cornell University. There Buck wrote her thesis on the 19th-century English essayists. In need of money, she also entered and won a history department contest with an article on "China and the West," a subject that would be a lifelong preoccupation.

The Bucks had brought back to the United States their daughter Carol whose slow development was a source of anxiety. Buck would later ex-

From the movie
The Good
Earth, *starring*
Luise Rainer.

press her gratitude to the doctor at the Mayo Clinic who told her bluntly that the child was mentally retarded and would never progress beyond a four-year-old level. The news was cruel. "It was as if my very flesh were torn. It was beyond belief, and yet I knew I had to . . . shape my life around it." Eventu-

ally, she would place Carol in the Training School at Vineland, New Jersey, and she herself became active in the affairs of the school.

Carol was a victim of phenylketonuria, an inability to assimilate protein. Tests to recognize the difficulty in newborns are now required in many states and a special early diet prescribed. Buck's *The Child Who Never Grew*, originally published in the *Ladies' Home Journal*, tells Carol's story and has been widely reprinted as a source of comfort and information for the parents of retarded children.

In 1926, the missionary couple returned to their post in China, but a new life was opening. In little more than a decade, Pearl Buck would find herself an internationally famous author. She had always known that she wanted to write. Now she was beginning to mine the rich ore of her Chinese life. She had already published articles on the East in *Atlantic* and *Forum* magazines. It was time to turn to fiction.

Buck's early books were not published in the order of their composition. What was to have been her first novel was destroyed in 1927 when Nanking was attacked by a marauding army. Buck, along with friends and family, narrowly escaped the widespread slaughter of foreigners; hidden in a hovel by a loyal Chinese friend, they eventually boarded English and American warships in the harbor. The danger reminded her of the perils of the Boxer Rebellion in her childhood. "I have had the strange and terrible experience of facing death because of my color," she would later write, exploring the origins of her deep sympathy for blacks and other minorities in the United States. That sympathy would be reinforced by the memory of her grandfathers, both Southern landholders, who had refused to own slaves.

In 1928, after a year spent in Japan, Buck returned to her vandalized home in Nanking and set about writing in earnest. Her short story "East Wind: West Wind" was accepted by *Asia Magazine*. With revision and additional material, it was published in 1930 as a novel under the imprint of the John Day Company and went into three printings in ten months. In 1930, she also rapidly completed *The Good Earth*, originally titled "Wang Lung," after the central figure in this epic tale of Chinese peasant life. *The Good Earth* was published in 1931 by John Day and was an instant bestseller in the United States. It would remain Buck's most popular and widely read novel, translated, according to one tally, into 30 languages, excluding pirated editions. Seven different versions appeared in China alone. The saga of a Chinese farming family clearly struck a universal chord.

Sons, the sequel to *The Good Earth*, was published in 1932 and *A House Divided*, the final volume of the trilogy, in 1935. An unrelated novel, *The Mother*, appeared in 1934. Even as she worked on these books, Buck labored almost daily on an English translation of the monumental Chinese classic *Shui Hu Chuan*. Under the English title *All Men Are Brothers*, the 600,000 word manuscript was published in 1933.

Meanwhile, Buck's personal life was undergoing important change. In 1934, she left her husband and her Chinese life behind and came to the United States with Carol and an adopted daughter. In 1935, she divorced John Lossing Buck and married Richard J. Walsh, her editor and president of the John Day Company, who had persistently sought her hand. The couple settled at Green Hills Farm near Perkasie, Bucks County, Pennsylvania, in a century-old, stone house. Both lovers of children, the couple adopted a large family, including some Caucasian children, some Amerasian, and some of mixed white and black heritage. In her later years, she claimed that she could remember no serious problems with any of the ten children she had raised.

A busy family life did not slow Buck's career. In 1936, she published *The Exile* and *Fighting Angel*, the much admired biographies of her missionary parents. In 1937, Metro-Goldwyn-Mayer's film version of *The Good Earth* premiered, starring Paul Muni, *Luise Rainer, and *Tilly Losch. *The New York Times* reported that $3 million had been spent on the production with 2 million feet of film exposed in China and 700,000 or 800,000 feet in Hollywood on the meticulously built replica of Chinese scenes. Though MGM chief Louis B. Mayer was quoted as saying, "Who wants to see a picture about Chinese farmers?" the movie was considered a classic man-and-wife struggle to live off the rugged land of China, and Rainer won an Academy Award for Best Actress. Wrote Nash and Ross in the *Motion Picture Guide*: "The actress' incredible performance . . . one where she never laughed, seldom spoke, and expressed everything in wide-eyed silence, pierced the heart of Pearl Buck's phlegmatic heroine and remains an artful classic." The story was also dramatized for Broadway in 1933, starring Claude Rains and *Alla Nazimova.

In 1938, already the recipient of the Pulitzer Prize and the Howells Medal, Buck became the first American woman to receive the Nobel Prize for Literature. The prize would not again go to an American woman until 1993 when *Toni Morrison became the Laureate. With the Nobel Prize behind her, Buck turned frequently to American subject matter, writing novels under the pseudonym of John Sedges. The acerbic Baltimore critic Henry L. Mencken, not an admirer, complained that she neglected her domestic duties to write stories "about her neighbors." She contributed also to children's literature with such books as *The Big Wave, Stories for Little Children, Matthew, Mark, Luke and John* and *One Bright Day.*

Over the years, Buck continued to be showered with honors. She received honorary degrees from Yale University, the University of West Virginia, St. Lawrence University, Howard University, Lincoln University, Women's Medical College of Pennsylvania, Combs College of Music, West Virginia State College, Bethany College, Delaware Valley College, Hahnemann Hospital and Muhlenburg College. Numerous awards hailed her service to humanity.

In 1941, Buck and her husband founded the East West Association, which for ten years brought Asian entertainers and scholars to American audiences. In 1949, she founded Welcome House as a non-profit adoption agency, first to aid children of mixed blood, later to help Amerasian children whose American soldier-fathers had abandoned them in the Orient. Still later, she founded and gave generously to the Pearl S. Buck Foundation to aid homeless Amerasian children in the lands of their birth.

Buck's other humanitarian interests were broad. She was a member of the national committee of the American Civil Liberties Union. She spoke out forcefully against censorship of books. She spoke for the rights of women and the development of their talents, which she saw as underutilized in mid-century American society. She was an ardent advocate of world peace and spoke with concern during the Korean War about the growing influence of the military in American life. She denounced racial prejudice on many occasions. In 1954, a letter from Buck to *The New York Times* led directly to the removal of immigrants from the Federal House of Detention in Manhattan and the Westchester Jail, where new arrivals to the United States were confined with criminals, following the closing of Ellis Island.

From the movie Dragon Seed, starring Aline MacMahon, Walter Huston, Turhan Bey, and Katharine Hepburn.

Despite widespread acclaim for her many contributions and the friendship of such luminaries as Sinclair Lewis and Theodore Dreiser, Buck's reception by literary critics has been ambivalent. She was for a time compared to Tolstoy, yet the comparison has not lasted. From the beginning, some intellectual Chinese emigres were incensed by her portrayal of Chinese peasant life, declaring it animalistic and inaccurate. J. Donald Adams, who was highly enthusiastic at the time of the publication of *The Mother*, tempered his praise later. Buck herself is said to have credited not the literati but the popular columnist Will Rogers with a large part of the immediate success of *The Good Earth*. "It's not only the greatest book about a people ever written," declared Rogers to his readers, "but the best book of our generation. Go get this and read it."

Since the 1930s, Buck has come to be largely ignored by American literary critics. Her concerns were for the most part not theirs. The traditional Chinese novel, whose history she traced in her Nobel Prize Lecture, was long and crowded, a blend of fact, fiction and folklore, intended for the general public who adored it. Buck herself sought to tell absorbing, didactic stories addressed to a large reading public, particularly in her later career. Though she is said to have been stung by the attacks of literary critics, she did not attempt to write for a cloistered and academic audience.

Her style and vocabulary were simple and concrete. She said that she often used Chinese idioms, and that, when writing about Chinese characters, she first composed her stories in Chinese, then translated them into English as she put the words down on paper. In the original version of *East Wind: West Wind*, she followed the Chinese tradition of including in her text words and phrases borrowed from admired older novels, unaware that in American literature this practice was not considered elegant but hackneyed and clichéd.

Western influences upon Buck's writing were the King James Bible read aloud in her childhood home and those Victorian novelists whom her parents considered acceptable reading. When in adulthood she became acquainted with the American literary scene, she admired her contemporaries, Sinclair Lewis and Theodore Dreiser, the latter of whom suggested to his publisher that she be commissioned to write a biographical sketch about him.

The critic Paul A. Doyle has called *The Good Earth* a *roman-fleuve*, detailing as it does in slow and steady flow many years in the life of a peasant family whose strength comes from the soil, in Buck's view the source of the great strength of the Chinese people. The novel seeks to portray life as it is actually lived, not as symbol, dream or melodrama. Doyle places Buck among the Naturalists, that late 19th-century and early 20th-century movement whose origins are generally traced to Emile Zola in France.

Unlike other Naturalists, however, Buck was not pessimistic about the fate of humankind. She decried young writers who produced "books of futility and despair." She believed that, as one of her characters said, "With his stomach full any man preferred to be good." In her view, human society could be improved by the efforts of concerned individuals. She herself was concerned. Her professional success gave her political power, and she used that power freely to help both persons and institutions.

Richard Walsh, Buck's husband of 25 years, died in 1960 after a series of debilitating strokes. Buck herself died in 1973 at Danby, Vermont, and is buried at Green Hills Farm. The old Stulting farmhouse in Hillsboro, in whose preservation she was greatly interested, has been restored and opened to the public as an historical museum by the Pearl S. Buck Birthplace Foundation.

SOURCES:
Buck, Pearl S. *My Several Worlds*. NY: John Day, 1954.
Doyle, Paul A. *Pearl S. Buck*. NY: Twayne, 1965.
Harris, Theodore F. *Pearl S. Buck: A Biography*. Vols. I and II. NY: John Day, 1969.
Nash, Jay Robert, and Stanley Ralph Ross. *The Motion Picture Guide*. Cinebooks, 1986.
Walsh, Richard J. *A Biographical Sketch of Pearl S. Buck*. NY: John Day, 1936.
Zinn, Lucille S., comp. *A Biographical Sketch of Pearl S. Buck*. Buckhannon, WV: Ralston Press, 1980.

SUGGESTED READING:
Brenni, Vito. "Pearl Buck: A Selected Bibliography," in *Bulletin of Bibliography*. Vol. XXII. May–August 1957, pp. 65–69; September–December 1957, pp. 94–96.
Buck, Pearl S. *A Bridge for Passing*. NY: John Day, 1962.
Conn, Peter S. *Pearl S. Buck: A Cultural Biography*. NY: Cambridge University Press, 1998.
Spencer, Cornelia (Grace S. Yaukey). *The Exile's Daughter: A Biography of Pearl S. Buck*. NY: Coward-McCann, 1944.

Margery Evernden,
Professor Emerita, English Department,
University of Pittsburgh, and freelance writer

Buckingham, duchess of.

See Beaufort, Joan (1379–1440) for sidebar on Neville, Anne (d. 1480).

See Woodville, Katherine (c. 1442–1512).

Buckman, Rosina (1881–1948)

New Zealand soprano whose operatic career was mainly in Great Britain. Born on March 16, 1881, in Blenheim, New Zealand; died in London, England, on December 31, 1948.

Rosina Buckman studied at the Birmingham and Midland School of Music in England, debuting in 1905. She then returned to her part of the world, appearing in 1911 with the Melba Grand Opera Company in Australia. In 1914, she was a flower maiden in the first English stage performance of *Parsifal* at Covent Garden. During World War I, Buckman was a member of the Beecham Opera Company where she appeared as Isolde, Butterfly, Mimi, and Aïda. In 1923, she sang in the only performance of Dame *Ethyl Smyth*'s *The Boatswain's Mate.* Her last performance was in 1925. Buckman's recordings enjoyed considerable popularity during the period, and an English language *Madame Butterfly* was especially well received.

Buczynska, Nadezhda Alekseyevna (1872–1952).

See Teffi, N.A.

Budberg, Moura (1892–1974)

Russian-born translator, motion-picture consultant, literary personality, and lover of Maxim Gorky and H.G. Wells. Name variations: Moura von Benckendorff; Baroness Marie Budberg. Born Maria Ignatievna Zakrevsky or Zakrevskaya in Kharkov, Ukraine, in 1892; died in Tuscany, Italy, on October 31, 1974; daughter of Count Ignaty Platonovich Zakrevsky and Countess Maria Boreisha Zakrevsky; sister of Alla Zakrevskaya and Assia Zakrevskaya; married Ioann (Djohn) von Benckendorff, 1911 (died, 1919); married Baron Nicolai Budberg; children: Pavel (Paul); Tania Alexander.

Born Maria Ignatievna Zakrevsky in Kharkov, Ukraine, in 1892, the woman who would be known throughout the European literary and artistic world as Baroness Moura Budberg grew up in tsarist Russia's gilded and doomed world of aristocratic privilege. As the youngest of three daughters born to Count Ignaty Platonovich Zakrevsky, a wealthy landowner and liberal-minded aristocrat, Budberg enjoyed the customary privileges of the Russian elite, including foreign governesses and innumerable servants. From one of their governesses, Irish-born **Margaret Wilson** who was

known to them as "Micky," Budberg and her sisters learned to speak virtually flawless English as well as French, German and Italian.

Prior to the revolutionary maelstrom that would commence in 1917, the idyllic world of the Zakrevsky family included summers at their Ukrainian estate and winters in the magical world of St. Petersburg, full of glittering balls and nights at the ballet and theater. Budberg's father, a lawyer and high state official whose progressive views often led to conflicts with his fellow aristocrats, died in 1905. There is little doubt that the intellectually independent Count Zakrevsky provided his youngest daughter with a lasting example of personal integrity and moral steadfastness. He also left behind family traditions that in later decades would be recounted, sometimes with considerable embellishment; one was the story of the Zakrevsky family's direct descendance from a rumored-but-unfounded child of Russian Empress *Elizabeth Petrovna*, supposedly born in 1742 during Elizabeth's secret and morganatic marriage to Aleksei Razumovsky. Although there was no documentary proof of her link to royalty, in later years Moura Budberg would delight her friends by putting on a false moustache, thus achieving a striking resemblance to Tsar Peter the Great.

In 1911, after completing her conventional upper-class education, Budberg married a promising young diplomat of Baltic German aristocratic ancestry, Ioann von Benckendorff, whose family owned large estates in Estonia. They moved to Berlin, where he had been assigned as a second secretary to the Russian Embassy. In these final years of peace in traditional, aristocratic Russia, Moura was a striking young woman with high cheekbones and a wide face that in later years prompted comparisons with *Marlene Dietrich*. At one Hohenzollern court reception, Budberg appeared wearing a silver Russian headdress and a dress of plum velvet with a three-yard train embroidered in gold. On her entrance, Kaiser Wilhelm II commented for all to hear, "Who is that? The Queen of Sheba?"

The start of World War I meant that Moura, her husband, and their young son Pavel had to return to Russia. For two more years, life remained largely the same as before while the von Benckendorffs entertained aristocrats and artists in their large rococo house. They enjoyed their dinners and dances, skating on the frozen Neva river, as well as watching *Anna Pavlova* and *Tamara Karsavina* dance and Fedor Chaliapin sing. Moura Budberg's world collapsed in 1917, when two revolutions first swept aside the cor-

Moura Budberg, with Maxim Gorky and H.G. Wells, 1920.

rupt Romanov Dynasty and then placed the Bolsheviks under V.I. Lenin in power as head of a radical proletarian state dedicated to the ideal of world revolution. A new woman, no longer passive or pampered but fiercely determined to survive and prevail, emerged in 1918, as it became clear to Moura that only those individuals who were supremely adaptive and resourceful would be able to survive. Her language skills enabled her to get a job as a translator with Maxim Gorky's World Literature publishing house.

Of even greater consequence for her survival was the intimate relationship she established with Bruce Lockhart, a British diplomat and intelligence agent. After a failed assassination attempt on Lenin in August 1918, Lockhart and Moura were both arrested and imprisoned for complicity in a plot to topple the Bolshevik regime. In later years, after Moura had successfully created a romantic life story about herself, she claimed to have been incarcerated on this and other occasions for periods of weeks or even months. In reality, according to her daughter **Tania Alexander**'s 1988 memoirs, Moura spent only a few days in prison. What remains undisputed is the raw courage she displayed on several occasions. When Lockhart was being interrogated in his cell by the deputy head of the dreaded Cheka (Secret Police in charge of the Red Terror), Moura risked her life by passing a message to him in a book. She took many risks during this time, yet somehow survived.

On April 18, 1919, her husband was found shot on the edge of a lake near the family estate in Kallijärv, Estonia. The murderers were never discovered, but it is likely that they were local peasants determined to divide up the land of a family of "aristocratic exploiters." Concentrating on her own survival and that of her children, after her mother's death in 1919 Moura moved in with Maxim Gorky, whose large Moscow flat was shared by a motley group of writers, artists and actors determined to outlive the terrible hardships of life in revolutionary Soviet Russia. Often spending more time vociferously discussing politics and the arts than worrying about subsistence, they all pooled their meager food rations, and Moura's French chef, whom she had brought with her when she moved in with the Gorky circle, performed feats of culinary alchemy to not only keep them alive but generally please their palates.

By this time, Moura had married her second husband, another Baltic German aristocrat. Baron Nicolai Budberg was handsome, charming and, as became obvious in a short time, an utterly irresponsible mate due to his compulsive gambling. Quickly recognizing that he would be unable to keep wolves from the door, Moura became increasingly intimate with Maxim Gorky, while at the same time cultivating what was to be a lifelong friendship with Gorky's wife **Ekaterina Peshkov**. (In 1903, Gorky had left Peshkov to be with *****Maria Andreeva**, a relationship that would terminate in 1920.) A crucial event in Moura's later life was her 1920 encounter with the British writer H.G. Wells, who came to Soviet Russia to see the new society being created there as well as to personally interview Lenin. During the brief time they were together (because of her excellent knowledge of English, she had been assigned to him as an interpreter), Wells and Moura were strongly attracted to one another both intellectually and physically, setting the stage for their intense and complex relationship of later years.

When Maxim Gorky and his entourage left Soviet Russia in 1921— partly for reasons of his poor health but also because of the great writer's growing ideological differences with the Leninist dictatorship—Moura Budberg accompanied him. By this time, rumors began to circulate that Moura had acted as a Soviet agent starting with her involvement with Lockhart. Largely because it added to her aura of glamour and mystery, she never disavowed these stories. In her memoirs, Moura's daughter made a strong case against the accusations of spying hurled against her mother, noting that her letters to Lockhart and other documentation completely refute these charges. While Moura Budberg did in fact engage in concealment (or gross exaggeration) of the facts of her life, the motives were much less ominous. Raised on great literature, she was determined to not only survive but to turn her life into a creation of her own making, part real and part self-created myth. In a 1970 interview, she acknowledged that with the revolution of 1917 her life had entered into a radical new phase, one that she decided to live "as though there had been no past, and life had begun on that very day." From the early 1920s to the end of her life, she was a superb manipulator, of friends, of lovers, and of images and myths about herself that with each passing day became larger than life. As the facts of her life became ever more elusive, she became ever more fascinating to her contemporaries.

After leaving Russia with the Gorky entourage, Moura lived with this creative but often unstable group of artists for almost the next decade, settling first in Germany and then moving to Czechoslovakia. While in Berlin, she quickly established contacts with major publishing firms, and her knowledge of both German and English played a significant role in the introduction of the works of several noted German writers of the day, including Thomas Mann, to audiences in the English-speaking world. By the mid-1920s, Moura and her children had moved with the Gorky group to Italy. They settled in Sorrento, where the climate proved beneficial to the tubercular Gorky. When Fascist police began harassing them, Moura went to Rome for a spirited encounter with Benito Mussolini. The Fascist dictator was evidently impressed by the complaints of the fearless Russian baroness, for he ordered his police to let the emigré intellectuals live in peace for the duration of their stay in Italy.

Moura Budberg moved to London in 1928, finding work as a literary agent and living at the heart of the city's intellectual life in an apartment near the British Museum. Over the next few years, she rekindled her relationship with the aging H.G. Wells, whose wife ❧➤ **Catherine Wells** had recently died. Growing tired of his current mistress, **Odette Keun**, he felt ready for one final passionate love affair in his life. As Wells described their 1920 encounter in his memoirs, "No other woman has ever had that much effectiveness for me." Although smitten with her, Wells was also distressed by the fact that she had lied to him about her continuing intimate relationship with Maxim Gorky. And he was quite clearly amazed by her seemingly indestructible capacity to enjoy herself: "She can drink quite enormous quantities of vodka, brandy or champagne without any apparent disorganization." In addition to remaining attractive, Budberg also

had a tendency to corpulence. Wells adored her and very much wanted to marry her, telling his friends, "You see that I have a wife but she won't marry me." Fiercely independent, Budberg refused to marry Wells though their relationship remained passionate. They were close until his death in 1946. She told friends that after Wells died no man mattered in her life.

By the 1940s, Moura Budberg had become one of the institutions of London's artistic and intellectual life. She greeted her many friends with a powerful bear hug, and they entered her "large Victorian apartment, its drawing room rather dim, a crowded reliquary of the past" with a tapestry of Tsar Nicholas II and his family—a gift from Wells—on one wall, and a small painting of Maxim Gorky on the mantelpiece. She had kept busy during the 1930s not only doing translations (in all she would translate over two dozen books) but also by serving as a consultant on films for Sir Alexander Korda. During World War II, her linguistic skills and extensive network of personal contacts served her well when she took a job as jack-of-all-trades for the monthly magazine published by French emigrés, *La France Libre*. Budberg raised substantial funding for the exile journal and persuaded a large number of distinguished writers, including Wells, George Bernard Shaw, and J.B. Priestly, to write articles for it. Within a short time, *La France Libre* had achieved a sterling reputation in both French exile and British intellectual circles as a major voice of French literary culture. The adversities of aging did not stop Moura Budberg, and she survived two painful hip surgeries ready to resume translation work and party-giving. Her London apartment had by now become a literary salon of some importance, and her place in the literary history of the city was assured.

In the early 1970s, a physically aging but intellectually strong Budberg presented a lecture in New York on the challenges of translating from Russian, and worked with, among others, **Vanessa Redgrave** on the film *The Sea Gull*. As she grew older, thoughts of Russia were never far from her mind and soul. A letter in 1958 from Gorky's widow, generous in spirit as always, invited Moura to stay with her in Moscow. Overcoming her initial misgivings, she flew to Moscow. The visit, immensely successful, would be followed by many more short visits to the Soviet Union. Moura Budberg remained an emigré, but reconciled at least part of herself with the sufferings that began for her in 1917. Still adventurous, less than two months before her death, Budberg moved to Tuscany to live

Catherine Wells. See Richardson, Dorothy for sidebar.

close to her son. It was here, still in exile from Russia, that she died on October 31, 1974.

Despite her fascinating life, Moura Budberg remains an elusive personality who has yet to find a biographer. Among those who have attempted to present the story of her life but given up in the attempt is **Rachel Lovat Dickson** who noted that Budberg was "a survivor of a revolution who used her brains, her looks and the vitality of her nature, not only to survive but to enjoy the risky process." Her ability to create deep and lasting friendships was legendary. The renowned actor Peter Ustinov, himself of Russian ancestry, noted that Bumberg "represented for me an indomitable side to the Russian character . . . [W]hen I was in Moura's company, I felt deeply and serenely Russian." She had refused to let the innumerable brutalities of the 20th century destroy her or her children. In the words of her daughter Tania Alexander, she was a woman "determined to be a survivor, and . . . she would never let anything get in the way of that; above all, she made it clear that she would have to be taken on her own terms, and that she could never be dictated to."

SOURCES:

Alexander, Tania. *Tania: Memories of a Lost World.* Bethesda, MD: Adler & Adler, 1988.

Andrew, Christopher. *Her Majesty's Secret Service: The Making of the British Intelligence Community.* NY: Penguin Books, 1987.

"Baroness Marie Budberg," in *The Times* [London]. November 2, 1974, p. 14.

"Baroness Moura Budberg Dies; Long a London Literary Figure," in *The New York Times Biographical Edition.* November 1974, p. 1542.

Budberg, Moura. "On Translating from Russian," in Gregory Rabassa, ed., *The World of Translation.* NY: PEN American Center, 1987, pp. 145–151.

Coren, Michael. *The Invisible Man: The Life and Liberties of H.G. Wells.* NY: Atheneum, 1993.

Knightley, Phillip. *The Second Oldest Profession: Spies and Spying in the Twentieth Century.* NY: Penguin Books, 1988.

Lockhart, R.H. Bruce. *Memoirs of a British Agent.* NY: Putnam, 1932.

Mackenzie, Norman, and Jeanne Mackenzie. *The Time Traveller: The Life of H.G. Wells.* London: Weidenfeld and Nicolson, 1973.

Smith, David C. *H.G. Wells: Desperately Mortal: A Biography.* New Haven, CT: Yale University Press, 1986.

Tynan, Kathleen. "The Astonishing History of Moura Budberg," in *Vogue.* Vol. 156, no. 6. October 1, 1970, pp. 162–163, 208–211.

Wells, H.G. *H.G. Wells in Love: Postscript to an Experiment in Autobiography.* Edited by G.P. Wells. London: Faber and Faber, 1984.

West, Anthony. *H.G. Wells: Aspects of a Life.* NY: New American Library, 1985.

John Haag, Associate Professor, University of Georgia, Athens, Georgia

Budd, Zola (b. 1966).

See Slaney, Mary Decker for sidebar.

Budzynska-Tylicka, Justyna

(1876–1936)

Polish physician, Socialist activist and birth-control pioneer. Born in 1876 in Lomza; died in Warsaw on June 8, 1936.

Born in the town of Lomza, Justyna Budzynska-Tylicka grew up in an area of Poland under Russian occupation. Repression of Polish national aspirations and culture by the Russian authorities only strengthened the determination of the Polish intellectuals to restore Poland as a free and sovereign state. Exposed to both nationalist and Marxist ideals in her youth, Justyna studied medicine in order to serve the poor peasantry of her district. The emergence of an industrial working class also dramatized the need for radical social reforms. Convinced that the achievement of national freedom alone would not be sufficient to raise the living standards of the masses, Budzynska-Tylicka became a militant Marxist, joining the Polish Socialist Party.

A feminist as well as a Socialist, she believed that women had to have full control over their reproductive destinies in order to be genuinely free. Accordingly, she advocated birth control, a position that placed her in conflict with both the Roman Catholic Church and a government that did not permit distribution of contraceptive information. Despite this formidable opposition, Budzynska-Tylicka refused to bow to religious or secular pressures, engaging in spirited debates with those who disagreed with her. A physician to the poor, she believed that only education would change the attitudes of women still strongly influenced by old traditions and the teachings of a patriarchal and ultra-conservative clergy. Her tireless work on behalf of the poor brought her to the attention of the leadership of the Socialist Party, and from 1931 through 1934 she served on the party's national council. An internationalist who was convinced that the aspirations of women throughout the world were morally and ideologically linked, she was for many years an active member of the Socialist Women's International. Justyna Budzynska-Tylicka died in Warsaw on June 8, 1936.

SOURCES:

"Budzynska-Tylicka, Justyna," *Wielka Encyklopedia Powszechna.* Warsaw: Panstwowe Wydawnictwo Naukowe, 1963, vol. 2, p. 201.

John Haag, Associate Professor, University of Georgia, Athens, Georgia

Buehrmann, Elizabeth (1886–1954)

American photographer. Born in 1886; died in 1954.

Elizabeth Buehrmann's career spanned the first half of the 19th century. In 1904, when she was elected an associate of Photo-Secession, a group intent on transforming photography into fine art, her business card noted her specialty was home portraiture. In 1908, her work was shown in the Art Crafts Exhibition at the Art Institute of Chicago; of her 61 photographs all but 15 were portraits. In 1910 and 1911, her work appeared at annual exhibitions of the works of the Art Students' League of Chicago at the Art Institute of Chicago. Buehrmann was also a member of the Photo-Club of Paris, through which she exhibited at each of the International Salons of Photography in 1910, 1912, and 1913. Her photographs appeared in *Vogue* and *Vanity Fair,* and her later career included advertising copy for some well-known products, including Corona typewriters, Packard automobiles, and Yuban coffee. Buehrmann retired to Miami, Florida, in the 1950s. Before her death in 1954, she contributed to an exhibition of ceramics at the Lowe Gallery, University of Miami.

Buell, Marjorie Henderson (1905–1993)

American cartoonist who created "Little Lulu." Name variations: Marge Henderson Buell; (pen name) Marge. Born in 1905; died in Elyria, Ohio, on May 30, 1993.

Using the pen name "Marge," Marjorie Henderson Buell was the original creator of "Little Lulu," which first appeared in June 1935 as a single-panel cartoon in the *Saturday Evening Post.* "Lulu" later became a comic-book series and a long-running newspaper strip produced by Western Publishing for the Chicago Tribune-New York News syndicate. Buell's character, the feisty little girl who could outwit any kid on the block, left Buell's hands in 1945 when Eastern Publishing Company obtained the rights to the feature for a series of special publications, followed by a long and successful series of comic books, written by John Stanley, whose storyboards were adapted into the artwork. The newspaper strip, which ran from 1955 to 1967, was first done by Woody Kimbrell and, for its last six years, by writer Del Connell and a stable of artists. The popularity of the comic books led to the merchandising of story and activity books, as well as a series of animated cartoons produced by Famous Studios. In 1972, Western Publishing assumed full ownership of *Little Lulu,* and the Marge byline was dropped.

Bueno, Maria (1939—)

Brazilian tennis superstar who, in her day, was one of the world's most graceful and proficient athletes, winning 62 titles in her career as an amateur. Name variations: (nicknames) Little Saber and Sao Paulo Swallow. Born Maria Esther Andion Bueno in Sao Paulo, Brazil, on October 11, 1939; daughter of a veterinarian who was also an amateur tennis player.

Ranked the world's best woman tennis player (1964); rated No. 1 in the world (1959, 1960, 1964 and 1966); won eight Wimbledon titles, three in singles (1959, 1960, 1964) and five in doubles (1958, 1960, 1963, 1965, 1966).

Born on October 11, 1939, in Sao Paulo, Brazil, Maria Bueno grew up in pleasant upper-middle-class surroundings. Her father was a veterinarian and amateur tennis player. When she was about five, Maria was given a junior-sized tennis racquet; from that time on, when not at school or at home, she could be found at the Clube de Regatas Tiete, a large sports club directly across the street from her family's white stucco house in downtown Sao Paulo. Entirely self-taught, by age 11 she was using Bill Tilden as one of her models. She attempted to duplicate his powerful service by studying his photographs, then imitating the same strokes on the court of the Clube. By 12, Maria Bueno had won a girls' tennis tournament in Sao Paulo. A superb all-around athlete, the same year she also won the city's 50-meter women's swimming championship. In 1954, at age 14, she became the women's tennis champion of Brazil. In 1955, Bueno represented her country at the Pan-American Games held that year in Mexico City, where she defeated **Maria Weiss**, the South American champion, in straight sets. After this victory, she went on to win several more international tournaments in Argentina and Venezuela.

By 1957, Maria Bueno was playing in the "sunshine circuit" in Florida and the Caribbean. Bowing to family wishes, she also completed work for a teacher's certificate during this period and briefly taught in an elementary school. Bueno's heart, however, was in tennis, not teaching. By December 1957, she was again competing, winning Florida's Orange Bowl junior championship. The next year, 1958, saw a whirlwind of activity, with Bueno winning 18 of the 32 tournaments in which she played.

Despite her formidable talent, Maria occasionally met a champion who was at least her equal and sometimes better. One such player was *Althea Gibson, who defeated Bueno in several tournaments, including the Caracas Invitational in March 1958. In April of that year, Bueno and Gibson teamed to win the women's doubles of the Good Neighbor Tournament, held in Miami Beach. In the summer of 1958, Bueno-Gibson won the women's doubles championship at Wimbledon. To top off a remarkable year, in September 1958, Maria Bueno was seeded fourth for the national singles championship. Althea Gibson won the crown.

By the time Maria Bueno appeared at Wimbledon in July 1959, many writers were predicting that she would be the next great star of tennis. She fulfilled those expectations with "a fluent and almost flawless performance," noted *The New York Times,* beating *Darlene Hard, who had defeated her in six earlier matches, by the score of 6–4, 6–3 in the finals. Bueno's triumph ended an unbroken string of U.S. victories for women tennis players that dated back to 1938. The year 1959 proved an excellent one for Bueno, as she won 19 of the 35 tournaments she entered. In January 1960, the Associated Press Annual Poll named her the leading female athlete of 1959.

At Wimbledon in July 1960, Bueno retained the singles title for the second consecutive year, scoring an 8–6, 6–0 victory over South Africa's **Sandra Reynolds**. A few days later, Bueno defeated Reynolds in Switzerland. As the top-seeded star and the Forest Hills defending champion, Bueno was expected to make a two-year sweep of both American and British titles. But the strain of playing was beginning to tell, for in September 1960, she lost the United States singles title to Darlene Hard. In her home country of Brazil, she had become an unchallenged national hero. In December 1960, the Brazilian post office issued a six-Cruzeiro air-mail stamp to honor Bueno for her second Wimbledon victory.

Shortly after winning the Italian championship in May 1961, Bueno came down with hepatitis and had to cancel all performances, missing both Wimbledon and Forest Hills that year. Thought to be fully recovered, she appeared in April 1962 at the Masters Invitational tournament in Florida, defeating her longtime rival Darlene Hard. But Bueno was still not fully recovered from her illness and lost a few weeks later in Italy to *Margaret Smith (Court). Summoning her last reserves of strength, the next day she teamed up with Hard to win the

doubles title against the Italian team of **Lea Pericoli** and **Silvana Lazzarino**. Although the aftermath of her illness made the quality of Bueno's playing in 1962 somewhat inconsistent, it was not her playing but her style of dress at Wimbledon in the summer of that year that brought her international publicity. Maria Bueno wore shocking pink panties under a "twist" tennis dress, a costume that the spectators reacted to with a mixture of cheers, gasps and boos. Some sportswriters suggested that the costume had interfered with her powers of concentration. In any event, in October 1962 Wimbledon officials ruled that henceforth only "all white" would be permissible dress.

Despite continuing victories and another singles triumph at Wimbledon in 1964, by the late 1960s Maria Bueno was coming to the end of her career due to a variety of arm and leg injuries. The dawn of a new era in tennis with the appearance of open tennis and prize money came too late for her. In 1974, she won the Japan Open, her lone pro title in singles. After a long period of virtual retirement, she felt sufficiently recovered in 1975 to undertake a pro tour. Bueno returned to Wimbledon for a personal triumph in the summer of 1976. Long past her prime, she won the respect of fans who remembered her from her glory days as well as those who now saw her for the first time. Traces of her old style remained, and she won three rounds. *Billie Jean King, who defeated Bueno at Wimbledon the following year, spoke for countless fans when she noted, "In her day she was so marvelous to watch. But it was painful to watch her today. I wanted to remember her as she was." Maria Bueno was philosophical and serene about the coming of the end of her career, "I have always loved tennis, and still enjoy playing. I've had my glory." Nicknamed the Little Saber and the Sao Paulo Swallow, she would continue to be regarded by admirers throughout the world as one of the great women tennis stars of all time, comparable to *Suzanne Lenglen, *Evonne Goolagong, *Alice Marble and *Helen Wills.

SOURCES:

"Bueno, Maria," *Current Biography 1965.* NY: H.W. Wilson, pp. 59–62.

Collins, Bud, and Zander Hollander, eds. *Bud Collins' Modern Encyclopedia of Tennis.* Detroit, MI: Gale Research, 1994.

Moran, Sheila. "The Swan Song of the 'Sao Paulo Swallow,'" in *Women Sports.* Vol. 4, no. 2. February 1977, pp. 35–36.

Robertson, Max, ed. *The Encyclopedia of Tennis.* London: George Allen & Unwin, 1974.

John Haag, Associate Professor, University of Georgia, Athens, Georgia

Buff, Charlotte (1753–1828)

Friend and companion of the German author Johann Wolfgang von Goethe. Name variations: Lotte Buff, Charlotte Kestner. Born in 1753; died in 1828; married Georg Christian Kestner (a court councilor), 1773.

Little is known of the enigmatic Charlotte Buff, companion of Goethe and the inspiration for Lotte in his first novel *Die Leiden des Jungen Werthers* (*The Sorrows of Young Werther*). At a party in Wetzlar in 1772, Goethe had met and fallen in love with Buff, the fiancée of Georg Kestner, whom she later married. The intensity of Goethe's affection for her remains unknown, although it is believed that he reveled in his status as the unhappy lover because it assured him his freedom; it is said that at one point, when Buff's marriage to Kestner appeared to be in doubt, Goethe fled. In *The Sorrows of Young Werther,* however, Werther is so overcome with his unhappy affair with Lotte that he commits suicide. The novel, published anonymously in 1774, was overwhelmingly received. Following the character's example, young men dressed as Werther and some even committed suicide with copies of the book in their pockets. Reportedly, Charlotte visited Goethe when he was an old man, appearing dressed in the clothing she had worn when they first met. This incident inspired Thomas Mann's novel *Lotte in Weimar.*

Buff, Lotte (1753–1828).

See Buff, Charlotte.

Buffalo-Calf-Road-Woman

(fl. 1876)

Native American.

On June 17, 1876, Buffalo-Calf-Road-Woman rescued her brother Chief Comes-in-Sight from George Crook's U.S. Cavalry by swooping him onto her horse in the battle of Rosebud Creek, in southern Montana; the event is known to Cheyennes as the Battle Where the Girl Saved Her Brother. The Indian charge, led by Crazy Horse, sent Crook and his men into hasty retreat, back across the Wyoming border.

Buffet, Marguerite (d. 1680)

French grammarian. Born in France; died in France in 1680; never married; no children.

Little is known about Marguerite Buffet's family background and childhood. She was an

Charlotte Buff

exceptionally well-educated woman of the French aristocracy, who produced written works outlining French grammar and other aspects of the language. Her only surviving work is *New Observations on the French Language* (published 1668), a work specifically designed by the author to instruct women in the skills of rhetoric and writing. Buffet believed that it was important for women to understand the structure of language and be able to use language effectively. She also advocated scholarship by women on other topics, and wrote that she hoped her own writings would inspire women to study.

SOURCES:

Buck, Claire, ed. *The Bloomsbury Guide to Women's Literature.* NY: Prentice Hall, 1992.

Laura York,
Riverside, California

Buffington, Adele (1900–1973)

American screenwriter who wrote scenarios for many of the silent screen's cowboy matinee idols, including Tom Mix, Tim McCoy, and Buck Jones. Name varia-

tions: (pseudonym) Jess Bowers. Born Adele Burgdorfer on February 12, 1900, in St. Louis, Missouri; died on November 23, 1973, in Woodland Hills, California; daughter of Adolph and Elizabeth (Friedrich) Burgdorfer; educated in public schools.

Filmography: River Woman *(1928);* Times Square *(1928);* Phantom Justice *(1929);* Swellhead City *(1930);* Just Like Heaven *(1930);* Extravagance *(1930);* Freighters of Destiny *(1930);* Aloha *(1931);* A Man's Land *(1932);* Ghost Valley *(1932);* Haunted Gold *(1932);* Forgotten Women *(1932);* High Speed *(1932);* The Eleventh Commandment *(1933);* The Iron Master *(1933);* West of Singapore *(1933);* Beggar's Holiday *(1934);* The Moonstone *(1934);* Picture Brides *(1934);* When Strangers Meet *(1934);* Cheaters *(1934);* Powdersmoke Range *(1935);* Keeper of the Bees *(1935);* Hi, Gaucho *(1936);* Circus Girl *(1937);* The Duke Comes Back *(1937);* Michael O'Halloran *(1937);* The Sheik Steps Out *(1937);* Any Man's Wife *(1937);* The Gunman from Bodie *(1941);* Forbidden Trails *(1941);* Arizona Bound *(1941);* Ghost Town Law *(1942);* Riders of the West *(1942);* West of the Law *(1942);* Dawn on the Great Divide *(1942);* Below the Border *(1942);* Down Texas Way *(1942);* Ghost Rider *(1943);* The Stranger from Pecos *(1943);* Six Gun Gospel *(1943);* Outlaws of Stampede Pass *(1943);* The Texas Kid *(1943);* Raiders of the Border *(1944);* Flame of the West *(1945);* Bad Men of the Border *(1945);* The Navajo Trail *(1945);* The Lost Trail *(1945);* Frontier Feud *(1945);* Wild Beauty *(1946);* Shadows on the Range *(1946);* Drifting Along *(1946);* Shadows of the West *(1949);* West of Eldorado *(1949);* Haunted Trails *(1949);* Western Renegade *(1949);* Raiders of the Dusk *(1949);* Range Land *(1949);* Crashing Thru *(1949);* West of Wyoming *(1950);* Gunslingers *(1950);* Jiggs and Maggie Out West *(1950);* Six Gun Mesa *(1950);* Arizona Territory *(1950);* Overland Telegraph *(1951);* Cow Country *(1953);* Born to the Saddle *(1953);* Bullwhip *(1956).*

At 16, Adele Buffington went to work as a cashier for a movie theater and apparently fell in love with the silents that flickered across the screen, telling the *Fort Wayne Journal Gazette* in 1919, "there came an hour when I simply had to do it—and I did . . . . When everyone else was asleep, I would write and write and write." Buffington sold her first script, *La Petite,* to a film company for $300. She was 19 years old.

Buffington went to work for Thomas Ince, the pioneering motion-picture director known for his realistic westerns, who was the first to employ Native American extras for Native American roles. She wrote scenarios for many of

the silent screen's cowboy matinee idols, such as Tom Mix, Colonel Tim McCoy, and Buck Jones. In the 1930s and '40s, Buffington worked with colleagues **Betty Burbridge** and **Olive Cooper** for Republic Pictures, a studio known for making hundreds of "B" westerns, nicknamed "horse operas" or "cow epics." Though the genre produced few memorable motion pictures, the fact that such films were authored by women like Buffington dispels any archaic notions that women "couldn't write action." By the time she retired, Buffington had more than 150 screen credits either under her own name or the pseudonym Jess Bowers. "It was a darn lot of 'horse operas,'" she told a reporter for the Los Angeles *Herald Examiner.* Buffington died of arterial sclerosis at the Motion Picture Country Hospital in Woodland Hills, California.

SOURCES:

Francke, Lizzie. *Script Girls: Women Screenwriters in Hollywood.* London: BFI Publishers, 1994.

McCreadie, Marsha. *The Women Who Write The Movies: From Frances Marion to Nora Ephron.* NY: Birchlane Press, 1994.

Obituary. *Variety.* December 5, 1973.

Vazzana, Eugene Michael. *Silent Film Necrology: Births and Deaths of over 9,000 Performers, Directors, Producers and Other Filmmakers of the Silent Era Through 1993.* Jefferson, NC: McFarland, 1995.

Deborah Jones,
Studio City, California

Bugarinovic, Melanija (1905–1986)

Serbian mezzo-soprano who sang with the Belgrade and Vienna operas. Name variations: Melanie, Melka, Milada. Born in Bela Crkva on June 29, 1905; died in Belgrade, Yugoslavia, on May 8, 1986.

Educated in Timisoara and at the Belgrade Conservatory, Melanija Bugarinovic performed regularly with the Belgrade Opera from 1930 to 1937. From 1938 to 1944, she sang with the Vienna Staatsoper and appeared in the role of *Herodias in the production of *Salome* conducted by Richard Strauss in 1942. Bugarinovic returned to Belgrade in 1946, singing there until 1961. She also appeared at Bayreuth in 1952–53. Bugarinovic's voice was dark in timbre and quite unusual, and she was well-known for her Wagnerian roles as Fricka, Erda, Brangäne, and Ortrud. Her recordings of Russian works with the Belgrade Opera are well known.

Bugbee, Emma (1888–1981)

American reporter who wrote for the New York Herald Tribune *for over half a century. Born on May 18, 1888, in Shippensburg, Pennsylvania; died on Octo-*

ber 6, 1981, in Warwick, Rhode Island; first of three children of Edwin Howard (a language teacher) and Emma Bugbee; graduated from Barnard College, New York; never married; no children.

At her retirement in 1966, Emma Bugbee, the grand dame of the *New York Herald Tribune*, estimated that she had spent 18,911 days as a newspaper reporter. In 56 years on the job—reporting mostly on women—she gained her greatest prominence as one of *Eleanor Roosevelt's "girls," a group of women reporters who traveled with the first lady. In 1962, when Eleanor Roosevelt died, Bugbee wrote an award-winning tribute about the woman she, and the country, had come to know and admire. Bugbee's retirement coincided with the announcement that the *Tribune* would merge with the *World Telegram and Sun* and the *Journal-American* to become the *World Journal Tribune*. Feeling that the best of New York journalism was behind her, she took her leave after filing her last assignment, the dedication of a United Nations' memorial to her friend Eleanor Roosevelt.

Emma Bugbee was born on May 18, 1888, in Shippensburg, Pennsylvania; she graduated from Barnard College and was on her way to a teaching career when a college classmate, a reporter at the *Tribune*, asked Bugbee to fill in for her while she was vacationing in Germany. When her friend decided to remain abroad, Bugbee was asked to stay. Although assigned to the city desk, the 22-year-old rookie wrote from a perch outside the all-male newsroom, from which, as a woman, she was barred. For four years, she worked without a byline, covering even major stories without credit. Her first byline came with an undercover story in the style of Nellie Bly (*Elizabeth Seaman) or Annie Laurie (*Winifred Sweet Black). Posing as a blue-bonneted Salvation Army collector, she rang a bell on the corner of Fifth Avenue and 42nd Street. Discouraged by the apathy of shoppers who rushed past her with their hands in their pockets, she led off her piece with, "Is it the hearts or the hands of New Yorkers that are so cold?"

Bugbee was a generalist, covering everything from the annual flower show and circus, to murders and local politics. She noted scores of women's "firsts" and was on hand for over half a century of women's events. In her book *Brilliant Bylines*, **Barbara Belford** notes that Bugbee's articles comprise a history of the women's movement: "She was there for the suffrage marches and rallies; for the 1924 convention, the first where women were voting delegates;

and for the introduction of the Equal Rights Amendment by the Women's Party in Washington in 1923. When she died at ninety-three, she was still optimistic about its passage."

In 1922, Bugbee was one of the founders of the Newspaper Women's Club of New York and served as its president for three terms. In 1936, she published the first in a series of five "Peggy" books, based on her experience as a reporter; these books inspired many young women to careers in journalism.

Bugbee's colleagues were possibly her biggest fans, and she was known as shrewd, warm, generous, and supportive, especially to her women associates. She was also unflappable, even under deadline pressure. Dick West, her copy editor for over 30 years, recalled her as "a lady who in a tumultuous, sophisticated world learned to adjust, but still preserved the virtues and manner of a simpler, homier time." When she retired, *Trib* columnist Jimmy Breslin wrote, "She left and took part of the business with her."

Emma Bugbee never married and spent several years of her retirement traveling and painting landscapes at her summer home in Connecticut. Her last 11 years were spent at a nursing home in Rhode Island, where she died on October 6, 1981.

SOURCES:
Belford, Barbara. *Brilliant Bylines*. NY: Columbia University Press, 1986.

Barbara Morgan,
Melrose, Massachusetts

Bühler, Charlotte (1893–1974)

German-born Austrian and American developmental psychologist often regarded as the "discoverer of the child." Name variations: Buhler or Buehler. Born in Berlin as Charlotte Malachowski on December 20, 1893; died in Stuttgart, Federal Republic of Germany, on February 3, 1974; daughter of Hermann Malachowski and Rose (Kristeller) Malachowski; attended Freiburg im Breisgau in 1913, the University of Kiel, 1914, the University of Berlin; granted Ph.D., University of Munich, 1918; married Karl Bühler, 1916; children: Ingeborg (b. 1917), Rolf (b. 1919).

One of the leading figures of child psychology in the first half of the 20th century, Charlotte Bühler was born Charlotte Bertha Malachowski in Berlin on December 20, 1893. Her parents, Hermann and **Rose Malachowski**, were members of the affluent and assimilated Berlin Jewish community, a group that proudly regarded themselves as "German citizens of the Jewish faith." Insulated from the cares of the less privileged and unaware of anti-Semitism, Charlotte grew up in an environment of physical luxury and emotional tension. A brilliant child, she quickly became aware of the stresses of her parents, particularly those of her bored and frustrated mother. Whereas Hermann Malachowski, a highly successful architect who helped to design and create the first department store in Germany, found an outlet for his energies, Rose Malachowski was a frustrated individual who believed that her plans for a singing career had been thwarted by marriage and motherhood. The emotional distance displayed by both parents, and the unhappiness of her mother, deeply affected the intellectually gifted Charlotte, who began to search for meaning in her life.

Although Charlotte and her family had adopted the Lutheran faith, like most bourgeois Jews this had been done largely for reasons of social and cultural assimilation. Rejecting her pastor's advice that Christianity ultimately had to be accepted on faith, Charlotte began to read extensively not in theology and metaphysics but in the field of psychology. While still in her teens, she had mastered much of the psychological literature; she had also begun to conduct her own experiments because she disagreed with such eminent scholars as Hermann Ebbinghaus, for whom thought could be explained exclusively in terms of associations. She began her university studies at Freiburg im Breisgau in 1913, moving to the University of Kiel the following year.

During this period, a geographer whom Charlotte had fallen in love with in Kiel became a shell-shock casualty in the early weeks of World War I. In later years, she would refer to her loss by describing herself as "a war victim by proxy." She continued her education at the University of Berlin, where she studied under the pioneer experimental psychologist Carl Stumpf. Showing her characteristic independence, she turned down Stumpf's offer of a graduate assistantship, rejecting what was an unprecedented honor for a woman for the simple reason that she wanted to study thought processes rather than the area of Stumpf's concentration, which was human feelings.

Continuing her studies at the University of Munich, Charlotte worked at first with Oswald Külpe, whose psychological laboratory was renowned throughout Europe for its innovative investigations of the human thought process. After Külpe's death in late 1915, she continued her research work with his chief assistant, Karl Bühler (1879–1963), a brilliant investigator with a strong background in both medicine and psychology. Charlotte was impressed by the fact that his experiments on thought processes were in essence more sophisticated versions of her own improvised probes of several years earlier. Charlotte and Karl Bühler were married on April 4, 1916. The births of two children, Ingeborg and Rolf, quickly followed in 1917 and 1919. Entrusting the care of her infants to a governess, Charlotte Bühler forged ahead with her academic career, earning her Ph.D. at the University of Munich in 1918 and publishing her first book, a probing study of children's fantasies and fairy tales, in the same year.

Despite the chaos and inflation that plagued Germany in the years after 1918, Charlotte and Karl Bühler combined their research efforts and made great progress in their various projects. In recognition of her work, in 1920 she received an appointment as the first female *privatdozent* at the Dresden Institute of Technology, where both she and her husband would teach until they accepted positions at the University of Vienna in 1922. Charlotte Bühler's incisive, and often controversial publications, brought her to the attention of leading personalities in her field; as a result of her new fame, she was the recipient in 1923 of one of the first Rockefeller exchange fellowships. Bühler went to the United States, working with Edward Thorndike at Columbia University. The behaviorist methods she encountered in the American psychological community reinforced her own commitment to a methodology of direct observation.

After returning to Vienna, Bühler continued to collaborate with her husband, now head of the university's psychological institute. She also founded her own institute dedicated to innovative investigations of the psychological development of children. From the beginning of her institute, Bühler spent significant time editing a series of research monographs in order to publicize the rapidly accumulating new insights into child psychology. By the late 1920s, she was in favor of a holistic view of human life and development, an ambitious and at the time highly innovative viewpoint. In a letter of July 1932 to Robert Havighurst, she explained the rationale for her decision: "My interest was in the whole of human life, which accompanied me from adolescence on. I then studied infancy to get an idea of life's earliest trends. But after some years, I decided that life as a whole could be better understood from its end than from its beginning. Thus my students and I studied *biographies,* which were well-enough documented to know them in great detail. We chose biographies, because these lives were closed and we could study their actual end, not only late periods."

For more than a decade, Charlotte and Karl Bühler lived the lives of busy, dedicated and highly respected Central European academics. When not delivering a lecture, she spent mornings writing at her desk before meeting with students and colleagues the remainder of the day. Her books became world-famous both in their original German-language editions as well as in translations into a number of languages including English. Both Charlotte and Karl Bühler admired and supported the social and educational agenda of Vienna's Social Democratic administration, which carried out far-reaching social reforms, turning an impoverished former capital of a defunct empire into a social laboratory known throughout the world as "Red Vienna." The Bühlers not only taught at the University of Vienna—which was often the scene of riots staged by anti-Semitic, pro-Nazi students—but also gave significant amounts of time and energy to the teacher-training work of the Vienna Municipal Pedagogical Institute, which was generously funded by the city administration in the hopes of democratizing the educational process in its very foundations. Although signs of political and social collapse became increasingly apparent with the onset of the world economic depression in 1929–1930, the Bühlers decided to remain at their posts, working to defend democratic ideals with the support of a group of creative and energetic graduate students including *Else Frenkel-Brunswik and Paul Lazarsfeld.

The appearance of the Nazi regime in Germany in 1933 only strengthened the Bühlers' resolve to remain in Vienna; both scholars were too deeply attached to European, and particularly Austrian, cultural ideals to abandon ship. Even the crushing of Red Vienna in February 1934 by a semi-Fascist Austrian government did not bring about their emigration, and offers from abroad brought polite refusals. Only the Nazi annexation of Austria in March 1938 brought them to the realization that in addition to their academic careers their very lives were now at risk. As a "full-blooded Jewess" who had achieved world fame as an educational reformer, Charlotte Bühler was a particular threat to the Nazi occupiers of Vienna: a despised personification of an alien intellectual presence. Although Karl Bühler qualified as a "pure Aryan," both his work and his choice of marriage partner made it clear that he too was an enemy of the new, intellectually and racially purified Third Reich.

Their world-class reputations enabled the Bühlers to find a place of refuge and an opportunity to continue their academic careers. The country that offered them sanctuary was Norway, and soon Charlotte, Karl, and their children were settled in one of the dwindling number of European countries that respected both intellectual freedom and basic human rights. Their time in Norway ended abruptly in 1940, when the entire Bühler family fled the invading forces of Nazi Germany. Arriving in the United States with little more than their lives, Charlotte and Karl struggled to reestablish themselves. Though Karl's work was respected in America, it was not as well known as Charlotte's due to his fewer publications in English-language translations, and he was never able to find a suitable academic position. Charlotte, however, showed great enterprise in building a new career while approaching the age of 50. She taught at several institutions, including the College of St. Catherine in St. Paul, Minnesota, Clark University in Worcester, Massachusetts, and the City College of New York. Although most of her colleagues and some of her students had heard of her work, neither Charlotte nor her husband would ever again enjoy the high status customarily granted to university professors of world distinction. Life in the New World was often difficult for them, but it was infinitely preferable to life in a Europe controlled by Nazi Germany, which was slipping inexorably into the horrors of total war and the Holocaust.

In 1945, the year that Charlotte Bühler became a U.S. citizen, she and her husband moved to Los Angeles, where their son Rolf had settled. Charlotte gave little indication of slowing down, working until 1953 as chief clinical psychologist at the Los Angeles County General Hospital. At the same time, she set up a successful private practice in both individual and group psychotherapy. Although she had never totally subscribed to Freudian orthodoxy during her 15 years in Vienna, Bühler showed that she was nothing if not a realist by adapting her own ideas to what at the time was a domination of American psychology by disciples of Freud. By the early 1960s, however, her misgivings about Freudianism surfaced once more, not only in writings and lectures but in her determination to transcend what she strongly believed to be the limitations of Freudianism. Always willing to work along with other distinguished thinkers in her field, she helped organize the Old Saybrook Conference, which in 1964 resulted in the birth of the humanistic psychology movement. Now in her seventh decade, Charlotte Bühler, while anything but weak-willed, exhibited intellectual and personal flexibility by working smoothly with other superstars in her field, including Viktor Frankl, Abraham Maslow, and Carl Rogers. Her enthusiastic involvement in the nascent movement of humanistic psychology helped her navigate the grief process that followed the death of her husband in October 1963.

Emphasizing the potentialities of the free development of the individual personality, and of growth and self-fulfillment as basic motives of human behavior, the ideals of humanistic psychology were immensely appealing to Charlotte Bühler during the last phase of her distinguished career. Although she could be curt and authoritarian in her relations with others, she continued to embrace humankind in the abstract, an irony that even some of her greatest admirers noted after her death, when they characterized her as a "visionary with gaping blind spots, she had a love of humanity and a sense of superiority to the commoner, a tremendous warmth and an imperious coldness."

After decades of relative indifference, her adopted homeland finally honored her during the last decade of her life with a number of tributes, including the presidency (in 1965–66) of the Association for Humanistic Psychology. Working with collaborators, she published two final books, *The Course of Human Life* (1968) and *An Introduction to Humanistic Psychology* (1972). By 1972, her formerly robust health was in decline, but in a display of iron will she decided to return to Europe to be with her children in Stuttgart. In Germany, during the last months of her life, she received long-overdue public recognition when on the occasion of her 80th birthday in December 1973 the newspaper *Die Welt* headlined a laudatory summation of her life's work under the banner, "The Discoverer of the Child."

Refusing to accept her increasing enfeeblement, she succeeded in setting up a short-lived private practice. To friends and family, she spoke of a yearning for a return to "her country, America" and for the many close friends and professional colleagues she had acquired over the decades. Following a series of strokes, Charlotte Bühler died in her sleep in Stuttgart on February 3, 1974. Although during their lifetimes neither she nor her husband achieved in the United States the eminence they had enjoyed in Europe, the ultimate impact of the American phase of their careers was both deep and lasting.

SOURCES:

Allen, Melanie. "Bühler, Charlotte Bertha," in Barbara Sicherman et al., eds. *Notable American Women: The Modern Period. A Biographical Dictionary.* Cambridge, MA: Belknap Press of Harvard University Press, 1980, pp. 119–121.

Bühler, Charlotte. *The First Year of Life.* Translated by Pearl Greenberg and Rowena Ripin. NY: John Day, 1930.

———. *From Birth to Maturity: An Outline of the Psychological Development of the Child.* London: Kegan Paul, Trench, Trubner, 1935.

———. *Kindheit und Jugend.* Leipzig: S. Hirzel Verlag, 1928.

———. *Das Märchen und die Phantasie des Kindes.* Leipzig: Verlag J. A. Barth, 1918.

———. *Psychologie im Leben unserer Zeit.* Munich: Droemer Knaur Verlag, 1962.

Charlotte Bühler collection, Archives of the American Psychiatric Association, Washington, D.C.

Coser, Lewis S. *Refugee Scholars in America: Their Impact and Their Experiences.* New Haven, CT: Yale University Press, 1984.

Fallend, Karl, and Johannes Reichmayr. "Das 'Psychologische Wien'," in Helene Maimann, ed. *Die ersten 100 Jahre: Österreichische Sozialdemokratie 1888–1988.* Vienna and Munich: Verlag Christian Brandstatter, 1988, pp. 138–142.

Fleming, Donald, and Bernard Bailyn, eds. *The Intellectual Migration: Europe and America, 1930–1960.* Cambridge, MA: Belknap Press of Harvard University Press, 1969.

Gruber, Helmut. *Red Vienna: Experiment in Working-Class Culture 1919–1934.* Oxford: Oxford University Press, 1991.

Havighurst, Robert J. "Charlotte Bühler, December 20, 1893-February 3, 1974," in *Human Development.* Vol. 17, no. 6, 1974, pp. 397–398.

Massarik, Fred. "Charlotte Bühler: A Reflection," in *Journal of Humanistic Psychology.* Vol. 14, no. 3. Summer 1974, pp. 4–6.

Pongratz, Ludwig J. et al., eds. *Psychologie in Selbstdarstellungen.* Berne: H. Huber Verlag, 1972.

Schenk-Danzinger, Lotte and Hans Thomae, eds. *Gegenwartsprobleme der Entwicklungspsychologie: Festschrift für Charlotte Bühler.* Göttingen: Verlag für Psychologie, 1963.

John Haag, Associate Professor,
University of Georgia, Athens, Georgia

Bulgaria, queen of.

Bulgaria, tsarina of.

Bullen, Nan (1507?–1536).

Buller, Annie (1896–1973)

Prominent speaker and organizer for the Communist Party in Canada who endured imprisonment and po-

litical repression to better the lives of Canadian workers. Pronunciation: BULL-er. *Born in December 1896 in Russia or Canada; died on January 19, 1973, in Toronto, Ontario; daughter of Jewish parents (her father was a carpenter); attended public school until age 13; attended the Rand School of Social Science in New York City in 1919; married Harry Guralnick, mid-1920s; children: one son, Jimmy.*

Began work in a tobacco factory (1910); joined the socialist youth movement (1917); left Montreal to attend the Rand School in New York (1919); arrested following the Estevan strike (1931); jailed for one year (1933); jailed for two years (1940); traveled to the Soviet Union (1955).

In defense of her part in organizing the Estevan strike of 1931, for which she was arrested along with 26 others, Annie Buller argued that it was not she who was on trial, but all of the working class, a position that reveals a great deal about how she viewed her life. Buller was a committed Marxist, who had already worked tirelessly for the building of unions, the production of working-class publications, and the raising of the consciousness of workers of Canada in the hope of bringing her country closer to socialism. As a dedicated organizer and mediator for the Communist Party, her efforts were to continue for 50 years. At the time of her trial, Buller probably realized that her conviction, and the imprisonment that would separate her from her husband and child, were inevitable, but saw the events as part of the overall march of workers towards socialism and a better life.

It is not clear whether Annie Buller was born in Russia or in Canada. Whatever the case, from an early age, she grew up in Montreal, Quebec, the daughter of Jewish parents of Russian ancestry. In a move typical of working-class children in early 20th-century Canada, she went to work at the age of 13, employed in a tobacco factory 12 hours a day for 6 days a week, a financial necessity for the family that ended her early formal education. She continued to study at home, and the reading of literary classics as well as political tracts became a lifelong habit.

After three years, Buller left the tobacco factory to work as a clerk in a five-and-dime store. Factory work, apart from being tedious, dirty, and unhealthy, held little status, and the move was a step up, if not necessarily in wages. By age 17, she had made a genuine advance in "respectability" for a young woman of the lower middle class when she became a clerk at Almy's department store. Her ascent continued when she was appointed the head buyer for the china and glassware department, making her the first woman to hold such a position in Canada.

The exposure she received in a store catering to the middle and upperclass undoubtedly helped Buller to recognize the great discrepancy between rich and poor, and during these same years she first became involved in the youth branch of the socialist movement. Interest in socialism was expanding and attracting activists like Buller, especially after the 1917 Russian Revolution held out the possibility that a workers' society could be accomplished. As a colony of Great Britain, Canada was then engaged in World War I, and socialists were theoretically opposed to war, viewing it as a battle between capitalists for markets and profit. Many socialists actually supported the war, but Buller maintained a pacifist stance and worked actively throughout 1918, collecting petitions against the war and conscription. After it ended, in 1918, her commitment to socialism had grown to the point that she decided to go to New York City to attend the Rand School of Social Science.

The Rand School was an adult education facility directed towards the study of Marxism, although it also held classes in the natural sciences and the humanities. Discussions there were characterized by vigorous debate as participants argued about how to interpret Marx and what constituted the best approach for socialism. Now in her early 20s, Buller was an assertive and outspoken woman, who began to develop the talent for oratory that would make her one of the most prominent representatives of the Canadian communist movement and a popular figure among Canadian workers. At the Rand School, Buller's commitment to communism also solidified. Many socialists stressed a social-democratic approach, believing that the lot of workers could best be improved through trade unions and pressure for factory legislation. While Buller accepted the need for these methods as the means to deal with immediate problems, she came to believe that a better life for workers could only be achieved through revolution, by which the workers would seize control of the state.

During this time, Buller met the two women who were to become her closest friends: **Bella Gould** (at the Rand School) and **Becky Buhay** (through the socialist youth movement). Despite frequent separations due to their commitments to communism, Buller and Buhay were to remain lifelong friends, writing to each other throughout their lives. Buhay once described

Buller as the person who gave her courage and strength. "I was starved for love and appreciation [and] she made me believe in myself."

Back in Montreal after a year, Buller and her two friends decided to set up a college like the Rand school. In the spring of 1920, they purchased a house on *Jeanne Mance Street in Montreal and began to hold classes. The education of workers was held to be one of the most important preconditions to revolution, and the college offered classes, hosted prominent guest speakers, and accommodated union meetings in its rooms until the mid-1920s. After it closed, much of Buller's activity remained educational. She was a regular contributor to communist publications and acted repeatedly as business manager for the party press throughout the 1920–30s, and undertook several speaking tours throughout the country during her lifetime.

Annie [Buller] is a part of the living history of Canada. . . . She will occupy a place of honor among Canada's fighters for peace, progress and socialism, among all those who strive for a better life.

—William Kashtan

Apart from her concern for their education, Buller believed that workers needed their own political party as well as effective unions. In February 1922, she became one of the founding members of the Communist Party of Canada (CPC). As business manager of the party newspaper, she tried to publicize the plight of Canadian workers and to encourage them in joining their respective unions. In 1929, her union involvement became more direct when she was sent to Winnipeg, Manitoba, to support workers in the needle trades.

By the late 1920s, the needle trades were infamous for poor working conditions and low wages. A union for the workers did exist but was organized on a "craft" basis and thus omitted all workers not considered skilled. Effectively, this denied membership to the dressmakers, who constituted the majority of workers in the business and were also predominantly female. The CPC, through its union division, the Workers' Unity League (WUL), wanted to organize all workers in the field, regardless of skill level, pay rate, or working location. In August 1928, the Industrial Union of Needle Trades Workers (IUNTW) was formed, and a year later Buller was sent to Winnipeg to help in its fight against wage cuts that were by then plaguing the industry as the country sank into depression.

The union undertook numerous strikes and work stoppages but generally failed to halt the wage cuts. In the economic climate of the early 1930s, most unions, communist or not, were unsuccessful in protecting wages; most were content to achieve recognition as the official bargaining unit from employers determined to obstruct their union activities. The IUNTW was successful in organizing the needle workers, many of whom had never been in a union before, but it is impossible to gauge how much more successful it would have been in protecting wages in the second half of the 1930s, when the economy improved. The CPC, like most other communist groups in the Western world, took its inspiration and its orders from the Communist Party in the Soviet Union. During 1935–36, the Canadian party was ordered by Moscow to disband unions under the WUL and join with non-Communist led unions in a "United Front."

There is no indication of whether Buller ever questioned the wisdom of this move by the Soviet leadership, which meant dismantling the institutions that had taken party workers a decade of hard effort to create. Throughout her life, communism in Canada would suffer many traumas as a result of orders from Moscow and actions of the Soviet Union in the international sphere. But communists were expected to commit themselves wholeheartedly to the "cause," and Buller appears to have remained dedicated to the principles of Marxism and the leadership of the Soviet Union, accepting all other matters, including family life, as secondary.

While in Montreal in the early 1920s, Buller had met and married Harry Guralnick, also a communist, who promoted the party cause through writing, translating, and organizing, and was also cultural director of the United Jewish People's Order and secretary of the Central Jewish Party Bureau. During the 1930s, both Buller and her husband, who had a son Jimmy, were to endure a great deal of hardship for the sake of their political concerns after the Canadian government initiated a variety of laws in order to crack down on the CPC and other groups they considered a threat to public order.

For Buller, the difficulties began with the famous Estevan strike of 1931. The Souris coalfields, near Estevan, Saskatchewan, had been mined since the 1890s. Like many coal mining enterprises, they involved dangerous conditions, hard work, and low pay, aggravated by the fact that the company owned the workers' town, charging high rates for substandard housing and the only goods available for buying through the company store. By the summer of 1931, the workers decided to join the Mine Workers' Union of Canada, a WUL affiliate. On September 7, after the employers refused to negotiate with the union, the workers went on strike. It was common practice to host speakers and other activities to maintain the unity of strikers. Buller, a well-known and popular speaker by then, was invited to appear before the miners on September 27. A parade was scheduled for the 29th, when the strikers were to march to the community of Estevan and hold a public meeting to try to elicit public support.

Met at the outskirts by a contingent of local police and the Royal Canadian Mounted Police (RCMP), the procession never made it into the town. A skirmish ensued, which ended with shots being fired at the unarmed miners, leaving three miners dead and 50 injured. As often happened, the state, represented through its police force, was on the side of the employers. The three men were buried in a common grave, and a monument was eventually erected bearing the inscription, "Murdered in Estevan September 29, 1931 by the RCMP." Local authorities later removed the reference to the Mounties.

Though Buller had helped with the parade preparations, she was not a participant. Organizers of the event realized that the government would respond with arrests, however, and arranged to have her smuggled to Winnipeg with the help of unionized railway workers. After the other organizers were arrested in Estevan, Buller continued to give speeches in Winnipeg and Toronto to raise funds in support of the Estevan strikers. Eventually, she was picked up in Toronto and charged with "inciting to riot."

Public outcry against the events in Estevan led the Federal government to step in and appoint a Conciliation Board to arbitrate between the workers and management, as well as a royal commission to investigate the conditions surrounding the incident. An agreement was reached between the miners and operators in which the miners won some concessions and agreed to return to work in October. In the spring of 1932, the report of the royal commission upheld the conditions of the agreement and recommended further concessions such as adequate medical care and the repair of the workers' houses. Meanwhile, the trials of the strike leaders continued, resulting in sentences of between three months and two years for most who were involved.

Buller's first trial ended in conviction but was appealed. The CPC had a legal division, but its lawyers were busy due to a rash of government arrests of suspected communists. For her second trial, beginning March 10, 1933, Buller decided to defend herself by proving: 1) that the speech she gave on the 27th had not been inflammatory, citing as evidence the fact that there were police spies present at the time of her speech with the power to arrest her if they had cause; 2) that the prosecution could not prove she was present at the riot; and 3) that there was no proof that she had incited a riot in any way.

Buller continued her argument by declaring that the string of events leading to the conflict had not been caused by the labor organizers, but by mine operators and the government, who had forced the workers into a position of strike through their failure to provide adequate working conditions as required by law. She ended by stating:

> When I face you here, I face you with my head erect. I face you as a worker with ideals and convictions. Those ideals and convictions are linked with the tide of human progress. You cannot stop that tide of progress any more than you can stop the tide of the sea with a pitchfork.

Nevertheless, Buller was convicted and sentenced to one year in jail, which she served at the women's prison in North Battleford, in solitary confinement. Undoubtedly, the condition of solitary confinement was the most difficult aspect of that year. After her release, she took a brief period of rest with her family before returning to her writing and organizing work for the party.

In the summer of 1935, Buller was one of the organizers for the "On-to-Ottawa" trek, a communist-organized march planned to draw attention to conditions in work camps established by the federal government to provide "relief" for young, unemployed men. The trek ended much as the Estevan strike had, with a riot between police and marchers in the town of Regina, but it did help to push the government to reassess the way its relief program was being administered. Also during this time, Buller worked on the campaign to raise funds in support of the loyalists in the Spanish Civil War.

In November 1939, the federal government banned the CPC, and by 1940, Buller and her husband once again faced the prospect of separation. As a British commonwealth nation, Canada was once more at war with Germany, while the Soviet Union, then allied with Germany under a "non-aggression pact," had become an enemy. Canadian communists, in line with orders from Moscow, openly opposed

Canada's role in the war as an act of aggression. Not long after, Harry became one of more than 100 prominent communists interned in camps by the federal government. Buller was arrested on charges related to an article she had written for the party newspaper, which had been banned and was publishing illegally. Sentenced to two years in the Women's Jail at Portage La Prairie, Manitoba, she was at least not placed in solitary confinement this time, and had the company of fellow inmates and visitors. Because she got along well with prison authorities, she was given some privileges, such as extended visits with friends, and she spent her time otherwise filling scrapbooks with newspaper and magazine clippings, cards and letters, and pictures. One scrapbook clipping that has survived includes the name of her son Jimmy in a list of graduates from a printing school, providing a vivid reminder that Buller was frequently forced to miss significant parts of her child's life.

In June 1941, due to the invasion of Russia by Hitler, the Communist Party line was switched in support of the war. With Russia as an ally, the Canadian government decided to release the interned communists in the summer of 1942. In December of that year, Buller completed her sentence and was reunited with Harry. She immediately resumed working for the party press in Toronto, as business manager of the *Tribune,* and also worked for a period as manager of *National Affairs Monthly,* another party publication.

In 1943, due to the continuing ban against the CPC, Canadian communists decided to establish a "new" party called the Labour Progressive Party (LPP), which renounced violence as a means of effecting change, and thereby hoped to avoid being banned. The LPP began running candidates in provincial and federal elections and did reasonably well until the Cold War began in 1948. Twice, Buller ran as a candidate. In 1932, she ran for the position of alderman in the city of Toronto. Later, in 1956, she was the party's candidate in Spadina Riding (Toronto) for federal election. In both cases, she did not win, which is understandable given the political climate of the time.

In 1955, Buller and her husband went to the Soviet Union, a trip that was undoubtedly one of the highlights of her life. Despite the problems communism was facing by the 1950s, Buller remained a dedicated believer and viewed the Soviet Union as a true socialist state. During her stay, she wrote articles for *The Tribune,* detailing the people she met and the places she saw. During a tour of a factory, she was greatly impressed by the organization and working conditions she witnessed.

On January 19, 1973, Annie Buller died at the age of 76, only a short time after the death of her husband Harry. Both were remembered by the party in warm tributes for their many years of service to the cause. Canadian society had changed greatly during their lives, and although no revolution had occurred, the standard of living and working conditions of most working people had improved remarkably, and Annie Buller had contributed to bringing about this change. As William Kashtan, general secretary of the CPC said at the funeral:

> If today the trade union movement has the strength it has, if the workers today are able to stand up with dignity and do not have to bend their knees to the corporations, no small cause for it lies in the self-sacrificing struggle of Annie and other Communists.

Although many of her activities were unsuccessful in achieving their immediate goals, Annie Buller undoubtedly affected the lives of many working Canadians, helping to educate them and encouraging them to act. For this reason, Annie Buller was known and respected by workers across Canada.

SOURCES:
Sangster, Joan. *Dreams of Equality: Women on the Canadian Left, 1920–1950.* Toronto: McClelland & Stewart, 1989.
Watson, Louise. *She Never Was Afraid: The Biography of Annie Buller.* Toronto: Progress Books, 1976.

COLLECTIONS:
Public Archives of Ontario, Multicultural History Society of Ontario, Annie Buller Papers.
Public Archives of Ontario, Communist Party of Canada Collection.

Catherine Briggs, Ph.D. Candidate, University of Waterloo, Waterloo, Ontario, Canada

Bullette, Julia (d. 1867)

English-born courtesan of Virginia City, Nevada, during the mining rush of the 1850s. Name variations: Julia Bulette. Born in London, England; died on January 20, 1867, in Virginia City, Nevada.

Julia Bullette, called the "Darling of the Comstock," was one of the most popular courtesans of Virginia City, Nevada, where she settled in order to cash in on the Western mining boom of the 1850s. Known for her community-minded spirit, she helped pump water for the local fire brigade, the Virginia Engine Company No. 1, which rewarded her with an honorary membership and showered her with attention and gifts. When Bullette was robbed and murdered by the notorious thief John Millian in 1867, her body was reportedly carried to Flowery Hill Cemetery in a black-plumed hearse, followed by thousands of grieving miners on foot; bringing up the rear, the fire brigade played a solemn rendition of "The Girl I Left Behind Me." Millian, a native of France, was arrested a few months later and subsequently hanged for his crime. The white picket fence that surrounded Bullette's grave was supposedly moved 200 feet away from the site so lazy visitors could view it with binoculars from a bar in town.

Bullinger, Anna (c. 1504–1564)

Swedish reformer, married to Heinrich Bullinger, who was a host to refugees during the 16th-century Reformation. Born Anna Adlischweiler around 1504 in Sweden; died in 1564; married Heinrich Bullinger (a church reformer), in 1529; children: eleven.

Anna Bullinger was living in a Zurich convent with her failing mother when she met and fell in love with Heinrich Bullinger who was to gain recognition in the church reform movement. The couple delayed marriage due to the illness of Anna's mother, giving Heinrich time to prepare his future wife for the upcoming nuptials with a small book entitled *Concerning Female Training, and How a Daughter Should Guide Her Conduct and Life*. The couple wed in 1529, after which Bullinger succeeded his father as pastor at Bremgarten, Argau, Switzerland. In 1531, as Roman Catholic armies were attacking Protestant ministers, Bullinger fled the city with his father and brother, leaving his young wife with their two small children to find her own way through the besieged city to join him in Zurich. There, Heinrich succeeded Swiss reformer Huldrych Zwingli as chief pastor, bringing both honor and increased responsibility to Anna. Managing on a small income, she cared for her ever increasing family (she would have 11 children), and made a home for many refugees, who praised her as a loving and caring host. Anna Bullinger died of the plague in 1564, after nursing her husband back to health from his own bout with the disease.

Bullowa, Emilie (1869–1942)

American lawyer, reformer and philanthropist, who was a founding member and first president of the National Association of Women Lawyers. Born in New York City in 1869; died in New York on October 25, 1942; oldest of six children of Morris Bullowa and Mary Bullowa; graduated from Law College of New York University, 1900; never married.

Born into a wealthy Jewish family in New York City in 1869, Emilie Bullowa was the oldest of six children. The early death of both her parents left her the head of a large family. After seeing her siblings well settled in various schools and universities (one brother and one sister became a physician), she started her own professional education, enrolling at the Law College of New York University. After graduating in 1900, Bullowa opened a law office at 34 Nassau Street in Lower Manhattan, from which she and her brother Ferdinand Bullowa would practice admiralty law for more than four decades.

Emilie Bullowa fought for the equal treatment of female lawyers and was a founding member and first president of the National Association of Women Lawyers. During World War I, having recently inherited a château in France, she turned the property over to French War Relief to house wounded soldiers and refugees. At the start of World War II, she showed similar generosity by donating a mobile field kitchen, as well as all her office furniture, to British War Relief.

Believing that democracy needed an economic as well as a philosophical foundation, Emilie Bullowa served in 1924 as a member of the platform committee of the Women's Democratic Union. She was sensitive to criticisms that the legal profession was unaffordable for the average citizen, declaring that "our democracy doesn't work if the people who can't afford to give compensation for legal aid can't get justice. It is just as important to help people in their rights as in their health and their housing." Having spent her life fighting for the rights of the weak and poor, Emilie Bullowa died in New York on October 25, 1942.

SOURCES:
"Emilie Bullowa, Lawyer 42 Years," in *The New York Times*. October 26, 1942, p. 15.

John Haag, Associate Professor,
University of Georgia, Athens, Georgia

Bülow, Frieda von (1857–1909)

German author, who was the creator of the German colonial novel. Name variations: Buelow, Bulow; Baroness von Bülow. Born Frieda Freifräulein von Bülow in Berlin, Germany, on October 12, 1857; died in Dornburg on March 12, 1909; daughter of Hugo Freiherr von Bülow (a diplomat); sister of Margarete von Bülow (1860–1884) and Albrecht von Bülow.

Selected writings: Allein ich will! Roman *(3rd ed., Dresden-Blasewitz: C. Reissner Verlag, 1911);* Im Lande der Verheissung: Ein deutscher Kolonial-Roman *(Berlin: F. Fontane, 1899);* Im Lande der Verheissung: Ein Kolonialroman um Carl Peter *(Dresden: Reissner Verlag, 1937);* Reiseskizzen und Tagebuchblätter aus Deutsch-Ostafrika *(Berlin: Walther & Apolant Verlag, 1889);* Tropenkoller: Episode aus dem deutschen Kolonialleben *(2nd ed., Berlin: F. Fontane, 1897).*

Older sister of novelist ***Margarete von Bülow**, Frieda von Bülow was born in Berlin on October 12, 1857. Her father Hugo von Bülow was a diplomat, and thus Frieda spent much of her youth in Smyrna, Turkey, as well as in England. When she returned to Germany, most of her time was spent in the province of Thuringia, as well as her native city of Berlin. In 1885, she accompanied her brother Albrecht to German East Africa, where he purchased land and attempted to create a successful career for himself as a plantation owner. During this time, Frieda von Bülow became a strong proponent of a German presence in Africa, at least in part because she had met and come under the influence of a ruthless colonial adventurer, Carl Peters (1856–1918). Returning to Europe in 1889, she was shocked in 1892 by the news of her brother's death in Africa and returned to his property the next year in an attempt to make the land a profitable undertaking.

Most of von Bülow's energy from the early 1890s to her death in 1909 went into convincing the German people that their national destiny included an ambitious agenda of colonial expansionism. Believing that German women should make their presence felt in the newly acquired German colonies, she founded and was tireless in propagandizing for the German Women's Guild for Nursing in the Colonies. Von Bülow was convinced that Germans were racially superior to Africans and thus fated to rule and "enlighten" them, and several of her novels dealt with the issue of racial roles in Africa. With her 1899 work *Im Lande der Verheissung*, she created the German colonial novel, which was not surprisingly populated with racist stereotypes, including the mulatto female Maria Beta, described as a "barbarian" whose "dark eyes glistened covetously." In contrast, the character of German baroness Maleen von Dietlas, whose "still healthy Nordic blood circulated in her veins," deserved to win the affections of the count, whose bloodline must remain pure. Frieda von Bülow died in Dornburg on March 12, 1909. The loss of Germany's colonial empire in

World War I effectively ended public interest in her writings, and even Nazi Germany's attempt to stir up public interest in a return of the lost colonies failed to restore her reputation either as a writer or propagandist.

SOURCES:

Hoechstetter, Sophie. *Frieda Freiin von Bülow: Ein Lebensbild.* Dresden: C. Reissner Verlag, 1910.

Müller, Fritz Ferdinand. *Deutschland-Zanzibar-Ostafrika: Geschichte einer deutschen Kolonialeroberung 1884–1890.* Berlin: 1959.

Warmbold, Joachim. "If only she didn't have Negro blood in her veins: The concept of *Métissage* in German colonial literature," in *Journal of Black Studies.* Vol. 23, no. 2. December 1992, pp. 200–209.

John Haag, Associate Professor, University of Georgia, Athens, Georgia

Bülow, Margarete von (1860–1884)

German novelist whose early death while attempting to save a drowning child cut short a highly promising literary career. Name variations: Buelow or Bulow. Born Margarete Freifräulein von Bülow in Berlin, Germany, on February 23, 1860; drowned in Berlin on January 2, 1884; daughter of Hugo Freiherr von Bülow (a diplomat); sister of Frieda von Bülow (1857–1909) and Albrecht von Bülow; grew up in various countries including England.

Selected writings: Novellen *(Berlin: Hertz Verlag, 1885);* Jonas Briccius: Erzählung *(Leipzig: Grunow Verlag, 1886);* Aus der Chronik derer von Riffelshausen: Erzählung *(Leipzig: Grunow Verlag, 1887);* Neue Novellen *(Berlin: Verlag Walther & Apolant, 1890);* Novellen einer Frühvollendeten: Ausgewähltes: Mit einer Einleitung von Adolf Bartels *(Leipzig: R. Voigtländer's Verlag, 1920).*

An act of spontaneous heroism cut short the life of a young artist who might otherwise have developed into one of Germany's major writers. On January 2, 1884, Margarete von Bülow died in Berlin while attempting to rescue a drowning child.

Born in Berlin on February 23, 1860, she was the daughter of Hugo von Bülow, a diplomat descended from a distinguished noble family. She grew up in Berlin and Thuringia as well as in Smyrna, Turkey, where her father was stationed as the German consul. Margarete von Bülow lived in England during the years 1876–1878, finally settling in Berlin in 1881 where she lived until her untimely death. A prolific writer as well as a sharp-eyed observer, she had a large number of unpublished manuscripts prepared for publication in the final months of her life. All of her novels and novellas were published posthumously to positive critical acclaim. Her realistic novellas of life in contemporary Berlin and Thuringia first appeared in print in 1885. A number of other works, mainly psychological novels, were published in the next few years, and a final collection of novellas, along with a biographical essay, appeared in 1890. Her sister *Frieda von Bülow wrote movingly of Margarete in her last novel, *Die Schwestern* (*The Sisters*, 1909).

SOURCES:
Bülow, Frieda von. *Die Schwestern: Geschichte einer Mädchenjugend. Roman.* Dresden: C. Reissner Verlag, 1909.

Hoechstetter, Sophie. *Frieda Freiin von Bülow: Ein Lebensbild.* Dresden: C. Reissner Verlag, 1910.

John Haag, Associate Professor, University of Georgia, Athens, Georgia

Bulwer-Lytton, Rosina, Lady (1802–1882)

*English novelist. Name variations: Lady Bulwer-Lytton. Born Rosina Doyle Wheeler in Ballywhire, County Limerick, Ireland, on November 2, 1802; died in Upper Sydenham, in London, England, on March 12, 1882; youngest daughter of Francis Wheeler and **Anna Doyle Wheeler** (the daughter of an archdeacon); married Edward George Earle Lytton Bulwer-Lytton, 1st baron Lytton, August 1827; children: one daughter (1828–1848); one son, Edward Robert Bulwer Lytton (1831–1891); grandmother of Lady *Constance Lytton.*

Despite his mother's wishes and the cessation of his yearly allowance, Edward Bulwer-Lytton married Rosina Wheeler, a popular member of the literary circle surrounding Lady *Caroline Lamb, in 1827. In 1836, Rosina legally separated from her husband because of his volatile temper (and possibly domestic violence), and was given custody of their two children. Two years later, they were taken from her. Rosina saw her daughter only once more before the young girl's death at age 20. In 1839, Lady Bulwer-Lytton attacked her husband in print with her book *Cheveley, or the Man of Honour,* which met with scandalous success, and she continued to publicly taunt her husband until his death in 1873. Her letters were edited by **Louisa Devey** as *Life of Rosina, Lady Lytton* (1887); see also Michael Sadleir's *Bulwer, a Panorama: Edward and Rosina, 1803–36* (1931).

Bunbury, Lady (1745–1826).
See Lennox Sisters for Sarah Lennox.

Bunbury, Selina (1802–1882)
Irish novelist and traveler. Born in Kilsaran, County Louth, Ireland, in 1802; died in Cheltenham in 1882.

Selina Bunbury was born in Kilsaran, County Louth, Ireland, in 1802; she was 17 when her father went bankrupt and her mother moved to Dublin with the children. While teaching in a primary school, Bunbury wrote books about Ireland, including *A Visit to My Birthplace* (1820) and *Tales of My Country* (1833). Then the family moved to Liverpool, where Selina kept house for her twin brother and continued writing, publishing many popular novels. Following her brother's marriage in 1845, Bunbury took to the road, publishing books on her travels throughout Europe. Though prolific, she hardly came close to the 100 titles that have been attributed to her.

Bundy, May Sutton (1887–1975).
See Sutton, May.

Bungu, Nonteta (c. 1875–1935).
See Nonteta Bungu.

Bunina, Anna Petrovna (1774–1829).
See Akhmatova, Anna for sidebar.

Bunke, Tamara (1937–1967)
Argentine-born revolutionary and Communist double agent in Cuba who was instrumental in planning the guerilla operation in Bolivia in which both she and Ché Guevara died. Name variations: (codename) Tania. Born Tamara Haydée Bunke on November 19, 1937, in Buenos Aires, Argentina; killed in ambush by Bolivian army patrol on August 31, 1967, at Vado del Yeso, Bolivia; daughter of Erich Otto Heinrich Bunke (a German Communist and teacher) and Esperanza Bider (a Polish Communist and teacher); educated in Argentina until 1948; graduated from Clara Zetkin Senior High School in East Germany; trained in East German and Soviet intelligence; married Mario Martínez Álvarez, briefly, to obtain Bolivian citizenship, 1966; children: none.

Moved with family to the German Democratic Republic (1948); joined GDR defense training program (1952); recruited for intelligence work by the East German Ministry of State Security (1958); went to Cuba as a translator (1961); recruited for Cuban intelligence (March 1963); sent to La Paz to establish a urban guerrilla network in Bolivia (October 1964); after deliberately revealing extent of Cuban involvement in Bolivia, joined Ché Guevara's guerrillas in the jungle (February 1967).

Inspired by ardent patriotism or motivated by the thrill of danger, women and men throughout history have chosen to engage in the difficult and demanding work of the intelligence agent. Following the overthrow of the Juan Batista dictatorship in Cuba in 1959, the Communist island revolution led by Fidel Castro inspired many idealistic revolutionaries and agents who believed that the model of society it proposed foreshadowed a new and better era for humankind. But this Caribbean island country off the U.S. coast was also caught up in struggles between internal warring Communist factions and a huge ideological conflict between East and West in ways that could result in the sacrifice of individual lives. Tamara Bunke, code name Tania, was one such dedicated Communist, who died not as a victim of the West, but because of infighting within her own party, while her actions also led directly to the death of the famed Cuban revolutionary Ché Guevara. Such is the tangled history that often surrounds the life of a double agent.

Tamara Bunke

Born in Buenos Aires, Argentina, on November 19, 1937, Tamara Bunke lived the outwardly normal childhood of many in her country; she swam, went horseback riding, and attended summer camp. Fluent only in Spanish (she did not learn German until adolescence), her cultural identity was Argentine. What made her household different from many others was the fact that her parents were dedicated Communists, engaged in clandestine activities, which required that she and her older brother, Olaf, learn to be close-mouthed and secretive from the earliest days of their childhood. In the privacy of her home, the blue-eyed little girl with pigtails was part of the revolution.

The ideology of the family was grounded in European events that began four years before her birth, when Adolf Hitler, at the head of Germany's Third Reich, had determined to wipe out both Jews and leftists. Tamara's father was Erich Otto Heinrich Bunke, a German and a Communist then living and teaching in Berlin; her mother Esperanza Bider was also a teacher and a Communist, and a Pole as well as a Jew. By 1935, many friends of the Bunkes had been rounded up by the Gestapo, and that year, shortly after the birth of her son Olaf, Esperanza was ordered to report to the Gestapo. Understanding the meaning of the summons, the couple arranged for Esperanza to escape the country within 24 hours, on her Polish passport with her son, fleeing first to Warsaw, then on to Switzerland, Luxembourg, France, and ultimately Argentina. The first choice of the Bunkes would have been to live in the USSR, but since there was no time to acquire the necessary papers, the couple reunited in Argentina and settled with other relatives among German refugees. As members of the Argentine Communist Party, they took up their underground work, learned Spanish, and became Argentine citizens.

In 1948, the Bunke family returned to Europe, moving to Stalinstadt in the German Democratic Republic to be closer to the center of Communist power. At age 11, Tamara lived for a while with a German family and found the adjustment to her new country a great shock. Teased about her accent, she was sometimes driven to tears, but she enjoyed sledding in winter and target shooting, and, in 1952, she joined the East German defense training program, the GDR Association for Sports and Skills. Trained in gymnastics, Morse code, target shooting and other skills useful to young revolutionaries, she developed a fondness for uniforms and handling weapons that was to last throughout her life.

After graduation from *Clara Zetkin Senior High School, Tamara joined Socialist Unity, the local name for the Communist Party; her Argentine background led to her placement as an interpreter for the Free German Youth's Latin American Bureau, for which she traveled to Prague, Vienna, and Moscow. At age 21, she was recruited for intelligence work by the East German Ministry of State Security (MFS), where she assisted Oberleutnant Guenther Maennel (who defected to the West in 1961); shortly thereafter, she was approached by the KGB to work as a double agent for Moscow.

Fluent in Spanish, dedicated to communism, intelligent and attractive, Tamara Bunke was the ideal candidate for the type of espionage work desired by the Soviets in Latin America, and especially Cuba. The small island country was heavily subsidized by the Soviet Union as a Communist foothold in the Western hemisphere, but since China was the great rival of the USSR in the Communist world, the Soviets were anxious about Maoist tendencies exhibited by some who were in power in Cuba. A Soviet agent who could document what was happening on a daily basis therefore seemed prudent, and Tamara had long shown an interest in advancing the Communist revolution in Latin America.

To older, mainline Communists, the revolution in Cuba often seemed undisciplined and unreliable, but to younger members of the party it was an inspiration. In late 1956, a group of 82 men led by Fidel Castro had invaded Cuba; among its members was an Argentine doctor, Ernesto "Ché" Guevara. In December of that year, all but 12 had been butchered in Oriente province by the troops of the ruling dictator, Juan Batista. This small group of survivors, including Fidel and Raúl Castro, Guevara, and Camilo Cienfuegos, formed the guerrilla movement dedicated to the overthrow of Batista that was finally successful on January 1, 1959. Guevara became a chief of staff of the Cuban revolution, appointed minister of industries and charged with introducing Communist reforms.

In 1961, Tamara Bunke arrived in Cuba to be a translator for the Ministry of Education. In a rare show of esteem toward a foreigner, she was invited to join the militia, and often dressed in uniform thereafter. A spontaneous and enthusiastic woman, popular with co-workers, she differed from many foreigners who came to help the revolution in her involvement in Cuban daily life. She also pursued her Communist ideals with the zeal of a religious believer, living by the maxim, "Anybody who can't do small things

will never be able to do great things." When she discovered that a domestic worker living in her building, named Elisa, had only a fifth-grade education, she spent up to three hours a day teaching the woman; she swapped her three-bedroom apartment for a two-bedroom apartment occupied by a Chilean family with four children; and she exchanged refrigerators with a neighboring family after theirs broke down, contending after it was fixed that they needed the larger one because they had children. As an important party functionary, she had many privileges, including an assigned maid, but the woman rarely had work to do because Bunke lived so simply.

At the same time, Tamara kept her activities strictly compartmentalized. Colleagues at work did not know her neighbors and neither knew her friends in the Young Communist League or other Latin American groups. Intense involvement as well as a close-mouthed nature were necessary for one in service to two bosses, one in Havana and one in Moscow. In March 1963, Tamara entered the phase of her life that inaugurated her identity as "Tania," the guerrilla. She was selected for a small and elite clandestine group and given the work of organizing a network to invade Latin America countries and subvert their governments, confronting the power and influence of the United States whenever possible.

A first step in this phase was to withdraw from public revolutionary work and stop associating with those who had become her comrades in Cuba. Her apartment was no longer open to friends and her life became further compartmentalized. Issued the first of many false identification papers, as Tamara Lorenzo, she was taught how to work in code, to make drops and pick-ups, to watch those around her to detect if she were under surveillance, and to mark clothing and personal items so that she would know if her belongings had been searched.

The full reasons for her selection to such a post are not fully known, but the appointment was probably influenced by her relationship with Ché Guevara. The actual nature of their association is not known, though they may have been lovers. What *is* known is that both were from Argentina, and therefore foreigners in Cuba, and both were ardent Communists. At the very least, she was a trusted ally of Guevara, and as such she was called to his office at the Ministry of Industries in March 1964, where she was informed that she would be sent to La Paz, Bolivia, to set up an urban guerrilla network.

First, however, on April 9, 1964, "Tania" left for Europe as Haydée Bidel Gonzalez. The objective of her travels over the next several months was to learn to be comfortable with different identities. In her first new guise, she was also to present herself as a nonpartisan after several years of living in the fervor of the Cuban Revolution. She was instructed to pose as an apolitical person, with slightly anti-Communist tendencies. In October 1964, she finally set out for Bolivia, where she was to establish residence as Laura Gutiérrez Bauer, an ethnologist. Since she played the accordion and guitar, the study of Bolivian folk music was a good cover. Bunke was a charming woman of 26 who quickly established herself in La Paz, making friends in the highest circles of government. To demonstrate a visible source of income, she devoted a few hours a day to teaching German to eight students; one of these pupils was López Muñoz, a journalist, whose influence eventually helped her to secure papers for Guevara to enter Bolivia as an anthropologist. She became a friend of **Anita Heinrich**, who was also of German background, and private secretary to the minister of government and justice, Antonia Arguedas Mendieta. Arguedas was a Communist, with a pipeline to the presidency, and his ministry controlled immigration, which proved helpful when papers were needed. No direct contact was established between Arguedas and Bunke, but it is possible that he was a part of the network she established. In mid-1966, Bunke married Mario Martínez Älvarez, a student of industrial engineering at San Andrés University, and thus obtained Bolivian citizenship. Much to the distress of Älvarez, who was genuinely in love with "Laura Bauer," she quickly sought a divorce and obtained a scholarship for him through Soviet contacts that allowed him to be packed off to Sofia, Bulgaria.

In her role as a musical ethnologist, Bunke had meanwhile traveled around Bolivia acquiring a vast collection of Bolivian folk music. The accumulated material documented a true talent and interest in this area while she was becoming highly familiar with the countryside. In mid-1966, she moved to Camiri, where she lived at the Hotel Oriente and started a radio program called "Advice to Women." The show was a huge hit among the lovelorn, though her audience sometimes found parts of her message unintelligible; it was only later realized that Bunke had used her program to send out coded messages to members of her network and the guerrillas awaiting word of when they were to launch their anti-government offensive.

Meanwhile, Bunke's information about Cuban activities was invaluable to the USSR, where the Soviets were eager to make Maoists like Ché Guevara toe the party line. In Cuba, Ché's popularity was also on the wane. He had always been viewed there as a foreigner, and his insistence on punctuality and efficiency, the norm in Argentina, had not won him allies. His relationship with Fidel Castro had also become tenuous, since he liked to take credit for guerrilla exploits, and Fidel had a way of eliminating those who tried to share the limelight. It was probably not by accident, therefore, that rumors of Guevara's death began to circulate in the mid-'60s. In 1965, Castro had sent Guevara to the Congo, to lead the mercenaries of the dictator Moïse Tshombe in Katanga province, but the outcome was not a success. In March 1966, Guevara returned secretly to Cuba, where he kept a low profile until leaving for Bolivia in early 1967.

Considerable money and effort had been invested by then, both to establish Bunke's network and to supply guerrilla bases in the Bolivian jungle. From the viewpoints of both Havana and Moscow, this was the perfect exploratory venture. If it succeeded, the U.S. would have another Vietnam on its hands; if it failed, a troublesome guerrilla leader would have been eliminated. Of all those involved in the plans, only Bunke belonged to an orthodox Communist organization loyal to Moscow. Her role was to reconcile the operation's two opposing objectives—the desire of Guevara to spread revolution and the determination of Moscow to extinguish a Maoist insurrection. Meanwhile, although it was not a declared aim, she might help Castro to eliminate a potentially dangerous rival. Her task was enormous, but she had made real inroads in Bolivia. Based on Bunke's clandestine activities, Guevara arrived in the country prepared to launch a guerrilla offensive.

Guevara's dream of a Bolivian revolution dated back to 1953, when a spontaneous revolt had put down a rightist coup against the government of Paz Estenssoro. A student at the time, Guevara had never forgotten how miners and peasants joined forces to quell the coup, and believed that the feat could be duplicated. Once the Communists were in control of Bolivia, his next objective would be to begin a revolution in Argentina, to be followed by a series of "Latin American Vietnams" he would help to create, which would overwhelm the U.S. and end its dominance in the hemisphere.

Guevara's romantic revolutionary notions were not well suited to the Bolivian jungle, nor to the Bolivian people, who held a deep resentment of foreigners of any ilk. Their hatred of outsiders extended even to members of the Bolivian Communist Party, and when threatened by outside influences, Bolivians from both the left and the right tended to unite not to overthrow their own government but to throw the intruders out.

In March 1967, Guevara set up camp near Ñancahuanzú, with some 40 men. There is considerable evidence that Castro knowingly sent Ché to his death on this ill-starred mission. At best, the Bolivian Communists were hostile allies, and by the time Guevara reached the country, the Bolivian government had documentation of the activities of Bunke's network. In late February, she had picked up two journalists in La Paz, to take them to interviews in the guerrilla area. Authorities in Ñancahuanzú were already suspicious of strange events in the area and therefore alert to unfamiliar vehicles. When the group stopped in Camiri for the night, she inexplicably left her jeep parked in a prominent place, containing documents and notebooks with names and addresses that gave away the entire enterprise. Throughout her intelligence career, Tamara Bunke had never committed such a gaffe, and it can only be concluded that this was a deliberate act: Moscow wanted Bolivian authorities to know what Guevara's troops were doing.

With the plans revealed, Bunke's cover was also blown, forcing her to move into the jungle with Guevara's forces. Meanwhile, chaos began to overtake the group. On March 14, two guerilla deserters, named Rocabado and Barrera, fell into the hands of the Bolivian army. Angered by an argument with Ché, they were ready to tell all they knew and confirmed what had been discovered in the jeep. On March 19, a Bolivian soldier discovered the guerrillas and was killed. In contradiction of a basic tenet of guerrilla warfare, which mandates that the fighters melt into the jungle, Guevara decided that the Bolivian troops should be ambushed when they came looking for the soldier. The camp was moved and valuable supplies, especially medicine, were lost in the process. On March 23, a Bolivian army patrol entered the area and was ambushed by some of the rebels, but it managed to kill and wound all who were not taken prisoner. With the presence of the invaders thus established, the guerrillas began to live as hunted animals.

News of the ambush electrified the country, unifying Bolivians of all political persuasions. The Bolivian army was mobilized to hunt down the intruders. By this time, Castro wanted no part of the venture and contact with Cuba was sporadic. In the jungle, Bunke became sick and ran a high fever. It is rumored that she may have been pregnant. Because her presence slowed the group's movements, Ché relegated her to a smaller group to unburden the main force. Although Ché never held her responsible for the jeep episode, some guerrillas viewed her as a traitor. Emotionally tormented, derided and sexually molested, suffering from hunger and exhaustion, she begged at times to be killed.

On August 30, as the Bolivian army drew closer to the rebels, Bunke's group bargained with a peasant for food. He alerted the army and led them to the camp the following day. Early on the morning of August 31, members of the Bolivian army waited for the guerrillas to pass by on the narrow path near the river in the Vado del Yeso. In the ambush that commenced at 5:20 AM, Bunke fell in a hail of bullets without firing a shot, and most of the group was slaughtered. Her body was discovered a week later, washed down the river. German nuns at a Christian school in nearby Valle Grande buried it in a modest coffin in the public cemetery. The other guerilla group eluded the army for five more weeks, until October 9, 1967, when Ché was finally captured and shot.

The life of the woman who has passed into history as Tania was so compartmentalized that even today it is impossible to discover all the facts. She was a dedicated daughter who wrote faithfully to her parents until her clandestine activities forbade further contact. She was an intelligent and charming person, who spoke several languages fluently, and could gather a creditable collection of material about folk music, while setting up an underground revolutionary network. She was also a double agent who could follow Ché Guevara's instructions while laying the groundwork for his demise. It is clear that she believed communism would create a better world, and accepted the view that the Moscow version of this doctrine was needed to accomplish this feat. Dead before her 30th birthday, she lies buried in a small Bolivian cemetery, where lighted candles and flowers appear from time to time on her grave, although no one knows who brings them.

SOURCES:

González, Luis J., and Gustavo A. Sánchez Salazar. *The Great Rebel: Che Guevara in Bolivia.* Translated from Spanish by Helen R. Lane. NY: Grove Press. 1969.

James, Daniel. *Ché Guevara.* NY: Stein and Day, 1969.

Marchetti, Victor, and John D. Marks. *The CIA and the Cult of Intelligence.* NY: Dell, 1974.

Rojas, Marta, and Mirta Rodríguez Calderón, eds. *Tania: The Unforgettable Guerrilla*. NY: Vintage Books, 1971.

Sauvage, Léo. *Che Guevara: The Failure of a Revolutionary*. Translated from Spanish by Raoul Frémont. Englewood Cliffs, NJ: Prentice-Hall, 1971.

"The Two Faces of Tania," in *Newsweek*. Vol. 72, no. 5. July 29, 1968, p. 45.

Karin Haag, freelance writer,
Athens, Georgia

Bunker, Carol Laise (1918–1991)

American diplomat. Born Carol Laise in 1918; died in Virginia in 1991; married diplomat Ellsworth Bunker, 1967.

Beginning her career with the State Department in 1948, Carol Laise Bunker rose to become ambassador to Nepal, where she served from 1966 to 1973. In 1967, she married Ellsworth Bunker, ambassador to Vietnam, with whom she maintained a commuter marriage, the first between two American ambassadors. She later went on to serve at the United Nations and as assistant secretary of state.

Buonaparte, Josephine (1763–1814).

See Josephine.

Buonoparte.

See Bonaparte.

Burbidge, Margaret (1919—)

English astronomer, distinguished for her research on the creation of galaxies and quasars, who became the first female director of the Royal Greenwich Observatory. Born Eleanor Margaret Peachey in Davenport, England, on August 12, 1919; daughter of Marjorie Stott Peachey and Stanley John Peachey; granted a B.Sc. from the University of London, 1939, Ph.D., 1943; married Geoffrey Burbidge (an astronomer), 1948; children: one daughter, Sarah Burbidge (b. 1956).

Awards: Shirley Farr Fellowship, Yerkes Observatory (1957); Helen B. Warner Prize of the American Astronomical Society (1959); member of the Royal Society of London (1964); president of the American Astronomical Society (1976); member of the American National Academy of the Arts and Sciences (1978); honorary D.Sc., Smith College (1963), University of Sussex (1970), University of Bristol (1972), University of Leicester (1972), City University, London (1974), University of Michigan (1978), Williams College (1979), State University of New York (1985), University of Notre Dame (1986), and University of Chicago; Bruce Gold Medal, Astronomical Society of the Pacific *(1982); president of the American Academy of the Arts and Sciences (1982); Lindsay Memorial Lecture, NASA (1985); Einstein Medal (1988).*

Enrolled at the University of London (1935); became assistant director of the London Observatory (1943–50); made acting director of the London Observatory (1950–51); became researcher, Yerkes Observatory (1951–53); became researcher, California Institute of Technology (1955–57); appointed associate professor, University of Chicago (1957–62); appointed associate research physicist, University of California at San Diego (1962–64); appointed professor, University of California (1964–84); served as Mauze Rockefeller professor, Massachusetts Institute of Technology (1968); became director of the Royal Greenwich Observatory (1971–73); made a member of the Anglo-Australian Telescope Board (1972–74); appointed *Virginia Gildersleeve professor, Barnard College (1974); appointed director of the Center for Astrophysics and Space Science, University of California (1979–88); named professor emeritus, University of California (1990).

Selected publications: "Distribution of Gas in Spiral and Irregular Galaxies," The Distribution and Motion of Inter-Stellar Matter in Galaxies: Proceedings of a Conference held at the Institute for Advanced Study (Princeton, N.J., April 1961); (with Geoffrey Burbidge) "Theories of the Origin of Radio Sources," IEEE Transactions of Military Electronics (Vol. 8. NY: Institute of Electrical and Electronic Engineers, 1964); (with Geoffrey Burbidge) Quasi-Stellar Objects (San Francisco: W.H. Freeman, 1967); "Radiogalaxies," Relativity Theory and Astrophysics: 2, Galactic Structures (J. Ehlers, ed. Providence, RI: American Mathematical Society, 1967); "Quasi-Stellar Objects," Annual Review of Astronomy and Astrophysics (Vol. 5, Palo Alto, CA: 1967); (with Geoffrey Burbidge) "Quasi-Stellar Objects-A Progress Report," Nature (London: Macmillan, 1969, vol. 224); (wrote foreword) Home is Where the Wind Blows (Mill Valley, CA: University Science Books, 1994).

Eleanor Margaret Burbidge was born in Davenport, England, on August 12, 1919. Little is known of her early life, save that she preferred to be called Margaret, and that her father Stanley Peachey was a lecturer in chemistry. In 1935, Margaret Burbidge enrolled at the University of London, graduating with a B.Sc. in 1939. She subsequently earned a Ph.D. in astrophysics. In 1943, she joined the Observatory of the University of London as assistant director. In 1948, she wed Geoffrey Burbidge, a co-worker and fellow astronomer. From 1950 until 1951, Margaret

Burbidge held the position of acting director at the Observatory of the University of London.

By the end of World War II optical astronomy in Britain was in decline. An increasing emphasis on theoretical and radio astronomy, as well as cloudy British skies and chronic underfunding, left British telescopes substandard and antiquated. In 1971, upon the retirement of Sir Richard Woolley as Astronomer Royal, Sir John Carrol referred to the "superannuated scrap heaps that constituted most of British astronomical equipment" at the time of Woolley's appointment in 1955. The lack of proper equipment initiated a "brain drain" among British optical astronomers. Promising young scientists such as Margaret and Geoffrey Burbidge, A. Dalgarno, T. Gold, and W.L.W. Sargent all departed for countries like the United States, where optical astronomy was taken seriously. Ironically, all five were subsequently elected as fellows of the Royal Society of London.

The Burbidges moved to the United States in 1951. While Geoffrey worked as a research fellow at the University of Chicago, Margaret

Margaret Burbidge

held a fellowship from the International Astronomical Union at the Yerkes Observatory in Williams Bay, Wisconsin. In 1955, the couple moved to California. There, Geoffrey held a Carnegie fellowship at the Mount Wilson Observatory, near Pasadena. Because women were ineligible for such fellowships, Margaret was forced to accept a junior teaching position at the California Institute of Technology. It was not the first time, nor the last, that gender bias interfered with her career.

Margaret Burbidge returned to the Yerkes Observatory in 1957 as a Shirley Farr fellow. She also held the position of associate professor at the University of Chicago. In 1962, she became an associate research physicist at the University of California. Two years later, she was promoted to the position of professor.

In 1959, along with William Fowler and Fred Hoyle, the Burbidges had been awarded the Helen B. Warner Prize for their paper "Synthesis of the Elements in Stars," published in the *Review of Modern Physics*. Commented Hoyle:

> Luck was certainly on our side, for we managed to find a whole series of results which pointed, I think conclusively, to the stars as being the main site of origin of chemical elements. We were able to go a long way towards understanding what might be called the "history of matter."

Margaret Burbidge's research built on results achieved by Paul Merrill, who had discovered spectral lines of unstable technetium in red stars. Due to the inherent instability of technetium, Merrill argued that its presence revealed the first evidence of the creation of elements. Margaret's research accepted the premise that most stars are largely composed of hydrogen. As stars grow, they produce helium from hydrogen. On earth, we see the released energy as starlight. Burbidge went on to argue that as stars mature they burn off some of their helium, producing other elements, such as oxygen and carbon. Oxygen and carbon may then trap hydrogen, which creates complex elements, such as silicon, argon, magnesium, sulphur, and calcium.

Margaret pointed to three other processes that may occur. One is the e-process, in which iron, cobalt, chromium, and nickel are formed due to extreme heat. When the "iron-peak" is reached, energy from the star is released. Beyond this point, additional energy is required to produce heavier elements. When an exploding star occurs, such as a supernova, the required amount of energy is released.

Burbidge also identified the r-process, in which the newly formed nuclei ensnare neutrons and are able to shed electrons. The resulting explosion produces elements such as bromine, krypton, selenium, xenon, tellurium, iridium, iodine, uranium, gold, and platinum. Margaret Burbidge's calculations provided a theoretical framework for measuring the production of different heavy elements in a supernova. She also theorized that a slower process, the s-process, also creates heavy elements in red giants.

Together with her husband, Margaret Burbidge published *Quasi-Stellar Objects* in 1967. Her research into quasars established that the ultraviolet radiation given off is the result of quasars receding at a great speed. This creates a spectrum shift towards red light, so that only a weak blue light is visible from the earth. During her research, she also discovered objects with red shifts, but no ultraviolet radiation. The Burbidges dubbed these quasi-stellar objects. Subsequent research by Margaret revealed that quasars and galaxies are intimately connected. Quasars tend to be located at the opposite end of bright galaxies, thus suggesting a yet to be determined dependent relationship, but one that put into question the Big-Bang Theory.

In 1971, Margaret Burbidge took a leave of absence as chair of astronomy at the University of California and returned to England, where she succeeded Sir Richard Woolley as the first female director of the Royal Greenwich Observatory. The circumstances of the appointment, however, were far from ideal. Tradition dictated that the positions of the director of the Royal Greenwich Observatory and that of Astronomer Royal be held concurrently. While Woolley retired as director of the observatory in 1971, he retained the title of Astronomer Royal. Although the staff of the Royal Greenwich Observatory protested to both the secretary of state for education and science, and to Prime Minister *Margaret Thatcher, no action by the British government was taken to remedy the situation.

On November 18, 1971, Margaret Burbidge held a news conference in London. As *The Times of London* reported:

> This attractive middle-aged woman brings to the job a charm not usually associated with the realms of advanced astronomy. Whether this factor, added to her reputation, will be enough to steer her through some difficult times ahead is an open question.

Burbidge made it clear during the news conference that gender bias was at the heart of the decision to exclude her from the position of Astronomer Royal. She argued that men and women should by treated equally in the field of astronomy. What should have been one of the crowning achievements of her career thus became another example of the discrimination she faced.

Burbidge promised to focus her energies on research, rather than allowing administrative duties to consume her time. "I would be a poor director if I got too involved in administration when there was such a very able administrative staff already at work," she told *The Times of London.*

It had taken considerable effort on the part of the Science Research Council to persuade Burbidge to return to Great Britain. She had arrived with the understanding that she would work to revive optical astronomy in the British Isles. The field, however, was in disarray. In an article entitled "Scandalous Muddle in British Astronomy," published in *Nature*, her husband Geoffrey argued that optical astronomy in Britain was on its death bed. He then catalogued a long list of errors that had led to the departure of elite astronomers from Britain over the years, including the Burbidges.

In the article, Geoffrey reported that radio-astronomy and theoretical astronomy were on a sound footing. Years of underfunding and neglect, however, had rendered optical astronomy third rate. Major mistakes, he alleged, included the mis-sighting of the Isaac Newton Telescope, Britain's largest. The mistake rendered the instrument virtually useless, contended Geoffrey.

Other errors in judgment, such as the failure of Britain to join the European South Observatory Project, had left British astronomy far behind international efforts. While Europeans, Americans, Canadians, and Russians were all building observatories in northern Chile, British astronomers had failed to grasp the observational opportunities that the Chilean site presented. Instead, the British Government decided to build a large Schmidt telescope jointly with Australia. The decision was condemned by Geoffrey, due to the poor observational conditions of the site. Margaret subsequently echoed many of the same concerns, though her position at the time precluded her from voicing these opinions as forcefully.

From 1972 to 1974, Margaret Burbidge served on the Anglo-Australian Telescope Board and advocated a management strategy common to major observatories around the world. It was rejected by the board, largely due to its American origins. As well, Burbidge sat on the board when the Australian National University, a major participant in the project, attempted to seize control of the observatory. Only a meeting between Margaret Thatcher and Australian prime minister Malcolm Fraser finally resolved the impasse.

Controversy arose in 1973 when Margaret officially reported that the new Isaac Newton 98-inch telescope at the Royal Greenwich Observatory should be moved to a better location. The new telescope, which cost £1 million, could only be used a quarter of the time. British skies, she said, were simply too cloudy. Geoffrey had predicted just such a situation the year before. Margaret was supported in her views by professors Hoyle, Ruyle, and Redman of Cambridge University. She also noted the propensity of British astronomers to squabble among themselves and confided to *The Times of London* that she found the situation "quite repugnant."

After 16 months as the director of the Royal Greenwich Observatory, Burbidge resigned. The task had been a thankless one. In her letter of resignation, she cited the lack of support among expatriate British astronomers as one of the primary reasons she had found it impossible to rebuild optical astronomy in the United Kingdom. As well, the sighting of the Isaac Newton Telescope and the Anglo-Australia Telescope had proved to be sources of major frustration. She then returned to the University of California.

In 1976, Margaret Burbidge became the first female president of the American Astronomical Society. She was elected to the American National Academy of Sciences in 1978 and awarded the Bruce Gold Medal of the Astronomical Society of the Pacific in 1982. From 1979 to 1988, she was director of the Center for Astrophysics and Space Science at the University of California and would eventually become professor emeritus at the University of California at San Diego. Burbidge also served as the president of the American Academy of the Arts and Sciences. In 1984, she and a team of astronomers perfected a faint object spectrograph for NASA's Space Shuttle. She also was a member of the team that worked on the Hubble Space Telescope. In 1985, Margaret Burbidge gave the Lindsay Memorial Lecture at NASA. For a lifetime of scientific achievement, she was awarded the Einstein Medal in 1988.

Margaret Burbidge has been the recipient of honorary doctorates from Smith College, the University of Sussex, the University of Bristol, the University of Leicester, City University, the

University of Notre Dame, the University of Chicago, the University of Michigan, and Williams College. On May 19, 1985, she was awarded an honorary Doctorate of Science from the State University of New York. Burbidge was lauded by the institution for her "vigorous role in the promotion of scientific research" and her "encouragement of women and minorities to embark on scientific careers."

Never one to anticipate the linear progress of astronomy, Margaret Burbidge acknowledged the uneven rate at which astronomical discoveries have been made:

> As one looks back over the advances in astronomy and astrophysics during the past 50 or 60 years, one sees that the pathway is marked by sudden leaps forward, both by new observational opportunities and by striking instances of perceptive theoretical insight. These discontinuities are followed and spaced by stolid observational or theoretical research that breaks no new ground but tracks along the newly opened pathways, as on a plateau following a major upward step.

Despite the uneven rate of astronomical advances, Margaret Burbidge's work has always been in the forefront of that quest. Her research led to the discovery of pulsars and the source of supernovas. As well, her subsequent observations led to the first accurate estimates of galactic masses. Her work with her husband and Fred Hoyle suggested that heavy elements were perpetually created from light ones within stars. This put into question the Big-Bang Theory, proposing that it may not be the sole explanation for the creation of the universe. Margaret Burbidge's contributions to the field of astronomy have ranged from spectroscopy to nycleosynthesis. In the long run, the quality of her research has overshadowed any professional impediments she may have faced as a woman.

SOURCES:

Gascoigne, S.C.B., K.M. Proust, and M.O. Robins. *The Creation of the Anglo-Australian Observatory.* Cambridge: Cambridge University Press, 1990.

Golemba, Beverly E. *Lesser-Known Women: A Biographical Dictionary.* Boulder, CO: Lynne Reinner, 1992.

Hoyle, Fred. *Home is Where the Wind Blows: Chapters from a Cosmologist's Life.* Mill Valley, CA: University Science Books, 1994.

Mitton, Simon, ed. *The Cambridge Encyclopaedia of Astronomy.* NY: Crown, 1977.

Porter, Ray. *The Hutchinson Dictionary of Scientific Biography.* Oxford: Helicon, 1994.

Ridpath, Ian, ed. *The Illustrated Encyclopedia of Astronomy and Space.* NY: Crown, 1979.

Hugh A. Stewart, M.A.,
University of Guelph,
Guelph, Ontario, Canada

Burchenal, Elizabeth (1876–1959)

American founder and educator who was head of the American Folk Dance Society. Born Flora Elizabeth Burchenal in Richmond, Indiana, around 1876; died in Brooklyn, New York, on November 21, 1959; the second of six children; obtained A.B. in English from Earlham College, Richmond, Indiana (1896); received diploma from Dr. Sargent's School of Physical Training (later part of Boston University), Boston, Massachusetts (1898).

As a child, Elizabeth Burchenal was strongly influenced by her mother, a musician and cultural enthusiast. In addition to six children, the Burchenal house was often filled with foreign visitors who were encouraged to join in the singing and dancing that provided the family entertainment. Burchenal recalled these early experiences as her first training in folk dancing, which would later become her life's passion.

After graduating from Earlham College, she studied at Boston's Dr. Sargent's School of Physical Training (later part of Boston University). Burchenal began her teaching career in Boston, moved on to Chicago, and took a position at Teacher's College at New York's Columbia University in 1903. At Columbia, she began to experiment with the theories of dance educator Melvin Gilbert, who advocated incorporating dance into physical-education classes. She subsequently worked for the city's public schools, holding positions as executive secretary of New York Public Schools Athletic League (Girls' Branch) and inspector of athletics for the New York Department of Education. During this period, she introduced innovative dancing programs for girls and organized folk festivals in Central Park that often attracted as many as 10,000 school children.

Retiring from the New York public-school system in 1916, Burchenal founded the American Folk Dance Society, through which she advocated her belief that folk dancing could be used to "bridge cultural and social gaps." As a national representative with the War Workers Community Service after World War I, she attempted to ease racial and ethnic problems through cultural and social programs that utilized dance. In 1928, she represented American folk dance at the first International Congress of Folk Arts, organized by the League of Nations in Prague, Czechoslovakia. A year later, the Folk Dance Society became a division of the National Committee of Folk Arts (NCFA), with Burchenal taking over directorship of the larger organization.

Throughout her career, Elizabeth Burchenal traveled and lectured in the U.S., Canada, and Europe and wrote numerous articles, as well as 15 books, on folk dancing. She established the Archive of American Folk Dance and was a fellow of the American Academy of Physical Education. In 1943, Boston University awarded her an honorary doctor of science degree. Burchenal remained active almost to her death at age 83 in Brooklyn, New York, where it is reported that her friends danced in tribute at her funeral.

Barbara Morgan,
Melrose, Massachusetts

Burdett-Coutts, Angela
(1814–1906)

English heiress who spent a large part of her fortune on various charitable causes, especially to help the very poor. Name variations: Baroness Burdett-Coutts of Highgate and Brookfield; took the name Coutts by royal license, 1837; surname sometimes unhyphenated; created baroness in 1871. Pronunciation: Coots. Born Angela Georgina Burdett on April 21, 1814, in London, England; died in London on December 30, 1906; daughter of Sir Francis (a politician) and Sophia

Angela Burdett-Coutts

(Coutts) Burdett; educated by private tutors; married William Ashmead-Bartlett, 1881; no children.

Awards: raised to the peerage (1871); Freedom of the City of London (1872); Freedom of the City of Edinburgh (1874); Order of Medjidie, conferred by the sultan of the Ottoman Empire (1878); Lady of Grace of the Order of St. John of Jerusalem (1888).

Selected publications: A Summary Account of Prizes for Common Things offered and awarded by Miss Burdett Coutts at the Whitlands Training Institution (Hatchard, 1856); (editor) Women's Mission: a series of congress papers on the philanthropic works of women (Sampson Low, 1893).

On Wednesday August 9, 1837, two days after her death, the relatives of ◄⏃ **Harriot Mellon**, duchess of St. Albans, gathered to hear the reading of her last will and testament. To the astonishment of those present, the greater part of her fortune, including the profits from half the shares in the banking house of Coutts, went to her stepgranddaughter, a tall, thin young woman, hardly pretty, although possessing a lively intelligence and much physical energy. Thus Angela Burdett was immediately transformed into the richest and, it was said, the most eligible heiress in England. Almost as immediately, numerous suitors appeared. "No young man of good family," according to the *Dictionary of National Biography,* "abstained from a proposal," but "she declined all advances and devoted herself exclusively to social entertainment and philanthropy, both of which she practiced at her sole discretion on a comprehensive scale and on the highest and most disinterested principles."

The birth of Angela Burdett was a result of the fusion between an older, aristocratic landed order and a newer, commercial elite. Her father,

---

⏃► **Mellon, Harriot** (c. 1777–1837)

*English actress and duchess of St. Albans. Born around 1777 in London, England; died in 1837; married Thomas Coutts (a banker), 1815 (d. 1822); stepgrandmother of **Angela Burdett-Coutts**; married William Aubrey de Vere, 9th duke of St. Albans, 1827.*

Harriot Mellon made her acting debut in 1787, and from 1795 to 1815 appeared at Drury Lane. In 1815, she married her elderly protector Thomas Coutts, a banker and sole partner of the banking firm, Coutts & Co., who left his entire estate to her when he died in 1822. In 1827, she married William Aubrey de Vere, the ninth duke of St. Albans.

Sir Francis Burdett (1770–1844), though born into a family that could be traced back over many generations, was a vigorous critic of the existing political order. His radicalism, at a time when the government was facing popular unrest at home and the turmoil of the French Revolutionary wars abroad, led to his arrest and a brief period of imprisonment. At the time of Angela's birth, he was the Member of Parliament for Westminster, the constituency at the center of London. The family of the woman he married in 1793, **Sophia Coutts**, had reluctantly agreed to the match, although the father of Sir Francis also had reservations about the suitability of the nouveau riche Coutts family. Sophia's father Thomas Coutts came from a Scottish family that had moved from trade into banking with so much success that King George III was a client. Sophia's mother had been a domestic servant in the Coutts' household, another reason for the disapproval of the Burdett family. What were widely regarded as irregular marriages twice more affected the course of Angela's life.

Sir Francis and Sophia Burdett had six children, one son and five daughters; Angela was the youngest. She received the education deemed appropriate to her social position: personal tutors and travel abroad (between the ages of 12 and 15, she mainly toured Europe with her mother and became fluent in French, German and Italian). Her father's London house was a center of literary and political debate, into which, as she became older, Angela was drawn.

In 1815, the wife of Thomas Coutts died. A few days later, and at the age of 80, he remarried. His second wife Harriot Mellon, a 38-year-old actress, inherited his entire fortune when he died in 1822. These events were the cause of much gossip, and further opportunity for disapproving comment arose in 1827 when Harriot married the much younger duke of St. Albans. At this time, Angela, still in her early teens, was on her European tour, but in later years she got on well with her stepgrandmother. The duchess was financially generous with her Coutts relations, who received a large part of her income. It is possible that these payments were made to forestall a legal challenge of the will left by Thomas Coutts, and Harriot might have undertaken to restore the family's inheritance in her own will. However, she did retain the freedom to decide which branch of the family would benefit. At one stage, she favored a cousin of Angela's, but he ruled himself out when he married one of Lucien Bonaparte's daughters—bigamously, as he later discovered, though Harriot's objection then was to a disreputably connected foreigner. She then decided that of her various relations Angela should be entrusted with her fortune, confident that she had the necessary qualities for the responsibilities that great wealth would bring. Her will did, however, limit the part that Angela could take in the running of Coutt's Bank and contained a provision to keep the family fortune from falling into the hands of a foreigner—this stipulation was, over 40 years later, to have its repercussions.

Angela entered into her inheritance at the age of 23 in 1837 when Harriot died (the duke of St. Albans was allowed the use of some family property during his lifetime; when he died in 1849 her wealth was further increased). Adding Coutts to her own name, Angela Burdett-Coutts moved from her father's house in St. James's Place to the substantial property adjoining Piccadilly that Harriot had occupied, 1 Stratton Place, where she lived for the remainder of her life. Burdett-Coutts was accompanied by her former governess **Hannah Meredith**, who until her death in 1878 assisted Angela's charitable work and was her closest friend.

During the 70 years following her inheritance, Burdett-Coutts supported a great range of charitable and other causes. In doing so, she to some extent reflected the conventional views of the time, and in retrospect some of her benevolence might seem misplaced. She advocated, for example, emigration as a solution to destitution but also as a means of extending the settlement of English stock in Canada, Australia, and South Africa. Her enthusiasm for colonization found an outlet in the financing of colonial bishoprics. In 1847, she endowed two bishoprics, in Cape Town and Adelaide, both of which were structured on the practices of the Church of England. A similar endowment was created in 1857 to provide British Columbia with a bishop; on this occasion, she made £50,000 available, a sum equivalent to several million pounds at present-day values.

In spite of her wealth, she lived in a relatively unostentatious style (although her collection of jewelry was worth a fortune). For some months of each year, she lived in Torquay, where the weather was milder. She also had a home in north London, Holly Lodge, the grounds of which were used for charitable garden parties. Much of her social entertaining was undertaken in connection with either her charitable efforts or to further other interests. Among the latter were the encouragement of scientific investigation; for example, she endowed the University of Oxford with two scholarships in 1861 for the study of

geology and presented the university with a collection of fossils. Kew Gardens, a leading botanical establishment, benefitted from her gifts of plant collections. Though progressive in such respects, her views on women's rights were not advanced. On the issue of women entering the medical profession, which was much discussed in the 1860s and 1870s, she told one correspondent that she feared it would lead to the breakdown of the "barriers of common decency."

She set a standard; her charity was given with style, without condescension and with kindness.

—Edna Healey

For many years, she collaborated closely with Charles Dickens, then equally prominent in the public eye as an author. He dedicated *Martin Chuzzlewit* to her and based one of the novel's most vivid characters, the old-fashioned nurse Sarah Gamp, on a woman she had hired to look after Hannah Meredith during an illness. Dickens encouraged Angela to give money to the Ragged Schools, which provided a basic education for London's poorest and most neglected children. They also worked together to establish a home in which prostitutes might be redeemed. This initiative led to the opening in 1847 of Urania Cottage. Women rescued from the streets were encouraged to learn respectable skills and were found situations (often, appropriate to her imperialist views, in the colonies). Her philanthropy operated whenever possible on the principle of "work, not alms." She encouraged schools that would provide practical training, in part by awarding prizes. Some of the educational provision was at a school attached to St. Stephen's Church, Westminster, a Gothic building endowed by her at a cost of more than £90,000 and opened in 1850, which commemorated her father, who was for many years Westminster's Member of Parliament. She assisted in the building of churches in poor areas in order that there should be not only the provision of spiritual values and the distribution of alms but also the coming into being of clubs and societies dedicated to self-improvement and mutual assistance through which the clergy could encourage their parishioners to better themselves in all respects.

Other efforts to help the poor included the erection of model dwellings. In 1862, four blocks of tenements, with accommodation for over 1,000 people, were opened in the Bethnal Green area of London, one of the poorest in the city. Angela Burdett-Coutts made a number of attempts to break the vested interests that controlled the capital's wholesale food markets in a way that caused higher prices. She paid over £200,000 for the construction of Columbia Market, a vast building, again in the Gothic style she and many Victorians favored, in the East End. It failed to serve the purpose for which it was designed and was one of her few unsuccessful projects.

On a more modest scale, she helped to initiate a Flower Girls' Brigade. This was intended to help the numerous girls, mostly in their early teens, who eked out a meager living by selling flowers in the better parts of London. In Clerkenwell, she set up a small workshop in which crippled girls were taught how to make artificial flowers as a means of supporting themselves. She tried to help unemployed weavers in the East End by training them for other forms of employment or by assisting them to emigrate. Though she realized that the enormous volume of hardship that existed would not be greatly reduced by these and by many other of her initiatives, the poor of London in particular held her in great regard.

Angela Burdett-Coutts' charity extended to animals. She was prominent in the Royal Society for the Prevention of Cruelty to Animals, both at the committee level and more publicly as a letter writer and speaker. She paid for drinking-troughs for the use of horses and, touched like many others by the story of Edinburgh's "Greyfriars Bobby," the dog that kept vigil over his master's grave, she erected in 1872 a fountain as a memorial. The costermongers of London were helped by the provision of stables for their donkeys. She encouraged the breeding of goats for the benefit of poor cottagers and became president of the British Goat Society; the milk from her own goats she sent to hospitals.

Though celebrated for her charitable work in the capital, she generously supported good causes in all parts of the United Kingdom, especially Ireland, where she believed fisheries would reduce poverty and accordingly helped with the purchase of boats. She admired *Florence Nightingale*'s medical work in the Crimean War and, with the help of Dickens, had a machine for drying clothes constructed and sent out to the Crimea. Some 20 years later, when the Russo-Turkish war was in progress, she helped to set up the Turkish Compassionate Fund, to which she contributed £2,000 for the aid of those peasants displaced by the advancing Russian army. At the end of the war, the sultan decorated her with the diamond star of the order of Medjidie and the grand cross and cordon of the Chafakar.

Convinced, as were many Victorians, of the civilizing influence of the British Empire, she supported various schemes for its extension. In the belief that the spread of missionary work would help to end the slave trade, she helped to finance the expeditions of David Livingstone, who became a friend, in East Africa. Her wealth and social position enabled her to befriend many politicians and builders of the British Empire. She encouraged Sir James Brooke, who had founded the kingdom of Sarawak, in Borneo, in 1842; she bought him a gunboat and put money into a model farm. In the late 1840s, she was so friendly with the old war hero and diplomat Arthur Wellesley, 1st duke of Wellington, that there were rumors of marriage, but he discouraged her overtures, pointing out the disparity in their ages. General Charles George Gordon was another friend, and she was one of those who pressed William Gladstone's government to mount an expedition to rescue Gordon from Khartoum. He died in 1885 at the hands of the Mahdi's forces before the grudgingly despatched help arrived, though she remained on cordial terms with Gladstone.

Queen *Victoria* had in 1871 conferred a unique honor, that of making Angela Burdett-Coutts a baroness: the raising of a woman to the peerage in recognition of her services had never happened before. Ten years later, however, the queen was far from pleased by an event that caused an immense stir in the upper reaches of English society. On February 12, 1881, the Baroness Burdett-Coutts, approaching her 67th birthday, married a man 27 years her junior, William Ashmead-Bartlett. He was American by birth, though he had lived most of his life in England and for some years had assisted the baroness in her good works. In particular, he had traveled on her behalf as an administrator of the fund to aid Turkish refugees and had caused her great anxiety with his falling ill. Many assumed Ashmead-Bartlett was merely a fortune hunter. Others dwelt on the motives of a woman who, having refused many offers of marriage in her youth, entered matrimony so late in life. Queen Victoria recorded in her journal on May 3, 1881, after the couple had been presented at court: "That poor foolish old woman Lady Burdett-Coutts was presented on her marriage with Mr Bartlett 40 years younger than herself. She looked like his grandmother and was all decked out with jewels—not edifying!" Elaborating on her theme, the queen wrote of the "mad marriage" as "a most lamentable act of self-abasement." Lady Burdett-Coutts seemingly ignored or was oblivious to such remarks. Perhaps, having grown up in the socially more relaxed atmosphere of pre-Victorian England, she underestimated the rigid proprieties that required those in the public sphere to have conventional private lives. If her husband, who took her surname, was embarrassed, her wealth ensured that he could live in an aristocratic style, of which he took full advantage. He was able to gain election in 1885 to the House of Commons, as MP for the Westminster constituency that he represented for many years.

After marriage there was some falling off in the amount of work undertaken by the baroness, though she still supported a great range of good causes. By marrying an alien she had, under the terms of her stepgrandmother's will, forfeited some of her income from Coutts' Bank. Nevertheless, among the ordinary people, she was regarded still with great respect and affection. Her example of charity work influenced others to take up similar causes. She always took a close interest in the schemes she supported and the good works she espoused. They involved a huge correspondence, innumerable visits and attendance at various meetings of committees or with groups of supporters. Many of the schemes she had initiated operated successfully for long periods. When organizers of the World Fair held in Chicago in 1893 required information on the philanthropic work of women, they turned to her, and she helped compile *Women's Mission,* which detailed the activities of some 300 individuals and organizations, an indication of the many-sided world of Victorian philanthropy.

In the longer term, many of the causes with which she was identified disappeared. As absolute poverty lessened, flower girls and others like them grew fewer; costermongers, and their donkeys, ceased to be a feature of metropolitan life; goats' milk was no longer of vital importance to cottage-dwelling peasants. The colorful exploits of Rajah Brooke and General Gordon, men once regarded as heroes of the British Empire, faded with the eclipse of that empire. In the 1950s, her model dwellings were pronounced unfit for human habitation and demolished. The Columbia Market building suffered the same fate in 1960, just a few years before legislation to preserve historic buildings that would probably have saved it. Historians with no particular respect for social status and those who believe in the insights offered by psychology have been less impressed than were the Victorians by private charity. From the age of 23, Angela's wealth tended to isolate her and led to a somewhat artificial style of life. Her enormous fondness for animals (she kept several pets as well as campaigning on behalf of animal charities) can be interpreted as a substitute for human affection and her controversial marriage, within three years of the death of her former governess and lifelong companion, gives further reason for regarding her as a "poor rich girl."

After Angela Burdett-Coutts died, of acute bronchitis on December 30, 1906, her private house in Stratton Street was opened to allow mourners to pass by her coffin. The decision that she should lie in state was unusual, yet over a period of two days tens of thousands paid their respects to a woman whose death was almost as much the end of an era as that of Queen Victoria a few years earlier. Her remains were interred in Westminster Abbey on January 5, 1907. William Ashmead-Bartlett, her widower, died in 1921.

SOURCES:

Anderson, J.P. "Burdett-Coutts, Angela Georgina," in *Dictionary of National Biography.* Second Supplement. London: Smith, Elder, 1912.

Healey, Edna. *Lady Unknown: The Life of Angela Burdett-Coutts.* London: Sidgwick & Jackson, 1978.

Johnson, Edgar, ed. *Letters from Charles Dickens to Angela Burdett-Coutts, 1841–1865.* London: Jonathan Cape, 1953.

Orton, Diana. *Made of Gold: A Biography of Angela Burdett-Coutts.* London: Hamish Hamilton, 1980.

Patterson, Clara Burdett. *Angela Burdett-Coutts and the Victorians.* John Murray, 1953.

Rutter, Owen, ed. *Rajah Brooke & Baroness Burdett-Coutts.* London: Hutchinson, 1935.

Wellington, Seventh Duke of, ed. *Wellington and his Friends: Letters of the First Duke of Wellington.* London: Macmillan, 1965.

SUGGESTED READING:

Owen, David. *English Philanthropy, 1660–1960.* Cambridge, MA: Harvard University Press, 1964.

COLLECTIONS:

Burdett-Coutts Papers, Bodleian Library, Oxford.

D.E. Martin, Lecturer in History, University of Sheffield, Sheffield, England

Buresova, Charlotte (1904—)

Czech-Jewish artist whose work documents her imprisonment at the Terezin-Theresienstadt concentration camp. Born in Prague, Czechoslovakia, in 1904; daughter of a tailor; married to a non-Jewish lawyer (divorced); children: one son.

Although Charlotte Buresova was born into modest circumstances in 1904 Prague, her parents did their utmost to foster her obvious artistic talents. By the age of six, she was drawing sketches of high quality, and her skills improved quickly as she excelled as well at her piano and French lessons. She married young, to a non-Jewish lawyer. By the 1930s, Buresova had become a leading artist in Prague and was part of that vibrant city's intellectual elite. When Nazi Germany occupied the Czech Republic in March 1939, Buresova divorced her husband with the intent of improving her son's chances of not being persecuted as a half-Jew under the new anti-Semitic racial legislation of the "Protectorate of Bohemia-Moravia," as the new occupation regime styled itself.

In 1942, the Jewish Buresova was deported to the Terezin-Theresienstadt concentration camp, 40 miles north of Prague. Established in late November 1941, this facility was a ghetto, a concentration camp, and a way station for Jews from Western and Central Europe en route to the extermination camp of Auschwitz. Although mostly populated by Czech Jews, Theresienstadt also incarcerated Jews from Germany, Austria, Denmark, and the Netherlands. This camp served as a propaganda facade designed to convince the outside world that Jews in Nazi-occupied Europe were living normal lives and even flourishing under the restrictions of the newly imposed racial laws of the Third Reich. In reality, living conditions at Theresienstadt were appalling, with heavy loss of life due to overcrowding and malnutrition.

Despite the terrible conditions, Buresova made heroic efforts to continue her work as an artist. Along with the many other artists imprisoned at Theresienstadt, she found ways to procure the materials necessary for her work. Not only paper and pencils, but even oils were found so that she was able to produce a significant number of sketches and paintings depicting the life around her. Hidden during the war, her work survived as a testimony of suffering and endurance. The Nazi administrators of Theresienstadt exploited the talents of the Jewish artists in the camp in a workshop called the *Lautscher Werkstätte*. Called the *Lautschana* by the artists forced to work in it, this facility produced a variety of artifacts such as toys, lamps, dolls, artificial flowers and other handicrafts, including leather goods. The Nazi staff sold these products outside the camp and pocketed the funds. The attractive, cheerful nature of these items, some of which survived the war and are now preserved in the Terezin Memorial Museum, stands in sharp contrast to the fate of their creators.

Despite the suffering that surrounded her, Charlotte Buresova refused to submit to despair. As in her 1942 oil painting "Deportation," the prisoners on their way to a terrible fate radiate a nobility and strength that have continued to move viewers. Buresova survived Theresienstadt and returned to her beloved Prague in 1945.

With virtually all of the city's prewar Jewish population murdered by the Nazis, she entered a transformed world of ghosts and painful memories, but she resumed her career, gaining new admirers for her powerful, truthful art.

In her 70s, Buresova gradually lost her eyesight but was able to see again after several operations. The terrible events of the 1940s continued to cast their shadow on her life and work into her old age, though she did not always dwell on her wartime experiences. Writing to a scholar, she noted, "Many people like to forget what happened. But I, though I was not damaged, cannot forget. It was terrible but it gave me much confidence and was a very hard school for my present life."

SOURCES:
Costanza, Mary S. *The Living Witness: Art in the Concentration Camps and Ghettos.* NY: The Free Press, 1982.
Feig, Konnilyn G. *Hitler's Death Camps: The Sanity of Madness.* London: Holmes & Meier Publishers, 1981.
Novitch, Miriam, Lucy Dawidowicz, and Tom L. Freudenheim. *Spiritual Resistance: Art from Concentration Camps 1940–1945.* Philadelphia: Jewish Publication Society of America, 1981.
Petrasova, Marketa. "Art in the Concentration Camp of Terezin," in *Judaica Bohemiae.* Vol 21, no. 1, 1985, pp. 50–61.
Starke, Käthe. *Der Führer schenkt den Juden eine Stadt: Bilder-Impressionen-Reportagen-Dokumente.* Berlin: Haude & Spenersche Verlagsbuchhandlung, 1975.
Yad Vashem Archives, Jerusalem.

John Haag, Associate Professor, University of Georgia, Athens, Georgia

Burger, Hildegard (1905–1943)

Austrian anti-Nazi activist and leading member of an underground Communist cell in Graz who was sentenced to death by the infamous People's Court. Born Hildegard Freihsl in Zeltweg, Austria, on November 6, 1905; executed in Graz on September 23, 1943; grew up in a militantly revolutionary family.

Born in Zeltweg, Austria, on November 6, 1905, Hildegard Freihsl grew up in a militantly Socialist family. Her father was a railway worker and committed trade unionist, while her mother, too, maintained distinctly radical political ideals. Hildegard's brother was also active in working-class organizations. Despite the imposition of a Fascist regime in Austria in 1934, Hildegard remained politically active by joining underground organizations. Convinced that only Communism could effectively fight domestic Fascism and German Nazism, after the German annexation of Austria in March 1938 she helped organize a tightly structured underground organization in Graz, the capital of the province of Styria. Her husband, much less politically militant, never approved of her dangerous activities.

In the fall of 1940, Hildegard Burger and Richard Zach, a young teacher, began producing and distributing an anti-Nazi newsletter, *Der rote Stosstrupp* (The Red Shock Troops). Her work included the perilous task of distributing this subversive literature in factories and workshops. Once the Graz office of the Gestapo had discovered copies of *Der rote Stosstrupp* in local industrial facilities, they were determined to destroy those responsible. Burger was arrested by the Gestapo in 1941. Because they were known to be militant anti-Nazis, her mother and brother were also arrested, and he was sent to the infamous Dachau concentration camp near Munich. Burger's husband, frightened for his own life though he had not participated in her activism, distanced himself from her, denouncing her as a traitor to the German Reich. At her trial before the infamous People's Court in Graz, Hildegard Burger was accused of high treason and of significantly contributing to "the Communist contamination of the Styrian industrial districts," and it was noted that even her volunteer work for the German Red Cross did not mitigate the destructive nature of her activities. Along with other members of her group who had been arrested, she was sentenced to death and "permanent loss of honor." Hildegard Burger was guillotined in Graz on August 23, 1943.

SOURCES:

Biographical file, Arbeitsgemeinschaft "Biografisches Lexikon der österreichischen Frau," Institut für Wissenschaft und Kunst, Vienna.

Weinzierl, Erika. *Emanzipation? Österreichische Frauen im 20. Jahrhundert.* Vienna and Munich: Verlag Jugend und Volk, 1975.

John Haag, Associate Professor,
University of Georgia, Athens, Georgia

Burgess, Renate (1910–1988)

German-born British art and medical historian. Born Renate Ruth Adelheid Bergius in Hanover, Germany, on August 2, 1910; died in London on August 15, 1988; daughter of Friedrich Bergius and Margarethe (Sachs) Bergius; educated in Berlin and Munich; received Ph.D. in art history, University of Munich, 1935; married Hans Burgess, 1950s.

Immigrated to Great Britain (1938); worked as a domestic, factory worker and office clerk (1938–44); worked as a nurse and midwife (1944–51); worked at General Nursing Council (1952–62); curator of paintings, prints and photographs at the Wellcome Institute for the History of Medicine (1964–80).

Renate Burgess was born in Hanover, Germany, on August 2, 1910, to Dr. Friedrich Bergius (1884–1949), a chemist whose innovations in the field of coal hydrogenation earned him a Nobel Prize in 1931, and **Margarethe Sachs Bergius**, who came from a cultured Jewish family. As a student in Berlin and Munich, Renate enrolled in art history, archaeology and French philology. She studied under the noted art historian Wilhelm Pinder and earned her degree in art history at the University of Munich in 1935. That year, the Nuremberg Laws stripped Renate of her German citizenship because of her part-Jewish ancestry. Unable to find a teaching post, she worked for the next 18 months in a Munich art gallery. Then, exercising considerable courage, she began teaching and doing social work for the Confessing Church (*Bekennende Kirche*), the branch of the Lutheran Church that rejected both Nazi racism and totalitarian attempts to create a unified state church.

Although she did not feel herself to be immediately threatened by Nazism, in 1938 Renate left Germany for England. Like the overwhelming majority of refugees from Nazi Germany, she arrived virtually penniless (having been allowed to leave with only ten Marks). The next years were difficult as she had to work at a series of jobs unrelated to art history—including domestic work, factory work, and routine secretarial tasks (for a while she worked for the Master of Downing College at Cambridge University)—but she remained undiscouraged. Theology was among her interests during these years, and she trained as a deaconess in the Church of England. Deciding against a life in the church, she took training in nursing and midwifery, working in several public-health hospitals as a nurse and midwife from 1944 to 1951. In the 1950s, she married Hans Burgess, a fellow refugee whose name was originally Juliusburger; the marriage would later end in divorce. From 1952 to 1962, Renate was a clerical officer and translator at the General Nursing Council.

Throughout these years, she retained a strong interest in art and art history, visiting London's galleries and museums. She also kept active as an art researcher, thanks to her mother's second husband, Dr. Werner Leibbrand, who occasionally called on her to carry out research projects at the Wellcome Institute for the History of Medicine, one of London's many superb research centers. In 1963, when Burgess applied for a typing job at the Wellcome Institute, her interviewer realized that she was qualified for the post of curator of the institute's vast collection of paintings, prints and photographs. Hired for the curatorial job, she began work on September 1, 1964.

At the age of 54, Renate Burgess began what would become a distinguished career in the area of medical bibliography and iconography. Her single greatest achievement during her career at the Wellcome Institute was the cataloguing of over 12,000 portraits and prints of physicians and other medical personages that had been collected by Sir Henry Wellcome between 1900 and 1936. With much of her time at the Wellcome Institute given to other researchers working there, she often spent evenings at the library of the British Museum to complete her research for the vast catalogue. When the catalogue, *Portraits of Doctors and Scientists in the Wellcome Institute,* was finally published in 1973, Burgess received accolades from reviewers and scholars as the world's leading expert on medical portraiture.

Burgess identified a number of notable paintings whose painters had hitherto remained unknown. Two of the most important were Adam Elsheimer's *St. Elizabeth Visiting a Hospital,* a canvas dating to 1598, and Joseph Wright of Derby's 1753 portrait of his brother, the surgeon Richard Wright. Burgess organized a number of exhibitions at the Wellcome Institute, including *Medicine in 1815, The History of Pharmacy, Chinese Medicine,* and *The Child in History.* Perhaps the most popular of her shows was the 1970 exhibition, *Dickens and Medicine,* which received the highest praise from both medical and literary experts. Although she officially retired from her post in 1980, Burgess continued working at the Wellcome Institute on an emeritus basis. She died in London on August 15, 1988.

SOURCES:

Bergius, Renate. *Französische und belgische Konsol-und Zwickelplastik im 14. und 15. Jahrhundert.* Würzburg: Konrad Triltsch Verlag, 1936.

"Dr. Renate Burgess," in *The Times* [London]. August 26, 1988, p. 14.

Schupbach, W. "Renate R.A. Burgess (1910–1988)," in *Medical History.* Vol. 33, no. 1. January 1989, pp. 120–123.

John Haag, Associate Professor,
University of Georgia, Athens, Georgia

Burgh, Elizabeth de (1295–1360).

See Clare, Elizabeth de.

Burgh, Elizabeth de (1332–1363).

See Elizabeth de Burgh.

Burghersh, Joan.

See Mohun, Joan.

Burgos, Julia de (1914–1953).

See de Burgos, Julia.

Burgundofara, Saint (d. 667).

See Fara.

Burgundy, duchess of.

See Hedwig (c. 915–965).
See Ermengarde of Anjou (1018–1076).
See Helia de Semur (fl. 1020–1046).
See Alix de Vergy (d. after 1218).
See Agnes Capet (1260–1327).
See Margaret of Flanders (1350–1405).
See Margaret of Bavaria (d. 1424).
See Isabeau of Bavaria for sidebar on Michelle Valois (d. 1422).
See Bonne of Artois (d. 1425).
See Isabella of Portugal (1397–1471).
See Margaret of York (1446–1503).
See Mary of Burgundy (1457–1482).
See Marie-Adélaide of Savoy (1685–1712).

Burgundy, queen of.

See Faileuba (fl. 586–587).
See Matilda Martel (943–c. 982).

Burian, Hildegarde.

See Burjan, Hildegarde.

Burjan, Hildegard (1883–1933)

Austrian social reformer who founded Caritas Socialis, to aid the poor, aged, and ill. Name variations: Burian. Born Hildegard Freund in Gorlitz an der Neisse, Silesia, on January 30. 1883; died in Vienna, Austria, on June 11, 1933; daughter of Adolf Freund (a merchant); studied in Berlin and Zurich; awarded Ph.D., University of Zurich, 1908; married Alexander Burjan, 1907; children: one daughter, Elisabeth.

Moved to Vienna (1909); converted to Roman Catholic faith and became involved in issues relating to social reform including abuses of child and domestic labor; active during World War I in alleviating the suffering of working-class families in Austria; founded "Caritas Socialis" (1918); elected as the only female deputy of the Christian Social Party to Austrian Parliament (1919); responsible for numerous social reforms during the First Austrian Republic (1919–33); founded "Bahnhofsmission" (1922); revived her "Soziale Hilfe" organization (1924); founded "St.-Elisabeth-Tisch" (1930); was close friend of Cardinal Piffl and Ignaz Seipel.

It is one of history's ironies that the social reformer Hildegard Burjan, one of the most influential and respected Roman Catholic women in 20th-century Austria, was born in the German Silesian city of Gorlitz an der Neisse, on January 30, 1883, into an assimilated, non-religious Jewish family that cherished the secular, humanistic values of 19th-century German culture. Her parents were strongly in favor of her receiving an excellent education, and when they moved to Berlin she was enrolled at the prestigious Charlottenschule. At age 16, she moved to Zurich to complete her secondary education at that city's respected Grossmunsterschule, graduating with honors.

Her studies at the University of Zurich brought her in contact with two powerful personalities, Professors Friedrich Wilhelm Foerster and Robert Saitschik. Both advocated a Christian humanism appropriate to an age of science, rationalism and rapid intellectual and social change. Deeply stirred by these ideas, she considered converting to Roman Catholicism at this time but some misgivings remained. In the spring of 1907, she married Hungarian-born Alexander Burjan, an engineering student. With Hildegard Burjan's 1908 graduation (magna cum laude in German philology) as a Doctor of Philosophy, a promising academic career appeared to be just on the horizon.

Events in the next several years were to radically change the course of Burjan's life. First, she and her husband moved to Berlin, where he began working for a major electric power corporation. Soon after their arrival in the German capital, Burjan became seriously ill. Barely surviving four major operations and seven months' hospitalization, Burjan believed that she owed her life to a "miracle" and to the nuns of Berlin's Catholic St. Hedwig's Hospital, whose compassion had seen her through the illness. Her previous doubts about Christianity evaporated, and she became an ardent convert to Roman Catholicism. Suddenly feeling out of place in Lutheran (and Socialist) Berlin, she informed her husband that she would prefer to live in a Catholic country, and when a career opportunity appeared for him in a telephone company in Vienna, they moved in the summer of 1909. Armed with suggestions concerning the Catholic world of Vienna, Frau Burjan quickly became part of the glittering social life of that imperial capital. More important for her, she became acquainted with leading Catholic prelates. The Burjans' first year in Vienna brought the birth of their daughter (and only child), Elisabeth. Strongly impressed by his wife's piety, Alexander Burjan also converted to the Roman Catholic faith.

Hildegard signed up for Countess **Lola Marschall**'s "social courses," which provided detailed insights into the serious problems of Vienna's poorer classes and the continuing need for both private charity and public legislation. At this time, she met and chose as her private confessor the Dominican monk Norbert Geggerle, forming a spiritual tie that would endure until her death more than two decades later. Impatient with purely theoretical discussions of the many social ills in Austria, Burjan gathered data on child labor and wrote a simple but eloquent pamphlet condemning this practice as totally unacceptable in a modern society on both moral and social grounds. This strong condemnation from a wealthy and socially prominent Catholic conservative with close ties to the hierarchy of the Austrian church stimulated public debate on this issue. Along with support from leading Social Democratic women like *Adelheid Popp, Burjan's agitation soon led to the abolition of child labor in Austria. During the years immediately preceding World War I, Burjan was also attentive to the sorry plight of Vienna's overworked and underpaid domestics, many of whom were poorly educated young women from rural areas.

The onset of World War I, greeted with immense enthusiasm by virtually all sectors of the population, soon led to major shortages of food, fuel and fiber. As is always the case in wartime, the poorer classes suffered the most. Burjan responded to their need by organizing the Verein "Soziale Hilfe" to purchase the basic elements of family survival on a wholesale basis in order to pass on the savings obtained to working women who found themselves increasingly hard-pressed to sustain their families. Supported by the Austrian church hierarchy, this organization appreciably improved the lives of at least 12,000 Austrian women. Burjan also organized sewing circles that enabled poor working women to produce articles of clothing that earned them modest but essential wages. The idea underlying these sewing circles was "education for self-help."

During the final phase of World War I, when the suffering of the masses in Vienna grew worse, Burjan founded a charitable organization named "Caritas Socialis," which would grow to become a major social agency of Austria's Roman Catholics in the next decades. By 1922, Caritas Socialis sisters were rendering assistance to the poor, aged and ill in Vienna and elsewhere in Austria. As the acknowledged founder of the organization, Hildegard Burjan had the role of an informal mother superior and general mentor. The beneficent role of Caritas Socialis in a society shattered by war was acknowledged even by its political adversaries. Although a bitter struggle raged between Catholic conservatives and Marxist Social Democrats, even militant socialists could find only words of praise for Hildegard Burjan.

The post-1918 Republic of Austria did not possess a viable economy and most of its citizens were demoralized by the immense problems faced by a new democracy in a Central Europe that smoldered with ethnic hatreds and class animosity. In this grim situation, Burjan founded, in 1922, the "Bahnhofsmission" to assist weary and impoverished travelers at train stations. In 1924, convinced that in time of peace the needs of society's outcasts and defeated must not be ignored, she revived her "Soziale Hilfe" organization. In 1930, as the world depression made conditions worse, she founded the "St.-Elisabeth-Tisch," which provided a simple but nourishing meal daily to some of Vienna's impoverished middle class.

By the early 1930s, Hildegard Burjan was in poor health, a result of her tireless work on behalf of the poor as well as the increasingly debilitating complications from her diabetes. She refused to cease her activities despite her physical decline. Burjan consulted on various social problems of the day with Chancellor Ignaz Seipel, a personal friend (and priest) whose own health was in rapid decline. She died on June 11, 1933, in Vienna, greatly mourned by Viennese of all faiths and virtually all political orientations. Only the growing Nazi Party despised both her and the Catholic Church to which she had been so devoted. With Burjan doubly cursed as a "blood-Jewess" and "disciple of Rome," the charitable organizations so closely linked with her name were banned in 1938 when Austria was annexed to Nazi Germany. After 1945, however, the Caritas Socialis organization was rapidly rebuilt, to the universal acclaim of the war-shattered people of Austria. Hildegard Burjan was proposed for sainthood after the Second Vatican Council, a slow process of beatification that still continues. In January 1983, her adopted country of Austria marked the occasion of the centenary of her birth by issuing a commemorative postage stamp in her honor. Her gravesite can still be visited in Vienna's Zentralfriedhof.

SOURCES:

Ackerl, Isabella, and Friedrich Weissensteiner. Österreichisches Personenlexikon. Vienna: Carl Ueberreuter Verlag, 1992.

Biographical file, Arbeitsgemeinschaft "Biografisches Lexikon der österreichischen Frau," Institut für Wissenschaft und Kunst, Vienna.

Burjan-Domanig, Irmgard. Hildegard Burjan: Eine Frau der sozialen Tat. Salzburg: Otto Müller Verlag, 1950.

Gellott, Laura S. "Mobilizing Conservative Women: The Viennese Katholische Frauenorganisation in the 1920s," in Austrian History Yearbook. Vol. 22, 1991, pp. 110–130.

Havelka, Hans. Der Wiener Zentralfriedhof. Vienna: J & V Edition, 1989.

Kuderer, Peter. Hildegard Burjan: Ein Leben werbender Liebe. Vienna: Selbstverlag der Caritas Socialis, 1953.

Rennhofer, Friedrich. Ignaz Seipel, Mensch und Staatsmann: Eine biographische Dokumentation. Vienna: Hermann Böhlaus Nachfolger, 1978.

Waach, Hildegard. Ein Pionier der Nächstenliebe, Hildegard Burjan: Skizze eines grossen Lebens. Vienna: Verlag Herder, 1958.

Weinzierl, Erika. Emanzipation? Österreichische Frauen im 20. Jahrhundert. Vienna and Munich: Verlag Jugend und Volk, 1975.

John Haag, Associate Professor,
University of Georgia, Athens, Georgia

Burk, Martha Jane (1852–1903).

See Cannary, Martha Jane (Calamity Jane).

Burka, Petra.

See Fleming, Peggy for sidebar.

Burke, Billie (1885–1970)

American actress who excelled in light comedy. Born Mary William Ethelbert Appleton Burke in Washington, D.C., on August 7, 1885; died in 1970; only daughter of William (a singing clown with Barnum and Bailey circus) and Blanche (Beatty) Hodkinson Burke (a widow with four grown children); educated in London and France; married Florenz Ziegfeld (the theatrical producer), 1914 (died, July 22, 1932); children: one daughter, Patricia Burke.

Feature films: Peggy (1916); (serial) Gloria's Romance (1916); The Mysterious Miss Terry (1917); Arms and the Girl (1917); The Land of Promise (1917); Eve's Daughter (1918); Let's Get a Divorce (1918); In Pursuit of Polly (1918); The Make-Believe Wife (1918); Good Gracious Annabelle! (1919); The Misleading Widow (1919); Sadie Love (1919); Wanted—A Husband (1919); Away Goes Prudence (1920); The Frisky Mrs. Johnson (1920); The Education of Elizabeth (1921); (unbilled cameo) Glorifying the American Girl (1929); A Bill of Divorcement (1932); Christopher Strong (1933); Dinner at Eight (1933); Only Yesterday (1933); Finishing School (1934); Where Sinners Meet (1934); We're Rich Again (1934); Forsaking All Others (1934); Only Eight Hours (1935); Society Doctor (1935); After Office Hours (1935); Becky Sharp (1935); Doubting Thomas

Billie
Burke

(1935); A Feather in Her Hat (1935); She Couldn't Take It (1935); Splendor (1935); My American Wife (1936); Piccadilly Jim (1936); Craig's Wife (1936); Parnell (1937); Topper (1937); The Bride Wore Red (1937); Navy Blue and Gold (1937); Everybody Sing (1938); Merrily We Live (1938); The Young in Heart (1938); Topper Takes a Trip (1939); Zenobia (1939); Bridal Suite (1939); The Wizard of Oz (1939); Eternally Yours (1939); Remember? (1939); The Ghost Comes Home (1940); And One Was Beautiful (1940); The Captain Is a Lady (1940); Irene (1940); Dulcy (1940); Hullabaloo (1940); Topper Returns (1941); One Night in Lisbon (1941); The Wild Man of Borneo (1941); The Man Who Came to Dinner (1942); What's Cookin' (1942); In This Our Life (1942); They All Kissed the Bride (1942); Girl Trouble (1942); Hi Diddle Diddle (1943); Gildersleeve on Broadway (1943); You're a Lucky Fellow Mr. Smith (1943); So's Your Uncle (1943); The Laramie Trail (1944); Swing Out Sister (1945); The Cheaters (1945); Breakfast in Hollywood (1946); The Bachelor's Daughters (1946); The Barkleys of Broadway (1949); And Baby Makes Three (1949); Father of the Bride (1950); Boy from Indiana (1950); Three Husbands (1950); Father's Little Dividend (1951); Small Town Girl (1953); The Young Philadelphians (1959); Sergeant Rutledge (1960); Pepe (1960).

Thanks to the cult status of the 1939 movie *The Wizard of Oz*, Billie Burke enjoys a once-a-year television comeback as the charming, ethereal, good witch Glinda, one of the twittery matron roles that so endeared her to audiences. Burke weathered the highs and lows of over five decades in show business, as well as a high-profile marriage to the notorious Florenz Ziegfeld. She once shared the formula for her longevity: "To survive in Hollywood, you need the ambition of a Latin American revolutionary, the ego of a grand opera tenor and the physical stamina of a cow pony."

Burke was born in Washington D.C. but at the age of eight followed her father's circus troupe—Billy Burke's Barnum & Great London Circus Songsters—to London, where she dutifully fulfilled her mother's wish that she become an actress. Borrowing her father's name, she made her first stage appearance in 1903 at the London Pavilion, singing "Mamie, I Have a Little Canoe," in a show called *The School Girl*. A hit, the show ran for two years and brought Burke some celebrity and better roles, including parts in *The Duchess of Dantzic, The Blue Moon*, and *Mrs. Ponderbury's Past*. In 1907, theater impresario Charles Frohman brought her back to New

York to co-star with John Drew in *My Wife*. The delicate-featured redhead soon became the toast of Broadway, with a string of admirers, including Mark Twain, Enrico Caruso, James Barrie and Somerset Maugham. It was Maugham who escorted her to a New Year's Eve party at the Astor Hotel where she met the renowned producer of the *Follies*, Florenz (Flo) Ziegfeld, who was newly divorced from actress *Anna Held. Burke would later say of that first encounter: "[E]ven if I had known then precisely what tortures and frustrations were in store for me during the next eighteen years because of this man, I should have kept right on falling in love." After a whirlwind courtship, the couple eloped (with Burke's mother in tow) and were married in the back room of a parsonage in Hoboken, New Jersey. After a weekend honeymoon, the newlyweds made their first home in a hotel room.

In 1915, film pioneer Thomas Ince offered Burke an unprecedented $300,000 to appear in the film *Peggy*. She accepted but turned down a subsequent five-year contract knowing that if she stayed in Hollywood her marriage would not survive. She finally signed on to do a number of silents with Famous Players-Lasky (Paramount) who were based in New York, where she could keep tabs on the philandering Ziegfeld.

After the birth of their daughter in 1916, they moved into a house, Burkely Crest, in Hastings-on-Hudson, which Ziegfeld, a master of overkill, outfitted with a menagerie that included a herd of deer, two bears, two lion cubs, a variety of birds, an elephant, and later a pony that had been previously owned by the prince of Wales. The couple's lavish lifestyle included dinners for 40, nightly motion pictures, and camping trips to Canada that, according to Burke, "closely resembled a rajah on safari with carpets, ices, cooks, and distinguished guests."

After a series of silents, the best of which are considered *In Pursuit of Polly, Good Gracious Annabelle!*, and *The Misleading Widow*, Burke grew weary of the movies and returned to Broadway in such hits as Booth Tarkington's *Intimate Strangers* and Noel Coward's *The Marquise*. Mothering responsibilities and the illness of her own mother also occupied much of her time, as did continuing problems with Ziegfeld, who took up gambling and *Marilyn Miller almost simultaneously. When the stock market crash of '29 and a string of failures on Broadway brought Ziegfeld close to financial disaster, Burke went back to work in earnest. Her first character role in Ivor Novello's play *The Truth Game*, followed by another in *The Vinegar Tree*, led to a new image for the actress as a scatter-brained comedienne.

After Ziegfeld's death in 1932, the movies beckoned Burke once again, and she embarked on the second phase of her career, playing what she referred to as "my silly women." "These characters," she wrote, "these bird-witted ladies whom I have characterized so often . . . derived from my part in *The Vinegar Tree*. I am neatly typed today, of course, possibly irrevocably typed, although I sincerely hope not, for I should like better parts."

With *Bill of Divorcement* considered her talkie debut, other memorable efforts of this period were *Topper*, its sequel *Merrily We Live* (which earned her an Academy Award nomination), and the role of Glinda in *The Wizard of Oz*. Burke cited Glinda as her favorite film part—nearest to her stage roles. In 1936, she was an advisor on the film *The Great Ziegfeld*, in which she was portrayed by *Myrna Loy. Burke tried a straight role in *The Cheaters* in 1945, but audiences did not want to take her seriously, perhaps because they'd grown accustomed to her comedy, perhaps because her voice, always slightly high pitched, became more "birdy" with age.

In 1949, Burke wrote the first of her memoirs, *With a Feather on My Nose*. By that time, she had moved to a modest home in West Los Angeles, next door to her daughter and three grandchildren. Still busy, she continued to work until her retirement in 1953, after which she was lured out for only a few plays in stock, including *The Solid Gold Cadillac*, and some very small movie roles. Her second autobiography, *With Powder on My Nose*, was published in 1959, 11 years before her death in 1970.

SOURCES:

Burke, Billie. *With a Feather on My Nose*. NY: Appleton-Century-Crofts, 1949.

Shipman, David. *The Great Movie Stars: The Golden Years*. Boston, MA: Little, Brown, 1995.

Barbara Morgan,
Melrose, Massachusetts

Burke, Martha Jane (1852–1903).

See Cannary, Martha Jane (Calamity Jane).

Burke, Selma Hortense

(1900–1995)

African-American sculptor who, among other works, created the profile of Franklin D. Roosevelt that appears on the U.S. dime. Born in Mooresville, North Carolina, in 1900; died on August 29, 1995, in Newtown, Pennsylvania; seventh of ten children of an African Methodist Episcopal Zion minister and Mary L. Burke; attended Slater Industrial and State Normal School (later Winston-Salem State University); attended Saint Agnes Training School for Nurses, Raleigh, North Carolina; attended Women's Medical College in Philadelphia, Pennsylvania; studied art at Sarah Lawrence College; MFA, Columbia College, 1941; twice married poet Claude McKay (twice divorced); married Herman Kobbe (an architect), late 1940s (died, 1950s).

Although Selma Burke is remembered as the sculptor who created the profile of Franklin D. Roosevelt that appears on the United States dime, she created many other critically acclaimed works in her lifetime. In a career that spanned the Harlem Renaissance, the Depression, and two world wars, Burke was still going strong in her 90s, sometimes working on three or four projects at a time.

As a child, Selma Burke's creative impulses were soon apparent as she worked with clay dug out of a dried-up river bed near her home, fashioning butterflies and other forms. To appease her mother's wish that she prepare for a field more lucrative than art, she attended nursing school but returned to her art studies when a wealthy woman for whom she was working urged her to follow her passion. Burke moved to Philadelphia and began studying sculpture at the Leonardo da Vinci School. She then worked at New York's Cooper Union before receiving scholarships to Sarah Lawrence and Columbia College, both of which she attended, earning her MFA at Columbia in 1941. She next traveled to Europe, where she studied architecture with Frank Lloyd Wright and Josef Hoffman. In Paris, she consulted with painter Henri Matisse, later recalling, "He said that I had a big talent and he wanted me to add size and volume to my drawings. He wanted me to open up as a person."

The sculpture that appears on the dime was Burke's winning entry in a 1943 competition to design a portrait of President Franklin Roosevelt for a plaque to adorn a new federal building in Washington (unveiled by President Harry S. Truman in 1945). Her portrait of Roosevelt was made on butcher paper in a 45-minute session with the president and was later criticized by *Eleanor Roosevelt as making her husband look too young. Said Burke to the first lady, "I've not done it for today, but for tomorrow and tomorrow."

Her other well-known works include the bust of Duke Ellington at the Performing Arts Center in Milwaukee; portraits of Booker T. Washington and *Mary McLeod Bethune; the eight-foot bronze statue of the Rev. Dr. Martin Luther King at Marshall Park, Charlotte, North Carolina; and sculptures of John Brown and President Calvin Coolidge. Calling Burke the "grand dame of African-American artists," **Nanette Acker-Clark,** director of the Afro-American Museum in Philadelphia, also regarded her as significant to American art in general.

Burke devoted much of her life to teaching art and sculpture. She taught at Livingston College, Swarthmore College, and Harvard University, as well as Friends Charter School in Pennsylvania and Harlem Center in New York. She founded the Selma Burke Art Center in Pittsburgh and the Selma Burke School of Sculpture in New York. The Selma Burke Gallery, which opened in 1983 at Winston-Salem State University, was her longtime dream; the gallery contains over 100 works from her private collection as well as works of other prominent artists such as Romare Bearden, Richard Satterwhite, and Claude Ward. In 1990, the gallery was moved to Johnson C. Smith University in Charlotte, North Carolina.

Burke was married to poet Claude McKay, whom she divorced, remarried, and divorced again. Her second marriage to architect Herman Kobbe ended with his death in the 1950s. Once telling an interviewer that "art was enough," Burke had no children. She died at the age of 94 in a nursing home and hospice in Newtown, Pennsylvania.

Barbara Morgan,
Melrose, Massachusetts

Burke, Yvonne Brathwaite (1932—)

First African-American woman to be elected to the California General Assembly and California's first black congresswoman (Democrat, 93rd–95th Congresses, January 3, 1973–January 3, 1979). Name variations: Yvonne Brathwaite. Born Pearl Yvonne Watson in Los Angeles, California, on October 5, 1932; only child of James T. (a janitor at MGM film studios) and Lola (Moore) Watson; attended University of California at Berkeley, 1949; granted B.A. degree from University of California at Los Angeles, 1953; J.D. degree, University of Southern California School of Law, 1956; married Louis Brathwaite in 1957 (divorced, 1964); married William A. Burke, June 14, 1972; children: (second marriage) Autumn Roxanne (b. 1973) and stepdaughter, Christine.

Yvonne Burke was the first black woman to be elected to the California General Assembly, as well as the first to represent California in the U.S. Congress. In 1973, she was the first congressional representative to be granted a maternity leave, and in 1976 the first woman selected to chair the Congressional Black Caucus. An outspoken and articulate advocate of social welfare, Burke described Congress as a way to make a difference. "I want to be able to look back and say there are people whose lives are better because I served there."

An only child, Burke grew up on the East Side of Los Angeles in what she called an "integrated slum with lots of yards and trees." Her parents struggled to provide her with a decent education, including music and speech lessons. From public school, she transferred to a model school affiliated with the University of Southern California where, as the only black student, she endured occasional racial taunts. At Manual Arts High School, she excelled. With the help of a scholarship from her father's union and her own part-time work, she graduated from the University of Southern California at Los Angeles before going on to law school, supporting herself by modeling. When the campus women's law society refused to admit blacks and Jews, Burke and two Jewish students started another professional society.

Admitted to the California state bar in 1956, Burke went into private practice. In 1957, she married Louis Brathwaite whom she later divorced. (She would marry William A. Burke in 1972.) In addition to her law practice, she served as the state's deputy corporations commissioner and as a hearing officer for the Los Angeles Police Commission. In 1965, she was an attorney for the McCone Commission, which was established to investigate the causes of the Watts' riot. She also worked with a NAACP legal defense team, preparing a report on housing conditions in the Los Angels area. Burke received the NAACP's Loren Miller Award in recognition of her efforts on behalf of the California legal system.

Her run for the California General Assembly required that she first defeat six male opponents in the primary and then endure a campaign in which her ultra-conservative opponent accused her of being a black militant and a Communist. Elected to the Assembly for three terms, she supported prison reform, child care for the underprivileged, equal job opportunities for women, and increased federal aid to education. She also introduced legislation to require licensing of nursing homes, to provide day care on college campuses and to in-

Yvonne Brathwaite Burke

sure truth in packaging and drug labeling. After trouncing her conservative Republican opponent with 73% of the vote in the November 1972 Congressional election, Burke remarked, "There is no longer any need for anyone to speak for all black women. I expect *Shirley Chisholm is feeling relieved." In her bid for reelection in 1974, Burke was elected to a second term, beating her opponent by over 66,000 votes.

During her tenure in Congress, Burke served on the Committee on Interior and Insular Affairs and later transferred to the Committee on Appropriations, where she called for additional federal funding of community nutrition programs. She also supported funding for the resettlement of Vietnamese refugees and supported the Humphrey-Hawking bill for full employment. In 1977, Burke joined several other members in securing a human-rights amendment to the foreign-aid bill, and she supported other efforts to pressure foreign governments guilty of human-rights violations. She also worked to restore planning grants from Housing and Urban Development. That same year, she introduced the Displaced Homemakers Act, which authorized job training for women entering the labor market.

Burke did not seek reelection for a third term in 1978, choosing instead to run for California attorney general. Failing to win the election, she was appointed to the Los Angeles County Board of Supervisors, where she served from June 1979 until her resignation in December 1980. She then returned to her Los Angeles law practice. In 1992, she was elected to a four-year term as a Los Angeles County Supervisor; she was re-elected in 1996.

SOURCES:

Moritz, Charles, ed. *Current Biography 1975*. NY: H.W. Wilson, 1976.

Office of the Historian. *Women in Congress, 1917–1990*. Commission on the Bicentenary of the U.S. House of Representatives, 1991.

Barbara Morgan,
Melrose, Massachusetts

Burke Sheridan, Margaret (1889–1958).

See Sheridan, Margaret Burke.

Burlin, Natalie Curtis (1875–1921)

American musicologist and student of Native American and African-American music. Born Natalie Curtis in New York City on April 26, 1875; died in Paris, France, on October 23, 1921; attended the National Conservatory of Music, New York; married Paul Burlin (a painter), July 1917.

Natalie Burlin considered a career as a concert pianist before turning her attention to the study of Native American music. She first became fascinated with the customs and lore of the Arizona Native Americans on a trip there in 1900. Visiting the villages and camps of the Zuñi, Hopi, and other tribes, she recorded their songs, poetry, and stories. In 1907, Burlin published a major work entitled *The Indians' Book*, which contained music and lore from 18 tribes, primarily Southwestern but also from as far away as Maine and British Columbia. The work enjoyed two later editions and remains a major source book for students and scholars.

Also interested in the performance and preservation of African-American music, Burlin joined David Mannes in 1911 to organize the Music School Settlement for Colored People in New York City. She was also instrumental in arranging the first concert of African-American music performed by black performers at Carnegie Hall, in March 1914. Burlin produced a number of volumes of African-American music, including the four-volume *Hampton Series Negro Folk-Songs* (1918–1919), the result of a period of study at the Hampton Institute in Virginia, and *Songs and Tales from the Dark Continent* (1920). Natalie Burlin was killed by an automobile while in Paris to address a congress of art historians.

Burnell, Jocelyn Bell (1943—)

Irish astronomer who discovered the first four pulsars.
Name variations: S.J. Bell; S. Jocelyn Bell Burnell; Jocelyn Bell-Burnell. Born Susan Jocelyn Bell on July 15, 1943, in Belfast, Northern Ireland; daughter of George Philip and Margaret Allison (Kennedy) Bell; attended Mount School, York; Glasgow University, B.Sc. 1965; Cambridge University, Ph.D., 1968; married Martin Burnell 1968 (divorced, 1989); children: Gavin.

Awards: honorary D.Sc. from universities of Heriot-Watt (1993), York (1994) Newcastle (1995) and Warwick (1995); Michelson Medal, Franklin Institute (1973); J. Robert Oppenheimer Memorial Prize, University of Miami (1978); Rennie Taylor Award, American Tentative Society (1978); Beatrice M. Tinsley Prize, American Astronomical Society (1987); Herschel Medal, Royal Astronomical Society (1989).

Was research fellow, University of Southampton (1968–73); served as research assistant, Mullard Space Science Lab, University College, London (1974–82); served as senior research fellow (1982–86), senior science officer (1986–89), Grade 7 (1989–91), Royal Observatory, Edinburgh; served as professor of physics, Open University, Milton Keynes (1991—).

Selected publications: (with A. Hewish, et al.) "Observation of a Rapidly Pulsating Radio Source" (Nature, 1968); Broken for Life (1989).

Jocelyn Bell Burnell's principal contribution to astronomy is her discovery of the first four pulsars during her Ph.D. research in radio astronomy, a discovery that netted a Nobel Prize for her thesis advisor.

Born Susan Jocelyn Bell on July 15, 1943, in Belfast, Northern Ireland, the eldest of four children of architect George Philip Bell and **Margaret Kennedy Bell**, both Quakers, she was raised in her family's country house surrounded by nannies and nursemaids. At age 11, she failed the college-preparatory placement exam; two years later, her family sent her to Mount School, a Quaker boarding school for girls in York, England. She would remain an active Quaker throughout her life. While there, Burnell became increasingly interested in astronomy and read through the astronomy shelves in the school library.

After graduating in 1961, she attended the University of Glasgow, majoring in physics rather than astronomy after considering future job prospects. As the only woman in her upper-level courses, she suffered considerable harassment. Graduating with honors in 1965, she began graduate studies at Cambridge University, arriving just as noted astronomer Antony Hewish began construction of a new radio telescope designed to study quasars. Hewish became Burnell's thesis advisor, and she spent two years constructing the 4.5 acre radio array. When the telescope began operation in July 1967, Burnell was in charge of data analysis. Several months later, she noticed a strange, rapidly varying signal that was later followed by the discovery of three similar signals. Burnell, Hewish, and their associates carefully analyzed the signals before publishing their results in 1968. Burnell completed her thesis that year, with the pulsars appearing in an appendix.

Upon graduation, Burnell switched to X-ray astronomy and took a position at the University of Southampton in order to be near soon-to-be husband Martin Burnell's government job. She resigned in 1973 after the birth of son Gavin. The following year, she began part-time work in X-ray astronomy at University College, London. During this time, her former thesis advisor Hewish was awarded the Nobel Prize in Physics in part for his "decisive role on the discovery of pulsars." Famed astronomer Fred Hoyle and others openly questioned the failure of the Nobel Committee to include Burnell in the award.

Burnell switched positions once again as her husband's job relocated in 1982, becoming Senior Research Fellow at the Royal Observatory in Edinburgh and, from 1986 to 1989, the manager of the international James Clerk Maxwell Telescope project. In 1989, the Burnells divorced. In 1991, Jocelyn signed on as professor of physics at the Open University at Milton Keynes.

The diagnosis of her son's juvenile diabetes was the major impetus for Burnell's published Swarthmore lecture, *Broken for Life* (1989). Although not a Nobel Prize recipient, she has received copious awards, including several honorary doctorates, the Michelson Medal (awarded jointly with Hewish in 1973), the first Beatrice Tinsley award of the American Astronomical Society (1987) and the Herschel Medal of the Royal Astronomical Society in 1989. The discovery of pulsars, Burnell wrote, "could not have been accomplished without a lot of luck and hard work. In return it has brought me enormous enjoyment, some undeserved fame, and opportunities to get to know many interesting people—marvelous rewards in themselves."

SOURCES:
Graham, Judith, ed. *Current Biography Yearbook 1995.* NY: H.W. Wilson, 1995.

Jones, Glyn. "When Stardom Beckoned," in *New Scientist.* July 18, 1992, p. 3639.
McGrayne, Sharon Bertsch. *Nobel Prize Women in Science.* Secaucus, NJ: Carol Publishing Group, 1993.
SUGGESTED READING:
Burnell, Jocelyn Bell. "Petit Four," in *New York Academy of Science Annals.* Vol. CCCII, 1976, p. 685–689.
Burnell, S. Jocelyn Bell. "Little Green Men, White Dwarfs, or What?" in *Sky and Telescope.* March 1978, p. 218–221.
Reed, George. "The Discovery of Pulsars: Was Credit Given Where it Was Due?" in *Astronomy.* Vol. 11, no. 12, 1983, p. 24–28.
Wade, Nicolas. "Discovery of Pulsars: a Graduate Student's Story," in *Science.* Vol. CLXXXIX, 1975, p. 358–364.

Kristine Larsen,
Associate Professor of Physics and Earth Sciences,
Central Connecticut State University,
New Britain, Connecticut

Burnett, Frances Hodgson
(1849–1924)

English-American author of novels and stories for children and adults, including **The Secret Garden, Little Lord Fauntleroy,** *and* **The Little Princess.** *Born Frances Eliza Hodgson on November 24, 1849, on York Street, Cheetham, Manchester, England; died on Long Island, New York, on October 29, 1924; third of five children of Edwin (a silversmith and dealer in hardware and interior furnishings) and Eliza (Boond) Hodgson (a homemaker); married Swan M. Burnett, September 19, 1873 (divorced, 1898); married Stephen Townesend (a physician and actor), 1900 (divorced, 1901); children: (first marriage) Lionel (1874–1890); Vivian (1876–1937).*

Immigrated to Tennessee (1865); published first stories at 17 and first novel, That Lass o'Lowrie's *(1877); published* Little Lord Fauntleroy *(1886); A* Little Princess *(1905); The Secret Garden (1911); wrote over 50 books, adapted several for the stage, published stories in* Peterson's Ladies' *Magazine, Scribner's, Harper's, and St. Nicholas.*

Frances Hodgson Burnett once recalled that her life was "founded and formed upon books," claiming that her love of reading dated from the age of three when she picked out a verse from the New Testament. The middle child of five, Burnett spent much of her early childhood either immersed in books or dramatizing them with her dolls. She described herself as a "story maniac," one who was reprimanded for neglecting the friends she visited because of her avid interest in any book she happened to see lying on a table in their home. It is not surprising, then, that a girl who was addicted to reading as a child would become a writer as an adult.

Frances
Hodgson
Burnett

The Hodgson family was prosperous when Frances was born in 1849 in Manchester, England. Her father's business flourished as long as the mills in the newly industrialized city flourished. When Frances was four, however, her father died of apoplexy, leaving her mother with five children to raise and a business to run. **Eliza Hodgson** not only had little commercial experience, but the economy of Manchester was affected negatively by the American Civil War and the decline in trade. In 1855, Eliza Hodgson sold their comfortable house and moved the family to smaller quarters in Islington Square, a marginal area of the city. Frances was one of the "Square children" as distinct from the working class "Street children." She described her neighborhood as "a sort of oasis in the midst of small thoroughfares and back streets where factory operatives lived and where the broadest Lancashire dialect throve." Although forbidden to play with the Street children (at least in part because she might start speaking in their lower-class accent), Burnett found their customs, manners, and language fascinating and the poverty of their lives engrossing. In the square at Islington, she first came to know many of the characters who would later appear in her books. The Islington house also had a back garden, which stimulated her imagination, "There were rosebushes and lilac-bushes and

From the movie Little Lord Fauntleroy, *starring Mary Pickford.*

rhododendrons, and there were laburnums and snowballs. Elephants and tigers might have lurked there, and there might have been fairies or gypsies." Burnett began to turn some of her material into stories, writing mostly on her slate (which had to be erased as soon as it was covered with writing) or between the lines of old account books donated by the cook. Her stories, she recalled, were "wildly romantic and preposterously sentimental," but Frances began, even at the age of ten or twelve, to develop her talents for description and plots.

Economic distress led Eliza Hodgson to accept her brother's invitation to move the family from Manchester to the United States in May 1865. Unfortunately, the Hodgsons discovered when they arrived in Knoxville, Tennessee, that, after the Civil War, hard times also existed on the other side of the Atlantic. The three girls and their mother settled in a log cabin in the tiny community of New Market. Due to her mother's poor health and the family's poverty, Burnett turned her energies toward earning a living. She started a small school, raised chickens, and gave piano lessons. In 1867, after they had moved closer to Knoxville, Frances submitted her first story to a publisher. Her purpose, she wrote, was "remuneration." *Godey's Ladies Book* accepted her manuscript on the condition that she submit an additional story. At age 17, she published her first two stories, netting a total of $35. Her work was popular with readers who enjoyed the tales of worthy heroes and heroines who overcame hardship and bad luck, and soon Frances had stories accepted by more prestigious magazines, such as *Scribner's* and *Harper's*. After her mother's death in 1870, Burnett became completely responsible for supporting her sisters with the proceeds from her writing.

I do not know whether many people realize how much more than is ever written there really is in a story.

—Frances Hodgson Burnett

In 1872, she became engaged to an old New Market acquaintance, Dr. Swan Burnett. Before they married, however, she spent a year in England, financed by the proceeds from her writing. During her lifetime, she crossed the Atlantic 33 times, building a life and reputation in both Europe and the United States. After their 1873 marriage, the Burnetts lived in Knoxville; their first son Lionel was born there in 1874. Frances longed for a more pleasant climate and a more cosmopolitan setting, and, in 1875, they moved to Paris, where her husband studied with French eye and ear surgeons, financed by the proceeds from Frances' writing. During this time, her first novel *That Lass o'Lowrie's* was published in *Scribner's* as a serial and also appeared as a book. In 1876, she gave birth to her second son Vivian. The family returned to the United States, settling in Washington D.C. where Burnett continued the frantic pace of her writing to pay the household expenses. By 1878, she was exhausted. "Write—write—write. Be sick, be tired, be weak and out of ideas, if you choose; but write! . . . Does anyone ever think I ought to be happy?" And although Burnett continued to produce an incredible amount of work, her fame was assured after the 1886 publication of her first full-length children's story, *Little Lord Fauntleroy*.

Like several of her other popular stories, *Little Lord Fauntleroy* was a modern version of the Cinderella myth, this time with a male hero. The title evokes an image of a simpering little boy in a velvet suit, with his hair in long golden curls. Had the story really featured such a title character, it is unlikely it would have achieved its phenomenal popularity. Some of the unfortunate associations of the name Lord Fauntleroy come from the illustrations by Reginald Birch in the original edition. Based on photographs of Burnett's younger son Vivian wearing curls and velvet, the image became a plague to small boys and a delight to late Victorian mothers. The notion of the hero as a sissy was not helped by the inexplicable practice of casting girls in the title role in several stage and screen adaptations, including a 1914 movie starring a quite womanly *Mary Pickford. When Vivian died during a boating mishap off Long Island Sound in 1937, one headline screamed: ORIGINAL "FAUNTLEROY" DIES IN BOAT; the newspaper's subhead went on to say, "Vivian Burnett, Author's Son who Devoted Life to Escaping 'Sissified' Role, is Stricken at Helm—Manoeuvres Yawl to get 2 Men and 2 Women from Overturned Craft, Then Collapses."

Most critics agree that the actual *Little Lord Fauntleroy* was better than its reputation would suggest. It is the story of a brave, virtuous, and democratic American boy who wins over and reforms his arrogant and aristocratic grandfather. It includes unbelievable coincidences and a rather maudlin relationship between the little lord and his mother, called "Dearest." But compared to much of the contemporary children's literature, Burnett's "rags to riches" story was refreshingly unsentimental.

The success of *Little Lord Fauntleroy* brought several changes to Burnett—financial success, which she would work feverishly to maintain, and an increasing focus on writing for children rather than adults. Among the more than 20 books she wrote for a juvenile audience, two others are particularly important: *Sara Crewe*, which was revised and expanded to become *A Little Princess*, and *The Secret Garden*. Another story of the reversal of fortune, *A Little Princess* tells of a rich, pampered girl who is transformed into a virtual servant at Miss Michin's school when her father dies bankrupt. But because Sara is an essentially noble character, she triumphs over economic circumstances. Unlike *Fauntleroy*, which is told from an adult point of view, *The Little Princess* is related in Sara's voice. It benefits from less sentimentality and more autobiographical detail. Burnett recognized the importance of descriptive detail to her young audience. "It is not enough to mention they have tea," she said, "you must specify the muffins."

In 1911, Burnett published *The Secret Garden,* her most enduring work. **Marghanita Laski** called it "the most satisfying children's book I know." Much of the satisfaction and continuing appeal of the book come from Burnett's development of the major characters, Mary and Colin, from sickly and utterly unattractive to warm and healthy children through their creative work in the garden. *The Secret Garden* provides readers with models who come to believe in themselves and who follow their own consciences rather than the advice of their elders. On the other hand, the book ends with Mary in a secondary role to Colin, who seems to be assuming his place as the "natural" heir to the manor.

Burnett herself never played a subordinate role in her adult life, particularly as she always provided the majority of her family's income.

With her earnings from *Little Lord Fauntleroy* and *Sara Crewe,* Frances and her sons set out in 1887 for 16 months in Europe. From this time, she and Swan Burnett spent little time together; they were usually on different sides of the Atlantic. The marriage ended in divorce in 1898.

Although Frances enjoyed increasing popularity and financial success, her personal life included considerable sorrow and suffering. Her older son Lionel died of consumption just before Christmas of 1890. Her second marriage, to Stephen Townesend, lasted only a year. He was ten years younger than Frances, and it seemed she married him mainly as a reward for his assistance in Lionel's last illness. "He talks about my 'duties as a wife' as if I had married him of my own accord," she wrote a friend, "as if I had not been forced and blackguarded and blackmailed into it." Some critics have suggested that Burnett was ambivalent about her non-traditional role as money earner, and that she tried to reconcile her fame and fortune with the conventional female role by playing a sort of fairy godmother.

From the movie The Secret Garden, *starring Kate Maberly, Andrew Knott, and Heydon Prowse.*

During these years, Burnett rented a country house in England, called Maytham Hall. Some of the setting for *The Secret Garden* was drawn from its "nicely timbered park and beautiful old walled kitchen garden." The house included 17 or 18 bedrooms, as well as a library, billiard room, morning room, smoking room, drawing room, and several dining rooms. Burnett's writing had brought her a very long way from the log cabin in Tennessee—a reversal of fortune not unlike the experience in many of her stories. She published her autobiography, *The One I Knew Best of All,* in 1893. It was originally intended as a children's book, but it became an adult book during the writing process. Burnett said the memoir, subtitled *A Memory of the Mind of a Child,* belonged to grown-ups, "especially those who are interested in children as a sort of psychological study."

In 1905, she became an American citizen, and, in 1908, began construction of a large house at Plandome, Long Island, overlooking Manhasset Bay. Frances Hodgson Burnett continued to write until the end of her life. Her last major children's book, *The Lost Prince,* appeared in 1915. Published during World War I, the story tells of the rightful heir to the throne of Samavia, who seeks to restore justice, peace, and freedom for everyone. She also wrote several more adult books, the last, *In the Garden,* was published posthumously in 1925.

Frances Hodgson Burnett died at her Long Island house in 1924. Anticipating perhaps that much of her work would become unfashionable in the postwar world, she defended her purpose: "There is enough . . . in all our lives that we cannot get away from. What we all want is more of the other things—life, love, hope—and an assurance that they are true. With the best that was in me I have tried to write more happiness into the world."

SOURCES:

Burnett, Constance Buel. *Happily Ever After: A Portrait of Frances Hodgson Burnett.* NY: Vanguard Press, 1965.

Burnett, Frances Hodgson. *The One I Knew Best.* NY: Scribner, 1893.

Commire, Anne, ed. *Yesterday's Authors of Books for Children.* Vol. 2, Detroit, MI: Gale Research, 1978.

Doyle, Brian, ed. "Frances Hodgson Burnett," in *The Who's Who of Children's Literature.* NY: Schocken, 1968.

"Frances Hodgson Burnett," *Children's Literature Review.* Vol. 24, 1991.

Thwaite, Ann. *Waiting for the Party.* NY: Scribner, 1974.

RELATED MEDIA:

THEATRE:

That Lass produced in New York in Autumn 1878.

*Elsie Leslie starred in the 1888 Broadway production of *Little Lord Fauntleroy.*

The Little Princess opened on Broadway in 1903.

FILMS:

Dawn of Tomorrow, Famous Players-Lasky Corp., 1924.

Little Lord Fauntleroy, starring Mary Pickford, 1914.

Little Lord Fauntleroy, starring Freddie Bartholomew and Mickey Rooney, Selznick International Pictures, 1936.

Louisiana, starring Jimmy Davis, Famous Players-Lasky, 1919.

The Little Princess, starring Mary Pickford and **Zasu Pitts,** Aircraft Pix, 1917.

The Little Princess, starring *Shirley Temple (Black),* Fox, 1939.

The Secret Garden, starring **Margaret O'Brien,** Metro-Goldwyn-Mayer, 1949.

The Secret Garden, starring **Kate Maberly** and **Maggie Smith,** Warner Bros., 1993.

RECORDINGS:

The Secret Garden, recorded by **Claire Bloom,** Caedmon; recorded by **Glenda Jackson,** Miller-Brody Productions.

Mary Welek Atwell, Associate Professor of Criminal Justice, Radford University, Radford, Virginia

Burnett, Hallie Southgate

(1908–1991)

American novelist and editor. Born Hallie Southgate in St. Louis, Missouri, on December 3, 1908; died in Raleigh, North Carolina, on September 4, 1991; daughter of John McKnight (a consulting engineer) and Elizabeth (Baker) Southgate; married Robert Abbott (divorced); married Whit Burnett (co-founder and editor of Story *magazine), 1942 (died April 22, 1973); married William Zeisel, 1977; children: (second marriage) John Southgate;* **Whitney Ann Burnett.**

Selected writings: A Woman in Possession *(Dutton, 1951);* This Heart, This Hunter *(Holt, 1953);* The Brain Pickers *(Messner, 1957);* The Watch on the Wall *(Morrow, 1965);* On Writing a Short Story *(Harper, 1983).*

Hallie Burnett's career began with her marriage in 1942 to Whit Burnett, who had co-founded and, for 11 years, co-edited the prestigious *Story,* a magazine of short stories published in book form, with his first wife *Martha Foley.* (Foley and Whit Burnett had just divorced in 1942.) As assistant editor of *Story,* Hallie brought to print the early short stories of notables like J.D. Salinger, Joseph Heller, Norman Mailer, and Truman Capote. Burnett regarded her first novel *A Woman in Possession,* as an experiment written around her duties as a wife and mother. Because of its satisfactory reception, she wrote a second novel, *This Heart, This Hunter* (1953), which had developed out of a short story. "It also grew from a long time interest in how men satisfied their desire for power," said Burnett. Both of the novels were set in college towns (perhaps drawn from the time of her first marriage when she was a faculty wife at Yale) and dealt with the emotional problems of intelligentsia. Henry Jackson, of the San Francisco *Chronicle*, praised Burnett's second novel as fulfilling the promise of her first, describing the work as "a truer novel than most, written with a simple warmth and knowledge that are rare." Hallie Burnett went on to write two additional novels and a textbook, and she edited several anthologies of fiction. She also taught literature and creative writing at the University of Missouri, Sarah Lawrence College, and Hunter College, among other schools.

SOURCES:

Candee, Marjorie Dent, ed. *Current Biography 1954.* NY: H.W. Wilson, 1954.

Moritz, Charles, ed. *Current Biography Yearbook 1991.* NY: H.W. Wilson, 1991.

Burnett, Ivy Compton (1884–1969).

See Compton-Burnett, Ivy.

Burney, Fanny (1752–1840)

English novelist, playwright, and diarist whose 18th-century "scribblings" and career reflect a society at once graced by wit and intellect, yet so ignorant of its assumptions concerning women that it missed, even discouraged, a rare dimension, preferring female sentiment to feminine insight. Name variations: Frances d'Arblay, Madame d'Arblay. Born Frances Burney at King's Lynn, England, on June 13, 1752; died in London on January 6, 1840; daughter of Charles (the musician) and Esther (Sleepe) Burney, who died when Fanny was ten; half-sister of Sarah Harriet Burney (1772–1844); married Alexandre d'Arblay, July 28, 1793; children: a son, Alexander (b. December 18, 1794).

Her education neglected in favor of her pretty sisters and talented brothers, Burney could not read at age eight, but was writing creatively at ten; burned her first novel, Caroline Evelyn (1767), but undertook the famous Early Diary (1768), though it was not published until long after her death; published most celebrated novel, Evelina, anonymously (1778), and became friends with Samuel Johnson and other literary and political figures; dissuaded from publication of comedy, The Witlings (1779); published Cecilia (1782) and served Queen Charlotte as second keeper of the robes (1786–91); published Camilla (1796); lived in France (1802–12); published The Wanderer

and returned to France (1814); published The Memoirs of Dr. Burney (1832); posthumous publication of Diary and Letters of Madame d'Arblay in seven volumes (1843–46) and The Early Diary of Frances Burney in two volumes (1889).

𝓕anny 𝓑urney

Gifted with acute observation and expression, Fanny Burney both adored and dissected the polished society into which she was born; conscious of her talent, she knew equally well that her work, whether good or indifferent, was judged differently because she was female, always because she was female.

Frances Burney, known to contemporaries and history as Fanny, was a shrewd observer of her times and a clever recorder of its charms and its follies. In her first published novel, *Evelina,* Fanny, aged 25, used the epistolary style to portray the mid-18th century English upper-middle class she knew so well through the innocent but sharp eyes of a 17-year-old girl. Superficially comical, the novel was also a challenge to the pretensions of her day, including that of masculine superiority; it is not certain, however, that she was as consciously feminist as some modern biographers wish her to have been. Fanny's talent was not employed solely to deflate insensitive men, though she could do that well; her targets also included pomposity, hypocrisy, self-righteousness, churlishness, and many women. New in her work was the woman who must and could make her way in an indifferent or hostile world. That is why she influenced later writers, including ***Jane Austen** and William Makepeace Thackeray, and why, while much of her writing is diminished by contrivance, her diaries and some of the works published during her life may still be read for enjoyment and instruction.

To Nobody, then, will I write my Journal! . . . No secret can I conceal from Nobody. . . . From Nobody I have nothing to fear.

—Fanny Burney, *Journal*, March 1768

Frances Burney was born on June 13, 1752, at King's Lynn, England. Her family was a large and illustrious one, and in her early life Fanny did not appear as promising as her brothers, James and Charles, or her attractive sisters, **Charlotte**, **Esther**, and **Susannah**. Her father Charles Burney, an accomplished musician and musicologist who moved the family to London in 1760, gained entry into higher levels of society by talent and force of character. Fanny's mother **Esther Sleepe Burney**, of French descent, died in 1761, but greatly influenced Fanny who never forgot her warmth and intelligence. When her father remarried in 1766, Fanny gained additional siblings, including ◄❧ **Sarah Burney**, to share the busy and apparently pleasant household.

Perhaps as a refuge from the others, Fanny, a quiet, modest child, began to write for herself

---

❧► **Burney, Sarah Harriet** (1772–1844)

English novelist. Born in 1772; died in 1844; daughter of Charles Burney (a musicologist) and his second wife; half-sister of Fanny Burney.

Novelist Sarah Burney's first success was with her novel *Clarentine,* published in 1798. While working as a governess and companion, she also wrote *Geraldine Fauconberg* (1808), *Traits of Nature* (1812), *The Shipwreck* (1815), and *Tales of Fancy* (1816–1829). Sarah's writing was often compared to that of her half-sister *Fanny Burney*. Wrote a critic for the *London Monthly Review* in 1813: "We have before remarked that together with family talents, we discern a family likeness in this lady's productions."

---

at age ten and authored several pieces, including a novel, *Caroline Evelyn*. This work, which she burned at age 15 in an act of contrition for writing such frivolity, was to serve as the foundation of her later published novel, *Evelina*. Fortunately, she did not destroy the journal she had also undertaken and to which she would add for the rest of her long and colorful life. It is in the journals, running to 12 volumes, that Fanny is best seen as a perceptive observer and able recorder of the late 18th-century English. Take, as an example, her description, in 1770, of a certain Miss Dalrymple:

> [S]he is about 28 or 9, rather handsome, lisps affectedly, simpers designedly, & lookes conceitedly. She is famed for never speaking ill to any ones Face, or well behind their Backs: an amiable Character.

By her early 20s, Fanny had had the opportunity to behold many of the most renowned personages of her day, including the celebrated actor David Garrick, who was a frequent visitor at the Burney house. Garrick had befriended Charles Burney and introduced him to a widening circle of English luminaries. Moreover, despite Fanny's unassuming ways, Garrick had singled her out from her siblings and particularly enjoyed her gift for mimicry. Indeed, that very ability to imitate and amuse indicated Fanny's fine cognizance of character and the satirist's capacity to seize upon the central flaw in speech, appearance, and manners to express disapproval or disdain. It was to be the talent that won her public approval, but it is unlikely that the great world really comprehended that Fanny's humor was a tool rather than an end in itself.

Fanny's biographers have agreed that she was enormously influenced by her intellectual father throughout her life and, in her young womanhood, by Samuel Crisp, a close family friend. So special was Crisp to her as a mentor and confidante that she called him "Daddy" Crisp. To a great extent, these men defined the role of women for Fanny, and it was a definition reinforced by the upper-middle-class world she inhabited. That role was essentially domestic, not public, subordinate, not dominant, and decidedly not political. But Fanny's native intelligence and sharp judgment allowed her to see the inconsistencies of such a system, if not overtly to rebel against it. Never one for radical political change in the style of her contemporary ***Mary Wollstonecraft**, Fanny opted instead for the vehicles of novels and plays to affirm women's capabilities and to persuade her readers that the female was mentally the equal of the male and certainly no more foolish. She started with *Evelina*.

Evelina emerged from Fanny's humorous exchanges with her brothers and sisters concerning the comings and goings of the great and those ambitious to be great in their society. She had it published anonymously in 1778 as *Evelina, or a Young Lady's Entrance into the World.* Couched in the form of the letters of a 17-year-old girl, the book is both a novel of manners and a clever reversal of the role of the author rather than the heroine. Evelina is conventionally young, innocent, and beautiful, the object of matrimonial manipulations. Burney, however, shrewdly evaluates the heroine, the hero Lord Orville, and a cast of worldly characters. Though weakened by contrived meetings, improbable resolutions, and some unconvincing characters, *Evelina* suggests that woman's path is difficult, is made the worse by male exploitation, springing from a failure or refusal to take women seriously, and must be traveled with circumspection.

Evelina was published without Charles Burney's knowledge, but when he learned of his daughter's accomplishment he was, to Fanny's relief, pleased. No doubt Charles saw the possible advantages to his family from the large and unexpected popularity of the book. Yet there is no reason to deny that he certainly took pride in the daughter who, as a child, and as an unmarried woman, seemed so unpromising. On her side, Fanny enjoyed the acclaim and accepted invitations to discuss her book with eminent personages. Indeed, she soon became a favorite of ☙➤ **Hester Thrale**, whose home at Streatham was a center of literary and political discourse. At Streatham, Burney was lionized by Samuel Johnson, Oliver Goldsmith, Edmund Burke, Joshua Reynolds, and others of similar fame. It is unlikely that such supporters saw in *Evelina* an indictment of conventions they took for granted. They loved its wit, its sentiment, and its wicked skewering of familiar types, and they loved Fanny for it. Fanny Burney had made her own entrance into the world.

Mrs. Thrale's lively and critical views and Johnson's magic language captivated Fanny. Johnson, particularly, was adored. In him was combined encyclopedic knowledge, strong opinions, and inimitable skill of expression. Burney could never hear of his faults and took great exception to James Boswell's famous biography for daring to display Johnson's less endearing attributes. In such a circle, Fanny's conservative political views were reinforced, yet while her shyness contrasted with Hester Thrale's assertiveness, her notice of the contrast between those things permitted of men and those of women was magnified.

In the spring of 1779, Burney finished a play, *The Witlings.* The play concerns the problems of two lovers, Cecilia and Beaufort, who are kept apart by family on the familiar ground of economic insufficiency. Beaufort's aunt, Lady Smatter, is a wonderfully satirical example of Blue Stocking pomposity, but Fanny does not really question the notion that happiness is impossible apart from economic well being. But it was not that truism that bothered Fanny's father. It was the lampooning of recognizable and influential individuals that alarmed him. With the powerful support of "Daddy" Crisp, the elder Charles dissuaded Fanny from allowing the play to be performed. She may not have agreed that the play's performance would have harmed her reputation, as her father and Crisp asserted, but she dutifully bowed to these gentlemen and their paternal views. Perhaps, given her background and her own doubts about the wisdom of undermining the established order, Fanny could not have defied her father. But it is a misfortune, as her biographer, Michael Adelstein, has noted, that Fanny lost the chance to use *The Witlings* to go on to other equally pithy satires of her times. It was a rich vein to mine, and in subsequent works Burney, choosing safer subjects, did not speak in her own adroit, spontaneous voice but in the more formal and conventional tone of the world she hoped to please.

In her next novel, *Cecilia, or Memoirs of an Heiress,* published in 1782, Fanny continued to deal with the economic problems of women but created a complex book fraught with plots, subplots, myriad characters, and boundless sentiment. The novel was an enormous popular success—Edmund Burke especially adored it—but the reviews were less favorable. While there are moments reminiscent of the fun of *Evelina,* the turgid characterizations and use of the intrusive omniscient view of the narrator indicate a falling off from Burney's previous works.

Cecilia was not a great book, but it nevertheless expanded her fame and brought her into even more refined social ranks. It also made her a more eligible marriage prospect. Fanny, who had firmly turned down the proposal of Thomas Barlow, a man of modest means, in 1775, apparently was quite attracted to a handsome cleric, George Cambridge, in the early 1780s. Cambridge made no offer, however, and Fanny, now a close associate of Mrs. *Mary Granville Delany, an elderly lady with impressive connections in both literary and royal circles, moved on

☙➤
Thrale, Hester (1741–1821). *See Piozzi, Hester Lynch.*

to charm the great families of the court. Eventually, she made the acquaintance of the royal family and was soon held in warm regard by George III and Queen *Charlotte of Mecklenburg-Strelitz. Their favor led to an offer of a position as second keeper of the robes for the queen. Many women would have been delighted with such a sign of approbation, but Fanny knew that the post would confine her, remove her from her friends, and deprive her of the independence she needed to write. On the other hand, the financial rewards would be substantial, her father wished her to accept the dignity, and Fanny knew all too well that the future of a female with no husband was very uncertain. Hesitantly, in 1786 she accepted the post.

Fanny Burney had doubted the sagacity of becoming the queen's close servant, and she soon had her doubts confirmed. The job involved many long hours of assisting the queen in her dressing and undressing, and Fanny was made miserable by her immediate supervisor, **Mrs. Schwellenberg**. Yet Fanny admired Charlotte, though she was hurt by the queen's apparent indifference to her unhappiness. For four years, Burney endured this duty, but, fortunately, she continued her diary. Among other interesting events recorded was Fanny's account of the celebrated parliamentary trial of Warren Hastings for official misconduct in India. Of particular notice is her fine record of the brilliant oratory of Edmund Burke. Restricting as her position was, Burney did not lose her gift for seeing deep into human character. She knew and admired Hastings, but she saw true greatness in Burke.

Less public was Fanny's relationship with Colonel Stephen Digby in these years. Digby, an official of the royal household, appeared to court Fanny, but disappointed her by marrying a wealthier woman. Now in her mid-30s, Burney had again experienced personally the problematic conduct of men toward women and the great attraction of money. Tired and downhearted, she began to lose her health by 1790. She could not go on in the queen's employ, and finally, with assistance from her friends, she was released. It renewed her zest for life and provided her with the chance to rekindle her interest in fiction and to meet the man she was to love for the remainder of her life.

Fanny Burney wrote several plays in the early 1790s, but only *Edwy and Elgiva,* an historical tragedy, reached the stage. Performed in London only one night in March 1795, it was so poorly received that it closed immediately. This failure proved again that while she knew human vanity well enough, her strength lay in depicting the absurdities of her times, not in serious drama. Yet just across the English Channel in France a vast, stark drama was in motion.

The French Revolution, beginning in 1789, had first attracted the English with its early generous sentiments. But as the revolution evolved into a massive and bloody struggle over the very fundamentals of political and social intercourse, Fanny and most of the others of her station sympathized with the beleaguered French monarchy, nobility, and clergy. When thousands of French aristocrats and clergy took refuge in England, Burney was willing to use her pen to drum up subscriptions for financial assistance for them. In 1793, she published *Brief Reflections Relative to the Emigrant French Clergy,* a pamphlet imploring her compatriots to give generously. The work is a standard one for its time, but it possesses interest in that Fanny, for all her justified concern about the devaluation of women, makes an argument for toleration of the French that she could and would as well apply to the masculine sex:

> Are we not all the creatures of one Creator? Does not the same sun give us warmth? And will not the days of the years of our pilgrimage be as short as theirs?

Perhaps it was this magnanimous view of the emigrants that led Fanny to the arms of Alexandre d'Arblay. D'Arblay was a destitute emigrant who undertook to teach Burney French and introduced her to other French travelers, including the slightly disreputable writer, Madame *Germaine de Staël. D'Arblay had lived an adventurous life before fleeing the revolution, and his kindness and charm appealed to Burney, but her father was uneasy with her growing fondness for a foreign and poor Catholic. At 41, however, Fanny decided to marry d'Arblay, and the wedding took place on July 28, 1793, at Mickleham. The couple were in love and were to remain so for the rest of their lives.

In the first years of their marriage, the d'Arblays suffered financial difficulties, but Fanny was content and overjoyed at the birth of their son Alexander in 1794. When Fanny published *Camilla* in June 1796, the first edition sold out, and the creditors were kept at bay. Indeed, the novel was such a commercial success that the d'Arblays were able to build a new residence at West Humble, which Fanny called Camilla Cottage. Actually, *Camilla* presents the familiar story of frustrated young love, the desperate need for money, and the obstacles to happiness for blameless women. Again, Fanny is heavy handed in her long admonishments to readers to be good, but there are sparks of the old Burney gift for characterization. Take, for example, when Lionel declaims to Camilla:

> He's just a girl's man, just the very thing, all sentiment, and poetry and heroics. But we, my little dear, we lads of spirit, hold all that amazing cheap. I assure you, I would as soon be seen trying on a lady's cap at a glass, as poring over a crazy old author when I could help it.

Still, *Camilla* was just another indication of Fanny Burney's decline as a writer. Having long since departed from her natural style and having given up caricature for tragedy, Burney's public writing lost its bite. Her fame remained, and her diary continued to be fresh and charming, but her best days as a writer of fiction were over.

In 1802, the d'Arblays sailed for France as Alexandre took service in Napoleon Bonaparte's government. When war with England resumed the next year, Fanny's husband was often away, but she made many friends and lived as well as she could among foreigners at Passy, near Paris. She was frequently desperate for news of her father and brothers and sisters, but she doggedly supported her husband. In fact, it is the French period of her life that displays Fanny Burney at her best as a dedicated and courageous person if not as a writer. Most indicative of her mature strength was the harrowing mastectomy she endured, without anesthesia, in 1811. Fanny has left a complete account of the operation to remove cancer. Nothing in all her fictional renditions of woman's suffering bears so powerful witness as the agony inflicted upon her living flesh and bone.

Fanny recovered from her illness and returned under dangerous circumstances to England in 1812 to forestall her son's conscription into the French army. Once again short of funds, she finished another novel, *The Wanderer,* in 1814. A story of love and misalliance set in the French Revolution, the novel lacks even the occasional insights of *Camilla.* It did nothing to revive her declining professional reputation.

Charles Burney also died in 1814 having long outlived his time. Fanny loved and respected him to the end, and the last great public work of her life was the meticulous collection and publication of his memoirs in 1832. After his death, however, she returned to France as her husband joined the forces of the restored French King, Louis XVIII, when the Emperor Napoleon escaped from exile in Elba and marched on Paris. Fanny was in Brussels when the epic battle of Waterloo occurred, and her report of the events surrounding the decisive military engagement of her age summons up the fear and eventual elation of those memorable June days.

On the morrow of victory, Fanny and her husband returned to England in joy, but d'Arblay was not well. Having been injured in 1815, his health declined, and Fanny's happiness in their reunion was replaced by lingering grief when he died in 1818. In fact, most of her old friends were going or were gone as the years slipped by. It was no longer the world of Evelina and Cecilia, and Fanny was becoming a relic of another age. New generations had new and even better authors to read, while time's passage ravaged Fanny's health as it had diminished her work. To her other sorrows, her son Alexander added new ones, first by failing as an Anglican cleric and then by dying young in 1837. Fanny, old and suffering from mental lapses, survived Alex by three years. Then, in 1840, at the age of 87, Fanny Burney relinquished her pen forever.

Fanny Burney was a good writer in an age of extraordinary writers. If she suffers in comparison with Fielding, Smollet, Goldsmith, Austen, and Thackeray, it is because she chose, after the publication of her first novel, to limit her true voice to her diaries. Even so, she was one of the best depictors of human character of her time and certainly a steady, if not spectacular, defender of the potential of women. Yet Fanny was quite acceptable to the establishment of her day. Her wit, sometimes broad and sometimes subtle, did slice through the pretensions and absurdities of the masculine world of 18th-century England, but she was careful to restrain it when warned or when she thought it would be too costly.

The most enduring of Burney's contributions is her journal and the early diary, both published posthumously. In them, the reader enters a world long past, as seen by one of its inhabitants, and one that is endlessly fascinating and civilized in a way later ages could not be. The diaries leave posterity a picture of that crowded stage, upon which tread so many unforgettable players, and many of them would be lost to us forever except for their quiet but gifted chronicler.

SOURCES:

Adelstein, Michael. *Fanny Burney.* Twayne, 1968.

Burney, Fanny. *Brief Reflections Relative To The Emigrant French Clergy (1793).* The Augustan Reprint Society, 1990.

———. *The Early Journals and Letters of Fanny Burney.* Vol. I. Edited by Lars E. Troide. McGill-Queens University Press, 1988.

———. *The Journals and Letters of Fanny Burney (Madame D'Arblay).* Vol. VI. Edited by Joyce Hemlow. Clarendon Press, 1975.

Cutting-Gray, Joanne. *Woman as 'Nobody' and the Novels of Fanny Burney.* FL: University Press of Florida, 1992.

Doody, Margaret Anne. *Frances Burney: The Life in the Works.* NJ: Rutgers University Press, 1988.

SUGGESTED READING:

Rogers, Katherine M. *Frances Burney: The World of "Female Difficulties."* Harvester Wheatsheaf, 1990.

C. David Rice, Ph.D., Professor of History,
Central Missouri State University,
Warrensburg, Missouri

Burney, Sarah Harriet (1772–1844).

See Burney, Fanny for sidebar.

Burns, Lucy (1879–1966)

American suffragist. Born in Brooklyn, New York, on July 28, 1879; died in 1966; graduated from Vassar College, 1902; graduate studies in Linguistics at Yale, Oxford, and the German universities of Berlin and Bonn.

In 1909, while working on her doctorate at Oxford, Lucy Burns became involved with the militant British suffragists, working as an organizer in Scotland until 1912. It was in Britain that she also met *Alice Paul with whom she joined forces; her organizational and persuasive skills proved the perfect complement to Paul's talent as a strategist. Returning to the United States, the pair opened a Washington office in January 1913.

Theodosia Burr

Hoping to breathe new life into the old National American Woman Suffrage Association and bring the suffrage issue to the forefront again, their first undertaking was an enormous parade held on the day prior to Woodrow Wilson's inauguration so as to attract influential politicians as well as the flood of journalists on hand in Washington. The event, attracting 5,000 marchers, was an enormous success, though the marchers were confronted by a jeering hostile crowd.

Burns proved especially valuable in the second phase of their plan, which was to build a new organization, the Congressional Union for Woman Suffrage. Using the techniques of the British militants, the group initiated a law-breaking campaign style that shocked the American public. Burns was arrested in 1913 for defacing public property with suffragist graffiti and would go on to eventually set a record as the suffragist who served the most time in jail. During the election of 1916, Burns took two dozen women across the country in a railroad car dubbed the "Suffrage Special" to campaign against the Democrats in states where women already had the vote. Undaunted, despite Wilson's reelection, she continued to lead demonstrations against his anti-suffrage stronghold. In 1917, when World War I began to dominate the news, Burns brought the suffrage issue back into focus by being arrested and imprisoned and going on a hunger strike for three weeks. In 1919, she organized another railroad-car campaign, filling the seats with women who had served time in jail for their suffrage activities.

After the vote was won in 1920, Lucy Burns abruptly abandoned the movement and returned to a lifestyle more in keeping with her strong Irish-Catholic background and deep family ties. Leaving Alice Paul to carry on with the National Woman's Party at the point of perhaps its greatest potential impact, Burns moved in with two unmarried sisters and spent the rest of her days caring for an orphaned niece. Although Lucy Burns lived until 1966, her years outside the cause obscured her contribution and left few who recalled her name.

Barbara Morgan,
Melrose, Massachusetts

Burr, Betty (1775–1865).

See Jumel, Eliza Bowen.

Burr, Theodosia (1783–1813)

*Daughter of Aaron Burr (vice president of the United States), who served as his hostess. Name variations: Theodosia Alston. Born on June 21, 1783, in Albany, New York; lost at sea in the Atlantic, January 1813; daughter of Aaron Burr (vice president of the United States under President Thomas Jefferson) and **Theodosia Bartow (Prevost) Burr**; married Joseph Alston, 1801.*

Theodosia Burr was the only daughter of Aaron Burr. Her mother, also named Theodosia, had five children from a previous marriage. Theodosia was doted upon as a child and, following the death of her mother when she was 11, grew even closer to her father. Their frequent correspondence, which began in her childhood, ultimately totaled thousands of letters. As she grew older, Theodosia took over as host of the Burr estate and, in 1801, married Joseph Alston, the same year Aaron Burr became vice president. Theodosia remained loyal and supportive as her father's career declined after his dual with Alexander Hamilton in 1804. When he was arrested for treason in 1807, Theodosia moved to Richmond to be near him; the following year, she traveled to New York under an assumed name to say goodbye before he left for England. Upon her father's return to New York in 1812, Theodosia set sail from South Carolina for a long-awaited reunion. The ship, *Patriot,* however, was lost at sea. The story of Theodosia Burr was fictionalized by **Anya Seton** in *My Theodosia* (Houghton Mifflin, 1941).

Burroughs, Nannie Helen

(c. 1878–1961)

African-American educator and school founder. Born in Orange, Virginia, on May 2, around 1878; died in Washington, D.C., in May 1961; older of two daughters of John (a farmer and preacher) and Jennie (Poindexter) Burroughs; attended M Street High School, Washington; awarded honorary A.M. from Eckstein-Norton University, Kentucky, 1907.

"The training of Negro women is absolutely necessary," said Nannie Burroughs at the Women's Convention of National Baptists in 1902, "not only for their own salvation and the salvation of the race, but because the hour in which we live demands it. If we lose sight of the demands of the hour we blight our hope of progress." Acting on her own words, Burroughs built a school and educated thousands of young black women in her lifetime.

The daughter of ex-slaves, Nannie Burroughs moved to Washington, D.C., with her widowed mother when she was five. While her mother worked as a cook, Burroughs attended public school, graduating from the M Street High School with honors in 1896. Unable to obtain a job as a domestic-science teacher in the District of Columbia public-school system, Burroughs worked at various jobs before finding employment as a secretary for the Foreign Mission Board of the National Baptist Convention, in Louisville, Kentucky. In her spare time, she organized the Woman's Industrial Club, which, in addition to offering moderately priced lunches to office workers in the area, held evening classes in typing, shorthand, bookkeeping, and

sewing for members. The night courses grew so popular that Burroughs finally hired teachers, leaving her free to supervise the operation.

In 1900, Burroughs attracted favorable attention at the annual meeting of the National Baptist Convention with a stirring speech entitled "Hindered from Helping" and was subsequently elected secretary of the National Baptist Woman's Convention, the newly formed auxiliary to the men's convention. Burroughs became a driving force within the organization (whose goal was to reinforce Christianity in the United States and ultimately to Christianize the world), especially as an inspirational speaker. Serving as secretary of the auxiliary until 1948 when she became president, Burroughs helped build the organization from the ground up.

The Baptist women eventually backed Burroughs' dream of establishing a school for young black women. In 1909, with seven students, she opened the Training School for Women and Girls located on a six-acre campus in suburban Washington. Like *Mary McLeod Bethune before her, Burroughs spent the rest of her life administering to, and raising money to sustain, the enterprise. By the end of its first year, the school had 31 students; 25 years later, the enrollment exceeded 2,000 women from the U.S., Africa, and the Caribbean Basin. In 1934, her school was named the National Trades and Professional School for Women.

Based on the three b's—the Bible, the bath, and the broom—Burroughs' educational philosophy was centered on Puritan ethic but also encompassed an innovative curriculum. She believed that black women could become self-sufficient wage earners. Thus, in addition to domestic arts and secretarial skills, she offered courses in unconventional occupations for women such as shoe repair, printing, barbering, and gardening. Vocational training was supplemented with classical academics, with emphasis on grammar and language. One of the most unique aspects of the school was its Department of Negro History established by Burroughs to instill a sense of racial pride in her students.

Burroughs was also an active participant in the club movement among black women during the late 19th and early 20th centuries. In 1896, she was a founding member of the National Association of Colored Women, a federation of more than 100 local women's clubs. She also founded the National Association of Wage Earners and served as its president. During the Depression, Burroughs organized a cooperative in northeast

Nannie
Helen
Burroughs

Washington (later called Cooperative Industries, Inc.), which provided facilities for a variety of services, including a medical clinic and variety store.

Sought after as a speaker and writer, Burroughs promoted her belief in self-help and self-

reliance for blacks. In an article for *Southern Workman* (July 1927), she encouraged self-pride: "No race is richer in soul quality and color than the Negro. Some day he will realize it and glorify them. He will popularize black." She was also outspoken in her feelings about the treatment of black women by black men, writing in a 1933 column of a black publication: "Stop making slaves and servants of our women. . . . The Negro mother is doing it all. The women are carrying the burden. The main reason is that the men lack manhood and energy. . . . [T]he men ought to get down on their knees to the Negro women. They've made possible all we have."

A champion of suffrage, Burroughs worked to register women after the vote was won in 1920 and remained devoted to the Baptist Women's Convention for more than a half century. It was through her school, however, with its motto of optimism—"We specialize in the wholly impossible"—that Burroughs dream was achieved. After her death from a stroke in 1961, the school was renamed the Nannie Burroughs School.

SOURCES:

Sicherman, Barbara, and Carol Hurd Green, eds. *Notable American Women: The Modern Period*. Cambridge, MA: Belknap Press of Harvard University Press, 1980.

Smith, Jessie Carney, ed. *Notable Black American Women*. Detroit, MI: Gale Research, 1992.

Barbara Morgan,
Melrose, Massachusetts

Burrows, Eva (1929—)

Australian-born general of the Salvation Army. Born Eva Evelyn Burrows on September 15, 1929, in an Australian mining town; daughter and one of nine children of Salvation Army officers; granted degrees in history and English and a graduate degree in education from Queensland University.

In 1986, Eva Burrows was appointed 13th general of the Salvation Army, the first woman elected to that high office since *Evangeline Booth** in 1934. Chosen over six male nominees by the denomination's 48-member high council, the second "General Eva," at 56, was also the youngest worldwide commander of the evangelical Christian group, founded in London by William and *Catherine Booth** in 1865.

On the day Burrows was born in 1929, one of nine children in a Salvation Army family, her father held her aloft and offered a prayer "dedicating her to the glory of God and the salvation of the world." After a brief period of rebellion in her teenage years, during which she viewed the Army's discipline as too rigid and refused to go to church, Burrows fulfilled her father's high expectations. While in college, she experienced a "divine compulsion" to rejoin the Army and, after finishing her university education and training, she spent 17 years at Howard Institute in Zimbabwe as a teacher and administrator. During this time, she also acted as an advisor to the Zimbabwe government on planning curriculums for African colleges. Leaving Africa in 1969, Burrows was an administrator at the International College for Officers in London and, in 1975, served as leader of Women's Social Services in Great Britain and Ireland. From 1977 to 1985, she was a territorial commander in Sri Lanka, Scotland, and southern Australia.

During her tenure as general, Burrows traveled extensively, commanding the Army's social-welfare operations in 86 countries and working to add to the organization's dwindling ranks. Her greatest concern, however, was to reinvest the Army's evangelical side. "In The Salvation Army, our social work is not a hook by which to angle souls," said Burrows. "It grows out of our compassion and love as an explanation of the Gospel. While we are speaking and helping people with their social needs, we also deal with the whole person, which includes their spiritual

*Eva
Burrows*

lives." Eva Burrows retired in 1993, while remaining active as an international speaker.

SOURCES:

Bourke, Dale Hanson. "A Heart for the World," in *Today's Christian Woman*. November–December, 1987.

Ostling, Richard N. "A New General Takes Charge," in *Time*. August 11, 1986, p. 34.

The War Cry. Vol. 108, no. 11, May 24, 1986.

Barbara Morgan,
Melrose, Massachusetts

Burton, Annie L.

African-American who wrote Memories of Childhood's Slavery Days. *Born on a plantation near Clayton, Alabama; birth and death date unknown; one of four children of a slave woman and a white plantation owner from Liverpool, England; married Samuel L. Burton, 1888.*

The available details of Annie L. Burton's life come from her 1909 autobiographical work *Memories of Childhood's Slavery Days*. Her narrative provides a glimpse into the world of the slave woman, while also relating the transition from slavery to freedom.

Raised in Alabama during the period of the Civil War, Annie Burton was the daughter of a slave woman and an English plantation owner whom Annie saw only a few times and from a distance. Her mother fled the plantation for a three-year period following a beating but returned at the end of the war to collect her children. Burton spent her early days of freedom eking out a living while residing with her mother, sister, and brother, as well as several other children her mother had brought along, in a small one-room log cabin. She then found work with a wealthy family who saw to it that she learned to read and write. Among the earliest black emigrants to the North during the postwar era, Burton arrived in Boston in 1879. She supported herself and her sister by working as a domestic and took over raising her nephew upon her sister's death. Burton moved to Georgia and eventually became a restaurateur in Jacksonville, Florida, and later in Boston, doing well enough financially to send her nephew through Hampton Institute. She married in 1888 and opened a rooming house with her husband. It was through an evening course at the Franklin School in Boston that Burton was encouraged to write her life story.

SUGGESTED READING:

Gates, Henry Louis, Jr., ed. *Six Women's Slave Narratives*. NY: Oxford University Press, 1988 (a collection of works of 19th-century black women by Annie L. Burton, "Old Elizabeth," Mattie J. Jackson, Lucy A. Delaney, and Kate Drumgoold).

Burton, Beryl (1937—)

English cycling champion. *Born in Yorkshire, England, in 1937; married cyclist Charles Burton; children: one daughter* **Denise Burton** *(also a cycling champion).*

Won the World Championship in the Pursuit (1959, 1960, 1962, 1963, 1966); won the World Championship Road Race (1960, 1967).

Introduced to the sport by her future husband Charles Burton, Beryl Burton became the foremost 20th-century cyclist, with a 20-year unbroken record as Best British All-Rounder (1958–1978). In pursuit and road-racing events, she won 80 English titles and seven world championships. **Galina Ermolaeva** of Russia has been the only woman to approach Burton's amazing success. Burton's unsurpassed speed records often beat the top-ranked male riders in open events. In 1967, for example, she raced a distance of 277.37 miles in 12 hours, beating the men's best distance cyclist by 10 miles. When Burton retired to take up farming, her daughter Denise took her place in cycling competition.

Burton, Isabel (1831–1896)

English traveler. *Name variations: Lady Burton. Born Isabel Arundell in London, England, in 1831; died of cancer in 1896; daughter of Henry Raymond Arundell; married Sir Richard Francis Burton (1821–1890, the English explorer and scholar), in 1861.*

Before her marriage, Lady Isabel Burton performed social work among London prostitutes. Married to explorer Richard Burton in 1861, she accompanied him as much as possible, sharing his posts at Santos, Brazil, and Damascus where they pioneered interracial receptions and went on archaeological expeditions. After her husband's death in 1890, Isabel wrote his biography, *The Life of Sir Richard Burton* (1893). Though she destroyed his journals and last incomplete work, *The Scented Garden Men's Hearts to Gladden*, she did prepare a memorial edition of his works. She also wrote *Inner Life of Syria* (1875), the success of which financed a trip to India, as well as *Arabia, Egypt, and India* (1879). Her own biography was written nearly a half a century after her death by **Jean Burton**. Entitled *Sir Richard Burton's Wife* (also called *Life of Lady Burton*), the work was published in 1942.

SUGGESTED READING:

Lovell, Mary S. *A Rage to Live: A Biography of Richard and Isabel Burton.* NY: W.W. Norton, 1998.

Burton, Lady (1831–1896).

See Burton, Isabel.

Burton, Sala (1925–1987)

U.S. Representative, Democrat of California, 98th–100th Congresses, June 21, 1983–February 1, 1987. Born Sala Galante in Bialystok, Poland, on April 1, 1925; died in Washington, D.C., on February 1, 1987; attended San Francisco University; married Philip Burton (a congressional representative from 1964 to 1983), in 1953.

Before the Nazi occupation, Sala Burton fled Poland with her parents in 1939 and made a new home in California. After attending San Francisco University, she took a job as associate director of the California Public Affairs Institute. She was active in the Democratic Party and worked with the NAACP in its efforts against job and housing discrimination.

After her marriage to Phillip Burton in 1953, her own political career paralleled her husband's rise in Congress. As a founder of the California Democratic Council, she served as its vice president from 1951 to 1954. She was president of the San Francisco Democratic Women's Forum from 1957 to 1959 and held memberships in both the San Francisco County and California State Democratic Central Committees. From 1972 to 1974, she served as president of the Democratic Wives of the House and Senate.

In 1983, she was elected to the House of Representatives to fill the vacancy left by the death of her husband and was appointed to his former seats on the Committee on Education and Labor and the Committee on Interior and Insular Affairs. During her second term, she was named to the Committee on Rules. Her assignments afforded her opportunities to advocate for a number of policies, including social-welfare programs, child nutrition assistance, and bilingual education. She also supported the Equal Rights Amendment and defended Soviet dissidents. Burton was reelected to the 100th Congress but had to be sworn in at her home due to illness. She died on February 1, 1987.

Burton, Virginia Lee (1909–1968)

American writer and illustrator of children's books. Born in Newton Centre, Massachusetts, on August

Sala Burton

30, 1909; died in Boston, Massachusetts, on October 15, 1968; daughter of Alfred E. Burton (first dean of Massachusetts Institute of Technology) and Lena Dalkeith (Yates) Burton; half-sister of Harold H. Burton, Justice of the Supreme Court; studied ballet privately in San Francisco, California; studied art at California School of Fine Arts and Boston Museum School; married George Demetrios (a sculptor and teacher), March 28, 1931; children: two sons.

Selected writings (all self-illustrated): Choo Choo *(1935);* Mike Mulligan and His Steam Shovel *(1939);* Calico, the Wonder Horse *(1941);* The Little House *(1942);* Katy and the Big Show *(1943);* Maybelle, the Cable Car *(1952);* Life Story *(1962).*

Illustrator: Arna Bontemps and Jack Conroy's Fast Sooner Hound *(1942); Anne Malcolmson's* Song of Robin Hood *(1947); Hans Christian Andersen's* The Emperor's New Clothes *(1949).*

Raised in Sonora, California, from the age of seven, Virginia Lee Burton wavered between a career in dance and art before finding her niche as a prize-winning illustrator of children's books. After a stint as a sketch artist for the *Boston Transcript,* Burton created her first self-illustrated children's book, *Choo Choo* (1935), inspired by an engine on the Gloucester Branch of the Boston & Maine line. This was followed with a series of books that she tested out on her own two sons, adjusting the stories to the boys' interest or lack thereof. In 1943, Burton's *The Little House* won the Caldecott Medal for the best-illustrated book for children. Her books were so popular that they remained in print after her death in 1968.

When working on a book, Burton created her illustrations first, pinning the sketched pages in sequence around the walls of her studio and adding text only after the final drawings were completed. In an article in *Horn Book,* Lee Kingman discussed Burton's process and her unrelenting revisions: "Suddenly, looking up, she might see, in a page supposedly completed days ago, an area or a line she knew needed changing. To do one book, she filled wastebaskets full of what other artists might well have considered satisfactory work." In addition to her own books, Burton illustrated stories by other authors. During the 1940s, she taught graphic design and organized the Folly Cove Designers, who became known for their linoleum block prints.

Bury, Charlotte (1775–1861)

English novelist who wrote romantic fiction, including a thinly veiled account of life at court with Caroline of Brunswick, princess of Wales and queen of England. Name variations: Charlotte Campbell; Lady Charlotte Bury. Born Charlotte Susan Maria Campbell in London, England, on January 28, 1775; died in London on March 31, 1861; daughter of *Elizabeth Gunning (1734–1790) and John Campbell, 5th duke of Argyll; educated by private tutors; married Col. John Campbell on June 14, 1796 (died, 1809); married Rev. Edward John Bury on March 17, 1818 (died, 1832); children: (first marriage) nine; (second marriage) two.

Selected works: Conduct is Fate *(1822);* Alla Giornata *(1826);* Flirtation, A Marriage in High Life *(1828);* The Exclusives *(1830);* Diary Illustrative of the Times of George IV *(1838);* The History of a Flirt *(1840).*

Born in London on January 28, 1775, the daughter of *Elizabeth Gunning and John Campbell, 5th duke of Argyll, Charlotte Campbell's lineage assured her a home at Inverary Castle, the family seat in Scotland. Known for her

beauty, she could have married suitors with more money or station, but she chose John Campbell, a poor cousin, moved with him to Edinburgh, and had nine children in thirteen years. Widowed in 1809 and soon destitute, she took a post as lady-in-waiting to *Caroline of Brunswick, then princess of Wales, who was separated from Prince George (George IV) and the subject of slander. In 1815, Charlotte left royal service upon publication of her first novel.

When she married the Reverend Edward John Bury, rector of Lichfield, in 1818, Charlotte's parents and children objected vehemently. Like Charlotte's first husband, Bury was poor; his tastes, however, were expensive. Lady Charlotte had two more children during her second marriage and began to publish prolifically to support the family. When her husband died in 1832, leaving Charlotte once again indebted, she increased her literary output but did not improve her situation. But in 1838, she published *Diary Illustrative of the Times of George IV,* an account of her experiences in Caroline of Brunswick's court and had her first bestseller. Public criticism for having violated the queen's privacy, albeit sympathetically, forced Charlotte into seclusion, but the book temporarily warded off creditors. Though a handful of novels followed, Charlotte Bury never enjoyed a steady income. She outlived eight of her children and died impoverished at her London home at age 86.

Crista Martin,
Boston, Massachusetts

Busch, Mae (1894–1946)

Australian-born actress. Born in Melbourne, Australia, on January 20, 1894; died in 1946; educated in a New Jersey convent; married Francis McDonald (an actor).

Selected filmography: The Agitator *(1912);* A One Night Stand *(1915);* A Favorite Fool *(1915);* A Bath House Blunder *(1916);* The Fair Barbarian *(1917);* Her Husband's Friend *(1920);* A Parisian Scandal *(1921);* The Love Charm *(1921);* Foolish Wives *(1922);* Only a Shop Girl *(1922);* Souls for Sale *(1923);* Name the Man *(1924);* The Shooting of Dan McGrew *(1924);* The Unholy Three *(1925);* Camille of the Barbary Coast *(1925);* The Miracle of Life *(1926);* San Francisco Fights *(1928);* While the City Sleeps *(1928); (played Oliver Hardy's wife in first Laurel & Hardy talking short)* A Man's Man *(1929);* Young Desire *(1930); (Laurel & Hardy short)* Chickens Come Home *(1931);* Wicked *(1931); (Laurel & Hardy short)* Their First Mistake *(1932);* Scarlet Dawn *(1932);* Blondie Johnson *(1933);* Dance Girl

Dance *(1933); (played Oliver Hardy's wife)* Sons of the Desert *(1933); (L&H short)* Oliver the Eighth *(1934); (L&H short)* Going Bye-Bye *(1934); (L&H short)* Them Thar Hills *(1934); (L&H short)* The Live Ghost *(1934); (L&H short)* Tit for Tat *(1935);* Stranded *(1935); (L&H feature)* The Bohemian Girl *(1936);* Daughter of Shanghai *(1937);* Prison Farm *(1938);* Nancy Drew—Detective *(1938);* Women without Names *(1940);* The Mad Monster *(1942); (bit part)* The Blue Dahlia *(1946).*

Mae Busch was born in Melbourne, Australia, on January 20, 1894. Her father was conductor of the Australian Symphony Orchestra; her mother was a grand-opera singer. Mae spent much of her childhood in Tahiti, where the Buschs owned property, until the family immigrated to the United States. Making her stage debut at age 17, Busch became a popular headliner in vaudeville. Her film debut was in a Mack Sennett Keystone comedy in 1912, and her first major movie success was her star turn in Erich von Stroheim's *Foolish Wives* in 1922. Throughout the 1930s, she appeared in Laurel and Hardy two-reel comedies, sometimes playing Hardy's wife, other times as a foil for their routines. She became a foil once again when Jackie Gleason began to use her name in a running gag on his popular television program with the phrase "and the ever-popular Mae Busch."

Mae
Busch

Bush, Barbara (1924—)

American first lady from 1989 to 1993. Born Barbara Pierce in Rye, New York, on June 8, 1924; third of four children of Marvin (a magazine publisher of Mc-Calls-Redbook) and Pauline (Robinson) Pierce; attended Smith College (1943–44); married George Herbert Walker Bush, January 6, 1945, in Rye, New York; children: George Walker Bush (b. 1946, governor of Texas); Robin (1949–1953, died of leukemia); John "Jeb" Ellis (b. 1953); Neil Mallon (b. 1955); Marvin Pierce (b. 1956); Dorothy Walker Bush (b. 1959).

Born in 1924, the third of four children, Barbara Bush spent a carefree childhood in an upper-middle-class neighborhood of Rye, New York. Particularly fond of her father, she recalled walking with him to the train station in the morning, where he would catch the commuter to his New York City office at the McCall Corporation. She remembered her mother as a great beauty, known for her immaculate house, beautiful flower garden, and exquisite needlework. Bush described her mother as having left the world "a more

beautiful place than she found it," but admits to not completely understanding or appreciating her until becoming a mother herself.

In 1945, at the age of 19, Barbara left Smith College to marry "the first man she ever kissed," George Herbert Walker ("Poppy") Bush. The couple had met at a dance four years earlier, and their lengthy courtship included a secret engagement, during which time George served as a Navy pilot in the South Pacific during World War II. One of the couple's first homes after the war was a married housing unit at Yale University, where George finished his education and Barbara gave birth to the first of their six children. Her life centered around the dictates of her husband's expansive career. From his early days as a Texas businessman to political posts as a Congressional representative, ambassador to the United Nations, U.S. Envoy in China, director of the CIA, and vice president, the Bushes had 29 homes in 17 cities. In her husband's absence, Barbara Bush shouldered most of the parenting duties; she also

blossomed from a shy housewife into a savvy political advisor and campaigner.

Yet, her image as matriarch was key. In a complete departure from the glamorous and aloof image fostered by First Lady *Nancy Reagan, Barbara Bush arrived on the scene with a shock of white hair, undisguised wrinkles, and wearing a size–14 dress with a triple strand of faux pearls. Her down-to-earth demeanor and obvious devotion to her husband and family—including 11 grandchildren—embodied the new administration's focus on American "family values."

Barbara Bush has few regrets about her "husband-centric" existence, though she was called upon to defend it on a number of occasions. During an interview for the "Today" show, **Jane Pauley** caught her off guard: "Mrs. Bush, people say your husband is a man of the '80s and you are a woman of the '40s. What do you say to that?" Bush was both devastated and infuriated by the question. During her husband's bid for presidential reelection in 1992, his party's "family values" campaign brought her under fire from opponents who argued that the image promoted of Barbara Bush, the typical American stay-at-home mom, was misleading. Citing her privileged background, a parade of household help, and the time dedicated to being a political wife, they questioned just how much hands-on mothering Bush had actually done.

Community service and volunteerism had always been important to the Bush family and provided the basis of the Bush administration's "thousand points of light" volunteer campaign. Involvement in two of her causes was inspired by personal experience. In 1953, the Bushes lost their three-and-a-half-year-old daughter Robin to leukemia. As part of what Barbara Bush described as the painful but necessary "dance back to real life," the Bright Star Foundation was started in Robin's name. Bush also continued her work and interest in Sloan-Kettering, where Robin had received new and experimental treatment.

The long, frustrating struggle with her son Neil's dyslexia led to Bush's efforts on behalf of literacy and learning disabilities, which became her main focus while in the White House. During her husband's vice presidency, she attended 500 literacy events across the country, and as first lady established the Barbara Bush Foundation for Family Literacy. With an intergenerational approach, the foundation attempts to keep illiteracy from being handed down from generation to generation. Proceeds from two of her books, *C. Fred's Story* and *Millie's Book* (insider books on Washington from the view of While House pets), have gone to the literacy foundation. No one was more surprised than Bush at the success of the second book. Selling more than 400,000 copies, *Millie* raised $1 million.

Bush considered the job of first lady as the best in America and, aside from a bout with the thyroid disorder Graves Disease, which was diagnosed during Bush's first year in the White House, she was energetic and well-traveled. In the first year alone, she witnessed the demolition of the Berlin Wall and lifting of the Iron Curtain, the American invasion into Panama, and chaos in Rumania. As the Bush administration confronted a number of domestic and foreign crises, Bush often accompanied the president on visits across the United States and abroad.

Although for the most part Barbara Bush was supportive—almost protective—of her husband, she maintained strong opinions on many controversial issues. More than once during her tenure, her opinions brought her outside the bounds of first-lady protocol, and she admitted to having to learn to "curb her mouth" by fielding questions of a controversial nature with the stock answer, "Let me tell you how George Bush feels."

The campaign for reelection brought serious attacks on administration policies, three national debates, and a bizarre chocolate-chip-cookie recipe contest between Barbara Bush and soon-to-be first lady **Hillary Clinton**. Through all the frustration and exhaustion, Bush believed that her husband was unfairly perceived as having more interest in foreign affairs than in the nation's struggling economy. Whatever the case, in the 1994 election, America opted for a Democratic president for the first time in 12 years.

For the most part, Bush takes pleasure in life after politics, with time divided between homes in Houston, Texas, and Kennebunkport, Maine. She admits to having less patience than her husband with drive-by tourists and the constant intrusion of well wishers. Plans for the house they built in Houston were changed to include a six-foot fence, and she is sometimes short with people who stop her when she is shopping or dining out. She fills her time with friends, family, travel, and a continuation of charitable work. Completing her biography, *Barbara Bush: A Memoir* (1994), she had remained active in her efforts on behalf of people with leukemia, the Crohn's and Colitis Foundation, and Boys and Girls Clubs. She is also ambassador at large for AmeriCares. Bush's number one cause, however, continues to be literacy.

SOURCES:

Bush, Barbara. *Barbara Bush: A Memoir.* NY: Scribner, 1994.

Gareffa, Peter, ed. *Newsmakers, 1989.* Detroit, MI: Gale Research, 1989.

Paletta, LuAnn. *The World Almanac of First Ladies.* NY: World Almanac, 1990.

Barbara Morgan,
Melrose, Massachusetts

Bushnell, Catherine (1825–1861).

See Hayes, Catherine.

Busoni, Anna (1833–1909)

Italian pianist. Born Anna Weiss in Trieste in 1833; died in 1909; married Ferdinando Busoni (a clarinettist); children: Feruccio Benvenuto Busoni (1866–1924).

Anna Busoni showed musical talent at an early age and made her debut as a soloist at 14. Married to Ferdinando Busoni, a clarinettist of limited talent, she gave lessons to their son Feruccio Benvenuto Busoni, a prodigy who gave his first concert at age seven. By the time Feruccio was 12, he and his mother were performing duet recitals in public. In later years, she concentrated on teaching.

Buss, Frances Mary (1827–1894)

English pioneer in women's education. Born in London in 1827; died in London on December 24, 1894; daughter of R.W. Buss (a painter and etcher who was one of the original illustrators of Pickwick Papers*).*

Frances Mary Buss

Educated at a school in Camden Town, England, Frances Mary Buss continued there as a teacher until she joined her mother in keeping a school in Kentish Town. In 1850, her school was moved to Camden Street; under a new name, the North London Collegiate School for Ladies, it rapidly increased in numbers and reputation. In 1864, Buss appeared before the Schools Inquiry Commission, which later singled out her school for exceptional commendation. Under her influence, pioneering work was done to put the education of girls on a proper intellectual footing. Shortly afterwards, the Brewers' Company and the Clothworkers' Company provided funds by which the existing North London Collegiate School, of which Buss was principal, was rehoused and a Camden School for Girls founded. Buss and *Dorothea Beale of Cheltenham became famous as the chief leaders in this branch of the educational reform movement. Buss played an active part in promoting the success of the Girls' Public Day School Company, encouraging the connection of the girls' schools with the university standard by examinations. She worked for the establishment of women's colleges and improved the training of teachers, while her energetic personality was known as a potent force among her pupils and colleagues.

Butcher, Joan (d. 1550).

See Bocher, Joan.

Butcher, Susan (1954—)

American sled-dog racer and four-time winner of the Iditarod. Born on December 26, 1954, in Cambridge, Massachusetts; daughter of Charlie and Agnes Butcher; married David Monson (1988 winner of the Yukon Quest).

Though she grew up in Cambridge, Massachusetts, Susan Butcher spent her happiest days at the family summer home in Brooklin, Maine, a sparsely populated town on the Atlantic seacoast. Her constant companion was a Siberian husky. To make her position on urban living clear, at age eight, she wrote an essay entitled "I Hate the City." At 16, Butcher, who had learned to sail and work as a skilled carpenter, was rejected when she applied to a boat-building school. The administrators, though regretful, informed her that she was the wrong gender.

After graduating from Warehouse Cooperative School near Cambridge, the teenaged Butcher moved to Boulder, Colorado, where she met a woman who bred and raced sled dogs. For several years, Butcher spent weekdays as a veterinary technician while racing Siberians in local weekend sprints. In March of 1973, she read about the inaugural running of the Alaskan Iditarod (brainchild of ❧ **Dorothy Page**), which was billed as The Last Great Race on Earth. Two years later, Butcher moved to Fairbanks, where she signed on as a veterinary technician at the University of Alaska musk-ox farm; she also acquired a 15-dog kennel and started training. When the musk-ox farm moved to Unalakleet, a fishing village on Norton Sound, Susan made the move as well. Fortunately for her, Joe Redington, Sr., the father of the Iditarod, just happened to be managing a fishing cannery there that summer of 1977. During the early part of 1978, Butcher lived in a tent near Knik to train her first sled-dog team and simulate conditions of the grueling race.

Each year in late February or early March, during the long Alaskan winter, the Iditarod begins in downtown Anchorage in southcentral Alaska and runs for 1,049 miles through the vast uninhabited wilderness. The historic Iditarod trail began as a mail-and-supply route from the coastal towns of Seward and Knik to interior mining camps—Flat, Ophir, Ruby—and the westcoast communities of Unalakleet, Elim, Golovin, White Mountain, and Nome. Until the arrival of the airplane in the 1920s, the only means of winter travel was by dog team.

Mushers come from Canada, Czechoslovakia, Great Britain, France, Germany, Switzerland, Norway, Italy, Japan, Austria, and Australia to cross the Alaska Range, head west along the winding Yukon River through the arctic tundra, then north up to Nome on the western Bering Sea coast. Fighting subzero temperatures, blizzards that wipe out visibility, long hours of darkness, and treacherous climbs over rough terrain, they cross frozen rivers, cut through dense forests, and scale jagged mountain ranges. Depending on the weather, the race takes anywhere from two to three weeks. Food and supplies are available at 26 checkpoints in small Eskimo villages. Mushers are equipped with an arctic parka, a heavy sleeping bag, an axe, snowshoes, musher food, dog food, and boots for each dog's feet to protect against cutting ice and hard-packed snow injuries. The care of the 12-to-18 dog team is strictly enforced and an integral part of the official rules. Each racer has a different strategy: some run their dogs at night, others by day.

When Susan Butcher entered the Iditarod in 1978, it was the first time three women ran and the first time women placed in the Top 20: Butcher placed 19th, **Varona Thompson** placed

❧▶ **Page, Dorothy G.** (d. 1989)
American mayor, considered the "Mother of the Iditarod." Born in Bessemer, Michigan; died in 1989; married Vondolee Page.

Following her marriage, Dorothy Page moved to Alaska by way of New Mexico in 1960, when her husband Von was hired as superintendent of schools of Dillingham. When Von accepted another superintendency in 1962, the couple moved to Wasilla. Immersing herself in its civic life, Page labored for the city's incorporation in 1974, then served on the Wasilla City Council for ten years. In 1986, she was elected mayor.

In 1964, she served as chair for the Wasilla-Knik Centennial Committee, working on projects to celebrate Alaska's 1967 Centennial Year. Page happily submerged herself in the state's history, heading two historical restoration ventures that turned the Knik Pool Hall and the Wasilla Community Hall into museums. Becoming aware of the importance of dog teams and the Iditarod trail in Alaskan history, she created the Sled Dog Mushers Hall of Fame in the Knik museum; this marked the beginning of interest in mushing.

In 1965, Page proposed a sled-dog race over part of the Iditarod trail and took her idea to Joe Redington, Sr., who had been involved with mushing in Alaska for years. Together, they headed a small group that planned the first short (60 miles) "Iditarod Trail International Championship Race" and convinced locals to clear years of overgrowth for the first nine miles of the trail. Fifty teams vied in 1967 for $25,000. The purse was partially amassed when Joe and **Vi Redington** donated an acre of their own land to sell. When the U.S. Army reopened the trail as a winter exercise in 1973, Page and Redington gathered other dog drivers and kennel clubs to organize the trans-Alaska race. Although the inaugural race was fraught with financial difficulties, Page induced musher Muktuk Marston to ante up $10,000; others, now convinced of the soundness of the race, began to contribute. For the next 16 years until her death in 1989, Dorothy Page worked arduously for the success of the Iditarod, edited the *Iditarod Trail Annual*, and created the monthly *Iditarod Runner*. "I don't ever want to see any high pressure people getting in and changing the spirit of the race," said Page. Headquarters for the Iditarod is still in Wasilla, Alaska. Population: 4,028 at the last census.

20th. The following year, Butcher crossed the finish in Nome in 9th place. A few months later, she and Redington assembled a team of dogs and spent 44 days climbing Mt. McKinley, the first to mush a team of dogs to the top.

Training 6,000 to 7,000 miles per year for the next seven years would pay off for Butcher. She finished 5th in 1980 and 1981, the first woman to place in the Top Five. (Seven women

had entered the 1980 race.) In 1982, after 16 days on the trail, despite injured dogs and constant storms, Butcher moved up to 2nd—the winner had crossed the line only 3 minutes and 46 seconds before her. In 1983, she placed 9th; in 1984, she again took 2nd. Alaskans began to

speculate that it was just a matter of time before Susan Butcher would win the Iditarod.

In 1985, Butcher felt her time had come. But snow in the Matanuska-Susitna Valley was very deep that year, and when the snow is deep the moose use the dog trails. Butcher was in the lead approaching the tent checkpoint at Rabbit Lake when a large cow moose, "eyes wild," stood in the middle of the trail 20 feet in front of her legendary lead dog Granite. Though Butcher tipped the sled over to stop, the moose charged into the team. Butcher was terrified, but she'd met up with moose before. Generally, they "come storming through," she noted, "hitting dogs, the sled and myself, but then they continue down the trail." So she braced for the momentary onslaught, but:

> fate would not have it that way. The moose stopped in the middle of the team and reared up on her hind legs, and with her full weight came crashing down on Johnnie and Ruff, two of my strongest team dogs. For the next five minutes, it was a nightmarish blur. I was hearing yelps of my beloved dogs, hearing the cow snorting and growling and the snap of her hind legs striking out against dog after dog all up and down the line. My mind was whirling with thoughts to protect my dogs and myself, but no solution came up. Then suddenly she stopped, square in front of me. . . . I pulled off my parka, waving it in her face, trying to scare her off. She charged me. I backed off. But again I tried. She backed off to the front of the team where she had a free avenue of escape, but instead she charged again. . . . I went slowly up through the team releasing necklines and tugs so the dogs tangled could retreat.

By the time another musher appeared and shot the moose, the animal had killed two of Butcher's dogs, Johnnie and Hyde, and injured 13 others. That year, to the surprise of all, ❧➤ **Libby Riddles** was the first woman to win the Iditarod. With Butcher's tender care, her dogs recovered (though she still felt the loss of Johnnie and Hyde); the following year, Susan Butcher finally won her first Iditarod, taking 11 days, 15 hours, 0 minutes, and 6 seconds. She repeated her win in 1987, setting a new record of 11:2:5:13. In 1988, when she again crossed the finish line first in 11:11:41:11, she was surrounded by cheering fans and T-shirts that read "Alaska: Where Men are Men and Women Win the Iditarod." Though she did not win in 1989, the women were accounted for: **DeeDee Jonrowe** finished 4th. Butcher returned to win in 1990, breaking her own record and setting a new record for the northern route, 11:1:53:23. She was now only the second person to win the race four times.

In 1991, Butcher's 3rd place finish was with first-rate style. Ordinarily, the run from Ophir to Iditarod, the halfway point in the race, takes about 12 hours, but the race was plagued by storms and that year it took 25 hours. For al-most 80 miles, Butcher and Jonrowe took turns in front so neither of their lead dogs would become discouraged. Both snowshoed ahead of their teams, leading them on. Just before she crossed the halfway line at Iditarod, Butcher stopped her team and asked the race judge if she could park her dogs and wait to cross. "We mushed 80 miles together," she said, "and I want it to be a tie." The two women crossed together and were the first to share the halfway prize. When Butcher hit another storm after leaving White Mountain in the lead, she turned back, feeling that her dogs had endured one storm too many.

Out of her last 14 races entered, Butcher has finished in the Top 10 in 11 of them. She has set the Iditarod speed record of 11:1:53:23, and records in four other races: the Norton Sound 200, the Kusko 300, the Arctic Coast 200, and the John Beargrease Race in Minnesota.

Susan Butcher lives north of Fairbanks in Manley with husband David Monson. Together they operate the Trail Breaker Kennels. "I pride myself in taking the best care and spending the most time with my dogs of all long distance racers," said Butcher. "My lead dog training and love of my animals are the reasons for my success. I have fantastic dogs to work with." Twice named Women's Sports Foundation's Profession-

❧➤ **Riddles, Libby** (1956—)
American sled-dog racer and the first woman to win the Iditarod. Born on April 1, 1956, in St. Cloud, Minnesota; daughter of Mary Riddles.

Libby Riddles, who began mushing in 1979, placed 18th in her first Iditarod in 1980 and 20th in 1981. While living in Teller, a village north of Nome, she trained her team by running into the cold winds that swept in from the Bering Sea. Though *Susan Butcher was the favorite in the 1985 race, Riddles pushed on when other mushers held back. The run from Shaktoolik to the next checkpoint is about 50 miles across the ice. With bad weather closing in, only a few hours of daylight left, and the possibility that she could lose the trail because of blowing snow, Riddles decided to take her chance. She was the only musher to leave that day; the others, because of darkness and blizzard conditions, waited until the following morning. Her perseverance paid off, and Riddles won this, only her second, Iditarod.

SUGGESTED READING:
Riddles, Libby. *Race Across Alaska: First Woman to Win the Iditarod Tells Her Story.* Stackpole Books, 1988.

al Sportswoman of the Year in 1987 and 1988, Butcher was also named Sled Dog Racer of the Decade in 1989 by the *Anchorage Times* and was selected Outstanding Female Athlete of the World by the International Academy of Sports.

SOURCES:
Stout, Peg. *Alaskan Women in the Iditarod.* State of Alaska: Alaska Department of Education, 1992. (Funded by Title IX.)
Woolum, Janet. *Outstanding Women Athletes: Who They Are and How They Influenced Sports in America.* Phoenix, AZ: Oryx Press, 1992.

SUGGESTED READING:
Nielsen, Nicki J. *The Iditarod: Women on the Trail.* Anchorage, AK: Wolfdog Publications, 1986.

RELATED MEDIA:
Alaska's Great Race: The Susan Butcher Story (57 min.), Pal Productions, 1989.

Bute, countess of.

See Montagu, Mary Wortley for sidebar on Mary (b. 1718).

Bute, Mary Ellen (1906–1983)

American avant-garde filmmaker. Born in Houston, Texas, in 1906; died in 1983; attended the Pennsylvania Academy and the Sorbonne, Paris; married Ted Nemuth.

Filmography: Rhythm in Light *(1934);* Synchrony No. 2 *(1936);* Evening Star *(1937);* Parabola *(1938);* Spook Sport *(1939);* Escape *(1940);* Tarantella *(1941);* Polka Graph *(1952);* Mood Contrasts *(1952);* Abstronics *(1954);* The Boy Who Saw Through *(1956);* Passages from Finnegan's Wake *(*Finnegan's Wake, *1965);* The Skin of Our Teeth *(unfinished, 1983).*

Mary Ellen Bute was one of the most original avant-garde filmmakers of her day. Trained initially as an artist, she found the traditional frame too confining and turned to musical composition to augment her painting. To this end, she became an experimental filmmaker.

Working with musician and electronics engineer Leon Theremin, in an effort to create "visual music," Bute began to experiment with optical devices that projected color and images synchronized to musical compositions. She made several films using drawings photographed at differing speeds of light. *Rhythm in Light,* shot in black and white in 1934, is scored to Edvard Grieg's *Anitra's Dance.* Her color film *Spook Sport,* shot in 1939, was animated by Norman McLaren, another well-known experimental filmmaker of her generation.

In the 1950s, Bute collaborated with her husband, director Ted Nemuth. Together they choreographed images with a beam of light using a custom made oscilloscope. The result was the film *Abstronics,* which was based on music by Aaron Copland.

In the early 1960s, when she decided to direct live-action features, Bute chose as her first work, *Passages from Finnegan's Wake,* also titled *Finnegan's Wake,* adapted from a play by **Mary Manning.** Bute had long been attracted to the work of writer James Joyce. "Considering the impossibility of translating what is essentially a literary mind game into filmic terms, the picture is a triumph," wrote Nash and Ross. At the time of her death in 1983 at age 77, Bute was working on an adaptation of Thornton Wilder's *The Skin of Our Teeth.*

SOURCES:
Aker, Ally. *Reel Women: Pioneers of the Cinema 1896 to the Present.* NY: Continuum, 1991.
Kuhn, Annette, ed. with Susannah Radstone. *The Women's Companion to International Film.* Berkeley, CA: University of California Press, 1994.
Nash, Jay Robert, and Stanley Ralph Ross. *The Motion Picture Guide.* Chicago, IL: Cinebooks, 1986.

Deborah Jones,
Studio City, California

Butler, Eleanor (c. 1738–1829).

See Ladies of Llangollen.

Butler, Elizabeth Beardsley (c. 1885–1911)

American labor investigator. Born around 1885; died of tuberculosis on August 2, 1911; graduated Barnard College, 1905; never married; no children.

Was executive assistant, the New Jersey Consumers' League and the New Jersey Child Labor Committee (1905); was assistant secretary, Rand School of Social Science (1907). Selected publications: Women and the Trades, *Pittsburgh, 1907–1908 (1909) and* Saleswomen in Mercantile Stores, *Baltimore, 1909 (published posthumously in 1912).*

Little is known about Elizabeth Beardsley Butler, who died at the young age of 26. Yet before her death she wrote two of the most comprehensive examinations of women's labor conditions in pre-World War I America. Her 1909 publication *Women and the Trades* set a standard for investigation and interpretation of industrial conditions. A "convinced socialist," Butler railed against the exploitation of the women workers she studied and advocated protective labor legislation and vocational training as a way to address the inequities of industrial capitalism.

Elizabeth Butler graduated from Barnard College in 1905 and then, like so many women college graduates interested in social reform, lived for a time at a settlement house. While at Whittier House, in Jersey City, she worked for the Consumers' League of New Jersey as well as that state's Child Labor Committee. She also investigated the conditions of labor in sweatshops and department stores around New Jersey. In New York City, she worked for the New York School of Philanthropy's Bureau of Social Research and for the Rand School of Social Science.

In 1907, Butler went to Pittsburgh to investigate women's work conditions. As part of the privately funded Pittsburgh Survey, she joined a team of similarly minded Progressive reformers who sought to expose the harsh conditions of labor and life for America's predominately immigrant and urban working class. In two years, Butler visited over 400 places of employment, collecting a massive amount of data that demonstrated not only the need for reform but the varied occupations of American women workers. Shortly after conducting a similar study of Baltimore retail clerks, a 26-year-old Butler died of tuberculosis in 1911. This highly contagious disease was one of the leading causes of death for young working-class women in this period, though it is not certain that Butler contracted the disease while conducting her investigations. During her short life, Elizabeth Beardsley Butler exposed the world to the harsh conditions faced by working women in turn-of-the-century America.

SOURCES:

Butler, Elizabeth Beardsley. *Women and the Trades, Pittsburgh, 1907–1908.* Introduction by Maurine Weiner Greenwald. Pittsburgh: University of Pittsburgh, 1984.

Kathleen Banks Nutter,
University of Massachusetts at Amherst

Butler, Elizabeth Thompson

(1846–1933)

One of the most successful English painters of military subjects in the 19th century, who brought a new realism to the depiction of war in British art. Name variations: Elizabeth Southerden Thompson; Lady Butler. Born Elizabeth Southerden Thompson on November 3, 1846, near Lausanne, Switzerland; died on October 2, 1933, at Gormanston Castle, County Meath, Ireland; daughter of Thomas James Thompson and Christiana (Weller) Thompson; sister of ❧▶ *Alice Meynell; studied at the Female School of Art, South Kensington (1866–1870), and Giuseppe Bellucci's Academy in Florence (1869); married Major William Butler on June 11, 1877; children: Elizabeth (b. 1879); Patrick (b. 1880); Richard; Eileen (b. 1883); Martin (b. 1887); and a daughter, Mary, who died in infancy.*

Visited the battlefield of Waterloo (1865); exhibited at the Society of Women Artists and the Dudley Gallery (1867); received commission for The Roll Call *(1872); had* Missing *accepted by the Royal Academy (1873), and* The Roll Call *(1874); traveled extensively (1885–92), including time in Egypt where her husband was serving; toured Palestine (1891) and published* Letters from the Holy Land *(1903); published* From Sketch-Book and Diary *(1909); exhibited watercolors at the Leicester Galleries (1912); exhibited at the Waterloo Centenary Exhibition held at the Leicester Galleries (1915); published* An Autobiography *(1922).*

Major works: The Roll Call *(1874, collection of Her Majesty the Queen);* The 28th Regiment at Quatre Bras *(1875, National Gallery of Victoria, Melbourne);* Balaclava *(1876, Manchester City Art Galleries);* The Defence of Rorke's Drift *(1880, collection of HMQ);* Scotland for Ever! *(1881, Leeds City Art Galleries);* "Steady the drums and fifes!" *(1897, collection of The Queens' Regiment, Canterbury). Signed works E.T. or E.S.T. before marriage, E.B. after.*

During the 1870s, painting in England reflected the growing public concern over the failure of Victorian prosperity to reach the working classes. The resulting school of painting, known as British Social Realism, emphasized the stark, unromanticized, depiction of the poor and disadvantaged members of society. At the same time, a series of reforms of the military, known as the Cardwell Reforms (after Edward Cardwell, the war minister), was eroding the system of privilege and elitism that had until then characterized the British army. So, when in 1874 a young artist, Elizabeth Thompson, exhibited her painting *The Roll Call* at the Royal Academy, its realistic portrayal of the enduring strength of the common British soldier resonated strongly with popular sentiments. Elizabeth Thompson, virtually overnight, became one of the most renowned British military painters of the 19th century, with her works reproduced in thousands of prints.

The parents of Elizabeth Thompson first met in 1844, when, after attending a piano recital by Christiana Weller, Thomas Thompson and Charles Dickens called on the Wellers the next day. Thomas Thompson's background was

See sidebar on the following page

❧▶ Meynell, Alice (1847–1922)

English poet and essayist. Born Alice Christiana Gertrude Thompson at Barnes, Surrey, England, on September 22, 1847 (some sources cite August 17); died on November 27, 1922; second daughter of Thomas and **Christiana Weller Thompson***; younger sister of* *Elizabeth Thompson Butler; married Wilfred Meynell (a journalist), 1877; children: eight, including Francis, Everard, and Viola Meynell (1886–1956).*

Alice Meynell shared with her sister Elizabeth a liberal education and a wide experience of travel. Their mother Christiana, who was an accomplished concert pianist, took an active interest in all the arts, and encouraged her daughters to sing, write, and draw. In 1872, Alice converted to Catholicism, as her mother had before her, after which she became involved with the Catholic literary circle in England. Her first book of poems, *Preludes,* was published in 1875, with illustrations by Elizabeth. Meynell was praised and encouraged by Tennyson and Ruskin, among others, but in later years she expressed dissatisfaction with her earliest work.

Journalist Wilfred Meynell read a review of *Preludes* and was so impressed by the poem included in it that he contacted Alice regarding the possibility of contributing to the magazine that he edited. In 1877, they were married, and for many years they shared various writing and editing projects. First, in 1880, they edited and wrote for *The Pen,* then from 1881 to 1898 they worked on *The Weekly Register.* From 1883 to 1895, they ran *Merry England,* a monthly founded by the Meynells themselves, which, unlike the other periodicals Wilfred Meynell had been involved with, was intended to find an audience beyond the Catholic community. In 1893, Alice Meynell's first book of essays, *The Rhythm of Life,* was published;

it contained mainly essays originally written for the *Dublin Review* and the *Scots Observer.* Also in 1893, the poems from *Preludes* were republished as *Poems.* She began writing weekly articles for the *Pall Mall Gazette* in 1894, some of which were collected as *The Color of Life* in 1896. Other volumes of poems and essays followed, as she remained a prolific writer of essays and journalism throughout her career, although her output of poetry was small. She wrote for *The Spectator, The Saturday Review, The Magazine of Art,* and *The Art Journal,* among others. Somehow Alice maintained this pace while raising eight children born in the years 1879 to 1891.

Alice Meynell, though she emphasized that she was not a militant, was an active and vocal supporter of the women's suffrage movement. She noted, in a letter to *The Times,* that "it is a fact of human life that 'sex' troubles man at least as much as it troubles woman, but it does not disfranchise man." When Alfred Austin, England's poet laureate, died in 1913, Alice Meynell was among those championed in the literary press to assume the post. In one poll, she came second to Rudyard Kipling in popularity, although in the end neither of them was chosen. Alice Meynell died on November 27, 1922, leaving behind a reputation as one of England's most thoughtful poets and insightful essayists.

The Meynell family was very close, and from a young age the children were closely involved with writing and editing. Francis Meynell worked as an editor on several Socialist newspapers. Everard Meynell was an accomplished writer, particularly on art, including volumes on Corot and Bellini; he also wrote a biography of Francis Thompson. ❧▶ **Viola Meynell** (1886–1956) was a writer, poet, and biographer.

William MacKenzie, University of Guelph, Guelph, Ontario, Canada

---

somewhat unusual for an English gentleman of leisure. His grandfather, Thomas Pepper Thompson, made the family fortune in Jamaican sugar, before returning to England. Thomas Thompson was the illegitimate son of Mary Edwards and James Thompson, himself the illegitimate son of Thomas Pepper Thompson. Curiously, the inheritance that came to Thomas Thompson from his grandfather was, should there be no direct heir, to pass to the heirs of Edward Moulton Barrett; this included *Elizabeth **Barrett Browning**, the poet. Whether they were related is unknown, but the Brownings apparently believed so. The Weller family was initially opposed to the relationship that developed between Thompson and Weller, but in the end they were married on October 21, 1845. The couple

embarked upon a lifestyle of travel that was to continue for most of their lives. Elizabeth, their first child, was born on November 3, 1846; she was always known to her family as Mimi. Alice, their second daughter, was born in 1847.

The Thompson sisters benefitted from their parents mobile lifestyle, traveling throughout Italy for the first of many times in 1851, where they became attached to Fanny and Tom, their father's children from his first marriage. In 1852, the family took up residence at the Villa dei Franchi in Sori, where they frequently returned over the years. It was here that Thomas Thompson began the education of his daughters, which he undertook entirely by himself. He had attended Trinity College, Cambridge, and was a demanding teacher. Both sisters were keen students of history, and avid linguists. They worked particularly hard on their Italian, learning first the Genoese and then the Tuscan dialect. The sisters were also included in the numerous festivities that attended the visits of friends, among them Dickens, at the Thompson household. They spent a year (1854–55) in England, but continued to travel Europe at a frenetic pace with their parents. Both of the sisters were avid readers, and Alice began to write poetry by the time she was nine. By 1860, Elizabeth was filling sketchbooks with her drawings, which already emphasized military topics; she sketched Garibaldi's troops while they were bivouacked near Genoa, where the Thompsons were staying.

Elizabeth first studied painting under W. Standish, in London in 1862. On her 19th birthday, she visited the site of the battle of Waterloo, where she felt the "awful glamour" that characterized her feelings about war. She enrolled briefly in the Female School of Art, South Kensington, but withdrew because of the school's emphasis on design over figure painting. However, she returned in 1866 and engaged in rigorous study of figure drawing; she also attended a private class, drawing female nudes. In 1869, she spent much of the summer studying in Florence under Giuseppe Bellucci at the Academy of Fine Arts, further refining her ability to draw figures.

While in London for the winter, the Thompsons were visited by John Ruskin, who examined some of Elizabeth's drawings and was also one of the first to read some of Alice's poetry. Elizabeth had already settled on military painting as her specialty and was pleased to be able to make use of local farms to observe and paint horses, an essential skill in military painting. In Italy for the summer of 1868, Elizabeth set up a studio to paint, while Alice continued to write poetry. It was while in Italy that Elizabeth painted and exhibited her first major work. Her *Magnificat* (now in the Church of St. Wilfred, Isle of Wight), using her mother as a model for the Virgin Mary, was included in the Pope's International Exhibition, although because of her gender she was not herself allowed into the exhibition.

In 1868, Thompson exhibited two paintings with the Society of Female Artists; in 1872, the society changed its name to the Society of Lady Artists, and Thompson was one of the 23 full members. By 1872, Elizabeth had for several years been moderately successful at exhibiting and selling watercolors of military topics, some inspired by the Franco-Prussian War. The first watercolor that she exhibited publicly, *Bavarian*

❧ **Meynell, Viola** (1886–1956)

*English writer, poet, and biographer. Born Viola Meynell at Phillimore Place, Kensington, in 1886; died in 1956; daughter of *Alice Meynell (1847–1922) and Wilfred Meynell; married John Dallyn, 1922; children: one son.*

Viola Meynell's first novel, *Lot Barrow*, was published in 1913. She produced 20 volumes of prose and poetry, as well as editing others, including selections from George Eliot (*Mary Anne Evans*). Viola wrote a memoir of her mother, as well as one on her father's association with Francis Thompson, the poet. Her short stories, perhaps her best work, were collected in 1957.

William MacKenzie, University of Guelph, Guelph, Ontario, Canada

---

Artillery Going into Action (1867), was based on an incident during the Austro-Prussian War of 1866. In the fall of 1872, Elizabeth was able to observe British soldiers on manoeuvres near Southampton, and this inspired a number of watercolors that were exhibited at the Dudley Gallery in London. One of these, *Soldiers Watering Horses* (1872), was purchased by Charles Galloway, who subsequently commissioned an oil painting from Thompson. Her first military oil painting, *Missing*, inspired by the Franco-Prussian War, was accepted by the Royal Academy in 1873; her earlier work, *The Magnificat*, had been turned down by them in 1871. In the fall of 1873, Elizabeth and Alice went on pilgrimage to Paray-le-Monial, Elizabeth having recently followed her mother and sister in converting to Catholicism. When she received her commission from Galloway, she set up her own studio in London in December 1873 and began work on *The Roll Call*. Also in 1874, Elizabeth joined the New Watercolor Society, which was admitting women gradually; this was faster than the Royal Academy, which admitted no women in the 19th century.

> *T*hank God, I never painted for the glory of war, but to portray its pathos and heroism.
> —Lady Butler

When the annual exhibition of the Royal Academy opened in 1874, indeed even before, the center of attention was *The Roll Call* by Elizabeth Thompson. The man who had commissioned it, Charles Galloway, was promptly inundated with requests to purchase the painting, all of which he declined, until Queen *Victoria expressed a desire to purchase the work. A relatively static composition for a military painting,

The Roll Call shows a scene from the Crimean War, a unit of Grenadier Guards mustering in the snow after an apparently gruelling engagement. The painting was not, as many of her others were, explicitly identified with a particular action; it was, instead, a tribute to the endurance and bravery of the common soldier. Elizabeth Thompson was the first British artist to utilize the realistic approach to military painting, which was then flourishing in France. Three of the principal artists of this movement, Meissonier, De Neuville, and Detaille, influenced her work. *The Roll Call* toured the country after the exhibition, attracting thousands of viewers, achieving a remarkable popularity. Thousands of engravings were sold by the Fine Art Society, which held the copyright to reproductions of the painting. Even after the turn of the century, *The Roll Call* still evoked enthusiastic responses from the public when it was exhibited.

Thompson's next two works, *The 28th Regiment at Quatre Bras of 1875*, a Napoleonic scene, and *Balaclava of 1876*, another Crimean scene, were both well received, and again, many engravings of these works were sold. Thompson's decision to exhibit the later work at the Fine Art Society, rather than the Royal Academy, elicited criticism from the press, but, like *The Roll Call*, *Balaclava* toured the country with great public success. Despite warnings from critics that a woman artist could not adequately deal with the subject, Thompson rapidly became the most prominent military painter in the nation. She contributed illustrations to a number of projects, including a volume of her sister's poems (1875) and an edition of Thackeray's ballads (1879). *The Return from Inkerman of 1877* was Thompson's third Crimean War subject, and it was also displayed by the Fine Arts Society. However, it did not receive the critical or public attention of her earlier work, and indeed she never again achieved the prominence she had in the early 1870s. This was partially due to the generation of painters who, after the success of Thompson, produced something of a glut of similar work.

In 1879, in the wake of her remarkable rise to prominence, Elizabeth Thompson was nominated for election as an associate of the Royal Academy. The success of *The Roll Call* initiated a public debate over the issue of women artists, and the lack of female associates of the Academy was one element of this debate. In the end, Thompson came very close to being the only woman prior to the 20th century accepted into the Academy; the man chosen instead won by 27 votes to her 25. Strangely, though, having come so close, she was never even nominated again. A combination of the decline in pressure for reform and the decline of her own popularity contributed to this oversight. There is also the fact that Thompson herself was skeptical about suffragist issues, with which her sister Alice was so closely involved, and was not inclined to lobby for membership.

As a result of her success, Elizabeth was welcomed into the social sphere of the prominent Catholics in England. Consequently, she met Major William Francis Butler (1838–1910), a distinguished soldier from a poor Irish Catholic family. They were married on June 11, 1877. After her marriage, Elizabeth continued her career as a professional painter, which was somewhat unusual for the times, but her efforts were hampered by the demands of being a soldier's wife. In 1879, she exhibited two paintings with the Royal Academy, *The Remnants of an Army* and *Listed for the Connaught Rangers*. Both of these departed from her pattern of displaying the triumph over adversity in war but were still well received. In the 1870s, she also contributed illustrations to the *Graphic*, the main outlet of Social Realist work, and later to the *Daily Graphic*. Thompson's last major success at the Royal Academy was *The Defence of Rorke's Drift*, January 22nd, 1879, which was commissioned by the queen in 1879, completed in 1880, and exhibited in 1881. The dramatic *Scotland for Ever!* of 1881 was again much reproduced, and served as the model for many subsequent military paintings by other artists. Its success came in spite of the fact that it was not exhibited at the Royal Academy.

Thompson did not exhibit for four years after 1881, and her work received little attention during the 1880s. She had turned to the painting of modern actions and her approach to such topics may have been influenced by her husband, who was extremely critical of British Imperial policy. Her work showed less emphasis on victory and more on perseverance. During the decade, Thompson contributed illustrations to *Merry England*, a monthly paper established in 1883 by Alice and her husband Wilfred Meynell, the editor. In 1886, William Butler was knighted, and Elizabeth became Lady Butler.

The 1890s saw something of a rise in Thompson's fortunes, as her own return to historical subjects was paralleled by a general rise in interest in such works. *Dawn of Waterloo* (1895), exhibited at the Royal Academy, showed not the glory of the battle, however, but the trepidation preceding it. Similarly, *"Steady the*

Drums and Fifes!" (1897) placed emphasis on the young musicians facing death in the imminent battle. In 1891, the Butlers toured Palestine on horseback for a month, during which Elizabeth kept up her family's tradition of voluminous correspondence. Elizabeth's mother, **Christiana Thompson**, eventually encouraged the publication of a collection of Elizabeth's letters to her, with 16 illustrations by Elizabeth, as *Letters From the Holy Land* (1903).

From the turn of the century until World War I, Thompson exhibited only six paintings, a substantial decline in production. Additionally, her work began to place less emphasis on the heroism of the British soldier at war. Possibly she shared some of her husband's growing disillusionment with British imperialism. Sir William Butler was appointed commander in chief in South Africa in 1898, but only remained in the position for less than a year because he felt that the War Office's policy of instigating war with the Boers was unreasonable. As a result, he was a target for accusations in the press during the Boer War. After his retirement in 1905, the family moved to Bansha Castle, County Tipperary, in Ireland. He died in 1910, and their youngest daughter, Eileen, married in 1911, after which Elizabeth lived alone at Bansha until she moved to Gormanston Castle.

In 1906, Elizabeth was granted a semi-private audience with the pope while in Rome, and Alice accompanied her. While Alice was closely involved in the women's suffrage movement, Elizabeth distanced herself from it. When she heard of Alice's intention to attend the demonstration in Hyde Park in 1912, she wrote her, commenting, "the papers say all the marchers will wear 'Caps of Liberty.' I hope there will be some exceptions if you are one of the marchers." In 1909, Thompson published her second book, *From Sketch Book and Diary*, which contained accounts of some of her experiences traveling in Europe and Africa over the years. It was illustrated with 28 color plates of her watercolors.

In 1913, she began to organize a Waterloo Centenary Exhibition to be held at the Leicester Galleries. The exhibition opened in 1915 and featured *Scotland for Ever!*, along with one other oil painting and 24 watercolors. In contrast to the prior decades, the war years saw Elizabeth Thompson (now known as Lady Butler) again producing studies of the stalwart British soldier. She avoided dealing with the more horrific realities of modern war, however, partially by choice and partially because she was not herself witness to any of it. The realism of the Official War Artists made her work seem outmoded, but she defended her approach with the philosophy that while war brought out the worst in man, it also brought out the best, and it behooves the artist to focus on that. Elizabeth mounted two war-related exhibitions, "Some Glimpses of the Great War" in 1917 and "Some Records of the Great War" in 1919, both at the Leicester Galleries. Her earlier work remained her most popular, though, as indicated by the reenactment of *The Roll Call*, which took place at the Aldershot Tattoo in 1909.

When the war ended, Thompson ceased to paint contemporary scenes and mostly produced versions of earlier works for the remainder of her career. In 1922, she moved to her daughter Eileen's home at Gormanston Castle, where she lived for the rest of her life. She died on October 2, 1933, and was buried in Stamullen, a nearby village. Her reputation had already faded by the end of her career, but at the peak of her success she was perhaps the best known, and most popular, painter in England.

SOURCES:

Badeni, June. *The Slender Tree: A Life of Alice Meynell*. Padstow, Cornwall: Tabb House, 1981.

Greer, Germaine. *The Obstacle Race*. London: Secker & Warburg, 1979.

Lalumia, Matthew. "Lady Elizabeth Thompson Butler in the 1870s," in *Woman's Art Journal*. Vol. 4, no. 1. Spring-Summer 1983, pp. 9–14.

Lalumia, Matthew Paul. *Realism and Politics in Victorian Art of the Crimean War*. Ann Arbor, MI: UMI Research Press, 1984.

Meynell, Alice. *Prose and Poetry*. London: Jonathan Cape, 1947.

Meynell, Viola. *Alice Meynell: A Memoir*. London: Jonathan Cape, 1929.

———. *Francis Thompson and Wilfred Meynell*. London: Hollis & Carter, 1952.

Nunn, Pamela Gerrish. *Victorian Women Artists*. London: The Women's Press, 1987.

Oldcastle, John (Wilfred Meynell). "Elizabeth Butler (nee Thompson)," in *The Magazine of Art*. 1897, pp. 257–262.

Usherwood, Paul, and Jenny Spencer-Smith. *Lady Butler, Battle Artist, 1846–1933*. London: Alan Sutton Publishing and the National Army Museum, 1987.

Yeldham, Charlotte. *Women Artists in Nineteenth-Century France and England*. NY: Garland, 1984.

Obituary. "Lady Butler," in *The Times*. October 3, 1933.

SUGGESTED READING:

Butler, Elizabeth. *From Sketch-Book and Diary*. London: Adam and Charles Black, Burns and Oates, 1909.

———. *Letters From the Holy Land*. London: Adam and Charles Black, 1903.

———. *An Autobiography*. London: Constable, 1922.

COLLECTIONS:

Some correspondence in the collection of Hermia Eden, Catherine Eden, and Elizabeth Hawkins at Greatham, Sussex, England.

Works in many private and regimental collections; notable collections held by the National Army Museum and Her Majesty the Queen.

William MacKenzie, graduate student,
University of Guelph, Guelph, Ontario, Canada

Butler, Helen May (1867–1957)

Composer, conductor, and politician, known as the "Female Sousa," who helped establish careers for women musicians and was the first American woman to lead a professional concert band. Name variations: Helen May Spahn, Helen May Young. Born Helen May Butler on May 17, 1867, in Keene, New Hampshire; died on June 16, 1957, in Covington, Kentucky; daughter of Lucius M. (an engineer) and Esther (Abbott) Butler; attended primary schools in Keene and secondary school in Providence, Rhode Island; married John Leslie Spahn, November 5, 1902 (divorced, 1908); married a Mr. Young, around 1910; children (first marriage) Leslie and Helen May.

Helen May Butler

Moved with family to Providence (c. 1890); began Talma Ladies Orchestra (1892); founded Talma Ladies Military Band (1896); initiated band tours with manager John Leslie Spahn (1898); led performance at Pan American Exposition in Buffalo, New York (1901); conducted at the New York Women's Exposition and White House Concert (1902); conducted at Willow Grove Park, St. Louis World's Fair (1904); composed "Cosmopolitan America" for Republican Convention (1904); conducted at Barnum & Bailey Show (1914); ran for U.S. Senate (1936).

Compositions: "Cosmopolitan America March" (1904); "The Billboard Girl March" (1904); "What Cheer March" (1904); "United States Indemnity Medley."

Marking the beginning of the popular music craze, 1892 was a banner year for American music in general and for band music in particular. The song that brought it about was "After The Ball" by Charles K. Harris, which touched the hearts of millions of Americans and sold at least that many copies in the form of sheet music and arrangements for orchestras and bands. Few professional orchestras were in existence in the U.S. and bands were the purveyors of America's

popular music. "After the Ball" was introduced by John Philip Sousa, leader of the professional concert band that earned him the title of "The March King," while much of the nation mourned the passing that year of Patrick S. Gilmore, "The Father of the Modern Concert Band." In the midst of these great musical traditions, Helen May Butler, at age 25, began her own "ladies" orchestra, which would evolve into one of the finest women's concert bands in the world.

Butler was born into a musical household and developed a great love for singing at an early age. In her youth, the family moved to Rhode Island, where she took up the study of the violin with **Adele Shepherdson** of Providence, and later with Bernard Listerman, the concert master of the Boston Symphony. Few women studied violin at that time, and Helen's skill on the instrument must have been exceptional for Listerman to take her on as a student. It is likely that her father contacted the concert master on her behalf, as he was supportive of her musical ventures throughout the years.

It was through a local social group, the Talma Ladies Club, that Butler first encouraged her friends to learn instruments and perform in ensemble in member homes. The small chamber orchestra included men in the beginning, but, as more women became proficient, the men were replaced. As the Talma Ladies Orchestra, the group accumulated enough funds from the sale of concert subscriptions to purchase its own theater.

With band music sweeping the country, Butler decided in 1896 to organize her players into an all-woman band. The project proved difficult, since there were few male musicians who would teach her to play the brass instruments. It took her father several inquiries before he found a bandmaster willing to take her on as a student of the cornet. D.W. Reeves was renowned for his skill as a cornetist, composer, and conductor and had performed as a cornet soloist in Europe and the United States. Marches he composed were later to be extremely popular. Reeves was leader of the American Band, located in Providence, which was considered one of the finest in the nation; compositions and arrangements by Reeves were often a part of Butler's concert programs.

After mastering the cornet, Butler began to teach other women how to perform on band instruments. Sometimes the women had difficulty purchasing their equipment, since many of the instrument makers would offer credit only to men, assuming they were the only ones capable of earning money through performing. Butler's father and brothers would then step in, making the contract arrangements for the instruments in their names. The band leader also taught violin, and the success of her studio served as a model for a number of her own musicians, who would return to teaching music when their touring days were over or after they married.

Happiness and unhappiness are habits. You can cultivate whichever habit you choose.
—Helen May Butler

In performance, the Talma Ladies Military Band wore handsome uniforms in military style. While the novelty of their enterprise was a selling point and guaranteed that the group received attention in the newspapers, once the audience had arrived Butler saw to it that they were treated to the sounds of an exceptional band. In later years, she would be able to say without exaggeration that the group had never received a poor review. Judging from its duration and success, Butler's band far exceeded all other women's ensembles in performing in its day.

In 1898, the ensemble had been together for two years when J. Leslie Spahn undertook its management. Experienced in promotion, Spahn obtained bookings with promoters and park managers who would have been uncomfortable speaking to women about work. He set about arranging a tour that took the band to cities including New York, Boston, and Washington, D.C. Routed along the railroad lines, the group often gave two concerts a day for close to 50 weeks a year. Spahn once wrote that he had the band busy for 54 weeks straight and was trying to make it 56.

With Spahn taking care of the management and travel details and Butler in charge of the artistic side, the two made a successful team. Butler was also careful in the selection of her performers. Players had to be excellent musicians; they also had to associate easily with the other band members. Care was taken to see that the single women were properly chaperoned. Traveling around the country at the turn of the century was inevitably rigorous, however, and it is a testament to Butler's good judgment that the band endured as long as it did.

Her first band members had been drawn from the New England area. Later she was able to choose from hundreds of women musicians who wrote to her, and she had the benefit of hearing worthy musicians everywhere the band toured. Butler did not find it difficult by then to hire exceptional performers. Although she bemoaned the fact that matrimony often took away her best musicians, the band was not made up exclusively of single women. A number of older married women were part of the traveling group. At its largest, it numbered 49 players and was sometimes known as "An Adamless garden of musical Eves." What had begun as the U.S. Talma Ladies Band eventually became Helen May Butler and her Greatest American Ladies Concert Band. Butler's conducting style led to her sobriquet as "The Female Sousa." In the design of its first uniforms, musical selections, tour routes, instrumentation and concert style, the ensemble was in fact modeled after Sousa's entourage.

A few women's orchestras had come into existence and would occasionally ask for "Butler's Band" to join them in a concert. In answer to one such request, Butler was quoted in the *New York World*:

> I am ready to play my twenty brass girls against the Bostonian's forty strings and let the public decide on its merits. But I will not combine with the orchestra—put my players in the background. Mine is the only woman's military band in the world, and I won't play second fiddle.

In 1903, Butler was chosen as the musical director for the International Women's Exposition held in New York City. The event took place at Madison Square Garden where the Butler Band performed daily concerts, costumed in the eye-catching uniforms of Algerian Zouaves, which included balloon trousers and red leggings, in a period when the wearing of "bloomers" by women was still considered something of a sight. It is quite likely that the exposition would have led Butler to make the acquaintance of the leading women's rights activists of the day, but she never considered herself an activist. Her credo seems to have been more along the line of an honest day's work for an honest day's pay.

Another event in 1903 was a performance on the White House lawn, which became a highlight in the band's history. Theodore Roosevelt had succeeded President William McKinley, who died in office, and Roosevelt invited the band to perform while they were on tour in Washington, D.C. Roosevelt remained a great supporter of the band throughout his life. In 1904, he was running for election when the commission to compose the official march for the Republican Convention was tendered to Butler. Her "Cosmopolitan America" went through several printed editions, was played by bands from coast to coast, and was also popular in a sheet-music edi-

tion for performance on parlor pianos. Butler followed this composition with a few other marches that year, while press releases sought to establish her as "The March Queen."

In 1902, Helen May Butler had married Spahn. After the birth of her daughter Helen May, Butler toured with the child. When the couple's second child, Leslie, was born, it was thought that it would be better for the children to be brought up in a home. Arrangements were made with a caring friend, while Leslie Spahn tried to arrange for band routes that made visits possible.

Though Butler's marriage to Spahn ended in 1908, the band continued to tour until 1914. Butler by then had married a Mr. Young and settled eventually in Cincinnati to raise her two children and run the Burlington Hotel with her husband. She continued to take a great interest in the band members, who would write to her and send their latest publicity photos or reviews, which served in part to maintain a wideranging network among the women musicians. Butler returned to playing the violin for various church and lodge functions, and became involved in teaching music again. Cincinnati was a lively cultural center, and a fitting place for her to settle. The Cincinnati Conservatory was close at hand, and though it is uncertain whether she actually taught there, it is known that she worked with young students, especially violinists.

A tall, stately woman, about 5'8" in height, Butler was attending a performance at the Cincinnati Zoo of John Philip Sousa's Band, when she was recognized in the crowd by Sousa's manager. Invited backstage, she met the bandleader she had long admired, and who had followed her career for a number of years. Sousa paid her the rare honor of inviting her to conduct his world famous band in "Semper Fidelis," his own march.

In her later years, Butler also became active in politics, as a member of the Republican Club and serving at the polls on election days. Her years of touring had given her opportunity to meet many leading political figures of the day, including William Jennings Bryan and Robert M. LaFollette as well as Roosevelt. In 1936, at age 69, she announced her candidacy for the U.S. Senate. According to the *Kentucky Post*, Butler had decided to run "not because she feels certain she can win the Republican nomination and eventually a seat in the Senate, but because she may open the way for some other woman."

Helen May Butler's passions carried on until her 89th year, when she finally began to slow down. By the time of her death, at age 90, women were accepted as performing musicians, working in ensembles alongside their male counterparts. In areas of public service, they were beginning to make important contributions to the nation that she had crossed dozens of times during her career.

SUGGESTED READING:

Hazen, Margaret Hindle and Robert M. *The Music Men.* Washington, DC: Smithsonian Institution, 1987.

COLLECTIONS:

Correspondence, papers, and memorabilia located in the Museum of American History, Smithsonian Institution; correspondence, papers, and memorabilia in the authors' collection, Waukesha, Wisconsin; papers and memorabilia located in the Robert Parkinson Library, Circus World Museum, Baraboo, Wisconsin; papers and memorabilia located in the Chautauqua Collection, University of Iowa Library.

Dr. Patricia Backhaus,
cornet soloist & conductor,
American Ladies Concert Band
and band historian, Waukesha, Wisconsin

Butler, Josephine (1828–1906)

President of the Ladies National Association who led a successful campaign to repeal the British Contagious Diseases Acts, which subjected women suspected of prostitution to enforced examination and imprisonment. Name variations: Josephine Grey. Born Josephine Elizabeth Grey on April 13, 1828, at Dilston, Northumberland, England; died on December 30, 1906, at Wooler, Northumberland; daughter of John and Hannah (Annett) Grey; educated at home and at Newcastle; married George Butler (a cleric), 1851; children: three sons and one daughter, Evangeline, who died in childhood.

Moved to husband's parish in Oxford (1851); drawn into education issues (1858); death of her daughter (1858); took up more social issues after move to Liverpool (1866); elected president of North of England Council for Promoting the Higher Education of Women (1867–73); made president of Ladies National Association for the Repeal of the Contagious Diseases Acts (1869-86); became founding member of National Vigilance Association (1885).

Selected publications: The Education and Employment of Women *(1868);* On the Moral Reclaimability of Prostitutes *(1870);* Rebecca Jarrett *(1886);* Personal Reminiscences of a Great Crusade *(1896).*

In 1870, **Catherine Pickles**, a young girl of 16, was arrested by military police. Suspected of being a prostitute, she was taken to a hospital and forcibly examined by a doctor for venereal disease. Although Catherine protested, the law was on the side of the military. Six years previously the British government, alarmed by the rise in venereal disease among its armed forces, had passed the first of a series of Contagious Diseases Acts (CDA's), which applied to many garrison towns and naval ports of England. The first of these acts, passed in 1864, gave the police power to apprehend any woman suspected of being a "common prostitute." In the words of the bill: "If it is proved to the Satisfaction of such Justice that the Woman so brought before him is a common Prostitute, and at the time of her Arrest in a public Place . . . the Justice may order her to be taken to a Certified Hospital, there to remain until cured."

Once arrested, women were ordered to undergo an internal examination at a certified hospital. If they refused, they could be imprisoned for one month. The internal examinations, although rarely lasting more than a minute, were conducted by doctors who were neither gentle

Josephine
Butler

nor particularly hygienic; one doctor at Plymouth apparently examined about 70 women a day. Catherine, like many falsely accused women, was found to be healthy and set free without an apology. But if she had been diseased, she could have been detained for treatment up to a period of three months or until she was pronounced cured. Treatment at the time was grim and generally ineffective. The only known medical remedy available was mercury, a highly toxic substance.

This punitive approach to treatment was considered justified because women, not men, were held responsible for the spread of syphilis and gonorrhea. Soldiers and sailors were never examined. Modern-day historians view the CDA's as consistent with a set of attitudes towards women, sexuality, and class that permeated Victorian society. Josephine Butler, dubbing the examinations like that endured by Catherine Pickles "instrumental rape," led a campaign to repeal the CDA's. Eventually modified, in 1866 and 1869, they remained in force, in essence, for 22 years.

It is injust to punish the sex who are the victims of a vice, and leave unpunished the sex who are the main cause both of the vice and its dreaded consequences.

—Josephine Butler

Josephine Grey Butler, was born on April 13, 1828, at Milfield Hill, Dilston, in the stunningly beautiful but windswept county of Northumberland, England, situated near the Scottish border. She was the fourth of six daughters in a family that also included three sons. Her mother **Hannah Annett Grey** was of humble birth, descended from silk weavers who had been driven out of France, but her father John Grey came from an aristocratic Liberal family. His cousin, Lord Grey, served as one of England's prime ministers.

By all accounts, Josephine had an idyllic childhood on her father's 34,356-acre farm. She was educated at first by a strict and uncompromising governess but later went to school in the nearby town of Newcastle-on-Tyne. Her most important educational influences were her mother and father. From her mother, Josephine learned moral behavior, religious commitment, and intellectual rigor. From an early age, her father taught her to care about social justice. A well-known social reformer, John Grey supported free trade, the abolition of slavery, and parliamentary reform. Josephine shared her father's interests and political fervor.

Josephine was aged 22, in 1851, when she married George Butler, a cleric of the Church of England. For the next five years, the couple lived in Oxford, enduring the damp lowland country of their surroundings and what they viewed as the narrow-mindedness of the dons. In 1857, when her husband was offered the post of vice-principal of Cheltenham College, Josephine Butler was relieved to exchange the university setting for the healthy atmosphere of a Cotswold spa town. For the first few years in their new home, she became absorbed in educational issues and the lives of her four children. When *Dorothea Beale was appointed principal of Cheltenham Ladies College in 1858, education for women was placed firmly on the social agenda.

Butler had become committed to advancing educational opportunities for women when she experienced her greatest tragedy. The couple's youngest child and only daughter, Evangeline, had run to the top of the stairs, excited by her parents' return home. With her parents looking on, she tumbled over the banister onto the tiled floor below, and died a few hours later. Wrote Butler:

> Never can I lose that memory—the fall, the sudden cry, and then the silence. It was pitiful to see her, helpless in her father's arms, her little drooping head resting on his shoulder and her beautiful golden hair, all stained with blood, falling over his arm.

Josephine Butler had never enjoyed robust health; a lesion on her lung had kept her fragile. After the shock of Eva's death, Butler became seriously ill, and she was never to recover fully from the loss of her daughter. When George was offered a job in Liverpool, he accepted it in hopes of helping his wife overcome her melancholy.

Liverpool was quite different from the genteel Cheltenham: it was a working port with a large number of desperate poor. Soon after her arrival, writes Butler, she became involved in philanthropic work, because she had "an irresistible desire to go forth and find some pain keener than my own—to meet with people more unhappy than myself. . . . I only knew that my heart ached night and day, and that the only solace would seem to be to find other hearts which ached night and day."

To secure the trust of the despondent women she found in the poverty-ridden port, Butler at first joined in picking oakum (unravelling old ropes) alongside the most destitute of women incarcerated in the Brownlow Hill workhouse. She brought many who were sick and dying to her home, where she nursed them until they regained health or else died. When her house could not accommodate any more people, she opened a "House of Rest" to look after women who had been discharged from hospital but were incurably ill and had no place else to go. Later, she established an industrial home where destitute young women were employed making envelopes in exchange for food and shelter. Many of those she helped were former prostitutes, forced to earn a living on the streets because of a lack of job opportunities, low pay, and poor self-esteem.

Butler also remained committed to educational reform. As an ardent supporter of women's rights, she advocated higher education for women. From 1867 to 1873, she was president of the North of England Council for Promoting the Higher Education of Women, and in 1868 she published a pamphlet, *Education and Employment of Women*. She was also instrumental in the establishment of Newnham, the first women's college at Cambridge University. Like many English feminists, Josephine Butler advocated equal opportunities in work and politics and supported women's right to vote. In her opinion, prostitution, unemployment, and low pay were intimately connected.

In the meantime, the first of the Contagious Diseases Acts was passed in 1864. When the government extended these acts in 1869, a few middle-class women signed a petition and initiated a campaign to remove them from the statute books. As an eminently respectable, middle-aged married woman, Josephine Butler was the ideal figure to lead such a campaign. In conjunction with a group of other well-known feminists, she founded the Ladies National Association (LNA) to fight for the repeal of the Contagious Diseases Acts.

In contrast to the view that the acts defended morality, Butler took the position that the acts supported immoral laws, which legalized prostitution and encouraged vice. In addition, she argued, it penalized women. The CDA's, she believed, reinforced the double standard that prevailed in Victorian England because women, not men, were held responsible for venereal disease. In *The Shield*, the journal of the LNA, Butler repeated statements that she herself had heard from prostitutes:

"It is men, men, only men, from the first to the last, that we have to do with! To please a man I did wrong at first, then I was flung about from man to man. Men police lay hands on us. By men we are examined, handled, doctored. . . . In the hospital it is a man

again who makes prayers and reads the Bible for us. We are had up before magistrates who are men, and we never get out of the hands of men till we die!"

"It did seem hard, ma'am, that the Magistrate on the bench who gave the casting vote for my imprisonment had paid me several shillings, a day or two before, in the street, to go with him."

With the founding of the LNA, Butler's life became devoted to its cause. When the repeal movement ran short of money, she sold her jewels and donated what she could: at one time, a sixpence was all that remained in her bank account. In her first year, she traveled an exhausting 3,700 miles to 99 meetings to persuade others to publicize the repeal movement. She proved to be a brilliant speaker who captivated opponents with charisma and charm. Members of the group used petitions, deputations, lobbying, conferences, leaflets, and talks to rally support. In 1871, a petition signed by 250,000 women was presented to Parliament. In 1874, Butler was called upon to travel to France, Italy, and Switzerland to help reformers in these countries campaign for their own deregulation.

The campaign faced heavy criticism, however. On many occasions Butler and her colleagues were in physical danger. In Colchester, opponents threw mud, flour, refuse, and even furniture at the repealers, tore their clothes and threatened to burn down the hotel where Butler was staying. Women who supported repeal were accused of dabbling in filth because they discussed sexual issues, and one M.P. claimed that they were worse than prostitutes. At first, neither political party in Parliament advocated repeal of the CDA's; other issues such as England's relationship with Ireland, suffrage, imperialism, religion, urbanization, and education were considered far more urgent concerns of the government. By 1874, the LNA had gained the support of James Stansfeld, a leading Liberal M.P. With Stansfeld's parliamentary influence combined with Butler's persuasive campaigning outside the House of Commons, the Contagious Diseases Acts were finally repealed in 1886. When Butler received the news, she was in Italy.

My husband and I were at the time staying with my sister in Naples. It was a great joy to us to receive a telegram on April 16th, signed by Mr Stuart and Mr Stansfeld, saying; "The Royal Assent has this day been given to the Repeal Bill." I thanked God at that moment that Queen Victoria had washed her hands of a stain that she had unconsciously contracted in the first endorsement of this legislation.

Josephine Butler also became associated with campaigns to protect young people, sometimes as young as ten, who were sold into prostitution. Her son George had even found padded cells where children were tortured. One Harley Street doctor was said to have sold over 100 children to his patients. By publicizing these injustices, Butler hoped to shock the English out of their complacency. With the support of W.T. Stead, editor of the *Pall Mall Gazette,* Butler persuaded **Rebecca Jarrett**, a reformed brothel keeper, to pretend to purchase a child for immoral purposes. A young girl named **Eliza Armstrong** was duly bought for £5, tested for virginity, and taken to a brothel. When the story was published in Stead's paper, it caused a national sensation, and the publicity surrounding the case prompted passage of a Criminal Law Amendment Act in 1885, which raised the age of consent from 12 to 16, introduced heavy penalties for child abuse, and gave police stronger powers to close brothels; unfortunately, it also made homosexuality illegal.

In the view of Josephine Butler, however, prostitution, white slavery, and child abuse would not be stopped by passing laws. To enforce the 1885 Act, she helped to found the National Vigilance Association (NVA) in the same year. This group sought the prosecution of men who had sexually abused girls under 16; campaigned to tighten up the CLAA further; and tried to stop pornography, indecent advertising, obscene literature and semi-nudity in music halls. Initially a feminist inspired organization, the NVA later became a repressive force in British pressure group politics, and in its latter stages, Butler withdrew her support.

When her husband died in London on March 14, 1890, Josephine Butler lost a dear friend and political ally. Despite her grief, she continued to help destitute women, carried on the fight against moral bigotry, and supported votes for women. When the British attempted to reintroduce compulsory examination of prostitutes in India, Butler criticized the government for imperialistic behavior. In January 1898, nearing the age of 70, she published the first edition of her monthly journal, the *Storm Bell,* where she recounted her experiences of rescue work and raised questions about ethical issues. To the end of her life, she remained committed to rescue work even though by 1900 it was heavily criticized.

I know it will be said, as it is often said: "But rescue work is such discouraging, such hopeless work. It is far better to act on pub-

lic opinion, to elevate the morality of men, to educate the young in principles of justice and purity, to strike at the root, at the causes of prostitution. What you are counselling is but ambulance work for picking up and helping the wounded. Is it not far better to abolish war?" All this is quite true. Nevertheless, can we, in the name of pity, neglect our wounded and leave them to die?

When Josephine Butler died on December 30, 1906, at Wooler, in her home county of Northumberland, many people mourned the passing of one of England's greatest social agitators. In 1921, the Josephine Butler Memorial House was opened in Liverpool to train women in aspects of social welfare, and a commemorative window was eventually placed in the Lady Chapel of Liverpool Cathedral. In the calendar of the Church of England, December 30th is sanctified as Josephine Butler Day, in memory of her work.

SOURCES:

Bartley, Paula, co-author and co-ed. "Women In History" series, Cambridge University Press.

Johnson, George and Lucy, eds. *Josephine E. Butler: An Autobiographical Memoir,* 1928.

Walkowitz, Judith. *Prostitution and Victorian Society,* 1980.

Paula Bartley, University of Wolverhampton, Dudley, United Kingdom, author and joint editor of "Women in History" series, Cambridge University Press

Butler, Lady (1846–1933).

See Butler, Elizabeth Thompson.

Butler, Mrs. (1809–1893).

See Kemble, Fanny.

Butler, Selena Sloan (1872–1964)

American child welfare activist who established the first black parent-teacher association. Born Selena Sloan in Thomasville, Georgia, on January 4, 1872; died in October 1964; daughter of Winnie (Williams) and William Sloan; graduated from Atlanta Baptist Female Seminary (now Spelman College), 1888; attended Emerson School of Oratory (now Emerson College), 1894; married Henry Rutherford Butler (a doctor), May 3, 1893; children: one son.

Selena Sloan Butler, the daughter of an African and Indian woman and a white man, was separated from her family and received her early education from the Thomas County missionaries. Following graduation from the Atlanta Baptist Female Seminary, she held a series of teaching positions before her marriage to Henry Rutherford Butler in 1893. While her husband continued his medical education at Harvard University,

Butler studied speech and elocution at Emerson School of Oratory. Upon their return to Atlanta in 1895, Selena resumed her teaching career; she also established and edited the *Woman's Advocate*, a monthly paper devoted to the interests of black American women.

Butler's interest in the parent-teacher relationship began when she and neighboring mothers could not find a preschool teacher for their children, and Butler set up a kindergarten program in her own home. In 1911, with the help of other concerned black women, she established the first black parent-teacher association in the country and patterned it after the National Congress of Parents and Teachers. Butler subsequently developed a state organization (Georgia Colored Parent-Teacher Association) in 1919 and served as its president for many years. Her efforts were expanded to the national level with the formation of the National Congress of Colored Parents and Teachers in 1926, which adopted the principles and objectives of the National Congress of Parents and Teachers. As the founding president of the new organization, Butler worked closely with the white National Congress, and the Congress assisted the new organization through an integrated advisory group. Although the new black association served primarily in states that maintained segregated schools, the relationship to its sister organization encouraged greater cooperation between black and white groups in local school systems. In Butler's words, the organization became "a conduit for effecting interracial work."

Active in other local and state organizations, Butler served as the first president of the Georgia Federation of Colored Women's Clubs. Both she and her husband were members of the Georgia Commission on Interracial Cooperation, which helped improve race relations during the years between the two world wars. After her husband's death in 1931, Butler traveled to London with her son; while there, she was active in the Nursery School Association of Great Britain. Returning to the U.S. at the onset of the Second World War, she established a Gray Lady Corps at Fort Huachuca, Arizona, where her son was stationed. Butler spent her later years with her son in Los Angeles and remained active in church and welfare organizations until her death in 1964.

Barbara Morgan,
Melrose, Massachusetts

Butt, Clara (1872–1936)

English contralto whose concert hall appearances, early recordings, and broadcasting career made her one of the first entertainment superstars beloved throughout the world. *Name variations: Madame Clara, Dame Clara. Born Clara Ellen Butt on February 1, 1872, in Southwick, Sussex, England; died on January 23, 1936, at her home at North Stoke, Oxfordshire; daughter of Henry (a captain in the Mercantile Marine) and Clara (Hook) Butt; attended Royal College of Music, 1890; married Robert Kennerley Rumford, June 26, 1900; children: Joy, Roy, and Victor.*

Moved with family to Bristol, England (1880); awarded scholarship to Royal College of Music (1890); was inspiration for songs by Britain's foremost composer, Sir Edward Elgar (1901); began recording career (1909); mobilized women for the war effort (1914–18); appointed a Dame of the British Empire (1920); seriously injured (1931), but continued recording career.

Late in January 1936, three of the best-known figures in Britain—King George V, Rudyard Kipling, and Dame Clara Butt—died within a matter of days. In their lifetimes, all three had become symbols of England's far-flung empire on which it was said that the sun never set, but it is likely that the one held closest in the hearts of many of her compatriots was "Dame Clara." Her magnificent contralto voice had dominated English music since the reign of Queen *Victoria, and songs that she sang had become universally loved, heard from the planters' bungalows scattered across Java and the Malay peninsula to isolated British outposts in Fiji, Borneo, and India, as well as households of Australia, Canada, Britain's former colonies in America, and throughout the British Isles. Long before the Beatles captivated the musical world, Clara Butt established a reputation of the kind they would strive to emulate.

Clara Ellen Butt was born at Southwick, Brighton, on February 1, 1873, the second child in a large but close-knit family, where she grew up as the eldest because of the early death of her brother Bertie. Her father was Henry Butt, a captain in the Mercantile Marine, who had a very pleasing baritone, and her mother, also named Clara, possessed a truly beautiful voice. The younger Clara eventually had three sisters and two brothers, and the family, like many Victorians, enjoyed musical evenings together at home. Butt began piano lessons at age eight, and, after the family moved to Bristol in 1880, she joined the family in singing at various churches and homes.

It was a Miss Cook, the headmistress at South Bristol High School, who first recognized the quality of the girl's voice. At her suggestion, 12-year-old Clara sang before Dan Rootham, the leading voice teacher in the West of England, who told her, "You have gold in your throat, my child." Butt's repertory was soon expanded to include Brahms' *German Requiem* and Handel's *Messiah*. Singing with the Bristol Festival Choir, she continued her church appearances and accepted a growing number of requests to perform.

At the age of 16, Clara was on the way to her full height of 6'2'', a tall girl with a beautiful and imposing figure, when Rootham had her try out for the Open Scholarship at the Royal College of Music in January 1890. At the audition, the first song she sang was the "Enchantress," delivered in a booming contralto that had acquired a power and beauty that was to mesmerize listeners throughout her lifetime. The judges were unprepared for the first dramatic octave leap that burst upon them without warning. At first, they stared, then jumped to their feet, talking between themselves. Furious at their rudeness and believing they were poking fun, Butt sang even louder. When a judge asked that she sing something softer, the girl chose "Woe unto

Clara Butt

them," a lovely air, and was mystified by a tear she saw roll down a judge's cheek. As she sat in the corridor, waiting for the results, she overheard someone say that one of the scholarships had gone to "a great tall girl, a singer." Only then did she realize the impact of her performance.

In February 1890, Butt took up residence at Alexandra House, which provided a comfortable home for female art and music students, and was located next door to the old College of Music and behind the Royal Albert Hall. For four happy years, she studied music and dance and made many friends. The royal sponsor and patron of the establishment was *Alexandra of Denmark (1844–1925), then princess of Wales, who paid occasional informal visits to the school, where it was customary for her to take tea in the best kept room. As housekeeping was not one of Butt's many talents, she earned the honor of playing host to the princess only once. But Alexandra liked to hear the young girl sing and would ask Clara for a song no matter where she saw her. Once, when the two chanced to meet in a shop on Baker Street, the princess requested and the student obliged. Such episodes became a joke between them.

Under the strict supervision of the Royal College, Clara was not allowed to perform publicly until she was 21; even so, private performances were allowed and her reputation spread. Her first public performance, in Gluck's *Orpheus,* was in December 1892. But, because her height proved limiting for operatic roles, it was virtually the only operatic appearance in her long musical career. When she next appeared, in a concert at the Royal Albert Hall, the reception was tremendous. "She has the most beautiful voice in all England," commented Canadian singer *Emma Albani. The press was equally enthusiastic, and the young singer was soon invited to appear in a command performance before Queen Victoria at Buckingham Palace. Only members of the household and a few guests were present, and the queen entered the vast hall leaning on the arm of her Indian servant as the orchestra played the national anthem. Butt was the only performer, and since no applause occurred at such events, she had no idea how she had been received, until she was given a second invitation, very soon, to sing at Windsor Castle. This time she was told by the queen, who, because her mother *Victoria of Coburg was German, always spoke German with her immediately family, "I have never liked the English language before, but in your mouth it is beautiful."

Clara Butt's entrance into the professional music world coincided with a time when enter-

tainment was becoming increasingly commercialized. In particular, the 1890s were the golden age of the English music hall. The grim and dirty theaters once filled with poor, rowdy patrons were being displaced by new entertainment palaces patronized by the scions of a wealthier middle class. Such theatrical outings were enjoyed by the entire family, and although programs included some classical works, the ballad became the most characteristic musical form. Heard onstage, songs like "Softly Awakes my Heart," "Abide with Me," and "The Lost Chord" gained huge audiences and sold thousands of copies in sheet music, foreshadowing the internationalization of popular music that has dominated the 20th century. With the arrival of the phonograph and the wireless radio, allowing singers to be heard at any place and at any time, the process was simply accelerated.

Launched at this time in her career, Clara Butt became the first of that new 20th-century breed, the entertainment superstar. Her popularity was instant and her first few years of public performance a triumphal progress. And because her father's financial fortunes had always been precarious, she felt under considerable financial pressure to provide for the members of her large family.

A strikingly beautiful young woman, Butt was often a weekend guest in aristocratic country homes. Once, while returning to London by special train, she was asked by Lord Royston to "bring him luck" by sitting next to him during a poker game. When the noble won, he offered to share his winnings, but Clara declined to accept, and when the train reached the station, some of the card players suggested giving the young singer a farewell kiss. Clara refused, but a member of the party, a Monsieur Plançon, grabbed and kissed her. She slapped his face and burst into tears. Shortly thereafter, when the singer's health began to deteriorate from overwork, she was approached by a famous host, **Mrs. Ronalds**, who said that someone interested in her well-being had offered to pay for her to have a year of study abroad. When Clara explained that she required funds not only for herself but also for her family, sufficient money was provided, and the timely gift allowed her study, travel, and rest at a point in her career when it was sorely needed. It was many years later before Butt learned that her benefactor had been Lord Royston, who had admired her spunk in the confrontation on the train.

In 1899, Clara Butt made a singing tour of Canada and the U.S. where she was greeted with wild enthusiasm. She had been joined by a young baritone, Robert Kennerley Rumford, who had been accompanying her on tour. The two frequently performed duets. Rumford was smitten with Clara and began to pencil messages in the margins of the sheet music they shared. Butt never knew what message she might find on the page in front of her during a performance. Eventually, these dispatches had their intended effect, and the couple announced their engagement. The news attracted as much notice in the press as a Royal betrothal. Though St. Paul's Cathedral was offered as a site for the wedding, an almost unprecedented honor for commoners, Clara decided to be married in Bristol, among her own. On Tuesday, June 26, 1900, workers were given a half holiday and church bells rang as the city turned out for the event. Thousands jammed the streets outside the cathedral for sight of the couple following the ceremony, and the queen was among the many who sent wedding gifts.

You are a much bigger person than I. I should look like a ridiculous little busybody making a pretentious bow in your limelight.

—George Bernard Shaw in a letter to Clara Butt (October 1927)

Since her professional name was well established, Clara became known as "Madame" Clara Butt. For several years, she and her husband gave no foreign concerts, while their family expanded to include a daughter Joy and sons, Roy and Victor. There were some musical engagements she could not refuse, and following the death of Queen Victoria, on January 22, 1901, she sang "Abide with Me" at the memorial service at Kensington Palace Chapel. Around this time, Britain's foremost composer, Sir Edward Elgar, also wrote the *Sea Pictures,* a group of orchestral songs specifically composed for the voice of Madame Clara. His choral *Coronation Ode,* written for the accession of King Edward VII to the throne, included the memorable solo, "Land of Hope and Glory," also composed for her; the song became a kind of unofficial English national anthem as well as the one most identified with Clara Butt. Even now her rendition of "Land of Hope and Glory" is the standard by which all other versions are measured.

In 1909, Butt began recording, and radio broadcasts of her records and singing soon followed. Not everyone approved of the popularization of her gift through the new technologies, but she welcomed it, recognizing its value to the vast audience beyond the usual reach of concerts, trapped on isolated farms and villages, in hospitals or old folks' homes. "I pray that when the day comes I may not be too old to sing a song that shall be heard in the back-blocks of Australia and New Zealand, on the Pacific slopes of America, in India, and the islands of the Southern Seas," she said. "We have tapped a wonderful source of pleasure and profit, it is true, but surely it is one of world-peace and unity as well. I would like my voice to do something to bring to pass the glorious day 'when war shall be no more.'"

By the time this was spoken, the singer was an outspoken supporter of the mobilization of women for England's labor force during World War I. At one point, she organized a demonstration of 30,000 to 50,000 women demanding to be mobilized for the war effort. Speaking to the press, she pointed out that 80,000 women had signed up for wartime duty but only 3,000 had been asked to contribute their labor. She found it ridiculous that the government was not putting this ready resource to better use.

To demonstrate personally what women could accomplish, Dame Clara also raised funds for various war charities, amounting to hundreds of thousands of English pounds. She organized a series of concerts at hospitals, workhouses, community halls, and other sites throughout the United Kingdom, paying the artists small sums to perform to raise money for the Red Cross. Butt also made concert appearances, because she believed in the healing powers of music. About these performances before soldiers and civilians, rich and poor, she said, "We are a nation in mourning. In this tremendous upheaval, when youth is dying for us, I want to give the people a week of beautiful thoughts." In 1920, when she was knighted, receiving the title of Dame of the British Empire, the honor was bestowed "in recognition of the important services rendered by her during the late War."

Known from that time on as "Dame Clara," this musical artist had the rare luck of being an extremely successful performer who led a happy life. Easygoing, with many friends, she had a happy marriage and a close-knit family. Her later years were clouded by tragedies, however; one son died undergoing surgery, and the other perished in Africa. In 1931, she was in an accident from which she never fully recovered, and she was stricken with cancer before the age of 60. With stoic disregard for her physical and emotional pain, she continued to give concerts and to record, and her magnificent voice lasted to the end.

In 1995, Sir Henry Wood established the Promenade Concerts, known affectionately in Great Britain as the "Proms." This annual program, broadcast worldwide, features popular and classical music performed by a large orchestra and chorus in the concert hall built by Queen Victoria in memory of her husband, Prince Albert. The audience joins in the singing and many of the songs are ones made famous by Dame Clara. A perennial favorite is Elgar's "Land of Hope and Glory," and as the voices of the massed choir and audience rise in unison, one has the sense of Clara Butt joining them, in the hall where the spirit of this artist still seems to hover.

SOURCES:

Aldrich, Richard. "Dame Clara Butt Sings," in *The New York Times*. December 14, 1923, p. 28.

Bradley, Ian. "Changing the Tune. Popular Music in the 1890s," in *History Today*. Vol. 42. July 1992, pp. 41–47.

Butt, Clara. "Joan of Arc Day," in *The Times*. April 26, 1917, p. 6.

"Clara Butt is Statuesque 'Orpheus,'" in *The New York Times*. August 8, 1920, p. 4.

"Clara Butt Sings Here Again," in *The New York Times*. March 27, 1922, p. 15.

"Dame Clara Butt. A Famous Contralto," in *The Times*. January 24, 1936, p. 16.

"Debut of Miss Butt," in *The New York Times*. October 26, 1899, p. 5.

Henderson, W.J. "Debut of Miss Clara Butt," in *The New York Times*. October 29, 1899, p. 16.

"Miss Butt's Second Recital," in *The New York Times*. November 22, 1899, p. 4.

"Mme. Butt and Rumford: English Contralto and Baritone Appear Together in a Song Recital," in *The New York Times*. April 1, 1914, p. 13.

"Mme Clara Butt Says Many Women, Eager to Work and Needed, Are not Being Employed," in *The New York Times*. July 18, 1915, p. 1.

"Mme. Clara Butt's Recital," in *The New York Times*. January 15, 1913, p. 13.

Ponder, Winfred. *Clara Butt: Her Life-Story*. NY: DaCapo Press, 1978.

"Shaw Would Have Wed Clara Butt, He Says," in *The New York Times*. April 17, 1928, p. 15.

"Two Voices that Have Come to Interest and Engross New York: Miss Frieda Hempel at the Opera and Mme. Clara Butt in Concert," in *The New York Times*. January 12, 1913, p. 9.

RECORDINGS:

Dame Clara Butt, Arabesque Recordings, no. 9027, 1980.

Karin Loewen Haag,
freelance writer and editor, Athens, Georgia

Butters, Mary (fl. 1839)

Irish woman accused of sorcery.

Mary Butters, of the town of Carrickfergus, County Antrim, was found guilty in 1839 of "making use of some noxious ingredients, in the manner of a charm, to recover or relieve from witchcraft a cow, the property of Alexander Montgomery."

Butterworth, Mary Peck
(1686–1775)

American counterfeiter. Born in Rehoboth, Massachusetts, on July 27, 1686; died in Rehoboth on February 7, 1775.

Around 1715, after Rhode Island had issued five-pound notes of credit, Mary Peck Butterworth, together with **Hannah Peck**, allegedly organized a counterfeiting ring involving a dozen or so citizens of Rehoboth, Massachusetts (then Plymouth Colony). The group was accused of counterfeiting the notes by transferring the image from muslin to clean paper, thus avoiding the use of copper plates and leaving no evidence. Ultimately, the charges against Butterworth were dropped, and she went free.

Butts, Mary (1890–1937)

British author. Born Mary Francis Butts in Poole, Dorset, England, on December 13, 1890; died in Sennen, Cornwall, England, on March 5, 1937; daughter of Mary Jane (Briggs) and Frederick John Butts (a naval captain); educated at St. Leonard's School and Westfield College of London University; married John Rodker (a poet), in 1918 (separated, 1920); married Gabriel W. Aitkin (writer), in 1930 (separated, 1934); children: (first marriage) daughter **Camilla Rodker** (b. 1920).

Selected works: Speed the Plough (1923); Ashe of Rings (1925); Armed with Madness (1928); The Crystal Cabinet (1937).

At the family estate Salterns, near Poole, Dorset, England, Mary Butts had a country upbringing. She enjoyed roaming the 50-acre grounds with her brother Tony (who would later be author William Plomer's lover) and was artistically influenced by family friend William Blake: 30 of his drawings adorned the walls of her home. In 1910, shortly after her father's death, Salterns was sold; both losses contributed to Butts' defiant nature.

Enrolled at Westfield College, she attended a horse race with a male professor and was sanctioned for the indiscretion; she left Westfield without a degree. In London, she lived sparsely, took odd jobs, worked for the pacifist cause, and published when she could. Her 1918 marriage to poet, conscientious objector, and publisher John

Rodker lasted two years. After the birth of their daughter Camilla, Butts left Rodker for painter Cecil Maitland, whom she had met while volunteering as a nurse; he had been recovering from a suicide attempt in the same hospital. Butts left her daughter Camilla with her great aunt and moved with Maitland to Paris where they were habitual frequenters of Left Bank bars and opium dens. They also explored black magic and mysticism with Aleister Crowley. Butts, who continued to publish stories and poems in little magazines, socialized with Ezra Pound, *Djuna Barnes, *Peggy Guggenheim, Jean Cocteau, and *Gertrude Stein.

Despite Maitland's affairs, depression, and alcoholism, Butts loved him deeply. "I've always wanted to make my lovers well, sense powers liberated in them," she wrote in her journal. When Maitland left her in 1925, her substance abuse increased. She took both male and female partners but held steadfast in her dedication to Maitland. A one-year affair with composer Virgil Thompson provided some stability, but Butts exhausted her friends with her continual requests for money to support her opium habit. One friend referred to her as a "storm goddess" for her red hair and turbulent life. In 1930, Butts returned to England in deep emotional distress.

She then married Gabriel Aitkin and moved to rural Sennen, Cornwall, where Camilla visited at holidays. The union collapsed in 1934 due to Aitkin's homosexuality and both partners' dependence on alcohol. Butts' autobiographical reflection on her childhood, *The Crystal Cabinet*, was released just prior to her March 5, 1937, death from a ruptured appendix. Her work was well-respected in her time by other writers, but talk of her personal life overshadowed her literary reputation. A half-century after her death, Butts' work experienced a modest revival.

SOURCES:

Ashbery, John. Preface. *From Altar to Chimney-Piece.* NY: McPherson, 1992.

Blain, Virginia, Pat Clements, and Isobel Grundy, eds. *The Feminist Companion to Literature in English.* New Haven, CT: Yale University Press, 1990.

Blondel, Nathalie. Afterword. *With and Without Buttons.* Manchester, England: Carcanet Press, 1991.

Buck, Claire, ed. *The Bloomsbury Guide to Women's Literature.* NJ: Prentice Hall, 1992.

Hanscombe, Gillian, and Virginia L. Smyers. *Writing for Their Lives: The Modernist Women 1910–1940.* Boston, MA: Northeastern University Press, 1987.

SUGGESTED READING:

Blondel, Nathalie. *Mary Butts: Scenes from the Life.* McPherson, 1997.

Crista Martin,
Boston, Massachusetts

Byckerdyke, Mary Ann (1817–1901).

See Bickerdyke, Mary Ann.

Bye, Karyn (1971—).

See Team USA: Women's Ice Hockey at Nagano.

Byers, Margaret (1832–1912)

Irish educationalist who founded the Ladies' Collegiate School (later Victoria College) in Belfast, in 1859, and took a leading part in campaigns to secure equality for women within the Irish education system. Born Margaret Morrow in April 1832 in Rathfriland, County Down, Ireland; died in Belfast on February 21, 1912; daughter of Andrew Morrow (a farmer) and Margaret (Herron) Morrow; educated in Nottingham, married Reverend John Byers, February 24, 1852 (died, 1853); children: son John (b. 1853).

Taught at the Ladies' Collegiate School in Cookstown, County Tyrone (1853–59); opened the Ladies Collegiate School, later Victoria College, in Belfast (1859); elected president of the Ulster Headmistresses' Association (1903); awarded honorary degree by Trinity College, Dublin (1905); appointed to the Senate of Queen's University, Belfast (1908).

In 1852, Margaret Byers embarked on what she must have anticipated would be a life of usefulness and adventure far away from her native Northern Ireland. At 20 years of age, and just married to a young Presbyterian minister, John Byers, she left with her husband for China, where he had been commissioned as a missionary. Shortly after their arrival, however, Reverend Byers fell ill. Far from home and heavily pregnant, Margaret's situation was already precarious, but worse was to come. On the day before her child was born, she was told by the doctors that her husband could not recover. With the birth safely over, the Byers decided to return home without delay, and it was left to Margaret to organize their departure, embarking with her dying husband and baby on a ship bound for New York. It was already too late for John Byers, however. He died during the voyage and was buried in New York, leaving his widow to continue her journey back to Ireland.

Little in Margaret's life before then could have equipped her for these ordeals. Born near the small town of Rathfriland in rural County Down in April 1832, she was the fourth child and only daughter of Andrew Morrow, a farmer, and **Margaret (Herron) Morrow.** Margaret Morrow is a shadowy figure in her daughter's youth, perhaps because she was already almost 50 years old at the time of her daughter's birth. However,

Andrew Morrow was a more forceful personality, an intelligent and religious man, active in his local Presbyterian church as an elder, and in his community as a temperance campaigner. The similarities between him and his daughter are striking, and it seems clear that he had a lasting influence on her character and beliefs. However, when she was eight her father died, and Margaret was sent to England, living for the next few years with relatives in Stoke-on-Trent. During this time, she attended a Ladies' College at Nottingham, where she qualified as a teacher, and where she, perhaps, came into contact with a more radical approach to female education than currently existed in Ireland. In the short term, however, she had little opportunity to put her training into practice. In 1852, she had returned to Ulster in order to marry John Byers, and, immediately after the wedding, the young couple left together for their new life in the Far East. According to some accounts, Margaret had an opportunity to observe the education system in the United States when she stayed with her husband at Princeton, but this was only a short break in their journey before continuing on to China.

Within a short time, Margaret was back in Ulster. Her experience in the interim had been a traumatic one. In just a year, she had traveled to the other side of the world and back, had gained and lost a husband, had become a mother, and in the process had become aware of her own capacities. Alone, and faced with the necessity of finding a means of supporting herself and her young son for the future, she continued to display remarkable courage and self-reliance. She refused the pension to which she was entitled as the widow of a Presbyterian minister and, according to one report, actually considered going out herself as a missionary to India, but felt that "greater work" was to be done at home. Having decided to become a teacher, she found a position in the Ladies' Collegiate School in Cookstown, County Tyrone, while her son John was probably cared for by her own family in Rathfriland. Cookstown, however, was not really large enough to support a girls' school, and within a few years Byers had decided to move to Belfast, then experiencing a period of great economic growth, with a prosperous mercantile and professional middle class.

By now, Byers had also developed her own views of what type of education best fitted girls for their future role in society. Then the great majority of girls' schools, both in Ireland and in England, favored a training that would prepare young women to be virtuous wives and mothers:

in effect, this implied a concentration not on academic learning, but on sound religious instruction and on the acquisition of accomplishments, such as drawing, music and decorative needlework. This approach, however, was increasingly under attack from those who believed that women themselves, and society in general, would benefit greatly from improvements in the area of female education. This movement promoted a view of female education as a preparation for work rather than for marriage, and demanded equal access for girls and boys to an exam-based system of education, and the first significant step in this direction was taken with the foundation in London in 1848 of Queen's College in Harley Street. Envisaged by its initiators as a means of improving the quality—and thus the status and pay—of female teachers and governesses, the institution offered lectures in a wide range of subjects, both at elementary and advanced level, and had an immediate success. Moreover, many of its former students went on to enter the field of education, and thus helped to promote the Queen's College ethos throughout the British Isles. By the 1860s, the movement had gained considerable ground in England, with the government-appointed Schools Enquiry Commission admitting the need for sweeping improvements in middle-class female education, and cautiously approving the idea of admitting girls and boys to the same state examinations.

Byers was to become the earliest, and one of the most effective proponents of this approach in Ireland. As she herself recalled it:

> My aim was to provide for girls an education adapted to their wants as thorough as that which is afforded to boys in schools of the highest order; in fact, to work out for girls a practical and well-considered plan of education, in which due regard should be given to the solid branches of learning, as well as to moral and religious training.

Her own experience, both as a young woman who had to earn her own livelihood, and as a teacher, had shown her the acute need for such a system. In 1859, therefore, she rented a house at 13 Wellington Place, in which she opened an "establishment for the Boarding and Education of Young Ladies." Subjects taught included history, natural science, and classical and modern languages, and, in an effort to bring girls' education into line with that of boys, particular stress was laid on instruction in English and in mathematics. This first school rapidly proved too small, and Byers went on to build new premises for her Ladies' Collegiate School at Pakenham Place. Having started with 35 students, she now had 60 boarders, as well as day pupils. In 1874, expansion forced another move to specially built premises at the Crescent, which in 1887, Queen *Victoria's Jubilee year, was renamed Victoria College and School.

In 1878, secondary education was transformed by the passage of legislation that established a state system of examinations. Initially, the measure was to apply only to boys, but Byers was among those who mounted an effective, and ultimately successful, campaign to have girls included in the scheme. As a result, girls were allowed to enter the examinations of the Intermediate Board of Education, and to compete for prizes, scholarships, and exhibitions on the same terms as boys. The first examinations were held in 1879, and from the beginning the Ladies' Collegiate showed itself to be one of the most successful schools in terms of the results obtained. In 1888, for instance, the college won 48 distinctions, more than any other girls' school in Ireland, and 25 more than its nearest competitor, Alexandra College in Dublin.

Fully aware that improved secondary education was meaningless without access to higher level education, Byers had been among the first to demand that Irish women be admitted to university examinations. Having failed to persuade Cambridge University and Trinity College, Dublin, to open centers in Belfast in which her pupils could sit for their examinations, she discovered a redoubtable ally in *Isabella Tod, founder in 1867 of the Belfast Ladies' Institute, a body established to provide "advanced classes" in a range of subjects and to expand the opportunities currently available to middle-class women. In 1869, in response to a petition from the Institute, Queen's College, Belfast, a constituent college of the Queen's University of Ireland (QCB), agreed to allow women to sit external examinations, and to be awarded certificates. The Ladies' Collegiate School was in a position to take immediate advantage of this concession. From now on, senior pupils of the school were routinely prepared for the QCB examinations, and, by 1874, 13 had received honors certificates from the Queen's University.

The opening up of the QCB examinations to women also had the effect of improving the quality of instruction available to girls in Northern Ireland. Firmly convinced that female teachers were best fitted to teach girls, Byers had nevertheless found difficulty, during her early years as a headmistress, in securing properly trained women, and it had been found necessary to employ lecturers from QCB in order to prepare

pupils for the first university-level examinations. As more women attained certificates, however, increasing numbers of women teachers, many of them former Victoria College pupils, became available. Byers was quick to take advantage of this development, and, by 1889, her school had 38 female teachers and teaching assistants as against only seven men.

With the establishment of the Royal University of Ireland (RUI) in 1879, women became entitled to sit for examinations and to take degrees on the same basis as men. As the RUI was purely an examining body, however, students had to obtain their instruction elsewhere. Again, Byers was quick to respond to this need, and, in 1881, she opened a separate university department at the Ladies' Collegiate, in which students over 18 were prepared for RUI degree examinations. The department's achievement was apparent both in the numbers of women passing through it, and in their academic performance. Thus, while in 1888, 18 pupils passed RUI exams, by 1902 the number had risen to 70. In the decade 1891–1900, 95 Victoria students graduated, more than from any other women's college in Ireland, while in terms of the results achieved, Victoria was consistently ahead of all the women's, and most of the men's establishments.

By this time, however, women were gradually being admitted on equal terms to university faculties, putting the future of the women's colleges, such as Victoria, in doubt. Byers herself favored the retention of the women's colleges, believing that, as at secondary level, women were best qualified to teach women, and fearing that female lecturers and students would be disadvantaged in an integrated environment. On the other hand, many students and graduates as well as members of staff rejected the isolation, restricted curricula and potential second-class status of women's colleges, and demanded the full admission of women to university institutions. In 1908, two new universities, Queen's University, Belfast, and the National University, were established to replace the old Royal University. Women had full equality within both these institutions, making the remaining women's colleges superfluous. Shortly afterwards, the remaining women's colleges, including the college department of Victoria, closed down, bringing to an end the first stage in the movement for women's higher education and, theoretically at least, establishing their full equality in the area of higher education.

While Byers had struggled hard to achieve such success and was convinced of the value of girls' participation on equal terms in public examinations, she had no desire for any fundamental reassessment of the conventional female role. On the contrary, she argued, education could better equip a girl to "perform any womanly duty," and the development of a "maternal instinct . . . guided by high intelligence" would be to the betterment of society as a whole. While anxious to fit girls to earn their own living if necessary, she saw marriage and motherhood as perhaps the most important roles a woman could fulfil, and for that reason saw subjects such as cookery, dressmaking, and needlework as having an important place on the curriculum. As she allegedly remarked, "I think . . . the best life for a girl, after all, is a good marriage." Above all, she believed that education should inculcate a strong Christian faith, that academic success was no substitute for "a high moral tone of the spirit," and that it could reinforce women's moral influence and potential for good in the world. "Always be ready," she told her pupils, "to do with alacrity and earnestness the duty that lies near to you and ever hold yourselves in readiness for future work."

In addition to her achievements in the field of education, Margaret Byers was involved in a number of philanthropic and reformist movements. She was a leading member of the Ladies' Temperance Union and secretary of the Belfast Woman's Temperance Association and first president of the Irish Women's Temperance Union. She was also associated with the Band of Hope, a children's temperance organization, and with the Prison Gate Mission for Women, which met and assisted women on their release from jail. In these areas also, she believed that women could offer powerful, but always discreet, leadership. As she remarked in 1878 of the work of the Belfast Women's Temperance Association, "Its plans and operations have been carried on as heretofore in a quiet, unobtrusive way. Its action has been none the less powerful for good because it has never been characterized by anything that was startling or sensational." Again, she saw wifehood as the most desirable option for a woman, and the home as her proper sphere of activity: many prominent men, she argued, have had their "flagging zeal in temperance work stimulated by the gentle approval and tender sympathy of her who, though she may shrink from public work, accomplishes, it may be, more by her personal influence at her own fireside."

Despite such views, Byers played a major part in opening up opportunities to women outside the home. Moreover, she herself enjoyed an active public role throughout her career, serving,

in 1903, as president of the Ulster Schoolmistresses' Association; in 1905, she was awarded an honorary degree by Trinity College, Dublin, the first Ulsterwoman to receive such an honor from any university, and, in 1908, she was appointed to the Senate of Queen's University, Belfast. By then, she had largely retired from active work, due to ill health, and she died on February 21, 1912. Her coffin, with her LL.D. robes on top, rested before her burial in the lecture hall of Victoria College, and it was the college that was to be her most visible legacy. Overcoming financial difficulties, it went on to consolidate its position as one of the leading girls' schools in Northern Ireland, and a fitting memorial to a woman who believed in the right, indeed the duty, of all women to utilize their capacities to their fullest extent.

SOURCES:

Breathnach, Eibhlin. "Women and Higher Education in Ireland, 1879–1910," in *Crane Bag.* Vol. IV, 1980, pp. 47–54.

Brozyna, Andrea Ebel, "'The Cursed Cup Hath Cast Her Down': Constructions of Female Piety in Ulster Evangelical Temperance Literature, 1863–1914," in *Coming into the Light*, pp. 154–178.

Jordan, Alison. *Margaret Byers: Pioneer of Women's Education and Founder of Victoria College, Belfast.*

———. "Opening the Gates of Learning: The Belfast Ladies' Institute, 1867–97," in Janice Holmes and Diane Urquhart, eds. *Coming into the Light: The Work, Politics and Religion of Women in Ulster, 1840–1940.* Institute of Irish Studies, Belfast: 1994, pp. 33–59.

O'Connor, Anne V. "The Revolution in Girls' Secondary Education in Ireland, 1860–1910," in *Girls Don't Do Honours.*

COLLECTIONS:

Papers of the Ladies' Collegiate School, Belfast, in the Public Record Office of Northern Ireland, Belfast.

Rosemary Raughter,
freelance writer in women's history, Dublin, Ireland

Byington, Spring (1886–1971)

American stage and film actress who starred in the popular television series "December Bride." Born in Colorado Springs, Colorado, on October 17, 1886; died on September 7, 1971; daughter of Edwin Lee (an English teacher) and Helene Byington (a physician).

Selected films: Little Women *(1933);* The Werewolf of London *(1935);* Way Down East *(1935);* Mutiny on the Bounty *(1935);* Ah! Wilderness *(1935); (first of the "Jones Family" series)* Every Saturday Night *(1936);* Dodsworth *(1936);* Theodora Goes Wild *(1936);* It's Love I'm After *(1937);* The Adventures of Tom Sawyer *(1938);* Jezebel *(1938);* You Can't Take It With You *(1938);* The Story of Alexander Graham Bell *(1939)*; A Child is Born *(1940)*; The Bluebird *(1940)*; Meet John Doe *(1941)*; The Devil and Miss Jones *(1941)*; When Ladies Meet *(1941)*; Roxie Hart *(1942)*; Rings on Her Fingers *(1942)*; Presenting Lily Mars *(1943)*; Heaven Can Wait *(1943)*; The Heavenly Body *(1944)*; I'll Be Seeing You *(1945)*; The Enchanted Cottage *(1945)*; Dragonwyck *(1946)*; Singapore *(1947)*; BF's Daughter *(1948)*; In the Good Old Summertime *(1949)*; Louisa *(1950)*; Walk Softly Stranger *(1950)*; According to Mrs. Hoyle *(1951)*; Angels in the Outfield *(1951)*; Because You're Mine *(1952)*; The Rocket Man *(1954)*; Please Don't Eat the Daisies *(1960)*.

Spring Byington is probably best remembered as Lily Ruskin, "America's favorite mother-in-law," in the popular television series "December Bride," which first appeared in 1954 after two successful years on the radio. Her career also included 20 appearances on the Broadway stage and 75 motion pictures.

Byington was 14 when she decided to be an actress. Through a friend of her mother's, she landed a three-year engagement with the Elitch Garden Stock Company in Denver. After numerous stock appearances, including tours in Argentina and Brazil, Byington made her Broadway debut in 1924 as Miss Hey in the satirical comedy *Beggar on Horseback*. The Broadway roles that followed, mostly minor character parts, were often singled out for praise. Brooks Atkinson of *The New York Times* described her role as Janet Cannot in *The Great Adventure* (1926): "A simple attractive performance, dignified and illuminating, without any of the superfluous scroll work which is often confused with acting." Notable also were her roles in *Be Your Age* (1928), *Ladies Don't Lie* (1929), and *Once in a Lifetime* (1932), Her comedic talent was again recognized by Atkinson in her portrayal of Mrs. Bridget Drake in *Rachel Crothers' comedy *When Ladies Meet* (1932), which he called, "a fresh, delightful performance in the exact key of high comedy."

Director Stuart Walker was responsible for Byington's first screen role, as Marmee in *Louisa May Alcott's *Little Women* (1933). She soon found her niche in supporting roles, playing mostly scatterbrained wives or loving moms. In *Louisa* (1950), Byington's first lead, she portrayed a crotchety widow who is transformed by a new love. The most memorable of her numerous film appearances was in *You Can't Take It With You*, a role that earned her an Academy Award nomination for Best Supporting Actress. She was also a regular in the "Jones Family" film series

(1936–40), which began with *Every Saturday Night*. Of her late success on "December Bride," which attained the third highest national rating among television shows of the time, Byington said, "TV keeps me young because it keeps me busy, keeps my mind alert, my senses sharp and my interest up." She continued to make movies until 1960, 11 years before her death in 1971.

SOURCES:

Candee, Marjorie Dent, ed. *Current Biography 1956*. NY: H.W. Wilson, 1956.
Halliwell, Leslie. *The Filmgoer's Companion*. 4th ed. NY: Hill and Wang, 1974.

Byns, Anna (d. 1575).

See Bijns, Anna.

Byrne, Jane (1934—)

American politician and first woman mayor of Chicago, Illinois. Born Jane Margaret Burke in Chicago, Illinois, on May 24, 1934; daughter and second oldest of six children of William (an executive with Inland Steel and co-founder of Gordon-Burke Steel) and Katherine (Nolan) Burke; attended Queen of All Saints grammar school; Saint Scholastica High School; B.A., Barat College of the Sacred Heart, 1955; attended University of Illinois and Chicago Teachers College (now Chicago State University); married William P. Byrne (a Marine Corps pilot), December 31, 1956 (died, May 1959); married Jan McMullen (a reporter), March 17, 1978; children: (first marriage) daughter Katherine.

Born in Chicago, Illinois, in 1934, Jane Byrne was the daughter of a wealthy steel executive. In 1956, she abandoned her dream of becoming a doctor to marry William Byrne, a marine pilot; he was killed in 1959, two years after the birth of the couple's daughter. As an antidote for the depression that followed, Byrne became involved in the 1960 campaign of John F. Kennedy, which would eventually bring her to the attention of politicians, including Chicago's controversial mayor, Richard Daley. Between 1963 and 1965, Jane Byrne worked as a substitute teacher in the Chicago public schools and continued to devote time to precinct and ward-level politics. She met Daley in November 1963 when she was invited to sit in President Kennedy's box during the Army-Air Force football game in Chicago; a year later, after the assassination of Kennedy, Daley recruited Byrne for his organization.

After serving in a relatively minor position with the Chicago operation of the federal antipoverty program in 1965, Byrne secured a position on the administrative staff of the Chicago Commission of Urban Opportunity and, in 1968, was appointed to the Daley Cabinet, as commissioner of consumer sales, weights, and measures. Her efforts to weed out corruption in her department won her public approval and the further admiration of Daley, who took her under his wing and began to carefully groom her for leadership. She became co-chair of the Cook County Democratic Committee and was appointed to the party's National Committee.

Upon Daley's death in 1976, Byrne immediately locked horns with his successor Mayor Michael Bilandic, charging him with collusion with officials to secure a rate increase for taxicab operations. After Bilandic was acquitted of any illegal activities, he fired Byrne from her commissioner's post in November 1977. Castigating him and what she called his "cabal of evil men," Byrne organized a challenge to him and his powerful Democratic organization. She aligned herself with the still-revered Daley and was aided by a record two-month snowfall that tied the city in knots and demonstrated the inefficiency of the Bilandic administration. Byrne mustered a huge voter turnout (800,000 Chicagoans went to the polls) and surprised all observers by defeating Bilandic in the Democratic primary election in February 1979. Party leaders were stunned when she went on to win election as mayor, with 82% of the vote, a greater margin than even Daley had accomplished. Inaugurated on April 19, 1979, she became the first woman to head the nation's second largest city.

Byrne's four-year tenure was tumultuous at best, beginning with shakeups in the city's police and sanitation operations, as well as the replacement of several commissioners and top government officials. Her years in office are recounted in her book *My Chicago* (1992). Byrne failed in her reelection bid in 1983, losing to Harold Washington who became the first black mayor of the city.

SOURCES:
Granger, Bill and Lori. *Fighting Jane: Mayor Jane Byrne and the Chicago Machine.* NY: Dial, 1980.
McHenry, Robert. *Famous American Women.* NY: Dover, 1980.
Moritz, Charles. ed. *Current Biography Yearbook 1980.* NY: H.W. Wilson, 1980.

SUGGESTED READING:
Byrne, Jane. *My Chicago.* NY: W.W. Norton, 1992.

Barbara Morgan,
Melrose, Massachusetts

Byron, Augusta (b. 1784).

See Lamb, Caroline for sidebar on Augusta Leigh.

Byron, Augusta Ada (1815–1852).

See Lovelace, Ada Byron.

Byron, Beverly Butcher (1932—)

U.S. Representative, Democrat of Maryland, 96th–101st Congresses, January 3, 1979–January 3, 1993. Born Beverly Barton Butcher in Baltimore, Maryland, on July 27, 1932; attended Hood College, Frederick, Maryland, 1963–64; married Goodloe E. Byron (a congressional representative, 1971–78).

See following page for photograph

Beverly Byron grew up in Washington, D.C., the daughter of a military man who served as an aide to General Dwight D. Eisenhower during World War II. After a year at Maryland's Hood College, Byron married Goodloe E. Byron and worked on his campaigns for the Maryland Legislature and the House of Representatives. When he died in 1978, one month before the general election, Byron agreed to run for his seat and won. Coincidentally, her mother-in-law, *Katharine E. Byron, had also succeeded her husband, William D. Byron, after his death in 1941.

Beverly Byron's tenure in Congress was distinguished by her seat on the Committee on Armed services and, in 1987, by appointment as the first woman to chair an Armed Services subcommittee: the Subcommittee on Military Personnel and Compensation. She also served on the Committee on Interior and Insular Affairs and the Select Committee on Aging. From 1983 to 1986, she chaired the House Special Panel on Arms Control and Disarmament. Byron also had a strong interest in promoting physical fitness and the improvement of national recreational areas. From 1979 to 1989, she served as chair of the Maryland Commission on Physical Fitness and was on the board of the American Hiking Society. Byron served six succeeding terms but was an unsuccessful candidate for renomination in 1992.

Byron, Katharine Edgar
(1903–1976)

*U.S. Representative, Democrat of Maryland, 77th Congress, May 27, 1941–January 43, 1943. Born in Detroit, Michigan, on October 25, 1903; died in Washington, D.C., on December 28, 1976; married William D. Byron (a congressional representative, 1939–41); children: five sons, including Goodloe E. Byron, who served in the House of Representatives from 1971 to 1978 and was succeeded upon his death by his wife *Beverly Byron.*

In 1941, with America on the brink of war, William D. Byron was killed in a plane crash less than two months after beginning his second term in the House of Representatives. Katharine Byron was elected to complete her husband's term in a special election. In the subsequent election, she edged out Republican A. Charles Stewart in a hotly contested battle over issues centering on reaction to the war in Europe. Byron, making appearances with prominent Democrats like first lady *Eleanor Roosevelt and Representative Estes Kefauver, endorsed America's support of nations fighting the Nazis and advocated battle preparedness for the United States.

Byron's congressional record included membership on the Committee on the Civil Service and the Committee on War Claims. In November 1941, during floor debate on the amendment of the Neutrality Act, she urged acceleration of the delivery of war materiel to Great Britain and the Soviet Union. On the day after the Japanese attack on Pearl Harbor, Byron was one of four representatives designated by Speaker Sam Rayburn to announce their support for a declaration

Beverly
Butcher
Byron

of war on the House floor. In 1942, Byron advocated maintenance of Works Projects Administration Programs as a necessary adjunct to national defense projects.

After filing for reelection, in August 1942 Byron withdrew her name, citing her wish to spend more time with her five sons. In later years, she continued her long-term association with the Red Cross. Katharine Byron died in Washington, D.C., on December 28, 1976.

Byron, Lady Noel (1792–1860).

See Lovelace, Ada Byron for sidebar on Anne Milbanke.

Byzantium, empress of.

See Eusebia of Macedonia (fl. 300).
See Faustina of Antioch (fl. 300s).
See Helena (c. 255–329) for sidebar on Helena (c. 320–?).
See Fausta (d. 324).
See Eudocia of Byzantium (d. 404).
See Pulcheria (c. 398–453).
See Ariadne for sidebar on Verina (fl. 437–483).
See Theodora (c. 500–548).
See Theodora (c. 500–548) for sidebar on Lupicinia-Euphemia (d. 523).
See Sophia (c. 525–after 600 CE) for sidebar on Constantina (fl. 582–602).
See Sophia (c. 525–after 600 CE) for sidebar on Ino-Anastasia.
See Fabia-Eudocia (fl. 600s).
See Fausta (fl. 600s).
See Martina (fl. 600s).
See Leontia (fl. 602–610).
See Irene (fl. 700s).
See Irene of the Khazars (fl. 700s).
See Maria (fl. 700s).
See Theodora of the Khazars (fl. 700s).
See Irene of Athens (752–803).
See Irene of Athens for sidebar on Theodote (fl. 795).
See Eudocia Decapolita (fl. 800s).
See Eudocia Ingerina (fl. 800s).
See Euphrosyne (fl. 800s).
See Irene of Athens for sidebar on Maria of Amnia (fl. 800s).
See Prokopia (fl. 800s).
See Thecla (fl. 800s).
See Theophano of Athens (fl. 800s).
See Theophano, Saint (866–893).

See Zoë Zautzina (d. 896).
See Theodora (early 900s).
See Theodora (late 900s).
See Zoë Carbopsina for sidebar on Eudocia Baiane (d. 902).
See Zoë Carbopsina (d. 920).
See Theophano (c. 940–?).
See Helena Lekapena (r. 945–959).
See Zoë Porphyrogenita for sidebar on Helena of Alypia (fl. 980s).
See Anna Comnena for sidebar on Catherine of Bulgaria (fl. 1050).
See Zoë Porphyrogenita (980–1050).
See Zoë Porphyrogenita for sidebar on Theodora Porphyrogenita (c. 989–1056).
See Eudocia Macrembolitissa (1021–1096).
See Maria of Alania (fl. 1070–1081).
See Priska-Irene of Hungary (c. 1085–1133).
See Marie of Antioch (fl. 1180–1183).
See Euphrosyne (d. 1203).
See Marie de Courtenay (fl. 1215).
See Irene of Brunswick. (fl. 1300s).
Anne of Savoy (c. 1320–1353).

Katharine Edgar Byron

C

Caballé, Montserrat (1933—)

Spanish soprano. Name variations: Caballe. Born on April 12, 1933, in Barcelona, Spain; studied at the Barcelona Conservatorio del Liceo and with Eugenia Kemeny, **Conchita Badia**, *and Napoleone Annovazzi.*

Awarded Liceo gold medal (1954); appeared in Barcelona, Basel and Vienna (late 1950s); debuted at the Teatro alla Scala (1960), and Mexico City, Chicago, and Metropolitan Opera (1965); debuted at Covent Garden (1970).

Montserrat Caballé

One of the 20th century's greatest prima donnas, Montserrat Caballé possessed an ethereal voice and sensitive musicality that combined to make her an exquisite vocalist. Hers was a luscious, finely trained soprano with very pure high notes and strong chest notes. She learned breath control from **Eugenia Kemeny**, who trained her pupils as if they were long distance runners. A combination of rich color and absolute steadiness gave her voice a peculiar charm. Though she won the Liceo gold medal for singing, Caballé was unable to launch her career in Italy so she went to Basel. In one seven-year period in the late 1950s and early 1960s, she sang 47 different operatic roles, an astonishing number, although Carmen came to dominate her repertoire. Her vast undertakings ranged from Mozart to Wagner and Strauss. Eventually, Cabellé's astounding voice won her attention, and she debuted at the Teatro alla Scala in 1960 and finally at the Met in 1965. She recorded extensively, which secured her place in the world of opera. Her career was marred during the last decade because of numerous cancellations due to bad health.

John Haag, Athens, Georgia

Caballero, Fernán (1796–1877).

See Böhl von Faber, Cecilia.

Cabarrus, Thérésa (1773–1835).

See Tallien, Thérésa.

Cable, Mildred, and Evangeline and Francesca French

British missionaries.

Cable, Mildred (1878–1952). Born Alice Mildred Cable in Guildford, England, in 1878; died in 1952.

French, Evangeline (1869–1960). Name variations: Eva. Born in Algiers in 1869; died in 1960.

French, Francesca (1871–1960). Born in Belgium in 1871; died in 1960.

Born in England in 1878, Mildred Cable attended Guildford High School and was inspired by the China Inland Mission, the organization for which she studied medicine. Evangeline French, born in Algiers, and her sister Francesca, born in Belgium, attended school in Geneva before their family relocated to England. In 1893, Evangeline was also inspired by the China Inland Mission lectures; she converted to Christianity and sailed to Shanghai to begin her work as a missionary. In 1902, Mildred Cable and Evangeline French met in Hwochow, becoming lifelong companions. Joined by Francesca French in China, they ran a girls' school while preparing for a journey through the Gobi Desert. To preach the gospel throughout the sparsely inhabited, often hostile Gobi, they embarked in 1923 from the City of Prodigals (Suchow) with only a tent, a kettle, a frying pan, and three sleeping bags, as well as a sizable load of Bibles. They traveled the Gobi for 16 years, until 1939, ending the journey in the City of Seagulls (Chuguchak). Their encounters with revolutionary generals, bandits, and lamas would inform their later narrative of the trek, *The Gobi Desert* (1942). Following her work in the desert, Mildred Cable worked for the Bible Society in England.

Cabrini, Frances Xavier

(1850–1917)

Italian saint, nun, charity entrepreneur, and champion of Italian immigrants to the United States. Name variations: Francesca Maria Cabrini (1850–1874); Sister Saveria or Xavier Angelica (1874–1879); Mother Francesca Saveria or Frances Xavier Cabrini (1879–1917). Born Francesca Maria Cabrini on July 15, 1850, at Sant'Angelo Lodigiano in the Lombardy region of Italy; died in Chicago, Illinois, on December 22, 1917; daughter of Agostino Cabrini (a Lombard farmer) and Stella Oldini Cabrini; never married; no children.

Taught school in Lombardy (1868–74); became orphanage worker and novice in Codogno (1877); took vows as a nun and promoted to superior (1877); founded Missionary Sisters of the Sacred Heart (1881); immigrated to New York (1889); founded a school in Nicaragua (1891); opened Columbus Hospital in New York City (1892); naturalized as U.S. citizen in Seattle (1909); named superior for life of the Missionary Sisters of the Sacred Heart (1910); beatified (November 1938); became first American citizen to be elevated to sainthood in the Roman Catholic Church (July 7, 1946).

In 1946, Pope Pius XII made Frances Cabrini a saint, the first American citizen to be honored in this way. Her work as a guardian angel to Italian immigrants in New York, Chicago, and other American cities bred tales of her supernatural virtues during her lifetime, and they have proliferated ever since. It is not always easy to untangle the history from the hagiography, but the extensive documentation of her life enables us to describe its principal features.

Francesca Maria Cabrini was born in 1850 at Sant'Angelo Lodigiano in Lombardy, the rich farm country of northern Italy, to a prosperous farm family. She was one of only four among her parents' 13 children to survive into adulthood, and her frail health caused them constant worry. At age seven, she fell into a stream and for several years suffered from bronchitis. She overcame this and a succession of other illnesses in growing to adulthood. Frances began her education at the village school where her sister Rosa was the schoolmistress. When she was 13, her parents sent her on to be educated by the Daughters of the Sacred Heart, a teaching order of nuns established earlier that century and dedicated to humane education in an unrepressive Christian atmosphere.

Cabrini was a good pupil and graduated at age 18, head of her class, to become an elementary schoolteacher in her own right in small towns near her birthplace. Inspired by tales of missionary daring, she declared her intention of becoming a nun and requested admission to the Daughters of the Sacred Heart, but her request was denied, possibly because of her health. In 1870, the year of the First Vatican Council, when the doctrine of papal infallibility was officially defined, both her parents died, leaving Frances and her sister Rosa to look after the family. In the same year, Frances suffered in a smallpox epidemic but recovered, unscarred. The newly unified and secular state of Italy forbade the teaching of religion in schools, but she did it anyway after negotiating with the mayor, who was impressed by her ability. Cabrini continued to nurse the ambition of becoming a nun.

B̶etween 1889 and her death at Chicago in 1917, the small nun crisscrossed America, seeking out Italian immigrants and establishing for them and their children a network of educational, health care and social service institutions.

—Mary Louise Sullivan, MSC

The first 20 years of her life had witnessed a succession of wars against Austria and the piecemeal unification of Italy. According to some tales, Austrian soldiers were billeted with the Cabrinis during one campaign. The family was pulled in two directions by the conflicts of the era. Frances' cousin Agostino Depretis was a prominent anticlerical politician who favored Italian unification and opposed papal political power, and, in 1876, when she was in her mid-20s, he became prime minister. Her parents, by contrast, had been devout upholders of the old papal tradition and opponents of the secular republicans, Giuseppe Garibaldi, Giuseppe Mazzini, and Camilla di Cavour, who unified Italy. Her career showed that she too would be a staunch papal loyalist.

Local church officials were impressed by Frances Cabrini's organizational powers and pleaded with her to sort out an administrative muddle at an orphanage in nearby Codogno. She went there and joined the Sisters of Providence, an order of charitable working sisters who ran the orphanage, taking the name of Sister Saveria Angelica in 1874. Three years later, just after she had taken her vows, the local bishop appointed her superior of the community, even though its founders and benefactors, **Antonia Tondini** and **Teresa Calza**, were still active in the group. These two women, apparently well-meaning at first but idle and undisciplined, had neglected their orphanage and spent some of the money they had pledged to its upkeep on bailing out dissolute relatives. Furious at Cabrini's promotion over their heads, they declined to follow her instructions and even made threats against her. Finally the local bishop enabled her to separate from the orphanage and its troublesome founders. Seven other young women, orphans who had grown up in her care and become novices under her inspiration, stuck with Cabrini, who now resumed her given name and became Mother Frances Xavier (Francesca Saveria) Cabrini. She learned from this bitter experience to assert her authority, govern with a firm hand, and make sure of dependable finances in all her subsequent charity work.

They renamed themselves the Institute of the Salesian Missionaries of the Sacred Heart. Mother Cabrini wrote a rule for the group in 1881, emphasizing modesty, humility, and daily silence except where speech was necessary in the work. For the next few years, these sisters were teachers in Lombardy despite Cabrini's eagerness for a more arduous field of endeavor—she dreamed of a mission to China. On a visit to Rome in 1888 where she opened another school, she won the attention of Bishop Giovanni Scalabrini of Piacenza, who ran a mission to prepare priests to minister to Italian immigrants in the New World. Economic conditions in Italy were forcing large numbers of peasants off the land, and the growing cities suffered periodic unemployment. America, which Italians believed to be a land of boundless wealth and opportunity, attracted thousands every year, and Scalabrini feared that their faith was endangered in a largely Protestant land so far from home. In his diocese, he founded a seminary to train priests who would emigrate to help the growing Italian-American community. He recognized in Mother Cabrini, with her mixture of piety and administrative ability, an ideal character to join in this effort and wrote a letter recommending her to Archbishop Michael Corrigan of New York.

With the approval of Scalabrini and Corrigan, and with a blessing from Pope Leo XIII who had told her that her missionary future lay "not to the East, but to the West," Mother Cabrini set out for America in 1889, her fare paid by the Congregation of Propaganda. Like Scalabrini, she knew that Italian immigrants to America faced severe hardships. They often had to take the hardest and lowest-paying work, and were frequently deceived and cheated by labor-bosses, *padrones,* in collusion with employers. Italian men were often used as strike breakers because they were willing to work for low wages, which they hoarded in order to buy boat tickets for their wives and children's emigration. American streets, alas, were not paved with gold. Steady employment was hard to find, especially for those slow to learn English, and the danger of unemployment hovered over every immigrant family. They crowded together in "little Italys," like New York's Italian Harlem, where they were packed into unhealthy tenement buildings, surrounded by dirt and smoke, always vulnerable to epidemics. It was a way of life totally different from that of rural southern Italy, from which many had come.

In addition to these problems with work and housing, Italian Catholics were often at odds with the American Catholic Church hierarchy. Most of the bishops were of Irish descent (the big Irish immigration had come 50 years earlier), and the Irish style of devotion was quite different from the Italian. Irish priests and bishops saw the church as the center of religious life, but for Italians the center was the *home.* Italians attended church for baptisms, weddings, and funerals but preferred the exuberant annual festivals in which they paraded statues of their favorite saints through the streets to the cooler worship services going on inside. Unable to pay pew rents, those Italians who did attend regularly were often relegated to church basements. Most of the American Catholic bishops in the late 19th century wanted the Italians to change their ways, conform to Irish-Catholic traditions, speak English, send their children to parochial schools, and give up devotional practices that seemed barbaric, such as some Italian women's custom of approaching a saint's altar on their knees, dragging their tongues along the church floor. Pope Leo XIII was aware of these ethnic tensions. Himself an Italian, upset at the Irish-Americans' high-handedness, he warned them not to get too carried away by "Americanization," and he signaled his faith in the New York Italians by turning their shrine at 115th Street into a Sanctuary of the Blessed Virgin Mary. He also welcomed Italian Catholics' efforts to set up Italian-language parishes whereas the American hierarchy had decided, at its Baltimore synod of 1884, to discourage cultural and linguistic fragmentation. These disagreements augured trouble for Mother Cabrini, and it is a measure of her skill and diplomacy that she was able to navigate through them and win a wide degree of support from both Italian and Irish Catholics.

Her first meeting with Archbishop Corrigan was not auspicious. He told her he had nowhere to put her at present, that a proposed orphanage

Frances Xavier Cabrini

was not yet built and had no proper funding, and that she should take her sisters back to Italy. Cabrini countered respectfully, showing him her letter from the pope and declaring that she would not return, so he put her group to work teaching Italian children at St. Joachin's Church on Mulberry Street. Other Catholic orders helped her out with donations, some of the Missionary Sisters went begging door to door, and they were able to establish a convent in the notorious Five Points district, then famous as a criminal slum. In the following years, the Missionary

Sisters' hard work and conciliatory attitude, their willingness to learn English and become American citizens, mollified Corrigan. They visited Italians in prison, acted as interpreters for immigrants negotiating with the authorities, and opened an orphanage on 59th Street similar to those they had built back in Italy. Cabrini, always alert to the need for money and influence, befriended some of New York's richest Italians, such as Count di Cesnola, director of the Metropolitan Museum of Art, and induced them to subsidize this and other charitable projects.

She soon realized that Father Felice Morelli, leader of the Scalabrinian priests in New York, was an incompetent administrator and severed her connection with his group in a dispute over a charity hospital. Next she acquired a pair of old houses in Manhattan and built her own hospital around them. From then on, her life became a long succession of charitable successes as she was invited by overstretched priests to help out in their parishes. First in New York, then in Chicago, Philadelphia, New Orleans, Denver, and Seattle, she filled in the gaps of a society, which as yet had no welfare system or social security and in which Italian-speaking immigrants (especially those from the south and Sicily) were cursed and despised by most other Americans. She was driven by the fear that Italians, without the support of Catholic schools, charities, and hospitals, might fall into the arms of the Protestant missionaries who challenged Catholicism in every city. Collaborating closely with the clergy, her sisters first helped in schooling, then established orphanages, hospitals, and cultural centers for adults. Cabrini wanted to adapt the Italians to American life, but she was also eager to preserve their Italian cultural traditions and, of course, the Catholic faith in which they were based. She had no medical training but understood basic principles of public health and led a fumigation campaign against the New Orleans yellow fever epidemic of 1905. She became an American citizen in 1909.

Mother Cabrini did not confine her activities to aiding the Italians, though they were always her first priority. Two of her first new novices were Irish-Americans and from then on Catholics of all ethnic groups joined the sisters. The newcomers learned Italian just as the Italian members were learning English, so that they could be of use in the "Little Italys" where much of the teaching and medical work was going on. Cabrini was not welcomed by every immigrant. Italian anticlericalism and atheism had crossed the ocean as surely as Catholicism. Italian radicals, of whom the best known were the anar-

chists Sacco and Vanzetti, had no love for the Missionary Sisters' message of humility and Christian charity. Some Italian government consuls, anticlericals, also tried to thwart her work. In New Orleans, 1905, for example, she persuaded a retired merchant marine sea captain, Salvatore Pizzati, to fund an orphanage. Fearful that he might change his mind under the influence of his anticlerical friend the local consul, she persuaded him to sign an ironclad contract committing his support. It held up under legal scrutiny and showed the consul that Cabrini's piety was very much this-worldly even if it was also supernatural.

As the years went by, more orders of teaching and nursing sisters joined in the work on behalf of immigrants, though few had an entrepreneurial flair to match Cabrini's. Historians Luciano Iorizzo and Salvatore Mondello note that by 1918, the year after Cabrini's death, "twenty six religious orders had founded schools, churches, and aid societies for the immigrant Italians." Cabrini always remembered that there was no surer friend for a Catholic leader than the pope. As a result, she was in constant correspondence with the Vatican and made more than a dozen trips back to Rome, shoring up her support, strengthening lines of influence and finance, and returning with batches of new recruits to the order.

When her American foundations were thriving, Cabrini, always a restless spirit, set out for other parts of the Americas. She trekked through tropical Nicaragua, preached to Mosquito Indians, and almost died of yellow fever. Later, she made a mule-back ride across the Andes from Chile to Argentina, and established foundations among the large Italian immigrant communities in Buenos Aires. In the first two decades of the 20th century, she began a long series of visits back and forth across the Atlantic, not only to Rome where she was already admired but also to London, Paris, and Madrid. In each place, she tried to make another foundation, school, hospital, or orphanage. Like *Mother Teresa, Cabrini mixed a saintly, charismatic presence with a hard head for business. When necessary, she could be a tough negotiator and drive a hard bargain, enabling her order to grow by leaps and bounds and to run on solid business principles. The original group of seven Missionary Sisters had grown to over a thousand by the time of her death.

Mother Cabrini died on December 22, 1917, at age 67, from the worsening of a chronic heart condition. Her body was preserved and put on display in the chapel at Mother Cabrini

High School, New York, where it still rests. Cardinal Mundelein of Chicago convened an investigation, ten years later, of alleged miracles being attributed to her intercession. The order she had founded campaigned hard for her canonization, and their work was rewarded with her beatification in 1938 and elevation to sainthood in 1946. By then, there were 3,700 Missionary Sisters of the Sacred Heart in the United States alone, and a thousand more in eight other countries around the world, running a wide array of educational and charitable institutions. Most of the writing about Mother Cabrini has been drenched in uncritical piety. Only recently have more rigorous historians begun to take a more impartial view of her life and work, and some of the stories about her still need to be taken with a pinch of salt. As **Mary Louise Sullivan** notes: "Cabrini was a modern woman. Her interests were extensive. She certainly did not adapt readily to the role expected of late nineteenth and early twentieth century women religious. She was an entrepreneur and world traveler, keenly aware of the currents of thought in the world of her time," who "foresaw the twentieth century as one of revolution."

SOURCES:

Borden, Lucille P. *Francesca Cabrini: Without Staff or Scrip.* NY: Macmillan, 1945.

Gallo, Patrick. *Old Bread, New Wine: A Portrait of the Italian-Americans.* Chicago, IL: Nelson-Hall, 1981.

Iorizzo, Luciano, and Salvatore Mondello. *The Italian-Americans.* NY: Twayne, 1971.

Maynard, Theodore. *Too Small a World.* Milwaukee, WI: Bruce, 1945.

Sullivan, Mary Louise, MSC. *Mother Cabrini: Italian Immigrant of the Century.* NY: Center for Migration Studies, 1992.

COLLECTIONS:

Cabriniana collection, Cabrini College, Radnor, Pennsylvania; Centro Cabriniano, Rome; Archives of the Missionaries of the Sacred Heart, Rome; Archives of the Archdiocese of New York.

Patrick Allitt, Assistant Professor of History, Emory University, Atlanta, Georgia

Caccini, Francesca (1587–c. 1626)

Italian composer, singer, and teacher. Name variations: Signorini, La Cecchina. Born in Florence on September 18, 1587; died around 1626 (some sources cite 1640), possibly in Florence; daughter of Giulio Caccini (c. 1546–1618, a revolutionary composer and instrumentalist) and a musical mother (name unknown); sister of **Settimia Caccini** *(c. 1591–c. 1638); married Giovanni Battista Signorini Malaspina; children: two.*

Known as "La Cecchina," Francesca Caccini was a skilled composer, singer, and instrumentalist who served the Medici court in Florence. Her 1625 *La liberazione di Ruggiero dall' isola d'Alcina* was the first known opera by a woman, and it also saw distinction as the first Italian opera to be performed abroad. She was born in Florence in 1587 and studied with her father Giulio Caccini. According to Monteverdi, Francesca was proficient on the lute, guitar, and harpsichord. At the Florentine court, she appeared with sister Settimia and their mother, taking part in lavish musical productions; during 1604–05, the three also appeared together in Paris. La Cecchina's composing apparently began at the prompting of poet Buonarroti. Among the festive ballets that comprised her early efforts was the 1615 *Il ballo delle zigane* (The Ballet of the Gypsies), a work, now lost, in which she also took part. In 1618, *Primo libro delle musiche*, a collection of skilled monodic writing that is said to be after her father's style, was published and showed her strong potential as a composer.

This promise was realized with her collaboration with Marco da Gagliano on the azione sacra *Il martirio di Sant'Agata* and with her *La liberazione di Ruggiero*, the latter of which was written for the visit to the Tuscan court of Poland's Prince Ladislas. In addition to being the first opera composed by a woman, *La liberazione di Ruggiero*, which was based on an episode of Ariosto's epic *Orlando furioso*, was one of the first operas not based on classical mythology. The work made a marked impression on the prince, as it was performed in Cracow in 1628, the same year a Polish translation was published there. The Cracow production is said to have had a fundamental influence on operatic development in Poland, with Prince Ladislas originating an Italian opera troupe as soon as he ascended the throne as Ladislas IV Vasa in 1632. Married to composer Giovanni Malaspina, La Cecchina passed her musical talent on to her two children, who were also performers at the Medici court.

Cäcilie, Fanny (1805–1847).

See Mendelssohn-Hensel, Fanny.

Cadière, Catherine (b. 1709).

See French Witches (14–16th centuries).

Cadilla de Martínez, Maria (1886–1951)

Puerto Rican writer, academic, and folklorist of the mid-20th century. Name variations: Maria Cadilla de

Martinez; Maria Tomasa Cadilla y Colón; Liana Cadilla de Martínez. Born on December 21, 1886, in Arecibo, Puerto Rico; died on August 21, 1951, in Arecibo; daughter of Armindo Cadilla y Fernandez (a navy official) and Catalina Colón y Nieves; received teaching certificate from the University of Puerto Rico, early 1900s; also attended the College of Agricultural and Mechanical Arts (Mayaguez), 1913; University of Puerto Rico, A.B., 1928, A.M., 1930; doctorate from the Universidad Central (Madrid), 1933; married Julio Tomas Martínez Mirabal, in 1903; children: María, Tomasita.

Studied in U.S. (1902); became professor of history (1916); published first book (1925); earned doctorate in Madrid (1933).

Selected writings: Cuentos a Lillian *(Stories for Lillian, 1925);* La Poesía Popular en Puerto Rico *(Popular Poetry in Puerto Rico, 1933);* La Mística de Unamuno *(Unamuno's Mystique, 1934);* Cantos y Juegos Infantiles de Puerto Rico *(Puerto Rican Songs and Children's Games, 1938);* Costumbres y Tradicionalismos de mi Tierra *(Customs and Traditions of My Country, 1939);* Raíces de la Tierra *(Roots from the Earth, 1941);* Rememorando el Pasado Heroico *(Remembering our Historic Past, 1946).*

Maria Cadilla de Martínez was a memorable figure in Puerto Rican cultural history. As a professor of history, author, and lover of art, music, and literature in all their forms, Cadilla was instrumental in focusing attention upon the indigenous Latin culture of her island, and her research, writings, and academic work helped the folk arts of Puerto Rico achieve recognition as an important part of its past.

Cadilla was born Maria Tomasa Cadilla y Colón on December 21, 1886, in Arecibo, Puerto Rico. She was the daughter of Armindo Cadilla y Fernandez, of Spanish heritage and an official in the navy, and **Catalina Colón y Nieves**, a native-born Puerto Rican. At the time of Cadilla's birth, the island was still part of the Spanish Empire, but after the Spanish-American War of 1898, it became an unincorporated territory of the United States.

Educated in Catholic schools, Cadilla began to write while still a teenager. She also displayed great interest in art and painted in her spare time; playing the piano was another great love. In 1902, she left Puerto Rico for a time to attend school at the Washington Institute, then returned the following year and wed architect Julio Tomas Martínez Mirabal. Her husband founded a school in Arecibo, and after earning her teaching credentials from the University of Puerto Rico she began to teach there. She also earned a certificate as an instructor in English and went on to pursue several degrees. She first took courses in agriculture and home economics at Mayaguez's College of Agricultural and Mechanical Arts around 1913, then later earned two degrees in education (an A.B. in 1928, and a master's two years later) from the University of Puerto Rico. She had already established herself in a teaching career at the same institution as a professor of Hispanic history and literature.

Before earning a doctorate in philosophy and literature from the University of Madrid in 1933, Cadilla had established herself as an author. Her first book, *Cuentos a Lillian* (Stories for Lillian), was published in 1925. Her doctoral thesis, *La Poesía Popular en Puerto Rico* (Popular Poetry in Puerto Rico), became a standard textbook in Latin American literature at the university level. She also published numerous essays, short stories, and poetry, but it was her recognition of Puerto Rican folklore and traditions that made Cadilla a leading academic of her day. Her teaching, preservation work, and several important books were a great influence upon a generation of writers and artists in her country, and throughout Latin America. Her writings include *Cantos y Juegos Infantiles de Puerto Rico* (Puerto Rican Songs and Children's Games, 1938), *Costumbres y Tradicionalismos de mi Tierra* (Customs and Traditions of My Country, 1939), *Raíces de la Tierra* (Roots from the Earth, 1941) and *Rememorando el Pasado Heroico* (Remembering our Historic Past, 1946).

Cadilla was an important women's-rights advocate in Puerto Rico. She served as vice-president of the island's Suffrage Association and was also involved in the Insular Association of Women Voters. She was the only female member of the Academy of History of Puerto Rico and was awarded numerous professional accolades during her lifetime, including the St. Louis Medal from France, and honors from the Folklore Society of Mexico and the Puerto Rican Atheneum. The mother of two children who survived into adulthood, María and Tomasita, Cadilla died in Arecibo on August 21, 1951. A high school in the city is named in her honor.

SOURCES:
Sicherman, Barbara, and Carol Hurd Green. *Notable American Women: The Modern Period.* Cambridge, MA: Belknap Press of Harvard University, 1980.

Votaw, Carmen Delgado. *Puerto Rican Women.* Washington, DC: National Conference of Puerto Rican Women, 1995.

Carol Brennan,
Grosse Pointe, Michigan

Cadilla y Colón, Maria Tomasa
(1886–1951).

See Cadilla de Martínez, Maria.

Cadiz, duchess of.

See Isabella II for sidebar on Louisa Carlotta of Naples (1804–1844).

Caduff, Sylvia (1937—)

Swiss conductor. Born in Chur, Switzerland, on January 7, 1937; attended the Lucerne Conservatory.

Was the first woman to win the Dimitri Mitropoulos Competition (1966); served as assistant conductor to Leonard Bernstein at the New York Philharmonic; was general director of the Orchestra of the City of Solingen, Germany, the first European woman to hold such a position.

Sylvia Caduff's childhood wish was to become a conductor. A symphony orchestra, she reasoned, was the only "instrument" that offered her all the possibilities she felt she needed to make music. Many thought such ambition for a woman was crazy, but she persisted. Though she studied music, Caduff agreed to earn a diploma in education and to teach in an elementary classroom to please her parents, but after a brief time at teaching, she devoted all her energies to her dream. While Caduff was studying at the Lucerne Conservatory, Herbert von Karajan came to teach a course. Caduff approached him, though she did not have a conducting diploma, and asked how he felt about women conducting. "If you are gifted why not conduct?," came his surprising response. "If you are gifted we can make you an example." After Caduff completed her schooling in Switzerland, she went to Berlin to study with von Karajan who was then conducting the Berlin Philharmonic. She became a first-class conductor during her three-year apprenticeship.

Caduff realized the unlikelihood of a woman being appointed to any position as a conductor, so she established her reputation by entering competitions. Following her selection as one of four finalists in the Guido Cantelli Conducting Competition, two judges encouraged her to enter competitions in the United States where, they felt, she would have a better chance of being judged on her own merit. "You should not have come to Italy," she was told, "for here a woman has no chance at all." Instead, she was encouraged to enter the Dimitri Mitropoulos International Competition, and the Swiss government, regarding her entry as an honor for the country, underwrote her travel

costs. There were 34 conductors representing 23 countries in the competition, where an unpaid jury graded performances over a two-week period. Speaking of Caduff's performance, one critic wrote that she "led the orchestra expertly and even passionately." In 1966, Sylvia Caduff was the first woman to win first-place in the Dimitri Mitropoulos International Competition, an achievement that gained her an assistantship to Leonard Bernstein at the New York Philharmonic. In 1967, in the *World Journal Tribune,* Miles Kastendieck discussed a performance conducted by Caduff when Bernstein fell ill, "At 29, Miss Caduff now has the distinction of being the first young lady to conduct the Philharmonic officially. . . . With her fire, vitality, and commanding beat, she can have the world at her feet; indeed, she had the Philharmonic playing for her in exciting fashion last night."

When Caduff returned to Europe, she made several guest appearances, including her British debut conducting the Royal Philharmonic Orchestra at the Royal Festival Hall in 1967. This invitation came only a few years after Sir Thomas Beecham had banned all women from holding a position in the orchestra. "Beecham would presumably have been horrified to see his orchestra last night," wrote one critic, "then astonished to hear it playing so well." For the next decade, Sylvia Caduff made many guest appearances. Though she had managed to break into the conducting world, she had not yet gained a permanent orchestra. In 1977, the City of Solingen, Germany, chose her from 12 candidates to be general music director. Caduff continued to perform as a guest conductor in addition to the 18-to-20 concerts a year she conducted in Solingen.

"I thought that when women orchestral conductors made music as good as everyone else we would be accepted," said Caduff. "But this is not so. Some people think women are not able to do something special." Breaking down the prejudice of the musical world proved a formidable task for women in the 20th century. First they struggled to be allowed to play in all-male orchestras and then to conduct and compose for these orchestras. Those places like the City of Solingen that were willing to break with tradition and offer women like Sylvia Caduff permanent positions were significant in helping women conductors to take their places at the podium.

SOURCES:

Le Page, Jane Weiner. "Sylvia Caduff: Orchestral Conductor," in *Women Composers, Conductors, and Musicians of the Twentieth Century: Selected Biogra-*

phies. Vol. II. Metuchen, NJ: Scarecrow Press, 1988, pp. 56–66.

John Haag,
Athens, Georgia

Caemmerer, Hanna von (1914–1971).

See Neumann, Hanna.

Caesar, Doris Porter (1892–1971)

American sculptor of bronze figures. Born Doris Porter in Brooklyn, New York, in 1892; died in Litchfield, Connecticut, in 1971: attended Spence School for girls and Art Students League; studied with George Bridgman and Alexander Archipenko; married, in 1913; children: two sons and a daughter.

The daughter of a brilliant and successful lawyer, Doris Porter Caesar began her art studies at the age of 16, dividing her time between a prestigious girls' school and the Art Students League. With her marriage in 1913, however, she traded her artistic ambitions for the responsibilities of a well-to-do housewife, and it wasn't until 1925 that she began to reemerge as a sculptor. Struggling to find her own personal style, she studied with Alexander Archipenko, the pioneering cubist. In 1927, having cast her first bronze piece, Caesar took it to E. Weyhe, a prospective dealer who ran a combination bookstore-art gallery on Lexington Avenue in New York City and was an enthusiast of German Expressionism. Influenced by Weyhe's personal collection, which contained the works of Wilhelm Barlach, Ernst Lehmbruck, and *Käthe Kollwitz, Caesar turned away from classical forms and distorted her figure pieces until they were almost "stick-like" in appearance. This Expressionistic distortion is evident in sculpture groups like *Mother and Child* (1947) and *Descent from the Cross* (1950). In the loose style of these works, the unsmoothed thumb marks in the clay remain as a textural element in the finished bronzes. Caesar's style was fully developed in the 1950s, during which time she produced only single, naked female figures, tense and tactile, smoother surfaced, but elongated in form. A work called *Torso* (1953) is indicative of this later style.

Caesar moved to Litchfield, Connecticut, in 1957, where she continued to work until her death at the age of 78. Forty of her pieces were part of a four-person show entitled *Four American Expressionists,* presented at the Whitney Museum in 1959.

COLLECTIONS:
Doris Caesar Collection, Syracuse University Library.

Caffyn, Kathleen (1853–1926)

Irish novelist. Name variations: Mrs. Mannington Caffyn; (pseudonym) Iota. Born Kathleen Goring in 1853 at Waterloo House, County Tipperary, Ireland; died in 1926; daughter of Louisa and William Hunt Goring; educated at home; married Stephen Mannington Caffyn (1850–1896).

Kathleen Caffyn authored 17 novels during a career in which she was noted for her skill at characterization and the intense romantic and sensual qualities of her books. Born in 1853 at Waterloo House, County Tipperary, she was the daughter of William and **Louisa Hunt Goring.** After receiving her education at home from English and German governesses, at the age of 21 Caffyn underwent nurses' training at St. Thomas' Hospital; she served a short nursing career before marrying the surgeon, writer, and inventor Mannington Caffyn. To accommodate Mannington's health, in 1880 the couple immigrated to Australia. Her stay there, which lasted several years, included Kathleen's contributions to some Australian newspapers. Caffyn's first novel, *A Yellow Aster* (1893), was enormously successful following the couple's return to Ireland. Usually writing under the pseudonym Iota, Caffyn wrote most of her books after her husband's death in 1896. Her works include: *A Comedy in Spasms, Children of Circumstances, A Quaker Grandmother, Poor Max, Anne Mauleverer, The Minx, The Happiness of Jill,* and *Dorinda and Her Daughter.*

Caffyn, Mrs. Mannington (1853–1926).

See Caffyn, Kathleen.

Cahina (r. ca. 695–703).

See Kahina.

Cahun, Claude (1894–1954)

French photographer. Born Lucy Schwob in France in 1894; died in Jersey, England, in 1954; daughter of Maurice Schwob; niece of Marcel Schwob, son of the publisher of Le Phare (The Lighthouse), a newspaper in Nantes, France.

Specializing in Surrealist photographs and photomontages, Claude Cahun launched her career in 1930, with the 200-page Surrealist text (*Cancelled Confessions*), containing 10 photomontages. In 1934, she was part of the *Surrealist Exhibition of Objects* at the Galerie Charles Ratton, in Paris, where she showed a mixed media construction. She was also associated with Georges Bataille's group, Contre-Attaque, founded in 1935. Her later work included illustrations for a book of poems, *The Pick-Axe Heart*, by **Lise Deharme**. For some time it was believed that Cahun, a Jew, died in a concentration camp during World War II. Recently, however, it was discovered that she moved to the Channel Islands in 1939, where she was arrested by the Nazis (1944) and subsequently indicted and imprisoned until February 1945.

SUGGESTED READING:

Rosemont, Penelope. *Surrealist Women: An International Anthology*. TX: University of Texas, 1998.

Cai Chang (1900–1990)

One of the first female members of the Chinese Communist Party, who rose to hold its most important post in the women's movement: chair of the National Women's Federation. Name variations: Ts'ai Ch'ang, or incorrectly Tsai Chang. Pronunciation: Cai (rhymes with sigh). Born Cai Chang in Hunan province, China, in 1900; died on September 11, 1990, in Beijing at age 90; daughter of mother Ge Jianhao (Ke chien-hao); both parents were modern in their outlook and encouraged Cai and her equally famous brother, Cai Hesen (1890–1931), to secure a modern education; sister-in-law of Xiang Jingyü (1895–1928); married Li Fuqun (the economist and revolutionary), in 1923; children: one daughter.

Cai Chang was born in the early 20th century, at a time when traditional, Confucian China was rapidly fading away but a new, modern China had yet to be born. Cai, like many of her contemporaries, came to believe that the Communist Party would be the best instrument with which to achieve progress in her homeland, particularly progress for China's long-downtrodden women. China was to be torn between two competing political parties, the Chinese Communist Party (CCP) and the Chinese Nationalist Party (usually known from the abbreviation of its Chinese name as the Guomindang or Kuomintang). These two parties competed with each other for more than 50 years. The struggle between the CCP and the Guomindang was frequently bloody. Cai Chang's brother and her noted sister-in-law, the Communist female leader *****Xiang Jingyü** (1895–1928), died in the struggle. Cai survived, despite almost constant exposure to the dangers of assassination or execution, and rose through the ranks of the women's movement to become China's most important female political leader.

Cai Chang was born in Hunan province in 1900. Others born in the province around that time included Xiang Jingyü, Mao Zedong, founder of the People's Republic of China, and noted female writer and political leader *****Ding Ling** (1904–1985). Like many of the young women who were attracted to Communism, Cai Chang had a progressive father. More important, her mother **Ge Jianhao** was determined to see Cai gain a modern education. In the old Confucian society, women were rarely schooled. Although Cai was not able to begin her formal learning until the age of 11, due to the poor circumstances of her family, her mother saw to it that she was able to attend a modern school for girls, the Zhou Nan Girls' Normal School in Changsha, the provincial capital. Scholar and journalist Nym Wales (*****Helen Foster Snow**), who studied the lives of many revolutionary Chinese women, termed it "the cradle of the Chinese Communist women's movement."

> *The Dean of Chinese Communist women was Cai Chang, petite and gentle, but nevertheless a "professional Revolutionary."*
>
> —**Nym Wales**

While at Zhou Nan, Cai Chang met many other radical Chinese women, including Xiang Jingyü, who was to be her inspiration. Cai Chang's older brother, Cai Hesen, was a fiery radical, as was his friend, Mao Zedong. As Changsha was the most modern city in Hunan and contained the best modern schools, progressive youth congregated there in great numbers. Ge Jianhao moved to Changsha after the death of Cai Chang's father. There, her home became a sort of radical salon where many of the future leaders of China met to argue and discuss their country's many problems.

The central challenge facing China at the time that Cai Chang graduated, about 1918, was what sort of government was to replace the Chinese monarchy, which had collapsed in 1911–12. China had gone through a brief period of Republican government led by Sun Yat-sen (1866–1925), but the country lacked a foundation of custom and practice in democratic government, and it was soon in the grips of regional military strongmen, known as "warlords."

Radical youth like Cai Chang and her friends read widely from translated works of Western literature, including books on government and political theory, as well as novels and plays. They believed that whatever replaced Confucianism as the animating value system of China, it would probably come from the West, which seemed to them to be the source of modernity itself. At the same time, they were angry and frustrated with the Western nations that had long been taking advantage of China's economic and political weakness. As a result, they were as much attracted to radical critiques of Western nations as to the West itself.

After graduation, Cai Chang worked briefly at Zhou Nan as an instructor of physical education. To engage in serious and extended physical activity, let alone systematic physical training, was very unusual for Chinese women. In the old society, the ideal woman had been a cloistered beauty, often pictured in novels as suffering from some debilitating disease or lingering illness. Although Cai Chang was physically small, she was an active and confident young woman. It may have been at this time that she built the rugged constitution that was to enable her to endure great hardship later in life.

The First World War created a need for vast numbers of unskilled laborers in Europe. At war's end, France took the lead in inviting Asian youth to come to Europe on work-study programs. In 1919, a large group of Hunanese scholars left for France, organized by Cai's brother Cai Hesen, and their mutual friend, Mao Zedong. In France, Cai Hesen soon became the leader of the increasingly radical community of Chinese young people; he also married Cai Chang's friend and classmate, Xiang Jingyü. Now their apartment became the center of the radical youth. While attending the Collège de Montargis, south of Paris, Cai Chang met and, in 1923, married Li Fuqun, another radical Chinese student from Hunan.

While in France, the Chinese students were well-placed to closely study the preeminent event then occurring in the world: the Russian Revolution. Because Russia seemed to them to be a backward agrarian and monarchical state much like their own traditional China, the students were particularly drawn to the Bolshevik revolution as a possible model for their own liberation. They soon founded a Socialist Youth League, then, in 1923, in China, the Chinese Communist Party (CCP). Mao was a founding member of the CCP, and many of the students in France soon joined as well. Also like other students, Cai Chang and her husband Li Fuqun went from France to the Soviet Union in 1924 where they attended a special school for Asian revolutionaries, the University of the Toilers of the East. Cai Chang remained there until the spring of 1925.

The Chinese Communist Party was only one of several groups competing for the support of Chinese people who wanted political reform and modernization. The most important one at that time was the Chinese Nationalist Party (Guomindang). The Guomindang, like the CCP, had substantial Soviet aid and modelled itself in many important regards upon the Communist Party of the Soviet Union. The Soviets, desiring to see a strong nationalist China, which might cause difficulty for the Western powers in their Asian colonies, forced the CCP and the Guomindang into an alliance for the purpose of a joint movement that would seize China from the warlords by military and political action. In this alliance, the Guomindang became the main military force, while the CCP took charge of organizing workers, peasants, and women to support the revolution. While this was a dynamic combination that the warlords could not hope to long stand against, it was an alliance doomed from the beginning. While the CCP and the Guomindang easily agreed on the need for revolution, the Guomindang envisioned only a political revolution that would see it at the head of a strong national government. But the idealists and radicals of the CCP wanted a complete social revolution that would create a modern, egalitarian and Chinese Communist society.

Because the CCP was inclined by its revolutionary doctrines to seek support from Chinese women, radical women such as Cai Chang were naturally drawn to it. The party, in turn, eagerly employed them in working among such groups of women as industrial workers and radical students. Cai Chang came to specialize in working among such women and rose quickly through the party ranks. The Guomindang, for its part, largely neglected such social issues as "the woman question" but rather relied upon its erstwhile ally, the CCP, for organizational work among women.

Like many Communists, Cai Chang held joint membership in both the Guomindang and the CCP and served in many posts for both parties. She was a propagandist for the Guomindang and headed a CCP women's bureau in south China. When the Northern Expedition, a joint CCP-Guomindang offensive, was launched in 1926, Cai Chang accompanied the armies into Wuhan, the first important city to be taken from the warlords. Seeing that victory was near, the two allies fell to plotting against each other. Chiang Kai-shek, the Guomindang military leader, seized the initiative by organizing a great massacre of radicals in Shanghai in 1927. All over China radical youth and workers and peasant organizers were rounded up and executed. In some cities, young women were shot as suspected Communists simply for having cut their hair short in the modern fashion. Cai Chang's girlhood friend Xiang Jingyü, then the leader of the CCP women's movement, was executed in 1928, and Cai's beloved older brother, Cai Hesen, in 1931. Other members of her immediate family and many friends also died in the series of purges. This gave the survivors a steely resolve, which saw them through decades of hardship and constant danger.

In 1934–35, the CCP was driven out of the south of China by Chiang Kai-shek and undertook the fabled "Long March" to a secure northern base area at Yenan. Along with Mao's wife ⚘▶ He Zizhen, Cai Chang was one of the very few women who participated in the Long March. It was a terrible ordeal. The troops were under almost constant attack from the Guomindang, warlords, and hostile minorities. They marched more than 6,000 miles through great swamps and over frozen mountains—some of the most difficult terrain in the world—under all weather conditions. This was the formative experience of the CCP. Throughout their lives, the veterans of the Long March were to be united by their common participation in the event, during which more than 100,000 of their comrades died; some figures suggest that only about 10% of those who began the march finished it. On the Long March, Mao Zedong gained full control over the CCP, and at the Yenan base Cai Chang became the leader of its important women's movement.

The political situation at the time was extremely complicated, particularly after the Japanese invasion of China, which soon became a theater of World War II. Cai Chang worked tirelessly. In 1938, American journalist Nym Wales interviewed Cai and had extensive conversations with her in French. Wales wrote that while Cai Chang had been beautiful at one time, her suffering, particularly the deaths of so many of her loved ones, had marked her face with "lines of sad experience." Wales found her to be gentle, "almost spiritual," but also a woman of "individual character and great determination." One of the few personal possessions that Cai Chang had carried throughout the hardships of the Long March was a tattered photograph of her mother Ge Jianhao. During the war, Cai Chang continued to rise in the leadership of the party. She had been an associate member of the leadership group of the CCP, the Central Committee, since 1928. In 1945, Cai Chang became the only full female member of the Central Committee.

After the defeat of Japan in 1945, the Guomindang and the CCP went through another brief period of uneasy truces marked with military clashes. In 1946, the civil war began in earnest. The CCP strategy of relying upon mass organizations rather than solely upon military power proved to be a wise choice. The Guomindang was quickly revealed to have been vitiated by factionalism and corruption; its sudden military collapse astonished foreign observers. The disciplined mass armies of the CCP were victorious by October of 1949, when the founding of the People's Republic of China was declared. Cai Chang and her female comrade-in-arms, *Deng Yingzhao (1903–1992), were present at the events. Deng Yingzhao, while herself an amazing woman, shared in part the high status of her husband, the new premier of China, Zhou Enlai. As Mao Zedong's closest confidant for many years, Zhou's position in the new China was second only to Mao. But Cai Chang had won her place in the revolutionary pantheon through her own life of arduous work.

For many Chinese women, particularly for Cai Chang, the signal event of the revolution was probably the creation of the All-China Women's Federation in 1949. The federation became the representative of Chinese women in the political process and took the lead in working to solve women's problems. As its first chair, Cai Chang served her country and her political party in many offices, both honorary and substantive, until growing less active through the 1960s. She was a member of the Central Committee from 1928 to 1982. Although still active and politically involved, Cai Chang's long career as a revolutionary had left her in increasingly frail health. Probably because of her relative retirement, and because of her great standing with the veterans of the Long March, including her childhood friend Mao Zedong, Cai Chang escaped the sort of political persecution that others suffered. On September 11, 1990, Cai Chang died in Beijing at the age of 90.

SOURCES:

Boorman, Howard L., ed. "Ts'ai Ch'ang," in *Biographical Dictionary of Republican China*. Vol. III. NY: Columbia University Press, 1970, pp. 282–283.

Klein, Donald W., and Anne B. Clark, eds. "Ts'ai Ch'ang," in *Biographic Dictionary of Chinese Communism 1921–1965*. Vol. II. Cambridge, MA: Harvard University Press, 1971, pp. 847–851.

Wales, Nym. *Inside Red China*. NY: 1939 (reprinted NY: Da Capo Press, 1977).

SUGGESTED READING:

Brandt, Conrad. *The French-Returned Elite of the Chinese Communist Party*. Reprint no. 13. Institute of International Studies, Berkeley, CA: University of California, 1961.

◀⚘
He Zizhen. See *Jiang Qing* for sidebar.

Chow Tse-tsung. *The May Fourth Movement: Intellectual Revolution in Modern China*. Stanford, CA: Stanford University Press, 1960.

Snow, Edgar. *The Battle for Asia*. NY: 1941.

Jeffrey G. Barlow, Professor in the Department of Social Studies, Pacific University, Forest Grove, Oregon

Caillaux, Henriette (?–1943)

French murderer of Le Figaro *editor Gaston Calmette. Born Henriette Rainouard; died in 1943; second wife of Joseph Caillaux (1863–1944, member of chamber of deputies, premier of France [1911–1912], French minister of finance).*

In March 1914, as France teetered on the brink of war with Germany, *Le Figaro*'s editor, Gaston Calmette, continued his two-month campaign against France's minister of finance Joseph Caillaux, husband of Henriette Caillaux. Calmette had printed some 138 articles and cartoons aimed at discrediting the minister's political and personal life, even suggesting that he was a traitor who was dealing with enemy agents of Germany. Calmette had also published letters Minister Caillaux had written years before to his first wife and to Henriette, when the latter was his mistress. In one particular missive, Joseph had confided to Henriette, "I have crushed the Income Tax Bill while appearing to defend it, thereby pleasing the Centre and the Right, without too much upsetting the Left." This disclosure in *Le Figaro* turned public opinion against Caillaux, leaving him branded as a hypocrite and one of the most ruthless politicians France had seen. Henriette was infuriated over the attack on her husband and further frustrated by the discovery that public figures could not sue for libel. She purchased a Browning revolver from a local gunsmith, visited the newspaper offices of *Le Figaro* on March 16, and calmly fired four bullets into editor Gaston Calmette, who died that night of his injuries.

Henriette Caillaux did not flee the scene of the crime. Immediately apprehended, she was incarcerated in a comfortable jail cell, with her meals catered by one of Paris' finest restaurants. For the four months up to her trial in July, the murder story so dominated the European press that attention was even diverted from the international political crisis. When she finally faced a jury, Henriette described Calmette's persecution and claimed that the killing had not been premeditated. "I lost my head when I found myself in the presence of the man who had done us much harm," she said. "The gun went off accidentally. The bullets seemed to follow each other automatically." The jury, seemingly mesmerized by the soft-spoken defendant, found her innocent of premeditated murder and sent her home, shocking the nation and the press. Her husband remained in public office, although he was later charged with treason for corresponding with Germany during the war. Henriette Caillaux died in 1943, her husband a year later.

SUGGESTED READING:

Berenson, Edward. *The Trial of Madame Caillaux*. Berkeley, CA: University of California Press, 1992.

Barbara Morgan,
Melrose, Massachusetts

Henriette Caillaux

Cai Yan (c. 162–239)

Chinese composer and poet. Name variations: Caiyan or Ts'ai Yen. Born around 162 CE, during the time of the Han Dynasty; died around 239 CE; daughter of the scholar and poet Cai (Ts'ai) I; widowed around 192; children: two sons.

Cai Yan, daughter of the famous scholar and poet Cai I (Ts'ai) I, wrote poetry that documents her difficult and tragic life during the time of the Han Dynasty. She had been married and widowed before being captured and taken North by the Huns. For the next 12 years, she was a captive and had two sons by a Hun chieftain. Cai Yan's family finally located her and ransomed their daughter back, but she had to return to China without her boys, a heartbreaking experience for her. Though attribution is uncertain, it is believed she wrote *Eighteen verses*, which describes the life she endured—war, barbarism, and grief. "A Tatar chief forced me to become his wife, And took me far away to Heaven's edge." The verses were meant to be accompanied by the lute and the Tatar horn. Cai Yan is the first Chinese female poet whose life and writings are documented.

John Haag,
Athens, Georgia

Cajanello, duchess of.

See Edgren, Anne Charlotte (1849–1892).

Calamity Jane (1852–1903).

See Cannary, Martha Jane.

Calderón de la Barca, Frances
(1804–1882)

Scottish-American woman of letters, traveler, and companion to the royal family of Spain, whose observations of Mexico in the age of Antonio López de Santa Anna are considered among the finest of the travel-literature genre. Name variations: Fanny Calderon. Pronunciation: Cal-der-OWN de la BAR-ca. Born Frances Erskine Inglis on December 23, 1804, in Edinburgh, Scotland; died on February 6, 1882, in Madrid, Spain; daughter of William Inglis (a prominent attorney) and Jane (Stein) Inglis (of a wealthy distilling family); married Angel Calderón de la Barca (an aristocratic Spanish civil servant and diplomat), on September 24, 1838; no children.

Moved with her widowed mother and four siblings to Boston, where she helped to operate the family's private school (1831); moved with family to New York where they established a second school on Staten Island (1837); moved with husband, Angel Calderón de la Barca, to Mexico City, where he was the first Spanish diplomat posted to Mexico (1839); stationed in Washington (1844–53); wrote much-respected Life in Mexico *(1843); after Angel's recall to Spain to serve as foreign minister, forced by revolution to flee to France (1854); returned to Spain in 1856, where Angel served as senator while Fanny attended the royal court and wrote her second book,* The Attaché in Madrid *(1856); after death of Angel, became tutor to Princess Maria Isabel Francisca, serving in the household of Spain's royal family as educator, friend and confidante (1861); awarded patent of nobility, as the Marquesa de Calderón de la Barca (1876).*

In the summer of 1840, Mexico was shaken to its foundations by a bloody revolution; a virtual civil war. Fanny and Angel Calderón de la Barca were caught at its epicenter, as their Mexico City mansion was just blocks away from the contested presidential palace. For weeks, bullets and cannonballs shrieked over and by their home, but Fanny remained typically unruffled. On July 19, she wrote, "Dr. Plane, a famous French physician, was shot this morning as he was coming out of the palace, and his body has just been carried past our door. . . . We pass our time on our balconies, listening to the thunder of the cannon, looking at the different parties of troops riding by . . . excessively tired of the whole affair."

Frances Erskine Inglis (pronounced "Ingalls") was born December 23, 1804, at Edinburgh, Scotland, the fifth of ten children in the wealthy and prominent family of William and **Jane Stein Inglis**. William Inglis was an attorney who traced his ancestry back to a family that had been elevated to the nobility in 1396, and Jane Stein's family had prospered in the business of highland whiskey distilleries. The child, universally called Fanny, grew up in a frenetic household of parents, servants, and five sisters and four brothers. Little is known about how she was educated, formally or by tutors, but it is clear that she grew up as a learned woman, fluent in a number of languages, conversant in the classics, and very much aware of world affairs.

When Fanny was in her teens, the family was struck by a succession of tragedies, including the death of her married sister, Catherine, followed by the death of an elder brother who was serving as a soldier in India. In 1828, William Inglis was bankrupted—a horrible stigma in that era—and forced to flee with his family to France in order to avoid creditors, and perhaps debtor's prison; broken in spirit and health, he died in 1830.

Unwilling to return to Scotland as social pariahs, the Inglis family used the last of their money to book passage for Boston. Jane Inglis set sail with her divorced daughter Richmond (and Richmond's four children), her 15-year-old son Duff, and daughters Fanny, Harriet, and Lydia. In Boston, the Inglis women opened a school on Mount Vernon Street that attracted the daughters of the city's elite and allowed the family to prosper again. But in 1833, an anonymous pamphlet was published, assaulting the character of some of Boston's finest families, and it soon became known that the author was 29-year-old Fanny. Many elite families showed their pique by withdrawing their children from the Inglis' school.

Financially strapped again, the Inglises held on out of stubborn pride and only left Boston at a time of their *own* choosing. In 1837, they moved to New York City and settled into a fashionable area of Staten Island, where they opened another school, catering to the children of government officials and diplomats. Once again the family prospered, and Fanny, by then in her early 30s, began to receive the attentions of a diplomat she had met casually in Boston. Angel Calderón de la Barca was minister plenipotentiary (ambassador) of Spain to the United States, a career diplomat, and smitten by the young Scottish woman. Now that she was closer to Washington, he visited her often, and the two were soon betrothed.

So it appears to me that when bullets are whizzing about our ears . . . it ought to be considered extremely natural, and quite feminine, to inquire into the cause of such phenomena.

—Fanny Calderón de la Barca

On September 24, 1838, the 33-year-old Fanny married the 48-year-old diplomat in a Catholic ceremony in New York. The following summer, Angel's tour in Washington was ended, and the couple spent some months on Staten Island with the Inglis clan. In late October 1839, they took ship for Mexico, where Angel had been posted as the country's first Spanish ambassador.

Fanny, whose linguistic gifts made learning a new language a trifle, was fluent in Spanish before their ship anchored in the Vera Cruz harbor. For her husband, the assignment to Mexico was employment; for her, it was an adventure, and she was eager to observe and record everything she could. During the four turbulent years she remained there, she kept a form of daily journal, copies of letters she wrote, and random jottings and musings. She was an exceptionally keen and witty observer, as has been recognized by later travelers and scholars ever since. In 1908, Charles Flandrau wrote in *Viva Mexico!*: "The most entertaining as well as the most essentially true book on Mexico that I have been able to find was written by . . . Madame Calderón de la

Barca." More recently, Selden Rodman wrote in his *Mexican Journal* in 1958: "She accepts Mexico, *from the heart,* without closing her eyes to its defects."

Her observations of people—such as "the melancholy and philosophic" dictator General Antonio López de Santa Anna, conqueror of the Alamo—and of the terrain, flora and fauna, religious and social customs, and a good deal more, were succinct and insightful. They have also proved to be extremely detailed and accurate. As Flandrau noted 60 years later, "From Madame Calderón, and from her only, was I able to learn the exact religious import of the nine dances" of the Christmas season. Today's scholars of 19th-century Mexico consider her book to be one of the major sources, if not *the* source, on the period.

When she first put them on paper, Fanny had no thought of publishing her writings. A lengthy correspondence with William Hickling Prescott led to the possibility. Prescott, conceivably the first true historian in the United States, was dedicated to the history of Mexico and South America, and had been a friend of the Calderóns since their first years in Washington. Nearly blind, he researched and wrote a number of stout volumes, including the monumental, three-volume *History of the Conquest of Mexico* (1843). After reading Fanny's papers, he all but demanded that she have them published, and she agreed, somewhat reluctantly. With the scholar's editorial advice, she arranged for the large volume, *Life in Mexico,* to be published by friends in Boston in late 1843; soon thereafter, it appeared in London.

In a transparent, but diplomatic, gesture of anonymity (she was, after all, wife of a serving diplomat), she had authorship credited to a "Madame C——— de la B———." The book was an instant success and has since become what one critic has termed "a quiet persistent classic," translated into a score of languages. To her relief, it was early applauded even in Mexico, which she observed with rather blunt frankness: "On first arriving in Mexico one cannot fail—especially if arrived from the United States where an ugly woman is a phoenix—to be struck at the first glance with the general absence of beauty and grace."

During the next nine years, Angel again represented Spain in Washington. In 1847, Fanny Calderón converted to Catholicism, which apparently played a role in the advancement of her husband to the highest of diplomatic positions. In 1853, he was recalled to Madrid, to serve as minister of foreign affairs. The exhilarating move into the exalted circles and having access to the royal court was not to last, however. When a revolution ousted the government in 1854, Angel was forced to flee for his life to France, disguised and using a false passport. Fanny Calderón soon followed, also traveling incognito, and for two years the couple lived quietly in Neuilly, then Paris, where she wrote, in complete anonymity, her very perceptive *The Attaché* in Madrid. When the governmental crisis was ended, the couple returned to Spain in 1856, the year *The Attaché* in Madrid first reached print in New York. Purportedly written by a German diplomat, it dealt with the turmoil into which Spain descended in 1854, and it was not known for many years that Fanny Calderón de la Barca was its real author.

The next five years were pleasant, placid ones for the couple, with Angel serving in the Spanish senate, Fanny reading a great deal, and summers spent in the cool, mountainous Basque provinces near the French border. This peaceful time of stability and contemplation was broken abruptly by Angel's unexpected death in the spring of 1861, just as the United States was entering its Civil War.

Not long after Angel's passing, the widow Calderón was summoned to the royal court, where Queen **Isabella II** (1830–1904) paid her the singular honor of asking her to tutor the nine-year-old "Infanta," ❧➤ **Maria Isabel Francisca** (b. 1851), known as Princess Isabel. With some reluctance, Fanny, now 57, assented, gave up her stately Madrid mansion, and moved into the gigantic royal palace to take up her new duties. Because Isabel was the oldest royal child, and her only brother was weak and chronically ill, it was apparent that Fanny was probably educating the future queen of Spain. In 1868, when the Infanta was married, at age 16, to Caetano de Borbón, a distant cousin, the duties of the former tutor were completed, and she took the opportunity to sail to the United States on an extended vacation visit.

That same year, yet another revolution swept through Spain, requiring the royal family to flee into exile in France. Young Isabel, who had developed an almost filial attachment to her former tutor, now wrote from France pleading that Calderón return to her side as confidant, educator, and companion. After some hesitation, Calderón's sense of duty to the royal family impelled her to travel to France to be at the teenager's side. Isabel's husband had by then developed a severe mental illness (probably acute depression) and was displaying, among other things, suicidal tendencies. Fanny found herself acting

as nursemaid to the prince while advising the princess, but in late 1871, despite all efforts, Caetano shot himself to death.

While Fanny was consoling the young Isabel in France, Queen Isabella II abdicated the throne of Spain to her—still sickly—son, Alphonso (XII). In 1874, Parliament officially proclaimed him king. Before long, Fanny was again living in Spain's royal palace, as companion to the princess; two years later, the young king (whom Fanny had briefly tutored in his tender years) brought Fanny, the Scottish-born tutor and daughter of a debtor, into the Spanish nobility, as the *Marquesa de Calderón*.

Nor was she alone and without family of her own in Madrid. By quirk of fate, one of her nieces had married a Spanish *marques* and lived in the capital; her widowed younger sister, Harriet, lived part of each year in Madrid, with a daughter who had married a Spanish diplomat; and her youngest sister, Lydia, lived there as well, married to yet another Spanish diplomat. When Lydia's husband died, she was appointed governess to a new generation of the children in the royal family.

After years of separation, the Inglis descendants were reunited in Madrid, living spirited, happy, and useful lives. Fanny remained remarkably healthy throughout her years, despite all of her travel and living in sometimes primitive circumstances. At age 77, she was still fully active, when she contracted "the chills" (probably pneumonia) and died soon after on February 6, 1882, in the royal palace she had called home for most of the past 20 years. At a funeral attended by Spain's royal family and members of her own family, she was buried in a ceremony befitting a marquesa.

SOURCES:
Calderón de la Barca, Fanny. *Life in Mexico*. Boston: Anchor Books, 1970.
————. *Life in Mexico During a Residence of Two Years in that Country*. NY: Everyman's Library, 1954.

SUGGESTED READING:
Becher, Carl C. *Cartas sobre México*. Mexico City: Nueva Biblioteca Mexicana, 1959.
Simpson, Lesley Byrd. *Many Mexicos*. Berkeley, CA: University of California Press, 1962.
Stephens, John L. *Incidents of Travel in Yucatan*. 2 vols. NY: Harper & Brothers, 1843 (1963).

John Hoyt Williams,
Professor of History, Indiana
State University, Terre Haute, Indiana

❧➤
Maria Isabel Francisca (1851–1931). See Isabella II for sidebar.

Calderone, Mary Steichen

(1904–1998)

American pioneer in the development of responsible sex education for children and adults. Name varia-

tions: Mary Steichen; Mary Steichen Martin. Pronunciation: STAI-ken. Born Mary Steichen in New York City, on July 1, 1904; died on October 24, 1998, in Kennett Square, Pennsylvania; daughter of Edward Steichen (the photographer) and Clara (Smith) Steichen (a homemaker); graduated Vassar College, B.A., 1925; University of Rochester Medical School, M.D., 1939; Columbia University, Master's Degree of Public Health, 1941; married W. Lon Martin, in 1926 (divorced 1933); married Frank Calderone, on November 27, 1941; children: (first marriage) Nell (d. 1935) and Linda; (second marriage) Francesca and Maria.

Became medical director of Planned Parenthood (1953); named first executive director of SIECUS (1965); became president of SIECUS (1975); retired from active involvement in SIECUS (1982); received numerous honorary degrees and dozens of awards and citations for her work in the field of public health including: the distinguished service award of the Mental Health Association of Nassau County (1958); the fourth annual award for distinguished service to humanity of the women's auxiliary of the Albert Einstein Medical Center in Philadelphia (1966); the Woman of Conscience Award of the National Council of Women (1968); the Woman of Achievement Award of the Albert Einstein College of Medicine of Yeshiva University (1969); the annual award from the Education Foundation for Human Sexuality (1973); and the Edward Browning Award for Prevention of Disease from the American Public Health Association (1980).

Publications: (with father Edward Steichen under name Mary Steichen Martin) The First Picture Book: Everyday Things for Babies *(1930) and* The Second Picture Book *(1931); (editor, under Mary Steichen Calderone)* Abortion in the United States *(1958) and* Release From Sexual Tensions *(1960); (editor)* Manual of Family Planning and Contraceptive Practice *(1964); (editor)* Sexuality and Human Values *(1974); (with Eric Johnson)* The Family Book About Sexuality *(1981); (with James W. Ramey)* Talking With Your Child About Sex *(1982).*

Mary Steichen Calderone was one of the pioneers of sexual education and reform in 20th-century America. During a time when important new discoveries about the nature of human sexuality were precluded from open public discussion because of rigid social and religious mores, she became a vociferous, tireless crusader. It was her firm belief that if ordinary people had access to information relating to human sexuality they would make responsible and rational decisions about sex. Calderone is credited with taking information on procreation and sexuality out of the exclusive domain of professional circles and putting it into homes and public schools across America.

Born in New York City on July 1, 1904, Mary Steichen Calderone was the elder of two daughters of **Clara Smith Steichen** and renowned photographer Edward Steichen. Mary spent her first ten years in France where artistic luminaries such as August Rodin and *Isadora Duncan were frequent guests in the Steichen home. Calderone was always close to her father and considered him one of the greatest influences on her life. She credited his "extension of photography into the area of human life and the human condition" as informing her own eventual decision to work in the area of public health.

Edward Steichen exercised little overt control over his daughters, instead insisting that the girls be given the freedom to make their own decisions. The result was that Calderone developed into a strong, independent thinker. Her father later recalled that Mary "always had a strong personality, almost as strong as my own." Her mother did not share his enthusiasm. She found it increasingly difficult to manage her high-spirited daughter, and their relationship was fraught with difficulties.

The outbreak of World War I forced the family to return to the United States. By this time, her parents had divorced, and her father's service in the army left her without an ally at home. After passing one unhappy year at a country school in Connecticut, Calderone was sent to New York to live with Dr. Leopold Stieglitz, brother of Alfred Stieglitz, another pioneer of early photography and an associate of her father. "This is where my academic intellectual life and my interest in medicine began, for Dr. Stieglitz loved to talk over his cases with me, and often I went on his rounds with him," Calderone later recalled.

While living with Leopold Stieglitz and his family, she attended the exclusive Brearley School. After graduating in 1922, she went to Vassar College where she majored in chemistry and began acting in college plays. She was graduated in 1925 and returned to New York eager to pursue a stage career. For three years, she studied under Richard Boleslavsky and *Maria Ouspenskaya of the American Laboratory Theater. It was during this interval that she was married for the first time to an actor, W. Lon Martin. The couple had two daughters before divorcing in 1933.

Calderone also decided to give up acting. She later described her decision to leave the theater in a characteristically straightforward way: "I gave up acting when I found I wasn't good enough. . . . I was ambitious and if I couldn't be as good as Katharine Cornell—that is, tops—I decided I wouldn't go on with it." The dual failure of marriage and career was followed by the death of her eight-year-old daughter Nell from pneumonia in 1935. These losses sent Calderone into a period of sadness and confusion for which she underwent psychoanalysis.

Emerging from this bleak period with a new direction and a renewed determination, she decided on a medical career in the field of public health, and, in 1934, at age 30, entered the University of Rochester Medical School. Calderone received her M.D. in 1939 and interned for one year at the Children's Hospital in New York City. Awarded a two-year fellowship by the Department of Health of New York City, she took graduate courses at the Columbia University School of Public Health and received a Master's Degree in Public Health in 1942. While at Columbia, she worked for Dr. Frank A. Calderone, a district health officer on New York's Lower East Side (he later became deputy commissioner of health for New York City). They wed on November 27, 1941, and the marriage produced two daughters.

For the next few years, Mary Calderone stayed home to raise her young daughters, working only part time as a physician to the public schools in Great Neck, New York. Then in 1953, she became medical director of the Planned Parenthood Federation of America, a position she held until 1964. It was in this capacity that Calderone first became aware of the critical need for sex education and family planning.

As medical director, she lectured widely to professional groups, urging them to recognize family planning as a basic public-health issue. She is credited with influencing the American Medical Association to adopt a policy in 1964 that permitted physicians to dispense birth-control information more freely. Yet Calderone began to wonder whether advising the medical community and handing out contraception to the public was enough. She was astonished by the thousands of letters that Planned Parenthood received from around the country asking basic questions about birth control, sex, and sexual problems. The letters reflected feelings of guilt, fear, and misunderstanding. Calderone became convinced that a pandemic of ignorance about sexuality existed and that the people she most needed to reach were ordinary men and women. She decided to wield her considerable influence

to educate people and challenge the prevailing social taboos and religious doctrines responsible for keeping the discussion of sexuality out of the public sphere.

In 1961, Calderone took part in the first North American Conference on Church and Family, sponsored by the National Council of Churches. The convention was attended by sociologists, religious leaders, family-life educators, and public-health officials. Calderone and five colleagues who took part in the conference established an informal committee to examine studies on human sexuality. Out of this committee was formed the Sex Information and Education Council of the United States, Inc. (SIECUS) in 1964. The stated purpose of the organization was to dignify human sexuality "by openness of approach, study, and scientific research . . . to the end that human beings may be aided toward responsible use of the sexual facility and towards assimilation of sex into their individual life patterns as a creative and re-creative force."

My motivation . . . is simple: to give ordinary people access to the facts scientists now have about the different aspects of sexuality common to all people everywhere. . . . Such knowledge, when understood, accepted and applied . . . can act to avoid or prevent many of the sexual dysfunctions easily observable in our society and elsewhere.

—Mary Steichen Calderone

Calderone resigned her position at Planned Parenthood and became executive director of SIECUS in 1965. Under her stewardship, SIECUS became a clearinghouse on sexuality, providing individuals and organizations with information on reproduction, premarital sex, masturbation, homosexuality, frigidity, and impotence. It provided training in sex education to doctors, ministers, and psychiatrists. As executive director, Calderone lectured widely to educators, parents, students, religious leaders, and professional groups, advocating a continuum of sex education in the public schools, beginning in kindergarten with the basic facts about procreation and masturbation. She argued that this instruction should continue as necessary throughout elementary school. At the high school level, she stressed the importance of integrating scientific information on reproduction and sexuality with social concerns about human relationships and responsibilities. She suggested that the curriculum should include discussions of sexual and mating behavior, psychological factors involved in the human sexual response, the relationship between family and society, and the institution of marriage. Frank discussion of venereal disease, divorce, and abortion were also to be included.

Though Calderone's specific ideas for sex education were not always implemented, her pioneering efforts paid off. In 1964, the year of SIECUS' inception, only 1% of the medical schools in the United States included sex education; ten years later, 95% included it (though the number eventually declined). The proliferation of sex-education courses in grade schools and high schools across America also testifies to the enormous impact of her work.

Throughout her career in the field of human sexuality, Calderone was a controversial figure. Her efforts to speak out about homosexual rights, abortion, sex for the handicapped and elderly, pornography (which she did not denounce), and sex education for children continually came under fire. She was accused of being subversive and immoral and was labeled an "aging sexual libertine" by the John Birch Society, while SIECUS was accused of being a Communist plot to overthrow the government. Her critics charged that educating children about sex at an early age encouraged experimentation and led to sexual dysfunction. Calderone scoffed at these charges, and instead insisted that it was the withholding of information that led to misunderstanding and warped attitudes. She wrote in *Clinical Pediatrics* in March 1966:

> Sexuality . . . as an attribute of life that lends the variety and color and excitement and creativity that adults know, is never presented to young people because we are so afraid that, if we do so we may stimulate them and lead them astray. My answer to that is that plenty of erotic stimuli reach them so continually in so many other ways that it is like the man living on a garbage dump who worries that the teaspoon of honey he has spilled may attract flies.

In spite of the resistance she received from many conservative and religious groups, Calderone maintained that her own faith informed her progressive attitude toward sexuality. As a devout Quaker, she believed "sexuality is a part of God because . . . it is part of being human." She disagreed with those who tried to keep it tied under the yoke of fear and sin. She called, instead, for teaching children that sexuality constitutes the deepest form of communication, and that, as in other human relations, one should enter into a sexual relationship with a sense of responsibility of the rights and well being of the other person. She also roundly criticized those who trivialized sex, engaging in it indiscriminately and thus equating "sexuality with genitality."

As she moved into old age, Calderone stayed active in public health and debate. She remained the executive director of SIECUS until 1975, when she was named president, the position she held until her retirement in 1982, at age 78. She subsequently held several academic appointments, including a lectureship in sexuality at New York University (1982–88). *The Family Book About Sexuality,* which she co-wrote with Eric Johnson, was published in 1981. *The New York Times* called it "a comprehensive family guide to sexuality, full of surprises, rich in facts and . . . stripped of propaganda." The book was named "Best Trade Book" by the American Medical Writers Association. The following year saw the publication of *Talking With Your Child About Sex,* which she co-wrote with James W. Ramey.

SOURCES:

Breasted, Mary. *Oh! Sex Education!* NY: Praeger Publishers, 1970.

Calderone, Mary Steichen. *Release From Sexual Tension.* NY: Random House, 1960.

——, ed. *Sexuality and Human Values.* NY: Association Press, 1974.

——, and Eric W. Johnson, eds. *The Family Book About Sexuality.* NY: Harper & Row, 1981.

Contemporary Authors: New Revision Series. Vol. 104. Detroit, MI: Gale Research, 1981.

Current Biography. NY: H.W. Wilson, 1967.

Freese, Arthur S. "Meet Mary Calderone," in *Modern Maturity.* August–September 1978, pp. 55–56.

Hottois, James, and Neal A. Milner. *The Sex Education Controversy: A Study of Politics, Education and Morality.* Lexington, KY: Lexington Books, 1975.

Mace, David. "A Quaker Portrait: Mary Steichen Calderone," in *Friends Journal.* March 15, 1971.

McGuire, William, and Leslie Wheeler. *American Social Leaders.* Santa Barbara, CA: ABC-CLIO, 1993.

Ohles, John F. *Biographical Dictionary of America's Educators.* Westport, CT: Greenwood Press, 1978.

Sex Information and Education Council of the U.S. *SIECUS Report.* May–July 1982. NY: Sex Information and Education Council of the U.S.

Suzanne Smith, freelance writer,
Decatur, Georgia

Caldicott, Helen (1938—)

Australian pediatrician, anti-nuclear campaigner, conservationist, and dynamic orator. Pronunciation: COLD-ee-cot. Born Helen Mary Broinowski on August 7, 1938, in Melbourne, Victoria, Australia; daughter of Philip Broinowski (a paint factory manager) and Mary Mona Enyd (Coffey) Broinowski (an interior designer); attended University of Adelaide Med-

Helen
Caldicott

ical School, Bachelor of Medicine and Bachelor of Surgery, 1961, Paediatrics, 1975; married William Caldicott, December 8, 1962 (divorced 1988); children: Phillip (b. 1964); **Penelope Mary Caldicott** (b. 1965); William (b. 1967).

Prizes and awards: British Medical Association Prize for Clinical Medicine (1960); prize for Surgical Anatomy (1961); Margaret Mead award for defense of the environment, Ghandi Peace Prize, Thomas Merton Peace Prize, and Boston Ethical Society's Hu-

manist of the Year (1980); UN Association for Australia Peace Medal Award (1985); Nobel Peace Prize, presented to Physicians for Social Responsibility (1985); (with Bishop Desmond Tutu and Los Angeles Mayor Tom Bradley) John-Roger Foundation Integrity Award (1985); nominated for Nobel Peace Prize (1986); Academy Award for best short documentary, If You Love This Planet *(1983); numerous honorary degrees.*

Brought about cessation of French atmospheric nuclear testing in the Pacific (1971–72); moved to U.S. (1977); published Nuclear Madness *(1978); resigned as pediatrician (1980); resurrected, and was national president of, Physicians for Social Responsibility (1978–83); founded Women's Party for Survival (WPFS, 1980); founded Women's Action for Nuclear Disarmament (WAND, 1980); published* Missile Envy *(1984); nominated for Nobel Peace Prize (1986); returned to Australia (1986); founded Green Labor political faction within the Australian Labor Party (1988); ran (unsuccessfully) for Parliament (1990); published* If You Love This Planet *(1992); published autobiography* A Desperate Passion *(1996).*

In 1938, the world was reluctantly heading towards World War II. Germany and Japan were building up their military forces while other nations watched uneasily. Nuclear fission, a process wherein an atom's nucleus is broken into pieces, releasing huge amounts of energy, had just been discovered, and the first atomic bomb was only seven years away. That same year, Helen Caldicott, who would become the brightest star in the anti-nuclear movement, was born in Melbourne, the capital of Victoria, Australia.

Christened Helen Mary Broinowski, she was the eldest child of Philip, the manager of a paint factory, and **Mary Broinowski**, an interior designer. They were intelligent parents and encouraged their first born—a younger brother Richard and sister Susan would soon follow—to become aware of world affairs. Where her father was loving, Caldicott's mother Mary, described by Caldicott as "intuitive and politically astute" and a voracious reader, was emotionally distant. At 18 months, Helen was left in the care of a stranger for two weeks. In her autobiography, *A Desperate Passion,* she claims this left her with an inordinate fear of abandonment that has remained throughout her life.

Soon after Helen's first birthday, in August 1939, Australia went to war, allied with Great Britain against Nazi Germany. For the next six years, her childhood was affected by wartime life, with clothing, gas and food rationing. When the atomic bomb was dropped on Hiroshima in 1945, a siren sounded in her primary school, and the teacher asked, "What's that?" Caldicott was the only child in the class who knew. "The war's ended," she replied. Caldicott was savvy enough to know the bomb would end the war but had no concept of what a bomb was—yet.

As a young child, Caldicott did not fit in at school and was often teased. "I was different," she recalled. "I don't know why. I just was. I've always been creative, and believed I could do whatever I wanted to do." She was going to be a doctor, because that way she could "help people more." She read widely. As a teenager, she read Australian author Nevil Shute's novel *On the Beach,* about the devastation after a nuclear war, and was shocked into activism for life. After that, she read everything she could about nuclear weapons, appalled that scientists made them in the first place. In the 1950s, when nuclear weapons testing was just beginning, most people were unaware that fallout from these tests (the radioactive dust that falls after an explosion) could cause cancer and genetic damage.

In 1954, the Broinowski family moved to Adelaide, the capital of South Australia. Two years later, Caldicott entered the University of Adelaide Medical School, where she learned more about the effects of radiation, especially on babies and children who are much more susceptible than adults. Horrified, she tried to raise concern among her fellow medical students, "but the guys would just look up from their poker games . . . so I shut up." In 1961, she graduated with a Bachelor of Medicine and Bachelor of Surgery, second in her class that final year. She married Bill Caldicott, also a doctor (radiology), in December 1962, and over the next several years as she worked as a general practitioner in Adelaide, the couple had three children: Phillip (born 1964), Penny (born 1965), and William (born 1967).

Between 1966 and 1969, the family lived in America, where she had a fellowship at Harvard Medical School in Boston. They returned to Adelaide in 1970, just after Caldicott's mother died, which was a terrible shock. Six months after she began working at the renal unit in Queen Elizabeth Hospital, Caldicott accidentally pricked her finger on a contaminated syringe needle and contracted serum hepatitis, which infects the liver. She was so ill that she nearly died. "Like many people who have faced death, you feel you've been saved for something," she said upon recovery. "Life becomes a gift. There had to be a reason why you didn't die then." After working in general practice for a few more years, Caldicott returned to medical school to study pediatrics. As an intern at the Queen Elizabeth Hospital, she set up a clinic for sufferers of cystic fibrosis and became a specialist in treating this hereditary, and often fatal, childhood disease.

She also became politically active. "Somehow I felt wary of adults—that they weren't making the world safe. Then one day I thought: 'My God, I'm an adult. I'm part of this.' That's when I began to realise that one person could make a difference." Her intense commitment to the world's survival, strengthened by her love for her children and young patients, was influenced by Bertrand Russell (1872–1970), British philosopher, mathematician, social critic, and writer. Russell's ban-the-bomb movement had given rise to the International Atmospheric Test Ban Treaty in 1962.

In 1971, Caldicott learned that the French had been doing atmospheric nuclear tests in the South Pacific, over their island colony of Mururoa, for the last five years, in direct contravention of this treaty. Incensed, especially since she fully realized that the dangerous fallout was upwind of Australia, she wrote a letter about the medical effects of radioactive drinking water to the Adelaide newspaper, *The Advertiser*. In doing so, she became the unofficial medical spokeswoman on radioactivity and was interviewed on television each time the French detonated a bomb.

In 1972, Caldicott received a leaked confidential report from a sympathizer in the state government of South Australia, which showed that the drinking water in that state *did* have a high level of radiation. She revealed these findings to the public and continued to speak out and gain support. Once they knew the facts, hundreds of thousands of Australians were outraged and demanded the French stop testing. Spontaneous and widespread boycotting of French products resulted; postal workers even refused to deliver mail from France.

With the support of Dr. Jim Cairns of the Australian Labor Party (ALP), the non-conservative party led at that time by Gough Whitlam, Caldicott headed a delegation to Paris in 1972. Their efforts were ultimately successful. The recently elected ALP, which had strong anti-nuclear policies, listened to the Australian public and, along with the New Zealand government, took France before the International Court of Justice in 1973. The court's ruling was ambigu-

ous and did not force an end to the testing, but France decided to conduct its future nuclear tests underground.

Two years later, huge uranium deposits were discovered in Australia. Uranium is bombarded with neutrons to produce plutonium—a deadly radioactive element named after Pluto, the Roman god of the dead—and is used as a reactor fuel and in nuclear weapons. As Caldicott pointed out repeatedly, there is no safe level of plutonium for the living—even one atom can cause cancer. Many people in the Australian government wanted to extract this mineral for sale to other countries. Caldicott did not agree.

> *When I was 15, I read Nevil Shute's On the Beach and that was it. I immediately began to question what humans were doing to their world, and I've never stopped.*
>
> —Helen Caldicott

In Australia, trade unions—comprised of workers in each trade, such as mining—wield considerable political power. Trade-union leaders represent their workers throughout the country, striving to ensure reasonable pay and working conditions for their members. To keep uranium in the ground, Helen Caldicott needed the mining, as well as other trade-union support, because the government and media were ignoring her. Each trade union laconically agreed to let her talk to their membership, predicting her failure. With every session, "I would convince them in ten minutes," said Caldicott. "I just talked about the effect [of uranium] on their testicles and what radiation does to the genes and sperm, and I'd talk about nuclear war and what it means to their children." The Australian Council of Trade Unions passed a resolution banning the mining, transportation, and sale of uranium, which lasted from 1975 to 1982.

The Caldicott family moved to the United States in 1975, returned to Adelaide briefly the following year, and then went back to Boston in 1977, where Caldicott was a fellow in cystic fibrosis and an associate in medicine at the Children's Hospital Medical Center and an instructor in pediatrics at the Harvard Medical School. Bill was also working at Harvard as a pediatric radiologist. Caldicott was getting more deeply involved in her anti-nuclear campaigning in her less-than-free time, which kept her away from her young family, causing conflict at home. "I tried to make sure they had a future. It's sad, and yet it's more important to do this for them now than make sure they cleaned their teeth." Bill carried much of the child-rearing load during these years. In 1976, Caldicott had offered to stop because, she said, the family was feeling "a bit rejected," but in the end they urged her to continue. As the anti-nuclear movement became "all-embracing," Caldicott felt guilty when she "refused invitations to speak."

During these years in America, she published her first book, *Nuclear Madness: What You Can Do,* in 1978. In it, she describes in laymen's terms the medical consequences of nuclear war. She also revived the dormant group Physicians for Social Responsibility (PSR) and totally energized the organization. This Boston-based group works to publicize the medical consequences of nuclear war. A PSR ad in the *New England Journal of Medicine,* in March 1979, happened to coincide with the Three Mile Island incident in Pennsylvania, where the nuclear reactor core suffered a partial meltdown, releasing radioactive material, and forcing the evacuation of thousands of residents. More than 500 doctors signed up, and thereafter membership increased steadily. Caldicott was the national president of PSR until 1983, when she would resign over differences in approach. She remained opposed to nuclear power as well as weapons, while she felt that PSR had become too conservative, focusing only on arms-control rather than being totally anti-nuclear. In the late 1980s, the group numbered around 30,000 and won the Nobel Peace Prize in 1985, as part of the umbrella organization International Physicians for the Prevention of Nuclear War.

During the 1980s, Caldicott also lead U.S. medical delegations to Russia to discuss nuclear issues with high-ranking officials and helped start British, German, and Swedish medical campaigns, as well as organizations for women to fight nuclear threats. In 1980, she had founded Women's Action for Nuclear Disarmament (WAND), an influential Washington-based lobby group. She is convinced that women can have, and need to have, more political power and effect for the world to be saved.

That same year, Caldicott resigned from her medical career, so that she could work on the anti-nuclear campaign full-time, and in 1984 her husband Bill also resigned to help in the cause—difficult decisions for both of them. The year 1980 also saw a change in Caldicott's spirituality. Raised as an agnostic, she was for many years an atheist but became a non-sectarian believer in God as the life force of the Universe. "Now I believe God is life," she wrote, "the DNA mole-

cule, reality. Prayer gives me strength. I know I'm on the side of truth, that I'm doing the right thing, and that inspires me."

The 1982 National Film Board of Canada's short documentary, *If You Love This Planet,* features an attractive, elegantly dressed woman, with auburn hair and intense pale-blue eyes, delivering one of her typically shocking, scientifically precise, medically accurate and emotional speeches about *exactly* what happens when a nuclear bomb lands on *your* city. Helen Caldicott at her best. (Caldicott was thinking of naming her 1996 autobiography, "If You Wear Pearls, You Can Say Anything," she told Hubert Herring of *The New York Times.* "If you look attractive, people consider you trustworthy, and they tend to believe your logic, however radical.") The documentary was classified as "foreign propaganda" by the American Justice Department, which inadvertently helped publicize the film, and it won an Oscar for best short-subject documentary in 1982.

That same year, following a lecture, Caldicott met Ronald Reagan's daughter, **Patti Davis.** An impressed Davis felt that Caldicott would be able to influence her father and arranged an unprecedented one-hour private meeting with the president to discuss nuclear issues. It was "the most shocking experience of my life," she said in her 1984 book, *Missile Envy,* "You expect the President to be intelligent and well-informed. I found the opposite." Caldicott would later call him a "nice old guy," but "everything he said to me was inaccurate."

In the 1984 election, she campaigned full-time for Walter Mondale, but Reagan was reelected. By 1986, Caldicott was exhausted mentally and physically. Dubbed Henny Penny, a Cold War Zelig, and a dupe for communists, she faced constant opposition and criticism in America and wanted to go home to Australia. She announced her resignation from her anti-nuclear campaigning. Wrote **Janine Perrett** in *The Australian:*

> There is no doubt that the demise of the "stirrer" who has been called everything from the mother of the anti-nuclear movement to a modern day Joan of Arc is not universally hailed as a tragedy. Along with the plaudits have been bitter criticism that her left-wing anti-nuclear policies are out of step with today's conservative mood.

Even so, her break from dismal and emotional public lectures came just before Chernobyl, the kind of nuclear disaster she had feared and predicted for years. Caldicott became quite discouraged. She felt that all the marches, meetings, lectures, and papers had little impact. She was ignored by Reagan and believed that if Chernobyl had happened in America, affecting thousands of Americans rather than Russians, it would have changed government policy in ways that she could not. "I suddenly realised that I was sort of arrogant to think I could save the world. I know I can't do it with my own intellect and ego." The Caldicotts moved back to Australia the same year, settling in Bermagui, a small town on the south coast of New South Wales (NSW). This was also the year Caldicott was nominated for the Nobel Peace Prize.

Back home, Caldicott spent time swimming, cooking, and reading (she was particularly interested in Gandhi). She occasionally gave a public lecture but was glad to be away from the depressing subject and constant nightmares—for a time. By 1988, she was back, talking with the Australian union movement about uranium mining once again. Around this time, she also "came to a sudden realisation," reported Wayne Crawford in *The Mercury*, "that while she was campaigning energetically to stop the world blowing itself up in an Armageddon-type holocaust, the earth was quietly disintegrating beneath her feet." She became a fervent conservationist and put all her skills as a speaker and campaigner into this new mission.

In 1988, her husband Bill left her unexpectedly. As traumatic as it was, the experience strengthened her. That same year, she founded the Green Labor Party, which developed strong conservationist policies, such as advocating the close-down of American bases in Australia, no port visits by nuclear ships, no uranium mining or wood chipping, environmental clean-ups, and limiting family size to one child per couple.

Caldicott had been a long-term and steadfast member of the Australian Labor Party and was chosen as the Green Labor candidate in the 1990 federal (national) election for the seat of North Sydney. In a drastic change, however, she resigned from the ALP, claiming that the NSW head office was trying to sabotage her campaign. She then moved to Byron Bay, on the coast in northern NSW, and campaigned as an Independent candidate for that seat. She lost in a close-run election.

In 1992, she brought out her next book, *If You Love This Planet,* and continued to develop her environmentally and spiritually peaceful lifestyle. A year later, she moved to Leongatha, Victoria, to join the "All One Voice" community, a non-religious group that is concerned about the state of the earth and employs bartering, permaculture, wind and solar power, and runs classes for children and adults. She bought and renovated the Koonwarra Store, where the community runs a shop and cafe, using organic produce. She also bought a home in East Hampton, Long Island, New York, and soon learned that there were three nuclear reactors 15 miles away across Long Island Sound, at the Millstone power plant in Connecticut.

The second edition of *Nuclear Madness,* including sections about Chernobyl and post-Cold War issues, was brought out in 1994, her autobiography in 1996. "I used to feel I had to save the world by myself," she wrote. "Now I see I am part of the whole. I keep myself clear, not angry but pretty clear. I feel so good now."

SOURCES:

Arnold, J., and D. Morris, eds. *Monash Biographical Dictionary of Twentieth Century Australia.* Port Melbourne: Reed Reference Publishing, 1994.

Atkinson, Alan. "For the Love of Peace—and Family," in *The Advertiser.* Adelaide, April 28, 1983, p. 2.

Baker, Candida. "The Candidates with Causes," in *The Age.* Melbourne, March 30, 1990, p. 13.

Buchanan, Rachel. "The Greening of Helen Caldicott," in *The Age.* Melbourne, July 30, 1993, p. 16.

Caldicott, Helen. *Nuclear Madness—What You Can Do!* Queensland: Jacaranda Press, 1978.

Contemporary Australians, 1995–96. Port Melbourne: Reed Reference Australia, 1995, pp. 66–67.

Crawford, Wayne. "A mission to save the Earth," in *The Mercury.* Hobart, February 15, 1989, pp. 15–17.

Dalley, Helen. "A Triumph in America for an Australian Anti-nuclear Crusader," in *The Australian Women's Weekly.* August 4, 1982, pp. 29–37.

Day, Samuel H., Jr. "Eclipse of the Peace Movement," in *The Progressive.* September 1996.

Game, Peter. "The Doctor's Fall-out with Reagan," in *The Herald.* Melbourne, March 6, 1986, p. 6.

Herring, Hubert B. "Dr. Helen Caldicott: The Whole Planet is Her Patient" (for The New York Times News Service), in *The* [New London] *Day,* November 11, 1996.

"I Never Thought Bill Would Leave Me," in *ITA.* December 1989, pp. 28–31.

Molony, John. *The Penguin Bicentennial History of Australia.* South Yarra, Australia: Viking Penguin, 1987.

Moritz, Charles, ed. *Current Biography Yearbook 1983.* NY: H.W. Wilson, 1984, pp. 41–45.

Perrett, Janine. "Helen Caldicott Tired of Fighting a Lone War," in *The Australian.* Canberra, May 27, 1986, p. 14.

Smith, Jillian. "A Voice Heard all over the World," in *The Advertiser.* Adelaide, May 6, 1989, p. 12.

Stocker, Carol. "The Fallout from Caldicott's Passion," in the *Boston Globe.* December 2, 1996.

Tarrant, Deborah. "Caldicott: the Power of Nuclear Anger," in *The Australian.* Canberra, May 2, 1984, p. 8.

Uglow, Jennifer, ed. *The Macmillan Dictionary of Women's Biography,* 2nd ed. London: Macmillan, 1989.

Whittaker, Mark, and Phil Teese. "Read Me My Rights, Says Peace Practitioner," in *The Australian*. Canberra, March 26, 1990, p. 3.

SUGGESTED READING:

Caldicott, Helen. *Missile Envy*. NY: Bantam Books, 1984.

————. *If You Love This Planet*. NY: W.W. Norton, 1992.

————, ed. *Nuclear Madness*. Rev. NY: W.W. Norton, 1994.

————. *A Desperate Passion* (autobiography). NY: W.W. Norton, 1996.

Shute, Nevil. *On the Beach*. Melbourne and London: Heinemann, 1957.

RELATED MEDIA:

If You Love This Planet (26 min.), produced by National Film Board of Canada, 1982 (Academy Award for Best Documentary short).

Eight Minutes to Midnight (60 mins.), documentary portrait of Caldicott produced by Physicians for Social Responsibility, 1981 (Academy Award nomination for Best Documentary).

Denise Sutherland, freelance writer, Canberra, Australia

Caldwell, Anne (1876–1936)

American lyricist. Name variations: Anne O'Dea. Born Anne Marsh Caldwell in Boston, Massachusetts, in 1876; died on October 22, 1936; educated in New Bedford and Fairhaven; married James O'Dea.

In an age when many creative occupations were closed to women in American musical theater, a number of women lyricists made contributions to the field that would prove of historical importance. Anne Caldwell was among this group, which also included *Rida Johnson Young and *Dorothy Donnelly, and she was a prolific Broadway lyricist from 1912. Her collaborations with Jerome Kern totaled eight musicals for which Caldwell wrote lyrics and often the librettos. Caldwell also provided lyrics for one of Kern's collaborations with Otto Harbach, *Criss Cross*, starring Fred Stone. Thomas Hischak lauded this musical farce for its "delightfully silly" songs, including "In Araby with You," "You Will, Won't You?" and "I Love My Little Susie," the latter of which was sung by Fred Stone to a camel. She also collaborated on songs for the films *Babes in Toyland* and *Flying Down to Rio*. Caldwell retired in 1928.

Caldwell, Mary Gwendolin

(1863–1909)

American philanthropist. Name variations: Mamie; Marquise des Monstiers-Mérinville. Born Mary Gwendolin Caldwell in Louisville, Kentucky, in 1863; died on October 5, 1909, aboard the German liner Kronprinzessin Cecile outside New York; elder of two daughters of William Shakespeare Caldwell (a constructor and operator of gas plants in the Midwest) and Mary Eliza (Breckinridge) Caldwell; attended Academy of the Sacred Heart, New York; married François Jean Louis, Marquis des Monstiers-Mérinville, on October 19, 1896 (separated 1905).

Born in Louisville, Kentucky, Mary Caldwell and her younger sister grew up in New York City, where their wealthy father took them to live after the death of their mother, and where he converted to Roman Catholicism. Upon his death in 1874, she and her sister became wards of Roman Catholic friends and also inherited several million dollars. While attending the Academy of the Sacred Heart in New York, Caldwell became acquainted with the Rev. John Lancaster Spalding, who later became the first bishop of Peoria, Illinois. Whether through her relationship with Spalding, or according the dictates of her father's will—it is not certain which—Caldwell made an offer in 1884 to donate $300,000 for the founding of a national Catholic school of philosophy and theology. The offer was accepted, with the stipulation that Caldwell be considered the founder of what became the Catholic University of America, incorporated in the District of Columbia in April 1887. Caldwell later made two smaller endowment gifts that were lost in the failure of a brokerage firm.

Mary Caldwell traveled extensively and became part of the international set. In 1889, she became engaged to Prince Joachim Joseph Napoleon Murat, the invalid grandson of the king of Naples, but marriage plans were terminated when the prince insisted on a settlement of half her fortune. She later married François Jean Louis, Marquis des Monstiers-Mérinville, a French noble, 30 years her senior. The marriage floundered, along with Caldwell's faith in the Catholic Church. By 1899, when she received the Laetare Medal from Notre Dame University, her attachment to Catholicism was considerably weakened, and in 1904 she stunned the church by renouncing her faith. Those close to her, however, were less surprised, citing an impulsive nature and poor health. (In 1902, she had suffered a stroke that left her paralyzed and impaired her speech.)

Caldwell separated from her husband in 1905, though she paid him $8,000 a year to refrain from filing for divorce in an effort to keep her title. Four years later, the 46-year-old Caldwell died of Bright's disease in her stateroom aboard the German liner *Kronprinzessin Cecile*.

Barbara Morgan, Melrose, Massachusetts

Caldwell, Sarah (1924—)

American operatic conductor and impresario, a leading figure on the Boston music scene and the first woman to conduct the orchestra of Metropolitan Opera, known for her innovative but never outlandish interpretations of operatic works. Born Sarah Caldwell in Maryville, Missouri, on March 6, 1924; daughter of parents who divorced when she was aged two (Caldwell avoids listing their names in biographical directories); stepdaughter of Henry Alexander; graduated from high school at age 14; attended the University of Arkansas, and the New England Conservatory of Music; never married; no children.

Entered the New England Conservatory of Music to continue violin studies (1942); won a scholarship as a violinist at the Berkshire Music Center at Tanglewood (1946); staged Vaughan Williams' Riders to the Sea *at Berkshire (1947); engaged as assistant to Boris Goldovsky, founder of the New England Opera Company (1947); headed Boston University's opera workshop (1952–60); founded the Opera Company of Boston (1958); organized a concert of music by women conductors (1976); became the first woman to conduct the orchestra of Metropolitan Opera in New York (1976); organized cultural exchanges involving several hundred Soviet and American musicians (1988 and 1991).*

For her new production of the *Barber of Seville*, Sarah Caldwell had engaged the soprano *Beverly Sills to sing the role of the beautiful Rosina. In the story, Rosina is kept a virtual prisoner by her guardian Dr. Bartolo, and Caldwell wanted to use some form of caged bird in the production to visually express Rosina's confinement. Her first thought was to make Rosina's entire room a bird cage complete with swing, but then she conceived the idea of having a bird in a gilded cage carried by Rosina. Caldwell then asked Sills to find a bird, a task a director would not ordinarily expect a prima donna to undertake. But in New York City, Sills found a rare music box in the shape of a bird and called Caldwell from the Madison Avenue shop to ask if the price of $185 was acceptable. Caldwell asked Sills, "Could you bring it close to the telephone?" So Sills wound up the bird and placed it next to the receiver. Then Caldwell directed the soprano, "Now sing." Sills replied, "Are you some kind of lunatic? I'm in a store full of people on Madison Avenue!" Nevertheless, she began to chirp into the telephone along with the mechanical bird, confirming for Caldwell that she could imitate the cadenza the bird was trilling. The purchase was quickly okayed, and when Sills appeared onstage as Rosina carrying the miniature cage, the charm of Caldwell's innovative scene almost brought the house down.

Sarah Caldwell was born in Maryville, Missouri, on March 6, 1924, a precocious child with theatrical instincts. Her mathematical and musi-

Sarah Caldwell

cal abilities were evident by age four. After the divorce of her parents when she was two years old, the early years of her childhood were somewhat unstable. Her mother moved to New York to complete her graduate degree in music at Columbia University, leaving Sarah to be raised by an assortment of relatives, involving moves to various places, including Kansas City. Sarah was not unhappy in this extended family, where her creativity appears to have been appreciated. Her favorite holiday was the Fourth of July, for which she loved to stage elaborate backyard fireworks displays. Not allowed to buy the fireworks until July 3, Sarah made the rounds of stores in Maryville in advance, setting aside her purchases. When she brought them home, "I would set them all out on the table and look them over: sparklers, snakes, cherry bombs, Roman candles, firecrackers. Then I'd make my plans." These displays became the first expression of Caldwell's innate theatrical talent.

When Sarah was 12, her mother married Henry Alexander, a professor of political science at the University of Arkansas, and the family moved to Fayetteville. As the young girl's love of music grew increasingly apparent, she was encouraged by her mother and began taking violin lessons. Caldwell graduated from high school at age 14 and entered the University of Arkansas; she also studied at Hendrix College. Urged by her stepfather initially to study psychology, she soon allowed her love of music to direct her academic course. In 1942, at age 18, she entered the prestigious New England Conservatory of Music, bolstered by a fistful of scholarships. She studied violin with Richard Burgin, concertmaster of the Boston Symphony Orchestra, and later with George Flourel, whom she found more congenial. In 1946, Caldwell won a scholarship to play in the student orchestra at Tanglewood, the world renowned music center in the Berkshires and summer home of the Boston Symphony.

After graduation from the New England Conservatory, Caldwell was offered positions in the string sections of the Minneapolis and Indianapolis orchestras, but she chose to stay in Boston. She became assistant to Boris Goldovsky, the Russian-born founder of the New England Opera Company, where she spent 11 seasons as a props manager, stage director, translator, chorus conductor, and conductor, learning the nuts and bolts of operatic production from Goldovsky and conducting her first opera there, Mozart's *La Finta Giardiniera*.

Of all the forms of dramatic presentation, opera is the most difficult, because it involves staging, singing, dancing, acting, orchestral playing, and costumes and sets. Caldwell and Goldovsky were very close, but a rift eventually developed between them. According to Caldwell:

> Whatever versatility is attributed to me stems directly from Boris. He trained me. But we developed differently. Coming from Philadelphia, where he had witnessed the painful birth and quick death of too many opera adventures, he was reluctant to rock the boat, to press trustees beyond a certain point. And he enjoyed traveling through the whole United States. As for me, I was fascinated with the idea of building a professional opera company at home.

The time came when Caldwell had grown beyond what her mentor could teach. In 1952, she was appointed director of Boston University's opera workshop, and, during her eight years of tenure there, she created the university's department of music and theater, while gradually becoming obsessed with the notion of founding an opera company.

Her timing, unfortunately, could not have been worse. In 1958, the magnificent Boston Opera House, built in 1909, with a spacious stage and the most advanced stage machinery available at the time, was demolished by the city of Boston to make room for a parking lot. During her entire career, Caldwell would never have the opportunity to mount a production in a facility that came close to the structure that was destroyed. Nevertheless, in the previous year, 1957, she had gathered together a group of supporters to found the Boston Opera Group, with a modest nest egg of $5,000.

Over the next few years, Caldwell produced opera anyplace she could—be it a gymnasium, hockey rink, old movie house, indoor track, or converted flower stall. More significantly, with her very limited funds, she was giving ingenious productions of operas no one else would touch. Acting as conductor, administrator, stage director, talent scout, principal researcher, and fund raiser, she drew increasing attention and often rave reviews. Among her particularly memorable productions were Verdi's *La Traviata* and *Falstaff*, Berlioz' *Benvenuto Cellini*, Massenet's *Don Quichotte*, Bellini's *I Capuletti ed i Montecchi*, as well as lesser known modern works such as Prokofiev's *War and Peace*, Schoenberg's *Moses and Aron*, Alban Berg's *Lulu* and Roger Sessions' *Montezuma*. Her shoestring productions were in and out of crises. Once, when trucks rolled up from St. Louis with the stage sets for *La Traviata*, the C.O.D. charge was $9,600, and the driver would not take a check. Caldwell phoned a supporter, the owner of a chain of local Stop & Shop stores, who had a store manager make the rounds of his stores to collect enough money to cash a check of that size. A few hours later, Caldwell was able to hand the driver $9,600 in bills stuffed in brown paper bags.

Like many people of genius, Caldwell had her eccentricities. She was a large woman, weighing almost 300 pounds, and some of her colleagues considered her commanding bulk to be an asset. Meeting Sarah Caldwell, one recognized her immediately as an unmovable force. Clothing meant nothing to her; as she said, "I'm afraid I do not relate well to possessions." To conduct rehearsals, she generally wore a flowered tent dress covered by a rain coat and houseshoes. For performances, she put on a black tent dress and kept on the houseshoes, stepping into street shoes only when she knew her feet could be seen by the audience. She frequently lost things, from purses to cars, and gave up driving because she could never remember where she had parked.

Although she worked hard to raise money, Caldwell did not always keep strict account of funds. A friend remembered getting into her car, and when they drove off with the windows down, $5 and $10 bills billowed up, "floating all over the car and out the window." Often working nonstop, she would catnap where she could and was once found sleeping on a pile of theater curtains in the aisle. With no home theater for the Boston Opera Company, she virtually moved into whatever facility it was using, in order to get the production up and going in the 10 to 12 days allotted her.

In a profession known for its excesses of temperament, Caldwell was beloved by all who worked with her, musicians and stagehands alike. A whirlwind of activity, she asked for the opinions and took the suggestions of everyone and almost never lost her temper. Her good relationships with cast and crew were a primary reason she could mount such fine productions with so little backing, and she was greatly respected for the infinite pains she took. When she decided to mount *Louise* by the French composer Gustave Charpentier, she wanted to use a sunrise over Montmartre as one of her settings, so she went with her assistants to Paris, where they rose early in the morning to watch the sun climb over the marketplace near the top of Montmartre; she worked extensively from Charpentier's original production notes.

Caldwell's productions were both daring and fun. In a scene that called for a Trojan horse, she was not satisfied that the one constructed looked large enough, so she hired dwarfs for the roles of the soldiers hidden inside, making it appear larger when they crawled out. Caldwell also liked children and enjoyed using them onstage. During rehearsals, there were often children in the theater, some belonging to members of the cast, others coming in off the street, whom she called her "knothole gang." She felt that animals could add flavor to a scene, and ponies, dogs, cats, bears, horses, monkeys, and llamas were only some of the creatures that turned up on her stage. For the orgy scene in *Moses and Aron,* she thought animals would add a pagan flavor. As she related:

> I had engaged some sheep and goats and a calf from a theatrical-animal supply house, but I hadn't thought about where they were to be kept. The only possible place was under a ramp in front of the stage. But during the final rehearsals the animals bleated and bawled to such an extent that the music could hardly be heard.

After the guest conductor told Caldwell, "It's either me or the animals," the creatures were sent back.

My passion in life is opera. I remember being told when I was quite young that the real trick of living was to find something you like to do best in all the world and find someone else to pay you to do it. And I love what I am doing.

—**Sarah Caldwell**

In 1958, Rudolf Bing, the renowned director of the Metropolitan Opera, became infamous for claiming, "There is no opera in America worth speaking of outside New York City." Bing had not reckoned, however, with the reputation Sarah Caldwell was in the process of building, which eventually attracted some of the greatest operatic voices to perform under her directions, including *Joan Sutherland, *Marilyn Horne, *Renata Tebaldi, Placido Domingo, Nicolai Gedda, and *Tatiana Troyanos to name only a few. With the musical instincts of a Mozart and the theatrical techniques of a P.T. Barnum, she attracted and widened an opera-going public of educated middle-class professionals, intellectuals, artists, and journalists eager to witness what she would do next. Lively as they were, her productions refrained from being bizarre nor outlandish. According to the critic Winthrop Sargent, her productions represented "nothing in the way of eccentricity and everything in the way of bringing to light all the musical and dramatic subtleties that a score contains." Breathing new life into an art form enjoyed for hundreds of years, she also became one of America's finest conductors.

The mid-1970s to the 1980s were a good time for Caldwell, even without the opera house she so desired. Since the late 1950s, it had been her dream for the city of Boston to construct a $10 million opera house, with three theaters. Without anything approaching such a space, gathering funds from wherever she could, she nevertheless produced wonderful opera for two decades. In 1976, she became the first woman conductor to lead the Metropolitan Opera orchestra, and that same year she played a pivotal role in organizing a series of concerts featuring the music of female composers, including *Thea Musgrave, *Pozzi Escot, and *Vivian Fine. In the late 1980s, Caldwell was active in an exchange involving several hundred Soviet and American musicians.

With her style of operating, however, and a consistent lack of adequate support, production deficits were inevitable. When recession hit New England, bills mounted until her company was $5 million in debt. While some blamed Caldwell's eccentricity and poor administrative capacities, others felt she simply had bad luck. Caldwell felt the problem was due to constant scrimping and saving. Attempting to save money, she locked herself into a downward spiral. Financial crisis led to artistic compromise that led to disappointing performances and a poor box office. Years of postponements, cancellations, replacements, and undependable announcements no doubt contributed to her problems, and administration was never Caldwell's forte. Also, her personal rise to fame took her out of Boston on guest appearances, and productions suffered from her lack of attention. Ultimately, Caldwell discovered what many of her musical predecessors knew—Bostonians loved opera, they just weren't willing to foot the bill for it.

In the early 1990s, with invitations from all over the world to appear as guest conductor, Caldwell took a sabbatical from opera. Then in her late 60s, she was personally more financially secure than she had ever been, but in her enforced semi-retirement, she went into a temporary depression. In a relatively short time, however, she signed with a new agent and began booking guest appearances, as well as working on a book. There were also a myriad of operas she still wanted to stage, including an "ecological" Ring cycle, a revival of her Turandot, and Robert Schumann's Genoveva. And an opera house for Boston was a dream she still refused to give up.

In Western cultural tradition, music has rarely been an easy profession for women. Operatic singers became increasingly common after the 18th century, but it is only in the 20th century that women have been accepted into major symphony orchestras. Opportunities to hear their compositions played, to stage operas, or to conduct have remained rarer still. Armed with outstanding gifts and seizing the role of impresario, Sarah Caldwell challenged centuries of European musical tradition. While her resources remained slender and acknowledgment of her work was sometimes slow, the career that began with childhood fireworks is defined today less by individual eccentricities than by a body of work of musical and theatrical genius.

SOURCES:
Appleton, Jane Scovell. "Sarah Caldwell: The Flamboyant of the Opera," in *Ms.* Vol. 3, no. 11. May 1975, pp. 26, 28, 30–31.
Dizikes, John. *Opera in America. A Cultural History.* New Haven, CT: Yale University Press, 1993.
Dyer, Richard. "Opera's Missing First Lady," in *Boston Globe.* September 20, 1992, p. B25.
———. "Sarah Caldwell: Her Genius Is Her Gimmick," in *The New York Times Biographical Service.* January 1976, pp. 17–18.
Eaton, Quaintance. "Renaissance Woman," in *Opera News.* Vol. 28, no. 23. April 18, 1964, pp. 26–29.
Henahan, Donal. "Prodigious Sarah," in *The New York Times Biographical Service.* October 1975, pp. 1249–1253.
Jones, Robert. "Walking into the Fire," in *Opera News.* Vol. 40, no. 14. February 14, 1976, pp. 11–21.
Le Page, Jane Weiner. *Women Composers, Conductors, and Musicians of the Twentieth Century.* Vol. II. Metuchen, NJ: Scarecrow Press, 1983.
Moritz, Charles, ed. *Current Biography Yearbook 1973.* NY: H.W. Wilson. 1973.
"Music's Wonder Woman" [cover story], in *Time.* Vol. 106, no. 19. November 10, 1975, pp. 52–60.
Porter, Andrew. "Caldwell in Command," in *The New Yorker.* Vol. 50, no. 46. January 6, 1975, pp. 61–63.
Sargent, Winthrop. "Infinite Pains," in *The New Yorker.* December 24, 1973, pp. 43–49.
Warrack, John, and West, Ewan. *The Oxford Dictionary of Opera.* NY: Oxford University Press, 1992.

John Haag, Associate Professor, University of Georgia, Athens, Georgia

Caldwell, Taylor (1900–1985)

English-American fiction writer whose historical romances were bestsellers and often adapted as motion pictures. Name variations: (pseudonym) Max Reiner. Born Janet Miriam Taylor Caldwell on September 7, 1900, in Prestwich, Manchester, England; died of lung cancer on August 30, 1985, in Greenwich, Connecticut; daughter of Anna (Marks or Markham) Caldwell and Arthur Francis Caldwell (a commercial artist); attended University of Buffalo, BA, 1931; married

William Fairfax Coombes (sometimes spelled Combs), on May 27, 1919 (divorced 1931); married Marcus Reback (a linguist and advisor to Herbert Hoover), on May 12, 1931 (died 1970); married William E. Stancell, on June 17, 1972; married William Robert Prestie, in 1978; children: (first marriage) Mary Margaret Coombes Fried; (second marriage) Judith Ann Reback Goodman (d. 1979).

Selected works: Dynasty of Death *(1938);* The Eagles Gather *(1940);* The Earth Is the Lord's *(1941); (under pseudonym Max Reiner)* Time No Longer *(1941);* The Arm and the Darkness *(1943);* This Side of Innocence *(1946);* Let Love Come Last *(1949);* Balance Wheel *(1951);* The Devil's Advocate *(1952);* Never Victorious, Never Defeated *(1954);* Tender Victory *(1956);* The Sound of Thunder *(1957);* Dear and Glorious Physician *(1959);* A Prologue to Love *(1961);* The Late Clara Beame *(1963);* A Pillar of Iron *(1965);* Testimony of Two Men *(1968);* Captains and the Kings *(1973);* Glory and Lightening *(1974); (with Jess Stearn)* The Romance of Atlantis *(1975);* Ceremony of the Innocent *(1977); (with Stearn)* I, Judas *(1977);* Bright Flows the River *(1978);* Answer as a Man *(1981).*

Taylor Caldwell's Scottish father Arthur, a commercial artist, moved his family from Manchester, England, to Buffalo, New York, in 1907, hoping to escape the increasing ethnic and religious diversity in England. He had a "strange antipathy for almost everyone but Scotsmen, Presbyterians and Caldwells," reported *Current Biography* in 1940, "and because in England his profession was full of Germans he brought his family to America." On the crossing, Caldwell was snubbed by first-class children but forbidden to play with those of the third class; her "first lesson in undemocracy," she noted.

Janet Taylor Caldwell, called Taylor by her family, was nine when she began writing fiction. Preferring writing to playing with others, she also illustrated her own stories, which she made into books. After their completion, she set these aside; they were later incinerated by her father to clear the home of clutter.

Caldwell's father did not believe in higher education for women, and she quit school at age 15 to begin working. Trained as a stenographer, she married at 19 and enlisted in the Naval Reserve where she served as a "yeomanette" (1918–19). By 1923, she was enrolled at the University of Buffalo and worked her way through night classes as a court reporter for the State Department of Labor (1923–24), and as

secretary to a board of special inquiry of the U.S. Immigration and Naturalization Service (1924–31), both in Buffalo. Following her graduation in 1931, she married her second husband, linguist Marcus Reback. Caldwell, who had one daughter with her first husband, had a second with Reback.

Beginning with *Dynasty of Death* in 1938, Caldwell became a popular romance novelist. She was also a founding member of the New York State Conservative Party, and her stories often reflected her conservative views. She and Reback, who advanced to an advisory position with Herbert Hoover, collaborated frequently as writers. Caldwell was often praised for her storytelling but more often criticized for her lack of style and tendency to overwrite. Several of Caldwell's novels became popular movies. Reback died in 1970. Caldwell lived in their Greenwich, Connecticut, home until her death in 1985.

SOURCES:
Block, Maxine, ed. *Current Biography 1940.* NY: H.W. Wilson, 1940, pp. 137–138.

Taylor Caldwell

Buck, Claire, ed. *The Bloomsbury Guide to Women's Literature.* NY: Prentice Hall, 1992.

Contemporary Literary Criticism. Vol. 28. Detroit, MI: Gale Research, 1984.

The Oxford Companion to American Literature. 5th ed. Oxford University Press, 1983.

SUGGESTED READING:

Caldwell, Taylor. *On Growing Up Tough.* Devin-Adair, 1971.

Stearn, Jess. *Search for a Soul: Taylor Caldwell's Psychic Lives.* Doubleday, 1973.

———. *In Search of Taylor Caldwell.* NY: Stein and Day, 1981.

Crista Martin,
Boston, Massachusetts

Calisher, Hortense (1911—)

American fiction writer. Born Hortense Calisher on December 20, 1911, in New York, New York; daughter of Hedwig (Lichstern) Calisher and Joseph Henry Calisher (a manufacturer); Barnard College, B.A., 1932; married Heaton Bennet Heffelfinger, in 1935 (divorced 1958); married Curtis Harnack, in 1959; children: (first marriage) Bennet and Peter Heffelfinger.

Selected works: In the Absence of Angels *(1951);* False Entries *(1961);* The New Yorkers *(1969);* Queenie *(1971);* Herself *(1972);* The Collected Stories of Hortense Calisher *(1975);* On Keeping Women *(1977);* Mysteries of Motion *(1973);* Saratoga Hot *(1985);* In the Palace of the Movie King *(1993).*

Born in New York City to parents who were separated in age by 22 years, Hortense Calisher was raised in a household of dichotomies. Her mother, a German-Jewish émigré, fretted over the details of daily life, especially those concerning finances, while her father, a Jewish manufacturer from Virginia, was easygoing and affectionate. Hortense's grandmother lived with the family as well, adding to the age disparity in the household. "The combination was odd all around," Calisher noted, "volcanic to meditative to fruitfully dull, bound to produce someone interested in character, society and time." After attending Hunter College High School, Calisher enrolled at Barnard College in 1928. She worked her way through college as a waitress and earned an English degree by 1932.

After graduation, she served as a social worker for the Department of Public Welfare in New York City, distributing emergency relief for the poor. She married Heaton Heffelfinger, an engineer, in 1935. After several moves, they settled in the Manhattan suburb of Nyack, where for 13 years Calisher was a housewife. She had two children, a daughter Bennet and a son Peter. Writing was a secret hobby until publication of her story "The Ginger Box" in 1948. By 1951, she had produced enough stories for her first collection, *In the Absence of Angels.* Calisher earned Guggenheim Fellowships (1952 and 1955) and began to teach at colleges throughout the country. Divorced in 1958, the following year Calisher met Curtis Harnack, then executive director of Yaddo, while she was teaching at the Iowa Writer's Workshop. They married in 1959. Calisher has published more than 15 volumes of fiction.

SOURCES:

Hellerman, Jeffrey, and Richard Layman, eds. *Dictionary of Literary Biography.* Vol. 2. Detroit, MI: Gale Research, 1978.

Snodgrass, Kathleen. *The Fiction of Hortense Calisher.* Newark: University of Delaware Press, 1993.

Current Biography 1973. NY: H.W. Wilson, pp. 74–77.

Crista Martin,
Boston, Massachusetts

Calkins, Mary Whiton (1863–1930)

American psychologist and philosopher who was the first woman president of both the American Psychological Association and the American Philosophical Association. Born Mary Whiton Calkins in Hartford, Connecticut, on March 30, 1863; died in Newton, Massachusetts, on February 26, 1930; daughter of Wolcott (a Presbyterian minister) and Charlotte Grosvenor (Whiton) Calkins; graduated from Smith College, 1885; never married; no children.

Became tutor in Greek, Wellesley College (1887), instructor in Greek, (1889), and instructor in psychology (1891); established first psychology laboratory at

*ortense
alisher*

*Mary
Whiton
Calkins*

women's college (1891); appointed associate professor in psychology, Wellesley College (1894); pioneered technique of paired-associate learning (1894–95); appointed associate professor of psychology and philosophy, Wellesley College (1896); completed requirements for a Ph.D. in psychology at Harvard University (1896); promoted to full professor, Wellesley College (1898); published An Introduction to Psychology *(1901); elected first woman president of the American Psychological Association (1905); published* The Persistent Problem of Philosophy *(1907); published* A First Book in Psychology *(1909); published* The Good Man and The Good *(1918); elected first woman president of the American Philosophical Association (1918); retired from active teaching (1919).*

In a time when women began to enter higher education in the face of strong societal opposition, psychologist and philosopher Mary Whiton Calkins established herself as a pioneer: first as one of a handful of female graduate students at Harvard University, then as a professor at an all-women's college, and finally as the first woman president of both the American Psychological Association and the American Philosophical Association. Though repeatedly denied many of the professional rights and privileges extended to her male counterparts because of her gender, Calkins nonetheless rose to the top of her profession. One of the preeminent psychologists and philosophers of her time, she created the paired-associate technique of learning, founded one of the first psychological laboratories in the country, and developed a theory of "self psychology," which she detailed in books and numerous published articles.

The roots of Mary Whiton Calkins' success in adulthood can be traced back to the loving and unconventional family into which she was born, the eldest of five children (a sister and three brothers followed) on March 30, 1863. Though in mid-19th century America the education of women was widely regarded as both a waste of time and potentially dangerous, Mary's devoted father Wolcott Calkins, a Presbyterian minister, and her mother **Charlotte Whiton Calkins**, an informally trained musician, believed wholeheartedly in the education of women. The result was an extremely nurturing family environment in which Calkins and her siblings flourished.

Mary Calkins was born in Hartford, Connecticut, but the family moved to Buffalo, New York, in 1866 when she was three. She spent the next 14 years in Buffalo. Her father took so

keen an interest in the education of his children that he painstakingly outlined and supervised their studies. He particularly encouraged professional aspirations in his extraordinarily bright and naturally precocious eldest daughter. In addition to her father, Calkins developed an important relationship with **Sophie Jewitt**, who had moved in with the Calkins family following the death of her own parents. The young girls became intellectual companions and best friends who read their way through the Calkins family library. Later on, their relationship took on a professional aspect when both joined the staff of Wellesley College.

Mary Calkins' mother was devoted to her children and singlehandedly nursed them through a series of potentially life threatening childhood illnesses. The anxiety of caring for them took its toll, and Charlotte Calkins suffered a breakdown during Mary's adolescence. Mary Calkins took her role as a dutiful daughter seriously; she supervised her mother's care and would continue to live with her parents in the house her father built in Newton, Massachusetts, where the family had moved in 1880, throughout her adult life. The education she received from her father was so thorough and advanced that Mary Calkins entered Smith College (then only a decade old) in 1882 as a sophomore. It was during this first year at Smith that her sister Maud died from what was diagnosed as inflammatory rheumatism. It was a terrible blow to the Calkins family. Following this tragedy, Mary took a year off from Smith and stayed at home taking private lessons in Greek. She reentered Smith in 1884 with senior standing and was graduated in the spring of 1885 with a concentration in classics and philosophy.

The Calkins family toured Europe for a year in 1886, thus furnishing Mary with a splendid opportunity for educational advancement. While in Leipzig, she studied briefly at the university there and encountered an American instructor, **Abby Leach**, who invited her along on a trip to Italy and Greece to visit historical sites and continue her studies in modern Greek and the classics.

While still abroad, Wolcott Calkins contacted the president of Wellesley College, a women's liberal arts college located near the Calkins home, seeking a teaching post for his daughter. In 1887, one week after returning home from Europe, Mary Calkins accepted a position at Wellesley as a tutor in Greek. This would not be the only time her father would intervene on her behalf and influence her professional career.

Her natural intelligence and talent as a teacher did not go unnoticed. In 1889, she was promoted to the rank of instructor. But Calkins' intellectual interests were moving away from the classics towards more modern disciplines. She was increasingly drawn to the new study of psychology, which then constituted a subfield of philosophy, and was offered a position in the Department of Philosophy on the condition that she study psychology for a year.

To that end, she approached the Department of Philosophy at Harvard, which was headed by the brilliant William James. Harvard was also one of the few institutions in the United States that possessed a laboratory for experimental psychology. At that time, psychology was primarily a laboratory science directed at exploring and explaining the workings of the mind and behavior. Most pioneering university psychologists studied human and animal behavior, sensation and perception, and learning and cognition. Though William James and Josiah Royce, another noteworthy professor in Harvard's philosophy department, agreed to accept Calkins as a student, she met with resistance from Harvard University president Charles W. Eliot who, backed by the trustees, roundly opposed co-education. Her request to attend seminars was refused because of gender. Her father once again interceded on her behalf. With a letter of support from the president of Wellesley, he petitioned Harvard on the grounds that his daughter's "admission did not involve the question of co-education in general, and cannot be quoted as an embarrassing precedent. For we ask only post-graduate and professional instruction for one who is already a member of a college faculty." On October 1, 1890, Harvard agreed to admit Calkins but noted that "by accepting this privilege Miss Calkins does not become a student of the University entitled to registration."

Mary Calkins credited the year she spent at Harvard as the most stimulating and rewarding intellectual experience of her life. The seminar she attended with William James, together with his monumental *The Principles of Psychology*, profoundly influenced her thinking and the trajectory of her career. She later wrote that her seminar with James and "my absorbed study of those brilliant, erudite and provocative volumes was my introduction to psychology." It was also under James' intellectual guidance that Calkins wrote her first important paper on association, which was subsequently published in the July 1892 edition of the *Philosophical Review*.

In 1890, Calkins also began working in the psychology laboratory at Clark University under the supervision of Edmund Sanford, her second important teacher. Calkins credited Sanford with educating her in the "details of laboratory experiments." Together, they conducted an experiment on dreams. Their conclusions, that dreams reproduce "in general the persons, places and events of recent sense perception" and that the dream is rarely "associated with that which is of paramount significance in one's waking experience," would later run counter to Sigmund Freud's theories of dreams, which would eventually dominate psychological thought.

In the fall of 1891, Calkins returned to Wellesley as an instructor in psychology in the Department of Philosophy. That same year, she established at Wellesley one of the first laboratories for experimental psychology in the country and the first ever at a women's college. Most of her laboratory work during this time was devoted to color theory, animal consciousness, space consciousness, association, and emotion.

I am a personalistic, introspective psychologist because in introspection I find the self.
—Mary Whiton Calkins

In 1892, Calkins again petitioned to enter Harvard University, this time to study under the German psychologist Hugo Munsterberg who was then beginning a three-year appointment. With Munsterberg's letter of support, Harvard granted permission, and she began to study with him in his laboratory in 1893 while concurrently holding her teaching position at Wellesley. In 1894, Calkins was named associate professor in psychology but took a leave of absence from Wellesley for the 1894–95 academic year to work full time with Munsterberg.

It was during this year at Harvard that she embarked upon an original laboratory investigation into the factors influencing memory. Her experiment demonstrated the importance of associative learning. Her technique, which was later modified by other psychologists and became known as paired-associate learning, showed that when certain objects, such as numerals, repeatedly appeared in conjunction with other objects, such as specific colors, they were more likely to be remembered later. Experimental subjects therefore could more consistently recall a number when they associated it with a corresponding color than in situations when numbers appeared by themselves and paired-associated learning was lacking.

By 1896, Mary Whiton Calkins had published dozens of scholarly articles on a wide variety of topics, including association, dream research, the conception of the psychic element, the doctrine of relational elements of experience, and a series of papers on the paired-associate technique she had invented. That same year, she presented a thesis on "experimental research on the association of ideas" to the philosophy department at Harvard. Though she had completed all the requirements for a Ph.D. and was recommended wholeheartedly by the Harvard faculty, the university declined her degree application because of her gender. Later, when she was offered a Radcliffe degree instead, she turned it down on the grounds that she had not attended Radcliffe College.

In 1898, Mary Calkins was promoted to full professor at Wellesley College. Two years later, she published an important paper, "Psychology as a Science of Selves," which was her first attempt to provide a systematic analysis of her emerging theory of the conscious self as the central fact of psychology. This new theory of "self psychology" was to be her most important contribution to psychology and one to which she devoted the next ten years of her life.

In 1901, she published her first book, *An Introduction to Psychology,* which offered a more detailed treatment of experience from the perspective of "self psychology." The book argued against the prevailing behaviorist psychology, which denied the actual existence of a self and which held that consciousness consisted of bodily reactions. Not surprisingly, her book drew considerable professional criticism, attacking Calkins' concept of the self as unscientific and unverified. Despite the criticism, her emerging position in the field of psychology could not be denied. In a 1903 list of the 50 most prominent psychologists in America, Calkins ranked 12th, and in 1905 she was the first woman elected president of the American Psychological Association.

She modified and defended her theories of self psychology in papers published in 1907 and 1908 in the *Journal of Philosophy* and in her 1909 book *A First Book in Psychology,* which went through four revised editions. In it, she championed the analytical integrity of the self and argued for introspection or self examination as the starting point in psychology. She offered a definition of the self as "persistent, unique, complex" and that which experiences, and which drives or is driven. As she later explained in an essay in the book *A History of Psychology in Autobiography:*

Whenever I try to take the opposite point of view, when, in other words, I attempt the study of mental processes, experiences and the like, I invariably find not a mere process, an experience, but a mind in process, a someone who is experiencing.

The first half of Mary Calkins' professional career was preoccupied with the study of psychology; the last half was devoted to philosophy, especially metaphysics. Influenced by philosopher Josiah Royce's idealism, she created her own system of "personalistic absolutism," which had two main principles: the first, that "the universe is through and through mental in character, that all that is real is ultimately mental, and accordingly personal in nature," and the second, that "the universe literally is one all-including (and accordingly complete) self of which all the lesser selves are genuine and identical parts, or members." She had already produced one book in philosophy in 1907, *The Persistent Problem of Philosophy,* which was reprinted five times, and over the next 20 years she published numerous articles in philosophical journals. In 1918, she published a study in ethics, *The Good Man and The Good,* which aimed at the general reader as well as professionals. That same year, she received further professional recognition as the first female elected president of the American Philosophical Association.

Throughout her life, Mary Whiton Calkins sought to achieve a balance between professional and social responsibilities. She allied herself with the political left and became involved in pacifist and socialist movements as well as causes such as the Sacco and Vanzetti case. As a woman who had enjoyed enormous professional success despite routine and institutionalized sexism, she was also highly sensitive to the obstacles that confronted all women in the workplace. She was an active suffragist and an outspoken feminist who decried the belief that there existed inherent differences in mental abilities of men and women.

Mary Whiton Calkins retired from Wellesley after more than 40 years of teaching with the title of research professor. She died the following year on February 26, 1930, in Newton, Massachusetts.

SOURCES:

Brozek, Josef. *Explorations in the History of Psychology in the United States.* Lewisburg: Bucknell University Press, 1984.

Calkins, Mary Whiton. *An Introduction to Psychology.* NY: Macmillan, 1901.

———. *The Good Man and the Good: An Introduction to Ethics.* NY: Macmillan, 1918.

Furumoto, Laurel. "Mary Whiton Calkins (1863–1930)," in *Psychology of Women Quarterly*. Vol 5, no. 1. Fall 1980, pp. 55–68.

Hilgard, R. Ernest. *Psychology in America: A Historical Survey*. NY: Harcourt Brace Jovanovich, 1987.

James, Edward T., ed. *Notable American Women 1607–1950: A Biographical Dictionary*. Vol 1. Cambridge: Belknap Press of Harvard University Press, 1971.

Murchison, Carl, ed. *A History of Psychology in Autobiography*. Worcester, MA: Clark University Press, 1930.

Scarborough, Elizabeth, and Laurel Furumoto. *Untold Lives: The First Generation of American Women Psychologists*. NY: Columbia University Press, 1987.

Suzanne Smith, freelance writer,
Decatur, Georgia

Callander, Caroline Henrietta
(1779–1851).

See Norton, Caroline for sidebar on Caroline Henrietta Sheridan.

Callas, Maria (1923–1977)

American opera singer whose powers of vocal interpretation sparked a revival of classical coloratura roles and gave rise to unforgettable recordings considered among the most significant contributions to opera performance in the 20th century. Name variations: Mary, Marianna. Pronunciation: Callas rhymes with palace. Born Maria Cecilia Sophia Anna Kalogeropoulos on December 2, 1923 (according to her birth certificate), in New York; died in Paris, France, on September 16, 1977; daughter of Georges (a chemist) and Evangelia "Litza" (Dimitriadu) Kalogeropoulos (Kalogeropoulos became "Kalous" and eventually "Callas" according to spellings adopted by Georges in New York); traveled to Greece with her mother for voice lessons, first under Maria Trivella at the National Conservatory and then under Elvira de Hidalgo; married Giovanni Battista Meneghini, in 1949; no children.

Family moved from Greece to New York (1923); spent childhood in New York; started musical training (1930); departed for Greece with mother and sister (1937) and studied under Trivella and de Hidalgo; made operatic debut during German occupation of Greece and sang at La Scala, Milan (1951); met Giovanni Battista Meneghini (1947); sang Norma for her American debut with the Chicago Lyric Opera (1954); made debut at the Metropolitan Opera (1956); with voice problems plaguing her performances, reduced number of engagements (late 1950s); quit opera altogether (1965) and collaborated, unsuccessfully, with Pier Paolo Pasolini, in Medea; taught master classes at the Juilliard school (1971–72); sang in public for the last time (1973) with Giuseppe di Stefano.

Selected discography (most performances were reissued by the EMI label): Bellini, Norma (1955), La Sonnambula (1957); Donizetti, Lucia di Lammermoor (1953, 1955); Cherubini, Medea (1957); Mascagni, Cavalleria Rusticana (1953); Ponchielli, La Gioconda; Puccini, Tosca (1953), Turandot (1957); Verdi, Macbeth (1952), Rigoletto (1955), La Traviata (1955, La Scala), Aïda (1955).

More than any other singer in the 20th century, Maria Callas represents the quintessential opera diva. Her meteoric rise from immigrant working-class origins to international fame is the material that operas are made of, and she blurred the distinctions between art and life, between what was performance and what was not. Callas remains one of the most important figures in the American culture of the second half of the 20th century.

In a remote part of Greece before the First World War, Evangelia "Litza" Dimitriadu, daughter of an army officer known as the Singing Commander, married Georges Kalogeropoulos, a chemist and owner of a pharmacy in Meligala. Within six months, Evangelia knew she had made a horrendous mistake, but she was determined to be the good wife. In June 1917, at age 18, she gave birth to her first daughter Yacinthy (soon to be known as Jackie); three years later, she had a son Vasily. In 1923, after Vasily died of typhoid fever, Georges sold his business and, only the day before they were set to sail, informed his pregnant wife that they were emigrating to America. Evangelia swallowed her resentment, and, in August 1923, the Kalogeropoulos family, including six-year-old Jackie, arrived in America, where the name Kalogeropoulos—meaning "the good brother"—became Kalous, then Callas, because these were easier to pronounce.

Transported to this new land, **Evangelia Callas** was set on saving her crumbling marriage and compensating for the lost Vasily by having another son. The birth of Maria Cecilia Sophia Anna the following December was therefore disappointing, and the couple's relationship continued to deteriorate. They moved a number of times, unable to meet their apartment rent, and had settled in Washington Heights when Georges found enough money to open a drugstore, the Splendid Pharmacy. Evangelia, who considered her family to be superior to her husband's, would provoke him by playing opera on the piano to reflect her musical taste. According to Steven Linakis, a cousin of Callas, Evangelia "had a devilish temper, calling her husband a *zo* and a *vlahos*—an animal and a peasant, in that order—reminding him of her . . . grandfather who was a commander in the Balkan War, and of her father, a colonel, who didn't want her to marry Georges." According to various accounts, one cause of the couple's constant bickering was Georges' pursuit of other women.

After the stock market crash of 1929 left Georges bankrupt, he was forced to sell the pharmacy and become a traveling salesman of pharmaceuticals. By this time, however, Evangelia had become convinced that her daughter Maria was going to develop a voice as fine as Evangelia's father, the colonel, and furious battles ensued when she insisted that Georges pay for piano lessons four times a week for his daughters.

Maria, known at school during these years as Mary Callas, was pressured by her mother to work hard at singing. From an early age, however, she was highly motivated and made great demands on herself. "Maria would sing at the drop of a hat," writes Linakis. "She sang for public school events at every opportunity and even once sang down to the street, where a crowd gathered." At age 11, she entered a radio contest, singing "La Paloma" on "Major Bowes' Amateur Hour," and won. The prize was a Bulova watch, which Callas still wore years later. Evangelia entered her in other contests and booked her on an endless run of children's shows. "Only when I was singing did I feel loved," said Callas. A guilt-ridden Evangelia showed her love the only way she knew how, with food: home-made bread, macaronada, fried potatoes, saganaki, and cream cake. Callas would eat herself to sleep.

It is what I do that interests me, not what I say.

—**Maria Callas**

Evangelia eventually saw the need for Maria to receive better voice training than she could arrange in New York. More estranged from her husband than ever, in 1937, she won his acceptance to take their daughters back to Greece. There, a trembling 13-year-old Maria auditioned for **Maria Trivella**, who taught at the Conservatory of Ethnikon. "This is talent," said Trivella, who then arranged a scholarship for the American-born girl to become her voice student.

In *My Daughter Maria Callas*, Evangelia Callas recalls that her daughter "practiced day and night and sometimes forgot to eat, which for Maria was miraculous." Caring more about her study of music than her appearance, the young girl was a sloppy dresser and gained considerable weight. But the voice was there and developing. In April 1939, at age 15, Maria Callas appeared in her first operatic role, as Santuzza in a student production of *Cavalleria Rusticana*. According to her mother, she "won first prize in opera at the conservatory for her performance . . . but . . . it was no thundering triumph." Throughout that year, as World War II engulfed Europe, Maria continued to perform in student recitals.

While still studying with Trivella, Maria had a chance to audition for *Elvira de Hidalgo, a Spanish soprano then teaching at the Odeon Athenon, who had sung at Milan's famed La Scala as well as the Metropolitan Opera in New York. While Callas' presence at the time gave off little suggestion of an aspiring singer, de Hidalgo was impressed by the ardor of her voice, and its idiosyncratic qualities, and took on the young Maria as a private student. "It is to this illustrious artist," Callas has written, "with a moved, devoted, and grateful heart, that I owe all my preparation and my artistic formation as an actress and musician."

In 1941, just months before the German Nazis occupied Greece, Maria made her professional operatic debut as Beatrice in the *Boccaccio*. Following the occupation, a curfew was imposed that at first threatened to make it difficult for the young singer to continue her voice lessons. Once the curfew proved perfunctory, she returned to her classes where she practiced from early in the morning until late at night, continuing to bring the same focus she'd shown with Trivella to lessons with de Hidalgo. Both had become surrogate mothers. In performance, Maria was also making impressive progress, particularly after a well-received appearance as a 17-year-old Tosca, where she substituted at the last minute for one of her rivals at the conservatory. When the singer who had fallen ill tried to use her husband to block Maria's entrance on stage, the unfortunate man went home that night with bloody scratches on his face, while the audience heard a performance that received much praise.

The following year, in August 1942, Callas appeared as Tosca at the Royal Theater in Athens, this time not as an understudy. In his review for *Vradnyni*, Alexandra Lalaouni wrote that Callas "not only sustains the role without failings and sings it correctly, but she is capable at the same time of performing it with a conviction that in many places overwhelms the audience." Other engagements soon followed, while Maria's personality and self-esteem continued to

be nurtured under de Hidalgo. Approaching 20, the young singer was increasingly self-absorbed, competitive, and deeply ambitious.

With war raging throughout Europe, her voice was a salvation to her and her family in a time of terrible scarcity. There were Italian soldiers in the occupying army that she befriended, who would bring her food in exchange for hearing her sing. Her appearance as Martha in *Tiefland*, at the Olympia Theater, won her a respectful review from Friedrich W. Herzog in

Deutsche Nachrichten in Griechenland, who noted that "what other singers must learn, she possesses by nature: the dramatic instinct, the intensity of her acting, and the freedom of interpretation." It was this expressiveness she brought to her acting as well as the voice that was to influence the way operatic roles are performed. After Callas, singing was no longer enough; opera buffs began to demand incisive acting along with estimable singing.

By October 1944, Germany was on its way to military defeat, and a jubilant Greece was freed from occupation. Shortly, however, a *coup d'état* brought the Communist Party to power, and for a month, until the government and the rebels reached agreement, there was so little food available to Maria and Evangelia that she was unable to sing. Then, on grounds that she had collaborated with the enemy by taking food and singing for the occupying forces, Callas was refused a new contract for the upcoming season at the Athens Opera. Informed by the company's director that she would not be hired, Callas' parting words, by her own account, were, "Let's hope that you won't have to regret this one day." Though Callas had not been especially heroic during the occupation, neither was she a collaborator.

Elvira de Hidalgo recommended that Maria go to Italy, but Callas instead returned to the United States, where she lived with her father while preparing for auditions in New York. After a number of rejections, she auditioned at the Met, where she was offered a contract for leading roles in two productions in the 1946–47 season. But "the administration," wrote Callas, "offered parts that I believed unsuited to my possibilities at that time": the lead in Puccini's *Madame Butterfly,* which she saw as inappropriate for her physical build, and a part in Beethoven's *Fidelio,* which she did not wish to sing in English. Thus, to the amazement of the Met staff, she turned down the most important offer she had yet received.

Astute as her judgment was, she was thrust back into the frustration of auditioning. Another promising chance seemed to present itself but failed at the last minute: Eddie Bagarozy and Ottavio Scotto were trying to launch the U. S. Opera Company in Chicago with a production of Puccini's *Turandot;* when the arrangement collapsed, so did Maria's lead role. But the disappointment in this case was brief. An audition for Giovanni Zenatello led to an offer to sing at the Verona Festival. In June 1947, Callas left for Verona to sing in *La Gioconda.* Her last public appearance had been two years earlier, in *Tiefland,* at the Athens Opera in 1945.

In Verona, the 23-year-old Callas met Giovanni Battista Meneghini, a businessman, aged 51, who took her on a shopping spree. From Verona, she went to Venice, where she was engaged by Tullio Serafim to sing in *Tristan und Isolde,* which became her first success outside her homeland. According to Beppe Broselli, reviewing the performance for the *Corriere del Papolo,* "her magnificent figure brought to the part an added appeal and irresistible grandeur. But the greatest fascination, the most moving quality was that projected by her voice, a majestic, splendid instrument, vibrant and warm, smooth and equalized in every register."

Deluged, now, with offers to sing, Callas spent most of 1948 touring Italy, managed by Serafin. It was during this time that she developed the role, with Serafin, for which she would come to be known: Norma. One of the most vocally challenging roles in the entire operatic repertoire, Bellini's Norma required Callas to bring together that particular combination of dramatic force and superb singing that were to make her an international star.

Meanwhile, her commitment to the preparation did not detract from her other performances. She had the devoted support by this time of Meneghini, who had become her friend and unofficial personal manager. Soon after they met, Meneghini had proposed marriage, but Callas delayed making up her mind, due in part to opposition from both their families—Meneghini's because he had become so absorbed with her career that he was neglecting his, and Callas' because of the difference in their ages. Callas, herself, was not sure what her expectations were for this man in her life. As Steven Linakis relates in *Diva: The Life and Death of Maria Callas,* it was his advice that she found most helpful in making up her mind. Wrote Linakis: "Maria said I was the only one who agreed with her about him. All I did was to tell her to take him for all he was worth." On April 21, 1949, after Maria's baptism certificate reached her from New York, accompanied by a warning from Evangelia that Meneghini might not live long enough to help in the raising of their children, the couple married.

A few months earlier, in January 1949, Callas was working under the guidance of Serafin when she did what was then considered unthinkable. Barely a week after appearing in the demanding role of Brünnhilde in Wagner's *Die*

Walküre, she sang the part of Elvira in *I Puritani* on short notice. The two roles make such different demands on the range of the soprano voice that the ability to sing both is considered almost impossible. Demonstrating that she could sing both impressively, Callas drew enormous attention, in what proved to be a turning point in her career. "A few days ago," according to a review by Mario Nordio, "we were startled to read that our magnificent Brünnhilde, Isolde, and Turandot would interpret Elvira. . . . Even the most skeptical . . . had to acknowledge the miracle that Maria Callas accomplished."

Leaving behind a mesmerized Italy as well as her new husband, Callas next appeared at the Teatro Colón in Argentina, singing *Turandot, Norma,* and *Aïda.* While the role of Norma gained critical praise locally, the others were considered less impressive. Callas returned to Italy to start her married life and found herself under the constant gaze of Italy's famed paparrazzi, who were hungry for stories about the great singer on her way to becoming a public personality. During this period, she made her debut at La Scala, replacing *Renata Tebaldi in the title role of Verdi's *Aïda* and received mixed reviews.

When Callas appeared as Aïda in Mexico's Palacio de Bellas Artes, her performance was praised for its vigor. Other successes followed, in Italy, in Spain, and in São Paulo, Brazil. At the beginning of 1952, she returned to La Scala to sing *Norma.* Although, as Newt Jenkins wrote in *Musical America* that "there was occasionally a slight tendency to shrillness and hardness on the high notes . . . her pitch was faultless," and the performance was deemed a success.

Callas carved one indelible image after another in the imagination of her adoring public, appearing in a variety of roles considered virtually impossible for a soprano in the 1950s. Encouraged by her capacity to handle them, producers and directors began to unearth the great but almost-forgotten *bel canto* roles of the great Italian tradition. Maria, at her artistic prime, also determined to create a new physical image of herself, and within a matter of months had slimmed down to a "new" Maria—the regal Callas still remembered today.

The early 1950s were also the years Callas became notorious for her temperament. Her famous rivalry with Tebaldi, another great soprano, dates from this time, and there were other singers who grew resentful of the public attention she drew. She had become an international figure of growing mythical proportions, with the public's attention so centered on her that no one sharing the stage with her was able to shine in performance.

Recordings she made with EMI at this early period of her international career are proof, nevertheless, that the attention Callas received from her audiences was deserved. She brought a keen musical mind to every role. Over a period of a few years, and while sharing the performance season at the Opera La Scala with Tebaldi—where they appeared in different productions, developing a rivalry that split the public into fanatical factions—she worked hard at perfecting the title roles of *Medea* and *Lucia di Lammermoor.* Effective collaborations with Herbert von Karajan, Luchino Visconti, Franco Zeffirelli and Leonard Bernstein met the high standards of the demanding La Scala in the first half of the decade. Finally, after a successful 1954–55 season, she sang in London and then made her way to the United States, where her first operatic appearance was in Chicago. Meneghini, who was now her manager, continued to reject offers from the Metropolitan Opera, so that Maria did not debut there until 1956.

In Chicago, meanwhile, the diva was a huge success. According to Ronald Eyer, writing about her in *Norma* for *Musical America,* "She molds a line as deftly as she tosses off cruelly difficult ornamentations in the highest register. And she brings to everything a passion, a profile of character and a youthful beauty that are rare in our lyric theater." In a review of *Lucia di Lammermoor,* **Claudia Cassidy** of the *Chicago Tribune* found the composer's "mad scene" to be a description of the operagoers' ecstatic response. "Near pandemonium broke out," she wrote; "there was an avalanche of applause, a roar of cheers growing steadily hoarser, a standing ovation, and the aisles were full of men pushing as close to the stage as possible."

While the cult of Callas continued to grow for years, the singer began to demonstrate vocal difficulties; toward the end of the decade, these became impossible to ignore. After the 1958–59 season, she reduced the number of performances from more than 55 a year to fewer than 10. As her voice declined, the public turned more attention to her difficult personality and strained relationships with other singers and administrators of the opera houses where she sang. Her emotional life was made similarly turbulent by a prolonged affair with the Greek shipping magnate Aristotle Onassis. When Callas ceased to perform, Onassis was held responsible for her abandonment of the stage, but it is doubtful that he determined the course of her career. As a great singer who had always set the highest standards for herself, Callas was faced with the tragic irony of a voice that had lost its glow at a relatively young age.

After appearances in New York, Paris, and London during the 1964–65 season, Maria Callas ceased to perform. Almost a decade passed before she was approached, in 1972, with an invitation to give master classes at the Juilliard School of Music. A few years earlier, she had tried film acting, appearing in Pier Paolo Pasolini's *Medea*, released in 1969.

During the master classes at Juilliard, which were open to the public, Callas met up again with an old friend, the tenor Giuseppe di Stefano. The two gave some recitals together, made a recording of duets, and gave a master class in Osaka, but this reemergence lasted only until 1973; the singer's last public appearance was November 11, 1974. Three years later, on September 16, 1977, she died in Paris, three months short of her 54th birthday. Her reputation as an extraordinary if troubled musical genius remains undiminished.

SOURCES:
Callas, Evangelia. *My Daughter Maria Callas*. NY: Arno Press, 1977.
Eckert, Thor, Jr. "Maria Callas," in *High Fidelity*. February 1989.
Linakis, Stephen. *Diva: The Life and Death of Maria Callas*. Englewood Cliffs, NJ: Prentice-Hall, 1980.
Lowe, David A., ed. *Callas: As They Saw Her*. NY: Ungar, 1986.
Rémy, Pierre-Jean. *Maria Callas: A Tribute*. London: Macdonald and Jane's, 1978.
Scott, Michael. *Maria Meneghini Callas*. NY: Simon and Schuster, 1991.
Stassinopoulos, Arianna. *Maria Callas: The Woman Behind the Legend*. NY: Simon and Schuster, 1981.
Stearns, David P. "Diva at Twilight," in *Opera News*. April 16, 1994.

SUGGESTED READING:
Ardoin, John. *The Callas Legacy: A Biography of a Career*. NY: Scribner, 1982.
Bret, David. *Maria Callas: The Tigress and the Lamb*. Robson-Parkwest, 1998.
Kesting, Jurgen. *Maria Callas*. Northeastern University Press, 1993.
Landrum, Gene N. *Profiles of Female Genius: Thirteen Creative Women Who Changed the World*. Amherst, NY: Prometheus, 1994.
Wineski, Henry. *Maria Callas: The Art Behind the Legend*. Garden City, NY: Doubleday, 1975.

RELATED MEDIA:
Master Class, a play by Terrence McNally based on master classes that Callas gave at Juilliard School in New York in 1971–72, starring **Zoe Caldwell**, opened on Broadway in November 1995.

Carlos Decena, freelance writer, Philadelphia, Pennsylvania

Callender, Marie (1907–1995)

American piemaker and businesswoman who turned a struggling business into a multimillion-dollar restaurant chain. Born in 1907 in South Dakota; died in Laguna Hills, California, on November 11, 1995; married Cal Callender, in 1924; children: one son, Donald Callender.

Steered by hard work, persistence, and some luck, Marie Callender's life is a classic American rags-to-riches story. Born in South Dakota in 1907, as a young girl she accompanied her poor but hardworking family when they moved to California in search of a better life. In 1924, she married Cal Callender; both she and her husband were 17 at the time. During the next decades, life was difficult for the couple and their young son Donald, as they worked long hours and struggled to make ends meet. The small family was a happy one, however, though they remained only a paycheck or two from economic disaster.

To raise additional money once their son was in school, Marie began to work part-time. In the mid-1940s, the family was living in the Long Beach area when she answered a newspaper advertisement for delicatessen help. She worked in the deli on a part-time basis, making salads and preparing simple hot meals. When her boss opened a snack bar, he asked her to bake pies there; the oven, however, was not the right type, so Marie and her mother—an experienced pie-baker—began to bake pies in her own kitchen. Work was so physically demanding that one Saturday in 1948, after producing countless pies and dragging one too many 100-pound sacks of flour around her kitchen, Marie announced to her boss that she was quitting.

So pleased was Callender's boss with the quality of her pies that he talked her into starting her own pie business, assuring her that he would be her steady customer. Marie and Cal took the risky plunge into a small-business venture. Their almost total lack of capital necessitated the sale of their only major asset, a new Chevrolet; once outstanding bills were paid, about $700 remained in the family treasury. With this modest sum, Marie purchased an old oven and three rolling pins. They rented an old Quonset Hut in Long Beach and began baking pies and other items on a wholesale basis for local shops. Marie, Cal and their son Don worked in the simple facility. Hours were long and gruelling, and during the early years of the business Cal baked all night, only to shower, eat breakfast, and deliver pies most of the day. Determined to help his parents succeed, Don quit college to assist in the fledgling enterprise.

The business grew only modestly for the next decade. In 1962, they moved into the retail food world with a small pie and coffee shop, called Marie Callender's, on Tustin Avenue in Orange, California. With little name recognition despite the quality of Marie's pies, the challenge was to pick up a loyal customer base before bankruptcy. Thanks to Don's ingenuity, the little shop began offering a free slice of pie and cup of coffee to all first-time customers. The line outside Marie Callender's was three blocks long during the first few days. Won over by the excellence of the pies, most of the customers became steadies and spread the word throughout the town. Another feature that intrigued customers was the pie oven, which Marie placed where it could be seen in the window from the street. Watching their pies going in and out the oven pleased patrons immensely, giving them a sense of participation in the baking process. In 1964, the shop added soup and sandwiches to the menu, and by the end of the 1960s a rapidly growing number of Callender restaurants were in operation in southern California.

By the 1970s, the Callender family was in charge of a veritable empire of restaurants. Don's marketing ability, along with Marie's insistence on high quality in all items sold (particularly in the pies), resulted in a huge success for the precarious enterprise that had begun decades earlier in a Quonset Hut. In 1986, Marie Callender proudly told a reporter that she always was certain that the quality of her pies was excellent: "everybody predicted we'd go broke, but we outlived 'em all. So we knew we had something better." Even when their restaurants became successful, the Callenders spent virtually no money on advertising, preferring to let word of mouth do the work of publicity for them. Quality control was maintained on an informal basis by Marie; even in "retirement," she continued to eat in a Marie Callender's restaurant every so often and report any substandard pies or other items to her son, who was CEO of the chain.

After Cal's death in 1984, when Marie was living in a retirement home and no longer active in the business, Don placed the Marie Callender chain on the market. A number of corporate leaders, including **Joan Kroc** of McDonald's, expressed an interest in the company that in 1985 had sales of $180 million, with 119 restaurants in California and 11 other states. In February 1986, Marie Callender's Pie Shops, Inc. was purchased by Ramada Inns for nearly $90 million in cash and stocks. As part of the deal, Don Callender remained as chief executive officer. Marie, who had long been living at Leisure World in Laguna Hills, told reporters, "I really have no feeling about it. I've been out of the business for too long." Yet, she continued to visit Marie Callender's pie shops, enjoying the pies and passing on whatever information her son might need to maintain the high standard of quality she had set in Long Beach many decades earlier. Marie Callender, a household name not only for her pies but also for a line of frozen dinners, died in a nursing home in Laguna Hills on November 11, 1995.

SOURCES:

Bauer, Bob. "Dinner time, frozen dinners, supermarket frozens," in *Supermarket News*. Vol. 45, no. 14. April 3, 1995, p. 36.

Cekola, Anne. "Restaurant Chain Founder Callender Dies," in *Los Angeles Times*. Orange County ed. November 12, 1995, Metro section, p. B1.

Horovitz, Bruce. "Ramada Inns purchases Callender's for $90 Million," in *Los Angeles Times*. February 7, 1986, business section, pt. IV, p. 3.

"Marie Callender, Restaurateur, 88," in *The New York Times Biographical Service*. November 1995, p. 1681.

Strauss, Duncan. "Pie in the Sky: Marie Callender had the Recipes and an Oven," in *Los Angeles Times Magazine*. June 15, 1986.

John Haag, Associate Professor,
University of Georgia, Athens, Georgia

Callil, Carmen (1938—)

Australian publisher. Born in Melbourne in 1938; attended Melbourne University.

Carmen Callil was the founder of Virago Press, a publishing house dedicated to the publication of women writers. She was born in Melbourne in 1938 and attended Melbourne University before settling in England in her mid-20s (1963). A position as a buyer's assistant at Marks and Spencer preceded her entry into the publishing world. After working for several firms, including Hutchinson, Batsford, and Andrew Deutsch, she founded her own company, Callil Book Publicity, in 1972. The same year, she founded Virago Press. Virago's most successful line, Modern Classics—"dedicated to the celebration of women writers and to the discovery and reprinting of their works"—was begun in 1978 and initially focused on English authors including *Emily Eden, *Antonia White, and *Margaret Kennedy; the list later widened to encompass works from various countries and time periods. Callil served on the Board of Directors for Britain's Channel 4 and was managing director of Hogarth Press and Chatto and Windus.

Calloway, Blanche (1902–1973)

African-American singer who was one of the most successful band leaders of the 1930s and the first black woman to lead an all-male band. Born on February 2, 1902, in Baltimore, Maryland; died on December 16, 1973, in Baltimore; one of four children of Cabell (a real-estate agent and lawyer) and Martha Eulalia (Reed) Calloway (a teacher); sister of entertainer Cab Calloway and band leader Elmer Calloway; attended Morgan State College.

After a brief stay at Morgan State College, Blanche Calloway began her professional career in Baltimore as a singer in local revues, stage shows, and nightclubs. In 1923, she joined the touring company of the Noble Sissle and Eubie Blake musical *Shuffle Along*. In 1927, when a subsequent tour in *Plantation Days* ended in Chicago, she took up residency there to work as a nightclub vocalist. Four years later, in 1931, she sang with the Andy Kirk band at Philadelphia's Pearl Theater.

Between 1931 and 1938, Calloway headed her own all-male band—Blanche Calloway and Her Joy Boys, and later Blanche Calloway and Her Orchestra—which included some of the top musicians of the day. Appearing at New York's exclusive black theaters, the band played the Lafayette, the Harlem Opera House, and the Apollo. With their theme song "Growlin' Dan," they performed across the United States and recorded frequently for Victor. In a survey conducted by the *Pittsburgh Courier* in 1931, Calloway's band ranked 9th of 38, only 5 slots behind Louis Armstrong. A reviewer for the *Courier* called her "one of the most progressive performers in the profession."

In 1938, bankruptcy forced Calloway to give up the band, after which she worked as a solo artist for several years. By 1944, she had tired of life on the road and settled in Philadelphia, where she became active in community and political affairs. After moving to Florida in 1953, she became a disc jockey on radio station WMEM out of Miami. She later founded and served as president of Afram House, a company specializing in cosmetics and hair preparations for blacks. Continuing her activity in politics, in 1958 Calloway was the first black woman in Miami to vote.

Details of her private life are difficult to track. One source claims that her bankruptcy was filed under the name Pinder, giving evidence of at least one marriage. Her story has been eclipsed by that of her immensely successful brother Cab, who ironically was known during his sister's heyday as Blanche's younger brother.

SUGGESTED READING:
Calloway, Cab, and Bryant Rolls. *Of Minnie the Moocher and Me.* NY: Crowell, 1976.

Barbara Morgan,
Melrose, Massachusetts

Calpurnia (c. 70 BCE–?)

Roman noblewoman, third wife of Julius Caesar. Born around 70 BCE; death date unknown; daughter of Lucius Calpurnius Piso Caesoninus; sister of Lucius Calpurnius Piso, the "pontifex"; became third wife of Julius Caesar (c. 100–44 BCE), military and political leader of Rome, in 59 BCE. Caesar was also married to *Cornelia (c. 100–68 BCE) and Pompeia (c. 87–?BCE).

A Roman noblewoman of the late Republic, Calpurnia was the daughter of Lucius Calpurnius Piso Caesoninus, who arranged her marriage to Julius Caesar, for reasons of mutual political expediency, during the latter's consulship in 59 BCE. Caesar embraced this marriage in order to anchor his standing with a faction sympathetic to his liberal policies as he strove to strengthen his hand (without creating too many waves) in the wake of the formation of the First Triumvirate, the political alliance bringing Caesar, Pompey, and Crassus together. Piso's motivation for arranging his daughter's marriage was considerably more concrete: his association with Caesar guaranteed his election to the consulship in the year following Caesar's. Although Calpurnia's marriage to Caesar was entirely political at its inception, there quickly developed a real affection between Calpurnia and her husband. Affection was one thing and politics another, however, for, despite his fondness for Calpurnia, Caesar considered divorcing her in 53 BCE to marry *Pompeia, the daughter of Pompey and *Mucia, in an effort to shore up their deteriorating political relationship. This marriage fell through, and Caesar remained united with Calpurnia who understood political realities and nursed no grudge against her husband of whom she continued to be fond. In 44, hearing rumors of Caesar's possible assassination, Calpurnia tried to prevent him from attending the meeting of the Senate where he would, in fact, be murdered. Though she must have been aware of his affair with *Cleopatra VII during the last years of his life, she remained a Caesarian partisan even after her husband's death. Thinking (erroneously) that Marc Antony represented the future of Caesar's faction, after Caesar's death Calpurnia surrendered his private papers and most of his enormous fortune to

Opposite page From the movie Julius Caesar, *starring Greer Garson as* Calpurnia.

Antony, to help avenge Caesar's murder. Calpurnia had no children with Caesar.

Calpurnia represented an important link between her family and that of Caesar, for her brother Lucius Calpurnius Piso, the "pontifex," long served the interests of Caesar's posthumously adopted son and heir, Octavian (later, Augustus). As a consular legate under that emperor's authority in Thrace, the younger Piso earned an *ornamenta triumphalia* as a reward for military accomplishment. Later, he served as the proconsul of Asia and for 20 years between 12 and 32 CE served as the city of Rome's *praefectus urbi* under both Augustus and his successor, Tiberius.

The date of Calpurnia's death is unknown, but her loyalty to Caesar, and her willingness to overlook his marital indiscretions, politically established her immediate family for the duration of their lives.

William S. Greenwalt,
Associate Professor of Classical History,
Santa Clara University, Santa Clara, California

Calvé, Emma (1858–1942)

*Spanish-born soprano who was considered the most vivid Carmen of her day. Name variations: Emma Calve. Born Emma de Roquer on August 15, 1858, in Décazeville, Spain; died on January 6, 1942, in Millau; daughter of a Spanish father and a French mother; trained in Paris, studying with Jules Puget, *Mathilde Marchesi, and Rosina Laborde; married tenor Galileo Gaspari.*

Debuted as Marguerite in Gounod's Faust in Brussels (1881 or 1882); performed at the Opéra-Comique in Paris (1880s); debuted at Teatro alla Scala (1887); created Suzel in Mascagni's L'amico Fritz in Rome (1891); debuted at Metropolitan Opera (1893); made debut in Boston (1912), Nice (1914).

"People do not go to the opera or the concert hall merely to hear sofeggios, trills and runs. They want to hear a human message from a human being who has experienced great things and trained the mind and soul in finer discipline than mere exercises. The singer must be a personality, must understand the bond of sympathy with mankind, which, even more than a beautiful voice, commands the attention and interest of the audience." This was Emma Calvé's guiding philosophy as an opera singer. Among the most accomplished sopranos, and perhaps the most inspired actress of her time, she despised the theatrical posturing so typical of the era. She was particularly influenced by *Eleanora Duse (1858–1924), the brilliant tragedian, and like

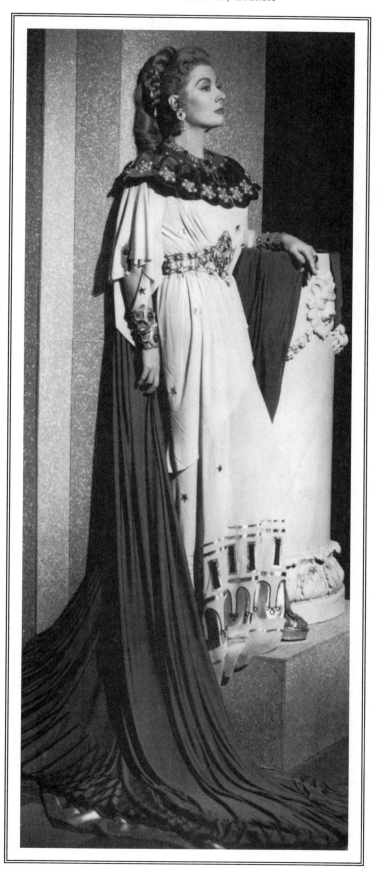

Emma
Calvé

In his account of women painters, Pliny the Elder mentions the subjects of three paintings after Calypso's name; it is possible that Calypso was not a painter at all but actually the subject of a portrait by *Irene. *See entries on Aristarete and Irene for further background information.*

Peter H. O'Brien,
Boston University

Cam, Helen M. (1885–1968)

English university professor and historian. Born Helen Maud Cam on August 22, 1885, in Abingdon, Berkshire, England; died in 1968; one of nine children of William Herbert (an educator and rector of two parishes) and Kate (Scott) Cam; schooled at home; attended Royal Holloway College; granted B.A., University of London, 1907; attended Bryn Mawr College, Philadelphia, 1908; granted M.A., University of London, 1909; never married; no children.

Calling herself a scholar by choice and a teacher by necessity, historian Helen M. Cam was appointed to a full professorship on the faculty of Harvard University in 1948, the first woman honored with such an appointment in the history of the institution. She was chosen by a committee representing 11 Harvard departments after a distinguished teaching career at Girton College of England's Cambridge University.

Cam was born into a family of modest means on August 22, 1885, in Abingdon, Berkshire, one of nine children of William Herbert Cam, an educator and rector of two parishes, and **Kate Scott Cam**. Because there was no day school available and they could not afford boarding schools, her parents educated all their young at home. By age 19, Helen qualified for a scholarship to Royal Holloway College of the University of London. After receiving her M.A. in history in 1909, she took a position as assistant mistress in history at Ladies' College, Cheltenham. From 1912 to 1921, she held teaching positions at Royal Holloway College, after which she was appointed a lecturer in history at Girton College, Cambridge, where she remained until 1929. That year, she accepted a post at the University of Cambridge, where in addition to lecturing on English medieval constitutional history, she tutored and conducted research. In 1940, she returned to Girton College where she was director of studies in history and law. At Harvard, Cam taught medieval English history to

Duse she paid close attention to every detail. Bernard Shaw who saw Calvé at Covent Garden described her Santuzza in Mascagni's *Cavalleria Rusticana* as "irresistibly moving and beautiful, and fully capable of sustaining the inevitable comparison with Duse's impersonation of the same part." Although Calvé performed the standard repertory as well as many contemporary works, she was particularly beloved for her portrayals of Santuzza and of Carmen, a role to which she remains inseparably linked. Calvé created the part of Bianca in Dubois' *Aben Hamlet*; Massenet's *Navarraise* and *Sapho* were written specially for her. Known as the "Singing Duse" for her dramatic powers, Emma Calvé was a superstar in her own era and is remembered for her great singing and her artistry on the opera stage.

John Haag, Athens, Georgia

Calypso (fl. c. 200 BCE)

Ancient Greek painter. Name variations: Kalypso. Pronunciation: cal-up-SO or cal-IP-so. Flourished around 200 BCE.

both Radcliffe (the university's women's affiliate) and Harvard students.

Cam was a well-published scholar, issuing a book every few years, notably *Local Government in Francia and England, 768–1934* (1912), *Liberties and Communities in Medieval England: Collected Studies in Administration and Topography* (1944), and *Law Finders and Law Makers in Medieval England* (1962). She also contributed articles to magazines such as the *English Historical Review, History, Speculum,* and the *Transactions of the Royal Historical Society.* In 1937, she was awarded a Litt. D. degree at the University of Cambridge on the basis of her published works.

Cam, who was a member of Britain's Conservative Party in her college days, became an energetic campaigner for the Labor Party. In addition to her political allegiance, she was widely traveled, having visited India, Burma, Persia, Iraq, Palestine, as well as most of the countries on the Continent. She was a member of many learned and public-service organizations, holding offices in nearly all of them. She also held honorary doctorates from Smith College, Mount Holyoke College, North Carolina University, and Oxford. Described as "vigorous-appearing," she relaxed by walking and painting with watercolors.

Barbara Morgan
, Melrose, Massachusetts

Camargo, Marie-Anne Cupis de

(1710–1770)

French-Spanish ballerina. Born Marie-Anne de Cupis (or Marie Anne Cuppi) in Brussels, Belgium, of Spanish descent on April 15, 1710; died in Paris on April 20, 1770; daughter of Ferdinand Joseph de Cupis (a violinist and dance master).

Though Marie-Anne Cupis de Camargo's father was descended from a noble Roman family, he earned a scanty living as violinist and dance-master. An excellent teacher, he trained his daughter from childhood for the stage. At ten, Camargo was given lessons by **Françoise Prévost*, then the first dancer at the Paris Opéra, and before long she had secured an engagement as *première danseuse,* first at Brussels and then at Rouen. When the season at Rouen foundered, she was invited to join the Paris Opéra, as was singer **Marie Pélissier**. No one was surprised when Françoise Prévost, who was well-known for her competitive jealousy, quickly relegated her ex-pupil to the *corps de ballet*. But Camargo did not remain there for any length of time. On a

long-remembered night, when one of the Dumoulin brothers failed to make his entrance, she took center stage to fill the void and brought down the house.

Under her Spanish maternal grandmother's name of Camargo, she made her Paris début in 1726, electrifying the audience with her technical feats and the *entrechat quatre,* up until then reserved for male dancers. At age 16, Camargo become the rage of Paris: new fashions bore her name; her hairstyle was copied by the ladies at court; and her shoemaker was in demand. On **Marie Sallé*'s return from London in 1727, the press and public touched off a rivalry between the two that became the subject of verse and prose. Aficionados took sides, some championing the grace and eloquence of Sallé, others the verve and technique of Camargo. While the sensitive Sallé fled to London, Camargo seemed to have relished the challenge.

She had many titled admirers and her liaisons were common gossip. At 23, she became the mistress of Louis de Bourbon, comte de Clermont, grandson of the great Condé. Dubious about her faithfulness when his duties in the King's Armies forced him to leave Paris, he asked her to retire from the stage while he was gone. From 1736 to 1741, she lived in retirement at the Château de Berny, a safe distance from the Opéra and its many temptations. On Clermont's return, their ardor had cooled. He took up with Mlle **Le Duc** of the *corps de ballet;* she took up with Mlle Le Duc's paramour, Bernard de Rieux.

In 1741, Camargo resumed her career, continuing at the Opéra for ten more years. In her time, she appeared in 78 ballets or operas, always to the delight of the public. Camargo was the first ballet dancer to shorten the skirt to what afterwards became the regulation length. On her death in April 1770, there was a magnificent funeral at the Église Saint-Roch, a somewhat surprising occurrence, since the church took a dim view of dancers. Years later, that same church would bar the gates to the ballerina **Louise Chameroy**.

There is a portrait of Camargo by Nicolas Lancret in the Wallace Collection, London. She was also the subject of an opera, a ballet choreographed by **Petipa**, and dishware created by Escoffier.

SOURCES:

Migel, Parmenia. *The Ballerinas: From the Court of Louis XIV to Pavlova.* NY: Macmillan, 1972.

❧➤
*See following
page for
illustration*

Cambridge, Ada (1844–1926)

Australian fiction writer and poet. Name variations: *Mrs. George Cross. Born Ada Cambridge on November 21, 1844, at Wiggenhall, St. Germains, Norfolk, England; died on July 19, 1926, at Elsternwick, Australia; daughter of Thomasine (Emerson) and Henry Cambridge (a farmer); educated at home; married Reverend George Frederick Cross (d. 1917), on April 25, 1870; children: Arthur Stuart (1871–1876); Edith Constance (1873–1884); Vera Lyon (b. 1876); Hugh Cambridge (1878–1902); Kenneth Stuart (1880–1967).*

Selected works: Hymns on the Litany *(1865);* Hymns on the Holy Communion *(1866);* The Manor House *(poems, 1875);* Unspoken Thoughts *(1887);* A Marked Man *(1890);* Thirty Years in Australia *(1903);* The Hand in the Dark *(1913).*

Ada Cambridge was the eldest daughter and second child in a family of ten children whose parents farmed 174 acres in England's Thorpland. Their father Henry, however, was more interested in hunting, and much of the farming fell to their mother Thomasine, while Ada, a caretaker at a young age, saw to household chores. Unable to make ends meet, the Cambridges moved to Downham Market in 1854, where Henry became a grain merchant. During her youth, Ada and her siblings had seven governesses, most of whom were less literate than their pupils who terrorized them into quitting. Ada maintained that one governess, with whom she was forced to share a bedroom, molested her. A maternal aunt took a special interest in Ada and pushed her to study languages and literature.

The family eventually moved to Ely, where the teenage Ada became devoutly religious and considered becoming a nun; she worked as a District Visitor for her church, checking on elderly and sick parishioners and, by age 22, had anonymously published two volumes of hymns. She also helped financially support her family with the publication of short stories in local magazines and newspapers.

Cambridge met her future husband George Cross, who had been born and raised in Ely, while he was completing his theology studies. Ada knew that George wanted to move to Australia and help establish the Church of England. During their seven-week engagement, she sewed her own wedding dress in grey so that it might be worn again, and they married in April of 1870. Cross was made a rector on the same day, and they sailed for Australia on June 1. The 80-day voyage brought Cross and Cambridge (who kept her maiden name for its established literary reputation) ashore at Hobson's Bay, from which they departed for his first parish, in Wangaratta. There, the couple had a son, Arthur Stuart, and Ada learned to handle a pistol in the event of attack by Aborigines. In January of 1872, the family moved to Yackandandah. They had a daughter, Edith, in November of 1873, and Ada began publishing in magazines once more to contribute to the family coffer. Although she taught Sunday school and led the choir, Cambridge shunned most of the traditional duties of a parson's wife, which she found boring. "After I could plead the claims of a profession of my own," she wrote, "my position in the scheme of things was finally and comfortably defined." The family suffered Edith's death of whooping cough in April of 1874, after which they moved as soon as Cross could obtain a new post. As well, their new home in Ballan proved a house of sadness with Arthur dying two years after his sister, and Cambridge was childless for two months until Vera was born. When Vera was one, they moved to Coleraine and added two sons, Hugh

and Kenneth. The seasons were harsh—flooding in winter, extreme heat in summer—and the parsonage was isolated. Loneliness and long hours working for extra income made Cambridge ill. She was frequently bedridden but wrote voluminously.

George Cross could not keep up the parsonage, so in December 1883 the family sold its belongings and boarded the school-age children. George began a series of traveling posts and Cambridge, her baby, and a nursemaid went "visiting" with friends and family for a year. Cross took an assignment in the Melbourne district of Beechworth, where they would stay for nine years. The country landscape soothed Ada, and the parishioners expected little of her. A near-fatal illness in March of 1886 left her with recurring periods of poor health, which were complicated by a back injury suffered in a carriage accident; still, her writing continued to flourish.

The 1887 poetry volume *Unspoken Thoughts,* which voiced Ada's increasing doubt in the organized religion her husband represented and the "relentless bonds" of marriage, deepened the emotional gap between the two. Ada withdrew the volume but not all copies were recovered. Of her increasingly feminist works, she remarked, "I am a woman's woman; I am even—although I detest the term—a woman's rights woman."

In 1893, the Beechworth years closed with a move to Williamstown. Ada continued to write and publish prolifically but the quality of her writing diminished; demands on her time from the parish had increased. Williamstown was Cross' longest post, and they remained there through their daughter Vera's marriage and son Hugh's death at age 23 of enteric fever.

Ada Cambridge lived in Australia nearly 30 years before she returned to her homeland. The trip was afforded by Cross' sister's estate, which George was called home to settle. They stayed five months, visiting family and old friends. When they returned to Australia, he worked for only a year more before retiring. In 1912, the couple returned to England to live. Cambridge destroyed most of her personal papers before they set sail.

To George Cross, Australia was a career, but it had become home to Cambridge. She returned to Malvern, Victoria, within months of George's death in February 1917, and "found a tiny home for myself here, under the wing of my only daughter who lives in the next street." In her final years, Cambridge's eyesight and general health failed. Her savings were depleted. When she could no longer afford her own home, she moved in with her son Kenneth with whom she stayed for three years before a series of strokes forced her into full-time nursing care. Cambridge's longtime publisher, George Robertson, arranged to purchase the rights for her entire catalog of writings in October 1924. He did it as a kindness, and the sum allowed Cambridge to live out her days in a private hospital in Elsternwick. She died on July 19, 1926, and was buried at Brighton Cemetery, Melbourne. Her tombstone incorrectly identifies her as 84 years old, instead of her true 81 years. Cambridge's sister, **Jenny Wylie**, was buried beside her five years later.

SOURCES:

Belby, Raymond, and Cecil Hadgraft. *Ada Cambridge, Tasma and Rosa Praed.* Melbourne: Oxford University Press, 1979.

Bradstock, Margaret, and Louise Wakeling. *Rattling the Orthodoxies: A Life of Ada Cambridge.* Victoria, Australia: Penguin Books, 1991.

Tate, Audrey. *Ada Cambridge.* Victoria, Australia: Melbourne University Press, 1991.

Crista Martin,
Boston, Massachusetts

Cambridge, countess of.

See Clifford, Maud (d. 1446).
See Mortimer, Anne (1390–1411).

Cameron, Mrs. Alan (1899–1973).

See Bowen, Elizabeth.

Cameron, Bessy (c. 1851–1895)

Aboriginal teacher. Born in King George Sound, Western Australia, around 1851; died on January 12, 1895; attended Annesfield School, Albany; attended a model school in Sydney; married Donald Cameron, on November 4, 1868; children: four who survived.

Her father's connections enabled Bessy Cameron to receive a formal education and have a short teaching career, a rare opportunity for an Aboriginal. Because her father was a servant of Henry Camfield, a government official, Cameron was educated at the native institution opened by Henry's wife, **Anne Camfield**, to instruct Aboriginal children in the "ways of civilized life" and Christianity. An excellent student, Cameron was then sent to Sydney, where she was trained as a teacher and also became an accomplished pianist. She returned to Albany in 1866 as an assistant to Anne Camfield as well as the salaried church organist.

In 1867, Cameron was chosen to become a teacher at Ramahyuck mission where, in addition to attending classes, she performed housework. When she became involved with a European man who wanted to marry her, the missionaries, afraid of losing her, relocated her to Lake Tyers mission and arranged her marriage to Donald Cameron, a seemingly more suitable native man. The couple were then put in charge of the mission's boarding house, a demotion in Cameron's eyes that sapped her initiative; she made known her displeasure, began to neglect her duties, and turned to reading. Removed from the mission house, the couple found themselves on their own in the mission village. With her four children, Bessy Cameron spent the next years living off and on again at Lake Tyers and Ramahyuck, finding it difficult to support her family outside the mission environment. At one point, she left her husband, though they later reconciled. In 1887, Cameron suffered a miscarriage and was allowed to return to Ramahyuck because she was seriously ill; she then left and returned yet again. Her final years were spent trying to keep her younger children and her grandchildren from being taken from her to be brought up "white."

Barbara Morgan,
Melrose, Massachusetts

Cameron, Donaldina (1869–1968)

American California mission superintendent and social reformer. Born Donaldina Mackenzie Cameron on July 26, 1869, in Otago Land District on the South Island of New Zealand; died on January 4, 1968, in Palo Alto, California; daughter of Allan Cameron (a sheep rancher) and Isabella Mackenzie; attended Castleman School for Girls and Los Angeles Normal School; never married; no children.

Donaldina Cameron was born on July 26, 1869, on a sheep station near the Clutha River in Otago Land District on the South Island of New Zealand. In 1871, her family moved to the San Joaquin Valley of California. Three years later, following the death of her mother, Cameron moved with her family to San Jose, California, then to Oakland in 1878, and to La Puente, near Los Angeles, in 1885. In 1887, after her father's death, Cameron left the Los Angeles Normal School where she was a student and returned to live with her siblings in La Puente.

In 1895, she began to work with Chinese women, joining **Margaret Culbertson**, under the auspices of the Presbyterian Church, at the mission home of the Woman's Occidental Board of Foreign Missions in San Francisco. In 1900, Cameron became superintendent of the home, a position to which she devoted the rest of her professional life.

Located on the fringe of San Francisco's Chinatown, the mission house provided her with a base of operations from which she effectively waged her campaign against Chinese female slavery. Cameron broke into brothels and gambling clubs, bringing the captive women and girls to the mission house. She developed educational programs and found jobs, homes, and schools for them. In 1925, she established a second mission house in Oakland as a refuge for young children. As the Chinese slave trade diminished, these mission houses grew into educational and community centers.

Obeying the National Board of Missions' mandatory retirement age of 65, in 1934 Cameron retired from the mission, but she remained in the San Francisco area and worked with the mission as a volunteer until 1939 when she returned to Oakland to care for her three remaining sisters. In 1942, she and her two surviving sisters moved to Palo Alto. That same year, the mission house at 920 Sacramento Street in San Francisco was renamed the Donaldina Cameron House. In and around the Palo Alto area, Cameron was very involved in civic activities in volunteer positions until her death from a pulmonary embolism at the age of 98 in 1968.

In 1969, the California State Legislature introduced a memorial tribute for her work. While regarded as a model of selfless missionary behavior by many, some critics propose that she was intolerant, unsympathetic, and possibly racist. They cite the fact that she never learned to speak Chinese and that she frequently referred to the Chinese as "heathens." Whatever the grounds and validity of these concerns, Cameron remains personally responsible for the rescue of thousands of Chinese women and young girls held as slaves in sweatshops and brothels, and she was primarily responsible for the eventual demise of the Chinese slave trade in America. She established educational and community organizations that taught, trained, and placed women in employment and safer living conditions, providing over the years employment and education for consecutive generations of Chinese-American women in San Francisco.

SOURCES:

Martin, Mildred Crowl. *Chinatown's Angry Angel: The Story of Donaldina Cameron.* Palo Alto, CA: Pacific Books, 1986.

McClain, Laurene, "Donaldina Cameron: A Reappraisal," in *Pacific History.* Vol. 27, no. 3, 1983, pp. 24–35.

Wilson, Carol Green. *Chinatown's Quest: The Life and Adventure of Donaldina Cameron.* Stanford, CA: Stanford University Press, 1958.

SUGGESTED READING:

Wilson, Carol Green. *Chinatown Quest: 100 Years of the Donaldina Cameron House, 1874–1974.* San Francisco: California Historical Society, 1974.

COLLECTIONS:

Papers relating to the Woman's Occidental Board of Foreign Mission are housed at the Donaldina Cameron House, San Francisco; personal papers held privately by her niece, Caroline Bailey.

Amanda Carson Banks,
Vanderbilt Divinity School

Julia
Margaret
Cameron

Cameron, Julia Margaret

(1815–1879)

*British Victorian portrait photographer who was one of the most prominent figures in the history of photography. Born Julia Margaret Pattle in Calcutta, India, on June 11, 1815; died in Kalutara, Ceylon (now Sri Lanka), on January 26, 1879; one of ten children, and third of six daughters, of James Pattle (an official of the East India Company) and Adeline (de l'Etang) Pattle; great-aunt of Virginia Woolf and *Vanessa Bell; educated in France and England; married Charles Hay*

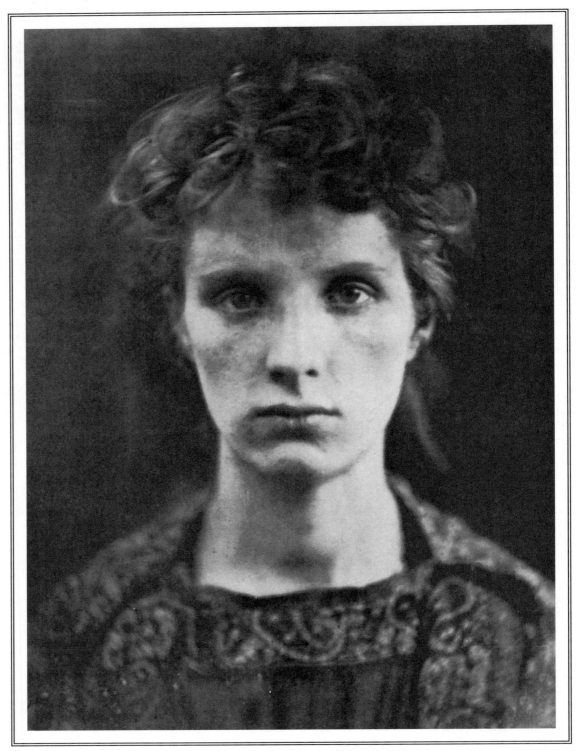

Cassiopeia.
*Photograph by
Julia Margaret
Cameron
(1866).*

Cameron (an official in the British Civil Service), in 1838; children: five sons and one daughter.

Julia Margaret Cameron, one of the most prominent figures in the history of photography, was one of ten children of James and **Adeline**

Pattle, an official of the East India Company. Although considered quite plain when compared to her five beautiful sisters, she was to be known for her abundance of wit and her extraordinary gift for capturing the beauty in others. Her career in photography, however, was something of an afterthought. In 1838, she married Charles Hay Cameron, a widower twenty years her senior, and ten years later moved with him to England, living first in London, then Putney, and finally settling on the Isle of Wight in a house next door to Alfred and *Emily Tennyson. In addition to raising six children, Cameron was active in philanthropic and artistic activities. As a member of the Society for Promoting Knowledge of Art, she used her home, "Dimbola," to entertain some of the most prominent scientists, artists, and literary figures of Victorian England.

Cameron did not take up photography until the age of 49, after receiving a camera and photographic equipment from her married daughter. She transformed a chicken coop into a studio and a coal bin into a darkroom and, by 1864, had produced her first portrait of a young girl, which she inscribed "Annie, my first success." In a biographical fragment, "Annals of My Glass House" (published in *The Photographic Journal*, 1927), Cameron elaborated on this early effort: "From the first moment," she wrote, "I handled my lens with a tender ardour. . . . I longed to arrest all beauty that came before me." She first displayed her work in 1864, at the 10th Exhibition of the Photographic Society in London. Many shows followed in London as well as in Edinburgh, Dublin, Berlin, Paris, and Vienna.

Cameron focused her camera on the luminaries of her social circle, including Sir John Herschel, Sir Henry Taylor, Charles Darwin, Henry Wadsworth Longfellow, Robert Browning, and *Ellen Terry. Most sat for her more than once, enduring long hours and uncomfortable postures. Tennyson, who posed up to 50 times, once remarked to Longfellow who was embarking on his first sitting, "You'll have to do whatever she tells you. I'll come back soon and see what is left of you." Cameron's soft-focused portraits, usually large, mostly heads or half-lengths (never full-lengths), are considered some of the finest contributions to early photography in England. Some critics compared her portraits to the paintings of Velasquez and Rembrandt, and one critic called her a "Whistler in photography."

Cameron was less successful with her allegorical, religious, and genre pictures, which were criticized harshly by professional photographers as being beyond the limits of the medium. She often posed her grandchildren with swans' wings and crowns of flowers, or draped parlor maids as Madonnas. She once pulled an unsuspecting tourist into service as Guinevere and on another occasion induced her husband to pose as Merlin in a hollow tree. Many works were influenced by the artists of the time, mostly Pre-Raphaelites such as Edward Burne-Jones, Dante Gabriel Rossetti, G.F. Watts, and Holman Hunt. Her photographs, in turn, influenced the work of these painters. It is believed that Cameron used two different, poorly defining landscape lenses, constructed for her by Sir John Herschel, to create her characteristic out-of-focus pictures. She may have also placed a piece of glass between the paper and the negative to achieve the soft, fuzzy effect she sought and for which she was often criticized by those who did not comprehend her intent.

Cameron illustrated Tennyson's *Idylls of the King*, which was published in different formats in 1874 and 1875. Decades after her death, America was introduced to her work through the periodical *Camera Work*, which published some photographs in a 1913 publication. Two years later, in 1915, her works were exhibited at the Albright Art Gallery in Buffalo, New York.

In 1875, after the death of her only daughter, Cameron and her husband embarked for Ceylon (later Sri Lanka), where four of their sons were employed. Years later, in 1919, Cameron's great-niece *Virginia Woolf, who held her great-aunt in high regard but also considered her somewhat of an eccentric, envisioned a burlesque with Cameron as the leading character. An entry in Woolf's diary contains notes on how her aunt's departure for Ceylon might appear in the little drama. ". . . & the last sight of Aunt Julia is on board ship, presenting porters with large photographs of Sir Henry Taylor and the Madonna in default of small change." In Ceylon, Cameron continued to photograph, mostly the native inhabitants. She died there in 1879, supposedly uttering the word "Beautiful!" with her last breath.

SOURCES:

Lukitsh, Joanne. *Cameron: Her Work and Career.* Rochester, NY: International Museum of Photography at George Eastman House, 1986.

Newhall, Beaumont and Nancy, eds. *Masters of Photography.* NY: Castle Books, 1958.

Williams, Val. *The Other Observers.* London, England: Virago Press, 1986.

Barbara Morgan,
Melrose, Massachusetts

Camille (1824–1847).

See Plessis, Alphonsine.

Cammermeyer, Margarethe

(1942—)

American chief nurse of the Washington National Guard who, discharged from duty on the grounds that she was a homosexual, dedicated herself to changing the military's prejudiced policy against gays. Name variations: Grethe Cammermeyer. Born in March 1942 in Oslo, Norway; daughter of a renowned neuropathologist and a nurse; became a U.S. citizen in 1960; University of Maryland, B.S., 1963; graduated from the Army Student Nurse Program, 1963; University of Washington, M.A., 1976, Ph.D., 1991; married Harvey Hawken, on August 14, 1965 (divorced 1980); lives with Diane Divelbess (a university professor and artist); children: four sons.

In March 1942, Margarethe Cammermeyer was born in Oslo, Norway, the eldest in a family of four children. Her mother, a nurse, and her father, a neuropathologist, were members of the underground anti-Nazi resistance during World War II. Margarethe was only months old when her mother packed her into the baby carriage with guns, hidden beneath her blankets, for distribution to resistance members. She was a young child in 1945 when she watched American soldiers marching through town, liberating Oslo. From that time forward, she had a love of things American, particularly the country's military. In 1951, a year after her father was offered a position in Washington, D.C., the family received permission from Norway to immigrate to America.

Cammermeyer entered the pre-med program at the University of Maryland in the fall of 1959, intending to become a doctor like her father and his father before him. But toward the end of her sophomore year, a graduate from the Army Student Nurse Program walked into a bowling party Cammermeyer was attending, and Cammermeyer, recalling the high esteem in which she had held the women of the Norwegian Resistance, knew that she wanted to serve her new country as a military nurse. In 1960, she became a U.S. citizen and joined the Army Student Nurse Program in 1961, graduating two years later. Cammermeyer continued her training at the Brooke Army Medical Center, Fort Sam Houston, then worked in a Georgia army hospital in the gynecology and obstetrics ward, before being sent to a U.S. base in Nuremberg, Germany, in March of 1964. There, she met a tank commander named Harvey Hawken, whom she married in Nuremberg on August 14, 1965.

After the couple returned to the United States in 1966, Hawken was assigned to duty in Vietnam. Cammermeyer volunteered for service there, both because she felt a duty to do so and to be close to her husband. From February 1967 to May 1968, she served in Vietnam during a period of some of the most intense fighting. She remarked of her efforts as head nurse of an intensive care ward: "My work was a mix of contradictions. I helped save men with such massive injuries that I can only wonder if they hated me for it. When we did make them 100 percent better, we were the agents that propelled them back out into combat and possible death. When we couldn't save them, I was there with them when they died." At one point, Cammermeyer risked disciplinary action when she refused orders to leave the wounded behind. For her efforts in Vietnam, she was awarded a Bronze Star.

Once they returned to the United States, Margarethe and Harvey lived on land they had purchased in Washington State near Puget Sound. Margarethe raised their four sons during the next decade, served as nurse at a military hospital, and did graduate work. She was forced to leave the military in 1968 with the birth of her first son because women were then not allowed to have dependents under 16 years of age. The regulation was changed in 1972, and Cammermeyer returned to the military. Specializing in neuroscience nursing with a focus on epilepsy and cognitive impairment, she earned her masters degree from the University of Washington in 1976. Although friends considered Harvey and Margarethe the perfect couple, strain on the marriage increased as Harvey resented the amount of time his wife dedicated to her work. They were divorced in 1980, and custody of the children was awarded to Harvey. Devastated, Cammermeyer chose not to contest the decision, fearing a nasty court battle.

She took a position in San Francisco at a veteran's hospital, and in 1985 the Veterans Administration presented her their Nurse of the Year award while the Women's Veterans Association named her Woman of the Year. To be near her sons, Cammermeyer returned to Washington, where, promoted to colonel, she was chief nurse of the Washington State National Guard. On July 4, 1987, she met Diane Divelbess, a university professor and artist. The relationship that developed between them took Cammermeyer to a new awareness in her life. "My relationship with Diane," she said, "evolved out of a mutual caring, trust, respect, and enjoyment of being together. It just felt right, and that rightness made me realize I am a lesbian." Cammermeyer did not expect this personal realization to impact her professional life. "At the time," said Cammermeyer, "there was not much talk about gays in the military. I never thought I'd have to choose between being honest and serving my country. I didn't think I'd lose my military career because of prejudice and hate."

Since joining the army in 1961, she had dreamed about becoming national chief nurse and an army general. The only thing standing between her and the new post was the War College, which she would need to attend, and which required a Top Secret security clearance. Her interview took place on April 28, 1989. During the session, she was asked a routine question about homosexuality and replied honestly, with the four words that were to change her life and make news across the nation: "I am a lesbian." The 45-minute session became an interrogation that went on for five hours.

She was notified seven months later that her security clearance had been withdrawn and that discharge was under consideration. Cammermeyer continued her work as chief nurse of the Washington National Guard while her lawyers awaited the army's next move. Although terrified of possible rejection and the shame they might feel, she decided to tell her sons, at least in part to warn them of the potential battle and publicity that her honesty with the government might yet provoke. Each son said that they already knew and had no conflict with her sexual identity. During the next few years, all four came to live with her in the home she shared with Diane.

Cammermeyer, a nearly three-decade army nurse with impeccable credentials, received a telegram on March 18, 1991, informing her that the army would recommend her discharge and that she could plead her case at an administrative hearing. She received her Ph.D. in nursing from the University of Washington two days later. On July 14, 1991, her legal defense team went into the hearing intending to reveal the army's anti-gay policy as irrational and founded exclusively on prejudice, and to illuminate the long history of gays and lesbians who served with honor in the military.

Witnesses testified that, even after Cammermeyer's unit learned that she was a lesbian, no breakdown in unit cohesion or morale occurred. The 1988 Defense Personnel Security Research and Education Center (PERSEREC) Report, commissioned by the Defense Department, was discussed in length by a former assistant secretary of defense, who remarked on the report's conclusion that the army's policy on homosexuals was founded upon prejudice and stereotype. The report—finding no evidence to uphold the military's claim that homosexuals presented poor security risks, nor that homosexuals were disruptive to the military's order, discipline, or morale—suggested that the policy should be extinguished. Last to testify was Cammermeyer:

> There are times when change can be made only by someone stepping forth, being willing perhaps to expose themselves and their vulnerability so that others become aware of the fact that there are differences in the world. So that people will understand these differences are okay and don't affect our ability to be part of an organization or to make a contribution. And so, I choose . . . to come before you and my family, and be vulnerable in hopes that perhaps it can influence making a change and allowing us to serve as we have in the past and will continue to do in the future.

The board deliberated for an hour. Its decision read: "Colonel Cammermeyer has proved to be a great asset [to the military] and the medical profession as a whole. She has consistently provided superb leadership. . . . Notwithstanding, the board finds Colonel Margarethe Cammermeyer is a homosexual." Cammermeyer was the highest ranking officer ever discharged for homosexuality.

Cammermeyer's last day in the military was June 11, 1992, on which she turned in a 300-page document, which was to become what writer **Laurie Lindop** has called "the definitive document on standard operating procedures for military nurses." That year, a report detailing the cost of the military's anti-gay policy was released from the U.S. government, which had spent $494 million to train and discharge gays and lesbians between 1980 and 1991. The cost of investigations against homosexuals, not included in this amount, increased the sum significantly, amounting to $2.5 million for the year 1990 alone.

In 1992, Cammermeyer was preparing to fight the policy in civil court when the newly elected president Bill Clinton informed her of his hope to lift the military's ban against homosexuals. Clinton prodded Congress to reevaluate the policy in 1993, and as Cammermeyer met individually in Washington with in excess of 50 senators she asked them to study the facts put forth in the PERSEREC report and to support lifting the ban on homosexuals with their votes. When it became apparent that there would not be enough votes to support lifting the ban, the Clinton administration agreed to a compromise, what is known as the "don't ask, don't tell, don't pursue" policy. No longer would recruits and military members asking for security clearances be asked if they were homosexuals. If, however, a recruit or military member makes a disclosure of their homosexuality, they could be investigated and discharged. Said Cammermeyer of the new "don't-ask-don't-tell" policy, "It's a travesty. It shows how incredibly backward our approach to human rights is."

Cammermeyer's case challenging the ban on homosexuals in the military and requesting reinstatement was tried in the spring of 1994, and the Pentagon was ordered by a federal judge to reinstate her. After Cammermeyer had been separated from the military for 25 months, Judge Zilly ruled that the military's policy by which her discharge had been justified was unconstitutional and "based solely on prejudice. Prejudice, whether founded on unsubstantiated fears, cultural myths, stereotypes or erroneous assumptions cannot be the basis of a discriminatory classification." This ruling affected the military's old ban on homosexuals that was in force at the time of Cammermeyer's discharge, not the new "don't-ask-don't-tell" policy. In July of 1994, Margarethe Cammermeyer reported back to the National Guard and was met by a standing ovation from her unit.

She served as chief nurse of the 164th MASH until May of 1996 and retired from the military on March 23, 1997. The Justice Department denied a motion to vacate the 1994 decision in November of 1997, and Cammermeyer's ruling became case law.

Cammermeyer was the 1995 Distinguished Alumna from the University of Washington School of Nursing, was recognized by the National Organization of Women with the Women of Power award, and received the Honorary Human Rights Award from the American Nurses Association, the Humanitarian Award by the Privacy Fund, and The *Hannah Solomon award from the Jewish Women League.

In the 1998 elections, Cammermeyer challenged U.S. Representative Jack Metcalf, R-Langley. After she announced her intentions to run, Metcalf let it be known that he had a "lot of respect for Grethe Cammermeyer" and would run against her politically not personally. Although she was not successful in her bid, Cammermeyer promised her supporters that she would find other ways to continue to serve her country.

Cammermeyer's autobiography, *Serving in Silence* (1994), was cited as an Outstanding Book on the subject of human rights in North America by the Gustavus Myers Center and was recognized by the National Education Association. The book was the basis of an award-winning television movie of the same name, which starred **Glenn Close**. **Barbra Streisand** served as an executive producer for the movie, which took three Emmy awards (Glenn Close for Best Actress, **Judy Davis** for Best Supporting Actress, and **Alison Cross** for Best Teleplay), three Golden Globe awards, and the prestigious Peabody award.

In her autobiography, Cammermeyer reviews the reasons she joined the U.S. military:

> My belief—born in my earliest years living across from Nazi headquarters—that there are values worth dying for, now found expression. The idea of liberty and justice for all is worth dying for—and worth living twenty-six years in uniform for. It's not an esoteric concept. American soldiers, many who gave their lives, rescued me and my parents, our town and country, from Nazi conquest and tyranny. Though I was only three when our liberation came, it was and remains the event that made the rest of my life, my freedom and my family's freedom, possible.

SOURCES:
Cammermeyer, Margarethe. *Serving in Silence*. NY: Penguin, 1994.
Clutter, Stephen. "Cammermeyer Challenges Metcalf," in *Seattle Times*, November 18, 1997.
Lindop, Laurie. *Champions of Equality*. NY: Twenty-first Century Books, 1997.
Mills, Kim I. "Lesbian Colonel No Longer Silent about Military Policy," in *The* [New London] *Day*. January 3, 1995.
Sanborn, Margaret. "Viking Welcomes to List Lesbian Army Nurse," in *Publisher's Weekly*. June 6, 1994.

RELATED MEDIA:
Serving in Silence, starring Judy Davis and Glenn Close, produced by Barbra Streisand and Glenn Close, 1995.

Campan, Jeanne Louise Henriette (1752–1822)

French educator and companion of Marie Antoinette.
Born Jeanne Louise Henriette Genet or Genest in Paris, France, in 1752; died in 1822; daughter of M. Genet or Genest (first clerk in the foreign office); married M. Campan; children: one son.

Because of her father's position as first clerk in the French foreign office, even though he was not a wealthy man, Jeanne Louise Henriette Campan grew up in cultivated society. By age 15, she could speak English and Italian, in addition to her mother tongue, and had gained such a high reputation for her erudition that she was appointed reader to the aunts of Louis XVI: *Adelaide (1732–1800), *Victoire (1733–1799), *Sophie (1734–1782), and *Louise Marie (1737–1787). At court, Campan was a widespread favorite, and when she married M. Campan, son of the secretary of the royal cabinet, the king gave her an annuity of 5,000 livres as dowry. Soon after, she was appointed first lady of the bedchamber by *Marie Antoinette, and she continued to be her faithful attendant until she was forcibly separated from Marie after the royal family attempted to escape Paris on June 20, 1792.

Though Madame Campan survived the Terror, her husband's failing health took most of her annuity. Determined to support herself, she established a girls' boarding school at St. Germain. The institution prospered and was patronized by *Hortense de Beauharnais, whose influence led to the appointment of Jeanne Campan as superintendent of the academy founded by Napoleon at Écouen for the education of the daughters and sisters of Legion of Honor members. Napoleon was pleased with the place accorded to domestic economy in the education of the girls. At Écouen, the pupils underwent a complete training in all branches of housework.

Campan held this post until it was abolished at the restoration of the Bourbons. Retiring to Mantes, she spent the rest of her life there with close friends, but she was saddened by the loss of her only son and by the lies circulated about her because of her connection with the Bonapartes. She died in 1822, leaving the valuable *Mémoires sur la vie privée de Marie Antoinette, suivis de souvenirs et anecdotes historiques sur les règnes de Louis XIV.-XV.* (Paris, 1823); a treatise *De l'Education des Femmes;* and one or two small instructive works, noted for their clear, natural style.

SUGGESTED READING:
Flammermont, Jules. *Les Mémoires de Madame de Campan.* Paris, 1886.

Campanini, Barbara (1721–1799)

Italian ballerina. Name variations: La Barbarina; Barberina Campanini; Countess de Campanini or Comtesse de Campanini. Born in Parma, Italy, in 1721; died in Germany on June 7, 1799; studied with Rinaldi Fossano, a Neapolitan comic dancer; married Carlo Luigi Cocceji also known as Charles-Louis de Cocceji (son of Frederick the Great's chancellor), in 1749 (separated 1759, divorced 1788).

Barbara Campanini arrived in France at age 16 and soon became the mistress of the Prince de Carignan, inspector general of the Paris Opéra. Two years later, in July 1739, she made her debut there in *Les Fêtes d'Herbe, ou Les Talents Lyriques.* With *Marie-Anne Cupis de Camargo retired and *Marie Sallé about to withdraw, it was an auspicious time. Successful in her Paris debut, Campanini next appeared in *Zaide, Reine de Grenade,* and *Momus Amoureux.* Known for her precision, elevation, and the acrobatic style of the Italian school, she executed her *entrechat huit* with ease. La Barbarina was soon adored and spoiled, and just as soon was said to be demanding.

Engaged for Covent Garden, she made her first appearance on October 25, 1740, and became an immediate favorite of the royal family: George II and *Caroline of Ansbach and the princesses *Amelia Sophia (1711–1786), *Caroline Elizabeth (1713–1757), and *Louise of England (1724–1751). For the next year, Campanini made a number of appearances at Covent Garden, Académie Royal, Versailles, and the Smock Alley Theatre in Dublin; she also became the mistress of Lord Arundel, the Marquis de Thebouville, and the Duc de Durfort. The French sent their chief designer Jean-Nicolas Servandoni to England to fetch her back, but when she arrived in France, she was quickly apprised of the ascent of **Marianne Cochois** in the eyes of the new director. Campanini returned to England for another 50 performances.

Frederick the Great, determined to foster an opera company to rival that of France, engaged Barbara Campanini as *première danseuse* for the 1744 season. Campanini was inaugurating a new affair with Lord Stuart Mackenzie, however, and was just as determined not to arrive on the stipulated date; she had to be escorted from the Austrian border to Berlin under guard. By the time she made her debut on May 13, all was forgiven. Frederick backed her with a corps de ballet and a three-year contract with the proviso

Jeanne Louise Campan

that she was not to marry. The 23-year-old La Barbarina was the hit of Berlin and granted the title, Comtesse de Campanini. By then, she was also Frederick's mistress as well as the secret wife of the son of the king's chancellor, Charles-Louis de Cocceji. Campanini eventually separated from her count but, with Frederick's approval, kept her title and settled down for a quiet life, endowing a convent for impoverished women, the Poor Ladies of Good Birth, and becoming its prioress until her death on June 7, 1799. Marianne Cochois filled the void for Frederick and would be Berlin's esteemed ballerina for the next ten years.

SOURCES:
Migel, Parmenia. *The Ballerinas: From the Court of Louis XIV to Pavlova*. NY: Macmillan, 1972.

Campbell, Beatrice Stella (1865–1940).

See Campbell, Mrs Patrick.

Campbell, Betty Becker (1903–1989).

See Becker-Pinkston, Elizabeth.

Campbell, Charlotte C. (1914–1993)

American medical mycologist and university professor. Born Charlotte Catherine Campbell in Winchester, Virginia, on December 4, 1914; died in Boston, Massachusetts, on October 8, 1993; daughter of Philip Edward and Mary (Ambrose) Campbell; attended Blackstone College, Virginia, 1934, and Ohio State University; graduated B.S., George Washington University, 1951; earned a diploma in medical technology from the University of Pennsylvania Hospital in Philadelphia; never married; no children.

Served as medical technician in Winchester (1938–41); taught during World War II at Walter Reed Army Institute of Research, Washington, D.C. (1941–48), becoming chief of medical mycology (1948); an outstanding pioneer in the field of medical mycology, was on the faculty of Harvard University (1962–73) and promoted to full professor (1970) despite the fact that she had never been awarded a doctorate.

Born and raised in rural Winchester, Virginia, Charlotte Catherine Campbell rode horseback from her family's farm to get to the local one-room seven-grade country school. Her native intelligence and leadership abilities were apparent in her early years, when she was elected the first female class president at Handley High School in Winchester. Two weeks after her graduation, Charlotte's father died, placing the family under severe financial pressure during the Great Depression. Unable to afford a college ed-

ucation, Campbell had no choice but to find work to support herself. Her first job was as a laboratory assistant in her hometown hospital. She was, however, focused on a career in medical research and continued to upgrade her professional skills, eventually earning a diploma in medical technology from the University of Pennsylvania Hospital in Philadelphia.

In 1941, with war already raging in several parts of the world, Campbell became an instructor in bacteriology and medical mycology at the Walter Reed Army Institute of Research in Washington, D.C. Her job was to teach military officers about the threats to human health posed by fungal infections such as histoplasmosis. The field was a new one at the time, and during these years she became an expert on histoplasmosis and other fungal diseases, publishing the results of her research. By the time she retired almost four decades later, Campbell had published 126 articles in the most eminent scientific journals in her field. Because of the excellence of her wartime work, she was promoted in 1948 to become the head of the mycology section of the Walter Reed research facility.

Despite her busy schedule, Campbell took college courses in the 1940s and early 1950s, earning from George Washington University in 1951 the B.S. degree, "with honors," that economic pressures during the depression had denied her. To friends, she simply noted, "it took me 18 years to get the degree; it was a real effort." During the next decade, she upgraded the research at Walter Reed while continuing to pursue her own research agenda, which concentrated on cultivation of *Histoplasma capsulatum* in yeastlike tissue form as well as perfecting the antigenic analysis of the organism and developing a complement fixation test using the yeast phase antigen. The test developed by her during these years is now routinely used for serological diagnosis of histoplasmosis.

In 1962, with her scientific reputation internationally anchored, Charlotte Campbell left Walter Reed after more than two decades of achievement. Nobel laureate Dr. Thomas T. Weller of Harvard University convinced her to accept the offer of associate professorship in the Harvard University School of Public Health. Though she had never earned a doctorate, Campbell's world reputation as a research superstar followed her to Harvard, and she was soon the center of a large circle of admiring colleagues and friends. Over the next few years, she established an outstanding teaching and research program in her increasingly important area, a fact that brought further professional recognition in 1970 when she was promoted to the rank of full professor. With this promotion, she entered the small group of only 17 women to enjoy that high distinction in the 334 years of Harvard history up to that time. The next year, Charlotte Campbell received an honorary doctorate from Lowell Institute of Technology in Lowell, Massachusetts.

In 1973, Campbell left Harvard for a prestigious post at Southern Illinois University. Retirement from academic life in 1977 did not significantly slow her down as she continued to maintain a strong interest in research and worked on projects aimed at promoting world peace and social justice. Believing that intellectual exchanges could lessen the tensions of the Cold War, she served as the coordinator of the US/USSR Exchange Program in Microbiology from 1977 to 1982. In 1982, she moved back to Boston, turning her home on 120 Pembroke Street into a center for informal gatherings, political debates, and reunions of former colleagues and students. Despite the growing infirmities of age, in her last years Charlotte Campbell was intensely active in her community; she organized soup kitchens for the homeless and worked as a volunteer at Brigham and Women's Hospital and with battered women at a local shelter.

In the final years of her career, Campbell received numerous awards to honor her pioneering work in the field of medical mycology. These included the **Rhoda Benham** Award from the Mycology Society of America, the International Society for Human and Animal Mycology Award for distinguished contributions to the field, and an honorary doctorate in 1991 from Shenandoah University in her home state of Virginia. Governed by intense intellectual curiosity, Campbell ignored her frail health even in the last months of her life, undertaking a strenuous trip to Siberia and Lake Baikal with several Harvard scientists. Shortly before her death, she sold her Boston home and contributed the sizable profit from the sale to a graduate-student endowment in medical mycology at the Harvard School of Public Health. Her plan had been to return to her childhood home in Winchester to spend her final years in Virginia, but her final illness intervened, and Campbell died in Boston on October 8, 1993, of complications after open-heart surgery. Her funeral at Trinity Church on Boston's Copley Square was a time to celebrate her life as well as mourn her death. Countless friends, colleagues and former students were in attendance as the bagpipes played. According to her wishes,

Campbell's ashes were taken to Virginia and scattered over the farm in Winchester where she had grown up. In the words of a colleague and fellow scientist, she was "simply a gracious, insightful, humorous woman of deep humility who knew the meaning of the word 'friend.'"

SOURCES:

Saxon, Wolfgang. "Charlotte Catherine Campbell, 78, Ex-Professor and Expert on Fungi," in *The New York Times*. October 12, 1993, p. C19.

Tewari, Ram P. "Charlotte C. Campbell 1914–1993," in *Mycopathologia*. Vol. 130, no. 1. April 1995, pp. 1–2.

John Haag, Associate Professor, University of Georgia, Athens, Georgia

Campbell, Dorothy I. (1883–1945).

See Hurd, Dorothy Iona.

Campbell, Helen Stuart
(1839–1918)

American writer and sociologist. Name variations: Helen Stuart Weeks Campbell; wrote under the names Campbell, Weeks (her married name), and several pseudonyms, some of which were male. Born in Lockport, New York, on July 4, 1839; died in 1918; married a man named Weeks (divorced 1871).

Selected works: The Problem of the Poor *(1882);* The What-to-do Club *(1884);* Miss Melinda's Opportunity *(1886);* Prisoners of Poverty *(1886).*

Born in 1839, Helen Stuart Campbell would contribute to the reform of 19th-century capitalism by addressing many of the social and economic problems facing women and the poor. Her career began during the Civil War when she started to write children's books under her married name, Weeks. In a move that was daring in her day, she divorced her husband in 1871. Her adult novels followed under a variety of pseudonyms, some of them male, until she settled into using the name Helen Stuart Campbell in the late 1870s. Also around this time, she began writing nonfiction, first in the emerging field of home economics. She published widely in newspapers and magazines and, from 1881 to 1884, served as literary editor of *Our Continent*, Philadelphia. Campbell's attention turned to the plight of women workers and the poor, and she published her best known work, *Prisoners of Poverty*, in 1886.

One of the primary points made in Campbell's articles concerned the impossibility of women meeting their financial needs given their meager wages; by reporting average earnings and analyzing budgets, she revealed a harsh economic reality for women, documenting that women's wages were at most half that of men's, virtually without exception, while their financial needs, including housing and clothing, were often higher. For Campbell, the economic dilemma faced by women had moral repercussions, as economics forced women into a position of vulnerability in regard to men. Budding social scientists regarded Campbell's methodology as more emotionally than statistically based, but her work on women wage-earners represented sound enough investigative work to win her a prize from the American Economic Association in 1891.

In addition to her efforts for better wages among women, Campbell used her writing to address the need for occupational health and safety regulations. Her concerns over what she termed "nicotine poisoning" among tobacco industry workers were far ahead of her time. Campbell, who died in 1918, was an adherent to Edward Bellamy's utopian ideals.

Campbell, Kate (1899–1986)

Australian pediatrician of international renown. Born Kate Isabel Campbell at Hawthorn, Melbourne, in 1899; died on July 12, 1986; only daughter and third of four children of Janet Duncan (Mill) Campbell (a schoolteacher) and Donald Campbell (a shipping clerk); attended Methodist Ladies' College; University of Melbourne, MB BS, 1922, MD, 1924.

Born just before the turn of the century in Hawthorn, Melbourne, Kate Campbell was to maintain a dedication to children's health care that would lead to an internationally acclaimed career in pediatrics. Her parents were determined that their only daughter receive a good education, and it was important to her mother that Kate have access to an independent livelihood. Kate's schooling began at the primary school in Hawthorn, after which she attended the Methodist Ladies' College on scholarship. With her parents' support, she entered the University of Melbourne medical school (1917), again with a scholarship, where she was one of 26 women in a class of 160 men; this was an unusually large number of women for the era, due to the absence of men who were away at war.

After graduation with her MB BS in 1922, Campbell turned her interest to health problems of babies and young children, and she applied to the Royal Children's Hospital for her residency. The hospital, however, was unwilling to admit female doctors and resisted her application until finally pressured to appoint her. In addition to her work at the Royal Children's Hospital, Campbell served as a resident medical officer at the Royal Women's Hospital until 1927. With a concentration on young children, she studied for her doctorate in medicine, graduating in 1924 with her MD.

During the early stages of the Infant Welfare movement in Victoria of the 1920s, Campbell maintained a general medical practice in Essendon for ten years and became an important voice in health care for children. Appointed medical officer for the Victorian Baby Health Centres Association, she would hold the post for more than 40 years. Campbell lectured nurses, and her ideas have been credited with preventing the rigidity of Truby King methods from prevailing in Victoria. In 1929, she was appointed the University of Melbourne's inaugural lecturer in neo-natal pediatrics and would continue in this capacity until 1965.

In private practice as a Collins St. specialist in pediatrics (from 1937), Campbell quickly became a nationally acclaimed pediatrician known for her brilliant diagnostic skills. Called the doyen of pediatrics by one admiring colleague, she was consulted by other specialists who were facing particularly difficult cases. Together with *Vera Scantlebury Brown and A. Elizabeth Wilmot, Campbell authored the *Guide to the Care of the Young Child* for the Department of Health; the publication saw six editions between 1947 and 1972. In 1947, she was particularly pleased with her part in introducing unrestricted visiting in children's hospitals.

In 1951, the cause of *retrolental fibroplasia*, a disease that results in blindness of premature babies, was discovered by Campbell, and this important breakthrough brought international recognition upon publication of her study in the *Medical Journal of Australia*. In 1964, she shared the first *Encyclopaedia Britannica* award for medicine. Additional honors followed with an honorary LLD (Melbourne) in 1966 and, for her services to Australian medicine, the DBE in 1971. In her 80s, Campbell described her special interests as "the newborn infant, child welfare, the status of women." She died on July 12, 1986, after more than a half century of work on behalf of children's health.

Campbell, Mrs. Patrick (1865–1940)

One of the most celebrated English actresses who passed into literary history when George Bernard Shaw created the role of Eliza in Pygmalion *for her.*

Mrs.
Patrick
Campbell

Name variations: Beatrice Tanner; Stella Campbell; Stella Tanner. Born Beatrice Rose Stella Tanner on February 9, 1865; died in Pau, France, on April 9, 1940; daughter of John and Maria Louisa Romanini Tanner; formal schooling at private schools, begun when she was ten, was erratic and ended when was 13; married Patrick Campbell (d. 1900), on June 21, 1884; married George Cornwallis-West, April 6, 1914 (separated); children: (first marriage) Alan Urquhart (b. 1885); Stella Tanner Campbell (b. 1886, an actress).

Made debut as Marie Graham in In His Power *with the Anomalies Dramatic Club of Norwood (1886), then as a French modiste in* Duty, *as Marie de Fontanges in* Plot and Passion *and as Alma Blake in* The Silver Shield *(all 1886); joined the Frank Green Company playing on tour as Lynne Loseby in* Bachelors *(1888–89); toured with the Millicent-Bandmann-Palmer Company as Rachel Denison in* Tares; *joined Ben Greet's Woodland Company for a season, playing a variety of classical and modern roles, as Rosalind in* As You Like It, *as Olivia in* Twelfth Night, *as Helena in* A Midsummer Night's Dream, *as the Princess of France in* Love's Labour's Lost, *the title role in* ***Adrienne Lecouvreur**, *as Lady Teazle in* The School for Scandal, *as Millicent Boycott in* The Money Spinner, *as Alma Blake in* The Silver Shield *(1889–90); made London debut as Helen in* The Hunchback *(March 13, 1889); on tour in Shakespearean roles and as Queen Eglamour in* Love-in-a-Mist, *as Stella Maris in* A Buried Talent; *on tour with* A Village Priest *(1890); first major London success as Astrea in* The Trumpet Call *(1891–92); as Elizabeth Cromwell in* The White Rose, *as Tress Purvis in* Lights of Home *(1892); as Belle Hamilton in* The Black Domino; *first triumph as Paula in* The Second Mrs. Tanqueray *(1893) and on tour (1894); as Dulcie Larandie in* The Masqueraders; *as Kate Cloud in* John-a-Dreams; *title role in* The Notorious Mrs. Ebbsmith *(1895); title role in* Fedora *(1895); as Juliet in* Romeo and Juliet *(1896); as Audrie Lesden in* Michael and His Lost Angel *(1896); as Militza in* For the Crown, *the title role in* Magda, *as Lady Hamilton in* Nelson's Enchantress *(1897); as Lady Teazle in* The School for Scandal; *as the Ratwife and then as Rita Allmers in* Little Eyolf *(1896); as Ophelia in* Hamlet, *as Lady Macbeth in* Macbeth, *as Vera Carlyon in* Carlyon Sahib; *on tour in Germany and Amsterdam (1898); as Mélisande in* Pelléas and Mélisande; *as Nanoya in* The Moonlight Blossom, *as the peasant girl in* The Sacrament of Judas, *as Sybil Temple-Martin in* The Canary *(1899); title role in* Mrs. Jordan; *on tour in repertory, as Percinet in* The Fantasticks, *as Hilda Daventry in* Mr. and Mrs. Daventry *(1900); title role in* Mariana, *as Clara Sang in* Beyond Human Power, *in first American tour in repertory (1901–02); as Beata in* The Joy of Living; *as Jeannie Halston in* Aunt Jeannie; *title role in* Undine *(1903) as the Queen in* Ruy Blas, *as Theodosia Hemming in* Warp and Woof, *as the Queen of Spain in* The Queen's Romance, *as Mélisande in* Pelléas and Mélisande *(opposite Sarah Bernhardt playing Pelléas); second American tour (1904), including the role of Zoraya in* The Sorceress; *(with Sarah Bernhardt) on tour in England, Scotland and Ireland with* Pelléas and Mélisande

(1905); as the Countess of Ellingham in The Whirlwind, *as Margaretta Sinclair in* The Macleans of Bairness, *as Greeba in* The Bondsman *(1906); title role in* Hedda Gabler; *third American tour including as new plays Von Hofmannsthal's adaptation of Sophocles'* Electra *and* The Moon of Yamato *(1907); as Phyllis Mortimore in* The Thunderbolt, *as Deirdre in* Deirdre of the Sorrows, *and the title role in* Lady Windemere's Fan *(in Dublin); on tour with* Electra *and* Deirdre *(1908); as Olive in* Olive Latimer's Husband, *as Fabia Sumner in* His Borrowed Plumes, *as Mierris in* False Gods, *and in* A Russian Tragedy *(1909); fourth American tour (winter–spring, 1910); title role in* Lady Patricia, *toured in music halls as Olga Weather in* The Bridge, *in* Bella Donna *(1911); as Leonora in* The Adored One *(1913); as Eliza Doolittle in* Pygmalion *(in London, then in New York and on a fifth American tour, 1914–15); in* The Law of the Sands *in London and on tour (1916–17); as Therese Bonnet in* Pro Patria, *as Madame La Grange in* The Thirteenth Chair *(1917); as* ***George Sand** *in* Madame Sand, *and revival of* Pygmalion *for British troops in Germany (1920); as* Hedda Gabler *(1922); toured the British provinces in repertory including* Voodoo *(1922–25); as Adela Rivers in* The Adventurous Age *(New York, 1927); returned to England touring in the title role in* Madame Kuranda *(1927); as Mrs. Alving in* Ghosts *(single performance, London, 1928); as Ella Rentheim in* John Gabriel Borkman; *as Anastasia Rakonitz in* The Matriarch *(1929); toured the States, where she appeared in one film and gave isolated performances in* Ghosts *(Los Angeles and San Francisco, 1930); small role in* The Sex Fable *(New York, 1931); as Clytemnestra in Sophocles'* Electra *(New York, 1932); in* The Thirteenth Chair *(brief English tour, 1932); Mrs. MacDonald in* A Party *(New York, 1933).*

Films: The Dancers *(First National, 1930);* Riptide *(MGM, 1934);* Outcast Lady *(MGM, 1934);* One More River *(Universal, 1934); (the pawnbroker)* Crime and Punishment *(Columbia, 1935).*

Mrs. Patrick Campbell was born Beatrice Rose Stella Tanner, the youngest of six children, on February 9, 1865; she was known as Stella. Her father John Tanner was a provider of military equipment for the British army in India but otherwise a ne'er-do-well, who, though frequently prosperous was just as frequently a failure and often absent. Her mother, born **Maria Louisa Romanini**, from whom Stella inherited her dark beauty, was the daughter of an Italian adventurer who had come to Bombay, where the couple were married in July 1852. Sent to private schools, Stella was soon bored with classwork, and her formal education ended when she was 13. Most of what she learned was derived from her association with her mother, her uncle Henry Tanner, and a one-year sojourn in Paris, when she was 15, during which she learned to speak French fluently enough to perform in the language in later years and developed a taste for luxury and sophisticated company that never left her.

In 1881, at age 17, Stella gave up a chance for a musical scholarship to marry a young man named Patrick Campbell by whom she was already pregnant. A handsome libertine like her father, Campbell drifted from one occupation to another and, after siring two children, migrated to the colonies virtually abandoning his family. His young wife, having no other means of earning a living and having experienced some success at dramatic readings, went on the stage to support her children. To assure her Victorian contemporaries of her respectability, Stella performed as Mrs. Patrick Campbell, inadvertently memorializing her shadowy husband for all time.

Mrs. Pat, as she came to be known by her contemporaries, made her debut on the stage with the Anomalies Dramatic Club of Norwood in a play entitled *In His Power,* replacing the star who had fallen ill. The success of her debut decided Campbell on an acting career, and she immediately appeared in other plays for the Anomalies Company. In 1888, she secured a contract, her first, with the Frank Green Company, opening in Liverpool on October 22 in *Bachelors.* This began a grueling tour of the provinces, which offered Campbell the opportunity to learn her craft by playing in a great variety of roles before vastly differing audiences. Moving on to Ben Greet's Woodland Company, she was soon playing Shakespearean roles, including Rosalind in *As You Like It* and Olivia in *Twelfth Night;* despite her total lack of experience with the Bard, she was a notable success. In the course of her association with Greet's company, she made her London debut in *The Hunchback* (March 3, 1889). In 1890, she had her first major London success in the role of Astrea in *The Trumpet Call,* which ran for 220 performances, and for which she received her first ovation.

Other roles on the London stage quickly followed, whereupon Mrs. Patrick Campbell became a star overnight in the role of Paula in Pinero's *The Second Mrs. Tanqueray* (1893), perhaps the first important "modern" play, inspired by the work of Henryk Ibsen, in English drama. That Campbell was the right actress for the role was beyond doubt when the play triumphed, even though the critics could see its faults. *The Second Mrs. Tanqueray* did more than make

Campbell a star; it opened up a new world of social contacts. She found herself sought after, not only by theatrical figures, artists and literati, but also by London "society," still wealthy and exclusive in the late Victorian age but willing to receive a fashionable actress. Mrs. Pat thoroughly enjoyed her new life and, in time, came to know everyone who mattered in England in the last years of Queen *Victoria's reign, from the prince of Wales to the playwright Oscar Wilde. She was said to have inspired Edward Burne-Jones to paint *The Vampire* and Rudyard Kipling to write the poem of the same name; the strange but talented Aubrey Beardsley drew her caricature, and she was thrice painted in oils, once by John Singer Sargent. Patrick Campbell, returning to London at this time as a penniless failure, was hard put to deal with the new situation and soon went back to South Africa, where, in 1900, he was killed in action during the Boer War.

For 20 years (1894–1914), Mrs. Patrick Campbell flourished as one of the great ladies of

Stella Campbell with her son Alan, known as Beo.

the English stage, appearing in no less than 43 roles, though not always to critical acclaim. In 1895, for example, she had a triumph in Pinero's *The Notorious Mrs. Ebbsmith*, appeared as Juliet to mixed reviews, and then failed in Sudermann's *Magda*. She then moved on to play Lady Teazle in Sheridan's *The School for Scandal*, only to turn to Ibsen to play the Ratwife and then Rita Allmers in the same production of *Little Eyolf*, performances that earned her universal praise. In 1898, she undertook a successful tour to Germany, where she was presented to the kaiser. Returning to London, Mrs. Campbell triumphed in *Pelléas et Mélisande*, the much-admired poetic drama by the Belgian playwright Maurice Maeterlinck, who was enjoying an enormous popularity at the time. Seeing her in this role, *The London Times* wrote that Mrs. Campbell was "an actress of rare physical grace, distinction and poetic charm," while the critic Walkley said of her performance that "the sheer physical pleasure of the thing is not to be described," and the playwright James Barrie wrote simply: "Mrs. Campbell is beyond comparison."

She expressed poetry with every gesture of her hands, and the objects which she touched in playing a scene suddenly seemed to gain immediate significance and life.

—John Gielgud

In 1900, Campbell undertook the responsibilities of manager and, at the Royalty Theater, staged a number of plays by a variety of dramatists, including both writers of traditional theater pieces as well as the practitioners of the new drama of social significance spawned by the Ibsen craze: Sudermann, Maeterlinck, Björnson, Echegaray, and Rostand. In 1901, Mrs. Pat made her first visit to America for six months of repertory in which she had an immediate and triumphant success in Chicago and New York. Everywhere she was taken up by high society, pursued by the press and admired by the critics. The following year, she returned to America for a second tour.

Perhaps the greatest triumph of Campbell's career occurred when the great French tragedienne *Sarah Bernhardt undertook (at age 60) the role of the youthful Pelléas in Maeterlinck's *Pelléas et Mélisande* and chose Mrs. Pat to play his beloved Mélisande. Thereafter, Campbell undertook to appear in several of Bernhardt's successes, among them *Fédora*, which she had to leave after a few weeks because of the strain that the part placed on her voice. Campbell's friendship with Bernhardt

was close, and she visited the great French actress a few days before her death in 1923.

Along the way, Campbell had her share of love affairs and close relationships with various men. At a celebration after the opening of *His Borrowed Plumes* on June 6, 1909, Campbell met George Cornwallis-West, the man who would become her second husband. At the time, he was the second husband of Lady *Jennie Jerome Churchill** and stepfather of Winston Churchill. Resentful of his wife's fame and the fact that she had far more money than he, Cornwallis-West had gradually edged into infidelity, and Mrs. Campbell was not the first of his outside interests. While pouring out his heart to her, he did not seem to notice that Campbell was similar to his wife and not much younger. Disappointed in her current theatrical venture and mindful of the gossip that was beginning to circulate around this affair, Mrs. Pat abruptly decided on an American tour in January 1910. With no engagement arranged and badly in need of money, she secured a turn in vaudeville, offering as her "act" a 20-minute Russian drama called *Expiation*. To everyone's surprise, she was an instant hit with her new audience, and Edward Albee, head of the circuit, booked her for ten weeks at her rather steep terms of $1,500 per week.

Returning to England, Campbell continued her relationship with Cornwallis-West, all the while becoming increasingly involved with the Anglo-Irish playwright, George Bernard Shaw. The greatest fruit of this latter relationship was the comedy *Pygmalion*, which Shaw wrote for his inamorata on a dare in 1914. One of Shaw's best plays, *Pygmalion* had a long success with its reincarnation as a Broadway musical and Hollywood film, *My Fair Lady*. Although, at close to 50, Campbell was too old by 30 years for the part of a young cockney girl, she nevertheless had an astonishing success in the role, the critics being unanimous that she had brought it off. It was her last great triumph, and she owed it all to G.B.S. Through the years, Shaw wrote her some 128 love letters, some of which Campbell would publish in 1922, but the rest of which he forbade her to put into print while his wife was alive, admonishing her that he would not "play the horse to your Lady Godiva." A few years after Shaw's death in 1950, the relationship between the English-Italian actress and the Anglo-Irish playwright would be embodied in Jerome Kilty's play, *Dear Liar*, which was based on their correspondence. In 1914, Mrs. Patrick Campbell not only reached what was perhaps the peak of her career but at last married George Cornwallis-West.

Poster for Pygmalion, *starring Mrs. Patrick Campbell as Eliza Doolittle (1914).*

Poster for Pygmalion, *starring Mrs. Patrick Campbell as Eliza Doolittle (1914).*

Stella Campbell was famed for her wit and notorious for her bad temper. She detested people who were afraid of her and usually responded to them by attempting to intimidate them further. Theater managers, hoteliers, steamship captains, waiters and chefs were treated with equal disdain, and directors hated working with her and seldom agreed to do so a second time. In 1907, she stunned New York by being the first woman to smoke in public. On her second visit, there was a turntable just in front of the theater where rumbling streetcars reversed direction. Annoyed that her audiences might miss the dialogue, Mrs. Pat demanded and got three cartloads of tanbark unloaded by the city and spread in front of the theater to hold down the noise while she performed. Her cavalier attitude towards her fellow cast members was legendary, and her regard for her audiences was not much higher. She changed her lines at will and, when on the stage, performed to perfection or walked through her roles. Never one to stand on ceremony, even with a giant such as George Bernard Shaw, Mrs. Pat freely antagonized the easily antagonized playwright by adding a final line to his *Pygmalion* that completely changed the author's intended ending.

As she grew older, Campbell's testiness matured into a ripe eccentricity that people increasingly refused to take seriously and that made her appear to a younger generation as an endearing "character" from an era long past. Though her education was spotty, Campbell had a passion for reading—especially Milton, Longfellow, Whitman, Keats, Tennyson, and Baudelaire—was a gifted pianist, loved chess, and was a sharp card player. Frequently ill, even in her youth, her constant ailments and collapses forced her to take time out from her career simply to recuperate. Though close to her extended family, Campbell's second marriage was a failure, Cornwallis-West deserting her in 1919, while her relationship with her daughter, a sometime actress performing under the name **Stella Tanner Campbell**, was troubled. Eventually, they ceased to communicate at all. Her beloved son was killed at the front in 1918, but she remained close to her daughter's son Patrick.

The First World War was a watershed in the history of the Western world. Nothing was the same afterwards. Trends that had been avantgarde in 1910 were now in the mainstream, and those artists whose careers spanned both sides of the great divide were often the worse for it. Always game, Ms. Pat acquired an automobile, bobbed her hair, and sailed gallantly on, but with far less success. Obese, but still a presence, she starred in a London revival of *Hedda Gabler* after which she went on a long provincial tour (1922–25) in repertory with *Hedda, The Second Mrs. Tanqueray, Magda,* and a dreadful melodrama set in old Virginia, titled *Voodoo,* whose sole distinguishing feature was that it had a very young Paul Robeson playing a pivotal role. In these years, Campbell played throughout England, Scotland, Ireland, and Wales, and not al-

ways to full houses. Told that her performance as Hedda was a *tour de force,* she quipped "that, I suppose, is why I am always forced to tour." When the long and arduous *tournée* was finished, Campbell appeared in London in H.F. Maltby's *What Might Happen,* an engagement for which she slimmed down and, now 60, made a sincere effort to please. Dissatisfied with the play, however, in spite of good reviews, and increasingly at odds with its author, she soon took to walking through the performances, and the play lasted but two weeks. In November, Campbell sailed for America to present *The Adventurous Age.* "I'm out of a job," she told reporters upon her arrival. "London wants flappers and I can't flap." The production opened in January 1927 and was a disaster. Alexander Woolcott called it a "recklessly ill-advised and acutely embarrassing evening." The general consensus was that Mrs. Patrick Campbell was a pathetic and overweight caricature of the dazzling beauty who had captivated New York a quarter of a century before, and the play lasted a bare six weeks. Penniless, Campbell wired Shaw for passage and returned to England.

Still possessed of her magnificent voice, if not her figure, and still her vibrant, energetic and witty self, Campbell now took to the lecture circuit. When Shaw suggested that she organize a benefit for herself to raise some badly needed funds, she recognized that she had made far too many enemies in the London theater to expect much response. Meanwhile, she was asked to appear in a one-performance revival of *Ghosts* as a part of the celebration of the centenary of Ibsen's birth. Playing her son Oswald was a young actor named John Gielgud, who after this engagement remained one of her closest friends. Critics objected that she did not begin to emote until the third act during which, however, she worked her magic as of old. The same complaint followed the opening of a revival of Ibsen's *John Gabriel Borkman,* in which she was described as giving a marvelous performance in the second and fourth acts and a disgraceful one in the rest of the play. As penniless as ever, Campbell was considering cashing in her insurance in 1929, when she was suddenly offered what proved to be the last important original role of her career, that of Anastasia Rakonitz in G.B. Stern's *The Matriarch* based on his novel *The Tents of Israel.* Though far from a masterpiece, the play afforded Campbell a triumph. The production ran for 249 performances, enabling her to put her financial affairs in order and, perhaps more important, to reinstate herself as one of the great actresses of the English stage.

After the closing of *The Matriarch,* Campbell toured briefly as the mother in *Ghosts,* everywhere receiving plaudits, but, in 1930, with no further offers forthcoming, she decided to take her lecture tour to the United States. The coming of talking films had created havoc in Hollywood as some of its brightest stars, unable to speak suitably, fell by the wayside and studios turned to the stage for performers who knew how to speak dialogue. Thrilled to have these artistes—*Ethel Barrymore, *Constance Collier, *Ruth Chatterton, George Arliss—the studios treated them with deferential awe, even if some of the imports, like Mrs. Pat, were superannuated. Campbell arrived in Hollywood in mid-1930 and was given star treatment, but her first role in *The Dancers* was poorly written and most of her scenes were cut. Returning to the stage, in November 1930 Campbell secured an engagement to perform in *Ghosts* in Los Angeles and San Francisco, and then undertook a lengthy lecture tour beginning in Chicago. In June 1931, she was back in New York to play a small part in *The Sex Fable,* which failed and, in January, appeared in four matinees playing Clytemnestra to *Blanche Yurka's Electra in Sophocles' tragedy. Returning to England, Campbell toured briefly in *The Thirteenth Chair,* then returned to the States for another lecture tour, which she cut short to appear in the New York production of *A Party,* an English play about herself, thinly disguised as a Mrs. MacDonald, written by Ivor Novello. This may have been the first time in theatrical history for any actress to have portrayed herself in a stage play. Though the play was nonsense, Campbell received good reviews, and, armed with a contract from MGM, she set out once again to conquer Hollywood.

Campbell appeared in four films in 1934, but her performance as the pawnbroker in a modern-dress version of *Crime and Punishment* remains the only true film record of her as an artist. Used to creating character in one piece, Mrs. Pat found it difficult to perform in scenes totally out of chronological order. Out of her element in Hollywood society, she resorted to her traditional ploy of using outrageous behavior as a defense, pretending never to have heard of famous stars when introduced to them or, in the case of the celebrated American actress of her own vintage, Mrs. *Leslie Carter, asserting to a companion in the actress' presence, "I thought she was dead." Cultivating her image as a character, Campbell insisted on traveling everywhere with her Pekinese dogs to whom she gave absurd names (Wush-Wush, Moonbeam), and it is Mrs. Pat whom *Marie Dressler was obviously sati-

rizing when she played the faded but still salty actress Carlotta Vance in the 1933 film comedy *Dinner at Eight.* Famed critic Alexander Woolcott could only shake his head at Mrs. Campbell's Hollywood antics, quipping that she was like a sinking ship firing on its rescuers.

Leaving Hollywood permanently, Campbell returned to New York and, in the summer of 1938, was invited to appear in *The Thirteenth Chair* at a summer theater in Milford, Connecticut, for $400 per week. Opening night was a triumph. Campbell received a standing ovation, but she would never perform again. That autumn, she decided to leave America for France rather than England, eventually settling in Paris. After the Second World War broke out on September 1, 1939, she moved to Pau, a resort in the foothills of the Pyrenees from where she could flee the country more easily if need be. That spring, Campbell caught a cold that quickly developed into a serious pulmonary congestion. She died on April 9, 1940, at age 75, and was buried in an unmarked grave in the municipal cemetery of Pau.

There seems to be no question that Mrs. Patrick Campbell was potentially one of the great actresses of her time. Paul Shiunkman called her the "last of the theatrical immortals," ranking her with Bernhardt, *Eleanora Duse, and *Ellen Terry; James Agate even went so far as to class her with Bernhardt, Duse, Terry, *Réjane, and *Madge Kendal as one of the half-dozen greatest actresses of all time. Agate called her "the best tragic or emotional actress in the country," adding that "in the sheer acting sense, by which one means the marriage of spirit and technical means to convey that spirit, Mrs. Campbell has no rival on our stage." In actual fact, Mrs. Pat was rarely as great as she might have been, and there is no doubt that she lacked discipline in her work and an overall vision in her career, or that her greatness as an actress came more through instinct than through a conscious understanding of her craft. Graham Robertson described her life as "a record of talent thrown away, wasted time, lost opportunities." Richard Findlater compared her with her contemporary *Janet Achurch (1864–1916) as "another case of burnt-out promise," concluding that, "If only she could have *cared* more: if only, like Ellen Terry, she had ever thought of being *useful*: if only she had believed, just a bit more, in the theater."

SOURCES:
Findlater, R. *The Player Queens.* NY: Taplinger, 1977.
Peters, Margot. *Mrs. Pat: The Life of Mrs. Patrick Campbell.* NY: 1984.

Philadelphia Free Library, Theater Collection.

SUGGESTED READING:

Campbell, Mrs. Patrick. *My Life and Some Letters*. London: 1922.

Dent, Alan. *Bernard Shaw and Mrs. Patrick Campbell: Their Correspondence*. London: 1952.

Robert H. Hewsen, Professor of History,
Rowan University of New Jersey,
Glassboro, New Jersey

Campbell, Stella (1865–1940).

See Campbell, Mrs. Patrick.

Campoamor, Clara (1888–1972)

Spanish lawyer, politician, and feminist at the time of Spain's Civil War. Born in Madrid, Spain, on February 12, 1888; died on April 30, 1972, in Lausanne, Switzerland; daughter of Manuel Campoamor Martínez and Pilar Rodríguez Martínez.

A native of Madrid, Clara Campoamor was born to working-class parents on February 12, 1888. Her father, Manuel Campoamor Martínez, died during her childhood, leaving her mother, **Pilar Rodríguez Martínez**, to raise the family under difficult economic circumstances. Clara Campoamor worked as a seamstress and then for the Spanish postal service before obtaining a position as teacher of typewriting. She also worked as a secretary for the newspaper *La Tribuna* and translated French for a publishing house. In 1923, she finished a university diploma by taking evening classes and the following year earned a law degree. These were significant accomplishments, given the few women who even gained admission to Spanish universities.

Increasingly drawn to politics, Campoamor championed women's rights. Affiliating with the Spanish Social Party, she worked to improve conditions for women. When Manuel Primo de Rivera, dictator from 1923–1930, nominated her to join the Junta of the Ateneo, she refused and also turned down the Great Cross of Alphonso XII, another attempt by the regime to win her support. Active in legal and education circles, Campoamor was more interested in female suffrage and other women's rights than adherence to a political party. After Primo de Rivera fell and Alphonso XIII abdicated in 1931, Spaniards declared the Second Republic, and Campoamor won election to the Constituent *Cortes* (Assembly). While another prominent female deputy, *Victoria Kent, urged the Cortes to postpone dealing with the issue of female suffrage, Campoamor refused to wait. Trying to win female support, she founded the Feminine Republican Union. Her insistence that the Republic grant suffrage alienated many male deputies and left Campoamor isolated, even within her own party.

She failed to win reelection in 1933, but the Lerroux government made her director of social services. Campoamor served, however, under a rightist minister and soon resigned. In 1934, she was part of the investigating commission sent to Oviedo following the brutal suppression of the miners' strike. She attempted to stand for election in 1936 but no party would support her.

When the Civil War began in July 1936, Campoamor immediately went into exile. She published her account of events in Spain in 1937: *La révolution espagnole vue par une républicaine*. Along with many other Spanish exiles, Campoamor made her way to Argentina. She attempted to return to her country, but the Franco government refused to grant her residence. Despondent over the failure of the Second Republic and what had happened to Spain, Campoamor abandoned politics. Instead she translated French novels into Spanish and wrote several biographies, including one of *Juana Ines de la Cruz, the 17th-century Mexican poet and intellectual. Another request to return to Spain was denied in 1951. Campoamor moved to Switzerland in 1955, where she worked in the legal office of **Antoinette Quinche**, a marital lawyer and longtime friend. Campoamor was discouraged and yearned to return to her homeland. Nearly blind, she died from cancer on April 30, 1972. After her death in Lausanne, Campoamor's cremated remains were buried in San Sebastian.

SOURCES:

Campoamor, Clara. *Mi pecado mortal: el voto feminino y yo*. Barcelona: laSal, 1981.

Capel, R.M. *El sufragio femenino en la II República*. Granada: Ed. Universidad de Granada, 1975.

Kendall W. Brown,
Chair, Department of History,
Brigham Young University, Provo, Utah

Camps, Miriam (1916–1994)

*American state department official and author on international affairs. Born Miriam Camp in Lynn, Massachusetts, in 1916; died of lung cancer, age 78, in Little Abingdon, Cambridge, England, on December 30, 1994; sister of Paul R. Camp and **Margaret Schwartz**; earned degrees at Mount Holyoke and Bryn Mawr colleges; married William Anthony Camps (a classicist at Cambridge University), in 1953.*

Miriam Camps was the first woman to be vice chair of the U.S. State Department's Planning Council. Born Miriam Camp in Lynn, Massachusetts, in 1916, she studied at Mount Holyoke and Bryn Mawr before joining the State Department during World War II and working at the U.S. embassy in London. From 1947 to 1953, she worked for the State Department in Washington, D.C., then resigned to marry William Camps, a classicist at Cambridge University. Miriam Camps returned to the State Department from 1968 to 1970 as vice chair of the Planning Council. Her books included *Britain and the European Community* (1964), *What Kind of Europe?* (1965), and *European Unification in the Sixties* (1966).

Canal, Marguerite (1890–1978)

French composer and teacher, who was the first woman in France to conduct orchestral concerts. Born in Toulouse, France, on January 29, 1890; died in Cépet, France, on January 27, 1978; married Maxime Jamin.

Born into a musical family in Toulouse in 1890, Marguerite Canal revealed her musicality in her earliest years and began her studies at the Paris Conservatory in 1903. Under the direction of Paul Vidal, Canal proved to be an outstanding pupil, earning first prizes in harmony, piano accompaniment and fugue. Drawn to composition, she began to write songs, some of them to accompany her own poems. Her phenomenal talents were recognized in 1917 and 1918 when she became the first woman to conduct orchestral concerts in France (at a series held at the Palais de Glace). In 1919, she was appointed teacher of solfège (music theory) for singers at the Paris Conservatory, and the next year she won the Premier Grand Prix de Rome for her dramatic scene for voice and orchestra, "Don Juan."

In the early 1920s, most observers of the French musical scene predicted a significant future as a composer for Marguerite Canal. During these years, she married Maxime Jamin, who became the publisher of several of her most important compositions. One of her most moving works from this productive phase was the 1922 Sonata for Violin and Piano, which is in the grand lyrical tradition of Franck and Fauré. Many critics felt that this touching piece was very likely an autobiographical evocation of the emotional life of a young woman. Another chamber music work that elicited much favorable critical comment was *Spleen*, a 1926 com-

position for cello and small ensemble. A great number of Canal's most important songs were written at this time, many of them of great beauty and sensitivity, and set to some of the best works of French poetry, including Baudelaire and Verlaine. One of her most delicately crafted vocal works was the song cycle, *Amours tristes*, set to her own verse and that of other poets.

Although her teaching responsibilities kept her busy, Canal was able in the early 1920s to make considerable progress toward the completion of her most ambitious project to date, a full-scale opera. Based on a Jack London story, *Tlass Atka (Le pays blanc)* was an ambitious work, but unfortunately the pressure of her teaching responsibilities and personal turmoil (she eventually was to be divorced from her husband Maxime Jamin) precipitated an artistic crisis that led to a greatly diminished output. A number of half-finished works, including a *Requiem*, were not brought to final state and remain unpublished. She continued to compose into the 1940s, but it was clear that Canal had made a decision to concentrate on teaching.

Marguerite Canal's compositions are sensitive and often poignant. Her songs, particularly those set to the verse of Paul Fort, display her love of the sea and the coast of Brittany. Others, including a 1948 setting of four lullabies derived from the poetry of *Marceline Desbordes-Valmore*, testify to her passionate love of children, and are a commentary on one of the great sadnesses of her life, never having had a child. Largely unknown even to connoisseurs of modern French music, the creative efforts of Marguerite Canal represent an aesthetic treasure yet to be discovered by music lovers. She died in Cépet, near her home city of Toulouse, on January 27, 1978.

John Haag, University of Georgia, Athens, Georgia

Canary, Martha Jane (1852–1903).

See Cannary, Martha Jane.

Candace.

Like the name pharaoh for earlier Egyptian kings, Candace is a hereditary name of the queens of Meroe, an extensive kingdom in Upper Nubia, ranging from just south of Aswan and the First Cataract of the Nile in modern-day Egypt to the north and well into Ethiopia to the south. Pronunciation: KANDA-see.

Candeille, Julie (1767–1834)

French singer, actress, and composer who wrote music and scripts for plays as well as six novels, sev-

eral on historical topics. Born Amélie Julie in Paris, France, on July 31, 1767; died in Paris on February 4, 1834; married to Jean Simons from 1798–1821.

Julie Candeille's father, who educated her, claimed his daughter was endowed with great talent, an observation that would prove correct over her multifaceted career. By age 13, she had already appeared in public as a composer and a pianist. At age 15, in 1782, she sang the title role in Gluck's *Iphigénie en Aulide*. By age 18, she was an established actress at the Comédie Française. Her greatest success as a singer and actress was in *Catherine, ou La belle fermiére*, which ran for 154 performances in 1792–93; Candeille wrote both the text and music. Over the next 35 years, she would revive this role many times. Though not as successful as *Catherine*, she also wrote *Bathilde, ou Le duc, Le commissionnaire, La bayadère ou Le Français à Surate*, and *Louise, ou La réconcilliation*. Her most important work for the stage was *Ida, ou L'orpheline de Berlin*, a two-act opéra comique given in 1807. In addition to writing plays, Julie Candeille composed music, mainly for the piano, and wrote novels, many on historical topics.

Canfield, Dorothy (1879–1958).

See Dorothy Canfield Fisher.

Cannary, Martha Jane (1852–1903)

Legendary frontierswoman, known as Calamity Jane, who did exactly as she pleased in her own colorful manner, thus significantly contributing to the lore of the Wild West. Name variations: Calamity Jane; Martha Jane Burk or Burke; Marthy Jane Canary. Born Martha or Marthy Jane Cannary on May 1, 1852, in Princeton, Missouri; died in Terry, South Dakota, on August 1, 1903; daughter of Robert and Charlotte Cannary; married Clinton Burk or Burke (1885?); also had a number of common-law husbands; children: number and names are uncertain; one woman, Jane McCormick, claimed Calamity Jane as her mother, though the veracity of this is questioned.

After living in Missouri in her early years, moved to Montana (1865); mother died (1866); moved to Utah where father died (1867); moved to Wyoming (1868); went on army expeditions (1872–73); with Wild Bill Hickok, came to Deadwood, South Dakota, where Hickok was murdered by Jack McCall (1876); nursed victims of smallpox epidemic in Deadwood (1878); worked as bullwhacker or teamster between Fort Pierre and Black Hills (1879); claimed to have married Clinton Burk (1885), though marriage proba-

bly occurred sometime in the 1890s; published her autobiography (1896); appeared on stage at the Palace Museum in Minneapolis (1896); appeared at the Pan-American Exposition in Buffalo, New York (1901).

Calamity Jane has become such a legendary figure that when tourists stroll through Deadwood's Mt. Moriah Cemetery in South Dakota and stumble upon her grave, they are astonished. To some, she exists only as a mythical or fictional figure like Wonder Woman. Though many of the facts and feats of her life have been fabricated, distorted, or exaggerated, thus making it difficult to determine the truth, Calamity Jane certainly existed. This uninhibited woman lived in a manner that places her in a class with Jesse James, Wild Bill Hickok, and Buffalo Bill. "Of all the half-legendary characters who roamed the frontier in the last quarter of the nineteenth century and whose exploits have provoked the imagination," writes her biographer **Roberta Sollid**, "one of the most amazing was Calamity Jane."

She was born Marthy Jane Cannary in Princeton, Missouri, on May 1, 1852, the eldest of six children of Robert and **Charlotte Cannary**. In frontier Missouri, young Martha Jane received little or no formal education. She grew up loving horses and became an expert rider, boasting an ability "to ride the most vicious and stubborn of horses."

In 1864, 13-year-old Cannary traveled with her family by wagon to Montana, which would become home; by this time, writes biographer **Doris Faber**, she could already "cuss as fiercely as any man" and had "learned to like the taste of whiskey." On the way, wrote Cannary in her autobiography, *Life and Adventures of Calamity Jane by Herself*, the family "had many exciting times fording streams for many of the streams in our way were noted for quicksands and boggy places, where, unless we were very careful, we would have lost horses and all."

In Montana, Martha Jane's mother helped supplement the family's meager income by serving as a washerwoman in surrounding mining camps. She died in 1866 from an ailment dubbed "washtub pneumonia." Soon after, the family moved again, this time to Salt Lake City, Utah, where Cannary's father died in 1867. With both parents dead, 15-year-old Martha Jane pulled up stakes with her siblings and left for Fort Bridger, Wyoming, in the spring of 1868.

In the late 1860s, the first transcontinental railroad was being built, so Cannary headed to

Piedmont, Wyoming, where construction crews were laying track for the Union Pacific. Many of the workmen were attracted to "this wayward girl," declared one writer. That beauty exists in the eye of the beholder certainly seems true in Cannary's case. Miguel Otero, one time governor of New Mexico, boasted that at age 20 Cannary was "extremely attractive," while another observer who met her in Cheyenne, Wyoming, characterized her as a "pretty, dark-eyed girl." Sollid claims that photographs of Cannary reveal she had "dark hair and high cheek bones"

and that she was slender as a young woman, more stocky later in life, but shortly before her death slimmer again. Sollid, however, concluded, "In no picture is her appearance striking or even attractive."

In the 1870s, the West was still wild, and white settlers and Native Americans were still at odds. The American government continued to send U.S. soldiers to subdue the tribes, utilizing scouts who knew the country through which the soldiers traveled. During that decade, Cannary seems to have served the army, though how and when is not always clear. In her autobiography, she states that in 1870 she joined General George Custer at Fort Russell and, working as a scout, headed for Arizona. There is no evidence, however, that Custer was ever at Fort Russell; in 1870, he was writing his memoirs at Leavenworth, Kansas. There is better evidence that she served with the soldiers of General George Crook whose headquarters were at Fort Fetterman, Wyoming.

If you scorn Martha Jane Cannary, you court calamity.

—Calamity Jane

Stories have been told concerning Cannary's attempt to disguise her gender. Up to the time she worked with the army, claims Cannary, "I had always worn the costume of my sex," but after donning the uniform of a soldier, "I soon got to be perfectly at home in men's clothes." It also seemed necessary if she were to gain acceptance. On one occasion it was rumored that one of the teamsters on a stagecoach was Calamity Jane. "Her sex was discovered," writes Sollid, "when the wagon-master noted she did not cuss her mules with the enthusiasm to be expected from a graduate of Patrick and Saulsbury's Black Hills Stage line, as she had represented herself to be."

Cannary claims that she derived her nickname as a result of a military campaign in which she was engaged. An officer named Captain Egan, she said, was in command of a post on Goose Creek, Wyoming, which today is the site of Sheridan. When the Indians ambushed and wounded Egan and he was about to fall from his horse, Cannary "galloped back with all haste to his side and got there in time to catch him as he was falling." Egan made it safely to the fort; after recovering, he rechristened his protector, "Calamity Jane, the heroine of the plains."

That she was called Calamity Jane is certain, though not everyone who knew Cannary accepts her version as to how her nickname was acquired. Some say she always seemed beset by calamity. As

one old-timer put it, "If she sat on a fence rail, it would rare up and buck her off." The *St. Paul Dispatch* maintained: "She got her name from a faculty she has had of producing a ruction at any time and place and on short notice."

Sometime between mid-June and mid-July of 1876, with Deadwood gripped by gold fever, Cannary rode into town with a party that included Wild Bill Hickok, Colorado Charles Otter, his brother Steve, and **Kittie Arnold**. The fact that the *Black Hills Pioneer* reported "Calamity Jane has arrived" seems to indicate that Cannary was by then a celebrity in her own right. Thus, Cannary was in Deadwood when one of the most famous killings in the history of the Wild West occurred: the murder of Wild Bill Hickok. On August 2, 1876, Hickok sat playing poker, facing the front door of the Number Ten Saloon, when Jack McCall snuck in through a rear entrance. McCall shot Hickok in the back of the head and then fled. Rushing to the scene, writes Cannary, "I at once started to look for the assassin." She found him at Shurdy's butcher shop, grabbed a meat cleaver, and "made him throw up his hands." McCall was tried, sentenced, and hanged.

Apparently, Cannary had a softer side, according to the testimony of several who saw her ministering to unfortunates victimized by the smallpox epidemic that beset Deadwood in 1878. **Dora DeFran**, a notorious madam of brothels in communities in South Dakota's Black Hills (Deadwood, Lead, Belle Forche, and Rapid City), reported that when the smallpox plague descended, eight men were quarantined in a little shack on the shoulder of a mountain called "White Rocks." Cannary volunteered to care for them. Her only medicines were epsom salts and cream of tartar. When three of them died, she recited the prayer "Now I Lay Me Down to Sleep" as they were laid to rest. "But her good nursing brought five of these men out of the shadow of death," wrote DeFran, "and many more later on, before the disease died out." That 1878 smallpox epidemic saw many "bedfast from the scourge," writes Lewis Crawford. "It was here that this outcast woman, true to the better instincts of her sex, ministered day and night among the sick and dying, with no thought of reward or of what the consequences might be to herself."

Cannary was a free spirit; no single occupation was hers for long. When she needed money, she could turn to bullwhacking at which she was an expert. In the old West, covered-wagon trains were formed to haul freight from one place to another; these trains were often drawn by oxen.

From the movie Calamity Jane, *starring Doris Day.*

A bullwhacker was simply a teamster who "whacked" the animals with a long whip to make them go. In 1879, "I went to Fort Pierre and drove trains from Rapid City to Fort Pierre for Frank Witcher," wrote Cannary, "then drove teams from Fort Pierre to Sturgis for Fred Evans." Oxen "were better fitted for the work than horses, owing to the rough nature of the country." Cannary was so good, one writer declared, that she offered to wager she could "knock a fly off an ox's ear with a sixteen-foot whip-lash three times out of five." Not only did she wield the whip with expertise, but as a bull-whacker she could "lash out with her voice as well as her whip."

Colorful tales are told of Calamity Jane, the gunslinger. That she was familiar with guns, wore them, and, on occasion, used them seems certain. However, there is little or no evidence that she was a killer who ruthlessly shot those who got in her way. Bozeman, Montana's *Avant Courier* boasted that Calamity Jane "could draw as quickly as any man who ever lived." On one occasion, reported the *Courier,* the cowboys in a saloon in Oakes, North Dakota, began to "chaff" her. Cannary smiled, whipped out two revolvers, shouting, "Dance, you tenderfeet, dance." Dance they did "with much vigor." "Calamity Jane was not a person to be trifled with," concluded the Bozeman newspaper.

From the movie The Plainsman, starring Gary Cooper and Jean Arthur.

O.W. Coursey in a publication titled *Beautiful Black Hills* described Cannary's intervention on behalf of a helpless mule, one of a pack train carrying army supplies from Laramie to Deadwood along the Black Hills Trail. When the mule went down, the driver "kicked it viciously with his heavy army boots and abused it mercilessly." When Calamity, dressed as a man, could no longer endure the plight of the mule, she cried out, "Don't you kick that mule again." The driver responded by jerking her hat off with a sharp flick of his whip. Calamity pulled her revolver "quicker than a flash," commanding the driver to "put that hat where you got it." Coursey reported: "Judging by the look in her eyes and the tone of her voice, he promptly obeyed."

"Husbands, Lawful and Casual" was a chapter title in Sollid's biography. There is "ample evidence," writes Sollid, that during the 1880s "Calamity Jane was mixed up in some manner with a young man named Robert Dorsett." Exactly what the relationship was or how long it lasted is unclear. A court record from November 1888 states that "Charles Townley, an unmarried man, and Jane Doe, alias Calamity Jane, an unmarried woman," did at various times "unlawfully bed, cohabit and live together and have carnal knowledge of each other without being then and there married."

In Cannary's autobiography, the only man she claimed as her husband was one "Mr. Clinton Burk" whom, she said, she married in August 1885. According to Cannary, she gave birth to a child on October 28, 1887. Other men with whom she had relationships included a Wyoming rancher named King and a certain William Steers, characterized by one newspaper as "a miserable stick" who "is one of the worthless curs unhung." Though Cannary seems to have longed for a relationship with Wild Bill Hickok, her love was not reciprocated.

In 1896, she was persuaded to tour some of America's major cities decked out in buckskin trousers and jacket "with all imaginable accompanying wild west accouterments." In January 1896, she was off for Minneapolis where she appeared at the Palace Museum. There she was billed as the "famous woman scout of the Wild West" who was the "heroine of a thousand thrilling adventures," "the Terror of evildoers in the Black Hills," and "the comrade of Buffalo Bill and Wild Bill Hickok."

No one seems to know how long her stand at the Palace Museum lasted. One paper in Deadwood states that Calamity Jane would begin her tour in Minneapolis and then move on to Chicago. There is no evidence that she appeared in Chicago or any other city after her Minneapolis debut. "Chances are," surmises Sollid, she was unable to "stay away from her liquor and conform to the restrictions imposed upon her by the management." (Cannary was reputed to have sworn never to go to bed with "a nickel in her pocket or sober.") On June 6, 1896, Deadwood's *Pioneer Times* reported that Calamity Jane was back in town.

In 1901, journalist **Josephine Brake** inveigled Cannary to appear at the Pan-American Exposition in Buffalo, New York, where promoters promised fairgoers "a wild-west woman straight from the cow country." (It was at this same exposition that Leon Czolgosz assassinated President William McKinley.) Again, there is uncertainty as to how Cannary fared as a showgirl. One old-timer described how the master of ceremonies with great fanfare introduced Calamity Jane, whereupon she tore into the ring on horseback attired in buckskin, boots, packing revolvers and stealing the show. Other descriptions of her performance were not quite as glowing.

About this time, she was also hawking her autobiography, *Life and Adventures of Calamity Jane by Herself.* Apparently sales were slim. Seemingly after Calamity's drinking embroiled her with the Buffalo police, William Cody (Buffalo Bill) had to loan her money to return home. "I expect she was no more tired of Buffalo than the Buffalo police were of her," said Cody, "for her sorrows seemed to need a good deal of drowning."

Upon returning to the West that she knew, the 51-year-old Cannary was ill and nearing her end. In early July 1903, she spent some time in Deadwood where she visited Wild Bill Hickok's grave at Mt. Moriah Cemetery, posing for a picture beside his tombstone. Later in July, she traveled from Spearfish to Terry, a small mining town near Deadwood and spent her last days in the Calloway Hotel where she was visited by several old friends. She requested that her funeral be conducted under the auspices of the Black Hills Pioneer Society and that she be buried in the Mt. Moriah Cemetery. "Bury me beside Wild Bill—the only man I ever loved," she is supposed to have said. She died on August 1, at five o'clock in the afternoon. Funeral services were held in Deadwood's First Methodist Church on August 4 after which Martha Jane Cannary's body was carried to the Mt. Moriah Cemetery. She was laid to rest next to Wild Bill Hickok.

SOURCES:

Ahearn, Robert G. *The Mythic West in Twentieth Century America.* Lawrence: University of Kansas Press, 1986.

Cannary, Martha Jane. *Life and Adventures of Calamity Jane by Herself.* Fairfield, WA: Galleon Press, 1969.

DeFran, Dora. *Low Down on Calamity Jane.* Stickney, SD: Argus Printers, 1981.

Faber, Doris. *Calamity Jane: Her Life and Legend.* Boston: Houghton Mifflin, 1992.

Klock, Irma M. *Here Comes Calamity Jane.* Deadwood, SD: Dakota Graphics, 1979.

Mueller, Ellen Crago. *Calamity Jane.* Laramie, WY: Jelm Mountain Press, 1981.

Sollid, Roberta B. *Calamity Jane: A Study in Historical Criticism.* Helena, MT: Historical Society of Montana, 1958.

SUGGESTED READING:

Clairmonte, Glenn. *Calamity Was the Name for Jane.* Denver, CO: Sage Books, 1959.

Horan, James D. *Desperate Women.* NY: Bonanza, 1962.

Jennewein, J. Leonard. *Calamity Jane of the Western Trails.* Huron, SD: Dakota Books, 1953.

Mumey, Nolie. *Calamity Jane: A History of Her Life and Adventures in the West.* Denver, CO: Range Press, 1950.

RELATED MEDIA:

The Plainsman, starring *Jean Arthur and Gary Cooper, produced and directed by Cecil B. DeMille, screenplay by Waldemar Young, Harold Lamb, Lynn Riggs, and *Jeanie Macpherson, edited by *Anne Bauchens, Paramount, 1937 (the best of the Calamity Jane films).

The Plainsman, starring Don Murray and **Abby Dalton,** directed by David Lowell Rich, Universal, 1966.

Calamity Jane, musical film starring ***Doris Day** and Howard Keel, Warner Bros., 1953.

Calamity Jane and Sam Bass, starring **Yvonne De Carlo** and Howard Duff, Universal, 1949 (in reality, Cannary never met outlaw Sam Bass).

Wild Bill, film written and directed by Walter Hill, starring Jeff Bridges as Hickock and **Ellen Barkin** as Calamity Jane, 1995.

Robert Bolt, Professor of History,
Calvin College, Grand Rapids, Michigan

Cannon, Annie Jump (1863–1941)

American astronomer who was the first to develop a simple spectral classification system and who classified more stars than anyone previously. Born Annie Jump Cannon on December 11, 1863, in Dover, Delaware; died of heart failure and arteriosclerosis in Cambridge, Massachusetts, on April 13, 1941; daughter of Wilson Lee (a state senator, merchant, and shipbuilder) and Mary Elizabeth (Jump) Cannon; graduated Wellesley College, B.S., 1884, M.A., 1907; special student in astronomy at Radcliffe College (1895–97).

Became assistant astronomer at Harvard College Observatory (1896–1911), curator of astronomical photographs (1911–38), William Cranch Bond Astronomer and Curator (1938–40); developed a simple spectral classification system (1901), that was adopted by the International Solar Union (1910); compiled Henry Draper Catalogues (1911–24); was first woman elected an officer of the American Astronomical Society (1912–19); designated America's leading female scientist by League of Women Voters (1922); was first woman to receive honorary doctorate from Oxford University (1925); awarded Henry Draper Gold Medal from the National Academy of Sciences (1931); saw first Annie Jump Cannon Prize awarded (1934).

Selected publications: "Classification of 1,122 Bright Southern Stars" in Annals of the Astronomical Observatory at Harvard College *(vol. 28, part 2, 1901); "Second Catalogue of Variable Stars," in* Annals of the Astronomical Observatory at Harvard College *(vol. 55, part 1, 1907); "Williamina Paton Fleming," in* Science *(vol. 33, June 30, 1911, pp. 987–988); (with Edward Pickering) "The Henry Draper Catalogue," in* Annals of the Astronomical Observatory at Harvard College *(vols. 91–99, 1918–24); "Henry Draper Extension," in* Annals of the Astronomical Observatory at Harvard College *(vols. 100 and 112, 1925 and 1949); "Sarah Frances Whiting," in* Popular Astronomy *(December 1927); "Biographical Memoir of Solon Irving Bailey, 1854–1931," in* Biographical Memoirs of the National Academy of Sciences *(Washington, D.C.: National Academy of Sciences, vol. 15,* 1932); "The Story of Starlight," in The Telescope *(vol. 8, May–June 1941, pp. 56–61).*

Young Annie Jump Cannon scribbled astronomical observations in her journal as molten wax dripped down her candlestick. Blowing out the flame, she gathered her notebooks and climbed down from the roof through the trapdoor into the attic, anxious to tell her mother about her star gazing and reassure her father that she had not burned the house down. She paused to admire the family candelabra that twinkled starlike as light beamed through its glass prisms. These luminary experiences impacted the girl who chose to study stars for her life work. As an adult, Annie Jump Cannon was considered the most famous woman astronomer in the world and was called the "Census Taker of the Sky." At Harvard University Observatory, she classified more stars than anyone had before—400,000 stellar bodies; she also discovered 300 variable stars, five novas, and a double star.

Born on December 11, 1863, at Dover, Delaware, Annie Cannon, oldest of three children from her father's second marriage, had a happy childhood. Her father Wilson Cannon, a state senator and wealthy merchant and shipbuilder of Scottish descent, was lieutenant governor when the Civil War began. A prominent Unionist, he deserted the Democratic Party to cast the deciding vote in the Delaware senate against secession. His convictions to preserve the Union caused many former political allies to shun him. Despite this ostracism, the Cannons were a prominent Dover family.

Annie's mother **Mary Jump Cannon** encouraged Annie to pursue scientific as well as cultural activities. She sparked her daughter's interest in stars, teaching her to recognize constellations. As a girl, Mary had taken an astronomy class at the Quaker Friend's School near Philadelphia. She fashioned an observatory in the Cannon's attic where she instructed Annie on how to determine stars' positions in the sky and how to record her observations in logbooks by candlelight.

Climbing up through that trap door, Annie would squat on the roof to peer at stars shining through tree branches and to memorize charts by the light of a tallow, using an astronomy book that probably was her mother's textbook. But Wilson Cannon discouraged Annie, believing the candlelight celestial sessions posed a dangerous fire risk. As Cannon would recall, "Father was more interested in the safety of the house than in the movements of the stars." In their large white house, Annie also became curious when their elaborate candelabra would cast sunlight into rainbow spectra on the room's walls.

Cannon attended local schools in Dover and the Wilmington Conference Academy where her teachers commented to Wilson that his daughter demonstrated unusual scientific ability. When she graduated at age 16 in 1880, her teachers urged him to consider enrolling her in an intellectually stimulating woman's college where she would have access to the academic opportunities becoming available to women in the late 19th century.

Despite contemporary opinions that higher education ruined women's minds and health,

Cannon's father embraced the idea and traveled to various colleges to meet teachers and students. He chose Wellesley in Massachusetts. Eager to study science, Annie Cannon traveled northeast even though most of Dover's citizens were aghast; few women had left Delaware to attend college. When Cannon matriculated, Wellesley had only been open for five years. She happily embraced collegiate life, enrolling in as many science classes as possible.

Studying under ❧▶ **Sarah F. Whiting**, head professor of physics and astronomy, Cannon broadened her interest in stars. She attended her

❧▶
*See sidebar
on the
following page*

Annie Jump Cannon

Whiting, Sarah F. (1847–1927)

American physicist and astronomer and first woman to study physics at the Massachusetts Institute of Technology. Born Sarah Frances Whiting in Wyoming, New Jersey, on August 23, 1847; died in 1927; daughter of a physics teacher; attended Ingham University.

While a professor of physics at Wellesley College in 1876, Sarah Whiting furthered her own studies by attending classes in physics at Massachusetts Institute of Technology (MIT) as a guest. She then developed, with the help of Harvard's E.C. Pickering, one of the first undergraduate teaching laboratories in physics in the country, while "meeting," she noted, "the somewhat nerve wearing experience of constantly being in places where a woman was not expected to be." In 1880, Whiting introduced an astronomy course, then called "applied physics," at Wellesley. A friend, **Sarah Elizabeth Whitin**, on the board of trustees at Wellesley from 1896 to 1917, donated an observatory that housed a 12-inch telescope and spectroscopic lab. Better known for her teaching than her research, Sarah Whiting was the first director of the Whitin Observatory. She retired in 1916.

SUGGESTED READING:

Shearer, Benjamin F., and Barbara S. Shearer. *Notable Women in the Physical Sciences.* Westport, CT: Greenwood Press, 1997.

first class in astronomy in Whiting's physics laboratory, located in a converted organ loft on the fifth floor of College Hall. Sarah Whiting encouraged her students and insured that they saw the Great Comet of 1882. Her specialty of spectroscopy motivated Cannon to pursue a "desire to continue the investigation of spectra." Under Whiting, Cannon focused on physics. But for all her joy and talent, she did not consider science a realistic career.

Cannon graduated Phi Beta Kappa with her bachelor's degree in 1884 and returned to Dover, a "dutiful daughter," to pursue a debutante's life. Happy at home with her sisters and mother, with whom she shared an especially strong bond, she practiced to be a consummate pianist, a skill that her mother encouraged. A beautiful young woman, Annie was a popular date and had several marriage offers, but she refused the young men, possibly still heartbroken over a beau who had died in college. She cooked gourmet meals, established a reading club, attended dances, and sailed and camped with friends near her home. She traveled throughout Europe, photographing the countryside with her Kamerette, an early box camera, a hobby that was considered extraordinary for women of that

era. In 1892, she saw and captured a Spanish solar eclipse on film.

In 1893, her mother died suddenly. Stunned and grief-stricken, Cannon quit her social activities and resumed her attic astronomy observations to curb her loneliness, to keep her mind busy, and to acquire a sense of purpose. In her journal, she admitted, "I am sometimes very dissatisfied with life here. I do want to accomplish something so badly." At age 30, in 1894, she left Dover and returned to Wellesley to enroll in postgraduate work in mathematics, physics, and astronomy.

Cannon assisted Whiting in the physics laboratory, which had the most current equipment and was one of the best in the country, conducting experiments verifying newly discovered x-rays, but by the spring of 1895, her academic interests had focused on the stars. She corresponded with Harvard Observatory director Edward C. Pickering and became a special astronomy student at Radcliffe College, studying astronomy and "Practical Research" under Pickering's supervision. In January 1896, he offered her a position, promising that "one or more telescopes will also be available for the observations on variable stars which you wish to make." A month later, Cannon began making observations at the Harvard College Observatory.

Pickering supported women who sought advanced education in astrophysics; he was angered that many male astronomers relegated intelligent women to subordinate positions, which was an inefficient use of their talents. Observation was considered men's work, while classifying plates was labeled a female task. Like many other fields, women filled lower positions while men had numerous opportunities at the top. The progressive Pickering made Harvard an exception, hiring women to use technology such as cameras and spectroscopes, and feminizing observation jobs so that women had access to expanded roles. He hired astronomer *Williamina Paton Fleming to oversee women assistants, who were paid 25 to 35 cents per hour to sort stellar spectra photographs. Cannon's beginning salary was $1,200 for seven hours per day, six days weekly, for eleven months. After her classes, Cannon examined photographic plates during the day; at night, she gazed through the telescope. Each plate had hundreds of spectra that she analyzed with a magnifying lens while reciting her identifications to a stenographer. When Cannon started, she could classify 5,000 stars per month, increasing the quantity to as many as 300 stars an hour as she acquired expertise. The skilled Cannon could soon identify stars at a glance.

Although she was not a pioneer in astronomy, Cannon simplified and perfected a stellar classification system that was used for a comprehensive survey of the heavens. Pickering, Fleming, and *Antonia Maury had developed preliminary classification methods to utilize the thousands of plates at Harvard, the largest collection in the world. They analyzed star characteristics in patterns revealed when starlight was photographed refracting through prisms, creating a spectrum. One system allocated each spectrum to a category labeled alphabetically from A to Q and another sequenced spectra types designated by Roman numerals in order of descending temperatures. Pickering realized Cannon had unique insights when examining the plates and asked her to help organize a more satisfactory system to record star information.

Cannon perfected classifying stars by the color of their spectra. She realized that elements in the stars' composition created different radiations and wavelengths, resulting in various colors forming the spectrum. Stars could be identified by their color and brightness. When starlight passed through a prism at the end of a telescope, it produced a ribbon of multicolored light, the star spectrum, which was crossed from top to bottom by dark lines and bands. This spectrum revealed the most about a star's characteristics such as composition, temperature, rotation speed, speed in space, and size. Cannon emphasized, "So it is not just a streak of light to me, but a gateway to a wonderful new world."

In 1901, she rearranged previous classification systems that had ranked stars according to their temperature and composition. She established ten categories designated by letters—her sequence being O, B, A, F, G, K, M, R, N, S—in which the first three stars were white or bluish, the next two were yellow, K was orange, and the final four categories were red. The sun, for example, was placed in category G because it was yellow. The Cannon sequence went from very hot white and blue stars to cool stars, with subdivisions identified by Arabic numeral. The spectra that did not fit into this system were classified as peculiar and described in detail.

This classification system is considered Cannon's greatest professional contribution. She showed that only a small number of spectral types existed and proved that with few exceptions, most spectra could be arranged into continuous series and that the majority of stars were in groups O to M. Cannon's system was so simple, expandable, and usable that in 1910 the International Solar Union adopted it as the official classification system for all observatories worldwide, and the "Harvard System," with some modifications, is still used. Harvard became a mecca for astronomers worldwide to learn Cannon's classification methods. Other classification systems have since been developed, but Cannon's information built their foundation.

Cannon had acquired her insight into spectral classification when she photographed the spectra of bright southern stars at Harvard's observatory station in Arequipa, Peru. In 1901, she published descriptions of the spectra of 1,122 stars, which became the basis for future star catalogs she would compile. Pickering, who was her most enthusiastic supporter, recommended that Cannon receive her master's degree in astronomy in 1907. Admiring her "keen sense, keen sight" and sincere interest in conducting original work, he assigned her increased responsibilities.

*W*here she found chaos she left cosmos.

—Cecilia H. Payne-Gaposchkin

Cannon's work was not just restricted to classification. She also interpreted photographs, finding unusual stars in the sky. "She had wonderful eyes," commented one of her assistants, **Margaret Mayall**, "and she could see things that very few people would recognize until she pointed it out." During her work, Cannon noted spectral peculiarities and discovered more than 300 rare variable stars, whose light intensity varied in a regular pattern that required several years to be completed. Athenian thinker Hipparchus had suggested a continuous sequence of stellar magnitudes in which each star's brightness was constant with time. Cannon's observation of variable stars, however, showed that their brightness varied, occasionally dimming, for many reasons such as being eclipsed by an orbiting star.

She photographed these stars for a permanent record of their existence and prepared an index card record with detailed information. Responsible for the observatory card catalogue of literature available on variable stars, she expanded its resources from 14,000 cards to a quarter million by her death, providing a foundation bibliography on variable stars for Harvard researchers. These cards included published references and unpublished information about both known and suspected variable stars. She observed five nova, which were infrequently seen because they would blaze up suddenly then die down, and one double star. In 1919, she also detected the first diffuse interstellar band, mysterious broad interstellar absorption lines in galactic spectra; astronomers have only recently begun to unravel their obscure origins. Of her work, biographer **Edna Yost** noted, "Truly her patience with detail in pursuit of truth was nothing short of prodigious."

In October 1911, after Fleming's death, Pickering appointed Cannon curator of astronomical photographs donated by the Henry Draper Memorial. Draper, a New York doctor, was also a pioneer in celestial photography, and his widow gave Harvard funds to classify stars in his photographs. Draper's memorial provided women more opportunities in astronomical work because hundreds of stars appeared on each plate. Although several women worked before her, Cannon performed the bulk of the work. The Draper work resulted in the largest compilation of astronomical data by one person. Cannon had to examine and approve the quality of each plate; Harvard Observatory's plate collection totaled half a million plates. Cannon's work on the project required classifying all stellar spectra brighter than the eighth magnitude from the North Pole to the South Pole and to reclassify all stars previously catalogued under old systems. To help with the laborious work, she hired several assistants. "It was evidently best that she should restrict her own work to those portions which could not readily be undertaken by the others," commented Pickering. "This included the classification, the revision, and the supervision of the whole."

A devoted Cannon analyzed the plates and insured that both the northern and southern hemispheres were completely photographed in square sections. After four years, she completed classifications on September 30, 1915, then patiently verified her arrangements until 1924. Publication was a long and costly process, with Pickering paying to have the first volume published. A total of ten volumes, several published posthumously by the observatory, indicate each star's position in the sky, brightness, visual and photographic magnitudes, and comments on peculiarities of each star and other pertinent information, listing a number and description so that other astronomers could recognize each star. The Draper catalogues are especially valuable because Cannon was the sole observer and classifier, thus her observations and information were consistent and accurate.

She catalogued the spectra of 300,000 stars. The Draper volumes centralized descriptions of stellar spectra. They helped transform astronomy from a hobby of stargazing into a scientific profession with a theoretical basis. Cannon worked until even the faintest stars were identi-

fied. She demanded that new plates be developed to show them and learned to photograph the heavens herself, exposing the plates until all stars were visible, even those that were 100 times fainter than the naked eye could see. In the *Yale Zone Catalogue* and *Cape Zone Catalogue* extensions, she classified the spectra of 47,000 fainter stars, many in the Milky Way regions.

When she concluded her work, she had classified approximately 400,000 stars according to their spectral type and arranged them in catalogues that were called "the bible of modern astronomy" because her work was the fundamental start for any astronomical investigation. The catalogues are considered her scientific legacy, providing sufficient data for advanced astrophysics research. Dr. Harlow Shapley, director of the Harvard Observatory from 1921 to 1952, predicted that her classification was "a structure that probably will never be duplicated in kind or extent by a single individual." And her vast work has not yet been matched by any astronomer.

Although she was a skilled observer who understood the underlying principles of classification and analyses of stars, Cannon did not create a concept or methodology for studying stellar spectra. She simplified and applied procedures. According to colleague *Cecilia Payne-Gaposchkin, "Cannon was not given to theorizing; it is probable that she never published a controversial word or a speculative thought. That was the strength of her scientific work—her classification was dispassionate and unbiased."

While astronomy became more businesslike and specialized, with discoveries becoming rarer, Cannon focused her life work on improving her field by identifying stars' characteristics revealed by their rainbow-hued spectra. Many stars she classified were so distant that their light would require millions of years to reach the earth, but through her observation the world community acquired immediate knowledge about them. Outlining stellar evolution, she also emphasized in her work that the universe is not static but ever changing with new and dying stars.

The Draper Catalogue provided the basis for research for which numerous men have been elected to the National Academy of Sciences, but Cannon was not selected for her original work. In 1923 when her name was under consideration, many male scientists used her deafness as an excuse for excluding Cannon from professional societies. Two explanations for her hearing impairment have been offered. Some sources state that she had scarlet fever after her college graduation, while others claim she gradually lost her hearing as she aged due to exposure to severely cold weather during her first winter at Wellesley. Occasionally wearing a hearing aid and reading lips, Cannon's deafness may have been a benefit, enabling her to concentrate so well on her work. Despite withholding membership, the National Academy of Science recognized her astronomy classifications in 1931 by awarding her the first Henry Draper Gold Medal given to a woman.

Cannon received numerous honors. In 1925, Oxford University bestowed a doctorate on Cannon who was the first woman to don those special Oxford robes. Cannon was the first person to receive an honorary doctorate in astronomy from the University of Groningen, the Netherlands. She was named an honorary member of the Royal Astronomical Society in 1914 because women were not permitted to join and was one of the few women elected an honorary member of the American Philosophical Society and American Academy of Arts and Sciences. A 1922 League of Women Voters' survey named her America's leading female scientist.

Other awards included the Nova Medal of the American Association of Variable Star Observers in 1922 and the *Ellen Richards Research prize from the Society to Aid Scientific Research by Women in 1932 for best experimental work by a woman. Because she did not think women had access to equal research opportunities and that many awards to women were long overdue, Cannon gave the $1,000 honorarium to establish the Annie Jump Cannon Prize of the American Astronomical Society, a triennial award granted to a woman who gave distinguished service to astronomy. Cecilia Payne-Gaposchkin received the first award in 1934.

Annie Jump Cannon was starred in the third edition of *American Men of Science*. She also was the first woman elected an officer of the American Astronomical Society (as treasurer from 1912–19), and in 1929 was included among 12 of the "greatest living American women" designated by the National League of Women Voters. "My success, if you would call it that," she said, "lies in the fact that I have kept at my work all these years. It is not genius, or anything like that, it is merely patience."

Having enormous enthusiasm for her work, Cannon shared a cordial relationship with her peers. She published at least 90 papers and catalogues in addition to the Draper work and wrote a biographical sketch for the National Academy of Sciences. In 1936, she classified 10,000 faint stars on photographs mailed to her by the Royal Observatory Cape of Good Hope. She shared her philosophy and revealed her delightful personality on radio broadcasts about astronomy. A popular lecturer, she managed to hear audience questions despite her deafness. She loved to travel to astronomical meetings, and according to Mayall, "No meeting of the American Astronomical Society was considered complete without her presence." Every three years, Cannon attended International Astronomical Union meetings around the globe.

Despite her many accolades, Harvard denied Cannon institutional honors. A 1911 visiting committee to the Observatory wrote: "It is an anomaly that, though she is recognized the world over as the greatest living expert in this line of work, and her services to the Observatory are so important, yet she holds no official position in the university." Shapley attempted to get her as much external recognition as possible to force Harvard to promote her. Finally, at age 75, Cannon was granted the rank of professor, being named William Cranch Bond Astronomer (Bond was the founder of the college observatory). She became one of the first women to have a titled corporation appointment at Harvard but still was not listed in the university catalogue.

An ardent Republican, pro-suffrage advocate, and member of the National Woman's Party, Cannon was upset at women's apathy toward voting. She supported women scientists, commenting: "It is hard to conceive of the time when mathematical or other scientific study by girls was so shocking to the conceptions of mankind that she must need do all her study secretly at night with a candle by her bedside." She believed that because astronomers shared ideas and goals they could create an international "diplomacy of the skies." "In these days of great trouble and unrest," she wrote during World War II, "it is good to have something outside our own planet, something fine and distant and comforting to troubled minds. Let people look to the stars for comfort and find solace as others have."

A Methodist as a child, Cannon converted to the Congregational Church in New England, enjoying worship services. Friends noted that although she was "a pure scientist of high rank, she was also a human being of the first order." She loved children and parties, often hosting social events at her "Star Cottage" home, an astronomical mecca nestled at the foot of Observatory Hill at 4 Bond Street. A charming host, known as Aunt Annie, she reveled in entertaining her observatory friends and hosting such events for their children as Easter egg rolling contests. Of special sentimental value, her parent's candelabrum sparkled in Star Cottage.

Cannon retired in September 1940, and Yale University commissioned her to conduct research at Harvard where she worked until several weeks before her death. On April 13, 1941, Cannon suffered heart failure; she was buried in her family's plot at Dover's Lakeside Cemetery. Portraits memorializing her hang at the University of Delaware and at the Wellesley College Observatory. At a memorial service at Harvard, Shapley spoke, dedicating a room in the Harvard Observatory and a memorial volume of the Draper Catalogue to Cannon. Several leading journals printed commentary from colleagues and peers, praising Cannon's productivity, lauding her as the "dean of women astronomers." Leon Campbell predicted: "The astronomical world will not soon forget Annie J. Cannon." Wrote Gaposchkin, "Where she found chaos she left cosmos."

SOURCES:

Campbell, Leon. "Annie Jump Cannon," in *Popular Astronomy*. Vol. 49. August 1941, pp. 345–347.

Jones, Bessie Z., and Lyle Boyd. *The Harvard College Observatory: The First Four Directorships, 1839–1919.* Cambridge: Harvard University Press, 1971.

Payne-Gaposchkin, Cecilia H. "Miss Cannon and Stellar Spectroscopy," in *The Telescope*. Vol. 8. May–June 1941, pp. 62–63.

Yost, Edna. *American Women of Science.* Rev. ed. Philadelphia, PA: J.B. Lippincott, 1955.

✤➤ Ayres, Anne (1816–1896)

Protestant religious. Name variations: Sister Anne. Born in London, England, on January 3, 1816; died at St. Luke's Hospital in New York, New York, on February 9, 1896; came to the United States in 1836.

In 1845, as Sister Anne, Anne Ayres became the first member of an American sisterhood in the Protestant Episcopal Church; she then founded the Sisterhood of the Holy Communion (1852), which was affiliated with the Church of the Holy Communion in New York City. The sisters did not wear habits and took vows, renewable in three-year terms, to remain celibate and to care for the poor.

In 1858, Ayres became the head of housekeeping and nursing at the newly constructed St. Luke's Hospital in New York. With William Augustus Muhlenberg, she also opened St. Johnland, a refuge for orphans, the homeless, and the handicapped, on Long Island in 1865. Ayres wrote *Evangelical Sisterhood* (1867) and *Life of William Augustus Muhlenberg* (1880).

SUGGESTED READING:

Kass-Simon, Gabriele, and Patricia Farnes, eds. *Women of Science: Righting the Record.* Bloomington, IN: Indiana University Press, 1990.

Mack, Pamela E. "Women in Astronomy in the United States, 1875–1920." B.A. honors thesis, Harvard University, 1977.

Rossiter, Margaret W. *Women Scientists in America: Struggles and Strategies to 1940.* Baltimore, MD: Johns Hopkins University Press, 1982.

COLLECTIONS:

Correspondence, photographs, memorabilia, obituaries, and 201 record books of Cannon's daily work, the Harvard College Observatory Papers, and Williamina Paton Fleming's journals are available at the Harvard University Archives, Cambridge, Massachusetts.

Cannon's alumnae records and the Sarah F. Whiting Papers are located at the Wellesley College Archives, Wellesley, Massachusetts.

Cannon's diary is held in the private collection of Margaret Mayall.

Elizabeth D. Schafer, Ph.D., freelance writer in history of technology and science, Loachapoka, Alabama

Cannon, Harriet Starr (1823–1896)

Superior of the first American Episcopal religious community. Born on May 7, 1823, in Charleston, South Carolina; died on April 5, 1896, in Peekskill, New York.

Harriet Starr Cannon, orphaned at 12 months, would later earn distinction for her work with poor children, prostitutes, homeless women and children, and orphans. Born in Charleston, South Carolina, in 1823, she was raised by an aunt in Bridgeport, Connecticut, where she was educated at local schools and received private instruction in music. In 1851, in her late 20s, Cannon moved in with her older sister in Brooklyn, New York, and gave music lessons to make a living. Her sister died only four years later, in 1855, and the loss to Cannon was great. In February 1856, she entered New York City's Episcopal Sisterhood of the Holy Communion, organized by ◄✤ Anne Ayres, and she became a full member in February of the following year. A ward in the recently established St. Luke's Hospital, which was staffed by the order, came under her charge in 1858; due to escalating disagreements with the rule of the order, however, she was asked to leave St. Luke's in 1863. Cannon was not alone in her opinion that the order's rule needed to be more traditionally monastic, and several others left with her.

In September, this small group was then invited by Bishop Horatio Potter to run the House of Mercy, a rescue house and reformatory for young women. The Sheltering Arms orphanage came under their care a year later, as did St. Barnabas' House for homeless women and children in February of 1865. In the same month, the informally associated sisters founded the first Episcopal religious community in the United States (1865), called the Community of St. Mary. Elected the community's first superior in September of 1865, Cannon took her life vows in February 1867.

The Roman-Catholic-like rule of Cannon's order prompted great suspicion, leading to the sisters' dismissal from both St. Barnabas' (1867) and Sheltering Arms (1870). Nonetheless, they proved successful with St. Mary's School in New York City (opened in 1868). The establishment of many helping institutions followed, including St. Gabriel's School in Peekskill, New York (1872), St. Mary's School in Memphis, Tennessee (1873), Kemper Hall in Kenosha, Wisconsin (1878), and St. Mary's Free Hospital for Poor Children in New York City (1870). Serving immigrant communities, city missions were established in New York (1880) and Chicago (1886). Also among the projects undertaken by Cannon's order was the management of the House of Mercy, a place of refuge for young prostitutes.

In her 70s, Harriet Starr Cannon died on April 5, 1896, at St. Mary's convent in Peekskill, New York.

Cannon, Ophelia Colley (1912–1996).

See Pearl, Minnie.

Canossa, Matilda of (1046–1115).

See Matilda of Tuscany.

Canova, Judy (1916–1983)

American comedian and singer. Born Juliet Canova on November 20, 1916, in Jacksonville, Florida; died of cancer on August 5, 1983, in Hollywood, California; married twice; children: two daughters, Diana Canova (b. June 1, 1953, a television actress) and Juliette Canova.

Selected films: In Caliente *(1935)*; Thrill of a Lifetime *(1937)*; Artists and Models *(1937)*; Scatterbrain *(1940)*; Puddin' Head *(1941)*; Sis Hopkins *(1941)*; Sleepytime Gal *(1942)*; Joan of the Ozarks *(1942)*; Chatterbox *(1943)*; Louisiana Hayride *(1944)*; Hit the Hay *(1945)*; Singin' in the Corn *(1946)*; Honeychile *(1951)*; WAC from Walla Walla *(1952)*; Oklahoma Annie *(1952)*; Untamed Heiress *(1954)*; Carolina Cannonball *(1955)*; The Adventures of Huckleberry Finn *(1960)*; Cannonball *(1976)*.

Judy Canova

Known for her hillbilly antics and an ear-splitting yodel, comedian Judy Canova was part of a family vaudeville team before landing a part on Broadway in Flo Ziegfeld's *Calling All Stars*, in 1934. Her break came the following year when Hollywood director Busby Berkeley gave her a small part in the movie *In Caliente*, starring **Wini Shaw**, a popular singer of the day. In one of the film's lush production numbers, a nightclub scene, Shaw sang "The Lady in Red." Just as the scene ended, Canova appeared, clad in a red dress resembling Shaw's, and offered her own fractured rendition of the same song. Reviewers loved it, and Canova went on to perform similar humorous bits in major films like *Thrill of a Lifetime* (1937) and *Artists and Models* (1937). Her popularity was such that during the 1940s she made a string of "programmers" (low-budget, full-length films that played the lower half of double bills), including *Scatterbrain* (1940), *Puddin' Head* (1941), *Singin' in the Corn* (1946), *Honeychile* (1951), *WAC from Walla Walla* (1952), and *Untamed Heiress* (1954).

From the war years into the 1950s, Canova also starred in a successful weekly half-hour radio show featuring her sidekick Pedro, whose expression "Pardon me for talking in your face, Señorita" became a popular phrase. In 1957, Canova formed her own television production company, but aside from a few guest appearances on the "Huckleberry Finn Show" in the late 1950s, she was seldom seen again. In 1960, she made her first appearance in a dramatic television role on "Alfred Hitchcock Presents." In 1976, she returned briefly to the screen in *Cannonball*.

Canova, who had actually been trained as a classical singer, was said to be nothing like her screen persona, often disappointing her fans with her sophisticated and subdued manner. She married twice and had two daughters, Juliette Canova and actress **Diana Canova**. Judy Canova spent her later years living in the San Fernando Valley with her second husband, a real-estate broker.

Barbara Morgan,
Melrose, Massachusetts

Cansino, Rita (1918–1987).

See Hayworth, Rita.

Canth, Minna (1844–1897)

Finnish playwright and author, a major representative of the realist school, who was an eloquent advocate for women's rights. Name variations: Ulrika Wilhelmina Canth. Born Ulrika Vilhelmina Johansson on March 19, 1844, in Tampere, Finland; died on May 12, 1897, in Kuopio, Finland; daughter of Gustaf Wilhelm Johannson or Johnson (inspector in a cotton mill, then shopkeeper) and Ulrika Johannson or Johnson; attended a teacher's college at Jyväskylä; married Johan Ferdinand Canth (a natural science instructor and newspaper editor), around 1864 (died around 1877); children: seven.

Born Ulrika Vilhelmina Johansson into a shopkeeper's family in Tampere, Finland, the future playwright and feminist attended a teacher's college at Jyväskylä where she met and married one of her teachers, Johan Ferdinand Canth. Marriage and motherhood—she was to have seven children—interrupted her studies, but she never gave up her youthful ambition of becoming a noted writer. After the death of her husband left her and her children in a precarious economic state (she was pregnant with her last when he died), Ulrika Canth supported her family by running the shop she had inherited from her father. Busy as she was, she used her nickname Minna, and began to submit articles to local newspapers; some of these pieces were short literary essays, while others dealt with such controversial issues of the day as temperance and women's suffrage. The sharp, incisive nature of her articles gave Minna Canth the confidence to tackle larger artistic forms, particularly drama.

By 1879, she had completed a folk play entitled *The Burglary*. The difficult years of widowhood and economic struggle had matured Canth, and in this and other plays her combination of powerfully depicted characters and a strong sense of social indignation appealed to a generation of Finns ready to change society and help create a new world based on justice and freedom. The founding of a professional Finnish-language theater in Helsinki in 1872 signaled the dawn of a new era in the nation's cultural life, free of Swedish domination over a people traditionally regarded as little more than ignorant peasants and fishermen. In the 1880s, Minna Canth became a leading member of the Young Finns, a movement organized to promote both social reforms and the heightening of national cultural awareness. Her plays *The Workman's Wife* (1885) and *Children of Misfortune* (1888) were often shocking in their depiction of brutal exploitation and human degradation. These tragedies, although didactic in intent, were recognized as significant works of art. Thanks to Canth, by the 1890s the Finnish stage could claim equality with that of Sweden.

Encouraged by the success of her plays, Canth turned to other literary forms. Her novellas *Poor Folk* (1886) and *The Sunken Rock* (1887) were generally well received by both critics and the reading public. Equally successful were her short stories "Hanna" and "Poor People" (both 1886) and "Lopo the Peddler" (1889). Canth's last plays revealed a depth and philosophical wisdom often lacking in her earlier efforts. In these final works, *The Vicar's Family* (1891), *Sylvi* (1893) and *Anna-Liisa* (1895), she became the voice of the long-oppressed Finnish people, particularly its women who had for centuries suffered not only from foreign oppression but also from the injustices at the hands of a patriarchal regime. With these plays, the tradition of Finnish literary realism reached its apex. While mercilessly exposing the hypocrisies of bourgeois society in these works, Canth also looked forward to a new age of reason by calling for social peace and reconciliation based on a spirit of national harmony. Minna Canth died in Kuopio on May 12, 1897, deeply mourned by her nation. She was honored on the centenary of her birth in 1944 with a commemorative postage stamp, and her works continue to be read and staged in Finland.

SOURCES:

Frenckell-Thesleff, Greta von. *Minna Canth och "det unga Finland."* Helsinki: H. Schildt, 1942.

Minna Canth

———. *Minna Canth: Suomentanut Tyyni Tuulio.* Helsinki: Otava, 1944.

Kannila, Helle. *Minna Canthin kirjeet.* Helsinki: Suomalaisen Kirjallisuuden Seuran Toimituksia, 1973.

Korhonen, Hilkka. "Hymyt ja naurut Canthin novellissa 'Salakari'," in *Kirjallisuudentutkijain Seuran Vuosikirja.* Vol. 22, 1967, pp. 24–34.

Lehtonen, Soila. "Jouko Turkka's *The Burglary*," in *The Drama Review.* Vol. 26, no. 2. Fall 1982, pp. 51–56.

Ravila, Paavo. *Finnish Literary Reader with Notes.* The Hague: Mouton, 1965.

Tuovinen, Elia, ed. *Taisteleva Minna: Minna Canthin lehtirkirjoituksia ja puheita 1874–1896.* Helsinki: Suomalaisen Kirjallisuuden Seura, 1994.

John Haag, Associate Professor, University of Georgia, Athens, Georgia

Cantofoli, Ginevra (1618–1672)

*Italian artist. Born at Bologna in 1618; died in 1672; pupil of *Elisabetta Sirani.*

Ginevra Cantofoli's paintings were historical in nature and may be seen in several churches in Bologna.

Capell-Coningsby, Catherine (1794–1882).

See Stephens, Catherine.

Capello, Bianca (1548–1587).

See Cappello, Bianca.

Capet, Gabrielle (1761–1817)

One of the most popular French miniature portraitists of the late 18th and early 19th centuries. Born Marie Gabrielle Capet on September 6, 1761, in Lyon, France; died in 1817.

It is unknown how Gabrielle Capet moved from a modest life in the provinces where her father was a *domestique,* or household servant, to Paris where she trained as a painter. There is speculation that her great talent inspired a local patron to sponsor her training and relocation. In Paris, Capet entered the studio of *Adelaide Labille-Guiard, and she would display lifelong devotion to her mentor, living in her household from 1782 and caring for Labille-Guiard during her final illness.

Capet's public debut came in the Exposition de la Jeunesse (1781), where she would exhibit for four years. Though she began with pastel and oil portraits, her specialty became portrait miniatures; some conjecture that the switch was made to avoid competition with Labille-Guiard and to forge her own identity as an artist. Her first dated miniature is from 1787, the same year in which Capet received a commission to paint the royal princesses. In 1791, in large part due to the efforts of Labille-Guiard, the official Salon was opened to women, and Capet, who would send work there until 1814, was one of 21 women and 236 men whose works were represented.

Capet's patrons were primarily educated bourgeois artists, writers, politicians and actors. Her miniature representing the sculptor Houdon at work on a bust of Voltaire, considered among her finest, was stolen from the museum in Caen. Though known primarily for the quality and popularity of her miniatures, Capet is also considered an excellent larger-scale portraitist in pastels and oil. Of the approximately 30 oil paintings, 35 pastel, and 85 miniatures of Capet's catalogued by Doria, the majority were in private French collections and are today untraceable.

Cappello, Bianca (1548–1587)

Grand duchess of Tuscany. Name variations: Bianca Capello; Bianca Bonaventuri; Bianca de Medici. Born in Venice in 1548; died suddenly in Tuscany during a colic epidemic in October 1587; daughter of Bartolommeo Cappello (a Venetian aristocrat); married Pietro Bonaventuri (a clerk), in 1563 (died 1572); became second wife of Francesco I also known as Francis I de Medici (1541–1587), grand duke of Tuscany, in June 1578; children: (first marriage) one daughter, **Pellegrina Bonaventuri** (who married Ulisse Bentivoglio); (second marriage) stepdaughter Marie de Medici (c. 1573–1642).

Bianca Cappello was born into a very wealthy family of the Venetian aristocracy. She was probably well educated, as that was the fashion for Italian noblewomen at the time, and was renowned for her beauty. It is certain that her father, the great Bartolommeo Cappello, had important dynastic plans for his beautiful daughter. However, Bianca rebelled against her parents' plans for her, and eloped to Florence with her lover, Pietro Bonaventuri, when she was 15. Their marriage in November 1563 caused great consternation in Venice and caught the attention of the Venetian authorities. The scandal arose partly because theirs was not a traditionally arranged marriage set up for the benefit of their families, and partly because Pietro was only a poor clerk in a banking firm and thus considered unworthy to marry the daughter of such a noble family.

Bartolommeo Cappello urged the Venetian city leaders to find Bianca and return her to

Bianca Cappello

Venice, and the city officials did their best to oblige. Fortunately for the young couple, however, the powerful Cosimo de Medici, duke of Florence and Tuscany, took their side (probably to anger his enemies in Venice), and they were allowed to remain safely in Florence. However, Bianca, raised in an opulent palace and used to luxury, did not get along with the Bonaventuris, who were indigent and apparently wanted her to perform the same manual labors they did. After only a few years of marriage, Bianca became the mistress of Cosimo de Medici's son and heir, Francesco de Medici, himself already married as well to *Joanna of Austria (1546–1578).

Pietro Bonaventuri seems to have made no great protest to his wife's affair, and for his silence he was rewarded with a clerkship at the duke's court. He himself was known to have many lovers during his time at court. He was murdered in 1572, apparently as the tragic consequence of one of his liaisons. Two years later, Francesco succeeded his father as duke of Tuscany and Florence. At this point, his relationship with Bianca became public knowledge, scandalizing Florence and infuriating his wife Joanna. This state of affairs continued until Joanna's untimely death in April of 1578. Francesco and Bianca married only two months later but did not make the news public until the following year.

Francesco's first wife had given birth to three daughters—*Eleonora de Medici (1567–1611), Caterina (1569–1584), and *Marie de Medici (c. 1573–1642)—but no living sons. Bianca knew that she needed a son to insure her position as Florence's "first lady," since only as the mother of the succeeding duke could she hope to retain her power if Francesco died before her. Bianca did not enjoy popularity in Florence, and was especially disliked by the Medici family. However, she and Francesco had no surviving children, although Bianca tried all sorts of ruses to pretend that she did have a son, including trying to convince the court that an orphaned boy was really her son by Francesco.

Bianca Cappello died suddenly at the age of 39 during a colic epidemic in October 1587. Her husband Francesco followed her in death from the same epidemic only a few days later.

Cappiani, Luisa (b. 1835).

See Farrar, Geraldine for sidebar.

Captain Molly.

See "Two Mollies."

Carabillo, Toni (1926–1997)

American feminist and historian. Born Virginia Ann Carabillo in Jackson Heights, New York, on March 26, 1926; died in Los Angeles, California, on October 28, 1997, after a long bout with cancer; daughter of Ann and Anthony Carabillo (a pharmacist); graduated from Middlebury College, 1948, and Columbia University, M.A., 1949; lived with Judith Meuli (a writer).

Toni Carabillo, feminist leader and historian, was born in Jackson Heights, New York, in 1926. Following graduation from Columbia University, she joined corporate America, working for System Development, a communications company, for 11 years. The job ended abruptly when she was involved in an inhouse survey by women employees that turned up a major disparity between the salaries of men and women and chances for advancement.

In 1967, Carabillo joined NOW and helped launch branches throughout California, serving over the years as president of the Los Angeles chapter, national vice president, and board member. She also co-edited NOW's national newsletter and newspaper. She would be a major fund raiser and organizer for the Equal Rights Amendment ratification during the early 1980s.

In 1969, Carabillo co-founded the Women's Heritage Corp., publishing the *Women's Heritage Calendar and Almanac* and a series of paperbacks, concerning such women as *Elizabeth Cady Stanton and *Lucy Stone. Along with Judith Meuli, who would be her life partner for 30 years, Carabillo opened a graphic arts company in Los Angeles in 1970. Together, they wrote *The Feminization of Power* (1988) and, with June Csida, *Feminist Chronicles, 1953–1993*, a textbook for college-level women's studies sources (1993).

In 1987, Carabillo teamed with Meuli, *Eleanor Smeal, *Peg Yorkin and Katherine Spillar to create the Feminist Majority Foundation, an organization designed to encourage women's empowerment by supporting professional women in the private and public sphere. Carabillo served as national vice president.

Caraway, Hattie Wyatt (1878–1950)

American politician who was the first woman to be elected to the U.S. Senate, serving from November 13, 1931–January 2, 1945. Born Hattie Ophelia Wyatt in Bakerville, Tennessee, on February 1, 1878; died in

Hattie Wyatt Caraway

Falls Church, Virginia, on December 21, 1950; daughter of William Carroll Wyatt and Lucy Mildred (Burch) Wyatt; attended public school; earned a B.A., Dickson (Tennessee) Normal College, 1896; married Thaddeus Horatius Caraway (d. 1931), in 1902; children: three sons, Paul Wyatt, Forrest, and Robert Easley.

Following the death of her husband, U.S. Senator Thaddeus Caraway, in 1931, Hattie Caraway, a devoted homemaker and mother of three sons, received a courtesy appointment to fill out the unexpired term. She later surprised Arkansas politicians by announcing her decision to run for election for a full six-year term. With the support of Senator Huey Long of Louisiana, she defeated seven primary challengers and, in November 1932, became the first woman elected to the U.S. Senate.

With a motherly demeanor that belied her political savvy, "Miss Hattie," as she came to be known, gained the respect of her constituents who elected her to a second term over John Mc-

Clellan, the powerful senator of the 1950s. Although she never delivered a speech on the Senate floor or participated in a debate ("I haven't the heart to take a minute away from the men," she once confided. "The poor dears love it so."), Caraway impressed her colleagues with her integrity and droll wit. Her tenure was marked by support of President Franklin Roosevelt's foreign policy and domestic economic programs. She was also attentive to the needs of her largely agricultural constituency, throwing her support behind farm relief and flood control. She never missed a vote and, unlike many in the Senate, actually studied the bills and listened attentively at committee hearings.

Caraway became the first woman to chair a Senate committee, the first woman senior Senator, and the first woman to conduct a Senate committee hearing. In May 1932, she established another precedent by presiding over the Senate in the absence of Vice-President John Nance Garner and the usual Senate president, pro tem. During her second term, in 1943, Caraway co-sponsored the *Lucretia Mott Equal Rights Amendment to the Constitution, thus becoming the first woman in the Senate to endorse the measure, which had previously been presented in the Senate 11 times.

Regarding the public's interest in her status as the lone woman senator, Caraway once remarked, "I'm really afraid that tourists are going to poke me with their umbrellas." She went on to declare that there was no reason why women shouldn't sit with men in the House and Senate. "Women are essentially practical because they've always had to be. . . . And women are much more realistic than men, particularly when it comes to public questions. Of course, having had the vote for such a short time is a distinct advantage, for we have no inheritance of political buncombe."

In 1944, after 13 years of service, Caraway was defeated in the Arkansas primary by Republican Representative William Fulbright. When the 78th Congress held its last session on December 19, 1944, the Senate rose in tribute to her, a rare occurrence. President Roosevelt subsequently appointed her to the Federal Employees' Compensation Committee, on which she served from 1946 until her death on December 21, 1950.

Barbara Morgan,
Melrose, Massachusetts

Carbery, Ethna (1866–1902).

See MacManus, Anna.

Cardny, Marion (fl. 1300s)

Mistress of Robert II, king of Scotland. Flourished in the 1300s; daughter of John Cardny; paramour of Robert II (1316–1390), king of Scotland (r. 1371–1390); children: (with Robert II) Alexander Stewart, canon of Glasgow; John Stuart of Arntullie; James Stuart of Kinfauns; Walter Stuart.

Carey, Catherine (1529–1569)

England's chief lady of the bedchamber during the reign of Henry VIII. Name variations: Katherine Carey. Born in 1529; died on June 18, 1569; daughter of William Carey and *Mary Boleyn (d. 1543, sister of *Anne Boleyn); married Sir Francis Knollys; children: *Lettice Knollys (c. 1541–1634); William Knollys (1547–1632); comptroller of Queen *Elizabeth I's household.

Carey, Mary (d. 1543).

See Boleyn, Anne for sidebar on Mary Boleyn.

Carey, Miriam E. (1858–1937)

American librarian. Born on February 21, 1858, in Peoria, Illinois; died on January 9, 1937, in Cheyenne, Wyoming; daughter and second of three children of Reverend Isaac Eddy (a Presbyterian minister); mother's name unknown; attended Rockford Seminary, 1876; attended Oberlin College, Ohio, 1877; attended library school of the University of Illinois, 1898.

Miriam E. Carey was the innovative force in the movement to establish libraries in state institutions throughout the United States. She began her work as a librarian at age 40, following many years of teaching and some time spent at Hull House in Chicago, where she was greatly influenced by the work of *Jane Addams. In 1899, after a year in library school, Carey took a job as director of the public library in Burlington, Iowa, where **Alice S. Tyler**, secretary of the library commission, and **Fanny Duren**, a young college graduate, were experimenting with the use of books in the new School for Delinquent Boys. Their work, and Tyler's convincing presentation to the Iowa Board of Control, eventually led to the creation of the position of supervisor for the Iowa State Institution Libraries, the first position of its kind in America. Appointed to the new post in 1906, Carey oversaw the pioneering program, which utilized books as a rehabilitative tool in prison wards and mental hospitals, as well as in tuberculosis sanitariums and schools for delinquent children. In 1913, after success with the Iowa plan, Carey was appointed to head the institutional libraries in Minnesota, where she organized libraries at 18 various institutions across the state.

During World War I, the American Library Association sent Carey to establish libraries in army camps and hospitals across five southern states, which would prove to be a great morale booster for soldiers in training, in action, or in hospitals, and helped spur a later national movement to establish civilian hospital libraries. From 1913 to 1923, Carey also served as chair of the Committee on Libraries in Correctional Institutions. After her retirement in 1927 at age 69, she taught at the newly established library school at the University of Minnesota and took up the study of Italian. She also wrote some short stories based on her prison experiences. Miriam E. Carey died on January 9, 1937, at age 78.

Barbara Morgan,
Melrose, Massachusetts

Caria, queen of.

See Artemisia II (c. 395–351 BCE).

Carinthia, duchess of.

See Maultasch, Margaret (1318–1369).

Carisbrooke, marquise of.

See Mountbatten, Irene (1890–1956).

Carlén, Emilia (1807–1892)

Swedish novelist and feminist. Name variations: Emilie Smith Flygare-Carlén; Emilia Carlen. Born Emilia Smith in Strömstad, Sweden, on August 8, 1807; died in Stockholm on February 5, 1892; youngest of 14 children of Rutger Smith (a merchant, shipowner, and retired sea captain); self-educated; married Axel Flygare (a doctor), in 1827 (died 1833); married Johan Gabriel Carlén (a lawyer and poet), in 1841; children: (first marriage) son Edvard Flygare (1820–1853), and three others (two died in childhood); (out of wedlock) daughter, Rosa Carlén (1836–1883), who was also a popular novelist.

Emilia Carlén

Emilia Carlén, considered Sweden's first regional

writer, was the youngest of a family of 14 children whose father, Rutger Smith, was a retired sea-captain. Rutger had settled down as a small merchant in Strömstad, and Emilia often accompanied him on the voyages he made along the coast; she would later become noted for her stories of seafarers, fishermen, and smugglers, with whom she came in frequent contact as a child.

In 1827, Emilia married an impoverished, elderly physician from Kronbergslän and lived with him in the province of Småland, The couple had four children, two of whom died in childhood. After her husband's death in 1833, she returned to her old home. While there, she fell in love with another man and was soon pregnant. When he died before they could get married, Emilia avoided the scrutiny of society by secretly giving birth, then adopting the child, future novelist ◄⅜ **Rosa Carlén**. Five years later, 30-year-old Emilia published her first novel, *Waldemar Klein* (1838), anonymously, and it met with great success.

On her father's advice, in 1839, she moved to Stockholm; shortly thereafter, in 1841, she married the jurist and poet Johan Gabriel Carlén (1814–1875). She produced one or two novels annually over the next 12 years, and her works were widely read. Carlén's son by her first marriage, Edvard Flygare (1820–1853), had published three books and shown great promise before his premature death in 1853. The tragedy silenced Carlén's pen for the next six years. She resumed her writing in 1858 and would continue until 1884. Carlén was honored by the Swedish Academy in 1862, and her house became a meeting place for Stockholm's literati until the death of her husband in 1875, when she completely retired from the world. With the considerable sum earned from her writing, she founded charitable endowments to aid teachers, established the Rutger Smith Fund for poor fishermen and their widows, and instituted an endowment for students to the University of Uppsala in memory of her son.

In her work, Emilia Carlén was most comfortable depicting fisherfolk and peasantry, but her writing embraced all facets of Swedish life; her stories were considered rich, her characters natural. As a novelist, she shared the limelight with her fellow countrywoman, *Fredrika Bremer. The most famous of Carlén's tales are *Rosen på Tistelön* (*The Rose of Tistelön*, 1842); *Enslingen på Johannisskäret* (1846; English translation published as *The Hermit of the Johannis Rock*, 4 vols., 1853); *Jungfrutornet* (*The Maiden's Tower*, 1848), and *Ett köpemanshus i skärgarden* (*The Merchant's House on the Cliffs*, 1859). She also wrote *Gustav Lindorm* (1835). Carlén's novels were collected in 31 volumes (Stockholm, 1869–1875).

Carlén, Rosa (1836–1883).
See Carlén, Emilia for sidebar.

Carles, Emilie (1900–1979)
French teacher, activist and autobiographer who was a fierce champion of the ideals of human freedom and a passionate defender of the natural environment of her beloved valley. Born Emilie Allais in 1900 in Val-des-Pres, France; died on July 29, 1979; daughter of Joseph Allais and Catherine (Vallier) Allais; married Jean Carles, in 1928; children: Georges, Janny, Michel.

Had a long career as a teacher (1918–62) in the remote Alpine region where she was born; in later life, became a French national celebrity with a best-selling book.

Born in 1900 in the remote French Alpine village of Val-des-Pres, Emilie Allais became a village schoolteacher. Although she never left her region except for a brief stay in Paris, she was involved with the major ideas of her century and spoke eloquently to the urbanized world about the increasingly threatened rural way of life. Like virtually everyone living in the French Alps a century ago, the Allais family was poor. Emilie's father Joseph eked out a living on the beautiful but bare land around their village, an alpine settlement in the Clarée Valley near Briancon and the Italian border. This region of short summers and long, bitterly cold winters made for a dangerous landscape. When Emilie was four, her mother was killed by lightning. Two years later, Emilie almost lost her life when she fell from a hayloft. Life was difficult: nearly all of the families in the area labored from dawn to dusk for the bare necessities. From her earliest years, Emilie was expected to contribute to the family's coffer by working both in the fields and in the stables. In later years, she would describe her mountainous world simply as "the harshest place on earth."

⅜► **Carlén, Rosa** (1836–1883)
*Swedish novelist. Name variations: Rosa Carlen. Born in Sweden in 1836; died in 1883; daughter of *Emilia Carlén.*

Rosa Carlén's first book, *Agnes Tell*, was well received in 1861. She followed with *Tuva* (1862), *Helena, a Woman's History* (1863), *Three Years and Three Days* (1864), and *The Gypsy's Son* (1866), which is regarded as her best work.

The village life that molded Emilie Allais was overwhelmingly communitarian, and group survival was the community's paramount goal. In this environment occurrences like the death of a beloved child "didn't amount to much" if the village was able to remain biologically viable; such a perspective was not callous, but hard-headedly realistic. Deeply rooted in tradition, the people of her valley had a deep and abiding sense of place and loyalty to their soil. While their conservatism could sometimes be narrow and intolerant, at other times it was a source of strength, allowing them to collectively defy the aggressively dislocating intrusions of the outside world.

Although geographically remote, Val-des-Pres was by no means cut off from the larger world. A bright girl, young Emilie was intensely curious about the larger universe, and education provided her means of escape. She was able to study in Paris from 1918 through 1920, supporting herself by working as a teacher and monitor in boarding schools. By the early 1920s, she had returned to her home region and was working as a substitute teacher not only in her native village of Val-des-Pres but also in one-room schoolhouses in the nearby communities of Les Gourniers and Queyras. From the outset of her career, Emilie loved teaching. A realist rather than a starry-eyed idealist when it came to her students, she was aware that many of them had been raised in narrow and closed-minded family environments.

Although Emilie Allais had decided to return to her native valley to teach, she was influenced almost as strongly by the outside world of ideas and ideals as she was by the unforgiving mountains and valleys of Val-des-Pres. During her stay in Paris, she had been deeply impressed by the ideas of anarchist friends who alerted her to the dangers of a central government that could easily turn tyrannical. The bloodbath of the recently terminated world war also left a deep mark on her, and she became increasingly receptive to pacifist thinking, which she saw as the best chance of avoiding another such catastrophe. Her attraction to radical ideas received additional encouragement when she met and married Jean Carles, a committed pacifist who worked as an innkeeper and house painter. They married in 1928 and had an extraordinarily happy marriage. Emilie would say of her husband: "through the warmth he radiated, the gifts he lavished on everyone, Jean Carles dealt out happiness." Their first child, a son, died in childbirth. While the parents grieved, the village's mayor had the infant's body buried in the far end of the cemetery "in the common grave re-served for people who've been drowned or hanged." Refusing to be broken by tragedy, Emilie and Jean continued to want a family. A year later, she gave birth to another son who was followed two years after by a healthy daughter.

Despite their surroundings, both Emilie and Jean were intensely involved with the important political and literary currents of the day. Jean subscribed to "all the progressive periodicals of the day" and introduced Emilie to the books of major authors. Sharing with her husband a deep love of liberty, Emilie worked hard to pass on the ideals of freedom to her students. At a time in France when extreme patriotism and intolerance was the norm, she introduced her students to ideas critical of existing society, such as anarchism and pacifism. If this meant telling them that even Napoleon Bonaparte was not a hero, but a tyrant whose lust for power deserved to be halted, she was equal to the task. Emilie Carles was fearless, and both she and her husband were enthusiastic supporters of the Popular Front government that in 1936 initiated major social reforms in France and attempted—but ultimately failed—to create an effective anti-Nazi coalition among the European powers. During these years, the Carles family managed a communal inn that catered to urban workers, many of whom were now enjoying the first paid vacations of their lives as a result of Popular Front social legislation.

Emilie Carles lost her teaching job in 1941 as a result of her well-known political views. Jean Carles joined the anti-Nazi *maquis* forces active in the mountains and was willing to accept the risks of working with them. But, true to his pacifist principles, he never carried a rifle during these dangerous years. With liberation in 1944, Emilie returned to her teaching job, working at the communal school in Val-des-Pres until her retirement in 1962. In the 1970s, she organized her friends and neighbors throughout the Clarée Valley in a united front of opposition to a superhighway planned to cut through the region. She also opposed the plans of various developers who argued that they would "improve" the area; Carles was convinced they would totally destroy its scenic beauties and remaining institutions of human solidarity. In addition to getting virtually all of her neighbors and former students to sign petitions against the highway, she also urged local farmers to drive their tractors in a dramatic demonstration in the town of Briancon. To top things off, the sprightly septuagenarian held a press conference in Paris to bring her and her neighbors' concerns to the attention of all of France. A canny practitioner of modern media politics, she brought the politicians and shady speculators of Paris to heel when it became clear that their goal was not the improvement but the despoliation of her valley.

In 1977, Emilie Carles was in her old age when she became a national celebrity in France with the publication of her autobiography, *Une Soupe aux herbes sauvages* (*A Soup of Wild Herbs*), in which she related her life in sharp, clear detail. Selling almost a quarter of a million copies in the first three months after publication, the book became one of the French literary world's most remarkable bestsellers. Carles appeared on national television recounting to an overwhelmingly urbanized nation tales of a virtually unknown world, including such vignettes of her youth as the proper methods of winter storage of food and the wolf stories told by superstitious peasants when they gathered in their stables at night to tell tall tales.

Emilie Carles was a last living link with a vanishing rural France of extreme poverty and self-reliance; she was also an extraordinary woman in her own right, a person of acute intellectual powers and high moral vision. Intellectually, she had liberated herself as a young woman from the stifling conservatism of rural life, while at the same time remaining deeply rooted in the better aspects of its values. She died on July 29, 1979, but her legacy of rural activism lived on. Carles' energized neighbors continued to fight for the preservation of the Clarée Valley, and in 1990 the French government named the valley a protected natural site.

SOURCES:

Carles, Emilie, with Robert Destanque. *Une Soupe aux herbes sauvages*. Definitive ed. Paris: Editions Robert Laffont, 1988.

———, with Robert Destanque. *A Life of Her Own: A Countrywoman in Twentieth-Century France*. Translated with an introduction and afterword by Avriel H. Goldberger. New Brunswick, NJ: Rutgers University Press, 1991.

———. *Mes Rubans de la St. Claude*. Paris: Encre, 1982.

Robinson, Lillian S. "A Soup of Wild Herbs," in *The Nation*. Vol. 253, no. 6. August 26–September 2, 1991, pp. 234–236.

Rose, Phyllis, ed. *The Norton Book of Women's Lives*. NY: W.W. Norton, 1993.

John Haag, Associate Professor,
University of Georgia, Athens, Georgia

Carlile.

Variant of Carlisle or Carlyle.

Carlisle.

Variant of Carlyle.

Carlisle, countess of.

See Hay, Lucy (1599–1660).
See Cavendish, Georgiana (1783–1858).
See Howard, Rosalind Frances (1845–1921).

Carlot.

See Edgren, Anne Charlotte (1849–1892).

Carlota.

Variant of Carlotta.

Carlota (1840–1927)

Belgian princess who accompanied Maximilian on an ill-fated adventure to Mexico, where she was crowned empress and witnessed royal splendor, civil war, personal tragedy, and ultimately dementia in an attempt to bring monarchical rule to the land of the Aztecs. Name variations: *Carlotta, Charlotte, Charlotte of Belgium, Charlotte Saxe-Coburg; Marie Charlotte of Saxe-Coburg.* Pronunciation: *Car-LOW-ta.* Born Marie Charlotte Amelie Augustine Victoire Clementine Leopoldine on June 7, 1840, at Laeken, Belgium; died at the castle of Bouchout, Belgium, on January 19, 1927; daughter of Leopold I (1790–1865), king of the Belgians (r. 1831–1865), and his third wife Princess Louise d'Orléans (1812–1850); married Archduke Maximilian von Habsburg, on July 27, 1857; children: none, except for the adoption of son Agustín de Iturbide in 1865.

After marriage to Archduke Maximilian and his appointment as Austrian viceroy of Lombardy-Venetia, the couple began residence in northeastern Italy; after the Austrians had been expelled from Lombardy (1859), they relocated to the palace of Miramar on the Adriatic coast near Trieste; bored with his idle life at the palace (and evidently exasperated by the ambitions of his wife), Maximilian made a grand tour of Brazil (1860); meanwhile agents of the Mexican conservative party and of Napoleon III began to float inquiries regarding the couple's possible interest in assuming the throne of Mexico; despite some early misgivings, which he soon recanted, Maximilian was won over by Carlota's enthusiasm (1863) and they embarked for Mexico to accept the crown; upon arrival in Mexico City, Carlota and Maximilian busied themselves with organizing court life, founding hospitals and scientific societies, and coordinating political and military affairs with their French sponsors; guerrilla actions against the monarchy kept Maximilian and the French from consolidating their hold on the country; Carlota, in deeply humiliating circumstances, was forced by Maximilian to agree to the adoption of a Mexican-born son (in an effort to placate the popu-

lace); this effort came to nothing (1867), and under steady U.S. pressure, the French expeditionary force that supported the Empire began to evacuate Mexico; hoping to buy time, Maximilian sent Carlota to Europe to negotiate with Napoleon III for further aid; by the time she arrived in Paris, Carlota was showing clear signs of severe mental strain; meanwhile, Maximilian, abandoned by all but his untrained Mexican conscripts, found himself surrounded by republican troops at Querétaro; after its fall, he faced the firing squad; upon hearing the news of his death, Carlota lost her mind and spent the next 60 years insane, dying as a mental recluse in a Belgian castle (1927).

The green, rain-soaked Belgian plain that surrounds the palace of Laeken presents a picturesque appearance, but it has none of the exotic quality of sweet jasmine and spiny cacti that one encounters at Chapultepec palace in Mexico City. Yet, despite the striking divergences in terrain and climate, the two edifices have the strongest of historical links. Between them, they provided the chief residences in the 1860s for the Empress Carlota, who, together with her Austrian consort Maximilian, painted one of the more colorful, though tragic, chapters in the long history of misunderstanding between the Old World and the New.

When Carlota was born in 1840, her father Leopold I had just entered his 50th year and was celebrating his tenth anniversary as king of the Belgians. The Great Powers had originally engineered his accession to the throne as an act of political expediency. Now, however, after nearly a decade of war, blockade, and complicated diplomacy before the independence and frontiers of Belgium could be recognized, Leopold had more than earned the respect of his subjects and of foreign powers. Duty was always uppermost in his mind. To that end, he proved willing to set aside his emotional life in order to pursue national ends. To cement an alliance with France, he married Princess ❧▶ **Louise d'Orléans**, the daughter of King Louis Philippe, a woman for whom he cared not at all. Carlota was their fourth child, their only daughter.

Leopold's relation with the young Carlota was cool. The rest of the family, however, always held her in high regard. A small-framed girl with dark brown eyes, she deeply impressed her tutors with her intelligence and precocity. At 13, she could speak perfect German and English as well as French. Though the king himself was a Protestant, he made sure that Carlota was raised in the Catholic faith of her mother (and of the

majority of his subjects). Carlota, in turn, became very devout indeed. Her undoubted devotion, however, never quite obscured her own ambition, and her conviction that Belgium was too small a realm to bother with.

By her 16th birthday, Carlota became eligible to act on her ambitions. She had several important suitors. One was the 24-year-old Prince George of Saxony, and the other was the late Portuguese Queen *Maria II da Gloria's eldest son, who had recently ascended his country's throne as Pedro V. This 19-year-old monarch had the strong support of Britain's Queen *Victoria, who fancied herself the grand matchmaker among the European royal houses. But Carlota would not cooperate; she hated the prospect of living her life in Lisbon. Neither had she any warm disposition toward Saxony. When the Austrian Archduke Maximilian paid her court in 1856, however, this was a very different matter.

Maximilian was both charming and handsome, with blue eyes that took Carlota's breath

❧▶ **Louise d'Orléans** (1812–1850)

*Queen of the Belgians. Name variations: Louise Bourbon; Louise of France; Louise of Orleans or Orléans; Louise-Marie d'Orleans; Louise Marie d'Orleans. Born Louise-Marie Bourbon-Penthievre on April 3, 1812, in Palermo, Sicily; died on October 10 (some sources cite the 11th), 1850, in Ostende, Belgium; interred in Laeken, Belgium; daughter of Louis Philippe I (1773–1850), citizen king of France (r. 1830–1850), and *Maria Amalia (1782–1866); became third wife of Leopold I, king of the Belgians (r. 1831–1865), on August 9, 1832; children: Leopold (b. 1833); Leopold II (1835–1909), king of the Belgians (r. 1865–1909); Philip (1837–1905), count of Flanders; *Carlota (1840–1927), empress of Mexico.*

Like so many royals, the gentle and loving Louise d'Orléans was used as a pawn in a political alliance; it is said that her father Louis Philippe wept when he had to sacrifice his favorite daughter to widower Leopold, 22 years her senior. (Leopold's first wife was morganatic wife *Karoline Bauer. His second wife, who had died in 1817, was *Charlotte Augusta, princess of Wales and daughter of George IV and *Caroline of Brunswick.) But the sweet-tempered Louise grew attached to Leopold and was a considerate wife. She was also popular with her subjects. When the king ensconced his Flemish paramour Arcadie Clairet de Viescourt (**Mme Meyer von Eppinghoven**) in the Rue Royale, Belgians were furious for their "good little Queen." Louise, who doted on her father, died a few months after his death in 1850, when her daughter Carlota was ten.

Carlota

learned to speak the language. They sponsored cultural events and scientific societies. Yet they could not easily stay in the good graces of their Italian subjects who, not surprisingly, regarded them as foreign interlopers, only the latest in a long line of outside exploiters. Most Lombards and Venetians therefore did everything in their power to undermine the Austrian regime. And in this they had the support of two foreign powers, Piedmont and France, whose respective leaders, Victor Emmanuel and Napoleon III, had motives that were far from disinterested.

Seeing the writing on the wall only at the last moment, Maximilian urged Franz Joseph to allow a measure of home rule to the Italians. This being refused, he went on to witness the French and Piedmontese invasion of 1859, which resulted in short order in the loss of Lombardy (though not Venetia). Austrian blundering had brought about the empire's defeat.

This whole period in many ways seemed a precursor to what Carlota and Maximilian would eventually see in Mexico. For the moment, the two sought to forget their disillusionment. They traveled to the island of Madeira, where she stayed while he went on to Brazil to tour the Amazon river valley. He returned some months later enamored of the American continent and its warm climate, though highly critical of the social injustices he saw there. Here again, he displayed the curious blend of liberal sentiment and autocratic *hauteur* that marked his politics and his life with Carlota.

The archduchess still held high ambitions, though in one respect, she was destined for immediate disappointment. It was said that Maximilian caught syphilis from a Viennese prostitute and that he passed on the disease to his wife, who, as a result, was barren. This personal tragedy was only the first of many she would know in her life.

In October 1861, the Austrian foreign minister came to Maximilian's palace of Miramar near Trieste with a surprising proposal—would he consider becoming emperor of Mexico?

For over a decade, the Mexican nation had been torn by a vicious civil war between Liberals and Conservatives. The latter party had recently suffered a major defeat, leaving power in the country in the hands of the full-blooded Indian president Benito Juárez. With the national economy a wreck, however, Juárez found it necessary to borrow heavily in Europe. And his government was manifestly unable to pay these debts. He declared a moratorium on debt payments in

away. He was also the younger brother of Franz Joseph, the emperor of Austria, a country of primary rather than tertiary importance in Europe. For Carlota, his proposal of marriage came as a reflection of deep affection as well as of political consideration. Maximilian, for his part, regarded her with fondness and passable respect but little more. His infidelities would later become almost scandalous, but at this stage he saw in Carlota the perfect consort: loyal, trustworthy, fiercely dedicated to their future greatness.

In the autumn of 1856, Franz Joseph decided that the time had come to liberalize his policies toward his Italian domains. Aside from some minor political concessions, the first move he made was to appoint his brother viceroy of Lombardy-Venetia. After their wedding in Brussels in the summer of 1857, Maximilian and Carlota immediately set out for Milan where he took up his viceregal duties.

The young couple did everything in their power to win the approval of the Italians. They

1861, which brought an immediate armed intervention by France, Spain, and Britain. The latter two countries withdrew their forces in quick order, but Napoleon III decided that the Mexican venture was his opportunity to extend French influence in a major way. To accomplish this, and at the same time avoid U.S. opposition, he required the appearance of Mexican support. The defeated Conservatives provided this support in exchange for Napoleon's assurances that he would find for them a European prince to act as emperor; they could thus realize one of their fondest political ambitions—to restore the monarchical system in Mexico.

Maximilian seemed a perfect candidate. He was, first of all, a Habsburg, a descendant of Charles V in whose name Mexico had been conquered in the 1500s. His majestic physical appearance was equally striking—some of Maximilian's Conservative supporters even argued that the Mexican masses would take him for the blonde Aztec god Quetzalcoatl, come back after all these years to free them from the tyranny of Juárez. This, to be sure, was nonsense, but it pleased the archduke's ears to hear it.

The quaintness of his prospective subjects might have amused Maximilian, but he was still unsure as to the wisdom of accepting the Mexican proposal. He had strong reservations about its legality. It was Carlota who finally convinced him that duty and honor demanded his presence in Mexico. The poor people needed a protector and had turned to him in desperation—he could not refuse. This suggested a curious irony; by appealing to Maximilian's liberal instincts, Carlota persuaded him to give in to the entreaties of Mexican reactionaries and French interventionists. Napoleon III, the same ruler who had humiliated the Austrians in Lombardy, now portrayed himself as the disinterested sponsor of Maximilian's New World venture. The French ruler did exact a price, however. He made the new empire pay the cost of French occupation— a concession that Carlota urged the archduke to make. Before the couple had even embarked for Mexico, therefore, they had tripled their new country's foreign debt.

Their arrival at the port of Veracruz in May 1864 had an eerie quality to it. They had expected to see throngs of cheering crowds. Instead, save for French troops, the streets seemed deserted, the result, they were told, of an outbreak of plague. The truth was more prosaic: Juarista feeling remained strong in many areas of the country and the bulk of the populace had no use whatsoever for the new imperial couple (and this despite the favorable results of a plebescite arranged by the French army).

Mexico City, with its more cosmopolitan environment, willingly gave Maximilian and Carlota a chance to prove themselves. And model liberal monarchs they turned out to be. They gave magnificent balls, founded scientific and cultural societies, and spent lavishly to refurbish the national palace and other public buildings. They issued contracts to European companies to construct railroads. Hospitals and orphanages received their generous patronage. Their imperial majesties even snubbed some of their erstwhile friends, arguing with justice that Conservative programs worked counter to the interests of the majority of the people.

> *W*herever she went she attracted regard, especially in Mexico City, where even the most irreconcilable enemies of the Empire admired her magnanimous heart.
>
> —José Luis Blasio

The proud Maximilian, now sporting a dashing *sombrero* and native costume, actually began to think of himself as a master builder as well as a Mexican patriot. His wife knew better. Carlota recognized the urgency of consolidating the monarchy and beginning the reconstruction of the economy. In her first letter to French Empress *Eugénie, she stressed the need for building from the ground up after the long spate of civil war and misgovernment:

> Everything in this country calls for reconstruction; nothing is to be found, either physical or moral, but what Nature provides. . . . Things will go on here, if your Majesties will stand by us, since they must go on, and we mean them to go on; but it is an appalling task, for when a country has spent forty years of its experience in destroying all that it possessed in the way of resources and government, everything cannot be set right in a day.

Carlota obviously grasped the seriousness of the challenge, realizing that governing Mexico required an immense effort and the time in which to implement change. She tried to supply the practical attitude to counterbalance Maximilian's visionary side. She was concerned to keep her husband's mind on the dangers that confronted them if they failed to take their task seriously.

This did not prove easy. Maximilian had an obsession with the outward forms of monarchy, the pomp and ritual of court life. He kept a focus on these details and forgot to keep an eye on the internal politics of Mexico. This was certainly not the case with Juárez, who, hidden in the mountain fastness of the interior, had succeeded in forging a guerrilla army that the French could not suppress. In addition, with the end of the U.S. Civil War, the Americans now turned their attention to Mexico. Refusing to recognize the Maximilian government, they began to supply Juárez with arms and munitions. Ulysses S. Grant went so far as to order General Philip Sheridan to amass a large army on the Texan frontier to directly pressure Napoleon III into evacuating Mexico as soon as possible.

Maximilian remained oblivious to all this for the longest time. But Carlota did not. She knew that time was conceivably running out, and she took the lead in badgering the French ambassador and military representatives for continued aid. She also agreed to a personal sacrifice that every fibre in her body rejected—she said yes to the adoption of a Mexican-born boy, the grandson of an earlier monarch, who would act as the crown prince. This action, her courtiers hoped, would solidify the imperial couple's links with the Mexican people. It clearly galled the empress to accept this condition, however much she recognized its necessity; she had become aware of Maximilian's infidelities with various Mexican women and her deep frustrations with their personal relationship were already beginning to tear at her. She now experienced bouts of depression and unreasoning fear. Had circumstances been different, she probably would have taken a long rest cure at a European sanitarium. Instead, as Napoleon III announced his intention to withdraw his troops, Maximilian sent Carlota as a special envoy to the court at Paris to beg for the intercession of Eugénie: French troops had to stay—only the final blow remained to strike against Juárez and then the Mexican Empire could stand on its own.

Before Carlota could present this appeal to the French, however, she began to suffer delusions. She raved in her sleep. She spoke while awake of unnamed assassins following her everywhere. Court physicians recommended immediate hospitalization and called in specialists from Vienna. These men, when they arrived, expressed their fears for her future.

Maximilian, when informed of his wife's condition, considered the course of abdication. Many of his closest advisers had pressed for this for some time. The French commander in Mexico, Marshal François Bazaine, offered to escort Maximilian and his party out of the country.

Still the emperor wavered, as so often in the past. In the end, conscious of his perceived obligation to his native troops, he rejected Bazaine's offer and set out to confront Juárez at the head of a conscript army.

In early 1867, as the last French troops set sail for Europe, Maximilian's levees found themselves trapped by the republican forces at the little central-Mexican town of Querétaro. At the last moment, a trusted lieutenant betrayed the emperor and delivered him into the hands of the Juaristas. A trial ensued a month thereafter, and Maximilian was sentenced to death. He faced the firing squad bravely, evidently with little rancor in his heart either for Juárez and for those Europeans who had deceived him so callously.

Though the news of his death was conveyed to Carlota in the most careful manner possible, still it was enough to unhinge her mind at the age of 26. Already there was in Europe much debate as to her role in the whole Mexican fiasco. The radical French journalist Georges Clemenceau, who would one day become president, was scornful of the sentiment her case had aroused:

> His wife is mad, you say. Nothing more just. This almost makes me believe in Providence. Was it not her ambitions that incited the fool? I regret that she *has* lost her reason and cannot realize that she killed her husband and that a people are avenging themselves.

Other commentators at the time were kinder, though it mattered not at all to Carlota. She spent the next 60 years in seclusion at the château of Bouchout in Belgium. Dynasties fell, republics were established, the automobile and airplane were invented, and a world war went by, and still the old empress "reigned" within its palace walls. Her insanity never abated. She died still pining for her lost husband in 1927.

SOURCES:

Haslip, Joan. *The Crown of Mexico: Maximilian and his Empress Carlota.* NY: Holt, Rinehart, Winston, 1971.

Hyde, H. Montgomery. *Mexican Empire.* NY: Macmillan, 1946.

O'Connor, Richard. *The Cactus Throne: The Tragedy of Maximilian and Carlotta.* NY: Putnam, 1971.

Ridley, Jasper. *Maximilian and Juárez.* Ticknor & Fields, 1992.

SUGGESTED READING:

Basch, Samuel. *Memories of Mexico: A History of the Last Ten Months of the Empire.* Trinity University Press, 1973.

Blasio, José Luis. *Maximilian Emperor of Mexico: Memoirs of his Private Secretary.* CT: Yale University Press, 1934.

Harding, Bertita. *The Phantom Crown.* London, 1935.

Thomas Whigham, Associate Professor of History, University of Georgia, Athens, Georgia

Carlota Joaquina (1775–1830)

Queen of Portugal as wife of John VI, renowned for political intrigue and a leading proponent of conservatism and absolutism against the rising tide of liberalism after 1822. Name variations: Carlotta, Charlotte or Joaquina Carlota de Borbon; Charlotte Bourbon; Charlotte of Spain. Born on April 25, 1775, in Aranjuez, Spain; died on January 7, 1830, in Queluz Palace outside Lisbon; daughter of Charles IV, king of Spain (r. 1788–1808), and Maria Luisa Teresa of Parma (1751–1819); sister of *Maria Luisa of Lucca and Etruria (1782–1824); betrothed to John, prince of Portugal in 1778; married Joao VI also known as John VI (d. March 10, 1826), king of Portugal (r. 1816–1826); children: *Teresa of Portugal (1793–1874); António Pio (1795–1801); ❧▶ Maria Isabel of Portugal (1797–1818); Peter IV (b. 1798), king of Portugal (r. 1826) also known as Pedro I, emperor of Brazil (r. 1826–1831); *Francisca of Portugal (1800–1834); Isabel Maria (1801–1876); Miguel also known as Michael I (1802–1866), king of Portugal (r. 1828–1834); Maria da Assumpção (1805–1834); Ana de Jesus Maria (1806–1857, who married Nuno José Sevro de Moura, 1st duke of Loulé).

Death of his older brother José made John the crown prince and Carlota Joaquina the crown princess of Portugal (1788); John declared regent due to insanity of his mother, Maria I (1792); John, Carlota Joaquina, and court fled to Brazil due to Napoleonic invasion (1807); Carlota Joaquina initially tried to claim regency of the Spanish River Plate territory and then unsuccessfully pressed for the right to rule it as empress (1808–12); acclaimed queen of Portugal (1816); liberal Revolution of 1820 in Portugal; returned to Portugal with John VI (1821); Rua Formosa Conspiracy to depose John VI in favor of Carlota Joaquina (April 1822); "Vilafrancada" movement (May 1822); "Abrilada" revolt headed by Carlota Joaquina and her son Michael against the liberal monarchy (1824); death of John VI brought to the throne Pedro IV, who as emperor of Brazil abdicated the Portuguese crown in favor of his daughter, Maria da Glória (1826); with Carlota Joaquina's support, Michael declared absolute monarch, leading to civil war (1828).

Little about Queen Carlota Joaquina matched the stereotypes of regal dignity or womanly submission to male authority associated with the Old Régime. Born April 25, 1775, in the Aranjuez Palace south of Madrid, she was the daughter of the Spanish crown prince Charles (the future Charles IV) and *Maria Luisa Teresa of Parma. When she was three, her grandfather,

Charles III, approved her engagement to the Portuguese prince, John (João), to fortify amicable relations between the two monarchies. As a ten-year-old, she left her beloved Spain to marry, although she and John then lived separately at different palaces for five years until Carlota Joaquina reached puberty. The separation was a foretaste of their conjugal life: despite giving birth to seven children, she hated her husband, often lived apart from him, and caused John frequent scandal and controversy.

The royal couple had little in common except their homeliness. Andoche Junot, Napoleon's officer assigned as a diplomat to the Portuguese court, reportedly told his wife after meeting John and Carlota Joaquina: "My God! How ugly he is! My God! How ugly the princess is! How ugly they all are!" Phlegmatic but thoughtful with an oversized head and drooping lip, the prince wore clothes till they literally fell from his body. A glutton, he stored boxes of roasted chicken in his pockets in the event hunger tempted. In 1792, he became regent and *de facto* ruler of Portugal due to the mental illness of his mother, *Maria I (1734–1816).

Carlota Joaquina was short, little more than four and a half feet tall, with a hooked nose, large uneven teeth, unruly hair, and "bluish" lips. Whereas her husband seemed lethargic to observers, she exuded energy. She loved hunting and was an excellent equestrian, even after a riding accident broke her leg and left her lame. John loved religious music and ritual. According to historian Neill Macaulay, "In music, the princess preferred the profane to the sacred. In men, she preferred almost anyone to Dom John." Generally biased against her, foreign diplomats found her conspiratorial, avid for power, vindictive, and mean. William Beckford, for example, wrote of

❧▶ Maria Isabel of Portugal (1797–1818)

Portuguese princess. Name variations: Marie-Isabel Braganza; Isabella of Portugal. Born on May 19, 1797, at Queluz; died on December 26, 1818, in Madrid; daughter of Carlota Joaquina (1775–1830) and John VI (1767–1826), king of Portugal (r. 1816–1826); became second wife of Fernando or Ferdinand VII (1784–1833), king of Spain (r. 1813–1833), on September 29, 1816; sister of Peter or Pedro IV, king of Portugal, and Michael I, king of Portugal. Ferdinand VII's first wife was *Maria Antonia of Naples (1784–1806); his third was *Maria Josepha of Saxony (1803–1829); his fourth was *Maria Cristina I of Naples (1806–1878).

"her restless intrigues of all hues, political as well as private—her wanton freaks of favouritism and atrocious acts of cruelty."

Her hatred of John perhaps reflected her dependence on him. Carlota Joaquina delighted in defying him, and John could not help but perceive her scorn. Disdaining Portugal and its ally, Great Britain, she clung haughtily to her Spanish heritage. She found Lisbon boring, with "a husband she considered an imbecile, an insane queen and a poor nobility, without the least brilliance." By the late 1790s, her estrangement from John reached the point that she resided at the Ramalhão estate while he stayed at the monastery-palace of Mafra. Her later children had questionable parentage. One rumor held Michael (Miguel) to be the son of a gardener at Ramalhão; another that the Marquis of Marialva had sired him. Certainly by 1802 when Michael was born, Carlota Joaquina and her husband could hardly tolerate joint appearances on state occasions. In 1806, John fell seriously ill. She unsuccessfully maneuvered to have him declared insane and herself regent. To achieve her objectives, she sought her parents' support, wildly asserting that the Portuguese people loved her and would back her with force.

> $\mathcal{S}$he was an ambitious woman who gave herself, with singular and stubborn ardor, to the most daring plans of conquest and grandeur, without being restrained by the difficulties of her position, her sex, nor much less the bad luck and dangers of her unfortunate undertakings.
>
> —Roberto Etcheparenborda

The following year, one of the most fateful in Portuguese history, opened new vistas for her schemes. Napoleon tried to intimidate John into breaking Portugal's alliance with Great Britain. When that failed, the French invaded. The British navy saved the royal family by escorting it, along with many courtiers, to Rio de Janeiro. Though Carlota Joaquina accompanied John to be with her children, she would have preferred staying in Europe, as her father Charles IV had aligned himself with Napoleon. During the voyage to Brazil, she refused to sail aboard the *Príncipe Real* with her husband, instead sailing on the *Afonso d'Albuquerque*. They arrived in Rio de Janeiro on March 7, 1808, to the delight of the Brazilians. John occupied the viceroy's palace, while Carlota Joaquina lived in apartments above the mint. She disliked Brazil, long-

ing for the pleasures and sophistication of Europe. She made little effort to ingratiate herself with her Spanish-American subjects. As her carriage passed in the street, she demanded that all kneel before it and ordered her guards to beat anyone who failed to show her proper deference.

Meanwhile, Napoleon turned on Spain and forced Charles IV and then her brother Ferdinand VII to abdicate. This sent shock waves through the Spanish-American colonies, raising questions as to who their legitimate ruler was. Sensing an opportunity for power, Carlota Joaquina declared herself ready to rule Spanish America as regent until her family regained the Spanish throne. She wrote to Buenos Aires, Lima, Santiago, and Montevideo, offering her leadership and protection. The British admiral Sir Sidney Smith encouraged these ambitions, as did José Presas, an Argentine sympathetic to Great Britain who served as her secretary from 1808 to 1812. As her political ambitions grew, she also offered herself as regent to the *junta* (committee) of patriotic Spaniards who had organized to govern the independent regions of Spain and lead the resistance against Napoleon. Neither Spain nor the colonies showed any inclination to submit to her. Nonetheless, she pressed her claims, assisted for a while by John who feared he might never be able to return to Portugal. Thus, acquisition of former Spanish territories attracted him also. When Buenos Aires declared itself independent in May 1810, Carlota Joaquina offered to sell her jewels to provide arms for loyal Montevideo. Representing the monarchy in Spain, the duke of Palmela persuaded the *junta* to recognize Carlota Joaquina as heir to the Spanish throne should her brother Ferdinand die.

Nothing came of her efforts, however, and John eventually removed the inflammatory Presas as her secretary. By early 1814, Portugal had been liberated, and Ferdinand returned to rule Spain. This opened the way for John and Carlota Joaquina to go back to Portugal, but the Brazilians objected. They feared losing the privileges and freedoms granted them by the monarchy since 1808. Across the Atlantic, the Portuguese insisted that the court return, while John vacillated. In 1816, his mother Maria died, and the prince-regent became King John VI, with his estranged wife as queen-consort.

Still they remained in Brazil, to the dismay of Portuguese conservatives who hoped the monarch would return and block the rising tide of liberalism. When the Riego Revolt forced Ferdinand VII to accept a liberal constitution in

1820, it provoked a liberal uprising in Oporto. The insurgents cast out the Council of Regency, which had been governing Portugal on John's behalf and invested sovereignty in the people and the *cortes* (representative assembly).

This at last forced John's hand. He and Carlota Joaquina returned in 1821, much to her delight: "At last we are going to a place fit for ladies and gentlemen to live in!" Their son Pedro remained in Brazil as regent to mollify the mounting nationalism among the Brazilians. He declared Brazil independent in September 1822. The monarchs found Portugal torn apart by conservatives yearning for the old days of royal absolutism and liberals anxious to maintain control of the nation. The liberal constitution required that the royal couple swear allegiance to it, which John did in November 1822. Conservatives, however, found a heroine in Carlota Joaquina. She absolutely refused, avowing that her religious views prevented her from taking any oaths. The queen was thus subject to loss of citizenship and exile. Aiding her resistance, conservative doctors found her too ill to travel, and she went into seclusion at the Ramalhão Palace outside Sintra.

Her refusal to take the oath was, according to her biographer Marcus Cheke, "the single most important action" of her life. It placed her at the head of the reactionary elements within Portugal. Carlota Joaquina's motivations were complicated. She undoubtedly held absolutist sentiments and despised the middle-class liberals. But her hatred for John strengthened her resolve and was perhaps as important as her political principles. His submission to the liberals' demands heightened her contempt for him. Regarding her exile, she wrote John: "Last night I received, by the hand of one of your ministers, the order to depart from your States. I pardon you. I pity you, from the bottom of my heart. All my disdain, all my hatred will be reserved for those who surround you." The queen also perceived the latent conservatism of the Portuguese peasantry and recognized that she could use it in her quest for political power. By this time, she had given up hope of ruling herself. She maneuvered instead to raise to the throne her favorite son, the 21-year-old Michael I. His charisma aided her cause.

Ramalhão became the center of conservative conspiracy against the liberal monarchy. The clergy, devout lay Catholics, and aristocrats intrigued with her. They took inspiration from events in Spain, where the French invaded to overthrow the liberal government and restore Carlota Joaquina's brother Ferdinand to absolute power. On May 27, 1823, a rebellion began north of Lisbon at Vila Franca de Xiram, headed by the absolutist Count of Amarante. The *Vilafrancada* spread to garrisons in Lisbon, and Michael joined the rebels. But John went to Vila Franca, and the troops invited him to rule as an absolute monarch. He accepted, frustrating Carlota Joaquina's ambitions. She then plotted, without success, to have him declared insane so that Michael could rule.

Nonetheless, the liberals were discredited, and Portugal shifted toward the conservatives. As historian H.V. Livermore notes, "The radical regime had . . . forced the separation of Brazil, imposed a doctrinaire form of government, humiliated the king, antagonized the nobility, the church and the merchants, and failed to produce any improvement in the economic situation." John tried to steer a middle course, but Carlota Joaquina and the other absolutists worked incessantly to seize control of the nation. Their machinations probably included the murder in February 1824 of the Marquis of Loulé, one of the king's confidants.

Tensions mounted, and in April the queen's partisans struck again. Placards appeared mysteriously in Lisbon, proclaiming "Long live the Queen!" and calling for John's abdication. On the night of April 29, the absolutists attempted another *coup d'état*. Michael gathered troops in Lisbon, ostensibly to protect his father's life. Carlota Joaquina's followers arrested a number of liberals, and the queen moved into Lisbon, to the Ajuda Palace. With the city in turmoil, John's position was precarious. Michael's forces continued their campaign of arrest and intimidation. The foreign diplomatic corps, however, refused to recognize the rebels and helped protect the king. John finally fled aboard the British *Windsor Castle* and from that refuge decreed the release of liberal prisoners and dismissed Michael from his military command.

Carlota Joaquina's gambit seemed on the verge of success. The *Abrilada,* as the tumult became known, nearly forced her husband's abdication. But she had not counted on Michael's impetuosity. Learning of his father's decree, Michael boarded the *Windsor Castle* and asked John's pardon. By submitting to the king, Michael undercut the rebellion. His mother reportedly remarked: "If when that old fool went on board the English ship Michael had come to me instead of obeying his father all would have been well: the Lisbon streets would have run with blood!" In the wake of the *Abrilada*'s collapse, Michael went abroad, eventually spending his exile in Vienna. His mother, however, rejected John's encouragement to accept her brother Ferdinand's invitation and go to Spain to live. She remained at Queluz Palace, forbidden by the king to appear in public. Stories circulated of her wandering the grounds in a tattered dressing gown, her haggard appearance more in keeping with phantasms than royalty.

Her prospects seemed dim, but John VI died less than two years later, on March 10, 1826. His death touched off rumors and accusations. Liberals claimed that Carlota Joaquina had poisoned him. Conservatives reported that the king had died from a plot hatched in the masonic lodges, and she apparently feared the radicals would also kill her. Meanwhile, John's demise created a crisis over the succession. The government organized a council of regency headed by one of John and Carlota Joaquina's daughters, ◄❧ **Isabel Maria** (1801–1876). It excluded Carlota Joaquina. Pedro (Pedro I), emperor of independent Brazil, was the king's heir. He was in South America, and the Brazilians showed no inclination to let him take the Portuguese crown out of fear that they would revert to colonial status. Pedro attempted to resolve the predicament by proclaiming a new constitution for Portugal and then abdicating in favor of his seven-year-old daughter, *Maria II da Glória.** He also proposed Maria da Glória's betrothal to his brother Michael.

When the Portuguese regency enacted Pedro's constitution with support from the British, it alienated nationalist and conservative opinion and offered new hope to Carlota Joaquina. She moved into the Ajuda Palace to await Michael, whom Pedro had appointed lieutenant general of Portugal and the Algarve. Michael had convinced the British and the Austrians that he would respect the constitution. Once in Portugal, however, he quickly adopted his old colors. Greeting his mother, he announced: "Mother, you see before you the same child you lost!" On February 26, he was to take an oath to the new constitution.

Amidst deafening shouts of "Long live the absolute king!" it was not clear whether Michael swore the oath. Liberals went into exile or hiding, after the absolutists crushed an uprising in Oporto. In late April, on his mother's birthday, an enthusiastic crowd acclaimed him king. Carlota Joaquina died not long afterward, on January 7, 1830. Her remains were buried at Sintra and then transferred to the Royal Pantheon in 1859.

When she died, Carlota Joaquina's cause seemed triumphant, her enemies vanquished. But in reality, Pedro held sway. His constitution survived, with some modification, into the 20th century. He himself returned to Portugal to fight for his daughter's right to rule. Her cause prevailed, following a war against Michael's forces. Michael returned to exile, and in 1834 Maria II da Glória, Carlota Joaquina's granddaughter, became ruler of Portugal in the name of constitutional monarchy. Had she lived to witness the triumph of liberalism, Carlota Joaquina might have reacted as she did when a British diplomat visited her: departing from the audience, he glanced around and discovered that the old queen was sticking out her tongue at him.

SOURCES:

Almeida Corrêa de Sá, José. D. *João VI e a Independência do Brasil: Ultimos Anos do Seu Reinado.* Lisbon: Sociedade Nacional de Tipografia, 1937.

Cheke, Marcus. *Carlota Joaquina, Queen of Portugal.* London: Sidgwick and Jackson, 1947.

Edmundo, Luiz. *A Côrte de D. João no Rio de Janeiro.* 2 ed. 3 vols. Rio de Janeiro: Conquista, 1957.

Etchepareborda, Roberto. *¿Qué fue el carlotismo?* Buenos Aires: Editorial Plus Ultra, 1971, p. 58.

Livermore, H.V. *A New History of Portugal.* Cambridge: Cambridge University Press, 1969.

Macaulay, Neill. *Dom Pedro: The Struggle for Liberty in Brazil and Portugal, 1798–1834.* Durham, NC: Duke University Press, 1986.

Serrão, Joaquim Veríssimo. *História de Portugal.* 12 vols. Lisbon: Editorial Verbo, 1977–1985, especially vol. 6–7.

SUGGESTED READING:

Fonseca Benevides, Francisco da. *Rainhas de Portugal; Estudos Históricos com Muitos Documentos.* 2 vols. Lisbon: Typographia Castro Irmão, 1878–1879.

Presas, José. *Memórias Secretas de D. Carlota Joaquina.* Rio de Janeiro: Edições de Ouro, 1966.

Kendall W. Brown, Chair, Department of History, Brigham Young University, Provo, Utah

❧► **Isabel Maria** (1801–1876)

Regent of Portugal from 1826–1828. Born on July 4, 1801, in Lisbon, Portugal; died on April 22, 1876, in Benfica, Lisbon; daughter of **Carlota Joaquina** (1775–1830) *and John VI (1767–1826), king of Portugal.*

Carlotta.

Variant of Carlota.

Carlovna, Anna (1718–1746).

See Anna Ivanovna for sidebar on Anna Leopoldovna.

Carlyle, Jane Welsh (1801–1866)

*Brilliant conversationalist and letter-writer whose correspondence is filled with entertaining and detailed accounts of her day-to-day experiences and of the many men and women, famous and not so famous, with whom she came into contact. Name variations: Jane Welsh Baillie; Jane Baillie Welsh; Mrs. Thomas Carlyle; known by close friends and family as Jeannie. Born Jane Baillie Welsh on July 14, 1801, in Haddington, near Edinburgh, Scotland; died in London on April 21, 1866; daughter of John Welsh (a country doctor) and Grace Baillie (Welsh) Welsh (de-*spite the same last name, parents were not related); educated at schools in Haddington, Miss Hall's finishing school in Edinburgh, and by a private tutor; married Thomas Carlyle, on October 17, 1826; no children.*

Childhood and young adult life spent in Haddington; first 18 months of married life at Comely Bank in Edinburgh followed by six years at an isolated farmhouse at Craigenputtock in Dumfriesshire; moved to London (1833); made many visits to family and friends in Scotland, Manchester, and near Liverpool and, after Thomas Carlyle had found fame, to country houses of the English aristocracy, especially

Jane Welsh Carlyle

that of Lord and Lady Ashburton in Hampshire; seriously injured in an accident (1863).

Selected publications: none in her lifetime but several collections of her letters are available, including (Charles R. Sanders, general ed.) The Collected Letters of Thomas and Jane Welsh Carlyle *(12 vols., 1970–85); (J.A. Froude, ed.)* Letters and Memorials of Jane Welsh Carlyle prepared for publication by Thomas Carlyle *(3 vols., 1883); (Alexander Carlyle, ed.)* New Letters and Memorials of Jane Welsh Carlyle *(2 vols., 1903); (Alexander Carlyle, ed.)* The Love Letters of Thomas Carlyle and Jane Welsh *(2 vols., 1909); (Leonard Huxley, ed.)* Jane Welsh Carlyle: Letters to Her Family, 1839–1863 *(1924); (Townsend Scudder, ed.)* Letters of Jane Welsh Carlyle to Joseph Neuberg, 1848–1862 *(1931); (Trudy Bliss, ed.)* Jane Welsh Carlyle: A New Selection of Her Letters *(1949).*

In the early evening of July 25, 1849, a slim, graceful, middle-aged woman, her smooth, raven-black hair parted in the center, stepped out of the train at the little station in Haddington, a lovely old country town 16 miles to the east of Edinburgh. Laden with two boxes, a writing-case and a carpet bag, she took the only vehicle, a dusty little omnibus, and was soon installed in the best room on the first floor of the George Inn. Having taken tea, she informed the landlord that she wished to visit the old village church and allowed herself to be shown over the schoolhouse, the playground, the village green and, finally, the cemetery. Alone in the churchyard, she slowly approached one of the graves. It was surrounded by nettles, the lettering overgrown with moss except for just two lines of the inscription that had recently been cleared. Then she slowly walked into the church and stood silently for a while before one of the pews. To her it looked untouched since she had last occupied it as a young woman. The green cloth was almost white with age. Her visit to the church accomplished, she spent a little more time wandering around the town before returning at long last to the inn. Even then, although it was very late, she sat writing furiously for two hours before going to bed.

The next morning she was up very early. Soon after six, she was to be found in front of an elegant but shabby house, which, with its façade of Corinthian pilasters topped by a stone balustrade and four stones urns, was sorely in need of a coat of paint. Here she stood for some time in quiet contemplation before making her way back to the churchyard. At that early hour it was still locked, but she scrambled over the wall and having rediscovered the same grave as the

evening before pulled out a pearl-handled button hook, a treasured possession that had belonged to her father, and started to scrape the moss out of the inscription. A few hours later she was back on the train. Very few people had recognized her. Indeed, when questioning one young shopkeeper, she had actually been told that he remembered a Miss Welsh whom he considered the "tastiest young lady in the whole place," but she had gone to England and died there. As she had written to her husband that morning, "I am so glad I came here on this incognito principle. It is the only way in which I could have got any good of the dear old place—God bless it! how changed it is and how changed am I!"

In fact, Jane Welsh had been living for the past 15 years in London, with her husband, the writer and historian, Thomas Carlyle. Their house stood in a flag-pathed street known as Cheyne Row, which ran down towards the river Thames at Chelsea, once the resort of the Court but now a quiet, unfashionable village. However, in 1849, with her husband away on a trip to Ireland, lonely, and feeling considerable bitterness at his infatuation with the brilliant Lady **Harriet Ashburton**, she made plans to visit her native Scotland. On the spur of the moment, she had suddenly decided to make Haddington, her childhood home, her first stop, to revisit her beloved father's grave and, perhaps, to relive some of her past happinesses and recapture her lost dreams.

Jane had been born in Haddington on July 14, 1801. Her father John Welsh, who came from a family of moorland sheep farmers, had studied to become a doctor at Edinburgh University and had a flourishing practice in the town where he was much admired for his striking good looks and highly respected for his professional wisdom. After two years in practice, he had married **Grace Welsh** who was not related to him but also came from a long-established farming family. Grace Welsh was a good-looking woman. She dressed well, managed the household admirably, and was an excellent hostess. However, she was also very temperamental—reputed to be capable of 15 different moods in an evening—and made heavy demands on the patience and goodwill of her family.

Jane grew up secure in the knowledge of her parents' love and affection, but, as their only child, it is probable that she was spoiled and overindulged. She was a lively, intelligent child, and her father took great pride in her scholastic achievements. He was happy for her to tackle subjects rarely taught to girls at that time, logic, arithmetic, algebra; Jane also had little difficulty in persuading him to allow her to learn Latin. By age ten, she was coming to grips with Virgil under the tutelage of the local schoolmaster, Edward Irving, who was shortly to embark on his fiery career as a revivalist preacher. She would read late into the night and then be up and about when Irving arrived at six to tutor her for two hours before breakfast. During the day, she attended the village school and, not to be outdone, pitted herself against the most daring of the boys, once actually hitting one of them who had upset her. She was determined to prove herself and bravely crawled across the Nungate bridge, face down on the parapet's narrow edge. On another occasion, accompanied by a groom who held the lantern for her, she went out before daybreak to skate on the frozen river. Eventually, though, Grace Welsh made sure that the more feminine and genteel accomplishments such as piano playing, dancing and singing, writing with a fine copper-plate, drawing and languages were not neglected by insisting that her daughter become a boarder at Mrs. Hemmings' newly opened establishment for girls in Haddington. The final year of Jane's formal education was spent at Miss Hall's finishing school in Edinburgh where she renewed her acquaintance with Edward Irving. By age 16, Jane had already written a novel and a five-act tragedy. She had developed a quick wit and was starting to acquire a reputation for being sharp and haughty. At the same time, she was beginning to suffer more and more from prostrating headaches, a foretaste of the ill-health that was to plague her for the rest of her life.

When she was 18, Jane's happy comfortable existence was suddenly shattered when her father caught typhus fever from a patient and within four days had died. Both Jane and her mother were devastated, and for Jane it felt that there was no one left who could appreciate her intellectual achievements. Life at Haddington became very dull. Occasionally, Irving paid a short visit, and, in 1821, he wrote asking if he could bring his friend, Thomas Carlyle, to meet Jane and her mother. Thomas was then 25, struggling to earn a living and make a name for himself as a writer. He and Irving stayed for three days, and it was to be the beginning of a five-year correspondence between Jane and Thomas. For four years, Jane was determined the relationship should remain one of intellectual friendship in which Thomas acted as teacher and mentor. He sent her books to read, corrected her German translations, encouraged her study of history. They rarely met, and even when

Thomas eventually succeeded in persuading her to marry him, during their 18-month engagement a year went by in which they did not see each other.

Why, after four years, did Jane finally agree to marry Thomas Carlyle? She was after all a rich and desirable heiress. He was a writer struggling to make a name for himself, the eldest of eight children of a stonemason, raised in a puritanical, impoverished family in the grim little village of Ecclefechan. His mother, whom he was very close to, was illiterate, but, in her 40s, she taught herself to read so that she might enjoy his letters at first hand. His rough, craggy physical appearance did not appeal to Jane. He was awkward. He had virtually no social graces. He had annoying habits such as a tendency to scratch the fender (fireplace screen) with his heavy walking boots and to crumble his cake into his tea. In September 1823, she still felt marriage was impossible, "Your Friend I will be, your truest most devoted friend, while I breathe the breath of life; but your wife! never never!"

[Jane Welsh Carlyle was] the most wonderful letter-writer in the English language.
—Sir Leslie Stephen, father of Virginia Woolf

However, she certainly found in him a substitute for her sadly missed father, "I had never heard the language of talent and genius but from my Father's lips—I had thought that I should never hear it more—you spoke like him—your eloquence awoke in my soul the slumbering admirations and ambitions that *His* first kindled there." She was certainly ambitious for intellectual fame for herself. She certainly recognized his genius and perhaps hoped that they would be able to work in partnership, and Thomas encouraged her to write, "sit down and write . . . begin to write something, if you can, without delay, never minding how shallow and poor it may seem." She certainly longed to escape from her difficult relationship with her mother and the boredom of her existence in Haddington. There were many social callers and many visits to relatives but, as it was, "a tea-party, a quarrel, or a *report* of a marriage now and then, are the only excitements this precious little borough affords." There were undoubtedly other suitors but they had little appeal. To **Eliza Stodart**, a childhood friend in Edinburgh, she wrote: "A visit from a man with any brains in his head would really be an act of mercy to us here." She certainly had high ideals. In 1822, she read Rousseau's *La Nouvelle Héloïse*. Her imagination was fired by Julie's passionate but doomed love for her tutor Saint-Preux and her resigned acceptance of Monsieur de Wolmar, the man chosen for her by her father. In another letter to Eliza, Jane poured out her belief that she would never find anyone who could live up to her expectations: "No lover will Jane Welsh ever find like St. Preux—no Husband like Wolmar . . . and to no man will she give her heart and pretty hand who bears to these no resemblance." She then went on to list all her past and present suitors and finished with the anguished cry, "Oh Lord Oh Lord! Where is the St. Preux? Where is the Wolmar?" There had been only one man whom she is thought to have loved passionately, her erstwhile tutor, Edward Irving, but he was betrothed to another. It seems it was only when Irving was finally beyond her reach, and she became aware she was in danger of losing the intellectual companionship of Carlyle as well, that the realization came to her that marriage to him was what she wanted.

Jane and Thomas Carlyle were married on October 17, 1826. Only four others were present, Thomas' brother and Jane's mother, grandfather, and aunt Jeannie. After a few months in Edinburgh, Thomas felt his health and writing would benefit from a move to the countryside. Shortly before their marriage, Jane had made her inheritance over to her mother as Thomas' pride would not allow him to be dependent upon his wife's income. Her inheritance had included her father's family's farm at Craigenputtock, a house tucked away in the southern Scottish moorlands, which they now decided to rent from Grace Welsh. During this period, the Carlyles were visited by the American writer Ralph Waldo Emerson who found them, "among wild and desolate heathery hills, and without a single companion in this region." It was at Craigenputtock that Thomas Carlyle labored away at what was to become his first masterpiece, *Sartor Resartus*.

While her husband was closeted in his small library room or going for long solitary walks across the heather-clad hills, Jane found herself having to struggle with the demands of running the house. With only one woman servant, she was obliged to undertake cooking, housework and routine sewing such as stitching nightshirts and darning socks. Scouring floors and blacking the grates, households task she had never had to do before, had to be tackled regularly. She also looked after the poultry and learned to milk the cows.

Friends and family came to visit occasionally but there were long periods when they were on their own. They were short of money. They both suffered from chronic ill health, and the harsh conditions did little to help. The winters were particularly hard, and in 1829 when Jane needed nursing through suspected diphtheria her mother had to struggle up to the farm through deep snowdrifts. Both Thomas and Jane gradually came to realize that neither of them was really suited to such an isolated existence and that they badly missed the stimulus of intellectual companionship with others. In 1834, therefore, after six years at Craigenputtock, they moved to Cheyne Row, and their home soon became the haunt of many of the foremost thinkers, writers, and artists of the time.

However, it was not an easy marriage. Both of them were plagued by insomnia and vaguely defined illnesses. It seems likely that the marriage was consummated but that sexual relations did not survive for long. Before many years had passed, they had separate bedrooms and even spent most of the day in different parts of the house. Thomas was often irritable, totally absorbed in his work. He would go for long walks and rides, alone or with others. Jane felt neglected and even more so when her husband became increasingly absorbed with the grand, wealthy, clever, high-spirited Lady Ashburton. But there were also many good times, especially in the earlier years. They exchanged long and affectionate letters when apart. In the evenings, if at home with no visitors, they would read together, study languages together, or she would make little stories for him out of the trials and tribulations of her day.

Jane's literary ambitions were never realized. Instead, she devoted herself to soothing the path of her "Lion." If he wanted to go off on travels of his own, she did not stand in his way. He was sensitive to the slightest sound, and, if anything disturbed his work or his sleep, she made it her mission to seek out and eradicate the source of the offending noise. Unlike most women of her day, she even managed his financial affairs and on one traumatic occasion went to fight his case before the Commissioners of Inland Revenue arguing, when told that Thomas should be there to swear his own statement, that she understood her "husband's affairs fully, better than he does himself." It is doubtful whether at that time it could have been otherwise. Thomas' own view of marriage was merely a reflection of contemporary thinking, which was constantly repeated in the literature of the day and subscribed to by many other eminent Victorian writers such as Coventry Patmore and John

Ruskin. Writing some six months before they were married, Thomas explained his objection to Jane's suggestion that her mother should be allowed to share their home on the grounds that:

> The Man should bear rule in the house and not the *Woman*. This is an eternal axiom, the Law of Nature herself which no mortal departs from unpunished. . . . Think not, Darling, that this comes of an imperious temper; that I shall be a harsh and tyrannical husband to thee. God forbid! But it is the nature of a man that if he be controlled by any thing but his own Reason, he feels himself degraded; and incited, be it justly or not, to rebellion and discord. It is the nature of a woman again (for she is essentially *passive* not *active*) to cling to the man for support and direction, to comply with his humours, and feel pleasure in doing so, simply because they are his.

However, between the rows with domestic staff, the household upheavals, the regular bouts of frenzied cleaning—"earthquaking" as she called it—the unending stream of visitors, the constant demands of her husband's career and ill-health, struggling with her own bouts of sickness and hypochondria, which were never fully explained or sympathized with, Jane Carlyle managed to find the time to write detailed accounts of her daily experiences. She poured out letters to her husband when they were apart, to her family, to her friends, to her husband's family. These sparkling, vibrant letters are the legacy she left behind. The editors of the definitive edition of *The Collected Letters of Thomas and Jane Welsh Carlyle* have found about 3,000 letters written by her and have estimated that in her most prolific period, 1841–45, judging only by the letters that have survived, she was writing on average 116 each year. To a Mrs. Russell, the wife of the doctor who attended her dying mother, Carlyle wrote: "I never sit down at night, beside a good fire, *alone,* without feeling a need of talking a little, on paper, to somebody that I like well enough, and that likes *me* well enough, to make it of no moment—whether I talk sense or nonsense, and with or without regard to the rules of grammar." She wrote about "everything and everybody," about herself, her difficulties with the maids, her problems with running the house, her travels, her family, the people she met, both celebrated and ordinary. She had a keen eye for a detail and was a brilliant story-teller, making great play, often in a mocking and mischievous way, of the trivia and absurdities of everyday life.

Jane Carlyle died on April 21, 1866, while out for a ride in her brougham in Hyde Park. Three years previously, she had had a fall in the street, and this had been followed by several months of intense pain and miserable illness, which was eventually only relieved by a long period of convalescence with family and friends in Scotland. Back in London, her health continued to be very poor, and it is probable that she died from heart failure. Thomas had just been triumphantly installed as rector of Edinburgh University, and the news of her death was brought to him by telegram as he stayed with his brother and sister in Dumfriesshire. Two days later, she was reunited with her father, buried alongside his grave in the churchyard at Haddington as she had wished. Thomas Carlyle was shattered by her death. It was only then that he realized how much she meant to him, and, full of remorse for the way he had neglected her, he set to work to write his reminiscence of her and to prepare her letters and "memorials" for publication. It was Thomas, consumed by his guilt, who by his selection and annotation of Jane's letters created the portrait of her as a neglected, self-sacrificing, genius manqué. This was the interpretation used by Thomas' disciple, James Anthony Froude, who in his biography, which created a sensation when it appeared in 1882, presented Jane as the long-suffering, sexually unfulfilled wife, deserted in middle-age for a more brilliant woman and allowed to sacrifice her literary ambitions on the altar of her husband's career. On the other hand, the work of Alexander Carlyle, Thomas' nephew, which was produced at the instigation of the Carlyle family as a riposte to Froude, attempted to vindicate Thomas and absolve him from responsibility for Jane's supposed hypochondria and failure to achieve fame as a writer. It was not, Alexander Carlyle argued, that Thomas never gave her the opportunity; the fault lay within *her* as she did not have the ability to make the necessary sustained effort.

Whatever the truth, the portrait that Thomas Carlyle and Froude drew from Jane's letters is without doubt too harsh an interpretation. Jane's letters also reveal a different story. True, she could be bitter, but she could also be bubbling over with joy and excitement. True, she was sometimes full of self-pity, but at others she was full of affection and concern. Moreover, she *may* have devoted herself constantly to her husband's well-being but her friends spoke highly of her own successes and abilities, both as a brilliant conversationalist and letter-writer. For some, she was "the cleverest woman in London" and many of those who called to see the Carlyles in Cheyne Row came to visit her in her own right. As her close friend, novelist *Geraldine Jewsbury wrote in 1849: "I do not feel that either you and I are to be called failures. We are indications of a development of womanhood which as yet is not recognized. It has, so far, no ready-made channels to run in, but still we have looked, and tried, and found that the present rules for women will not hold us."

SOURCES:

Brysson Morrison, N. *True Minds: The Marriage of Thomas & Jane Carlyle.* London: J.M. Dent, 1974.

Burdett, Osbert. *The Two Carlyles.* London: Faber & Faber, 1930.

Simpson, Alan, and Mary McQueen, eds. *I Too Am Here: Selections from the Letters of Jane Welsh Carlyle.* Cambridge, England: Cambridge University Press, 1977.

Surtees, Virginia. *Jane Welsh Carlyle.* Salisbury: Michael Russell, 1976.

SUGGESTED READING:

Christianson, Aileen. "Jane Welsh Carlyle and Her Friendships with Women in the 1840s," in *Prose Studies.* Vol. 10, no. 3. December 1987, pp. 283–295.

Froude, James Anthony. *My Relations with Carlyle.* 1903.

Holme, Thea. *The Carlyles at Home.* London: Oxford University Press, 1965.

Ireland, Mrs. Alexander, ed. *Selections from the Letters of Geraldine Endsor Jewsbury to Jane Welsh Carlyle.* 1892.

Rose, Phyllis. *Parallel Lives: Five Victorian Marriages.* London: Vintage, 1994.

Vicinus, Martha. *Suffer and Be Still: Women in the Victorian Age.* Bloomington, IN: Indiana University Press, 1982.

COLLECTIONS:

Substantial numbers of Jane Carlyle's letters are held by The National Library of Scotland at Edinburgh, the University of Edinburgh, the New York Public Library, and the Ashburton collection at Castle Ashby, Northamptonshire, England. Others are to be found in some 30 libraries and private collections in English-speaking countries.

The Carlyle house in Cheyne Row has been preserved by The National Trust and still contains furniture, books, personal relics and portraits.

Sylvia Dunkley, part-time tutor
in women's history and in social history,
Division of Adult Continuing Education,
University of Sheffield, Sheffield, England

Carlyle, Mrs. Thomas (1801–1866).

See Carlyle, Jane Welsh.

Carmen Sylva (1843–1916).

See Elizabeth of Wied.

Carmichael, Elizabeth (fl. 1530s)

*Mistress of James V, king of Scotland. Name variations: Katherine. Flourished around 1530; daughter of Sir John Carmichael; mistress of James V (1512–1542), king of Scotland (r. 1513–1542); chil-*dren: (with James V) John Stewart (b. around 1531), prior of Coldinghame.

Carnegie, Caroline (1934—)

Duchess of Fife. Born Caroline Cecily Dewar on February 12, 1934, in Bardowie Castle, Milngavie, Strathclyde, Scotland; elder daughter of Alexander Dewar, 3rd baron Forteviot, and **Cynthia Starkie**; *married James Carnegie, 3rd duke of Fife, September 11, 1956 (divorced 1966); children:* **Alexandra Carnegie** *(b. 1959); David Carnegie, earl of Macduff; and one other.*

Carnegie, Hattie (1886–1956)

Austrian-born American fashion designer and retailer. Born Henrietta Kanengeiser in Vienna, Austria, on March 14, 1886; died in New York City on February 22, 1956; one of six brothers and sisters; married an Englishman while in her teens; married a second time; married John Zanft (a motion-picture executive); no children.

Immigrated to New York with her family (1897); opened her own business (1909); was in control of a fashion empire (by mid-1920s), which lasted until her death.

Born in Vienna, the second in a large family of seven children, Henrietta Kanengeiser grew up as one of millions of poor but ambitious immigrants in New York City. After attending public school for only two years, she began working as a messenger at Macy's department store. Only 4'10" in height, Henrietta displayed unlimited energy and ambition as well as a knack for stylish dressing despite a wardrobe that consisted of no more than a skirt and three blouses. Her first contact with the fashion world took place when a neighborhood shopowner noticed her flair for dressing and provided Henrietta with a free wardrobe in exchange for her enthusiastic promotion of the shop's line of merchandise. In 1909, she opened her own business in partnership with a seamstress named **Rose Roth**, and the venture prompted Henrietta Kanengeiser to transform herself into Hattie Carnegie. (At the time, industrialist Andrew Carnegie was the richest man in the United States, and his name was synonymous with the ultimate in American business success.) Situated on East 10th Street in Manhattan, their little hat shop was called Carnegie-Ladies' Hatter. During the next few years, while Rose Roth made dresses, Hattie Carnegie designed and sold hats. Now a professional in the world of fashion, Carnegie could not sew, an ability she would never acquire. Although she had a sharp eye for fashion, Hattie would also never become a fashion designer. Instead, as she branched out from hats to dresses she would later employ the very best fashion designers.

Thanks to her energy and shrewd entrepreneurial instincts, their business grew rapidly, and by 1913 the Carnegie-Roth partnership had become successful enough to be incorporated with a capital of $100,000. Success also made possible a move from East 10th Street to a boutique on 86th Street and Broadway, in what was at the time Manhattan's fashionable Upper West Side. Situated near exclusive Riverside Drive, her new shop was located on the second floor of a building over a restaurant, a laundry and a delicatessen. Carnegie was very purposeful about her business strategy, aiming for the high end of the market, and her clothes were only for the affluent, starting at $75. While Rose Roth worked hard behind the scenes, Hattie mixed with her customers wearing her designs at all of the socially correct places, including the smart restaurants, the theater, and the opera.

By the end of World War I in 1918, Hattie Carnegie was having more and more disagreements with Rose Roth and decided to buy out her partner. Continuing to display the confidence that had made her a success, she changed the emphasis of her business from American designs to stylish adaptations of Paris originals. This strategy was so dramatically successful that in 1923 she opened the retail shop at 42 East 49th Street that became almost immediately a fount of fashion wisdom for America's well-dressed matrons and their daughters, both pre- or post-debutantes. With this success, she branched out to create a veritable fashion empire. Her millinery business was headquartered at 29 West 57th Street, while her popular lines of perfumes, jewelry and cosmetics were manufactured under her watchful eye at a factory located at 412 East 59th Street. Carnegie relied on two of her brothers to help build up and manage her complex business enterprises. Her brother Tony managed the wholesale dress business while financial affairs were handled by her brother Herman.

Whereas the prices of her dresses were stratospherically high and unaffordable to all but a few of America's women, Carnegie realized the potential market embodied by middle-class women who desired to dress fashionably. The models of original Hattie Carnegie dresses were sold to manufacturers who sold them at lower and relatively affordable prices, and her fashion line soon became so popular that many

of her designs were pirated by unscrupulous entrepreneurs. Although annoyed by her business competitors, legal and illegal, Carnegie forged ahead with new ideas. She purchased a building at 711 5th Avenue to house her offices and wholesale business. Here were created the dresses that would be sold in major stores throughout the United States.

In little over a decade's time, Carnegie had gone from impoverished immigrant to fashion mogul. Starting in 1919, she made the first of what would total 142 buying trips to Europe by the start of World War II in September 1939, more than seven trips annually. These buying sprees made her well-known in Paris and other European fashion centers. If a dress caught her eye, Carnegie bought it regardless of cost; only weeks or months later did she contend with the problem of how to pay for her European purchases. In virtually every instance, however, her instincts were excellent and the dresses she brought to the United States were snapped up by her affluent customers. With an eye for talent as well as dresses, she discovered a large number of highly gifted designers including Travis Banton, Bruno, *Madeleine Vionnet, Jean Louis, *Claire McCardell, Norman Norell, Pauline Potter and *Pauline Trigére. Madeleine Vionnet, who was discovered in Paris, was launched by Carnegie on a career that placed the French designer at the very peak of the world of haute couture. Norman Norell worked for Carnegie from 1928 through 1941, producing one successful dress after another.

Hattie Carnegie and her team of designers and seamstresses were responsible for creating both custom-made clothing and high-priced ready-to-wear items for women with both the taste for and means to afford quality dresses. She made a permanent mark on American fashion in the era of depression and war from the early 1930s through the late 1940s. Her "little Carnegie suit" became an unchallenged status symbol, as was also true for the "little black dress" that American women relied on for an entire generation. Sensing a need for elegance in a nation that was still defining itself, Carnegie brought style to the minority of women privileged enough to wear a suit in the morning, a cocktail dress in the afternoon, and an evening dress at night. Among the honors she received were the Neiman-Marcus Award in 1939 and the American Fashion Critics' Award in 1948, the latter for her "consistent contribution to American elegance."

The celebrities who patronized the Carnegie salon included *Tallulah Bankhead, *Constance

Bennett, *Oona O'Neill Chaplin, *Joan Crawford, *Marlene Dietrich, Barbara Hutton, *Gertrude Lawrence and *Wallis Warfield, the Duchess of Windsor. But it was average women of means with a desire to dress stylishly who enabled Hattie Carnegie to prosper for more than three decades. The brand loyalty of her patrons helped her establish retail shops not only in Manhattan but also in Southampton, N.Y., and Palm Beach, Florida. Her multimillion-dollar corporate interests included a custom and wholesale dress business, a millinery business, and a nationally distributed wholesale lines of jewelry, cosmetics and perfume. Having exemplified the American dream, Hattie Carnegie died in New York City, her name truly a household word, on February 22, 1956; she left behind a name synonymous with quality and a fashion empire worth more than $8 million. For three decades, she had reigned, in the words of Hilton Als, as "the pioneering spirit of Seventh Avenue ready-to-wear."

SOURCES:

Als, Hilton. "So Very Hattie," in *The New Yorker*. Vol. 72, no. 3. March 11, 1996, pp. 80–81.

"Designer's Will Filed," in *The New York Times*. March 9, 1956, p. 8.

"Hattie Carnegie dies here at 69," in *The New York Times*. February 23, 1956, p. 27.

"Luxury, Inc.," in *The New Yorker*. Vol. 10, no. 7. March 31, 1934, pp. 23–27.

Schiro, Anne-Marie. "To Hattie Carnegie, Style's God Was in the Details," in *The New York Times*. March 1, 1996, p. B10.

Stegemeyer, Anne. *Who's Who in Fashion*. 3rd ed. NY: Fairchild Publications, 1996.

John Haag, Associate Professor, University of Georgia, Athens, Georgia

Carnegie, Maud (1893–1945)

*Countess of Southesk. Name variations: Maud Duff. Born Maud Alexandra Victoria Georgina Bertha on April 3, 1893, in Richmond upon Thames, Surrey, England; died on December 14, 1945, in London, England; daughter of *Louise Victoria (1867–1931), princess Royal and duchess of Fife, and Alexander Duff, 1st duke of Fife; married Charles Carnegie, 11th earl of Southesk, on November 12, 1923; children: James Carnegie (b. 1929), 3rd duke of Fife.*

Carner, JoAnne (1939—)

American golfer. Name variations: JoAnne Gunderson; The Great Gundy. Born Joanne Gunderson on April 4, 1939, in Kirkland, Washington; graduated from Arizona State University; married Don Carner, around 1965.

Top money-winner and winner of five Vare trophies; winnings include USGA Amateur (1957, 1960, 1962, 1966, 1968); LPGA Burdine (1969); U.S. Open (1971, 1976); Bluegrass Invitational (1971); Desert Inn Classic, Hoosier Open, Dallas Civitan (1974); American Defender Classic, All-American Sports Classic (1975); Orange Blossom Classic (1976); LPGA team championship (with Judy Rankin) and Borden Classic (1977); Colgate Triple Crown (1978, 1979); Peter Jackson Classic (1978); Honda Civic Classic (1979, 1980); Women's Kemper Open (1979); Whirlpool Championship and Sunstar '80 (1980); Lady Keystone Open (1980, 1981); S&H Golf Classic (1981); McDonald's Classic (1982); Chevrolet World Championship (1982, 1983); Henredon Classic (1982); Portland Ping (1983); Corning (1984); Safeco Classic (1985), becoming the oldest winner ever on the LPGA tour.

In the early 1980s, JoAnne Carner was number one in career earnings on the LPGA professional circuit. A gallery favorite who was equally good at match and stroke play, she was one of the longest drivers on the women's tour, often achieving distances off the tee of 275 yards. Carner earned over $1.6 million.

She began playing golf at age 10 and, at 17, won the U.S. Girls' Junior championship in 1956. In 1957, 1960, 1962, 1966, and 1968, she won the U.S. Amateur championship, as well as the Women's Western, The Doherty Challenge Cup, the Intercollegiate, the Trans-Mississippi, the Pacific Northwest, the Southwest, the Northwest, and the Eastern—all under the name of JoAnne Gunderson. She married Don Carner around 1965 and did not turn pro until 1970, winning the Wendell West Open and designated Rookie of the Year. In 1971 and 1976, she won the U.S. Women's Open. In 1974, she was named LPGA Player of the Year because of her six victories. In 1975, she won the du Maurier Classic in Canada. In the 1970s, she was earning over $100,000 a year in purses. She was awarded five Vare trophies in 1975, 1976, 1981, 1982, and 1983. Said *Nancy Lopez: "Now we are talking about one of the really great ones. . . . She has the sort of personality that I wanted to have when I came onto the tour. She seemed to make every shot exciting, from the long ones right down to the putts. The crowds like her very much—*exciting* is really the right word for her."

Though a motorcycle accident threatened to end her career, Carner came battling back. In 1981, she won the Bob Jones Award, ousted *Kathy Whitworth from the top of the all-time money winners with $1,042,544, and was elected to the LPGA Hall of Fame. In 1983, she again led in earnings, and in 1985 she won the Safeco Classic at age 46, becoming the oldest winner in LPGA Tour history. Carner also finished as runner-up in an LPGA Tournament each year from 1986–90, and then again in 1992 at age 53.

Karin Loewen Haag,
Athens, Georgia

Carney, Winifred (1887–1943)

Irish suffragist, socialist and labor organizer. Born in Bangor, County Down, Ireland, on December 4, 1887; died in Belfast, Northern Ireland, on November 21, 1943; daughter of Alfred Carney and Sarah (Cassidy) Carney; educated at Christian Brothers School, Donegall Street, Belfast; qualified as secretary; married George McBride (labor organizer), in 1928.

Winnie Carney came from a Catholic, lower-middle-class family in the coastal town of Bangor, just south of Belfast. She was educated and later became a junior teacher at the Christian Brothers School in Belfast. She then qualified as a secretary and shorthand typist and in her early 20s became involved in the Gaelic League, which was concerned with the revival of the Irish language, and in suffrage and socialist activities. It was through her friend **Marie Johnson** (b. 1874), wife of the labor leader Thomas Johnson, that she met James Connolly in the summer of 1912. Connolly was the Ulster provincial secretary of the Irish Transport and General Workers Union (ITGWU), and in 1912 he helped to organize the Textile Workers Union, which functioned as the women's section of the ITGWU. Appointed secretary of the Textile Workers Union, Carney was responsible for the insurance section. She became Connolly's trusted associate and confidante, accompanying him to the factory-gate meetings of the "mill-girls" who made up the membership. She also typed the many articles Connolly wrote for the labor press and was probably the person most familiar with his ideas.

Throughout his career, Connolly had close working relationships with many active feminists including *Elizabeth Gurley Flynn, *Constance Markievicz, *Hanna Sheehy-Skeffington, and *Helena Moloney. In contrast to some other labor organizers, he always treated women on an equal basis and in December 1915 he urged women to protect themselves: "If you want a thing done do it yourself . . . don't whine about men protecting you. If men wanted to protect you there would be no war and no prostitution." Carney took his advice to heart and joined the Belfast branch of Cumann na mBan (The Women's League) where she taught first aid and

learned rifle-shooting. In 1914, she joined the Irish Citizen Army (ICA), a workers militia founded after the lockout of Dublin workers the previous year. Unlike the Irish Volunteers also founded in 1913, the ICA accepted women as full members and soldiers.

After the outbreak of the First World War, plans for a rebellion against British rule in Ireland were prepared and Connolly decided to join forces with the Irish Volunteers. The rebellion was planned for Easter 1916. The week before, Connolly wired Carney to come to Dublin. On Easter Monday, she joined the garrison at the General Post Office in Dublin with the rank of adjutant. For a week, she helped Connolly to maintain contact with the other insurrectionary centers in Dublin, and when the order came to evacuate the Post Office because of heavy shelling she refused to leave because Connolly had been wounded. As the surrender was being discussed the following Saturday, she asked Connolly, "Is there no other way?" Connolly shook his head.

Of the 77 women arrested after the rebellion, only 6 were imprisoned for a long period and Carney was among them. She was distressed but not surprised when she heard that Connolly was executed on May 12. To the end of her life, she regarded her work with him as one of the high points of her career and was scathing about those of his successors who did not live up to his ideals. After her release from prison on Christmas 1916, colleagues in the ITGWU found her restless and impatient about the political future in Ireland. In 1917, she was the Belfast delegate at the Cumann na mBan convention and in 1918 was one of only two women nominated by the Sinn Fein party to contest the general election: Constance Markievicz was nominated for the St. Patrick's Division in Dublin and Winnie Carney was nominated for the Victoria Division of Belfast.

As the Victoria Division was predominantly unionist in political sympathies, Carney—a feminist, socialist republican—had little chance of winning, a view shared by many Sinn Fein party workers who gave her little help. She won only 395 votes, later writing that she was amazed to get even that many considering the minimal support she received. The experience confirmed her dissatisfaction with Sinn Fein as being too conservative in its social aims, and she returned to work for the ITGWU in Belfast. When the Irish civil war broke out in 1922, she supported the republican side and sheltered many republicans in her home, which led to police raids. Arrested in July 1922, she was released after three weeks and fined for possessing seditious papers. She continued to work for the ITGWU both in Belfast and Dublin until 1928.

In 1924, she joined the Northern Ireland Labor Party and was associated with the radical wing, which later became the Revolutionary Workers Groups. The party had members of both nationalist and unionist sympathies, and among the latter was George McBride, a textile engineer from a staunchly unionist, working-class background in Belfast, who was active in the labor movement. Despite their different backgrounds, Carney and McBride shared many socialist and cultural interests and in 1928 they married. Her marriage alienated many of her family and friends who could not understand why she married "an Orangeman" who was moreover ten years her junior. They lived in north Belfast where Winnie nursed her mother until her mother's death in 1933. She joined the Belfast Socialist Party in the 1930s but her health was poor, and Carney died in November 1943. Her grave remained unmarked as her family did not want McBride's name to appear on it.

SOURCES:
Ward, Margaret. *In Their Own Voice: Women and Irish Nationalism*. Dublin: Attic Press, 1995.
Woggon, Helga. "Silent Radical: Winnie Carney 1887–1943," in *Labour History News*. Vol. 1. Dublin, 1986.

Deirdre McMahon, Lecturer in History,
Mary Immaculate College,
University of Limerick, Limerick, Ireland

Carolina.
Variant of Caroline.

Carolina, Queen of the Two Sicilies (1752–1814).
See Maria Carolina.

Caroline.
Variant of Carolina.

Caroline (1768–1821).
See Caroline of Brunswick.

Caroline (1793–1812)
*Tuscan noblewoman. Born in 1793; died in 1812; daughter of Ferdinand III, grand duke of Tuscany (r. 1790–1802 and 1814–1824) and *Louisa Amelia (1773–1802); sister of Leopold II, grand duke of Tuscany (r. 1824–1859).*

Caroline Amelia Augusta or Caroline Amelia Elizabeth (1768–1821).
See Caroline of Brunswick.

Caroline Amelia of Augustenburg (1796–1881)
*Queen of Denmark. Name variations: Caroline Amalie of Augustenborg; Caroline Amelia of Schleswig-Holstein. Born on June 22, 1796, in Copenhagen, Denmark; died on March 9, 1881, in Amalienborg, Copenhagen; daughter of Frederick Christian, duke of Schleswig-Holstein, and *Louise Augusta (1771–1843); became second wife of Christian VIII (1786–1848), king of Denmark (r. 1839–1848), on May 22, 1815; children: (stepchild) Frederick VII (1808–1863), king of Denmark (r. 1848–1863).*

Caroline Augusta of Bavaria (1792–1873)
*Bavarian princess. Name variations: Karoline Augusta or Auguste; Charlotta Augusta; Charlotte of Bavaria. Born on February 8, 1792, in Mannheim; died on February 9, 1873, in Vienna; daughter of *Wilhelmine of Darmstadt (1765–1796) and Maximilian I Joseph, elector of Bavaria (r. 1799–1805), king of Bavaria (r. 1805–1825); married William I (1781–1864), king of Wurttemberg (r. 1816–1864), on June 8, 1808 (annulled in 1814); married Francis I (1768–1835), emperor of Austria, also known as Francis II, the last Holy Roman emperor (r. 1792–1806). Francis' other wives were *Maria Teresa of Naples (1772–1807), *Elizabeth of Wurttemberg (1767–1790), and *Maria Ludovica of Modena (1787–1816).*

Caroline Elizabeth (1713–1757).
See Caroline of Ansbach for sidebar.

Caroline Louise of Saxe-Weimar (1786–1816)
*Duchess of Mecklenburg-Schwerin. Born on July 18, 1786; died on January 20, 1816; daughter of Charles Augustus (b. 1757), duke of Saxe-Weimar and Eis, and *Louise of Hesse-Darmstadt (d. 1830); became second wife of Frederick Louis (1778–1819), duke of Mecklenburg-Schwerin; children: Albert of Mecklenburg-Schwerin (b. 1812); *Helene Louise of Mecklenburg-Schwerin (1814–1858).*

Caroline Matilda (1751–1775)
Queen of Denmark and wife of the mad and profligate monarch Christian VII, who formed a romantic and political liaison with the brilliant statesman Count Johann Friedrich von Struensee. Name variations: Caroline Mathilde; Caroline Guelph. Born on

July 11, 1751, at Leicester House, St. Martin's, London, England; died of scarlet fever on May 11, 1775, in Celle Castle, Brunswick, Germany; posthumous daughter of Frederick Louis, prince of Wales (eldest son of King George II of Great Britain) and Augusta of Saxe-Gotha (1719–1772); sister of George III, king of England; married her cousin Christian VII (son of Frederick V of Denmark), king of Denmark and Norway (r. 1766–1808), on November 8, 1766 (divorced 1772); children: (with Christian VII) Frederick VI (b. 1768), king of Denmark and Norway (r. 1808–1839); (with Johann Struensee) Louise Augusta (1771–1843).

Her brother became King George III of England (1751); betrothed to Christian VII (January 10, 1765); married Christian by proxy (October 1, 1766), in actuality (November 8, 1766); following a palace revolt staged by Christian's stepmother and his half-brother, the heir presumptive, her lover was executed and she was exiled to Celle in Germany (1772); conspiracy formed to liberate her, but she died of scarlet fever before her rescuers could intervene (1775).

When Caroline Matilda was born on July 11, 1751, her father, Frederick Louis, prince of Wales, had been dead for four months and her brother, George (III), had been named successor to the throne of England. A lively, pretty girl, the youngest of nine and her mother's last child, Caroline Matilda responded to her siblings' benevolent indulgence and her mother ❧ **Augusta of Saxe-Gotha**'s strict and loving care with a desire to please and a will to obey authority. She learned languages—German, English, and French—easily, and she sang beautifully.

Until she was nine, Matilda, as she preferred to be called, had experienced only the warm and tender benefits of love. Now, she was introduced to the notion that love may inflict hurt as well. Her favorite brother, George, had fallen in love with an unsuitable girl, Lady ***Sarah Lennox**. He courted her despite his fear of his mother's wrath but succumbed to authority when the earl of Bute, his mother's close friend and fellow dynasty builder, threatened to withdraw his affection and approval. George consequently renounced Sarah—with no thought of taking her for a mistress—then dutifully married Princess ***Charlotte of Mecklenburg-Strelitz** (1744–1818) and remained faithful to her. Caroline Matilda's quiet life continued at Carlton House outside London and at Kew, surrounded by the Kew Gardens, which her mother had established with Bute's help in 1759. George's submissiveness had cast a shadow on his sister's path, however, and Matilda's progressive distancing herself from Bute sug-

gests a decreasing willingness to accept authority unquestioned. She realized that George felt differently when, two years later, he made Bute his prime minister. It would be Caroline Matilda's fate to demonstrate that when women of royalty are no longer willing to sacrifice themselves to uphold a throne, a kingdom is placed in present or permanent peril.

Matilda's good health and robust appearance—promising a long and fruitful life—were the qualities that convinced the Danish envoy, Count Bothmar, that she must be the bride of his sovereign, Prince Christian VII of Denmark. He had come for her elder sister, ***Louisa Anne** (1749–1768), but found her too frail for the task. George resisted the match, thinking his little sister Matilda too young for marriage, but Bothmar had an ally in the Princess Dowager Augusta, who thought her youngest daughter a perfect fit for the Danish crown. Her ambitions easily overruled the fact that Matilda had lived a secluded existence and was totally untrained in manners at court. Caroline Matilda informed the Danish ambassador that she knew plants better than people and could make greater use of the flowers nature produced than of those decorating the speech of courtiers. Only 15 years old, she had no inclination to marry a distant prince, but her mother lectured her on the duty of royalty, and George was reminded of England's anti-French and Protestant cause, which a union with Denmark would serve. Against such inducement, Matilda's tears and increasing depression could produce no argument. George consented, and, on January 10, 1765, the betrothal was announced in both countries. On October 1, 1766, Caroline Matilda was married by proxy at Carlton House, and the next day she departed for Denmark.

She had a rough crossing. Her ship did not reach Rotterdam until October 11th. She proceeded from there to Utrecht in a Dutch vessel and then went overland to the English colony of Hanover and on to Hamburg, from where she sailed down the Elbe to Altona, the frontier city between Denmark and Germany. Her tears re-

Caroline Matilda

❧ See sidebar on the following page

Augusta of Saxe-Gotha (1719–1772)

*Princess of Wales and mother of George III of England. Name variations: Augusta of Saxe-Coburg, Augusta of Saxe-Gotha-Altenburg. Born Augusta, princess of Saxe-Coburg-Gotha, on November 30, 1719, in Gotha, Thuringia, Germany; died on February 8, 1772, at Carlton House, London, England; buried at Westminster Abbey; daughter of Frederick II, duke of Saxe-Gotha-Altenburg, and *Madeleine of Anhalt-Zerbst (1679–1740); married Frederick Louis, prince of Wales (1706–1751, son of George II and *Caroline of Ansbach), on April 27, 1736; children: *Augusta Guelph (1737–1813), princess royal; George William Frederick (1738–1820), later George III, king of England; Edward Augustus (1739–1767), duke of Albany and York; *Elizabeth Caroline (1740–1759); William Henry (1743–1805), duke of Gloucester; Henry Frederick (b. 1745), duke of Cumberland; *Louisa Anne (1749–1768); Frederick William (1750–1765); *Caroline Matilda (1751–1775).*

When the 17-year-old Augusta of Saxe-Gotha arrived in Greenwich, England, for her marriage to Frederick Louis, prince of Wales, she was clutching her doll. It didn't help that Frederick was out of favor with his father George II, king of England. To the consternation of the king, Frederick was exceedingly influential at court. George's growing antipathy caused him to have Frederick and Augusta evicted from their palace apartments and moved to lodgings at Leicester House.

In a time span of less than 14 years, Augusta gave birth to nine children, before the death of her husband in 1751. (She was pregnant with Caroline Matilda at the time of his death.) Her first born, the future George III, was then only 13. Augusta was heavily influential in the life of her royal son and heavily influenced by her close friend the earl of Bute. Both were largely responsible for George III's views on politics.

turned as she bade farewell to her English train in Altona to give herself into the hands of Danish courtiers whose language she did not speak. Even so, Danish historians describe her pleasure at being the center of attention in the cities through which she journeyed. They admired her lively and mild disposition, her beautiful blue eyes, flawless skin, pretty hands and feet, and lovely voice.

All alone among Danish courtiers and ladies, she traveled up through Schleswig Holstein, across Funen and on to Sealand, where Christian VII, her future husband, met her at the ancient city of Roskilde, 20 miles south of Copenhagen. He found her actual visage much improved over the portrait that had been painted during her time of sorrow and tears. Noting

her blue eyes, exquisite coloring, and sweet expression, he kissed her hand and cheek. With a second breach of etiquette, he handed Caroline Matilda into her gilded equipage and sat down beside her. Together, they rode to the castle of Frederiksborg where she was to reside until the wedding ceremony on November 8th.

Seemingly, all was well. Caroline Matilda had found favor with Christian, and his people had cheered them all the way to the capital. She was accepted also by the king's grandmother *Sophia of Bayreuth, and his stepmother, the queen dowager, **Maria Juliana of Brunswick** (1729–1796). The second wife of Frederick V, Maria Juliana wanted her own son, Christian's half brother and heir presumptive, to inherit the throne. She had had to resign herself to Christian marrying and possibly begetting an heir and had fashioned her hopes for a bride who would at least be pleasant and at best barren. Finally, Matilda found in her Mistress of the Robes, **Madame de Plessen**, the maternal guardian she needed. She reminded Matilda of her mother; like her, she was formal, strict and knowledgeable. Madame de Plessen was also observant; on the trip from Altona to Copenhagen, she had realized that Matilda was untrained in courtly etiquette, and she had made herself indispensable as teacher and guide.

The warring factions at court, at whose center Caroline Matilda would be placed, declared themselves almost immediately. The initial defeat was suffered by Madame de Plessen. As the wedding party drew to a close, the king's sister and her husband led the guests in a wild dance through all the ground floor apartments of the palace. When they came to the double doors of Matilda's rooms, however, they found her Mistress of the Robes denying them entry. Christian thrust Madame de Plessen aside, and with his wife and several hundred couples he danced through the bedrooms and galleries until they had finished their rounds. Though Madame de Plessen had yielded temporarily, her fierce standards of behavior and her sense of respect owed women of royalty dictated her further instructions to the young queen with the result that in a matter of weeks, Caroline Matilda found herself alone with her Mistress of the Robes behind the double doors. Arguably, she herself had pushed the king away when on Madame de Plessen's advice she would show Christian his place by keeping him waiting while she finished a game of chess or simply locked the doors against his advances.

A sensible, confident, and intelligent man would have understood the situation of a 15-

year-old bride in a strange country taking motherly advice from a mature woman; but Christian was neither sensible nor confident, and his intelligence did not help him. He had become king at the demise of his father, who had whored and drunk himself to death. His primary teacher, Rewentlow, who had wanted to make a man of the small and slender prince, had beat him into submission like a dog. The Swiss teacher, Reverdil, who joined the court in 1760 as Christian's teacher in French and geometry, had been horrified at Rewentlow's methods and tried to teach his pupil in a more humanitarian way. But he was too late. Christian, who had been mostly left with servants when not in the care of Rewentlow, had learned from them the intemperance that would characterize his later behavior. He had the notion that he was destined to be someone great; above all, he wanted to be tough, untouchable, and invulnerable. He thought he saw the world in a different light from that of everybody else and wanted to prepare himself to be a part of that world by becoming "harder" all over. Reverdil discovered that when Christian felt his stomach or his head, he was testing them to see if they were getting harder. To that end, he frequently engaged in combat with his pages and courtiers. He would revel through the nights with his companions and get into brawls with the night watchmen. On one occasion, Reverdil surprised Christian who was strapped to the floor enjoying a whipping by his Groom of the Chamber, Christian Holck. Or he would entertain himself with boys, among them a young black lad. Christian would play horse and the boy would be his rider.

Considering Christian's behavior, the Danes were understandably eager to get their sovereign married, and they put high hopes in Caroline Matilda's ability to settle him down. She might, in fact, have been able to do so, or at least mitigate his behavioral excesses by a relationship of playful encounters befitting their ages—15 and 17—had not the territorial strife at court been so pervasive. Reverdil tried to bring the king and queen together, insisting among other things that Christian sleep with his wife. But the king's young men, especially Christian Holck, tried to keep them apart for fear the queen might gain control over the king at their expense. They mocked her and called her names, in which endeavors they were aided by Christian's notion of marriage as a ridiculous affair and husbands as ludicrous creatures who could not possibly be "tough." Expectedly, Madame de Plessen despised them and advised the queen to put up with none of Christian's sexual games. She urged

Matilda to let him know it was a matter of her discretion whether or not she would welcome him in her bed. The king quickly tired of waiting and returned to his nights of excess in the city.

Nonetheless, Caroline Matilda did get pregnant, and in January 1768, she gave birth to a son, the future Frederick VI. Immediately after, Christian dismissed Madame de Plessen unbeknownst to Matilda who grieved at the loss of the only person she considered a true friend. He also denied the queen permission to accompany him on a grand tour of Germany, England, and France, which lasted from May of 1768 to January of 1769. She had hoped to revisit England and her relatives; instead, she spent her time caring for her little son and waiting on Christian's grandmother and his stepmother, Maria Juliana.

How fortunate you are, to marry where you wish! If I were a widow, I would marry the man I loved and give up my throne and my country.
—Caroline Matilda, speaking to her ladies

This interlude of relative tranquility would be the last Caroline Matilda would enjoy at the Danish court. It was extended for a brief time after the king's return by Christian's temporary attentiveness to his wife and her acceptance of his favors. They dined together and appeared in public as a happy couple. Christian's increasing melancholia and bouts of delusion, however, tired him of the queen's company, and again he found his chief companion in Christian Holck.

Matilda could not compete with her husband's courtier. And to her increasing despair, she saw herself further outnumbered with Christian's addition of yet another young man to his retinue: Johann Frederick Struensee, a German physician he had met on his journey. In contrast to the king, Struensee was a tall man, well built and broad shouldered. He had a full, sensuous face, a large nose, daring blue eyes and a steady gaze, which, joined with a calm demeanor, would quiet Christian and temporarily rescue him from himself. Struensee quickly grasped the situation at the Danish court: the king's attachment to a group of courtiers and a famous courtesan **Catherine Bootlet** who fed his masochistic tendencies, and the queen's emotional, social, and political isolation. Madame de Plessen's replacement by the sister of the courtier on whom Christian depended the most, and whom Matilda hated above all men, had put the enemy inside the doors of her apartments. The jealousy of her stepmother had increased with the birth of Matilda's son, the crown prince Frederick, an event that had temporarily dashed Maria Juliana's hopes albeit not her designs on the crown. Finally, Matilda was a pawn in the warring influences of Russian and French ambassadors vying for Danish support in their pro- and anti-English politics. Her only consolation lay in the baby prince as the one human being she could love and expect love from in return. That his health from the first had been delicate intensified her devotion.

As Christian's attendant on a second journey to England and France, Struensee had added opportunity to study the king and offer remedies as needed. By the time they returned to Copenhagen, he had become indispensable. Christian subsequently tried to introduce his physician to Matilda, but she refused to even talk to the gallant doctor whom she considered another of the king's favorites who would turn him against her.

Then Matilda fell ill of some undiagnosed disease. She thought it dropsy and was unwilling to seek help. It took steady persuasion from both her brother and her husband—who was temporarily better—to permit Struensee to examine her. They appealed to her sense of duty as wife, mother, and queen, and ultimately she relented; she spent two hours with the physician on his first visit and called him back each day thereafter. Caroline Matilda was not only cured within a fortnight; she was given prescriptions for exercise, fresh air, and distraction as a prevention of future depression. Specifically, she was urged to take up riding, which to her delight and surprise proved to be a sport for which she had a special aptitude.

Struensee's next step was to convince the queen that she needed to resume her relationship with the king. Christian's show of sanity, he explained, was only temporary. Consequently, said Struensee, the one closest to the king would be the person with the greatest influence, for Christian would continue to be invested with official authority. That person, he pointed out, might be Christian Holck, Prime Minister Bernstorff, or herself. Struensee's calm and reasonable manner was persuasive; it steadied Matilda's physical and emotional health and promised a relationship of trust and mutual dependence, which, kept within bounds, might have guided the entire court.

But again, something happened that changed Matilda's attitude, this time not from antipathy to sympathy, but from respect and confidence to love and adoration. Copenhagen was attacked by smallpox; 1,200 children died, and Matilda was frantic at the thought of losing her son. She looked to Struensee, who calmly announced that the crown prince had to be inoculated, a practice that was novel in Danish court circles and relatively untried elsewhere as well. Together, the mother and physician brought the two-year-old boy to the country for his vaccination, and for ten days and nights they watched his reaction. Courtiers began to whisper they were lovers, but Matilda was oblivious to the gossip. She had from childhood seen her widowed mother in the company of the earl of Bute who had assisted her in her endeavors, and she saw nothing amiss. The rapid recovery of the young prince sealed the fate of his mother before she even realized the extent of her infatuation with his physician. Gradually, not only Christian's but Matilda's reliance on Struensee became total, and together Struensee and Matilda became Christian's guardians. Holck saw his power reduced and unsuccessfully appealed to Bernstorff to side with him against their common enemy before it was too late. But the prime minister assured the noble that an upstart doctor could in no way unseat either of them. He even agreed to Matilda's suggestion that Struensee be made Christian's reader and private secretary, a post that carried with it the designation of councillor. It furthermore entailed a key to the royal apartments, and soon Struensee could be seen dining with the king and queen, reading to the queen, riding, walking, and playing cards with her. Their becoming lovers in May 1770, just prior to Matilda's 19th birthday, seems the logical corollary of those activities performed in the context of a court that was girded all about with bickering parties and presided over by a king who was descending into madness. Christian was well contented in the company of his wife and her lover, who were kind to him, and asked nothing by way of his participation.

In 1770, Prime Minister Bernstorff arranged a trip to Holstein for Christian and Matilda in hopes of distracting public attention from the latter's relationship with Struensee. The couple refused to go without their doctor, however, so all three of them left, after Christian—*read* Struensee—had given orders that no decision be made until their return, especially pertaining to support of Russian alliances. Bernstorff then realized the degree to which the doctor had involved himself in politics and the extent of his power. In panic, the Danish prime minister appealed to George III of England who arranged for his mother to have a visit with his wayward sister on her way back to Copenhagen. Matilda reluctantly agreed to meet at her sister *Augusta Guelph's palace in Brunswick but sent a last minute notice that she was too ill to make the journey. Her mother therefore suggested Lüneburg for the rendezvous, and they met in June 1770. Princess Dowager Augusta quickly assessed the situation—a determined young woman in love, an almost entirely withdrawn husband, and an all-powerful lover—but her appeals were to no avail. She had seen her daughter for the last time.

When Prime Minister Bernstorff was dismissed in 1770, George III again appealed to his sister in the name of Danish-English connections but received the reply that he was to communicate with her only through her ministers, and his ambassador was denied access. Meanwhile, Struensee had started his reforms to bring Denmark into the 20th century. He began by addressing the problem of the national debt, followed by arrangements for freedom of the press, and in an amazingly short period of time he became known throughout Europe as a champion reformer. The subjects he aimed to reform, however, were offended at his issuing decrees and regulations in German because he had not learned Danish. They were also scandalized by his relationship with the queen and highly critical of his treating crown prince Frederick like a common child. Struensee had replaced the boy's diet of spiced meats, ale, and pastries with one of boiled rice, bread, milk, and vegetables and ordered exercise outdoors in all kinds of weather. Matilda spent much time with her son, playing and gardening with him, for which both were criticized, accused of behaving like peasants. Struensee's felicitous treatment of the young prince, which helped him grow into a ro-

bust, intelligent man further incurred the wrath of Queen Dowager Maria Juliana whose hopes of advancement for her own son were once again diminished. Maria Juliana's ambition remained unreduced; it found response in others' dissatisfaction with Struensee's rule and the queen's behavior, and ultimately resulted in plans for a *coup d'état*.

From then on, events accelerated. On July 1, 1771, Matilda was delivered of a baby girl. News of the princess were proclaimed from the balcony of Christiansborg palace, and two weeks later, Christian conferred on Struensee the titles of privy cabinet minister and count, invested with absolute power in Christian's name. The court physician and political reformer had reached the pinnacle of power, but his stay there was to be brief.

On January 17, 1772, Queen Dowager Maria Juliana's group of conspirators, armed with Christian's signatures on their warrants for arrest, apprehended Struensee and brought him to Copenhagen's citadel. Matilda tried to gain access to the king but found his doors barred. Accompanied by a maid and her baby daughter ❧▶ Louise Augusta, Matilda was escorted to the castle of Kronborg. She had been denied her request to say goodbye to her four-year-old son.

The English ambassador Sir Robert Murray Keith dispatched a message to George describing his sister's imprisonment in a heavily barred room, without either fireplace or shutters, as flagrantly illegal; she had not yet been accused of any crime. The queen dowager he threatened with an English declaration of war, which effected a speedy removal of Matilda to Kronborg's royal apartments. But George ignored his sister's pleas for rescue, despite his knowledge that were she tried for adultery, she might be charged with high treason.

Struensee and Matilda were mutually tricked into signing documents of admission of

❧▶ **Louise Augusta** (1771–1843)
*Duchess of Schleswig-Holstein. Name variations: Louise Augusta Oldenburg. Born on July 7, 1771; died on January 13, 1843; legitimized daughter of *Caroline Matilda (1751-1775) and Johann Struensee; married Frederick Christian, duke of Schleswig-Holstein, on May 27, 1786; children: *Caroline Amelia of Augustenburg (1796–1881); Christian Charles (b. 1798), duke of Schleswig-Holstein; Frederick Emile (b. 1800), prince of Nöer.*

adultery. He was shown her forged signature whereupon he, too, signed. Her hand was guided by one of her judges as she collapsed in the process of writing her name. She had acted throughout with composure and dignity, but on seeing her lover's signature on the incriminating document, she fell back in her chair and covered her face with her hands.

Struensee was brutally executed. His body was quartered and laid upon a wheel, while his head and right hand were cut off and raised on poles. Matilda was rescued from the lifelong imprisonment Maria Juliana had planned for her at a remote castle in northern Jutland by her brother. Though George had finally decided it was his duty to help her, his queen Charlotte refused to welcome Matilda back to England, so Matilda settled on Celle in the English colony of Hanover. There she would have a miniature court and be granted an allowance of £8,000 a year. George sent an escort of two sloops and a frigate to transport her there but ignored her pleas for permission to take with her into exile her ten-month-old daughter, who, she bravely ventured, had no connection with the Danish royal family despite the court's confirmation of her legitimacy.

In the fall of 1772, Caroline Matilda was installed at the castle of Celle, a luxurious but lonely place set in the middle of heavy forested land and the nearest house 15 miles away. Books, music, needlework, cards, and—increasingly—religion took up her time. Matilda was joined there by her old friend Madame de Plessen, whose loyalty remained unconditional. When de Plessen took a house in Celle, they met almost every day. Planning her garden became another resource and, to mitigate the loss of her children, Matilda adopted a four-year-old orphan.

Yet the last phase in Matilda's life was not entirely without drama. A group of Danish exiles from Queen Dowager Maria Juliana's court, who had taken refuge in Altona, formed a plot to return their one time queen to Copenhagen and invest her with supreme power during the king's incapacity and her son's minority. They needed someone outside their circle, however, who could contact Matilda without raising suspicions about their undertaking. They found their man in Nathaniel Waxhall, a "high-minded but egocentric enthusiast." He had read about his countrywoman's fate at the Danish court and yearned to come to her rescue. George, with accustomed reticence, pledged his approval of the plans for his sister's restoration if they were successfully executed.

However, just before midnight on May 11, Carolina Matilda died in her sleep, having been infected by scarlet fever or possibly typhoid. A week later, this rather laconic message appeared in a Copenhagen paper: "Yesterday we were informed by intelligence from Celle that Queen Caroline Matilda after a few days' illness the night before last at eleven o'clock exchanged temporality for eternity." Christian's comment on learning the news: "Too bad, she had pretty calves" sums up his condition.

SOURCES:

Bech, Svend Cedergreen. *Brev fra Dorothea*. Copenhagen: Politikens Forlag, 1975.

Chapman, Hester W. *Caroline Matilda*. London: Jonathan Cape, 1971.

Lange, Victor. *Fra Struensetiden*. Copenhagen: Jacob Lunds Boghandel, 1926.

Reverdil, Salomon. *Struense og det danske hof*. Copenhagen: Host og Son, 1916.

Inga Wiehl, Yakima Valley Community College, Yakima, Washington

Caroline Matilda of Denmark
(1912—)

Danish royal. Name variations: Caroline-Matilda Louise Oldenburg. Born on April 27, 1912; daughter of Harald (b. 1876, son of **Louise of Sweden** *and Frederick VIII, king of Denmark), and* **Helen of Schleswig-Holstein** *(1888–1962); married Prince Knud Christian Frederik (b. 1900, son of Christian X, king of Denmark); on September 8, 1933; children:* **Elizabeth Caroline-Matilde** *(b. 1935); Ingolf Christian Frederik Knud (b. 1940); Christian Frederik Francis (b. 1942).*

Caroline Matilda of Schleswig-Holstein (1860–1932)

Duchess of Schleswig-Holstein. Name variations: Victoria Frederica of Schleswig-Holstein. Born Victoria Fredericka Augusta Mary Carolina Matilda on January 25, 1860; died on February 20, 1932; daughter of Frederick, duke of Schleswig-Holstein-Sonderburg-Augustenburg, and **Adelaide of Hohenlohe-Langenburg** *(1835–1900); married Frederick Ferdinand (1855–1934), duke of Schleswig-Holstein-Glucksburg (r. 1855–1934), on March 19, 1885; children:* **Victoria Adelaide of Schleswig-Holstein** *(1885–1970);* **Alexandra Victoria of Schleswig-Holstein** *(1887–1957, who married Augustus William, the son of Kaiser Wilhelm II);* **Helen of Schleswig-Holstein** *(1888–1962); Karoline-Mathilde of Schleswig-Holstein (b. 1894, who married Hans, count of Solms-Baruth); Adelaide of Holstein-Schleswig (b. 1899); Wilhelm Fredrich also known as Frederick (1891–1965), duke of Schleswig-Holstein (r. 1934–1965).*

Caroline of Ansbach (1683–1737)

Queen of England. Name variations: Wilhelmina Carolina, Caroline the Good, Caroline of Brandenburg-Ansbach or Anspach. Born Wilhelmina Charlotte Caroline in Ansbach, Germany, on March 1, 1683; died at St. James' Palace, London, England, on November 20, 1737; daughter of John Frederick, margrave of Brandenburg-Ansbach (d. 1686) and *Eleanor of Saxe-Eisenach (1662–1696); married George II (1683–1760), king of Great Britain and Ireland (r. 1727–1760), on August 22, 1705; children: Frederick, prince of Wales (1701–1751, father of George III and husband of *Augusta of Saxe-Coburg-Gotha); ⚜➤ Anne (1709–1759); ⚜➤ Amelia Sophia (1711–1786), ⚜➤ Caroline Elizabeth (1713–1757); George (died as an infant); William Augustus (1721–1765), duke of Cumberland (called the Butcher of Culloden); *Mary of Hesse-Cassel (1723–1772); *Louise of England (1724–1751).

Born in the tiny state of Ansbach in the Bavarian Highlands on March 1, 1683, the Princess Caroline grew up mainly at Dresden and Berlin, where she enjoyed the close friendship of *Sophie Charlotte of Hanover (1668–1705), wife of Frederick I of Prussia. After turning down a proposal from the king of Spain, in August 1705 Caroline married the Hanoverian prince, George Augustus, whose father would become King George I of England in 1714. Son and father were continually at odds. Though the early years of her married life were spent in Hanover, Caroline took a strong interest in the approaching accession of the Hanoverian dynasty to the British throne. She was on very friendly terms with the old electress *Sophia (1630–1714), and she corresponded with Baron Gottfried von Leibnitz, whose acquaintance she had made in Berlin.

In October 1714, Caroline followed her husband and father-in-law to London. As princess of Wales, she was accessible and accepted; she took the first place at court, filling a difficult position with tact and success. "Caroline's enthusiasm and willingness to go halfway to meet everyone made her and George extremely popular," wrote historian **Barbara Softly**, "and the sight of the little princesses, Caroline's daughters, bouncing excitedly up and down in their carriage, brought roars of approval from the crowds."

When the squabbles between the prince of Wales and his unpopular father escalated to serious proportions, Caroline sided with her husband, and the conflict reached a climax in 1717. Driven from court, ostracized by the

➤ **Anne** (1709–1759)

Princess of Orange. Name variations: Anne Guelph; Anne of England, princess royal. Born on October 22 (some sources cite November 2), 1709, in Hanover, Lower Saxony, Germany; died on January 12, 1759, in The Hague, Netherlands; daughter of George II (1683–1760), king of Great Britain and Ireland (r. 1727–1760), and *Caroline of Ansbach (1683–1737); married William IV, prince of Orange (r. 1748–1751), on March 25, 1734; children: son (1735–1735); daughter (1736–1736); daughter (1739–1739); *Caroline of Orange (1743–1787); Anne Marie (1746–1746); William V (1748–1806), prince of Orange (r. 1751–1795, deposed).

➤ **Amelia Sophia** (1711–1786)

English princess. Name variations: Amelia Guelph. Born Amelia Sophia Eleanor on June 10, 1711, in Herrenhausen, Germany; died on October 31, 1786, in London, England; buried in Westminster Abbey, London; daughter of George II (1683–1760), king of Great Britain and Ireland (r. 1727–1760) and *Caroline of Ansbach (1683–1737).

➤ **Caroline Elizabeth** (1713–1757)

Princess royal. Name variations: Caroline Guelph. Born Caroline Elizabeth in Hanover, Lower Saxony, Germany, on June 10, 1713; died at St. James' Palace, London, England, on December 28, 1757; buried at Westminster Abbey, London; daughter of George II (1683–1760), king of Great Britain and Ireland (r. 1727–1760) and *Caroline of Ansbach (1683–1737).

king, deprived even of the custody of their children, the prince and princess took up their residence in London at Leicester House and in the country at Richmond. They surrounded themselves with a distinguished circle. Caroline had a taste for art and literature, once rescuing some Holbein drawings from a dusty cupboard, and their London home was the meeting place of noted celebrities of the day: Lord Chesterfield, poet Alexander Pope, playwright John Gay, Lord Hervey and his much-admired wife, *Mary Hervey.

A formal reconciliation with George I took place in 1720. On his death in October 1727, George II and his queen were crowned. During the rest of her life, Queen Caroline's influence in English politics was chiefly exercised in support of her friend Sir Robert Walpole, a minister whom she kept in power and in control of church patronage. Caroline was exceedingly tolerant, and the bishops appointed by her were distinguished more for their learning than for

Caroline of Ansbach

George II (ed. by J.W. Croker, 1884) and W.H. Wilkins' *Caroline the Illustrious* (1904).
SOURCES:
Lofts, Norah. *Queens of England.* NY: Doubleday, 1977.
Softly, Barbara. *The Queens of England.* NY: Bell, 1979.

Caroline of Austria (1801–1832)

Austrian princess. Name variations: Karolina Ferdinanda. Born on April 8, 1801, in Vienna; died on May 22, 1832, in Dresden; daughter of *Maria Teresa of Naples (1772–1807)* and Francis I, emperor of Austria (r. 1804–1835), also known as Francis II, Holy Roman emperor (r. 1792–1806); became first wife of Frederick Augustus II (1797–1854), king of Saxony (r. 1836–1854), on October 7, 1819. Frederick Augustus' second wife was *Maria of Bavaria (1805–1877).*

Caroline of Baden (1776–1841)

Queen of Bavaria and electress of Bavaria. Born on July 13, 1776, in Karlsruhe; died on November 13, 1841, in Munich, Germany; daughter of *Amalie of Hesse-Darmstadt (1754–1832)* and Charles Louis of Padua, prince of Padua and Baden; became second wife of Maximilian I Joseph, elector of Bavaria (r. 1799–1805), king of Bavaria (r. 1805–1825); children: Maximilian (1800–1803); *Elizabeth of Bavaria (1801–1873,* who married Frederick William IV of Prussia); *Amalia of Bavaria (1801–1877); *Sophie of Bavaria (1805–1872); *Maria of Bavaria (1805–1877,* who married Frederick Augustus II of Saxony); *Ludovica (1808–1892,* who married Duke Maximilian Joseph of Bavaria); Maximiliana (1810–1821).

Caroline of Birkenfeld-Zweibrucken (1721–1774)

Landgravine of Hesse-Darmstadt. Name variations: Caroline of Zweibrücken-Birkenfeld. Born on March 9, 1721; died on March 30, 1774; married Ludwig IX also known as Louis IX (b. 1719), landgrave of Hesse-Darmstadt, on August 12, 1741; children: *Caroline of Hesse-Darmstadt (1746–1821); *Frederica of Hesse (1751–1805); Louis I (b. 1753), grand duke of Hesse; *Amalie of Hesse-Darmstadt (1754–1832); *Natalie of Hesse-Darmstadt (1755–1776).

Caroline of Bourbon (1822–1869)

Duchess of Aumâle. Name variations: Caroline de Bourbon. Born on April 26, 1822; died on December 6, 1869; daughter of Leopold (b. 1790), prince of Salerno, and *Clementine of Austria (1798–1881);* married Henry (1822–1897), duke of Aumâle, on November

their doctrines. During the king's absences from England, she was regent of the kingdom on four occasions. Went an ill-metered rhyme of the day: "You may strut, dapper George, but 'twill all be in vain,/ We know 'tis Queen Caroline, not you, that reign."

On the whole, Caroline's relations with her husband, with whom she had eight children, were satisfactory. A clever and patient woman, she was complaisant towards the king, flattering his vanity and acknowledging his mistresses, including *Henrietta Howard, countess of Suffolk, and Caroline retained her influence over him to the end. At 54, on November 20, 1737, she died of an internal complaint that she had hidden for years. Her grieving husband ordered that upon his death the sides of their coffins were to be removed so that they might spend eternity together.

Caroline of Ansbach appears in Sir Walter Scott's *Heart of Midlothian.* She is also detailed in Lord Hervey's *Memoirs of the Reign of*

25, 1844; children: Louis Philippe (b. 1845), prince of Conde; Henry (b. 1852); Franz (b. 1854), duke of Guise; and two other children who died in infancy.

Caroline of Brandenburg-Ansbach
(1683–1737).

See Caroline of Ansbach.

Caroline of Brunswick (1768–1821)

Queen of Great Britain and Ireland who was locked out of Westminster by her husband George IV on coronation day. Name variations: Caroline Amelia Augusta; Caroline Amelia Elizabeth; Queen Caroline; Caroline Amelia of Brunswick-Wolfenbuttel; Princess of Wales. Born Caroline Amelia Augusta on May 17, 1768, in Brunswick, Lower Saxony, Germany; died at Brandenburg House, Hammersmith, London, England, on August 7, 1821; buried in Brunswick, Lower Saxony, Germany; second daughter of Charles William Ferdinand Bevern, duke of Brunswick-Wolfenbüttel, and Augusta Guelph (1737–1813, sister of George III, king of England); married George IV (1762–1821), king of England (r. 1820–1830), on April 8, 1795; children: Charlotte Augusta (1796–1817, who married Leopold I, king of the Belgians); (adopted) William Austin and Edwina Kent.

Born in Germany on May 17, 1768, Caroline of Brunswick was the second daughter of the duke of Brunswick-Wolfenbüttel and *Augusta Guelph, sister of King George III of England. The education of the fun-loving, vivacious, and outspoken Caroline did little to prepare her for a future as queen and long-suffering wife of a disreputable monarch.

Her marriage to the dissolute and much-opposed George, prince of Wales (future King George IV), was arranged in 1795 by his father George III who was also her uncle. The 33-year-old prince, who disliked his cousin intensely, had a preference for older, sophisticated, highly cultivated women. His 27-year-old bride-to-be did not fit this criteria; so candid was Caroline as a teenager that she was often accused of inappropriate utterances, especially about sex, so much so that her parents hired a moral guardian to police her tongue.

As if the prince's lack of affection for Caroline weren't enough, he was already illegally wed to the Roman Catholic widow *Maria Anne Fitzherbert and was in the process of replacing their ten-year liaison with a stable of mistresses. George III, however, offered to pay off his son's

huge debt if he acquiesced. Agreeing in word, if not in deed, the prince heartlessly named his mistress **Frances, countess of Jersey**, Lady of the Bedchamber to the German princess who was to be his bride. He then sent Lady Jersey and her retinue to greet Caroline as she arrived in England, aware that the group would delight in mocking a foreign princess. They did not disappoint, telling all who would hear that the German princess was in need of a wash, especially when it came to body linen. (Personal cleanliness was just becoming fashionable in England's upper ranks.)

Caroline of Brunswick

At first sight of his bride-to-be, the prince reportedly staggered backward and asked for brandy. Caroline, on her part, found her future husband to be "very fat and not half as handsome as his portrait." Unfortunately, with Caroline's propensity for blunt truths, this was said to his face. At the wedding, the prince of Wales was deep into his cups. Caroline was quoted as saying, with a hint of a German accent: "Judge what it was to have a drunken husband on one's wedding day and one who passed the greatest part of his bridal night under the grate, where he fell and where I left him. If anybody say to me at dis moment—will you pass your life over again or be killed? I would choose death, for you know, a little sooner or later we must all die, but to live a life of wretchedness twice over—oh, mine God, no!"

Days into the marriage, as soon as the royal couple had done their all for England to conceive a legal heir, the prince deserted his wife for his mistresses, who over the years included Lady Jersey, Mrs. Perdita Robinson (*Mary Robinson), Countess von Hardenburg, ❧▶ Anna Maria Crouch, and ❧▶ Lady Melbourne. As soon as Caroline's daughter ❧▶ Charlotte Augusta, the princess royale, was born on January 7, 1796, she was taken from her mother, and Caroline was given permission to see her for about two hours a week.

Thus, Caroline, princess of Wales, resided alone at Blackheath, entertaining writers and artists, selling produce from her garden to subsi-

❧▶
Melbourne, Lady. See Lamb, Caroline for sidebar on Melbourne, Elizabeth.

❧▶
See sidebars on the following page

Crouch, Anna Maria (1763–1805)

English opera singer. Born in 1763; died in 1805; married to a lieutenant in the Royal Navy.

A beautiful and talented singer, Anna Maria Crouch triumphed in the role of Polly Peachum in John Gay's *The Beggar's Opera.* Her relationship with George IV was brief and profitable. Her husband, a navy lieutenant, received £400 per annum for not suing the king, while Anna Maria received a £12,000 bond.

SUGGESTED READING:

Young, M.J. *Memoirs of Mrs. Crouch.* London, 1806.

Charlotte Augusta (1796–1817)

Princess of Wales. Name variations: Charlotte Augusta of Wales; Charlotte of Wales, Charlotte Guelph; Princess Charlotte. Born Charlotte Augusta at Carlton House, London, England, on January 7, 1796; died in childbirth in Esher, Surrey, England, on November 6, 1817; buried at St. George's Chapel, Windsor, Berkshire, England; daughter of George IV (1762–1821), king of England (r. 1820–1830), and *Caroline of Brunswick (1768–1821); married Leopold of Saxe-Coburg-Saalfeld, also known as Leopold I (b. 1790), king of the Belgians (r. 1831–1865), on May 2, 1816; children: a son who died at birth.

Throughout all the rumors, innuendo, investigations, and trials revolving around her royal parents, Charlotte Augusta sided with her mother *Caroline of Brunswick, rather than her father George IV. The cheerful and popular princess once said of them: "My mother was bad, but she would not have been as bad as she was if my father had not been infinitely worse."

When Charlotte's father planned to marry her off to Prince William of Orange, she fled in a hackney carriage to the house of her mother. Ordering her return, George IV promised a more suitable suitor, and Prince Leopold of Saxe-Coburg-Saalfeld (the future king of the Belgians) was happy to accept the honor. Though brief, theirs was a happy marriage. But at age 20, Charlotte died in childbirth, along with her still-born child, over ten years before Leopold came to the throne. Leopold's second wife was *Louise d'Orleans (1812–1850).

dize the education of nine local orphans. To replace the loss of her daughter, she adopted William Austin, the four-month-old son of a destitute woman, and a girl, **Edwina Kent**. Sexually frustrated, socially ignored, mocked by her husband's mistresses, and supported with meager finances, Caroline lapsed into rebellious conduct. But the sympathies of the people of England were strongly in her favor: she was thought to have been badly treated by her profligate husband.

Rumors abounded that the adopted children were her own, rumors possibly started by her husband. (The prince of Wales was no stranger to slander; it was he who went around convincing others that his father George III was insane.) About 1806, gossip regarding Caroline's behavior was circulated so openly that George III ordered an investigation. The princess was acquitted of any serious offense when two English ladies of her household testified that, though she may have been foolish in her indiscretions, she had never committed adultery. Even so, various improprieties in her deportment were pointed out and censured. When the acquittal was announced, English subjects put lights in every window in support of the decision.

In 1814, Caroline left England with her adopted children to escape the persecutions of the king and his friends and traveled on the Continent, living principally in Italy. The prince of Wales continued to try to shed his wife, even after their only daughter Charlotte Augusta died in childbirth in 1817, age 20, leaving no heirs.

On the accession of the prince to the throne of England as George IV in 1820, orders were given that the English ambassadors should halt the recognition of the princess as queen at any foreign court. Her name was also formally omitted from the liturgy, meaning that British subjects could not pray for her in church, and that she must not be thought of as queen. These acts once again roused widespread pity for the princess of Wales among the English. She immediately made arrangements to return to England to claim her rights as queen, rejecting a proposal that she should receive an annuity of £50,000 a year on condition of renouncing her title and remaining abroad.

When further efforts at compromise proved fruitless, Caroline arrived in England on June 6, 1820; the usual crowds came out to greet her and accompany her to London, bearing signs "The queen forever; the king in the river!" Intent on denying Caroline the crown on the grounds of adultery, the openly adulterous George IV had sent spies to glean information while she was overseas and claimed that she had lived in sin with Bartolomo Pergami, a chamberlain in the royal household. One month later, a bill to dissolve her marriage with the king was brought into the House of Lords. The so-called Trial of Queen Caroline began on August 17, 1820. The queen maintained that the only adultery she had committed was on her wedding night with the husband of Mrs. Fitzherbert. The public interest was intense, and the queen's counsel highly skilled. Though Caroline's behavior had often been scandalous, indiscreet, a bid for attention (e.g., she had a predilection for exposing her ample bosom), no one could prove adultery. The ministers felt that the narrowness of their majority would lead essentially to defeat of the bill. On November 10, after passing the third reading, the legislation was abandoned.

Though Caroline defeated her husband's efforts to divorce her and was permitted to assume the title of queen, she was forcibly prevented from attending the coronation ceremony in Westminster Abbey on July 19, 1821, when her husband ordered the doors chained during the service. Caroline, arriving at the door in regal robes with friends in attendance, was refused admittance since she had no ticket. The crowd outside, up until that time firmly on her side, reacted with laughter. The details of her behavior served up at the trial had cost the queen her constituency. The humiliation as she drove away is thought to have hastened her death, which took place less than three weeks later, on August 7. She was 53.

Caroline had requested that she be buried in Brunswick with her parents. When George, in his last act of cruelty, wanted to have the funeral procession bypass the city of London, the crowd's sympathy turned toward Caroline once more. "Dawn in London on August 14th was wet and drizzly," writes Stanley H. Palmer. "Dirt streets became muddy pools. The hearse, elaborately decorated and drawn by eight horses, moved away from Caroline's residence, Brandenburgh House, at 8 a.m. The first test of the procession came in Kensington. A crowd had shut the gates to the Gardens, through which the hearse was to have gone, and chanted, 'The City, the City . . . the City or death!'" During what is now known as the Caroline Riots, the military entourage accompanying the coffin ran into barricades at every turn. Serving as targets for stones, the nervous guards fired into the crowd, killing two and wounding several others. But, after seven hours of thwarted passage, the mob successfully diverted the procession through the streets of the city until the humiliated queen's coffin was placed on board a ship bound for her native country.

SOURCES AND SUGGESTED READING:

Carlton, Charles. *Royal Mistresses*. London: Routledge, 1990.

Clerici, Graziano Paolo. *A Queen of Indiscretions: The Tragedy of Caroline of Brunswick, Queen of England*. Translated by F. Chapman. London, 1907.

Fraser, Flora. *The Unruly Queen: The Life of Queen Caroline*. NY: Knopf, 1996.

Palmer, Stanley H. "Before the Bobbies: The Caroline Riots of 1821," in *History Today*. October 1977.

Caroline of Hesse-Darmstadt
(1746–1821)

*Landgravine of Hesse-Homburg. Name variations: Caroline von Hessen-Darmstadt. Born on March 2, 1746; died on September 18, 1821; daughter of Ludwig IX, landgrave of Hesse-Darmstadt, and *Caroline of Birkenfeld-Zweibrucken (1721–1774); sister of *Frederica of Hesse (1751–1805), Grand Duke Louis I, *Amalie of Hesse-Darmstadt (1754–1832), and *Natalie of Hesse-Darmstadt (1755–1776); married Frederick Louis V (1748–1820), landgrave of Hesse-Homburg (r. 1751–1820), on September 27, 1768; children: Frederick VI (b. 1769), landgrave of Hesse-Homburg; *Mary of Hesse-Homburg (1785–1846).*

Caroline of Mecklenburg-Strelitz (1821–1876)

Princess of Mecklenburg-Strelitz. Born on January 10, 1821; died on June 1, 1876; daughter of George (b. 1779), duke of Mecklenburg-Strelitz; became second wife of Frederick VII (1808–1863), king of Denmark (r. 1848–1863), on June 10, 1841 (divorced 1846).

Caroline of Naples (1798–1870)

*Duchess of Berry. Name variations: Caroline Ferdinande Louise of Naples; Caroline of Naples; Marie Caroline Ferdinande Louise of Naples; Maria Carolina de Bourbon; Marie-Caroline de Bourbon-Sicile; duchesse de Berry; princess of the Two Sicilies. Born Marie Caroline Ferdinande Louise on November 5, 1798; died on April 17, 1870; daughter of Francis I, king of Two Sicilies (r. 1825–1830) and *Maria Clementina of Austria (1777–1801); married Charles Ferdinand (1778–1820), duke of Berry (second son of Charles X, king of France); married Ettore, count Lucchesi-Palli, in 1831; children: (first marriage) *Louise of Bourbon-Berry (1819–1864), duchess of Parma; Henry V (1820–1883), duke of Bordeaux and count of Chambord (who married *Therese [1817–1886]); (second marriage) Clementina de Campofranco (b. 1835).*

Charles Ferdinand, son of Charles X, king of France, lived in exile in England from 1789 to 1814 where he married **Anna Brown** (d. 1876) in 1806. When Brown's family refused to acknowledge the marriage, he returned to France in 1814 and married Caroline of Naples two years later. Charles Ferdinand was assassinated in Paris on February 13, 1820. In 1832, Caroline promoted an unsuccessful attempt at revolution in favor of her son Henry, count of Chambord, in 1832. Henry was proclaimed Henry V, king of

France, by Legitimists but was compelled to live in exile in Lower Austria.

Caroline of Nassau (fl. 1730s)

Countess of Zweibrucken. Married Christian III, count of Zweibrucken (r. 1733–1735); children: Christian IV (r. 1735–1775), count of Zweibrucken; Frederick Michael (d. 1767).

Caroline of Nassau-Usingen (1762–1823)

Landgravine of Hesse-Cassel. Name variations: Caroline Polyxena of Nassau-Usingen. Born Caroline Polyxene on April 4, 1762; died on March 28, 1823; daughter of Charles William, prince of Nassau-Usingen, and **Caroline Felizitas of Leiningen-Heidesheim** *(b. 1734); married Frederick III, landgrave of Hesse-Cassel, on December 2, 1786; children: eight, including William, landgrave of Hesse-Cassel (1787–1867);* ***Mary of Hesse-Cassel** *(1796–1880, who married George, grand duke of Mecklenburg-Strelitz);* ***Augusta of Hesse-Cassel** *(1797–1889, who married Adolphus Guelph, 1st duke of Cambridge).*

Caroline of Orange (1743–1787)

Princess of Nassau-Weilburg. Name variations: Wilhelmina Caroline of Nassau-Dietz. Born on February 28, 1743; died on May 6, 1787; daughter of William IV, prince of Orange (r. 1748–1751), and ***Anne** *(1709–1759, daughter of King George II of England and* ***Caroline of Ansbach**); *married Charles, prince of Nassau-Weilburg, on March 5, 1760; children: nine, including Frederick William (1768–1816);* **Henrietta of Nassau-Weilburg** *(1780–1857).*

Caroline of Parma (1770–1804)

Princess of Parma. Born on November 22, 1770; died on March 1, 1804; daughter of ***Maria Amalia** *(1746–1804) and Ferdinand I (1751–1802), duke of Parma (r. 1765–1802); married Maximilian of Saxony (son of Frederick Christian and* ***Maria Antonia of Austria**), *duke of Saxony (r. 1830–1838), on May 9, 1792; children: Frederick Augustus II (1797–1854), king of Saxony (r. 1836–1854); John (1801–1873), king of Saxony (r. 1854–1873);* ***Amalie of Saxony** *(1794–1870);* ***Maria Josepha of Saxony** *(1803–1829).*

Caroline of Saxony (1833–1907)

Queen of Saxony. Born Caroline Frederica Francisca on August 5, 1833; died on December 15, 1907; daughter of Prince Gustavus Vasa (b. 1799) and ***Louise of Baden** *(1811–1854); married Albert (1828–1902), king of Saxony (r. 1873–1902), on June 18, 1853.*

Caroline of Sicily (1820–1861)

Sicilian princess. Born on February 29, 1820; died on January 13, 1861; daughter of ***Marie Isabella of Spain** *(1789–1848) and Francis I, king of Two Sicilies (r. 1825–1830); married Charles of Molina, on July 10, 1850.*

Carpenter, Iris (1906—)

British journalist and war correspondent who was one of the few women to report the Allied invasion of Europe from D-Day in June 1944 to the surrender of Germany in May 1945. Born in England in 1906; daughter of a cinema entrepreneur; married Charles Scruby (a developer); married Russell F. Akers, Jr. (an American colonel), in 1946; children: (first marriage) one son, one daughter.

Retired from journalism (early 1930s) to raise a family; start of World War II motivated her to return to the profession to cover the Battle of Britain; facing strong discrimination by British military authorities and determined to be a combat reporter, was hired by the Boston Globe *and was accredited with the 1st American Army; her reports from the front lines and hospitals in France and Germany described in graphic prose some of the bloodiest fighting on the Western front, including the Battle of the Bulge as well as the liberation of Nazi concentration camps; remained in the U.S., working for Voice of America.*

Iris Carpenter was one of the most intrepid and respected women war correspondents of World War II. With her powerful stories appearing in the *Boston Globe*, many of her loyal readers were unaware that Carpenter was not an American, but a British-born journalist. Born into a wealthy family (her father was a cinema magnate), she used her father's connections to land a job in 1924 as a film critic for a British publication called *The Picture Show*. Her talent pushed her up the professional ladder, and she signed on with London's *Daily Express*. Following her marriage to Charles Scruby, a wealthy developer, Carpenter quit journalism in 1933 to devote her energy to raising a young son and daughter.

The start of World War II in September 1939 ended Iris Carpenter's life of secure domesticity. From the outset, the conflict came uncomfortably close to her private life when five German planes were shot down in the woods behind her home. Determined not to sit out the war, she reported on the conflict in several roles, including as a broadcaster for the BBC as well as a print reporter for both the *Daily Express* and the *Daily Herald*. Ignoring the dangers around her, Carpenter turned in colorful and perceptive articles documenting the heroism and destruction of the Battle of Britain. By 1942, the United States had joined the war effort, and it was clear that one day Hitler's Fortress Europe would be invaded by an Allied armada. A tested veteran war correspondent, Carpenter believed that she had earned a right to be part of the first wave of troops liberating the Nazi-occupied European Continent.

Her application to be accredited with the British Expeditionary Force for its coming invasion of Europe was vetoed. Carpenter's book, *No Woman's World*, notes the hostile attitudes of the British high command toward female reporters at the front: "The only chance a newspaper girl had in talking to troops was by touring camps with the Red Cross doughnut girls." Refusing to be excluded from one of the greatest stories of the war, she decided to find a job with an American newspaper and report on American participation in the upcoming invasion. Her meeting with Carlyle Holt of the *Boston Globe* was a persuasive one, and she was hired as that newspaper's accredited correspondent with the U.S. 1st Army. On D-Day plus four, Iris Carpenter became one of the first women to land on the Allies' precarious Normandy airstrip. Though she and a handful of other women had now appeared on the scene, the British War Office continued to place obstacles in their way, reflecting the openly hostile attitudes of Field Marshall Bernard Montgomery, whose position was a flat: "We will not tolerate them."

Taking advantage of the American military's greater receptivity to female reporters, Carpenter followed the troops beyond the immediate area of France's rapidly expanding Normandy beachhead. On her first return to London to file some stories, she discovered that she had broken a rule by advancing with the troops and was subject to a court-martial and subsequent disaccreditation if found guilty. Fortunately she had saved her typed orders (in triplicate), satisfying her accusers that she had not consciously broken the rules, which were now recast to redefine the beachhead as being four miles inland from Omaha Beach to the city of Cherbourg. Despite Carpenter's escape from punishment, institutional hostility toward women journalists remained strong. The Public Relations Division (PRD) of Supreme Headquarters Allied Expedi-

tionary Forces (SHAEF) had full jurisdiction over female reporters, dictating that they could only write about subjects the PRD approved, which included such topics as the Women's Army Corps (WACS), wounded soldiers and hospital life. Women reporters, regarded as little more than a nuisance, were severely restricted in their access to the front lines, being ordered to go no farther than the areas designated for nurses and Red Cross staff. Whereas male correspondents were usually assigned to camps that had jeeps and drivers as well as teletype and radio transmitters, women reporters enjoyed few of these professional advantages. The hospitals to which they were assigned, often situated in areas more exposed to enemy shelling, rarely had jeeps, making it difficult for reporters to get their stories to the local press camp.

As the Germans retreated, Carpenter followed the Allied forces through the shattered French city of Caen and across the River Orne, reporting not only the exploits of American troops but the involvement of the local population against their Nazi oppressors. She was perceptive in her observations of both the evil and altruistic traits that the end of foreign occupation brought out in the French—some displayed malevolence, others heroism. In her constant search for good stories, she ignored the dangers of the war. Only in her memoirs could she look back on the dangers of her exhilarating, perilous job, noting that "No combat soldier, however experienced or well trained, did a better job of inching out in retreat with the fanny well down than this correspondent." Despite the courage and competence of female war correspondents like Carpenter during the first weeks of the invasion, SHAEF continued its policy of discrimination and none of them were present for the exhilarating first hours of the liberation of Paris. Arriving in Paris after having been "quarantined" along with other women reporters by a PR officer, Carpenter more than made up for her frustration by reporting on the final stages of mopping-up operations by French resistance forces of holdout German troops, which she called "head-hunting."

Soon after leaving liberated Paris, Carpenter suffered a shattered eardrum during a bombing raid on St. Lô, which became infected. A painful and dangerous case of mastoiditis was suspected, but she refused to submit to an operation, fearing that by the time she had fully recovered the war would be over. She ameliorated her condition by remaining with a field hospital as it moved toward the front; in this manner, she maintained medical treatment and stayed close enough to the action to continue reporting.

Carpenter's stories of wounded soldiers and of the skillful, compassionate medical and nursing staff were among the best published during the final phase of the war in Europe. The horror of war was never far from her reportage: "Time was taken out to bury the men, but carcasses of cattle were everywhere. I don't know why the sight of a flock of sheep bowled stiffly on their sides, or a cow with the soft, flabby folds of her neck stretched taut to the sky, or a horse with his four legs jutting from a bloated belly, should seem more sadly to heighten the horridness of war than anything it does to men. I know only that it did. Maybe it's because animals are so unresponsible for it all."

In her reporting on the carnage of the battle of the Hürtgen Forest, Carpenter again pointed up the animal life sacrificed to the war. Wounded American soldiers sought shelter in a barn while the war raged around them: "Every time another crash shook the trembling structure, the surviving animals burrowed into the hay among the wounded, squealed and whinnied and bleated. A youngster with a dangling bloody mess of coat-sleeve where his left arm should have been had the other one firmly around a frightened pig. 'Silly, isn't it?' he cracked. 'Me, with pork my favorite meat!'" Once in Germany, Carpenter began to write not only of American and Allied soldiers but of the German civilian population as well, who, she said, "were Germans, but that made them no less pitiable" as they wandered the roads with a handful of salvaged possessions. Determined to see as much as she could, Carpenter moved from place to place by cub plane in what were often dangerous forays, not only because of enemy fire but hostile weather; on one trip, she spent three hours in a wild storm, finally finding a safe airfield with only a few minutes of fuel left in the tank.

The war ended for Iris Carpenter with scenes both horrific and exhilarating. She reported on the concentration camps at Buchenwald, Dachau and Nordhausen, telling of monstrous deeds her readers could not always easily accept as part of the human experience in the 20th century. More optimistic were her reports from Torgau on the Elbe river, where American and Soviet troops met and celebrated a hard-won victory, hopefully foreshadowing a new era of peace and cooperation. The war ended for Carpenter in Weimar, the city of both Goethe and Schiller as well as Buchenwald. After composing her last dispatches, she came to the United States in early June 1945 and consciously began the transition to a world at peace. Wrote Carpenter after seeing the New York skyline: "I was afraid that the sensation of combat would deprive me of the quality of being excited about anything else . . . but I am excited."

The Allied victory in Europe brought other changes to Carpenter's life. She divorced her husband and married an American officer, Colonel Russell F. ("Red") Akers, Jr. Her son came to the United States while her daughter remained in school in England. Iris and "Red" settled down in the Washington, D.C., area, he remaining in the military and she finding a job with the Voice of America. Her war memoirs, *No Woman's World*, were published in 1946, receiving positive reviews. Carpenter remained in the United States, living out a long retirement in her beloved state of Virginia.

SOURCES:

Beasley, Maurine H. "Women and Journalism in World War II: Discrimination and Progress," in *American Journalism*. Vol. 12, no. 3. Summer 1995, pp. 321–333.

Carpenter, Iris. *No Woman's World*. Boston, MA: Houghton Mifflin, 1946.

Edwards, Julia. *Women of the World: The Great Foreign Correspondents*. Boston, MA: Houghton Mifflin, 1988.

Wagner, Lilya. *Women War Correspondents of World War II*. NY: Greenwood Press, 1989.

COLLECTIONS:

MSS. Collection #147, Archives and Special Collections, Ohio University Libraries, Athens, Ohio.

John Haag, Associate Professor, University of Georgia, Athens, Georgia

Carpenter, Karen (1950–1983)

American pop singer, known for her pure voice, whose death at age 32 helped bring anorexia nervosa to national consciousness. Born in East Haven, Connecticut, on March 2, 1950; died of heart failure brought about by anorexia nervosa on February 4, 1983; daughter of Harold Bertram Carpenter (a pressman) and Agnes Reuwer (Tatum) Carpenter; sister of Richard Carpenter (1946—); married Tom Burris (a real-estate developer), on August 31, 1980 (separated).

Selected singles: "Close to You," "We've Only Just Begun," "Top of the World," "Yesterday Once More," "Rainy Days and Mondays," "I Need to be in Love," "Hurting Each Other," "Goodbye to Love," "Solitaire," "I Won't Last a Day without You," and "Please Mr Postman."

Albums: Ticket to Ride; A Song for You (1972, featuring "Hurting Each Other," "It's Going to Take Some Time," "I Won't Last a Day without You,"

"Goodbye to Love," "Top of the World"); The Now and Then Album (1973, "Yesterday Once More," "Da Doo Ron Ron," "One Fine Day," "Sing," "This Masquerade," "Jambalaya," "I Can't Make Music"); Horizon (June 1975, "I Can Dream, Can't I," "Desperado," "Solitaire," "Only Yesterday," "[I'm Caught between] Goodbye and I Love You," "Aurora," and "Eventide"); A Kind of Hush (1976, "I Need to be in Love," "Sandy," "One More Time," "Breaking Up is Hard to Do"); Passage (1977, "Don't Cry for Me, Argentina," "Calling Occupants of Interplanetary Craft," "All You Get from Love is a Love Song," "I Just Fall in Love Again," "Sweet Sweet Smile"); Voice of the Heart (released posthumously, "Your Baby Doesn't Love You Anymore," "Now," "Ordinary Fool," "Look to Your Dreams").

"There must be . . . for every woman a correct weight, which cannot be discovered with reference to a weight chart or to any statistical norm," writes author **Kim Chernin**. "If we should evolve an aesthetic for women that was appropriate to women it would reflect this diversity, would conceive, indeed celebrate and even love, slenderness in a woman intended by nature to be slim, and love the rounded cheeks of another, the plump arms, broad shoulders, [large] hips, full thighs . . . of a woman made that way according to her nature." But Madison Avenue has a slim definition of what is beautiful in a woman, and Karen Carpenter hated her hips. On February 4, 1983, she died of heart failure brought about by anorexia nervosa. "With her life and death," notes Chernin, "a generation of young women found their exemplar, the representative figure who spoke symbolically to their lives."

She was born 32 years earlier, on March 2, 1950, in East Haven, Connecticut, the daughter of Harold and **Agnes Reuwer Carpenter**. Her brother Richard, three years older, was the first to fall under the spell of music, while Karen was more interested in baseball, basketball, badminton, ballet and tap dancing lessons. But she worshipped her brother: "I idolized him so much and we were so close . . . that if he listened to music, I did. I did everything he did. . . . Every record we've ever listened to is embedded in my mind." She grew up to the eclectic sounds of Perry Como, Harry James, Frankie Laine, *Theresa Brewer, Al Jolson, Spike Jones, Les Paul and **Mary Ford**, the Crew Cuts, and Tchaikovsky's First Piano Concerto. Throughout their youth, Karen and Richard sang along with records in their basement, then analyzed the arrangements.

By 13, Richard was studying piano at the Yale Music School. Karen put down the accordion and flute after a few lessons and continued with outdoor pursuits. Her brother began forming small bands, picking up work. At 16, he was featured on a record, though it was not sold nationally. Karen sat in on basement practice sessions, poised behind the drummer, watching intensely. As she entered puberty, her body began to change; now slightly chubby, she could be hurt by childish teasing. Recalled a childhood friend: "I think she always felt she was unattractive. Especially when she became a woman she had large hips. No matter how thin she got on top, her hips were always big."

In June 1963, in an effort to avoid the snow and further Richard's career, the family moved to the suburb of Downey, on the fringe of Orange County, California. Their father Harold got a job as a pressman, while their mother Agnes worked in the stockroom at North American Aviation. The money was tight, but the family was thrifty. Hardly eager students, Karen and Richard joined the band to avoid physical education classes at Downey High School. Though Karen was handed a glockenspiel, she surprised her parents with a request for a set of drums. This was no passing fad. "When I went to high school," she said, "I had no idea that I could do a blasted thing. I just kinda hung around and watched [Richard] be good." She taught herself the beat of Joe Morello who drummed for Dave Brubeck; she also followed the rhythms of Ringo Starr. Soon hooked, she practiced before and after school, getting better and better. When Richard began attending California State, Long Beach, he formed The Richard Carpenter Trio with Karen on drums and Wes Jacobs on bass. Though a female singing drummer was rare, Karen also began to do vocals.

By 1966, they were taking on regular weekend club work, playing old-style traditional pop. Karen was not enamored of her voice and preferred thinking of herself as a drummer. It was Richard who believed in her potential as a singer and convinced her to take instruction. In the fall of 1967, she joined him at Cal State, where both studied for degrees in music.

The turning point had come in May 1966, while attending a friend's audition for a small recording label named Magic Lamp. Before the session was over, Karen and Richard were also asked to audition. Karen, who had just turned 16, "was nervous as hell," said Richard. "When I heard the playback in the booth I just flipped because Karen's voice had recorded so well.

When I heard it come out of those speakers, I thought: 'My God!' She had her sound." They began hanging out at the studio, experimenting, analyzing the Beach Boys' "Good Vibrations" and the Beatles' "Eleanor Rigby," and learning how to stack vocal parts on a four-track. Though the small label released a single with Karen as a solo, the recording company folded the following year, and the 500 records pressed are now collector's items.

On June 24, 1966, The Richard Carpenter Trio made the finals of the prestigious "Battle of the Bands" at the Hollywood Bowl, taking three awards. Richard, who was now experimenting with a "choral approach to pop," teamed up with fellow student and lyricist John Bettis. The twosome would compose hit after hit for the next 12 years. Karen, still struggling with baby fat (she weighed 145), preferred singing from her position behind the drums. With their career looming, she went on a Stillman water diet prescribed by a doctor. Though she hated it, she stuck to it rigidly. Losing 25 pounds in six months, she remained at her new weight, 120, from 1967 to 1973. "She kept trying to get rid of the hips," said her then boyfriend Gary Sims, a guitarist who had joined the band along with several others. The new group, called Spectrum, quickly sank. Richard began to believe that success was to be found in a simple duo, he and Karen, calling themselves Carpenters, minus the *The*.

But they could not get a recording contract. Though not yet aware, Karen was fighting her image on two fronts: weight and the vogue of the day. This Age of Aquarius—a time of Beatle haircuts, Haight-Ashbury fashion, and a hippie drug culture—appeared less than accommodating to the old-fashioned love songs of the non-smoking, non-drinking, square-looking Carpenters. Then a friend of a friend managed to put one of their tapes into the hands of Herb Alpert of Tijuana Brass fame, who was founder and one-half of the operation of A&M records—the house of Joe Cocker, Cat Stevens, the Sandpipers, and Burt Bacharach and *Dionne Warwick*.

Alpert put on their tape in early 1969, while sitting in his garden in Lake Arrowhead: "I remember staring up at the speakers thinking *Patti Page*'s voice was in my lap," said Alpert. "It had so much *presence*." He was stunned by the soulful, haunting, purity of voice. Karen had always been struck by the clarity of Page, so had Alpert. Taken with Karen's voice, the harmonies, and Richard's arrangements, Alpert offered them a contract. With 19-year-old Karen underage, and her parents doing the signing, the Carpenters quit college and joined A&M on April 22, 1969. Alpert's associates thought he had gone mad.

The Carpenters' first album, *Offering*, was released on October 9, 1969, but the marketing people at A&M didn't know how to package this staid, brother-sister act in the same month that hundreds of thousands throughout the nation were participating in the first Moratorium Day to protest the Vietnam War and 35 black coeds seized control of the school-administration office at Vassar. Though the album included a slower version of "Ticket to Ride," which sold modestly as a single, its respectable but hardly earth-shattering sales fueled the naysayers at A&M. Convinced that their superb musicianship and "seductive delicacy" would find an audience, Alpert gave them another chance. Their next single, a Hal David-Burt Bacharach reject called "Close to You," was recorded three times before Richard was satisfied with the sound. It made its debut at number 56 on the Billboard charts; by July 22, 1970, it was number one and would quickly sell one million copies. Three months later, "We've Only Just Begun" by Paul Williams and Roger Nichols was released, and the single went gold. An album featuring both hits sold 5 million copies and grabbed six Grammy nominations, including Record of the Year and Album of the Year. Karen and Richard won Grammys as Best New Artist and Best Contemporary Vocal Group. In January 1971, "For All We Know" ("Love, look at the two of us/ strangers in many ways"), from the movie *Lovers and Other Strangers*, was released, becoming their third million-selling record.

The bashful 20-year-old Karen, who still considered herself a drummer who sang, was now in the limelight. When Richard demanded that she come out from behind the drums, they reached a compromise: for the love songs, center stage; for the novelty songs, behind the drums. "Pulling her out from behind the drums was a big deal, very hard for Karen to do," said John Bettis. "Karen's whole view of show business grew up with Richard standing right there beside her." As the critics began to take potshots at the "tomboy" who was most comfortable in T-shirts and jeans, Karen went shopping for dresses and a new image.

In an age when it was uncool to identify with the projected innocence of the Carpenters, the duo would often be critiqued on their image rather than their music. They were portrayed as goody two shoes, said Karen, "and because we came out in the middle of the hard-rock things, we didn't dress funny, and we smiled, we ended up with titles like 'Vitamin-swallowing, Colgate-smiling, bland Middle America.' . . . They never touched our music. We would get critics reviewing our concerts, they'd review the AUDIENCE."

Released in 1972, *A Song for You* album contained the hit single "Top of the World." Next came "Rainy Days and Mondays" (another Williams-Nichols song), which was their fourth million seller, followed by "Superstar" (by Leon Russell and **Bonnie Bramlett**), which also went gold. Yet, while their recordings sold and won Grammys, the Carpenters remained objects of derision. "The criticism of us was divisive," said Richard, "making it appear like two camps. People who liked us were cast as having no musical sophistication or any idea about what was hip. They could not appreciate Led Zeppelin *and* the Carpenters, and that was wrong. Not so. If someone really likes music, they can tell something done well in any genre."

Karen Carpenter was a perfectionist, with a demanding yardstick, who never measured up to her own expectations. Convinced that she owed her success to her brother, she was bothered that the spotlight was on her and that she got all the credit. She bemoaned her appearance. Because she was so unsure of herself, she was shattered when critics ignored all the work they poured into their music and turned to her looks. "Take hairdo's," wrote one, "Karen, who never really had one before, has added a few curls and looks positively done up. Not gorgeous, but at least she's trying." Her voice, said Henry Mancini, was "the manifestation of everything within her. Maybe if she had more self-esteem, it wouldn't have been the same voice."

The next five years (1970–75) were spent on grueling road tours—U.S., Europe, Japan, Australia. Though Karen was a caring friend and played the mother on tour, the Carpenters were both perfectionists and expected the best out of themselves and the band. It was a lonely time. They seldom stayed anywhere at length, eroding the potential for long-term romances. In February 1975, she would meet Terry Ellis, the British recording executive who had founded Chrysalis with Chris Wright. She and Ellis began to live together, but the living arrangements were over quickly, and Karen remained forever saddened by the loss. She would also maintain a brief relationship with Tom Bahler, co-producer of *The Wiz* (with Quincy Jones) who would write "She's Out of My Life," a hit for Michael Jackson in 1980.

Viewing replays of herself in concert during August 1973, Karen was appalled by her appearance. She hired a personal workout doctor, bought a "hip cycle," and went on a high carbohydrate diet. Rather than drop weight, she gained muscle and talked of her fleshy arms, her thick butt. She hated her "hourglass" figure and sought to "do something" to control her body. By 1974, she had lost some weight, but her family began to notice that dieting had become an obsession. Her food portions were tiny; she would stab at dressing-less salads and make soup with bouillon cubes, cutting them in half. Down to 115 pounds, she wanted to weigh 105. In 1975, anorexia nervosa was still a phrase in the clinic stage; the public was unaware of the insidious disease.

During their 1975 tour, audiences gasped as she came on stage. She was now down to 80 pounds. Though she was exhausted between shows, her voice was still surprisingly strong. But the singer who had been known for her humor was now easily upset and caught every bug in sight. She became too ill to finish the tour. Still, she could not slow down. "I go to bed at night with a pad by the bed," said Karen, "and the minute I lie down it's the only quiet time of the day. My mind starts going. 'This has gotta be done; you've gotta call this person.' I find myself with a flashlight in bed writing down about fifty things that have to be done by ten o'clock next morning. . . . It's going, going, GO." The new album, *Horizon,* released in June 1975, sapped more of their energy.

Though it was hard for her, in late 1976 Karen moved out of her parents' house, despite her mother's protests, and bought a condo in Century City. She was 27 years old. But she returned to Downey two or three times a week with an endless need to please her parents and her brother. When her parents visited her, they would take her across the street to Hamburger Hamlet, where her mother would demand that she order something substantial to eat. Karen would obey, but she had learned the methods common to an anorexic, pushing food under a lettuce leaf, slipping meat into her purse, or buttering a roll for an inordinate amount of time, only to take a small bite. They began to notice that her refrigerator was invariably empty. "No milk, no bread, nothing," her secretary **Evelyn Wallace** told biographer Ray Coleman. "If I'd have had to live there, I'd have starved to death." Agnes Carpenter denied that her daughter was deeply troubled and saw Karen's lack of eating as symptomatic of a personality trait she recognized in herself—stubbornness.

Richard was popping Quaaludes, prescribed by his doctor because he was too revved to sleep.

By late 1978, he was taking 25 a day and could barely play the piano with his shaking hands; his weight dropped to 139. Because of his panic attacks and obvious addiction, the duo had to end their live performances at the MGM Grand a week early. It was to be their last concert.

Meanwhile, the sales of their records began to taper off. Before the *Horizon* album, all their records had gone platinum; *Horizon* only went gold. Their next, *A Kind of Hush,* was not up to Richard's usual standards, except for Karen's rendition of "I Need to be in Love." Though it also went gold, their career was beginning to slide. They signed with master agent Jerry Weintraub, whose wife, singer **Jane Morgan**, was a fan. Morgan, who had recorded the 1950 hits "Fascination" and "The Day the Rain Came Down," regarded Karen as a superb vocalist. On December 8, 1976, with the push of Weintraub, the Carpenters aired their first TV special to good ratings. Karen had gone from a size 14 to a size 2; Weintraub began calling her "a Biafra child."

On January 10, 1979, Richard flew to Topeka, Kansas, to seek treatment in the chemical dependency unit at the Menninger clinic. When his sister visited, he begged her to face up to her own disease. Karen said she'd think about it. Richard returned home with his addiction under control. "Doing something out of the family" became important for Karen, said her close friend **Olivia Newton-John**, "a show of strength, of independence." On May 1, 1979, Karen flew to New York to make her solo album, but the producer was wrong for her needs, and the album would eventually be scrapped. That same year, Richard bullied her into seeking help. Karen went to an internist in Beverly Hills, gained weight to 106 pounds, "and got some color back into her cheeks," he said. Then, exhibiting her strong will, she quit and conned the doctor into telling her family she was not anorexic.

Within two months of meeting Tom Burris, a divorced real-estate developer nine years her senior with an 18-year-old son, Karen was engaged. They married in 1980. She clearly wanted children, but after 15 months the marriage was pretty much over, reaffirming her long held belief that she had traded in marriage and motherhood for success. She would die six hours before an appointment with her lawyer to sign divorce papers.

By 1981, Karen Carpenter's relentless battle with her body was in its seventh year. Starting with continual dieting from mid-1974, she was, by 1978, sometimes packing only 79 pounds on her 5'4" frame. She brushed friends' comments off, saying she was in control and that the weight loss was actually caused by a gastrointestinal problem that caused colitis. In reality, she was disappearing after meals to the bathroom, was taking 80 to 90 laxative tablets a night, and was ingesting 10 thyroid pills a day to race her heart and burn more calories. The only person she turned to was **Cherry Boone** O'Neill, daughter of singer Pat Boone. Known to have conquered anorexia, Cherry had written the bestseller *Starving for Attention* and was happily married by the time Karen came to her. Boone was emphatic: see a specialist.

In November 1981, Carpenter moved to New York. She lived there for a year, seeing specialist Steven Levenkron, author of *The Best Little Girl in the World,* five days a week. He later spoke of the desperateness of her situation: anorexics "do lots of terrible things to themselves, but this was unique. Ten thyroid pills would speed up her metabolic rate so that her heart was beating 120 to 150 beats a minute. You run the heart at that rate while you're emaciated, and you wear out that little muscle. So now I had somebody who had been emaciated for six or seven years, worked very hard doing singing tours, and had taken enormous quantities of laxatives and God knows how many bottles of thyroid, all of which cause enormous cardiac stress. So she had pushed herself to the physical limits."

Until a visit to her aunt's house in Connecticut, Karen had taken care to avoid mirrors. On these sojourns from New York, reports Coleman, she slept "in her cousin's pretty bedroom, which had a long mirror on the back of the door. Stepping out of the shower, Karen slumped into a chair in her aunt's bedroom next door—and wept. She had caught sight of her pathetic frame in that mirror and realized just how thin she had become." Said Levenkron, "Here was a lovely person who didn't want to die but was unstoppable. She would sit here and say, 'Why do I have this horrible illness? I do love my life, I love my career, I love my family—why do I have this?'"

After an eight-week stay in a New York hospital, where she was fed by a tube, Karen gained weight and was released on November 8, 1982. That Thanksgiving, having gained a total of 30 pounds, she quit treatment against Levenkron's advice and left for home. She now weighed 108. Within weeks, Richard and her friends noticed that the problem was unchanged. Karen's mother, however, continued to believe that her stubborn daughter was just not using common sense.

Karen continued to return home to Downey weekly, staying the night. On the evening of Feb-

ruary 3, 1983, she arrived there intending to shop locally for a washing machine the following morning. That night, when she went out to dinner with her parents, they were amazed at her appetite, though they noticed she was tired. The next morning, they found her dead, lying on the floor of the wardrobe closet of her brother's room where she had spent the night. The autopsy report stated pulmonary edema (heart failure) brought on by emetine cardiotoxicity (emetine poisoning caused by using ipecac syrup to induce vomiting). Neither her family, experts, nor her biographer saw any proof of Karen taking ipecac. She was buried in a mausoleum in Forest Lawn Cemetery in Cypress, California.

Karen Carpenter was the first celebrity to die of the effects of anorexia nervosa. As of 1995, the National Association of Anorexia Nervosa and Associated Disorders, founded in 1976, estimated that eight million people suffered from eating disorders in the United States, 95% of them women, 6% of the serious cases were fatal. Gymnasts, such as *Cathy Rigby, are especially susceptible, along with performers like actress **Tracey Gold**. Striking primarily females between the ages 18 and mid-20s, it can affect rich and poor, young and old, black and white. It can also affect males. In England, by the end of the 20th century, over 60,000 were battling the disease, including *Diana Spencer, Princess of Wales. Said model **Christine Alt** about her teen years, "I remember looking at Karen Carpenter's picture in *People* and thinking: 'God, how lucky she was because she died thin.'"

While striving endlessly to please her brother, her family, her listeners, Karen Carpenter used her body as a means of exercising control over her own life. Her death at age 32 silenced one of the most talented singers of her generation. "Twenty years later," writes Coleman, "while many of the artists who jeered at them have burned out, their music has grown in stature. . . . Their CD sales are booming. . . . Karen and Richard Carpenter's craft is now admired openly—particularly by a young audience that even considers it 'cool' to admit it, pointing out the beauty of that voice and the quality of those songs and arrangements. If they were not particularly timely when they began, [they] have confirmed their appeal as timeless."

SOURCES:
Chernin, Kim. *The Hungry Self: Women, Eating, and Identity.* NY: Harper and Row, 1986.
———. *The Obsession: Reflections on the Tyranny of Slenderness.* NY: Harper and Row, 1981.
Coleman, Ray. *The Carpenters: The Untold Story.* NY: HarperCollins, 1994.

Carpenter, Mary (1807–1877)

English philanthropist and social reformer who was especially influential in juvenile delinquency and prison reform. Born on April 3, 1807, in Exeter, England; died on June 14, 1877, in Bristol, England; daughter of Lant Carpenter (1780–1840; a Unitarian minister and master of a boarding school in Exeter and Bristol, who had *Harriet Martineau as a pupil) and Anna Penn; sister of William Benjamin (1813–1885, a physiologist).

Selected publications: Ragged Schools: Their Principles and Modes of Operation (1850); Reformatory Schools for the Children of the Perishing and Dangerous Classes and for Juvenile Offenders (1851); Juvenile Delinquents: Conditions and Treatment (1853); On Reformatory Schools (1855); Our Convicts: How They are Made and Should Be Treated (1864); Six Months in India (1868).

Born on April 3, 1807, in Exeter, Mary Carpenter was the eldest of six children of Dr. Lant Carpenter, a Unitarian minister, and **Anna Penn**. In 1817, the family moved to Bristol, where Dr. Carpenter was called to the ministry of Lewin's Mead Meeting. Mary's early childhood years were happy. She was educated in her father's school for boys, learning Latin, Greek and mathematics, and other subjects not generally taught to girls of her day. She early showed an aptitude for teaching, taking a class in the Sunday school, and afterwards helping her father with his pupils. She developed a strong character as well as a distinct sense of duty and desire to reform. Her father's strict religious and moral education affected her greatly.

At age 20, Carpenter left home to work as a governess on the Isle of Wight and then at Odsey. By 1829, however, she returned home to assist her mother in opening a school for girls after her father's ill health necessitated the closure of his school for boys. She worked at this school with her mother and sister until 1848, though these were not particularly happy years. Carpenter did not enjoy teaching young girls, and she yearned to become a wife and mother. Her harsh self-criticism manifested itself in depression and physical illness. Nonetheless, she maintained her interest in reform issues throughout this difficult time, and her focus turned increasingly towards juvenile delinquents. Her father's death in 1840 pained Carpenter deeply but also spurred her on to greater philanthropic works. In 1846, she opened her first Ragged School in Bristol, and in 1850 she published the first of many works on the subject of delinquent children.

In December 1851, she organized a conference for reformatory school workers. Though she disliked the public spotlight and did not speak at this meeting, her influence was felt; a parliamentary committee of inquiry was formed (at which she gave evidence), and in 1854 Parliament passed the Reformatory Schools Act. During these years, Carpenter opened a reformatory school for boys in 1852 and one for girls, Red Lodge, in 1854. She also published two books on school reform, *Reformatory Schools for the Children of the Perishing and Dangerous Classes, and for Juvenile Offenders*, and *Juvenile Delinquents, their Condition and Treatment*. Once the principle of reformatory schools was established, Carpenter returned to her plea for free dayschools, contending that the ragged schools were entitled to financial aid from the annual parliamentary grant. From that time on, she was drawn into dialogues on the subject with leading thinkers and workers.

After the death of her mother in 1856, Carpenter bought a house near Red Lodge. Two years later, she adopted a five-year-old, but the girl did not remain with her for long, mostly because Carpenter, at age 51, found herself incapable of caring for a small child. An attempt at living with a female companion also failed when, from 1858 until 1859, Carpenter lived with the Irish feminist ***Frances Power Cobbe**. The two women proved incompatible, and after Cobbe's departure Carpenter never again lived with anyone.

By 1864, her interests turned to the problems facing women in India; she left England for India in 1866, the first of many trips she would undertake over the next ten years. She visited Calcutta, Madras and Bombay, and inaugurated the Bengal Social Science Association. While there, she spoke to governmental officials about educational and prison reform. Her attempt to found a female normal school was unsuccessful at the time, owing to the inadequate previous education of the women, but afterwards such colleges were founded by the government. A start, however, was made with a model Hindu girls' school, and here she had the co-operation of local leaders. As she was highly respected for her expertise in these areas, Carpenter also traveled to North America in 1873 where she spoke on prison reform in the United States and Canada.

By the end of her life, Mary Carpenter began to work for women's rights. She became a member of the Bristol Committee for the repeal of the Contagious Diseases Acts and, just before her death, signed a petition advocating the admission of women to medical schools. She also spoke on behalf of the Bristol and West of England Society for Women's Suffrage. She died on June 14, 1877, in Bristol. Her interest was in the "children themselves, in their souls," Cobbe once said, "and not, as philanthropy too often becomes, an interest in her own institution."

SOURCES:

Banks, Olive. "Mary Carpenter," in *Biographical Dictionary of British Feminists, Volume I 1800–1930*. NY: New York University Press, 1985, pp. 46–48.

Manton, Jo. *Mary Carpenter and the Children of the Streets*. London: Heinemann, 1976.

Margaret McIntyre, University of Guelph, Guelph, Ontario, Canada

Carpenter-Phinney, Connie

(1957—)

American cyclist who won more national and international cycling titles than any American cyclist, male or female. Name variations: Connie Carpenter. Born Connie Carpenter in Madison, Wisconsin, on February 26, 1957; married Davis Phinney (a professional cyclist).

Winner of the first Olympic gold medal for the U.S. in cycling in the Los Angeles Olympics (1984), the first cycling medal for the U.S. since 1912.

Connie Carpenter-Phinney began her cycling career as a speed skater on the frozen lakes and ponds of Wisconsin. At 14, she made the U.S. Olympic speed-skating team with *Anne Henning, *Diane Holum, and *Sheila Young. She finished seventh in the 1,500 meters (88th of a second out of medal contention). Her speed-skating career was short lived, however, because of an ankle injury in 1976.

Her older brother Chuck and Sheila Young, world champion speed skater and cyclist, introduced her to cycling. In her first year (1976), Carpenter won the national championship in road race and pursuit, titles she would win again in 1977 and 1978. At her first international competition, the world championship road race (1977), she won a silver medal. She also won the Coors International Classic in 1977, 1981, and 1982, as well as three national titles in 1981. In 1983, she injured her wrist but managed to defend her national pursuit title.

In the 1984 Los Angeles Olympics, site of the first women's cycling event in the history of the Games, her main competition for the grueling 79.2-kilometer road race was her roommate, *Rebecca Twigg. Because of all the "media hype" over their supposed rivalry, Carpenter-Phinney

leaned over to Twigg just before the race and advised: "If one of us isn't the winner, we'll have to crawl home." Only five women remained in contention during the last 800 meters. At 100 meters, Carpenter-Phinney and Twigg became the leading competitors, passing Germany's **Sandra Schumacher**. When the two reached the finish line in an all-out sprint, Carpenter-Phinney forced herself forward, a technique she calls "throwing her bike," to win the race by less than half-a-wheel length; her gold medal time was 2:11:14. The United States had not won a gold medal in an international cycling event since 1912.

Between 1976 and 1984, Carpenter-Phinney won 12 national championships, four world championships, and three Coors International Classics. No American cyclist, male or female, had ever been so victorious. She was inducted into the International Women's Sports Hall of Fame in 1990, having retired from competitive cycling to conduct cycling training camps in Colorado with her husband.

Karin L. Haag, Athens, Georgia

Carr, Catherine (1954—).

See Belote, Melissa for sidebar.

Carr, Emily (1871–1945)

Canadian painter of totem poles and forest scenes who belatedly achieved both international and national recognition as one of her nation's greatest artists. Name variations: Millie. Born Emily Carr on December 13, 1871, in Victoria, British Columbia (Canada); died in Victoria on March 2, 1945; daughter of Richard and Emily (Sauders) Carr; attended the California School of Design (later renamed the Mark Hopkins Institute of Art) in San Francisco, California, for over two years, the Westminster School of Art in England for two years, and the Academie Colarossi in Paris, France, for several months; never married; no children.

Left home for art school in San Francisco (1891); began a period of study and travel in England (1899); left Victoria to study in France (1910); first national exhibit of her work held (1927); had most productive and creative period of painting (1928–36); suffered serious heart attack, beginning of declining health (1937); published first book (1941); received Governor General's Award for Klee Wyck (1942).

Selected paintings: Tanoo, Q.C. Islands (Provincial Archives British Columbia, 1913); Indian Church (Art Gallery of Ontario, 1929); Blunden Harbour (National Gallery of Canada, 1930); Forest, British Columbia (Vancouver Art Gallery, 1931); Above the

Gravel Pit *(Vancouver Art Gallery, 1936)*; *Cedar (Vancouver Art Gallery, 1942)*.

Selected publications: Klee Wyck *(1941)*; The Book of Small *(1942)*; The House of All Sorts *(1944)*; Growing Pains *(1946)*; The Heart of a Peacock *(1953)*; Pause: A Sketchbook *(1953)*; Hundreds and Thousands: The Journals of Emily Carr *(1966)*.

To her contemporaries, both friends and acquaintances, Emily Carr was undoubtedly an eccentric woman. Never married, she operated a boarding house, raised dogs, and produced curio pottery to make a living. She could often be found sketching in some wooded area dressed in bizarre clothing and smoking a cigar while surrounded by a curious array of birds and animals. All of these factors were unusual, even outrageous, for a woman living in the conservative society of early 20th-century Canada. But Carr was also an oddity because of her art. She produced paintings that many of her time could not understand nor appreciate. Rejecting traditional methods of painting realistic images, she sought to capture the emotions that the objects evoked. Consequently, her paintings never achieved wide popular appeal during her lifetime. By the late 1920s, the artistic community had begun to recognize her creative genius, however, and Emily Carr is now viewed as one of Canada's greatest artists. Her paintings provide a vivid testimonial to the inherent beauty and mysticalness of nature.

I drove ahead through . . . life, to get time and money to push further into art, not the art of making pictures and becoming a great artist, but art to use as a means of expressing myself, putting into visibility what gripped me in nature.

—Emily Carr

Emily's parents, Richard and Emily Sauders Carr, were originally from England but met in San Francisco where Richard had made a small fortune as a merchant during the California Gold Rush of 1849–54. The couple immigrated to Victoria, British Columbia, in 1863 because of reports of a new gold rush in the area of the Fraser and Thompson rivers. On arrival, the Carrs brought with them two small daughters. By 1875, their family was complete with six children: five girls and one boy. The fifth child (and fifth girl) had been born in 1871 and was named Emily.

Emily Carr had an average childhood. In the 1870s, Victoria was a frontier town, born of the gold rush, and had only existed for a couple of decades. Thus, it lacked the characteristics and services of a settled area. Seizing opportunities, Richard Carr established a wholesale business from which he prospered in the following years. The family was not wealthy but comfortable. The Carrs built a proper house, with large gardens, in the prestigious area of town. Richard Carr provided all of his children with an education, including both public and high school. In this frontier environment, young Emily could always find a stretch of wilderness in which to retreat. From a young age, she displayed the love of outdoors, which would characterize her adult life and paintings. She also displayed her love of animals. She was continually picking up strays, both wild and domesticated, and bringing them home. Rebellious and non-conformist in nature, she preferred climbing trees to the more appropriate feminine preoccupations of the time. Never particularly interested in academics, Carr graduated from public school 11th in a class of 13 in 1888.

Family life was tumultuous at times. Richard Carr was stern with his children. A religious man, his family was expected to observe daily prayers and all-day church attendance on Sundays. As a teenager, it seems Emily's relationship with her father was tense, perhaps even hostile. In her youth, however, she appears to have spent considerable time with her father, walking and sharing common interests. Her relationship with her mother is more uncertain. A frail woman, her mother became increasingly ill (and eventually bed-ridden) after the birth of her last child in 1875. She died in 1886. Emily Carr's most important female relationships seems to have been with her sisters. Throughout most of their lives, the five Carr sisters remained in close proximity, often living together. As the youngest (and most cantankerous), Emily was often treated as a difficult child by her siblings, even during her adult years. But despite frequent fighting, she looked to them, throughout her life, for support, love, and companionship.

After the death of Richard Carr in 1888, various opportunities became available to Emily. She entered high school that fall but quit after only one year. Her father had left a significant estate in trust for his children. After convincing the estate administrator of the seriousness of her interest in art, Carr was given the money necessary to relocate to San Francisco where she enrolled in the California School of Design (later renamed the Mark Hopkins Institute of Art) in the fall of 1891. Due to problems with family finances, she was forced to leave just a few months shy of completing her third year and did not receive her university certificate. In 1899,

Emily Carr

she again left Victoria, this time for London, England, where she enrolled in the Westminster School of Art for two years. In the spring of 1901, Carr continued her art education by traveling through the English countryside, studying under a number of art instructors. Both of these periods were important to her development and gave her the means to get away from Victoria and the watchful eyes of her sisters. Living alone, she had the opportunity to develop her independence as well as to meet new people and travel. By this time, Carr had committed herself to a lifelong career as an artist. She had begun her struggle to capture the beauty of nature, particularly of forests, a theme that

would dominate her work as a mature artist. But her painting style remained traditional. She struggled to capture images exactly as they appeared (like a photograph). At this point, she was still unaware, or at least had not been influenced, by the impressionist work being done in France.

Carr's return to her native city of Victoria meant living with her sisters in the family home, at least for a brief period. Since childhood, she had been strong willed and had tended towards behavior deemed inappropriate. With age, she had become increasingly eccentric. Her sisters were more conventional; they attended church and participated in charitable organizations, activities that were fitting for middle-class women of the time. But Emily Carr did not enjoy such ventures and was generally intolerant with the middle-class "society" ladies with whom her sisters associated. Since returning from England in 1904, she had acquired some habits that her sisters found repulsive. Emily Carr smoked, swore on occasion, played cards, and insisted on riding horses astride rather than sidesaddle. Furthermore, her love of animals continued; at any given moment, she could be found living among a large assortment of pets. Into advanced age, Carr's house, studio, and yard was littered with cages containing parrots, finches, cockatoos, squirrels, chipmunks, raccoons, numerous dogs and cats, and even at one time, a monkey named "Woo." Add to this, Carr could be moody, cantankerous, and rude, so much so that she offended many people and made others wary of approaching her. Still, she and her sisters remained close, even if their relations were often strained.

Contributing to this image of eccentricity was her connubial state. By 1904, when she turned 33, it was becoming clear that Emily Carr would not marry. An attractive woman, she had her share of suitors during her early adulthood. One man, William "Mayo" Paddon, was so enamored he followed her to England to propose. Although it appears they were in love, Carr refused his overture for reasons that are not clear. Many years later, she addressed this issue in her journal. Speaking of the "love" she had "killed," she argued: "I think it was a bad, dreadful thing to do. I did it in self-defence because it was killing me, sapping the life from me." Whatever the reason, Carr attracted no further suitors after her return from England.

She had a number of important friendships, however, including one with Lawren Harris, a prominent Canadian artist and member of the Group of Seven. Another lifelong friendship was with **Sophie Frank**, a Squamish Indian of the Salish nation who lived on the North Vancouver Reserve. Mired in poverty and sometimes alcohol, Sophie had 20 children of which only one survived. Though the Canadian artist and the Native Indian were worlds apart in background and life experiences, the friendship endured. Carr also interacted well with children (at least until old age). During sojourns between art schools, she successfully taught art to children to make a living. Her classes were so popular that parents began to seek her out, especially in Vancouver where she lived from 1906 to 1910. Playful and relaxed, Carr's sessions were appealing to children, especially given the atmosphere of her studio, which was always filled with animals crawling over desks and chirping in cages.

With savings accumulated from teaching, Carr left for France in 1910 to pursue art classes one final time. This year of study was crucial because it marked her departure from traditional methods to impressionism. It is not evident whether Carr was aware of this *new* way of painting previous to 1910, but it is clear that her time in France convinced her of its utility. After 1910, she began a gradual transformation in style. She no longer attempted to achieve an exact, photographic image of the item being portrayed. Impressionism gave her the freedom to experiment with color, form, and perspective to convey an emotion or an idea. After 14 months studying at both the Academie Colarossi in Paris and in the countryside under several private instructors, Carr headed back to western Canada to try her new methods on the subject matter she loved the most, the natural environment and Native peoples of British Columbia.

During her lifetime, Emily Carr was known primarily for her paintings of Native life and particularly of the totem poles of British Columbia's coastal Indians. This subject matter dominated much of her early work. Her fascination with Native images began in 1898 when she spent the summer at Ucluetet, a remote Native village on the Northern British Columbian coast where one of her sisters was training as a missionary. It was here that the Indians nicknamed her "Klee Wyck" ("the one who tends to laugh"), a sign that she interacted well with the people of the village. Over the next 30 years, Carr made several extensive trips into Indian country. By 1907, her stated purpose was to create a permanent record of the totem poles that were fast disappearing from the landscape. Some of her trips, such as the one in the summer of 1912, were so extensive that they took her to remote areas beyond the reach of modern services like trains and hotels. On occasion, Carr slept in vacant buildings or on the beach. Often, she had to travel by canoe or gas-powered launch through bug-infested wilderness to reach the sites that interested her. From these trips, she acquired a reputation for having lived among the Indians. This was not uncommon for male artists but unique for a woman.

Throughout her travels, Carr acquired a large number of sketches that she used over the years to create some of her most celebrated paintings. The gradual evolution of her work is evident in these renderings. The work derived from her 1912 trip into Indian country is traditional in method despite her conversion to impressionism in 1910. Her dedication to preserving a record of the totem poles compelled her to paint them as she saw them (rather than as she felt about the images). The totems were rapidly disappearing, and Carr had little time to paint all she wanted. Paintings such as *Tanoo, Q.C. Islands, 1913* are vivid reproductions of the images she saw in 1912. By the late 1920s, her Indian paintings were much more impressionistic. Her final trip was in 1928, after which many of her paintings were reworkings of earlier sketches, or, as in the case of one of her best works *Blunden Harbour, 1930,* they came from photographs. In these later paintings, much of the background detail is removed. Form and color are often exaggerated, creating mystical, awe-inspiring central images.

A second theme, found primarily in Carr's later paintings, is the British Columbia forest. Having become a subject of interest in the 1920s, it dominated her work after 1930. In the generally impressionistic forest paintings, she struggled to show the existence of God in nature. On November 12, 1931, she wrote of the feelings she was trying to capture:

> Go out there into the glory of the woods. See God in every particle of them expressing glory and strength and power, tenderness and protection. . . . [G]o into the woods alone and look at the earth crowded with growth. . . . Feel this growth, the surging upward, this expansion, the pulsing life, all working with the same idea, the same urge to express the God in themselves—life, life, life, which *is* God, for without Him there is no life.

In the 1930s, Carr produced some of her most acclaimed paintings, many of which sought to represent God through the beauty and majesty of the forest.

During her life, Emily Carr struggled to achieve recognition as an artist. Like many others, she was never able to support herself financially from sales of work. Though, on occasion, sporadic sales gave her extra income, she could not rely on them for her needs. But she did receive national recognition in the form of critical praise and invitations to exhibit. Up until 1927, most of Carr's work was displayed in local exhibits in the Victoria and Vancouver areas, for which she received mixed reviews. "Discovery" came in 1927 when the director of the National Gallery of Canada viewed her work on Native sites and decided to include it in the Exhibition of Canadian West Coast Art. This brought Carr's work to national attention, in particular giving her exposure in Central Canada (as the exhibit traveled through Canada's major centers). Her work was praised and eventually purchased by the National Gallery and the National Museum. This exhibit also brought Carr into contact with major Canadian artists, including the prominent Group of Seven. From them, in particular Lawren Harris, she received praise, encouragement, and constructive criticism. With national fame, Carr also began to receive more praise and recognition in British Columbia.

Still, Carr had to make a living. In 1913, she used the remainder of her inheritance to build a boarding house near the family home. From this, she hoped to make enough income to live on. Often, however, the rents did not suffice, forcing her to grow vegetables and raise chickens and rabbits in the back garden for extra money. She did not like being a landlord, a fact revealed in her often scathing treatment of former tenants in her memoir *The House of All Sorts.* Not only did boarding-house life require a great deal of cooking and cleaning, which took time away from painting, but it also required constant interaction with people, which Carr often found difficult. Much more enjoyable and financially successful was her raising of dogs. From 1917 to 1921, Carr ran a kennel, breeding Bobtail sheepdogs. During the latter half of the 1920s, she switched to Belgian griffons, which were smaller and easier to manage. After 1924, she was also successful at selling pottery, which she fired in her back garden and painted with Native motifs. It not only sold well but was displayed at arts-and-crafts shows throughout western Canada. Along with her pottery, Carr also turned to creating hooked rugs with Indian motifs. Despite her efforts at subsistence and the apparent success of her art, she was financially insecure throughout her life. There were few jobs available to women in the early 20th century; most turned to marriage for support. Given the limitations placed before her, Carr was reasonably successful living as a single, self-supporting woman.

In 1935, she gave up the boardinghouse and moved into a small house on her own. Two years later, in early January 1937, she suffered a major heart attack. It was the end of the most productive artistic period in her life and led to a permanent change in lifestyle. Physically, she was no longer able to pursue many of her interests and was forced to get rid of most of her animals and move in with her one remaining sister Alice, who was near blind and also in poor health. While Carr continued to exhibit her paintings, her illness meant she was unable to withstand the rigors of going into the woods to sketch. Although she occasionally visited wooded areas on the outskirts of Victoria over the next few years, most of her painting was done from existing sketches. Oftentimes, Carr even found the act of painting to be taxing. Thus, from 1937 to 1945, she suffered through a long and frustrating period of increasing invalidism.

Her mind, however, remained active even as her body was failing. Always a woman of unlimited energy, she turned her attention to a new interest—writing memoirs. Carr had expressed some interest in writing short stories previous to 1937 by taking courses and writing some narratives, which reflected her early experiences. From 1927 to 1941, she had also kept a journal that was eventually published under the title *Hundreds and Thousands*. Her most prolific writing period covered the years 1934 to 1942 when she compiled a wide assortment of stories. She wrote about her experiences in the Indian villages, about her childhood, and about her adventures as a landlady. Essentially, the stories were memoirs (and were intended to be), but they had a literary merit that drew the reader into her experiences. The quality of the writing was recognized by Ira Dilworth, a broadcasting executive and choir conductor, who took it upon himself to assist Carr by editing the tales and bringing them to publishers. In 1941, his efforts paid off with the publication of *Klee Wyck*. Dilworth also became an important friend. Confined and isolated by her poor health, Carr was visited by Dilworth and often received letters. She achieved early recognition for her writing when *Klee Wyck* was given the Governor General's Award for nonfiction in 1942. Carr was further overjoyed when told the book was to be issued for use in the schools. Over the next few years, with Dilworth's help, Carr worked hard to ensure her other stories were edited and compiled into their final form. She succeeded in seeing *The Book of Small* and *The House of All Sorts* published during her lifetime.

Carr's productivity during these years is amazing given the state of her health. The heart attack in 1937 had been followed by a major stroke in 1940, another heart attack in 1942, and another stroke in 1944. At times, she had such difficulty breathing that she was confined to sitting in bed for long periods. Yet, she defied doctor's orders and continued to write and edit. During a few respites of improved health, she actually resumed painting, including an eight-day sketching trip to Mount Douglas Park near Victoria, during which she produced *Cedar* (1942), visible proof of her continuing creative genius.

Carr's acclaim, both as a writer and an artist, was growing during the 1940s. A national exhibit of her paintings in 1944 resulted in 38 of the 60 works being sold within the first two months. Both *The Book of Small* and *The House of All Sorts* also received critical praise. To top it off, Carr received news in early 1945 that the University of British Columbia was going to confer the honorary degree of Doctor of Letters on her in May. She was proud and perhaps a little amused by this news, given her school performance as a child. Emily Carr did not live to see the degree conferred, however, for she died only a few days later on March 2, 1945.

SOURCES:

Carr, Emily. *Hundreds and Thousands: The Journals of Emily Carr*. Toronto: Clarke, Irwin, 1966.

MacEwan, Grant. . . . *And Mighty Women Too*. Saskatoon: Western Producer Prairie Books, 1975.

Tippett, Maria. *Emily Carr: A Biography*. Toronto: Oxford University Press, 1979.

SUGGESTED READING:

Carr, Emily. *The Emily Carr Omnibus*. Introduction by Doris Shadbolt. University of Washington, 1993.

COLLECTIONS:

Journals, manuscripts, and letters of Emily Carr located in the National Archives of Canada, Ottawa, Ontario.

Catherine Briggs, Ph.D. candidate, University of Waterloo, Waterloo, Ontario, Canada

Carr, Emma Perry (1880–1972)

American chemist and university professor. Born on July 23, 1880, in Holmesville, Ohio; died in 1972 in Evanston, Illinois; third of five children of Edmund Cone (a physician) and Anna Mary (Jack) Carr; attended Ohio State University, 1898; transferred to Mount Holyoke College for two years; University of Chicago, B.S., 1905, Ph.D. in chemistry, 1910.

Emma Perry Carr, an influential organic and physical chemist, headed the chemistry department at Mount Holyoke College for over 30 years. Attracted to chemistry early in her academic career, Carr was one of only a handful of women students entering Ohio State University in 1898. She studied there with the noted scientist William McPherson, then transferred to Mount Holyoke in Massachusetts where she studied for two years and served as a chemistry assistant for another three. She did her advanced work with Alexander Smith and Julius Steiglitz at the University of Chicago, receiving her Ph.D. in 1910. Carr then returned to Mount Holyoke as an associate professor of chemistry; within three years, she was named full professor and chair of the department. Although the college was not a well-endowed research university, she

built the chemistry department into a unique and important research facility.

With her colleague, organic chemist **Dorothy Hahn** (1876–1950), Carr initiated a series of group research projects in the application of physical chemistry to organic problems, the most important of which involved the synthesis and analysis of complex organic compounds by absorption spectra of organic compounds. Since ultraviolet absorption spectroscopy was new in the United States, she traveled to Ireland and Germany to study innovative techniques with scientists in the field. During the 1930s, Carr received grants from the National Research Council and the Rockefeller Foundation that allowed her to pursue a group research investigation of simple unsaturated hydrocarbons. The study ultimately contributed to the understanding of the carbon-carbon double bond, an important link in chemistry. For her contribution, Carr was awarded numerous honorary degrees and, in 1937, was chosen by the American Chemical Society as the first recipient of the Garvan Medal for distinguished service in chemistry by an American woman. Carr was also an inspirational teacher and mentor, and the work of her research group stimulated the interest of women in chemistry and chemical research. Between 1920 and 1980, 93 Mount Holyoke graduates would go on to receive doctorate degrees in the discipline.

Carr retired from Mount Holyoke in 1946 and was succeeded by **Mary Lura Sherrill** (1888–1968), with whom she later shared the James Flack Norris Award of the American Chemical Society (1957) for distinguished achievement in the teaching of chemistry. Although well into her 70s, Carr remained active in the laboratory work on the spectrographic program, continuing to reinterpret her original conclusions in light of new discoveries in the field. She also remained active in the South Hadley community and, in 1948, was elected as a representative to the Town Meeting. In 1964, Carr took up residence in a rest home in Evanston, Illinois. She died there in 1972.

Barbara Morgan,
Melrose, Massachusetts

Emma Perry Carr

Carr-Boyd, Ann (1938—)

Australian composer. Born in Sydney, Australia, in 1938; daughter of Norbert (a teacher, composer, musician) and Nyora Wentzel (an artist); studied with Donald Peart at Sydney University; received her master's degree from Sydney University in 1963.

Won the Sydney Moss Scholarship and went to London where she studied with Peter Racine Fricker and Alexander Goehr; after writing several works, her orchestral composition Gold *won the Maggs Award in Melbourne (1975) and was premiered by the National Training Orchestra; began composing for the harpsichord; broadcast a series of programs on women composers on Australian television (1980s).*

Ann Carr-Boyd established her reputation with compositions written for the harpsichord. Speaking of her compositions *Suite for Veronique* and *Lullaby for Nuck* written for this instrument, the reviewer W.L. Hoffman noted, "the works played utilized the harpsichord, either as a solo instrument or in ensemble, and the harpsichord is still rarely heard as a transmitter of contemporary music. . . . The harpsichord, with its limited dynamic range and lack of tonal contrast, throws emphasis on the music, both in its content and in the playing of it." This creative departure was typical for Carr-Boyd whose approach to modern music was distinctly her own.

Her grandfather, a violinist, came to Australia from Bohemia in 1888 with the Cowen orchestra and appeared in a centenary celebration concert in Melbourne. He stayed on, and Carr-Boyd's father and uncle were founders of the Sydney Symphony Orchestra. She was born in Sydney in 1938 and completed her degree there before going on to London. Her String Quartet was performed at the Royal College of Music, followed by other performances. Carr-Boyd actively promoted the work of women composers and implemented a series of television programs on the subject. Known to sometimes lapse into jazz, her music could be lighthearted and entertaining.

John Haag,
Athens, Georgia

Carr-Cook, Madge (1856–1933).

See Belmont, Eleanor Robson for sidebar.

Carré, Mathilde (1908–c. 1970)

French spy and triple agent, known as La Chatte ("The Cat"). Name variations: Carre. Born Mathilde-Lucie Bélard in Chateauroux, France, in 1908 (some sources cite 1910); studied law at the Sorbonne; married Maurice Carré (a schoolteacher), in 1933 (divorced 1939).

Joined Army Nurse Corps at start of World War II; became leading member of the Interallié spy network; arrested and interrogated by the Germans (November 1941); turned against her former comrades and began working for the Gestapo; as a result, the Interallié network was destroyed; arrested in England (June 1942) and returned to France after the war; found guilty of treason and sentenced to death (1949); upon appeal, the sentence was reduced to life imprisonment; released (1954) and lived in seclusion under a new identity until her death.

Known as "the cat" and despised by her former comrades in the French resistance movement because of her treachery, Mathilde Carré lived a prewar existence that was almost dull in its conventional contours. Born as Mathilde-Lucie Bélard in 1908 into a bourgeois family in Chateauroux, she earned a law degree at the Sorbonne. After graduation, she married Maurice Carré, a schoolteacher, and moved with him to Oran, Algeria. They divorced after six years (1939), and she returned to France on the eve of World War II. During the brief struggle to hold back the German onslaught (1939–1940), resulting in a catastrophic defeat for the French in June 1940, Mathilde Carré served as a member of the French Army's nurse corps. After the defeat, she was evacuated to the southern city of Toulouse. Here she met a Polish military intelligence officer, Captain Roman Garby-Czerniawski, who remained in France as part of a network to spy on the Germans and transmit the data to the Polish embassy in Madrid. Garby-Czerniawski had been recruited by the overall chief of Polish intelligence in France, Colonel Wincenty Zarembski, the man responsible for brilliantly improvising the creation of an anti-German spy operation.

Using the papers of a Frenchman killed in the fighting, Garby-Czerniawski (code-named "Valentin") was a bold operative who quickly organized an effective network of agents that called itself Interallié. From his headquarters in Paris, he masterminded a rapidly growing organization, and by the time wireless contact was established with London in early 1941 the ring consisted of agents operating in almost all of the German-occupied zone of France. He and Mathilde Carré had become lovers, and she quickly emerged as one of Interallié's most valuable members. Cool-headed and capable of inspiring confidence in her fellow spies, Carré became known to them as La Chatte (The Cat), which was also her code name.

By late summer 1941, the Interallié network was operating at maximum effectiveness when it had operatives working in 14 designated districts of German-controlled France, each with its own couriers and chief agents. At full strength, Interallié could boast of roughly 120 agents strategically located in the heart of industrial centers, British channel ports and Luftwaffe airfields. Besides the ring's main transmitter in Paris, they were now able to use three additional transmitters to send intelligence data to England. Unfortunately, their luck ran out in November 1941. This was in part due to the arrival in Paris of Sergeant Hugo Bleicher, a former Gestapo agent who had been assigned to work for the Abwehr, the German military intelligence service. Specially chosen to wipe out Interallié, Bleicher possessed talents as an intelligence agent that guaranteed doom for the Allied spy network. The fatal blow came after a major lapse of security in Cherbourg in early November 1941, which provided the Germans with crucial information about the ring and enabled them to round up most of the members. Harsh interrogation methods including physical torture provided Bleicher's men with major pieces of information. Garby-Czerniawski was arrested early in the morning of November 17, 1941, and a few hours later Bleicher arrested an unsuspecting Mathilde Carré.

When Garby-Czerniawski refused to reveal any useful information to his German interrogators despite many hours of brutal torture, Bleicher decided to concentrate on Carré. His strategy, which was very different in her case, emphasized a psychological offensive against the prisoner rather than the infliction of physical pain. First he initiated a dramatic change in her surroundings, having her moved from a bleak prison cell to a place of startling contrast, the five-star Hotel Edouard VII on the exclusive Avenue de l'Opéra; the hotel also happened to be Abwehr headquarters in Paris. Over a sumptuous meal, Bleicher was able to convince Carré that by working for him she would not only save herself from torture and probable death but also save the lives of her comrades whom he would protect from execution. All that was required was that Carré now begin working for the Abwehr, helping them to deceive the British by feeding them false information via Interallié transmitters. In her memoirs, written at the end of her life, Mathilde Carré would later admit that within hours of being interrogated by Hugo Bleicher she would commit "the greatest act of cowardice in my life . . . a purely animal cowardice," which consisted not only of promising

to collaborate with the Germans but also of becoming Hugo Bleicher's mistress.

Within days of "turning," Carré was working to assist Bleicher in rounding up the remaining members of Interallié who still remained at large. Now operating as a double agent, The Cat led Bleicher to the homes and meeting places of a number of men and women who had only days before been her trusted comrades. She cold-bloodedly identified one of them, Claude Jouffret, by greeting him with a kiss at the Café Louis XIV. Bleicher's agents seized the four radio transmitters of the Interallié network, moving to a Paris suburb so as to continue sending messages to London as if nothing had happened. Since Carré provided the Abwehr with all necessary codes, transmission schedules and pre-arranged security checks, there was little that might arouse the suspicions of British intelligence. However, one of the few members of Interallié who still remained free, Pierre de Vomécourt, began to suspect that Carré was, in some way he could not define, acting in a suspicious manner. To test her loyalty, in January 1942 he asked her to procure some forged identity documents. She showed up the next day, bringing with her a perfect set of papers complete with authentic German stamps. On top of this, she produced a photograph and with an air of studied casualness asked De Vomécourt if he recognized the man in the photo, who was an agent of Britain's Special Operations Executive (SOE).

His suspicions confirmed, De Vomécourt vehemently accused Mathilde Carré of treachery and working for the Nazis. Confronted by the facts, she broke down in tears and confessed. Within the rules governing the precarious world of espionage, it would not have been unreasonable for De Vomécourt to kill Carré, warn the remaining members of Interallié of her treason, and flee himself. But his plans were considerably more complex. De Vomécourt persuaded Carré to once more work for the Allies, making her a triple agent. Soon after this dramatic change in her loyalties, she informed Bleicher that De Vomécourt was planning to go to England for an important meeting with British intelligence chiefs, and that she was being considered for inclusion on this important mission. Though she convinced Bleicher, he in turn had considerable difficulty convincing his superiors of the value to the Abwehr of allowing Carré to make a secret trip to Britain. Eventually, Bleicher received permission for Carré and De Vomécourt to leave France. After two failed attempts by British intelligence agents to locate the two key Interallié agents on an isolated beach, they were finally picked up and taken to London in late February 1942.

Safely arrived across the channel at Dartmouth, Carré was debriefed by British intelligence. She broke down almost immediately, admitting her capitulation under Bleicher's interrogations and her work for the Abwehr. She also explained her return to the Interallié fold under De Vomécourt's leadership several months previously. Not surprisingly, Britain's SOE imprisoned Carré for the duration of World War II, first at Holloway and then in the "D" wing of Aylesbury prison. Returned to France after the war, she spent three years at La Sante and Rennes. Her January 1949 trial, which lasted four days, resulted in a death sentence, but upon appeal this was reduced to life imprisonment. Her defense attorney did not dispute her treasonous behavior but argued that the judges should "consider that this woman was faced with the choice of life or death. Do not forget that from the beginning of the resistance she was a heroine. Would you put to death those who at the beginning sowed the seed of faith and later overestimated their own strength?" Carré was released from prison in September 1954 and attempted to resume her life with a new identity. By the early 1960s, when she published her memoirs, her health had begun to fail and she was rapidly losing her eyesight. Virtually forgotten by the world, Mathilde Carré died in total obscurity in the early 1970s.

SOURCES:

Buranelli, Vincent and Nan. *Spy/Counterspy: An Encyclopedia of Espionage.* NY: McGraw-Hill, 1982.

Carré, Mathilde. *I was "The Cat": The Truth about the Most Remarkable Woman Spy since Mata Hari—by Herself.* Translated by Mervyn Savill. London: Souvenir Press, 1960.

———. *J'ai été "La Chatte."* Préface d'Albert Naud. Paris: Morgan, 1959.

Cookridge, E.H. *Set Europe Ablaze.* London: Pan Books, 1966.

Franklin, Charles. *The Great Spies.* NY: Hart Publishing, 1967.

Fuller, Jean Overton. *The German Penetration of SOE: France 1941–1944.* London: William Kimber, 1975.

Keegan, John, ed. *Who Was Who in World War II.* NY: Thomas Y. Crowell, 1978.

Mahoney, M.H. *Women in Espionage: A Biographical Dictionary.* Santa Barbara, CA: ABC-Clio, 1993.

Miller, Russell. *The Resistance.* Alexandria, Virginia: Time-Life Books, 1979.

Minney, Rubeigh J. *Carve Her Name with Pride.* London: Collins, 1965.

Paine, Lauran. *German Military Intelligence in World War II: The Abwehr.* NY: Stein and Day, 1984.

———. *Mathilde Carré, Double Agent.* London: Hale, 1976.

Richelson, Jeffrey T. *A Century of Spies: Intelligence in the Twentieth Century.* Oxford: Oxford University Press, 1995.

Seth, Ronald. *Encyclopedia of Espionage.* Garden City, NY: Doubleday, 1974.

Singer, Kurt D. *Spies for Democracy.* Minneapolis, MN: Dennison, 1960.

West, Nigel, ed. *The Faber Book of Treachery.* London: Faber and Faber, 1995.

Wighton, Charles. *The World's Greatest Spies: True-Life Dramas of Outstanding Secret Agents.* NY: Taplinger, 1966.

Young, George Gordon. *The Cat with Two Faces.* Reprint ed. London: White Lion, 1975.

John Haag, Associate Professor,
University of Georgia, Athens, Georgia

Carrel, Felicite (fl. 1860s)

Italian mountaineer who attempted to climb the Matterhorn. Flourished in the 1860s; daughter of J.A. Carrel (Italian guide and mountaineer).

In 1867, Felicite Carrel attempted to climb the Matterhorn (14,690 ft.), along with Caesar Carrel, J.J. and J.P. Maquignaz, and her father J.A. Carrel. In the appendix to *Scrambles amongst the Alps* by Edward Whymper, all names of those who ascended the Matterhorn are carefully listed, including the Carrels, except for the neglected Felicite who is cited as "and a daughter of the last named." The party made the fourth attempt at the mountain (third from the Italian side). Leaving Breuil at 5 AM on September 12, 1867, they reached the shoulder of the final peak after 7 AM the following day. They then passed a cleft, which had stopped another climber seven years before, and arrived at the base of the last precipice within 350 feet of the summit. Writes Whymper: "J.J. and J.P. Maquignaz alone ascended; the others had had enough and returned." Despite Whymper's exclusion, the point she reached is now known as Col Felicite.

Carreño, Teresa (1853–1917)

Most famous woman pianist of the late 19th century, who also sang operatic roles, conducted an orchestra, and introduced the music of Edward MacDowell and Edvard Grieg to audiences throughout Europe and the Americas. Name variations: Teresa Carreno. Pronunciation: Kah-RAIN-Yo. Born Maria Teresa Carreño in Caracas, Venezuela, on December 22, 1853; died in New York City on June 12, 1917; daughter of Manuel Antonio Carreño (a pianist and Venezuelan minister of finance); married Émile Sauret, in 1872; married Giovanni Tagliapietra, in 1875; married Eugen d'Albert, in 1895; married Arturo Tagliapietra,

Teresa
Carreño

in 1902; children: (first marriage) two, including Emelita Sauret Tauscher; (second marriage) three, including Teresita Carreño Tagliapietra (a pianist) and Giovanni Tagliapietra, Jr. (a baritone singer); (third marriage) Herta and Eugenia.

Gave first piano concert at age nine, New York City, followed by a performance tour of Cuba (1862); performed solo with the Boston Philharmonic (1863); performed at the White House for President Abraham Lincoln (1863); taught Edward MacDowell, the American composer (1872); began operatic career (1872); appeared at first Telephone Concert (April 2, 1877); composed Hymn for Bolivar (1883); established as one of Europe's greatest pianists with a series of concerts in Berlin (1889); gave second performance at the White House, for President Woodrow Wilson (1916). Telefunken issued 25 LPs from piano rolls, featuring early performers including Carreño (1961), re-released on CD (1990s).

An 1862 portrait of the child prodigy featured on the sheet music of her opus 1, "Gottschalk Waltz," reveals a small dark-eyed girl sitting pensively at a Chickering piano, her dress gleaming with medals recently awarded her in Boston. Large audiences were turning out to hear nine-year-old Teresa Carreño, who had made her concert debut in New York that same year. Three years earlier, at age six, she had arrived in the United States from Venezuela with her family, following her father's loss of his position as minister of finance during a period of political upheaval. Now, thanks to the gifted child, the family was restored to prosperity.

Born in Caracas, Venezuela, on December 22, 1853, Teresa Carreño had spent her earliest years in an atmosphere of culture and affluence. Her mother was a niece of the country's great national hero, Simon Bolivar, and her grandfather was a recognized composer. Her father, Manuel Antonio Carreño, was a pianist as well as the Venezuelan minister of finance, and when Teresa showed a gift for playing the piano at an astonishingly early age, he was the one who began to guide her progress.

After the family's move to New York, the attempts of Señor Carreño to enter business proved unprofitable, and when Teresa's first public recital was planned, in 1862, the concert was a deliberate attempt to rescue the family from financial straits. The nine-year-old girl arrived onstage at New York's Irving Hall with her father at her side and sat alongside him at the piano, her legs still too short to reach the floor. The brilliance of her playing caused a musical

sensation, and before the year was out she made her first concert tour, in Cuba. In January 1863, she soloed with the Boston Philharmonic, then went on to play 20 concerts in that city. Invited to the White House, she performed for President Abraham Lincoln, who asked her to play his favorite piece, "Listen to the Mocking Bird," and she was sufficiently unintimidated by the president of the United States to complain about the quality of the piano.

Teresa made another tour of Cuba in 1865. Her abilities had been recognized by then by some of the leading musicians of the times. The famous American pianist Louis Moreau Gottschalk, for whom she had named her waltz, gave her lessons, and when the great Russian pianist and composer, Anton Rubinstein, gave a series of concerts in the United States, he invited Señor Carreño to bring his daughter to play for him. Rubinstein was so impressed that he suggested the family follow him to Europe so Teresa could study with him. The child had received a similar offer from the composer and pianist Franz Liszt, which had been declined, but in 1866, the Carreño family sailed for Paris, where she studied under both Rubinstein and George Matthias.

At age 18, Carreño was a seasoned performer well-known throughout Europe and America. That year, 1872, she began to give informal piano lessons to Edward MacDowell, then 12 years old, establishing a relationship that was to have important consequences. Throughout Carreño's performing years, MacDowell would continue to send her his newest compositions at intervals, and she would introduce his works to the public through her playing. His *Hexentanz* and *Baracarolle* would become her program staples. On July 5, 1888, Carreño would play MacDowell's *First Piano Concerto* in Chicago under the direction of Theodore Thomas. After MacDowell dedicated his Second Concerto to her, she performed it every year from 1908 to 1914. Carreño also became a personal friend of MacDowell's parents, particularly his mother, and his wife ***Marian MacDowell**. Letters to MacDowell from his mother stress the importance of Carreño's support to the moody young composer, and her featuring of his work in her concerts did much to secure his place in the musical world.

In 1873, Carreño married Émile Sauret, an attractive French violinist, who performed in a concert company. Their union was short-lived but produced two children, whom Carreño was soon supporting on her own. The death of her beloved father in 1874 was a great blow, magnified by her mother's death shortly thereafter. Carreño plunged into performing to earn money, but she was also devoted to family life and was praised by contemporaries for her tenderness as a mother.

Carreño had been on tour in England as a piano soloist with James Henry Mapleson's opera company in 1872 when a backstage crisis inaugurated her operatic career. The company was in Edinburgh when one of the principals could not go on, and Mapleson persuaded Car-

reño to sing the role of the queen in *Les Huguenots*. Her well-received performance precipitated a series of singing engagements, and Carreño returned to America in 1875 to study singing with **Mme. Ruderdorff**. That year, she married the baritone, Giovanni Tagliapietra, and in 1876 she sang the role of Zerlina in Mozart's *Don Giovanni* in Boston and New York. The couple moved to Venezuela and organized an opera company, where Carreño sang and also conducted the orchestra. The sojourn in Venezuela lasted two years, and three children were born to this marriage.

Carreño, the child prodigy, around age nine.

Teresa Carreño was an intense, dynamic woman, always open to new and interesting experiences. She was therefore the perfect choice to participate in the inaugural Telephone Concert on April 2, 1877, in New York City. The event was the brainchild of Elisha Gray, the inventor who had filed a patent on the telephone only hours after Alexander Graham Bell, precipitating years of legal conflict before Bell was finally awarded the patent. The concert was designed to demonstrate how music could be transmitted long distance, and a group of outstanding artists, among whom Carreño was the most eminent, had been invited to take part on the stage at Steinway Hall. Curious no doubt about what his rival was up to, Alexander Graham Bell was in the audience, and an advertising banner trumpeted, "Transmission of Music by Telegraph! Triumph of American Science!" A telephonic apparatus attended by an operator was set up on stage, and 16 sounding boxes were scattered throughout the hall. Frederick Boscovitz, also a well-known pianist, sat at another apparatus in Philadelphia, some 90 miles away, and played a group of pieces that were transmitted to New York. Though the music that was produced sounded faint and far away, reviewers found that the "effect of the telephone music was on the whole very pleasant."

They called her "The Walküre of the Piano," and there was something wild about her from the moment she emerged from Venezuela.

—**Harold C. Schonberg**

Though she did not perform over the telephone that evening, Carreño's presence lent credence to the event. She needed no gimmicks, however, to promote her career. Her performances were usually sellouts. She had large hands and was a forceful player, and, like other musicians in the late 19th century, she was willing to take interpretive liberties. At the end of the Grieg piano concerto, for instance, she would play in octaves rather than arpeggios for the simple reason that she had good octaves. Edvard Grieg was a fairly close friend of hers but did not always approve of such tampering; he wrote disgustedly to a friend, "the devil is in the virtuosos who always want to improve on everything." On the other hand, Carreño was a star, and Grieg was happy for her to perform his work. Thundering through the Beethoven Emperor Concerto, the Rubinstein D minor, the Liszt E flat, and the Tchaikovsky B flat minor, she had the power and technique to play these bold works, and left her audiences mesmerized.

In 1877, the same year as the Telephone Concert, Thomas Edison took out a patent on a talking machine. Recorded sound was in its infancy, and early phonograph records were of such poor quality, many musicians preferred to record on piano rolls manufactured for player pianos. The technology was ultimately limited, but some piano roll recordings are actually superior to phonograph records of the same period, and this is the medium in which Carreño's playing has been preserved. In 1961, Telefunken issued 25 LP's from piano rolls, featuring 23 performers playing 80 pieces, which were released on CDs. Flawed as they are, they reveal Carreño's free style, which was not always note perfect (also a norm for the period), and hint at the brilliance of her performances.

Carreño's concert career reached new heights during a series of concerts she gave in Berlin during the fall of 1889. She was the idol of Europe, hailed as "The Walküre of the Piano" for her dual career, and dubbed "The Empress of the Piano" for her performance of large works. Her interest in composing, begun as a child and young adult, continued throughout her life. One of her most famous pieces is the "Teresita Waltz," inspired by the first steps taken by one of her daughters, which she often played as an encore. She composed the *Hymn for Bolivar* for chorus and orchestra for the centenary celebration of the birth of Simon Bolivar, which was first performed in Caraças in 1885. Other compositions were songs for voice and piano, a choral work, a string quartet, and a serenade for string orchestra as well as orchestral music. The serenade is described as "a remarkable four-movement piece, full of feeling and high ambition . . . [which] stands as testimony to Carreño's continuing aspirations as a composer."

Like her career, Carreño's personal life was packed with adventure. Her marriage to Giovanni Tagliapietra ended, and in 1892 she married the composer and pianist Eugen d'Albert, who was 11 years her junior. Carreño was the second of his six wives, and each spouse occupied a separate wing of a castle in Germany. The confusion of such living arrangements was reflected in a German review, which read: "Frau Carreño yesterday played for the first time the second concerto of her third husband at the fourth Philharmonic concert." Their marriage produced two children, and d'Albert was the most talented of her husbands, but they remained together only three years. The union had a lasting impact on her playing, however, which was transformed from her original forceful and impetuous style into that of a thoughtful, and even profound, performer.

In 1902, Carreño married Arturo Tagliapietra, the brother of her second husband. It was to be her longest and happiest marriage. Meanwhile, her interest in new composers continued. Adding the works of Edvard Grieg to her repertoire, she was one of the first to give the Norwegian composer considerable exposure. She also became acquainted with the young American *Amy Beach whose reputation as a composer continues to grow steadily. Carreño never actually performed Beach's concerto, which premiered in Boston on April 6, 1900, but a score and complete set of orchestra parts is in the Carreño collection, as well as correspondence between the two women. Carreño did take part in performances of Beach's Violin Sonata in Germany, and the correspondence indicates that Beach hoped Carreño would play the same role in her life as she had in MacDowell's. Apparently Carreño's manager was not supportive of Beach's work, and meanwhile the pianist was being constantly admonished by MacDowell's mother to perform the pieces of her son.

Carreño had many pupils beside MacDowell. In describing her teaching technique, **Ruth Payne Burgess** writes that Carreño stressed using the weight of the whole arm and wrist to bring forth a rich, full tone from the instrument. She stressed exercises that students had to master before they were allowed to play actual pieces, and she often admonished, "Squeeze the notes. Do not hit them." An intense performer, she also said, "Express emotion, feeling in your playing, but not hysterics." While on tour she would send her students "lesson letters" full of advice. Burgess, who was also a friend and frequent visitor in the Carreño home, described her teacher as generous, compassionate, and full of love for her children.

Five of Carreño's seven children lived to adulthood. The eldest, **Emelita Sauret Tauscher**, married a German and lived in Berlin. **Teresita Carreño Tagliapietra**, for whom the waltz was named, married an Englishman and also performed as a pianist. A son, Giovanni Tagliapietra, Jr., became a baritone singer like his father. The two daughters of Eugen d'Albert, Herta and Eugenia, both married and lived in Berlin.

As Carreño grew older, her hectic schedule subsided. Some 50 years after she had played for President Lincoln, she was invited to perform at the White House again, this time for President Woodrow Wilson, in 1916. The following year, she was on tour in Cuba when she fell ill and returned to New York. Over several months of illness, she became paralyzed and died on June 12, 1917, at age 63. Her honorary pallbearers included Ignace Jan Paderewski, Walter Damrosch, and Charles Steinway. Edward MacDowell's widow, Marian, was in attendance and many other pupils and fellow performers. Her ashes were later returned to Venezuela where a theater was founded in her name and a museum was established, containing some of her belongings. On June 12, 1938, Venezuela issued a postage stamp with her portrait. In 1940, **Marta Milinowski**, a former pupil and a professor of music, responsible for preserving the Carreño's papers at Vassar, published *Teresa Carreño: "By the Grace of God."*

Few child prodigies have successful careers as adults. Teresa Carreño not only flourished professionally, but she encouraged new artists and lived a rich, even tempestuous, personal life. A century beyond the height of her career, the Empress of the Piano has few rivals in achievement.

SOURCES:

Burgess, Ruth Payne. "Teresa Carreño as a Teacher," in *The Etude*. Vol. 48, no. 11, pp. 779–781, 826.

Davis, Peter G. "Music by Women Composers," in *The New York Times*. April 13, 1980, p. D26.

Holoman, Jan. "From Shadow to Substance," in *Saturday Review of Literature*. Vol. 45, no. 21. May 26, 1962, pp. 46–47, 57.

Klein, Alvin. "Reprising a Tempestuous Pianist's Life," in *The New York Times*. February 10, 1991, sec. XII–LI, p. 11.

K.M. "Chamberworks by Women Composers," in *High Fidelity*. May 1980, pp. 87–88.

Kammer, Rafael. "Foreign Market," in *The American Record Guide*. Vol. 27, no. 6. January 1961, pp. 457–465.

Mann, Brian. "The Carreño Collection at Vassar College," in *Notes*. June 1991, pp. 1064–1083.

"Mme. Carreno Here after Long Absence," in *The New York Times*. October 28, 1916, p. 11.

"Mme Carreno's Recital," in *New York Tribune*. October 28, 1916, p. 9.

"Mme Teresa Carreno, Famous Pianist, Dies," in *The New York Times*. June 13, 1917, p. 13.

"Musicians Gather at Carreno's Bier," in *The New York Times*. June 15, 1917, p. 9.

Schonberg, Harold C. *The Great Pianists*. Simon and Schuster, 1963.

———. "When Music was Broadcast by Telephone," in *The New York Times*. May 11, 1975, sec. II, p. 17.

"The Telephone Concert," in *New York Daily Tribune*. April 3, 1877, p. 5.

"Teresa Carreno and the Venezuela Hymn," in *The New York Times*. June 17, 1917, p. 10.

RELATED MEDIA:

In 1989, pianist-actress **Pamela Ross** starred in her own full-length production, *Carreño!*, loosely based on the artist's life.

COLLECTIONS:

The Carreño Collection at Vassar College has the most extensive holdings of the artist's compositions, some 42 in all, 26 published, the rest in manuscript, as well as letters, manuscripts, programs, scrapbooks and clippings documenting her life.

Karin Haag, freelance writer, Athens, Georgia

Carrick, countess of.

See Marjorie of Carrick (c. 1254–1292).

Carriera, Rosalba (1675–1757)

Italian portrait painter who was known for her miniatures and pastels. Born in Venice, Italy, on October 7, 1675; died in Venice in 1757; eldest of three daughters of Andrea (a Venetian clerk) and Alba (Foresti) Carriera (a lacemaker); sister-in-law of Giovanni Antonio Pellegrini (1675–1741).

Selected works: Horace Walpole *(Lord Walpole Collection, Wotterton Hall, Norfolk);* Allegory of Painting *(National Gallery of Art, Washington, D.C.);* Africa *(from the cycle* The Four Continents, *Gemäldegalerie, Dresden);* Abbé Leblond *(Gallerie dell'Accademia, Venice);* Cardinal Melchior de Polignac *(Gallerie dell'Accademia, Venice);* Robert, Lord Walpole *(Victoria and Albert Museum, London);* Woman at Her Dressing Table *(Cleveland Museum of Art);* Portrait of a Man *(National Gallery, London).*

Of the few women painters who gained renown during the 18th century, none enjoyed the international reputation and success of Rosalba Carriera, an artist who made her name as a miniaturist, before popularizing pastel as a medium for serious portraiture. Unfortunately, as the Rococo style went out of fashion, the aesthetic value of her art declined, and her historical significance was eclipsed by Maurice Quentin de la Tour, who, largely influenced by Carriera, went on to become the acknowledged 18th-century master of the pastel medium.

The details of Carriera's early life are not well documented. She was born in Venice, Italy, on October 7, 1675, the eldest daughter Andrea Carriera, a modest Venetian official, and **Alba Foresti Carriera**, a lacemaker. Following her father's death in 1719, she lived most of her life with her widowed mother and unmarried sister **Giovanna Carriera**, who became her assistant. Her sister Angela married the painter Giovanni Antonio Pellegrini, who acted as Carriera's agent and was largely responsible for her popularity in England.

Carriera displayed an early interest in art, perhaps influenced by her grandfather, a painter. She probably began by designing lace patterns for her mother, then graduated to decorating the lids of snuff boxes and painting miniatures on ivory (2x3 or 3x4 inches in size). Her miniature portraits gained her entrance into the Academy of Saint Luke, Rome, in 1705. By one account, her miniature of a girl holding a dove so impressed an official of the Academy that he sat and stared at it for half an hour, mesmerized by the white-on-white technique of the dove. Her work was of such merit that she was made an *accademico di merito*, a title reserved for a few special artists for whom the normal tests for admission were waived. By this time, she had also sent work to Paris and was receiving as many commissions as she could handle. In these early years, she also showed a musical inclination and was known to have considerable skill on the violin.

A friend is credited with sending Carriera the pastels that would alter the course of her work. Although black, white, and red chalk had long been used for sketching, pastels—crayons made of a dried paste comprised of ground and mixed pigment, chalk, and gum—were just beginning to gain recognition. They were used at first to make copies of oil paintings, and artists liked the speed and versatility they provided, as well as the color range and versatility. On the practical side, pastels were less expensive than paint and did not require sitters to spend hours posing in smelly studios. There is evidence that Carriera was using pastels for portraits as early as 1703, though she is said to have complained to one patron in 1706 that she was so busy painting miniatures that she did not have time to learn pastel technique. Whereas she established her reputation in the medium of pastel, she would produce works in both media for most of her career.

Characterized by their light, delicate, and elegant effect, Carriera's Rococo-style portraits were a perfect match for pastels. Working small, she increased her speed, turning out an enormous number of portraits. Her sister Giovanna also helped by filling in the backgrounds and draperies of the pictures. Most unique about Carriera's work, whether in paint or pastel, was her ability to flatter her subject without losing their sense of individuality. As **Germaine Greer** writes in *The Obstacle Race:* "She eschewed pompous detail and concentrated instead upon the expressiveness of the countenances she observed." In *Women Artists: 1550–1950,* **Ann Sutherland Harris** and **Linda Nochlin** elaborate: "In an age when it was far more important for a woman to be physically attractive than it is now, Rosalba's ability to render all her female subjects charming without reducing their features to bland stereotypes was much appreciated." Men also seemed to admire Carriera's talent, as an impressive number sat for her, including the artist Antoine Watteau, and her informal portrait of Lord Robert Walpole is considered to be one of her best miniatures.

Carriera became well recognized in Italy, where she was elected to membership in the academies of Bologna and Florence, as well as Saint Luke's in Rome. Her informal small portraits, however, were more popular with foreign clients—from Germany, France, and England— than with the Venetians. While this was due in part to Venice's economic decline, it also reflect-

ed the city's ceremonial tradition of large, full-length, formal oil portraiture, though there were apparently few artists around at the time to paint them.

In 1720, at the urging of her friend Pierre Crozat, a wealthy Parisian banker and art collector, Carriera and her family visited Paris, and she took the city by storm. One of her first sitters was the young king Louis XV, after which she was besieged by noble patrons and entertained by the cream of Parisian society. In October of that year, she was made a member of the French

Rosalba Carriera, Self-Portrait, Holding Portrait of Her Sister *(1715).*

Academy, in spite of a 1706 rule forbidding the admission of any more women. Establishing a fashion for pastel portraits that persisted in France well into the 19th century, Carriera not only influenced the artist Maurice Quentin de la Tour but also several talented women as well, including **Marie Suzanne Giroust-Roslin (1734–1772)**, ☙ **Magdalene Basseporte**, and **Theresa Concordia Mengs (1725–1808)**. There is evidence that Carriera actually taught the medium to Basseporte, who later gave up the genre to become a flower portraitist. In Italy, she trained **Felicità** and **Angioletta Sartori**, **Antoinette Legru**, and **Marianna Carlevaris**.

Carriera's diary entries from Paris describe processions of visitors, sittings, and a round of excursions to see the city's sights and art collections. According to Greer, the artist had no difficulty charming her wealthy patrons and handled her busy social calendar with grace and some flair. She is described as not particularly pretty but stylish in dress, articulate, and personable. Other biographers, however, point out that Carriera was not gregarious by nature and soon wearied of the social whirl of Paris. She returned to Venice in the spring of 1721, where she settled into a quiet life on the Grand Canal and dedicated herself to her work. She left the city only rarely: once in 1723, on a commission assignment to Modena, and to Vienna for six months to work for Holy Roman Emperor Charles VI.

In 1737, the artist was devastated by the death of her sister Giovanna from tuberculosis and lapsed into a depression that kept her from working for several months. Her greatest personal tragedy, however, was the gradual loss of her eyesight, which became of serious consequence in 1746 (her later self-portraits show a weakness in her left eye). Several cataract operations only delayed the inevitable, and her worsening condition contributed to a deepening depression in her later years. One of the best and most moving of her many self-portraits was made shortly before she went blind and is described by Harris and Nochlin: "She faces us almost directly but her gaze is withdrawn, her lips firmly set. The choice of dark fur robes and the somber mood can be read, in retrospect, as signs of her approaching isolation from her profession and her unhappy last years." After a decade of total blindness, Carriera died in 1757, in a state of complete mental collapse.

SOURCES:

Greer, Germaine. *The Obstacle Race*. NY: Farrar, Straus, 1979.

Harris, Ann Sutherland, and Linda Nochlin. *Women Artists: 1550–1950*. Los Angeles County Museum of Art, 1976.

Barbara Morgan,
Melrose, Massachusetts

Carrington, Dora (1893–1932)

English painter and decorative artist who lived for nearly half her life with Lytton Strachey. Name variations: Dora Carrington Partridge. Born Dora de Houghton Carrington on March 29, 1893, in Hereford, England, in a house called Ivy Lodge; committed suicide on March 11, 1932, at Ham Spray near Ham, Wiltshire; fourth child of Samuel (a civil engineer with the East India Railway Company) and Charlotte (Houghton) Carrington (a governess); attended Bedford High School, 1903–10, and Slade School of Art, London, 1910–14; married Ralph Partridge, May 31, 1921; no children.

Attended Slade School of Art and met Mark Gertler (1910); met Lytton Strachey (1915); moved into Tidmarsh Mill with Lytton Strachey (1917); her father died (December 1918); fell in love with Gerald Brenan (1921); moved to Ham Spray (July 1924); earned money painting glass pictures and tiles (1924—); started affair with Beakus Penrose (1928); death of Strachey (January 1932); committed suicide (March 11, 1932).

Selected paintings (unless otherwise stated, all the following are in private collections): Hills in Snow at Hurstbourne Tarrant (1916); Giles Lytton Strachey (1916); The Mill at Tidmarsh, Berkshire (1918); Mrs Box, Farmer's Wife at Welcombe, Cornwall (1919); Lady Strachey (Scottish Portrait Gallery, Edinburgh, 1920); Farm at Watendlath (Tate Gallery, London, 1921); Mountain Ranges from Yegen, Andalusia (c. 1924).

Dora Carrington was once described by Lady *Ottoline Morrell as "a wild moorland pony." Others recall her amazing blue eyes and her blonde hair with its Dutch-boy cut. But

---

☙ **Basseporte, Magdalene** (?–c. 1780)

French artist. Name variations: Madeleine Basseporte. Born Frances Magdalene Basseporte; died around 1780.

Magdalene Basseporte painted subjects from natural history in watercolors, executing three books of flowers, which were engraved by Avril. She also engraved some plates for the Crozat College and for others, including *The Martyrdom of S. Fidelio de Sigmaringa* (after the work of P.A. Robert) and *Diana and Endymion* (after a design by Sebastiano Conca).

"tens of thousands of young women have china-blue eyes, talk in little gasps and have sex trouble," wrote David Garnett, "but one does not want to wade through their correspondence." She fascinated her friends, many of whom were writers. *Katherine Mansfield featured her in a short story. D.H. Lawrence characterized her in *Women in Love* and "None of That"; Aldous Huxley used her in *Chrome Yellow*, Wyndham Lewis in *The Apes of God*. But each portrayed only one facet of her complexity. She was also "the most neglected serious painter of her time," wrote John Rothenstein.

After her death, she quickly disappeared from the public mind. Carrington had always been incredibly diffident about her painting, and little had survived. Her name did not resurface until the publishing of her friends' letters and diaries in the 1960s and her own in 1970. It was kept alive by the emergence of interest in women artists in the 1980s and was brought to the forefront again by the release of a feature film, *Carrington,* starring **Emma Thompson**, in 1995. Her oil painting "Farm at Watendlath" was reproduced on the front cover of *The National Trust Magazine* for Autumn 1995 and an exhibition of her work was held at the Barbican, London, from September to December 1995.

There is no shortage of information about Dora Carrington's life, for she was part of a group who kept extensive diaries and wrote letters to and about each other constantly. The difficulty lies in trying to distinguish between fact and opinion, between the significant and the trivial. Throughout her days, Carrington enjoyed parties, dancing, amateur theatricals, home movies, tobogganing, kite-flying, and games of Pooh-sticks. She cycled for miles, learned to ride a motor bike, and drove a car. She was thrilled one day to be taken up in an airplane. Friends testify to Carrington's fun-loving nature; her letters are often wryly humorous, and there are examples of her utilitarian work that display a keen wit. Yet from an early age, she was dogged by self-doubt: a sense of frustration over what she felt she was capable of in contrast to what she actually achieved became dominant. An inability to knowingly cause others distress often made her indecisive in her relationships. And the nightmares to which she was prey seem to have become more frequent and horrific in later life.

Dora's father Samuel Carrington was born into a family with a tradition of service in India. He was educated at Cheltenham College, trained as an engineer, and, at 25, joined the East India

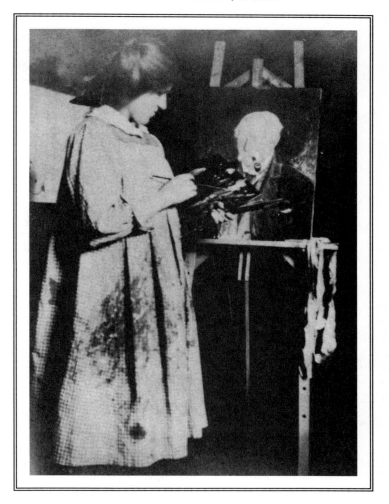

Dora Carrington

Railway Company as a civil engineer. He suffered the customary tropical diseases, supervised the building of many railway stations, and traveled to many other parts of the world. He seems to have been a fair-minded man who treated the locals under his supervision with kindness and respect. He was said to have once personally supported a whole district when it was stricken by famine. After 30 years, he returned to England intent upon marrying and raising a family. Samuel was comfortably off and still physically active, though rather deaf owing to the accumulated quinine he had been obliged to take during his life in the tropics.

Dora's mother, **Charlotte Houghton Carrington**, had been a governess, already in her 30s, when she met Samuel Carrington. The Carringtons disapproved of Charlotte because she was "from a less affluent stratum of the middle class," but she was already related to them by marriage. Her brother had married Samuel's niece. When her brother died, she stepped in to help her widowed sister-in-law bring up the children. Possibly, the Carringtons felt that with Samuel's money he could have attracted a more elevated "catch" and were disappointed. However, there is no evidence that Samuel was dissatisfied with his choice. Charlotte gave birth to six children in the space of five years. Dora, the fourth, was born when her father was 61.

In a much-quoted letter to Gerald Brenan, Carrington declared that she had an "awful childhood," but there seems to be little evidence to support such a claim. At first, the family moved house frequently; by the time Dora was ten, she had lived in at least five different houses. The blonde child with the striking blue eyes tended towards plumpness and inward-turning feet. The latter possibly caused her to fall down often—a habit, which earned her the nickname of Dumpty from her siblings.

Her life was a series of unresolved, opposing tensions . . . : she loved truth but constantly lied; she rejected her lovers but continually lured them back; she was happiest when she painted, but her painting frequently depressed her.

—**Gretchen Gerzina**

In later life, Carrington remembered such escapades as locking her younger brother Noel outside the garden gate and cutting a square out of the front of her dress. She wanted to test the theory that if a hole was cut in folded material, the hole would double when unfolded. Both activities were punished: because of the first, she missed a party; because of the second, she was spanked on her bare bottom by her nurse. "I turned my head round as I lay on her knee, and saw my bottom," she said. "I was mortified. . . . I thought it very large, and pink." Other early memories included frequently wetting herself because she was too embarrassed to ask, "May I go to the lavatory," having a friend when she was six "called Carol who had a red pinafore, and short black hair" (it was unusual for little girls to wear their hair short at that time), and attending a gymnasium to try to straighten her pigeon toes.

In 1903, the Carringtons moved to Bedford. For family men who had retired from colonial or military service, it was a popular place of residence because of its inexpensive private schools. Dora and her sister, then aged 14, were sent to Bedford High School. Though she scored well in physical education, Carrington could never become enthusiastic about competitive games. School records show that her spelling was poor (recent writers have suggested that she may have

been dyslexic), but that she was good in natural history and drawing. These characteristics were to remain with her throughout her life. At first, she learned music as an "extra" but, as her artistic talents became more obvious, her parents allowed her to drop these lessons in favor of extra art.

As Dora matured, she lost her puppy fat and her hair grew long and luxuriant. From the age of 12, her drawings were entered for the annual schools' competition organized by the Royal Drawing Society of Great Britain and Ireland, and every year she won prizes. She inherited her artistic ability from both sides of the family— both Samuel and his mother were competent drawers and Charlotte had attended Lambeth Art School in her youth. Charlotte hung the walls of her homes with reproductions of famous paintings and attended the Royal Academy's Summer Exhibition in London every year, bringing the catalogue home for the children to peruse. Samuel encouraged Dora's talents by keeping her supplied with materials, and Charlotte boasted of her daughter's ability to her friends. At age 17, Carrington left Bedford High School to study at the Slade School of Art in London.

It is impossible to gain an unbiased view of the elder Carringtons and their life together, as Dora, the main source of information, so clearly favored her father. She saw him as open-handed and open-minded and her mother as repressive and narrow in outlook. Charlotte certainly lacked her husband's liberal background, but there seems no evidence to suggest that he disapproved of her provincial outlook. Charlotte was responsible for the upbringing and moral guidance of five children; Samuel was accorded the indulgence more befitting a wealthy grandfather. Dora loved to hear the stories of his adventures in India and appears to have blamed her mother, rather than his age or inclination, for his more mundane lifestyle in England. In various letters she said that she hated her mother, that her mother put her father in a cage, and that she wished her mother, not her father, had died in 1918, though he was 82 years old by then and paralyzed by a stroke.

It does, however, seem to have been mainly her mother's fault that Carrington should have experienced sexual difficulties as she matured into a woman. In accordance with much middle-class thinking at the time, any discussion within the family of bodily functions was strictly taboo. One of Carrington's early memories was of being punished, along with two of her brothers, after the eldest boy knowingly allowed them to peep through cracks in the walls as he used the

From the movie Carrington, *starring Emma Thompson.*

outside lavatory. Dora seems to have been totally unprepared when she started menstruating at age 14 and never came to terms with this symbol of her femininity. *Virginia Woolf** wrote of Charlotte's struggle to explain the facts of life to Dora on the eve of her wedding when she was already 28 years of age and had had a number of sexual relationships. Charlotte seemed either unwilling or unable to accept that Dora's lifestyle changed dramatically after she left the puritanical confines of her Bedford home for the far-more-liberal atmosphere of the Slade.

As her brother Noel recalled over 60 years later, "even after one term she returned a very changed young person." Since women artists at Slade were determined to be equal to men, Carrington adopted the Slade convention of using just a surname. She would be known only as Carrington, even by her brother, for the rest of her life. In her second year, she cut her thick hair into a daring short bob, threw herself into social activities, attended dances and concerts, exhibitions and picnics. Popular, she gathered about her a large circle of friends, many of whom were older and drawn from every strata of society. Some of these she kept until the end of her life. She was attractive to men and enjoyed their attentions while steadfastly avoiding any sexual involvement. By 1912, two erstwhile friends, Mark Gertler and C.R.W. Nevinson, were bitterly quarrelling over her, while she seemed unable to comprehend their sexual feelings and wished all three could remain good friends.

Meanwhile, she was proving a very promising student. She won two prestigious prizes for nude studies and was awarded a scholarship worth £30 *per annum* for two years. In the summer of 1913, she painted a fresco in Ashridge House, Hertfordshire, and toward the end of 1914 sold a drawing that she was exhibiting at the New English. While still refusing sexual intimacy with Gertler, they were often in one another's company, and it was through his widening circle of friends that Carrington first became involved with the Bloomsbury Group, a set of intellectuals loosely grouped round that section of London after which they are named. They dedicated themselves to pacifism, art, and literature, as well as witty, high-flown conversation. Notes **Carolyn G. Heilbrun**: they lived "their lives as though reason and passion might be equal ideas."

Not all of them were rich, however, and Roger Fry, one of the earliest group members, instigated the Omega Workshop where artistic talents could be put to utilitarian use in order to make money. It is thought that Carrington was glad of the opportunity to fulfill commissions as she was permanently poor. She later remembered this as a period of "walking from Waterloo to Hampstead because I hadn't a penny. Eating two-penny soup packets meal after meal, in a smelly studio in Brompton Rd."

It was through her acquaintance with the Bloomsbury Group that Carrington met the man who was to determine the pattern of the rest of her life. She was spending a few days with a group of "Bloomsberries" at Asheham House near Lewes, the home of Virginia and Leonard Woolf. One of the party was Lytton Strachey, who belonged to an old, respected family, was 35, and homosexual. In appearance, Strachey was tall and thin with straight hair, a straggly red beard and spectacles. At first, Carrington found him repulsive and was shocked when he tried to kiss her. But, so the story goes, as she crept into his bedroom that night, intending to punish him by cutting off his beard, she fell irrevocably in love with him when he opened his eyes and looked at her.

Since her early days at the Slade, Carrington had been concerned about the paucity of her education, and, in Lytton Strachey, she found the teacher she had been seeking. He lent her books, read to her, and formed her mind. Despite the obvious differences between them, Strachey and Carrington had a fair amount in common. Both had fathers who had lived in India and married wives much younger than themselves. Both felt their mothers to be overbearing, and both, though irked by much within their family homes, were forced to remain on intimate terms with them because of financial dependency. Indeed, for many years Carrington seems to have led a double life: one as the reluctantly dutiful daughter at Hurstbourne Tarrant near Andover in Hampshire where her parents had moved in 1914, the other as the free-thinking artist among a like-minded circle of friends.

Carrington began to see more and more of Strachey while still carrying on her stormy relationship with Gertler. By 1917, she was cycling round the countryside in search of a home for them to share—Strachey in order to finish his book, *Eminent Victorians*, she as his housekeeper. By November, she was busy preparing the house she had found at Tidmarsh Mill near Pangbourne, Berkshire, for Strachey's arrival in December. Since Lytton was still extremely short of money, the rent was to be paid by friends who would then be free to use the house as a country retreat. Once there, writes **Gretchen Gerzina**, "Lytton read, wrote, or corrected proofs; Carrington painted and gardened and wrote her famous letters." They both, however, still spent much time in London and in the country homes of others. They seem, at this point, to have kept a careful balance between their need for independence and their need for each other.

Around this time, Carrington approached Roger Fry for advice about her work. Friends agree that something destructive took place during the interview. Despite her talent and success at the Slade, Fry evidently discouraged her from attempting to be a serious painter. "Although she would continue to paint throughout her life, she never again did so with confidence," writes Gerzina, "and from then on satisfaction with her work eluded her. Only recently has she begun to be taken seriously as a major figure of her period, whose work deserves careful attention."

Already by 1915, she had begun to doubt her own ability. In a letter to Gertler, she commented, "My work disappoints me terribly. I feel so good, so powerful before I start and then when it's finished I realise each time it is nothing but a failure." Predictably, she began a picture full of enthusiasm only to lose confidence as she proceeded, and she would leave it unfinished or paint over it at a later date. She seems to have painted very much for herself alone and was frequently so emotionally tied up with the finished product that she could not bear to expose it to public view. Of her portrait of Strachey, Carrington wrote in her diary in 1917: "Looking at your picture now tonight it looks wonderfully good and I am happy. But then I dread showing it. It's marvellous having it all to myself . . . and I hate the indecency of showing them what I have loved." This, of course refers particularly to Strachey, but it seems to be applicable to much of her painting. Aware of the problem, Lytton wrote to her on July 22, 1919: "Don't you think the time has come to think seriously of beginning to show your pictures? Unless you do I cannot see how you can hope to sell them, and that will really be essential if you ever want to stand on your own legs." Nevertheless, some noteworthy paintings do exist, both from this time and later.

In 1918, Carrington made a new friend, Rex Partridge, a pal of her brother Noel. By the end of 1919, Partridge was in love with Carrington, Strachey was in love with Partridge (he had peremptorily changed Rex's name to Ralph), and Carrington was enjoying Partridge's physical attractions while still remaining emotionally dependent on Strachey.

Carrington, Strachey, and Partridge set up a virtual *ménage a trois* at Tidmarsh. One of their visitors was Gerald Brenan, a friend of Ralph Partridge and Noel Carrington. When Brenan went to live in Spain, Dora Carrington added him to her list of correspondents, and in the spring of 1920 all three went to visit him in his remote home at Yegen, Andalusia. On their return, Carrington's painting was going well, and she was further heartened by praise from the French artist, Simon Bussy. Strachey suggested a one-woman show. She did send three pictures to the London Group show in the autumn, but the whole exhibition was a failure. However, **Lady Strachey** paid her £25 for a commissioned portrait of herself.

On May 21, 1921, in an effort to maintain the status quo at Tidmarsh, Carrington married Ralph Partridge. He had threatened to leave if she didn't marry him, and she feared Lytton would leave if Ralph went. Even so, life was far from smooth. All three continued to travel both together and separately, returning intermittently to Tidmarsh. Relations became even more complicated when Carrington and Brenan's friendship escalated into an affair in May 1922. Despite having already been unfaithful himself, Ralph was insanely jealous. Nevertheless, Carrington continued to juggle her relationships with all three men, and, at the end of 1923, Strachey began negotiations to purchase a new house for himself, Partridge, and Carrington near the village of Ham in Wiltshire. It was about this time that Ralph began to take an interest in the woman who was later to become his second wife, **Frances Marshall**.

Carrington's life became even more complicated when she gave way to a bisexuality, which until now she had resisted, by embarking upon an affair with ❧▶ **Henrietta Bingham**. "For the first time in her life, Carrington was in active pursuit of a particular lover," writes Gerzina. "Men had always been attracted to her, but she

---

❧▶ **Bingham, Henrietta** (1901–1968)
American socialite. Born Henrietta Worth Bingham in 1901; died in 1968; daughter of Judge Robert Worth Bingham (American ambassador to the Court of St. James), and Eleanor E. Miller Bingham; aunt of Sallie Bingham.

When Henrietta Bingham was ten, she was in an automobile accident in which her mother **Eleanor Miller Bingham** was killed. Her father Judge Robert Worth Bingham, an American ambassador to the Court of St. James, subsequently married twice more, but both marriages were unsuccessful. (In 1917, he was all but accused of murdering his second wife, **Mary Lily Flagler Bingham**, one of the richest women in America. That autumn, the scandal made the front page of newspapers throughout the nation.)

At the time she met *Dora Carrington, Henrietta was living in England with her friend **Mina Kirstein** and taking courses at the London School of Economics. Henrietta married briefly while in her 50s and died an alcoholic in 1968.

SUGGESTED READING:
Brenner, Marie. *House of Dreams: The Bingham Family of Louisville*. NY: Random House, 1988.

had never taken on the chase herself." However, life settled down at Ham Spray, and Carrington was able to paint a number of pictures (mainly portraits and flower studies) in the new studio that Lytton had had built for her. Towards the end of 1924, she began to create small pictures—a blend of paint and silver foil, covered in glass, which was then sometimes partly painted. Later, she began to paint tiles for bathrooms and fireplaces. Both pictures and tiles proved popular and provided her with a much-needed source of personal income. As ever, there was an unending stream of visitors, but at first Carrington seemed able to enjoy it all.

As the years passed, however, difficulties once again arose. Ralph and Frances took up residence together in London but still came to Ham Spray sufficiently often to ensure that Strachey kept the house. In the autumn of 1926, Carrington found a long visit to her mother, in order to nurse her after pneumonia, particularly irksome. Carrington began to drink more heavily and vacillated between the solitude of Ham Spray and the gregariousness of parties and travel. By 1928, she had once again quarrelled with Gerald Brenan and was seeking to stave off her loneliness by instigating an affair with Bernard (Beakus) Penrose who was, according to Frances Partridge, "a well-off young man, romantic about the sea." During this period, Carrington decorated rooms for **Dadie Rylands, Dorelia John**, a Cambridge don, and at Ham Spray. In the latter, she created an amusing *trompe l'oeil* bookcase to disguise an unused door. Yet her attempt to raise her spirits with Beakus was not entirely successful; in November 1929, she found she was pregnant and had an abortion. In 1930, Brenan finally broke free and became engaged to an American poet, Gamel Woolsey. Carrington and Beakus' affair was slowly winding down.

In July 1931, Carrington won a competition in the *Weekend Observer*, which had been announced in these words: "Mr Lytton Strachey has just published a set of six thumbnail sketches of six English Historians. Let us suppose that to these a seventh is added—that of Mr Strachey himself. We offer a First Prize of TWO GUINEAS and a Second Prize of HALF-A-GUINEA for the last 250 words of this essay." Not surprisingly, Carrington was able to imitate his style perfectly. In October, she painted another *trompe l'oeil*—this time on the outside wall of Biddesdon, the home of Bryan Guinness. By November, Strachey, who had always been something of a hypochondriac, was seriously ill. In her autobiography, Carrington writes that on

January 20, 1932, Strachey said, "Darling Carrington, I love her. I always wanted to marry Carrington and never did." The following day, Ralph prevented her from killing herself with car-exhaust fumes. On January 24, Lytton died of undiagnosed stomach cancer.

Carrington sank into a profound depression. "Oh darling Lytton you are dead," she wrote in her diary, "& I can tell you nothing." She spent her days reading his letters to her and nights going through his clothes. Friends were worried. When she asked to borrow a shotgun to kill the rabbits overrunning the Ham Spray garden, they were even more concerned. Leonard and Virginia Woolf came to see her on March 10th, ostensibly for lunch but actually to check on her. At one point, Carrington broke down and sobbed in Virginia's arms. As she walked them to their car, Carrington kissed Virginia, who said: "Then you will come & see us next week—or not—just as you like." Replied Carrington: "I will come." Then she paused, "Or not." They were the last to see her alive. The next day, Carrington shot herself while dressed in Lytton's purple silk dressing gown.

SOURCES AND SUGGESTED READING:

Brenan, Gerald. *Personal Record 1920–1972*. London: Jonathan Cape, 1974.

Carrington, Noel, ed. *Mark Gertler: Selected Letters*. London: Hart Davis, 1965.

Caws, Mary Ann. *Women of Bloomsbury: Virginia, Vanessa, and Carrington*. London: Routledge, 1990.

Garnett, David, ed. *Carrington: Letters and Extracts from her Diaries*. London: Jonathan Cape, 1970.

Gerzina, Gretchen Holbrook. *Carrington: A Life of Dora Carrington 1893–1932*. London: John Murray, 1989.

Grimes, Teresa, Judith Collins, and Oriana Baddely. *Five Women Painters*. Oxford: Lennard, 1989.

Hill, Jane. *The Art of Dora Carrington*. London: Herbert, 1994.

Holroyd, Michael. *Lytton Strachey: A Critical Biography*. London: Heinemann, 1968.

Partridge, Frances. *Love in Bloomsbury: Memories*. London: Gollancz, 1981.

Woodeson, John. *Mark Gertler: Biography of a Painter, 1891–1939*. London: Sidgwick and Jackson, 1972.

RELATED MEDIA:

Carrington, film produced by Polygram Filmed Entertainment, written and directed by Christopher Hampton, starring Emma Thompson and Jonathan Pryce, 1995.

Barbara Evans, Research Associate in Women's Studies at Nene 1College, Northampton, England

Carrington, Leonora (1917—)

English painter who developed sensibilities that were independent of earlier Surrealist influences. Born in 1917 in Lancashire; daughter of a wealthy textile

manufacturer and an Irish mother; attended schools in England, Florence, and Paris; studied at the Amedée Ozenfant Academy, London, 1936; lived with Max Ernst for two years at St. Martin d'Ardèche; married Renato LeDuc; married Enrique "Chiqui" Weisz.

Selected writings: numerous short stories, including "The House of Fear," "The Oval Lady," "As They Rode Along the Edge," "The Debutante," "White Rabbits," "Waiting," "The Seventh Horse," "The Bird Superior Max Ernst"; plays, including Une Chemise de Nuit de Flanelle *(written in 1945 and)* Penelope *(1946); and two novels,* Down Below *(1944) and* The Hearing Trumpet *(published in French, 1974).*

Numerous exhibitions, including first one-woman exhibition at the Pierre Matisse Gallery, New York (1948); retrospective exhibitions at the Museo Nacional de Arte Moderno (Mexico Center, 1960) and the Center for Inter-American Relations (New York, 1976); exhibitions in Paris (1938), Amsterdam (1938), New York (1942), and Paris (1947). Painted a mural, The Magic World of the Mayans, *for the National Museum of Anthropology (Mexico City, 1963).*

Women artists associated with the Surrealist movement were working at a time in history when women were seldom encouraged to construct professional identities for themselves as artists. On the path to artistic maturity, their efforts to achieve some accord between their ideas and their own lives often involved the renouncement of the conventions that had dictated their upbringings. With few role models available to women in the visual arts, and conflicting attitudes toward their existence and purpose as artists, women like Leonora Carrington performed high-wire acts of imagination, without a net. Writes Whitney Chadwick in *Women Artists and the Surrealist Movement,* "Young, beautiful, and rebellious, they became an embodiment of their age and a herald of the future as they explored more fully than any group of women before them the interior sources of woman's creative imagination."

Poet André Breton was the father of the Surrealist Movement, an artistic revolution that was to dramatically change the face of art history. Returning to Paris after World War I to confront a culture that he held responsible for the massacre of thousands upon thousands of young men, Breton blamed the educational system for its glorification of war and a literary establishment, which he viewed as detached from social and political truths. He was inspired by the poet Guillaume Apollinaire's call for an art of revolt and gave birth to a movement that was

dedicated to no less than the transformation of human values through art. Apollinaire was the first effective champion of an art of revolt in the 20th century. His writings helped shape the Surrealist revolution but did little to construct a new image of women. Chadwick has described him as the "first French poet of this century to integrate erotic and poetic expression," and goes on to say that he "nevertheless confused love and war, invoked Symbolist polarities to express the duality of feminine nature (purity/impurity, for example), and constructed an image of his longtime companion, the painter *Marie Laurencin, as an eternal child." This image of the *femme-enfant,* or woman-child, was to become a powerfully charged and defining image of Surrealist expression of the day. At one and the same time, it identified woman as close to the sources of imagination and creativity while ascribing to her a role that put a check on her artistic independence as well as her cultural, political, and spiritual liberation. This image, writes Chadwick, worked to "exclude women artists from the possibility of a profound personal identification with the theoretical side of Surrealism." Under Breton, Surrealist theory gave to women a poetic role, as that of the muse. Some women artists of the day embraced this notion; others rejected it. Remarked Carrington in 1983, "I didn't have time to be anyone's muse. . . . I was too busy rebelling against my family and learning to be an artist."

Leonora Carrington, a woman of rebellious spirit and boundless imagination, was born into a family of means. Her father was a wealthy textile manufacturer, and her mother, a relative of the writer *Maria Edgeworth, was the daughter of an Irish country doctor. The family lived a life of Catholic piety in a remote area of Lancashire, where Carrington grew up in the two-fisted grip of Catholic piety and capitalist gain. She was raised in the mansion Crookhey Hall, where, as a lonely child, she lived out an imaginary relationship with the rocking horse that stood in the corner of the nursery. Her rebellion was not to be against the family as an institution, but against her own family. Crookhey Hall would provide the subject matter for a later painting of the same name, which shows a ghostly figure fleeing the building. Educated by governesses, tutors, and at convent schools, she was repeatedly expelled for unorthodox behavior and her habit of writing backward in mirror script; the nuns thought her mentally deficient. At a clinic in Spain, she repeatedly climbed onto the roof so as to be nearer to the stars, causing the staff to despair. The expulsions served to further her hatred of the church and her family, and at 14, when she was introduced to the local priest, Carrington wreaked havoc at the assembly by pulling up her dress. Wearing nothing underneath, she demanded: "Well, what do you think of that."

Her rejection of Catholicism had begun at a young age. An early story, "As They Rode Along the Edge," shows what **Helen Byatt** describes as St. Alexander's "perverse penance of wearing underwear filled with scorpions and adders" in contrast with the "half-human and wildly sexual heroine, who has a rampant affair with a wild boar." But Carrington's distaste for Catholicism extended to all religions, in which she saw no equality for women.

The difficult child was sent by the family to Florence where she attended Miss Penrose's boarding school. There she learned to paint. On class trips to Rome and Siena, Carrington studied the Italian masters. Her time in Florence, as well as a stay living with a family in Paris, gave her a glimpse of freedom.

I felt that, through the agency of the Sun, I was an androgyne, the Moon, the Holy Ghost, a gypsy, an acrobat, Leonora Carrington and a woman. I was also destined to be, later, Elizabeth of England. I was she who revealed religions and bore on her shoulders the freedom and the sins of the earth changed into Knowledge, the equal between them. . . . The son was the Sun and I the Moon, an essential element of the Trinity, with the microscopic knowledge of the earth, its plants and creatures.

—**Leonora Carrington**

Her parents, however, planned her debut into society. Back in England, she was presented at the Court of King George V, and during the event she sat reading Aldous Huxley. Although her parents were strongly opposed to Carrington's decision to become an artist, they finally permitted her to study in London with Amedée Ozenfant. Her paintings in class were remembered by fellow student and friend **Ursula Goldfinger** as showing qualities at odds with Ozenfant's strict formal geometry. Carrington stayed in the family suite of an exclusive hotel in London. In the lobby, while groups of matrons gathered for afternoon tea, she and a friend moved through the crowds speaking in loud voices about invented syphilitic symptoms.

In 1936, a copy of *Surrealism,* written by Herbert Read, was given to Carrington by her mother who thought that as an art student she might find it of interest. The following year, Carrington met the Surrealist Max Ernst at a London party at the time of his 1937 exhibition opening at the Mayor Gallery. Carrington and Ernst returned to Paris together, and he left his wife, **Marie-Berthe Aurenche**, for her.

Paintings executed early in her life with Ernst were often satirical of the English upper-class society into which she had been born, drew on images from childhood, and included magical birds and animals. Over time, Carrington's work would mature into a visionary art inspired by Celtic mythology and the ideas and language of alchemical transformation. "It is an art of sensibility rather than hallucination," writes Chadwick, "one in which animal guides lead the way out of a world of men who don't know magic, fear the night, and have no mental powers except intellect."

Carrington's life with Ernst intensified her associations with nature. Moving in part to escape the jealous eye of Aurenche, they renovated a group of buildings that were in ruins at St. Martin d'Ardèche and in the process covered walls with cement casts of mythical animals and birds. As Carrington's work continued its exploration of magical animals, the image of the white horse became a focal point.

In 1937, Carrington wrote "The House of Fear," the first of her short stories to be published, for which Ernst contributed the introduction and collages. This story presented the horse as a guide who conducts the heroine into a world of ceremony and rituals presided over by Fear. In his introduction, Ernst presents Carrington as "The Bride of the Wind," writing: "Who is the Bride of the Wind? Does she know how to read? How to write French without errors . . . ? She is warmed by her intense life, by her mystery, by her poetry. She has read nothing, but she had drunk everything. She does not know how to read. Meanwhile the nightingale has seen her, seated on the stone of Spring . . . animals gathered around . . . she is reading 'The House of Fear.'"

Two paintings, *Self-Portrait* and *Portrait of Max Ernst,* often dated between 1937 and 1940, are thought by Whitney to have been executed in late 1938 or early 1939. These works evidence Carrington's early fascination with alchemical transformation of matter and spirit. While a student at Ozenfant's academy, she had begun her first reading about alchemy, finding works on

Leonora
Carrington

the subject in the used bookstalls around London. *Self-Portrait* depicts Carrington perched on the edge of a Victorian chair, the only piece of furniture in the room, surrounded by animals. A white rocking horse floats behind her, another horse gallops outside the open window, as a hyena with three breasts and a human-like expression approaches the artist. The distinctions between animal and human are blurred, as are those between animate and inanimate as the arms and legs of the chair parody those of Carrington's own. Images in this painting would reappear often in Carrington's later works and in her writings, with the hyena making an appearance in her early short story, "The Debutante," published in 1940 in Breton's *Anthology of Black Humor*.

The image of the magical white horse had come down to her from the Celtic legends, which she had first heard from her Irish mother. Carrington's play *Penelope* (written in 1946 and first performed in Mexico in 1957) tells of a young girl who falls in love with Tartar (named after the underworld of Greek mythology, Tartarus), her hobbyhorse. Her father prohibits the heroine's imaginative play with Tartar, and the heroine escapes by transforming into a white colt who flies off into a different realm. As intermediaries between the unconscious and the natural world, Carrington's magical animals served to "replace male Surrealists' reliance on the image of woman as the mediating link between man and the 'marvelous,' and suggest the powerful role played by Nature as a source of creative power for the woman artist," writes Chadwick.

At St. Martin d'Ardèche, Carrington and Ernst spent their last summer together in 1939. When not painting or writing in the small upstairs bedroom, Carrington looked after the birds and little animals that made their nests in the deteriorating walls of the studio and house. She cooked and maintained her garden and vineyards. The house was full of guests, including Roland Penrose, *Lee Miller, *Peggy Guggenheim, and *Leonor Fini who came accompanied by the writers André Pieyre de Mandiargues and Federico Veneziano. Carrington and Fini's friendship dated from Carrington's arrival in France, and Fini's previous relationship with Ernst did not deter their affection and respect for each other. A later painting by Fini, *The Alcove: An Interior with Three Women*, included a full-length portrait of Carrington presented as a woman warrior. That summer, there were group games and swimming expeditions. There was a visit to the market to procure a large bird, still alive, which was later found in the bed of an unwanted guest.

For Carrington, the following months precipitated a journey into loss, anxiety, and mental breakdown. Ernst was interned as an enemy alien by the Nazis. "I begin therefore with the moment when Max was taken away to a concentration camp," writes Carrington in *Down Below* (1944), her account of this time:

> I wept for several hours, down in the village; then I went up again to my house where, for twenty-four hours, I indulged in voluntary vomitings induced by drinking orange blossom water and interrupted by a short nap. I hoped that my sorrow would be allayed by those violent spasms which tore my stomach apart like so many earthquakes. . . . I had realized the injustice of society . . . . My stomach was the seat of that society, but also the place in which I was united with all the elements of the earth. It was . . . the *mirror* of the earth, the reflection of which is just as real as the person reflected.

Alternatively fasting and working at hard labor in her vineyards, Carrington spent the next three weeks engaged in an act of purification. Physical deprivation combined with the shock of her familiar world collapsing. The village was not hospitable, as the people of St. Martin d'Ardèche neither trusted nor liked the Englishwoman. In 1940, the village was occupied by German troops, to whom the villagers told stories in order to try to force Carrington out. Convinced that if she did not leave she would face arrest, and confused by the recent events, Carrington sold their house to the cousin of a German officer who paid with a bottle of brandy. She fled to Spain with her friends, hoping to secure a visa for Ernst in Madrid. The trip was a nightmare, filled with anxiety and increasing delusions.

In Madrid, Carrington was found at the British embassy issuing threats to kill Hitler and calling for the metaphysical liberation of humanity. Her family intervened, and she was institutionalized. Her writings about this time in *Down Below* recount the administration of cardiazol, a shock-inducing drug, and the violence and pain of having her clothes ripped off and her body strapped naked to the bed. Whereas Carrington's early painting made use of a magical realism based on autobiographical detail, in *Down Below* she relied heavily on the language of alchemy, which was to become of increasing importance to her as a means of creative exploration.

Carrington has expressed anger at Surrealist attitudes toward madness, seeing in them an inappropriate humor that was opposed to the anguish involved in a loss of inner connection with the outside world. G. Ornstein, in "Leonora Carrington's Visionary Art for the New Age" (*Chrysalis* 3, 1978), has argued that Carrington's experience during her breakdown may be more accurately seen as a breakthrough to new strata of awareness.

Following her confinement, Carrington was released into the care of a nurse who saw her to Lisbon where passage had been arranged by her family to England or South Africa. Her departure from Lisbon was to be in the company of one of her former nannies. Carrington took a ride with the nanny to a hilltop tearoom, then escaped via a back door and made her way to the Mexican consulate. There, her refuge was arranged by Renato LeDuc, a Mexican diplomat whom Carrington had met through Picasso in Paris. Later, Carrington would wed LeDuc in a marriage of convenience that would facilitate her journey to New York.

Carrington had not heard from Ernst since leaving France. She feared that he had died during his internment. Ernst, however, had been released in the winter of 1940 and returned to St. Martin to find that Carrington had left the country and relinquished the house. When Carrington met him in 1940 in a Lisbon market, he was with Peggy Guggenheim, who had come to his aid. Guggenheim would later recall the two months in Lisbon when the three of them worked to take the reins of their lives, as she held onto Ernst, her new love. Carrington was devastated by her loss of him. The traumatic events of 1940 informed Carrington's work for the next several years. Her short stories "White Rabbits," "The Seventh Horse," and "Waiting" date from this period. After her arrival in New York in 1941, "Waiting" was published later that year in *View* magazine. It is the story of two women attached to one man. One asks, "Do you fondly believe that the past dies?" The other replies, "Yes, if the present cuts its throat."

Carrington and Ernst met often in New York, the first time was by chance at the Pierre Matisse gallery, which pained them both deeply. Ernst's son Jimmy recorded his father's unhappiness: "I don't recall ever again seeing such a strange mixture of desolation and euphoria in my father's face as when he returned from his first meeting with Leonora in New York. One moment he was the man I remembered from Paris—alive, glowing, witty and at peace—and then I saw in his face the dreadful nightmare that so often comes with waking. Each day that he saw her, and it was often, ended the same way." Carrington's presence found its way into a number of Ernst's paintings during this period, works like *Napoleon in the Desert* and *Europe After the Rain*. In 1942, Carrington wrote the story "The Bird Superior Max Ernst" for a special number of *View* that was dedicated to him.

Carrington arrived in Mexico in 1942 to begin a new life in the world André Breton called the Surrealist place *par excellence*. She moved into an apartment with Renato LeDuc on Rosa Moreno, in an abandoned building that had once housed the Russian Embassy. To Car-

rington, Mexico was an extraordinary land. Their home was widely visited, and bullfighters were among her husband's friends. Although she and LeDuc would end their marriage of convenience, they remained close friends.

A few blocks from their apartment lived the painter *Remedios Varo and her husband, poet Benjamin Peret. Carrington had first met Varo at Breton's home in Paris. "Remedios's presence in Mexico," she said, "changed my life." The two women became the center of a collection of European artists, including photographers *Kati Horna and Eva Sulzer, and two Hungarians Günther Gerzso and Enrique "Chiqui" Weisz whom Carrington took as her second husband. Luis Buñel also traveled in this group, as did a number of former Surrealists now living in Mexico, including *Alice Rahon, Wolfgang Paalen, and Gordon Onslow-Ford. This active group of exiled painters and writers paved the way for the remarkable creativity that took place in Mexico for the following decade. Although Carrington would remain for decades and give birth to her two sons in Mexico, she was not entirely at ease in this land that would pervade her life and work. "I felt at home," she remarked, "but as one does in a familiar swimming pool that has sharks in it."

Carrington saw Varo and her husband Peret nearly every day. The close relationship that matured between Carrington and Varo was significant to the history of women artists, and their work developed sensibilities that were independent of earlier Surrealist influences. Together, they shared a journey to discover the source of their creative lives. "For the first time in the history of the collective movement called Surrealism," writes Chadwick, "two women would collaborate in attempting to develop a new pictorial language that spoke more directly to their own needs."

Carrington's new imagery was expressed through writing during her early years in Mexico in both short stories and plays. By 1945 her production of paintings was significant. Among her paintings of 1947 were *The Old Maids, Night Nursery Everything, Neighborly Advice,* and *The House Opposite;* the alchemist's chamber in *The House Opposite* shows a black-and-white tile floor, which reappears in a 1958 work by Varo, *Alchemy or the Useless Science. Crookhey Hall* also dates from this period. While Carrington's consciousness of painters such as Bosch and Breughel increased, she became more drawn to the technical side of painting. She revived a medieval technique by working with egg tempera on gessoed wooden panels. Carrington and Varo developed what Chadwick has called "their highly personalized vision of the woman creator whose creative and magical powers were a higher development of traditional domestic activities like cooking."

Producing a number of watercolors, Carrington often covered them with the same mirror writing for which she had earlier been forced out of school. Many of Carrington's watercolor sketches include messages to friends. One addressed to Varo reads: "Remedios, I told you that I made a spell against (the evil eye) there it is—yesterday evening I had 38° of fever, autosuggestion perhaps—I don't feel well enough to go out—Come see me if you can? Both of you come to drink some of our tequila? . . . Leonora." Stories, dreams, and magic potions were shared between the two artists. Images that appeared in the work of one were often echoed in the work of the other, but their individual sensibilities remained unmistakable. Whereas Varo's women may be seen as magicians, scientists, alchemists, Carrington's protagonists have been described as sibyls, priestesses, sorceresses. Both artists portrayed secret quests toward enlightenment. Carrington's variations on the quest to psychic awareness grow from various pre-Christian sources, including the Celtic stories and fairy tales first told to her in childhood. The year 1948 brought the publication of Robert Graves' *The White Goddess*. Carrington called her reading of this work "the greatest revelation in my life."

Carrington and Varo made spiritual investigations into Tibetan Tantrism (in the mid-70s Carrington would study under a lama in Canada), Zen Buddhism, Jung's work, and the Russian mystic Gurdjieff. Although Carrington and Varo took their spiritual inquiries seriously, they also maintained a level of detachment as evidenced in Carrington's parody of Gurdjieff through her character of Dr. Gambit in *The Hearing Trumpet*, her novel, which was written in English in Mexico and circulated for years underground before it was finally published in French (1974). Her longest work, the novel features Marian Leatherby as Carrington's main character, a 92-year-old, deaf, toothless woman whose face is graced with a small beard, in which she takes pride. Said Carrington in an interview with **Germaine Rouvre**, "I wanted to appear like a nice old lady so that I could poke fun at sinister things." A magical horn, the hearing trumpet, provides Marian with extraordinary powers of hearing. Writes Byatt: "Her audacious

voice sounds a distinctive and witty presence, rubbing against the seriousness of the book's quest for the ultimate knowledge. The landscape is not just a personal one; *The Hearing Trumpet* is a melting pot for an eclectic mass of images, symbols and allusion, Carrington's version of Jung's collective unconscious."

Edward James first met Carrington in Mexico in 1944, becoming her friend and the most prominent collector of her paintings. "I painted for myself," said Carrington: "I never believed that anyone would exhibit or buy my work." It was James who arranged her 1948 Exhibition at the Pierre Matisse Gallery in New York. He wrote of her studio:

Leonora Carrington's studio had everything most conducive to make it the true matrix of true art. Small in the extreme, it was an ill-furnished and not very well lighted room. It had nothing to endow it with the title of studio at all, save a few almost worn-out paint brushes and a number of gesso panels, set on a dog-and-cat populated floor, leaning face-averted against a white-washed and peeling wall. The place was a combined kitchen, nursery, bedroom, kennel and junkstore. The disorder was apocalyptic: the appurtenances of the poorest. My hopes and expectations began to swell.

Visitors to Carrington's studio often found magic in her environs, with one guest calling it "the most dream-saturated place I know." Her study was compared to that of a 16th-century magician, with a guest remarking on what Byatt has called, its "apocalyptic disorder of boxes and jars overflowing with aromatics and spices, the dusty books, pictures of fantastic animals with human eyes, and the strange dolls with birds' heads hanging from the ceiling."

Although Carrington had spent a great deal of her life in the company of Surrealists, she found the theoretical and judgmental side of Surrealism highly distasteful. Asked her feelings about the Surrealist identification of woman and muse, Leonora Carrington responded with one word, "bullshit." Léonor Fini, who refused to officially join the Surrealist group, maintained that Carrington, a "true revolutionary," was nonetheless never a Surrealist. Carrington found in the Feminist movement a place to articulate her ideas. On the occasion of her 1976 retrospective exhibition at the Center for Inter-American Relations, New York, Carrington's commentary included the following thoughts:

The furies, who have a sanctuary buried many fathoms under education and brain washing, have told females that they will return, return from under the fear, shame, and finally through the crack in the prison door, Fury. I do not know of any religion that does not declare women to be feeble-minded, unclean, generally inferior creatures to males, although most Humans assume that we are the cream of all species. Women, alas, but thank God, Homo Sapiens. . . . Most of us, I hope, are now aware that a woman should not have to demand Rights. The Rights were there from the beginning; they must be Taken Back Again, including the mysteries which were ours and which were violated, stolen or destroyed, leaving us with the thankless hope of pleasing a male animal, probably of one's own species.

SOURCES:

Byatt, Helen. "Introduction" in *The Hearing Trumpet*. Boston, MA: Exact Change, 1996.

Chadwick, Whitney. *Women Artists and the Surrealist Movement*. NY: Little, Brown, 1985.

Carroll, Anna Ella (1815–1894)

American who wrote books and pamphlets supporting political causes and claimed authorship of the Union's Tennessee Campaign during the Civil War. Born on August 29, 1815, in Somerset County, Maryland; died on February 19, 1894 (gravestone misdated as 1893), in Washington D.C.; daughter of Thomas King Carroll (a lawyer and legislator) and Julianna Stevenson; attended Miss Margaret Mercer's boarding school in West River, Maryland (did not graduate); never married; no children.

Began career by writing promotional material for hire, then wrote books and pamphlets in support of political candidates and parties; during Civil War, assisted the federal government in procuring and delivering military correspondence; claimed sole authorship of the Tennessee Campaign to split the Confederate forces; spent much of her later years seeking recognition and compensation for both her controversial claim and her written work for the government.

As Americans experienced the escalating tensions that would eventually result in the Civil War, one woman insisted that her thoughts on the matter be known. Through her writing, Anna Ella Carroll entered the male-dominated arena of politics and government. Her opinions were to influence elections and policy, while her contributions to military strategy would embroil her in controversy.

When Anna Carroll was born on August 29, 1815, the family resided at Kingston Hall, their ancestral plantation located on Maryland's Eastern Shore. It is perhaps no coincidence that Anna would make a name for herself. Her lineage boasted of the Reverend John Carroll, the

first Catholic archbishop in the United States, and Charles Carroll, a signer of the Declaration of Independence. These, along with many other distinguished predecessors, would give her the advantage of a respected and influential family. In following the high expectations of his ancestors, Anna's father Thomas King Carroll had received a master's degree in law from the University of Pennsylvania. At 21 years of age, he was the youngest man elected to the Maryland legislature. Anna benefitted greatly from the attentions of her well-educated father, in whose personal library she was known to indulge. She much preferred the world of deep, analytical thought to the expected feminine pursuits of needlework, music, and domestic tasks. Her mother was kept busy with eight Carroll children, of which Anna was the eldest.

Anna attended Miss **Margaret Mercer**'s boarding school in West River, Maryland, at the age of 15. Along with the expected curriculum, Mercer attempted a balance with "the refinements and delicacy which communicate an ap-

Anna Ella Carroll

propriate and attractive grace to the female character." Unfortunately, Carroll was unable to finish her schooling because of financial difficulties and had to return home. Thomas Carroll, who had a history of poor financial planning, faced bankruptcy and the loss of their Kingston Hall plantation. The family rented a house, and Anna started a briefly successful school for girls.

Now a mature woman of 30, Anna Carroll moved to Baltimore to make a living and help support her parents and siblings. Though the nature of her employment is unclear, sources suggest that she was a contributing political writer for local newspapers; she also wrote promotional material for railroad interests. As she hustled to find jobs, she augmented the social network formed over the years from her father's friends and connections. After the death of her mother in 1849, Anna's name had enough influence to get her father appointed as a naval officer in Baltimore.

Her whole course was the most remarkable in the war; she found herself, got no pay, and did the great work that made others famous.

—Edwin M. Stanton, Secretary of War

This success gave Carroll the confidence and credibility to expand her political connections, and to offer advice to any diplomat or distinguished gentleman she deemed in need of it. After a cordial but brief correspondence, her tone would often change to requesting, if not demanding, a position be filled by one of her friends or relatives, or a candidate of her choice. This, she rationalized, would certainly be in the best interest of the nation. Much to her chagrin, only a very small minority took her advice.

In spite of a reputation as a nuisance (doubtless exacerbated by bias against her gender), Carroll's political image continued to hold a certain credibility. In 1855, she became involved in the American Party, otherwise known as the "Know-Nothings." This seemingly self-deprecating name was actually the stated answer given by party members when questioned about their internal administration ("We know nothing about that"). Wasting little time, she drafted an unwilling Millard Fillmore as the Know-Nothing candidate for president in 1856 and proceeded to promote him with a barrage of articles, pamphlets, and books in what was to be her most prolific period. Titles such as "The Great American Battle," "The Star of the West," and "Who Shall be President?" addressed many of the controversial issues of the time.

The Know-Nothing agenda, which included an anti-Catholic movement, alleged that there had been a large-scale purchasing of Catholic votes, especially those of new immigrants—a grand, Papal conspiracy to gain control of American life and government. The party also cultivated a strong sense of nativism, with little tolerance for those new to the United States. Carroll addressed such issues with a multitude of exclamation points, unsubstantiated evidence, and threats of the horrible consequences if the Know-Nothing candidate or point of view were not supported. Millard Fillmore lost the election to James Buchanan and the Democrats.

Not only did Fillmore have to deal with his failed election bid, but Carroll began to test his patience. After receiving a request for a letter of introduction for her upcoming book tour, Fillmore graciously yielded. When she altered and published his letter to imply a stronger endorsement of her political accomplishments, a flabbergasted Fillmore demanded his letter back. The published letter, she replied, "has done you more good than that of any letter you ever wrote in your whole life before. No one living has done so much for you." Carroll's desire for recognition would cause her to overstate her social or political contributions over and over. While this behavior may be deemed unseemly or even dishonorable, certainly many persons in government and business have benefitted by adopting such a strategy. For Carroll, it became a consistent dynamic in her tactical career maneuvers.

In the late 1850s, she continued applying her political pen, most notably in addressing the anti-Catholic issue. She assisted in the gubernatorial elections in Maryland and began planning for the 1860 presidential elections. While still a Know-Nothing, she began to be welcomed by the Republicans. With headstrong resolve, Carroll decided to support the experienced politician and pro-Unionist, John Minor Botts of Virginia. As his campaign manager, she presented Botts as an attractive compromise candidate who would unite Republicans and Know-Nothings to win the presidency. This was easier said than done, as closed-door politics and party affiliations effectively killed the nomination. Carroll rallied and decided to support her old friend Thomas Corwin for speaker of the house. Corwin's eventual defeat was another addition to a string of political disappointments for Anna. This was followed by personal tragedy with the death of both her sister Julianna and her close friend and suspected lover John Causin.

As the fractured North and South headed toward Civil War, Carroll's strength and sense of purpose rose to meet her new goal, saving the Union. She wrote letters and pamphlets for the Union cause and successfully worked to keep her home state of Maryland from seceding. Her support for the North soon expanded to support for the president, as Abraham Lincoln's actions were openly questioned by John C. Breckinridge. A former Kentucky senator and vice-president under Buchanan, Breckinridge argued that Lincoln exercised powers that he did not have, and that, in effect, the war was illegal. In her highly regarded work, "Reply to Breckinridge," Carroll claimed that Lincoln's actions were in defense of the Constitution and the Union and therefore justifiable.

Her pamphlets were widely distributed and earned her a meeting with the assistant secretary of war, Thomas A. Scott. Evidently, an agreement was made in which Carroll would be paid for any such future contributions, if approved by Scott's office. With this sanction, she continued her work by writing "The War Powers of the General Government." This again supported Lincoln's position and also addressed the divisive topic of slavery.

Although slavery had been a part of everyday life even for Carroll, she was convinced that it was wrong. When her father considered selling and hence separating the few remaining slaves he owned, she solicited for contributions to purchase them herself and then set them free. As a political pragmatist, however, her opinion was not that of a true abolitionist. Fear of bipartisan strife and an economic collapse of the South, if full freedom was granted, caused her to adopt a more gradual approach. Slavery should not be stopped by the government but by the "preservation of the Union, and with that silent progress of intelligence and virtue which the Union alone can guarantee." In addition, Carroll sided with the popular notion of colonization for freed slaves. She was hired by a business interest as a lobbyist, to convince the government to colonize a section of land in British Honduras, Central America. Lincoln's Emancipation Proclamation would eventually prove such prospects to be in vain.

In the fall of 1861, the stage was set for a protracted political battle that would become Carroll's central focus in life; a controversy that continues. Legend has it that while she and her good friend Lemuel D. Evans visited St. Louis, ostensibly to research another pamphlet, Carroll stumbled upon what appeared to be a previously overlooked strategic alternative for the Union. Control of the Mississippi River had been considered the key to winning the war. The Confederate forces were strong, however, and taking the river would be difficult and costly. Why not push up the Tennessee and Cumberland rivers, which ran roughly parallel to and east of the Mississippi? There would be less resistance, and, if accomplished, the South would effectively be split. Carroll sought the help of seasoned riverboat pilot Captain Charles M. Scott, who could answer her specific and detailed questions. A plan was written, and Carroll returned to Washington for a meeting with Thomas Scott. Apparently, Scott was impressed with the scheme and promised to present it to the president. Lincoln was equally interested and began military preparations.

At this point, history can validate the resulting events: the operation began on February 6, 1862, when Fort Henry on the Tennessee River was captured, soon to be followed by Fort Donelson on the Cumberland River and the surrender of Nashville. Union general Ulysses Grant continued up the Tennessee where on April 6–7, 1862, he would win the bloody battle of Shiloh near Pittsburg Landing. The surrender of New Orleans that same month marked the successful end of the Campaign and a great advantage for the Union.

Few knew of Carroll's alleged authorship, and she kept strangely silent. During Congressional hearings to congratulate those responsible, she sat and watched anonymously from the gallery. Years later, in March of 1870, Carroll would voice her claim as originator of the plan, in hopes of both personal recognition and monetary reward. In the meantime, another dispute began regarding payment for her writing.

After completion of "Reply to Breckinridge" in 1861, Carroll encountered difficulty when she approached the War Department for payment. While Scott had dealt with her in good faith, evidently it was not within his authority to have granted the agreement to begin with. In remorse, he gave her $1,250 from his own pocket to cover her expenses. Subsequently, Carroll, who was always struggling financially, presented him with another bill for later works written in support of the administration. Her original charge was $5,000, which quickly grew to the sum of $50,000 and included the provision that Carroll visit Europe to distribute Union propaganda. An exasperated Lincoln considered her request "the most outrageous one ever made to any government on earth." In September of 1862, Carroll received $750 and was told in no uncertain terms that she no longer worked for the government. This only strengthened her resolve, and she persisted in her requests for compensation.

Following the Tennessee Campaign, Carroll continued to give the government military advice and wrote politically supportive pamphlets for which invoices were futilely submitted. Her opinions, however, became less notable, and her contributions to the political world decreased, never again to attain their former status. In March of 1870, she gave up pursuing the War Department and petitioned the U.S. Senate. Along with her request for "compensation commensurate with the service" of writing for the government, she now desired recognition for influencing the government "to adopt the Tennessee River instead of the Mississippi" strategy. Her bill now totaled $250,000.

Years of political wrangling followed, including confrontations with the riverboat pilot Captain Charles M. Scott, who disputed Carroll's claim. In the winter of 1871–72, her now intimate friend Lemuel Evans wrote an anonymous pamphlet in her support, stating that Carroll "must be given the credit of having solved the problem of the military destruction of the 'Southern Confederacy.'" He went on to suggest that her contributions warranted a rank of major general, with retroactive pay dating back to late 1861.

On February 18, 1879, after years of effort, the Senate Committee on Military Affairs ruled against her claim, citing a lack of supporting evidence. She would receive no more than the $1,250 and $750 already paid out, and if additional funds were desired for her strategic contributions, "the deficit should be supplied from the large store of gratitude which . . . republics should bestow upon their citizens." Carroll's vain search for monetary compensation now ruled her life. She sought support from the National Woman Suffrage Association who publicized her story and lowered her dollar request hoping for a compromise. In dire financial need and following a decline in health, Anna Ella Carroll died on February 19, 1894, in Washington D.C.

Some believe that Anna Carroll was a victim of male-dominated politics while others dismiss her every assertion. The truth can probably be found in the title of Janet L. Coryell's biography, *Neither Heroine nor Fool: Anna Carroll of Maryland.* To date there are several theories on the authorship of the Tennessee Campaign, none of which seem more valid than the next. Conflicts regarding the government contract for Carroll's writing have many possible explanations as well, including prejudice, overstepped authority, misunderstanding, or a willful interpretation by Anna Carroll herself.

Be that as it may, the influential nature of her written opinions and her tenacious drive to be included in the political machinery, attest to her intellect and desire to serve. Without the gender restrictions of her day, one could easily imagine Anna Ella Carroll to have been a leading politician of her time.

SOURCES:

Armstrong, Walter P. "The Story of Anna Ella Carroll," in *American Bar Association Journal.* Vol. 35. March 1949, p. 198.

Bowman, John S., ed. *The Civil War Almanac.* NY: World Almanac, 1983.

Coryell, Janet L. *Neither Heroine nor Fool: Anna Carroll of Maryland.* Kent, OH: Kent State University Press, 1990.

Denney, Robert E. *The Civil War Years; A Day-by-Day Chronicle of the Life of a Nation.* NY: Sterling, 1992.

Greenbie, Marjorie Barstow. *My Dear Lady.* NY: Arno Press, 1974.

James, Edward T., ed. *Notable American Women 1607–1950.* Vol. I. Cambridge, MA: Belknap Press of Harvard University Press, 1971.

McPherson, James M., ed. *Battle Chronicles of the Civil War, 1862.* NY: Macmillan, 1989.

Ward, Geoffrey C. *The Civil War: An Illustrated History.* NY: Alfred A. Knopf, 1990.

Wise, Winifred E. *Lincoln's Secret Weapon.* Philadelphia, PA: Chilton, 1961.

COLLECTIONS:

Papers and correspondence kept at the Maryland Historical Society.

Matthew Lee,
Colorado Springs, Colorado

Carroll, Madeleine (1906–1987)

British actress. Born Marie-Madeleine Bernadette O'-Carroll in West Bromwich, Staffordshire, England, on February 26, 1906; died at her home in Marbella, Spain, on October 2, 1987; one of two daughters of John and Hélène (Tuaillon) Carroll; her sister Marguerite was killed at age 19 in the London blitz, 1940; awarded B.A. from Birmingham College; post-graduate study in Paris; married British Captain Philip Astley, in 1931 (divorced 1939); married Sterling Hayden (an actor), in 1942 (divorced); married producer-director Henri Lavorel (divorced); married Andrew Heiskell (a magazine publisher), in 1950 (divorced 1965).

Selected films: The Guns of Loos (1928); The First Born (1928); What Money Can't Buy (1929); The American Prisoner (1929); Atlantic (1930); Young Woodley (1930); Escape (1930); The W Plan (1930); Madame Guillotine (1931); Kissing Cup's

Madeleine
Carroll

Race *(1931)*; French Leave *(1931)*; Fascination *(1932)*; School for Scandal *(1933)*; Sleeping Car *(1933)*; I Was a Spy *(1933)*; The World Moves On *(1934)*; Loves of a Dictator *(1935)*; The Thirty-Nine Steps *(1935)*; The Case Against Mrs. Ames *(1936)*; Secret Agent *(1936)*; The General Died at Dawn *(1936)*; Lloyds of London *(1936)*; On the Avenue *(1937)*; The Prisoner of Zenda *(1937)*; It's All Yours *(1938)*; Blockade *(1938)*; Honeymoon in Bali *(1939)*; Cafe Society *(1939)*; My Son, My Son! *(1940)*; Safari *(1940)*; North West Mounted Police *(1940)*; Virginia *(1941)*; One Night in Lisbon *(1941)*; Bahama Passage *(1942)*;

My Favorite Blonde *(1942)*; White Cradle Inn *(1946)*; Don't Trust Your Husband *(1948)*; The Fan *(1949)*.

English-born Madeleine Carroll was a French teacher in a girls' school at Hove before making her debut in London's West End in 1927, playing a minor role in *The Lash*. In 1928, while rehearsing for another play, she made her first screen test and was chosen from among 150 applicants for the leading role in the British film *Guns of Loos*, about World War I. She began to win a following after her second movie, *The First Born*, which resulted in roles in a string of British plays and motion pictures, including her first talkie *The American Prisoner*. After three films in 1931—*Kissing Cup's Race, Fascination,* and *The Written Law*—she married army officer Philip Astley (they would divorce in 1939) and concentrated on stage work. A generous contract offer lured her back to film in 1933, when she made two of her best movies of the period, *Sleeping Car*, with Ivor Novello, and *I Was a Spy*, which *Film Weekly* readers voted the Best Film of the Year. In 1936, her role in the Alfred Hitchcock thriller, *Thirty-Nine Steps,* brought her to the attention of American audiences.

Signing with Paramount, Carroll made her American debut in *The Case Against Mrs. Ames*, which was followed by *The General Died at Dawn*, with Gary Cooper. Hollywood made the most of her cool blonde beauty and ladylike demeanor, providing her with prime roles in historical, adventure, romance, and comedy films. Notable among these were *Lloyds of London* (1936), *The Prisoner of Zenda* (1937), and *Blockade* (1938), a highly controversial film about the Spanish Civil War that was banned by the Catholic Church. Some consider her performance in the drama *My Son, My Son!* (1940), opposite Brian Aherne, to be her best work and proof that she could shine given the right material. She was also the perfect foil for Bob Hope in the comedy *My Favorite Blonde* (1942). Carroll's beautifully modulated and well-trained voice also made her popular on a variety of radio programs, including "Madeleine Carroll Reads," a 15-minute, five-day-a-week CBS show in 1942, during which the actress read chapters from books.

Near the onset of the war in Europe, Carroll traveled to France to convert her home near Paris into an orphanage for French children. When her sister was killed in a 1940 bombing raid in London, Carroll commented, "the personal loss drove home the full meaning of the hideous fate that has closed in on the people of Europe." During the war years, she was active in the Allied Relief fund and served as a hospital assistant in the overseas branch of the American Red Cross. After the war, Carroll was honored by the French government and the American Legion. In 1948, the National Conference of Christians and Jews named her "Woman of the Year."

Before returning to Hollywood, she and her third husband Henri Lavorel (Carroll was married to actor Sterling Hayden during the war), a producer of films for the United Nations, formed a production company that made pictures aimed at promoting an atmosphere of understanding among peoples of the world. In 1948, in an interview with the *Christian Science Monitor*, Carroll commented that she and her husband believed "wars are started at the top but can be prevented at the bottom, if all men and women will rid themselves of distrust and suspicion of that which is foreign." Set in a children's school in France, their film *Children's Republic* was shown during an International Film Festival at Nice.

In 1948, Carroll made her American stage debut as Congresswoman Agatha Reed in *Goodbye, My Fancy*. Reviewer John Lardner in the *New York Star* called her "a performer virtually matchless today for her combination of honesty, intelligence, and sheer scenic zing." (The role in the movie version went to *Joan Crawford.) Carroll's postwar pictures were disappointing, though a 1950 television appearance on "Robert Montgomery Presents" in Somerset Maugham's *The Letter* was notable.

One of her last stage appearances was in 1964, in a pre-Broadway road tour of *Beekman Place*, although she was ultimately replaced by *Arlene Francis. Carroll's fourth marriage, to *Life* magazine publisher Andrew Heiskell, ended in 1965, after which she spent time in London, Paris, and Marbella, Spain, where she died in 1987.

Barbara Morgan,
Melrose, Massachusetts

Carson, Rachel (1907–1964)

American marine biologist who alerted the world to the dangers of chemical pollution, altering its destructive course. Born Rachel Louise Carson in Springdale, Pennsylvania, on May 27, 1907; died of cancer at her home in Silver Spring, Maryland, on April 14, 1964; daughter of Robert Warden Carson and Maria Carson; attended Pennsylvania College for Women in Pittsburgh (became Chatham College in 1955), B.A., 1929; Johns Hopkins, M.A. in marine zoology, 1932; never

Rachel
Carson

married; children: brought up two nieces, then adopted Roger Christie, son of one of the nieces.

Selected writings: (illustrated by Howard Frech) Under the Sea Wind (Simon and Schuster, 1941); The Sea Around Us (Oxford University Press, 1951); (illustrated by Bob Hines) The Edge of the Sea (Houghton Mifflin, 1955); Silent Spring (1961).

"If I had influence with the good fairy who is supposed to preside over the christening of all children," wrote Rachel Carson, "I should ask that her gift to each . . . be a sense of wonder so indestructible that it would last throughout life." Carson had such wonder, and it lasted until the day she died. She longed to be remembered for her love of nature, rather than for her dark warning.

The woman who wrote so eloquently of the ocean was born on May 27, 1907, far from its shores, 18 miles from Pittsburgh, Pennsylvania. Seven years earlier, her father Robert Warden Carson had purchased 65 heavily wooded acres in the town of Springdale, near the banks of the Allegheny River. In its pastoral setting, his white clapboard, two-story house was surrounded by the region's industries—coal mining, iron smelting, and steel and chemical manufacturing—and by their byproducts—slag heaps, black soot, industrial housing, low wages, unemployment, and strikes. Rachel's stern-looking, gentle mother **Maria Carson** was convinced that when people savaged their environment, the ugliness infiltrated their lives. Love of nature became a mother-daughter bond.

From the age of two on, Rachel roamed the family woods and ten-acre apple orchard. There were chickens, as well as rabbits, pigs, cows, horses, and always a dog, always a cat. At first, Rachel loved to tag along as brother Robert, eight years her senior, went hunting; soon, however, she pattered behind him, questioning his need to kill, putting a large damper on Robert's day.

At six, she entered the Springdale Grammar School. Despite poor attendance, Rachel maintained a B average. There were many deadly diseases plaguing the children of turn-of-the-century America: smallpox, tuberculosis, diphtheria, scarlet fever, and whooping cough. With the first sign of an outbreak, Maria preferred to tutor her brood at home. This was due, no doubt, to the chronic illness of her eldest daughter Marian, who was ten years older than Rachel and suffered from diabetes.

Rachel longed to be a writer. She was enthralled by the works of **Beatrix Potter* and

doted on **Gene Stratton Porter*'s *Freckles*, the story of an orphan boy who loved nature. In a September 1918 issue of *St. Nicholas* magazine, 10-year-old Rachel Carson had her first story in print, the tale of a Canadian aviator, inspired by a letter from her brother who was then in the U.S. Army Aviation Service. A year later, *St. Nicholas* published two more. Maria Carson, an educated, talented woman who could sing and play the piano and had dreamed of a performing career, determined that her daughter would have her own chance at her dreams.

Though the Carsons appeared well-off, they were land poor. Rachel's father, who worked for the local power company, had intended to subdivide some of his property into building lots. Instead, because of economic downturns and World War I, he was forced to sell off the land bit by bit and borrow on the lots remaining.

In May 1925, 18-year-old Rachel graduated from Parnassus High School in New Kensington. That fall on a tiny scholarship, she entered the Pennsylvania College for Women (now Chatham College) in Pittsburgh to study literature. The school, noted for high academic standards, was comprised mainly of students from prosperous homes in the area. Though she made friends easily, Carson was selective and a hater of small talk. At first, she turned her attention to her studies and joined the student paper, "The Arrow." She eventually became part of a small group, mostly writers and hockey players. The slight, blue-eyed, 5'4" Carson was considered "a whale of a goalie" by teammates; the hockey squad would win the 1927–28 school championship.

Required to take biology as a sophomore, Carson arrived in class, writes Philip Sterling, as "an intellectual tourist," but was soon caught up in the intense passion her teacher **Mary Scott Skinker** had for the marvels found beneath the microscope. The two developed a lifelong friendship, and Carson realized that art and science were not necessarily at odds. When she changed her major from English to science, her friends and English teachers were fearful that she was throwing away a chance for stardom as a writer in order to become an obscure biology teacher in some remote high school; opportunities for women in science were severely limited in the 1920s. "You ought to see the reactions I get," she wrote a friend. "I've gotten bawled out and called all sorts of blankety-blank names." Carson never earned less than an A minus in her science courses.

But she was falling behind in tuition. Rachel's earnings from tutoring and her mother's sale of the good china was not enough. The school's president **Cora Coolidge** and dean **Mary Marks** arranged for private financial help from some of their well-heeled friends. By the time she graduated, magna cum laude, in 1929, Carson owed the school $1,600, a substantial amount for the time, and used two of her father's lots, held in her name, as collateral.

Carson had begun to believe that her future was linked to the sea. Intent on studying marine biology, she was granted a year's scholarship at Johns Hopkins in zoology and spent the summer before graduate school on a fellowship at Woods Hole Marine Biological Laboratory in Cape Cod where she began her master's thesis project: studying the cranial nerves of a turtle. Carson was warned again and again, by those who cared, that her career choices would be limited. There was no room in the male-dominated field of marine biology for a woman, no matter how bright, no matter how well-trained.

At Johns Hopkins, she worked a 46-hour week with classroom study and evening lab work. In early January 1930, she found a house just outside Baltimore and convinced her family to move there, two months after the Wall Street crash. By June, Carson had found summer work as a teaching assistant to help make ends meet. That autumn, while her father found a job in Baltimore as a radio-repairs estimator, she worked as a lab assistant to a geneticist.

Following her June graduation in 1932, the warnings proved true: she found no work in science for the next two years. When her father died on July 6, 1935, Rachel became the sole support of her mother. She began writing seven-minute radio "fish tales" for the U.S. Bureau of Fisheries. She then took a civil-service exam for the position of junior aquatic biologist, grade P-1, achieved the highest score, and was assigned to the office of Elmer Higgins, head of the bureau's Division of Scientific Inquiry. It was her first full-time job. Rachel and her mother moved to Silver Spring, Maryland, to be closer to her office in Washington D.C. The household had expanded. Rachel's sister Marian had died of complications from diabetes at age 40, leaving behind two daughters, **Virginia** and **Marjorie Williams**, who were of elementary school age. Rachel and her mother were determined to raise them. Rachel would be responsible for the money; her mother would care for the house.

Higgins had asked Carson to gather her "fish tales" for a government pamphlet and write an introduction, but when she turned in the work, he found it unsuitable. What she had written, he said, was a piece of literature, far too good for a U.S. government pamphlet. Higgins encouraged her to write a more pedestrian overview of fish and send her original material to the *Atlantic Monthly*. The experience provided the inspiration: Carson would combine her love of writing and her love of biology. In early 1936, she began to sell articles to *The Baltimore Sun*'s Sunday magazine. In September 1937, the *Atlantic Monthly* published her introduction, now titled "Undersea," under the name R.L. Carson.

The always encouraging Higgins pointed out that the introduction was in actuality an outline for a book on marine ecology. Break it down into subdivisions, he said, and write a full chapter on each. Meanwhile, author Hendrik Willem van Loon had read her article in the *Atlantic* and was so impressed with its lively prose that he bandied the name R.L. Carson about the offices of Quincy Howe, editor-in-chief of Simon and Schuster. Howe contacted Carson and asked for a book outline and sample chapter. For the next three years, Rachel worked nights and weekends, writing from the viewpoint of her main character, the sea, and peripheral characters, the sea's inhabitants and the birds who lived by the shore. She would always be a slow writer. "Writing is largely a matter of . . . hard work," she said, "of writing and rewriting endlessly until you are satisfied that you have said what you want to say. . . . For me, that usually means many, many revisions." Finally, her mother typed the manuscript and sent it to New York. *Under the Sea Wind*, published in 1941, had a swift, spectacular reception from dazzled New York critics and renowned marine scientists, then was abruptly forgotten. The Japanese bombing of Pearl Harbor quickly diverted interest.

> The central problem of our age has become the contamination of man's total environment with substances of incredible potential for harm.
>
> —Rachel Carson, *Silent Spring*, 1961

With men going off to war, Carson was upgraded at the U.S. Bureau to assistant to the chief of the Office of Information in the Fish and Wildlife Service; for the next two years (1942–44), she and her family lived in Evanston, Illinois, close to her Chicago office, where the Bureau had been moved to make room for wartime agencies in Washington. Because of meat shortages, Carson was in charge of enticing America to eat seafood as a dinner-time staple.

Between 1943 and 1945, she put out four pamphlets extolling the nutritional value of fish. Personally, Carson never cared for fish—at least, not on a platter.

Following the war, the Fish and Wildlife Service turned to wildlife conservation. Carson planned a series of 12 booklets, collected under the title *Conservation in Action* (1947–50). Independent, affable, but certainly not meek, she became editor-in-chief of the Bureau's Information Division, supervising a staff of six. Wildlife artist Bob Hines, who then worked for her, remarked that she had "the sweetest, quietest 'no' any of us had ever heard. But it was like Gibraltar." Said Hines:

> She knew how to get things done the quickest, simplest, most direct way. . . . She had no patience with dishonesty or shirking in any form and she didn't appreciate anybody being dumb. She always showed much more tolerance for a dull-minded person who was honest than for a bright one who wasn't. She didn't like shoddy behavior. She was just so doggone good she couldn't see why other people couldn't try to be the same. She had *standards*, high ones.

Once when he brought her a drawing of a mullet, she held it up and said, "We'd better fix this one, Bob. You've put one spine too many in the dorsal fin."

The quick disappearance of her first book had been a major disappointment to Carson, mentally and financially; she had little interest in trying again. Instead, aided by her job, she studied the sea through summers spent at Woods Hole and job-related excursions to eastern fishery stations, marine wildlife refuges, Atlantic beaches, and California's Pacific coast. Before long, she needed a better outlet than government pamphlets to contain all that she had learned. Carson wanted to write a book that she herself had "searched for on library shelves but never found," a book for anyone who "has stood on the shore alone with the waves and his thoughts, or has felt from afar the fascination of the sea."

Her work began the summer of 1948. After six months of early morning sessions before going to her office, she had enough pages to show a publisher and sought out agent **Marie Rodell** in New York. Oxford University Press, though skeptical about its commercial prospects, offered a contract in May 1949. Carson took the next step in the research. Though she called herself an "indifferent swimmer," she dove in full metal helmet and lead weights off the Florida coast. Then, though sailors believed that women on board were bad luck, she and Rodell were the first women to voyage on the *Albatross III*, the Fish and Wildlife survey ship, spending ten days trawling the fishing grounds of George's Bank off Cape Cod. A fellowship allowed her to take a leave from work without pay. Carson had never known freedom to just write. When the money ran out, she returned to work but continued to squeeze out writing hours. With no time for nature walks, no time for sleep, no time for life, she slogged on. "I feel now that I'd die if this went on much longer." *The Sea Around Us* was typed by Maria Carson, then 81, and delivered in July 1950.

Soon, there were rumblings of the success to come—Yale reprinted a chapter in its *Yale Review*; *The New Yorker* bought the right to reprint sections; *Nature Magazine* took a chapter; Reader's Digest purchased reprint rights in condensed form—all before the July 2, 1951, publication date. *The Sea Around Us* spent 81 weeks on *The New York Times*' bestseller list; there was not an unfavorable review in sight. Wrote a *New York Times* critic: "Great poets from Homer . . . down to Masefield have tried to evoke the deep mystery and endless fascination of the ocean, but the slender, gentle [Carson] seems to have the best of it. Once or twice in a generation does the world get a physical scientist with literary genius. . . . Miss Carson has written a classic." The shy, private Carson put up with a few luncheons to promote the book but just as quickly returned to the edge of the sea.

In December, RCA-Victor released Debussy's *La Mer*, conducted by Arturo Toscanini, with a commentary written by Carson; women's page editors across the nation voted her "Woman of the Year in Literature"; and RKO wanted to turn the book into a documentary. (They did; she hated the film because of scientific errors in the script; and it won an Oscar in 1953.) In January 1952, she was awarded the Henry G. Bryant medal of the Philadelphia Geographical Society, the first conferred on a woman; that same month, she received the National Book Award for best nonfiction book of 1951. "The truth is," she told an ex-classmate as she stood through one of many reception lines, "I'm much more at home . . . on shipboard in sneakers than on hardwood floors in high heels."

With her success, Carson bought a tract of wooded land in West Southport, Maine, along the west shore of Boothbay Harbor. There she built a one-story cottage, just above the rocks overlooking Sheepscot Bay. Carson could be found investigating tidal flats or tide pools at low tide with pail in hand, a hat on to protect her fair skin, binoculars dangling from around her neck, and specimen bottles, a magnifying glass, a spiral notebook, and camera, all contained in a canvas sack slung across her shoulder. In Southport, she met Stanley and **Dorothy Freeman**, who wintered in West Bridgewater, Massachusetts, but summered in a cottage about a half mile down the shore. Kindred spirits, they became fast friends. A large egg-shaped tide pool in one of the beach rocks could be seen from the Freeman house. "On clear nights," wrote Sterling, "Rachel and the Freemans sometimes sat on the seaward verandah to watch the moon. They would follow its steady progress as it lighted point after point along the water. When at last the moon could see itself reflected in the tide pool, they would applaud."

For Rachel and Dorothy it was far more than friendship. Their letters, begun in 1952, were published in 1995 by Dorothy's daughter Martha, as *Always, Rachel*. In 1954, Rachel wrote Dorothy for their yearly Christmas eve missive:

> I have been remembering that my very first message to you was a Christmas greeting. Christmas, 1952. . . . I didn't know then that you would claim my heart—that I would freely give you a lifetime's love and devotion. I had at least some idea of that when Christmas came again, in 1953. Now I know, and you know. . . . We passed through a phase when we asked "why" and tried to find reasons and explanations for this wonderful experience. I am glad to remember we decided long ago that there was something beyond the sum of all the "reasons" we could put forth—a mystery beyond all explainable mysteries.

Carson took another leave of absence from her government job and started *The Edge of the Sea* for editor Paul Brooks at Houghton Mifflin, to be illustrated by Hines. Meanwhile, with the success of *The Sea Around Us*, Oxford reissued *Under the Sea Wind*. She now had two books on the bestseller list simultaneously. Finally financially solvent, Carson resigned from the Fish and Wildlife Service.

Published in 1955, *The Edge of the Sea*, which described three living eco-communities along the Atlantic coast, was almost as successful: 23 weeks on the bestseller list. In 1956, Carson purchased a plot of land in Silver Spring, and was in the process of building a house for her extended family: her ailing 89-year-old mother, now crippled with arthritis, an ailing and unmarried Marjorie, and Marjorie's small son Roger Christie. For someone who meant to

be unfettered in order to write, Carson had a great deal of responsibility. She was catching frequent colds and losing weight. On January 30, 1957, her young niece Marjorie succumbed to complications from diabetes, and Carson officially adopted Marjorie's five-year-old son Roger Christie.

Grandaunt and grandnephew already possessed a loving and close relationship, a hint of which might be found in the opening of *A Sense of Wonder*:

> One stormy night when my nephew Roger was about 20 months old I wrapped him in a blanket and carried him down to the beach in the rainy darkness. Out there, just at the edge of where-we-couldn't-see, big waves were thundering in, dimly seen white shapes that boomed and shouted and threw great handfuls of froth at us. Together we laughed for pure joy—he a baby meeting for the first time the tumult of Oceanus, I with the salt of a half a lifetime of sea love in me. But I think we felt the same spine-tingling response to the vast, roaring ocean and the wild night around us.

But this majesty was being threatened. The postwar era had brought chemical sludge, nuclear waste in leaking containers beneath the ocean floor, unfiltered sewage pouring into streams and lakes. As far back as 1946, Elmer Higgins had warned of the dangers of DDT (dichloro-diphenyl-trichloro-ethane) to fish and wildlife. Carson had long been aware of the dangers and had often expressed a desire to tackle the subject, but none of her editors had shown interest.

In January 1958, Carson received a letter from **Olga Owens Huckins**, a friend and book editor for *The Boston Post*: "The mosquito control plane flew over our small town last summer. Since we live close to the marshes we were treated to several lethal doses. . . . The 'harmless' show bath killed seven of our lovely song-birds outright." Though Huckins scrubbed the bird bath thoroughly, "YOU CAN NEVER KILL DDT," she added. "On the following day one robin dropped suddenly from a branch in our woods. . . . All of these birds died horribly." Air spraying, summarized Huckins, was "inhuman, undemocratic, and probably unconstitutional."

Then a Long Island group fought against the spraying of DDT in their area for gypsy moths; they lost. The spraying went forth anyway, saturating gardens, ponds, and humans with DDT. Birds, fish, crabs, and a family horse were found dead. Carson urged fellow-writer E.B. White to "take up your pen against this nonsense." White, who had other commitments, reversed the plea, encouraging her to take up the cause. "I could never again listen happily to a thrush song if I had not done all I could," she wrote.

For the rest of 1958, she pored over books and papers on pesticide. That December, her mother died just shy of her 90th birthday. "Her love of life and of all living things was her outstanding quality," Carson wrote Freeman. "And while gentle and compassionate, she could fight fiercely against anything she believed wrong." Rachel might have been describing herself. Dorothy Freeman dreaded the clamor the DDT book would provoke and feared for Rachel. Before it was remotely near completion, corporations were threatening lawsuits. On June 28, 1958, Rachel wrote Dorothy: "You do know, I think, how deeply I believe in the importance of what I am doing. Knowing what I do, there would be no future peace for me if I keep silent. I wish I could feel that you *want* me to do it." Rachel checked and double checked her data. Fighting fatigue, she wrote through, "a catalogue of illnesses," flu, a sinus infection, heart trouble, arthritis, and an ulcer. In 1960, she was diagnosed with breast cancer and had surgery that April. Carson felt an urgent need to finish the book and judiciously conserved her energy in order to wade through the mountain of technical research and correspondence she had accumulated for her "extremely complex jigsaw puzzle." Collecting evidence, seeking to build up an incontrovertible case against the use of chemicals as they were then being used, she felt like she was running as fast as she could to stay in place.

The surgery had not been entirely successful; the cancer mestastisized. She told her publisher it was arthritis, and only a few friends knew the truth. I know "that if my time were to be limited," she wrote Dorothy, "the thing I wanted above all else was to finish this book." Finally, after four years, the book was completed. *Silent Spring* was slated to appear initially between the pages of *The New Yorker* in June 1961 as a condensation in three-weekly installments. Exhausted and apprehensive, Carson sent the pages to *The New Yorker*. When its editor William Shawn called one evening, "Suddenly I knew from his reaction that my message would get across," a relieved Carson wrote Freeman. "After Roger was asleep, I took Jeffie [the cat] into the study and played the Beethoven violin concerto—one of my favorites, you know. And suddenly the tension of four years was broken and I let the tears come."

Carson opened *Silent Spring* by drawing a deadly picture of what one American town would be like if chemical spraying continued unabated. At first, the town lives in harmony with its surroundings: "the orchards, the foxes, the deer, the birds." One day "everywhere was a shadow of death."

> There was a strange stillness. . . . In the gutters under the eaves and between the shingles of the roofs, a white granular powder still showed a few patches; some weeks before it had fallen like snow upon the roofs and the lawns, the fields and the streams. No witchcraft, no enemy action had silenced the rebirth of new life in this stricken world. The people had done it themselves.

In many areas of America, she wrote, this was not science fiction. The voices of spring were truly being silenced.

Pesticides, she pointed out, not only killed pests, but birds, fish, and small animals, rabbits, squirrels, muskrats, ladybugs, beetles that eat spider mites. Pesticides infiltrated the river systems, the water supply, the soil, and life's food chain. DDT could be found in fish in Japan, seals in the antarctic, stored in the fatty tissue of animals, poultry, cattle, and in sprayed vegetables. Carson was not against pest control, a fact intentionally ignored by future foes. Instead, she recommended biological ways to kill pests, including sterilization and ultrasonic vibrations.

The New Yorker appearance resulted in an avalanche of mail to Congress and other federal agencies, long before the book's official end-of-September publication. William Proxmire, in the Senate, and John V. Lindsay, in the House, read sections into the *Congressional Record*. Citing Carson's book, President John F. Kennedy formed a group to look into the pesticide issue. U.S. Supreme Court Justice William O. Douglas called *Silent Spring* "the most important chronicle of this century." Many years before, Upton Sinclair's *The Jungle* had changed the face of the meat-packing industry. *Silent Spring* was about to alter the course of pesticide forever.

Though many scientists applauded her scholarship, the chemical and food-processing industry, standing to lose millions, threw much of its power and money at Carson, poring carefully over the pages of *Silent Spring,* looking for cracks, minute errors they could enlarge to cloud the debate. Unable to refute her allegations, they dismissed her science background. They portrayed her as an alarmist, a middle-aged kook, a communist, a new-age faddist, one far out of the American mainstream, threatening Americans who needed these chemicals to protect their quality of life. Mostly, they called her hysterical.

Governmental backing for her ideas was slow to come. The chemical industry had effectively lobbied the government for years. Since the Department of Agriculture had championed pesticides, it found it hard to back down now. Only the Department of the Interior sided with Carson, admitting that there were questions that needed to be answered. For that, the Department of the Interior came under fire.

To those who would drown out her truths in diversions, a seriously ill Carson had no choice but to respond through essays, interviews, articles, and correspondence. Though she shrugged off personal attacks, she felt compelled to answer attacks on her scientific stand one by one. From September to December, her calendar was a jumble of luncheons, talks, lectures. In a speech to the Women's National Press Club on December 5, she said:

> One obvious way to try to weaken a cause is to discredit the person who champions it. So the masters of invective and insinuation have been busy: I am a bird lover—a cat lover—a fish lover—a priestess of nature—a devotee of a mystical cult having to do with laws of the universe which my critics consider themselves immune to.

Their methods, she noted, were to attack statements she never made. Thus to their claim that she was against controlling insects, she countered that it was only because the industry controlled them badly and dangerously. In 1963, two years after the first publication of *Silent Spring,* the United States sprinkled, sprayed, and dropped 900 million pounds of pesticides on the land.

But Carson was growing weaker and weaker, canceling major appearances throughout March of 1963. On April 3, CBS News presented "The Silent Spring of Rachel Carson," in which Carson, filmed earlier at her Maryland home, went head-to-head with Dr. Robert White-Stevens, research executive for the American Cyanamid Company. White-Stevens suggested that her book was one of gross distortion, that she preferred the dark ages. Once again, Carson maintained that it was not her aim to rule out pesticides, but to use them after their hazards had been thoroughly investigated. She claimed that the nation was being fed "tranquilizing pills of half truths." On the same show, three government representatives found themselves agreeing with her by program's end, calling for stricter control and more investigation. White-Stevens was the lone hold out, claiming that balance of nature was not a major force in the survival of man; man, he said, had effectively disrupted the balance of nature with its cities,

roads, and lifestyle. For that reason, the modern scientist was learning to control nature. Carson replied that to some people, "the balance of nature is something that was repealed as soon as man came on the scene. You might just as well assume that you could repeal the law of gravity." There is nothing wrong with trying to tilt the balance of nature in people's favor, noted Carson, but, if we do, we had better know what we're doing.

The president's advisory report was issued on May 15; in essence, though it was careful to skirt any bias against chemicals, the report agreed with her, and CBS aired, "The Verdict on 'The Silent Spring of Rachel Carson.'" At show's end, Eric Sevareid wrapped it up:

> Miss Carson is a scientist and a poet of nature. The men who wrote this report are scientists, period. [Her] book and this report deal with the same facts, the same issues. The first was a cry of alarm from a quietly passionate woman. The second is a sober warning by dispassionate judges. But the cry and the warning bear the same essential message: There is danger in the air, and in the waters and in the soil, and the leaves and the grass.

Senator Abraham Ribicoff began governmental hearings. The first week Stewart Udall sat before the Senate subcommittee on "Activities Relating to the Use of Pesticides" and testified that though her "critics have protested the inadequacy of certain data cited in her book, they have not, to my knowledge, challenged the fact that she raises genuine issues." Two weeks later, on June 4, 1963, Carson gave testimony. At the end of the day, Senator Ernest Gruening of Alaska addressed her: "Miss Carson, every once in a while in the history of mankind a book has appeared which has substantially altered the course of history. . . . Your book is of that important character, and I feel you have rendered a tremendous service."

That summer, Rachel Carson returned to the quiet of her home in Maine, then to her home in Silver Spring for the winter; soon the 56-year-old was using a cane, then a wheelchair, the cancer having spread to her bones. Each day's mail contained the announcement of an award. "Now all the 'honors' have to be received for me by someone else," she wrote Dorothy on March 2, 1963. "And all the opportunities to travel to foreign lands—all expenses paid—have to be passed up. Sweden is the latest." In January 1964, she shared Dorothy's loss when Stanley Freeman died of a heart attack. In February, Rachel underwent another round of surgery, then returned home under a nurse's care. She died on April 14, 1964, age 56, 18 months after the publication of *Silent Spring*. Before she died, Rachel left two notes for Dorothy to be delivered after her death; one closed with, "Never forget, dear one, how deeply I have loved you all these years. Rachel."

Rachel Carson's childhood home in Pennsylvania is open to the public. The Rachel Carson Seacoast Preserve, a wildlife refuge along the Maine coast proposed by the Secretary of the Interior Walter Hickel, was dedicated in 1970. In 1979, a young falcon named Rachel was one of three released into the wild to forestall the extinction of its species. The following year, President Jimmy Carter awarded Rachel Carson the Presidential Medal of Freedom; it was accepted by Roger Christie.

SOURCES:

Freeman, Martha, ed. *Always, Rachel: The Letters of Rachel Carson and Dorothy Freeman, 1952–1964.* Boston, MA: Beacon Press, 1995.

Sterling, Philip. *Sea and Earth: The Life of Rachel Carson.* NY: Thomas Y. Crowell, 1970.

Wadsworth, Ginger. *Rachel Carson: Voice for the Earth* (juvenile). MN: Lerner, 1992.

SUGGESTED READING:

Lear, Linda. *Rachel Carson: Witness for Nature.* NY: Henry Holt, 1997.

Cartamandia (fl. 43–69 CE).

See Cartimandua.

Carte, Bridget D'Oyly (1908–1985)

English theatrical manager and proprietor of the D'Oyly Carte Opera Company. Name variations: Dame Bridget D'Oyly Carte. Born in 1908; died in 1985; educated privately and at Darlington Hall; granddaughter of Richard D'Oyly Carte (1844–1901) who, with his father, built the Savoy Theatre in 1876 to present Gilbert and Sullivan operas.

From 1938 to 1947, Dame Bridget D'Oyly Carte worked in London in child welfare. In 1948, she became the manager of the D'Oyly Carte Opera Company, presenting operas in England, America, and Canada until the copyright expired in 1961, the year she endowed the D'Oyly Carte Opera Trust. She continued to offer operas until the Arts Council withdrew support in 1981. D'Oyly Carte was chair and managing director of Bridget D'Oyly Carte, Ltd., president of the Savoy Company, and director of the Savoy Theatre. She was named Dame of the British Empire (DBE) in 1975. With the support of a bequest from Dame Bridget's es-

tate following her death in 1985, a new company was formed in 1988.

Carter, Angela (1940–1992)

British novelist, one of the most creative of her generation, whose writings are sensuous in language and rich in imagination, creating a strange and dangerously beautiful world. Born Angela Olive Stalker in Eastbourne, England, May 7, 1940; died in London on February 16, 1992; daughter of Hugh Alexander Stalker and Olive (Farthing) Stalker; married Paul Carter; married Mark Pierce; children: one son.

Writing in *The New York Times* soon after her death in February 1992, Angela Carter's good friend Salman Rushdie insisted with passionate conviction that she was a great writer whose books rightly belonged "at the center of the literature of her time, at the heart." Only the passage of time can confirm whether Rushdie's judgment is accurate, but her literary stature is strong and shows no sign of weakening. For a writer whose reputation is based on her highly imaginative prose, Carter's early years were conventional to the point of dullness. Her middle-class family (her father was a journalist) moved to Yorkshire soon after her birth, because Eastbourne was on the Channel coast and dangerously close to Nazi-occupied France. Angela spent her first years in Yorkshire, but the family moved back to London after the war.

A sensitive child, Carter found it difficult to accept the social and educational conventions of society and developed anorexia nervosa. By her late teens, she had found work as a journalist with a local newspaper. In 1960, she married Paul Carter, an industrial chemist. The Carters moved to Bristol, where, soon bored with domesticity, Angela enrolled at the university to earn a degree in English literature. Enthralled by the world of ideas and words, Carter emerged so confident in her powers as a writer that during a summer vacation she ventured to write a novel. Published in 1966 under the title *Shadow Dance*, her first novel was a powerful study of a group of vicious misfits who live in a decaying urban Britain, including a protagonist named Honeybuzzard. Encouraged by critical responses to her work, she published *The Magic Toyshop* and *Several Perceptions* in 1967 and 1969, the former a fantastic modern tale incorporating parts of the Leda-and-the-swan motif, the latter a brilliant recreation of the world inhabited by schizophrenics.

By 1969, Carter had decided to separate from her husband. Financially this was made easier by the fact that she had won the Somerset Maugham Award that year. She moved to Japan, taking a job with the English language division of the NHK broadcasting company. Despite her work, she was able to find the time and energy to continue writing, publishing *Love* in 1971 and *The Infernal Desire Machines of Dr. Hoffman* the next year. Neither was a great success, but Carter refused to be discouraged. Indeed, she became known as a much more powerful, and even sharply polemical, writer when she published *The Passion of New Eve* in 1977. In this work, an insensitive male is captured by a tribe of wandering Amazons and surgically changed into a woman in order that he learn firsthand about male domination and exploitation of women. With the appearance of this work, Angela Carter became famous in the United Kingdom and began to develop a reputation in other English-speaking countries as well.

Although she considered herself to be a feminist, Carter sometimes disagreed with specific political aspects of feminism. An independent thinker, she clearly was concerned about issues that activist women consider central to their agendas. One of these was the issue of pornography, which she examined with intellectual energy and skill in her 1979 study *The Sadeian Woman*. Among the ideas presented in this volume is the notion that Sade's character Juliette can be viewed as a sexual dominatrix, while Sade's character Justine is a forerunner of the Marilyn Monroe good-bad girl. Throughout these years, while producing her finely crafted novels, Carter also wrote a series of brilliant short stories as well as plays, screenplays, children's books, and edited works and translations (of the fairy tales of Charles Perrault). Three collections of short stories, *Fireworks: Nine Profane Pieces* (1974), *The Bloody Chamber and Other Stories* (1979) and *Saints and Strangers* (1986), all contained her familiar themes of betrayal, claustrophobia and murder. They range from hideous fairy tales to dissections of the lives of famous criminals, including *Lizzie **Borden**, and many display touches of sardonic humor.

In her 1985 novel *Nights at the Circus*, Angela Carter reached new heights of imaginative power. Set in the London of 1899, the main character is trapeze artist Sophie Fevvers, who is 6'2'' tall and boasts a pair of wings that, when spread out, span 6 feet. The novel, Carter's eighth, received rave reviews in the United States as well as in Britain. *Time* called the book "a three-ring extravaganza."

By the time *Wise Children* was published in 1991, Angela Carter was battling cancer. Her personal life in her last decade was happy, and she had chosen to became a mother in the early 1980s. By 1991, she was a world-famous writer with a constantly growing tribe of enthusiastic readers. Some, like the reviewer **Carole Angier** in her review of *Wise Children*, noted that they had never read a Carter book before, having had "the impression of a dark and difficult writer, intellectual and feminist, interested in the sinister and supernatural. But I was mostly wrong, or she has mostly changed." Several reviewers spoke of *Wise Children*, which would be her last novel, as being her finest as well. *Wise Children* is a breathtaking "paean to bastardy" that chronicles the adventures of identical twins, illegitimate offspring and a slew of actors, the entire volume being a virtuoso literary performance that ends with "a completely preposterous happy ending."

Angela Carter died in London on February 16, 1992. Her readers and friends mourned her passing with great intensity but were consoled by the fact that in her relatively short but highly productive life she left behind a large body of extraordinary writings. Her friend Salman Rushdie eulogized her and her achievements: "Angela Carter was a thumber of noses, a defiler of sacred cows. She loved nothing so much as cussed—but also blithe—nonconformity. Her books unshackle us, toppling the statues of the pompous, demolishing the temples and commissariats of righteousness. They draw their strength, their vitality, from all that is unrighteous, illegitimate, low. They are without equal, and without rival."

SOURCES:

Angier, Carole. "Song and Dance," in *New Statesman & Society*. Vol. 4, no. 155. June 14, 1991, pp. 38–39.

Carter, Angela. *Burning Your Boats: The Collected Short Stories*. With an Introduction by Salman Rushdie. NY: Henry Holt, 1996.

———. *The Sadeian Woman and the Ideology of Pornography*. NY: Pantheon Books, 1988.

———. *Shaking a Leg: Collected Writings*. Edited by Jenny Uglow. Penguin, 1998.

Gray, Paul. "On the Wings of a New Age," in *Time*. Vol. 125, no. 8. February 25, 1985, p. 87.

Kinmonth, Patrick. "Step Into My Cauldron: A Chat with Angela Carter," in *Vogue*. Vol 175. February 1985, p. 224.

Mooney, Louise, ed. *The Annual Obituary 1992*. Detroit, MI: St. James Press, 1993.

Mortimer, John Clifford. *In Character*. NY: Penguin Books, 1984.

Richardson, Lynda. "Angela Carter, 51, British Writer Of Fantasy With Modern Morals," in *The New York Times Biographical Service*. February 1992, p. 211.

Rushdie, Salman. "Angela Carter, 1940–92: A Very Good Wizard and a Very Good Friend," in *The New York Times Book Review*. March 8, 1992, p. 5.

Smith, Amanda. "PW Interviews Angela Carter," in *Publishers Weekly*. Vol. 227, no. 1. January 4, 1985, pp. 74–75.

John Haag, University of Georgia,
Athens, Georgia

Carter, Anita (1933–1999).

See Carter, Maybelle for sidebar.

Carter, Betty (1929–1999)

American jazz great, regarded as one of the few true jazz singers in the 1960s, 1970s, and 1980s. Name variations: Lorene Carter. Born Lillie Mae Jones on May 16, 1929, in Flint, Michigan; died of pancreatic cancer at her home in Brooklyn, New York, on September 26, 1998; father was a defense-plant worker and choir director; grew up in Detroit; studied piano at the Detroit Conservatory; married; children: two sons, Myles and Kagle.

Betty Carter grew up on welfare during the depression and became interested in jazz while at Northwestern High School in Detroit. After studying piano at the Detroit Conservatory, she won an amateur show at 16, singing "The Man I Love" (1945). She went professional the following year, using the stage name Lorene Carter. Carter quickly began to perform with America's best jazz artists. While still a teenager, she sang with Charlie Parker. From 1948 to 1951, she toured with Lionel Hampton. By the time she toured with Miles Davis in 1958–59, she was calling herself Betty Be-Bop Carter. In 1961, Carter and Ray Charles made an album on the ABC Paramount label; her duet with Charles, "Baby, It's Cold Outside," became a jazz classic. She toured with Charles' show visiting Japan, France, and Great Britain from 1963 to 1968. Record companies, however, did not support her, so she was finally forced to start her own company, Bet-Car Records and Lil-Jay Productions, to provide fans with her sound. Carter would not make concessions to public taste, preferring complex renditions of popular songs, and she continued to make albums that are now collector's items. Forming her own trio from 1975 to 1980, Carter won great acclaim at the Newport Jazz Festivals and at Carnegie Hall in 1977 and 1978. In 1988, she released *Look What I Got!* (Polygram/Verve) to rave reviews.

Known as the godmother of jazz because she taught and nurtured young musical talent, Carter guided pianists John Hicks and Mulgrew Miller, bassists Buster Williams and Dave Holland, and drummers Jack DeJohnette and Lewis Nash. "I'm not an instrument teacher," she said. "But what I can give young musicians is a concept—of knowing how to deal with an audience, and to encourage them to be an individual and not use others to copy from, which is especially important in jazz." Carter also founded "Jazz Ahead" in 1993, a music program that brought about 20 young musicians to New York during Spring Break for a weekend of concerts. "She's wary of the syndrome which makes millionaires of singers and leaves musicians in the pits," writes Mark Jacobsen in the *Village Voice*. "She decided it was, for the most part, musicians who are responsible for creation in jazz, and resolved to take her lumps with them rather than go to Vegas and wear chiffon." In October 1997, President Bill Clinton presented Carter with the National Medal of Arts.

SOURCES:
Jacobson, Mark. "Don't Call Me Man," in *Village Voice*. August 18, 1975, p. 100.

Smith, Jessie Carney. *Notable Black American Women*. Gale Research, 1992.

John Haag,
Athens, Georgia

Carter, Carlene (b. 1955).

See Carter, Maybelle for sidebar.

Carter, Caroline Louise (1862–1937).

See Carter, Mrs. Leslie.

Carter, Elizabeth (1717–1806)

English intellectual, poet and translator, best known for her translation of Epictetus. Name variations: (pen name) Eliza. Born Elizabeth Carter on December 16, 1717, in Deal, Kent, England; died in Clarges Street, Piccadilly, on February 19, 1806; eldest daughter of Nicolas Carter (a curate) and Margaret Carter; educated at home by her father; read Latin, Greek, Hebrew, French, Italian, German, Spanish, Arabic, and Portuguese and was considered to be the most learned member of the Bluestocking Circle; never married.

Selected works: Poems on Particular Occasions *(1736 or 1738); translated several philosophical works, most notably* All of the Works of Epictetus *(1758);* Poems on Several Occasions *(1762);* Memoirs of the Life of Mrs. Elizabeth Carter, with a New Edition of Her Poems *(1807);* Series of Letters between Mrs. Elizabeth Carter and Miss Catherine Talbot from the year 1741 to 1770, to which are added, letters from Mrs. Elizabeth Carter to Mrs. Vesey, between the years 1763 and 1787 *(1809);* Letters from Mrs. Elizabeth Carter, to Mrs. Montagu, between the Years 1755 and 1800: Chiefly upon Literary and Moral Subjects *(1817); contributed to the* Gentlemen's Magazine *and* The Rambler.

Elizabeth Carter was born in Deal, a town on the English seaside, where she would live for most of her life, except for wintering in London. Her father Nicholas was the curate of Deal and preached at Canterbury Cathedral; he believed in educating all his children, both girls and boys alike. Not considered a gifted student, Elizabeth persisted despite her father's impatience. Although languages did not come easily to her at first, she studied early in the morning and late into the night, taking snuff, and chewing green tea to keep awake; in this manner, she learned nine languages (Latin, Greek, Hebrew, French, German, Italian, Spanish, Portuguese, and some Arabic) as well as classics, astronomy, geography, music and history. As a tutor, she prepared her younger brother for university. Ultimately, her translations would be such a financial success as to enable her to purchase her own home, where she spent eight to twelve hours a day studying.

She began publishing her work at the age of 17 (in 1734), in the *Gentlemen's Magazine,* a publication owned by a friend of her father's, Edward Cave. Cave also published a volume of her poetry entitled *Poems upon Particular Occasions* (in 1736 or 1738) and suggested to Carter that she pursue translation, probably because, as her publisher, he could profit greatly from the attention that was drawn by a woman scholar. An expert linguist, in 1739 she translated from the French an attack on Alexander Pope's *Essay on Man* by J.P. de Crousaz. Her translation from the Italian of Francesco Algarotti's *Newtonianismo per le Dame* appeared the same year under the title of *Sir Isaac Newton's Philosophy explained for the use of the Ladies, in six Dialogues on Light and Colour.*

Carter's friends came to include *Catherine Talbot, who probably gave some help in the translation of Epictetus, and who introduced her to a much larger intellectual and social circle in London, including Lady **Mary Coke**. A seasoned Greek and Latin scholar, Carter counted among her friends the distinguished men of the day, Edmund Burke, David Garrick, Bishop Butler, Richard Savage, Samuel Richardson, Horace Walpole, and Samuel Johnson (remarked Johnson of a celebrated male intellectual: he "understood Greek better than any one whom he had ever known except Elizabeth Carter"). From March 1750 to March 1752, Carter wrote for Johnson's *The Rambler.*

Carter received financial support from several people, and she published at her own expense a collection of pieces on religion by Talbot. In general, Carter preferred the company of women, although she considered the feminism of *Mary Wollstonecraft too zealous. She came to be included among the women intellectuals of the time who were known as "bluestockings" and became friends with intellectual women, including *Hannah More and *Elizabeth Vesey, leaders of literary society.

Destined to span roughly two generations, the Bluestocking Circle became one of London's most celebrated societies for members of the leisured gentry. The Circle began during the 1750s and 1760s as a conversation among friends, both females and males, who were interested in literature and other intellectual pursuits. Rather than wear the white silk stockings then worn by London's fashion-conscious gentry, one member of the Circle, Benjamin Stillingfleet, started to attend their evening meetings dressed in blue worsted stockings, ordinarily worn only by peasants. From Stillingfleet's provocative choice, *Elizabeth Montagu, an early member, coined the society's name.

A "bluestocking philosophy," concerned with literature rather than politics, emerged as a means of what members called "rational entertainment" for women, and the Circle evolved into London's most famous women's-only society. With Montagu, Talbot and *Hester Mulso Chapone, Carter was among the first generation of bluestockings. In addition to their meetings, members communicated through letters, discussing their personal and professional activities and ideas at length. Eventually, as political turmoil in Europe of the late 1790s destabilized society, more conservative men and women openly scorned the accomplishments of intellectual women, and "bluestocking" became a term of ridicule.

Although Carter's favorite philosopher was Plato, she was sympathetic to Stoicism and is best known for translating the collected works of the Roman Stoic philosopher Epictetus. The translation was begun in 1749, with the encouragement and sheet-by-sheet scrutiny of her friend Catherine Talbot. The first translation of Epictetus to appear in English, the work took nine years to complete. Highly acclaimed on its publication in 1758, her translation was considered by some to be better than the original. She made more than £1,000 from the publication, which continued in popularity for some time (through four editions in her lifetime). The excellence of the translation was given particular notice because it was very difficult scholarship, and unusual due to its authorship by a woman. As was often the case when women made significant contributions in what were perceived to be male spheres, some doubted that a woman could have authored it.

In 1763, Carter undertook a continental tour with Edward and Elizabeth Montagu and Sir William Pulteney, 1st earl of Bath, an account of which can be found in her letters. The great success of her translation of Epictetus gave her the financial independence to purchase a home. An annuity was bestowed on her by Pulteney and his wife, who had inherited Lord Bath's fortune, and Carter had another annuity from Montagu. Her father came to live with her until his death in 1774; all the while, she continued her studies, especially of the Bible. Remaining single, she helped raise her father's large family by his second wife. After his death in 1774, she remained in Deal, a venerated woman who lived to be 88, retaining the vigor of her intellect and the clearness of her judgment until the end.

Elizabeth Carter's *Memoirs* were published in 1807; her correspondence with Talbot and Vesey in 1808; and her letters to Montagu in 1817.

Mrs. Leslie Carter

SOURCES:
Buck, Claire, ed. *Bloomsbury Guide to Women's Literature.* NY: Prentice Hall, 1992.
Carter, Elizabeth. *Memoirs,* 1807.
Gaussen, Alice C.C. *A Woman of Wit and Wisdom: A Memoir of Elizabeth Carter.* 1906.
Kersey, Ethel M. *Women Philosophers: a Bio-critical Source Book.* NY: Greenwood Press, 1989.
Stenton, Doris Mary. *The Englishwoman in History.* NY: Macmillan, 1957.
Talbot, Catherine. *Letters between Mrs. Elizabeth Carter and Miss CT,* 1808.

Catherine Hundleby, M.A. Philosophy,
University of Guelph

Carter, Helen (b. 1927).

See Carter, Maybelle for sidebar.

Carter, Jeanette (b. 1923).

See Carter, Maybelle for sidebar.

Carter, June (b. 1929).

See Carter, Maybelle for sidebar.

Carter, Mrs. Leslie (1862–1937)

American actress. Name variations: Caroline Louise Carter. Born Caroline Louise Dudley in Lexington, Kentucky, on June 10, 1862; died in Santa Monica, California, on November 13, 1937; married Leslie Carter, in May 26, 1880 (divorced 1889); married William L. Payne (an actor), on July 13, 1906.

Some believe that Mrs. Leslie Carter's acting career was ignited from the ashes of her scandalous private life. After her nine-year marriage to wealthy Chicagoan Leslie Carter ended in a sensational divorce case in which she was found guilty of adultery, she persuaded famed theatrical producer David Belasco to launch her on a stage career. No doubt intrigued as much by her notoriety as her acting ability, he starred her as the central character in his 1890 production of *The Ugly Duckling.* Critics found promise in her fiery red hair, green eyes, and willowy figure, though her performance was considered a tad unrestrained. Her second effort, in the title role of Audran's operetta *Miss Helyett* (1891), was well received, but her real success came with her portrayal of the determined Maryland Calvert in *The Heart of Maryland* (1895). Roles as a prostitute in *Zaza* (1899) and a courtesan in *Du Barry* (1901) expanded her following. Carter continued to use her ex-husband's name throughout her career.

Carter's performance in the title role of *Andrea* (1905) was considered her finest by far. William Winter, who had previously been critical of her overacting, overwrote glowingly of her portrayal of the tragic heroine. "No denotement in Mrs. Carter's acting of *Du Barry* had even remotely indicated such depth of tragical feeling and such power of dramatic expression as she revealed in the scene of the tempest, in pronouncing *Kaeso's* doom, and, above all, in the terrible, piteous, tragic self-conflict through which the Woman became the incarnation of Fate and the minister of death."

In 1906, secure in her partnership with Belasco, Carter suddenly married a young actor, William L. Payne, an act that so offended the producer that he dissolved their relationship and never spoke to her again. After the break, she toured on her own and with other managements, but her career went into decline until 1921, when she won generous notices as Lady Catherine in Somerset Maugham's *The Circle*, opposite John Drew. Her last New York performance was in a 1928 revival of *She Stoops To Conquer*. Carter also made one movie, *The Vanishing Pioneer*, when she was in her 70s.

Carter kept up an impassioned, although one-sided, correspondence with Belasco until his death in 1931, but he never forgave her. The actress made some stage appearances in California before her death on November 13, 1937, in Santa Monica.

Barbara Morgan,
Melrose, Massachusetts

Carter, Maybelle (1909–1978)

American guitarist, autoharp player, and singer from southwestern Virginia who—with the Carter Family, the Carter Sisters, and as a solo performer—popularized country and folk music over a 50-year career. Name variations: (nicknamed) Mother Maybelle, Queen Mother of Country Music, and Queen of the Autoharp. Born Maybelle Addington in Nickelsville, Virginia, on May 10, 1909; died on October 23, 1978; one of ten children of Margaret Addington; married Ezra J. Carter, March 13, 1926; children: Helen Myrl (b. September 12, 1927); Valerie June (known as June Carter Cash, b. June 23, 1929); Ina Anita (known as Anita Carter, b. March 31, 1933; d. July 29, 1999).

Selected discography: The Best of the Carter Family *(Columbia CS-9119);* Carter Family Album *(Liberty 7230);* Country's First Family *(Columbia KC-34266);* 50 Years of Country Music *(Camden ACL-2-0782);* Happiest Days of All *(Camden ACL-1-0501);* Lonesome Pine Special *(Camden 2473);* Mid the Green Fields of Virginia *(Victor ANL 1-1107);* More Golden Gems from the Carter Family *(Camden 11554);* Mother Maybelle Carter *(Columbia CG-32436);* My Old Cottage Home *(Camden ACL-1-*0047)*;* Original and Great Carter Family *(Camden 586);* Precious Memories *(Camden X-9020);* Stars of the Grand Ole Opry *(Victor CPL-2-0466);* Three Generations *(Columbia KC-33084);* World's Favorite Hymns *(Columbia C-32246);* Jimmie Rodgers Visits the Carter Family *(Victor 23574). Inducted into the Country Music Hall of Fame (1970).*

August 1–4, 1927, was dubbed by *Billboard*: "Four days that shook the country music world." During this time, two separate recording sessions were held in a studio in Bristol, southwestern Virginia. Both sessions featured unknowns: the Carter family—comprised of ❧▶ **Sarah Carter**, her husband A.P. and her younger cousin Maybelle— performed for the first two days; on the third, a frail youth named Jimmie Rodgers stepped up to the mike.

On August 3, the Carter Family drove home from Bristol in a borrowed Model T. It took most of the day and three tire patches to travel across the 26 miles of rolling hills and mountains, back to Maces Springs, a rural village in a section of Appalachia known as "Poor Valley." Despite the heat, the group felt good. Maybelle had little idea what to expect, but she thought the sessions went well. Sarah, with three children to care for, was relieved by the payment the work provided. A.P., the group's dreamer, was thrilled with the sessions but could not have predicted their historical significance. So they all "went home and planted corn," recalled Sarah. Maybelle, 18 years old and eight months pregnant, prepared for the arrival of her first child.

Maybelle's ancestral roots could be traced back several generations to early English, Scotch, and Irish settlers. Family legend claims that she was a descendent of William Addington, an aide to General George Washington during the Revolutionary War. Born May 10, 1909, she was raised in the Nickelsville area of Virginia where her family owned a mill and a general store. "Momma" **Margaret Addington** led the Fair Oak Methodist Church women's chorus, while blue-eyed Maybelle, one of ten Addington children, sang in church as well as with her sisters, brothers, aunts, and uncles. She learned gospel songs, traditional family ballads, and community square-dance melodies.

The youngest, shyest member of the Carter family, Maybelle began to play the autoharp not long after she began to sing. "I have loved music all my life," she would later recall. "I guess I was just born that way. My sister used to play the banjo some, my mother played the banjo and I

❧▶
*See sidebar
on the
following page*

Carter, Sarah (1898–1979)

American musician who was lead singer and instrumentalist for the Carter Family. Born Sarah Dougherty in Flat Woods, Virginia, on July 21, 1899; died on January 8, 1979; one of ten orphaned daughters of Elizabeth and Sevier Dougherty; married A.P. (Alvin Pleasant) Carter (a bandleader), on June 18, 1915 (divorced 1933); married Coy Bayes, in 1939; children: (first marriage) **Gladys Carter** (b. 1919); *Jeanette Carter (b. 1923); Joe (b. 1927). Inducted into the Country Music Hall of Fame (October 1970).

After the death of their mother, Sarah Dougherty and her nine siblings were sent to live among various relatives. Young Sarah moved in with her childless Aunt Melinda and Uncle Millburn, who lived in the mountains, 125 miles away from the nearest large city. Her childhood included hard work on the homestead, school in a one-room schoolhouse, singing at church, and living among musicians.

A tall, attractive black-haired teenager, she developed a powerful, high, sometimes masculine sounding, singing voice. Her notes rang with loneliness and regret, echoed by hope and promise. Music teacher Eb Easterland taught Sarah to play the autoharp; eventually, she played the guitar, banjo, and fiddle but never developed a passion for a particular instrument. Instruments would remain primarily a background for her voice. Along with Uncle Millburn, who played the fiddle and sang, and his friend Ap Harris, Sarah began to sing for small gatherings. She also played and performed with her cousin **Madge Addington**, and eventually with Madge's younger sister *Maybelle Carter.

It's said that Sarah's future husband Alvin Pleasant (A.P.) Carter first heard Sarah when she was 15 singing the mournful railroad disaster ballad "Engine 143" on her aunt's porch. A.P. stopped to visit while making his rounds selling fruit trees, and, when he joined in, his baritone voice blended beautifully with Sarah's. They exchanged visits and letters for a year, then married on June 18, 1915, a month before her 17th birthday.

A.P. and Sarah moved to a cabin built on land in Maces Springs, which was given to A.P. by his father. Sarah cultivated a garden and raised goats. Music was naturally woven into their lives as they played for friends, relatives and neighbors. Their first Christmas, the couple sang together at the New Hope Methodist Church.

The Carters' homemade music began to have a special sound, particularly after the talented instrumentalist Maybelle joined the group (Maybelle had become a Carter by marriage to A.P.'s brother Ezra). But day-to-day life remained difficult, and Sarah delivered her third child at age 27. A.P. worked several jobs but had no reliable income. By the year 1940, family income in their part of Virginia reportedly averaged only $200 per annum. Like most of their neighbors, A.P. and Sarah were poor.

As word spread that a handful of hill musicians from Scott County had made records and as the Carters local popularity began to build, A.P. set his sights on making a living with their music. Sarah sometimes found herself attending to chores while A.P. went out looking for songs, and she remained ambivalent and deeply conflicted about the notion of singing, which she regarded as simple and free, for pay.

Ultimately, Sarah recorded because she needed money. She said that the first $25 check they received was, "more than I would have made if I had taken in the entire town's laundry." Sarah sang with the Carter Family from 1927 to 1943. Although the income made her life easier, her career did not make her happier. In an interview, she named A.P.'s younger sister **Sylvia**, who watched the kids and handled family problems while the band toured, "the unsung hero of the Carter Family."

As the Family became nationally successful, the demands on the band increased and her marriage disintegrated. After 17 years of marriage, she shocked her family and the community by separating from and then divorcing A.P. For a time, the personal distance saved their professional lives. Sarah continued to live in Cooper Creek with the children, or in separate residences in Texas and North Carolina, as she continued to perform with the band.

In 1938, just prior to leaving for Texas to perform with the Carter Family on border-station radio, Sarah ran into Coy Bayes, an old acquaintance. Coy, a native of Wise County and A.P.'s first cousin, was a big, hardworking electrician, mechanic, and tree farmer who had been successful in the timber business in California. Sarah and Coy corresponded for a year. They became engaged in 1939 and married that winter in Texas.

Sarah sang with the Carter Family until 1943 when the group officially disbanded, then lived privately with Coy in California. She came out of retirement briefly to play a reunion concert and to tour on the folk circuit with Maybelle for a year in the mid-1960s. Sarah Carter outlived both A.P. and Maybelle. She passed away in 1979, at the age of 81.

Jesse T. Raiford

Maybelle Carter

would pull the autoharp down off the table to the floor and try to play it." An American invention from the 1800s, literally an automatic harp, the autoharp is easy to play and transport and provides a bright background for nearly any style of music. By age 12, Maybelle had taught herself to pick out melodies instead of merely strumming the harp, a revolutionary achievement that gained her modest local fame. Maybelle next mastered the banjo, in a day when female banjo players were rare, and played with her brothers at square dances. Finally, she took up the instrument that would make her famous. Her unique guitar style, which incorporated the famous "Carter lick," was probably adapted from a banjo technique called "frailing."

"When I was about twelve or thirteen," she recalled, "one of my older brothers gave me a guitar and I started trying to pick it, and came up with my own style, because there weren't many guitar pickers around."

Guitar players generally strum chords fingered across all strings or pick out a melody using individual notes, predominately on the higher sounding strings. Maybelle taught herself to pick out a melody on the bass strings while simultaneously strumming a rhythm on the treble strings. The easy-to-listen-to, hard-to-learn, "Carter lick" continues to influence both bluegrass and folk music and, to a lesser degree, modern country music. Beginning guitarists routinely learn Maybelle's style and struggle to imitate her version of "Wildwood Flower." Upbeat and warm, her musicianship reflected her easygoing personality. Maybelle's techniques, although neither flashy nor complicated, redefined the roles of autoharp and guitar. The best guitarists of her time—Chet Atkins, Les Paul, Joe Maphis, Merle Travis, Lester Flatt and Doc Watson—considered her to be a "musician's musician."

When her cousin Sarah Dougherty married A.P. Carter, six-year-old Maybelle had danced to the music. Sarah, 11 years older than her cousin, treated Maybelle like a younger sister. As Maybelle's skills increased, the three began to play together. They arranged and performed in their own style: family songs, church songs, parlor tunes, traditional songs, and songs that A.P. wrote or gathered as he traveled for work. Maybelle's musicianship, Sarah's voice, A.P.'s vast repertoire, and the group's ability to harmonize were the elements that would make them famous. Ezra (Eck) Carter, A.P.'s younger brother, reportedly fell in love with six-year-old Maybelle when he first watched her perform at a school. They met again 11 years later, courted for four months, and eloped in 1926.

A.P.'s initial goals for the three Appalachian musicians may have seemed grandiose, but his timing was right. As they built their local reputation, the country was changing. Commercial radio broadcasting started in Pittsburgh in 1920. Back then, musicians played live or recorded live at the station for playback because records would be prohibited on radio until 1948. By 1922, Fort Worth's WBAP and Atlanta's WSB both began to feature fiddle songs. Stations experimented with formats such as the Barn Dance—featuring fiddlers and hillbilly bands—and country music began to reach across the south. In 1925, the Grand Ole Opry in Nashville, Tennessee, which would become the longest-running radio show in America, copied the barn-dance format.

By the 1920s, records were moderately expensive, but the recording industry had little competition in rural areas. Movies played only in town, radios required electricity, but wind-up Victrolas were available for ten dollars. Electronic advancements permitted record companies to transcribe local talent on location, and the high-volume sales of regional tests startled record executives. As record sales grew, companies sought stars. The person most responsible for the discovery of talent and growth of the in-dustry was RCA Victor talent scout Ralph Peer. Urbane, wealthy and well educated, he had a passion for horticulture and merely a business interest in music. After successfully experimenting with the "Negro" market, he ventured to Atlanta and recorded Fiddlin' John Carson. When Carson's records sold well, Peer began to look for additional talent in the South.

When A.P. heard that Peer was coming to Bristol, he arranged the historic August 1–4 session through record-store owner Cecil McClister. The Carters arrived with A.P. in dirty coveralls and Sarah and Maybelle in faded calico dresses. Peer, though taken back by their appearance, loved their sound. "The moment I heard Sarah's voice," he later said, "I knew it was going to be wonderful." He also recognized Maybelle's instrumental abilities and noted the band's professional polish. The Carters recorded 12 songs and signed a five-year exclusive contract with RCA Victor. A day later, Peer recorded Jimmie Rodgers, a well-traveled, self-promoting, colorful character, who drew from a range of styles and was called "The Singing Brakeman." In four days' time, Peer had signed the two dominant country music performers of the 1920s and '30s.

After Bristol, Maybelle gave birth to a daughter in the one-room Clinch Mountain cabin that she and her husband Eck had built with the help of their neighbors. With her mother-in-law serving as midwife, Maybelle survived the delivery without aspirin or doctor. Scott County life was hard and isolated. Jobs were scarce, even before the Depression of 1929. There were no televisions and few telephones or radios. Mail deliveries came two or three times a week, and neighbors shared month-old newspapers. Amid the poverty and isolation, people made, grew, or bartered for what they needed, or they did without. After work and chores, families and friends often gathered on the porch or by the fire to make music.

Maybelle raised her daughter, Sarah tended to her family, A.P. went back to work, and their records began to sell. The warm Carter harmonies hooked Southern listeners. Maybelle first heard a Carter Family record while visiting McClister's store. Cecil had sold 200 and reported sales of 2,000 in Atlanta.

The trip to Bristol established a pattern. For the next 15 years, the Carters would modestly venture out of the hills to play music—music that was indigenous to their southern mountain areas—and then return to their insular homes in

June
Carter
Cash

the Virginia hills to work other jobs, to raise children, to gather and write new songs. Each time they visited a recording studio, performed a concert, or sang live over the radio, they helped shape music history and preserved a portion of rural southern American heritage. The Carter Family music, set into wax molds spinning at 78 revolutions per minute at the Bristol recording studio, was simple, traditional, rural, and religious. The songs cataloged the hopes and sorrows of rural living, lamented the call of the city, and longed for places or loved ones left behind. Many of the tunes contained the traditional lyrics and melodies their European ancestors had carried across the ocean and up into the moun-

tains. Their music, called by many names—traditional country music, mountain music, and hillbilly music—was similar in many ways to the commercial country music, bluegrass, and modern folk music that the Carters preceded and inspired.

Although it took some time before royalties trickled back to Scott County, concert requests picked up and A.P. devoted more time to managing the band. Instead of the vaudeville circuit or promotional tours to capitalize on their fame, the Carters continued to do casual, well-rehearsed and carefully presented performances. Kerosene lamps and lanterns brought by the spectators often lit their staging areas. Too modest to sell their own records at their concerts, they continued to perform as if playing for friends, usually to crowds of less than 200.

Despite their growing popularity, music income did not pay the bills. A.P. traveled to Detroit for work, and Maybelle traveled with Eck as his work advanced with the railroad. Then a telegram came from Peer requesting another recording session. On May 7, 1928, the Carter Family boarded a train bound for Camden, New Jersey. The sessions at Victor's main recording studio were a turning point for the Carters, and music became their vocation.

After their second child, ◄ June Carter (Cash), was born in 1929, Maybelle and Eck moved to Bluefield, West Virginia, and then to Washington, D.C., where Eck continued his railroad work. Although this prevented the Carter Family from practicing regularly, Maybelle was

Cash, June Carter (1929—)

American Grammy Award-winning country music songwriter, singer, entertainer and actress. Name variations: June Carter. Born Valerie June Carter in Maces Springs, Virginia, on June 23, 1929; daughter of Maybelle Carter (1909–1978) and Ezra Carter; married Carl Smith, in 1952 (divorced); married Rip Nix, in 1960 (divorced); married Johnny Cash, in 1968; children: Rebecca Carlene Smith (b. September 29, 1955, later known as Carlene Carter); Rosie Nix; John Carter Cash (b. 1970).

Although in the beginning, June Carter Cash's sisters had to work with her to help develop her musical talents, the slowest to develop ultimately became the most talented performer and the most famous of the Carter Sisters. "While everyone was dating," writes Cash, "I was busy riding everywhere in our old Cadillac, setting up the PA system, and taking money at the door." After high school, she bypassed college to go on the road, performing as many as five shows a day with her mother and sisters. Her mother Maybelle's smile and sense of humor, her tomboy outlook, and the road-show education took June a long way.

A.P. Carter initially noted June's potential and encouraged her to introduce comedy into performances. June's solo career flourished while she was still a member of the Carter Sisters. "Baby, It's Cold Outside," recorded with Homer and Jethro, made the top ten in 1949. In the early 1950s, she signed with Columbia and recorded a number of hits that made the country music charts.

In 1952, June married honky-tonk performer Carl Smith, whom she divorced two years after her daughter Rebecca Carlene Smith (Rebecca would later change her name to *Carlene Carter) was born. Carl recorded a song called "Just Wait Till I Get You Alone," and as an answer song—a country music tradition of a later song responding to an earlier hit—June recorded "You Flopped When You Got Me Alone."

In 1954, June left the Carter Sisters and the Grand Ole Opry and moved to New York to study dramatics at the Actor's Studio. She then appeared on television shows hosted by Tennessee Ernie Ford, Jack Paar, and Garry Moore, as well as on episodes of "Jim Bowie," "Gunsmoke," and "Little House on the Prairie." In 1958, she starred in a movie called *Country Music Holiday*. In 1960, she married wealthy contractor Rip Nix; the couple had a daughter named **Rosie Nix** before they divorced.

Elvis Presley, with whom Mother Maybelle & the Carter Sisters had toured as an opening act, suggested to Johnny Cash that he hire June. She joined Johnny Cash's touring troupe in 1961. In 1962, she signed an exclusive five-year personal appearance contract and started writing songs for him. The following year, she coauthored "The Matador" (1963), a huge hit. She and Merle Kilgore co-wrote "Ring of Fire," and Johnny Cash turned it into a number-one recording. In 1964, June and Johnny released the successful duet "It Ain't Me, Babe."

In 1967, the pair produced two country music hits: "Jackson" and "Guitar Pickin' Man." The following year, they began touring as a singing team. They married that March, in Franklin, Kentucky, after Johnny proposed on stage before a huge audience in London, Ontario. June, by then deeply religious, helped him fight a drug habit and encouraged him to convert to Christianity. The following year, they earned the "Vocal Group of the Year" award (1969) from the Country Music Association, and a Grammy for "If I Were a Carpenter." In June 1970, their son John Carter Cash was born.

June played the role of Mary Magdalene in a 20th Century-Fox movie called *Gospel Road* (1972), the concept for which reportedly originated from one of June's dreams. Her husband narrated the film. June's autobiography, *Among My Klediments* was published in 1979 and was followed by *From the Heart* in 1987.

SUGGESTED READING:

Cash, June Carter. *Among My Klediments*. Grand Rapids, MI: Zondervan, 1979.

Jesse T. Raiford

able to perform at most of their concerts. During the Depression, record sales slowed but were steady enough to prove the existence of a long-term country music market. At a time when unemployment in America reached above 30%, the Carter Family members established what they regarded as a reasonable degree of economic comfort.

In 1931, Peer brought the Carters and Jimmie Rodgers together in Louisville, Kentucky, for a meeting of country music's royalty. Rodgers, whose professional success had awed the Carters, now suffered from tuberculosis, which left him too weak to both sing and play. Somewhat reluctantly, Maybelle faked his guitar style, and they recorded four songs together. Rodgers would die two years later.

The Family gained momentum after a third recording session in Camden. The Sears Roebuck Catalog began to list Carter Family recordings. But royalties, equally divided between the three, still did not fully support either family. As musicians were soon to learn, concerts increased record sales, and A.P. set up larger gatherings while the group's schedule expanded. They traveled in his new Model T throughout North Carolina, South Carolina, Virginia, West Virginia, and Kentucky, into Pennsylvania, Maryland, and Alabama.

By 1932, larger venues and a crowded schedule made it harder to linger with the crowds or to slip back home to their familiar lifestyles. "Keep on the Sunny Side" was their theme song, but it became increasingly difficult to follow their own advice. The professional grind strained both marriages. Eck had adjusted his work schedule so that Maybelle could be closer to the band, but she missed being a full-time wife and mother. A.P.'s obsession with show business and Sarah's need for a normal life became irreconcilable; the couple separated in 1933. While taking a much needed break, Maybelle and Eck built a larger home with income from Eck's job and royalty payments. They were comfortable enough to afford the luxury of cleaning women, and Maybelle began to study classical guitar. On March 31, 1933, she gave birth to a girl named ✥▶ Anita. Although Sarah and A.P. lived apart, they sang together and remained friends.

The Carters left Victor in 1934 and went on hiatus. By 1935, Maybelle began to miss the stage and encouraged Sarah and A.P. to perform again. That year, they signed with the American Record Company, while Peer continued to advise the group. Concert bookings, record sales, and royalty income increased. They did occasional appearances on radio shows, and eventually the Barn Dance on WLS in Chicago featured them as regulars.

John Romulus Brinkley—a politician, radio pioneer, and self-proclaimed doctor of medicine—brought the Carter Family to a huge audience in 1937. Though his station XERA was located in Mexico, allowing him to skirt U.S. standards, it sat near the Texas border and the town of Del Rio, Texas. Thus, his 100,000-watt station reached most of North America. Performing six days a week on the radio from June

Carter, Anita (1933–1999)

American backup singer of Carter Sister fame and modest solo star. Born Ina Anita Carter in Maces Springs, Virginia, on March 31, 1933; died July 29, 1999; daughter of Maybelle Carter (1909–1978) and Ezra Carter; married Dale Potter (divorced); married Don Davis (divorced); married Robert Wooten (divorced); children: Lorrie Frances; John Christopher.

Like all of *Maybelle Carter's daughters, Anita was an accomplished musician. Proficient on the guitar, the autoharp, the gitarro, and the bass, she also worked as a songwriter. While singing with Mother Maybelle & the Carter Sisters, Anita performed solo when she dueted with Hank Snow on "Blue Island/Down the Trail of Aching Hearts" in 1951. She recorded for Columbia Records (1953 and 1954), and between 1955 and 1957 joined with *Kitty Wells' daughter Ruby Wright and yodeler Don Winter's daughter Rita Robbins to produce several songs for RCA—under the name 'Nita, Rita and Ruby—aimed at the teen market.

After 1960, when Maybelle toured on the folk-music circuit and *June Carter (Cash) was working with Johnny Cash, Anita devoted more time to a solo career. She was a sought after back-up singer and in 1965 and 1966 had a couple of medium successes with her own records. In 1968, she recorded a top-five country single, "I Got You," with Waylon Jennings and in 1969 teamed with Johnny Darrell on "The Coming of the Roads." Anita worked for United Artists and Jennings and had several hits listed on the country charts into the 1970s.

Eventually shifting her attention to television production, Anita worked as a talent coordinator and consultant. She also performed on *The Unbroken Circle*, a tribute to Mother Maybelle Carter (produced in 1979); served as an associate producer on the movie *County Gold* (1982); and worked on the 1986 CBS-TV movie *Stage Coach*. Anita married and divorced three different musicians, one of them twice, and had two children.

Jesse T. Raiford

1938 to October 1940 required tremendous effort, but the work paid well. Carter Family broadcasts exceeded expectations, and their national exposure increased record sales as royalties finally began to mount.

That first year in Texas, Maybelle lived with her daughter Anita while Eck traveled with the railroad. Daughters June and ◀❧ **Helen** stayed with their Aunt Sylvia. With so many radio hours to fill, family members joined the shows. First ◀❧ **Jeanette**, daughter of A.P. and Sarah, and then Maybelle's daughter Anita, sang on the air. After a contract renewal, Maybelle's two other daughters, June and Helen, moved to Texas and joined the broadcasts. Sarah, A.P. and Maybelle performed two days a week, leaving the other three days for their daughters. The second year, performances were transcribed (an early recording technique) in the XERA engineer's basement studio and sent to other stations, giving the Carters their largest audience ever. Despite success, life in the barren countryside of Texas and the strain on A.P., who arranged every program, eventually became unbearable. After Sarah remarried in the winter of 1939, A.P. was distracted and distant. Ultimately, the work in Texas ended in 1940 due to a Mexican-American transmission agreement that affected XERA.

After the Carter Family recorded their final album together, it looked like the end for the Carter Family when Sarah moved to California in 1941 and avoided performing. But in 1942 she surprised everyone by accepting work with the band on WBT in Charlotte, North Carolina, one of the largest stations in the Southeast. Since Charlotte was one of the stops on Eck's Southern Railroad run as a mail clerk, the whole family moved. Sarah and A.P.'s children, **Gladys**, Jeanette, and Joe, made appearances with them

---

❧▶ **Carter, Helen** (1927–1998)

American musician who became known as the most capable instrumentalist of the Carter Sisters. Born Helen Myrl Carter in Maces Springs, Virginia, on September 12, 1927; died in Nashville, Tennessee, on June 2, 1998; first daughter of Maybelle and Ezra Carter; married Glen Jones, in 1950; children: Glen Daniel; Kenneth Burton; David Lawrence; Kevin Carter.

When the Carter Family made their first recordings in 1927, Maybelle Carter was eight months pregnant with Helen. Surrounded by music and musicians, Helen became proficient on the accordion, guitar, autoharp, piano and mandolin. She also sang and learned to write songs.

In 1950, Helen married pilot and inventor Glen Jones, with whom she would have four children, and signed with Tennessee Records. The most talented musician of Maybelle's three daughters, she had a hit as a songwriter in 1959 with "Poor Old Heartsick Me," but had the majority of her success working alongside her mother and sisters as part of the Carter Family and the Carter Sisters. Although Helen had the most stability away from the music of all the Carter Sisters, she was the least publicly known.

❧▶ **Carter, Jeanette** (1923—)

American musician who opened the Carter Family "Fold," a performance center in Maces Springs, Virginia, and the Carter Family Museum. Born Jeanette Carter in Maces Springs, Virginia, on July 2, 1923; middle daughter of Sarah Carter (1898–1979) and A.P. Carter; married and divorced twice; children: Dale, Don, Rita.

Jeanette Carter grew up surrounded by musicians and, at age four, accompanied the Carter Family on their historic trip to Bristol, southwestern Virginia, for their first recording session. She learned to sing, write songs and play the autoharp. By age 15, she became the first Carter Family sibling to perform on the radio. Jeanette occasionally played with, or filled in for, her aunt *Maybelle Carter, or her mother *Sarah Carter, and she began to perform as a soloist during the Carter Family radio broadcasts in 1938.

After her parents divorced and the Carter Family disbanded, Jeanette remained in Maces Springs. She wrote and recorded with her father A.P. when he attempted a comeback in the mid-1950s. After A.P. passed away in 1960, she also recorded a few songs on her own but without much success.

At age 51, Jeanette, who had promised her father that she would devote her life to the perpetuation of old-time music, converted A.P.'s old store into a "hoe-down" venue (1974), where up to 200 could gather for old-time country music playing and dancing. As the venue grew in popularity, her brother Joe built the "Fold," an outside theater overlooking the valley with seats for 400. The store was converted into the Carter Family Museum. In 1975, Jeanette sponsored the first Annual Carter Family Memorial Festival, held in Hiltons, Virginia.

Jesse T. Raiford

on the air. Maybelle's children went to school during the week and then joined the Saturday night shows. But when old tensions flared, the group rejected a contract renewal and disbanded for good. Sarah returned to California with her new husband Coy, A.P. went back to his cabin, and Maybelle, Eck, and their daughters returned to Scott County.

Historians call the Carter Family the first nationally prominent stars of country music. Lacking in self-promotion, the modest threesome became seminal country-music influences, later to be dubbed "patron saints of folk music" and "country music's first family." Performers as diverse as Bob Dylan, Woody Guthrie, Merle Haggard, Leadbelly, The Stanley Brothers, Hank Thompson, *Kitty Wells, *Dottie West, and Clarence White owe homage to the Carters. Bluegrass guitarist Lester Flatt compiled a commemorative album for Maybelle, who with Sarah did most of the picking and singing, assuming a forefront status in an age when bands relegated women to backup singing and accompanist roles. Folk artist **Joan Baez** began her ca-

reer singing Carter classics. Elvis Presley's "Are You Lonesome Tonight," The Kingston Trio's "Worried Man," Roy Acuff's "Wabash Cannonball," **Linda Ronstadt**'s "I Never Will Marry," **Emmylou Harris'** "Hello Stranger," and *Minnie Pearl's "Jealous Hearted Me" were all introduced first by the Carter Family. Ten years before Bill Monroe invented bluegrass, Maybelle was strumming the standard guitar rhythms, and the Carters were singing the essential bluegrass vocal harmony foundations. Carter Family songs remain gospel standards.

The Carter's collective works exceed 250 recorded songs. Famous songs first written or popularized by the family include: "Keep on the Sunny Side," "I'm Thinking Tonight of My Blue Eyes," "John Hardy," "Gold Watch and Chain," "Lonesome Valley," "Cowboy Jack," "Engine 143," "Foggy Mountain Top," "My Heart's Tonight in Texas," "Black Jack David," "Rambling Boy," "Bury Me Beneath the Weeping Willow," "Coal Miner's Blues," "You Are My Flower," and "I Have No One to Love Me."

June, Maybelle, Anita, and Helen Carter.

After the Carter Family disbanded, Maybelle was still not through with show business. After six-months' vacation, Eck encouraged Maybelle, who missed the music, to return to the stage. Maybelle and her daughters abandoned old-time music for an all-female format. Instead of Maybelle and the staid Sarah in straight-back chairs with A.P. standing behind to introduce songs, Mother Maybelle & the Carter Sisters added comedy, a dance routine, and pop songs to the mix of Carter Family classics. Maybelle's easygoing personality and keen sense of humor added to the act. Helen sometimes played the accordion; Anita, on bass, occasionally stood on her head; and June "hoofed away," doing what she called "one of the silliest looking vaudeville jigs that a girl could ever do."

The daughters' first public appearance had been on the WOPI radio program "Popeye Club" in 1937, when Anita was just four, singing "Beautiful Brown Eyes." The three sisters gained experience on the radio in Mexico, but June remembered touring and working live audiences as the influences that taught them to be performers. In 1943, Maybelle assumed A.P.'s role, booking shows, fixing flat tires, sometimes driving through the night. Her daughters bounced between states and schools, while the concerts helped land radio offers.

Mother Maybelle & the Carter Sisters first appeared on WRNL and then the Old Dominion Barn Dance on WRVA in Richmond, Virginia. June blossomed on WRVA and developed as a comedian. When they moved to WNOX in Knoxville, Tennessee, in 1948, Eck quit to work full time with his wife and daughters. The same year, they released their first record, "The Kneeling Drunkard's Pleas." In 1949, they moved to the Ozark Jubilee in Springfield, Missouri, where they reached huge audiences on Si Siman's KWTO. The group briefly turned to gospel music, but June and Anita's public divorces made it difficult to maintain a full-time repertoire of religious music, despite the wholesome, country sweetheart image they maintained on stage.

By the late 1940s, the Carter Sisters were known throughout the country. As the family Packard traveled as far as Bakersfield, California, Maybelle wrote songs and rearranged country music standards. Their success led to an invitation that Maybelle considered the high point of her career: in 1950, they joined the Grand Ole Opry, which was by then the Mecca of country music.

In 1952, host *Kate Smith introduced the Carter Sisters on the first national country music television show. During the same year, A.P. Carter, with his son Joe and daughter Jeanette, formed a new Carter Family band and opened an outdoor arena in Maces Springs. They played together until 1956 but, unlike the Carter Sisters, were unable to adapt to the expanded business of country music that ironically A.P. had helped pioneer.

In 1956 and 1957, Mother Maybelle & the Carter Sisters toured as the opening act for Elvis Presley. When A.P. died in 1960, they reclaimed the Carter Family name, recorded for Decca, and then had several hits for Columbia. In 1961, Maybelle, Anita, and Helen joined June in a limited association with Johnny Cash. They backed up Cash on the 1963 hit "Busted" and had a top-40 success with "A Song to Momma," narrated by Cash.

Maybelle's popularity increased as folk music became popular in the 1960s. She toured campuses and concert halls on the folk circuit and headlined at the Newport Folk Festival in 1963. Maybelle also talked Sarah into recording the album "An Historic Reunion" in 1966, and the following year Sarah joined Maybelle at the Newport Folk Festival. In 1967, the group left the Opry to join sister June on ABC television's *The Johnny Cash Show* and stayed until 1969. In 1970, Maybelle, Sarah, and A.P. were inducted into the Country Music Hall of Fame.

The following year, Merle Haggard invited the Carters to perform along with **Bonnie Owens** on his double album "Land of Many Churches." Also in 1971, Maybelle played a major role on a record that united musicians from different camps and brought traditional country and bluegrass music to a new urban audience. The concept album borrowed its title, "Will The Circle Be Unbroken," from a famous Carter Family song. Released during the early 1970s, the successful triple album appeared in stores at a time when the Vietnam War, the civil-rights movement, and campus unrest polarized America. The media took note as long-haired, liberal California musicians and conservative Southern musicians warmed to each other in the studio.

In 1972, the Carter Family had a top-50 hit, "Travelin' Minstrel Band," and a top-40 single, "The World Needs a Melody." The following year, working with Cash and the Oak Ridge Boys, they had their last country chart entry, "Praise the Lord and Pass the Soup." At age 64, Maybelle, a living legend in the world of bluegrass and folk music, became the oldest woman listed on the national country charts. Throughout her life, as the world and the music business changed, Maybelle maintained her country ways, smiling disposition, and intense love of music. Her spirit lingers in the oldest Carter Family 78's and colors modern renditions of Carter Family songs by new artists. "God, the first time I heard the Carters sing 'Gold Watch and Chain,'" said Emmylou Harris, "I thought about my grandparents and I cried."

In the mid-1970s, Maybelle began to suffer from arthritis and a form of Parkinson's disease. In 1976, she missed a note on the autoharp and never again played it in public. Her final public appearance was with Sarah at the Carter Family Reunion at Jeanette Carter's "Fold," an outdoor stage in the mountains of Southern Virginia, not far from where Carter music first echoed among the hills. Maybelle Carter died at the age of 69, on October 23, 1978.

Helen and Anita continued to tour as the Carter Family. In 1980, MCN named them Gospel "Act of the Year" at the Cover awards. In 1988, along with Maybelle's granddaughter ❧▶ **Carlene Carter**, they recorded Maybelle's most famous song, "Wildwood Flower," on Mercury. In June of 1992, they appeared on the Nitty Gritty Dirt Band's "Will the Circle Be Unbroken, Vol. 2" and received Gold Records for their contributions.

SOURCES:

Artis, Bob. *Bluegrass.* NY: Hawthorne Books, 1975.

Brown, Charles T. *Music USA: America's Country & Western Tradition.* NJ: Prentice-Hall, 1986.

Bufwack, Mary A., and Robert K. Oermann. *Finding Her Voice: An Illustrated History of Women in Country Music.* NY: Henry Holt, 1993.

Byworth, Tony. *The History of Country & Western Music.* NY: Exeter Books, 1984.

❧▶ Carter, Carlene (1955—)

American rock and country music singer, songwriter, guitar and piano player who was heir to the Carter Family legacy. Born Rebecca Carlene Smith in Madison, Tennessee, September 26, 1955; daughter of June Carter Cash (b. 1929) and Carl Smith; stepsister of Rosanne Cash (1955—); married Joe Simpkins, in 1970 (divorced); married Jack Routh, in 1974 (divorced); married Nick Lowe, in 1979 (divorced); children: Tiffany and Jackson.

Carlene Carter was born Rebecca Carlene Smith in Madison, Tennessee, in 1955. Her parents, *June Carter (Cash) and honky-tonk star Carl Smith, divorced when Carlene was two. Her mother married Rip Nix, a wealthy contractor, when Carlene was six, but they soon divorced; she then married country music superstar Johnny Cash when Carlene was 12. Carlene hated growing up in the spotlight. While tour groups stopped to gaze at her house, family indiscretions made the tabloids. Dropping out of high school at age 15 to become a teenage mother, Carlene married and divorced twice before turning 20. The wilder side of her early career was reportedly urged on by cocaine. "I was caught up in that southern-woman idea that once you had your man, then your life was figured out," she said. "Then one day it dawned on me that my life is what I make it."

Although Carlene rebelled against the family fame, she absorbed the stagecraft and the music that was her legacy. She first appeared on stage at the age of four, singing with her half sister **Rosie Nix** and with four of Johnny Cash's daughters, including **Rosanne Cash.** For a short time, Carlene sang the Coasters' rock-and-roll classic "Charlie Brown" in the family road show. She began playing piano at age six, studied classical music, and, at age ten, started strumming the guitar after instructions from her grandmother *Maybelle Carter. At age 17, Carlene and Maybelle sang before an audience of over 10,000 in Morgantown, West Virginia. Carlene was close to her upbeat grandmother and was inspired by Maybelle's love of, and dedication to, her music.

In 1977, Carlene recorded her first album, a collection of piano-based pop songs performed with Graham Parker's former band Rumor. Two years later, she married rock star Nick Lowe. Her next two albums were *Two Sides of Every Woman* (1979) and *Musical Shapes* (1980). Critics praised the single "Musical Shapes," calling it a "fusion of rock and country." Carlene followed with the albums *Blue Nun* (1981) and *C'est C Bon* (1983), neither of which fared well.

In 1985, the same year that Carlene appeared in the London version of the Broadway show *Pump Boys and Dinettes,* the Carter Family toured England. When Anita couldn't perform because of an illness, Carlene filled in. Her marriage to Nick Lowe folded, and in 1987 and 1988 she toured regularly with the Carter Family. Eventually, her music style turned from rock-and-roll back to her country roots.

In 1988, Carlene moved in with Howie Epstein, a successful record producer and member of Tom Petty's band, the Heartbreakers. Epstein produced her album *I Fell in Love* in 1990, a highly successful and pivotal country album for which Carlene co-wrote most of the songs, as well as *Little Love Letters* in 1993. In 1994, she appeared on the soundtrack of the feature film *Maverick* and in 1995 released *Little Acts of Treason.*

Jesse T. Raiford

Cantwell, Robert. *Bluegrass Breakdown: The Making of the Old Southern Sound.* Chicago: University of Illinois Press, 1984.

Hagen, Chet. *Grand Ole Opry.* NY: Henry Holt, 1989.

Kingsbury, Paul. *The Country Music Foundation's Country: The Music and the Musicians.* NY: Cross River Press, 1988.

Krishef, Robert K. *The Carter Family.* Minneapolis, MN: Lerner, 1978.

Mason, Michael. *The Country Music Book.* NY: Scribner, 1985.

McCloud, Barry. *Definitive Country: The Ultimate Encyclopedia of Country Music and Its Performers.* NY: Berkely, 1995.

Orgill, Michael. *Anchored In Love: The Carter Family Story.* Old Tappan, NJ: Fleming H. Revell, 1975.

Rosenberg, Neil V. *Blue Grass: A History.* Chicago: University of Illinois Press, 1985.

Jesse T. Raiford,
President of Raiford Communications, Inc., New York City

Carter, Rosalynn (1927—)

American first lady from 1977 to 1981. Born Eleanor Rosalynn Smith on August 18, 1927, in Plains, Georgia; oldest of four children of Wilburn Edgar (an auto mechanic) and Frances Alletta (Murray) Smith (a seamstress); attended Georgia Southwestern College; married James Earl Carter, known as Jimmy Carter (president of the United States), on July 7, 1946, in Plains, Georgia; children: John (b. 1947); James Earl III, known as Chip (b. 1950); Donnel Jeffrey (b. 1952); Amy Carter (b. 1967).

Rosalynn Eleanor Smith and Jimmy Carter grew up three miles apart in Plains, Georgia, a small hardworking community where religious dedication and community service were the way of life. When Rosalynn was 13, her father died after a long bout with leukemia, leaving her mother **Allie Smith** with four young children to support. While Allie went to work in the post office and took in sewing, Rosalynn, the eldest, helped with the younger children and earned extra money working in the local beauty parlor giving shampoos. Rosalynn was valedictorian of the Plains High School class of 1944 and briefly commuted to Georgia Southwestern College, where she was president of her sophomore class. She is said to have fallen in love with a photograph of Jimmy Carter even before his sister **Ruth Carter** arranged for the two to meet when he was home on leave from Annapolis Naval Academy. The two wed in an informal ceremony shortly after his graduation, and Rosalynn, barely 18, embarked on a new life as a navy wife.

For over seven years, each spent in a different city, Rosalynn juggled households and three young sons, while her husband was away at sea.

Relishing her new-found independence, she was hard-pressed to give it up when Jimmy decided to leave the navy after his father's death and return home to run the family peanut business. With his brother Billy still in high school, Jimmy saw himself as the only one to carry on his father's lifelong work. Rosalynn adamantly opposed the move, and they made an interminably silent trip back to Plains. It was the first real crisis of the marriage, and Rosalynn experienced a difficult period of adjustment before she resigned herself to life in her hometown. Gradually adopting the business as her own, she worked long hours beside her husband to turn a profit (the first year brought in only $254); she also studied accounting in order to take over the bookkeeping and tax preparation. Any spare time was filled with children, church, and community activities.

Jimmy Carter's political career began in 1962 with a successful run for a Georgia state senate seat. While her husband stumped county to county, Rosalynn both ran the warehouse and campaigned, making phone calls and door-to-door visits. Four years later, his 1966 run for Congress suddenly shifted to a gubernatorial race when the Democratic candidate dropped out due to illness. During this difficult and sometimes dangerous period in Georgia's history, the state was struggling with approaching integration, and Jimmy Carter's liberal views were not popular. He was defeated by Lester Maddox, a staunch segregationist. The disappointment of her husband's loss would remain with Rosalynn a long time.

With plans for a second run for governor underway a month later, Rosalynn found herself pregnant again at age 40. A much hoped for daughter, Amy Lynn, was born in October 1967. The family was further surprised by news that Carter's unpredictable and colorful mother, **Lillian Carter** ("Miss Lillian"), was joining the Peace Corps at age 68 and would travel to India to assist in a family-planning program.

In 1970, the formally announced campaign that would land Jimmy the governor's seat was underway and demanded Rosalynn's full-time attention. Reluctantly, she left Amy behind to go on the road. Rosalynn overcame her retiring nature to make campaign appearances at factories, livestock sales, rodeos, and even a rattlesnake roundup. With an eye toward practicality, she started her day at fire stations because the food was good, and she learned to double back to the last appearance to pick up discarded campaign literature so it could be recycled.

Rosalynn Carter

Religious faith had always guided the Carters' lives. After his first unsuccessful run for governor, Jimmy had an intimate conversation with his sister Ruth Carter, who devoted her life to Christian work, and decided, "her much deeper religious life and convictions were what he wanted and needed." During the 1976 campaign, his effort to reaffirm his faith was widely reported as Jimmy Carter's "born again" experience, which Rosalynn maintained was overblown by reporters who did not know what "born again" meant.

Rosalynn also credited a profound renewal of her own faith for helping her through the difficult transition from a simple life in Plains to a public life as first lady of Georgia; her beliefs allowed her to accept the new responsibilities on her own terms while releasing many of the pressures and demands that made her feel frustrated and trapped. As her new outlook brought some order to her busy day-to-day life in the governor's mansion, she worked on projects she regarded as particularly important in Georgia. Appointed to the Governor's Commission to Improve Services for the Mentally and Emotionally Handicapped, she visited every mental health facility in the state. She also acted as honorary chair of the state's Special Olympics and worked with *Lady Bird Johnson to start the Georgia Highway Wildflower Program. Rosalynn pushed for passage of the Equal Rights Amendment in Georgia and for judicial reforms for women prisoners.

Since Georgia law prevented Jimmy from succeeding himself as governor, in 1975 he announced to the family that he would run for the presidency. Rosalynn, now a seasoned campaigner, took the decision in stride, though she knew it would be an uphill struggle. She served as an advisor, wrote and delivered speeches, helped make staff decisions, and traveled independently in 40 states in order to double the campaign mileage. During one junket, her luggage and best wig were stolen, and she was forced to wear the same outfit for days in a row, washing it out nightly in her hotel room. It was during this 1976 campaign that one reporter referred to her as the "steel magnolia," a name that stuck. The election of outsider Jimmy Carter as president was somewhat of a political miracle. On the brink of his victory, the world was still asking "Jimmy Who?"

The Carters, ever mindful of their humble beginnings, were the first to walk the one-and-a-half miles back to the White House after the inauguration, and that evening Rosalynn wore the same dress she had worn to Jimmy's inauguration ball as governor. She chose the Thaddeus Stevens School for Amy to attend, the first public school for a presidential child since 1906. As first lady, Rosalynn continued to function as a full partner with her husband, acting as his emissary on an unprecedented trip to Latin America. She was also Jimmy's envoy to the Cambodian refugee camps. She toured Central and South America, met the pope in Rome, and attended the inauguration of President Jose Lopez Portillo of Mexico. Like *Eleanor Roosevelt before her,

Rosalynn was often considered too influential and powerful. Her attendance at Cabinet meetings, though at her husband's invitation, drew particular criticism.

Using her influence as first lady, Rosalynn was anxious to continue her work in the area of mental health. When the president signed the Executive Order creating the President's Commission on Mental Health, she became honorary chair. The work of the commission resulted in the 1980 Mental Health Systems Act, which was passed and funded by Congress to become the first major reform of federal publicly funded mental-health programs since the Community Mental Health Centers Act of 1963. Included in the Systems Act were provisions for housing, insurance coverage, distribution of mental-health personnel, advocacy for mental patients, research and professional recruitment. Rosalynn was also deeply committed to the Equal Rights Amendment and was enormously disappointed that it failed to be ratified during her tenure.

With another campaign on the horizon, Rosalynn was confident that her husband would be elected to another term. Even when the Iranian unrest erupted on November 4, 1979, and 50 Americans were taken hostage at the American Embassy in Iran, she held fast to her belief that Americans would not be taken in by the rhetoric of the Republican nominee, Ronald Reagan. The hostage situation, however, stretched into 444 days, preventing President Carter from campaigning and setting the stage for defeat. Rosalynn felt strongly that her husband had been victimized by the crisis, and she had difficulty overcoming her bitterness at the loss. The day after the inauguration of Reagan, Jimmy Carter flew to Wiesbaden to welcome the hostages back to freedom. For a number of years, Rosalynn would long to return to the world of politics. "Nothing is more thrilling," she wrote, "than the urgency of a campaign—the planning, the strategy sessions, getting out among people you'd never otherwise meet—and the tremendous energy it takes that makes a victory ever so sweet and a loss so devastating."

Back home in Plains, Georgia, the Carters became active in the Habitat for Humanity housing campaign and the Friendship Force, a group that promotes friendship around the world. Rosalynn keeps an office in the Jimmy Carter Presidential Center in Atlanta, Georgia, a nonprofit institution founded in 1982, where she created the Carter Center's Mental Health Task Force, an advisory body that promotes positive change in the mental-health field, which she chairs. She also hosts a yearly symposium on Mental Health Policy, bringing together leaders of the nation's mental-health organizations to address critical issues. In 1991, with **Betty Bumpers** (wife of U.S. Senator Dale Bumpers of Arkansas), Rosalynn launched a nationwide campaign to publicize the need for early childhood immunizations.

In 1984, Rosalynn completed her autobiography, *First Lady from Plains,* which was followed in 1987 by a book co-authored with her husband, *Everything to Gain: Making the Most of the Rest of Your Life.* She published a solo book on the subject of care giving, *Helping Yourself Help Others,* in 1995.

SOURCES:
Carter, Rosalynn. *First Lady from Plains.* Boston, MA: Houghton Mifflin, 1984.
Melick, Arden David. *Wives of the Presidents.* Maplewood, NJ: Hammond, 1977.
Paletta, LuAnn. *The World Almanac of First Ladies.* NY: World Almanac, 1990.

SUGGESTED READING:
Carter, Rosalynn. *Helping Yourself Help Others.* NY: Random House, 1995.

Barbara Morgan,
Melrose, Massachusetts

Carter, Sarah (1898–1979).

See Carter, Maybelle for sidebar.

Carter, Violet Bonham (1887–1969).

See Bonham-Carter, Violet.

Cartimandua (fl. 43–69 CE)

Queen of the Brigantes in central Britain and a Roman ally. Name variations: Cartamandia; Cartumandia. Pronunciation: Car-ti-man-DOO-ah. Dates of birth and death unknown; married Venutius (divorced); married Vellocatus.

Ruled Brigantes probably from 43 CE; handed over the British chieftain Caratacus to the Romans (51); divorced her husband Venutius and married Vellocatus; overthrown by Venutius and sought refuge with the Romans (69).

Knowledge of Queen Cartimandua has come down to us from the Roman historian Tacitus, complete with his male and imperialist prejudices. He relates her role in native British affairs from 51 to 69 CE in three separate accounts. The first, in the *Annals* (12. 36), he briefly mentions that in 51 she handed over to the Romans the defeated British chieftain Caratacus, who had sought refuge with the Brigantes. The second account a few chapters later (12. 40)

tells us that Cartimandua's husband, Venutius, had long been a Roman ally because of his marriage to her. A divorce between the two soon led to civil war among the Brigantes. When Cartimandua detained his brother and other relatives, Venutius sent a band of picked troops into her territory and the Romans were forced to intervene. Tacitus notes that Venutius' followers did not want to be ruled by a woman (12. 40. 3).

Tacitus' third account is found in his *Histories,* which describes the struggle for succession in the Roman empire after the death of Nero in 68. His portrait here of Cartimandua becomes less than flattering. Tacitus informs us that when Venutius took advantage of the civil war in Rome to stage a revolt, he was motivated not only by hatred for the Romans, but by a desire for revenge against Cartimandua. Tacitus writes that her betrayal of Caratacus (which, he adds here, was done by a trick) had "adorned the triumphal parade of Claudius Caesar" (an event that he reports in some detail in the *Annals*) and that resources and wealth—from her association with Rome, it is implied—had corrupted her. He mentions that she was already powerful in social standing and that she now sought to extend her rule. Divorcing Venutius, she married his armor-bearer Vellocatus and shared the throne with him. According to Tacitus, this was a moral crime that shook her rule. Venutius found backing among the Brigantes while Vellocatus had only Cartimandua's lust and savagery to support him. As in the *Annals,* Tacitus mentions an invasion by Venutius' forces and a Roman intervention. The Romans were able to save Cartimandua but not her kingdom: rule passed to Venutius.

Tacitus' account has cast the actions of this Celtic queen from a Roman mold. It is highly likely that Cartimandua's divorce and remarriage were political, as well as personal, decisions. In Latin, the term for Vellocatus, armor-bearer (*armigerum* [*Histories* 3. 45]), has connotations of slavery. For a Roman wife to reject her husband and marry a slave or a free, poor man would have indeed been, to the Roman upper crust, a moral crime. But this does not necessarily mean that Vellocatus occupied such a low status among the Brigantes; the social position of such a person in Brigantine society is unclear. Tacitus' references to the lust and savagery of the queen is in keeping with the way he (and other Roman historians) depict women in general. Indeed, women whom he does not describe with these characteristics receive scant attention in his works.

As to the desire of the Brigantes not to be ruled by a woman, this may well reflect Tacitus' feelings about the conduct of powerful women in the imperial family more than it reflects a reality of Celtic Britain. It was, after all, a woman, *Boudica, who led the famous revolt against the Romans (*Annals* 14. 31, 35, 37). Tacitus has Boudica say: "It is customary for we Britons to fight under the leadership of women" (12. 35. 1). In his monograph on the Roman general Agricola, he says that the Britons made no distinction between men and women in military command (*Agricola* 16). Finally, Tacitus has the British chieftain Calgacus brag that the Brigantes burned a Roman colony and stormed a Roman camp under the leadership of an unnamed woman between 71 and 83 CE.

Cartumandia tuke Caratacus, the King of Scottis, with tressoun in hir awain place, and delyuerit him to Ostorius, the Roman legat.

—The Buik of the Croniclis of Scotland

Aside from Tacitus, little is certain about Cartimandua. She seems to have ruled the Brigantes from at least 43 CE. We know that the Brigantes were the most important buffer for the Romans between the British lowlands and unconquered highlands of modern Scotland. Cartimandua's territory appears to have stretched from coast to coast and to have included areas of what is now northern England such as Manchester, Leeds, and Newcastle-upon-Tyne and a part of Yorkshire.

Cartimandua lived on in British literature for centuries. In the medieval Welsh collection of poetry known as the *Triads*, she is worked into Arthurian legend and is equated with one Aregwedd Foeddawg who is generally considered a deceitful Roman collaborator. In the *Buik of the Croniclis of Scotland* composed in 1535 for the instruction of the future King James, she is "this wickit woman" who sells Caratacus to the Romans. Her motivation is to rule Brigantia in peace. When her husband Venutius revolts, she throws him and his family into prison. After he is freed, Venutius seeks revenge and burns Cartimandua to death. *The Croniclis* refers to Tacitus as a source. Finally, in 1759 William Mason published his successful tragedy *Caratacus*, which featured Cartimandua's sons.

SOURCES:

Boece, Hector. *The Buik of the Croniclis of Scotland: Rerum Britannicarum Medii Aevi Scriptores.* Edited by William B. Turnball. Vol. 1, no. 6. London: Longman, Brown, 1858.

Bromwich, Rachel, ed. *Trioedd Ynys Prydein: The Welsh Triads.* Cardiff: University of Wales Press, 1978.

Tacitus. *Annals* 12. 36, 40; *Histories* 3. 45

SUGGESTED READING:

Casson, T.E. "Cartimandua, in History, Legend and Romance," in *Transactions of the Cumberland and Westmoreland Antiquitarian and Archaeological Society.* Vol. 44, 1945, pp. 68–80.

Richmond, I.A. "Queen Cartimandua," in *Journal of Roman Studies.* Vol. 44, 1954, pp. 127–60.

Webster, Graham. *Rome Against Caratacus: The Roman Campaigns in Britain AD 48–58.* Totowa, NJ: Barnes and Noble, 1981.

Alexander Ingle,
Department of Classical Studies,
Boston University, Boston, Massachusetts

Cartland, Barbara (b. 1901)

*British popular novelist. Name variations: Dame Barbara Cartland; Barbara McCorquodale. Born in Edgbaston, Birmingham, England, on July 9, 1901; daughter of Bertram Cartland (a major in the Worcestershire regiment) and Polly (Scobell) Cartland; attended Malvern Girls' College and Abbey House, Netley Abbey, Hampshire, England; married Alexander George McCorquodale, in 1927 (divorced 1933); married Hugh McCorquodale, on December 28, 1936 (died, December 29, 1963); children: (first marriage) Raine McCorquodale (who upon marriage became Countess Spencer and the stepmother of *Diana Spencer, Princess of Wales); (second marriage) Ian and Glen.*

Awards: Gold Medal of the City of Paris for Achievement (1988), for selling 25 million books in France; Dame of the Order of the British Empire (1991).

Destined to see over 600 million copies of her novels in print, Barbara Cartland began her career writing for the *Daily Express* as a gossip columnist. After publication of her first novel, *Jigsaw,* in 1925, Cartland went on to become a prolific author of romance novels who brought readers stories of fairy-tale love set against 19th-century backdrops. Though her plots have been called repetitive and highly unrealistic by detractors, the popularity of her work is undeniable, a fact attested to by her citation in the *Guinness Book of World Records* as the bestselling author in the world.

In addition to her romantic fiction—works like *The Ruthless Rake* (1975), *The Penniless Peer* (1976) and *The Cruel Count* (1976)—Cartland published several volumes of autobiography, including *We Danced All Night 1919–1929* (1971) and *I Search for Rainbows* (1967). She also authored fictionalized historical biographies, including *The Private Life of Elizabeth Empress of Austria* (1959), *The Private Life of Charles II: The Women He Loved* (1958), and *Josephine, Empress of France* (1961). Her advice books, which espouse ideas about the "inferior" social role of women as well as ideas on women's infidelity, have met with controversy. Among these works are *Love, Life and Sex* (1957), *The Etiquette Book* (1962), *Look Lovely, Be Lovely* (1958) and *Barbara Cartland's Book of Beauty and Health* (1971).

Known to write an average of 23 books a year, Cartland traveled the world searching for exotic settings for her stories. She has lent her voice to a number of charitable causes and to England's Conservative Party. In 1991, she was created Dame of the British Empire.

SUGGESTED READING:

Cartland, Barbara. *I Reach for the Stars: An Autobiography.* Parkwest, 1995.

Cartumandia (fl. 43–69 CE).

See Cartimandua.

Carus-Wilson, Eleanora Mary

(1897–1977)

English medieval economic historian. Born Eleanora Mary Carus-Wilson on December 27, 1897, in Mon-

Barbara Cartland

*treal, Canada; died in 1977; daughter of **Mary L.G. (Petrie) Carus-Wilson** and Ashley Carus-Wilson (professor of electrical engineering at McGill University, Montreal); attended St. Paul's Girls' School; Westfield College, London, B.A., 1921, M.A., 1926.*

Eleanora Carus-Wilson began her impressive academic career at her alma mater, London's Westfield College, where she was a part-time lecturer and did research under *Eileen Power. During the war years, 1939–1945, she worked in the Ministry of Food, after which she joined the London School of Economics, becoming a professor of economic history in 1948. From 1953 to 1965, Carus-Wilson was at London University, where she carried out a major study in medieval trade. From 1964 to 1965, she was a Ford's lecturer in English history at Oxford.

Carus-Wilson's publications include *England's Export Trade 1275–1547* (1963), written in collaboration with her pupil, **Olive Coleman**. She also contributed a chapter on the cloth industry to *Cambridge Economic History of Europe* (Vol. II, 1952) and authored a controversial article titled "An Industrial Revolution of the Thirteenth Century" for the *Economic History Review* (Vol. XI, 1941). In addition to her academic duties, Carus-Wilson served as president of both the Economic History Society and the Society of Medieval Archaeology (1966–69). She was awarded an honorary LL.D. from Smith College in 1968 and became an honorary fellow, LSE, in 1969. She also served as a governor of Westfield College and as president of the Westfield College Association.

Carvajal, Luisa de (1568–1614)

Portuguese missionary who worked in England. Name variations: Carvajal de Mendoza. Born at Jaraicejo in Estremadura, Portugal, on January 2, 1568; died in London, England, on January 2, 1614; daughter of Francisco de Carvajal (a Portuguese aristocrat) and Maria de Mendoza; never married; no children.

Luisa de Carvajal was born into a wealthy, pious, aristocratic family of Portugal. In 1572, her mother contracted a fever while visiting the poor and both her parents died of it. Orphaned, Luisa and her brother were taken in by their great aunt **Maria Chacon**, governess of the young children of Philip II, king of Spain and soon to be king of Portugal. When Chacon died, they lived with their maternal uncle, Francisco Hurtado de Mendoza, count of Almazan. The count, who was named viceroy of Navarre by Philip II, was an able public servant in whom religious zeal was carried to the point of inhuman asceticism. Under his tutelage, Luisa showed signs of a religious calling of her own and, even as a girl, practiced some of the mortifications her uncle practiced. She often went without eating. When Luisa was 17, her uncle instructed her to surrender her will to two female servants whom he set over her, and by whom she was repeatedly scourged while naked, trampled upon and otherwise ill-treated.

When she reached adulthood, Luisa refused to enter a religious house. Instead, she decided to dedicate her life to the conversion of England back to the Catholic faith. The execution of the Jesuit emissary priest, Henry Walpole, in 1596 had moved her deeply. This was an era of great spiritual upheaval in England, which under the reign of *Elizabeth I was outwardly Protestant but facing a counter-reformation from its Catholic adherents. In Portugal, Luisa spent many years studying English and theology to prepare herself. She devoted her share of the family inheritance to found a college at Louvain for English Jesuits (transferred to Watten near Saint Omer in 1612, the college survived until the suppression of the Order). In 1605, at age 37, she was finally allowed to move to England. Initially, she worked from the house of the Spanish ambassador, another Catholic who supported her efforts. A highly visible missionary, Luisa worked among London's poor to win converts while acting as midwife and nurse to many in order to win their confidence. Her remarkable success led the English authorities to arrest her in 1608, although she was soon released on orders of King James I himself, who wanted to maintain good relations with Spain.

After her release, Luisa established an underground nunnery at Spitalfields. Again, she was under the watch of the English authorities, and in 1613 she was arrested by the archbishop of Canterbury. Similarly, she was quickly released, but this time she was not allowed to resume her missionary work. The Portuguese government (ruled by Spain from 1580 to 1640), having determined that Luisa posed a threat to Spanish-English relations, recalled her to Portugal immediately following her release. Infuriated by the order, Luisa refused to leave England. How that conflict might have been played out is unknown, as Luisa died in the Spanish ambassador's house on her birthday, January 2, 1614, at age 46, before any further actions could be taken by the Portuguese authorities. Luisa de Carvajal's body remained on display in England for several months before being returned to Portugal for burial. In Madrid during 1632, *La Vida y Virtudes de la Venerable Virgen Doña Luisa de Carvajal y Mendoza* by the Licentiate Lorenzo Muñoz appeared. This work was founded on her own papers, which were collected by Michael Walpole, her English confessor.

Laura York,
Riverside, California

Carvalho, Dinora de (1905—)

Brazilian composer, conductor, pianist, and professor who founded the Women's Orchestra of São Paulo and wrote many pieces for orchestra. Name variations: Dinora Gontijo de Carvalho Murici. Born in Uberaba, Minas Gerais, Brazil, on June 1, 1905; daughter of Vincente Gontijo (a musician); studied with Maria Machado, Carlino Crescenzo, Francesco Franceshini, Martin Braunwieser.

Dinora de Carvalho was admitted to the São Paulo Conservatory at age six to study piano under **Maria Machado** and Carlino Crescenzo. At age seven, she gave her first piano recital and wrote her first composition, a valse entitled *Serenata ão Luar,* as well as a piano nocturne. Her success as a concert pianist won her a scholarship in Europe where she studied with Isidor Philipp. Returning to Brazil in 1929, she studied with Lamberto Baldi and Martin Braunwieser. In 1939, Carvalho was nominated federal inspector for advanced music education at the São Paulo Conservatory. That same year, she established the Women's Orchestra of São Paulo, the first of its kind in South America. She also directed this orchestra. Throughout her career, Carvalho continued to compose and in 1960 the Municipal Theater of São Paulo sponsored the Dinora de Carvalho Festival in which many of her compositions were played. She was the first woman to be nominated to the Brazilian Academy of Music.

John Haag,
Athens, Georgia

Carvalho, Marie (1827–1895).

See Miolan-Carvalho, Marie.

Carven (b. 1909)

French fashion designer. Name variations: Carven Grog. Born Carmen Tommaso in Chateauroux, France, in 1909.

At age 87, French fashion designer Carven was awarded France's highest recognition, Officer of the Legion of Honor. Said Culture Minister Philippe Douste-Blazy at the ceremony, "Sorry this is so late in coming." Carven, born Carmen Tommaso, opened her fashion house on the Champs-Élysees in 1944; the five-foot-tall Carven specialized in clothes for the petite woman.

Cary, Alice (1820–1871)

*American poet and short story writer who hosted a popular New York literary salon for 15 years. Name variations: Patty Lee. Born Alice Patty Lee Cary on April 26, 1820, in Mount Healthy, near Cincinnati, Ohio; died on February 12, 1871, in New York, New York; daughter of Elizabeth (Jessup) and Robert Cary; sister of poet **Phoebe Cary** (1824–1871); educated at home; never married; no children.*

Selected works: Lyra *(1852);* Poems *(1855);* Ballads, Lyrics, Hymns *(1866);* Lover's Diary *(1868);* Clovernook Sketches *(1987);* Poetical Works of Alice and Phoebe Cary *(1886).*

Alice Cary was born in Mount Healthy, Ohio, in 1820, the fourth of Robert and **Elizabeth Cary**'s eight children. By 1836, she had lost her mother and three older siblings, including her closest companion Rhoda, and by age 17 was in charge of the Ohio farm house and her four younger brothers and sisters. The loss of her sister Rhoda, who had shared Alice's passion for stories and writing, made the demands of farm life even harder. Together the sisters had read and reread the family's six books (including a Bible and a cookbook). The largely self-educated Cary was further isolated when her father remarried and moved with his wife to a new house, leaving Alice to govern the family.

Cary began submitting her poetry to local papers, and "The Child of Sorrow" (1838) in Cincinnati's Universalist newspaper, *Sentinel,* was her first publication. For ten years, her work was widely printed and read locally, always without payment. Editors Rufus Griswold, an arbiter of American verse, and Gamahiel Bailey helped bring Cary and her poet

Alice Cary

sister *Phoebe Cary to national readership in 1849; they also saw to it that the sisters began receiving payment for their work.

In the summer of 1850, Cary made her first trip East, visiting New York and Massachusetts. In November, she moved to Manhattan permanently. It is believed that she was drawn to the city in part by a romance with Griswold; however, Cary also knew New York as a literary hub. She rented a house on East 22nd Street, and in the spring of 1851 Phoebe and their younger sister **Elmina** joined her. Elmina's death in 1862 was another emotional blow for Cary. Although she had the weakest bond with Phoebe, the sister with whom she would remain the longest, the two worked together in what has been described as "unbroken partnership."

In 1868–69, Alice served as the earliest president of Sorosis, the first professional woman's club organized in New York. Cary began regular publication in magazines (*National Magazine, Atlantic Monthly, National Era*) and in anthologies that were sufficient to support the household. She bought the East 22nd Street home and began inviting a literary circle home for Sunday-evening gatherings. Her salon existed for 15 years. Alice Cary always signed her pieces, an uncommon practice for women at the time. Her work includes prose sketches and novels, now almost forgotten, and volumes of verse; her lyrical poem *Pictures of Memory* was greatly admired by Edgar Allan Poe. In late 1869, Cary suffered an illness that left her paralyzed and in constant pain. Phoebe cared for her until Alice's death at home on February 12, 1871. She was buried at Greenwood Cemetery.

Crista Martin,
Boston, Massachusetts

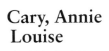

Annie
Louise
Cary

Cary, Annie Louise

(1841–1921)

*American contralto. Born Ann Louisa Cary in Wayne, Maine, on October 22, 1841; died in Norwalk, Connecticut, on April 3, 1921; grew up in Yarmouth and Gorham; graduated from Gorham Seminary, 1860; studied in Milan under Giovanni Corsi; studied with *Pauline Viar-*

dot in Baden-Baden and Giovanni Bottesini in Paris; married Charles M. Raymond (a New York banker), in 1882.

Made her debut as an operatic contralto in Copenhagen (1868); made her London debut at Covent Garden in Donizetti's Lucrezia Borgia *(1870); appeared in the American premieres of Verdi's* Requiem *(1874), Bach's* Magnificat *(1875) and Christmas Oratorio *(1877), and Boito's* Mefistofele *(1880).*

Born in Wayne, Maine, on October 22, 1841, the contralto Annie Louise Cary began to study abroad in 1866. She had a successful European career for several years, singing in Stockholm, Paris, and London. In 1870, she made her New York debut at Steinway Hall in Flotow's *Martha*, with a company that featured *Christine Nilsson. Cary's success with the public was instantaneous, and for years she was the most popular, as well as the most preeminent, contralto in America. In New York, she created the part of Amneris in *Aïda* in 1873. The following year, she became the first American woman to sing a Wagnerian role in the United States when she undertook *Lohengrin*. Her tours in Russia in 1875–77, her only return to Europe, were a series of continuous triumphs.

In 1882, Cary married Charles M. Raymond of Brooklyn and retired from public life, singing only occasionally for charity. At her death, she bequeathed $50,000 to the Peoples' Symphony Orchestra of New York and the same amount to charitable and educational institutions.

Cary, Diana Serra (b. 1917).

See Montgomery, Peggy.

Cary, Elisabeth Luther (1867–1936)

American art critic. Born in Brooklyn, New York, on May 18, 1867; died in Brooklyn on July 13, 1936; educated at home by her father, a newspaper editor; studied painting with local teachers.

Selected works: Tennyson: His Homes, His Friends, and His Work *(1898);* Browning, Poet and Man *(1899);* The Rossettis: Dante Gabriel and Christina *(1900);* William Morris, Poet, Craftsman, Socialist *(1902);* Emerson, Poet and Thinker *(1904);* The Novels of Henry James *(1905);* The Art of William Blake *(1907);* Honoré Daumier *(1907);* The Works of James McNeill Whistler *(1907);* Artists Past and Present: Random Studies *(1909).*

Elizabeth Cary, art critic for *The New York Times* for 28 years, began with an early interest

in literature. Her career got under way with the publication of three translations from the French: *Recollections of Middle Life* by Francisque Sarcey (1893), *Russian Portraits* by E. Melchior de Vogüé (1895), and *The Land of Tawny Beasts* by "Pierre Maël" (Charles Causse and Charles Vincent). Cary's original writings focused on literary figures until 1907, when she published the first of several books dealing with art and artists. In 1905, she started writing and publishing a monthly art periodical called the *Script,* which eventually came to the attention of Adolph S. Ochs, publisher of *The New York Times.* Ochs was so impressed with Cary's work that he invited her to become the art critic for his newspaper, the first position of its kind. Through the turbulent period of early 20th-century art, she melded traditional art standards with an open-minded interest in new modes of expression, and her reviews were popular with both the paper's readership and the art world. After 1927, Cary concentrated more on feature articles, often writing on her particular interest, printmaking.

Cary, Mary Ann Shadd

(1823–1893)

American teacher, journalist, and lawyer who championed the cause of racial integration in Canada and the U.S. Pronunciation: KAR-e. Born Mary Ann Shadd on October 9, 1823, in Wilmington, Delaware; died of cancer at her home in Washington, D.C., on June 5, 1893; daughter of black abolitionist Abraham Doros Shadd (a shoemaker) and Harriet (Parnell) Shadd; attended Price's Boarding School, 1833–39; graduated, LL.B., Howard University, 1883; married Thomas F. Cary of Toronto, in 1856; children: Sarah and Linton.

Taught school in Delaware, Pennsylvania, and New York (1840–51); moved to Canada (1851); wrote Notes on Canada West *(1852); helped found* Provincial Freeman *(1853), then de facto editor (1854–58); recruiting officer for black volunteers in Indiana (1863); moved to Washington, D.C. (1869), and taught next 15 years in public schools; served as public school principal (1872–74).*

In 1853, Mary Shadd helped to found the *Provincial Freeman,* a weekly journal devoted to bettering conditions of North Americans of African descent. The newspaper began regular publication in 1854 with Mary Shadd listed as its "publishing agent." This title, however, failed to accurately represent Shadd's role. She was, as

the *Provincial Freeman* itself reported in 1855, "the first colored woman on the American continent to establish and edit a weekly newspaper."

Mary Ann Shadd was the oldest of 13 children born to a free black family in Wilmington, Delaware. Her father, black abolitionist Abraham Doros Shadd, was a successful shoemaker. Her mother, **Harriet (Parnell) Shadd,** who like her husband had never been a slave, was born in North Carolina. In 1833, the year the Shadd family moved to West Chester, Pennsylvania, Abraham was named one of six African-American members of the board of managers of the new American Anti-Slavery Society. That same year, he became president of the national Convention for the Improvement of Free People of Color in the United States. Abraham Shadd believed that education and self-reliance would provide the key to achieving racial equality, a notion his daughter Mary would come to share. He was an agent for *The Liberator* and *The Emancipator,* whose home was a stop on the un-

Mary Ann Shadd Cary

derground railroad where the Shadds "entertained and forwarded" runaways.

Though raised as a Roman Catholic, at the age of ten Mary began attending a Society of Friends school for free black children. She started teaching school at the age of 16 and ultimately held positions in segregated schools in Wilmington, West Chester, New York City, and Norristown, Pennsylvania. She also published *Hints to the Colored People of the North* (1849), a pamphlet that called on African-Americans to push forward independently to bring about the abolition of slavery, with or without white support. In 1851, she moved to Windsor, Canada, where she founded an integrated school with the aid of the American Missionary Association. A 40-page pamphlet promoting black migration that she wrote in 1852, *Notes on Canada West*, enjoyed a wide circulation in the United States.

Self-reliance is the fine road to independence.
—Mary Ann Shadd Cary

Mary Shadd became a bitter critic of efforts that promoted racial segregation in Canada. The chief target of her wrath was the Refugee Home Society, an organization based in Detroit that sought to establish new settlements for runaway slaves and free black migrants. The society purchased land and then resold plots in organized, segregated communities. Mary Shadd accused the group, however, of charging more for land than the government did. She believed that most officers and agents were not anti-slavery men and had created the Refugee Home Society solely for their own economic benefit.

Shadd continued to attack the Refugee Home Society and to promote racial integration when the *Provincial Freeman* began regular publication in 1854, the year she moved to Chatham, Ontario. First published in Toronto, the *Freeman* was printed in Chatham beginning in 1855. In her writings for the journal, Shadd often contrasted the better life of blacks in Canada to that of African-Americans living in the United States. But her primary message was a call for full racial integration of Canadian and American societies. She was one of a very few black women who lectured extensively in North America. "Tall and slim" and possessing "an intellectual countenance," as contemporaries observed, Shadd was an effective speaker who refused to back down even in the face of the most combative audience. Inconsistent with prevailing notions of the period about feminine behavior, she could be direct, uncompromising, and abrasive.

Mary Shadd married Thomas F. Cary of Toronto in 1856, and they had two children before his death in 1860. During her marriage, Mary lived in Chatham most of the time while her husband remained in Toronto tending to his barbering and bathhouse businesses. Thomas shared his wife's commitment to achieving racial justice.

In 1858, John Brown visited Chatham, where he met with Thomas and Mary, Mary's brother Isaac Shadd, and Osborne P. Anderson. While there, the radical anti-slavery activist shared his plan for an "assault" on the evil institution. Mary Shadd supported Brown's ideas and would later write a favorable eulogy for the *New York Weekly Anglo-African* after his execution. Her friend Osborne Anderson was with Brown at Harper's Ferry and, as a survivor of the ordeal, recorded his experience in *A Voice from Harper's Ferry*, which Mary Shadd edited.

After the *Provincial Freeman* went under in 1858, she returned to teaching school. But in 1863, the year of the Emancipation Proclamation, Shadd was appointed a recruiting officer for black volunteers in Indiana. She returned to the United States for good by 1869, when she undertook a brief stint as a teacher in a Detroit school and then moved on to Washington, D.C. Shadd continued to support herself by teaching, served as a principal of a public school in the early 1870s, and went to Howard University to study law, receiving the degree in 1883. She also wrote for the *New National Era* and other journals on a variety of subjects, including women's rights. Lecturing frequently throughout the country promoting racial and gender equality, she delivered a well publicized address at the National Woman's Suffrage Association's annual convention in 1878. An activist of many talents and interests, she died in Washington in 1893.

SOURCES:

Bearden, Jim, and Linda Jean Butler. *Shadd: The Life and Times of Mary Ann Shadd*. Toronto: NC Press, 1977.

Silverman, Jason H. "Mary Ann Shadd and the Search for Equality," in *Black Leaders of the Nineteenth Century*. Leon Litwack and August Meier, eds. Urbana: University of Illinois Press, 1988, pp. 87–100.

SUGGESTED READING:

Winks, Robin. *The Blacks in Canada*. New Haven, CT: Yale University Press, 1971.

Sterling, Dorothy, ed. *We Are Your Sisters: Black Women in the Nineteenth Century*. NY: W.W. Norton, 1984.

COLLECTIONS:

Mary Ann Shadd Cary Papers, Manuscript Division, Moorland-Spingarn Research Center, Howard University, Washington, D.C.

Mary Ann Shadd Cary, Pre-Confederation Section, Manuscript Division, Public Archives of Canada. Ottawa, Ontario, Canada.

John Craig, Professor of History,
Slippery Rock University,
Slippery Rock, Pennsylvania

Cary, Phoebe (1824–1871)

American poet who, in a literary partnership with sister Alice, was less known for her poetry than for her support of her more famous sibling. Born Phoebe Cary on September 4, 1824, in Mount Healthy, near Cincinnati, Ohio; died on July 31, 1871, in New York, New York; daughter of Elizabeth (Jessup) and Robert Cary; sister of poet Alice Cary (1820–1871); educated at home; never married; no children.

Selected works: Poems and Parodies *(1854);* Poems of Faith, Hope, and Love *(1868);* Poetical Works of Alice and Phoebe Cary *(1886).*

Phoebe Cary lived in the shadow of her adored older sister *Alice Cary. Raised by Alice from age 11, Phoebe emulated her and eventually followed her to New York, where their publishing careers mirrored their personalities: Alice always more apparent and ambitious than Phoebe.

In New York, Phoebe let her sister direct their lives socially and financially while she tended to their more basic needs and comforts. She wrote poetry and hymns when the inclination struck, and went for a eight-year period without writing at all. Both sisters were abolitionists. Phoebe worked briefly as assistant editor on *Susan B. Anthony's suffragist newspaper *The Revolution*. When Alice Cary became chronically ill in 1869, Phoebe acted as her full-time nurse. Alice died on February 12, 1871; Phoebe died six months later.

Crista Martin,
Boston, Massachusetts

Casa, Lisa Della (b. 1919).

See Della Casa, Lisa.

Casadesus, Gaby (b. 1901)

French pianist. Born in 1901; married Robert Casadesus (1899–1972, a pianist); children: son Jean (1927–1972).

A superb pianist who studied with the renowned Louis Diemer (1843–1919) at the Paris Conservatory, Gaby Casadesus enjoyed a career as a duo-pianist with her husband Robert that took her all over the world. Her recordings of his solo piano music have delighted both crit-

ics and listeners. Casadesus' recording of Gabriel Fauré's *Ballade* for Piano and Orchestra was one of the first to appear in the long-playing record format. Her life was marred by personal tragedy in 1972, the year in which both her husband and her son Jean died.

Casals, Rosemary (1948—)

International tennis star of the 1960s and 1970s. Name variations: Rosie. Born in San Francisco, California, on September 16, 1948; youngest of two daughters of Manuel Casals y Bordas (owner of a stamp-machine business); attended George Washington High School, San Francisco; never married; no children.

𝒫hoebe
𝒞ary

Described as a born tennis player and one of the fastest on the courts, Rosemary (Rosie) Casals is the daughter of San Salvadorian immigrants, who settled in San Francisco before she was born. In her paternal lineage, which reaches back to Barcelona, Spain, she is the grandniece of the late cellist Pablo Casals, an association that she has never exploited. "I get wild when people keep bringing up Pablo," she told Hugh McIlvanney of the *Observer* (July 9, 1967). "I've never met the man. . . . When I'm asked about him I feel that he is taking part of my identity away. If people know me I want it to be because of what I've done."

Casals' father taught her the fundamentals of tennis when she was eight and remained her chief mentor throughout her career. Once an outstanding soccer player, he had turned to tennis after suffering a serious injury on the playing field. Casals credits him with instinctively knowing what was wrong with her game and with encouraging her without too much pressure. Before tennis began to consume much of her time, Casals was a bright student who loved to read. By the time she entered George Washington High School, however, she had been winning tournaments for several years and had little interest in academics.

By age 15, Casals had won every trophy in California and was ready for national and inter-

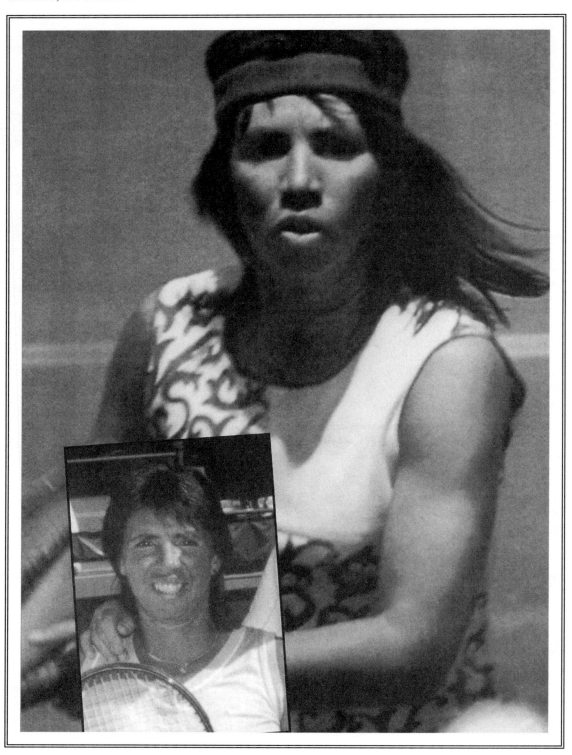

*R*osemary *C*asals

national competition. Opportunity arrived by way of a phone call from *Billie Jean King, who had noticed her talent and asked her to be her doubles partner at Forest Hills. The two Californians became known as the world's best women's doubles team, winning numerous titles in the United States as well as five Wimbledon titles. In 1966, Casals also had two singles victories over King and wins over **Kerry Melville** and *Maria Bueno, giving her international status. Small, at 5'2'', she was nicknamed "Rosebud" and credited in newspaper articles with daring and courage, although some called her game erratic. **Kim Chapin** observed: "Her forehand is hit with tremendous overspin; . . . Her service is rarely tempered and is hit with all the twist and body gymnastics of a Tony Trabert. . . . The missing fraction is her backhand, which so far tends to be a defensive chop."

In 1967, Casals won the women's singles crown in the Wills Invitational tournament in New Zealand, defeating **Françoise Durr** of France in straight sets. At Wimbledon, she was called the tournament's most improved player, which she attributed to better concentration. "I realized that most of my reason for losing was lack of concentration. You just can't allow your mind to drift away. You've got to control your mind as well as your play." Although losing to Britain's **Ann Hayden Jones** in the semi-finals at Wimbledon that year, Casals beat Billie Jean King in the semi-finals of the national clay court matches in Milwaukee. In November, she won over *Margaret Court in the quarterfinals of the Victoria championships in Melbourne. In the semifinals of the U.S. championships, however, she lost to Maria Bueno. In 1968, she once again reached the semifinals in the U.S. championships, but once again was beaten, this time by **Nancy Richey**.

In February 1968, Casals became one of the first woman players to sign a professional contract and join the pro tour. Despite the hardships of life on the road, she went on to win more than 30 national titles and to become one of the world's top money winners. She also contributed substantially to the growth of women's tennis. In 1970, she and Billie Jean King led a group of female players in a protest against discrimination. Demanding bigger purses for women, equal exposure in center-court matches, and better coverage by the news media, the group threatened to boycott future tournaments unless their requests were met. The protest was effective, and in 1973, Casals won a total of $115,000 in prize money, including the biggest single prize in the history of women's sports, the Family Circle Tournament. Defeating **Nancy Gunter** in the final match, she took home $30,000. A sports writer for *The New York Times* called it one of the best efforts of her career: "[N]ever has she displayed such commitment of purpose and concentration as she did during this four-day tournament." Phil Elderkin, in the *Christian Science Monitor,* remarked on her powerful legs and the "dash of Pancho Gonzales in her serve."

Casals captured the attention of many Americans not even interested in tennis in Sep-

tember 1973, during the celebrated "battle of the sexes" match, when Billie Jean King trounced tennis hustler and avowed "male chauvinist" Bobbie Riggs in a highly publicized match. Hired by ABC, along with Howard Cosell and tennis pro, Gene Scott, to comment on the match, Casals' acerbic commentary even outdid Cosell, who built his reputation on the put-down. Although some admired her spunk, most felt she was brash and "unladylike" in her presentation. (Some even mistook her for Cosell's daughter because their last names sounded similar.) Although her image suffered, the television appearance boosted her career considerably, raising public curiosity about the intense young tennis star. She went on to win two additional Wimbledon doubles titles and was the winner of the 1988 Virginia Slims of California with her partner *Martina Navratilova.

During the 1970s, Casals had a reputation for nonconformity. According to newspaper accounts, she kept late hours, had an enormous appetite, and smoked an occasional cigar. She retired from competitive tennis to run a company in Sausalito, California, that organizes tournaments, special charity events, and corporate outings. Casals was inducted into the International Tennis Hall of Fame in 1996, and is on the Board of Directors of the Women's International Tennis Association. In her spare time, she enjoys golf, poetry, and by her own admission "plays a mean game of table tennis."

SOURCES:
Chapin, Kim. *Sports Illustrated.* October 24, 1966.
Current Biography. NY: H.W. Wilson, 1974.
Elderkin, Phil. *Christian Science Monitor.* August 27, 1973.
Meade, Marion. *Women in Sports: Tennis.* NY: Harvey House, 1975.
The New York Times. May 6, 1973.

Barbara Morgan,
Melrose, Massachusetts

Casanova, Danielle (1909–1943)

French resistance leader and political activist. Born Vincentella Périni on January 9, 1909, in Ajaccio, Corsica; died in Auschwitz (Oswiecim), German-occupied Poland, on May 10, 1943; daughter of Olivier Périni and Marie Hyacinthe (Versini) Périni; had three sisters and one brother; married Laurent Casanova (1906–1972).

After Napoleon Bonaparte, Danielle Casanova is probably the best-known Corsican. Her name is instantly recognizable to most French men and women as a heroine of the World War II resistance. Born in Ajaccio, Vin-

3,00

HOMMAGE A LA FEMME
DANIELLE
CASANOVA

REPUBLIQUE FRANÇAISE

SAINSON-BETEMPS

POSTES 1983

Danielle Casanova

centella Périni grew up in a large family. One of four girls, she also had a brother, André. The family had strong political convictions, her parents being school teachers known for their republican and leftist loyalties. Vincentella and her siblings were by no means political conformists, however, exhibiting the flinty independence of an island people long accustomed to fighting and dying for their beliefs. While two of her sisters remained relatively indifferent to politics, her younger sister **Emma** was also drawn to radical ideas from an early age, becoming a militant Communist in the 1930s. Brother André, on the other hand, was a political moderate who became a colonial administrator in French Morocco where he served until his early death in 1942.

Always able to depend on her family for support, Vincentella moved to Paris in November 1927 to study dentistry. A serious pupil, she remained passionately interested in politics, joining the Federal Union of Students. Soon she became leader of that organization's section of dental students. In 1928, Périni joined the Young Communist League. Increasingly at home in the rough-and-tumble of Parisian student politics, she worked to shed her provincial identity, preferring the more sophisticated name of "Lella" to Vincentella. Active in two arrondisements, she emerged as the unchallenged political powerhouse of the activist medical students of the French capital, and by 1930 had become a

force to be reckoned with as secretary of region IV of the Young Communist League.

Known to her friends from this point on as Danielle, it was during this period in her life that Périni met Algerian-born Laurent Casanova. Three years her senior, Casanova was a militant Communist whose family had migrated to north Africa from Corsica. Besides their shared Corsican roots, Danielle and Laurent were convinced that Marxism alone could save France from social chaos and Fascism. The couple was married in December 1933, having, however, little time for youthful diversions. Danielle struggled to establish her dental practice, fortunately receiving assistance from her grandmother, who provided a much-needed financial subsidy to equip her office. In the depths of the depression, clients at first were scarce, and Danielle had to share her office in a working-class district with a masseur, who used the office several days a week. Soon, however, she found a more stable work environment in "La Bellevilloise," a workers' dental cooperative.

During these years, Danielle Casanova was politically more active than ever, serving even before her marriage as a member of the central committee of the Young Communist League of France. Having impressed the inner circles of the French Communist Party with her leadership qualities, she was chosen in 1936 to be a member of the French delegation to an international youth congress in Moscow. There, she was elected to the central committee of the World Youth Congress. The Soviet party line at the time was one of cooperation with all anti-Fascist forces, and Danielle was able to forge ties to various organizations determined to fight Fascism both in France and abroad. Within the French party, her star was rising, because her husband, whose area of responsibility was clandestine work among the French military, had become a close collaborator of Maurice Thorez, the head of the party. But much of her influence derived from the fact that she was an indefatigable worker and a loyal party member whose faith in Marxism was absolute and who never questioned the Stalinist system of "democratic centralism."

The mid-1930s saw Danielle Casanova using every ounce of energy to bring about the creation of a Communist France. In March 1936, she added to her already numerous posts that of secretary of the Young Girls' Union of France, an organization that thrived during the Popular Front period when Communist ideological rigidity was relaxed in order to more effectively fight the threat of Fascism. The start of civil war in Spain in the summer of 1936 brought a host of new tasks, including collecting and shipping relief supplies to the Spanish Republican forces and the French volunteers of the International Brigades. On one occasion, Casanova personally accompanied a shipment of condensed milk for malnourished Spanish children in the war zone.

Throughout these years, Casanova was one of the most energetic leaders of the French Communist movement, organizing new units of the party and spreading the message that Fascism could be halted if all strata of France mobilized its latent strength. Probably the last gasp of optimism during this period took place in October 1938 when Danielle served as leader of the French delegation to the United States to attend a World Congress of Youth for Peace, which was held at Vassar College. Within months, the hopes that had sustained Danielle and her generation were shattered. In March 1939, Nazi Germany marched into Prague, snuffing out the remnants of Czech independence and a few weeks later the Spanish Republic capitulated to the forces of General Franco's Fascist hordes. In August 1939, Hitler and Stalin signed a non-aggression pact that made war inevitable.

Their intense loyalty to the Stalinist party meant that for Danielle and her husband there was no question as to what they would do once war was declared. Laurent had been in Moscow for several months in 1939 and Danielle prepared for underground work. Her clandestine work began within weeks of the start of hostilities due to the fact that the Communist Party was banned as a defeatist organization. Having fled from her home, Danielle lived under an assumed identity, organizing a program of systematic propaganda designed to weaken the French armed forces. After the defeat of France in June 1940, her responsibilities were shifted away from the military and in October Casanova was placed in charge of women's committees in Paris and the German-occupied zone of France. Starting with the German attack on the Soviet Union in June 1941, Casanova's task was to organize Young Communist cadres into effective partisan fighters.

Although Danielle's organization could boast of some successes, the Gestapo spared no effort to smash her own and other resistance groups. During a mass roundup in mid-February 1942, she was arrested along with a large number of other resistance activists. She was imprisoned and interrogated, first in La Santé in Paris and then in the prison of Romainville/ Seine. Convinced that they could not benefit by keeping her a prisoner in France, her German jailers deported Danielle to Auschwitz on January 24, 1943. Weakened in body but not in spirit, she died of typhus at Auschwitz on May 10, 1943.

Danielle Casanova did not disappear from French national consciousness with her death in a Nazi extermination camp. With liberation in 1944, the French sought to rehabilitate their national honor, an often difficult task given the fact that many men and women had in fact collaborated with the enemy or remained indifferent. The Communist Party, on the threshold of power in the immediate postwar years, had many martyrs they could point to, and Danielle Casanova was obviously one of the most attractive. A remarkable woman by any yardstick, even anti-Communists had to admit that she had shown great courage as a resistance leader and thus helped to salvage the nation's tattered honor.

The post-war leaders of the French Communist movement, which included her husband (who had survived the war, escaping German captivity to resume underground work), used her memory to enhance the legitimacy of their claim that their party had always opposed the Germans—which was not true during the period of the Hitler-Stalin pact of 1939–41. Maurice Thorez and others compared Danielle to Joan of Arc, thus attempting to create a cult around her martyrdom. Her name was mentioned reverentially at all Communist mass meetings, and a painting commissioned by the party depicted her death in Auschwitz.

Laurent Casanova died in 1972 and by the early 1980s the divisive passions of a generation earlier were being transformed into unifying national mythologies. For most French, Danielle Casanova had lived and died as a courageous patriot despite the sometimes duplicitous policies of her party. Few objected when she was honored with a commemorative postage stamp in 1983, and most Corsicans were pleased when a large car ferry bearing her name was launched in 1989. Many French men and women live on streets named after her. With the passage of time and with changing views of history, Danielle Casanova, the Corsican revolutionary, has become an honored Frenchwoman, parallelling in many ways the historical evolution of the reputation of an earlier Corsican rebel, Napoleon Bonaparte.

SOURCES:
Beard, Roger. "Passion of Another Casanova," in *Financial Times* [London]. January 24, 1987, p. XVII.
Bell, David S., Douglas Johnson, and Peter Morris, eds. *Biographical Dictionary of French Political Leaders since 1870.* NY: Simon & Schuster, 1990.
Chatel, Nicole, and Annie Boulineau. *Des Femmes dans la Résistance.* Paris: Julliard, 1972.
Le Figaro, May 23, 1989.
Macdonald, Alastair. "Paris Honours 1944 Uprising Amid Memories of Jewish Roundup," in *The Reuter Library Report.* August 24, 1992.
Maitron, Jean, and Cl. Pennetier. "Casanova Vincentella née Périni, dite Danielle Casanova," in Jean Maitron, ed. *Dictionnaire Biographique du Mouvement Ouvrier Français.* Vol. 21. Paris: Les éditions ouvriéres, 1984, pp. 253–254.
Le P.C.F. dans la Résistance. Paris: Editions Sociales, 1967.
Rossiter, Margaret L. *Women in the Resistance.* NY: Praeger, 1986.
Rousseau, Renee. *Les Femmes rouges: Chronique des annees Vermeersch.* Paris: Albin Michel, 1983.
Téry, Simone. *Danielle: The Wonderful Story of Danielle Casanova.* Translated by Helen Simon Travis. NY: International Publishers, 1953.
Union des Femmes françaises. *Les Femmes dans la Résistance.* Paris: Editions du Rocher, 1977.
Weitz, Margaret Collins. *Sisters in the Resistance: How Women Fought to Free France, 1940–1945.* NY: John Wiley, 1995.

John Haag, University of Georgia, Athens, Georgia

Casares, Maria (1922–1996)

Spanish-born French actress, best known for starring in the plays of Shakespeare and the existentialists. Name variations: *Maria Casares Quiroga; Casarès.* Born Maria Casarès Quiroga in La Coruña, Spain, on November 21, 1922; died at her home outside La Rochelle in the western Brittany region of France, on November 22, 1996; daughter of Santiago Casares Quiroga, a pro-Republic politician and diplomat; studied acting at the Paris Conservatoire.

Filmography: Les Enfants du Paradis *(Children of Paradise, 1945);* Les Dames du Bois de Boulogne *(Ladies of the Park, 1945);* Roger-la-Honte *(1946);* La Septième Porte *(1946);* La Revenche de Roger-la-Honte *(1946);* L'Amour autour de la Maison *(1946);* La Chartreuse de Parme *(1948);* Bagarres *(The Wench, 1948);* L'Homme qui revient de Loin *(1949);* Orphée *(Orpheus, 1950);* Ombre et Lumière *(1951);* Testament d'Orphée *(Testament of Orpheus, 1960);* La Reine verte *(1964);* La Lectrice *(1989);* Les Chevaliers de la table ronde *(1990).*

Born in La Coruña, Spain, in 1922, Maria Casares immigrated to France in 1936. Her father was a pro-Republic politician when the Spanish Civil War began in July 1936, and Maria and her mother took refuge north of the Pyrenees after Francisco Franco's victory. In her new homeland, she studied acting at the Conservatoire in Paris. During World War II, she performed at the Mathurins theater, working with director Marcel Herrand. While there, she appeared in J.M. Synge's *Deidre des douleurs* (*Deidre of the Sorrows*) and existentialist plays such as Albert Camus' *La Malentendu* and Jean-Paul Sartre's *Le Diable et le Bon Dieu.* From 1945 to 1949, Casares starred in important films, such as *Les Dames du Bois de Boulogne,* Jean Cocteau's *Orphée, Les Enfants du Paradis,* and *La Chartreuse de Parme.* Preferring the stage, however, she returned to theater. Independent by nature, Casares often changed companies and constantly explored new roles. She excelled at both classical and modern drama and earned distinction as one of France's foremost actresses, appearing in nearly every classic female stage role, from Medea to Lady Macbeth. In 1988, she won the coveted Molière Prize for best comedienne; in 1990, she was awarded the National Grand Prix of Theater.

SOURCES:
Casarés, Maria. *Residente privilegiada.* Barcelona: Editorial Argos Vergara, 1981.
Dussane, Beatrix. *Maria Casarés.* Paris: Calmann-Lévy, 1953.

Kendall W. Brown, Provo, Utah

Casely-Hayford, Adelaide (1868–1960)

Sierra Leonean writer and educator who was active in encouraging her nation to avoid relinquishing traditional values and customs. Born Adelaide Smith on June 2, 1868, in Sierra Leone, Africa; died on January

From the movie Les Enfants du Paradis, *starring Maria Casares and Jean-Louis Barrault.*

24, 1960, in Freetown, Sierra Leone, Africa; daughter of Anne (Spilsbury) Smith and William Smith, Jr. (a registrar); educated at Jersey Ladies' College and the Stuttgart Conservatory; married Joseph E. Casely-Hayford (a lawyer), on September 10, 1903, in Shep-erd's Bush, England; children: Gladys Casely-Hayford (1904–1950, a poet).

Selected works: short stories, including "Savages?," "Mista Courifer," and "Two West African Simpletons."

Adelaide Casely-Hayford's paternal grandparents were of an elite Fanti family in Sierra Leone. Her father William Smith, Jr., had seven children before he married Adelaide's mother **Anne Spilsbury** in 1858. William retired in 1871 from his post as registrar in the court of Sierra Leone, and the next year moved his family to St. Helier on the British Isle of Jersey, so that his children would have a English education. Adelaide's mother died four years later, and money was limited without the income from her family estate. Nevertheless, Adelaide and her siblings were afforded two years at Jersey Ladies' College because her father volunteered on the school committee. He married again in 1883, and Adelaide, who was not fond of her stepmother, left for the Stuttgart Conservatory in Germany in 1885.

She studied piano for three years and returned to England before moving to Freetown, Sierra Leone, in 1892 at her father's urging. William Smith wanted his children to return to their homeland, but Adelaide observed, "Africa at the time did not attract us because we were . . . strangers." She spent a short time teaching and returned to England in 1894 when her stepmother died. Adelaide and her sister Emma lived and traveled with their father until his death in August 1905. After their mother's estate was settled in November 1897, leaving Adelaide and Emma financially self-sufficient, the sisters moved back to Freetown to be near the rest of their family. They established a school but were shunned for months because of their British ways. Finally, their enrollment grew, and the school was Sierra Leone's first private secondary school for girls. They closed the school in 1900 when their sister Nettie was widowed and wished to take her children to England. The Smith sisters returned to Jersey and took in bachelor guests to help pay the rent.

Sierra Leonean lawyer Joseph Casely-Hayford visited Adelaide Smith in July of 1903. Within weeks of their meeting, he proposed. Smith had previously had a romance in Freetown, which ended in 1899 with the suitor's death of tuberculosis. "From that experience," she said, "I knew I could only offer a second best affection . . . . He told me plainly that his first wife, whom he adored, had died two years previously, and that he too had nothing but a second-best affection to offer me. I honoured him for his frank avowal and accepted his offer in the right spirit." They were married in September 1903, and after a brief honeymoon in Stratford-on-Avon they returned to Africa were they were joined by Joseph's five-year-old son, Archie. Joseph traveled regularly but sent daily telegrams home. Their daughter, *****Gladys Casely-Hayford**, was born in 1904, with a malformed hip joint. When Gladys was only months old, Adelaide took the two children to England seeking medical advice. Over the next six years, the Casely-Hayfords were together for only months; by the time Adelaide returned to Freetown to stay, Joseph had taken a home up the coast in Accra. The Casely-Hayfords, however, never divorced. "I was married for 27 years," Adelaide later observed, "and have been a neglected widow for 23."

Casely-Hayford took a job teaching music and began campaigning for an Industrial and Technical Training School (ITTS) that would give African girls the skills to support themselves rather than depend on husbands. To increase funds, she ventured to the United States in July 1920, touring 36 cities and observing African-American schools. The trip raised £1,800 but cost £1,200. In 1923, the school opened, with **Mrs. Ejesa Osora** as co-headmistress. An initial enrollment of 81 waned when Osora left to begin her own school. Casely-Hayford shut down ITTS in 1924 and reopened it in 1926 after another U.S. fundraising tour. In Casely-Hayford's view, "education meted out to us had, either consciously or unconsciously, taught us to despise ourselves." Her goal with the ITTS was an "education which would instill into us a love of country, a pride of race, an enthusiasm for the black man's capabilities and a genuine admiration for Africa's wonderful art work." In order to keep the school open, Casely-Hayford reorganized to accept younger children who were then fed into the popular Annie Walsh Memorial secondary school. ITTS existed until 1940. Her daughter Gladys' refusal to assume leadership of the school left a permanent rift in their relationship.

Near the end of her life, Casely-Hayford began writing short fiction that reflected her ideals. In England, she was honored twice for her achievements—with the King's Silver Jubilee Medal in 1935 and with the Medal of the British Empire in 1950. Casely-Hayford died in Freetown on January 24, 1960.

SOURCES:

Cromwell, Adelaide M. *An African Victorian Feminist.* London: Frank Cass, 1986.

Fister, Barbara. *Third World Women's Literature.* Westport, CT: Greenwood Press, 1995.

Okonkwo, Rina. *Heroes of West African Nationalism.* Enugu, Nigeria: Delata Publications, 1985.

Crista Martin,
Boston, Massachusetts

Casely-Hayford, Gladys
(1904–1950)

Sierra Leonean poet, one of the first to write in Krio, a Sierra Leonean Creole. Name variations: Aquah Luluah. Born Gladys May Casely-Hayford in 1904 in Axim, Ghana, Africa; died in 1950 in Accra, Sierra Leone, Africa; daughter of Adelaide Casely-Hayford (1868–1960) and Joseph E. Casely-Hayford (a lawyer and author); educated at Penrhos College, Wales; married Arthur Hunter, around 1936; children: Kobina (b. 1940).

Selected Works: Take Um So (1948).

*Adelaide Casely-Hayford believed an encounter with a chimpanzee while she was pregnant with Gladys was a defining factor in her daughter's disposition. "I am quite sure that this fright affected the delicate mechanisms of my unborn child's brain, and was largely responsible for the eccentricity which developed in her later years." There were other possibilities: Gladys was born with a malformed hip joint, and she often had to compete with their burgeoning careers for her parents' attention. Raised in Sierra Leone, she went to Penrhos College in Wales in 1915 to complete her secondary education and returned to Freetown at age 22 to teach in her mother's Industrial Technical and Training School (ITTS). Adelaide wanted her daughter Gladys to receive a prestigious college degree and obtained her admission to Columbia University. En route in 1929, Gladys detoured to Germany, performing with a jazz troupe and touring. A failed romance with one of her co-musicians made her restless to relocate. Her mother obtained Gladys admission to Radcliffe College, which she declined, and then Ruskin College in Oxford, which she accepted. Gladys Casely-Hayford's poetic talents were admired at Ruskin, but the stress of her failed affair and her difficult relationship with her mother brought a mental breakdown in 1932. Gladys was hospitalized in Oxford. When Adelaide appeared at her bedside, a doctor advised them to have a less competitive relationship. Said Adelaide, "As far as I can see Gladys is just a little eccentric. At times she is absent-minded and she also has fits of depression, which I am sure will disappear as time goes on, and sometimes she is not as polite as I would like her to be."

They returned to Freetown. Gladys resumed teaching at ITTS but increasingly withdrew from Adelaide, first moving to Accra, where her father's family lived, then marrying Arthur Hunter, whom her mother had not met. Hunter was, in turn, sweet natured, abusive and adulterous. Adelaide paid for him to go to England to learn the printing business. On his return, he eschewed work as a printer. Gladys' son Kobina Hunter was born in 1940. From age ten on, he would live alternately with his grandmother or his half-uncle.

Gladys' poetry, sometimes published under the name Aquah Luluah, drew critical acclaim, and her writings in Krio, a Sierra Leonean Creole, were revolutionary. Her work addressed both her personal emotions and her resolves for her country. "As we pass onward, through evolution rise,/ May we retain our vision, the truth may light our eyes." Gladys Casely-Hayford died in 1950 of blackwater fever. Her poems had appeared in a collection, *Take Um So* (1948), and in international magazines, such as the *Atlantic Monthly*.

SOURCES:
Cromwell, Adelaide M. *An African Victorian Feminist*. London: Frank Cass, 1986.

Fister, Barbara. *Third World Women's Literature*. Westport, CT: Greenwood Press, 1995.

Okonkwo, Rina. *Heroes of West African Nationalism*. Enugu, Nigeria: Delata Publications, 1985.

Crista Martin,
Boston, Massachusetts

Casgrain, Thérèse (1896–1981)

French-Canadian feminist, humanist, pacifist, and social reformer who led the feminist movement in Quebec throughout much of her life. Pronunciation: Ter-ACE CAS-gra. Born Thérèse Forget on July 11, 1896, in Quebec, Canada; died in Quebec at age 85 in 1981; daughter of Blanche (MacDonald) and Sir Rodolphe Forget (a financier); attended convent school of the Dames du Sacré-Coeur in Sault-aux-Récollets; married Pierre Casgrain, in 1916; children: Rodolphe, Hélène, Paul, Renée.

Joined Provincial Suffrage Committee (1921); elected president of the Suffrage Committee (1928); vote for women is achieved in Quebec (1940); won the battle over Family Allowance checks (1945); joined Cooperative Commonwealth Federation (1946); elected to leadership of Quebec CCF (1951–57); toured Asia and the East (1956); formed Quebec branch of Voice of Women (1961); appointed to Canadian Senate (1970).

In her autobiography *A Woman in a Man's World*, Thérèse Casgrain reflects fondly on the country house where she spent the summers of her childhood. Located on a hill in the rural community of Saint-Irénée (Quebec), the estate consisted of a main house and many auxiliary buildings built on various levels interconnected by pathways and steps. The main house, used extensively for entertaining, was huge. With 16 bedrooms, Casgrain claims there was barely enough room for the guests and family. The grounds were beautifully landscaped with gardens, walkways, and an orchard. Tennis courts, an indoor swimming pool, a yacht and stables provided entertainment for the family and their guests. The size and splendor of this home graphically depicts the wealth and comfort within which Casgrain lived her life. She never rose to challenge the disparity between rich and poor in Canada. Still, at an early age, she devoted herself to a number of social and political issues, challenging the values of the existing society and forcing many changes. An important leader in the Quebec feminist movement, she fought to improve the legal, political, and social position of women in Quebec. Of particular importance was her contribution to the suffrage cause. Not content to achieve social reform exclusively through private charitable activities, she moved eventually to join the Cooperative Commonwealth Federation (CCF), a socialist party dedicated to improving the lives of workers, farmers, and the disadvantaged. Charming, confident and intelligent, Casgrain had unbounded energy that she used to alter the social inequities in Quebec society.

Thérèse Casgrain was born into a well-established, prominent and wealthy Quebec family. From colonial times, family members of both parents had been influential in the legal, political, and economic elite of the province. Casgrain's father Sir Rodolphe Forget was a wealthy Quebec financier and a member of the Federal Parliament from 1904 to 1917. Her mother **Blanche MacDonald Forget** lived the life of a woman in her socio-economic position. A house full of servants gave her time for leisure, social and charitable activities, and travel. Reflecting back on this from the perspective acquired as an adult, Casgrain spoke of the lifestyle and charitable actions of women like her mother: "Women, especially those of the comfortable classes, enjoyed playing the role of lady bountiful and distributed food baskets in the homes of needy families every Christmas. They never dreamed, however, of trying to find out why these people were in need." As an adult, Casgrain would deviate from her mother's path. Yet, in the early years, her life conformed to societal expectations for a young female of her class and social position.

At age eight, Casgrain was sent to the convent school at Sault-aux-Récollets (outside Montreal) where she boarded from September to June. At this time, the majority of schools in Quebec were run by the Roman Catholic Church. Girls, in particular, were educated by nuns from numerous religious orders. The school attended by Casgrain was run by the order of the Dames du Sacré-Coeur and was considered one of the best. Here, she would have learned the skills deemed important for a woman—domestic skills such as cooking, reading and writing, languages, and music. The purpose of a girl's education, it was believed, was to prepare her for her eventual role as a wife and mother.

Summers were spent at the country house or touring her father's riding (county) of Charlevoix during the years he was a Member of Parliament. One summer, the family accompanied Forget on a business trip to Paris, France. Detained beyond their scheduled return date, the family narrowly escaped death: their original return booking was on the *Titanic*. In 1913, Casgrain was awed by the spectacle of the 65th Regiment performing their yearly manoeuvres on the grounds of the country estate. As a finale, mass was held on the grounds during which a royal salute was fired from the top of the hill at the moment of the elevation of the Host. Discussing these events in her memoirs, Casgrain reveals a childhood that was peaceful, happy and comfortable.

After graduating from convent school, Casgrain's days were filled with shopping, party-going, and game playing. Her studies of literature, music and domestic skills continued on a less formal basis. All of these activities were directed towards providing her with the skills necessary for an upper-class wife. On reaching marriageable age, she, like her peers, began attending approved social events intended to give her the opportunity to meet an acceptable husband. At the annual oyster supper held to raise funds for the deaf, she met Pierre Casgrain, a young, independently wealthy lawyer from a good family. She did not feel that she had made an impression on him until the next day when a bouquet of roses arrived. On the first date, chaperoned by her eldest brother Gilles, Casgrain felt awkward and shy. She politely declined several items offered to her until a kick from Gilles under the table induced her to accept some ice cream. Apparently if she had not accepted, Pierre would have felt rejected and not asked her out again.

On January 19, 1916, they were married. It appears the relationship was happy and affectionate. Four children—Rodolphe, Hélène, Paul, and Renée—were born. Although the marriage was traditional in the sense that Casgrain speaks

Thérèse
Casgrain

of seeking his "permission" to pursue her interests, he was supportive, regardless of how much she deviated from the norms of acceptable behavior for women. Pierre not only supported her decision to join the CCF but expressed interest in her activities despite his lifelong affiliation with the mainstream Liberal Party. Pierre had a prominent and successful career as a lawyer and a politician. From 1917 to 1940, he was a Liberal Member of the Federal Parliament, serving in the prestigious post of speaker of the house from 1936 to 1940 and as secretary of state during the Second World War. On his retirement from politics, he was appointed a judge of the Quebec Superior Court.

During the early years of her marriage, Casgrain continued to fill the role expected. At this time, social services (the provision of support for the poor, etc.) were provided by private charities staffed and supported by middle- and upper-class women. Like her mother, Casgrain fulfilled this social function. Due to her unbounded energy, self-confidence and intelligence, however, she went beyond the requirements, creating charities and providing leadership. In 1926, she founded the Ligue de la jeunesse féminine (Young Women's League), which organized young volunteers for social work. She also created the Fédération des oeuvres de charité canadiennes-françaises (Federation of French-Canadian Charitable Workers). During the war, her leadership skills were called upon by the federal government when she was put in charge of administering half of Canada at the Consumer Branch of the Wartime Prices and Trade Board. Despite the prominent role that Casgrain assumed in these organizations, they remained within the rubric of acceptable activity for women.

Canadian women are still considered second-class citizens and they are too often deprived of the treatment and consideration they deserve as human beings. To try to rectify these wrongs became my goal.

—Thérèse Casgrain

Rebellion against the limitations of both her gender and her class began not long after marriage. She had begun to tire of the continuous circuit of parties and social gatherings that filled her time. As well, she probably needed a wider range of activities to satisfy her. In her autobiography, Casgrain maintains that the opportunity came in 1921 when her husband became ill just before a campaign speech. Before the assembled crowd, Casgrain stepped up to the podium and gave a brief explanation. It was not the content of the speech but the act of giving it in public that helped raise her confidence and bring her more into public activity. Afterwards, several women involved in the women's movement came to see Casgrain, inducing her to join. For the next 60 years she remained one of the most prominent figures in the Quebec feminist movement.

In 1921, women in Quebec were in a peculiar situation. They could vote in federal elections but not provincially. Manitoba had been the first province to grant women the vote in 1916, and all the others, except Quebec, had followed suit. But the Quebec government had refused to extend the franchise, a situation that continued until 1940. The feminist movement that Casgrain joined in 1921 was just in the process of reviving after several years of inactivity. There was widespread opposition to female suffrage, particularly from the Catholic Church, which continued to exert considerable influence over attitudes in Quebec society. Thus, the newly formed Comité provincial pour le Suffrage féminin (Provincial Suffrage Committee) decided to pursue an educational rather than political campaign to teach the public that, in their view, female suffrage would not alter sex roles but would lead to a general improvement in society. Women, it was argued, deserved the vote because many political issues touched on the areas of home and family life, which were women's concerns. However, due to virulent opposition, the committee's activities were sporadic and low key until 1927 when the committee, along with a new suffrage group, began to increase their pressure on the Quebec government. Annually, for the next 13 years, the women had a sympathetic member of Parliament introduce a bill to grant the vote to women. They knew it would be rejected but believed it was good publicity. The jeers, sarcasm and vulgarities of some politicians during debate undoubtedly brought the issue to public consciousness, raising awareness and often sympathy.

Recalling these years, Casgrain wrote in her autobiography of a conversation with the premier of Quebec, L.A. Taschereau. Popular opinion held that women who wanted the vote were unattractive spinsters, unable to attract a husband and deprived of children. According to Casgrain their encounter went as follows:

[H]e said to me with a smile, "Of course now that you're campaigning for the woman's vote, there'll be no question of your having any more children. But if such a thing should occur, I'd like to be godfather. If it's a boy we'll make him a bishop." "And if it's a girl," I retorted, "she'll be a suffragette." At that moment, as it happened, I was pregnant.

Apparently, when the little girl was born, Premier Taschereau and his wife were appointed the godparents. The story is interesting, not only because it reveals the belief that a "feminist" woman would reject motherhood but also because of the friendly relations between Casgrain and her opponent. As leader of the suffrage movement (Casgrain became president in 1928 of the Provincial Committee), she was effective because of her social connections to the most influential people in the province.

Eleven years of persistence bore fruit at the Liberal Party convention in 1938. The Provincial Committee (renamed the Ligue des droits de la femme [League for Women's Rights] in 1929) was able to force the party to include women's suffrage in their platform. Casgrain was understandably skeptical about the sincerity behind Liberal support. After all, it was the Liberals who had jeered and repeatedly voted against women's suffrage during their years in power in the 1920s and early 1930s. Now out of power, it was questionable whether they really intended to fulfill their promise if they won the next election. Still, when the election was called in the autumn of 1939, Casgrain and the League came out in support of the Liberals and worked hard to ensure a Liberal victory in 1940. Casgrain also worked to ensure the Liberals kept their promise by encouraging women to write to the Liberal leader, resulting in a barrage of letters, telegrams, and petitions. Their efforts succeeded when the Liberals won the election. On April 25, 1940, Quebec women were granted the privilege to vote in provincial elections and to stand for election; they were the last women in Canada to achieve this right.

Casgrain was not only dedicated to women's suffrage, she also worked to increase female access to the professions and to improve the position of women in law. Legal inequality was of particular concern. Married women, under the Quebec Civil Code, had few rights. The husband was the head of the family. As such, he had total control over all family assets and was free to dispose of it, including his wife's wages and inherited property, as he saw fit. Quebec feminists, including Casgrain, had hoped to change this when the government appointed a commission to study marriage laws in 1929; they were not rewarded. The commission recommended few changes, leaving married women in the same position. In 1945, the same issues arose again, but this time Casgrain achieved success. In 1945, the federal government introduced a "family allowance" program for all of Canada which provided families with children a small monthly check. The check was to be made payable to the mother because of the belief that she would use it for the benefit of the children. When this was discovered, the Quebec premier Maurice Duplessis, several Quebec cabinet ministers, and the clergy intervened to ensure that checks going to Quebec families would be paid to the fathers. They argued that, by law, the husband was the head of the family and its adminis-

trator, and, thus, payments had to be made to the fathers or they would violate Quebec statutes. When Casgrain heard of the change indirectly, she had little time; the first checks were due to be issued in two months. Immediately, she formed a committee and began a publicity campaign through the radio and newspapers urging mothers to protest to the government. Though the church opposed her actions and asked her to stop, she refused. In July 1945, when the first checks were paid out, they were sent to mothers in Quebec as in the rest of the country. Casgrain may not have actually changed the laws regarding marriage, but she had dealt a serious blow by challenging the foundation on which they were based.

It was around this time that Casgrain made the decision to join the Cooperative Commonwealth Federation. Created in 1932, the CCF was a socialist party formed from a coalition of farmer, worker, and intellectual groups dedicated to reform. In the post World War II atmosphere, it was growing in popularity in Canada but continued to be marginal in Quebec. Casgrain joined because she was attracted to the philosophy that emphasized working for the good of all people rather than the few. At some point, she had become disillusioned with the Liberals, the party of her husband, believing that it only worked for the interests of the wealthy. Working for the CCF was difficult. Quebeckers generally rejected the CCF (believing that it was a manifestation of western and English Canadian concerns), funds were severely limited, and it received continuous abuse from the mainstream parties and the church. Eight times Casgrain ran as a candidate but was not elected. Although the CCF was unable to achieve electoral success in Quebec, in many ways it was a positive experience for her.

Within the party, Casgrain achieved prominence as a politician and as a figure known to Canadians. In 1942, she had run as a Liberal candidate in her husband's old riding of Charlevoix-Saguenay. Her defeat was particularly disappointing because she had not received any aid from Liberal Party members, either through endorsements or by visits to the riding during her campaign. In the CCF, her experience was much different. In 1948, she was elected, in absentia, to one of the posts of vice-president in the national party, a post she held until 1963. From 1951 to 1957, she was leader of the party in Quebec. To Casgrain, this success meant that the party did not discriminate against women. As such, it allowed her to serve in the prominent, leadership roles that were not accessible to women in the mainstream parties. This opportunity, combined with a sincere attraction to the policies of the party (such as free access to education), motivated her to perform the time-consuming and unrewarding task of building the party in Quebec.

After relinquishing party leadership in Quebec in 1957, Casgrain's interests shifted towards international concerns. As a delegate for the CCF (which amalgamated into the New Democratic Party [NDP] in 1961), she attended numerous socialist conferences such as the International Socialist Council held in 1963. Having turned 60 in 1956, Casgrain remained energetic and involved. Her new interest in international affairs meant that traveling became a significant part of her life. When appointed the CCF delegate to the Congress of Socialist Nations of Asia in 1956, Casgrain decided to tour Asia and the East. Accompanied by a friend and the mother of Pierre Trudeau (future prime minister of Canada), she traveled from Paris and Rome to India, Greece, Iran, Ceylon, Burma, Thailand, Hong Kong and Japan. Throughout the trip, the well-known Casgrain was treated with diplomatic courtesy in most of these countries.

In these later years, significant interest and activity was devoted to the peace movement, particularly the cause of nuclear disarmament. In 1961, Casgrain formed a branch of "Voice of Women" in Quebec. This too provided her with opportunities to travel, as in 1965 when she went to Russia by invitation of the Committee of Soviet Women. At home, Voice of Women attempted to affect foreign policy by petitioning the government to reject nuclear weapons for Canada, to halt the export of materials used in the creation of nuclear weapons, and to transform the Canadian economy to only peace-time production. In this capacity, Casgrain again ran for Parliament as an NDP (Peace) candidate in 1962 and 1963. NDP policy, unlike that of the other parties, was clearly opposed to war and the development of destructive potential.

In 1970, Casgrain's desire to sit in Parliament was finally realized when she was appointed to the Canadian Senate (the upper chamber of the federal government). Although she knew she could only serve for one year due to mandatory retirement at age 75, Casgrain was honored and enthusiastic. She believed, despite the lesser powers of the Senate (as compared to those of the elected House of Commons), that Senators were able to influence government policy. As she stated in her autobiography, as a senator her opinions would suddenly become respectable in the eyes of many.

To list every one of Casgrain's activities throughout her life would be a momentous, and confusing, task. At any one time, she was involved in numerous activities and organizations. Social connections due to her class position allowed her access to the most influential people in the country. However, it was the boundless energy combined with sincere devotion to social reform, women's rights, and international peace that allowed her to influence the development of Canadian society. Many of the issues that Casgrain fought for were achieved within the span of her lifetime. In 1969, the Civil Code was amended giving married women control over their own property. Women's suffrage and access to the professions, such as law and medicine, had been achieved. As well, a wide range of social reforms ensuring universal access to health and education and the provision of social welfare had evolved. Although by 1970 Casgrain spoke of the many obstacles to overcome, especially in the area of women's rights, she must have recognized how fundamentally Quebec and Canada had changed.

SOURCES:

Casgrain, Thérèse F. *A Woman in a Man's World*. Translated by Joyce Marshall. Toronto: McClelland and Stewart, 1972.

Trofimenkoff, Susan Mann. "Thérèse Casgrain and the CCF in Quebec," in *Canadian Historical Review*. Vol. LXVI, no. 2, 1985, pp. 125–153.

COLLECTIONS:

Thérèse Casgrain Papers located in the Public Archives of Canada (PAC), Ottawa, Ontario; CCF Papers located in the PAC, Ottawa, Ontario.

Catherine Briggs, Ph.D. Candidate,
University of Waterloo,
Waterloo, Ontario, Canada

Cash, June Carter (b. 1929).

See Carter, Maybelline for sidebar.

Cashin, Bonnie (b. 1915)

American fashion designer. Born in Oakland, California, in 1915; studied painting at the Art Students League (New York) and in Paris.

Awards: Neiman-Marcus award (1950); Coty Award (1961); New York City Fashion Critics Winnie award; Sports Illustrated award; named Woman of the Year by the Lighthouse of the Blind (1961).

Selected films—as costume designer: Claudia (1943); Ladies of Washington (1944); The Eve of St. Mark (1944); Home in Indiana (1944); In the Meantime, Darling (1944); Laura (1944); Keys of the Kingdom (1944); A Tree Grows in Brooklyn (1944); The Bullfighters (1945); Billy Rose's Diamond Horseshoe

(Diamond Horseshoe, GB, 1945); Where Do We Go from Here? (1945); Junior Miss (1945); The Caribbean Mystery (1945); The House on 92nd Street (1945); Fallen Angel (1945); Do You Love Me? (1946); Cluny Brown (1946); Anna and the King of Siam (1946); Claudia and David (1946); Three Little Girls in Blue (1946); (with Charles LeMaire) I Wonder Who's Kissing Her Now? (1947); (with LeMaire) Nightmare Alley (1947); (with LeMaire) Scudda Hoo! Scudda Hay! (1948); (with LeMaire) Give My Regards to Broadway (1948); (with LeMaire) The Iron Curtain (1948); (with LeMaire) Cry of the City (1948); (with LeMaire) The Luck of the Irish (1948); (with LeMaire) Unfaithfully Yours (1948); (with LeMaire) The Snake Pit (1948); (with LeMaire) Mr. Belvedere Goes to College (1949); (with LeMaire) It Happens Every Spring (1949); (with LeMaire) You're My Everything (1949).

Bonnie Cashin followed the same path as her mother, who was also a fashion designer, and began her career as a designer for New York's Roxy Theater in the 1930s. While working there, she studied painting at the Art Student's League and brought in extra money by designing sports clothes for a manufacturer; from this time on, Cashin would continue to divide her time between designing for showbusiness and the rag trade. After studying in Paris, she returned to her native California to work for 20th Century-Fox. Cashin's fame came early with the dress she designed for one of Hollywood's most elegant actresses, *Gene Tierney, in the 1944 film Laura. Whereas many American films of the '40s were marked by an over-dressing offered by filmmakers as an antidote to war-time austerity, Cashin avoided this stylistic trap for Laura and the result was costuming that would not look dated to later audiences.

Cashin returned to New York in 1949 and in 1952 founded her own firm, Bonnie Cashin Designs, Inc., in Briarcliff Manor, New York. Her designs—executed in sturdy materials of natural and bright colors, sometimes with leather and brass trimmings—followed an independent, informal direction. In a 1953 collaboration with manufacturers Phillip Sills and Ballantyne, she produced classic, simple sportswear. Cashin also served as head of Innovative Design Fund, a foundation that encourages younger designers. Known as one of America's most original and successful designers, she received numerous awards and honors, including a Neiman-Marcus Award (1950) and a Coty Award (1961). Many of her originals are housed at New York's Brooklyn Museum.

Cashman, Mel (1891–1979)

Australian union organizer. Born Ellen Imelda Cashman on November 19, 1891, at Gladesville, Sydney; died in 1979; daughter of Ellen and Edward (Ned) Cashman (a hotel licensee); attended St. Joseph's School, Hunter's Hill.

Mel Cashman left school to begin work at an early age. Employed first in the clothing trade, she then took a job in the printing industry. Ten years later, she was a forewoman earning slightly over £1 a week but lost her job upon joining the Women and Girls' Printing Trades Union. In 1914, she became president of the union and, three years later, in 1917, became secretary. Shortly thereafter, the women's union amalgamated with the men's, becoming the Printing Industry Employee's Union of Australia. Appointed organizing secretary of the Women and Girls' Section, from 1918 Cashman also served in this capacity for the Cardboard Box and Carton Section. Earning only £1 per week, she protested the difference between her own wage and the wage paid to male organizers, and as a result of her agitation her salary was increased to 95% that of the rate paid to men. Greatly restricted in the range of work the union permitted them to perform, women were confined primarily to sewing, folding, numbering, and making paper bags.

Able to rely on the women's vote, Cashman was always elected to the Board of Management. Among her activities for the union were the organization of social events, debates, and physical activities and camps for women. Cashman also wrote a column for the Printer. In 1918, she gave evidence to the cost of living inquiry, and for the 1926 inquiry represented employees as an assessor. Additionally, at arbitration hearings, Cashman appeared for her union. In 1940, following one in a series of attempts to limit the voting rights of women union members, Cashman resigned her post.

Appointed a Commonwealth arbitration inspector, she was transferred in 1914 to the Department of Labour and National Service where her job was to survey clothing industry conditions. Wartime brought the creation of the Women's Employment Board to regulate the stipulations under which women could be employed in "male" work, and Cashman joined the Board as the representative for the Commonwealth. Voting with the majority, she usually sought between 60% and 95% of the rate paid to men. She resumed her appointment as arbitration inspector in 1944 but resigned after being hospitalized in 1952. She resided with her niece Ellen Brown until Ellen died in 1978, a year before Cashman's death.

SOURCES:
Radi, Heather, ed. *200 Australian Women*. NSW, Australia: Women's Redress Press, 1988.

Cashman, Nellie (1844–1925)

American miner and philanthropist. Born in County Cork, Ireland, in 1844; died on January 4, 1925, in St. Joseph's Hospital, Victoria; one of two daughters of Patrick and Frances "Fanny" (Cronin) Cashman.

Of the thousands lured by the gold-rush fever of the 19th century, few had the staying power or generous spirit of Nellie Cashman. An Irish immigrant who spent her childhood in Boston, Cashman first followed gold miners into British Columbia, Canada, where, during the early 1870s, she operated a boarding house while learning elementary mining techniques

Nellie Cashman

and geology. For the next 50 years, the precious metal led her to Arizona, Nevada, Mexico, the Canadian Yukon, and north of the Arctic Circle in Alaska. In addition to successfully prospecting and running mines (at one time she owned 11 mines in the Koyukuk District of Alaska), she operated boarding houses, restaurants, and supply depots.

The quality that truly established Nellie Cashman's place in mining lore was her charity, which earned her the titles "Angel of Tombstone" and "Saint of the Sourdoughs" while sometimes obscuring her career as a successful miner. As early as 1874, while visiting Victoria, she led a dangerous, some called it insane, rescue effort to free a group of miners trapped by a severe winter storm. Later, during the glory days of Tombstone, Arizona, she helped establish the town's first hospital and its first Roman Catholic Church. Although she was known to be tough and aggressive in defending her claims, she was also big-hearted. Upon the deaths of her sister and brother-in-law, Cashman took in her nieces and nephews and brought them up as her own.

Around 1889, Cashman was active in the gold camp at Harqua Hala, Arizona, and came close to marrying Mike Sullivan, one of the original discoverers of gold in that area. Along with mining, she contributed a number of excellent articles for Tucson's *Arizona Daily Star*, in which she discussed history, techniques, types of claims, and personalities in the field.

Cashman spent the last 20 years of her life on Nolan Creek, in the Koyukuk River Basin of Alaska, then the farthest north of any mining camp in the world. She was among about eight women who joined a group of approximately 200 miners to brave the harsh environment and isolation in hopes of striking the "big bonanza." Once a year, she would leave for supplies and equipment, traveling hundreds of miles to Fairbanks, by sled, boat, or wagon. Her spirit of adventure apparently never died. In 1921, during one of her trips to the outside, she was interviewed for *Sunset*, a California publication. Then 76, Cashman told the writer that, although she loved Alaska, she was not so tied to it that she wouldn't pull up stakes if something turned up somewhere else.

Nellie Cashman died on January 4, 1925, in St. Joseph's Hospital in Victoria—one of the hospitals she had helped fund some 40 years earlier. The U.S. Postal Service honored her with a stamp in 1944 as part of its "Legends of the West" series.

SOURCES:

Chaput, Don. "In Search of Silver & Gold," in *American History*. February 1996.

SUGGESTED READING:

Chaput, Don. *Nellie Cashman and the North American Mining Frontier*. Tucson, AZ: Westernlore Press, 1995.

Barbara Morgan,
Melrose, Massachusetts

Casilda (d. about 1007)

Moorish saint. Died around 1007; daughter of Aldemon, Moorish king of Toledo; widowed.

Casilda was the daughter of Aldemon, the Moorish king of Toledo who hated the Christians and had a predilection for keeping many imprisoned and in chains. Casilda, a catechumen (a student of Christianity), secretly visited these prisoners and brought them food. Legend has it that one day, while on her way to the prison with a basket filled with loaves of bread, she ran into her father who insisted on seeing the contents of the basket. It is said that when she lifted the cloth, the basket contained red roses; the flowers then returned to bread as soon as Aldemon walked on. When Casilda succumbed to what was thought to be an incurable illness, she traveled to bathe in Lake St. Vincent, received baptism, and built a small chapel and a house by the lake where she passed her years in retreat.

Caslavska, Vera (1942—)

Czech gymnast who won four silver and seven Olympic gold medals. Name variations: Caslavska-Odlozil; Čáslavská. Born in Prague, Czechoslovakia, on May 3, 1942; married Josef Odlozil, a national track champion and Olympic athlete, while she was competing in Mexico City, 1968.

One of the top gymnasts in the world (1960s); won 15 world and European championships; won a silver in all-around team in Rome Olympics (1960); won a silver medal for all-around team and gold medals in balance beam, horse vault, all-around individual in Tokyo (1964); won a silver medal in all-around team and balance beam, gold medals in floor exercises, horse vault, uneven parallel bars, and all-around individual in Mexico City (1968), making her the first woman to win four individual gold medals in a summer Game.

Originally an ice skater before switching to gymnastics, Vera Caslavska burst onto the international gymnastics' scene with a silver medal at the 1958 world championships. For the next six years, Caslavska and *Larissa Latynina of the Soviet Union were the top gymnasts in the world.

In 1960, competing in her first Olympics, Caslavska shared a team silver. At the Tokyo Games in 1964, the Czech gymnast won gold medals in all-around (Latynina placed 2nd), side horse vault (Latynina placed 2nd), and balance beam (Latynina placed 3rd) as well as a team silver. The floor exercises went to her rival, Latynina.

Two months before the 1968 Olympics, Soviet tanks rolled into Czechoslovakia, putting an end to the Prague Spring, a brief period during the Cold War when Caslavska's country enjoyed greater political freedom. When the Olympics arrived, Caslavska was determined to be the best gymnast in the world as a symbol of Czech resistance to Soviet dominance. At that Olympic competition in Mexico City, her "Mexican Hat Dance" routine for the floor exercise was wildly popular with the crowd, and she tied for first place with **Larissa Petrik** (USSR). Sharing the podium and first place with the Soviet, Caslavska bowed her head when the Czech national anthem was played, a grim reminder to a watching world of events taking place in Prague.

The gymnastic star of the Mexico City games, Caslavska took gold medals in the uneven bars, the side horse vault, the floor exercise, and the individual all-around, a title she secured in a close contest with the favorite, another Soviet gymnast, *Natalia Kuchinskaya. Caslavska had become the first woman to win four individual gold medals in a summer Game. Later, the gymnast announced that she would present her gold medals to Alexander Dubcek, Ludvik Svoboda, and Oldrich Cernik, Czech leaders who had been ousted after the Soviet occupation. When a hardline Soviet-backed regime returned to power in Czechoslovakia, Caslavska and her husband, Czech-runner Josef Odlozil, were harassed, humiliated, and repeatedly denied employment.

Karin Loewen Haag,
Athens, Georgia

Cass, Mama (1941–1974).

See Elliott, Cass.

Cassandane (fl. 500s BCE).

See Atossa for sidebar.

Cassandra (possibly fl. around 1200 BCE)

Trojan woman, possibly mythical, who became a prototype for historical sibyls.

Although the historicity of Cassandra's life is questionable, she became a prototype for the historical sibyls (female prophets widely dispersed throughout the Mediterranean world in antiquity). In the alleged manner of Cassandra, the sibyls successfully utilized oracular madness for centuries. Nevertheless—unlike Cassandra—sibyls were highly regarded and closely heeded until the advent of Christianity.

Legendary child of King Priam and Queen Hecuba of Troy, Cassandra was renowned as their most beautiful daughter. Whether or not there is any germ of historical truth behind the stories associated with her is unknown. Myth maintains that her beauty was so great as to attract the lust of the god Apollo, who, in bargaining for her sexual favors, is said to have bestowed upon her the power of prophesy. Granted a seer's insight and the god's promise never to revoke the precious gift, Cassandra thereafter spurned Apollo's advances. Not to be tricked by a mere mortal, however, Apollo qualified his "benefaction" by ensuring that no one would ever believe her foretellings. The most common theme running through the "life" of Cassandra associates her great beauty with ruination—of both her city and her self. At the time of her brother Paris' birth, she was thought by some to have predicted that he would be the ruin of Troy. This is said to have led to Paris' exposure, but eventual rescue by a shepherd brought her prediction to pass. (As in other myths, mere mortals could not escape fate.) The destinies of Cassandra and Paris remained intertwined; some believed that Cassandra foretold that Paris' journey to Sparta, where he met and abducted Helen, would lead to disaster for Troy. Another prophesy ignored by those Cassandra would try to save was her prediction that the Trojan horse would lead to Troy's fall. Another tale that associated Cassandra with Troy's destruction told that she was the first of her people (except Priam) to see her brother Hector's dead body as it was returned to Troy.

Cassandra's tragedy was that her fate was so linked with that of her city—and that she, like Troy, would be destroyed by beauty. Apollo was not the only male smitten by Cassandra, but unlike Apollo those mortal men who fell under her spell suffered the severest of consequences. Two would-be suitors, Coroebus of Phrygia and Othryoneus of Cabesus, fell to Greek spears before they could win Cassandra as a wife.

Cassandra's rape by the Locrian Ajax (the "lesser" Ajax, one of the second rank of Greek heroes at Troy) had far-reaching consequences. After Troy had fallen, Ajax is reported to have raped her at an altar of Athena, knocking over the image of the goddess in the process. When the Greek horde refused to punish Ajax for his impiety, the irate Athena (angry more for where the rape occurred than for the rape itself) convinced Zeus and Poseidon to attack the homeward-bound Greek armada with a great storm, in which many perished and many others were swept far from home (in Odysseus' case, for ten years). Ajax himself was either drowned or struck by a thunderbolt immediately after the tempest. One Greek who was undisturbed by the fleet's fate was King Agamemnon, but he, too, made the mistake of loving Cassandra, whom he made his slave and by whom he is said to have fathered two sons (Teledamus and Pelops). Although she was not responsible for the murderous wrath of Agamemnon's wife, Clytemnestra, Cassandra's very beauty enhanced that queen's ire, with the result that Cassandra and her hated master were murdered by Clytemnestra shortly after their arrival at Mycenae. Thus, myth has Cassandra end her days as the reluctant concubine of a hated enemy, murdered in a foreign land for reasons only hazily understood. Thought to be buried near Amyclae, Cassandra was as isolated in death from the bosom of her homeland and people as she had been during life after her unfortunate tryst with a randy god.

William S. Greenwalt,
Associate Professor of Classical History,
Santa Clara University, Santa Clara, California

Cassandra (1892–1985).

See Tabouis, Geneviève.

Cassatt, Mary (1844–1926)

American artist and grande dame of the Impressionists. Born Mary Stevenson Cassatt in Allegheny City, Pennsylvania, on May 22, 1844; died at Château de Beaufresne (Oise), France, on June 14, 1926; fourth child of Robert Simpson Cassatt and Katherine Kelso Johnston; enrolled in Pennsylvania Academy of Fine Arts, 1861; graduated, 1865; never married; no children.

Moved to Paris, France (1866); first painting exhibited in the Salon, Paris (1868); had work in Salon exhibits (1872–76); met Edgar Degas (1877); exhibited with Impressionists (1879–86); submitted murals for Women's Building, Chicago World's Fair (1893); held first one-woman show, Paris (1893); bought Château de Beaufresne (early 1890s); named honorary president of Paris Art League (1904); awarded Lippincott Prize by the Pennsylvania Academy and the N.W. Harris Prize by the Art Institute of Chicago (1904); received France's Legion of Honor (1904);

toured Egypt (1910); awarded the Gold Medal of Honor by the Pennsylvania Academy (1914).

In 1866, 22-year-old Mary Cassatt told her father that she wanted to study art in Paris. "I would rather see you dead," he responded. A few months later, the determined, self-assured young woman took up residence in France where she lived and worked for the rest of her life. From a traditional Victorian upper-middle-class family, Cassatt rejected the colorful bohemian lifestyle common among her Parisian artist friends. Yet she joined the now famous Impressionist painters, Edgar Degas, Edouard Manet, Claude Monet, Auguste Renoir, and Camille Pissarro, who rebelled against the officially sanctioned "true" art accorded the blessing of the French Academy of Fine Arts. "I recognized my true masters," Cassatt recalled. "I hated conventional art. Now I began to live."

The Cassatt family was typically bourgeois, financially comfortable, and unremarkable. Robert Cassatt was a moderately successful stockbroker and one-time mayor of Allegheny City, Pennsylvania, restless and unfocused. **Katherine Cassatt** was more intelligent than he, well-read, aloof, and rather tart. Mary inherited her father's stubbornness and her mother's sharp-edged personality. One of five children (three boys, two girls), Cassatt was brought up in a closely knit family. In the fall of 1851, the Cassatts sailed for Europe, living in Paris and Germany for four years. According to Cassatt's biographer **Nancy Hale:** "It was in France that she learned art could be an exciting cultural issue." From Paris, the family moved to Heidelberg, then to Darmstadt where Alexander (Aleck), the eldest son, could study engineering in the excellent German schools. However, when another son, Robert, age 13, died in Darmstadt in 1855, the family returned to Paris and sailed home to Philadelphia. But the lure of Paris remained strong; to Cassatt, "Paris is the place where people are happy." By contrast, Philadelphia was a cultural wasteland in her eyes, an opinion that determined her future decisions.

Once she had decided to be an artist, Cassatt persuaded her father to allow her to enroll in the Pennsylvania Academy of the Fine Arts in Philadelphia. He agreed only because he hoped this would improve Cassatt's marriage prospects. If she were adept at drawing and painting, Robert Cassatt reasoned, his daughter, who was rather plain, might attract suitors. Critical of her training at the Academy, Mary claimed it was too academic and restrictive. However, she acquired

a solid grounding in technique and graduated at the head of the class of women students in 1865. Confident in her ability and choice of career, she approached her father about furthering her studies in Europe. According to her biographers, she was "not a very inventive painter" and needed strong influences around her. She found her inspiration in Paris, the cultural capital of Europe, and among the most brilliant artists of the time, the Impressionists.

Cassatt lived with family friends in Paris, not on her own. It was unusual for any young, unmarried woman at that time to live separated from her family. Although Robert Cassatt was convinced that women lacked common sense, he "trusted" his daughter, meaning that since she was "plain," she would not attract male admirers. Actually Cassatt preferred men to women as friends. She was often described as having a "man's mind" and as viewing art from a male perspective. She considered this a compliment. In fact, her male friends were fellow artists for whom she felt no sexual attraction, only a professional attachment. Mary Cassatt never regarded herself as a "dabbler" in art, an amateur; lady-like timidity and modesty were not part of her character. In a letter to her brother Aleck's fiancée, **Lois Buchanan** (niece of President Buchanan), Cassatt compares herself to an American friend, Miss Gordon, who, though she "calls herself a painter she is only an amateur and you must know how we professionals despise amateurs." And, writes Hale, "it was on that mysterious, indisputable sense of superiority that she operated for the rest of her life." Buchanan resented Cassatt's superior attitude and envied her talent, which afforded her so much freedom.

It was not that her pictures told about her, so much as that they were her; just as the other side of the moon, hidden, is still the moon.

—Nancy Hale

In 1870, Cassatt reluctantly returned to Philadelphia when the Franco-Prussian War forced foreigners to leave France. Convinced that her paintings would sell in America but not in philistine Philadelphia, she traveled to Chicago in 1871, to consult with an art dealer. The devastating Chicago fire of that year destroyed her commercial hopes and her pictures. With peace restored, Cassatt sailed for Europe in 1872. Rather than remain in Paris, she went to Italy to further her studies of the great Masters. In Parma, she was particularly impressed with the work of Correggio whose renderings of cherubs and babies had a great influence on her future work. During her two years in Italy and Spain, Cassatt slowly developed a personal technique that would bring her recognition from the official Paris art world and the group of artists calling themselves the Independents.

In 1872, Mary Cassatt submitted a work done in Spain, During the *Carnival,* signed Mary Stevenson, to the Paris Salon. For the next four years, she exhibited in the prestigious Salon shows. Her portrait, *Ida,* in the 1874 exhibit was the first to carry her signature, Mary Cassatt. Edgar Degas, a member of the Independents-impressionists, attended the exhibit; on seeing Cassatt's work, he said, "There is someone who feels as I do." He was right. Cassatt admired the work of this group but hesitated to join a movement that was rejected by the art critics of the Salon and ridiculed by the public. She was overtly ambitious, craving recognition and financial security. But without consciously modifying her technique, Cassatt was becoming an Impressionist painter. When one of her two submissions to the 1874 Salon was rejected by the jury panel as being "too bright," she dutifully toned it down, and it was accepted the next year. However, having to conform to conventional art standards disgusted her, and when the Salon jury rejected a painting in 1877, she never submitted another.

Mary Cassatt asserted her independence, artistic and social, in an age when young women were traditionally tightly corseted, both literally and figuratively. Stubborn, opinionated, and certain of her talent, Cassatt made a life of her own choosing while remaining a member of her rather dull, bourgeois family. In 1877, the Cassatts, including her sister **Lydia** (age 40), moved to Paris, renting a large apartment in Montmartre, an artistic district of Paris. The Cassatts had not come to Paris to absorb culture; money and position defined who one was. Although Mary had exhibited in Salon shows and had sold some of her pictures, Robert Cassatt did not consider this sufficient. One painted to make money, why else paint? His son Aleck was a vice-president of the Pennsylvania Railroad, and Gardner, the youngest child, was in banking, both very wealthy men. Cassatt, too, was proud of her brothers, but she rebelled against painting "pot-boilers" to earn money.

Mary accepted, and never resented, the more restricted lifestyle imposed on her. Family meant love and security. Her profession meant freedom, creation, and recognition. She comfortably inhabited these two worlds, distinct and fulfilling. Her interest in the Impressionists provided stimulus for her art and for friendships. In 1877, Cassatt finally met Degas, who asked her to join the Impressionist group. "I accepted with joy," she recalled. She was one of the few Americans in Paris who sincerely appreciated the importance of this movement. Mary had learned much by copying the Old Masters in the Louvre museum, and she learned from Degas, too. "He was the first to recognize what I had attempted to do. He *knew*," she stated. Degas and Cassatt were similar in many ways; they were dogmatic, egocentric, bad-tempered, and strong-willed. Good breeding, intelligence, and taste were also important to these prickly personalities.

From the mid-1870s, Cassatt turned from the Old Masters for inspiration to her contemporaries—Manet, Sisley, Pissarro, Monet, and Renoir. Their originality and rebellion against academically sanctioned art bound them together. Unlike their fellow artists, however, Cassatt and Degas lived lives of respectability and decorum, eschewing sexual or romantic liaisons. Cassatt

Self-Portrait, *by*
Mary Cassatt
(1880).

sought equality, not love, from Degas. There is no evidence of an affair, something Cassatt vehemently denied. "What a repulsive idea," she declared. Degas was an astute critic of Cassatt's work, suggesting to her "the maternal theme which was to occupy her talents to some degree for the rest of her career." She wanted to learn from Degas, to share ideas about art, but she would not be dependent on him. She had liberated herself from societal strictures, from marriage, because she knew that "a woman artist must be . . . capable of making the primary sacrifices."

Mary Cassatt and Edgar Degas exhibited with the Impressionists from 1879 to 1886, adhering to the Impressionist principle of not showing in juried exhibits. Her experience in 1878 confirmed her objections to juries. Her painting, *The Blue Room,* for which Degas painted some of the background, was rejected for the American section of the Great Exhibition in Paris by a jury of three men, "of whom one was a pharmacist," Cassatt fumed. In 1879, she exhibited her marvelous work, *The Loge,* a sensitive depiction of Lydia in a box at the Opéra. Several paintings of Lydia and of Katherine Cassatt and her grandchildren earned good reviews from French critics. Mary's reputation as an Impressionist was made in France. But not in America where the Impressionists were simply ignored. Similarly, Cassatt's parents were largely ignorant of and indifferent to art in general. Mary not only created, she collected art. With earnings from exhibitions, she purchased Impressionist paintings and encouraged her brothers in America to buy from the artists or her own art dealer in Paris, the Durand-Ruel Gallery. However, they never displayed a taste for or interest in art. Her parents had little contact with French culture or French people except for Cassatt's artist and writer friends, and they had no contact with the extensive American colony in Paris. The Cassatts lived a comfortable life in France; they hired servants, kept a carriage and horses, and spent summers in the country.

Cassatt used family members as models for some of her best pictures; Lydia posed for *The Garden* and *The Cup of Tea,* and Katherine sat for *Reading Le Figaro* (1882), one of Mary Cassatt's finest works. Women and children were her forte. Portraits of her brother Aleck and of her father on horseback are, in contrast, stiff and prosaic. It is curious that she could never capture men on canvas since she liked men better than women; she liked horses, too, but her few paintings that include horses are not memorable. Nancy Hale attributes Cassatt's success in portraying women and children to her memory rather than personal experience which, she says, accounts for the absence of sentimentality in her portraits. The 1880s were Cassatt's most creative period, producing 12 pictures in 1889 alone, placing great emphasis on design and on delicate texture, with landscapes and still life simply serving as background to her individualized figures. In her work, as with other Impressionists, light was a major element, interior light and the light of Paris. Degas judged Cassatt to be a master draftswoman, essential to producing "good" art. Cassatt agreed, and nothing irritated her more

than hearing people say "only a woman" could have painted a particular picture. If her horses and men were wooden, lifeless images, her women and children evoked positive responses from viewers. However, when she did a portrait of Mrs. Riddle, her mother's cousin, the woman's daughter rejected it because the nose was too large. *Lady at the Tea Table* was relegated to a closet for many years before being exhibited by Durand-Ruel in 1914, causing a great sensation; Cassatt gave it to the Metropolitan Museum of Art in New York in 1923. In 1886, Durand-Ruel organized an exhibit of Impressionist paintings in New York for the American Art Association, including two by Mary Cassatt. This was the first major showing of these artists in the United States, and, as Cassatt had predicted, Americans did not appreciate them.

Mary Cassatt's ascendancy in the French art world was the result of hard work and her strong will; "none but those who have painted a picture know what it costs in time and strength," she declared. She earned a good income and was able to contribute to family expenses. In 1887, she found a large apartment for herself and her parents (Lydia died of Bright's disease in 1882) at 10, rue de Marignan, off the Champs-Élysées, large enough to accommodate Cassatt's studio and servants' quarters. Since her family had moved to Paris a decade earlier, Cassatt had been responsible for finding their apartments in Paris and villas for their summer holidays. Cassatt's brothers, Aleck and Gardner, and their families, often visited for extended periods, her nieces and nephews serving as models for some of her best paintings. Aleck's wife, Lois Buchanan, disliked the Cassatts, especially Mary: "I cannot abide Mary and never will," she wrote to her sister. No doubt Cassatt's abrasive personality and superior attitude made her a difficult relative and friend, but the family attributed this to artistic temperament.

Close ties with the French Impressionists were abruptly severed in 1891 with the formation of a new group, the Society of French Painters-Engravers. As an American, Cassatt was excluded, as was Pissarro who was born in the West Indies. Barred from exhibiting with the Society, Cassatt arranged a one-woman show next door at Durand-Ruel's gallery. But public attention had shifted to Pointillism and neo-impressionism, and her show attracted little attention. Cassatt's work sold well in France, but in America she and the Impressionists had not yet found a market. The reaction of the untutored American public was confirmed for Cassatt when she painted a series of murals depicting *The Modern Woman* for the Women's Building at the Chicago World's Fair of 1893. Her panels were described by critics as "erratic and ridiculous," to which she reacted angrily: "After all, give me France. Women do not have to fight for recognition here if they do serious work." In contrast to the American reception of her work, the Luxemburg Palace museum in Paris purchased a set of her etchings, and the French government invited her to contribute a picture for the national collection. Curiously, Cassatt declined the government request, though it was an honor. Another one-woman show, comprising 98 items, at the Durand-Ruel gallery received great acclaim from French critics, who rated *The Boating Party* as one of her best paintings. In New York, two years later, the same exhibit aroused scant interest. American art critics disparaged Impressionist art in general; a review several years earlier summed up their attitude. "[Impressionism] is founded neither on the laws of Nature nor the dictates of common sense. We can see in it only the uneasy striving after notoriety of a restless vanity, that prefers celebrity for ill doing rather than [pursuing] the paths of true Art."

Cassatt produced a large number of fine works in the 1880s and 1890s; over 200 pieces of graphic art, aquatints, pastels, a few drawings, watercolors, and *gouaches* attest to her assertion that art entailed hard work. She continued using the mother-and-child theme, but, writes Hale, "she varied her interpretation constantly and through change of scale, mood, and tone avoided monotony." William Wiser described Mary Cassatt as an "intimist, a delineator of intimate life and a brilliant interpreter of character in portraiture." Her *Young Women Picking Fruit, Woman Arranging Her Veil,* and *Young Girl in Large Hat* illustrate her adept handling of female subjects in a natural, non-formulaic, manner.

Mary Cassatt's contribution to the world of art was not limited to her own creations. She was, Wiser stated, "the first to introduce American wealth to European art." In 1873, Cassatt had met ✒➤ **Louisine Elder (Havemeyer)**, an American in Paris, who shared Cassatt's love of art. Cassatt convinced her to purchase a Degas for $100 (sold by Havemeyer's grandson in 1965 for $410,000). After Louisine married the wealthy Henry O. Havemeyer, Cassatt acted as their guide and advisor during their numerous sojourns in Europe. An artist and connoisseur, Cassatt advised her friends wisely; in Spain, she recognized a fake Goya being offered by a Spanish noblewoman. She later found the original in

Havemeyer, Louisine (1855–1929)

American art collector. Born Louisine Waldron Elder in Philadelphia, Pennsylvania, in 1855; died of heart disease on January 6, 1929; daughter of George W. Elder (a sugar refiner); married Henry Osborne Havemeyer (a mogul in the sugar industry), in 1883 (died 1907); children: **Adaline Havemeyer Frelinghuysen** (b. 1884); Horace Havemeyer (b. 1886); **Electra Havemeyer Webb** (b. 1888, also a collector).

The Havemeyers of Philadelphia were an extraordinary team of art collectors. "He was the plunger, she was the thrifty one," wrote *Aline B. Saarinen in *The Proud Possessors.* "He brought to collecting the nerve. . . . She brought to it so eager a desire to be an 'original' that she encouraged their venturing into the vanguard." He bought by the car load; she preferred hunting down one object at a time. In the beginning, Henry Havemeyer's interests were primarily with Persian and Oriental pottery, rugs, tea jars, three-dimensional objects. It was Louisine Havemeyer and *Mary Cassatt who convinced him to move into paintings.

The daughter of George Elder, a sugar refiner who had been in business with Henry Havemeyer's father, Louisine spent her girlhood wandering European galleries and museums. The Elders belonged to the same Philadelphia set as the Cassatts. When Mary Cassatt arrived in Paris, she looked up Louisine and the two joined hands for purchasing expeditions. Though Louisine had only a small allowance, she saved and spent wisely (with the help of Cassatt)—a habit held for a lifetime. (In 1913, Louisine bid $40,000 on a Daumier but took a bus to the auction.)

When the Havemeyers were married in 1883, he was 36 and she 29. He had been married earlier to her aunt. It was Louisine who tracked and stored the vast collection—which included Greco's *View of Toledo,* Goya's *Women on a Balcony,* Manet's *Le Bal de l'Opéra,* Daumier's *Third Class Carriage,* and Courbet's *Landscape and Deer*—in their Fifth Avenue mansion, interiors by Tiffany, at 1 East 66th Street.

Following Henry's death in 1907, Louisine continued collecting; she also carried on with her Sunday musicales and Tuesday at homes. The famous collection was viewed by many callers, including Lord Kitchener. Also a feminist, Havemeyer lectured in support of enfranchisement and better education for women ("Women were good ballast on the *Mayflower,* why not on the Ship of State") and once lent the collection for a suffragist benefit. To the horror of relatives, she also spent a night in the lock-up with 28 other campaigners.

On her death in 1929, Louisine Havemeyer bequeathed 142 works of art from "The H.O. Havemeyer Collection" to the Metropolitan Museum of Art; by 1930, her children had increased the bequest to 1,972 items. It was "one of the most magnificent donations ever made to a museum of art," said Edward Robinson, then director of the museum.

SOURCES:
Saarinen, Aline B. *The Proud Possessors.* NY: Random House, 1958.

France, and the Havemeyers added it to their extensive collection, which eventually became a part of the Metropolitan Museum of Art in New York. Cassatt's advice was also sought by her friend James Stillman, a retired American banker who lived in Paris. As with the Havemeyers, Cassatt traveled with Stillman to various museums and galleries in Europe to purchase individual pieces of art. They enjoyed a longterm friendship, but Cassatt, as usual, avoided a romantic entanglement or even the hint of impropriety in their relationship. To Cassatt's great disappointment, the few pieces of art she persuaded her brothers to purchase were later disposed of by their heirs; Lois Buchanan destroyed the portrait Cassatt had done of her years earlier.

After Cassatt's father died in 1891, she bought a 17th-century manor house, Château de Beaufresne, with 45 acres of gardens and parks near Mesnil-Théribus (Oise) with her own money. Known locally as "The Empress" for her aristocratic demeanor, Cassatt became quite active in local affairs with a special interest in politics. At Beaufresne, she "lived the life of a well-to-do, cultivated American"; seven servants, including her German housekeeper Mathilde, provided her with all the comforts she demanded. Cassatt refused to hire French servants because under French law they could be dismissed only for gross misbehavior; she felt this restricted her freedom of action. Dressed by the best French dressmakers, she preferred English shoes to the "frivolous" French footwear, and had a passion for old jewelry. Elegant and distinguished, she impressed the local villagers by her charity and concern for them. A local button factory was the chief employer in the area, and Cassatt thought young women should have access to better opportunities. She trained some young women as domestics and placed them with families in Paris; one of them attended the Cordon Bleu cooking school in Paris, at Cassatt's expense, and was employed by Baron Rothschild's family. Cassatt lived on at the château and in the apartment on the rue de Marignan after her mother's death in 1895. At age 50, she remained a good conversationalist and enjoyed visits from her small circle of friends, including Degas whose acrid remarks and inflexible opinions matched her own. Cassatt's interest in spiritualism was shared by **Mrs. Montgomery Sears**, an American living in Paris, and Cassatt often attended the Thursday evening seances at her house.

To Mary Cassatt, decorum and respectability were essential elements of social discourse; those who violated her sensibilities were quickly dismissed. On meeting Leo and *Gertrude Stein*, American expatriates and art collectors, she promptly dismissed them as social deviants. Sears had persuaded Cassatt to attend a Stein "evening at home," frequented by artists and writers, and to see their collection of modern art, which included Matisses, Picassos, and Cubists. Cassatt was unimpressed: "I have never seen so many dreadful paintings in one place . . . [and] so many dreadful people gathered together, and I want to be taken home." The "prim Philadelphia spinster" had no use for the frumpy Americans or for the avant-garde art of the early 20th century. She even dismissed Monet's famous water-lilies as nothing but "glorified wall paper." Cassatt's friendship with Degas was shaken by the nationally divisive Dreyfus Affair. Alfred Dreyfus, a Jewish army captain, was accused of selling secrets to the Germans; he was tried, found guilty, and sent to prison on Devil's Island. Cassatt and Degas embodied the prejudices of their time and class, but she slowly realized that Dreyfus might have been falsely accused, which was later proven to be the case. Degas refused to consider the possibility, and his virulent anti-Semitism led him to break with his old friend Pissarro, a Jew. To Cassatt, Pissarro was an artist and a friend, "so not a Jew at all." She attended his funeral in 1904; Degas did not.

Like many expatriates, Cassatt lived all her adult life in France while retaining her American identity. She never considered living in the United States but made two extended visits in 1898–99 and in 1908–09. She suffered from debilitating seasickness and had to be carried from the ship after her final voyage, followed by weeks of bedrest. Cassatt vowed never to return, and she didn't. Moreover, she remained critical of the inadequate attention paid to collecting major artists by American museum directors; she attributed this to lack of taste, not lack of money. Her dismissal of most modern art—all lines and squiggles—did not mean she took a narrow view of art. On a cruise up the Nile River with Gardner and his family in the fall of 1910, she was impressed with the majestic Egyptian art, "all strength, no room . . . for grace, for children, none. Only intellect and strength," she wrote. But exposure to this ancient art never influenced her techniques as had an earlier Japanese exposition of woodcut prints in Paris.

Mary Cassatt had definite ideas about most subjects, and she also held to a rigid set of principles from which she refused to deviate. In 1904, she finally received recognition from the American art world that she had so long coveted. The Pennsylvania Academy awarded her the Lippincott Prize of $300 for her painting *Caress*. She declined the offer, informing the Academy that "I must stick to my principles . . . no jury, no medals, no awards." She suggested the money be given instead to a young, struggling artist. Her principles were obviously not taken seriously by the Academy—they asked her to serve as a juror that same year; she, of course, refused. Ten years later, Cassatt did accept the Gold Medal of Honor from them; no money was involved and it was given for her entire production, not a specific picture. The Art Institute of Chicago also presented her with a prize, the N.W. Harris Prize of $500 for *Caress*. Again, she refused to accept it. The prize money was awarded to an art student, as she directed. And France honored her; Mary Cassatt was made Chevalier of the Legion of Honor, which she proudly accepted.

Cassatt's brother Gardner had fallen ill during their trip to Egypt and died in Paris in April 1911. Devastated by his death, she suffered what she called a "breakdown." Alone and depressed, her health deteriorated. Cataracts and diabetes, for which she was given radium treatments, restricted her ability to work. A series of operations failed to save her sight. Friends and relatives noticed a change in her personality. Short-tempered and vindictive, she lashed out at all around her. When war came in August 1914, Cassatt was at her château. She left for the south of France but returned to Beaufresne in 1915, which was at times only 50 miles from the front lines. The faithful Mathilde was interned and deported as an enemy national, leaving Cassatt more isolated than ever, but she never considered returning to the United States, a "hopeless cultural vacuum of a society dedicated primarily to material gain. Its politics were ridiculous, its ambitions shameful." Ravaged by war, France was still more congenial. Amidst the horrendous carnage, the death of Degas in 1917 was barely noticed by most of the nation. However, Cassatt was saddened by the loss of "my oldest friend here and the last great artist of the 19th century. I see no one to replace him."

Nearly blind and raging against her disabilities, Cassatt did not find the postwar years happy. Unable to paint, she systematically began to dispose of her numerous works. She wrote a friend that she realized "the absurdity of keeping a picture to leave a nephew or niece, who care nothing for art, and certainly not for my pictures." Cassatt had offered *The Boating Party* to her niece Ellen Mary, who never bothered to reply. Durand-Ruel sold it for 10,000 francs.

Furthermore, she wrote, her family "secretly resent my reputation, for which I care little." Even Louisine Havemeyer did not escape Cassatt's vitriol. Cassatt sent two sets of dry-point plates to Louisine who was to negotiate a purchase by William Ivins, curator of prints at the Metropolitan Museum of Art in New York. Ivins said the plates were old and worn and that the Museum already had a set of these prints. Cassatt insisted they had never been printed and that Louisine and Ivins were conspiring to defraud her. Refusing to admit she was wrong, Cassatt ended her 50-year friendship with Havemeyer.

Mary Cassatt died at Beaufresne and was buried there alongside her parents, her sister Lydia, and brother Robbie. Her longtime art dealer, Durand-Ruel said of her, "In Paris, she has always been appreciated as a great painter. . . . It was her *own* country that failed to value her." Fortunately, this is no longer true.

SOURCES:

Hale, Nancy. *Mary Cassatt*. Reading, MA: Addison-Wesley, 1987.

Sweet, Frederick A. *Mary Cassatt: Impressionist from Pennsylvania*. Norman: University of Oklahoma Press, 1966.

Wiser, William. *The Great Good Place: American Expatriate Women in Paris*. NY: W.W. Norton, 1991.

SUGGESTED READING:

Dillon, Millicent. *After Egypt: Isadora Duncan and Mary Cassatt*. NY: Dutton, 1990.

Mathews, Nancy Mowll. *Mary Cassatt: A Life*. NY: Villard Books, 1994.

Pollack, Griselda. *Mary Cassatt*. NY: Harper and Row, 1980.

Jeanne A. Ojala, Professor of History, University of Utah, Salt Lake City, Utah

Cassian, Nina (1924—)

Rumanian poet, translator and composer whose work was scrutinized and subjected to political stricture. Born on November 27, 1924, in Galati, Rumania; educated at public schools; married Vladimir (Jany) Colin (1921–1991, a poet), in January 1943 (divorced); married Al. I. (Ali) Stefanescu (1915–1983), in 1948; no children.

Selected works: La Scala 1/1 (On the Scale of One to One, 1947); Nica fara frica (Fearless Niki, 1952); Numaratoarea in versa (Countdown, 1983); Life Sentence (1990).

Nina Cassian was born on November 27, 1924, in Galati, Rumania. Her Jewish father was a French-German translator despite having little formal education, and the family moved often following job opportunities. He encouraged her schooling, and she enrolled at the Pompilian Institute as a teen. Expelled when Fascism took hold in Rumania, she finished her education at a high school for Jewish girls. As a reaction against Fascism, she became a Communist.

Her brief marriage to poet Vladimir Colin ended before the 1947 publication of her first verse collection, *La Scala 1/1*, under the name Nina Cassian. She met and married Al. I. Stefanescu as her popularity rose. When her poetry came under political scrutiny, the government deemed her too lofty and demanded that she reduce her vocabulary and figurative language. Her style thus stifled, she turned to translating, writing children's books, and composing music. In the decades after Stalin's death, as government strictures tightened and loosened, Cassian's poetry followed suit.

After her husband died in 1983, Cassian obtained a visiting professorship at New York University. Upon her arrival in the United States in 1985, she was granted a Fulbright Fellowship (she had won the fellowship several years earlier but Rumania had refused to advise her of it). Shortly into her stay, Cassian learned that a long-standing friend in Rumania, Gheorghe Ursu, had been imprisoned; his primary offense centered around his diary, which contained a copy of her unpublished satirization of President Nicolae Ceausescu and other authorities. Cassian requested and was granted U.S. political asylum; her friend was tortured to death; and Cassian's home and possessions in Bucharest were seized. In her home country, Cassian's poetry was withdrawn from publication, and the author was erased from her country's recorded history.

SOURCES:
Smith, William Jay. "Introduction," in *Life Sentence*. London: Anvil Press, 1990.

Crista Martin,
Boston, Massachusetts

Castellanos, Rosario (1925–1974)

Mexican writer who published many volumes of poetry and two novels, which are part of her "Chiapas Cycle" of fiction. Born in Mexico City, Mexico, on May 25, 1925; grew up on her wealthy parents' coffee plantation near the town of Comitán close to the Mexico-Guatamala border; died the result of an accident in Tel Aviv, Israel, August 7, 1974; studied at National University; married Ricardo Guerra, in 1958 (divorced 1971); children: one son, Gabriel.

Became deeply aware of both the suffering of the Indian population of Chiapas province and the subordinate position of women in a culture dominated by the concept of machismo; *educated in Mexico City and became a member of the literary "Generation of 1950."*

Selected works: Another Way to Be: Selected Works of Rosario Castellanos *(University of Georgia Press, 1990);* Book of Lamentations *(Marsilio, 1996);* City of Kings *(Latin American Literary Review Press, 1993);* Meditation on the Threshold: A Bilingual Anthology of Poetry *(Bilingual Press/Editorial Bilingüe, 1988);* The Nine Guardians: A Novel *(Readers International, 1992);* A Rosario Castellanos Reader: An Anthology of Her Poetry, Short Fiction, Essays, and Journals *(University of Texas Press, 1988);* The Selected Poems of Rosario Castellanos *(Graywolf Press, 1988).*

Although she enjoyed an excellent reputation in her own country as a poet and novelist in her lifetime, it is only since her accidental death in 1974 that Rosario Castellanos has become known to the world as not only one of Mexico's major writers but as its strongest and most persuasive feminist voice. Born into an elite landowning family while they were visiting Mexico City, she spent her formative years on her parents' coffee plantation near the small town of Comitán, situated in the cool highlands of Chiapas. Despite her position in the privileged landowning oligarchy of Chiapas province, the young girl was burdened in her earliest years by a somber family environment. Her father was melancholy and introverted, her mother remote and emotionally unresponsive. Typical of Mexico's *machismo* culture, her parents clearly favored her brother Benjamin. On one occasion, her mother told her, "Your father and I love you because we're obliged to." Rosario was only eight when her brother died suddenly from an untreated appendicitis; his death left her profoundly guilt-ridden because she had often wished for him to die.

Sensitive and highly observant, Rosario remained in the background of the Castellanos clan, learning about the world not from her parents but from her nurse and maid, Rufina. An uneducated peasant woman of Indian blood, Rufina not only took care of Rosario but loved her. Instructing her in the myths, legends and folk wisdom that constituted her own world, Rufina provided her young charge with an alternative environment that was then supplemented by literature. In 1941, the government program of agrarian reform resulted in the appropriation of her family's land. Rosario and her parents moved to Mexico City, where she began her studies at the National University. Her literary interests blossomed, and she joined a group of

Rosario Castellanos

other young writers who came to be known as the "Generation of the 1950s." Even before her graduation, she published her first book in 1948, a long poem, "Trajectory of Dust," which was her powerful response to the death of both of her parents the same year.

Castellanos' master's degree in philosophy, "On Feminine Culture" (1950), is now seen as a landmark in the history of Mexican feminism. Given the confinements for women in Mexican culture, feminist ideals were profoundly subversive of the existing social and gender structure, but Castellanos was determined to explore new areas of thinking whatever the cost. Never afraid

to probe her own despair, in the early 1950s a bout with tuberculosis inspired another book of poetry.

Her first novel, *Balún-Canán* (1957), translated as *The Nine Guardians* (1959), received the Chiapas Prize in 1958 and is clearly autobiographical, describing events in Chiapas during the turbulent 1930s through the eyes of a seven-year old Indian girl. This sensitive work shows the profound differences between the magical, mythical world of the Indians and the rational, scientific Ladino (non-Indian) way of life. Tzotil Indian myths are blended with stories of the traditional system of oppression of Indians and women to create a rich tapestry of life in a pre-industrial world. The small Chiapas town of Comitán, which is depicted in this novel, struggles with the basic problems of Mexican society, namely the oppression of the Indian majority and the subjugation of women. Possessing little wealth or power, the "obscure" individuals depicted are often profoundly wise in their judgments and capable of deep understanding of human problems.

Throughout the next decades, Castellanos became a successful academic, teaching first at the Institute of Indian Affairs in her native state of Chiapas, then later in Mexico City at the National University where she held a chair in journalism from 1960 through 1966. Castellanos' confidence as a writer was strengthened by the positive critical response to her first novel, and she continued to explore the world of Chiapas in *Los convidados de agosto* (*The Guests of August*), a collection of short stories published in 1964. As in *Balún-Canán*, the dilemmas of being female in male-dominated Mexican society are explored with great power and sensitivity. Individuals in the story attempt to give some meaning to their desperate situations, lest their frustrated existences "like water, seem to filter through the fingers of the hand." Abandoned by fathers and lovers, Castellanos' women often accept their passive role, resignedly waiting for something to happen rather than initiating action. The 1962 novel, *Oficio de tienblas* (*Book of Lamentations*), is also set in Chiapas and further explores many of these same themes. The work's central character, an Indian woman who becomes a priestess and healer, is embroiled in a tragic uprising against Spanish rule. One of the main themes of this book, which many critics believe to be Castellanos' best novel, is that the Spanish language itself has served for centuries as a primary tool in the oppression and exploitation of Mexico's indigenous population and its women. Castellanos tells us that only a systematic effort of understanding and organized resistance by the oppressed will eventually overthrow the system controlled by the male elite.

In 1966, Castellanos resigned from the university in protest over government meddling in the internal affairs of her institution, and was a visiting fellow at the universities of Wisconsin, Indiana and Colorado. With the political situation in Mexico somewhat stabilized, she returned home in 1967 to once again teach at the National University, this time specializing in literature courses. By now, Castellanos was Mexico's leading woman writer and one of the country's best-known intellectuals abroad. That same year, 1967, she was named Mexico's Woman of the Year, also receiving a major literary award, the Carlos Trouyet Prize, for her oeuvre.

The year 1971 marked a major transition in the writer's life. After 13 years of marriage, she divorced Ricardo Guerra, a philosophy professor whom she had met at the university. The pain of separation was considerably lessened by the fact that she retained custody of her son Gabriel. She left her university post to begin a career as a diplomat, a new phase in her life. Appointed Mexican ambassador to Israel in 1971 by President Luis Echeverria, she was clearly enthusiastic about the possibilities presented by the opportunity. In addition to her diplomatic duties, she had sufficient energy left over to teach a literature course at the University of Tel Aviv. These activities were brought to a sudden and tragic end on August 7, 1974, in Tel Aviv when Rosario Castellanos was accidentally electrocuted while trying to plug in a lamp. Her body was flown to Mexico City where she received a state funeral. She was buried in the Rotunda de los Hombres Ilustros, a tomb in which repose the nation's most revered artists and leaders.

Despite the serious and often tragic nature of her subjects, Castellanos often used humor in her writings. In her posthumously staged drama, *The Eternal Feminine*, a farce set in a beauty parlor, the hair driers and other paraphernalia of the shop are depicted as being used by *machismo* society to keep women in their place. Though Castellanos took a more serious tone in her feminist writings, she was neither pompous nor preachy. Despite a life that was often unhappy and painful, she drew strength and pleasure from writing and communicating. Her friend and colleague **Elena Poniatowska** spoke for many when she claimed: "I believe that Rosario Castellanos was a great Mexican writer, if not great in all she wrote, great in her aspirations. And great above all for the love she inspired and continues to inspire in us. Before her, no one except Sor *Juana [Inés de la Cruz]** truly devoted herself to her vocation. No woman lived to write like her. Rosario is faithfully that: a creator, a maker of books. Her books—poetry and prose—are the diary of her life."

SOURCES:

Anderson, Helene M. "Rosario Castellanos and the Structures of Power," in Doris Meyer and Margarite Fernández Olmos, eds., *Contemporary Women Authors of Latin America: Introductory Essays*. NY: Brooklyn College Press, 1983, pp. 22–32.

Bruckner, D.J.R. "Woman's Many Lives In 'El Eterno Femenino'," in *The New York Times*. March 25, 1990, p. 63.

Castellanos, Rosario. *Another Way to Be: Selected Works of Rosario Castellanos*. Edited and translated by Myralyn F. Allgood. Athens, GA: University of Georgia Press, 1990.

———. *Book of Lamentations*. Translated by Alma Guillermoprieto. Marsilio, 1996.

———. *City of Kings*. Translated by Robert S. Rudder and Gloria Chacón de Arjona. Pittsburgh, PA: Latin American Literary Review Press, 1993.

———. *Meditation on the Threshold: A Bilingual Anthology of Poetry*. Translated and with an Introduction by Julian Palley. Tempe, AZ: Bilingual Press/Editorial Bilingüe, 1988.

———. *The Nine Guardians: A Novel*. Translated and with a preface by Irene Nicholson. Columbia, LA: Readers International, 1992.

———. *A Rosario Castellanos Reader: An Anthology of Her Poetry, Short Fiction, Essays, and Journals*. Edited and with a critical introduction by Maureen Ahern. Translated by Maureen Ahern and others. Austin: University of Texas Press, 1988.

———. *The Selected Poems of Rosario Castellanos*. Edited by Cecilia Vicuña and Magda Bogin. Translated by Magda Bogin. Saint Paul, MN: Graywolf Press, 1988.

Donahue, Francis. "Feminists in Latin America," in *Arizona Quarterly*. Vol. 41, no. 1. Spring 1985, pp. 38–60.

Fox-Lockert, Lucia. *Women Novelists in Spain and Spanish America*. Metuchen, NJ: Scarecrow Press, 1979.

Magill, Frank N., ed. *Masterpieces of Latino Literature*. NY: HarperCollins, 1994.

Meyer, Doris, ed. *Lives on the Line: The Testimony of Contemporary Latin American Authors*. Berkeley, CA: University of California Press, 1988.

Miller, Beth Kurti. *Rosario Castellanos: Una conciencia feminista en Mexico*. Chiapas: UNACH/Universidad Autonoma de Chiapas, 1983.

Rodriguez-Peralta, Phyllis. "Images of Women in Rosario Castellanos' Prose," in *Latin American Literary Review*. Vol. 6, Fall-Winter 1977, pp. 68–80.

Sommers, Joseph. "The Changing View of the Indian in Mexican Literature," in *Hispania*. Vol. 47, no. 1. March 1964, pp. 47–55.

"A Woman Who Knew Latin," in *The Nation*. Vol. 248, no. 25. June 26, 1989, pp. 891–893.

John Haag, Associate Professor,
University of Georgia, Athens, Georgia

Castiglione, Virginie, Countess de (b. 1837)

Florentine noblewoman sent to France to influence Napoleon III. Name variations: Virginia Oldoini or Oldoïni; Contessa Virginie di Castiglione. Born in Florence on March 22, 1837; died after 1875; daughter of Marchese Filippo Oldoini (a diplomat and erstwhile tutor to Prince Louis Napoleon) and an invalided mother; granddaughter of jurist Lamporecchi; cousin of Count Camillo di Cavour; married the Count Francesco di Castiglione, in 1851 (some sources cite 1855); children: (with Castiglione) one son; (with Napoleon III) *one son, known in later life as Dr. Hugenschmidt, a dentist.*

Emperor Napoleon III had a habit of listening to the views of his many paramours on affairs of state. After consulting with his advisers and Empress *Eugenie, he was known to do an about-face the morning after a night of love, and Eugenie once told a friend that she hated these "influences by night."

In 1855, one Virginie Oldoïni, countess de Castiglione, arrived from Italy: a present to Napoleon from Count Camillo Cavour, an Italian aristocrat and master manipulator of Europe's diplomatic scene, and the chief counsel to the king of Sardinia. Cavour and his king, Victor Emmanuel II, were intent on the unification of Italy. Because Emperor Francis Joseph of Austria held Italy's rich northern provinces, Cavour needed the help of the French military to take on the Austrian emperor. Thus, the Countess Castiglione was sent to Napoleon with instructions to obtain a Franco-Italian alliance, stipulating that if Austria made war, France would join with Italy in combat.

The daughter of a diplomat, Virginie di Castiglione grew up lonely in a large palazzo in Florence, the home of her grandfather, Lamporecchi, a well-known jurist. By age 12, she was a great beauty, and her ailing mother was actively seeking suitors for marriage. At age 14, in 1851 (some sources claim age 18), she became the wife of a young widower, Count Francesco di Castiglione, equerry to Victor Emmanuel. Francesco was also the king's procurer. Thus, the countess was soon involved with the king, as well as others, including her cousin Count Camillo Cavour. Cavour soon realized that her talents could be put to better use. He groomed her for espionage, provided her with an eye-catching wardrobe and a codebook, and sent the 20-year-old to Paris. "A beautiful countess has just been enrolled in the Italian diplomatic corps," Cavour wrote to the foreign minister of Turin: "I have invited her to flirt with the emperor, and I promised her that if she succeeds, I will get her brother the position of secretary to the embassy in St. Petersburg."

Cavour sent word ahead that Paris was about to visited by the "most beautiful woman in Europe." Because of the advance notice, when the countess made her first public appearance—a tardy, contrived entrance at a Tuileries ball—the dancing stopped, along with the orchestra. After she made her obeisance to the emperor and empress, Napoleon asked her to dance; their affair began soon after. The countess spent weekends at his villa at St. Cloud and could be seen strolling the evening paths at Compiègne. As a member of the Florentine nobility, Castiglione easily accessed the French upper strata, getting to know Princess *Mathilde (1820–1904) and Countess **Marianne Walewska**. Looking back, Lady Holland (*Mary Fox) wrote that, in all her years of entertaining, she could recall only one woman: "as being absolutely faultless, alike in figure and feature, from the crown of her head to the sole of her foot," *la belle* Castiglione.

Eugenie, who always knew of her husband's affairs, knew immediately. At a time when French actresses appeared at Parisian balls in sparing attire, Countess Castiglione outdid them. She pioneered the see-through top, sometimes wearing little more than her beauty, and quickly became a Paris sensation. On the streets, citizens climbed lampposts to see her; in England, those of quality stood on chairs to glimpse her latest outrage. When the countess arrived at one ball as the Queen of Hearts in a gown so low-cut that only decorative hearts covered her breasts, Eugenie commented, "You wear your heart rather low down, don't you?," and sent her home.

Even so, Castiglione had the emperor firmly in her pocket. Napoleon loved the intrigue, sending missives back and forth between Florence and Paris. But she was also in league with two of Napoleon's enemies: Thiers and the duke d'Aumale. Much that has been handed down of the countess comes from the many letters she sent back to Florence and to one of the duke d'Aumale's secretaries, a man named Estancelin with whom she had a 45-year relationship.

By night, she and Napoleon III plotted French-Italian strategy, while he blithely bypassed his ministers. By day, she carried documents from one embassy to another or drove to the border to deliver information in person to her husband who, in turn, met with Cavour. She was ambitious and calculating. Despite the warnings of his police, Napoleon continued his evening talks. His ministers brought in **Marguerite Beranger**, an ex-circus rider, to counter the effects of the countess, but to no avail.

In 1858, with none of his ministers the wiser, Napoleon had a secret meeting with Cavour at Plombières, France, and offered the Italian diplomat all that he was after: the services of the French military. Soon, the countess told Napoleon that Austria had infiltrated Italian borders, and Napoleon immediately led his troops to Italy. The French were quickly victorious. But to the countess' and Cavour's fury, with a war only partially won, Napoleon made peace with Francis Joseph of Austria and brought his troops back to France. Eugenie had called him home.

"I would have made him a conqueror," the countess fumed to a friend, "in word, in deed, in private and in public . . . but my Napoleon did not dare, and I abandoned him and his concerns." Some say Napoleon was getting bored with his countess, possibly because she might have been involved in a half-hearted attempt on his life. There are two versions to the story. In the first, Napoleon left Castiglione's house in the Avenue Montaigne one early morning and was attacked by three Italian thugs but saved by his driver. In another version, as the emperor entered the countess' room during an assignation, her maidservant signaled someone in the shadows of the darkened stairwell. A man appeared and climbed the stairs. As luck would have it, a member of Napoleon's secret police was standing in a separate shadow. When the man, armed with a revolver and a poisoned stiletto, turned the handle to enter the room, the constabulary stabbed him in the back and killed him. Though this might have been a French setup to put the countess in a negative light, Castiglione was quickly banished from France, and Eugenie had one less mistress to deal with.

In Turin, the countess lived in an isolated hilltop house with her small son. To all appearances, she was haughty, self-absorbed, and vain (she sat for 190 photograph sessions), a cold-hearted beauty who did not suffer anyone gladly and received few visitors. But a French diplomat, Henri d'Ideville, was granted an interview and returned often. Eventually, the countess spoke candidly with him. Henri wrote that he discovered a warm, generous, intelligent person. When asked why she wore the haughty mask, she responded: "I scarcely began my life, when my role was ended."

Eventually the countess returned to Paris where she entertained and tried to maintain her beauty, hiding her age and that of her son, dressing him as a groom in her household (he lived with the servants), conspiring with Thiers to overthrow the French empire. Reportedly, Lord Hertford gave her £20,000 for one night of love. In 1867, her often absent husband fell from a horse, landed under the wheels of the wedding coach during the nuptials of Victor Emmanuel's brother, and died. The countess continued shuffling between delegations but now more openly. She is credited with bringing about a reconciliation be-

tween Victor Emmanuel and the pope, and helping France work out the terms of the armistice with Prussia after the Franco-Prussian war.

Late in life, she wrote Estancelin: "What I wanted was a serious, deep, lasting bond, to be handed down by us to our descendants, to be hidden under no iron mask, without fear, shame, or scruples: no half-love, no carefully concealed affection; a connection accepted by the world, admitted by society, received at court, recognized by our families, sanctified by time."

On Christmas Eve, 1875, she moved to the Place Vendôme, painted the rooms black, the shutters black, the ceiling black, put locks on every outer and inner door, and removed all mirrors. She lived in deep seclusion, no longer left the house, except in the dark of night to walk her dogs. "The more I see of men, the more I love dogs," she wrote Estancelin. She continued her correspondence with him until her letters became unintelligible.

SOURCES:
Kelen, Betty. *The Mistresses: Domestic Scandals of 19th Century Monarchs.* NY: Barnes and Noble, 1966.

Castile, queen of.

See Blanche of Navarre (d. 1158).

See Blanche of Castile (1188–1252) for sidebar on Eleanor of Castile (1162–1214).

See Juana la Loca (1479–1555).

Castile and Léon, queen of.

See Sancha of Leon (1013–1067).

See Urraca (c. 1079–1126) for sidebar on Constance of Burgundy (1046–c. 1093).

See Agnes of Poitou (1052–1078).

See Urraca (c. 1079–1126).

See Bertha of Burgundy (d. 1097).

See Berengaria of Provence (1108–1149).

See Ryksa of Poland (d. 1185).

See Beatrice of Swabia (1198–1235).

See Eleanor of Castile (1241–1290) for sidebar on Joanna of Ponthieu (d. 1279).

See Yolande of Aragon (d. 1300).

See Constance of Portugal (1290–1313).

See Maria de Molina (d. 1321).

See Guzman, Leonora de for sidebar on Maria of Portugal (1313–1357).

See Marie de Padilla (1335–1365).

See Blanche of Bourbon (c. 1338–1361).

See Castro, Juana de (d. 1374).

See Joanna of Castile (1339–1381).

See Eleanor of Aragon (1358–1382).

See Beatrice of Portugal (1372–after 1409).

See Catherine of Lancaster (1372–1418).

See Maria of Aragon (1403–1445).

See Eleanor of Navarre for sidebar on Blanche of Navarre (1424–1464).

See Isabel of Portugal (1428–1496).

See Joanna of Portugal (1439–1475).

See Isabella I (1451–1504).

Castle, Barbara (1910—)

British political leader and author who became the most powerful woman in British politics prior to the appointment of Margaret Thatcher as prime minister.

Name variations: Baroness of Blackburn. Born Barbara Anne Betts in Chesterfield, England, on October 6, 1910; daughter of Frank Betts (a government official) and Annie Rebecca (Farrand) Betts; attended St. Hugh's College, Oxford University; married Edward (Ted) Castle (a journalist), in 1944 (died 1979).

Began working life as a journalist; elected member of House of Commons (1945–79); held several important ministerial posts (1964–76); served as member of national executive committee of Labour Party (1950–79) as well as chair of the party (1958–59); member of European Parliament (1979–89); created life peer (1990) with title of Baroness Castle of Blackburn of Ibstone in the County of Buckinghamshire; well known as the author of diaries detailing the nuts and bolts of cabinet decision-making (1960s and 1970s), as well as a biography of the Pankhurst sisters; published autobiography (1993).

One of the United Kingdom's most respected, and sometimes feared, politicians of the day, the Labourite Barbara Castle predicted in a 1972 interview with *The New York Times* that the moment had come for her country to accept the appointment of a woman to its highest political post: "I'm certain we shall have a woman Prime Minister in Britain before very long; the mood is right. Two of the ablest prime ministers in the world are women—*Indira Gandhi* and *Golda Meir*. I think it would have an immensely unifying and stimulating effect on political life." By the end of the 1970s, in a nation known as much for its steadfast traditionalism as for its democratic innovations, *Margaret Thatcher* had indeed been chosen to guide Britain through the countless challenges faced during the closing decades of the 20th century. Many students of British political history assert that Barbara Castle, Thatcher's political opposite in virtually all facets of political theory and practice, was equally qualified to become Britain's first female prime minister.

She was born Barbara Anne Betts in 1910 to parents whose strong marriage made a lasting impact on her. In the Yorkshire industrial town of Bradford where Barbara grew up, her father Frank was a government tax inspector who spent his leisure hours reading and writing; he was also a passionate socialist whose activism in the Independent Labour Party included editing a vigorous local leftist journal, the *Bradford Pioneer*. All aspects of politics were discussed in the Betts home, and Barbara Castle was to always regard her father, an idealistic and intellectually curious man, as one of the most powerful influences in her life. Already having joined the Labour Party in 1927, Barbara entered St. Hugh's College, Oxford University, on a scholarship. Her political militancy undiminished, she served as secretary-treasurer of the university's Labour Club. During her university years, she felt stifled by her studies and was only an indifferent scholar. Politics was her passion, and her opinions were both strongly felt and eloquently argued. Morally outraged by the human suffering caused by the economic depression of the 1930s, she became increasingly critical of the leadership of the Labour Party, particularly that of the prime minister, Ramsay MacDonald, who as leader of a national government abandoned socialism as an achievable goal. Decades later, as a member of the British government, Castle would be one of the most vocal representatives of the party's left wing, continuing to dream of the creation of a socialist commonwealth.

As a young university graduate during the depths of the depression, Castle struggled to find a niche in society. She worked for a while in Manchester, selling grocery supplies to local shops, but seized the opportunity to return to the infinitely more stimulating intellectual life of London, finding work as an assistant editor of *Town and County Councillor*, a journal for local government officials. During these years, she spent her leisure hours as an active member of the Socialist League and in 1937 entered political life as a member of London's St. Pancras borough council. Sensing the imminence of war, she took the lead in her council in pushing for civil-defense measures. In her personal life, she fell in love with a gifted left-wing journalist, William Mellor. Mellor, however, was married and never divorced his wife. Personal disappointments were largely forgotten as the second world conflagration in a generation began to make its mark on the United Kingdom. In 1940, she was appointed to the Metropolitan Water Board, and starting in 1941 she worked as a full-time administrative officer in the Ministry of Food. For the next several years, she would gain valuable experience as a bureaucrat, also serving in her spare time as an air-raid warden.

Despite the considerable demands of her several jobs and the uncertainties of wartime, she was never far removed from the world of politics in the early 1940s. Within the Labour Party, she came under the sway of Aneurin Bevan, leader of the left wing, an eloquent Welshman and ardent champion of working-class interests. Optimistic about the postwar future of a Britain advancing toward a socialist so-

ciety, she was active in the Fabian Society. Castle also carried out some of the research that was incorporated into the Beveridge Report, a historic document outlining the post-1945 welfare state that would provide social security for all citizens "from the cradle to the grave." Castle was one of the authors of the influential 1943 anthology *Social Security*, which became a key document for the post-war welfare state. She quit her government job in 1944 and began writing a column for the *Daily Mirror*, giving advice to the men and women who were beginning a return to civilian life. Also in 1944, she married the journalist Edward Cyril (Ted) Castle.

Having proven her loyalty to the Labour Party, Barbara Castle was chosen to run for Parliament in July 1945. The election, which swept Winston Churchill and his Conservatives from office, constituted a veritable peaceful revolution. Elected as M.P. for Blackburn, an industrial city in Lancashire, Castle became Britain's youngest woman member of Parliament; she was well liked by her constituents, serving uninterruptedly from 1945 through 1979. Although knowledgeable in many areas, Castle realized early on that there was much yet to learn, and as a junior legislator she spent the next few years as parliamentary private secretary to the president of the Board of Trade, working first for Sir Stafford Cripps and from 1947 through 1951 for Harold Wilson. During the next years, she experienced firsthand the problems of an increasingly interdependent world environment by traveling to a number of war-ravaged nations on the Continent. An early supporter of the United Nations, she served in 1949–50 as an alternate British delegate to the United Nations General Assembly. In 1950, Castle was elected to the national executive committee of the Labour Party, a post she would serve in until 1979.

The fine prospects Barbara Castle appeared to have in 1950 were dashed in 1951 when the Labour Party was defeated at the polls by Churchill and his resurgent Conservatives. The entire decade would prove to be a time of troubles for the Labourites, split internally between moderate and activist wings and facing an electorate now considerably disenchanted with some if not all aspects of the welfare state. Even though her party was defeated at the polls in 1951, 1955 and 1959, Barbara Castle remained popular with her constituents and was returned to her parliamentary seat at each election. The prospect of political success or failure in no way moderated her position when she felt that certain things had to be said. Concerned about the threat of a world nuclear conflagration, she criticized the American dominance of the Western alliance. On one occasion, she took on Prime Minister Churchill himself for not standing up to the Americans on the matter of the potential use of nuclear weapons in the Korean war. Not mincing her words, Castle addressed Parliament: "We used to think of [Churchill] as a bulldog sitting on the Union Jack. He has become a lapdog sitting on the Stars and Stripes of America."

Although she regarded herself as a committed socialist, Castle sometimes spoke during this period as a somewhat aggrieved British patriot saddened by the dramatic decline of her nation's power vis-a-vis the United States. By the mid-1950s, sensing that the time had arrived to make dramatic moves to end the Cold War, she spoke out strongly in favor of such measures as allowing the sale of British machine tools to the Soviet Union and full diplomatic recognition of the People's Republic of China. Her 1954 trip to China as a part of a Labour Party delegation brought considerable disapproval, not so much in Britain but from hardliners in a United States still strongly influenced by McCarthyism.

By the late 1950s, Barbara Castle had become a well-known personality on the British political stage. While not always popular with the more conservative elements within her party, the articulate Labourite was liked by her peers and the media. Never lacking confidence, she dared to speak out on unpopular issues that sometimes baffled the so-called experts. While visiting the violence-racked British colony of Cyprus in September 1958, Castle was quoted in the press as saying that, in their searches of the civilian population, British troops on the island were "permitted to be very tough." Since terrorism on Cyprus had claimed some British civilian lives, her statement was highly controversial back in Britain with the Labourite leadership quickly distancing itself from her views. Despite the furor, Castle did not back off from her engagement in the tragic Cyprus situation; she interviewed Cypriote leader Archbishop Makarios in Athens, and the main theme of their discussions centered around the urgent necessity of full independence for the colony.

The British Foreign Office was furious at what they saw as Castle's "meddling" in a highly volatile situation, but the entire incident only served to enhance her already solid reputation for courage and integrity. By the end of the 1950s, it was apparent to many intelligent observers of the British political scene that Barbara Castle was an individual to watch. In January 1959, the *Toronto Globe and Mail* wrote of her as combining the traits of a journalist and a "dash of the actress" as well as exhibiting "slim, smart good looks and her striking copper-colored hair, pale skin and bright blue eyes [which] mark her out from her dowdier, worthier and altogether less exciting rivals." But Castle would not continue her political ascent during the next two decades because of her appearance, but rather because of her skills and convictions.

Within the Labour Party, Barbara Castle's reputation was very high indeed in the late 1950s. Having already served as vice-chair of the party's national executive committee in 1957–58, in October 1958 she was elected chair of the committee for 1958–59. The fact that the Labourites were once again defeated in the national elections of 1959 doubtless affected Castle's prospects within the party for she was not re-elected as chair of the national executive committee nor was she named to the shadow cabinet. Her manifold talents, however, could not be ignored, and party leader Hugh Gaitskell appointed her to be Labour's chief spokesperson in the area of public works. Refusing to trim her sails lest she offend powerful elements within her party, Castle continued to speak out on matters she believed to be of vital interest to her nation and the world at large. Deeply concerned over the potential of a nuclear armageddon, in 1961, she strongly criticized the British decision to allow the stationing of American Polaris submarines in Scotland's Holy Loch.

Morally outraged by state-sanctioned racism in South Africa, in 1963 Castle became honorary president of the British Anti-Apartheid Movement. She joined the campaign against racism in South Africa at a time when it was by no means certain that the system of Apartheid could ever be toppled. During one anti-Apartheid protest against the shipment of British arms to South Africa in May 1963, with little more than a dozen idealistic demonstrators on hand, she brushed aside the harsh reality of the indifference of most of her compatriots, promising those present that more demonstrators, namely those from Durham, Nottingham and Manchester, "were expected later."

The Labour Party was finally returned to power in October 1964 after more than a dozen years in the political wilderness. One of the first acts of the new prime minister, Harold Wilson, was to create a new ministry, that of Overseas Development, and appoint his friend and colleague Barbara Castle as its first head. Only the fourth woman in British history to hold cabinet rank, Castle was also the only woman minister in Wilson's cabinet. (She was the first woman to serve in the British cabinet since *Florence Horsbrugh, who had held the post of Minister of Education a decade earlier.) Castle exhibited both imagination and sensitivity in her role as the administrator of British foreign-aid programs. Respected by the governments of the Commonwealth, Minister Castle became in November 1964 the chair of the consultative committee of the Colombo Plan, a multinational organization for the economic development of southeast Asia; she was the first woman to hold this important post. Despite budgetary pressures, she was successful during her brief term in office in raising the amount of funds Britain gave to underdeveloped nations. Most observers gave Castle high marks for her tenure as Minister of Overseas Development, noting her "tireless zest for hard work, and her power of swift decision"—qualities that enabled her to both capture and hold the loyalty of her civil servants.

Most important was the positive evaluation of her work by Prime Minister Harold Wilson who in December 1965 appointed her Minister of Transport. Now in charge of a vast empire of transportation affairs, she personally did not know how to drive an automobile, a detail that provided the press, with whom she enjoyed a good relationship, ample sport at the time of her appointment. With this promotion, Castle took on what was very likely the highest position ever held up to that time by a woman in the British democratic system. As before, she wasted little time in effecting change. Refusing to accept as inevitable the statistically high number of deaths and injuries on British roads and highways, she imposed a general speed limit of 70 miles per hour throughout the United Kingdom. Despite some opposition, she was able to win the public over to her position, namely that reducing speeds saved lives.

Convinced that her country was basically stuck in the 19th century where transport was concerned, Castle worked hard during her first months as Minister of Transport to draw up a coherent master plan to coordinate and modernize the country's railroads, ports, and canals as well as its trucking and bus lines. In a series of white papers that began to be issued in the summer of 1966, she announced a number of different plans to coordinate the various aspects of the British transportation system. While accepting that automobiles constituted a major part of a modern nation's life, she also remained convinced that mass transportation, whether railroads or busses, should remain in public hands in order to stay competitive with cars. Conceding that automobiles were a dominant form of transportation, Barbara Castle also noted, "But that doesn't mean public transport should be a Cinderella."

Castle visited the United States in 1966 to study urban transportation's problems and possible solutions. One of the major achievements of her tenure was the Road Safety Act, which went into effect in October 1967 and imposed stiff penalties on drivers who failed a breath test for intoxication. Enraged, some pub owners commented on these changes by introducing a new drink called "the Bloody Barbara," consisting of only tomato juice and tonic. The reforms were accepted by the public, however, at least in part because of the persuasiveness of Castle, who skewered critics through a series of interviews that won over the nation to the goal of fewer highway fatalities.

In April 1968, much of her agenda in the transportation arena achieved, Castle became part of a cabinet restructuring and accepted the important portfolio of first secretary of state for Employment and Productivity. Formerly known as the Ministry of Labour, the organization she took over faced the daunting tasks of significantly improving British industrial productivity and overcoming generations of class tensions and suspicions within the nation's social fabric. Castle was given special responsibility for policy regarding prices and incomes, in effect serving as national chief of labor relations. No woman in Britain had ever achieved such a high-ranking political position before her.

By the 1960s, Castle was becoming increasingly concerned by the rapid deterioration of Britain's industrial position within an increasingly competitive world economy. The retention of outmoded union rules encouraged countless wildcat strikes, which cut deeply into national productivity. Scarcely concealed under the facade of British civility were lingering class hatreds from an earlier age of social injustice and industrial strife. These resentments, which had smoldered since Victorian times, now increasingly burst forth in major national strikes fueled more by powerful emotions than purely rational economic goals.

Hoping to break this vicious cycle of distrust and destructive behavior for the good of the nation, in January 1969 Castle issued a policy statement outlining a new course of industrial relations. Published as a pamphlet entitled *In Place of Strife: A Policy of Industrial Relations* (its memorable title was suggested by her journalist husband Ted), the white paper issued by her ministry called for drastic revisions in national labor laws. Although she was quite aware that there would be strong resistance to these reform proposals from the unions, Castle felt that she was in the right both because of the clear necessity of the changes and because of the apparent support she had from within the leadership of the government and the Labour Party. But once the unions began to fight back, and point out how many votes they could muster in an election, most of Castle's fair-weather allies in the cause of labor law reform now deserted her, including such powerful Labour leaders as Roy Jenkins and James Callaghan.

Revealing a lack of political backbone, most of the Labour Party leaders ran for cover when union opposition to the reforms outlined in the pages of *In Place of Strife* became a matter of arm-twisting and pressure tactics. Only Castle's old political mentor and friend Prime Minister Harold Wilson remained steadfast in his support. Due to her strong performance in her two previous posts, she was increasingly being mentioned in the late 1960s as the individual with the strongest chance of becoming Britain's first woman Prime Minister. Harold Wilson agreed with this high assessment, once calling her "the best man in the Cabinet." Most political observers regarded her during these years as the first woman in British politics to be treated by men as their equal. Nonetheless, the bitter feelings unleashed by her proposals for major labor union reforms effectively destroyed whatever chances Castle had of achieving the very summit of British political life.

A realist, with her party deeply divided by the labor reform issue in the closing months of 1969, Castle admitted she had been defeated. Even during this tense period she rarely missed an opportunity to communicate directly with workers her strong belief that they themselves could turn around the nation's declining economic productivity. Thus, in November 1969, she urged dockworkers to lift their eight-month ban on the handling of container ships, noting that their intransigence would likely cost them their jobs if shippers decided to use Antwerp rather than London as their port of entry.

Refusing to bow under the pressure of the militants in the left wing of her party, Castle made it known to them that Labour had to be concerned about the issue of inflation, which impacted on the entire national economic well-being, as much as they needed to be concerned about the issue of justice for union members. Such senti-

ments created deep and permanent distrust of Castle on the extreme left of her party, but she continued to prefer what she saw as the truth of the issue over political expediency. After she spent almost two years attempting to increase industrial productivity through persuading the unions to accept some reform measures, her effectiveness had largely evaporated. Accepting her diminished influence on this front, Castle returned to her other responsibilities as a member of Parliament and leading member of her party. Before leaving her post, however, she introduced a bill in January 1970 in the House of Commons to require employers to give women equal pay for equal work, the changes to be phased in until finally completed at the end of 1975, when it would become law as the Equal Pay Act.

Starting in 1964, Castle began to keep a detailed diary of her daily activities. As a former journalist, she had been trained in shorthand and thus was able to record verbatim countless exchanges in the Cabinet Room of the British government. This documentation not only fixed her important place in modern British history but was recognized immediately after the publication of the first segment in 1980 as a major source of information for future historians of British political life. By the early 1970s, she had become an internationally recognized political figure whose expertise and courage made her a desirable lecturer. One of the many tangible honors she received during these years took place in August 1969 when she was a luncheon guest at Lloyd's of London, the first woman ever invited to this prestigious and exclusive group.

After ending her Cabinet career in 1976 as secretary of state for Social Services, Barbara Castle began a second distinguished career as a member of the European Parliament, serving in this post until 1989. Advancing age did little to reduce her energy or capacity for making bold and controversial statements. In a 1993 interview, she noted: "any government I'd been a member of would have been ashamed to get the country into this mess." Reporters loved her, while sometimes her colleagues in the Labour Party winced at her typically frank assessments of the party's tactical errors. When Castle was involved in a public issue, one could be certain of two things: that she would be outspoken and that her motives would be based on a grand perspective of the issues involved. In December 1996, Baroness Castle of Blackburn, a title granted her in 1990, threatened to walk out on the pension policy review panel of which she

506   *Women in World History*

was a member, stating in no uncertain terms: "I shall not indefinitely go on lending myself to this farce. The review body clearly has no real say in policy making."

In the 1990s, Barbara Castle, a diminutive redhead whose willpower and critical judgment was undiminished despite her weakened eyesight, had become one of the surviving legends of Old Labour, a rare blend of the idealistic and pragmatic elements of politics. At her 84th birthday celebrations in 1994, session chair Robin Cook affectionately described Barbara Castle as "one of our youngest members in spirit." Castle participated with great fervor in a half-century of British politics, giving it a rare energy and zest.

SOURCES:

Baxter, Sarah. "Fortified Castle," in *New Statesman and Society.* Vol. 6, no. 256. June 11, 1993, p. 23.

"The Best Man," in *Time.* Vol. 91, no. 22. May 31, 1968, pp. 27–28.

Castle, Barbara. *The Castle Diaries 1964–70.* London: Weidenfeld and Nicolson, 1984.

———. *The Castle Diaries 1964–76.* London: Macmillan, 1993.

———. *The Castle Diaries 1974–76.* London: Weidenfeld and Nicolson, 1980.

———. *Fighting All the Way.* London: Macmillan, 1993.

———. *Sylvia and Christabel Pankhurst.* London: Penguin, 1987.

"Castle, Barbara (Anne Betts)," *Current Biography 1967.* NY: H.W. Wilson, pp. 58–60.

"Chief's Call for Arms Ban," in *The Times* [London]. May 21, 1963, p. 16.

De'ath, Wilfred. *Barbara Castle: A Portrait from Life.* Brighton: Clifton Books, 1970.

Great Britain. Department of Employment and Productivity. *In Place of Strife: A Policy for Industrial Relations.* London: Her Majesty's Stationery Office, 1969.

Halligan, Liam. "Labour Pensions Review 'A Sham,'" in *Financial Times* [London]. December 2, 1996, p. 7.

Hammel, Lisa. "Barbara Castle: 'Women in Politics'—Lecture Topic She Knows Well," in *The New York Times Biographical Edition.* February 1972, p. 269.

"Mrs. Castle's Recipe," in *Time.* Vol. 93, no. 5. January 31, 1969, p. 63.

National Union of Teachers. *"In Place of Strife": A Commentary on the Government White Paper prepared by the Executive of the National Union of Teachers.* London: National Union of Teachers, [1970].

"Profile of Barbara Castle: Tigress in the Tank," in *New Statesman.* Vol. 71, no. 1817. January 7, 1966, pp. 12–13.

Rose, Paul B. "Barbara Castle: Labour's Fearless Fighter," in *Contemporary Review.* Vol. 263, no. 1532. September 1993, pp. 127–131.

"She Masterminds Plans for British Transport," in *Business Week.* No. 1905. March 5, 1966, pp. 90–92, 94, 99.

Vallance, Elizabeth. *Women in the House: A Study of Women Members of Parliament.* London: Athlone Press, 1979.

Vaughan, Margaret. "The Fiery Fighter Who Was Too Honest to Win," in *The Herald* [Glasgow]. June 11, 1993, p. 17.

John Haag, Associate Professor,
University of Georgia, Athens, Georgia

Castle, Irene (c. 1893–1969)

American dancer who started the bobbed-hair fad of the 1920s and, with her husband, the "Castle Walk" dance craze. Born Irene Foote around 1893; died at her home in Eureka Springs, Arkansas, on January 25, 1969; married British-born Vernon Blythe Castle, in 1911 (killed in an aviation accident in Texas on February 15, 1918); married Robert E. Treman (dates unknown); married Frederick McLaughlin (dates unknown); married George Enzinger, in 1946; children: two.

Selected writings: (with Vernon Castle) Modern Dancing *(1914);* My Memories of Vernon Castle *(1918).*

Selected films: (with Vernon Castle) The Whirl of Life *(1915);* Patria *(1917);* The Hillcrest Mystery *(1918);* The Invisible Bond *(1919);* The Broadway Bride *(1921);* No Trespassing *(1922).*

The husband-and-wife dancing team of Irene and Vernon Castle literally invented modern social dancing; in the process, they became one of the most famous and admired couples of their day. The dances they developed and introduced, including the fox trot, turkey trot, one-step, and the Castle Walk, became standards in ballrooms throughout the nation. At the peak of their career, they were making an unheard of $30,000 a week doing one-night stands. By one account, while appearing in Chicago, they danced the Castle Walk down the aisle at the city's first "tango wedding." In 1914, they performed in Irving Berlin's first musical *Watch Your Step,* the same year their book *Modern Dancing* was published. (In 1918, Irene would write *My Memories of Vernon Castle.*) Irene Castle, slender and elegant, was one of the most photographed women in America; she was also one of the few women at the time to bob her hair without losing her reputation.

After Vernon's untimely death in an air crash in 1918, Irene continued to perform on stage and in films. A popular figure on the vaudeville circuit throughout the 1920s, she became less active in the 1930s, though the New York World's Fair of 1939 honored her with Irene Castle Day, for which she created a special dance—the World's Fair Hop. That year also marked the release of the movie musical *The*

Story of Vernon and Irene Castle, starring Fred Astaire and *Ginger Rogers**. During her later years, Castle became a devoted animal-rights activist, operating a shelter, Orphans of the Storm, out of her Illinois home. One of her last appearances was at her 71st birthday party, which was hosted by *Dance Magazine* in New York City.

Castlemain, countess of.

See Villiers, Barbara (c. 1641–1709).

Castles, Amy (1880–1951)

Well-known Australian soprano who faded into obscurity, but whose brilliance as a vocalist can still be heard on later released CD's. Born in Melbourne, Australia, on July 25, 1880; died in Melbourne on November 19, 1951.

Born in Melbourne, Australia, in 1880, Amy Castles was able to study in London with *Mathilde Marchesi**, thanks to popular support for overseas studies. She later trained with Jacques Bruhy before making her debut in Cologne in 1907. In 1909–10, she toured Australia, and in 1912 the Vienna Hofoper awarded her a four-year contract. Castles struggled as a singer for several reasons: World War I cut short her Vienna contract, making concerts on the Continent all but impossible; she was diabetic with attendant health problems; and Australian singer *Nellie Melba** (1861–1931) was a superstar who overshadowed other singers from the outback. Eventually, Castles gave up an international career and faded into obscurity. Her recordings reissued on CD document the brilliance of her voice.

Castro, Agnes de (c. 1320–1355).

See Castro, Inez de.

Castro, Inez de (c. 1320–1355)

Spanish mistress and probably wife of Peter I of Portugal. Name variations: Ines de Castro or Inês de Castro; Ines di Castro; sometimes Anglicized as Agnes; called Collo de Garza (Heron's Neck). Born in Spanish Galicia around 1320 (some sources cite 1327); stabbed to death on January 7, 1355, at Coimbra, Spain; daughter, possibly illegitimate, of Pedro Fernandez de Castro of Castile and Alonca also known as Aldonca or Aldonza Soares de Villadares of Portugal; the reigning house of Portugal directly descended from her brother, Alvaro Perez de Castro; presumably became the third wife of Pedro I also known as Peter I

(1320–1367), king of Portugal (r. 1357–1367), probably in 1354; children: (with Peter I) probably *Beatrice of Portugal (c. 1347–1381), countess of Albuquerque; Affonso (b. 1348, died young); John, duke of Valencia (c. 1349–1397); Diniz or Denis, count of Villar-Dompardo (c. 1354–1397).

Inez de Castro was born into an aristocratic Spanish family, the daughter of Pedro Fernandez de Castro and Alonca Soares de Villadares, a noble Portuguese woman. Tradition maintains that her father and mother were unmarried, and that Inez and her two brothers were consequently considered of "bastard birth." As a child, she was sent to be educated in the palaces of Juan Manuel, duke of Penafiel. Many young noblewomen of the late medieval age experienced the same fate; their parents placed them in the homes of those who were even wealthier and more prestigious in the hope that they would become well-educated and attract suitable offers of marriage. Inez grew up with and became lady-in-waiting to her cousin ❧▶ Constance of Castile (1323–1345), the daughter of *Constance of Aragon (d. 1327) and Duke Juan Manuel. In 1341, she and Constance moved to Lisbon upon Constance's marriage to Peter, prince of Portugal.

It was at Lisbon shortly after his marriage that Prince Peter fell deeply in love with Inez. Despite his married state and Inez's position as lady-in-waiting to his wife, the two soon became lovers. Given that many royal men had love affairs with little scandal or consequence in their era, the two might have remained happily together, yet tragedy awaited them instead. After Constance died in 1345 during childbirth, their relationship was almost that of husband and wife. Peter claimed that he and Inez married in 1354, although this would have been a secret marriage and thus cannot be proven.

Inez's paternal relatives, the Castro family, were gaining power and prestige during the same years as Peter and Inez's affair. Eventually, enemies of the Castros convinced Peter's father, King Alphonso IV of Portugal, that the affair between his son and the daughter of the hated Castros could prove dangerous to the security of his throne. Their proposed solution was to have Inez murdered. King Alphonso first refused the plan but later yielded. The king was among those who went secretly in 1355 to the palace of Coimbra where Inez and Peter lived. Inez's beauty and her tears are said to have dissuaded the king, but those who accompanied him were resolute and stabbed Inez to death. Her body was then immediately buried in the church of Santa

❧▶ **Constance of Castile** (1323–1345)

*Queen of Portugal. Name variations: Constance of Aragon; Constance Manuel; (Spanish) Constance de Castilla. Born in 1323; died on November 13, 1345, in Santarum, during childbirth; daughter of Juan Manuel de Villena, duke of Penafiel, and *Constance of Aragon (d. 1327); married Alphonso XI, king of Castile and Leon, on March 28, 1325 (annulled in 1327); became second wife of Pedro I also known as Peter I (1320–1367), king of Portugal (r. 1357–1367), on August 24, 1336; children: (second marriage) Luiz (1340–1340); Maria of Portugal (1343–1367, who married Fernando also known as Ferdinand of Aragon, marquis of Tortosa); Fernao also known as Fernando or Ferdinand I the Handsome (1345–1383), king of Portugal (r. 1367–1383, who married *Leonora Telles).*

Clara. It seems Alphonso misread his son's passion for Inez, for the murder nearly cost Alphonso the throne that the misdeed was meant to secure. Prince Peter revolted against his father as soon as he learned of Inez's murder, and the three men who had committed the crime fled to Castile. Peter ended the revolt after winning guarantees of his father's good will. In 1357, Alphonso died, and Peter succeeded to the throne of Portugal. He had the three murderers brought from exile into Portugal and tortured to death, and belatedly had Inez's body buried in a magnificent tomb at Alcobaca. Many stories were told of Peter's undying love for his murdered wife, including one that had Prince Peter crowning Inez's corpse and setting it beside him at his coronation, the authenticity of which is highly questionable at best. These stories made the love between Inez and Peter the stuff of legends in their own time and for several centuries to follow. Around 1558, António Ferreira, the Lisbon humanist and younger son of a noble at the Court of the duke of Coimbra, wrote *Inês de Castro*; it was the first dramatic tragedy in Portuguese. At Naples, *Elizabeth Billington appeared as the hero in *Inez di Castro,* an opera written for her by F. Bianchi. As well, *Aphra Behn wrote *The History of Agnes de Castro.*

Laura York,
Riverside, California

Castro, Rosalía de (1837–1885)

Galician writer, best known for her poetry and for her contribution to the revival of the Galician language in Spain. Name variations: María Rosalía Rita; Rosalía Castro de Murguía; Rosalia de Castro. Born on February 24, 1837, in Santiago de Compostela, Spain;

Opposite page

Irene and Vernon Castle.

died in Padrón, Galicia, Spain, on July 15, 1885, of uterine or stomach cancer; daughter of María Teresa da Cruz de Castro y Abadía (of noble family) and José Martínez Viojo (a priest); attended school in Santiago where she learned music, drawing and French; married Manuel Martínez Murguía on October 10, 1858, in Madrid; children: Alejandra (b. 1859); Aurea (b. 1869); twins Gala and Ovidio (b. 1871 or 1872); Amara (b. 1874); Adriano (b. 1875, died in infancy); Valentina (1877–1877).

Began composing verses at age 11 or 12; published first book of poetry (1857); enjoyed first publicly acclaimed poetry collection Cantares gallegos *(Galician Songs, 1863); published second poetry collection* Follas novas *(New Leaves, 1880); published last poetry collection and book,* En las orillas del Sar *(On the Banks of the River Sar, 1884).*

Poetry: La flor *(The Flower, 1857);* A mi madre *(To my Mother, 1863);* Cantares gallegos *(Galician Songs, 1863);* Follas novas *(New Leaves, 1880);* En las orillas del Sar *(On the Banks of the River Sar, 1884).* Prose: La hija del mar *(The Daughter of the Sea, 1859);* Flavio *(1861);* El cadiceño: Descripción de un tipo *(The Man from Cádiz: Description of a Type, 1863);* Ruinas: Desdichas de tres vidas ejemplares *(Ruins: Misfortunes of Three Exemplary Lives, 1866);* El caballero de las botas azules *(The Gentleman of the Blue Boots, 1867);* El primer loco *(The First Madman, 1881);* Conto gallego: Os dous amigos e a viuda *(Galician Tale: The Two Friends and The Widow, 1923).* Nonfiction: Las literatas *(Literary Women, 1866);* Lieders *(1858);* "El Domingo de Ramos" *(Palm Sunday, 1881);* "Padrón y las inundaciones" *(Padrón and the Floods, 1881).*

Rosalía de Castro is one of the few women as well as one of the few regional writers in Spain to have a position in the literary canon of Spanish literature. As one of the protagonists of the cultural revival in Galicia, a region of Spain situated at the northwestern corner of the Iberian peninsula, in the 19th century, she remains the best-known and most popular poet of Galicia. Her first collection of poems in the language of her native region, *Cantares gallegos* (Galician Songs), constituted a crucial turning point for the literary status of the Galician language, which had been relegated to the oral tradition since the 15th century, when Castilian had become the literary language of Spain.

It was the rich oral tradition into which she was born that inspired Rosalía de Castro to write much of her poetry. She expressed a vivid concern in her work for the sorrows and predicament of her fellow Galicians. In the pro-

logue to her second poetry collection in the Galician language, *Follas novas* (New Leaves), she voiced this empathy: "My natural disposition (for not in vain am I a woman) [is] to feel other people's sorrows as my own." It is to the Galician women, however, that she particularly directs her sympathies:

> What always really moved me and, therefore, could not but be present in my poetry, were the innumerable worries of our women: loving beings to their people and to strangers, full of sentiment, strong in body as they have tender hearts and also so miserable that they seemed to have been born to deal with all the worries of the most humble and most fragile part of humanity. In the fields they share with their men half of the hard chores; in the home they courageously endure the hardships of motherhood, housework and the difficulties of poverty. Alone most of the time and having to work from dawn to sunset to barely make a living for them and their children, they seem to be condemned to never find rest if it is not in the grave.

Rosalía de Castro was born in Santiago de Compostela, in Galicia, in 1837. Her mother, **María Teresa da Cruz de Castro y Abadía** was of a noble family from the village of Padrón. Her father, José Martínez Viojo, was a seminarian from the same village, who later served as a priest. Castro's birth certificate records her as a child of "unknown parents"; the mysterious circumstances surrounding her birth are related to what was then regarded as the scandalous nature of her origin; she was the daughter of unmarried parents and, what is more, her father was soon to become a priest. She spent her early childhood in the countryside with her godmother **María Francisca Martínez** who, some speculate, was related to Castro's father. At the age of nine or ten, the child joined her mother to live in Santiago de Compostela, where she received the education befitting a lady of her time, including lessons in music, drawing and French. In her youth, she took part in events at the Lyceum, a meeting place for young artists and writers, and she was well received when she played the leading role in a local amateur theater production.

At age 19, Rosalía de Castro moved to Madrid, some argue for reasons related to family legal matters while others speculate that she was fleeing the provincial atmosphere of Santiago, to perhaps seek work as an actress. The cultural vitality of Madrid seems to have inspired her; one year later, in 1857, Castro published her first collection of poetry, *La flor* (The Flower). This book was warmly reviewed by the writer and historian, Manuel Martínez de Murguía, who became her husband the following year. Immediately after the marriage, Castro and Murguía returned to live in Santiago de Compostela; reports on the character of Castro's husband are contradictory, but he seems to have been supportive and to have encouraged her to write. In 1859, Castro had her first child, Alejandra, and published her first novel, *La hija del mar* (The Daughter of the Sea). Her second novel, *Flavio*, followed two years later.

A year after the death of her mother in 1862, Castro published a brief volume of poems, entitled *A mi madre* (To my Mother). Aware of the oppressive social conditions for women at the time, the poet had never reproached her mother for having abandoned her in her early childhood. In one of her nonfiction pieces, *Lieders*, written several years earlier, in 1858, Castro had explicitly denounced the unfair treatment of women:

> Oh woman! . . . Why do men pour on you the filth of their whims, afterwards despising and abhorring in your deadening tiredness the horror of their misconduct and heated desires? . . . [T]hey transmit everything to you, everything, . . . and in spite of it, they despise you.

In 1863, Rosalía de Castro published *Cantares gallegos* (Galician Songs), her first collection of poetry written in Galician. In 1886, Murguía would give an account of the genesis of this work in his *Los precursores*: The poems were written at the beginning of a period, lasting up to 1870, when Castro was living away from Galicia, traveling throughout other regions of Spain. According to her husband, it was in the dry lands of Castile that Castro especially longed for the exuberance of the Galician countryside and felt the need to write "a book in which the landscape and whole life of the people of our country would be reflected with all its poetry and purity." This book, based on Galician popular lyrics, particularly appealed to those in sympathy with the Galician regionalist movement, which was led by Murguía. Castro was reluctant to have the poems published and at first wanted them to appear under her husband's name. Ultimately, however, they were published under her name and won her widespread recognition for her literary accomplishment.

In the prologue to the collection, the poet acknowledges the influence of another collection of popular poetry, *El libro de los cantares* (The Book of Songs), written by Antonio Trueba in 1852. Castro surpassed her predecessor, however, in what was her own personal tribute to the already existing body of folk songs from the Galician oral tradition. Each poem is introduced by a popular refrain, followed by an elaboration on its theme, motif or tone, resulting in a lyrical work of powerful creativity. Although many critics regard this book as a collection of folk songs, it should be appreciated for its highly artistic value. In the prologue of *Cantares gallegos*, Castro wrote that she wanted to defend her homeland and Galician language from those who "despise" the land and who "mock" the language, but her poetic themes deal in particular with the everyday life of the Galician people. Love is a frequent theme; it is common to hear the voice of a girl or a woman singing to her lover, or the melancholy and sorrow in remembrance of something or someone that has been lost; the theme of emigration is also present, as Galicians are known as an emigrant people, often forced by economic conditions into leaving their homeland for unknown destinations, usually in Central or South America.

In an age when poets declaimed, Rosalía de Castro had the courage to write honestly and realistically about issues that troubled her.

—Jack Shreve

Cantares gallegos was followed by a number of prose works, including the novelette *Ruinas* (Ruins) and the article "Las literatas" (Literary Women) in 1866. The latter is one of the most vivid and direct accounts of the conditions for a woman writer in 19th-century Spain:

> Above all, my friend, you do not know what it is to be a writer. . . . In the street they point at you permanently, and not for a good reason; everywhere they gossip about you. . . . Women point out the most hidden of your imperfections and men tell you unceasingly that a talented woman is a true nuisance . . . that women should leave the pen and mend their husbands' socks, if they have husbands, and, if not, then women should mend their menservants'. It would be easy for some women to open their wardrobes and show them the careful mendings and prove to them that the writing of a few pages does not prevent them from attending their household chores. . . . [I]t is a fact that men look upon women writers worse than they would the devil.

In 1867, Castro published her best-known novel, *El caballero de las botas azules* (The Gentleman of the Blue Boots), which is a satirical analysis of 19th-century Spanish society and of the popular novels of the time. Two years later, she gave birth to her second child, Aurea, and afterward poor health compelled her to return to Galicia. In 1871, the family moved to La Coruña and later to Santiago de Compostela, following Murguía's job opportunities. While living in Santiago, Castro had twins, Gala and Ovidio, in 1872, and a daughter, Amara, was born in La Coruña in 1874; a sixth child, Adriano, was born in 1875 but died before the age of two; a seventh child, Valentina, was stillborn in 1877.

In 1880, poems written in Castile and the Galician cities of Santiago and La Coruña were published in *Follas novas* (New Leaves), Castro's second collection written in Galician. In the foreword to the new volume, the poet eloquently declares her intention to express the sorrows of those least favored by Galician society, particularly its country women. She prefers "instead of personal compositions, those that with more or less success express the tribulations of the ones who suffer around me." The poems in *Follas novas,* which reflect less of the gaiety of the Galician people found in her earlier volume, can be grouped in three categories: those similar to *Cantares gallegos* in their concern with popular roots; those of social content, particularly the issue of emigration, and those that are intimate and personal. Thus, a whole section of the book is dedicated to "The Widows of the Living and The Widows of The Dead," referring to the women left behind when the men of Galicia are forced to emigrate. It is in the third category, however, that Castro's outlook becomes truly revolutionary, as she uses her native tongue not only to portray picturesque scenes of her homeland, but to express metaphysical, spiritual, and highly subjective themes, for which the Galician language had previously been considered unfit.

El primer loco (The First Madman), subtitled *Cuento extraño* (Strange Tale), was Castro's last novel, published in 1881. The book, which offers a psychological analysis of the Romantic temperament and madness, appeared in the same year as two articles: "Padrón y las inundaciones" (Padrón and the Floods) and "Domingo de Ramos" (Palm Sunday). In the latter, Castro vividly describes the ceremonies and festivities related to the observance of the religious holiday. In the final years of her life, the poet was quite ill and had little energy to travel, but her love for the sea drove her to a last journey to the seaport of Carril on the Atlantic coast. On July 15, 1885, she died in the Galician village of Padrón, of either uterine or stomach cancer. It is said that just before her death she asked her eldest daughter, Alejandra, to open the window for she wanted to see the ocean. A number of her works in progress were subsequently lost when members of her family carried out her request to destroy her manuscripts.

A year before her death, Castro published her last poetry collection, *En las orillas del Sar* (On the Banks of the River Sar), written in Castilian. In the Introduction to *Rosalía de Castro: Obras completas,* Victoriano García Martí notes that this collection of poetry differs from her other two major collections, in that the late poems are about "disillusion imposed by the passing of time, the inevitable loss of youthful hopes." This final collection was the work that finally earned Castro acclaim throughout Spain. Praised at first for its innovative experiments with meter, which anticipated the modernist poetry of the Nicaraguan poet, Rubén Darío, that was yet to come in the early 20th century, the book also earned the recognition of the writers of the Generation of 1898, including Antonio Machado, Juan Ramón Jiménez and Miguel de Unamuno, who admired the work for its subjective, personal, and existentialist mood. The volume also addresses some very contemporary concerns: the long poem "Los robles" (The Oak Trees) has an ecological theme, denouncing the deforestation that was occurring in Galicia in the late 19th century. Most of the poems share a tone of despair and desolation scarcely present in Castro's earlier collections.

Due in large part to the tremendous impact of *Cantares gallegos,* Rosalía de Castro has been mythologized by the Galician people. She is often referred to as *la santiña,* "the little saint," or *la nai gallega,* "the Galician mother," and she is also popularly known as *la chorona,* "the sorrowful woman." She has become a symbol representing all that is Galician. Her contribution to an imminent feminist sentiment in Spain should also not be ignored. Although she was far from being an outright advocate for the rights of women, the unjust treatment of women, especially of Galician country women, was a frequent concern of hers. Castro's decrial of the oppression of women was actually part of a broader concern for all oppressed people. Some critics see her as a Romantic and others as a Realist; however difficult it may be to reconcile these opinions, her poetry is truly original.

SOURCES:

Castro, Rosalía de. *Rosalía de Castro. Obras completas.* 2 vols. Edited by Arturo del Hoyo. Madrid: Aguilar, 1988.

Kulp-Hill, Kathleen. *Rosalía de Castro.* Boston: Twayne, 1977.

Murguía, Manuel. *Los Precursores.* La Coruña: Imprenta de "La Voz de Galicia," 1886.

SUGGESTED READING:

Brenan, Gerald. *The Literature of The Spanish People: From Roman Times to The Present Day.* Cambridge: Cambridge University Press, 1970.

Castro, Rosalía de. *Poems.* Edited and translated by Anna-Marie Aldaz, Barbara N. Gantt, and Anne C.

Bromley. NY: State University of New York Press, 1991.

Davies, Catherine. "Rosalía de Castro's Later Poetry and Anti-Regionalism in Spain," in *The Modern Language Review.* Vol. 79, no. 3. July 1984, pp. 609–619.

Kulp, Kathleen K. *Manner and Mood in Rosalía de Castro: A Study of Themes and Style.* Madrid: Ediciones José Porrúa Turanzas, 1968.

Stevens, Shelley. *Rosalía de Castro and The Galician Revival.* London: Tamesis Books, 1986.

Ingrid Martínez-Rico,
Assistant Professor of Spanish,
Gettysburg College, Gettysburg, Pennsylvania

Cat, The (1908–c. 1970).

See Carré, Mathilde.

Català, Víctor (1869–1966).

See Albert, Caterina.

Catalani, Angelica (1780–1849)

Italian opera singer. Born in Senigallia, Italy, on May 10, 1780; died of cholera in Paris, France, on June 12, 1849; educated at the convent of Santa Lucia, at Gubbio; studied in Senigallia with her tradesman father and Morandi; debuted in Venice in 1797; married Paul Valabrègue (a French diplomat who later became her manager), in 1804.

When only seven years old, Angelica Catalani attracted general attention for the power and purity of her voice. In 1797, she made her debut in Venice in Mayr's *Lodoïska*, and from then on every impresario in Europe was eager to sign her. In 1802, she sang in Rome at La Scala to great success. One of the last of the bel cantos, she next appeared in Madrid and Paris to large acclaim. Catalani was married in 1804 and her husband Paul Valabrègue took over her management; two years later, she made her first appearance in London, at the King's Theatre. A prima donna without rival, she remained in England for the next seven years and appeared as Susanna in the first London production of Mozart's *Le nozze di Figaro* (The Marriage of Figaro). Offered management of the Théâtre Italien at the Salle Favart in Paris, Catalani and her husband moved to that city, but their stewardship from 1814 to 1818 resulted in financial failure. Catalani's continental tours, however, continued to be enormously successful until she retired in 1828. During her 30-year career, noted most for her singing of popular songs, she amassed a large fortune, receiving at its height up to 200 guineas for one rendition of "Rule Britannia." In 1830, she settled in Florence, Italy, and established a tuition-free singing school for girls. Angelica Catalani died of cholera in Paris on June 12, 1849.

SUGGESTED READING:
Escudier, M. and L. *Vie et aventures des cantatrices célèbres.* Paris, 1856.

Catalina.

Variant of Catherine.

Catalina (1403–1439)

*Duchess of Villena. Born in 1403; died on October 19, 1439, in Saragosa; daughter of *Catherine of Lancaster (1372–1418) and Enrique also known as Henry III (1379–1406), king of Castile (r. 1390–1406); married Henry of Aragon (1399–1445), duke of Villena, on July 12, 1420.*

Catalinda de Albret (c. 1470–1517).

See Margaret of Angoulême for sidebar on Catherine de Foix.

Catargi, Marie

Mother of the king of Serbia. Married Milosh of Serbia (d. 1861); children: Milan II (I), prince of Serbia (r. 1868–1882), king of Serbia (r. 1882–1889).

Catarina.

Spanish variant for Catharine or Catherine.

Catchpole, Margaret (1762–1819)

English pioneer and convict who became a well-known midwife in Australia and was the subject of a play, a film, and a historical novel. Born in Nactom, Suffolk, England, on March 10, 1762; died in Richmond, Australia, on May 13, 1819; buried at St. Peter's Church, Richmond; illegitimate daughter of Elizabeth Catchpole and a father unknown, possibly Richard Marjoram; never married; no children.

Baptized (March 14, 1762); left the service of the Cobbold family (1795); stole a horse (May 23, 1797) and arrested; sentenced to death, then sentence commuted to transportation for seven years (1797); escaped Ipswich jail (March 25, 1800); recaptured, sentenced to death, and had sentence commuted to transportation for life (1800); left England (May 27, 1801); arrived in Australia (December 20, 1801); employed by James Palmer (1802–04); appointed overseer by the Rouse family of a property at Richmond (1804); recorded the Hawkesbury River floods (1806 and 1809); pardoned by Governor Macquarie (January 31, 1814).

Born on March 10, 1762, in Nactom, England, Margaret Catchpole was the illegitimate daughter and youngest of six children of **Elizabeth Catchpole**. Margaret's baptism was recorded in the register of Hoo, 15 miles from Nactom: "Margaret, natural daughter of Elizabeth Catchpole was bapt. 14 March, 1762." As a young woman, Catchpole, whose father worked for a celebrated breeder of Suffolk cart horses, became a skilled and accomplished equestrian. She once mounted a spirited horse and rode bareback to call a doctor to the bedside of her father's employer.

Given the financial constraints of the family's rural existence, Margaret Catchpole had little in the way of formal education. She was by all reports, however, an intelligent, pretty, and resourceful young woman, employed by various families of the locality as a servant. Later she became a nurse and cook in the household of John Cobbold, a wealthy Suffolk brewer, and was taught to read and write by his wife. Catchpole became a valued member of the household and was responsible for saving the lives of the Cobbold children on three separate occasions. Even after her deportation to Australia, Catchpole would maintain contact with the family.

Along the picturesque coastline of Suffolk, the age old profession of smuggling was a common occupation. Margaret met and fell in love with William Laud, a sailor and smuggler from Landguard Fort. Since the Cobbolds disapproved of the liaison, the relationship with Laud led to friction with her employers. In 1795, Catchpole left their service. She was seriously ill for several months and thereafter unemployed. On the night of May 23, 1797, she stole a gelding from the Cobbold coach house. Disguised as a sailor, she covered the distance from Ipswich to London in ten hours, riding 70 miles in order to help William Laud, who was sought by the police.

On the information of John Cobbold, Margaret Catchpole was arrested for horse theft in London. She was returned to Suffolk and pleaded guilty. Crimes against property were treated particularly severely by contemporary English law. Catchpole was sentenced to death by Chief Baron MacDonald of the Suffolk Summer Assizes. Due to the intersession of John Cobbold, however, the death sentence was commuted. Instead, Catchpole was sentenced to be transported to Australia, commonly referred to as going "Bay side"; the length of the punishment was to be seven years.

For two years, Catchpole was a model prisoner in the Ipswich jail. Then William Laud was arrested on smuggling charges and housed in the same jail. Somehow Catchpole managed to pay the fine for his release. In return, Laud promised to break her out of prison. Then she and Laud planned to marry. On the night of March 25, 1800, Catchpole made a daring escape, using a rope smuggled into the jail by Laud to scale a 22-foot wall topped with spikes.

The police surprised Catchpole and Laud at Suffolk Beach. During the ensuing struggle, Laud was killed, and Catchpole was recaptured. Once again Chief Baron MacDonald pronounced the death sentence, and once again the sentence was commuted to transportation. Given her attempted escape, however, the sentence of transportation was extended to life.

Margaret Catchpole set sail for New South Wales on May 27, 1801, aboard the *Nile*. For many convicts, the prospect of exile to such a remote and forbidding land was a heartrending experience. Catchpole wrote to Mrs. Cobbold two days before her departure.

> I have taken the liberty, my good lady, of troubling you with a few lines as it will be the last time I shall trouble you in this sorrowful confinement. My sorrows are very great. To think I must be banished out of my own country and from all my dearest friends forever. It is very hard indeed for anyone to think on it and much more for me to endure the hardship of it.

On December 20, 1801, the ship carrying Catchpole dropped anchor in Botany Bay. "We had not one died," wrote Catchpole, "no not all the passage out, in so many women."

Conditions in the colony of New South Wales had improved since the first convict ships arrived in 1788. Nevertheless, it was still a rough and rowdy outpost of the British Empire—a penal colony from which there was little or no chance of return. Margaret Catchpole's first impressions of Australia, however, were by no means completely unfavorable. On January 21, 1801, she wrote to Mrs. Cobbold:

> It is a great deal more like England than I ever expected to have seen, for here is garden stuff of all kinds, except gooseberries and currant and apples. The gardens are very beautiful, all planted with geraniums and they run 7 or 8 foot high. It is a very woody country for if I go out any distance from here it means going through woods for miles. But there are very beautiful and very pretty birds.

Since servants were scarce in the penal colony, it was a common practice for military officers and government officials to select servants from among the women gathered on the decks of newly arrived vessels. Margaret Catchpole's previous experience recommended her to James Palmer, the colony's commissary.

For the first 18 mouths of her life in Australia, Margaret Catchpole worked as a cook for Palmer. He and his wife had been in Australia since 1788. It was during these early months that Catchpole wrote to her uncle in England:

> I am well beloved by all that know me and that is a comfort for I always go into better company than myself, that is among free people where they make as much of me as if I were a lady—because I am the commissary's cook. . . . I have at this time a man that keeps me company and would marry me if I like. But I am not for marrying. He is a gardener. He came out as a botanist and is to be allowed one hundred pounds per year . . . and a man to fetch wood and water and one to go out with him to select seeds and see skins and all sorts of curiosities.

Men outnumbered women in New South Wales six to one. Many people have speculated as to the identity of Margaret Catchpole's suitor. Some have suggested that it was James Gordon, a botanist working for the War Office. Others claim it was George Caley, a natural history collector employed by Sir Joseph Banks. Either way, it must have been through one of these two that Margaret Catchpole obtained two specimens of the lyrebird, or native pheasant, which she sent to Mrs. Cobbold, who then donated them to the Ipswich museum where they are still on display.

Over the years Catchpole was employed by various prominent colonial families, including the Skinners, the Faithfulls, the Woods, the Dights, and the Rouses. Indeed, it was Mrs. Palmer who suggested that Catchpole travel to Richmond to nurse Mrs. Dight and Mrs. Rouse during their pregnancies, and Catchpole subsequently delivered two of the Rouse children. She wrote:

> I went there to nurse Mrs. Rouse, a very respectful person. They come from England free. They respect me as one of their own family, for Mrs. Rouse with her last child had told her husband that she almost died because I was not there. Mr. Rouse did live up at Richmond on his farm.

When Mr. Rouse was appointed superintendent of Public Works at Parramatta in 1804, he hired Catchpole to manage his 40-acre farm at Richmond, near the junction of the Grose and Hawkesbury rivers. Rouse paid her in livestock and gain, since there was little money in circulation at the time. By the turn of the century, all of the Cumberland Plain had been explored. The land was remote, but fertile. "The crop of wheat is very good in this country for it produces fourteen bushels per acre," writes Catchpole; "it is a very fruitful place indeed." The overseeing of the Rouse farm was an extraordinary responsibility to place upon a convicted criminal, particularly a woman. Catchpole clearly enjoyed the trust and challenges of her position. As she wrote, "I am living all alone as before in a very honest way of life. There is not one woman in the colony that lives like myself."

Margaret Catchpole was the first female convict chronicler of Australia's early frontier history. In 1806 and 1809, she recorded the disastrous Hawkesbury River floods. During the flood of 1806, six of her pigs were killed, causing considerable financial hardship. Such natural disasters, however, had even more perilous consequences as Catchpole described:

> This place has been so flooded that I thought once all must be lost . . . as you well know I have a good spirit. I was trying to save what I could and then I and Mrs. Dight and her three children went up to the loft for safety. We had not been there above one hour before the chimney went down and the middle wall went. Then I expected the next chimney to go and all the walls and then to be crushed to death, for the water was above five feet deep in the house.

In Catchpole's letters, one senses the everyday difficulties of life on the Australian frontier. In a dispatch dated October 8, 1806, she described how she collected a package that had been sent to her from England. "Dear Uncle, you must think I can walk well, for when I heard there was a box for me I set off and walked fifty miles in two days."

Like many convicts, Margaret Catchpole often dreamt of returning to what she described as her "own native land." On January 31, 1814, she was officially pardoned by Governor John Macquarie, on behalf of the British government. Nevertheless, she chose to remain in Australia. She thrived on the challenges of pioneer life, and a measure of independence that she could never have achieved in England. For the rest of her life, Catchpole farmed and ran a small store in Richmond. In a letter dated September 2, 1811, she described her home:

> I rent a little farm of about fifteen acres, but half of it is standing timber. And on the cleared ground, I hire men to put in my corn, and I work a great deal myself. I have got thirty sheep and forty goats, thirty pigs, and two dogs; they care of me for I live alone, not one in the house. There is a house within twenty roods of me.

Catchpole became one of the colony's best known midwives. "It is a wonderful country to have children in," wrote Catchpole. "Very old women have them that never had none before." She also frequently acted as a nurse. But in May 1819, when she nursed a shepherd ill with influenza, she caught the disease herself. Margaret Catchpole died on May 13, 1819, and was buried by Reverend Henry Fulton in the graveyard of St. Peter's Church in Richmond.

The correspondence of Margaret Catchpole describes the aboriginal inhabitants of Australia, the geography of this new land, and its unusual wildlife. She also chronicled the early struggles of convict laborers at Coal River, and the often brutal realities of penal life:

> But God only knows how it might be for here is many a one that has been here for many years and they have their poor head shaved and sent up to the Coal River and there carry coals from daylight in the morning, till dark at night, and half starved. . . . It is very cruel indeed.

For many Australian women, letter writing was an integral part of their lives. Correspondences were a socially acceptable form of expression, during a period when women were denied access to the literary professions. Such long lived correspondences served to ease the sense of isolation that women felt in the New World and to maintain family ties. The anxiety that accompanied such long-distance communication is revealed in one of Catchpole's letters.

> With great joy I received your letters for I thought you had forgot me. But when I saw the date they had been [traveling] a long time. They should have come in the *Dromedary* almost two years ago. I received my box on 28th August, 1811, and it makes me very happy to hear my dear cousins are doing so well. A great blessing and comfort to you and a source of happiness to me.

For many years, Catchpole corresponded with Mrs. Cobbold. The letters formed the basis of Mrs. Cobbold's son's fictionalized account of Catchpole's life, entitled *The History of Margaret Catchpole* (1885), as well as a stage play. Richard Cobbold took many liberties with the facts, including penning some of the letters between his mother and Margaret himself, cleaning up the spelling (Catchpole's style tended toward "i tak grat kear of my self"), and possibly inventing William Laud. He transposed the married life of ❧➤ **Mary Reibey** to that of Margaret, who never married. To this day, the two are often confused.

In 1911, Australian film pioneer Raymond Longford produced the silent film *The Romantic Story of Margaret Catchpole*. The silent film was based on Richard Cobbold's book, and starred *Lottie Lyell, another pioneer of Australian cinema. The picture was infused with a sense of doom and foreboding and derived much of its impact from the breathtaking footage of the Australian wilderness.

In total, 162,000 convicts were transported to Australia. Most of them were sentenced for crimes against property, such as theft, burglary, and larceny; 25,000 were female. Female convicts were often publicly maligned as prostitutes and women of ill-repute. Margaret Catchpole's story illustrates the fallacy of such portrayals. But as Robert Hughes noted:

> There was rarely a comment . . . a tract or a letter home that missed the chance to describe the degeneracy, incorrigibility and worthlessness of women convicts in Australia. . . . Convict men might in the end redeem themselves through work and penance, but women almost never.

The deportation of female convicts to Australia was part of a deliberate colonization policy sponsored by the British government. Women often endured terrible hardships and abusive treatment, as the colony was perpetually short of females. Nonetheless, as with Margaret Catchpole, convict women showed themselves to be equal to their male counterparts in stamina and determination, when facing the deprivations of frontier life. For many women, life in Australia offered a measure of independence scarcely imaginable in Britain. For those who chose to marry, a vast array of suitors were available. For others, such as Margaret Catchpole, it was possible to fashion a life outside the control of fathers, brothers, uncles, and husbands. Both groups richly deserve the title of "Mothers of the Nation."

SOURCES:

"Catchpole, Margaret," in *Australian Dictionary of Biography*. Vol. 1. Edited by A.G.L. Shaw and C.M.H. Clark. Melbourne: Melbourne University Press, 1966, pp. 215–216.

Hughes, Robert. *The Fatal Shore*. London: William Collins, 1986.

Rienits, Thea and Rex. *A Pictorial History of Australia*. Sydney: Paul Hamlyn, 1969.

Spender, Dale, ed. *The Penguin Anthology of Australian Women's Writing*. Victoria: Penguin Books, 1988.

Walkins, Morgan George. "Catchpole, Margaret (1773–1841)," in *The Dictionary of National Biography*. Edited by Sir Leslie Stephen and Sir Sidney Lee. Vol. III. Oxford: Oxford University Press, 1917, p. 1187.

SUGGESTED READING:

Chisholm, Alec H. *The Australian Encyclopaedia*. Vol. 2. Sydney: Halstead, 1958, pp. 285–286.

RELATED MEDIA:

The Romantic Story of Margaret Catchpole, a fictionalized account starring Lottie Lyell, Raymond Longford, Augustus Neville, Australia, 1911.

Hugh A. Stewart, M.A.,
University of Guelph, Guelph, Ontario, Canada

Caterina.

> *Italian variant for Catharine or Catherine.*

Caterina Benincasa (1347–1380).

> See Catherine of Siena.

Caterina Cornaro (1454–1510).

> See Cornaro, Caterina.

Caterina di Iacopo (1347–1380).

> See Catherine of Siena.

Caterina Sforza (1462–1509).

> See Sforza, Caterina.

Catharina.

> *Variant of Catharine or Catherine.*

Catharine.

> *Variant of Catherine.*

Cather, Willa (1873–1947)

American novelist and short-story writer whose work celebrated the complexities of life in the New World—the American west, midwest, southwest, south, and occasionally the urban east and Canada. Name variations: Willa S., Willa Sibert, Willie, William, Wilella. Pronunciation: CATH-er (like rather). Born on December 7, 1873 (some sources cite 1876, but 1873 is documented), in Back Creek Valley (near Winchester), Virginia; died in New York City on April 24, 1947; eldest of seven children of Virginia (Boak) Cather and Charles Cather (land investments and insurance agent); University of Nebraska, Lincoln, B.A., 1895; never married; lived in partnership with Edith Lewis, 1908–47; no children.

Awards: honorary degrees at Nebraska, California, Columbia, Yale, Smith, Creighton, Michigan; Pulitzer Prize (1922); Prix Femina Americaine (1931); elected member of American Academy of Arts and Letters (1938), and National Institute of Arts and Letters (1944).

Family moved to Webster County, Nebraska (1883), then settled in Red Cloud (1884); became journalist and published early stories during undergraduate years in Lincoln, Nebraska (1891–95); moved to Pittsburgh, Pennsylvania (1896) to become managing editor of Home Monthly *magazine and newspaper columnist; lived with Pittsburgh socialite Isabelle McClung Hambourg (1901–06); taught high school Latin and English, published volume of poems* April Twilights *(1903) and stories* The Troll Garden *(1905); moved to New York City as editor for* McClure's *Magazine (1906); published first novel* Alexander's Bridge *(1912); left editing to write fiction after successful "second first novel"* O Pioneers! *(1913).*

Reibey, Mary (1777–1855)

Australian entrepreneur. Name variations: Mary Raby or Raiby; Mary Haydock. Born Molly Haydock on May 12, 1777, at Bury, Lancashire, England; died at Newtown, a suburb of Sydney, Australia, on May 30, 1855; daughter of James Haydock and Jane (Law) Haydock; married Thomas Reibey (Raby, or Raiby), in September 1794; children: three sons and four daughters.

Orphaned when young, Mary Reibey was brought up in Cheshire by her grandfather who taught her to read and write. After his death, none of her relatives would take her, so she was sent into service from which she ran away. In August 1791, while in male disguise and using the name James Burrow, the name of the dead son of a neighbor, she was arrested for trying to sell a horse that had been stolen. Despite her age, the 13-year-old was sentenced to seven years transportation and continued the disguise throughout her imprisonment, only confessing when she was about to sail. Her relatives, given one more chance to claim her and assure her good conduct, refused.

On October 7, 1792, Reibey sailed from England with the Third Fleet on the ship *Royal Admiral*. Arriving in New South Wales (Sydney, Australia), she was possibly assigned as a nursemaid to the family of Lieutenant Francis Grose, then commandant of the colony. Two years later, she married Thomas Reibey, a junior officer for the East India Company on the trading ship *Britannia*. Granted permission to settle, Thomas was given land on the Hawkesbury River, where the couple took up farming. Thomas then bought a house at the Rocks, Sydney, and began transporting grain up the river. The business grew, as did his fleet, his cargo, and the value of his properties. By 1809, he was trading with China and India. In his frequent absences, Mary ran a hotel, as well as the business, while bringing up their three sons and four daughters.

On the death of her husband in April 1811, having inherited substantial property, she opened new warehouses, bought more ships, and purchased 2,000 acres in Van Diemen's Land, which she entailed to her sons. Accepted into Sydney society, Reibey was also celebrated on her 1820 return visit to Lancashire, England, with her daughters. Despite a couple of disreputable sons-in-law, Mary and her children added to their substantial wealth, and she became a noted philanthropist and religious worker. She died in the Sydney suburb of Newtown on May 30, 1855.

SUGGESTED READING:

Irvine, Nance. *Mary Reibey: Molly Incognita*, 1982.

Novels: Alexander's Bridge *(1912),* O Pioneers! *(1913),* The Song of the Lark *(1915),* My Antonia *(1918),* One of Ours *(1922),* A Lost Lady *(1923),* The Professor's House *(1925),* My Mortal Enemy *(1926),* Death Comes for the Archbishop *(1927),* Shadows on the Rock *(1931),* Lucy Gayheart *(1935),* Sapphira and the Slave Girl *(1940); short stories:* The Troll Garden *(1905),* Youth and the Bright Medusa *(1920),* Obscure Destinies *(1932),* The Old Beauty and Others *(posthumously 1948); poems:* April Twilights *(1903),* April Twilights and Other Poems *(1923); essays:* Not Under Forty *(1936),* Willa Cather on Writing *(posthumously 1949).*

In a 1908 letter to her friend, New England short-story writer *Sarah Orne Jewett, Willa Cather quoted Samuel Goldsmith to describe her current state of mind. She felt like a panic-stricken rabbit, she said, pursued by horses and hounds and panting "for the place from which at first she flew." At 35, Cather had not yet produced a publishable novel. An executive and editor in the whirlwind atmosphere of the New York offices of *McClure's Magazine,* she hardly had time to write anything at all. Every day brought a rush of important people and exciting news, but working for Samuel S. McClure was like racing through life on a train, she told Jewett, never getting off to know the people or seeing in any detail the towns she passed through. This life seemed superficial and shallow, and Cather felt torn apart by a split personality—efficient and authoritative on the outside, harried and anxious within. Worse, with no time to concentrate on her own writing, Cather feared for her soul.

In a 1925 letter to another friend, *Dorothy Canfield Fisher, the Vermont short-story writer and novelist, Cather still described herself as needing to race off, but now it was for a good reason. At last, her fiction came first, and she ran in order to write what she wanted. Now she was a "wild turkey," she told Fisher, a "crafty bird" who would light out for new territory the moment anyone discovered her home feeding ground. No matter how hard the critics might try, they would never be able to hold her to one subject or force her to repeat indefinitely the same story. She wanted to be free, she declared, free to experiment with her fiction, to dive in deep, to surprise.

What had transformed Cather from the scared rabbit to the wily bird were six novels, a volume of short stories, and a Pulitzer Prize. With them came fame, some fortune, a great deal of controversy, and numerous critics quite willing to tell Cather she must write only nostalgic novels about women in the American West. The uproar began in 1922 when Cather won the Pulitzer for *One of Ours,* the story of a young Nebraskan whose life ended heroically on a French battlefield in World War I. What could a woman know about men and war, the critics

sputtered. Cather should write about women and eulogize the frontier, as she had with her great triad of triumphant heroines—Alexandra Bergson in *O Pioneers!,* Thea Kronberg in *The Song of the Lark,* and Antonia Shimerda in *My Antonia*—and more recently with Marian Forester in *The Lost Lady.*

After one false start with the cosmopolitan *Alexander's Bridge,* Cather had in fact gone back to the "place from which at first she flew" for the early novels, to her own felt experience as an adolescent and young woman growing up on the Nebraska frontier. But when Cather turned to contemporary themes and less fortunate characters, like the sacrificial hero of *One of Ours* and the disaffected protagonist of *The Professor's House,* the critics balked. No woman could write about war, they said, or understand the lives of men. But the critics could no longer subdue Willa Cather, the "crafty bird" who had taken charge of her art. If she was still desperate for time and the space in which to do her work, Cather was no longer torn about what that work would be.

The oldest of seven children, Cather seems always to have been sure of her ambition, but she was also aware at an early age of inequities in class, race, and gender, and of oppression, disruption, and disaster: cultural shadows that underscore even the most hopeful of her novels. When Cather was born in the mountainous northwest corner of Virginia, the United States was still in the process of healing from the Civil War. Eight years had passed since Lee signed the treaty at Appomattox, but the area around Willow Shade, the Cather family home, had been the site of fierce fighting, and families like Cather's, wrenched apart during the war by divided loyalties, were just beginning to reunite. As sheep farmers, the Cathers also sought, like so many during the economic turmoil of the postwar years, to better their lot by heading West. Following a pattern typical of pioneer settlers, Cather's uncle and then her grandfather scouted out land and settled their families first, leaving behind Cather's mother and father, who took charge of Willow Shade until they too, in April 1883, were ready to try homesteading in Webster County, Nebraska.

Cather's family settled first on the Divide near the newly named settlement of Catherton, but by September 1884 they decided to move into the town of Red Cloud, where the children could attend school and Cather's father could open an office in the booming business of land investments. Cather lived in Red Cloud for only

*W*illa
*C*ather

six years, but those were important, formative years for the young writer. Red Cloud and its people served as the setting and provided models for several characters in her short stories and novels, including *O Pioneers!,* Song of the Lark, *My Antonia,* and *Lucy Gayheart.* Populated by settlers from New England, Missouri, Kentucky, West Virginia, and Virginia, the Divide was also filled with French Canadians, Germans, Bohemians, Swedes, Danes, and Swiss. Cather spent her days attending school and playing with her peers, but she also rode her pony across the plains, listened for hours to stories in the kitchens of immigrant women, made house calls by buggy and practiced dissection with the local doctor, read all the literary masterpieces available in a small midwestern town, and absorbed the multiplicity of cultures and values her neighbors represented.

An excellent student, Cather also readied herself to attend the University of Nebraska, one of the early land-grant colleges in the United States, which admitted women as well as men. Cather studied Latin and Greek with a tutor and, after graduating from Red Cloud high school, attended the university's high school in Lincoln in order to matriculate as a regular student at the university. Cather quickly made her mark in Lincoln. Years before, she had already declared her ambition in "this man's world" of the 1880s and 1890s by cutting her hair short and signing her name, William Cather, M.D. In Lincoln, Cather found other young women serious about careers and issues related to the New Woman, and her writing drew immediate attention from professors. When her short stories began to appear in both local and college publications, Cather shifted from science to literature, and, during the depression of 1893, she began earning her own living as a columnist and critic for the *Nebraska State Journal,* Lincoln's leading daily newspaper. After graduating in 1895, Cather became associate editor of *The Courier,* which focused on social items and news of the state's General Federation of Women's Clubs. That job lasted only a few months, however, and Cather found herself back in Red Cloud. By January, she was ready to call Red Cloud Siberia and consider herself in exile. She applied for a teaching job at the university, although she knew they would not hire her because of her sex, and worked hard on the short fiction she hoped would spring her release.

That is happiness: to be dissolved into something complete and great.

—Willa Cather's epitaph and a line from *My Antonia*

Journalism, writing, and teaching are separate but related career directions. Cather achieved success in all of them. In August 1896, she left Nebraska for a job as interim editor for a new family magazine, the *Home Monthly,* in Pittsburgh, Pennsylvania. She filled its pages with her own stories, written under a variety of pseudonyms, and then in 1897 shifted to a job at the *Pittsburgh Leader,* a newspaper, all the while contributing columns to the *Nebraska State Journal* and *The Courier.* In 1900, Cather left the *Leader* to write fiction for *The Library,* but that publication soon folded, and she considered moving back to Nebraska. By December, however, she had taken on a temporary writing assignment in Washington, D.C., and in March 1901 she returned to Pittsburgh, took a position teaching English and Latin in a local high school, and moved into the comfortable home of Judge Samuel A. McClung at the invitation of his socialite daughter, **Isabelle McClung,** whom Cather had met several years before. Teaching, Cather thought, would give her time to write, and the McClung's Squirrel Hill home would provide an ideal setting. By 1903, Cather had traveled with Isabelle to Europe, accepted a job chairing the English department at another Pitts-

burgh high school, and published a volume of poems, *April Twilights.*

In 1903, Cather also met S.S. McClure, the magazine editor and book publisher, and **Edith Lewis,** the fellow Nebraskan with whom she would share a home for nearly 40 years. Cather also began to work on her first volume of short stories, *The Troll Garden,* to be published by McClure in 1905. In 1906, at McClure's insistence, Cather left Pittsburgh for New York City and teaching for journalism. The most famous muckraking magazine of its day, *McClure's Magazine* had just lost its entire editorial staff. She was to replace one of its best-known writers, **Ida Tarbell.* Cather began by reworking a controversial biography of **Mary Baker Eddy,* the founder of Christian Science. Within two years, with Edith Lewis as her assistant, Cather had taken over much of the daily work of the office and by 1910, when she was associate editor, S.S. McClure encouraged Cather to stop writing fiction altogether and devote herself to journalism.

Had it not been for the timely advice and support of Sarah Orne Jewett, Edith Lewis, and Isabelle McClung, Cather might never have written her great novels. Contrary to McClure's advice, Jewett encouraged Cather to leave journalism for fiction. Edith Lewis, as always, provided Cather with editorial and personal support, and Isabelle McClung once again supplied Cather with a place to write, this time a cottage in upstate New York. By the time *O Pioneers!* appeared to quiet, but appreciative, reviews in 1913, Cather was 40 years old. For the first time in her life, she had written what she wanted to write instead of what she thought others wanted-ed. *O Pioneers!* was nothing like the stylish imitation of Henry James she had done for her first novel, *Alexander's Bridge.* It was also unlike the new genre of westerns, Owen Wister's *The Virginian,* for example, or Zane Grey's *Riders of the Purple Sage. O Pioneers!* was about immigrants on the Great Plains. Its main character was a hard-working woman, not a gunslinger. In only a few short stories had Cather hinted at the direction she might take in *O Pioneers!,* but when she finished it, she knew she had found home ground. The writing of *O Pioneers!* was entirely spontaneous, she declared, "like taking a ride through a familiar country on a horse that knew the way, on a fine morning when you felt like riding."

It was a ride in a country Cather would return to time and again. Not Nebraska or the past, necessarily, but territory familiar to her imagination. According to her own judgment,

Cather did that best in *My Antonia* and *Death Comes for the Archbishop.* Contemporary critical taste would also include *The Lost Lady* and *The Professor's House.* Cather always strove, as she said of Sarah Orne Jewett, to write novels that seem to be "not stories at all, but life itself." Deceptively simple, with beautifully cadenced prose, her novels are also rich in their complexity, filled with timeless oppositions—male/female, hope/despair, ancient/modern, art/life, urban/rural, native/foreign, Old World/New World—that are resolved symbolically through the feminine principle and Cather's own artistic "gift of sympathy."

Cather explores themes of diversity, change, and division and celebrates continuity, permanence, and universal values. Her fiction often feels autobiographical, but Cather's method was to fuse personal experience with contemporary and historical research. *My Antonia* and *The Lost Lady,* both set in Nebraska, focus on people (**Annie Pavelka Sedilak** and **Lyra Garber [Anderson]**) and places (Red Cloud and Lincoln) Cather knew well. *The Song of the Lark* intermixes details from Cather's youth with the childhood of *****Olive Fremstad,** the Metropolitan Opera star whose career the novel traces. *Death Comes for the Archbishop,* on the other hand, focuses on historical figures (Jean Baptiste Lamy and Joseph P. Machebeuf) and places (Santa Fe and Taos). The same is true of the symbolic "Tom Outland" section of *The Professor's House,* which portrays the discovery of Mesa Verde, and *Shadows on the Rock,* which records the settling of Quebec, Canada.

Whatever Cather's method, the clarity of her prose and her insights into people, times, and places are often breathtaking in their simplicity. "Art," she would say, "should simplify. That, indeed, is very nearly the whole of the higher artistic process." Great artists refine and distill until the composition of a work becomes "so simple that it seems inevitable." Art, Cather said elsewhere, is also "concrete and personal and rather childish . . . too terribly human to be very 'great,' perhaps." But as Stephen Tennant suggests in his introduction to Cather's essays on writing, Cather's own greatness "lies in the arrow-like flight of her faith in man ultimately— the eternal vision behind her work—juxtaposed to the homely, simple facts of life. . . . She understood the hearts of people—and wished always to understand them better."

On April 24, 1947, when Cather died of a cerebral hemorrhage, she had soared far from the actual "place from which at first she flew." A professional writer of international renown, she had lived and worked for more than 40 years in New York City, first in Greenwich Village and then on the upper East Side, with journalist and advertising writer Edith Lewis. At Cather's request, she was buried near Mt. Monadnock in Jaffrey Center, New Hampshire, a favorite vacation and writing retreat, where 25 years later Edith Lewis rejoined her.

SOURCES:

Bennett, Mildred R. *The World of Willa Cather.* Lincoln: University of Nebraska Press, 1961.

Brown, E.K. *Willa Cather: A Critical Biography.* Lincoln: University of Nebraska Press, 1987.

Cather, Willa. *Not Under Forty.* Lincoln: University of Nebraska Press, 1936.

———. *Willa Cather on Writing: Critical Studies on Writing as an Art.* Foreword by Stephen Tennant. Lincoln: University of Nebraska Press, 1976.

Lee, Hermione. *Willa Cather: Double Lives.* NY: Pantheon Books, 1989.

O'Brien, Sharon. *Willa Cather: The Emerging Voice.* NY: Oxford University Press, 1987.

Woodress, James. *Willa Cather: A Literary Life.* Lincoln: University of Nebraska Press, 1987.

SUGGESTED READING:

Lewis, Edith. *Willa Cather Living: A Personal Record.* Athens: Ohio University Press, 1953.

Sergeant, Elizabeth Shepley. *Willa Cather: A Memoir.* Athens: Ohio University Press, 1992.

RELATED MEDIA:

"My Antonia," television movie, starring Jason Robards and *****Eva Marie Saint,** premiered on USA Network, March 29, 1995.

"Marian Seldes as Willa Cather" (95 min.), audio cassette of Merkin Concert Hall performance in New York City, 1996.

Susan A. Hallgarth, editor,
National Council for Research on Women,
and faculty, Empire State College/State
University of New York (SUNY)

Catherina.

Variant of Catherine.

Catherina of Saxe-Lauenburg or Luneburg (1513–1535).

See Katarina of Saxe-Luneburg.

Catherine.

Variant of Catharine, Katharine, Katherine, or Ekaterina.

Catherine (?–305).

See Catherine of Alexandria.

Catherine (c. 1420–1493)

*Austrian royal. Name variations: Katharina. Born around 1420 in Wiener Neustadt; died on September 11, 1493, at Hochbaden Castle; daughter of *****Cimbur-**

ca of Masovia (c. 1396–1429) and Ernest the Iron of Habsburg (1377–1424), duke of Inner Austria.

Catherine, Countess Palatine
(1584–1638).

See Christina of Sweden for sidebar.

Catherine, Queen of Portugal
(1507–1578).

See Juana la Loca for sidebar.

Catherine I (1684–1727)

Lithuanian peasant who became the second wife of Tsar Peter the Great of Russia and succeeded him as empress of Russia from 1725 to 1727. Name variations: Catherine Skavronsky; Marta, Marfa, or Martha Skovoronski (Skavronska or Skavronskii, Skovortskii, Skowronska); Yekaterina Alexseyevna. Born Marta Skovoronski on April 5, 1684, in Marienburg or Jacobstadt, in the Swedish controlled province of Livonia, now part of Latvia; died on May 6, 1727, in St. Petersburg, Russia; daughter of Samuel Skovoronski and his peasant wife; married Johann Raabe; married Peter I the Great (1672–1725), tsar of Russia (r. 1682–1725), on February 9, 1712; children: 12, including Paul (1704–1707); Peter (1705–1707); Catherine (1706–1708); Anne Petrovna (1708–1728); *Elizabeth Petrovna (1709–1762); Margaret (1714–1715); Peter Petrovitch (1715–1719); Natalia (1718–1725).

Family moved to Latvia (1690s); Catherine became prisoner and paramour of General Boris P. Shermatov (1702); became servant and mistress of Alexander D. Menshikov (1704–05); became mistress and companion of Emperor Peter the Great (1705–12); married Peter the Great (1712); crowned as empress-consort (1724); succeeded Peter the Great as empress of Russia (1725–27).

Born to a peasant family, Marta Skovoronski survived an arduous life before becoming the mistress and finally, rechristened Catherine, the wife of Peter I the Great. After 12 difficult years of marriage, she was crowned empress-consort in a magnificent ceremony in May 1724. This astonishing story reached its zenith less than a year later when Catherine succeeded Peter on the Russian imperial throne.

The circumstances of the Empress Catherine's birth and infancy are somewhat obscure and based on mostly unreliable sources. Marta Skovoronski was probably born in April 1684 in the Swedish-controlled province of Livonia, now part of Latvia. She was born near the town of Marienburg but other sources suggest that her actual birthplace was the nearby village of Jacobstadt. Her father Samuel Skovoronski was a Lithuanian Catholic peasant who herded cattle for his master. The name of Marta's mother is unknown, but she and Samuel had several other children.

Life during Marta's childhood years in the Baltic region was extremely harsh. The area was plundered in almost continuous wars between Sweden, Poland, and Russia. When Marta was two, her father died during a plague that ravaged the Baltic provinces; her mother died about a year later. It is possible that the orphaned Skovoronski children may have lived for a few years with an aunt; then, though Catholic by birth, Marta went to live with a Lutheran pastor in the village of Ringen. When the plague reached Ringen and took the life of the pastor, the district superintendent for the Lutheran parish of Marienburg, Pastor Ernst Glück, took Marta into his home. She did the daily chores as a household servant and looked after the pastor's younger children. Although Pastor Glück provided lessons for his children, Marta received no formal education and remained illiterate. She survived her unfortunate circumstances by hiding her meager aspirations and substantial discontent under a mantle of submission and pleasantness. She also converted to the Lutheran faith.

In 1702, during her 18th year, Marta was attracted to Johann Raabe, a young dragoon in the Swedish occupation army. The Glücks negotiated with Raabe's commanding officer and a wedding date was established but had to be moved forward because war between Sweden and Russia was disrupting the peaceful life of Marienburg. A few days after the wedding, the Swedish commander withdrew his forces from Marienburg to escape the advance of Russian troops under Count Boris Shermatov. Raabe was among those withdrawn, but Marta remained behind. They never saw each other again.

Pastor Glück led a delegation, which included Marta, from Marienburg to the Russian camp to plead for mercy for the town. Detained by the Russians, Marta was assigned to the baggage train and temporarily fell under the protection of a German mercenary, Brigadier Bauer. She eventually caught the eye of Shermatov, and he added her to his collection of serving maids. Marta attended the aristocratic Shermatov at his table, made his bed and almost certainly shared it on occasions.

Considering her circumstances, Marta was fortunate to have served in the retinue of the

Catherine I

gentlemanly Shermatov. But in late 1703 or early 1704, she caught the eye of Alexander Dmitrievitch Menshikov, a young officer. An energetic, clever, and brave youth, Menshikov had risen from a street peddler to a place of affection with Tsar Peter I. Marta, who was by now used to being passed from one to another, found that she and her new master were two of a kind. Both were ambitious, and for the rest of their lives they remained connected. Marta saw Menshikov as a means to improve her status, and he hoped to use her charm and physical beauty to advance his ambitions at court. Sentiment between them played a part in their relationship, but advancement and a mutual fear of falling back into poverty sustained their friendship.

Marta, assigned to Menshikov's house as a servant, was an attractive woman with a lithe figure, a tilted nose and velvety black eyes. Blonde at birth, she dyed her hair black and wore it in a long and tumbling style. In 1705, when Tsar Peter visited Menshikov, he was attracted to Marta as she served the dinner. Told by Menshikov to see the tsar to his room, Marta spent the night, and Peter rewarded her with a gold ducat when he left the following morning. Menshikov was aware that Peter had sent his wife *Eudoxia Lopukhina to a convent and had recently dismissed *Anna Mons, his mistress of 12 years. Hoping to use Marta for his advantage, Menshikov again invited Peter to his home, was at first evasive when Peter asked for her, then produced a sophisticated Marta in a satin gown and flamboyant coiffure. Peter stayed for several days. Soon after his departure, the captain of the guards returned to Menshikov's home with orders to escort Marta to Moscow, and she became the mistress of one of the most powerful men in the world. Moreover, Peter the Great was no ordinary man. He was a tireless worker with prodigious appetites in everything he undertook. Standing 6'8", the tsar was temperamental, easily enraged, and suffered from occasional fits.

The nature of Marta's relationship with Peter between 1703 and 1710 is uncertain. Though Peter had Marta reside at the lavish house of Menshikov's sister and fiancé in the German suburb of Moscow, his public duties and the Great Northern War with Sweden (1700–21) made him an infrequent visitor to the city. During his long periods away, Marta improved her spoken Russian; she also gave birth to a son towards the end of 1704. On the tsar's insistence, both Marta and the child were baptized into the Russian Orthodox Church. The boy was named Paul, and Marta was given the name Catherine Alekseevna, the patronymic coming from Peter's son, Alexis Petrovitch, who served as Marta's godfather.

Anne Petrovna.
See Elizabeth Petrovna for sidebar.

*H*er amazing physical endurance was allied with a strong common sense and a simple honesty, which held [Catherine I] from being carried away by her new, exalted position, first as mistress, then as wife of the great Tsar.

—Ian Grey

Perhaps sensing his desire for a permanent relationship, Catherine devoted her efforts to understanding the moods and habits of the tsar. She made every effort to be agreeable. Gradually Peter visited Catherine more frequently during times of despair, realizing that she could calm his rages and soothe his stressful spirit. Catherine discovered that his bouts of rage, often dangerous to those around him, could be frightening. His eyes would stand out from the sockets and his mouth and face would twitch violently. Even Menshikov avoided the tsar during those spells, but Catherine would cradle Peter's head in her lap until he fell asleep. In truth, her ability to mother Peter was the strongest factor in their relationship as evidenced by the tsar calling her "mother."

A second son, Peter, soon followed the first child. In 1706, Tsar Peter took Catherine to the secluded fortress encampment where he was building his dream capital, St. Petersburg. While he worked on his new city, they lived in a small log cabin and were extremely happy. Catherine came to see Peter as her hero as well as her lover and protector. She never complained about the cramped and austere quarters and endured the same hardships that he faced. The interlude was brief. War and diplomacy soon forced Peter to leave, and the couple entered a long and tense time of intermittent separation.

It was one of the most tragic periods of both their lives. Catherine gave birth to a daughter, Catherine, on December 27, 1706, but Peter could not return to her until May. During the months that followed, both of their sons died. The following January, Peter once again had to return to the front to face another Swedish offensive. A month later, in February 1708, Catherine gave birth to a second daughter whom she named ◄ Anne (Petrovna). After a short visit, Peter again returned to his army and the war.

It was apparent to Catherine that Peter planned to marry her. He was hesitant, however, because a marriage would remind the public of his divorce from Eudoxia. There was also the problem of Catherine's humble origins, which would make her unacceptable to the nobility as a consort for the tsar. Catherine gave birth to another daughter, *Elizabeth Petrovna, just before Peter victoriously returned from the war in December 1709.

The year 1710 was a happy one; the couple returned to their spartan life of solitude and work at St. Petersburg. Though Peter left briefly to launch his new navy, he had Catherine seated beside him in the place of honor at an official function on his return. By December, an inevitable war with Turkey led Catherine to request permission to accompany Peter to the front and to provide inheritances for their daughters in case they did not survive. Though Peter refused Catherine's first request, he recognized their daughter Anne as a princess at a court banquet. On March 7, 1711, Peter informed the members of the royal family that Catherine was his "consort," and upon his death she would be provided for as an imperial dowager. He acknowledged that his first wife still lived, but when time permitted he intended to wed Catherine.

Catherine continued to insist on traveling with Peter, and he finally relented. When he left for the Turkish border in June 1711, she was with him. But the campaign bogged down on the Pruth River, and the Russians were soon surrounded by a powerful Turkish army. Tradition, perhaps fostered by Peter to make Catherine more acceptable to the Russian people, gives Catherine credit for negotiating a truce. Unconfirmed sources suggest that she and other women bribed the Turks with their jewelry. The following year, wearing a brocade gown that glittered with gems, Catherine married Peter on February 9, 1712, at Menshikov's chapel in St. Petersburg. His wedding gift was an ebony and ivory candelabrum carved by his own hands. Most of the day was celebrated by an elaborate banquet that was concluded with a massive firework display. Peter also legitimized their daughters, Anne and Elizabeth. Catherine gave birth to two more children, Peter Petrovitch in 1715 and Natalia in 1718. Both died without surviving their childhood.

Catherine's marriage brought few changes to her life. By choice, the royal couple had only a few servants and lived a less than magnificent lifestyle. Peter, always preoccupied with his realm, was often away but would return when possible to his family. Catherine, who felt that hers was a supportive role, had no political or social aspirations and always endeavored to please her husband. Though she gave her advice if Peter requested it, she rarely pursued an agenda or openly disagreed with his views.

Catherine did attempt to improve Peter's attitude toward his son by his first marriage. Disappointed with Alexis, Peter had made up his mind to disinherit his eldest son and heir. Alexis, who fled from Russia, was later lured back by a promise of reconciliation. Instead, Peter had him arrested, tried and sentenced to death for high treason. There is evidence that Catherine unsuccessfully pleaded to Peter for mercy for Alexis, who died in June 1718 while undergoing judicial torture.

With the death of his only living son, Peter was burdened with concerns about the succession. His only surviving male heir was his grandson Peter Alexivitch (Peter II), the son of Alexis and ❧▶ **Charlotte of Brunswick-Wolfenbüttel**. Resolute that his grandson would never reign, Peter issued a decree in February 1722, authorizing that Russian tsars appoint their own successors in order to exclude undesirable successors in the dynasty. Peter revealed his desire to have Catherine succeed him by crowning her empress-consort in an elaborate ceremony in the Uspensky Cathedral in Moscow on May 7,

1724. Catherine's coronation crown was fashioned by Paris jewelers using over 2,500 precious stones. Peter even stripped jewels from his own crown and purchased a massive ruby from China to cap the diadem. Yet he never formally proclaimed her as successor, and there were those who feared he might even choose a foreign relative to succeed him.

The only breach in Catherine and Peter's relationship occurred that same year. It has been traditionally believed that gossip among jealous courtiers drove Peter to suspect Catherine of taking a lover, and his eye fell upon William Mons, Catherine's chamberlain and the brother of Peter's former mistress. Much of this incident is debatable because Peter never held a formal inquiry in order to prevent embarrassment for his court. In November 1724, he had Mons, whom he also suspected of corruption, arrested and then exacted his vengeance on the entire family. Though most of them were exiled, William Mons was beheaded in Trinity Square. No incontrovertible evidence ever surfaced that proved there was a liaison between Catherine and Mons. Some scholars believe that Peter never suspected Catherine of having an affair but was instead angry over her defense of Mons' corrupt behavior. Peter and Catherine's children finally brought about a reconciliation, and at Princess Anne's betrothal ceremonies things seemed almost normal again. Peter was already very ill. Several weeks before, he had caught pneumonia rescuing some capsized sailors. After a long illness, he fell into a coma just as he was attempting to name his successor in writing; his only words were that "everything should be left to. . . ." He died on January 28, 1725.

Several candidates for the throne emerged. The stronger claims belonged to Catherine, who had nursed Peter in his last weeks, and Peter the Great's grandson, Peter Alexivitch, son of Alex-

❧▶ **Charlotte of Brunswick-Wolfenbüttel** (1694–1715)

German princess. Born on August 29, 1694; died in childbirth on November 2, 1715; daughter of Ludwig Rudolf, duke of Brunswick-Wolfenbüttel; sister of *Elizabeth Christina of Brunswick-Wolfenbüttel (1691–1750, the mother of *Maria Theresa of Austria); married Alexis Petrovitch (d. June 1718 while undergoing judicial inquiry authorized by his father Peter I the Great), on October 25, 1711; children: Natalie (1714–1728); Peter Alexivitch also known as Peter II (1715–1730), tsar of Russia.

is. Even as Peter was dying, the Russian nobles were forming factions to support their candidates. The old nobility, the Golitzins, Repnins, and Dolgorukis, supported Peter Alexivitch. The "new party," consisting of men like Menshikov who had risen from obscurity under Peter's reign, preferred Catherine. The Semenovski and Preobrazhenski imperial guard regiments remained loyal to Menshikov and those other leaders supporting Catherine, Procurator-General Pavel Iaguzhinski, Senator Peter Tolstoi, and Admiral Fyodor Apraksin. The opposition faction collapsed and the prominent figures of the state proclaimed Catherine the empress of Russia. The Senate and Holy Synod, which had controlled the bureaucracy during Peter's reign, proclaimed her succession the same day.

Catherine, almost totally illiterate, had no desire for power nor the qualities of a monarch. Her supporters viewed her as a suitable figurehead who would maintain the Petrine reforms and provide for their position and security. Catherine had always relied on strong men, and she became dependent upon her old friend Menshikov as her chief advisor. She took almost no part in government and in February 1726 began transferring authority to the Supreme Privy Council. In a sense, this council, dominated by Menshikov, became both an associate and advisor of the empress.

Catherine made every effort to complete several projects instituted by her husband. In 1725, she opened the Academy of Sciences, which had been one of Peter's dreams. His plan to explore the northern Pacific region was continued when she financed the expedition of Vitus Bering. Still in mourning for Peter, she permitted the marriage of her daughter Anne and the duke of Holstein to go forward. While 400 wedding guests celebrated, Catherine spent the day alone. Like Peter, she sought the affection of her soldiers and frequently dined with her officers, reviewed parades, and visited military hospitals.

Catherine attempted to distance herself from politics. She relied on the Supreme Privy Council but only occasionally attended the twice-a-week meetings. She signed the papers the council placed before her, entertained diplomats, and enjoyed making public appearances at banquets, balls, and parades. She loved the trappings of monarchy, and her taste for life became more self-indulgent and luxurious. She spent fortunes on clothing imported from abroad. Lavish improvements were added to the numerous royal palaces, and she traveled in gilded coaches and barges.

In November 1726, Catherine suffered a serious chill while being evacuated from a flood in St. Petersburg. Though she seemed to have recovered, she soon began to suffer fainting spells. By the middle of April, she was seriously ill and even had occasional hallucinations of talking to Peter in her sleep. Her physicians diagnosed an abscessed lung, but they had no treatment that could cure her. Some of her supporters believed she was being slowly poisoned, but it is more likely that she was in the terminal stage of tuberculosis.

While Catherine favored naming her daughter Anne as her successor, her advisors, led by Menshikov, convinced her that Peter Alexivitch had the best claim. Shortly before her death, she apparently assented to naming Peter as heir to the throne and sanctioned his marriage to Menshikov's daughter (though the marriage never took place). Catherine also nominated her daughters, Anne and Elizabeth, Peter's aunts to the Privy Council. Following her death, the Supreme Privy Council confirmed a last testament by Catherine, long believed a forgery, naming Peter as her successor. Catherine fell into a coma and died during the evening of May 6, 1727, in the third year of her brief reign.

SOURCES:

Longworth, Philip. *The Three Empresses: Catherine I, Anne and Elizabeth of Russia.* NY: Holt, Rinehart and Winston, 1973.

Massie, Robert K. *Peter the Great: His Life and World.* NY: Alfred A. Knopf, 1980.

Mottley, John. *History of the Life and Reign of the Empress Catherine of Russia.* London: n.p., 1744.

———. *The History of the Russian Empire from its Foundation to the Death of the Empress Catherine.* 2 vols. London: n.p. 1757.

Strong, Phil. *Marta of Moscow: The Fabulous Life of Russia's First Empress.* Garden City: Doubleday, Doran, 1945.

SUGGESTED READING:

de Jonge, Alex. *Fire and Water: A Life of Peter the Great.* NY: Coward, McCann, 1980.

Grey, Ian. *Peter the Great: Emperor of all Russia.* Philadelphia, PA: J.B. Lippincott, 1960.

Phillip E. Koerper, Professor of History, Jacksonville State University, Jacksonville, Alabama

Catherine II the Great (1729–1796)

An enlightened despot, who seized the throne from her husband Tsar Peter III and ruled Russia as empress and autocrat of All the Russias for over 34 years. Name variations: Sophia Augusta Frederika, princess of Anhalt-Zerbst; Catherine Alexeievna, Alekseyevna, or Alekseevna, grand duchess of Russia; Catherine II, empress of All the Russias; (nickname) Figchen. Born in Stettin, Pomerania, on April 21,

Catherine II
the Great

1729; died of a cerebral stroke in the Winter Palace in St. Petersburg, Russia, on November 6, 1796; daughter of Prince Christian Augustus von Anhalt-Zerbst and Johanna Elizabeth of Holstein-Gottorp (1712–1760); married Peter Fedorovich, grand duke of Russia, later Peter III, tsar of Russia (r. 1762–1762), on Friday, August 21, 1745, in St. Petersburg; secretly married her lover, Gregory Potemkin in 1774, in St. Petersburg (?); children: Paul Petrovich also known as Paul I (b. September 20, 1754), tsar of Russia; (with Stanislas Poniatowski, later king of Poland) Anna Petrovna (1757–1758);

(with Gregory Orlov) Count Alexei Gregorevich Bobrinski (b. April 11, 1762), and two more sons born in 1763 and 1771.

Coup against her husband, Tsar Peter III (June 28, 1762); declared empress (June 29, 1762); murder of Peter III at Ropsha (July 5, 1762); Catherine crowned in Moscow (September 22, 1762); meeting of the Great Commission on Codification (December 1766–June 1768); war with Turkey (1768–74); Pugachev Rebellion (1773–74); Charter to the Nobility (April 21, 1785); annexation of the Crimea (1783); second war with Turkey (1787–92); partitions of Poland (1772, 1793, 1795).

The Empress Catherine II has been admired for her liberal ideas, reviled as a usurper and nymphomaniac, praised as an Enlightened Despot and worthy successor of Peter the Great (r. 1682–1725), and condemned for neglect of the Russian masses and aggression against Turkey and Poland. According to a recent article by James Cracraft, "Empress Catherine II was easily the most humane and literate ruler in all of Russian history as well as one of the most active. . . [and] by the standards of her own or almost any other time, her reign was the most successful."

All I hope, all that I wish is that this country in which God has cast me, should prosper. . . . The glory of this country is my glory.

—Catherine the Great

The young Princess Sophia, from a minor German principality, was shy, plain, and exhibited few qualities that later marked her personal life or her autocratic reign as empress of All the Russias. Lacking beauty and a fortune, her future was not promising. However, her life and ultimately the history of a vast empire changed forever when the formidable Empress *Elizabeth Petrovna of Russia selected her as a prospective bride for her nephew and heir, the Grand Duke Peter Fedorovich (born Charles Peter Ulrich of Holstein). In January 1744, Sophia and her mother, Princess *Johanna Elizabeth of Holstein-Gottorp, set out on a journey that brought them to Moscow. Russia in the 18th century was at once immense and exotic, reputedly rich but barbarous by Western European standards. Equally mysterious was Sophia's future husband who, like herself, was Lutheran and German by birth; grandson of Peter the Great, he had been brought to Russia in 1742. Lonely and immature both physically and emotionally, Peter was irascible and cruel, and hated all things Russian.

In stark contrast to this infantile boy, the young Sophia was intelligent, ambitious and calculating, and eager to please the lusty Elizabeth and her court. As Catherine noted years later in her memoirs: "I felt little more than indifference towards [Peter], though I was not indifferent to the Russian crown." Sophia succeeded in impressing the empress and even won approval from the grand duke. Almost immediately, she began instruction in the Russian Orthodox Church and to study the Russian language, thereby shedding her Lutheranism and her native tongue. "I wanted to be Russian in order that the Russians should love me," she admitted in her memoirs.

Six months after her arrival, on June 28, Sophia was received into the Orthodox Church and was given the name Catherine Alexeievna. The next day, Catherine and Peter exchanged rings at a solemn ceremony in the Kremlin and became officially betrothed. Despite Elizabeth's sense of urgency regarding their marriage, she judged Peter as yet unable to produce an heir. Catherine also thought Peter immature and uninteresting, but she never contemplated abandoning the position of grand duchess or future empress. Catherine attended fancy dress balls, visited the theater, played games with her ladies-in-waiting, and traveled extensively with Elizabeth and her court; while Peter played with his toy soldiers, tortured animals, and engaged in childish behavior at public functions.

Peter was rather sickly and, in November 1744, he contracted measles and later that winter came down with smallpox. When Catherine saw him the following February, his bloated, pockmarked face horrified her. But nothing deterred Elizabeth from making plans for an elaborate wedding, and the couple were married by the bishop of Novgorod in St. Petersburg on August 21, 1745, a marriage singularly lacking in prospects of happiness or even compatibility. This arranged marriage would not be consummated for several years, which frustrated and eventually angered the empress. Actually, Peter and Catherine had only a vague idea of sexuality, no experience, and almost a total lack of interest in one another. But to Elizabeth whose sexual exploits were legendary, this ignorance was unacceptable. She resorted to isolating the couple, forcing them to live together under close supervision. For nine years, Catherine endured living with a man for whom she felt increasing contempt, surrounded by Elizabeth's spies. Peter continued to engage in juvenile pursuits and to ignore his wife. Catherine, however, slowly emerged from this long ordeal as a mature, self-assured woman; bored with the trivialities of the "Little Court" and the inane conversation of her companions, she immersed herself in reading the great literature of Greece and Rome, as well as the famous French writers of the 18th century Age of Enlightenment—Voltaire, Montesquieu, and Diderot. And she developed an interest in writing; she was not happy unless she had written something every day, according to historian Bernard Pares.

After years of coercion and enforced isolation, a bizarre sequence of events led to the birth of an heir. Through Catherine's chief lady-in-waiting, **Mme Choglokov**, two young nobles were introduced into the household of the little court. Undoubtedly with Elizabeth's blessing, Mme Choglokov implied that Catherine must take the initiative, choose one as a lover, and get pregnant. Still a virgin at 23 and eager for affection, Catherine promptly fell in love with Serge Saltikov who became her lover in the summer of 1752. A son was born two years later. Fortunately by then Peter had had sexual relations with another woman, and with Catherine, one must assume. The handsome, refined Saltikov affected Catherine's life in profound ways: their affair aroused Catherine's sensuality that had been repressed by her abnormal marital situation, it involved her in court politics for the first time to protect herself and her lover, and it guaranteed a continuation of the Romanov dynasty. Catherine's position in the royal family was more secure after she gave birth to Paul Petrovich in September 1754. Petrovich meant son of Peter, but was he? There is no solid evidence that he was not Peter's child and though Catherine suggested that Saltikov was the father, Paul's paternity remains uncertain. To Catherine, motherhood was no less aberrant than marriage. Elizabeth, who had never wed, took charge of the newborn heir, denying Catherine any contact with him for months at a time. Ignored and alone, she lived in a dismal, cramped room in the Winter Palace in St. Petersburg. Saltikov was dispatched to a post at the court of the king of Sweden; though he assumed the affair was over, Catherine did not, and word of his liaisons caused her great pain.

From the movie The Scarlet Empress, *starring Marlene Dietrich as Catherine II the Great.*

However, the future empress had no intention of allowing others to dictate her fate. She began to assert herself and to take an active role in influencing court policies through friends and favorites. Her first foray into international affairs involved her with the newly appointed British ambassador, Sir Charles Hanbury-Williams. He arrived in the capital in 1755, accompanied by a charming, educated Polish aristocrat, Count Stanislas Poniatowski. Catherine was attracted to the count, and Hanbury-Williams encouraged their friendship, which he hoped would win Catherine's support for British interests. He was aware of Elizabeth's deteriorating health, and he seriously doubted that Peter would reign as tsar. Catherine had already gained a reputation at court for being intelligent, sensible, and mature, but always in need of money. Her financial insolvency involved her in a risky and nearly disastrous political venture. Britain and Prussia were allies, and Hanbury-Williams used Catherine to try to convince the Empress Elizabeth not to make war on Prussia. His diplomatic maneuver failed; Catherine was reprimanded for interfering in affairs of state, which Elizabeth had forbidden her to do.

Catherine's position was precarious. She was pregnant by Poniatowski, and Peter openly questioned whether he was responsible. Equally serious was his declared love for his mistress, **Elizabeth Vorontsova**. At court, the powerful Shuvalov family was preparing to assert its influence over Peter when the ailing empress died. In either case, Catherine would be thrust aside. But Catherine was shrewd and tough, and she actively garnered support among Peter's adversaries and made peace with the empress. Even Elizabeth considered Peter deficient and puerile, and perhaps she realized that only Catherine could save Russia from disaster under his reign. But already some of Catherine's friends at court were planning to install her as co-ruler, an arrangement not favored by her. After the birth of her daughter ◄ᣟ **Anna Petrovna** in December 1757, and her reconciliation with Elizabeth, Catherine gave serious thought to her situation and decided upon a course of action. She wanted to wield power, not behind the throne, but on the throne.

ᣟ▶ **Anna Petrovna** (1757–1758)

*Princess of Russia. Born on December 9, 1757; died on March 8, 1758; daughter of *Catherine II the Great (1729–1796) and Stanislas Poniatowski, later king of Poland.*

The crown changed hands on Christmas Day 1761, eleven days before Elizabeth died. Few applauded the ascension of Peter III, and Catherine still felt vulnerable. The royal couple continued to occupy separate residences and lead independent lives. Peter repeatedly stated that he wished to marry his mistress and threatened to have Catherine arrested. Curiously, Catherine did nothing; she was pregnant by her current lover, Gregory Orlov, who would play a major role in subsequent events. However, she also had secured powerful allies, including Orlov's four brothers and Count Nikita Panin, former ambassador to Sweden and tutor to the Tsarovich Paul. During Peter's brief reign of six months, he managed to alienate important segments of Russian society, in particular the army and the church, both of which he set out to "Prussianize."

In April 1762, Catherine gave birth, in secret, to a son, Alexei Gregorevich Bobrinski. She was 33 years old, a warm, ebullient, and self-confident woman. Orlov matched her lusty nature, and their affair, lasting almost 14 years, was directly responsible for placing Catherine on the throne. The sexual life of the great Catherine has been savagely criticized by contemporaries and by posterity. Europe delighted in, but was scandalized by, her succession of lovers, 55 by some accounts. The editor of her memoirs remarked that her attitude towards love was unfeminine, "she loved like a man, and worked like a man." In fact, Catherine described her mind and temperament as more male than female. Pleasure to her was not sinful, and she sought pleasure from a series of handsome, virile, young men ("temporaries" or "housepets") up to the time of her death.

As Catherine grew more assertive, she publicly stated her disapproval of Peter's peace treaty with Prussia. His tactless disregard for everything Russian, and his open devotion to all things Prussian could no longer be tolerated. Preparation for war with Denmark, which would only benefit his native Holstein was viewed with alarm. So, too, was Peter's stated intention to marry Elizabeth Vorontsova. Meanwhile, a plot laid by Catherine's supporters and led by the Orlov brothers was put into action. Catherine was in residence at Peterhof and would have to be rescued before Peter and his entourage arrived to celebrate the feast days of Saints Peter and Paul, on June 29.

Gregory Orlov ensured the allegiance of the Ismailov Regiment and several others in St. Petersburg for Catherine, while his brother Alexei conducted her safely to the capital. Shortly before 8:00 AM, Catherine arrived in St. Petersburg, where the officers and soldiers swore an oath to her. In the Kazan Cathedral, Catherine was crowned and received the blessing of the church; the entire affair had taken only four hours. Peter was informed of the coup by Catherine herself, as she led 14,000 troops to Peterhof. He was placed under house arrest at Ropsha, near Petersburg. Writing to Catherine, he asked to share power with her, which she refused, and Peter quietly abdicated. Alexei Orlov was appointed to guard him, but on July 5, Peter died under mysterious circumstances. It has been assumed that Alexei Orlov suffocated or strangled Peter. Orlov denied this, but it is certain that Catherine gave no orders to murder Peter. No one was punished. In a public statement, Catherine claimed that Peter died of hemorrhoidal colic; in her memoirs, she noted, "I had him opened up. . . . The cause of death was established as inflammation of the bowels and apoplexy. He had an inordinately small heart, quite withered."

The coronation of Catherine II took place on September 22, 1762, in Moscow, the traditional, historical capital of pre-Petrine Russia, thereby identifying herself with her Russian predecessors, and as autocrat and heir of the Westernizer, Peter I the Great. She would "civilize Russia" through education, enlightened laws, and administration. Often working 15 hours a day, employing four secretaries, Catherine attempted to drag Russia into the Age of Enlightenment. However, she was ever mindful of Russian realities and her own insecurity on the throne because of other claimants such as the deposed Ivan IV and her son Paul who were objects of plots to replace her. Her support came from the privileged landed gentry whom she must appease. In spite of all obstacles, she made sincere efforts to improve conditions in her empire.

The gentry enjoyed a monopoly of rights that would be enhanced during Catherine's reign. At her insistence, they eagerly embraced Western ideas and ways in vogue at the time, separating them from their native traditions, their Russian roots. Bernard Pares claims that Catherine gave the nobility "their soul: certainly she gave them their style." That style was European. On the other hand, serfdom continued to bind the masses to legal servitude.

One of the most important attempts to modernize Russia was Catherine's proposal to assemble a Great Commission of elected delegates from all classes and parts of her realm to discuss a new law code. Prior to the meeting,

Catherine spent almost two years compiling an *Instruction* (*Nakaz*) based on liberal, humanitarian principles. The 500-odd articles reveal how Catherine viewed her role and what she considered beneficial for her subjects. Borrowing from several writers of the Age of Enlightenment, issues such as equality before the law, taxation, capital punishment, personal liberty, and justice were included. From December 1766 to June 1768, the Commission of 564 delegates met in Moscow, but nothing constructive came from the 203 sessions held because of the privileged gentry whom Catherine could not afford to offend. In principle, Catherine opposed serfdom and had written that serfs should be freed when estates were sold, a gradual rather than sudden emancipation, to avoid social and economic instability. In fact, nothing of the sort was ever carried out; social stability overrode humanitarian considerations.

Catherine attended many of the sessions and responded to the numerous demands for administrative reform; subsequently Russia was divided into 50 *gubernii* (provinces) headed by governors and subdivided into districts, and on the national level, she reorganized her own administration. In 1785, Catherine granted charters to towns that implemented self-government through an elected mayor and a town council (*duma*). That same year, she issued her Charter to the Nobility, inaugurating the "golden age of the nobility," which lasted in large measure until the 1917 Revolution. Hereditary nobility had exclusive rights to own peasant villages with absolute authority over their serfs, were exempt from personal taxes and capital punishment, and could elect their own provincial and district officials and convene assemblies every three years.

Catherine took special interest in agriculture and trade. Roads and canals were built and improved, trade treaties were negotiated. However, towns failed to flourish due to lack of industry and heavy taxes. Trade generally remained in the hands of foreigners. Catherine had founded the Free Economic Society to investigate the conditions of agriculture; its findings confirmed what she already knew: serfdom was uneconomical, not to mention morally reprehensible. In practice, Catherine had to choose between principle and the possible, and it was not possible to tamper with aristocratic privilege.

During her long reign, Catherine had the habit of recording her thoughts on a myriad of subjects. A sentence or short paragraph would be devoted to education, to relocating factories from Moscow to outlying villages to boost local economies, thoughts on the production of oysters, and the causes of high infant mortality in Russia. Often her words were translated into action. She had Foundling Hospitals built in Moscow and St. Petersburg. And in 1771, when Moscow was ravaged by bubonic plague, which killed about 100,000 people, and riots broke out, she sent Gregory Orlov to restore order and enforce a quarantine of the city. Catherine was also well acquainted with the scientific advances of the time and as an example to others, she and her family were inoculated against smallpox in 1768. To Catherine, disease and ignorance were enemies of progress and happiness, which could be conquered through education. "Domestic education is still a muddy stream," she wrote. "When oh when will it become a torrent?" Catherine established schools—the Smolny Institute for daughters of the gentry, an Academy of Beaux Arts, a School of Mining, and a College of Medicine—and built a public library in St. Petersburg.

But these measures did nothing to improve the widespread misery of the masses. In May 1773, a massive rebellion, led by Emelian Pugachev, broke out. Claiming to be Peter III, Pugachev and an army of Cossacks and peasants pillaged and murdered gentry, clergy, and officials. When the rebels controlled almost one-third of Russia, Catherine sent an army to crush the revolt, the largest in Russia to this time. Pugachev was brought to Moscow in an iron cage, tried, and executed in January 1775. Catherine's reaction led to extending serfdom to newly acquired areas, and to expanding the nobles' legal authority over their serfs.

Catherine's rule was autocratic; she functioned as her own minister of foreign and domestic affairs, of finance and war. And she directed her private life with the same decisiveness that she displayed in governing. Behavior at court was regulated by a list of "Ten Commandments," compiled and enforced by the empress. Her lovers were also required to live by her rules. When Gregory Orlov, the father of three of her sons, engaged in an affair with a distant adolescent relative, Catherine terminated their relationship, then made him a prince and showered him with riches. Orlov was "replaced" by a long, undistinguished series of virile young "temporaries." When they bored her or became too greedy, she discarded them as she did old gowns. But in 1774, Catherine fell in love with Gregory Potemkin whose ability and judgment matched her own. More than a lover, he acted as her trusted advisor during the last half of her reign. However, Catherine continued to rely on young lovers

to amuse and serve her. As she explained to Potemkin, "The trouble is that my heart is loath to remain even one hour without love."

If Catherine's sexual exploits shocked and titillated courts from London to Constantinople, her aggressive foreign policy made Europe tremble. She is reported to have said, "If I could live to be a hundred, I should wish to unite the whole of Europe under the scepter of Russia." A master of diplomacy, Catherine forged alliances, made war, negotiated treaties, and expanded the Russian land mass. With the cooperation of Frederick the Great of Prussia, she placed her former lover, Stanislaus Poniatowski, on the throne of Poland and controlled him through her ambassador in Warsaw. But this did not prevent Catherine, along with Austria and Prussia, from partitioning Poland until even the name disappeared from the map in 1795. Russia gained six million people and over 180,000 square miles, a Machiavellian feat of diplomacy. Similar success against the Turks in two wars resulted in Russian expansion to the Black Sea and into the Caucasus region and the Balkans. Her unrealized "Greek Plan" would have established a reconstituted Christian-Byzantine state under an Orthodox ruler in Constantinople, namely one of her adored grandsons, Alexander or Constantine. Catherine never lost sight of Russian interests and her desire to make the empire into a great power; she achieved what Peter the Great had begun.

Catherine became more conservative as she aged. Alarmed by the revolution that shook France, and Europe, after 1789, she tightened censorship laws to prevent "godless ideas" from infecting her realm. With amazing prescience, she predicted the rise of a strong man in France, but did not live to see Napoleon Bonaparte assume power.

There is little doubt that Catherine merited the appellation "the Great." She presided over a brilliant court with tact and ease, corresponded with great thinkers and powerful monarchs as equals, and revelled in their admiration; she collected art, built palaces, wrote plays and satirical articles, and worked on a comprehensive chronicle of Russian history, but her lively and intimate letters best reflect her personality. As empress, she assembled one of the greatest art collections in Europe, and she built the Hermitage in St. Petersburg to house it. Her ambassadors and agents searched out and bid on entire collections as well as single pieces. By 1785, she had bought 2,658 paintings. In addition, she acquired the entire library and papers of Voltaire and of the

French philosophe, Denis Diderot, who had visited her for five months in 1773; both collections are housed in the National Library in St. Petersburg. As one of her biographers noted, "Life was never too much for her; the problem rather, was time—time to devour it all."

In a brief section of her memoirs, entitled "Achievements," Catherine listed her accomplishments in ruling Russia, a most impressive précis of the reign of this most remarkable woman "who warmed both hands before the fire of life." Her people viewed her as the embodiment of Russia, a true Russian. In the epitaph she wrote for herself, Catherine reflects this: "Enthroned in Russia she desired nothing but the best for her country and tried to procure for her subjects happiness, liberty, and wealth. She forgave easily and hated no one." Through her ability and perseverance, the Russian colossus became a major force in European history.

SOURCES:

Alexander, John T. *Catherine the Great: Life and Legend.* Oxford: Oxford University Press, 1989.

Bruun, Geoffrey. *The Enlightened Despots.* NY: Rinehart and Winston, 1967.

Coughlan, Robert. *Elizabeth and Catherine: Empresses of All the Russias.* NY: Putnam, 1974.

Kitzlvetter, Aleksander A. "Portrait of an Enlightened Autocrat," in *Catherine the Great: A Profile.* Edited by Marc Raeff. NY: Hill and Wang, 1972.

Maroger, Dominique, ed. *The Memoirs of Catherine the Great.* Trans. by *Moura Budberg. NY: Macmillan, 1955.

Oldenbourg, Zoé. *Catherine the Great.* Trans. by Anne Carter. NY: Pantheon Books, 1965.

Pares, Bernard. *A History of Russia* (chapters XIII-XV). NY: Vintage Books, 1965.

SUGGESTED READING:

Anthony, Katherine. *Catherine the Great.* Garden City, NY: Garden City Publishing, 1925.

Cronin, Vincent. *Catherine, Empress of All the Russias.* London: Collins, 1978.

Grey, Ian. *Catherine the Great: Autocrat and Empress of All Russia.* Philadelphia, PA: Lippincott, 1962.

Madariaga, Isabel de. *Russia in the Age of Catherine the Great.* New Haven, CT: Yale University Press, 1981.

Oliva, Lawrence Jay, ed. *Catherine the Great.* Englewood Cliffs, NJ: Prentice-Hall, 1971.

Thomson, Gladys Scott. *Catherine the Great and the Expansion of Russia.* NY: Collier Books, 1962.

Troyat, Henri. *Catherine the Great.* NY: Dutton, 1981.

RELATED MEDIA:

Great Catherine, film adapted from George Bernard Shaw's short play of 1913, starring *Jeanne Moreau (1967).

The Scarlet Empress, film by Josef von Sternberg, starring *Marlene Dietrich (1934).

Catherine the Great, film starring *Elisabeth Bergner and Douglas Fairbanks, Jr., directed by Alexander Korda, 1934.

Catherine was Great, Mike Todd's Broadway production, starring *Mae West (1944).

Two-part television presentation, "Meeting of Minds," with Steve Allen, and **Jayne Meadows** Allen as Catherine (1980).

Segment on Catherine the Great (played by **Valentina Azovskaya**), in Peter Ustinov's "Ustinov in Russia" (1987).

Jeanne A. Ojala, Professor of History, University of Utah, Salt Lake City, Utah

Catherine Agnes de Saint Paul, Mere (1593–1671).

See Arnauld, Jeanne Catherine in entry on Port Royal des Champs, Abbesses of.

Catherine Charlotte of Hildburghausen (1787–1847)

*Princess of Saxe-Hildburghausen and duchess of Wurttemberg. Name variations: Charlotte of Saxe-Hildburghausen. Born Catherine Charlotte Georgina on June 17, 1787; died on December 12, 1847; daughter of Duke Frederick; married Paul Charles Frederick (1785–1852), duke of Wurttemberg, on September 28, 1805; children: *Helene of Wurttemberg (1807–1873, who married Grand Duke Michael of Russia); Frederick Charles (1808–1870); Paul (1809–1810); *Pauline of Wurttemberg (1810–1856); August (1813–1885).*

Catherine Cornaro (1454–1510).

See Cornaro, Caterina.

Catherine de Bora (1499–1550).

See Bora, Katharina von.

Catherine de Clermont (fl. 16th c.)

French military hero. Flourished 16th century in Clermont, France.

Very few facts remain about Catherine de Clermont, a noblewoman who became countess of Clermont. In the medieval period in Europe, noblewomen were often expected to defend their castles from enemy attack in the absence of husbands or fathers. Loyal to the monarchy, Catherine was a fearless leader who commanded her own troops in the defense of her estates and successfully brought Clermont back under the authority of the French king.

Catherine de Courtenay (d. 1307)

*Countess of Valois. Name variations: Katherina de Courtenay. Died on January 3, 1307; daughter of *Beatrice of Anjou (d. 1275) and Philipp de Courte-*

nay, titular emperor of Constantinople; became second wife of Charles of Valois also known as Charles I (1270–1325), count of Valois and duke of Anjou (son of Philip III the Bold, king of France), on February 8, 1301; children: *Jeanne of Valois, countess of Beaumont (b. 1304, who married Robert III of Artois); stepchildren: Philip VI of Valois (1293–1350), king of France (r. 1328–1350); *Jeanne of Valois (c. 1294–1342, mother of *Philippa of Hainault).

Catherine de Foix, Queen of Navarre (c. 1470–1517).

See Margaret of Angoulême for sidebar.

Catherine de France (1428–1446).

See Mary of Burgundy for sidebar.

Catherine de Medici (1519–1589).

See Medici, Catherine de.

Catherine de Ruet (c. 1350–1403).

See Beaufort, Joan (c. 1379–1440) for sidebar on Catherine Swynford.

Catherine Frederica of Wurttemberg (1821–1898)

Princess of Wurttemberg. Born on August 24, 1821; died on December 6, 1898; daughter of *Pauline of Wurttemberg (1800–1873) and William I (1781–1864), king of Wurttemberg (r. 1816–1864); married her cousin Frederick Charles Augustus (1808–1870), on November 20, 1845; children: William II (1848–1921), king of Wurttemberg (r. 1891–1918, abdicated).

Catherine Howard (1520/22–1542).

See Six Wives of Henry VIII.

Catherine Jagello (1525–1583)

Queen of Sweden. Name variations: Catherine of Poland; Catherine Jagellonica or Jagiello. Born in 1525; died on November 16, 1583; daughter of Sigismund I, king of Poland (r. 1506–1548), and *Bona Sforza (1493–1557); sister of Sigismund II, king of Poland (r. 1548–1572); married John III Vasa (1537–1592), duke of Finland and king of Sweden (r. 1568–1592), on October 4, 1562; children: Zygmunt III also known as Sigismund III (1566–1632), king of Poland (r. 1587–1632), king of Sweden (r. 1592–1599); Isabella (1564–1566); Anna (1568–1625); John (d. 1618). Following Catherine Jagello's death, John III married Gunila Bjelke on

February 21, 1585. The couple had one child: John, duke of East Gotland, born on April 18, 1589.

Catherine Labouré (1806–1875).

See Labouré, Catherine.

Catherine of Achaea (d. 1465)

Byzantine royal and member of the powerful Paleologi family. Died in 1465; married Thomas Paleologus (younger brother of Constantine IX, emperor of Byzantium), despot of Morea (present-day Greece); children: *Sophia of Byzantium (1448–1503); and two sons.

Catherine of Alexandria (?–305)

Christian martyr and saint. Name variations: Catharine, Katharine, Katherine, Katerin; (Spanish) Catarina; (Italian) Caterina; (Portuguese) Catharina. Born in Alexandria, date unknown; according to tradition, tortured on the wheel and beheaded at Alexandria on November 25, 305 CE; daughter of Costus, king of Cilicia, and Sabinella, a Samaritan princess; educated at home.

The historical details of Catherine of Alexandria's life are uncertain, but she is distinguished as the patron saint of philosophers, literature, schools, wheelwrights, spinners, and mechanics. Her feast day is November 25, and she is portrayed with a book, a crown, and a wheel, which represent knowledge, royalty, and her miraculous escape from death.

Born in Alexandria to royalty, Catherine was schooled from the age of seven and then educated at home, where, because of her great wisdom, her tutors are said to have become her pupils. Despite the wishes of her family that she marry, Catherine chose to remain a virgin. Shortly after her baptism, she had a religious vision (probably of marriage to Christ), which sealed her Christian faith.

When the Emperor Maximin Daia, admiring her great beauty, attempted to seduce the 17-year-old woman, he could not overcome the religious devotion that now underscored her vow of chastity. He called on 50 pagan philosophers to dispute Catherine, all of whom were then converted to Christianity by her. Maximin Daia had them put to death, and Catherine was whipped and imprisoned.

During Maximin Daia's absence, his wife Empress ✤ Constance, with her attendant

Catherine of Alexandria

Porphyrius, visited Catherine, and they were also converted to Christianity by her arguments. Porphyrius, in turn, is said to have converted 100 soldiers. Upon his return, Maximin had his wife, Porphyrius, and the soldiers put to death, and Catherine was condemned to be broken on the wheel, which involved the use of two iron wheels covered with sharp blades between which Catherine was supposed to die. When the wheels broke in answer to her prayer, the onlookers were killed and maimed by the flying razored spikes. Her escape from death earned the spiked wheel the name "Catherine wheel" and earned Catherine her place as patron saint of wheelwrights. She was subsequently beheaded. Relics of Catherine's life are scattered throughout European churches. In the 10th century, a cult, the Order of the Knights of Saint Catherine, arose at Mount Sinai, where it was thought that her body had been discovered. The body remains there, and what is believed to be the head is housed in Rome.

SOURCES:

Baring-Gould, S. *The Lives of the Saints*. London: John C. Nimmo, 1897.

Caxton, William. *The Golden Legend or Lives of the Saints*. NY: AMS Press, 1900.

Kersey, Ethel M. *Women Philosophers: a Bio-critical Source Book*. NY: Greenwood Press, 1989.

Catherine Hundleby, M.A. Philosophy,
University of Guelph

Catherine of Aragon (1485–1536).

See Six Wives of Henry VIII.

Catherine of Bologna (1413–1463)

Italian saint and artist. Name variations: Caterina da Vigri; Caterina de' Vigri; Caterina dei Vigri. Born on September 8, 1413, in Bologna, Italy; died at Bologna on March 9, 1463; never married; no children.

A revered holy woman, Catherine of Bologna was recognized as much for her relationship to God as for her artistic works. Details of her early life are unknown. She entered a convent of Poor Clares (Franciscan nuns) in Bologna and eventually her education and piety led her to become its abbess. Acting as the convent's administrative and spiritual director, she was also an instructor of novices.

Catherine's primary expressions of faith were revealed through her art. She painted

❧➤ **Constance** (d. 305 CE)

Roman empress. Martyred in 305 CE; married Maximin Daia, the Eastern emperor and governor of Egypt and Syria (r. 305–313).

miniatures on manuscripts produced in the convent scriptorium and worked as a calligrapher. The abbess, who earned a widespread reputation for her great learning and intelligence, also showed talent in the field of music; she wrote numerous songs for the nuns to sing during services and played several instruments herself. In her later life, Catherine began receiving visions, descriptions of which were published for the spiritual benefit of others. Catherine was extraordinarily popular. Soon after she died in 1463, at age 50, her followers pressed for sainthood, leading to her canonization in 1492.

Laura York,
Riverside, California

Catherine of Bourbon (d. 1469)

*Duchess of Guelders. Name variations: Katherina de Bourbon. Died on May 21, 1469; daughter of *Agnes of Burgundy (d. 1476) and Charles I (b. 1401), duke of Bourbon (r. 1434–1456); married Adolf (b. 1438), duke of Guelders, on December 18, 1463; children: *Philippa of Guelders (d. 1547).*

Catherine of Bourbon

(c. 1555–1604)

*French Huguenot reformer and princess of Navarre. Name variations: Catherine, princess de Navarre; Catherine of Navarre; Catherine de Bourbon; duchesse de Bar; duchess of Bar. Born around 1555; died in 1604; daughter of *Jeanne d'Albret (1528–1572) and Antoine, duke of Bourbon; sister of Henry of Navarre (1553–1610), the future Henry VI, king of France (r. 1589–1610); married the duc de Bar.*

Catherine of Braganza

The highly educated, some say brilliant, Catherine of Bourbon spent much of her life in Navarre where she acted as regent for her absent brother Henry from 1585 to 1593. In 1593, she journeyed to France, fell in love with the country, and remained there until her death. Catherine was intent on marrying her distant cousin, the Comte de Soisson, but Henry questioned his loyalty. Instead, he contracted a marriage for her to the duc de Bar.

Though a staunch Huguenot reformer who was against her brother's conversion to Catholicism, Catherine became a good friend of her brother's mistress, the Catholic *Gabrielle d'Estrées, and surprisingly championed their marriage. It was chiefly through the efforts of Catherine and Gabrielle that the Edict of Nantes came to be written, providing religious freedom and restoring order to France. Berger de Xivrey wrote the biography *Catherine of Navarre, Duchesse de Bar.*

Catherine of Braganza (1638–1705)

*Queen of England and regent of Portugal. Name variations: Bragança. Born Catherine Henriqueta de Bragança on November 25, 1638, at Vila Viçosa, Lisbon, Portugal; died on December 1, 1705, at Bemposta Palace, Lisbon; interred at Belém Monastery, Lisbon; daughter of John IV, king of Portugal (r. 1640–1656), and **Luisa de Guzmán** (1613–1666); sister of Alphonso VI (1643–1683), king of Portugal (r. 1656–1667), and Peter II (1648–1706), king of Portugal (r. 1667–1706); married Charles II (1630–1685), king of England (r. 1661–1685), on May 21, 1662, in Portsmouth; children: four failed pregnancies.*

A Catholic princess of the Portuguese royal family, Catherine of Braganza was betrothed to Charles II, king of England, while still a child. In May 1662, she left the convent where she had received a modest education and traveled to England to meet and marry him. Charles seemed pleased with his young bride, writing in a letter after their first meeting that she was as "good a woman as ever was born," although her "face is not so exact as to be called a beauty." As Charles did not speak Spanish and Catherine knew no English or French, they could not converse at first.

However, Catherine soon adapted to her new homeland, although her somber Catholic upbringing and modest clothing were the subject of derision at the elegant English court. Queen Catherine remained in England for the next 20 years, during which time she was often pregnant. Unfortunately, none of her pregnancies came to term, and after two decades she had still not fulfilled what was considered the primary function of a queen—to produce an heir for the throne. She reportedly felt ashamed and embarrassed at this failure, especially as Charles became well known for his many mistresses and many illegitimate children.

Eventually, Catherine found her situation unbearable and left England to return to her native land. Charles is said to have missed her presence and to have begged her forgiveness on his deathbed for his offenses toward her. Back in Portugal, Catherine began taking an active role in the reign of her brother Peter II, now king of Portugal; in 1704, she was named regent in her brother's absence.

Laura York,
Riverside, California

Catherine of Brittany (1428–c. 1476)

Princess of Orange. Born in 1428; died around 1476; daughter of *Marguerite of Orleans (d. 1466) and Richard of Brittany, count d'Etampes; married William VIII, prince of Orange, in 1438; children: John IV the Good, prince of Orange.

Catherine of Brunswick-Wolfenbuttel (1488–1563)

Duchess of Saxe-Lüneburg. Name variations: Katharina of Brunswick-Wolfenbüttel. Born in 1488; died on June 19, 1563; daughter of Henry I the Elder, duke of Brunswick, and *Catherine of Pomerania (d. 1526); married Magnus, duke of Saxe-Lüneburg, on November 20, 1509; children: *Katarina of Saxe-Lüneburg (1513–1535); *Dorothea of Saxe-Lauenburg (1511–1571).

Catherine of Bulgaria (fl. 1050).

See Anna Comnena for sidebar.

Catherine of Burgundy (1378–1425)

Duchess of Austria. Name variations: Katharina. Born in 1378; died on January 26, 1425 (some sources cite 1426), in Dijon, France; daughter of *Margaret of Flanders (1350–1405) and Philip the Bold (1342–1404), duke of Burgundy (r. 1363–1404); married Leopold IV (1371–1411), duke of Austria (r. 1386–1411).

Catherine of Clermont (fl. 16th c.).

See Catherine de Clermont.

Catherine of Cleves (1417–1479)

Duchess of Guelders. Name variations: Katherine von Kleve. Born on May 25, 1417; died on February 10, 1479; daughter of Adolf of Cleves (d. 1492) and Beatriz; married Arnold, duke of Guelders, in 1430; children: Adolf (b. 1438), duke of Guelders; *Mary of Guelders (1433–1463).

Catherine of Cleves (fl. 1550s)

Duchess of Guise. Name variations: Catherine de Cleves. Flourished in the 1550s; married Henry I of Lorraine le Balafré, 3rd duke of Guise (r. 1550–1588); children: fourteen, including Charles of Lorraine (1554–1611), 4th duke of Guise; Claude, duke of Chevreuse (who married *Marie de Rohan-Montbazon, duchesse de Chevreuse); Louis, 3rd cardinal of Guise (d. 1621).

One of three daughters of Nevers ("three princesses who cannot be lauded enough either for their beauty or their virtues," wrote St.-Beuve), Catherine of Cleves had 14 children. Her husband, Henry of Lorraine, 3rd duke of Guise, fought against the Huguenots and took an active part in the St. Bartholomew's Day Massacre. To Catherine of Cleves' long-held sorrow, he was assassinated by the Royal Guard at Blois in December 1588. Her brother-in-law, Louis, 2nd cardinal Guise, was assassinated the following day.

Catherine of Courtenay (d. 1307).

See Catherine de Courtenay.

Catherine of Custrin (1549–1602)

Electress of Brandenburg. Name variations: Catherine von Brandenburg-Kustrin or Cüstrin. Born on August 10, 1549; died on September 30, 1602; married Joachim Frederick (1546–1608), elector of Brandenburg (r. 1598–1608), on January 8, 1570; children: John Sigismund (1572–1619), elector of Brandenburg (r. 1608–1619); *Anna Catherina of Brandenburg (1575–1612, who married Christian IV, king of Denmark).

Catherine of France (1401–1437).

See Catherine of Valois.

Catherine of Genoa (1447–1510)

Italian mystic who, thwarted in her desire to become a nun, continued to deepen her religious fervor into a remarkable mysticism, one side of a "double life," which was combined with an active role in the secular world. Name variations: Catherine or Caterinetta Adorno; Catherine Fieschi; Caterinetta Fieschi. Born in autumn 1447 in Genoa, northern Italy; died on September 15, 1510, at the

Pammatone Hospital, Genoa; daughter of Giacomo Fieschi, viceroy of Naples, and Francesca di Negro; married Giuliano Adorno, on January 13, 1463; children: none.

As daughter of noble parents in one of Italy's most important cities, demonstrated early in life that she was more concerned with the life of the spirit than bodily pleasures; attempted to become a nun (1460), at age 13; pressured into marriage by her family at age 16 (1463); distanced herself from her spiritual impulse, first isolating herself in misery and then attempting to live the social life expected of her (1463–73); received a powerful, transforming vision, which she called her "conversion" (1473); devoting herself to the life of the spirit, fasted for up to six weeks at a time, existing only on salt water and the eucharist; spent hours each day in prayer and continued to receive intimate visions of God and revelations concerning the nature of divine love and sin and other mysteries of her faith, combining this intense spirituality with an active physical life of service to the poor and sick (1473–96); served as director of the Pammatone Hospital in Genoa (1490–96); died age 63, her physical vitality apparently burned away by her consuming love of God (1510).

The plague struck early in the spring of 1493, and the people of Genoa died in the thousands throughout that summer. Four-fifths of those who remained in the city perished. Catherine of Genoa, director of the great Pammatone Hospital, did not for a moment consider leaving her post. Instead, as the building filled to bursting with the sick and dying, she had tents set up in the grounds, and she tirelessly cared for the hundreds who sought her spiritual and material comfort.

Catherine Fieschi was born into a powerful and wealthy Genoese family, the youngest of five children, three boys and two girls. Her mother **Francesca di Negro** was of noble blood, and her father was the former viceroy of Naples. Despite her powerful family connections—Pope Innocent IV was a relative on her father's side—Catherine was denied permission to enter into the Augustinian convent of Santa Maria Delle Grazie in 1460 because she was only 13.

As a child, she seems already to have been inclined to simplicity and piety. The author of the earliest and most detailed biography of Catherine, who was probably her friend and disciple Ettore Vernazza, records in the *Vita e Dottrina* how devout she was. At the age of about eight "beginning to dislike the soft indulgence of her bed, she laid herself down humbly to sleep on straw, with a block of hard wood under her head, in the place of pillows of down." An image of the suffering Christ, which she kept in her room, caused her to be convulsed with grief. Unimpressed by riches, "she led a very simple life, seldom speaking with any one, very obedient to her parents, well skilled in the way of divine precepts, and zealous in the practice of the virtues."

Catherine seems to have decided to follow her older sister **Limbania Fieschi** into the religious life, and it was to her sister's convent that she unsuccessfully applied in 1460. The early death of her father in 1461 meant that control of the family's affairs passed to Catherine's oldest brother, and it was he who decided that the pious, almost reclusive young woman should marry. Beautiful and wealthy, she was certainly not without suitors. At age 16, Catherine was married off, against her wishes, to Giuliano Adorno. The match was made purely for political reasons; the marriage represented a healing of a long-standing feud between two powerful families.

With her ambition of devoting herself to God thwarted, Catherine endured ten years of great unhappiness. For the first five years of her marriage, she withdrew from society almost entirely and lapsed into a lonely, melancholy state during which she took little interest in anything. Whether her husband's behavior was the cause of her withdrawal or whether Catherine's obvious unhappiness provoked her husband to neglect her, we cannot be sure. Certainly the couple did not spend much time together, and Giuliano, while squandering the family's fortune, acquired a mistress and an illegitimate daughter.

Perhaps at the urging of her family, perhaps in an attempt to save her faltering marriage, Catherine came out of seclusion after five years, and between 1467 and 1473 she became more involved in the life appropriate to her social class in the busy, cosmopolitan port city of Genoa. According to her biographer, she became "devoted to external affairs and feminine amusements, seeking solace for hard life, as women are prone to do, in the diversions and vanities of the world, yet not to a sinful extent." But involvement in the world satisfied Catherine no more than withdrawal from it had done, and her life was to be utterly transformed once again as the result of a mystical experience she received on the feast day of St. Benedict, March 22, 1473.

The night before St. Benedict's day, Catherine had gone, in desperation, to the church named after the saint and had prayed that God might keep her sick in bed for three months, so disgusted was she with all the worldliness that surrounded her. The next day, she went to the convent of Santa Maria delle Grazie, persuaded by her sister to make her Lenten confession. Her biographer describes the event in minute detail:

> The moment she knelt before [the priest], she was wounded so forcibly with the love of God, and received so clear a revelation of her misery and faults, and of the goodness of God, that she had well nigh fallen to the ground. Overpowered by these emotions . . . she was so drawn away by her purified affections from the miseries of the world, that she became almost beside herself; and without ceasing, internally repeated to herself, in the ardor of love: "No more world, no more sin." And at that moment if she had possessed a thousand worlds, she would have thrown them all away.

Catherine was overcome by the feeling that all her imperfections were being burned away by God's love and that a bright light was illuminating her soul so that she could understand God's goodness, physical manifestations of her spiritual experience, which were to stay with her for the rest of her life. On this occasion, she "lost entirely all consciousness through this sweet wound of love, so that she could not speak." Unable to complete her confession, Catherine was taken home where she had more visions, including one of the bleeding Christ carrying his cross, "and this vision so inflamed her heart, that she was more than ever lost in love and grief."

In discussing the impact of these visions, Friedrich von Hugel, author of *The Mystical Element of Religion,* a massive and complex study of Catherine and her ideas, has observed: "Something profoundly real and important took place in the soul of that sad and weary woman." She had begun the first stage of what was to be a spiritual journey, a journey that was in many ways to resemble, and in other significant ways to be markedly different from, other such mystical progressions.

And to him who seeks to know what it is that I know and feel, I can only reply that it transcends all utterance.

—Catherine of Genoa

In order to more clearly understand the nature of Catherine's spiritual transformation, it is essential to examine a little of the devotional context of Western Europe during the later Middle Ages. The medieval period is often, somewhat simplistically, presented as an "Age of Faith." It was that, but it was also much more. By the mid-12th century, popular devotion was beginning to assume a more personal and less institutional character. While the services of the church—the Mass and sacraments—were still central to the Catholic faith, private prayer and other individual devotional practices were becoming more important. At this time also the first well-known and influential female mystic *Hildegard of Bingen (1098–1179) emerged.

By the late medieval period, mystics had become a familiar part of the spiritual landscape, increasing in numbers during the 14th and early 15th centuries as the institutional church was assailed, first by the relocation of the papacy from Rome to Avignon and then by the Great Schism. The Schism was a bitter dispute, which saw the church, the "body of Christ" on earth, with two heads. For almost four decades, two, and occasionally three opposing popes, claimed rightful jurisdiction.

For the mystics, the troubles of the church establishment were peripheral, if not irrelevant, to their spiritual progress. These women, and most of the mystics we know about were female, were able to develop an intense familiarity with God by entering ecstatic states that we might call trances or out-of-body experiences. In such situations, God would reveal himself, usually speaking directly to the mystic, who would recall and record the nature of her visions once her trance-like interlude was over.

Should we then regard Catherine as being simply part of a trend towards the personal in the spiritual realm, which increasingly, and most interactively, expressed itself in mysticism? In the years that followed her "conversion" in 1473, her theology unfolded, and it seems logical to place it in the tradition of the revelations of Hildegard, *Julian of Norwich and *Catherine of Siena. Yet Hildegard was a German abbess, Mother Julian was an anchoress (recluse), and Catherine of Siena was a Dominican nun. Women traditionally chose between marriage or the life of the spirit, hence the convent or the anchoress' cell. The best that a pious married woman of the time might be expected to do, in terms of her spiritual development, would be to give money to the church and to the poor, to purchase or commission elaborate Books of Hours or, if she were extremely pious, to pray regularly and perform occasional tasks of a charitable nature. Catherine was to prove a notable exception to such stereotypical expectations.

One early, tangible sign of the change in Catherine's life, the shaping of her new spiritual identity, occurred in May 1474: "The Lord gave her the desire for holy communion, which she never lost during her whole life. . . . [S]he was often summoned to receive it, by priest inspired by God to give it to her." The faithful believed the body of Christ was present in the bread, consecrated during the ceremony of the Mass, and although devotion to the eucharist had grown in intensity as part of the increasingly personal trend in religious devotion, it was still considered somewhat irregular to receive it frequently. Catherine's biographer reveals that she "envied no one in this world" but the priests "who received whenever they wished, without causing remarks from anyone."

Particularly fervent devotion to the eucharist can be observed in the lives of many late medieval mystics, with Catherine of Siena being a notable example. Another element that many of the female mystics shared was the practice of rigorous fasting. Catherine's *Vita* describes this next step in her spiritual journey:

> Some time after her conversion, on the day of the Annunciation of our Lady [March 25 1476], her Love spoke within her, saying that he wished her to keep the fast in his company in the desert, and immediately she became unable to eat, so that she was with-

out food for the body until Easter, and with the exception of the three feast days, on which she had the grace to be able to eat, she took nothing during the whole of Lent.

The recent work of historian **Caroline Bynum Walker** has persuasively documented the significance of fasting in the lives of female mystics. Walker suggests that since medieval society allowed women such little influence in the political and economic spheres, and often denied them control of decisions affecting their own lives, fasting represented an act of defiance, as well as an act of devotion. For the next 23 years, Catherine's biographer tells us, during Lent and Advent, the six penitential weeks before Easter and Christmas, "she took nothing but a tumblerful of water, vinegar and pounded salt." She described feeling as if the fire of love that was within her instantly dried up the moisture, and her biographer could not have been alone in reacting in amazement: "How wonderful! For no one, however healthy, could bear a drink of this kind, fasting; but she described the sweetness that proceeded from her burning heart as so great, that even this harsh beverage refreshed her." He records also that, during these times of fasting, "she slept better, and felt stronger and more active," although she insisted that the fasting was not a penitential act on her part, for she did not choose it. Rather, she said, she was physically unable to swallow food, much as she might try. Yet, on the days preceding and following the penitential periods, she was able to eat quite normally.

Such bodily deprivation would have been considered exceptional, even for the most devout recluse, but Catherine had still to maintain her involvement with the world. A few months after Catherine's conversion in the spring of 1473, her husband's extravagances resulted in the loss of his fortune. He was forced to sell or rent his various palaces, and by the autumn his misfortunes, no doubt combined with Catherine's influence, lead to Giuliano's own conversion. It was probably at this time that he told his wife about the existence of his illegitimate daughter whom Catherine accepted and provided for in her will. Giuliano became a lay member of the Franciscan order and spent the rest of his life working with his wife among the poor and sick of Genoa. Having made a vow to abstain from sexual intercourse, the couple moved to a small house, close to the famous Hospital of the Pammatone.

Thus began Catherine's new double life: the interior life of penance and fasting, and the exterior life of active service. To mortify her flesh, she wore a hair shirt, never ate meat or fruit, and slept on thorns. When her relatives came to visit, she spoke as little as possible; as much as she could, she denied herself all earthy pleasures. Her biographer records that sometimes "she was found in a remote place, prostrate on the earth, her face covered with her hands, so completely lost in the sweetness of divine love, that she was insensible to the loudest cry." And yet, "she would be aroused suddenly by the voices of persons calling her, and attend to their smallest wants." With a group of charitable women of the city, the *Donne della Misericordia,* she visited the poor and sick, cleaning their houses and their vermin-infested clothes.

In 1479, Giuliano and Catherine moved inside the hospital where both were to spend the rest of their lives. She was appointed director (*rettora*) of the hospital in 1490 and expertly fulfilled this burdensome office for six years. Despite the growing intensity of her internal, devotional life, she directed the hospital through its time of gravest crisis and, says her *Vita*, "her accounts were never found wrong by a single *danaro* (farthing)."

Von Hugel describes Catherine's tireless activity in 1493, the year of the plague:

> Throughout the weeks and months of the visitation she was daily in the midst, superintending, ordering, stimulating, steadying, consoling, strengthening this vast crowd of panic-stricken poor and severely strained workers.

The *Vita* gives a vivid account of the death of a pious woman in Catherine's care. During her final days, the woman lost her ability to speak, but Catherine visited her constantly, urging her to "Call Jesus." The dying woman moved her lips "and Catherine, when she saw her mouth so filled, as it were, with Jesus, could not restrain herself from kissing her, and in this way took the fever, and only narrowly escaped death." As soon as she recovered, however, Catherine devoted herself once again to the running of the hospital and the care of the sick.

In 1496, her own health broke down, but there was no discernable medical ailment to account for the weakness and pain she suffered. She could no longer administer the hospital and was forced to abandon her great fasts during Lent and Advent. In the autumn of the following year, her husband Giuliano died. Catherine remarked to a friend a short time later that, although her husband "was of somewhat wayward nature, whence I suffered much mental pain," God had assured her of his salvation. Giuliano carefully provided for "his beloved wife and heiress" Catherine in his will, affirming that she had "ever behaved herself well and laudably towards himself," wanting "to provide the means for her continuing to lead, after his death, her quiet, peaceful and spiritual mode of life."

Despite her increasing frailty, Catherine resolutely continued her spiritual mode of life, but she also remained closely involved with worldly matters. Administration of the complex provisions of her late husband's will forced her to travel, and the frequent changes in her own will, reflecting the deaths of family members or their changing economic circumstances, makes it clear that she vigorously maintained her external interests. From 1506 onwards, she weakened still further, and she was thought to be near death for much of the year 1510. She complained of intense pain in her heart and of the feeling that she was being burned by fire. She was sometimes heard to whisper: "Now my heart seems as if in ashes, I am consuming with love." The physicians who were called could not identify a physical cause nor find any remedies to assist her. On September 10, 1510, less than a week before Catherine's death, they concluded that her illness must be "a supernatural and divine thing, since neither the pulse, nor any of the secretions, nor any other symptom, showed any trace of any infirmity."

By September 12, Catherine was unable to eat or drink; for the next three days, she consumed only the eucharist. She began to vomit blood, black spots appeared all over her body and the following day she lost the ability to speak. At dawn on Sunday September 15, when she was asked by friends who were with her whether she wished to communicate, she pointed towards the sky. "And at this moment, this blessed soul gently expired, in great peace and tranquility, and flew to her tender and much desired Love."

Catherine of Genoa was buried next to one of the walls of the hospital chapel, but when the area was flooded some 18 months later, the coffin was dug up and opened. Her body was found to be perfectly intact, and great crowds flocked to see it. The body was subsequently placed in a marble tomb inside the church, where it may still be seen, resting in its crystal casket. Such was her reputation that she immediately began to be called "blessed," and she was made a Saint of the Catholic Church by Pope Clement XII on May 18, 1733. An indication of her continuing importance in the Catholic Church is the decision of Pope Pius XII to proclaim Catherine Patroness of the Hospitals in Italy in 1944.

We know more about Catherine of Genoa's exterior and interior lives than we do about most women of her time, yet this knowledge is based almost entirely on three sources, all previously thought to have been written by Catherine herself. *The Vita e Dottrina* was probably the work of her closest disciple Ettore Vernazza; *The Spiritual Dialogue,* also sometimes entitled *The Pure Love of God,* was compiled from Catherine's teachings, perhaps by Vernazza's daughter **Mother Battistina**; and the *Trattato,* sometimes entitled *The Treatise on Purgatory,* is a collection of Catherine's sayings and teachings on purgation and purgatory, the only one of the three still thought to be actually written by the saint. While the *Vita* is the best guide to Catherine's exterior life, it is *The Dialogue* which best reflects her "inner history," with various allegorical figures reflecting aspects of her character and struggling for control. At the heart of *The Dialogue* is the conflict between the Soul and the Body, vividly and often poetically depicted in terms of a painful progress towards union with God, with the voice of God sometimes taking part in the discussion.

Catherine's great admirer and biographer von Hugel has observed that she had "a highly nervous, delicately poised, immensely sensitive and impressionable psycho-physical organism and temperament." Her strong mind and will, he concludes, having discovered the support of religion, were able to shape this fragmented, conflicting personality into a strong, coherent whole. She became a saint, he suggests, because she had to, in order to harmonize the potential chaos within her. While, almost a century after von Hugel's analysis appeared, we may be less inclined to agree with his view that Catherine espoused her faith "to prevent herself going to pieces," it is clear that her sensitivity and religious devotion combined to produce one of the most coherent mystical voices of the Christian church.

Like those of her namesake Catherine of Siena, Catherine of Genoa's spiritual insights are compelling and eloquent. Like her namesake, she lived a life of intense physical deprivation. However, almost unique among mystics, Catherine of Genoa was actively "of the world," as a married woman, a hospital director, and a widow. Even after her husband's death, she never became a nun or even joined any of the religious orders that allowed men and women to continue to live independent lives. It was as if such created structures were irrelevant to her active, individual life of spirituality and service. As Catherine, in the allegorical guise of the Soul, recounted in *The Dialogue:*

She said that no human tongue could describe how inflamed she was with that glowing fire. The love that God manifested to her made her instinctively reject whatever was displeasing to him. . . . She heeded not the world, the flesh, nor the devil. All devils who opposed her were not so strong as this soul in her union with God, who is the true strength of those who fear, love, and serve him; and so much more because she did not perceive how she could be injured by self, it being in the hands of God and upheld by his goodness.

SOURCES:
Catherine of Genoa. *Life and Doctrine of Saint Catherine of Genoa.* NY: Christian Press Association, 1907.
————. *Purgation and Purgatory: The Spiritual Dialogue.* Translation and notes by Serge Hughes. Introduction by Benedict J. Groeschel. NY: Paulist Press, 1979.
————. *Treatise on Purgatory: The Dialogue.* Translated by Charlotte Balfour and Helen Douglas Irvine. London: Sheed & Ward, 1946.

SUGGESTED READING:
Butler's Lives of the Saints. Edited, revised, and supplemented by Herbert Thurston and Donald Attwater. London: Burns Oates and Washbourne, 1956.
Deen, Edith. *Great Women of the Christian Faith.* NY: Harper and Row, 1959.
von Hugel, Friedrich. *The Mystical Element of Religion, as Studied in St. Catherine of Genoa and her Friends.* 2 vols. London: J.M. Dent, 1908.

(Dr.) Kathleen Garay,
Assistant Professor of History and Women's Studies,
McMaster University, Hamilton, Canada

Catherine of Gorizia (fl. late 1300s)

Duchess of Bavaria. Flourished in the late 1300s; married John II of Munich (c. 1341–1397), duke of Bavaria (r. 1375–1397); children: Ernest or Ernst (b. 1373), duke of Bavaria (r. 1397–1438); William II (b. 1375), duke of Bavaria (r. 1397–1435); *Sophia of Bavaria (fl. 1390s–1400s), queen of Bohemia.

Catherine of Guise (1552–c. 1594)

Duchess of Montpensier. Name variations: Caterina de Lorraine; Catherine Marie of Lorraine; Catherine Marie de Lorraine. Born in 1552; died around 1594; daughter of Francis (1519–1563), 2nd duke of Guise, and *Anne of Ferrara (1531–1607); sister of Henry, 3rd duke of Guise, and Louis, 2nd cardinal of Guise; married Louis de Bourbon (d. 1582), duke of Montpensier.

Catherine of Habsburg (c. 1254–1282)

German princess. Name variations: Catherine of Hapsburg; Katharina. Born around 1254; died on

*April 4, 1282, in Landshut; daughter of Rudolf I (1218–1291), Holy Roman emperor (r. 1273–1291), and *Anna of Hohenberg (c. 1230–1281); sister of *Clementia of Habsburg (d. 1293) and Albert I, Holy Roman emperor (r. 1298–1308, but not crowned); married Otho of Bavaria, also known as Otto III, duke of Lower Bavaria (r. 1290–1312), king of Hungary (r. 1305–1308).*

Catherine of Habsburg
(1533–1572)

*Queen of Poland. Name variations: Catherine of Austria; Caterina of Austria; Catherine Gonzaga, duchess of Mantua; Catherine of Hapsburg. Born in 1533; died in 1572; daughter of Ferdinand I, Holy Roman emperor (r. 1558–1564), and *Anna of Bohemia and Hungary (1503–1547); sister of *Elizabeth of Habsburg (d. 1545), Maximilian II (1527–1576), Holy Roman emperor (r. 1564–1576), and *Eleonora of Austria (1534–1594); married Francesco Gonzaga (1533–1550), 2nd duke of Mantua (r. 1540–1550), in 1549 (17-year old Francesco fell into a lake that same year and died of a fever shortly thereafter); third wife of Sigismund II, king of Poland (r. 1548–1572). For more information see Sforza, Bona (1493–1557).*

Catherine of Lancaster (1372–1418)

*Queen of Castile and Léon. Name variations: Catalina; Katherine of Lancaster; Katherine Plantagenet. Born in Hertford, Hertfordshire, England, in 1372 (some sources cite 1373); died in Valladolid, Castile and Leon, Spain, on June 2, 1418; daughter of *Constance of Castile (1354–1394) and John of Gaunt, 1st duke of Lancaster (his first wife was *Blanche of Lancaster); half-sister of *Joan Beaufort (c. 1379–1440), Henry IV, king of England (r. 1399–1413), and *Philippa of Lancaster (c. 1359–1415); married Enrique also known as Henry III (b. 1379), king of Castile and Léon (r. 1390–1406); children: four, including Juan also known as John II (1405–1454), king of Castile (r. 1406–1454); *Catalina (1403–1439, who married Henry of Aragon, duke of Villena); *Maria of Castile (1401–1458).*

Catherine of La Rochelle (fl. 1429).

See Women Prophets and Visionaries in France at the End of the Middle Ages.

Catherine of Lorraine

Duchess of Nevers. Name variations: Catherine or Katherine de Lorraine. Daughter of Charles, duke of

*Maine; married Charles II Gonzaga, duke of Nevers (r. 1601–1637); children: two, including *Anne de Gonzaga (1616–1684).*

Catherine of Mecklenburg-Schwerin (1692–1733)

*Duchess of Mecklenburg-Schwerin. Name variations: Yekaterina Ivanova or Ivanovna Romanov. Born on July 25, 1692; died on June 25, 1733; daughter of Ivan V (1666–1696), tsar of Russia (r. 1682–1689), and *Praskovya Saltykova (1664–1723); elder sister of *Anna Ivanovna (1693–1740); niece of Peter I the Great; married Charles Leopold, duke of Mecklenburg-Schwerin, on April 19, 1716; children: *Anna Leopoldovna (1718–1746).*

Catherine of Navarre (c. 1470–1517).
See Margaret of Angoulême for sidebar on Catherine de Foix.

Catherine of Navarre (c. 1555–1604).
See Catherine of Bourbon.

Catherine of Poland (1525–1583).
See Catherine Jagello.

Catherine of Pomerania (d. 1426)

*Danish royal. Name variations: Katharina. Died on March 4, 1426; daughter of *Marie of Mecklenburg and Vratislas of Pomerania (d. 1394); sister of Erik of Pomerania also known as Eric VII, king of Denmark, Norway, and Sweden (r. 1397–1439); married Johan or John of Bavaria (son of Emperor Rupert), count of Neumarkt, on August 15, 1407; children: Christopher III of Bavaria (1416–1448), king of Denmark, Norway, and Sweden (r. 1439–1448).*

Catherine of Pomerania (d. 1526)

*Duchess of Brunswick. Name variations: Katharina of Pommerania. Died in 1526; daughter of Sophia of Pomerania and Eric II of Pomerania; married Henry I the Elder, duke of Brunswick, in August 1486; children: *Catherine of Brunswick-Wolfenbuttel (1488–1563); Henry II the Younger, duke of Brunswick.*

Catherine of Portugal (1540–1614)

*Duchess of Braganza. Name variations: Catarina; Katherine of Portugal. Born on January 18, 1540, in Lisbon; died on November 15, 1614; daughter of Duarte, duke of Guimaraes, and *Isabella of Braganza (c. 1512–1576); married Joao also known as John I*

(1544–1583), duke of Braganza, on December 8, 1563; children: Theodosius II, duke of Braganza (1568–1630), who married *Anne of Velasquez*; Duarte (1569–1627); Alexander of Evora (1570–1608), archbishop of Evora; Filipe (1581–1608); *Maria of Braganza (1565–1592)*; *Serafina of Braganza (1566–1604, who married John Fernandez-Pacheco, duke of Escalona)*; Cherubina of Braganza (1572–1580); Angelica of Braganza (1573–1576); Maria (1573–1573); Isabella (1578–1582).

Catherine of Ricci (c. 1522–1589)

Italian saint and Dominican nun who was noted for her wisdom. Name variations: Catherine de Ricci. Born in Florence, Italy, around 1522; died on February 2, 1589.

Catherine of Ricci took the veil among the Dominican nuns at Prato, Tuscany, in 1535. She was made perpetual prioress seven years later, at the age of 25. Though they never met, Catherine was a great friend of, and correspondent with, St. Philip Neri; their letters "flew back and forth like homing pigeons," writes *Phyllis McGinley* in *Saint-Watching*. Catherine of Ricci was canonized in 1746; her feast day is on February 3.

SOURCES:
McGinley, Phyllis. *Saint-Watching*. NY: Viking, 1969.

Catherine of Russia (1788–1819)

*Queen of Wurttemberg. Name variations: Catherine Pavlovna, Grand Duchess; Catherine Romanov. Born on May 21, 1788; died on January 19, 1819; daughter of *Sophia Dorothea of Wurttemberg (1759–1828)* and Paul I (1754–1801), tsar of Russia (r. 1796–1801, son of *Catherine II the Great*); married George, duke of Oldenburg, on August 3, 1809; married William I (1781–1864), king of Wurttemberg (r. 1816–1864), on January 24, 1816; children: (first marriage) Alexander (b. 1810); Peter (b. 1812), duke of Oldenburg; (second marriage) Maria (1816–1887, who married Count Neipperg); *Sophia of Wurttemberg (1818–1877, who married William III, king of the Netherlands).*

Catherine of Saxe-Lauenburg or Lüneburg (1513–1535).

See Katarina of Saxe-Lüneburg.

Catherine of Saxony (1421–1476)

Electress of Brandenburg. Name variations: Katharina of Saxony. Born in 1421; died on August 23, 1476; daughter of Fredrick I the Warlike (b. 1370), elector of Saxony; sister of *Anna of Saxony (1420–1462)*; married Frederick II the Iron (1413–1471), elector of Brandenburg (r. 1440–1470, abdicated), on June 11, 1441; children: *Dorothea of Brandenburg (1446–1519)*; *Margaret of Brandenburg (c. 1450–1489)*.

Catherine of Siena (1347–1380)

Roman Catholic saint, and co-patron (with Francis of Assisi) of Italy, who was declared a Doctor of the Roman Catholic Church. Name variations: Caterina di Iacopo (YAH-co-po) or Giacomo (JAH-co-mo) di Benincasa; Caterina or Catherina Benincasa; St. Catherine (or Katherine) of Siena; Caterina da Siena; also spelled Sienna. Born Catherine di Benincasa in Siena, Italy, in 1347; died in Rome, on April 30, 1380; daughter of Lapa Piacenti and Iacopo (or Giacomo) di Benincasa (a well-to-do wool-dyer); never married; no children.

Wrote letters (382 survive) to various European leaders, urging peace between states and submission to papal authority (1370–80); wrote the Dialogue of Divine Providence, *a didactic religious work; undertook commissions at behest of pope; led a religious group in Siena; canonized (1461); declared Doctor of Roman Catholic Church (1970).*

Racked with convulsions, tormented by visions of devils and of her beloved church in ruin, a young woman lay drifting in and out of a coma in an austere cell in a church in Rome. Long unable to eat, she had decided three months before that she could not tolerate even water crossing her lips. Though she relented after a few days and began drinking a little, even eating a small amount of bread, it was not enough. Catherine of Siena died on April 30, 1380. Anyone seeing her pitiful end might have thought her a person of little consequence, another religious woman ill-equipped to live in the world. Yet Catherine, a child of the newly emerging middle class, who had never officially joined a religious order, had in her day held great influence in the balance of powers in Europe and in the direction of the Roman Catholic Church.

Born Catherine di Benincasa in Siena, central Italy, in 1347, she and a twin sister, who died in infancy, were the 23rd and 24th of 25 children of Iacopo di Benincasa and **Lapa Piacenti**, herself the daughter of a poet and a quilt-maker. (The last of the children, another girl named for Catherine's dead twin, also died soon after birth.) The Republic of Tuscany—of which

Siena was one of the most important cities—was the home of a new social category in Europe; neither peasant nor noble, the middle class was emerging as a force with which to be reckoned. Like its neighbor Florence, Siena's wealth was largely based on the wool trade, and Iacopo was engaged in the lucrative trade of wool-dyeing.

Raised like most girls of her station, Catherine received no formal schooling and probably never learned to read or write, but she prized the written word. Her mystical experiences began at an early age. At age six, she claimed a vision of the Virgin Mary; at age seven, she declared that she heard voices telling her to devote herself and her life to God. But her parents, eager to make a good marriage for her, did not support her aspirations for a contemplative, cloistered life; they urged her to concentrate on attracting a husband. Many young children went through a religious phase; actions that would seem extreme to modern parents (for example, stopping on each step of the stairway to recite a Hail Mary) were not unusual in her day.

As Catherine aged, however, her continual refusal to entertain thoughts of marriage grew worrisome. After her sister Bonaventura, to whom Catherine was quite attached, died in childbirth, 15-year-old Catherine was even more adamant that she would never marry. It was also when her denial of food began, for at that time she announced that she would eat nothing other than bread, vegetables, and water.

As she approached marriageable age (in the Italian High Middle Ages, women of the lower and middle classes tended to marry in their late teens or early twenties), her family began to pressure her to marry. In response, she cut off her hair in defiance. Long, loose hair was the symbol of a girl's virginity; at her marriage, a young woman would bind up her hair to indicate her new state. Thus, with short hair like that of a nun, Catherine could not participate in a marriage ceremony until her hair grew out. While waiting, her parents set her to work in their house as a maid, perhaps intending to show their daughter what life would be like with the low status of an unmarried woman. To their chagrin, she willingly performed the menial, unpleasant tasks assigned to her and even requested more from the family housemaid. When Catherine was 18, her parents finally relented and allowed her to join the Dominican order but only as a tertiary: a lay sister who did not reside in the convent and was expected to live "in the world."

The Dominican order was noted for its service to the poor and sick, distinguishing it-

self by tending to plague victims. In Catherine's infancy, in the years 1347–51, the Black Death had killed about one-third of the people of Europe, and the Dominicans' nursing of the ill in a 1361–63 recurrence may have inspired Catherine to ally herself with this order. Whatever her motivation, she took tertiary orders and withdrew to her room in the house of her parents, determined to spend the rest of her life in meditation and prayer. It appears that her lifelong antipathy toward food worsened at this point. After her father died in 1368, she could not even tolerate bread, except, occasionally, the Host.

When Catherine was 21, her life of solitude ended abruptly after she experienced a mystical vision. Though she did not detail the experience, she apparently felt the stigmata (the wounds of Christ at his crucifixion experienced by religious mystics as pain in the palms of the hands, soles of the feet, forehead, and left side), although with no visible wounds. From then on, she returned to the outside world, determined to serve others. Three years later, in 1370, when Catherine fell dangerously ill, was not expected to live, but miraculously recovered, she was convinced that God had a plan for her.

Catherine of Siena

Her constant dedication to serving God and her ongoing mystical visions had gained the young woman many disciples. Since she was not a nun and had no formal education (though some think she learned to read and write after she took her tertiary vows), she could not found a new order. Instead, she gathered an informal group around her, a small religious community, comprised of men and women of all ages, from all social classes, some in the religious life, some not, who had been inspired by tales of her holiness. She called the group her family. Family relationships were, indeed, central to her conception of humanity. Catherine once exclaimed of the many nieces and nephews playing in her mother's kitchen, "If decency allowed it, I would never stop kissing them." She called all her followers, regardless of age, her children. They called her "mamma" and worked with her to help fulfill her goal. But this group was apparently too small to satisfy her longing to change the world, and she soon broadened her scope. She took to nursing the ill (even in the years without plague, many diseases ravaged Europe, worsened by the cycles of famine that gripped the continent). At one point, in an effort to ally herself with the suffering of Jesus, she drank the water she had used to bathe the sores of a leper, claiming that it was miraculously transformed into the blood of Christ as she swallowed it.

Cursed are ye, the lukewarm!

—Catherine of Siena

The first known letters of Catherine of Siena (it is unclear whether she wrote or dictated them) date from shortly after her 1370 illness and recovery. The early ones are addressed to religious figures in her area, urging them to serve God. Even though she never officially joined a religious order, she was most anxious that the leaders of spiritual communities never cease in their efforts toward holiness, and she took the tone of their superior in addressing them, calling abbesses "my daughter" (though she sometimes addressed priests more respectfully, as "father") and referring to herself as "your mother." Her advice was sought in such matters as which bride to choose, whether or not to go on Crusade, whom to promote as master of the Dominican order, how to settle a family feud. Certain themes recur in these letters: her passion for the blood of Christ, the need to submit utterly to the will of God, the necessity for trusting in redemption, the irrelevance of the opinions of one's neighbors.

One of her most widely read letters was written to her spiritual advisor (appointed to her in 1374), Raimondo da Capua, concerning the forthcoming execution of a young man convicted of speaking out against the Sienese government. Since he refused to be absolved of his sin, his punishment could not be carried out because his executioners would be committing a mortal sin by consigning his soul to Hell. The authorities could have used torture; instead, they called on Catherine who spent the night in his cell, praying and consoling him until he finally broke down, confessed, and begged forgiveness. He also begged Catherine to be with him at his beheading. She agreed. Preceding him to the place of execution, she placed her own neck in the block in order to understand the sensation he was soon to feel. When the young man was brought forth, he laughed with joy at seeing her and asked for her blessing, which she willingly gave. Catherine then held his neck in place on the block and kept her eyes fixed on his. As his head was cut off and she was sprayed in his blood, she claimed to have seen the blood of Christ flow with the young man's as he was received into Heaven. Catherine then cradled his head in her lap until the body was removed for burial.

While thus engaged in ministering to those in need, Catherine felt compelled to expand her sphere of influence. She had a strong base of support from her own followers and the people of Siena and surrounding areas who were familiar with her visions and who believed she had a special connection to God. This popularity gave her words credence and led even the upper classes to put faith in her spiritual authority. Thus, she turned to politics.

The great political event of her day was the friction between the individual states of Europe. Earlier attempts at a unified Europe (under either the pope or an emperor) had failed, and the various republics, kingdoms, duchies of Europe were locked in conflict. Siena and Florence, the major forces in Tuscany, had managed to gain representative governments for themselves, but at the cost of years of bloodshed and political repression. Complicating the situation was the question of the papacy. When a French archbishop was elected Pope Clement V in 1305, he decided to reside not in Rome, the traditional seat of the papacy, but in Avignon, in southern France. This transfer of residence was significant because the popes who lived in France for the next 72 years were seen (sometimes correctly) as puppets of the French king against the states of Italy.

Catherine was a stubborn person, not at all timid about speaking her mind to those whom others deemed her superiors. She gave orders rather than requests. When called to the apparent deathbed of a young man, she brusquely told him, "I command you in the name of our Lord Jesus Christ, not to die!" and to another, "I command you, in virtue of holy obedience, to suffer this fever no longer" (the record is unclear as to the fate of either sufferer). Raimondo da Capua mentions her disconcerting habit (then unusual in a woman) of maintaining eye contact with the person to whom she was speaking. Thus, when she decided to do something about the state of the papacy and its relation to Italy, it was in her character to take a direct approach, unusual though this course of action was for a woman of her day. She began by writing letters to various European leaders—Bernabò Visconti, the despotic ruler of Milan; the *condottiere* John Hawkwood; *Joanna I, the queen of Naples; a Sienese senator; queen mother ❧➤ Elizabeth of Pomerania (1347–1393); and at last to Pope Gregory XI and important figures in his court at Avignon. She urged these leaders to end the schism in the church, to stop warring with each other, and to settle their differences. Her exhortations so impressed Pope Gregory that when he declared a Crusade in 1375, he asked her to encourage soldiers to join him. Catherine was apparently so successful at this that when Gregory had need of a mediator between himself and the government of Florence in 1378 she served in this capacity.

Unfortunately, that same year Gregory died, and his successor Urban VI was immediately challenged by an anti-pope. Catherine saw this as a personal failure of diplomacy on her part. Forty years of this "Great Schism" were to pass before the rival claims were settled, and Catherine spent her last years trying to bolster support for Urban's claim to the position. She wrote in her usual authoritative style to leaders of both church and state, urging them not to recognize the false claimant and to help Urban maintain control of the Holy See. While she was in Rome, her "family" of followers in Siena was unable to hold together without her, and they disbanded.

Perhaps haunted by her sense of failure and her dismay at the loss of her followers, Catherine became unable to tolerate even the small amount of food and water she had allowed herself, refusing even water after January 29, 1380. Unable to move from her bed, she cried out in agony at visions of devils tormenting her. Although she was eventually persuaded to take sips of water throughout the day, she never recovered, and died three months after beginning her self-imposed fast.

Catherine's letters and her *Dialogue of Divine Providence*, a somewhat rambling collection of religious advice written around 1377, have never lost their popularity and influence. After her death, they were widely circulated throughout Europe. An edition of her letters is among the very early works printed in Italian (1492).

Catherine of Siena's political importance and religious activism led her to be canonized 80 years after her death; she was declared a saint of the Roman Catholic Church in 1461. When the country of Italy was unified in 1870, Catherine and St. Francis of Assisi shared its patronage. In 1970, she and St. *Teresa of Avila were declared Doctors of the Church, the first women to be so honored.

SOURCES:

Attwater, Donald. *The Penguin Dictionary of Saints*. Baltimore, MD: Penguin, 1965.

Fatula, Mary Anne, O.P. *Catherine of Siena's Way: The Way of the Christian Mystics*. Vol. 4. Wilmington, DE: Michael Glazier, 1989.

Foster, Kenelm, O.P., and Mary John Ronayne, O.P., ed. and trans. *I, Catherine: Selected Writings of St. Catherine of Siena*. London: Collins, 1980.

Noffke, Suzanne, O.P., ed. *The Letters of St. Catherine of Siena*. 2 vols. *Medieval and Renaissance Texts and Studies*, Vol. 52 and 53. Binghamton, NY: Center for Medieval and Early Renaissance Studies, State University at Binghamton, 1988.

Previté-Orton, C.W. *The Shorter Cambridge Medieval History*. Cambridge: Cambridge University Press, 1952.

SUGGESTED READING:

Bell, Rudolph M. *Holy Anorexia*. Chicago, IL: The University of Chicago Press, 1985.

Tracy Barrett, Vanderbilt University, Nashville, Tennessee

Elizabeth of Pomerania (1347–1393). See Anne of Bohemia for sidebar.

Catherine of Spain (1567–1597)

*Duchess of Savoy. Name variations: Katherine Michela. Born in 1567; died in 1597; daughter of Philip II (1527–1598), king of Spain (r. 1556–1598), and king of Portugal as Philip I (r. 1580–1598), and *Elizabeth of Valois (1545–1568); married Charles Emmanuel I the Great (1562–1630), duke of Savoy (r. 1580–1630); children: Victor Amadeus I (1587–1637), duke of Savoy (r. 1630–1637); *Margaret of Savoy (fl. 1609–1612, who married Francesco IV Gonzaga of Mantua); Philibert, prince of Oneglia; Cardinal Maurice; Thomas Francis, prince of Carignan or Carignano (d. 1656).*

Catherine of Sweden (c. 1330–1381)

Swedish saint. Name variations: Karin. Born in 1330 or 1331 in Sweden; died on March 24, 1381 at Vadstena (or Wadstena), Sweden; daughter of (Saint)

Bridget of Sweden (1303–1373) and Sir Ulf Gudmarsson, prince of Nericia (a knight); married Count Eggard, a Swedish knight (widowed); no children.

Holy woman and saint, Catherine of Sweden was the beloved daughter of Saint *Bridget of Sweden. Bridget first raised the family and then began a second career as a religious reformer and mystic; Catherine was the only one of her siblings to follow her mother's religious path so closely. She married but her husband, a Swedish noble, did not live long. Deciding against remarriage, the childless widow then became her mother's most important ally in the religious work they both felt called to perform. Catherine was usually overshadowed by her mother's tremendous fame, but achieved a reputation for herself as equally committed to the faith and to serving others. Mother and daughter traveled across Europe together on pilgrimages, and even rode as far as Jerusalem, a popular destination for adventurous European Christians. Like Bridget, Catherine became an important political voice in the struggle over returning the pope to Rome from Avignon.

After Bridget's death, Catherine of Sweden remained influential, establishing the Birgittine order of nuns as her mother had wished. Later she moved to the abbey of Vadstena as a nun, where she became known as a healer and miracle worker. Her final efforts were devoted to achieving her mother's canonization, testifying on Bridget's behalf before ecclesiastical courts in Rome. After her own death around age 51, Catherine of Sweden was canonized for her crucial reforming work and untiring devotion to serving others. Her feast day is March 24.

Laura York,
Riverside, California

Catherine of Tarento (fl. early 1300s)

Empress of Constantinople. Name variations: Catherine of Valois. Flourished in the early 1300s; possibly daughter of Philip III the Bold, king of France; married Philipp or Philip of Tarento (d. 1332), prince of Tarent; children: Louis of Tarento; Robert II of Constantinople; Philip II of Constantinople; Margaret Balliol (fl. 1300s, who married Edward Balliol).

Catherine of Valois (fl. early 1300s).

See Catherine of Tarento.

Catherine of Valois (1401–1437)

Queen of England, by her peace-treaty marriage to Henry V, who was widowed at 21, maintained a se-

*cret liaison with Welsh commoner Owen Tudor, and became the grandmother of the first Tudor monarch, Henry VII. Name variations: Catharine; Catherine de Valois; Katherine of France; Fair Kate of France. Born Catherine on October 27, 1401, at the Hôtel de St. Pôl, Paris, France; died of breast cancer on January 3, 1437, at Bermondsey Abbey, London, after a lengthy illness; buried in Westminster Abbey; daughter of Charles VI the Mad (1368–1422), king of France (r. 1380–1422), and Isabeau of Bavaria (1371–1435); sister of *Isabella of Valois (c. 1389–1409) and Charles VII, king of France (r. 1422–1461); married Henry V, king of England (r. 1413–1422), at Troyes, France, on June 2, 1420 (died, August 31, 1422); secretly married Owen Tudor (Owen ap Meredyth ap Tudur) sometime before 1429; children: (first marriage) Henry VI (b. December 2, 1421), king of England (r. 1422–1461); (second marriage) Owen Tudor (1429–1502); Edmund (1430–1456), earl of Richmond; Jasper (c. 1431–1495), earl of Pembroke; Tacinda Tudor (who married Reginald Grey, Lord Grey de Wilton); Margaret (1436–1436).*

Sent to a convent at Poissy when young; first chosen as a wife for Henry V (1413), but no dowry could be agreed upon; finally engaged to Henry V after the Treaty of Troyes (May 21, 1420); crowned queen of England in Westminster Abbey, London (February 24, 1421); publicly supported her son, the child monarch, until 1428; spent the rest of her life in seclusion, away from the public eye.

Catherine of Valois spent her earliest years in the Hôtel de St. Pôl where her father Charles VI, king of France, suffered from prolonged and increasingly frequent bouts of insanity, and her mother *Isabeau of Bavaria carried on a life of deceit and greed. Stories circulated that Queen Isabeau had an affair with the king's brother Louis, duke of Orléans, and that together they pilfered money from the royal household. Eventually, Isabeau was imprisoned at Tours, and Catherine was removed from the influences of her mother. It is believed that Catherine was then raised at the convent of Poissy, where her sister *Marie (1393–1438) became a nun.

As early as 1413, the idea of a peacekeeping marriage to unite England and France was being discussed. An English embassy arrived in Paris on April 8, 1414, to arrange a marriage between Henry (V) and Catherine, with the sole intent that both the crown and kingdom of France be yielded to England through this union. King Henry demanded the outrageous dowry of 2,000,000 gold crowns, in addition to Normandy and the territory that had belonged to *Eleanor of Aquitaine, making the conditions for marriage totally unacceptable to the French. Charles VI refused to pay more than 600,000 crowns. A second embassy returned in March 1415. By then, Henry had reduced the dowry to a mere 1,000,000 crowns, but with the addition of a trousseau of clothes and jewels. Again, Charles countered with a lower offer of 800,000 crowns. A truce between the English and French lasted until June 1415, but by July of that year all negotiations were completely broken off. By October, though seriously outnumbered, Henry V had decimated the French army at Agincourt.

After numerous defeats, the French were eager, if not desperate, to settle on this marriage for the sake of peace. On June 1, 1419, the princess Catherine, wearing apparel supplied by the Bergundians at a cost of 3,000 florins, was escorted into the English king's presence just outside the west gate of the French city of Meulan. Henry had never met his intended face to face, though Isabeau had sent him her portrait. As described by one chronicler, he was immedi-

ately struck by Catherine's charm and beauty. Following this initial meeting, Henry sent her a gift of jewelry worth 100,000 crowns, which, early sources claim, was later stolen by robbers.

After the signing of the Treaty of Troyes on May 21, 1420, the royal couple became officially engaged. The mad Charles VI would retain the French crown during his lifetime, but, because of his marriage to Catherine, Henry would inherit the throne. Twelve days later, their marriage took place at the nearby parish church of St. Jean, a humble site for such a monumental union. Catherine was only 18, while Henry was 33. The marriage did not put a stop to war, however, and Henry began the siege of Sens in July 1420. Special quarters were built near Henry's tent to accommodate his bride.

The newly married couple delayed their ceremonial entrance into Paris until December 1420, where, during Christmas festivities, they stayed at the royal palace of the Louvre. But the celebrations were cut short when the English Parliament sent Henry, who had been absent

From the movie Henry V, starring Kenneth Branagh as Henry V and Emma Thompson as Catherine of Valois.

from England for more than three years, an urgent request to return home with his wife. The royal party slowly made its way to Calais for the channel crossing, stopping at Rouen for an official welcome on New Year's Eve, and did not arrive on English soil until February 1, 1421. Twenty days later, they were welcomed in London by extravagant medieval pageantry, including minstrels, jesters, and decorations. Free wine was dispersed to the public. After spending the night in the royal palace of the Tower of London, Catherine was crowned queen of England on February 23, 1421, at Westminster Abbey. Following her coronation, a great banquet was held in Westminster Hall, and, since it was Lent, all manner of fish and shellfish were on the menu. As was the custom, Henry absented himself from the festivities so that all eyes could be focused on the new queen, who was accompanied by the bishop of Winchester, King James I of Scotland, and the archbishop of Canterbury, Henry Beaufort. The king and queen then traveled together for several months through the midlands and north of England, visiting many sacred shrines. In addition, Henry used this trip to raise both money and men for his next campaign in France (the Dauphin still controlled most of France south of the Loire), while Catherine donated £1,333 to the cause.

By June 1421, Henry had returned to France with his armed men to continue his campaign through the country. A pregnant Catherine stayed behind and gave birth to a son, Henry VI, on December 2, 1421, at Windsor Castle. That winter, the troops in France were ravaged by a dysentery-like disease. It is believed that this debilitating illness eventually caused Henry's death on August 31, 1422. On October 5, Catherine joined the extensive procession of mourners for Henry in Rouen. By early November, the funeral cortege finally reached Calais and crossed the channel. After a funeral in St. Paul's Cathedral, London, Henry was buried on November 7, in Westminster Abbey. Catherine later commissioned a silver effigy for her husband's tomb.

King Henry had died before laying eyes on his heir and namesake. Thus, at the age of nine months, Henry VI became king of England. Just a few months later, on October 21, 1422, he would become king of France on the death of King Charles VI. Turning from mourning to a preoccupation with her young son, Catherine accompanied him to all public appearances and to Parliament, where he sat on her knee. While she held the title of dowager-queen, the country was actually run by the protector of the realm, Henry VI's uncle Humphrey, duke of Gloucester, and the royal council. Catherine, as a young widow, quickly developed the reputation of a vivacious and passionate woman. Instead of returning to her native land, she remained in England and took an interest in Edmund Beaufort, nephew of Henry Beaufort, bishop of Winchester. But this relationship was discouraged and judged an undesirable match for the young queen, because Edmund had a lower social status. Indeed, in 1428, possibly to prevent a union between Catherine and Edmund, Parliament enacted a statute prohibiting a dowager-queen of England from remarrying without consent of king or council. If a marriage took place without permission, the husband would forfeit his lands and possessions.

From 1427 to 1430, Catherine lived in the royal household. The issue of social status did not stop her from falling in love with a Welsh royal servant by the name of Owen Tudor who was either keeper of the queen's wardrobe or household. Their liaison was kept secret from the public for many years, even though it led to four children, three sons and a daughter Margaret who died shortly after her birth. Their marriage, which was never revealed until after Catherine's death, has never been verified by church or legal documents. It is believed, however, that they were married before the birth of their first child in around 1430.

Soon after her fourth pregnancy, with Owen Tudor imprisoned in Newgate (he would later escape), a despondent Catherine fell ill and entered Bermondsey Abbey in London to rest and recover. She never left the abbey alive. On January 1, 1437, she had her last will drawn up, then died two days later on January 3. In her will, Henry VI is the only descendent recognized; no mention is made of Owen Tudor or her three sons. In 1452, Parliament officially would declare Catherine and Owen's marriage valid, to remove any doubt about the legitimacy of their offspring. Catherine and Owen's first son, Edmund Tudor, eventually married *Margaret Beaufort, and was the father of Henry VII, the first monarch of the Tudor line.

Until an effigy could be prepared, Catherine's body lay in state at St. Paul's Cathedral, before being interred in Westminster Abbey's Lady Chapel, her corpse loosely wrapped and open to view through the lid of the coffin. But the inscription on her tomb only mentioned her marriage to Henry and their one son. After her grandson Henry VII became king in 1485, he had the Lady Chapel destroyed, and Catherine's remains were placed at last beside the tomb of her first husband Henry V. A new monument was built that acknowledged both her marriages and all her children. No doubt, this was done not only for historical accuracy but also to legitimize Henry VII's new position as king. Her corpse could still be seen in this new location. Diarist Samuel Pepys recorded on February 24, 1668, that on his birthday he took the liberty of kissing the queen on the lips. It was not until 1878 that Catherine's body was hidden beneath a marble altar slab.

SOURCES:

Griffiths, Ralph A., and Roger S. Thomas. *The Making of the Tudor Dynasty.* NY: St. Martin's Press, 1985.

Hutchison, Harold F. *King Henry V.* NY: John Day, 1967.

Jarman, Rosemary H. *Crispin's Day: The Glory of Agincourt.* Boston, MA: Little, Brown, 1979.

Strickland, Agnes. *Lives of the Queens of England.* Vol III. Philadelphia: Blanchard and Lea, 1857.

Williams, Jeanne U. "Katherine of Valois, 1401–1437," M.A. diss., University of Washington, 1966.

SUGGESTED READING:

Griffiths, Ralph A. "Queen Katherine of Valois and a Missing Statute of the Realm," in *Law Quarterly Review.* Vol. 93, 1977, pp. 248–58.

Jacob, E.F. *The Fifteenth Century (1399–1485).* Oxford: Oxford University Press, 1961.

RELATED MEDIA:

Henry V (138 min. film), adapted from the play by William Shakespeare, directed by Kenneth Branagh, starring Kenneth Branagh as Henry V and **Emma Thompson** as Catherine of Valois, with Paul Scofield, Derek Jacobi, **Judi Dench**, produced by the BBC, Samuel Goldwyn Co., and Renaissance Films, 1989.

Karen E. Mura, Assistant Professor of English, Susquehanna University, Selinsgrove, Pennsylvania

Catherine of Vendôme

(r. 1374–1412)

Countess of Vendôme. Name variations: Vendome. Born before 1360 in Vendôme; died in 1412 in Vendôme; daughter of Bouchard VI, count of Vendôme, and *Jeanne de Castile (r. 1366–1374); sister of Bouchard VII; married Jean I, duke of Bourbon, before 1374 (d. 1393); children: Louis (c. 1376–1346), later count of Bourbon (who married Jeanne de Montfort-Laval).

Daughter of the noble house of Vendôme, Catherine was betrothed and married to the French noble Jean, duke of Bourbon, to seal an alliance between Bourbon and Vendôme. She resided at the court of Bourbon until 1374, bearing only one surviving child, Louis. Upon the death of her brother Bouchard VII in 1374,

Catherine was her father's only living child, and she succeeded her brother as ruler of Vendôme. She governed for 38 years, until her death in 1412. Catherine was succeeded by her son Louis.

Catherine of Wurttemberg

(1783–1835)

Queen of Westphalia and second wife of Jérôme Bonaparte. Born Sophia Dorothea Frederica Catherine on February 21, 1783; died on November 28, 1835; daughter of Frederick II (1754–1816), duke of Wurttemberg (r. 1797–1802), elector of Wurttemberg (r. 1802–1806), also known as Frederick I, king of Wurttemberg (r. 1806–1816), and *Augusta of Brunswick-Wolfenbuttel (1764–1788); married Jérôme Bonaparte (1784–1860), king of Westphalia, on August 23, 1807; daughter-in-law of Letizia Bonaparte (1750–1836); sister-in-law of Napoleon I (1769–1821), emperor of France; children: Jérôme Napoléon; *Mathilde, princess of Westphalia (1820–1904); Napoléon Joseph also known as Plon-Plon.

Intelligent, plump, and given to blushing, Catherine of Wurttemberg did not want to marry Jérôme Bonaparte but fell deeply in love with him after the nuptials. Though Jérôme treated her badly almost from the beginning, she remained devoted to him through battle, imprisonment, and exile, even when her father offered her anything she wanted if she would divorce him. She continued to be a favorite of her mother-in-law *Letizia Bonaparte, for whom she had the greatest respect. In 1840, five years after her death, Jérôme would marry his third wife, *Giustina Bartolini-Badelli.

Catherine Parr (1512–1548).

See Six Wives of Henry VIII.

Catherine Romanov (1878–1959)

Russian princess. Name variations: Ekaterina Iurevskaya. Born in 1878; died in 1959; daughter of *Ekaterina Dolgorukova (1847–1922) and Alexander II (1818–1881), tsar of Russia (r. 1855–1881); married Alexander VI, prince Bariatinsky; married Serge, Prince Obelensky; children: (first marriage) Andrei (b. 1902); Alexander (b. 1905).

Catherine Skovronsky (1684–1727).

See Catherine I of Russia.

Catherine the Great (1729–1796).

See Catherine II the Great.

Catherwood, Ethel (1910–1987).

See Balas, Iolanda for sidebar.

Catlett, Elizabeth (1915—)

African-American sculptor and printmaker. Born in Washington, D.C., on April 15, 1915; B.A., Howard University, 1936; M.F.A. in sculpture, University of Iowa, 1940; married Charles White (an artist), in 1941 (divorced); married Francisco Mora (an artist), in 1947; children: three.

Selected works: The Negro Woman (series of paintings and prints, 1946–47); Olmec Bather (cast bronze statue, 1966); Reclining Woman (sculpture, 1968); Homage to My Young Black Sisters (mahogany, 1968); Black Unity (sculpture, 1968); Malcolm Speaks for Us (linocut, 1969); Target Practice (bronze sculpture, 1970); Homage to the Panthers (linoleum cut, 1970); Black Flag (cedar, 1970); Black Woman Speaks (Spanish cedar with polychromed eyes and ears, 1970); Magic Mask (mahogany, 1971); Louis Armstrong (bronze sculpture, 1976); Bronze Head (1976); Maternity (black marble, 1980); Torres Bodet (life-size bronze, 1981); Vasconcelos (life-size bronze, 1981).

"I have gradually reached the conclusion," wrote African-American artist Elizabeth Catlett, "that art is important only to the extent that it aids in the liberation of our people." To that end, Catlett carried the politics of her work into her battles in the civil-rights arena.

Catlett's father died before she was born, and she was raised by her mother in Washington, D.C., in a comfortable, middle-class home. Excelling in art, she set her sights on Carnegie Institute of Technology after high school, but Carnegie had never accepted a black student. In spite of an outstanding entrance exam, Catlett was turned down. Instead, she went to Howard University, one of the first black institutions to establish an art department. After earning her B.A., she worked briefly in the mural division of the Federal Art Project before taking a job teaching elementary and high school in Durham, North Carolina, for $59 a month. In Durham, she worked with NAACP attorney Thurgood Marshall in a campaign conducted by the state teachers' association to equalize wages for all teachers.

Catlett sought her graduate degree at the University of Iowa, living in Iowa City's black ghetto because she was unwelcome in the university dormitories; she graduated as the first M.F.A. candidate in sculpture from the university. She then took a position as chair of the art department at Dillard University. There, she fought for higher wages for teachers, worked to establish life classes with nude models, and pushed to get black students admitted to the local museum to view a Pablo Picasso exhibit.

She met and married artist Charles White in 1941; soon after, the couple moved to New York, where Catlett flourished in the cultural atmosphere of the Harlem Renaissance. She continued studies in several mediums, working with French sculptor Ossip Zadkine, who would profoundly influence her subsequent work, and learning lithography at the Art Students League. During this period, she exhibited around the country, including at the Institute of Contemporary Art in Boston, the Baltimore Museum of Art, the Newark (New Jersey) Museum, and the Albany Institute of History and Art.

In 1946, after receiving a Rosenwald fellowship, she moved with her husband to Mexico. There, Catlett worked with the famous Taller de Grafica Popular (TGP), a collaborative of printmakers, on a volume depicting life throughout the Mexican republic. It was here that Catlett made a firm commitment to art as an aid to socio-political change and executed a series of prints and paintings on the theme *The Negro Woman*, depicting black women as laborers, farm workers, artists, and in a variety of other roles. She earned her first solo exhibition, at the Barnett-Aden Gallery, Washington, D.C., in 1948. Women, and the recurring theme of motherhood, would continue to dominate Catlett's work, with many of her works, such as *Black Woman Speaks* and *Homage to My Young Black Sisters*, intended as political statements about black women in society and their determined effort to elevate their position in cultures that subjugated them.

Remaining in Mexico, Catlett divorced White and later married Mexican artist Francisco Mora, also a member of the TGP, with whom she shared a commitment to the practice of social art. During the McCarthy era in the 1950s, the couple's art and leftist politics resulted in accusations of Communism, which ultimately led Catlett to become a citizen of Mexico. In 1959, she became the first woman professor of sculpture at Mexico's national university and continued to exhibit and win prizes in both Mexico and America. In the 1970s, she had 17 one-woman shows, most of them in the United States.

Catlett's sculptures are, for the most part, realistic in style, reflecting her training in the modern tradition and in African art, but her later work became increasingly abstract, in the manner of postwar sculptors Henry Moore and Constantin Brancusi. One of her larger works, *Olmec Bather*, a nine-foot-tall cast bronze, commissioned by Mexico's National Polytechnic institute, is a tribute to Mexico's great historical civilizations. Also well known is her *Black Unity;* seen from one side, this piece consists of two black walnut heads, seen from the other, the piece becomes a large clenched fist. Her bronze sculpture *Target Practice* achieves its powerful impact by presenting a view of the sculpture of a black man through the sights of a rifle.

Though primarily known as a sculptor, Catlett is also recognized for her prints, particularly her lithography and linoleum prints. She preferred these processes because many originals can be made at a relatively low cost, thus making art accessible to the working class as well as the elite.

During the 1960s and 1970s, Catlett sought to inform the public as to the significance of black achievement with a series of works portraying great figures in black history. Her depictions ranged from 19th-century abolitionists like *Harriet Tubman to more contemporary heroes represented in *Homage to the Panthers* and *Malcolm Speaks for Us*. In 1973, she was commissioned by Jackson State College in Mississippi to create a bust of *Phillis Wheatley, and two years later she created a ten-foot-tall bronze sculpture of Louis Armstrong for the City Park of New Orleans.

Through the decade of the 1980s, Catlett had more solo exhibitions and was included in four traveling survey exhibitions: "Amistad II: Afro-American Exhibition" (1975–77); "Two Centuries of Black American Art" (1976–77); "Forever Free: Art by African-American Women" (1981); and "The Art of Black America, Art Museum Association" (1985–86). In 1981, she completed two life-size bronze sculptures, *Torres Bodet* and *Vasconcelos*, commissioned by the secretary of education in Mexico City. That year, the Women's Caucus for Art honored Catlett with one of their coveted prizes.

SUGGESTED READING:

Dover, Cedric. *American Negro Art*. Greenwich, CT: New York Graphic Society, 1960.

Fax, Elton Clay. *Seventeen Black Artists*. NY: Dodd, Mead, 1971.

Lewis, Samella. *The Art of Elizabeth Catlett*. Claremont, CA: Hancraft Studios, 1984.

COLLECTIONS:

Printed material in the Archives of American Art, Smithsonian Institution, Washington, D.C.

RELATED MEDIA:

Elizabeth Catlett, film by June Mora, Contemporary Crafts, Los Angeles, California.

Barbara Morgan,
Melrose, Massachusetts

Catley, Ann (1745–1789)

English actress and singer. Name variations: Ann Lascelles. Born near Tower Hill, in London, England, in 1745; died at Ealing on December 14, 1789; daughter of a hackney-coachman; studied under Charles Macklin; married Francis Lascelles (a major-general).

From her first professional appearance at Vauxhall in 1762, Ann Catley's voice, beauty, and idiosyncratic manners brought her fame and notoriety. In 1763, an action was taken against Sir Francis Blake Delaval in the Court of King's Bench, accusing him of purchasing Catley from her singing master for improper purposes; her father had undertaken legal proceedings to regain her custody. From 1763 to 1770, she was an immensely popular performer in Dublin; after 1770, she beguiled the audiences of London. Women eagerly copied her dress; to be "Catleyfied" became synonymous with dressing becomingly. In 1784, Catley made her last appearance, having then married Major-General Francis Lascelles. Following the actress' death in 1789, *The Life and Memoirs of the late Miss Ann Catley, the celebrated actress* was published by a Miss Ambrose. The book was advertised as a "brief narrative of the life of Miss Ann Catley, containing the adventures of that lady in her public character of a singer, and private one of a courtezan, in England, Ireland, &c. With many curious anecdotes."

Caton-Thompson, Gertrude (1888–1985)

English archaeologist. Born on February 1, 1888 (some sources cite 1889), in London, England; died on April 18, 1985, in Hereford, Worcester, England; educated at the Links School, Eastbourne, and at Newnham College, Cambridge; trained at the British School of Archaeology in Egypt, studying under Flinders Petrie.

Together with the young British woman archaeologist **Elinor W. Gardner**, Gertrude Caton-Thompson worked on a number of projects in Egypt, especially in Northern Fayum (1924–28).

Her investigations pushed back the beginnings of Egyptian culture as far as 5000 BCE, into the Neolithic era, and were reported in her book *The Desert Fayum*. In 1928–29, she traveled to Rhodesia to excavate the ruins at Zimbabwe (the name would eventually be adopted by that country when it ceased to be subjugated by colonial rule). Caton-Thompson worked on the early site of Kharga Oasis in Egypt (1930–33), later publishing *Kharga Oasis in Pre-history*, and the tombs and temples of Hureidha in the Hadramaut of southern Arabia (1937–38), which resulted in *The Tombs and Moon Temple of Hureidha, Hadramaut*. She was president of the British Prehistoric Society, vice-president of the Royal Anthropological Institute, governor of Bedford College (University of London), and a fellow of Newnham College (Cambridge). Gertrude Caton-Thompson retired in 1957.

Catt, Carrie Chapman (1859–1947)

Activist for women's rights and crusader for world peace who was president of National American Woman Suffrage Association, founder and first president of the International Woman Suffrage Alliance, and organizer of the League of Women Voters. Born Carrie Clinton Lane on January 9, 1859, in Ripon, Wisconsin; died on March 9, 1947, in New Rochelle, New York, of a heart attack; daughter of Lucius (a farmer) and Maria (Clinton) Lane; attended public schools in Wisconsin and Iowa through high school; received a B.S. in the General Science Course for Women at Iowa State Agricultural College (now Iowa State University) in 1880; married Leo Chapman, February 12, 1885 (died 1886); married George Catt (d. 1905), on June 10, 1890; no children.

Began teaching high school in Mason City, Iowa (1881); promoted to principal and city school superintendent (1883); resigned to marry Leo Chapman, editor of the Mason City [Iowa] Republican *(1885); widowed, after a year as husband's business partner (1886); established suffrage clubs in Iowa (1887–90); elected secretary of Iowa Woman Suffrage Association (1889); played major role in successful campaign for woman suffrage in Colorado (1893); elected president of National American Woman Suffrage Association (1900–04 and 1916–20); founded International Woman Suffrage Alliance (1902); traveled to Europe, Africa, and Asia, observing conditions of women, speaking, and organizing women's rights groups; helped to found the Woman's Peace Party (1915); while continuing work on the international scene, organized and led the unsuccessful "Victory in 1915" New York suffrage campaign (1915); led the success-ful "Victory in 1917" campaign (1917); assisted in creating the League of Women Voters (1919); given "Distinguished Service" award of the National American Woman Suffrage Association (1920); founded the Committee on the Cause and Cure of War (1925); helped to establish the Protest Committee of Non-Jewish Women Against the Persecution of Jews in Germany (1933); awarded American Hebrew Medal (1933); honored with the Chi Omega Achievement Award (1941).*

Selected publications: The Home Defense *(NY: National American Woman Suffrage Publishing, 1918);* How to Work for Suffrage in an Election District *(NY: National American Woman Suffrage Publishing, 1917);* Then and Now *(NY: Leslie Woman Suffrage Continuing Committee, 1939);* War Aims *(NY: National American Woman Suffrage Association, 1918); (with Nettie Rogers Shuler)* Woman Suffrage and Politics: The Inner Story of the Suffrage Movement *(NY: Scribner, 1923);* Women in the Industries and Professions *(NY: Putnam, 1901).*

August 27, 1920, was a triumphant summer day for Carrie Chapman Catt and millions of women across the United States. Arriving at New York City's Pennsylvania Station on a train from Washington D.C., she was greeted by a mob of suffragists, presented with a huge bouquet of flowers addressed "To Mrs. Carrie Chapman Catt from the enfranchised women of the United States," and extended official congratulations by Governor Alfred E. Smith, who welcomed her as New York State's "distinguished citizen." Banners waved, a band played "Hail the Conquering Hero Comes," and Catt acknowledged that "This is a glorious and wonderful day."

The reason for celebration was summed up in the events of the day before, when Catt, *Harriet Taylor Upton and *Maud Wood Park, all leaders of the woman suffrage movement, had met with Secretary of State Bainbridge Colby to see the document that they, and thousands of women, had fought for since the mid-19th century: the proclamation, signed by Colby, announcing that the 19th Amendment, granting equal suffrage to men and women, was now a part of the American Constitution. Following their meeting, the group visited Woodrow Wilson and *Edith Bolling Wilson at the White House, offering the president a gift of appreciation in the form of a book compiled by the National American Woman Suffrage Association, acknowledging his work for suffrage.

For Catt, at age 61, the event marked the climax of decades of struggle, spent organizing women and speaking out for women's rights. Even then, however, she did not consider her work to be done. There were more battles to be fought on behalf of women, and there would be more time now to devote to another of her favorite causes, the goal of world peace.

Carrie Clinton Lane was born on January 9, 1859, in Ripon, Wisconsin, on the family farm. She was the second of three children and the only daughter of Lucius and **Maria Clinton Lane**. Her parents had grown up in the Potsdam, New York, area and were both high school graduates, which was somewhat unusual for that day. After high school, Maria Lane attended a woman's school, Oread Collegiate Institute, in Worcester, Massachusetts. Lucius, meanwhile, traveled with a cousin to California in 1850 to join the gold rush and earn enough money to wed. He failed to gain his fortune but returned to New York to marry Maria. The Lanes moved to Cleveland, Ohio, where Lucius bought a partnership in a coal business but soon found city life not to his liking. He sold his partnership to purchase the Ripon farm.

Carrie Chapman Catt

In 1866, when Carrie was seven, the family purchased and moved to a farm near Charles City, Iowa, a community that only a few years earlier had been part of the American frontier. Maria is said to have disliked the drudgery of farm life, but, in the patriarchal society of the 19th century, she followed her husband's lead. Carrie's elementary education was in a one-room schoolhouse in Charles City, and later she rode horseback to attend a high school five miles from home and boarded with friends who lived nearer the school during the winter.

Carrie was a bright, self-confident, independent child, who excelled in her studies and stood firm in her opinions and actions, whether or not they conformed with social convention. On election day, 1872, at age 13, she asked her mother why she was not dressing to go to town to vote as her father and the hired hand were doing and was shocked to learn that women could not vote. She was further mortified when members of her family, and later a neighbor boy, laughed at her for thinking that women were capable of voting. This single incident was to have a profound effect on the course of Catt's life.

Roll up your sleeves, set your mind to making history and wage such a fight for liberty that the whole world will respect our sex.

—**Carrie Chapman Catt**

While in high school, she was introduced to Charles Darwin's *Origin of Species*. The book led to her lifelong interest in evolutionary science, and to a philosophy she was able to embrace. Skeptical of traditional religion for most of her life, she retained a faith in human potential and saw evolutionary science as offering the idea of a constantly evolving and improving world, progressing toward a free and peaceful society. It was a philosophy that grew especially popular during the Progressive Era, around 1890 to 1920, and became the impulse behind social reforms of the period.

As Carrie neared the completion of high school, she longed to attend college, a highly unusual step for a young woman of her day. Since her father refused to provide financial support for more education, Carrie taught school for a year to earn enough money to enter Iowa State Agricultural College, then supported herself with work in the Iowa State Library and in the college kitchen. When she graduated on November 10, 1880, she was the only woman among 18 graduates.

Carrie aspired to become a lawyer, a profession only recently opened to women. She began reading law in the offices of a Charles City attorney and, in 1881, accepted a high-school teaching job at Mason City, Iowa, intent on earning enough money to study law at the university. Apparently a popular teacher, however, she enjoyed teaching so much that she gave up the idea of a law career. Less than two years later, she was appointed principal and superintendent of Mason City schools. Iowa was a progressive state, and it was not particularly unusual for a woman to be appointed principal or school superintendent, but it was unusual for anyone to rise as fast as Carrie did to such a position.

Married women were not allowed to teach, however, and at the end of the 1884 school year, Carrie resigned her job to marry Leo Chapman, editor of the *Mason City Republican*. The wedding took place on February 12, 1885, and Carrie Chapman became her husband's business partner. Soon a "Woman's World" section appeared in the newspaper. In contrast to the usual articles on food or fashion covered in "women's" columns, this new segment was devoted to women's political and labor issues and reminded women that if they wanted the vote, they needed to organize.

When Leo subjected a local Republican candidate to in-print vitriolic assaults, the newspaper became the center of a controversy. Leo was sued for libel, and, after a local judge ruled in favor of the complainant, the couple was forced to sell the newspaper. In May 1886, Carrie stayed with her parents, while her husband departed for San Francisco to find work. In August, after receiving a telegram advising that Leo was ill with typhoid fever, she left on the first westbound train, but Leo died while she was en route.

Widowed at age 27, with no home and few financial resources, Carrie remained in San Francisco for a year, electing to continue in the field of journalism rather than return to teaching. Writing freelance articles and canvassing for ads, she earned barely enough to meet basic needs. At this low period, a male associate suddenly grabbed her and began kissing her when she was working one evening. Though she managed to break away, the assault left her feeling frightened and outraged. Realizing the vulnerability of working women, she determined to do something about it.

One bright spot during the year in San Francisco was her reacquaintance with George Catt, a student she had met at Iowa State when she was a junior and he was a freshman. Since then, he had become a civil engineer for a bridge-building firm in the area. **Jacqueline Van Voris**, in *Carrie Catt: A Public Life*, speculates that it was George Catt who inspired Carrie to take on her next career, as a public lecturer. Lecturing was popular entertainment during the late 19th century, and an accomplished speaker could both influence public opinion and make a good living. Carrie prepared three lectures, hired an agent, and perfected her speeches delivering them along the West Coast, then returned to Iowa to embark on her new career.

In two of her lectures, "America for Americans" and "The American Sovereign," Catt revealed the nativist sentiments she held to some degree throughout most of the pre-suffrage years. She resented the fact that recent male immigrants were eligible to vote while native-born American women were not. In her opinion, these men were not only ignorant of American culture and institutions, but their practice of clinging to their own ethnic groups, and their susceptibility to exploitation by local political bosses who bought and sold their votes, made their franchise a threat to American society. As more and more immigrants arrived from Southern and Eastern Europe, many Americans feared the consequences of unassimilated ethnic groups, and such anti-foreign sentiments became widely held. Catt's suspicions of foreigners lessened during the early decades of the 20th century, when she began to involve herself in international issues.

Her return to Iowa in 1887 also marked the beginning of Catt's devotion to organizing women for suffrage. With other suffragists of her time, she shared the belief that the vote would bring women the power to eventually break down other barriers against their sex. She joined the Iowa branch of the Women's Christian Temperance Union (WCTU) and became the head of its suffrage section. When the local WCTU began to break apart, she focused solely upon the issue of woman suffrage, putting all her energy into organizing women and creating suffrage clubs. In 1889, she was elected secretary of the Iowa Woman Suffrage Association and, a year later, was an Iowa delegate and a minor speaker at the convention of the National American Woman Suffrage Association (NAWSA) in Washington, D.C. During the 1860s, a split had occurred between the two leading groups of suffragists over what methods to employ to achieve female suffrage. In 1890, the two main organizations—the American Woman Suffrage Association, led by *Lucy Stone and Henry B. Blackwell, and the National Woman Suffrage Association, led by *Susan B. Anthony and *Elizabeth Cady Stanton—reconciled their differences to form a united front as the National American Woman Suffrage Association, together for the first time since 1869.

Shortly after the convention, on June 10, 1890, Carrie surprised her suffragist friends when she married George Catt, in Seattle, Washington. Those who feared the marriage would put an end to Carrie Catt's suffrage career, soon found there was nothing to worry about. George Catt was not the typical 19th-century husband and gave full support to his wife's reform work. Catt once said of him, "My husband used to say that he was as much a reformer as I, but that he couldn't work at reforming and earn a living at the same time; but what he could do was to earn living enough for two and free me from all economic burden, and thus I could reform for two."

Before he finally moved his business to New York City in 1892, George Catt's work required him to move frequently about the country. Carrie accompanied him but also devoted time to her own business travels, especially making trips to states before an upcoming vote on the issue of woman suffrage, to organize women for a campaign in favor of the vote. More often than not, however, victory eluded the suffragists. In 1890, the vote for women went down to bitter defeat in South Dakota, but two weeks later Catt was back to campaigning in Kansas City, Missouri, along with Susan B. Anthony. Catt often worked herself to exhaustion. When she became too ill to lecture or travel, she wrote articles from her bed.

As the decade progressed, the aging leaders among the suffragists began to look closely at younger NAWSA members, in search of women competent to become the movement's next leaders. In 1893, Catt played a major role in the campaign to bring women the vote in Colorado, the first state to achieve woman suffrage through the ballot box. The only other state then granting women the vote was Wyoming, which had been admitted to the Union in 1890 as a full-adult suffrage state. Catt's work in Colorado, and her untiring organizing work throughout the country, made a strong impression on the suffragist leadership. In 1900, when 80-year-old Susan B. Anthony announced her retirement from the presidency of NAWSA, Carrie Chapman Catt was elected her successor and held the position from 1900 to 1904.

As NAWSA's president, Catt played a leading role in bringing about the dream, shared by

Anthony and Stanton, of founding an international woman's suffrage organization. The International Woman Suffrage Alliance (IWSA), which Catt worked to create, was officially recognized at a congress held in Washington, D.C., in 1902. Eight countries—Australia, Denmark, Germany, Great Britain, Holland, Norway, Sweden, and the United States—were affiliated with the organization at its founding. Catt was elected first president of the international alliance and held the position until 1923.

In 1904, Catt resigned the presidency of NAWSA because of physical exhaustion and family illness. In 1905, following several years of poor health, George Catt died in New York. Devastated by the loss, Catt became deathly ill herself and for a while lost all interest in suffrage work. But during the spring of 1906, she traveled to Copenhagen to prepare for the third congress of the IWSA scheduled to be held there in August.

Catt accepted the vice-presidency of NAWSA, under Dr. *Anna Howard Shaw, who was president from 1905 to 1915, but, until the onset of the World War I in 1914, Catt devoted most of her energies to the IWSA. She traveled to Europe on a number of occasions, to lecture, organize, and participate in IWSA conventions. In April 1911, she began an 18-month journey around the world. From Stockholm, Sweden, she traveled to several countries in Europe, then to Africa, including stops in South Africa and Egypt and places in between, then continued eastward to India, Sumatra, the Philippines, China, Korea, and Japan, and various other countries along the way. She managed some sightseeing, but her main purpose was to lecture, found suffrage organizations, and observe the conditions faced by women of diverse cultures. The hardships were many on a journey across three continents, loaded down with heavy trunks, and wearing the cumbersome clothing of the era, but Catt felt the trip was worthwhile and was pleased to find strongholds of feminism scattered around the world. Upon her return, she noted that she and her companions "left the seeds of revolution behind us, and the hope of liberty in many souls. But we have got much more than we gave—an experience so upsetting to all our preconceived notions that it is difficult to estimate its influence upon us."

Catt returned to the United States in November 1911 at a time when American women, after a lull of 14 years following the Idaho vote for woman suffrage in 1896, were once again making progress toward enfranchisement. In 1910, women had won the vote in the state of Washington, and in 1911 in California. In 1912, they gained three more Western states, and in 1913 they finally had a victory east of the Mississippi, in Illinois. These successes gave the suffragists encouragement, but, to reach their goal of a national amendment, they would have to win the most populous state of the union, the Empire State of New York.

Catt led the Empire State Campaign Committee, an organization comprised of members of most of the state's suffrage societies. To be sure that no one in the state was unaware of the suffragists' cause, she started a school to train volunteers in organization, public speaking, parliamentary practice, and suffrage history. Catt saw that workers were assigned to every voting precinct in New York State. Their slogan was "Victory in 1915," and when the campaign failed, they rallied with a new slogan, "Victory in 1917," and finally won that year.

When Anna Howard Shaw resigned from the presidency of NAWSA in 1915, Catt's energy and organizational skills still so impressed the membership that she was once again pressured to become their leader. The association was in disarray, and Catt was viewed as the one person who could save it. She reassumed the position but with reluctance, partly because her concerns were now divided between the suffrage movement and her interest in peace.

The onset of WWI brought a suspension of activities of the IWSA, leaving Catt with few responsibilities as president of the international organization. A lifetime pacifist, she had helped to establish the national Woman's Peace Party early in 1915 but then chose to expend her energies in the New York suffrage campaign. Catt believed, as did many pacifist women, that the potential for world peace would be much greater once women had the vote. Their main argument was that mothers, who gave life, were much more reluctant than men to see lives lost in wars. For the next five years, therefore, as leader of the Empire State Campaign Committee and president of NAWSA, her focus was on winning the vote for women.

Early in 1917, Catt announced NAWSA's support of President Wilson and volunteered the group's services to the U.S. government in the event of the nation's participation in the war. This move shocked Catt's pacifist friends, and the Woman's Peace Party denounced her actions, but whether or not she intended it so, her announcement was politically astute. It appears that by 1917 Catt had come to believe that

WWI was a necessary war, and by handing the government the support of NAWSA's more than two million members, she knew she could call upon the president in the future for his personal attention in woman suffrage matters. On the other hand, if NAWSA had acted in opposition to public opinion by obstructing the war effort, they would probably have lost the little influence that they had worked so hard to gain in the nation's capital.

Until passage of the 19th Amendment in 1920, Catt worked tirelessly as the bill made its way through Congress and on to state legislatures for ratification. In March 1919, sensing that victory was near, she used NAWSA's 50th Anniversary, the "Jubilee Convention," in St. Louis, to establish the League of Woman Voters (LWV) as the organization's successor. As most women had little political experience, the purpose of the LWV was to educate American women to become informed voters. As Catt traveled from state to state, still urging ratification of the suffrage amendment, she advertised and recruited for the new organization.

It was during this time, while on tour in the South, that Catt made a comment that has spurred accusations of racism in the 1990s, especially on the campus of Iowa State University in opposition to a building named in her honor. Reputedly, she exhorted Southerners to ratify the amendment, because "White supremacy will be strengthened, not weakened, by women's suffrage." Said professor **Jane Cox**: "That was a speech she made in 1919 in Mississippi and also in South Carolina. I view this as one of the ways she used to try to persuade white Southern men. It was a waste of time, of course. Neither of those states voted for it." In light of her future humanitarian work for the Jews of Germany, long before others joined in, it is a puzzling blot on an otherwise extraordinary career.

In 1918, following the armistice ending WWI, Catt had set out to revive the International Woman Suffrage Alliance, helping to plan its Eighth Congress, held in Geneva in June 1920. In 1923, when she resigned from the organization at the Rome Congress, at age 64, there were delegates from 43 countries in attendance, and in 25 of these countries women had equal suffrage, extended in most cases during or immediately after the recent war.

After returning from Rome to the U.S., Catt devoted the remainder of her life to the cause of peace. She could recall many wars fought during her own lifetime—the American Civil War, Na-

tive American wars, the Spanish-American War, and World War I. She hated war and decided to do everything she could to prevent future conflicts. Believing that an international forum would enable nations to negotiate for peace, she campaigned for American participation in the League of Nations and took advantage of every possible opportunity to lecture on the cause of peace. In 1925, she led in establishing the Committee on the Cause and Cure of War (CCCW) and served as the group's chair until 1932. Drawing from the membership of major women's organizations, the CCCW claimed over five million members at the outset. By 1930, over eight million women had joined, a time when the adult female population of the United States numbered approximately 37 million.

During the "Red Scare" that followed the Russian Revolution and World War I, some members of "super-patriotic" organizations, such as the Daughters of the American Revolution, accused Catt of being a Communist sympathizer due to her pacifism and her promotion of improved international relations. Such accusations were unfounded, and Catt found herself in good company, as other popular and admired women, including *Eleanor Roosevelt and social worker *Jane Addams were similarly accused.

With the rise of Hitler and the Nazi Party in Germany, Catt became concerned over the persecution of Germany's Jews. In 1933, she helped to establish the Protest Committee of Non-Jewish Women Against the Persecution of Jews in Germany, which mounted a campaign for signatures to a letter protesting the German government's crimes against the Jewish people, and quickly obtained the signatures of thousands of Americans. She also participated in lobbying Congress to amend the country's immigration laws to aid Jews and other refugees in escaping to the United States. In recognition of her work, Catt received the American Hebrew Medal for 1933, the first woman to receive the award.

Catt remained active in the CCCW until the late 1930s, when she realized that war was once again imminent. Eleanor Roosevelt had great respect for Catt, and when people wrote her to inquire how they could best work for peace, the first lady often referred them to Catt. Catt was 80 years old when World War II broke out. Although age and ill health often prevented her from publicly campaigning, she continued to correspond with influential people to express her views in support of war refugees and her ideas regarding programs for maintaining peace in the postwar years.

Carrie Chapman Catt died of a heart attack in her home in New Rochelle, New York, on March 9, 1947, at the age of 88. Having lived through three major wars, she must have been disappointed that she never saw the realization of her dream of world peace. But she had also been born in a time when the idea of woman suffrage was considered a joke by most members of both sexes, and in this respect she lived to see the results of her efforts. Although she may have been disappointed that the vote did not bring about the rapid breakdown of other barriers to women, nor any noticeable changes in the nation's political status quo, by the time of her death, women had equal voting rights in most developed countries around the world.

SOURCES:

Correspondence in Eleanor Roosevelt papers, Franklin Delano Roosevelt Library, Hyde Park, New York.

Flexner, Eleanor. *Century of Struggle: The Woman's Rights Movement in the United States.* NY: Atheneum, 1970.

Fowler, Robert Booth. *Carrie Catt: Feminist Politician.* Boston, MA: Northeastern University Press, 1986.

Munns, Roger. "Iowa Students Oppose Plan to Name Building for Suffragette Now Accused of Being a Racist," in *The* [New London] *Day.* April 18, 1996.

Peck, Mary. *Carrie Chapman Catt.* NY: H.W. Wilson, 1944.

Van Voris, Jacqueline. *Carrie Chapman Catt: A Public Life.* NY: The Feminist Press at the City University of New York, 1987.

SUGGESTED READING:

Cott, Nancy F. *The Grounding of Modern Feminism.* New Haven, CT: Yale University Press, 1987.

COLLECTIONS:

Correspondence, papers, and memorabilia located in the Catt Papers, Blackwell Papers and National American Suffrage Association Papers, Library of Congress; at the Sophia Smith Library, Smith College; and the Schlesinger Library, Radcliffe College.

June Melby Benowitz, Ph.D. candidate, University of Texas at Austin

Cattanei, Vannozza (fl. 1440–1490).

See Borgia, Lucrezia for sidebar.

Cattaneo, Simonetta (d. 1476).

See Vespucci, Simonetta.

Cattarina.

Variant of Catherine.

Cattle Kate (1861–1889).

See Watson, Ellen.

Cauer, Minna (1841–1922)

German feminist leader and writer. Born on November 1, 1841, in Freyenstein-Ostprignitz, Germany; died in Berlin on August 3, 1922; daughter of Alexan-

der Schelle and Juliane (Wolfschmidt) Schelle; married August Latzel (d. 1866); married Eduard Cauer; children: (first marriage) son (died in infancy).

Minna Cauer was born Wilhelmina Theodore Marie Schelle in 1841, the daughter of **Juliane Wolfschmidt Schelle** and Alexander Schelle, a Lutheran minister. She grew up in the small Silesian town of Freyenstein and in 1862 married a physician, August Latzel. Within the next five years, however, her life turned to horror when both her two-year old son and her mentally unstable husband died. Refusing to be crushed by these events, Minna prepared herself to be a schoolteacher, passing the examinations in 1867, a year after her husband's death. After teaching in Paris for a year, she married Eduard Cauer, an educator 18 years her senior. The years of her second marriage were spent in Berlin, where her husband was a school inspector, and the Cauers moved in influential liberal circles. She and her husband became close friends of the liberal-minded Frederick William, crown prince of Prussia, and his wife *Victoria Adelaide, whose mother was Queen *Victoria of Great Britain. Theirs was a happy marriage, ending only with Eduard's death in 1881.

Widowed a second time and without children, Minna Cauer was determined at the age of 40 not to drift or succumb to the forces of depression. Instead, she methodically began to inform herself on all aspects of the major political and social issues of the day. Free of material pressures, she was free to slowly enter the public arena at a time when German women were becoming increasingly assertive. In 1889, she played a key role in transforming the German Academic Alliance, an educational reform organization founded the year before, into a national organization, the Women's Welfare Association (Verein Frauenwohl). At first, the organization's goals were confined to the expansion of women's opportunities in education and the professions. Within a few years, however, Cauer realized that many needs remained unaddressed and the activities of the Verein Frauenwohl were expanded to include voluntary work in nurseries, homes for the blind, and other institutions. Determined that her organization gain a national reputation in the field of social reform, she worked tirelessly to spread the message that new areas of social work needed the skills of idealistic and skilled women.

Although respected by thousands of feminists for her energy and organizing skills, Minna Cauer often found herself in the middle of the turbulent internal struggles of the German women's movement. On one such occasion, in December 1894, her leadership as president of the Women's Welfare Association was seriously challenged by *Helene Lange, who found Cauer's strategies too radical, calling for a return of the organization to the older, more sedate pattern of calls for moderate reform. After a stormy meeting, Cauer and her faction emerged triumphant. For the next two decades, she would be the leading voice of the left wing of the bourgeois German women's movement, demanding in no uncertain terms that German women be granted the right to vote. Starting in 1895, she served as editor of the journal *Die Frauenbewegung,* which provided her with an important platform for bringing progressive ideas to the attention of women throughout the German Reich, whether they lived in Berlin, Munich, or a small town or village.

Refusing to compromise on basic issues or mince words in her writings, Minna Cauer was the impatient voice of the growing group of German women who in the years before 1914 demanded full civil rights. As early as 1904, she told her fellow crusaders that the only time she would believe the promises of politicians on the issue of female suffrage was the day on which they actually wrote this demand into their party platforms. She was deeply convinced that the women of Germany had long since earned the right to full political equality with males. Although she was not a Social Democrat, she was willing to be identified with the much-reviled "reds" by calling for the members of her organization to take to the streets to dramatize their demands. In 1910, she drew headlines in the national press when she provided strong evidence of her militancy by participating in Berlin demonstrations and then calling the city's police chief "a psychopath." For good measure, she characterized the Reich government as "a Junker clique," reminding her fellow militants that in 1848 Germany's women had been forced to pay with their blood in their attempt to free themselves. An anxious Imperial German government surrounded the hall in which she spoke, and the police dispersed Cauer's audience when they emerged into the street.

The start of World War I in the summer of 1914 was a blow to the aspirations of Minna Cauer as Germany became a nation in arms. The immediate aims of the suffrage movement had to be temporarily shelved in order to support the national war effort. By 1915, however, Cauer had regained some of her earlier optimism, arguing that Germany's women could play a major role in the war effort, thus strengthening their case for receiving the ballot once peace was restored. Arguing that all of the nation's women belong to "a greater whole," she noted that only by subordinating the needs of the individual to that of the totality could victory be assured. As it became clear that Germany would lose the war, Cauer's profound sense of nationalism become increasingly assertive. Fearful of revolution from the extreme left, she accepted some of the traditional authoritarian arguments of the ruling elite.

Moving away from the ideals of liberal feminism, Minna Cauer sought comfort in the idea that her threatened fatherland would survive its time of troubles, including the humiliating defeat of November 1918. Deeply alarmed by the appearance of a reborn Polish state that threatened to seize the area in which she was born and grew up in, she pledged the resources of her organization to the struggle to keep Upper Silesia within the borders of the new German republic. In her final years, Cauer did her best to keep from losing hope for her nation. Women had received the right to vote in 1919, but sadly this took place in a time of national chaos and upheaval. One of the last blows that she had to endure came only a few weeks before her death. Her friend Walter Rathenau, Germany's foreign minister, was assassinated in Berlin because he was Jewish and too conciliatory toward Germany's former enemies. Minna Cauer died in despair, barely realizing that she had in fact fought the good fight to raise the political consciousness of Germany's women. Starting in the 1980s, her impressive career has begun to be reevaluated by scholars, most of whom agree that Cauer must be recognized as a major figure in the history of the political emancipation of German women.

SOURCES:

Altbach, Edith Hoshino et al., eds. *German Feminism: Readings in Politics and Literature.* Albany, NY: State University of New York Press, 1984.

Cauer, Minna Schelle. *Die Frauen in den Vereinigten Staaten von Nordamerika.* Berlin: R. Lesser, 1893.

———. *Die Frau im 19. Jahrhundert.* Berlin: S. Cronbach, 1898

Evans, Richard J. *The Feminist Movement in Germany 1894–1933.* Beverly Hills, CA: SAGE Publications, 1976.

Jank, Dagmar. *Vollendet, was wir begonnen! Anmerkungen zu Leben und Werk der Fraunrechtlerin Minna Cauer, 1841–1922.* Berlin: Universitätsbibliothek der Freien Universität Berlin, 1991.

Lüders, Else. *Ein Leben des Kampfes um Recht und Freiheit: Minna Cauer zum 70. Geburtstag.* Berlin: W.&S. Loewenthal, 1911.

———. *Minna Cauer: Leben und Werk.* Gotha and Stuttgart: Friedrich Andreas Perthes, 1925.

Naumann, Gerlinde. *Minna Cauer: Eine Kämpferin für Frieden, Demokratie und Emanzipation*. Berlin: Sekretariat des Zentralvorstandes der Liberal-Demokratischen Partei Deutschlands im Buchverlag Der Morgen, 1988.

John Haag, University of Georgia,
Athens, Georgia

Caulier, Madeleine (d. 1712)

French peasant who was noted for her bravery during the siege of Lille. Died in the battle of Denain on July 24, 1712.

During the War of the Spanish Succession, the city of Lille, France, was besieged on August 12, 1708, by the Imperialists under Austria's Prince Eugene of Savoy. The city was defended by a French garrison under the command of Marshal Louis de Boufflers. On September 8, Madeleine Caulier carried an important order from the duke of Burgundy to Boufflers. Though Boufflers repulsed several assaults, he had to surrender on October 25, having lost 7,000 soldiers. Caulier was permitted to enlist in a regiment of dragoons as a reward for her bravery. Four years later, in a French attack led by Marshal Villiers during the same war, Madeleine Caulier fell in the battle of Denain on July 24, 1712.

Caulkins, Tracy (1963—)

American swimmer and Olympic gold medalist. Born in Winona, Minnesota, on January 11, 1963; daughter of Martha Caulkins (a junior-high art teacher) and Thomas Caulkins (a group testing coordinator for the public schools); grew up in Nashville, Tennessee; attended Harpeth Hall Academy; attended University of Florida, 1981–1985.

❧➤ **Pollack, Andrea** (1961—)

East German Olympic swimmer. Born on May 8, 1961.

In 1976, Andrea Pollack won two silvers (in the 100-meter butterfly and 4x100-meter freestyle) and two golds (in the 200-meter butterfly and the 4x100 medley relay) in the Montreal Olympics. That year, the powerful East German women's swimming team won 11 out of 13 events. In the Moscow Olympics in 1980, Pollack won another silver in the 100-meter butterfly. Andrea Pollack set two world records in the butterfly within a day of each other, with a time of 59.46 in the 100 meters on July 3, 1978, and a time of 2:09.87 in the 200 meters on July 4, 1978.

Was the youngest recipient of the Sullivan Memorial Trophy at 16 (1979); won 48 titles, becoming the most victorious woman swimmer in history (1981), eclipsing the records of Ann Curtis; won 200-meter and 400-meter individual medleys in the Pan American Games (1982); won three gold medals—the 200-meter individual medley, 400-meter individual medley, and the 400-meter relay—in the Summer Olympics, Los Angeles (1984); set NCAA records in four individual events (200-meter individual medley, 400-meter individual medley, 100-meter breaststroke, and 200-meter butterfly) and two relay events (800-meter freestyle and 400-meter freestyle); awarded Broderick Cup as outstanding collegiate athlete of the year (1983, 1984); selected by U.S. Olympic Committee as "female athlete of the year" (1984); elected to the Women's Sports Hall of Fame (1986); inducted into the International Swimming Hall of Fame (1990).

In 1980, when President Jimmy Carter called for a boycott of the Olympic games because of the Soviet Union's invasion of Afghanistan, countless American athletic careers were affected, including that of swimmer Tracy Caulkins. She would overcome this temporary setback, however, and, unlike other athletes who peaked during the boycotted games, win Olympic gold in 1984.

Caulkins was eight when she began swimming at the Seven Hills Club in Nashville, Tennessee, the city to which her family had moved subsequent to her birth in Minnesota. By age ten, she had made the nation's top ten in her age bracket in several events; at 12, she qualified for the senior nationals. Because her frequent school absences due to national competition were frowned upon, she left public junior high school to attend the private Harpeth Hall Academy in Nashville where she could both study and swim competitively. In 1976, Caulkins failed in her attempt to make the Olympic swim team. A year later, she defeated East Germany's ◀❧ **Andrea Pollack** in the 200-meter butterfly at the U.S.-East Germany meet, a particularly sweet victory as Pollack had recently won the Olympic gold medal in that event.

In 1977, Caulkins won the U.S. Amateur Athletic Union (AAU) championship, setting records in the 100-meter and 100-yard short course breaststroke and in the 200- and 400-meter long-course individual medley. In 1977 and 1978, she was named SW Swimmer of the Year. During 1978, she broke or tied 27 American and world swimming records, and in the world championships (West Berlin, Germany), she won three gold medals in both individual medleys and the 200-meter butterfly and a silver in the 100-meter breaststroke. At 16, she was the youngest recipient of the Sullivan Memorial Trophy as the outstanding American amateur athlete.

In 1980, Caulkins qualified for the Olympic swimming team, but the American boycott ended her hopes of participating. That same year, she was named American Swimmer of the Year and won the J.H. Kiphuth Award. In 1981, she eclipsed the records held by *Ann Curtis, the outstanding female swimmer of the 1940s. The following year, Caulkins was the top amateur swimmer, male or female. Her awards included *World's* American Female Swimmer in 1981, WSF Amateur Athlete of the Year in 1981, the Southland Olympia Award in 1982, the Broderick Award as best collegiate woman swimmer in 1982, and The Swimming All-American teams award in 1982 and 1983.

The dolphin kick was Caulkin's specialty, and she gained leverage from her hyperextended knees. Known for her carefree personality, she made winning look easy and, by early 1984, had 48 national and 62 American swimming titles. During her career at the University of Florida from 1981 to 1985, she won 12 NCAA titles. When the 1984 Los Angeles Games arrived, Caulkins was ready. She set an Olympic record in the 200-meter individual medley in 2:12.64, winning a gold medal. In the 400-meter individual medley, she won another gold in 4:39.24. The 400-meter medley relay was hers for a third gold. In 1986, Caulkins was elected to the Women's Sports Hall of Fame.

Karin L. Haag,
Athens, Georgia

Caux, Marchioness de (1843–1919).

See Patti, Adelina.

Cavalcanti, Ginevra.

See Medici, Ginevra de.

Cavalieri, Caterina (1760–1801)

Austrian soprano, best known for performing Mozart's music during his lifetime. Name variations: Katharina or Catherina. Born in Vienna, Austria, on February 19, 1760; died in Vienna on June 30, 1801.

Debuted at the Kärntnertortheater in Vienna (1775); career based entirely in Vienna.

On September 26, 1781, Mozart wrote to his father, "I have sacrificed Konstanze's aria a little to the flexible throat of Mlle Cavalieri."

The talented young composer was eager to ingratiate himself with Caterina Cavalieri and her protector, the court composer Salieri. Although Salieri was the senior composer, Cavalieri gladly sang the younger Mozart's works, which gained her a place in musical history. She possessed an impressive upper range that was combined with an extraordinary stamina and flexibility. She also possessed a very strong chest voice. After her debut in Vienna, Cavalieri sang 18 leading roles with the Italian group of singers to which she belonged. When Joseph II inaugurated opera buffa at the Burgtheater, Cavalieri was given many new roles. She played Donna Elvira in the first Vienna production of *Don Giovanni* in 1788. Mozart rewrote "Dove sono" in *Le nozze di Figaro* (*Marriage of Figaro*) in 1789 to accommodate the singer. Some criticized Cavalieri for lack of animation and accuracy whereas others maintained that she screamed her roles. Despite these flaws, Caterina Cavalieri had some of music's greatest works written for her by one of the world's most talented composers. Her character has been fictionalized in the movie *Amadeus,* directed by Milos Forman, from Peter Shaffer's screenplay based on his own play.

John Haag,
Athens, Georgia

Cavalieri, Lina (1874–1944)

Italian soprano. Born on December 25, 1874, in Viterbo, Italy; killed in a bombing raid on February 7, 1944, in Florence; married Prince Alexander Baritinsky in the 1890s; married Winthrop Chandler, in 1907; married French tenor Lucien Muratore (divorced 1927); married Giuseppe Campari.

Began career as a cafe singer before studying with **Maddelena Mariani-Masi**; *debuted in Naples as Mimi in La Bohème (1900), and Metropolitan Opera as Fedora (1906); appeared at Covent Garden (1906); performed mostly in Paris, Monte Carlo, and St. Petersburg.*

Lina Cavalieri

Lina Cavalieri was born in Viterbo, Italy, on December 25, 1874, and grew up in the slums of Rome. She began her career in cafes before moving into variety theaters and eventually onto the opera stage. Appearing on Italy's lesser stages, Cavalieri graduated to theaters in Naples and Lisbon and then secured engagements in Poland and Russia. She achieved great stardom in Russia and from 1904 to 1913 was featured at the glamorous international Italian seasons in St. Petersburg. While there, she married Count Alexander Baritinsky, but this marriage was nullified by the tsar on the grounds that Baritinsky had married beneath his station. Despite this ruling, the tsar, who adored the singer, gave her a generous settlement and many jewels.

A master at self-promotion, Cavalieri developed a great persona that attracted a wide public. Her voice was small scale but she made the most of all of her assets, particularly her great beauty. When she married Lucien Muratore, a French tenor matinee idol, her singing days were almost over. She ultimately settled in Paris where she eventually opened a successful beauty salon. Cavalieri's autobiography, *Le mie veritá* was published in Rome (1936). During World War II, she was killed in a bombing raid on February 7, 1944, in Florence, reputedly because she returned to her villa to retrieve her jewels. Cavalieri understood public relations in its infancy and it is for her abilities in this regard, rather than her somewhat weak voice, that she was known. An Italian film of her life, *La donna più bella del mondo*, starred *Gina Lollobrigida in 1957.

SUGGESTED READING:

Cavalieri, Lina. *Le mie veritá* (autobiography). Rome, 1936.

John Haag,
Athens, Georgia

Cavanagh, Kit (1667–1739)

Irish-born English soldier. Name variations: Christian Davies; Christopher Welsh; Mother Ross. Born Christian Cavanagh in Dublin, Ireland, in 1667; died in 1739 in England; daughter of a prosperous brewer; married Richard Welsh (a servant and soldier); married Hugh Jones (a soldier); married a man named Davies; no children.

Born in Dublin, Ireland, to a prosperous brewer, Kit Cavanagh grew up, writes one historian, favoring "manly Employments, such as handling a rake, flail, pitchfork, and riding horses bareback." When her first husband Richard Welsh was drafted in 1692, she was determined to find him. A year later, under the name of Christopher Welsh, she disguised herself as a

man and joined the British army as a dragoon (mounted soldier).

Throughout the next ten years, she served under John Churchill, duke of Marlborough. After fighting the French in Holland, she transferred to her husband's cavalry regiment, the Scots Greys, eventually finding Richard and convincing him to keep her secret. During the War of the Spanish Succession, she distinguished herself on the battlefield while fighting the French on the Continent in the campaigns of 1702 and 1703. She was wounded several times. When Cavanagh suffered a skull fracture in 1706 at the battle of Ramillies, her gender was discovered during an ensuing operation. Though she was discharged, the army allowed her to remain with the dragoons as an officer's cook and to be open about her true sex.

It is said that when her husband was killed in 1709 along with 25,000 others at the battle of Malplaquet, it was Cavanagh who found his body. Deeply distraught, she was consoled by a captain named Ross. Though their relationship is unknown, she was soon nicknamed Mother Ross. Three months later, she married Hugh Jones, a grenadier with the Royal Greys, who was soon killed in battle (1710). In 1712, she retired from the army and opened an inn. Cavanagh was granted a lifetime pension of a shilling a day by Queen *Anne and married another soldier, a dissolute fellow named Davies. When she died in Chelsea Hospital in 1739, Kit Cavanagh was given a regular military burial. One year later, an autobiography appeared. Though there is no proof, many believed that it was actually authored by Daniel Defoe.

SOURCES:

The Life and Adventures of Mother Ross. Conjectured author: Daniel Defoe. London: Peter Davies, 1928.

Laura York,
Riverside, California

Cavell, Edith (1865–1915)

English nurse and hero of World War I who was executed by the Germans for assisting fugitive Allied soldiers escaping from German-occupied Belgium. Name variations: Nurse Cavell. Born Edith Louisa Cavell on December 4, 1865, in Swardeston, Norfolk, England; died by execution at the Tir National near Brussels, Belgium, on October 12, 1915; daughter of the Reverend Frederick Cavell, vicar of Swardeston, and Louisa Sophia Walming Cavell; attended a school in Somerset and in Brussels, Belgium; studied nursing at the London Hospital; never married; no children.

Edith
Cavell

Served as governess for a Brussels family (1890); entered nurses training at London Hospital (1895); appointed matron of nurses training school at Berkendael Medical Institute in Belgium (1907); changed nursing school into a Red Cross Hospital during World War I (1914); aided Allied soldiers trapped in Belgium (1914–15); accused of aiding the enemy (1915); tried for treason and executed (1915).

The prisoner, an obscure 49-year-old English nurse named Edith Cavell, was led to the firing range posts at 7:00 AM on October 12, 1915, in Brussels, Belgium. As a nurse serving in a foreign land, the English woman was theoretically nonpolitical, but she had been accused of aiding the enemy by the German occupiers of Belgium and had refused to defend herself throughout her trial, even admitting guilt. After she had been tied to the post and blindfolded, shots rang out, and Edith Cavell died a horrendous death. The world was shocked. To many, she was a martyr who had resolutely done her duty.

Edith Louisa Cavell was born on December 4, 1865, in the small village of Swardeston, four miles from Norwich, the daughter of **Louisa Walming Cavell** and Frederick Cavell. A grim, bewhiskered, pious man who prayed in a doomsday voice with a fierce demeanor, Frederick was vicar to a parish of 300 that was as poor in finances as it was in attendance. Louisa, the daughter of his housekeeper, had been sent to finishing school by Cavell before he married her. Her warmth and charm made her the perfect spouse. Edith, and an older sister Florence, spent their youth in a large 18th-century brick farmhouse that faced the village common.

From an early age, Edith showed a remarkable aptitude for art, painting watercolors of nature, especially dogs, which she adored. While her village friends attended the elementary school, Edith was tutored by her father, an education that included German philosophy. When Edith was 16, Frederick arranged for her to spend a few months at Norwich High School. She was then sent to three different boarding schools in as many years, in Kensington, Clevedon near Bristol, and at Laurel Court in Peterborough. At Laurel Court, she studied all subjects and was exceptional in French. The headmistress, **Margaret Gibson**, had a great impact on Edith and would later recommend her as a governess for M. François, a prominent attorney from Brussels, Belgium.

In the five years preceding her sojourn in Brussels, Edith held positions as governess for several families. She continued to grow artistically and intellectually and delighted her charges with sketches of animals to accompany nursery tunes. Cavell was also extremely athletic and loved lawn tennis and ice skating. In 1888, she was left a small competency, which she used to travel to Germany and Austria. While in Bavaria, she visited a Free Hospital maintained by a Dr. Wolfenberg, an encounter that would lead to her interest in the medical and nursing profession. Impressed with the work being done there, Cavell contributed money for the purchase of much needed medical equipment. Those

associated with the infirmary adored her and called her the "English Angel."

Edith Cavell arrived in Brussels in 1890 and remained as governess to the four children of the François family for five years. She easily bridged the differences between the small village of Swardeston and the cosmopolitan life of Brussels. Her sketches of dogs, her illustrated nursery rhymes and original poems delighted the François children. Cavell traveled with the family by yacht and carriage throughout Belgium and the adjacent countries. She painted, decorated dinner party menus with illustrations, and involved herself in every aspect of her duties to the children. During long summer holidays, she returned to Swardeston to spend time with her family. She was romantically attracted to her second cousin, Eddy Cavell, but he was reluctant to pursue marriage with his close relative. Years later, during the last hours of her life, Edith Cavell would write on the flyleaf of *The Imitation of Christ,* "With love to E.D. Cavell," with instructions to give the book to her cousin.

In June 1895, Edith received word that her father was seriously ill with circulatory problems. Despite the efforts of the François family to retain her services, she resigned her position and returned to Swardeston. For nearly a year, Cavell nursed her father while he slowly responded to her efforts. As he resumed his duties and planned his retirement, Edith, now 30, decided to pursue a long-held desire to enter the nursing profession.

On December 6, 1895, she applied for an appointment as Assistant Nurse, Class II, at Fountains Fever Hospital in Tooting. Although she confessed to her lack of training, she began work on December 12. After seven months at Fountains, her superiors were impressed enough to support her application for a six-week nurses' training program at Tredeger House. On completion, she spent two years in training at the London Hospital. Extremely proficient, she was given supervision over other nurses assigned to combat a typhoid epidemic in Maidstone, Kent, in October 1897. Her organizational skills, energy and dedication in this pre-vaccine outbreak was praised by her superiors, and she was given the silver medal for her efforts, the only award she received in her lifetime. Cavell was granted her nursing certificate and was appointed for a third year on the private nursing staff. She worked in several hospitals in London, Sussex, and Gloucestershire during that year. Having attained the position of staff nurse, she worked in poor-law nursing in infirmaries at St. Pancras,

Highgate, and Shoreditch. Subsequently, she served nine months as temporary matron of the Ashton New Road District Home as Queen's District Nurse in Manchester. Her kindness to the poor and laboring classes in the mine and mills of Manchester led the people to call her the "poor man's Nightingale."

Edith Cavell emerged from her training and nursing experience as a quiet, strict, overly serious professional with little humor but great compassion and patience. She was an attractive woman, 5'3", about 150 pounds, with dark brown hair and aquiline features. At times shy, she was tender towards animals and devoted to improving everything. One nurse observed that "next to Miss Cavell, other women seem so weak, so thin."

In 1907, Edith Cavell was invited by Doctor Antoine Depage, one of the most eminent surgeons in Europe, to move to Brussels and become matron of Belgium's first training program for nurses. Depage envisioned an extensive, modern school based on the English system.

Prior to 1907, the only available nurses in Belgium were sisters from the Catholic religious orders. The offer to Edith came as a direct result of her employment with the François family. **Mme Graux**, a member of the committee supporting Depage's nursing school, was the mother-in-law of one of the children formerly under Edith's governance. On the recommendation of Graux, Depage offered the appointment. Cavell accepted the position and arrived in Brussels in August.

The nursing school opened on October 1, 1907, as the École Belge d'Infirmières Diplômées Clinique, but in time it became popularly known as the Berkendael Institut, from the street bordering the school's buildings. Cavell's initial class of probationers, which numbered 13, were uniformed in blue cotton dresses, white collars, high white aprons and caps. She became a close friend with Mme **Marie Depage**, who often served as a peacemaker between the imperturbable Cavell and Marie's volatile husband Antoine. Edith staffed the school with excellent graduate assistants from England, Holland, France, Germany, and Switzerland. She was re-

From the movie Nurse Edith Cavell, *starring Anna Neagle as Edith Cavell.*

spected, trusted and admired by her staff, the students and doctors. All business, her conversations tended to center on her patients, students, and the school. Some students actually feared her curt manner, and as time passed her occasional smile was seldom seen. Cavell was impressive with her clipped French accent, her knowledge of nursing, and her emphasis on hygiene and preventative medicine. She knew anatomy like Gray and used her artistic skills to illustrate her lectures. Edith's duties continued to expand. Her skills as a surgeon's assistant were sought for all major operations. By 1912, she was also matron of St. Gilles Hospital and carried out similar responsibilities at the St. Pierre and St. Jean hospitals. In addition, she supervised a sanitarium established by Dr. Depage. She and her students worked nine hours a day, six-and-a-half days a week.

I know now that patriotism is not enough. I must have no hatred and no bitterness toward anyone.

—Edith Cavell

Years passed at the school, and Cavell became a lonely, gaunt, gray woman. She had spent almost all her vacations in Swardeston but even that changed following Reverend Cavell's death in June 1910. Her mother tried to live with her in Brussels but, unable to adjust to a foreign country, returned to England. Edith's constant companions were her two dogs, a mongrel named Don and a collie named Josh. Although she kept them immaculate and hygienically scrubbed, the dogs were a humorous diversion since the irascible Dr. Depage disapproved of their presence.

On July 14, 1914, just two weeks after the assassination of Archduke Franz Ferdinand and his morganatic wife *Sophie Chotek in Sarajevo, Bosnia, Cavell traveled to Norwich to visit her mother. They spent a few days at a Norfolk seaside resort during Edith's last visit to her beloved England. The trip back to Brussels found the railway carriages and boat overcrowded. By the time she arrived back at the Beckendall Institute on August 3, the Great War or World War I had begun. Though she could have remained in Britain, Cavell believed her duty was with her nurses in Brussels.

German troops violated Belgian neutrality when they crossed the border on August 3. Although she had only arrived that day, Edith Cavell had already draped Red Cross flags across the school. Bewildered refugees and battle-weary troops soon filled the streets of Brussels. As the German assault continued, tales blending truth and propaganda circulated, telling of burning villages, executions, and rape. In time, almost everyone, including Cavell, came to believe the stories of savagery. By August 20, nearly 20,000 Germans had entered Brussels. Dr. Depage had been called away to set up military hospitals, and Edith was in charge of the institute. She and her staff devoted themselves to the care of the wounded, both Allies and Germans. They continued their nursing duties encumbered by curfews, restrictions, and shortages of necessities. The fighting moved swiftly away and centered around the battle of Mons and Charleroi in late August and early September.

Several hundred Allied survivors from these battles eventually reached Brussels. Throughout Belgium, resistance to the German invaders began to evolve. Many French and Belgian civilians sheltered and fed the Allied troops. Eventually, they organized networks to help them escape to their own lines. The underground system was led by Prince Reginald deCroy and his sister, Princess **Marie deCroy**, and consisted of an amateurish group of Belgian nationalists, including Philippe Baucq, an architect, Herman Capiau, an engineer, Albert Libiez, a lawyer, **Louise Thuliez**, a school teacher, and eventually Edith Cavell.

Herman Capiau, a friend of Madame Depage, came to the institute one night and informed Cavell that two wounded English soldiers were hiding in a Brussels convent. She agreed to shelter them and administer medical treatment. The soldiers eventually left the institute with the help of the Belgian underground. During the next nine months, over 200 soldiers passed through Cavell's hospital in their flight to freedom, moving about in the guise of doctors, nurses, patients, visitors, and domestics. Her involvement took a dramatic toll on Edith Cavell. Because her staff was entangled in her actions, her concern for their safety affected her health and produced a visible strain on her weary face.

The Germans eventually infiltrated the underground, and many refugees were arrested or killed. One informer, Georges Gaston Quien, who had passed through Cavell's hospital, was the betrayer of the network. On August 5, 1915, Otto Meyer and other members of the secret police arrested Cavell and another nurse, **Elizabeth Wilkins**. After being questioned, nurse Wilkins was released but Edith was detained. Led to believe that other members of the underground had supplied the authorities with ample evidence, she freely admitted her role in the escape operations.

Edith Cavell, condemned on the charge that she had conducted enemy soldiers back to their lines where they could once more take up arms against Germany, was held in solitary confinement for two months in the prison of St. Gilles. It was nine weeks before she and 35 others were brought to trial. At first, because of German secrecy and efficiency, support for Cavell was slow in developing. Nurse Wilkins and the hospital staff pled her case to foreign embassies. During the weeks preceding the trial, Brand Whitlock, the U.S. ambassador in Brussels, was the most energetic on her behalf. Whitlock, representing British interests, wrote an impassioned letter to Baron von der Lancken, the German political minister in Brussels, stating that he was instructed to take charge of her defense and requesting that an attaché of the U.S. legation be permitted to consult with Cavell to arrange for her defense. When von der Lancken failed to reply, Whitlock wrote again and was informed that nurse Cavell had already confessed her guilt and was legally represented by Thomas Braun. At the last minute, Braun was replaced by Sadi Kirschen, a member of the Brussels bar, who did everything possible, under the circumstances, to defend Edith.

The trial was a foregone conclusion. Under German legal procedures, Edith Cavell was not permitted to meet with her advocate before the trial, nor could the defense have access to documents pertaining to the case. She was officially charged with enabling no less than 130 people to escape from Belgium. Had she confessed to merely assisting the men to escape to Holland, the charges would have constituted nothing more than an attempt to conduct soldiers to their homelands. That was not a capital offense under German military law. But Edith Cavell was alleged to have signed a confession the day before her trial that she had actually assisted Belgian men of military age to reach the front, and that she had provided funds and guides, or helped conceal French and British soldiers in order that they might cross the Belgian borders to Holland. Her confession was not surprising since she had been in solitary confinement for two months without benefit of legal counsel and suffered some self-doubts about the morality of her own actions.

The trial, which opened on October 7, 1915, lasted for only two days, but none of the 35 defendants were denied legal rights. Possibly because she did not want to compromise the Berkendael Institute or dishonor the uniform of the nursing profession, Cavell wore civilian clothing for the trial. Some have speculated that her uniform, much honored by Germans, might have stood her in good stead and earned her sympathy. She did little to defend herself. Asked a dozen questions, her entire defense, spoken in French, consisted of 130 words and took less than four minutes. The trial ended on Friday, October 8, and the prisoners heard nothing until they were summoned back to court on Monday afternoon, October 11. Nine defendants were acquitted, but most received prison sentences ranging from two to fifteen years at hard labor. Five death sentences were pronounced, but three of them were commuted. Edith Cavell and Philippe Baucq were sentenced to immediate execution. When it was suggested that she appeal for mercy, Cavell replied serenely: "It is useless; I am English and they want my life."

The American embassy was informed unofficially at eight o'clock on Monday evening, October 11, that the sentence had been pronounced on Edith Cavell and that her execution would take place the following morning. From his sickbed, Whitlock wrote a letter to the German authorities, pleading for mercy; he also dispatched Hugh Gibson, the American embassy attaché, and Marquis de Villabobar, the Spanish ambassador, to see Baron von der Lancken. Continuous attempts to persuade the German officials to commute or delay the execution were in vain.

Edith Cavell wrote farewell letters at St. Gilles prison to her nurses, her family, and the note to Eddy Cavell in her copy of *Imitation of Christ*, which she had also used for a final diary. The Reverend Horace Stirling Gahan, chaplain of Christ Church in Brussels, was permitted to celebrate communion with her and to carry away her last messages. The guards came for her at 6:00 AM on October 12, 1915, and she was driven to the Tir National, a rifle range near the city. As they approached the execution site, she declined an offer of smelling salts from Pastor Paul le Seur, the German army chaplain. When they reached the execution post, le Seur squeezed her hand and recited the Grace of the Anglican Church to her in English. She asked the chaplain to have Reverend Gahan inform her loved ones that "my soul I believe is safe, and that I am glad to die for my country." She was then bound to the execution post and her eyes, full of tears, according to the soldier who put on the bandage, were blindfolded. She and Baucq were shot dead by firing squad at 7:00 AM and buried near the place of execution.

The execution of Edith Cavell—a woman and a nurse—aroused widespread indignation around the world. There was no evidence that she was a spy and many considered her death to have been a judicial murder. Prime Minister Herbert H. Asquith, speaking in the House of Commons, said that Edith Cavell faced a worse ordeal in her last hours than that of a soldier on a battlefield. Even the Germans realized too late the propaganda victory they had presented to the Allies and Kaiser Wilhelm II announced that no woman was to be executed without his approval.

Following the end of World War I, Edith Cavell's body was returned to England and commemorative services were held at Westminster Abbey on May 15, 1919. When the solemn ceremony was completed, the funeral continued by train to Norwich, where her body was laid to rest in Life's Green, just outside the south transept of the cathedral. A statue in her honor stands in Saint Martin's Place near Trafalgar Square in London.

SOURCES:

Grey, Elizabeth. *Friend Within The Gates: The Story of Nurse Edith Cavell.* Boston, MA: Houghton Mifflin, 1961.

Hoehling, A.A. *A Whisper of Eternity: The Mystery of Edith Cavell.* NY: Thomas Yoseloff, 1957.

Judson, Helen. *Edith Cavell.* NY: Macmillan, 1941.

Ryder, Rowland. *Edith Cavell.* NY: Stein and Day, 1975.

Til, Jacqueline van. *With Edith Cavell in Belgium.* NY: H.W. Bridges, 1922.

SUGGESTED READING:

Berkeley, Reginald. *Dawn* (novel). London: London Book Co., 1928.

DeCroy, Marie. *Memoirs of Marie deCroy.* London: Macmillan, 1932.

Got, Ambroise. *The Case of Miss Cavell.* London: Hodder and Stoughton, 1920.

RELATED MEDIA:

Dawn (silent film), starring *Sybil Thorndike, 1928.

Bechofer, C.E., and C.S. Forester, *Nurse Cavell,* (3-act play), London: Bodley Head, 1933.

Nurse Edith Cavell (95 min.), based on the novel *Dawn,* produced by Imperadio/ RKO, directed by Herbert Wilcox, starring *Anna Neagle, *Edna May Oliver, and *May Robson, 1939.

Phillip E. Koerper, Professor of History, Jacksonville State University, Jacksonville, Alabama

Cavendish, Ada (1839–1895)

English actress. Born in 1839; died in 1895.

Ada Cavendish made her acting debut at the New Royalty in 1863. She went on to play Juliet, Beatrice, Rosalind, and Lady Teazle on the London and New York stage.

Cavendish, Christiana (1595–1675)

Countess of Devonshire. Born in 1595; died in 1675; daughter of Edward Bruce, Baron Kinloss; married

William Cavendish, 2nd earl of Devonshire (c. 1591–1628, MP for Derby).

Christiana Cavendish, countess of Devonshire, was an ardent supporter of the Royalist cause.

Cavendish, Elizabeth (d. 1582).

See Stuart, Arabella for sidebar.

Cavendish, Elizabeth, duchess of Devonshire (1758–1824).

See Lamb, Caroline for sidebar.

Cavendish, Georgiana, duchess of Devonshire (1757–1806).

See Lamb, Caroline for sidebar.

Cavendish, Georgiana (1783–1858)

*Countess of Carlisle. Name variations: Lady Morpeth. Born in 1783; died in 1858; daughter of *Georgiana Cavendish (1757–1806), and William, 5th duke of Devonshire, June 6, 1774; married George, Viscount Morpeth (later 6th earl of Carlisle), March 21, 1801; children: five daughters and four sons.*

Cavendish, Harriet (1785–1862).

See Leveson-Gower, Harriet.

Cavendish, Henrietta

Countess of Oxford and Mortimer. Daughter of John Holles, duke of Newcastle; married Edward, 2nd earl of Oxford and Mortimer. Henrietta Street in Cavendish Square, London, was named after her.

Cavendish, Margaret (1623–1673)

English philosopher, duchess of Newcastle, and first woman to write about science. Name variations: Duchess of Newcastle upon Tyne. Born Margaret Lucas in Essex, England, in 1623 (some sources cite 1624); died on December 15, 1673 (some sources cite 1674); buried in Westminster Abbey; daughter of Thomas and Elizabeth Lucas; had three brothers—including Sir William, Lord John Lucas—and four sisters; educated at home; served in the court of Queen Henrietta Maria; married William Cavendish (1592–1676), marquis of Newcastle, later duke of Newcastle, in December 1645.

Published many philosophical works as well as biography and utopian science fiction; first woman to attend a meeting of the Royal Society (May 23, 1667).

Selected works: Poems and Fancies *(1653);* Philosophical Fancies *(1653, reprinted as* Philosophical and Physical Opinions, *1655);* Philosophical Letters: or Modest Reflections upon some Opinions in Natural Philosophy Maintained by Several Famous and Learned Authors of This Age *(1655);* Observations Upon Experimental Philosophy *(1666);* Grounds of Natural Philosophy *(1668);* The Description of a New World, Called the Blazing World *(1668);* The Life of William Cavendish, Duke of Newcastle, to Which Is Added the True Relation of My Birth, Breeding and Life *(1886).*

Margaret Cavendish is known both for her philosophy and her unusual character. Her prolific writing was considered unseemly for a woman of the time, especially because of the confidence she displayed in her own ideas. Of the 600 books published in English by women between 1475 and 1700, Cavendish was responsible for 21. Her style was forthright, if not confrontational; her manner of appearance was also unique, earning her a reputation for outlandish apparel. The combination of her personal and literary styles prompted biographer Samuel Pepys to dub her "Mad Madge."

Margaret was born in 1623 in Essex, England, one of eight children of Thomas and **Elizabeth Lucas**. They were an extremely wealthy family but without stature. Even after the death of Thomas in 1625, Elizabeth kept a good distance from her affluent neighbors, though she was also indifferent to the poor. More forceful and ambitious than her husband, Elizabeth proved to be a shrewd entrepreneur, and when she assumed control of the family business it continued to prosper. But the family's association with the High Church led to difficulties. The Lucases, particularly Elizabeth and her son Lord John Lucas, became the target of riots in 1640 and 1641. They were nearly lynched, and their manor was looted.

Elizabeth Lucas was inordinately tolerant and supportive of her daughter. Provided with a great deal of freedom as well as care, nevertheless, Margaret suffered from social isolation. Her siblings were all older, distant and cold, and her only friend was her serving woman, **Elizabeth Champlain**, who would remain a good friend for the rest of Margaret's life. As a result, Margaret did not learn the social graces, particularly the expected skills of women. Though she did not feel denied in this way, Margaret did regret not securing a better education; the only schooling the future philosopher received was

Margaret Cavendish

tutoring at home, which was not of a high quality. A happy, confident child, Margaret recorded her thoughts from the age of 12 in what she came to refer to as "Baby Books."

After petitioning the king at Oxford with her sisters in 1642, Margaret became a maid of honor in Queen *Henrietta Maria's Court, a move that was sanctioned by her mother, who hoped she would find a rich husband. Soon after, however, Margaret began to abhor the arrogance and superficiality of the other nobles, advising those who would attain such heights to:

> be bold, rude, and vain, talk much without sense, swear much without cause, brag much without reason, accoutre your self fantastically, behave your self carelessly, and imploy time idly; and be sure you raile of all Women generally, but praise every particular one.

Despite her confidence, Margaret's lack of social skills proved a great disadvantage. In addition, her mother, who had earlier suffered the stigma of having a child out of wedlock, made sure that her daughter's behavior would not encourage sexual advances and lead to a similar humiliation. This only served to enhance Margaret's shyness and social ineptitude. Even so, Elizabeth would not allow Margaret to leave the Court, as this would seem an admission of failure, so Margaret accompanied the queen to France for five years.

Margaret met her future husband, William Cavendish, the marquis of Newcastle, in April 1645 while at Court in France. Renowned for his flair with women, the marquis gave Margaret the attention for which she craved. He was attracted by her demureness and ample figure—which was enhanced by the clothing that seemed so fashionably incorrect to others—and began to send her romantic poetry. Margaret had few romantic inclinations, however. She admired his prestige but resisted all physical advances. The marquis, who had also been a victim of Court malice, accepted Margaret's view of herself as one maligned because of her virtue. They married in December 1645, shortly after their first meeting.

In the first few years of their marriage, the couple suffered from debt, political misfortune, and disappointment over their failure to conceive children. (William already had several from an earlier marriage but was eager for more sons.) Margaret became obsessed with fame. Fascinated by the philosophical views of her husband's brother, Sir Charles Cavendish, she began to write her own philosophy, publishing her first book, *Poems and Fancies,* in 1653. Her husband supported her intellectual work, and, despite their financial problems, she was given her leisure and never made to perform household tasks. Though William's financial situation improved, he fell into political disfavor; this redoubled Margaret's intellectual efforts in her desire for social recognition.

Through William and Charles, Margaret had access to the intellectual group known as the Newcastle Circle. She was also exposed to science through her brother, John, who was one of the original members of the Royal Society. Although William was more of a dilettante than a serious thinker, he was a generous patron of intellectuals. Charles was actively involved in the Newcastle Circle, which included Thomas Hobbes, Kenelm Digby, and, during exile from France in the 1640s and 1650s, French philosophers Pierre Gassendi and René Descartes as well as French mathematicians Marin Mersenne and Gilles Personne de Roberval. While Margaret may never have conversed directly with these men, she was exposed to their theories by William and Charles, and her considerations may also have been relayed back to the group. Charles discussed with her science and math, relating the advances of the day.

In England—as everywhere else, with the exception of Italy—women could not receive university education at the time, and women intellectuals were ridiculed. Margaret was unaware of the existence of the English philosopher, *Anne Finch (1631–1679), a contemporary with similar interests. Margaret's lack of education, however, did not hinder her in engaging in the philosophy of nature, as science was then still fairly accessible to the non-professional. She was particularly influenced by Hobbes' atomism, the doctrine that reality consists of minute independent particles. Rather than Hobbes' version— that atoms are inanimate, passive and subject to the manipulation of humanity—she saw atoms as self-propelling, intelligent, energized particles, and humanity as part of nature. According to Cavendish, nature was not subject to, but constitutive of, human life; the mind and the body were not distinct; and dominion over nature was an illusion because of the independence of atoms.

Whereas, it was not unusual for women to spend time writing, it was rare for a woman to publish her work, and Cavendish's publications met with opposition from many quarters. In regard to the philosophical content, her work was "at once so extreme and so fanciful that she shocked the enemies of atomism and embarrassed its friends."

> Small Atomes of themselves a World may make,
> As being subtle, and of every shape
> And as they dance about, fit places finde
> Such Formes as best agree make every kinde . . .
> So Atomes, as they dance, find places fit
> They there remaine, lye close and fast will sticke.

Although well aware of her own limitations and addressing her writing to women, Cavendish's work was in no way simplified or soft-handed, but ambitious and boldly directed toward the ideas of the key philosophers of the time, including Descartes, Hobbes, Henry More, and Jan van Helmont. In her early writings, she was careful to apologize for her lack of scholarly background, citing this as a plight of her sex. She ascribed to the notion of women's inborn inferiority: "It cannot be expected I should write so wisely or wittily as men, being of the effeminate sex, whose brains nature has mixed with the coldest and softest elements." Some ridiculed her writing style for its lack of seriousness (she experimented with many forms, including rhyme, plays and oration), while others objected that the ideas and writing could not be her own, given her lack of education. Cavendish protested that her ideas were original, citing her scant exposure to books as evidence that she could not have plagiarized.

Margaret Cavendish later undertook an extensive reading program, having apparently abandoned the idea that the quality of her ideas was unhindered by lack of scholarship. She discarded the Hobbesian system of similar atoms for a hierarchical view of nature, in which different kinds of atoms interact mechanically, a view more in line with those of Descartes and Francis Bacon.

In 1665, William became duke of Newcastle; two years later, he and Margaret traveled to London for an extended stay. While there, Margaret's request to visit the Royal Society to observe science in practice caused a great deal of debate among its members because of her eccentricity and gender. A man of her stature would have had little trouble achieving membership, never mind a visit, but no woman was given full membership in the Society until 1945. Margaret had always enjoyed using fashion as a means of personal expression. With the elevation to the rank of duchess, she began to dress even more flamboyantly, including adopting some of the styles of men, earning the nickname "Queen of *Sheba."

Her mode of dress caused a sensation when she was allowed to visit the Society on May 23, although she remained quiet during the visit. A great performance was put on for her benefit, including demonstrations by Robert Boyle and Robert Hooke, and she reported that she was much impressed. The visit is not mentioned in her memoirs, but it seems to have ended her philosophical work. After this, she published only second and third editions of her writing, attempting nothing new.

Instead, she turned her attentions to the family business. Her influence on her husband became a source of concern for those dependent on him, and they conspired to undermine her sway by convincing William that she was having an affair. They forged a letter, but Margaret was soon able to show the real source. Her husband's trust and love for her continued unabated until her death at age 50, on December 15, 1673. She was buried in Westminster Abbey, and the famous inscription on her tomb declares that she belonged to a family of which "all the brothers were valiant and all the sisters virtuous." In 1676, William published *Letters and Poems in Honor of the Incomparable Princess, Margaret, Duchess of Newcastle.*

SOURCES:

Kersey, Ethel M. *Women Philosophers: a Bio-critical Source Book.* NY: Greenwood Press, 1989.

Mendelson, Sara Heller. *The Mental World of Stuart Women: Three Studies.* Brighton, Sussex, England: Harvester Press, 1987.

Waithe, Mary Ellen, ed. *A History of Women Philosophers, vol. 3.* Boston: Martinus Nijhoff, 1987.

SUGGESTED READING:

Atherton, Margaret. *Women Philosophers of the Early Modern Period.* Indianapolis, IN: Hackett, 1994.

Grant, Douglas. *Margaret the First: a Biography of Margaret Cavendish, Duchess of Newcastle.* Toronto: University of Toronto Press, 1957.

Jones, Kathleen. *A Glorious Fame: The Life of Margaret Cavendish, Duchess of Newcastle, 1623–1673.* London: Bloomsbury, 1988.

Catherine Hundleby, M.A. Philosophy,
University of Guelph

Cavendish, Mary (d. 1632).

See Stuart, Arabella for sidebar on Mary Talbot.

Cavendish-Bentinck, Nina (b. 1870).

See Elizabeth Bowes-Lyon for sidebar.

Cawley, Evonne Goolagong (b. 1951).

See Goolagong, Evonne.

Caylus, Marthe M. (1673–1729)

French writer of memoirs. Pronunciation: KAY-lüs. *Name variations: Marquise or Comtesse de Caylus. Born Marie Marguerite Le Valois de Villette de Murçay in Poitou, France, in 1673; died in Paris on April 15, 1729; niece of Mme de Maintenon (1635–1719); married J.-Anne de Tubières (d. 1704), comte de Caylus, in 1686; children: son Anne Claude Philippe de Tubières, Comte de Caylus (an archaeologist who published* Recueil d'Antiquités Egyptiennes, Étrusques, Grecques, Romaines, et Gauloises *[7 vols. 1752–67]).*

A French woman of fashion and niece of *Mme de Maintenon, the Marquise de Caylus was one of the brilliant wits and social leaders of the court of Louis XIV. Long a fixture of the court, she passed her declining years dictating her famous *Souvenirs* (My Recollections), which contained valuable insight into the life of the king. With additional notes and a preface, they were edited in 1770 by Voltaire who regarded them as masterpieces of candor and wit. Sainte-Beuve assigned to her a distinguished place in his *Portraits of Celebrated Women.*

Ceausescu, Elena (1916–1989)

Rumanian political leader who was co-leader of Rumania for almost two decades along with her hus-

band Nicolae Ceausescu. Name variations: Ceauçescu. Pronunciation: Chaow-u-SESH-coo or Shaow-CHESS-coo. Born Elena Petrescu on January 7, 1916, in the village of Petresti near Scornicesti in the Oltenia region; executed along with husband on December 25, 1989; married Nicolae Ceausescu, president of Rumania (1974–1989), in 1944; children: two sons, Nicolae (popularly known as Nicu, d. 1996) and Valentin (adopted); and daughter Zoia Ceausescu.

Member of central committee of Rumanian Communist Party (1965–89); received numerous Rumanian and foreign decorations and honorary degrees; arrested along with her husband (December 1989); found guilty of several offenses by an improvised political tribunal and executed along with him (December 25, 1989).

One of the most powerful women in Eastern Europe during the final decades of Communist rule, Elena Ceausescu was a key member of a regime of corruption and clan rule that left Rumania with a legacy of economic, social and moral devastation. Unlike many of the Communist leaders of the region who grew up in urban bourgeois homes, she was born into grinding rural poverty on January 7, 1916. Elena Petrescu was a poor student at school, attending classes for only four years and barely becoming literate. Like many thousands of young Rumanians in the 1930s, she moved to the capital city of Bucharest in order to find work and be less of a burden on her impoverished family. Elena found employment as an unskilled worker at Bucharest's Jacquard textile factory, where in 1939 she met a young Communist militant named Nicolae Ceausescu. Two years younger than Elena, he was a slender and handsome young man from a background similar to hers, as he too had been born in an impoverished village. Both were active Communists, and, the year they met, Elena was elected "Queen of Labor" by her politically active fellow workers. Little is know of her activities during the war years, but later, during his trial after the collapse of the Ceausescu regime, her brother-in-law accused her of consorting with German officers, a story that may or may not be true and cannot be corroborated.

The collapse of the pro-German government in Rumania in 1944 and the liberation of the country by Soviet forces presented tremendous career opportunities for the country's small Communist movement. In 1944, Nicolae Ceausescu married Elena Petrescu, but they did not immediately become a political team. Instead, she concentrated on raising a family and advancing her husband's political career. She gave birth

to a son Nicolae (known as Nicu), and a daughter **Zoia Ceausescu**, and in 1946 the Ceausescus also adopted a small boy, Valentin, whose parents could not support him because of a local famine in the province of Moldavia. Determined to play a role in the Communization of Rumania, Elena got a job in the Foreign Ministry in the 1940s, but her performance of her tasks—selecting and clipping foreign newspapers—left much to be desired since her knowledge of foreign languages was rudimentary at best. Although she continued to receive a salary, she often did not show up at work, and her supervisors did not mind her absence in view of the poor quality of her job performance.

Refusing to be discouraged by her ineffectiveness at the Foreign Ministry, Elena Ceausescu attended night classes in chemistry at the University of Bucharest; there was, however, never any evidence that she completed a course of study. Given her scanty educational background (her formal education had ended after four years of dismal performance in primary school), it is unlikely that she acquired much knowledge of chemistry. During the 1950s and 1960s, her husband's political career prospered dramatically, and in March 1965 he effectively became the leading political figure in Rumania with his accession to the post of first secretary of the country's ruling Communist Party. A year earlier, in 1964, Elena had become director of the Central Chemical Research Institute. Although she knew virtually nothing about chemistry, she received a doctoral degree on the basis of a dissertation that had actually been written by members of the institute who had to bow to the formidable political power of the Ceausescus.

At first, the regime of Nicolae Ceausescu gave the impression of taking serious steps toward political and economic liberalization. The United States and other Western nations were pleased by what appeared to be Rumania's relative independence of the Soviet Union, which included endorsement of the idea of polycentrism in the Communist world and refusal to participate in such Moscow-dominated policies as the 1968 invasion of Czechoslovakia to crush a liberal Communist movement in the bud. Nicolae enjoyed considerable popularity as well with his own people during these years. Although they lacked political freedom, Rumanians could look forward to lives centered around economic security and modest increases in their standard of living, which were in most cases significantly higher than those of the pre-1945 era for average workers and farmers. For many Rumanians during these years, Nicolae Ceausescu was a national hero, bringing international respect as well as domestic prosperity to his nation.

By the early 1970s, however, there were increasingly negative forces at work, not the least of which involved the growing megalomania of both Nicolae and Elena Ceausescu. Elena was sharing power with her husband by this time and, flushed with success, the couple became increasingly convinced that they could do no wrong. On a trip to the Far East in May 1971, a glimpse of the Chinese Communist and North Korean dictatorships clearly whetted their appetites for power. Elena was strongly impressed by the example of *Jiang Qing, Mao Zedong's widow. On their return to Rumania, a personality cult was increasingly imposed on Rumania. Nicolae became known as the Conducator, supreme leader, and was praised to the sky by sycophants in the party and media. Elena, too, was the object of ever-increasing flattery by craven journalists and court poets, one of which, Virgil Teodorescu, composed a dithyramb praising her:

> Her face is lit up by eyes that look far into the
>   distance
> Being a beautiful gift of diligent nature,
> And the gentle energy radiating from her features,
> Is a perpetual model for the arts.

In addition to the personality cult, the Ceausescus imposed a clan oligarchy on Rumania in which over 30 members of Nicolae and Elena's families received titles and perquisites of power. These individuals included Elena's son Nicu, who by 1982 had become a candidate member of the ruling political executive committee of the central committee of the Communist Party. Daughter Zoia, with a doctorate in mathematics, quickly advanced to the post of secretary general of the Communist Party. Adopted son Valentin remained largely aloof from politics, becoming a student of nuclear physics. Elena's brother Gheorghe Petrescu, on the other hand, served for two decades until his death in 1987 on the central committee of the Communist Party as well as on numerous other government ministries and councils, thus becoming entitled to luxurious living quarters and other material rewards the Rumanian masses could only dream of. The boundless corruption of the family resulted in the awarding of high state posts to Nicolae's brothers Florea, Ilie, Ion, Nicolae Andruta and Marin. Large sums of money—perhaps totaling as much as $1 billion—were believed to have been deposited in Swiss and other foreign banks by the Ceausescu clan during the decades they dominated Rumania.

Elena Ceausescu's power increased dramatically in the early 1970s, particularly after she became a member of the ruling political executive committee of the party's central committee in June 1973. From this point on, it can be said that along with her husband she was co-ruler of Rumania. Elena became virtual dictator of Rumania's scientific community in 1979 when she received the post of president of the National Council for Science and Technology. In March 1980, her power received full public recognition when she was appointed a first deputy prime minister. Numerous other posts bestowed on her and her family simply ratified an already existing power reality, namely that the Ceausescu clan had total domination over Rumania, an arrangement that proved tremendously rewarding, materially as well as psychologically, to a small but insatiably greedy oligarchy. Ordinary members of the Communist Party received far fewer perks, mainly in the area of preferential treatment with housing and certain food staples. The key to the regime's hold on power was the Securitate, a massive system of secret police and informers whose eyes and ears kept the population frightened, fragmented and submissive.

The Ceausescus lived in one of Bucharest's elite neighborhoods in the Villa Primavera, a handsome 40-room building set among fir trees. Inside, however, the visitor was overwhelmed with an excess of silver, porcelain and crystal chandeliers. Furniture was gilded, elaborately carved and inlaid, the wallpaper was silk, and the bathrooms glittered with exquisite marble and gold fixtures. The couple's elaborate and huge closets bulged with a great excess of clothing. Elena owned hundreds of pairs of expensive shoes, some with diamond-encrusted heels designed by Charles Jourdan; several of her closets contained dozens of couture gowns and mink coats. A large number of palaces throughout the country, 21 in all, formerly owned by the royal family of Rumania were reserved for Nicolae and Elena. There were also 41 residential villas and 20 hunting lodges that were maintained for the exclusive use of the Ceausescu clan and their guests. Unlike some other Communist states, where the luxuries enjoyed by the ruling elites was kept secret, in Rumania the sumptuous lifestyle of the Ceausescus was regularly presented to the public through the media to create an image of uncrowned royalty. Toward the end of his regime, Nicolae, who sometimes appeared at state ceremonies with scepter in hand, was granted among other titles that of "Genius of the Carpathians."

While the Ceausescus lived in ostentatious luxury, the ordinary Rumanians sank inexorably into a nightmare world of increasing hardships and privation. By the early 1980s, with the regime's decision to rapidly repay Rumania's huge foreign debt, harsh austerity measures were imposed on the nation. The suffering of the Rumanian populace had become almost intolerable by the time of the unusually harsh winter of 1985. Only one room per residence could be lit at night and the use of household electrical appliances was banned. Home heating was cut to 39–48 degrees Fahrenheit while burst water pipes left entire apartment buildings without water for weeks at a time. To add to the general misery, the driving of both private cars and taxis was banned in order to cut back on domestic petroleum consumption. All restaurants were ordered to close by 6:00 PM every night and television use was limited to two hours daily. In contrast to these privations, the regime went ahead with vast projects designed to radically change the face of Rumania. Central to these plans were industrial projects reminiscent of the Soviet Stalin era; in addition to being environmentally destructive, the new industries became increasingly inefficient, creating products for which there was no world market.

The immensely vain Elena Ceausescu, determined to be accepted both at home and abroad as nothing less than a world-class scientist, brought about the virtual destruction of the Rumanian Academy of Sciences. During the Ceausescu era, the Academy lost control of all the 50 institutes originally under its jurisdiction. By 1989, the Academy's normal membership of 230 had evaporated to a total of only 93 cowed and submissive members with an average age of over 70; for more than a decade, Elena had refused to allow the election of new members. The Academy's scientific work was crippled because the Academy was denied the foreign currency needed to subscribe to foreign scientific journals and retain membership in international scientific organizations and academies. To the end of her life, Elena Ceausescu maintained her pose as a distinguished chemist when accompanying her husband on his foreign trips, and, amazingly, foreign scientific academies and universities responded to her craving for academic respectability by bestowing on her a vast number of honorary degrees, awards and memberships. In many cases, a combination of Cold War pressures (the belief that Rumania deserved to be rewarded for its independence of Moscow), lack of moral spine and plain ignorance were responsible for such behavior on the part of respected institutions of learning.

Determined to retain power as long as possible, Elena and Nicolae Ceausescu watched their weight carefully as they grew older and took other steps designed to preserve and enhance their health. The menus at the Villa Primavera recorded the calorie count of each of their five daily meals. Elena and her husband were convinced that organically produced food would ensure them long and healthy lives. The Ceausescus also employed a foodtaster to guard against poisoning by their political enemies. Their palatial Villa Neptune on the Black Sea featured a swimming pool inlaid with fine mosaics, a sauna, massage showers, and a plenitude of bathroom scales, testifying to a belief that with the passage of time they could hold onto both their health and power. As they grew older, however, factions within the Communist upper ruling elite began to hatch plots for the removal of the Ceausescu clan from power.

Increasingly isolated from their own people, Elena and Nicolae Ceausescu lived in this fantasy world through the 1980s. The economic life of the country was in a shambles. A plan of economic and social "systematization" destroyed much of the country's village life. Huge building projects in Bucharest resulted in the destruction of many historic buildings in order to create vast spaces on which to build some of the largest buildings in the world, including a "House of the People" meant to serve as a presidential palace, as well as a "House of Science"; the latter would presumably have provided office space for Elena Ceausescu, who preferred to be addressed as "Comrade Academician Doctor Engineer."

By 1989, the regime was in a profound crisis. The Ceausescus probably could have held on to power in a stable environment, but the mood of that year was a revolutionary one. The peaceful transfer of power by the Communists in Poland during the summer of that year, the upheaval in East Germany in October and the opening up of the Berlin Wall in early November should have made clear to the Ceausescus how precarious their power was, but they did not heed the warnings. A Communist Party congress in November ritualistically reaffirmed Nicolae's dictatorship and Elena continued to control the scientific and cultural life of an exhausted nation. The collapse came suddenly. During Nicolae's ill-advised state visit to Iran, long festering minority problems erupted when many thousands of the oppressed Hungarian minority demonstrated for cultural autonomy and freer conditions. The Securitate forces, with the approval of Elena and her son Nicu, responded by savagely attacking the demonstrators. Hundreds of dead and wounded resulted from this bloody massacre, which pushed the patience of the populace to the breaking point.

Initially, it appeared that the regime would survive on the basis of terror and the vastly superior power it possessed in the Securitate and armed forces. But when a huge rally in Bucharest on December 21 designed to show public support for the regime turned into an anti-Ceausescu demonstration, Nicolae and Elena lost their nerve and fled the capital by helicopter. Betrayed, they were captured on the morning of December 22. The new government, which called itself the National Salvation Front, at first announced that there would be a public trial of the couple but then quickly reneged on its promise. A secret trial held at Tirgoviste north of Bucharest on Christmas day, December 25, 1989, resulted in a death penalty for both Nicolae and Elena Ceausescu, who were found guilty on ill-specified charges of "genocide against the Rumanian people." At the trial, which was videotaped, Elena denied charges of corruption. When it became clear to her that she and her husband were to be executed, she screamed "Don't tie us up!" and as three paratroopers approached to tie her hands behind her back she said, "Children, I brought you up and raised you. Stop, my boy, you're hurting me." Her husband struggled briefly with the soldiers but said nothing as tears rolled down his cheeks. It appears that the Ceausescus were thereupon executed.

Various stories surfaced in the world press after the execution of the Ceausescus on Christmas day, 1989. The official line taken by the National Liberation Front was that the execution had to be carried out immediately after the trial's conclusion because of a serious threat from Securitate forces who, refusing to lay down their arms, might have attempted to liberate the Ceausescus and restore them to power. Later, however, it became clear that Securitate resistance had been no more than sporadic and that dramatic television footage of destruction in Bucharest misrepresented the extent of fighting in the capital. When the National Salvation Front failed to either bring Securitate "terrorists" to trial or indeed even mention them again, many grew suspicious about the circumstances surrounding the death of the Ceausescus. The question now was not whether their regime had been corrupt and repressive but whether the new Rumanian government had eliminated the hated Ceausescu clan in a planned coup d'etat, rather than as the result of a spontaneous mass uprising, and was thus in fact little more than a thinly veiled continuation of the old Communist order.

Both the nature and actions of the tribunal became increasingly suspicious in March 1990, when its presiding officer, Major General Gica Popa, shot himself in the heart; the official cause given was "a severe nervous breakdown," but not until his unexpected suicide had Popa or any of the other members of the tribunal been publicly identified as having served on it. The growing suspicions about what took place on Christmas day, 1989, gained support in April 1990, when French television broadcast both the official as well as pirated versions of the trial and execution of the Ceausescus. Major discrepancies between the two versions made it clear that several questions about the trial and execution needed to be answered by the new Rumanian government. Among them was the issue of Victor Stanculescu, one of the members of the 10-man military tribunal, who was a former Securitate general. Stanculescu admitted in 1990 that he had promised the Ceausescus a helicopter to carry them away to safety when he in fact delivered them to the hastily assembled tribunal. The behavior of both Nicolae and Elena on the trial tape makes it appear likely that reports that they had been told that the trial was a formality and after its conclusion they would be able to return to Bucharest were correct, for not until the announcement of the death verdict did they panic and cease their defiance of the tribunal.

Finally, French forensic pathologists who viewed the pirated tape noted that as soon as the dust from what appeared to have been the Ceausescus' execution had settled, military doctors appeared on the scene to be certain death had occurred. On the official tape, Elena lay over a stream of blood, yet when a doctor lifts her head it is stiff with no running blood; also, the blood on her head and on the ground could clearly be seen to have coagulated. Rigor mortis had set, suggesting that when the tape was made she had already been dead four or five hours. In contrast, Nicolae's body was less rigid and his head bobbed when lifted by the doctors; like his wife, no blood trickled from his head wounds. Experts concluded on the basis of this evidence that he was killed well after his wife. In other words, there was compelling evidence that the official Rumanian tape of the execution was a fabrication, and that both Ceausescus had been killed well before their official "execution," then their bodies were propped against the wall some hours later at which point soldiers were ordered to fire on them. The French report prompted a series of vehement denials from a representative of the state-controlled Rumanian television network, who told the Paris newspaper *Libération*, "the place was surrounded by Securitate who wanted to free them." Having earlier been told many different versions of the trial and execution, few chose to believe this latest Rumanian spin on an increasingly elusive truth.

In death as in life, Elena Ceausescu remained linked to a system of lies, corruption and deception. Even her final hours remained a mystery. The Ceausescus left a profoundly negative legacy to their people, a society of material impoverishment and a political culture that was morally depleted and spiritually devastated. The dynastic neo-Stalinism imposed by the Ceausescu clan had paralyzed an entire nation's civil society and traumatized its populace by the irrational sacrifices imposed during the Ceausescu era. Burdened by its history, as the 20th century came to an end Rumania faced immense difficulties as it attempted to meet the challenges of political freedom, economic competition and individual moral responsibility.

Maria Cebotari

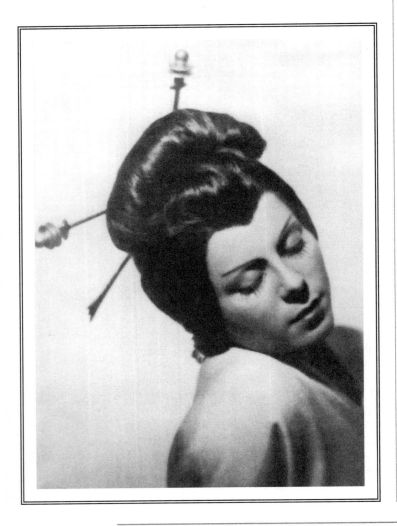

SOURCES:

Almond, Mark. *Decline without Fall: Romania under Ceausescu.* London: Alliance Publishers/Institute for European Defence & Strategic Studies, 1988.

———. *The Rise and Fall of Nicolae and Elena Ceausescu.* London: Chapmans, 1992.

Behr, Edward. *Kiss the Hand You Cannot Bite: The Rise and Fall of the Ceausescus.* NY: Villard Books, 1991.

Binder, David. "Bucharest Seizes Communist Assets," in *The New York Times.* January 19, 1990, p. 6.

Calinescu, Matei, and Vladimir Tismaneanu. "The 1989 Revolution and Romania's Future," in *Problems of Communism.* Vol. 40, no. 1. January–April 1991, pp. 42–59.

Clogg, Richard. "Let us now praise a famous woman," in *New Scientist.* Vol. 125, no. 1700. January 20, 1990, pp. 65–66.

"Executions called fake, Ceausescus dead when shot, forensic experts say," in *Baltimore Sun.* April 30, 1990, p. 12.

Fischer, Mary Ellen. *Nicolae Ceausescu: A Study in Political Leadership.* Boulder, CO: Lynne Rienner, 1989.

Frankland, Mark. *The Patriots' Revolution: How Eastern Europe Won Its Freedom.* London: Sinclair-Stevenson, 1990.

Galloway, George. *Downfall: The Ceausescus and the Romanian Revolution.* London: Macdonald Futura, 1991.

Held, Joseph. *Dictionary of East European History Since 1945.* Westport, CT: Greenwood Press, 1994.

"The Hole in the Map," in *The Economist.* Vol. 312, no. 7615. August 12, 1989, Eastern Europe Survey, p. 15.

"In Honor of Elena Ceausescu, D. Chem. Eng., Member of the Academy of the Socialist Republic of Romania," in *Revue Roumaine de Chimie.* Vol. 34, no. 7. July 1989, pp. I–VII.

Kaplan, Robert D. *Balkan Ghosts: A Journey Through History.* NY: St. Martin's Press, 1993.

Kligman, Gail. "The Politics of Reproduction in Ceausescu's Romania: A Case Study in Political Culture," in *East European Politics and Society.* Vol. 6, no. 3, 1992, pp. 364–418.

Ratesh, Nestor. *Romania: The Entangled Revolution.* NY: Frederick A. Praeger, 1991.

Sweeney, John. *The Life and Evil Times of Nicolae Ceausescu.* London: Hutchinson, 1991.

Tanner, Marcus. "Life on the baby-farm," in *People* [London]. Vol. 16, no. 3, 1989, pp. 10–12.

RELATED MEDIA:

"Romania: The Damned Dynasty," video cassette, Derry, NH: Chip Taylor Communications, 1992.

John Haag, Associate Professor,
University of Georgia, Athens, Georgia

Cebotari, Maria (1910–1949)

Bessarabian soprano. Born Maria Cebotari in Kishinev, Bessarabia, Russia, on February 10, 1910; died on June 9, 1949, in Vienna, Austria; married Count Alexander Virubov (divorced 1938); married Gustav Diessl (a film actor); studied at the Kishinev Conservatory (1924–29) and at the Hochschule für Musik in Berlin with Oskar Daniel.

Made debut at the Dresden Staatsoper as Mimi (1931) and sang there until 1936; appeared at Covent Garden (1936 and 1947); appeared in Berlin (1936–44) and in Vienna (1946–49); appeared in six films between 1933 and 1941.

Maria Cebotari was born in Kishinev, Bessarabia, Russia, on February 10, 1910. She sang in a church choir and then studied at the Kishinev Conservatory from 1924 until 1929. Joining a troupe of itinerant Russian actors who visited her small town, Cebotari later married the troupe's leader. She made her operatic debut in Paris and then studied in Berlin, joining the Dresden Opera in 1931. Although she performed in Germany, Austria, Switzerland, Italy, France, and Rumania, Cebotari never appeared in the United States because of the outbreak of World War II. She specialized in the music of Richard Strauss, Mozart, Verdi, and Puccini and sang many Russian operas. In addition to appearing in six films, Cebotari made many recordings. In the early 1970s, BASF re-released many radio tapes on which she could be heard. Her commercial recordings continue to reappear with great regularity despite her untimely death at the early age of 39 on June 9, 1949.

SUGGESTED READING:

Mingotti, A. *Maria Cebotari*. Salzburg, 1950.

John Haag,
Athens, Georgia

Cecchi D'Amico, Suso (1914—)

Italian screenwriter. Born in Rome, Italy, in 1914; daughter of Emilio Cecchi (1884–1966), producer, writer, director; married Fedele D'Amico (a music critic).

Filmography: Ladri di biciclette (Bicycle Thief, 1948); Miracoloe a Milano (Miracle in Milan, 1950); Bellissima (1951); I vinti (The Vanquished, 1952); Siamo donne (We the Women, 1953); La signora senza camelie (Camille Without Camellias, 1953); Tempi Nostri (Anatomy of Love, 1953); Senso (1954); Peccato che sia una canaglia (Too Bad She Is Bad, 1955); Le amiche (The Girl Friend, 1955); Le notti biache (White Nights, 1957); La sfida (The Challenge, 1958); I magliari (1959); Rocco e i suoi (Rocco and His Brothers, 1960); Il lavoro (The Job, 1962); Salvatore Giuliano (1962); Il Gattopardo (The Leopard, 1963); Taming of the Shrew (adaptation, 1964); Gli indifferenti (Time of Indifference, 1964); Vaghe stelle dell'Orsa (Sandra, 1965); Lo Straniero (The Stranger, 1967); Ludwig (1974); Cruppo di famiglia in un interno (Conversation Piece, 1974); L'innnocente (The Innocent, 1976); La Slovia (The Story, 1986); Oci ciornie (Dark Eyes, 1987).

Considered Italy's most distinguished screenwriter, Cecchi D'Amico received a classical education in which she specialized in languages, launching her career as a translator of plays. After the Second World War, she started to write screenplays, beginning with a collaboration with her father, the distinguished Emilio Cecchi, for director Renato Castellani's film *Mio figlio professore* (*Professor, My Son*). A second project in 1946, a collaboration with Luigi Zampa on *Vivere in pace* (*To Live in Peace*), brought her a Silver Ribbon (Italy's equivalent to an Academy Award).

In 1948, Cecchi D'Amico wrote the classic Italian neo-realist film called *Ladri di biciclette* (*Bicycle Thief*) for Italian auteur Vittorio De Sica. She became a writer most associated with neo-realism, the film genre that emerged from postwar Italy, as did directors De Sica, Roberto Rossellini (*Open City*) and Luchino Visconti (*The Earth Trembles*). Most notable among this film style's definable characteristics is the preference for location shooting and non-professional actors. The subjects concern matters of everyday, middle-class life with themes that express a hopefulness (attributed to the defeat of Fascism) tempered with a certain disillusionment.

Widely considered the perfect example of neo-realism, *Bicycle Thief* is a standard in film schools where it is used to typify the genre. The film, shot in the back alleys of postwar Rome among the working class and the poor, is the moving story of a poor man's (Ricci) struggle for survival. Ricci is offered a job on the condition that he supply his own bicycle. His hopes for employment, however, are dashed when his bicycle is stolen. While the filmmakers follow Ricci's desperate search for his bicycle, his moving relationship with his young son is revealed. In the end, Ricci is met with defeat. In the final shot, he takes his son by the hand and the two disappear into a crowd of their peers, the recently liberated people of Rome, who, released from their suffering under Fascism, are now victimized by poverty. Considered a classic, *Bicycle Thief* won the American Academy Award for Best Foreign Film in 1949.

Along with De Sica, Cecchi D'Amico has had many long-standing collaborations with the great Italian directors of the day, including Franco Zefferelli and Michelangelo Antonioni. The relationship most satisfying to her, and for which she is most known, has been with Luchino Visconti. From *Bellissima*, starring *Anna

Magnani (1951), to *The Innocent* (1976), Cecchi D'Amico was Visconti's most important collaborator.

Unlike some dramatic writers, Cecchi D'Amico has also written social satire and comedy, and she has worked in television. In 1989, she collaborated with director Nikita Mikhalov on the film *Dark Eyes* for which its star, Marcello Mastroianni, won the Best Actor award at the prestigious Cannes Film Festival.

SOURCES:
Bergan, Ronald, and Robin Karney, eds. *The Holt Foreign Film Guide.* NY: Henry Holt, 1988.

Konigsberg, Ira. *The Complete Film Dictionary.* NY: Penguin Books, 1987.

Kuhn, Annette, and Susannah Radstone, eds. *The Women's Companion to International Film.* Los Angeles, CA: University of California Press, 1990.

Vincendeau, Ginette, ed. *Encyclopedia of European Cinema.* London: Cassell Press and the British Film Institute, 1995.

Deborah Jones,
Studio City, California

Cecilia (c. 154–c. 207)

Christian martyr, patron saint of music, and legendary inventor of the pipe organ. Born in Rome;

From the movie Bicycle Thief, screenplay by Suso Cecchi D'Amico, 1948.

conflicting dates of birth are around 154 or 177 or 207 CE; conflicting dates of death are around 177 or 200 or 230 CE; any of the three sets of dates yields a lifespan of 23 years; member of a noble Roman family; martyred for her faith.

Cecilia's status as the patron saint of music is somewhat ironic as, from the 5th century, obstacles were placed in women's path in the performing and composing of music. The church, for example, preferred male sopranos to female, and each year thousands of young boys in Europe, particularly in Italy, were castrated so that they would retain their soprano voices. These male sopranos not only performed church liturgy but also appeared on stage where they became wildly popular as opera stars. Much of the vocal music written by Handel, Haydn, and Mozart was written for male sopranos. Only in the 18th century were women allowed to perform, and finally by the middle of the 19th century castration of young male singers stopped. Women were also prohibited from playing certain instruments. In Sweden, for example, they were not allowed to play the pipe organ until the 19th century. These restrictions and prohibitions continued in orchestras where female players were not allowed (the Vienna Philharmonic Orchestra continued to be an all-male institution throughout the 20th century). In the 1920s and 1930s in Europe and America, all-women orchestras were created until major symphony orchestras were finally integrated. Once women insisted that all auditions be held behind curtains so the judges could not determine their sex, their talent placed them in symphonies of first rank. Throughout the centuries of discrimination, St. Cecilia remained the patron saint of music.

Where the facts of St. Cecilia's life are unknown, only legend exists. The accepted legend is that she was a member of a noble Roman family. It is said Cecilia converted her home into a church where some 400 converts were baptized. Compelled to violate her vows of celibacy, Cecilia was forced to marry the pagan Valerianus, a Roman noble. Eventually, she converted both him and his brother Tiburtius to Christianity. When Valerianus and Tiburtius refused to make a sacrifice to Jupiter, they were executed. Like her husband, Cecilia was given the choice of a sacrifice to the gods or death. She chose death, but two attempts to execute her, by suffocation and beheading, miraculously failed before the penalty was carried out. Her body is said to have been buried in the 4th-century church of St. Cecilia in Trastevere. A cypress coffin was opened in that church in 1599 and found to contain the

bones of a young woman, which were identified as Cecilia's. She was canonized in the 16th century. Many paintings show her playing the organ, the viola, the pedal harp, the clavichord, the virginal spinet, and the viol. She lent respectability to music, which was originally condemned by the church as being frivolous and degrading. Composers from the time of Henry Purcell in the 17th century composed works in her honor, and many academies and schools of music bore her name although she was never identified as having been a composer. Her feast day is November 22.

It is a mystery why the church continued to identify St. Cecilia as the patron saint of music while at the same time going to great lengths to keep women from contributing to this important field of human endeavor. In retrospect, however, her elevation seems only just, as women continued to create music and foster the field's growth despite discrimination.

John Haag,
Athens, Georgia

*C*ecilia
(c.154–c.207)

Cecilia (c. 1059–1126).

See Matilda of Flanders for sidebar.

Cecilia (1469–1507)

English princess. Name variations: Cecily Planta-genet. Born Cecilia on March 20, 1469; died on August 24, 1507, at Quarr Abbey, Isle of Wight, England; third daughter of Edward IV, king of England, and Elizabeth Woodville; betrothed to James IV, king of Scots, 1474; betrothed to Alexander Stewart, 1st duke of Albany, 1482; married John Welles, 1st viscount Welles, in December 1487; married Thomas Kymbe or Kyne, of the Isle of Wight, in 1502; children: (first marriage) two; (second marriage) two.

The daughter of Edward IV, king of England, and **Elizabeth Woodville**, Cecilia became a pawn in England's struggles with Scotland and the War of the Roses. To secure an alliance with Scotland in 1474, she was betrothed as a five-year-old to the future James IV, son of James III, king of Scots. In 1482, she was 13 years old when she was betrothed to James IV's brother, Alexander Stewart, 1st duke of Albany. Following the death of her father the king in 1483, Cecilia's 13-year-old brother Edward V became king, though his uncle, Richard, duke of Gloucester, had other plans. By force, he became the young king's protector and eventually usurped the throne as Richard III. Fearing for her children's lives, Elizabeth Woodville fled the palace and sought sanctuary in Westminster Abbey—accompanied by her son Richard, duke of York, Cecilia, and her other daughters. But Richard III soon sent both of Cecilia's brothers to the Tower of London; the fate of young Richard and Edward is still unknown. In 1484, Cecilia surrendered to her uncle. In 1486, she was "taken into favor" by Richard's successor, Henry VII, and married John Welles, 1st viscount Welles, in December 1487.

Cecilia of Baden (1839–1891)

Princess of Baden. Name variations: Cecily of Baden; Cecily Augusta Zahringen; after marriage became Olga Feodorovna. Born Cecilia Augusta on September 20, 1839; died on April 12, 1891; daughter of Leopold, grand duke of Baden, and Sophia of Sweden (1801–1875); married Michael Nicholaevitch (son of Nicholas I of Russia and Charlotte of Prussia), on August 16, 1857; children: Nicholas (1859–1919); Anastasia Romanova (1860–1922), who married Frederick Francis III, grand duke of Mecklenburg-Schwerin); Michael (1861–1929);

George (1863–1919); Alexander (1866–1933); Sergius (1869–1918); Alexi (b. 1875).

Cecilia of France (fl. 1100s)

*Princess of Antioch. Name variations: Cecilia Capet. Flourished in the 1100s; daughter of *Bertrada of Montfort (d. after 1117) and Philip I the Fair (1052–1108), king of France (r. 1060–1108); married Tancred, prince of Antioch (r. 1111–1112).*

Cecilia of Mecklenburg-Schwerin (1886–1954)

*Duchess of Mecklenburg. Name variations: Cecily von Mecklenburg-Schwerin. Born on September 20, 1886, in Schwerin, Germany; died on May 6, 1954, in Bad Kissingen, Germany; daughter of *Anastasia Romanova (1860–1922), and Frederick Francis III, grand duke of Mecklenburg-Schwerin; married William or Wilhelm also known as Frederick William (1882–1951), crown prince of Prussia, on June 6, 1905; children: William Frederick (1906–1940, who married Dorothea de Salviati); Prince Louis Ferdinand of Prussia (1907–1994, who married *Kira of Russia); Hubert (1909–1950, who married Magdalene Pauline, Princess Reuss); Frederick (1911–1966, who married Brigid, Lady Guinness); Alexandrine Irene (1915–1980), princess of Prussia; Cecilia (1917–1975), princess of Prussia (who married Captain Clyde Kenneth Harris).*

Cecilia Renata of Austria (1611–1644)

*Queen of Poland. Name variations: Cecilia Renata of Hungary; Cecilie Renate; Cecily Habsburg or Hapsburg; Cacilia Renata. Born on July 16, 1611, in Graz; died on March 24, 1644, in Vilna; daughter of Ferdinand II (1578–1637), king of Bohemia and Hungary and Holy Roman emperor (r. 1619–1637), and *Maria Anna of Bavaria (1574–1616); sister of Ferdinand III (r. 1637–1657); became first wife of Wladyslaw also known as Ladislas IV (1595–1648), king of Poland (r. 1632–1648), tsar of Russia (1610–1634), on September 13, 1637; children: Casimir Sigismund (b. 1640).*

Cecily.

Variant of Cecilia.

Cecily Neville (1415–1495).

See Neville, Cecily.

Celeste, Madame (1815–1882)

French dancer and actress. Name variations: Mme Célesté; Celeste-Elliott. Born in Paris, France, on August 16, 1815 (some sources cite 1814); died in Paris on February 12, 1882; trained in Paris; married a Mr. Elliott in America.

As a little girl, Madame Celeste was a pupil in the ballet class at the Paris Opéra. At 15, she had an offer from America and made her debut at the Bowery Theatre in New York City. Returning to England in 1831, she appeared at Liverpool as Fenella in *Masaniello*, and also in London. When she appeared again in America in 1834, Celeste aroused such enthusiasm that her admirers carried her on their shoulders and unharnessed the horses from her carriage in order to pull it themselves. It is even said that President Andrew Jackson introduced her to his Cabinet as an adopted citizen of the Union. Having made a large fortune, Mme Celeste returned to England in 1837. She gave up dancing and now appeared as an actress, first at Drury Lane and then at the Haymarket. In 1844, she joined Benjamin Webster in the management of the Adelphi and afterwards took over the sole management of the Lyceum until 1861. After a third visit to the United States from 1865 to 1868, she retired in 1870.

Cenci, Beatrice (1577–1599).

See Beatrice of Cenci.

Centlivre, Susanna (c. 1669–1723)

Successful British playwright whose major comedies became stock pieces of the English theater throughout the 18th century. Name variations: Susan Centlivre; Susanna Carroll; (pseudonym) R.M. Born Susan Freeman around 1669 (some sources cite 1667), probably in Whaplode, England; died on December 1, 1723, in London; probably daughter of William and Anne Freeman; possibly married to "nephew of Sir Stephen Fox," date unknown, widowed; married to a Mr. Carroll, date unknown, widowed; married Joseph Centlivre, on April 23, 1707.

Plays: The Perjur'd Husband, or, The Adventures of Venice *(1700);* The Beau's Duel: or, A Soldier for the Ladies *(1702);* The Stolen Heiress; or, The Salamanca Doctor Outplotted *(1702);* Love's Contrivance, or, Le Médecin Malgré Lui *(1703);* The Gamester *(1705);* The Bassett Table *(1705);* Love at a Venture *(1706);* The Platonick Lady *(1706);* The Busy Body *(1709);* The Man's Bewitched: or, The Devil to Do About Her *(1709);* A Bickerstaff's Burying: or, Work for the Upholders *(1710);* Marplot: or, The Second Part of The Busy Body *(1710);* The Perplexed Lovers *(1712);* The Wonder: A Woman Keeps a Secret *(1714);* A Gotham Election *(1715);* A Wife Well Managed *(1715);* The Cruel Gift: or The Royal Resentment *(1716);* A Bold Stroke for a Wife *(1718);* The Artifice *(1722).*

Madame Celeste

The beginning of the 18th century in England was a period of political and artistic transition. The bawdy years of the Restoration, after Charles II ascended to the throne of England, encouraged extravagant behavior and artistic license. After the repressive days of the Commonwealth under Cromwell, the British theater saw its first actresses grace the stage, and a growing number of rivaling theaters caused the king to issue two royal patents, one to Drury Lane and the other to Lincoln's Inn Fields. The plays of the Restoration were filled with sexual innuendo and lewd behavior that mirrored the society of Charles II's reign. However, with his death in 1685, and the succession of his son James II, the climate in England began to change. James II, who had hoped to establish an absolute monarchy and return the country to Catholicism, reigned until 1688 when he was forced to flee to France. When James finally had a male heir, "Bonnie Prince Charlie," the people, fearing a Catholic takeover, entreated William III of Orange (Holland), a devout Protestant and husband of James II's daughter, *Mary II (1662–1694)*, to become king of England. William's arrival, and the departure of James II, secured Parliamentary rule in England and the hopes of a Protestant country. The reign of William and Mary and the subsequent rule of *Anne*, Mary's sister, from 1702–1714, saw a change in society. The bawdiness of the Restoration gave way to a greater sense of decorum. The new middle-class audience preferred farce, comedy of manners and intrigue. The "celebrated Mrs. Centlivre" gained her reputation as a playwright of worth in this climate of change. She has been acclaimed as one of the best comic playwrights of her age. Of the 19 plays that she

Susanna
Centlivre

wrote, four became stock pieces: *The Gamester, The Busy Body, The Wonder: A Woman Keeps a Secret,* and *A Bold Stroke for a Wife.* These comedies continued to be staged in England and the United States throughout the 18th and 19th centuries.

While Susanna Centlivre's literary career is easily documented, the early years of her life remain somewhat obscure. Several accounts of her birth and youthful years have been recorded, but there is uncertainty as to the factual accuracy they represent. **Nancy Cotton**, in *Woman Playwrights in England*, has combined the various accounts into an amusing amalgamation:

> She was precocious, composing a song before she was seven, and self-educated, with a flair for languages, mastering French before she was twelve; nonetheless, she had a wicked stepmother who drove her at the age of fourteen to run away from home with a company of strolling players or, alternatively, with Anthony Hammond, who dressed her in boy's clothes and took her with him to

Cambridge for several months as his lover. At the same time, or shortly thereafter, she married, "or something like it," a nephew of Sir Stephen Fox and was widowed in a year. She then married an army officer named Carroll, who was killed in a duel eighteen months later.

The adventures associated with the young Susanna cannot be proved categorically; what can be assumed, however, is that she was self-educated, read at least one foreign language (French), and that she developed a very independent spirit.

Starting in 1700, when as Susanna Carroll she began publishing epistolary writing, an accounting of her life is more complete. At the turn of the century, fictional letter writing was popular and financially rewarding. Her contributions were published in *Familiar and Courtly Letters Written by Monsieur Voiture* (London, 1700), *Volume II of Voiture's Letters* (London, 1701), and *Letters of Wit, Politicks and Morality* (London, 1701). Once she began writing plays in 1700, she wrote often, as this provided her only means of financial support.

In the first year of the new century, Centlivre published her first play, *The Perjur'd Husband; or, The Adventures of Venice,* which premiered at the Theatre Royal in Drury Lane. This unsuccessful tragicomedy, which failed to be performed a sixth night—the second of two nights that the playwright kept the evening receipts less house expenses—was criticized for several indecorous expressions used in the subplot. In the Preface to the play, which was published subsequent to the first performance, Susanna Carroll defended the language in the piece, insisting that the characters were merely reflecting the manners and morals of London and that, until those were reformed, the stage would continue to follow suit. It is not "reasonable," she wrote, "to expect a Person, whose inclinations are always forming Projects to the Dishonour of her Husband, should deliver her Commands to her Confident in the Words of a Psalm." This entangled love story focused on Count Bassino, a visitor to Venice. Having left his wife Placentia in Turin, he met and fell in love with Aurelia, who was engaged to Alonzo. Aurelia returned Bassino's affection and agreed to marry him, though she did not know that he was already married. Bassino's friend, Armando, tried to dissuade him from pursuing this romance. Placentia, having learned about Aurelia, traveled to Venice. Disguised as a man and unable to stop the relationship, Placentia stabs and kills Aurelia. Bassino, not recognizing Placentia, stabs and kills her. Alonzo enters and stabs Bassino in revenge for his lost Aurelia. Alonzo and Bassino's friend,

Armando, are left to mourn the dead. The unrelated subplot, and the part that offended some critics, dealt with the Pizalto family. The young Lady Pizalto attempts to take a lover, while her older and lecherous husband tries to have an affair with the maid. Disguises and mistaken identities generate considerable humor and form the basis for subsequent comic devices used in Centlivre's more mature work. Although this first attempt at playwriting was not well received, she was not deterred.

Until her first major success in 1705, she experimented with different styles in her quest to find not only what she excelled at, but also what would please the ever changing audiences of London. Because playwriting was her means of financial gain, pleasing the audiences was of major importance. Although it was not a lucrative profession, there were three avenues for financial reward: theatrical benefits, the sale of copyright, and patronage. F.P. Lock estimates, in his book *Susanna Centlivre*, that "Centlivre might have grossed anything from 50 to 100 pounds from those of her early plays that reached a third night and perhaps from 100 to 150 pounds from her more successful later ones. How well she could live on these receipts would depend entirely on how frugal or extravagant she chose to be."

Her next two plays, *The Beau's Duel; or, A Soldier for the Ladies* and *The Stolen Heiress; or, The Salamanca Doctor Outplotted*, both staged in 1702, showed her capabilities in writing "intrigue comedy." Unfortunately, neither piece was particularly successful. Finally, in June of 1703, commercial success came her way with *Love's Contrivance; or, Le Médecin Malgré Lui*. Adapted from several plays by Molière, this series of farcical scenes brought continuous laughter from the audiences. The play was filled with numerous delightful comic roles and was restaged for many years. In fact, the last act was frequently staged on its own as an Afterpiece to the regular theatrical presentations of the evening. In the Preface to the play, she acknowledged that comedies should entertain, not strive to educate the audience: laughter was her goal. She also did not adhere to the classical rules of writing, believing that anything was acceptable as long as it pleased the audience. On this account, given the changing tastes of the populace, she did temper the language and innuendo in her plays, explaining in the Preface: "tho' I did not observe the Rules of Drama, I took peculiar Care to dress my Thoughts in such a modest Stile, that it might not give Offence to any."

Centlivre not only had to contend with the fickle taste of the London audiences with regard to the content of her plays, but she also had to deal with the apparent lack of acceptance of work written by women in general. After the *Perjur'd Husband*, she printed her next plays anonymously. In the Prologue to her second play, *The Beau's Duel*, she refers to "Our Female Author" and for the third play, *The Heiress*, the author is referred to as a man. *Love's Contrivance*, her fourth play and first commercial success, was written by "R.M." Even for her first major success, *The Gamester*, the author was anonymous and subsequent plays were penned "By the Author of the *Gamester*." When *The Platonick Lady* was printed in 1706, she used the Dedication to rail against those who would deny women a place in the literary annals of the English stage: "the Vulgar World . . . think it a proof of their Sense, to dislike every thing that is writ by Women. . . .And why this Wrath against the Womens Works? Perhaps you'll answer, because they meddle with things out of their Sphere: But I say, no; for since the Poet is born, why not a Woman as well as a Man?"

My Bookseller . . . told me, of a Spark that had seen my *Gamester* three or four times, and lik'd it extremely: Having bought one of the Books, ask'd who the Author was; and being told, a Woman, threw down the Book, and put up his Money, saying, he had spent too much after it already, and was sure if the Town had known that, it wou'd never have run ten days. . . . It is such as these that rob us of that which inspires the Poet, Praise.

—Susanna Centlivre, Dedication, *The Platonick Lady*, 1706.

Finally, in 1705, Centlivre found both commercial and artistic success with *The Gamester*, in which she took advantage of the common 18th-century vice of gambling. This play clearly established her reputation for comedy writing. The characters Valere and Angelica are young lovers; Valere is addicted to gambling, and despite Angelica's pleas and his father's entreaties he cannot abandon the sport. He makes and breaks numerous promises, and Angelica repeatedly forgives him. She gives Valere a miniature of herself, warning him that if he loses it he will lose her love as well. Upon discovering that Valere has again broken his promise not to gamble, Angelica disguises herself as a man and encounters him at the gaming tables where, upon losing, he gives the miniature to this apparent stranger in lieu of money. He is so remorseful after handing it over that he vows never to enter a gambling establishment again. Angelica, believing him to be sincere, willingly forgives his past indiscretions. Remaining in the repertoire of London theaters for at least half a century, *The Gamester* saw 75 London productions. The play was particularly popular with audiences because of its local color and Centlivre's command of the gambling lingo of the day.

Her plays were produced with great regularity until 1706, when she left London with a company of traveling players to pursue a short-lived career as an actress. While performing at Windsor, she met Joseph Centlivre, whom she married on April 23, 1707. Joseph, one of the royal cooks for Queen Anne, and previously for William and Mary, had the title of Yeoman of the Mouth; he was a widower with two children. The financial security of this marriage enabled Susanna Centlivre to concentrate on her writing. No longer having to write to provide herself with financial security, she could write to perfect her craft, which she did with great success. The Centlivres resided in Buckingham Court until their deaths.

Although Centlivre wrote a number of other comedies (*The Bassett Table, Love at a Venture, The Platonick Lady*), she did not receive the same critical acclaim that accompanied *The Gamester* until 1709 with *The Busy Body*. This was the first play that she wrote following her marriage to Joseph Centlivre. F.P. Lock cites John Mottley's *A Compleat List of All the English Dramatic Poets,* published in 1747, as asserting that "when it was first offered to the Players, [it] was received very cooly, and it was with great Difficulty, that the Author could prevail upon them to think of acting it." Mottley goes on to report that the play was considered "a silly thing wrote by a Woman, [and] that the Players had no Opinion of it." The opening night audience at The Theatre Royal in Drury Lane was small indeed, but "agreeably surprized" as noted by Mottley; Nancy Cook, in *Women Playwrights in England,* reports that the second night the house was larger and the laughter stronger; for the third night, the Benefit performance for the playwright, the theater was crowded with an appreciative audience. The play was staged for 13 consecutive performances and continued to be staged in London throughout the 18th and well into the 19th centuries. The plot deals with two pairs of lovers, each try-

ing to overcome the obsessive behavior of parents or guardians. Throughout the various plot twists and counterplots, Marplot, a friend and busybody, continually disrupts and almost ruins the plans of Sir George Airy and Miranda, and Charles Gripe and Isabinda. Cook explains that "in his impertinent but good-natured eagerness to discover his friends' secrets, Marplot repeatedly brings the young lovers near to disaster."

For the next five years, Centlivre wrote a number of comedies that achieved limited acclaim: *The Man's Bewitched: or, The Devil to Do about Her; A Bickerstaff's Burying; Marplot;* and *The Perplexed Lovers.* Her next major success was *The Wonder: A Woman Keeps a Secret,* which opened April 27, 1714, at the Theatre Royal in Drury Lane and played six nights. Subsequently, it was restaged at least 232 times in London throughout the 18th century. This much-celebrated comedy of intrigue focuses on two pairs of lovers: Felix and Violante, and Colonel Britton and Isabella. Violante's grandfather has left her a sizeable sum of money in his will; in an attempt to get control of this fortune, Don Pedro, Violante's father, arranges for Violante to enter a nunnery. Since she is in love with Felix, she is opposed to her father's intentions. Felix is Isabella's brother. Their father, Don Lopez, wants Isabella to wed an old but wealthy gentleman. Isabella, in her attempt to avoid this unwanted marriage, decides to run away from home; she jumps from her balcony and is unexpectedly caught by one Colonel Britton. Britton takes her to the safety of a neighbor's home, which happens to be Violante's. Violante agrees to keep Isabella's whereabouts a secret from Don Lopez and Felix, and Isabella and the Colonel soon fall in love. The comedy focuses on Violante's attempts to keep the promise she has made regarding Isabella's whereabouts. This leads to many misunderstandings, particularly between Felix and Violante when Felix becomes convinced that Violante is being unfaithful. Violante is able to parry Felix's accusations and displays tremendous strength of character by keeping a secret and remaining loyal to her friend Isabella. F.P. Lock in his detailed study, *Susanna Centlivre,* writes: "Love and friendship are often at odds in the play. Centlivre uses the conflict to challenge the idea that friendship is a peculiarly male virtue. Violante's ability to keep the secret, to put Isabella's interests before her love for Felix, shows considerable strength of character: more than Felix shows when he is placed in difficult circumstances."

The outright sale of Centlivre's plays generated income as did gifts from well-to-do patrons.

Because she was an ardent Whig, one whose loyalty to Parliamentary rule and a Protestant succession never wavered, favor was bestowed upon her. For example, after George I was crowned king of England, her support for the Hanoverian rule was rewarded when the prince of Wales commanded a performance of *The Wonder* on December 16, 1714. F.P. Lock reports: "in 1717, the prince commanded performances of *The Cruel Gift* (May 3) and of *The Busy Body* (October 23). On March 17, 1720, the king himself commanded a performance of *The Busy Body* for the author's benefit."

The next two pieces that Centlivre wrote, both in 1715, were satirical farces that were not produced in her lifetime. *A Gotham Election* looks at the Tory corruption in a local election, and *A Wife Well Managed* makes fun of Catholicism through the activities of a less than pious priest. Given the political situation at the time, it is not surprising that the Master of Revels, who was charged with licensing all theatrics, would not approve of *A Gotham Election*. Centlivre didn't even submit *A Wife Well Managed*. With George I's ascension to the throne of England, the cries of the Jacobites to reinstate James III and Catholicism to England were tempered. When the Jacobite rebellion flared in 1715, political references became unwelcome on the stage.

The last years of Centlivre's writing career included three full-length plays: *The Cruel Gift* (1716), *A Bold Stroke for a Wife* (1718), and *The Artifice* (1722). Of these, *A Bold Stroke for a Wife* was deemed a comic success when it was produced at Lincoln's Inn Fields on February 3, 1718, running for six nights. It was repeated throughout the 18th century for 236 London performances. Instead of the usual dual pair of lovers, this piece centers on the adventures of Colonel Fainwell in his attempt to marry Anne Lovely. Before the vows can be said, he must get the permission of four different and difficult-to-please guardians—"an old beau," "a kind of silly virtuoso," "a changebroker," and "a Quaker [hosier]." The lengths to which the Colonel must resort in order to convince these gentlemen resulted in a comedy that pleased audiences well into the 19th century.

Centlivre wrote during a time when few writers, either male or female, were able to earn a living in the theater. George Farquahar, for example, a noted comic writer of the time, died in poverty. Others eventually abandoned the theater for more stable employment. Her early years of writing, from 1700 to 1709, were marked with considerable effort; her plays were staged with regularity in London and while only a few during that time period were deemed artistically successful she was still able to stay afloat financially. When she married Joseph Centlivre, she gained a sense of financial security. From this point forward, she wrote less frequently, but more artfully. She was a highly acclaimed writer of the comedy of intrigue, and her plays follow the trends of an age that had moved from bawdy, sexual innuendo to a more decorous approach to love and marriage. Her plays were restaged throughout the 18th and 19th centuries, providing vehicles for the great comedic actors of the age. Although she was not formally educated, her knowledge of English, French (particularly Molière) and Spanish literature provided the sources for many of her plays. Centlivre overcame the prejudice against women and succeeded where others had failed. She died on December 1, 1723, and was buried in St Paul's, Covent Garden.

SOURCES:

Cotton, Nancy. *Women Playwrights in England c. 1363–1750.* Lewisburg, PA: Bucknell University Press, 1980.

Lock, F.P. *Susanna Centlivre.* Boston: Twayne, 1979.

SUGGESTED READING:

Bowyer, John Wilson. *The Celebrated Mrs. Centlivre.* Durham, NC: Duke University Press, 1952.

COLLECTIONS:

Four Celebrated Comedies. London: Printed for W. Mears, 1735.

The Dramatic Works of the Celebrated Mrs. Centlivre with a New Account of Her Life. London: J. Pearson, 1872.

The Plays of Susanna Centlivre. Edited by Richard C. Frushell. 3 vols. NY: Garland, 1982.

The Works of the Celebrated Mrs. Centlivre. 3 vols. London: Printed for J. Knapton, C. Hitch & L. Hawes, 1760–1761.

Anita DuPratt, Professor of Theatre, California State University Bakersfield, Bakersfield, California

Cereta, Laura, of Brescia

(1469–1499)

Italian scholar. Born Laura Cereta in 1469, in Brescia, Italy; died in 1499 and buried at the Church of San Domenico in Brescia; daughter of Veronica di Leno and Silvestro Cereta (a jurisprudent and humanist); eldest of six children; educated for two years at a convent school and then at home by her father; married Pietro Serina at age 15.

Taught philosophy for seven years at the University of Padua. Works: 84 pieces comprised mostly of letters, orations, and essays, including one parody of funeral orations.

Laura Cereta was educated in a convent school for two years and then at home by her father Silvestro Cereta, a staunch supporter of her scholarship at a time when the education of women was a much disputed issue. A jurisprudent who generally worked for the public administration of Brescia, he was also a humanist and a very capable tutor for his daughter in her studies of mathematics, astrology, and religion.

As was usual for learned women in Renaissance Italy, from an early age Laura was involved in public argumentation, orations and debates. Also in line with the fashion of the time, her philosophizing was concerned mostly with ethics, rather than metaphysics (the study of the nature of reality) or epistemology (the theory of knowledge). She had a great love of learning, exalting it as characteristically human, and a desire to seek the truth, although her intellectual activities were also motivated by the wish to immortalize her name.

When she was 15, Brescia married Pietro Serina, a man who shared her thirst for learning. In only 18 months, however, she was widowed and would mourn the death of her husband for several years while seeking solace in religion.

Around the time of her marriage, she probably wrote all of the 84 pieces left behind after her death. These included mostly letters (to family members and local professionals), orations, and "disputations" (a type of essay popular at the time) in Latin. The letters concern malice, death, fate, chance, war, the contemporary political problems with Turkey, marriage, the importance of leading an active life, and the happiness gained from self-control. She also wrote a parody of the elaborate funeral orations popular at the time, about the death of an ass.

Cereta probably taught philosophy for seven years at the University of Padua. With a strong belief in her own intellectual capabilities, she argued that women should be educated. She felt isolated as a female scholar and thought that her scholarship suffered from lack of time and harassment by others who were jealous of her intellect. At the end of her life, she was pressured to abandon scholarship and enter a religious order. She died in 1499, at age 30, and was buried at the Church of San Domenico in Brescia.

SOURCES:

Kersey, Ethel M. *Women Philosophers: a Bio-critical Source Book.* NY: Greenwood Press, 1989.

Russell, Rinalda. "Laura Cereta," in Katherina M. Wilson, ed., *An Encyclopedia of Continental Women Writers.* NY: Garland, 1991.

Catherine Hundleby, M.A.
Philosophy, University of Guelph

Cerrito, Fanny (1817–1909)

Italian ballerina and choreographer. Born Francesca Cerrito in Naples, Italy, in 1817; died on May 6, 1909; studied at the Ballet School of the Royal Theaters; married dancer and choreographer Arthur Saint-Léon, in April 17, 1845; children: (with the Marqués de Bedmar, a Spanish noble) Matilde (b. 1853).

Fanny Cerrito, considered one of the finest ballerina's of the Italian Romantic school, was the daughter of modest Neapolitans who doted on her. Although it was always her wish to dance, she was short and plump as a child and showed little outstanding talent. However, as a student at the Ballet School of the Royal Theaters, she worked so hard on her technique and physical appearance that by age 15 she was ranked as a solo dancer. She made her debut in July 1832, dancing a *pas de deux* in *L'Oroscopo.* Cerrito subsequently toured Italy and Austria (in Vienna they converted her name from Francesca to Fanny, which she used from then on), before becoming the prima ballerina at La Scala in Milan. There, she studied with the renowned Carlo Blasis, whose precepts influence the teaching of classical ballet to this day.

Originally scheduled for April 30, 1840, her London debut at Her Majesty's Theatre was postponed due to a rowdy demonstration over the failure of the management to produce a favored tenor for the same show. On May 2, with Queen *Victoria in attendance and a promise that the tenor in question would soon appear, Cerrito's debut took place. She was an instant success, as much for her opulent figure as for her dancing.

Waiflike slimness was not always *de rigeur* for ballerinas. In the 19th century, they were admired for their ample bosoms, wide hips, and sturdy legs. One critic, quoted in Parmenia Migel's *The Ballerinas,* took a ballerina to task for what was later to be considered a dancer's great attribute:

> We are grieved to utter unpleasant truths about Mlle Fitzjames. . . . The sight of her abnormally thin body is quite painful. . . . Mlle Louise Fitzjames has no body at all; she is not even substantial enough to play the part of a shadow; she is as transparent as a lantern pane, so that the *corps de ballet* girls who hover behind her are quite visible through her.

Cerrito's dancing was praised as spectacular, especially her leaps and point work, and even the appearance of her serious rival *Marie Taglioni could not eclipse her success. Amid ac-

Fanny
Cerrito

colades, she returned to La Scala and a successful tour of several Italian cities.

The year 1843 was a turning point for Cerrito. After excelling in Perrot's *Ondine*, in which she also presented some of her own choreography, she was asked by Queen Victoria to dance the *pas de deux* with *Fanny Elssler** at a Royal Command performance. The success of this performance led to the sensational *pas de quatre* with Marie Taglioni, *Carlotta Grisi**, and *Lucille Grahn**, staged by Perrot in 1844. Cerrito danced other notable roles in Perrot's ballets, including a goddess in *Le Jugement de Pâris* (1846), *Air in Les Eléments* (1847), and

Spring in *Les Quatre Saisons* (1848).

In 1847, during her brief marriage to her dancing partner Arthur Saint-Léon, she made a successful debut at the Paris Opera, dancing *La Fille de Marbre*, which had been choreographed by her husband especially for her. Saint-Léon was apparently not as gifted a choreographer as Perrot but understood how to take advantage of his wife's particular talents as well as his own. Although Cerrito left him in 1851 and became involved with a Spanish noble, Marqués de Bedmar, she stayed at the Opera, where she starred and also choreographed. In 1853, at age 36, she had a child, Matilde. The

Marqués de Bedmar became a devoted and generous father to the child, whose parenting continued after his affair with Cerrito had ended.

Motherhood did not prompt Cerrito to retire, and she remained busier than ever, but her greatest joy was now her daughter. Her career included two seasons in Russia between 1855 and 1857, where she made an appearance at the coronation celebration for Alexander II. Although she grew quite round (Cerrito lost her adorable plumpness early in her career, prompting critics to extol her dancing "in spite" of her figure), she did not stop dancing until 1857, after which she remained active in the ballet world for another half century. Fanny Cerrito lived in Paris until her death a week shy of her 92nd birthday. Not long afterward, Paris witnessed the arrival of *Anna Pavlova, one of the greatest dancers of modern times.

SOURCES:

Migel, Parmenia. *The Ballerinas: From the Court of Louis XIV to Pavlova.* NY: Macmillan, 1972.

Barbara Morgan,
Melrose, Massachusetts

Cezelli, Constance de (d. 1617).

See Constance de Cezelli.

Chabi (fl. 13th c.)

*Empress of China. Flourished in the 13th century; empress-consort and second wife of Kublai Khan (1215–1294, also called Shih-tsu, Mongol founder of China's Yüan dynasty who was one of the most famous rulers of all time). Khan's four wives were: **Tele-gun, Chabi, Tarakhan**, and **Bayaghuchun**. He had at least twelve sons with his wives (Dorji, Chen-chin, Manggala, Nomukhan, Khoridai, Hugechi, A'urugchi, Ayachi, Kokochu, Khudlugh Temur, Toghon, Temechi) and at least two daughters (**Miao-yen, Hu-tu-lu Chieh-li-mi-shih**).*

Chabrillan, Céleste de (1824–1909)

Parisian-born dancer, courtesan, novelist and autobiographer whose five volumes of memoirs scandalized France. Name variations: Comtesse de Moreton de Chabrillan; Celeste or Céleste Mogador, Mme Mogador, La Mogador. Born Céleste Vénard in Paris, France, on December 27, 1824; died in 1909; married Lionel, Comte de Chabrillan, around 1853.

Born in Paris in 1824, Céleste de Chabrillan was the daughter of working-class parents. Her father died when she was young, and she was

raped in adolescence by one of her mother's suitors. When her mother remarried, Céleste was "rescued" from a miserable life by a Parisian prostitute. "On Sept 26 at 9 pm," according to her own account, she assumed that profession, taking the name Madame Mogador. Though a large woman with a pockmarked face, Céleste was known for her charm and had great success as a courtesan. By 1846, now known as the Queen of the Prado, she was also working as an actress at the Variétés and as an equestrian at the Hippodrome circus.

Around 1853, Céleste married the Comte de Chabrillan who had made his fortune in the gold fields of Australia in 1852. In 1853–54, her memoirs titled *Adieux au Monde* (Goodbye World) appeared in France. The five volumes, describing her life as a courtesan, caused a sensation. Despite her intentions to portray the world of prostitution as a condemnation of vice, the volumes were considered scandalous and were at first banned. This only added to the mystique, and *Adieux au Monde* became a bestseller, bringing her notoriety.

Around 1854, the count was made a semi-official at the French Consulate in Melbourne, and the couple moved to Australia to start life anew. Melbourne society, however, was aware of her writings and spurned the pair. Miserable, Céleste returned to Paris alone in 1856. Her memoirs were reissued in 1858 against her will (she wanted to spare her husband further embarrassment) and seized once more.

Following a serious illness, and in desperate need of money, Céleste tried her hand at novels. *Les Voleurs d'Or* (1857) concerned the gold-rush days in Victoria. (Translated by **Lucy** and **Caroline Moorehead**, it would be published in Australia in 1970 as *The Gold Robbers*.) Céleste followed this with *Sapho* (1858) and *Miss Pewel* (1859). In 1863, she took over the directorship of the Folies Marigny theater and produced one of her own plays, but the venture failed within a year. Céleste de Chabrillan died in poverty in 1909.

SUGGESTED READING:

Haldane, Charlotte. *Daughter of Paris: The Life Story of Céleste Mogador*, 1961.

Chacel, Rosa (1898–1994)

Spanish writer. Name variations: Rosa Clotilde Cecilia María del Carmen Chacel Arimón. Born in Valladolid, northcentral Spain, on June 3, 1898; died of heart and lung failure, age 96, in Madrid on August 3, 1994; daughter of Francisco Chacel Barbero and Rosa Cruz Arimón Pacheco; studied art in Madrid and

spent six years in Rome; married Timoteo Pérez Rubio (a painter), in April 1922; children: Carlos.

Rosa Chacel was born in Valladolid, Spain, on June 3, 1898, the daughter of Francisco Chacel Barbero and Rosa Cruz Arimón Pacheco. Her mother, a teacher by profession, instructed Rosa at home, and her education progressed rapidly although she missed interaction with other children. When she was ten years old, her family moved to Madrid, where she studied sculpture in the Fine Arts School of San Fernando. After a six-year engagement, she married Timoteo Pérez Rubio, a painter, in 1922. Her first experience outside Spain came in 1927 when Timoteo received an art scholarship, and she accompanied him to Italy, Germany, and France.

Intrigued by the intellectual and artistic currents of the time, Chacel studied literature and then began writing. Her first book, *Estación, ida y vuelta* (*Season of Departure and Return*), was published in 1930, the same year as the birth of her only child Carlos. When the Spanish Civil War began, she supported the Republic against Franco's Nationalists, working in a hospital, and she also published a book of sonnets, *A la orilla de un pozo.*

In late 1936, displaced by the Nationalist victory, she left Spain for refuge in France. Then with the outbreak of the Second World War, she and her family moved to Buenos Aires in 1940. There, Chacel continued to write, and her works began to attract critical attention, including a fellowship from the Guggenheim Foundation. In 1962, she returned to Spain for several months but found her homeland now unappealing. The family moved to Rio de Janeiro in 1964. Over the following years, she spent greater amounts of time in Spain, participating in literary conferences. After 1974, she and her husband split their time between Brazil and Spain. Meanwhile, her critical acclaim promoted Chacel's standing with the reading public. Saddened by her husband's death in 1977, Chacel nonetheless continued actively in literary and cultural circles. Among her many awards and recognitions was the National Prize for Spanish Letters presented to her by the Spanish Ministry of Culture in 1987.

Chacel's chief works include novels: *Teresa* (1941), *Memorias de Leticia Valle* (*Memoirs of Leticia Valle*, 1946), *Ofrenda a una virgen loca* (1960), *La sinrazón* (1960), *Barrio de Maravillas* (1976); autobiographical works: *Desde el amanecer* (1972), *Alcancía* (1982); and a compilation of literary criticism: *Los títulos* (1981).

SOURCES:

Mateo, María Asunción. *Retrato de Rosa Chacel.* Galería de Grandes Contemporáneos. Barcelona: Círculo de Lectores, 1993.

Kendall W. Brown,
Provo, Utah

Chadwick, Cassie L. (1859–1907)

Canadian swindler who defrauded rich Americans and Ohio banks out of an estimated $2 million. Name variations: Constance Cassandra Chadwick; alias Lydia de Vere. Born Elizabeth Bigley in Strathroy, Ontario, Canada, in 1859; died in prison in 1907; daughter of an Ontario railway worker; married Dr. Leroy Chadwick.

Canadian con-artist Cassie L. Chadwick plied her trade in the United States for a number years until her illicit machinations caused the failure of one Ohio bank and the near failure of several others. At first, she was known as Lydia de Vere in San Francisco where she bilked the unsuspecting by passing herself off as a clairvoyant. Following a move to Cleveland in 1886, she married a respected Ohio physician, Leroy Chadwick, whom she had met in a whore house on Euclid Avenue where she assured him that she was only there to instruct the girls in etiquette. She then set up her greatest con.

In the lobby of the New York's posh Holland House hotel, she was introduced to an Ohio banker named Dillon and told him that she was the illegitimate daughter of Andrew Carnegie. To prove her assertion, she took Dillon on a carriage ride to Carnegie's Fifth Avenue mansion. While Dillon remained in the carriage, she ascended the steps, was admitted into the mansion, and stayed nearly 30 minutes. When Chadwick reemerged, she turned to the mansion and waved to a well-dressed man at the window. She tripped as she entered the carriage and dropped a piece of paper. The banker picked it up. To his dismay, he was holding a promissory note for $2 million signed by Andrew Carnegie, the same man, said Chadwick, who had waved at the window. As Dillon pumped Chadwick for details, she swore the banker to silence and told him that Carnegie, out of shame for her illegitimacy, had given her even more notes, worth $7 million, but because of her own shame she was frightened of drawing on them. She also told him that she would inherit $400 million on Carnegie's death.

In actuality, the man at the window was Carnegie's butler whom she had managed to occupy by claiming that she was interested in the credentials of a maid she intended to employ. The promissory notes were fake. Returning to Ohio, Dillon convinced Chadwick to put the notes in a safe-deposit box in a local bank for safe keeping. He then shared her secret with most every lender in greater Cleveland and beyond. Bankers, eager to partake in the millions to be gleaned, encouraged her to take out loans of up to $1 million at usurious interest rates of 25%. Rather than demand payment on the interest, they let the debts compound annually, convinced they would reap their reward after probate. Chadwick meanwhile became known as the "Queen of Ohio." She bought diamond necklaces, filled 30 closets with clothes, had a gold organ installed in her living room, and entertained lavishly, spending $100,000 for a dinner party. Even millionaires loaned her money, including a Massachusetts entrepreneur named Herbert Newton. When Newton became nervous and called in the loan for $190,000, Chadwick was indignant, explaining that all her securities, all $10 million, were in the Wade Park National Bank in Cleveland. Newton pressed his case with the police. On inspection, the notes were found to be obvious forgeries.

The scam placed several Ohio banks in trouble. A run on the Citizen's National Bank of Oberlin, which had loaned her $200,000, forced a bankruptcy. When queried about his daughter in hopes he could save the banks, Andrew Carnegie issued a press release: "Mr. Carnegie does not know Mrs. Chadwick of Cleveland. . . . Mr. Carnegie has not signed a note for more than thirty years." Cassie Chadwick was arrested on December 7, 1904, at her suite in Cleveland's Hotel Breslin. At the time, she was ensconced in bed, along with her money belt containing $100,000. Tried and convicted of fraud and sentenced to ten years, Cassie Chadwick died in jail three years later.

Chadwick, Florence (1918–1995)

American marathon swimmer who holds the women's record for swimming the English Channel. Born Florence May Chadwick on November 9, 1918, in San Diego, California; died on March 15, 1995, in San Diego; daughter and one of two children of Richard William Chadwick (a police officer, later a restaurateur) and Mary Chadwick (a restaurateur with her husband); graduated from Point Loma Junior and Senior High School, San Diego, 1936; attended San Diego State College, Southwestern University of Law at Los Angeles, and the Balboa Law School, San Diego; abandoned study of law to attend Dickenson Business College, San Diego; never married; no children.

Won second place in national backstroke championships at age 13; became model for Catalina swimwear and appeared in movie Bathing Beauty *with Esther Williams; made her first swim of the English Channel, from France to England, in 13 hours 20 minutes, breaking the 1926 record of Gertrude Ederle (1950); elected to International Hall of Fame for swimming (1970); served as president of San Diego Stadium Authority and member of the board of directors San Diego Hall of Champions.*

Major swims: Cape Gris-Nez, France, to Dover, England (August 8, 1950); English Channel from England to France (1951, 1953); English Channel from England to France in 13 hours and 55 minutes, 11 minutes faster than the existing men's record (1955); Catalina to California coast in 13 hours and 47 minutes, breaking the record set in 1927 by George Young (1952); Straits of Gibraltar, Dardanelles, Bosporus (1953).

On August 8, 1950, when Florence Chadwick made her first record-breaking swim of the English Channel, she was 32 years old, an age when most of her fellow athletes were thinking about retiring. Chadwick, on the other hand, was only beginning. Having long postponed her childhood dream of swimming the channel, she now embraced the challenge wholeheartedly. She made three additional crossings, becoming the first woman to make the swim in both directions and capturing a place among the premier distance swimmers of all time. It was not until she was 50 that Chadwick finally traded her swimsuit for a business suit and settled into a new career as a stockbroker.

Florence Chadwick was born on November 9, 1918, in San Diego, California, where her father was a detective and narcotics agent. Her uncle, who taught her to swim when she was a child, also sparked her competitive spirit. "He entered me in a race, which I lost," she once recalled. "I was six years old, but I decided to work harder and prove somehow that his confidence was not misplaced." Chadwick was just eight when American *Gertrude Ederle made her successful swim across the English Channel in 1926. The event galvanized interest in long-distance swimming in the United States, and Ederle became the idol of many youthful swimmers, including young Florence.

Chadwick gradually grew to prefer rough-water swimming over traditional lap-swimming, and at the age of ten became the first child to swim across the channel at the mouth of San Diego Bay. (During the next 18 years, she would win the annual 2½-mile race ten times.) At age 13, she finished second to *Eleanor Holm in the U.S. National Championships in the backstroke. Chadwick continued to swim competitively throughout high school, where she was also president of the Associated Student body. After graduation, she pursued the study of law for a number of years, before abandoning it for business college. She eventually left college to accept a contract to promote Catalina swimwear.

With the onset of World War II, Chadwick became a troop entertainer through the United Service Organizations (USO), producing, directing, and appearing in a number of aquashows for the benefit of America's soldiers and sailors. The aquashow was an outgrowth of American's love affair with swimming. Although female athleticism was suspect during the period, women swimmers were an exception, mostly because they didn't grunt or sweat noticeably while performing, and because they maintained an idealized female body type, without bulky muscle development. Both men and women embraced the sport and enjoyed watching swimmers perform, making aquashows a profitable entertainment. Even show business great Billy Rose produced his own Aquacade, starring champion swimmers Eleanor Holm and *Esther Williams. In 1945, Chadwick relinquished her amateur standing to appear in the MGM movie *Bathing Beauty*, with Williams, who, now billed as "Hollywood's Mermaid," starred in a series of films during the 1940s and '50s that featured spectacular underwater scenes and were box-office bonanzas. After completing her stint in the movies, Chadwick returned to San Diego where she worked as a professional swimming instructor at the La Jolla Beach and Tennis Club. Teaching provided her with the time and financial support to continue her own intensive training for her long-dreamed-of chance to swim the English Channel.

In June 1948, partly in order to raise money for her channel swim, she went to Saudi Arabia as a statistician with the Arabian-American Oil Company. There, she began training in earnest, using the 150-foot pool at Dhahran. Later, when she was transferred to an office in Ras Al Mishab, she trained in the choppy waters of the Persian Gulf. On her free days, she would spend as many as ten hours in the water. (At 5'6" and 141 pounds, Chadwick was said to have possessed an unusually high tolerance for cold temperatures, which gave her an edge in her long-distance swims.) In June 1950, having saved $5,000, Chadwick left her job and traveled to Wissant on the French coast for final preparations for her channel attempt.

When she entered the water on August 8, 1950, Chadwick became the 12th woman to attempt the 19-mile channel swim. She left Cape Gris-Nez at 2:37 AM, accompanied by a party of 15 (including her father, officials, crew, and friends) in an escort fishing boat. With lumps of sugar as her only nourishment throughout the swim, Chadwick made the crossing in 13 hours and 20 minutes, beating Ederle's record by 1 hour and 11 minutes. Met by reporters when she reached shore, Chadwick flashed her glorious smile and commented, "I feel fine. I am quite prepared to swim back." Arriving in the U.S., Chadwick spent a few eventful days in New York, where she made a number of radio and television appearances before traveling home to San Diego. There, she was greeted with a ticker-tape parade and a public luncheon in her honor.

Chadwick made good on her proposal to "swim back," making the more arduous channel crossing from England to France in 1951, and again in 1953 and 1955. Continuing to improve through training, Chadwick, at 37, made the 1955 swim in 13 hours and 55 minutes, 11 minutes faster than the existing men's record. She also swam across the Strait of Gibraltar, the Dardanelles, and the Bosporus, swims that were completed before satellite and radio-tracking systems allowed the distance swimmer to take advantage of the shortest courses across the open sea. Between channel swims, Chadwick returned to her home waters in September 1952, where she swam the 21 miles from Catalina Island to the California coast, breaking the time record established in 1927 by the Canadian George Young.

Chadwick made the most of her success and notoriety and, for an extended period, was the world's highest-paid woman athlete. She established Florence Chadwick Swimming Schools in New York, New Jersey, and California and was the aquatic director at Grossinger's, the posh Catskills' resort, for a number of years. In 1960, well into her 40s, she made an unsuccessful attempt to cross the Irish Sea. Shortly thereafter, she began to rethink the future, and a possible move into the business of finance, which had held her interest since the early 1920s.

In 1968, Chadwick moved back to San Diego to begin a career as a stockbroker. She became active in San Diego society as well, serving as president of the San Diego Stadium Authority, and as a member of the board of directors of the San Diego Hall of Champions. She also wrote a monthly column on women's investment issues for *The Moneypaper*, a financial publication especially geared to women's needs and interests. Chadwick ended her business career as vice-president of First Wall Street Corporation in San Diego. The champion swimmer was inducted into the International Hall of Fame for swimming in 1970. She died in the city of her birth on March 15, 1995, at the age of

Florence
Chadwick

76. The following year, she was inducted into the Women's Sports Hall of Fame.

SOURCES:

Besford, Pat. *Encyclopaedia of Swimming.* London: Robert Hale, 1976.

Conlon, Robert J. *Great Women Athletes of the 20th Century.* Jefferson, NC: McFarland, 1991.

Current Biography 1950. NY: H.W. Wilson, 1950.

Graham, Judith, ed. *Current Biography 1995.* NY: H.W. Wilson, 1995.

Guttmann, Allen. *Women's Sports: A History.* NY: Columbia University Press, 1991.

Katz, Ephraim. *The Film Encyclopedia.* NY: Harper-Collins, 1994.

Lamparski, Richard. *Whatever Became of . . . ?* 5th Series. NY: Crown, 1974.

Witty, Elizabeth. "Chadwick Out of Water But Still Swimming," in Futures: *The Magazine of Commodities and Options.* October 1986, pp. 64–66.

Wanda Ellen Wakefield, historian,
SUNY, Buffalo, New York

Chaffee, Suzy (1946—)

American skier, influential in the creation of freestyle skiing, who is known as the "Mother of the Hotdog." Name variations: Suzy Chapstick (from a popular advertising campaign that she endorsed). Born in Rutland, Vermont, on November 29, 1946.

One of the more unusual events of the Winter Olympics is the freestyle mogul, a competition in which skiers race over treacherous terrain, sometimes jumping, sometimes flipping. A relatively new sport in the 1990s, the freestyle mogul has become tremendously popular with audiences worldwide. In the sport's early years, Suzy Chaffee greatly appreciated the event's potential and worked hard to see freestyle skiing made a part of the Olympics.

Raised in Rutland, Vermont, where skiing was an everyday sport, Chaffee was on the slopes by age three, an auspicious beginning for the woman who would become America's number-one ranked female skier by 1967. At age 22, in 1968, she was captain of the U.S. Olympic Ski Team in the Grenoble Winter Games. Although she won many national and international championships, Chaffee was dissatisfied with traditional events. She lost her heart to "hotdog" or freestyle skiing, marked by unusual or flamboyant maneuvers, once solely the terrain of daredevil males.

When she began competing in freestyle, there was no separate division for women, so she skied head-to-head with men. From 1971 to 1973, she was the World Freestyle champion. She thrived on tip rolls, outriggers, royals, worm turns, and 360s as she encouraged creativity, musical accompaniment and the use of short skis in the sport. She also urged other women to participate. When the International Freestyle Association was formed in 1973, Chaffee's concepts became central to the sport.

By 1974–75, women hotdoggers had their own competitions. **Genia Fuller, Marion Post,** and **Karen Huntoon** performed midair flips, airborne leaps, and catlike groundwork of great precision. Freestyle skiing was dangerous, so, while the stunts were spectacular, safety was always a concern. Organized contests included several areas: Stunt Ballet used short skis to produce spins and gymnastic moves to music. Freestyle Mogul involved the challenge of a treacherous course demanding an aggressive approach; Aerial Acrobatic, with its gainers, kickouts, spread eagles, and flips, has been likened to a springboard competition on skis.

When Chaffee became a member of the U.S. Olympic Committee, she used her position to push for the acceptance of freestyle skiing. Eventually, the Mother of the Hotdog prevailed. Largely thanks to Chaffee's effort American women did exceptionally well in Freestyle Mogul events in the 1994 Winter Olympics.

Karin L. Haag,
Athens, Georgia

Chafik, Doria (1908–1975).
See Shafik, Doria.

Chain, Anne Beloff (1921–1991).
See Beloff-Chain, Anne.

Challans, Mary (1905–1983).
See Renault, Mary.

Chalpaida (c. 654–c. 714).
See Alphaida.

Chambers, Dorothea Lambert (1878–1960)

British tennis champion and seven-time singles winner at Wimbledon. Name variations: Dorothea Katharine Chambers; Dorothea Lambert-Chambers; Mrs. Robert Lambert Chambers; Dorothea Katherine Douglass. Born Dorothea Katharine Douglass at Ealing, Middlesex, England, in September 1878; died in January 1960; married Robert Lambert Chambers, 1907.

Singles winner at Wimbledon (1903, 1904, 1906, 1910, 1911, 1913, and 1914); All-England badminton doubles champion (1903) and mixed champion (1904); won an Olympic gold medal in singles tennis in London (1908).

Possibly the most outstanding woman tennis player before World War I, Dorothea Lambert Chambers was one of the first athletes to take up tennis as a serious sport and was a forerunner to the modern-day dedicated professional. The daughter of a cleric, she won her first Wimbledon title by default in 1903, when **Muriel Robb** did not defend her title. Chambers retained the Wimbledon title in 1904 against **Charlotte Sherry** but lost it in 1905 to American *May Sutton. The following year, she regained the title but lost to Sutton again in 1907. Chambers was the All-England badminton doubles champion in 1903 and mixed champion in 1904. In the London Olympics in 1908, she won the gold medal in singles tennis.

After leaving competition to have a child, Chambers returned to Wimbledon with renewed determination in 1910 and won the title, as she would three more time times in the next four years. Her 1911 win over **Dora Boothby**, by a score of 6–0, 6–0, was the only shut out of its kind in a Wimbledon singles final. Following World War I, which halted competition, Chambers returned to the courts, blessedly free of the long skirts and petticoats that had restricted play early in her career. Now 40 years old, she faced the brilliant young Frenchwoman *Suzanne Lenglen in one of the most exciting of all women's finals at Wimbledon, with Lenglen barely squeaking out the win in the final set. The following year, Chambers again faced Lenglen in the finals but was defeated 6–3, 6–0.

In 1925, at age 46, Chambers was selected to play for Great Britain in the Wightman Cup at Forest Hills. On the first day, partnered with **Ermyntrude Harvey**, she won a doubles match against Americans *Molla Mallory and May Sutton. On the second day, in searing heat, Chambers won her singles match against **Eleanor Goss**, a woman half her age, in a game that J. Arthur Batley, the British Team manager, called "the brainiest display of lawn tennis one could wish to see." It was Great Britain's first Wightman victory on American soil, a feat that was not to be repeated again for 50 years. In 1928, Chambers turned to coaching.

Barbara Morgan,
Melrose, Massachusetts

Chambers, Norah (1905–1989).

See Women POWs of Sumatra for sidebar.

Chambrun, Comtesse de or Josée de (c. 1911—).

See Laval, Josée.

Chaminade, Cécile (1857–1944)

French composer and pianist, recognized as the first professional woman composer, whose work has been rediscovered in recent years, appearing on major labels. Pronunciation: SHAH-mee-nod. Born Cécile Louise Stéphanie Chaminade in Paris, France, on August 8, 1857; died in Monte Carlo, Monaco, on April 13, 1944 (some sources cite the 18th); third of six children of Hippolyte Chaminade (a manager of a British

insurance firm in Paris who played the violin) and a mother who was an amateur pianist; studied in Paris with various teachers, including Benjamin Godard Félix Le Couppey, Augustin Savard, and Martin Marsick; married Louis-Mathieu Carbonel (a music publisher), on August 29, 1901.

Was composing by age seven; gave first concert ten years later (1875); much of her early life was spent concertizing; had become the first professional woman composer (1900); appeared in Great Britain, Europe and the U.S. on international concert tours (1890s–1914); was the first female composer to receive the Chevalier of the Legion of Honor (1913).

Cécile Louise Stéphanie Chaminade was born in Paris on August 8, 1857, the third of six children. The Chaminades were a prosperous family who valued music highly. Her father Hippolyte Chaminade, a manager of a British insurance firm in Paris, played the violin, while her mother, an amateur pianist whose name was never cited in biographies, gave young Cécile her

Dorothea Lambert Chambers

first lessons on the keyboard. Life in France's Second Empire in the early 1860s was pleasant indeed. The family lived on the fashionable Rue Brochant, spending their holidays at the Château de la Farge, their villa in Périgord. In 1865, property was purchased in Le Vésinet, a village west of Paris, and many vacations were spent there.

Cécile's musical gifts revealed themselves early. She composed by the age of seven, and around that time some of her piano mazurkas appeared in print in a magazine. Georges Bizet, the famous composer of "Carmen" who was also a neighbor, noticed the little girl's musical talent when he visited the Chaminade home in August 1869. Cécile's parents took their daughter's abilities seriously. Félix Le Couppey (1811–1887), a professor at the Paris Conservatoire, was enthusiastic about her potential, advising her parents to enroll her at the Conservatoire for instruction in musical theory. Cécile's father decided against this, holding that a young woman of her social standing should not embark on a musical career. Instead, she studied piano privately with Le Couppey. Her progress was rapid and other eminent teachers were engaged to instruct her, including Augustin Savard (1841–1881), who taught counterpoint, harmony and fugue, Martin Marsick (1848–1924) who taught violin, and the noted composer Benjamin Godard (1849–1895). The family's pleasant life was interrupted by the Franco-Prussian War of 1870–71. The Chaminades took refuge from the siege of Paris in nearby Angoulême, avoiding the bloody Commune and the even bloodier suppression that followed Emperor Napoleon III's military debacle. Despite the lost war, there was a renascence of French musical life in the 1870s. Leading composers included César Franck, Camille Saint-Säens, Emanuel Chabrier, Henri Duparc, and Vincent D'Indy who experimented vigorously with new forms and sonorities, preparing French music for the next chapter of Gallic musical achievement, that of Debussy and Ravel.

Chaminade's first public recital was in 1875, following years of private concertizing in salons at Le Vésinet. She accompanied her violin teacher, Marsick, in a Mozart violin sonata and the performance was an unqualified success. A reviewer wrote glowingly of the "magnificent skill" of both the long-dead composer and "this child . . . so brilliantly and truly talented." Two years later, in 1877, she made her professional debut at the Salle Pleyel in Paris. The young musician continued to compose as well as concer-

tize. Around this time, the composer Ambroise Thomas heard some of her compositions and declared that she should be known as a composer pure and simple, rather than by the then-pejorative designation of *woman-composer*. When Chaminade published her Opus 1, a piano etude, it also received favorable reviews. On April 25, 1878, at Le Vésinet, she introduced a style of performing that would henceforth mark her career. With the blessing of her distinguished teacher Le Couppey, Chaminade performed her own piano solos and songs at the keyboard. Reviews of the 15 works were highly complimentary, praising Chaminade for her "remarkable virtuosity" as a performer, as well as for her skill as a composer of piano pieces of "dense, taut workmanship [and] an astonishing mastery of harmony," works that were demonstrably of "elegant and delicate design."

Chaminade's next major recital took place in February 1880 at the Salle Erard in Paris where she performed her Piano Trio No. 1, Op. 11. Romantic in spirit and broadly Brahmsian in style, this work was published at the time of its successful premiere by the respected music firm Durand, Schoenewerk & Cie. From then on, she was much in demand as a recitalist. In many of these recitals, her own compositions occupied a major portion of the program. Chaminade's growing confidence in her own creative gifts resulted in the composition of an *opéra-comique*, *La Sévillane*. Although the premiere performance of this large-scale work took place in the intimate setting of her parents' home in 1882, critics who were present were highly enthusiastic about its dramatic and musical qualities.

In April 1881, Cécile Chaminade presented a public performance of her first full-scale symphonic work, the Suite for Orchestra, Op. 20, before the National Society of Music in Paris. Although the reviews were mixed, all agreed that the work's orchestration deserved high praise for its color and originality. The *Petit Journal* predicted a bright future for the young composer, but this foray into major works of orchestral and operatic music was not sustained. Most of her energies went into composing works for solo piano, pieces that she could perform in recitals. Still, ambitious compositions such as the Piano Trio No. 2, Op. 34, continued to appear.

During the early years of her musical career, Chaminade performed and composed for amusement. The daughter of wealth and privilege, her drive to succeed was personal. All this would change in the 1880s, however. Family crisis was precipitated by the marriage in 1886 of

Cécile
Chaminade

her younger sister **Henriette** to the pianist and composer Moritz Moszkowski (1854–1925). The marriage was considered a scandal because Moszkowski was German and Jewish, and Cécile's father broke all ties with Henriette. At the same time, the family began to suffer from a series of poor investments made by Hippolyte Chaminade. When he died in 1887, a death perhaps precipitated by his younger daughter's marriage, his estate was divided up and the family's opulent Paris house was sold. It soon became apparent that the Chaminades could survive economically only if Cécile marketed her compositions successfully and aggressively. She focused almost exclusively on the more commercial solo piano pieces and songs, spending much less time on large-scale compositions like symphonic works, operas, concertos, and chamber music. Although several major compositions were completed in the late 1880s, these smaller works would become Chaminade's musical legacy.

Around that time, Chaminade wrote the full-length ballet *Callirhoë*, which was originally offered to Benjamin Godard; since he was occupied with another project, he suggested that Chaminade be given the commission. The ballet premiered in Marseille in March 1888 to a cheering reception. One local reviewer claimed that the work's success was "without precedent" in that city. The canny young composer took advantage of her ballet's popularity, publishing a piano arrangement soon after its orchestral premiere. Several movements became independent compositions of immense appeal, and the *Scarf Dance* became particularly well-known. Throughout her career, Chaminade's work was received with raves outside Paris, while her success in the capital was always less certain.

In April 1888, her choral symphony *Les Amazones,* conceived as a dramatic work for large orchestra, soloists, and vast choral forces, premiered in Antwerp. Chaminade was highly praised, one critic noting that she had succeeded in avoiding too slavish a reliance on the great orchestral master of the day, namely Richard Wagner. Another major achievement of this period was her *Concertstück for Piano and Orchestra,* which was also successfully launched in Antwerp along with *Les Amazones.* This success was repeated in Paris where she appeared as a soloist with the Lamoureux Orchestra in January 1889. *Concertstück* was performed in a number of European countries as well as in the United States, where the distinguished conductor Theodore Thomas included it on one of his Chicago orchestral programs in December 1896.

There is no sex in art. Genius is an independent quality. The woman of the future, with her broader outlook, her greater opportunities, will go far, I believe, in creative work of every description.

—Cécile Chaminade, 1908

By the early 1890s, Chaminade's goal was to lure audiences to her recitals and then to sell large quantities of her compositions as sheet music so that she and her aging mother could enjoy financial security. During this period, she produced a number of charming piano works and over 60 songs while becoming a major star on the international touring circuit. On her first concert tour abroad to Great Britain in June 1892, she discovered foreigners were considerably more sympathetic than a sometimes fickle Parisian public. Although Chaminade never learned English, she managed to charm her audiences on many trips to the British Isles. One of her most fervent fans was Queen *Victoria. On at least one occasion, Chaminade was invited to chat with Her Majesty at Windsor Castle, and one of her compositions, the song *Reste,* was dedicated to Princess ◄❧ Beatrice, the aged-sovereign's daughter. While in London during the

Beatrice. See Queen Victoria for sidebar.
❧▶

1897 Diamond Jubilee celebrating the 60th anniversary of Victoria's reign, Chaminade received a Jubilee Medal. At Victoria's funeral in January 1901, the ceremonies included a performance of Chaminade's *Prélude* for organ, Op. 78. Most London critics were as enthusiastic about Chaminade as their sovereign. London's *Daily Chronicle* of June 24, 1892, declared that "both as composer and executant her success was beyond question," while the same concert prompted the *Daily Telegraph* to characterize it "a complete success." Chaminade concertized in London in 1893, 1894–95, as well as in 1897 and 1899. She returned again in 1902, 1907–08, for concerts and to record piano rolls for the Aeolian Company in 1913–14. Her last trips to London took place in 1922 and 1924 when she was in her 60s and in declining health.

When the 20th century dawned, Cécile Chaminade was known throughout Europe and the New World. She toured France, Belgium, Switzerland, and Great Britain as well as Germany, Austria-Hungary, and less-traveled places including Rumania, Bulgaria, Serbia, Greece, and Turkey. During her 1896 tour of the Balkan region, she performed a benefit concert in Athens to raise funds for the music conservatory in that city. Throughout the 1890s, she gave "Chaminade Festivals" that customarily filled concert halls and elicited rave reviews. Her reputation in the United States was stellar as well, and by 1898 at least four Chaminade Clubs had been founded to disseminate her compositions.

For most of her life Cécile Chaminade was a single career woman, so her marriage to the music publisher Louis-Mathieu Carbonel, on August 29, 1901, was a surprise to many. Her husband, whose business was in Marseille rather than Paris, was more than 20 years her senior and had in fact long been a friend of her mother. During Chaminade's 1899 tour of Eastern Europe and the Balkans, Louis-Mathieu had taken her mother's place as her traveling companion. Announcement of their marriage plans in July 1901 greatly upset the Chaminade family, even more so when they realized this would not be a conventional marriage. Cécile married only on condition that the marriage remain a purely platonic union without sexual relations. Furthermore, each partner continued to reside in her or his former home, she in Paris and he in Marseille. Her husband visited regularly and accompanied her on her concert tours. The arrangement worked well until 1903, when her aging husband fell ill with a lung disease. Cécile spent the next few years nursing her ailing spouse, but he never fully recovered and died in early 1907. Because Chaminade was an intensely private individual who destroyed her diaries before she died, her motives for this unusual marriage are unknown. Some evidence suggests that in the summer of 1888 she fell in love with and even became engaged to a "Dr. L." Some unspecified tragedy in his family prevented the marriage, however. A number of other men fell in love with her, including her teacher Benjamin Godard, who proposed to her on three occasions. Her rejection to other suitors was always the same: "I am wedded to my music." In an interview published in the *New York Herald* in November 1908, she stated that marriage "must adopt itself to one's career" because it was "difficult to reconcile the domestic life with the artistic. A woman should choose one or the other."

Chaminade's career continued to blossom. Well-known in the United States and Canada, she decided a tour of North America would enhance her earnings there. The mass-circulation press, including the *Century Magazine, The Etude,* and *The Ladies' Home Journal,* all featured articles about her life. Chaminade Clubs continued to appear, distributing her music and creating an ever-growing number of fans eager to see her perform in person. In 1908, a year after her husband's death, she traveled to the New World to expand her immense popularity. Chaminade arrived in New York City on October 17, 1908, for a two-month tour of America. A lengthy interview with her appeared the next day in the *New York Sun,* in which she discussed her first impressions of New York, her opinions about contemporary French composition, and her marriage. In another interview published several days later in the *Evening World,* she was described as the "World's Greatest Woman Composer." Her first recital in Carnegie Hall on October 24 was a tremendous popular and financial success. Many in the audience were members of Chaminade Clubs and gave her a rousing reception. The sold-out recital grossed $5,000—a huge sum in 1908. Commenting in the next day's *New York Times,* Richard Aldrich dismissed Chaminade's playing as "dull" and her compositions "small in compass, unpretentious in idea, aiming chiefly at attractive melody and rhythmic grace and claiming immediate acceptance by those whose knowledge and taste in music are not erudite." After such negative assessments, Aldrich backed off somewhat, noting that her compositions were "agreeable" and showed some distinction. A more positive note was struck by Reginald De Koven in *The World.* This critic regretted that none of Chaminade's

orchestral works were on the program, but he was generally pleased by her interpretations, which were those of "a real artist," and which were made effective through their "grace and delicacy . . . and a fluent technique." Just before Chaminade departed for Philadelphia, she granted an interview to the *Washington Post* in which she spoke at length of the creative abilities and opportunities for women in music.

Her *Concertstück* with the Philadelphia Orchestra, on November 6, elicited three quite different reviews. For the reviewer of the *Evening Bulletin,* the work itself was "a somewhat ambitious composition," but the performance by the composer was vitiated by her lack of pianistic power. *The Philadelphia Inquirer* was much more negative regarding the *Concertstück* as a "vague, formless, incoherent, vacillating piece of work, without any thematic backbone or logical harmonic development." In strong contrast, the *Ledger* hailed the work as "a composition which does not suffer by comparison with the musical handiwork of man." Furthermore, this paper's critic was certain that Chaminade played as "she composes, like a woman sentient to every influence of nature."

After Philadelphia, Chaminade toured Louisville, Cincinnati, Milwaukee, Minneapolis, Chicago, and St. Louis—receiving positive reviews, enjoying full houses. On December 3, she performed in Indianapolis and then went on to Washington, D.C., for a December 8 recital at the New National Theater. Much of Washington society turned out for the recital, including the first lady, *Edith Kermit Roosevelt. The critic for the *Washington Post* was delighted that Chaminade performed works largely unknown to an audience familiar with many of her pieces. This critic felt her *"Troisieme Valse"* was musically the equal of any of the Chopin waltzes customarily performed in concerts. Another pleasant aspect of the Washington leg of her tour was a luncheon at the French embassy and a meeting with Edith and President Theodore Roosevelt at the White House.

The tour ended with a return to Philadelphia, a performance in Boston on December 12, and a final recital in New York's Carnegie Hall on December 15. On Christmas Eve, a tired but considerably richer Cécile Chaminade set sail for France. Despite some negative reviews, the tour was a success. Even a sometimes lukewarm admirer like Lawrence Gilman wrote in the November 14, 1908, issue of *Harper's Weekly* that since she was a "maker of adored and ingenious music, let us offer gladly the salutation that is due the skillful and self-respecting craftsman, the music-maker of true and honorable talent." Paris was forced to take note of her success, and the December 1908 issue of *Paris Musical et Artistique* praised her as "more than just a French woman"; indeed, she was a "Parisian woman" who created an impressive reputation "in all the countries of the world." In 1913, the French government awarded her its highest honor, Chevalier of the Legion of Honor. Although a number of French women had received this award before, Cécile Chaminade was the first female composer to receive it. Showing a shrewd sense of public relations, she asked that the presentation ceremony take place at a Paris orphanage in which she had been actively involved. To assure maximum public interest, the award ceremony was filmed and shown as a news item in cinema theaters.

World War I began a declining phase in the composer's career. After 1910, she composed fewer and fewer piano works and songs. Her large-scale works were now rarely if ever performed in concert. In 1915, she moved to a seaside villa at Tamaris, near Toulon, a home purchased in 1903 by her husband. She spent the war years ministering to wounded soldiers in a convalescent home in nearby Les Sablettes. A strong mystical streak in her personality became even more pronounced during the war when millions of lives were snuffed out and some meaning had to be salvaged from the general carnage. After her mother's death in 1912, Chaminade attended séances. Following a visit to Beethoven's birthplace in Bonn, she saw a flame that, she said, allowed her to experience the soul of the great composer. Strong-willed and eccentric, she adhered to a strange diet that may well have brought on serious health problems.

The world Chaminade had known disappeared with World War I. Her delicate and charming music seemed an echo from a dead world. Refusing to adapt to the radically changed mood of the postwar era, Chaminade became increasingly reclusive and in 1925 abandoned a Paris she no longer understood, selling her family property at Le Vésinet. Living year-round in her villa near Toulon, she became a recluse. After one final work appeared in 1928, she never composed again. Advancing years and her diet may have combined to cause deteriorating health. Attended by her niece, she moved to Monte Carlo, Monaco, in 1936. Several years later, her left foot had to be amputated. Stubbornly refusing to use a wheelchair, she became a bedridden invalid. Contacts with friends and fans dwindled, causing in-

creasing despondency. In 1939, *The Etude* requested readers to communicate with Chaminade on her birthday. When several thousand did so, she was grateful and summed up her feelings in a 1942 letter to a friend in the United States: "Not to be forgotten, to live in the heart and memory of those who understand you—that is the supreme consolation for an artist."

World War II isolated Chaminade even more. Although she remained physically protected in Monaco, many of her compositions were out of print after the Nazi occupiers of France liquidated her publisher, Enoch, because it was a Jewish-owned enterprise. This act brought on a serious drop in royalty income. In the last months of her life, Radio Monte Carlo broadcast a concert of her works, and the day after she died, on April 13, 1944, the station aired a memorial program that included tributes and recordings of her immensely popular song "L'Anneau d'Argent" ("The Silver Ring") and the stirring finale of the *Concertstück*. Despite the war, a number of French publications wrote obituaries of varying length and accuracy, and in the United States, where she had been so immensely popular a generation earlier, short accounts of her career appeared in *The New York Times*, the *New York Herald Tribune*, and *Time*, while warm tributes could be found in the music journals *The Etude* and *Musical America*.

For a generation after her death, Cécile Chaminade remained an obscure, slightly ridiculous figure from the vanished world of Queen Victoria. Nicolas Slonimsky's mocking remarks in his highly regarded chronicle of musical events in the 20th century accurately reflected a widely held perspective on the composer's work. Unfortunately, many of these critics had never heard Chaminade's music. By the late 1970s, this changed when gifted musicians began to make excellent recordings of her major compositions. James Galway performed her charming Concertino for Flute and Orchestra, Op. 107. In the early 1990s, two superb recordings of Chaminade piano compositions, by the British pianists Peter Jacobs and Eric Parkin, received much critical praise. New ears were more sympathetic, and salon music regained its place as a valid form of musical expression.

Cécile Chaminade had few if any rivals as a composer of salon music. An accomplished artist, she possessed impressive business abilities, shrewdly gauging her market and becoming one of the first, if not indeed, *the* first fully professional female composer. For several decades, she earned a substantial annual income not only from recitals but from the publication of her compositions. For example, her song "L'Anneau d'Argent" was performed in countless countries for many decades, selling an immense number of copies. The greatest singers of the day, including *Clara Butt and John McCormack, made this work even more well known. Her signature piece, *Pas des écharpes*, Op. 37 (*Scarf Dance*), had sold well over five-million copies by the time of her death in 1944. Opera singers of note, including *Emma Albani, added Chaminade's song "L'Eté" to their recital programs, and the Viennese violin virtuoso Fritz Kreisler dazzled countless audiences with the colorful and playful *Sérénade Espagnole*. In recent years, stars like *Joan Sutherland and Itzhak Perlman included Chaminade works in their repertoire, often presenting them as encores. Finally, Cécile Chaminade is fully acknowledged as a genuine master of her craft, a superb musician who understood her gifts and her limits, establishing a reputation that continues to grow.

SOURCES:

Briscoe, James, ed. *Historical Anthology of Music by Women*. Bloomington, IN: Indiana University Press, 1987.

Citron, Marcia J. *Cécile Chaminade: A Bio-Bibliography*. NY: Greenwood Press, 1988.

Demuth, Norman. *French Piano Music: A Survey with Notes on Its Performance*. London: Museum Press, 1959.

Faurot, Albert. *Concert Piano Repertoire: A Manual of Solo Literature for Artists and Performers*. Metuchen, NJ: Scarecrow Press, 1974.

Hinson, Maurice. *Guide to the Pianist's Repertoire*. 2nd rev. ed. Bloomington: Indiana University Press, 1987.

Jezic, Diane Peacock. *Women Composers: The Lost Tradition Found*. 2nd ed. NY: The Feminist Press, 1994.

Johnson, Rose-Marie. *Violin Music by Women Composers: A Bio-Bibliographical Guide*. NY: Greenwood Press, 1989.

Kerr, Laura. *Scarf Dance: The Story of Cecile Chaminade*. NY: Abelard Press, 1953.

Meggett, Joan M. *Keyboard Music by Women Composers: A Catalog and Bibliography*. Westport, CT: Greenwood Press, 1981.

Olivier, Antje, and Karin Weingartz-Perschel. *Komponistinnen von A-Z*. Düsseldorf: Tokkata Verlag für Frauenforschung, 1988.

Slonimsky, Nicolas. *Music since 1900*. 4th ed. NY: Scribner, 1971.

Stern, Susan. *Women Composers: A Handbook*. Metuchen, NJ: Scarecrow Press, 1978.

Weissweiler, Eva. *Komponistinnen aus 500 Jahren*. Frankfurt am Main: Fischer Taschenbuch Verlag, 1981.

RELATED MEDIA:

Jacobs, Peter. *Piano Music by Cécile Chaminade* (Hyperion CD CDA66584, released 1992).

Parkin, Eric. *Chaminade: Piano Works* (Chandos CD CHAN 8888, released 1991).

John Haag, Associate Professor, University of Georgia, Athens, Georgia

Chamorro, Violeta (1929—)

Nicaraguan political leader, president of Nicaragua from 1990 to 1996, who was thrust into politics as a result of her husband's assassination and the triumph of the Sandinista revolution. Born Violeta Barrios in Rivas, Nicaragua, on October 18, 1929; daughter of Carlos Barrios and Amelia (Sacasa) Barrios; married Pedro Joaquin Chamorro Cardenal; children: Pedro Joaquin ("Quinto"); Carlos Fernando; Claudia Chamorro; Cristiana Chamorro.

For over a decade, the impoverished Central American nation of Nicaragua was the subject of countless newspaper and magazine articles, television reports and books in the United States and Europe that often differed sharply in their explanations of what was taking place in an area of the world heretofore largely ignored. A land of great social contrasts, Nicaragua was where the Panama Canal had almost been built had it not been discovered that the area was seismically very active and thus unsuitable for a safe path between the seas. A typical "banana republic," it had experienced in the late 1920s and early 1930s a temporarily successful uprising against its socially indifferent landowning oligarchy. Led by General Augusto César Sandino, this popular insurrection terrified not only the Nicaraguan elite classes but their American business allies as well. The murder of Sandino in 1934 ended the threat of social revolution as the Somoza clan established themselves at the top of the semi-feudal pyramid that was Nicaraguan society. United States corporate interests breathed a sigh of relief with the restoration of "order and normalcy." What was restored, or more correctly retained, was a plantation economy in which the vast majority of the people remained landless, illiterate and exploited.

Anastasio Somoza, the founder of the dynasty that was to rule and mercilessly exploit Nicaragua for the next 45 years, received the seal of approval of Franklin D. Roosevelt and succeeding Washington administrations. Roosevelt once admitted that Somoza "is a bastard, but he's *our* bastard." For decades, U.S. policy was to back the ruling oligarchies in Latin America, including the Somoza family, which ignored the needs of their nation's impoverished masses, enriching themselves, their friends and cronies to an obscene degree. When bribes did not quiet potential opponents, terror and murder invariably did. The onset of the Cold War and the appearance of a revolutionary government in Cuba in 1959 enabled the Somozas to argue more than ever that only their kind of rule would keep Nicaragua from succumbing to Marxism.

It was into this world of glaring social injustices that Violeta Barrios was born in 1929 in Rivas, a small town near the Costa Rican-Nicaraguan border. Both of her parents were members of the landowning elite. She grew up on a sprawling cattle ranch, enjoying a carefree life with numerous servants and total economic security; her early years were pleasant and intellectually unchallenging. Few in her circle ever questioned the social or economic system that gave them so much abundance, while most of their fellow Nicaraguans lived in conditions of squalor.

When the time came for decisions to be made about Violeta's education, it was clear that, since she had shown little evidence of strong intellectual interests, the best course would be to prepare her for the traditional role of marriage and motherhood. She spent two years at a Roman Catholic girls high school in San Antonio, Texas, and then went to Blackstone College in Southside, Virginia, where she took some secretarial courses. Despite her exposure to English during these years in the United States, Violeta Barrios never mastered the language, and could only speak it in broken fashion in later years. In 1948, her father died, and Violeta dropped out of college to return to life on the ranch in Rivas.

That year the life of Violeta Barrios changed forever when she met a charming and dynamic young man named Pedro Joaquin Chamorro. Five years her senior, he was descended from one of Nicaragua's most distinguished families. A great-uncle had been the country's first president, and three other Chamorros at four different times had held the highest office, one of them as recently as 1926. Pedro's family was wealthy and highly influential, his father being publisher of *La Prensa*, the only afternoon daily in the capital city of Managua. Although only a few years older than Violeta, Pedro's life had been infinitely more exciting. When they met, he and his family had recently returned to Nicaragua from an extended period of political exile. In 1944, while he was a law student, he had participated in a failed uprising against the Somoza dictatorship. The regime's punishment for the impetuous rebel from the prominent family was to shut down *La Prensa* and banish the entire family from Nicaragua. While Pedro's parents lived in New York City, he completed his legal studies in Mexico City.

Violeta Barrios and Pedro Chamorro were married in 1950. The same year, with the full backing of the landed interests and the United States, General Anastasio Somoza Garcia, known as "Tacho," was reelected president in an election that was a travesty of democracy. With his father's death in 1952, Pedro became publisher of *La Prensa*. His strong, religiously based sense of justice quickly became apparent both in the editorials of his paper and his own political actions. He joined the Internal Front, an organization of liberals from the ruling class who believed the nation needed both democracy and fundamental social reforms. Impatient with the pace of change and convinced that the Somoza clan would never relinquish control, in 1954 Pedro Chamorro joined an ill-fated rebellion. Confident in their hold on power, Somoza decided to punish Chamorro with mild sanctions. Sentenced to two years in jail, Pedro was able to spend the second year of his term under house arrest.

During the early years of her marriage, Violeta Chamorro showed little interest in politics, concentrating on raising her family of four, two boys and two girls who arrived in quick succession; a fifth child, a daughter, had died soon after birth. In 1956, only months after Pedro had resumed full control of *La Prensa*, Tacho Somoza was assassinated. As expected, he was succeeded by his son, Luis. Within hours, both Violeta and Pedro Chamorro found themselves under arrest. She was soon released, but Pedro was found guilty by a military court of having known about the assassination plot and failed to report. As punishment, he was to be banished for 40 months to the small town of San Carlos del Rio on the shores of Lake Nicaragua.

After leaving her children in the care of her mother-in-law, Violeta joined Pedro at his isolated place of exile, but he had no intention of spending over three years cut off from the world. One midnight, he and Violeta fled by canoe, eluding searchlights sweeping across the San Juan River, the boundary between Nicaragua and Costa Rica. After three hours, they entered a river tributary and thus escaped to freedom.

In San José, Costa Rica, the family was reunited. Besides writing fierce denunciations of the Somoza tyranny for the local press, Pedro also wrote a book-length indictment of their bloody, corrupt rule. He believed that only an uprising would topple the dynasty that ruled his country, and he now organized a military rebellion. Violeta kept in the background but did not try to stop him. Pedro went to Cuba to get arms from Fidel Castro, who had recently led a successful guerilla campaign against the corrupt Batista dictatorship, but was rebuffed. Undis-

couraged, Pedro led a small band of rebels into Nicaragua, but the rebellion was quickly snuffed by the better armed Somoza forces and Pedro and his men were forced to surrender. A sentence of nine years in prison was handed down by a military tribunal.

In the arbitrariness that was central to his and his clan's regime, Luis Somoza declared a general amnesty in 1960 that resulted in Pedro Chamorro being released from prison. He no longer plotted armed insurrection but continued during the next years to attack the regime on the pages of *La Prensa*. Violeta agreed with her husband. For several years in the 1960s, the Somozas were content to respect the letter of the constitution by ruling the country through puppet presidents. But in 1967, General Anastasio Somoza Debayle, known as "Tachito," announced he would run for the highest office. Mass protests followed and Pedro was arrested on the basis of "evidence" of involvement in terrorist activities found at his *La Prensa* office. He was released in 45 days.

Few were surprised when Tachito won the election, nor when, at the end of his term in 1972, Somoza turned over power to a hand-picked triumvirate guaranteed to do his bidding. Nature intervened at this point to dramatically alter the course of Nicaraguan history. A devastating earthquake destroyed Managua in December 1972, and both the corruption and incompetence of the Somoza dynasty was now revealed to the eyes of the world. Little reconstruction took place for years and vast sums of assistance funds from abroad was stolen by the Somozas and their cronies. In the middle of this situation, Tachito once more ran for the presidency, an election he of course won handily. Once in office, he brutally suppressed all stirrings of opposition. An outraged Pedro Chamorro now founded a coalition of anti-Somoza elements as the Democratic Union of Liberation (UDEL), organizing meetings throughout the country.

As Pedro Chamorro's political activism increased, his wife became ever more supportive. She often traveled with him to rural areas where they attended meetings and met with the poor. A novelist throughout his career, Pedro's book *Jesus Marchena* reflects his concern for the poor peasants, and is set in the area in which Violeta grew up. A passionate man, Pedro became increasingly impatient with the slow pace of change and his rhetoric became angrier. He was aware of the dangers involved in being leader of the opposition in a cruel dictatorship, often telling his wife that he expected to be killed. On January 10, 1978, Violeta was in Miami, shopping for a trousseau with her daughter **Cristiana** when a telephone call from her brother-in-law told her that Pedro had been assassinated by gunmen while driving to work.

Violeta returned home for the funeral, and despite her grief displayed strength and fortitude during the days of mourning. She turned her husband into a martyr, parking the bullet-ridden Saab he had been driving on the patio of their home; his blood-stained clothes were displayed in a glass case inside the house. Both remained there decades after Pedro Chamorro's martyrdom. The political consequences of the murder were immediate and dramatic. UDEL called for a general strike, which was largely successful in shutting down economic life. Somoza cracked down by proclaiming a state of siege. But what had been a spark of rebellion now turned into a strong flame of revolution, with bourgeois moderates seeking to collaborate with the decade-old Sandinista Liberation Front (FSLN).

As publisher of *La Prensa,* Violeta Chamorro continued to attack the Somoza regime. But it was deeds, not words, that counted now. A small force of FSLN rebels dramatically seized the National Palace in August 1979, forcing Somoza to release political prisoners, pay a ransom, and guarantee safe conduct. He agreed to their demands but soon attacked FSLN outposts in rural areas. He also burned down the *La Prensa* building. Violeta continued to publish in another city and returned to Managua some months later. Respected by anti-Somoza Nicaraguans as the "noble widow," she was neither an intellectual nor a leader, but her honesty and courage in the face of the dictatorship was nevertheless an inspiration when hopes seemed to fade.

Somoza wanted the United States to save his regime, but the Carter administration refused to assist him, and thus the butcheries and thieving that he and his family had presided over for more than a generation ended in July 1979, when he fled to Miami. The new "government of national reconstruction" was dominated by the radical Sandinistas, but they asked the more moderate Violeta Chamorro to join it as a member of its provisional executive junta. The prestige that she, the memory of her martyred husband, and *La Prensa* represented were all desired by the new government led by Daniel Ortega. But her view of the new, increasingly militant Ortega administration soon soured, and she resigned from the junta after only nine months.

After 1980, the situation within Nicaragua became part of international power politics and an increasingly tense renewed Cold War. The ultra-conservative administration of Ronald Reagan perceived the Sandinistas as Moscow's tool in the Americas, and Washington's response went far beyond verbal bursts of moral outrage. Full-scale economic warfare was declared to bring a defiantly radical Nicaragua to its knees, and the manpower and treasury of the Central Intelligence Agency were tapped to create a counter-revolutionary force, the Contras, comprised mainly of the remnants of Somoza's brutal National Guard.

The drawing of political lines both within Nicaragua and outside impacted strongly on the Chamorro family. While Violeta became increasingly disenchanted with Sandinista policies, criticizing them caustically in *La Prensa,* her son Carlos became an enthusiastic supporter of Daniel Ortega's line, becoming editor of the Sandinista party paper. Daughter **Claudia Chamorro** also became an enthusiastic Sandinista. Violeta's brother-in-law, Xavier Chamorro, also broke ranks with her by resigning from *La Prensa* to found a pro-revolutionary journal. Two of her children, however, were not swept up in the revolutionary currents of the day. Son Pedro Joaquin (known as "Quinto") and daughter **Cristiana Chamorro** and her husband Antonio became well-known anti-Sandinistas. Eventually "Quinto" became a Contra leader based in Miami. Despite these bitter political divisions, the family remained close, largely due to the strong personality of Doña Violeta, who remained an enduring symbol of clan stability and continuity.

After the 1984 election of Daniel Ortega as Nicaraguan president, pressure against *La Prensa* increased significantly. The paper was frequently shut down for brief periods, culminating in a major crackdown that began in 1986 when it was banned for fifteen months. Refusing to bow to the pressure, Violeta Chamorro published her critiques in other journals, demanding that the outside world exert pressure to bring about "a civilized government in Nicaragua, based on the right to free elections and respect for the fundamental rights of man." A hard-pressed *La Prensa* was kept afloat with substantial funding from the American Central Intelligence Agency.

Violeta realistically accepted the fact that massive intervention by the United States would not evaporate, but at the same time tried to create attitudes that would begin a process of superpower disengagement from Nicaraguan internal affairs. In an open letter to President Ortega published in *The New York Times,* she argued that "the grave crisis affecting Nicaragua must be resolved among ourselves, the Nicaraguans, without the interference of Cubans, Soviets, or Americans." Relaxation of Cold War tensions resulting from the appearance on the international scene of Mikhail Gorbachev made possible a resolution of the bloody and destructive unrest and social chaos that were destroying Nicaragua.

The Sandinistas, who had been immensely popular with the Nicaraguan masses in the first years of their rule, now had little to offer but more uncertainty and privation. Raids by the Contras, American trade sanctions, and the devastation of Hurricane Joan in 1988 all helped to demolish an already precarious economy. Living standards by the late 1980s were lower than the abysmal situation of a decade earlier, with Nicaragua now approaching the level of Haiti as one of the poorest societies in the Western Hemisphere. By August 1989, the inflation had reached an annual rate of 11,445%. For most Nicaraguans, the basics of survival had become unaffordable.

In 1989, Costa Rican President Oscar Arias persuaded his fellow heads of state of Central America, including Nicaragua, to sign an accord calling for the disbanding of the Contra forces in return for open and free national elections as well as other concessions from the Sandinistas. Convinced that they could win free elections, the Sandinistas signed the accord. Burying past differences, the anti-Sandinista forces created a coalition of 14 parties calling itself the National Opposition Union (UNO). Although her political skills were known to be modest, UNO chose Chamorro as their presidential candidate. She in turn chose her Sandinista son-in-law Antonio as her campaign manager, to underline her hopes that she was not running for office to triumph over an enemy but was engaged in the first steps of a process of national reconciliation.

If Chamorro did not grasp many details of economics or political maneuvering, there were times when she did act decisively. One such occasion was her choice of Alfredo César as her personal adviser. A businessman and politician disliked by many in the UNO leadership for his alleged opportunism, César had a good understanding of the Nicaraguan masses. He advised Violeta to run a simple campaign based on the slogan "UNO! Yes, it can change things!" The complacently confident Sandinistas relied on slick slogans that usually backfired, and despite advice from an American consulting firm that caused Daniel Ortega to abandon his army fatigues and designer glasses for contacts and casual garb, this image change also seemed to fizzle.

During the campaign, Violeta Chamorro, dressed in pristine white, was presented as an attractive grandmother with white hair. Her deeply traditional Roman Catholic piety was reflected in her speeches and appealed to conservative peasants who often linked her with *Mary the Virgin, mother of Jesus. Although she would later recall with distaste being "rolled out like some traveling circus attraction," she also fully realized "the importance of symbolism and the value of making the right gestures." She told a reporter at the time, "I have enormous confidence in God. He will illuminate and show me how to do what my conscience dictates." The genuine and essentially unsophisticated faith that radiated from Chamorro appears to have made a much stronger case with potential supporters than did her virtually nonexistent resumé. One UNO leader noted that "She is an icon like the Virgin of Fatima. She doesn't have to talk; she can just lead the procession."

In order to be seen firsthand by thousands of potential voters, Violeta let herself be driven through villages in her four-wheel-drive pickup truck, equipped with a canopy to protect her from the sun and "pillows to mitigate the blows from the potholes on the road." A fractured kneecap only heightened her appeal as she campaigned in a wheelchair or on crutches, stressing her message of national reconciliation and hope for a better future.

Internationally supervised free elections held on February 25, 1990, resulted in a UNO victory with 55.2% of the votes cast. While still president-elect, she made clear that hers would not be a vindictive victory: "Here we will not have victors or vanquished." Still on crutches when she took the presidential oath of office on April 25, Violeta Chamorro invoked the memory of her martyred husband: "This is the hour that his blood has borne the fruit of his dreams. We have reached the promised land. This is the Nicaragua sought by the exiles expelled by dictators. This is the Nicaragua without tyrants, without ideologies that destroy reality, without lies that conceal our history."

Acting as both head of state and government, Chamorro began her presidency wielding great power resting on a popular mandate. Rather than using her authority to crush the losing side in the election, she took steps from the first day of her administration to heal the nation's wounds. One measure was a general amnesty for all political crimes, which included those individuals responsible for her husband's assassination. There would be no rollback on Sandinista land reforms already in place, which meant that land titles already handed out to peasants would be respected. Within a few months after assuming the presidency, Chamorro had been able to disarm the last remnants of what had been a Contra guerilla army of 17,000 men. After abolishing military conscription, she was able to pressure the commanders of the Sandinista armed forces to trim their numbers, the largest in Central America, down to a more reasonable 28,000.

The six years of Violeta Chamorro's presidency were spent in attempts to heal the wounds resulting from the bitter struggles of the 1980s. By the end of her term in the fall of 1996, her government had achieved significant constitutional reforms including a permanent prohibition of obligatory military service and guarantees of private property rights. For only the second time in Nicaraguan history (her coming to power was the first), one chief executive passed power to the next in a peaceful and constitutional fashion. These were remarkable achievements, and gave hope that political democracy had at least a fair chance of becoming permanently rooted in Nicaragua.

What remained only a dream for the vast majority of Nicaraguans when Chamorro left office in 1996 was prosperity and social justice. The national economy was still essentially stagnant, with the damage of more than a decade of civil war still weighing down the lives of most farmers, workers and traders. The oligarchic structure of society, which produced a Violeta Chamorro, a woman who wished for the physical betterment of her poorer fellow-citizens but could offer no clear map to the future, remained largely intact. The privileged were still rich, and many of the poor in the 1990s were becoming even poorer. Unemployment was more than 50% of the potential work force, with infant mortality on the level of some of the poorest African states. These problems would have to be addressed by the next generation of Nicaraguans, hopefully in an atmosphere of political stability and democratic social reform.

SOURCES:

Chamorro, Violeta Barrios de, with Sonia Cruz de Baltodano and Guido Fernandez. *Dreams of the Heart: The Autobiography of President Violeta Barrios de Chamorro of Nicaragua*. NY: Simon and Schuster, 1996.

Kagan, Robert. "After the Deluge, and Before," in *New Republic*. Vol. 215, no. 17. October 21, 1996, pp. 36–41.

Veeser, H. Aram. "Addicted to Privilege," in *Nation*. Vol. 263, no. 9. September 30, 1996, pp. 27–30.

John Haag, University of Georgia,
Athens, Georgia

Champagne, countess of.

See Maud of Normandy (d. 1107).
See Marie de Champagne (1145–1198).
See Adele of Champagne for sidebar on Maud Carinthia (c. 1105–1160).
See Joan I of Navarre (1273–1305).

Champagneux, Madame (1781–1858).
See Roland, Madame for sidebar.

Champaigne, countess of.
See Champagne, countess of.

Champion, Kate (1861–1889).
See Watson, Ellen.

Champmesle, Marie (c. 1642–1698)

French actress. Name variations: Marie Desmares; Marie de Champmeslé. Born Marie Desmares in Rouen, France, in 1642 (some sources cite 1641 or 1644; died in Auteuil, France, on May 15, 1698; sister of actor Nicolas Desmares (c. 1650–1714); aunt of actress ✥➤ Christine Desmares (1682–1753); married Charles Chevillet (1645–1701), who called himself sieur de Champmeslé or lord of Champmeslé, in 1666; no children.

Little is known about Marie Champmesle's family or childhood, except that she was born in Rouen in 1642. Because she became an actress instead of marrying young, the norm for aristocratic women, it is unlikely that Marie came from a wealthy family. It seems more likely that her roots were in the lower bourgeoisie; very few women pursued independent careers if they came from well-to-do families. Marie began acting in the early 1660s, making her first appearance in Rouen with Charles Chevillet, known as the lord of Champmeslé. They appeared in many plays together and married in 1666.

Marie quickly became known as a talented dramatic actress in Rouen. In 1669, she and her husband moved to Paris to further their careers, both performing at the Théâtre du Marais, where Marie appeared as Venus in Boyer's *Fête de Venus*. She had great success at Paris' Hôtel de Bourgogne as Hermione in Racine's *Andromaque*. Her friendship with one of France's most talented playwrights dates from this production. Jean-Baptiste Racine admired Champmesle immensely and would write some of his finest tragedies for her. Though she was also the original Berenice, Monimia, and Phédre in his works, her repertoire was not confined to Racine's plays, and many indifferent plays—such as Thomas Corneille's *Ariane and Comte d'Essex*—owed their success to "her natural manner of acting, and her pathetic rendering of the hapless heroine."

When she and her husband left the Hôtel de Bourgogne, her Phédre, the culmination of Champmesle's triumphs, was selected to open the Comédie Française in Paris on August 26, 1680.

✥➤ **Desmares, Christine** (1682–1753)

*French actress. Born Christine Antoinette Charlotte Desmares in 1682; died in 1753; daughter of actor Nicolas Desmares (c. 1650–1714); niece of *Marie Champmesle (c. 1642–1698).*

Marie Champmesle's niece, Christine Desmares, to whom Denmark's king Christian V and his queen *Charlotte Amalia of Hesse stood sponsors, was a fine actress in both tragedy and ingenue parts. Christine made her debut at the Comédie Française in 1699, in La Grange Chancel's *Oreste et Pylade*, and was immediately received as *societaire*. She retired in 1721.

She and her husband would remain as principal players for the next 30 years. With **Mme Guérin** as the leading comedy actress, Marie played the great tragic love parts. In addition to acting, Charles wrote many of the plays in which Marie starred; his *Parisien* (1682) gave Guérin one of her greatest successes. Champmesle attracted many admirers as the leading actress in the Comédie's tragic dramas; one devoted fan was the great French novelist Jean de la Fontaine, who dedicated his novel *Belphégor* to her. The French critic and poet Nicolas Boileau-Despréaux immortalized the actress in verse. Champmesle continued to work up until her death on May 15, 1698, at age 56.

Laura York,
Riverside, California

Champseix, Léodile (1832–1900).
See Léo, André.

Chandler, Dorothy Buffum
(1901–1997)

American newspaper executive, civic activist, and the major force behind the building of Los Angeles' Music Center. Name variations: Buffy. Born Dorothy Buffum in Lafayette, Illinois, on May 19, 1901; died on July 6, 1997; one of three children of Charles Abel (owner of a chain of department stores) and Fern (Smith) Buffum; graduated from Long Beach High School, 1919; attended Stanford University, in Palo Alto, California; married Norman Chandler (publisher of the Los Angeles Times from 1944 to 1960), on August 30, 1922; children: Otis Chandler (publisher of the Los Angeles Times from 1960 to 1980); Camilla Chandler.

Dorothy Chandler, wife of Norman Chandler, president and publisher of the Los Angeles-based Times-Mirror Company, became administrative assistant to her husband in 1948. She helped him establish an afternoon paper, the *Los Angeles Mirror*, and worked with the women's department of the *Los Angeles Times*. Although Chandler became a director of the company in 1955 (she retired in 1976), it was her long involvement in civic affairs that prompted *Life* magazine to refer to her in a 1956 article as the "great lady of the West."

In 1950, Chandler initiated the *Los Angeles Times* Women of the Year Awards, which were presented annually to southern California's outstanding women. She was a recipient of this award in 1951 in recognition of her work in fund-raising for the financially distressed Hollywood Bowl. She was active with the Southern California Symphony Association and served as director of the San Francisco Opera Association. Chandler also raised funds for the Los Angeles Philharmonic Orchestra and helped make possible the orchestra's tour of the Orient in 1956. She chaired the board of the Civic Auditorium and Music Center Association of Los Angeles County and served on the boards of Children's Hospital, Occidental College, and the University of California. Named to President Dwight Eisenhower's U.S. Committee on Education Beyond the High School, Chandler traveled to the USSR in 1955 and later appeared before an Education and Labor subcommittee to urge adoption of a more liberal cultural-exchange program. In the early 1960s, Chandler raised a "staggering $18.5 million," wrote a *Time* magazine correspondent, to build the Los Angeles Music Center, "and organized a company to float another $13.7 million in bonds to finish the job." The Music Center now houses the Dorothy Chandler Pavilion, from which the Academy of Motion Picture Arts and Sciences has held its yearly awards ceremony.

SUGGESTED READING:

Time (cover story on Dorothy Chandler). December 18, 1964.

Barbara Morgan,
Melrose, Massachusetts

Chandler, Elizabeth Margaret

(1807–1834)

American abolitionist and writer. Born on December 24, 1807, at Centre, near Wilmington, Delaware; died of fever on November 22, 1834; daughter of Thomas Chandler (a Quaker farmer); educated at the Friends' schools in Philadelphia; never married.

Elizabeth Margaret Chandler's writing called upon women to stand beside men in the battle against slavery, "the only means of avoid-

ing participation in guilt." She was born near Wilmington, Delaware, in 1807. After the death of both her parents when she was still a child, Chandler was raised in Philadelphia by Quaker relatives. She was 18 when her poem "The Slave Ship" won a literary prize and was spotted by anti-slavery leader Benjamin Lundy. Chandler began writing for his paper, the *Genius of Universal Emancipation*, to which she contributed for the rest of her short life. A supporter of the free produce movement (in which women refused to purchase goods produced by slave labor), she called upon women to think independently from men. While her writing touched upon a variety of reform issues, she was primarily concerned with the immediate abolishment of slavery, and many of her poems, set to music, were rendered at anti-slavery meetings.

In 1830, Chandler and her aunt and brother moved to the territory of Michigan, settling near the village of Tecumseh, Lenawee County, on the river Raisin. She named her farm Hazlebank and continued contributing poetry on the subject of slavery until 1834 when she succumbed to remittent fever on November 22; she was in her 20s when she died. Two years later, in 1836, Benjamin Lundy published *The Political Works of Elizabeth Margaret Chandler*. Included in this volume is an 1830 letter from Chandler to abolitionist friends; the letter reads in part:

> Your cause is a righteous one, and *worth every effort*. There are times when I feel as if I could go unflinching to the stake or the rack, if I might by that means advance it. I never expected to do "great things" in this cause—I have never indulged in speculations as to the effect of what I attempted to do, yet I sometimes feel as if I had been a mere idle dreamer, as I had wasted my time in nothingness—so disproportioned does the magnitude of the cause appear to all that I have done; so like a drop in the ocean are my puny efforts.

Chanel, Coco (1883–1971)

French fashion innovator, patron of the arts, entrepreneur, and creator of the little black dress and the Chanel suit. Name variations: Gabrielle Bonheur Chanel. Born Gabrielle Bonheur Chanel on August 19, 1883, in Saumur, France; died on January 10, 1971, in Paris, France; daughter of Albert Chanel and Jeanne (Devolle) Chanel; attended Aubazine Orphanage and Notre Dame Finishing School, Moulins; never married; no children.

Raised by nuns (1895–1901); employed as a shop assistant, seamstress, and music-hall performer,

Coco
Chanel

(1901–06); lived with Étienne Balsan at Royallieu
(1906–09); moved to Paris (1909);
met Arthur Capel (1909); opened shop in
Deauville (1913); introduced casual sports wear;
opened fashion house, Biarritz, (1915); created the
jersey dress; met Pablo Picasso (1917); reimbursed
Arthur Capel (1918); worked on ballets with Sergi Diaghilev and Pablo Picasso; introduced Chanel no. 5
perfume (1921); entertained a romance with Grand
Duke Dimitri (1922–24); had a relationship with
Duke of Westminster (1924–30); created the little
black dress (1926); accepted contract from Samuel
Goldwyn (1930); closed House of Chanel (1939); had
a relationship with Hans Gunther Spatz (1940–50);
arrested in Paris (1946);
moved to Switzerland (1946);
made fashion comeback (1954); introduced the Chanel suit (1956); inspired
Broadway musical Coco (1969).

Because her father Albert Chanel was an
itinerant merchant, Gabrielle "Coco" Chanel
was born in a hospice in Saumur, a remote town
in southwestern France, on August 19, 1883.
Over one year later, in November 1884, her parents married. When her mother **Jeanne Devolle
Chanel** died at age 32, in February 1895, leaving
behind five children, Gabrielle was 11. Her father soon abandoned his young family, and
Gabrielle never saw him again. For the next six

years, Albert's daughters lived in a bleak orphanage at Aubazine. In later years, Gabrielle never spoke of this period of her life.

As an adolescent, she was enthralled by the novels of Pierre Decourcelle, which she would smuggle into the orphanage. The writer's heroines were always intelligent and independent, with a flair for fashion and a wardrobe to match. At 18, she and her sister **Julie Chanel** were sent to a finishing school in Moulins. After graduation, Gabrielle was employed as a shop assistant, a seamstress, and a music-hall performer, where she gained her lifelong nickname from the refrain of a popular song: "I've lost my poor Coco. Coco, my lovable dog."

Coco blossomed into an attractive young woman with many admirers. One was Étienne Balsan, a former army officer and horse breeder. In 1906, he invited her to live at Royallieu, his estate near Paris. At age 23, happy to escape the past and the provinces, she gladly accepted. By age 25, Chanel was familiar with the charms of luxury and leisure. She often took long rides in the forest of Compiègne and dressed with unfailing instinct for fashion. Among the regular visitors to Royallieu were the courtesan ❧ **Emilienne d'Alençon** and the actress *Gabrielle Dorziat**, both of whom later became her clients. But Chanel soon grew tried of the idle pleasures of Royallieu, and in 1909 Balsan lent her his pied-a-terre in Paris. After she began to buy hats in Paris shops and remodel them according to her minimalist tastes, what began as a hobby mushroomed into a business.

It was during her first stay in Paris that she met Arthur Capel, an English friend of Balsan, who became her financier and lover. "He had a very strong personality," she recalled years later, "and was an ardent and concentrated man; he made me what I am, developed what was unique in me, to the exclusion of the rest." Throughout her life, Capel remained one of her few true loves.

On rue Cambon, Chanel opened a small shop; soon, the names rue Cambon and Chanel became synonymous. Her success was so rapid that by 1910 famous actresses and celebrities were often photographed donning her headgear. In 1913, Coco and Arthur Capel vacationed at Deauville, where he encouraged her to open a boutique. With her reputation as a milliner firmly established, she added a line of accessories, as well as beachwear and sports clothes of her own design. The clothes were casual, comfortable, and classic, and the Baroness *Mathilde de Rothschild** became a client, setting a trend for others to follow.

With the outbreak of World War I, the coastal resort was soon deserted by fashionable society, but Coco refused to panic. Soon, she was doing a brisk trade in outfitting newly arrived nurses, as well as returning wealthy clients who had fled the French capital in the face of a German advance. A year later, Coco and Arthur moved on to Biarritz, a fashionable resort near the Spanish border. There, she opened her first *maison de couture*, complete with its own dressmakers and high fashion collections, which she would operate until 1922. Nearby Spain offered a clientele of wealthy aristocrats, and, by 1918, Chanel had paid off her debt to Capel and was financially independent. Shortly afterward, Capel died in an automobile accident on the Côte d'Azur.

With the shortage of textiles caused by the war and an increasing demand for practical women's fashions, Chanel adapted the jersey, a style of sweater originally worn by the mariners of the Channel islands, into a dress, creating a fashion revolution. "In inventing the jersey, I liberated the body, I eliminated the waistline," she noted, "and created a new silhouette. . . . To the great indignation of couturiers, I shortened dresses." Along with social emancipation, the war created a demand for functional simplicity that extended into the postwar era.

In May 1917, *Misia Sert** introduced Chanel into French high society, and Coco became an instant success. "She seemed to have an infinite grace," recalled the socialite. Pablo Picasso, who also met Chanel in 1917, claimed she had more good sense than any other woman he had ever known. In turn, Chanel was mesmerized by Picasso's intensity: "He was wicked. He fascinated me the way a hawk would; he filled me with a terrible fear. I would feel it when he came in: something would curl up inside me: he'd arrived. I couldn't see him yet but already I knew he was in the room." The two would collaborate on several theater and ballet projects. Chanel became a patron of the Paris art scene, financing Les Ballets Russes, the company of Sergi Diaghilev, as well as designing costumes. She lent Igor Stravinsky her villa in 1920, so that he could finish his Concertina for String Quartet and write his symphonies for wind instruments. Stravinsky gave her his most treasured possession as a gift, a Russian icon that Chanel kept on her night-table until the end of her life.

She met Ernest Beaux, one of the most celebrated perfumers of his generation. Many great perfume houses had opened their doors in Paris during the late 18th century. Beaux presented

❧▶
Alençon, Emilienne d'.
See Uzès, Anne, Duchesse d' for sidebar.

Chanel with a series of perfume samples made of natural ingredients, and she selected one. On May 5, 1921, the same day she unveiled a new collection, her perfume went on sale. Chanel no. 5 was to become world famous.

The Roaring '20s marked a period of liberalization in the lifestyles of women. Chanel created dresses that were synonymous with luxury and simplicity. She never worked from sketches, but on models, using scissors and needles to create her fashions. The youthful, slender look of Chanel's "little black dress" became the uniform of a generation, with its geometric austerity and its functionality. "Women think of all colors except the absence of color," she commented. "Black has it all."

Before World War I, Chanel had met the Grand Duke Dimitri (Romanov), a tall and handsome member of the Russian nobility, who was a co-conspirator in the murder of the politically powerful monk Rasputin. In 1922, Chanel and the grand duke became seriously involved, and she supported him financially. In return, he gave her the Romanov pearls, which she copied, legitimizing the wearing of false pearls in the world of high fashion.

The Duke of Westminster, the richest man in England, was also sincerely in love with Coco; their affair lasted from 1924 to 1930. She accompanied him on his yachts, visited his many houses, and he showered her with flowers and jewelry. But Chanel, bored with the life of the idle rich, continued to turn down his marriage proposals. Work was something she could not do without. Her visits to Britain inspired many of her fashion ideas. "I had the tweeds brought over from Scotland," she said; "homespuns overthrew the crepes and muslins."

In the summer of 1930, Chanel accepted a contract from Sam Goldwyn, the Hollywood magnate, to design movie wardrobes for the stars of his studio. Coco soon saw through the glitter and pretence of Hollywood and dropped the contract, but among the clients she acquired during her American sojourn were ***Marlene Dietrich** and ***Greta Garbo**. ***Gloria Swanson** wore her creations in the film *Tonight or Never*.

From the movie Chanel Solitaire, *starring Marie-France Pisier.*

Despite the worldwide Great Depression and the rise of Nazism in Germany, Chanel continued her brilliant career. In 1933, she turned 50, still dictating fashion. "Be a caterpillar by day and a butterfly at night," she said. "There is nothing more comfortable than a caterpillar and nothing more made for love than a butterfly. We need dresses that crawl and dresses that fly." Chanel excelled in the use of transparent materials for evening gowns—tulle, net, muslin—all in her favorite colors: white, black, pink, and navy blue.

When war was declared on September 3, 1939, Coco closed her fashion house, leaving open only the perfume boutique, which sold all of its stock of Chanel no. 5 to German soldiers wishing to impress their sweethearts back home. After a brief sojourn in the south, she returned to Paris, where she lived out the war in seclusion. During the German occupation, she became involved with Hans Spatz, a German diplomat and suspected Gestapo agent. With the liberation of Paris, popular indignation among the public and the press was overwhelming. Chanel was openly labeled as a collaborator and arrested after two weeks but not charged. In 1946, she and Spatz moved to Lausanne, Switzerland, becoming neighbors of Charlie Chaplin.

Fashion is architecture: it is a matter of proportion.
—Coco Chanel

In 1947, Christian Dior's "New Look" swept Paris, but Chanel rejected it as nostalgic. In 1950, Spatz faded from her life, and in 1953 she secretly began to plan her return. Chanel was assured of the support of the Wertheimer brothers, who owned the rights to Chanel no. 5. Postwar America had also developed a large and growing ready-to-wear market and a mechanized fashion industry that was geared to mass production, which Coco eyed with interest.

On February 5, 1954, at age 70, Chanel unveiled her new collection, which the fashion critics dismissed as dated. Undeterred, Chanel had the support of the American press, and by 1956 she was back in designing form. Her tailored wool suit, henceforth associated with her name, became the universal success that her "little black dress" had enjoyed. "These post-war suits of Chanel were designed God knows when," wrote the editor of *Vogue* years later, "but the tailoring, the line, the shoulders, the underarms, the jupe—never too short, never making a fool of a woman when she sits down—is even today the right thing to wear." When combined with American mass production techniques, Coco captured the U.S. and European markets. Along with her tailored suits and evening gowns, she created short, airy dresses, worn without a hat, for cocktail or garden parties.

By 1958, the women's weekly *Elle* was declaring that "all the movie people want to be dressed by Chanel." Coco designed the flowing costumes for Louis Malle's film *The Lovers* (1958); the clothes worn by *Delphine Seyrig in *The Last Year at Marienbad* (1961); and the costumes of *Romy Schneider in Luchino Visconti's film, *Boccaccio '70* (1962).

The last years of Chanel's life saw her at the peak of her fame. By 1968, the House of Chanel payroll totalled 400 employees; her celebrated clientele included *Sophia Loren, Catherine Deneuve, and *Elizabeth Taylor; and *Time* Magazine estimated that Coco's fashion empire, including perfume, was worth $160 million a year. A Broadway musical appeared in 1969 entitled "Coco," starring *Katharine Hepburn. In the meantime, Chanel continued policing fashion, lashing out at the Mao suits and miniskirts of the era. "Do you think that a woman looks any younger because she shows her knees and her thighs? It's gaudy and it's indecent; two things I hate." The spring collection of 1971, her last, stuck to classic styling, and was heralded by the critics as a definitive success.

In later years, Coco Chanel was a lonely figure, sustained by her work. She spoke of retirement, though never seriously, but work became increasingly difficult in her 80s, because of arthritis. Asked by the press why she never married, she replied: "The two men I loved never understood. They were rich, and never realized that a woman, even a rich woman, wants to do things. I would never be able to abandon the House of Chanel. It was my child." When she died on January 10, 1971, the funeral, held at the church of the Madeleine in Paris, brought out the Paris fashion community, as well as artists, socialites, and politicians. Her casket was draped with garlands of roses, gardenias, and orchids.

Coco Chanel created a fashion look for the ages. She ruled the fashion industry for nearly six decades, showing that innovations can be basic, and that casual can be classic. Not just a creative dynamo, Chanel also built a vast business empire. Her heart, however, remained in fashion. She was a woman who refused the traditional role; instead, she defined her role:

I wonder why I went into this profession, and why I played a revolutionary role. It was not to create what pleased me; what I wanted above all was to put out of fashion what did not please me. . . . I have been the instrument of Fate for a necessary cleaning operation.

SOURCES:

Charles-Roux, Edmonde. *Chanel.* Trans. by Nancy Amphoux. NY: Alfred A. Knopf, 1975.

Galante, Pierre. *Les Années Chanel.* Paris: Paris-Match, 1972.

Haedrich, Marcel. *Coco Chanel: Her Life, Her Secrets.* Trans. by Charles L. Markmann. Boston, MA: Little, Brown, 1972.

Kenneth, Francis. *Coco: The Life and Loves of Gabrielle Chanel.* London: Victor Gollancz, 1989.

Millbank, Caroline. *Couture: The Great Designers.* NY: Stewart, Tabori, and Chang, 1988.

Steele, Valerie. *Paris Fashion: A Cultural History.* NY: Oxford University Press, 1988.

SUGGESTED READING:

Madsen, Axel. *Chanel: A Woman of Her Own.* NY: Henry Holt, 1990.

Wallach, Janet. *Chanel: Her Style and Her Life.* NY: Doubleday, 1998.

RELATED MEDIA:

Chanel Solitaire (124 min film), starring **Marie Pisier,** Timothy Dalton, Rutger Hauer, **Karen Black,** and **Brigitte Fossey,** directed by George Kaczender, FR/GB, 1981.

The musical *Coco,* book and lyrics by Alan Jay Lerner, music by Andre Previn, opened at the Mark Hellinger Theatre on Broadway on December 18, 1969, starring Katharine Hepburn.

Hugh A. Stewart, M.A., University of Guelph, Guelph, Ontario, Canada

Chang, Eileen (1920–1995)

Chinese novelist and short story writer, considered by critics to be one of the greatest figures of modern Chinese literature. Born Chang Ai-ling (Zhang Ailing) in Shanghai on September 30, 1920; found dead in her apartment in Los Angeles, California, on September 8, 1995; married Hu Lan Cheng; married Ferdinand Reyher.

Eileen Chang, who was to become one of the greatest figures of 20th-century Chinese literature through her powerful depictions of a traditional society in the throes of moral and social decay, grew up in the highest levels of that same society. She was born Chang Ai-ling (Zhang Ailing) in Shanghai in 1920 into an elite family with a distinguished lineage that included statesmen of the Imperial court as well as classical scholars. Despite her affluence, she grew up in emotional turmoil. Her father was a domestic tyrant who tormented his daughter by locking her up in the house for months at a time. A profoundly troubled man, Chang's father derived pleasure from the mental torture he inflicted on his child, who eventually was able to flee and join her mother, a woman of cosmopolitan education who had studied painting in France and had already fled from her abusive husband. After having lost both wife and daughter, Chang Ai-ling's father lived openly with his concubine and rapidly declined into a haze of opium addiction.

Determined to put her life in order, Chang enrolled at the University of Hong Kong in 1938 where she studied literature and English. During these years, she continued her intensive investigations, already begun in her earliest years, of Chinese literary classics including the 18th-century novel *Dream of the Red Chamber.* Starting in 1937, China was embroiled in a bloody war with Japan, and although she had the means to leave, Chang decided to remain in Hong Kong. She was still there in December 1941 when Japanese invasion brought panic to the city. In 1942, she returned to Shanghai, now under a harsh regime of Japanese occupation. Here, she made her living by turning out both novels and film scripts. Although they were all conceived of as commercial products and their literary quality varied greatly, these apprentice writings were nevertheless all superbly crafted and gave evidence of Chang's deep study of the great works of modern Western literature, particularly the French naturalist school of Emile Zola and others. Her romance *Love in a Lost City* caught the mood of the city in wartime and made her an overnight cultural celebrity.

In her personal life, Chang did not show the deliberation and order so apparent in her art. Although much desired because of her beauty and stylishness (she designed her own elegant dresses), she had been unlucky in her amours; she then fell recklessly in love with **Hu Lan Cheng,** who unfortunately was not only married but served as a high official of the pro-Japanese puppet Chinese regime as well. Unable to rein in her emotions even though many of her friends urged caution, the affair ended in inevitable calamity: her lover fled for his life when Japan lost the war and their Chinese collaborators were reviled as traitors.

The end of the war did not bring peace either to China or to Chang. Growing politicization of literature and the rapid collapse of the Nationalist regime made ideology attractive to the majority of Chinese writers and Chang's aristocratic disdain for politics served to isolate her within intellectual circles. Although they would later be held in high esteem, the books she published during these tumultuous years found little critical or popular support. *Rumors,* a collection of essays, and *Strange Stories,* a collection of her short stories, were viewed as showing indifference to the great events transforming the lives of hundreds of millions of Chinese. With misgivings, but hoping to make the best of the radically new situation, she decided to remain in China as Mao Zedong's Red Army swept all before it.

The birth of the Chinese People's Republic in 1949 created a radically new environment for bourgeois intellectuals like Chang Ai-ling. Although by no means dogmatically opposed to the sorely-needed reforms the Communists would bring to a corrupt and morally exhausted society, she remained independent in spirit so that try as she might, she could neither accept Communist goals nor join the party. In 1952, Chang left the mainland for Hong Kong, where a collection of her short stories appeared in print in 1954. The next year would mark a turning point in Chang's career, transforming her into an international literary star. She moved to the United States in 1955, settling in Los Angeles, and published *The Rice-Sprout Song,* a novel about the harsh impact of the Korean War on China's peasantry. To mark her entrance onto the stage of world literature with a work that she had first written in English and then herself translated into Chinese, Chang Ai-ling now signed her writings with her newly adopted Western name of Eileen Chang.

The Rice-Sprout Song was a great success in part for the wrong reasons, having been viewed in a strongly political context by many American critics. With anti-Communism still a dominant feature of intellectual life, some Americans read Chang's novel more as an ideological tract than as commentary on a tragic phase of modern Chinese history. Chinese Communist cultural bureaucrats were outraged, banning all of her works—a measure that remained in place for three decades. Although an effective piece of literature, *The Rice-Sprout Song* was by no means Eileen Chang's best work, having been written at least in part in anger. Western readers would not be able to read her best work for at least another decade.

Critics agree that Chang's greatest work is her 1944 novella *The Golden Cangue,* which relates the life of a beautiful girl who marries for money and finds herself the object of her husband's abuse (*cangue* refers to a form of restraint resembling the stocks used in colonial America). When expanded into a full-length novel as *The Rouge of the North,* the story takes on added depth and psychological subtlety, showing how the once-compassionate girl was transformed into a despotic matriarch. Chang's subtle use of the Chinese vernacular, effectively translated into English, impressed Western critics who hailed the novel as a masterpiece when it was published in 1967. Unfortunately for Chang, her work continued to be viewed in light of the Cold War, rather than simply literary art. Feeling that her efforts were misunderstood by both critics and readers, by the 1960s she rapidly lost confidence in her abilities as a writer.

In the 1960s, Eileen Chang was a writer-in-residence at the University of California, Berkeley. By this time she had essentially abandoned her own writing, concentrating instead on teaching and working on a translation from the Shanghai dialect into Mandarin Chinese of *The Lives of Shanghai Beauties,* a classic novel of the Qing dynasty. A loner throughout her life, Chang now became a recluse, rarely emerging from her Los Angeles apartment. She was married a second time to Ferdinand Reyher, a Hollywood screenwriter who had been a close friend of Bertolt Brecht. After Reyher's death in 1967, Chang withdrew into ever more strict hermit-like seclusion. She never read the innumerable scholarly articles praising her writings, she granted no interviews, and she disappointed countless readers by no longer even considering a resumption of her writing career. Literary fanatics went so far as to search her garbage for signs of renewed writing activity, but to no avail. Totally alone but with her work by no means forgotten by the literary world, Eileen Chang died on an unknown date in early September 1995 in her Los Angeles apartment. Her body was discovered on September 8. Unfortunately for her many readers, no literary manuscripts were found among her effects.

SOURCES:

Chang, Eileen. *Naked Earth: A Novel about China.* Hong Kong: Union Press, 1964.
———. *Red Rose, White Rose* (1995 motion picture, directed by Stanley Kwan).
———. *The Rice-Sprout Song.* NY: Scribner, 1955.
———. *The Rouge of the North.* London: Cassell, 1967.
"Eileen Chang," in *Daily Telegraph* [London]. September 20, 1995, p. 21.
"Eileen Chang," in *The Times* [London]. September 18, 1995, p. 21.
Hsia, Chih-tsing. *A History of Modern Chinese Fiction.* 2nd ed. New Haven, CT: Yale University Press, 1971.
———, ed. *Twentieth-Century Chinese Stories.* NY: Columbia University Press, 1971.
Lau, Joseph S.M., C.T. Hsia and Leo Ou-Fan Lee, eds. *Modern Chinese Stories and Novellas 1919–1949.* NY: Columbia University Press, 1981.
Thomas, Robert McG., Jr. "Eileen Chang, 74, Chinese Writer Revered Outside the Mainland," in *The New York Times Biographical Service.* September 1995, p. 1352.

Tsai, Nai-huei Shen. "Patriarchy and Female Subjectivity: Eileen Chang's *The Golden Cangue* and *The Rouge of the North*." M.A. Thesis, University of California, San Diego, 1992.

Tseng, Sally. "An Analysis of Eileen Chang's *The Rice-Sprout Song*: Irony." M.A. Thesis, University of Toronto, 1992.

Weissman, Dorothy Tsungsu. "Chang, Eileen," in Martin Tucker, ed. *Literary Exile in the Twentieth Century: An Analysis and Biographical Dictionary*. NY: Greenwood Press, 1991, p. 177.

Zhao, Henry. "Shanghai Classic," in *The Guardian*. October 6, 1995, p. 17.

John Haag, University of Georgia, Athens, Georgia

Chang Cai (1900–1990).

See Cai Chang.

Chanler, Margaret (b. 1862).

See Farrand, Beatrix Jones for sidebar.

Chanler, Mrs. Winthrop (b. 1862).

See Farrand, Beatrix Jones for sidebar.

Channing, Carol (1921—)

Tony Award-winning actress best known for her roles as Lorelei Lee in Gentlemen Prefer Blondes *and Dolly Levi in* Hello, Dolly! *Born on January 31, 1921, in Seattle, Washington; only child of George Channing and Adelaide (Glazer) Channing; attended local schools in Seattle and San Francisco, and Bennington College in Vermont; married briefly to novelist Theodore Naidish; married Alexander Carson (an ex-football player from Canada); married Charles Lowe (her manager), around 1957 (divorced 1998); children: (second marriage) son, Channing Lowe (who would be adopted by her third husband).*

Found first job on Broadway in her junior year in college; gained stardom with her creation of Lorelei Lee in Gentlemen Prefer Blondes *(1949); cast as Dolly Levi in* Hello, Dolly! *(1964), a role for which she received the Tony Award as Best Actress in a Musical and which she has since played more than 4,000 times on Broadway and on tour; awarded the Tony Award for Lifetime Achievement (1995).*

Stage: No For an Answer; *(lead understudy)* Let's Face It; Lend an Ear; Gentlemen Prefer Blondes; Wonderful Town; Show Girl; *(tour)* The Millionairess; Pygmalion; Hello, Dolly!; Lorelei; Jerry's Girls; *(tour)* Legends.

Filmography: Paid in Full *(1950);* The First Traveling Saleslady *(1956);* Thoroughly Modern Millie *(1967);* Skidoo *(1968); (voice only)* Shinbone Alley *(1971);* Sgt. Pepper's Lonely Hearts Club Band *(1978); (voice only)* Happily Ever After *(1985); (voice only)* Thumbelina *(1992).*

On October 19, 1995, Dolly Gallagher Levi reappeared on Broadway, sweeping down the famous steps leading to the Harmonia Gardens Restaurant and the welcoming arms of its cadre of waiters in pin-striped vests. Carol Channing has stopped counting exactly how many times she has made the same entrance in *Hello, Dolly!*, although estimates stand at more than 4,500. She *is* Dolly Levi, readily admitting that she sometimes doesn't know where one persona ends and the other begins. Both she and Dolly are strong-willed, capable women wrapped in a pleasing façade of wide-eyed innocence. "World, beware," wrote Vincent Canby in his *New York Times* review of the new production. "It's possible this woman is a substance that should be legally controlled."

For Carol Channing, Dolly's 30th anniversary appearance on Broadway was only the midpoint of a tour of more than 40 American cities, with even more to come in Europe, Japan, and the Far East, all undertaken in her 74th year. She has been called "the greatest comedienne since *Bea Lillie" and has a reputation as the understudy's nightmare for never missing a performance—except once, so she could accept her 1995 Tony Award for Lifetime Achievement. When journalist **Leslie Bennetts** asked why she drove herself so hard, Channing's reply was simple: "It's happiness," she said. "What am I supposed to save myself for? This is pleasure."

Her early childhood bore little sign of what was to come. Carol Channing was born on January 31, 1921, in Seattle, Washington, the only child of George and **Adelaide Channing**. Soon after Carol's birth, her father, a well-known Christian Science lecturer, took a teaching position in San Francisco, the city Channing would consider her hometown. Her parents' marriage was a strained one, and Adelaide often took her frustrations and anger out on her daughter. "Nobody understands if you're frightened of your mother," Channing once told Bennetts, claiming that her mother was, at the least, eccentric and possibly mentally unbalanced. "She would go to school and tell the teachers things I never said about them. I was absolutely petrified." Adelaide deliberately kept Carol away from other children and was jealous of any achievements her daughter could claim—even going so far, Channing later claimed, as to persuade one of her teachers to refrain from giving the girl an award for public speaking. "She completely possessed me," said Channing.

But Adelaide couldn't prevent her daughter from being elected class secretary at her grammar school, and it was then that the first indication of Channing's future talent came to light. Afraid of saying something in her acceptance speech that would make her seem above everyone else, Channing began imitating familiar school figures, gently but accurately enough to bring howls of laughter to the auditorium. She was utterly amazed that the same things *she* found funny everyone else did, too. "This is the most delicious feeling I ever had," she remembers thinking. "We're all alike!" Her imitations became a regular feature of Friday morning assembly at Commodore Slope Grammar School, enjoyed as much by the teachers as by their pupils.

When Channing was in her early teens, she was taken to see *As Thousands Cheer,* a musical revue in which *Ethel Waters sang "Summertime" from *Porgy and Bess.* It was Channing's first exposure to professional theater, and Waters' performance affected her profoundly. "It was like being in love," she later said, and the experience convinced her that she should pursue a career on the stage. Not long after, she found a summer job with the dance company of the San Francisco Opera and returned there each season until she was too tall for the troupe.

By now, however, she was ready for college. When her parents moved to Boston, Channing entered Bennington in Vermont, as a dance and drama major. New York was only a few hours away by train, and her visits there on weekends and holidays were frequent. By the time she was 19 and a junior at Bennington, Channing felt she was ready for a career. In 1940, William Morris was the biggest agency in the business, and Channing managed to get an appointment with no less than its president, the legendary Abe Lastfogel.

Her biggest hit during Bennington drama evenings had always been her stirring recitation of the funeral chant from *Orestes.* This failed to impress Lastfogel, who suggested she forget the "ethnic music" and try something more classical—"like Ethel Merman," recounted Channing to the 1975 graduating class at Bennington. She hit on a Yiddish song she had learned in an Eastern European seminar at Bennington. Lastfogel, still not entirely sold on this wide-eyed young woman from Vermont, nevertheless sent her off to audition for a very off-Broadway musical called *No For an Answer.* The answer in her case was yes. It was her first paid job in New York, though a short-lived one, the show closing after only a few performances. Her only job on Broadway was as an understudy for *Eve Arden who, like Channing years later, never missed a performance. For the next six years, Channing

was on the road—a tour of the borscht belt through the Catskills (she was fired, she claims, for going flat during one number), and an endless round of nightclub engagements that eventually brought her back to the West Coast. Along the way, there was a brief marriage to novelist Theodore Naidish who, she later said, died of drug abuse.

It was in her home territory that her fortunes would change; in San Francisco, Channing auditioned for a young director and choreographer named Gower Champion, then about to begin rehearsals for a show called *Lend an Ear.* After a successful run in California, the production was brought to Broadway in 1948. It was a hit and won her the Theatre World Award. But it was her next show that would make her a star overnight.

Over 20 years before, *Anita Loos had published a novel featuring a good-hearted golddigger named Lorelei Lee. On December 8, 1949, the musical version of *Gentlemen Prefer Blondes* premiered on Broadway, with a libretto by Loos, music by Jule Styne, and starring Carol Channing as Lorelei. The show introduced her signature song, "Diamonds Are a Girl's Best Friend," along with "I'm Just a Little Girl from Little Rock," and defined her stage persona as the not-so-dumb dumb blonde. In 1976, when Channing was touring a comedy act with George Burns, the venerable comedian would say of her: "We all know today that the dumb blonde isn't dumb. She never was. Channing makes us understand that joke. Her dumb blonde becomes larger than life—like Jimmy Carter's teeth." Audiences loved the mixture of innocence, calculation, and kindness Channing brought to the role of Lorelei. In a pattern that has repeated itself throughout her professional life, Channing went on the road with the show and brought Lorelei to audiences across the country and overseas. Along the way, she met and married an ex-football player from Canada, Alexander Carson.

As the London tour of *Gentlemen Prefer Blondes* was being put together, Channing discovered she was pregnant and subsequently had to withdraw from the production. She admits that the unplanned pregnancy was a blow to her professional hopes. "I was upset," she told journalist Bennetts. "I knew how ambitious I was." Her son Channing (in future, a successful political cartoonist) was born in 1953 and would spend much of his childhood, like his mother, on the road. Three years after his birth, while her marriage was suffering from her husband's excessive drinking, Channing met and fell in love with television producer Charles Lowe, and it is hard to overstate his influence on her future. Lowe expedited her divorce from Alexander Carson; married Channing and legally adopted her son; and in time took over the management of Channing's career, a successful collaboration that lasted for 40 years and was one of the most remarkable relationships in show business. Their secret, Channing explains, was simple—fill up the theatre, whatever it takes. But Channing made headlines in 1998 when she filed for divorce, claiming that Lowe was squandering her money and had not made love to her since the first year of their marriage.

With the tour of *Gentlemen Prefer Blondes* over, Channing returned to Broadway for a revue called *Show Girls*; for the role of Eliza Doolittle in Shaw's *Pygmalion*; and for the *Betty Comden-Adolph Green musical, *Wonderful Town*. Then came an offer to take the lead role in a musical to be produced by David Merrick and scored by her friend Jerry Herman, based on Thornton Wilder's book *The Matchmaker*. Wilder had originally written it in 1938 as a dramatic play, called *The Merchant of Yonkers*, which had starred *Ruth Gordon*. It was Channing's good fortune that Gower Cham-

*Carol
Channing*

pion had been asked to direct and choreograph the musical version, for he had insisted on Channing for the lead. On January 16, 1964, Channing took her first steps down those famous stairs as Dolly Gallagher Levi in the premier of *Hello, Dolly!*

The safest place in the world is the middle of a stage.
—Carol Channing

"I worked very hard in the beginning to become Dolly," Channing has said. "I was madly in love with the character, but I had never played anyone like her before." Even with her hard work, the road to Broadway wasn't a smooth one. Reviews were generally negative when the show tried out in Detroit, and librettist Michael Stewart had to trim many of the show's subplots and bolster the main storyline dealing with Dolly's grief for her dead husband and how she overcomes it. Because the cutting meant dropping several musical numbers, the show had to be restaged; as late as the critics' preview in New York, the cast was working with an entirely new ending for the first act with no costumes ready for its new closing number ("Before the Parade Passes By"). But by opening night, none of the frustrations and headaches mattered. The show was an instant success, and Carol Channing had won that rare thing for any musical comedy star—a second triumph, not to mention her first Tony Award. She would play Dolly for three years, finally closing—after 1,273 performances—in Houston, Texas, on June 11, 1967. By then, the show had grossed some $17 million at the box office, a record at the time. In a closing curtain speech, Channing said, "Maybe David Merrick will have a grand *Hello, Dolly* reunion in the year 2000, and we'll all come back!" But it wouldn't take that long. Channing toured with the show again in 1978, including another Broadway run, and eagerly accepted plans for the 30th anniversary tour in 1994–95.

Although some performers might have adopted a more leisurely pace after two huge successes, Channing was not one of them. She continued to tour her nightclub act. Along with spoofs of *Marlene Dietrich and **Brigitte Bardot**, she featured such characters as the excessively sibilant Cecilia Sisson, a silent film diva mystified by her inability to make it in talkies, and Cuddles Heffelfinger, the chorine with little talent but big ambitions. There were, to be sure, some disappointments to offset the renown of Dolly and Lorelei Lee. A 1973 sequel to *Gentlemen Prefer Blondes*, called *Lorelei*, was a disappointment; as was an ill-fated show called *Legends*, in which

Channing co-starred with *Mary Martin. The show folded after doing badly on tour and never opened in New York. Hollywood, always baffled by Channing's wide-eyed bewilderment and gravelly voice, also proved a source of frustration. The film versions of both *Gentlemen Prefer Blondes* and *Hello, Dolly!* were cast without her. *Marilyn Monroe appeared on screen as Lorelei, while **Barbra Streisand**, whose chance at a Tony Award for her portrayal of *Fanny Brice in *Funny Girl* was lost to Channing's Dolly, starred in the film version of *Hello, Dolly!* Privately hurt by the announcement, a day later she sent a typical Channing telegram to Streisand's dressing room: "So happy for you and Dolly, dearest Barbra. Love, Carol." Undaunted, Channing continued to accept the occasional film role and was nominated for an Oscar as Best Supporting Actress for her performance in 1967's *Thoroughly Modern Millie*. She appeared regularly on television specials and chat shows throughout the '70s and had her own weekly "The Carol Channing Show" on ABC.

But it was the stage that never let her down. Since *Lend an Ear* in 1948, Channing has never stopped working and touring, traveling with up to 20 suitcases in tow—one of which amounts to a small, portable kitchen, for Channing prefers to travel with her own food supply because of what she says are allergies to sprays and preservatives in commercially prepared food. She is notorious for appearing at the most sophisticated restaurants with a large handbag containing her foil-wrapped meals, and recalls with relish dining on her own roast pork with Princess *Margaret Rose who, she remembers, was "stuck with shrimp scampi, the poor dear." Another suitcase once contained 20 pairs of false eyelashes, the loss of which on one occasion in Detroit resulted in a virtual civic emergency, with appeals on radio and television for their return, which happily took place. (She has since given up the false eyelashes because, she says, the years of adhesive have irritated her lashes and eyelids.)

Channing has also been active politically for the Democratic Party, especially during Lyndon Johnson's Great Society period of the 1960s. (Asked why she was a Democrat, Channing said it was because "the Republicans never spoke to me.") She appeared at the 1964 Democratic National Convention that nominated Johnson, singing "Hello, Lyndon," and the 1976 convention that nominated Jimmy Carter, singing "Peanuts Are a Girl's Best Friend." Later, during the Nixon years, she ended up on the infamous Enemies List, which was published only a week after she had appeared at a luncheon given by *Pat Nixon, to whom Channing gave one of her signature "diamonds"—actually a rhinestone. "I guess the President had the diamond appraised," she suggested. The publication of the list was not without its advantages. The box office for the Cincinnati production of *Lorelei* shot up by $10,000 the day after.

Like her father, Channing has been a devout Christian Scientist all her life, and even her religious faith is grounds for some ribbing. "We Christian Scientists don't believe in age," she says. "It's my favorite part of the whole religion." To this day, Channing is unsure of her own parents' ages, although she thinks her mother was close to one hundred at her death. Despite the lightheartedness, her spiritual beliefs have informed her public life with a reputation for caring and hard work. "It's when we take the plunge we've been afraid to take," she once wrote, "deliberately putting ourselves in other people's shoes, involving ourselves in their struggles, that we make contact again with God." Nor does she abandon her faith when she steps onto a stage; she says it helps her face an audience that may not be in the most receptive mood. "These are the times I use a little trick," she says. "'*I care about you*' I say to myself as I face the audience. '*I know you're tired from working hard and that you've paid a high price for your seats.*' The first thing you know, the laughter comes bouncing back and forth from audience to stage, like anodes and cathodes, and down near the orchestra pit comes a bridge of love you could walk over." That bridge has supported Carol Channing during a career of more than 50 years, and shows no sign of weakening.

SOURCES:

Bennetts, Leslie. "All Lips and Lashes," in *Vanity Fair*. No. 422. October 1995.

Cagle, Jess. "Hello Again," in *Entertainment Weekly*. No. 277. June 2, 1995.

Flatow, Sheryl. "As If She Never Said Goodbye," in *Playbill*. Vol. 95, no. 9. September 1995.

King, Larry. Transcript of interview on "Larry King Live," CNN, November 28, 1994.

Tynan, William. "Hello, Dolly!" *Time*. Vol. 144, no. 12. September 19, 1994.

Norman Powers, writer/producer, Chelsea Lane Productions, New York, New York

Chantal, Jane de (1572–1641).

See Chantal, Jeanne de.

Chantal, Jeanne de (1572–1641)

French saint and co-founder, along with Francis de Sales, of the Order of the Visitation of Holy Mary, whose many letters survived, providing a detailed picture of the religious ideas and ideals of her age. Name variations: Saint Jane Chantal; Jeanne Chantal; Jane de Chantal or Jeanne de Chantal; Jane Frances de Chantal; Madame de Chantal; Jeanne-Françoise, baroness de Chantal; Jeanne de Rabutin-Chantal. Born Jeanne-Françoise Frémiot in Dijon, France, on January 23, 1572; died in Moulins, France, on December 13, 1641; daughter of Bénigne Frémiot and Marguerite de Berbisey Frémiot; grandmother of Marie de Sévigné (1626–1696); married Baron Christophe de Rabutin-Chantal; children: Celse-Bénigne de Rabutin-Chantal (1596–1627, father of Marie de Sévigné); and five others, of which three survived infancy. Canonized as a saint of the Roman Catholic church in 1767.

Born in 1572 into the highest strata of the French nobility, Jeanne-Françoise Frémiot lost her mother **Marguerite de Berbisey Frémiot** at the age of 18 months. Fortunately, her father Bénigne Frémiot, president of the Burgundian parliament, which met at Dijon, was a man of integrity who concerned himself with his daughter's education and moral development. Jeanne was educated at home by tutors who imparted the usual skills of a girl of the aristocracy—reading, writing, dancing and performance on musical instruments. By her mid-teens, Jeanne-Françoise had blossomed into a beautiful young woman with good sense and a happy, lively temperament.

At age 21, she married Baron Christophe de Rabutin-Chantal, thus becoming linked with one of the most ancient and illustrious families of Burgundy. Within the next few years, she lived on her husband's estate in Monthelon, giving birth to six children, two of whom died in infancy; a boy and three girls would survive. After seven years of marriage, her husband was killed in a hunting accident. After the initial shock of losing her spouse, Chantal returned to her father's home in Dijon. Here she sought solace for her loss and turned to a priest who encouraged a spiritual regimen that was austere and very likely excessive. Because she had left her children behind, her father-in-law threatened to disinherit his grandchildren unless she returned to his castle at Monthelon near Dijon. This she did in 1602, spending almost the entire decade that followed supervising the education of her children while attempting each day to exercise the Christian virtues of patience and humility. She would return every year to her own estates at Bourbilly near Semur-en-Auxois to supervise the wine harvest.

In 1604 while visiting her father, Jeanne de Chantal met Francis de Sales (1567–1622) who had recently been appointed the bishop of Geneva. Deeply impressed by the piety and broad learning of this fellow aristocrat, she asked that he serve as her spiritual director. After some hesitation, he consented and presented her with a spiritual agenda based on his principles. From this point on, they were in contact with one another through a mutual correspondence that lasted almost two decades, ending only with his death.

After her first meeting with Francis de Sales, Chantal made a double vow—to remain unmarried and to obey him. She wished at this stage to enter upon a religious life, but he counseled patience. In 1607, he informed her of his plan for founding a group of women who would practice those virtues of humility, piety and mutual charity that were exemplified in *Mary the Virgin's visit to *Elizabeth. The plan also called for a community of women who would engage part of the time in the carrying out of works of mercy for the sick and poor.

After almost three years of preparation and consultation with Chantal, Bishop de Sales established the first convent in Annecy adhering to their rules in March 1610. Jeanne de Chantal was the co-founder and superior of what would henceforth be known as the Order of the Visitation of Holy Mary. Changes agreed to during the next few years included the elimination of external works of charity and subordination of the cloister to the authority of the bishop of Lyons. In April 1618, Pope Paul V elevated what was still officially an institute of the church to an officially sanctioned religious Order.

By the time Francis de Sales died in December 1622, there were 12 other monasteries besides the original one. At the time of her death in 1641, there were 80 monastic houses in the Order. Jeanne de Chantal spent the last years of her life collecting her correspondence with de Sales. She was still alive in 1627 when the process of his canonization was opened; in 1662, de Sales was beatified, and he was canonized a saint by Pope Alexander VII in 1665.

After a long, richly rewarding life, Jeanne de Chantal died in Moulins on December 13, 1641. She was beatified in 1751, and Pope Clement XIII declared her a saint of the church on July 16, 1767. Besides her considerable achievements in the religious sphere, Jeanne de Chantal represents a significant link with a vibrant and complex period in European history. One scholar has written admiringly of "[t]his foundress in a great age [who] wrote good and vivid letters [that] are of considerable spiritual but also literary and

historical value; they reflect moreover the religious and cultural climate of France in the reign of Louis XIII." Some scholars have argued that her letter-writing talent was a genetic quality that was passed on to her descendants. Jeanne's granddaughter Marie de Rabutin-Chantal, known to literary history as *Marie de Sévigné (1626–1696), left behind an equally valuable treasure trove of correspondence. To be both a saintly human being and superb letter-writer, as was Jeanne de Chantal, makes her an unusually appealing personality to a contemporary era that has only rarely produced individuals who are able to combine such qualities.

SOURCES:

Bougaud, Émile. *St. Chantal and the Foundation of the Visitation.* Translated from the 11th French edition by a Visitandine. 2 vols. NY: Benziger Brothers, 1895.

Ravier, Andre. *Saint Jeanne de Chantal: Noble Lady, Holy Woman.* Translated by Mary Emily Hamilton. San Francisco, CA: Ignatius Press, 1989.

Sanders, Ella Katharine. *Sainte Chantal, 1572–1641: A Study in Vocation.* NY: Macmillan, 1928.

Stopp, Elisabeth. "François de Sales and Jeanne de Chantal: Two Unpublished Letters," in *French Studies.* Vol. 18, 1964, pp. 17–23.

———. *Madame de Chantal: Portrait of a Saint.* Westminster, MD: Newman Press, 1963.

Wright, Wendy M., and Joseph E. Power, eds. Francis de Sales, *Jane de Chantal: Letters of Spiritual Direction.* Translated by Peronne Marie Thibert. NY: Paulist Press, 1988.

———. *Bond of Perfection: Jeanne de Chantal and François de Sales.* NY: Paulist Press, 1985.

———. *A Retreat with Francis de Sales, Jane de Chantal, and Aelred of Rievaulx: Befriending each other in God.* Cincinnati, OH: St. Anthony Messenger Press, 1996.

John Haag, University of Georgia, Athens, Georgia

Chantal, Marie de Rabutin (1626–1696).

See Sévigné, Marie de.

Chapelle, Dickey (1919–1972)

American photojournalist and the first American woman reporter killed in action. Name variations: Dickey Meyer. Born Georgette Louise Meyer in Shorewood, Wisconsin, a suburb of Milwaukee, in 1919; killed at the front near Chu Lai, South Vietnam, on November 4, 1972; daughter of Edna and Paul Gerhard Meyer (a traveling salesman for a steel company); granted full scholarship to Massachusetts Institute of Technology, 1935, but dropped out her second year; married Tony Chapelle, in October 2, 1940 (annulled, July 1956); children: (stepson) Ron Chapelle.

Georgie Lou Meyer, who would jettison the "Georgie Lou" for "Dickey" by her senior year in high school, was raised in Shorewood, an affluent suburb of Milwaukee, Wisconsin, where she was born in 1919. A roustabout with a penchant for getting herself into unlikely places, she found her heroes among the doers of her age: Admiral Byrd hurtling his dogsleds toward the South Pole and Baron von Richthofen performing in air battles over Germany. Two books that profoundly affected her were Yancey's *Aerial Navigation and Meteorology,* 4th edition, and an account by Richard Harding Davis of his experiences as a combat reporter in World War I. Dickey's father was a patient, quiet man, while her mother was described as a controlling, overprotective woman who went on emotional binges. **Edna Meyer,** like her daughter, was said to be a nonstop talker.

Dickey loved airplanes, and set her sights early on a career in aeronautical engineering, possibly because she was forbidden by her mother ever to enter a plane. Her first published article, at age 14, was "Why We Want to Fly," which landed in the *United States Air Service* magazine. In 1935, Dickey graduated from high school, valedictorian of her class at age 16, after skipping a grade; that autumn, she was one of seven girls entering the freshman class of the Massachusetts Institute of Technology (MIT), Cambridge.

At MIT, "her hair was kept as short as a boy's," Chapelle wrote in a third-person self-assessment. "She dressed in trousers, a man's shirt and tie, and a battered blue raincoat. It was a perfect time for an overprotected girl to bust loose, to shock, to rebel, to be seen living in the manner of a young savage." Admitted on full scholarship, the "young savage" also moonlighted as a "flying girl reporter for the *Boston Traveler,*" but signs of her immaturity soon outstripped her daring; by 1937, she was on the train home to Wisconsin, having flunked out.

With planes still on her mind, Dickey negotiated her services as a secretary in exchange for flying lessons. "I was the least-promising flight student who ever near-crashed a trainer on each circuit of the field," she wrote. Because her parents wanted her away from pilots, she took a job as a typist in the accounting department of the *Milwaukee Journal.* When they discovered that she was still hanging around the airport, they packed her off to a grandparent in Coral Gables, Florida, which allowed her to maneuver her way into a job as assistant on an air show in Miami and led to her being hired in 1939 as a correspondent for *The New York Times* and Associated Press (AP) to cover a Cuban air show. This

Dickey Chapelle

she parlayed into a position as secretary to the public relations director of the New York branch of the company that was soon to become Trans World Airlines (TWA).

By 1940, Dickey Meyer had also joined the Women Fliers of America (WFA), when she signed up for a photography course run by Tony Chapelle, a WWI navy photographer who directed TWA's publicity photos. Tony was more than 20 years her senior and secretive about his past; it would be six years after their 1940 marriage before she discovered that his second wife was just getting around to divorcing him.

Professionally, Tony took his third wife under his wing, piloting her in flights over the George Washington Bridge while Chapelle hung over the side of the plane taking aerial shots with an eight-pound Speed Graphic camera. She had sold a few photos to newspapers when she made her first major sale, a story on "spec" about a woman in an aircraft plant. When *Look* magazine published the story in the spring of 1941, Chapelle quit her job to work freelance.

In December 1941, the bombing of Pearl Harbor drew the United States into World War II. Tony was soon sent by the navy to the Canal

Zone, Panama, to be an instructor in aerial photography, and the following June, Chapelle parlayed her few sales and a firm magazine assignment into accreditation as a war correspondent. Joining her husband, she completed the assignments but found them rejected. In 1943, she returned to New York, where she began to write for *Life Story* magazine (known later as *Today's Woman*). In the spring of 1945, she got the opportunity she had been waiting for: an assignment to cover the Pacific Theater.

At 25, Chapelle was the first woman photographer accredited to the Pacific Fleet and the youngest of all women correspondents. Authorized by the magazine, along with McBride Publishing, she proceeded to Honolulu, where she soon discovered the rules against women on the military front. "No woman correspondent was allowed to spend the night with the troops, unless navy nurses were already there," wrote her biographer **Roberta Ostroff**. "If she went against these orders, scrupulously drawn to prevent women from covering combat, she would lose her accreditation."

Nevertheless, Chapelle soon hitched a ride in a C-47 troop transport plane to the island of Guam, just as the American flag was being raised on neighboring Iwo Jima. On Guam, she begged Admiral Harold Miller, public relations officer for the Pacific Fleet, to allow her onto Iwo, still under combat, but her pleas were met with a resounding no. He did agree, however, to let her accompany a hospital ship to the island to pick up casualties; en route, the ship came under Japanese air attack. Writes Ostroff:

> Racing to a prearranged security station, up three ladders to the ship's flying bridge, [Chapelle] squeezed under the mount of the ship's searchlight. As the public address system blared its instructions to take cover, the zeke [kamikaze] came into focus in her viewfinder.

But she had left behind her telephoto lens. "In short," wrote the humbled Chapelle, "I'd fluffed the coverage of my own baptism by fire." She promised herself that she would never make such a mistake again.

That same day, Chapelle watched the grim work of corpsmen loading 552 casualties onto the hospital ship.

> When I first began to work on the welldeck, I tried only to keep out of the way of stretcher bearers and to keep on focusing, framing, lighting, and shooting pictures. The shapeless, dirty, bloody, green bundles being lifted and carried before me were not, repeat, not, human as I was human. . . . There must be

something better that a woman could do with these men than to photograph them. I haven't cringed at their wounds, but at my lens.

The ship returned to Guam with a total of 753 casualties, and Chapelle's photographs reached print in December 1945 in *Cosmopolitan.*

Guided by her Guam tentmate, **Barbara Finch**, a correspondent for Reuters, Chapelle managed to board another hospital ship just off Okinawa, which was poised for the invasion of that island. But she "prided herself on not writing up anything she could not personally see and verify. . . . She called it 'eyeballing.'" With the help of the marines, and despite the warnings of the naysaying admiral, Chapelle managed to maneuver her way off the ship and to the front, where she remained "overnight" for six days. The furious admiral withdrew her accreditation and had her escorted back to Guam, then home.

Stateside, Chapelle became a staff photographer and associate editor for *Seventeen,* where she quickly grew bored. On November 14, 1947, with the Cold War underway, she and her husband Tony embarked on a Danish freighter for Eastern and Central Europe, hired by the American Friends Service, the Quaker group that was one the major charitable organizations providing aid to Europe's postwar survivors. Gone for six years, the Chapelles made a total of 10,000 pictures used by a dozen agencies—including CARE, Save the Children, the United Nation's Children's Emergency Fund (UNICEF)—to encourage donations.

Photographically, Chapelle does not compare to later women photographers like **Susan Meiselas** (1948—), **Mary Ellen Mark** (1940—), and *Eve Arnold. "The value of her photos was their authenticity," according to Ostroff, "which meant the world to her. They were quality snapshots of events she eyewitnessed, events few photographers had the courage to seek out. The frames did not yield poetry, but reality. They were I think her way of seeing and then proving to disbelieving editors that she indeed was there. Her writing for publication had the same utilitarian quality. The value of what she wrote was where it originated, in the eye of the storm."

Through the 1950s, Chapelle was where the action was. She was a small birdlike woman with a smoky voice—one of the few voices, as one friend put it, that could be heard under machine-gun fire. In September 1955, back in the States, she spent three months bunked in a marine women's barracks at Camp Pendleton, writing about the women's *esprit de corps*. In October 1956, when Hungarian freedom fighters rose up against the Russians who controlled their country's communist dictatorship, Chapelle looked for a way to cover the uprising and the aftermath, in which thousands of Hungarians fled their country to escape Russian reprisals. By November 15, Chapelle was in Vienna, on secret assignment for Leo Cherne's International Rescue Committee (IRC) and the editors of *Life* magazine.

At the Hungarian border, near the small wooden footbridge at Andau, Chapelle became friends with the writer James Michener, who was also there for the story, and his wife **Mari**. "On the frontier, Dickey and I sometimes went far behind the Russian lines," said Michener. "I was cautious, she was totally fearless. I would draw back from spots of danger, she would always crowd forward. I was older than she, more experienced. It was her first time in the situation, yet she was quite extraordinary in her personal courage." With each expedition, according to Michener, Chapelle would go deeper and deeper into Hungary, to bring out Hungarians. She saved "hundreds, maybe," said the writer. "If she were a man, they would have called her a hero."

On the evening of December 4, Chapelle walked into Hungary illegally, carrying antibiotics for Hungarian patriots under one arm and a Minox camera taped under the other. Arrested that night, she was driven to Budapest, but she managed to toss the Minox out the window before she reached AVO headquarters (Hungarian secret police). Chapelle was held for five weeks at the state prison in solitary confinement before being moved to Marco Street Prison where she was put in a cell with eight other women. Out of diplomatic necessity, she was disowned by everyone. *Life* had warned her that if the trip did not go smoothly, it would disavow any involvement with her; and though two of her photos had appeared in its December 3rd issue, the magazine kept its word. Overseas press reports of her capture identified her to the American public only as a freelance photographer.

Brought to trial on January 26, 1957, Chapelle was sentenced by the Communists to 50 days in prison; since she had already served 53, she was ordered to leave the country immediately. Crediting the American embassy for her release, she returned to the U.S., recognized as something of a Cold War celebrity. Her exploits became fodder for episodes appearing in the Steve Canyon comic strip into the 1960s.

Chapelle returned to her old job as press liaison at the Research Institute of America (RIA), which was also run by Leo Cherne, but according to Orloff, the captivity had left her humiliated. "She was no longer the bright-eyed, enthusiastic employee." Apart from her wounded pride, she held herself to blame for the imprisonment of two freedom fighters who had accompanied her on the venture. When fellow reporters in the Overseas Press Club suspected her of having gone to Hungary for her own self-aggrandizement, she could not argue her case without exposing the IRC and *Life*. "I knew the conditions under which I'd been employed," Chapelle wrote later. "I'm proud of taking my medicine and coming back for more. . . . *I* made the mistakes; *I* was punished. End of story." Ironically, in writing his *Bridge at Andau*, Michener disguised the identity of "a brave and daring photographer whose pictures helped tell the story of Hungary's mass flight to freedom," by referring to the photojournalist as a male. Six years later, Chapelle would finally be honored by the IRC.

> *C*ourage is not the absence of fear but the control of fear.
>
> —Dickey Chapelle

For the next four years, *Reader's Digest* was her main sponsor. In July 1957, she covered the Algerian War from the side of the FLN, who were rebelling against the French. In November 1958, she set out for Cuba to interview Fidel Castro and his insurgents. The Cuban military force was the first in her memory to include women fighters and the first to minimize her restrictions, allowing her to witness five military actions. Chapelle was not blind to the faults of Fidel; she worried about his ego and the Communist tendencies of his brother Raoul, but she also fumed at U.S. indifference to the terrorism of Cuba's ruling dictator, Fulgencio Batista. In a *Reader's Digest* article, she delineated the U.S. role in arming Batista's forces. According to Ostroff, "She did not fare well in issues falling outside her midwestern morality of black and white, good guy against bad guy, and toward the end of her life, the indistinguishable grays the world had become sent her searching harder, further, for the moral certainty of her youth." By January 1960, when Castro had been in power in Cuba for a year, she would go off him. "While the sky is the limit in attacking the United States," she would grouse, "no Castro leader ever attacks Soviet Russia or Red China."

In 1958, Chapelle covered the Lebanese Civil War, the marine maneuvers on Crete, and the marines' final assault landing in Beirut on July 17, worrying less in each case about getting shot than getting future work. Despite her credentials, scrambling for assignments had always been a chore. "She was a woman, and most photo editors were male," said her agent, **Nancy Palmer**. "Most of them simply didn't believe she shot half the pictures she did. And I must say that women editors were not much better. So she worked cheaper than the male photographers, because she wanted the assignments." In May 1959, Chapelle was 40 years old when she signed up for parachute training. Two months later, as part of a story, she jumped with the troops of the First Special Forces of the 82nd Airborne.

In 1961, when she first arrived in Vietnam, there were fewer than 12 accredited reporters from the West. Dressed in fatigues, jungle boots, an Australian hat, and black harlequin glasses, with two battered Leica cameras draped around her neck, she liked going into action behind the "point man," the man who led the patrol, the first man the enemy was likely to pick off. Chapelle's only concern was keeping up. "She did not stay in the safety of the rear battalion, as many reporters did when covering conflicts, but kept up with the foot soldier or jumped with the parachutists. Besides, she preferred staying with the troops twenty-four hours a day, sleeping in a foxhole. Unlike the correspondents, who didn't know what to make of her, the marines accepted her as she was. She traveled with enough supplies in her small combat pack for three weeks in the field."

On May 3, 1961, Chapelle landed in Vientiane, Laos, to gather military intelligence for *Reader's Digest* on a ceasefire. While there, she wrote a piece on the U.S. Green Berets, but it was turned down by the *Digest* to protect the activities of the CIA. In June, she arrived in Saigon. Parachuting with Vietnamese airborne, she earned her second set of wings, for completing six jumps, one with two cameras and full field gear. "With them," writes Ostroff, "she walked nearly two hundred miles through head-high jungle and knee-deep swamp. She was fired on from ambush, watched the airborne return fire seven times, and slept seventeen nights in the field." Returning to the United States on November 7, 1961, Chapelle reported to the Pentagon in Washington, where she turned in 1,000 photos for clearance, only to have 800 of them manage to get lost by the Defense Department in censorship.

On April 1962, Chapelle was given the highest honor of the Overseas Press Club, the George Polk Award, "for the best reporting in any medium requiring exceptional courage and enterprise abroad." The following year, one of her photos would be chosen Photograph of the Year by the Press Photographers' Association. That year, Chapelle's autobiography, *What's a Woman Doing Here?* hit the bookstores with a title she hated. For one thing, as she told her publisher, the military's greeting was generally: "What the hell are you doing here?" Writes Ostroff:

> Reading the edited version, she discovered that all her hard-earned reporting on war from the grubby perspective of the soldier in a foxhole had been scrupulously disinfected by her editor in New York. She felt burning indignation at being portrayed as a dizzy, if gutsy, broad who just happened to show up whenever she heard the sound of guns. To her, her sex had nothing whatsoever to do with her role as a military observer, and now she felt as though the publisher were making *that* the only point.

In Chapelle's words, they "feminized the hell out of it."

Meanwhile, though she was in favor of America's role in the war in Vietnam, she was pushing the U.S. government to admit that there actually was a war going on and that the United States was in on it. On November 4, 1965, she was in the field, covering forced resettlement of the country's peasants for the *National Observer* and New York's WOR Radio. On morning patrol for a search-and-clear mission on the front near Chu Lai, South Vietnam, Chapelle was in her usual spot, directly behind the man on point, when he tripped a booby trap that killed them both. "Guess it was bound to happen," she said, just before she died. As Father John McNamara administered last rites to Dickey Chapelle, fellow journalist Henri Huet shot the AP photo that went out over the wire service around the world.

The body of the first American woman reporter killed in action was brought back to Milwaukee by an honor guard of six marines. The 82nd Airborne named a drop zone after her, and the marines named a hospital in Vietnam in her memory. At her funeral, the Women's National Press Club presented a memorial scroll, asserting that Dickey Chapelle was "the kind of reporter all women in journalism openly or secretly aspire to be. She was always where the action was."

SOURCES:
Ostroff, Roberta. *Fire in the Wind: The Life of Dickey Chapelle*. NY: Ballantine Books, 1992.

SUGGESTED READING:
Chapelle, Dickey. *What's a Woman Doing Here?* (autobiography). NY: Morrow, 1962.
Los Angeles Times (obituary). November 21, 1965.
National Geographic (farewell tribute). February 1966.

Archives of the Wisconsin State Historical Society at the University of Wisconsin, Madison.

Chapin, Augusta (1836–1905)

American minister. Name variations: Reverend Augusta J. Chapin. Born Augusta J. Chapin in Lakeville, New York, in 1836; her ancestors settled in Springfield, Massachusetts, in the 17th century; died in New York, New York, on June 30, 1905; attended Olivet College, Michigan; A.M. from the University of Michigan, Ann Arbor; granted honorary doctor of divinity by Lombard University, Galesburg, Illinois, in 1893; never married.

The daughter of parents who pioneered in Michigan, Augusta Chapin began attending school at age three; by fourteen, she was a teacher. Chapin applied to the University of Michigan but was refused admittance several time because of her gender. In 1852, she entered a small school in Michigan, Olivet College, where she developed what would be a lifelong interest in theology. Chapin received her degree and preached her first sermon around 1856, beginning the life of an itinerant minister, a "circuit rider" who taught school to support her efforts.

In 1863, in Malone, New York, *Olympia Brown* became the first ordained woman in America; Chapin's ordainment followed six months later, in December 1863, by the Universalists at Lansing, Michigan. In 1864, she received her first pastorate. Her career as a preacher would continue until 1901, and Chapin was ordained by congregations in Iowa, Illinois, Nebraska, Pennsylvania, and rural New York, finding increased opportunity in remote locations. In 1893, she received the first honorary doctorate of divinity given to an American woman, from Lombard University in Galesburg, Illinois. She also received her A.M. from the school that earlier rejected her application, the University of Michigan.

A feminist who spoke at national suffrage conventions, Chapin was a member of the first executive committee of the Association for the Advancement of Women. At the Columbian Exposition in 1893, she served as chair of the general committee for women. Chapin was 65 when she retired to New York City, where she died four years later, in 1905.

Chaplin, Mildred Harris (1901–1944).

See Weber, Lois for sidebar on Mildred Harris.

Chaplin, Oona O'Neill
(1925–1991)

Well-known daughter of Eugene O'Neill and wife of Charlie Chaplin. Born Oona O'Neill on May 14, 1925; died in 1991; only daughter and youngest of two children of Agnes Boulton (1893–1968, a writer) and Eugene O'Neill (a playwright); attended Brearley School, New York; married Charlie Chaplin (the film actor), on June 16, 1943; children: eight, including Geraldine Chaplin.

The product of the intense, tempestuous union of playwright Eugene O'Neill and his second wife, writer *Agnes Boulton, Oona O'Neill Chaplin was raised primarily by her mother after her father deserted the family when she was just two. The divorce that followed left Eugene angry and bitter toward Boulton and had a scarring effect on his relationship with Oona and her older brother Shane. Despite her splintered family, Oona grew into a bright and self-assured young woman, as well as a great beauty. While still a senior at Brearley, a swank private school in New York, she was voted "New York's Number One Debutante" and counted the then unknown writer J.D. Salinger among a string of admirers.

At the age of 17, Oona left New York for Hollywood, hoping to break into acting. There she met and fell deeply in love with the legendary English-born screen actor Charles Chaplin, who offered to coach her for a screen career. "What blue eyes he has!" she wrote to her girlhood friend **Carol Matthau**, wife of actor Walter Matthau. Charlie, at age 53, was something less than the ideal suitor. The veteran of three failed marriages with women half his age, he had two teenage sons—one Oona's age and one a year younger—and was embroiled in a paternity suit brought against him by a young actress named **Joan Berry**, who claimed he was the father of her unborn child. (A blood test later cleared Chaplin of the charge.) His career was also on the skids, the result of unfavorable headlines criticizing him for his womanizing and for his support of Russia in its plight with the Nazis. Although many believed that Oona merely saw Chaplin as the father she had never had, she denied it at the time, claiming that Charlie made her more mature while she kept him young. The two eloped in 1943, much to the consternation of Oona's father Eugene, who was so infuriated by the marriage that he disowned his daughter.

Against all odds, the couple proved to be a perfect match. "It was a great, great love affair," said Carol Matthau, "not only because of the intensity but because of the lasting intensity." Oona helped revive Charles' interest in work and also produced eight children, the oldest, Geraldine, born when Charles was 55, and the youngest, Christopher, when he was 73. Charles, however, always remained Oona's top priority, and the children, who were raised by a legion of nurses, were frequently denied access to their parents. "Sometimes I felt like I was intruding on their intimacy," said daughter Jane, "but now I understand a love like that. It's once in a lifetime."

In 1953, after Chaplin was blacklisted in Hollywood for his leftist leanings, the family moved to Switzerland, settling on a 37-acre estate overlooking Lake Geneva. It became their world apart until Chaplin's death on Christmas Day, 1977. Oona, who never recovered from the loss of her husband, lapsed into alcoholism and remained something of a tragic figure until her death of cancer in 1991.

SOURCES:
Gelb, Arthur and Barbara. *O'Neill*. NY: Harper and Row, 1962.
"Charlie Chaplin and Oona O'Neill," in *People*. February 12, 1996, p. 173.

SUGGESTED READING:
Scovell, Jane. *Oona: Living in the Shadows*. Warner Books, 1998.

Barbara Morgan,
Melrose, Massachusetts

Chapman, Maria (1806–1885).

See Grimké, Angelina E. for sidebar.

Chapone, Hester (1727–1801)

Literary figure in Georgian England. Name variations: Hester Mulso. Born Hester Mulso on October 27, 1727, in Twywell, Northamptonshire, England; died on December 25, 1801, in Hadley, Middlesex, England; daughter of Thomas Mulso (a farmer and landowner) and Hester (Thomas) Mulso; married John Chapone (an attorney), in 1760 (he died ten months later); no children.

Published first poem, "To Peace: Written During the Late Rebellion" (1745); began writing for The Rambler *(1750); widowed (c. 1761); wrote educational treatise for young women (1773).*

Selected writings: Letters on the Improvement of the Mind (1773); Miscellanies in Verse and Prose (1775); A Letter to a New-Married Lady (1777).

Hester Mulso challenged conventions of her time to earn recognition as a writer and advocate educational opportunities for women in Georgian England. She was born in 1727 in Northamptonshire (where her father was a prosperous farmer) and was the only daughter among the four Mulso offspring. Known as a precocious child, Hester, familiarly called Hecky, wrote a romance entitled *The Loves of Amoret and Melissan* at the age of nine. Her beautiful voice earned her the name of the "linnet."

Her brothers, who all entered the ministry as adults, were educated from an early age, and Mulso also displayed an interest in learning, which her mother strongly discouraged. But when her mother died, Chapone was able to study—apparently unimpeded by her father—literature and languages; by her early adulthood, she was versed in French, Italian, and Latin. At the age of just 18, she wrote the poem "To Peace: Written During the Late Rebellion," which established her as a literary figure of the day. Beginning in 1750, she penned fiction for *The Rambler*, a well-known journal published by Samuel Johnson, the respected novelist, essayist and author of the first *Dictionary of the English Language*.

Chapone was a contemporary and friend of *Mary Wollstonecraft, author of *On the Vindication of the Rights of Women*, as well as of the writer *Elizabeth Montagu; Samuel Richardson, a popular novelist of the era with whom she corresponded on the subject of "filial obedience," was also an influential acquaintance of hers. Though she signed her letters as his "ever obliged and affectionate child," Chapone's biographer indicates that "her letters show with what dignity, tempered with proper humility, she could maintain her own well-grounded opinion," as she admired Richardson's views with discrimination.

Chapone was esteemed for her spirited conversational skills among the literati with whom she socialized. She—along with *Elizabeth Carter, Elizabeth Montagu and *Catherine Talbot—was among the first generation of Bluestockings. Destined to span roughly two generations, the Bluestocking Circle became one of London's most celebrated societies for members of the leisured gentry. The circle began during the 1750s and 1760s as a conversation among friends, both women and men, who were interested in literature and other intellectual pursuits. Rather than wear the white silk stockings then worn by London's fashion-conscious gentry, one member of the circle, Benjamin Stillingfleet, started to attend their evening meetings dressed in blue worsted stockings, ordinarily worn only by peasants. From Stillingfleet's provocative choice, Montagu, an early member, coined the society's name.

A "bluestocking philosophy," concerned with literature rather than politics, emerged as a means of what members called "rational entertainment" for women, and the circle evolved into London's most famous women-only society. In addition to their meetings, members communicated through letters, discussing their personal and professional activities and ideas at length. Eventually, as political turmoil in Europe of the late 1790s destabilized society, conservatives openly scorned the accomplishments of intellectual women, and "bluestocking" became a term of ridicule.

Against her father's wishes, Hester wed lawyer John Chapone in 1760, but it may have been an unhappy marriage. When he died less than a year later, she was devastated and mourned his passing deeply. For the rest of her life, Chapone earned a living as a writer; her most famous work had similarities to Wollstonecraft's later *Vindication*, published in 1792: in Chapone's 1773 work, *Letters on the Improvement of the Mind*, she argued for a self-education course for young women and presented a general curriculum that included science, history, and philosophy. She had written it for her niece, and the book remained popular in Britain, the United States, and even France well into the next century; its 25th edition was issued more than 70 years later in 1844. Chapone also wrote *Miscellanies in Verse and Prose* (1775) and *A Letter to a New-Married Lady* (1777). She died in 1801, and her collected writings were published in the four-volume *Works* in 1807 and the two-volume *Posthumous Works*, also in 1807; her descendants later wrote a biography of her, *Memoirs of Mrs. J. Chapone, from Various Authentic Sources* (1839).

Carol Brennan,
Grosse Pointe, Michigan

Charaoui, Hoda (1879–1947).

See Shaarawi, Huda.

Charito (fl. 300s)

Byzantine and Roman empress. Flourished around 350; married Jovian, Byzantine and Roman emperor (r. 363–364).

Charles, Elizabeth (1828–1896)

English author. Born at Tavistock on January 2, 1828; died at Hampstead on March 28, 1896; daughter of John Rundle (a Member of Parliament); married Andrew Paton Charles, in 1851.

Over the course of her career, Elizabeth Charles wrote some 50 books, primarily of a semi-religious nature. Some of her early poems won praise from Alfred Lord Tennyson, who read them in manuscript. Charles' best known book, titled *The Chronicles of the Schönberg-Cotta Family*, was written to order for an editor who was looking for a story about Martin Luther. Published in 1862, this work was translated into most of the European languages, Arabic, and many Indian dialects. In addition to writing, Charles took an active role in the operation of various charitable institutions. Arthur Stanley, dean of Westminster, Archibald Tait, archbishop of Canterbury, Charles Kingsley, a writer and cleric, and Edward Pusey, an Anglican theologian, were among her friends and correspondents. She died at Hampstead on March 28, 1896.

Charles, Eugenia (1919—)

Prime minister of the island nation of Dominica, and first female head of state in the Caribbean, who took a major leadership role in regional and international affairs. Name variations: Dame Eugenia Charles. Pronunciation: You-JEEN-yuh Charles. Born Mary Eugenia Charles in Roseau, Dominica, in 1919; daughter of wealthy planter and political figure J.B. Charles; attended Catholic school in Grenada and went on to study law at the University of Toronto and in England; never married; no children.

Born into a successful, well-to-do family, grew up in an environment of relative privilege; sent to the best schools in the British Caribbean and to the University of Toronto (late 1940s), where she earned a bachelor's degree; qualified as a barrister in Britain (1947); returned to Dominica to open a law practice (1949); entered politics (1968) and then only to protest the passage of a controversial sedition law by the Edward Oliver LeBlanc government; became the chief focus of loyal opposition, creating the Dominica Freedom Party along the way; during years in the opposition, saw her influence on the island's politics grow (1968–78); in the wake of violence between various partisan factions, her DFP organization came out on top (1979); elected prime minister (1980), a position she held for 15 years (1980–1995); under her leadership, Dominica's government became the most conservative in the region, firmly committed to free enterprise and attracting foreign, particularly American, investment to the island; her greatest moment in terms of international exposure came during the U.S. intervention on the island of Grenada—an effort that she vociferously defended as chair of the newly established Organization of Eastern Caribbean States (1983).

For those visitors to the Caribbean islands who are accustomed to white sandy beaches crowded with tourists, the lonely, verdant appearance of the island of Dominica will cause some degree of surprise. Not a single white sandy beach is to be seen. Instead, the visitor will encounter a mountainous 298-square mile island ribboned by no less than 365 rivers that cascade through the landscape in uncounted waterfalls. The beauty presented by this picture seems to suggest an otherworldly, rather than a tropical identity. The problems of the island—the lack of roads and reliable electricity, and the pervasive poverty of the inhabitants—are not, however, in any sense otherworldly but instead have called out for remedies in the here and now. From 1980 to 1995, the person most willing to answer this call was the island's prime minister, Eugenia Charles.

Miss Charles, as she is universally known on Dominica, was born in 1919. At that time, save for the Falkland Islands of the South Atlantic, the island was perhaps the most isolated of British possessions; it was, for instance, one of the last bastions of the Red Carib Indians, a tiny but historically important group that had died out everywhere else but continued to live in squalor on a remote reservation on Dominica. Eugenia's childhood bore little resemblance to these human relics of a bygone time. Instead, she lived a life of relative privilege, with all of the few luxuries the island had to offer.

Her remote ancestors had come to the Caribbean from Africa as slaves more than a hundred years earlier. Through manumission and ultimate emancipation in the 1840s, they came to enter the considerable population of those freed from bondage who worked in agriculture. But with a difference. Whereas some ex-slaves tended to be improvident, Eugenia's forefathers were recognized for their industriousness and common sense. Her father, in particular, was generally regarded as a phenomenon on the island. Having started with only modest wealth, J.B. Charles worked as a mason for the colonial government for many decades. At the same time, he began to buy parcels of land, first only some peripheral properties along the hillsides, and ultimately some of the choicest pieces of land on Dominica. He became a millionaire land speculator and planter, one of the richest men on the island. He added to his elementary school education with periodic visits to New York, where he sold his limes, and to London, where he sold his cocoa. But his first love was always his family. To his daughter, who was the youngest of three children, the elder Charles passed on the attributes that had given him so much success: shrewdness, charm, and most important, a penchant for hard work.

That young Eugenia should so resemble her father was in some ways unusual. In the home, her mother was clearly the dominant force. In fact, females were normally more influential on the island than males. The reason was historical. Dominican society had long been noteworthy for its high incidence of illegitimacy; and with so many men working overseas or on plantations on adjacent islands, a sort of matriarchy developed, with some strong and experienced women controlling the marketplace and the church. From her own mother and from these other strong women in public life, Eugenia drew some important inspiration—easily as much as from her better-known father. The market women would later come to look upon her as one of their own.

During the 1920s, Charles benefitted from her father's extensive library, her lessons from tutors, and her many walks around the island. Her parents encouraged her to excel in letters and in the sciences. She also took an early fancy to gardening. But perhaps she gained most from listening to the discussions and arguments in the marketplace, where clients and saleswomen debated the value of different items and judged what price was possible and what was not. The art of the possible became her *metier*.

Eugenia received her primary schooling and most of her secondary schooling at home in the Dominican capital Roseau. In her late teens, however, her parents sent her to a Roman Catholic convent in Saint John's, Grenada, there to complete her secondary education. This was the first time that she had been away for any length of time from Dominica, but she adapted to the rigors of convent learning nonetheless.

World War II brought many changes to the Caribbean basin. Wartime demands for raw materials transformed the economies of many islands. Technicians and investors primarily from the United States came into the region in great numbers. They spent lavishly, sometimes with government money and sometimes with their own, providing the early basis for what would one day be a massive tourist industry in the Caribbean. But it was the exploitation of raw materials that ultimately encouraged Eugenia Charles to enter public life—for the men and women who worked in the mines, in agriculture, and in transport formed labor unions and self-

help groups during the war and these unions in the end became political associations.

Charles spent the war years in Grenada and at home on Dominica. In 1946, she attended the University of Toronto, where, amidst the unac-

customed snows, she received a bachelor's degree before moving on to London to study to be a barrister. At this time, she evinced an interest in staying in England to work on urban social problems, especially juvenile delinquency. Though she herself had no children—and, in fact, would never marry—she always maintained a deep affection for children and a special sensitivity to their particular problems.

In the end, however, she decided against a career in juvenile law and social work. As she remarked in an interview many years later, the crucial moment came in London in 1949: "My parents came to see me, and they looked as if they needed someone to be home. So I went home." She never looked back. Instead, she settled into island life and throughout the 1950s gained some modest success as a lawyer specializing in business law. While she handled the legal affairs of her father's various concerns and those of his associates, she largely ignored politics. Then events overtook her.

The 1950s was a problematic time for Britain's Caribbean colonies. The same labor unions that had come together with colonial authorities to forward the struggle against Nazism now broke with those same authorities. Most labor leaders were decidedly leftist, with Cominform connections and militant agendas (indeed, Cheddi Jagan, who would soon be elected prime minister of British Guiana, was an active communist; so was Aimé Cesaire, the anti-imperialist poet of the nearby French island of Martinique). In their encounters with the colonial governments of their respective islands, these leaders stressed a heightened sense of class struggle, with direct confrontation as their chief tool. Interestingly, independence was not at this time one of their main goals, though the same cannot be said of their desire for political power.

Charles viewed the growth of militant unionism in the Caribbean with some trepidation. She felt deeply skeptical about the socialist programs the unionists advocated and resented their hatred of the rich. She felt that the elites and the poor together could forge a more prosperous future. She had seen how a common-sense approach to economic hardship could work wonders. Her own father had created a self-help organization on Dominica in the 1930s. This "Penny Bank" association provided small financial incentives to poor people who showed frugality during the worst times of the Depression. "It taught people thrift before the credit union people [came on the scene]; people could save a penny," she noted.

Charles feared that in the end the labor leaders would offer their followers nothing but demagoguery. Words instead of results. Even independence, then a decidedly distant objective, could be used to dupe the masses into thinking that their very precarious future would in fact be golden. She knew better. Dominica had some advantages, but the island could not hope to compete even regionally without a long period of preparation and hard work. Redistribution meant little under such circumstances, and independence—if anything—meant even less. Therefore, against the general trend in the Caribbean basin at that time, Charles began to speak out against the left, arguing initially that independence was undesirable, and that Dominica's future would be best assured by a continued close relation with Britain and, if possible, with a still closer relation with the United States.

In the beginning, these opinions appeared only in letters to the editor in island dailies. Charles, who had a thriving legal practice, which represented some important planters on the island, had little time for political activism. Slowly, however, the political side of her character manifested itself more and more. She began to organize town meetings where she was generally heckled as "a lackey of the bourgeoisie." But she continued to speak out and gradually earned the grudging respect of many of her opponents. Some of these individuals, such as the writer *Phyllis Allfrey**, would later join her in a political association when they became disillusioned with socialist politics.

Charles became president of the Dominica Employer's Federation in the mid-1960s, a position that provided an excellent platform for her to champion the view of business interests on the island. She became actively involved in politics in 1968, when the government of the autocratic Premier E.O. LeBlanc passed a Seditious and Undesirable Publication Act. Charles, who stood to be censured under this new legislation, publicly attacked it and its author. The conservative Dominica Freedom Party (DFP), which she founded and over which she still presides, grew out of this protest. The legislation failed to become law, and she was now in politics for good.

In 1970, her party won two seats in the island legislature. She herself was defeated but served nonetheless in the House of Assembly as an appointed member. She was finally elected in 1975 and remained leader of the opposition for five years. During this time, LeBlanc was replaced by the eccentric Patrick John, whose plans for the island included purging Dominica's "pseudo-intellectuals," promoting terrorist attacks on Rastafarians (few of which ever came to Dominica), negotiating with South African agents to launder money and arms exports through the island, even suggesting to the United States that the U.S. Navy open a submarine base there. But the only immediate plan he made for the island that came to fruition was to bring independence to Dominica in November 1978. Charles strongly opposed this move, arguing that the island was not ready and that John was setting Dominica up to prostitute itself to the highest bidder. After all, she noted, the British had not been so bad: "It wasn't them who brought class hatred among us—it was our own people."

In the wake of independence, the John government was convulsed by demonstrations and a general strike. Though Charles did not instigate these actions, she strongly supported them through the Committee for National Salvation, a coalition group that included both leftists and conservatives. John tried to fight back, first through a prohibition on strikes and finally through physical attacks on the demonstrators. His ultimate use of violence brought chaos within the Parliament. Charles' old opponents in the Labor Party then abandoned John and formed new opposition parties loosely aligned with the conservatives.

John was ousted from office in mid-1979. Within a few months, Charles led her DFP to a landslide victory in an all-island election. From 1980 to June 1995, she held the office of prime minister. As head of government, she led a democratic regime that was widely regarded as the most conservative in the Caribbean, firmly committed to private enterprise and to attracting foreign investment, unswervingly pro-West, and especially pro-United States in foreign policy. She ultimately became president of the Organization of Eastern Caribbean States and from that vantagepoint, the strongest regional proponent of American intervention on the nearby island of Grenada in 1983. Her timely support earned her the undying friendship of President Ronald Reagan, who reserved a special place for Dominica in his Caribbean Basin Initiative.

Her father, who died at age 107 in 1982, got only a glimmer of the fame that Charles would ultimately enjoy, but he was inordinately proud of the progress his island home was making under her leadership. Though she had many detractors, her administration was widely viewed as moderately progressive, while she was seen as a consummate pragmatist. "They called me an old woman. I reminded [my opponents] that I had more stamina and energy than they had at 35." By all accounts, that energy and that force of personality remained undiminished for a great many years.

SOURCES:

Richards, Peter. "Leading the Way: An Interview with Eugenia Charles," in *Americas*. Vol. 37, no. 5. September–October 1985, pp. 28–30.

Thomas, Jo. "Quietly she Makes History as a Caribbean Leader," in *The New York Times*. December 1, 1980.

Walter, Greg. "President Reagan Finds a Fast Friend in Eugenia Charles, Dominica's Plucky PM," in *People Weekly*. November 14, 1983.

SUGGESTED READING:

Smith, Linden. "The Political Situation in Dominica," in *Bulletin of Eastern Caribbean Affairs*. Vol. 5, no. 3. July–August 1979.

Thomas Whigham,
Associate Professor of History,
University of Georgia, Athens, Georgia

Charlieu, Louise (c. 1523–1566).

See Labé, Louise.

Charlotte.

Variant of Carlota.

Charlotte (1516–1524)

French princess. Born in 1516; died at age eight in 1524; daughter of *Claude de France (1499–1524) and Francis, duc d'Angoulême, later Francis I, king of France (r. 1515–1547).

Upon the death of eight-year-old Charlotte in 1524, her aunt *Margaret of Angoulême wrote an essay in her honor titled: *A dialogue in the form of a nocturnal vision between the right honourable and excellent Princess, my Lady Marguerite of France, only sister of our Sire the King, by the grace of God Queen of Navarre and Duchess of Alençon and Berry, and the Holy Soul of the deceased Madame Charlotte of France, eldest daughter of the said Sire and niece of the said Lady and Queen.*

Charlotte (1896–1985)

Grand duchess of Luxemburg. Name variations: Duchess of Nassau; Princess of Bourbon-Parma; Countess-Palatine of the Rhine; Countess of Sayn, Königstein, Katzenelnbogen, and Dietz; Burgravine of Hammerstein; Lady of Mahlberg, Wiesbaden, Idstein, Merenberg, Limburg, and Eppstein; Grand Duchess of Luxembourg. Born Charlotte Aldegonde Elise Marie Wilhelmine at the castle Colmar-Berg in northern Luxemburg on January 23, 1896; died in 1985; second of six daughters of William IV (1852–1912), grand duke of Luxemburg (of the House of Nassau) and *Marie-Anne of Braganza (an infanta of Portugal); younger sister of **Marie Adelaide of Luxemburg**; privately educated by tutors; married Felix, prince of Bourbon-Parma, on November 6, 1919; children: son Jean or John, grand duke of Luxemburg (b. 1921, who married Princess *Josephine-Charlotte of Belgium in 1953);

Charlotte

(1896–1985)

Elisabeth (b. 1922); Marie Adelaide (b. 1924); Marie Gabrielle (b. 1925); Charles (b. 1927); Alix (b. 1929).

During his reign as grand duke of Luxemburg (1905–12), William IV, with the consent of The Hague Tribunal, created a family statute in 1907, enabling his six daughters to succeed to the throne of Luxemburg (an independent duchy founded in 1815, bounded by France, Belgium, and Germany). Upon his death in 1912, his eldest ◄❧ **Marie Adelaide** replaced him, but she suffered from poor health and was not popular. On September 28, 1919, following the German subjugation of Luxemburg in which the sisters and their mother were essentially prisoners of the German occupiers, Charlotte, grand duchess

of Luxemburg, won overwhelmingly in a referendum vote to rule the country and continue its sovereignty, forcing her sister to abdicate. Marie Adelaide entered a convent in Italy, where she would die five years later in 1924.

Charlotte was a progressive and an advocate of republicanism. She encouraged the 1919 emendation of Luxemburg's constitution, which established universal suffrage and proportional representation, though the grand duchess, as head of state, retained a great deal of constitutional power. The country went on to enjoy prosperity and political stability under the leadership of premiers Pierre Dupong and Joseph Bech.

During World War II in 1940, when Luxemburg once again suffered German occupation and violation of their neutrality, Charlotte set up a government-in-exile in London, then joined her husband and children who had fled to Montreal. From Canada, she frequently broadcast to her nation, now under control by Nazi *gauleiter* Gustav Simon; she also made repeated visits to Washington, D.C., and London to work closely with the Allies. Her son and husband joined the British army, witnessing the liberation of Luxemburg in September 1944.

In 1948, Charlotte and the grand duchy of Luxemburg abandoned the policy of unarmed neutrality and joined in a customs union with Belgium and the Netherlands. Ten years later (February 3, 1958), the accord was expanded into the Benelux Economic Union. During her reign, Luxemburg prospered, ranking sixth in world production of steel while undergoing little unemployment. On November 12, 1964, the unpretentious Charlotte abdicated in favor of her son, who ascended the throne as Grand Duke Jean. The popular grand duchess had ruled her country for 45 years, from 1919 to 1964.

Charlotte, Countess of Derby (1599–1664).

See Charlotte Stanley in entry titled Siege Warfare and Women.

Charlotte, Duchess of Saxe-Hildburghausen (1769–1818).

See Louise of Prussia for sidebar.

Charlotte, Empress of Mexico (1840–1927).

See Carlota.

Charlotte, Queen of Portugal (1775–1830).

See Carlota Joaquina.

❧► **Marie Adelaide of Luxemburg** (1894–1924)

Grand duchess of Luxemburg. Name variations: Maria Adélaïde; Marie Adélaïde, Marie Adelaide, Marie-Adelaide. Born on June 14, 1894; died on January 24, 1924; daughter of William IV (1852–1912), grand duke of Luxemburg, and *Marie-Anne of Braganza. Reigned from 1912 to 1919.

Charlotte-Aglae (1700–1761)

*Duchess of Modena. Name variations: Charlotte d'Orléans; Charlotte of Orleans; Charlotte of Orléans. Born on December 22, 1700; died on January 19, 1761; daughter of *Françoise-Marie de Bourbon (1677–1749) and Philippe II also known as Philip Bourbon-Orléans (1674–1723), 2nd duke of Orléans (r. 1701–1723); married Francesco or Francis III, duke of Modena (r. 1748–1780), on June 21, 1720; possibly mother of Ercole III Rinaldo (1727–1803), duke of Modena. Charlotte-Aglae was the subject of a painting by *Angelica Kauffmann.*

Charlotte Amalia of Hesse (1650–1714)

*Queen of Denmark and Norway. Name variations: Charlotte Amalie of Hesse-Cassel; Charlotte Amelia. Born on April 27, 1650, in Cassel; died on March 27, 1714, in Copenhagen, Denmark; married Christian V (1646–1699), king of Norway and Denmark (r. 1670–1699), on June 25, 1667; children: Frederik or Frederick IV (1671–1730), king of Norway and Denmark (r. 1699–1730); Christian William (b. 1672); Christian (b. 1675); *Sophie Hedwig (1677–1735); Christiane Charlotte (1679–1689); Charles (b. 1680); William (b. 1687).*

Charlotte Amalie (1706–1782)

*Danish princess. Name variations: Charlotte Amalie Oldenburg. Born on October 6, 1706; died on October 28, 1782; daughter of *Louise of Mecklenburg-Gustrow (1667–1721) and Frederick IV (1671–1730), king of Denmark and Norway (r. 1699–1730).*

Charlotte Augusta (1796–1817).

See Caroline of Brunswick for sidebar.

Charlotte Augusta Matilda (1766–1828)

*Princess royal. Name variations: Charlotte Guelph; Charlotte Hanover. Born Charlotte Augusta Matilda on September 29, 1766, at Buckingham Palace, London, England; died on October 6, 1828, at Ludwigsburg Palace, Stuttgart, Germany; buried at Ludwigsburg Palace; daughter of George III (1738–1820), king of England (r. 1760–1820) and *Charlotte of Mecklenburg-Strelitz (1744–1818); married Frederick II (1754–1816), duke of Wurttemberg (r. 1797–1802), elector of Wurttemberg (r. 1802–1806), also known as Frederick I, king of Wurttemberg (r. 1806–1816), on* May 18, 1797, at Chapel Royal, St. James's Palace; children: Paul of Wurttemberg (b. 1798). Frederick's first wife was *Augusta of Brunswick-Wolfenbuttel.

Charlotte de Montmorency (fl. 1600–1621).

See Longueville, Anne for sidebar.

Charlotte Elizabeth of Bavaria (1652–1722)

*Duchess of Orleans. Name variations: Elisabeth Charlotte of Orleans; Elizabeth Charlotte of Bohemia; Elizabeth Charlotte of the Palatinate; Elizabeth-Charlotte of Bourbon Orleans. Born in Heidelberg, Baden, on May 27, 1652; died in St. Cloud, France, on December 8, 1722 (some sources cite 1712); daughter of *Charlotte of Hesse (1627–1687) and Charles I, Elector Palatine; became second wife of Philip (1540–1701), duke of Orléans (r. 1660–1701, brother of King Louis XIV of France), on November 16 or 21, 1671, at Metz; children: Alexander (b. 1673); Philip or Philippe (b. 1674), 2nd duke of Orleans; *Elizabeth-Charlotte (1676–1744, who married Leopold, duke of Lorraine, and was the mother of Emperor Francis I).*

The daughter of a minor German prince and the intended bride of Louis XIV's homosexual brother Philip, duke of Orléans, Charlotte Elizabeth, princess of the Palatinate, had much to overcome as she entered the court of Versailles in 1671. Ungainly and plain in appearance, with a brash and assertive manner, she initially appeared to have only political expediency in her favor. (Louis XIV, known as the Sun King, was eager to annex large parts of the Palatinate and had his eye on the electoral vote he might obtain should Philip become the elector through a Palatinate marriage.) The groom-to-be had already rid himself of his first wife *Henrietta Anne of England, who died under mysterious circumstances, and aside from his aversion to women in general, he had a particular dislike of his intended bride. "Am I supposed to sleep with that?," he wailed upon first setting eyes on her. Charlotte Elizabeth, who had hoped to marry a German prince if she married at all, had her own misgivings. A sense of duty on the part of both participants prevailed, however, and a marriage contract was signed on November 16, 1671, following Charlotte Elizabeth's secret conversion to Catholicism.

Regally known as Madame after her marriage, Charlotte Elizabeth became a formidable force in court life, largely because of her flourishing relationship with the king, whom she came to call the "Great Man." Louis, for his part, respected her keen intelligence and appreciated her sincerity and lack of pretense. Charlotte also developed a surprisingly good relationship with her husband, although she detested two of his scheming confidants, the Chevalier de Lorraine and the Marquis d'Effiat. She dutifully gave birth to three children, after which she and Philip agreed to live separate lives. While he occupied himself with his wardrobe and his social calendar, she tended the family, which included his two daughters from a previous marriage—*Marie Louise d'Orleans (1662–1689) and ◄✧ Anne-Marie d'Bourbon-Orleans (1669–1728). Motherhood became Charlotte's overriding concern, and she approached it with an unconventional, and quite modern, combination of love and discipline. The children, in turn, remained devoted to her for as long as she lived.

In addition to her status as one of the best-read members of court, Charlotte distinguished herself as one of the most prolific letter writers of all time. Indeed, as she grew older, she often spent 10-to-12 hours a day writing letters that sometimes stretched to 30 pages in length. Witty and candid, she detailed day-to-day life at court, as well as observations on the relatives and courtiers of Louis XIV. As historian Nis A. Petersen points out, Charlotte's correspondence is not only engaging and informative but has the particular edge of an outsider, or, "a very square peg in a round hole. . . . It was this sense of detachment," he writes, "that give Madame's observations their special flavour—that make them of interest to the casual reader and historian alike."

Charlotte used her correspondence to criticize many of the prevailing practices of the day. She mistrusted doctors and had no faith in the frequent use of purging and bloodletting, which she avoided until shortly before her death. She treated her own illnesses "in the German manner," with a wholesome diet, fresh air, and exercise. She avoided the vast quantities of greasy, overcooked, over spicy foods consumed by the royal family and also eschewed chocolate, coffee, tea, and tobacco, delicacies of the time. She particularly detested the use of snuff by the court ladies, proclaiming that their dirty noses looked as though "they had poked them in dung." She was equally outspoken about the lack of personal hygiene of a certain member of court and described in detail the slovenly habits of the **Princess d'Harcourt**, a great lady of the court,

and ****Madame de Montespan**, the king's former mistress. Charlotte was meticulous about her own regimen which was simple and practical. She wore no make-up or perfume, refused to don a wig, and limited her wardrobe to three principal items: a state robe for formal functions; a riding habit, tailored like a man's but with a long, flowing skirt; and a night shift. These were augmented with a few pieces designed for comfort, like a quilted dressing robe and otter-skin stockings to ward off the winter chill. Once, when she wound an old fur around her neck for additional warmth, she was dumbfounded when the ladies of the court began sporting fur pieces of their own. (To this day, a fur tippet worn over the shoulders is known as a "Palatine.")

Perhaps the most interesting of Charlotte's voluminous correspondence are the letters devoted to the discussion of court morals. Although she abided by a strict code of ethics and felt that others might do well to emulate her, she was tolerant of others. Regarding her husband's homosexuality, or the "Italian Vice," as it was then termed, she was resigned. She found homosexuality to be common at court, and, according to Petersen, surmised that "if the King were really to punish all those guilty he would decimate all the great houses of France and would also have to close the College of Jesuits." She was not so tolerant of actual vices such as gambling, drinking, and adultery, the latter of which she found particularly repugnant among the royal family because of the embarrassing offspring it produced. Referring to them as "mousedroppings among the pepper," she was intensely disturbed by the arranged marriage of Louis' illegitimate daughter ◄✧ **Françoise-Marie de Bourbon**, comtesse de Blois, the product of his liaison with Madame de Montespan, to her son Philip.

It was Madame's view that rather than seeking hedonistic diversions, royalty should seek to do good, administer justice, and spare their subjects the burdens of excessive taxation. She also believed that religion had no place in politics and was appalled at the persecution of the Huguenots during the close of Louis' reign. Blaming the king's actions on his lack of information (unlike her, he hated to read), and the influence of his last mistress and second wife ****Madame de Maintenon**, Charlotte was frustrated by his behavior. "I must own," she wrote, "that when I hear the Great Man praised in a sermon for his persecution of the reformed, I am always impatient. I cannot hear bad actions being praised."

Charlotte, who had hoped to outlive her tormentors, also survived her admirers, includ-

Anne-Marie d'Bourbon-Orleans (1669–1728). See Henrietta Anne for sidebar.

Françoise-Marie de Bourbon. See Montespan, Françoise, Marquise de for sidebar.

ing her husband, whom she lost in 1701, and the king, who died in 1715. The death in 1714, of her beloved aunt, *Sophia, Electress of Hanover, to whom she wrote many of her most scathing letters, was particularly devastating. Though broken in spirit during her later years, Charlotte faced her own death with her usual good sense and courage, saying that it was "only the last absurdity we are capable of committing, so we put it off as long as possible." In 1722, she attended the coronation of Louis XV, agreeing against her better judgment to be bled and purged before making the trip from Paris to Reims. She died soon after, on December 8, 1722. Just before she slipped away, one of her ladies-in-waiting sought to kiss her hand. "You may kiss me properly on the lips," Charlotte was said to have whispered. "I am going to the land where all are equal."

SOURCES:

Petersen, Nis A. "Madame: Elisabeth Charlotte of Orleans," in *History Today*. Vol. XXVII, no. 2. February 1977.

Barbara Morgan,
Melrose, Massachusetts

Charlotte Frederica of Mecklenburg-Schwerin (1784–1840)

*Princess of Mecklenburg-Schwerin. Name variations: Charlotte Frederikke; Charlotte of Mecklenburg-Schwerin; Charlotte von Mecklenburg-Schwerin. Born on December 4, 1784, in Ludwigslust; died on July 13, 1840, in Rome, Italy; daughter of Frederick Francis, duke of Mecklenburg-Schwerin, and *Louise of Saxe-Gotha (1756–1808); became first wife of Christian VIII (1786–1848), king of Denmark (r. 1839–1848), on June 21, 1806 (divorced 1810); children: Frederik or Frederick VII (b. 1808), king of Denmark (r. 1848–1863).*

Charlotte of Bavaria (1792–1873).

See Caroline Augusta of Bavaria.

Charlotte of Belgium (1840–1927).

See Carlota.

Charlotte of Bourbon (d. 1582)

*Princess of Orange and countess of Nassau. Name variations: Charlotte Bourbon; Charlotte of Bourbon-Montpensier; Charlotte de Montpensier. Died in 1582; possibly daughter of Louis, duke of Montpensier; became third wife of William I the Silent (1533–1584), prince of Orange, count of Nassau (r. 1544–1584), stadholder of Holland, Zealand, and Utrecht (r. 1572–1584); children: *Louisa Juliana of*

Orange (1576–1644); Amalia (who married Frederick Casimir of Zweibrücken); Elizabeth; Catherine Belgica; Brabantina; Flanderina; Antwerpina. William the Silent's first wife was *Anna of Egmont (1533–1558); his second was *Anna of Saxony (1544–1577); his fourth was *Louise de Coligny (1555–1620).*

Charlotte of Brunswick-Wolfenbüttel (d. 1715).

See Catherine I of Russia for sidebar.

Charlotte of Hesse (1627–1687)

*Landgrave of Hesse-Cassel. Name variations: Charlotte of Hesse-Cassel. Born on November 20, 1627, in Cassel, Germany; died on March 16, 1687, in Cassel; daughter of William V (b. 1602), landgrave of Hesse, and Amelia of Hanau; married Karl Ludwig also known as Charles I Louis (1617–1680), elector Palatine of the Rhine (r. 1648–1680), on February 22, 1650 (divorced); children: Charles II (1651–1685), elector Palatine of the Rhine; Frederick Simmern; *Charlotte Elizabeth of Bavaria (1652–1722); Charlotte Wittelsbach (1659–1696, who married Meinhard, duke of Leinster). Charles I Louis' second wife was Marie Susanne Louise Raugräfin.*

Charlotte of Lusignan (1442–1487)

Queen of Cyprus. Name variations: Carlotta; Charlotte of Cyprus. Born on Cyprus in 1442; died in Rome, Italy, on July 16, 1487; daughter of John II, king of Cyprus (r. 1432–1458), and Helen Paleologina; married Joao de Coimbra also known as John of Portugal (1431–1457); married Louis of Savoy; children: none.

Charlotte of Lusignan was the eldest daughter and heiress of King John II. Although John claimed the title king of Jerusalem, in reality his domain encompassed only the small island of Cyprus off the coast of Jerusalem. Charlotte first married John of Portugal, but after he was murdered she returned to Cyprus in 1457 (some sources claim he was poisoned by his mother-in-law *Helen Paleologina). She then married the French noble Louis of Savoy.

On her father's death, Charlotte became queen of Cyprus in 1458. She ruled alone for several years before her illegitimate half-brother James wrested control of the government from her and established himself as King James II. Forced to flee to Rome for safety, she and her husband then moved to Rhodes, where she began to plot to regain her throne. But James died in 1473, leaving Cyprus in the hands of her widow, the Italian noble *Caterina Cornaro. Caterina claimed the regency of Cyprus in the name of her infant son James III and ruled the island kingdom from Italy. Charlotte continued to intrigue for her reinstatement until her death in 1487.

Laura York,
Riverside, California

Charlotte of Mecklenburg-Strelitz (1744–1818)

*Queen consort of England. Name variations: Charlotte Sophia or Charlotte-Sophia. Born a princess on May 19, 1744, in Mirow, Mecklenburg-Strelitz, Germany; died on November 17, 1818, in Kew Palace, Surrey; interred at St. George's Chapel, Windsor Castle; daughter of Charles Louise Frederick (b. 1708), duke of Mecklenburg-Strelitz and *Elizabeth of Saxe-Hildburghausen (1713–1761); married George III (1738–1820), king of England (r. 1761–1820), on September 8, 1761; children: George IV (1762–1830), prince of Wales and king*

Charlotte
of Mecklenburg
Strelitz

*of England (r. 1820–1830); Frederick Augustus (1763–1827), duke of York; William IV (1765–1837), duke of Clarence; *Charlotte Augusta Matilda (1766–1828); Edward Augustus (1767–1820), duke of Kent; *Augusta Guelph (1768–1840); *Elizabeth (1770–1840); Ernest Augustus (1771–1851), duke of Cumberland; Augustus Frederick (1773–1843), duke of Sussex; Adolphus Frederick (1774–1850), duke of Cambridge; *Mary (1776–1857), duchess of Gloucester; *Sophia Matilda (1777–1848); Octavius (1779–1783); Alfred (1780–1782); *Amelia (1783–1810).*

Charlotte of Mecklenburg-Strelitz was a shy, plain queen who spoke English haltingly but for some reason "suited George." Eighteen when she married George III, king of England, she and her husband settled down to quiet living. "Life at Charlotte's court," writes **Norah Lofts**, "even when she was not pregnant—she had fifteen children—sounds stultifyingly dull." But the queen was terrified by the king's illness—then thought mental, now thought physical in nature—which began in 1804. As a result of his violent episodes, Charlotte refused to be alone with him. She died in 1818.

SOURCES:
Lofts, Norah. *Queens of England.* NY: Doubleday, 1977.

RELATED MEDIA:
The Madness of King George, (110 min. film), starring Nigel Hawthorne as George and **Helen Mirren** as Charlotte, Channel Four Films, 1994.

Charlotte of Mexico (1840–1927).
See Carlota.

Charlotte of Montmorency (fl. 1600–1621).
See Longueville, Anne for sidebar.

Charlotte of Oldenburg (1759–1818)

*Queen of Sweden. Name variations: Hedwig of Oldenburg. Born on March 22, 1759; died on June 20, 1818; daughter of August, duke of Oldenburg, and *Friederike of Hesse-Cassel (1722–1787); married Karl or Charles XIII (1748–1818), king of Sweden (r. 1809–1818), on July 7, 1774; children: Charles XIV John (b. 1763), king of Sweden; Charles Adolf (b. 1798).*

Charlotte of Prussia (1798–1860)

*Empress of Russia. Name variations: Alexandra Feodorovna; Charlotte Hohenzollern; Louise Charlotte of Prussia. Born on July 13, 1798; died on November 1, 1860; daughter of Frederick William III, king of Prussia (r. 1797–1840), and *Louise of Prussia (1776–1810);*

married Nicholas I (1796–1855), tsar of Russia (r. 1825–1855), on July 13, 1817; children: Alexander II, tsar of Russia (r. 1855–1881); Constantine Nicholaevitch (who married *Alexandra of Saxe-Altenburg); Nicholas Nicholaevitch (1831–1891), grand duke (who married *Alexandra of Oldenburg); Michael Nicholaevitch (who married *Cecilia of Baden); *Maria Nikolaevna (1819–1876); *Olga of Russia (1822–1892, who married Charles I of Württemberg); *Alexandra Nikolaevna (1825–1844, who married Frederick William, landgrave of Hesse-Cassel); and two others.

Charlotte of Savoy (c. 1442–1483)

Queen of France. Name variations: Charlotte d'Savoie. Born in 1442 (some sources cite 1439, 1440 or 1445); died on December 1, 1483 (some sources cite 1515); daughter of Louis I, prince of Piedmont and duke of Savoy, and *Anne of Lusignan; sister of *Bona of Savoy (c. 1450–c. 1505); became second wife of Louis XI (1423–1483), king of France (r. 1461–1483), in March 1451; children: Joachim (b. 1459, died at age four months); *Anne of Beaujeu (c. 1460–1522); Francis (1466–1466); Charles VIII (1470–1498), king of France (r. 1483–1498); Francis (1473–1473); *Jeanne de France (c. 1464–1505).

In March 1451, 28-year-old Louis (XI), then dauphin of France, married nine-year-old Charlotte of Savoy against his father's wishes. His father Charles VII, king of France, promptly deprived his son of his pension and confiscated his French lands. The king was also furious with Charlotte's father, the duke of Savoy, for entering into this marriage conspiracy, and threatened an invasion if the duke did not repudiate the 28-year-old dauphin. In the middle of this tempest, the English landed at Guienne, and father and son were forced to make up, at least temporarily. The marriage, however, was not consummated until 1457.

It was considered an agreeable union, despite the fact that Louis was rarely in the company of his wife. The patient and submissive Charlotte led a secluded existence with her children and her ladies-in-waiting at the royal castle in Amboise, on the Loire. Wrote Philippe de Commynes, Charlotte "was not one of those women in whom a man would take great pleasure but in all a very good lady." Despite a few dalliances, Louis was more faithful to Charlotte than was the norm for princes of his day. Louis died on August 30, 1483; Charlotte died three months later, on December 1.

Previously, in 1436, a 13-year-old Louis had married the charming Scottish princess and poet

*Margaret of Scotland (1425–1445), daughter of James I and *Joan Beaufort. It is said that her marriage to Louis was so wretched that when she died at age 20, her parting words were: "Oh! fie on life! Speak to me no more of it."

Charlotte of Saxe-Hildburghausen (1787–1847).

See Catherine Charlotte of Hildburghausen.

Charlotte of Saxe-Meiningen (1860–1919)

German princess. Name variations: Charlotte Hohenzollern. Born Victoria Elizabeth Augusta Charlotte on July 24, 1860, in Potsdam, Brandenburg, Germany; died on October 1, 1919, in Baden-Baden, Germany; daughter of Frederick III (1831–1888), emperor of Germany (r. 1888), and *Victoria Adelaide (1840–1901), princess royal (and daughter of Queen *Victoria of England); sister of Kaiser Wilhelm II (r. 1888–1918); married Bernard III (b. 1851), duke of Saxe-Meiningen and Hildburghausen, on February 18, 1878; children: Feodora of Saxe-Meiningen (1879–1945, who married Henry III, prince of Reuss), duchess of Saxony.

Charlotte of Vendôme

Duchess of Nevers. Name variations: Charlotte of Vendome. Married Engelbert, duke of Nevers; children: Charles I, duke of Nevers (d. 1521).

Charlotte of Wales (1796–1817).

See Caroline of Brunswick for sidebar on Charlotte Augusta.

Charlotte Oldenburg (1789–1864)

Danish royal. Name variations: Louise Charlotte of Denmark. Born on October 30, 1789; died on March 28, 1864; daughter of Frederick (1753–1805), prince of Denmark (son of Frederick V of Denmark and *Maria Juliana of Brunswick) and *Sophia of Mecklenburg (1758–1794); sister of Christian VIII, king of Denmark (r. 1839–1848); married William, landgrave of Hesse-Cassel, November 10, 1810; children: Caroline Frederica of Hesse-Cassel (1811–1829); Marie Louise Charlotte of Hesse-Cassel (1814–1895, who married Frederick Augustus, prince of Anhalt-Dessau); *Louise of Hesse-Cassel (1817–1898, wife of Christian IX of Denmark); Frederick William (1820–1884), landgrave of Hesse; Augusta Frederica Marie

(1823–1889, who married Charles Frederick, lord of Dallund); Sophie Wilhemina Augusta (1827–1827).

Charlotte Saxe-Coburg (1840–1927).

See Carlota.

Charolois, countess of (d. 1465).

See Mary of Burgundy for sidebar on Isabelle of Bourbon.

Charriere, Isabelle de (1740–1805)

Dutch-born author of plays, stories, novels and essays, which were largely romantic reflections on her liaisons. Name variations: Isabelle de Charrière; Zelide or Zélide; Abbe de la Tour. Born Isabelle Agnès Elisabeth van Tuyll van Seeroskerken van Zuylen in 1740 at Zuylen, Netherlands; died in 1805; daughter of the Lord of Zuylen; educated at home; married Charles-Emmanuel de Charriere (a mathematician), on February 17, 1771, in Zuylen; no children.

Selected works: Lettres de Mistress Henley *(The Letters of Mistress Henley, 1784);* Lettres neuchâteloises *(Letters from Neuchâtel, 1784);* Lettres trouvées dans des portfeuilles d'emigrés *(Letters from an Émigré's Wallet, 1793);* Trois Femmes *(Three Women, 1797).*

Aristocratic life, at her family's castle at Zuylen and mansion in Utrecht, held little interest for Isabelle van Tuyll, the first of seven children. Her young mother had little time for her, and her strict father kept her in social isolation. A childhood governess taught her to speak better French than Dutch, and she longed for a romance that would take her to France. Countless suitors sought to marry her, but she rejected them in 1771 in favor of her brother's former tutor, Charles-Emmanuel de Charriere. His family home in Neuchâtel, Netherlands, on France's border, intrigued her, and she found in him an intellectual peer.

Still Isabelle de Charriere was not in love. In 1762, she had begun a correspondence with David-Louis Constant d'Hermenches. Although his marriage prevented an amorous relationship, she had her strongest emotional bond with him. Married life, shared with an elderly father-in-law and two unmarried sisters-in-law, did not curb her restlessness. "Excessively emotional, and not less fastidious," she wrote, "[I] cannot be happy either with or without love."

De Charriere often wintered in Geneva and tried numerous spas in an attempt to cure a lifelong illness. In 1787, she and her husband moved to Paris in hopes of finding a community for her.

There she met Benjamin Constant, the nephew of d'Hermenches. The two began an affair that lasted several years (1787–1796), until Constant was called away from Paris by his family. Although de Charriere wrote a number of novels and some political tracts, she is perhaps best remembered for her liaison with him. Her letters to him would be printed in the *Revue suisse* of April 1844.

Monsieur de Charriere regularly transcribed his wife's plays and fictional stories, which were veiled accounts of her search for love and intellectual companionship. The de Charrieres returned to Neuchâtel where Isabelle lived out her days. Her scandalous 16-year correspondence with d'Hermenches was published; it documents her lifelong discontent.

SOURCES:
Allison, Jenene J. *Revealing Differences.* University of Delaware Press, 1995.
Scott, Geoffrey. *The Portrait of Zélide.* NY: Scribner, 1927.

Crista Martin,
Boston, Massachusetts

Chartres, countess of.

See Maud of Normandy (d. 1017).
See Maud of Normandy (d. 1107).
See Adela of Blois (1062–c. 1137).
See Marie de Chatillon (r. 1230–1241).

Chartres, duchess of.

See Louise Marie of Bourbon (1753–1821).
See Helene Louise of Mecklenburg-Schwerin (1814–1858).
See Françoise d'Orléans (1844–1925).

Chase, Agnes Meara (1869–1963)

American botanist. Name variations: Mary Agnes Meara Chase. Born Mary Agnes Meara in Iroquois County, Illinois, on April 20, 1869; died in Bethesda, Maryland, in 1963; fifth of six children of Martin J. (a railroad engineer) and Mary (Brannick) Meara; attended public grammar school in Chicago; married William Ingraham Chase, in 1888 (died 1889).

Lacking formal education, Agnes Meara turned a passionate hobby into a distinguished career as a botanist and international authority on grasses. She was known as a woman of unflagging energy and interests, who also devoted herself to a number of reform movements.

Chase was a teenager when she landed a position as a newspaper proofreader to help her widowed mother keep the family of six together. She fell in love and married her editor, William

Chase. When he died less than a year later, 19-year-old Agnes was on her own. She worked a variety of jobs, while expanding her growing interest in botany. On a plant collecting trip in 1898, she met bryologist Ellsworth Hill, who instructed her in plant lore, taught her how to use a microscope, and enlisted her as an illustrator. While working for Hill, Chase also illustrated two publications for the Field Museum of Natural History: *Plantae Utowanae* (1900) and *Plantae Yucatamae* (1904). With Hill's encouragement, she applied for a position with the U.S. Department of Agriculture (USDA), working as a meat inspector at the Chicago Stockyards before obtaining a position as a botanical artist with the Bureau of Plant Industry (1903) in Washington, D.C.

At the Bureau, she met Albert Spear Hitchcock, a specialist in the study of grasses, and they began a long collaboration. With Hitchcock as a mentor, Chase moved up quickly through the ranks and, at his death in 1936, succeeded him as principal scientist in charge of systematic agrostology. Over the years, her various collecting trips yielded over 4,500 specimens, most of which she donated to the Smithsonian and the National Herbarium. In addition, she identified new species and extended the ranges of previously described ones. Her work in agrostology had practical applications in agriculture, where her information was applied to crop development. Fully dedicated to her work, Chase eschewed lunch hours and worked on Saturdays. Although she never remarried, she built an extended family of friends and co-workers with whom she shared living quarters in the Washington area. One such friend, **Mary Wright Gill**, illustrated a children's book that Chase wrote about an orphaned squirrel she had adopted named Toodles.

Agnes Chase was as devoted to political causes as to her work and was associated with a number of reform movements during her lifetime. She was a suffragist (jailed in 1918 and again in 1919 while protesting), a prohibitionist, and a socialist. She supported the Fellowship of Reconciliation, the NAACP, the National Woman's Party, and the Women's International League for Peace and Freedom, and gave a portion of her salary to groups such as the Quakers and the National Wildlife Federation.

Following her mandatory retirement at age 70, she remained active, working as a volunteer at the Smithsonian Institution revising Hitchcock's *Manual of the Grasses of the United States*, as well as compiling a massive index to grass species. She continued to take field trips, including one to Venezuela when she was 71 to assist in developing a range-management program. At age 91, Chase wrote in a letter to her goddaughter, "If I had any sense I'd quit the herbarium and grasses, but it would be easier to stop breathing." She died at a nursing home in Bethesda, Maryland, at age 94.

COLLECTIONS:
Chase's papers located at the Hunt Institute for Botanical Documentation at Carnegie-Mellon University.

Barbara Morgan,
Melrose, Massachusetts

Chase, Edna Woolman (1877–1957)

American editor of Vogue *magazine. Born on March 14, 1877, in Asbury Park, New Jersey; died of a heart attack on March 20, 1957, in Sarasota, Florida; daughter of Franklyn Alloway and Laura (Woolman) Alloway; married Francis Dane Chase, in 1904 (divorced); married Richard T. Newton (an English automotive engineer and inventor), in 1921 (died 1950); children: (first marriage) *Ilka Chase (1905–1978). Editor of* Vogue *magazine (1914–52).*

America's "high priestess of fashion" for most of the first half of the 20th century, Edna Woolman Chase was born in 1877 in Asbury Park, New Jersey. After her parents divorced, she was raised in the country by her Quaker grandparents but maintained a relationship with her mother, who lived in New York City with a second husband and visited often. As a teenager, Edna moved in with her mother in New York, where, through newspapers, she voraciously tracked every detail of the lives of high-society debutantes.

In 1895, *Vogue* was a small but refined weekly society magazine, and Edna was 18 and in need of Christmas money. A friend who worked at the magazine got her a temporary job there addressing envelopes. A diligent and eager worker, Edna quickly grasped the mechanisms of the publishing business as well as *Vogue*'s editorial approach. She was soon noticed by the magazine's founder and publisher, Arthur Baldwin Turnure, who came to depend on her bright mind and conscientious work ethic. In 1904, she married Francis Chase and they had a daughter, Ilka, in 1905. Francis had trouble supporting his family, and eventually Edna Chase divorced him; she would marry once more in 1921.

After Turnure died in 1906, Chase developed a bond with her new boss, Condé Nast, and continued accepting ever-greater responsibilities from the magazine's editor, **Marie Harrison**. Chase also began displaying a keen instinct for delighting and influencing *Vogue* readers. In 1914, she easily slid into the editor's chair when Harrison retired. While Nast expanded the *Vogue* empire by acquiring and establishing international editions, Chase elevated its reputation and riches with her inventive ideas and hustle.

In 1929, Chase became editor-in-chief of all *Vogue* editions and controlled virtually every aspect of the magazine. A perfectionist, she brought in only the most talented artists and editors to help *Vogue* achieve its goal of being *the* high-society authority on matters of style and elegance. She balanced all the demands of running a large, influential fashion publication: artistic, financial, topical, and even political. She was fiercely loyal to the magazine and never apologized for its openly snobbish, and to some, frivolous nature. During her tenure, her pronouncements on fashion were a powerful force in the fashion industry worldwide.

In 1952, at 75, Chase retired from active editorship, and two years later co-wrote her autobiography, *Always in Vogue*, with her actress daughter Ilka. Edna Chase was always proud of having made *Vogue* a training ground that helped young women launch successful careers in a time when their professional options were limited. She died of a heart attack while on vacation in Florida in 1957.

SOURCES:
"Chase, Edna Woolman," in *Current Biography 1940.* Edited by Maxine Block. NY: H.W. Wilson, p. 160.

SUGGESTED READING:
Chase, Edna Woolman, and Ilka Chase. *Always in Vogue.* Garden City, NY: Doubleday, 1954.

Jacquie Maurice, Calgary, Alberta, Canada

Chase, Ilka (1905–1978)

American actress and author. Born on April 8, 1905, in New York, New York; died on February 15, 1978, in Mexico City, Mexico; daughter of Francis Dane (a hotel manager) and Edna Woolman Chase (editor Vogue *magazine; maiden name, Alloway); attended Mrs. Dow's School, Briarcliff Manor, New York; attended a private school at Groslay, near Paris, France; married Louis Calhern (an actor), in 1926 (divorced 1926); married William B. Murray (a radio executive), on July 13, 1935 (divorced 1946); married Norton Sager Brown (a physician), on December 7, 1946; no children.*

Theater: made professional debut as Polly Carter in The Proud Princess *(Cox Theater, Cincinnati, Ohio, 1924); made Broadway debut as Sister Francesca and the Maid in* The Red Falcon *(Broadhurst Theater, New York, October 1924); appeared as Mrs. Castro in* Shall We Join the Ladies? *(Empire Theater, New York, January 1925); with the Henry Miller Co., appeared in* Embers, The Swan, *and* The Grand Duchess and the Waiter *(San Francisco, California, April–May 1925); appeared as Lia in* Antonia *(Empire Theater, New York, October 1925), Madame Cleremont in* Embers *(Henry Miller Theater, New York, February 1926), Frances Drayton in* Loose Ankles *(Biltmore Theater, New York, August 1926), Consuelo Pratt in* The Happy Husband *(Empire Theater, New York, May 1928), Grace Macomber in* The Animal Kingdom *(Broadhurst Theater, New York, January 1932), Elinor Branch in* Forsaking All Others *(Times Square Theater, New York, March 1932), Lucy Hillman in* Days without End *(Henry Miller Theater, New York, January 1934), Marion Langdon in* Wife Insurance *(Ethel Barrymore Theater, New York, April 1934), Lady Cattering in* While Parents Sleep *(Playhouse Theater, New York, June 1934), Sylvia Temple in* Small Miracle *(John Golden Theater, New York, September 1934), Dona Isabella in* Revenge with Music *(New Amsterdam Theater, New York, November 1934), Eleanor Sloan in* On to Fortune *(Fulton Theater, New York, February 1935), Sylvia Farren in* Co-Respondent Unknown *(Ritz Theater, New York, February 1936), Sylvia Fowler in* The Women *(Ethel Barrymore Theater, New York, December 1936); appeared in* Keep Off the Grass *(Broadhurst Theater, New York, May 23, 1940), as Jean Harding in* Beverly Hills *(Fulton Theater, New York, November 1940); toured in Stock as Carlotta in* Love in Our Time *(Summer 1943), and as Marion Froude in* Biography *(Summer 1943); appeared as Devon Wainwright in* In Bed We Cry *(Belasco Theater, New York, November 1944), Susan in a stock production of* Susan and God *(Summer 1945); appeared in* Laughter From a Cloud *(Boston, Massachusetts, August 1947), in* The First Lady *(Empress Theater, St. Louis, Missouri, October 1952), in the Farewell Tribute to the Empire Theater (New York, May 1953); appeared as Mrs. Banks in* Barefoot in the Park *(Biltmore Theater, New York, May 1966).*

Selected filmography: Paris Bound *(1929);* Red Hot Rhythm *(1929);* The Careless Age *(1929);* South Sea Rose *(1929);* Why Leave Home *(1929);* On Your Back *(1930);* The Big Party *(1930);* Let's Go Places *(1930);* Rich People *(1930);* The Floradora Girl *(1930);* The Lady Consents *(1936);* Soak the Rich *(1936);* Stronger Than Desire *(1939);* Now, Voyager *(1942);* No Time for Love *(1943);* Miss Tatlock's Millions *(1948);* Johnny Dark *(1954);* It Should Happen to You *(1954);* The Big Knife *(1955);* Oceans *(1960).*

Selected writings: (novels) In Bed We Cry *(1943),* I Love Miss Tilli Bean *(1946),* New York 22: That Dis-

Opposite page

𝒪lka

𝒞hase

trict of the City which Lies Between Fiftieth and Sixtieth Streets, Fifth Avenue, and the East River *(1951)*, The Island Players *(1956)*, Three Men on the Left Hand *(1960)*, The Sounds of Home *(1971)*; *(autobiography)* Past Imperfect *(1942)*, Free Admission *(1948)*, *(with mother, Edna Woolman Chase)* Always in Vogue *(1954)*; *(travel)* The Carthaginian Rose *(1961)*, Elephants Arrive at Half-Past Five *(1963)*, Second Spring and Two Potatoes *(1965)*, Fresh from the Laundry *(1967)*, The Varied Airs of Spring *(1969)*, Around the World and Other Places *(1971)*, Worlds Apart *(1972)*; *(other)* The Care and Feeding of Friends *(1973)*.

As an actress, Ilka Chase performed in over 20 Broadway plays, 30 movies, and was a radio and television personality; as a writer, she penned a half-dozen or so novels, two biographies, seven travel books, and an entertainment guide. Once, during a lull in her social calendar, she embarked on a lecture tour, speaking on the philosophy of being a woman. With the publication of her autobiography *Past Imperfect* (1942), Chase took aim at the sophisticated New York society in which she traveled. Described by one critic as "just about pulling the skin off many of her contemporaries," the book, along with her second autobiography *Free Admission* (1948), provides clear-cut examples of Chase's wit and cynicism.

The only child of longtime *Vogue* editor *Edna Woolman Chase** and her first husband Francis Dane, Ilka Chase was born in New York City on April 8, 1905, and was named for a Hungarian friend of her mother's. In love with the theater from an early age, she made her stage debut at eight in a convent-school production of *Puss in Boots*. Later, at Mrs. Dow's in Briarcliff Manor, New York, she appeared in her first classic drama, as Malvolio in *Twelfth Night*. At 16, Chase chose to attend school in France (Groslay, outside of Paris), rather than a college in the States, and although the theater was forgotten amid the glamour of her first trip abroad, her passion was rekindled when she saw **Vera Sergine** play the lead role in a production of Rostand's *L'Aiglon*.

Returning to New York, Chase put her career plans on hold in order to make her society debut, but after three months of awkward party-going she joined the Stuart Walker stock company. For the next few years, she endured a series of bit parts—mostly maids—with Walker, then with companies headed by Henry Miller and George Cukor. While touring in Rochester with Cukor, she met and fell in love with the elegant actor Louis Calhern. They were married in 1926 but

divorced less than a year later, after which Calhern remarried his ex-wife **Julia Hoyt**. (Purportedly, Chase sent Hoyt a box of her unused calling cards, elegantly engraved "Mrs. Louis Calhern," with a note saying, "I hope these reach you in time.") Following the divorce, Chase stayed in London with her mother, trying, without success, to find work on the English stage.

Returning to the United States, Chase went to Hollywood, where she launched her movie career with a role in the Pathé production *Paris Bound* (1929). She ultimately appeared in some 30 movies—notably *Fast and Loose* (1930) and *The Animal Kingdom* (1942)—but she did not take to the California climate and felt out of place in the Hollywood milieu. It was there, however, that she met her future husband, William Murray, an advertising executive. After a five-year courtship, during which he obtained a divorce from his first wife, they married in July 1935 and settled into a posh New York apartment.

Memorable among Chase's numerous stage roles was that of Sylvia Fowler in *Clare Boothe Luce*'s vitriolic play *The Women* (1936), which Chase described as having "the fetid atmosphere of a badly ventilated women's washroom." Among the 33 females in the cast, Chase was praised by critic Brooks Atkinson as "the mother of all the vultures." After the show closed in 1938, Chase embarked on a radio program, "Luncheon at the Waldorf," which was conceived as the educated woman's alternative to soap operas. Within an interview format, Chase conversed with various luminaries, ranging from the Harvard anthropologist Dr. Earnest A. Hooton to cosmetic maven *Elizabeth Arden*. Encountering censorship and sponsor problems, the show was eventually given a night slot as "Penthouse Party" and lasted until 1945. Chase went on to a short-lived television program of her own and made frequent guest appearances.

SOURCES:

Block, Maxine, ed. *Current Biography 1942.* NY: H.W. Wilson, 1942.

Mainiero, Lina, ed. *American Women Writers.* NY: Frederick Ungar, 1979.

McGill, Raymond D., ed. *Notable Names in the American Theater.* Clifton, NJ: James T. White, 1976.

Moritz, Charles, ed. *Current Biography 1978.* NY: H.W. Wilson, 1978.

Barbara Morgan,
Melrose, Massachusetts

Chase, Lucia (1907—)

American dancer who was a founder and co-director of the American Ballet Theatre. Pronunciation: LOO-shuh. Name variations: Lucia Chase Ewing. Born on March 24, 1907, in Waterbury, Connecticut; third of five daughters of Irving Hall Chase (president of the Waterbury Watch Company, manufacturer of Ingersoll watches) and Elizabeth Hosmer (Kellogg) Chase; graduated from St. Margaret's School, Waterbury; attended Theatre Guild School in New York City; studied ballet at the Vestoff Serova School; married Thomas Ewing, Jr. (d. 1933), in 1926; children: Thomas (d. 1963); Alexander Cochran Ewing (at one time business manager for the Robert Joffrey Ballet; chancellor of North Carolina School of the Arts).

In 1940, New England heiress Lucia Chase became a principal dancer and founding member of the Ballet Theatre, later to be called the American Ballet Theatre (ABT). Set on developing a world-class American ballet company, the maverick enterprise broke with tradition from the beginning. "The young Ballet Theatre grew like Topsy," wrote dance historian Robert Coe. It avoided a unified style of dancing by hiring the best and brightest performers, including Russian and English artists, and by eliminating the role of a single company choreographer, a new concept. The group employed young and innovative choreographers, such as Michel Fokine, *Agnes de Mille*, Antony Tudor, and Eugene Loring, to create a varied dance gallery appealing to the eclectic tastes of the American audience. During the 1940s, the company used as many as 32 choreographers, creating a repertory that included influences from France and Russia, as well as Hollywood, Broadway, and modern-dance companies. With renowned theatrical designer Oliver Smith, Chase became co-director of the company in 1945. Throughout her near 40-year association with the ABT, she not only provided generous financial support (almost single-handedly pulling it through the lean years of the 1950s and 1960s) but also guided the careers of countless extraordinarily talented dancers and choreographers.

Born in Connecticut in 1907, an imaginative Chase knew from age three that she wanted to be an actress, and she was encouraged by her parents. She often appeared in children's plays in her hometown of Waterbury and, after graduating from St. Margaret's School, enrolled at the Theatre Guild School in New York City. There, her acting instructor, Rouben Mamoulian, cultivated the pantomimic skills that would later serve her so well as a dramatic dancer. Chase also took singing lessons at the school and studied both tap and ballet. Her fledgling pursuit, however, was cut short by her marriage in 1926 to Thomas Ewing, Jr., vice president of the Alexander Smith and Sons Carpet Company, a business established by his grandfather in the 1800s. Chase had two sons (the eldest of whom was lost at sea in a sailing accident in 1963). Aside from giving an occasional voice or dance recital, she forgot about her professional career until 1933, the year her husband died of pneumonia.

Chase picked up her ballet studies with Mikhail Mordkin, formerly of the Bolshoi Theatre and one of *Anna Pavlova's most brilliant partners. In 1937, when Mordkin established the Mordkin Ballet Company for some of his more ambitious students, Chase became one of its principal dancers, performing the title role in *Giselle*, Lise in *La Fille Mal Gardée*, and leading roles in *The Goldfish*, *Trepak*, and other ballets. When Mordkin's business manager Richard Pleasant founded Ballet Theatre, Chase was not only a major financial backer and charter member of the new group but also a dancer in the company. During the initial sold-out season in 1940, she created the roles of the Girl in Eugene Loring's *The Great American Goof* and Minerva in Antony Tudor's *Judgment of Paris*. Dance critic **Grace Robert** praised the latter as "one of the more compelling performances in the contemporary theatre." In subsequent ballets, Chase made her mark in a number of other performances, including the title role in *Princess Aurora*, the Greedy One in Agnes de Mille's *Three Virgins and the Devil*, the Nurse in *Romeo and Juliet*, and Pallas Athena in *Helen of Troy*.

Chase's dancing career peaked in 1960, when she and *Nora Kaye, another of Ballet Theatre's stunning dramatic dancers, performed in Tudor's *Pillar of Fire*, which was considered one of the masterpieces of the company. (Chase also performed in Tudor's *Dark Elegies*, another of her more distinctive roles.) After 1960, Chase made only occasional appearances on stage, typically as the Princess Mother in *Swan Lake* and the Stepmother in de Mille's *Fall River Legend*, a ballet based on the story of *Lizzie Borden. Most critics concur that Chase's greatest strength as a dancer lay in her roles. "Coming too late to the classic technique to become a truly proficient classicist," writes **Olga Maynar** in *Dance* magazine, "she drew on her talents and training to make herself a fine character dancer." Foremost dance critic Walter Terry agreed: "She is a superb dramatic dancer and a brilliant comedienne," he wrote, "and her presence in these capacities would enhance any company, whether she controlled it or not."

From the earliest days of Ballet Theatre, Chase supported Richard Pleasant's goal of cre-

Lucia Chase

ating a truly American ballet company, but with his resignation in 1941 she watched the young company begin to flounder. His replacement, Sol Hurok, brought a decidedly Russian element to the company that Chase and her associates found contrary to its American spirit. In 1945, when she was asked to take over management of the company, she agreed, with the condition that Oliver Smith, who had mounted the company's production of *Fancy Free* (1944), share the job. (*Fancy Free*, choreographed by former chorus member Jerome Robbins and scored by the young Leonard Bernstein, was a runaway hit. It ran for two weeks of an extended Metropolitan Opera House season.)

During the late 1940s, Ballet Theatre continued to be a showcase for international ballet stars and choreographers, and, as Coe points out, "a stronghold of a new kind of dance-theater realism, inspired in part by experiments in modern dance, by the naturalism of the American theater, and by an unabashed engagement with the historical experience of the nation." Chase was continually cited as the pivotal figure in the growth of the company, which enjoyed a well-received London performance and a successful American tour, performing a new George

Balanchine ballet, *Theme and Variations*, and an upgraded production of *Giselle*. While Smith, as artistic director, handled the music and the staging, Chase was responsible for the dozens of dancers, overseeing promotion of students from the Ballet Theatre School to the company, assigning featured roles, negotiating contracts, and, with Smith, selecting and casting each ballet. Believing that no one person could oversee the staging of both classical and modern ballet, she also hired an individual choreographer for each specific work and followed their progress by attending regular rehearsals. "You have to know what your dancers are doing," she once told John Gruen of *Dance* magazine. "You have to see how they're coming over. Dancers come and tell me how well they're doing, but I prefer to see for myself."

Entering the 1950s, as the company began to experience financial woes in spite of a dedicated campaign to secure public and private grants, it continued receiving financial transfusions from Chase. During most of the decade, the company toured, performing in Europe and South America, as well the United States. By 1959, however, bookings were down, and the company disbanded until 1960, when it celebrated its 20th anniversary with the performance of *Pas de Deux*, a new ballet choreographed by Herbert Ross, along with choreographer *Birgit Cullberg's *The Lady from the Sea*, *Pillar of Fire*, and *Giselle*. The 1960s brought further overseas tours in the Soviet Union, South America, and an international dance festival in Cuba.

The American Ballet Theatre celebrated its 25th year in 1965, with a soldout performance at the Lincoln Center for the Performing Arts in New York City. Chase raised the money for the performance, which showcased six new ballets, including Jerome Robbins' *Les Noces*, Glen Tetley's *Sargasso*, and Agnes de Mille's *The Wind in the Mountains* and *The Four Marys*. Although critics praised this as their most exciting season to date, Chase admitted in an interview for the *Washington Post* that she had serious doubts about the company's future. "We were determined to go out in a blaze of glory," she said. Near financial collapse by November 1965, the company was rescued at the last minute by an emergency grant from the National Council on the Arts. Earlier, in 1963, they had been conspicuously ignored by the Ford Foundation, in favor of Balanchine's New York City Ballet and the School of American Ballet. Chase, no longer able to pour large sums of her own money into the faltering company, insisted that even without her the company must go on.

She told the *New York World Journal Tribune* in October 1966: "I feel that there should be at least two great ballet companies in America.... We can and should be friendly rivals, just like Yale and Harvard.... We are very different from the New York City Ballet. We are not a one-choreographer company, and I know that for us, our cornerstone was and is right."

In 1968, the ABT became the official ballet company of the Kennedy Center for the Performing Arts in Washington D.C., which had become its home base in late 1962. Chase, believing the company deserved such an honor, cited its performances in each of the 50 states and its representation of the nation in 55 different countries during 15 international tours. In preparation for the Washington premiere (followed by performances in New York, Chicago, Los Angeles, Houston, and Dallas), Chase revived *Petrouchka* and *Romeo and Juliet* and asked David Blair, of the Royal Ballet, to design a new *Sleeping Beauty*. The modern-dance portion of the repertory included two works by José Limon, *The Moor's Pavane* and *The Traitor*, as well as a new Alvin Ailey ballet, *The River*, scored by Duke Ellington.

Throughout the 1970s, Chase resorted to more revivals, often at the expense of new works, and began contracting more and more foreign stars to dance them. According to Coe, critics began to argue "that America's exemplary ballet company had surrendered itself to the cultural imagination of Europe and the charisma of foreigners." There was also increasing dissension among the company's dancers, who resented outsiders being brought in for plum roles. In 1974, *Cynthia Gregory resigned briefly in protest after the announcement that nine guest stars were contracted for the coming season. More disastrous to the company, however, was the overwhelming financial burden of mounting the classical ballets and importing foreign dancers.

Amid growing problems, in January 1975 the ABT presented a gala 35th-anniversary performance at Manhattan's City Center. The program, under the direction of Tony-award-winning choreographer Donald Sadler, was interwoven with current dancers and returning alumni; Chase recreated her original role in a scene from *Pillar of Fire*. The audience honored Chase and Smith for their three decades as co-directors with a standing ovation. "The whole evening was, of course, a source of renewed satisfaction to Lucia Chase," writes Charles Payne, "a convincing confirmation that thirty-five years had been well spent. She would continue to resist any suggestion that she was solely responsible for the success and survival of Ballet Theatre, and certainly there were hundreds of other contributors. But of Lucia Chase alone could it be said that had she not been there, Ballet Theatre would never have been alive to celebrate its Thirty-fifth Anniversary."

When she stepped down in the late 1970s to make way for Mikhail Baryshnikov, Lucia Chase was still trim and petite, looking years younger than her age and enjoying an active personal life at her home in New York and at the family's oceanside retreat in Narragansett, Rhode Island. She had received the Capezio and the *Dance* magazine awards, as well as the Handel Medallion, the highest cultural citation New York City can bestow. Of her many years with the American Ballet Theatre, she was most fulfilled by its status as a showcase for American ballet throughout the world.

SOURCES:

Coe, Robert. *Dance in America*. NY: E.P. Dutton, 1985.
Current Biography. NY: H.W. Wilson, 1947.
Dance Magazine. August 1971.
Moritz, Charles, ed. *Current Biography 1975*. NY: H.W. Wilson, 1975.
Payne, Charles. *The American Ballet Theatre*. NY: Alfred A. Knopf, 1978.

Barbara Morgan,
Melrose, Massachusetts

Chase, Mary Agnes Meara (1869–1963).

See Chase, Agnes Meara.

Chase, Mary Coyle (1907–1981)

American playwright, who won the Pulitzer Prize in 1945 for her comedy Harvey, *one of Broadway's four longest running shows. Born Mary Coyle on February 25, 1907, in West Denver, Colorado; died of a heart attack on October 21, 1981, in Denver; daughter of Frank Coyle (a salesman for a flour mill) and Mary (McDonough) Coyle; attended West Denver High School, 1922, Denver University, 1929-23 (majored in classics), University of Colorado at Boulder, 1923-24; no degree; married Robert Lamont Chase (a newspaper reporter), June 7, 1928; children: Michael Lamont, Colin Robert, and Barry Jerome.*

Worked as reporter for Rocky Mountain News *(1924–31); was freelance correspondent, International News Service and United Press (1932–36); awarded Pulitzer Prize in Drama for* Harvey *(1945); awarded Honorary Doctor of Letters, Denver University (1947); named runner-up New York Drama Critics Circle Award for* Mrs. McThing *(1951–52); appointed to honorary committee of the American National*

Theater and Academy (ANTA, 1981); during lifetime, worked for numerous social causes and was proudest of founding House of Hope, a home for women alcoholics in Denver; member of the Dramatists Guild, the board of trustees of the Bonfils Theater, the Denver Center for the Performing Arts, and the Christian Science Church; given an honorary life membership in the Women's Press Club of Denver.

Plays: Me Third, *first produced in Denver, Colo. at the Federal Theater (1936), first produced in New York as* Now You've Done It *(1937);* Too Much Business *(one-act, Samuel French, 1940);* A Slip of a Girl, *first produced in Camp Hall, Colo. (1941);* Harvey *(three-act), first produced in New York at the 48th Street Theater, November 1, 1944, starring Frank Fay and Josephine Hull (Dramatists Play Service, 1950);* The Next Half Hour *(previously titled "The Banshee"), first produced in New York, October 29, 1945, starring Fay Bainter;* Mrs. McThing *(two-act), first produced by ANTA at the Martin Beck Theater on Broadway in February 20, 1952, starring Helen Hayes and Brandon de Wilde (Oxford University Press, 1952, rev. ed., Dramatists Play Service, 1954);* Bernardine *(two-act), first produced at The Playhouse on Broadway on October 16, 1952, starring John*

Mary Coyle Chase

Kerr (Oxford University Press, 1953, rev. ed., Dramatists Play Service, 1954); Midgie Purvis (two-act), first produced on Broadway in 1961 (Dramatists Play Service, 1963); The Prize Play (Dramatists Play Service, 1961); The Dog Sitters (three-act, Dramatists Play Service, 1963); Mickey (two-act, based on her novel Loretta Mason Potts, Dramatists Play Service, 1963); Cocktails with Mimi (Dramatists Play Service, 1974).

Novels for children: (illustrated by Harold Berson) Loretta Mason Potts (Lippincott, 1958); (illus. by Don Bolognese) The Wicked Pigeon Ladies in the Garden (Knopf, 1968); also contributed to magazines.

It is only when I am writing that I feel really complete. When I am in one of my writing trances, I am cushioned against the sadnesses and griefs of the world.

—Mary Chase

One of the most famous and imaginative characters in dramatic literature is a rabbit. Not a garden-variety rabbit but a statuesque, 6'½" rabbit, who walks erectly, talks intelligently, thinks whimsically, and is totally invisible to a great majority of people—but not all. This is the premise of Mary Chase's timeless comic fantasy that poses the question: Is Elwood P. Dowd demented because he insists that Harvey, known as a pooka in Celtic mythology, is his constant companion?

Chase's original and highly unorthodox play opened on November 1, 1944, at the 48th Street Theater and delighted Broadway audiences for the next five years. Since then it has been translated into numerous languages, has been produced throughout the world, and has kept audiences laughing. Yet according to John Toohey, when the play opened in New York, the author and her husband were so low on funds they had to borrow $300 from a Denver bank in order to attend. "Money has never been anything you made," Chase once said. "It has merely been something you owed." Happily, *Harvey* changed their lives. Or was it the luck of the Irish? Just before the tryout in Boston, Chase was certain the play would be a success because—as she later confided to Wallis Reef in a *Saturday Evening Post* interview—she had received three good omens:

A member of the cast gave me a two-dollar bill. . . . Then, a short time later, Josephine Hull gave me a four-leaf clover. Then, as I was walking to the theater on opening night in Boston, a huge truck drove slowly next to the curb. The driver turned his head and said casually, "Hello, Love." It wasn't an at-

tempted pickup; he didn't even smile. I noticed he wore a dirty leather jacket and his face was solemn and well shaped under the grime, and his eyes were dark and thoughtful. He didn't stop, but drove on without another glance. Somehow, it seemed like a benediction.

Though born in West Denver, Colorado, on February 25, 1907, Mary Coyle was steeped in the Irish tradition, the folklore, and the search for the rainbow. At age 16, her mother **Mary McDonough (Coyle)** had immigrated from Ulster County, Ireland, to keep house for her four brothers, who were unsuccessfully swept up in the Colorado gold fever of the 1880s and '90s. While McDonough attended parochial school, she met her future husband Frank Coyle who had been just as swept up and just as unsuccessful in the Oklahoma land rush. After their marriage, Frank Coyle settled for a salesman's job with a flour mill.

When Mary was born, her circle of admirers included her parents, two brothers, an older sister, and four uncles. Irish folk and fairy tales were told as often as Irish politics were discussed and Irish folk songs sung. Mary heard the English language with an Irish lilt, fostering in her a fondness for rhythm, the poetic turn of phrase, and always the mysterious mystical fairy folk—the leprechauns and pookas.

She recalled a day when her mother chased away some youths as they tossed snowballs at an old woman who was attempting to navigate a slippery surface with her cane. Outraged, Mary McDonough Coyle cautioned her daughter, "Never be unkind or indifferent to a person others say is crazy. Often they have a deep wisdom. We pay them a great respect in the old country and we call them fairy people, and it could be, they are sometimes." In many of Chase's plays, there is a mysterious, magical and sometimes muddled character who is often the wisest: Mrs. McThing, Midgie Purvis, Elwood P. Dowd.

Another Chase theme might have germinated during another youthful incident: while shaking down a gum machine, her older brother was shot and wounded by a police officer. Though the officer was later discharged, Denver's Sunday paper carried the story and the damage to the family name was done. Under the guise of respectability, Mary was instantly ostracized. Perhaps this is why she relished exposing the hypocrisy and prejudices of so-called polite society.

Although her family was poor and her undergarments were often sewn from the mill's floursacks, Mary was rich in imagination and in her insatiable preoccupation with language and literature. By age eight, she had read *A Tale of Two Cities;* by ten, she was reading Thomas De Quincy and at fifteen she began Xenophon's *Anabasis* in Greek. From the moment she saw her first play—Shakespeare's *Macbeth* performed by the Denham Theater Stock Company—she was mesmerized by the theater. She would sometimes play hooky from school to walk the five miles to see a play at a Denver theater; she also devoured books on plays and playwriting. Despite her love of books, she was impatient with college. After studying the classics for two and a half years at Denver University, she transferred to the University of Colorado at Boulder but never earned a degree.

By all accounts, Mary Chase was high-spirited, athletic, adventurous and fond of practical jokes, "which contrasted nicely with her Madonna appearance," wrote longtime friend **Wallis Reef.** She had "wide grey eyes, rich brown hair with hints of red in it, and a white, imperious face." But close friends claimed that although most anecdotes concerning Chase were amusing, she seldom smiled and her eyes contained a hint of melancholy.

From the movie Harvey, *starring James Stewart, based on the play by Mary Coyle Chase.*

While still at college, she talked the *Rocky Mountain News* into giving her a summer job and soon worked there full-time. Journalists were notorious for doing whatever was necessary to get the story, and Mary rapidly became known as an aggressive reporter. Once, on a particularly sensational socialite divorce story, the *Rocky Mountain News* wanted a photograph of the husband but requests to the family were turned down flat. Then Chase remembered seeing the gentleman's picture at the Denver Country Club. She jumped on a bus, strolled into the club, and removed the portrait from the wall. Racing out the front door with the manager in hot pursuit, Chase hailed a passing coal truck. "To the Rocky Mountain News—as fast as you can," she ordered. Either enchanted by her looks or stunned by the request, the driver delivered her to the newspaper's door, where she triumphantly handed the picture over to be copied. A few minutes later, the irate club manager arrived.

Like other newswomen of her era, Chase was restricted to covering society news and items for the women's page, but she longed to be a street reporter, she said, so she could "study people, meet life and later put it into plays. I wanted to see how people reacted under stress, how they spoke in times of crisis." Though she worked demanding hours, she also fought for human rights. She once walked with Chicano paper handlers who were striking for a raise, served them coffee and sandwiches, and persuaded the police not to break up the strike. (The strikers got their raise.) In 1928, she married Robert L. Chase, an admiring fellow reporter who would later become an associate editor. Three years later, Chase was consigned to freelance writing when a practical joke backfired, unfortunately on the city editor, and she was discharged from the *Rocky Mountain News* for her fourth and final time.

Her first play *Me Third* (about a Western politician whose campaign slogan was "God first, the People Second, Me Third") was finished about the time her third son arrived. Presented by Denver's Federal Theater as a WPA project and praised by Denver critics, it was purchased by New York City producer Brock Pemberton and renamed *Now You've Done It*. Though the New York offering of this rowdy political piece lasted less than two months and was a financial loss, Pemberton urged Chase to continue writing.

Chase is reputed to have had the ability to completely concentrate on the writing task at hand. After her children had gone to sleep and her husband had gone to his night shift at the newspaper, she would work on a miniature stage, manipulating characters by blocking empty thread spools. She also continued her involvement in social causes, forming a local chapter of the American Newspaper Guild and fighting for the rights of Denver's Spanish Americans who, says Reef:

> had been getting kicked around. All this was done with a gaiety that astounded some of her dead-serious associates. She was likely to show up in a picket line wearing a fifty-dollar hat, fantastic earrings, and a dress best described as slinky. The effect on employers was amazing. At one time, she was running a quiet and effective lobby for an oleomargarine concern and writing a weekly radio program for the Teamster's Union. The group of people whose activities seem to revolve about Mrs. Chase would, on a chart, be a sort of vertical section of Denver's social and economic life.

After two years of hard work, Chase completed the script of *Harvey* (earlier titles were "The White Rabbit" and "The Pooka"). Initially, the play's pooka—a Celtic spirit that takes animal form—was a canary before it became a man-sized rabbit, and the play's protagonist was a female before it became the amiable Elwood P. Dowd. Chase rewrote the play, tried it out on friends, rewrote the play, read it to her cleaning woman, rewrote the play 50 times before sending it on to New York. And, according to John Gassner, there were 18 more versions prior to its Broadway opening. Chase cautioned Pemberton, the play's producer:

> It must be bold humor with a folk-lore quality to it. It must be the kind of production about which the audience will say later, "It's a play about a man who goes around with a 6-foot rabbit," rather then, "It's a play about a woman who tries to get her brother in a sanitarium."

In those days, previews were held on the road in places known as tryout towns, where writers would hole up in bleak hotel rooms frantically revising, rewriting, and repairing the flaws of the new script. It was a time of high stress, and under such duress Pemberton insisted that the audience needed to have a brief glimpse of the pooka. Chase was equally adamant that the mythological creature should be invisible; but the producer's wishes prevailed. In Boston, an anonymous actor in a $650 rubber rabbit suit pursued the director of Chumley's Rest (the sanitarium) at the end of Act II. The decision proved to be a disaster, ruining the effect of the play. From then on, Harvey the Pooka never appeared again to anyone—not even during the curtain call—except on the extraordinary stage of the imagination.

When the play opened in New York City, the critics were enthusiastic. Lewis Nichols in *The New York Times* found it a "delightful evening—one of the treats of the fall theater." Burton Rascoe in the *World-Telegram* couldn't recall another opening where he laughed "so hard and so continuously. . . . The whole fantasy is delicious, subtle, clever and very funny." John Chapman of the *Daily News,* thought it "the most delightful, droll, endearing, funny and touching piece of stage whimsy I ever saw." *Time* crowned it the funniest fantasy Broadway "has seen for years."

Though *Harvey* certainly provided an opportunity for a war-weary audience to escape, there was wisdom as well as whimsy. Consider the comments of the cab driver outside the sanitarium who compares his arriving fares with his departing fares, after they've had the miracle injection to make them "normal."

> I've been drivin' this route fifteen years. I've brought 'em out here to get that stuff and drove 'em back after they had it. It changes 'em. . . . On the way out here they sit back and enjoy the ride. They talk to me. Sometimes we stop and watch the sunsets and look at the birds flyin'. Sometimes we stop and watch the birds when there ain't no birds and look at the sunsets when it's rainin'. We have a swell time and I always get a big tip. But afterward. . . . They crab, crab, crab. They yell at me to watch the lights, watch the brakes, watch the intersection. They scream at me to hurry. They got no faith—in me or my buggy—yet it's the same cab—the same driver—and we're goin' back over the very same road. It's no fun—and no tips.

Unaware of *Harvey*'s impending success, Chase returned to Denver the day after the opening to catch up on her house cleaning. "From then on, the telephone never stopped ringing," she said. Three years later, when her husband tracked her down in a local movie house to tell her *Harvey* had won the Pulitzer Prize for 1947, she screamed so loud that she nearly started a panic in the theater. But success had its downside, noted Chase in an interview in *Cosmopolitan:*

> Any precipitous change is a terrible shock in itself, whether you lose all your money or make a fortune. But nobody seems to realize this. If you lose everything overnight, everyone gives you sympathy. But if you make a great deal of money, no one sympathizes or even seems to understand what a shattering thing has happened to you. I became deeply unhappy, and suspicious of everyone. A poi-

son took possession of me, a kind of soul sickness.

Harvey was also produced in London and was revived in New York in 1970. When it was made into a film in 1962 starring James Stewart, Universal-International paid $1 million for script rights, a then unheard of sum. A decade later, *Harvey* had been translated into many languages and was a "Hallmark Hall of Fame" television broadcast.

Her following play, *The Next Half Hour,* was about a banshee, the Irish spirit who allegedly warns families about the impending death of a relative. But it was wartime and Pemberton thought the timing was poor for such a topic. In the fall of 1945, it was brought to Broadway, directed by George S. Kaufman, but it only lasted a week.

Seven years later *Mrs. McThing,* which was intended for children and a two-week run at the ANTA Theater during the holiday season, became an unexpected success. Starring the venerable *Helen Hayes, it was a runner-up in the 1951–52 season for the New York Drama Critics Circle Award. In this unusual play, a lonely house and its lonelier inhabitants, leading altogether superficial lives, are threatened. It takes fierce love and respect and just a touch of magic to teach them how to transform a mansion into a home. Mrs. McThing—sometimes ugly, sometimes beautiful—holds the power. Brooks Atkinson of *The New York Times* expressed gratitude to Ireland for "Mrs. Chase's rich make-believe sense of humor and her compassion for the needs of adults and children." Comparing *Mrs. McThing* to *Harvey,* he believed that it was "a richer play with a broader point of view, a greater area of compassion, and a more innocent sense of comedy."

Bernardine, which explores the fragility of adolescent egos, opened on Broadway in autumn of 1952; *Midgie Purvis,* created for *Tallulah Bankhead, opened in 1961. In the play, a well-to-do matron dons a cleaning woman's attire and discovers the superficiality of her previous existence. The show, full of hilarious mistaken identity, was clearly a tour de force for Bankhead, who was obliged to perform rapid-fire character changes. But underneath the comedy is a force for life; Midgie Purvis' plea could just as easily be that of Mary Chase:

> And when I do go—really go—finally go. . . . I don't want anybody acting like I haven't gone. I don't want anybody saying—we won't act like she's gone. We'll act like she's only stepped into another room. That's the

way she'd want it. Well—that's not the way I want it. I want them to scream and yell and howl—for months. I want one of those stars up there to go out—when I go out and never turn on again—I want somebody some place—to miss me.

Although Mary Chase died, age 75, of a heart attack on October 21, 1981, the gentle charm of her Irish pooka will continue to capture the affection of audiences.

SOURCES:

Barnes, Clive. *50 Best Plays of the American Theatre.* NY: Crown, 1970.

Chase, Mary. *Bernardine.* NY: Dramatists Play Service, 1954.

———. *Harvey.* NY: Dramatists Play Service, 1945.

———. *Mrs. McThing.* NY: Dramatists Play Service, 1954.

Chinoy, Helen Krich, and Londa Walsh Jenkins. *Women in American Theatre.* NY: Theatre Communications Group, 1987.

Harris, Eleanor. "Mary Chase—Success Almost Ruined Her," in *Cosmopolitan.* February 1954.

"Harvey is Winner of Pulitzer Prize," in *The New York Times.* May 8, 1952.

Mackay, Barbara. "Harvey Author Mary Chase Dies," in *Denver Post.* October 21, 1981.

Melrose, Frances. "Mary Chase Colorado's Pulitzer Prize Winner Dies," in *Rocky Mountain News.* October 21, 1981.

Mitgang, Herbert. "Mary Chase," in *The New York Times.* October 23, 1981.

Miller, Jordan. *American Dramatic Literature.* NY: McGraw-Hill, 1961.

Reef, Wallis M. "She Didn't Write it for Money—She Says," in *Saturday Evening Post.* September 1, 1945.

Rothe, Anna, ed. *Current Biography.* NY: H.W. Wilson, 1945.

Robinson, Alice, Vera Roberts, and Millie Barringer. *Notable Women in American Theatre.* Westport, CT: Greenwood Press, 1990.

Sherwin, Mary. *Comedy Tonight.* NY: Doubleday, 1977.

Toohey, John L. *A History of the Pulitzer Prize Plays.* NY: Citadel Press, 1967.

RELATED MEDIA:

Sorority House (film), screenplay by Mary Chase, RKO-Radio, 1938.

Harvey (film), starring James Stewart and Josephine Hull, Universal, 1950.

Bernardine (film), starring Pat Boone and *Janet Gaynor, 20th Century-Fox, 1957.

"Harvey" (television special), starring James Stewart, "Hallmark Hall of Fame," 1972.

Joanna H. Kraus, Professor of Theatre,
State University of New York College at Brockport,
and author of *Remember My Name* (Samuel French),
Tenure Track (Players Press), *The Ice Wolf* in *New Women's Theatre*
(Vintage Books) and *Tall Boy's Journey* (Carolrhoda Books)

Chase, Mary Ellen (1887–1973)

American writer and educator. Born on February 24, 1887, in Blue Hill, Maine; died on July 28, 1973, in Northampton, Massachusetts; attended University of Maine, graduated 1909; University of Minnesota, Ph.D. 1922.

Selected writings: His Birthday *(1915); (juvenile)* The Girl from the Bighorn Country *(1916); (juvenile)* Virginia of Elk Creek Valley *(1917); (with W.F.K. Del Plaine)* The Art of Narration *(1926); (juvenile)* Mary Christmas *(1926);* Thomas Hardy from Serial to Novel *(1927); (novel)* Uplands *(1927); (with M.E. Macgregor)* The Writing of Informal Essays *(1928);* Constructive Theme Writing *(1929);* The Golden Asse and Other Essays *(1929); (juvenile)* The Silver Shell *(1930); (autobiography)* A Goodly Heritage *(1932); (novel)* Mary Peters *(1934); (novel)* Silas Crockett *(1935); (essays)* This England *(1936); (juvenile)* It's All About Me *(1937); (novel)* Dawn in Lyonesse *(1938); (autobiography)* The Goodly Fellowship *(1939); (novel)* Windswept *(1941);* The Bible and the Common Reader *(1944); (biography)* Jonathan Fisher, Maine Parson *(1948); (novel)* The Plum Tree *(1949); (biography)* *Abby Aldrich Rockefeller *(1950); (autobiography)* Recipe for a Magic

Childhood *(1951); (autobiography)* The White Gate: Adventures in the Imagination of a Child *(1954); (novel)* The Edge of Darkness *(1957).*

Mary Ellen Chase was born in 1887 in Blue Hill, Maine, where she attended local public schools. Following her graduation from the University of Maine (1909), she worked for nine years as a school teacher. Her first novel, *His Birthday,* was published in 1915, and she followed this with two children's books: *The Girl from the Bighorn Country* (1916) and *Virginia of Elk Creek Valley* (1917). In 1918, Chase began working as an instructor at the University of Minnesota where she earned her Ph.D. in English (1922). The year she completed her graduate work, she was appointed an assistant professor at the university.

Chase became associate professor at Smith College in 1926 and would advance to full professor three years later (1929). Although she authored a number of academic writings, her novels, set on the coast of Maine, were considered more important. In 1955, she retired from Smith College. Chase died on July 28, 1973, in Northampton, Massachusetts.

Châteaubriant, Comtesse de
(c. 1490–1537)

French mistress of King Francis I. Name variations: Madame de Chateaubrant or Chateaubriand; Françoise de Foix. Born around 1490; died at Châteaubriant, France, on October 16, 1537.

Comtesse de Châteaubriant was the first of many mistresses of Francis I, king of France (r. 1515–1547). The love poems and letters attributed to the pair may not be genuine, however, and the countess had little, if any, political influence. Her successor was the more powerful Anne d'Heilly, *duchesse d'Étampes.

Châteauroux, Marie Anne de Mailly-Nesle, Duchesse de.

See Pompadour, Jeanne-Antoinette for sidebar.

Châtelet, Émilie du (1706–1749)

French scientist, philosopher, and enlightenment feminist, beloved by Voltaire. Name variations: Emilie du Chatelet; Marquise du Chatelet or Chastellet; Marquise du Châtelet-Laumont; Émilie de Châtelet. Pronunciation: SHA-te-let. Born Gabrielle-Émilie Le Tonnelier de Breteuil on December 17, 1706, in

Paris, France; died in Lunéville, France, on September 7, 1749; buried at Church of Saint-Jacques; daughter of Gabrielle-Anne de Froulay and Louis-Nicholas Le Tonnelier de Breteuil, baron of Preuilly; educated by tutors; married Florent-Claude, marquis du Châtelet-Laumont, 1725; children: (with Marquis du Châtelet) Françoise Gabrielle Pauline (b. 1726), Louis Marie Florent (b. 1727), and an unnamed son who died in infancy; (with Marquis de Saint-Lambert) unnamed daughter (b. September 1, 1749, who died in infancy).

Father died (1728); met Voltaire in Paris (1733); government ordered Voltaire's arrest (June 10, 1734); moved with Voltaire to Cirey (1734); began translation of Bernard Mandeville's Fable of the Bees *(1735); Voltaire allowed to return to Paris briefly (March 1735); began work on* Grammaire raisonnée *(1736); entered the French Academy of Sciences essay competition (1737); had dispute with Academy of Science over the dynamic force in matter (1739); published the* Institutions de physique *(1740); began work on* Discours sur le bonheur *(1744); was guest at the court of Stanislas Leszczynski, ex-king of Poland (1748); met poet Marquis de Saint-Lambert (1748); completed translation of Isaac Newton's* Principia Mathematica

Émilie du Châtelet

from Latin into French (1749); made second visit to Lunéville (1749).

Publications: Lettres sur le Elément de la philosophie de Newton *(1738);* Institutions de physique *(1740);* Dissertation sur la nature et la propagation du feu *(1744);* Discours sur le bonheur *(1750);* Principes Mathématique de la philosophie naturelle, par M. Newton, traduits par feue Madame la Marquise du Châtelet *(1759).*

Eighteenth-century France offered few educational opportunities for women. Young girls were customarily sent to convents to await the age of marriage. Their education was rudimentary; domestic skills and social graces comprised the bulk of their instruction. As adults, woman were expected to be decorous. They were not frowned upon if they were bright, but in general it was considered unnecessary. Scholarship was the exclusive preserve of the male aristocracy. It is therefore ironic that such an age should produce a woman of the stature of Émilie du Châtelet.

The daughter of **Gabrielle-Anne de Froulay** and Louis-Nicholas Le Tonnelier de Breteuil, baron de Preuilly and chief of protocol at the court of Louis XV, Émilie was born in the family's fashionable Paris home overlooking the Tuileries Gardens. Her father initially despaired of his daughter's prospects.

> My youngest is an odd creature destined to become the homeliest of women. Were it not for the low opinion I hold of several bishops, I would prepare her for a religious life and let her hide in a convent.

Since the family consensus was that Émilie had little chance of securing a husband, it was decided that she would be provided with a good education. Her early intellectual promise was soon evident, and in the spirit of Renaissance Humanism her father saw to it that she received the finest tutoring available. Émilie acquired a thorough grounding in languages, Latin, English and Italian, and also studied the writings of Virgil, Milton, Tasso, Horace, and Cicero. But her true passion was mathematics. Years after her death, Voltaire described her skills of calculations: "I saw her, one day, divide a nine-figure number by nine other figures, in her head, without any help, in the presence of a geometer unable to keep up with her."

Paternal prognostications aside, by age 19, Émilie was an exceptionally tall and surprisingly attractive young woman, and her father arranged a match with the Marquis du Châtelet-Laumont, an uninspiring, if up-and-coming young army officer, who owned a number of country estates. For the Marquis du Châtelet, marriage seems to have been largely a means of securing an heir.

The freedom granted to married women in 18th-century France was considerably greater than the freedom accorded to single women. Throughout their marriage, the marquis was frequently away with his regiment. Left to her own devices, Mme du Châtelet threw herself into the whirlwind of Parisian social life. Her time was taken up by theater, expensive clothes, gambling, and romantic liaisons. In an age when lovers were almost a social obligation, she had affairs with the Marquis de Guébriant, whom she supposedly took poison over, and Louis François Armand de Vignerot du Plessis, Duc de Richelieu, a notorious wit and infamous womanizer. Richelieu, however, was to remain a lifelong friend.

Descriptions of Émilie du Châtelet varied according to the partisanship of the observer. ◀❧ **Mme du Deffand** described her as thin and flat chested, with large limbs, a small head, bad teeth, coarse hair, and a weather-beaten complexion. Conversely, Cideville, a friend of Voltaire's and an admirer of Émilie, dwelt at length on her large soft eyes, and her witty and intelligent expression. No doubt the truth of the matter lies somewhere between. While Émilie du Châtelet was no *❧**Madame de Pompadour**, she was nevertheless a handsome woman who attracted her share of admirers.

In the eyes of fashionable Parisian society, Mme du Châtelet scorned the conventions of her class in two unforgivable ways. Firstly, she refused to neglect her intellectual pursuits and recruited the best European minds to tutor her. Secondly, she stole Voltaire's heart and company from their midst. Already considered one of the most notable thinkers of the 18th century, Voltaire met Émilie when he was 39. She was 27, and the mother of three. Voltaire appreciated Mme du Châtelet's brilliant scientific mind, and this seems to have formed the basis of their attraction.

During the first year of their relationship, Voltaire's *Lettres philosophique*, also known as the *Lettres sur Les Anglais*, were published in France without his permission. The bold re-examination of literature, religion, government, science, and human nature, which was being undertaken by enlightenment scholars such as Voltaire, was aggressively countered by official censorship, the burning of subversive books, imprisonment and exile. On June 10, 1734, Voltaire's *Let-*

❧▶

du Deffand, Mme. *See "Salonnières."*

tres were condemned to be publicly burned and an order for his arrest was issued. The violent reaction of the government forced him to flee.

At length, the crisis abated and Émilie suggested that Voltaire retire with her to Cirey, the ancestral château of the du Châtelets. Here the pair lived for the next 15 years. Their first year in the country was far from idyllic, however. The estate was in disrepair, verging on collapse, and Voltaire wrote amusingly of the renovations:

> Mme. du Châtelet is going to put windows where I have put doors. She is changing staircases into chimneys and chimneys into staircases. Where I have instructed the workmen to construct a library, she tells them to place a salon. My salon she will make into a bath closet. She is going to plant lime trees where I proposed to place elms, and where I have planted herbs and vegetables (at last, my own kitchen gardens, and I was already taking great pride in them!) nothing will make her happy but a flower bed.

Of these new domestic arrangements, Émilie asked the Duc de Richelieu to explain the situation to her husband, the marquis: "Speak to him of Voltaire, simply but with concern and friendship and try, in particular, to make him feel that it is madness to be jealous of a wife with whom one is satisfied, whom one esteems and who behaves well." Like many husbands of the day, the Marquis du Châtelet chose to ignore the situation. When not away with the army, he took up residence with his wife and Voltaire, and although the two men inhabited the same house, they lived in disparate, unrelated universes. Thus friction, impolite at the best of times, was kept to a minimum.

Of the tutors that Émilie employed over the years, perhaps the most influential was Pierre-Louis de Maupertuis, a highly respected astronomer and mathematician. Both Maupertuis and Voltaire acknowledged an intellectual debt of gratitude to Descartes. However, both men had also traveled to England at the turn of the century and had been exposed to the work of Isaac Newton. Newton's theory of universal gravity and his laws of motion fired both with messianic zeal and a desire to convert the nationalistic scientific community of France.

Mme du Châtelet was a determined and demanding scholar. In 1734, she hired Samuel Koenig, a protégé of Maupertuis, to teach her algebra for three hours a day. She was also writing her first book, the *Institutions de physique* (*Institution of Physics*), intent on a modern replacement for Rohault's textbook on physics, which had been written 80 years before. Mme du

Châtelet's work challenged Descartes' assertion that the acquisition of knowledge was based upon an innate "inner sentiment." Rather, Émilie argued that the acquisition of knowledge was dependant upon logic and rationality. The *Institutions de physique* established Émilie du Châtelet's reputation as a scientist and a scholar. Upon its publication, however, a scandal erupted concerning the book's authorship. Koenig claimed that the ideas contained in the *Institutions de physique* were simply a recapitulation of his own lessons to Mme du Châtelet. Naturally, she was infuriated:

> I didn't have time to look for the ideas I needed in the big quarto volumes. I begged M. Koenig to make extracts for me of the chapters I required, which he was kind enough to do and on this I partly based my work. . . . No sooner had I left than M. Koenig told everyone . . . that I had written a book that was worth nothing, that he had made me write another and that I had not paid him enough for his trouble.

In 1752, after her death, Koenig showed his true colors by publishing a forged letter from Leibnitz. This, however, came too late to vindicate Émilie.

> *I* found, in 1733, a young woman who thought as I did, and who decided to stay several years in the country, cultivating her mind.
>
> —Voltaire

Mme du Châtelet and Voltaire set up a scientific laboratory at Cirey. Their first experiment was an investigation of the properties of fire. In 1738, when the French Academy of Sciences announced an essay competition on the subject, Voltaire was determined to win. Émilie entered the competition secretly. She wrote to Maupertuis shortly after submitting her entry.

> I believe that you will have been very surprised that I was bold enough to write a memoir for the Académe. . . . I did not tell M. de Voltaire because I did not wish to displease him. Moreover, I opposed almost all his ideas in my work.

Neither essay won the competition, though Émilie's did preempt future research by postulating that fire had no weight and that both heat and light came from the same source. The Academy was so impressed by both works that they agreed to publish them.

The Cirey years were productive and stimulating. In 1739, Mme du Châtelet entered into a spirited public debate with the Academy of Science over the nature of kinetic energy. Debates such as that served to enliven the atmosphere at

Cirey. "The letters that flew back and forth became so technical," wrote Samuel Edwards, "that only a few people in all Europe had the educational background to understand them." By 1747, young scientists where beginning to arrive from all over Europe to study with Émilie.

When they were not working, Mme du Châtelet and Voltaire entertained house guests. They staged amateur performances of Voltaire's plays, in a small private theater at Cirey. Émilie loved to act and sing, although she is reputed to have lacked talent in both areas. The couple also traveled extensively.

By the mid-1840s, the relationship between Mme du Châtelet and Voltaire had begun to cool, although they still lived and worked together. But Mme du Châtelet began to speak of her relationship with Voltaire in terms of "friendship." A tinge of sadness can be detected in her *Discours sur le bonheur* or essays on happiness, begun in 1744.

> I was happy for ten years in the love of a man who subjugated my soul, and these ten years I passed alone with him, without a single moment of distaste or lassitude. When age, illness, perhaps also the satiety of sensual enjoyment diminished his inclination, it was long before I noticed anything. . . . The certainty that it was impossible to expect the return of his desire for me and his passion, which is not in nature, as I well know, insensibly led my heart to an untroubled feeling of friendship, and this sentiment joined to a passion for study, gave me happiness enough.

It was not illness, or age, however, that had dampened Voltaire's ardor, but his niece, the young widow ✿▶ **Mme Denis**. Voltaire was falling in love.

There were interludes away from Cirey: in Brussels, Mme du Châtelet was involved in a protracted lawsuit; she also sojourned at the Lunéville court of Stanislas Leszczynski, ex-king of Poland. Here Émilie indulged her taste for dancing and gambling, while still maintaining a rigorous work schedule. Voltaire and du Châtelet traveled there in 1748 and again in 1749. It was at Lunéville that Émilie met, and fell in love with, the Marquis de Saint-Lambert, a minor poet.

The situation began to unravel when Mme du Châtelet discovered that she was pregnant. At Cirey, Émilie, Voltaire, and Saint-Lambert plotted on how to inform her husband. But the Marquis accepted the inevitable and hurried off to rejoin his troops. Émilie wrote to her friend ◀✿ **Mme Boufflers:**

There were three Mme Boufflers; **Marie Boufflers** *(1706–1747) was the friend of Émilie du Châtelet.*

✿▶

I am pregnant and you can imagine the distressing state I am in, how much I fear for my health, even for my life, how ridiculous I find it to give birth at the age of forty, not having had children for the past seventeen years, how upset I am for my son.

Because Émilie preferred having the baby in Lunéville, Stanislas agreed to make a small house available for her during her pregnancy. Voltaire reluctantly agreed to accompany her.

At the same time, Émilie worked 17-hour days in order to complete her translation of Newton's *Principia Mathematica*. Her commentary at the beginning of the book was partially based upon experiments that she had conducted at Cirey, and upon discussions with such eminent scientists of the day as Clairault, Bernoulli, and Maupertuis.

On September 4, 1749, Mme du Châtelet gave birth to a daughter. Her devotion to her work is reflected in the letter that Voltaire wrote to Comte d'Argental immediately after the event: "Mme du Châtelet informs you, Sir, that this night, being at her desk and scribbling a notice about Newton, she felt a little call. The little call was a daughter, who appeared in the instant. She was laid on a quarto tome of geometry."

On September 4, all seemed well. On September 5th, while the new mother was resting, she felt pangs of indigestion but not enough to "curtail the party atmosphere in her suite." The following day, she began to have difficulty breathing and physicians were called in; they diagnosed stomach upset because of rich food. On September 7, Mme du Châtelet went into a coma and died. Overcome with grief, Voltaire dashed from the room, tripped, and fell down a flight of stairs.

Émilie du Châtelet accomplished her metamorphosis from social butterfly to scholar in a society that cast a cool eye on such grand ambitions. And yet she was never deterred by the criticism of her peers. Her mind was an enviable example of depth and flexibility. From mathematics, algebra and geometry, to physics, metaphysics, moral philosophy, and theology, she exhibited a breadth of interest that distinguished her, not only as a true enlightenment scholar, but a scholar for all seasons. She is best known for *Institutions de physique*, and her translation and analysis of Newton's masterpiece, the *Principia Mathematica*, published after her death. Together with Voltaire and others, her work served to popularize Newton's ideas throughout continental Europe.

However, her other achievements deserve equal attention. Works such as her essay on the nature of fire, presented to the Academy of Sciences in 1738, and an incomplete manuscript on Newtonian optics, were both influential and timely. As well, she sought to explore the logic of grammar in an unfinished work, *Grammaire raisonnée*, or the reason of Grammar.

Mme du Châtelet was often incensed by the treatment women received. On one occasion, she is even said to have penetrated an exclusive café in the guise of a man. Of particular concern to her was the state of women's education, a subject dear to her heart. As she wrote in the preface to her unfinished translation of Bernard Mandeville's *The Fable of the Bees:* "If I were a king I would redress an abuse which cuts back, as it were, one half of human kind. I would have women participate in all human rights, especially those of the mind. There is no place where we are trained to think."

Émilie's essay *Discours sur le bonheur* was her only foray into the realm of moral philosophy. From it, it is possible to divine the subtleties and passions that drove her: her zest for life, her love of romance, and her devotion to learning. Although many of Mme du Châtelet's critics focused primarily on the social details of her life, it was Maupertuis, her friend and tutor, who summed up her true contribution. Thus, it seems fitting that he should have the last word.

> Society is losing a noble and pleasant figure of a woman who is rightly regretted, the more so because, having great wit, she never put it to bad use. . . . How marvellous, besides, to have been able to ally the pleasing qualities of her sex with that sublime science which we believe to be meant only for us.

SOURCES:

Barber, William H., ed. "Mme. du Châtelet and Leibnitzianism: The Genesis of the Institutions de physique," in *The Age of the Enlightenment: Studies Presented to Theodore Besterman.* Edinburgh: Oliver and Boyd, 1967.

Besterman, Theodore. *Voltaire.* London: Longmans, 1969.

Davis, Herman S. "Women Astronomers, 400 A.D.–1750," in *Popular Astronomy.* Simon Newcomb, ed. NY: Harper, 1878.

Edwards, Samuel. *The Divine Mistress: A Biography of Émilie de Châtelet, the Beloved of Voltaire.* NY: David McKay, 1970.

Mitford, Nancy. *Voltaire in Love.* NY: Harper, 1957.

Vaillot, René. *Avec Madame Du Châtelet: 1734–1749.* Oxford: Voltaire Foundation, Taylor Institution, 1988.

Wade, Ira Owen. *Studies on Voltaire, With Some Unpublished Papers of Mme. du Châtelet.* Princeton, NJ: Princeton University Press, 1947.

———. *The Intellectual Development of Voltaire.* Princeton, NJ: Princeton University Press, 1969.

Denis, Louise (c. 1710–1790)

French author. Born Louise Mignot Arouet around 1710; died in 1790; daughter of Voltaire's oldest brother; married the middle-class M. Denis, 1738 (died 1744); married a Sieur du Vivier, 1779.

When Voltaire's oldest brother died in 1738, Voltaire's niece, the independent Louise Arouet—then 26 and unmarried—paid a visit to Cirey, in Lorraine. A handsome woman, similar to Émilie du Châtelet in temperament, her passion was music rather than science. There was no love lost between Mme Arouet and Mme du Châtelet. Intellectually equal, Louise demanded proof of Émilie's every assertion. Mme du Châtelet complained to few, however, and was relieved when Louise returned to Paris to marry M. Denis. When Denis died in 1744, Mme Denis paid another visit to Cirey. Voltaire sought out his comforting niece, and she lived with the philosopher until his death in 1778. In 1779, when she was 70, she married a Sieur du Vivier, who was about 60. Louise wrote several works and a play, "La coquette punie," but her literary work has been largely overshadowed by her relationship with Voltaire.

SUGGESTED READING:

Ehrman, Esther. *Mme du Châtelet.* Lemington Spa: Berg Publishers, 1986.

Hugh A. Stewart, M.A., University of Guelph, Guelph, Ontario, Canada

Châtillon, Madame de (fl. 1498–1525).

See Margaret of Angoulême for sidebar on *Louise de Montmorency.*

Chatterton, Ruth (1893–1961)

American actress, best known for her performance in **Dodsworth.** *Born on December 24, 1893, in New York City; died in Redding, Connecticut, on November 24, 1961; daughter of an architect; married Ralph Forbes (a British actor), in 1924 (divorced 1932); married George Brent (an actor), in 1932 (divorced 1934); married Barry Thomson (an actor), in 1942 (died 1960).*

Filmography: Sins of the Fathers (1928); The Doctor's Secret (1929); The Dummy (1929); Madame X (1929); Charming Sinners (1929); The Laughing Lady (1929); Sarah and Son (1930); Paramount on Parade (1930); The Lady of Scandal (The High Road, 1930); Anybody's Woman (1930); The Right to Love (1930); Unfaithful (1931); The Magnificent Lie (1931); Once a Lady (1931); Tomorrow and Tomorrow (1932); The Rich Are Always with Us (1932); The Crash (1932); Frisco Jenny (1933); Lilly Turner (1933); Female (1933); Journal of a Crime (1934); Lady of Secrets

(1936); Girls' Dormitory (1936); Dodsworth (1936); The Rat (UK, 1938); A Royal Divorce (UK, 1938).

Ruth Chatterton—now best remembered for the film *Dodsworth*—was popular in movies during the 1930s, when she was often referred to as the First Lady of the Screen. Drama critic James Agate once quipped: "As an actress la Chatterton seems to me to knock La Garbo silly." Hollywood was only a brief interlude in Chatterton's career, and some believe she became trapped in a series of overly melodramatic films in which she played tense, misunderstood, and sometimes misguided women. Her career, however, also included stage acting, playwriting (*Monsieur Brotonneau*), directing, and, in her later years, some literary success as the author of four novels. A liberated spirit somewhat ahead of her time, she was a licensed pilot and flew her own plane cross-country.

Chatterton was born in New York City on December 24, 1893, the daughter of a successful

Ruth Chatterton

architect. She reportedly took her first stage role at age 14 to earn money after her parents separated. Her Broadway debut came in 1911 in *The Great Name,* and she triumphed at 20 as the star of *Daddy Long Legs* (1914), the dramatization of *Jean Webster's popular book. Chatterton went on to become one of Broadway's leading ladies, shunning movie offers until she was well into her 30s. With her debut film performance as Emil Jannings' second wife in *Sins of the Fathers* (1928), she signed with Paramount, who found her stage background a great asset in the new talkies. She won an Oscar nomination as Best Actress for her role in *Madame X* (1929), which she made on loan to MGM. *Picturegoer* called her performance "the most poignant thing the Talkies have given us to date." Back at Paramount, she received another Oscar nomination for her role as a German immigrant in *Sarah and Son* (1930).

After *The Right to Love* (1930), a tour de force in which she played both mother and daughter, Chatterton made a series of duds before signing with Warner Bros. Her first movie for the new studio was a comedy, *The Rich Are Always with Us* (1932), co-starring George Brent, who became her second husband. (Chatterton was chastized in the media for marrying Brent less than 24 hours after her divorce from British actor Ralph Forbes became final.) By 1934, both her marriage and her Warner's contract were finished, and her career was in such a rut that the major studios lost interest. As one of the oldest female stars of her time, other than character actors like *Marie Dressler, she also encountered age discrimination. After a two-year absence from the screen, she starred in the forgettable *Lady of Secrets* (1936) for Columbia and had a supporting role in *Girls' Dormitory* for 20th Century-Fox. That same year, however, cast as the vapid, self-centered wife of Walter Houston in MGM's *Dodsworth*, Chatterton played what may have been her finest movie role; according to Hollywood lore, though, she hated it and gave director William Wyler a difficult time during filming. After losing the lead in Goldwyn's *Stella Dallas* to *Barbara Stanwyck, Chatterton left Hollywood, explaining that she was just too lazy to fight for good roles. She made two British films before returning to the stage in a London revival of *The Constant Wife,* after which she toured the United States in *West of Broadway.* Chatterton appeared on Broadway again in *Leave Her to Heaven* (1940).

During the 1940s and 1950s, she did stage work, television, and radio, including an appearance in the New York City Center revival of

Idiot's Delight in 1951. Her last stage appearance was in St. Louis in 1956 in *The Chalk Garden*. During the 1950s, she also published four novels, most notably *Homeward Borne*. Chatterton suffered a cerebral hemorrhage and died in 1961 in Redding, Connecticut.

Barbara Morgan,
Melrose, Massachusetts

Chattopadhyaya, Kamaladevi

(1903–1988)

Indian independence leader, feminist and eloquent advocate of Indian cultural and artistic autonomy. Name variations: Kamala Devi Chattopadhyay. Born into a wealthy family in Mangalore, a city in the southern Indian province of Karnataka, in 1903; died in Bombay, India, on October 29, 1988; educated locally at St. Mary's College before attending Bedford College, London, and the London School of Economics; married Harindranath Chattopadhyay (a poet and dramatist), in 1919.

Joined the independence movement at an early age and was imprisoned many times; elected to All-India Congress (1927), becoming organizing secretary and president of All-India Women's Conference; imprisoned (1930, 1932, 1934, 1942); after achievement of Indian freedom (1947), continued to call for social justice; founded the Indian Cooperative Union (1948) to assist refugees uprooted by the partition; established the first co-operative at Chattarpur, near Delhi; helped build the city of Faridabad (or Fari Debad); leader of many craft organizations in India and internationally; developed the Cottage Industries Emporium; became chair of All-India Handicrafts, Ltd. (1952); helped found the World Crafts Council of which she was senior vice-president; served as president of the Centre of India.

Typical of virtually all of the leaders of India's independence movement, Kamaladevi Chattopadhyaya came from a wealthy upper-caste family. She was born in 1903 in Mangalore, a city in the southern Indian province of Karnataka. Her father was an upper-echelon official in the Madras Civil Service and one of her uncles was a leading lawyer in the region. Her family believed that women should receive the best possible education, which in Kamaladevi's case meant a Roman Catholic convent and then St. Mary's College in Mangalore. Her higher education took place at the London School of Economics. Married young to a much older man of her family's choice, she became a widow within a few years. Exhibiting the strong independence

that would mark her life, she next married Harin Chattopadhyay, a man of her own choice. Kamaladevi and her husband spent the next few years traveling widely in Europe, visiting museums, studying various aspects of theatrical production, and meeting many of the leading directors and artists of the day.

On her return to India, Chattopadhyaya began producing and staging plays. She pioneered in the Indian theater and also performed in a number of leading roles. Unable to remain indifferent to the political and social turmoil that gripped India in the years after World War I, the sophisticated and confident Chattopadhyaya also became an active member of Mohandas K. (Mahatma) Gandhi's Congress Party, passionately supporting its goal of Indian independence from Great Britain. Her eloquence and courage quickly made her one of the leading women of the national movement, and she counted among her close friends such leaders as Mahatma and Kasturba Gandhi, Jawaharlal Nehru, and *Sarojini Naidu. Kamaladevi was imprisoned many times for varying terms of incarceration in the infamous prisons of Terawada, Belgaum and Vellore. In later years, as one of India's best-known political prisoners, she proudly noted that she had spent a total of five years of her life in British jails.

By the early 1930s, Kamaladevi Chattopadhyaya had become an inspiring leader and repository of both practical advice and elevated philosophical truths, particularly among the young women and men of Karnataka. Her talents as both a journalist and an orator spread the nationalist message to the most remote villages and impoverished city slums. As a leader of the Salt March in Bombay in 1930, she became an internationally recognized leader of resistance to imperialism. Her organizational talents found an outlet when she organized the movement's Women's Volunteer Wing. At the same time, she became a key figure in the All-India Women's Conference. While devoting most of her energy to organizing the struggle against British rule, Chattopadhyaya also investigated the root causes of her nation's poverty and lack of development. Even before the achievement of Indian independence in August 1947, she had concluded that political freedom alone would not bring about a national renaissance of her country; only a profound social and cultural transformation, she reasoned, would bring about this desired goal.

The achievement of Indian independence in 1947 brought with it a great human tragedy, the bloody partition of the Indian subcontinent into the sovereign and hostile states of India and Pakistan—the former mostly Hindu, the latter almost exclusively Muslim. Communal violence resulted in the massacres of hundreds of thousands and the creation of millions of destitute refugees who had to be absorbed by the hard-pressed fledgling nation of India. Chattopadhyaya's response to these tragic events was to found in 1948 the Indian Cooperative Union, the stated purpose of which was to create livelihoods for the refugees whose lives had been shattered by partition. The first cooperative was founded at Chattarpur near Delhi. After the basic idea had been shown to work, the national organization played a leading role in building the new city of Faridabad to rehabilitate not just individuals but entire families and communities.

In addition to providing moral support, the Cooperative Union offered desperately needed tools, seeds and loans to thousands of displaced persons whose fear and despair began to be replaced by hope and faith in a better future. As soon as a reasonable degree of rehabilitation had been achieved, consumer and handloom cooperatives were established. By the early 1950s, a central Cottage Industries Emporium located in New Delhi had been developed as an outlet for the products of over 700 cooperatives. Often directly inspired and encouraged by Chattopadhyaya, new designs for craft products were first seen here. Once a significant flow of production began to reach the market, increasingly attractive products could be offered to wholesalers for distribution not only throughout India but abroad as well.

Not satisfied with the achievements of the Indian Cooperative Union, Chattopadhyaya divided her time between the never-ending tasks of guiding India's cooperative movement to new achievements and a disciplined writing agenda that would produce more than a dozen books and countless articles over her lifetime. Convinced that the Congress Party, which had spearheaded Indian independence, was now incapable of leading a national social rebirth, she joined the Congress Socialist Party in 1948, declaring, "Socialism is not a mere negative pretext against Poverty. . . . It is much more, the positive passion for happy human relations." Her non-Marxist definition of Socialism allowed Chattopadhyaya to see the social problems of India as moral issues that could be solved through leadership from above and energy from below. Although remaining in many ways an upper-caste intellectual, she strongly sympathized with the struggles of the working masses, particularly the village women who continued to bear so many of the burdens

and injustices of traditional Indian society. Traveling throughout the country, she spread the message of the All-India Women's Conference, namely that the women's movement "is essentially a social movement. . . . It is in the nature of our society which is at fault and our drive has to be directed against faulty social institutions."

Remaining in almost constant touch with thousands of people from the 1940s until her death in 1988, Kamaladevi Chattopadhyaya had an extraordinary capacity to remember and file away information, data that would then emerge years or even decades later in her books on such diverse subjects as tribal cultures and carpets. Although extremely well-read, she derived much of her knowledge from observation and conversation. By the 1950s, although retaining her passionate interest in politics and social reform, she had reallocated much of her time and energy into what she clearly regarded as a crusade for a cultural revival in India. Following Gandhi's teachings, she believed that immense cultural strengths resided in the subcontinent's thousands of villages. From her earliest years, she believed that the essence of true culture was the pursuit of beauty, and she noted proudly, "our tradition is to make *utility* items, indeed decorated as richly as one would want them to be." She also pointed out with considerable delight that the Hindi language had only one word—*shilpa*—for both art and craft, and that this covered the range from a plain reproduction to an artifact universally regarded as a masterpiece of artistic inspiration.

Emphasizing a holistic view of arts, crafts, social change and justice, Chattopadhyaya fused her trained intellect and her love of beautiful objects to point out to her sophisticated audiences, both in India and abroad, that urban women and men who complacently regard themselves as advanced have much to learn from so-called primitive peoples. In the preface to her 1978 study of tribalism in India, she pointed out the essentially religious roots of the traditions of craft excellence in tribal societies:

In line with this tradition of the tribal is their insistence on excellence in work. No matter how humble the object, it is exquisitely wrought, the makers taking real pride in their performance and achievement. Unfortunately, we are fast losing this pride in work and a sense of reward in the excellence put into the job itself, for now the commercial element has come in to distort natural elements. An awareness of an undeclared kinship with these communities, who still preserve and cherish some of the elements and values that have faded out of our lives, should reorient our policy towards the process of rapid detribalization. It should see that the tested and tried values are sought to be saved so that some of the ancient wisdom is retrieved and preserved.

Despite advancing years, Chattopadhyaya spent the last decades of her busy life writing books, lecturing, traveling and meeting with the young and old to both teach and learn. She served long terms as the vice president of the World Crafts Council and was the highly regarded chair of the All-India Handicrafts Board. She also provided valuable advice as a member of the Crafts Council of India, the All-India Design Center, the National Theater Center, and the Indian Council for Cultural Relations. Her autobiography, *Inner Recesses, Outer Spaces*, was published to rave reviews in 1986 and won her the 1988 Padma Vibushan Prize for literary excellence in the English language. In this volume, she expressed not only strong views on matters of society and culture but also a poignant nostalgia for the fleeting events of human existence, "the trifles we usually brush or throw away." In 1987, she received one of her most cherished awards, the Charles Eames Award of the National Institute of Design in Ahmedabad; surrounded by colleagues and friends, she was honored "for laying the foundations of a genuine Indian design movement."

Born to a life of privilege, Kamaladevi Chattopadhyaya decided while still in her youth that she would live a life of service to her nation. Her knack for combining idealism, practicality, and persuasion led her to the realization of this goal. Indefatigable and optimistic to the end of her days, she died fully in harness in Bombay on October 29, 1988, while visiting that metropolis to inaugurate a craft exhibition. With her passing, one of the very last leaders of an extraordinary generation of Indian intellectuals left the scene. Though the women of India lost one of their most remarkable pioneers, the craft movement she had helped inaugurate a half century earlier continued to thrive in the villages and artisan workshops of her nation.

SOURCES:

Chattopadhyaya, Kamaladevi. *Carpets and Floor Coverings of India.* Bombay: D.B. Taraporevala Sons, 1969.
———. *Inner Recesses, Outer Spaces—Memoirs.* New Delhi: Navarang, 1986.
———. *Tribalism in India.* New Delhi: Vikas Publishing, 1978.
Kalapesi, Roshan. "Obituaries," in *American Craft.* Vol. 49, no. 3. June–July 1989, p. 66.
Murthy, H.V. Srinivasa, "Chattopadhyaya, Kamaladevi (1903—)," in S.P. Sen, ed., *Dictionary of National Biography.* Vol. 1. Calcutta: Institute of Historical Studies, 1972, pp. 277–278.
O'Neill, Lois Decker, ed. *The Women's Book of World Records and Achievements.* Garden City, NY: Anchor Press/Doubleday, 1979.

John Haag, Associate Professor,
University of Georgia, Athens, Georgia

Chattopadhyaya, Sarojini (1879–1949).

See Naidu, Sarojini.

Chaucer, Alice (fl. 1400s).

See Margaret of Anjou for sidebar.

Chauvin, Jeanne (1862–1926)

France's first woman lawyer. Pronunciation: JHAN show-VAN. Name variations: Mlle Chauvin. Born in Jargeau (Loiret), France, on August 22, 1862; died at Provins (Seine-et-Marne), on September 28, 1926; sister of Émile Chauvin (1870–1933), a prominent deputy (1898–1909) from Seine-et-Marne; never married.

Jeanne Chauvin was one of the first females to pass the baccalaureate examination. She enrolled in the Faculty of Law and the Faculty of Letters at the Sorbonne and became the first woman to complete legal training. Chauvin defended her thesis, "Des professions accessibles aux femmes en droit roman at en droit français" (On the Professions Accessible to Women in Roman and French Law), in a private session on July 2, 1892, after rioting caused cancellation of a public defense.

Because as a woman she lacked full political rights, Chauvin was not allowed to practice until René Viviani and the feminist daily *La Fronde* (published by ***Marguerite Durand**) undertook a campaign that resulted in passage of a bill by the Chamber on June 30, 1899, and by the Senate on November 14, 1900, admitting women to the bar. Chauvin took the oath on December 19, 1900, shortly after **Olga Petit**.

Though she seldom appeared in court, mainly earning her living teaching law in the girls' lycées in Paris, Chauvin was the first woman to plead a case (1907). She linked her personal goals to the cause of women's emancipation and, when ***Jeanne Schmahl** founded L'Avant-courrière (1893), Chauvin drafted the bills for which the organization ultimately obtained passage: the right of women to bear legal witness to public and private acts (1897) and the so-called "Schmahl Law" on the right of women to control their own income (1907). In 1900, at the Congress of Feminine Works and Institutions, Chauvin presented the most aggressive report of the meeting, calling for numerous changes in the Civil Code.

SOURCES:

Dictionnaire de biographie française. A. Balteau, M. Barroux, M. Prévost et al., directeurs. Paris: Letouzey et Ané, 1933-.

Hause, Steven C., with Anne R. Kenney. *Women's Suffrage and Social Politics in the French Third Republic.* Princeton, NJ: Princeton University Press, 1984.

Klejman, Laurence, and Florence Rochefort. *L'Égalité en marche: Le féminisme sous la troisième république.* Paris: Presses de la Fondation nationale des sciences politiques, 1989.

David S. Newhall,
Professor of History Emeritus,
Centre College, author of *Clemenceau: A Life at War* (Edwin Mellen Press, 1991)

Chaworth, Maud (1282–c. 1322)

Countess of Lancaster. Born in 1282; died before December 3, 1322; daughter of Patrick Chaworth and *Isabel Beauchamp; married Henry (1281–1345), earl of Lancaster, in 1298; children: Blanche (c. 1305–1380); Maud Plantagenet (c. 1310–c. 1377); Joan (c. 1312–c. 1345); Henry of Grosmont, 1st duke of Lancaster (c. 1314–1361); Isabel (c. 1317–1347); *Eleanor Plantagenet (c. 1318–1372); *Mary Percy (1320–1362). Henry's second wife was *Alice de Joinville.

Chekhova or Chekova, Olga
(1870–1959).

See Knipper-Chekova, Olga.

Chelles, abbess of.

See Bertille (d. 705/713).
See Gisela of Chelles (781–814).
See Louise-Adelaide (1698–1743).

Chen, Joyce (1918–1994)

Chinese-born American cooking teacher, author, television personality and restaurateur who played a major role in introducing Americans to authentic Chinese cuisine starting in the 1950s. Born in Beijing, China, in 1918; died in Lexington, Massachusetts, in August 1994; immigrated to the United States in 1949; married; children: Helen Chen; Henry; Stephen.

In the mid-20th century, Chinese restaurants had as their staple dishes such offerings as chow mein, chop suey, and, oddly enough, French bread. The great majority of Americans, lacking contact with authentic Chinese culture, accepted this sort of cuisine as the genuine article. Joyce Chen, a recently arrived immigrant from China, was determined to radically change this situation. A pioneer of Chinese cooking in the United States, she would face a daunting task when opening a Chinese restaurant in Cambridge, Massachusetts, during the 1950s.

Born in 1918 into a prosperous family, Chen was interested in food even as a child and watched as the family cook prepared delicious meals in the kitchen. Whereas most upper-class women in China did not cook or take an interest in food preparation, the Chen family women were exceptions, with Joyce's mother encouraging this interest by telling her daughter, "You never know what the future will bring, and you don't want to eat raw rice."

The future turned out to be highly uncertain for Joyce Chen, her husband, and her two children when they fled mainland China in 1949 after the Communist takeover. Having settled in Cambridge, Massachusetts, the Chen family began what was for them a difficult but exhilarating adventure of Americanization. Joyce Chen was determined to help her family succeed economically while remaining proud of their Chinese heritage. She found a means of doing both, first by teaching Chinese cooking in her home and at adult education centers in her neighborhood. In 1958, she opened a Chinese restaurant in Cambridge. Introducing the American palate to genuine Chinese food was not always a simple matter, and one of Chen's early customers registered his suspicion by grumbling, "What kind of Chinese restaurant is this that doesn't serve French bread?" Her strategy was simple and involved offering a buffet that began with standard American foods such as ham, roast beef and turkey but then moved on to authentic Chinese dishes not often then found in Chinese restaurants, such as hot-and-sour soup and moo shu pork. Slowly, the doubters were won over, and the non-Chinese foods were phased out of the buffet line.

Within a few years, Joyce Chen had emerged as America's "godmother of Chinese cooking." Her Cambridge restaurant was a hit, regularly attracting such local culinary and academic luminaries as *Julia Child, James Beard, Henry Kissinger and John Kenneth Galbraith. Both students and faculty at Harvard and M.I.T. became regular patrons at the Joyce Chen restaurant, and by word of mouth her cooking became known throughout the United States. The next step in her career was a television program on the Public Broadcasting System, "Joyce Chen Cooks." A cookbook written in 1964 was privately published after commercial publishers lost interest when Chen insisted on color pictures of the various dishes. This edition was a hit with diners at her restaurant, selling more than 6,000 copies to satisfied customers. The commercial edition that followed was a great success.

Chen continually worked to improve the offerings at her restaurant and spread the message of Chinese cuisine throughout the United States. In her own words, she spoke of a "desire to open a Chinese restaurant which would make American customers happy and Chinese customers proud." Chen displayed considerable savvy in winning over new devotees to Chinese cuisine, coining the term "Peking ravioli" for dumplings, which likely made this dish more intriguing for the large number of New Englanders of Italian descent. After creating a large clientele, she disseminated her intense pride in Chinese civiliza-

tion in a series of special culinary events in which she presented different foods and explained the cultural context in which those foods evolved. As time went by and her audiences became more knowledgeable, Joyce Chen gave increasingly specialized talks about Chinese cuisine, including one entitled "Breakfast in Shanghai," a popular presentation featuring authentic breakfast foods and a talk on the role of breakfast in China.

By the end of her life, Joyce Chen had not only made Chinese food a major aspect of America's cuisine but had also created a thriving busi-

Joyce Chen

ness empire that included a successful restaurant and a cookware firm, Joyce Chen Products, that marketed such previously unknown items as a flat-bottomed wok, the polyethylene cutting board, and the "Peking Pan" (a stir-fry pan with rounded sides, a flat bottom and a Western-style skillet). Her children, Helen, Henry and Stephen, kept her legacy alive after her death and worked hard to make the companies she founded grow and thrive. Remarked her daughter **Helen Chen**, Joyce Chen "accomplished a beginning. She was never one to sit back and say, 'Now we've done it.' Her mind was always turning out new ideas."

SOURCES:

"Joyce Chen merges with Keilen," in *HFN: The Weekly Newspaper for the Home Furnishing Network.* Vol. 69, no. 9. February 27, 1995, p. 27.

"Joyce Chen, 76, U.S. Popularizer Of Mandarin Cuisine," in *The New York Times Biographical Service.* August 1994, p. 1287.

Weiland, Jeanne. "Joyce Chen: Joyce Chen Inc. founder and first to introduce authentic Chinese cooking to U.S. restaurants," in *Nation's Restaurant News.* Vol. 30. February 1996, p. 56.

John Haag, Associate Professor, University of Georgia, Athens, Georgia

Cheney, Amy (1867–1944).

See Beach, Amy Cheney.

Cheney, Dorothy (b. 1917).

See Sutton, May for sidebar.

Cheney, Ednah Dow (1824–1904)

Boston abolitionist, suffragist, and author. Born Ednah Dow Littlehale on June 27, 1824, in Beacon Hill, Boston, Massachusetts; died in 1904; married Seth Wells Cheney (an American engraver), in 1853 (died 1856); children: one daughter.

Educated in excellent private schools, acquainted with Ralph Waldo Emerson and Bronson Alcott, and deeply influenced by *Margaret Fuller, Ednah Dow Cheney helped relocate freed slaves and organized Boston teachers to serve in the South after the Civil War. She was secretary, then president, of the New England Hospital for Women and Children, as well as president of the New England Woman's Club and the Massachusetts Woman Suffrage Association. Cheney authored *Handbook of American History for Colored People* (1866), *Gleanings in the Field of Art* (1881), *Life of Louisa M. Alcott* (1889), and several stories, including "Nora's Return," a sequel to Ibsen's "A Doll's House"; her reminiscences were published in 1902.

Chen Lu (1976—)

Chinese figure skater. Last name: Chen; first name: Lu; (nickname) Lulu. Born in Changchun, Jilin Province, northeast China, on November 24, 1976; daughter of a hockey skater and a ping-pong player; raised in Jilin Province.

Placed 3rd at the World Championships (1993), 1st (1995), 2nd (1996), and 25th (1997); won a bronze medal at the Winter Olympics in Lillehammer (1994); finished 1st at the Karl Schafer Memorial figure-skating championship in Vienna, Austria (1997); won a bronze medal in Nagano (1998).

Lovely Lu Chen, China's first figure-skating champion, was born in northeast China in 1977; her father, a former member of China's national hockey team, taught her to skate on a patch of ice in her backyard. Her mother was a competitive ping-pong player. But her nation was isolated from the world of figure skating; there were no indoor rinks, no organized training; the sport was virtually unknown. Her coach Li Mingzhu learned technique by studying videos.

In her first Olympics at Albertville, Lu Chen placed a surprising 6th. Then came Lillehammer in 1994 and the Kerrigan-Harding circus. While Ukraine's **Oksana Baiul** took gold and **Nancy Kerrigan** took silver, Lu Chen beat out France's **Surya Bonaly** for the bronze, becoming the first female figure skater to compete in the Olympic Games for China. "She's always serene and in control," said *Peggy Fleming. "She's effortless and haunting. She literally takes your breath away."

Following their skater's success at Lillehammer, the Chinese sent her to train in California; Lu Chen took to her new home with ease and became a beloved and serious contender in international figure skating, winning the World Championship in 1995, taking silver medals in both Skate America and the Trophee de France that same year. But just as she was making a life for herself in America, the Chinese ordered her to return home to Beijing in the fall of 1996, then restricted her travel. Instantly, Lu Chen all but disappeared from the skating circuit. The following season was abysmal: she left her long time coach, appeared at only two international tournaments, battled the Chinese Figure Skating Federation, and, amazingly, came in an appalling 25th at the 1997 World Championships that March in Lausanne, Switzerland, not even qualifying for the finals. Lu Chen was not only suffering from injuries but seemingly a broken spirit. She looked uncomfortable when reporters asked what was going on, and would not answer questions about her Chinese handlers. "China is my country," she would answer, diffidently. "I love my country." In 1998, Lu Chen seemed to regain her sense of purpose and returned to the Olympics at Nagano. Though she struggled in the warmups, she came in fourth in the compulsories, then took the bronze medal once more with an elegant performance. (**Tara Lipinski** and **Michelle Kwan** of the U.S. placed 1st and 2nd.) Lu Chen turned professional following the 1998 Olympic games; she was 21.

Chenowith, Alice (1853–1925).

See Gardener, Helen Hamilton.

Chéri, Rose (1824–1861)

Celebrated French comedian. Name variations: Cheri. Born Rose Marie Cizos at Étampes, France, on October 27, 1824; died at Passy, near Paris, on September 22, 1861; married M. Lemoine Montigny, in May 1847.

The celebrated French comedian Rose Chéri first appeared at the Gymnase on March 30, 1842. In 1846, the role of Clarissa Harlowe placed her in the first rank of her profession. She married M. Lemoine Montigny in May 1847 and continued to perform under the name Rose Chéri.

Chernysheva, Liubov Pavlovna (1890–1976).

See Tchernicheva, Lubov.

Chervinskaya, Lidiya Davydovna (1907–1988)

Russian emigré poet and literary critic who was one of the most original and distinguished poets of the Russian emigration of the interwar decades. Name variations: Lidia Chervinskaia. Born in Russia in 1907; died in Paris, France, in July 1988; moved to Paris in the early 1920s; published three volumes of verse and a large body of essays and criticism.

Born in Russia in 1907, Lidiya Chervinskaya experienced the hardship and chaos of war and revolution, fleeing her native land for France in the early 1920s. Bare survival was of paramount importance to most of the Russian emigrés in Paris, but for Chervinskaya things of the spirit were equally if not even more important. By the end of the 1920s, she was writing a series of poems on the most basic aspects of life, including the nature of God, sin, loneliness, the difficulties of human communication, and the ultimate separation of human beings from one another, namely death. By 1934, a volume of poems, entitled *Approaches*, was published in Paris, but like her two other books of verse, published in 1937 and 1956, they received encouraging reviews in the Russian emigré press but sold relatively few copies.

Lidiya Chervinskaya's poems are considered by critics to be the most outstanding examples of the "Parisian note" (*Parizhkaia nota*) of the Russian emigré literary scene. Highly emotional, the poems written during this period refer to moods of love and longing, hope and despair, joy and deep sadness. The musicality of her verses was enhanced by skillful use of repetition, anaphora and rhetorical questions. Sometimes the scenery of Paris appears, but the essence of her work from this period inhabits a world of vague impressions and half-shadows. Much of the inspiration for Chervinskaya's poetry came from her often flamboyant personal life, which led to her being called the "Greta Garbo of Russian Montparnasse."

After surviving the difficult war years, Chervinskaya lived for a number of years in Munich, where she worked for Radio Liberty, which broadcast news and cultural programs to the Soviet Union. During this mature phase of her poetry, she increasingly defined pain not as having to part from a lover, but rather in terms of a generalized suffering, some of which was now derived from the continuing separation from her Russian homeland. The lost mother country was gone forever, as was "a lost language, once glorious and powerful." Lidiya Chervinskaya died in Paris in 1988, still longing for her beloved Russia. As one admiring critic has written, hers "is the poetry of belated regrets, pangs of conscience, and the domination of merciless intellect."

SOURCES:

Couvée, Petra. "Chervinskaia, Lidia Davidovna," in Marina Ledkovsky *et al.*, eds. *Dictionary of Russian Women Writers*. Westport, CT: Greenwood Press, 1994, pp. 130–131.

Kasack, Wolfgang. *Dictionary of Russian Literature Since 1917*. Translated by Maria Carlson and Jane T. Hedges. NY: Columbia University Press, 1988.

Pachmuss, Temira, ed. and trans. *A Russian Cultural Revival: A Critical Anthology of Emigré Literature before 1939*. Knoxville: University of Tennessee Press, 1981.

Terras, Victor, ed. *Handbook of Russian Literature*. New Haven, CT: Yale University Press, 1985.

John Haag, University of Georgia, Athens, Georgia

Chesnut, Mary Boykin (1823–1886)

Southern intellectual, socialite, and candid diarist of the American Civil War. Born Mary Boykin Miller on March 31, 1823, in Statesburg, South Carolina; died of a heart attack on November 22, 1886, in Camden, South Carolina; eldest child of Stephen Decatur Miller (a governor, U.S. senator, and U.S. congressional representative) and Mary (Boykin) Miller; attended private schools in Camden and at Madame Talvande's School in Charleston, South Carolina, excelling in French, literature and history; married James Chesnut, Jr. (a U.S. senator from Camden, South Carolina), on June 23, 1840 (died 1885); no children.

Moved to Washington, D.C., when James Chesnut elected to U.S. Senate (1858); moved to Charleston after James resigned his office and departed to assist in the draft of South Carolina's Ordinance of Secession (1860); briefly resided in Montgomery, Alabama, for the Confederate Provisional Congress; began and kept a private diary, later to be published as A Diary From Dixie, *written in Charleston, Camden, Columbia, Montgomery, and Richmond (1861–65); witnessed the attack on Fort Sumpter (April 12, 1861); observed the decline and collapse of the Confederate government in Richmond and took flight as a war refugee (1865); laboriously revised and re-revised wartime diaries for possible publication (1881–84).*

Selected literary works: Two Years of my Life *(unpublished novel);* The Bright Side of Richmond *(unpublished short story);* The Captain and the Colonel *(unpublished novel);* "The Arrest of a Spy" *(short story, 1885);* A Diary From Dixie *(published posthumously, 1905).*

Mary Boykin Chesnut was one of the most remarkable women of the Civil War era. Though she was well acquainted with many notables, she was not herself a celebrity. By the time of her death, few people in America knew her name. The publication, 19 years later, of a work based on her Civil War diaries has nonetheless made Mary Boykin Chesnut famous as the author of the most insightful view of the inner circle of Confederate society. Comparatively little is known of Chesnut except for the person depicted in the diaries. They reveal her, however, quite fully. According to Bell Irvin Wiley, "Mary Chesnut enjoys the distinction of being one of the most amply portrayed women in American history. This is because of the frankness and fullness of her journal."

It is the quality of her journals, rather than her deeds, which assures Mary Chesnut's place in history. The writer of these diaries was a woman of intelligence, wit, and charm. She recognized the historic importance of the events unfolding around her and resolved to keep a daily record of those momentous days. She possessed the rigorous mind, the skill at writing, and the necessary intimate contact with Southerners in power to make such an undertaking successful. Mary Boykin Chesnut was a woman of her times and lived a life that was characteristic of many antebellum Southern women of the privileged class, but the private Mary Chesnut was anything but typical. She possessed ideas and attitudes significantly unrepresentative of her gender, class, and region.

Mary Boykin Miller was the first child of Stephen Decatur Miller, a lawyer who had already served in the U.S. House of Representatives. At the time of her birth, he was a senator in the South Carolina Legislature. By Mary's fifth birthday, he had been elected governor of their state. The political atmosphere of her home life doubtless had a potent effect on Mary, who was quickly maturing into a young sophisticate who loved nothing better than reading speeches and engaging in rousing debate. Within eight years of her birth, three siblings (Stephen Decatur, Jr., 1825, Catherine, 1827, and Sarah Amelia, 1831) were added to the family. A powerful influence in Mary's youth was her maternal grandmother, **Mary Whitaker Boykin**, who undertook to teach Mary the art of plantation household management.

South Carolina law prevented Governor Miller from seeking a second term, so in 1830, he successfully campaigned for the U.S. Senate. He was a "firebreathing nullifier," a radical states' rights advocate whose politics reflected the mood of South Carolina at the time. His campaign slogan expressed the widespread hostility felt in South Carolina against the U.S. Congress: "Three ways to reform Congress; the ballot box, the jury box and the cartridge box!" Because of poor health, Miller resigned his seat in the Senate and returned home to Statesburg in 1833. In 1835, he sold his property and made preparations to move to Mississippi, where he owned plantations being managed by overseers. This was an unexpected change for one so successful in politics and so inexperienced as an agriculturalist. In all likelihood, the rising popularity of John C. Calhoun in South Carolina was pushing Miller out of the limelight. For whatever reason, Miller decided to try his hand at planting in the deep south.

Chesnut did not accompany the rest of her family at first. At age 12, she was enrolled at

Madame Talvande's French School for Young Ladies in Charleston. There, she received the usual instruction deemed necessary for women of her position. Fortunately, she also gained a more serious academic background in history, rhetoric, natural science, German, and a mastery of French. In Charleston, Chesnut learned to love the city, an affection that would be abiding. As she grew older, her need for the bustle and stimulation of urban life, and her loathing of the boredom of quiet plantation life, developed into an illness. When residing in the country, chronic headaches invariably plagued her, but the symptoms would disappear upon arrival in Washington, Richmond, or Charleston. Her own words confirm that her illness was probably psychosomatic. "I am always ill. The name of my disease is longing to get away from here and go to Richmond." On another occasion she brooded, "We go home Monday . . . already I feel the dread stillness and torpor of our Sahara."

While in Charleston, 13-year-old Mary met and was courted by James Chesnut, Jr., the 21-year-old son of one of South Carolina's wealthiest families. James, of Mulberry Plantation near Camden, was a recent graduate of Princeton University and was in Charleston reading law in the office of James L. Petrigru. James became Mary's regular escort, accompanying her to dances, on strolls along the Battery, and to the theater, to see "whatever was worth seeing," she wrote, "and a good deal besides."

As her diary reveals, Mary came to detest slavery as an abominable social evil. Her first revulsion of bondage occurred when she came upon the captured Seminole chief Osceola being exhibited on the street. "They were like a monkey show," she recalled. "Osceola [had] the saddest face I ever saw. It seemed to me that my country had not dealt magnanimously with these aborigines of the soil."

In 1838, Mary's father died in Mississippi. After a brief sojourn there to assist her mother in settling the estate, she returned to Camden and became engaged to James. On June 23, 1840, the 17-year-old Mary married James, who was then 25. Although there is scant information about Chesnut during the next 20 years, it is known that life at Mulberry Plantation was not pleasant for her. Frustrated that she was not mistress of her own household, she lived in submission to her mother-in-law's close ordering of the home, feeling she had no specific role in the scheme of things. To make matters worse, Chesnut's inability to become pregnant increased her insecurity and unhappiness. She lamented that her mother-in-law, "was bragging to me with exquisite taste—me a childless wretch, of her twenty-seven grandchildren, and Col. Chesnut, a man who rarely wounds me, said to her, 'You have not been a useless woman in this world' because she had so many children. And what of me! God help me— no good have I done—to myself or anyone else— with the power I boast of so—the power to make myself loved. Where am I now. Where are my friends. I am allowed to have none."

> There surely was never anyone like her— physically and intellectually so perfectly fearless— fearless of facts and fearless of the truth—never afraid where it would lead her or land her.
>
> —L.S.W. Perkins

Outlets for Mary's creativity were few, and she was beset by recurring bouts of depression. She sublimated her despondency over her childlessness by occasionally "borrowing" one or more of her nieces or nephews for extended visits. Excursions to the city were fairly reliable therapy for Chesnut's depression, but they were not frequent. Like many women of her time, she took opium to help her cope with her problems. Her diary contains several references to its effect on her:

> Yesterday on the cars we had a mad woman raving at being separated from her daughter. It excited me so, I quickly took opium and that I kept it up. It enables me to retain every particle of mind or sense or brains I ever have, and so quiets my nerves that I can calmly reason and take rational views of things otherwise maddening.
>
> Mrs. Davis . . . sat with me and told me unutterable stories of the war—but I forget after so much opium. Mr. Chesnut . . . sat up and gave me such a scolding.
>
> Came home disheartened and miserable . . . was so ill I had to take morphine to go down. I know I talked sad nonsense all the evening. I felt mad with suspense and anxiety and morphine!

From 1842 to 1852, James Chesnut served in the South Carolina legislature; he then served one term in the state senate, from 1854 to 1858. In 1858, he was elected to the U.S. Senate. Here, finally, Mary found an environment in which she could thrive. Unquestionably, Washington was her element. The love of things political, fostered in childhood, came to fruition, and Mary easily won friends among Washington's elite. Her natural wit and spirited conversation made her a focal point of many social gatherings, a role she relished.

She met virtually every political and military leader who would soon command the Confederacy. Among those, Jefferson and *Varina Howell Davis became her closest friends. Mary defended Jefferson Davis against a multitude of critics and was his loyal supporter in the last dark days of the rebellion. She and Varina were especially close throughout their lives, except for a brief estrangement in 1861. The reasons for the rift were trivial, but Mary was angry enough to thoroughly castigate the Davises in her private journal. "We dined with the President," she wrote. "Mrs. Davis and himself are coarse talking people." A few days later, she added, "I think it provokes Mrs. Davis that men praise me so. . . . Mrs. Davis and Jeff Davis prove themselves anything but well bred by their talk." The conflict, however, was short-lived and soon the Chesnuts and Davises resumed cordial relations. Over 20 years later, in a letter to Varina, Mary said, "How I wish you could read over my journal. I have been two years overlooking it—copying—leaving myself out." Mary deleted a great deal more than herself, although she did strike out many of her more vainglorious statements. She also removed the critical comments about the Davises and quite a few others who were still living at the time.

By 1860, hostility between North and South had escalated. As a protest against the election of Abraham Lincoln, James resigned his seat in the Senate. The Chesnuts left Washington (Mary, reluctantly) and returned to South Carolina so that James could participate in the drafting of South Carolina's Ordinance of Secession. Then, in February of 1861, James and Mary traveled to Montgomery, Alabama, where the Confederate Provisional Congress organized a government and elected Jefferson Davis president. Realizing the historic significance of her times, Mary began keeping a journal on February 18, 1861, and made regular entries until June 26, 1865. Even though gaps exist in the extant manuscripts of Mary Boykin Chesnut's diary, it remains the most complete and forthright insider's view of the Confederacy. Chesnut's diary allows her a suitable format for her commentary on the events of the conflict. As well, it gives her ample opportunity to make personal evaluations of military commanders, political leaders, and their wives.

The diary was written in brief moments of privacy, whenever Chesnut could get away from the crowd of family and friends by whom she was usually surrounded. The journal was hastily scrawled upon whatever was available. The extant portions of Mary's diary are written on loose pieces of paper, pads, notebooks, and even a book bound with red leather. No one, not even her husband, was allowed to see it. This explains the remarkable candor with which Mary described people she encountered. At the time, Chesnut did not intend to publish, but when she finally decided to prepare it for the public in the 1880s, she deemed it necessary to revise substantially.

An example of Chesnut's redaction may be seen early in the diary, from her comments on the bombardment of Fort Sumpter. She was in Charleston on April 12, 1861, because James was involved in the negotiations between Confederate General Pierre Beauregard and Major Richard H. Anderson, who commanded the fort. Her original account said, "The live-long night I toss about—at half past four we hear the booming of the cannon. I start up, dress and rush to my sister's in misery. We go onto the housetop and see the shells bursting." By 1881, her actions as she recorded them, were more pious. "At half past four, I sprang out of bed and on my knees, prostrate I prayed as I never prayed before."

Although these references to fervent prayer were emendations, Chesnut's religious impulse was genuine. She was an essentially secular person who systematically read classic works of theological and devotional literature. Her religious reading regimen sprang from her desire to overcome feelings of resentment toward a number of relatives and acquaintances. On December 1, 1861, she wrote, "Went to church and made this resolution which only with God's help I can keep—not to be so bitter—not to abuse people and not to hate them so." Mary attended both Presbyterian and Episcopal churches but found that worship services at the church for slaves on Mulberry Plantation more closely approximated her conception of the true meaning of Christianity. She was keenly critical of the practice of advancing religious arguments to support political positions. She was especially opposed to mixing religion with war rhetoric.

> One poor young man found dead with a shot through his heart had a Bible in his pocket in which was written: "Given to the defender of his country by the Bible Society." How dare men mix up the Bible so with their own bad passions.

Though Mary Boykin Chesnut was a loyal supporter of the Southern cause, she was not an uncritical one. Her keen powers of observation were more than matched by a willingness to face facts about Southern shortcomings. Her attitude about the South's peculiar institution is a case in point. Raised as a beneficiary of the slave system, Chesnut was an unlikely critic of slavery. The Boykins, the Millers, and the Chesnuts all held slaves, but they considered it a responsibility to treat them as humanely as possible, steadfastly refusing to use corporal punishment or allow families to be broken up. Mary's diary makes it plain that she loathed slavery, although an incongruity exists between these feelings and Chesnut's fondness for her affluent life, which was only possible because of slavery. On March 18, 1861, she wrote:

> I wonder if it be a sin to think slavery a curse to any land. Sumner said not one word of this hated institution which is not true. Men and women are punished when their masters and mistresses are brutes and not when they do wrong. . . . God forgive us, but ours is a monstrous system and wrong and iniquity.

The single most important consideration in her condemnation of slavery was her conviction that it undermined the sexual morality of Southern men. She vented anger at the common practice of slave holders keeping mistresses among their female slaves.

> This only I see: Like the patriarchs of old, our men live all in one house with their wives and their concubines, and the Mulattoes one sees in every family exactly resemble the white children—and every lady tells you who is the father of all the Mulatto children in everybody's household, but those in her own, she seems to think drop from the clouds or pretends so to think.

In another enlightening passage, Chesnut equates slavery with marriage. She was never reluctant to express antipathy to the monolithic authority of men in her society.

> South Carolina slave holder as I am, my very soul is sickened—it is too dreadful. I tried to reason—this is not worse than the willing sale most women make of themselves in marriage—nor can the consequences be worse. The Bible authorizes marriage and slavery—poor women! Poor slaves!

She often groused at the double standard that so restricted the lives of women in her time.

> I think these times make all women feel their humiliation in the affairs of the world. With men, it is on to the field—glory, honor, praise and power. Women can only stay at home. . . . Women are to be violated, ravished and all manner of humiliation. How are the daughters of Eve punished.

At another time, she complained:

> Dogmatic man rarely speaks at home but to find fault. . . . At every word the infatuated fool of a woman recoils as if she has received a slap in the face; and for dear life she begins to excuse herself for what is no fault of hers.

Not only did Chesnut think that slavery undermined morals, but she also believed that Southern principles of states' rights and high individualism undermined the war effort. Though loyal to Jefferson Davis, she was nonetheless outspoken in her criticism of many Confederate leaders, calling them quarrelsome and self-serving. She recognized that factionalism and dissension were rife in the government. Individual states looked to their own interests. Worse yet were the politicians and generals who sought to advance their own careers more than the common cause of the South. In her diary, in her parlor, and at her dining-room table, Mary Chesnut took to task scores of Southern luminaries:

> One of the first things which depressed me was the kind of men put into office at this crisis. Invariably, some of the sleeping dead, head long forgotten or passed over, young and active spirits are ignored.
>
> We are abusing one another as fiercely as ever we abused the yankees.
>
> Every man in South Carolina was willing for a monarchy if he (himself) could be king—but not otherwise.
>
> Oh, if I could put some of my reckless spirit into these discrete, cautious, lazy men.

Chesnut still considered Southerners, with all their flaws, as superior to Northerners, whom she judged to be self-righteous, hypocritical, materialistic, and power mad. She remained hopeful and supportive of the Confederacy even though she knew the odds against Southern victory grew slimmer every day. Acting out her patriotism, Chesnut made her contribution to the war effort by nursing wounded soldiers in the hospitals.

After General Robert E. Lee surrendered his army on April 9, 1865, it was only a short time before the complete collapse of the Confederacy, and the Chesnuts found themselves war refugees in flight before approaching federal troops. Mary continued her diary for a brief period after the war, terminating it in June of 1865, after the Chesnuts had returned to Camden. Even though James still owned property, he was otherwise nearly penniless and encumbered with an immense debt. Reconstruction was a harsh experience for former Confederates and their families. Mary's depression was deeper than it had been during the bleakest hours of war. "I write, myself now the wife of Damocles—for the sword seems suspended by a glittering hair—ready to fall and crush me," she lamented. "I could tear my hair and cry aloud for all that is past and gone." Eventually, her morale rebounded when she realized that for the first time in her life, it would be necessary for her to work to support her family. She began a small butter-and-egg business that supplemented what James earned through farming and legal fees.

In the 1870s, at the urging of friends who were already established writers, Chesnut began to consider the possibility of creating income through writing. After finding employment as a translator of French works into English, she soon determined to try her hand at fiction. First, she wrote a short novel based on her youth at Madame Talvande's school. *Two Years of My Life*, as she entitled it, was never submitted to a publisher. Chesnut's second attempt was a full-length novel of the Civil War to which she gave the title, *The Captain and the Colonel*. This work, semi-autobiographical like the first, was based on her Civil War diary. By 1875, she recognized that it was not nearly as interesting as the diary on which it was based. Another project abandoned. In 1883, Chesnut wrote a 3,000-word sketch entitled, "The Arrest of a Spy," which was published as part of a series, "Our Women in the War," in *The Charleston Weekly News and Courier*. For this essay, she was paid ten dollars.

Chesnut wanted to collect and publish her husband's papers, but friends advised her that her own recollections would be more interesting than those of "a dozen generals." It was Varina Howell Davis who most strongly encouraged Mary to publish a form of her wartime diary: "I think your diaries would sell better than any confederate history of a grave character. Between us, no one is so tired of confederate history as the confederates—they do not want to tell the truth or to hear it."

Chesnut wrote voluminously in the 1870s, but her health was in decline. She developed cardiac and respiratory problems that periodically drove her to bed. Between 1881 and 1884, she devoted herself to the task of revising, and revising again, her Civil War journal. Beyond simply deleting potentially embarrassing passages, she worked to make her prose as interesting as possible, since she believed that to be boring was the greatest sin of all. The book was essentially complete by 1884, although Chesnut had not yet written an introduction or a conclusion.

Serious blows were dealt Chesnut in 1885, which she called, "the black year of my life." The two persons dearest to her, her mother and husband, died in the month of February, only eight days apart. Her father-in-law, James Chesnut, Sr., had bequeathed his plantation to James, Jr., only

for his lifetime. It was not his, then, to leave to Mary. Old Colonel Chesnut's will made it plain that at the time of his son's death, Mulberry would revert to a male heir who bore the name Chesnut. James Chesnut, Jr. did, however, leave Mary a large debt that brought her to virtual destitution. She wrote to her old friend, Varina Davis, a letter that unfortunately has not survived, but which evidently was a scorching denunciation of James Chesnut, Sr., and his troublesome will. Varina's reply was to the point:

> The miseries that old men entail by their unbridled wills would be understood by mankind if the sex were reversed and women did it. The world would not hold the tirades that men would utter to condemn, or the books full of statutes which they would enact against us.

Mary's heart condition continued to worsen through 1885 and 1886. References to "my poor weak heart" are frequent in her final correspondence. In an 1886 letter to old friend **Virginia Clay**, she still has her sense of humor. Referring to an earthquake recently felt in Charleston, she exclaims, "Earthquakes for all and angina pectoris for me." On November 22, 1886, Mary Boykin Chesnut suffered a severe heart attack and died that day at the age of 63. She was buried next to James Chesnut, Jr., at Knights Hill in Camden, South Carolina.

Chesnut bequeathed her diaries to **Isabella Martin**, a South Carolina teacher with whom she had developed a cordial friendship. Eighteen years after Mary's death, Isabella Martin showed the journal to **Myrta Lockett Avary**, an experienced editor, and the two of them jointly edited the first edition of Chesnut's journal in 1904, which they entitled, *A Diary From Dixie*.

SOURCES:
Chesnut, Mary Boykin. *A Diary From Dixie*. Edited by Isabella D. Martin and Myrta Lockett Avary. NY: Peter Smith, 1929.
———. *A Diary From Dixie*. Edited by Ben Ames Williams. Boston, MA: Houghton Mifflin, 1949.
Muhlenfeld, Elizabeth. *Mary Boykin Chesnut: A Biography*. Baton Rouge: Louisiana State University Press, 1981.
Wiley, Bell Irvin. *Confederate Women*. CT: Greenwood Press, 1975.
Woodward, C. Vann, and Elizabeth Muhlfeld. *The Private Mary Chesnut: The Unpublished Civil War Diaries*. NY: Oxford University Press, 1984.
———. *Mary Chesnut's Civil War*. New Haven, CT: Yale University Press, 1981.

Peter Harrison Branum, Ph.D. in Philosophy, Auburn University, Auburn, Alabama

Chester, countess of.

See Matilda de Blois (d. 1120).

See Bertrada of Evreux (fl. 1170s).
See Constance of Brittany (1161–1201).
See Ellen of Wales (d. 1253).

Chevenix, Helen (1886–1963)

Irish suffragist, labor organizer, and pacifist. Born in Blackrock, County Dublin, on November 13, 1886; died in Dublin on March 4, 1963; daughter of Henry Chevenix and Charlotte Sophia (Ormsby) Chevenix; educated at Alexandra College Dublin; graduated with B.A. from Trinity College, University of Dublin, 1909; never married.

Helen Chevenix came from a comfortable, south Dublin family. Her academic career at both Alexandra College and Trinity College was distinguished, and she won several prizes and scholarships. Graduating in 1909, one of the first generation of women to graduate after Trinity opened the college fully to women students, Chevenix soon became interested in the suffrage movement. In 1911, at the inaugural meeting of the Irishwomen's Suffrage Federation, she met *Louie Bennett. She and Bennett, who came from a similarly comfortable middle-class family, became close friends and co-workers for the rest of their lives. Chevenix was impressed by Bennett's leadership gifts, her shrewd common sense and her persuasive abilities. They were both described after Chevenix's death as "two of the most remarkable Irish women of this century."

The Irishwomen's Suffrage Federation was an umbrella group that coordinated the various suffrage organizations active in Ireland at the time. In June 1912, Chevenix was on the platform at a mass meeting of women's groups that demanded the inclusion of female suffrage in the Home Rule Bill for Ireland then before the British Parliament. But suffrage was not the only concern for Chevenix and Bennett who were keenly interested in social and labor issues. They subsequently helped to set up the Irish Women's Reform League, which became an affiliated body of the Suffrage Federation, and used the League to highlight the various social and economic problems faced by women. They were also drawn to pacifism by the radical journalist and writer Francis Sheehy-Skeffington, husband of *Hanna Sheehy-Skeffington. During the First World War, Chevenix was active in the Irish section of the Women's International League for Peace and Freedom, which was established in 1915. Francis Sheehy-Skeffington was subsequently murdered during the 1916 Easter Rising

in Dublin, but his murder only confirmed Chevenix in her pacifism, and for the rest of her life she remained active in various pacifist organizations: the Fellowship of Reconciliation, the Women's International League for Peace and Freedom, and the Irish Pacifist League.

In 1913, the mass lockout of workers belonging to the Irish Transport and General Workers' Union created major labor unrest in Dublin and mobilized women like *Delia Larkin and *Helena Molony to organize women workers. They were encouraged in this by James Connolly, the Marxist labor leader. The Women Workers' Cooperative Society was set up, but in 1916, following the Easter Rising, Helena Molony was arrested and the Society disintegrated. From jail, Molony urged Bennett and Chevenix to organize women workers again, as Connolly had wished. They got to work, beginning with the women in the printing trade and moving on to the laundry workers for whom conditions and pay were particularly bad. The working week for laundry workers averaged 60 hours; wages were between five to ten shillings a week; and health services, canteen and cloakroom facilities were non-existent. Bennett and Chevenix, through hard bargaining and persuasion of employers, secured an extra week's holiday and gradual improvements in pay and conditions.

The Irish Women Workers' Union was established in 1916 with Bennett as general secretary and Chevenix as assistant secretary. At the conference of the Irish Trade Union Congress (ITUC) the following year, the union was accepted as an independent union and not, as previously, as an affiliate of the Irish Transport and General Workers Union. Despite this acceptance, the new union was regarded with disfavor by a number of male labor leaders who were hostile to the organization of women workers and regarded them as a threat. Chevenix and Bennett were subsequently elected presidents of the ITUC, the first two women to be elected to the post. Chevenix was also an active member of the Irish Labor Party and was a regular delegate at its annual conferences.

When civil war broke out in Dublin in the summer of 1922, following the disputed terms of independence set out in the 1921 Anglo-Irish Treaty, Chevenix and Bennett were active, through the Women's International League for Peace and Freedom (WLPF), in trying to mediate a settlement, though without success. For the second time in six years, the center of Dublin was reduced to rubble and, as both women were aware, the poorest people suffered the most. When the WLPF held its fifth International Congress in Dublin in 1926 (which was in part a tribute to the work of its Irish section), it was the first occasion since the end of the civil war in 1923 that leaders of the opposing sides met together.

Chevenix was for a time a member of Dublin Corporation where she worked hard on the housing committee to secure provision for working-class women. She was also a prominent member of the Irish Housewives Association and pressed for the reduction of retail prices, particularly during World War II when high prices in staples like bread affected the poor. She was interested in the problem of child labor and campaigned strongly for the provision of school meals as well as for the raising of the school-leaving age to 16.

After the Second World War, Chevenix continued her dedicated pacifism as vice-president of the Irish Campaign for Nuclear Disarmament. This led to her being branded as a Communist, and at one trade-union congress there were protests when she presented a resolution on world peace on behalf of the Women Workers' Union. As her frail, gentle figure made its way to the platform and began to speak in a whisper, which gradually grew stronger, the hubbub in the hall died down, and she was listened to attentively. In recognition of her work, she was appointed to the consultative Health Council set up by the Irish government under the 1953 Health Act. Only a few days before her death in 1963, she would be appointed a member of the Industrial Accidents Commission.

When Louie Bennett died in November 1956, Chevenix succeeded her as general secretary of the Women Workers' Union. Chevenix wrote a tribute to her old friend that could equally apply to herself: "To her political labels mattered little. What mattered was human life; physical, cultural, spiritual. In her whole being was answered the prayer of Rabindranath Tagore: 'Give me the strength never to disown the poor nor bow my knees before insolent might.'"

SOURCES:
Fox, R.M. *Louie Bennett: Her Life and Times*. Talbot Press, 1958.
Cullen Owens, R. *Smashing Times: A History of the Irish Women's Suffrage Movement 1889–1922*. Attic Press, 1984.
Obituary of Helen Chevenix, in *Irish Times*. March 5, 1963.

Deirdre McMahon, Lecturer in History,
Mary Immaculate College,
University of Limerick, Limerick, Ireland

Chevreuse, Duchesse de (1600–1679).

See Rohan-Montbazon, Marie de.

Chézy, Helmina von (1783–1856)

German musician and writer known for her librettos and incidental music as well as for her Viennese salon. Name variations: Chezy. Born Wilhelmina Christiane Klencke in Berlin, Germany, on January 26, 1783; died in Geneva, Switzerland, on January 28, 1856; married twice; children: two sons.

In Vienna, an eccentric, overweight, strangely dressed woman held an open house for artists and intellectuals. Although some made fun of Helmina von Chézy, these young people loved and appreciated her eccentricities. Von Chézy had written the libretto for Carl Maria von Weber's *Euryanthe* and for her own play *Rosamunde* for which Franz Schubert had written the music. A talented poet as well as musician, she also wrote the text for E.J.O. von Hettersdorf's *Singspiel Eginhard und Emma*.

Helmina von Chézy had two brief, unhappy marriages. Between them, she traveled to Paris to live with Friedrich and Dorothea Schlegel (*Dorothea Mendelssohn*), steeping herself in Romantic literature. Von Chézy returned to Germany in 1810, bringing her two young sons with her; from there, she went to Vienna, living in Austria from 1823 to 1833, when she received commissions for dramatic and musical work. Some of her dramas were severely criticized. Despite a rather strange personality and uneven gifts, Helmina von Chézy always had a wide circle of friends and admirers. She wrote *Poems* (1812), *Heart Notes during a Pilgrimage* (1833), and similar romantic stanzas, as well as the novel *Emma's Ordeals* (1827).

John Haag,
Athens, Georgia

Chiang Ch'ing (1914–1991).
See Jiang Qing.

Chiang Kai-shek, Madame (b. 1898).
See Song, Meiling.

Chiang Mei-ling or May-ling (b. 1898).
See Song, Meiling.

Chiara.
Variant of Clare.

Chiara di Favorone (c. 1194–1253).
See Clare of Assisi.

Chica, Elena (1828–1888)

Rumanian author. Name variations: (pseudonym) Dora d'Istria; Helene Ghica or Elena Ghika. Born in Bucharest, Rumania, in 1828; died in 1888; married Russian Prince Koltzoff- or Kolzow-Massalsky.

Elena Chica received a classical education and acquired an extensive knowledge of modern languages and literature. At age 15, under the pseudonym Dora d'Istria, she began a translation of the *Iliad*, and not long afterward wrote several pieces for the theater. Her 1855 work, *La Vie Monastique dans l'Église Orientale* (*Monastic Life in the Eastern Church*), alleges monasticism to be the principal obstacle to civilization in Eastern and Southern Europe. In 1864, she published the two-volume *Des Femmes par une Femme* (*Women, by a Woman*), which was translated into Russian, Italian, and English. Her studies on Albanian poetry gave rise to a nationalistic and literary movement among the Albanians. In April 1868, the Greek Chamber of Deputies named her "high citizeness of Greece." Chica also wrote the four-volume *German Switzerland*.

Chi Cheng Reel (b. 1944).

See Reel, Chi Cheng.

Chichibu Setsuko (1909–1995)

Princess of Japan who was deeply involved in the restoration of ties of friendship between Britain and Japan. Name variations: Princess Chichibu; Chichibu no Miya Setsuko. Born Matsudaira Setsuko in Walton-on-Thames, England, on September 9, 1909; died on August 25, 1995; daughter of Matsudaira Tsuneo (a diplomat); educated in Western schools; married Prince Yasuhito Chichibu (d. 1953, a younger brother of Emperor Hirohito), in 1928; no children.

Likely the most Westernized member of the Japanese imperial family in her generation, Princess Setsuko Chichibu was a highly respected member of a clan that until 1945 were regarded in Japan as divine or semi-divine. She was born Matsudaira Setsuko in Walton-on-Thames, England, in 1909 when her diplomat father Matsudaira Tsuneo worked on assignment as attaché at the Japanese Embassy in London. Her upbringing would be thoroughly Western. At the age of eight months, she returned to Japan with her parents, where she was raised in a privileged environment. Though her father had renounced his inherited title thus technically making himself and his daughter commoners, the family contin-

ued to move in aristocratic circles, and Setsuko grew up in what was essentially an extremely restricted elite environment. In 1925, her father was appointed Japanese ambassador to the United States, and she moved with her family to Washington, D.C. Her Western-oriented education, which had begun in Japan, continued in Washington at the Friends School, a highly regarded institution run by the Quakers.

Setsuko's life changed dramatically several years after she had come to the United States. As an emissary for the Empress Dowager *Sadako, Count Kabayama arrived in Washington with a proposal, suggesting that Setsuko marry Prince Yasuhito Chichibu, a younger brother of the emperor, Hirohito. The offer, which came as a complete surprise, was deeply upsetting for Setsuko; she had only met the prince briefly on a few occasions. Furthermore, she and her family were living the lives of commoners, had become familiar with Western ways, and she was unfamiliar with the rigid ceremonial patterns of the Japanese imperial court. But the empress dowager believed Setsuko to be the perfect match for the prince and refused to be dissuaded. Eventually, Setsuko and her parents accepted the proposal, and she was married to Prince Chichibu in September 1928.

Despite her fears, Setsuko's marriage proved to be a happy one. Both she and her husband were modern in their thinking (he had studied at Magdalen College, Oxford) and shared a love of sports. Although the prince taught at the Imperial Military Academy, he was not an extreme militarist and became alarmed by events in Japan in the 1930s. He was not a policymaker, and the prince and princess, who had no children, centered their lives on friends and travel. They visited the West on several occasions in the 1930s, the most important trip being in 1937 when they attended the coronation of King George VI as official representatives of Emperor Hirohito and the imperial Japanese government.

The drift toward war saddened both Princess Chichibu and her husband, and he received the news of the outbreak of war against the United States and Great Britain in December 1941 in stunned silence. By this time, he was already in poor health, suffering from overwork and the early stages of tuberculosis. Withdrawing from a world intent on destroying itself, the couple spent the rest of the war in their mountain villa in Gotemba, with a splendid view of the sacred Mount Fuji. The princess spent much of her time raising vegetables and wondering what had happened to their friends in the West.

The defeat of Japan in 1945 created a new, more democratic society in which the princess became one of the most active and respected members of the imperial family. After the death of her husband in 1953, she became increasingly active in various aspects of public life, serving as patron of the national anti-tuberculosis association and working to raise funds for the Japanese Red Cross. One particular interest of hers was a fund to provide for children who had been orphaned as the result of traffic accidents. Among the organizations dearest to her heart was the Japan-Britain Society. The princess succeeded her late husband as patron of this friendship organization, serving it well not only because she had been born in England and spoke English perfectly, but also because she had developed so many friendships with men and women in that far-off island nation. Whenever members of the British royal family visited Japan in the postwar years, they made a special point of visiting Princess Chichibu, who returned the courtesy by making numerous trips to Britain.

Despite her aristocratic roots, Princess Chichibu mixed with ordinary women and men and projected considerable charm and warmth on her foreign travels, thus helping to rebuild the ties of Japanese-British friendship that had been so badly damaged by the hatreds of World War II. One of the ways in which she endeared herself to Britishers was through her love of gardening. A knowledgeable gardener, for many years she grew English roses in Japan. When in Britain, she pleased her hosts by making long tours of their gardens, obviously enjoying the experience. Princess Chichibu published her memoirs in Japan in 1991, and they appeared in an English translation in 1996.

SOURCES:

Chichibu no Miya Setsuko. *The Silver Drum: A Japanese Imperial Memoir.* Translated by Dorothy Britton. Folkestone, Kent: Global Books, 1996.

"Princess Chichibu," in *The Times* [London]. September 11, 1995, p. 21.

John Haag, Associate Professor, University of Georgia, Athens, Georgia

Chick, Harriette (1875–1977)

British nutritionist who made important contributions to public health—particularly by discovering the nutritional origins of a number of diseases including rickets and pellagra—and who was a co-discoverer of the standard Chick-Martin test for disinfectants.

Name variations: Dame Harriette Chick. Born in London, England, on January 6, 1875; died at age 102 in Cambridge, England, on July 9, 1977; one of six daughters and four sons of Samuel Chick and Emma (Hooley) Chick; attended University College, London, graduating with a doctorate in 1904; postgraduate work at the hygiene institutes in Vienna and Munich; never married.

Awarded Commander of the British Empire (1932) and Dame of the British Empire (1949).

Harriette Chick was one of the key figures in the development of nutritional science in the 20th century. She was born into a large, affluent British family in 1875, a year in which the British Empire was unchallenged and Queen *Victoria had been on the throne for 38 years. Harriette's father Samuel was a prosperous lace merchant and property owner. Both he and his wife were devout Methodists who staunchly believed that their seven daughters, as well as their four sons, should cultivate their minds along with their souls. Of the seven Chick girls, five became university graduates in various fields including medicine, physics, chemistry, botany, medicine and English. After receiving an excellent education that encompassed the basics of science at Notting Hill High School, Harriette enrolled at University College, London, graduating with a doctorate in 1904 on the basis of research on green algae in polluted waters. Determined to make research her life's work, she did postgraduate work at the leading Hygiene Institutes of the Continent, those in Vienna and Munich.

Upon Chick's return to England, she worked for some time in Liverpool and then applied for a research fellowship at London's noted Lister Institute of Preventive Medicine. Despite her obvious qualifications, two members of the institute staff were strongly opposed to having a woman even as a junior colleague, and they implored the director, Sir Charles Martin, to turn down her application. Their objections were ignored, and in 1905 Chick began a highly productive relationship of four decades with the Lister Institute. Among her first major research achievements was a collaborative effort with Martin that resulted in what became known as the Chick-Martin test for disinfectants. This replaced an earlier, much less satisfactory procedure that was carried out in distilled water; the Chick-Martin test, on the other hand, was realistic in that it added organic matter (3% dried human feces). In the next several years, the research team of Chick and Martin produced work of at least equal significance, including pioneering investigations of the nature of proteins. Three of their important papers, which appeared in the *Journal of Hygiene* in 1908, demonstrated conclusively that heat coagulation was an orderly process governed by known chemical laws.

The start of World War I in 1914 created new priorities for researchers, and at first Chick was involved in the task of testing and bottling tetanus antitoxin for the British troops on the Western front. This emergency task completed, she returned to her laboratory at the Lister Institute to prepare serums for the treatment of typhoid, paratyphoid and dysentery, diseases that were killing and disabling thousands of Allied troops on several fronts of the war. During this period, she became increasingly involved in research into vitamins, work that resulted in the publication of a number of important monographs between 1919 and 1932. The sufferings brought on by the war did not end with the armistice that was signed in November 1918. In the spring of 1919, Harriette Chick began to receive alarming reports of widespread nutritional deficiencies among the populations of the former enemy nations Germany and Austria-Hungary. She arrived in Vienna to find a population on the brink, due to more than four years of near-starvation conditions.

Working with two other dedicated scientists, **Margaret Hume** and ✋▶ **Elsie Dalyell**, Chick and her staff catalogued a vast range of malnutrition-induced diseases including scurvy, rickets and xerophthalmia in infants, as well as osteomalacia in the elderly. Along with the internationally recognized Professor Clemens von Pirquet and his staff at the University of Vienna's Pediatric Clinic, over the next several years Chick and her team made important discoveries in the relationship between nutrition and disease. During this period, Harriette Chick and her colleagues were able to prove conclusively that rickets was caused exclusively by dietary deficiencies, and that these deficiencies could be prevented or their effects overcome by regular ingestion of cod liver oil, which contained large amounts of the needed fat-soluble preventive vitamins. Regular exposure to ultraviolet light, if necessary through a sun lamp in the winter, was also discovered to be a crucial prevention measure. Marshaling vast amounts of clinical evidence, Chick argued her case convincingly to the sometimes skeptical and conservative Viennese physicians, including Professor von Pirquet, who had at first believed that the cause of rickets was an infection. These important contributions to public health would remain foundation stones of modern medical therapeutics.

Chick returned to London in 1922 to continue her research at the Lister Institute, becoming the director of its division of nutrition.

Throughout the next two decades, she would work tirelessly studying an exciting new field of investigation, the nutritional value of proteins. First working with rats, she methodically investigated the role of vitamins in human health. In time, she would make important discoveries regarding the nutritional role of B-vitamins, and her papers in this area—including the values of different kinds of flour, brown and white bread, and potatoes—were of pioneering significance. During these years, she began to receive many honors. In 1932, she was appointed a Commander of the British Empire, and the next year she received an honorary doctorate in science from the University of Manchester. Another important honor was the position of secretary of the League of Nations health section committee on the physiological bases of nutrition, a post she held from 1934 through 1937.

Although she was close to retirement when World War II began in September 1939, Chick refused to leave her research, insisting instead on moving her rats and other experimental animals in her own car to Cambridge, where her laboratory was reconstituted in the home of Sir Charles Martin. Harriette continued her research throughout the war years and did not retire from the Lister Institute until 1945, five years later than would have been customary. Although officially retired, she maintained close contact with the nutrition division of the institute until it was disbanded in 1949. That same year, King George

✋▶ **Dalyell, Elsie (1881–1948)**

Australian pathologist. Born Elsie Dalyell on December 13, 1881, in Newtown, Sydney, Australia; died in 1948; second daughter of Jean (McGregor) Dalyell and James Melville Dalyell (a mining engineer); attended Sydney Girls' High School.

Following her graduation from Sydney Girls' High School, Elsie Dalyell became a pupil-teacher for the Department of Public Instruction in 1897, while studying arts and science for a year at the University of Sydney. In 1905, after a hysterectomy, Dalyell quit teaching and undertook second-year medicine, graduating with an MB (bachelor of medicine) first class with honors from the university in 1909 and a degree in chemistry in 1910. She was then appointed medical officer at the Royal Prince Alfred Hospital. In 1911, Dalyell became the first woman on the full-time medical-school staff as demonstrator in pathology. The next year, in 1912, she became the first woman elected to a Beit fellowship. Dalyell served out her fellowship at the Lister Institute of Preventive Medicine in London.

VI granted Harriette Chick the title of Dame of the British Empire. Dame Harriette remained active during the later decades of her long life, and her service to the field of nutritional research included her pioneering efforts in the 1940s as a founding member of the Nutrition Society. Highly respected by her peers, she served as president of the Nutrition Society from 1956 through 1959.

In 1974, shortly before her 100th birthday, she gave a lecture on her years in Vienna to the British Nutrition Foundation. On this occasion, she not only received an award, but was able despite her extreme age to give a lively introduction to the lecture, the bulk of which was then read by a younger colleague. A year later, when she was 100 years of age, Chick attended the annual general meeting of the Lister Institute, which was held in the laboratories in Chelsea where she had carried out so much of her path-breaking research. Short in stature, always neatly dressed, Harriette Chick was interested in lively conversation and debate even in the tenth decade of her long and productive life. Physically and mentally active to the end, she died suddenly in Cambridge on July 9, 1977. The warm tribute to her in London's *Times* summed up a remarkable life rich in achievements: "Dame Harriette was a person of quiet charm, of great determination, and of much courage. She had all the best and most sterling qualities of the Victorians—upright, honest, and at all times determined to do her duty."

SOURCES:

Chick, Harriette, Margaret Hume, and Marjorie MacFarlane. *War on Disease: A History of the Lister Institute.* London: André Deutsch, 1971.

"Dame Harriette Chick: Strides in nutrition that overtook disease," in *The Times* [London]. July 11, 1977, p. 14.

Sinclair, H.M. "Chick, Dame Harriette," in Lord Blake and C. S. Nicholls, eds., *The Dictionary of National Biography 1971–1980.* Oxford: Oxford University Press, 1986, pp. 142–143.

John Haag, Associate Professor, University of Georgia, Athens, Georgia

Chien-Shiung Wu (1912–1997).

See Wu Chien-Shiung.

Child, Julia (1912–)

American cooking teacher, cookbook author, and television personality who almost single-handedly pioneered the epicurean cooking revolution of the 1960s and 1970s in the United States, taking the mystery out of the preparation of French cuisine. Born Julia McWilliams in Pasadena, California, on August 15, 1912; daughter of John and Carolyn (Weston) McWilliams; Smith College, B.A., 1934; married Paul Child (an artist-sculptor), in September 1946 (died, May 1994).

Selected writings: (with Simone Beck and Louisette Bertholle) Mastering the Art of French Cooking (Vol. I, 1961); The French Chef Cookbook (Alfred A. Knopf, 1968); (with Simone Beck) Mastering the Art of French Cooking (Vol. II, 1970, rev. ed., Alfred A, Knopf, 1983); From Julia Child's Kitchen (Alfred A. Knopf, 1975); (with E.S. Yntema) Julia Child and Company (Alfred A. Knopf, 1978); (with Yntema) Julia Child and More Company (Alfred A. Knopf, 1979); The Way to Cook (Alfred A. Knopf, 1989); Cooking at Home with the Master Chefs (1993); (with Nancy Verde Barr) In Julia's Kitchen with Master Chefs (Alfred A. Knopf, 1996).

Julia Child was very much a late bloomer, not finding her métier as the most famous chef in America until she was well into middle age. Raised in Pasadena, California, she graduated from Smith College in 1934 with a degree in history, then worked as a copywriter for an ad agency in New York. During World War II, she joined the Office of Strategic Services, serving as a clerk in a document center in Ceylon, where she met her husband Paul Child, an artist-sculptor. After the war, the couple settled in Washington, D.C. They lived there until 1948, when Paul was assigned to the American Embassy in Paris as the exhibits officer for the U.S. Information Agency.

Child's experience in Paris changed her life. "From the beginning, I fell in love with everything I saw," she said. After taking French lessons at Berlitz and studying at the famed Cordon Bleu, she began giving informal cooking lessons in her Left Bank apartment. With the assistance of established French chefs **Simone Beck** and **Louisette Bertholle**, the classes eventually developed into *L'École des Trois Gourmandes*. The success of the school prompted the three women to collaborate on a cookbook adapting French culinary techniques to American kitchens. Twelve years in preparation, *Mastering the Art of French Cooking* was published in 1961, a year after Paul's retirement and the couple's move to Cambridge, Massachusetts. *The New York Times* hailed it as the "finest volume on French cooking ever published in English." A second volume, co-authored with Beck, was published in 1970.

It was Child's appearance as a guest on a Boston educational television show called "I've Been Reading," whisking eggs while she chatted about her book, that led to "The French Chef," a cooking show that ran for nine years and turned her into a national institution. In an interview for an article in *The Boston Globe* (March 6, 1997), Child told Jack Thomas that the moment was just right. "At the time," she said, "French cooking was the cat's whiskers. Most of what people ate in this country was a kind of terrible ladies'-magazine food, awful!" Combining a hearty and authoritative manner with a droll sense of humor, Child attracted an ever-increasing number of aspiring gourmets. Thomas wrote that watching the show was "the equivalent of tuning to Wyeth on art or Updike on writing. . . . She'd mince an onion with blinding speed and, using a cleaver, amputate the wings of a chicken—THWACK! THWACK!—with the authority of an executioner." On camera, nothing rattled her, even the inevitable mishaps. During one show, after a flipped omelet rained down on the stove, she told viewers, "Well, that didn't go very well. See, when I flipped it, I didn't have the courage to do it the way I should have. But you can always pick it up," she confided while returning pieces of egg to the pan, "and if you're alone, who's going to see!" By 1966, the series was carried on 104 stations, and Child appeared on the cover of *Time* magazine, and in cartoons in *The New Yorker*. The television show also led to the publication of her first solo book, *The French Chef Cookbook,* in 1968. Seven subsequent television programs (including a second series of "The French Chef"), as well as six one-hour videos called *The Way to Cook,* provided the basis for nine additional cookbooks.

Child has twice received awards from the French government, including the prestigious National Order of Merit in 1976. In the United States, she has been the recipient of a Peabody Award (1966) and an Emmy (1966) for "The French Chef" series. In 1997, slowed only slightly by some stiffness in her knees, Child still kept an exhausting schedule. Appearing weekly in a PBS series, "Baking with Julia," and promoting a companion cookbook, she was also active in the Association of Culinary Professionals and the American Institute of Wine & Food, which she founded with vintner Robert Mondavi in 1981. That year, she spent 200 days on the road, appearing at culinary events around the country. In his article for the *Globe*, Jack Thomas asked Child to speculate on her obituary. "It would say that Julia Child encouraged home cooking and the pleasure of food," she told him over a second glass of luncheon wine, "that she made it a respectable hobby, something fun and creative and not drudgery."

Julia Child

SOURCES:

"From Omelets to America," in *Maclean's*. Vol. 106, no. 49. December 6, 1993, p. 48.

Green, Carol Hurd, and Mary Grimley Mason. *American Women Writers*. NY: Continuum, 1994.

McHenry, Robert, ed. *Famous American Women*. NY: Dover, 1983.

Thomas, Jack. "Julia Child: Still Cookin'," in *The Boston Globe*. March 6, 1997, pp. E1 and E4–5.

SUGGESTED READING:

Bridges, Linda. "The Food Police," in *National Review*. Vol. 44, no. 20. October 19, 1992, pp. 64–65.

Chesnoff, Richard Z. "The Real Joy of Cooking," in *U.S. News & World Report*. Vol. 119, no. 12. September 25, 1995, p. 79.

"Child, Julia," in *Current Biography 1967*. NY: H.W. Wilson, pp. 66–69.

Davidson, Susy, "Views from Twin Peaks," in *Food Arts*. Vol 4, no. 10. December 1991, pp. 54–57.

"Eat, Drink and Be Sensible," in *Newsweek*. Vol. 117, no. 21. May 27, 1991, p. 52.

Fitch, Noël Riley. *Appetite for Life: The Biography of Julia Child*. NY: Doubleday, 1997.

Gilbert, Lynn, and Gaylen Moore. *Particular Passions: Talks with Women Who Have Shaped Our Times*. NY: Clarkson N. Potter, 1981.

Hall, Trish. "Simone Beck, a Cook, Dies at 87; Co-Wrote Book With Julia Child," in *The New York Times Biographical Service*, December 1991, p. 1391.

Lawson, Carol. "Julia Child Boiling, Answers Her Critics," in *The New York Times*. June 20, 1990, p. C8.

O'Neill, Molly. "Savoring the World According to Julia," in *The New York Times Biographical Service*. October 1989, pp. 996–997.

Saxon, Wolfgang. "Paul Child, Artist, Dies at 92," in *The New York Times Biographical Service*. May 1994, p. 708.

Shapiro, Laura. "Once More, It's 'Bon Appétit!'," in *Newsweek*. Vol. 114, no. 15. October 9, 1989, pp. 114–115 and 117.

"Silver Spoon: Julia Child," in *Food Arts*. Vol. 3, no. 10. December 1990, p. 88.

Whitcomb, Meg. "Julia Child: Life Started Cooking at 50," in *50 plus*. Vol. 20, no. 2. February 1980, pp. 20–23.

COLLECTIONS:

Julia Child's papers are at the Schlesinger Library, Radcliffe College, Cambridge Massachusetts.

Barbara Morgan,
Melrose, Massachusetts

Child, Lydia Maria (1802–1880)

American author who used her writings to attack slavery and advance the cause of women's rights. Born Lydia Maria Francis on February 11, 1802, in Medford, Massachusetts; died in Wayland, Massachusetts, on October 20, 1880; daughter of David Convers Francis (a baker) and Susannah (Rand) Francis; sister of Convers Francis (1795–1863, a Unitarian minister); educated in Norridgewock, Maine; married David Lee Child (1794–1874, a Boston lawyer and journalist); children: none.

Lydia Maria Child

Taught school in Watertown, Massachusetts; published her first novel (1824); became an abolitionist (1833); wrote numerous volumes of fiction, light verse, children's stories, as well as serious works on abolition, women's history, and comparative religion.

Selected works: Hobomok *(1824);* The Frugal Housewife *(1830);* An Appeal in Favor of that Class of Americans Called Africans *(1833);* History of the Condition of Women *(2 vols., 1835);* The Family Nurse *(1837);* Flowers For Children *(1844);* Letters from New York *(1843, Vol. 1, 1845, Vol. 2);* Correspondence between Lydia Maria Child, Governor Wise and Mrs. Mason *(1860); (editor)* Incidents in a Life of a Slave Girl *(1861);* Looking Toward Sunset *(1864).*

By the time she was 30, Lydia Maria Child had enjoyed as much literary acclaim as any young writer could hope for. At age 22, she had dashed off her first novel in only six weeks and had become an overnight celebrity in Boston. Her second novel also sold well, and she had then written two popular nonfiction works, both providing household hints to American women. At the same time, she had founded her own children's magazine, the first of its kind in America, which enjoyed praise from literary critics and financial support from subscribing parents. Surprised by her own success, Child told a friend, "It seems as if the public was resolved to give me a flourish of trumpets, let me write what I will."

Yet Lydia Child knew that this was not quite true. There was one topic, close to her heart, that the American public did not want her to write about—the evils of slavery. But in 1833, she decided to obey the dictates of her conscience, no matter what the consequences might be for her career as a writer. "I am fully aware of the unpopularity of the task I have undertaken," she boldly announced in the preface to her book, *An Appeal in Favor of that Class of Americans Called Africans.* Even the title was shocking at the time—few other whites thought of the slaves as fellow Americans. "Though I expect ridicule and censure," the young author wrote, "I do not fear them. Should [the Appeal] be the means of advancing even one single hour of the inevitable progress of truth and justice, I would not exchange the consciousness for all Rothschild's wealth or Sir Walter's fame."

Just as Child had predicted, the publication of her radical ideas about slavery proved to be a devastating setback to her literary career. Editors shunned her, parents canceled their subscriptions to her magazine, and she was ostracized by many Bostonians who had, up to that point, praised her as a rare talent. While Child suffered in the short-term, her act of courage and self-sacrifice have since earned her a special place in American history, as one of the earliest and most steadfast opponents of slavery. Her *Appeal* was a spark that helped ignite the abolition movement.

When Lydia was 12, her mother died of tuberculosis. Her father, a successful baker and real-estate speculator, had little time to care for his daughter. So Child turned for guidance to her

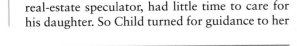

older brother Convers Francis, a serious young divinity student at Harvard. Their relationship nurtured a love of learning in Lydia that would stay with her the rest of her life. At a time when young women were not encouraged to be interested in such things, she spent many hours poring over her brother's library of classical literature, science, and theology. More concerned about philosophy than fashion, she was perceived by her relatives as eccentric. Her father decided that his daughter needed a feminine role model, so he sent her at the age of 14 to live with her married sister in Norridgewock, a village in central Maine.

Lydia attended the local school there, although she often knew as much as her teachers. She learned more from her visits to a band of Abenaki Indians who had settled nearby. One of the few white settlers to befriend the tribe, she enjoyed hearing their traditional stories and learning some of their skills. The experience gave her a respect for other cultures, and a perspective on racism that would echo throughout her career as a reformer.

At age 18, Child returned to the Boston area, living with her brother and his wife in Watertown. Convers had become a leading Unitarian minister, and his home became a gathering place for restless young intellectuals, such as transcendentalist Ralph Waldo Emerson, the radical Unitarian preacher Theodore Parker, and the Quaker poet and abolitionist John Greenleaf Whittier. Child thoroughly enjoyed these evenings of intellectual stimulation and developed lifelong friendships with Parker and Whittier.

For several years, she supported herself by running a school for girls. But she found her true calling when she read an article in a literary magazine by the Unitarian intellectual John Palfrey. Like many of America's cultural elite, Palfrey regretted that his young nation had not yet distinguished itself in the arts, that its writers had produced nothing more than second-rate copies of British literature. He called on American writers to declare their cultural independence by producing a native literature, and he suggested that the rich and romantic past of New England could provide the themes. That very night Child wrote the first chapter of *Hobomok*, a novel she finished six weeks later. Drawing on her knowledge of Indian culture, she spun the tale of an ill-fated marriage between a young white woman and an Indian chief. Through a strange twist of fate, the heroine discovers that her first husband, a white man

she had presumed lost at sea, is actually still alive. His return to New England puts all three characters into an awkward dilemma, until the noble savage Hobomok graciously agrees to disappear silently into the wilderness.

Modern critics do not feel that *Hobomok* truly answered Palfrey's call for a new American literature; the plot is standard melodrama, the characters wooden, and the depictions of native life are more romantic than real. But, according to biographer **Helene Baer**, the moral of the book was one that Child would make the centerpiece of her life's work—that the nobility of a human soul "rests in the conscience, not in the color of the skin."

Whatever its literary failings, *Hobomok* was a commercial success. Since it was not considered proper for women to write books, Child had published it under the patriotic but unrevealing name, "An American." Before long, her true identity was discovered and, at 24, she began to enjoy some of the privileges of literary celebrity, including an open invitation to use the Athenaeum, an exclusive lending library that rarely extended borrowing privileges to women.

> *No* man or woman of that period rendered more substantial service to the cause of freedom, or made such a "great renunciation" in doing it.
>
> —John Greenleaf Whittier

Child next published *The Rebels*, a novel about the Revolution, which was the first American book to use actual people and events from New England history. Like her first novel, this work enjoyed commercial success at the time but does not hold much interest for the modern reader. At the same time, she founded and wrote most of the *Juvenile Miscellany*, a bi-monthly children's magazine that was the nation's first. The prestigious *North American Review* praised her as a national treasure. "In all her works nothing can be found which does not commend itself, by its tone of healthy morality and good sense. Few female writers if any have done more or better things for our literature."

In the midst of these early years of literary success, Lydia met a young lawyer named David Child, a scholar who could speak six different languages, and an idealist with a reputation for providing free legal services for the poor. Lydia's family warned her about the pitfalls of joining her fate with an impractical reformer, but they underestimated her own deep streak of romantic idealism. She married him in 1828, when she was 26.

Just as her family had warned, David turned out to be a better philanthropist than a provider. He gave away much of his income to various causes and spent more time promoting the Whig Party than his own career. For the time being, Child's writing brought in enough income to keep them afloat, but they often hovered on the edge of debt. Marriage to David inspired household economy, and Lydia set aside novel writing to produce *The Frugal Housewife,* a bestselling book of cost-saving tips for women.

In 1832, David joined William Lloyd Garrison in the formation of the New England Anti-Slavery Society. When Lydia was introduced to Garrison, she was also won to the cause. Years later, she wrote, "I little thought then that the whole pattern of my life-web would be changed by that introduction." While others had criticized slavery before, none did so with Garrison's uncompromising courage. In his mind, the institution was a sin against God that demanded an immediate end. Though he rejected the use of violence himself, he fearlessly exposed himself to mob attack in order to make his convictions heard. Garrison's example made Child a lifelong abolitionist. "He got hold of the strings of my conscience," she wrote, "and pulled me into reform."

The result was the aforementioned *An Appeal in Favor of that Class of Americans Called Africans.* Though notorious, it was her most important work. In it, she marshalled fact and feeling in an all-out war on slavery. She recounted the history of slavery, reprinted statistics about its spread, but also used her artistic powers to touch her readers' sympathetic emotions. Thirty years before slavery brought the Union to war, most Bostonians preferred to ignore the issue, particularly since many shared in the profits from slave labor, a fact Child was quick to point out. Bostonians were stung by her attack and scandalized that a woman would dare to express herself on a controversial political issue. Not only did the book sell poorly, but Child lost her market for her other writings, and even had her borrowing privileges at the Athenaeum withdrawn. "Her praises were suddenly silenced," her friend Whittier later recalled, adding that "no woman in this country . . . sacrificed so much for principles as Mrs. Child."

Though most readers hated the book, a few were ready to respond to Child's appeal. The great Unitarian minister, William Ellery Channing, had always opposed slavery but had hesitated to carry the controversy into his pulpit. Child's courageous decision to speak out inspired him to do the same. Wendell Phillips read the *Appeal* while a young man in law school; the book, he later said, "obliged" him to become an abolitionist. For the next 30 years, he served as the movement's most powerful orator.

Concern for the slave led many abolitionist women to think about the limits on their own liberties. Inspired by her friendship with transcendentalist philosopher *Margaret Fuller, Child began to research women's history. "From the beginning of time," she found, women had been "perpetually insulted by literature, law and custom." She set down her findings in a series of works she called "The Ladies' Library." Biographer Baer describes the work as a "long, humorless dose," but at the dawn of the women's rights movement in America many early leaders found the work inspiring.

Because of the backlash against her *Appeal,* Lydia lost most of her writing opportunities, and the Childs' plummeting financial situation was made worse by one of David's new reform schemes. Convinced that Northerners would never unite against slavery as long as they needed Southern products, he decided to help free the slaves by learning how to grow sugar beets. The Dutch already knew how to turn beets into sugar, and David hoped to convince New England farmers to try this as an alternative to cane sugar raised by slaves on the Southern delta. He left his wife behind, dependent on her family, for more than a year, while he studied beet technology in Holland. Returning to New England, he sank a large sum of money, borrowed from Lydia's father, into a lonely farm in Western Massachusetts. The two shared a shack at the edge of their beet field and sank deeper into debt. "If this won't drive poetry out of a mortal," she complained to a friend, "I know not what will."

On the verge of bankruptcy, Child agreed to rescue the family's finances by leaving David and his farm and taking a job in New York as editor of an important abolitionist journal, the *National Anti-Slavery Standard.* The transition from a lonely beet farm in rural New England to America's largest city revived her literary inspiration, particularly as Margaret Fuller had also moved to New York and the two were able to renew their studies together. In addition to editing the *Standard,* Child produced a series of sketches about life in the city, describing both the beauty and the squalor of the growing metropolis. Giving free reign to her inclinations as a sentimental novelist, she sometimes described the city's glamorous social life, rhapsodizing about "the sad music of the moon, the birth and death of flowers, and above all, the rose-colored dreams of youthful love." In other pieces, she returned to her job as reformer, reporting about wretched slum conditions, the threat of prostitution to young country girls, and the state of New York's prison system. Gathered into a book called *Letters from New York,* these essays revived Child's literary career, and still stand as some of her best writing.

In 1844, after several years as editor, Child quit her post at the *Standard.* By the mid-1840s, the abolitionist movement was divided. Some wanted to pursue their goals gradually, through political compromise, while others still held to Garrison's view that no compromise was acceptable short of an immediate end to slavery. As an independent-minded editor, Child had not done enough to please either group. Feeling overworked and unappreciated, she was glad to jump off what she called the "anti-slavery treadmill."

At the same time, she faced a crisis in her marriage. After years of effort, David's sugar beet experiment collapsed in bankruptcy. Frustrated with her husband's financial incompetence, she decided to separate her own finances from his. "Water pumped into a sieve for fourteen years is enough to break the most energetic spirit," is the way she summed up her decision to stop subsidizing her husband's grand schemes. Yet, in spite of this act of independence, she longed to resume a more conventional life with David. For years, she had stretched the bounds of proper middle-class behavior, living apart and placing her literary career ahead of her role as David's wife and caregiver. In 1850, the two reunited under the same roof, to care for her aging father in his home in Wayland, Massachusetts. They lived there for the next 26 years, until David's death, enjoying an intimate and stable relationship.

Through the 1850s, Child continued to write prolifically. She produced several volumes of children's verse, including her best known creation, a ditty that begins, "Over the river and through the woods/ To Grandmother's house we go." At the other end of the literary spectrum, she labored for eight years on a meticulously researched three-volume work on comparative religion, a field of investigation begun years before with Margaret Fuller. The work, which sold poorly, was a testimony to her liberal religious convictions. No religious faith, she argued, has a monopoly on God's truth; all have something to teach us. The final authority for each individual, she insisted, was "the voice of God in the silence of our souls."

Although she had withdrawn from organized abolitionism, Child continued to promote the cause in her own way. Her Wayland farmhouse became a station on the underground railroad, and she continued to write articles for anti-slavery journals. Following the political currents that were sweeping the nation towards the Civil War, she keenly resented her inability to vote. "Why should women be politically mute?" she demanded to know.

Child returned to the public spotlight in 1859, in the aftermath of John Brown's failed attempt to incite a slave rebellion in Harper's Ferry, Virginia. Brown was badly wounded in his capture and was held in a Virginia jail, awaiting trial. Child wrote to Virginia's Governor Wise, asking for permission to come to his aid. "He needs a mother or a sister to dress his wounds and speak soothingly to him. Will you allow me to perform that mission of humanity?" Wise agreed, but Brown cordially refused her offer. Child's request outraged many Southerners, and she was publicly rebuked by a letter from a Mrs. Mason, who charged her with trying to aid a bloodthirsty murderer. Child replied with a stinging attack on slavery. Brown's noble but misguided deeds meant little, she suggested, when compared to the massive inhumanity of human bondage. The exchange was widely read in 1860 and, on the eve of the Civil War, delivered a decisive propaganda victory for the cause of abolition.

Through the war, Child continued to do her part by darning socks for soldiers and raising funds to help escaped slaves resettle. She also helped *Harriet Jacobs, a young woman recently escaped from slavery, tell her life story, editing her *Incidents in the Life of a Slave Girl,* and sponsoring its publication. Looking forward to the time when slaves would be educated to become citizens, Child prepared the *Freedman's Book,* a collection of stories and poems she had written praising African-Americans and their contribution to American culture. Lacking a publisher, she raised the money for the book herself and had it distributed in the South.

Child spent her final years in relative seclusion, refusing every effort to honor her for years of selfless devotion to reform. When asked if she would cooperate in the writing of her biography, she snapped, "I detest notoriety. This mousing around after my private sentiments seems to me like surgeons politely asking me to be dissected before I am dead."

David Child died in 1874. In the last years of her life, Lydia maintained her seclusion. Her writing slowed to a trickle, as the fertile imagination that had produced more than 40 volumes and countless stories and poems at last began to slow down. She died in 1880, at the age of 78, and was buried beside her husband in Wayland. When her friends and admirers gathered to honor her at last, they looked back on a remarkable career of unswerving commitment to the principle of human equality, regardless of race, gender, or religious faith. Lydia Child had done her part to turn America's slaves into citizens. And she had spoken out against the oppression of women, adding her voice to the fledgling women's rights movement. Speaking of the vast change in the public role of women that had occurred during Child's lifetime, Wendell Phillips told the crowd gathered at her grave, "She was the kind of woman one would choose to represent woman's entrance into broader life."

SOURCES:

Baer, Helene G. *The Heart is Like Heaven: The Life of Lydia Maria Child*. Philadelphia, PA: University of Pennsylvania Press, 1964.

Clifford, Deborah Pickman. *Crusader for Freedom: A Life of Lydia Maria Child*. Boston, MA: Beacon Press, 1992.

Cowie, Alexander. *The Rise of the American Novel*. NY: American Book, 1948, pp. 177–84.

SUGGESTED READING:

Karcher, Carolyn L. *The First Woman in the Republic: A Cultural Biography of Lydia Maria Child*. NC: Duke University Press, 1994.

Ernest Freeberg,
historian, Bath, Maine

Child-Villiers, Margaret Elizabeth
(1849–1945).

See Villiers, Margaret Elizabeth Child-.

Childress, Alice (1916–1994)

African-American actress and playwright. Born Alice Herndon Childress on October 12, 1916, in Charleston, South Carolina; died on August 14, 1994, in Astoria, Queens, New York; daughter of Florence Childress; educated at Wadleigh High School, New York, and Radcliffe Institute for Independent Study (1968); married Nathan Woodard (a musician), on July 17, 1957; children: Jean R. Childress (1935–1990).

Selected works: Florence (play, 1949); Gold through the Trees (1952); Trouble in Mind (play, 1955); Like One of the Family . . . Conversations from a Domestic's Life (1956); A Hero Ain't Nothin' but a Sandwich (1973); Rainbow Jordan (1981); Gullah (play, 1984).

Eliza Campbell White, the daughter of an African slave freed under the Emancipation Proclamation, taught her granddaughter Alice Childress to approach her life as an education. Childress moved with her mother from Charleston, South Carolina, to her grandmother's home in Harlem, New York, in 1921. There, she went to public school intermittently, studied the people, and frequented the museums and libraries of New York. Childress was encouraged by her mother to make up stories about the people she watched and to study the behavior and culture of New York City's melting pot.

Both her mother and grandmother died when she was a teenager, and Childress was forced to quit Wadleigh High as a sophomore to support herself. At age 19, she gave birth to a baby daughter, Jean. With no one else to care for the child, Childress brought Jean with her to work at jobs including those of a machinist, photo retoucher, domestic, salesperson, and insurance agent.

Childress loved the theater, and made her acting debut in 1940. The following year, she joined the American Negro Theater (ANT). ANT required of members a commitment of four nights a week of work performed on a volunteer basis. Childress acted, did set construction and make-up, directed, and eventually began contributing scripts. In 1944, she received a Tony nomination for her portrayal of Blanche in *Anna Lucasta*. In 1949, her first play, *Florence*, was staged. Written literally overnight, the play was fueled by Childress' frustration at a paucity of parts for black women and became the first of her ten dramas. *Gold Through the Trees*, staged in 1952, was the first professionally produced play in New York by an African-American woman.

Childress' fiction career began with a serialized column, "Here's Mildred," in the newspapers *Freedom* and *Baltimore Afro-American*. The fictitious Mildred was a domestic in an uptown New York apartment whose relegated position of anonymity allowed her to comment on the comings and goings of the building's inhabitants. The columns were collected as Childress' first book, *Like One of the Family . . . Conversations from a Domestic's Life* (1956). She is best recognized for her adolescent fiction, *A Hero Ain't Nothin' but a Sandwich* (1973), later produced as a movie, and for *Rainbow Jordan* (1981).

In July 1957, Childress married musician Nathan Woodard. They collaborated to incorporate music in Childress' later plays, which depict life in the Gullah Islands of South Carolina. Childress and Woodard also traveled extensively, first to Cambridge, Massachusetts, where Childress was playwright-in-residence at Radcliffe's Institute for Independent Study. In 1971, she went to Russia to study the culture; in 1973, she explored the theater arts in China; and in 1974, she participated in Ghana's summer drama festival.

Childress' daughter Jean developed cancer in her 50s and Alice nursed her until Jean's death in 1990. Childress died at age 77 in 1994. She is recognized as a trailblazer for African-American women in drama, ahead of her more famous peer **Lorraine Hansberry**, for her creation of a catalog of leading characters.

SOURCES:

David, Thadious M., and Trudier Harris, eds. *Dictionary of Literary Biography, Vol. 38.* Detroit, MI: Gale Research, 1985.

Jennings, LaVinia Delois. *Alice Childress.* NY: Twayne Publishers, 1995.

Crista Martin,
Boston, Massachusetts

Chilswintha.

See Galswintha.

Chiltrud (fl. 700s)

Frankish princess. Born between 726 and 740; daughter of Charles Martel (c. 690–741), mayor of Austrasia and Neustria (r. 714–741); and *Sunnichild (d. 741); married Odilo, duke of Bavaria, in 749; children: Tassilo III, duke of Bavaria.

Chimay, Princess de (1773–1835).

See Tallien, Thérésia.

Chimnechild (r. 662–675).

See Himnechildis.

China, empress of.

See Cixi for sidebar on Lü Hou (r. 195–180 BCE).
See Wu Zetian (624–705).
See Chabi (fl. 13th c.).
See Cixi (1835–1908).

Chinchon, Ana, countess of (1576–1639)

Spanish countess who gave the world a quinine called Cinchona. Born at Astorga, Castile, in 1576; died at Cartagena, Columbia, in December 1639; daughter of the 8th marquis of Astorga; married Luis de Velasco, marquis of Salinas (died); married Luis Geronymo de Cabrera, count of Chinchon (viceroy of Peru).

Ana, countess of Chinchon, was born in Castile in 1576, the daughter of the 8th marquis of Astorga. She married Luis de Velasco, marquis of Salinas, twice viceroy of Mexico and once of Peru. After his death, she married

Alice
Childress

Luis Geronymo de Cabrera, count of Chinchon, who was appointed viceroy of Peru in 1629. During her second residence in Lima, the countess was attacked with a tertian ague (a form of fever occurring every other day) and was cured by some powdered Peruvian bark that had been sent to her physician by the *corregidor* (chief magistrate) of Loxa, Juan Lopez de Canizares. When the countess set sail for Spain, she carried a quantity of the bark with her. Though she died on the voyage at Cartegena in December 1639, it was through her cure that the medicinal cinchona bark was first introduced into Europe. In honor of her, Linnaeus named the genus of quinine-bearing plants *Cinchona*, though it should have been written *Chinchona*.

Ching Hsi Kai (fl. 1807–1810).

See Ching Shih.

Chingling Soong (1893–1981).

See Song Qingling in entry on The Song Sisters.

Ching Shih (fl. 1807–1810)

Chinese pirate who built one of the largest pirate fleets in history. Name variations: Ching Hsi Kai; Ching Yih Saou. Flourished from 1807 to 1810; married Ching Yih (d. 1807).

The famine of 1799 drove many Chinese to piracy. The early years of the 19th century saw the rise of the pirate Ching Yih, who by 1805 maintained almost complete control of the coast around Canton with a fleet of 500 to 700 junks. Ching Yih's fleet held sway over the corrupt, demoralized imperial navy, and attacks on European trading vessels took place seemingly without effort. A European hostage, John Turner, who was held for ransom by Ching Yih (1806–07), observed the fleet first-hand during his five-month imprisonment. The vessels were divided into six squadrons, each of which flew a flag of a different color as it cruised for victims along its designated stretch of the China coast. Rules of engagement were simple: if a ship surrendered without resistance, only its cargo was taken; if the crew resisted, they were fair game for torture, murder, and hostage taking. Turner witnessed scenes of atrocity—bodies cut to pieces, disembowelment, cannibalism—at the hands of Ching Yih's fleet. In 1807, Ching Yih died in a typhoon. His widow, Ching Shih, succeeded him. Whereas incidents of female captains were not uncommon, Ching Shih would prove no ordinary captain.

An exceptional leader, Ching Shih was known to possess abilities as an administrator and businesswoman that equalled her successes as pirate chief. At the height of her power, the number of those under her command reached some 70,000 to 80,000 men, women, and children upon more than 2,000 vessels, as she built a pirate fleet of unprecedented size. Of her war junks, the largest weighed almost 600 tons, mounted up to 30 guns, and carried 300–400 men. The pirates who served her were kept to a set of rules governing all aspects of pirate life. Among these rules were:

> No pirate might go ashore without permission. Punishment for a first offence was perforation of the ears; a repetition attracted the death penalty.
>
> All plundered goods must be registered before distribution. The ship responsible for the taking of a particular piece of booty received a fifth of its value, the remainder became part of the general fund.
>
> Abuse of women was forbidden, although women were taken as slaves and concubines. Those not kept for ransom were sold to the pirates as wives for $40 each.
>
> Country people were to be paid for provisions and stores taken from them.

While it appears that these rules were not always followed, Ching Shih was, at least for a time, known for her sympathy to peasants. Encouraging her fleet to prey upon Portuguese, English, and Mandarin ships, she insisted that the coastal peasants not be attacked, and molestation of peasants carried the death penalty.

Ching Shih worked in conjunction with her second in command, Chang Paou (Pao), a lieutenant of her late husband, who is said to have been her lover. She sailed in his junk, heading the Red Squadron. As the chief division of her fleet, this squadron was as large as the other five collectively. A brilliant engineer of military tactics, Ching Shih won out over the Mandarin navy in their attempts to rid the waters of the "wasps of the sea." One navy fleet sent to destroy her retreated upon first sight of Ching Shih's ships. For three masterful years, her control over the waters was so complete that she alone, for a fee, could provide a vessel safe passage.

In September 1809, Ching Shih captured Richard Glasspoole, fourth officer of the East Indian marquis of Ely. Remaining her prisoner until he was ransomed in December, he witnessed life aboard the pirate junks and noted an atmosphere of dirt, overcrowding, and boredom in which rats, considered a delicacy, were encouraged to breed. "We lived," he said, "three weeks on caterpillars boiled in rice." This landscape was replete with extreme violence. After the Chinese government attempted to starve the pirates out of commission by forbidding all ships to enter Ching Shih's waters, her previous policies of protection toward the villagers were abandoned as her pirates stormed the coastal regions, plundering. In October 1809, they torched entire settlements west of Bocca Tigris; inhabitants were kidnapped for ransom or murdered. Glasspoole's men, threatened with death, were coerced into participating in the slaughter and were provided with $20 for each head with which they returned. Apparently Glasspoole too participated in the attack, remaining on board manning one of the large guns. He noted that slung around the necks of returning pirates were pairs of heads tied together by pigtails. Ching Shih, it is said, regarded Glasspoole as a favorite and would sprinkle him with garlic water before battle as a guard against injury.

Despite all efforts by Mandarin and foreign ships to hunt her down, Ching Shih held strong. Her downfall, however, was a result of dissension among her own pirates. Kwo Po Tai, commander of the Black Squadron, was jealous of the relationship between Ching Shih and her lieutenant Chang Paou, and he refused to come to Chang Paou's assistance in battle. Chang Paou survived this betrayal to do battle with Kwo Po Tai directly. At Lantao, near the future colony of Hong Kong, the Red and Black Squadrons met in battle. Many ships were blown up, fully crewed, and Chang Paou, his decks soaked in blood, retreated.

Foreseeing that the fracture in pirate alliance would break up the fleet, Kwo Po Tai surrendered. Made a naval mandarin, he was employed to bring down the other pirates. Ching Shih's fleet had been weakened. She and Chang Paou, learning of Kwo Po Tai's pardon, likewise surrendered. Accepting an amnesty offered in 1810, they sailed toward Bocca Tigris, and the fleet was surrendered at Canton. Like his adversary, Chang Paou was appointed a naval mandarin. His men were offered a choice—return to their homes or join the imperial navy—and several thousand sailed under his command against their former partners of the Yellow and Green squadrons. Ching Shih, chief of perhaps the largest pirate fleet ever amassed, now fades from view. It is thought, however, that her abilities were turned to the smuggling trade and that she lived out her days on land in prosperity.

SOURCES:
Cordingly, David, and John Falconer. *Pirates*. London: Artabras, 1992.

Ching Yih Saou (fl. 1807–1810).
See Ching Shih.

Chionia of Thessalonica (d. 304).
See Irene, Chionia, and Agape of Thessalonica.

Chirwa, Vera (1933—)
Malawi lawyer and politician. Born in 1933; married Orton Chirwa (a lawyer and politician).

Vera Chirwa and her husband Orton, both lawyers, played prominent roles in Malawi's bid for independence from Britain in 1964, but political unrest forced them into exile shortly thereafter. In 1981, while staying in Zambia, the Chirwas were abducted by Malawi security officials, charged with treason, and sentenced to death. Malawi's courts, buckling under international outrage, commuted their sentence to life in prison. For 11 years, the Chirwas were separated and held incommunicado. Orton died in 1992. In 1993, as a result of efforts by Amnesty International, Senator Paul Simon, and then senator Al Gore, Vera Chirwa was released.

Chisholm, Caroline (1808–1877)
British-born philanthropist, known as "The Emigrant's Friend," who is famous throughout the world as a result of her selfless devotion to the welfare of Australia's early settlers. Pronunciation: CHIS-um. Born Caroline Jones on May 10, 1808, in Wootton, near Northampton, England; died in London on March 25, 1877; daughter of William (a yeoman farmer) and Sarah Jones; married Archibald Chisholm (captain in the forces of the East India Company), December 27, 1830; children: Archibald (b. 1836); William (b. 1837); Henry (b. 1839); Sydney (b. 1846); Caroline (b. 1848); Monica (b. 1851).

Traveled to India to join her husband (1832); founded The Female School of Industry for the Daughters of European Soldiers in Madras; traveled to Australia (March 1838); established the Female Immigrants Home in Sydney (1841); formed branches to settle immigrants throughout New South Wales (1842); prosecuted the captain of the ship Carthaginian (1842); gave evidence to New South Wales Legislative Council's Select Committee on Immigration (1845); sailed for England (1846); lobbied the Colonial Office on behalf of emigrants; gave evidence before House of Lords committees on the Execution of the Criminal Law and Colonization from Ireland (1847); established the Family Colonization Loan Society (1849); traveled to Melbourne, Australia (1854); established Shelter Sheds for immigrants on the routes to the Victorian goldfields (1854); fell ill with a kidney disease and moved to Sydney NSW (1857); founded her Educational Establishment for Young Ladies in Sydney (1862); returned to England (1866); bedridden until her death (1871–77).

Other than the queen of England, only one woman has ever been featured on Australia's bank notes. Such is the standing of Caroline Chisholm that, when a new plastic $5 note was issued in Australia, there was a huge public outcry that her image would no longer appear. In a time when women were strictly confined to the home and purely ornamental roles, Chisholm made a place for herself in public affairs and the early history of Australia.

She was known as "The Emigrant's Friend," and, though she never held any official positions, she was a self-appointed advocate of immigrants arriving in the then fledgling colony. Chisholm was so charismatic and of such moral and intellectual stature that she managed to break through the barriers that otherwise prevented women from influencing government and social policy. Her main concern was always the welfare of the poor and downtrodden of both the new colony and the mother country, England. She was so determined to help them that she thought nothing of transgressing gender roles of the time.

During her childhood, as a yeoman farmer's daughter in Northamptonshire, England, Chisholm's charitable instincts were grounded in the neighborliness of her parents. Her father often brought home people down on their luck. Since she grew up during the Napoleonic Wars, there were many poor widows and wounded soldiers roaming the countryside. "My first attempt at colonization was carried on in a wash hand basin, before I was seven years old," Chisholm wrote years later. "I made boats of broad beans; expended all my money in touchwood dolls; removed families, located them in the bed quilt, and sent boats filled with wheat (of which I kept a store in the thimble case) back to their friends."

Her love of humanity was so strong that she gave her best to all who asked her help no matter to what class or creed they belonged.

—Margaret Kiddle

When she was only six years old, her father died. The large number of people at his funeral praised his benevolence and readiness to support the poor and weak. In the postwar years, there was even greater poverty, and, though a widow herself, her mother often sent Caroline out with baskets of food for the old, poor, and sick of the district. Together with some cousins, young Chisholm was educated by a governess. She excelled at arithmetic, a skill much used in her later life, when she made meticulous calculations of costs for her migrant shelters, ships, and the economics of migration schemes.

An extremely intelligent young woman, she was bored by the male suitors she encountered until she met Lieutenant Archibald Chisholm, a Scot on leave from army service in India. When Archy soon asked for her hand in marriage, Caroline hesitated, concerned that her unconventional ways and strong "calling" to help the needy might hinder his career in the army. He replied, "I will help you always," and, true to his word, supported his wife throughout her life, contributing money, time, and effort. When posted abroad in army service, he agreed to live apart so that she would not have to leave her work. Archy seemed content to stand in her shadow, while working for her on the many projects she initiated.

Since Archy was a Catholic, Caroline converted to Catholicism in order to marry in his church. This was to have major implications in later years when her work was often challenged by Protestant fanatics. When she cared for and promoted immigration for the Irish who were among the poorest of the poor, especially at the time of the famine, they accused her of being a tool of the papists. Caroline Chisholm, however, served all comers with equal zeal no matter what their religious persuasions and won many accolades for her lack of a partisan approach in a time when this was extremely rare.

Following their marriage, the couple lived in Brighton for two years; then Archy was called back to service in India. She followed him there after a few months and lived in Madras for over six years. The role of an officer's wife was one of superficial socializing, but Chisholm soon found a more worthwhile occupation. Having noticed that the children of the common soldier, especially the young girls, lived neglected and aimless lives with the prospect of early degradation all too prevalent, she decided to open a school for them. At first, she requested and was given use of a room in the barracks within the fort. When this proved impractical, she persuaded the newly promoted Captain Archibald Chisholm to move out of the privileged environment of the fort and into a poor area where she secured use of a large building on the waterfront. Impressed by her sincerity and skill, officers contributed financial support for her Female School of Industry for the Daughters of European Soldiers. Caroline Chisholm was no naive bleeding heart. Her endeavors were characterized by a shrewd assessment of human nature and strict rules, coupled with kindness and attention to the needs of her charges. The girls were trained in the three Rs, as well as domestic management.

Chisholm gave birth to two sons during her time in India. At the end of seven years service, Captain Chisholm was again due for extended leave, and they decided to explore Australia, or New Holland as it was known then, hoping it might offer a better future for their sons than

Caroline
Chisholm

Britain. The school that Caroline had set up continued after her departure.

By the end of the Napoleonic Wars in Europe, free immigration slowly began to transform Australia from a reputedly desolate penal colony to a thriving, prospering, proud member of the British Empire. Sydney stretched at its seams, bustling with activity and opportunity. Initially, all immigration had been unassisted, but in 1831 the Home government had instituted a system of assisted immigration. This new step was taken because the majority of the free immigrants had been single men, and since the transported convicts were predominantly male as well, a poor male-female ratio existed in the colony. The disparity between the sexes was, according to some, "causing grave moral evils," and assisted immigration, it was hoped, would provide a balance between the sexes and encourage civilized conduct in this less than civilized outpost of the Empire. The British government, however, emptied the slums, tenements, orphanages and asylums of England, and by 1835 this system was suffering severe criticism. A program of bounties was instituted, by which agents of Australian settlers in England would offer bounties to qualified immigrants. Gradually, bounties were handed out by shipping companies and shipowners. These shipowners were granted bounty permits in

their name, with no mention of specific immigrants, by the governor of Australia. Spotting an opportunity for immense profit, shipowners packed as many immigrants as possible on their ships, without regard for their suitability or comfort. Regardless of the obvious corruption of this system, the settlers were contented with these new immigrants.

One of the main flaws associated with assisted immigration and the bounties was the lack of provision for immigrants after disembarkation. Whereas in 1838, when Chisholm arrived in Australia, less than 7,000 immigrants entered the country, by 1841, a surge in immigration swelled the number of newcomers to over 20,000. Even in the best of times, such a number would have overwhelmed the system. In the depressionary times of the early 1840s, the effects were disastrous. Immigrants—largely taken from large urban centers in England, Scotland, and Ireland—preferred starvation in Sydney to an uncertain future in the bush. Although a demand existed in the interior for labor, these immigrants were unwilling, without assistance, to venture far from Sydney's familiar trappings.

Within a few days of arriving in Australia, the Chisholms took a house outside Sydney on the Hawkesbury River where they settled down happily in an idyllic rural environment. During visits to the city, Caroline was soon aware of the plight of the poor immigrants, many of whom were unable to find work on their arrival. Young female immigrants, homeless and friendless, became easy prey for those men prone to ruthlessness. The assumption at the time was that the women were naturally immoral. Chisholm, who could see that they were victims who had been heartlessly treated, began to shelter the girls in her own home while training them for a new start. She also used her connections to find them jobs.

Early in 1840, Archy left to return to his post in India. Shortly after, Caroline visited those camped near the disused government Immigration Barracks and witnessed a married "gentleman" seducing a homeless waif. There and then, she resolved to devote "all my leisure time in endeavouring to serve these poor girls, and felt determined, with God's blessing, never to rest until decent protection was afforded them." She worked to secure an interview with Sir George Gipps, the governor of the colony, requesting access to the Immigration Barracks. Gipps, shocked at her temerity, refused. Undaunted, Chisholm collected detailed information and became an expert on the employment needs of the colony and situation of immigrants. In 1842, she authored *Female Immigration Considered in a Brief Account of the Sydney Immigrants Home,* the first book published in Australia by a woman. Because her work received a great deal of publicity, Gipps finally had to give in; she soon had the barracks furnished and was sheltering her flock.

Intent on providing comfort and protection in the short term and gainful employment in the long, Chisholm boarded arriving ships to collect girls before the madams and hucksters wooed them away. Also, possibly protected by her fame as a selfless benefactor, she often walked into the rough Rocks area where no unaccompanied woman other than herself dared go. "She cast aside all fear and even ventured there at night," wrote biographer **Mary Hoban**. "She was a well-known figure now in all parts of Sydney, and if a girl wanted protection, she had only to join the black-clad lady and walk away with her."

Chisholm periodically led parties of female immigrants on expeditions into the bush. She not only escorted them but stilled their fears of the wilderness and rode ahead to secure a camp or lodging for the night. On the journey, she would approach settlers for offers of safe employment and would invariably find positions

for her charges. The settlers were grateful for her efforts in supplying much needed helpers. Often men in need of work, and their families, joined her parties. Because of Chisholm's reputation and moral authority, employers tended to trust the women she recommended, while the women tried to live up to Chisholm's expectations. Many would invoke her name as protection from exploitation. In the relatively lawless and rough interior, "I'll tell Mrs. Chisholm" served as a shield.

Over the years, she made many expeditions into the bush and established regional Female Immigrant Homes. Wherever she went people offered her free accommodation, often supplying her entire expedition with food and horses. When traveling by ship along the coast (a common mode of conveyance in the days before made roads), she was given free passage for herself and her charges. In one famous incident, Chisholm tackled the appalling conditions on the emigrant transport ships. After hearing of a particularly shocking incident on the *Carthaginian*, she sued the captain. Though it was unheard of for a woman to take a captain to court, she won the case, causing other captains to improve conditions.

Eventually, a financial depression and inflated land prices slowed the arrival of new immigrants. Chisholm closed down her Female Immigrant's Home and returned to her house on the Hawkesbury. Those who needed her still came to ask for help, and many of her female immigrants came to introduce their new husbands. They usually brought a piece of their wedding cake—hence the subtitle of one of her biographies, *Fifty-One Pieces of Wedding Cake.* But Chisholm continued to agitate on the subject of immigration and employment in the colony. She wrote articles, letters, and pamphlets to espouse her ideas, which were often ignored or opposed. Determined, she took her concerns to higher powers. When she audaciously wrote to Lord Stanley, the English colonial secretary, she began by saying: "The novelty of receiving a letter from a lady, regarding Immigration to this colony, will, I feel assured, ensure my letter a reading. . . . It is perhaps as well I tell you at the commencement that I am neither a visionary or an enthusiast, I am a practical worker of my own plans." Though she was an enthusiast who envisaged many novel plans, her practicality and the extensive research and factual knowledge with which she backed her ideas won respect. She was heard in forums where women had not before appeared. Over the years, she was called to give evidence to a number of government enquiries both in Australia and England.

Caroline Chisholm was deeply religious and had a strong commitment to women's traditional roles, despite her own activities, which were nonetheless an expression of woman's role as nurturer. She just extended her concept of family to everyone who needed her. Her work for Australia was based on creating and reuniting families and settling them on land of their own. The wisdom of some of her policies have been questioned because small holdings are not viable on the arid soils of Australia. Though she may have made mistakes, she never stinted in her efforts for the lower classes and was often the lone voice representing them in government and society.

She campaigned to find ways to transport family members to Australia that had been left behind by the emancipists (released convicts) and emigrants who could not afford ship's passage for all their children. The better to pursue this task, she decided to go to England and encourage the poor there to migrate to the "lucky country" where their standard of living could be greatly improved. Before she left, she conducted a detailed survey of successful small farm settlers in New South Wales.

In 1845, Captain Chisholm retired from the army and returned to Australia. The following April, determined to take her fight directly to the British, Caroline and her family sailed for England armed with a bundle of Voluntary Statements and countless letters and small amounts of money for relatives throughout the British Isles. During her six years in Australia, Caroline Chisholm had settled 11,000 people. Amazingly, to all of these, she gave some degree of personal attention.

As soon as she arrived in England, she found her fame preceded her. People gathered to see her, while letters arrived sometimes addressed only to "Mrs. Chisholm, The Emigrant's Friend, London." Determined to set up a system for national emigration to Australia, she approached the Colonial Office, and, though she had, as the *Illustrated London News* reported in 1877, "neither rank nor influence and an income scarcely amounting to a competency," she was heard. Chisholm persuaded them to send a shipload of children to Australia, to be reunited with their parents.

All the same, her wider ambitions were often blocked by the slow wheels of bureaucracy and the interests of the Australian squatters who were the upper class of the new colony and wanted to maintain a monopoly on land. They had far more influence in the halls of British Parliament than she did. Resolved to provide a means of escape for the paupers suffering in the newly industrialized wastelands of England, she decided to set up her own emigration system. Traveling the length and breadth of England, she visited relatives of those she'd helped in New South Wales (NSW) and expounded on the virtues of emigrating to Australia. In 1849, she raised the initial capital to establish the Family Colonization Loan Society, which loaned money to families to be repaid after their successful settlement in Australia.

To ensure safe conditions, she personally oversaw the outfitting of ships for her emigrants. One benefactor built a ship for the Society, which was christened the *Caroline Chisholm*. Her energy and capacity for work was enormous. From 1846 to 1847, she processed 4,071 applications for emigration, and her house was constantly crowded with inquirers. Each day, she looked at an average of 140 letters, saw 30 to 40 hopefuls in the morning, went to the docks and gave directions for the fitting of her ships, went to town to transact business, and in the evening saw another 40 to 60 candidates. After 9:30 PM, she went to visit female immigrants boarded near her house to see them settled for the night. In between, she found time for her family. By the early 1850s, Caroline Chisholm was one of the most famous women in Britain.

In 1854, with the advent of the Crimean War, ships became scarce, and Chisholm decided to return to New South Wales. On arrival, she faced a new problem. With the discovery of gold near Melbourne, vast tracts of land were deemed off-limits by the local government. Her call for opening of the land, and the sale of tracts of land at an affordable price, initially fell on deaf ears. She set off to the goldfields to survey conditions and initiate the establishment of cheap hostels called Shelter Sheds on the roads. But the pace of Caroline Chisholm's efforts eventually caught up with her. In 1857, she fell ill with a kidney disease, was forced to leave this fight half-fought, and moved to Sydney for medical treatment. Though she continued some level of agitation for her concerns, she began to fade from view. Her work, for which she had always refused any government pay lest it compromise her, had impoverished the Chisholms, even though a number of testimonial sums were given her by the public. Archibald Chisholm's pension from the Honorable East India Company had all but dried up. In an effort to address her family's economic hardship, she opened an Educational Establishment For Young Ladies at Rathbone House, Newtown, Sydney, in 1862, which subsequently closed in 1864. Too ill to work, she asked a priest for a loan.

Then, in 1866, she and Archy returned to England so that one of their daughters might complete schooling. In 1871, until her death, Chisholm became bedridden. Though granted a government pension of £100 per annum, the family could only afford a dingy apartment, where Caroline spent her last years in pain and poverty until she died in her sleep on March 25, 1877, aged 69. Though somewhat neglected in her dying years, her fame as a great benefactor has lived on. Caroline Chisholm changed the course of Australia's history and helped ensure its future prosperity by successfully settling so many willing workers.

SOURCES:

Hoban, Mary C. *Fifty-One Pieces of Wedding Cake: A Biography of Caroline Chisholm*. Lowden, 1973.

Kiddle, Margaret. *Caroline Chisholm*. Melbourne: Melbourne University Press, 1957.

COLLECTIONS:

Kyneton Historical Society, Kyneton, Victoria, Australia; Latrobe Collection, State Library of Victoria, Australia; Mitchell Library, Sydney, New South Wales, Australia; National Library of Australia, Canberra; Northamptonshire Record Society, England; Royal Historical Society of Victoria, Australia.

Chris Sitka, freelance writer and researcher, Sydney, Australia

Chisholm, Shirley (1924—)

First African-American woman elected to U.S. House of Representatives (1968) and first African-American woman candidate for the presidency of the U.S. (1972). Pronunciation: CHIZ-um. Born Shirley Anita St. Hill on November 30, 1924, in the Bedford-Stuyvesant section of Brooklyn, New York; daughter of Charles Christopher St. Hill (an unskilled laborer in a burlap-bag factory) and Ruby (Seale) St. Hill (a seamstress and domestic born in Barbados); attended elementary school in Barbados, completed in Brooklyn; graduated from Girls' High School in Brooklyn (1942); Brooklyn College, B.A. cum laude in sociology (1946); Columbia University, M.A. in education (1953); married Conrad Chisholm, on October 8, 1949 (divorced, February 1977); married Arthur Hardwick, Jr., on November 26, 1977; no children.

From age 3 to 11, spent the years in Barbados with maternal grandmother (1927–35); returned to Brooklyn and completed elementary and high school;

worked in various child-care centers and completed M.A. in education; became director of the large Hamilton-Madison Child Care Center in Lower Manhattan (1953–59); began work for the New York City Division of Day Care, and gained recognition as a child-care expert (1959); was active in Democratic Party politics (1950–80), founding, with others, the reform-oriented Unity Democratic Club in Brooklyn (early 1960s); elected to New York State Assembly (1964); elected to U.S. House of Representatives (1968) and served seven terms (retiring in 1982); in Congress, concentrated on issues related to jobs, housing, education and welfare; ran for the Democratic nomination for president of the U.S. (1972); taught courses on politics, race, and women at Mt. Holyoke College in Massachusetts; lecturer and author (since 1982).

Selected publications: Unbought and Unbossed *(Houghton Mifflin, 1970);* The Good Fight *(Harper and Row, 1973).*

On Wednesday night, July 12, 1972, at the Democratic National Convention, Percy Sutton, black president of the borough of Manhattan in New York City, moved to place in nomination the name of Shirley Chisholm for the top office in the land; the motion was seconded by Charles Evers, the black mayor of Fayette, Mississippi. Thus, Shirley Chisholm became the first African-American female nominated for president of the United States, paving the way for the later nominations of both minority and female candidates for national office.

Her presidential campaign capped her efforts in early childhood education and politics, in which she served as an outspoken champion of the rights of the disadvantaged—including the poor, women, and minorities. During the 1950s, '60s and '70s, her career played out against the turbulent backdrop of changing demands and roles of both women and minorities in American society.

Shirley Chisholm was a native of the district she would later represent in the U.S. Congress, the Bedford-Stuyvesant section of Brooklyn, New York. She was born Shirley St. Hill on November 30, 1924, to Charles St. Hill and **Ruby St. Hill**, both impoverished immigrants. Her father came from Guyana and worked as a laborer in a burlap-bag factory, while her mother, a native of Barbados, was employed as a seamstress and domestic worker.

In an effort to educate each of their children, the St. Hills sent three-year-old Shirley and two other daughters to live with their maternal

$\mathcal{S}$hirley
$\mathcal{C}$hisholm

grandmother in Barbados. "What an important gift my parents had given me by seeing to it that I had my earliest education in the strict, traditional, British-style schools of Barbados," noted Chisholm. "If I speak and write easily now, that early education is the main reason." While the move was intended to be temporary, Shirley was eleven before the family was reunited in Brooklyn. Thus, her grandmother, a "very stern and determined person who constantly preached from morning to night the virtues of pride, courage and faith," had a major impact on her childhood.

Readjusting to the American school system proved challenging. As a junior-high student, Shirley had to master U.S. history and geography, which she had not studied in Barbados' schools. Frustrated, she became a discipline problem, but the rebellion was short lived. With the help of a tutor, she not only caught up but surpassed her natural grade level. She also got along well with her classmates, most of whom were white.

But when the family moved to a larger apartment—in a neighborhood that was more racially mixed—Shirley encountered her first racial slurs. While attending Girls' High School in Brooklyn, she managed to sidestep the many racial incidents she observed, experiencing, instead, discrimination because of gender. Despite the fact that most of the information doled out in history classes centered around white males, Chisholm's historical heroes were *Harriet Tubman, a slave who became a famous "conductor" on the Underground Railroad, and *Susan B. Anthony, a white woman who fought against slavery.

Chisholm's mother, who worked as a maid to a white family, left Shirley in charge of her three younger sisters, a position that she took seriously, causing tension between Shirley and her sisters. It would later contribute to her awareness for the need for day care. Meanwhile, her father was actively involved in the labor movement, and much of the family kitchen-table talk revolved around unions. His awareness of racial issues also had a profound effect. Charles St. Hill, wrote Chisholm, was "a very proud black man, who instilled pride in his children, a pride in ourselves and our race" that was not then fashionable. He was a great admirer of Marcus Garvey, who would influence many black separatists. Garvey argued that blacks would never achieve full equality in white societies.

In 1942, Chisholm graduated with honors from Girls' High School in Brooklyn. While she received scholarship offers from many prestigious private colleges, her parents argued that, for financial reasons, she should attend a college nearer to home, so she entered Brooklyn College and majored in sociology. There, her political interests began to slowly surface. She received much encouragement, especially from a blind political science professor, Louis Warsoff, and tentatively joined the college chapter of the National Association for the Advancement of Colored People (NAACP). Through community involvement with hospitals, the

Urban League, and other service organizations, she began to feel how "useless it was for blacks to sit and talk with the leading 'people' in the community."

During her senior year, Chisholm became involved in Democratic Party politics but was soon disillusioned. "Political organizations are formed to keep the powerful in power," she wrote. "Their first rule is 'Don't rock the boat.'" She was soon convinced that blacks—or others interested in major change—would need to develop their own organizations. She joined forces with Mac Holder, who formed the Bedford-Stuyvesant Political League, a splinter group, to elect an outstanding black lawyer, Lewis S. Flagg, to a judgeship. Chisholm would remain active in the league until 1958.

Though Chisholm graduated from Brooklyn College cum laude in 1946, she had great difficulty finding a teaching job. The experience only served to intensify her feelings regarding discrimination against both blacks and women. She went to work at Mt. Calvary Child Care Center in Harlem and enrolled in classes at Columbia University, where she received a master's degree in education in 1953. That year, she was appointed director of a private nursery school in Brooklyn. Six years later, she went to work for the New York City Division of Day Care, clearly having established herself as a leading advocate for children and poor women, as well as an expert on early childhood education. Chisholm also continued to be active in the Democratic reform movement in Bedford-Stuyvesant.

While studying at Columbia, she had met Conrad Chisholm, a detective with a private security company. They married in 1949, when she was 25, and moved into a house in Brooklyn. They were unable to have children. "Probably few men could have stayed happily married to me for more than twenty years," recalled Chisholm. "I don't think Conrad has ever had a moment of insecurity or jealousy over the fact that I have always been a public figure."

In the early 1960s, spurred on by the Civil Rights Movement, many African-Americans became more politically active. Shirley Chisholm was drawn back into Democratic politics in Brooklyn and formed, with about six others, a new organization named the Unity Democratic Club. Their goal was to take over the 17th (state) Assembly District and remove the failing, but still potent, white machine that had dominated the party, even as the area itself became increasingly populated by minorities. Similar political rebellions were occurring in many districts of New York City in 1960. By 1962, Chisholm's group controlled the Democratic Party in her district.

In 1964, asked to run by those in her district, Chisholm was elected to the New York State Assembly, largely because of the Unity Democratic Club's organization and her own strong campaign arguments on behalf of women, blacks, and hispanics. During her tenure, she adopted the legislative style that would guide her later in the U.S. Congress. As a woman and a minority member, she was well aware that most legislative weapons (the rules and a fraternal power structure) were not available to her. She would have to adopt strong stances on issues and confront the leaders of the assembly and important committees directly if she wanted to make a difference. "There is little place in the political scheme of things for an independent, creative personality, for a fighter," she wrote. "Anyone who takes that role must pay a price." Nevertheless, "Being a maverick," she wrote, "hasn't kept me from being an effective legislator." Chisholm believed that her colleagues supported her on issues, because they felt there was "no personal vindictiveness" in her rebellions, that she was fighting for things she believed in. "They respect me as a person even when I horrify them as a politician."

In the assembly, she promoted day-care services and civil-rights training for law-enforcement personnel, along with many programs for the urban poor. She successfully sponsored SEEK, a plan that enabled minority students lacking necessary academic requirements to enter state universities with remedial help. Chisholm, who had to run twice because of changing district boundaries, won reelection in 1965 and 1966 and enhanced her political reputation in her district. Her vote-getting strength was soon a given.

In 1968, a new Congressional district, which included Bedford-Stuyvesant, was created by court-ordered reapportionment. Shirley Chisholm, the first candidate to file for the Democratic nomination for U.S. Representative, was opposed in the primary of June 1968 by two other black candidates. With the slogan "unbought and unbossed," she succeeded in beating out party regulars with support from women, some of whom conducted a door-to-door campaign on her behalf. Some observers also give credit for her narrow primary victory (799 votes) to her ability to speak to Puerto Rican audiences in Spanish.

In the 1968 general election for the U.S. House of Representatives seat, Chisholm was opposed by James Farmer, the former director of the Congress of Racial Equality (CORE) and a civil-rights leader of national reputation. Chisholm asserted throughout the campaign that she would win because she knew her constituents and their needs better than Farmer, a resident of Manhattan. Despite the fact that both candidates campaigned strongly on basic issues, such as local control of schools, opposition to the Vietnam War, employment, and housing, Chisholm defeated Farmer that November by a margin of 2.5 votes to 1. Asked to comment on her election as the first black woman in Congress, she replied, "It's sad, really; it should have happened years ago." Only nine blacks were sent to Congress in 1968.

Shirley Chisholm announced that she did not intend to be "a quiet freshman Congressman," and she was not. In a rousing first speech on the House floor, delivered March 26, 1969, she declared that she would vote against any defense spending bill, "until the time comes when our values and priorities have been turned right-side up again." She fought against the leaders of her own party to obtain committee assignments that would let her work on the domestic policy proposals she considered vital. By the end of her first term, she had succeeded in being appointed to the House Education and Labor Committee.

During her early years in the House, Chisholm received some 3,000 invitations to speak, becoming a celebrated advocate of women, minorities, and domestic priorities. She was amazed, however, that she often encountered "harsher criticism" in fighting for the rights of women than in fighting for civil rights for blacks. In the early 1970s, the women's movement gained national attention. Women began to demand and demonstrate for equal rights, just as blacks had done during the 1960s. This prompted some to ask, "Why not a woman president?" Women's groups, black women, even college students, who were unusually active politically during this era, began to urge Chisholm to run for president. Almost every politician, however, black or white, urged her to refrain.

On January 25, 1972, Shirley Chisholm announced her candidacy:

> I stand before you today as a candidate for the Democratic nomination for the presi-

dency of the United States. I am not the candidate of black America, although I am black and proud. I am not the candidate for the women's movement of this country, although I am a woman, and I am equally proud of that. I am not the candidate of any political bosses or special interests. . . . I am the candidate of the People.

Chisholm thus became the first black woman, and only the second woman, to seek the presidency (the first was *Victoria Woodhull).

The campaign suffered from internal conflicts and a lack of a strong national organization. With limited financial backing, Chisholm had to devote hours to fund-raising. Women's groups supporting her claimed that blacks were trying to take over the campaign, while blacks complained that women were doing the same. Women portrayed Chisholm as a women's candidate, while blacks presented her as a black candidate. In her first primary, in Florida, she won only 4% of the vote. What political scientists **Sandra Baxter** and **Marjorie Lansing** have called the "double whammy," the combined effect of being black and female, seemed overwhelming to the Chisholm candidacy.

The mere fact that a black woman dared to run for President, *seriously,* not expecting to win, but sincerely trying to, is what it was all about. "It can be done"; that was what I was trying to say, by doing it.

—Shirley Chisholm

Still, she pressed on. Charged with lack of experience and lack of a clear platform, Chisholm responded that she was forced to discuss herself often in the campaign, rather than issues, because she was continually being bombarded with questions regarding her qualifications to serve as president. She urged blacks to vote for her in the primaries in order to strengthen their position within the Democratic Party and their bargaining power at the national convention. Her actual percentage of primary votes received, in the ten primaries she entered, averaged about 3%.

At the national convention, during the roll-call vote on the presidential nomination, Chisholm received 151.25 votes. Much of her support came from southern black delegates, who had hoped for a show of unity behind the Chisholm candidacy. Black unity, however, never evolved at the convention, partially because Chisholm was not endorsed by key black political groups such as the Black Congressional Cau-

cus. Similarly, women delegates split their votes among many candidates. "Even more than the blacks, I think, [women] showed the effects of their past exclusion from the political process," wrote Chisholm, "and unlike blacks, they found it hard to believe that they had a great deal to learn." In reflecting on her presidential campaign in her autobiography *The Good Fight,* Chisholm expressed disappointment that more of her issue positions were not adopted by the 1972 Democratic Convention. She also expressed pride in how much was accomplished:

with next to no money, with a haphazard, volunteer organization, and with no planning worthy of the name. The only way I can explain it is that there must have been a lot of people who were fed up with traditional candidates and campaigns, and eager to throw themselves into an effort to change the way things are done, and open up national politics to full participation by women, minorities and other excluded groups.

Chisholm returned to the Congress after her presidential campaign, serving in the House of Representatives until 1982. She continued to fight for changes in economic and social policy that she felt essential to the advancement of minorities and the poor. In addition, she staunchly supported the "women's agenda" of the 1970s, including fair-credit laws, child-care legislation, and abortion rights. In the early 1980s, she began teaching at Mt. Holyoke College and continued to speak out on the issues:

What I hope most is that now there will be others who will feel themselves as capable of running for high political office as any wealthy, good-looking white male. Their way will still be hard, but it is essential that they travel it. We Americans have a chance to become someday a nation in which all racial stocks and classes can exist in their own selfhoods, but meet on a basis of respect and equality and live together, socially, economically, and politically. It can still happen. I hope I did a little to make it happen.

SOURCES:

Baxter, Sandra, and Marjorie Lansing. *Women and Politics.* Ann Arbor: University of Michigan Press, 1980.

Chisholm, Shirley. *The Good Fight.* NY: Harper and Row, 1973.

———. *Unbought and Unbossed.* Boston, MA: Houghton Mifflin, 1970.

Haskins, Jim. *One More River to Cross: The Stories of Twelve Black Americans.* NY: Scholastic, 1992.

SUGGESTED READING:

LeVeness, Frank P., and Jane P. Sweeney, eds. *Women Leaders in Contemporary U.S. Politics.* Boulder, CO: Lynne Rienner, 1987.

Jacqueline DeLaat,
Associate Professor of Political Science,
Marietta College, Marietta, Ohio

Ch'iu Chin (c. 1875–1907).
See Qiu Jin.

Chiyo, Uno (b. 1897).
See Uno Chiyo.

Chizhova, Nadezhda (1945—)

Russian shot putter. Name variations: Nadyezhda. Born on September 29, 1945, in the Soviet Union.

Nadyezhda Chizhova won the Olympic bronze medal for the shot put in Mexico City in 1968. In the Munich games in 1972, she took the gold in the shot put. Four years later, in Montreal, she completed her necklace set in the same event, capturing a silver (1976).

Chlothilde.
See Clotilda.

Chodziesner, Gertrud (1894–1943).
See Kolmar, Gertrud.

Chojnowska-Liskiewicz, Krystyna (1937—)

Polish yachtswoman who in 1978 became the first woman to sail solo around the world. Born in Warsaw, Poland, in 1937; educated as a shipbuilding engineer; married.

Arrived in the harbor of Las Palmas, the Canary Islands (April 21, 1978), where her epic voyage of over 28,500 miles had begun more than two years earlier.

The first woman to sail solo around the world came from a country better known for its music, theater, and tragic history than for significant maritime achievements. Educated as a shipbuilding engineer, Krystyna Chojnowska-Liskiewicz first experienced the sea more from a technological perspective than from a perspective of courage or endurance. She began sailing while in school and in 1966 received a captain's certificate. In March 1976, she set sail from the harbor of Las Palmas, the Canary Islands, in her 32-foot yacht *Mazurek*. Her entire voyage, which covered more than 28,500 miles, saw her crossing the Atlantic, going through the Panama Canal, then crossing the Pacific to Australia.

A serious kidney ailment forced Chojnowska-Liskiewicz into hospital in Australia. After several weeks' hospitalization, she resumed her voyage, crossing the Indian Ocean. She arrived in Cape Town, South Africa, in early 1978, re-provisioned her supplies and checked out her vessel, before leaving on the final leg of her voyage on February 5. Fierce storms in the South Atlantic gave rise to fears that she was lost, and she was unable to establish radio contact with a Polish Antarctic station in early March. Sailing conditions improved considerably over the next few weeks, and in mid-April she was able to assure an anxious world (and her husband) that she was well and looking forward to the final stage of her voyage. Sounding relieved that her long adventure was about to come to an end, she described the final leg of the journey as being "like a stroll." The courageous voyager frankly admitted over her radio to the Polish press agency PAP: "I think I can do without sailing for some time now."

In addition to the dangers of her trip, Krystyna Chojnowska-Liskiewicz also found herself in a competitive situation, because a similar feat was being attempted at almost exactly the same time by *Naomi James of the U.K. as well as by France's **Brigitte Oudry**. The last weeks of her trip were uneventful, and Krystyna Chojnowska-Liskiewicz, the first woman to sail solo around the world, arrived safely at the harbor of Las Palmas on April 21, 1978. "There were times when I thought I would never manage it," she remarked, "but now it is all over." A decade later, Australia's *Kay Cottee would also sail around the world, doing so not only solo but also nonstop. But it was Krystyna Chojnowska-Liskiewicz who had broken a major barrier, proving that women on the high seas could muster every bit as much courage and resourcefulness as men.

SOURCES:
"Polish woman sails round the world single handed," in *The Times* [London]. March 22, 1978, p. 9.
"Round-world sail," in *The Times* [London]. April 22, 1978, p. 4.

John Haag, Associate Professor, University of Georgia, Athens, Georgia

Cholmondeley, Elizabeth or Anne (1866–1941).
See Arnim, Elizabeth von.

Choms, Wladyslawa Laryssa (1891–1966)

Polish rescuer who saved the lives of many hundreds of Jews and became known as the "Angel of Lvov" during the Holocaust. Name variations: Angel of Lvov. Born in Poland in 1891; died in 1966; lived before World War II in Drohobycz (Drogobych), Eastern Galicia; married Friedrich Choms; children: one son.

Before World War II, Wladyslawa Choms lived in Drohobycz, a town in a section of Poland that was populated by a mixture of Ukrainians, Poles and Jews. In an atmosphere where ethnic tensions and rivalries were often passionate and disruptive, traditional hatreds and prejudices held no appeal for Choms. In 1927, she was elected head of the municipal social welfare council and became intimately acquainted with the problems of poverty in her town. Contrary to the prevailing prejudices of Poles and Ukrainians, many of the Jews of Drohobycz were not wealthy capitalists; in fact, they were terribly poor. As time went by, Choms became increasingly sympathetic to the economic plight of Jews as well as to their political aspirations. She sympathized with the Zionist students who were often attacked by Ukrainian and Polish anti-Semitic student fraternities armed with clubs, brass knuckles, and sticks sporting razor blades. Although she was Polish and Roman Catholic, many Poles in Drohobycz, particularly those in the violently anti-Semitic National Democratic Party ("Endeks"), regarded her as a traitor and as "the Jews' mother."

Choms' attitudes placed her squarely at odds with the great majority of her fellow Poles, but she had a few friends who quietly supported her beliefs. The likemindedness of her husband Friedrich, a major in the Polish Army, was to be crucial to her later activities. Perhaps even more than his wife, Friedrich Choms felt out of place among his peers, as the spirit of the Polish military in the 1920s and 1930s was, with few exceptions, highly anti-Semitic and intolerantly nationalistic. Unable to abide by the oppressive atmosphere promoted by his fellow officers, Friedrich resigned from the military, a difficult decision in the middle of an economic depression. In 1934, Wladyslawa and her husband visited Palestine and were greatly impressed by the achievements of Zionist pioneers, many of whom had migrated from Poland to build a Jewish state. On their return to Poland, the Choms family, including their small son, settled in the city of Lvov (Lviv; Lemberg), which was similar to Drohobycz in its ethnically mixed population of Poles, Jews and Ukrainians.

With the start of World War II, the Nazi German attack on Poland in September 1939 resulted in the occupation and partitioning of the country. The western and central sections were either annexed to Germany or turned into a colony named the Generalgouvernement. Both Poles and Jews were harshly treated from the outset of the occupation, but the conditions the Jews endured were usually dramatically worse and included the creation of ghetto districts in the major towns and cities. From late September 1939 to late June 1941, Lvov was part of a region newly annexed to the Soviet Union as part of the Ukrainian Soviet Socialist Republic. Though conditions here were not easy, Jews did not need to fear because of their religion, since Stalin's goal was the consolidation of his power rather than a complete social transformation. Under these fluid conditions, Wladyslawa Choms could continue her work of amelioration among the Jewish community. The defeat of Poland had radically altered her family life, with both her husband and son fleeing the country to fight the Nazis. Not until after the war would she learn that her husband had survived as a prisoner of war in Germany. Her son escaped to England, but like many other young Polish aviators he lost his life in combat as a pilot in the Royal Air Force in 1941.

The Nazi occupation of Lvov, which began on June 30, 1941, was a tragedy for virtually all of that city's inhabitants but particularly for its Jews. At first, thousands of Jews were massacred in a bloody pogrom carried out by gangs of Ukrainians; soon, however, the terror became systematized, bureaucratic violence carried out by German occupation forces determined to exterminate Jews, Bolshevik sympathizers, and any form of Polish resistance. Under this regime of mass murder, Wladyslawa Choms was both defiant and practical in her resistance. She collected money and jewelry from wealthy Jews, using these resources to create a permanent fund for extending aid to endangered Jewish families and individuals. Building on the friendships and alliances she had nurtured in Lvov over the years, she created a tight circle of Polish women and men who daily risked their lives working together to outwit the Nazi occupiers and save as many Jewish lives as possible.

After the Nazis built a ghetto for Lvov's Jewish population, it became even more difficult for Choms and her circle to assist the increasingly threatened Jews. Bold efforts, nonetheless, continued. Under her leadership, the group smuggled food to those in need, provided them with medical care, and arranged for the procurement of false identity papers and the subsequent movement of Jews from the ghetto to safer locations within the city. On many occasions, entire families were moved, sometimes to areas as far away as Warsaw.

In the spring of 1943, a branch of the national organization Council for Aid to the Jews (Zegota) was created in Lvov with Choms elected chair. As a member of the Democratic Party, she enjoyed the confidence of the various factions within the underground movement—groups, which were often suspicious of each other's motives—and none doubted her sincerity or courage. Within the complex and dangerous efforts to aid Jews, her word was law. Choms' intimate knowledge of Lvov and her superb instincts for conspiratorial work enabled Zegota activities on behalf of the city's Jews to flourish despite German and Ukrainian nationalists who spent almost every waking hour in a search for Jewish men, women and children. As the Germans deported more and more Jews to death camps and the overall situation grew increasingly desperate, Choms and her group responded with every means at their disposal to rescue Jews, particularly children. Jewish infants were given for safekeeping to 60 trusted Polish families, who had volunteered for a task that if discovered could bring the death penalty.

Always aware of the enormous danger her work entailed, Choms periodically changed her name and address, but this did not prevent close calls. With each scrape with disaster, both her immediate collaborators and superiors in the Zegota organization in Warsaw feared she would soon fall prey to the Germans. While masterminding her large and complex assistance network, Choms also personally saved the lives of **Klara Chotiner-Lustig** and her small child, who appeared on her doorstep, hungry, frightened and exhausted. Choms took them into her own apartment until Klara had regained some strength, then found a safe place for the two at a neighbor's home. Soon forged papers made it possible for mother and child to receive legal food rations. A grateful Klara Chotiner-Lustig then became a member of the Choms group, joining them in the preparation of forged identity documents for other endangered Jews.

Long before the Polish underground central command ordered Choms to leave Lvov in November 1943 for Warsaw, the Jews of that city had come to know her as the "angel of Lvov." Her countless interventions, each of which could have cost her and her co-workers their lives, had resulted in the saving of many hundreds of Jews. In Warsaw, Choms continued her resistance activities and survived the bloodbath of the 1944 uprising that essentially leveled a once beautiful city. After the war, Choms began the painful work of restoring her own life. She left Poland to search for her husband, whom she found in occupied Germany where he had survived Nazism after years as a slave laborer. News of her beloved son's death was a profound blow. In the 1940s, many of her Jewish friends left Poland for Israel, a move Wladyslawa and Friedrich considered before deciding to remain in Europe, at least in part because of Friedrich's fragile health. After his death in France in 1951, she pondered a move to Israel, a step she finally took in 1963. Although she was not Jewish, Choms felt at home in Israel, where many of those whose lives she had saved now lived. A network of friendships made the burdens of growing old and the loss of her husband and son easier to bear.

On May 22, 1963, Wladyslawa Choms received the award of the "Righteous among the Nations" in the Hall of Remembrance at Yad Vashem in Jerusalem, where Israel and the Jewish people pay homage to the victims and heroes of the Holocaust. Visitors to Yad Vashem can still see the tree planted in her honor.

SOURCES:

Bartoszewski, Wladyslaw, and Zofia Lewin. *The Samaritans: Heroes of the Holocaust.* Edited by Alexander T. Jordan. NY: Twayne Publishers, 1970.

Bauminger, Arieh L. *The Righteous Among the Nations.* Jerusalem: Yad Vashem, 1990.

Bronowski, Alexander. *They Were Few.* Translated by Murray Raveh. NY: Peter Lang, 1991.

Paldiel, Mordecai. "Choms, Wladyslawa (1891–1966)," in Yisrael Gutman, ed. *Encyclopedia of the Holocaust,* Vol. 1, pp. 289–290.

Silver, Eric. *The Book of the Just: The Unsung Heroes Who Rescued Jews from Hitler.* NY: Grove Press, 1992.

John Haag, Associate Professor, University of Georgia, Athens, Georgia

Chopin, Kate (1850–1904)

American writer, originally characterized as a local colorist, who is now acknowledged as a pioneering American realist, best known for her 1899 novel, **The Awakening.** *Pronunciation: SHOW-pan. Born Katherine O'Flaherty on February 8, 1850, in St. Louis, Missouri (some sources, notably Chopin herself, cite 1851); died at home in St. Louis on August 22, 1904; daughter of Thomas (a merchant) and Eliza (Faris) O'Flaherty; attended the Sacred Heart Academy off and on from 1855 until she graduated in June 1868; married Oscar Chopin, in 1870 (died 1882); children: Jean Baptiste (b. 1871); Oscar Charles (b. 1873); George Francis (b. 1874); Frederick (b. 1876); Felix Andrew (b. 1878); Lelia (b. 1879).*

After European honeymoon, moved with Oscar Chopin to New Orleans, Louisiana; moved to Cloutierville (1879); husband died (1882); returned to St. Louis (1884); mother died (1885); published love poems (1889); began At Fault *(1889), which was self-published (1890); published "Desiree's Baby" in* Vogue, *and Houghton Mifflin accepted* Bayou Folk *(1893); attended Indiana Conference of Western Association of Writers and wrote critical article, "The Western Association of Writers" (1894); sent de Maupassant translation collection to Houghton Mifflin (1895), rejected; her grandmother Athenaise Charleville Faris died (1897); published* The Awakening *(1899); her* A Vocation and a Voice *rejected by publisher Herbert S. Stone (1900); published "Polly" in* Youth's Companion *(1902), last publication during her lifetime.*

Selected publications: stories, poems, reviews and articles published in literary journals, newspapers, and large circulation magazines (1889–1902); (stories) Bayou Folk *(Houghton Mifflin, 1894); (stories)* A Night in Acadie *(Way and Williams, 1897); (novel)* The Awakening *(Herbert S. Stone, 1899).*

Katherine O'Flaherty was born in St. Louis, Missouri, on February 8, 1850, two years after the convention for women's rights had met in Seneca Falls, New York, to call for woman's suffrage. While the mature Kate Chopin was not a feminist advocate, nor a champion of women's rights *per se*, her life as an artist might be understood as an example of how certain freedoms and economic rights are necessary to artistic integrity and creative production. The work for which Chopin is best known, *The Awakening*, tells another side of that story, of a woman's frustration and diminishment as she discovers that marriage means she is no more than "a valuable piece of [her husband's] personal property" with no voice or autonomy of her own. In *The Awakening*, the artistic Edna Pontellier wants "to swim out where no woman has ever swum before," but at the novel's close she finds that she does not have the strength or the skills to persevere; "exhaustion presses down upon her, and she sinks in the sea's sensuous, enfolding embrace."

It is possible to make interesting and useful connections between Chopin's life and the story and setting of the novel. But the connections between Kate Chopin and her creation, Edna Pontellier, are more imaginative mirrors than descriptions of actual like experience. Unlike Edna, who lost her mother when she was a baby, Kate Chopin was a beloved child in an extended family with a strong maternal influence that continued to nurture her as she matured and raised her own family. Chopin, an artist who did "dare and defy" the narrow role of woman as mother/wife in the 19th century, *understood* Edna's frustrations and longings. When Edna Pontellier tells Robert Lebrun: "I always feel so sorry for women who don't like to walk; they miss so much—so many rare little glimpses of life; and we women learn so little of life on the whole," we can imagine Chopin speaking here, giving to her character's longings the shape and taste of her own love of exploration, expression, and solitude.

St. Louis in the 1850s was both a Southern city and a frontier town, later christened "Gateway to the West." Its society was Southern (many families, including the O'Flaherty's, were slave-holding), and heavily French and Catholic, though there was a rich representation of diversity: German immigrants, fur trappers and traders, Indians, steamboatmen, con artists. While a girl would not have had the mobility of her brothers and could not have moved freely through the streets, nor fully explore what she found there, the young Kate did likely visit the levee and the docks with her father Thomas O'Flaherty. St. Louis, like many American cities in the late 19th and early 20th centuries was so polluted by the soft coal that was burned for heat and energy that candles and street lamps would have been necessary for illumination during the afternoon. Sewers were open; disease and infant mortality were a reality, especially in the summer heat. Crime, as noted by **Emily Toth**, included the assault, seduction and abandonment of women, of which the young Kate would have been ignorant, but which serve to remind that the city and the 19th century were not safe "places" for women, nor places where they were taken seriously or respected. But there was culture here, and opportunity for women as well as men. St. Louis had a museum, libraries, several newspapers, a telegraph system, access to products from Europe and the other states, a university, and a seminary for girls. For the O'Flaherty family, life in St. Louis offered rich possibilities for a rewarding social, familial, and intellectual life.

Kate's extended family included half-brothers from Thomas O'Flaherty's first marriage. Her mother **Eliza Faris (O'Flaherty)** was 23 years younger than her husband, and, like O'Flaherty's first wife, she was of French Creole ancestry. By the time Kate was born, Thomas O'Flaherty, an Irishman who had immigrated to the United States in 1823, was a prosperous merchant who was prominent in the St. Louis business and social world, both by virtue of his industry, and through his marriages. Kate was enrolled briefly in Sacred Heart Academy in 1855 but left in November when her father was tragically killed in the collapse of the new Gasconade Bridge carrying the inaugural train of the Pacific Railroad into St. Louis. Several months later, a significant part of Kate's education began when her maternal great-grandmother joined the O'Flaherty household. Mme. Charleville taught Kate her French, and she also told sophisticated stories of Creole life in which strong, vocal women were frequently involved in interracial marriage or extramarital romance. The plots of these stories resisted a popular 19th-century compulsion to moralize and introduced Kate to a formative and complex understanding of the relationships between men and women, which would later be the subject of her fiction.

In 1859, Kate was re-enrolled in Sacred Heart Academy where her special subjects were literature and piano—both of which are featured prominently in the plots of her stories 30 years later. The education at Sacred Heart was traditional in that the school's express mission was to train young women to enter the domestic and social spheres as good wives and mothers. But there was solid intellectual grounding here, too. Chopin was already well read in the French classics, as well as some Dickens, *Ivanhoe*, and *Paul and Virginia*. In her academics, she later read Dante, Cervantes, Goethe, and Coleridge. At the same time, Kate and her best friend **Kitty Garesche**, who later became a Sacred Heart nun and teacher, were reading novels by women: *Days of Bruce, Zaidee, Queechy, Orphans of Moscow; or, The Young Governess*. Chopin also had a teacher, Mme. O'Meara, who encouraged her to write.

Though Kate Chopin's reading was varied, and her views of the world shaped by creative, unusual women, there were limits to the broad-mindedness of her childhood. It is unlikely that Kate or Kitty would have read *Uncle Tom's Cabin*. Kitty Garesche wrote that she did not think she and Kate had ever seen a slave sale, "though I think we wanted to," but their families were slave-holding; Kate's brother George fought for the South, was captured and imprisoned, and later died of typhoid while traveling to rejoin his regiment; Kitty Garesche's family was banished from the city because of their pro-slavery politics. Toth recounts a story of a fero-

cious Kate who yanked down a union flag that had been pinned to their porch after the Union army made its home in St. Louis. But the mature Chopin's stories, like "Desiree's Baby" and "La Belle Zoraide," indicate that her sophisticated understanding of the way in which patriarchal law disenfranchised women, while protecting their abusers, included stories of black women's lives. Chopin would live in Louisiana after her marriage. While Louisiana law did not allow married women to own property, and this would have included their children, black women were much more at risk in this system than were their white counterparts. Many critics suggest that Chopin's handling of racial issues is simply a background for her stories, and her black characters are caricatures, but it is also true that, like a number of women writing in the United States in the late 19th century, the point of view of her stories calls attention to women's longings, women's angers and experiences in women's voices, both black and white.

Chopin's early reading habits became a lifelong vocation. And, as her taste matured, she gravitated towards writers like Madame *Germaine de Staël* who explored a tension in women's lives between desire and virtue. At the same time, in her late adolescence, Chopin was a social success. Kitty Garesche recalls that Kate had a "droll gift for mimicry" and "was the object of much admiration." But she also remembers that Kate's "intellect predominated and kept the passions cool." Chopin herself wrote in her commonplace book on New Year's Day, 1868: "parties, operas concerts, skating and amusements ad infinitum have so taken up my time that my dear reading and writing that I love so well have suffered much neglect." The next year would begin a time of activism for women in St. Louis; the young Kate Chopin read about these passionate women and their work. In 1869, she was jotting in her journal that women's "duties" and "rights" were issues in conflict. At the same time, she noted that a woman, like herself, with intellectual needs and interests, is rarely taken seriously. The questions raised in that year about women's rights within and beyond the confines of the home would also appear later in the mature Kate Chopin's work.

In June 1870, Kate married Oscar Chopin, a French Creole from Natchitoches, Louisiana. After a three month European honeymoon, which culminated in leaving Paris just before that city was closed by siege during the Franco-Prussian War, the Chopins settled in New Orleans in the American Quarter where they lived for nine years. Oscar was a cotton factor (agent), and Kate lived a life not unlike Edna Pontellier's, which included a receiving day, the endless social range of "calls," and summertime visits to the Creole culture of Grande Isle where much of the drama of *The Awakening* occurs. Kate Chopin's talent for sketching local color is a significant gift, for the Grand Isle she recorded ceased to exist when in 1893 the island was besieged by a hurricane. Two thousand people were killed, the coast was devastated, and the hotel and cabins she described were destroyed. During the New Orleans years, Chopin also gave birth to her four sons, returning for several of the births to St. Louis where she had the company and support of her mother and grandmother.

> *The artist must possess the courageous soul that dares and defies.*
>
> —**Kate Chopin**, *The Awakening*

The young Chopins moved to Cloutierville, Louisiana, in 1879, after excessive rainfall ruined the cotton crop; Chopin described Cloutierville as a "little French village, which was simply two long rows of very old frame houses, facing each other closely across a dusty roadway." There, Oscar worked as a merchant, and Kate was known as a gracious hostess who, nevertheless, shocked many of her neighbors with her chic town clothes, her penchant for cigarettes, and for wandering off alone on horse or on foot.

The couple's last child, Lelia, was born during the Cloutierville years, and though many critics have wanted to read Chopin's marriage-weary heroines autobiographically, there is no evidence to suggest that Kate Chopin was unhappily married. What is more likely: her early introduction to a sophisticated understanding of women's passions enabled her to contemplate paradox. A woman might know that she lived in a culture that circumscribed her activities and monitored her desires, but she could also choose to live in such a way that she questioned the tyranny of the 19th-century family structure, while loving her own. Chopin was critical of the Creole mother-women she would have encountered in New Orleans and at Grand Isle, describing them in *The Awakening* as women who "esteemed it a privilege to efface themselves as individuals and grow wings as ministering angels," but her son, Felix Chopin, remembers that she was always available to her children. It is possible that had Oscar not died when Kate was

just 33 she would never have written a story for publication despite all the seeds that had been sown for the fruit of her ten strong writing years. But he did. And after maintaining her husband's business in Cloutierville for a few more years and possibly having an affair with a married man (which according to Toth may have begun before the death of her husband), Kate Chopin returned with her children to St. Louis and the company of the strong women in her own family.

It was devastating to Chopin when her mother died in 1885. Her daughter told Daniel Rankin that the "tragic death of her father early in her life . . . the loss of her young husband and mother, left a stamp of sadness on her which was never lost." It was Kate Chopin's St. Louis obstetrician, Frederick Kolbenheyer, who urged her to write. He was a man noted for his intellectual pursuits, and someone she trusted. Chopin's first published work was love poems, elegies for her husband. They were sentimental, but they were deeply felt, and they were a beginning. She was at the same time trying her hand at short stories, which were profoundly influenced by the stories of the French writer, Guy de Maupassant. Chopin credits him with her own literary awakening, writing in an essay for *The Atlantic*:

> I had been in the woods, in the fields, groping around; looking for something big, satisfying, convincing and finding nothing but—myself [when] I stumbled upon Maupassant. I read his stories and marveled at them. Here was life, not fiction; for where were the plots . . . that in a vague, unthinking way I had fancied were essential to the art of story making. Here was a man who had escaped from tradition and authority, who had entered into himself and looked out upon life . . . with his own eyes; and who, in a direct and simple way, told us what he saw. When a man does this, he gives us the best that he can; something valuable for it is genuine and spontaneous.

What she saw in Maupassant was a vision and a sensibility similar to her own, and the literary corollary to the early stories told her by her great-grandmother that refused to reduce the complexities of human interaction to a socially acceptable moral.

As her writing skills sharpened, Chopin's themes emerged clearly. Her first novel, *At Fault*, published at her own expense, introduces her exploration of the tensions between passion and convention. Early stories, "Wiser Than a God" and "A Point at Issue," explore conflicts between artistic integrity and social mores. Later, in tales like "The Story of an Hour," Chopin began clearly to describe her ideas about a woman's experience of marriage. And, as always, she embraced paradox. In "The Story of an Hour" a wife weeps, and then feels delirious with the sudden possibility of freedom when she hears of her husband's sudden death in a train accident. She falls dead at the end of this brief, terse story when she discovers he's alive. But in other narratives, also collected in *Bayou Folk,* young wives awaken to sensual pleasure—both inside and outside their marriages. "Athenaise" is a good example, convincing, erotic and subtle in its portrayal of a young wife's rebellion against her marriage. In so many of Chopin's stories, the shadowy, sensual and autonomous self lurks just behind the woman whose responses are muted, or socially correct. And Chopin often suggests that there has been an extramarital liaison that facilitates her characters' awakenings.

Early reviewers praised *Bayou Folk,* lauding Chopin's ear for the regional voice and flavor of Louisiana; few noted her implied criticism of marriage, nor her exploration of women's sensual lives. These were not considered appropriate subjects for women who wrote during the 19th century; women were routinely disparaged for any perceived censure of social mores either by public (critical) censure, inability to publish, or by editors who would request more "wholesome" material. In the end, in *The Awakening,* it is Edna Pontellier who brings the longing for autonomy, and artistic integrity, and sensual insistence together. While she is "forced to admit that there are none better" than her husband, Edna also realizes that generous as he is, he cannot understand her. She cannot "make an indenture, not a mark" upon her marriage. When he complains that she doesn't comply with his idea of a woman, and that she ought to be able to paint as a hobby while still attending to all of the household duties, Edna responds with a challenge: "I'm not a painter. It isn't on account of painting that I let things go." Just before she drowns, while standing before "the inviting waves," Edna attempts to cast convention away as she casts her "unpleasant, pricking garments from her." And though she cannot sustain her gesture and live, she is clear in her last thoughts that while she loves her family, "they needn't think they could possess her, body and soul." Chopin's radical insistence here is upon the necessity of autonomy to the human soul. It is the ability to be alone, without a label that condones aloneness, like "artist," or "business man," that Edna longs for.

Though Chopin was accustomed to critics misreading her work, she wasn't prepared for the acrimonious reviews *The Awakening* received. Few critics doubted the strength of her writing, few quibbled with the style, but nearly all responded to the story of Edna Pontellier with such bitter protestations that it appears as if Edna, or Kate Chopin, had personally offended. Though Edna does not have the emotional strength to conceive of herself outside a romantic relationship, what she strives to articulate before she swims to her death is the right of the human being, particularly the female human being, simply to be herself, something Kate Chopin always insisted upon. (This insistence was also clear when Chopin wrote an essay describing the concerns of the Western Association of Writers as provincial, thus alienating a group to which she belonged.) Chopin's ability to create her own self, independent of sexual and material, or other relationships, depended in part on those maternal and female friendships that nurtured her in her writing, in her education, and in her ability to be a loving mother. She had models in her mother, and grandmothers, and friends that the motherless and friendless Edna did not.

Though she remained intellectually engaged, Chopin wrote and published very little after the hostile reaction to *The Awakening,* and she died at home in 1904 after a day of exploring at the St. Louis World's Fair. While it is a myth that the book was ever banned, it was out of print and unread for a long time. Daniel Rankin's edition of *Kate Chopin and Her Creole Stories* did much to revive interest in Chopin's work. And the growing awareness of readers and students of women's work has brought all of Chopin's oeuvre into print.

Kate Chopin crossed boundaries. In both her work and her life she insists upon the necessity of autonomy, complexity, and paradox. In her ten writing years, she produced three novels, over 100 short stories, a translation of de Maupassant's stories, a play, and numerous reviews, articles, and essays for the most prestigious and popular journals and magazines in the country. Her life was richly intellectual, sensual and familial, while her exploration of women's lives is as relevant at the conclusion of the 20th century as it was at the turn of the 19th century. It was she who had the courage to dare and defy social convention, as well as the courage to describe herself as an artist with a particular and important vision.

SOURCES:

Chopin, Kate. *The Awakening.* Edited by Nancy A. Walker. NY: Bedford Books of St. Martin's Press, 1993.
Martin, Wendy, ed. *New Essays on "The Awakening."* Cambridge: Cambridge University Press, 1988.

Toth, Emily. *Kate Chopin*. NY: William Morrow, 1990.

SUGGESTED READING:

Rankin, Daniel. *Kate Chopin and Her Creole Stories.* Philadelphia, PA: University of Pennsylvania Press, 1932.

Seyersted, Per, ed. *The Complete Works of Kate Chopin.* 2 vols. Baton Rouge, LA: Louisiana State University Press, 1969.

———. *Kate Chopin: A Critical Biography*. Baton Rouge, LA: Louisiana State University Press, 1969.

———, and Emily Toth, eds. *A Kate Chopin Miscellany.* Natchitoches, LA: Northwestern State University Press, 1979.

———, and Emily Toth, eds. *Kate Chopin's Private Papers.* Bloomington, IN: Indiana University Press, forthcoming.

RELATED MEDIA:

The Joy That Kills (VHS, 56 minutes), an adaptation of a short story produced by Films for the Humanities, 1988, was a Blue Ribbon Winner at the American Film Festival.

COLLECTIONS:

Primary collection of Kate Chopin materials located at the Missouri Historical Society, St. Louis, Missouri, includes most extant manuscripts, stories, poems, clippings, the de Maupassant translations, diaries, letters, notebooks, and photographs.

Other materials can be found in several collections housed at Northwestern State University.

Susan Morehouse,
Assistant Professor of Creative Writing,
Alfred University, Alfred, New York

Chotek, Sophie (1868–1914)

German-born Austrian aristocrat whose assassination in Sarajevo with husband Archduke Franz Ferdinand triggered the chain of events that hurled the world into the first total war in history. Name variations: Sophia, countess of Chotek; Sophie of Hohenberg; Sophie von Hohenberg; duchess of Hohenberg, Hohenburg or Hohenbourg. Born in Stuttgart, Germany, on March 1, 1868; assassinated in Sarajevo, Bosnia, on June 28, 1914; daughter of Count Bohuslav Chotek of Chotkova and Wognin and Countess Wilhelmine Chotek; had four sisters and three brothers; married Francis Ferdinand also known as Franz Ferdinand (1863–1914), archduke of Austria (r. 1896–1914); children: Sofie (b. 1901); Max (b. 1902); Ernst (b. 1904).

Sophie Chotek was born into one of the most distinguished families of the Czech nobility. Her ancestors had been barons of Bohemia since 1556, counts of Bohemia since 1723, and counts of the Holy Roman Empire (*Reichsgrafenstand*) since 1745. Her father, Count Bohuslav, was a successful diplomat of the Austro-Hungarian Empire, ending his career with posts in Brussels and Dresden. Sophie's mother, Countess **Wilhelmine Chotek**, could point with pride to her own family tree, that of the illustrious Kinskys, who had long served many Habsburg rulers over the centuries. Despite this illustrious lineage, the Choteks were not deemed eligible to enter the very highest circles of the Austrian-Hungarian aristocracy through marriage. Jealously preserving their status, in 1825 the ruling houses of Austria, Baden, Bavaria, Hanover, Hesse, Prussia and Württemberg published a schedule of those noble families that would henceforth be eligible for marriage into their august circle. Despite their excellent record of service to the Austrian crown, neither the Chotek nor Kinsky families—and, indeed, others at least as illustrious—were included on the Austrian list of 14 "princely houses domiciled in the Monarchy" and six families headed by counts who were included for special historical or genealogical reasons.

As the fourth of the five Chotek daughters, Sophie had by her late teens blossomed into an attractive and intelligent young woman. Given the fact that her father was not wealthy, she followed the path taken by several of her sisters, namely looked for suitable employment. The opportunity soon presented itself when Sophie was hired by the Belgian-born Archduchess *Isabella of Croy-Dulmen*, whose husband Archduke Friedrich was one of the wealthiest members of the Habsburg imperial family. In 1894, Sophie met Archduke Franz Ferdinand, who had been heir to the throne of Austria-Hungary since the death of the intellectually mediocre and politically inept Archduke Karl Ludwig (Charles Louis) in May 1896. When Archduchess Isabella discovered that Franz Ferdinand had come to her estate to see Sophie rather than one of her own eligible daughters, she fired Sophie on the spot. But once ignited, Franz Ferdinand's passion for Sophie did not cool off. Although he had been involved in several passionate affairs, Franz Ferdinand now found himself hopelessly in love with the charming, "wholesome, womanly yet strikingly dignified" Sophie Chotek. The fact that her family tree did not make her "of equally high birth" (*ebenbürtig*) to the Habsburg clan was contemptuously dismissed by the archduke as a matter of "some triviality in the family tree."

Once he knew about his strong-willed nephew's plans to marry Fräulein Chotek, Emperor Franz Joseph made it clear that he did not approve of the match. But Franz Ferdinand was equally determined to marry his beloved "Sopherl." Accepting the reality that the Chotek family could never qualify as a members of the very highest nobility, on June 28, 1900, Franz Ferdinand swore on a Bible and signed an Act of Renunciation that took away all rights to succession to the throne for any children that he and Sophie might have, thus making theirs a morganatic marriage. This solemn declaration was not only written into the Habsburg family records, but raised to the status of a legally binding agreement by the parliaments of both Austria and Hungary, and sanctioned by a law of December 4, 1900.

On July 1, 1900, Franz Ferdinand married Sophie. With her marriage, she automatically was raised to the rank of a princess—a very minor title in the scheme of Austrian nobility. Happily, the couple quickly raised a family: in 1901, daughter Sofie was born, followed in 1902 and 1904 by sons Max and Ernst. Although Sophie had agreed to the morganatic union, it soon became evident that she was not happy with the consequences. An inflexible tradition of imperial Habsburg court etiquette and protocol kept Sophie from riding in the same coach in public with her husband. At the begin-

nings of official ceremonies and events, she had to wait until higher-ranking women had made their entrances before she could herself enter and rejoin Franz Ferdinand.

Never ceasing to look upon these restrictions as deeply hurtful personal slights, Sophie felt totally justified in asserting her full rights as the wife of the heir to one of Europe's great powers. In 1905, the emperor Franz Joseph relented somewhat by elevating her to the title of duchess of Hohenberg, thus allowing her to be addressed as "Your Serene Highness." In 1909, the emperor further increased the status of the duchess by permitting her to be addressed as "Highness" *ad personam*, thus making her status in public somewhat less socially awkward than before.

Both Franz Ferdinand and Sophie were devout Roman Catholics. In his case, it was largely a matter of sticking to socially prescribed external rituals, but where Sophie was concerned religion was an important part of her daily routine. She rarely neglected either confession or Holy Communion, and both she and her spouse were

Sophie Chotek (with umbrella) and Franz Ferdinand in Sarajevo, shortly before their assassination.

active in Vienna's Roman Catholic circles. This included the political arm of the church, the Christian Social Party of Dr. Karl Lueger (1844–1910), who as lord mayor of Vienna governed on a demagogic anti-Semitic and anti-Socialist platform. Commenting on Austrian politics, Pope Pius X noted that "the Archduke sees through the eyes of his wife." Sophie not only agreed with Franz Ferdinand, who regarded Jews as a threat to the social order because they were customarily too liberal and sympathetic to Marxism, but gave him the confidence to pursue a course of action that soon diverged significantly from those of the emperor.

At times, the duchess of Hohenberg was able to engage in the kind of public actions that her husband would never dare be involved in. In April 1901, she took part in a militantly Catholic street demonstration in Vienna that her husband doubtless approved of. As reported in London's *Daily Mail*, the Viennese public was astonished to see Sophie lead "a procession of 200 fashionable and aristocratic ladies" who marched to several churches where they were addressed by a Jesuit priest who gave "an inflammatory sermon." Again asserting her rights as the wife of the heir to the throne, in 1913 Sophia, accompanied by her children, ostentatiously went with Franz Ferdinand to the military maneuvers then taking place in Bohemia. Her presence on this occasion served to unleash a storm of protest in Parliament, where some deputies accused her of meddling to the extent of determining how the troops should march during the exercises.

One of the most astute observers of the Viennese court scene, Baron Albert von Margutti, described the duchess as "a woman of high intelligence, extraordinarily ambitious, resolute and yet vain, and without the slightest intention of accommodating herself to the position of a morganatic wife kept carefully in the background. On the contrary, she strained every nerve, with a zeal that was not always coupled with the necessary tact—especially after she had presented her husband with a daughter and two sons—to assert her full rights as the wife of the heir to the throne."

Having settled down in his marriage and content with his private life, starting in 1906 Franz Ferdinand devoted the bulk of his energy to political affairs. His military affairs office in Vienna's Belvedere Palace, where he and his family lived, developed into a sort of shadow government of the aging Franz Joseph. Above all, Franz Ferdinand feared that growing nationality tensions would inevitably result in the self-destruc-

tion of the venerable Habsburg state he hoped to one day rule. One of his concepts was to bring the Czechs into full partnership in the monarchy with the Austro-Germans and Hungarians that already dominated it. His foreign policy was predicated on eliminating the threats from Italy and Serbia, and he was sympathetic to the idea of preventive war against these two states.

By 1914, it was clear that "something had to be done" in the Balkans to assure the continued existence of Austria-Hungary. Serbian self-confidence had grown in two regional wars, and Serbian-backed nationalist agitation had begun to destabilize Bosnia-Herzegovina, seized by Austria-Hungary from Turkey in 1878 and officially annexed to the Habsburg state as recently as 1908. In 1913, the governor of Bosnia-Herzegovina, General Oskar Potiorek, responded to the nationalist activities in his province by cracking down with more police repression, press censorship and a temporary suspension of the regional assembly. Hoping to show how well the situation was now in hand, he invited Franz Ferdinand, who was inspector-general of the Austrian armed forces, to visit the capital city of Sarajevo. The date chosen by Potiorek, June 28, 1914, St. Vitus' Day, was particularly provocative to Serbian nationalist elements because it was also a day sacred to South Slav nationalists, being the anniversary of the fateful battle of Kosovo, June 28, 1389, when Serbia surrendered its freedom to the Ottoman Empire.

General Potiorek may have innocently chosen the date, but some have suggested that it was done to deliberately provoke already incensed Bosnian Serbs. Personally, Potiorek had reasons to resent Franz Ferdinand, having been twice denied promotion by him. More ominous was the fact that a newspaper announcement in mid-March 1914 of plans for the visit was read by diehard enemies of the Habsburg state, including a young Bosnian Serb nationalist Gavrilo Princip (1894–1918). Son of a postman and in fragile health, young Princip was a militant Serbian nationalist who had since 1912 been an active member of the Black Hand (*Ujedinjenje ili Smrt*—"Union or Death"), a secret nationalist organization determined to create by any means possible a Greater Serbian state, clearly at the expense of a Habsburg monarchy that was both multinational and increasingly vulnerable.

In the Serbian capital of Belgrade, the leadership of the Black Hand, which had recruited its leaders from within the higher echelons of the government and military, decided to plot the assassination of the archduke, heir-apparent to the

Postage stamp of Sophie Chotek and Franz Ferdinand issued on June 28, 1917.

throne of hated Austria-Hungary. Besides Princip, two other Bosnian Serbs, Nedjelko Vaso Cabrinovic and Trifko Grabez, were trained to kill Franz Ferdinand on his official visit to Sarajevo. In an attempt to divert attention from Serbia's own deep involvement in Black Hand activities, the Serbian minister to Vienna, Jovan Jovanovic, issued a vague warning about a possible assassination attempt on June 5, 1914, to the Austrian minister of finance, Dr. Leon von Bilinski. Bilinski unfortunately did not understand the diplomatic innuendo and completely missed the warning. By early June, Princip and his colleagues were already in Sarajevo, where over the next days they would recruit four additional young men as members of the conspiracy.

Franz Ferdinand was determined to take Sophie along with him on his trip to Sarajevo, particularly in view of the fact that away from the Viennese Court a number of social taboos relating to her subordinate status could be ignored. For one thing, she would be able to ride next to him in an automobile, something that remained *verboten* (forbidden) to them in Vienna. Scheduled as it was for the last days of June, the trip would coincide with their 14th wedding anniversary. Franz Ferdinand was indifferent to his own security, intensely disliking the presence of personal guards when in public. Raised in a medieval intellectual environment, he was extremely superstitious, once telling Count Ottokar Czernin how a

fortuneteller had predicted "that he would let loose a world war." When Franz Ferdinand and Sophie departed from the estate at Chlumetz on June 23, their private rail car had to be left behind because of axle problems. He told Sophie: "Well, our journey starts with an extremely promising omen. Here our car burns and down there they will throw bombs at us." When the electricity in another rail car failed and candles were substituted for light bulbs, Franz Ferdinand said to his secretary: "Is it not like a grave?"

In Sarajevo, June 28, 1914, was a hot and sunny day. After reviewing troops at a nearby army camp, the archduke and Sophie headed for City Hall for a reception hosted by the mayor. Franz Ferdinand and Sophie rode in the second of a six-car motorcade. The driver and the car's owner, Count Franz Harrach, sat in the front seat while Franz Ferdinand and Sophie were in back. With friendly cheering crowds on the sidewalks, the motorcade traveled along the wide avenue called Appel Quay, which followed the north bank of the River Miljacka. Amid the crowd were the seven Black Hand assassins. While the first lost his nerve, the second, Cabrinovic, withdrew a bomb from his coat pocket, striking its percussion cap against a lamp post, and hurled it at Franz Ferdinand's vehicle.

The alert driver stepped on the accelerator while at the same time Franz Ferdinand caught a brief glimpse of the object and raised his arm to deflect it away from Sophie. Glancing off the archduke's arm, the bomb exploded with great ferocity, injuring members of the crowd and passengers in the third car, including General Potiorek's chief adjutant, Lieutenant Colonel Merizzi, who suffered a deep flesh wound to the back of his head. Fortunately, Sophie only received a barely noticeable graze wound near her shoulder blade. Several bomb fragments had become embedded in the car, but the only injuries sustained by Franz Ferdinand's group were Sophie's negligible scratches. In his determination to commit suicide, would-be assassin Cabrinovic swallowed cyanide and jumped into the river. But he failed to kill himself because the poison the Black Hand had given him was old and no longer lethal, and the river contained only a few inches of water. He was taken into custody.

Arriving at the City Hall, a furious Franz Ferdinand confronted the mayor who had begun a welcoming address, sputtering, "Herr Bürgermeister, one comes here for a visit and is received by bombs! It is outrageous!" The mayor found himself at a loss for words, but the duchess of Hohenberg managed to calm the situation by whispering a few words into her husband's ear. After some hesitation, a considerably more composed Franz Ferdinand informed the mayor he could complete his interrupted speech. Although he believed there was more violence on hand in Sarajevo, having told this to Count Harrach after the bomb attack, the archduke turned down his staff's plan to remain in the City Hall until the city's streets had been cleared by troops. Habsburg pride prevailed, and Franz Ferdinand decided to complete the day with the scheduled visit to the National Museum as well as a brief visit to the hospital to see the wounded Merizzi. Although both an aide and Franz Ferdinand himself tried to dissuade Sophie from joining the party, she determinedly refused, insisting that "as long as the Archduke shows himself in public today I will not leave him."

Placing security first, the new plan was for the motorcade to avoid the narrow streets of the old city of Sarajevo, driving swiftly instead along the Appel Quay directly to the hospital. Unfortunately, neither the driver of the mayor's car nor the driver of Franz Ferdinand and Sophie's car had been told of the changed plans (Merizzi had been in charge of this detail, but he was now hospitalized). Six of the seven conspirators remained in the crowds, hoping to find a second opportunity to strike.

The opportunity soon presented itself when the first two cars of the motorcade mistakenly turned at Franz Joseph Strasse, with the imperial Habsburg vehicle briefly stopping in front of Moritz Schiller's delicatessen, where a few moments earlier Gavrilo Princip had stopped to buy a sandwich. When it came to a complete stop no more than five feet from him, Princip immediately recognized the car's illustrious occupants. He quickly raised his revolver, but for a split second hesitated from any action when he saw Sophie seated on the near side of vehicle. But then seized by "a strange feeling" and "greatly agitated," he fired two shots in quick succession. Most likely he intended to hit Franz Ferdinand and Governor Potiorek, but the bullet meant for Potiorek hit Sophie instead. Count Harrach, who had been riding on the car's left running board so as to shield the precious couple from assassins, now unfortunately found himself placed in a position useless to afford any protection. Intending to commit suicide with a third shot, Princip turned his gun on himself, but a spectator stopped him. With a crowd on top of him, Princip also swallowed cyanide, but like that taken by Cabrinovic, his portion was also old and only made him ill. Had both men died by poison, the Black Hand involvement would most likely have remained murky and the political crisis of the next weeks might possibly have been averted.

The car turned around quickly and sped down the Appel Quay to the Konak, a walled fortress from Turkish times that served as Military Governor Potiorek's residence across the river. The first impression of the entourage was that there had been no injuries to the car's passengers. But as the vehicle sped to the safety of the Konak, it became obvious that both Franz Ferdinand and Sophie had been grievously injured in the Franz Joseph Strasse. As the car neared the Lateiner Bridge, a stream of blood shot from Franz Ferdinand's mouth. He had been shot in the neck and was bleeding profusely. Seeing this, Sophie called out to her husband, "For heaven's sake, what has happened to you!" Thereupon she fell over, unconscious and sinking fast. Still optimistic, Potiorek and Harrach believed that she had simply fainted from the excitement. Seeing his wife, Franz Ferdinand pleaded with her, "Sopherl! Sopherl! Sterbe nicht! Bleibe am Leben für unsere Kinder!" ("Sophie dear! Sophie dear! Don't die! Stay alive for our children!"). When Count Harrach asked the archduke if he was in great pain, he answered, "It is nothing." He repeated the phrase six or seven more times, each time slipping further into a state of unconsciousness.

By the time the car arrived at the Konak, both Franz Ferdinand and Sophie were unconscious and barely alive. Their wounds were mortal. Franz Ferdinand died from a bullet that severed his jugular vein and lodged in his spine. Sophie, who died first, succumbed to a bullet that had entered her abdomen from the right side, causing massive internal trauma and bleeding. The couple were declared dead by 11:30 AM, June 28, 1914. The archduke's body was laid out in the governor's bedroom. His collar was open, and a gold chain could be seen from which hung seven gold and platinum amulets, each one meant to ward off a different form of evil. Around the neck of the duchess of Hohenberg was a golden chain, with a scapular of holy relics that she had firmly believed would serve as protection from ill health and misfortunes.

The bodies were taken back to Vienna from Sarajevo by rail to the coast, then by sea to the port of Trieste on board the battleship *Viribus Unitis*. From Trieste to Vienna, the caskets went by train. Even in death and laying in state in Vienna, Sophie Chotek remained an inferior member of the ancient Habsburg clan. At first, the Court chamberlain, Prince Montenuovo, decided that the duchess' casket would not be permitted to be placed next to that of Franz Ferdinand. Only the personal intervention of the Emperor Franz Joseph himself made it possible for her to lie next to her husband in the imperial chapel. But her coffin was set conspicuously lower than that of Franz Ferdinand, and with far less decoration. Some historians have suggested that the fact that Franz Ferdinand and Sophie did not receive a grand state funeral in Vienna made it impossible for the European heads of state to meet in an informal summit conference that might still have averted a major war.

Since Sophie could not be buried in Vienna's Capuchin Crypt, reserved only for "true" members of the imperial family, it was decided that she and the archduke would be buried at his favorite castle, Artstetten. Located in the romantic Pöchlarn region of Lower Austria near the Danube, less than two hours' drive from Vienna, Artstetten had been the site of Franz Ferdinand's happy childhood. But a darker side of his personality had revealed itself soon after his marriage to Sophie, when he ordered a crypt built underneath the castle church. Years later, the archduke's private secretary wrote that in ordering the crypt's construction while still a young man, Franz Ferdinand appeared to be possessed "by an intimation of his impending fate . . . and could hardly await its completion." Sophie and Franz Ferdinand's coffins arrived at the modest Pöchlarn train station at 2:00 AM just as a violent thunderstorm broke out. The ceremony had to be held inside a crowded waiting room. To reach Artstetten, the two hearses, each drawn by eight black horses, had to cross the Danube on a ferry. The thunderstorm continued unabated as they crossed the Danube, and only the quick-witted intervention of bystanders kept the hearses from slipping into the raging river.

Among the few mourners present that stormy night was a certain "Herr Burg," who happened to be Franz Ferdinand's younger brother Ferdinand Karl. The emperor had granted Ferdinand Karl no more than one day's stay in Austria to attend his brother's funeral. Stripped of his noble name and military rank and exiled from the Habsburg realms for life, Ferdinand Karl had, like his brother, chosen to marry for love—in his case, he had married far below his exalted aristocratic status, the daughter of a Viennese university professor. Sophie and Franz Ferdinand still rest in the crypt of the castle church at Artstetten. A plaque over their graves serves to remind visitors of a grim fact that places their personal tragedies in the context of a much larger, global catastrophe that began in the summer of 1914: "Here Lie the First Two Victims of the [First] World War." Only in death, on June 28, 1917, the third anniversary of her and Franz Ferdinand's assassination, did Austria-Hungary recognize Sophie as being fully equal to her husband, when the postal administration of Bosnia-Herzegovina honored her on a series of postage stamps meant to raise funds to build a memorial church in Sarajevo.

SOURCES:

Brook-Shepherd, Gordon. *Victims at Sarajevo: The Romance and Tragedy of Franz Ferdinand and Sophie*. London: Harvill Press, 1984.

Cassels, Lavender. *The Archduke and the Assassin: Sarajevo, June 28th 1914*. NY: Stein and Day, 1985.

Danszky, Eduard Paul. *Krone und Herz: Ein Roman um Franz Ferdinand und Sophie von Hohenberg*. 2 vols. Vienna-Mödling: St. Gabriel-Verlag, 1952–53.

Dedijer, Vladimir. *The Road to Sarajevo*. NY: Simon and Schuster, 1966.

Hamann, Brigitte, ed. *Die Habsburger: Ein biographisches Lexikon*. Munich: Verlag Piper, 1988.

Kiszling, Rudolf. *Erzherzog Franz Ferdinand von Österreich-Este*. Graz and Cologne: Böhlau Verlag, 1953.

Knappman, Edward W., ed. *Great World Trials*. Detroit, MI: Gale Research, 1997.

Madjera, Wolfgang. *Gedenkblatt zur Erinnerung an seine k. u. k. Hoheit den durchlauchtigsten Erzherzog-Thronfolger Franz Ferdinand und höchstseine Gemahlin, die durchlauchtige Frau Herzogin Sophie von Hohenberg, 28. Juni, 1914*. Vienna: Gerlach and Wiedling, 1914.

Margutti, Albert Alexander Vinzenz, Freiherr von. *The Emperor Francis Joseph and His Times*. London: Hutchinson, 1921.

Pauli, Hertha Ernestine. *The Secret of Sarajevo: The Story of Franz Ferdinand and Sophie.* NY: Appleton-Century, 1965.

Pohl, Walter, and Karl Vocelka. *Die Habsburger: Eine europäische Familiengeschichte.* Edited by Brigitte Vacha. Graz: Verlag Styria, 1992.

Pozzi, Henri. *Black Hand over Europe.* Translated by Ksenija Horvaf. Zagreb: Croatian Information Centre, 1994.

Remak, Joachim. *Sarajevo: The Story of a Political Murder.* NY: Criterion Books, 1959.

Tötschinger, Gerhard. *Auf den Spuren der Habsburger.* Vienna: Amalthea Verlag, 1992.

Weissensteiner, Friedrich. *Franz Ferdinand: Der verhinderte Herrscher.* Vienna: Österreichischer Bundesverlag, 1983.

RELATED MEDIA:

"The Hapsburgs: A European Family History" (4 videocassettes), Princeton, NJ: Films for the Humanities, 1998.

John Haag, Associate Professor of History,
University of Georgia, Athens, Georgia

Chrestienne.

Variant of Christina or Christine.

Christensen, Inger (1935—)

Danish poet, dramatist and novelist whose works are concerned with the issue of how we may be free while living in community. Born Inger Christensen in Jutland, town of Vejle, Denmark, in 1935, where she grew up and graduated from high school in 1954; daughter of a tailor; received her teaching diploma, 1958; married to Poul Borum (a Danish author) for several years. (Christensen is shy and slow to give out biographical information.)

Awarded a three-year stipend from the Danish Art Foundation (1966); received the Danish Critics' Award (1969), the Golden Laurels (1970), the Aarestrup Medal (1973), the Kjeld Abell Prize and Tagea Brandt's Travel Award (1978); became member of the Danish Academy (1978).

Selected works: (poems) Lys *(Light, 1962); (poems)* Gras *(Grass, 1963); (novel)* Evighedsmaskinen *(The Perpetual Movement Machine, 1964); (novel)* Azorno *(1967); (poems)* Det *(That, 1969); (play)* Intriganterne *(The Schemers, 1972); (novel)* Det malede varelse *(The Painted Room, 1976); (poems)* Brev i april *(Letter in April, 1979); (poems)* Alfabet *(Alphabet, 1981); and numerous essays.*

Inger Christensen grew up on an ordinary street in Vejle, a middle-size town on the eastern coast of the Jutland peninsula. She was a child of the working class—her father was a tailor—and she cherished the experiences to which that position in society gave her entry. Writing about the summers of her childhood, spent partially in Vejle and partially in the summerhouse owned by the tailors' union, she has described her encounter with the heat of a summer's day; because the air and her own skin had the same temperature, she felt one with the universe.

From these summers, the poet recalls three events that taught her of aesthetic experiences: viewing a broad meadow of cress, bouncing a huge rubber ball against a hot wall at high noon, sitting in the kitchen eating strawberries during an evening thunderstorm. Trivial incidents in themselves, for Christensen, these moments conveyed the meaning of beauty: openness without limits, energy spent to no purpose, and the safety in knowing we are not alone. All three situations relate to the major theme found throughout her writing: the question of how we become free human beings even as we live in community with one another.

Like other writers of her time, Christensen is preoccupied with contemporary people and their alienation from self and nature. We have invested our brains in technology, she argues, but forgotten to embrace "in a fragrant meadow/ in a sun warmed bed" despite our deeper knowledge that only as lovers and children can we regain the doubly lost paradise. Her poetry shows that the road to our loss is caused by misguided choices, and it suggests a corrective to a reality built on a false premise. The means of that poetry is language, whose function is to make meaning.

The language of greed and economic power, Christensen writes, is restrictive; consequently, the language of the poet must liberate the imagination by being open, like a meadow, encouraging writer and reader to let go of prejudices to explore the unknown. Only by raising our consciousness to a vision and acceptance of passion can we hope to break down the chains that prevent us from being free. Understandably, Christensen's first two collections of poems, *Light* and *Grass*, deal with her own process of liberation, demonstrated in their form; *Grass*, especially, explores methods of invention of a new language to express and embody love.

The immediate contrast between the titles *Light* and *Grass* suggests the contrast between the poems of the former, which focus on cosmic and visionary themes, and the latter, which celebrates the concrete, earthbound world. Light shows the cold ice-bound landscapes of the writer's unconscious and her relationship with people in the world, both of which undergo a change as the poems progress from winter to summer, evening to morning, darkness to light in a shifting array of colors from white-black to blue and finally red. Christensen sees the anxiety that attends the writer's—and humankind's—sojourn in the chilling land of ice as the condition for change and continued development. It affords the individual the opportunity to see the condition in which he lives, and it gives birth to his anxiety, which is both his condemnation and his salvation.

Like her compatriot Søren Kierkegaard, the existential philosopher, Christensen sees anxiety, or *angst,* as a condition for change. The ability to tolerate this *angst,* provoking polarities of destruction and creation, she sees as sustained by love, because only love can engender new and continuous life. "Light" and "grass," the cosmic and the earthly, she finds co-existing in the act of love between a man and a woman. She seeks erotic love as an awakening. It is no lasting panacea; rather it must be experienced over and over to make the poet—and the reader—ready for change, and for the repeated encounters with the lies and deception that are part of everything human. Those must be confronted and fought and relationships of love started over both in terms of human intercourse and poetic expression.

Beginning with her novels, Christensen expands her area of concern to include society itself. She focuses on the roles people play—mandated by themselves or by others—and shows their debilitating effect. With *The Perpetual Movement Machine* and *Azorno,* she dramatizes the frustration of the artist's relationship to society. Her main character in *Perpetual Movement Machine* is a Christ-like figure, a mythical incarnation of love. For those in power, Ulrik Kent serves as a lightning rod for the increasingly vocal dissatisfaction of the oppressed; for the writer, he is a savior with connections to a world the powerful have denied him. Eventually executed and buried, he claws himself out and lives in isolation near the town dump. Again he is beaten and raped, and again executed, and subsequently resumes life by the river at the outskirts of town. There, people flock to hear his tale about a perpetual movement machine that goes round and round, indifferent to up and down, like a life in which beginning and end are uncertain. Only after the individual has set himself outside society, Christensen suggests, does he make connection with utopia, a connection that for Ulrik Kent is facilitated by his love of the character Coy. Their love initiates him into the cosmos as an individual and a collective being, "not just a man, but everyman," who appears and reappears in a variety of figures and professions, emblematic of the process of human life.

Azorno, Christensen's second novel, shows how we choose to plot our lives as main characters, just as we play minor roles in the dramas of others. We shape lives and we are shaped in turn. At our peril, we assign roles to one another in our love relationships that are too narrow, because as Christensen shows, not only society, but individuals and lovers may imprison one another.

> *I* am passionate about continuation.
> —**Inger Christensen**

Liberation, in the language of Inger Christensen, clearly does not mean separation from others. It means voluntarily seeking and building community while being tolerant of other people's individual needs and characteristics. "I believe we put too much emphasis on self realization," she writes. "As a counterbalance to the complexity of the world, we start cultivating the individual and the complexity of the individual," a direction that she is concerned may lead to self-sufficiency and subsequently to the destruction of the world in which we live. In contrast, she urges, it should be humanly possible to engage in the lives of others, even of strangers, and to become curious about what is going on in the world, asking questions about what we are about and what constitutes a mass society: "What is this city, is it a piece of art, a mobile, building blocks or what?"

A highly reflective writer of essays, Inger Christensen voices her awareness of the difficulties inherent in human communication. Verbal intercourse she finds problematic because:

> only very few things are worth talking about—and those we don't talk about. Those we cannot talk about; for instance, life, death and love. We are afraid to be alone and afraid to be together, afraid for what is past, what has stopped and what is all too orderly and afraid of that which is not past, what is floating along and what is messy—and we are afraid of our sexuality and afraid of death. . . . [W]e make war because we are afraid to tell one another we are afraid of each other and everything. It seems to me that we obstinately insist on walking into the rain—and equally obstinately continue to refuse inventing rubber boots and rain coats. . . . We must change if the world is going to change.

She urges her readers to talk about things ordinarily left unspoken, even to themselves. As a writer, she sets herself the task of thinking about the impossible, the "incomplete" and "irregular," attempting a classless language that does not yet exist.

The collections of poems titled *Det* (*That*), from 1967, is a demonstration of Christensen's artistic development as well as a response to the 1960s and its demands for a liberation of the imagination and celebration of the senses. "I have tried to write about a world that does not exist so that it may exist," she comments. *Det* is a poetic drama, divided into three parts, "Prologos," "Logos," and "Epilogos," an amalgam of the literary genres Christensen has been exploring. As such, it reflects the world as in a mirror and demonstrates, in the balance of formlessness and structure, the author's center of energy and insights. The published text appears "typed," suggesting the ongoing artistic process taking place even as we read.

This dramatic poem reveals the writer's uncertainty and *angst* as she invests her artistic powers in promoting the collective liberation she espouses. She writes that we must live in the "interregnum" of the unconscious, where the transformation of the soul, triggered by our anxiety, must take place. The poem attacks the church, the military, and capitalist society, which suppress human sexuality and creativity and exploit their energies. In that world, lovers and lunatics have the greatest revolutionary powers; the former due to their talent for transformation, the latter because of their inability to adjust to a sick society, both of which bespeak their basic health.

In the poems *Letter in April,* Christensen's belief that we must trust liberation of ourselves and others as the basis on which we can build human relationships and stake our future brings her to a confrontation between adult resignation and childlike capacity for wonder. She concludes that she must create her own sense of wonder or die. The mature poet realizes that, unlike the child who wonders at the unknown, the adult must wonder at the repetitive nature of the world and its phenomena, and experience her renewal through experiencing those.

With a shift in focus to ecological issues, Inger Christensen signals her sensitivity to the concerns of the late '70s and early '80s. The poems titled *Alfabet* (*Alphabet*) speak of the lethal rays and general pollution that are endangering the earth and that have afflicted words as well. The sequence is systematically structured, beginning with the letter "a," "apricot trees exist, apricot trees exist" and advancing through the letters of the alphabet. Increasing numbers of lines and words denote destruction, until the poem ends with "n," leaving the reader with a feeling of descent into horrors too great to list.

Our antidote to those horrors, according to Christensen, is care, care for people and all living substances, including air, water and the earth, "care which prevents fabrication of elements which threaten those of which people are made, care which cannot be ignored, neither with money or arguments." With utmost logic, she argues that if accident rules, we could be anyone else; consequently, we are responsible for the actions of everyone else.

Inger Christensen's writing is considered difficult reading. In a striking example of the intricacy of her thought, she explains her use of "systems" in her poetry:

> By using a system you are trying to reveal the rhythm of the universe. In the Creation story, there is silence, and then there are patterns. . . . And a useful benefit of a system is that you can't just write the first thing that comes into your mind; because of the resistance in the system, you get onto the track of something that you wouldn't otherwise have thought of. The gift is that you're forced to put much more of the world into the poem. Sometimes it feels as though the poem is carrying you along. You have access to a universe that begins to carry you. It carries you into something that you otherwise would never have been able to see or write. For me there was a shift from "I" to "it." The important thing became not "I" and psychological considerations but collective concerns: the way the world is set up. Boundaries between different individuals dissolved through osmosis, that's how I experienced it. You can express your own experience and emotions more effectively by starting somewhere else.

Christensen's ideas challenge the reader's expectations, forcing the viewer to see his or her imprisonment in the world of machines, and Christensen's experimentation with different forms of expression bring additional and demanding surprises. Yet the effort to understand her work is well rewarded. As one of her critics put it, "She is an intellectual, she is a philosopher, a philosopher, even, who deals with the most essential things in life. Of people like her we do not have too many."

SOURCES:

Christensen, Inger. *Del af Labyrinten.* Gylling: Narayna Press, 1982.
Dansk Litteraturhistorie. Edited by Torben Brostrom and Jens Kistrup. Copenhagen: Politikens Forlag, 1977.

Danske Digtere i det 20. aarhundrede. Vol. 4. Edited by Torben Brostrom and Mette Winge. Copenhagen: G.E.C. Gads Forlag, 1982.

The Nordic Poetry Festival Anthology. Edited by Kajsa Leander and Ernst Malmsten. Sweden, 1993.

Tegnverden. Ed. Iben Holk. Aarhus: Centrum, 1983.

Inga Wiehl, Yakima Valley Community College, Yakima, Washington

Christian (d. 1246)

Countess of Aumale. Name variations: Christian de Forz; Christina de Galloway. Died in 1246; daughter of Alan, lord of Galloway, and *Margaret (d. 1228), countess of Huntingdon; sister of *Devorgilla (d. 1290); aunt of John Balliol, king of Scots (r. 1292–1296); married William de Forz, 1st count of Aumale, before 1234; children: William de Forz, 2nd count of Aumale (d. 1260).

Christian Bruce (d. 1356).

See Bruce, Christian.

Christian de Plessetis (c. 1250–?)

Baroness Segrave. Name variations: Christian Segrave. Born around 1250; married John Segrave (1256–1325), 2nd baron Segrave, 1270; children: Stephen Segrave (d. 1325); *Margaret Segrave (c. 1280–?).

Christian of Schleswig-Holstein, Princess (1846–1923).

See Queen Victoria for sidebar on Helena.

Christians, Mady (1900–1951)

Austrian-born actress who, after a distinguished career in Europe, fled Fascism (1933), and created a strong reputation in the U.S., but fell victim to Cold War McCarthyism. Name variations: Margarete Christians. Born Marguerita or Margarethe Maria Christians in Vienna, Austria, on January 19, 1900; facing the end of her career after being blacklisted, died of a stress-induced stroke in South Norwalk, Connecticut, on October 28, 1951; daughter of Rudolf Christians and Bertha (Klein) Christians; married Sven von Müller (editor of the Hamburger Fremdenblatt*).*

Selected films—in U.S.: Audrey (1916); Wicked Woman (1934); Escapade (1935); Come and Get It (1936); Seventh Heaven (1937); The Woman I Love (1937); Heidi (1937); Address Unknown (1944); Tender Comrade (1944); All My Sons (1948); Letter From an Unknown Woman (1948).

In Germany: Der Mann ohne Namen (1920); Das Weib des Pharao (The Loves of Pharaoh, 1921); Malmaison *(1922);* Die Budden-brooks *(1923);* Das Spiel der Königin *(Ein Glas Wasser, 1923);* Der verlorene Schuh *(1923);* Der Wetterwart *(1923);* Die Finanzen des Grossherzogs *(The Grand Duke's Finances, 1923);* Mensch gegen Mensch *(1924);* Der Abenteurer *(1925);* Der Fanner aus Texas *(1925);* Die Verrufenen *(Slums of Berlin, 1925);* Ein Walzertraum *(The Waltz Dream, 1925);* Nanette macht alles *(1926);* Die Königin vom Moulin Rouge *(1926);* Grand Hotel *(1927);* Königin Luise *(Queen Luise, 1927);* Der Sohn der Hagar *(Out of the Mist, 1927); (UK)* The Runaway Princess *(1928); (Fr.)* Duel *(1928);* Das brennende Herz *(The Burning Heart, 1929);* Dich hab'ich geliebt *(Because I Loved You, 1929);* Die Frau von der man spricht *(1931);* Friederike *(1932);* Der Schwarze Husar *(1932); (portrayed Empress *Eugenie)* Ich und die Kaiserin *(and in English version,* The Only Girl *[Heart Song], 1933).*

A versatile and strong actress, Mady Christians became well-known and loved in the United States for her portrayal of a Norwegian-

Mady Christians

American matriarch in the play *I Remember Mama*. Highly regarded by critics for her ability to present superb performances even within mediocre plays and films, Christians was a stage veteran long before she came to America.

On January 19, 1900, she was born Marguerita Maria Christians into a theatrical family in Vienna; her father Rudolf Christians was a noted actor and her mother **Bertha Klein Christians** was an opera singer and recitalist. In 1912, the Christians moved to New York, where Rudolf became manager of the Irving Place Theater, which specialized in German-language repertory.

Bitten by the acting bug, at age 16 Mady was able to persuade her somewhat skeptical father to give her a role as a heroine in one of his productions, a one-act operetta. The role was challenging, calling on her to be both a bride of 17 and an old woman. Her father's response to the first-night performance was by no means supportive when he simply advised her: "Mady, I think you'd better get married." Confident in

Mady Christians as a European film star, 1920s.

her own talents, Mady refused to halt her career, noting that her performance had been praised in a local newspaper. Of greater importance was the fact that her mother, convinced of her daughter's talents, backed Mady's stage ambitions. To advance Mady's future, and also escape from an America on the brink of war and seething with anti-German hysteria, Bertha Christians returned to Vienna with her daughter.

Enrolled in Max Reinhardt's famous acting seminar, Mady Christians was now fully in her element. She had many small parts, but few critics could detect star quality in her. Fortunately, her mother and Max Reinhardt were convinced that her talents were deep and genuine, and that stardom was imminent. She alternated between engagements at Berlin's Deutsches Theater and Vienna's Theater in der Josefstadt. It took several difficult years to turn the corner, but a role in Tolstoy's *The Light Shines in Darkness* revealed her talents to both Berlin's critics and ordinary theatergoers. Now an unchallenged star, Christians signed a long-term contract with Reinhardt and was able to appear at not only the major theaters of Germany and Austria but throughout the rest of Europe as well. Performing in up to 45 plays a year, Christians led an often hectic life, but her professionalism carried all before it. Whether in plays by Shakespeare, Pirandello, Goethe, or Lessing, her characterizations were strong and well-focused. Before stardom arrived, she had married Dr. Sven von Müller, editor of one of Germany's most respected newspapers, the *Hamburger Fremdenblatt*. Both were too busy and interested in their respective careers to create a stable marriage, and some years later they were divorced.

Having seen anti-German intolerance in action in the United States in her youth, Mady Christians now witnessed infinitely greater explosions of hatred and brutality as Germany slid into the abyss of Fascism in the early 1930s. Many of her friends and colleagues in the theater were threatened by the rise of Hitlerism, either because they were Jewish or politically on the Left, or often because both elements were combined in the same individual. Always interested in artistic growth, Christians trained her fine soprano voice to the point where she was able to appear in 1932 in two sound films, the Franz Lehár operettas *Friederike* and *The Black Hussar*. But these were to be her last European triumphs. With Adolf Hitler and his brown-shirted hordes in control of Germany, artistic freedom was quickly extinguished. For Mady Christians, there was no choice but to emigrate. Her native

Austria, also abandoning democracy for Fascism, no longer offered a place of refuge. Despite its economic depression, free America beckoned.

Arriving in New York in 1933, Christians had to face the fact that she was relatively unknown in the United States even though she had toured there and many of her films had received favorable reviews. Although she quickly landed major parts in Broadway plays, most of these turned out to be flops. Fortunately, the brilliance of her acting rose above the mediocrity of the plays in which she found herself cast. Leading New York critic Brooks Atkinson clearly recognized the situation when he wrote that it "would be worth sitting through fifty bad plays to see her perform."

During these often difficult years, Christians remained reasonably solvent by also appearing in films. In one of these, *Heidi* (1937), which boasted *Shirley Temple (Black) as its star, the European refugee attracted the attention of critics with her sharp characterization of Heidi's aunt who sends the little girl to two ogres who eventually sell her to the Roma (gypsies).

Moving from one ill-fated role to the next, Christians managed to persevere and eventually found herself in a stage production matching her talent, a presentation of *Hamlet* that opened in October 1938. Starring Maurice Evans, this was triumphant Shakespeare, and Christians' portrayal of Hamlet's mother Gertrude was widely acclaimed. Soon, other quality situations were offered her, including a role in Shaw's *Heartbreak House* as presented by Orson Welles' Mercury Theater, and another fine part, this time in *Henry IV.*

By the fall of 1939, Europe was engulfed in the opening salvoes of the Second World War. Mady Christians was concerned about the fate of humane values and the survival of democracy itself. She had visited Germany briefly in 1938 to attend her mother's funeral and knew only too well how menacing a force Hitler's Germany had become. Although not interested in the minutiae of world politics, she took a stand, warning all she met about the evils of Fascism, and joining organizations that assisted refugees and combatted Nazism on American soil. In later years, the idealism she displayed during these years would provide an excuse for witchhunters to destroy her career and, with it, her life.

An established star, Mady Christians was now offered excellent scripts of new plays and leading roles in films. She was brilliant as Sara Mueller in *Lillian Hellman's anti-Fascist play

Watch on the Rhine, which opened to excellent reviews in April 1941. Brooks Atkinson characterized her acting in the Mueller role as being "full of womanly affection and a crusader's resignation to realities." The anti-Nazi activist Kurt Mueller's wife was seen as being masterfully depicted by a Mady Christians "taut with womanly anxiety in a clearly resolved performance." Atkinson could barely contain his enthusiasm for the quality of Christians' performance, praising it again some months after his initial review. On this occasion, he noted that as "a fine actress with unusual range in the parts she can play," she was now offering New York's theater patrons "a rich, emotional performance."

Christians was able again in 1943 to find in the film *Address Unknown* a vehicle for her strongly anti-Nazi sentiments. Even more important for her growing reputation as one of America's eminent actresses was her starring role in the play *I Remember Mama.* Opening on Broadway in October 1944, *I Remember Mama* boasted several other refugees from Hitlerism in its cast, Adrienne Gessner and Oscar Homolka. Based on an adaptation by John Van Druten of Kathryn Forbes' book *Mama's Bank Account,* *I Remember Mama* was a delightful evening of theater, at least in part because its producers were none other than Richard Rodgers and Oscar Hammerstein II.

The central character of this play about a Norwegian-American family in San Francisco, the strong-willed individual who keeps the family stable and happy, is of course Mama. Normally caustic critics gushed words of praise for Mady Christians' portrayal of Mama. "Mama in her hands is warm and honest," wrote Lewis Nichols of *The New York Times*; "her deceits,

Forbes, Kathryn. See Dunne, Irene for sidebar on McLean, Kathyn.

Gessner, Adrienne (1896–1987)
Austrian actress. Born Adrienne Geiringer in Maria Schutz am Semmering, Austria, on July 23, 1896; died in Vienna, on June 23, 1987; married Ernst Lothar.

Adrienne Gessner was a distinguished actress and major star on the Vienna stage before Hitler's minions marched into Austria in 1938. That year, Gessner and her husband Ernst Lothar sailed for America where she soon appeared on Broadway. Her U.S. stage credits include *Another Sun, Claudia,* and *Thank You, Svoboda.* She also portrayed Aunt Trinka in *I Remember Mama.* Gessner returned to Austria, where her career continued to even greater heights of acclaim, and she became one of the leading actresses of the Burgtheater and Salzburg Festival.

such as talk of the bank account which wasn't there, are in the world's best interests." As the key player in a super-hit, Christians did not miss a single day of the show's 720 performances. She then went on tour with it.

The Allied victory over Fascism, and U.S. possession of the ultimate weapon of mass destruction, the atomic bomb, should have provided a sense of security for Americans. But in fact the onset of the Cold War quickly created an all-pervasive sense of paranoia in all sectors of American society, including the entertainment world. Mady Christians was naïve about politics and proceeded with her career as if nothing had changed. She continued to search for roles that gave her an opportunity to project the deep humanity that was the essence of her being.

Confident that she was suited to the part, Christians co-starred as Edward G. Robinson's wife in Arthur Miller's *All My Sons*, released in its screen version in early 1948. Some conservatives did not take kindly to the central character of this drama, a manufacturer of defective weapons in wartime who rationalizes his actions as having made him prosperous so that he could benefit his family. Radical, and even anti-capitalist sentiments were seen lurking in Miller's story, and not only Miller but those artists who had appeared in *All My Sons* were seen as subversives by some politicians who felt that ideological differences threatened Americanism.

In 1948, Mady Christians appeared in what would be her last film, *A Letter from an Unknown Woman*, turning in another excellent performance. The next year, she unwittingly made her last stage appearance, in Strindberg's *The Father*. In 1950, catastrophe struck. The notorious Hollywood blacklist, which effectively made it impossible for artists to find employment in the entertainment industry, appeared in its final and most comprehensive form as a "subversive dictionary" entitled *Red Channels*.

Professional red-hunters, determined to root out assorted doctrinaire "reds" and leftists as well as liberals who were "soft on Communism," were indifferent to the impact their lists might have on the careers and lives of the individuals they stigmatized. For an artist, the price of once having briefly belonged to the Communist Party, or having been too vehement in opposing Fascism by supporting refugees from Europe, was professional annihilation. In 1950, witch-hunting was both popular and profitable in a country made ever more fearful by a world in which the Soviets now had nuclear weapons,

China had been "lost" to Communists, and an inconclusive war was raging in Korea. Senator Joseph McCarthy of Wisconsin seized the opportunity to become a national figure at this time by asserting that the government and the country in general were in dire peril, riddled with subversive traitors and their various allies and dupes. The American mood was that of a witch-hunt.

Along with hundreds of other artists, Mady Christians was now branded for her "un-American activities" in years past. Her alleged transgressions included having shown too much compassion for the anti-Franco veterans of the Spanish Civil War as well as far too much sympathy for leftist German writers who had fled for their lives from Hitler's wrath. Furthermore, she had joined organizations such as the American Committee for the Protection of Foreign Born, now stigmatized as Communist fronts by the attorney general of the United States in his well-known and much-feared list.

The frightened actress was visited by investigators, anonymous men working for vast and essentially secret organs of state like the FBI. At the same time, her phone ceased to ring with job offers, and some who had once been her friends or colleagues were suddenly cool and distant. Her health suffered as a result of growing anxiety and uncertainty, and her blood pressure skyrocketed to dangerous levels.

A brief respite from her travails took place when Christians was offered a television role in "The Mother" on the "Somerset Maugham Theatre." But a week before rehearsals were to begin, the producer informed her that it had all been "a mistake" and while she would be paid her salary she could not appear in the role. A recurrence of hypertension put the actress into a New York hospital. Upon her release, she wrote one of her remaining friends: "I cannot bear yet to think of the things which led to my breakdown. One day I shall put them down in a record of something unbelievable." A few days later, on October 28, 1951, Mady Christians collapsed at the home of a friend in Connecticut. She died that same day of a massive cerebral hemorrhage in Norwalk Hospital.

Defying the blacklist that had hastened her death, 300 of Christians' friends and colleagues attended her funeral services in Manhattan. A moving eulogy noting both the dead artist's professional brilliance and private humanity was delivered by her close friend, producer-director *Margaret Webster. Christians was buried in a private service at Ferncliff Cemetery, Ardsley, New York, but the issues raised by her tragic death were by no means gone and forgotten. In a moving, angry letter to *The New York Times*, her good friend the playwright Elmer Rice asserted that "a fine, vital, liberal, warm-hearted human being" had both her life and career snuffed out by "relentless, sadistic persecution." Rice singled out as the men responsible for his friend's death the "small-souled witch-hunters who make a fine art of character assassination." Bitterly, the playwright concluded by noting that it would useless to appeal "to the consciences of the McCarthyites: obviously they have none. But perhaps the martyrdom of Mady Christians will set freedom-loving citizens thinking about what is happening to art and to democracy in America."

In response to the Rice letter, others appeared in the same newspaper in succeeding weeks, including one from John Van Druten, who praised Rice for what he had written earlier and described Christians as having been to him "a true and deeply valued friend" whose death was triggered by persecution that was known to the theater world but very likely not by the public at large. More letters followed in succeeding weeks, the sometimes acidic exchange being ended in late November by a moving letter from Margaret Webster, who dismissed the notion that Christians had ever behaved in a disloyal fashion. Defending the reputation of a woman no longer able to speak for herself, Webster described her close friend as having been "deeply in love with her country, conscious of her responsibilities toward it and concerned for its welfare. She was a fine actress of great gifts which she devoted to the service of her profession and its members. She was a warm-hearted human being who always held out a helping hand to anyone who needed it. It is thus that she would want to be, and should be, and will be remembered."

SOURCES:

Ceplair, Larry, and Steven Englund. *The Inquisition in Hollywood: Politics in the Film Community, 1930–1960*. Garden City, NY: Anchor Press/Doubleday, 1980.

"Drama Mailbag," in *The New York Times*. November 4, 11, 18, 25, 1951, section II, p. 3.

Kanfer, Stefan. *A Journal of the Plague Years*. NY: Atheneum, 1973.

"Mady Christians, Actress, Is Dead," in *The New York Times*. October 29, 1951, p. 23.

Navasky, Victor S. *Naming Names*. NY: Penguin Books, 1981.

Red Channels. NY: American Business Consultants, 1950.

Schrecker, Ellen. *The Age of McCarthyism: A Brief History with Documents*. Boston and NY: Bedford Books of St. Martin's Press, 1994.

"300 at Christians Rites," in *The New York Times*. November 1, 1951, p. 29.

Vaughn, Robert. *Only Victims: A Study of Show Business Blacklisting*. NY: Putnam, 1972.

John Haag, University of Georgia, Athens, Georgia

Christie, Agatha (1890–1976)

English novelist and dramatist, mainly of detection stories and thrillers, whose sales continue to break all records. Name variations: Agatha Christie Mallowan; Lady Mallowan; (pseudonym) Mary Westmacott. Born Agatha Mary Clarissa Miller on September 15, 1890, in Torquay, Devon, England; died on January 12, 1976, at Wallingford, Berkshire; daughter of Frederick Alvah and **Clarissa Margaret (Boehmer) Miller**; *educated at home and at various finishing schools; married Archibald Christie, on December 24, 1914 (divorced, April 1928); married Max Mallowan, on September 11, 1930; children: (first marriage) Rosalind (b. 1919).*

Published first novel, The Mysterious Affair at Styles *(1920); published* The Murder of Roger Ackroyd *(1926); had first stage adaptation produced (1928); had first film adaptation released (1928); had first play produced (1930); published first Mary Westmacott novel,* Giant's Bread *(March 1930); had radio play commissioned for Queen Mary's 80th birthday (1947); saw her play* The Mousetrap *begin London run (November 25, 1952); received the Grand Masters Award of the Mystery Writers of America (1954); awarded the CBE (January 1, 1956); became president of the Detection Club (1957); received an honorary Doctorate of Letters from Exeter University (1961); given the Order of Dame Commander of the British Empire (January 1, 1971); was subject of wax model placed in* *Madame Tussaud's*, London (1972).*

Selected writings: (short story collection) The Mysterious Mr. Quin *(1930); (under pseudonym Mary Westmacott)* Unfinished Portrait *(1934);* The ABC Murders *(1936);* The Body in the Library *(1942); (autobiography)* Come, Tell Me How You Live *(1946); (play)* Murder on the Nile *(1945); (play)* Witness for the Prosecution *(1953); (short story collection)* The Adventure of the Christmas Pudding *(1960);* By the Pricking of My Thumbs *(1968); (poetry)* Poems *(1973).*

Though Agatha Christie's first novel did not appear until she was 30 years old, she would go on to write just under 100 books, mainly detective stories and thrillers. Owing to the fact that most English publications were soon followed by publication in America, often bearing a different title, this number can appear to be even greater. Nevertheless, her popularity was, and still is, phenomenal. By the time she died, over four million copies of her books had been sold worldwide. By now, over a billion copies have been printed in English alone, and she has been translated into more languages than Shakespeare. Her celebrated play, The *Mousetrap*, made theatrical history by having an unbroken London run for over 40 years. Television programs, featuring her characters Hercule Poirot, played by David Suchet, and Miss Marple, played by *Joan Hickson, have had huge ratings over the years.

Agatha's mother Clarissa Boehmer had had a troubled childhood. On the early death of her father, her mother kept the three boys, and Clarissa was sent to live with an aunt. Though the aunt was of a kindly disposition, she did not really understand children, while Clarissa, despite having every material advantage, felt rejected by her own mother. She was fond of her stepuncle, a rich American, however, and particularly fond of his son Fred by a previous marriage. Though Fred was a good deal older than Clarissa and often away in America, she idolized him, even as a child. Unbelievably, Fred kept all of Clarissa's letters and poems and the pocket book she embroidered for him. Finally, he returned from his philandering in America and married his young stepcousin.

Frederick Alvah Miller never worked; his income was generated through property in New York. At first, he and his wife traveled between England and America, but they eventually settled in Torquay, Devon, in a house named Ashfield. It remained in the family for many years. In her autobiography, Agatha Christie recalled, "looking back I feel that our house was a truly happy house." She was a solitary child, as her brother and sister were a few years older, but she seems to have been contented with her own company and professed satisfaction with her upbringing: "I had a very happy childhood. I had a home and a garden that I loved; a wise and patient Nanny; as father and mother two people who loved each other dearly and made a success of their marriage and of parenthood."

The domestic arrangements were typical of the well-to-do of the period; there were sufficient servants to run the household smoothly. Agatha said that as a child the servants were far more real to her than her mother's friends or her distant relations. Frederick Miller spent each day at his club, while dinner was usually taken in the company of friends. According to Agatha, "There was one big dinner party at our home every week, and he and my mother went out to dinner usually another two or three times a week."

Agatha's day followed the strict routine of many other upper- and middle-class children of the age. She lived in the nursery with her nurse, was taken for a daily walk, and after tea would be "put into starched muslin" and taken downstairs to her mother "to be played with." The rest of the time "good" children were expected to entertain themselves so Agatha played indoors or in the garden. Like many solitary children, she peopled her life with imaginary characters. At first, there were "the Kittens," later a family who were "not quite children and not quite dogs, but indeterminate creatures between the two." Outdoors, she endowed her hoop with a personality of its own. Later still, she invented a number of female companions who remained with her for several years. She had plenty of toys, but, apart from her dolls' house and her rockinghorse, these left little impression on her in later years. She also had pets—a canary called Goldie and a Yorkshire terrier called Tony.

Christie claims to remember little of her siblings Madge and Monty while she was a child—possibly because they were both at school. Madge was generally kind and read to Agatha, though they did play one game in which the older girl pretended to be mad, which both terrified and fascinated the younger. Monty avoided his kid sister when he could, teased her when he couldn't, and called her "the scrawny chicken." Occasionally, he condescended to show her his white mice or to allowed her to "help" when he was making things. Once he took her out in his boat, but the experiment was never repeated as Agatha, always a poor sailor, became seasick.

As a little girl, Christie was indulged by her grandmothers and her uncles. Grannie B. was her paternal grandmother; Auntie-Grannie was her paternal stepgrandmother. Grannie B. was poor, "sitting all day in the window of her house, sewing." Auntie-Grannie was rich and lived in a large house in Ealing. When Agatha and her Nanny paid extended visits, Agatha particularly remembered playing a game that she called "A Chicken from Mr. Whitely's":

> Needless to say, I was the chicken. Selected by Grannie with appeals to the shopman as to whether I was really young and tender, brought home, trussed up, skewered (yells of delight from my skewered self), put in the oven, done to a turn, brought on the table

Agatha Christie

dished up, great show of sharpening the carving knife, when suddenly the chicken comes alive and "It's me!"—grand climax—to be repeated *ad lib.*

On a Sunday, when Grannie B. and two of her sons came for a splendid lunch, they would all play school with their little visitor.

Clarissa Miller seems to have been somewhat indecisive. She flirted with several religious sects before coming full circle and returning to the Church of England. While Madge and Monty were young, their mother had ardently believed in formal education for both boys and girls. Monty had gone to Harrow. Madge had attended Roedean, though the line had been drawn when a mistress had wished her to go to the ladies' college at Girton, and she was "finished" in Paris instead. However, by the time Agatha was old enough for school, Clarissa no longer believed that children should be taught. She was very disappointed when Agatha was found to be able to read before the age of five. The little girl went on to write and to learn arithmetic from her father. French she learned from a maid whom Clarissa Miller engaged in France and brought back to England. Later, Agatha attended school in Torquay for a little while and various establishments of an educational nature in France. It was during this time that she toyed with the possibility of a musical career but found that her temperament was unsuited to public performance.

It was still the fashion at this time for young girls to "come out" into society, a costly business. Madge had made her society debut in New York, but by the time Agatha was old enough the family's financial position had changed. Frederick Miller had died, not exactly ruined but in straitened circumstances, owing, Christie thought, to the bad management of his American financial advisers. Ashfield was expensive to run, and it was often cheaper to rent out the house and live abroad. Agatha "came out" in Cairo, where her mother had gone for her health. Since several British regiments were stationed in Egypt, there was a lively social life. Christie later claimed that for three months she "went to five dances every week." Though she flirted, no one really touched her heart.

Agatha Christie's pleasure and genius lay in the dovetailing of events and the posing of a puzzle.

—Jessica Mann

Once back in England, Christie went to country house parties, attended race meetings, was driven about in the cars of friends, and, in 1909, even flew in an airplane. She fell in love several times, had a number of proposals of marriage, and eventually became engaged to Reggie Lucy, a major in the Gunners and a member of a family with whom she had been friendly for many years. During her late teens, she had had a few poems printed, mainly in *The Poetry Review,* and then at her mother's suggestion started to write stories, but none of them was accepted for publication. When she progressed to a novel, she sent it to Eden Philpotts for advice. A well-known writer at the time and a near neighbor of the Millers, Philpotts made some suggestions and arranged for his own literary agent, Hughes Massie, to criticize the book. Massie advised her "to stop thinking about it any more and to write another book."

Shortly before Christmas 1912, Agatha met Archie Christie. In her autobiography, she describes him as "a tall fair young man, with crisp, curly hair, a rather interesting nose, turned up not down, and a great air of careless confidence about him." After what might justifiably be termed a whirlwind romance, Agatha wrote a farewell to Reggie who was abroad with his regiment and became engaged to Archie. In 1914, war broke out between England and Germany. Archie was in the Flying Corps where his life was in great danger while Agatha worked as a voluntary nurse in Torquay. When Archie was handed an unexpected leave over Christmas 1914, he and Agatha hastily arranged to be married on Christmas Eve. The next day, Archie returned to his unit; he and Agatha were not to meet again for the next six months.

After about a year, Christie left nursing to work in the hospital dispensary. It was here, during slack periods, that she began planning her first detective story. Called *The Mysterious Affair at Styles,* it contained the Belgian investigator who later became so famous—Hercule Poirot. Though the book was finished during a fortnight's holiday at a hotel on Dartmoor, taken especially for the purpose, it was not published until 1920. By then, the war was well over, and the Christies were living in London where Archie had a job in the City. A daughter had been born to them the previous year. Christie's contract with Bodley Head gave her a small royalty, but only after 2,000 copies had been sold; all monies accrued by subsidiary rights were shared on a 50/50 basis. It also committed her to offer her next five novels to the same publisher. At the time, none of this worried her. She and Archie were elated, and they celebrated at the Hammersmith Palais de Danse.

In 1923, the Christies gave up their conventional lifestyle to tour the world. Archie went as financial adviser to the British Empire Mission, an organization set up to prepare for the forthcoming Empire Exhibition, with all expenses paid and a fee of £1,000. Christie was allowed to accompany him virtually free of charge. While Madge looked after their daughter Rosalind, the couple visited South Africa, Australia, New Zealand, Hawaii, and Canada. On their return, Archie took another City job.

Since *The Mysterious Affair at Styles,* Christie had continued writing. Her second novel, a thriller, introduced Tommy and Tuppence Beresford who were to become popular investigators with Christie fans. With £500 that she received from the "Evening News" for the serial rights of *The Man in the Brown Suit,* Christie was able to buy a car. The Christies also moved to Sunningdale where Archie could more easily indulge his passion for golf. Agatha acquired Hughes Massie Ltd. as her literary agent and wrote a series of 12 short stories for *The Sketch.* As soon as Bodley Head had published the contracted books, Christie left them for Collins who remained her publishers in England for the rest of her life. From then until her death, Agatha Christie wrote at least one detective book or thriller every year. Miss Marple, her other popular investigator, was not created until 1930, but her reputation as a successful crime writer became fully established with the publication of *The Murder of Roger Ackroyd* in the spring of 1926.

That year also brought sadness. For some time, the Christies' marriage had been less than happy: golf had virtually taken over Archie's leisure hours and now he had fallen in love with a young woman named **Nancy Neele** and wanted a divorce. Christie was distraught. On December 3, after quarrelling with her husband, she disappeared and was missing for several days. A full-scale search was mounted involving hundreds of police and thousands of ordinary citizens. *The Daily News* offered £100 reward for information about her—a large sum in those days. Ten days later, she was found to be staying at a spa, the Hydro Hotel in Harrogate, Yorkshire, under an assumed name. Archie went to bring her home and issued a statement to the effect that his wife was suffering loss of memory and was to receive medical treatment. The Christies divorced in April 1928.

In the autumn of 1929, Christie holidayed alone, traveling to Damascus and Baghdad, and

From the movie Agatha, *starring Vanessa Redgrave as Christie.*

as far as Istanbul on the Orient Express. While there, she visited the excavations at Ur, where Leonard Woolley was leading a dig under the joint auspices of the British Museum and the Museum of the University of Pennsylvania. In March 1930, Christie returned and this time met Woolley's assistant, Max Mallowan. Max was part Austrian, part French, and 14 years younger than Christie. At the instigation of Woolley's wife, Max escorted Christie home, showing her something of the desert on the way. By September of the same year, they had married, choosing a small church in Edinburgh for the ceremony in order to avoid publicity.

From now on, except for a break during the Second World War when she returned to dispensing, Christie was to spend part of her life in England and part on digs abroad with her husband. She became skilled at documenting, cleaning, assembling, and photographing finds. She even undertook the developing of the film—a hot and uncomfortable activity as the darkroom was sometimes little more than a closet. Yet, even under these circumstances, she continued writing. **Alison Light**, in her book *Forever England,* notes, "in order to gauge what nostalgia in the work of Agatha Christie really means one needs to imagine her a stout woman in her early forties, in a hot tent or on a dusty verandah, looking across the desert, and settling down to write about murder in the vicarage."

As well as stories, Christie wrote plays, an outgrowth of her dissatisfaction with the adaptations of her works by others. The first play to be staged by another was *Alibi,* Michael Morton's adaptation of *The Murder of Roger Ackroyd.* Her own first play was *Black Coffee,* staged in 1930 and turned into a film in 1931. Undoubtedly her most popular play was *The Mousetrap,* which began its London run on November 25, 1952. Christie continued to write poetry and published two collections of poems, *The Road of Dreams* in 1924 and *Poems* in 1973. Although best remembered for her thrillers and her mysteries, Christie also wrote six serious novels using the pseudonym, Mary Westmacott. It is claimed

From the movie Death on the Nile, *starring Peter Ustinov as Hercule Poirot.*

that all these novels are, to a greater or lesser degree, autobiographical. The first Mary Westmacott novel, *Giant's Bread,* was published as early as 1930 but until 1949 very few people were aware that Mary Westmacott and Agatha Christie were in fact the same person.

In later life, Christie had several honors bestowed upon her but the one that, according to her *Autobiography,* afforded her the most pleasure was "dining with the Queen at Buckingham Palace." After her husband was knighted in 1968 and she was made Dame Commander of the British Empire in 1971, Christie was handed a name problem. She solved the dilemma by being Lady Mallowan when appearing in the capacity of Max's wife and Dame Agatha when appearing in her own right.

Even after her death, one "new" Agatha Christie was published. Many years earlier, she had written two books containing the deaths of Hercule Poirot and Miss Marple, *Curtain* and *Sleeping Murder.* Intended for posthumous publication, their author's rights were assigned to Rosalind and to Max. In 1975, Christie was too infirm to write her annual "Christie for Christmas" and was persuaded to release *Curtain* instead. In January 1976, she died, and the other book, *Sleeping Murder,* was published in October of the same year. *An Autobiography* was published in 1977.

SOURCES:
Christie, Agatha. *An Autobiography.* London: Collins, 1977.

Mann, Jessica. *Deadlier than the Male: An Investigation into Feminine Crime Writing.* London: David and Charles, 1981.

Osborne, Charles. *The Life and Crimes of Agatha Christie.* London: Michael O'Mara, 1990 (1st pub. in 1982).

SUGGESTED READING:
Mallowan, Agatha Christie. *Come, Tell Me How You Live.* London: Collins, 1946.

Mallowan, Max. *Memoirs.* London: Collins, 1977.

RELATED MEDIA:
Miss Marple series of films, starring ***Margaret Rutherford**; Miss Marple series for television, starring Joan Hickson.

Agatha (98 min.), film starring **Vanessa Redgrave** and Dustin Hoffman, produced by Warner Bros., 1979, screenplay by **Kathleen Tynan** based on her story (a fictionalization of the disappearance and search for Christie).

Endless Night, also titled *Agatha Christie's Endless Night* (99 min.) British film, starring **Hayley Mills,** Hywel Bennet, and **Britt Eckland,** 1971.

And Then There Were None (97 min.), film starring Barry Fitzgerald, Walter Huston, ***Judith Anderson,** produced by 20th Century-Fox, 1945.

Ten Little Indians, film starring Hugh O'Brien and **Shirley Eaton,** Seven Arts, 1965.

Ten Little Indians, film starring Oliver Reed, **Elke Sommer,** and ***Stephane Audran,** 1975.

Murder on the Orient Express, film starring Albert Finney, **Lauren Bacall,** ***Ingrid Bergman,** Sean Connery, ***Wendy Hiller,** and Vanessa Redgrave, produced by Paramount, 1974.

Evil Under the Sun (102 min.), starring Peter Ustinov, **Maggie Smith, Diana Rigg,** produced by EMI/ Universal, 1982.

Barbara Evans,
Research Associate in Women's Studies
at Nene College, Northampton, England

Christina.
Variant of Christine.

Christina (fl. 1086).
See Margaret, Saint for sidebar.

Christina, Queen (1626–1689).
See Christina of Sweden.

Christina I of Naples, Queen of Spain (1806–1878).
See Isabella II for sidebar on Maria Christina I.

Christina Bernadotte (b. 1943)
Swedish royal. Name variations: Christina of Sweden. Born Christina Louise Helen on August 3, 1943, at Haga Palace, Stockholm, Sweden; daughter of Gustavus Adolphus (1906–1947), duke of Westerbotten, and *Sybilla of Saxe-Coburg-Gotha (1908–1972); sister of Carl XVI Gustavus, king of Sweden; married Tod Gösta Magnuson, on June 15, 1974; children: Carl Gustaf (b. 1975); Tord Oscar (b. 1977); Victor Edmund (b. 1980).

Christina Casimir (fl. 1640–1660)
Margravine of Baden-Durlach. Name variations: Christina von Simmern. Flourished from 1640 to 1660; daughter of *Catherine (1584–1638), countess Palatine, and John Casimir of Zweibrücken (b. 1589), count Palatine; married Frederick VI, margrave of Baden-Durlach, on May 15, 1640; children: *Christine of Baden-Durlach (1645–1705); Frederick VII (1647–1709), margrave of Baden-Durlach; *Johanna Elizabeth of Baden-Durlach (1651–1680).

Christina of Denmark (1521–1590)
Duchess of Milan. Name variations: Christine, duchesse de Lorraine; Christierna Sforza. Born in 1521; died on December 10, 1590; daughter of Christian II (1481–1559), king of Norway and Denmark (r. 1513–1523), and *Elisabeth of Habsburg (1501–1526); niece of Charles V, Holy Roman emper-

or; married Francesco Maria Sforza, duke of Milan (r. 1521–1535), on May 4, 1534; married Francis I (1517–1545), duke of Lorraine (r. 1544–1545, son of *Renée of Montpensier), on July 10, 1541; children: (second marriage) Charles II the Great, duke of Lorraine (r. 1545–1608, who married *Claude de France [1547–1575]).

Christina of Holstein-Gottorp
(1573–1625)

Queen of Sweden. Born on April 13, 1573; died on December 8, 1625; daughter of Adolf (1526–1586), duke of Holstein-Gottorp (r. 1544–1586), and *Christine of Hesse (1543–1604); became second wife of Charles IX (1550–1611), king of Sweden (r. 1604–1611), on August 27, 1592; grandmother of *Christina of Sweden; children: Gustavus Adolphus II (1594–1632), king of Sweden (r. 1611–1632, who married *Maria Eleonora of Brandenburg); Marie Elizabeth (1596–1618, who married John, duke of East Gotland); Charles Philip, duke of Sodermann-land (b. 1601). Charles IX's first wife was *Anna Maria of the Palatinate (1561–1589).

Christina of Sardinia (1812–1836)

Queen of the Two Sicilies. Name variations: Christine of Sardinia. Born on November 14, 1812; died on January 31, 1836; daughter of *Maria Teresa of Austria (1773–1832) and Victor Emmanuel I (b. 1759), king of Sardinia (r. 1802–1821); married Ferdinand II of Naples (b. 1810), king of the Two Sicilies (r. 1830–1859), on November 21, 1832; children: Francis II (1836–1894), king of the Two Sicilies (r. 1859–1860), king of Sicily (r. 1859–1894).

Christina of Saxony (1461–1521)

Queen of Norway and Denmark. Name variations: Christine. Born on December 25, 1461; died on December 8, 1521; daughter of Ernest (b. 1441), elector of Saxony; sister of *Margaret of Saxony (1469–1528); married John I or Johannes also known as Hans, king of Norway and Denmark (r. 1481–1513), on September 6, 1478; children: Johann (died young); Ernst (died young); Christian II (b. 1481), king of Norway and Denmark (r. 1513–1523); *Elizabeth of Denmark (1485–1555, who married Joachim I of Brandenburg); Franz (1497–1511).

Christina of Saxony married Hans, king of Norway and Denmark, who reigned from 1481 to 1513. Hans was also king of Sweden from 1497 to 1501, but the Union was breaking up; Sweden's regent, Sten Sture was vying for power. Hans and Christina of Saxony arrived to stay in Stockholm palace in January 1501. In August, Hans left the castle, accompanied by his mistress **Adele Ironbeard**, leaving the palace in the charge of Christina. By September, the castle was under siege. Christina held out doggedly until the garrison of 1,000 had been reduced to 70 defenders, none of whom could stand upright. All others had been killed by weapon, starvation, or disease. Though Christina continued to hold out in hopes of her husband's promised fleet, she was obliged to surrender on May 6, 1502. At first, Sten Sture promised her safe passage home, then changed his mind and imprisoned her until that October when she was freed. The Union was shattered.

Christina of Sweden (d. 1122)

Grand Princess of Kiev. Name variations: Kristina of Sweden; Kristina Ingesdottir. Died on January 18, 1122 (some sources cite 1120); daughter of Inge I the Elder, co-regent or king of Sweden (r. 1080–1110, 1112–1125), and *Helen (fl. 1100s); married Mstislav I (b. 1076), grand prince of Kiev (r. 1125–1132), in 1095; children: *Ingeborg of Russia; Malmfrid of Novgorod; Izyaslav II also known as Yziaslav II, prince of Kiev (r. 1146–1154); Rostislav I (d. 1167), prince of Kiev; *Marie of Kiev (d. 1179); *Irene of Kiev.

Christina of Sweden (1626–1689)

Queen of Sweden and learned ruler who crossed gender boundaries, supported knowledge and art, and fascinated people with her unconventional ways. Name variations: Kristina Augusta Wasa; Christina Maria Alexandra Vasa; Christina Alexandra. Pronunciation: VAH-sa. Born Kristina Augusta Wasa on December 8, 1626 (December 18, by the Gregorian calendar now in use), in Stockholm, Sweden; died in Rome on April 19, 1689 (Gregorian); daughter of Gustavus II Adolphus (1594–1632), king of Sweden (r. 1611–1632), and Maria Eleonora of Brandenburg (1599–1655); never married; probably the most important romantic relationship in Christina's life, though discounted by most biographers writing from 1900s to 1960s, was with Countess Ebba Sparre; no children.

Became queen of Sweden (1632); began to reign (1644); abdicated (1654); moved to Rome (1655).

The astrologers had predicted a son, and King Gustavus II Adolphus, the great Swedish hero, was elated when told of the arrival of his long-awaited heir. Born with the placenta

Christina of Sweden

See sidebar
on the
following page

wrapped around its body, only its head and limbs showing, the baby was covered with hair, its voice loud and vigorous, and in those first moments no one had realized that a girl had been born. When the women attending the birth realized their mistake, they wondered how to break the news to the king. Finally, ❧▶ **Catherine**, the king's older sister, carried the baby to the father "in such a condition that he could see . . . for himself what she dared not tell him." The king took his daughter in his arms, saying, "I hope that this girl will be as good as a son to me.

I only pray that God will preserve her," then ordered a grand celebration appropriate for a male successor to the throne. Soon after, he laughed, "She will be clever. She took us all in!"

As a matter of fact, Christina of Sweden *could* inherit the Swedish throne. Written into the pact her great grandfather Gustavus I Vasa had made with the Swedish people was a clause stating that if a king should die without leaving a male heir, the crown could pass to an unmarried daughter. When Christina was one year old, her father had the government explicitly affirm her as his heir, since, as the proclamation said, the idea that a woman could be monarch, writes Christina in her autobiography, was one "not fully understood by many simple people of all degrees."

Christina's mother, ◄⅜ **Maria Eleonora of Brandenburg**, was bitterly disappointed, both

⅜► **Catherine** (1584–1638)

Countess Palatine. Name variations: Katarina; Catherine Vasa. Born on November 19, 1584; died on December 13, 1638; daughter of Charles IX, king of Sweden, and *Anna Maria of the Palatinate (1561–1589); half-sister of Gustavus II Adolphus (1594–1632); aunt of *Christina of Sweden (1626–1689), queen of Sweden; married John Casimir of Zweibrücken (b. 1589), count Palatine, on June 11, 1615; children: Charles X Gustavus (1622–1660), king of Sweden (r. 1654–1660); *Christina Casimir (who married Frederick of Baden-Durlach).

⅜► **Maria Eleonora of Brandenburg** (1599–1655)

Queen of Sweden. Name variations: Maria Eleanora Hohenzollern. Born on November 11, 1599; died on March 28, 1655; daughter of John Sigismund (1572–1619), elector of Brandenburg (r. 1608–1619), and *Anna of Prussia; sister of George William, elector of Brandenburg (r. 1619–1640); married Gustavus II Adolphus (1594–1632), king of Sweden (r. 1611–1632), on November 25, 1620; children: Christine (1623–1624); *Christina of Sweden (1626–1689).

To solidify his position with the Protestant north German states, Gustavus married Maria Eleonora, sister of George William, elector of Brandenburg, on November 25, 1620. According to historians, the marriage failed on all counts: not only did it not bring German support for Gustavus' war in Poland, but he and the mentally unbalanced Maria Eleonora never produced a male heir. Sadly, most of what is known of Maria Eleanora is seen through the eyes and writings of her not-so-doting daughter. In the early years, Maria accompanied her husband on Swedish campaigns against Germany.

that Christina was a girl, and that, being a girl, she was not pretty. Christina always believed that her mother disliked her to the point of wishing her dead; she even blamed her mother for an accident in her infancy that left her with one shoulder higher than the other.

Queen Maria Eleonora loved her husband but found his subjects uncultured and unemotional. The king was away at foreign wars most summers, wars against Russia, Denmark, and Poland. Each time he left, she wept inconsolably, afraid she would never see him again. There was good reason for her fears, for King Gustavus II Adolphus approached war-making with the same zest and skill he showed in the rest of his life, and he had many close calls with enemy bullets and cannonballs. Sometimes, Maria Eleonora followed him to Europe, staying in towns behind the lines, leaving Christina in Stockholm in her Aunt Catherine's care.

When Gustavus Adolphus was home in Sweden, he kept the young princess near him for many hours daily. Since he was a busy king, this probably means that she accompanied him in some of his activities, as he directed the copper mines, saw to the ships, and reviewed the troops. As a boy, he had watched his own father do the work of ruling; this no doubt seemed to him a natural way to learn.

In June of 1630, when Christina was three and a half years old, her father set sail to join a war already underway in Germany. When he left, Christina cried for three days and nights; such grief in so young a child was feared a bad omen. After a year, the queen followed her husband to Europe, leaving her daughter once more in Catherine's care.

The war in Germany was to become the Thirty Years' War, remembered for the devastation it brought the people on whose farms, towns, and cities it was fought. It began as a war of Catholic against Protestant, a war the Catholics were winning. By stepping in to save the Protestant side, the vigorous young king of Sweden gained his country the status of a great European power.

In December 1632, Christina had been living for a year and a half with her aunt's family, which included several cousins near her own age. On the evening of her sixth birthday, the fateful news arrived from Germany that Gustavus Adolphus had been killed in battle. Christina was now the queen of Sweden. "I was such a child," she tells us, "that I knew neither my misfortune nor my fortune." But she remembers how enchanted she was when all the household came to kneel before her and kiss her hand, even her uncle, and later the mayor.

For six months, Christina enjoyed her life as queen. She writes proudly of the dignity with which she received a Russian delegation. But in July, her mother returned, bringing the king's body. This began a time that Christina was to recall with horror. Maria Eleonora had ignored her child previously, whereas now she nearly suffocated her. Christina looked like her father; the grieving queen fastened on her, keeping her con-

stantly with her in rooms that were draped for mourning in black velvet, shutting out all light and air. At night, the two of them slept in a bed at whose head hung a small gold casket containing her father's heart. Maria Eleonora wept constantly and spent long hours with the embalmed body displayed in state in the great hall. Aunt Catherine was sent away. It was a full year before the old king was finally buried in Stockholm.

Christina's main source of pleasure and escape were the hours she spent at her studies. She was a good student and liked her tutors, espe-

From the movie Queen Christina, *starring Greta Garbo as Christina.*

cially Johannes Matthiae. He had been her father's chaplain and was now her preceptor, in charge of her moral development. He was kind and open-minded, unlike many of the Swedish Lutheran clergy of the day, and he won the suspicious child's trust. She also liked and trusted Axel Banér, her governor, who had been her father's intimate friend. Gustavus Adolphus had left some unusual instructions for his daughter's education: she was to be raised as a boy in every respect, even to physical training. She was to be taught nothing of womanly ways, "except modesty and virtue." This plan "agreed wonderfully with my own inclinations," Christina writes. She learned languages, literature, mathematics, astronomy, geography, politics, history, and, what is probably unique for a girl in her times, learned to "handle any weapon passably well." She became a first-rate rider and an excellent shot.

To be obliged to obey none is a greater happiness than to command the whole world.

—**Queen Christina of Sweden**

During Christina's minority, the work of ruling the country was handled by a High Council of nobles headed by Chancellor Axel Oxenstierna. Dedicated to preserving the old king's dynasty, Oxenstierna was a superb diplomat who "knew the strengths and weaknesses of every European state." He spent several hours a day with the young queen, passing on as much as he could of political wisdom. He had returned from Europe, where the war still raged on, when Christina was nine years old. Seeing at once the harm inflicted on Christina by her mother, he forced the old queen to move away from Stockholm, many miles up Lake Mälaren to Gripsholm Castle. Aunt Catherine again became Christina's guardian, moving with her family to the Three Crowns Castle where Christina lived. For a while, two girl cousins shared Christina's lessons; she once wrote to her uncle complaining that one of them giggled too much.

Already, as a child, Christina had begun to have serious questions about the religion in which she was being raised. When six years old, she heard a terrifying sermon on the Last Judgment: the end of the world, the preacher said, could come at any moment; everyone caught unprepared would be cast into the tortures of hell. Emerging from church crying, Christina ran to her preceptor, demanding, "Why has no one ever told me about this terrible day? Will it come in the night tonight?" Matthiae reassured her, "It will come. But don't worry about it. Just be

good and obey your teachers, and you will go to paradise." This reply, she writes, "stirred up reflections in my mind that I shall never forget; for one of my age they were out of the ordinary." Three times she listened to the annual sermon, feeling a little less frightened, and a bit more skeptical on each hearing. Then she asked Matthiae frankly if religion were not all just fables, "like this famous Day of Judgment which never comes." Shocked, Matthiae threatened her with a beating if she said anything of the kind again. "I promise I will never again say anything like that," she told him icily, "for I do not want a beating. I also assure you that if you did have me beaten, you would later regret it." Unable to completely trust her thoughts to anyone, Christina tells us she was "unbelievably secretive," a trait she would make good use of later.

When Christina was ten, a French dancing master arrived at court, and she and her cousins began lessons in the new art of ballet. She studied and exercised for 12 hours a day. At age 11, her heroes were Julius Caesar, Cyrus, and especially Alexander the Great. She dreamed of outshining her own father just as Alexander had surpassed his. It was useless for her ladies-in-waiting or her foster mother to try to teach her stitchery or ladylike decorum; she had, she writes, "an invincible antipathy to all women are and say."

Several people close to Christina died during her early adolescence, including her Aunt Catherine. When Christina was 15, she became secretly engaged to marry Catherine's son Charles (X), four years older than herself. She cared for his hunting dogs and wrote dutiful love letters while he was away studying at the university, taking the grand tour of Europe, and training to be a soldier. She began to attend meetings of the High Council, listening and learning. On her 18th birthday, Christina became the ruler of Sweden in fact, as well as in name.

The winter also witnessed the arrival at court of a new lady-in-waiting. Though the same age as Christina, the recently orphaned **Ebba Sparre** had been placed under her protection. Soon, the two were constant companions and bedmates. At that time, bedmates were common in Sweden, for the nights were often cold. But from the few surviving letters Christina wrote to Ebba much later, it is clear that from the beginning Christina was in love with her, and that her love was probably returned. By all accounts, Ebba was beautiful, and Christina's pet name for her was "Belle."

Perhaps it was both Christina's assuming the royal power and the coming of Belle that contributed to her decision not to marry Charles. When he returned to Stockholm, she informed him that she had changed her mind and did not consider herself bound by promises made when she was hardly more than a girl. Afterwards, Christina did have a succession of male "favorites," whose friendship she valued and whose interests she forwarded. Popular opinion often linked her to them romantically, especially to the young noble, Magnus De la Gardie, and later to the Spanish ambassador, Pimentel. The truth of these rumors is not known. What is clear is that Belle was by Christina's side for all the years she ruled.

As monarch, Christina's first efforts went toward halting the wars in Europe that her country had been waging all her life, depleting its population and resources. She first urged Chancellor Oxenstierna to conclude a truce with Denmark, which he did. Then she turned her attentions to the stalled peace negotiations among the combatants in the Thirty Years' War. She insisted that Sweden drop its excessive demands and offer terms the enemy could accept. It took nearly four years, but in 1648 the Peace of Westphalia earned Christina the gratitude of her own suffering people, and that of much of Europe. She was, however, happy that peace had been delayed long enough for her troops to capture Rudolph II's castle in Prague, sending her its incomparable booty of art treasures, scientific instruments, rare books, even a lion. The queen feasted her delighted eyes on the rich colors of the painters of Italy such as Titian and Correggio.

Christina slept only three or four hours a night, waking early in order to have time to read and study before taking up the rounds of royal duties and pleasures that occupied her days and evenings. She gathered around her a distinguished circle of scholars, collected books and art works and news of the cultures to the south, and bought one of Pascal's calculating machines. She even succeeded in bringing the famous René Descartes to Sweden to talk philosophy. Unfortunately, she could only see him at five o'clock in the morning. In the depths of the Swedish winter, Descartes caught pneumonia and died.

There were strains between Christina and her subjects. The Swedes at court often resented the foreigners (some of them Catholic) she brought to Stockholm. Too, she often shocked with her unorthodox ways: she swore notably, wore men's jackets, hats, and comfortable flat shoes, and enjoyed nude paintings. She was even rumored to have doubts about religion. Christina spent a great deal of money on her rare books, collections, scholars, and on the elaborate ballets she staged and often danced in herself in her new theater. She also gave away crown lands to her friends and favorites. Thus, taxes were as high as in wartime.

Above all, there was the question of Christina's marriage, and the need for an heir, so that the country might avoid civil war. Over the years, she had several inquiries from European princes who sought such an attractive alliance; but she found she could not imagine marrying anyone. Gradually, she convinced the government that she wouldn't marry and persuaded them to declare her cousin Charles heir to the throne. In the midst of all this, Christina continued to study, reading omnivorously and learning new languages; she eventually knew nine, and something of two or three more. In Europe, she was becoming famous, the young woman who was Sweden's "philosopher king," "the Diana of the North."

Christina was strong and vigorous, enjoyed hunting, and was able to walk or ride for ten hours at a stretch. But her body frequently gave out. She sometimes fainted and had monthly spells of pain, sickness, and severe headache, in addition to bouts with serious diseases such as measles and pleurisy. When she was 21, a malarial fever brought Christina so near death that she formed the resolution to abdicate. It took her six more years to work out the details and to be sure in her own mind: How would she support herself? Where would she live? How would she get the country to agree? But in June of 1654, in a solemn ceremony, she lifted the crown from her own head.

Christina headed south. Near the border with Denmark, she cut her hair and donned men's clothes, entering Europe at first disguised as "Count von Dohna." Belle stayed behind. Though Ebba had married, she had continued as companion and bedmate. From Belgium, Christina wrote, saying how much she missed her. Then, the queen, for so she continued to be called, traveled to Hamburg, Amsterdam, and Brussels, enjoying life and soaking up culture. Within 18 months, she converted to Catholicism—much to the shock of her former subjects—and moved to Rome. She also changed her name from Kristina Augusta Wasa to Christina Maria Alexandra Vasa and was thereafter known as Christina Alexandra. Whether or not her conversion was sincere has been debated ever since. She once remarked, "After all, one must have some religion or other. But as for me, my religion is that of the philosophers."

Christina probably chose to live in Rome to avoid living on any other monarch's territory. Rome was a great center of culture and learning, where so many of the heroes of her youth had walked, from Caesar to Marcus Aurelius. She also hoped Rome would be more open to new ideas than was her native land; but she soon learned that most popes were not like the free-thinking Catholics who had sought her out in Sweden.

Still, she was able to find like-minded souls in Rome, particularly Cardinal Decio Azzolino. They may have been lovers for a while (there are letters in which Christina sounds like a rejected lover). Eventually, however, they became dear and lifelong friends. Christina put her political skills to work on various schemes, some more admirable than others. She cultivated peace between Spain and France. She dreamed of a united Europe where there would be freedom of religion. She also plotted to make herself the ruler of Naples and later applied for the throne of Poland when it became vacant. She argued for raising a new crusade against the advancing Turks. With Azzolino, she schemed to elect liberal popes. Once she ordered a man put to death, one of her retinue who had betrayed her plans for Naples. Legally, as a sort of "queen-at-large," she had the right to do so; but it did shock people.

Eventually, Christina settled down to be what she had left Sweden to become, the queen of the arts and sciences. She is remembered as a patron of artists, astronomers, composers, singers, alchemists, philosophers, actors, archaeologists, and assorted rogues. The sculptor Bernini, the composer Scarlatti, and the astronomer Cassini were among those she befriended and supported. She founded a public theater. Over the years, she led several "academies," where thinkers gathered to discuss philosophical questions; they met in her palace, which was a virtual temple to the arts, or in her large hillside garden. At the top of the hill was an astronomical observatory; her basement harbored an alchemical laboratory. Christina had fine collections of ancient Roman statues and of paintings by the Italian masters. The best singers and musicians in Rome made music in her halls and gardens. Remarkably free from some of the prejudices of her contemporaries, she had many Jews for friends, and near the end of her life declared all the Jews of the Roman ghetto to be under her protection.

Christina has been seen as male-identified and not a feminist. She believed that women rarely made good rulers: "Their virtues make them unfit to rule, as well as their faults," she said. It's true she preferred the company of men, with whom she could discuss the things that interested her, from military strategy to philosophy. She once said, "It's not that I like so much that they are men; but at least they are not women!" On the other hand, from Sweden, she had corresponded enthusiastically with some of the *précieuses,* a circle of educated, aristocratic French women who urged women not to marry. She was very taken with her visitor **Madame de Brégy,** who walked the streets of Stockholm in men's clothing, even when she was clearly pregnant. After Christina abdicated, she visited the scholar *Anna Maria van Schurmann, and she wanted to meet Descartes' friend, the philosopher Princess *Elizabeth of Bohemia (1596–1662), though, unbelievably, considerations of protocol prevented this. In Rome, she made retreats in nunneries and liked to read *Catherine of Genoa.

In her late 40s, Christina studied quietism, a Catholic form of mysticism that stressed simple meditation and the seeking of inner guidance. Her outer life, however, remained anything but quiet; and she was involved in controversies to the end.

When Christina died in 1689, age 62, she was buried in St. Peter's Cathedral, wearing a silver mask, a replica of her face. She also left us her image in paintings, engravings, coins, and medals, and her thoughts in letters, maxims, an unfinished autobiography, and in notes scribbled down the margins of her books. Her life spanned Renaissance Sweden through Baroque Rome and has left a unique record of a woman who used both privilege and strength of character to challenge the parameters of "woman" in her time.

SOURCES:

Åkerman, Susanna. *Queen Christina of Sweden and Her Circle: The Transformation of a Seventeenth-Century Philosophical Libertine.* NY: E.J. Brill, 1991.

Clarke, M.L. "The Making of a Queen: The Education of Christina of Sweden," in *History Today.* Vol. 28, 1978, pp. 228–235.

Goldsmith, Margaret. *Christina of Sweden: A Psychological Biography.* Garden City, NY: Doubleday, Doran, 1933.

MacKenzie, Faith Compton. *The Sibyl of the North: The Tale of Christina, Queen of Sweden.* Boston: Houghton Mifflin, 1931.

Masson, Georgina. *Queen Christina.* NY: Farrar, Straus and Giroux, 1968.

Rodén, Marie Louise. *Queen Christina of Sweden at Rome, 1655–1689.* Rome: Biblioteca Apostilica Vaticana, 1989.

Stolpe, Sven. *Christina of Sweden.* Edited by Eric Randall, translated by Eric Randall and Ruth Mary Bethell. NY: Macmillan, 1966.

Queen Christina (97 min.), film starring *Greta Garbo and John Gilbert, directed by Rouben Mamoulian, M-G-M, 1933.

The Abdication, film starring *Liv Ullmann, Harvey, 1974.

COLLECTIONS:

Papers located at Biblioteca Apostolica Vaticana, Archivio Storico Communali, Jesi, and Archivio Segreto Vaticano, Rome; Bibliothèque Nationale, Paris; Bibliothèque de l' école de médecine de Montpellier, Montpellier; Bodleian Library, Oxford; British Library, London; Kunglia Biblioteket, and Riksarkivet, Stockholm; Uppsala Universitets Bibliotek, Uppsala.

Tangren Alexander, a philosopher at Southern Oregon State College, who is currently working on a historical novel about Christina, *Her Majesty, The King*

Christina Stigsdottir (fl. 1160s)

Queen of Sweden. Name variations: Kristina Stigsdottir. Flourished in the 1160s; daughter of Stig Whiteleather and **Margaret Knutsdottir** *(daughter of Knut Lavard, duke of South Jutland, and* *Ingeborg of Russia); married Karl Sverkersson also known as Charles VII, king of Sweden (r. 1161–1167), in 1163; children: Sverker II the Younger, king of Sweden (r. 1195–1208); possibly* **Sophie Karlsson** *(d. 1252, who possibly married Henry Burwin II, prince of Mecklenburg-Rostok).*

Christina the Astonishing

(c. 1150–c. 1224)

French saint. Born around 1150 into a peasant family in Brusthem, in Liége, France; died around 1224.

Born into a peasant family in Brusthem, France, Christina the Astonishing was orphaned at age 15. Her life comes down from two eminent scholars of the time: Thomas de Cantimpré (d. 1270), professor of theology at Louvain, and Cardinal Jacques de Vitry (d. 1244). Writes Vitry who knew her personally:

> In her the divine operations were truly marvellous. She had been dead a long time and had obtained the grace of resuming her flesh in order to suffer her purgatory here below. Thus for many years she underwent extraordinary trials, sometimes rolling in the fire, sometimes remaining in icy water in the middle of winter, sometimes going as though despite herself into the tombs of the dead. In the end she was favoured with sublime graces and enjoyed profound peace. Often, her spirit in ecstasy, she led the souls of the dead to purgatory; sometimes she even led them out of purgatory to paradise.

Christina spent her last days in the convent of St. Catherine at Saint Trond. Her feast day is celebrated on July 24.

Christine.

Variant of Christina.

Christine de Pizan (c. 1363–c. 1431)

Writer, lyric poet, historian, and scholar of the royal French court, who argued passionately against the negative views of women propounded by male writers, and urged men and women to respect and admire all women for their many virtues. Name variations: Chrystyne; Christine de Pisan; Christine of Pisa; Christine of Pisan. Pronunciation: puh-ZAHN. Born between 1363 and 1365 in Venice, Italy; died after 1429, possibly 1431 or 1434, at convent of Poissy, France; daughter of Tommaso di Benvenuto da Pizzano (a physician and astrologer); mother's name unknown; married Sir Etienne du Castel, in 1380; children: two sons, including the eldest Jean, and a daughter.

Family moved to France (about 1368); married (1380); widowed (1390); began composing poetry (1390); retired to convent of Poissy (1418); last known composition, Song of Joan of Arc, *finished (July 1429).*

Selected writings: One Hundred Ballads, Virelays, Rondeaux *(1390–1400);* Epistle to the God of Love *(1399);* Epistle to Othea *(1400);* The Book of the Mutations of Fortune *(1400–03);* Epistles on the Debate of the "Romance of the Rose" *(1401–03);* The Book of the Way of Long Study *(1402–03);* The Book of the Deeds and Good Customs of the Wise King Charles V *(1404);* The Book of the City of Ladies *(1405);* The Book of the Three Virtues *(*The Treasure of the City of Ladies*) (1405);* The Vision of Christine *(1405);* The Book of Feats of Arms and Chivalry *(1410);* The Book of Peace *(1412–14);* Song of Joan of Arc *(1429).*

One of the most remarkable of all medieval women, the Italian scholar Christine de Pizan was an internationally known writer, poet, and feminist at the French royal court. Yet despite her prolific output of poetry and prose and the far-reaching fame and admiration she enjoyed during her life, Christine and her works are known to few today, and only some of her works have been made into modern editions. She has been consistently "rediscovered" in every century since her death, but she has still been unable to take her place among the finest of medieval writers, most likely because her sex and her feminist attacks on the misogynist writers of her time have found little favor with the male historians and literary critics who have encountered her.

Unfortunately we do not know Christine's mother's name, but her father, Tommaso di Benvenuto da Pizzano, was a well-to-do physician and astrologer in Bologna who became a municipal bureaucrat in Venice. He married in Venice where Christine was born in 1365. Tommaso enjoyed a widespread reputation for his knowledge and soon received invitations to join the courts of King Louis I of Hungary and Charles V of France as court astrologer. Tommaso chose France because it was known as a country of scholars, and shortly after Christine's birth he left for Paris. The next year, King Charles paid for Tommaso's wife and children to travel to Paris as well. Thus Christine left her homeland as a young child and was taken to France, where she would spend the rest of her life.

Christine de Pizan is at once one of the outstanding writers of world literature and one of the most neglected.

—Earl Jeffrey Richards

Because of her father's high position, Christine grew up close to the center of French court society, a closed, highly structured social setting with rigid rules of protocol, hierarchy, and etiquette. Tommaso strongly encouraged his intelligent daughter to study and learn as much as possible and taught her himself when he could. Christine's mother, as Christine herself records, was not in favor of her daughter's studies but did not go against Tommaso's wishes by keeping Christine from her reading. Christine thus gained an education rare for medieval women, being allowed to study in the king's library the great Greek and Roman authors, from Ovid to Boethius to Aristotle, as well as many medieval writers. She learned to read French, Italian, and Latin. At this time, only a few noblewomen were allowed a formal education in the classics; for Christine, daughter of a bourgeois, to have surpassed even her social betters in her learning makes her even more unique in medieval history.

Tommaso was shown great favor by King Charles, who admired him immensely. He soon became an advisor to the king on all political and state matters and was granted by Charles many gifts of land, pensions, and money. Thus, Christine's childhood was spent in relative luxury, made secure by the king's affection for her father. Being the daughter of a royal favorite, Christine had no lack of suitors when she entered her teen years, the age when most medieval women were betrothed and married. Tommaso chose a bright young noble from Picardy for his only daughter. Etienne du Castel was 25 years old at the time of his marriage to 15-year-old Christine in 1380; despite the difference in age and the prearranged nature of their marriage, Christine and Etienne fell deeply in love and were quite happy together, as Christine records in her autobiography. Her new husband even supported her studies and, like her father, encouraged her to learn. Christine gave birth to three children, two sons and a daughter, although the name of only one, the eldest boy Jean, is known. Soon after the wedding, Etienne's quick mind and his connection to Tommaso led Charles to appoint him as his personal secretary and notary.

The year 1380 proved to be a great turning point in Christine's life. It marked her marriage and the end of her childhood, and it came to mark as well the beginning of a downturn in her fortunes and those of her family. For, on September 16, 1380, their great and kindly benefactor King Charles V suddenly died. It was not uncommon in court society for a person's fortunes to rise with the good will of a king and fall with his death, but this could not have been consolation to Tommaso, his wife, and their children, who went from living very well to financial hardship. The new king, Charles VI, was only a child; his uncle, Philip the Bold, duke of Burgundy, who acted as regent, had little use for his dead brother's astrologer. Tommaso retained his position but at a much-reduced salary, and all his pensions, annuities, and other stipends were immediately cut off. "Now the door to our misfortunes opened up, and I, still young, entered in," wrote Christine in *The Vision of Christine*.

Tommaso began suffering from ill health after Charles V's death and died around 1385. Etienne and Christine found themselves at the head of her family, which included their three children, Christine's brothers, and her mother. And yet another tragedy awaited Christine. Etienne had managed to retain his position in the new administration and spent much time traveling with the young king and his advisors across the kingdom. In 1390, Etienne died while in Beauvais with the royal court when an unspecified epidemic, possibly the bubonic plague, broke out suddenly.

Christine was devastated when she heard the news. As Etienne had not been an inheritor of his family wealth, nor had Tommaso left much to his own family, she also faced financial ruin. Only 25 years old, Christine had no resources except herself and had been left to care for her entire family. Her choices were narrowly circumscribed; she could remarry, but this was unlikely, as she could not bring a dowry to a new husband. Instead, she spent most of the next several years pursuing one lawsuit after another, trying to salvage what was left of her father's fortune. To escape from her financial worries, Christine used her spare time to continue her studies, reading as much history, science, and poetry as she could. She also began composing poetry herself.

Although many medieval women faced the kind of frightening situation Christine did as a widow, she was particularly fortunate in two ways: she had received an exceptional education, and she had friends at the royal court and among France's nobility. When it seemed her many lawsuits were to come to little fruition, it was to those wealthy friends that Christine turned to for help, not asking for gifts or charity, but for commissions to write for them. She received several, and her writing career began.

Christine proved to be one of the most talented scholars and writers of the Middle Ages and was well-rewarded for it during her lifetime. In the beginning, she concentrated on poetry, many of her works expressing her previous happiness in marriage and her desolation on her husband's death. For the first decade of her career, the young widow wrote on "universal" themes, such as love, grief, and the consolation of her faith in times of need. These poems established Christine as a gifted writer and earned her the patronage and admiration of many of France's most powerful figures, including King Charles VI and his wife, *Isabeau of Bavaria (1371–1435).

In May 1399, Christine composed a work in verse that was to change the course of her writing life. *The Epistle to the God of Love* was a spirited attack on the popular *Romance of the Rose,* a long misogynist poem that details the seduction of a lady by her lover and included many negative stereotypes about women's evil nature. In the *Epistle,* women from every social class complain to Cupid, God of Love, about the unjustified hatred and slander they receive at men's hands. They defend women's good nature against male writers both ancient and contemporary, including Jean de Meung, author of the *Romance.* Christine's work sparked a heated literary debate (which came to be called the "Quarrel of *The Romance of the Rose*"), in

which France's leading thinkers and writers argued about the "true nature" of womankind. Some writers, including the chancellor of the University of Paris and the provost of Paris, sided with Christine that woman's nature is basically good and equal to man's, while other equally respected men agreed that the Romance represented women as they were, conniving, mean-spirited, greedy, insatiable in lust. *The Epistle* demonstrates Christine's developing consciousness of the slander against womankind; its wide reception led her to continue defending women in her writing.

Christine's growing reputation spread outside France. She received invitations from Gian Galeazzo Visconti, the duke of Milan, and King Henry IV of England to live and write at their courts, but she declined them both, preferring to stay in Paris. Her output between 1399 and 1405 was prolific: nine book-length works in verse and six book-length prose works were completed in six years, along with other small works of poetry and short stories. These major works ranged from *The Book of the Mutations of Fortune*—a poem over 23,000 lines long, which details the reversals and changes in fortune of various historical, mythical, and Biblical figures—to *The Book of the Deeds and Good Customs of the Wise King Charles V,* commissioned as the official biography of the late king by Philip the Bold.

Christine was a unique writer for her time in many ways. Not only was she a secular woman writer, but she also wrote several major works on commission at a time when most writers completed a work and then presented it to a potential patron, hoping for rewards. She was also closely involved with the copying and illumination of her work, unusual for a vernacular writer in the 15th century, and supervised the illustration of her manuscripts herself. Her writing style after 1400 changed from the traditional forms of lyric poetry to a complicated prose style. She wrote in French but chose ancient Latin prose as her model, creating what Earl Jeffrey Richards calls, in his introduction to the *Book of the City of Ladies,* an "experimental and innovative" style whose syntax was a "hallmark of stylistic refinement." Thus, Christine challenged herself as well as her readers.

At age 40, Christine found herself in a situation that must have been a far cry from what she had been brought up to expect. Instead of a quiet domestic existence, she was supporting herself and her family through her own labors. She had been a principal protagonist in the most celebrated literary debate of the Middle Ages and had found friends, protectors, and patrons among the highest of France's elite. The duke of Berry eventually collected a copy of almost everything she had written; the king and queen each rewarded her for her work; the powerful Duke Louis of Orléans and his duchess *Valentina Visconti counted themselves among her admirers and owned several of her writings. And her works were being copied and translated into foreign languages, which increased her international reputation.

The same year that found 40-year-old Christine at the pinnacle of fame, 1405, proved to be an extremely busy one. She completed three of her most important prose works, including *The Book of the City of Ladies*, *The Book of the Three Virtues*, and *The Vision of Christine*. *The City of Ladies* was her final comment on the arguments raised by the "Quarrel of *The Romance of the Rose*." Here, Christine made her most reasoned and articulate argument in defense of women and advocated equality in the education of men and women. In the book, the characters Reason, Rectitude, and Justice appear to Christine when she is feeling despair about being a woman because authorities have written that women are sinful and immoral. The three allegorical Virtues console her and order her to construct, with their help, a new city where women from every social class can live together without men, and can reach their highest potential for true nobility—which for Christine meant nobility of the heart, rather than nobility of birth.

While they are building the new City of Ladies, the Virtues give Christine's character a new history of women, showing what important contributions wise and good women have made to the world. When the city is complete, the Virtues invite all women to come there, and ask *Mary the Virgin, as the most perfect of all women, to preside over it as their queen. Christine followed the *City of Ladies* with *The Book of the Three Virtues* (also called *The Treasure of the City of Ladies*) in which the Virtues again appear and give advice on appropriate conduct and behavior to the women of each social class. Christine also completed her autobiographical work, *The Vision of Christine*, in 1405. It is from this work that almost all the biographical details extant of her life are recorded.

After 1405, Christine began writing on other topics, in part spurred by the growing political crisis in France, which was being torn apart by a civil war. In 1407, Christine's patron Louis, duke of Orléans, was murdered on the orders of his cousin John, duke of Burgundy (another of Christine's patrons). Paris quickly became a chaotic, unstable city, with nobles and commoners taking sides in the brewing conflict between the royal houses. Christine remained in Paris despite the conflicts but used her writing to protest for peace and good government. In 1407, she completed *The Book of the Body Politic*, which details recommendations for the proper behavior of each social class in dealing with the others, a work intended for the use of the king.

Three years later, she wrote *The Book of Feats of Arms and Chivalry*, a military handbook spelling out, among other things, battle strategies, techniques for besieging a castle, and the moral behavior of a wise and noble knight. In the work, realizing that as a woman with no military experience she might not be qualified to write on the subject, she calls on Minerva, goddess of war, to aid her and oversee her pen. This book was both accurate and practical, so much so that years later King Henry VII of England had it translated into English and given to his captains for their instruction.

Christine continued her writing in the areas of conflict and peace with *The Book of Peace*, written between 1412 and 1414. The fighting between the House of Orléans and the House of Burgundy had spread across the kingdom and was complicated by incursions of English forces; the king, Charles VI, had been mentally incapacitated for several years and his queen Isabeau was completely disinterested in providing even a semblance of leadership and authority. Christine wrote *The Book of Peace* for the king's son, the Dauphin Louis (Louis, duke of Guienne), and in it urges him to work for resolution and peace in his kingdom because of the great harm and suffering the civil war was causing. Unfortunately, the dauphin was not moved by the work, and the civil unrest continued.

By 1418, Christine was forced to leave Paris; it had become simply too dangerous a place, where armed men of all ranks wandered the streets and many Parisians were attacked and robbed at random. Now 53 years old, Christine retired to the convent of Poissy, some miles outside of Paris where her daughter had been placed in the 1390s. Christine described it as having immense grounds and beautiful gardens, where the abbess and her associates ate off gold plates with crystal goblets. (Poissy was a convent for noblewomen, who brought large endowments when they entered. Christine, as a bourgeois, had had to petition to get her daughter admitted.)

Between 1418 and 1429, Christine did not publish any works; we have no idea how she spent her time. Presumably, she kept up her lifelong passion for knowledge and study, as the abbey had a fine library. In 1429, however, at age 64, she broke her silence with one last work, *The Song of *Joan of Arc*, the only work known to have been written on that remarkable peasant during her lifetime. As **Sarah Lawson** writes in her introduction to *The Treasure of the City of Ladies*, the *Song*'s unique subject and author "should have been enough by itself to ensure Christine's fame."

It is unclear exactly how many years Christine lived after 1429, since the records of the convent were eventually lost. But she left an impressive body of work behind: over 20 volumes of writing, which inspired, challenged, amused, and provoked her many readers during her life, and many of which remain as fresh and stimulating as the day they were penned. Christine de Pizan is finally being made the subject of study and translation by several scholars; it is hoped that her works will be as accessible and widely read as those of contemporary male medieval writers.

SOURCES:

Christine de Pizan. *The Book of the City of Ladies*. Translated by Earl Jeffrey Richards. NY: Persea Books, 1982.

———. *The Treasure of the City of Ladies*. Translated by Sarah Lawson. NY: Penguin Books, 1985.

SUGGESTED READING:

Cherewatuk, Karen, and Ulrike Wiethaus, eds. *Dear Sister: Medieval Women and the Epistolary Genre*. Philadelphia, PA: University of Pennsylvania Press, 1993.

Wilson, Katharina, ed. *Medieval Women Writers*. Athens, GA: University of Georgia Press, 1984.

Laura York, freelance writer
in medieval history and women's history,
Riverside, California

Christine of Baden-Durlach

(1645–1705)

*Duchess of Saxe-Gotha. Born on April 22, 1645; died on December 21, 1705; daughter of *Christina Casimir and Frederick VI, margrave of Baden-Durlach; married Albert, margrave of Ansbach, on August 6, 1665; married Frederick I, duke of Saxe-Gotha, on August 2, 1681.*

Christine of Bourbon (1779–1849).

See Maria Carolina for sidebar.

Christine of France (1606–1663)

Duchess and regent of Savoy. Name variations: Christine of Savoy; Christine of Bourbon; Chrestienne or

*Christina. Born in 1606; died in 1663 in Savoy; daughter of Henry IV the Great (1553–1610), king of France (r. 1589–1610), and Marie de Medici (c. 1573–1642); sister of *Elizabeth Valois (1602–1644, who married Philip IV, king of Spain), *Henrietta Maria (1609–1669, who married Charles I, king of England), and Louis XIII, king of France (r. 1610–1643); married Victor Amadeus I (d. 1637), duke of Savoy (r. 1630–1637); children: Francis Hyacinth, duke of Savoy (r. 1637–1638); *Henrietta of Savoy (c. 1630–?); Charles Emmanuel II (1634–1675), duke of Savoy (r. 1638–1675).*

The daughter of Henry IV and Queen *Marie de Medici, Christine was a French princess whose marriage to Victor Amadeus I, duke of Savoy, was arranged as part of a political alliance between France and Savoy. At that time, Savoy was an independent duchy bordering on Italy, in what is now southeast France. Christine gave birth to three children and, when Victor Amadeus died in 1637, their eldest son, Francis, succeeded as duke, although he was still young. The succession brought civil war to Savoy, as the lesser nobility saw an opportunity to increase their own power while a boy ruled the duchy and so rebelled against Francis' authority. After the young duke's death in 1638, Christine took over the government of the duchy as regent for her younger son, Charles Emmanuel. Proving an effective and capable ruler, she quelled the nobles' rebellion and reestablished peace. She ruled for ten years as regent, and, although she technically resigned her authority when her son came of age to rule, Christine remained the most influential and powerful figure in Savoy politics for the next 15 years.

Laura York,
Riverside, California

Christine of Gandersheim (d. 919)

*Abbess of Gandersheim. Name variations: Christina. Died in 919; daughter of Ludolf or Liudolf (c. 806–866), count of Saxony, and *Oda (806–913); sister of abbesses *Gerberga (d. 896) and *Hathumoda (d. 874).*

Christine of Hesse (1543–1604)

*Duchess of Holstein-Gottorp. Born on June 29, 1543; died on May 13, 1604; daughter of Philip I, landgrave of Hesse, and *Christine of Saxony (1505–1549); married Adolf (1526–1586), duke of Holstein-Gottorp (r. 1544–1586), on December 17, 1564; children: *Sophie of Holstein-Gottorp (1569–1634); *Christina* *of Holstein-Gottorp (1573–1625); Johann Adolf, duke of Holstein-Gottorp (b. 1575).*

Christine of Hesse-Cassel (1933—)

*Princess. Born Christina Marguerite on January 10, 1933, in Schloss Kronberg; daughter of Christopher Ernest, prince of Hesse, and *Sophia of Greece (b. 1914); married Andrei or Andrej Karadjordjevic (son of Alexander I, king of Yugoslavia), on August 1, 1956 (divorced 1962); married Robert Floris van Eyck, on December 3, 1962 (divorced 1986); children: (first marriage) Princess Tatiana Maria (b. 1957, who married Gregory Thune-Larsen); Christopher, known as Marko (b. 1960); (second marriage) Helen Sophia van Eyck (b. 1963); Mark Nicholas van Eyck (b. 1966). Andrei's second wife was *Kira of Leiningen (b. 1930).*

Christine of Lorraine (c. 1571–1637)

*Grand duchess of Tuscany. Name variations: Christina of Lorraine; Christine de Medici. Born around 1571; died in 1637 (some sources cite 1636); daughter of *Claude de France (1547–1575) and Charles II, duke of Lorraine (r. 1545–1608); granddaughter of *Catherine de Medici (1519–1589); married Ferdinand I de Medici (1549–1609), grand duke of Tuscany (r. 1587–1609); children: Cosimo II (1590–1620), grand duke of Tuscany (r. 1609–1620, who married *Maria Magdalena of Austria); *Eleonora de Medici (1591–1617); *Caterina de Medici (1593–1629, who married Ferdinand also known as Fernando Gonzaga, 6th duke of Mantua); Francesco (d. 1614); Carlo, cardinal (d. 1666); twins *Maddalena de Medici (1600–1633) and Lorenzo (1600–1648); *Claudia de Medici (1604–1648, who married Federigo della Rovere, hereditary prince of Urbino, and Leopold of Austrian Tyrol).*

Although she was born and raised in France, Christine's life is closely linked to the story of the Medici, one of the most wealthy and powerful patrician families of Italy. Her mother *Claude de France was a princess of the royal house of France; her father, Duke Charles II, ruled the small province of Lorraine in what is now eastern France. Christine was part of the Medici lineage on her mother's side, since Claude was the daughter of Queen *Catherine de Medici. After Christine's mother died, Christine was raised by her grandmother, forging a strong bond of affection between Christine and Catherine. When she was about 16, Christine's Medici links were reinforced in 1587 when Catherine de Medici agreed to a marriage between Christine and the head of the Medici family, 40-year-old Grand Duke Ferdinand I of Tuscany.

Christine's husband had been a cardinal in Rome before the 1587 death of his brother, Francesco, forced him to resign as cardinal and succeed Francesco as grand duke. Despite the sudden turn in fortune, which led him from ecclesiastical to secular office, Ferdinand showed himself to be a talented politician during his two decades as duke. One of his first political moves was to try to strengthen Tuscany's diplomatic relations with France. His negotiations with France's *de facto* ruler and his own relative, Queen Catherine, led to his marriage with Christine as a guarantee of new friendship between the two states. Although they were married by proxy in 1587, Christine did not leave France until 1589; her journey was delayed first by the death of her father, then by the death of Queen Catherine, whom Christine refused to leave during her final illness.

Christine and Ferdinand had eight children in their 31-year marriage, including five sons and three daughters. The couple were well-suited for one another. They both supported the political aims of the Medici family, of which they were the most prominent members, and they shared the traditional Medici interest in promoting the arts and keeping a magnificent, opulent court. Christine's role at court was very public; as the wife of the grand duke and the mother of his heir, she had a great political responsibility to uphold the honor of the family, provide for a secure succession by bearing several sons, and to preside over a sumptuous court of aristocrats, scholars, scientists, and ladies-in-waiting whose collective purpose, like hers, was to glorify the grand duke.

After Ferdinand's death in February 1609, their eldest son Cosimo succeeded his father as Cosimo II. Although the new grand duke had a wife, Archduchess *Maria Magdalena of Austria, Christine did not lose her important place at court. Instead, she and Maria Magdalena shared the role of being the most prominent woman in Florence and a leader of its social and cultural life. Cosimo apparently respected his mother's ability more than he did that of his wife. Before his early death in 1620, he wrote a will in which Christine and Maria Magdalena were named joint regents of Tuscany for the young Ferdinand II. Yet it was understood by his courtiers that Christine was the senior regent and that Maria's nomination was more a formality than a recognition of her governing ability. Christine and Maria served well together, but the results of their reign are mixed. For example, the years of Ferdinand II's long minority were relatively peaceful, but the regents nearly emptied the Medici treasury, and Christine allowed the clerics of Tuscany to interfere in its administration much more than previous rulers had.

After Maria died in 1631, Christine's position at court was strengthened, as now she was again the undisputed first lady of Florence. She did not relinquish the reins of government even after her grandson had reached adulthood. Ferdinand II did not begin to rule for himself until after Christine died about age 66, in 1637.

SOURCES:
Micheletti, Emma. *The Medici of Florence*. Florence: Scala, 1980.
Young, George F. *The Medici*. 2nd ed. NY: E.P. Dutton, 1911.

Laura York,
Riverside, California

Christine of Pisa (c. 1363–c. 1431).

See Christine de Pizan.

Christine of Savoy (1606–1663).

See Christine of France.

Christine of Saxony (1505–1549)

Landgravine of Hesse. Born on December 25, 1505; died on April 15, 1549; daughter of *Barbara of Poland (1478–1534) and George the Bearded, duke of Saxony; married Philip I, landgrave of Hesse, on December 11, 1523; children: *Agnes of Hesse (1527–1555); William IV the Wise (b. 1532); Barbara of Hesse (1536–1597, who married George I, stadholder in Mompelgard); Elisabeth of Hesse (1539–1582, who married Louis VI, elector of the Palatinate); *Christine of Hesse (1543–1604); George I the Pious (b. 1547), landgrave of Hesse-Darmstadt.

Christman, Elisabeth (1881–1975)

American labor leader. Born in Germany on September 2, 1881; died of cerebral arteriosclerosis in Delphi, Indiana, on April 26, 1975; daughter of Henry Christman (a laborer) and Barbara (Guth) Christman; educated in a German Lutheran school until age 13 when she began work in a Chicago glove factory; never married; no children.

Co-founded Operators Local 1 of the International Glove Workers Union of America (IGWUA, 1902); joined the Chicago Women's Trade Union League (WTUL, 1904); elected to WTUL executive board (1910–29); served as treasurer of Local 1 (1905–11) and president (1912–17); served as

IGWUA secretary-treasurer (1913–31); was administrator, WTUL Training School for Women Organizers (1914–26); served as chief of women field representatives for the National War Labor Board (1917–18); elected to the WTUL's national executive board (1919); served as NWTUL secretary-treasurer and editor of the WTUL monthly journal Life and Labor Bulletin *(1921–50); appointed member, the 1921 National Unemployment Conference (1921); appointed member, National Organization on Unemployment Relief (1931); became first woman appointed to a National Recovery Administration code authority (1934); appointed member, National Commission on Vocational Guidance (1936); appointed to the Women's Bureau advisory committee (1940); served as director of Women's Bureau investigation of women's wages in war industries (1942–43).*

Soon after Elisabeth Christman was born in Germany on September 2, 1881, her parents immigrated to America and settled in Chicago. There, her father Henry Christman worked as a laborer and as a clarinet player in a union band. Her mother **Barbara Guth Christman** instilled in her six children, of whom Elisabeth was the oldest, a sense of independence and a devotion to the Lutheran faith. Elisabeth attended a German Lutheran school until the age of 13 when she went to work in the Eisendrath Glove Factory in Chicago. After years of long hours and low pay, Christman joined her co-worker, ***Agnes Nestor**, in leading a successful ten-day strike in 1902. Out of this strike was born Glove Workers Local 1. Christman helped her local and 27 others form the International Glove Workers Union of America (IGWUA). She would serve in a number of official capacities both for her local and the International.

However, it was as a member of the Women's Trade Union League (WTUL) that Elisabeth Christman tirelessly sought to address the needs of working women. Founded in Boston in 1903, the WTUL was a cross-class alliance of middle- and upper-class reformers and working-class women devoted to organizing women into trade unions and educating the public regarding the frequently harsh conditions under which America's women worked in this period. As a leader in the Chicago WTUL and on the national level, Christman was one of the few working-class women who directed the day-to-day policies of the WTUL until its demise in 1950. "Good times or bad," she once said, "the Labor Movement can not afford to stand still."

Elisabeth Christman also brought her talents to government, first during World War I when she worked with the National War Labor Board. Although a lifelong Democrat, Christman was appointed by two Republican presidents to commissions addressing unemployment, in 1921 and again in 1931. She would continue to serve the government in a number of advisory positions throughout the New Deal and during World War II. For most of her long life, Elisabeth Christman devoted her energies to the organization of working women. Near the end of her life, she advised women hospital workers while she was herself a hospital patient. She died in her niece's home in Delphi, Indiana, a few months before her 94th birthday.

SOURCES:

Boone, Gladys. *The Women's Trade Union Leagues in Great Britain and the United States of America.* NY: Columbia University Press, 1942.

Sicherman, Barbara, and Carol Hurd Green, eds. *Notable American Women, The Modern Period.* Cambridge, MA: Belknap Press of Harvard University Press, 1980, pp. 148–150.

Kathleen Banks Nutter,
Department of History,
University of Massachusetts at Amherst

Christopher, Mary (1907–1998).

See West, Dorothy.

Chrodielde (fl. 590)

French nun and warrior. Flourished 590 in Poitiers, France; never married; no children.

A nun with an unusual life story, Chrodielde fought a war to become an abbess. She joined the convent of St. *Radegund of Poitiers (518–587) as a child and nothing is known of her family background. Chrodielde began her military career around 590, when she tried to force the abbess, **Leubevere of Cheribert**, out of office in an effort to become abbess herself, and Leubevere defended her position with force. While the position of abbess may seem to contemporary minds a weak motivation for a war, in medieval times an abbess was not simply the austere head of a convent who gave sermons and counseled her nuns. Instead, the abbess of a large establishment like the abbey of St. Radegund had the same duties as a wealthy noblewoman: she was a spiritual leader but also managed the estates of the abbey (which included supervising the agricultural and manufacturing processes which brought the abbey income), entertained and provided for traveling nobility, and often had authority over an attached monastery as well.

Though Chrodielde's political efforts to discredit Leubevere were unsuccessful, she was determined to become abbess, and soon Leubevere found herself keeping an army to ward off attacks by Chrodielde's armed supporters. After several battles, Chrodielde was evicted from the convent. She took refuge in a cathedral and raised an even larger army, as more people from Poitiers and the countryside took up her cause. Leubevere meanwhile continued to defend herself and was supported by the church hierarchy.

When it became clear that neither side would capitulate, King Childebert of France was forced to send peacekeeping troops to Poitiers. These troops managed to quell the violence and to defeat Chrodielde's army, although this was no easy task. Chrodielde's political and military career came to an end when she was excommunicated for her warlike behavior.

SOURCES:

King, William C. *Woman: Her Position, Influence, and Achievement Throughout the Civilized World.* Springfield: King-Richardson, 1900.

Laura York, Riverside, California

Chrotrud (d. 724)

*Frankish noblewoman. Name variations: Rothrude; Rotrou of Belgium; Rotrude. Died in 724; daughter of St. Leutwinus; married Charles Martel, mayor of Austrasia and Neustria (r. 714–741); children: Carloman, mayor of Austrasia (d. 754); Pepin III the Short (715–768), mayor of Neustria (r. 741), king of the Franks (r. 747–768); Grifon; Bernard, count of St. Quentin. Charles Martel's second wife was *Sunnichild (d. 741).*

Chrystyne.

Variant of Christine.

Chudleigh, Elizabeth (1720–1788)

English adventurer and bigamist. Name variations: Elizabeth Chudleigh (1720–44); Mrs. Hervey (in secret, 1744—); Duchess of Kingston (1769–1788, she continued to call herself duchess and expected others to do likewise even after her conviction for bigamy); Countess of Bristol (her actual title after 1775 but one she refused to acknowledge). Born Elizabeth Chudleigh in Devonshire, England, in 1720; died in France in 1788; daughter of Colonel Thomas Chudleigh and Harriet (nee Chudleigh); married Augustus John Hervey, in 1747; married the duke of Kingston, in 1769; children: (first marriage) son, Henry Augustus Hervey (b. 1747, died in infancy).

Elizabeth Chudleigh is the only woman in British history to be tried and convicted of bigamy in an open trial before the House of Lords. Long known as an "adventuress" and sexual intriguer at the courts of kings George II and George III, her trial for wrongful marriage to a duke when she was already wife of an earl was the scandal-sensation of 1776.

She was born, probably in 1720, to a minor but honorable family of the English gentry, in Devonshire. Her father was lieutenant-governor of the Royal Hospital in Chelsea but died when she was still a child, after losing most of his money in a wild speculation scheme of the era, the South Sea Bubble. Her childhood and early teens were spent, therefore, in straitened conditions of genteel poverty. Her doughty mother once calmly withstood the threats of a highwayman until her lagging escort could come up and shoot the villain dead.

Elizabeth grew into a strikingly beautiful girl and had the luck to survive an attack of smallpox at age 15 without losing her good looks. She was high-spirited, witty, playful, and flirtatious. Soon afterwards, she attracted the notice of a leading Whig politician, William Pulteney (later the earl of Bath), a 50ish man who had a large fortune, a seat in the House of Commons, and a wife of long standing. Alleging that he aimed to further her education, he spent hours alone with her. "This intimacy," said her first biographer John Fyvie, "notwithstanding the difference of age between the parties, was not considered by all as being strictly platonic." Her mother co-operated with Pulteney's suggestion that they move to London and go to court. He was made earl of Bath by King George II, and Elizabeth was given an income of £400 and a job as maid of honor to ✥➤ **Augusta of Saxe-Gotha**, wife of the prince of Wales.

At the prince's court—which had a reputation for vice and sexual intrigue—Elizabeth met the wealthiest and most eligible men of her generation, one of whom, James, duke of Hamilton, proposed to her in 1743, asking her to wait until he returned from his Grand Tour of the Continent. But when she met another young suitor, Augustus John Hervey, at a horse-race, they fell madly in love and married, even though he was a poor younger son and had to earn his living as a naval officer. The service took place secretly at 10 PM on an August night of 1744, in an isolated Hampshire church, lit only by a single candle and in the presence of a few close friends and servants. They kept the wedding secret—even from Elizabeth's mother—as she would lose her job and income if known to be married. But the couple fell out very soon after the wedding, pos-

sibly due to some form of sexual abuse on his part, and when Hervey returned to the fleet she resolved to have nothing more to do with him.

At the prince's court, her intrigues continued and her name was linked romantically (or sexually) with those of many prominent courtiers. Gossips wrote, claimed Fyvie, that she always had "a train of captives at her heels." King George II was also strongly attracted to her, but, rumors notwithstanding, she does not seem to have had an affair with him. Even so, through his favor she was able to secure for her mother a job as housekeeper at Windsor Castle, which she held for the rest of her life with the princely stipend of £800 per year. Elizabeth was a witty speaker and provocatively flirtatious. She appeared at a court masque as Iphigenia, so scantily clad that even the more rakish courtiers were shocked. One observer, *Mary Wortley Montagu*, wrote that "her dress, or rather undress, was remarkable. She was Iphigenia for the sacrifice, but so naked that the Maids of Honor, not of maids the strictest, were so offended that they would not speak to her." Princess Augusta, to whom she was still maid of honor, hastened to cover her with a blanket.

Chudleigh at first refused to see her husband on his return to England, but he threatened to expose their real relationship. When they met alone, Hervey apparently forced himself upon her, and nine months later she gave birth to a son, after an unexplained absence from court. She tried to scotch rumors by exaggerating them, telling Lord Chesterfield, for example: "The world says I have had twins." Chesterfield answered, dead pan: "Well, I make a point of believing only one half of what the world says." In any event, the child, who had been consigned to a wet nurse, did not long survive.

Meanwhile, Elizabeth was becoming involved with the Duke of Kingston, a man of ancient lineage, vast estates, and the immense income of £17,000 per year. He had raised a regiment to help suppress Bonnie Prince Charlie's rebellion in 1745, was still nominally in the army, but was more of a sportsman and dandy than an officer. He dismissed his long-term French mistress, who returned to Paris and later wrote a malicious book about Elizabeth, and devoted himself to his new love. It was 1750 and Elizabeth was now aged 30. She settled down with the duke, and, despite her numerous flirtations with other men, he loved and kept her in fine style. She was an extravagant spender, filling the duke's houses, and the houses he gave her, with gaudy, costly ornaments. Horace Walpole,

➤✥
Augusta of Saxe-Gotha. *See Caroline Matilda for sidebar.*

Elizabeth
Chudleigh

Austria, electress of Saxony (1724–1780), before responding to the duke's entreaties for her return. Then, to her dismay, her husband showed up again, saying he planned to sue her for divorce (an elaborate, highly public, and costly procedure in that era) because he wanted to marry someone else. She would have liked to be divorced but was determined not to appear as the guilty party, lest it jeopardize her prospects of getting the duke to marry her. She warned Hervey that if he tried to publicize their marriage he would recover not just his bride but her £16,000 in debts, which he was quite unable to pay. They now colluded in a legal scheme. She sued *him* on grounds of his "jactitation of marriage." Jactitation is the malicious declaration that you are married to someone when you are not. Hervey put up a deliberately weak defense and so, in 1768, the court found in her favor and declared that the couple had never been married.

But there is an extra ironic layer to this part of the story. According to one of the many rumors that swirled about her, Elizabeth had heard in 1759 that Hervey's childless older brother, the earl of Bristol, was on his deathbed. If he died, Hervey would become the new earl and gain a huge fortune while his wife would become a countess. Enticed by *that* prospect, she gathered the surviving witnesses to her original marriage and got them to sign an oath that it *had* taken place. But fortune deceived her, the earl recovered, and now, nine years later, she was swearing in public that she had *not* married Hervey. At different moments, in other words, she was determined to prove both that she had married Hervey and that she had not.

If she was *not* married to Hervey, as the 1768 court had declared, Elizabeth was free to marry the duke of Kingston. She did so, in 1770, and they lived on together, entertaining in the finest style as before. Society letters of the time describe her as bossing the duke around and denying him even the liberty to take a breath of fresh air without her express permission. In 1773, however, the old duke died. He left his estates and income to Elizabeth, the duchess, for the duration of her life, specifying that on her death it would all go to Charles Medows, the younger of his two nephews. The older of the two, Evelyn Medows, had fallen out with the duke years before and now found himself excluded from the will. This exclusion gave him a motive to prove that Elizabeth's marriage to the duke had been bigamous, and that, by law, the will was invalid.

Another sordid episode of the early 1770s was Samuel Foote's play, *A Trip to Calais*. Foote,

whose massive collection of gossipy letters is one of our best sources on her life, wrote a friend, after one of Elizabeth's lavish parties thrown to celebrate the queen's (*Caroline of Ansbach) birthday: "Oh, that you had been at her ball t'other night! History could never describe it and keep her countenance. . . . A scaffold was erected in Hyde Park for fireworks. To show the illumination without to more advantage the company were received in an apartment totally dark, where they remained for two hours. If this gave rise to any more birthdays, who could help it?" She heaped up cherries and strawberries for her guests and presented elaborate illuminated tableaux of the royal family, who willingly turned a blind eye to her shady reputation for the sake of enjoying her entertainments.

Elizabeth and the duke split up for a few months in 1764 when he had a fling with a hatmaker. She spent the time touring Europe, got drunk at a dance in the court of King Frederick II of Prussia, and befriended *Maria Antonia of an unscrupulous popular writer of the times, had talked with one of Elizabeth's servants (who had herself attempted unsuccessfully to blackmail her mistress), and now wrote a thinly veiled account of her life, naming the Chudleigh character Lady Kitty Crocodile. Foote anticipated that she, hearing of its rehearsals, would pay him to suppress it rather than be held up to the ridicule of London society. Sure enough, she summoned him, asked him to read some of it, and, after hearing the more incriminating passages, asked him in a tone of barely suppressed fury how much it would cost to suppress. He

suggested £2,000, which further enraged her. An unseemly bargaining period followed, in which she offered as much as £1,600, but Foote stubbornly held out for the full amount.

Under this provocation, Chudleigh appealed to the duke of Newcastle, one of the political grandees of the Whig Party, describing the blackmail. Foote retaliated by telling a political friend of his own, Lord Hertford, that Chudleigh was indeed a bigamist and that there were living witnesses who could prove it. With Evelyn Medows, the disinherited nephew, and Samuel Foote forc-

The trial of Elizabeth Chudleigh, Duchess of Kingston.

ing the issue, a Grand Jury considered the evidence and found reason to proceed with a trial. Messengers took the summons to Elizabeth, who was on one of her periodic tours of the Continent, and warned her that if she did not go back to England to face the prosecution she would be made an outlaw. First, she met with one of her bankers in Rome to collect some money and jewels to pay for her defense, then threatened him with loaded pistols when he declined to hand them over forthwith. She returned to England, where she appealed, as a member of the nobility, for the right to be tried by her peers, the House of Lords in Westminster Hall. But if she was not in fact a duchess, was she part of the nobility? Yes, ironically, for in 1775 the earl of Bristol had finally died, which made Hervey the new earl and herself the new countess. This was a vital matter: in the 18th century, the punishment for bigamy was to have one's hand seared by fire *unless* one belonged to the aristocracy.

"The trial," wrote historian Lewis Melville, "was a tremendous affair—it was the event of the year. A peeress, a reputed duchess who was at least a countess, a woman of immense notoriety in more than one country, charged with bigamy, and tried by her peers. There had never before been anything like it, nor was such an affair likely to happen again. Everyone begged, coaxed, or threatened those in authority to be allowed to be present. It was joyously anticipated that there would be 'scenes' in court."

Elizabeth, now aged 56, was no longer much of a beauty. One witness of the case, *Hannah More, wrote that "she is large and ill-shaped. There was nothing white but her face and had it not been for that she would have looked like a ball of bombazine." She had gained weight steadily but was still an artful manipulator of occasions and persons. She appeared at court dressed in modest black clothes, avoided the selfish tantrums for which she was also becoming notorious, and prompted the Law Lords to treat her courteously. The trial lasted for a week in April 1776 (and caused a far greater stir than the war then raging in England's American colonies), but the evidence against her was overwhelming, whereas her own defense was flimsy. She was convicted of bigamy but, because of her rank, spared the grisly punishment she would have suffered if still a commoner.

Chudleigh realized that Evelyn Medows would now sue for the old duke's will to be overturned and that he would try to prevent her from leaving the country. To outwit him, she invited a large group of friends and sympathizers to a din-

ner party at her London house and told her coachman to drive her well-known coach around the popular streets of town, so that Medows would think she was still accessible. Meanwhile, she fled to Dover in a hired coach and then sailed across the English Channel to France, carrying as many assets from her estates as she could liquidize. Medows was thwarted. So was her one real husband, the earl of Bristol. Hervey tried to revive divorce proceedings in 1777, but his legal advisors told him that his earlier legal misconduct, when he had tried to obtain Elizabeth's collusion to a divorce bill, would prejudice his case.

Chudleigh spent the remaining 12 years of her life traveling throughout Europe. She had houses in Paris and Rome, befriended the pope and the Russian royal family, and bought a large estate outside St. Petersburg. She became increasingly tight-fisted, despite her ostentatious wealth, and often tried to leave her lodgings without paying the bill. Strong in constitution and untiring in her travels, she enjoyed almost constant good health and was still drinking and eating heartily the day before her sudden death in 1788. "According to one account," wrote Melville, "the immediate cause of death was the breaking of a blood-vessel as the result of a violent outburst of rage on hearing that a lawsuit in Paris had gone against her."

Elizabeth had little education, and what letters we still have over her signature were probably drafted by her lawyers rather than by Chudleigh herself. In fact, our only sources on her life are the gossipy letters of her detractors and the record of her scandalous court case—no sympathetic account of her life by a contemporary survives, and it may be that a modern biographer would interpret her life less harshly than those of her own time and place.

Chudleigh's reputation lived on, partly because William Thackeray based two of his characters on her: first Beatrix in *Henry Esmond* and later Baroness Bernstein in *The Virginians*. She had seemed larger than life in her own times, and, after the earnest evangelical reforms of the early Victorian era, she became, in retrospect, a representative symbol of the fascinating, sexy, decadent world of 18th-century society.

SOURCES:

Fyvie, John. *Wits, Beaux, and Beauties of the Georgian Era*. London: John Lane-Bodley Head, 1909.

Lewis, W.S., ed. *The Correspondence of Horace Walpole*. New Haven, CT: Yale University Press, 1937–83.

Melville, Lewis, ed. *The Trial of the Duchess of Kingston*. Edinburgh, UK: William Hodge, 1927.

Patrick Allitt, Assistant Professor of History, Emory University, Atlanta, Georgia

Chudleigh, Mary Lee (1656–1710)

English poet and essayist. Name variations: Lady Mary Lee Chudleigh. Born in August 1656 in Devon, England; died on December 15, 1710; buried in Ashton, Devonshire; daughter of Richard Lee, Esq., of Winsdale; married Sir George Chudleigh; children: several, including Eliza Marie, George, and Thomas.

Selected works: The Ladies Defence; or, the Bride-Woman's Counsellor answered: A Poem. In a Dialogue between Sir John Brute, Sir William Loveall, Melissa and a Parson *(1700);* Essays Upon Several Subjects in Prose and Verse. Written by Lady Chudleigh *(1710).*

Though Mary Lee Chudleigh studied literature and history, while showing a particular enthusiasm for philosophy and divinity, her education veered from the norm in that she did not learn languages. She was highly motivated in her studies, valuing her intellect for aid in living a virtuous life. Writing offered her a means of finding solace, particularly after the deaths of her mother and young daughter Eliza Marie, and Chudleigh claimed that her true self was revealed in her poetry.

In 1700, she published the poem "The Ladies Defence" anonymously, and she was later concerned about acknowledging authorship of this feminist piece when it was included in a subsequent edition of her poetry. The work was an attack aimed explicitly at John Sprint, author of *The Bride-Woman's Counsellor,* who advised women to be subservient to their husbands. The other woman who challenged Sprint, under the pseudonym "Eugenia," was a close friend of Chudleigh, and to her Chudleigh dedicated the first edition of her poems.

Though Chudleigh applied John Locke's epistemology to argue for the equal education of women, her defense of women does not necessarily indicate that her own marriage accommodated her views. Indeed, her poetry displays bitterness about women's plight in marriage:

> When she the word *obey* has said,
> And Man by Law supreme has made,
> Then all that's kind is laid aside,
> And nothing left but State and Pride . . .
>
> Value yourselves, and Men despise,
> You must be proud, if you'll be wise.

A longtime sufferer of rheumatism, Chudleigh was confined to her bed for several years before her death in 1710. That same year, she published *Essays upon Several Subjects,* which included treatments of knowledge, pride, humility, life, death, fear, and grief.

SOURCES:

Ballard, George. *Memoirs of Several Ladies of Great Britain Who Have Been Celebrated for Their Writings or Skill in the Learned Languages, Arts and Sciences.* Detroit, MI: Wayne State University Press, 1985.

Kersey, Ethel M. *Women Philosophers: a Bio-critical Source Book.* NY: Greenwood Press, 1989.

Stenton, Doris Mary. *The English Woman in History.* NY: Macmillan, 1957.

SUGGESTED READING:

Smith, Hilda L. *Reason's Disciples: Seventeenth Century English Feminists.* Chicago: University of Illinois Press, 1982.

Catherine Hundleby, M.A. Philosophy,
University of Guelph, Guelph, Ontario, Canada

Chukovskaya, Lidiya (1907–1996)

Russian novelist, critic, memoirist, poet and dissident, whose writings preserve the history of Russian literature and culture and document the tragedies of Stalinist and post-Stalinist repression in the Soviet Union. Name variations: Lydia, Lidija, Lidiia, or Lidia Chukovskaia, Chukovskaja. Pronunciation: LEE-dia Kor-NAY-yevna Choo-KOVE-skaya. Born Lidiya Korneyevna Chukovskaya on March 24, 1907 (some sources cite March 23), in St. Petersburg, Russia; died at her home in Moscow on February 7, 1996; daughter of Kornei Ivanovich Chukovsky or Chukovskii (a Russian critic, translator, and popular author of children's verse and fairy tales) and **Maria (Borisovna) Chukovsky;** *married Tsezar' Vol'pe; married Matvei Petrovich Bronshtein also known as Matvey Bronshteyn (a physicist); children: (first marriage) daughter Elena (b. 1932). Expelled from Soviet Writers' Union (1974).*

Selected writings: The Decembrist Nikolai Bestuzhev: Investigator of Buratia *(Moscow, 1950);* In the Editor's Laboratory *(Moscow, 1960, 1963);* Hertsen's "Past and Thoughts" *(Moscow, 1966);* The Open Word *(New York, 1976);* On This Side of Death *(Paris, 1978);* The Process of Expulsion *(Paris, 1979);* Sofia Petrovna *(published as* The Deserted House, *Paris, 1965, published as* Sofia Petrovna *in New York, 1967, 1972, Moscow, 1989);* Going Under *(London, 1972, Moscow, 1989);* Notes on Anna Akhmatova *(Vol. I, Paris 1976, 1984, Vol. II, Paris 1980);* To the Memory of Childhood *(New York, 1983, Moscow, 1989). Collected and edited* The Children Are Called Upon to Speak *(Tashkent, 1942).*

On a cold day in February 1938, Lidiya Chukovskaya reached the front of a long line of wives, mothers, and other relatives of Soviet citizens in prison. She held out some money and named her husband, but the voice behind the

*Lidiya
Chukovskaya*

window snapped, "He's been sent out!" and her hand was brushed aside. After two or three days in another line, Chukovskaya was told that she could find out about her husband's sentence in Moscow; that same night, she took the express train from Leningrad. In the morning, a friend from Leningrad called to say that Chukovskaya's five-year-old daughter and her nanny had moved to the apartment of Chukovskaya's father—in other words, in the careful language of that period, she must not return home, because overnight the secret police had come to arrest her, too, as the wife of an "enemy of the people."

Chukovskaya returned to Leningrad only to meet her father and daughter on the street. Taking some money, she departed again and spent several months with acquaintances in distant cities, moving frequently, determined to survive, to care for her daughter and work for her husband's release. At last she heard from her family that Pëtr Ivanovich (a code name for the Soviet secret police, the NKVD) "had calmed down and stopped chasing other men's wives." She re-

turned to her apartment in Leningrad to find her husband's belongings plundered and his room occupied by an NKVD man, who was soon replaced by his sister, a professional prostitute. There seemed to be no further danger of arrest, so Chukovskaya brought her daughter back home. It was during these difficult days that she began to visit the great poet *Anna Akhmatova.

Matvei Bronshtein's sentence was "ten years of imprisonment without the right of correspondence." The folk wisdom surrounding arrest, prison, labor camps and exile finally concluded that these words really meant immediate execution. Bronshtein's death in February 1938 was confirmed only in 1957, when innocent victims of the great purges were "rehabilitated." Chukovskaya's literary work became a lasting memorial to her husband and countless other victims of Stalinist terror in the Soviet Union.

Lidiya Chukovskaya's life breaks into four distinct parts: childhood before the 1917 Revolution, youth and adulthood following the Revolution, Stalinist repression, and finally open dissidence. Until she was ten years old, she lived mainly at the family's *dacha* (summer house) in Kuokkala, Finland, not far from St. Petersburg. Unlike most other Russians, who only spent the summer in their dachas, the Chukovsky family lived in Kuokkala year round. Chukovskaya describes her happy childhood in *To the Memory of Childhood,* which is in reality a tribute to her father who taught her that writers are special and important people whose contribution to culture sets them apart. Lidiya's mother was not an artist, and so she barely appears in this recollection of childhood or any of Chukovskaya's writings.

Lidiya's father, born Nikolai Vasil'evich Korneichukov, was the illegitimate son of a university student and a peasant woman, **Ekaterina Osipovna Korneichukova**, who supported herself and her two children doing laundry. Nikolai grew up in Odessa, bitterly aware of his poverty and the circumstances of his birth; he was expelled from school after a government decree prohibited education for "cooks' children." Though he educated himself, he always felt secondary in talent and importance to the many poets and artists he knew. After 1917, he changed his name legally to Kornei Ivanovich Chukovsky, the literary pseudonym he had been using for more than a decade. His new first name, not the old one, formed Chukovskaya's patronymic, "Korneyevna." Chukovsky was a prominent literary critic before the 1917 Revolution, but in the Soviet period he became best known for children's poems and translations. He was the second Russian ever to receive an honorary doctorate from Oxford University (1962).

Chukovsky worked hard to give his children an artistic education, passing on his almost religious love of literature. Lidiya relished reading girls' books, *The Little Princess* and *Little Women,* but she soon learned to prefer the poems of Pushkin, Nekrasov, and the great Ukrainian Shevchenko. Still, when famous poets, singers, actors, and painters visited the dacha, the children were most interested in the important questions: what were their dogs or horses like, how did they play croquet? Lidiya enjoyed family games, rowing on the Gulf of Finland while her father recited poetry, and learning English through nonsense translations. Chukovskaya and her brothers Kolya (Nikolai, 1904–1965) and Boba (Boris, 1910–1941) were the first source for their father's influential writings on childhood language acquisition, and his famous rhymed fairy tales began in the nonsense rhymes he made up to amuse them. At the same time, Lidiya had to obey the iron rule of the household: her father must not be disturbed while working. One afternoon she happened to see the headmaster of the local primary school methodically whipping another pupil with a belt. Upset and stuttering, she told her family what she had seen, and from then on she and her brothers took their lessons at home with a tutor, preparing for high school.

At some point after Tsar Nicholas II's abdication in 1917, the Chukovsky family moved to Petrograd. (St. Petersburg was renamed during World War I to sound less German.) Chukovskaya gives few details of the next part of her life. After finishing preparatory school in Petrograd, she attended the former Tenishev school, a famous and excellent institution whose earlier alumni included Osip Mandelstam and Vladimir Nabokov. She later recalled her embarrassment, during Russia's Civil War (1919–21), when she had no shoes and could go outside only with her father's galoshes over her house slippers; the enormous galoshes constantly fell off her feet. At school, she formed lasting friendships with other girls who liked literature: they sat together for hours, reciting poems by Blok and Akhmatova from memory. Chukovskaya completed her formal advanced studies in literature at the Leningrad Institute for the History of the Arts.

In 1927, Chukovskaya began work at the Leningrad State Publishing House in the branch for children's literature, directed by her father's friend, the poet Samuil Marshak. She married Tsezar' Vol'pe, an up-and-coming critic and edi-

tor, and their daughter Elena (called by the affectionate nickname Liusha) was born in 1932. Chukovskaya admitted with shame that she did not "open her eyes" as millions of peasants died or were exiled during the collectivization of Soviet agriculture, but there was one family tragedy in this period: her little sister Maria, born in 1920, died painfully of tuberculosis in 1931.

> *W*here the word has not perished,
> there the future is saved.
>
> —**Lidiya Chukovskaya**

Lidiya was a talented and hard-working editor who enjoyed her job and her co-workers. In 1937, however, members of the staff of the children's section were denounced as "wreckers" by a colleague. Abruptly, Chukovskaya and those she cared for were thrown out of work. Some of the editors were arrested and spent years in prison or camp. When her obviously innocent second husband, promising astrophysicist Matvei Petrovich Bronshtein, was arrested in 1937, an exhausted and humiliated Chukovskaya tried to find out what was happening to him. This, and her own near-arrest in 1938, finally convinced her that the Soviet state was committing horrendous crimes, that she could only survive physically and morally by doing all she could to stay free and to preserve the people and writing she loved. With her talents and connections, she continued her critical and editorial work in children's literature to support her daughter through the Stalinist period. Personal tragedy and the threat to Russian culture provoked her, in spite of the danger, to begin her best creative writing, a psychological release from the pressures of caution and silence. Writing about the terror meant risking arrest and torture, for herself and her family. Chukovskaya's courage, in this third part of her life, prepared her for her later dissident activity.

Chukovskaya's first novel, *Sofia Petrovna,* is the only known prose work about the terror that was written in the Soviet Union between 1939 and 1940. The heroine is an "ordinary" Soviet woman very unlike the author, a hard-working and self-righteous citizen with middle-class tastes. Sofia Petrovna's world collapses when her only son is arrested on false charges in 1937. Though she is driven from her job because she is a relative of an enemy of the people, she continues to believe that her son's arrest is a single mistake in the state's pursuit of wreckers and foreign spies. She stands for hours in lines to learn his fate, hoping to argue his innocence; his devoted best friend is also arrested and the young woman she hoped would become her daughter-in-law, unemployed and desperate, commits suicide. In the end, a letter arrives from her son begging for help, telling of how he was beaten until he went deaf in one ear and confessed. Sofia Petrovna, unbalanced as her world collapses, burns the letter that may be her last link with her son. This was strong stuff, and Chukovskaya asked a friend to keep the notebook containing the only copy of the novel. "If they had caught him with it, they would have drawn and quartered him," she noted. The friend starved to death during the blockade of Leningrad in the Second World War, but his sister kept the notebook and later returned it to Lidiya.

Chukovskaya and Anna Akhmatova began meeting to exchange advice about the prison system in hushed voices. Though they had met before 1938, they now had something in common: Akhmatova's son Lev was also arrested. Soon, Chukovskaya was keeping regular notes of their conversations, especially Akhmatova's thoughts about poetry, to preserve all she could of the great poet's life and work. Since this, too, meant risking her life and freedom, Lidiya abbreviated the most dangerous details in code. She began to help preserve Akhmatova's own dangerous poems: Akhmatova would write on a scrap of paper, Chukovskaya would memorize the words quickly, and then Akhmatova would burn the paper over an ashtray. In May 1941, the secret police somehow heard about *Sofia Petrovna*, and Chukovskaya left Leningrad for a second time, claiming she needed to have a serious operation in a Moscow hospital. At the end of July 1941, after Hitler's Germany attacked the Soviet Union, Chukovskaya was evacuated with her daughter and nephew to the city of Chistopol' in Central Asia, where she briefly met *Marina Tsvetaeva, a few days before that poet's suicide, and learned of her younger brother's death in battle near Moscow. Anna Akhmatova, evacuated from Leningrad, joined the Chukovskaya party in Chistopol', and they traveled together to Tashkent. Chukovskaya continued to record their conversations until she began to notice that Akhmatova was treating her rudely. Convinced that someone must have told Anna lies, Lidiya stopped visiting, offended. Both friendship and notes broke off for a decade.

After the liberation of Leningrad in 1944, Chukovskaya tried to return, but the secret police clearly wanted to keep her out of the city, and someone else was living in her apartment. She settled in Moscow, staying partly in an apartment in the city, partly at her father's dacha in the nearby writers' colony of Peredelkino, and wrote her second novel, *Going Under*, between 1949 and 1955. Its heroine Nina Sergeyevna, a writer much like Chukovskaya, is vacationing at a writer's sanatorium in the late 1940s, before Stalin's death, working on a translation and at the same time "going under" into her memories of the 1930s, when her husband was arrested and killed. The novel is written in an unobtrusive but gripping style. Nina feels a survivor's guilt and sadly testifies to declining moral and cultural standards, even among educated Russians; the anti-Semitism of the early 1950s (the midnight arrest of the poet Veksler, a hero of World War II); and the unpleasantness of life in communal apartments. More than Chukovskaya's other writings, *Going Under* also shows how oppression works to distance people from each other: Nina Sergeyevna is not afraid to say that she loves Pasternak's poetry and does not believe the charges aired in the latest newspaper, but she harshly judges writers who do not dare tell the truth in their conversation and their writing.

Like *Going Under*, the poems Chukovskaya began to write in 1936 are somewhat autobiographical, documenting and mourning the losses of friends, loved ones, and her beloved city of Leningrad. Throughout her writing, Chukovskaya advocates the writer's prerogative to use her own life experience as the basis for literature, even if so doing demands bravery and honesty. Like *Nadezhda Mandelstam, another memoirist and judge of her generation, Chukovskaya is both judgmental and quick to criticize her own compromises.

In 1952, Chukovskaya began to meet Akhmatova anew in Moscow, where Akhmatova spent weeks at a time visiting friends. Lidiya's notes pick up in the second volume of *Notes on Anna Akhmatova*, and she continued meeting the poet regularly until Akhmatova's death in 1966. One of the most important writers of the 20th century, Anna Akhmatova was a living link with the prerevolutionary literary tradition but also a woman whose personal losses let her speak for all survivors of the Stalinist period. The *Notes* provide intimate details about Akhmatova—her poor health, her irritation at petty humiliations, even her panic at crossing the busy city streets—but ultimately present her as a monumental cultural figure. Along the way, Chukovskaya recounts her own life to help explain literary history or the context of Akhmatova's words.

Chukovskaya's mother died in 1955, and her father's health became fragile; worn out by the stresses of the Stalinist terror, Lidiya too had various illnesses. Her weak eyes were further irritated when she did too much close reading, but her work as an editor and scholar and her love of literature meant that she spent hours reading every day. In the late 1950s, she experienced prickly relations with her older brother, a successful writer with an official position in the Soviet Writers' Union. She felt that his speeches condemning Boris Pasternak for publishing his novel *Doctor Zhivago* in the West were a betrayal of Russian poetry and of a family friend.

Stalin's death was eventually followed by a brief "thaw," when writing and conversation about the decades of repression were allowed and even encouraged. Chukovskaya began to submit *Sofia Petrovna* to different state publishing houses, and, in September 1962, the novel was accepted. Editors and workers at the publishing house praised the book in her presence, told how they had wept reading it, and asked for copies for relatives and friends. The illustrations were done and she had received 60% of her royalties, when suddenly the political climate changed. In 1963, the book was "stopped." Chukovskaya, stung by the hypocrisy of the upper-level staff when she inquired about the book's fate, sued the publishing house for the remaining royalties and received them. The experience made her even more convinced that working to protect her career as a writer made her a collaborator in the general lie and silence about the horrors of the past, and she gradually began to protest openly. She had already championed Boris Pasternak. But after 1966, she had more and more trouble publishing her work, as she was publicly speaking out and writing open letters to defend dissidents such as writer Aleksandr Solzhenitsyn (who often visited the Peredelkino dacha to work or to evade surveillance), poet Joseph Brodsky, and physicist Andrei Sakharov. "Ideas should be fought with ideas," she wrote, "not with camps and prisons." In October 1969, Kornei Chukovsky died, and his age and fame could no longer protect his daughter. Always concerned with preserving the past, she made the dacha an unofficial museum where her father's books and belongings were kept untouched in the three rooms where he had lived. Lidiya worked with her father's longtime secretary, **Klara Israilevna Lozovskaya,** trying to maintain the place and receiving visits from other writers, foreign students, scholars, correspondents, and bus loads of school children.

Chukovskaya's writings spread through *samizdat*, the unofficial typed "publication" of unpublishable works and documents in multiple-carbon copies. This made her "open letters" addressed to (but not published in) the country's leading newspapers available to a wide circle of readers. When the *samizdat* texts began to appear in print in the West, the Soviet literary establishment moved to throw her out of its organizations. (In 1967, *Sofia Petrovna* was smuggled out of Russia and published in the West under the title *The Deserted House.*) It was impossible to make a living as a writer outside the official literary system, and it was the royalties from overseas publications that paid for medication for her failing eyes. Despite Kornei Chukovsky's fame, the museum-dacha in Peredelkino was falling apart—the Writers' Union, the owner from which Lidiya rented the building, refused to repair it to show its disfavor. Students and friends volunteered to help with repairs and clear the yard.

Chukovskaya angrily details her exclusion from the Writers' Union in 1974 in *The Process of Expulsion.* Called to a meeting with the union's secretary Yuri F. Strekhinin, she was asked about her continual criticism of the Stalinist regime:

> "How do you know these things," he asked.
> "From my life," she replied. "From mothers, wives, sisters. In order not to see, you have to shut your eyes and cover your ears. It's all around. . . . They put one of my friends who was completely healthy in an insane asylum."
> "Why does all this happen around you and nothing like that happens around me?" asked another writer in attendance.
> "I don't know—maybe you are living on an island. You make a special effort not to see."

The expulsion deprived her of any legal right to publish her work. Her name was purged, her books were removed from library shelves, and she was completely deprived of her livelihood. By now, Chukovskaya was a frail old woman in terrible health; she had a weak heart and was almost blind, able to read even her own handwriting only by using a special magnifying glass. However, her protests gave a moral and cultural example for others, and she kept right on working.

Unlike so many of her contemporaries, Lidiya Chukovskaya lived to see her vindication: her novels were published in Moscow in 1989, her writings are now available in Russia, and the "dangerous" poems she helped Akhmatova to preserve and conceal for decades have been published in many editions. The writers in whose defense she wrote so many letters have been welcomed back to Russia. Even her vision improved after several operations on her cataracts. The crisis of Russian culture in the early 1990s is foreseen in Chukovskaya's critical open letters from the decades before: she argued then that by artificially cutting the masses off from the intelligentsia, especially from the greatest writers, the rulers of the country were preparing an ignorant and embittered populace that would eventually turn violent. Even in 1995, one year before her death, when Boris Yeltsin awarded her the State Prize for Literature, she refused the money because of Russia's handling of Chechnya. Said her longtime friend and translator **Sylvia Rubashova**: "She was very uncompromising." Solzhenitsyn used another term, "incorruptible." Following her death on February 7, 1996, Chukovskaya was buried in the cemetery of Peredelkino, a few feet from the grave of Boris Pasternak.

Lidiya Chukovskaya was devoted to the highest achievements of Russian literature and culture, loved and supported those who produced that culture, and was convinced that a network of writers, appreciating the dissident's work, would come forward to offer support at crucial moments. Her judgments can be harsh and abrasive, though she was aware that it is easy to succumb to compromise and silence when loved ones are held hostage by an oppressive regime. The monstrosity of Stalinism is almost too grotesque to understand, but Chukovskaya's writing attempted to document and explain it, while raising a monument to those who died. Throughout the entire Stalinist period until the mid-1980s, preserving and documenting the Russian cultural, historical and literary heritage was as radical a challenge as any purely creative work. In working to serve her country and its art, defining her artistic mission in terms of selflessness, Lidiya Chukovskaya discovered a powerful, memorable voice as a writer.

SOURCES:

Chukovskaia, Lidia. *To the Memory of Childhood*. Trans. by Eliza Kellogg Klose. Evanston, IL: Northwestern University Press, 1988).

Holmgren, Beth. *Women's Works in Stalin's Time: On Lidiia Chukovskaia and Nadezhda Mandelstam*. Bloomington: Indiana University Press, 1993.

The [London] Times (obituary). March 2, 1996.

Van Gelder, Lawrence. "Lidiya Chukovskaya, Champion of Dissidents and Chronicler of Stalinist Abuses, Dies at 88," in *The New York Times*. February 9, 1996.

SUGGESTED READING:

Holmgren, Beth. "Chukovskaia, Lidiia Korneevna," in *Dictionary of Russian Women Writers*. Edited by Marina Ledkovsky, Charlotte Rosenthal, and Mary Zirin. Westport, CT: Greenwood Press, 1994, pp. 133–137.

Lydia Korneevna Chukovskaya: A Tribute by Bella Hirshon. Melbourne, Australia: University of Melbourne, 1987.

Russell, John. "High Spirits" (review of *To the Memory of Childhood*), in *New York Review of Books*. February 15, 1990, pp. 12–16.

Sandler, Stephanie. "Reading Loyalty in Chukovskaia's *Zapiski ob Anne Akhmatovoi*," in *The Speech of Unknown Eyes: Akhmatova's Readers on Her Poetry*. Vol. II. Edited by Wendy Rosslyn. Nottingham: Astra Press, 1990, pp. 267–282.

Sibelan Forrester,
Assistant Professor of Russian,
Swarthmore College, Swarthmore, Pennsylvania

Chunsina

Queen of the Franks. Second wife of Chlothar also known as Clothaire, Clotar, or Lothair I (497–561), king of Soissons (r. 511), king of the Franks (r. 558–561); children: Chrammus (d. 560). Lothair I's first wife was *Guntheuca; his 3rd wife was *Ingunde; his 4th was Aregunde (sister of Ingunde); his 5th was *Radegund (518–587); his 7th was *Vuldetrade.

Church, Marguerite Stitt

(1892–1990)

U.S. Republican Congresswoman who served six terms. Born Marguerite Stitt in New York City on September 13, 1892; died in Evanston, Illinois, on May 26, 1990; graduated from Wellesley College, 1914; master's degree in political science from Columbia University; married Ralph Church (an Illinois state legislator), in 1918.

Marguerite Church's political career was sparked by her marriage to Illinois state legislator Ralph Church in 1918, after which she worked in a number of family and children's welfare organizations. With her husband's election to the House of Representatives in 1934, she became more involved in his career, campaigning and accompanying him on investigative trips. She was active in the Republican presidential campaigns of 1940 and 1944 and, during and after World War II, made several inspection tours in Europe at her husband's request. After his death in March 1950, party leaders convinced her to run for election to his seat. Her November 1950 victory was followed by six successive terms.

Church's tenure was marked by her thoughtful attention to constituent services. As a member of the Committee on Foreign Affairs, she traveled extensively, particularly in Asia, and through her work on Government Operations helped pass the act that placed the federal budget on a system of annual expenditures. In 1962, at age 70, Church voluntarily withdrew from elective politics but remained active in the political campaigns of Barry Goldwater (1964) and Richard Nixon (1968). She also served on the national boards of the Girl Scouts of America and the U.S. Capitol Historical Society. She died in 1990, at the age of 98.

Barbara Morgan,
Melrose, Massachusetts

Churchill, Anne (1684–1716).

See Churchill, Sarah Jennings for sidebar.

Churchill, Arabella (1648–1714)

*English mistress of King James II of England. Born in 1648; died in 1714; eldest daughter of Sir Winston Churchill of Wootton Bassett, Wiltshire, and Elizabeth Drake; sister of John Churchill, duke of Marlborough (1650–1722); had long affair with James II, king of England (r. 1685–1688, deposed); children: (with James II) five, including **Henrietta FitzJames** (b. 1667); James Fitzjames, duke of Berwick-upon-Tweed (1670–1734); **Arabella (Ignatia) FitzJames** (b. 1674) who became a nun at Pontoise; and Henry Fitzjames, duke of Albemarle (d. 1702).*

Born in 1648, Arabella Churchill was the daughter of 🐝▶ **Elizabeth Drake** and Winston Churchill, a royalist and Member of Parliament. She first met James II, king of England, when she fell off a horse while out hunting in 1669. What the married James saw in her was the subject of much conjecture; one contemporary described her as "a tall creature, pale faced and nothing but skin and bone." Over the next ten years, their affair produced five children. Their first son James FitzJames, became the duke of Berwick and distinguished himself as a French military leader. Arabella used her influence to advance the interests of her brother John Churchill, 1st duke of Marlborough, who, as a general, would win some of the most renowned battles in European history.

Churchill, Clementine (1885–1977)

Political partner and wife of British prime minister Winston S. Churchill, remembered for her courage, compassion, and service during the dark hours of World War II. Name variations: Lady Clementine Churchill; Baroness Spencer-Churchill; (nickname) Clemmie. Born Clementine Ogilvy Hozier on April 1, 1885, in London, England; died at her home in London on December 12, 1977; daughter of Colonel (Sir)

Henry Montague Hozier (a career military officer) and Lady Henrietta Blanche Ogilvy (daughter of the 10th earl of Airlie); educated at home, Berkhamsted Girls' School, and Sorbonne, Paris; married Sir Winston Spencer Churchill, on September 12, 1908; children: Diana (1909–1963); Randolph (1911–1968); Sarah (1914–1982); Marigold (died at age three); Mary (b. 1922).

Honored for World War I service by King George V (1918); lived with Winston at No. 10 Downing Street while he was prime minister (1940–45); appointed chair British Red Cross Aid to Russia (1939); elevated to rank of Dame, Grand Cross Order of the British Empire (1946); lived at No. 10 Downing Street as wife of the prime minister (1951–55); widowed (1965); created Baroness Spencer-Churchill (1966).

When Clementine Hozier was introduced to Winston S. Churchill at a dance, she was nonplussed: he stared at her without saying a word. Four years later, they married, and she became his ever-present partner in elections, conferences,

Marguerite Stitt Church

◀🐝
Elizabeth Drake.
See Churchill, Sarah Jennings for sidebar.

ceremonies, and public appearances in the centers of world power. Her life with Winston was often difficult as he struggled in the political wilderness of the 1930s only to emerge as the century's greatest statesman. The perfect consort to deal with her husband's tempestuous career, energetic spirit, deep depressions, and fragile health, she was his "Clemmie," and she directed his home, advised him on his speeches, campaigned beside him, and lectured him on his health and work schedules as though he were a schoolboy. Winston would later write that he married Clemmie and lived happily ever after.

My marriage was the most fortunate and joyous event which happened to me in the whole of my life, for what can be more glorious than to be united in one's walk through life with a being incapable of an ignoble thought.

—Winston S. Churchill

Clementine Ogilvy Hozier was born on April 1, 1885, at her parents' home on Grosvenor Street, Mayfair, London. She was the second daughter of Sir Henry Montague Hozier and Lady **Blanche Ogilvy Hozier**. Her father, a retired dragoon colonel, was the third son of the lord of Newlands and Mauldslie Castle, Scotland. Lady Blanche was a daughter of the 10th earl of Airlie. When Clementine was nine, her father resigned his commission to accept a position at Lloyd's; he also separated from his wife. Lady Blanche was left to care for Clementine and her three other children on a small allowance from her relatives. Clementine was educated at home by governesses and then attended Berkhamsted Girls' School in Hertfordshire and the Sorbonne in Paris. She was well read in English and fluent in both German and French. After her return from France, she lived with her mother in a rental house in Kensington and gave French lessons to supplement the family income.

Clementine's mother knew the Churchill family, including Lord Randolph Churchill, Winston's father. It was her friendship with Lady Randolph Churchill (***Jennie Jerome Churchill**) that led to the introduction of Clementine to the silent Winston at that dance in 1904. Four years later, they met again at a dinner party, struck up a friendship, and began an exchange of letters. Winston, a member of the Liberal Party, was seeking a new seat in Parliament to confirm his Cabinet appointment as president of the Board of Trade. Since he was seeking the seat in nearby Dundee, Scotland, the Hozier family provided support for his campaign. The correspondence

continued, and Winston openly courted Clementine that summer. During a visit to Blenheim Palace, the Churchill ancestral home, he proposed to her in a Greek Temple during a rainstorm in August 1908. Both Jennie Churchill and Blanche Hozier were pleased with the match.

Their wedding, the social event of the season, took place at St. Margaret's Church, Westminster, on September 12, 1908. Clementine wore a white ivory satin dress and a lace de Venise veil, which was held in place by a coronet of fresh orange blossoms loaned to her by Jennie. Over one thousand guests filled the church, including many dignitaries and members of the British Cabinet. The newlyweds honeymooned at Blenheim Palace and later at Lake Maggiore in Italy.

When the Churchills returned to London, they established their first residence at Eccleston Square, Westminster. Winston was nearly 34, and Clementine was 23. Their marriage, which endured for 57 years, produced five children: one son and four daughters. The early months of their marriage were distinguished by austerity and a distinct shortage of money that made them appear middle class to their friends. Both had been unhappy as children, and they now found happiness in their own private world. Winston received the love from Clementine so long denied to him from his often distant mother and relatives. Clementine found the dedication and love that she had missed from her absent father. She dedicated herself to both Winston and his career.

Clementine immediately accepted an active role in Winston's political life. Seldom far from her husband's side, she involved herself in his constituency and accepted the turbulence and excitement of election campaigns. She found time to hear him rehearse his important speeches and rarely missed being present when he delivered them in the House of Commons. Clementine did not hesitate to criticize him or rap his knuckles with a fork for sulking at the dinner table, and Winston would often turn to her after one of his eloquent oratories to ask if it was all right.

Life with Winston was difficult, and Clementine needed all her firmness of character and keen intelligence to cope with his fiery temperament, impetuous actions, and disregard for his own physical well-being. He resented the incompetence of others, criticism of his own policies, and lack of foresight in contemporary leaders. One of Clementine's greatest challenges was contending with his periods of deep depression that he called "the black dog." She would be largely responsible for keeping up his spirits dur-

*C*lementine
*C*hurchill

ing the 1930s when he was virtually a prophet without honor as he warned about the threat of Fascism. Rather than argue with him, she often wrote notes explaining her views on the matter. She also had to deal with his unashamed propensity toward tardiness, often setting his bedside clock ahead to get him to places on time. Like a naughty boy, he found great delight in catching her advancing the clock.

Clementine was quite tall, fine featured, aristocratic and dressed with classic taste. Extremely athletic, she had played tennis at championship level during school days, loved horseback riding, croquet, hiking, and took up skiing at age 40. She was a talented organizer, capable administrator, gracious host, and competent public speaker. Her wit was extremely sharp, and she could be both caustic and warm in her public responses. She did not approve of all of Winston's friends, partly because she was reserved, and gave her friendship and trust carefully. She also felt that many of them, such as Lord Beaverbrook, did not have Winston's best interests at heart.

During the pre-World War I era, in addition to running the home and raising their young family, Clementine had often made non-political speeches for charities, fund-raising events, and public dedications. During the First World War, she organized and chaired, under the auspices of the Young Mens' Christian Association, canteens for the munitions workers in London. For her service, she was created a Commander Order of the British Empire by King George V. She solidly supported and shared the anguish Winston felt following his resignation as lord of the admiralty after the failure of the Dardanelles campaign. Singly, she maintained their home while her husband served as an officer on the front lines in France.

Winston returned to the Cabinet before war's end as munitions minister, but, following a change of political tide in England and appendicitis during the 1922 campaign, he was out of Parliament for two years. During this time, he used the proceeds from his lucrative writing to purchase Chartwell Manor, near Westerham, Kent. Although Winston loved Chartwell until his death, Clementine was never fond of the sprawling estate. During the period between the two wars, the Churchills were financially strapped, making Clementine's management of the large and expensive Chartwell very difficult.

Clementine was at heart a staunch and sincere liberal in politics. Although disappointed when Winston rejoined the Conservative Party in 1924, she remained unwaveringly at his side publicly. While she worked for him in his district, she never gave up her independent views. But, no matter how critical or outspoken she was to him in private, she put her loyalty to Winston above all else. From the beginning, she was a dedicated mother, but she delegated the care and education of her children to others so that Winston could receive her full attention.

Shortly after the outbreak of the Second World War in 1939, Clementine, now wife of the first lord of the admiralty, once again took up volunteer work for the war effort. From 1940 to 1946, she served as chair of the Council of the Fullmer Chase Maternity Hospital for the Wives of Junior Officers. From 1941 to 1947, she was president of the Young Women's Christian Association War Time Fund. She was also a member of the advisory committee of the British War Relief Society of America in 1942 and director of the Knitted Garments for the Royal Navy Organization. Her major volunteer contribution during the war was as chair of the Red Cross Aid to Russia Fund. Popularly known as "Mrs. Churchill's Fund," the organization under her leadership raised nearly £8 million. In 1945, Clementine journeyed to Moscow as a guest of the Russian Red Cross to visit several of the hospitals aided by her work. During her visit, she traveled extensively to Stalingrad, Leningrad, and other cities with the Red Cross, was received by Premier Joseph Stalin, delivered a message from Winston to Stalin over Moscow Radio, and on May 7 was awarded the Order of the Red Banner of Labour by N.M. Shverkin on behalf of the Supreme Soviet. While there, she learned of the death of President Franklin D. Roosevelt and Germany's surrender.

Clementine had moved to No. 10 Downing Street in May 1940 when Winston accepted the burden of leadership as wartime prime minister. In addition to her numerous volunteer efforts, she had the responsibilities of Britain's political "first lady." She brought to her new residence her serene charm, outstanding courage, and years of experience as a hostess. She accompanied Winston on his inspection tours of bombed British cities and once, when bombs were falling, told a friend to simply ignore them. While looking after the prime minister's health, she accompanied him on many of his important wartime trips, including the 1942 trip to the Quebec conference to meet with Roosevelt, and subsequent missions to Washington, Yugoslavia, and the Soviet Union.

In the July 1945 general election, Winston's Epping district was partitioned, and he sought re-election to Parliament in the division of Wanstead and Woodford. Clementine enthusiastically toured the constituency, often holding an umbrella over her husband's head, and delivered six speeches on behalf of Winston on the eve of the election. Winston won his seat by a large margin, but the nation provided a landslide for the Labour Party, which replaced him with Clement Attlee as prime minister. Although Winston was deeply disappointed, Clementine privately felt that his health would benefit from the removal of such heavy burdens of office.

Clementine's general health had also suffered during the war. Winston, now leader of the Opposition, continued to place many demands on her. They were also celebrities who were admired not only by the British but throughout the world. On the King's Birthday Honor List announced June 12, 1946, Clementine was elevated to the title of Dame, Grand Cross Order of the British Empire, and characteristically asked the monarch if she could still be known as Mrs. Churchill. During the same month, she was awarded an honorary LL.D. from Glasgow University and the honorary D.C.L. from Oxford.

In the autumn of 1951, Winston led the Conservatives back to power, and he and

Clementine returned to the prime minister's residence. Like her husband, she viewed his return to power as a vindication for the 1945 election, but she also viewed his victory with trepidation because of his advanced age and problematic health. When Winston was to be awarded the Nobel Prize for Literature in 1953, he was unable to attend because of the Big Three Conference in Bermuda. Swedish authorities, choosing to disregard protocol, specifically requested that Clementine, rather than the British ambassador, represent Winston at the Stockholm ceremonies. Elegantly dressed with a diamond tiara crowning her white hair, Clementine performed so brilliantly that nearly 1,000 Swedish students serenaded her with the song "Clementine" at the ball following the awards.

Winston Churchill suffered a stroke in June 1953. Although not his first stroke, the severity led many to doubt that he could continue as prime minister. Once again, Clementine consoled him and directed his recovery. After two more years of active politics, he resigned as prime minister on April 5, 1955. The evening before his departure, Clementine and Winston entertained Queen *Elizabeth II and her husband, Prince Phillip, at Downing Street. Although Winston retained his seat in Parliament until 1964, life for both of them slowed considerably.

Freed from the burdens of leadership, the Churchills spent more time at Chartwell with their grandchildren and extended family—pets and racing horses. Winston pursued his interest in painting, while Clementine began to enjoy Chartwell for the first time. Because Winston had arranged for the estate to become a National Trust for the public, Clementine began to make major improvements so that it would reflect the history and beauty that it represented. Although Winston's health was poor, they traveled to France, the Riviera and took several cruises with their old friends. But the last decade of Winston's life was not congenial for him; his enjoyment had been drained away by his many strokes. Clementine's health was also failing, and she had some hospital stays for her nerves and anxiety. When Winston Churchill died on January 24, 1965, following a severe stroke, he was in his 91st year.

The entire nation rallied to Clementine with a sincere and abiding sympathy. During the great pageantry and ceremony of the state funeral, she presented a figure of tremendous dignity and poise. Everyone admired her resolve to actively continue life as she had lived it before Winston's death. She made the final preparations for Chartwell's National Trust status, sold their Hyde Park Gate apartment, and moved into a smaller apartment in Prince's Gate. With her beloved Winston at rest, her health improved. In May 1965, a lifetime peerage was conferred on Clementine, and she took the title of Baroness Spencer-Churchill of Chartwell. Though Spencer Churchill had been Winston's family name, he had never used the hyphen. She attended the House of Lords' sessions until deafness rendered her attendance pointless. Until the year before her death, she was also a regular participant at Westminster Abbey for the Service of Thanksgiving commemorating the Battle of Britain. As her classic looks were refined with age, she was a striking figure at the Abbey, dressed in black with her row of medals displayed on her dress.

Clementine Churchill died suddenly of a heart attack at her home on December 12, 1977, at age 93. Of her five children, only two survived her: *Sarah Churchill, the actress, who was born in 1914, and ☘▶ Mary, wife of British politician Christopher Soames, born in 1922. A daughter, Marigold, born in 1918, had died of pneumonia at three years of age. *Diana Churchill, born in 1909, had died in 1963, and Clementine's only son Randolph, born in 1911, had died in 1968. Special services for Clementine Churchill were held in Westminster Abbey on January 24, 1978, the 13th anniversary of her husband's death. Five weeks earlier, on De-

☘▶ Churchill, Mary (1922—)

Youngest of the Churchill daughters. Name variations: Lady Soames. Born in 1922; youngest daughter of Winston and Clementine Churchill; married British politician, Christopher Soames; children: five.

During World War II, Mary Churchill worked for the Red Cross and the Auxiliary Territorial Service in Britain; she also accompanied her father as an aide on several of his conferences overseas. In 1946, she married Christopher Soames, who was subsequently a Member of Parliament for 16 years. The Soames were then assigned by the British government to posts on the Continent, where Christopher served first as ambassador to Paris and then as vice president of the European Commission in Brussels. Mary was a vice president of the Church Army and served as United Kingdom chair of the International Year of the Child, 1979. The couple have five children and live in Hampshire. Mary Soames wrote of her mother and father in her book *Clementine Churchill: The Biography of a Marriage* (Boston: Houghton Mifflin, 1979).

cember 15, 1977, her ashes had been laid to rest in Sir Winston Churchill's grave at Bladon Church near Blenheim Palace.

SOURCES:

Fishman, Jack. *My Darling Clementine: The Story of Lady Churchill*. NY: David McKay, 1963.

Gilbert, Martin. *Churchill: A Life*. NY: Henry Holt, 1991.

Moran, Lord. *Winston Churchill: The Struggle for Survival 1940–1965*. Boston, MA: Houghton Mifflin, 1966.

Soames, Mary. *Clementine Churchill: The Biography of a Marriage*. Boston, MA: Houghton Mifflin, 1979.

———. *Family Album*. Boston, MA: Houghton Mifflin, 1982.

SUGGESTED READING:

Blake, Lord, and C.S. Nicholls, eds. *Dictionary of National Biography 1971–1980*. Oxford: Oxford University Press, 1986.

Bonham-Carter, Violet. *Winston Churchill: An Intimate Portrait*. NY: Harcourt, Brace and World, 1965.

Candee, Marjorie Dent, ed. *Current Biography, 1953*. NY: H.W. Wilson, 1954.

COLLECTIONS:

Most of Clementine Churchill's papers are in The Baroness Spencer-Churchill Collection owned by the Sunday Times/ Thompson Trust.

Phillip E. Koerper, Professor of History, Jacksonville State University, Jacksonville, Alabama

Churchill, Deborah (1677–1708)

British pickpocket and prostitute. Born in 1677; hanged at Tyburn on December 17, 1708; married John Churchill (an army ensign).

Deborah Churchill, who came from a good family and had an excellent education, turned to a life of crime, leading one chronicler to remark on her descent into "all manner of filthiness and uncleanness which afterward proved her shame and ruin." She married an ensign in the army before becoming a prostitute on the streets of London, picking the pockets of her clients. With Richard Hunt, her procurer and lover, she blackmailed rich merchants, and although she was arrested many times Churchill escaped any harsh punishment due to Hunt's bribery of officials.

Her downfall came in early 1708 when she was walking through Drury Lane on the prowl for a pick-pocket victim. She was shadowed by three male friends, Richard Hunt, William Lewis, and a youngster named John Boy, when she propositioned Martin Were, a merchant. When Were discovered Churchill's hand in his pocket, he pushed her down, whereupon her male companions came to her aid and complied with Churchill's demand that they kill Were by stabbing him with their swords. Of the four, only Churchill was caught by officials. Tried for the murder, she was condemned on February 26, 1708. Churchill convinced the prison authorities that she was pregnant, and she received a seven-month reprieve until they realized she had lied. On Friday, December 17, 1708, she was transported by coach to Tyburn where she was hanged.

Churchill, Diana Spencer

(1909–1963)

Eldest daughter and least known of the Churchill children. Name variations: Diana Sandys; Mrs. Duncan Sandys. Born Diana Spencer Churchill on July 11, 1909, at Eccleston Square, London, England; died on October 19, 1963, at Chester Row, London, England; daughter of Sir Winston S. Churchill (prime minister of England) and Lady Clementine Hozier Spencer-Churchill; attended Notting Hill High School, London, as a day student; studied at the Royal Academy of Arts; married John Milner Bailey (1932–1935), in December 1932; married Duncan Sandys (1935–1960), on September 16, 1935; children: (second marriage) Julian Sandys (b. 1936); Edwina Sandys (b. 1938); Celia Sandys (b. 1943).

Diana Spencer Churchill was born on July 11, 1909, at Eccleston Square in London, England, to Winston S. and *Clementine Churchill. Her father proudly told parliamentarian David Lloyd George that she was the prettiest child ever seen. After some tutoring at home, Diana was enrolled, along with her younger sister *Sarah, as a day student at Notting Hill High School in London. Dressed alike, the girls campaigned with their parents during elections, shared the cruelties and catcalls of politics, and even encountered bricks heaved at their father's open-top automobile. On April 28, 1925, Diana accompanied her father, now chancellor of the exchequer, from their residence at No. 11 Downing Street to present his first budget to Parliament.

In December 1932, Diana married John Milner Bailey, son of Sir Abe Bailey, the South African gold-mining millionaire and long-standing friend of Winston. Though the wedding that took place at St. Margaret's Church in Westminster was a dazzler, the marriage was not enthusiastically received in the Churchill home and a strained relationship developed between Diana and her mother that lasted most of her life. Diana and John separated barely a year later and divorced in early 1935. Diana lived alone in London but visited the Churchill home at Chartwell in Kent on weekends.

During a political campaign for her brother, Randolph, in the summer of 1935, Diana met Duncan Sandys, a diplomat who had left the Foreign Office to enter the political arena. They married on September 16, 1935. Their union produced a son Julian and two daughters Celia and Edwina. During World War II, Diana served in the Women's Royal Naval Service (WRNS) in London, while Duncan, a Territorial Officer, was also stationed near London with an anti-aircraft regiment. Diana worked as a nurse during the London air raids.

In 1953, Diana suffered a nervous breakdown, which affected her health for several years, but Winston had a soothing influence on his daughter. In 1955, she represented him in Copenhagen for Denmark's tenth anniversary of their liberation from Nazi occupation. Diana spoke briefly and unveiled a bust of Sir Winston at Liberty College, Copenhagen University.

By 1957, Diana and Duncan had separated, and she lived in a small house on Chester Row, London, with her two daughters. Their 25-year marriage ended in divorce in 1960. When Duncan remarried in 1962, Diana announced that she would revert to the name of Diana Churchill. Following the divorce, she and her mother developed a warmer relationship, and Diana and the children were regular visitors at Chartwell. Diana also accompanied her father on his numerous visits to southern France. In the summer of 1962, Diana became an unpaid volunteer in the Samaritans, an organization that counseled those contemplating suicide or suffering from despair. With her daughter Edwina's marriage and the birth of a grandchild, Diana's life seemed more tranquil and settled, but, during the night of October 19–20, 1963, she took a massive overdose of sleeping pills and died. Following an inquest, Diana was cremated and a memorial service was held at St. Stephen's Church in London on October 31, 1963. Her ashes lie near her parents at Bladon Cemetery, near Blenheim Palace, Norfolk.

Phillip E. Koerper, Professor of History, Jacksonville State University, Jacksonville, Alabama

Churchill, Elizabeth (fl. 1625–1650).

See Churchill, Sarah Jennings for sidebar on Elizabeth Drake.

Churchill, Fanny (d. 1899).

See Churchill, Jennie Jerome for sidebar.

Churchill, Henrietta (1681–1733).

See Churchill, Sarah Jennings for sidebar.

Churchill, Jennie Jerome
(1854–1921)

American-born public figure, wife of Lord Randolph Churchill, and mother of Sir Winston S. Churchill, who was influential in Britain's royal and political affairs for an entire generation. Name variations: Jennie Jerome; Lady Jennie Jerome Spencer Churchill; Lady Randolph Churchill; Mrs. George Cornwallis-West. Born Jeanette Jerome on January 9, 1854, in Brooklyn, New York; died on June 29, 1921, in London, England; daughter of Leonard Walter Jerome and Clara (Hall) Jerome; married Lord Randolph Churchill, in 1874; married George Cornwallis-West, in 1900; married Montague Porch, 1918; children: (first marriage) Winston Spencer Churchill (1874–1965); John Strange Churchill (b. 1880).

Mother moved family to Paris (1868); married Lord Randolph Churchill (1874); Lord Randolph died (1895); served as chair and nurse on hospital ship Maine *during Anglo-Boer War (1899–1900); founded and edited the* Anglo-Saxon Review *(1899); published her reminiscences (1908); had two plays produced (1914); served on several hospital boards (1915–19).*

Selected publications: Reminiscences of Lady Randolph Churchill *(Century, 1908);* Small Talks on Big Subjects *(Pearson, 1916).*

Jennie Jerome Churchill was destined to play a prominent and influential part in English court and political life for an entire generation. Born in America, she married Randolph Churchill, an English politician of first-rate political talent, and she was the mother of Sir Winston S. Churchill, a parliamentarian who proved to be a greater public figure than his father. Her part in public affairs can be found in the two careers with which she was so intimately associated.

Jeanette Jerome was born on January 9, 1854, in Brooklyn, New York. Her father Leonard Jerome was a self-made Wall Street millionaire and her mother **Clara Hall Jerome** was an attractive, fashion-conscious woman said to be one-quarter Iroquois Indian. Leonard dabbled in journalism, telegraphs, railroads, and horses. In an attempt to bring respectability to horse-racing, he was the founder of the New York Jockey Club and built the Jerome Park Racecourse. He also once owned *The New York Times.* Following the birth of their first child in 1851, Leonard served as American Consul in Trieste and later lived with his family in Paris before returning to America in 1860. He had a passion for music and was the patron of many aspiring young singers. Because of his fondness for the singer *Jennie

Lind, he named his second daughter Jennie. But Leonard was a philanderer and Clara, exasperated by her husband's lifestyle, moved to Paris in 1868 to educate her three daughters, **Clara**, Jennie, and **Leonie**. The Jeromes' wealth was a passport to Parisian society and the court of French Emperor Napoleon III. When the German army advanced on Paris during the Franco-Prussian War in 1870, the Jerome women were among the last foreigners to flee to London, England. English society was quite cold and lacked the elegance for the debut of young Jennie, but the Jeromes gravitated to the most exclusive events. One of these was the Cowes Regatta on the Isle of Wight in August of each year.

My mother always seemed to be a fairy princess; a radiant being possessed of limitless riches and power.

—Winston S. Churchill

On August 12, 1873, 19-year-old Jennie Jerome attended a Cowes Regatta ball given by the Prince and Princess of Wales (the future Edward VII and *Alexandra of Denmark) on H.M.S. *Ariadne* in honor of the heir to the Russian throne. It was a splendid evening for Jennie because she met and enchanted 24-year-old Lord Randolph Churchill, the younger son of John Spencer Churchill, the seventh duke of Marlborough. Randolph was short and slender with a walrus mustache, popping eyes and a refined, almost foppish demeanor. His personality, which reflected the superiority of class, matched that of the pampered Jennie. Theirs was a love match from the start. Two nights later, when Randolph proposed under starlight, in a garden overlooking the harbor and yachts, Jennie accepted without hesitation.

When Jennie conveyed to her mother her intentions to wed the younger son of an English duke, Clara opposed the idea as precipitate and hasty. Randolph's mother ❦▶ **Fanny Churchill**, duchess of Marlborough, was also deeply disappointed at the news. The duke of Marlborough, hoping his son would marry into the upper nobility, tried to discourage Randolph and expressed his dissatisfaction with Leonard Jerome's speculating and sporting background. At first, Jennie's father was happy for her, but he withdrew his consent after hearing of the duke's opposition. The young couple went through a cooling-off period, but separation did not dampen their ardor.

In time, the young lovers' obdurate endurance finally wore down parental objections.

Randolph won over his parents by agreeing to seek a seat in Parliament. But Jennie's father had suffered some financial reversals, and there were some ungentlemanly negotiations over the dowry. When Leonard Jerome and the duke finally reached a satisfactory agreement, the amount of £50,000 ($250,000) went to Randolph with the Leonard-generated stipulation that Randolph give Jennie £1,000 a year. The duke also paid off Randolph's debts and increased his allowance to £1,100 a year. The marriage was briefly delayed while Randolph contested the seat for Woodstock in the General Election on February 3, 1874. Woodstock, virtually a Churchill "family borough," included Blenheim Palace. Randolph, running as a conservative, outpolled his Liberal opponent by 165 votes.

On April 15, 1874, Jennie, in a dress of white satin and a long train lavishly trimmed with Alençon lace, wed Randolph in a simple ceremony in the British Embassy in Paris before a handful of people. With her dark hair, striking eyebrows, flashing dark eyes and fair features, Jennie possessed a natural beauty. While her family attended the wedding, the Marlboroughs sent their warmest greetings and patiently awaited the couple's arrival at Blenheim Palace, following their French honeymoon. In early May, the duke and duchess were waiting on the palace steps to greet them as they arrived amidst the cheering servants. During the visit, Jennie became more comfortable with her new family and the overwhelming splendor and size of Blenheim. Later in the month, the couple moved into their London home on Curzon Street.

Jennie quickly learned that London was dominated by social rituals. Arriving in London in the family coach, the duchess escorted her daughter-in-law on initial visits to the city's social leaders. The Churchills' early days of marriage were dominated by a constant gala of regattas, operas, hunts, balls and visits to the theater. Their attendance at fashionable functions were only interrupted briefly by the birth of a son on November 30, 1874. Jennie was out on a shooting party at Blenheim, became ill, and was rushed back to the palace where she prematurely delivered a son at one-thirty in the morning. He was named Winston Leonard Spencer Churchill, after his English and American grandfathers. The Churchill's second child, John (Jack) Strange Churchill, was also born prematurely in Dublin, Ireland, on February 4, 1880. The children were relegated to the nursery, while Jennie and Randolph resumed their active public lives.

Randolph's father was appointed viceroy of Ireland by Prime Minister Benjamin Disraeli in 1876. Jennie and Randolph accompanied the Marlboroughs to Dublin, where Randolph served as his father's private secretary. For the next four years, Randolph's attendance in Parliament was irregular, but he gained a close understanding of Irish problems during a critical era. When Disraeli's government fell in 1880, Jennie and Randolph returned to the intensity of domestic politics and the feverish social life of London.

Randolph was a captivating speaker, and he could often dominate debates in the House of Commons. He soon became the leader of a new clique of independent conservatives, known as the "Fourth Party," who favored social welfare, education reforms, and fairness towards Ireland. As his influence increased, Jennie's role also grew. She helped him prepare speeches, salved his sagging confidence, and campaigned beside him. She was an excellent host, and in their electrically lighted new home in Connaught Place they and their friends formed the Primrose League in 1883 to discuss the contemporary issues of the nation. Dismissed by critics at first, the League membership grew into the millions, and the duchess of Marlborough became president of the Ladies Council while Jennie served as a dame. It was the first serious involvement of women in English politics, and Jennie was an indefatigable recruiter, organizer and speaker.

Randolph rose rapidly in the Conservative Party. In 1885, he joined Lord Salisbury's Cabinet as secretary of state for India, and, in 1886, he became chancellor of the exchequer and leader of the House of Commons. Virtually assured of the prime ministership by virtue of his position, Randolph had little time for political campaigns. Jennie was a natural at electioneering and relished the responsibility with enthusiasm. She delivered fiery speeches, canvassed households from door-to-door, and chaired public meetings. Her beauty and spirit drew crowds wherever she went. She was a major asset to Randolph's political career.

But there were dark shadows, bad decisions and personal problems that threatened the Churchills' meteoric rise to power. Jennie was courted and won by many of the upper-class men of her day. Among her paramours were the prince of Wales (later Edward VII), the marques of Breteuil, and even the son of the German chancellor Otto von Bismarck, Herbert. She truly loved Count Charles Kinsky but lost his love to another woman. Her own marriage was

◆ Churchill, Fanny (d. 1899)
Seventh duchess of Marlborough. Name variations: Lady Frances Emily Vane. Born Frances Anne Emily Vane; died on April 16, 1899; eldest daughter of Charles William Stewart (b. 1778), 3rd marquis of Londonderry, and Frances Anne Emily Vane-Tempest (d. 1865); married John Winston Spencer Churchill (1822–1883), 7th duke of Marlborough (r. 1857–1883), on July 12, 1843; children: George Charles Spencer Churchill (1844–1892), 8th duke of Marlborough (r. 1883–1892); Frederick (1846–1850); Randolph Henry Spencer Churchill (1849–1895); Charles (1856–1858); Augustus (1858–1859); Cornelia Spencer Churchill (d. 1927, who married Ivor Bertie Guest, 1st baron Wimborne); Rosamond Spencer Churchill (d. 1920, who married William Henry Fellowes, 2nd baron de Ramsey); Fanny Spencer Churchill (d. 1904); Anne Emily Spencer Churchill (d. 1923, who married James Henry Robert, 7th duke of Roxburghe); Georgiana Spencer Churchill (d. 1906); Sarah Isabella Spencer Churchill (d. 1929).

An awesome presence, Fanny, the seventh duchess of Marlborough, was described in *The Complete Peerage* as "a woman of remarkable character and capacity." She was also domineering. "She ruled Blenheim and nearly all those in it with a firm hand," wrote *Jennie Churchill, "At the rustle of her silk dress, the household trembled." During the Irish potato famine in 1877, the duchess started a Famine Fund for Ireland's aged and infirm.

a romantic tragedy. Randolph, who had contracted syphilis as a young man, gradually became more unpredictable, petulant, and eventually went insane. In December 1886, he threatened to resign as chancellor of the exchequer in a Cabinet disagreement over military expenditures. To nearly everyone's surprise, Lord Salisbury accepted Randolph's resignation and his political career was virtually over. Though Randolph lingered in Parliament, he never held a Cabinet position again. His health declined into a tragic insanity and after a prolonged illness he died on January 24, 1895, at the age of 45.

Jennie, after a proper period of mourning, launched herself back into English society. She maintained her social position but widened the scope of her activities and took more interest in her sons. While Winston was serving as an officer in India, she often assisted him by utilizing her numerous contacts in government. She was concerned about her lack of money and often reflected on the need to remarry. In 1899, she founded and edited *The Anglo-Saxon Review*.

One of the best designed and beautiful journals of the day, it contained articles from such prominent writers as Algernon Swinburne, Henry James, Cecil Rhodes, and Lord Rosebury. Unfortunately her efforts failed financially in 1901 after ten issues.

When the Anglo-Boer War broke out in South Africa in 1899, Jennie was personally concerned, since both of her sons and a handsome young officer named George Cornwallis-West were on military duty there. She originated and promoted a plan to provide a hospital ship to assist the wounded in the war and formed a committee of wealthy American women living in Britain to raise the necessary funds for outfitting a ship. She convinced financier Bernard N. Baker, owner of the Baltimore Atlantic Transport Company who was captivated by her charm, to donate a ship. Baker also provided an entire crew at considerable personal expense. Jennie christened the vessel *The Maine*, secured American nurses, and convinced the British Admiralty to designate the ship as a British military hospital ship and to escort it to South Africa. Wearing a white nurse's uniform, she served as representative of the executive committee governing the vessel and accompanied *The Maine* to South Africa. One of her first patients was her son, Jack, who was slightly wounded in battle. King Edward VII, pleased with the personal sacrifice of one of his friends, gave Jennie Royal Orders. In 1901, he made her Lady of Grace of St. John of Jerusalem; the following year, he invested her with the Order of the Royal Red Cross.

Despite the doubts and concerns of their families, 46-year-old Jennie married 26-year-old George Cornwallis-West in London on July 28, 1900. George, who was just 16 days older than her son Winston, had no money and resigned his commission to seek more lucrative employment. Though they were happy for a time, arguments over money and his propensity for other women weakened the marriage. After the failure of *The Anglo-Saxon Review*, Jennie tried her hand at writing plays. In 1909, her first play, *Borrowed Plumes,* which ran briefly at the Haymarket Theater, received poor reviews and lost money. She also lost her husband to the play's leading actress, the legendary *Mrs. Patrick Campbell. In July 1914, their divorce was finalized, and he married Campbell the following day. Jennie chose to return to her more famous name, Lady Randolph Churchill.

Jennie was at one of the low points in her life. She had loved her second husband, but he had not returned her affections. She had also put every effort into Winston's military career, using her influence to gain him opportunities, but Winston had resigned his commission to seek a career in journalism and politics. Jennie had campaigned as energetically for Winston as she had earlier for Randolph, and he had won a parliamentary seat in Oldham on the second try in September 1900. Like his father, Winston rose rapidly to Cabinet status as president of the Board of Trade, undersecretary for colonies, home secretary, and first lord of the admiralty. During World War I, he received the full blame for the disastrous Dardanelles Campaign and was forced to resign from the Cabinet. His political future appeared to have been cut short just as abruptly as his father's career had ended. Jennie was crushed by his fall from power. She had served as one of his political mentors, hosted necessary dinners, and provided him with political connections to the power-brokers of government. She had lived a second political career only to see Winston suffer the same hurt and disappointment that his father had suffered earlier.

Her spirit, which she had always relied on to overcome disappointment, was unable to bring her the inner peace and happiness she sought. She had been pleased with the reception of her memoirs, *The Reminiscences of Lady Randolph Churchill,* which were published in 1908. But a second play, *The Bill,* had not been well-received in 1913. Though Jennie gained some satisfaction when several articles she had written were published in *Pearson's Magazine* in 1915, and later edited into a book entitled *Small Talks on Big Subjects* (1916), she continued, with somewhat less enjoyment, to attend parties, balls, and the theater. But she was spending her time with another generation. The splendor and excitement of the Edwardian age had given way to a less formal and less sophisticated society. Many of her old friends, including King Edward VII, had passed away and were replaced by acquaintances like Scott and *Zelda Fitzgerald, James Joyce, Pablo Picasso and Igor Stravinsky.

In 1914, Jennie attended her nephew Hugh Frewen's wedding in Rome and was introduced to Hugh's friend, Montague Phippen Porch, a young man serving in the colonial service in Nigeria. Porch, a graduate of Oxford and member of the landed gentry who had served in the Boer War, was a darkly handsome and intelligent man, slightly built with a glorious moustache and premature white hair. He was also 37, three years younger than Winston. They casually spent some time together sightseeing in Rome before Jennie returned to London.

Opposite page

Jennie Jerome Churchill

WOMEN IN WORLD HISTORY

During World War I, Jennie took part in many volunteer activities. She translated a French book, *My Return to Paris,* into English for the French Parliamentary Committee. She also edited and wrote the preface for *Women's War Work,* wrote several political articles for the *London Daily Chronicle* on the impact of the war on Ireland, organized luncheons for French diplomats, and, in 1917, helped recruit singers for *Margaret Lloyd George's Welsh Memorial Matinee.

Since their initial meeting in Rome, Jennie had corresponded with Porch. In 1918, he came home on leave to England, and the couple set out to visit Jennie's sister Leonie at her castle in Ireland. By the time they arrived in Ireland, Jennie and Montague had an "understanding." They were married on June 1, 1918, in a simple, unheralded ceremony at the Registry Office on Harrow Road. Winston was the first to sign the register and assured Porch that he would never regret marrying Jennie. Porch later wrote that, indeed, he never did.

After spending some time visiting her new husband's family in Bath, Jennie continued her volunteer war service by working at Lancaster Gate Hospital while Porch returned to Nigeria. At war's end, Porch resigned his Nigerian position, returned to London, and the couple traveled in France. It seemed that life had improved considerably for Jennie. Winston had overcome his political setback and was back in the British Cabinet. His wife *Clementine had taken over Jennie's old role of campaigning and hosting political dinners. Jack had his own business interests and was doing well.

In early 1921, Porch, unable to make money in London, returned to Nigeria where he hoped to use his knowledge of the country for profitable investment opportunities. Jennie remained in London and volunteered time to the Young Women's Christian Association, the Shakespeare Union, and other organizations. She continued to amaze everyone by acting in a movie, taking an airplane ride, and learning the newest dances.

In June 1921, Jennie visited her friend Lady **Frances Horner** at Mells Manor in Somerset. As she hurried down a staircase in new high-heeled shoes, she slipped and fell down the stairs, breaking an ankle. After nearly two weeks, gangrene set in, and her leg had to be amputated. Jennie calmly instructed the doctor to make certain he amputated high enough to contain the infection, and her leg was removed just above the knee. Though she seemed to be making progress,

on the morning of June 29 the main artery in the thigh of the amputated leg began to hemorrhage. She went into a coma before Winston and Jack arrived at the hospital and died shortly thereafter at age 67. A memorial service was held at St. Margaret's Church, Westminster, before the funeral train left Paddington Station on the morning of July 2. That afternoon, Jennie was buried beside Randolph Churchill in the small cemetery at Bladon Church near Blenheim Palace. Montague Porch, still unaware of her death, was on his way to London from Nigeria.

SOURCES:

Churchill, Peregrine, and Julian Mitchell. *Jennie: Lady Randolph Churchill, a Portrait with Letters.* NY: St. Martin's Press, 1974.

Cornwallis-West, Mrs. George (Churchill, Jennie). *The Reminiscences of Lady Randolph Churchill.* NY: Century, 1908.

Kraus, René. *Young Lady Churchill.* NY: Putnam, 1943.

Leslie, Anita. *Lady Randolph Churchill: The Story of Jennie Jerome.* NY: Scribner, 1969.

Martin, Ralph G. *Jennie: The Life of Lady Randolph Churchill.* 2 vols. Englewood Cliffs, NJ: Prentice Hall, 1969–71.

SUGGESTED READING:

Churchill, Lady Randolph. *Small Talks on Big Subjects.* London: Pearson, 1916.

Churchill, Winston S. *Lord Randolph Churchill.* 2 vols. London: Macmillan, 1906.

Foster, R.F. *Lord Randolph Churchill: A Political Life.* Oxford: Clarendon Press, 1981.

Gilbert, Martin. *Churchill: A Life.* NY: Henry Holt, 1991.

James, Robert Rhodes. *Lord Randolph Churchill.* NY: A.S. Barnes, 1960.

Leslie, Anita. *The Remarkable Mr. Jerome.* NY: Henry Holt, 1954.

COLLECTIONS:

Lady Churchill's letters and papers are located in several collections but most are in the Churchill Papers, Blenheim Palace, England.

Phillip E. Koerper, Professor of History, Jacksonville State University, Jacksonville, Alabama

Churchill, Mary (1689–1751).

See Churchill, Sarah Jennings for sidebar.

Churchill, Mary (1922—).

See Churchill, Clementine for sidebar.

Churchill, Odette (1912–1995).

See Sansom, Odette.

Churchill, Pamela (1920–1997).

See Harriman, Pamela.

Churchill, Lady Randolph (1854–1921).

See Churchill, Jennie Jerome.

Churchill, Sarah (1914–1982)

English actress, author, painter and daughter of Clementine and Winston Churchill. Born Sarah Millicent Hermione Churchill on October 7, 1914, at Admiralty House in London, England; died on September 24, 1982, in London, England; daughter of Sir Winston S. Churchill (prime minister of England) and Lady Clementine Hozier Churchill; attended Notting Hill High School, London, as a day student, North Foreland Lodge boarding School, Broadstairs, and De Vos School of Dance; married Vic Oliver, in 1936 (divorced 1945); married Anthony Beauchamp, in 1949 (divorced 1955); married Baron Henry Audley, in 1963; no children.

Publications: The Empty Spaces (Leslie Frewin, 1966); The Prince With Many Castles, and Other Stories (Leslie Frewin, 1967); A Thread in the Tapestry (Andrè Deutsch, 1967); The Unwanted Statue, and Other Poems (Leslie Frewin, 1969); Keep on Dancing (Weidenfeld, 1981).

Sarah Churchill was born on October 7, 1914, at Admiralty House in London to Winston and *Clementine Churchill. At the time of her birth, her father was first lord of the admiralty, and his political career would always have an influence on her life. She was educated at Notting Hill School, London, and North Foreland Lodge Boarding School in Broadstairs, and studied ballet for two years with the De Vos School of Dance. A beautiful young woman who had inherited her father's pale complexion and red hair, she made her acting debut at age 21, with her parents' consent, as a member of the chorus line in C.B. Cochran's musical *Follow the Sun* at the Adelphi Theater in London on February 4, 1936. During the play's run, Sarah fell in love with the show's star, Vic Oliver, a popular and charming Austrian-born comedian. The Churchills tried to dissuade their daughter from marrying Oliver who had been married twice before and was 17 years her senior. But a headstrong Sarah ran away to New York and married him on December 25, 1936.

In December 1939, she made her first dramatic performance at the Mercury Theater playing Lucrezia in *Mandragola*. In addition to other stage appearances, Sarah was in the feature film *Who's Your Lady Friend?* (1937), *Spring Meeting* (1941), and *He Found His Star* (1941). During the first two years of World War II, Sarah had several dramatic roles on the London stage. In 1941, she separated from Oliver and served for a brief period in the Women's Auxiliary Air Force (WAAF). She was commissioned and worked in the highly secret photographic intelligence sector at Medmenham, Buckinghamshire, until 1945. During the war, she was twice excused from her duties to accompany her father, now prime minister, to the 1943 Teheran Conference and the 1945 Yalta Conference where Churchill, Franklin D. Roosevelt, and Joseph Stalin held wartime summit discussions.

After the war, Sarah resumed her theatrical career with stage performances in *Gaslight* (1946), *Barretts of Wimpole Street* (1948), and *House of Sand* (1949). Now divorced from Oliver, she made her debut in the United States as Tracy Lord in Philip Barry's *The Philadelphia Story* (1949). Her first New York appearance came in the Broadway production of *Gramercy Ghost* in 1951. She continued her film career with several successful screen appearances in *When in Rome* (1947), *All Over Town* (1949), and *Serious Charge* (1959). Her best-known screen role was opposite Fred Astaire in *Royal Wedding* in 1951. It was seven years before Sarah returned to the London stage in the title role of *Peter Pan* in 1958. She later played the role of Eliza in *Pygmalion* (1961) and in several other plays over the next nine years, appearing on stage for the last time in 1971.

Sarah had married Anthony Beauchamp, a photographer, in 1949, but their rocky marriage ended in separation in 1955. In August 1957, Beauchamp committed suicide with an overdose of sleeping pills. Though they had been separated for two years, his death greatly affected Sarah. She entered a period of alcohol abuse and dreadful publicity that would probably have been ignored had her name not been Churchill. She finally found peace with Baron Henry Audley. They married in 1963 but her happiness was quickly shattered when he died of a massive heart attack later that year in Spain.

Like her father, Sarah took up painting later in life and became a respected amateur artist. While never reaching the success of Sir Winston, her works were displayed alongside his in an exhibition in London. She published three books of poetry, the short memoir *A Thread in the Tapestry*, principally about her father (1967), and a longer autobiography, *Keep on Dancing* (1981). After a long illness, Sarah Churchill died at her London home on September 24, 1982. Funeral services were held on September 30 at St. Michael's in London.

SUGGESTED READING:
Churchill, Sarah. *Keep on Dancing*. London: Weidenfield, 1981.

Phillip E. Koerper, Professor of History, Jacksonville State University, Jacksonville, Alabama

Churchill, Sarah Jennings

(1660–1744)

Duchess of Marlborough, Keeper of the Privy Purse for Queen Anne of England, and wife of John Churchill, first duke of Marlborough, who used her wealth and connections to further the cause of the Whig Party.
Name variations: Sarah Jennings. Born on May 29, 1660, in St. Albans, Hertfordshire, England; died on October 18, 1744, at Marlborough House in London; daughter of Richard Jennings (Jenyns) and Frances Thornhurst; sister of *Frances Jennings (d. 1730); received no formal education; married John Churchill (1650–1722), 1st duke of Marlborough (r. 1702–1722), on October 1, 1677 or 1678; children: Harriet (b. October 1679, died in infancy); Henrietta Churchill (1681–1733), 2nd duchess of Marlborough; Anne Churchill (1684–1716), countess of Sunderland; John (b. January 12, 1686–1703) 1st marquis of Blandford; Elizabeth Churchill (b. March 15, 1687–1714), countess of Bridgwater; Mary Churchill (1689–1751), duchess of Montagu; Charles (b. August 19, 1690, died in infancy).

Sarah Jennings Churchill

From age 12 to 17, was attendant at court of Mary of Modena (1662–67); appointed lady of the bedchamber to Anne, princess of Denmark, later Queen Anne (1683); named first lady of the bedchamber for Anne (1685); Glorious Revolution and flight of James II brought William III and Mary II to the throne (1688); replaced as lady of the bedchamber by Abigail Hill, later Lady Abigail Masham (1700); William III succeeded by Queen Anne (1702); appointed Groom of the Stole, Keeper of the Privy Purse, mistress of the robes, and together with her husband created duke and duchess of Marlborough (1702); Battle of Blenheim; Marlboroughs created prince and princess of Mindelheim by Emperor Leopold (1704); Anne began castle of Blenheim (1705); dismissed from offices in favor of Abigail Masham (1711); Queen Anne succeeded by George I (1714); Duke of Marlborough died (1721); published vindication of herself in Account of the Conduct of the Dowager Duchess of Marlborough from her First Comming to Court to the Year 1710 *(1742).*

Sarah Jennings Churchill, duchess of Marlborough, made a decisive impact on English politics during the reign of Queen *Anne. From Anne's accession in 1702 until an irreparable quarrel separated them in 1711, Sarah was the power behind the English throne. Her fall from favor shook the nation and resulted in the eclipse of the Whigs and a resurgence of the Tories. Remembered by contemporaries as "a torpedo in petticoats," Sarah moved beyond the traditional bounds of 18th-century womanhood to exercise incredible political and economic power.

> She knew favour and disfavour, eminence and exile, happiness and bitterness; she was wife, mother, grandmother, [and] was forever wishing she had been a man.
>
> —David Green

Sarah Jennings was born on May 29, 1660, in a small house in St. Albans. Her father Richard Jennings had lost most of his possessions during the English Civil War because of his Royalist sympathies, but when Charles II was restored to the English throne in 1660 the Jennings family was rehabilitated. Until his death in 1668, Richard sat in the House of Commons during the reign of Charles II. Sarah's mother **Frances Thornhurst** was the daughter of Sir Gifford Thornhurst. A shadowy figure, she developed in later years a reputation for witchcraft and seems to have been chronically in debt.

Taken to visit the royal court at a very young age, Sarah captivated James' youngest daughter Anne, who was four years her junior. The quiet and painfully shy Anne, whose mother had died while she was still an infant, idolized her bold and independent friend. When Sarah was 12 and returned to court to attend *Mary of Modena, James' young new wife, Sarah and Anne became inseparable. Rapidly becoming a great beauty in her own right, Sarah captivated the court with her charm and wit.

When only 15, she caught the eye of John Churchill. Ten years her senior, John was a page who had done little to distinguish himself beyond having a three-year affair with *Barbara Villiers, duchess of Cleveland, one of Charles II's many mistresses. John wooed the cynical Sarah with all his might, pouring out his anguish in a series of ardent letters, proclaiming his undying love: "Give me leave to do what I cannot help which is to adore you as long as I live. Could you ever love me I think . . . it would make me immortal." Although he could offer neither title nor substantial wealth, he was as handsome as she was beautiful. Sarah even admitted in later years that John "was naturally genteel without the least affectation, and handsome as an angel tho' ever so carelessly dress'd." After months of wavering, Sarah finally consented to John's proposal. She became Sarah Jennings Churchill when they were married secretly, sometime in the winter of 1677–78.

The penniless couple moved in with John's mother, ❧ **Elizabeth Drake**. Sarah was wretched in these circumstances, and as soon as he was able, in 1683, John built her a modest home called Holywell House. Sarah's first child Harriet was born in October 1679 but died soon afterward. There followed a succession of six other children: ❧ **Henrietta** in 1681, Anne in 1684, John ("Jack") in 1686, **Elizabeth** in 1687, ❧ **Mary** in 1689, and finally Charles, who also died in infancy, in 1690. John was an adoring husband and an affectionate and indulgent father, though Sarah observed that "by reason of his indulgent gentleness that is natural to him he could not manage matters so as was convenient to our circumstances," obliging her to take primary responsibility for the management, education, and discipline of their children.

Sarah attended court as often as she could, but family responsibilities sometimes forced her to stay away for months at a time. Anne insisted that Sarah write every day, and she sent letters to Sarah daily, occasionally twice a day. Impatient with the formality with which Sarah had to address her in correspondence, Anne hit upon an idea that would allow them to converse as equals: pen names. Sarah chose Mrs. Freeman and Anne took Mrs. Morley. In her letters, Anne pined for Sarah's companionship, insisting: "I would live on bread and water between four walls, with her, without repining," and assuring her that she "would go round the world on my bare knees to do her the least service and she may be assured the last command from her shall be obeyed . . . by your faithful Morley."

When Charles II died in 1685 and was succeeded by his brother James II, John Churchill distinguished himself by leading a successful defense against an attempted invasion by one of Charles II's illegitimate sons, James Scott, duke of Monmouth. James rewarded John by making the Churchills baron and baroness of Sandridge. Then Anne, who had married Prince George of Denmark in 1683, was given her own household, and she insisted that Sarah be made lady of

the bedchamber, though Sarah still seldom attended court. Anne clung to Sarah for friendship and support, insisting that Sarah keep up close correspondence with her when she could not be present, and describing Sarah's frequent absences as "a sort of death."

James II proved a troublesome monarch. An avowed Roman Catholic, he aroused deep-seated suspicion within the hearts of the English nobility when he began placing Catholic friends in prominent government positions. Rumors of his intention to impose "popery" on his subjects created ripples of unrest throughout the country. Belief that James would not long outlive his brother and would soon be succeeded by his Anglican daughters, Mary (*Mary II, 1662–1694) and Anne, encouraged the majority of the English nobility grudgingly to accept his unpopular friends. Suspicion turned into alarm when James' wife, Mary of Modena, announced in late 1689 that she was pregnant. Although Mary

Drake, Elizabeth (fl. 1625–1650)

*Name variations: Elizabeth Churchill. Born Elizabeth Drake, a descendant of the seafarer Sir Francis Drake; daughter of Lady Eleanor Drake; married Winston Churchill (a West Country Lawyer); children: *Arabella Churchill (1648–1714, mistress of King James II of England); John Churchill, 1st duke of Marlborough (1650–1722).*

During the English Civil War (1642–51), when a West Country lawyer by the name of Winston Churchill became a Royalist cavalry captain and took up arms in defense of crown and his Anglican church, his fortunes fell along with those he championed. Facing destitution, Winston and his wife Elizabeth Drake took refuge with her mother, the staunch Parliamentarian Lady **Eleanor Drake**. On May 26, 1650, while living under Lady Drake's roof, Asche House in Devonshire, Elizabeth gave birth to a son, John Churchill, the future first duke of Marlborough.

As Royalists, the Churchills entertained few prospects. Elizabeth's family enjoyed a measure of social prestige. The century before, it had produced the great Elizabethan admiral, Sir Francis Drake. Through marriage, Elizabeth was related to the Villiers family, including *Barbara Villiers. George Villiers, the duke of Buckingham, had been the intimate friend of both James I and Charles I. But during the Puritan Commonwealth, such affiliations offered no advantage.

The Stuart Restoration in 1660 produced an immediate improvement in the Churchill family fortunes. Elected a member of Parliament for Weymouth, Winston Churchill took his seat in the Convention Parliament in 1661. Making a mark for himself, he quickly earned an entrée to Charles II's court and substantial royal preferments. In 1662, Winston Churchill became commissioner for Irish Land Claims and the following year obtained a knighthood and a posting in London.

Churchill, Henrietta (1681–1733)

*Second duchess of Marlborough. Born on July 19, 1681; died on October 23, 1733; acceded as duchess of Marlborough, 1722; daughter of *Sarah Jennings Churchill (1660–1744) and John Churchill (1650–1722), 1st duke of Marlborough (r. 1702–1722); married Francis Godolphin, 2nd earl of Godolphin, on April 23, 1698; children: William, marquess of Blandford; Henrietta Godolphin (d. 1776, who married Thomas Pelham-Holles, 1st duke of Newcastle); Mary Godolphin (d. 1764, who married Thomas Osborne, 4th duke of Leeds).*

Churchill, Mary (1689–1751)

*Duchess of Montagu. Born on July 15, 1689; died in 1751; daughter of *Sarah Jennings Churchill (1660–1744) and John Churchill (1650–1722), 1st duke of Marlborough (r. 1702–1722); married John Montagu, 2nd duke of Montagu.*

was only in her mid-30s, the possibility that she would conceive after two decades of barrenness astounded the nation. Many preferred to think of the pregnancy as a sham, a "popish plot" foisted on the English by James and his Catholic cronies. James' own daughters, Mary and Anne, refused to believe that the pregnancy was real. When Mary of Modena gave birth to a son in June of 1688, a panicked contingent of nobles hastily composed a note to William, stadtholder of Holland, and husband to James' daughter Mary, asking him to come to the aid of England and the Protestant Church against the tyrannical James. They offered as reward a joint monarchy under William (III) and Mary.

When William invaded England, Sarah and John Churchill faced a difficult decision. They supported William, believing that James was determined to restore the Roman Catholic Church in England. Sarah helped smuggle Anne out of London until the danger of an armed uprising passed. The expected rebellion, however, never materialized—James escaped with his wife and child to France, informally abdicating his authority by throwing the seals of office into the Thames. William and Mary were warmly welcomed in London, where they were crowned William III and Mary II. Anne was elevated to the position of heir apparent.

Jealous over Sarah's domination of Anne, Mary insisted that Anne dismiss her and terminate her allowance of £1,000 per year. Anne steadfastly refused. John was relieved of all his appointments, and, in the spring of 1692, he was imprisoned in the Tower. Though released after two months, he remained out of favor with the royal court for six years. Anne still resisted any attempts to displace Sarah. To punish her for her obstinance, William and Mary forced Anne out of her lodgings at court, and Anne and her husband George moved into a house owned by the Duke and Duchess of Somerset. When Anne still would not waver, William and Mary decreed that she and George were not to be saluted and took their guard away. Sarah prevailed on Anne to relent, but Anne remained adamant. The incident created a permanent schism between Anne and Mary, until Mary's death from smallpox in 1694.

John, who was reinstated to his offices in 1698, was made a member of William's Privy Council and governor to William, duke of Gloucester, Anne's only surviving son after 17 pregnancies. William died in 1700, at age 11. Meanwhile, Sarah was busy with her own brood of children, who were nearing adulthood, invest-

ing an incredible amount of energy in securing proper matches for them.

When William III died childless in 1702, Anne became queen of England. At 37, she was prematurely aged; multiple pregnancies, gout and arthritis had made her a virtual cripple. Leaning on Sarah more than ever to assist her in fulfilling the rigorous political and ceremonial duties of a monarch, Anne made her friend Groom of the Stole, Keeper of the Privy Purse (a sum from the public revenues allotted to the sovereign for personal expenses), and mistress of the robes. Anne also made John a duke. When Sarah protested that their income was insufficient to support such a high office, Anne granted John £5,000 per year for life.

Sarah attacked her new responsibilities with zeal, eliminating the use of bribes in the royal household and applying strict economy to the Privy Purse and the queen's wardrobe. She attended Anne closely until 1703, but, when her only son Jack died of smallpox at 17, Sarah was inconsolable. For months, while John was in Europe, fighting against the French, Sarah haunted Westminster Abbey dressed in black. In the summer of 1704, John led the English in a glorious victory against the French at Blenheim, becoming a national hero overnight. The Holy Roman Emperor Leopold I gave him the tiny principality of Mindelheim.

Anne enthusiastically proposed to finance the building of a splendid residence for the Churchills to be called Blenheim, and the first stone was laid in June 1705. Thrilled at the prospect, John hired all the best architects in England, including Christopher Wren and Sir John Vanbrugh, to design the magnificent structure. Sarah was less than enthusiastic about the enterprise, confessing, "I mortally hate all Grandeur and Architecture." The construction of Blenheim progressed slowly; it was not put into livable condition until 1719 and was under construction for 20 more years.

Sarah's position near the queen encouraged her to take a more active role in politics. An ardent Whig, she began badgering Anne to make her son-in-law Charles Spencer, Lord Sunderland, secretary of state. Anne refused, believing Sunderland "a brazen Freethinker and at heart a Republican." A moderate Tory, Anne despised political factionalism and wanted a cooperative ministry of the best talents available; she found Sarah's diatribes distressing. Sarah sent Whiggish political treatises to Anne to "instruct" her on the principles of liberty and wrote to her in an increasingly spiteful tone. Beleaguered by ambitious office-seekers and scorned by her girlhood friend, Anne eventually turned elsewhere for support.

Anne found friendship and comfort in one of her ladies of the bedchamber, ❧▶ **Abigail Masham**. A poor relation of Sarah's, Abigail had been placed in Anne's court at Sarah's request. Sarah never considered Abigail a potential threat, convinced that her unaristocratic background would prevent Anne from viewing Abigail as anything more than a glorified household servant. Sarah, however, was so often absent from court that she had little opportunity to observe Anne's growing intimacy with Abigail, and she continued to badger Anne with strident letters.

Sensing Abigail's potential as a political pawn, Robert Harley, the leader of the Tory faction, cultivated her friendship. The gambit paid off—Anne's relationship with Sarah grew increasingly cold and formal. Though John tirelessly worked to heal the growing breach between them, the queen abruptly broke off relations with Sarah early in 1710. In January 1711, Anne dismissed Sarah from all her offices, despite John's pleas on Sarah's behalf. The queen demanded the gold key, which was the symbol of the Keeper of the Privy Purse. When John returned home with the news, Sarah took the key and "threw it into the middle of the room and bid him to take it up and carry it to whom he pleased."

Abigail was made Keeper of the Privy Purse; Harley was made earl of Oxford and Mortimer; and Sarah's other offices were given to the wives of leading Tory politicians. In 1712, Sarah wrote a vindication of herself but held off publishing it, believing it to be too politically controversial. In the heated atmosphere, the Churchills were keenly aware of the danger of being out of favor. John hastily made plans for them to tour Europe, a retreat Sarah wryly referred to as "a sort of pilgrimage." They toured their principality of Mindelheim and were welcomed enthusiastically throughout Europe, but Sarah expressed impatience with the unfamiliar surroundings and longed to return to England. On March 31, 1713, the Treaty of Utrecht was signed, ending the long war with France. The treaty proved highly unpopular, but the blame for its provisions was placed squarely on Harley and his lieutenant, Henry St. John, whom Anne had made Viscount Bolingbroke.

By 1714, John judged it safe to return. Anne fell desperately ill in July, and soon afterward Harley fell out of favor with Abigail and Boling-broke. Anne's successor, according to the 1701 Act of Succession, was to be George (I), prince of Hanover, a distant relative preferred by Parliament over 86 claimants with closer blood ties by virtue of being the only Protestant. As Anne's condition worsened through July, Bolingbroke began secret negotiations with James II's son, James Stuart, known as "the Old Pretender," who had grown up at the French court and was conspiring to return to England and claim his birthright by force. Anne's intentions in the matter were unknown. She did not recognize James, but she also expressed many unflattering comments about George of Hanover. Anne breathed her last on August 1, 1714. The Churchills landed in Dover on the following day.

Within days of Anne's death, John sided with the supporters of George of Hanover, Harley was clapped in the Tower (where he languished for two years before being acquitted and released), and Bolingbroke fled to France to join the Old Pretender's court. George of Hanover landed in England on September 18. He immediately restored John as captain-general of the armed forces.

After her fall from favor, Sarah gave up politics and devoted her energies to her family. Shortly before their return to England, she and John had received word that their daughter Elizabeth, countess of Bridgwater, had died of smallpox in March. In April of 1716, another daughter, ❧▶ **Anne Churchill**, countess of Sunderland, died of pleuritic fever. Sarah was devastated. Elizabeth and Anne had been her favorites; Sarah's relationship with her remaining two daughters, Henrietta and Mary, was strained. Sarah took in the youngest of Anne's and Elizabeth's children to see to their upbringing.

◀❧ *Abigail Masham.* *See Queen Anne for sidebar.*

❧▶ **Churchill, Anne** (1684–1716)
*Countess of Sunderland. Born on February 27, 1684; died on April 15, 1716; interred at Brington, Northamptonshire, England; daughter of *Sarah Jennings Churchill (1660–1744) and John Churchill (1650–1722), 1st duke of Marlborough (r. 1702–1722); married Charles Spencer, 3rd earl of Sunderland, on January 2, 1699; children: Robert (b. 1700); Robert (b. 1701), 4th earl of Sunderland; Charles (b. 1706), 3rd duke of Marlborough; John, known as Jack of Althorp (b. 1708), a member of Parliament; **Anne Spencer** (d. 1769), viscountess Bateman; **Diana Spencer** (1708–1735), duchess of Bedford (who married John Russell, 4th duke of Bedford).*

In May 1716, John suffered a stroke, which impaired his speech and sapped his energy. He had a second stroke in November. Sarah dedicated her time and attention to nursing him and caring for her grandchildren. John continued to weaken and finally died in June of 1721. Sarah's grief at losing him was made more bitter by the outbreak of open hostility with Henrietta and Mary at their father's deathbed and funeral. Sarah later wrote that her husband's death made her feel as though her "soul was tearing from [her] body."

After John's death, Sarah became obsessed with finishing Blenheim as a monument to the courage and greatness of her beloved husband. She exasperated the architects and builders engaged in the project with demands for speed and frugality. Before it was finished, she had fired all the well-known architects involved. Her arguments with the Blenheim contractors drew her into a mass of litigation as she approached her 60s.

Legal entanglements, the raising and placement of her grandchildren, and continued arguments with her daughters filled her attention during the last decades of her life. She became increasingly absorbed with vindicating herself for posterity. In the 1720s, she began keeping what she called her "Green Book," entitled "An Account of the Cruell Usage of My Children." It contained excerpts from her struggles with her daughters as well as her grandchildren. Sarah's Green Book circulated only among her closest friends, whom she hoped to convince of her unfailing love and attention to her children and their horrible disrespect for her.

But the intervening years had robbed her of much of her earlier vitriol. While polishing her political self-justification, *An Account of the Conduct of the Dowager Duchess of Marlborough from her First Comming to Court to the Year 1710*, for its 1742 publication, she was visited by Voltaire who asked to see it. Sarah replied, "Wait a little, I am altering my account of Queen Anne's character. I have begun to love her again since the present lot have become our governors."

Sarah's health began failing in the 1730s, and she complained often of arthritis and gout. Yet she still outlived all of her children, except Mary, and many of her grandchildren. Sarah died on October 18, 1744, after living through six reigns. John's body was moved and interred next to hers at Blenheim chapel. On a scrap of paper among her writings she had once written:

I forsee the world will interpret whatever I do that may look discontented and particular to my having lost the queen's favor and my great Employments. That may vex me a little . . . but I hope you will never think my mis-fortunes can be one grain heavier upon that account, for as long as I can live in quiet and safety with the Dear Duke of Marlborough I shall have very little more to wish for.

Sarah Jennings Churchill died a phenomenally wealthy woman. Her possessions included no fewer than 30 estates. Her outspoken nature and scathing pen earned her more than a few enemies, but her power and influence were unequalled by any other 18th-century Englishwoman. As the progenitor of a dynasty that eventually produced Winston Churchill, Sarah left behind a reputation larger than life and proved herself the equal of anyone who served as an English politician.

SOURCES:

Green, David. *Sarah, Duchess of Marlborough*. NY: Scribner, 1967.

Harris, Frances. *A Passion for Government: Life of Sarah, Duchess of Marlborough*. Oxford University Press, 1991.

Marlborough, Sarah J. *Letters of Sarah, Duchess of Marlborough*. AMS Press (reprint of the 1875 edition).

SUGGESTED READING:

Churchill, Winston S. *Marlborough: His Life and Times*. 2 vols. London: George G. Harrap, 1933.

Jones, J.R. *Marlborough*. Cambridge: Cambridge University Press, 1993.

Trevelyan, George Macaulay. *England Under Queen Anne*. 3 vols. London: Longmans, 1931.

COLLECTIONS:

Correspondence, papers and memorabilia located at Blenheim Estate, London, England.

Kimberly Estep Spangler,
Assistant Professor of History, Chair,
Division of Religion and Humanities,
Friends University, Wichita, Kansas

Chute, Marchette (1909–1994)

American children's poet and biographer. Born Marchette Gaylord Chute on August 16, 1909, in Hazlewood, Minnesota; died on May 6, 1994, in New Jersey; daughter of Edith Mary (Pickburn) Chute and William Young Chute (realtor); educated at University of Minnesota, B.A., 1930; never married, no children.

Selected works: Rhymes about Ourselves *(1932);* Rhymes about the Country *(1941);* The Innocent Wayfaring *(1943);* Geoffrey Chaucer of England *(1946);* Shakespeare of London *(1950);* Ben Jonson of Westminster *(1953).*

Marchette Chute's mother Edith homeschooled Marchette and her two sisters, Mary (**M.G. Chute**) and Beatrice (✤➤ **B.J. Chute**). When

Marchette was 11, the Chutes moved to Minneapolis, where the daughters were permitted to attend public school. Marchette went on to the University of Minnesota. After graduation, she returned home to live and work as an author, illustrator and children's tutor. Her first book, a collection of children's verse, was published in 1932.

The Chute sisters, all writers, and their mother moved to the beach in San Clemente, California, after Marchette's father died in 1939. Two years later, they relocated to New York City where, during the war, Marchette volunteered as a civil-defense worker. She began her biographies of classic authors at the New York Public Library, researching from nine in the morning until lunch, then writing at home in the afternoon.

From 1950 until her sister Beatrice's death in 1987, the two shared a Manhattan apartment. Chute then moved to her sister Mary's New Jersey home where she resided until her death of pneumonia at age 84.

SUGGESTED READING:
Serafin, Steve, ed. *Dictionary of Literary Biography.* Vol. 103. Detroit, MI: Gale Research, 1991.

Crista Martin,
Boston, Massachusetts

Chytilova, Vera (1929—)

Czech film director. Born on February 2, 1929, in Ostrava, Czechoslovakia (Czech Republic); educated at Charles University and Film Faculty, Academy of Music and Art (FAMU), 1957–1962; married Jaroslav Kucera (a cinematographer); children: two.

Filmography: Ceiling (short, 1961); A Bagful of Fleas (short, 1962); Something Different (1965); Automat (1966); Daisies (1969); The Fruit of Paradise (1969); The Apple Game (1976); Inexorable Time (short, 1978); Panelstory (1979); Calamity (1980); The Very Late Afternoon of a Faun (1983); Prague, the Restless Heart of Europe (short, 1985); Wolf's Cabin (1986); The Jester and the Queen (1987); Tainted Horseplay (1988); The Liberator (short, 1991); My Inhabitants of Prague Understand Me (1991); Inheritance (1992).

In 1978, when Vera Chytilova's film *The Apple Game* found its way to the United States, David Andelman wrote in *The New York Times:* "Chytilova cannot be classified as a dissident; she's a compassionate, committed woman, a director long considered in the first rank of Czechoslovakian filmmakers who once were numbered among the best in the world." It had taken the "non-dissident" Chytilova seven years to make *The Apple Game:* six to be granted permission from the authorities to make the film

Marchette Chute

❧▶ Chute, B.J. (1913–1987)

American writer. Name variations: Joy Chute. Born Beatrice Joy Chute in Minneapolis, Minnesota, on January 13, 1913; died in 1987; daughter of William Young Chute (a realtor) and Edith Mary (Pickburn) Chute; attended private schools through grades, public high school, and took extensive courses from the University of Minnesota.

B.J. Chute worked as her father's secretary for ten years before she began writing professionally. Her books include *The Fields Are White* (1950), *The End of Loving* (1953), *Greenwillow* (1956), *Journey to Christmas* (1958), and *The Moon and the Thorn* (1961).

and one year of production. *Apple Game* is a simple, powerful love triangle that weaves in and out of the delivery rooms and wards in a maternity hospital in Czechoslovakia. Hardly a threat to state security, the film did not carry forward the socialist agenda of those in power. Though it won top awards at several international film festivals, Czechoslovakian authorities considered it frivolous. When they finally allowed it to be released, it was shown at only one theater in Prague. But with word of mouth, the lines to see the film went around the block.

Chytilova didn't grow up with a strong desire to become a film director. She studied philosophy and architecture in college and worked several jobs (in drafting, modeling, and film continuity) before landing a coveted spot at FAMU (Film Faculty, Academy of Music and Art), Prague's film school, where she studied directing. She came of age with Milos Forman, best known in the West for *Amadeus,* and Jaromil Jires (*The Cry*) during what's been called the Czechoslovakian "New Wave." Leaning heavily on the French-style *cinema verité*, which literally means "camera truth," Chytilova and her colleagues often used non-actors and improvisation in their films to give the effect of authenticity.

The early 1960s saw a positive resurgence of Czech writers and a relaxation of bureaucratic control over the arts, now referred to as the Prague Spring. During this time, Czech native Franz Kafka was once again recognized as an important writer, and Western plays by writers such as Edward Albee, Samuel Beckett and Ionesco were put into production. Czech filmmakers like Jan Nemec (*Diamonds of the Night*) were allowed to depict the state of affairs in Czechoslovakia as Kafkaesque and surreal. But no filmmaker pushed the envelope like *Chytilova. Daisies* and *The Fruit of Paradise* (both 1969) provoked the audience and enraged the censors. In particular, *Daisies,* which featured two teenaged girls in a nihilistic orgy that culminated in a Kafkaesque food fight, went way beyond what the censors could tolerate or even comprehend. While Chytilova was commenting on the destructiveness of a conformity based on apathy, the censors were complaining about the waste of food.

With the 1968 Soviet invasion of Czechoslovakia, Chytilova was fired from Barrandov Studios. The head of the studios was arrested and many of the films that had been produced were not allowed to be released. Directors like Forman and Nemec went into exile in the West. Though Chytilova was not officially "blacklisted," she and the leading Czech directors who remained in their homeland were not allowed to work as Czechoslovakia went into a cultural dark age.

"What I most value in a person is courage," Chytilova told David Andelman in a *New York Times* interview. In 1975, she took a stand, though these were still dangerous times. She wrote to Czechoslovakian President Gustav Husak, telling him in effect that she had been censured. Perhaps because she attributed her censure to male chauvinism in the industry rather than politics, the letter did not land her in jail, and Chytilova was allowed to work again. *The Apple Game* was released in 1976, with critics both in and out of Czechoslovakia hailing this work as the best film to come out of that nation in the previous ten years.

Between 1976 and 1992, Chytilova made 11 more films. Though still virtually unknown to Western audiences, she has been widely regarded as one of the best filmmakers in Europe (a retrospective of her work aired on French television in 1989) and certainly one of the few Eastern European filmmakers whose films depict women as an oppressed class. *Calamity,* produced after *The Apple Game,* illustrates her dedication to feminism. "It's . . . about courage," she said. "In a sense it's about myself. All my films are. Like the heroine, I also feel a victim, like all women who are victims. . . . We are still a bit primitive in our treatment of women."

During the 1980s, Chytilova found inspiration while working with an avant-garde theater group called SKLEP (The Cellar). *The Jester and the Queen,* made in 1987, is a filmed version of their play. With the release of her 1989 film *Tainted Horseplay,* Chytilova became the first Eastern European filmmaker to deal with the subject of AIDS.

SOURCES:

Andelman, David. Interview. *The New York Times.* Sunday, March 12, 1978.

Hames, Peter. "The Return of Vera Chytilova," in *Sight and Sound.* Volume 3, 1979.

Lyon, Christopher, ed. *The International Dictionary of Films and Filmmakers: Volume 2.* Chicago: Macmillan, 1984.

Deborah Jones,
Studio City, California

Ci'an (1837–1881).

See Cixi for sidebar.

Ciano, Edda (1910–1995)

Italian anti-fascist. Name variations: Edda Mussolini. Pronunciation: CHEE-anno. Born in Italy on Septem-

ber 1, 1910; died of cardiac arrest related to lung and kidney failure in Rome, Italy, on April 8, 1995; firstborn child of Benito Mussolini (1883–1945) and Rachele (Guidi) Mussolini; married Count Galeazzo Ciano (a future Italian foreign minister), in 1930; children: two.

Edda Mussolini Ciano was the firstborn child of Italian dictator Benito Mussolini and his wife *Rachele Guidi. The eldest of five, she had one sister **Anna Maria** and three brothers, Vittorio, Bruno, and Romano (father of right-wing lawmaker Allessandra Mussolini). Edda was considered the stubborn one in the family; she was the first Italian woman to wear pants and the first to drive a car.

This same inflexibility was to have a profound effect on her life and the short life of the man she married: Count Galeazzo Ciano. In 1943, as foreign minister and a member of the Fascist Grand Council, Galeazzo voted against his father-in-law following the Allied invasion of Italy, a vote that led to Mussolini's arrest and would eventually topple his regime. Despite Edda's pleadings, when the Germans freed Mussolini in 1944, the dictator had her husband executed. "I prefer to be the wife of a victim of fascism," she said, "than the daughter of Il Duce." With that, she renounced her birth name and never used it again. Her father was executed by Italian partisans in 1945.

Cibber, Susannah (1714–1766).
See Clive, Kitty for sidebar.

Cibò, Caterina (fl. 1533)

*Duchess of Camerino. Name variations: Catherine Cibo or Cybo. Flourished around 1533; daughter of *Maddalena de Medici (d. 1519) and Franceschetto Cybo, Cibo, or Cibó.*

In 1533, Caterina Cibò accompanied *Catherine de Medici (1519–1589) to France on Catherine's wedding journey.

Cibo or Cibò, Maddalena
(d. 1519).
See Medici, Maddalena de.

Cicely.
Variant of Cecilia or Cecily.

Cidie (1880–1961).
See Sarfatti, Margherita.

Cigna, Gina (b. 1900)

*French-Italian coloratura soprano. Name variations: Genoveffa Sens. Born on March 6, 1900, in Angères, France; daughter of an Italian mother and French father; studied at the Paris Conservatory with *Emma Calvé, Darclée, and Storchio; married Maurice Sens (French opera singer); children: one son.*

Debuted under name Genoveffa Sens at Teatro alla Scala, singing there every season thereafter under her own name (1929–43); debuted at the Metropolitan Opera as Aïda (1937); abandoned her singing career after an automobile accident (1947); became a voice teacher and taught at the Royal Conservatory in Toronto, Canada (1953–57).

Gina Cigna was born on March 6, 1900, in Angères, France, and studied at the Paris Conservatory. Her career spanned 20 years, from 1927 until an automobile accident in 1947. Cigna specialized in heavy dramatic Italian heroines, particularly those of Verdi, Puccini, Mascagni, Zandonai, Giordano, and Ponchielli.

Gina Cigna

She debuted at the Metropolitan Opera in 1937, mid-point in her career, and she performed at the Teatro alla Scala every season from 1929 until 1943. One of her most celebrated roles was as Bellini's Norma.

Gina Cigna's voice was not always perfectly even or connected. At times, she exploited the breaks that often occurred in the middle and lower registers, using them for dramatic effect. Sustaining an even, controlled legato was not easy for her. Characteristically, she subdivided long lines into shorter phrases, defining each phrase with great vitality. Her tones were not always sustained, and her dynamics were not always controlled according to the tenets of bel canto.

Excelling in ensembles, Cigna's singing was focused, deliberate, responsible, and intense. As an actress, she portrayed complex layers of emotions. Her naturally clean sensitive soprano had a pleasing vibrata, which, combined with her acting abilities, made her a memorable performer. Retiring after an auto accident in 1947, she turned to teaching. Cigna's last position was at the Toronto Conservatory in 1957.

John Haag,
Athens, Georgia

Çiller, Tansu (1946–)

Prime minister of Turkey. Name variations: Ciller. Pronunciation: (CHILL-air). Born in Istanbul, Turkey, in 1946; attended American College for Girls, Istanbul; graduated from Robert College, 1967, with a degree in economics; graduated University of New Hampshire, master's degree in economics; graduated University of Connecticut, doctorate in economics; attended Yale University, post-doctoral studies, 1971; married banker and businessman Ozer Çiller (who took his wife's surname at the behest of her father, who did not have a son), in 1963; children: two sons.

Tansu Çiller, a United States-trained economist and former university professor, became the first woman prime minister of Turkey on June 14, 1993, following *Benazir Bhutto of Pakistan and Khaleda Zia of Bangladesh as the third woman to head a predominantly Muslim country. Çiller, a member of the moderate-right True Path Party, is often compared to *Margaret Thatcher. To many young Turkish women, she is a symbol of women's ability to achieve professional and political success in a male-dominated society.

Born in Istanbul into a wealthy family, Çiller finished her post-doctoral studies at Yale University in 1971 and stayed in the United States to begin her academic career at Franklin and Marshall College in Lancaster, Pennsylvania. She returned to Turkey in 1974 and quickly worked her way up the academic ladder at her alma mater, Robert College (now Bosporus University). In 1983, at age 36, she was promoted to full professor, the youngest person in Turkey to hold that title. During this time, her husband Ozer amassed a fortune as a successful businessman.

Çiller eased her way into politics during the 1980s, working as a consultant for the World Bank's Chamber of Industry and Trade Board of the State Planning Organization, and as an adviser to the Istanbul Metropolitan Municipality. She gained public notice for a report she prepared for the Turkish Association of Industrialists and Businessmen, in which she was highly critical of the economic policies of President Turgut Özal and the ruling Motherland Party. As a result, she was drafted by Süleyman Demirel, head of the True Path Party, who was looking for ways to broaden support among business leaders and urban intellectuals. After the party's victory in the 1991 election, she was appointed minister of state for the economy and elected a deputy of the General Assembly, where she introduced a controversial plan to privatize many of Turkey's State Economic Enterprises, SEEs (large state-owned monopolies that employ much of the Turkish population but are an inefficient drain on government budgets), through the formation of a professional nonpartisan agency set up to implement reforms. No less controversial was her anti-inflation policy, aimed at lowering interest rates and thus curbing inflation. Her harsh economic plan did not win the support of the governor of the Turkish Central Bank, and public clashes with him, coupled with her growing reputation for being difficult to work with, caused Çiller to fall out of favor with the party leadership.

Upon the sudden death of President Özal in April 1993, Demirel was elected to the presidency, leaving the position of prime minister vacant. Çiller resigned her Cabinet post to run for office, conducting an effective and successful populist campaign, even without party support. To many, her victory as a political outsider reflected the public's desire for reform and change.

As leader of the government, Çiller was beset with problems. She faced renewed hostilities between Turkish government forces and guerrillas affiliated with the Kurdish Worker's Party, which was considered by many—including Çiller—as a terrorist organization from which citizens must be protected. She also

Tansu
Çiller

worked to resolve the ethnic conflict between the Azerbaijanis and the Armenians over control of Nagorno-Karabkh, resolving that Turkey would not stand by in the face of Armenian aggression. In February 1994, she joined Benazir Bhutto in Sarajevo (in the former Yugoslav republic of Bosnia) to draw attention to the plight of Bosnian Muslims and to issue a joint plea for an end to the civil war between the republic's Muslim and Serb populations. Four months later, she sent armed forces to join U.N. peacekeeping troops in Bosnia.

The Turkish economy continued to be among Çiller's top concerns, and several months into office she issued a "White Book" of her administration's accomplishments, which was criticized by detractors as an unconvincing document. In spite of the belief of some that Çiller's promises for sweeping reform and restructuring were empty, she received a vote of confidence from the True Path Party when they reelected her in 1993. However, by 1994, her unorthodox anti-inflation policy was deemed a failure when the credit-rating agencies Moody's and Standard & Poor's downgraded her country's creditworthiness, thus precipitating the devaluation of the Turkish lira. According to a writer for the *Economist* (February 5, 1994): "What turned things into a crisis was

Mrs. Çiller's failure to make the treasury and central bank work in harness."

In spite of gloomy predictions, Çiller's party rallied during the municipal elections in March 1994, winning a plurality of the popular vote. In April 1994, she announced a three-month austerity plan providing for the sale or close of the SEEs; a raise in taxes, especially on the wealthy; a freeze on wages; and the doubling of prices of some staple goods. These measures, the most daring in Turkey's history, were announced to the public with the plea from Çiller for unity among citizens to "disperse the dark clouds hanging over the country." By summer 1994, a recovery of the Turkish economy appeared to be on the horizon.

Çiller remained realistic about the challenges facing her. In 1993, after her first year in office, she said to *Maclean's* (July 12, 1993), "I am brave, I have no time to lose. Turkey is at a critical point. We are up against a wall. We will either climb over it, or be crushed at the bottom." By 1996, Çiller was no longer prime minister but still the leader of the True Path Party.

SOURCES:
Graham, Judith. *Current Biography.* Vol. 55, no. 9. NY: H.W. Wilson, 1994.

Barbara Morgan,
Melrose, Massachusetts

Cimburca of Masovia
(c. 1396–1429)

*Duchess of Inner Austria. Name variations: Cimburgis of Mazovia; Cymbarka; Cymburga. Born between 1394 and 1397; died on September 28, 1429, in Turnitz near Lilienfeld; second wife of Ernest the Iron of Habsburg (d. 1424), duke of Inner Austria (son of *Virida Visconti and Leopold III of Habsburg); children: Friedrich IV the Fair also known as Frederick III (1415–1493), king of Germany and Holy Roman emperor (r. 1440–1493); *Margaret of Saxony (c. 1416–1486, who married Frederick II of Saxony); Albrecht or Albert VI (1418–1463); *Catherine (c. 1420–1493).*

Cimburgis (c. 1396–1429).
See Cimburca of Masovia.

Cinthia.
Variant of Cynthia.

Cinti-Damoreau, Laure (1801–1863)
French soprano. Name variations: Madame Damoreau; Laure Cinthie Montalant; Mademoiselle Cinti.

Born in Paris, France, on February 6, 1801; died in Chantilly, France, on February 25, 1863; studied in Paris with Plantade and Catalani.

In 1819, Laure Cinti-Damoreau made her first appearance as Cherubino in *Le Nozzo di Figaro* in Paris. In 1822, her pure, distinct voice could be heard in London, and in 1826 at the Grand Opéra in Paris where she created leading roles in Rossini's *Le siège de Corinth*, Moïse, *Le Comte Ory* and *Guillaume Tell*. From that time on, she sang to great success in both in Europe and the United States. In 1834, Cinti-Damoreau was made professor of singing at the Conservatoire, Paris, and taught there until her retirement in 1856.

Cintrón, Conchita (1922—)
Latin-American bullfighter. Name variations: Cintron. Born in Chile in 1922; daughter of a Puerto Rican father and an Irish-American mother (both U.S. citizens); raised in Peru.

Though women have been active in the *corridas* since the 17th century, it was usually on horseback, "Portuguese style." The first mention of a *torera*, or woman bullfighter, was in 1654, and Francisco Goya portrayed a *torera* in action in his painting *La Pajuelera*. The first woman of modern times to achieve success as a *torera* was Conchita Cintrón who began to slay bulls on horseback at age 12. At 15, in Mexico, she made her first appearance in the arena on foot. During a career that spanned 25 years, Cintrón was gored only twice while mastering over 1,200 bulls. Acclaimed in Mexico for her bravery as well as her beauty, she would open the way for women bullfighters in other parts of the world.

France, Portugal, and Spain resisted having women in the ring. In Spain, bullfighting by women on foot was banned from 1908 to 1973. (The first woman to appear there as a *torera* after 1973 was **Maria de Los Angeles**.) In 1949, in her farewell appearance in Spain, Cintrón challenged the law of the ring by dismounting from her horse and executing a collection of perfect passes; she then tossed her sword to the ground and refused to kill the bull. Though she was taken in custody by outraged authorities, she was soon released because of the demands of the crowd.

In 1951, Cintrón married and retired in Lisbon, reporting on bullfighting for newspapers. Three years later, in Ciudad Juarez, Mexico, Texas-born **Patricia McCormick** made her debut in January 20, 1952. Over 40 years later, in 1996, **Cristina Sánchez** (1972—), who was badly gored three times, became Spain's first female *matador de toros*—a bullfighter of the first rank. No female bullfighter before her had been allowed to take on fully grown bulls weighing over 1,300 pounds.

Cisneros, Eleonora de (1878–1934)

International opera star who claimed to be the first American-trained singer to perform at the Metropolitan Opera. Born Eleanor Broadfoot in Brooklyn, New York, on November 1, 1878; died in New York on February 3, 1934.

Mezzo-soprano Eleonora de Cisneros studied with Francesco Fanciulli and **Adeline Murio-Celli** in New York before going to Paris to study with Angelo Tabadello. She then appeared at the Metropolitan Opera during the 1899–1900 season, claiming to be the first American-trained singer to do so. Because the world of opera and classical music was biased against native performers in the United States, one way to gain entry was to train in Europe. As the 20th century progressed, however, this prejudice slowly began to wane. In 1902, Cisneros sang Brünnhilde, Ortrud, Venus, Delilah, and Amneris in Turin. For four years from 1904 to 1908, she performed regularly at Covent Garden, making her debut at La Scala in 1906. In the United States, she appeared at the Manhattan Opera and the Chicago-Philadelphia Opera Company. During the 1920s, most of Cisneros' performances were in Europe. Eleonora de Cisneros was remembered for the remarkable volume and range of her voice.

John Haag,
Athens, Georgia

Cisse, Jeanne-Martin (1926—)

Guinean diplomat who was the first woman appointed as a permanent representative to the U.N. Name variations: Jeanne Martin Cisse. Born in 1926; married; six children.

Before entering politics, Guinean diplomat Jeanne-Martin Cisse began her career as a teacher in 1945 and from 1954 to 1958 served as a school director. Becoming a member of the Democratic Party in 1959, Cisse worked in the Federal Office of the Kinda Region. She served as the first African secretary, second vice-president, and first vice-president of the National Assembly of Guinea. Cisse also served on the Assembly's Na-

Jeanne-Martin Cisse

tional and Regional Women's Committees, becoming secretary-general of the Conference of African Women, a post she held from 1962 to 1972. Cisse was the first woman to be appointed a permanent representative to the United Nations (1972–76) and was also the first woman who presided over the UN Security Council. From 1976 to 1984, she was minister of social affairs in Guinea. In 1975, the Lenin Peace Prize was awarded to Cisse, whose career has been largely dedicated to improving conditions for African women. Her work has been geared toward helping women become politically, economically, and socially active in their own countries.

Cixi (1835–1908)

Manchu empress-dowager of China who dominated politics for half a century until her death, just three years before the 2,000-year-old imperial system was overthrown by the Republican Revolution. Name variations: Tz'u-hsi, and its alternate spellings, Tse-Hi, Tsu-Hsi, Tze Hsi, Tzu Hsi, T'zu Hsi, Tsze Hsi An; Xi-

aoqin Xian Huanghou; Xi Taihou (empress-dowager of the Western Palace); Imperial Concubine Yi; Yehonala; Nala Taihou (empress-dowager Nala); Lao Fuoye (Old Buddha); Venerable Ancestor. Pronunciation: TSE-shee. Born Yehonala, or Yehe Nara, but first name at birth not confirmed, on November 29, 1835, in Taiyuan, Shanxi province, China; died on November 15, 1908, in Beijing; buried in the Qing imperial mausoleum; daughter of a Manchu official, Huizheng; married as lowly ranked concubine of Xianfeng emperor (r. 1851–1861) in 1851 (died 1861): children: one son, T'ung Chih, the Tongzhi emperor (1856–1875).

Ruled de facto three times as empress-dowager regent, as co-regent to her son, the Tongzhi emperor (1861–73), and twice as regent to her nephew, the Guangxu emperor (1875–89, 1898–1908); dominated politics for half a century during failed self-strengthening and reform measures to cope with China's critical decline in the backdrop of Western imperialism and internal rebellion; died one day after the death of the legitimate Guangxu emperor.

Cixi, best known as China's empress-dowager or Old Buddha, was the de facto ruler of China for half a century during a tumultuous period of internal and external crises that demanded social and political changes to Qing (Ch'ing) China (1644–1911). Her life spanned the glorious reign of Queen *Victoria in the United Kingdom, but Cixi's appraisal in history and literature has been mainly negative and denunciatory. She has been portrayed as an ignorant, extravagant, murderous, and ultraconservative woman who epitomized the incompetence of the Chinese empire and exacerbated the difficulties of modernizing initiatives. Surprisingly, despite the enormous controversy surrounding Cixi's historical role and the appearance of numerous popular, unreliable biographies and novels both in Chinese and Western languages, a published academic and comprehensive study of her life has not yet appeared. Nevertheless recent scholars, including Luke Kwong and **Sue Fawn Chung**, have convincingly provided some balanced and positive views of Cixi's historical role in 1898–1900.

Cixi was preceded by two other powerful women in Chinese history who ruled as regents to their emperor sons: Empress ☙ **Lü Hou** (r. 195–180 BCE) and Empress-Emperor *Wu Zetian of the Tang (624–705). While condemning Lü and Wu for murderous plots and sexual scandals, historians have generally acknowledged the competence of their rulership. But whereas Lü and Wu ruled during a period of ascending dynastic fortunes, Cixi's life and times were characterized by the intrusive presence of foreign powers and the decline of Qing China through the Opium Wars, Taiping Rebellion, Sino-French War, Sino-Japanese War, and the Boxer Uprising.

The Qing, China's last dynasty, was founded by the non-Chinese Manchu minority, which constituted only one or two percent of China's population. In order to consolidate Manchu minority power, the conquerors represented themselves as defenders of Chinese culture but adopted a banner system of hereditary military establishment that favored the Manchu minority. As daughter of a minor official in the eminent Yehonala Manchu banner, Cixi was selected at the age of 16 to serve as a low-ranking concubine to the Xianfeng emperor (Hsien Feng, r. 1851–1861). From 1851 until her death in 1908, except for the flights to Jehol in 1860 and Xian in 1900, and excursions to the summer palaces, she resided in the imperial palaces known as the Forbidden City in Beijing. Her status and rank in the harem soared in 1856, when she gave birth to the Xianfeng emperor's only son, T'ung Chih, the future Tongzhi emperor. A

☙ Lü Hou (r. 195–180 BCE)

Chinese empress and regent of China. *Name variations: Empress Lu or Lü; Lu Hou of the Han. Reigned from 195 to 180 BCE; murdered in 180 BCE; married Gao Zu (Kao Tsu) who became the Han emperor Liu Pang (r. 220–195 BCE); children: Hui Ti.*

Following her marriage to the peasant Gao Zu, Lü Hou persuaded her husband to seek the throne, and he became the first Han emperor Liu Pang, reigning from 220 to 195 BCE. It was Lü Hou who began the Chinese tradition that the mother of a son deemed heir apparent be recognized as an empress. Following the death of her husband in 195 BCE, Empress Lü waited until her son Hui Ti was safely ensconced on the throne, then dismissed her husband's relatives who were in positions of power to make way for her own family. A few years later, when her son died, she expropriated even more power, choosing another child as his successor. Before long, the child balked under her authority. Lü Hou had him imprisoned and designated a third child as emperor of the Han. In 180 BCE, her deceased husband's loyal ministers had Lü Hou put to death and massacred her entire family. They then installed Wen Ti, a son of Emperor Liu Pang's with another wife, on the throne of China. Though Empress *Wu Zetian would later rule in name and in fact, Empress Lü ruled in fact but not name, as was the case of *Cixi and many other empress-dowagers in Chinese and Korean history.

Cixi

Manchu, Cixi had some proficiency in the Chinese language and first became involved in state affairs by classifying memorials for the Xianfeng emperor.

As a child of four, Cixi had lived through the first Opium War of 1839, when the British crushed the Chinese forces, acquired Hong Kong island, and opened China to Western trade. By 1860, the second Opium War, fought between China and a joint British-French force, had escalated into the occupation of Beijing and the burning of the summer palaces located in the outskirts of the city. Cixi fled north to Jehol, Manchuria, with her son, along with the Xianfeng emperor and his empress, ❧▶ **Ci'an** (1837–1881). Ci'an, a Manchu aristocrat, was two years younger than Cixi but as empress was senior in rank.

In August 1861, the Xianfeng emperor died in Jehol, leaving a regency of eight princes to take over the administration on behalf of Cixi's six-year-old son, the Tongzhi emperor. In collaboration with Prince Gong (1833–1898), the deceased emperor's brother and a key personality in the Qing government, Cixi returned to Beijing with Ci'an, the deceased emperor's empress. The regency of the eight princes was overthrown and replaced by Cixi and Ci'an as co-regents, ruling

❧▶
See sidebar on the following page

Ci'an (1837–1881)

Chinese queen and regent. Name variations: *Tz'u-an, Cian. Born in 1837; died in 1881.*

Ci'an, a Manchu aristocrat, was two years younger than Cixi, but as senior consort to the Xianfeng (Hsien-feng) emperor she was much higher in rank. Until Ci'an's death in 1881, she served as regent with Cixi, though Cixi had usurped her power long before. It is said that while Ci'an had the virtues, Cixi had the talent in reading and writing.

from behind the screen due to concern for propriety. The regency of the two empress-dowagers was set up despite the protest of the Qing court: although a normal procedure in the Chinese dynastic system, it violated Qing dynastic laws. Cixi was the biological mother of the Tongzhi emperor, but Ci'an, as Xianfeng's empress, was observed to be the official mother who made decisions over the Tongzhi emperor's upbringing, including the choice of empress.

During the Tongzhi regency of 1861–1873, Cixi, rather than Ci'an, played the dominant role in direct involvement with state affairs. The Taiping Rebellion, a pseudo-Christian revolt which devastated much of the Chinese empire, was suppressed in 1864. The regency then launched a "self-strengthening" movement to revitalize the dynasty by entrusting high-ranking officials with the modernization of the military and the navy. In 1873, the Tongzhi emperor, now at the age of majority, ended the regency but embarked on a life of debauchery. In early 1875, he died without heir from a sexually transmitted disease, which was officially recorded as smallpox; his pregnant empress **Akute** soon passed away as well.

I have 400 million people, all dependent on my judgment.

—Cixi

With both her husband and only son predeceasing her, Cixi then designated her four-year-old nephew (the son of her own sister and the half-brother of the Xianfeng emperor) as the Guangxu emperor (Kuang Hus, r. 1875–1908). This choice violated the Manchu generational rule and set the Qing court in an uproar, but Cixi achieved a compromise by promising that Guangxu's successor would continue the lines of both the Guangxu and Tongzhi emperors. Because the enthronement of the Guangxu emperor was entirely due to Cixi's designation, she

was regarded as his official mother to whom the emperor's filial piety and obedience must be directed. As the Guangxu emperor was a minor, the co-regency of Cixi and Ci'an was in effect. The sudden death of Ci'an in 1881 left Cixi the sole regent to deal with the Sino-French War of 1884, which tore Vietnam away from China's sphere of influence.

To consolidate her authority over the Guangxu emperor, Cixi married him to her niece (her brother's daughter) in 1889, the same year that the Guangxu emperor terminated Cixi's regency by virtue of his adulthood. But Cixi still retained real power due to her firm control over high-ranking Manchu and Chinese officials. Officially, she had retired to the new summer palaces being constructed with funds earmarked for the navy. While the navy sorely needed more ships to deter foreign incursion, an immobile marble boat—now a prime tourist attraction—was built in the summer palaces. In 1895, the poorly financed Chinese navy was no match for the Japanese naval forces, and the Sino-Japanese war concluded with the disastrous loss of Taiwan and the huge reparations payable to Japan. To the chagrin of the Guangxu emperor and his court, other powers including Germany, encouraged by the gains of Japan, demanded more concessions from China.

By 1898, the Guangxu emperor had been exposed to Western ideas and foreign languages and had come under the influence of several progressive advisors and reform-minded intellectuals, including Kang Youwei (1858–1927) and Liang Qichao (1873–1929). From June to September 1898—known as the Hundred Day Reform—the Guangxu emperor proclaimed sweeping political and social reforms to transform China into a modern nation-state. As the decrees became more radical and an anti-Cixi plot leaked out, Cixi and the conservatives in the government became alarmed. In September 1898, she returned to Beijing from the summer palaces, placed the Guangxu emperor under house arrest, and secured his signature to approve her regency on his behalf. For the remainder of his reign to 1908, although he remained emperor in name, he was rendered powerless. Cixi immediately revoked the reforms, purged the reformers, and executed six prominent intellectuals without trial. Kang Youwei and Liang Qichao escaped and founded societies to protect the Guangxu emperor. Their influential writings portrayed Cixi as a domineering, corrupt, selfish, and incompetent woman who thwarted the reforms that could have molded China into a respectable member of the global community of equal nation-states. Recent appraisals of this event now show that Cixi was not against the general idea of reform but that her hostility was due to the conspiracy to remove her and her clansman Ronglu (Jung Lu, 1836–1903), a powerful military figure.

After stripping power from the Guangxu emperor, Cixi's desperation with the demanding Western authorities drove the Qing court to a bizarre episode in 1900—the Boxer Uprising. In her half-a-century of residence in the imperial places, Cixi had witnessed the opium trade's burden on the Chinese economy, the outflow of foreign currency, and the continued scramble for concessions by the foreign powers. Natural disasters such as droughts, floods, and epidemics exacerbated the unprecedented population increase as peasant refugees flooded the cities or became involved in banditry and secret societies, one of which was the anti-foreign and anti-Christian Boxer movement. In May 1900, the Boxers started to kill foreigners, missionaries, and Chinese converts, murdering the German

ambassador in the chaos. Relying on poor advice from Manchu officials, Cixi joined the Boxers' fanaticism by declaring war on the foreign governments. The foreign powers responded with an allied expeditionary column that overpowered the Boxer forces, sacked Beijing, and looted the imperial palaces. Accompanied by the Guangxu emperor, Cixi took refuge in the ancient Chinese capital of Xian—her second flight out of Beijing. In January 1902, Cixi and her entourage returned to Beijing, after signing a humiliating settlement with the allied forces.

In 1901, Cixi and the Qing government finally launched a drastic modernization program, reminiscent of the political and social reforms that the Guangxu emperor had wanted to implement in 1898. The civil-service examination system was abolished in 1905 and replaced with a national school system and a modern syllabus. Cixi endorsed the concept of a constitutional monarchy and supported the nine-year plan to prepare for constitutional government. She adopted a more open attitude to foreign governments and entertained diplomats and mis-

From the movie 55 Days at Peking, *starring Flora Robson as Cixi.*

sionaries in the imperial palaces. Her portrait was painted by Western artists, who were among the authors of the earliest Cixi biographies that were based on these brief, personal encounters. One memoir of Cixi's court life was authored by Cixi's Western-educated lady-in-waiting, **Derling.**

On November 15, 1908, shortly after appointing Henry Puyi (Xuantong emperor, r. 1908–1911) to succeed both the Guangxu and Tongzhi emperors, Cixi died from amoebic dysentery, within a day after the death of the Guangxu emperor. The grand scale of Cixi's funerary rituals—unprecedented for an empress or empress-dowager—rivaled that reserved for emperors, and 39 representatives from 14 countries offered condolences. The rituals continued for a full year before the actual burial in the Eastern Mausoleum. In 1928, her tomb was looted and her skeleton strewn about, but the tomb was restored in 1949 as well as in 1979 by the current government.

As a Manchu minority and a woman ruling a vast country of 400 million for half a century, during a lengthy and critical period of Chinese and world history, Cixi's achievements were extraordinary. No other Manchu woman in history had acquired and exercised political power, not to mention breaking dynastic laws by her own regency and the appointment of three emperors (Tongzhi, Guangxu, Puyi). Meticulous in her attire and hairstyle, she was a woman who, despite a limited education, appreciated and promoted traditional music, theater, opera, and calligraphy.

Historical and literary sources in both Chinese and Western languages disagree among themselves about Cixi's capabilities and intelligence. Her eventful life and attributes have been tarnished by accusations of her extreme brutality and scandalous sexuality. With little documentation, traditional historians have implicated Cixi in no less than five murders committed, they say, to fulfill her thirst for power: her own son Tongzhi and his empress Akute (1875), the co-regent Ci'an (1881), and the Guangxu emperor (1908) and his favorite concubine **Zhenfei** (1900). This cruelty extended to some eunuchs and maids, whom she reportedly flogged to death. At the same time, she supposedly favored several powerful and abusive eunuchs who served as her spies and executors in the palaces. Again without conclusive evidence, traditional sources have represented Cixi as a sexually promiscuous woman who had a pregnancy and a lifelong affair with her clansman and powerful military figure, Ronglu. Rumors of Cixi's sexual excesses included sexual trysts with her eunuchs.

These depictions of cruelty and promiscuity lack substantiation and are typical of the portrayal of powerful women rulers in Chinese history. A revisionist reassessment of Cixi and the legacy of her rule is long overdue and will likely focus on newly opened archives that may indicate the exact nature of her political role and relationship with the high-ranking officials. With so many factors involved in China's history during Cixi's lifetime, it may be a futile exercise to speculate what might have otherwise been China's experience in the 19th century had there been a different ruler, or a male sovereign, in control.

SOURCES:

Chung, Sue Fawn. "The Much Maligned Empress Dowager: A Revisionist Study of the Empress Dowager Tz'u-hsi (1835–1908)," in *Modern Asian Studies.* Vol. 13, no. 2, 1979, pp. 177–96.

Cohen, Paul, and John E. Schrecker, eds. *Reform in Nineteenth-Century China.* Cambridge: East Asian Research Center, Harvard University, 1976.

Griessler, Margareta T.J. "The Last Dynastic Funeral: Ritual Sequence at the Demise of the Empress Dowager Cixi," in *Oriens Extremus.* Vol. 34, no. 1/2, pp. 7–35.

Hummel, Arthur W. *Eminent Chinese of the Ch'ing Period (1644–1912).* Washington: Government Printing Office, 1943.

Kwong, Luke S.K. *A Mosaic of the Hundred Days: Personalities, Politics, and Ideas of 1898.* Cambridge: Council on East Asian Studies, Harvard University, 1984.

Tang, Zhijun, and Benjamin Elman. "The 1898 Reforms Revisited," also Rejoinder by Luke S.K. Kwong, in *Late Imperial China.* Vol. 8, no. 1, 1987, pp. 205–219.

Zhao Ersun, *et al. Qingshi gao* (Draft History of the Qing Dynasty). Beijing: Zhonghua shuju, 1977.

SUGGESTED READING:

Bland, J.O.P., and E. Backhouse. *China Under the Empress Dowager.* Boston: Houghton Mifflin, 1914.

Der Ling. *Two Years in the Forbidden City.* NY: Dodd, Mead, 1931.

Haldane, Charlotte. *The Last Great Empress of China.* Indianapolis: Bobbs-Merrill, 1965.

Hussy, Harry. *Venerable Ancestor: The Life and Times of Tz'u-Hsi, 1835-1908.* Westport, CT: Greenwood Press, 1949.

Seagrave, Sterling. *Dragon Lady: The Life and Legend of the Last Empress of China.* NY: Vintage Books, 1992.

Warner, Marina. *Dragon Empress: Life and Times of Tz'u-hsi 1835-1908 Empress Dowager of China.* London: Weidenfeld and Nicolson, 1972.

Jennifer W. Jay,
Associate Professor of History and Classics,
University of Alberta, Edmonton, Canada

Claflin, Tennessee (1846–1923)

Sister of Victoria Claflin Woodhull (the first woman candidate for the presidency), who was important in her own right, as a securities broker, spiritualist, and crusader for social reform. Name variations: Tennessee Cook, Lady Cook. Born in Homer, Ohio, on October 26, 1846 (some sources cite 1845); died on January 18, 1923; one of seven children of Roxanna (Hummel) Claflin and Reuben Buckman ("Buck") Claflin; sister of Victoria Woodhull (1838–1927) and Utica Claflin Brooker (d. 1873); married John Bartels; married Francis Cook (a wealthy, elderly widower, who held the title of Visconde de Montserrate bestowed by the king of Portugal), in October 1885.

In a period during which spiritualism (the belief that the spirits of the dead can and do communicate with the living) enjoyed a great vogue, the Claflin sisters were major attractions, touring the countryside and offering performances in which they claimed to have contacted the spirits of the deceased, who through them would speak to large, enthralled audiences. In time, *Victoria Woodhull would become a national figure, overshadowing her sister Tennessee. But, in their youth, it was Tennessee who was better known.

Tennessee Claflin was born in 1846 to Reuben (Buck) Claflin and **Roxanna Claflin** in Homer, Ohio. Buck made a living running a mill and trading whatever he came upon, while "Roxy" stayed home and gave birth to seven children, of whom Tennessee was the last. Roxy was a spiritualist, given to speaking in tongues at revival meetings in Homer. Victoria followed in her path, preaching to her fellow students, exhorting them to repent. But it was Tennessee who attracted the most attention. When only five or six years old, she showed signs of having second sight. She read the minds of her playmates, told a farmer where he could find a lost calf, and predicted a fire in a nearby seminary. For the sisters, this led to invitations to speak and demonstrate their powers outside the area. By 1852, they had traveled throughout the region and had displayed their abilities as far east as New York.

Their father Buck exploited the sisters' gifts. Acting as their agent, he booked the girls into shows, advertising them as child fortunetellers. They expanded into spiritualism, tipping tables, commanding spirits to speak through them at well-advertised seances. Buck discovered Tennessee had the gift of magnetic healing and advertised her as "The Wonder Child." When Victoria married Canning Woodhull and had a child, she semi-retired, so Buck, now proclaiming himself "The American King of Cancer," took to the road as a healer with Tennessee. Declaring her the "prophetess" who "astonished

people through her wondrous cures and mysterious revelations during her travels in the United States," Buck opened a cancer clinic and advertised Tennessee's powers along with fraudulent testimonials. This plan, however, backfired. A former patient repudiated the claims, there was an investigation of the clinic, and Tennessee, barely 18 years old, was indicted for manslaughter. With this, the Claflins fled to Cincinnati, where they were joined by Woodhull and her family. Above the door of their new home was a sign: "Tennessee Claflin and Victoria Woodhull, Clairvoyants." They were plagued by problems; neighbors claimed their home was a house of prostitution, and Tennessee was charged with adultery and figured in a blackmail case. The family moved to Chicago.

*T*ennessee
*C*laflin

There, Tennessee married John Bartels, but since her name was so well-known she did not take his name, and instead signed herself, "Tennie C. Claflin." The sisters continued to tour, but Bartels soon departed the scene. Then, Victoria Woodhull met James Blood, with whom she fell in love. According to some accounts, they married in 1866, only to divorce two years later though they continued to live together. Through Blood, the sisters became involved with other movements of the time—free love, women's rights, and politics. Claflin, who had been wilder than Woodhull, settled down, largely because of Blood's influence.

The family moved from Chicago to Pittsburgh where they stayed until 1868 when Woodhull had a visitation from the spirit of Demosthenes. He told her to go to New York, and they did, to a new home at 17 Great Jones Street. It was there that Buck arranged for Claflin, and later Woodhull, to have an audience with Commodore Cornelius Vanderbilt, one of America's wealthiest men, who at age 74 had become quite interested in spiritualism. While attracted to both women, Vanderbilt was drawn more closely to Claflin, whose "magnetic healing" seemed to alleviate all his physical distress.

Vanderbilt reciprocated with gifts and tips on stock, which were dispatched to Blood, who made purchases or sales as the information dictated. Soon Vanderbilt's interest turned to infatuation. He proposed marriage to Claflin, who rejected him. But the friendship continued.

In 1869, Vanderbilt helped the sisters open a brokerage house, making them the nation's first female brokers. Woodhull, Claflin & Co. opened on January 19, 1870, in the Hoffman House, a hotel near Wall Street. They soon moved to 44 Broad Street, across from the New York Stock Exchange. All the city's newspapers took note of the occasion. In one account, Claflin was described as: "to all appearances the photograph of a business woman—keen, shrewd, whole-souled." Another wrote of "The Queens of Finance," and a third described their offices as: "the Palace of Female Sovereigns of Wall Street."

*W*ere I to notice what is said by what we call society, I could not leave my apartment except in fantastic walking-dress and ball-room costume. But I despise what squeamy, crying girls or powdered, counter-jumping dandies say of me.

—Tennessee Claflin, 1871

The sisters were a huge success. Fueled by tips from Vanderbilt and his associates, they prospered. As far as the public was concerned, however, most of their information came from the spirits they daily contacted for that purpose. They hired additional brokers and soon became known as the hottest house on the Street. Not content with this, in May the sisters came out with *Woodhull & Claflin's Weekly*, which was not a business newspaper but rather a journal of opinion. The motto seemed to say it all: "Upward and Onward." It was considered a liberal publication, the first American periodical to publish Karl Marx's *Communist Manifesto*.

In 1872, Woodhull announced her intention to run for the presidency, "subject to ratification of the national convention" of the National Women's Suffrage Association. Soon after, Claflin announced she would be a candidate for a seat in the New York legislature. Since the district in which she ran was populated largely by German immigrants, Claflin learned the language and stumped the district delivering speeches in translation. She inveighed against the corruption of the Boss Tweed organization and accepted support of labor unions, but her race was overshadowed by Woodhull's presidential bid.

On November 2, shortly before the election, the *Weekly* broke its most sensational story, that of an affair between popular preacher Henry Ward Beecher and Mrs. Theodore (*Elizabeth) Tilton. That Woodhull had an affair with Theodore Tilton only complicated matters. Woodhull and Claflin were jailed on the trumped-up charge of having published an obscene newspaper. In the interim, the election was held, and Woodhull received no votes. Though Woodhull and Claflin were found not guilty, the struggle with Beecher continued.

Vanderbilt died in 1877, leaving a fortune of over $90 million and a messy fight over his will. Fearing they might be embroiled in the struggle, Woodhull, Claflin, and their families journeyed to England, where they lectured on political and religious subjects. Woodhull soon married John Biddulph Martin, a banker. Claflin met Francis Cook, a wealthy, elderly widower interested in spiritualism, who held the title of Visconde de Montserrate bestowed by the king of Portugal. Claflin informed Cook that she had a message from his departed wife, urging him to marry Claflin. So he did, in October 1885. Soon after, Cook was rewarded for his contributions to the arts by being made a baronet, which meant that Claflin now became Lady Cook.

Lady Cook became known in London society for her lavish parties. She dispensed the Cook fortune by making contributions to schools and charities. Her husband died in 1901, leaving her well taken care of. John Martin had died earlier, and Woodhull was also in good financial shape. At this point, the sisters grew apart. Lady Cook became involved with women's suffrage concerns in England. For a while, she hoped to found a bank, and on another occasion she wanted to erect a home for unwed mothers, but nothing came of these plans. Gradually, she faded from sight. She died while visiting with the conductor, Sir Thomas Beecham (who had married her grandniece, Lady **Utica Welles Beecham**), on January 18, 1923, at the age of 77.

SOURCES:

Johnson, Johanna. *Mrs. Satan: The Incredible Saga of Victoria C. Woodhull.* NY: Putnam, 1967.

Marberry, M.M. *Vicky: A Biography of Victoria C. Woodhull.* NY: Funk and Wagnalls, 1967.

SUGGESTED READING:

Sachs, Emanie. *The Terrible Siren: Victoria Woodhull.* NY: Harper, 1928.

Wilson, Forrest. *Crusader in Crinoline.* Philadelphia, PA: Lippincott, 1941.

Robert Sobel,
Lawrence Stessin Professor of Business History,
New College of Hofstra University, Hempstead, New York

Claflin, Victoria (1838–1927).

See Woodhull, Victoria.

Claire.

Variant of Clare.

Claire, Ina (1892–1985)

American actress and Broadway star of the 1920s. *Born Ina Fagan on October 15, 1892, in Washington, D.C.; died from the effects of a stroke at her home in San Francisco, California, on February 21, 1985; married James Whittaker (a critic), in 1919 (divorced 1925); married John Gilbert (the actor), in 1929 (divorced 1931); married William R. Wallace (an attorney), in 1939 (died 1976).*

Filmography: Wild Goose Chase *(1915);* The Puppet Crown *(1915);* Polly with a Past *(1920);* The Awful Truth *(1929); (portrayed* *Ethel Barrymore)* The Royal Family of Broadway *(1931);* Rebound *(1931);* The Greeks Had a Name for It *(1932);* Ninotchka *(1939);* Stage Door Canteen *(1943);* Claudia *(1943).*

Later typed as a well-dressed, well-bred sophisticate, Ina Claire started out on the road as a vaudeville comedian, at age 13, accompanied by her mother. In 1909, she gained notice in New York with her impersonation of the Scottish entertainer Sir Harry Lauder. Two years later, she made her Broadway debut in *Jumping Jupiter.* By 1915, Claire was a featured star in the *Ziegfeld Follies* and returned to the Follies the following year. Her 1917 performance in *Polly with a Past* firmly established her as a consummate comedienne. Sealing her reputation in 1919 with *The Gold Diggers,* which ran for two years, Ina Claire was well-known in New York circles for her ready wit.

Though Claire made her screen debut in the silent *Wild Goose Chase* in 1915, she preferred the stage and was a reigning Broadway star throughout the 1920s. In 1922, she played the lead in *The Awful Truth* on Broadway, then starred in the film version in 1929, her first talkie. (The movie would be remade in 1937 with *Irene Dunne.) Though she did other films, Claire was content to stay in New York, performing in *The Last of Mrs. Cheyney* (1925) and S.N. Behrman's smash hit *Biography* (1932). Ina Claire retired in 1954, after a successful run in T.S. Eliot's *The Confidential Clerk.*

Clairmont, Claire (1798–1879).

See Shelley, Mary for sidebar.

Ina
Claire

Clairon, Mlle (1723–1802)

French actress. Name variations: La Clairon; Claire Hippolyte Clairon. Born Claire Hippolyte Josèphe Légris de Latude near Condé, in Hainault, France, in 1723; died in Paris, France, on January 18, 1802 (some sources cite 1803).

Commonly known as La Clairon, Mlle Clairon made her first appearance in 1743 at the Comédie Français, Paris, as Phêdre. A triumph, she remained at the Comédie for 22 years, dividing the honors with her rival *Marie Dumesnil. Some of Clairon's greatest achievements were in the classical roles of tragedy, including Medea, and she originated many of the parts in Voltaire's plays. She is also remembered as an innovator who endeavored to bring about a more sensible style of costuming than was then conventional on the stage, as well as a natural style. In 1765, she retired and trained dramatic pupils. In her old age, Clairon wrote a book of memoirs, published in Paris in 1799, which offers

many details concerning her art and is known for its lively anecdotes.

Mlle Clairon was of small stature and noted for a beauty at once vivacious and dignified; she was also gifted with a remarkable voice. Oliver Goldsmith claimed that she had "the most perfect female figure" he had ever seen on any stage, and David Garrick noted, "She has everything that art and a good understanding with great natural spirit can give her." She died, poor and forgotten, in the winter of 1802.

Clampitt, Amy (1920–1994)

American poet. Born in New Providence, Iowa, on June 15, 1920; died of ovarian cancer at her home in Lenox, Massachusetts, on September 10, 1994; oldest of five children of Pauline (Felt) and Ray Justin Clampitt; graduated from Grinnell College, B.A. with honors, 1941; studied at Columbia University on a graduate fellowship, and at the New School for Social Research.

Awards: Guggenheim Fellowship, 1982; honorary doctorate from Grinnell College; award in literature from the American Academy and Institute of Arts and Letters. Writer-in-residence at the University of Wisconsin (Milwaukee), the College of William and Mary, and Amherst College.

Selected publications: Multitudes, Multitudes *(self-published, 1974);* The Isthmus *(Coalition of Publishers for Employment, 1981);* The Kingfisher *(Alfred A. Knopf, 1983);* What the Light Was Like *(Knopf, 1985);* Archaic Figure *(Alfred A. Knopf, 1987);* Westward *(Alfred A. Knopf, 1990).*

Often compared to *Elizabeth Bishop, *Marianne Moore and Gerard Manley Hopkins, Amy Clampitt published her first major collection of poetry, *The Kingfisher,* when she was 63. Nominated for the National Book Critics Circle Award, this work was an auspicious debut. She "immediately merits consideration as one of our most distinguished contemporary poets," wrote Richard Tillinghast in *The New York Times Book Review.* Clampitt treated her themes of travel, science, psychology, art, and metaphysics in a style that offered long strings of dependent clauses, rich but often obscure vocabulary, and esoteric allusions. These elements combined in what poet Alfred Corn termed a "baroque profusion, the romance of the adjective, labyrinthine syntax, a festival lexicon."

Clampitt's preoccupation with the natural world echoed a childhood spent growing up in the Midwest on a 125-acre farm. "I was always aware that my parents were unhappy," she recalled. "So I grew up with all these layers and interminglings. There was the natural world that was frightening and beautiful, and the adult world that was frightening and painful."

After college, she worked as a secretary and writer at Oxford University Press in New York (1943–51) and then as a reference librarian at the National Audubon Society (1952–59). Unhappy with this job, she returned to Iowa in 1959 to live with her parents and worked in a contractor's office. In the early 1960s, she gave New York another try. Through the 1960s to 1970s, she earned a living as a freelance writer, editor, and researcher, while taking part in the Vietnam protests and writing a series of unpublished novels. In 1977, she returned to the world of nine-to-five, becoming an editor at E.P. Dutton, a post she would hold until 1982.

Though Clampitt fell in love with poetry in college, reading especially the work of Gerard Manley Hopkins, it was not until the 1960s that she began to write poetry herself. At her own expense, she published a chapbook *Multitudes, Multitudes* in 1974. When Howard Moss, poetry editor of *The New Yorker,* became aware of the chapbook, he began to publish her poetry regularly, as did the *Atlantic Monthly,* the *Kenyon Review, Prairie Schooner,* and the *Yale Review.* In 1981, a second small collection, *The Isthmus,* was published.

Clampitt's 1987 collection, *Archaic Figure,* explores "the ancient consciousness of women" and contains a series of biographical poems on *****Dorothy Wordsworth,** George Eliot (*****Mary Anne Evans**) and *****Margaret Fuller.** "A central concern," wrote Clampitt, "is with the experience of women, as individuals and as a part of history." Despite this, the poet was accused of lacking an interest in people. "The truth is I don't write so much about human relations," replied Clampitt. "I don't think that's my primary subject. When I write about the emotional experience of people, it's more about the sense of deprivation."

Though she had residences in New York and Lenox, Massachusetts, Clampitt preferred the life of a nomad, remarking, "I don't want to be locked in. I want to be able to roam around and be part of a landscape." She died in her 70s at the Lenox home on September 10, 1994.

SOURCES:
Contemporary Authors. Vol. 110. Detroit, MI: Gale Research, 1984.
Current Biography 1992. NY: H.W. Wilson, 1993.
Morrisoe, Patricia. *New York.* October 15, 1984.

Clapp, Louise Brough (b. 1923).
See Brough, Louise.

Clara.
Variant of Clare.

Clara (c. 1194–1253).
See Clare of Assisi.

Clara (1697–1744)

Italian saint. Name variations: *Clara Isabella Fornari.* Born Anna Felicia Fornari in Rome on June 25, 1697; died in 1744.

Born in Rome in 1697, Anna Fornari entered the novitiate of the Poor Clares of Todi. A year later, she professed her vows and was given the name Clara Isabella. Contemporaries—fellow nuns, her confessor, and her doctor—maintain that from the start of her novitiate, the devil was intent on driving her to despair and suicide: he struck her, threw her down the stairs, and tried to destroy her faith. Clara's hands, feet, and side were marked with the stigmata, the wounds of Christ on the cross, which sometimes bled.

Ecstatic visions were said to be interspersed with the devil's persecutions. Clara claimed prolonged visitations from St. *****Clare of Assisi,** St. *****Catherine of Siena,** Jesus Christ, and *****Mary the Virgin.** During one of these visitations, Christ placed a ring on her finger, in honor of their spiritual marriage. A few months before her death, Clara felt abandoned by God but renewed her faith once more before she died in 1744.

Clare.
Variant of Clara.

Clare (c. 1194–1253).
See Clare of Assisi.

Clare, Amicia de (1220–1283)

English noblewoman. Born on May 27, 1220; died in 1283; daughter of Gilbert de Clare, 5th earl of Hertford, 1st of Gloucester, and Lady *****Isabel Marshall** (1200–1240); married Baldwin de Reviers, 6th earl of Devon, in 1226; married Robert de Guines, in 1247.

Clare, countess of.
See Clare, Elizabeth de (1295–1360).

Clare, Eleanor de (1292–1337).
See Isabella of France for sidebar.

Clare, Elizabeth de (1295–1360)

Countess of Clare. Name variations: *Elizabeth de Burgh.* Born in England in 1295 (some sources cite 1291); died on November 4, 1360, in England; third daughter of Joan of Acre, princess of England, and Gilbert de Clare, 9th earl of Clare, 7th earl of Hertford, 3rd earl of Gloucester (1243–1295); married John de Burgh (d. 1313), lord of Ulster, in 1308; married Theobald de Verdon (d. 1316), in 1316; married Roger Damory (d. 1322), baron of Armoy, in 1317; children: (first marriage) William de Burgh, 3rd earl of Ulster (1312–1333); grandmother of *****Elizabeth de Burgh** (1332–1362).

Elizabeth de Clare was a powerful and wealthy English noblewoman whose life exemplifies the activities of highborn widows who wished to leave their mark on their society. She was descended from the English royal house, the daughter of the Princess *****Joan of Acre** (herself the daughter of King Edward I Longshanks and *****Eleanor of Castile**), and Gilbert de Clare, earl of Gloucester, an important noble. Around 1308, Elizabeth married the heir of Ulster, John de Burgh, who died five years later. When Elizabeth's brother, who had inherited the family properties, died in 1314, the vast holdings of the de Clares (probably the wealthiest of the kingdom) were split between Elizabeth and her two sisters, *Margaret de Clare (c. 1293–1342) and ◄ Eleanor de Clare (1292–1337). Two years later, the young widow was kidnapped and forced to marry Theobald de Verdon, a noble who wanted her rich estates for himself. Fortunately for Elizabeth, he died several months later; the next year, she married the knight Roger Damory.

Elizabeth seems to have been destined to widowhood, for Roger was executed in 1322 by order of the powerful and greedy Lord Hugh Despenser, who at the time had control of the ineffectual king Edward II. Despenser had the wealthy heiress Elizabeth forcibly taken to Barking Abbey after her husband's death, and kept there until she granted him all her holdings in Wales. The next year, all her holdings were seized by Despenser and Elizabeth was incarcerated again. When Edward III succeeded his father in 1327 and Despenser lost power, Elizabeth was restored to all her proper inheritance. After the chaos and tragedies of her youth, she settled down to a life of managing her estates from her main residence at Clare Castle in Suffolk, also building a reputation as a generous founder and pious noblewoman.

Although her widowed years were relatively peaceful and independent of male control, Elizabeth was by no means unoccupied. She oversaw all the activities of a large household of over 200 employees, ranging in class from her most important land managers to the accountants, reeves, auditors, laundresses and gardeners. Not everyone at Clare Castle had a strictly practical function; Elizabeth had no less than four goldsmiths who created jewelry and art pieces for her and handled the maintenance of her precious ornaments, plates, and jewelry. Her officers managed the income from her various estates in Wales, Dorset, East Anglia, and Ireland. She entertained visitors on a regular basis both at Clare Castle and in her London house, seeing local nobility as well as members of the royal family and the nuns of the Franciscan convents that she supported.

Elizabeth's generosity and piety were well-known. Household records reveal the distribution of a daily money allowance to about 800 of the local poor. The widow also became an important supporter of various religious houses, and had a particular fondness for the Franciscan nuns, called Minoresses. In addition, she was a great supporter of education, giving grants for (male) clerks to attend the large colleges like Oxford. In 1336, she founded Clare College (still in existence) at Cambridge; originally named University Hall, it was renamed after her primary title, Lady of Clare, in her honor. She provided the funds for the buildings as well as stipends for the scholars and set out the statutes for the college, prescribing the number of students allowed and the courses each must take. On her death, Elizabeth left Clare College some books, more money, gold, and vestments. Her will also provided generous pensions for her servants, bequests to the Minoress houses, and gifts of her jewelry and other precious items to her friends, notably Countess *Marie de St. Pol, with whom Elizabeth had developed an intimate relationship. The great widow died at age 65.

Laura York,
Riverside, California

Clare, Isabel de (d. 1217).

See Isabella of Angoulême for sidebar on Avisa of Gloucester.

Clare, Isabel de (c. 1174–1220)

*Countess of Pembroke. Name variations: Isabel Marshall, countess Strigoil. Born around 1174; died in 1220; interred at Tintern Abbey; daughter of Richard de Clare (b. 1130), 2nd earl of Pembroke, and Aoife (Eva) MacMurrough, countess of Ireland; married William Marshall, 1st earl of Pembroke, in August 1189; children: William Marshall, 2nd earl of Pembroke; Richard Marshall, 3rd earl of Pembroke; *Maud Marshall (d. 1248); Gilbert Marshall, 4th earl of Pembroke; *Sybilla Marshall; *Isabel Marshall (1200–1240); Joan Marshall (d. after 1234, who married Warine de Monchensy, lord of Swanscombe); *Eve de Braose; Walter Marshall, 5th earl of Pembroke; Anselme Marshal, 6th earl of Pembroke (some sources cite him as 9th earl of Pembroke).*

Clare, Isabel de (1200–1240).

See Marshall, Isabel.

Clare, Isabel de (1226–1254)

*Scottish noblewoman. Name variations: Isobel de Clare. Born on November 8, 1226; died in 1254; daughter of Gilbert de Clare, 5th earl of Hertford, 1st earl of Gloucester, and Lady *Isabel Marshall (1200–1240); married Robert Bruce (1210–1295), lord of Annandale, on May 12, 1240; children: Robert Bruce (1253–1304), earl of Carrick (who married *Marjorie of Carrick); William Bruce; Bernard of Conington and Exton; Richard Bruce.*

Clare, Eleanor de (1292–1337).

See Isabella of France for sidebar.

Opposite page

Clare of Assisi

Clare, Margaret de (1249–1313)

*Countess of Cornwall. Name variations: Marguerite de Clere. Born in 1249; died in February 1313; buried at Chertsey Abbey, Surrey, England; daughter of Richard de Clare, 6th earl of Hertford, 2nd earl of Gloucester, and *Maud Lacey; married Edmund Plantagenet, 2nd earl of Cornwall, October 6, 1272 (divorced 1293).*

Clare, Margaret de (fl. 1280–1322).

See Siege Warfare and Women for sidebar.

Clare, Margaret de (c. 1293–1342)

*Countess of Cornwall and Gloucester. Born around 1293; died in 1342; daughter of Gilbert de Clare, 7th earl of Hertford, 3rd of Gloucester, and *Joan of Acre (1272–1307); married Piers Gaveston, earl of Cornwall, in 1307; married Hugh Audley, earl of Gloucester, in 1317; children: (second marriage) *Margaret Audley (who married Ralph Stafford, 1st earl of Stafford).*

Clare, Maud de (fl. 1230–1250).

See Lacey, Maud.

Clare dei Sciffi (c. 1194–1253).

See Clare of Assisi.

Clare of Assisi (c. 1194–1253)

Founder of the Franciscan nuns, a community that formed a refuge for women desiring to pursue the religious life by renouncing the world. Name variations: St. Clare; St. Clara; Santa Clara d'Assisi; Claire d'Assise; Clare dei Sciffi; Chiara di Favorone. Born in 1193 or 1194 in Assisi, Umbria, in Central Italy; died after a long illness, on August 11, 1253, in Assisi; daughter of Ortolana and Favorone (or Favarone) Offreduccio (a noble and crusader); privately educated.

Met Francis (later St. Francis of Assisi) and entered religious life (1212); became abbess of the Poor Ladies (1215); canonized as St. Clare (1255).

On the night of Palm Sunday, in the year 1212, a 17-year-old girl was removing, with her bare hands, the heavy beams that covered the "door of the dead" in her family's luxurious home in Assisi, Italy. This door, intended for use only when transporting a corpse from the house to the cemetery, was customarily kept barred; in this Christian country, some superstitions still lingered, including the fear that the dead would try to find the way back to their homes through

the door by which they had left. With a strength that she later recalled as astonishing, the runaway Clare removed the heavy masonry blocking the exit and pulled off the beams that had been hammered in with a force intended to keep out even the most persistent ghost. Once outdoors, Clare met with a female companion, and they made their way to a spot where a young man was waiting.

Despite appearances, this was not a lovers' meeting. The site of the rendezvous was the Church of Santa Maria degli Angeli, and the young man expecting the girls was Francis, later to be known as St. Francis of Assisi, whose religious fervor was attracting followers from all over Italy. He welcomed Clare and, in hasty silence, cut off her long blonde hair and gave her, in place of the fine robes she was wearing, a coarse nun's habit and veil. Then they fled through the night to a nearby Benedictine convent, where he left her in charge of the nuns.

These Benedictines were among the few in the religious life whom Francis and Clare could trust. At the time, the Church of Rome was in turmoil. While people with genuine religious fervor strove to live decent lives, the Crusades were in full swing, drawing the devout (as well as profiteers) to leave their homes and attempt to "redeem" Jerusalem from the non-Christian "infidels" who held it. In fact, Clare's father, Favorone Offreduccio, had gone on Crusade, and it is likely that Clare's mother, **Ortolana**, had accompanied him. The devout who could afford it (including Ortolana) made pilgrimages to holy sites to see the relics of the martyrs and pray for the redemption of their souls.

Though some religious orders genuinely tried to emulate the life of Christ and provide a sanctuary for those seeking refuge from the outside world, many were hotbeds of corruption, with members taking orders, not out of conviction, but out of a lack of ability to make any other way in life. Some monks and nuns genuinely felt a calling to the religious life; others were sent there by parents who were unable to care for them. Many of the latter were girls whose prospects for marriage were small, either for lack of a dowry or because they were handicapped or mentally ill. Not surprisingly, people warehoused in monasteries out of necessity, rather than callings, were not likely to live exceptionally holy lives.

In addition, the church was busy attempting to stamp out various heresies, splinter-groups whose views differed from those of the orthodox church. While not as intolerant as it would later become during the age of the inquisitions, the church was zealous in its efforts to ensure that all Christians follow a certain course of belief and conduct. Assisi, located in Central Italy less than 100 miles northeast of Rome, managed to stay out of most of these controversies. Though not particularly noted for its holiness, Assisi had the requisite share of churches and monasteries in its vicinity. But at this time, when the merchant-class was beginning to emerge as a powerful force, most of the citizens of Assisi were more interested in commerce than religion.

In the midst of this confusion, Francis, a young man of Assisi's newly important merchant class, underwent a religious conversion while recovering from a serious illness. He renounced his worldly life and embraced the principles of Poverty, Chastity, and Obedience. The pope approved his new monastic order in 1209. In a short time, men of the area (and later, from all over Europe) were giving away their possessions and joining him.

Although, by necessity, all his followers were men, Francis was also mindful of the spiritual needs of women. It was said that in the early days of his religious life, while he was rebuilding the church of San Damiano (St. Damian), Francis "used to call with a loud voice in the joy of the Spirit to those living near or passing by the church and would say to them in French: 'Come and help me in [this] project for the church of San Damiano which will be in the future a monastery of women by whose fame and life our heavenly Father will be glorified throughout the entire Church.'"

While this inspiring religious activity was going on, Clare was growing up in Assisi as an unusually pious child. It was said that, shortly before her birth, her mother prayed to the ***Mary the Virgin** for a safe delivery and received a vision in which she was told, "Fear not, for thou wilt safely give birth to a light which will shine on all the earth." When her baby girl was born, Ortolana named the child "Chiara," or "Bright."

Clare is said to have secretly worn an instrument of torture, a hair shirt, under her clothes. Made of knotted horsehairs, or a boarskin, with the coarse fur turned to the inside, a hair shirt caused enough pain to make the wearer mindful of the weakness of the flesh. Clare enjoyed repeating prayers from a very young age and was certainly aware of the travels made by her parents in service of their religion.

In an age when few people, especially women, could read and write, Clare was literate in both Italian and Latin. Usually only girls destined for the convent were taught to read, but her parents' later resistance to her taking the veil indicates that they intended a good marriage for her, as well as, most likely, for their three other daughters and their son. Clare was quite artistic; an unusually beautiful embroidered religious vestment, known to date from the 13th century, is said to be the work of her hands. She had a lifelong interest in music, was attentive to the beauties of nature, and the religious life attracted her from an early age.

Even if her parents had been in favor of it, a girl of Clare's social class, with a desire to take the veil as a nun, would have had a difficult adjustment. She made a start by selling her possessions and distributing the proceeds among the poor. Evidently, this was not enough to satisfy her. Clare's situation was complicated by the powerful attraction exerted by Francis. While men of all ages were coming to join him, he held a particular fascination for the young that must have been felt by Clare as well as other girls. Consequently, when she felt the desire to leave her family, renounce all thought of married life, and devote herself to God, it was natural for her to turn to Francis for advice. He told her to go to church that Palm Sunday as usual, and she would learn what she had to do.

On that Sunday, when the faithful approached the altar to receive their palm-fronds from the hands of the bishop, Clare was struck by a sudden attack of shyness or indecision and held back. Seeing her, the bishop took the unusual step of descending from the altar, making his way through the crowds. He handed her the palm and, leaning over, said a few words in her ear. What he said has not been recorded, but that night she took the desperate measure of leaving her home through the "door of the dead" (perhaps symbolizing her recognition that she would henceforth be dead to her family and to the world) and meeting Francis to begin her spiritual life.

Though his monastic order had been recognized by the pope several years earlier, Francis had no authority to make someone a nun. Indeed, Clare's family did not recognize his legitimacy in this area. Accordingly, the men of her family stormed the convent to force her return home. Clare knelt at the altar and held onto it, aware that anyone attempting to tear her away would be guilty of sacrilege. They left without her, but when her sister ❧▸ **Agnes of Assisi** ran off to join her a few days later, they used such force that Agnes was left unconscious before her relatives decided to give in and leave her.

When Francis began his reforms, the young women of Assisi had been swept up by the same fervor as the men, but until now they had lacked a leader and a place to go. Clare's courageous flight and devotion to her principles inspired them, and many (eventually including two more of her sisters) soon joined her. The bishop allowed them to live in the vacant monastery of San Damiano; and, while they were waiting to petition the pope for recognition as a new order, they took their rule from that of Francis. Their major emphasis was on poverty, which would prove a major hurdle in the pope's approval of their order. By embracing this principle, the nuns would not be allowed to earn money and would thus be dependent upon the charity of their neighbors for survival. The pope was reluctant to allow an unproven group of women, many of whom were accustomed to what went for a luxurious life in the Middle Ages, to risk privation. But both Francis and Clare insisted that "embracing Lady Poverty" was essential to their conception of a devout life.

While waiting for papal approval, the Sisters acquired the name of the Poor Ladies of San Damiano (later known as the Poor Clares or the Clarisses). As their leader, Clare set up a temporary rule taken from that of Francis, with whom she was in frequent communication. Though mindful of the possible problems if the two

---

❧▸ **Agnes of Assisi** (1207–1232)

Italian abbess. Name variations: (Italian) Agnese. Pronunciation: ah-NYAY-zay. Born in Assisi, Umbria, in Central Italy, in 1207; died in 1232; daughter of Favorone (or Favarone) Offreduccio (a noble and Crusader) and **Ortolana**; *sister of Clare of Assisi.*

Born into a wealthy Italian family, Agnes of Assisi was about 13 years younger than her holy sister, *Clare of Assisi, yet the sisters seem to have been made closer by their common commitment to serve God and their admiration for the reformer Francis of Assisi. When Clare founded the Poor Clares (the Franciscan order for women) and established a convent at San Damiano, Agnes proved an important assistant. She joined the convent as a nun and helped her sister in the role of spiritual advisor. Although sometimes overshadowed by Clare, Agnes drew admiration from the people of Italy for her own selfless devotion to serving the poor and the sick. She founded a convent in the town of Monticelli (near Florence) and became its abbess in 1219. Agnes died quite young from an undiagnosed illness, about age 25.

Laura York, Riverside, California

groups had too much contact with each other, she urged Francis to allow his Brothers and her Sisters to meet for a meal. He agreed on condition that they meet at the Church of Santa Maria degli Angeli, where he had first welcomed her into the religious life.

The powerful impact of these two on the city of Assisi is illustrated by the tale told of this dinner. One of the stories of the life of St. Francis relates that after the meal had been underway for a short time, the church appeared to be on fire to the people of Assisi. Rushing to put out the flames, they found nothing burning; the Brothers and Sisters were still seated, unmoving, at the table, apparently rapt in contemplation. The people withdrew, having witnessed a spiritual—not an actual—fire.

In recognition of Francis' importance in her religious life, Clare referred to herself as his *pianticella* (little plant). Nonetheless, they treated each other as equals; he referred to her as "mother and sister," just as she referred to him as "father and brother." In addition to infrequent meetings for meals, Clare also advised Francis on his spiritual life. At one point, he contemplated withdrawing from the world to live as a hermit. Clare and Francis' trusted Brother Sylvester convinced him that he was needed to continue preaching and leading new initiates to the religious life.

That Clare loved the world she had left is obvious; she urged her Sisters, when out in the forest, to note and thank God for every tree. But she led a life of extreme self-denial and humility in her convent, from which she never stirred until her death. When Sisters returned to the convent from necessary errands, she washed their feet with her own hands. She continued to wear hair shirts (one of the new Sisters attempted to put one on and was so uncomfortable that she immediately removed it) and slept on a pile of twigs with a rock or log for a pillow. Though she slept without a blanket, on cold nights she rose from her bed and made certain that the other women had coverings. While all the Sisters ate frugally (only one meal a day except on rare occasions, such as Christmas, when they might have two), she fasted continuously. In fact, she became so weakened from lack of food that the bishop and Francis made her promise to eat at least one and a half ounces of bread daily.

But despite their devotion to frugality, when the Poor Ladies were granted their charter as a religious Franciscan community in 1215, the pope did not permit them to adopt poverty as one of their guiding principles. Clare gave much of her energy to changing this policy, and, in 1228, he finally acceded. In 1218, their official Rule had finally been approved, with the permission to become cloistered, meaning that the nuns were to have extremely limited contact with the outside world. Theirs was not a service order, a teaching order, or a missionary order; their purpose was to contemplate God and provide an example for others by leading holy lives.

With the official sanction on their rule, followers began to flock in from all over Italy. Clare's sister Agnes founded a convent in the town of Monticelli (near Florence) and became its abbess in 1219. As time went on, more convents of the Poor Ladies were formed through Italy and later the rest of Europe and the world.

In 1226, Clare's mother Ortolana joined the convent, calling her own daughter "Mother" (Clare's father had evidently died several years earlier). That same year, Francis died. Without his support, Clare's influence with the pope declined; in 1230, the pope restricted the rights of the Franciscan Brothers to visit with Clare's Poor Ladies. The loss of Francis' support became evident in the functioning of the convent as well; in 1235, the pope had to make a public appeal for provisions for the Sisters.

Clare was in poor health for the last 28 or 29 years of her life. It is not clear what specific ailment she suffered from, although it is likely that the hard life she forced on herself, especially her refusal to eat sufficiently, contributed to her invalidism. Although she had told the nuns not to disturb her if she was absent from functions of the convent, a young sister became concerned when she did not appear for several meals. Going to her room, the sister reminded her that she had promised Francis to eat at least a little bread every day. Clare, rapt in divine visions, had lost track of time and was unaware that two days had passed since she had left her cell.

In 1252, the pope visited Clare at San Damiano. She died in 1253 and was almost immediately canonized. The Church of St. Clare was built in Assisi in the year 1260. In 1850, her body was found and moved to her church where it continues to dwell, an object of extreme veneration.

SOURCES:

Armstrong, Regis J., O.F.M., Cap. and Ignatius C. Brady, O.F.M. *Francis and Clare: The Complete Works.* NY: Paulist Press, 1982.

Clare of Assisi, Saint. *Claire d'Assise: Écrits. Introduction, Texte Latin, Traduction, Notes et Index.* Edited and translated by Marie-France Becker, Jean-

François Godet, Thaddée Matura. Paris: Les Éditions du Cerf, 1985.
———. *Early Documents*. Edited and translated by Regis J. Armstrong, O.F.M., Cap. NY: Paulist Press, 1988.
de Robeck, Nesta. *St. Clare of Assisi*. Milwaukee, WI: Bruce, 1951.

SUGGESTED READING:
Nichols, John A., and Lillian Thomas Shank, eds. *Distant Echos: Medieval Religious Women*. Vol. 1. Cistercian Studies Series, 71. Kalamazoo, MI: Cistercian Publications, 1984.
Roggen, Heribert. *The Spirit of Saint Clare*. Chicago: Franciscan Herald Press, 1971.

Tracy Barrett, Vanderbilt University, Nashville, Tennessee

Clarence, duchess of.

See Visconti, Violet (c. 1353–1386).
See Neville, Isabel (1451–1476).
See Adelaide of Saxe-Meiningen (1792–1849).

Claricia of Augsburg (fl. 1220)

German manuscript illuminator. Flourished in 1220 in Augsburg, Germany.

Claricia worked as a manuscript illuminator at the convent of Augsburg. She is one of the very few women illuminators who actually signed one of her creations, an ornate initial Q in the text of a Psalter. For the tail of the Q, she even painted a whimsical portrait of herself dangling happily from the body of the letter, a young woman with long braided hair and wearing secular clothing. These clues tell us that Claricia was not a nun but probably a student of professional illumination at the Augsburg convent at the time she worked on the Psalter. Her convent education and vocational training indicate that she was born into an artisan family with the means to pay for her education, although no other details are known about her life.

Laura York,
Riverside, California

Clarinda (1759–1841).

See Maclehose, Agnes.

Clark.

Variant of Clarke, Clerk, and Clerke.

Clark, Arizona Donnie (1872–1935).

See Barker, Ma.

Clark, Eleanor (1913–1996)

American author and travel essayist. Name variations: Eleanor Clark Warren. Born in Los Angeles, California, on July 6, 1913; raised from four weeks on in Roxbury, Connecticut; died in Boston, Massachusetts, on February 16, 1996; daughter of Frederick Huntington (an engineer) and Eleanor (Phelps) Clark; attended Rosemary Hall School; graduated from Vassar College, 1934; married Jan Frankle (Czech secretary to Leon Trotsky), in 1937 (divorced 1938); married Robert Penn Warren (1905–1989, author and Pulitzer Prize winner); children: (second marriage) Rosanna Warren; Gabriel Penn Warren.

See
following page
for photograph

Following graduation from Vassar, Eleanor Clark moved to New York, where she wrote fiction, reviewed for *The New Republic*, worked for the *Partisan Review,* and edited *New Letters in America* for Norton. In 1937, she became a translator for Leon Trotsky while he was in Mexico and, that same year, married Trotsky's secretary Jan Frankle. The marriage lasted one year. In 1939, Clark was involved with poet Louis MacNeice. From 1943 to 1946, she worked for the Office of Strategic Services in Washington, D.C., interviewing French and Italian refugees. During this period, she met Robert Penn Warren (1944).

Most of the latter '40s and early '50s were spent in Italy where Clark finished her first book *Rome and a Villa* (1952); Anatole Broyard would later refer to it as "perhaps the finest book ever to be written about a city." On returning home, she married Warren, and the couple settled on Redding Road in Fairfield, Connecticut, where they lived for 37 years. When Warren died in 1989, Clark moved to Cambridge, then to Boston, while struggling with emphysema.

Considered a master stylist, Clark wrote four novels (including *The Bitter Box,* 1946, and *Baldur's Gate,* 1970), three travel memoirs, children's books, essays, and a memoir about her failing sight, *Eyes, Etc.* Her 1964 book *The Oysters of Locmariaquer,* an account of oystering in Brittany, received the National Book Award.

Clark, Georgia Neese (1900–1989)

First woman treasurer of the United States. Born on January 27, 1900, in Richland, Kansas; died in 1989; daughter of a businessman; B.A. in economics from Washburn College (now Washburn University); married George M. Clark (a theatrical manager), in January 1929 (divorced); married A.J. Gray, in January 1953.

The signature of Georgia Neese Clark was the first of any woman's to appear on U.S. currency. Appointed treasurer by Harry Truman in 1949, she served in that capacity until 1953.

Eleanor Clark with husband Robert Penn Warren.

The daughter of a wealthy businessman, Clark graduated in 1921 from Washburn College (now Washburn University of Topeka) with a B.A. in economics. She spent the 1920s in New York pursuing a career in the theater and was with Earl Carroll's company for a time. Clark worked with various touring stock companies and in 1929 married her manager, from whom she would later be divorced. In 1930, Clark returned to Kansas to care for her ailing father. During the Depression, she took over his business interests, replacing him as president of the Richland State Bank after his death in 1937.

During the Roosevelt years, Clark became active in Democratic politics. In 1936, she was elected to the Democratic National Committee, and in 1948 she put her efforts to the candidacy of Harry Truman. Predicted to lose, Truman was especially thankful to those who had stood by him. When he appointed Clark treasurer in 1949, she became the first woman to hold the position in U.S. history. She left the treasury in 1953, when the Republicans took the presidency. Dwight Eisenhower was careful to appoint a woman to replace her, and the post has been regularly filled by a woman since that time. Clark returned to Kansas and married A.J. Gray. She was to remain a member of the Democratic National Committee for some years. The Richland Bank, of which Clark retained presidency, relocated in 1964 and was renamed the Capital City State Bank. In 1967, for a few months Clark served as chair of the advisory council of the Small Business Administration.

Clark, Marguerite (1883–1940)

American stage and silent-screen actress. Born Helen Marguerite Clark in Avondale, Ohio, on February 22, 1883; died in New York City on September 25, 1940; educated in public schools and in a convent school in St. Martin, Ohio; married Harry P. Williams (a New Orleans businessman), in August 1918 (died 1936).

Selected films: Wildflower *(1914);* The Goose Girl *(1915);* Molly Make-Believe *(1916);* Snow White *(1917);* Prunella *(1918);* Mrs. Wiggs of the Cabbage Patch *(1918);* All-of-a-Sudden Peggy *(1920);* Scrambled Wives *(1921).*

Marguerite Clark, who at one time rivaled *Mary Pickford as the darling of silent pictures, began her career on the stage, making her New York debut in 1900 in the chorus of *The Belle of Bohemia*. With the role of Polly, opposite De-Wolf Hopper in *Mr. Pickwick* (1903), her popularity continued to grow and would continue to do so over the next decade. She had roles in *Babes in Toyland, The Pied Piper, Baby Mine,* and *Snow White* (a production for children), and in 1914 signed on with Adolph Zukor's Famous Players (which later became Paramount). Her first film effort, *Wildflower* (1914), was a huge success, and she went on to perform a succession of innocent maiden roles well into her 30s, becoming one of the most beloved and highly paid stars of the silent era. In two of her films, *The Prince and the Pauper* and *Topsy and Eva,* she played double roles. Her performances in the stage and film versions of *Snow White* were said to have influenced the future Walt Disney animated version. Clark retired from films after her marriage to New Orleans businessman Harry P. Williams, appearing in her last movie, *Scrambled Wives,* in 1921. After her husband's death in 1936, she managed his air-service business before selling it to a larger airline. The actress died in September 25, 1940, in New York City.

Clark, Mattie Moss (1929–1998)

Gospel singer. Born in 1929; died in 1998; children: Jackie Clark; Denise Clark; Elbernita (called Twinkie); Dorinda; Karen.

Mattie Moss Clark, America's leading female choir director, trained gospel headliners Donald Vails, Rance Allen, and **Beverly Glenn.** As national minister of music for the Churches of God in Christ, she directed many choirs, the most famous of which was the Churches of God in Christ Southwest Michigan State Choir. Her most prominent pupils, however, were her daughters, a famed gospel group known as the **Clark Sisters:** Jackie, Denise, Elbernita (called Twinkie), Dorinda, and Karen.

Clark, Septima Poinsette (1898–1987)

African-American educator, civil-rights activist, humanitarian, training director for Southern Christian Leadership Conference, and driving force behind the influential Citizenship Schools. Born Septima Poinsette on May 3, 1898, in Charleston, South Carolina; died on December 15, 1987, on John's Island, South Carolina; daughter of Peter Porcher Poinsette (born a slave on the Poinsette plantation, later worked as a caterer on a steamship) and Victoria Warren Anderson Poinsette (freeborn in Charleston and reared in Haiti); graduated (12th grade) from Avery Normal Institute, a private school to train black teachers in Charleston, S.C., 1916; awarded A.B., Benedict College, 1942; granted M.A., Hampton Institute, 1946; married Nerie David Clark, May 1920 (died of kidney failure in December 1925); children: daughter (who died within a month of birth); son, Nerie David, Jr. (b. 1925).

Awards: Martin Luther King Award from SCLC (1970); Race Relations Award from National Education Association (1976); the Septima P. Clark Expressway named after her in Charleston (1978); honorary Doctor of Humane Letters, College of Charleston

(1978); received Order of the Palmetto from Governor Richard Riley (1982).

Unable to teach in Charleston public schools because of race, obtained a position at the Promiseland School on John's Island, South Carolina; took a position with Avery Normal School and joined in a political crusade to change the law barring black teachers in the Charleston public schools (1919); enrolled in college, earning her bachelor's degree (1942) and master's (1946); as a longtime member of the NAACP, refused to renounce her affiliation when South Carolina passed a law prohibiting NAACP membership for state or city employees; thus, fired from her teaching job at the Henry Archer School (1956); hired as director of education for Highlander Folk School (HFS) in Tennessee by Myles Horton for adult literacy programs; taught skills to enable deep South blacks to qualify to vote and become effective citizens in her Citizenship Schools, based at HFS; because of harassment by Tennessee officials at Highlander, her citizenship training was moved to the Southern Christian Leadership Conference (SCLC), where she continued to conduct literacy training programs that substantially increased the rolls of black voters (early 1960s); retired from SCLC (1970), age 72; elected to the Charleston School Board (1976).

Septima Clark had been teaching successfully for 40 years when she was suddenly fired for being a member of the National Association for the Advancement of Colored People (NAACP). At age 58, Septima Clark was about to become a legend of the civil-rights era.

Septima Poinsette Clark was born just as the prejudicial "Jim Crow" codes of the South were being solidified, two years after the 1896 *Plessy* v. *Ferguson* decision by the U.S. Supreme Court. In that decision, the Court found no violation of the Constitution in the new segregation laws being imposed throughout the South. Having witnessed the transition from slavery to freedom, it must have been particularly hard for her parents' generation to bear this dramatic retreat from the march to freedom. Clark told **Grace McFadden** that her mother had been a proud woman because she had been free-born, never a slave. "I never gave a white woman a drink of water," Septima recalled her mother saying. In contrast, Septima's father, an extremely gentle man, had experienced slavery on the Joel Poinsette plantation near Georgetown, South Carolina. Fortunately, Clark inherited a bit of both personalities. "His nonviolence helped me to work with the people" in rough places of Mississippi and Texas, noted Clark,

"and her haughtiness helped me to stay, enduring the harassment."

After a secure childhood in Charleston, Septima attended Avery Normal Institute through the 12th grade, graduating in 1916 with a license to teach. Her first position was in a small school on John's Island, where she and another teacher taught 132 children. Though the white teacher at the whites-only school on the island had only three pupils, she received a salary of $85 per month, compared to Septima's $35. This experience figured significantly in Clark's efforts on behalf of salary equalization, which she began after returning to teach at her alma mater, the Avery Normal Institute, in 1919. Inspired by the rhetoric of black leaders Edwin Halston and Thomas Ezekiel Miller, whom she heard address the issue of unequal pay for black teachers at NAACP meetings, Clark participated in a petition drive, going door to door for signatures. In addition to equal pay, the campaign worked to secure for blacks the right to teach in the Charleston public schools and the right to be named as school principals. As she has written in her autobiography, *Echo in My Soul*, the petition-drive proved effective in prompting the state legislature to enact their demands into law in 1920.

Septima married Nerie Clark in 1920. It was not a happy union. During the early years of their marriage, Nerie was in the navy, and a daughter died soon after birth. In 1925, after the birth of their son Nerie, Jr., the couple separated. That same year, Nerie Clark died of kidney failure; Septima remained close to his parents.

To provide for Nerie, Jr., Septima Clark moved in with her in-laws in Hickory, North Carolina. Then, in 1929, she moved to Columbia, South Carolina. Unable to support her son, she sent him back to Hickory to live with his paternal grandparents until he completed high school. During this period, Clark returned to school to earn an A.B. from Benedict College (1942). In the summer of 1944, she began working toward her M.A. at Hampton Institute. Taking courses for three summers, she earned the degree in 1946. Earlier, in 1937, she had taken a course, under W.E.B. Du Bois at Atlanta University, entitled "Interpersonal Relationships of Human Beings." Du Bois predicted a time when the segregation laws of the South would be abolished. His example of teaching and activism provided Clark with an inspiring model for her later work at Highlander and with the Southern Christian Leadership Conference (SCLC) Citizenship Schools.

In Columbia, Clark began working with Wil Lou Gray of the South Carolina Adult Education Program, who was developing a literacy training program for the U.S. army at Camp Jackson. The emphasis was on practical literacy, that is, students learned to sign their names, read paychecks, maps, bus schedules, and the like, as well as basic arithmetic. Clark would use this model for citizenship training at the Highlander School and for the SCLC, more than 20 years later.

It was while teaching in the elementary level at the Booker T. Washington School in Columbia that Clark resumed her political fight for better wages for South Carolina's black teachers. Another renowned civil-rights leader, ❧➤ **Modjeska M. Simkins**, was a math teacher in the same school. They, along with principal J. Andrew Simmons, challenged the lower pay scale for black teachers in federal court. Assisted by the NAACP, which sent Thurgood Marshall to represent them, the case was argued before Judge Julius Waties Waring of the District Court for the Eastern District of South Carolina. Waring issued a favorable ruling requiring equal salaries for black and white teachers. As a result, Clark's salary was increased. "When I went to Columbia, my salary was $65 a month. When I left I was getting almost $400 a month," she wrote in *Echo*.

In 1947, Septima moved back to Charleston to be nearer her mother, who had suffered a stroke. That year, Judge Waring was involved in another case brought by the NAACP, *Elmore* v. *Rice*, in which he ruled that the Southern practice of holding "whites only" primaries violated the U.S. Constitution. Waring's pro-civil-rights decisions made him extremely unpopular in the white community of Charleston and elsewhere in the state. To make matters worse, Clark developed a friendship with the Warings after she extended an invitation to Mrs. Waring to speak out against segregation before the (black) YWCA, an event reported in the newspapers. After repeated harassments and a number of violent threats against the Warings by white supremacists, the couple decided to leave the South and move to New York City in 1950. Septima Clark was also criticized by her family and friends, and by the administration of her school, for having transgressed the racial code when she visited the Warings' home and entered through the front door.

In 1954, Clark paid a visit to the Highlander School, run by Myles Horton, near Chattanooga, Tennessee. There, she found blacks and whites living and working together. The experi-

❧➤ **Simkins, Modjeska M. (b. 1899)**
African-American civil-rights activist and educator. Born Mary Modjeska Monteith on December 5, 1899, in South Carolina; eldest child of Henry Clarence Monteith and Rachel Evelyn (Hull) Monteith; Benedict College, A.B., 1921; also attended Columbia University, Morehouse College, University of Michigan, and Eastern Michigan University (then Michigan State Normal School); married Andrew Whitfield Simkins (a businessman).

In 1931, after teaching at the Booker T. Washington School in Columbia, South Carolina, Modjeska Simkins was named "Director of Negro Work" for the South Carolina Tuberculosis Association. For the next 11 years, she set up clinics for TB testing at schools, churches, and sometimes on the plantations; she also circulated a newsletter and held conferences. When a jittery state senate demanded that all state employees, including Simkins, break from the NAACP, she refused and was discreetly fired. She then began her long campaign as an agitator for civil rights.

ence had a powerful impact on her, she told **Cynthia Brown**, because that "wasn't done" in South Carolina. When she returned to Highlander in the summer of 1955, escorting groups from South Carolina to attend integration workshops, she chanced to meet *****Rosa Parks**, an attendee from Montgomery, Alabama. Parks appeared meek and timid, writes Clark in *Ready from Within*; thus, she was surprised when Parks made headlines that year by refusing to move to the back of the bus, that refusal precipitated the year-long Montgomery Bus Boycott.

> ⁀he greatest evil in our country today is not racism but ignorance.
> —**Septima Poinsette Clark**

The NAACP continued to win segregation cases, the most noteworthy being the *Brown* v. *Board of Education of Topeka, Kansas* Supreme Court case of 1954, declaring segregated school systems illegal. Subsequently, Southern state policymakers initiated campaigns of repression against the NAACP and other civil-rights organizations. In South Carolina, in April of 1956, the state legislature passed a law making it illegal for employees of the state or city governments to belong to a civil-rights group. Since Clark would not renounce or hide her NAACP membership, she was fired from her teaching position at the Henry Archer School in Charleston (as were ten other blacks). The 58-year-old Clark, with 40 years experience as a teacher, also lost her pension. (Twenty years later, the state legislature would yield to pressure from the National Education Association and grant her a small pension of $3,600 per year.)

Myles Horton took this opportunity to recruit Clark to work at the Highlander School, located on a 200-acre farm about 50 miles to the northeast of Chattanooga, outside the town of Monteagle. Hired full-time to direct the workshops, Clark expanded this into a general program of citizenship training that eventually qualified thousands of Southern blacks to pass the literacy tests that enabled them to vote.

The Highlander School, like other organizations promoting integration and civil rights, soon drew fire from the authorities. It had often been called a "communist" organization by its critics, including the local paper. In 1957, when Martin Luther King, Jr. addressed a group assembled in honor of Highlander's 25th anniversary, a photograph was published of King standing near another man, apparently unknown to King, who was there to report the event for *The Daily Worker*, an American Communist Party newspaper. Reproduced widely, the photograph even adorned billboards, said Clark, to prove that King was a communist and Highlander was a "communist training center."

Such publicity attracted the attention of the Tennessee state legislature, which debated the legality of the Highlander organization. In July of 1959, the state police raided Highlander on a warrant for illegally selling liquor. They seized some dusty jugs from the basement as evidence and, because she was the manager of Highlander at the time, locked Clark in jail overnight. As a result of the raid, Highlander had its charter revoked. A panel of admittedly biased jurors, writes **Donna Langston**, found the school guilty on three trumped-up charges. The school property, valued at $175,000, was confiscated by the state.

Clark did not remain idle long. She developed "Citizenship Schools" in a number of places throughout the South. Her prototype was set up on John's Island, off the South Carolina coast, where most of the island's black population could not read or write. Secretly, Highlander paid for the rental of a classroom and for minimal supplies, fearing that whites would put an end to the schools if they learned of them. As William Ayers writes in the *Harvard Educational Review*: "Learning to read in the South of *Ella Baker and Septima Clark was a subversive

activity, an activity that many thought could change the fundamental structure of the Jim Crow system."

The training programs began by teaching the non-traditional students to write their names in cursive script, as required on the ballot forms. It then moved to practical reading and writing, drawing content from the daily routines of the students. The schools were organized around work schedules. Classes were more often held during winter months because there was less field work to be done then. Clark hoped that graduates would become the next wave of teachers, thereby multiplying the effect of her efforts. By 1961, 82 teachers from the Citizenship Schools were holding classes in Alabama, Georgia, South Carolina, and Tennessee.

Though she began having health problems soon after her ouster in Charleston, Clark did not let it slow her work. In 1957, working at Highlander with some women from Montgomery, she suffered a heart attack and spent four days in the Sewanee hospital, integrating it in the process. It was the "first time a black person had ever been in the Sewanee hospital," she told Brown. She experienced a second heart attack in January of 1961, which forced her to rest for several weeks.

That summer, King invited Clark to move to the SCLC headquarters in Atlanta. From that base, she organized Citizenship Schools, assisted by the United Church of Christ (UCC) organization of New York, and by Andrew Young, who was working for the UCC at that time. Through them, the SCLC acquired use of the Dorchester Cooperative Community Center in McIntosh, Georgia, located about 40 miles south of Savannah, as a home base. At Dorchester, Clark, Young, and **Dorothy Cotton** created a well-structured program for teacher training, inviting up to 70 individuals for weeklong training sessions. The Marshall Field Foundation, which had supported Clark's work at Highlander, contributed a $250,000 grant to the SCLC for the Citizenship Schools project, enabling Clark to bring in more trainees and pay them a small stipend.

Her work with the SCLC brought her notoriety. By 1963, the FBI regarded her with suspicion. That spring, as the Birmingham protests resulted in mass arrests of nonviolent demonstrators, officials wondered at the resolve and organization evidenced by the marchers. FBI officials suspected a conspiracy and "took note of a report from the Savannah office that the Negroes," writes Taylor Branch, "'were all trained' at Septima Clark's Dorchester retreat." This was false. Only a small percentage of the protestors at Birmingham had been to the Dorchester literacy and voter registration training sessions.

As newly literate black voters tried to register, they encountered more barriers, like tests without objective answers, the correctness of an answer depending on the whim of the registrar. It has been reported that even highly educated black citizens, some with doctoral degrees, were denied the right to vote in this way. Responding to such procedural devices, Clark participated in protests and in lobbying Washington to have these practices stopped. Eventually, in 1965, Congress passed the Voting Rights Act, and the federal government subsequently moved with a firm hand to end voting discrimination in the South. This greatly simplified the work of the teachers at the Citizenship Schools. The new requirement simply called for a ballot form signed in cursive writing, a skill relatively easy to teach. Preparing for the next election in 1966, Clark set up 150 Citizenship Schools in Selma, Alabama, from May 18 to August 15, 1965, paying teachers $1.25 an hour for two hours of teaching every weekday morning. They registered over 7,000, and the new voters soon made themselves heard. By 1972, Andrew Young of Georgia and *Barbara Jordan of Texas became the first African-Americans elected to the U.S. Congress from any of the 11 states of the "Deep South" in the 20th century, and the number of black officeholders at all levels began to increase steadily.

When the Voting Rights Act was passed in 1965, Clark was 67 years old and ready to reduce her level of activity. The following year, after ten years of full-time civil-rights work, she bought a house for herself and her sister, which needed substantial repairs. She turned her attentions to that task. Though Clark officially retired from the SCLC in 1970, she remained active and, in 1976, became the first African-American woman to be elected to the Charleston School Board, the same board that had fired her 20 years earlier.

Late in life, Septima Clark received much deserved recognition for her work. A portion of the cross-town expressway in Charleston, from Spring Street to Coming Street, was named the Septima P. Clark Expressway in 1978. That year, she was honored by the College of Charleston, which bestowed upon her an honorary doctorate. In 1982, South Carolina governor Richard Riley awarded her the Order of the Palmetto. "If I were young again, starting all over," wrote Clark, "I'd do the same things over and over

again. We do have problems. But I have lived so long that I have seen great progress."

SOURCES:
Ayers, William. "'We Who Believe in Freedom Cannot Rest Until It's Done': Two Dauntless Women of the Civil Rights Movement and the Education of a People," in *Harvard Educational Review*. Vol. 59, no. 4. November 1989.
Branch, Taylor. *Parting the Waters: America in the King Years 1954–1963*. NY: Simon and Schuster, 1988.
Clark, Septima P. *Echo In My Soul*. NY: E.P. Dutton, 1962.
———. *Ready from Within* (as told to Cynthia Stokes Brown). Navarro, CA: Wild Trees Press, 1986.
Crawford, Vicki, *et al*, eds. *Black Women in United States History: Trailblazers and Torchbearers, 1941–1965*. Brooklyn, NY: Carlson, 1990.
Langston, Donna. "The Women of Highlander," in *Black Women in United States History*. Edited by Vicki Crawford, *et al*. Brooklyn, NY: Carlson, 1990.
McFadden, Grace Jordan. "Clark, Septima Poinsette," in *Black Women in America, Vol 1*. Brooklyn, NY: Carlson, 1993.
Salem, Dorothy C., ed. "Clark, Septima," in *African-American Women: A Biographical Dictionary*. NY: Garland, 1993.

SUGGESTED READING:
McFadden, Grace Jordan. *Oral Recollections of Septima Poinsette Clark*. Columbia: USC Instructional Services Center, 1980.

COLLECTIONS:
Septima Clark Collection, Robert Scott Small Library, Charleston, South Carolina; Highlander Folk School files, State Historical Society of Wisconsin, Madison; Southern Oral History Program Collection, Southern Historical Collection, University of North Carolina-Chapel Hill; Papers of the Southern Christian Leadership Conference, 1954–1970, Archives of the Martin Luther King, Jr., Center for Social Change, Atlanta, Georgia.

Michael D. Cary,
Chair, Department of History and Political Science,
Seton Hill College, Greensburg, Pennsylvania

Clark, Sharon Stouder (b. 1948).

See Stouder, Sharon.

Clark Sisters (fl. 1940s)

Singing swing specialists of the 1940s. Inspired and coached by Sy Oliver.

The four Clark Sisters—Ann, Jean, Peggy, and Mary Clark—starred as "The Sentimentalists" with Tommy Dorsey's orchestra, doing the vocals on "Chicago" and "The Sunny Side of the Street." They sang as instrumentalists, delivering the big-band orchestral stylings of the swing years. Their albums include *Sing, Sing, Sing!* and *The Clark Sisters Swing Again* on Dot Records.

Clarke.

Variant of Clark, Clerk, and Clerke.

Clarke, Edith (1883–1959)

American engineer. Born on February 10, 1883, in Howard County, Maryland; died on October 29, 1959, in Olney, Maryland; daughter of a lawyer-farmer; A.B. in math and astronomy from Vassar College, 1908; civil engineering courses at the University of Wisconsin, 1911–12; M.S. in electrical engineering from Massachusetts Institute of Technology (1919).

Edith Clarke's career as an engineer would be marked by many firsts. She was to gain prominence as the first woman elected to the Society of Electrical Engineers, the first woman to earn a master's degree from the Massachusetts Institute of Technology (MIT), the first woman to address the American institute of Electrical Engineers, and the first woman to teach electrical engineering in an American university. Clarke was born on February 10, 1883, in Maryland where her father was a lawyer and a gentleman farmer. When Edith was seven, her father died, and her mother took charge of the farm until her own death five years later. Edith's uncle was appointed guardian over the orphaned children, the eldest of whom, **Mary**, reared her siblings. Edith used her share of the inheritance for college tuition at Vassar, a decision that earned her rebukes from some relatives.

Although Clarke wanted to study engineering, Vassar had not opened this field to women in the early 1900s. She studied instead math and physics, graduating in 1908 with an A.B. in math and astronomy. After teaching math and physics for three years, Clarke became seriously ill. "Thinking I was going to die," she would later tell a reporter, "I just decided to do what I really wanted to do—study engineering." A year's training at the University of Wisconsin's School of Engineering was followed by seven years (1912–18) of work for the American Telephone & Telegraph Company (AT&T). She was accepted to study electrical engineering at MIT from which she would earn her M.S. (1919). During her days at MIT, Clarke became interested in symmetrical components, a complicated mathematical technique invented by Charles Fortescue for quick computing. She developed a convenient version of the technique that made it workable, and the new components, named "Clarke components," streamlined complex equations in the pre-computer age when equations had to be worked out by hand.

Upon graduation from MIT in 1919, Clarke could not find a job better than her old position at AT&T, which involved supervising a group of "girls" in a computing pool. Instead, she traveled to Constantinople where she spent a year teaching engineering as a visiting professor of physics at the Istanbul Woman's College in Turkey (1920). When Clarke returned, she was finally hired as an electrical engineer by General Electric (GE). During a career with GE that would span 23 years, she analyzed power transmission problems that were submitted by power companies from across the United States. Clarke is credited with placing circuit theory on firm mathematical ground during her time at GE. In February 1926, she became the first woman to address the American Institute of Electrical Engineers (AIEE), speaking at its convention in New York on "Steady-State Stability in Transmission Systems." In 1940, she was among the only three women members of AIEE, an organization that had a membership of 17,000 (**Vivien Kellems** and **Mabel McFerran Rockwell** shared this distinction with Clarke). Destined to be called the "foremost woman engineer in history," in 1943 Clarke published what would become the major textbook in her field, *Circuit Analysis of AC Power Systems, Symmetrical and Related Components.*

Clarke was 62 when she left GE. She then served as a professor at the University of Texas, Austin, where, in addition to teaching, she published and received honors from the AIEE (of which she was elected fellow in 1948) and from the Society of Women Engineers, which awarded her its Achievement Award in 1954. She taught at the University of Texas until 1959, the year of her death in Olney, Maryland, on October 29.

Clarke, Mrs. Edward (1906–1983).
See Lutyens, Elisabeth.

Clarke, Helen Archibald (1860–1926).
See joint entry under Porter, Charlotte Endymion (1857–1942).

Clarke, Kathleen (1878–1972)

Irish republican activist. Name variations: Mrs. Tom Clarke. Born Kathleen Daly in Limerick, Ireland, on April 11, 1878; died in Liverpool, England, on September 29, 1972; daughter of Edward Daly and Catherine (O'Mara) Daly; educated privately; married Thomas J. Clarke, on July 16, 1901 (died May 3, 1916); children: three sons, John Daly, Thomas and Emmet.

Kathleen Clarke was born into a family that had long been prominent in Irish republican circles, and she remained a dedicated republican throughout her long life while witnessing the execution of both her husband and her only brother for the sake of the republican cause. Both her father Edward and her uncle John were prominent Fenians, members of the secret revolutionary brotherhood dedicated to the overthrow of British rule in Ireland and to the establishment of an independent Irish republic. Her father had been arrested at the age of 17 in 1865 for suspected Fenian activities, and in 1884 John Daly was arrested and convicted for dynamiting activities in England and sentenced to penal servitude for life. While in Portland Prison, he met Thomas Clarke who had been sentenced to penal servitude in 1883, also for dynamite activities, and they became close friends.

Kathleen Clarke came from a large family of nine girls and one boy; her only brother Edward (Ned) was born five months after her father's death in 1890. She recalled that at bedtime, the first prayer was "always for Irish freedom." Her grandmother lived until the age of 97 and died "a rebel against England to her last breath." Her aunt **Ellen Daly** was a formative influence in her childhood and told her many stories from Irish history, especially about the Fenians who were active in the 1860s and 1870s. She painted the Fenian period, recalled her niece, "in the most glowing and romantic colours."

At the age of 16, Kathleen was apprenticed to a dressmaker. Two years later, displaying the determination and independence that was a marked feature of her character, she rented premises and set up her own prospering business. In 1896, her uncle John was released from prison and returned to Limerick where he established his own bakery. In 1899, he was elected mayor of Limerick and set up a branch of the Irish Labor Party in the city. Kathleen refused to go into the bakery business as some of her sisters did, preferring her own independence.

Thomas Clarke was eventually released from prison in October 1898 and when he came to stay with John Daly early the following year he was given the Freedom of Limerick. In poor health after his 15 years in prison, he looked much older than his 40 years. Kathleen Clarke recalled in her autobiography that her first impression of him was one of keen disappointment after what she had heard of him from her uncle. But they became friends and, in the summer of 1899, became engaged, though the betrothal, while welcomed by her uncle, was opposed by her mother and her aunt because of Thomas Clarke's lack of prospects. These looked so unpromising that at one point Thomas offered to release her from the engagement. He went to the United States in 1900 and obtained employ-

ment. Kathleen gave up her business and joined him in New York where they were married in July 1901. Their first son was born the following year when Thomas started work for the American counterpart organization of the Fenians, Clan na Gael. The Clan was setting up a newspaper, the *Gaelic American*, of which Thomas became general manager. He also started the Brooklyn Gaelic Society and was involved with the Clan na Gael Volunteers. He and Kathleen ran an ice cream and candy store, and in 1906 they bought a small farm on Long Island.

By 1907, Thomas was anxious to return to Ireland and help reorganize the republican cause. Though reluctant to leave America, Kathleen agreed. They left in November 1907 and over the next two years opened several shops in Dublin. Their shop in O'Connell Street, Dublin's principal street, soon became the center for the reorganization of revolutionary republicanism in Ireland, attracting a number of young organizers, among them Sean MacDermott who became one of Thomas' closest associates. A new journal, *Irish Freedom,* was founded and with this, as Kathleen Clarke recalled, "the work towards the Rising began." She was deep in her husband's confidence and became an ever more trusted confidante as the plans for a rebellion against British rule gradually took shape.

Kathleen was present at the first meeting in April 1914 of the women's auxiliary organization of the Irish Volunteers, Cumann na mBan (the Women's Club). She and **Aine Ceannt**, wife of Eamon Ceannt who was also to be executed in 1916, started the Central Branch of Cumann na mBan of which Kathleen Clarke was later president. When the First World War broke out, both the Irish Volunteers and Cumann na mBan split over whether to support the British war effort. The membership of the Central Branch declined from 200 to about 24. Kathleen Clarke remained with the anti-British group and ran classes and lectures in first aid, rifle practice, and signalling, preparations for a rebellion that she now knew her husband and his associates were planning to take place during the war.

The Rising was planned for Easter 1916. Shortly before it was due to occur, Thomas Clarke told his wife that in the event of the arrest of the leaders, she had been chosen as the custodian of their plans, which she was to pass on to the next in command. She memorized the names of all the key men in the organization around the country and, knowing what was being planned, feared for the future. Knowledge of the key role her husband played in these events made her extremely protective of his reputation in later life; in her autobiography, she was disparaging of, among others, Patrick Pearse and Roger Casement whom she felt did not deserve the prominence they attracted after 1916.

Thomas Clarke was the first signatory of the Proclamation of the Irish Republic, read by Patrick Pearse outside the General Post Office in O'Connell Street on Easter Monday, 1916. "I felt Tom would not come through," wrote Kathleen, "and I think he knew he would not, but neither of us would admit it." They had three sons and she was expecting a fourth child but decided not to tell him of her pregnancy. On the previous Thursday, Kathleen had gone down to Limerick with dispatches for the local Irish Volunteers and left her children with her mother so that she would be free for the Rising. Thomas had told her not to get involved and to hold herself in readiness for what might happen afterwards.

After a week of intense fighting, the rebels surrendered on the Saturday after the proclamation and the following day the Clarke house was raided and Kathleen Clarke was arrested and escorted to Dublin Castle. She was taken to see her husband in Kilmainham Jail the night before he was shot for his part in the rebellion. To her horror, he told her that her only brother Ned, who had taken part in the Rising, was also to be executed. They had a poignant farewell, repeated a few days later when she saw her brother the night before his death. Kathleen subsequently miscarried the baby she was expecting.

She was released from detention and within days of her husband's death she set up the Irish Republican Prisoners Dependants' Fund (IRPDF), to help not just the families of the executed men but also those of the hundreds of men and women who had been deported and interned without trial. Thomas Clarke had left her over £3,000 pounds of republican funds, which she distributed to the dependants with the help of Cumann na mBan. The IRPDF later merged with Irish National Aid to form the National Aid and Volunteers' Dependants' Fund (NAVDF); as secretary of the new organization, Kathleen Clarke chose a young man who had just been released from internment in England, Michael Collins, whom she remembered for "his forceful personality, his wonderful magnetism and his organizing ability." She was more waspish about other survivors of the Rising, especially Eoin MacNeill (who had tried to cancel the plans at the last minute) and Cathal Brugha. Clarke was also noticeably cool towards some of the other prominent women in the move-

ment, including **Mary MacSwiney** and *Count-ess Markievicz.

When the British government started to release the rebellion prisoners in 1917, they began to reorganize the Sinn Fein party as a political movement. At its first conference in October 1917, Kathleen Clarke was elected to the executive and became vice-president of Cumann na mBan. In May 1918, she was arrested with other Sinn Fein leaders, including Eamon de Valera, on suspicion of plotting with the Germans. No proof was ever produced and there was no trial. She was imprisoned at Holloway Jail in London and was not released until February 1919 by which time her health had deteriorated seriously, in part through anxiety for her children. Her fellow prisoners included *Maud Gonne and Countess Markievicz, and she was considerably annoyed when she heard that the countess had been chosen, while she had not, to represent Sinn Fein in the parliamentary elections of December 1918; she regarded this selection as an insult to her husband's memory and her own ability. The Sinn Fein leaders, she noted caustically, were "not over-eager to put women into places of honor or power." However, in the 1919 municipal elections for Dublin Corporation, she was elected an alderman. By now the Irish war of independence was at its height, and she served on the executive committee of the White Cross organization, which helped to alleviate distress among the families and dependants affected by the war. Her own home in Dublin was continually raided by British forces. As a further deliberate reprisal, her mother's home in Limerick was burned to the ground along with its contents. In May 1921, she was elected to the Irish republican parliament, the Dail.

When the Anglo-Irish Treaty was signed in December 1921, Clarke rejected the terms for Irish independence demanded by the British government. In her speech to the Dail explaining the reasons for her rejection of the treaty, she recalled her last visit to her husband before his execution. She would never go back on the oath she had taken to the Irish republic, she told the Dail, and she regarded the treaty as "a surrender of all our ideals." Increasingly disturbed as the country lurched towards civil war in 1922, she retained her affection for Michael Collins although he had signed the treaty she opposed. In the general elections of June 1922, she lost her Dail seat. When the civil war broke out, she sympathized with the republicans but took no active part in the war, although this did not prevent her house from being raided by the forces of the new Irish government.

She became involved with a new dependants' fund, this time for republican prisoners, and toured America for money on their behalf. The civil war ended in May 1923 but the republicans remained in a political limbo, refusing to take their seats in the new Irish Parliament. This policy of abstention was finally opposed by de Valera, the republican leader, and Kathleen Clarke supported him when he decided to set up a new political party, Fianna Fail. She was on the first executive of Fianna Fail and was briefly elected to the Irish Parliament in 1927 though she did not take her seat. De Valera then decided to end the policy of abstention and Fianna Fail entered the Parliament in late 1927. In 1928, Kathleen Clarke accepted nomination for the Irish senate where she served until 1936. In 1930, she was again elected to Dublin Corporation.

Fianna Fail won the general election in 1932, but over the following years Kathleen Clarke experienced growing disillusionment with the party and its leader, de Valera, whom she regarded as socially conservative, especially in relation to women. She opposed the clauses of his 1937 constitution, which concerned women and was censured by the party. In June 1939, despite opposition from within her own party, she was elected the first woman Lord Mayor of Dublin, and controversy attended one of her first actions in office—the removal of a large portrait of Queen *Victoria. She condemned the bombing campaign that the Irish Republican Army initiated in Britain in 1939–40 but opposed de Valera's policy of internment and arrests of IRA men. When IRA men were executed in 1940, she ordered the flag of Dublin City Hall to be flown at half-mast. Her term as Lord Mayor finished in 1941 and her uncomfortable membership in Fianna Fail was finally terminated in 1943.

Clarke stood as a candidate in the 1948 general election for the new republican party, Clann na Poblachta, but was defeated. This marked her effective retirement from political life although she continued to serve on the boards of several Dublin hospitals. In 1965, she moved to England to live with her youngest son, Dr. Emmet Daly, but returned to Dublin the following year for the 50th anniversary celebrations of the 1916 Rising. She was conferred with an honorary doctorate of the National University of Ireland by its chancellor, Eamon de Valera. When she died in September 1972, Kathleen Clarke was given a state funeral.

SOURCES:
Clarke, Kathleen. *Revolutionary Woman: An Autobiography.* O'Brien Press, 1991.

Ward, Margaret. *Unmanageable Revolutionaries: Women and Irish Nationalism.* Brandon, 1983.

Deirdre McMahon, Dublin, Ireland,
Assistant Editor, *Dance Theatre Journal* (London),
and author of *Republicans and Imperialists*
(Yale University Press, 1984)

Clarke, Mary Anne (c. 1776–1852)

English mistress of Frederick, duke of York, second son of George III. Name variations: Maryanne Clark. Born Mary Anne Thompson, either in London or at Oxford, around 1776; died at her estate at Boulogne on June 21, 1852; daughter of a man named Thompson (an impoverished bricklayer); received a modest education at Ham; married a man named Clarke (a proprietor of a stonemasonry business), around 1794.

Known for her wit and beauty, Mary Anne Clarke was married before she was 18. She left her husband, the proprietor of a stonemasonry business, when he took to drink and went bankrupt. After liaisons with Sir Charles Milner and Sir James Brudenell, in 1804 she became mistress of Frederick Augustus, duke of York and Albany, second son of King George III. Frederick, who was then commander-in-chief of the British army, settled Clarke in a large, expensive house in Gloucester Place, a fashionable district, with three carriages, ten horses, 20 servants, and an allowance of £1,000 per annum. The duke's promised allowance was not regularly paid, however, and to escape financial difficulties Clarke used the duke's position to sell army commissions, promotions, and transfers, undercutting the government, which was also in the business of selling the same. Her machinations brought on a public scandal in early 1809, when Colonel Gwillym Wardle, the M.P. for Salisbury, made a startling speech in the House of Commons. Eight charges of abuse of military patronage were levied against the duke, and a committee of inquiry was selected. Mary Anne Clarke appeared before the committee to give evidence. Though it was fairly obvious that the duke of York was aware of her dealings, he had not financially benefitted and was cleared of the charges. He resigned his appointment as commander-in-chief and terminated his affair with Clarke, who subsequently secured from him a considerable cash sum and a pension: the price for her withholding publication of his many letters to her. In 1814, she was imprisoned for nine months for libelling the Irish chancellor of the exchequer. Following her release, Clarke, who had been shrewd with her money, moved to Paris and set up an elegant salon where she entertained comfortably for several decades.

Clarke, Mary Cowden (1809–1898)

English Shakespearean scholar. Name variations: *Mary Cowden-Clarke. Born Mary Victoria Novello in London, England, on June 22, 1809; died in Italy on January 12, 1898; daughter of Vincent Novello (a composer and organist) and Mary Sabilla Hehl; educated at home and in France; married Charles Cowden Clarke (a literary historian), in 1828.*

Mary Cowden Clarke was the daughter of **Mary Sabilla Hehl** and Vincent Novello, a composer and organist. In her youth, she frequently met her father's associates, including Shelley, Coleridge, Charles and *Mary Anne Lamb, Keats, Leigh Hunt, Hazlitt and other literary celebrities of the day. Their influence undoubtedly fueled the early development of her intellectual powers, and by her 15th year she was a contributor to magazines. In 1828, she married Charles Cowden Clarke, a literary historian, and soon began the *Complete Concordance to Shakespeare*, with which her name was to become associated. After 16 years of uninterrupted labor, this work was published in London in 1846, in a large octavo of 860 pages, and remained the standard concordance until the end of the 19th century.

Clarke's services to Shakespearean literature became widely acknowledged. Among the tokens of appreciation bestowed upon her was a memorial from America consisting of a chair ornamented with small figures of tragedy and comedy carved from the Shakespeare mulberry tree, as well as a replica of the Stratford bust of the great dramatist. Nearly every state in the Union contributed. The author of many novels and essays, Clarke collaborated with her husband on *The Shakespeare Key* (1879) and *Recollections of Writers* (1898). She was also the editor of the *Musical Times* (1853–56).

SUGGESTED READING:
Altick, R.D. *The Cowden Clarkes.*
Clarke, Mary Cowden. *My Long Life.* 1896.

Clarke, Mary Goulden (d. 1910).

See Pankhurst, Emmeline for sidebar.

Clarke, Maryanne (c. 1776–1852).

See Clarke, Mary Anne.

Clarke, Rebecca (1886–1979)

English composer who created over 58 songs and 20 instrumental or chamber works. Name variations: *(pseudonym) Anthony Trent. Born in Harrow, England, on August 27, 1886; died in New York City on October 13, 1979; studied with Sir Frederick Bridge,* Sir Charles Stanford, and Lionel Tetris, and at the Royal College of Music; married James Friskin (a pianist), in 1944.

For a number of years, Rebecca Clarke submitted her compositions under the name of Anthony Trent, reporting that publishers were more interested in modern compositions by someone presumed to be male. Despite this prejudice against women composers, she also composed under her own name. Trained at the Royal College of Music in London, Clarke was a concert violinist as well as a composer, influenced by Dame *Ethel Smyth as well as Sir Edgar Elgar, Ralph Vaughn Williams, and Gustav Holst. She founded an all women's piano quartet, the English Ensemble, in 1913. In 1919, she won second place for her viola sonata at the Berkshire Festival in Tanglewood, Massachusetts, established by *Elizabeth Sprague Coolidge. Clarke won the second prize again in the same competition in 1921. Her work was widely published by Winthrop Rogers and the Oxford University Press in Great Britain and by G. Schirmer in the United States. She was particularly known for her chamber music, which favored English musical themes and texts by William Shakespeare, William Butler Yeats, and William Blake. In August 1942, Clarke was the only woman among more than 30 composers present at the International Society for Contemporary Music in San Francisco where her Prelude, Allegro, and Pastorale for clarinet and viola was enthusiastically received. In addition to composing, Clarke toured widely as a concert violinist with her husband, pianist James Friskin. In recent years, several of her important chamber music compositions, including the Piano Trio, the Viola Sonata, and the Prelude for Viola and Clarinet, have been recorded.

John Haag,
Athens, Georgia

Clarke, Sara J. (1823–1904).

See Lippincott, Sara Clarke.

Clarke, Shirley (1925–1997)

American filmmaker and pioneer of the independent film movement. Born Shirley Brumberg, on October 2, 1925, in New York, New York; died after a long illness in Boston, Massachusetts, on September 23, 1997; attended Stephens College, Bennington College, Johns Hopkins University, and University of North Carolina; married Bert Clarke (divorced 1963); children: Wendy Clarke (b. 1951).

Filmography: Dance in the Sun *(1953);* Bullfight *(1955);* In Paris Parks *(1955);* A Moment in Love *(1957);* Loops *(1958);* Skyscraper *(1959);* Bridges-Go-Round *(1959);* A Scary Time *(1960);* The Connection *(1960);* The Cool World *(1964);* Robert Frost: A Lover's Quarrel with the World *(1964);* Man in the Polar Regions *(1967);* Vosnesensky *(not completed, 1967);* Portrait of Jason *(1967);* 24 Frames Per Second *(1977);* Initiation *(1978);* Four Journeys Into Mystic Time *(1980); (in collaboration with Sam Shepard)* Savage/Love *(1981);* Tongues *(1983); and a portrait of jazz musician Ornette Coleman,* Ornette: Made In America *(1986).*

In the mid-1960s, Shirley Clarke, and the avant-gardists who had formed the New American Cinema Group, spoke before would-be filmmakers at the New York Film Festival. A photograph of Clarke, shot at the event, presents a petite woman, her dark hair bobbed in a Beatle cut and a look in her eye so intense and passionate it belies her fragile appearance. Taking people by surprise on all fronts was Clarke's trademark. Her appearance and her upper-class background contradicted her career choices and certainly the subject matter she chose to explore. The advice she gave to students that day revealed a commitment to individual expression that was without artistic naivete. "I'll tell you something I learned the hard way," she told them. "Independent films need special treatment. [They] need to be treated not as one of a bucket of films but for what each individual film is saying."

Born to a wealthy Jewish family, Shirley Brumberg may have grown up on Park Avenue but she never felt as though she belonged. The eldest of three daughters in an intensely competitive family, Clarke rebelled against the expectations set by the Brumbergs and by the elite circles in which they lived. Her resistance to family pressures was probably due in part to a learning disability; she was unable to read until the fifth grade, unable to write until the seventh. As she told journalist **Marjorie Rosen** in an interview for *Ms.* magazine: "Until I discovered dance at 14, I was the outsider. But the child that observes has many advantages, she identifies with 'out' people." Though formal education was difficult (she attended four colleges), Clarke found her niche in the company of professional dancers like *Hanya Holm, *Doris Humphrey and modern-dance's great master, *Martha Graham. By age 17, Clarke's original choreography was presented at the 92nd Street YMHA in New York, a facility renowned for its commitment to new works by dancers, writers, and performance artists.

Still living at home with her parents, Clarke longed for independence, and Bert Clarke seemed to offer a way out. He was older, sophisticated, and supportive, and Shirley thought she was in love. But the marriage was a disappointment. Though they would divorce in 1963, they remained friends, and Bert financed many of Shirley's early dance films.

In 1951, during a long recovery that followed the birth of their daughter Wendy, Clarke began to rethink her creative direction. In an interview for *Dance Perspectives,* she told **Gretchen Berg,** "I got tired of rehearsing for six months for one performance at the 'Y' and wanted to preserve forever what everyone had worked so hard to achieve." Thinking it would be a simple matter to put dance on film, Clarke learned quickly how difficult it is to capture a live performance. Her first attempts, she admits, were horrendous, so she took a look at *Choreography for a Camera,* directed by *Maya Deren, a woman often called the mother of the avant-garde. Clarke articulated what Deren already knew, "that one had to destroy one art to be true to the other; dance as it existed had to be transformed into good film. Dance was not only a human being whirling in space, but also someone walking down the street, or your hair waving in the breeze."

> *There are no unrealized dreams, just the courage to do what I know I have to do.*
>
> —**Shirley Clarke**

Clarke began to develop what John Martin, *The New York Times'* dance critic, dubbed "Cine-Dance." Rather than documenting a dance as it exists on stage, Cine-dance can only exist on film. Clarke's early films are innovative examples of this unique genre. Documenting the development of *Dances in the Sun,* one of her first films, she told Berg: "I had seen the dance in the theatre and I had gotten the feeling of a place [the beach]. So I shot the identical dance on stage and [then] on the beach and I intercut the two. . . . The movements seemed enormous in time and space." Clarke knew she was onto something and wanted to continue to experiment with screen images set to music. While in Paris, she made *In Paris Parks,* a film about children playing in the park. Though the children never dance *per se,* the images seem to have a kinetic quality because they're supported by a musical score.

Bullfight, Clarke's third film, was even more ambitious. It cross cut three elements: a dancer, a bullfighter, and the audience watching both.

Though Clarke admits the idea was not entirely successful, she discovered that she could no longer rely on dances that had been specifically choreographed for the stage. For a dance to work on film, it had to be choreographed for film. With that idea in mind, Clarke made *A Moment in Love*. Eight minutes long, its simple premise involves a romantic encounter by a young couple in a wooded glen. The dance takes off with a leap into space. Through the use of technology, the young dancer-lovers are transformed into blossoming flowers.

Clarke's theories were taking wing. In her next movie, *Bridges-Go-Round*, she began to reinvent the entire definition of dance. In this film, the dancers are the bridges of Manhattan. Henry Breitrose in *Film Quarterly* called Clarke an "instinctive filmmaker"; the bridges "are manipulated in a complex but extremely arresting way."

In 1959, Willard Van Dyke, a filmmaker who had hired Clarke to make 15 two-and-a-half-minute films for the Brussel's World's Fair, commissioned her to make a short about the construction of a skyscraper. After a year of work, *Skyscraper,* which Clarke refers to as a musical comedy documenting the construction of a building, won a prize at the prestigious film festival in Venice, Italy, and was nominated for an American Academy Award for Best Short Subject. That same year, Clarke and fellow filmmakers Donn Alan Pennebaker, Willard Van Dyke, and Ricky Leacock started a filmmakers co-op in order to share space and equipment. Clarke was also invited to teach a filmmaking course at Northwestern. Though she had been uninterested in academia as a student, she found the atmosphere conducive for an experimental filmmaker and a good place to expose her work. At term's end, she returned to New York and taught film courses at Columbia.

In 1960, Clarke was asked to make a film for UNICEF, the United Nations' organization for children. Since her previous films had been creative, if somewhat whimsical, the United Nations' film unit most likely felt comfortable having Clarke at the helm. What they couldn't have known was Clarke's penchant for realism. Instead of showing the successes of UNICEF, Clarke's film, *A Scary Time,* was a searing look at the true-life horrors suffered by the world's impoverished children. The result was so overwhelming, the UN refused to release the film. According to Clarke, if internationally renowned filmmaker Roberto Rossellini had not come to her aid, the film would have been destroyed.

On September 28, Clarke and 23 independent filmmakers met at 165 West 46th Street and announced they would form The New American Cinema Group. Whereas Clarke's earlier co-op shared space and equipment, this group went much further. Their aim was to overturn the negative aspects of working independently, much of which had to do with the difficulty of distributing low-budget films and the struggle independents were having with the craft unions. Each member of the group pledged to put aside a certain amount of film profits in order to help other members finish films, aid in distribution, or stand as a bond for film labs. The coalition was an important step in the development of an independent film community that continues to grow.

Clarke then set out to make a feature film. Having seen Jack Gelber's play *The Connection* at the Living Theatre, she was so moved by its honesty she optioned it. Raising money, however, to fund a film that deals with hard-core heroin junkies proved daunting. Nevertheless, she and her co-producer Lewis Allen managed to raise the necessary capital, as they had always done, by forming a limited partnership. The film was shot on location in a gritty Harlem tenement. **Dorothy Oshlag** in *Sight and Sound* noted that the film works on several levels. On its surface, we watch as a group of heroin junkies wait for their "connection." A documentary filmmaker comes on the scene; he wants to photograph their lives. But on another level, Clarke uses the camera to pry into the junkies' private emotions to the point where the camera functions as another character.

Reactions to *The Connection* were explosive. Completed in early 1961, it won a prize at the Cannes Film Festival. "*The Connection* appears to be one of those legendary 'firsts' like *Citizen Kane* or *Breathless,* which not only succeed filmically, but also set the standards for other film work," wrote critic Jay Jacobs in *The Reporter.* No doubt Jacobs was correct. Films of the 1990s, such as the highly controversial *Kids,* directed by Larry Clark, and to some extent *Leaving Las Vegas,* directed by Mike Figgis, owe a debt of gratitude to Clarke's uncompromising look into the underbelly of life, specifically the drug culture. But its release in the United States was held up for 18 months while Clarke did battle with the Supreme Court. The problem: she refused to edit out the word "shit" used by the junkies themselves as the term for heroin. Clarke eventually won the battle, and the film was distributed.

The merit of *The Connection* was debated for over a year. Front-line New York critics largely dismissed the film (Brendan Gill of *The New Yorker* called it a "stunt"). In his October 11, 1962, column, Jonas Mekas of the *Village Voice* took the critics to task for "butchering what may be the best film made in this country this year. I don't even want to read what you have to say: to describe your criteria I could use the same word *The Connection* uses for heroin."

But Clarke's reputation was growing, and she was asked by President John F. Kennedy to make a documentary on poet laureate, Robert Frost. Her first reaction was that it wasn't her kind of film, but, after she met "Frostie," he interested her so much she could not resist. Frost died before the film was completed. Colin Young wrote in *Film Quarterly* that *Robert Frost: A Lover's Quarrel with the World* is "a confrontation of two views of Frost—his public performance and his private thoughts." Though it won an Academy Award for Best Documentary, Clarke felt that the film was Frost's rather than hers, and she was more than ready to make another full-length feature.

She optioned a novel by Warren Miller called *A Cool World*, returning to Harlem to shoot the story of a "rumble" between two rival African-American gangs, the Royal Pythons and the Wolves. Clarke hired locals to play the roles, many of whom had police records. When asked how she became interested in what was called at the time the "Negro problem" she replied, "this is America's key problem. Without a solution to it, we will never have a free country." James Farmer, National Director of the Congress for Racial Equality (CORE), recommended that all Americans see the film because "it is the truth." Released in 1963, the film was less controversial than its predecessors, though some cities (Boston in particular) refused to distribute it. That the subject matter was explored at all certainly blazed the trail for future filmmakers. Both *Clockers,* directed by Spike Lee, and *Boyz N the Hood,* directed by John Singleton, are direct descendants of *A Cool World.*

Personally, Clarke's life was chaotic. Her marriage with Bert Clarke was over. For a time, she lived with Carl Lee, one of the black actors who appeared in *The Connection,* and she was having a bitter public dispute with Fred Wiseman, the producer of *Cool World.* In an interview for *Take One,* Clarke told **Susan Rice** that Wiseman cheated her on royalties. Apparently she made no money from the film nor would Wiseman allow her to have a print. Thankfully,

none of these situations seemed to impact on the spirit of her daughter Wendy. Always close, Wendy studied at her mother's knee, eventually becoming a filmmaker in her own right.

While waiting for her next feature project, Clarke accepted a challenging assignment from the organizers of Montreal's World Expo. The theme for the 1967 fair was "Man and His World." Clarke's section, "Man and the Polar Regions," was to be viewed on a carousel of 11 moving screens. Mid-project, she told Berg, "This is even wilder than a dance film and it will take me several years to digest the possibilities. It should provide an enormous kinetic kick for the audience. . . . 1, 2 or 3 screens keep appearing and disappearing . . . this should be violently kinetic!"

Clarke's next film was the controversial *Portrait of Jason.* Jason Holliday was a 33-year-old black male prostitute whose dream was to become a nightclub entertainer. Clarke turned the camera on Holliday for 12 hours and let him reminisce about his life as a prostitute, his incarceration, his time spent in a mental hospital, and the emotional torture he endured as a child while living with his family. She then sifted it down to two hours. Mekas of the *Voice* cited the result as "one of the important, very important contemporary films." Clarke told Berg: "It reveals the humor and pathos, the joys and pains of Jason, a unique and extraordinary human being. Somehow all of Jason's problems and ambiguities seem to explain our own." Though hailed by Charles Hartman in *Film Society Review* as "a giant figure of American independent film," Clarke was vilified in several corners. Critic John Simon said *Jason*'s "100-minute outpouring of a drug-and-drink-sodden, goaded, taunted Negro male whore strikes me not as cinema verité but as egregious lack of cinema-charité." *Variety* called the film "more sociology than art and pretty superficial at that." It wasn't until the 1990s, with the release of a film called *Paris Burning,* that the rest of the world was ready to explore that subject matter. *Paris Burning* takes up where *Jason* leaves off by looking deeply into the lives of a "family" of transvestite nightclub performers who are also caught up in the drug-prostitution subculture.

In 1969, after nearly 20 years toiling as an independent, Clarke was asked to work on a movie in Hollywood. Academy Award-winning actress *****Shelley Winters**, who had written the script, wanted Clarke to direct. Unfortunately, negotiations broke down when the producers, who had claimed to love the "real" look of

Clarke's movies, insisted upon using fake locations to film the movie. Clarke passed.

Before abandoning Hollywood completely, she accepted a role in director *Agnes Varda's film *Lion's Love*. Clarke played a filmmaker who attempts suicide when her pet project is refused funding by the Hollywood power establishment. Though Varda and Clarke were good friends, Clarke was incapable of playing the role as Varda wished. Depressed, Clarke returned to New York, and, as she described to Rosen, "By 1970 I was lying on my back staring out the window, saying things like, 'If it weren't for my daughter, I wouldn't bother staying alive.'" At that point, she also recognized her career, if she was going to have one, would have to take another turn. Ultimately, she stopped making independent films because she couldn't find a suitable producer, and Hollywood wouldn't take a chance on her projects because they were not "commercial."

By fluke, Clarke was given a grant to make a piece on videotape. It was a happy turn of events. Videotape offered what film never could, especially for the experimental artist, portability, spontaneity, and multiplication of images via several monitors. Immediately, videotape became the overriding passion in her life. She took her equipment everywhere. In Syracuse, New York, in 1972, Clarke held a "video ball" during an art show put on by John Lennon and **Yoko Ono**, offering participants the chance to view themselves on tape. In the mid-1970s, Clarke became the artistic director of the TP Videospace Troupe, which toured the United States, teaching workshops and performing.

In the late 1970s, she accepted a teaching position at the University of California, Los Angeles (UCLA). Once again, academic life allowed her a base from which to work. During that period, she made several films, including *Savage/Love*, a co-production with playwright-actor Sam Shepard released in 1981. When asked what the future held for her, she told Rosen, "Fortunately, despite constant complaint and anger and bitterness, at heart I'm an eternal optimist."

That Clarke's work was virtually ignored by the commercially driven Hollywood market is not a surprise. She was not a "success" by Hollywood standards, though with two Oscar nominations and one statuette she could hardly be called a failure. Her greatest contribution to the filmmaking community was her innovative spirit, her drive to expose the truth, no matter how unsavory, and her willingness to not only identify with society's outcasts but to uncover the dark side. In doing so, in taking her audience to a place in themselves that they feared the most, Clarke challenged everyone.

SOURCES:
Berg, Gretchen. "Interview with Shirley Clarke," in *Film Culture*. Vol. 44, 1967, pp. 52–55 (originally published in *Dance Perspectives*).
Breitrose, Henry. "Films of Shirley Clarke," in *Film Quarterly*. Volume 13, no. 4. Summer 1960.
"Filmmakers Cooperative," in *Film Culture: New York Film Festival*. Vol. 42, 1966.
Heck-Rabi, Louise. "Shirley Clarke: Reality Rendered," in *Women Filmmakers: A Critical Approach*. London: Scarecrow Press, 1984.
Jacobs, Jay. "Song Without Words," in *The Reporter*. November 8, 1962, p. 50.
Mekas, Jonas. "Movie Journal," in *The Village Voice*. October 11, 1962, p. 13.
Oshlag, Dorothy. "Filming The Connection," in *Sight and Sound*. Spring 1961.
Rosen, Marjorie, "Shirley Clarke: Videospace Explorer," in *Ms*. April 1975, pp. 107–110.
Young, Colin. "Robert Frost: A Lover's Quarrel with the World," in *Film Quarterly*. Vol. 17. Spring 1964.

Deborah Jones, freelance writer, Studio City, California

Clarke, Mrs. Tom (1878–1972).

See Clarke, Kathleen.

Clary, Désirée (1777–1860).

See Désirée.

Clary, Julie (1771–1845).

See Bonaparte, Julie Clary.

Claude.

Variant of Claudia.

Claude de France (1499–1524)

*French queen. Name variations: Claudia; Queen Claude; Claude Valois; Claude de Valois; Claude of France. Born on October 14, 1499, in Romorantin, France; died on July 20, 1524, in Blois, Anjou, France; eldest daughter of Louis XII (1462–1515), king of France (r. 1498–1515), and Anne of Brittany (c. 1477–1514); sister of *Renée of France (1510–1575); married Francis, duc d'Angoulême, later Francis I, king of France (r. 1515–1547), on May 18, 1515; children: (three sons) Francis (1518–1536); Henry II (1519–1559), king of France (r. 1547–1559); Charles (1522–1545); (four daughters) Louise (1515–1517); Charlotte (1516–1524); *Madeleine of France (1520–1537, who married James V, king of Scotland in 1537 and died a few months later); *Margaret of Savoy (1523–1574).*

A favorite daughter of Louis XII, king of France, and *Anne of Brittany, Claude de France inherited two duchys: Milan and Brittany. Saint-Beuve maintains that if her mother had not died in 1514, Claude would have never married Francis I, king of France, for Anne "forsaw the evil treatment she was certain to receive." Saint-Beuve goes on to note that Claude's husband, the king, gave her "a disease that shortened her days." Claude was also treated harshly by the regent *Louise of Savoy (1476–1531). But Claude "strengthened her soul as much as she could," continued Saint-Beuve, "by her sound mind and gentle patience and great wisdom." Following Claude's death, Francis married *Eleanor of Portugal (1498–1558) in 1529, the sister of his adversary Charles V, in the interest of gaining the peace.

Claude de France (1547–1575)

*French princess and duchess of Lorraine. Name variations: Claudia; Claude of France. Born on November 12, 1547; died in 1575; daughter of *Catherine de Medici (1519–1589) and Henry II (b. 1519), king of France (r. 1547–1559); sister of Francis II, king of France, *Elizabeth of Valois, queen of Spain, Charles IX, king of France, Henry III, king of France, *Margaret of Valois, and half-sister of *Diane de France (1538–1619); married Charles II, duke of Lorraine (r. 1545–1608); children: Henry I, duke of Lorraine (r. 1608–1624); *Christine of Lorraine (c. 1571–1637, who married Ferdinand I, grand duke of Tuscany); Francis II, duke of Lorraine (r. 1624–1625).*

Claude des Armoises.

See Women Prophets and Visionaries in France at the End of the Middle Ages.

Claude of France.

See Claude de France.

Claudel, Camille (1864–1943)

French sculptor, primarily of small-scale works, noted for their detail and expressive quality. Pronunciation: Kah-MEE Klo-DEL. Born Camille Claudel on December 8, 1864, in Fère-en-Tardenois, France; died on November 19, 1943, in Montdevergues, France; daughter of Louis-Prosper Claudel and Louise-Athénaïse (Cervaux) Claudel; sister of Paul Claudel (renowned poet and diplomat); entered the Académie Colarossi in 1881; tutored by sculptor Alfred Boucher and Auguste Rodin; never married.

Moved with family from Fère-en-Tardenois to Bar-le-Duc (1870), to Nogent-sur-Seine (1876), to Paris (1882); began work as an assistant in the studio of Rodin (1885), began affair; had first major exhibition (1888–89); left Rodin's studio (1893); broke with him (1898); continued to exhibit (1898–1908) but showed signs of mental instability; committed to asylum at Ville-Evrard (1913); transferred to asylum at Montdevergues (1914), lived there until her death (1943).

Sculptures: La Vieille Hélène (1882); Young Roman or My Brother at Age Sixteen (1884); Giganti (1885); Bust of Auguste Rodin (1888); The Waltz (1891–1905); Clotho (1893); Sakuntala or Abandon (plaster 1888, marble 1905); The Gossips (1897); The Age of Maturity (first version, plaster, c. 1894); The Age of Maturity (second version, bronze, 1898); The Wave (1900); Perseus and the Gorgon (1902); The Flute Player or The Little Siren; Deep Thought or Woman Kneeling before a Hearth (1905).

Camille Claudel's reputation as an artist has long been entwined with that of Auguste Rodin, the most respected French sculptor at the end of the 19th century. For some, she is no more than an episode—albeit an important one—in his life. Indeed, before anyone had written any serious work about Claudel, one could always find a few pages or a chapter devoted to her turbulent affair with Rodin in any biography of that artist. Further, as the sister of Paul Claudel, the renowned poet and diplomat, her name was also well-known. Yet she was most often portrayed as a cross he and his family had to bear and not as the talented artist she was. Indeed, Paul Claudel found in his sister an example of the dangers of art: "I witness the tragedy of my sister's life, and I don't encourage anyone to follow the path of the arts," he told a reporter just a few months before her death. It is perhaps not surprising that the accomplishments of a woman associated with two such major figures should become subsumed to theirs, especially since her life did not fit into an easily constructed narrative. Nonetheless, her brother characterized her as a "genius," and Rodin recognized that she was "abundantly gifted." In line with these judgments, renewed interest in her work in recent decades allows a more complete glimpse into her life and her originality.

Camille Claudel was born into a comfortable, middle-class family in a small town in the Champagne region. Louis-Prosper Claudel, her father, was a civil servant who held the office of registrar of mortgages, a position that found him frequently being transferred from district to district. The family's move to Paris in 1882 was occasioned by the fact that Claudel had already left home for Paris to study in a private art school the year before. Although the Claudels moved a number of times, they always kept the house in

Villeneuve that came to the family when Louis-Prosper married Louise-Athénaïse Cervaux. That house would remain their preferred place to pass the summer vacations and serve as an anchor to the family.

All that has happened to me is more than a novel, it is an epic. . . . [I]t would need a Homer to recount it.

—Camille Claudel

By all accounts, Camille Claudel was headstrong and independent as a young girl, dominating her brother and sister, her schoolmates, and the servants. She was closer to Paul than to her sister **Louise**, though in most matters later in life Paul would side with his mother and Louise. From an early age, Camille showed an interest in sculpting; she would model bones from clay and bake them in the oven. She turned the house into her atelier and even taught one of the maids how to prepare marble blocks for sculpting. This desire and determination to become a sculptor, an activity her mother considered completely inappropriate for a young woman, engendered frequent family disputes. Claudel's father, while not certain of her abilities, encouraged her to pursue her goals, and she began sculpting in earnest. The family's moves took them to Nogent-sur-Seine, a town that happened to be the home of two well-known sculptors, Paul Dubois (later the director of the École de Beaux-Arts in Paris) and Alfred Boucher. Claudel's father called upon Boucher to assess his daughter's works, and Boucher immediately recognized the talent of the now 15-year-old Claudel. He offered Camille both encouragement and served as an occasional tutor until the family moved again, this time to Wassy-sur-Blaise. Claudel longed to go to Paris where she could study and exhibit her work. Although women were not allowed to attend the Beaux-Arts, a number of private schools did accept female pupils. It is likely that the intervention of Boucher and Dubois facilitated Camille's acceptance into the Académie Colarossi in 1881. She moved to Paris and persuaded her father to rent an apartment there for the family.

Camille Claudel soon left the Parisian sculpting school to work again with Boucher and to pursue a more independent, and unfortunately more costly, program of study. She used her ingenuity to come up with a way to supplement the limited funds her parents had to contribute to her studies. Claudel organized a group of students, made up primarily of young English women (including **Jennie Lipscomb** with whom

she would remain fast friends), into a sort of cooperative: they shared the expenses for rent of her studio on the rue Notre-Dame-des-Champs in Montparnasse, and for tutors' as well as models' fees. This period marks the beginning of Claudel's exploration of portraiture. Her earliest extant works date from this interval and include a bronze bust of her brother, finished in 1881. The next year, she completed a terra cotta head entitled *La Vieille Hélène*. These two works demonstrate the range of Claudel's vision from the idealized portrait of her brother to the highly naturalistic head of the family servant. Meanwhile, Boucher's talents garnered him the Prix de Rome, and he left Paris for Italy in 1883. At his urging, Auguste Rodin took over as tutor to Camille and her "school."

The association between Rodin and Claudel—first as mentor-pupil, then master-artist and assistant, then collaborators and lovers—coincides with the production of some of Rodin's greatest achievements. For Camille, however, the time was not without difficulties. The discovery of her liaison with Rodin did little to improve Claudel's relations with her family. Although she still had her father's support, the gap between Claudel and the other members of her family widened. Her successes in her early exhibitions somewhat mollified the family, and they were happier when she moved out of Rodin's studio and into a new one of her own. She traveled to England more than once during this period to see her friend Jennie Lipscomb and exhibited with her at Nottingham in 1886. L'Islette, a château near Azay-le-Rideau in the Loire valley, became a favorite hideaway where Claudel would stay alone or with Rodin as a break from city life. She attempted to steer a difficult course, one that created the fewest tensions with her family and that would allow her to balance her career as an artist with the demands of Rodin, who frequently asked her to model for him or to assist him in his work.

The relationship between Rodin and Claudel is reflected differently in their works. It is perhaps easier to see Rodin's influence on her style than Claudel's on his. Her *Bust of Rodin*, a bronze exhibited at the Salon of 1892, earned praise, most notably from Rodin who judged it to be "the finest sculptured head since Donatello." It also resembles most closely Rodin's own techniques. However, *La Vieille Hélène*, completed before Claudel ever met Rodin, was not dissimilar in style. Thus, while Rodin's influence is present, it is not incongruent with Camille's own stylistic choices. Rodin, on the other hand, executed a number of portraits and busts of Claudel. Her

Camille
Claudel

image appeared in some of his most striking works, among them *Thought* and *The Dawn*. It is easy to understand why Camille has often been called Rodin's muse: she inspired many of his works while they were together and continued to do so even after their separation.

Claudel's own sculptures often seem to be symbolic representations of moments in her life, what Paul called the "confessional" aspects of her works. *Sakuntala*, which received honorable mention at the Salon of 1888, draws its inspiration from Hindu mythology. It is the name of a hermit maiden who secretly bears a child. According to some sources, Claudel gave birth to two children with Rodin; in contrast, Paul Claudel refers in his correspondence to an abortion. Whatever the truth is, it seems certain that this sculpture parallels in some sense Camille's experiences. The figures in the sculpture hover between naturalism and idealism and thus differ from the majority of pairs of lovers that Rodin sculpted (for example, his most famous couple in *The Kiss*).

Claudel then fashioned a new version of realism in sculpture that portrays the mythic. *The Waltz*, exhibited in 1893 and generally considered her masterpiece, depicts another couple, moving in complete harmony to the strains of some far-away music. A cast of the statuette was in the collection of the composer Claude Debussy. In this piece, Camille seems to have transcribed the music of Debussy who once played for her and, in so doing, created a piece unlike any other.

Claudel produced two versions of *The Age of Maturity:* the first (c. 1894) depicts a man caught between two women, one older, one younger, each holding on to him. In the second version (1898), the younger woman no longer holds onto the man. Claudel was the younger woman; **Rose Beuret**, Rodin's older mistress, was the older woman; the figure in the middle was Rodin. The works are noteworthy not only for their biographical content but for their stylistic differences. The earlier of the two is smaller and much closer in style to Rodin. The second version changes the proportions and displays the gap between figures, which appears frequently in Claudel's work. The unusual composition makes it all the more remarkable.

Clotho is one of Claudel's most enigmatic pieces: a skeletal old woman tangled in the fateful threads she spins. The vacant stare on Clotho's face renders the work all the more disturbing. The sculpture again recalls Donatello, yet the tree-like braids of Clotho's hair display the ornamental quality of the nascent Art Nouveau style.

From the period before Claudel's last major show in 1908 at the gallery of her longtime supporter Eugène Blot to her commitment by her brother Paul to an insane asylum in 1913, it becomes extremely difficult to sort out what happened in her life. Camille had become a recluse in her studio on the Ile-Saint-Louis. Although she continued to exhibit, these exhibits did nothing to change her temperament. *The Age of Maturity,* a marble *Sakuntala, Perseus and the Gorgon, The Gossips, The Wave,* and *Deep Thought* were all shown from 1902 to 1908. Despite the fact that these works did not receive unanimous praise from her contemporaries, each marks a significant part of her output. The final version of the *Age of Maturity* reaffirms Claudel's style of sculpture as a play of void and weight while *Sakuntala* demonstrated again her skill in marble. Of the new works, in *Perseus and the Gorgon* Claudel achieved her ambition of creating a monumental group while retaining the same enigmatic quality as the smaller-scale *Clotho. The Gossips, The Wave,* and *Deep Thought or Woman Kneeling before a Hearth* all are examples of Claudel's mastery of the small scale piece and are highly successful juxtapositions of bronze and onyx or marble. *Deep Thought* brings Claudel closest to the decorative arts tradition that dominated the Art Nouveau movement. This period saw the completion of many long-term projects and the beginnings of some experimentation. Paradoxically, her production began to decline. As Camille began to recycle images and figures in new groupings, it seemed as if her creative talents were on the wane. Finally, in 1906, she began to destroy the clay, plaster, and wax models of her works after they were cast.

Things might well have continued outside of an asylum were it not for the death of her father in 1913. Within a week, her brother was able to get an order signed, committing Camille to a public insane asylum just outside Paris. With the onset of World War I and the impending threat to the safety of Paris, Claudel was transferred to another public asylum in Montdevergues, in southern France, just outside Avignon. It was there that she spent the remaining three decades of her life, virtually cut-off from all family and friends. Neither her mother nor her sister ever came to visit. On the contrary, her mother refused to let her be released into her family's custody. Lacking any real psychiatric evidence, we can surmise that Claudel suffered from a persecution complex and may well have been manic-depressive. The mood swings she manifested would seem to bear out the latter conclusion, and her repeated accusations against Rodin's treachery concerning her career (which, in fact, was quite untrue) support the former. The question remains, however, as to whether Camille Claudel was truly "insane" as her brother asserted. Jennie Lipscomb maintained that Claudel was sane, and she as well as others, including some members of Claudel's family, saw the confinement as a convenient way for Paul and his mother to push aside someone who was a liability, both financially and socially. In a letter to Blot, Claudel wrote of her confinement: "I live in a world that is so curious, so strange. Of the dream which was my life, this is a nightmare." The nightmare ended on October 19, 1943, when Camille Claudel died at age 79.

Eight years after her death and over four decades after her last exhibition, the Musée Rodin in Paris organized a special exhibition of Camille Claudel's sculptures. Paul Claudel's introduction to the catalogue, "My Sister Camille," was a paean to his sister's genius and the eulogy she never received at her death. In 1951, Camille Claudel had once again begun to receive the recognition she had so long been denied.

SOURCES:
Grunfeld, Frederic C. *Rodin*. NY: Holt, 1987.
Paris, Reine-Marie. *Camille: The Life of Camille Claudel, Rodin's Muse and Mistress*. Translated by Liliane E. Tuck. NY: Seaver Books, 1988.
Schmoll, J.A. *Auguste Rodin and Camille Claudel*. Translated by John Ormond. Munich: Prestel Verlag, 1994.

SUGGESTED READING:
Delbée, Anne. *Camille Claudel: une femme*. Translated by Carol Cosman. San Francisco, CA: Mercury House, 1992.
Paris, Reine-Marie, and Arnaud de la Chapelle. *Catalogue raisonné*. Paris: A. Biro, 1991.

RELATED MEDIA:
Camille Claudel (173 min), starring **Isabel Adjani** and **Gérard Depardieu**, directed by Bruno Nuytten, produced in France.

Edith J. Benkov, Professor of French,
San Diego State University,
San Diego, California

Claudia.

Variant of Claude or Clodia.

Claudia (c. 94–post 45 BCE).

See Clodia.

Claudia (fl. 26–36 CE)

Biblical woman. Name variations: Claudia Procula. Flourished around 26–36 CE; married Pontius Pilate, the Roman procurator of Judea during the time of Jesus' ministry and Crucifixion.

Referred to in the Bible as Pilate's wife, Claudia asked that Jesus' life be spared. While her husband ascended the judgment seat to hear the accusations against Jesus, she sent a message through a servant imploring Pilate to "have nothing to do with that righteous man, for I have suffered much over Him in a dream." Although Pilate was perplexed by this incident, he eventually yielded to the crowd and sent Jesus away to be scourged.

Claudia Acte (fl. 55–69 CE).

See Acte.

Claudia Antonia (27–66 CE)

Roman noblewoman. Born in 27 CE; died in 66 CE; daughter of Tiberius Claudius Nero Germanicus (10 BCE–54 CE), also known as the Roman Emperor Claudius (r. 41–54 CE), and his second wife Paetina; married Gnaeus Pompey; married Faustus Cornelius Sulla Felix, also known as Sulla (a consul).

The daughter of Tiberius Claudius Nero Germanicus (the Roman emperor, Claudius) and his second wife **Paetina**, Claudia Antonia was the oldest of Claudius' children to survive childhood. Before her father became a political force, she was raised on the fringe of the imperial court under the reigns of Tiberius and Caligula (respectively, the uncle and nephew of her father), and she would remain an imperial pawn throughout her life. Claudia's political importance increased enormously after Caligula's assassination elevated her father to the imperial throne in 41 CE. Never taken seriously in a political sense until the Praetorian Guard (seeking a supposedly malleable emperor from the Julio-Claudian house) forced his accession, Claudius fooled everyone by ruling well until his weakness for beautiful women and the encroachment of senility combined to undermine the effectiveness of his declining years.

As the daughter of the emperor, Claudia's political importance was manifest; whomever she married was guaranteed a close connection to the imperial house and thus a status with the potential to affect the imperial succession. Had her mother Paetina continued as Claudius' wife, Claudia Antonia's interests would have been well served. However, by the time of his political rise in 41, Claudius was madly smitten with the beautiful but notorious *****Messalina**, his second cousin. Messalina was around 15 when she married Claudius (in 38 CE); he was 48. Although Messalina gave birth to a daughter (*****Octavia**) and a son (Britannicus), she was scandalously prone to adultery, though for a time her hold over Claudius was so great that he was inclined to overlook her indiscretions. After Claudia's mother was replaced by Messalina, Claudia (just slightly younger than Messalina) constituted a threat to the successional aspirations of Britannicus, if for no other reason than that a husband of hers could function as a focal point of political opposition to Messalina's son. Claudia's first husband Gnaeus Pompey was executed at Messalina's command. In 48, Claudia realized a degree of revenge for this murder, for in that year Messalina herself was executed for treason.

In 49, Claudius again married—this time to his niece *Agrippina the Younger. The ramifications of this union for the succession were enormous, for in the year 50 Agrippina convinced Claudius to adopt Nero (her son by a previous marriage) and to establish him as the "guardian" of the younger Britannicus. In 53, Nero strengthened his status at court by marrying Octavia, Claudius' daughter by Messalina. In the next year, the ground having been carefully prepared, Agrippina (in collusion with Nero) murdered the now mentally befuddled Claudius to set into motion the process that would establish Nero on the throne; this process included Britannicus' death in 55, and even Agrippina's in 59. Since Nero had insured through marriage that no political opposition could focus on Octavia, when court intrigue did mount against the increasingly irresponsible Nero, it sought alternative ties to Nero's imperial predecessor. With Octavia out of the picture, the most obvious link to the legitimacy of Claudius was Claudia Antonia, whose second husband, Faustus Cornelius Sulla Felix, was a prominent figure at the imperial court. An associate of Claudius late in his reign, Sulla had been rewarded with a consulship in 52. Such an honor insured Nero's enmity—an animosity only heightened when many at court began to turn to Sulla as a potential imperial candidate. Such promotion, however, only assured Sulla's exile (58) and eventual murder (62) at Nero's command.

After the loss of a second husband to imperial jealousy, Claudia Antonia refused all subsequent offers of marriage, knowing full well a husband would be considered a political threat by Nero. Ironically, it was Claudia's refusal of a third suitor, which led to her death. Although married to Octavia, Nero prominently adopted as his mistress a woman named ❧ Poppaea Sabina (probably beginning in 58). In 62, as Nero's relationship with Poppaea intensified, he decided to "legitimate" their association (spurred both by political intrigue and by the promise of their first child—a daughter named Claudia) by marrying Poppaea. In order to do so, Nero first divorced Octavia. Shortly thereafter, to insure that she would be put to no political use, Nero ordered her death. These actions horrified the Roman elite, but not as much as what followed. In 65, angry at her husband's dallying at the Circus Maximus, Poppaea, pregnant a second time, raged at Nero. Unused to

such treatment, Nero responded with a kick to Poppaea's abdomen, causing her death. Probably contrite about the killing, and certainly bothered by the intensified rumblings about his outrageous behavior, Nero sought to shore up his crumbling standing by proposing marriage to Claudia Antonia (eight years his senior). Bearing a grudge against Nero for the loss of Sulla, however, Claudia refused and Nero was forced to "console" himself in 66 with a marriage to another of his mistresses, one *Statilia Messalina. Within a year, this happy couple undertook a grand tour of Greece, where Nero would so embarrass the Roman elite as to number his days. Before abandoning Italy for the east, however, he took vengeance upon Claudia by ordering her death on the grounds that she had incited revolution against him. In fact, Claudia Antonia had done nothing but refuse his hand, but in the mind of Nero that was enough to prove treason. Claudia's death brought the direct line of Claudius to an end, and was a harbinger to the demise of the Julio-Claudian dynasty—an end realized when Nero himself was forced to commit suicide in 68.

William S. Greenwalt, Associate Professor
of Classical History, Santa Clara University,
Santa Clara, California

Claudia de Medici (1604–1648).
See Medici, Claudia de.

Claudia Felicitas

Florentine noblewoman. Born in Florence; daughter of *Anna de Medici (b. 1616) and Ferdinand, archduke of Austrian Tyrol; granddaughter of *Claudia de Medici (1604–1648); second wife of Leopold I, Holy Roman emperor (r. 1658–1705). Leopold's first wife was *Margaret Theresa of Spain (1651–1673); his third was *Eleanor of Pfalz-Neuburg (1655–1720).

In the Uffizi Gallery, there is a portrait of Claudia Felicitas dressed as *Galla Placidia.

Claudia of Tuscany (1604–1648).
See Medici, Claudia de.

Claudia Quinta (fl. 220–206 BCE)
Roman woman. Flourished between 220–206 BCE.

In 206 BCE, the ship conveying the image of the goddess Cybele grounded in the shallows at the mouth of the Tiber River. In Roman legend, when the oracles announced

*Poppaea Sabina
(d. 65). See
Agrippina the
Younger for
sidebar.*

that only a chaste woman could move the ship, Claudia Quinta cleared herself from an accusation of faithlessness by stepping forward from among the matrons who had accompanied Scipio to receive the image. The ship was tied to her girdle by a long rope, and she dragged it out of the shallows.

Claudine (1451–1514)

Ruler of Monaco. Born in 1451 in Monaco; died in 1514 in Monaco; daughter of Catalan Grimaldi, ruler of Monaco; married Lambert Grimaldi (a Genovese noble and cousin); children: John (later John II of Monaco), Lucien, and Augustin.

Claudine was born into the ruling Grimaldi family of Monaco, a small independent principality on the Mediterranean coast south of France. The Grimaldis were one of the leading families of Genoa; before Claudine's birth, they had seized Monaco from the French and set themselves up as its ruling clan. As her father's only legitimate heir, Claudine succeeded her father as ruler on his death in 1657. Since she was only six years old, the government was run in her name by regents, who arranged her marriage to her cousin Lambert Grimaldi. Lambert was named seigneur, or lord, of Monaco, and co-ruled with Claudine when she came of age. The couple had three sons, all of whom succeeded their mother.

Laura York,
Riverside, California

Clauss-Szárvady, Wilhelmina (1834–1907)

Czech pianist, known throughout 19th-century Europe for her renditions of Bach and Beethoven. Name variations: Wilhelmine. Born in Prague, Czechoslovakia, on December 13, 1834; died in Paris, France, on November 1, 1907.

Wilhelmina Clauss-Szárvady studied in Prague. When she began to tour in 1849, her playing caused a stir; some spoke of her as being the artistic rival of *Clara Schumann. The feared Viennese critic Eduard Hanslick wrote in 1855 of the "characteristic reflective quality" of her pianism. Clauss-Szarvady's great reputation was based mostly on her playing of Bach and Beethoven, though she played some Chopin as well.

Clavers, Mrs. Mary (1801–1864).

See Kirkland, Caroline Matilda.

Clelia.

See Cloelia.

Clemence of Hungary (1293–1328)

*Queen of France. Name variations: Clemence d'Anjou. Born in 1293; died in 1328; daughter of Charles Martel of Hungary and *Clementia of Habsburg (d. 1293); became second wife of Louis X (1289–1316), king of France (r. 1314–1316), in August 1315; children: John I the Posthumous (1316–1316), king of France (r. 1316).*

Clemence of Hungary's son, John I the Posthumous, was king of France for six days: from the day of his birth on November 14, 1316, to the day of his death on November 19. Her husband Louis X had died the preceding May. Since Louis had left behind no other male heirs, his brother Philip of Valois declared himself Philip VI, king of France.

Clementia

Duchess of Lower Lorraine. Daughter of Guillaume de Bourgogne also known as William, count of Burgundy; became second wife of Godfrey I (d. 1139), duke of Lower Lorraine, after 1121.

Clementia of Habsburg (d. 1293)

*German royal. Birth date unknown; died after February 2, 1293; daughter of Rudolf I (1218–1291), Holy Roman emperor (r. 1273–1291), and *Anna of Hohenberg (c. 1230–1281); married Charles Martel of Hungary; children: Charles Robert of Anjou (1288–1342) also known as Charles I, king of Hungary (r. 1307–1342, who married Elizabeth of Poland, 1305–1380); *Clemence of Hungary (1293–1328).*

Clementina of Austria (1777–1801).

See Maria Clementina of Austria.

Clementina of Zahringen (fl. 1150s)

*Countess of Savoy. Flourished in the 1150s; daughter of Conrad I, duke of Zahringen; became first wife of Henry XII also known as Henry V the Lion (1129–1195), duke of Saxony and Bavaria (r. 1156–1195), around 1150 (divorced 1162); married Humbert III, count of Savoy, around 1164; children: (first marriage) possibly Gertrude of Saxony (c. 1155–1196, who married Canute IV, king of Denmark). Henry V's second wife was *Matilda of England (1156–1189).*

Clementina Sobieski (1702–1735).

See Sobieski, Clementina.

Clementine of Austria (1798–1881)

Princess of Salerno. Born on March 1, 1798; died on September 3, 1881; daughter of *Maria Teresa of Naples (1772–1807) and Francis I (1768–1835), emperor of Austria (r. 1804–1835), also known as Frances II, Holy Roman emperor (r. 1792–1806); sister-in-law of Napoleon Bonaparte; married Leopold, prince of Salerno, on July 28, 1816; children: *Caroline of Bourbon (1822–1869); Ludwig Karl also known as Louis Charles (b. 1824).

Clementine of Belgium (1872–1955)

Belgian princess. Born on July 30, 1872; died on March 8, 1955; daughter of Leopold II (b. 1835), king of Belgium (r. 1865–1909), and *Maria Henrietta of Austria (1836–1902); married Prince Victor (son of Prince Napoleon and *Clotilde of Savoy), on November 14, 1901; children: Clotilde (b. 1912); Louis Napoleon (b. 1914).

Clementine of Orleans (1817–1907)

Princess of Saxe-Coburg. Name variations: Clementine Bourbon; Clémentine of Orléans or Clémentine d'Orléans. Born Marie Clémentine Caroline Leopoldine Clotilde d'Orléans on June 3, 1817, in Neuilly-sur-Seine; died on February 16, 1907, in Vienna, Austria; second daughter of *Maria Amalia (1782–1866) and Louis Philippe I (1773–1850), the Citizen King of France (r. 1830–1848); sister of *Louise d'Orleans (1812–1850, queen of Belgium); married Augustus, prince of Saxe-Coburg-Gotha, on April 20, 1843; children: Prince Philip of Saxe-Coburg-Gotha (1844–1921); August of Saxe-Coburg-Gotha (1845–1907); *Clotilde of Saxe-Coburg-Gotha (1846–1927); *Amalie of Saxe-Coburg-Gotha (1848–1894); Ferdinand I (1861–1948), prince of Bulgaria (r. 1887–1908), tsar of Bulgaria (r. 1908–1918). Clémentine of Orléans was a close friend of *Maria II Da Gloria (1819–1853), queen of Portugal.

Cleobulina of Rhodes (fl. 570 BCE)

Greek philosopher and poet. Name variations: Eumetis. Flourished around 570 BCE; daughter of Cleobulus of Rhodes (one of the "Seven Sages" and ruler of Rhodes); children: (son) Thales of Miletos (philosopher and mathematician).

Works: riddles in hexameter verse.

Cleobulina belonged to a line of Greek intellectuals that included her father Cleobulus (fl. 600 BCE), who was known as one of "Seven Wise Men" or "Seven Sages." He nicknamed her "Eumetis" ("of good counsel"). Thales of Miletos (c. 585 BCE), who is held to be the father of Western philosophy, is generally considered to have been Cleobulina's son. We know of Thales having praised her as a woman "wise and far-famed," with "a statesman's mind," whose influence on Cleobulus made him rule Rhodes more fairly. Her fame was so great that she was the subject of a satire, "Cleobulina," by the Athenian dramatist of the next century, Cratinus. Despite his disparagement of the intellectual capabilities of women, Aristotle quotes one of her riddles (written in her usual style of hexameter)—concerning how brass might be attached to flesh, probably as part of a medical practice—in his *Poetics* and his *Rhetoric*. Several of her other rhymes survive.

Catherine Hundleby, M.A.
Philosophy, University of Guelph

Cleopatra (354 BCE–?).

See Olympias for sidebar.

Cleopatra (fl. 1st c. BCE)

Egyptian physician and author. Flourished in the 1st century BCE.

Cleopatra was a physician and author who is known from references in the work of Galen (fl. 2nd century CE), the ancient world's greatest medical authority. Since Galen confused her with *Cleopatra VII of Egypt (in fact, crediting the latter as the author of the texts he cites), it is probable that she lived and worked as a medical authority in Alexandria in the 1st century BCE, and that she was associated with the Ptolemaic court. Virtually nothing is known of the medical Cleopatra, other than that she is one of few ancient women who broke the gender barrier to practice medicine and be taken seriously as an authority in the field.

William S. Greenwalt,
Associate Professor of Classical History,
Santa Clara University, Santa Clara, California

Cleopatra I (c. 210–176 BCE)

Queen of Egypt. Born around 210 BCE in Syria; died in 176 BCE; daughter of Antiochus III, a Seleucid king, and his cousin-wife, Laodice III; married Ptolemy V Epiphanes, king of Egypt, in 196 BCE; children: Ptolemy VI Philometor; Cleopatra II (c. 183–116 BCE); Ptolemy VIII Euergetes II.

Cleopatra I was the daughter of the Seleucid king Antiochus III and his cousin-wife, ✥▶ **Laodice III**. Her political importance began in 196 BCE with her betrothal to the young king of Egypt, Ptolemy V Epiphanes, when both were about 14. This betrothal was arranged in the interests of Antiochus after he had defeated the Egyptians in battle at Panium, a victory that resecured for Syria the control over Palestine, which had been lost to Egypt 22 years earlier at the Battle of Raphia. The youth of the principals delayed their marriage, but when it occurred in 193, it was again scheduled for the benefit of Antiochus, who thereby expected to strengthen ties with Egypt as he embarked upon what would be an unsuccessful war with Rome. The site of the marriage was as symbolic as its timing, for Antiochus chose to deliver his daughter to Ptolemy V at Raphia, in order to demonstrate his hegemony over Egypt at the site of Egypt's last significant victory over a Seleucid army. Hoping, however, to ease the longstanding animosity between Syria and Egypt over Palestine, and hoping to lay the foundation for a lasting friendship between the two powers as both were beginning to be overshadowed by Rome in the international arena, Antiochus returned Palestine to Ptolemy as Cleopatra's marriage dower. Nonetheless, she, not her husband, controlled the region's revenues until her death.

Ptolemy V's reign was a troubled time for the Greeks and Macedonians who ruled Egypt, both because the indigenous population of Egypt resented the rule of a foreign regime and also because the native population at that time was in a position to flex its political and military muscle. Ironically, it had been the Battle of Raphia, which inaugurated a new age of unrest, because, in order to defeat the Seleucid army in 218, Ptolemy V's father had been forced to conscript native Egyptian soldiers into his army—an epic turning point that inhibited the Greco-Macedonian elite's ability to rule solely in its own interests. It is against this background that Ptolemy V's relationship with Cleopatra is best viewed, for Syria had become an essential ally against indigenous Egyptians.

Under influence of the Seleucid court, Ptolemy V manifested a more responsible sense of kingship than his hedonistic father ever had. Although Antiochus clearly intended for Cleopatra I to effectively link Ptolemy V's interests to his own, it is equally clear that she quickly assumed a more Egyptian perspective on affairs, much to the delight of the Greeks in Egypt. So well did she come to identify with Ptolemy instead of her

✥▶ **Laodice III** (fl. 200 BCE)
Syrian queen. Flourished around 200 BCE; married her cousin, the Seleucid king Antiochus III (r. 223–287); children: Cleopatra I (c. 210–176 BCE); Seleucus IV (r. 187–176 BCE); Antiochus IV Epiphanes (r. 175–164 BCE).

father, that when the Romans ejected Antiochus from Greece in 190, Cleopatra with her husband sent an embassy to congratulate the Romans on their victory. Ptolemy V came to value Cleopatra's insight and strength of character, even if these were incapable of overcoming all vestiges of his well-documented cruelty. (Especially noteworthy in this regard was the torture he mandated as punishment for an unsuccessful Egyptian rebellion in 184–183 BCE.) Iconographically represented as an equal of her husband, Cleopatra I received many honorific titles on his approval. She and her husband produced three offspring: Ptolemy VI Philometor, *Cleopatra II, and Ptolemy VIII Euergetes II.

When Ptolemy V died in 180, perhaps the victim of poisoning (his cruelty had manifested itself at court as well as among those less able to retaliate), Cleopatra seized the reigns of power and ruled, without male oversight, as the first female regent in Ptolemaic history. Nominally ruling on behalf of her older son, Ptolemy VI (a boy of about five when his father died), Cleopatra did so at least as competently as any of her immediate predecessors. However, to maintain an uncontested control of the court, Cleopatra I built up a faction comprised of eunuchs, ex-slaves, and others whose lowly status undermined the loyalty of many to the royal government. The net effect of this policy would be to accelerate the decline of the Ptolemaic dynasty once Cleopatra I was no longer on the scene. Nevertheless, as long as she lived Cleopatra reigned supreme—coining money in her own name and generally ruling well. After the death of her father, she wisely maintained cordial relations with her brother, Seleucus IV (who succeeded in 187), and reestablished domestic order within Egypt itself. Cleopatra I introduced her famous name into the Ptolemaic dynasty, and her responsible rule would foster future intermarriages between the Ptolemaic and Seleucid houses.

After her death in 176, Cleopatra was famed as a good influence on her children (she was praised as kind and intelligent); priesthoods were established in her memory. For all of her ability, however, she proved to be but a brief respite from the devolution of the Ptolemaic house. Nevertheless, her example subsequently motivated those of her successors (such as her famous namesake, *Cleopatra VII) who possessed both the character and talent essential for responsible rule.

William S. Greenwalt,
Associate Professor of Classical History,
Santa Clara University, Santa Clara, California

Cleopatra II (c. 183–116 BCE)

Co-ruler of Egypt (176–130 BCE and 118–116 BCE) and sole ruler of Upper Egypt (130–118 BCE). Name variations: Cleopatra II Philometor or Philomater ("Mother-loving"). Born around 183 BCE; died in 116 BCE; daughter of Ptolemy V Epiphanes and Cleopatra I (c. 210–176 BCE); sister of Ptolemy VI Philometor and Ptolemy VIII Euergetes II; married brother Ptolemy VI Philometor, in 176 BCE (died 145 BCE); married brother Ptolemy VIII Euergetes II, in 144 BCE; children: (first marriage) Ptolemy Eupator; Ptolemy VII Neos Philopator; Cleopatra III Euergetis; Cleopatra Thea; (second marriage) Ptolemy Memphites.

The daughter of Ptolemy V Epiphanes and *Cleopatra I, Cleopatra II had two brothers, Ptolemy VI Philometor and Ptolemy VIII Euergetes II. She was probably the middle of the three siblings. Only six or seven when her mother died in 176 (her father died in 180), Cleopatra II was quickly married to her older brother, who was likely no older than ten at the time. This underage marriage was arranged by Eulaeus (a eunuch) and Lenaeus (an ex-slave), two regents who, in lieu of anyone better situated, assumed their authority after Cleopatra I's death. Brother-sister marriages were common in ancient Egypt, and this one was quickly devised because the regents' lowly status and the monarchs' young ages called into jeopardy the stability of the Ptolemaic court and the peace of Egypt. Since the most compelling support of the new regime was its association with the popularity of Cleopatra I, it followed that a union of her daughter to her older son could have the potential to strengthen the dynasty's staying power. To make the link between the newly married couple and their deceased mother even more patent, both Cleopatra II and Ptolemy VI began to be designated as "Philometor," that is, "Mother-loving."

Although this policy seems to have won Egypt over to the regency of the two underage monarchs, the precariousness of the new arrangement encouraged the Seleucid king Antiochus IV (enthroned, 175) to invade Palestine in 171 to re-cover that region when Egypt was least able to defend it. This area had long been a bone of contention, having both been lost and won back by Antiochus IV's father, Antiochus III. Although Antiochus III had recovered Palestine in war (200), he endowered his daughter Cleopatra I with Palestine when he gave her in marriage to Ptolemy V, and the region reverted back to Ptolemaic control.

When Antiochus IV decided to exploit the weak reign of his nephew and niece to reclaim Palestine, he was opposed by Ptolemy VI (170). Declaring himself and his sister-wife Cleopatra II no longer subject to a regency (although he was still in his mid-teens), Ptolemy VI followed with an attack of his own on Palestine. This campaign, led as it was by an inexperienced general, was a disaster. Defeated by Antiochus IV, Ptolemy VI fled Palestine in such confusion that he did not even trust in his ability to return to Egypt. Rather, he headed for sanctuary on the sacred Aegean island of Samothrace—a destination he never reached, for the fleet of Antiochus captured him anyway. The military failure, all the more damaging because of Ptolemy VI's "cowardly" flight, led to a revolution in Alexandria where the population briefly replaced Ptolemy VI, both as king and as the husband of Cleopatra II, with their brother Ptolemy VIII.

After the capture of Ptolemy VI, Antiochus seems to have had ambitions on the Egyptian throne for himself until he learned of the accession of Ptolemy VIII. Thereafter, he invaded Egypt to return his recent antagonist, Ptolemy VI, to the throne. Initially successful, Antiochus left Egypt in 169 with Ptolemy VI reunited with Cleopatra and reinstalled on the throne, and with a strong Seleucid garrison in Pelusium (the fortress that defended Egypt's frontier from Syria). For Antiochus, there was influence to be gained through a manipulation of the rivalry engulfing the Ptolemaic house, that is, until more calculating heads held sway in Alexandria. Knowing that they needed a foreign champion to check Antiochus IV's ambitions in Egypt, Ptolemy VI and Cleopatra II sent an embassy to Rome to request protection from Seleucid Syria. Responding favorably to the request, in 168 the Romans sent an embassy under Gaius Popillius Laenus to demand that the newly returned Antiochus IV leave Egypt for good. Knowing that the Romans had already soundly defeated his father, and also knowing that they had recently crushed the Macedonians in Europe under Perseus, Antiochus caved in to the Roman ambassador and left Egypt permanently. In the next year, his garrison on Cyprus was also expelled and that island was returned to its Ptolemaic masters. With the foreign threat eased, Rome then worked out a compromise intended to keep Syria out of Egypt's affairs: it was agreed that Egypt should be ruled by the trinity of siblings—Ptolemy VI, Cleopatra II, and Ptolemy VIII. This Roman action began a long association between Rome and the Ptolemies, which had the effect of establishing Rome's right to intercede in Egyptian affairs—a right that was to grow until Egypt became a part of the Roman Empire.

Cleopatra II was initially cited as a full equal of her husband in the original petition against Antiochus IV before the Roman Senate, and her status was confirmed in Egyptian documents shortly thereafter. This made Cleopatra II the first Ptolemaic queen to gain full political equality with a reigning king—actually, in this case, with two kings. Exactly why she became so established is a matter of conjecture, but most likely she had a talent for political affairs and was considered by all concerned as essential to the continued collaboration of Ptolemy VI and Ptolemy VIII. In addition, Cleopatra II clearly was more popular among her subjects than either of her brothers, thus conjuring up images of her mother whose memory was a significant legitimizing factor behind this generation of Ptolemies.

The three monarchs collectively ruled all of Egypt's possessions until violence flared between Ptolemies VI and VIII in 164. This forced Ptolemy VI—never popular with the inhabitants of Alexandria after his early failures in Palestine—out of Egypt proper until Rome brought him back to Alexandria and Cleopatra. Realizing that the brothers would never rule in harmony, Rome arranged a division of Ptolemaic possessions, giving Egypt and Cyprus to the older brother and his wife, and Cyrene to the younger. Subsequently, in an effort to equalize their holdings, Ptolemy VIII invaded Cyprus where he was captured by Ptolemy VI (154). Under Roman pressure, however, Ptolemy VI and Cleopatra "forgave" their younger brother, and in order to win a "reconciliation" betrothed one of their daughters (*Cleopatra III Euergetis) to her uncle.

Back in Egypt proper, with all opposition to their rule overcome, Cleopatra and Ptolemy VI ruled peacefully and apparently with competence as joint monarchs until Ptolemy VI's death in 145. His death occurred as a result of Egypt's reinvolvement in the affairs of the Seleucid Empire. Hoping to improve their standing through a deft manipulation of marriage politics, Ptolemy VI and Cleopatra initially betrothed their daughter *Cleopatra Thea to a pretender, Alexander Balas, who had seized the Syrian throne from its king Demetrius I (150). When that marriage proved to be politically barren, the same daughter was forced to abandon her first husband to marry Demetrius II (145), the son of Demetrius I and thus the enemy of Alexander Balas. The latter took both personal and political affront at the Egyptian change of heart. Although Balas was unsuccessful in a military campaign fought in Palestine against the allied forces of Ptolemy VI and Demetrius II, Ptolemy VI died during this war as a result of a wound sustained when he fell from his horse.

Before his death, Ptolemy VI fathered four children with Cleopatra II: Ptolemy Eupator, Ptolemy VII Neos Philopator, Cleopatra III Euergetis, and Cleopatra Thea. The first of these predeceased both of his parents. Of the remaining children, Cleopatra III was promised to Ptolemy VIII (154), Cleopatra Thea became enmeshed in Seleucid politics, and Ptolemy Neos Philopator was established as the heir to his parents' joint throne.

As a result of Ptolemy VI's demise, Cleopatra II served briefly as regent for Ptolemy Neos Philopator, the younger of her sons. However, this arrangement did not last for long because Ptolemy VIII returned to Egypt to reclaim it as his own. Although Cleopatra II (with the help of a band of Jewish mercenaries) attempted to hold out against her brother, the Greek citizens of Alexandria weighed in decisively behind the return of Ptolemy VIII. As a result, Cleopatra II married her brother Ptolemy VIII (144), and the life of her younger son with Ptolemy VI was forfeited. Ptolemy VIII arranged for his murder.

Life at the Ptolemaic court became even more surreal. Not long after his return to Egypt and his marriage to Cleopatra II, Ptolemy VIII married the long-promised Cleopatra III (142), the daughter of his wife. Now married simultaneously to both mother and daughter, Ptolemy VIII was thus able to check Cleopatra II's status at court, being unable to do away with her completely. Although he certainly preferred the company of Cleopatra III, Ptolemy VIII nevertheless had a son (Ptolemy Memphites) with Cleopatra II. (In addition, the number of Ptolemy VIII's mistresses were legion, with their offspring granted positions of authority.) Eventually, tensions at court erupted into civil war (132), and Ptolemy VIII was driven temporarily to Cyprus with Cleopatra III and his children. Not the type to miss an opportunity for vengeance, while in exile Ptolemy VIII sent as a birthday gift to

Cleopatra II the dismembered body of their son, Ptolemy Memphites.

Loathe to reconcile with Ptolemy VIII, Cleopatra II was forced to defend Egypt against his efforts to return. He finally engineered a successful return in 127, driving her to Syria and the shelter of her son-in-law, King Demetrius II. Cleopatra II, however, managed to abscond with most of the Egyptian treasury. After Demetrius' domestic fortunes flagged, Cleopatra II—not one to abandon the prerogatives of a royal life—made her peace with Ptolemy VIII and returned home to her husband and daughter (124). Since Cleopatra II had the Egyptian treasury in hand, and since important regions in Upper Egypt remained loyal to her alone even after Ptolemy VIII and Cleopatra III controlled Lower Egypt, Cleopatra II was made "welcome" by her brother and daughter. Thereafter, a balance reigned between the interests and factions of Cleopatra II and of Ptolemy VIII-Cleopatra III. The greatest achievement of this period came in the Edict of 118 (collectively ordained by Ptolemy and both Cleopatras), which constituted a serious reform of Egyptian law, which had been long neglected amid the various plots and gambits of the royal house.

Although Cleopatra II died in 116 exhausted by years of trials and tribulations, she had the satisfaction of outliving Ptolemy VIII by a few months.

William S. Greenwalt,
Associate Professor of Classical History,
Santa Clara University, Santa Clara, California

Cleopatra III (c. 155–101 BCE)

Queen of Egypt. Name variations: Cleopatra III Euergetis. Born around 155 BCE in Egypt; died in 101 BCE; daughter of Ptolemy VI Philometor and Cleopatra II (c. 183–116 BCE); married her uncle-stepfather Ptolemy VIII Euergetes; children: two sons, Ptolemy IX Philometor Soter II and Ptolemy X Alexander I; three daughters, Cleopatra Selene, Cleopatra IV, and Cleopatra Tryphaena (d. after 112 BCE).

Cleopatra III was the daughter of Ptolemy VI Philometor and *Cleopatra II of Egypt, who were brother and sister as well as husband and wife. Cleopatra III's political life began when she was very young, for as an infant she was betrothed (but not sent) to her uncle Ptolemy VIII Euergetes (the younger sibling of her parents), then established on Cyprus. The death of her father Ptolemy VI in 145 BCE brought on the reign of Cleopatra III's brother, Ptolemy VII Neos

Philopator under her mother's regency. This government quickly failed, however, because the death of Ptolemy VI also sparked the return of Cleopatra III's uncle Ptolemy VIII to Egypt. In short succession, Ptolemy VIII married Cleopatra III's mother, murdered her brother, and elevated himself to the Egyptian throne on a par with Cleopatra II, his sister and new wife. At the first opportunity (probably in 142), Ptolemy VIII then married the young Cleopatra III who had been betrothed to him over a decade earlier. It is not known how willing a partner Cleopatra III was in her union with Ptolemy VIII; but, emerging as a woman of ruthless character, she would have five children with him, likely overcoming any initial qualms for the sake of power. Although polygamy had long been known among the Macedonians, Ptolemy VIII's union with Cleopatra III nevertheless raised eyebrows, for, as a result of this second marriage, he was wed to both mother and daughter simultaneously. Whereas the debauchery of Ptolemy VIII was infamous—distinctly pot-bellied, he was an exhibitionist who enjoyed wearing see-through gowns while lolling about the palace—he married Cleopatra III less for her charms than for politics, seeking to play daughter off against mother in order to check the latter's influence within Egypt's royal administration.

In the years that followed, the rivalry between Cleopatra III and her mother intensified, with both producing children with Ptolemy VIII: Cleopatra II had a son, Ptolemy Memphites; Cleopatra III had two sons, Ptolemy IX Philometor Soter II and Ptolemy X Alexander I, and three daughters, *Cleopatra Selene, *Cleopatra IV, and ◀❧ Cleopatra Tryphaena (d. after 112 BCE). The number of children born to Cleopatra III clearly demonstrates that Ptolemy VIII marginalized Cleopatra II, probably in an attempt to replace her in the affections of their subjects with her daughter. Tensions among the triple monarchs exploded into civil war in 132, with Cleopatra II enjoying initial success by driving Ptolemy VIII, Cleopatra III and their children to Cyprus; but the exiles also whisked away Cleopatra II's son Ptolemy Memphites, whom Ptolemy VIII brutally murdered to send his dismembered remains back to Cleopatra II as a birthday present. Despite Cleopatra II's early success, in 127 the forces of Ptolemy VIII and Cleopatra III drove her from Egypt to Syria. Their victory, however, was a hollow one, since Cleopatra II managed to smuggle the Egyptian treasury to Asia, and since most of Upper Egypt remained loyal to the exiled queen. For three years, both sides did everything within their power to overcome the other, but neither had the strength to do so decisively. As a result of their stalemate, and with Seleucid affairs turning against Cleopatra II's interests, a reconciliation was arranged. Cleopatra II returned to Egypt to rule again at the side of Ptolemy VIII and Cleopatra III, who, for their part, "welcomed" Cleopatra's return for the wealth she had in hand and for the peace she brought to Upper Egypt. The three monarchs then collectively reigned for eight relatively quiet years. Of note from this period was the Edict of 118, which made a significant effort to reform Egyptian law after years of neglect and irresponsible rule.

In 116, Ptolemy VIII died, leaving the two Cleopatras to rule with Cleopatra III's older son, Ptolemy IX. Three months later, Cleopatra II also died. Thereafter, the independent personality of Cleopatra III fully emerged as she strove to arrange Ptolemaic affairs to her own liking. Seizing control of the court, she made certain her subjects knew of her status by demanding that she always be awarded first mention in official documents. Though she did not care much for the older of her two sons (perhaps because she found him difficult to manipulate), she was incapable of disassociating him from royal authority because of his popularity among the Greeks of Alexandria. Cleopatra III nevertheless fostered the interests of the younger son Ptolemy X Alexander as much as possible. For example, Cleopatra took pains for him to escape the shadow of his older brother's status, by establishing him in Cyprus (116) where he could cultivate an independent power base. As much as she inclined toward her younger son, Cleopatra III also jealously guarded her control of Ptolemy IX; when he began to rely on the support of his sister-wife, Cleopatra IV, in an attempt to liberate himself somewhat from their mother's influence, Cleopatra III quickly arranged their divorce. Cleopatra III then forced Ptolemy IX to marry another, more tractable younger sister named Cleopatra Selene (115–114). Intrigue thereafter followed intrigue as Cleopatra III and Ptolemy IX sparred for control of Egypt.

Attempts by Cleopatra III to oust Ptolemy IX in 110 and 108 in favor of the younger Ptolemy Alexander failed, but in 107 she took decisive action after Ptolemy IX sent troops to a Syrian ally in order to war upon the Jews of Palestine without Cleopatra III's approval (Jews made up a large part of her support in Alexandria, thus inclining her to look favorably on Jews elsewhere). Staging the events carefully, Cleopatra III had some of her own supporters roughed up so that they could claim that they had received their wounds defending her from an assassination attempt planned by Ptolemy IX. Fanning passions thereafter, Cleopatra III inflamed the city of Alexandria against Ptolemy IX, forcing him to flee for the relative safety of Cyprus.

Seizing the moment, Cleopatra III had Ptolemy Alexander recalled to Egypt where he was installed as her colleague, Ptolemy X. Hoping to stave off an attempted return of Ptolemy IX, Cleopatra III ordered him seized before he could establish himself. When this order failed to be carried out, Cleopatra was so displeased that she had the officer responsible executed. Though Ptolemy IX would live to return to Egypt some time after his mother's death, he came to flourish on Cyprus while she was still in power in Egypt to such an extent that Cleopatra III did everything she could (including marrying her daughter Cleopatra Selene to the Seleucid Antiochus VIII in 102) to secure Egypt against his return.

Meanwhile her relationship with her younger son Ptolemy X, who proved not to be as docile as she expected, began to deteriorate. By 103, Ptolemy X had become so disgusted with his mother's will to dominate his life that he withdrew from Alexandria to raise an army against her. Unable to hold out against two hostile sons, Cleopatra III attempted a reconciliation with the younger. Feigning a willingness to comply, he returned to the city in 101, only to murder his mother shortly after his return.

An imperious queen whose career did little to foster the health and well-being of Egypt, Cleopatra III nevertheless was not an entirely political being. She was a devoted follower of the goddess Isis and lavished funds to foster that goddess' worship. Also, realizing the potential political and economical benefits to be had from the establishment of a regular trade between India and Egypt, she sponsored voyages of exploration and trade under the maritime adventurer, Eudoxus of Cyzicus.

William S. Greenwalt,
Associate Professor of Classical History,
Santa Clara University, Santa Clara, California

Cleopatra IV (c. 135–112 BCE)

Queen of Egypt. Born around 135 BCE; died in 112 BCE; daughter of Ptolemy VIII Euergetes II and Cleopatra III (c. 155–101 BCE); married full brother, Ptolemy IX Philometor Soter II (divorced 115 BCE); married Antiochus IX Philopator Cyzicenus, a Seleucid king, in 113 BCE; children: (first marriage) possibly **Cleopatra Berenice III**.

Cleopatra IV was the daughter of Ptolemy VIII Euergetes II and his niece-wife, *Cleopatra III Euergetis of Egypt. She was first married to her full brother, Ptolemy IX Philometor Soter II, and subsequently to the Seleucid Antiochus IX Philopator Cyzicenus. Cleopatra IV was the middle of three sisters, *Cleopatra Selene being the younger, and ◄⚜ Cleopatra Tryphaena, who first married the Seleucid king Antiochus VIII Philometor Grypus, being the older. The marriage of Cleopatra IV to her first husband Ptolemy IX was congenial to both; but when Ptolemy IX, under Cleopatra IV's influence, began to challenge their mother's control of Egyptian affairs, Cleopatra III forced their divorce and Ptolemy IX's remarriage to Cleopatra Selene (115).

Furious that her political ambitions had been frustrated by her mother's interference, Cleopatra IV fled Egypt for Cyprus where she raised an army loyal to herself. She then led this army to Seleucid Syria where she offered it to her cousin, Antiochus IX Cyzicenus who was engaged in a civil war against his half-brother Antiochus VIII Grypus (both were sons of *Cleopatra Thea, the sister of Cleopatra III). Antiochus IX subsequently married Cleopatra IV (113), but, in the conflict that followed, she was trapped in Antioch by his brother Antiochus VIII (112). Seeking sanctuary, Cleopatra IV escaped to an altar of Artemis where she pleaded in vain for her life. At the insistence of her own sister Cleopatra Tryphaena, Cleopatra IV was executed before she could even be dragged from the sacred precinct. It is reported that Tryphaena insisted upon Cleopatra IV's murder because she feared that her husband, the rival Antiochus VIII, might be susceptible to her charms. Antiochus IX, doubly angered by the loss of Cleopatra IV and the impiety of her demise, made sure that when the tables were turned and Cleopatra Tryphaena had fallen into his hands, she was similarly shown no mercy.

William S. Greenwalt,
Associate Professor of Classical History,
Santa Clara University, Santa Clara, California

⚜► **Cleopatra Tryphaena** (d. after 112 BCE)
*Queen of Syria. Condemned to death by Antiochus IX Cyzicenus after 112 BCE; daughter of Ptolemy VIII Euergetes II and *Cleopatra III Euergetis (c. 155–101 BCE) of Egypt; sister of *Cleopatra IV and *Cleopatra Selene; married Antiochus VIII Grypus, Seleucid king (r. 125–96 BCE); children: Seleucus VI and Antiochus X Eusebes Philopator.*

Cleopatra V Selene (c. 40 BCE–?).
See Cleopatra VII for sidebar.

Cleopatra V Tryphaena
(c. 95–c. 57 BCE)

*Queen of Egypt. Name variations: Cleopatra VI Tryphaena or Tryphaeana. Born around 95 BCE; died around 57 BCE; illegitimate daughter of Ptolemy IX Philometor Soter II Lathyros of Egypt and an unknown mother; married possibly full-brother Ptolemy XII Theos Philopator Philadelphus Neos Dionysus, in 80 BCE; children: possibly two sons, Ptolemy XIII and Ptolemy XIV; and three daughters, *Berenice IV (d. 55 BCE), *Arsinoe IV (d. 41 BCE), and *Cleopatra VII (69–30 BCE).*

Cleopatra V Tryphaena was the illegitimate daughter of Ptolemy IX Philometor Soter II Lathyros of Egypt by an unknown mother, and the (perhaps full) sister-wife of Ptolemy XII Theos Philopator Philadelphus Neos Dionysus (as the Ptolemaic dynasty devolved, the titles associated with those who sought kingship grew), whom the citizens of Alexandria nicknamed *Auletes* (the flute player). Cleopatra V Tryphaena married Auletes in late 80 immediately after his initial attempt to secure the vacant Ptolemaic throne, an attempt that was disputed as a result of his own illegitimacy. Their marriage attempted to bolster his claim to the throne, as if the half claims of two illegitimate siblings could combine to constitute one legitimate stake. Never popular in Egypt, Auletes depended on the friendship of Rome to maintain power and heavily "lobbied" the Roman Senate, spending a fortune in bribes to insure his restoration. A hedonistic roué, Auletes was expelled from Egypt in 59, only to return backed by Roman military might four years later. Cleopatra V Tryphaena is a shadowy figure throughout most of Auletes' reign because she maintained a low profile, unlike other women of her line. Auletes fathered at least five children—two sons, Ptolemy XIII and Ptolemy XIV; and three daughters, *Berenice IV, *Arsinoe IV, and *Cleopatra VII—some, or all of whom, may have been by Cleopatra V Tryphaena. Since Auletes was a noted womanizer, there is no way to know how many children Cleopatra V Tryphaena had. In lieu of better evidence, it is possible that Cleopatra V was the mother of Cleopatra VII (the identity of whose mother is nowhere revealed), the most famous queen produced by the Ptolemaic dynasty.

When Auletes was temporarily deposed by his Alexandrian subjects in 59, Cleopatra V

Tryphaena reigned as regent on behalf of her (probable) daughter, Berenice IV. However, Cleopatra did not live to see Egypt politically settled, for she died (probably in 57) before the Romans restored her husband Auletes to the Ptolemaic throne (55).

William S. Greenwalt,
Associate Professor of Classical History,
Santa Clara University, Santa Clara, California

Cleopatra VI Tryphaena (c. 95–c. 57 BCE).

See Cleopatra V Tryphaena.

Cleopatra VII (69–30 BCE)

Queen of Egypt, mistress of Julius Caesar, eventual wife of Mark Antony, who was the last—but certainly not the least—of the Ptolemaic dynasty to rule Egypt. Name variations: sometimes known as Cleopatra VI. Born in 69 BCE; committed suicide on August 10, 30 BCE; daughter of Ptolemy XII (king of Egypt) and possibly Cleopatra V Tryphaena (c. 95–c. 57 BCE); sister of Ptolemy XIII, Ptolemy XIV, *Berenice IV (d. 55 BCE) and Arsinoe IV (d. 41 BCE); married brother Ptolemy XIII, in 51 BCE; married brother Ptolemy XIV, in 47 BCE; children: (with Julius Caesar) Ptolemy XV Caesar (Caesarion); (with Marc Antony) twins Alexander Helios and Cleopatra V Selene (b. around 40 BCE) and another Ptolemy (b. 36 BCE).

Ascended to the throne (51 BCE) as co-ruler with her brother-husband, Ptolemy XIII; became lover of Caesar; pregnant with Caesar's child and married brother Ptolemy XIV (47 BCE); traveled to Rome to be with Caesar (46 BCE) but remained no more than his mistress at the time of his assassination (44 BCE); returned to Egypt; seeing her salvation in Antony, seduced him; with Antony, was in open war against Octavian, concluding in Octavian's victory (31 BCE); along with Antony, forced into suicide (30 BCE).

Cleopatra VII was of the Ptolemaic royal house, founded in Egypt by Ptolemy I at the end of the 4th century BCE. Ptolemy I had been a Macedonian general in the army of Alexander the Great, through whose conquests Egypt had come within the Greek political orbit. Alexander seized Egypt from the Persians in 333 BCE and thereafter founded Alexandria, the city that bore his name, from which his political successors ruled Egypt. When Alexander's direct line died out in 310 BCE, Ptolemy I took possession of the rich kingdom centered on the Nile River valley. Ptolemy I's dynasty, however, did not sustain the political and military talent that had enabled him to wrest Egypt from his many rivals. By the

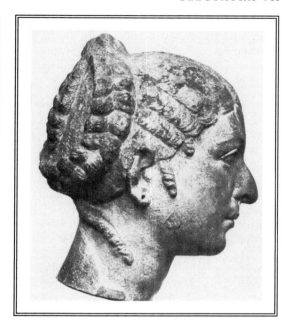

Cleopatra VII

middle of the 1st century BCE, until Cleopatra VII later revived its fortunes somewhat, degeneracy was the dynasty's norm.

Cleopatra's father Ptolemy XII, the "Flute-Player," was a pro-Roman hedonist who was unpopular with the Greek inhabitants of Alexandria (few native Egyptians were allowed inside the city, and its large Jewish population did not wield political clout), because they knew that he could not maintain his rule without foreign backing and that Rome craved Egypt for its enviable wealth. After Ptolemy XII came to the throne in 80 BCE, his domestic authority deteriorated, leading to his expulsion from Egypt in 58 BCE. He remained exiled in Rome until forcibly reinstated by a Roman show of power, obtained at enormous cost, in 55 BCE. Thereafter, Ptolemy XII ruled under Rome's thumb until 51 BCE. Officially married to his sister, *Cleopatra V Tryphaena (since the reign of Ptolemy II, brother/sister royal marriage had been a Ptolemaic custom), he nevertheless fathered several children with other women of acknowledged status at the Alexandrian court. These offspring were considered fully legitimate and raised with all due honor. Among these was Cleopatra VII (born 69 BCE), whose mother may, or may not, have been Cleopatra V.

We know little of Cleopatra VII's youth. The intelligence that would later seem so impressive to her contemporaries probably made her a precocious child, and modern scholars often note that her father must have early recognized this intelligence and promoted her education. Her father's example would have shown her that Roman senators were the most profound threat to an independent Egypt, but that these senators could be manipulated to the benefit of her nation. Her later policy would exploit this rationale.

Cleopatra had remained in Egypt during her father's exile. When she was 14, she met a young Marc Antony, a junior officer among the Romans responsible for her father's return; it is likely they took little notice of each other at the time. In Alexandria, Cleopatra developed the taste for reading, doubtless exposed to that city's famed Library, which fueled her curiosity and provided her with the intellectual range that her paramours would find so enticing. As a child, she learned the language of the native Egyptians—the first of her dynasty to have taken the time to do so. Her unique interest in her kingdom's non-Greek population marked a political sagacity long dormant among the Ptolemies. From an early age, Cleopatra understood that both her own future and Egypt's depended largely upon her ability to tap the loyalty of the ancient land's entire population.

$\mathcal{F}$or her beauty was not without compare, nor such as to enthrall those who saw her. Her conversation, however, was irresistibly charming, and her demeanor . . . was utterly arousing.

—Plutarch, *Life of Antony*

Upon their father's death in 51 BCE, Cleopatra VII (then 17) and her brother, Ptolemy XIII (then around 11), married and jointly acceded to the throne. This, however, was no love match. In a marriage fostered by tradition and by palace power brokers—intended more to consolidate the influence of a political clique than to enhance the strength of Egypt—Cleopatra soon chafed under the restraints thrust upon her. As a result, the sibling/spouses and their respective factions feuded, with Ptolemy's bloc gaining the initial advantage. Cleopatra was expelled from Alexandria, probably fleeing first to Arabia before establishing herself amidst a garrison at Pelusium, on Egypt's northeastern coast.

Meanwhile, Rome's situation paralleled Egypt's somewhat since a civil war between Julius Caesar and Pompeius Magnus (Pompey) foretold the final collapse of its Republican constitution. When war erupted (49 BCE), both Ptolemy XIII and Cleopatra backed Pompey with money, ships, men, and supplies. Their rationale was simple: both thought Pompey would

win, and each sought to curry favor, which could thereafter be turned to personal benefit. In addition to the rendering of military aid, Cleopatra is also said to have fostered her interests by having a willing advocate within Pompey's camp; she is reported to have seduced his son.

Caesar, however, surprised everyone with a lightning-swift campaign that ended in Greece with a victory over Pompey (48 BCE). Defeated in battle but not captured, Pompey fled to Alexandria where he hoped to restore his fortunes. Before his arrival, Ptolemy XIII reconsidered the situation and decided that it was Caesar who must now be wooed. At Ptolemy's command, assassins killed Pompey as he attempted to step onto Egyptian soil.

Caesar quickly made for Alexandria and the hornet's nest of political conspiracy that city represented. Needing to secure Egypt swiftly, and grateful for the "service" rendered by the young king, Caesar seemed about to proclaim his support for Ptolemy XIII in the latter's struggle against Cleopatra. But, at night, Cleopatra had herself hidden in a bed-roll and smuggled into Caesar's room. Described as "imperious, determined, courageous, ambitious, intensely alive," by biographer **Eleanor Goltz Huzar**, Cleopatra has been called Caesar's female counterpart, even in intelligence and education. The next morning Caesar became her avid proponent.

Intrigue followed during which Caesar tried to reconcile the political marriage of Ptolemy XIII and Cleopatra (while Caesar remained her lover), as well as to accommodate the concerns of two younger siblings—***Arsinoe IV** and Ptolemy XIV. Arsinoe, securing armed backing, was the first to rebel; soon, Ptolemy XIII joined the revolt and besieged Caesar and Cleopatra in Alexandria. The resulting clash almost cost Caesar and Cleopatra their lives. Caesar, however, heroically organized and led a harried defense. Some of Alexandria burned in the process, with perhaps a portion of the famous Library engulfed by the conflagration. Eventually, Caesar was reinforced and rallied to defeat his foes, after which the fleeing Ptolemy XIII abetted a quick resolution of the conflict by unheroically drowning in the Nile during the course of a naval campaign.

Thereafter, Caesar imposed order throughout the city and the realm. He took his time with the latter, in the process taking a leisurely cruise up the Nile with Cleopatra at his side. But by early 47 BCE, events beyond Egypt intruded upon the momentary respite in his military responsibilities. Consequently, Caesar left Egypt for Syria, leaving Cleopatra in Alexandria with two significant mementos of his visit and political settlement: a new brother/husband, Ptolemy XIV (about age 11); and a son, Ptolemy XV Caesar, known as Caesarion. In light of Cleopatra's pregnancy (known before Caesar left Egypt, though the boy was not born until after Caesar's departure), and the fact that the child's father was in the process of becoming the sole ruler of the Roman world while still without a legitimate heir, few imagined that Ptolemy XIV would remain Cleopatra's spouse and co-regent for long. In fact, we can be fairly certain that Cleopatra hoped to see her union with Caesar officially acknowledged, so as to fuse Rome with Egypt and allow both to be ruled by a royal house established by their offspring.

In 46 BCE, the lovers reunited in Rome, where Caesar erected a golden statue of Cleopatra in the temple of Venus Genetrix. With Cleopatra came Caesarion and Ptolemy XIV, with whom Cleopatra probably did not consummate her marriage. Officially, Cleopatra's status remained undefined. Despite his obvious infatuation, since 59 BCE Caesar had been married to *Calpurnia, whose impeccable Senatorial connections made her rejection in favor of a foreign queen a delicate matter. Equally dangerous would have been a public acknowledgement of Caesarion's paternity. With the civil war so recently won, the situation in Rome was fraught with ambiguity. Would Caesar agree to a continuation of traditional constitutional constraints upon his authority or would he now aspire to kingship? All the city's ruling elite were extremely nervous about Caesar's long-term ambitions. Whatever Caesar's intention, he did not need to stir up unnecessary opposition: the wisest course, therefore, was one of delay and political consolidation. This meant that Cleopatra would have to await a more settled political climate before Caesar could afford to endow her and her son with the legitimacy she sought.

That climate never materialized. On March 15, 44 BCE, a republican coterie assassinated Caesar. With his death, Cleopatra lost a golden opportunity to elevate Egypt above servile de-

Augustus Caesar and Cleopatra *by August von Heckel.*

pendency and to augment her personal majesty. After the assassination, Cleopatra and Caesarion promptly returned to the relative safety of Egypt, anticipating the renewal of Roman civil war. This was an especially dangerous time for both, for whoever emerged triumphant from the looming carnage would be unlikely to tolerate the potential threat of Caesarion (unacknowledged as he was) to some day lay claim to Caesar's legacy. As dangerous as the times were for Cleopatra and Caesarion, they proved even more so for Cleopatra's husband Ptolemy XIV who had mysteriously died shortly after Caesar, probably poisoned at Cleopatra's command. Cleopatra then claimed joint rule with her son Caesarion, still a toddler, and coins from the period show her suckling him in the guise of the Egyptian goddess Isis nursing her divine son Horus.

By default, Mark Antony became the sole leader of the loyal Caesarian faction immediately after Caesar's murder. Nonetheless, he proceeded cautiously, not knowing the extent of the conspiracy, nor precisely how the Roman mob might react to developments. The assassins, whose anti-Caesarian propaganda held sway for a time, nonetheless lost control of the situation when they allowed Caesar's will to be read publicly. That document contained two especially important provisions: a generous legacy from Caesar's private fortune to every Roman citizen and the posthumous adoption as Caesar's heir—not of Caesarion but of Caesar's little known greatnephew, Octavian (the future Caesar Augustus). Knowing that his true friends expected his faction to continue but also realizing that they would not willingly follow the unacknowledged son of a foreign queen, Caesar had hoped to avoid another civil war by passing over Caesarion in favor of another blood relative. All political calculations were at once refigured.

After Caesar's will was read, the assassins were hounded to the provinces where they prepared for war. Mark Antony also mobilized, but, needing money to do so, he refused to distribute the largesse promised in Caesar's will. Antony's failure here opened the door for Octavian (whom Antony tried to ignore), who borrowed heavily to pay off his "father's" debt. Public sympathy then swung to Octavian. Machinations followed, but after a short time a compromise alliance (the "Second Triumvirate") was arranged between Antony, Octavian, and a Lepidus (a partisan soon outpaced by his colleagues) through which the Caesarian party was reunited. Unified and armed, the Caesarian junta sought vengeance for Caesar's death. The final blow came in 42 BCE, with Antony hailed as the triumvir most responsible for victory against the assassins. Thereafter, much remained to be settled to the new junta's liking and so the Roman world was divided among them into three parts, with Antony taking the East.

Now that Octavian was Caesar's legal heir, Cleopatra and her son Caesarion had much to fear. In Egypt, she supported the Caesarians but not as enthusiastically as she might. When she finally collected a fleet for use against the assassins, foul weather prevented its deployment before the war ended. Held accountable for her apathy, Cleopatra was summoned to Tarsus by Antony to explain her passivity. A more golden opportunity for her to win a champion, split the ruling coalition, and rejuvenate the dream recently shattered by Caesar's death could not have been conjured. Although Antony (now married to *Fulvia) knew Cleopatra from Egypt and Rome, he was unprepared for what was coming—for she would soon loose upon him the full impact of her charm.

Cleopatra approached Tarsus leisurely, with many gifts and theatrical pomp. The last part of her trip was taken on a perfumed barge complete with silver oars and purple sails. Dressed as Venus, she planted rumors that Venus incarnate was coming to mate with Bacchus, then paraded to Antony's quarters escorted by boys attired as "Lusts" and girls arrayed as "Graces." While they feasted, Cleopatra's sophisticated wit and irresistible allure intoxicated Antony, who became her lover. Antony was so overawed by Cleopatra that she was accused of employing witchcraft or magic to enthrall him, since she was not known for her beauty. After this renewal of their acquaintance, Antony accepted an invitation to visit Alexandria. Meanwhile, Antony's wife and brother, outraged by the way Octavian was arranging Italian affairs against Antony's interests, though some suggested that Fulvia acted more to recall Antony from Cleopatra's arms, engaged Antony's nominal ally in open war (41 BCE).

Grace Macurdy voiced a common perspective among modern historians of antiquity when she called Antony "strong in action and weak in will, gallant and brave where physical courage was required, but incapable of self-control and victim of his appetites." After months of immoderation, with Italy in an uproar and conditions deteriorating on Rome's Parthian frontier in the east, Antony felt constrained to stir (40 BCE). Since the domestic situation was the more pressing, Antony proceed-

From the movie Cleopatra, *starring Claudette Colbert.*

ed to Italy via Greece. In Egypt, Cleopatra re- mained, pregnant with the twins Alexander He- lios (sun) and ✥➤ **Cleopatra V Selene** (moon) who would be born after their father's depar- ture. Passing through Athens, Antony met and rebuffed his wife Fulvia, who died shortly thereafter. In Italy, political reality combined with his geographical distance from Cleopatra to persuade Antony to embrace a renewal of his alliance with Octavian—this time cemented by Antony's marriage to Octavian's sister, the well- educated and beautiful *Octavia.

See sidebar on the following page

❧▸ **Cleopatra V Selene** (c. 40 BCE–?)

Queen of Cyrene and Numidia. Name variations: Cleopatra of Cyrene. Born around 40 BCE; daughter of *Cleopatra VII (69–30 BCE, queen of Egypt) and Marc Antony; married Rome's Mauritanian client king, Juba II, king of Numidia; children: Ptolemy Caesarion. Ruled Cyrene around 33–31 BCE.

With the Triumvirate rejuvenated, Antony and his wife Octavia ventured to rule the East from Greece. For three years, they lived in apparent contentment, though the political ambitions of both Antony and Octavian put great strain on the marriage. Antony saw Octavia bear two children, even as she diplomatically intervened to prevent a breach between her brother and husband. Both Octavian and Antony, however, coveted the unfettered power of Caesar. Of the two, Octavian made the most out of the years of peace, carefully consolidating his personal following while simultaneously working loyal clients into positions of power. Though Antony was a capable leader, he lacked Octavian's aptitude for political manipulation. Over time, he saw himself being edged out of power and came to realize that only success in war could reestablish his power base in Rome. The East, where trouble had been festering with the Parthians since the 50s BCE, gave him his opportunity.

Going to war against Parthia in 37 BCE, Antony left behind Octavia (burdened with her third pregnancy) to continue her mediation with her brother Octavian while caring for her children. This separation provided Cleopatra with another opportunity to advance her political ambitions. She met Antony at Antioch in Syria with military support; once they were reunited, Antony again succumbed to her magnetism. Cleopatra forced Antony to burn many of his Roman bridges by inducing him to publicly acknowledge his paternity of their twins and their third child, another Ptolemy, born in 36 BCE. Even more inflammatory, she convinced Antony to grant her authority over Phoenicia, Coele Syria, Cyprus, parts of Cilicia, and important revenues from the spice trade—all considered by Romans to be possessions of the Roman Imperium. The two traveled eastward together as far as the Euphrates frontier, permitting Cleopatra to cement her emotional hold over Antony. Before fighting began, she returned to Egypt via Judea, where she was feted by Herod the Great. Within a year, an unsuccessful Antony returned from Parthia with a tattered army. Depressed at the failure of his invasion and needing the comfort of Cleopatra's companionship, Antony summoned her to meet him in Phoenicia. She did so bearing material aid for the army and emotional solace for its general.

Despite his obviously insulting behavior, when news of Antony's loss reached Rome, Octavia also organized and personally led a relief effort. At Athens, however, she received an order to proceed no further, clearly at the instigation of Cleopatra, who feared Antony's emotional inconstancy. Octavia returned to Rome (35 BCE), where remarkably she resisted her brother's insistence that she abandon Antony's interests. Rather, she maintained his Roman house (until formally divorced in 32 BCE) and continued to look after their children.

After wintering in Alexandria, Antony relieved some of his frustration by subduing Armenia, for which he celebrated a Triumph in Alexandria, not Rome. Compounding the shock of this innovation, he also delivered the traditional thanksgiving offering not to Jupiter, but to Cleopatra dressed as the Egyptian goddess Isis. There followed an incredible scene in which Antony proclaimed himself and Cleopatra the king and queen of the East. Then he dispersed both Roman lands and others not under his control. To Cleopatra and Caesarion (whom he publicly declared Caesar's son and rightful heir—implicitly disinheriting Octavian), he gave Egypt, Cyprus, Libya, and Coele Syria. To Alexander Helios, he conferred Armenia, Media and Parthia. Cyrenaica went to Cleopatra Selene, and Phoenicia, Syria, and Cilicia to the younger Ptolemy. Cleopatra subsequently let it be known that she anticipated the day when she would dispense justice from the Capitol in Rome. Clearly, a Rubicon had been crossed; the forthcoming encounter would be for the possession of the entire Roman world.

During the period of mobilization that followed, Octavian carefully prepared his ground through an adept manipulation of propaganda. Wanting all of Rome behind him, he accused Cleopatra of having seduced Antony from his responsibilities and his heritage. Although Antony and Cleopatra apparently went through some sort of marriage ceremony before 36 BCE, Roman law and Octavian refused to recognize their union. She was depicted as archetypically evil—a demon against which all Romans had the patriotic obligation to fight. She thus was unfavorably contrasted with every virtue traditionally associated with "proper" Roman matrons (not surprisingly associated with Octavia, who piously bore Antony's inconstancy). Immoral and foreign, Cleopatra, if successful, would replace Rome's respect for law with oriental despotism, it was claimed. What news filtered back to Rome of Antony and Cleopatra's ostentation (he openly sported a golden scepter and royal attire, while she reportedly consumed pearls with her vintage wine) only seemed to confirm Octavian's allegations.

In 32 BCE, Rome declared war, not against Antony, but against Cleopatra alone. Although some of Antony's friends attempted negotiations dependent upon a rejection of Cleopatra, all efforts to disassociate Antony from her failed. Perhaps to insure that distance would not erode her control over Antony, Cleopatra remained at his side (albeit with a considerable military contingent).

After some strategic maneuvering, the showdown came on September 2, 31 BCE, when Octavian's navy, commanded by Marcus Agrippa, defeated his enemies at Actium, off the western coast of Greece. Antony and Cleopatra fled immediately to Egypt to attempt a defensive stand and ward off possible rebellion. In Egypt, disappointment fed feverish carousing and atrocities against any who might have had the wherewithal or inclination to side with Octavian. By the spring of 30 BCE, Octavian's noose around Egypt began to tighten and frantic but unsuccessful negotiations were undertaken. Octavian, however, would neither allow Antony to live as a private citizen, nor permit Cleopatra's children to continue as Egypt's rulers. Whatever truth, if any, lay behind the charges that Octavian attempted to bargain with Cleopatra for Antony's murder is no longer recoverable. In the end, all alternatives were cut off but unconditional surrender. When Antony heard a false report of Cleopatra's suicide, he attempted to take his life and ultimately died in her arms. Cleopatra was captured, but, a queen to the very last, she smuggled a poisonous asp to her room and sought death in its bite—at the time, a symbol of Egyptian royal authority over 3,000 years old. She died on August 10, 30 BCE, thinking she had seen her son Caesarion to safety. Caesarion, however, was quickly murdered. Cleopatra's children by Antony were sent to be raised by Octavia in Rome. Eventually, Cleopatra Selene married Rome's Mauritanian client king, Juba II. Although the fates of Cleopatra Selene's brothers are uncertain, they perhaps went with her to north Africa. Regardless, she alone of her siblings knew the prerogatives of royal power. When Cleopatra Selene's son Ptolemy Caesarion was executed by Caligula, the line of Ptolemies ended.

From the movie Cleopatra, *starring Elizabeth Taylor.*

Though Cleopatra had only two known lovers, one of whom she married, Octavian's portrait of her as an evil harlot unfortunately prevails. Rather, she was the last ptolemaic ruler of Egypt, whose only crime seems to have been her desire to safeguard her country's independence and rebuild its power in the East.

SOURCES:

[Caesar], *Alexandrian War*. Loeb Classical Library. Cambridge, MA: Harvard University Press, 1922.

Cassius Dio. *Dio's Roman History*. Vols. IV, V, VI. NY: Putnam, 1914, 1916, 1917.

Huzar, Eleanor Goltz. *Mark Antony: A Biography*. Croom Helm, 1978.

Plutarch. *Life of Caesar*. Loeb Classical Library. Cambridge, MA: Harvard University Press, 1917.

———. *Life of Antony*. Loeb Classical Library. Cambridge, MA: Harvard University Press, 1920.

SUGGESTED READING:

Appian. *Appian's Roman History*. Vols. III and IV. Macmillan, 1913.

Bevan, E.R. *The House of Ptolemy*. Ares (reprint), 1968.

Grant, Michael. *Cleopatra*. 2nd ed. NY: Macmillan, 1974.

Lindsay, Jack. *Cleopatra*. NY: Coward, 1970.

Macurdy, Grace H. *Hellenistic Queens*. CT: Greenwood, 1975.

Pomeroy, Sarah Borges. *Women In Hellenistic Egypt from Alexander to Cleopatra*. Schocken, 1984.

William S. Greenwalt,
Associate Professor of Classical History,
Santa Clara University, Santa Clara, California

Cleopatra Berenice III (c. 115–80 BCE)

Queen of Egypt and one of the most beloved Ptolemies of the last century of that dynasty's rule in Egypt. Name variations: Berenice III. Born Berenice but took the name Cleopatra when she married. Born Berenice around 115 BCE; murdered in 80 BCE; daughter of Ptolemy IX Philometer Soter II Lathyros (meaning Ptolemy the Mother Loving; also known by the population of Alexandria as "Physcon," that is, the "Pot-Bellied") and Cleopatra IV or Cleopatra Selene; married her uncle Ptolemy X Alexander I, in 102 or 101 BCE (died 88 BCE); married her father Ptolemy IX (died 80 BCE); married Ptolemy XI Alexander II, in 80 BCE; children: (first marriage) one daughter.

Few royal dynasties anywhere in the world have ever achieved the level of decadence attained by Egypt's Ptolemaic dynasty during the last century of its existence (c. 130–30 BCE). General incompetency, however, did not prevent the emergence of a monarch worthy of the royal title. Although the most famous member of the Ptolemaic house was its last scion, *Cleopatra VII, Cleopatra Berenice III overcame the prevailing faults of her line to act as a responsible queen, when every obstacle imaginable stood in her way.

Due to omissions in the extant evidence, we do not know the precise kinship relations among important members of Cleopatra Berenice III's close family. As a result, we cannot be absolutely certain about the factions that split the royal house, which presents a problem for interpreting the politics of the Ptolemaic court during the three generations prior to Egypt's absorption into the Roman Empire.

To understand Cleopatra Berenice III, one must first understand her dynastic context. Her father was Ptolemy IX Philometer Soter II Lathyros (that is, Ptolemy the "Mother Loving," "Savior" and, oddly enough, "Chickpea"). Cleopatra Berenice III's paternal grandparents were Ptolemy VIII Euergetes II Physcon (the "Benefactor" and "Pot-Bellied") and *Cleopatra III. Cleopatra Berenice III's mother is not known for certain, but the two most likely possibilities are her father's first and second wives, *Cleopatra IV and *Cleopatra Selene, respectively. If Cleopatra

Berenice III's mother was Cleopatra IV, then Berenice was born before 116 BCE when her father Ptolemy IX assumed the Egyptian throne. If Cleopatra Berenice III's mother was Cleopatra Selene, then she was born after 115 BCE, thus after her father became the king of Egypt.

Cleopatra Berenice III's story begins either about the time of her birth or slightly earlier (depending upon which of these women was her mother). In 116 BCE, Ptolemy VIII died, leaving his wife, Cleopatra III, to rule Egypt in conjunction with whichever of their two sons she preferred. Although the deceased king had hoped that his older son, Ptolemy IX, would follow in his footsteps, Cleopatra III favored the elevation of her younger son, Ptolemy X Alexander I (hereafter, Ptolemy X). Obviously the court was divided into at least two significant factions, but it is impossible to say whether these were distinguished primarily by policy disagreements, or merely by personalities.

It should by now be clear that "Ptolemy" was an established dynastic name—as would become "Cleopatra" after the elevation of Berenice Cleopatra III, for, although other Cleopatras preceded her on the throne, Berenice was the first to take the name upon her accession. It should also be noted that as far as royal was conceived and symbolized in Egypt, queens were as important as their male consorts. Both kings and queens were the objects of worship both by the Ptolemies' Greek subjects and by indigenous Egyptians. In fact, royal power was largely associated with a unification of male-female opposites come together in (supposedly) perfect harmony, following, on one plane, the model of the Osiris and Isis. The union of these two deities (who were both brother and sister and husband and wife) represented the perfect union upon which all proper order was thought to rest. In one aspect, Osiris represented all of the good that accompanies well-arranged social order, while Isis represented primal nature perfectly managed. The masculine and the feminine thus intimately wed were thought essential for the health and well being of Egypt. Although the importance of Osiris and Isis to Egypt was greater than royal legitimacy alone, and although Ptolemaic kings and queens were frequently associated with other divinities (for example, Ptolemaic queens were often styled "Aphrodite"), it is clear that the inhabitants of Egypt expected royal authority to be shared by a man and a woman.

Although Cleopatra III would have had it otherwise, Ptolemy IX (with the support of the Alexandrian population and a developing Ptolemaic tradition of primogeniture) assumed his father's kingship. Nevertheless, hoping to secure an advantage over Ptolemy IX upon his accession, Cleopatra III forced him to divorce his sister-wife, Cleopatra IV (whom he loved), and to marry another of his sisters (and another daughter of Cleopatra III), Cleopatra Selene. This demand antagonized Ptolemy IX, but perhaps was justified by the aftermath, for clearly Cleopatra IV had little love for her mother: split from her brother-husband, Cleopatra IV went to Cyprus (long a possession of the Ptolemaic house) where she raised an army, seemingly to overthrow her mother Cleopatra III. On Cyprus, Cleopatra IV met up with her younger brother, Ptolemy X, who had previously made his way to the island having had his royal ambitions temporarily frustrated by the accession of his older brother. Although no source says so, the two might have made common cause, and perhaps were married (see below for a possible child from this possible union). If so, Cleopatra IV's ambition soon took another tangent, for she abandoned an attempt to return to Egypt in favor of venturing with her army to Syria, where she offered herself and her troops to Antiochus IX Cyzicenus, himself locked in a dynastic struggle against his half-brother, Antiochus VIII Grypus, for a control of the Seleucid Empire. Thus wed, we will leave Cleopatra IV to her own entry, although perhaps it should be mentioned that Grypus was already married to her sister ❧ **Cleopatra Tryphaena** and that Cleopatra IV soon met her death at the hands of said sister.

Why Cleopatra Selene was more to the liking of Cleopatra III than Cleopatra IV is not said, but it is certain that Cleopatra III believed Selene more malleable in her interests than the more independently minded, Cleopatra IV. Regardless, for several years after Cleopatra IV's exile, Ptolemy IX vied with his mother for superiority in Egypt, where for a time, since neither was able to be rid of the other, their supporting factions appear to have been evenly balanced. Cleopatra III made at least two unsuccessful attempts (in 110/9 and 108 BCE) to oust Ptolemy IX in favor of Ptolemy X, before finally achieving that aim in 107 BCE. In addition, as their relationship deteriorated Cleopatra III for the second time broke up Ptolemy IX's marriage—this time by forcing Cleopatra Selene to abandon her husband. Cleopatra's eventual success in ousting Ptolemy IX involved turning the loyalties of Alexandria's citizenry, for after having had a number of her own eunuchs wounded, she publicly accused Ptolemy IX of plotting her murder. Hoping that an enraged mob would tear Ptole-

my IX to pieces, Cleopatra was partially frustrated. Instead of losing his life, Ptolemy IX fled to Cyprus where by 105 BCE he had established himself as a king in exile, and where he almost immediately began plotting his return to Egypt. For his part, Ptolemy claimed that he left Egypt not because he was the weaker party, but because he was too "pious" to fight with his mother, and as a result he assumed as an official title, "the Mother-Loving." This propaganda would eventually bear fruit in Egypt, but it did not prevent Ptolemy IX from plotting against his mother while she lived. Chief among his attempts to unseat her involved a use of Syria as a staging ground. With the dynastic rivalries of the Seleucid Empire already intertwined with those of Egypt, Ptolemy IX sought Seleucid complicity in a conquest of Egypt between 103 and 101 BCE. This effort was successfully turned away by Cleopatra III and Ptolemy X, with the result that Ptolemy IX returned to rule Cyprus until after Ptolemy X's death in 88 BCE.

Ptolemy X's fortunes were initially the reverse of his older brother's. Openly antagonistic to Ptolemy IX's accession in 116, Ptolemy X initially fled Egypt for Cyprus where, from 114 until 107 BCE, he ruled as king. From Cyprus, Ptolemy X intrigued with his mother until she engineered his return to Egypt in 107 (after which, as noted, Ptolemy IX replaced him on Cyprus). In Egypt, Ptolemy X ruled alongside his mother until late 101 BCE, when, seemingly tired of Cleopatra III's continual manipulation, he planned her murder. Knowing that matricide would be difficult to justify to an Alexandrian population that had previously expressed a preference for his older brother, Ptolemy X had paved the way for Cleopatra III's death by marrying Ptolemy IX's daughter, his niece—Cleopatra Berenice III, either in 102 or 101 BCE. (The marriage occurred before October 31, 101, for it is attested on that date in a papyrus fragment.) At the time of her marriage, Cleopatra Berenice III was at most about 15 and perhaps no more than 13. Nonetheless, she had already proved herself to be popular at court and with the people of Alexandria. Cleopatra Berenice III had not fled Egypt with her father, but remained with Cleopatra III (her grandmother) and Cleopatra Selene (possibly her mother) in Alexandria after his flight.

Ptolemy X's marriage to Cleopatra Berenice III (upon which, Berenice adopted the name "Cleopatra") was considered a diplomatic triumph by Cleopatra III, whose relationship with her younger son had gradually been slipping since his return to Egypt, which is proven by at least

❧
*Cleopatra
Tryphaena
(d. after 112 BCE).*
See Cleopatra IV
for sidebar.

two incidents. The first of these involved religion. Although it was tradition for the Ptolemaic king to preside as a priest over a cult honoring Alexander the Great, Cleopatra III replaced Ptolemy X with herself in this capacity in 104 BCE. Then, in the next year came certain disagreements between Cleopatra III and Ptolemy X over how the war against Ptolemy IX should be waged in Syria. In addition, this marriage also had the advantage of trumping the aspirations of Ptolemy IX after his aborted invasion of Egypt, for it redirected what was left of his support in Alexandria to Ptolemy X through the person of the popular Cleopatra Berenice III. Whatever hope the old queen might have invested in this union, however, she herself was at last subjugated, for Ptolemy X, fortified by the support brought to him by his new wife, murdered his mother.

For a reason that is not explained but which probably had something to do with cutting Ptolemy IX out of the succession as much as possible, Cleopatra Berenice III was hailed in official titulature (for both Greek and Egyptian audiences) as Ptolemy X's "sister." Hence, she became "Philadelphus" ("Brother-Loving"). Perhaps also Ptolemy X thus chose to claim a closer intimacy with his new wife because he felt that her popularity could fortify his rule. Why Cleopatra Berenice III was so popular can only be gleaned from a variety of fragmented sources, but it appears to have been the case that she was somewhat modest in her personal behavior, that she was reverent of the gods (both Greek and Egyptian) while simultaneously giving the influential Jewish population of Alexandria its due, and that she did what she could to limit Egypt's foreign involvements.

On the other hand, Ptolemy X's reputation sank after the murder of his mother. Not only was that deed resented, so was the revolting nature of his behavior and his undisguised loathing of the inhabitants of Alexandria. No longer kept in check by the worthy rivalry of his mother, Ptolemy X went to seed in the decade after her death. Always prone to heaviness, Ptolemy X came to be so obese that, when sober, he could no longer even walk without his body being supported by a slave under each arm. Emphasizing his pathetically sober incapacity, moreover, was Ptolemy X's surprising agility when he was drunk—a not infrequent occurrence. While inebriated, he was credited with being especially adept at a game that involved a kind of dance from drinking couch to drinking couch—perhaps not the most useful talent for one who would be king. Yet, while Ptolemy X appeared

to rot before his peoples' eyes, the reputation of his wife grew. Noted for her loyalty and piety, Cleopatra Berenice III produced at least one daughter by Ptolemy X, but none of her children (if she ever gave birth to more than one child) is known to have survived her.

However, not even Cleopatra Berenice III's popularity sufficiently masked her husband's debauchery, so that by the end of the 90s BCE many began to scorn the monarch who was best known for murdering his mother. Cleopatra Berenice's success as the royal consort of Ptolemy X should not be under-appreciated. On whim, the population of Alexandria was capable of acting the role of a mob and taking the matter of political succession into its own hands. By 89 BCE, the patience of Alexandria's population with Ptolemy X had been exhausted, and he was driven from Egypt. Temporarily elevated above a stupor, Ptolemy X raised a mercenary army in Syria, which he "triumphantly" led back to Alexandria. However, in order to pay his new army, Ptolemy X was reduced to plundering the revered tomb of Alexander the Great, which had been a sacred monument in Alexandria since its construction during the time of the first Ptolemy. In fact, Alexander's remains were not only worshipped by the local population, they also were the anchor of the Ptolemaic royal burial-ground, and thus, an important element in the legitimization of the entire dynasty. None of this counted much to Ptolemy X, who seized the gold coffin in which Alexander had rested for almost 200 years and had it melted down so that he could mint its gold and pay off his foreign troops. (Ultimately a new coffin would be piously recrafted from alabaster, but the memory of what happened to the original sarcophagus shamed the Alexandrians for centuries.) This impiety infuriated an Alexandrian mob that drove Ptolemy from Egypt a second time—this time, however, he was accompanied by Cleopatra Berenice III and their daughter. First, the royal family made their way to Syria. From there, they made their way to Lycia in Anatolia to prepare an invasion of Cyprus—by this date, long the possession of Ptolemy IX (Cleopatra Berenice's father and Ptolemy X's brother). Here fate intervened, for the Alexandrians raised a navy (surely with the connivance of Ptolemy IX) and won a naval battle off the coast of Cyprus against Ptolemy X, in which the latter also lost his life.

Playing upon his brother's infamy, and his own propaganda, which increasingly emphasized his piety toward his mother (even as he waged war against her), in 88 BCE Ptolemy IX made his way back to Egypt as king. With him came his daughter, Cleopatra Berenice III, whom he married. This was an unprecedented incest as far as the Ptolemaic dynasty was concerned (although there were pre-Ptolemaic precedents for such marriages—during the New Kingdom both Akhenaten and Ramses the Great married daughters), for although brother-sister marriages were common from the reign of the second Ptolemy, no father-daughter union had previously occurred. Whatever else induced Ptolemy IX to take his daughter as his wife, there was an excellent political reason to break with precedent. Shortly after Ptolemy IX's return to Alexandria, there was a revolt against his authority in Upper (that is, southern) Egypt, led by the influential priests in the ancient city of Thebes. This revolt lasted three years and only succumbed as Ptolemy IX virtually razed the city of Thebes in 85 BCE. It is clear that Ptolemy IX was only able to amass the resources to defeat this revolt by exploiting his daughter-wife's popularity, especially in Alexandria. In addition, Ptolemy IX—who took pains to dot the "i's" and cross the "t's" by embracing every ritual associated with royal legitimacy—needed a wife before he underwent for a second time the native Egyptian ritual at Memphis that would elevate him again to the status of a pharaoh. Who could be trusted more than his daughter during a period before Ptolemy IX's authority had been firmly reestablished?

Ptolemy IX's instincts concerning Cleopatra Berenice III proved accurate, for after the reduction of Thebes, he ruled without incident with his daughter-wife at his side, and she clearly was the primary reason for his welcome home. The rest of his reign (85–80 BCE) saw Ptolemy IX striving desperately to keep his realm free from entangling foreign alliances—especially difficult with the expansion of Rome. Rome had come to dominate the Mediterranean, having extended its direct and indirect control throughout the East as well as the West. Roman greed had become infamous enough to spark widespread resentment. A champion of this resentment in the person of Mithradates, a hellenized king of Pontus (in north central Anatolia), had arisen, and in 88 BCE Rome found itself fighting a major war in Greece and in Asia Minor. For its part, Rome sent its most ruthless general, Lucius Cornelius Sulla, to regain control of the eastern provinces and client kingships. As a result of the widespread destruction brought on by this conflict (epitomized well by Sulla's sack of the city of Athens), it was becoming increasingly clear that anyone not actively supporting Rome was its enemy. Never-

theless, Ptolemy IX generally succeeded in his neutrality while the war was being fought, although he betrayed his basic philhellenic sympathies by financially assisting in the reconstruction of Athens after Sulla's army had its way. For this help, Athens erected bronze statues honoring not only Ptolemy IX, but Cleopatra Berenice III as well, specifically noting that the latter was her husband's only "legitimate" offspring. (Obviously, she took some active role in the Egyptian philanthropy.) Another indication of Cleopatra Berenice III's prominence at the time came in the form that her and Ptolemy IX's official titulature took, for both came to be hailed as "the gods Philadelphus Philometores Soteres." Since the first of these epithets was originally Cleopatra Berenice III's, it appears that Ptolemy IX hoped to bask at home in the glow of his daughter-wife's popularity.

Although Ptolemy IX apparently had at least two other children, when he died in March of 80 BCE, Cleopatra Berenice III was his only surviving offspring. For about six months, she ruled Egypt by herself, but foreign politics in conjunction with the preference of the Egyptians to have both a male and a female ruler conspired to force Cleopatra Berenice III to accept a joint-monarch. This was no criticism of Cleopatra Berenice III, but not even one so beloved (she is praised as one "dear to her people and established in their affections") to those over whom she ruled could escape the weight of tradition.

The male elevated to equality with Cleopatra Berenice III was Ptolemy XI Alexander II, whose name clearly denotes his paternity, for his father was Ptolemy X, Cleopatra Berenice III's late and unlamented husband. The new Ptolemy (hereafter, Ptolemy XI) was the only living male of the royal family in 80 BCE, probably having been born about 105 BCE to an unknown mother. Perhaps Ptolemy XI's mother had been Cleopatra IV who had briefly known her brother on Cyprus before she went on to Syria. Whether or not Cleopatra IV was Ptolemy XI's mother, most believe that Ptolemy XI was born before his father married Cleopatra Berenice III in 102 or 101 BCE, thus making it unlikely that Cleopatra Berenice III was Ptolemy XI's mother. (Although this possibility cannot absolutely be ruled out, for he is referred to in Egyptian texts as her *sr,* a term that can mean either *son* or *stepson.*) Regardless, Ptolemy was not only associated with Cleopatra Berenice III because he was the only living male Ptolemy, he was so also through the agency of Sulla—at the time, the sole master of Rome.

In 103 BCE, as Cleopatra III was preparing to fight with Ptolemy X against Ptolemy IX in Syria, she had deposited the young Ptolemy XI (and much treasure) in the sanctuary of Asclepius on the island of Cos (in the Aegean). She did so to minimize potential losses, not yet knowing that her war would be successful and that she would keep Egypt. There Ptolemy XI remained, for what reason we cannot be certain. Apparently, however, Ptolemy XI posed an embarrassment, not to Cleopatra III, but to Ptolemy X. This embarrassment seems not to have disappeared when Ptolemy IX returned to Egypt, but whatever the long term fate of Ptolemy XI might have been, shortly after Ptolemy IX resumed his kingship in Egypt the great anti-Roman crusade led by Mithradates broke out. In 88 BCE, Mithradates plucked Ptolemy XI from Cos, and "entertained" him, until Ptolemy XI escaped to Sulla in 84 BCE. Thereafter he returned with Sulla to Rome, where Ptolemy was bombarded with Roman "hospitality" until such time as he would become useful. This time came in the fall of 80 BCE, when Sulla decided to return Ptolemy XI to Egypt, thus to increase Rome's leverage there. There, Ptolemy assumed his status by marrying Cleopatra Berenice III. After a joint rule of only 19 days, Ptolemy XI assassinated his newly acquired bride. This murder of a beloved monarch—certainly the most responsible to have been associated with the Ptolemaic throne in over a generation—incensed the Alexandrian people, who immediately avenged Cleopatra Berenice III by killing Ptolemy XI, who had attempted to hide in a public gymnasium.

Thus did Cleopatra Berenice III die, and, along with her, the last vestige of Ptolemaic independence. After her death and that of Ptolemy XI, the only existing scions of the royal house were two illegitimate sons of Ptolemy IX by common concubines. Although the Ptolemaic dynasty would continue for another 50 years through one of these—Ptolemy XII (the self-styled "New Dionysus, Father Loving, Sister Loving, Flute Player")—his claim to the Ptolemaic throne could only be enforced through the intervention of Rome, an intervention that cost both Ptolemy XII and Egypt dearly: Ptolemy XII by rendering huge bribes to the likes of Crassus, Pompey and Caesar, and Egypt by being forced to accept a Roman financial "advisor" through whom the wealth of the land was increasingly funneled to Rome.

SOURCES:
Justin, *Epitome of the Philippic History*, esp. Book 39. Translated by J.C. Yardley. Atlanta: Scholars Press, 1994.

SUGGESTED READING:
Bevan. Edwyn R. *The House of Ptolemy*. Chicago, IL: Ares Press, 1995.
Macurdy, Grace H. *Hellenistic Queens*. Baltimore, MD: Jonns Hopkins Press, 1932.
Pomeroy, Sarah B. *Women in Hellenistic Egypt*. NY: Schocken Books, 1984.
Whitehorne, John. *Cleopatras*. Routledge, NY, 1994.

William S. Greenwalt,
Associate Professor of Classical History,
Santa Clara University, Santa Clara, California

Cleopatra of Cyrene.

See Cleopatra V Selene.

Cleopatra Selene (c. 130–69 BCE)

Queen of Egypt and Syria. Born around 130 BCE; died in 69 BCE; youngest daughter of Ptolemy VIII Euergetes II and Cleopatra III Euergetis (c. 155–101 BCE) of Egypt; sister of Cleopatra IV (c. 135–112 BCE) and Cleopatra Tryphaena (d. after 112 BCE); married Ptolemy IX Philometor Soter II, in 115 BCE (divorced 107 BCE); married Antiochus VIII Grypus, 103 BCE (killed 96 BCE); married Antiochus IX Cyzicenus, in 96 BCE (killed 95 BCE); married Antiochus X Eusebes Philopator; children: (first marriage) probably two sons, possibly *Cleopatra Berenice III; (third marriage) two sons, including Antiochus XIII Asiaticus.

Cleopatra Selene was the youngest daughter of Ptolemy VIII Euergetes II and *Cleopatra III Euergetis of Egypt, and she was the sister of *Cleopatra IV. Selene's sister was married to their brother Ptolemy IX Philometor Soter II until their mother decided to limit the influence of Cleopatra IV by replacing her as Ptolemy's wife with Selene. Thus, Selene married her brother Ptolemy IX in 115 BCE and the marriage lasted until 107, when their mother Cleopatra III finally ousted Ptolemy IX from Egypt in favor of his younger brother, Ptolemy X. From his base on Cyprus, Ptolemy IX thereafter began to make common cause with the Seleucid Antiochus IX Cyzicenus in his wars against the Jews of Palestine and Cyzicenus' royal rival for the Seleucid kingdom, Antiochus VIII Grypus. By 103, Ptolemy IX's military success in these conflicts was such that Cleopatra III feared his imminent return to Egypt; to forestall that eventuality, she weighed in heavily on the side of Antiochus VIII—securing his allegiance through a marriage to Cleopatra Selene.

While she probably had two sons with Ptolemy IX before his exile, Cleopatra Selene had no children with Antiochus VIII though they remained married until 96, when he was assassinated by Heracleon, an overly ambitious military aide. This murder caused Cleopatra Selene to abandon her previous Seleucid commitments in order to marry her former enemy, Antiochus IX. This union lasted only about a year, for in 95 Seleucus VI, the son and heir of Antiochus VIII and ☙➤ **Cleopatra Tryphaena** (sister of Selene), seeking his father's royal status, defeated Antiochus IX in battle. Immediately thereafter, Cleopatra Selene's third husband was either executed or committed suicide.

Into this picture (made even more complicated by the intrigues of Cleopatra Selene's ex-husband Ptolemy IX) came Antiochus X Eusebes Philopator—another son of Antiochus VIII and Cleopatra Tryphaena. To enhance his claim, Antiochus X married Cleopatra Selene, his much older aunt-stepmother. Despite the difference in their ages, Cleopatra Selene had two sons with Antiochus X, although we know the name of only one: Antiochus XIII Asiaticus. With Cleopatra Selene's support, Antiochus X routed Seleucus VI, after which he was forced to do battle with other dynastic claimants. These were the least of his worries, however, because in 89 Antiochus X was forced on the defensive in the east by an invasion of the Parthian king, Mithradates II. Not up to the challenge, Antiochus X died a victim of Parthian arms in 88.

After this death of her fourth husband, Cleopatra Selene then retreated to the coastal fortress of Ptolemais and sanctuary so that she could foster the royal claims of her young sons by Antiochus X. Amid the general chaos into which the Seleucid kingdom was swept, Selene bided her time. However, her time never came, for in 75 the Roman Senate (without whose help, Selene's sons had little chance against their innumerable rivals) refused to back the royal claims of her children. Antiochus XIII would eventually rule Syria between 69 and 64 at the whim of the Roman general Lucullus, but when Pompey, Lucullus' replacement in the east, rearranged Seleucid affairs to his liking, he decided to dethrone Cleopatra Selene's son in favor of converting Syria into a Roman province.

Regardless, by this time Cleopatra Selene was dead. The king of Armenia, Tigranes, taking advantage of the region's chaos, had swept down upon Palestine and captured the fortress of Ptolemais in 69. Along with the city, Tigranes had taken Cleopatra Selene. Although his success in this area was short-lived, when Tigranes returned eastward he deported Selene to the city

of Seleucia on the Tigris River, where he shortly afterwards had her executed.

William S. Greenwalt,
Associate Professor of Classical History,
Santa Clara University, Santa Clara, California

Cleopatra Thea (c. 165–121 BCE)

Queen of Syria. Born around 165 BCE; died in 121 BCE; daughter of Ptolemy VI and Cleopatra II (c. 183–116 BCE) of Egypt; probably the older sister of Cleopatra III; married Alexander Balas, pretender to the Seleucid throne (r. 150–145 BCE), in 150 BCE (died 145 BCE); married Demetrius II Nicator, Seleucid king (r. 145–138), in 146 BCE (died 125 BCE); married Antiochus VII Sidetes (died 129); children: (first marriage) Antiochus VI Epiphanes; (second marriage) sons Antiochus VIII Philometor Grypus and Seleucus V, and a daughter Laodice (fl. 129 BCE); (third marriage) Antiochus IX Philopator Cyzicenus (r. 96–95 BCE).

The daughter of Ptolemy VI and *Cleopatra II of Egypt (and probably the older sister of that kingdom's *Cleopatra III), Cleopatra Thea renewed the link between Ptolemaic and Seleucid interests. As a result, she made her mark in Syria, where in succession she wed three Seleucid monarchs: Alexander Balas (d. 145), Demetrius II Nicator (d. 125), and Antiochus VII Sidetes (d. 129), the latter two of whom were brothers. Cleopatra Thea's first husband, Alexander Balas, usurped the Seleucid throne from his cousin, Demetrius I. Thereafter, the friendship of Cleopatra's father Ptolemy VI—made manifest through the gift of his daughter—helped Balas maintain his power for a time. Cleopatra Thea's marriage to him in 150 BCE was accompanied by great pageantry, and she soon gave birth to Balas' son, Antiochus VI Epiphanes. An irresponsible monarch, Balas abandoned himself to debauchery, with the result that he lost control of his subjects and was challenged by royal pretenders, despite support from powerful foreign allies. By 146, Ptolemy VI had so lost faith in Balas' competency that he dissolved Cleopatra Thea's marriage in order to give her to the young Demetrius II (a few years her junior), whom the Egyptian monarch hoped would prove to be a more dependable ally.

A Seleucid dynastic war followed. Campaigning in Asia on behalf of his new son-in-law, Ptolemy VI died in 145 as a result of wounds he sustained when he fell from a horse. However, before breathing his last, Ptolemy learned of Balas' assassination by Balas' own disaffected troops. Unfortunately for the Seleucid kingdom,

◄☙
Cleopatra Tryphaena. See *Cleopatra IV for sidebar.*

these two deaths did not secure a peace, for Balas' faction, led by Diodotus Tryphon, continued to agitate against Demetrius II in the interests of Cleopatra Thea's very young son, Antiochus VI, by her first marriage. For a time, Cleopatra Thea's second husband Demetrius held the upper hand against the forces of her son, but this he lost when he failed to live up to the expectations of the citizens of Antioch (the Seleucid kingdom's capital city). As a result, Diodotus established Antiochus VI in Antioch, where the youth "reigned" until 141 when Diodotus had him murdered so as to claim the throne for himself.

Before Demetrius fled Antioch in 144, he fathered two sons (Antiochus VIII Philometor Grypus and Seleucus V) and a daughter (*Laodice) with Cleopatra Thea. After fleeing the city, Cleopatra Thea's husband hoped to recoup his losses through a successful campaign against the Parthians who had established themselves in a kingdom to the east of the Seleucid realm. In this venture Demetrius was no more successful than he had been elsewhere, however, for he was captured and imprisoned by the Parthians in 140, and he would remain in captivity until he was released (to wreak havoc back at home) in 131.

Hating Diodotus for the actions he had taken to unseat both Demetrius II and Antiochus VI, Cleopatra Thea acted decisively against his reign in 138. In that year, holed up in Seleucia-in-Pieria against Diodotus, and fearing that Demetrius II would never survive imprisonment, Cleopatra Thea proposed matrimony to Demetrius II's younger brother Antiochus VII, who until this time had lived privately and in relative safety in the Pamphylian city of Side. Accepting Cleopatra Thea's offer, Antiochus VII successfully rallied various anti-Diodotan interests. Within the year, he married Cleopatra Thea, defeated Diodotus in battle (Diodotus then committed suicide), and established himself on the Seleucid throne. Antiochus VII began as a vigorous monarch who restored order throughout much of his realm, even earning the respect of his Jewish subjects (frequently at odds with their Seleucid masters) because of his regard for their religion.

Antiochus VII and Cleopatra had a son, Antiochus IX Philopator Cyzicenus, and the couple seemed content with their relationship until fortune intervened. Having secured the western portion of his Seleucid domains, in 131 Antiochus VII was ready to flex his muscle in the unsettled east, which had received little Seleucid attention since Demetrius II's military debacle and imprisonment in 140. That failure had eroded Antioch's control over its eastern lands, but even more disturbing to Antiochus in 131 was the news that he received from the Parthian court. Far from abusing their captive, the Parthians treated Demetrius II with extreme favor, so much so that the Parthian king, Phraates, had arranged for Demetrius to marry a Parthian princess. This marriage infuriated Cleopatra Thea, less for reasons of the heart than because she understood its political implications for herself and her children. Phraates acted as he did in order to create an ally against an expected attack from the west, for if any assault was unleashed upon his realm from that quarter Phraates could free Demetrius II and support his claim (and that of anticipated half-Parthian children) to the Seleucid throne. As such, he could incite a civil war, which at a bare minimum could be expected to undercut effective Seleucid action in the east.

Antiochus undoubtedly suspected the purpose for which his brother was being kept, but, feeling strong enough by 131 to act decisively, he demanded Demetrius' release: nominally out of "brotherly love," but in fact in the hopes of quickly laying hands on Demetrius so that he could be put under wraps. Phraates complied with Antiochus' demand, but in the end it did not matter, because Antiochus VII was killed attacking Parthia in 129. With Antiochus on this inauspicious invasion went two of Cleopatra Thea's children by Demetrius II, Seleucus V and Laodice. Both were captured after Antiochus' death: Seleucus soon to be returned to Syria, while Laodice remained in Parthia to marry Phraates II, thus transfusing some Seleucid blood into the Parthian royal house.

Then began a struggle between Cleopatra Thea and Demetrius II for control of the Seleucid throne. Alienated from her second husband, and fearing that Demetrius would attempt to secure the future succession of the kingdom through the line of his Parthian wife, Cleopatra Thea entered the political fray on behalf on her children. She sent two sons (Grypus and Antiochus IX) away for safekeeping (to Athens and Cyzicus respectively), and then went about soliciting the support needed to repel Demetrius. With both Seleucid factions seeking allies, it was inevitable that support was sought from Egypt, where Cleopatra II (Cleopatra Thea's mother) was engaged in a war with her brother-husband Ptolemy VIII over royal authority. When Cleopatra II was temporarily driven from Egypt to Syria by Ptolemy VIII, she sought Syrian support from Demetrius, not her daughter. When Demetrius agreed to an alliance with Cleopatra II, Cleopatra Thea and those of her children still in Syria fled to Ptolemais, on the coast beyond Demetrius' control. Ptolemy VIII then jumped into the Seleucid fray to back one Alexander Zabinas, a purported son of Alexander Balas, who, in part as a result of his Egyptian backing, drove Demetrius from Antioch (127). Seeking some success, Demetrius then moved against Cleopatra Thea in Ptolemais, but he failed to breach that city's defenses. Thereafter, Demetrius took up residence in Tyre where he was murdered by the local governor at Cleopatra Thea's command. Cleopatra Thea's son Seleucus V, learning of his mother's complicity in his father's death, denounced Cleopatra Thea in a fury and assumed the throne on his own authority (126). This reign, however, was extremely short-lived, for Cleopatra Thea took the life of her alienated son with her own hand.

With Seleucus V exterminated, Cleopatra Thea assumed royal authority, fully exercising the prerogatives of rule. Still faced with the royal claims of Alexander Zabinas, and thus needing a masculine associate upon whom she could rely, in 125 she raised another son, Antiochus VIII Grypus, to the position of co-monarch, and then quickly formed an Egyptian association of her own by marrying him to ❧➤ **Cleopatra Tryphaena** (Thea's niece). In 123, Cleopatra Thea's boldness appeared to pay off, for Antiochus VIII defeated and executed Alexander Zabinas. However, this military victory created a tension between an overbearing mother and her ambitious son, who increasingly sought to be free of her control. By 121, Antiochus VIII had completely tired of Cleopatra Thea's presence and had her poisoned. Antiochus justified his matricide by claiming that he had merely turned the tables on Thea, that is, that he had merely forced her to drink a suspicious cup of wine that she had intended for him.

William S. Greenwalt,
Associate Professor of Classical History,
Santa Clara University, Santa Clara, California

Cleopatra Tryphaena (d. after 112 BCE).

See Cleopatra IV for sidebar.

Clerk.

Variant of Clark, Clarke, and Clerke.

Clerke, Agnes Mary (1842–1907)

Prolific Irish-born writer of popular astronomy articles and books. Pronunciation: Clark. Born Agnes Mary Clerke on February 10, 1842, in Skibbereen,

County Cork; died on January 20, 1907, in London; daughter of John William (a bank manager) and Catherine Mary (Deasy) Clerke; sister of Ellen Mary Clerke (1840–1906) and Aubrey St. John Clerke; received home schooling by parents; self-study in Italy and London; never married; no children.

Awards: Acton Prize (1892); honorary member, Royal Astronomical Society (1903).

Selected publications: A Popular History of Astronomy during the Nineteenth Century (1885); The System of the Stars (1891); Problems in Astrophysics (1903); The Herschels and Modern Astronomy (1895); Modern Cosmogonies (1906). Freelance astronomy writer (1877–1907).

A self-taught Irish astronomy writer, Agnes Mary Clerke contributed significantly to the popular astronomy literature of the late 19th and early 20th centuries. She was born on February 10, 1842, in Skibbereen, County Cork, Ireland, the daughter of John William Clerke, a bank manager, and Catherine Mary Deasy Clerke. Her brother Aubrey St. John Clerke was educated at a boarding school and later at Trinity College, becoming a barrister. Agnes and her older sister ❧➤ **Ellen Mary** were educated at home. Ellen would also become a successful writer, though never achieving the fame of her sister. The family relocated to Dublin in 1861 when Aubrey entered college. Agnes and Ellen then resided in Italy from 1867 to 1877 where they studied in the libraries. During these years, Agnes began to write. Her first two articles— "Brigandage in Sicily" (concerning the rise of the Mafia) and "Copernicus in Italy"—were published in 1877 in the *Edinburgh Review*. She would continue to contribute articles to the *Review* until her death. In 1877, the entire family moved to London.

While writing popularized science articles, in 1881 Clerke began her most famous work, *A Popular History of Astronomy during the Nineteenth Century*, which was published in 1885 to

➤❧
*Cleopatra
Tryphaena
(d. after 112 BCE).*
See Cleopatra IV
for sidebar.

❧➤ **Clerke, Ellen Mary** (1840–1906)
*Irish-born translator. Born in 1840; died in March 1906; daughter of John William and Catherine Mary Deasy Clerke; sister of *Agnes Mary Clerke (1842–1907).*

Ellen Mary Clerke published poetry, novels, and astronomical pamphlets. In 1899, she published her translation of Italian verse, *Fable and Song in Italy*.

rave reviews. She became well known in astronomical circles and spent two months working at the Cape of Good Hope Observatory in 1888 at the invitation of director David Gill. Clerke made further observations aboard the yacht *Palatine* in the Baltic Sea. Her experiences were incorporated in her 1891 work, *The System of the Stars.* A prolific writer, Clerke made numerous contributions to popular journals and the *Encyclopaedia Britannica,* and authored a number of popular books, including *The Herschels and Modern Astronomy* and *Modern Cosmogonies.* Wrote T.J.J. See of her work: "In the line of popular writing Miss Clerke had no superior. Her style was classic, her imagery clear, her thought lucid, original and suggestive."

Clerke never held an official astronomical position, although she turned down a position at the Royal Observatory in Greenwich and she was nominated to succeed *Maria Mitchell as professor of astronomy at Vassar College. She was awarded the Acton Prize in 1892 and was the fourth woman elected an honorary member of the Royal Astronomical Society (1903). None of the Clerke children married, and Ellen and Agnes were close until Ellen's death in March 1906. Agnes died in London shortly after her sister, on January 20, 1907, from pneumonia.

SOURCES:

Bruck, M.T. "Agnes Mary Clerke, Chronicler of Astronomy," in *Quarterly Journal of the Royal Astronomical Society.* Vol. XXXV, no. 1. March 1994, p. 59–80.

Dent, Elsie A. "Agnes Mary Clerke," in *The Journal of the Royal Astronomical Society of Canada.* Vol. I, no. 2. March–April 1907, p. 81–84.

Huggins, Margaret Lindsay. "Agnes Mary Clerke," in *Astrophysical Journal.* Vol. 25, 1907, p. 226–230.

Macpherson, Hector, Jr. *Astronomers of Today.* London: Gall and Inglis, 1905.

See, T.J.J. "Some Recollections of Miss Agnes M. Clerke," in *Popular Astronomy.* Vol. XV, no. 6. June–July 1907, p. 323–326.

SUGGESTED READING:

Bruck, Mary T. "Companions in Astronomy: Margaret Lindsay Huggins and Agnes Mary Clerke," *in Irish Astronomical Journal.* Vol. 20, no. 2, 1991, p. 70–77.

Weitzenhoffer, Kenneth. "The Prolific Pen of Agnes Clerke," in *Sky and Telescope.* Vol. LXX, no. 3. September 1985, p. 211–212.

Kristine Larsen,
Associate Professor of Physics and Earth Sciences,
Central Connecticut State University, New Britain, Connecticut

Clermont, countess of.

See Marie of Hainault (fl. 1300).
See Guzman, Leonora de (1310–1351).
See Maria Theresa of Wurttemberg.

Clermont-Tonnerre, duchesse de
(fl. 1875–1935).

See Barney, Natalie Clifford for sidebar on Gramont, Elizabeth de.

Cleusa, Mother (c. 1931–1998).

See Millet, Cleusa.

Cleveland, duchess of (c. 1641–1709).

See Villiers, Barbara.

Cleveland, Emeline Horton
(1829–1878)

American physician and the first woman on record to perform major surgery. Born Emeline Horton in Ashford, Connecticut, on September 22, 1829; died of tuberculosis in Philadelphia, Pennsylvania, on December 8, 1878; graduated from Oberlin College, 1853; M.D. from the Female (later Woman's) Medical College of Pennsylvania, 1855; advanced training in obstetrics at the school of the Maternité hospital in Paris, 1860–1861; married Rev. Giles B. Cleveland, in March 1854; children: son (b. 1865).

Born in 1829 in Connecticut, Emeline Horton grew up in Madison County, New York, from 1831. She attended local schools and then worked as a teacher to earn money so that she could attend college. After graduating from Oberlin College in 1853, she married a childhood friend and fellow Oberlin graduate, Reverend Giles Cleveland. Her husband's ill health prevented them from pursuing their plan to become missionaries; it also meant that the couple would rely on Emeline's earnings as their main source of income. In 1855, she received her M.D. from the Female (later Woman's) Medical College of Pennsylvania. Following a year of private practice in New York's Oneida valley, Cleveland became a demonstrator of anatomy at the Female Medical College (1856) before being named professor of anatomy and histology.

The support of the college's Dr. *Ann Preston helped Cleveland to take advanced training (1860–1861) in obstetrics at the school of the Maternité in Paris, from which she received a diploma. She returned to the college (rechartered Woman's Medical College) as chief resident, a position she was to hold until 1868. Her early efforts included the establishment of training courses for nurses and, in a pioneering venture, for nurses aides. Cleveland established an outstanding reputation among her male colleagues, several of whom consulted her and one of whom read a paper of Cleveland's to the Philadelphia

Obstetrical Society. While carrying on an extensive private practice, she also served as professor of obstetrics and diseases of women and children. Finally admitted as a member of several local medical societies, Cleveland was responsible for helping women physicians gain acceptance to societies that had vehemently resisted the entrance of women into the male-dominated field of medicine. Her service at the college culminated with her succeeding Dr. Preston as dean, and she served in this capacity from 1872 to 1874. Cleveland has historical significance as the first woman physician on record to practice as a surgeon, which she did in 1875, at age 46, with her first of several ovariotomies. She was appointed gynecologist to the department for the insane at Pennsylvania Hospital in 1878. That year, she died of tuberculosis on December 8.

Cleveland, Frances Folsom

(1864–1947)

The youngest of America's first ladies, and one of the most popular women ever to serve in this capacity. Name variations: Frances F. Preston. Born on July 21, 1864, in Buffalo, New York; died on October 29, 1947, in Baltimore, Maryland; only child of Oscar (an attorney) and Emma Cornelia (Harmon) Folsom; graduated from Wells College in Aurora, New York, June 1885; married (Stephen) Grover Cleveland (U.S. president), on June 2, 1886, at the first wedding ceremony to take place in the White House (died 1908); married Thomas Jex Preston, Jr. (an archeology professor), on February 10, 1913; children: (first marriage) **Ruth Cleveland** *(1891–1904, died of diphtheria at age 12);* **Esther Cleveland** *(1893–1980, only presidential child ever born in the White House); Marion Cleveland (b. 1895); Richard Cleveland (1897–1974); Francis Cleveland (b. 1903).*

Frances ("Frank") Folsom Cleveland was the youngest first lady and the first to be married in the White House. The 21-year-old exchanged vows with President Grover Cleveland, 28 years her senior, on June 2, 1886, in a small ceremony in the Blue Room. The celebration included a 21-gun salute and music by The Marine Band, under the direction of John Philip Sousa. It is reported that the word "obey" was eliminated from the wedding vows, and that the groom was so nervous he forgot to kiss the bride.

Frances was born in Buffalo, New York, the only child of Oscar and **Emma Folsom**. Her early schooling included **Madame Brecker's** Kindergarten, the Medina (New York) Academy,

and Central High School in Buffalo. When she was 11, her father was killed in a carriage accident. With no will on file, Grover Cleveland (known to her family as "Uncle Cleve"), law partner and close family friend, took over administration of the sizable estate, caring for Frances and her mother as though they were his own family. It is not clear when fatherly concern took a romantic turn, but, when Frances left to attend Wells College in New York, Uncle Cleve wrote to her dutifully. At the time of her graduation in June 1885, and a subsequent yearlong European tour with her mother, rumors of their engagement abounded. Upon her return, the newly inaugurated president announced his intentions, and wedding plans went forward.

Frances
Folsom
Cleveland

Frances took over the duties of first lady from Cleveland's sister, ✤▶ **Rose Elizabeth Cleveland**, who had acted as her brother's hostess for 15 months of his first term. In spite of her youth, Frances possessed such tact, charm and beauty that she quickly won popularity. She graciously presided over an increased social calendar and held several weekly receptions, includ-

---

✤▶ **Cleveland, Rose Elizabeth** (b. 1846)

American writer. Born in Fayetteville, New York, in 1846; daughter of Richard Falley (a Presbyterian minister) and Anne (Neal) Cleveland; sister of Grover Cleveland.

After the presidential inauguration of her brother Grover Cleveland in 1885, Rose Elizabeth Cleveland became the "mistress of the White House," remaining there until 1886. "Miss Cleveland carries an atmosphere of female college about her, thicker than the snow storm outside my window," wrote Henry Adams to his wife *Clover Adams. "She listens seriously and asks serious questions. . . . We talked chiefly of George Eliot's biography, which she takes in an earnest spirit." Rose Cleveland published a book of essays and lectures entitled *George Eliot's Poetry, and Other Studies* (1885); and a novel, *The Long Run* (1886).

ing one on Saturday afternoons, so women with jobs could attend. The stylish first lady was widely emulated and started a fashion trend when she refused to wear a bustle.

Grover Cleveland's 1888 bid for reelection was difficult. Rumors of improprieties involving an illegitimate child, which had marked the 1884 campaign, resurfaced. When trumped-up charges about drunken wife-beating also found their way into the press, Frances made a public statement that she was happily married. Cleveland lost the election, however, and the couple moved to New York City, where they lived quietly and began a family that would come to include five children over the next 12 years.

The Clevelands returned to the White House in 1893 for an unprecedented second term. The couple faced a nation in the throes of economic depression and labor turmoil, which resulted in a more restrained social climate. Frances supported her husband through the political storms of this term, and there is evidence that she also saw him through an unpublicized bout with cancer and an operation in which a portion of his jaw was removed.

At the end of the second term, the family retired to "Westland," a home near Princeton University, where Grover became a law professor. Frances was offered the presidency of the National Society of the Daughters of the American Revolution but declined, not wanting to involve herself in the politics of the post. Grover Cleveland died in 1908. In 1913, Frances married Thomas Jex Preston, Jr., an archeology professor. She remained a prominent figure in the Princeton community and served as trustee of various national charities and women's organizations. During World War I, she headed the National Security League's speaker's bureau and was secretary of its Bureau of Patriotism through Education. She also led the Needlework Guild of America in a clothing drive for the poor during the Depression. Frances Cleveland died on October 29, 1947, at age 83. She is buried in Princeton, New Jersey, beside her first husband.

SOURCES:

James, Edward T., ed. *Notable American Women, 1607–1950.* Cambridge, MA: Belknap Press of Harvard University Press, 1971, pp. 350–351.

Klapthor, Margaret Brown. *The First Ladies.* Washington, D.C.: The White House Historical Association, 1979.

Paletta, LuAnn. *The World Almanac of First Ladies.* NY: World Almanac, 1990.

Barbara Morgan, Melrose, Massachusetts

Cleveland, Rose Elizabeth (b. 1846).

See Cleveland, Frances for sidebar.

Cleves, Anne of (1515–1557).

See Six Wives of Henry VIII.

Cleves, duchess of.

See Mary of Burgundy (c. 1400–1463).
See Elizabeth of Nevers (fl. 1460).
See Maria of Julich-Berg (fl. 1515).
See Mary (1531–1581).
See Elizabeth Charlotte of the Palatinate (fl. 1620).

Cleyre, Voltairine de (1866–1912).

See de Cleyre, Voltairine.

Clicquot, Mme (1777–1866).

See Uzès, Anne, duchesse d' for sidebar.

Clidat, France (1932—)

French pianist. Born in Nantes, France, in 1932.

Born in Nantes in 1932, France Clidat studied in Paris with Lazare-Lévy (1882–1964) from 1948 through 1950, winning a first prize at the end of her course of study. Clidat's enthusiasm for the piano music of Franz Liszt led to a prize-winning series of 24 long-playing recordings of the Hungarian master's works. Her repertoire was extensive, including the complete works of the eccentric French composer Erik Satie and the daunting Third Concerto of Sergei Rachmaninoff.

Clifford, Anne (1590–1676)

Countess of Dorset, Pembroke, and Montgomery, who was a diarist and biographer. Name variations: Lady Anne Clifford. Born in Yorkshire, England, on January 30, 1590; died in Westmoreland, England, on March 22, 1676; only surviving child of George Clifford, 3rd earl of Cumberland (a naval commander and buccaneer), and Margaret (Russell) Clifford (c. 1560–1616); educated by Samuel Daniel, the poet; married Richard Sackville, Lord Buckhurst, earl of Dorset (claimed the barony of Clifford in 1628), in February 1609 (died 1624); married Philip Herbert, earl of Pembroke and Montgomery, in 1630 (died 1650); children: (first marriage) three sons, all of whom died in infancy; two daughters.

Anne Clifford's life was marred by two unhappy marriages and an extensive lawsuit to regain her inheritance. Her first marriage to Richard Sackville, a spendthrift and philanderer, produced three sons, all of whom tragically died in infancy, and two daughters. Widowed in

1624, she later married Philip Herbert, earl of Pembroke and Montgomery, from whom she was separated.

Upon the death of her father George Clifford, 3rd earl of Cumberland, in 1605, Anne's male cousin commandeered the lands and title that were rightfully hers. Clifford, along with her mother ✤▶ **Margaret Clifford**, initiated a legal battle to regain the estates. Even though Clifford's first husband and the king tried to persuade her to accept a cash settlement, she continued her lawsuits. But it wasn't until 1643, when her cousin died with no male heir, that Anne Clifford inherited the Clifford estates after a 38-year struggle.

For the rest of her life, she rebuilt her six castles, secured a reputation for "bounty and hospitality," and continued to defend her rights. When the secretary of state for King Charles II wrote to her, naming his own candidate for one of her pocket boroughs, she replied: "I have been bullied by a usurper, I have been neglected by a court, but I will not be dictated to by a subject; your man shan't stand." Clifford engaged in numerous other charitable activities and also embarked on an extensive family history, including her own autobiography and the biographies of her parents. The work, edited by J.P. Gilson, was published in 1916. Her extensive diary, which she kept until her death, was published in 1923. In a funeral sermon, published in 1677, Edward Rainbow, bishop of Carlisle, remarked on Clifford's penetrating wit and quoted John Donne's remark that "she knew well how to discourse on all things, from predestination to slea-silk."

SOURCES:

Blodgett, Harriet. *The English Woman's Diary*. London: Fourth Estate, 1991.

Shattock, Joanne. *The Oxford Guide to British Women Writers*. Oxford: Oxford University Press, 1993.

SUGGESTED READING:

Holmes, Martin. *Proud Northern Lady: Lady Anne Clifford 1590–1676*, 1975.

Sackville-West, Vita, ed. *The Diary of Lady Anne Clifford*, 1923.

Williamson, George. *Lady Anne Clifford, Countess of Dorset, Pembroke and Montgomery*, 1922 (2nd edition, 1967).

Barbara Morgan,
Melrose, Massachusetts

Clifford, Lady Jane (d. 1679).

See Seymour, Jane.

Clifford, Margaret (d. 1596)

Countess of Derby. Died on September 29, 1596; daughter of Henry Clifford, 2nd earl of Cumberland,

✤▶ **Clifford, Margaret** (c. 1560–1616)

Countess of Cumberland. Born Margaret Russell around 1560; died in 1616; youngest daughter of Francis Russell, earl of Bedford; married George Clifford, 3rd earl of Cumberland, in 1577 (separated); children: *Anne Clifford (1590–1676), countess of Dorset.

and *Eleanor Brandon (c. 1520–1547); married Henry Stanley, 4th earl of Derby, on February 7, 1555.

Clifford, Margaret (c. 1560–1616).

See Clifford, Anne for sidebar.

Clifford, Maud (d. 1446)

Countess of Cambridge. Name variations: Maud Neville. Died on August 26, 1446; daughter of Thomas Clifford, 4th baron Clifford; married Richard of Conisbrough, 2nd earl of Cambridge, around 1413; married John Neville, 6th baron Latimer.

Anne Clifford

Clifford, Rosamund (c. 1145–1176)

Mistress of King Henry II of England. Name variations: Rosamond; Rosamonde; "Fair Rosamund." Born around 1145 in Wales; died at Godstow convent, England, in 1176; believed to be the daughter of Sir Walter de Clifford, a Norman knight, of the family of Fitz-Ponce (evidence for paternity is only an entry made by the jurors of the manor of Corfham in a Hundred Roll of the second year of the reign of Edward I, great grandson of Henry II); never married; no children (there is no evidence for the belief that she was the mother of Henry's natural son William Longsword, earl of Salisbury).

Rosamund Clifford's affair with King Henry II of England and her death made her a popular figure in legends and ballads in her own time and for centuries afterwards. She was the daughter of Walter de Clifford, a Norman knight in King Henry's service and one of the important marcher lords who kept watch over the border between Wales and England. King Henry, who was well-known for his many affairs, met Rosamund in 1165, probably at her father's castle when he was warring against the Welsh. They soon became lovers, and Henry moved Rosamund, probably about 20 years old, from her childhood home to his own favorite castle of Woodstock in Oxfordshire. At the time, Henry's powerful queen, *Eleanor of Aquitaine, posed no threat to their relationship, for she was across the English Channel acting as regent in the province of Angers. Many legends have been told of Henry hiding his beautiful mistress in a secret tower near Woodstock, and of him building a maze around it that he alone could negotiate.

When Queen Eleanor returned to England, she took up residence at Oxford castle and probably first discovered Rosamund's existence at that time. The affair seems to have roused the queen's ire, not because Henry was unfaithful (he had never been faithful), but because Rosamund was accorded the privileges Eleanor herself was owed; in Eleanor's absence, Henry had flaunted the young woman as a wife and queen, allowing her to preside over his court and use Eleanor's throne. It was the insult to her personal power as a monarch that began the royal couple's estrangement and started the processes by which Eleanor later encouraged rebellion by her sons against their father.

Rosamund remained at Woodstock until about 1176, and Henry was abroad much of the time. Although the reasons are unclear, Rosamund then left Henry and Woodstock for the convent at Godstow, probably due to an ongoing illness. Some months later, she died at the nunnery, still a relatively young woman; it is thought she may have taken the veil before her death. Dramatic stories of Eleanor murdering Rosamund out of jealousy were first concocted by Eleanor's feudal enemies and later by chroniclers trying to tarnish the image of this powerful political leader. Actually, at the time of Rosamund's death Eleanor was being held prisoner in Salisbury tower for her treason against Henry and so was probably unaware that Henry's mistress had died.

Rosamund's tomb at Godstow was the cause of some controversy. Whereas some felt she was a great sinner and should not have been buried in sacred ground, the nuns of Godstow had loved her deeply and kept candles burning around the tomb until 1191, when a bishop ordered the tomb moved out of the church, lest other young women become convinced that one could be rewarded in heaven for adultery.

Laura York,
Riverside, California

Cline, Genevieve (1879–1959)

First woman to be appointed a U.S. federal judge. Born on July 27, 1879 (some sources cite 1878) in Warren, Ohio; died in 1959 in Cleveland, Ohio; educated at Spencerian College, Oberlin College, and Baldwin-Wallace Law School, LL.B., 1921.

After completing a one-year business program at Oberlin College in Ohio, Genevieve Cline went to work for her brother John who was an Ohio prosecutor. She attended Baldwin-Wallace Law School, from which she received her L.L.B. in 1921, and was active in politics as a Republican during her years in school. Appointed by President Warren Harding, in 1922 Cline began to serve as appraiser of merchandise at the port of Cleveland, the first woman to be appointed to such a position at a large port city. She worked in this capacity, appraising merchandise that was shipped from foreign ports, until 1928. Cline's appointment to the U.S. Customs Court by President Calvin Coolidge was confirmed on May 25, 1928. The first woman appointed as a U.S. federal judge, Cline sat on the Customs Court until her retirement 25 years later, in 1953. In 1927, she served as vice president of the Ohio branch of the National Association of Women Lawyers.

Cline, Nancy Lieberman (b. 1958).

See Lieberman-Cline, Nancy.

Cline, Patsy (1932–1963)

Legendary American pop, rock, and country singer who pushed the boundaries for women in country music. Name variations: Virginia Dick. Born Virginia Patterson Hensley in Winchester, Virginia, on September 8, 1932; died in a plane crash on March 5, 1963; daughter of Samuel Lawrence Hensley (a master blacksmith) and Hilda Virginia (Patterson) Hensley; married Gerald Cline, on March 7, 1953; married Charlie Dick (a linotype operator), in 1957; children: (second marriage) Julia Simadore Dick (b. August 25, 1958); Allen Randolph (b. January 22, 1961).

Discography: "Walkin' after Midnight," "Don't Ever Leave Me," "Then You'll Know," "Try Again," "Today, Tomorrow, and Forever," "Fingerprints," "Too Many Secrets," **Lillian Claiborne**'s *"A Stranger in My Arms," "That Wonderful Someone," "In Care of the Blues," "Hungry for Love," "I Can't Forget," "Stop the World," "Walking Dreams," "Cry Not for Me," "If I Could See the World," "Just out of Reach," "I Can See an Angel," "Come on In," "Never No More," "If I Could Only Stay Asleep," "Crazy," "She's Got You," "Seven Lonely Days," "I Love You So Much It Hurts Me," "Have You Ever Been Lonely," "Foolin' Around," "South of the Border," "Who Can I Count On," "When I Get Through with You," "Leavin' on Your Mind," "Blue Moon of Kentucky," "Faded Love," "Someday (You'll Want Me to Want You)," "Always," "Sweet Dreams (of You)," "Does Your Heart Beat for Me?," "Bill Bailey," "Lovesick Blues," "There He Goes."*

She sang in clubs. She sang in firehalls. She sang in gin mills and juke joints. She sang in the annual minstrel show and on the roof of the refreshment stand at the Winchester Royal Drive-In. She sang at county fairs in towns called Brunswick, Barryville, Warrenton, Elkton, and Martinsburg. But in her hometown of Winchester, population 15,000, the conventional wisdom was that she wouldn't amount to a hill of beans.

Patsy Cline was born in Winchester, apple capital of Virginia. Proud of being the oldest English colonial settlement west of the Blue Ridge, the town venerated its genteel, well-bred ladies, a circumstance that "put Patsy on a collision course with Southern Womanhood," writes her biographer **Margaret Jones**. In May 1957, with her career on the rise, the 25-year-old Cline was selected queen Shenandoah XXX of the Apple Blossom Festival. She wore makeup, dressed like a cowgirl, had a womanly figure, and was from Kent Street—the wrong side of the tracks. Winchester was not about to have this singer with her newfound pop success shoved down their throats; Cline was greeted with cat calls from the curb. "Sonsabitches," she muttered, "I'll show them yet."

Descended from prime "hillbilly" stock, Cline's paternal grandfather was a major landowner. Her father Sam Hensley, who lost the family property in the Depression, was a master blacksmith and a talented singer and piano player, whose sisters attended the Shenandoah Conservatory of Music and whose brother was a guitarist. Sam was also known for his uncontrollable temper. Following his return from World War I and a tour of the Argonne Forest, he took to periodic drinking. Then his first wife and one of his children were killed in an auto accident, and he sent his surviving son and daughter to live with the local music teacher, **Sally Mann**. At age 43, Sam Hensley was essentially a bachelor and a mean drunk when he married 15-year-old **Hilda Patterson** six days before the birth of their daughter Virginia Patterson Hensley on September 8, 1932. The bride's stepfather, a guard on a prison chain gang, provided the motivation. Called Ginny at first, then Patsy, a corruption of her middle name, the child was precocious; at age four, she won a street-fair talent contest with her tap dancing.

Though charming to others, Sam Hensley terrorized his family. Patsy was aware that her teenaged mother, who worked at the apple processing plant, lived in constant fear. Often the beneficiary of her father's temper, Patsy had the fire to go toe to toe with him, though she lost every round. Mother and daughter formed an alliance that would last for the rest of their lives.

There was a more serious problem. In later years, careful to avoid particulars, Cline spoke tearfully of a relative who made frequent sexual advances toward her. Prefacing her admission with "take this to your grave," she confided in *Loretta Lynn that the abuser was her father. Knowledge of the incest would become public after Cline's death, when in 1985, her mother disclosed the abuse to producer Bernard Schwartz while he was filming Cline's bio-pic *Sweet Dreams,* with **Jessica Lange**. Though discreet scenes were shot and Lange wanted the scenes in the movie, director Karel Reisz left most of this footage on the cutting-room floor. Instead, the film became a love story between Cline and Charlie Dick.

When Patsy was about seven, a younger brother Sam, Jr., known as John, was born (1939), followed by a sister Sylvia Mae (1944).

During Patsy's youth, the family moved 19 times—from Lexington to Norfolk, from Norfolk to Frederick County. Sam would find a large Victorian house that Hilda would fix up. Spending freely, Sam would get behind on the rent; they'd move again.

Music was Patsy's solace. To mother and daughter religion was "problematic," but Patsy loved to sing gospel. At times, Sam Hensley would find religion and join the choir. Patsy was given an old upright, at age eight, and learned to play piano by ear. Her influences were the women with the booming voices: *Kate Smith and *Helen Morgan. The singer who had the most impact was Rubye Blevins, known professionally as *Patsy Montana, the first country-singing woman to don cowgirl clothes, complete with a six shooter. In 1936, Montana sold a million copies of "I Want to Be a Cowboy's Sweetheart." By the 7th grade, Cline was wearing a scarf around her neck, country style. By 16, she was listening to Grand Ole Opry on Nashville's WSM radio and begging to wear cowboy boots and a fringed vest.

In 1948, the Hensleys moved from Gore, Virginia, to a run-down duplex in Winchester. That December, Patsy re-enrolled at Handley High School for the 9th grade, just before Sam abandoned the household. To help support her mother and siblings, the 16-year-old Cline dropped out of school and lied about her age to get work—at the Rockingham Poultry butchering chickens, at the Greyhound Bus depot as a countergirl, finally at the local drugstore as a sodajerk. Her mother filled the gap by taking in sewing.

But Cline had a dream. She began to make the rounds for singing jobs, both pop and country. Driven, she made cheap discs and sent them to magazine advertisers. She entered an amateur contest at the local movie house and took first prize. With no connections, she walked into WINC, Winchester's radio station, and asked to sing with a local hillbilly band, the Melody Playboys, who played on a Saturday morning show. It was her first radio broadcast. Then she was offered a job fronting a band at Yorks Inn, a high-class nightclub. Cline would arrive home at 3 AM then roust out of bed early the next morning for her post at the drugstore. She sang anywhere, with anybody, to anyone. When she landed an audition for the Opry, she and Hilda, with no money for a hotel, slept in the car in Nashville. Though impressed, the Opry told her she was too young; besides, girls singing solo . . . well, it wasn't considered a nice thing to do. In 1948, "girl singers were rare and girl soloists were an anomaly," writes Jones:

> The girls worked with their husbands, like cowgirl **Texas Ruby**, or **Annie Lu**, or their families, like the **Cackle Sisters** or the **Poe Sisters**. And if they didn't have any family, they invented them. . . . It was said that girls would never be stars [of the Opry] because the good old boys in the audience with their wives 'would get their ears slapped down if they stared at a strange female.'. . . The only way a woman could get a star billing was if she cultivated a homely image, like Sarah Ophelia Colley, who, as *Minnie Pearl, was the Opry's reigning female icon.

Cline's experience at the Opry made her more determined. Turning away from the pop music she loved, she majored in country, while her mother sewed fringe on cowgirl outfits. In 1952, *Kitty Wells broke ground with her smash hit "It Wasn't God Who Made Honky-Tonk Angels," releasing the first important country recording by a woman since Patsy Montana. That year, bandleader Bill Peer took Cline in hand. Quitting her drugstore job, she began singing full time at his Moose Lodge in Brunswick, Maryland. Under pressure from Peer, she reluctantly began an affair with him, to the consternation of her mother and the ruination of her reputation in Winchester.

On March 7, 1953, Patsy married Gerald Cline, a regular at Moose Lodge. Seven years her senior, Gerald was a short, heavy-set, big spender from a well-off family; he also owned a Buick. For Patsy, he looked like a first-class ticket out of town. "She thought she could learn to love him," said a friend. But Gerald's expected wealth would remain just that. In reality, he wasn't the Cline Construction Company; he was only working for his family. Though he treated her well, Gerald had little interest in his wife's ambitions. He was also deadly dull. During their marriage, Cline continued her relationship with Peer.

Then, on September 30, 1954, she signed a two-year, 16-side contract with Bill McCall and his 4 Star records (Decca was his distributor). Since McCall was one of the biggest shysters in the business, Cline's royalties turned out to be half the going rate and the fine print would handcuff her for years. When she was broke and needed an advance, McCall would gladly oblige, but only if she signed an extension on her contract. Cline, who would receive little in royalties, was generally broke.

That year, she took first at the National Country Music Championships, caught the attention of Connie B. Gay, a deejay, producer,

and power broker in country music, and joined his daily "Town and Country" television show in Washington D.C. as a regular, becoming a regional star. Between that and the nightclubs, 22-year-old Cline was finally making enough money on singing alone to help support her family. But the response to her first single for 4 Star, "A Church, a Courtroom and Then Goodbye," was tepid.

By 1956, she was separated from Gerald. That April, on Friday the 13th, she met Charlie

Dick, a Winchester man with a wild-boy reputation, and formed an instant attachment. Her mother's response was just as instant: total dislike. Charlie Dick was decent when sober but a mean drunk, and he was drunk often. He, too, had not lived a storybook life: Dick was 15 and in his bedroom when his father shot himself in the downstairs kitchen.

By now, Cline had recorded four singles, all duds. When Donn Hecht urged her to record his song "Walkin' after Midnight," originally written for *Kay Starr, she demurred, convinced it was another dud; besides, she didn't think it was country. They compromised. Cline agreed to record "Walkin'" if she could choose the flip side, "A Poor Man's Roses"; still, she was not keen on the deal.

She was a tough-talking survivor— a strong woman in country music when strong women weren't wanted or tolerated.

—Gerry Woods

Early in 1957, she brought her mother by Greyhound to New York on borrowed money, stayed at the Dixie Hotel across from the bus station, and tried out for Arthur Godfrey's "Talent Scouts," an enormously popular prime-time TV show of the 1950s. Godfrey, with his red hair, easy manner, and nasal patter, made headlines if he sneezed. It was his producer and sometime regular singer **Janette Davis**, however, who nixed four of Cline's offerings and convinced her to sing the yet unreleased "Walkin' after Midnight." Wearing a linen dress, which prohibited sitting for fear of wrinkles, and singing a song she had no faith in, Patsy Cline went on "Talent Scouts" the night of January 21 and won. The next day, Gerald Cline filed for divorce.

Following Cline's appearance, Decca had to race to press the master for "Walkin' after Midnight" to satisfy eager distributors; it was an instant crossover hit, both country and pop. The song peaked at No. 12 on the pop charts and No. 2 on country, but when her royalty statements arrived from 4 Star, she saw no money after "expenses." Cline needed an advance; McCall gladly extended her contract. "Walkin'" sold 2.5 million records in her lifetime, and she made $900 from the royalties.

She was, however, finally making money on bookings. Though shy, and fearful of her grammar, Cline was invited to become a regular on Godfrey's show, performing every three months for about a year and a half, at $1,000 a week.

She was also named *Billboard*'s "Most Promising Country & Western Female Artist" for 1957. Moving up, she rented a brick house for her family on the same street as before and, for a friend, signed records at McCrory's 5&10 in Winchester. In April 1957, she cut eight more songs and had recording dates in May, December, and February (1958). None of these recordings made the charts. She knew the songs were not good enough—everyone at the sessions knew—but Cline, and the talent around her, had no say; 4 Star chose the material. Cline was so broke that she'd record anything for the 50 bucks a side.

She became close with *June Carter (Cash)*, seeking her out to discuss problems of the heart. Charlie Dick was Cline's passion, and he was cheating on her. Their relationship was in constant turmoil; they had mammoth fights. Even so, when Charlie was drafted in 1957, she married him. "That was the only time Patsy ever went against her mother," said a friend. For awhile, she lived off-base in Fayetteville, North Carolina, where he was stationed at Fort Bragg. When Cline gave birth to **Julia Simadore Dick** on August 25, 1958, Charlie encouraged her to stay home and raise a family, to let him become the breadwinner. Tired after a heady year, she agreed. Between fights, she would return home to mother, while Charlie lived on the base. After one year, she missed singing—not the business, just singing.

She took to the road, long before there were touring buses. Charlie was out of the army, hanging around her shows, flirting with women, getting drunk and, at some of her appearances, making scenes. Her weight fluctuated, she started smoking, drinking a little more. Sometimes she showed up at sessions with a bruised face. When asked, she'd reply: "I can hand it back."

Cline's new manager Randy Hughes advised her to ride out the contract with 4 Star, no extensions. With his encouragement, she moved to Nashville. Though she and Charlie couldn't afford a phone, her hopes were high. "We haven't had a fuss since we been here," she wrote her mother. When another baby, Allan Randolph, arrived on January 22, 1961, Charlie was passed out from an evening revel, and she had to ask a neighbor to take her to the hospital.

Finally out of 4 Star's clutches, Cline signed with Decca for three years, and Owen Bradley, a well-known arranger-producer, was free to choose her material. Bradley liked a ballad called "I Fall to Pieces," but once again Patsy wasn't sure, especially when she heard that *Brenda Lee had turned it down. Another compromise was reached: they would record one of his, one of hers. More comfortable with swing, she hated Bradley's slow arrangement, but session musicians urged her to try it. During the playback, Cline reluctantly admitted, "I like that, even if it isn't me."

Though her new record was released with slight promotion from Decca, Pamper Music (publishers of "I Fall to Pieces") gave it their all for six months. Across the nation, Cline did a host of sock hops. Soon tiring of the road, she took a gig at the Winchester Drive-In theater, just to come home. The event was a fiasco. As she sang on the roof of the refreshment stand, she heard more horns than cheers. "Why do people in Winchester treat me like this?" she asked, leaving the stage in tears.

On May 22, 1961, "I Fall to Pieces" made the charts. By August 7, it was No. 1 on country charts; by September 12, it peaked at No. 12 on the pop charts. Cline was thrilled; the repossessors could no longer threaten to take her refrigerator. On the strength of the song, she bought her mother a car and made a down payment on a modest home in Madison, a suburb of Nashville.

Throughout her life, Cline maintained she had premonitions. In April 1961, certain that an accident was imminent, she made out a will, leaving everything to her mother, including her children. To Charlie, she left "whatever make car we have at the time of my death." On June 14, a rainy day in Nashville, she was driving with her brother John on a two-lane road when a passing car came roaring toward them as they topped a hill. In the head-on collision, Cline was thrown through the windshield onto the hood, while John, who had been at the wheel, had a puncture in his chest and cracked ribs. In the other car, a woman and her six-year-old son were killed. Unaware of how badly she was injured, Cline told the ambulances at the scene to take care of the others.

The admitting physician said Cline was a "gory mess" on arrival at the hospital. Her scalp was peeled back; she had a deep gash across her forehead from temple to temple, crossing the right eyebrow, the bridge of her nose, and left eyebrow; she also had a dislocated hip, a broken wrist, and enormous blood loss. Twice, the doctors thought they lost her. Cline, who claimed a near-death experience, told a visiting minister, "All my life I have been reaching for God and today I touched him." Most agree that the hard-talking, cussing singer changed after the accident, and she made a pact with God to make her marriage work for the kid's sake. Charlie was at the hospital throughout.

While in the hospital, Cline heard Loretta Lynn sing "I'm a Honky Tonk Girl" on Opry radio. That night, Lynn, who had only been singing for six months and was still pretty green, dedicated her next song to Patsy Cline, saying "I love her and love her singing," Lynn then sang "I Fall to Pieces." Touched, Patsy sent Charlie to bring Lynn to the hospital. They were close friends from then on. Wrote Lynn:

> [Patsy] was my protector. . . . She taught me how to get on and off the stage, how to wear makeup, how to start a show and how to leave people wanting more at the end. She made sure I had clothes to wear and many times when she bought an outfit for herself, she'd buy one for me just like it. She bought curtains for my house because I was too broke to buy 'em. She protected me with the radio stations all she could. She'd tell those disk jockeys, "If you want to talk to me, you'll have to talk to both of us." . . . Maybe she saw something of herself in me, 'cause she and I both grew up the hard way, had to be women when we were children, and she was a woman, a wise, older woman, even though she was so young when she died.

Known for her generosity to other female singers, Cline had a tendency to take kid stars, like Brenda Lee, *Dottie West, and 13-year old Barbara Mandrell, under her wing. Many looked up to her. "She was the first woman in country music to step out of the boundaries they had been placed in," wrote Lynn.

Because of the accident, deejays could not resist the irony, and "I Fall to Pieces" received a great deal of airplay. Letters poured into her hospital room. After a small amount of cosmetic surgery (she was frightened of, and avoided, the major one needed), Cline pulled her bangs down over the scar across her forehead, drew on eyebrows in place of those that were no longer there, and returned to the stage on crutches.

She was brought a song called "Crazy" by a newcomer named Willie Nelson. In August 1961, still on crutches—with sore ribs, painful breathing, and severe headaches from her head injury—she had another recording session. Slowing Nelson's tempo, she attempted "Crazy," but her ribs hurt so much that she couldn't hold her breath long enough to sustain the notes. Returning two weeks later, she tried again. Decca released "Crazy" on October 16. The song was an instant hit, in Europe as well as America, and even cracked the tough sophisticated New York market. In fact, the Grand Old Opry, with Cline aboard, played Carnegie Hall in November 1961, much to the distaste of New York columnist *Dorothy Kilgallen. *Billboard* named Cline "Favorite Female Artist" for two years running (1961 and 1962), an honor that had been given only to Kitty Wells for the preceding nine years. In December 1961, Cline recorded "She's Got You," her third smash hit in a row.

In 1962, she toured off and on with the Johnny Cash Show, one highlight of which was playing the Hollywood Bowl. With money finally coming in, Charlie quit his job and stayed home to take care of the kids. He continued to cheat on Cline, and she began to look for love elsewhere. She also bought a split-level house for the family, nothing grand, on Nella Drive in Madison. The following year, "Leavin' on Your Mind" was released, and Cline recorded an album that included "Blue Moon of Kentucky," "Someday (You'll Want Me to Want You)," and "Sweet Dreams (of You)." That January, the 30-year-old had another premonition. Write this down, Cline told June Cash, "I'm going out soon." She then instructed Cash on everything she wanted her mother, husband, and children to know.

On Sunday, March 2, 1963, Cline and her manager Randy Hughes flew to Kansas City for a couple of shows at the Memorial Building. Hughes had only recently taken up flying. Though he had little experience and was not rated for instruments, he sometimes transported them to dates. The next morning, Monday, was rainy and foggy. Hughes, Cline, and singers Lloyd "Cowboy" Copas and Hawk Hawkins sat at the airport, waiting out the weather. Though Dottie West, who had appeared with them the night before, offered her friend a ride back to Nashville, Cline decided to wait. The group flew out on Tuesday. The only thing that could be concluded about the crash near Camden, Tennessee, was that it was raining at the time, and Hughes must have thought he was gaining altitude when in reality he was nosediving at 120 miles per hour into a hillside. In Cline's hometown, the *Winchester Star* gave the tragedy a banner headline: PATSY CLINE, 3 OTHERS KILLED IN PLANE CRASH. Writes her biographer Margaret Jones: "Hit records, awards, appearances on network television notwithstanding, her demise was, by far, the biggest press she'd received from the hometown newspaper."

In March 1995, along with *Peggy Lee, Henry Mancini, Curtis Mayfield, and **Barbra

Streisand, Patsy Cline was inducted into Grammy's Hall of Fame by the National Academy of Recording Arts and Sciences. Over time, her *Greatest Hits* album was No. 1 on *Billboard*'s chart for 165 weeks, going multiplatinum in 1992. In 1986, 23 years after her death, the Winchester City Council met to vote on changing the name of Pleasant Valley Road to Patsy Cline Boulevard. The vote was 11–1, against.

SOURCES:
Jones, Margaret. *Patsy: The Life and Times of Patsy Cline.* Foreword by Loretta Lynn. NY: Harper-Collins, 1994.
Woods, Gerry. "Patsy Cline, The Legend Continues," in *Country Weekly.* March 7, 1995.

SUGGESTED READING:
Nassour, Ellis. *Honky Tonk Angel: The Intimate Story of Patsy Cline.* St. Martin's, 1993 (rev. abridgement of 1981 version published as *Patsy Cline*).

RELATED MEDIA:
Sweet Dreams (115 min.), starring Jessica Lange and Ed Harris, produced by Bernard Schwartz for Tri-Star, 1985.
Coal Miner's Daughter (125 min.), a musical biography of Loretta Lynn, starring **Sissy Spacek** (who won an Academy Award for Best Actress), Tommy Lee Jones, and **Beverly D'Angelo** (who portrayed Cline), produced by Bernard Schwartz for Universal, 1980.
Patsy Cline: The Birth of a Star, audio collection of her TV appearances with Arthur Godfrey, produced by Razor & Tie Records, 1996.
Always . . . Patsy Cline, stage show first produced in Nashville, starring **Mandy Barnett**.

Clisby, Harriet (1830–1931)

Australian doctor and feminist. Born Harriet Jemima Winifred Clisby in 1830 in London, England; died in 1931; daughter of a corn merchant; graduated from New York Medical College for Women, 1865.

In 1838, Harriet Clisby's father, a corn merchant, took his family from London to South Australia where they farmed until moving to Adelaide in 1845. Harriet began work as a journalist and joined the Swedenborgian New Church in 1847. The link between spiritual health and physical health was to be of concern to Clisby for the rest of her long life; accordingly, she became a vegetarian and practiced gymnastics.

After traveling to Melbourne in 1856, the next year Clisby began working as editor of the *Southern Photographic Harmonia*, a publication written in shorthand. *The Interpreter*, a literary journal, which was the first Australian journal produced by women, benefitted from Clisby's work with *Caroline Dexter and was published in 1861. Clisby, who had read *Elizabeth Blackwell's 1852 work *Laws of Life,* was prompted to train as a doctor. A friend provided her tuition for two years' of physiology and anatomy before Clisby moved on to England where she worked as a nurse at Guy's Hospital in London. She did not have the funds to follow *Elizabeth Garrett Anderson's advice for training in America until a friend finally financed her studies at the New York Medical College for Women. Clisby graduated from the program in 1865. She lectured and was for many years involved with feminist and Christian groups, founding in 1871 the Women's Educational and Industrial Union in Boston. In Geneva, to which she later retired, Clisby founded L'Union des Femmes. She died in 1931, having lived a century.

Clisson, Jeanne de (fl. 1343).

See Jeanne de Belleville.

Clive, Caroline (1801–1873)

English author. Name variations: (pseudonym) V; Mrs. Archer Clive. Born Caroline Meysey-Wigley in Brompton Green, London, England, on June 24, 1801; died on July 13, 1873, at Whitfield, Herefordshire; second daughter of Edmund Meysey-Wigley, M.P. for Worcester, and Anna Maria Watkins Meysey; married Reverend Archer Clive, in 1840; children: one son; one daughter.

Illness left Caroline Clive lame at age three, depriving her of many of the usual activities of childhood. At age 39, she married the Reverend Archer Clive, rector of Solihull in Warwickshire. Under the signature V, Caroline Clive published eight volumes of poetry. She is best known as the author of *Paul Ferroll* (1855), a sympathetic portrait of a man who murders his wife to marry his first love. This work was followed with the less successful *Why Paul Ferroll Killed his Wife* (1860). In 1865, Clive suffered a stroke while traveling in Europe. In July 1873, she was writing in her bedroom surrounded by books and papers, when her dress caught on fire, and she was burned to death.

Clive, Catherine (1711–1785).

See Clive, Kitty.

Clive, Kitty (1711–1785)

English-Irish actress and leading lady at London's Drury Lane for 40 years, who was particularly noted for her performances in comedy roles, and as a singer. Name variations: Catherine (Kitty) Raftor; Mrs.

Catherine Clive. Born Catherine Raftor on November 15, 1711, in London, England; died at Twickenham, near London, on December 6, 1785; daughter of William Raftor (a lawyer) and his wife, the erstwhile Miss Daniel (given name unknown); married George Clive, in 1733; no children.

Became a member of the company of London's Drury Lane Theatre at age 17 (1728); first appeared as Nell in The Devil to Pay, *one of her most famous roles (1730–31); publicly defended her right to the part of Polly in* The Beggar's Opera *(1735–36); joined the Covent Garden company, and published* The Case of Mrs. Clive *(1744); returned to Drury Lane (1745–46), remaining there until her retirement; made her final appearance on stage, opposite David Garrick, in* Lethe *(April 24, 1769).*

Selected works (published and/or performed): The Case of Mrs. Clive Submitted to the Public *(1744);* The Rehearsal, or Bayes in Petticoats *(1753);* Every Woman in her Humour *(1760);* Sketch of a Fine Lady's Return from a Rout *(1763);* The Faithful Irishwoman *(1765).*

In January 1729, the curtain rose at London's Drury Lane Theatre on the first performance of a new piece. Written by actor-manager Colley Cibber in the currently popular form of ballad opera, *Love is a Riddle* was an attempt to emulate the spectacular success of John Gay's *The Beggar's Opera*. Kitty Raftor, the actress taking the leading part of Phillida, was one of the newest and least experienced members of the company, having joined it only the year before, but she had already achieved considerable popularity with both the public and the critics. On this occasion, however, she faced a daunting prospect, since some of Cibber's rivals, determined to wreck the performance, had whipped up the always volatile audience to a state of extreme hostility. To go on stage at all required considerable courage, to quell the riot appeared impossible. Within only a few moments of her entrance, however, Kitty had succeeded in winning over the audience to her side, and in alarming the instigators of the riot. According to the theatrical historian, William Chetwood, who was acting as prompter, "When Miss Raftor came on . . . the monstrous roar subsided; a person in the stage-box next to my post called out to his companion in the following elegant style: 'Zounds! You take care, or this charming little devil will save all!'"

In any event, the reprieve was only temporary. The piece was an abysmal failure, closing after only two nights. For Kitty Clive, however, it was only the beginning of a long and triumphant career as the undisputed mistress of English comedy. Having entered a profession that was still widely regarded as disreputable, she compelled respect for her qualities as a woman, her shrewdness, her intelligence, and her strength of character, as well as for the art in which she was acknowledged to be supreme. Even the author of *The Rosciad,* a savage satire on the theater of the time, made her one of the rare exceptions from his censures.

> Original in spirit and in ease,
> She pleas'd by hiding all attempts to please.
> No comic actress ever yet could raise
> On humour's base, more merit or more praise.

According to Kitty Clive's own account, given to Chetwood, her fascination with the stage had begun in childhood, when she and a friend "used to tag after" the famous actor, Robert Wilks, as he strolled through the streets of London, "and gape at him as a wonder." Unlike many of her fellow actors, however, she had not been born into the profession. Her father William Raftor was a lawyer, originally from Kilkenny in Ireland, who in 1690 had taken up arms on behalf of the ousted king, James II. The defeat of the Jacobites forced Raftor into exile, but he later succeeded in obtaining a pardon and settled in London, where he married a Miss Daniel, with whom he had a number of children. In spite of the fact that Miss Daniel is said to have brought "a handsome fortune" to her marriage, the Raftors seem to have been far from prosperous. Kitty's education was probably rudimentary: her later correspondence, while demonstrating wit, a lively intelligence, and a good command of language, also reveals that her spelling was, even by the erratic standards of the time, highly idiosyncratic.

Although Clive's first performance, and her subsequent career are well documented, accounts of her entry into acting vary. According to one version of events, she was employed as maidservant to a woman who lived in Church Row, Houndsditch. Singing one day as she washed the doorstep, Kitty was overheard by some members of the fashionable Beef-steak Club, whose meetings were held at the Bull Tavern, just across the street. Impressed by the young woman's talent, they introduced her to the management of Drury Lane Theatre, where she was immediately engaged as a player.

However, Chetwood, who was himself working at Drury Lane at this time, has a different version of events. According to him, the young Kitty was lodging at the same house as

himself and the actor, Theophilus Cibber. As Chetwood remembered, "Miss Raftor had a facetious turn of humour and infinite spirits, with a voice and manner in singing songs of pleasantry peculiar to herself. Those talents . . . we . . . thought a sufficient passport to the theatre." Chetwood and Cibber recommended her to the latter's father, Colley Cibber, then manager at Drury Lane, who "the moment he heard her sing, put her down in the list of performers at twenty shillings per week," and gave her the minor role of the page, Ismenes, in Nat Lee's tragedy *Mithridates.*

Despite her inexperience, Clive had an almost immediate success in this, and in the other small parts that Cibber assigned to her. Even at this early stage, her musical skills and her ability to put over a song were apparent, and as Ismenes, Chetwood recorded, her performance won her "extraordinary applause." In the following, 1728–29, season, she began to emerge in more prominent roles in comedy, appearing in January 1729 as Phillida in Cibber's ill-fated *Love is a Riddle.* Other early parts included Honoria in *Love Makes a Man,* Rosella in *The Village Opera,* Bonvira in the *History of Bonduca,* and Maria in *Whig and Tory.*

Unlike the great majority of her contemporaries, Kitty did not have to serve a long apprenticeship in provincial theaters or in a "strolling" company and was remarkable in her almost instantaneous success: as Chetwood remarked, "never any person of her age flew to perfection with such rapidity." Although not a beauty, she had a remarkably mobile and expressive face, and an ability to create an immediate rapport with her audience. While appearing in a great range of parts, both in new plays and in established works, her particular forte was low comedy, and one of her most successful parts was as Nell in Coffey's *The Devil to Pay,* which fully utilized her talents as a singer and comedian. She first played the part in August 1731, and it remained a favorite with her, and with her public, throughout her career. In the 1731–32 season, she took on the role of Polly Peachum in *The Beggar's Opera,* and began her successful collaboration with Henry Fielding, appearing in his *The Old Debauchees, The Covent Garden Tragedy, The Lottery* and, in 1732–33, his adaptation of Moliere's *The Miser.*

In 1733, when she was 22 and already one of Drury Lane's leading ladies, Kitty secretly married George Clive, an apparently undistinguished young man from an aristocratic family. The marriage hardly lasted a year; by 1735, the couple were living separately, although they never divorced, and Kitty retained her husband's surname as her own stage name. Little is known of the Clives' marriage, and nothing of the reason for their separation. However, George Clive's bitterness seems to have lasted longer than Kitty's. When he died many years later, leaving his considerable fortune to his landlady, his widow philosophically noted that "he has not left me even the shilling he has cut me off with."

Throughout her marriage, and afterwards, Kitty remained at Drury Lane, steadily adding to her repertoire, regularly reviving favorite roles, and defending those that she regarded as her own against all rivals. In 1735–36, a public row erupted, when the management attempted to give the part of Polly Peachum in *The Beggar's Opera* to ❧▸ **Susannah Cibber**, leaving Clive with the secondary role of Lucy. The affair was delightedly covered in the London journals, in street ballads, and even made its way onto the stage in the form of a farce, *The Beggars' Pantomime, or the Contending Columbines*, dedicated by the author, Woodward, to the two ladies "who had a violent contention for Polly." As assertive as ever, Kitty went into print to defend herself, alleging, in a letter published in the *Daily Post*, that "there was a design formed against me, to deprive me by degrees of every part in which I had the happiness to appear with any reputation; and at length, by this method to make me so little useful to the stage, as not to deserve the salary I now have, which is much inferior to that of several other performers."

Despite her complaints, Clive was now a celebrated figure in London theatrical and intellectual circles and a leading member of the Drury Lane company. Off stage, her strong will and her temper were legendary: as Samuel Foote tactfully expressed it in 1747: "This lady has now and then perhaps . . . expressed herself behind the scenes in too loud and forcible a manner." In fact, Clive's tirades were notorious, allowing her to overawe even her most celebrated colleagues, and giving her a voice in a profession in which women had traditionally had little influence. Moreover, as Foote admitted, her tantrums were commonly "owing to an earnestness for the success of the business," that is, to her sense of duty towards her audience and her art. According to her colleague, Tate Wilkinson, Clive "was . . . passionate, cross and vulgar," but he, too, went on to acknowledge her supreme skills as an actress, as well as her generosity and her common sense. Her wit and intelligence were as evident in private life as in the

❧▸ **Cibber, Susannah** (1714–1766)

English singer and actress. Born Susannah Maria Arne in London, England, in February 1714; died at Westminster, on January 30, 1766; buried in Westminster Abbey; daughter of a Covent Garden upholsterer; sister of the composer Thomas Arne; married Theophilus Cibber (1703–1758, an actor-manager), in 1834 (divorced); children: two who died in infancy.

An eminent actress and singer, Susannah Cibber made her debut at age 18 at the Haymarket in the opera *Amelia* by Lumpé. In 1834, she became the second wife of the notorious Theophilus Cibber, an actor-manager and son of Colley Cibber. Theophilus directed her in her first success as a tragic actress in Voltaire's *Zaire*, which opened in 1736. Theirs was a miserable marriage: their two children died in infancy and Theophilus claimed all her wages. It is said he also encouraged an affair with William Sloper, so that he might sue for damages to pay his debts. In 1739, Theophilus brought an action against Sloper for £5,000. In the sensational trial, the jury gave their opinion of the cuckolded husband by awarding him £10. When Susannah continued to live with Sloper, Theophilus brought another action against the man for detaining his wife. This time, he was awarded £500 in damages. Four letters from Theophilus to Susannah and Sloper, relating to the divorce case, were published, as well as *Tryal of William Sloper Esq. for Criminal Conversation with Mrs. Cibber* (London, 1739). All the notoriety put Susannah's career on hold for 14 years. Returning to the theater in 1753, she became Garrick's most famous partner at the Drury Lane and was truly mourned at the time of her death in 1766. (Theophilus had drowned in 1758 while crossing the Irish sea to fulfill an engagement in Dublin.)

theater, and enabled her to mix on equal terms with the most gifted personalities of her time, among them Dr. Samuel Johnson who, according to Boswell, "had a very high opinion of Mrs. Clive's comic powers, and conversed more with her than any of the actresses. He said 'Clive, sir, is a good thing to sit by; she always understands what you say.'" Kitty reciprocated his compliment, declaring that "I love to sit by Dr Johnson; he always entertains me."

Almost as noteworthy was her exemplary private life, in an era when women players were popularly regarded as little better than prostitutes, and when the parts that they played were generally written to exploit their sexuality. Despite her separation from her husband, she never became an object of scandal, and indeed made something of a parade of her virtue, particularly in disputes with her rival, *Peg Woffington, who was reputed to have had numerous lovers. Clive also had a strong sense of family loyalty, and from an early age she supported her father and other relatives, including her brother Jemmy, whom she assisted in a generally unsuccessful stage career, and who lived with her for most of her life. As her friend Fielding wrote to her, "Great favourite as you are with your audience, you would be much more so were they acquainted with your private character . . . did they see you, who can charm them on the stage with personating the foolish and vicious characters of your sex, acting in real life the part of the best wife, the best daughter, the best sister, and the best friend."

As an actress, Clive was outstanding in comedy. According to Thomas Davies, who saw her often, "a more extensive walk in comedy than hers cannot be imagined. . . . To a strong and melodious voice, with an ear for music, she added all the sprightly action requisite. . . . Her mirth was so genuine, that . . . her audience was sure to accompany her." Fielding agreed with this assessment, drawing a parallel between the real woman and the actress when he declared that "Mrs Clive is esteemed by all an excellent comic actress; and as she has a prodigious fund of natural spirit and humour off the stage, she makes the most of the poet's on it. Nothing, though ever so barren . . . can be flat in her hands." Her comic and singing talents were combined in one of her most popular pieces, her "mimic comic opera song," in which she imitated the performance of some of the leading prima donnas of the time, whom she allegedly described as "a set of Italian squalling devils who come over to England to get our bread from us." Songs were often introduced into her plays in order to exploit her popularity as a singer, but she was reportedly as effective in the works of great composers such as Purcell and Handel as in more ephemeral works, and, in 1743, she was chosen by the latter to sing Dalila in his oratorio *Samson*.

She did, however, have her weaknesses: as *The Dramatic Censor* summed it up, "Mrs Clive, peculiarly happy in low humour . . . was always the joy of her audience when she kept clear of anything serious and genteel." Her Ophelia was comprehensively damned, as was her Portia in *The Merchant of Venice*, in which she appeared for the first time in 1740–41. Nevertheless, the critics noted with disgust that her faithful public was amused by her interpretation of the part. According to *The Censor*, "The applause she received . . . was disgraceful both to herself and the audience," and Benjamin Victor deplored the "comic finishings" that she added

to the courtroom scene, while admitting her power to entertain even in such a performance. Characteristically, Kitty refused to admit defeat and, braving unanimously unfavorable reviews, revived the part on a number of other occasions.

In summer 1741, Clive visited Dublin for the only time in her career, appearing at the Aungier Street Theatre, to great acclaim, as Lappet in *The Miser*. Back in London, she fell ill, and at one stage it was reported that "her life has been despaired of," but shortly afterwards she was back on stage, apparently fully recovered. In 1743–44, she was once more involved in controversy when she was among the leading players, including Charles Macklin and David Garrick, who seceded from Charles Fleetwood's Drury Lane to set up a new company at the Haymarket. This venture was not a success, and shortly afterwards she moved to Covent Garden, where she remained for just two seasons. The period was a troubled one in the London theatrical world, with actors attempting to assert their rights against the powerful theater managers, and, in October 1744, Clive made her own contribution to the debate. In *The Case of Mrs. Clive Submitted to the Public*, she accused Fleetwood and John Rich, the manager of Covent Garden, of uniting in a cartel to keep down actors' salaries. While confidently leaving her audience to judge her performances, she nevertheless put forward a strong justification for her own claims, and incidentally offered an insight into the heavy demands made on even the leading actresses of the time.

> I may venture to affirm that my labour and application have been greater than any other performer on the stage. I have not only acted in almost all the plays, but in farces and musical entertainments; and very frequently two parts in a night, even to the prejudice of my health. I have been at great expense in masters for singing . . . [M]y additional expenses in belonging to the theatre amount to upwards of one hundred pounds a year in clothes and other necessaries; and the pretended great salaries of ten and twelve pounds a week . . . will, upon enquiry, appear to be no more than half as much; since they performed last season, at the theaters, very seldom above three or four days a week.

Aware that there would be those who considered the affair to be trivial, and her own stance unduly assertive, she reminded her readers that, "however trifling such things may appear to them, to me, who am so much concerned in 'em, they are of great importance, such as my liberty and livelihood depend on."

With the resignation of Fleetwood from Drury Lane, the way was open for Clive's return there for the 1745–46 season. Opening in *The Merchant of Venice*, to the usual adverse critical reaction, she went on to play some of her more popular parts, such as Lady Fanciful in *The Provok'd Wife* and Hoyden in *The Relapse*. She also finally relinquished the part of Polly Peachum in *The Beggar's Opera*, coaching her replacement in the role and appearing herself as Lucy. For the remainder of her career, Kitty was to remain at Drury Lane, which from 1747, under the management of David Garrick, achieved a new distinction and dynamism. Clive's relations with Garrick were always stormy, and she frequently felt the force of her spectacular temper, as she asserted her rights against both real and imagined slights. On the other hand, she could not fail to respect his genius as an actor. Her conflicting feelings are well represented by an eyewitness account of a performance of *King Lear*, in which Garrick acted the king. According to John Taylor, Clive "stood behind the scenes to observe him, and in spite of the roughness of her nature, was so deeply affected, that she sobbed one minute and abused him the next, and at length . . . turned from the place with the following . . . tribute: 'D—n him, I believe he could act a gridiron.'" Garrick, for his part, admired both Clive's artistry and her wit: it is said that a whispered remark from her, during a performance of Arthur Murphy's *The Way to Keep Him*, reduced him to hilarity and forced him to leave the stage—the single occasion in his career on which he laughed out of his part.

Now in her middle years, and with her standing as an actor unassailable, Clive expanded her sphere of activity by turning author. Her farce, *The Rehearsal, or Bayes in Petticoats*, was included in the 1749–50 season, with Clive in the title part. The role was a "breeches" one, not a genre in which she had ever excelled, and her performance was poorly received. Unlike Woffington, who scored her most brilliant successes in male roles, Kitty was physically unsuited to such parts, "the concealing petticoat," as Fielding put it, "better suiting her turn of make than the breeches." However, she did go on to produce three more farces, *Every Woman in her Humour*, *Sketch of a Fine Lady's Return from a Rout*, and *The Faithful Irishwoman*, none of which received good reviews. Indeed, her final attempt, *The Faithful Irishwoman*, produced in 1764–65, had only one performance, and of her works, only *The Rehearsal* was actually printed.

By now, Clive was playing fewer new characters, although in 1757–58 she appeared for the first time as Lady Wishfort in William Congreve's *The Way of the World*, a role that was to be one of her most celebrated and frequently revived. In 1761–62, she played Lady Beverly, a part that had been specially written for her, in William Whitehead's *The School for Lovers*, and, in 1763–64, she appeared as Mrs. Friendly in *Frances Sheridan's *The Dupe*. Other notable performances were her Widow Blackacre in *The Plain Dealer*, Mrs. Heidelberg in *The Clandestine Marriage*, Lady Fuz in Garrick's *A Peep behind the Curtain*, and, in 1768–69, Mrs. Winifred in ❧➤ **Elizabeth Griffith**'s *The School for Rakes*. According to her friend Griffith, Clive was unwell at the time and agreed to undertake the part only out of "kindness to the author, and attention to the public"; nonetheless, the play was a great success, due in no small part to her own performance.

Now 57, Kitty was as confident as ever of her powers against the challenge of the new generation: as she assured Garrick when he fretted

---

❧➤ **Griffith, Elizabeth** (c. 1720–1793)

British-Irish playwright and novelist. Born in Glamorganshire, Wales, around 1720; died in Millicent, Nass, County Kildare, Ireland, on January 5, 1793; daughter of Thomas Griffith (a well-known Dublin actor-manager) and Jane (Foxcroft) Griffith (daughter of a Yorkshire cleric); married Richard Griffith, around 1752; children: two.

Born in Wales, brought up in Ireland, Elizabeth Griffith was educated and trained by her actor-manager father for the theater. Five years after his death in 1744, she made her debut as an actress with Thomas Sheridan's Dublin company. In 1753, a now-married Griffith moved to London and minor roles at Covent Garden. When her husband's linen factory failed in the 1750s, Griffith determined to support the family by writing and published her courtship letters by subscription. The success of *A Series of Genuine Letters between Henry and Frances*, published in 1757, gave impetus to her continued writings. Her first comedy, *The Platonic Wife*, an adaptation of a play by Marmontel, ran for six nights at the Drury Lane in 1765. *The School for Rakes*, an adaptation of Beaumarchais' *Eugénie*, written at the urging of David Garrick, opened at the Drury Lane with *Kitty Clive in the lead in February 1769. Griffith's next play, 1772's *A Wife in the Right*, was a failure, owing to the drunkenness of her lead actor. Her last, *The Times*, opened at the Drury Lane in 1779. Elizabeth Griffith also wrote three successful novels.

SUGGESTED READING:

Eshelman, D. *Elizabeth Griffith: A Biographical and Critical Study*, 1949.

about the onset of old age, her audience "had rather see *the* Garrick and *the* Clive at a hundred and four, than any of the moderns; the ancients, you know, have always been admired." However, she had already decided to retire, perhaps feeling that it would be more dignified to do so while her reputation was at its height than to risk decline and obscurity. Her final benefit was held on April 24, 1769, the bill announcing that it would be "the last time of her appearing on the stage." The plays were *The Wonder,* in which she played opposite Garrick, and Garrick's own *Lethe,* with Clive reviving her celebrated "Fine Lady," and closing with an epilogue written for her by her friend, Horace Walpole. The occasion was a suitably triumphant farewell performance, with two of the greatest figures of the 18th-century theater playing together for the last time on the stage that Kitty had graced for so long.

For about 30 years, Clive had been engaged in an intimate platonic friendship with the author, wit and connoisseur, Horace Walpole, who in 1748 had bought a "country box," beside the Thames at Twickenham, which he named Strawberry Hill and transformed into "a little Gothic castle." Kitty visited him there often, and while she was still acting had written to him that "tho' I am now representing women of quality and cobblers' wives etc. etc. to crowded houses, the character I am most desirous to act well is a good sort of country gentlewoman at Twickenham." Her wish was realized when she accepted Walpole's offer of a cottage, moving there sometime before her retirement in 1769. Little Strawberry Hill, as her house became known, was "a little box, contiguous to Mr Walpole's garden, and close almost to the chapel," and there was constant movement between the two houses, with Clive and Walpole spending much of their time together, gossiping, playing cards, and entertaining a constant stream of visitors. As Clive wrote to her friend, the actress ◀ Jane Pope: "I have ten times more business now than I had when I played the fool as you do. I have engagements every day of my life. Routs, either at home or abroad every night. . . . I am in such good health, and such fine spirits that it is impossible for any one to be happier."

In later years, the attacks of illness to which she had always been subject became more frequent, and according to Walpole she was sometimes "extremely confused." Kitty Clive died on December 6, 1785, and was buried in Twickenham churchyard. Walpole set up a memorial to her in the garden beside her house, with his own verse engraved on it.

> Ye smiles and jests still hover round!
> This is mirth's consecrated ground.
> Here lived the laughter-loving dame,
> A matchless actress, Clive by name;
> The comic muse with her retired,
> And shed a tear when she expired.

Clive would almost certainly have mocked such hyperbole, but in her own time she was, indeed, incomparable, the supreme comic actress of her generation, described by Tate Wilkinson as "a diamond of the first water." For Victor, she was "this laughter-loving, joy-exciting actress" and "a true comic genius," while Chetwood, in his *General History of the Stage,* considered that "of all actresses who have appeared in the comic vein, Mrs. Clive's superior talents have always been pre-eminent." While those talents disappeared with the woman herself, Clive's professionalism, her energy and obvious intelligence, and her fearless independence can still excite admiration in generations for whom the magic of her performances must be only hearsay.

SOURCES:

Fitzgerald, Percy. *The Life of Mrs. Catherine Clive.* London, 1888.

Fyvie, John. *Comedy Queens of the Georgian Era.* London: Archibald Constable, 1906.

Highfill, Philip H., Kalman A. Burnim, and Edward A. Laughans, eds. *A Biographical Dictionary of Actors, Actresses . . . and other Stage Personnel in London, 1660–1800.* IL: Southern Illinois University Press, 1975.

Parsons, Mrs. Clement. *Garrick and his Circle.* London: Methuen, 1906.

SUGGESTED READING:

Ferris, Lesley. *Acting Women: Images of Women in Theatre.* London: Macmillan, 1990.

Howe, Elizabeth. *The First English Actresses.* Oxford: Cambridge University Press, 1992.

Rosemary Raughter,
freelance writer in women's history,
Dublin, Ireland

❧▶ Pope, Jane (1742–1818)

English actress. Born in 1742; died on July 30, 1818; daughter of a London theatrical wigmaker.

Actress Jane Pope began her career in a Lilliputian company for David Garrick in 1756, at age 14, then quickly shifted into ingenue roles. She originated the part of Mrs. Candour in *The School for Scandal* in 1777 and thereafter tackled many other important parts. A lifelong friend of *Kitty Clive, Pope erected the monument at Twickenham to Clive's memory. She was not only an admirable actress, but, like her friend Clive, led an irreproachable life, for which she was praised by all the literary critics of her day.

Clodia.

Variant of Claudia.

Clodia (c. 94–post 45 BCE)

Roman aristocratic matron who influenced politics and patronized literature and the arts during the Roman Republic. Name variations: Claudia; Clodia Metelli; possibly Lesbia. Pronunciation: CLO-di-a. Born Claudia, probably in Rome, around 94 BCE; date and place of death unknown, probably after 45 BCE; daughter of Appius Claudius Pulcher (consul in 79 BCE) and a mother whose name is not known for certain, but who may have been Metella; married Quintus Caecilius Metellus Celer (consul in 60 BCE), sometime before 62 BCE (died 59 BCE); no evidence for remarriage; lovers: possibly the poet Gaius Valerius Catullus and Marcus Caelius Rufus; children: possibly Metella.

Independence, leisure, and the enjoyment of life characterize the opportunities available to women from aristocratic families during the Late Roman Republic (133–43 BCE). Much as Roman women were enjoying their increasing freedom, however, Roman men were becoming alarmed at the growing power these women wielded, especially over the men in their family. Unfortunately, only the men's writings and points of view have been preserved, with the result that some of Rome's most colorful women are seen in an almost completely negative light. Such is the case with Clodia, a fiercely independent woman who was, for a while, at the center of political debate in Rome. Although the sources are sparse and scattered, sometimes merely conjectured, and often heavily biased, there is still enough material to piece together an outline of a life lived fully, passionately, and well.

Clodia was born around 94 BCE, one of six children of Appius Claudius Pulcher (consul in 79 BCE) and perhaps the sole child of his first wife, who may have been Metella. The Claudian family was an old and respected aristocratic dynasty and the Metellan clan was one of the most powerful in Rome during the last century of the Republic. So Clodia should have been born to all the advantages of the powerful and wealthy upper class. Yet her father may have left the household penniless when he died in 76, since one of her elder brothers complained that he had to give away one of his sisters in marriage without a dowry because the family could not afford it. Clodia's name sounds like the name of a lower-class, plebeian woman, but her original name was Claudia (according to the Roman custom of naming girls after their father's family, or

middle name). She probably changed it to Clodia when her youngest brother changed his from Publius Claudius Pulcher to Publius Clodius Pulcher, hereafter referred to as Clodius.

In 62 BCE, Clodia enters the historical record where she is mentioned as married to her cousin, Quintus Metellus Celer, the future consul of 60 BCE. She had probably been married for some years already, since women were usually married early, or at least before the age of 18. At this point, we can distinguish her from her two sisters, who were also called Claudia or Clodia, by observing the Roman practice of placing the husband's name after the wife's: Clodia Metelli. The consul of 63, Marcus Tullius Cicero (106-43 BCE), Rome's greatest leader and orator, mentions in a letter to Metellus that he has spoken with Clodia about Metellus' brother, Nepos, who was making political trouble for him. Cicero hoped Clodia could assuage Nepos and encourage him to drop his attack. Thus, Clodia was already involved with the politics of the day, though it was as an influential background player.

Shortly thereafter, Clodia became embroiled in the revolutionary political machinations of her brother, Clodius, which were opposed by her husband. Clodius, an ambitious politician, is best known for his demagoguery during the late 60s and most of the 50s. Though born into an aristocratic family, he recognized that he could gain power faster by being elected tribune and appealing to the lower classes as well as to those who felt disenfranchised. Yet patricians could not become tribunes, for the tribunate was designed to allow the plebeians access to magistracies. Thus, Clodius contrived to have himself adopted by a plebeian family. He had already provoked citywide scandal by sneaking into a religious ceremony restricted to women, but he had an ally in Julius Caesar, who helped enable his adoption. Metellus, a fiercely conservative, sometimes snobbish aristocrat, could not sanction Clodius' populist activities and opposed Clodius' transference to the plebeian class. Forced to make a choice between her husband or her brother, Clodia preferred to support her brother and thus placed a strain on her marriage. In another letter, Cicero alleges that Clodius and Clodia were having an incestuous relationship, a rumor that the gossip mills at Rome probably encouraged to account for her support. It does seem certain that Clodius committed incest with another sister, **Clodia Luculli**, so perhaps that tainted the perception of Clodia Metelli's relationship with her brother. Whatever the facts, when Clodia's husband Metellus died suddenly in 59 BCE, she was suspected of poisoning him.

When a Roman woman lost her husband, she was expected to marry again soon. There is no evidence that Clodia did so. In fact, what we know about her life suggests that she prized her independence more than her good reputation according to traditional conservative expectations. In the early to mid-50s, she continued to support her brother's revolutionary schemes and enjoyed a comfortable lifestyle, hosting sumptuous banquets, giving lavish parties at her resort on the Italian coast, and entertaining young men of artistic and literary talent.

Everything we know about Clodia suggests a woman motivated by the love of pleasure and the love of sway.

—T.P. Wiseman

There is a tradition that Clodia was the lover of the lyric poet Catullus. In several of his poems, Catullus calls his girlfriend "Lesbia," a sophisticated reference to the greatest woman poet in the ancient world, *Sappho, who had lived on the isle Lesbos. One ancient writer actually claimed that Lesbia was Clodia. Which Clodia is not mentioned, however, and it may as well be Clodia Luculli as Clodia Metelli. Perhaps we can never know for sure, but there is a certain *joie de vivre* and independence in Catullus' Lesbia that suits Clodia Metelli:

Let us live, my Lesbia, and let us love,
and pay no attention to gossip of wrinkled old men.
Suns may rise and suns may set,
but for us, when once the brief light goes down,
there will be one everlasting night for sleep.
Give me a thousand kisses, then a hundred,
a thousand more, add a hundred,
another thousand, and another hundred.
Then, when we've kissed many thousands of times,
we'll forget the number, so even we don't know it,
and so no wicked person can cast the evil eye upon it,
when he knows the number of our multitudinous kisses.

Lesbia is having an affair with Catullus while she is married, she argues with her husband, and she is accused of committing incest with her brother, who is called *pulcher,* "pretty," which could refer to Clodia's brother, Publius Clodius Pulcher. The evidence is circumstantial, and, intentionally so, for it was a great social embarrassment for a married Roman woman to have an affair. It was also illegal, though it happened. Catullus maintains propriety by giving his lover a pseudonym, but it seems a thin veneer.

The relationship between Lesbia and Catullus was passionate and tempestuous. Finally, Lesbia left him and took other lovers. One lover mentioned by Catullus is a certain Rufus. The name is intriguing because, in the early to mid-50s, Clodia was the lover of Marcus Caelius Rufus. The evidence for this comes from a courtroom speech by Cicero in defense of Caelius in the year 56. After the few notes about Clodia in Cicero's private correspondence, the speech for Caelius provides most of our information about her. It also illustrates the difficulties of writing about ancient women, since the source is intentionally biased. Clodia appeared for the prosecution, and Cicero, appearing for the defense, attacked her vehemently. She and Caelius had been lovers, but he jilted her, and she is represented as a jealous, vindictive, and scorned woman. Cicero gives a negative interpretation of her character and actions. Clodia's independence, rare for a woman in a traditional patriarchal society, is made to seem like an attempt to gain control over men. Her patronage of young men with artistic talent and her grand parties are made to look like shameless and decadent living. Accusations of incest with her brother are relayed as jokes that men make at a woman's expense. She is called a two-bit whore, virtually accused of poisoning her husband, and likened to husband-slaying Clytemnestra and the witch, the mythological mistress of poisons, Medea.

This portrait has influenced perceptions of Clodia for centuries, and it still affects our views of her today. But due weight must be given to the nature of Cicero's attack as a source for Clodia's activities. It was customary in Roman judicial speeches to attack an opponent's character, and character assassination was considered most likely to influence a jury. Yet Cicero and Clodia appeared to be on tolerably good terms just a couple of years after the speech; so it seems that Clodia did not carry a grudge on this matter (the same as men who were ruthlessly attacked in court, yet maintained their friendship with the author of the attack). What Cicero said was meant to play upon Roman attitudes toward women in order to win the case.

Clodia was caught up in the political machinations of her brother throughout the 50s, although her support began to wane by the end of the decade. In 59, she was part of Clodius' close circle of confidants, but in the next couple of years she confided in people sympathetic to Clodius' enemies. Clodius was becoming wild and reckless, a political firebrand, a liability. His ambitions may have offended his sister, who seems to retire quietly from history.

The last mention of Clodia comes in the mid-40s BCE. Once again, it is Cicero who provides the information. Cicero was looking to purchase some property upon which he might dedicate a shrine to his recently deceased daughter, *Tullia. He considers asking Clodia about her house by the Tiber River. In private correspondence, he assumes she will not sell, for she does not need the money and she likes the place. If she does want to sell, he says, she will want cash on the spot. Clodia probably did not need the money, but she was known for a certain amount of financial savvy.

Clodia did not sell her house and gardens to Cicero. She may have had a daughter, but aside from an obscure reference to the girl in the early 40s, nothing is known about her except that she was married and divorced young. No grandchildren are mentioned, and we hear of no descendants under the Roman Empire.

Clodia has been called the "first political strategist" among women at Rome, and Richard Bauman in *Women and Politics in Ancient Rome* sums up her life:

> Clodia is known to have been beautiful and she is generally assumed to have been intelligent, educated and witty. There is no need to quarrel with that assessment, but the point is that those qualities are only peripheral to her consequence. Determination, at times bordering on ruthlessness, a profound understanding of politics and politicians and consummate skill in manipulating them, and indifference to, and even contempt for, the traditional curbs on women's political mobility . . . these are the marks of the great feminine political strategist.

Clodia's "consequence" may be understood in various ways. Her political influence was not long lasting; nor was that of most men. She survives as one of a very few of the countless Roman women who were mentioned by contemporary male writers. As such, she provides a window onto the lives of other ancient Roman women. She also provides a warning. Clodia was politically active and independent, as were many Roman women of the late Republic. Most of the comments about her come from a man who often needed to oppose her in public, though he may have privately gotten along with her. Once the biases of the sources are considered, Clodia emerges as an intelligent woman who knew how to gain power and possessions to make her life pleasant. She appears as a woman who lived her life as fully as possible within a male-dominated society. Clodia fought for and maintained her ability to live beyond the constraints.

SOURCES:

(All original sources are in Latin. The following are English translations, often presented parallel to the Latin text.)

Catullus, Tibullus, Pervigilium Veneris. Translated by F. W. Cornish, *et al.* 2nd ed., revised by G. P. Goold. Loeb Classical Library. Cambridge, MA: Harvard University Press, 1988.

Cicero: Pro Caelio, De Provinciis Consularibus, Pro Balbo. Translated by R. Gardner. Loeb Classical Library, *Cicero,* Vol. 13. Cambridge, MA: Harvard University Press, 1958.

Cicero's Letters to Atticus. 7 vols. Edited and Translated by D.R. Shackleton Bailey. Cambridge Classical Texts and Commentaries, Vols. 3–9. Cambridge: Cambridge University Press, 1965–70.

Cicero's Letters to His Friends. Translated by D.R. Shackleton Bailey. American Philological Association Classical Resources Series, no. 1. Atlanta: Scholar's Press, 1988 (without Latin text).

SUGGESTED READING:

Bauman, Richard A. *Women and Politics in Ancient Rome.* London: Routledge, 1992.

Skinner, Marilyn B. "Clodia Metelli," in *Transactions of the American Philological Association.* Vol. 113, 1983, pp. 273–287.

Wiseman, T.P. *Catullus and His World: A Reappraisal.* Cambridge: Cambridge University Press, 1985.

———. "Clodia: Some Imaginary Lives," in *Arion.* New series, Vol. 2, 1975, pp. 96–115.

Robert W. Cape, Jr.,
Visiting Assistant Professor of Foreign
Languages and Classics,
Skidmore College, Saratoga Springs, New York

Clodia (c. 60 BCE–?).

See Fulvia for sidebar.

Cloe.

Variant of Chloe.

Cloelia (c. 508 BCE)

Semi-historical hero celebrated by ancient Roman writers for leading an escape from an Etruscan camp and swimming across the Tiber River. Name variations: Clelia. Pronunciation: KLOY-lee-ah. No sources identify her date of birth or death, her family connections or any other accomplishment beside the circumstances of her escape from the Etruscans in the early years of the Roman Republic.

According to most versions of the story, the fledgling Roman state surrendered Cloelia and other young women as hostages in a treaty with the Etruscan king Porsena. Cloelia soon led an escape of these women from the Etruscan camp. In all surviving accounts, she swam across the Tiber to the safety of Rome, usually with the rest of the hostages. Though the Romans, respecting their treaty with the Etruscans, returned Cloelia and the others, Porsena was so impressed with Cloelia's courage that he freed her. Even more graciously, he allowed Cloelia to take with her any of the hostages whom she might choose. She picked the younger children (there are boys among the hostages in some versions of the story) since they were the most exposed to harm, that is, to sexual abuse. In some versions of the story, Cloelia made her escape partly on horse, and a statue of a woman on horseback in the Via Sacra in Rome was said to portray her.

Cloelia reappears in Roman historical writing (including historical episodes in poetry) as a figure willing to die for the city republic of Rome. The story seems to exemplify the acquisition of *virtus* (manly courage, virtue; in Greek *arete*) and *fortitudo* (bravery) by women in the minds of Roman writers. Florus, in discussing the heroes of the early republic, says that women as well as men deserved praise for their *virtus* (*Epitoma* 1. 4. 7). In Livy's treatment of Cloelia's story, he tells us that the public respect paid to male heroes in the wars against the Etruscans inspired Roman women to emulate these heroes (2. 16. 6). Livy paints Cloelia as a military leader leading a breakout from a prisoner-of-war camp under a stream of arrows.

After her chains were burst Cloelia sailed over the river.

—Virgil

It is noteworthy that two ancient works of military history, Florus' *Epitoma* and Polyaenus' *Strategika* (31), mention Cloelia. The 1st century Greco-Roman writer Plutarch in his *Bravery of Women* (14) has Cloelia lead a group of women who swim closely together through the deep eddies and rapid currents of the Tiber. Their escape was one of "enormous toil." (Plutarch also relates the story that Cloelia led the group slowly across the river on horseback.) When she is returned to Porsena, not only do her comrades keep silent on her account, but Cloelia voluntarily takes responsibility for the escape.

Women could render selfless service to the state. In what was regarded as a high social and moral stance by the Romans, the Cloelia story is a milestone in the development of women's political personality in the ancient world. Livy remarks that a new type of virtue for women was marked by a new genre of statue: that of horse and rider. The statue that is said to portray Cloelia provides an important epilogue to her story: the durable monument—inscription, statue, grave—was an advertisement of status and

public personality in the Roman world. The Cloelia story is certainly older than the time of Livy (59 BC–17 CE). According to Florus, it was recorded in the *annales*, the official documents of the acts of the Roman Senate. It is noteworthy, however, that the surviving ancient writers of the Cloelia story lived during the empire, that is, during an age when a few rich and powerful women, especially in the imperial family, were publicly celebrated and even granted public authority by the Senate.

The story does not appear to have been active in the Middle Ages. In the Renaissance, the Tuscan painter Domenico Beccafumi revived the equestrian motif in his *La Fuga di Clelia* (1523) now in the Uffizi gallery in Florence. In the painting, several young women with Cloelia in the lead are shown on horseback riding away from the Etruscan tents. None rides sidesaddle. Though *La Fuga di Clelia* turns the legend into a love story, it is relatively faithful to Cloelia's story. In the 18th century, the same libretto was sung in two operas based on the legend of Cloelia: Johann Adolph Haase's version of *Il Trionfo di Clelia* was performed in Vienna in 1762 and Christoph Willibald Gluck's version in Bologna the next year.

SOURCES:
Haase, Johann Adolph. *Il Trionfo di Clelia*. NY: Garland, 1981.
Livy. *History of Rome* 2. 13. 6
Pliny the Elder. *Natural History* 34. 28
Plutarch. *Bravery of Women* 14 Valerius Maximus Memorable Words and Deeds 3. 2. 2.

Alexander Ingle,
Department of Classical Studies,
Boston University

Clooney, Rosemary (1928—)

American singer and actress. Born on May 23, 1928, in Maysville, Kentucky; one of four children, three girls and a boy, of Andrew Clooney (a house painter) and Frances (Guilfoyle) Clooney; sister of Betty Clooney (a singer who died of a brain aneurysm in August 1976) and Nick Clooney (an actor and television host); aunt of George Clooney (an actor); attended Lady of Mercy Academy, Cincinnati, Ohio; married José Ferrer (an actor-producer-director), on July 13, 1953 (divorced); children: Miguel (b. 1955); **Maria Ferrer**; *Gabriel;* **Monsita Ferrer** *(b. 1960); Rafael.*

Filmography: The Stars Are Singing *(1953);* Here Come the Girls *(1953);* Red Garters *(1954);* White Christmas *(1954);* Deep in My Heart *(1954).*

Radio series: "Songs for Sale" *(1950–51);* "The Rosemary Clooney Show" *(1954–55);* "The Ford

Road Show with Bing Crosby and Rosemary Clooney" (1958–1962).

Television: "Songs for Sale" (1950–51); "The Johnny Johnston Show" (1951); "The Rosemary Clooney Show" (1956–57); "The Lux Show Starring Rosemary Clooney" (1957–58); "Rosie: The Rosemary Clooney Story" (1982, voice only); "Sister Margaret and the Saturday Night Ladies" (1987).

Album discography: (with Duke Ellington) Blue Rose; Children's Favorites; Clap Hands, Here Comes Rosie; (with Betty Clooney) The Clooney Sisters; Clooney Tunes; Come on-a My House; Country Hits from the Heart; (with Benny Goodman) A Date with the King; Deep in My Heart; Everything's Coming up Rosie; Fancy Meeting You Here; (with José Ferrer) The Ferrers Sing Selections from "Oh Captain!"; Greatest Hits; Here's to My Lady; (with Harry James) Hollywood Hits; (with Harry James) Hollywood's Best; Hymns from the Heart; Look My Way; Love; Mixed Emotions; (with The Hi-Los) Now Hear This; Red Garters; (with Bing Crosby) Rendezvous; (with The Hi-Los) Ring Around Rosie; Rosemary Clooney and Dick Haymes; Rosemary Clooney in High Fidelity; Rosemary Clooney on Stage; Rosemary Clooney

Rosemary Clooney

Sings Ballads; Rosemary Clooney Sings the Lyrics of Ira Gershwin; Rosemary Clooney Sings the Lyrics of Johnny Mercer; Rosemary Clooney Sings the Music of Cole Porter; Rosemary Clooney Sings the Music of Harold Arlen; Rosemary Clooney Sings the Music of Irving Berlin; Rosemary Clooney Sings the Music of Jimmy Van Heusen; Rosemary Clooney Swings Softly; Rosie Sings Bing; Rosie Solves the Swingin' Riddle; Rosie's Greatest Hits; Show Tunes; Songs for Children; The Story of Celeste; Leo the Lion; Swing Around Rosie; Jasmine; Tenderly; Thanks for Nothing; (with Bing Crosby) That Travelin' Two Beat; (with Perez Prado) A Touch of Tabasco; The Uncollected Rosemary Clooney; While We're Young; White Christmas; With Love; Young at Heart.

One of America's leading popular singers of the 1950s, Rosemary Clooney was born in Maysville, Kentucky, one of four children of Andrew and **Frances Guilfoyle Clooney**. Andrew was a house painter and heavy drinker. Through a series of parental separations and reconciliations, the children were farmed out to various relatives and shunted from school to school. At an early age, music came to be the only constant in Rosemary's life. While living with her paternal grandfather Andrew J. Clooney, the mayor of Maysville, she and her younger sister **Betty Clooney** frequently sang at his political rallies. Later, at their maternal grandparents in Cincinnati, Ohio, they made their professional debut on the local radio station WLW. The Clooney Sisters continued to sing at the station for two years, then were hired by Cincinnati bandleader Barney Rapp to appear with his group. In 1945, still teenagers, the girls signed on with Tony Pastor and embarked on a cross-country tour with his band, accompanied by their uncle George Guilfoyle who acted as chaperon. Rosemary made her first recording with the Pastor group, an unlikely tune titled "I'm Sorry I didn't Say I'm Sorry When I Made You Cry Last Night," which was considered "revolutionary" by the disc jockeys because of Rosemary's soft, whispery style. She later attributed the whisper to sheer terror.

By 1949, Betty had wearied of the grueling road schedule and went home to pursue a more normal life. Refining and polishing her style and gaining confidence, Rosemary left Pastor and went out on her own later that same year. Through Joe Shribman, who later left Pastor to become her manager, she brokered a contract with Columbia Records and produced a series of soft, sentimental recordings, including "Beautiful Brown Eyes" and a duet with Guy Mitchell

of "You're Just in Love." Between recording dates, Clooney made night club and television appearances. In 1950, after winning first place on "Arthur Godfrey's Talent Scouts," she was hired for "Songs for Sale," a showcase for aspiring songwriters that was simulcast on radio and television.

Clooney's break came when Columbia's Mitch Miller urged her to record a novelty number called "Come on-a My House," adapted from an old Armenian folk song by William Saroyan and Ross Bagdasarian. Thinking the song ill-suited to her style, Clooney initially refused, but Miller was persistent. After some bickering back and forth, she gave in. The tune flew off the charts, selling a million copies and paving the way for subsequent novelty numbers like "Botcha Me," "Mangos," "Mambo Italiano," "This Ole House," and a duet with *Marlene Dietrich: "Too Old to Cut the Mustard." "I always wanted to sing sad ballads, but I didn't get many opportunities," she later recalled. "At the same time, you can't quarrel with success. If it hadn't been for 'Come On-a My House,' I probably wouldn't have gotten anywhere."

In 1953, Clooney married actor-producer-director José Ferrer, whom she had met on a television talk show in 1950, when he was separated, but not yet divorced, from actress **Phyllis Hill**. Meanwhile, at the suggestion of Bing Crosby, Clooney had been tested by Paramount and placed under contract, thus launching what appeared to be a promising second career in films. She first appeared in *The Stars Are Singing* (1953), followed by four more movies including the perennial favorite *White Christmas* (1954). Clooney's slightly wooden film persona, however, never matched the warmth of her singing voice, and after giving birth to her first child in February 1955 she gave up the screen to concentrate on her recording career. She was also a frequent guest on the television variety show circuit and successfully played the London Palladium and the Sands Hotel in Las Vegas. In January 1956, Clooney was contracted to star in the syndicated half-hour television program "The Rosemary Clooney Show," featuring the Nelson Riddle Orchestra and The Hi-Los, who would later join Clooney on some popular recordings. It lasted a season and segued into a new half-hour variety series, "The Lux Show Starring Rosemary Clooney," which was on the air from 1957 to 1958.

As radio became a dying medium and rock 'n' roll started to take over the pop charts, Clooney's career began to slip, severely unnerving her. There were additional emotional upheavals that would plague the singer throughout the '60s. In 1961, a year after the birth of her fifth child, her marriage began an agonizing five-year decline: she and Ferrer divorced, remarried, and divorced again. Although Clooney continued to make guest appearances on television and to perform on the nightclub circuit, an increased reliance on drugs and alcohol made her erratic and often incoherent on stage. In 1968, following the break-up of a two-year romantic relationship, and the assassination of her friend Robert Kennedy, she had a nervous breakdown. At a performance in Reno, she lost control, lashing out hysterically at the audience and later tearing up her hotel room. She was taken to a local hospital and later flown to Los Angeles, where friends and relatives convinced her to get help. Confined to a mental hospital for weeks, she then underwent years of extensive therapy on an outpatient basis. "I learned to cook and put in a vegetable garden in the yard of my home," she says of her recovery. "I went through analysis and group therapy. I was lucky I survived." Clooney rounded out her therapy with a no-holds-barred autobiography, *This for Remembrance*, written with Raymond Strait. "It turned out to be the best thing I could do," she said. "Tell all and learn to live with it." The book became the basis for a television film "Escape from Madness" (1978).

A healthy but heavier Clooney emerged professionally again in the 1970s, helped immensely by her friend Bing Crosby, who made several tours with her (including the London Palladium), before his death in October 1977. In 1982, the singer undertook a tour in "Four Girls Four," a revue that alternately featured old-timers *Margaret Whiting, *Helen O'Connell, Rose Marie, *Martha Raye, and *Kay Starr, and that same year she provided the soundtrack singing voices for her character and that of her sister in a television film "Rosie: The Rosemary Clooney Story," with Sondra Locke in the title role. Clooney appeared in another television film in 1987, "Sister Margaret and the Saturday Night Ladies," and continued to make television guest appearances when not on tour.

In later years, Clooney's voice was thought to be better than ever, more resonant, with a new-found depth of emotion. Always known for her impeccable phrasing, she was compared to *Ella Fitzgerald, Frank Sinatra, and Mel Tormé in their prime. In her second go-around, she became more selective about recording choices; her later albums include a series of jazz tributes to such composers as Johnny Mercer, Cole Porter, Harold Arlen, Irving Berlin, and Jimmy Van Heusen. But Clooney still includes "Come On-a My House" in her concert and nightclub performances. "Maybe I'm getting sentimental," she says, "but I'm actually fond of that song now."

SOURCES:

Candee, Marjorie Dent, ed. *Current Biography 1957*. NY: H.W. Wilson, 1957.

Hemming, Roy, and David Hajdu. *Discovering Great Singers of Classic Pop*. NY: Newmarket, 1991.

Parish, James Robert, and Michael R. Pitts. *Hollywood Songsters*. NY: Garland, 1991.

Barbara Morgan,
Melrose, Massachusetts

Clothilde.

Variant of Clotilda or Clotilde.

Clotilda (470–545)

*Queen of the Franks and saint. Name variations: Chlotilda; Chlotilde; Chlothilde; Chrotechildis; Clothild; Clothilda; Clothilde; Clothildis; Clodechildis; Clotilde; Hlotechilde or Hluodhild. Born around 470 in Lyon (some sources cite 474 or 475); died in June 545 in Tours, France; daughter of Childeric also known as Chilperic II, king of the Burgundians, king of Lyon, and Queen Caretena; married Chlodovechs or Clodovic also known as Clovis I (465–511), king of the Franks (r. 481–511), around 490 or 493 (d. 511); children: Ingomer (b. around 494, died young); Clotimir also known as Clodomir or Chlodomer (495–524), king of Orléans (r. 511–524); Childebert I (d. 558), king of Paris (r. 511–558); Chlothar, Clothaire, Clotar also known as Lothair I (497–561), king of Soissons (r. 511), king of the Franks (r. 558–561); and several daughters including Clotilda (other names unknown, possibly died young); great-grandmother of *Bertha of Kent (c. 565–c. 616). Thierry, Theodoric or Theuderic I (c. 490–534), king of Reims and Metz (r. 511–534), was the son of Clovis and Amalaberga or a mistress.*

Few 6th-century historical sources touching on the life of the Frankish queen Clotilda have survived, making it difficult to reconstruct the details of her life. Adding to this difficulty are the many legends and traditions interwoven in biographies of this early medieval saint, stories that are often not easily separated from historical fact. Although much information survives about her husband Clovis, Clotilda's life must be pieced together from a few main sources, primarily the chronicles of the 6th-century monk Gregory of Tours, who wrote years after her death.

It is known that Clotilda was born around 470, the daughter of King Chilperic II of Burgundy and Queen **Caretena**. The 5th-century kingdom of Burgundy encompassed modern-day southeastern France. It was one of many small monarchies that arose from the political vacuum left by the collapsing Western Roman empire. Known as the "barbarian kingdoms," these small states were a mix of native Germanic culture, adopted Roman beliefs, and, eventually, Christianity. The Burgundian people had adopted Christianity, but they appear to have been divided between Arianism (which worshipped Christ as a secondary deity) and Catholicism, worshipping the Father and the Son as equal in importance. Clotilda was raised in the Catholic faith by her parents, a fact that was to play an important role in the future of the Franks, Burgundy's neighbors to the west.

There is some confusion over the fate of Clotilda's father Chilperic, who died around 490. According to Gregory of Tours, King Chilperic and his wife Caretena were killed by Chilperic's brother Gundobad (or Gundobald) in a dynastic struggle for control of Burgundy. Actually, Chilperic died in battle, and his widow took her two daughters to live at the court of Chilperic's brother King Godegisil of Geneva. Godegisil and his followers were Catholics, and Clotilda and her sister **Sedeluna** benefited from an excellent education provided by their uncle's advisor, the future saint Avitus of Burgundy. Sedeluna eventually founded a church and monastery near Geneva, where she became a nun under the name of Chrona.

In the history of the modern world, Saint Clotilda occupies a place of honor.

—Godefroi Kurth

A different future awaited Clotilda. Around 493, a messenger from the court of the Frankish king Clovis came to Geneva to ask for a Burgundian princess as a royal bride. Clovis was then 28 years old and had reigned over the Franks for 12 years. His realm was the most populous and powerful of the barbarian kingdoms, constantly engaging its enemies in an effort to expand their territory. Clovis, chosen king when he was only 16, had proven himself an ambitious and ruthless leader, single-minded in his desire to unite the small tribes of Frankish people into one state. He was remarkably successful in ending Roman control of Gaul and uniting the Franks, owing mostly to a strong army and a willingness to use it. Although many of the Franks were Christians, both Arian and Catholic, Clovis and his soldiers remained loyal to the warlike Germanic gods worshipped by their ancestors.

Clovis had repudiated his first wife, the Visigothic princess **Amalaberga**, when his alliance with her father became undesirable. He then sought a marriage alliance with the Burgundian kingdom. Popular tradition holds that it was 22-year-old Clotilda's widespread reputation for beauty and virtue that led Clovis to seek her hand from King Godegisil, but it is important to recognize Clovis' need for an alliance with the Burgundians as his prime motivation. It is also possible that Clotilda's Catholicism made her more desirable as a queen, since Clovis may have seen this as a means of bonding him to his Christian subjects.

Godegisil welcomed the opportunity to make friends with the powerful Frankish king; the alliance seemed to promise peace and security for his subjects. Clotilda's own thoughts on marrying a pagan king whom she had never met are unrecorded, but it is known that she consented to the arrangement. Thus in 493 Clotilda left Geneva and her mother and sister, whom she never saw again, and traveled to Clovis' capital at Soissons. The marriage was performed by Remigius, the Catholic bishop of Rheims; he was Clovis' supporter and soon to be a close friend and advisor to the newly crowned Queen Clotilda.

Many legends were later created about the betrothal and marriage of Clovis and Clotilda in popular tradition. Resembling other medieval nuptial legends, some describe a secret betrothal; others hold that King Gundobad, who feared Clovis' revenge on him because of his (supposed) murder of Clotilda's parents, tried to stop the wedding. Others describe Clotilda as seeking vengeance for her parents' death by burning Gundobad's villages as she passed through them on her way to Soissons. Such stories grew out of the later popular belief that Clovis' marriage had transformed France's future: that by marrying a Catholic, Clovis had truly founded the French nation. Understandably, an event of such historical importance became an imaginative story of high drama and intrigue.

Clotilda established a Christian court at the ancient Roman palace in Soissons. Soissons was only one of the royal residences; frequent travel around the region—to quell uprisings, ensure loyalty, dispense justice, and collect tribute—was a necessary part of kingship in the early Middle Ages. The king never traveled alone, and so Clotilda, along with their children, attendants, soldiers, and courtiers, spent the better part of each year on the road. But in the final years of their marriage, Clotilda and Clovis established an essentially permanent capital in Paris. We unfortunately know little of Clotilda's married life or of her relationship with Clovis. Gregory of Tours informs us that they were a loving couple who agreed on most matters—except for the fundamental question of religious belief—and that they enjoyed great popularity among their subjects.

According to Gregory of Tours, and most of Clotilda's later Catholic biographers, the queen's most cherished goal was the conversion of her husband to Catholicism. While it is not known exactly how Clotilda sought to convert Clovis, it is clear that his conversion was indeed of utmost importance to her and that her efforts were aided by Bishop Remigius. When their first child, Ingomer, was born around 494, Clotilda persuaded Clovis to have him baptized, showing Clotilda's influence on her pagan husband; but Clovis blamed the baby's early death on the anger of his gods for allowing the baptism. Nonetheless, Clotilda persuaded him to have their second child, Chlodomer, baptized as well, in 495. Sons Childebert and Lothair (I) were also baptized. Her last child was her only surviving daughter, also named **Clotilda**. As she was born after Clovis' conversion to Christianity, Clotilda's hope to raise a Catholic family was indeed realized. There is no evidence that any of her children gave up their mother's faith to worship the ancestral gods of the Franks.

Much has been written of Clovis' conversion, which probably occurred in 496. Indeed, his conversion is often considered the defining moment of his reign. Before him, no Christian monarch ruled over the people who founded France; after him, no pagan monarch did. Most of the credit for this turn of events has been given to Clotilda, unyielding in her determination to bring her husband to her faith. Like Clovis' marriage to Clotilda, numerous legends surround the king's decision to accept his wife's faith. The most widely told version places the momentous event during the Franks' battle against the Alemanni in 496 at Tolbiac. His army facing defeat, Clovis called on "the god of Clotilda" to aid him, promising to be baptized and forsake his old gods if he won the battle. When word of his miraculous victory reached Clotilda, she called on Bishop Remigius to help instruct Clovis in her faith.

Clovis still hesitated to commit himself to the new faith, however, despite Clotilda's urgings, because he feared his pagan subjects would reject him. But Clotilda saw her efforts rewarded when Clovis finally yielded and allowed Remigius to baptize him and his soldiers on Christmas Day 496. Clovis must have seen the political advantages of his conversion. By proclaiming his new faith across Europe, he secured the powerful friendship of the pope and the Eastern Roman emperor. They became allies in his constant struggle against the Arian-led Visigoths and Burgundians who surrounded the Frankish kingdom. Having such allies legitimized Clovis' rule, helping him conquer his enemies and expand his state.

Clovis' conversion began a new phase in Clotilda's married life. No longer concerned with bringing her faith to her husband, Clotilda turned her attentions to educating her children, presiding over an increasingly larger and more pious court, and bringing her faith to their subjects. Clovis became her partner in this, and the Catholic king and queen worked to strengthen the church within their kingdom. Together they founded a church in Paris dedicated to the apostles Peter and Paul; they also formed a friendship with *Geneviève of Paris (c. 422–512), the great spiritual leader of the city. After Geneviève's death and canonization, Clotilda and Clovis had her buried in the royal vault in their church, which was renamed in her honor.

Clotilda was about 40 when Clovis died in 511. Earlier that year, he had summoned and presided over the first Catholic council of bishops in Western Europe, his last important act as king and one that certainly pleased his devout queen. But the legacy of Clovis and Clotilda's rule—a strong and united Frankish kingdom supported by, and supportive of, the Catholic church—was not to last long. Clotilda's three surviving sons, along with Clovis' son from his first marriage, immediately divided the realm into four small and quarrelsome kingdoms. Her eldest son was only 16 years old; all four were immature, rash, ambitious, and competitive. Like their father, they were warrior-kings, which was to cause their pious mother much grief.

Although she continued to enjoy her previous rank and wealth, Queen Clotilda retired from an active political life. She moved from Paris to Tours; the town had been part of her dowry and now it provided her with a royal income. For the most part, her remaining years were filled with charitable works; she founded monasteries and churches, endowed convents, and gave away her own lands to support these new religious establishments. Two of her foundations in particular, Chelles and Notre Dame des Andelys in Touraine, became renowned as centers of learning in later centuries, and revered Clotilda as their patron saint.

Around 523 all three sons joined together to declare war on the Burgundians, their mother's people, for reasons that are unclear. Popular tradition attributes this war to Clotilda herself, still attempting to revenge her parents' supposed murder by attacking the sons of their murderer. This portrayal of Clotilda as cruel and vengeful, though common in biographies of her, is starkly at odds with the equally common but more substantiated portrayal of her as a pious and benevolent queen. In the course of the war, Clotilda learned to her sorrow that her eldest son Chlodomer had murdered her first cousin, King Sigismund; this was followed by the murder of Chlodomer himself by another Burgundian cousin. Clotilda, advanced in age for her time at 52 years old, adopted and raised Chlodomer's three children. She was devoted to the little princes, which soon led to more familial troubles.

Clotilda's two sons were jealous of their nephews, and feared that Clotilda would seek kingdoms for her grandsons at her sons' expense. Lothair and Childebert resolved to eliminate this threat. They requested their mother to send the boys to them so that, as they told her, they might make the boys kings. Clotilda, trusting in her sons, sent Theodoald, Gonthier, and Clodoald to Paris. There they were imprisoned and the two eldest murdered by their uncles. The youngest, five-year-old Clodoald, was smuggled to a monastery and became a monk, canonized after his death as Saint Cloud.

When Clotilda learned of the murders and of the subsequent flight of her sons from Paris, she went in mourning to the capital city to see the children buried next to Clovis in the royal vault. After returning to Tours, the queen discovered that her daughter Clotilda, who had been given in marriage to Amalaric, the king of the Visigoths in Spain, was being abused by her Arian husband in part because of her Catholic faith. Lothair and Childebert also heard of this outrage against their sister, and used it as a pretext for invading the Visigothic kingdom. Amalaric was killed in the ensuing battles, and although Clotilda was rescued and brought back to Gaul by her brothers, she unfortunately died soon afterwards. Thus in the course of a few months, Queen Clotilda had suffered the loss of her eldest son, her only daughter, and two of her grandchildren.

In Tours, Clotilda returned to her efforts to relieve the suffering of the poor and her religious activities. Her relationship with her remaining sons was bitter; she rarely saw them, but because they were the only surviving members of her family, she felt that she could not abandon them, despite their horrendous deeds. In 544, war broke out between Lothair and Childebert. According to Gregory of Tours, the distraught queen prayed for days that God would end the conflict, until at last, as the armies were about to engage, God sent a terrible storm, which caused both armies to flee and make peace. This was only one of the numerous miracles attributed to Clotilda in the years after her death.

Clotilda died, age 74, around June 3, 545, not long after her sons reconciled. Her sons were reportedly with her when she died, and they led the large mourning procession that took her body from Tours to Paris. The popular queen was buried next to her husband in the Church of Saint Geneviève in Paris. Clotilda was soon canonized and has been revered for bringing Catholicism to the French people. She became one of Paris' patron saints, and as recently as 1857, a new church in that city was dedicated to her.

SOURCES:

Gregory of Tours. *The History of the Franks*. Trans. by Lewis Thorpe. London: Penguin Books, 1974.

Kurth, Godefroi. *Saint Clotilda*. Trans. by V.M. Crawford. London: Duckworth, 1906.

Wood, Ian. *The Merovingian Kingdoms, 450–751*. London: Longman, 1994.

SUGGESTED READING:

Bachrach, Bernard S. *Merovingian Military Organization*. University of Minnesota Press, 1972.

Bury, J.B. *The Invasion of Europe by the Barbarians*. Norton, 1967.

Geary, Patrick J. *Before France and Germany: The Creation and Transformation of the Merovingian World*. Oxford University Press, 1988.

James, Edward. *The Origins of France: From Clovis to the Capetians, 500–1000*. St. Martin's Press, 1982.

Lasko, Peter. *The Kingdom of the Franks: North-west Europe before Charlemagne*. McGraw-Hill, 1971.

Sergeant, Lewis. *The Franks*. Putnam, 1898.

Scherman, Katharine. *The Birth of France: Warriors, Bishops and Long-Haired Kings*. NY: Random House, 1987.

Simonde de Sismondi, J.C.L. *The French Under the Merovingians and the Carlovingians*. Trans. by William Bellingham. London: W. & T. Piper, 1850 (1975).

Wallace-Hadrill, J.M. *The Long-Haired Kings: And Other Studies in Frankish History*. London: Methuen, 1962.

Zollner, Erich. *Geschichte der Franken Bis zur Mitte des 6. Jahrhunderts*. Munich: C.H. Beck Verlag, 1970.

Laura York, M.A. in History,
University of California, Riverside, California

Clotilde.

Variant of Clotilda.

Clotilde (d. 691)

Queen of Neustria, Burgundy, and the Franks. Flourished around 682 and 683; married Thierry or Theoderic III (654–691), king of Neustria and Burgundy (r. 673/75–691), king of the Franks (r. 687–691), in 675; children: Clovis III (682–695), king of the Franks (r. 691–695); Childebert III (c. 683–711), king of the Franks (r. 695–711).

Clotilde of Sardinia (1759–1802).

See Marie Clotilde.

Clotilde of Savoy (1843–1911)

*Italian princess. Name variations: Clothilde. Born on March 2, 1843; died on June 25, 1911; daughter of Victor Emmanuel II, king of Italy (r. 1849–1878), and *Marie Adelaide of Austria (1822–1855); sister of *Maria Pia (1847–1911), queen of Portugal; married Prince Napoleon Joseph Charles Paul Bonaparte (Plon-Plon), on January 30, 1859; children: Prince Victor (b. 1862); Louis (1864–1932); *Marie Laetitia (1866–1890, who married Amadeus, king of Spain).*

Clotilde of Saxe-Coburg-Gotha (1846–1927)

*Archduchess. Name variations: Klothilde. Born on July 8, 1846, in Neuilly; died on June 3, 1927, in Alcsut, Hungary; daughter of *Clementine of Orleans (1817–1907) and Augustus, Prince of Saxe-Coburg-Gotha; married Archduke Josef Karl Ludwig also known as Joseph Charles Louis (1833–1905), on May 12, 1864; children: *Maria Dorothea of Austria (1867–1932); *Margaret Clementine (1870–1955); Josef August also known as Joseph of Alcsut (1872–1962); Ladislaus or Ladislas (1875–1895); Elisabeth Clotilde (1883–1958); Clotilde (1884–1903).*

Clotsinda

*Queen of the Lombards. Daughter of *Ingunde (fl. 517) and Chlothar also known as Clothaire, Clotar, or Lothair I (497–561), king of Soissons (r. 511), king of the Franks (r. 558–561); married a Lombard king.*

Clough, Jemima (1820–1892)

English educator. Born Anne Jemima Clough at Liverpool, England, on January 20, 1820; died in Cambridge, England, on February 27, 1892; daughter of a cotton merchant; sister of the poet Arthur Hugh Clough.

Born in Liverpool, Jemima Clough was two years old when she moved with her family to Charleston, South Carolina. In her mid-teens, she returned to England (1836), where she was engaged as a teacher though her ambition was to write. She was prompted by her father's business failure to open a school in 1841, which she ran until 1846. Clough studied in London and worked at both the Borough Road and the Home and Colonial schools before opening her own small school in 1852 at Ambleside in Westmoreland. Ten years later, she gave up this venture to educate the children of her brother Arthur Hugh Clough, who died in 1861, living for a time with his widow. Intensely interested in the education of women, Clough made friends with *Emily Davies, *Barbara Bodichon, and *Frances Mary Buss. She helped found the North of England council for promoting the higher education of women, of which she acted as secretary (1867–70) and president (1873–74).

When a house for the residence of women students at Cambridge was opened, she was chosen as its first principal. Originating with five students in 1871 in Regent Street, Cambridge, this hostel continued at Merton Hall, Cambridge, in 1872, and led to the building of Newnham Hall (opened in 1875), as well as to the establishment of Newnham College for women (1880). Clough's magnetism and ambitious goals, together with her stewardship of Newnham College, led her to be regarded as one of the foremost leaders of the women's educational movement. Two portraits of Jemima Clough are located at Newnham College, one by Sir W.B. Richmond, the other by J.J. Shannon.

SOURCES:
Clough, Blanche Athena. *Memoir of Anne Jemima Clough*, 1897.

Clouzot, Vera (1921–1960)

Brazilian-born actress who starred in several French films directed by her husband Henri-Georges Clouzot. Born Vera Amado Gibson in Brazil in 1921; died on December 15, 1960; daughter of Gilberto Amado and Alice de Rego Barros Gibson; married Leo Lapara, in 1938; married Henri-Georges Clouzot, on January 15, 1950.

Vera Clouzot was born in 1921 in Brazil, the daughter of Gilberto Amado and Alice de Rego Barros Gibson. Her father was a writer and politician who also served as a Brazilian representative to the United Nations. A cousin, Jorge Amado, became one of Brazil's greatest novelists of the 20th century. Vera married a Brazilian co-median, Leo Lapara, in 1938 and spent several years touring the Americas and Europe with a troupe managed by Louis Jouvert, owner of the Athénée in Paris. In 1949, however, Vera divorced, tired of sacrificing her marital life to Leo's work. She reportedly complained to him: "It's not with me you are married. It's with the boss."

Shortly thereafter, she met French film director Henri-Georges Clouzot and became a "script girl" on the set of *Miquette et sa mère*. They married on January 15, 1950, shortly after he com-pleted *Miquette et sa mère* and *Retour a la vie*. A visit to Brazil followed. Accompanied by Clouzot's film crew, they arrived in Rio de Janeiro on April 17, 1950, on a delayed honeymoon.

Returning to France, she became well-known as the female lead in many of his subsequent films. Her first role was Linda, the servant girl who loved Mario in *La salaire de la peur* (The Wages of Fear, 1952). Perhaps her most famous performance came in *Les diaboliques* (The Fiends, 1954), in which she portrayed Christina Delasalle, a former South American heiress whose

From the movie Les diaboliques, *starring Vera Clouzot.*

husband uses her money to operate a boarding school. Because of his cruelty and treachery, Christina and her husband's mistress (played by *Simone Signoret) plot and carry out his murder, with unforeseen consequences. Throughout her marriage, Vera read constantly, searching for material suitable for new film projects. Her husband's films were usually thrillers, often combining philosophical themes with suspense. As was true with many actors, Vera found her husband to be a hard taskmaster as a director.

While filming *La salaire de la peur*, Vera suffered a pulmonary edema, and she experienced recurring problems thereafter. In pain and emotional distress, she turned to morphine and other opium derivatives. Neither Henri-Georges nor psychiatrists could conquer her addiction. The couple gradually became estranged. Not yet 40, on December 15, 1960, she died alone in the George V Hotel in Paris, victim of a heart attack.

SOURCES:

Bocquet, José-Luis, and Marc Godin. *Henri Georges Clouzot cinéaste*. Sèvre: La Sirène, 1993.

Lacassin, Francis, and Ramond Bellour. *Le Procès Clouzot*. Paris: Eric Losfeld, Le Terrain Vague, 1964.

Pilard, Philippe. *Henri-Georges Clouzot*. Paris: Editions Seghers, 1969.

"Vera Clouzot," in *The New York Times*. Vol. 38, no. 4, December 16, 1960.

Kendall W. Brown, Professor of History, Brigham Young University, Provo, Utah

Coachman, Alice (1923—)

First African-American woman to win an Olympic gold medal. Born on November 9, 1923, in Albany, Georgia; daughter of Fred Coachman and Evelyn Jackson; attended Tuskegee Institute High School; Albany State, BA in Home Economics, 1949; married Frank Davis (divorced); children: Richmond and Diane.

Won an Olympic gold medal for the women's high jump, 5'6½", setting an Olympic record (1948); holds record for most consecutive Amateur Athletic Union (AAU) championships in outdoor high jump (1939–48); was AAU champion, 50 meters (1943–47); was AAU champion, 100 meters (1942, 1945, 1946); was AAU champion, indoor high jump (1941, 1945, 1946); was AAU champion, indoor 50 meters (1945, 1946).

By the last event on the last day of Olympic competition at the 1948 London Games, the U.S. team had been all but shut out in women's track and field. They had watched victory after victory go to the Netherlands. If the women's team wanted to take home a gold medal, it would have to be in the high jump. As the bar was raised past the 5'3" mark, the competition was narrowed to three jumpers: *Micheline Ostermeyer of France, Dorothy Tyler of Great Britain, and Alice Coachman of the United States. Though it was late in the afternoon, Wembley stadium was packed with 65,000 spectators who had come to witness this final Olympic contest. The jumpers were given three attempts to clear the bar at each subsequent height and soon Micheline Ostermeyer was eliminated. The battle between Coachman and Tyler continued. When the bar was raised to 5'6½", Coachman and Tyler both cleared the height. Tyler, however, had more misses, and Alice Coachman was declared the winner, setting a new Olympic record. Recalling her victory, Coachman remarked in an interview with *Essence* magazine, "I've always believed that I could do whatever I set my mind to do; I've had that strong will, that oneness of purpose, all my life. That morning I knew I had the ability; I just called upon myself and the Lord to let the best come through."

Coachman was born in Albany, Georgia, in 1923, the fifth of ten children. Because her family had little money, she picked cotton, plums, and pecans to help out. Her natural athletic ability showed itself early on. At Monroe Street Elementary School, she roughhoused, ran and jumped with the boys. Though she was spanked repeatedly by her parents to discourage her ath-

Tyler, Dorothy J. (1920—)

English high jumper. Name variations: competed as Dorothy Odam in 1936; as Dorothy Tyler in 1948; Odam-Tyler. Born Dorothy Odam in Great Britain on March 14, 1920; married; children: two.

Won a silver medal in the high jump in the Berlin Olympics (1936); won a silver medal in the high jump in the London Olympics (1948).

Britain's Dorothy Tyler came in second in the high jump finals in the 1948 Olympic Games in London with 5'6¼". At the time, she was the only Olympic athlete to equal the winning height in the high jump in two successive Olympics and still lose first place under the "tie-break" rules; Tyler had the most failures at the winning height. In the 1936 Olympics, in another long drawn out duel, 16-year-old Tyler, then competing as Dorothy Odam, had placed second to *Ibolya Csák of Hungary in a jump off. Both competitors had a jump of 5'3" but Tyler had the greater number of failures. Had a later rule applied for deciding ties, Tyler would have been the champion.

letic play, Coachman endured and once in high school earned a place on the track team. "Back then," Coachman recalled in a *New York Times* interview, "there was a sense that women weren't supposed to be running like that. My father wanted his girls to be dainty, sitting on the front porch."

But the front porch was no place for a talented athlete like Coachman. After a short tenure at the local high school, she attracted the attention of recruiters from the Tuskegee Institute in Alabama, a refuge for women's track and field. As a spectator sport, track and field had generated little interest in the United States. To compensate, Major Cleveland Abbot developed a series of races, known as the Tuskegee Relays, which served as a venue for African-American girls in the southern U.S. to compete. The relays also benefited the institute as coaches recruited talented new athletes to participate in its summer track program.

I was good at three things: running, jumping, and fighting.

—Alice Coachman

The institute's recruitment strategy paid off; beginning in 1937, the Tuskegee Institute began to dominate women's track and field in the United States and would continue to do so for the next 20 years. That domination would not have been possible without Alice Coachman. After a heated family debate, she was finally granted permission by her parents to enroll at Tuskegee High School in 1939. During her seven-year tenure at Tuskegee, she played basketball, and was an all-conference guard who led her team to three straight Southeastern Intercollegiate Athletic Association (SIAC) women's titles. Coachman's real strength, however, was in track and field. She would win 25 Amateur Athletic Union (AAU) championships, including the U.S. Outdoor 50 meters (from 1943 to 1947), the 100 meters (1942, 1945 and 1946), the indoor 50 meters (1945 and 1946), and the high jump (from 1939 to 1948).

The high jump was Coachman's specialty. Using a combination of forms—part straight jump, part western roll—she dominated the competition in an event that is uniquely challenging for athletes. The high jump requires athletes to convert horizontal momentum to a vertical momentum in attempts to clear an ever increasing height. The event's apparatus consists of a bamboo or aluminum crosspiece called the bar, which rests across two upright poles called

standards. As Coachman cleared the bar, she was often photographed on her side, a position reminiscent of the western-roll style of jumping, but her approaching run and takeoff utilized elements of the straight jump.

After graduating with her high school diploma in 1943, Coachman remained at the Tuskegee Institute to earn a trade degree in dressmaking and continue competing in track-and-field events. During this period, she worked part-time as a waitress at the Gordon Hotel. She received her degree in 1946. That same year, she became the only African-American woman named to the U.S. National Amateur Athletic Union Team. Because of her race, Coachman was studied closely by the public and the organizers of the competition. According to Michael Davis, author of *Black American Women in Olympic Track and Field*, one newspaper reported: "Miss Coachman was under careful scrutiny before being selected to go on the trip. The committee found her to be quiet, ladylike, reserved and most desirable. In addition to athletic prowess, she's a fine person to know on and off the track." In the U.S.-Canada meet, she won the 100 meters and ran the last leg of the 400-meter relay team. She also continued her dominance in the high jump, taking first place.

In 1947, Coachman entered Albany State College. Her amazing string of AAU championships had made her well known on the women's track-and-field circuit. When it was announced that the Olympic Games were to be held in London, England, after an 11-year hiatus (the 1940 and 1944 Olympic Games were cancelled because of World War II), Alice Coachman was among the foremost Tuskegee alumni to compete in the Olympic trials held in Providence, Rhode Island, at Brown University. The high jump trials were conducted in near darkness. She resorted to tying a white handkerchief on the high jump bar to mark the distance she had to clear. As officials lit matches so she could see, Coachman, who was suffering from a sore back, soared over the bar setting a new American Olympic trials record of 5'4¾". That record would not be broken until the Olympic trials of 1960.

Despite her joy at winning the trials, Coachman was distressed by the thought of overseas travel. Boarding the SS *America* to sail for London, she was homesick. Her coach selected 14-year-old *Mae Faggs, an energetic member of the team, to be her bunkmate, which improved her spirits. During the voyage, Coachman and the U.S. team were entertained by well-known celebrities, but they also charmed the other passengers with their own program. Coachman danced to the "St. Louis Blues," while other team members harmonized.

The singing and dancing ended when they arrived in London. The track-and-field competition was fierce, and the team from America saw their best athletes eliminated in heat after heat. The competition was dominated by *Fanny Blankers-Koen of the Netherlands, a 30-year-old mother of two, who won the 80-meter hurdles, the 100 and 200 meters, and ran the winning anchor on the 400-meter relay team. The best the U.S. team had been able to eke out was a bronze medal won by *Audrey Patterson-Tyler in the 200 meters. When it came time for the high jump competition, Coachman, America's best hope for bringing home a gold medal, had her work cut out for her. In a preliminary jump, she had suffered a hip injury. Once competition was underway, every time she cleared a new height the European women came back and matched it. She would later recall her victory over Dorothy Tyler as the toughest of her career. Reflecting on her gold-medal performance, Coachman told

Alice Coachman

Essence magazine, "It all came together and I was so glad. When I got to England my picture was everywhere, and everyone seemed to know all about me. All those people were waiting to see the American girl run, and I gave them something to remember me by." Standing on the Olympic platform, she received her medal before a stadium full of spectators, which included King George VI and Queen *Elizabeth (Bowes-Lyon). Hers was the only gold medal of the games for the U.S. women's track and field team. It was also the first Olympic gold medal ever won by an African-American woman.

When she returned to the States, Coachman was taken to the White House to meet President Harry S. Truman. She then continued home to Albany, Georgia, where an Alice Coachman Day was scheduled to honor her accomplishment. The parade from Atlanta to Albany would culminate in an indoor ceremony. Along the route, thousands stood shoulder to shoulder to cheer Coachman as her car passed. Reporters from *Life* and *Time* as well as Movietone News covered her homecoming. But in the Georgia of the 1940s, the honoring of a black champion, even an athlete as remarkable as Coachman, could not take place without prejudice. Marion E. Jackson wrote in his sports column for the *Atlanta Daily World*:

> Let me write now that until the parade terminated at the auditorium, Georgia had seen democracy in action. It was not a homecoming for a Negro Olympic star, but a champion of champions. As I watched the faces of thousands of Georgians from all over the state it was interesting to note, that all of their prejudices, preferences, passions and hates were momentarily swept from their countenances as if a heavy rainstorm had drenched a mountainous street. They came to applaud, cheer and praise an agile, slim and speedy star whose flying feet had brought her acclaim not only from her home state, but from the forums of the world. And then my dream was shattered. Reality returned and I knew that Georgia would not make Alice's welcome a wholehearted one. Mayor James W. "Taxi" Smith droned on about Georgia's other Olympic Champion (Forrest "Spec" Towns who had won the 110-meter hurdles in the 1936 Olympics). He never shook her hand nor did he look at her. Alice never got a chance to speak.

Albany's Municipal Auditorium was segregated. The stage where Alice Coachman sat was separated in the middle by a baby grand piano. On one side sat the mayor and other prominent white members of the community, while the Olympic hero sat on the other side with other African-American dignitaries. It is rumored that two white women surreptitiously handed Coachman a dozen American beauty roses before melting back into the crowd to avoid being recognized. If Coachman was bitter, she didn't show it to the outside world.

After the celebrations and acclamation died down, Coachman hung up her track shoes and quietly retired. "I had accomplished what I wanted to do," she told *The New York Times*. "It was time for me to start looking for a husband. That was the climax. I won the gold medal. I proved to my mother, my father, my coach and everybody else that I had gone to the end of my rope."

Coachman graduated from Albany State College in 1949 with a degree in home economics and a minor in science. She went on to marry and divorce Frank Davis and raise two children. In addition to teaching physical education at Albany State, she worked at South Carolina State College and her old alma mater, Tuskegee High School. Coachman also worked for a number of social-service programs, including the Turner Job Corporation, which encourages high school athletes who drop out to return to school. "Most of the kids I teach will never get a gold medal," she said. "But, if by example I can help turn one of them around, that will be my greatest reward."

She also founded her own organization, The Alice Coachman Foundation, which aided former Olympic athletes who hit hard times. A private person, Coachman spoke to school groups but kept out of the public eye, not sharing her personal archives with anyone, except her daughter and son. She has made some of her memorabilia available for an exhibit presented by Avon entitled "The Olympic Women," displayed at the 1996 Olympic Games in Atlanta, Georgia. "When the going gets tough and you feel like throwing your hands in the air," she told an interviewer for *The New York Times*, "listen to that voice that tells you 'Keep going. Hang in there.' Guts and determination will pull you through."

SOURCES:
Bernstein, Margaret E. "That Championship Season," in *Essence*. Vol. 15. July 1984, p 56.
Davis, Michael D. *Black American Women in Olympic Track and Field*. Jefferson: McFarland, 1992.
"Great Olympic Moments," in *Ebony*. Vol. 47, no. 1. November 1990, p 44.
Hickok, Ralph. *The Encyclopedia of North American Sports History*. NY: Facts on File, 1992.
Hine, Darlene C., ed. *Black Women in American: An Historical Encyclopedia*. Brooklyn: Carlson, 1993.
Jackson, Tenley A. "Olympic Mind Power," in *Essence*. Vol. 15. July 1984, p 63.
Page, James A. *Black Olympian Medalists*. Englewood, NJ: Libraries Unlimited, 1991.

Rhoden, William C. "Good Things Happen for One Who Waits," in *The New York Times*. April 27, 1995.

Smith, Jessie Carney, ed. *Notable Black American Women*. Detroit, MI: Gale Research, 1992.

"Tuskegee Girl Beats Stella Walsh in Track," in *Chicago Tribune*. July 1, 1945.

COLLECTIONS:

Photographs and news clippings of Alice Coachman are available in the Fisk University Library, Special Collections, Nashville, Tennessee.

RELATED MEDIA:

"Black Olympians: 1904–1984—Athletics and Social Change in America," part of the "America: A Cultural Mosaic" series, published by Modern Education Video Network (includes a brief look at Coachman).

"Sports Profile," Nguzo Saba Films, produced by **Carol Munday Lawrence**; directed by Robert N. Zagone, released by Beacon Films, 1982 (looks at life and career of Coachman).

Gaynol Langs, Independent Scholar,
Redmond, Washington

Coates, Anne V. (1925—)

British film editor. Born in Reigate, England, in 1925; attended Bartrum College; married director Douglas Hickox.

Selected films: The Pickwick Papers *(1952);* Lost *(*Tears for Simon, *1955);* The Horse's Mouth *(1958);* Tunes of Glory *(1960);* Lawrence of Arabia *(1962);* Becket *(1964);* Those Magnificent Men in Their Flying Machines *(1965);* Hotel Paradiso *(1966);* The Bofors Gun *(1968);* The Italian Job *(1969);* The Adventurers *(1970);* Request to the Nation *(*The Nelson Affair, *1973);* Murder on the Orient Express *(1974);* The Eagle Has Landed *(1976); (also co-producer)* The Medusa Touch *(1978);* The Elephant Man *(1980);* Ragtime *(1981);* The Pirates of Penzance *(1983);* Greystoke: The Legend of Tarzan *(1984);* Lord of the Apes *(1984);* Lady Jane *(1986);* Raw Deal *(1986);* Masters of the Universe *(1987); (co-editor)* Farewell to the King *(1989);* Listen to Me *(1989);* I Love You to Death *(1990).*

Leaving a career in nursing in the early 1950s to work in movies, British film editor Anne Coates has been associated with numerous major productions for close to four decades, including several for Hollywood. She won an Academy Award for editing *Lawrence of Arabia* (1962) and was nominated for Oscars for *Becket* (1964) and *The Elephant Man* (1980).

Coates, Florence Nicholson
(1850–1927)

American poet. Born Florence Van Leer Earle on July 1, 1850, in Philadelphia, Pennsylvania; died on April 6, 1927, in Philadelphia; married William Nicholson, in 1872 (died); married Edward H. Coates (a Philadelphia financier), in January 1879.

Selected works: Poems *(1898);* Mine and Thine *(1904);* Lyrics of Life *(1909);* The Unconquered Air and Other Poems *(1912); collected* Poems, *(2 vols., 1916);* Pro Patria *(1917).*

After attending private schools in New England and the Convent of the Sacred Heart in Paris, Florence Coates traveled to Brussels, where she studied music. After the death of her first husband, she married Philadelphia financier Edward H. Coates in January of 1879. She credited Matthew Arnold, a correspondent who was a frequent visitor to their home, with influencing her literary interests. Beginning in the 1890s, Coates' poems could be seen in leading magazines. Praised for their refinement of sentiment and thought, her poems were esteemed more for their crafting than for their originality or feeling. William Butler Yeats, Edmund Clarence Stedman, and Thomas Hardy were among the distinguished followers of Coates' work. The British consul in America forwarded her "Ode on the Coronation of King George V" (1911) to the king himself.

In addition to her literary achievements, Coates is known for her social leadership. Among the organizations in which she held membership were the Colonial Dames of America, the Society of Mayflower Descendants, the Browning Club (president 1895–1903, 1907–1908), and the New Century Club. The state Federation of Women's Clubs elected her "poet laureate of Pennsylvania" in 1915.

Coates, Gloria (1938—)

American composer and programmer who produced and organized the German-American Contemporary Concert Series in Munich. Born Gloria Kannenberg on October 10, 1938, in Wausau, Wisconsin; daughter of **Natalie Zanon** *(an Italian coloratura) and Roland Kannenberg (a state senator); married Francis Mitchell Coates, Jr., in 1959 (divorced 1969); children: one daughter,* **Alexandra Coates.**

Selected works: Music on Open Strings *(1974);* Planets *(1974);* Chamber Symphony *or* Transitions *(1976);* Sinfonietta della Notte *(1982);* L'Anima della Terra *(1982);* Symphony No. 3 *(1984);* Three Mystical Songs *(1985).*

Gloria Coates came from a musical background and composed her first melody on a toy piano at age three. At six, she began taking lessons and soon wanted to play the classical concertos she was hearing on the radio. When her piano teacher told her she was too young, Gloria babysat to earn money and bought sheet music by Massenet, Grieg, and Tchaikovsky, which she quickly learned.

As she grew older, Coates studied music theory with Lenard Siem and began to compose; at 13, she won a superior rating for "My Heart Yearns" in the National Federation of Music Clubs Composition Contest. There were those, however, who did not encourage her lofty aims. In high school, when Coates was told to choose a topic for an essay on her intended career, she asked to write about becoming an opera singer or a composer. Rejecting both choices, the teacher instructed her to be realistic and choose between being a music teacher or a music therapist. The message was clear: women belonged in the classroom, not on the stage.

Despite such warnings, Coates was a talented singer and actress who was drawn to the stage; she won an apprenticeship at the Brookside Playhouse in Petersburg, Pennsylvania, following her first year in college. That summer, she decided to quit school and devote herself completely to the arts. Moving to Milwaukee, she took a job as a waitress and began to study singing with **Nene Baalstad**, the Norwegian opera singer. Next Coates moved to Chicago where she studied with Alexander Tcherrepnin and acted with the Chicago Stage Guild; she then conducted a choir in Wausau before heading to New York City. There she studied voice and art and played the lead in an off-Broadway musical, *Dacota*.

Coates married in 1959 and moved to Baton Rouge, Louisiana, with her husband, an attorney. She continued her studies; became the music, art, and drama critic for the *Louisiana State Times*; and produced and moderated a daily television program. All the while, she continued to compose.

In 1969, Coates ended her marriage. Accompanied by her five-year-old daughter Alexandra and her dog Beatle, Coates boarded a Greek freighter bound for Europe. She settled in Munich and organized radio programs for West German Radio about contemporary American music. In 1971, she started a German-American Concert Series for the Amerika Haus. Additional radio work came her way while she continued composing. "I live very simply," she said. "I have no car and no luxuries, but my life is never dull." Her responsibilities, however, were many:

As the years went by, my responsibilities as a mother, as an organizer of concerts, musicologist, and most of all, as a composer increased so that I felt like an apple tree with its branches so heavy with fruit that they were curved to the ground. Gradually, as my daughter left for college..., I had more time to organize my life and write larger compositions.

In 1981, Coates was a guest of the Soviet Composers Union at the First International Festival of New Music in Moscow. Composing played an increasingly important role in her life; by 1978, she had 58 commissions and could not fulfill them all. Her String Quartet No. II for the 1972 Olympics in Munich was recorded in 1977 and 1983, along with her String Quartets, I and III. One of her most popular works was a music song cycle based on poems by *Emily Dickinson. In 1982, Coates received a Norlin Foundation Fellowship from the MacDowell Colony in Peterborough, New Hampshire, which allowed her to spend several months working on an orchestral piece based on texts by Leonardo da Vinci. A visual artist as well as a composer, Coates has many works in private collections as well as in European exhibits. Her daughter Alexandra is a harpist.

John Haag,
Athens, Georgia

Cobb, Jerrie (b. 1931).

See Astronauts: Women in Space.

Cobb, Jewell Plummer (1924—)

African-American educator, administrator, and cell biologist who pioneered programs for the inclusion of women and minorities in the sciences. Born on January 17, 1924, in Chicago, Illinois; daughter of Carriebel (Cole) Plummer and Frank V. Plummer; awarded B.S.C., Talladega College, Alabama, 1941, M.S.C., New York University, 1947, Ph.D. New York University, 1950; married Roy Paul Cobb, in 1954 (divorced 1967); children: Roy Jonathan Cobb (b. 1957).

Awards: Key Pin Award, New York University (1952); research grant from the American Cancer Society (1969); honorary Ph.D., Wheaton College (1971); honorary Ph.D., Lowell Technical Institute (1972); honorary Ph.D., Pennsylvania Medical College (1975).

Enrolled at the University of Michigan (1941); transferred to Talladega College (1942), graduated (1944); enrolled at New York University (1944), graduated (1950); became fellow of the National Cancer Institute, Harlem Hospital (1950); was instructor at Uni-

WOMEN IN WORLD HISTORY

versity of Illinois (1952); was instructor at New York University (1955); was visiting lecturer at Hunter College (1956–57); promoted to assistant professor, New York University (1956); was professor of biology at Sarah Lawrence College, Bronxville, New York (1960); appointed dean of Connecticut College and Sarah Lawrence (1969); appointed the only minority member on the National Science Board (1974); appointed dean of biology at Douglass College, Rutgers University (1976); appointed president of California State University at Fullerton (1981); appointed Trustee Professor of the California State College, Los Angeles (1990).

Jewell Plummer Cobb was born in Chicago, Illinois, on January 17, 1924, the only child of an upper-middle-class couple, Frank Plummer and **Carriebel Cole Plummer**. Jewell's parents could scarcely have been better role models; they placed great emphasis on academic achievements. Frank was a founder of the Alpha Phi Alpha fraternity at Cornell University and subsequently earned a degree in medicine from Rush Medical School. He spent his internship at Provident Hospital, which serviced the black community. As the segregationist laws of the United States forbade African-American doctors from

Jewell Plummer Cobb

treating white patients, Provident hospital served a pivotal role in Frank's training. In 1923, he opened a practice in Chicago and became a fixture of the growing African-American community. His office was located on 59th and State Street, within easy reach of the city's many stockyard employees.

Carriebel Cole Plummer moved to Washington, D.C., from the south while still a child. A great admirer of *Isadora Duncan (Jewell's middle name), Carriebel studied interpretive dance and received a degree in physical education from Sargeants, a college affiliated with Harvard University. After marrying Frank, Carriebel taught physical education and dance in the Chicago public school system for many years. In 1944, she also received a Bachelor of Arts from the YMCA College, which subsequently became Roosevelt University.

While financially privileged, Jewell became aware at an early age of the social restrictions placed on African-Americans. As **Dona Irvin** notes:

> From her earliest memory she heard discussions of racial matters—the hopes and frustrations of her family and associates. She became familiar with the aspirations, successes, and talents of the black people. . . . Cobb never lost sight of the fact that she was a black person living in a white-dominated society. Through the years the Plummer family changed their place of residence more than once, always to a better location, and always after the white population had fled, thereby making a choice part of the city available to minorities for the first time.

As a young girl, Cobb attended the racially segregated schools of Chicago. She was fortunate, however, that the family possessed an extensive library, which helped to supplement her education. Among the books were works concerning African-Americans, magazines on current events, and scientific journals. The Plummers also made frequent trips to New York City to attend cultural events, such as the ballet, concerts, and the theater. At the age of four, Cobb was taken by her mother to see *Porgy and Bess*.

Family friends embraced a wide range of Chicago's African-American cultural elite. The historian Carter Woodson was a friend of Cobb's mother. Writer and librarian Arna Bontemps was a frequent visitor to the Plummer household, as was Cobb's uncle Bob Cole who was a well-known producer of musicals in New York. The famous anthropologist **Allison Davis** and **Alpha White**, director of the YWCA, both lived in the vicinity of the Plummer residence. The Plummers

were also prominent members of Saint Edmund's Episcopal Church. Jewell was confirmed at Saint Edmund's, took communion there, and sang in the choir. The church was the social focus for many prominent African-American families. During the summers, the Plummers traveled to Idle Wild, a resort in northern Michigan, where prosperous African-American families maintained summer homes. There she played with school friends in idyllic surroundings.

Despite the segregation of the Chicago school system, Cobb flourished academically. Initially, she enrolled in Sexton Elementary school and was later transferred to Betsy Ross Elementary School. As a secondary student, she attended Englewood High School. Growing up, however, Cobb was unaware of the full extent to which race played a role in the Chicago school system. Writes Irvin:

> Decades later Cobb learned about the gerrymandering of the school districts in Chicago to prevent extensive integration by black children. In one instance the removal of non-white students resulted in enough space to found a community college in the building.

Throughout her educational career, Jewell Plummer Cobb remained an honors student. Fascinated by biology, she devoured Paul de Kruif's *Microbe Hunters*. Her parents insisted that she enroll in college-preparatory courses, which included five years of science. Cobb took courses in zoology, botany, physics, chemistry, and mathematics. Despite the overcrowded and dilapidated conditions of Chicago's segregated school system, several of Cobb's peers also showed strong academic abilities. Many undertook careers in education or the social sciences.

After graduating with honors in 1941, Cobb enrolled at the University of Michigan in Ann Arbor. Many of her summertime playmates from Idle Wild were also students there. The glamour of the University of Michigan's football team, headed by Tom Harmon, also attracted her. She met many African-American students from the south, who had been denied admission to their own state universities. Classes at the University of Michigan were not segregated, though dormitories, fraternities, sororities, and campus social life were. Cobb joined the African-American sorority Alpha Kappa.

For her second year of college, Cobb decided to transfer to Talladega College in Alabama with the encouragement of its dean of women, ❧▶ **Hilda Davis**. Talladega did not accept transfer credits, but students were allowed to take examinations for courses whenever they felt prepared to do so. In the more racially supportive environment of Talladega, Cobb entered the accelerated program, graduating three years later, in 1944, with a B.Sc. Her major was biology. America's involvement in World War II affected enrollment at the college. Only four of the thirty-two graduates that year were men.

That same year, with the encouragement of a bacteriology professor from Talladega, Cobb applied for a teaching fellowship at New York University (NYU) but was unsuccessful. When she arrived in New York, however, her excellent credentials spoke for themselves, and the decision was reversed. Following graduate research in biology. she completed her Ph.D dissertation in cell physiology in 1950. Her principle area of research was pigment cells and their effects of melanin.

In 1950, Cobb was awarded a post-doctoral fellowship at the National Cancer Institute. Instead of pursuing a medical career, she chose to focus on the theoretical approach to biology. As a cell biologist, she investigated the growth of cancer tumors in tissue cultures with Dr. Louis T. Wright at Harlem Hospital. Along with her research assistant **Dorothy Walker Jones**, a professor of biology at Howard University, Cobb also studied the effects of chemotherapy on cancer cells. She designed new experiments to compare the *in vivo* effects of chemotherapeutic agents (cells growing in the cancer patient) with *in vitro* effects of the same tissue obtained from the patient (cells growing in flasks, test tubes, or dishes).

In 1952, she moved to the University of Illinois, where she taught in the College of Medicine. Cobb also established the first tissue culture laboratory at the university, began a course in cell biology, and generated substantial research data on cancer cytology and bladder cancer. Research grants were provided by the Damon Runyon Fund and the National Institute of Health.

In 1954, Jewell Plummer married Roy Cobb. Three years later their son Roy Jonathan Cobb was born. The couple divorced in 1967. As a child, Cobb's son often visited her laboratory on weekends. Following in the footsteps of his great grandfather Robert Plummer, who had been a pharmacist, and his grandfather Frank, the boy would go on to graduate from Cornell Medical School and become a radiologist, specializing in magnetic resonance imaging (MRI).

From 1955 to 1956, Cobb taught at New York University and was promoted to assistant professor in 1956. She performed extensive re-

search on the pigmentation of cells, particularly the influence of melanin on skin color. One of her primary research efforts sought to learn how melanin protected human skin from the ultraviolet rays of the sun. In 1960, Cobb moved to Sarah Lawrence College, where she was appointed professor of biology. While there, she continued her experiments on melanin, as well as working on mouse melanoma. Maintaining a heavy teaching schedule, she also found time to hold the position of dean.

While retaining her position as dean at Sarah Lawrence, Cobb assumed the duties of professor of biology, as well as those of dean at Connecticut College, in 1969. At Conn College, she established privately funded scholarship programs for minority and female students in the fields of premedicine and predentistry; the highly successful programs served as pioneering models for 20 similar programs established across America. Ninety percent of the students who participated in the Conn College experiment were accepted into medical or dental school. Upon her departure, however, the program was discontinued.

Over the years, Cobb has shown great concern regarding the stature of women in the sciences. In her 1979 article, "Filters for Women in Science," published in the *Annals of the New York Academy of Sciences*, Cobb tried to unravel the reasons that "women, who constitute 52 percent of the population, make up only 20 percent of the scientists but less than one percent of the engineers." She used the analogy of a filter to demonstrate the institutional barriers that

❧ Davis, Hilda (b. 1905)

African-American educator. Born Hilda Andrea Davis on May 24, 1905, in Washington, D.C.; fourth child of Louis Alexander Davis and Ruth Gertrude (Cooke) Davis; graduated Howard University, 1925; attended Radcliffe, 1929–31; attended Alice Freeman Palmer course for Deans of Women at Boston University, 1932; earned a doctorate in human development at the University of Chicago.

In 1932, Hilda Davis signed on as dean of women and assistant professor of English at Shaw University, a liberal arts college in Raleigh, North Carolina, founded for blacks in 1865. Four years later, she became director of women's activities and associate professor of English at Talladega College in Alabama. Before long, she was dean of women and would soon be known as one of the most beloved deans in the south.

women face in gaining entry to scientific professions. She advocated increased support for girls' science programs at the elementary and secondary levels, and called for a revision of the traditional assumption that women cannot compete with their male peers in the scientific realm. For women already enrolled in the university system, Cobb advocated the formation of discussion groups comprised of undergraduate and graduate students. As well, she favored programs that help to financially support female graduate students, especially single mothers. She noted that in one recent year only four doctorates in mathematics were awarded to African-American students in the entire United States. From 1974 to 1980, Cobb was the only minority member on the National Science Board. Even so, she was instrumental in the creation of the Women and Minorities in Science Committee, designed to foster career awareness programs, teach refresher courses, and provide grant money for guest speakers at the secondary-school level.

It was not until she moved to Douglas College at Rutgers University in 1976, that the burdens of administration forced her to give up research. Cobb, however, continued to maintain a lively interest in cell biology and managed to keep abreast of developments in her field. Rutgers University named a residence hall in her honor. In 1981, Cobb moved to the California State University at Fullerton, where she assumed the office of president. Once established there, she quickly founded a privately funded gerontology center. In order to transform the university from a commuter campus to one more firmly rooted in the community, Cobb built a series of apartment complexes, also named in her honor, to serve the student body. As well, she lobbied the government of California for the construction of a new computer-sciences and engineering facility. In order to increase the number of female and minority students in the sciences, Cobb established programs similar to those she had pioneered at Connecticut College.

In 1990, Cobb was appointed Trustee Professor of the California State College in Los Angeles. She worked with a consortium of six colleges to encourage the participation of minority students in the sciences. The group devoted much of its time to corporate fund raising, as federal funding for such programs was on the decline. It also worked individually with students to help upgrade their educational skills.

That same year, Cobb retired as president of California State University. She continued, however, to serve as president emeritus and as a trustee. She has been honored for her work by the NAACP, and the American Medical Association. Her portrait also hangs in the National Sciences Academy in Washington, D.C., and she has been awarded several honorary degrees. Jewell Plummer Cobb's career has served to promote the inclusion of women and minorities in the sciences. As a result, she has influenced an entire generation of American scientists and opened the door of science to non-traditional practitioners.

SOURCES:

Hawkins, Walter L. *African-American Biographies*. Jefferson, NC: MacFarland, 1992.

Irvin, Dona L. "Jewell Plummer Cobb," in *Notable Black American Women*. Edited by Jessie Carney Smith. Detroit: Gale Research, 1992.

Taha, Kelle S. "Cobb, Jewel Plummer," in *African-American Women*. Edited by Dorothy C. Salmen. NY: Garland, 1993.

SUGGESTED READING:

Thompson, Kathleen. "Cobb, Jewell Plummer," in *Black Women in America*. Edited by Darlene Clark Hine. NY: Carlson, 1993.

Hugh A. Stewart, M.A.,
University of Guelph, Guelph, Ontario, Canada

Cobbe, Frances Power (1822–1904)

Prolific Irish writer, journalist, and feminist who wrote and spoke on a wide range of issues but is best known for her work on wife abuse and antivivisection. Born Frances Power Cobbe in Dublin, Ireland, on December 4, 1822; died at Hengwrt, Wales, on April 5, 1904; daughter of Charles and Frances (Conway) Cobbe; never married; no children; lifelong companion of Mary Lloyd.

Lived at home with her family in Ireland for 36 years; left home after her father died (1857); lived and worked with Mary Carpenter (1858–59); moved to London and began writing for several newspapers; published several hundred pamphlets on various reform causes, including wife abuse, suffrage, post-secondary education for women, and antivivisection; founded antivivisection association, Victoria Street Society (1875); left London with her lifelong companion Mary Lloyd and settled in Wales; founded the British Union for the Abolition of Vivisection (1898).

Selected publications: Essays on the Theory of Intuitive Morals *(1855);* Essays on the Pursuits of Women *(1863); (editor)* The Collected Works of Theodore Parker *(14 vols., 1863–66);* Studies New and Old of Ethical and Social Subjects *(1866); "The Rights of Man and the Claims of Brutes," in* Fraser's Magazine *(1870);* Darwinism in Morals, and Other Essays *(1872); "Wife Torture in England," in* Contemporary

Review *(1878);* The Duties of Women *(1881);* The Life of Frances Power Cobbe *(2 vols., 1894).*

Since the mid-18th century, the doctrine of separate spheres for women and men had been gaining strength and influence. Women were assigned to the private and tranquil world of the home where, as wives and mothers, they fulfilled their destinies as caregivers and the guardians of morality. The public sphere, on the other hand, was the preserve of men and was concerned with the busy world of economics and politics. By the 19th century, however, there were many women who chose not to marry and who, though they were increasingly seen as being redundant and a social problem, were joining the growing number of married women whose philanthropic activities grew into a widespread movement for the reform of women's political, economic, and legal rights. Frances Power Cobbe was an important participant in the middle-class women's movement of 19th-century England.

She was born in Dublin on December 4, 1822, the only daughter of Charles Cobbe, an Anglo-Irish landowner, and **Frances Conway Cobbe**. The young girl grew up on a large estate and was, for the great majority of her childhood, educated at home. At age 14, Frances Cobb was sent away for two years to a fashionable boarding school in Brighton where she was not only miserably homesick but found the experience intellectually unfulfilling. In later years, she condemned the boarding-school system as one that had been "devised to attain the maximum of cost and labour and the minimum of solid results." Upon her return home to Ireland, Cobbe occupied herself with a relentless schedule of reading and studying along with the management of the household.

Frances' mother, whom she adored, was bedridden during most of the girl's adolescence and her father remained a distant and remote figure. As a young teenager with a voracious appetite for learning, Cobbe began to doubt basic beliefs that she had been raised to follow, many of which centered around religion. As early as age 11, she questioned the validity of Christ's miracles; by her early 20s, she had abandoned many of the basic precepts of Christianity. When her beloved mother died in 1847, 25-year-old Frances had reached a crisis in her religious faith. In addition, she was now living alone in the great family estate house with her father who had ignored her throughout most of her childhood. Soon after her mother died, Cobbe announced to him that she had rejected traditional Christianity and would no longer participate in family prayers or attend church. Outraged, her father banished her from the house. She lived with one of her brothers for a short while until she was readmitted to her father's house a few months later.

Cobbe's relationship with her father was never easy. Historian **Barbara Caine** has determined that it was "through the rebellion she staged against her father's attempt to dictate her religious beliefs and observances, that Cobbe established the basis for her feminist beliefs." Frances finally settled upon a new set of religious beliefs, which were heavily influenced by the works of Theodore Parker, an American theologian. For Cobbe, God was no longer a harsh, masculine judge, but a being that, as Caine asserts, "combined both masculine and feminine qualities and thus incorporated reverence for women as well as for men." Cobbe believed that God was a rational being and that moral law was readily available to everyone through intuition.

I have felt all my life an irresistible impulse to rush in where-ever anyone is oppressed and try to deliver him, her, or *it,* as the case may be, from the adversary!
—**Frances Power Cobbe**

These religious and philosophical convictions were presented in her first published book, *Essays on the Theory of Intuitive Morals.* Like many Victorian women writers, Cobbe produced this work in secret, working late into the night when her household duties were completed and she was out of sight from her father's watchful eye. Though he soon discovered her work, she was determined to publish it in spite of his disapproval. In 1855, her wish was fulfilled, but she bowed to her father's authority by having the work published anonymously.

Immediately after the death of her father in 1857, Cobbe traveled throughout Europe and the East. During this trip, she met several unmarried women in Italy who were living together independently and who had developed close and sometimes intimate relationships. Cobbe would return to Italy several times over the course of the next 20 years, meeting and corresponding with many famous and influential writers, poets, and philosophers of the 19th century, including Theodore Parker whom she met in Florence shortly before he died. Some years later, she would edit all 14 volumes of his works.

Cobbe's skill at writing was to hold her in good stead. The family estate now passed into the hands of her eldest brother who moved into the house with his wife. Frances' father left her a legacy of £200 per year, which was less than she had received when she was living at home and was far less than she needed to maintain her current standard of living. Nonetheless, and in spite of receiving an invitation to remain in the house where she had spent the past 35 years, Frances refused to become dependent upon her brother and set out to make her own living by writing.

She also took up a philanthropic enterprise. Thus, in November 1858 she joined *Mary Carpenter, whose work with delinquent children she had long admired, in Bristol. The two women lived together in Carpenter's school for girls, Red Lodge House. Cobbe, however, soon became dismayed not only by the amount of work that Carpenter expected, but also by the asceticism of Carpenter's lifestyle. Long accustomed to bountiful meals, good wine, and lengthy conversation about literature, politics, and religion, Cobbe found Carpenter's sparse dinners, and relentless focus upon her children, uncomfortable and alienating. The women were incompatible in temperament. The more Frances demanded a close companionship with Mary, the more Mary strove for privacy and independence. The scheme was short-lived, and Cobbe left Red Lodge in 1859, obviously hurt by Carpenter's rejection of her affections. Looking back upon the experience many years later, Cobbe concluded: "I could be of no real comfort or service as an inmate of her house; she cannot bear the idea that anyone might expect companionship from her. She would have liked me better if I had been a delinquent."

Cobbe soon found a more amicable companion in **Mary Lloyd** whom she had met sometime in 1858 or 1859. The two women lived together for the next 34 years in what can only be described as a "female marriage." After her return to London, Cobbe began what became a lengthy and prolific career in journalism. She wrote essays and articles for several publications, including *Macmillan's Magazine, Fraser's Magazine, Modern Review, Cornhill Magazine,* and the *Quarterly Review*. From 1868 until 1875, she was the lead writer for the *Echo* and later for the *Standard*. Although she noted that her eldest brother made more money every year from the family property than she had received for life, Cobbe found journalism "a delightful profession, full of interest, and promise of ever-extending usefulness. It is pre-eminently healthy, being so full of variety and calling for so many different mental faculties one after another."

Cobbe wrote on a variety of topics during her lengthy career as a journalist, but she is best known for her work on women's issues and anti-vivisection. She first became interested in the rights of women when she worked with Mary Carpenter. Although many of her ideas about the roles of women were conservative, her desire to help raise the status of women was of the utmost importance. "I am a woman," she noted. "Nothing concerning the interests of women is alien to me." As such, she joined many of the new women's organizations that were being formed in the 1860s and '70s and met and corresponded with some of the leading figures in the 19th-century women's movement in England. She joined the Society for Women's Suffrage and the Married Women's Property Rights Group. In 1862, she read a paper at the Social Science Congress advocating admission of women to universities. At the time, she remembered being "the butt of ridicule," but her wishes were prophetic. Although it took another 50 years before Oxford and Cambridge Universities admitted women, the 1870s saw the establishment of several women's colleges that provided higher education for young women.

Cobbe felt most proud of her work on behalf of battered women. In 1878, she wrote an influential pamphlet entitled "Wife Torture in England." In the article, she recognized that the ultimate cause of wife abuse was women's inferior legal, social, and economic status:

> The notion that a man's wife is his PROPERTY, in the sense in which a horse is his property, is the fatal root of incalculable evil and misery. I conceive then, that the common idea of the inferiority of women, and the special notion of the rights of husbands, form the undercurrent of feeling which induces a man, when for any reason he is infuriated, to wreak his violence on his wife.

She worked continuously to bring wife abuse to the attention of Parliament. The debate centered upon a split among M.P.s as to whether flogging should be used as punishment for men convicted of brutal assault. Cobbe, however, saw punishment as ineffectual, since she knew that husbands would be even more brutal towards their wives after returning home from a flogging. Instead, she advocated giving the wife the power to separate from her husband; the power to implement an Act of Parliament whereby a wife could obtain a separation order when her husband was convicted of an aggravated assault upon her. Although Cobbe received the support of several male M.P.s for this legislation, she was well aware that women, without parliamentary representation, were at the mercy of men. The reason why women were still being abused was caused, she claimed, by "the simple fact that, under our present constitution, women, having no votes, can only exceptionally and through favour bring pressure to bear to force attention even to the most crying of injustices under which they suffer." Fortunately, Cobbe's influence captured the attention of enough like-minded M.P.s, and, on May 27, 1878, an Act of Parliament was passed whereby wives were allowed to separate from a husband convicted of aggravated assault.

Frances Power Cobbe continued to write about women's issues throughout the 1870s until her attention and energy was directed towards the antivivisection movement. Vivisection (experimentation upon live animals) was a common practice in most medical schools of Western Europe. To Cobbe, however, it represented the most abhorrent form of cruelty. Throughout her life, she held a great affection for animals; she had cared for dogs since childhood. While growing up in Ireland, she knew that the hunting, shooting, and fishing that her father and brothers enjoyed were acceptable sports; she, herself, had learned to fish. From age 16, however, when she began to question the basis of Christianity, she gave up fishing because she could "no longer take pleasure in giving pain to any creature of God."

In 1870, she published an article in *Fraser's Magazine*, entitled "The Rights of Man and the Claims of Brutes," in which she outlined the moral questions involved in vivisection. By 1874, she had drafted a petition to obtain parliamentary legislation to regulate experimentation upon only those animals that were under complete anaesthesia. In May 1875, the government established a Royal Commission to investigate the issue. Cobbe, however, was impatient and, at age 53, formed her own antivivisection association the same year. Although several antivivisection organizations were established over the next few years, Cobbe's Victoria Street Society for the Protection of Animals was the most prestigious, because she was able to attract influential political and literary figures to sit on its committees. The Society counted as its members Dr. George Hoggan, Leslie Stephen, the **countess of Camperdown**, Lord Shaftesbury, the archbishop of York, the marquis of Bute, and the bishops of Gloucester, Bristol, and Manchester.

In August 1876, the British Government passed the Vivisection Act, which limited experimentation upon live animals to licensed persons.

Much to Cobbe's anger and dismay, the Act rescinded a clause that would have incorporated her plea to have experiments performed under anesthesia. Undaunted, Cobbe continued to write and petition, and in 1876 the Victoria Street Society decided to work for the total prohibition of vivisection. Throughout the 1870s and '80s, Cobbe worked tirelessly on the antivivisection campaign and by her own estimation published over 400 pamphlets, books, and leaflets. She founded and wrote for the journal *Zoophilist* and until 1884 was the secretary, as well as the driving force, behind the Victoria Street Society. In 1884, she finally resigned and was paid an annuity of £100 per year as a token for her efforts.

Cobbe's work in the antivivisection movement was closely related to her work in the women's movement. She was a prominent member of the philanthropic activities of many 19th-century middle-class Englishwomen who entered the public sphere out of a sense of duty to reform society. Cobbe herself felt that philanthropy was a necessary activity for women.

> Every woman who has any margin of time or money to spare should adopt some one public interest, some philanthropic undertaking, or some special agitation of reform, and give to that cause whatever time and work she may be able to afford.

After she retired from the Victoria Street Society and received a large legacy from a female friend, Cobbe and her lifelong companion Mary Lloyd left London and moved to Hengwrt in Wales. Although Cobbe rarely mentions Lloyd in her autobiography, Mary's death in 1896 touched her deeply. In a letter to fellow-feminist *Millicent Garrett Fawcett, Cobbe wrote:

> The end of such a friendship—thirty-four years of mutual affection—is of course a mortal blow, and I have yet to learn how I am to live without the one who has shared all my thoughts and feelings so long.

Cobbe's last years were spent alone in Wales. She continued to campaign for the abolition of vivisection and in 1898 formed the British Union for the Abolition of Vivisection after she learned that her compatriots in the Victoria Street Society had altered their approach by continuing to support experimentation under anesthetics. Frances Power Cobbe died, aged 82, at Hengwrt on April 5, 1904.

SOURCES:

Banks, Olive. "Frances Power Cobbe," in *Biographical Dictionary of British Feminists, Volume I, 1800–1930*. NY: New York University Press, 1985, pp. 53–55.

Caine, Barbara. *Victorian Feminists*. Oxford: Oxford University Press, 1992.

Cobbe, Frances Power. *Life of Frances Power Cobbe*. 2 Vols. Cambridge, MA: Riverside Press, 1984.

SUGGESTED READING:

French, Richard. *Antivivisection and Medical Science in Victorian England*. Princeton, NJ: Princeton University Press, 1975.

Spender, Dale. *Women of Ideas and What Men Have Done to Them*. London: Routledge and Kegan Paul, 1983.

Margaret McIntyre, Trent University, Peterborough, Canada

Cobham, Eleanor (d. 1452)

Duchess of Gloucester. Died on August 7, 1452 (some sources cite 1446); daughter of Reginald Cobham, 2nd baron Cobham; became second wife of Humphrey, duke of Gloucester, 1431 (divorced 1441).

Eleanor Cobham was originally the mistress, then the wife, of Humphrey, duke of Gloucester, who was the son of *Mary de Bohun and Henry IV, king of England. After Cobham fell in with Roger Bolingbroke, who dabbled in the black art, she was tried for conspiracy to kill King Henry VI by magic, so that her husband might have the crown. Imprisoned in 1441, she was sentenced to walk the streets for three days while bareheaded and carrying a burning candle. She was afterward confined to Chester Castle, Kenilworth, then the Isle of Man, and is said to have remained in Peel Castle until her death in 1452. Eleanor Cobham figures in Shakespeare's play *Henry VI, part 2*, when her ears are boxed by the English queen, *Margaret of Anjou (1430–1482).

Coca, Imogene (b. 1909)

American actress and comedian who was the star of television's groundbreaking comedy "Your Show of Shows." Born on November 18, 1909, in Philadelphia, Pennsylvania; only child of Joseph (a musical conductor) and Sadie (Brady) Coca (a dancer and vaudeville actress); married Robert Burton (an actor-musician), in 1935 (deceased); married King Donovan (an actor).

Imogene Coca, who would capture America's heart as the pixilated co-star of the 1950s television program "Your Show of Shows," was a veteran performer before she finished grammar school. She told Ed Wallace of the *New York World-Telegram*: "I began as one of those horrible little children who sing with no voice." Thrust into vaudeville by her father at 14, she was a full time trouper—a tap, acrobatic, and ballet dancer. Deciding to forego high school for her career, she made her New York debut a year later in the chorus of the short-run musical *When You Smile*. Most of her early years were taken up with night club and vaudeville gigs, including a stint as Leonard Sillman's dancing partner in a vaudeville act booked at the Palace in New York. With the decline of vaudeville, Coca moved on to a series of minor stage roles. In 1934, Sillman drafted her for his *New Faces* revue and quite by accident discovered her flair for comedy. During a rehearsal break in the drafty theater, she put on an oversized man's polo coat and gave her rendition of a seductive fan dance. Sillman loved it and included the number in the show along with several other pantomimes. The reviewers hailed Coca as a rising young comedian.

She became a regular in Sillman's shows from 1935 to 1938, appearing in feature spots in seven productions. (In the 1935 revue *Fools Rush In*, Coca met her husband Bob Burton.) In 1938, she toured as a singer with George Olsen's orchestra before returning to New York for her first outstanding stage role in the 1939 production *Straw Hat Revue*. With a cast that included her husband and Danny Kaye, Coca appeared in 8 of the show's 25 sketches. This success was followed by a dry spell that lasted through the war years and discouraged the actress so greatly that she almost abandoned her career. When her husband joined the army, Coca went to live with her mother in Philadelphia.

Night club work sustained her through 1944 and 1945, during which time she polished some of her best routines, including a satire of Phil Spitalny's all-girl orchestra featuring Evelyn and her Magic Violin as well as a riotous take on 20 years of Hollywood *femmes fatales*. Reviewing her act at the night club Le Ruban Bleu, **Virginia Forbes** wrote in the *New York Sun*: "Miss Coca has the light lunatic touch which she uses to satirize fur fashion shows and torch singers in general. Her properties include everything from a voluminous evening wrap, probably made by Worth about 1910, to jack-in-the-box toys. 'Drunk with love,' which relates her adventures in a quaint little cocktail lounge, is hilarious." With a series of good reviews, bookings started to pick up, and Coca began to play the better clubs like New York's Blue Angel and Chicago's Palmer House. In 1948, she was tapped as a summer replacement for *Helen Hayes in *Happy Birthday*. After signing the contract, Coca felt out of her league filling Hayes' shoes and, had it been possible, would have canceled the booking.

Coca's big break finally came with her first television appearance in January 1949 in Max Liebman's "Admiral Broadway Revue," with a cast that included star comedians Sid Caesar and **Mary McCarty**. An instant hit, Coca was then cast in Liebman's 90-minute weekly revue "Your Show of Shows," which first aired on February 24, 1950, and is now considered one of the classics of television's heyday. Coca performed individually on the program—pantomimes, monologues, impersonations, original songs and dances—and also partnered with Caesar, Carl Reiner, and Howie Morris in a variety of come-

dy skits. Coca's solos included an inspired satire of a ballet, complete with a portrayal of her handsome partner and the accompanying *corps de ballet*. Ernest Haverman, in a 1951 article for *Life* magazine, called her humor "a matter of subtle and almost imperceptible shadings, balanced between dignity and absurdity."

Coca's career peaked with "Your Show of Shows," which went off the air in 1954. Later television endeavors—including a reuniting with Caesar in 1958 and two series, "Grindle" and "It's About Time"—were never as successful. In

Imogene Coca

1958, she appeared in the stage show *The Girls in 509*, where she met her second husband King Donovan; in 1963, she could be seen in the film *Under the Yum-Yum Tree*. She also took on a variety of stage roles, mostly in touring companies. In 1977, Coca joined Sid Caesar again for a cabaret tour. It was not until 1978, however, that Coca struck gold with the role of Letitia Primrose in the Cy Coleman musical *On the Twentieth Century*, which also proved to be a comeback success for lyricists *Betty Comden and Adolph Green. (The show boasted a superb set by Robin Wagner that included several replicas of the 1930s streamlined train the Twentieth Century Limited.) In addition to its Broadway run, the show had a successful tour.

Barbara Morgan,
Melrose, Massachusetts

Cochran, Barbara (1951—)

American skier. Born Barbara Ann Cochran in Claremont, New Hampshire, on January 4, 1951; daughter of Gordon S. ("Mickey") and Virginia Cochran; sister of skiers Marilyn Cochrane Brown *(b. 1950, who won a giant slalom in Austria, placed 2nd in two World Cup events in Italy and Czechoslovakia, and was the first American to win the French championship),* Linda Cochran *(b. 1954, who took 1st in European Cup giant slalom in 1975 and was the top American finisher in the 1976 Winter Olympics in Innsbruck, Austria, placing sixth), and Robert Cochrane.*

Won the U.S. Giant Slalom national championship (1969); took second in the world championship (1970); won the gold medal in slalom at the 1972 Sapporo Olympics with a combined time of 1:31.24.

Barbara Cochran was born into a skiing family. By 1973, all four Cochran siblings from Richmond, Vermont, were on the U.S. ski team that was coached by their father Mickey Cochran, a former international skier. In 1966, Barbara Cochran was junior national champion in the giant slalom. In 1970, she skied second in slalom, and third in giant slalom to become 5th overall in the World Cup. In 1971, she won the World Cup slalom and giant slalom back to back. Cochran entered the 1972 Olympics in Sapporo with her brother Robert and her sister Marilyn. Combatting thick clouds and heavy snow on Mount Teine, the 21-year-old Barbara, in a surprising upset, won the gold in slalom by 0.02 seconds, the first American skier to win gold since *Andrea Mead Lawrence won two gold medals in 1952. From 1972, no American woman won a gold medal again in skiing until 1984 when *Debbie Armstrong came in first in the giant slalom.

Karin Loewen Haag,
Athens, Georgia

Cochran, Jacqueline (c. 1910–1980)

American aviator, businesswoman, and one of the world's most famous woman fliers, who held the greatest number of speed, distance, and altitude records of any pilot, male or female. Born possibly in 1910, probably somewhere in northern Florida; died at her home in Indio, California, on August 9, 1980; orphaned, parents unknown; married Floyd B. Odlum (a financier), May 11, 1936.

Received primary education until age 9, when she began working in a cotton factory (c. 1919); received three years of nurse's training, Columbus, Georgia; was owner of cosmetics manufacturing company (1935 on); held many aviation records and awards; served as director of Women Pilots, Women's Airforce Service Pilots (1943–44).

Selected publications: The Stars at Noon *(Little, Brown, 1954); (published posthumously with co-author Maryann Bucknum Brinley)* Jackie Cochran: An Autobiography *(Bantam, 1987).*

From the start, everything had gone wrong. To Jacqueline Cochran, still in her mid-30s, the Bendix transcontinental air race of 1946 appeared jinxed. Once she left Los Angeles en route nonstop to Cleveland, she found the radio dead. Facing bad weather near the Grand Canyon, she tried to climb to 30,000 feet, but at 27,000 feet the engine cut, then surged on and off alarmingly. The only answer was to dive head-on into the storm at such a speed that her Mustang-51 was difficult to control. Flying solely on instruments, Cochran decided to jettison the external fuel-tanks over the Rockies, rather than risk dropping them in poor visibility upon a populated area. The drop mechanism, however, had not been tested. Hence, most of the tanks stayed firmly attached, wrenching the aircraft violently and damaging the wings. "The plane made a violent jerk—almost a collision in the air," Cochran said later. Moreover, a bad cut on her head had left her bleeding. "The main question was whether the plane would not disintegrate before I could get to Cleveland." She was able to keep control and landed only six minutes behind the winner.

Jacqueline Cochran's life in the air was always fraught with danger. One time, she crashlanded when the nose of her plane caught fire 10,000 feet in the air. Another time, doubled up

Jacqueline
Cochran

with pain, she climbed in her plane at midnight, flew from Albuquerque to California, landed at the Long Beach airport, and two hours later was on the operating table. Then there was the incident when she crash-landed at Indianapolis with such impact that the plane split in two on the runway. The two halves bounced several feet in the air and collided.

To avoid unnecessary weight, Cochran often calculated her fuel to the last few gallons; in doing so, she landed five times with only enough petrol for two more minutes in the air. For example, during a record flight from New York to Miami, she had to circle an airfield because a naval squadron was flying over it in formation. The engine cut just as her wheels touched the ground. With characteristic understatement, she said about her competitive flying, "All in all, the races were no picnics." Such risks, however, usually paid off. Cochran's name practically became synonymous with women in aviation. She was the first woman to break the sound barrier, the first woman to make a blind landing (that is flying solely by instruments), and the first woman to fly a British bomber. Few, however, realize that she also held practically all the men's records for propeller-driven planes. As jet pilot Chuck Yeager said, "She didn't set women's records. She set records, period. . . . Sometimes Jackie Cochran couldn't believe what she had accomplished."

Generous, egotistical, penny-pinching, compassionate, sensitive, aggressive—indeed, an explosive study in contradictions—Jackie was consistent only in the overflowing energy with which she attacked the challenge of being alive.

—Maryann Bucknum Brinley

Jacqueline Cochran was probably born in northern Florida, possibly around 1910. (She never knew her real age or the identity of her parents.) Orphaned in infancy, she lived with a poor family in sawmill camp towns of northern Florida and southern Georgia—Bagdad, Sampson, Millville, Panama City. The first sentence in her 1954 autobiography reads: "I am a refugee from Sawdust Road, which is located in the South close by Tobacco Road of theater and movie fame." Life, she continued, was "bleak and bitter and harsh":

> Until I was eight years old, I had no shoes. My bed was usually a pallet on the floor and sometimes just the floor. Food at best consisted of the barest essentials. . . . My dresses in the first seven years of my life were usually made from cast-off flour sacks.

At times close to starvation, Cochran often ate what she could steal or scrounge, and used a device of her own invention to "hook" stray chickens. On learning, at age six, that her "mother" and "father" were not her real parents, she grew even more independent, determined not to follow in their footsteps. She recalled: "My only reaction was happiness. I was glad that I wasn't related by blood to those shiftless people. Just knowing I wasn't really

one of them gave me incentive to get away and improve my lot."

She worked from the time she was seven. Once she stopped going to school because a teacher hit her, another time because her foster family needed another wage-earner. She learned her ABCs by watching railroad boxcars, sounding out the words written on their sides. A Roman Catholic priest befriended her, and a teacher, Miss Bostwick, taught her habits of cleanliness and paid her for doing odd jobs. At age seven, Cochran became a rent-out housekeeper, earning ten cents a day (if she was paid). She even served as midwife to an 18-year-old mother.

At nine, Cochran began work in the cotton mills of Columbus, Georgia, on a 12-hour night shift. Her first job: pushing a four-wheeled cart up the aisles that delivered spools of bobbins to the weavers. Her salary: six cents an hour. Soon, she was promoted to inspection room supervisor, where she had charge of 15 other children. The lighting was poor, ventilation bad, and sanitary conditions atrocious. "Human beings did not count—only yardage," she recalled.

By age 13, she left home to find work at a Columbus beauty shop. Here, Cochran learned how to give permanent waves for $1.50 a day. Then, at about age 15, she moved to Montgomery, Alabama, where she was employed in the beauty shop of a department store. One of her customers, a woman judge in the juvenile court, arranged for Cochran to seek nurse's training in a local Roman Catholic hospital. Formal requirements were waived. Although her grades were low in academic subjects, she excelled in nursing. At the end of three years in training, she worked for a country doctor in Bonifay, Florida, for three dollars a day. Before long, however, she moved to Pensacola, where she became a partner in a local beauty shop. While in Pensacola, she chose the name Cochran by scanning a telephone book. (In her autobiography, she never identifies her foster parents or offers her original name.)

In about 1928, Cochran worked nine months in a beauty operators' school in Philadelphia, after which she struck out for New York. She was immediately hired by the famous hair stylist Antoine at his Saks-Fifth Avenue salon, although in the winters she worked at his Miami Beach salon.

At a dinner party in Miami in 1932, Cochran met Floyd Bostwick Odlum, one of the wealthiest people in America. The founder of the Atlas Corporation, a giant holding company,

Odlum held major interests in RKO and Paramount pictures, Greyhound bus, United Fruit, and Bonwit Teller and Franklin Simon department stores over the course of his career. Although Odlum was 14 years older than Cochran, the couple were married on May 11, 1936, in Kingman, Arizona. Appropriately for the husband of what was then called an "aviatrix," he would head the Consolidated Vultee Aircraft Corporation, which built the B-36 intercontinental bomber and the Convair.

It was from Cochran's first conversation with Odlum that she got the idea of becoming an airplane pilot. In the summer of 1932, she took flying lessons at Roosevelt Field on Long Island. An exceptionally quick learner, she made her first solo flight after only three days of instruction. She later recalled:

> I was getting ready to land when suddenly the motor quit. I can remember thinking how considerate it was of my teacher to have arranged for the motor to stop while I was up there so I wouldn't have any trouble landing.

She was well aware of her ignorance, not even knowing how to read a compass or a map. Within three weeks, however, she obtained her pilot's license. Cochran took the examination orally, as she was still barely literate. In less than three weeks, she rented a Fairchild plane and traveled solo to Montreal. "Flying was now in my blood," she recalled.

In 1933, Cochran went to San Diego, where Ted Marshall, a friend and naval officer, taught flying according to military standards. She bought an old Travelair plane with a Gypsy motor for $1,200 and earned a commercial pilot's license. Because forced landings were the usual practice, she landed on many of California's beaches and open fields. At one point, she was briefly part of a flying circus.

In 1934, Cochran was the only American woman entrant in the McRobertson London-to-Melbourne air race. She started from England in a "Gee Bee" racing plane that was neither finished nor tested, sitting on a cracker box as the pilot's seat was not ready. After a forced landing in Bucharest, she had to abandon the race.

In 1937, she entered the Bendix Cross-Country Air Race, the major long-distance competition in the world. She placed third overall, first in the women's division, and covered the distance between Los Angeles and Cleveland in 10 hours, 19 minutes. That year, she set three major speed records: women's national, women's world, and New York-to-Miami.

Entering the Bendix race again in 1938, she won first place. The flight was a difficult one. Departing from Burbank, California, and piloting a craft she had never flown before, she ran into bad weather. Because a wad of paper was blocking the fuel pipe, she had to fly the plane with one wing higher than the other, which was the only way she could ensure an adequate gas supply. After reaching Cleveland in just over eight hours and receiving her trophy from Vincent Bendix, she climbed back into her Seversky Pursuit Plane and flew to Bendix Airport in New Jersey, in the process setting a new women's west-to-east transcontinental record of a little over ten hours.

In 1939 and 1940, Cochran set more records: women's national altitude record; international open-class speed record for both men and women; the New York-to-Miami Air Race record of 1939; world speed record for 100 and for 2,000 kilometers. In August 1939, she made the first blind landing ever performed by a female pilot.

As United States involvement in World War II approached, Cochran was convinced that woman pilots would be needed. Encouraged by General Henry H. ("Hap") Arnold, deputy chief of staff for air, and Lord Beaverbrook, British supply minister, she was the first woman to pilot a bomber to England, doing so on June 17, 1941. She sought to prove to U.S. and British officials that women could handle such heavy aircraft. Because of the opposition of the British military pilots, who fought the very idea of a civilian—much less a woman—at the controls, Cochran was required to relinquish the lever to a male copilot on takeoff and landing. In March 1942, while serving with the British Air Transport Auxiliary, she took a group of 25 American women pilots to England for training. She held the honorary title of flight captain.

That September, the U.S. Army Air Force recalled Cochran from Britain to direct its own women's pilot-training program. In August 1943, her unit was merged with the Women's Auxiliary Ferrying Squadron, headed by pilot ❧▶ **Nancy Love**. The new organization, named the Women's Airforce Service Pilots (WASP), was headed by Cochran, who was given the title Director of Women Pilots.

Cochran insisted on a strict military schedule, although technically her fliers remained civilians. WASPs not only did ferry duty; they towed targets for student anti-aircraft gunners, took part in smoke-laying, flew test flights, and

❧▶
See sidebar
on the
following page

❧▶ Love, Nancy (b. 1914)

American aviator and director of the Women's Auxiliary Ferry Squadron (WAFS). Born Nancy Harkness in Houghton, Michigan; attended Vassar; married Robert Love (a pilot).

Nancy Love learned to fly at age 16, was awarded her pilot's license one month after her first flight, and, in 1933, at age 19, received her transport rating. While at Vassar, she launched a flying school and transported passengers at the Poughkeepsie airport, but she was forced to leave school in her sophomore year because of the financial drain caused by the Depression. Even so, she continued to fly. In 1935, along with **Blanche Noyes**, *Louise Thaden, *Helen Richey, and **Helen Mac-Closkey**, Love was hired by the Bureau of Air Commerce. Love then worked with her husband Robert as a Beechcraft distributor; she also served as a test pilot for the Gwinn Air Car Company (1937–38), testing the durability of tricycle landing gear by performing hard landings.

At the onset of World War II, before Americans were engaged in the war, Love joined 32 male pilots to ferry much-needed American planes to Canada for shipment to France. Unfortunately, France capitulated before the planes could set out from Canada. When her husband was called to Washington as deputy chief of Air Transport Command (ATC), Love went with him. Aware of the contributions women could make to the air-ferrying service, she sought out Lieutenant Colonel Robert Olds. Olds was impressed with her idea and asked for a list of all women with advanced ratings; Love returned with 49 names. On September 10, 1942, the WAFS was formed with Love as the director. Twenty-seven women signed on. *See also entry on Fort, Cornelia.*

simulated gas attacks and low-level strafing. They flew nearly every type of plane used by the Army Air Force, from small trainers to B-29 Superfortresses. Some 1,074 WASP women flew 60 million miles. Only 38 fatalities resulted, or one to every 16,000 miles of flying.

Although well-connected with Washington's circles of power, Cochran was unable to keep her program intact, much less realize her goal of having it placed under the aegis of the semi-autonomous Army Air Corps. The opposition of unemployed male pilots and the Women's Army Corps (WAC) was too much for her. Cochran was so bitter that she called WAC director Colonel *Oveta Culp Hobby "the woman I love to hate." When, in December 1944, the WASPS were disbanded, Cochran's final report claimed that her pilots had proved conclusively that women were as fit as men to be pilots. In 1945, Army Air Force chief Arnold awarded her the Distinguished Service Medal, normally only bestowed upon full-fledged members of the armed forces.

When Cochran's WASP work was completed, the editor of *Liberty* magazine appointed her correspondent to the Pacific Theater. She witnessed the Japanese surrender of the Philippines at Baguio. In the process, she became so bitter at General Yamashita Tomoyuki, whom she held responsible for the atrocious treatment of war prisoners, that she said she wished she could have been present "when the rope tightened" around his neck. Soon she was the first American woman to enter postwar Japan. Going on to Shanghai, she was decorated by *Song Meiling, the wife of China's Generalissimo Chiang Kaishek, and spent two hours with Communist leader Mao Zedong.

For a year and a half after the Japanese surrender, Cochran worked as Arnold's special assistant, touring the country on behalf of a separate autonomous U.S. air arm. In 1948, she was commissioned a lieutenant colonel in the Air Force Reserves, retiring in 1970 at the rank of full colonel. In the summer of 1950, the U.S. chief of staff, General Hoyt S. ("Van") Vandenberg, offered her the directorship of the new Woman's Air Force. Cochran refused the offer while agreeing to serve as consultant, in which capacity she made various inspection tours in the United States and overseas.

After World War II, Cochran's primary focus was on her racing career. She finished second in the 1946 Bendix race, third in 1948. By the 1950s, Cochran experienced a new challenge: jets. "I had been in the center of aviation," she wrote later. "The jet phase was threatening to pass me by. I wanted a real touch of it." She took lessons from Air Force Captain Charles (Chuck) Yeager, who was establishing many records in this field. In spring 1953, Cochran flew a Canadian-built Sabrejet F-86, the fastest plane in the world, to become the first woman to soar faster than the speed of sound. She climbed to nearly 50,000 feet, breaking through the sonic barrier while diving at nearly 700 miles per hour. She wrote of the experience:

> As I climbed for this dive past the barrier, I noticed that the sky above was growing darker until it became a dark blue. The sun was a bright globe there above but there are no dust particles at the height to catch and reflect the sun's rays, so there is not what we know as "sunshine" down on the surface. Yellow has given way to blue. The gates of heaven are not brilliantly lighted. The stars can be seen at noon.

That same year, Cochran set several jet records for both men and women, including 15, 100, and 500 kilometers. On June 6, 1960, piloting an A3J plane, she was the first woman to fly at Mach 2, twice the speed of sound. She achieved another "first" for women on June 15, when she made an arrested landing in a jet on an aircraft carrier, the USS *Independence,* and was also catapulted from the carrier. By 1961, she was breaking her own 100- and 500-kilometer records of 1953, while setting an altitude record of 55,253 feet.

By now, setting records was becoming a pattern: 1961 (1,000 kilometer closed course; a new altitude record of 55,253 feet); 1962 (69 inter-city and straight-line distance records for Lockheed in a Jet Star; nine international speed, distance, and altitude records in a Northrop T-38 military jet); 1963 (15–25 and 100-kilometer courses in a Lockheed F-104G Starfighter); 1964 (15-25, 100-, and 500-kilometer courses in the same Starfighter model).

During her career, Cochran received many honors. In 1938, she was given the General William E. Mitchell Award for her contribution to the progress of American aviation. In April 1938, she was awarded the first of 15 Clifford Burke Harmon international trophies as the world's outstanding female pilot of 1937. Later, the Harmon selection committee named her the outstanding woman pilot of the 1940s. Other such tributes include the French Legion of Honor (1949), the French Air Medal (1951), the gold medal of the Fédération Aéronautique Internationale (1953), the gold medal of the International Flying Organization (1954), and the Distinguished Flying Cross with two oak-leaf clusters (1969). In 1958–59, she was elected president of the Fédération Aéronautique Internationale, the only woman to have held that office; she was reelected for the 1960–61 term.

Though many know of Cochran's flying exploits, few are aware of her activities in business and politics. In 1935, she started Jacqueline Cochran Cosmetics, which began with a beauty salon in Chicago and a laboratory in New Jersey. The company prospered, selling millions of dollars' worth of her products each year through thousands of outlets. Among her best-known products were Flowing Velvet and Shining Hour creams. In March 1961, she sold a major interest to Andrew A. Lynn, who became president and chief executive.

In 1952, Cochran was an early supporter of Dwight D. Eisenhower's presidential candidacy. Indeed, the famous slogan "I like Ike" was coined at a meeting in her New York City apartment. On February 11, Cochran made a special flight to Paris, where Eisenhower was on duty as supreme commander of the North Atlantic Treaty Organization. Her purpose: to show him newsreel films of an "Ike" rally in New York that she had co-chaired.

Four years later, Cochran took part in a colorful political contest in California. She contended for the 29th District Congressional seat against Dalip S. Saund, a Democrat born in India. Cochran genuinely suspected Saund of being a Communist, much less an illegal alien. Although Cochran was a flamboyant campaigner, piloting her own Lockheed Lodestar around the district, Saund won the election by about 3,000 votes.

Her autobiography, *The Stars at Noon* (1954), reveals her social views:

> Every generation has its rough roads and its barriers to surmount. . . . What I have done without special advantage, others can do. I hear too much about the desire for security—at least with satisfaction. It doesn't come from a private pension fund or a Government promise of poor bed and board after most of life has been spent idling around waiting for such a payoff.

At the same time, Cochran was somewhat close to Lyndon Johnson. In 1948, when Johnson was campaigning for the Senate, he fell ill from kidney stones. Cochran was attending a clambake in Dallas as the guest of Secretary of the Air Force Stuart Symington. Symington suggested she visit the ailing Johnson. Once Cochran saw his condition, she warned *Lady Bird Johnson: "Either you get proper medical aid for this man or he's going to be dead within twenty-four hours. I think he is dying." Within an hour, Cochran was personally flying the future president to the Mayo Clinic in Rochester, Minnesota, where he recovered.

By and large, Cochran's conservativism was bolstered by her frequent trips. Her personal prestige plus her husband's business influence gave her access to most of the world's leaders. In 1950, the Odlums met with Generalissimo Francisco Franco, whose regime—she claimed—"gives considerable freedom to the people of Spain." Several years later, however, she was horrified when South Korean president Syngman Rhee told her that the United States was a "yellow" nation that refused to summarily execute suspected Communists. She replied: "If you weren't an elderly man, and if I were strong enough, I'd knock you right on the nose. . . . I love my country and I'm leaving. . . . Good day."

Cochran always believed that she possessed unique psychic powers. She and her husband Floyd claimed to be able to communicate with each other while separated, in fact even in their sleep. In May 1937, on the basis of an intuitive hunch, Cochran tried to persuade her friend *Amelia Earhart not to make her fatal round-the-world flight. When on July 2, Earhart was thought to be lost over the Pacific, her husband, George Putnam, enlisted Cochran's supposed power in the search for her aircraft. Cochran claimed to know just where Earhart had crashed, although her assertions were never confirmed. A devout Roman Catholic, with a firm belief in an afterlife, Cochran lit a candle for Earhart when her senses told her that Amelia was no longer alive. Shaken by the experience, she seldom attempted to use such powers thereafter.

Through her life, Cochran suffered from health problems. A faulty appendicitis procedure led to seven further abdominal operations. She also underwent eye and foot surgery and miscarried twice. "My body simply wouldn't behave," she said. At their 600-acre ranch in California's Imperial Valley, Jacqueline and Floyd played host to hundreds of celebrities, often entertaining former president Eisenhower. In 1970, she experienced a major heart attack, and for the rest of her life she lived with a pacemaker. She was finally forced to give up competitive flying. In June 1976, Floyd Odlum died at age 84. He had suffered from arthritis for many years and was bedridden at their ranch. After Floyd's death, Jacqueline declined rapidly, suffering from heart and kidney disease. Jacqueline Cochran died on August 9, 1980, at her home in Indio, California.

SOURCES:

Cochran, Jacqueline. *The Stars at Noon.* Boston, MA: Little, Brown, 1954.

———, and Maryann Bucknum Brinley. *Jackie Cochran: An Autobiography.* NY: Bantam, 1987.

SUGGESTED READING:

Lomax, Judy. *Women of the Air.* NY: Dodd, Mead, 1987.

COLLECTIONS:

Both the Dwight D. Eisenhower Presidential Library, Abilene, Kansas, and the Lyndon B. Johnson Presidential Library, Austin, Texas, have many items dealing with Cochran. One should also consult the Columbia University Oral History Project and the National Air and Space Museum, Smithsonian Institution.

Justus D. Doenecke,
Professor of History, New College of the
University of South Florida, Sarasota, Florida

Cockburn, Alicia (1713–1794)

Scottish poet and author of the well-known Scottish ballad, "Flowers of the Forest." Name variations: Alison Cockburn. Born Alicia Rutherford or Rutherfurd on October 8, 1713; died in 1794; daughter of Robert Rutherfurd of Fairnalee, Selkirkshire; married in 1731.

There are two versions of the song "Flowers of the Forest," one by Alicia Cockburn, the other by **Jean Elliot** (1727–1805). Both versions were based on an ancient Border ballad. Cockburn's first line, "I've seen the smiling of Fortune beguiling," is said to have been written before her marriage in 1731. Though her song was not published until 1765, it was composed many years before Jean Elliot's companion verses, written in 1756, which begin, "I've heard them liltin' at our ewe-milkin'." Biographer Robert Chambers claims that Cockburn's ballad was written on the occasion of a great commercial disaster that ruined the fortunes of some Selkirkshire lairds. Later biographers, however, have thought it probable that it was written on the departure to London of a man named John Aikman, with whom Cockburn shared an early attachment.

In 1731, she was married to Patrick Cockburn of Ormiston, and following her marriage she associated with the intellectual and aristocratic celebrities of her day. In 1745, she expressed her predilection for Whiggism in a lampoon about Prince Charlie and narrowly escaped being arrested by the Highland guard as she was driving through Edinburgh in the family coach with the parody in her pocket. Cockburn was an indefatigable letter writer and a composer of parodies, squibs, toasts, and character sketches (then a favorite form of composition), but the "Flowers of the Forest" is considered her only work of great literary merit. At her house on Castlehill, and afterwards in Crichton Street, she received many illustrious friends, among whom were novelist Henry Mackenzie, historian William Robertson, philosopher David Hume, judge and pioneer anthropologist Lord James Monboddo, as well as the Keiths of Ravelston, the Balcarres, and Lady *Anne Lindsay, author of "Auld Robin Gray." As a Rutherford, Cockburn was related to Sir Walter Scott's mother with whom she had an intimate friendship. In a letter written by Cockburn in 1777, she describes a barely six-year-old Walter Scott, during one of her visits, remarking that he liked Cockburn because she was a "virtuoso like himself." Alicia Cockburn died on November 22, 1794. Her *Letters and Memorials,* with notes by T. Craig Brown, was published in 1900.

Cockburn, Catherine Trotter (1679–1749)

English playwright, essayist, poet, and philosopher. Born on August 16, 1679; died on May 11, 1749, in

Long Horsley, Northumberland; daughter of Scottish parents, her father a naval commander; mostly self-taught at home; converted from the Church of England to the Roman Catholic Church, then back to the Church of England in 1707; married Patrick Cockburn (a cleric), in 1708.

Selected works: Agnes de Castro *(1695);* Fatal Friendship *(1698);* Love at a Loss *(1700);* The Unhappy Penitent *(1701);* Revolutions of Sweden; A Defense of the Essay of Human Understanding *(1702);* A Discourse Concerning a Guide in Controversies, in Two Letters: Written to one of the Church of Rome, by a Person Lately Converted from the Communion *(1707);* Olinda's Adventures *(1718); two papers in defense of Locke, against Dr. Holdsworth (1726, 1727); "Remarks upon Some Writers in the Controversy Concerning the Foundations of Moral Duty" in* History of the Works of the Learned *(1743);* Remarks upon the Principles and Reasonings of Dr. Rutherford's Essay on the Nature and Obligations of Virtue, in Vindication of the Contrary Principles and Reasonings Inforced in the Writings of the Late Dr. Samuel Clarke *(1747).*

Catherine Trotter Cockburn's early life was not easy, though she was recognized as a child prodigy. While she was very young, her father, a Scottish naval commander, went down with his ship and the family's fortune. Catherine taught herself French, Latin, Greek and logic and supplemented her mother's earnings with her own, to support the Trotter family. She wrote five plays, becoming a popular playwright while still under 20 years of age. Even her last play, on an unusually dry subject, *Revolutions of Sweden*, met with great success.

Cockburn lived passionately. Published in 1718, her fictionalized autobiography, *Olinda's Adventures*, depicts the young life of an intelligent, confident, impassioned, and gregarious woman. Her dramatic works generally concern intense relationships, and her personal friendships and romances were known for a similar intensity. Her first play, *Agnes de Castro* (based on the life of *Inez de Castro from a novel by *Aphra Behn), was produced when she was only 17 at the Drury Lane Theatre in London. The play concerns love and friendship, as does *Fatal Friendship*, a play that appeared to enthusiastic reception three years later, in 1698. Other plays include a tragedy, *The Unhappy Penitent*, and a comedy, *Love at a Loss*.

Abandoning her dramatic writing, Cockburn became a follower of John Locke's epistemology (theory of knowledge), as set forth in his *Essay Concerning Human Understanding*.

Catherine Trotter Cockburn

Locke argues that at birth the mind is empty and absorbs information onto a blank surface, a *tabula rasa*. Many intellectuals of the time considered this position to be incompatible with a religious understanding of morality. *A Defense of the Essay of Human Understanding* was published anonymously by Catherine Cockburn in 1702 and argues that Locke provides a sound epistemology on which to base morality and religion.

Although her *Defense* was published anonymously, Locke discovered her authorship through his correspondent, George Burnet of Kemnay, Scotland, who was also a friend of hers. She had chosen to publish anonymously to avoid the inevitable attacks against a woman writing a scholarly work, and because she was humble about Locke's potential reception: "I am more afraid of appearing before him I defend than of public censure." But her fears were unfounded. Locke sent her a letter of thanks, some books and money.

George Burnet had also been at court at Hanover with G.W. Leibniz, and he kept Cockburn up to date with the philosophical issues of the day. In particular, he showed her the letters of *Damaris Cudworth Masham, who defended Locke. Where Burnet was critical of Masham, Cockburn defended her ideas and chided him for his imputation that Masham might not have originated the ideas put forth in her letters: "I pray," she wrote to Burnet, "be more equitable to her sex." Masham and Trotter soon began a direct correspondence.

It seems, however, that Cockburn could not reconcile Locke's epistemology with all Christian religion. She had converted to Roman Catholicism from the Church of England in 1707 but found her recent epistemological awareness incompatible with her new faith. Her 1707 publication, *A Discourse Concerning a Guide in Controversies*, sought to explain why she felt compelled philosophically to return to the Church of England. Both the 1707 and 1728 editions included a preface written anonymously by her friend, Gilbert Burnet, the bishop of Salisbury.

Catherine Cockburn became well known for her artistic and analytic abilities. Her collected works became a popular item among intellectuals. Fame, however, came at price, and she did not escape criticism; she was parodied as the main character in a farcical play. In 1708, she married Patrick Cockburn, a poor but educated Scottish cleric, and they went to the vicarage at Long Horsley, Northumberland. The demands on her time from a large family and a small income kept her away from intellectual work, and her public career was put aside for many years.

Cockburn resumed philosophical writing in her later years; she also corresponded with a niece, for whom she served as a mentor, on a variety of intellectual subjects. She continued to publish, including additional work in defense of Locke, throughout a painful illness that ended in her death, at age 71, on May 11, 1749.

SOURCES:

Atherton, Margaret. *Women Philosophers of the Early Modern Period*. Indianapolis: Hackett, 1994.

Kersey, Ethel M. *Women Philosophers: a Bio-critical Source Book*. NY: Greenwood Press, 1989.

Stenton, Doris May. *The English Woman in History*. NY: Macmillan, 1957.

Waithe, Mary Ellen, ed. *A History of Women Philosophers*, vol. 3. Boston: Martinus Nijhoff, 1987.

Catherine Hundleby,
M.A. Philosophy,
University of Guelph

Coffee, Lenore (c. 1897–1984)

American screenwriter. Name variations: Lenore Cowen. Born around 1897 in San Francisco, California; died on July 2, 1984, in Woodland Hills, California; educated at Convent school of the Dominican Order, San Rafael, California; married William Joyce Cowen (an English motion picture director), June 8, 1924; children: daughter Toni (b. January 29, 1927) and son Garry (b. February 2, 1930).

Filmography (credited): The Better Wife *(1919);* The Forbidden Woman *(1920);* Alias Ladyfingers *(1921);* The Face Between *(1922);* The Light That Failed *(1922);* Sherlock Brown *(1922);* Daytime Wives *(1923);* The Six-Fifty *(1923);* Temptation *(1923);* Thundering Dawn *(1923);* Bread *(1924);* Fools' Highway *(1924);* The Rose of Paris *(1924);* East Lynne *(1925);* Hell's Highroad *(1925);* The Volga Boatman *(1926);* The Angel of Broadway *(1927);* Chicago *(1927);* Lonesome Ladies *(1927);* The Night of Love *(1927);* Desert Nights *(1929);* The Bishop Murder Case *(1930);* Mother's Cry! *(1930);* Possessed *(1931);* The Squaw Man *(1931);* Night Court *(1932);* Downstairs *(1932);* Torch Singer *(1933);* All Men Are Enemies *(1934);* Four Frightened People *(1934);* Evelyn Prentice *(1934);* Vanessa: Her Love Story *(1935);* The Age of Indiscretion *(1935);* Suzy *(1936);* White Banners *(1938);* Four Daughters *(Oscar nomination, 1938);* Good Girls Go to Paris *(1939);* The Way of All Flesh *(1940);* My Son, My Son *(1940);* The Great Lie *(1941);* The Gay Sisters *(1942);* Old Acquaintance *(1943);* Till We Meet Again *(1944);* Marriage Is a Private Affair *(1944);* Tomorrow Is Forever *(1946);* The Guilt of Janet Ames *(1946);* Beyond the Forest *(1949);* Lightning Strikes Twice *(1951);* Sudden Fear *(1952);* The End of the Affair *(1955);* Footsteps in the Fog *(1955);* Another Time, Another Place *(1958);* Cash McCall *(1958).*

Novels include Weep No More; *produced plays include* Family Portraits; *memoirs published as* Storyline: Reflections of a Hollywood Screenwriter *(1973).*

The story of Lenore Coffee's entrance into the film business reads like one of her movie scripts. In her early 20s, while employed as an advertising copywriter for a San Francisco department store, Coffee launched an ad campaign so successful that her boss gave her a three-week paid holiday. During her time off, Coffee, who was an avid movie fan, wrote a story for silent-screen star *Clara Kimball Young and mailed it to Garson Studios, the film company employing the star. The studio quickly sent Coffee $100 for her story. Instead of cashing the check, the astute Coffee sent a telegram to the studio that read, "offer accepted providing I am given screen recognition." The studio agreed and Coffee received her first screen credit on *The Better Wife* in 1919.

In an interview with author Pat McGilligan for the book *Backstory*, Coffee describes what happened next. When she met Garson Studios chief, Henry Garson, he asked her how she learned to write movies. "I said 'seeing pictures.'" He said, 'You must come to Hollywood.'" Coffee begged off, saying she couldn't afford it as she was the sole support of her mother. Garson responded immediately, "I think you're going a long way in this business. I'll pay your fare and your mother's fare. . . . I'll give you fifty dollars a week on a year's contract."

Garson's assessment of Coffee's talent proved accurate. Her career spanned four decades and, though she writes in her memoirs that she considered the silent era to be her own "golden age," Coffee was in constant demand in the 1930s and 1940s when Warner Bros. and MGM were producing what were referred to as "women's pictures." During that time, Coffee wrote for many of the leading ladies of the day, including *Claudette Colbert (*Tomorrow Is Forever*) and *Deborah Kerr (*The End of the Affair*), but the two stars for whom Coffee wrote the most were *Joan Crawford and *Bette Davis. Coffee's insights into the abilities of these fine actresses allowed her to tailor-make characters for them. "Bette spits out her words," Coffee told an interviewer, "Joan doesn't. I gave Bette short speeches, short sentences." In her memoirs, Coffee describes the women's different approach: Bette "*thought* herself into a part. Joan *felt* herself into one. Bette's talent was basically intellectual, Joan's emotional."

Coffee worked with many of the leading directors of the early years, including Charles (King) Vidor, *Lois Weber, Michael Curtiz and George Fitzmaurice. Her favorite director was the legendary Cecil B. DeMille, or "C.B." as everyone called him. Coffee enjoyed working for DeMille and relays a story regarding their collaboration on *The Volga Boatman*, a classic silent film made in 1926. When, in preproduction, DeMille asked her opinion of the movie's outline, she replied candidly, "When you have a story like this, founded on capitalism and communism, you have to prove . . . both [capitalists and communists] behave equally badly when they are in power." DeMille agreed with Coffee. In a scene that shows capitalists attacking a boat, DeMille also showed the Bolsheviks behaving with equal aggressiveness by enslaving the nobility.

In the early days of the motion-picture industry, writers and actors were contracted to one studio. The major companies, MGM, Paramount, Warner Bros., and Universal turned out hundreds of pictures a year. Often times writers were called in to rewrite dialogue or even whole scripts without receiving credit. Coffee estimates that she worked on over 80 films in some capacity, though she received screen credit on only about half of them. At MGM, she worked with the legendary Irving Thalberg. "He had what is now called 'love/hate' feelings towards women," she wrote in her memoirs, "and he had the same thing towards writers. He said to me, 'What's all this business of being a writer; just putting one word after another.' My reply was, 'Pardon me, Mr. Thalberg, putting one *right* word after another.'"

Unlike her colleagues, Coffee rarely went into the studio to work, preferring instead to stay at her sprawling Mandeville Canyon estate, shared with her husband, English director William Joyce Cowen. She wrote in longhand and then dictated the work to a secretary at the studio. At first the studio did not take to her work habits and insisted that she come to the lot like everybody else. Recalled Coffee, "I wrote the first 20 pages and turned them in. Then I let time pass. They said, 'Where's the rest?' I said, 'I can't work away from home so let's call it off.' They liked the first pages I sent so much they told me I could work at home."

Though writers were often assigned particular scripts, Coffee sold original story ideas to her bosses. She was said to have been a master at the art of the "pitch," a nerve-wracking session in which the writer tells her story to a roomful of studio executives. The trick of the pitch is not only to tell a good story but to convince the studio heads the picture will be the next blockbuster hit. Though Coffee's background in advertising must have served her well, she still had much to overcome, including a serious stutter and, before a cataract operation, terrible eyesight. "Also I suffered from a nervous disease," said Coffee. "I used to excuse myself from meetings at the studio, slip out to the bathroom and shoot myself in the arm with a hypodermic of medicine. I was very good with a needle, as they say."

In 1959, after 40 years in the business, Coffee and husband moved to his beloved England. At 62, Coffee had had enough of Hollywood but not of writing. Her intention was to work on a second career as a playwright and novelist. But when her husband died not long after the move, she seemed to lose her will to write. Though she never again wrote fiction, in 1973 Coffee published her memoirs, *Storyline: Reflections of a Hollywood Screenwriter.*

Twenty years later, ill health and advancing poverty brought her back to the Motion Picture Retirement Home in Woodland Hills, a suburb of Los Angeles. Having outlived all her contemporaries, Coffee died July 2, 1984. Not long before her death when Pat McGilligan asked her how she viewed her time in Hollywood, she said, "I look back on my forty years in Hollywood with nothing but pleasure. If you can work forty years in Hollywood without getting your throat cut, you can count yourself lucky."

SOURCES:

Coffee, Lenore. *Storyline: Reflections of a Hollywood Screenwriter.* London: Cassell, 1973.

McCreadie, Marsha. *The Women Who Write The Movies: From Frances Marion to Nora Ephron.* NY: Birchlane Press, 1994.

McGilligan, Pat. "Lenore Coffee: Easy Smiler, Easy Weeper," in *Backstory.* n.d.

Deborah Jones,
Studio City, California

Coghlan, Rose (1852–1932).

See Elliott, Maxine for sidebar.

Cohen, Harriet (1895–1967)

English pianist who made the first recording of the Piano Quintet of Sir Edward Elgar. Born in London, England, on December 2, 1895; died in London, on November 13, 1967; daughter of musicians. The Harriet Cohen Medal was created in her memory.

One of Harriet Cohen's first memories was "playing on Paderewski's knee in the artist's room of the Queen's Hall at the age of six." She was born the daughter of musicians: her father was a well-known composer of orchestral and military music; her mother studied under the noted teacher Tobias Matthay (1858–1945). Also a student of Matthay, Harriet Cohen made her first solo appearance at the age of 13 and developed into a very individual performer who toured widely. She made a specialty of early keyboard music, and her Bach playing was highly regarded. Cohen made the first recording of the *Piano Quintet* of Sir Edward Elgar. Although she had small hands, she was the major exponent of the thick and complicated piano music of Sir Arnold Bax. Her romantic relationship with Bax, who called her "Tania," inspired him to compose a number of his best works, including his greatest orchestral composition, the moody and passionate tone poem of 1917, *Tintagel.* The great Hungarian composer Béla Bar-

tok dedicated his *Six Dances in Bulgarian Rhythms* to her.

"Her playing is clear, well shaped and very varied," wrote French critic Maurice Imbert. "She has a subtle touch and a strong sense of rhythm. She plays with sympathy, yet expresses herself with authority. The delicacy, grace, playfulness and tenderness of her interpretations, which are, at the same time, of a most expressive power, or full of animation, of fire, of color, prove the extent of her intelligence and convince one that she has cultivated the spirit. Everything has a personal accent."

In 1938, Cohen was made a Commander of the Order of the British Empire for her services to British musical life. Though a hand injury in 1948 cut short her concert career, she continued to play with her left hand until 1961. That same year, the Harriet Cohen International Prize Medal was founded. She is the author of her memoirs and a book on piano music entitled *Music's Handmaid.*

SOURCES:

Cohen, Harriet. *A Bundle of Time.* London: Faber and Faber, 1969.

Foreman, Lewis. *Bax: A Composer and His Times.* 2nd ed. Aldershot: Scolar Press, 1988.

Stevens, Halsey. *The Life and Music of Bela Bartok.* NY: Oxford University Press, 1953.

John Haag,
Athens, Georgia

Cohen, Rose (1880–1925)

Russian-born American author whose 1918 autobiography Out of the Shadow *provides a classic account of the lives of Jewish immigrants in New York City at the end of the 19th century. Born Rahel Gollup in Belarus on April 4, 1880; died under mysterious circumstances, most likely a suicide, in New York City, 1925; one of six children of Abraham (a tailor) and Annie Gollup.*

First published in 1918 and reprinted in 1995, Rose Cohen's *Out of the Shadow* remains one of the best firsthand accounts of what it was like to be a Russian-Jewish immigrant to America in the closing decade of the 19th century. Rose Cohen was born Rahel Gollup in a small village in Belarus in 1880 into a poor and deeply religious Orthodox Jewish family. She grew up in the Pale of Settlement, an area of tsarist Russia stretching from the Baltic to the Black Sea. Jews in the Pale were not permitted to own land and by the early 1880s found themselves increasingly subject to not only legal discrimination but bloody terroristic pogroms as well. The result of this rapidly deteriorating situation led to a mass exodus of Jewish emigration to Western Europe and North America. When she was ten, her father Abraham immigrated to the United States, after having first been subjected to arrest at the Russian border because his papers were not in order. After having established himself precariously, in 1892 he was able to send steamship tickets for Rose and her unmarried aunt Masha. A year later, the family was finally reunited when her mother Annie, two brothers, George and Michael, and two sisters, Sarah and Bertham, also arrived in the United States.

Although they had escaped the pogroms and grinding poverty of the Jewish shtetls of tsarist Russia, the reunited family found itself living on the lowest rung of New York City's immigrant ladder. Being old enough to work, Rose joined her father in the shop where he toiled. Soon, however, she had work of her own, stitching sleeve linings for men's coats. Underpaid and overworked, many of her fellow-workers were drawn to collective action, and Rose (or Rosie), as Rahel now called herself, was soon attending mass rallies. She joined the union, gaining a sense of solidarity with her fellow toilers. But most of all, Rose was fired by the desire for self-improvement and self-knowledge.

Life during the 1890s was exciting for Rose Cohen as she found herself subjected to the complex process of Americanization that in varying degrees changed the lives of the millions of the immigrants who had come to the new world. She worked briefly as a domestic servant, but did not care for this kind of life. A new environment was revealed to Rose when she found work during summers at a camp in Connecticut that brought immigrant children into an invigorating world of fresh air, nourishing food, and never-ending activities. During one of her frequent illnesses in this phase of her life, Cohen was visited by the noted settlement worker *Lillian Wald, who decades later would write a glowing review of *Out of the Shadow*. From then on, Rose became acquainted with not only assimilated German Jews like Wald, but non-Jews as well who funded medical facilities at the uptown Presbyterian Hospital where sick immigrants could regain their health. This was a new, exciting, and challenging world for a young woman who had grown up in a restrictive Orthodox Jewish ghetto.

By 1902, the family finances had reached the point where Abraham Gollup could quit working for a boss and open up his own grocery on 1st Street. Having turned down one suitor, a grocer, Rose eventually married, gave birth to a daughter, and enthusiastically continued to seek mastery of the English language and American ways. Along with many other immigrants, she attended the Breadwinner's College, a night school sponsored by the Educational Alliance, as well as the Rand School. Both of these institutions had been able to speed the Americanization of thousands of immigrants. Drawn to books, words and self-expression, Rose Cohen learned a great deal from her teachers, particularly Joseph Gollomb, a Russian-Jewish immigrant like herself. Perhaps inspired by his student, in 1935 Gollomb would publish an autobiographical novel entitled *Unquiet*.

Upon its publication in 1918, *Out of the Shadow* was showered with enthusiastic reviews. *The New York Times* praised it for its simplicity of style and sincerity, while in her laudatory review Lillian Wald held that its greatest value lay in the fact that it was "a social document transcending in value many volumes that have been brought forth by academically trained searchers for data on the conditions that the writer has experienced." Encouraged by the positive reception accorded her book, Cohen published a number of articles in literary journals during the next few years. All were essentially autobiographical in nature, continuing to explore her remarkable cultural odyssey, which had brought her from a life "among the Russian peasants" to years of struggle and intellectual challenges "among the Jews of Cherry Street" to her present life, "among the Americans." One of these pieces, the short story entitled "Natalka's Portion," was so highly rated by both editors and readers that it was reprinted at least six times, including an appearance in the prestigious anthology *Best Short Stories of 1922*.

Even greater successes now appeared possible for the woman who had begun life as a member of an oppressed community in benighted Russia. Rose Cohen spent the summers of 1923 and 1924 as an artist-in-residence at the MacDowell Colony in Peterborough, New Hampshire. Here, after hopefully productive days writing in her studio, she spent her dinner hours and evenings meeting and discussing various artistic problems with such cultural stars as the poet Edwin Arlington Robinson, the painter *Lilla Cabot Perry, and the playwright Thornton Wilder. All of this attention should have led to more books from Cohen, but after 1922 she published no more. The clues that might explain her mysterious artistic silence are scant, but besides the possibility of declining physical health there are also some suggestions that her cultural odyssey had been paid for with psychic toll. A brief *New York Times* notice in September 1922 noted a failed suicide attempt in the East River by a "Rose Cohen, 40, of 25 Decatur Street, Brooklyn."

In her 1927 short story, "Wild Winter Love," *Anzia Yezierska, herself a writer of Russian-Jewish background, presents as the protagonist an author named Ruth Raefsky who writes a book entitled *Out of the Ghetto*. The book's success, however, accelerates the disintegration of the author's marriage. After an ill-fated affair with an older, married Gentile, "Ruth Raefsky" commits suicide. It is not known whether Yezierska based all, part, or none of this story on the life of Rose Cohen, but the two writers knew each other, and it is possible that the tragic story of Ruth Raefsky is in fact that of Rose Cohen. At this point, what matters is that her remarkable autobiography is once more accessible, for it is a document of sincerity and passion that speaks for the millions of otherwise mute immigrants of Cohen's generation, telling of their dreams, struggles, victories and disappointments.

SOURCES:

Birmingham, Stephen. *"The Rest of Us": The Rise of America's Eastern European Jews*. NY: Berkley Books, 1985.

Cohen, Rose. *Out of the Shadow: A Russian Jewish Girlhood on the Lower East Side*. With an Introduction by Thomas Dublin. Ithaca, NY: Cornell University Press, 1995.

———. *A travers la nuit*. Translated by S. Godet. Paris: Renaissance du livre, [1924].

Ewen, Elizabeth. *Immigrant Women in the Land of Dollars: Life and Culture on the Lower East Side 1890–1925*. NY: Monthly Review Press, 1985.

Glenn, Susan A. *Daughters of the Shtetl: Life and Labor in the Immigrant Generation*. Ithaca, NY: Cornell University Press, 1990.

Goren, Arthur A. "Jews," in Stephan Thernstrom, ed. *Harvard Encyclopedia of American Ethnic Groups*. Cambridge, MA: The Belknap Press of Harvard University Press, 1980, pp. 571–598.

Howe, Irving, and Harold Libo. *World of Our Fathers*. NY: Harcourt Brace Jovanovich, 1976.

———, and Kenneth Libo. *How We Lived: A Documentary History of Immigrant Jews in America 1880–1930*. NY: Richard Marek, 1979.

Rischin, Moses. *The Promised City: New York's Jews, 1870–1914*. Cambridge, MA: Harvard University Press, 1977.

Sanders, Ronald. *The Downtown Jews: Portraits of an Immigrant Generation*. NY: Harper and Row, 1969.

———. *Shores of Refuge: A Hundred Years of Jewish Emigration*. NY: Henry Holt, 1988.

Shepard, Richard F., and Vicki Gold Levi. *Live and Be Well: A Celebration of Yiddish Culture in America from the First Immigrant to the Second World War*. NY: Ballantine Books, 1982.

John Haag, Associate Professor,
University of Georgia, Athens, Georgia

Cohen, Tiffany (1966—)

American distance freestyle swimmer who won the Olympic gold in 1984. Born in Culver City, California, on June 11, 1966; daughter of Shirley and Robert Cohen; graduated University of Texas, 1988.

Tiffany Cohen was ten when she began swimming for California's Culver City Swim Team under Bruce Kocsis. In 1980, at age 14, after winning several junior championships, she joined the Mission Viejo Nadadores, one of America's most prestigious aquatic clubs. Starting in 1981, Cohen won three consecutive 400-meter national outdoor championships and finished second in the 400 and 800 meters against the Soviet Union. In 1982, she won National Indoor titles at 500, 1,000, and 1,650 yards and took a bronze in the 200-meter freestyle championships. In 1983, at the Pan American and Pan Pacific Games, she won the 800 and 1,500 meters at the National Outdoor championships.

The following year, Cohen graduated from high school just in time for the 1984 Los Angeles Olympics. She established Olympic records of 4:7.10 in the 400 meter and 8:24.95 in the 800 meter to win the gold. Earlier that year, she had defeated East Germany's **Astrid Strauss** in the 200-meter freestyle. After the Olympics, Cohen entered the University of Texas where she won the NCAA titles in the 500 and 1,650-yard freestyles. In the 1985 SWC championships, she outscored all competitors and won the 200 and 500-meter freestyle, as well as the 400-meter individual medley. She then captured the 500, 1,000, and 1,650 yard freestyles at the Los Angeles indoor championships. In the 1,000-yard freestyle, she was clocked at 9:28.32 to set an American record. The following year, 1986, Cohen won the 400- and 800-meter freestyle and the 200-meter butterfly in the 1986 National Outdoor at Santa Clara, California. Tiffany Cohen graduated from the University of Texas in 1988 with a degree in journalism and retired from swimming.

Karin L. Haag,
Athens, Georgia

Cohn, Fannia (c. 1885–1962)

American labor educator and organizer. Born Fannia Mary Cohn in Minsk, Russia, on April 5, 1885 (some sources cite 1888); died of a stroke in New York City, on December 24, 1962; daughter of Hyman and Anna Rozofsky Cohn; privately educated in Russia; never married; no children.

Was a member of the Russian Socialist Revolutionary Party (1901–04); immigrated to the U.S.

(1904); joined the International Ladies' Garment Workers Union (ILGWU, 1909); served as member, executive board of the Kimono, Wrappers, and Housedress Workers Union 41 (1909–14) and chair (1911–14); worked as ILGWU organizer in Chicago (1915–16); served as ILGWU vice-president (1916–25); served as executive secretary of the ILGWU education department (1918–62); co-founded Brookwood Labor College and the Workers' Education Bureau (1921); served as member of the board of directors, Brookwood Labor College (1926–28) and vice-president of the College (1932–37). Publications: several articles in Labor Age, American Federationalist, Justice, and Workers' Education Bureau.

Unlike so many of her fellow Eastern European immigrants who were involved in the labor movement in the first decades of the 20th century, Fannia Cohn came from a prosperous family. Born in Minsk, Russia, on April 5, probably in 1885, Cohn enjoyed a comfortable childhood. Her father ran the family's flour-mill business and was able to provide all of his children with a private education. Despite their prosperity, her parents were involved with radical politics and apparently approved of their daughter Fannia's membership in the illegal Socialist Revolutionary party, beginning in 1901. She came to America three years later, initially with plans of becoming a pharmacist and joining a relative's drug supply company. However, in 1905, seeing the harsh conditions many of her less fortunate fellow Eastern European immigrants lived and worked in, Fannia Cohn decided to become a trade unionist.

After a brief career as a sleevemaker in a New York City garment factory, Cohn soon rose up through the ranks of the International Ladies' Garment Workers' Union (ILGWU). She organized locals in New York and Chicago as well as led a number of critical strikes, including the successful 1915 Chicago white goods workers' strike. Recognized by the ILGWU as one of its most talented organizers, Cohn was elected vice president by the union in 1916. The first woman to hold that office, she remained vice president until 1925. However, it was in the area of worker education that Fannia Cohn focused most of her energies for the next several decades. In 1918, she became executive secretary of the ILGWU's educational department. Although she valued trade unionism in and of itself, Cohn felt that educated workers would make the best union members. Further, she was well aware of the advantages of her own education and sought to provide that opportunity to all.

By the late 1920s, however, the workers' education movement was divided by internal disputes. While Cohn claimed to be politically neutral, some ILGWU leaders objected to the apparent affiliation between Brookwood Labor College, of which Cohn served on the board of directors (1926–28) and as vice-president (1932–37), and the American Communist Party. The union cut the funding for their educational department and Cohn, left without a salary, had to turn to her family for help. By the 1930s, she was further marginalized as a new, non-immigrant population became active in the ILGWU. Nonetheless, the union allowed her to keep the title of executive secretary of the ILGWU's educational department until forcing her into retirement in August 1962. By then in her mid–70s and increasingly frustrated and bitter, Fannia Cohn died only four months later.

SOURCES:

Kessler-Harris, Alice. "Organizing the Unorganizable: Three Jewish Women and Their Union," in *Labor History*. Vol. 17, 1976, pp. 5–23.

Sicherman, Barbara, and Carol Hurd Green, eds. *Notable American Woman: The Modern Period*. Cambridge, MA: Belknap Press of Harvard University Press, 1980, pp. 154–155.

COLLECTIONS:

Fannia Cohn Papers, New York Public Library.

Kathleen Banks Nutter,
Department of History,
University of Massachusetts at Amherst

Cohn, Marianne (1921–1944)

German-Jewish hero of the French resistance movement who smuggled Jewish children to safety in Switzerland. Born in Mannheim, Germany, in 1921; killed by a French militia unit on July 8, 1944.

Born in Mannheim, Germany, in 1921, Marianne Cohn fled the Nazi regime with her parents in 1935, and after a brief stay in Spain they were able to settle in France. Feeling accepted in France but also determined to maintain her Jewish identity, Marianne became a member of the Eclaireurs Israélites de France (French Jewish Scouts; EIF), a pluralist and traditionalist Jewish scouting organization founded by Robert Gamzon in 1923. In the ranks of the EIF, Jewish consciousness was fostered through hiking, friendship, and the study of Jewish history and traditions. Marianne and her family were interned for some months after the start of war in the notorious Gurs camp but were eventually released. Realizing the danger of being captured by the German forces, the Cohn family found refuge in the Maison EIF, located in the southern town of Moissac. Here Marianne and her mother cared for children while her father taught a course in accounting.

After the full impact of the German occupation began to be felt in the final months of 1940, Cohn's contacts were to prove invaluable for both her own survival and that of thousands of Jewish children. In the summer of 1942, the Vichy regime that governed the southern zone of France not occupied by German forces issued a decree expelling foreign-born Jews. Already an active member of the French Jewish resistance movement, Cohn now dedicated herself to the rescue of endangered Jewish children. Determined that no more refugees enter their country, Swiss officials declared that those individuals fleeing occupied France "only" because of racial reasons—i.e., Jews—would not be considered as political refugees and thus would be denied sanctuary. In practice, however, some Swiss border officials defied official directives by admitting certain categories of refugees, the great majority of which were Jews on the run. These included parents with children under the age of 6, unaccompanied children up to the age of 16, as well as ill and infirm adults. Using various stratagems, women and men like Marianne Cohn were able to evade German and French Fascist police to bring Jewish children to the Swiss border and safety.

Working tirelessly as a member of the underground section of EIF known as Sixième, and now using "Marianne Colin" as her conspiratorial name, Cohn was in her early 20s and successfully carrying out many missions before her luck finally ran out in the late spring of 1944. On May 31, having come to within 200 meters of the Swiss frontier, Marianne and her group of 28 children ranging from age 4 to 15 were arrested. Along with 11 of the older girls and boys, Cohn was imprisoned in the nearby town of Annemasse. When word of the arrest reached Jean Deffaugt, the town's mayor and a secret member of the resistance, he bravely went to the local Gestapo officials and vociferously registered his outrage at the arrest of the young woman and her group of children. Remarkably, the Germans—possibly impressed by Deffaugt's advocacy for the imprisoned Jews or perhaps also convinced that the war was lost and it might be prudent to distance themselves from atrocities—agreed to let the younger children remain at liberty in a local youth shelter.

Hoping to save Cohn's life, Deffaugt and members of her resistance unit worked out an escape plan for her. When she was told of the plan, however, she vehemently refused to participate, arguing that, if she escaped, the children still in German custody would pay for her freedom with their lives. Cohn's parents and sister had been able to escape the Nazi dragnet and were living in hiding in a French Alpine village. On July 1, 1944, Marianne Cohn wrote a letter to her father for his birthday, reassuring him that it would be the last time she was not with him to celebrate; at the same time she apologized to him for all of the anxiety her underground work had caused her family to endure. A week later, on July 8, French militia took Cohn and five other resistance prisoners to an isolated spot in Ville-la-Grande outside of Annemasse, murdering them with axes and leaving their mutilated bodies to be discovered more than a month later after the area had been liberated.

The children Cohn was attempting to rescue when they were captured in May survived. Her decision to remain in prison without doubt served to extend their lives. Of equal importance was continuing courageous intervention on their behalf by Mayor Deffaugt. On July 22, two weeks after Cohn's death, Deffaugt responded to the local Gestapo chief's demand for the 28 children with an effective combination of pleas for mercy, threats of bloody reprisals by the armed resistance, and promises of postwar protection (which did in fact take place when the Nazi official was allowed to escape to Switzerland). The Gestapo chief handed over the children to Deffaugt, and they were not sent to Lyon, where they would have fallen into the hands of the dreaded Klaus Barbie and immediately been shipped off to Auschwitz. Marianne Cohn did not die in vain, and her last mission was a total success. While under torture in prison, she wrote defiantly, "Tomorrow I will Betray, Not Today," a moving poem that survived her and continues to radiate much of her humanity and courage:

> "Tomorrow I will betray, not today
> Tear out my nails today,
> I will not betray
>
> You do not know the limits of my courage
> I know them
> You are five rough hands with rings
> You have hobnailed boots on your feet
> Today I have nothing to say
> Tomorrow I will betray
> I need the night to decide
> I need at least one night
> To deny, to abjure, to betray"

Jean Deffaugt preserved the story of Marianne Cohn's defiance for posterity. He was honored in 1968 in Jerusalem by being named one of the "Just among the Peoples" and having a tree planted in his honor at Yad Vashem.

SOURCES:

Courtois, Stephane, Denis Peschanski, and Adam Rayski. *L'Affice Rouge: Immigranten und Juden in der französischen Résistance*. Edited by Ahlrich Meyer, translated by Tom Wehmer. "Schwarze Risse," 1994.

Hammel, Frédéric Chimon. *Souviens-toi d'Amelek: Témoignage sur la lutte des Juifs en France (1938–1944)*. Paris: CLKH, 1982.

Latour, Anny. *The Jewish Resistance in France (1940–1944)*. Translated by Irene R. Ilton. NY: Holocaust Library, 1981.

Lustiger, Arno. *Zum Kampf auf Leben und Tod! Das Buch vom Widerstand der Juden 1933–1945*. Cologne: Kiepenheuer and Witsch, 1994.

Paldiel, Mordecai. *The Path of the Righteous: Gentile Rescuers of Jews During the Holocaust*. Hoboken, NJ: KTAV, 1993.

Paucker, Arnold. "Resistance of German and Austrian Jews to the Nazi Regime 1933–1945," *Leo Baeck Institute Year Book*. Vol. 40. London: Secker and Warburg, 1995, pp. 3–20.

Zuccotti, Susan. *The Holocaust, the French, and the Jews*. NY: Basic Books, 1993.

John Haag, Associate Professor, University of Georgia, Athens, Georgia

Coignet, Clarisse (1823–?)

French political activist, philosopher, educator and historian. Born in 1823; death date unknown.

Selected works: many works on morality and politics, including La Morale independante dans son principe et dans son objet *(1869) and* De Kant a Bergson; reconciliation de la religion et de la science dans un spiritualisme nouveau *(1911); many historical works, particularly on the history of morals and culture, including historical biographies of* **Elisa Grimhail Lemonnier** *(1856)* Francis I *(1885),* Francis Scepau *(1886),* Victor Considerant *(1895),* *Catherine de Medici *(1895) and* François de Guise *(1895).*

Clarisse Coignet played a significant role in France's political movement, known as "La Morale independante," which began in the 18th century. She had already published a number of works on education when she assumed editorship of the weekly newspaper *La Morale independante* (1865–70). Coignet believed in the liberal ideals of the French Revolution, as they were fostered by La Morale independante, and she argued for secularizing moral education. The issue of how morality should be taught was very popular and became the primary concern of many of the periodicals of the time. Writing under the name "C. Coignet," she was often mistaken for a male author, even in her correspondence. Coignet was not a feminist; she did, however, argue for women's suffrage only where it seemed likely to encourage liberalism, for instance in England but not in France.

Catherine Hundleby, M.A. Philosophy, University of Guelph

Coke, Alexandra

Countess of Airlie. Born Alexandra Mary Bridget Coke; daughter of the 3rd earl of Leicester; married David Ogilvy, on July 17, 1917; children: David Ogilvy, 13th earl of Airlie; Angus Ogilvy (husband of Princess Alexandra of Kent).

Coke, Jane Elizabeth (1777–1863).

See Digby el Mesrab, Jane for sidebar.

Colbert, Claudette (1903–1996)

American film actress, famed for her warmth, dignified bearing, and charm, who made 62 films, playing sirens, comic roles, and serious dramatic parts alike. Name variations: Claudette Chauchoin (pronounced clo-DET sho-SHWAHN); called "Lily" as a child. Born Claudette Chauchoin in Paris, France, on September 13, 1903 (not the 1905 as listed on her early passport; a mistake she did not correct until she was 75); died on the Caribbean Island of Barbados on July 30, 1996; came to U.S. with family in 1910; daughter of Georges Chauchoin and Jeanne (Loew) Chauchoin; attended New York City public schools; married Norman Foster (an actor), on March 13, 1928 (divorced 1934); married Joel Pressman (a surgeon), in 1936 (died 1968); children: none. Spent her last years between her New York apartment and her retirement home on the Caribbean Island of Barbados.

Awards: Sarah Siddons Society (Chicago, Best Actress of the Year, 1980); Lincoln Center (New York) tribute (1984); Legion of Honor (France, 1988); Hollywood Press Association Golden Globe for her role as the elder Mrs. Grenville in "The Two Mrs. Grenvilles"; included in the Kennedy Center Honors (Washington, 1989).

Made first stage appearance in The Wild Westcotts *and* We've Got To Have Money *(both 1923); appeared in* The Marionette Man, The Cat Came Back, High Stakes, *and* Leah Kleschma *(1924),* A Kiss in a Taxi *(1925),* Ghost Train *and* The Pearl of Great Price *(1926),* The Barker, *New York, (1927),* London *(1928),* Fast Life, Tin Pan Alley, *and* Dynamo *(1928),* See Naples and Die *(1929); returned to the stage in* Janus *(1956),* The Marriage-Go-Round *(1958),* Julia, Jake and Uncle Joe *(1961),* The Irregular Verb to Love *(1963),* The Kingfisher *(1979),* A Talent for Murder *(1981),* Aren't We All *(1985).*

Filmography: For the Love of Mike (1927); The Hole in the Wall (1929); The Lady Lies (1929); Manslaughter (1930); The Big Pond (La Grande Mer, 1930); Young Man of Manhattan (1930); L'Enigmatique Monsieur Parkes (1931); The Smiling Lieutenant (Le Lieutenant sourient, 1931), Secrets of a Secretary (1931), Honor Among Lovers (1931); His Woman (1931); The Wiser Sex (1932); (unbilled guest) Make Me a Star (1932); Misleading Lady (1932); The Man From Yesterday (1932); The Phantom President (1932); The Sign of the Cross (1932); Tonight is Ours (1933); I Cover the Waterfront (1933); Three-Cornered Moon (1933); Torch Singer (1933); Four Frightened People (1934); It Happened One Night (1934); Cleopatra (1934); Imitation of Life (1934); The Gilded Lily (1935); Private Worlds (1935); She Married Her Boss (1935); The Bride Comes Home (1935); Under Two Flags (1936); Maid in Salem (1937); I Met Him in Paris (1937); Tovarich (1937); Bluebeard's Eighth Wife (1938); Zaza (1939); Midnight (1939); It's a Wonderful World (1939); Drums Along the Mohawk (1939); Boom Town (1940); Arise my Love (1940); Skylark (1941); Remember the Day (1941); The Palm Beach Story (1942); No Time for Love (1943); So Proudly We Hail (1943); Since You Went Away (1944); Practically Yours (1944); Guest Wife (1945); Without Reservations (1946); Tomorrow is Forever (1946); The Secret Heart (1946); The Egg and I (1947); Sleep, My Love (1948); Family Honeymoon (1949); Three Came Home (1950); The Secret Fury (1951); Thunder on the Hill (1951); Let's Make it Legal (1951); The Planter's Wife (also known as Outpost in Malaya, 1952); The Texas Lady (1955); Si Versailles m'était conté (French, 1957); Parrish (1960). *Appeared in the television miniseries, "The Two Mrs. Grenvilles" (1987).*

Born Claudette Chauchoin in Paris on September 13, 1903, Claudette Colbert was called Lily as a child so that biographies occasionally give her real name as Lily Chauchoin. Her father Georges was an office worker; her mother **Jeanne Chauchoin**, who lived to be 94 and was, by her daughter's own admission, the dominant force in her life, was a native of the Isle of Jersey and was raised bi-lingually in French and English. A marvelous singer, Jeanne Chauchoin had longed for a career in opera and enthusiastically supported her daughter's decision to go on the stage. It was Claudette's grandmother **Marie Loew**, who encouraged the family to migrate to the United States, and she accompanied them when they decided to do so in 1910, when Claudette was six. They must be counted among the enormous wave of immigration that engulfed the East Coast cities of America in the decade immediately prior to the First World War, an immigration, however, that contained relatively few natives of France. In later years, Colbert recalled the importance of her mother and grandmother's ability to speak English in getting the family settled in its new homeland.

Once in New York, the Chauchoins took an apartment in the East 50s where Claudette and her brother Charles attended public school. The family attempted to preserve as much of its French heritage as it could at home; Claudette was raised French-speaking, and she and her brother, who later became her agent, were not allowed to play in the city streets.

Colbert's early goal was to become a fashion designer, but, after graduating from Washington Irving High School in 1921, her first employment was as a stenographer in a New York office. She was "discovered," however, at a party in New York by the playwright **Anne Morrison**, who, struck by her beauty, offered to secure her a part in her new play, *The Wild Westcotts,* starring *Cornelia Otis Skinner, Elliot Nugent and *Edna May Oliver. Agreeing to give the theater a try, Claudette made her debut in this production in Stamford, Connecticut, in 1923, at age 19, changing her surname from Chauchoin to the equally French but at least pronounceable Colbert. Originally only three lines, her part was quickly expanded after the Connecticut opening, but the play was not a success in New York. Nevertheless, Colbert received excellent reviews and decided that she never wanted to do anything but act again. The producer Al Woods now took an interest in her career and, placing her under contract, saw to it that she found regular work on the New York stage. Although the parts she played were small in plays now long-forgotten—*We've Got to Have Money* (1923), *The Marionette Man, The Cat Came Back, High Stakes,* and *Leah Kleschma* (all in 1924)—they were excellent "acting classes" for a neophyte, and Colbert gradually developed her natural talents, scoring her first success in the farce *A Kiss in a Taxi* in 1925. This was followed by the mystery play, *Ghost Train,* and the expensively mounted but short-lived spectacle, *The Pearl of Great Price* (both 1926).

In 1927, Colbert had her first striking success as Lou, the snake charmer, in Kenyon Nicholson's drama of circus life, *The Barker,* starring Walter Huston and Norman Foster, the latter of whom she married on March 13, 1928. The play not only ran 172 performances in New York but also served as the vehicle for Colbert's

Claudette
Colbert

London debut the following year. Upon her return to the States, Colbert found herself a "name" in the New York theater and was invited to appear in her initial silent film *For the Love o' Mike*, produced by First National Studios in New York. Since talkies had made their appearance the previous year, the film was poorly received, but it was directed by Frank Capra, who would be greatly influential in her movie career. Disappointed in the film and swearing never to appear in another, Colbert resumed her stage career, appearing successively in *Fast Life* and *Tin Pan Alley* (1928); before the end of the decade, her photograph was being featured in such magazines as *Theater* and *Theater Arts*.

I can say immodestly that I was a very good comedienne, but I was always fighting that image too. I just never had the luck to play bitches.

—Claudette Colbert

Colbert was appearing in one of Eugene O'Neill's less distinguished plays, the drama *Dynamo*, when Paramount Studios bought out her contract from Woods. She thus joined the exodus of stage artists to the world of filmmaking, where talking films required the services of actors who knew how to speak. Signed by Paramount to a double contract (fourteen years instead of the conventional seven), Colbert was immediately cast in *The Hole in the Wall*, co-starring Edward G. Robinson, and in *The Lady Lies* (both filmed in New York during the day in 1929, while she appeared on Broadway at night in Elmer Rice's *See Naples and Die*). *The Lady Lies* was a hit, and thereafter Colbert was cast in one picture after another. Her ability to speak flawless French was an early asset, for she recreated her role in *The Hole in the Wall* in the French version of the film and also appeared in the French version of *Slightly Scarlet*, released as *L'Enigmatique Mr. Parkes*, with Adolph Menjou. She did not move to California until 1932.

For a few years, Paramount was not exactly sure what to do with Claudette Colbert or how to utilize her skills. Her first serious film was a remake of the *Leatrice Joy silent vehicle *Manslaughter*, about a woman convicted of manslaughter by her lawyer fiancé (played by Fredric March). Colbert's obvious beauty soon led to her being cast by Cecil B. DeMille as a siren in his Biblical epics. In *The Sign of the Cross* (a left-handed 1932 version of *Quo Vadis* by the Polish writer Henry Sienkiewicz), Colbert played opposite Charles Laughton's Nero as Nero's empress, the evil *Poppaea Sabina, a part that she had boldly demanded in order to free herself of the rut into which her movie career had quickly fallen. She was required to bathe in a tub of milk. In De Mille's *Cleopatra* in 1934, she made love to Henry Wilcoxin behind a drawn curtain on the royal barge, while a drummer beat out a steady rhythm for the oarsmen. Years later, Colbert was to remark that she enjoyed playing vixens much more than "goody-goodies" and that she had more fun playing Poppaea than any other role. This grandiose but false start, during which her annual salary soared to the, at that time, impressive sum of $25,000 per year, was quickly rectified, however, when, in the same year, Frank Capra, now at Columbia, borrowed her from Paramount to cast her opposite Clark Gable as the runaway heiress in *It Happened One Night*. Her part, declined by *Myrna Loy, *Constance Bennett and *Miriam Hopkins, revealed to audiences for the first time Colbert's marvelous comic talents. The film went on to win every major Academy Award for 1934, including Best Picture of the Year, and became one of the great classics of the 1930s. Colbert, whose train was to leave Los Angeles for New York the night of the Oscar presentation, was reluctantly talked into attending. As she sat inside the Biltmore Hotel ballroom, a taxi waited outside. When Colbert won for Best Actress over *Grace Moore and *Norma Shearer, she raced to the podium, tossed a kiss at emcee Irwin Cobb, snatched her Oscar, thanked "Frank Capra for this," and rushed out the door. In so doing, she brought down the house.

Besides her skill at epic and comedy, Colbert also possessed great talent for drama and melodrama and this, too, was made clear in 1934, when she moved audiences deeply in *Fannie Hurst's melodrama *Imitation of Life*. This was the story of a white woman (Colbert), who goes into business selling pancake mix prepared by her black cook (*Louise Beavers), whose daughter, able to pass for white, grows up as Colbert's daughter's best friend. Colbert's role was not a major one and many other actresses could have handled it as easily, yet the sincerity and conviction that she brought to the part made it a "Claudette Colbert film" to be remembered. Although it might have been considered risky for an actress of 31 (posing as 29) to play the mother of a grown daughter, Colbert actually welcomed the opportunity, for it gave her a chance to move back and forth between mature and younger roles without the public assuming that she was getting on in years.

Imitation of Life was followed by *The Gilded Lily,* not an important picture but one that introduced Fred MacMurray, an unknown actor whom Colbert chose as her leading man. The two worked well together and were to be co-starred in several other films in later years, most notably *No Time for Love* (1943), *Practically Yours* (1944), and *The Egg and I* (1947).

Although she had rarely been seen in costume films, Colbert now appeared in a cluster of them: *Maid in Salem* (1937), *Bluebeard's Eighth Wife* (1938), *Drums Along the Mohawk,* and *Zaza* (1939). *Drums Along the Mohawk* cast her opposite Henry Fonda in the role of a pioneer woman in upstate New York during the American Revolution. Directed by John Ford, it is not considered to have been one of his best films, but it served as Colbert's first exposure in Technicolor, one of the rare color films she ever made. *Zaza*, on the other hand, based on a Broadway play starring **Clara Bloodgood** that had shocked New York at the turn of the century, was perhaps the poorest film of her career and certainly her greatest flop.

In the 1940s, Colbert continued to act as frequently as ever until her contract with Para-mount ran out in 1944. Her roles ranged from light comedy, such as *Arise My Love* (1940) and *Skylark* (1941), to nostalgia in *Remember the Day* (1941), slapstick farce in *The Palm Beach Story* (1942), and hard-hitting drama, such as *No Time for Love* (1943). Colbert's major World War II film roles, however, were as an army nurse in *So Proudly We Hail,* about the war in the Pacific (1943), and in *Since You Went Away,* in which she portrayed Anne Hilton, the wife of an American officer, who has just left for foreign duty. The film, also starring **Shirley Temple (Black)* and **Jennifer Jones*, begins with Colbert's return from seeing her husband off at the station and ends with the news that, having been earlier listed as missing in action, he is about to come home. The film was a sincere attempt to depict the American homefront during the war years and was so sincerely done, and lathered so little with easy sentimentality, that it stands as a remarkable documentary of the homefront as it really was.

After the war, free from her Paramount contract and able to freelance in Hollywood,

From the movie It Happened One Night, *starring Clark Gable and Claudette Colbert.*

Colbert chose films that she considered best suited to her, for example, the drama *Tomorrow is Forever,* in which she was allowed to select her co-star, in this case Orson Welles. Nevertheless, the last decade of her career saw her appear in one mediocre film after another although always receiving high praise from the critics for her unfailingly good performances and the spark that she brought to even her poorest roles. In *Three Came Home* (1950), Colbert's last significant film, she played real-life American author ◄⅋ **Agnes Newton Keith,** who wrote *Land Below the Wind,* an insightful and sympathetic description of British Borneo. Keith and her family had endured four years of Japanese internment during World War II. Colbert's true co-star in the film was the eminent Japanese actor Sessue Hayakawa, who had been appearing in American films since 1916 and whose performance of an understanding semi-sympathetic prison camp commander gave depth to a role that could easily have become a typical wartime stereotyped Japanese villain. Despite its box-office success and critical acclaim, however, this film was always a sore spot in Colbert's memory for, due to a dislocated disc that took place during its filming, she was unable to play the role of Margo Channing in *All About Eve* (1950), a film in which she had already been cast, and which would certainly have crowned her career. The part, that of an aging Broadway actress pushed out of her place in the theater by a younger but talented upstart, went, of course, to **Bette Davis** and has since gone on to become a part of motion-picture history. Few viewers of this film are now aware that **Anne Baxter,** as the wicked and conniving Eve, was cast in her role precisely because of her physical resemblance to Colbert, the actress whom she wished to emulate and eventually replace. Forty years later, Colbert still bitterly nursed her disappointment, claiming that the loss of this role was the worst thing that ever happened in her career.

Thereafter, Colbert's screen career inevitably declined, Hollywood typically having few roles of importance for an actress past the age of 45. A series of undistinguished roles in equally undistinguished films, of which *Let's Make it Legal* (1952) was perhaps the best, followed one upon the other, culminating in *The Texas Lady* (1955), and in a single French film *Si Versailles m'était conté* (1957). Thereafter, she retired from films except for *Parrish* (1960), a vehicle for the then popular but short-lived matinee idol, Troy Donahue. Though Colbert received excellent reviews, she devoted her last professional years to the stage, touring in *The Kingfisher* and *A Talent for Murder,* and appearing in a television miniseries, "The Two Mrs. Grenvilles," in 1987. In 1985, at age 82, she starred with Rex Harrison in a critically praised revival of Frederick Lonsdale's comedy, *Aren't We All,* receiving rave reviews and an opening-night standing ovation.

Of modest height (5'4½") and slight build (around 108 pounds), Claudette Colbert seemed more of a presence on screen than off. She was noted for her keen fashion sense and was always quietly but tastefully outfitted. That Colbert was a beautiful woman is readily apparent, but more than that she possessed a sweetness of expression and mischievous eye that made her appear to be a woman of great warmth and likability, equally popular with female as well as male audiences. "Audiences always sound like they're glad to see me," she once told an interviewer, "and I'm damned glad to see them." She had a beautifully modulated voice and exquisite diction and spoke with no trace of an accent, either of Paris or New York. Having discovered early in life that she looked best with her brown hair worn in bangs, she kept to this style all her life, simply altering the rest of her hair to suit the current mode.

⅋► **Keith, Agnes Newton** (b. 1901)

American writer of Asia and Africa. Born in Oak Park, Illinois, on July 6, 1901; daughter of Joseph Gilbert and Grace (Goodwillie) Newton; married Henry George Keith (in British Commonwealth government service in Asia), on July 23, 1934; children: Jean Alison Keith; Henry George Keith.

Agnes Newton Keith began her career as a reporter for the *San Francisco Examiner* in 1924. Soon after, she was attacked with an iron bar by a drug addict outside the *Examiner* office and lost the use of her sight for several years. She did not return to writing until after her 1934 marriage to Henry George Keith, who was in the British Commonwealth government service in Asia. The couple moved to Borneo where they lived until 1952. It was while there that the Keiths were interned in the Japanese concentration camp on Berhala Island, North Borneo, during World War II. The commandant of the camp, a Colonel Suga, had read her book about Borneo, *Land Below the Wind,* in the Japanese translation. Treating her with a modicum of respect, he demanded she write a book about her experiences in camp. She did, but later wrote the uncensored version known as *Three Came Home.* Aside from Suga, life in the camp with her two children was harrowing; she called it "the darkest hours of all my life."

Colbert was married twice. Following her divorce from Norman Foster in 1934, she married the surgeon Joel Pressman, who, after his retirement from private practice, served on the faculty of the University of California at Los Angeles Medical School. During the more than 30 years of her second marriage, she insisted that their non-related careers made the relationship work. In Hollywood society, which, in those days, was divided into different "sets," the Pressmans enjoyed the company of, among others, Gary Cooper, Jack Benny, Danny Kaye, and George Burns and *Gracie Allen. Widowed in 1968, Colbert never remarried and, in recalling her husband, always stressed that what he had done for a living was far more important than her own achievements on stage or screen.

Colbert's early taste for design never left her. Her home in Holmby Hills, built and decorated under her supervision soon after her arrival in Hollywood, was dear to her, and it was there that she lived with each of her husbands. Later, in 1960, after her return to the stage, she pur-chased a penthouse in New York and finally, three years later, sold the house in California to purchase a vacation home near Bridgetown, Barbados, which she named Belle Rive (beautiful shore), after the plantation in Tennessee Williams' play *A Streetcar Named Desire*. There, she installed her mother until the formidable old woman died in her 90s, and there she lived six months of the year—off season to avoid the tourists—spending the rest of her time in New York and Paris. Unlike other movie stars of her generation, such as *Marlene Dietrich and *Greta Garbo, who became reclusive after their careers faded, Colbert remained very much a part of the active scene. She had always made friends easily and was a good friend in return, and at her homes in New York and Barbados she played host to such luminaries as Anthony Eden, Noel Coward, and Cole Porter. A delightful and earthy storyteller, Colbert was an excellent interview and, in her later years, several magazines featured articles about her that were enlivened with her many anecdotes and reminiscences. She declined all offers, however, to write her mem-

From the movie Three Came Home, *starring Colbert as Agnes Newton Keith.*

oirs, which is perhaps to be regretted for she was a woman of remarkable intelligence.

In March 1993, she suffered a serious stroke, which left her confined to a wheelchair at her home in Barbados, but friends say she remained feisty and good-humored. She died on July 30, 1996, just short of her 93rd birthday, and left her estate to a female friend who had cared for her during the last three years of her life.

Colbert played opposite some of the foremost leading men in Hollywood, including Clark Gable, Gary Cooper, Melvyn Douglas, Maurice Chevalier, Ray Milland, John Wayne, Jimmy Stewart, David Niven, Henry Fonda, Fredric March, Joseph Cotton, Orson Welles and Spencer Tracy, and performed for some of its greatest directors, Lubitsch, Capra, Cukor, Sturges, Mankiewicz, and Litvak. Despite her French background, Colbert presented, perhaps consciously, the image of the quintessential American woman of breeding and refinement and rarely attempted roles that required her to descend from this ideal. She was noted for her seductiveness in her early roles, the delightfulness of her comic art with its marvelous sense of timing, and eventually for her portrayal of mature women made wise by the passing of years. Beyond this, however, she will be remembered for her dignity, her warmth, and the sincerity that she brought to all of her portrayals. In the Golden Age of Hollywood, Claudette Colbert was one of its finest actresses and one of the most admirable and respected women to achieve stardom.

SOURCES:
Current Biography. NY: H.W. Wilson, 1945, 1964.
Emerson, William K. *Claudette Colbert.* NY: Pyramid, 1976.
The Free Library of Philadelphia, Theater Collection.
Scott, Allan. "Claudette Colbert" in *Close-ups: The Movie Star Book.* Edited by Danny Peary. New York, 1978.
Shipman, David. *The Great Movie Stars: The Golden Years.* Rev. ed. New York, 1979.

Robert H. Hewsen,
Professor of History,
Rowan University of New Jersey

Colbran, Isabella (1785–1845)

Spanish soprano who was greatly loved in Italy. Born in Madrid, Spain, on February 2, 1785; died in Castenaso, Bologna, on October 7, 1845; studied in Madrid with Pareja, in Naples with Marinelli and Crescentini; married Gioacchino Rossini (who wrote several operas for her), in 1822. Made debut in Spain in 1806.

Probably no one had a greater influence on Gioacchino Rossini than Isabella Colbran, the great Italian soprano. *Elisabetta, regina d'Inghilterra* (1815), *Otello* (1816), *Armida* (1817), *Mosè in Egitto, Ricciardo e Zoraide* (1818), *Ermione, La donna del lago* (1819), *Maometto II* (1820), and *Zelmira* (1822) all contained parts written to display her special vocal and dramatic gifts. Colbran lived with Rossini for a number of years before the couple married at Castenaso in 1822. In 1823, Rossini wrote *Semiramide,* the final opera he composed for Colbran. A year later, she and Rossini traveled to London where she appeared in *Zelmira*; but her reputation had outlasted her voice, and the appearance was a disaster. Colbran retired from the stage and remained married to Rossini until 1837 when the couple separated formally. A brilliant and powerful singer in her prime, Isabella Colbran was one of the most famous in Europe. She is particularly remembered, however, as a great inspiration to Rossini and her legacy lives in his operas.

SUGGESTED READING:
Stendhal. *La vie de Rossini.* Paris, 1824.

John Haag,
Athens, Georgia

Colden, Jane (1724–1766)

*First American woman botanist who was an early student of the Linnaean method of plant classification. Name variations: Jenny Colden. Born on March 27, 1724, in New York City; died on March 10, 1766, in New York City; daughter of Cadwallader Colden (surveyor general, lieutenant governor, and acting governor of the Province of New York) and Alice (Christy) Colden; sister of **Alice Colden** and Alexander Colden, who succeeded his father as surveyor general; educated by her scholar father and her well-educated gardener mother with the help of the scientific library at the family estate of Coldengham in Ulster (now Orange) County, New York; married Dr. William Farquhar, in 1759; children: one (died in infancy).*

Considered to have been "the first lady on either side of the Atlantic" to master the new Linnaean method of plant nomenclature; created Flora—Nov Eboracensis (Botanic Manuscript), a compendium of drawings and descriptions of some 340 plants observed in Ulster County, possibly the most extensive botanical study of a single area carried out up to that time; corresponded with Dr. Alexander Garden, John Bartram, Peter Collinson, and other leading botanists of the period; contributed to Edinburgh Essays.

With some 300,000 plants known to modern botany, modern-day taxonomy (the classification of plants and animals) is a minor branch of the science. In the 18th century, when whole continents were accessible for the first time to Western students, the search for new and exotic plants and for their orderly classification was a worldwide passion. Long years of hardship, fortunes, and sometimes even life itself were sacrificed in the pursuit. "This was a great time for the science," H.W. Rickett has written, "when, upon the stimulus of [Linnaeus'] writing, many persons all over the world were contributing descriptions of species previously unknown. It is safe to say that Jane Colden was the only feminine member of that company."

Of the family into which Jane Colden, the first American woman botanist, was born, an early historian wrote that they "rose up like some mountain elevation, clad with the evergreens of wealth and adorned with the stately trees of honorable station." The wealth and honorable station were won by Jane Colden's father, Cadwallader, the son of an obscure Scotch dominie (schoolmaster). Sent to the University of Edinburgh to prepare himself for a clerical life, Cadwallader quickly turned to science. With a medical training gained in Edinburgh and London, he set out in 1716 to seek his fortune in the New World. He joined an aunt in Philadelphia where he proceeded to "practice physic" and engage in trade in the Indies.

In 1718, he abandoned active medical practice and accepted the position of surveyor general of the Province of New York and was soon thereafter granted a 3,000-acre wilderness estate, making him one of the great landowners of the colony. For more than half a century, he served as surveyor general, lieutenant governor and, for brief periods during the Stamp Act Protests, acting governor.

During his long years of political activity, Cadwallader wrote the still useful *History of the Five Indian Nations of Canada,* thought and wrote extensively on a wide range of medical and scientific subjects, and corresponded voluminously with leading scholars on both sides of the Atlantic. His interests ranged from the cause and treatment of diseases such as cancer, smallpox, and yellow fever to sanitation, education, physics, chemistry, and what is now called psychology. He was America's first materialist philosopher, a Deist who believed in a Guiding Intelligence that did not intervene in or break established material laws. Benjamin Franklin once warned Cadwallader that if his religious views were generally known he would share the fate of Galileo.

This doughty and omnivorously curious little man, quintessentially American in so many ways, was in politics a Tory and, according to **Alice Keys,** a "martinet." His goal as a colonial administrator was to drive, not lead. Through all the tumultuous years preceding the American Revolution, he remained implacably loyal to the king of England. His written oath of allegiance, still preserved by the Historical Society of Newburgh, was signed in a bold and resolute hand. His sons were to pay a price for their Tory allegiance, but he himself died in 1776 before the outbreak of full-scale war.

Notable women of the 18th century were characteristically the daughters of notable and sympathetic fathers. Jane Colden had a strong and congenial mother as well. **Alice Christy Colden** was, like her husband, a Scottish parson's child, a capable and cultivated woman. She gave birth to ten children, raised eight to adulthood, educated them all without help of schools or tutors, managed the family affairs during her husband's long absences as surveyor and politician, kept his voluminous records, and aided in the lively flow of his correspondence. Her "free" time she seems to have spent in her garden.

Jane, her parents' second daughter and fifth child, was born in 1724 in New York City, a metropolis of 8,000 inhabitants. Soon thereafter, Cadwallader moved his wife and family of young children up the Hudson to the remote wilderness estate previously granted him. The manor named Coldengham, which he already had under partial cultivation, was nine miles from the tiny riverside settlement of Newburgh. There, so Dr. Colden claimed, the only neighbors were wolves, bears, and other wild beasts. He seems not to have mentioned the nearby Native Americans who were not yet considered the threat that they would later become.

Although the site was remote and undramatic, much of it under dense forest cover, it was an ideal setting for botanical exploration. From the blood-root and Jack-in-the-pulpit of early spring through summer's brilliant loose strife to the golden rod of autumn—all to be seen in modern-day Orange County—a succession of flowering plants awaited a talented observer.

At Coldengham, Jane grew up in a self-sufficient, close-knit family. She early learned from her mother to practice "economy and virtue." There still exists a "Memorandum of Cheese Making in 1756," written in Alice's hand on five sheets of foolscap. It is a careful and painstakingly detailed account of a year's cheese-making, including methods, purchases, and amounts bought, also failures. The latter must have been rare, since one guest to the manor wrote, "She makes the best cheese I have eaten in America."

Cadwallader had further plans for his diligent Jane. "I have a daughter," he wrote to a European correspondent, "who has an inclination to reading and a curiosity for natural philosophy or natural history and a sufficient capacity for attaining a competent knowledge." To Gronovius, the noted Dutch botanist, he wrote:

> I (often) thought that Botany is an amusement which may be made greater to the Ladies who are often at a loss to fill up their time (and that) it would be made agreeable to them (it would prevent their employing so much of their time in trifling amusements as they do). Their natural curiosity and the pleasure they take in the beauty and variety of dress seems to fit them for it (far more than men). The chief reason that few or none of them have hitherto applied themselves to this study I believe is because all the books of any value are wrote in Latin and so filled with technical words that the obtaining the necessary previous knowledge (attended with) so (much) tiresome and disagreeable that they are discouraged at the first set out and give it over before they can receive any pleasure in the pursuit.

Although he opined that Latin was not for women, Cadwallader ordered Tournefort's *Institutiones Herbariae* and Morison's *Historia Plantarum* from Peter Collinson in Edinburgh. These he must have translated into English for Jane as he translated botanical terminology and parts of Linnaeus' work. He found his pupil "ingenious," quick to learn and apply the new Linnaean system.

Only 17 years Jane's senior, Carl Linnaeus had become famous well beyond his native Sweden by the age of 30. Like a number of other botanists, Cadwallader among them, Linnaeus was a physician by training and a close student of Aristotle. He took from the Greek philosopher the idea of an orderly pattern of plant and animal life, but he rejected the early 18th-century chaos of nomenclature, including the many religious names inherited from the monastery gardens of the Middle Ages. Rational naming he considered essential to any true scientific study, and he created a system by which each plant was to be identified by a universally accepted two-part Latin name, first the genus, second the species. Plants could for the first time be traced from author to author and botanical knowledge be reliably exchanged.

Linnaeus' taxonomy has been modified with time, but the brilliance of his basic concept reached round the scientific world. A pre-Darwinian, like his contemporaries, Linnaeus had no notion of evolving species, believing that God had created animals and plants in an unchanging, coherent, and beautiful pattern. He considered himself blessed in having the ability and opportunity to observe and reveal the divine mysteries through his explorations and writings. In Pennsylvania, Quaker John Bartram, whom Linnaeus considered the world's greatest natural botanist, wrote, "It is through this telescope, I see God in his glory." Cadwallader must have shared this point of view and transmitted it to his daughter.

Confident of Jane's facility in observation and classification, he wrote to numerous scientist friends offering her services in procuring and exchanging seeds and dried plants. Soon Colden herself was carrying on correspondence with the leading botanists of the day. By the 1750s, though she had never been as far from home as Bartram's botanical gardens in Philadelphia, she had become something of an international phenomenon.

Earlier Cadwallader had written *Plantae Coldenghamiae*, a paper on the plants at Coldengham, which Linnaeus had published. Colden set about expanding her father's work. She outlined for herself a project by which she would report on some 340 local plants, sketching and classifying each by the Linnaean system. Although never quite completed, Colden's was probably the most extensive botanical study of a single area accomplished up to that time. The drawings were done in pen and ink, washed with neutral tints. Simple, even crude in execution, they are not useful for identification, but some remain useful for confirmation. Any representations in color, which one visitor to Coldengham claimed to have seen and admired, have vanished.

It is Colden's plant descriptions that are remarkable for detail and accuracy. Her father stated that she had noted "particulars" that no other botanist, including himself, had observed. He believed, too, that three or four plants were entirely her new discoveries. Each detailed essay typically used as outline a list of 18th-century botanical terms. Each noted in addition the site where plants grew, their color, time of blooming and fruiting. Also included was occasional medicinal information, some gained from the "Indians" and "our Country People." "This pedicularis is called by the Country People Betony," she wrote, "and they make Thee of the Leaves, et use it for the Fever and Ague et for sikness of the Stomak."

> One ounce of the (Asclepius) Root, chiped into small pieces, to which put a pint and a half of boiling water, & let it stew for about

one hour, of this Decoction drink half a Tea cup full, every hour or two, and you bin certainly cured from the bloody Flux [dysentery], and better is when you boil the Root in Claret than in Water. This cure was learned from the Indians. [Poke Weed root] is very useful in the treatment of cancirs.

The infrequent images in Colden's writing were plain country images. One leaf was "awl-shaped," another "the size of a goose quill," another resembled "the lips of a hare." As candid as her father, who may have lost election to the Royal Society by seeming to disagree with Newton's explanation of gravity, she declared that Linnaeus had missed details that she had noted.

Despite its wilderness location, noted visitors came to Coldengham. Peter Kalm, a Finnish botanist and apostle of Linnaeus, spent a night on his way to plant collecting in Canada. John Bartram, Royal Botanist for the colonies, spent two days and brought with him his teenaged son William. William himself was to become a naturalist and nature writer whose accounts of his travels in the New World would in turn inspire the English Romantic poets, Wordsworth and Coleridge. Dr. Alexander Garden came from South Carolina.

Visits led to correspondence. Bartram wrote to "Respected Friend Jane Colden," discussing plant specimen with her. Garden, after whom the gardenia or Cape Jasmine was named, sent "seeds, mostly Persian . . . a pretty parcell . . . from . . . the Physician to the Prince Royal of Russia." In one letter to Cadwallader, Garden made the mistake of referring to Jane as "your lovely daughter" but apologized profusely when both father and daughter were affronted, on what grounds it is unclear.

In 1748 and 1749, Jane Colden and her sister Alice petitioned and received warrant for a patent for a larger piece of land than their father's original estate. Whether they intended to carve out their own estate or whether this was a legal manoeuvre on Cadwallader's part is not known. Whatever the plans, they did not come to fruition. The threat of Indian raids on the New York frontier increased, and in 1756 Cadwallader moved with his daughters to Spring Hill, an estate on Long Island. There, Jane Colden helped to create, so the sparse records suggest, one of the great gardens in the Colonies.

Colden's scientific studies were apparently at an end. At age 35, in 1759, she married Dr. William Farquhar, "a widower; a very worthy good Scotchman, and for some years before the Revolutionary War a practitioner of medicine, distinguished for his knowledge and ability, in New York City and vicinity." The marriage seems to have been a happy one, though fleeting. In 1766, Colden gave birth; she died, along with her child, soon after.

The adventures of Colden's *Botanic Manuscript,* labeled *Nov Eboracum* by Latinists of the period, are shrouded in some mystery. It appears that during the American Revolution, a decade or more after Colden's death, the manuscript fell into the hands of Captain Frederick von Wangenheim, a Hessian officer who happened also to be a Prussian-trained forester. Recognizing the unique quality of the work, von Wangenheim carried the manuscript back across the Atlantic to the University of Göttingen. It passed from there to the University of Marberg, then to Sir Joseph Banks, president of the British Royal Society, and upon his death to its permanent home in the British Museum where it remains today.

A condensed version of the *Botanic Manuscript* was published in 1963 under the auspices of the Garden Clubs of Dutchess and Orange counties. The original manuscript was on display for the first time in the United States in 1976 as part of the traveling Bicentennial exhibit "Remember the Ladies." A wildflower sanctuary at General Knox headquarters at Vails Gate, New York, bears Jane Colden's name.

SOURCES:

Colden, Jane. *Botanic Manuscript.* NY: Chanticleer Press, 1963.

Dexter, Elisabeth. *Colonial Women of Affairs: A Study of Women in Business and the Professions in America before 1776.* Boston, MA: Houghton Mifflin, 1924.

Edward, James, ed. *Notable American Women 1607–1950.* Cambridge, MA: Harvard University Press, 1974.

Hagberg, Knut. *Carl Linnaeus.* London: Jonathan Cape, 1952.

Keys, Alice. *Cadwallader Colden.* NY: AMS Press, 1967.

Vail, Anne Murray. "Jane Colden, an Early New York Botanist," in *Torreya.* 1907.

COLLECTIONS:

The Letters and Papers of Cadwallader Colden, N.Y. Historical Society Collections, vols. L–LVI, LXVII–LXVIII, 1917–23, 1934–35.

Margery Evernden, Professor Emerita, English Department, University of Pittsburgh, and freelance writer

$\mathcal{A}$CKNOWLEDGMENTS

Photographs and illustrations appearing in *Women in World History, Volume 3,* were received from the following sources:

Photograph by Joseph Abeles: **p. 683**; Courtesy of the Arkansas History Commission: **p. 358**; Basilica of St. Clare, painter identified only as "Maestro di S. Chiara": **p. 783**; Photograph by Cecil Beaton: **p. 5**; Bronston Productions (1963): **p. 775**; Engraving by John C. Buttre: **p. 833**; Courtesy of the Carter Family Collection: **pp. 451, 453** (photograph by Alan Meisser), **457**; Courtesy of the Chen Family: **p. 663**; Columbia Pictures Corporation: **pp. 22, 897** (1934); Courtesy of the Contemporary Forum: **p. 73**; Courtesy of the Embassy of Luxembourg: **p. 634**; Courtesy of the Embassy of Nicaragua, photograph by Rebecca Hammel ©1991: **p. 605**; Courtesy of the Embassy of the Commonwealth of Dominica: **p. 631**; Courtesy of the Embassy of Turkey: **p. 769**; EMI Films: **p. 720**; French commemorative postage stamp, issued March 8, 1983: **p. 474**; Galleria degli Uffizi (Florence): **p. 417**; Portrait by Gostl: **p. 527**; Grammercy Pictures (1995): **p. 421**; J. Gurney and Sons (New York): **p. 413**; Harvard College Observatory: **p. 347**; Harvard University, Fogg Art Museum, portrait by Hubert Vos: **p. 773**; Courtesy of Holyoke College: **p. 407**; Imperadio/RKO: **p. 567**; Courtesy of the International Swimming Hall of Fame: **p. 595**; state portrait from the studio of Jervas: **p. 388**; Courtesy of Julia Child's Kitchen, photograph by James Scherer: **p. 677**; Photograph by A. Karzanov: **p. 742**; Painting by Charles Le Brun: **p. 41**; Courtesy of the Library of Congress: **pp. 115, 171, 205, 222** (photograph by Frances Benjamin Johnson), **234** (Nannie Helen Burroughs Collection), **301, 341, 411, 497, 555, 565, 611, 652, 717, 749, 863, 875, 877**; Mary Pickford Corp.: **p. 223**; Mayer-Burstyn/De Sica: **p. 580**; Media Home Entertainment, Inc.: **p. 613**; Metro-Goldwyn-Mayer: **pp. 138, 173** (1937), **175** (1944), **315** (1952); Photograph by Lee Miller: **p. 427**; Mora (New York): **p. 468**; Museum of London: **p. 90**; Photographs by Nadar: **pp. 591, 757**; National Archives of Canada (PA-127238): **p. 481**; National Museum of American Art, Smithsonian Institution (Washington, D.C.): **pp. 86, 88**; National Portrait Gallery, Smithsonian Institution (Washington, D.C.): **p. 489**; Courtesy of Nebraska State Historical Society: **p. 519**; Courtesy of the New York Botanical Garden: **p. 54**; Courtesy of New York Historical Society: **p. 777**; Norman Rockwell Family Trust: **p. 26**; Odham's Press (London): **p. 96**; Opera Company of Boston: **p. 297**; Osterreichische Nationalbibliothek (Vienna): **p. 703**; From the movie *Pandora's Box*: **p. 79**; Paramount: **pp. 344** (1937), **435** (photograph by Eugene Robert Richee), **821** (1934); Engraving by George Parker from a painting by John Vanderlyn: **p. 232**; Courtesy of the Perkins School for the Blind (Watertown, Massachusetts): **p. 35**; Rachel Carson Council, Inc.: **p. 437**; *The Ecstasy of St. Cecilia* by Raphael: **p. 581**; Renaissance Films (1989): **p. 549**; Painting by George Richmond (1850): **p. 62**; Courtesy of the Royal Norwegian Embassy (Washington, D.C.): **p. 148**; Courtesy of the Salvation Army: **p. 235**; Samuel Goldwyn: **p. 67**; Sister Vision Press: **p. 121**; Engraving by H.W. Smith: **p. 471**; ©Paul Souders: **p. 244**; Courtesy of the State Historical Society of Wisconsin: **p. 623**; Photograph by Edward Steichen: **p. 643**; Film by Josef von Sternberg: **p. 529**; Engraving by F.T. Stuart: **p. 678**; Courtesy of Mary Louise Sullivan, M.S.C.: **p. 275**; Photograph by Robert S. Tait (1855): **p. 371**; *The Times*: **p. 201**; Twentieth Century-Fox Corporation: **pp. 66, 823** (1963), **895** (1950); Courtesy of the U.S. House of Representatives: **pp. 168, 237, 270, 271, 747**; Courtesy of the United Nations: **p. 71**; Detail of an engraving after a painting by Van Loo: **p. 780**; Photographs by Thomas Victor: **pp. 302, 788**; Courtesy of Virago Press: **p. 48**; Warner Bros.: **pp. 225** (©1993, photograph by Murray Close), **343** (1953), **719**; Warner Bros.-Seven Arts: **p. 860**; Courtesy of the Wellesley College Archives (Wellesley, Massachusetts): **p. 303**; Courtesy of Wide World: **p. 291**; Engraving by J.A.J. Wilcox: **p. 467**.